Management Decision

Management Team Decision

Develop Your Career Potential

Biz Flix

Management Workplace

Management 5e

Australia • Brazil • Canada • Mexico • Singapore • Spain • United Kingdom • United States

Management 5e
Chuck R. Williams,
Jim Jawahar,
Charles E. Bamford

VP/Editorial Director: Jack W. Calhoun

Editor-in-Chief: Melissa S. Acuña

Executive Editor: Joe Sabatino

Developmental Editor: Jamie Bryant, B-Books

Marketing Manager: Clint Kernen

Sr. Content Project Manager: Tamborah Moore

Manager, Editorial Media: John Barans

Technology Project Manager: Kristen Meere

Sr. Marketing Coordinator: Sarah Rose

Sr. Marketing Communications Manager: Jim Overly

Sr. Manufacturing Coordinator: Doug Wilke

Editorial Assistant: Ruth Belanger

Production House: Lachina Publishing Services

Sr. Art Director: Tippy McIntosh

Internal and Cover Designer: Trish and Ted Knapke

Cover Image: © Photonica, Jan Stromme

Sr. Image Permissions Manager: Deanna Ettinger

Photo Researcher: Susan Van Etten

Library of Congress Control Number: 2007939235

Student Edition ISBN 13: 978-0-324-56840-0
Student Edition ISBN 10: 0-324-56840-1
Instructor's Edition ISBN 13: 978-0-324-57902-4
Instructor's Edition ISBN 10: 0-324-57902-0

South-Western Cengage Learning
5191 Natorp Boulevard
Mason, OH 45040
USA

Cengage Learning products are represented in Canada by Nelson Education, Ltd.

Printed in Canada
1 2 3 4 5 6 7 11 10 09 08 07

BRIEF CONTENTS

CONTENTS

1 INTRODUCTION TO MANAGEMENT 2

THE END OF EACH CHAPTER CONTAINS THE FOLLOWING MATERIAL:

Key Terms
Self Assessment
Management Decision
Management Team Decision
Practice Being a Manager (an experiential exercise)
Develop Your Career Potential
Reel to Real

3

ORGANIZING 306

4

LEADING 468

WHAT'S NEW IN 5E?

ABOUT THIS EDITION

If you walk down the aisle of the business section in your local bookstore (or surf the "Business" page at Amazon.com), you'll find hundreds of books that explain precisely what companies need to do to be successful.

Unfortunately, these books tend to be faddish, changing every few years. Lately, the best-selling business books have emphasized technology, leadership, and dealing with change, whereas ten years ago the hot topics were reengineering, going global, mergers, and management buyouts.

One thing that hasn't changed, though, and never will, is the importance of good management. **Management** is getting work done through others. Organizations can't succeed for long without it. Well-managed companies are competitive because their work forces are smarter, better trained, more motivated, and more committed. Furthermore, good management leads to satisfied employees who, in turn, provide better service to customers. Because employees tend to treat customers the same way that their managers treat them, good management can improve customer satisfaction. Finally, companies that practice good management consistently have greater revenues and profits than companies that don't.

My goal in writing the first edition of ***Management*** was to write a textbook that students would enjoy, that students would refer to for practical, theory-driven advice, and that encouraged students to put theory-driven knowledge into practice for themselves. For the fifth edition, my goal was to update the content to reflect the changing face of management and to keep the text relevant, fresh, and interesting for students. In short, the ideas and concepts you'll learn about in this book can improve the performance of the organization and department where you work, help you solve job-related problems, and improve your own job performance, even if you're not a manager.

So welcome to ***Management,*** 5e! Please take a few minutes to read the preface and familiarize yourself with the approach (combining theory with specific stories and examples), features, pedagogy, and end-of-chapter assignments in ***Management***. This is time well spent. After all, besides your instructor, this book will be your primary learning tool.

Combining Theory with Specific, Up-to-Date Stories and Examples

Say "theory" to college students and they assume that you're talking about complex, arcane ideas and terms that have nothing to do with the "real world," but which need to be memorized for a test and then forgotten (at least until the final exam). However, students needn't be wary of theoretical ideas and concepts. Theories are simply good ideas. And good theories are simply good ideas that have been tested through rigorous scientific study and analysis.

Where textbooks go wrong is that they stop at theory and read like dictionaries. Or, they focus on theoretical issues related to research rather than practice. However, good management theories (i.e., good ideas) needn't be complex, difficult to understand, or irrelevant. In fact, the late Rensis Likert, of the University of Michigan, once said that there is nothing as practical as a good theory.

So, to make sure that you're exposed to good ideas (i.e., good theories), that you can refer to for practical, theory-driven advice, and which encourage you to put theory-driven knowledge into practice for yourselves, each chapter in this book contains 50 to 60 specific stories and examples that illustrate how managers are using management ideas in their organizations. Let's use an example from Chapter 8 on Global Management to show you what I mean. One of the key issues in Global Management is successfully preparing employees for international assignments. In fact, the difficulty of adjusting to language, cultural, and social differences in another country is the primary reason that so many businesspersons fail in international assignments. Consequently, you'll read this passage in Chapter 8.

> *For example, although there have recently been disagreements among researchers about these numbers, it is probably safe to say that 5 to 20 percent of American expatriates sent abroad by their companies will return to the United States before they have successfully completed international assignments. Of those who do complete their international assignments, about one-third are judged by their companies to be no better than marginally effective.*

In other words, this is fairly standard, research-based information. You'll find it in most textbooks. Is it important for students to know this information? You bet! Is it likely that students will find this and the thousands of other pieces of theory and research-based facts throughout the book particularly compelling or interesting (and thus easier to learn)? Ah, there's the problem. However, what if we combined theory and research with specific, "real world" stories and examples that illustrated good or poor use of those theories? For instance, the passage shown below is also in Chapter 8, where it follows the research-based information about the difficulty of adjusting to foreign cultures.

> *In his book* Blunders in International Business, *David Ricks tells the story of an American manager working in the South Pacific who, by hiring too many local workers from one native group, unknowingly upset the balance of power in the island's traditional status system. The islanders met on their own and quickly worked out a solution to the problem. After concluding their meeting at 3 AM, they calmly went to his home to discuss their solution with him (time was not important in their culture). But since the American didn't speak their language, and couldn't understand why they would show*

up in mass outside his home at 3 AM, he called in the Marines, who were stationed nearby, to disburse what he thought was a riot.

After reading this passage, students have a vivid understanding about what can go wrong if people don't receive cultural and language training before traveling or moving to another country. Why does this help students learn? Because the first passage cites theory and research on the effectiveness of cross-cultural training and the second brings the theory and research alive by indicating what can go wrong if you don't get that cross-cultural training.

Moreover, the stories and examples you'll read in each chapter are relevant and up-to-date. You'll read how Wal-Mart has started using software to schedule shifts for its 1.3 million workers. What used to take a store manager an entire day now takes only an hour, freeing up Wal-Mart managers to, well, manage. You'll learn how surgeons and nurses at the Veterans Health Administration are using safety pauses in the operating room to overcome organizational silence and reduce mistakes. The surgical team pauses for a moment, is asked if anyone has concerns or comments, and then addresses them if need be. You'll also learn how companies incorporate flexibility into their planning process so they can react appropriately and quickly when disruptions occur. For example, Virgin Atlantic spent considerable time and effort developing a reclining seat for first-class passengers, but before the company was able to bring the new seat to market, British Airways unveiled its fully flat bed for business class. In an instant, Virgin Atlantic's original plan was all but useless, but the VA team regrouped, was allocated additional resources, and developed a suite (not just a seat) that helped it increase its market share amoung transatlantic passengers. You'll also read about how companies use outsourcing to increase productivity—even companies you might not associate with outsourcing, like McDonald's. Some franchises have all but eliminated the 10-second idle time a drive-thru employee experiences between orders waiting for the first car to pull away and the next one to pull up to the speaker. How? By outsourcing the order taking function to remote call centers. A call center employee can take an order from a hungry patron at one location and immediately after take an order from another hungry patron at a completely different location, perhaps a completely different state. As these stories show, each chapter has been updated with dozens of new real world business examples, straight from the latest pages of *BusinessWeek, Fortune, Forbes, Fast Company,* and *Inc.,* as well as the *Wall Street Journal,* the *New York Times,* and other leading newspapers, to help you understand how management concepts are being used.

In short, research *and* theory and stories and examples are important for effective learning. Therefore, this book contains over a thousand specific examples and stories to make management theories and ideas more interesting. So, to get more out of this book, read and understand the theories and theoretical ideas. Then read the stories or examples to learn how those ideas should or should not be used in practice. You'll find that both are current and up-to-date.

So What's New?

If you are already familiar with the previous editions' approach of reinforcing research and theory with stories and examples you may be asking yourself, "So what's new?" The answer is quite a bit.

To keep pace with the evolution of management, the Fourth Edition underwent a rigorous review process that identified areas where I could strengthen and refine the text. Reviewers gave wonderful feedback about which boxed features were not being used in class, so I have streamlined each chapter to focus on the main content, retaining only the most popular boxes from the Fourth Edition, "What Really Works?" and "Doing the Right Thing." To each chapter, I've also added a short box on current management issues or interesting management facts. Titled "Management Fact" and "Management Trend," these boxes provide short examples and issues that get students thinking beyond the book.

For this edition, all eighteen of the "What Would You Do?" chapter-opening cases are new, and feature companies like Sony, PETA, StubHub, Whirlpool, Walgreens, Louis Vuitton, Tommy Hilfiger, and Radio Shack, among others.

What *brand new* things will you find in ***Management***, 5e? To start, you'll find:

Practice Being a Manager—Working through management issues before you even get to the workplace can be a beneficial way to practice being a manager. A new experiential exercise at the end of each chapter gives students a context in which to explore management issues and problems with other students. The guided exercises are supported by detailed teaching notes and role-playing instructions in the Instructor Manual.

Self Assessments—The Fourth Edition contained a self-assessment appendix, but for this edition, I wanted to better integrate the assessments into the chapters themselves. The chapter-ending cases and assignments now begin with a related assessment questionnaire to help students consider how their own perspectives influence their management skills. Basic scoring information follows each questionnaire, and the Instructor Manual contains directions for using the assessment tools in class.

Reel to Real Videos—When we asked professors how they used video in the classroom, we discovered two distinct preferences. Some like to use short video examples to reinforce certain points in the chapter; others like longer video cases that looked at various companies in-depth. In response to this feedback, each chapter of ***Management***, 5e contains two video options. The first is a film clip from a popular Hollywood movie that relates to the chapter content. For example, students will see a "Biz Flix" clip from *In Good Company* for Chapter 2 on History of Management, from *The Bourne Identity* for Chapter 5 on Planning, from *October Sky* for Chapter 7 on Innovation, and from *Casino* for Chapter 18 on Managing Service and Manufacturing Operations, to name a few. The second video option is comprised of longer segments, called "Management Workplace," which are an average of 12 minutes and provide a deeper look at a single company, its operations, and how it addresses various management issues every day. In the Fifth Edition, we go inside Original Penguin (apparel), Lonely Planet (travel guides), Organic Valley (organic dairy products), Timbuk2 (backpacks and bags), PepsiCo, NEADS (training service animals), and Peapod (online grocer). Both the "Biz Flix" and the "Management Workplace" videos guide students on what to look for and think about as they watch the video. Detailed teaching notes for both videos are in each chapter of the Instructor Manual.

CengageNOW for Williams—***Management***, 5e has a dedicated CengageNOW study tool that tightly integrates the material in the text with a myriad of review opportunities. Students can test their understanding, concentrate their review on their weakest areas, and then verify their progress using the latest technology.

So what *is* new in *Management*, 5e? Quite a bit.

Book Features

A tremendous amount of time and thought went into planning this textbook. I reviewed over 25 top selling textbooks in Management, Marketing, Finance, Statistics, and Economics. I asked more than 200 students and dozens of professors what they specifically liked and disliked about their textbooks. And, I pulled some of my favorite books (many of which were not about business) from my bookshelf to figure out what made them great books. Only then did I create the plan and organization for ***Management***. The Fifth Edition retains the popular features of previous editions and adds some new ones. So take a few minutes now to familiarize yourself with these features. Doing so will help you get more out of the book and your management class.

What Would You Do?—Each chapter opens with an engaging case outlining actual management problems facing a well-known company. After students read the case, they are presented several questions to help guide their thinking about the issues, and are ultimately asked "If you were the manager at this company, what would you do?" Putting students in the place of the manager personalizes the dilemma and forces students to solve common managerial problems. The solution to the case, or "What Really Happened?" is in the Instructor Manual. Allowing students to compare what they would have done to what the managers really did provides a great learning opportunity.

Doing the Right Thing—At the U.S. Military Academy, there is a strict code of conduct: "A cadet will not lie, cheat or steal, nor tolerate those who do." The code is concise and unmistakable. Regrettably, there is no equivalent code for managers because there's no doubt they need one. Numerous studies and well-known corporate scandals make clear the distressing state of managerial ethics in today's business world. Lying to stockholders about profits, cheating to win business, and stealing from companies have become all too common. And, because managers set the standard for others in the workplace, unethical behavior and practices quickly spread when they don't do the right thing. Therefore, in each chapter, you'll find practical, useful advice to help you become a more ethical manager or businessperson by "Doing the Right Thing." Topics include ethical competitive analysis, avoiding the slippery slope of cheating, dealing with gifts from suppliers, avoiding conflicts of interest, not cheating on travel expenses, enforcing fair and safe working conditions in foreign factories, giving credit rather than taking it, and many more.

What Really Works?—Some studies show that two drinks a day increases life expectancy by decreasing your chances of having a heart attack. Yet other studies show that two drinks a day will shorten your life expectancy. For years, we've "buttered" our morning toast with margarine instead of butter because it was supposed to be better for our health. However, new studies now show that the trans-fatty acids in margarine may be just as bad for our arteries as butter. Confusing scientific results like these frustrate ordinary people who want to "eat right" and "live right." It also makes many people question just how useful most scientific research really is.

Managers also have trouble figuring out what works, based on the scientific research published in journals like the *Academy of Management Journal*, the *Academy of Management Review*, the *Strategic Management Journal*, the *Journal of Applied Psychology*, and *Administrative Science Quarterly*. It's common for the *Wall Street Journal* to quote a management research article from one of these journals that says that total quality management is the best thing since sliced bread (without butter or margarine). Then, just six months later, the *Wall Street Journal* will quote a different article from the same journal that says that total quality management doesn't work. If management professors and researchers have trouble deciding what works and what doesn't, how can practicing managers know?

Thankfully, a research tool called *meta-analysis*, which is a study of studies, is helping management scholars understand how well their research supports management theories. Fortunately, meta-analysis is also useful for practicing managers, because it shows what works and the conditions under which management techniques may work better or worse in the "real world." Meta-analysis is based on the simple idea that if one study shows that a management technique doesn't work and another study shows that it does, an average of those results is probably the best estimate of how well that management practice works (or doesn't work). Fortunately, you don't need a Ph.D. to understand the statistics reported in a meta-analysis. In fact, one primary advantage of meta-analysis over traditional significance tests is that you can convert meta-analysis statistics into intuitive numbers that anyone can easily understand. Indeed, each meta-analysis reported in the "What Really Works?" sections of this textbook is accompanied by an easy-to-understand statistic called the *probability of success*. As its name suggests, the probability of success uses a bar graph and a percentage (0 percent to 100 percent) to indicate the likelihood that a management technique will actually work.

Of course, no idea or technique works every time and in every circumstance. However, in today's competitive, fast-changing, global marketplace, few managers can afford to overlook proven management strategies like those discussed in the "What Really Works?" feature of this book.

Pedagogy

Pedagogical features are meant to reinforce learning, but they don't have to be boring. Accordingly, the teaching tools used in ***Management*** will help students learn and hold their interest, too.

Chapter Outline and Numbering System, Learning Objectives, and Section Reviews—Because of their busy schedules, very few students have the opportunity to read a chapter from beginning to end in one sitting. Typically, it takes students anywhere from two to five study sessions to completely read a chapter. Accordingly, at the beginning of each chapter, you'll find a detailed chapter outline in which each major part in the chapter is broken out into numbered sections and subsections. For example, the outline for the first part of Chapter 4, on Ethics and Social Responsibility, looks like this:

What Is Ethical and Unethical Workplace Behavior?

1. Ethics and the Nature of Management Jobs
2. Workplace Deviance
3. U.S. Sentencing Commission Guidelines
    3.1 Who, What, and Why?
    3.2 Determining the Punishment

The numbered information contained in the chapter outline is then repeated in the chapter as learning objectives (at the beginning of major parts of the chapter) and as numbered headings and subheadings (throughout the chapter) to help students remember precisely where they are in terms of the chapter outline. Finally, instead of a big summary at the end of the chapter, students will find detailed reviews at the end of each section.

Together, the chapter outline, numbering system, learning objectives, section headings (which mark the beginning of a section), and section reviews (which mark the end of a section) allow students to break the chapter into smaller, self-contained sections that can be read in their entirety over multiple study sessions. Furthermore, the numbered headings and outline should make it easier for instructors and students to know what is being assigned or discussed in class ("In section 3.1 of chapter 3...").

Study Tip—Knowing how to study effectively is not an innate talent. So, to prepare students for studying the material, a detailed study tip appears in the chapter opener. Eighteen different tips give students many options for reviewing key concepts and mastering chapter content. Students are challenged to write their own tests and exchange them in a study group, explain the chapter concepts to a friend who is not in class, cut up the text glossary to make a quiz-bowl game, and much more.

Student Resources—The ***Management*** package has many resources to help reinforce the concepts in each chapter. For that reason, the opening of each chapter includes a list of various study tools and where they can be found. Each list contains information about CengageNOW and the student website.

Key Terms—Key terms appear in boldface in the text, with definitions in the margins to make it easy for students to check their understanding. A complete alphabetical list of key terms appears at the end of each chapter as a study checklist, with page citations for easy reference.

End-of-Chapter Assignments

In most textbooks, there are only two or three end-of-chapter assignments. By contrast, at the end of each chapter in ***Management***, there are five assignments from which to choose. (But if you count the opening case, "What Would You Do?," and its answer, "What Really Happened?," it's really six assignments.) This gives instructors more choice in selecting just the right assignment for their classes. It also gives students a greater variety of activities, making it less likely that they'll repeat the same kind of assignment chapter after chapter.

Self Assessment—As described above, each chapter has a "Self Assessment" questionnaire that helps students explore their own management perspectives.

Management Decision—"Management Decision" assignments are focused on a particular decision. Students must decide what to do in the given situation and then answer several questions to explain their choices. For example, students must decide whether to give a new employee a raise before company policy allows, if the company should permit camera phones in the office, whether to use personality tests as part of hiring and promotion decisions, if creating a workplace blog is worth the effort, whether to mine employees' personal data to find out how to motivate them, and more. Some "Management Decision" features have optional extensions that turn the exercises into mini-projects. Information on how to do that is in the Instructor Manual.

Management Team Decision—"Management Team Decision" assignments are similar to "Management Decision" assignments in that students face a problem, must decide what to do, and then answer several questions to explain their choices. The difference, however, is that "Management Team Decision" assignments are designed to be completed by student teams or groups. Teams have the opportunity to practice the group decision-making techniques outlined in Chapter 5 (Planning and Decision Making). Student management teams will decide whether to implement a shopper card program at a chain of independent supermarkets, consider the pros and cons of becoming a Wal-Mart supplier, build a balanced scorecard for H&R Block, map a strategy for Paramount Pictures, determine the role of innovation at Colgate-Palmolive, and more.

Practice Being a Manager Experiential Exercises—The end of each chapter contains an experiential exercise to give students the opportunity to role play management scenarios, discuss management dilemmas, and resolve management problems. Some of the exercises have components that require individual, take-home preparation, but most are designed to be started and completed during the class session.

Develop Your Career Potential—"Develop Your Career Potential" assignments have one purpose: to help students develop their present and future capabilities as managers. What students learn through these assignments is not traditional "book-learning" based on memorization and regurgitation, but practical knowledge and skills that help managers perform their jobs better. Assignments include interviewing managers, dealing with the press, conducting a personal SWOT analysis, learning from failure, developing leadership skills, 360-degree feedback, and more.

Instructor Supplements

Comprehensive Instructor Manual—The instructor manual to accompany the Fifth Edition has been completely redone to help instructors in every type of class. In addition to the chapter outlines, additional activities, and solutions you expect, the new manual includes one pedagogy grid and three lesson plans per chapter.

Each chapter of the instructor manual opens with a pedagogy grid that details all of the pedagogy in the chapter and the companies and teaching points presented. By giving you all the options you have in the chapter and the chapter content addressed by each option, you will be able to decide what you want to emphasize in class and the work you want to assign your students. Following the pedagogy grid is a series of three lesson plans: a lecture lesson plan, including lists of PowerPoint slides; a group-work lesson plan for professors who have smaller sections and/or more time during the semester; and a complete video lesson plan, including pre-viewing, viewing, and post-viewing activities for both "BizFlix" and "Management Workplace." The purpose of the video-only lesson plan is to illustrate how to teach using video without "losing time."

Each type of lesson plan includes pre-class preparation for the professor and for students, how to organize the content for the chapter during the class period, a list of possible assignments, and more.

A detailed chapter outline (lecture notes) is still part of the instructor manual. The lecture notes include additional examples, teaching notes for key concepts and for feature boxes, prompts where relevant PowerPoint slides and transparencies correspond to chapter content, as well as prompts for where to show the video. Solutions for chapter features are included.

In addition to all of these teaching tools, an appendix titled "Teaching Your First Management Course" can be found at the end of the instructor manual. This appendix is designed specifically to meet the needs and concerns of the first-time instructor.

Certified Test Bank—The Test Bank for the Fifth Edition of ***Management*** builds on the solid foundation of previous editions. A team of professors reviewed the entire test bank to verify the quality of each question. Then an editorial professional verified that the question concepts and wording matched the presentation in the text, as well as corrected grammatical and typographical errors and page references.

Each test bank chapter contains at least 150 questions in a variety of types: true-false, multiple-choice, short-answer, and critical-thinking questions, and a scenario section that asks students to answer questions based on detailed management situations, including on the chapter-opening "What Would You Do?" case. Thorough solutions are provided for each question, including difficulty ratings, AACSB tags, and page references where solutions appear in the text.

A computerized version of the text bank is available on your Instructor Resource CD-ROM and by special request. ExamView allows to you create, edit, store, print, and otherwise customize your quizzes, tests, and exams. The system is menu-driven making it quick and easy to use.

Course Pre- and Post-Assessments—To help you better determine your students' baseline understanding of management principles, we have created an assessment test for your use at the beginning of the term. The 200-question pre-test covers the basic management concepts that students need to understand. As a conclusion to your course, you can administer the 200-question post-test. These tests are designed to help you track your students' proficiency levels semester to semester. Pre- and post-assessments are also broken down by chapter, so if you prefer, you can administer throughout the semester for each chapter of the text. Assessment tests are available in both Word and ExamView formats.

ExamView—A computerized version of the Test Bank (called ExamView) is available on your Instructor Resource CD-ROM and by special request. ExamView allows you to add or edit questions, instructions, and answers. You can create, edit, store, print, and otherwise customize all your quizzes, tests, and exams. The system is menu-driven, making it quick and easy to use.

Reel to Real Video—Nothing helps students master management concepts like seeing them put into practice in the real world. New "Management Workplace" videos give an extensive look into the workings of interesting and successful companies like Original Penguin, Lonely Planet, PepsiCo, Organic Valley, and Peapod. In addition to these longer segments, each chapter has a movie clip that ties into the management concepts presented in the chapter. Clips are short, so you can view and review them easily and quickly.

Both the "Biz Flix" and "Management Workplace" videos are available on DVD. The Instructor Manual includes detailed teaching notes so that you can incorporate video into your class in a meaningful way.

PowerPoint® Slides—A rich set of PowerPoint slides, with teaching notes, will make class preparations easy and interesting. The approximately 30 to 50 slides per chapter cover all key concepts, terms, features, cases, and even some exhibits from the text. Animations and transitions add movement to many of the slides, allowing instructors to show one point at a time and adding a dynamic feel that will hold student interest throughout the presentation. Ample teaching notes offer additional insights and examples plus important points to cover in lectures. For instructors wishing to integrate various media, we have also created a set of video PowerPoint slides in which the "BizFlix" movie clips are embedded in appropriate slides. And to support the Self Assessment questionnaires, we have created a separate set of PowerPoint files that enable professors to use the assessment inventories in the classroom setting. In each Self Assessment PowerPoint chapter, individual assessment items are placed on separate slides. Excel spreadsheets embedded on each slide allow instructors to use the data from a simple show of hands to create distributions for each assessment item. Students can see where they fit in the distribution, making the assessment tool more interesting and relevant.

Who Wants to Be a Manager?—Games are an increasingly popular classroom review tool, so the Fifth Edition of ***Management*** includes a quiz game that uses JoinIn™ clicker technology. Each chapter has two rounds of 25 questions each, organized into 5 categories. Category names are fun, but the questions in each category are serious review of chapter concepts. A mixture of true-false and multiple choice questions keep students working through this enjoyable classroom review.

Instructor Resource CD-ROM (IRCD)—For your convenience, the Instructor Manual, Test Bank, ExamView Software, PowerPoint presentations, and Who Wants to Be a Manager are available on a single CD-ROM, the IRCD.

The Business and Company Resource Center—Put a complete business library at your fingertips with the Business & Company Resource Center (BCRC). The BCRC is a premier online business research tool that allows you to seamlessly search thousands of periodicals, journals, references, financial information, industry reports, company histories, and much more. The BCRC is a powerful and time-saving research tool for students—whether they are completing a case analysis, preparing for a presentation, creating a business plan, or writing a reaction paper. Instructors can use the BCRC like an online coursepack, quickly and easily assigning readings and research projects without the inconvenience of library reserves, permissions, and printed materials. BCRC filters out the "junk" information students often find when searching the Internet, providing only the high quality, safe, and reliable news and information sources. Visit **academic.cengage.com/bcrc** to learn more about how this powerful electronic tool integrates a diverse collection of resources to reflect the natural research process and contact your local representative for pricing and optional bundling information for the Business & Company Resource Center with your text.

Web Tutor™ (for both WebCT®, and Blackboard®)—Online learning is growing at a rapid pace. Whether you are looking to offer courses at distance or to offer a Web-enhanced classroom, South-Western/Cengage Learning offers you a solution with WebTutor. WebTutor provides instructors with text-specific content that interacts with the two leading systems of higher education course management—WebCT and Blackboard.

WebTutor is a turnkey solution for instructors who want to begin using technology like Blackboard or WebCT but who do not have Web-ready content available, or who do not want to be burdened with developing their own content. WebTutor uses the Internet to turn everyone in your class into a front-row student. WebTutor offers interactive study guide features such as quizzes, concept reviews, flashcards, discussion forums, additional video clips, and more. Instructor tools are also provided to facilitate communication between students and faculty.

Williams Website (academic.cengage.com/management/williams)—The Williams website contains a wealth of resources for both instructors and students. Here is what's available only for professors at the Instructor Resource page of the Williams website:

- The full PowerPoint presentations with teaching notes.
- Files for the full Test Bank.
- Files for the full Instructor Manual are also available online. If you don't have your materials on hand, you can download the chapters you need and customize them to suit your lesson plan.

Here is what's available for students at the Williams website:

- An abridged set of PowerPoint slides to help with review
- A quiz for each chapter
- Key terms with definitions

Student Supplements

CengageNOW for Management, 5e—**CengageNOW for *Management*, 5e** is an online assessment-driven and student-centered tutorial that provides students with a personalized learning plan. Based on a diagnostic Pre-Test, a customized learning path is generated for each student that targets their study needs and helps them to visualize, organize, practice, and master the material in the text. Media resources enhance problem-solving skills and improve conceptual understanding. An access code to CengageNOW for Williams can be bundled with new textbooks.

InfoTrac—Packaged free with every new copy of ***Management*, 5e** is a password for the InfoTrac database by Gale Research. InfoTrac enables students to connect with the real world of management through academic journals, business and popular magazines and newspapers, and a vast array of government publications. InfoTrac was used to create the end-of-chapter activities in each chapter; students can use InfoTrac for working through the "Management Decisions" at the end of each chapter.

Wall Street Journal Edition—This *Wall Street Journal* edition makes it easy to bring the real world into the classroom, providing numerous opportunities to relate economic concepts to daily news stories. New copies of ***Management*, 5e** can include an optional card entitling students to subscriptions to the *Wall Street Journal* and **WSJ.com**, giving students access to many articles used as examples in this textbook. Contact your local representative about pricing and optional bundling information.

Acknowledgments

Let's face it, writing a textbook is a long and lonely process. It's surely the most difficult (and rewarding) project I've ever tackled. And, as I sat in front of my computer with a rough outline on the left side of my desk, a two-foot stack of journal articles on the floor, and a blank screen in front of me, it was easy at times to feel isolated. But, as I found out, a book like this doesn't get done without the help of many other talented people.

First, I'd like to thank the outstanding team of supplement authors: Thomas K. and Betty Pritchett (Kennesaw State University), for the outstanding test bank; Eric Brengle (B-books, Ltd.), for the superb PowerPoint slide designs; and Teri Irvin (B-books, Ltd.) for her detailed video lesson plans.

I'd like to thank the world-class team at Cengage Learning for the outstanding support (and patience) they provided while I wrote this book; Joe Sabatino, who heads the Management group at Cengage Learning, was calm, collected, and continuously positive through the major ups and downs of this project; Clint Kernen, who was in charge of marketing the book, did an outstanding job of developing marketing themes and approaches; and Tamborah Moore, who managed the production process, was consistently upbeat and positive with me when I deserved otherwise. Authors are prone to complain about their publishers. But that hasn't been my experience at all. Pure and simple, everyone at Cengage Learning has been great to work with throughout the entire project. However, special thanks on this team goes to Jamie Gleich Bryant, of B-books, Ltd., who was my developmental editor and with whom I had the most contact while writing the book. Jamie and her team worked with reviewers, edited the manuscript, managed the development of supplements, provided superb feedback and guidance at every stage of the book, and nudged and prodded me to write faster, make improvements, and maintain the high quality standards that were set when I began writing. Jamie's enthusiasm, professionalism, commitment, and attention to detail made me a better writer, made this a better book, and made me appreciate my good fortune to work with such an outstanding talent. Thanks, Jamie, and here's to many more editions.

I'd like to thank an excellent set of reviewers whose diligent and thoughtful comments helped shape the earlier editions and whose rigorous feedback improved the Fifth Edition.

Ali Abu-Rahma
United States International University

William Acar
Kent State University

David C. Adams
Manhattanville College

Bruce R. Barringer
University of Central Florida

Gayle Baugh
University of West Florida

James Bell
University of Texas, Austin

Greg Blundel
Kent State University, Stark

Katharine A. Bohley
University of Indianapolis

Santanu Borah
University of North Alabama

Angela Boston
University of Texas, Arlington

Michael Boyd
Owensboro Community College

Jon L. Bryan
Bridgewater State College

Wayne Buchanan
Defiance College

Bruce Byars
University of North Dakota, Grand Forks

Diane P. Caggiano
Fitchburg State College

David Cassidy
College of Eastern Utah

Dan Cochran
Mississippi State University

C. Brad Cox
Midlands Technical College

Kathy Daruty
Pierce College

Nicolette DeVille Christensen
Guilford College

Michael DiVecchio
Central Pennsylvania College

Jennifer Dose
University of Minnesota-Morris

Jason Duan
Cameron University

Joyce A. Ezrow
Anne Arundel Community College

Kimborough Ferrell
Spring Hill College

Charles R. Franz
University of Missouri-Columbia

Paul R. Gagnon
Central Connecticut State University

Franco Gandolfi
Cedarville University

Janice Gates
Western Illinois University

Anu A. Gokhale
Illinois State University

Barry Allen Gold
Pace University

Martin Grossman
Bridgewater State College

Susan C. Hanlon
University of Akron

Russell F. Hardy
New Mexico State University

David Hennessey
Mount Mercy College

Dorothy Hetmer-Hinds
Trinity Valley Community College

Roger W. Hutt
Arizona State University at the Polytechnic Campus

Joseph Izzo
Alderson Broaddus College

Jim Jawahar
Illinois State University

Kathleen Jones
University of North Dakota

Paul N. Keaton
University of Wisconsin-La Crosse

Ellen Ernst Kossek
Michigan State University

Nancy E. Kucinski
Hardin-Simmons University

Lowell H. Lamberton
Central Oregon Community College
Linfield College

Donald R. Leavitt
Western Baptist College

Lee W. Lee
Central Connecticut State University

Jerrold Leong
Oklahoma State University

Randy Lewis
Texas Christian University

Bob Livingston
Cerritos College

Linda Livingstone
Baylor University

Thomas P. Loughman
Columbus State University

Larry Maes
Davenport University

George Marron
Arizona State University

Lynda Martin
Oklahoma State University

David McCalman
University of Central Arkansas

Robert McGowan
University of Denver

Don Mosley
University of South Alabama

Sherry Moss
Florida International University

Jaideep Motwani
Grand Valley State University

Victoria T. Mullennex
Davis & Elkins College

John J. Nader
Grand Valley State University

Charlie Nagelschmidt
Champlain College

Patrick J. Nedry
Monroe County Community College

Stephanie Newport
Austin Peay State University

Don A. Okhomina
Fayetteville State University

James S. O'Rourke, IV
University of Notre Dame

Rhonda S. Palladi
Georgia State University

Lynne Patten
Clark Atlanta University

Jane Pettinger
Minnesota State University, Moorhead

Clifton D. Petty
Drury University

John Poirier
Bryant University

David M. Porter, Jr.
UCLA

Michael Provitera
Barry University

Abe Qastin
Lakeland College

Robert Raspberry
Southern Methodist University

Levi Richard
Citrus Community College

Kim Rocha
Barton College

Linda Ross
Cleveland Community College

Penni F. Sikkila
Baker College

Amit Shah
Frostburg State University

Thomas Shaughnessy
Illinois Central College

Michelle Slagle
University of South Alabama

James Smas
Kent State University

James O. Smith
East Carolina University

Charlotte Nix Speegle
Cisco Junior College

Gregory K. Stephens
Texas Christian University

John Striebich
Monroe Community College

Joseph Tagliaferre
Pennsylvania State University

Jennie Carter Thomas
Belmont University

Neal F. Thomson
Columbus State University

James Thornton
Champlain College

Mary Jo Vaughan
Mercer University

Michael Wakefield
Colorado State University, Pueblo

James Whelan
Manhattan College

Joann White
Jackson State University

Xiang Yi
Western Illinois University

Finally, my family deserves the greatest thanks of all for their love, patience, and support. Writing a textbook is an enormous project with incredible stresses and pressures on authors as well as their loved ones. However, throughout this project, my wife, Jenny, was unwavering in her support of my writing. She listened patiently, encouraged me when I was discouraged, read and commented on most of what I wrote, gave me the time to write, and took wonderful care of me and our family during this long process. My children, two in college and one in a business career, also deserve special thanks for their patience and for understanding why Dad was locked away at the computer for all of this time.

Meet the Author:

Chuck Williams
University of the Pacific

Chuck Williams is Dean of the Eberhard School of Business at the University of the Pacific. Previously, Chuck was associate professor of Management at the M.J. Neeley School of Business at Texas Christian University, where he has also served as an associate dean and the chair of the Management Department. He received his B.A. in Psychology from Valparaiso University, and specialized in the areas of Organizational Behavior, Human Resources, and Strategic Management while earning his M.B.A and Ph.D. in Business Administration from Michigan State University. Previously, he taught at Michigan State University and was on the faculty of Oklahoma State University.

His research interests include employee recruitment and turnover, performance appraisal, and employee training and goal-setting. Chuck has published research in the *Journal of Applied Psychology*, the *Academy of Management Journal*, *Human Resource Management Review*, *Personnel Psychology*, and the *Organizational Research Methods Journal*. He was a member of the *Journal of Management*'s Editorial Board, and serves as a reviewer for numerous other academic journals. He was also the webmaster for the Research Methods Division of the Academy of Management (**http://www.aom.pace.edu/rmd**). Chuck is a co-recipient of the Society for Human Resource Management's Yoder-Heneman Research Award.

Chuck has consulted for a number of organizations, General Motors, IBM, JCPenney, Tandy Corporation, Trism Trucking, Central Bank and Trust, StuartBacon, the City of Fort Worth, the American Cancer Society, and others. He has taught in executive development programs at Oklahoma State University, the University of Oklahoma, and Texas Christian University.

Chuck teaches a number of different courses, but has been privileged to teach his favorite course, Introduction to Management, for nearly 20 years. His teaching philosophy is based on four principles: (1) courses should be engaging and interesting; (2) there's nothing as practical as a good theory; (3) students learn by doing; and (4) students learn when they are challenged. The undergraduate students at TCU's Neeley School of Business named him instructor of the year. He was also a recipient of TCU's Dean's Teaching Award.

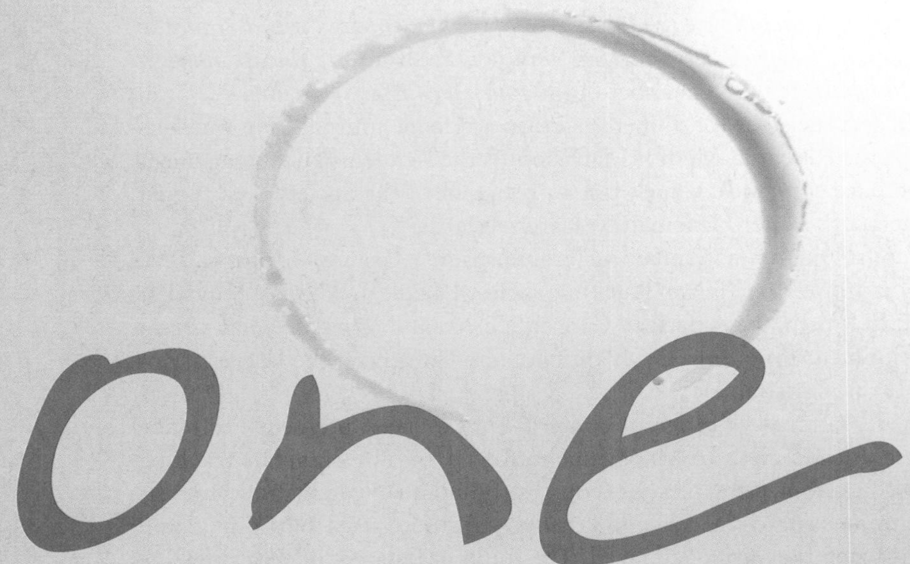
one

PART 1

Introduction to Management

Chapter 1

Management

This chapter begins by defining management and discussing the functions of management. We look at what managers do, what it takes to be a manager, what companies look for in their managers, the most serious mistakes managers make, and what it is like to make the tough transition from being a worker to being a manager.

Chapter 2

The History of Management

This chapter reviews the historical origins of management ideas and practice and the historical changes that produced the need for managers. You'll learn about various schools of management thought and the key contributions made by important management theorists.

Chapter 3

Organizational Environments and Cultures

Chapter 3 examines the internal and external forces that affect business, including how those forces affect the decisions and performance of a company. We cover the general environment that affects all organizations and the specific environment unique to each company.

Chapter 4

Ethics and Social Responsibility

This chapter examines ethical behavior in the workplace and explains how unethical behavior can expose a business to legal penalties. You'll read about the influences on ethical decision making and learn the practical steps that managers can take to improve ethical decision making.

Management

Learning Outcomes:

1 Describe what management is.
2 Explain the four functions of management.
3 Describe different kinds of managers.
4 Explain the major roles and subroles that managers perform in their jobs.
5 Explain what companies look for in managers.
6 Discuss the top mistakes that managers make in their jobs.
7 Describe the transition that employees go through when they are promoted to management.
8 Explain how and why companies can create competitive advantage through people.

© VEER

In This Chapter:

What Would You Do?

Nortel Headquarters, Toronto, Ontario, Canada.[1] When people use the Internet or make calls on their cell phones, the companies providing the Internet and cell phone service are probably using network or CDMA (code division multiple access) products made by Nortel Networks. And with its products used everywhere in the world, Nortel should be performing better. At least that's what you thought before deciding to become Nortel's new CEO and began working 100 hours a week to turn around this financially struggling company. You had hoped that your 25 years at GE, where you ran five of its key businesses, and your five years as the president and chief operating officer at Motorola would have prepared you to be Nortel's new CEO. But you underestimated the magnitude of the problems.

The most serious problem occurred six months after you started. After the previous management team overreported earnings to trigger corporate bonuses, Nortel had supposedly solved the company's financial-reporting problems. But now, for the third year in a row, Nortel incorrectly overestimated its profits and had to report, yet again, that it had earned substantially less than first reported. A financial analyst summed up the seriousness of the problem this way, "If you get three speeding tickets in a year, in many states you get your license pulled. . . . It's a big deal. It's a red flag." To no one's surprise, Wall Street hammered Nortel's stock price. Soon after, shareholders who had seen the value of Nortel stock lose $30 billion brought two class-action lawsuits against the company, seeking $9 billion in damages. The lawsuits, if successful, would put Nortel out of business. Restating earnings also had demoralizing effects within the company; the percentage of employees highly satisfied with their jobs dropped from 51 percent before to 40 percent after.

In addition, Nortel was running out of cash. Your job as CEO was to persuade skeptical financial companies to lend Nortel $2 billion to keep the company afloat. But before you could ask for more money, you had to cut costs by reducing retiree benefits and by laying off 1,900 employees and 350 managers. On top of that, Nortel's key cellular technology, CDMA, was aging, and losing out to newer, more powerful cell phone standards and equipment.

With problems mounting, you began losing sleep. Could you, in the end, fix the problems and return Nortel to profitability? With 35 percent of CEOs ultimately fired from their jobs, could you save yours? To do so, Nortel would have to get better, and fast. With billions in losses, and the need for an immediate $2 billion cash infusion, what steps must you take right now to ensure Nortel's short-term survival? Then, how should you deal with the $9 billion class-action suit that could put you out of business? Finally, if you solve those crises, what does Nortel need to do in the long run to become a more efficient company?

If you were the new CEO of Nortel Networks, what would you do?

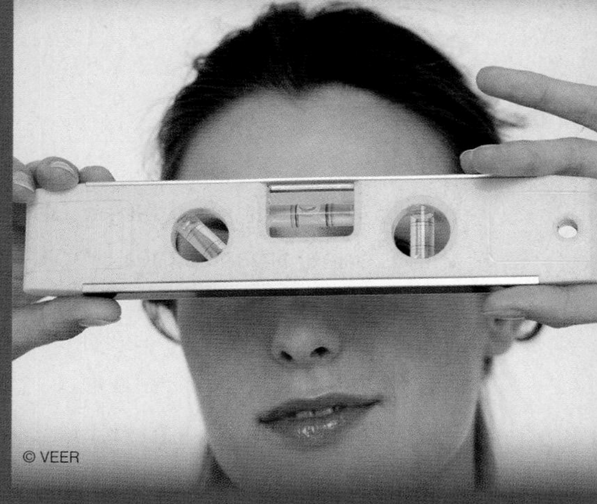

© VEER

Activities + Videos

CengageNOW Audio study guide, electronic flashcards, author FAQ videos, On the Job and Biz Flix videos, concept tutorial, and concept exercise

Web (academic.cengage.com/management/williams) Quiz, PowerPoint slides, and glossary terms for this chapter

© VEER

Study Tip

Use your textbook more like a notebook and less like a reference book. The margins are a great place for writing questions, highlighting important concepts, and adding examples to help you remember the material. Writing in your book makes it a better study tool.

Each chapter opener contains an activities and videos list that alerts you to the materials outside your book that can help you better understand assignments, work on group projects, and study for tests and exams.

"What's New" Companies

Nortel Networks
General Motors
United Parcel Service
Wal-Mart
AT&T
ExxonMobil
Google
Yahoo!
Xerox
Continental Airlines
Whirlpool
Norfolk Southern
Lloyds Pharmacy
Hewlett-Packard
Kikkoman
CDW
J.M. Smucker
And others . . .

The management issues facing Nortel are fundamental to any organization: How do we plan to get things done, organize the company to be efficient and effective, lead and motivate employees, and put in place controls to make sure our plans are followed and our goals are met? Good management is basic to starting a business, growing a business, and maintaining a business once it has achieved some measure of success.

We begin this chapter by defining management and discussing the functions of management. Next, we look at what managers do by examining the four kinds of managers and reviewing the various roles that managers play. Then we investigate what it takes to be a manager by reviewing management skills, what companies look for in their managers, the most serious mistakes managers make, and what it is like to make the tough transition from being a worker to being a manager. We finish this chapter by examining the competitive advantage that companies gain from good management. In other words, we end the chapter by learning how to establish a competitive advantage through people.

WHAT IS MANAGEMENT?

Mistake #1. A high-level bank manager reduces a marketing manager to tears by angrily criticizing her in front of others for a mistake that wasn't hers.[2] Mistake #2. Six months after he attacked a female coworker but wasn't fired, a Dairy Queen employee sits next to a customer, bites her, and declares, "I am like Dracula."[3] Mistake #3. Guidant recalled 50,000 heart defibrillators after 45 failed and two people died. However, Guidant continued to sell these defective products for three years, knowing that they might short-circuit. Patients were told that if they heard a beeping noise, their defibrillator was malfunctioning and they should see their doctor or go to an emergency room.[4]

Ah, bad managers and bad management. Is it any wonder that companies pay management consultants nearly $150 billion a year for advice with basic management issues, such as how to lead people effectively, organize the company efficiently, and manage large-scale projects and processes?[5] This textbook will help you understand some of the basic issues that management consultants help companies resolve (and it won't cost you billions of dollars).

After reading the next two sections, you should be able to

1. *describe what management is.*
2. *explain the four functions of management.*

1 Management Is . . .

Many of today's managers got their start welding on the factory floor, clearing dishes off tables, helping customers fit a suit, or wiping up a spill in aisle 3. Similarly, lots of you will start at the bottom and work your way up. There's no better way to get to know your competition, your customers, and your business. But whether you begin your career at the entry level or as a supervisor, your job as a manager is not to do the work, but to help others do theirs. **Management** is getting work done through others. Pat Carrigan, a former elementary school principal who became a manager at a GENERAL MOTORS car parts plant, says, "I've never made a part in my life, and I don't really have any plans to make one. That's not my job. My job is to create an environment where people who do make them can make them right, can make them right the first time, can make them at a competitive cost, and can do so with some sense of responsibility and pride in what they're doing. I don't have to know how to make a part to do any of those things."[6]

Pat Carrigan's description of managerial responsibilities suggests that managers also have to be concerned with efficiency and effectiveness in the work process. **Efficiency** is getting work done with a minimum of effort, expense, or waste. For example, UNITED PARCEL SERVICE, which delivers over 3.5 billion packages a year, will save 14 million gallons of fuel annually when it fully implements its new PAL software. PAL, which stands for Pre-Load Assistance Label, is part of an overall computerized route and load planning system that shows truck loaders where to put packages on the delivery truck (to maximize the number of packages per truck), determines how many packages and stops a UPS driver has and what routes should be taken (to minimize travel time, distances, and fuel costs), and tells drivers exactly where your package is on the truck when they stop in front of your house (to minimize search time at each stop).[7]

management getting work done through others

efficiency getting work done with a minimum of effort, expense, or waste

effectiveness accomplishing tasks that help fulfill organizational objectives

By itself, efficiency is not enough to ensure success. Managers must also strive for **effectiveness,** which is accomplishing tasks that help fulfill organizational objectives, such as customer service and satisfaction. WAL-MART's new computerized scheduling system measures trends in store sales and customer traffic so it can have more employees on the job whenever its stores are busy. Tests in 39 stores indicated that 70 percent of customers reported improved checkout times and service using this scheduling system. Wal-Mart spokesperson Sarah Clark said, "The advantages are simple: We will benefit by improving the shopping experience by having the right number of associates to meet our customers' needs when they shop our stores."[8] The computerized system also frees managers to manage instead of calculating schedules. Normally, it takes a Wal-Mart manager a full day to schedule the weekly shift for a single store. By contrast, in that time the computerized scheduling system can calculate the schedules for all of Wal-Mart's 1.3 million workers.

UPS saves 14 million gallons of fuel each year, not to mention time, by planning its routes to minimize left-hand turns, which take longer to make than right-hand turns.

Review 1: Management Is . . .

Good management is working through others to accomplish tasks that help fulfill organizational objectives as efficiently as possible.

mgmt: fact

History of Management

Management as a field of study may be just 125 years old, but management ideas and practices have actually been used from the earliest times of recorded history. Early on, the Greeks learned that they could improve the productivity of repetitious tasks by performing them to music. The basic idea was to use a flute, drum, or song lyrics to pace people to work in unison using the same efficient motion, stimulate them to work faster and longer, and make the boring work more fun.

2 Management Functions

Henri Fayol, who was a managing director (CEO) of a large steel company in the early 1900s, was one of the founders of the field of management. You'll learn more about Fayol and management's other key contributors when you read about the history of management in Chapter 2. Based on his 20 years of experience as a CEO, Fayol argued that "the success of an enterprise generally depends much more on the administrative ability of its leaders than on their technical ability."[9] In other words, eBay, the world's largest online auction company, succeeds because of CEO Meg Whitman's capabilities as a manager and not because of her abilities to write computer code.

According to Fayol, to be successful, managers need to perform five managerial functions: planning, organizing, coordinating, commanding, and controlling.[10] Today, though, most management textbooks have dropped the coordinating function and refer to Fayol's commanding function as "leading." Consequently, Fayol's management functions are known today as planning, organizing, leading, and controlling. Studies indicate that managers who perform these management functions well are more successful. For example, the more time that CEOs spend planning, the more profitable their companies are.[11] Over a 25-year period, **AT&T** found that employees with better planning and decision-making skills were more likely to be promoted into management jobs, to be successful as managers, and to be promoted into upper levels of management.[12]

The evidence is clear. Managers serve their companies well when they plan, organize, lead, and control. Consequently, as shown in Exhibit 1.1, this textbook is organized based on the functions of management. Furthermore, throughout this text, the major sections within each chapter are numbered using a single digit: 1, 2, 3, and so on. The subsections are consecutively numbered, beginning with the major section number. For example, "2.1" indicates the first subsection under the second major section. This numbering system should help you easily see the relationships among topics and follow the topic sequence. It will also help your instructor refer to specific topics during class discussion.

Now let's take a closer look at each of the management functions: ***2.1 planning****,* ***2.2 organizing****,* ***2.3 leading****, and* ***2.4 controlling****.*

2.1 Planning

Planning is determining organizational goals and a means for achieving them. As you'll learn in Chapter 5, planning is one of the best ways to improve performance. It encourages people to work harder, to work hard for extended periods, to engage in behaviors directly related to goal accomplishment, and to think of better ways to do their jobs. But most importantly, companies that plan have larger profits and faster growth than companies that don't plan.

planning determining organizational goals and a means for achieving them

For example, the question, "What business are we in?" is at the heart of strategic planning, which you'll learn about in Chapter 6. If you can answer the question "What business are you in?" in two sentences or less, chances are you have a very clear plans for your business. **ExxonMobil** CEO Rex Tillerson states clearly and simply that "conventional oil and gas . . . is the business we are in." When asked why ExxonMobil is not heavily investing in ethanol, a crop-based renewable source of fuel, he replies, "We are not in those other businesses."[13] Likewise, **Google**, which makes its money from search-based Internet advertising, says that it is not in the advertising business. Its business is to "organize the world's information and make it universally accessible and useful."[14] So when Google spent $1.65 billion to buy YouTube, it was adhering to its business by helping users access and organize video content. You'll learn more about planning in Chapter 5 on planning and decision making, Chapter 6 on organizational strategy, Chapter 7 on innovation and change, and Chapter 8 on global management.

Part 1: Introduction to Management

Chapter 1: Management
Chapter 2: The History of Management
Chapter 3: Organizational Environments and Cultures
Chapter 4: Ethics and Social Responsibility

Part 2: Planning

Chapter 5: Planning and Decision Making
Chapter 6: Organizational Strategy
Chapter 7: Innovation and Change
Chapter 8: Global Management

Part 3: Organizing

Chapter 9: Designing Adaptive Organizations
Chapter 10: Managing Teams
Chapter 11: Managing Human Resource Systems
Chapter 12: Managing Individuals and a Diverse Work Force

Part 4: Leading

Chapter 13: Motivation
Chapter 14: Leadership
Chapter 15: Managing Communication

Part 5: Controlling

Chapter 16: Control
Chapter 17: Managing Information
Chapter 18: Managing Service and Manufacturing Operations

Exhibit 1.1
Management Functions and Organization of the Textbook

2.2 Organizing

Organizing is deciding where decisions will be made, who will do what jobs and tasks, and who will work for whom in the company.

Go to **Yahoo!**'s home page and take a look at the vast number of topics, news, mail, messenger, shopping (from autos and finance to Hot Jobs, music, and real estate), small business, and featured services (downloads, mobile, voice, and personal websites). How would you organize this vast array of topics and activities? Yahoo! does it with two customer groups, audience and advertiser/publisher, and one technology group. The audience group has responsibility for Yahoo!'s products in search, media, communities and communications. The advertising/publishing group helps large advertisers and agencies, small- and medium-sized businesses, local advertisers, resellers, and publishers connect with their target customers across the Internet. Finally, the technology group supports the entire organization by creating technological capabilities and platforms. Yahoo!'s CEO said, "We believe having a more customer-focused organization, supported by robust technology, will speed the development of leading-edge experiences for our most valuable audience segments."[15]

You'll learn more about organizing in Chapter 9 on designing organizations, Chapter 10 on managing teams, Chapter 11 on managing human resources, and Chapter 12 on managing individuals and a diverse work force.

organizing deciding where decisions will be made, who will do what jobs and tasks, and who will work for whom

META-ANALYSIS

what *really* works.

Some studies show that having two drinks a day increases life expectancy by decreasing the chances of having a heart attack. Yet other studies show that having two drinks a day shortens life expectancy. For years, we've "buttered" our morning toast with margarine instead of butter because margarine was supposed to be better for our health. Now, however, new studies show that the trans-fatty acids in margarine may be just as bad for our arteries as butter. Confusing scientific results like these frustrate ordinary people who want to "eat right" and "live right." They also make many people question just how useful most scientific research really is.

Managers also find themselves questioning the conflicting scientific research published in journals like the *Academy of Management Journal,* the *Academy of Management Review,* the *Strategic Management Journal,* the *Journal of Applied Psychology,* and *Administrative Science Quarterly*. The *Wall Street Journal* may quote a management research article from one of these journals that says that total quality management is the best thing since sliced bread (without butter or margarine). Then, just six months later, the *Wall Street Journal* will quote a different article from the same journal that says that total quality management doesn't work. If management professors and researchers have trouble deciding what works and what doesn't, how can practicing managers know?

Thankfully, a research tool called **meta-analysis**, which is a study of studies, is helping management scholars understand how well their research supports management theories. Meta-analysis is also useful for practicing managers because it shows what works and the conditions under which management techniques may work better or worse in the "real world." Meta-analysis is based on the simple idea that if one study shows that a management technique doesn't work and another study shows that it does, an average of those results is probably the best estimate of how well that management practice works (or doesn't work). For example, medical researchers Richard Peto and Rory Collins averaged all of the different results from several hundred studies investigating the relationship between aspirin and heart attacks. Their analysis, based on more than 120,000 patients from numerous studies, showed that aspirin lowered the incidence of heart attacks by an average of 4 percent. Prior to this study, doctors prescribed aspirin as a preventive measure for only 38 percent of heart-attack victims. Today, because of the meta-analysis results, doctors prescribe aspirin for 72 percent of heart-attack victims.

Fortunately, you don't need a Ph.D. to understand the statistics reported in a meta-analysis. In fact, one primary advantage of meta-analysis over traditional significance tests is that you can convert meta-analysis statistics into intuitive numbers that anyone can easily understand.

Each meta-analysis reported in the "What Really Works" sections of this textbook is accompanied by an easy-to-understand statistic called the *probability of success*. As its name suggests, the probability of success shows how often a management technique will work.

For example, meta-analyses suggest that the best predictor of a job applicant's on-the-job performance is a test of general mental ability. In other words, smarter people tend to be better workers. The average correlation (one of those often-misunderstood statistics) between scores on general mental ability tests and job performance is .60. However, very few people understand what a correlation of .60 means. What most managers want to know is how often they will hire the right person if they choose job applicants based on general mental ability test scores. Likewise, they want to know how much difference a cognitive ability test makes when hiring new workers. The probability of success may be high, but if the difference isn't really that large, is it worth a manager's time to have job applicants take a general mental ability test?

Well, our user-friendly statistics indicate that it's wise to have job applicants take a general mental ability test. In fact, the probability of success, shown in graphical form here, is 76 percent. This means that an employee hired on the basis of a good score on a general mental ability test stands a 76 percent chance of being a better performer than someone picked at random from the pool of all job applicants. So chances are you're going to be right much more often than wrong if you use a general mental ability test to make hiring decisions.[16]

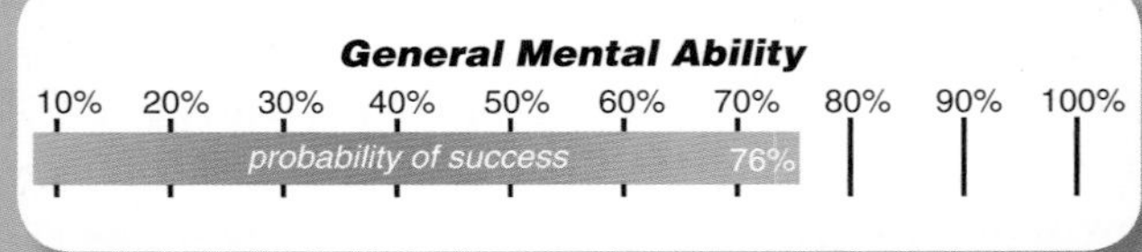

In summary, each "What Really Works" section in this textbook is based on meta-analysis research, which provides the best scientific evidence that management professors and researchers have about what works and what doesn't work in management. We will use the easy-to-understand index known as the *probability of success* to indicate how well a management idea or strategy is likely to work in the workplace. Of course, no idea or technique works every time and in every circumstance. Nevertheless, the management ideas and strategies discussed in the "What Really Works" sections can usually make a meaningful difference where you work. In today's competitive, fast-changing, global marketplace, few managers can afford to overlook proven management strategies like the ones discussed in "What Really Works."

2.3 Leading

Our third management function, **leading**, involves inspiring and motivating workers to work hard to achieve organizational goals.

When Anne Mulcahy became **Xerox**'s CEO, the company was on the brink of bankruptcy—it was $17.1 billion in debt and had only $154 million in cash. In addition, three years of steeply declining revenues and increasing losses had dropped the company's stock price from $64 a share to just $4.43. Mulcahy admits that the responsibility of turning the company around frightened her: "Nothing spooked me as much as waking up in the middle of the night and thinking about 96,000 people and retirees and what would happen if this thing went south."[17] Still, she took the job.

Mulcahy, who traveled to two and sometimes three cities a day to talk to Xerox managers and employees, implored them to "save each dollar as if it were your own." And at each stop, she reminded them, "Remember, by my calculations, there are [she fills in the number] selling days left in the quarter."[18] Mulcahy said, "One of the things I care most about at Xerox is the morale and motivation at the company. I think it is absolutely critical to being able to deliver results. People have to feel engaged, motivated and feel they are making a contribution to something that is important. I spend the vast majority of my time with customers and employees, and there is nothing more important for any of us to do as leaders than communicate and engage with our two most important constituencies."[19]

> "People have to feel engaged, motivated and feel they are making a contribution to something that is important."
>
> ANNE MULCAHY, CEO, XEROX

Today, as a result of Mulcahy's leadership and the hard work of dedicated Xerox employees, Xerox is back on its feet, having returned to profitability and financial stability.[20] You'll learn more about leading in Chapter 13 on motivation, Chapter 14 on leadership, and Chapter 15 on managing communication.

2.4 Controlling

The last function of management, **controlling**, is monitoring progress toward goal achievement and taking corrective action when progress isn't being made. The basic control process involves setting standards to achieve goals, comparing actual performance to those standards, and then making changes to return performance to those standards.

Needing to cut costs (the standard) to restore profitability (the goal), **Continental Airlines** started giving passengers small cups of their soft drinks instead of an entire can (one corrective action among many). Company spokesperson Rahsaan Johnson defended the move, saying, "Flight attendants have been telling us that the trash bags they carry were so heavy because of all the [wasted] liquid. We were pouring almost half away."[21] Although Continental will still give entire soft drink cans to customers who request them, serving smaller drinks saves the company $100,000 a year in costs.

You'll learn more about the control function in Chapter 16 on control, Chapter 17 on managing information, and Chapter 18 on managing service and manufacturing operations.

meta-analysis a study of studies, a statistical approach that provides one of the best scientific estimates of how well management theories and practices work

leading inspiring and motivating workers to work hard to achieve organizational goals

controlling monitoring progress toward goal achievement and taking corrective action when needed

Review 2: Management Functions

Henri Fayol's classic management functions are known today as planning, organizing, leading, and controlling. Planning is determining organizational goals and a means for achieving them. Organizing is deciding where decisions will be made, who will do what jobs and tasks, and who will work for whom. Leading is inspiring and motivating workers to work hard to achieve organizational goals. Controlling is monitoring progress toward goal achievement and taking corrective action when needed. Studies show that performing these management functions well leads to better managerial performance.

WHAT DO MANAGERS DO?

Not all managerial jobs are the same. The demands and requirements placed on the CEO of Sony are significantly different from those placed on the manager of your local Wendy's restaurant.

After reading the next two sections, you should be able to

3 describe different kinds of managers.

4 explain the major roles and subroles that managers perform in their jobs.

3 Kinds of Managers

*As shown in Exhibit 1.2, there are four kinds of managers, each with different jobs and responsibilities: **3.1 top managers, 3.2 middle managers, 3.3 first-line managers,** and **3.4 team leaders.***

3.1 Top Managers

Top managers hold positions like chief executive officer (CEO), chief operating officer (COO), chief financial officer (CFO), and chief information officer (CIO), and are responsible for the overall direction of the organization. Top managers have the following responsibilities.[22] First, they are responsible for creating a context for change. In fact, the CEOs of Walt Disney, Fannie Mae, Boeing, Morgan Stanley, American International Group, Merck, and Pfizer were all fired within a year's time precisely because they had not moved fast enough to bring about significant changes in their companies. Indeed, in both Europe and the United States, 35 percent of all CEOs are eventually fired because of their inability to successfully change their companies.[23] Creating a context for change includes forming a long-range vision or mission for the company. As one CEO said, "The CEO has to think about the future more than anyone."

"What's New" Company

Second, much more than used to be the case, top managers are responsible for developing employees' commitment to and ownership of the company's performance. Trusting that his 61,000 employees could dramatically increase product innovation at WHIRLPOOL appliances, then-CEO David Whitwam put $135 million directly into their hands and told them to come up with new ideas. Furthermore, he encouraged them to go to their bosses with their ideas. And if

top managers executives responsible for the overall direction of the organization their bosses wouldn't listen, they were to bring their new product ideas directly to him. Employees flocked to an in-house website with a course on innovation and a list of all the new suggestions and ideas, racking up 300,000 hits on the site each month. Of the commitment displayed by his workers, Whitwam says, "I had never seen a strategy that was so energizing to so many people." Today, revenue from innovative products has quadrupled. And instead of cutting prices to maintain sales, Whirlpool's prices are now rising 5 percent per year because customers are willing to pay more for its innovative products, such as the Duet washer and dryer, which were designed based on employees' ideas.[24]

JOBS

Top Managers
- CEO
- COO
- CFO
- CIO
- Vice President
- Corporate Head

Middle Managers
- General Manager
- Plant Manager
- Regional Manager
- Divisional Manager

First-Line Managers
- Office Manager
- Shift Supervisor
- Department Manager

Team Leaders
- Team Leader
- Team Contact
- Group Facilitator

RESPONSIBILITIES AND DUTIES

Top Managers:
- change
- commitment
- culture
- environment

Middle Managers:
- resources
- objectives
- coordination
- subunit performance
- strategy implementation

First-Line Managers:
- nonmanagerial worker supervision
- teaching and training
- scheduling

Team Leaders:
- facilitation
- external relationships
- internal relationships

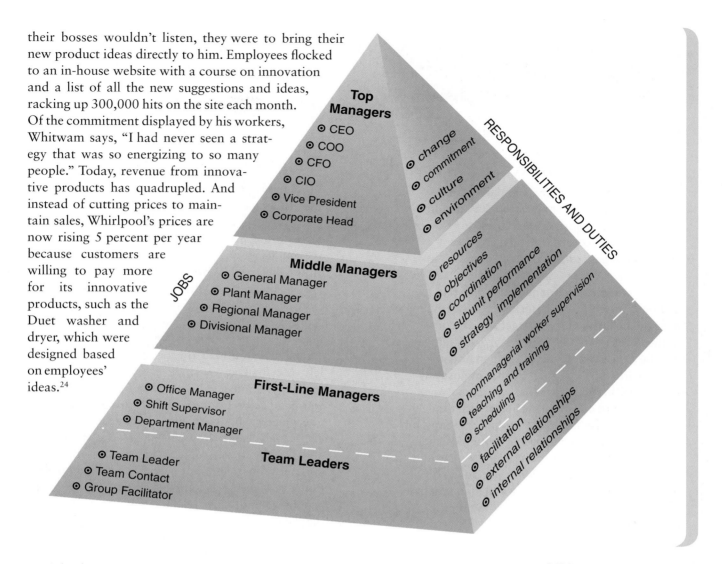

Exhibit 1.2

Jobs and Responsibilities of Four Kinds of Managers

Third, top managers are responsible for creating a positive organizational culture through language and action. Top managers impart company values, strategies, and lessons through what they do and say to others, both inside and outside the company. One CEO said, "I write memos to the board and our operating committee. I'm sure they get the impression I dash them off, but usually they've been drafted 10 or 20 times. The bigger you get, the more your ability to communicate becomes important. So what I write, I write very carefully. I labor over it."[25] Above all, no matter what they communicate, it's critical for CEOs to send and reinforce clear, consistent messages.[26] A former *Fortune* 500 CEO said, "I tried to [use] exactly the same words every time so that I didn't produce a lot of, 'Last time you said this, this time you said that.' You've got to say the same thing over and over and over."[27]

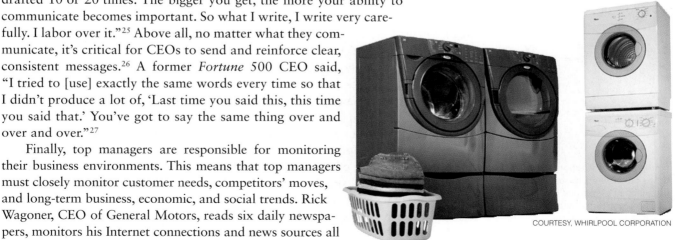

COURTESY, WHIRLPOOL CORPORATION

Finally, top managers are responsible for monitoring their business environments. This means that top managers must closely monitor customer needs, competitors' moves, and long-term business, economic, and social trends. Rick Wagoner, CEO of General Motors, reads six daily newspapers, monitors his Internet connections and news sources all day, and skims a variety of magazines from all over the world. Says Wagoner, "You've gotta know what the hell is going on in your business. If you've got a problem in China, you've gotta get into it and make sure that it's getting fixed. You've got to be on top of your business enough to know where are the problems, where are the opportunities."[28]

doing the right thing

Tell and Show People That Ethics Matter

Because managers set the standard for others in the workplace, unethical behavior and practices quickly spread when they don't do the right thing. One of the most important things managers can do is to tell people that ethics matter. When Charles Holliday, Jr., CEO of DuPont, was a young manager, he was told by DuPont's then-CEO Dick Heckert, "This company lives by the letter of its contracts and the intent of those contracts." Says Holliday, "I still remember the expression on his face when he said those words, and I've lived by that philosophy ever since." In today's business world, however, with one-third of workers reporting that they've seen their bosses lie, steal from the company, or break the law, talk clearly isn't enough. Holliday says, "Just saying you're ethical isn't very useful. You have to earn trust by what you do every day." So, tell the people whom you manage that ethics matter. Then show them by doing the right thing yourself.[30]

3.2 Middle Managers

Middle managers hold positions like plant manager, regional manager, or divisional manager. They are responsible for setting objectives consistent with top management's goals and for planning and implementing subunit strategies for achieving those objectives.[29] One specific middle management responsibility is to plan and allocate resources to meet objectives. Another major responsibility is to coordinate and link groups, departments, and divisions within a company. After a hurricane destroyed five miles of railroad tracks outside New Orleans, Jeff McCracken, a chief engineer at **Norfolk Southern**, consulted with three bridge companies, and managed a team of 100 employees and dozens of engineers who, by sleeping in campers and working around the clock, rebuilt the tracks in less than a week. McCracken said, "It was a colossal job that took more than 400 moves with heavy equipment." But McCracken was happiest about "working with people from all parts of the company—and getting the job done without anyone getting hurt."[31]

A third responsibility of middle management is to monitor and manage the performance of the subunits and individual managers who report to them. Graeme Betts is the manager of the Southwest region for **Lloyds Pharmacy** in England. While Betts works with people at all levels, from health-care assistants to board directors, he spends most of his time with the nine area managers who report to him. In terms of monitoring and managing the performance of his area managers and, in turn, the store managers who report to them, Betts says, "We have 231 pharmacies, and as a [management] team our task is to ensure that our pharmacies are as good as they can be, and are offering a great service to our customers. To this end we are focused on providing an efficient [drug] dispensing service, and continually developing new professional services such as . . . smoking cessation and medicines-use reviews."[32]

Finally, middle managers are also responsible for implementing the changes or strategies generated by top managers. Wal-Mart's strategy reflects its advertising slogan, "Always Low Prices." When Wal-Mart began selling groceries in its new 200,000-square-foot supercenters, it made purchasing manager Brian Wilson responsible for buying perishable goods more cheaply than Wal-Mart's competitors. When small produce suppliers had trouble meeting Wal-Mart's needs, Wilson worked closely with them and connected them to RetailLink, Wal-Mart's computer network, "which allows our suppliers immediate access to all information needed

middle managers responsible for setting objectives consistent with top management's goals and for planning and implementing subunit strategies for achieving these objectives to help run the business." Over time, these steps helped the produce suppliers lower costs and deliver the enormous quantities of fresh fruits and vegetables that Wal-Mart's supercenters need.[33] They also helped Wal-Mart become the world's largest grocer.[34]

3.3 First-Line Managers

First-line managers hold positions like office manager, shift supervisor, or department manager. The primary responsibility of first-line managers is to manage the performance of entry-level employees, who are directly responsible for producing a company's goods and services. Thus, first-line managers are the only managers who don't supervise other managers. First-line managers have the following responsibilities.

First-line managers encourage, monitor, and reward the performance of their workers. For example, Jeff Dexheimer requires the waiters and waitresses he supervises at the upscale Melting Pot restaurant in St. Louis to memorize a complex menu and a 400-item wine list. Says Dexheimer, "They've got to know every liquor, every beer, every food item, as well as the sauces it comes with." To reduce turnover and keep his 65 employees motivated, Dexheimer gives out $25 nightly rewards for "best attitude" or for selling the most wine. Since his employees are young and mostly single, he makes sure they work only one night each weekend. And once a week, after the restaurant closes, he takes his entire staff out for drinks. Says Dexheimer, as a manager, "I don't make myself successful. My employees make me successful."[35]

First-line managers teach entry-level employees how to do their jobs. Damian Mogavero's company, Avero LLC, helps restaurants analyze sales data for each member of a restaurant's wait staff. Restaurant managers who use these data, says Mogavero, will often take their top-selling server to lunch each week as a reward. The best managers, however, will also take their poorest-selling servers out to lunch to talk about what they can do to improve their performance.[36] Likewise, Coca-Cola manager Tom Mattia says, "I try to make every interaction I have with someone on my team a teaching experience. There are always specific work issues that need to get addressed, but then I try to explain my thinking behind an approach so people can get more experience."[37]

First-line managers also make detailed schedules and operating plans based on middle management's intermediate-range plans. In fact, in contrast to the long-term plans of top managers (three to five years out) and the intermediate plans of middle managers (6 to 18 months out), first-line managers engage in plans and actions that typically produce results within two weeks.[38] For example, consider the typical convenience store manager (for example, 7-Eleven) who starts the day by driving by competitors' stores to inspect their gasoline prices and then checks the outside of his or her store for anything that might need maintenance, such as burned-out lights or signs, or restocking, like windshield washer fluid and paper towels. Then comes an inside check, where the manager determines what needs to be done for that day (Are there enough coffee and donuts for breakfast or enough sandwiches for lunch?). Once today is planned, the manager turns to weekend orders. After accounting for the weather (hot or cold) and the sales trends at the same time last year, the manager makes sure the store will have enough beer, soft drinks, and Sunday papers on hand. Finally, the manager looks 7 to 10 days ahead for hiring needs. Because of strict hiring procedures (basic math tests, drug tests, and background checks), it can take that long to hire new employees. Said one convenience-store manager, "I have to continually interview, even if I am fully staffed."[39]

first-line managers train and supervise the performance of nonmanagerial employees who are directly responsible for producing the company's products or services

3.4 Team Leaders

The fourth kind of manager is a team leader. This relatively new kind of management job developed as companies shifted to self-managing teams, which, by definition, have no formal supervisor. In traditional management hierarchies, first-line managers are responsible for the performance of nonmanagerial employees and have the authority to hire and fire workers, make job assignments, and control resources. Team leaders play a very different role because in this new structure, teams now perform nearly all of the functions performed by first-line managers under traditional hierarchies.[40] Instead of directing individuals' work, **team leaders** facilitate team activities toward goal accomplishment. For example, HEWLETT-PACKARD's ad for a team leader position says, "Job seeker must enjoy coaching, working with people, and bringing about improvement through hands-off guidance and leadership."[41] Team leaders who fail to understand this key difference often struggle in their roles. A team leader at Texas Instruments said, "I didn't buy into teams, partly because there was no clear plan on what I was supposed to do. . . . I never let the operators [team members] do any scheduling or any ordering of parts because that was mine. I figured as long as I had that, I had a job."[42]

"WHAT'S NEW" COMPANY

Team leaders fulfill the following responsibilities.[43] First, team leaders are responsible for facilitating team performance. This doesn't mean team leaders are responsible for team performance. They aren't. The team is. Team leaders help their team members plan and schedule work, learn to solve problems, and work effectively with each other. Management consultant Franklin Jonath says, "The idea is for the team leader to be at the service of the group. It should be clear that the team members own the outcome. The leader is there to bring intellectual, emotional, and spiritual resources to the team. Through his or her actions, the leader should be able to show the others how to think about the work that they're doing in the context of their lives. It's a tall order, but the best teams have such leaders."[44]

team leaders managers responsible for facilitating team activities toward goal accomplishment

Second, team leaders are responsible for managing external relationships. Team leaders act as the bridge or liaison between their teams and other teams, departments, and divisions in a company. For example, if a member of Team A complains about the quality of Team B's work, Team A's leader is responsible for solving the problem by initiating a meeting with Team B's leader. Together, these team leaders are responsible for getting members of both teams to work together to solve the problem. If it's done right, the problem is solved without involving company management or blaming members of the other team.[45]

Even first-line managers perform the functions of management.

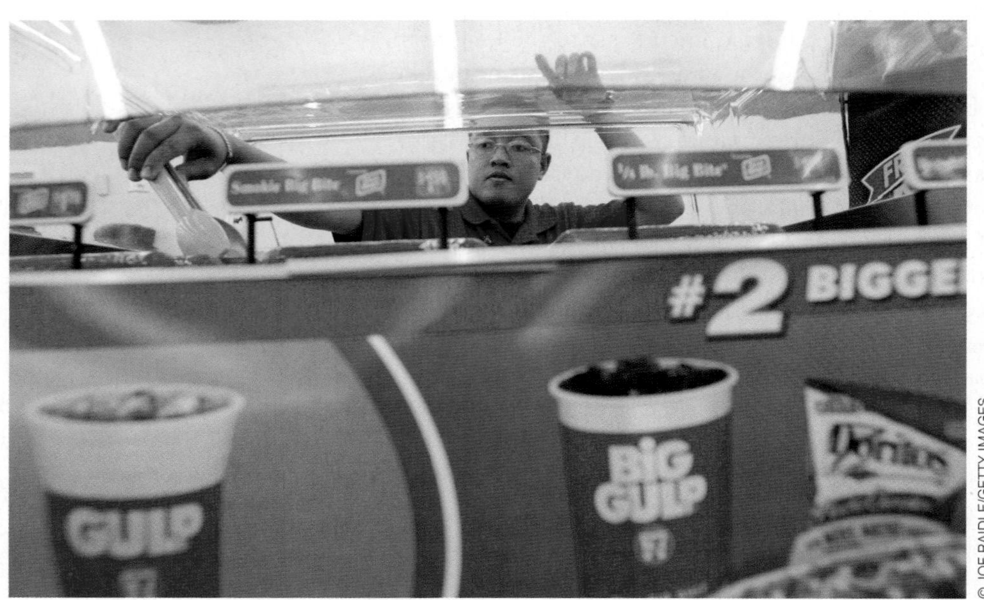

© JOE RAIDLE/GETTY IMAGES

Third, team leaders are responsible for internal team relationships. Getting along with others is much more important in team structures because team members can't get work done without the help of their teammates. For example, studies show that it's not the surgeon, but the interactions between the surgeon and all operating room team members that determine surgical outcomes. However, at 20 hospitals, 60 percent of the operating room team members—nurses, technicians, and other doctors—agreed with the statement, "In the ORs here, it is difficult to speak up if I perceive a problem with patient care."[46] And when operating room team members don't speak up, serious mistakes can occur, no matter how talented the surgeon. Consequently, surgeons are using "safety pauses" to better involve members of their surgical teams. The surgeon will pause, ask if anyone has concerns or comments, and address them if need be. Studies show that safety pauses reduce mistakes, such as operating on the wrong leg or beginning surgery with key surgical instruments missing.[47] You will learn more about teams in Chapter 10.

Review 3: Kinds of Managers

There are four different kinds of managers. Top managers are responsible for creating a context for change, developing attitudes of commitment and ownership, creating a positive organizational culture through words and actions, and monitoring their company's business environments. Middle managers are responsible for planning and allocating resources, coordinating and linking groups and departments, monitoring and managing the performance of subunits and managers, and implementing the changes or strategies generated by top managers. First-line managers are responsible for managing the performance of nonmanagerial employees, teaching direct reports how to do their jobs, and making detailed schedules and operating plans based on middle management's intermediate-range plans. Team leaders are responsible for facilitating team performance, managing external relationships, and facilitating internal team relationships.

4 Managerial Roles

So far, we have described managerial work by focusing on the functions of management and by examining the four kinds of managerial jobs. Although those are valid and accurate ways of categorizing managerial work, if you followed managers around as they perform their jobs, you probably would not use the terms *planning*, *organizing*, *leading*, and *controlling* to describe what they do.

In fact, that's exactly the conclusion that management researcher Henry Mintzberg came to when he followed around five American CEOs. Mintzberg spent a week shadowing each of the CEOs. He analyzed their mail, whom they talked to, and what they did. Mintzberg concluded that managers fulfill three major roles while performing their jobs:[48]

- *interpersonal roles*
- *informational roles*
- *decisional roles*

*In other words, managers talk to people, gather and give information, and make decisions. Furthermore, as shown in Exhibit 1.3, these three major roles can be subdivided into 10 subroles. Let's examine each major role—**4.1 interpersonal**, **4.2 informational**, and **4.3 decisional roles**—and their 10 subroles.*

Interpersonal Roles

- Figurehead
- Leader
- Liaison

Informational Roles

- Monitor
- Disseminator
- Spokesperson

Decisional Roles

- Entrepreneur
- Disturbance Handler
- Resource Allocator
- Negotiator

Source: Reprinted by permission of *Harvard Business Review* (an Exhibit) from "The Manager's Job: Folklore and Fact." By Mintzberg, H., *Harvard Business Review*, July–August 1975.

Exhibit 1.3

Mintzberg's Managerial Roles and Subroles

4.1 Interpersonal Roles

More than anything else, management jobs are people-intensive. Estimates vary with the level of management, but most managers spend between two-thirds and four-fifths of their time in face-to-face communication with others.[49] If you're a loner, or if you consider dealing with people a pain, then you may not be cut out for management work. In fulfilling the interpersonal role of management, managers perform three subroles: figurehead, leader, and liaison.

In the **figurehead role**, managers perform ceremonial duties like greeting company visitors, speaking at the opening of a new facility, or representing the company at a community luncheon to support local charities. For example, when Japan-based **KIKKOMAN** Corporation, the world's largest soy sauce maker, opened its first soy sauce manufacturing plant in Europe (in Hoogezand Sappemeer, the Netherlands), its CEO, Yuzaburo Mogi, gave a speech pledging that Kikkoman would be a good corporate citizen by donating to a local environmental conservation and water quality project and to the Rembrandt House Art Gallery.[50]

In the **leader role**, managers motivate and encourage workers to accomplish organizational objectives. At **CDW** (Computer Discount Warehouse), new CEO John Edwardson promised CDW's 2,750 workers that he would shave his head if the company met its third-quarter goals. Despite the industry downturn in computer sales, company employees responded. After announcing at a company function that the third-quarter goals had been met, Edwardson, as promised, had his head shaved to the harmonic sounds of a barbershop quartet.[51] At **J.M. SMUCKER**, that's right, the jelly and jam company, managers regularly thank employees with celebratory lunches and gift certificates. Tonie Williams, director of marketing for peanut butter, says she's been thanked more in her two years at Smucker than she was in her nine years at Nestlé, Kraft, and Procter & Gamble combined.[52] *Fortune* magazine recently included both CDW and Smucker in its annual list of the top 100 places to work in the United States.[53]

In the **liaison role**, managers deal with people outside their units. Studies consistently indicate that managers spend as much time with "outsiders" as they do with their own subordinates and their own bosses. In addition to his normal duties, Rajesh Hukku, chairman of j-Flex Solutions, a maker of financial-services software, regularly goes on sales calls, helps close sales deals, and markets his product to potential customers at industry conventions and forums.[54] The same holds true for the convenience store managers discussed earlier. From dealing with vendors who make store deliveries and set up product displays, to working with computer technicians who help with computer glitches and satellite connections to headquarters, to ordering from sales representatives who supply the mops and deli aprons used in the store, to calling the sheriff about stolen credit cards, even first-line managers spend much of their time dealing with outsiders.[55]

figurehead role the interpersonal role managers play when they perform ceremonial duties

leader role the interpersonal role managers play when they motivate and encourage workers to accomplish organizational objectives

liaison role the interpersonal role managers play when they deal with people outside their units

4.2 Informational Roles

Not only do managers spend most of their time in face-to-face contact with others, but they spend time obtaining and sharing information. Indeed, Mintzberg found that the managers in his study spent 40 percent of their time giving and getting information from others. In this regard, management can be viewed as processing information, gathering information by scanning the business environment and listening to others in face-to-face conversations, and then sharing that information with people inside and outside the company. Mintzberg described three informational subroles: monitor, disseminator, and spokesperson.

> More than anything else, management jobs are people-intensive.

In the **monitor role**, managers scan their environment for information, actively contact others for information, and, because of their personal contacts, receive a great deal of unsolicited information. Besides receiving firsthand information, managers monitor their environment by reading local newspapers and the *Wall Street Journal* to keep track of customers, competitors, and technological changes that may affect their businesses. Now, managers can also take advantage of electronic monitoring and distribution services that track the news wires (Associated Press, Reuters, and so on.) for stories related to their businesses. These services deliver customized electronic newspapers that include only stories on topics the managers specify. Business Wire (**http://www.businesswire.com**) offers services such as IndustryTrak, which monitors and distributes daily news headlines from major industries (for example, automotive, banking and financial, health, high tech).[56] CyberAlert (**http://www.cyberalert.com**) keeps round-the-clock track of new stories in categories chosen by each subscriber.[57] FNS NewsClips Online (**http://www.news-clips.com**) provides subscribers daily electronic news clips from more than 5,000 online news sites.[58]

Because of their numerous personal contacts and their access to subordinates, managers are often hubs for the distribution of critical information. In the **disseminator role**, managers share the information they have collected with their subordinates and others in the company. Although there will never be a complete substitute for face-to-face dissemination of information, the primary methods of communication in large companies like Continental Airlines and Cisco Systems are e-mail and voice mail. At Continental Airlines, the CEO broadcasts a voice mail message to all employees every Friday.[59] John Chambers, Cisco's CEO, says that 90 percent of his communication with employees is through e-mail and voice mail. Says Chambers, "If you don't have the ability to interface with customers, employees, and suppliers, you can't manage your business."[60]

In contrast to the disseminator role, in which managers distribute information to employees inside the company, in the **spokesperson role**, managers share information with people outside their departments and companies. One of the most common ways CEOs serve as spokespeople for their companies is at annual meetings with company shareholders or the board of directors. For example, at a Microsoft annual shareholder meeting, CEO Steve Ballmer told investors that Microsoft intended to offer its own Internet search service, **http://www.live.com**. Ballmer vowed that although Microsoft was late to the search engine business, "We will catch up, and we will surpass" Google and Yahoo in the Internet search and advertising business.[61]

monitor role the informational role managers play when they scan their environment for information

disseminator role the informational role managers play when they share information with others in their departments or companies

spokesperson role the informational role managers play when they share information with people outside their departments or companies

4.3 Decisional Roles

According to Mintzberg, the time managers spend obtaining and sharing information is not an end in itself. The time spent talking to and obtaining and sharing information with people inside and outside the company is useful to managers because it helps them make good decisions. Mintzberg found that managers engage in four decisional subroles: entrepreneur, disturbance handler, resource allocator, and negotiator.

In the **entrepreneur role**, managers adapt themselves, their subordinates, and their units to change. **Veterans Affairs (VA) hospitals** had long had a

entrepreneur role the decisional role managers play when they adapt themselves, their subordinates, and their units to change reputation for red tape, inefficiency, and second-class medical treatment. Today, though, independent groups rank VA hospitals as some of the best in the country. Improvements began 15 years ago when the VA's leadership instituted a culture of accountability and change aimed at improving its entire system. Procedures and outcomes were constantly evaluated. Doctors, nurses, staffers, and administrators met regularly to review possible improvements. For example, after a VA nurse in Topeka, Kansas, noticed that rental car companies used hand held bar-code scanners to check in returned cars, she suggested using bar codes on patients' ID bracelets and their bottled medicines. Today, the VA's bar-code scanners are tied to an electronic records system that prevents nurses from handing out the wrong medicines and automatically alerts the hospital pharmacy to possibly harmful drug interactions or dangerous patient allergies.[62]

In the **disturbance handler role**, managers respond to pressures and problems so severe that they demand immediate attention and action. Managers often play the role of disturbance handler when the board of a failing company hires a new CEO, who is charged with turning the company around. After **FORD MOTOR COMPANY**'s market share shrank from 25 percent to 16 percent and the company lost $7 billion in nine months, Alan Mulally came from Boeing to become Ford's new CEO. Mulally quickly arranged $23.5 billion in financing to cover the losses. He plans to cut costs by reducing the number of cars Ford produces, standardizing the use of shared parts across Ford vehicles, and laying off half of Ford's 82,000 factory workers. Mulally said, "I've seen this movie before [at Boeing]. Some very good and loyal people are going to leave this company between now and next summer, and that's going to be tough on everyone. [But] As demoralizing as a slide down may be, the ride back up is infinitely more exhilarating."[63]

In the **resource allocator role**, managers decide who will get what resources and how many resources they will get. For instance, E-Trade Financial, which is known for its online stock trading accounts, increased its marketing budget by $46 million to make potential customers more aware of its additional banking, loan, and mortgage services.[64] Hoping to revive sales of its luxury cars, General Motors invested $4 billion in its Cadillac division, or nearly 10 percent of its total capital budget for a division that accounts for only 4 percent of GM sales.[65] In these instances, top managers acted as resource allocators by changing budgets (E-Trade) or redirecting long-term investment in the company (GM).

In the **negotiator role**, managers negotiate schedules, projects, goals, outcomes, resources, and employee raises. When Sprint bought Nextel (another cell phone company), the Federal Communications Commission required it to buy new radios for police and firefighters because its cell phone tower transmissions were interfering with emergency service communications in hundreds of locations. **SPRINT NEXTEL**, which will spend $2.8 billion to fix the problem, has, for instance, been negotiating with law-enforcement agencies in Maryland and Washington to replace 35,000 radios. Unfortunately, progress has been slow, as it took Sprint a year to negotiate a $609,000 deal with the city of Fairfax, Virginia, just to develop plans to replace its radios. Furthermore, some emergency service providers don't want new radios. Instead, they're requiring Sprint to replace the crystals in their ancient radios, which would retune them to a new communications band. Since no one makes radio crystals any more, Sprint has had to grow the crystals itself in its research and development labs.[66] Negotiating, as you can see from Sprint's dilemma, is a key to success and a basic part of managerial work.

disturbance handler role the decisional role managers play when they respond to severe problems that demand immediate action

resource allocator role the decisional role managers play when they decide who gets what resources

negotiator role the decisional role managers play when they negotiate schedules, projects, goals, outcomes, resources, and employee raises

Review 4: **Managerial Roles**

Managers perform interpersonal, informational, and decisional roles in their jobs. In fulfilling the interpersonal role, managers act as figureheads by performing ceremonial duties, as leaders by motivating and encouraging workers, and as liaisons by dealing with people outside their units. In performing their informational role, managers act as monitors by scanning their environment for information, as disseminators by sharing information with others in the company, and as spokespeople by sharing information with people outside their departments or companies. In fulfilling decisional roles, managers act as entrepreneurs by adapting their units to incremental change, as disturbance handlers by responding to larger problems that demand immediate action, as resource allocators by deciding resource recipients and amounts, and as negotiators by bargaining with others about schedules, projects, goals, outcomes, and resources.

WHAT DOES IT TAKE TO BE A MANAGER?

I didn't have the slightest idea what my job was. I walked in giggling and laughing because I had been promoted and had no idea what principles or style to be guided by. After the first day, I felt like I had run into a brick wall. (Sales Representative #1)

Suddenly, I found myself saying, boy, I can't be responsible for getting all that revenue. I don't have the time. Suddenly you've got to go from [taking care of] yourself and say now I'm the manager, and what does a manager do? It takes a while thinking about it for it to really hit you . . . a manager gets things done through other people. That's a very, very hard transition to make.[67] *(Sales Representative #2)*

The above statements were made by two star sales representatives, who, on the basis of their superior performance, were promoted to the position of sales manager. As their comments indicate, at first they did not feel confident about their ability to do their jobs as managers. Like most new managers, these sales managers suddenly realized that the knowledge, skills, and abilities that led to success early in their careers (and were probably responsible for their promotion into the ranks of management) would not necessarily help them succeed as managers. As sales representatives, they were responsible only for managing their own performance. But as sales managers, they were now directly responsible for supervising all of the sales representatives in their sales territories. Furthermore, they were now directly accountable for whether those sales representatives achieved their sales goals.

If performance in nonmanagerial jobs doesn't necessarily prepare you for a managerial job, then what does it take to be a manager?

After reading the next three sections, you should be able to

5 explain what companies look for in managers.
6 discuss the top mistakes that managers make in their jobs.
7 describe the transition that employees go through when they are promoted to management.

5 What Companies Look for in Managers

Broadly speaking, when companies look for employees who would be good managers, they look for individuals who have technical skills, human skills, conceptual skills, and the motivation to manage.[68] Exhibit 1.4 shows the relative importance of these four skills to the jobs of team leaders, first-line managers, middle managers, and top managers.

Technical skills are the ability to apply the specialized procedures, techniques, and knowledge required to get the job done. For the sales managers described above, technical skills are the ability to find new sales prospects, develop accurate sales pitches based on customer needs, and close the sale. For a nurse supervisor, technical skills include being able to insert an IV or operate a crash cart if a patient goes into cardiac arrest.

technical skills the ability to apply the specialized procedures, techniques, and knowledge required to get the job done

human skills the ability to work well with others

conceptual skills the ability to see the organization as a whole, understand how the different parts affect each other, and recognize how the company fits into or is affected by its external environment

Technical skills are most important for team leaders and lower-level managers because they supervise the workers who produce products or serve customers. Team leaders and first-line managers need technical knowledge and skills to train new employees and help employees solve problems. Technical knowledge and skills are also needed to troubleshoot problems that employees can't handle. Technical skills become less important as managers rise through the managerial ranks, but they are still important.

Human skills can be summarized as the ability to work well with others. Managers with human skills work effectively within groups, encourage others to express their thoughts and feelings, are sensitive to others' needs and viewpoints, and are good listeners and communicators. Human skills are equally important at all levels of management, from first-line supervisors to CEOs. However, because lower-level managers spend much of their time solving technical problems, upper-level managers may actually spend more time dealing directly with people. On average, first-line managers spend 57 percent of their time with people, but that percentage increases to 63 percent for middle managers and 78 percent for top managers.[69]

Exhibit 1.4

Relative Importance of Managerial Skills to Different Managerial Jobs

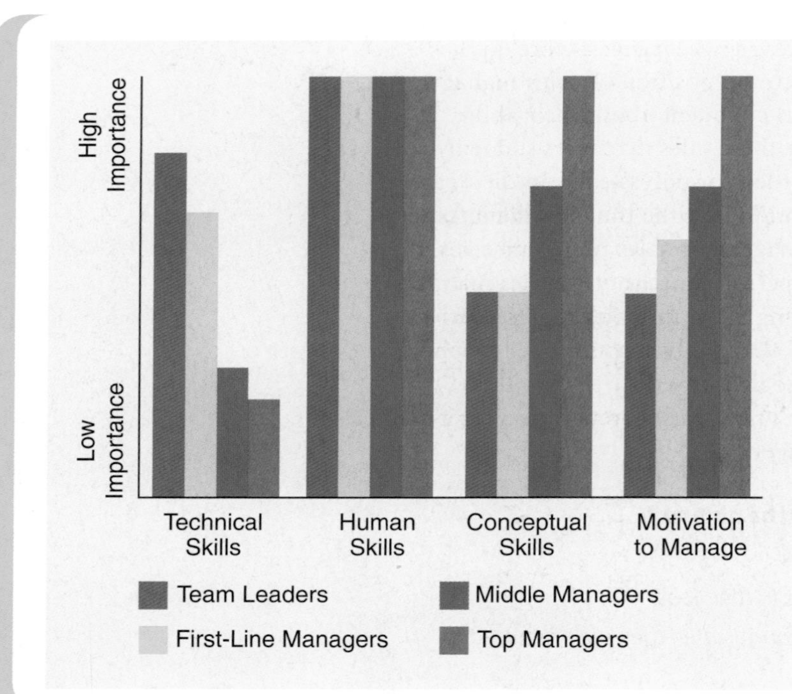

Conceptual skills are the ability to see the organization as a whole, to understand how the different parts of the company affect each other, and to recognize how the company fits into or is affected by its external environment, such as the local community, social and economic forces, customers, and the competition. Good managers have to be able to recognize, understand, and reconcile multiple complex problems and perspectives. In other words, managers have to be smart! In fact, intelligence makes so much difference for managerial performance that managers with above-average intelligence typically outperform managers of average intelligence by approximately 48 percent.[70] Clearly, companies need to be careful to promote smart workers into management. Conceptual skills increase in importance as managers rise through the management hierarchy.

Good management involves much more than intelligence, however. For example, making the department genius a manager can be disastrous if that genius lacks technical skills, human skills, or one other factor known as the motivation to manage. **Motivation to manage** is an assessment of how motivated employees are to interact with superiors, participate in competitive situations, behave assertively toward others, tell others what to do, reward good behavior and punish poor behavior, perform actions that are highly visible to others, and handle and organize administrative tasks. Managers typically have a stronger motivation to manage than their subordinates, and managers at higher levels usually have a stronger motivation to manage than managers at lower levels. Furthermore, managers with a stronger motivation to manage are promoted faster, are rated as better managers by their employees, and earn more money than managers with a weak motivation to manage.[71]

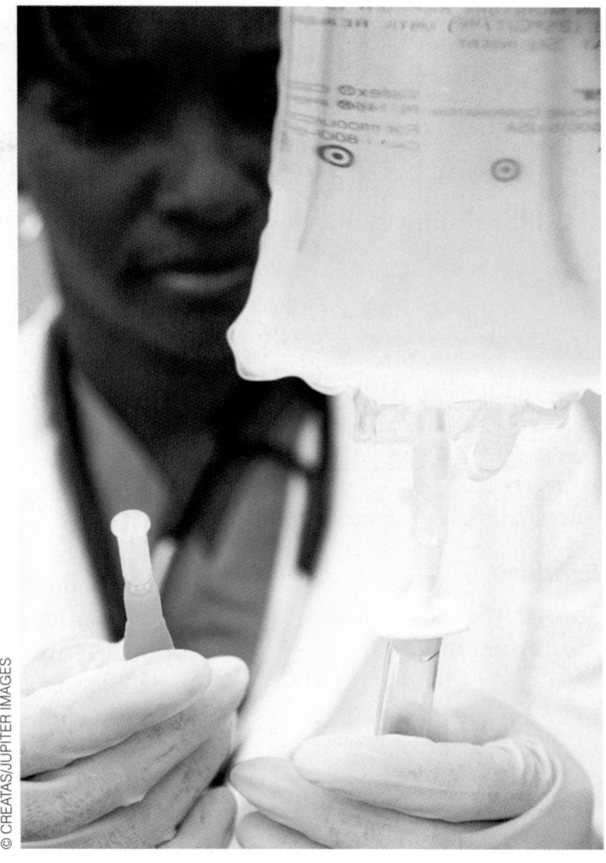
© CREATAS/JUPITER IMAGES

Technical skills are most important at the lower levels of management, but even top managers need technical skills

Review 5: What Companies Look for in Managers

Companies do not want one-dimensional managers. They want managers with a balance of skills. They want managers who know their stuff (technical skills), are equally comfortable working with blue-collar and white-collar employees (human skills), are able to assess the complexities of today's competitive marketplace and position their companies for success (conceptual skills), and want to assume positions of leadership and power (motivation to manage). Technical skills are most important for lower-level managers, human skills are equally important at all levels of management, and conceptual skills and motivation to manage increase in importance as managers rise through the managerial ranks.

6 Mistakes Managers Make

Another way to understand what it takes to be a manager is to look at the mistakes managers make. In other words, we can learn just as much from what managers shouldn't do as from what they should do. Exhibit 1.5 lists the top 10 mistakes managers make.

Several studies of U.S. and British managers have compared "arrivers," or managers who made it all the way to the top of their companies, with "derailers," managers who were successful early in their careers but were knocked off the fast track by the time they reached the middle to upper levels of management.[72] The researchers found that there were only a few differences between arrivers and derailers. For the most part, both groups were talented and both groups had weaknesses. But what distinguished derailers from arrivers was that derailers possessed two or more "fatal flaws" with respect to the way that they managed people! Although arrivers were by no means perfect, they usually had no more than one fatal flaw or had found ways to minimize the effects of their flaws on the people with whom they worked.

The number one mistake made by derailers was that they were insensitive to others by virtue of their abrasive, intimidating, and bullying management style. The authors of one study described a manager who walked into his subordinate's office and interrupted a meeting by saying, "I need to see you." When the subordinate tried to explain that he was not available because he was in the middle of a meeting, the

motivation to manage an assessment of how enthusiastic employees are about managing the work of others

1. Insensitive to others: abrasive, intimidating, bullying style.
2. Cold, aloof, arrogant.
3. Betrayal of trust.
4. Overly ambitious: thinking of next job, playing politics.
5. Specific performance problems with the business.
6. Overmanaging: unable to delegate or build a team.
7. Unable to staff effectively.
8. Unable to think strategically.
9. Unable to adapt to boss with different style.
10. Overdependent on advocate or mentor.

Source: M. W. McCall, Jr. & M. M. Lombardo, "What Makes a Top Executive?" *Psychology Today*, February 1983, 26–31.

Exhibit 1.5

Top 10 Mistakes That Managers Make

manager barked, "I don't give a damn. I said I wanted to see you now."[73] Not surprisingly, only 25 percent of derailers were rated by others as being good with people, compared with 75 percent of arrivers.

The second mistake was that derailers were often cold, aloof, or arrogant. Although this sounds like insensitivity to others, it has more to do with derailed managers being so smart, so expert in their areas of knowledge, that they treated others with contempt because they weren't experts, too. For example, **AT&T** called in an industrial psychologist to counsel its vice president of human resources because she had been blamed for "ruffling too many feathers" at the company.[74] Interviews with the vice president's coworkers and subordinates revealed that they thought she was brilliant, was "smarter and faster than other people," "generates a lot of ideas," and "loves to deal with complex issues." Unfortunately, these smarts were accompanied by a cold, aloof, and arrogant management style. The people she worked with complained that she does "too much too fast," treats coworkers with "disdain," "impairs teamwork," "doesn't always show her warm side," and has "burned too many bridges."[75]

The third and fourth mistakes made by the derailers, betraying a trust and being overly ambitious, reflect a lack of concern for coworkers and subordinates. Betraying a trust doesn't mean being dishonest. Instead, it means making others look bad by not doing what you said you would do when you said you would do it. That mistake, in itself, is not fatal because managers and their workers aren't machines. Tasks go undone in every company every single business day. There's always too much to do and not enough time, people, money, or resources to do it. The fatal betrayal of trust is failing to inform others when things will not be done on time. This failure to admit mistakes, quickly inform others of the mistakes, take responsibility for the mistakes, and then fix them without blaming others clearly distinguished the behavior of derailers from arrivers.

The fourth mistake, as mentioned above, was being overly political and ambitious. Managers who always have their eye on their next job rarely establish more than superficial relationships with peers and coworkers. In their haste to gain credit for successes that would be noticed by upper management, they make the fatal mistake of treating people as though they don't matter. An employee with an overly ambitious boss described him this way, "He treats employees coldly, even cruelly. He assigns blame without regard to responsibility, and takes all the credit for himself. I once had such a boss, and he gave me a new definition of shared risk: If something I did was successful, he took the credit. If it wasn't, I got the blame."[76]

The fatal mistakes of being unable to delegate, build a team, and staff effectively indicate that many derailed managers were unable to make the most basic transition to managerial work: to quit being hands-on doers and get work done through others. Two things go wrong when managers make these mistakes. First, when managers meddle in decisions that their subordinates should be making—when they can't stop being doers—they alienate the people who work for them. Rich Dowd, founder of Dowd Associates, an executive search firm, admits to constantly monitoring and interrupting employees because they weren't doing the job "in the way I saw fit, even when their work was outstanding." According to Richard Kilburg of Johns Hopkins University, when managers interfere with workers decisions, "You . . . have a tendency to lose your most creative people. They're able to say, 'Screw this. I'm not staying here.'"[77] Indeed, one employee told Dowd that if he was going to do her job for her, she would quit. Second, because they are trying to do their subordinates' jobs in addition to their own, managers who fail to delegate will not have enough time to do much of anything well.

© INSPIRE STOCK/JUPITER IMAGES

Review 6: Mistakes Managers Make

Another way to understand what it takes to be a manager is to look at the top mistakes managers make. Five of the most important mistakes made by managers are being abrasive and intimidating; being cold, aloof, or arrogant; betraying trust; being overly ambitious; and failing to build a team and then delegate to that team.

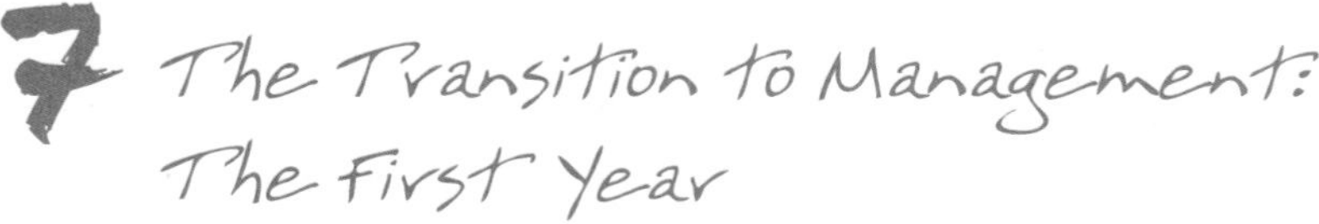

7 The Transition to Management: The First Year

In her book *Becoming a Manager: Mastery of a New Identity*, Harvard Business School professor Linda Hill followed the development of 19 people in their first year as managers. Her study found that becoming a manager produced a profound psychological transition that changed the way these managers viewed themselves and others. As shown in Exhibit 1.6, the evolution of the managers' thoughts, expectations, and realities over the course of their first year in management reveals the magnitude of the changes they experienced.

Initially, the managers in Hill's study believed that their job was to exercise formal authority and to manage tasks—basically being the boss, telling others what to do, making decisions, and getting things done. One manager said, "Being the manager means running my own office, using my ideas and thoughts." Another said, "[The office is] my baby. It's my job to make sure it works." In fact, most of the new managers were attracted to management positions because they wanted to be "in charge." Surprisingly, the new managers did not believe that their job was to manage people. The only aspects of people management mentioned by the new managers were hiring and firing.

After six months, most of the new managers had concluded that their initial expectations about managerial work were wrong. Management wasn't being "the boss." It wasn't just about making decisions and telling others what to do. The first surprise was the fast pace and heavy workload involved in being a manager. Said one manager, "This job is much harder than you think. It is 40 to 50 percent more work than being a producer! Who would have ever guessed?" The pace of managerial work was startling, too. Another manager said, "You have eight or nine people looking for your time . . . coming into and

Managers who fail to delegate will not have enough time to do much of anything well.

MANAGERS' INITIAL EXPECTATIONS	AFTER SIX MONTHS AS A MANAGER	AFTER A YEAR AS A MANAGER
JAN FEB MAR	APR MAY JUN	JUL AUG SEP OCT NOV DEC
Be the boss	Initial expectations were wrong	No longer "doer"
Have formal authority	Fast pace	Communicating, listening, and giving positive reinforcement
Manage tasks	Heavy workload	Learning to adapt to and control stress
Job is not managing people	Job is to be problem-solver and troubleshooter for subordinates	Job is people development

Source: L. A. Hill, *Becoming a Manager: Mastery of a New Identity* (Boston: Harvard Business School Press, 1992).

Exhibit 1.6

The Transition to Management: Initial Expectations, after Six Months, and after a Year

out of your office all day long." A somewhat frustrated manager declared that management was "a job that never ended . . . a job you couldn't get your hands around."

Informal descriptions like this are consistent with studies indicating that the average first-line manager spends no more than two minutes on a task before being interrupted by a request from a subordinate, a phone call, or an e-mail. The pace is somewhat less hurried for top managers, who spend an average of approximately nine minutes on a task before having to switch to another. In practice, this means that supervisors may perform 30 different tasks per hour, while top managers perform seven different tasks per hour, with each task typically different from the one that preceded it. A manager described this frenetic level of activity by saying, "The only time you are in control is when you shut your door, and then I feel I am not doing the job I'm supposed to be doing, which is being with the people."

The other major surprise after six months on the job was that the managers' expectations about what they should do as managers were very different from their subordinates' expectations. Initially, the managers defined their jobs as helping their subordinates perform their jobs well. For the managers, who still defined themselves as doers rather than managers, assisting their subordinates meant going out on sales calls or handling customer complaints. One manager said, "I like going out with the rep, who may need me to lend him my credibility as manager. I like the challenge, the joy in closing. I go out with the reps and we make the call and talk about the customer; it's fun." But when the managers "assisted" in this way, their subordinates were resentful and viewed their help as interference. The subordinates wanted their managers to help them by solving problems that they couldn't solve. Once the managers realized this contradiction, they embraced their role as problem-solver and troubleshooter. Thus, they could help without interfering with their subordinates' jobs.

After a year on the job, most of the managers thought of themselves as managers and no longer as doers. In making the transition, they finally realized that people management was the most important part of their jobs. One manager summarized the lesson that had taken him a year to learn by saying, "As many demands as managers have on their time, I think their primary responsibility is people development. Not production, but people development." Another indication of how much their views had changed was that most of the managers now regretted the rather heavy-handed approach they had used in their early attempts to manage their subordinates. "I wasn't good at managing . . . , so I was bossy like a first-grade teacher." "Now I see that I started out as a drill sergeant. I was inflexible, just a lot of how-to's." By the end of the year, most of the managers had abandoned their authoritarian approach for one based on communication, listening, and positive reinforcement. One manager explained, "Last night at five I handed out an award in the boardroom just to the individual.

It was the first time in his career that he had [earned] $100,000, and I gave him a piece of glass [a small award] and said I'd heard a rumor that somebody here just crossed over $100,000 and I said congratulations, shook his hand, and walked away. It was not public in the sense that I gathered everybody around. But I knew and he did too."

Finally, after beginning their year as managers in frustration, the managers came to feel comfortable with their subordinates, with the demands of their jobs, and with their emerging managerial styles. While being managers had made them acutely aware of their limitations and their need to develop as people, it also provided them with an unexpected reward of coaching and developing the people who worked for them. One manager said, "It gives me the best feeling to see somebody do something well after I have helped them. I get excited." Another stated, "I realize now that when I accepted the position of branch manager that it is truly an exciting vocation. It is truly awesome, even at this level; it can be terribly challenging and terribly exciting."

Review 7: The Transition to Management: The First Year

Managers often begin their jobs by using more formal authority and less people management. However, most managers find that being a manager has little to do with "bossing" their subordinates. After six months on the job, the managers were surprised at the fast pace and heavy workload and that "helping" their subordinates was viewed as interference. After a year on the job, most of the managers had come to think of themselves not as doers, but as managers who get things done through others. And because they finally realized that people management was the most important part of their job, most of them had abandoned their authoritarian approach for one based on communication, listening, and positive reinforcement.

WHY MANAGEMENT MATTERS

If you walk down the aisle of the business section in your local bookstore, you'll find hundreds of books that explain precisely what companies need to do to be successful. Unfortunately, the best-selling business books tend to be faddish, changing dramatically every few years. One thing that hasn't changed, though, is the importance of good people and good management: Companies can't succeed for long without them.

After reading this section, you should be able to

8 explain how and why companies can create competitive advantage through people.

8 Competitive Advantage through People

In his books, *Competitive Advantage through People* and *The Human Equation: Building Profits by Putting People First*, Stanford University business professor Jeffrey Pfeffer contends that what separates top-performing companies from their competitors is the way they treat their work forces—in other words, their management.[78]

Pfeffer found that managers in top-performing companies used ideas like employment security, selective hiring, self-managed teams and decentralization, high pay contingent on company performance, extensive training, reduced status distinctions (between managers and employees), and extensive sharing of financial information to achieve financial performance that, on average, was 40 percent higher than that of other companies. These ideas, which are explained in detail in Exhibit 1.7, help organizations develop work forces that are smarter, better trained, more motivated, and more committed than their competitors' work forces. And, as indicated by the phenomenal growth and return on investment earned by these companies, smarter, better trained, and more committed work forces provide superior products and service to customers, who keep buying and, by telling others about their positive experiences, bring in new customers.

Pfeffer also argues that companies that invest in their people will create long-lasting competitive advantages that are difficult for other companies to duplicate. Indeed, other studies clearly demonstrate that sound management practices can produce substantial advantages in four critical areas of organizational performance: sales revenues, profits, stock market returns, and customer satisfaction.

In terms of sales revenues and profits, a study of nearly 1,000 U.S. firms found that companies that use *just some* of the ideas shown in Exhibit 1.7 had $27,044 more sales per employee and $3,814 more profit per employee than companies that didn't. For a 100-person company, these differences amount to $2.7 million more in sales and nearly $400,000 more in annual profit! For a 1,000-person company, the difference grows to $27 million more in sales and $4 million more in annual profit!

Another study investigating the effect of investing in people on company sales found that poorly performing companies that adopted management techniques as

Exhibit 1.7

Competitive Advantage through People: Management Practices

1. Employment Security—Employment security is the ultimate form of commitment that companies can make to their workers. Employees can innovate and increase company productivity without fearing the loss of their jobs.
2. Selective Hiring—If employees are the basis for a company's competitive advantage, and those employees have employment security, then the company needs to aggressively recruit and selectively screen applicants in order to hire the most talented employees available.
3. Self-Managed Teams and Decentralization—Self-managed teams are responsible for their own hiring, purchasing, job assignments, and production. Self-managed teams can often produce enormous increases in productivity through increased employee commitment and creativity. Decentralization allows employees who are closest to (and most knowledgeable about) problems, production, and customers to make timely decisions. Decentralization increases employee satisfaction and commitment.
4. High Wages Contingent on Organizational Performance—High wages are needed to attract and retain talented workers and to indicate that the organization values its workers. Employees, like company founders, shareholders, and managers, need to share in the financial rewards when the company is successful. Why? Because employees who have a financial stake in their companies are more likely to take a long-run view of the business and think like business owners.
5. Training and Skill Development—Like a high-tech company that spends millions of dollars to upgrade computers or research and development labs, a company whose competitive advantage is based on its people must invest in the training and skill development of its people.
6. Reduction of Status Differences—These are fancy words that indicate that the company treats everyone, no matter what the job, as equal. There are no reserved parking spaces. Everyone eats in the same cafeteria and has similar benefits. The result: much improved communication as employees focus on problems and solutions rather than on how they are less valued than managers.
7. Sharing Information—If employees are to make decisions that are good for the long-run health and success of the company, they need to be given information about costs, finances, productivity, development times, and strategies that was previously known only by company managers.

Source: J. Pfeffer, *The Human Equation: Building Profits by Putting People First* (Boston: Harvard Business School Press, 1996).

simple as setting expectations (establishing goals, results, and schedules), coaching (informal, ongoing discussions between managers and subordinates about what is being done well and what could be done better), reviewing (annual, formal discussion about results), and rewarding (adjusting salaries and bonuses based on employee performance and results) were able to improve their average return on investment from 5.1 percent to 19.7 percent and increase sales by $94,000 per employee![79] So, in addition to significantly improving the profitability of healthy companies, sound management practices can turn around failing companies.

In 2007,* Fortune *ranked Google as America's Best Company to Work for. One of the perks at the Googleplex: Free—and good—food at the cafeteria. And that includes a company sushi chef.

To determine the effect of investing in people on stock market performance, researchers matched companies on *Fortune* magazine's list of "100 Best Companies to Work for in America" with companies that were similar in industry, size, and—this is key—operating performance. In other words, both sets of companies were equally good performers; the key difference was how well they treated their employees. For both sets of companies, the researchers found that employee attitudes such as job satisfaction changed little from year to year. The people who worked for the "100 Best" companies were consistently much more satisfied with their jobs and employers year after year than were employees in the matched companies. More importantly, those stable differences in employee attitudes were strongly related to differences in stock market performance. Over a three-year period, an investment in the "100 Best Companies to Work for" would have resulted in an 82 percent cumulative stock return compared with just 37 percent for the matched companies.[80] This difference is remarkable given that both sets of companies were equally good performers at the beginning of the period.

Finally, research also indicates that managers have an important effect on customer satisfaction. Many people find this surprising. They don't understand how managers, who are largely responsible for what goes on inside the company, can affect what goes on outside the company. They wonder how managers, who often interact with customers under negative conditions (when customers are angry or dissatisfied), can actually improve customer satisfaction. It turns out that managers influence customer satisfaction through employee satisfaction. When employees are satisfied with their jobs, their bosses, and the companies they work for, they provide much better service to customers.[81] In turn, customers are more satisfied, too. You will learn more about the service-profit chain in Chapter 18 on managing service and manufacturing operation.

Review 8: Competitive Advantage through People

Why does management matter? Well-managed companies are competitive because their work forces are smarter, better trained, more motivated, and more committed. Furthermore, companies that practice good management consistently have greater sales revenues, profits, and stock market performance than companies that don't. Finally, good management matters because good management leads to satisfied employees who, in turn, provide better service to customers. Because employees tend to treat customers the same way that their managers treat them, good management can improve customer satisfaction.

SELF ASSESSMENT

© VEER

Each chapter has a related self-assessment to help you consider how your own perspectives influence your management skills. Each assessment tool starts with a short description and ends with basic scoring information. (Your instructor will have interpretations of your scores.) As you advance through the book, take time to review your assessment scores together. Doing so will help you see patterns in your own perceptions and behaviors and give you insights into how those perceptions may affect your performance as a manager.

Is Management for You?

As you learned in Section 7 of this chapter, many managers begin their careers in management with specific ideas about what it means to be the boss. Although you may want to be a manager because of excitement, status, power, or rewards, knowing how to manage is not automatic; it requires specific skills and competencies, as well as a desire to manage. This assessment is meant to establish your baseline ability in the skills covered in the chapter. It will not tell you whether you should or should not be a manager, or whether you have "what it takes" to be a manager. It will, however, give you feedback on general skills that influence your overall managerial style.

Be candid as you complete the assessment by circling the appropriate responses.[82]

ML = Most like me
SL = Somewhat like me
NS = Not sure
SU = Somewhat unlike me
MU = Most unlike me

1. I can get others to do what I want them to do.
   ML SL NS SU MU
2. I frequently evaluate my job performance.
   ML SL NS SU MU
3. I prefer not to get involved in office politics.
   ML SL NS SU MU
4. I like the freedom that open-ended goals provide me.
   ML SL NS SU MU
5. I work best when things are orderly and calm.
   ML SL NS SU MU
6. I enjoy making oral presentations to groups of people.
   ML SL NS SU MU
7. I am confident in my abilities to accomplish difficult tasks.
   ML SL NS SU MU
8. I do not like to write.
   ML SL NS SU MU
9. I like solving difficult puzzles.
   ML SL NS SU MU
10. I am an organized person.
    ML SL NS SU MU
11. I have difficulty telling others they made a mistake.
    ML SL NS SU MU
12. I like to work set hours each day.
    ML SL NS SU MU
13. I view paperwork as a trivial task.
    ML SL NS SU MU
14. I like to help others learn new things.
    ML SL NS SU MU
15. I prefer to work alone.
    ML SL NS SU MU
16. I believe it is who you know, not what you know, that counts.
    ML SL NS SU MU
17. I enjoy doing several things at once.
    ML SL NS SU MU
18. I am good at managing money.
    ML SL NS SU MU
19. I would rather back down from an argument than let it get out of hand.
    ML SL NS SU MU
20. I am computer literate.
    ML SL NS SU MU

Scoring

Start by reversing your scores for items 5, 8, 11, 15, and 16. For example, if you used ML, change it to MU, and vice versa; if you used SL, change it to SU, and vice versa. Now assign each answer a point value.

KEY TERMS

conceptual skills 22
controlling 11
disseminator role 19
disturbance handler role 20
effectiveness 7
efficiency 7
entrepreneur role 19
figurehead role 18
first-line managers 15
leader role 18
leading 11
liaison role 18
management 7
meta-analysis 10
middle managers 14
monitor role 19
motivation to manage 23
negotiator role 20
organizing 9
people skills 22
planning 8
resource allocator role 20
spokesperson role 19
team leaders 16
technical skills 22
top managers 12

Number of ML answers ____ times 5 points each = ____
Number of SL answers ____ times 4 points each = ____
Number of NS answers ____ times 3 points each = ____
Number of SU answers ____ times 2 points each = ____
Number of MU answers ____ times 1 point each = ____
TOTAL = ____

You can find the interpretation for your score at: **academic.cengage.com/management/williams.**

MANAGEMENT DECISION

Making decisions is part of every manager's job. To give you practice at managerial decision making, each chapter contains a "Management Decision" assignment focused on a particular decision. You'll need to decide what to do in the given situation and then answer several questions to explain your choices.

Betting on an Employee

Although you've been in your new executive management position for barely a year, you have had abundant opportunities for decision making.[83] You have had the final say on a new advertising campaign, an employee washroom remodel, and the selection of the company's uniform vendor. You've met with community leaders to discuss your company's participation in a fundraiser for the local food pantry and with the press to announce your company's plan to bring 50 new jobs to the area. Surprisingly, however, you've had little experience with human resources issues.

But that changed this morning, when a colleague mentioned that a relatively new executive assistant named Andrew had taken a second job with another company in the evenings. Andrew has been at your company for only three months, but in that time has proved to be reliable, resourceful, and intelligent.

"He's doing well, though. Doesn't he like his job here?" you asked your colleague.

"He does, but he can earn an extra $250 a week at the second job. He says he's saving to go back to school," she responded.

"Oh," you replied. "Well, I'll talk to him."

Andrew is fast becoming a valuable employee, but the company has a policy against moonlighting. You expect your employees to give their best each day on the job. If they spend what would otherwise be leisure time working for someone else, they won't be fresh, alert, and productive when they come to work for you. At the same time, you remember how you worked several jobs to save money for graduate school. If you had been able to make enough money at one job, you wouldn't have pushed yourself to work three. You think briefly about giving Andrew a raise, but then recall that the company's policy is not to review new employees for raises or promotions until they've spent at least six months on the job. Andrew is only halfway there. Still, it would be a shame to see such a promising employee lose his spark from overwork and fatigue.

Questions

1. How is this decision emblematic of your job as a manager and your transition into that position?
2. What are the advantages and disadvantages to giving Andrew a raise before the customary period?
3. Do you break the company policy and give Andrew a raise three months early, or not? If not, how do you handle the moonlighting situation? Explain your decision.
4. Regardless of Andrew's situation, would it be better in the long run for your company to continue or end its "no moonlighting" policy?

MANAGEMENT TEAM DECISION

From sports to school to work to civic involvement, working in teams is increasingly part of our experience. But although working in teams is more and more common, making decisions as teams is not necessarily any easier. You will learn more about managing teams in Chapter 10, but to give you more experience with teamwork, a "Management Team Decision" exercise designed for a group of three to five students is included in each chapter. As a group, you must come to a mutually agreeable decision on the scenario presented. Each "Management Team Decision" will focus on a management topic presented in the chapter. For Chapter 1, you'll work with the management function of planning and organizing, as you decide whether to let a team member have a night off.

Baggage Claims—Is RFID the Ticket?

What a trip![84] You're exhausted from changing planes (three times because of cancellations) and trying to corral your colleagues as well as their luggage. And after all the cramped seats, complaining travelers, long lines, and marginal food, your team still hasn't come to a decision about what do to—at your own airport.

Last month, you and your management team from Hartsfield-Jackson Atlanta International Airport began discussing using radio-frequency identification (RFID) tags in the airport's baggage-handling operations. Recent reports on lost luggage have caused more than a ripple of concern, with roughly one in every 150 U.S. passengers losing a bag in any given year. U.S. airlines spent an estimated $400 million to replace mishandled luggage in a recent year, yet passengers are regularly incensed that the airlines give only partial reimbursements for lost bags and belongings. The cost of lost luggage, however, is not just the $400 million in reimbursements. There's the time and expense of staffing large customer-service departments to take complaints, process claims, track down and identify missing baggage, and deliver found bags to either the owner's travel destination or home. Multiple deliveries are often made, as the bag arrives at the passenger's destination after he or she has left for another destination or returned home. The International Air Transport Association estimates that airlines worldwide could save $760 million a year by reducing lost luggage.

Your team would love to reduce the costs associated with lost luggage at Hartsfield-Jackson (ATL), which consistently wins the title of world's busiest passenger airport. Nearly 6.5 million travelers pass through the airport in a given month and bring about 75 metric tons of luggage with them. That's more than the either the monthly amount of mail or commercial freight (think FedEx and UPS) that passes through the airport's facilities!

Thirty-one airlines take off and land at ATL, but Delta accounts for over 58 percent of passenger volume. As (bad) luck would have it, Delta has a dismal ranking for lost luggage, reporting 6.8 mishandled bags per 1,000, second only to US Airways' 7.7 losses per 1,000. Company-wide, Delta handles 1.3 bags per passenger, and there's no reason to think this number is any lower in Atlanta, its biggest hub. That means Delta alone puts over 160,000 bags into the ATL system each day!

To manage this tremendous flow of personal belongings, ATL uses the bar-coding system in use at the majority of U.S. airports. Adhesive paper tags are very economical at 4 cents each, but they also rip, smudge, get misread, or get torn off completely. Scanners even have trouble with twisted tags. Baggage sorting with bar-coded tags is only 80 to 90 percent accurate. And once they're printed, that's it. If a passenger's destination changes due to, say, inclement weather, flight cancellations, or being rerouted, the bar-code label can't change to reflect the new itinerary.

Armed with all this, well, baggage, your team went on a trip to Las Vegas's McCarran International Airport, which has been using radio-frequency identification tags to manage its bag handling. McCarran is the fifth-busiest airport in the United States, and it handles more than 70,000 outbound bags per day. Using bar-code readers, as many as 7,000 bags per day were not read properly and tossed into an "unknown" pile to be hand sorted. There was also the headache of lost luggage for passengers on quick three- and four-day excursions to consider. In the end, the airport decided to invest in a system based on RFID tags. Tags costs 21 cents apiece, or five times the cost of a bar-code tag, but the accuracy of the RFID system has cut the number of hand-sorted bags by 90 percent, and the tags can be rewritten electronically mid-travel if itineraries change. The RFID system has enabled the airport to let inbound passengers on long flights check their bags all the way to their casino or hotel, so that their luggage is waiting for them when they arrive.

What to do? ATL is already in the middle of a $5.4 billion campaign to improve facilities. Management does a great job managing the finances of the airport, and Hartsfield Jackson is considered a good risk (meaning a safe bet) for lenders. The hardware required to start using RFID is cheaper than maintaining the hardware that manages the system of traditional bar-code tags, but the difference in the cost of the tags is substantial if decreasing. And who's going to foot the bill? Should the airlines, which are nearly all suffering financially, be expected to pay for the program that will ultimately benefit them as well? Delta already stopped paying its $3.4 million annual rent to the airport as part of its bankruptcy restructuring. If they don't pay for the hardware required to read the tags, should airlines at least pay for the tags themselves?

Maybe you need to take another trip, this time to Furth, Germany, where Siemens, a provider of industrial software, has built a mock airport to demonstrate how automated technology can help airports improve efficiencies in nearly every aspect of their organization.

Siemens's automated luggage belts equipped with RFID readers can move at up to 30 feet per second, which means that passengers wouldn't have to wait hours for their bags to show up at the carousel, as they often do now. Even though the people at McCarran were helpful, their airport has less than half the traffic of Hartsfield-Jackson. Perhaps consulting with the folks at Siemens will help you better frame the issues for your massive operations. Or maybe you'd be better off visiting Denver International Airport, which is known for its notoriously flawed—and inefficient—automated baggage handling system.

Form a team of four or five students to act as the management team of Hartsfield-Jackson International Airport to determine if the tradeoffs of implementing RFID are worth the costs.

Questions

1. Implementing RFID is a complex situation that draws on many managerial roles. Describe the ways that the management team from Hartsfield-Jackson will fulfill Mintzberg's managerial roles and subroles (see Exhibit 1.3) as it thinks through the decision.
2. Additional information gathering at Siemens's mock airport is a good idea, but who to send? Identify how many and which type of managers to recommend for a fact-finding team and to tour the facility at Furth, Germany. Estimate how much money will be required to fund such a trip.
3. Do you implement RFID at Hartsfield-Jackson immediately, or do you schedule a trip to Furth, Germany, before deciding? Or do you decide not to implement RFID at all?

Finding a Management Job

Management is a wide ranging and exciting area of work. One way to gain a sense of the possibilities is to study the advertisements for management job openings. Companies advertise their management openings in a variety of ways, including print advertisements in such newspapers as the *Wall Street Journal* (especially its Friday career section) and online ads at job sites like Monster.com and CareerBuilder.com.

Step 1: Find a job you'd like to have. Search through the newspaper and online ads and locate several detailed job descriptions for management positions. Select the one that you find most appealing—a job that you could picture yourself interviewing for either in the near future or later in your career. Do not be too concerned about your current qualifications in making your selection, but you should see realistic prospects of meeting the qualifications over time (if a job requires an MBA, for example, you should see yourself completing this degree sometime in the future). Print your selected detailed job description and bring it to your next class session.

Step 2: Share your job description. In class, your professor will assign you to a pair or group of three. Write your name on your selected management job description, and exchange your job description with your partner(s). Each member of the pair or triad should now have a job description other than their own.

Step 3: Think like a hiring manager. Read the job description you received from your partner. Imagine that you are the manager responsible for hiring someone to fill this position. A human resources specialist in your company has already screened the applicants' resume and background. Thus, you may assume that your partner has met all the basic qualifications for the job. Your job as a senior manager is to ask questions that might get beyond the resume to the person—what might you ask to learn if someone is well-suited to thrive in this management job, and in your company?

Step 4: Take turns interviewing. Each member of the group should be briefly interviewed (5–10 minutes) for the job they selected.

Step 5: Debrief. Discuss your experiences with your partner(s). What was it like to be interviewed for your selected position? What was it like to role-play interviewing someone for a management position? Now imagine the real thing. Brainstorm about how you might prepare yourself over time to be the top candidate for an attractive management position, and to be a senior manager responsible for hiring the best qualified managers for your company.

Step 6: Discuss with the class. Share your interview experiences and brainstorming ideas with the class. Do you hear any similarities across the pairs/triads? What ideas or questions are most significant to you as you consider management job interviews?

DEVELOP YOUR CAREER POTENTIAL

Interview Two Managers

Welcome to the first "Develop Your Career Potential" activity! These assignments have one purpose: to help you develop your present and future capabilities as a manager. What you will learn through these assignments is not traditional "book learning" based on memorization and regurgitation, but practical knowledge and skills that help managers perform their jobs better. Lessons from some of the assignments—for example, goal setting—can be used for immediate benefit. Other lessons will obviously take time to accomplish, but you can still benefit now by making specific plans for future improvement.

Step 1: Interview two practicing managers. In her book *Becoming a Manager: Mastery of a New Identity*, Harvard Business School professor Linda Hill conducted extensive interviews with 19 people in their first year as managers.[85] To learn firsthand what it's like to be a manager, interview two managers that you know, asking them some of the same questions, listed below, that Hill asked her managers. Be sure to interview managers with different levels of experience. Interview one person with at least five years' experience as a manager and then interview another person with no more than two years' experience as a manager. Ask the managers these questions:

1. Briefly describe your current position and responsibilities.
2. What do your subordinates expect from you on the job?
3. What are the major stresses and challenges you face on the job?
4. What, if anything, do you dislike about the job?
5. What do you like best about your job?
6. What are the critical differences between average managers and top-performing managers?
7. Think about the skills and knowledge that you need to be effective in your job. What are they, and how did you acquire them?
8. What have been your biggest mistakes thus far? Could you have avoided them? If so, how?

Step 2: Prepare to discuss your findings. Prepare to discuss your findings in class or write a report (if assigned by your instructor). What conclusions can you draw from your interview data?

BIZ FLIX

8 Mile

Jimmy "B-Rabbit" Smith, Jr. (Eminem), wants to be a successful rapper and to prove that a white man can create moving sounds. He works days at a plant run by the North Detroit Stamping Company and pursues his music at night, sometimes on the plant's grounds. The film's title refers to Detroit's northern boundary, which divides the city's white and African American populations. This film gives a gritty look at Detroit's hip-hop culture in 1995 and Jimmy's desire to be accepted by it. Eminem's original songs "Lose Yourself" and "8 Mile" received Golden Globe and Academy Award nominations. This scene is an edited composite of two brief sequences that show Jimmy interacting with his manager, Manny, at the stamping plant.

What to Watch for and Ask Yourself

1. What kind of manager is Manny?
2. What management function is Manny fulfilling when he considers giving Jimmy extra shifts?
3. What managerial roles do you see in the clip?

© VEER

MANAGEMENT WORKPLACE

Original Penguin

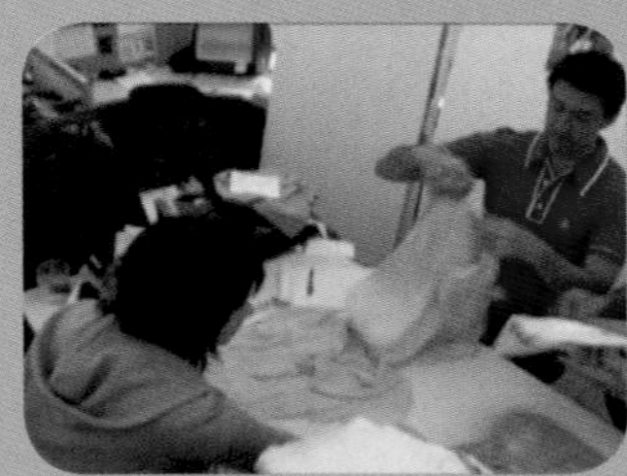

Penguins have always been cool. But golf shirts with a little flapping bird printed on them experienced a lull in coolness. In fact, their popularity remained frozen for two decades, largely because they were worn by aging golfers. Now the penguins are back, flapping furiously—and, many would argue, coolly—not just on golf shirts but also on a wide array of men's and women's clothing and accessories, including shirts, shoes, hats, belts, neckties, handbags, and even bathing suits. These items represent the extreme makeover of a 50-year-old brand of clothing called Original Penguin. Now owned by Perry Ellis International, the Original Penguin brand of clothing is experiencing rejuvenation—thanks largely to Penguin's vice president, Chris Kolbe. This video allows you to follow Kolbe around the management workplace to see what his job entails.

What to Watch for and Ask Yourself

1. Describe the conceptual skills you think Chris Kolbe needs for his job as vice president of Original Penguin.
2. Which management roles does Kolbe fulfill in the course of the video segment?
3. What do you think is the most difficult part of Kolbe's job? Why?

© VEER

CHAPTER 2

The History of Management

© STONE/GETTY IMAGES

Learning Outcomes:

1 Explain the origins of management.
2 Explain the history of scientific management.
3 Discuss the history of bureaucratic and administrative management.
4 Explain the history of human relations management.
5 Discuss the history of operations, information, systems, and contingency management.

In This Chapter:

WHAT WOULD YOU DO?

ISG Steelton–International Steel Group, Steelton, Pennsylvania.[1] As the day-shift supervisor at the steel plant, you summon the six college students who are working for you this summer doing whatever you need done (sweeping up, sandblasting the inside of boilers that are down for maintenance, running errands, and so forth). You walk them across the plant to a field where the company stores scrap-metal "leftovers." The area, about the size of a football field, is stacked with organized piles of metal. You explain that everything they see has just been sold. Metal prices, which have been depressed, have finally risen enough that the company can earn a small profit by selling its scrap.

You point out that railroad tracks divide the field into parallel sectors, like the lines on a football field, so that each stack of metal is no more than 15 feet from a track. Each stack contains 390 pieces of metal. Each piece weighs 92 pounds and is about a yard long and just over 4 inches high and 4 inches wide. You tell the students that working as a team, they are to pick up each piece, walk up a ramp to a railroad car that will be positioned next to each stack, and then neatly position and stack the metal for shipment. That's right, you repeat, *92* pounds, *walk* up the ramp, and *carry* the metal onto the rail car. Anticipating their questions, you explain that a forklift could be used only if the metal was stored on wooden pallets (it isn't), if the pallets could withstand the weight of the metal (they would be crushed), and if you, as their supervisor, had forklifts and people trained to run them (you don't). In other words, the only way to get the metal into the rail cars is for the students to carry it.

Based on an old report from the last time the company sold some of the metal, you know that over an eight-hour shift, workers typically loaded about 30 pieces of metal parts per hour. At that pace, though, it will take your six students six weeks to load all of the metal, and the purchasing manager who sold it says it must be shipped in two weeks. That means that without more workers (there's a hiring freeze) and without forklifts, all of the metal has to be loaded by hand by these six workers in two weeks. But how do you do that? What would motivate the students to work much, much harder than they have all summer? They've gotten used to a leisurely pace and easy job assignments. Motivation might help, but motivation will only get so much done. After all, short of illegal steroids, nothing is going to work once muscle fatigue kicks in from carrying those 92-pound pieces of metal up a ramp all day long. What can you change about the way the work is done to deal with the unavoidable physical fatigue? **If you were the supervisor in charge, what would you do?**

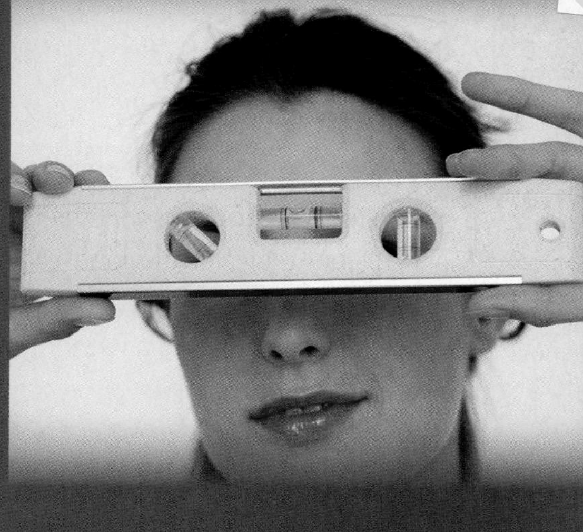

ACTIVITIES + VIDEOS

CengageNOW Audio study guide, electronic flashcards, author FAQ videos, On the Job and Biz Flix videos, concept tutorial, and concept exercise

Web (academic.cengage.com/management/williams) Quiz, PowerPoint slides, and glossary terms for this chapter

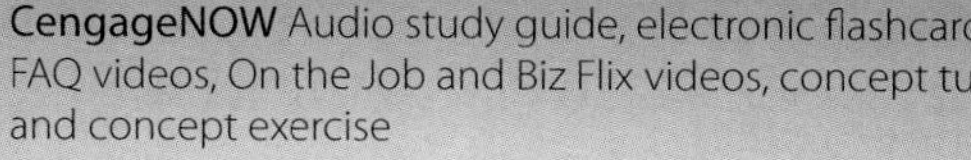

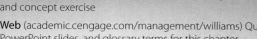

Study Tip

Build a management time line. On a blank sheet of paper, construct a time line that shows the evolution of management theory. Draw a line that divides the paper down the middle. Then, place management theories on one side and overall historical events on the other. This will help you see what was happening in management as a part of what was happening in the world in general. Examining theories in context can help you identify trends that are likely to emerge in the future.

"WHAT'S NEW" COMPANIES

- *ISG Steelton*
- *Ford Motor Company*
- *Chicago Harvester*
- *Pullman Company*
- *Midvale Steel Company*
- *Comambault*
- *Western Electric Company*
- *AT&T*
- *New Jersey Bell Telephone*
- *Beretta*
- *Oldsmobile Motor Works*

Certainly, the problems that the ISG steel plant supervisor is facing in the *What Would You Do?* case are difficult, but they aren't unique. Each day, managers are asked to solve challenging problems and are given only a limited amount of time, people, or resources. Yet it's still their responsibility to get things done on time and within budget. Furthermore, most of the management practices and ideas that today's managers use to solve their daily problems have their roots in the people and ideas you'll read about in this chapter on the history of management. Indeed, by reading the theories in this chapter, you will be able to figure out a solution to the ISG supervisor's problems.

We begin this chapter by reviewing the origins of management ideas and practice throughout history and the historical changes that produced the need for managers. Next, you'll learn about various schools of management thought. Beginning with scientific management, you'll learn about the key contributions made by Frederick Taylor, Frank and Lillian Gilbreth, and Henry Gantt. Next, you'll read about Max Weber and bureaucratic management and then about Henri Fayol and administrative management. Following that, you'll learn about human relations management and the ideas of Mary Parker Follett (constructive conflict and coordination), Elton Mayo (Hawthorne Studies), and Chester Barnard (cooperation and acceptance of authority). Finally, you'll learn about the history of operations management, information management, systems management, and contingency management.

IN THE BEGINNING

In this textbook, you learn that *management* is getting work done through others, that *strategic* plans are overall plans that clarify how a company will serve customers and position itself against competitors over the next two to five years, and that *just-in-time inventory* is a system in which the parts needed to make something arrive from suppliers just as they are needed at each stage of production. Today's managers would undoubtedly view those ideas and many of the others presented in the book as self-evident. For example, tell today's managers to "reward workers for improved production or performance," "set specific goals to increase motivation," or "innovate to create and sustain a competitive advantage," and they'll respond, "Duh! Who doesn't know that?" A mere 125 years ago, however, business ideas and practices were so different that today's widely accepted management ideas would have been as "self-evident" as space travel, cell phones, and the Internet. In fact, 125 years ago, management wasn't yet a field of study, and there were no management jobs and no management careers. Now, of course, managers and management are such an integral part of the business world that it's hard to imagine organizations without them. So if there were no managers 125 years ago, but you can't walk down the hall today without bumping into one, where did management come from?

After reading the next section, you should be able to

1 explain the origins of management.

1 The Origins of Management

Management as a field of study may be just 125 years old, but management ideas and practices have actually been used from the earliest times of recorded history. For example, 2,500 years before management researchers called it *job enrichment*, the Greeks learned that they could improve the productivity of boring repetitious tasks by performing them to music. The basic idea was to use a flute, drum, or song lyrics to pace people to work in unison using the same efficient motions, stimulate them to work faster and longer, and make the boring work more fun.[2] Although we can find the seeds of many of today's management ideas throughout history, not until the last two centuries did systematic changes in the nature of work and organizations create a compelling need for managers.

Let's begin our discussion of the origins of management by learning about ***1.1 management ideas and practice throughout history*** *and* ***1.2 why we need managers today.***

1.1 Management Ideas and Practice throughout History

Examples of management thought and practice can be found throughout history.[3] For example, as shown in Exhibit 2.1, in 5000 BC in an early instance of managing information, which is part of the control function, Sumerian priests developed a formal system of writing (scripts) that allowed them to record and keep track of the goods, flocks and herds of animals, coins, land, and buildings that were contributed to their temples. Furthermore, to encourage honesty in such dealings, the Sumerians instituted managerial controls that required all priests to submit written accounts of the transactions, donations, and payments they handled to the chief priest. And just like clay or stone tablets and animal-skin documents, these scripts were first used to manage the business of Sumerian temples.[4] Only later were the scripts used for religious purposes.

A thousand years after the Sumerians, the Egyptians recognized the need for planning, organizing, and controlling; for submitting written requests; and for consulting staff for advice before making decisions. The practical problems they encountered while building the great pyramids no doubt led to the development of these management ideas. The enormity of the task they faced is evident in the pyramid of King Cheops, which contains 2.3 million blocks of stone. Each block had to be quarried, cut to precise size and shape, cured (hardened in the sun), transported by boat for two to three days, moved onto the construction site, numbered to identify where it would be placed, and then shaped and smoothed so that it would fit perfectly into place. It took 20,000 workers 23 years to complete this pyramid; more than 8,000 were needed just to quarry the stones and transport them. A typical "quarry expedition" might include 100 army officers, 50 government and religious officials, and 200 members of the king's court to lead the expedition; 130 stonemasons to cut the stones; and 5,000 soldiers, 800 barbarians, and 2,000 bond servants to transport the stones on and off the ships.[5]

The remainder of Exhibit 2.1 shows how other management ideas and practices throughout history are clearly related to the management functions in the textbook. Besides the achievements of the Sumerians and Egyptians, we might note King Hammurabi, who established controls by using witnesses and written documents; King Nebuchadnezzar, who pioneered techniques for producing goods and using wages to motivate workers; Sun Tzu, author of *The Art of War*, who emphasized the importance of strategy and identifying and attacking an opponent's weaknesses;

Exhibit 2.1

Management Ideas and Practice throughout History

Time	Individual or Group	Planning	Organizing	Leading	Controlling	Contributions to Management Thought and Practice
5000 BC	Sumerians				√	Record keeping.
4000 BC to 2000 BC	Egyptians	√	√		√	Recognized the need for planning, organizing, and controlling when building the pyramids. Submitted requests in writing. Made decisions after consulting staff for advice.
1800 BC	Hammurabi				√	Established controls by using witnesses (to vouch for what was said or done) and writing to document transactions.
600 BC	Nebuchadnezzar		√	√		Wage incentives and production control.
500 BC	Sun Tzu	√		√		Strategy; identifying and attacking opponent's weaknesses.
400 BC	Xenophon	√	√	√	√	Recognized management as a separate art.
400 BC	Cyrus		√	√	√	Human relations and motion study.
175 BC	Cato the Elder		√			Job descriptions.
284	Diocletian		√			Delegation of authority.
900	Alfarabi			√		Listed leadership traits.
1100	Ghazali			√		Listed managerial traits.
1418	Barbarigo		√			Different organizational forms/structures.
1436	Venetians				√	Numbering, standardization, and interchangeability of parts.
1500	Sir Thomas More			√		Critical of poor management and leadership.
1525	Machiavelli		√	√		Cohesiveness, power, and leadership in organizations.

Source: C. S. George, Jr., *The History of Management Thought* (Englewood Cliffs, NJ: Prentice-Hall, 1972).

Xenophon, who recognized management as a distinct and separate art; King Cyrus, who recognized the importance of human relations and used motion study to eliminate wasteful steps and improve productivity; Cato the Elder, who espoused the importance of job descriptions; Diocletian, a Roman emperor, who mastered the art of delegation by dividing the widespread Roman Empire into 101 provinces, which were then grouped into 13 dioceses, which were in turn grouped into four geographic divisions; Alfarabi and Ghazali, who began defining what it takes to be a good leader or manager; Barbarigo, who discussed the different ways in which organizations could be structured; the Venetians, who used numbering and standardization to make parts interchangeable; Sir Thomas More, who, in his book *Utopia*, emphasized the negative societal consequences associated with poor leadership; and Machiavelli, who wrote about the importance of cohesion, power, and leadership in organizations.

© SUPERSTOCK

Management ideas have been in use from well before the Romans, but only recently has management become a profession and a topic of study.

1.2 Why We Need Managers Today

Working from 8 AM to 5 PM, coffee breaks, lunch hours, crushing rush hour traffic, and punching a time clock are things we associate with today's working world. Work hasn't always been this way, however. In fact, the design of jobs and organizations has changed dramatically over the last 500 years.

For most of humankind's history, people didn't commute to work. In fact, travel of any kind was arduous and extremely rare.[6] Work usually occurred in homes or on farms. For example, in 1720, almost 80 percent of the 5.5 million people in England lived and worked in the country. Indeed, as recently as 1870, two-thirds of Americans earned their living from agriculture. Even most of those who didn't earn their living from agriculture didn't commute to work. Blacksmiths, furniture makers, leather-goods makers, and other skilled tradesmen or craftsmen, who formed trade guilds (the historical predecessors of labor unions) in England as early as 1093, typically worked out of shops in or next to their homes.[7] Likewise, cottage workers worked with each other out of small homes that were often built in a semicircle. A family in each cottage would complete a different production step with work passed from one cottage to the next until production was complete. For example, textile work was a common "cottage industry": Families in different cottages would shear the sheep; clean the wool; comb, bleach, and dye it; spin it into yarn; and weave the yarn into cloth. Yet with no commute, no bosses (workers determined the amount and pace of their work), and no common building (from the time of the ancient Egyptians, Greeks, and Romans through the middle of the 19th century, it was rare for more than 12 people to work together under one roof), cottage work was very different from today's jobs and companies.[8] And because these work groups were small and typically self-organized, there wasn't a strong need for management.

During the Industrial Revolution (1750–1900), however, jobs and organizations changed dramatically.[9] First, thanks to the availability of power (steam engines and later electricity) and numerous inventions, such as Darby's coke-smelting process and Cort's puddling and rolling process (both for making iron) and Hargreave's spinning jenny and Arkwright's water frame (both for spinning cotton), low-paid, unskilled laborers running machines began to replace high-paid, skilled artisans. Whereas artisans made entire goods by themselves by hand, this new production system was based on a division of labor: Each worker, interacting with machines, performed separate, highly specialized tasks that were but a small part of all the steps required to make manufactured goods. Mass production was born as rope- and chain-driven assembly lines moved work to stationary workers who concentrated on performing one small task over and over again. While workers focused on their singular tasks, managers were needed to effectively coordinate the different parts of the production system and optimize its overall performance. Productivity skyrocketed at companies that understood this. For example, at **FORD MOTOR COMPANY**, the time required to assemble a car dropped from 12.5 man-hours to just 93 minutes after switching to mass production.[10]

"What's New" Company

Second, instead of being performed in fields, homes, or small shops, jobs occurred in large, formal organizations where hundreds, if not thousands, of people worked under one roof.[11] In 1849, for example, with just 123 workers, **CHICAGO HARVESTER** (the predecessor of International Harvester) ran the largest factory in the United States. In 1870, the **PULLMAN COMPANY**, a manufacturer of railroad sleeping cars, was the largest factory, with only 200 employees. Yet by 1913, Henry Ford employed 12,000 employees in his Highland Park, Michigan, factory alone. With the number of people working in manufacturing having quintupled from 1860 to 1890, and with individual factories employing so many workers under one roof, companies now had a strong need for disciplinary rules (to impose order and structure). For the first time, they needed managers who knew how to organize large groups, work with employees, and make good decisions.

"What's New" Company

"What's New" Company

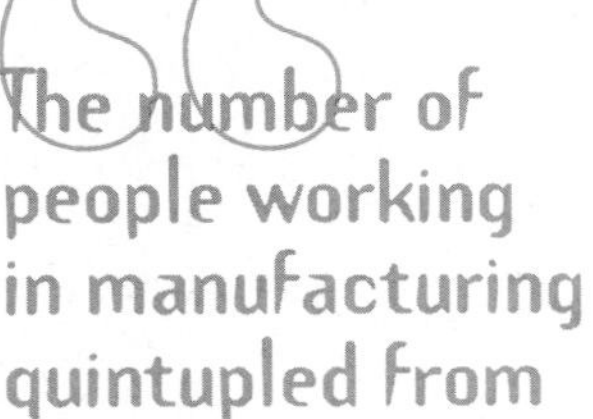
The number of people working in manufacturing quintupled from 1860 to 1890.

Review 1: The Origins of Management

Management as a field of study may be just 125 years old, but management ideas and practices have actually been used since the beginning of recorded history. From the Sumerians in 5000 BC to 16th-century Europe, there are historical antecedents for each of the functions of management discussed in this textbook: planning, organizing, leading, and controlling. Despite these early examples of management ideas, there was no compelling need for managers until systematic changes in the nature of work and organizations occurred during the last two centuries. As work shifted from families to factories, from skilled laborers to specialized, unskilled laborers, from small, self-organized groups to large factories employing thousands under one roof, and from unique, small batches of production to large standardized mass production, managers were needed to impose order and structure, to motivate and direct large groups of workers, and to plan and make decisions that optimized overall company performance by effectively coordinating the different parts of organizational systems.

THE EVOLUTION OF MANAGEMENT

Before 1880, business educators taught only basic bookkeeping and secretarial skills, and no one published books or articles about management.[12] Over the next 25 years, however, things changed dramatically. In 1881, Joseph Wharton gave the University of Pennsylvania $100,000 to establish a department to educate students for careers in management. By 1911, 30 business schools, including those at Harvard, the University of Chicago, and the University of California, had been established to teach managers how to run businesses.[13] In 1886, Henry Towne, president of the Yale and Towne Manufacturing Company, presented his ideas about management to the American Society of Engineers. In his talk, entitled "The Engineer as Economist," he emphasized that managing people and work processes was just as important as engineering work, which focused on machines.[14] Towne also argued that management should be recognized as a separate field of study with its own professional associations, journals, and literature where management ideas could be exchanged and developed. Today, because of the forethought and efforts of Joseph Wharton and Henry Towne, if you have a question about management you can turn to dozens of academic journals (such as the Academy of Management's *Journal* or *Review*, *Administrative Science Quarterly*, the *Strategic Management Journal*, and the *Journal of Applied Psychology*), hundreds of business school and practitioner journals (such as *Harvard Business Review*, *Sloan Management Review*, and the *Academy of Management Perspectives*), and thousands of books and articles. In the next four sections, you will learn about other important contributors to the field of management and how their ideas shaped our current understanding of management theory and practice.

After reading the next four sections, which review the different schools of management thought, you should be able to

2 explain the history of scientific management.
3 discuss the history of bureaucratic and administrative management.
4 explain the history of human relations management.
5 discuss the history of operations, information, systems, and contingency management.

2 Scientific Management

Before scientific management, organizational decision making could best be described as "seat of the pants." Decisions were made haphazardly without any systematic study, thought, or collection of information. Customer orders were transmitted verbally from sales representatives to shop floor supervisors. They were not written down. If the "managers" hired by the company founder or owner decided that workers should work twice as fast, little or no thought was given to worker motivation. If workers resisted, "managers" often resorted to physical beatings to get workers to work faster, harder, or longer. In general, with no incentives for "managers" to cooperate with workers and vice versa, managers and workers gamed the system trying to systematically take advantage of each other. Likewise, nothing was standardized. Each worker did the same job in his or her own way with different methods and different tools. In short, there were no procedures to standardize operations, no standards by which to judge whether performance was good or bad, and no follow-up to determine if productivity or quality actually improved when changes were made.[15]

This all changed, however, with the advent of **scientific management**, which, in contrast to the unsystematic "seat-of-the-pants" approach, thoroughly studied and tested different work methods to identify the best, most efficient ways to complete a job.

scientific management thoroughly studying and testing different work methods to identify the best, most efficient way to complete a job

Let's find out more about scientific management by learning about ***2.1 Frederick W. Taylor, the father of scientific management****;* ***2.2 Frank and Lillian Gilbreth and motion studies****; and* ***2.3 Henry Gantt and his Gantt charts****.*

© BETTMANN/CORBIS

Frederick Taylor is known today as the "father of scientific management." One of his many contributions to modern management is the common practice of giving employees rest breaks throughout the day.

2.1 Father of Scientific Management: Frederick W. Taylor

Frederick W. Taylor (1856–1915), the "father of scientific management," began his career as a worker at **Midvale Steel Company**. He was later promoted to patternmaker, supervisor, and then chief engineer.

At Midvale, Taylor was deeply affected by his three-year struggle to get the men who worked for him to do, as he called it, "a fair day's work." Taylor, who had worked alongside the men as a coworker before becoming their boss, said, "We who were the workmen of that shop had the quantity output carefully agreed upon for everything that was turned out in the shop. We limited the output to about, I should think, one-third of what we could very well have done." Taylor explained that as soon as he became the boss, "the men who were working under me ... knew that I was onto the whole game of **soldiering**, or deliberately restricting output."[16] When Taylor told his workers, "I have accepted a job under the management of this company and I am on the other side of the fence ... I am going to try to get a bigger output," the workers responded, "We warn you, Fred, if you try to bust any of these rates [a **rate buster** was someone who worked faster than the group] we will have you over the fence in six weeks."[17]

Over the next three years, Taylor tried everything he could think of to improve output. By doing the job himself, he showed workers that it was possible to produce more output. He hired new "intelligent" workers and trained them himself, hoping they would produce more. But they would not because of "very heavy social pressure" from the other workers. Pushed by Taylor, the workers began breaking their machines so that they couldn't produce. Taylor responded by fining them every time they broke a machine and for any violation of the rules, no matter how small, such as being late to work. Tensions became so severe that some of the workers threatened to shoot him. Looking back at the situation, Taylor reflected, "It is a horrid life for any man to live, not to be able to look any workman in the face all day long without seeing hostility there and feeling that every man around one is his virtual enemy." He said, "I made up my mind either to get out of the business entirely and go into some other line of work, or to find some remedy for this unbearable condition."[18] The remedy that Taylor eventually developed was scientific management.

soldiering when workers deliberately slow their pace or restrict their work outputs

rate buster a group member whose work pace is significantly faster than the normal pace in his or her group

Taylor, who once described scientific management as "seventy-five percent science and twenty-five percent common sense," emphasized that the goal of scientific management was to use systematic study to find the "one best way" of doing each task. To do that, managers must follow the four principles shown in Exhibit 2.2.[19] First, "develop a science" for each element of work. Study it. Analyze it. Determine the "one best way" to do the work. For example, one of Taylor's controversial proposals at the time was to give rest breaks to factory workers doing physical labor. We take morning, lunch, and

Exhibit 2.2

Taylor's Four Principles of Scientific Management

First	Develop a science for each element of a man's work, which replaces the old rule-of-thumb method.
Second	Scientifically select and then train, teach, and develop the workman, whereas in the past he chose his own work and trained himself as best he could.
Third	Heartily cooperate with the men so as to ensure all of the work being done is in accordance with the principles of the science which has been developed.
Fourth	There is an almost equal division of the work and the responsibility between the management and the workmen. The management take over all the work for which they are better fitted than the workmen, while in the past almost all of the work and the greater part of the responsibility were thrown upon the men.

Source: F. W. Taylor, *The Principles of Scientific Management* (New York: Harper, 1911).

afternoon breaks for granted, but in Taylor's day, factory workers were expected to work without stopping.[20] When Taylor said that breaks would increase worker productivity, no one believed him. Nonetheless, through systematic experiments, he showed that workers receiving frequent rest breaks were able to greatly increase their daily output.

Second, scientifically select, train, teach, and develop workers to help them reach their full potential. Before Taylor, supervisors often hired on the basis of favoritism and nepotism. Who you knew was often more important than what you could do. By contrast, Taylor instructed supervisors to hire "first class" workers on the basis of their aptitude to do a job well. In one of the first applications of this principle, physical reaction times were used to select bicycle ball-bearing inspectors who had to be able to examine and reject poor-quality ball bearings as fast as they were produced on a production line. For similar reasons, Taylor also recommended that companies train and develop their workers—a rare practice at the time.

Third, cooperate with employees to ensure implementation of the scientific principles. Labor unrest was widespread at the time; the number of labor strikes against companies doubled between 1893 and 1904. As Taylor knew from personal experience, more often than not workers and management viewed each other as the enemy. Taylor's advice ran contrary to the common wisdom of the day. He said, "The majority of these men believe that the fundamental interests of employees and employers are necessarily antagonistic. Scientific management, on the contrary, has for its very foundation the firm conviction that the true interests of the two are one and the same; that prosperity for the employer cannot exist through a long term of years unless it is accompanied by prosperity for the employee and vice versa; and that it is possible to give the workman what he most wants—high wages—and the employer what he wants—a low labor cost—for his manufactures."[21]

The fourth principle of scientific management was to divide the work and the responsibility equally between management and workers. Prior to Taylor, workers alone were held responsible for productivity and performance. But, said Taylor, "Almost every act of the workman should be preceded by one or more preparatory acts of the management which enable him to do his work better and quicker than he otherwise could. And each man should daily be taught by and receive the most friendly help from those who are over him, instead of being, at the one extreme, driven or coerced by his bosses, and at the other left to his own unaided devices."[22]

Above all, Taylor felt these principles could be used to determine a "fair day's work," that is, what an average worker could produce at a reasonable pace, day in and day out. Once that was determined, it was management's responsibility to pay workers fairly for that fair day's work. In essence, Taylor was trying to align management and employees so that what was good for employees was also good for management. In this way, he felt, workers and managers could avoid the conflicts that he had experienced at Midvale Steel. And one of the best ways, according to Taylor, to align management and employees was to use incentives to motivate workers. As Taylor wrote:

> *In order to have any hope of obtaining the initiative of his workmen the manager must give some special incentive to his men beyond that which is given to the average of the trade. This incentive can be given in several different ways, as, for example, the hope of rapid promotion or advancement; higher wages, either in the form of generous piecework prices or of a premium or bonus of some kind for good and rapid work; shorter hours of labor; better surroundings and working conditions than are ordinarily given, etc., and, above all, this special incentive should be accompanied by that personal consideration for, and friendly contact with, his workmen which comes only from a genuine and kindly interest in the welfare of those under him. It is only by giving a special inducement or "incentive" of this kind that the employer can hope even approximately to get the "initiative" of his workmen.*[23]

"Almost every act of the workman should be preceded by one or more preparatory acts of the management."

FREDERICK W. TAYLOR,
MIDVALE STEEL COMPANY

Although Taylor remains a controversial figure among some academics who believe that his ideas were bad for workers, nearly a century later it is inarguable that his key ideas have stood the test of time.[24] These include using systematic analysis to identify the best methods; scientifically selecting, training, and developing workers; promoting cooperation between management and labor; developing standardized approaches and tools; setting specific tasks or goals and then rewarding workers with financial incentives; and giving workers shorter work hours and frequent breaks. In fact, his ideas are so well accepted and widely used that we take most of them for granted. As eminent management scholar Edwin Locke says, "The point is not, as is often claimed, that he was 'right in the context of his time,' but is now outdated, but that *most of his insights are still valid today*."[25]

2.2 Motion Studies: Frank and Lillian Gilbreth

The husband and wife team Frank and Lillian Gilbreth are best known for their use of motion studies to simplify work, but they also made significant contributions to the employment of disabled workers and industrial psychology. Like Frederick Taylor, their early experiences significantly shaped their interests and contributions to management.

Though admitted to MIT, Frank Gilbreth (1868–1924) began his career as an apprentice bricklayer. While learning the trade, he noticed the bricklayers using three different sets of motions—one to teach others how to lay bricks, a second to work at a slow pace, and a third to work at a fast pace.[26] Wondering which was best, he studied the various approaches and began eliminating unnecessary motions. For example, by designing a stand that could be raised to waist height, he eliminated the need to bend over to pick up each brick. Turning to grab a brick was faster and easier than bending down. By having lower-paid workers place all the bricks with their most attractive side up, bricklayers didn't waste time turning a brick over to find it. By mixing a more consistent mortar, bricklayers no longer had to tap each brick numerous times to put it in the right position. Together, Gilbreth's improvements raised productivity from 120 to 350 bricks per hour and from 1,000 bricks to 2,700 bricks per day.

As a result of his experience with bricklaying, Gilbreth and his wife Lillian developed a long-term interest in using motion study to simplify work, improve productivity, and reduce the level of effort required to safely perform a job. Indeed, Frank Gilbreth said, "The greatest waste in the world comes from needless, ill-directed, and ineffective motions."[27] The Gilbreths' motion study, however, is different from Frederick W. Taylor's time study.[28] Taylor developed time study to put an end to soldiering and to determine what could be considered a fair day's work. **Time study** worked by timing how long it took a "first-class man" to complete each part of his job. After allowing for rest periods, a standard time was established, and a worker's pay would increase or decrease depending on whether the worker exceeded or fell below that standard. By contrast, **motion study**, as we saw in Frank Gilbreth's analysis of bricklaying, broke each task or job into separate motions and then eliminated those that were unnecessary or repetitive. Because many motions were completed very quickly, the Gilbreths used motion-picture films, then a relatively new technology, to analyze jobs. Most film cameras, however, were hand-cranked and thus variable in their film speed, so Frank Gilbreth invented the microchronometer, a large clock that could record time to 1/2,000th of a second. By placing the microchronometer next to the worker in the camera's field of vision and attaching a flashing strobe light to the worker's hands to better identify the direction and sequence of key movements, the Gilbreths could use film to detect and precisely time even the slightest, fastest movements. Motion study typically yielded

time study timing how long it takes good workers to complete each part of their jobs

motion study breaking each task or job into its separate motions and then eliminating those that are unnecessary or repetitive production increases of 25 to 300 percent.[29] It is even used in hospitals to clearly identify the large amount of time that surgeons wasted looking for the next surgical instrument they needed. Frank Gilbreth improved this process by making a nurse responsible for organizing, retrieving, and handing surgical instruments to surgeons, a process still in use today.[30]

One of the Gilbreths' most overlooked accomplishments was the critical role they played in rehabilitating and employing disabled workers.[31] After World War I, there were 13 million wounded and disabled soldiers in the United States and Europe. Frank Gilbreth worried, "What is to be done with the millions of cripples, when their injuries have been remedied as far as possible, and when they are obliged to become again a part of the working community?"[32] Sensitive to this issue because of Frank's recovery from a rheumatism attack that had left him temporarily paralyzed from the neck down, the Gilbreths applied motion study to identify the kinds of tasks that disabled workers could effectively perform. Nearly 75 years before the Americans with Disabilities Act became law (see Chapter 12 for more information), the Gilbreths argued that the government, employers, and engineers had an important role to play in employing disabled workers. The government's job, they said, was to provide vocational training. Indeed, in 1918, the U.S. Congress passed the Vocational Rehabilitation Act, adopting most of the Gilbreths' key recommendations. Employers, they said, should identify jobs that disabled people could perform. To help employers do this, the Gilbreths created a large slide show of pictures documenting the hundreds of ways in which disabled people could effectively perform jobs. Also, according to the Gilbreths, engineers had a responsibility to adapt and design machines so that disabled workers could use them.

Lillian Gilbreth (1878–1972) was an important contributor to management as well. She was the first woman to receive a Ph.D. in Industrial Psychology, as well as the first woman to become a member of the Society of Industrial Engineers and the American Society of Mechanical Engineers. When Frank died in 1924, she continued the work of their management consulting company (which they had shared for over a dozen years) on her own. Lillian, who was concerned with the human side of work, was one of the first contributors to

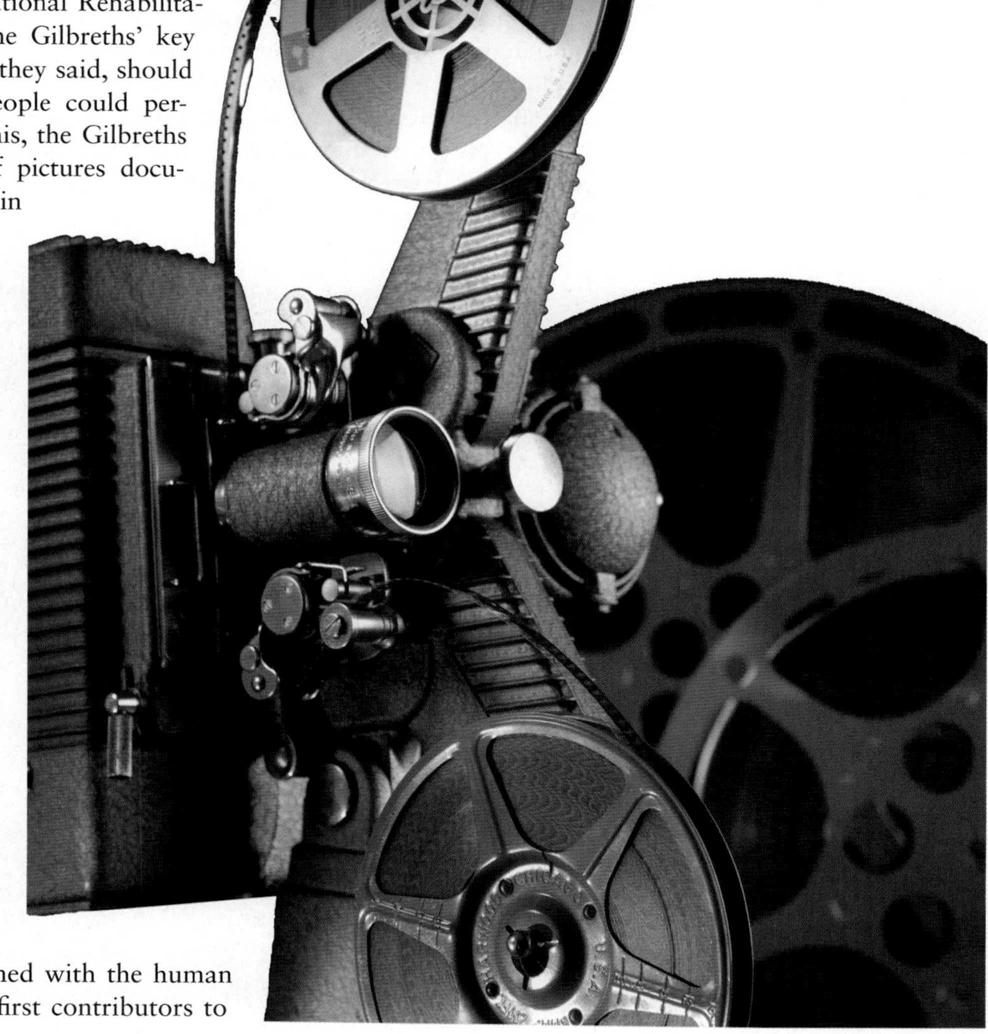

industrial psychology, originating ways to improve office communication, incentive programs, job satisfaction, and management training. Her work also convinced the government to enact laws regarding workplace safety, ergonomics, and child labor.

2.3 Charts: Henry Gantt

Henry Gantt (1861–1919) was first a protégé and then an associate of Frederick Taylor. Gantt is best known for the Gantt chart, but he also made significant contributions to management with respect to pay-for-performance plans and the training and development of workers. As shown in Exhibit 2.3, a **Gantt chart**, which shows time in various units on the *x*-axis and tasks on the *y*-axis, visually indicates what tasks must be completed at which times in order to complete a project. For example, Exhibit 2.3 shows that to start construction on a new company headquarters by the week of November 18, the following tasks must be completed by the following dates: architectural firm selected by October 7, architectural planning done by November 4, permits obtained from the city by November 11, site preparation finished by November 18, and loans and financing finalized by November 18. Though simple and straightforward, Gantt charts were revolutionary in the era of "seat of the pants" management because of the detailed planning information they provided to managers. As Gantt wrote, "By using the graphical forms [the Gantt chart] its value is very much increased, for the general appearance of the sheet is sufficient to tell how closely the schedule is being lived up to; in other words, whether the plant is being run efficiently or not." Gantt said, "Such sheets show at a glance where the delays occur, and indicate what must have our attention in order to keep up the proper output." Today, the use of Gantt charts is so widespread that nearly all project management software and computer spreadsheets have the capability to create charts that track and visually display the progress being made on a project.

Gantt chart a graphical chart that shows which tasks must be completed at which times in order to complete a project or task

Exhibit 2.3

Gantt Chart for Starting Construction on a New Headquarters

Current Week				↓					
Weeks	23 Sep to 30 Sep	30 Sep to 7 Oct	7 Oct to 14 Oct	14 Oct to 21 Oct	21 Oct to 28 Oct	28 Oct to 4 Nov	4 Nov to 11 Nov	11 Nov to 18 Nov	18 Nov to 25 Nov
Tasks									
Interview and select architectural firm	Architect by October 7								
Hold weekly planning meetings with architects			Weekly planning with architects by November 4						
Obtain permits and approval from city					Permits & approval by November 11				
Begin preparing site for construction					Site construction done by November 18				
Finalize loans and financing							Financing finalized by November 18		
Begin construction									Start building

Tasks
Weeks 23 Sep to 30 Sep 30 Sep to 7 Oct 7 Oct to 14 Oct 14 Oct to 21 Oct 21 Oct to 28 Oct 28 Oct to 4 Nov 4 Nov to 11 Nov 11 Nov to 18 Nov 18 Nov to 25 Nov
Current Week

Gantt, who was much more sympathetic toward workers than Frederick Taylor was, introduced a significant change to Taylor's well-known piece-rate reward system. Unlike Taylor's system, in which payment was completely dependent on production—if you produced at substandard levels, you got substandard pay—Gantt's task and bonus system did not punish workers for not achieving higher levels of production. Workers who produced more received a daily bonus, but those who didn't simply received their standard daily pay. The key, according to Gantt, was that his task and bonus system didn't punish workers for lower production as they took time to learn how to increase their production efficiency. Production usually doubled under Gantt's system.[33]

Finally, Gantt, along with Taylor, was one of the first to strongly recommend that companies train and develop their workers.[34] In his work with companies, he found that workers achieved their best performance levels if they were trained first. At the time, however, supervisors, fearing that they could lose their jobs to more knowledgeable workers, were reluctant to teach workers what they knew. Gantt overcame the supervisors' resistance by rewarding them with bonuses for properly training all of their workers. Said Gantt, "This is the first recorded attempt to make it in the financial interest of the foreman to teach the individual worker, and the importance of it cannot be overestimated, for it changes the foreman from a driver of men to their friend and helper."[35] Thus, Gantt's approach to training was straightforward: "(1) a scientific investigation in detail of each piece of work, and the determination of the best method and the shortest time in which the work can be done. (2) A teacher capable of teaching the best method and the shortest time. (3) Reward for both teacher and pupil when the latter is successful."[36]

Review 2: Scientific Management

In contrast to "seat of the pants" management, scientific management recommended studying and testing different work methods to identify the best, most efficient ways to complete a job. According to Frederick W. Taylor, the "father of scientific management," managers should follow four scientific management principles. First, study each element of work to determine the "one best way" to do it. Second, scientifically select, train, teach, and develop workers to reach their full potential. Third, cooperate with employees to ensure implementation of the scientific principles. Fourth, divide the work and the responsibility equally between management and workers. Above all, Taylor felt these principles could be used to align managers and employees by determining a "fair day's work," what an average worker could produce at a reasonable pace, and "a fair day's pay," what management should pay workers for that effort. Taylor felt that incentives were one of the best ways to align management and employees.

The husband and wife team of Frank and Lillian Gilbreth are best known for their use of motion studies to simplify work. Whereas Taylor used time study to determine "a fair day's work," based on how long it took a "first-class man" to complete each part of his job, Frank Gilbreth used film cameras and microchronometers to conduct motion study to improve efficiency by categorizing and eliminating unnecessary or repetitive motions. The Gilbreths also made significant contributions to the employment of disabled workers, encouraging the government to rehabilitate them, employers to identify jobs that they could perform, and engineers to adapt and design machines they could use. Lillian Gilbreth, one of the first contributors to industrial psychology, originated ways to improve office communication, incentive programs, job satisfaction, and management training. She also convinced the government to enact laws regarding workplace safety, ergonomics, and child labor. Henry Gantt is best known for the Gantt chart, which graphically indicates when a series of tasks must be completed to perform a job or project, but he also developed ideas regarding pay-for-performance plans (where workers were rewarded for producing more, but were not punished if they didn't) and worker training (all workers should be trained and their managers should be rewarded for training them).

3 Bureaucratic and Administrative Management

The field of scientific management, which quickly developed in the United States between 1895 and 1920, focused on improving the efficiency of manufacturing facilities and their workers. At about the same time, equally important ideas were developing in Europe. German sociologist Max Weber's ideas about bureaucratic management, which presented a new way to run entire organizations, were published in *The Theory of Economic and Social Organization* in 1922. Henri Fayol, an experienced French CEO, published his ideas about administrative management, including how and what managers should do in their jobs, in *General and Industrial Management* in 1916. Though developed at the same time as scientific management, the ideas of Weber and Fayol would not begin to influence American ideas about management until after World War II, when their books were translated into English and published in the United States in 1947 and 1949, respectively.

Let's find out more about Weber's and Fayol's contributions to management by learning about ***3.1 bureaucratic management*** *and* ***3.2 administrative management****.*

3.1 Bureaucratic Management: Max Weber

Today, when we hear the term *bureaucracy*, we think of inefficiency and red tape, incompetence and ineffectiveness, and rigid administrators blindly enforcing nonsensical rules. When German sociologist Max Weber (1864–1920) first proposed the idea of bureaucratic organizations, however, monarchies and patriarchies, not bureaucracies, were associated with these problems. In monarchies, where kings, queens, sultans, and emperors ruled, and patriarchies, where a council of elders, wise men, or male heads of extended families ruled, the top leaders typically achieved their positions by virtue of birthright. For example, when the queen died, her oldest son became king, regardless of his intelligence, experience, education, or desire. Likewise, promotion to prominent positions of authority in monarchies and patriarchies was based on who you knew, who you were (heredity), or ancient rules and traditions. In short, for much of humankind's history, people often rose to positions of wealth and power because of family, political connections, or personal loyalty.

It was against this historical background of monarchical and patriarchic rule that Weber proposed the then new idea of bureaucracy. *Bureaucracy* comes from the French word *bureaucratie*. Since *bureau* means desk or office and *cratie* or *cracy* means to rule, *bureaucracy* literally means to rule from a desk or office. According to Weber, however, **bureaucracy** is "the exercise of control on the basis of knowledge."[37] So, in a bureaucracy, rather than ruling by virtue of favoritism, or personal or family connections, people would lead by virtue of their rational-legal authority—in other words, their knowledge, expertise, or experience. Furthermore,

bureaucracy the exercise of control on the basis of knowledge, expertise, or experience the aim of bureaucracy is to achieve an organization's goals in the most efficient way possible.

Exhibit 2.4 shows the seven elements that, according to Weber, characterize bureaucracies. First, instead of hiring people because of their family or political connections, or personal loyalty, they should be hired because their technical training or education qualifies them to do their jobs well. Second, along the same lines, promotion within the company would no longer be based on who you knew or who you were (heredity), but on your experience or achievements. And to further limit the influence of personal connections in the promotion process, managers, rather than organizational owners, should decide who gets promoted. Third, each position or job is part of a chain of command that clarifies who reports to whom throughout the organization. Those higher in the chain of command have the right, if they so choose, to give commands, take action, and make decisions concerning activities occurring anywhere below them in the chain. Unlike many monarchies or patriarchies, however, those lower in the chain of command are protected by a grievance procedure that gives them the right to appeal the decisions of those in higher positions. Fourth, to increase efficiency and effectiveness, tasks and responsibilities are separated and assigned to those best qualified to complete them. Furthermore, authority is vested in positions, not people. If you move to a different job, your authority increases or decreases commensurate with the responsibilities of that job. And, to reduce confusion and conflict, the authority of each position or job is also clearly divided and defined. Fifth, because of his strong distaste for favoritism, Weber felt that an organization's rules and procedures should apply to all members, regardless of their position or status. Sixth, to ensure consistency and fairness over time and across different leaders and supervisors, all rules, procedures, and decisions should be recorded in writing. Finally, to reduce favoritism, "professional" managers rather than company owners should manage or supervise the organization.

When viewed in historical context, Weber's ideas about bureaucracy represent a tremendous improvement in how organizations should be run. Fairness supplanted favoritism, the goal of efficiency replaced the goal of personal gain, and logical rules and procedures took the place of traditions or arbitrary decision making. Today, however, after more than a century of experience we recognize that bureaucracy has limitations as well. In bureaucracies, managers are supposed to influence employee behavior by fairly rewarding or punishing employees for compliance or noncompliance with organizational policies, rules, and procedures. In reality, however, most employees would

Exhibit 2.4
Elements of Bureaucratic Organizations

Qualification-based hiring	Employees are hired on the basis of their technical training or educational background.
Merit-based promotion	Promotion is based on experience or achievement. Managers, not organizational owners, decide who is promoted.
Chain of commands	Each job occurs within a hierarchy, the chain of command, in which each position reports and is accountable to a higher position. A grievance procedure and a right to appeal protect people in lower positions.
Division of labor	Tasks, responsibilities, and authority are clearly divided and defined.
Impartial application of rules and procedures	Rules and procedures apply to all members of the organization and will be applied in an impartial manner, regardless of one's position or status
Recorded in writing	All administrative decisions, acts, rules, or procedure will be recorded in writing.
Managers separate from owners	The owners of an organization should not manage or supervise the organization.

Source: M. Weber, *The Theory of Economic and Social Organization,* trans. A. Henderson & T. Parsons (New York: Free Press, 1947), 329–334.

argue that bureaucratic managers emphasize punishment for noncompliance much more than rewards for compliance. Ironically, bureaucratic management was created to prevent just this type of managerial behavior. By encouraging managers to apply well-thought-out rules, policies, and procedures impartially and consistently to everyone in the organization, bureaucratic control is supposed to make companies more efficient, effective, and fair. Perversely, as you'll read in Chapter 16 on control, it can sometimes have just the opposite effect. Managers who use bureaucratic control often put following the rules above all else. Another limitation of bureaucratically controlled companies is that due to their rule- and policy-driven decision making, they can be highly resistant to change and slow to respond to customers and competitors. Despite its advantages over monarchical and patriarchic organizational forms, even Weber recognized bureaucracy's limitations. He called it the "iron cage" and said, "Once fully established, bureaucracy is among those social structures which are the hardest to destroy."[38]

"Once fully established, bureaucracy is among those social structures which are the hardest to destroy."

MAX WEBER, SOCIOLOGIST

3.2 Administrative Management: Henri Fayol

Though his work was not translated and widely recognized in the United States until 1949, Frenchman Henri Fayol (1841–1925) was as important a contributor to the field of management as Frederick Taylor. Like Taylor and Frank and Lillian Gilbreth, Fayol's work experience significantly shaped his thoughts and ideas about management. But whereas Taylor's ideas changed companies from the shop floor up, Fayol's ideas, which were shaped by his experience as a managing director (CEO), generally changed companies from the board of directors down.[39] Fayol is best known for developing five functions of managers and 14 principles of management, as well as for his belief that management could and should be taught to others.

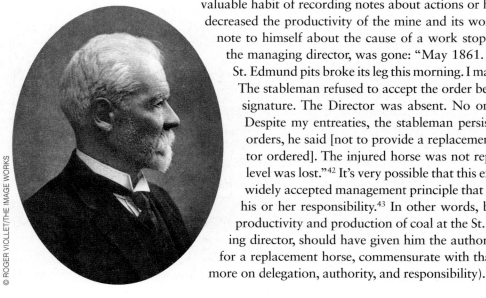

Henri Fayol conceived of the principles which today have been distilled into the four functions of management.

Like his father, Henri Fayol enrolled in France's National School of Mines, graduating with an engineering degree at the age of 19.[40] His first job as a mining engineer was spent learning how to contain and put out underground fires. In this job, he began the valuable habit of recording notes about actions or happenings that either improved or decreased the productivity of the mine and its workers.[41] For instance, he wrote this note to himself about the cause of a work stoppage that occurred when his boss, the managing director, was gone: "May 1861. The horse on the sixth level of the St. Edmund pits broke its leg this morning. I made out an order for its replacement. The stableman refused to accept the order because it did not bear the Director's signature. The Director was absent. No one was designated to replace him. Despite my entreaties, the stableman persisted in his refusal. He had express orders, he said [not to provide a replacement horse unless the managing director ordered]. The injured horse was not replaced and production at the sixth level was lost."[42] It's very possible that this experience helped him form the now widely accepted management principle that a manager's authority should equal his or her responsibility.[43] In other words, because he was responsible for the productivity and production of coal at the St. Edmund's pit, his boss, the managing director, should have given him the authority to take actions, such as signing for a replacement horse, commensurate with that responsibility (see Chapter 9 for more on delegation, authority, and responsibility).

It's likely, however, that the most formative events in Fayol's business career came during his 20 plus years as the managing director (CEO) of Compagnie de Commentry-Fourchambault-Decazeville, commonly known as **COMAMBAULT**, a vertically integrated steel company that owned several coal and iron ore mines and employed 10,000 to 13,000 workers. Fayol was initially hired by the board of directors to shut the "hopeless" steel company down. The company was facing increased competition from English and German steel companies, which had lower costs, and from new steel mills in northern and eastern France, which were closer to major markets and thus could avoid the large shipping costs incurred by Fayol's company, which was located in central France.[44] In the five years before Fayol became CEO, production had dropped more than 60 percent, from 38,000 to 15,000 annual metric tons. The company had exhausted a key supply of coal needed for steel production, had already shut one steel mill down, and was losing money at another.[45] The company had quit paying dividends to shareholders and had no cash to invest in new technology, such as blast furnaces, that could lower its costs and increase productivity. Therefore, the board hired Fayol as CEO to quickly dissolve and liquidate the business. But after "four months of reflection and study," he presented the board with a plan, backed by detailed facts and figures, to save the company.[46] With little to lose, the board agreed. Fayol then began the process of turning the company around by obtaining supplies of key resources, such as coal and iron ore; using research to develop new steel alloy products; carefully selecting key subordinates in research, purchasing, manufacturing, and sales and then delegating responsibility to them; and cutting costs by moving the company to a better location closer to key markets.[47] Looking back 10 years later, Fayol attributed his and the company's success to changes in management practices. He wrote, "When I assumed the responsibility for the restoration of Decazeville, I did not rely on my technical superiority.... I relied on my ability as an organizer [and my] skill in handling men (*manoeuvrier des hommes*)."[48] Fayol concluded, "With the same [coal] mines, the same [steel] mills, the same financial resources, the same markets, the same Board of Directors and the same personnel, solely *with the application of a new way of running the company* [italics added], the firm experienced a rise [in its performance] comparable to its earlier decline."[49]

Based on his experience as a CEO, Fayol argued that "the success of an enterprise generally depends much more on the administrative ability of its leaders than on their technical ability."[50] And, as you learned in Chapter 1, Fayol argued that this means that if managers are to be successful, they need to perform five managerial functions or elements: planning, organizing, coordinating, commanding, and controlling.[51] Today, though, most management textbooks have dropped the coordinating function and now refer to Fayol's commanding function as "leading." Consequently, Fayol's management functions are widely known as planning (determining organizational goals and a means for achieving them), organizing (deciding where decisions will be made, who will do what jobs and tasks, and who will work for whom), leading (inspiring and motivating workers to work hard to achieve organizational goals), and controlling (monitoring progress toward goal achievement and taking corrective action when needed). In addition, according to Fayol, effective management is based on the 14 principles in Exhibit 2.5.

Finally, along with Joseph Wharton, Fayol was one of the first to argue that management could and should be taught to others. In short, Fayol believed that the principles of management could be taught in colleges and universities and that managers are not born but can be made through a combination of education and experience.

1.	**Division of work**	Increase production by dividing work so that each worker completes smaller tasks or job elements.
2.	**Authority and responsibility**	A manager's authority, which is the "right to give orders," should be commensurate with the manager's responsibility. However, organizations should enact controls to prevent managers from abusing their authority.
3.	**Discipline**	Clearly defined rules and procedures are needed at all organizational levels to ensure order and proper behavior.
4.	**Unity of command**	To avoid confusion and conflict, each employee should report to and receive orders from just one boss.
5.	**Unity of direction**	One person and one plan should be used in deciding the activities to be used to accomplish each organizational objective.
6.	**Subordination of individual interests to the general interest**	Employees must put the organization's interests and goals before their own.
7.	**Remuneration**	Compensation should be fair and satisfactory to both the employees and the organization; that is, don't overpay or underpay employees.
8.	**Centralization**	Avoid too much centralization or decentralization. Strike a balance depending on the circumstances and employees involved.
9.	**Scalar chain**	From the top to the bottom of an organization, each position is part of a vertical chain of authority in which each worker reports to just one boss. For the sake of simplicity, communication outside normal work groups or departments should follow the vertical chain of authority.
10.	**Order**	To avoid conflicts and confusion, order can be obtained by having a place for everyone and having everyone in their place; in other words, there should be no overlapping responsibilities.
11.	**Equity**	Kind, fair, and just treatment for all will develop devotion and loyalty. This does not exclude discipline, if warranted, and consideration of the broader general interest of the organization.
12.	**Stability of tenure of personnel**	Low turnover, meaning a stable work force with high tenure, benefits an organization by improving performance, lowering costs, and giving employees, especially managers, time to learn their jobs.
13.	**Initiative**	Because it is a "great source of strength for business," managers should encourage the development of initiative, the ability to develop and implement a plan, in others.
14.	**Esprit de corps**	Develop a strong sense of morale and unity among workers that encourages coordination of efforts.

Sources: H. Fayol, *General and Industrial Management* (London: Pittman & Sons, 1949); M. Fells, "Fayol Stands the Test of Time," *Journal of Management History* 6 (2000): 345–360; C. Rodrigues, "Fayol's 14 Principles of Management Then and Now: A Framework for Managing Today's Organizations Effectively," *Management Decision* 39 (2001): 880–889.

Exhibit 2.5

Fayol's 14 Principles of Management

Review 3: Bureaucratic and Administrative Management

Today, when we hear *bureaucracy*, we think of inefficiency and red tape. Yet according to German sociologist Max Weber, bureaucracy, that is, running organizations on the basis of knowledge, fairness, and logical rules and procedures, would accomplish organizational goals much more efficiently than monarchies and patriarchies, where decisions were made on the basis of personal or family connections, personal gain, and arbitrary decision making. Bureaucracies are characterized by seven elements: qualification-based hiring;

merit-based promotion; chain of command; division of labor; impartial application of rules and procedures; recording rules, procedures, and decisions in writing; and separating managers from owners. Nonetheless, bureaucracies are often inefficient and can be highly resistant to change.

The Frenchman Henri Fayol, whose ideas were shaped by his 20-plus years of experience as a CEO, is best known for developing five management functions (planning, organizing, coordinating, commanding, and controlling) and 14 principles of management (division of work, authority and responsibility, discipline, unity of command, unity of direction, subordination of individual interests to the general interest, remuneration, centralization, scalar chain, order, equity, stability of tenure of personnel, initiative, and esprit de corps). He is also known for his belief that management could and should be taught to others.

4 Human Relations Management

As we have seen, scientific management focused on improving the efficiency of manufacturing facilities and their workers; bureaucratic management focused on using knowledge, fairness, and logical rules and procedures to increase the efficiency of the entire organization; and administrative management focused on how and what managers should do in their jobs. In contrast, the human relations approach to management focused on the psychological and social aspects of work. Under the human relations management approach, people were more than just extensions of machines; they were valuable organizational resources whose needs were important and whose efforts, motivation, and performance were affected by the work they did and their relationships with their bosses, coworkers, and work groups. In other words, according to human relations management, efficiency alone is not enough to produce organizational success. Success also depends on treating workers well.

Let's find out more about human relations management by learning about ***4.1 Mary Parker Follett's theories of constructive conflict and coordination****;* ***4.2 Elton Mayo's Hawthorne Studies****; and* ***4.3 Chester Barnard's theories of cooperation and acceptance of authority****.*

4.1 Constructive Conflict and Coordination: Mary Parker Follett

Mary Parker Follett (1868–1933) was a social worker with a degree in political science who, in her 50s, after 25 years of working with schools and nonprofit organizations, began lecturing and writing about management and working extensively as a consultant for business and government leaders in the United States and Europe. Although her contributions were overlooked for decades, perhaps because she was a woman or perhaps because they were so different, many of today's "new" management ideas can clearly be traced to her work.

Follett is known for developing ideas regarding constructive conflict and coordination. Constructive conflict, also called cognitive conflict, which is discussed in Chapter 5 on decision making and Chapter 10 on teams, is one of Follett's most important contributions. Unlike most people, then and now, who view conflict as bad, Follett believed that conflict could be beneficial. She said that conflict is "the appearance of difference, difference of opinions, of interests. For that is what conflict means—difference." She went on to say, "As conflict—difference—is here in this world, as we cannot avoid it, we should, I think, use it to work for us. Instead of condemning it, we should set it to work for us. Thus we shall not be afraid of conflict, but shall recognize that there is a destructive way of dealing with such moments and a constructive way."[52]

Follett believed that managers could deal with conflict in three ways: domination, compromise, and integration. She said, "**Domination**, obviously, is a victory of one side over the other. This is the easiest way of dealing with conflict, the easiest for the moment but not usually successful in the long run.... As for the second way of dealing with conflict, that of **compromise**, we understand [it] well, for it is the way we settle most of our controversies; each side gives up a little in order to have peace, or, to speak more accurately, in order that the activity which has been interrupted by the conflict may go on." Follett continued, "Yet no one really wants to compromise, because that means a giving up of something. Is there then any other method of ending conflict? There is a way beginning now to be recognized at least, and even occasionally followed: when two desires are *integrated*, that means that a solution has been found in which both desires have found a place that neither side has had to sacrifice anything." So, rather than one side dominating the other or both sides compromising, the point of **integrative conflict resolution** is to have both parties indicate their preferences and then work together to find an alternative that meets the needs of both. According to Follett, "Integration involves invention, and the clever thing is to recognize this, and not to let one's thinking stay within the boundaries of two alternatives which are mutually exclusive." Indeed, Follett's ideas about the positive use of conflict and an integrative approach to conflict resolution predate accepted thinking in the negotiation and conflict resolution literature by six decades (see the best-selling book *Getting to Yes: Negotiating Agreement without Giving In* by Roger Fisher, William Ury, and Bruce Patton).

Follett's writing on the role of coordination in organizations is another of her important contributions. According to Follett, there are four fundamental principles of organizations:

1. *Coordination as reciprocal relating all the factors in a situation.*
2. *Coordination by direct contact of the responsible people concerned.*
3. *Coordination in the early stages.*
4. *Coordination as a continuing process.*

Follett's first principle recognizes that most things that occur in organizations are interrelated. Make just one change in an organization, and other changes, some expected but some not, will occur. Cut costs, and quality may be affected. Change the raw ingredients used to make a product, and manufacturing procedures may no longer work. Marketing offers customers special incentives to buy more products, and operations has to work overtime to keep up with the increased demand. Accordingly, because of these interrelations, leaders at different levels and in different parts of the organization must coordinate their efforts to solve problems and produce the best overall outcomes in an integrative way. In short, managers cannot manage their part of the organization while ignoring its other parts. What each manager does affects other parts of the organization and vice versa.

domination an approach to dealing with conflict in which one party satisfies its desires and objectives at the expense of the other party's desires and objectives

compromise an approach to dealing with conflict in which both parties give up some of what they want in order to reach agreement on a plan to reduce or settle the conflict

integrative conflict resolution an approach to dealing with conflict in which both parties indicate their preferences and then work together to find an alternative the meets the needs of both

Follett explains her second principle, coordination by direct contact of the people concerned, and her third principle, coordination in the early stages, this way: "Direct contact must begin in the earliest stages of the process.... If the heads of departments confront each other with finished policies, agreement will be found difficult.... But if these heads meet while they are forming their policies, meet and discuss the questions involved, a successful co-relation is far more likely to be reached. Their thinking has not become crystallized. They can still modify one another."[53] In other words, better outcomes will be achieved if the people affected by organizational issues and problems meet early and directly to address them. Working with those involved or affected will produce more effective solutions than will isolating or ignoring them.

With respect to her fourth principle, coordination as a continuing process, Follett said: "It is a fallacy to think that we can solve problems—in any final sense. The belief that we can do so is a drag upon our thinking. What we need is a process for meeting problems. When we think we have solved one, well, by the very process of solving, new elements or forces come into the situation and you have a new problem on your hands to be solved." Consequently, there is always a need for early, integrative coordination of the people affected by organizational situations, problems, or issues. The need for coordination never goes away.

Exhibit 2.6 summarizes, in Follett's own words, her contributions to management regarding power ("with" not "over" others), the giving of orders (discussing instructions and resentment), authority (flowing from job knowledge and experience, not position), leadership (that leaders make the team and that aggressive, dominating leaders may be harmful), coordination, and control (should be based on facts, information, and coordination). In the end, Follett's contributions added significantly to our understanding of the human, social, and psychological sides of management. Peter Parker, the former chairman of the London School of Economics, said about Follett: "People often puzzle about who is the father of management. I don't know who the father was, but I have no doubt about who was the mother."[54]

4.2 Hawthorne Studies: Elton Mayo

Australian-born Elton Mayo (1880–1948) is best known for his role in the famous Hawthorne Studies at the **Western Electric Company**. His ideas became popular during the early 20th century when labor unrest, dissatisfaction, and protests (some of them violent) were widespread in the United States, Europe, and Asia. In 1919 alone, for example, more than four million American workers went on strike.[55] Working conditions contributed to the unrest. Millions of workers in large factories toiled at boring, repetitive, unsafe jobs for low pay. Employee turnover was high and absenteeism was rampant. With employee turnover approaching 380 percent in his automobile factories, Henry Ford had to double the daily wage of his manufacturing workers from $2.50, the going wage at the time, to $5.00 to keep enough workers at their jobs. Workers joined labor unions to force companies to improve their pay and working conditions. In 1913, the federal government created the U.S. Department of Labor "to foster, promote and develop the welfare of working people, to improve their working conditions and to enhance their opportunities for profitable employment." In 1935, Congress passed the National Labor Relations Act (also known as the Wagner Act), which gave workers the legal right to form unions and collectively bargain with their employers, but prevented companies from engaging in unfair labor practices to "bust" unions. In this historical context, Mayo's work on the Hawthorne Studies proved highly relevant as managers looked for ways to increase productivity and also to improve worker satisfaction and working conditions.[56]

The Hawthorne Studies were conducted in several stages between 1924 and 1932 at a Western Electric plant in Chicago. Although Mayo didn't join the studies until 1928, he played a significant role thereafter, writing about the results in his book, *The Human Problems of an Industrial Civilization*.[57] The first stage of the Hawthorne Studies investigated the effects of lighting levels and incentives on employee productivity in the Relay Test Assembly Room, where workers took approximately a minute to

Exhibit 2.6

Some of Mary Parker Follett's Key Contributions to Management

Constructive conflict	• "As conflict—difference—is here in this world, as we cannot avoid it, we should,I think, use it to work for us. Instead of condemning it, we should set it to work for us."
Power	• "Power might be defined as simply the ability to make things happen, to be a causal agent, to initiate change." • "It seems to me that whereas power usually means *power-over,* the power of some person or group over some other person or group, it is possible to develop the conception of *power-with,* a jointly developed power, a co-active, not a coercive power."
The giving of orders	• "Probably more industrial trouble has been caused by the manner in which orders have been given than in any other way." • "But even if instructions are properly framed, are not given in an overbearing manner, there are many people who react violently against anything that they feel is a command. It is often the command that is resented, not the thing commanded." • "An advantage of not exacting blind obedience, of discussing your instructions with your subordinates, is that if there is any resentment, any come-back, you get it out into the open, and when it is in the open you can deal with it."
Authority	• "Indeed there are many indications in the present reorganization of industry that we are beginning to rid ourselves of the over and under idea, that we are coming to a different conception of authority, many indications that there is an increasing tendency to let the job itself, rather than the position occupied in a hierarchy, dictate the kind and amount of authority." • "Authority should go with knowledge and experience, that is where obedience is due, no matter whether it is up the line or down."
Leadership	• "Of the greatest importance is the ability to grasp a total situation. . . . Out of a welter of facts, experience, desires, aims, the leader must find the unifying thread. He must see a whole, not a mere kaleidoscope of pieces. . . . The higher up you go, the more ability you have to have of this kind." • "The leader makes the team. This is pre-eminently the leadership quality—the ability to organize all the forces there are in an enterprise and make them serve a common purpose." • "[It is wrong to assume] that you cannot be a good leader unless you are aggressive, masterful, dominating. But I think not only that these characteristics are not the qualities essential to leadership but, on the contrary, that they often militate directly against leadership."
Coordination	• "One which I consider a very important trend in business management is a system of cross-functioning between the different departments. . . . Each department is expected to get in touch with certain others." • "Many businesses are now organized in such a way that you do not have an ascending and descending ladder of authority. You have a degree of cross-functioning, of inter-relation of departments, which means a horizontal rather than a vertical authority." • "The most important thing to remember about unity is—that there is no such thing. There is only unifying. You cannot get unity and expect it to last a day—or five minutes. Every man in a business should be taking part in a certain process and that process is unifying."
Control	• "Control is coming more and more to mean fact-control rather than man-control." • "Central control is coming more and more to mean the co-relation of many controls rather than a superimposed control."

Source: M. P. Follett, *Mary Parker Follett—Prophet of Management: A Celebration of Writings from the 1920s,* ed. P. Graham (Boston: Harvard Business School Press, 1995).

put "together a coil, armature, contact springs, and insulators in a fixture and secure the parts by means of four machine screws."[58] Two groups of six experienced female workers, five to do the work and one to supply needed parts, were separated from the main part of the factory by a 10-foot partition and placed at a standard work bench with the necessary parts and tools. Over the next five years, the experimenters introduced various levels and combinations of lighting, financial incentives, and rest pauses (work breaks) to study the effect on productivity. Curiously, however, whether they increased or decreased the lighting, paid workers based on individual production or group production, or increased or decreased the number and length of rest pauses, production levels increased. In fact, Mayo and his fellow researchers were surprised that production steadily increased from 2,400 relays per day at the beginning of the study to 3,000 relays per day five years later. The question, however, was why?

© BETTMANN/CORBIS

Although Mayo's studies used several variables, like lighting and incentives to increase productivity, it turned out that productivity increased no matter what changes were made. Mayo concluded that paying more attention to the workers and the development of the workers into a cohesive group produced higher levels of productivity and job satisfaction.

Mayo and his colleagues eventually concluded that two things accounted for the results. First, substantially more attention was paid to these workers than to workers in the rest of the plant. Mayo wrote, "Before every change of program [in the study], the group is consulted. Their comments are listened to and discussed; sometimes their objections are allowed to negate a suggestion. The group unquestionably develops a sense of participation in the critical determinations and becomes something of a social unit."[59]

The "Hawthorne Effect" cannot be understood, however, without giving equal importance to the "social units," which became intensely cohesive groups. (For years, the "Hawthorne Effect" has been *incorrectly* defined as increasing productivity by paying more attention to workers.[60]) Mayo said, "What actually happened was that six individuals became a team and the team gave itself wholeheartedly and spontaneously to cooperation in the experiment. The consequence was that they felt themselves to be participating freely and without afterthought, and were happy in the knowledge that they were working without coercion from above or limits from below."[61] Together, the increased attention from management and the development of a cohesive work group led to significantly higher levels of job satisfaction *and* productivity. Mayo and his research colleagues concluded:

- *"There has been an important increase in contentment among the girls working in the test-room conditions."*
- *"There has been a decrease in absences of about 80 percent among the girls since entering the test-room group."*
- *"The changed working conditions have resulted in creating an eagerness on the part of the operators to come to work in the morning."*
- *"The operators have no clear idea as to why they are able to produce more in the test room; but as shown in the replies to the questionnaires... there is the feeling that better output is in some way related to the distinctly pleasanter, freer, and happier work conditions."*[62]

For the first time, human factors related to work were found to be more important than the physical conditions or design of the work. In short, workers' feelings and attitudes affected their work.

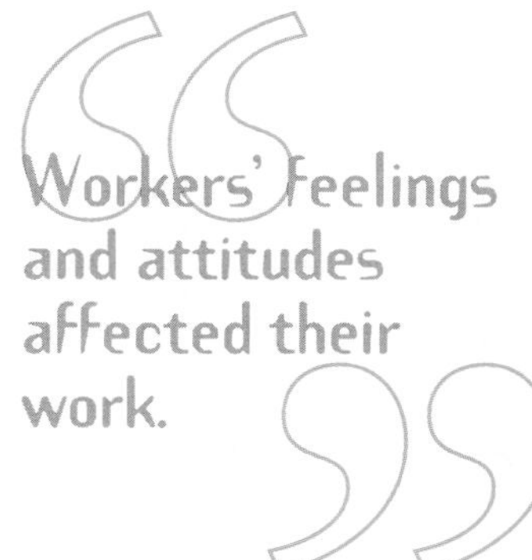
Workers' feelings
and attitudes
affected their
work.

The next stage of the Hawthorne Studies was conducted in the Bank Wiring Room, where "the group consisted of nine wiremen, three solderers, and two inspectors. Each of these groups performed a specific task and collaborated with the other two in completion of each unit of equipment. The task consisted of setting up the banks of terminals side-by-side on frames, wiring the corresponding terminals from bank to bank, soldering the connections, and inspecting with a test set for short circuits or breaks in the wire. One solderman serviced the work of the three wireman."[63] In contrast to the results from the Relay Test Assembly Room, where productivity increased no matter what the researchers did, productivity dropped in the Bank Wiring Room. Again, the question was why?

Interestingly, Mayo and his colleagues found that group effects were just as responsible for the decline in performance in the Bank Wiring Room as they were for the increased performance in the Relay Test Assembly Room. The difference was that the workers in the Bank Wiring Room had been an existing work group for some time and had already developed strong negative norms that governed their behavior. For instance, despite a group financial incentive for production, the group members decided that they would wire only 6,000 to 6,600 connections a day (depending on the kind of equipment they were wiring), well below the production goal of 7,300 connections that management had set for them. Individual workers who worked at a faster pace were socially ostracized from the group, or "binged," hit on the arm, until they slowed their work pace. Thus, the group's behavior was reminiscent of the soldiering that Frederick Taylor had observed. Mayo concluded, "Work [was] done in accord with the group's conception of a day's work; this was exceeded by only one individual who was cordially disliked."[64]

In the end, the Hawthorne Studies demonstrated that the workplace was more complex than previously thought, that workers were not just extensions of machines, and that financial incentives weren't necessarily the most important motivator for workers. By highlighting the crucial role, positive or negative, that groups, group norms, and group behavior play at work, Mayo strengthened Mary Parker Follett's point about reciprocal relating—make just one change in an organization and others, some expected and some unexpected, will occur. Thanks to Mayo and his colleagues and their work on the Hawthorne Studies, managers better understood the effect that group social interactions and employee satisfaction and attitudes had on individual and group performance.

4.3 Cooperation and Acceptance of Authority: Chester Barnard

"What's New" Company

Like Henri Fayol, Chester Barnard (1886–1961) had experiences as a top executive that shaped his views of management. Barnard began his career in 1909 as an engineer and translator for **AT&T**, becoming a general manager at Pennsylvania Bell Telephone in 1922 and then president of **New Jersey Bell Telephone** in 1927.[65] Furthermore, like Fayol's views, Barnard's ideas, published in his classic book, *The Functions of the Executive*, influenced companies from the board of directors down. Barnard is best known for his ideas about cooperation, the executive functions that promote it, and the acceptance of authority.

In *The Functions of the Executive*, Barnard proposed a comprehensive theory of cooperation in formal organizations. In fact, he defines an **organization** as a "system of consciously coordinated activities or forces of two or more persons."[66] In other words, "organization" occurs whenever two people work together for some purpose. Thus, organization occurs when classmates work together to complete a class project, when Habitat for Humanity volunteers donate their time to build a house, and when managers work with subordinates to reduce costs, improve quality, or increase sales. Why did Barnard place so much emphasis on cooperation? Because, he said, it is the

organization a system of consciously coordinated activities or forces created by two or more people "abnormal, not the normal, condition." "Failure to cooperate, failure of cooperation, failure of organization, disorganization, disintegration, destruction of organization—and reorganization—are characteristic facts of human history."[67]

Barnard argued that managers can gain others' cooperation by completing three executive functions: securing essential services from individuals, formulating an organization's purpose and objectives, and providing a system of communication. By "securing essential services from individuals," Barnard meant that managers must find ways to encourage workers to *willingly* cooperate with each other and management to achieve organizational goals. According to Barnard, managers can gain workers' willing cooperation by offering them *material incentives*, such as money or tangible rewards; *nonmaterial incentives*, such as recognition, prestige, personal power, improved working conditions, or satisfaction of personal ideals or needs; and *associational incentives*, such as the chance to work with people they like or to be more directly involved or associated with key events or processes in the organization.[68]

By "formulating an organization's purpose and objectives," top executives unify people in the company by making clear what needs to be accomplished. If the organization's purpose is clear, then each person in each job at each level of the company should understand how his or her daily activities, behaviors, and choices contribute to the accomplishment of that purpose. This is the ultimate form of cooperation in an organization. If, however, the organization's purpose is not clear, then departmental or personal objectives may become more important than organizational objectives. The result is a less cohesive organization in which workers are less likely to cooperate to accomplish the organization's goals.

By "providing a system of communication," Barnard meant that managers must create an organizational structure with a clear hierarchy (one that delineates responsibilities, tasks, and jobs) and hire and promote the right people into management, that is, talented people with the right skills and education who will put the organization's needs before their own. Those managers, in turn, are responsible for promoting cooperation by effectively communicating the organization's purpose and objectives and by minimizing organizational politics.

Finally, the extent to which people willingly cooperate in an organization depends on how workers perceive executive authority and whether they're willing to accept it. According to Barnard, for many managerial requests or directives, there

doing the right thing

A Dangerous Mix: Power, Authority, and Autonomy

Because of their authority to hire, fire, and reward employees, nearly all managers have the power to influence those who work for them. With jobs, promotions, or pay raises on the line, few will challenge what the boss wants, unless, as Chester Barnard suggested, they're asked to do something wrong. Even then, the boss's power and authority can be enough to get some subordinates to comply. Most dangerous of all, though, are managers who have power, authority, *and* autonomy. Adding the freedom and independence of autonomy to power and authority is like dropping a tank of gasoline on an already burning fire. An explosion is sure to result. Why? The reason is that managers with autonomy may begin to believe that the "rules" don't apply to them. When that happens, they're much more likely to engage in questionable, unethical, or illegal behavior. According to Wake Forest University professors John Dunkelberg and Debra Ragin Jessup, who studied six managers who engaged in spectacular cases of unethical and illegal behavior, "The desire to commit unethical acts is nothing without the autonomy to do so. Autonomy is the factor in the equation that sends intelligent successful people over the ethical edge. They believe they are invincible because no one is looking over their shoulder." The solution, say Dunkelberg and Jessup, is to make sure that even the most powerful people in the company haves checks, balances, and controls on their autonomy.[69]

is a *zone of indifference*, in which acceptance of managerial authority is automatic. For example, if your boss asks you for a copy of the monthly inventory report, and compiling and writing that report is part of your job, you think nothing of the request and automatically send it. In general, people will be indifferent to managerial directives or orders if they (1) are understood, (2) are consistent with the purpose of the organization, (3) are compatible with the people's personal interests, and (4) can actually be carried out by those people. Acceptance of managerial authority (that is, cooperation) is not automatic, however. Ask people to do things contrary to the organization's purpose or to their own benefit and they'll put up a fight. So, while many people assume that managers have the authority to do whatever they want, Barnard, referring to the "fiction of superior authority," believed that workers ultimately grant managers their authority. Consequently, rather than threatening workers to force cooperation, Barnard maintained that it is more effective to induce their willing cooperation through incentives, clearly formulated organizational objectives, and effective communication throughout the organization.

Review 4: **Human Relations Management**

Unlike most people who view conflict as bad, Mary Parker Follett, the "mother of modern management," believed that conflict could be a good thing, that it should be embraced and not avoided, and that of the three ways of dealing with conflict—domination, compromise, and integration—the latter was the best because it focuses on developing creative methods for meeting conflicting parties' needs. Follett also used four principles to emphasize the importance of coordination in organizations. She believed that the best overall outcomes are achieved when leaders and workers at different levels and in different parts of the organization directly coordinate their efforts to solve problems in an integrative way.

Elton Mayo is best known for his role in the Hawthorne Studies at the Western Electric Company. In the first stage of the Hawthorne Studies, production went up because the increased attention paid to the workers in the study and their development into a cohesive work group led to significantly higher levels of job satisfaction and productivity. In the second stage, productivity dropped because the workers had already developed strong negative norms, in which individual "rate busters" who worked faster than the rest of the team or cooperated with management were ostracized or "binged." The Hawthorne Studies demonstrated that workers' feelings and attitudes affected their work, that financial incentives weren't necessarily the most important motivator for workers, and that group norms and behavior play a critical role in behavior at work.

Chester Barnard, president of New Jersey Bell Telephone, emphasized the critical importance of willing cooperation in organizations and said that managers could gain workers' willing cooperation through three executive functions: securing essential services from individuals (through material, nonmaterial, and associational incentives), unifying the people in the organization by clearly formulating the organization's purpose and objectives, and providing a system of communication. Finally, although most managerial requests or directives will be accepted because they fall within the zone of indifference, Barnard maintains that it is more effective to induce cooperation through incentives, clearly formulating organizational objectives, and effective communication throughout the organization. Ultimately, he says, workers grant managers their authority, not the other way around.

In this last section, we review four other significant historical approaches to management that have influenced how today's managers produce goods and services on a daily basis, gather and manage the information they need to understand their businesses and make good decisions, understand how the different parts of the company work together as a whole, and recognize when and where particular management practices are likely to work.

To better understand these ideas, let's learn about ***5.1 operations management, 5.2 information management, 5.3 systems management****, and* ***5.4 contingency management****.*

5.1 Operations Management

In Chapter 18, you will learn about *operations management*, which involves managing the daily production of goods and services. In general, operations management uses a quantitative or mathematical approach to find ways to increase productivity, improve quality, and manage or reduce costly inventories. The most commonly used operations management tools and methods are quality control, forecasting techniques, capacity planning, productivity measurement and improvement, linear programming, scheduling systems, inventory systems, work measurement techniques (similar to the Gilbreths' motion studies), project management (similar to Gantt's charts), and cost-benefit analysis.[70]

Today, with those tools and techniques, we take it for granted that manufactured goods will be made with standardized, interchangeable parts; that the design of those parts will be based on specific, detailed plans; and that manufacturing companies will aggressively manage inventories to keep costs low and increase productivity. Surprisingly, these key elements of operations management have some rather strange origins: guns, geometry, and fire.

Since 1526, in Gardone, Italy, the descendants of Bartolomeo Beretta have been making world-renowned **BERETTA** firearms and gun barrels. Throughout most of the company's history, skilled craftsmen made the lock, stock, and barrel of a Beretta gun by hand. After each part was made, a skilled gun finisher assembled the parts into a complete gun. The gun finisher did not simply screw the different parts of a gun together, as is done today, however. Instead, each handmade part required extensive finishing and adjusting so that it would fit together with the other handmade gun parts. This was necessary because, even when made by the same skilled craftsman, no two parts were alike. In fact, gun finishers played a role similar to that of fine watchmakers, who meticulously assembled expensive watches—without them, the product simply wouldn't work. Today, we would say that these parts were low quality because they varied so much from part to part. You'll learn more about variation and quality in Chapter 18 on managing service and manufacturing operations.

All this changed in 1791, however, when the U.S. government, worried about a possible war with France, ordered 40,000 muskets from private gun contractors. Like Beretta, all but one contractor built handmade muskets assembled by skilled gun finishers who made sure that all the parts fit together. Thus, each musket was unique. If a part broke, a replacement part had to be handcrafted. But one contractor, Eli Whitney of New Haven, Connecticut, who is better known for his invention of the cotton gin, determined that if gun parts were made accurately enough, guns could be made with standardized, interchangeable parts. So he designed machine tools that allowed unskilled workers to make each gun part the same as the next. Said Whitney, "The tools which I contemplate to make are similar to an engraving on copper plate from which may be taken a great number of impressions perceptibly alike." Years passed before Whitney delivered his 10,000 muskets to the U.S. government. In 1801, however, he demonstrated the superiority of interchangeable parts to President-elect Thomas Jefferson by quickly and easily assembling complete muskets from randomly picked piles of musket parts.

Today, because of Whitney's ideas, most products, from cars to toasters to space shuttles, are manufactured using standardized, interchangeable parts. But even with this advance, manufacturers still faced the significant limitation that they could not produce a part unless they had seen or examined it firsthand. Thanks to Gaspard Monge, a Frenchman of modest beginnings, this soon changed.

In Monge's time, maps were crude, often inaccurate, and almost never up-to-date. In 1762, however, as a 16-year-old, Monge drew a large-scale map of the town of Beaune, France. He developed new surveying tools and systematic methods of observation so that every feature on the map was in proportion and correctly placed. Monge's advanced skills as a draftsman led to his appointment to the prestigious Ècole Militaire de Mézières, a military institute, where one of his first assignments was to determine the proper placement of cannons for a military fortress. This task normally involved long, complicated mathematical computations, but using the geometrical principles he had developed as a draftsman, Monge calculated his estimates so quickly that, at first, commanders refused to believe they were accurate. Soon, however, they realized the importance of his breakthrough and protected it as a military secret for more than a decade.[71]

Monge's greatest achievement, however, was his book *Descriptive Geometry*. In it, he explained techniques for drawing three-dimensional objects on paper. For the first time, precise drawings permitted manufacturers to make standardized, interchangeable parts without first examining a prototype. Today, thanks to Monge, manufacturers rely on CAD (computer-aided design) and CAM (computer-aided manufacturing) to take three-dimensional designs straight from the computer to the factory floor.

"Once standardized, interchangeable parts became the norm, and parts could be made from design drawings alone, manufacturers ran into a costly problem that they had never faced before: too much inventory."

Once standardized, interchangeable parts became the norm, and parts could be made from design drawings alone, manufacturers ran into a costly problem that they had never faced before: too much inventory. *Inventory* is the amount and number of raw materials, parts, and finished products that a company has in its possession. In fact, large factories were accumulating parts inventories sufficient for two to three months, much more than they needed on a daily basis to run their manufacturing operations. A solution to this problem was found in 1905 when the **Oldsmobile Motor Works** in Detroit burned down. At a time when cars were far too expensive for most Americans, Oldsmobile had become the leading automobile manufacturer in the United States by being the first to produce an affordable car. When the Oldsmobile factory burned down, management rented a new production facility to get production up and running as quickly as possible. But because the new facility was much smaller, there was no room to store large stockpiles of inventory

(which the company couldn't afford anyway as it was short on funds). Therefore, the company made do with what it called "hand-to-mouth inventories," in which each production station had only enough parts on hand to do a short production run. Fortunately, since all of its parts suppliers were close by, Oldsmobile could place orders in the morning and receive them in the afternoon (even without telephones), just like today's computerized, just-in-time inventory systems. So, contrary to common belief, just-in-time inventory systems were not invented by Japanese manufacturers. Instead, they were invented out of necessity a century ago because of a fire. You can learn more about just-in-time inventory management in Chapter 18.

5.2 Information Management

The earliest recorded use of written information occurred nearly 60,000 years ago when Cro-Magnons, from whom modern humans descended, created and recorded a lunar calendar. The calendar consisted of 28 symbols carved into a reindeer antler and indicated when the waters would be high. The calendar was used to track and kill deer, bison, and elk that would gather at river crossings. For most of recorded history, information has been costly, difficult to obtain, and slow to spread. Because of the immense labor and time it took to hand-copy information, books, manuscripts, and written documents of any kind were rare and extremely expensive. Word of Joan of Arc's death in 1431 took 18 months to travel from France across Europe to Constantinople (now Istanbul, Turkey). Most people literally heard news and information from the town crier (Hear ye! Hear ye!) or from minstrel and acting groups who relayed information as they traveled from town to town.

Moreover, as you will learn in Chapter 17, accurate, timely, relevant, and complete information has been important to businesses throughout history. Indeed, 99 percent of the clay tablets and animal-skin documents unearthed in our earliest cities are business and economic texts. Traders, craftspeople, and local businesspeople used them to keep track of trades, orders, and how much money (or gold, pigs, or chickens) was owed to whom.

Consequently, throughout history, organizations have pushed for and quickly adopted new information technologies that reduce the cost or increase the speed with which they can acquire, store, retrieve, or communicate information. The first "technologies" to truly revolutionize the business use of information were paper and the printing press. In the 14th century, water-powered machines were created to pulverize rags into pulp to make paper. Paper prices, which were already lower than those of animal-skin parchments, dropped dramatically. Less than a half-century later, Johannes Gutenberg invented the printing press, which greatly reduced the cost and time needed to copy written information. For instance, in 1483 in Florence, Italy, a scribe would charge one florin (an Italian unit of money) to hand-copy one document page. By contrast, a printer would set up and print 1,025 copies of the same document for just three florins. Within 50 years of its invention, Gutenberg's printing press cut the cost of information by 99.8 percent!

What Gutenberg's printing press did for publishing, the manual typewriter did for daily communication. Before 1850, most business correspondence was written by hand and copied using the "letter press." With the ink still wet, the letter would be placed into a tissue-paper "book." A hand press would then be used to squeeze the "book" and copy the still-wet ink onto the tissue paper. By the 1870s, manual typewriters made it cheaper, easier, and faster to produce and copy business correspondence. Of course, in the 1980s, slightly more than a century later, typewriters were replaced by personal computers and word processing software for identical reasons.

During the Renaissance, the Medici were at the forefront of managing information and ensuring that information was delivered speedily.

As the volume of printed information increased, businesses needed new ways to organize and make sense of it. Vertical file cabinets and the Woodruff file, invented in 1868, represented major advances in information storage and retrieval. Once sales orders or business correspondence were put in the proper file drawer, they could be found easily and quickly by anyone familiar with the system. The cash register, invented in 1879, kept sales clerks honest by recording all sales transactions on a roll of paper securely locked inside the machine. But managers soon realized that its most important contribution was better management and control of their business. For example, department stores could track performance and sales by installing separate cash registers in the food, clothing, and hardware departments. Time clocks, introduced in the 1890s, helped businesses keep track of worker hours and costs.

Finally, businesses have always looked for information technologies that would speed access to timely information. For instance, the Medici family, which opened banks throughout Europe in the early 1400s, used posting messengers to keep in contact with their more than 40 "branch" managers. The post messengers, who predated the U.S. Postal Service Pony Express by 400 years, could travel 90 miles per day, twice what average riders could cover, because the Medicis were willing to pay for the expense of providing them with fresh horses. This need for timely information also led companies to quickly adopt the telegraph in the 1860s, the telephone in the 1880s, and, of course, Internet technologies in the last decade. See Chapter 17 for more on how companies are using today's technologies to lower the cost and increase the speed with which accurate, timely, relevant, and complete information is acquired.

5.3 Systems Management

Today's companies are much more complex than they used to be. They are larger and employ more people. They most likely manufacture, service, *and* finance what they sell, not only in their home markets but in foreign markets throughout the world, too. They also operate in complex, fast-changing, competitive, global environments that can quickly turn competitive advantages into competitive disadvantages.

How, then, can managers make sense of this complexity, both within and outside their organizations? One way to deal with organizational and environmental complexity is to take a systems view of organizations, which derived from theoretical models in biology and social psychology in the 1950s and 1960s.[72] A **system** is a set of interrelated elements or parts that function as a whole. So rather than viewing one part of an organization as separate from the other parts, a systems approach encourages managers to complicate their thinking by looking for connections between the different parts of the organization. Indeed, one of the more important ideas in the systems approach to management is that organizational systems are composed of parts or **subsystems,** which are simply smaller systems within larger systems. Subsystems and their connections matter in systems theory because of the possibility for managers to create synergy. **Synergy** occurs when two or more subsystems working together can produce more than they can working apart. In other words, synergy occurs when 1 + 1 = 3.

system a set of interrelated elements or parts that function as a whole

subsystems smaller systems that operate within the context of a larger system

synergy when two or more subsystems working together can produce more than they can working apart

Whereas **closed systems** can function without interacting with their environments, nearly all organizations should be viewed as **open systems** that interact with their environments and depend on them for survival. Therefore, rather than viewing what goes on within the organization as separate from what goes on outside it, the systems approach also encourages managers to look for connections between the different parts of the organization and the different parts of its environment. Successful interaction with organizational environments is critical because open systems tend toward **entropy**, which is the inevitable and steady deterioration of a system.

As shown in Exhibit 2.7, organizations operate in two kinds of complex environments. The *general environment* consists of the economy and the technological, sociocultural, and political/legal trends that indirectly affect all organizations. Changes in any sector of the general environment eventually affect most organizations. In addition, each organization has a specific environment that is unique to that firm's industry and directly affects the way it conducts day-to-day business. The *specific environment* includes customers, competitors, suppliers, industry regulation, and advocacy groups. Both the general and specific environments are discussed in detail in Chapter 3. As Exhibit 2.7 shows, organizational systems obtain inputs from the general and specific environments. Managers and workers then use their management knowledge and manufacturing techniques to transform those inputs into outputs, such as products and services, which are then consumed by persons or organizations in the environment, which, in turn, provide feedback to the organization, allowing managers and workers to modify and improve their products or services.

closed systems systems that can sustain themselves without interacting with their environments

open systems systems that can sustain themselves only by interacting with their environments, on which they depend for their survival

entropy the inevitable and steady deterioration of a system

A systems view of organizations offers several advantages. First, it forces managers to view their organizations as part of and subject to the competitive, economic, social, technological, and legal/regulatory forces in their environments.[73] Second, it also forces managers to be aware of how the environment affects specific parts of the organization. Third, because of the complexity and difficulty of trying to achieve synergies between different parts of the organization, the systems view encourages managers to focus on better communication and cooperation within the organization. Finally, it makes managers acutely aware that good internal management of the organization may not be enough to ensure survival. Survival also depends on making sure that the organization continues to satisfy critical environmental stakeholders, such as shareholders, employees, customers, suppliers, governments, and local communities. For more on ideas related to the systems view of management, see Chapter 3 on environments and cultures, Chapter 4 on ethics and social responsibility, Chapter 6 on organizational strategy, and Chapter 8 on global management.

Fad Jumping

Management consultants are seemingly everywhere, and many make a living trying to convince companies that the latest management idea holds the key to previously unattainable success. Managers may be tempted to adopt these ideas and implement them across their organizations without considering their company's industry, business model, financials, workforce, or culture. But embracing one-stop, quick-fix management programs can be detrimental to a business and its employees. That's not to say all of the latest management ideas are bunk. Instead of jumping from fad to fad to fad, however, try cherry-picking the best ideas that are the most appropriate for your business. And really, just learn to manage.

5.4 Contingency Management

Earlier you learned that the goal of scientific management was to use systematic study to find the "one best way" of doing each task and then use that "one best way" everywhere. The problem, as you may have gathered from reading about the various approaches to management, is that

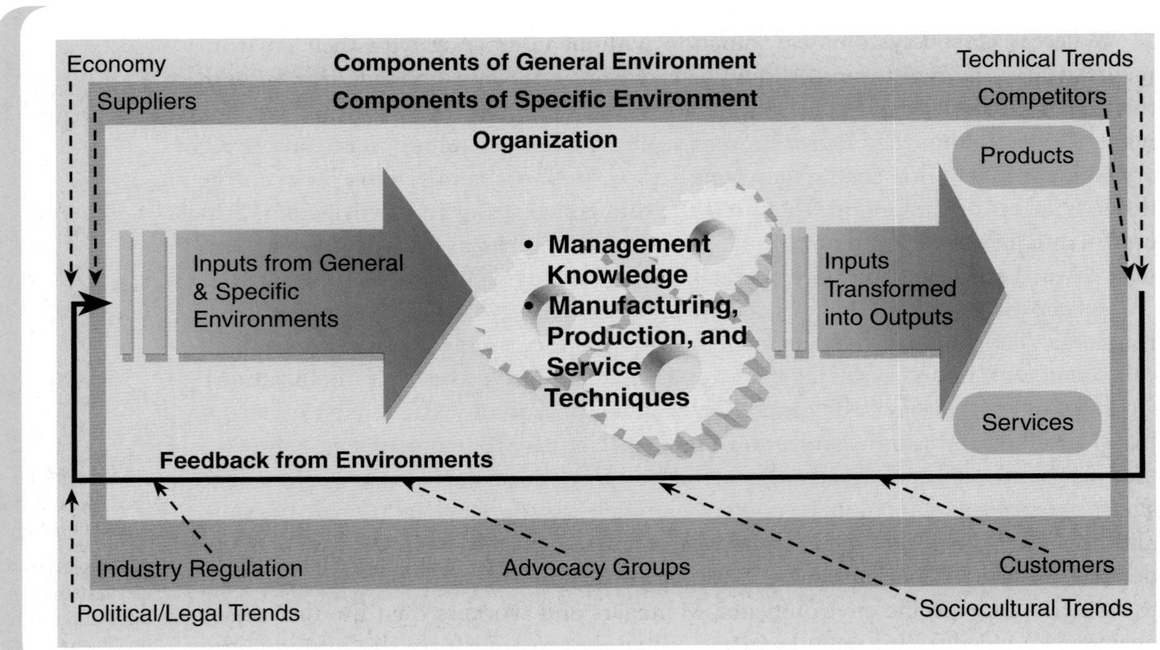

Exhibit 2.7

Systems View of Organizations

no one in management seems to agree on what that "one best way" is. Furthermore, more than 100 years of management research has shown that there are clear boundaries or limitations to most management theories and practices. No management ideas or practices are universal. Though they may work much of the time, none works all the time. But then how is a manager to decide what theory to use? Well, it depends on the situation. The **contingency approach** to management precisely states that there are no universal management theories and that the most effective management theory or idea depends on the kinds of problems or situations that managers or organizations are facing at a particular time.[74] In short, the "best way" depends on the situation.

One of the practical implications of the contingency approach to management is that management is much harder than it looks. In fact, because of the clarity and obviousness of management theories (OK, most of them), students and workers often wrongly assume that if management would take just a few simple steps, then a company's problems would be quickly and easily solved. If this were true, few companies would have problems. A second implication of the contingency approach is that managers need to look for key contingencies that differentiate today's situation or problems from yesterday's situation or problems. Moreover, it means that managers need to spend more time analyzing problems, situations, and employees before taking action to fix them. Finally, it means that as you read this text and learn about management ideas and practices, you need to pay particular attention to qualifying phrases such as "usually," "in these situations," "for this to work," and "under these circumstances." Doing so will help you identify the key contingencies that will help you become a better manager.

contingency approach holds that there are no universal management theories and that the most effective management theory or idea depends on the kinds of problems or situations that managers are facing at a particular time and place

Review 5: *Operations, Information, Systems, and Contingency Management*

Operations management uses a quantitative or mathematical approach to find ways to increase productivity, improve quality, and manage or reduce costly inventories. The manufacture of standardized, interchangeable parts, the graphical and computerized design of parts, and the accidental discovery of just-in-time management were some of the most important historical events in operations management.

For most of recorded history, information has been costly, difficult to obtain, and slow to spread. Consequently, throughout history, organizations have pushed for and quickly adopted new information technologies that reduce the cost or increase the speed with which they can acquire, store, retrieve, or communicate information. Historically, some of the most important technologies that have revolutionized information management were the use of horses in Italy in the 1400s, the creation of paper and the printing press in the 14th and 15th centuries, the manual typewriter in 1850, vertical file cabinets for storage of information and the telegraph in the 1860s, cash registers in 1879, the telephone in the 1880s, time clocks in the 1890s, the personal computer in the 1980s, and the Internet in the 1990s.

A system is a set of interrelated elements or parts that function as a whole. Organizational systems obtain inputs from the general and specific environments. Managers and workers then use their management knowledge and manufacturing techniques to transform those inputs into outputs, such as products and services, which are then consumed by persons or organizations in the environment, which, in turn, provide feedback to the organization, allowing managers and workers to modify and improve their products or services. Organizational systems must also address the issues of synergy, open versus closed systems, and entropy.

Finally, the contingency approach to management precisely states that there are no universal management theories. The most effective management theory or idea depends on the kinds of problems or situations that managers or organizations are facing at a particular time. This means that management is much harder than it looks and that managers need to look for key contingencies by spending more time analyzing problems and situations before they take action to fix them.

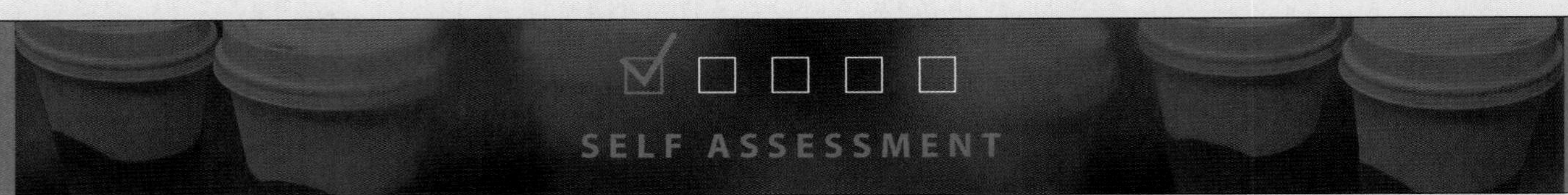

Dealing with Conflict

Conflict is an inevitable part of work life (and life in general), and the success of individual employees, teams, and entire organizations depends on how they manage interpersonal conflict. How do you deal with conflict? Do you look for it, avoid it, or something in between? This 20-question assessment is designed to provide insight into how you manage conflict.[75] This information will provide you with a baseline for future development of conflict-management skills.

You can also use this self-assessment as a precursor to doing the Management Team Decision below. At a minimum it will raise your awareness of how you handle differences of opinion before you begin working in a team. It may even inspire you to make conscious changes in your conflict-management style, helping you—and your team—be more effective.

Rate each statement using the following scale:

1 Strongly disagree
2 Disagree
3 Not sure
4 Agree
5 Strongly agree

When I have a conflict at work, I do the following:

1. I give in to the wishes of the other party.
   1 2 3 4 5
2. I try to realize a middle-of-the-road solution.
   1 2 3 4 5
3. I push my own point of view.
   1 2 3 4 5
4. I examine issues until I find a solution that really satisfies me and the other party.
   1 2 3 4 5
5. I avoid a confrontation about our differences.
   1 2 3 4 5
6. I concur with the other party.
   1 2 3 4 5
7. I emphasize that we have to find a compromise solution.
   1 2 3 4 5
8. I search for gains.
   1 2 3 4 5
9. I stand for my own and other's goals and interests.
   1 2 3 4 5
10. I avoid differences of opinion as much as possible.
    1 2 3 4 5
11. I try to accommodate the other party.
    1 2 3 4 5
12. I insist we both give in a little.
    1 2 3 4 5
13. I fight for a good outcome for myself.
    1 2 3 4 5
14. I examine ideas from both sides to find a mutually optimal solution.
    1 2 3 4 5
15. I try to make differences loom less severe.
    1 2 3 4 5
16. I adapt to the other parties' goals and interests.
    1 2 3 4 5
17. I strive whenever possible toward a 50–50 compromise.
    1 2 3 4 5
18. I do everything to win.
    1 2 3 4 5
19. I work out a solution that serves my own as well as other's interests as much as possible.
    1 2 3 4 5
20. I try to avoid a confrontation with the other person.
    1 2 3 4 5

KEY TERMS

This inventory can be broken down into five sections:

(A) Add together your scores for items 1, 6, 11, and 16: _____

(B) Add together your scores for items 2, 7, 12, and 17: _____

(C) Add together your scores for items 3, 8, 13, and 18: _____

(D) Add together your scores for items 4, 9, 14, and 19: _____

(E) Add together your scores for items 5, 10, 15, and 20: _____

You can find the interpretation for your score at: **academic.cengage.com/management/williams.**

Scripted Service

It has been two years since you took over your family's chain of specialty neighborhood bakeries located in areas with high foot traffic.[76] Throughout the city, your stores are *the* choice for birthday cakes, Christmas cookies, Valentine's Day cupcakes, and the daily doughnut. Even though sales are steady, you want to grow and are having a difficult time figuring out exactly how to increase revenues. For the past three weeks, you have spent each day in a different store, stocking cases, slicing bread, and generally pitching in where needed, but mostly you have been observing.

As luck would have it, about 80 percent of your stores are located near or next to a Starbucks. On your way to the stores each morning, you have stopped to get your morning coffee, and at each Starbucks, you have been greeted quickly, chatted with the clerk, ordered, heard your order repeated across the bar, used a loaded Starbucks card to pay, been asked if you want your balance, and been told to have a nice day. Today is the same. As you wait for your coffee, you think about the contrast between this prescribed sequence and what you have been seeing in your own stores. Even though your clerks serve customers efficiently, they do so in various ways. Some clerks are outgoing, talking and laughing with the customer while assembling the order. Other clerks are more reserved, filling the order quickly but with little conversation and barely a smile.

Now that you have noticed these differences, everywhere you shop you've been paying attention to sales speech patterns, which appear scripted and repetitive but pleasantly predictable. From the grocery ("Do you have any coupons?" and "Paper or plastic?") to the fast-food restaurant ("Do you want fries with that?" and "For here or to go?"), the patterns are most noticeable during busy periods. Clerks follow the same speech sequence with every customer.

A little research reveals that numerous companies require employees to follow a script. At McDonald's, the script is concerned with speech: for example, workers must say "May I help you, ma'am?" instead of "Can I help someone?" At Olive Garden, the script adds actions to the words: greet the table within 30 seconds of sitdown; take the drink order within three minutes; during ordering, suggest five items (drink, side dish, dessert, specials, and special offers); after food arrives, check back within three minutes. At Starbucks, things are more relaxed, but there is still a script to guide employee interactions with customers looking for a latte.

After a week of observing these scripted encounters, you begin to wonder if you should write a sales script for your bakery staff. If interactions were standardized, you might be able to increase efficiency and sales revenue. A script might be a great help during the morning and the after-school rush, as well as a useful training tool for new hires; it might help them feel more confident behind the counter. Since you want to grow, a script could also help you get up and running faster in new locations. But how would your current employees feel about it? They all have different ways of working with customers. About half of them have been with you for many years and know the ropes already. And how would your customers respond? The bakery could lose some of its neighborly appeal when customers recognize the canned speech.

You hear the barista call out, "Triple-shot venti extra-hot latte," so you go collect your coffee. She looks you right in the eye, smiles, and says, "Have a nice day!"

Questions

1. Which historical management technique best describes scripted service speech and scripted employee behavior? Explain your choice.
2. Do you implement a customer-encounter script at your bakeries? Why or why not?
3. Imagine that you have decided to implement a script for your frontline employees. Write the service script for bakery clerks.

Peer Review for Conflict Resolution

Your troubles began when the teenage clerk at one of your convenience stores wrestled a gun away from a would-be robber. On hearing the story, your friends said, "How brave!" and "Did you give him an award?" but you and the other managers in the company all had a very different reaction. You know you will have to fire the employee for violating a long-standing and well-known company policy against heroism. Convenience store robberies are a common occurrence, and if your (mostly young) workers, manning dozens of stores, begin to attempt behind-the-counter vigilantism, you will have a serious problem on your hands.

Despite the unanimous mind-set of your management team, you realize that firing the employee outright may create negative fallout among the other employees. At least one employee in particular is likely to vocally protest the firing. As you sit with your team trying to decide how to resolve this issue, one of your managers proposes implementing a peer review process at the company. A panel of employees would be responsible for arbitrating disputes and resolving any disagreements between how managers enforce the rules and how employees experience those rules being enforced.

Advocates trumpet the benefits of peer review systems. Peer reviews are practical and cost-effective, particularly compared with formal legal arbitration, and they allow disputes to be resolved internally. Because peer reviews give employees some say in the outcome of disputes, the employees are more likely to find the decisions credible and acceptable. Many managers also like peer reviews because they help to avert the backlash that a manager may experience for unilaterally disciplining an employee who has violated company rules.

Detractors, however, say that peer reviews may give employees too much control over the management decision process. Review panels effectively diffuse the decision-making function throughout the organization in a way that is counter to the centralized decision making of traditionally structured companies. In addition, creating and maintaining peer review systems requires a commitment of time and resources. Employees lose work hours (and thus productivity) when they participate on panels. And management should consult with a knowledgeable attorney to make sure that review panel procedures conform to National Labor Relations Board (NLRB) dictates about work teams. The process must be shared with all employees, who also must be trained in the process. And what will you do if employees reverse a management decision?

Nonetheless, the number of companies using peer review systems is increasing as their popularity grows. One consultant alone has over 500 companies, including Kodak, Hooters, Marriott, and Red Lobster, using his peer review process.

For this exercise, assemble a team of five students to act as the management team for the convenience store chain in this scenario.

Questions

1. Which historical management theory gives the best justification for implementing peer review systems? Which theory would not support peer reviews?
2. Do you implement a peer review process in the convenience store scenario? Explain your decision.
3. Regardless of your answer in question 2, as a team draw up guidelines for a peer review process. What would you need to consider if you were to create a review panel? For example, do you need to set restrictions on the ratio of employees to managers on the panel (will there even be managers on the panel?). How many years of service should an employee have to participate? Should the panel include a mix of employees from different departments?
4. Now, following the guidelines you established in question 3, imagine that your team is the review panel for the convenience store clerk who foiled a robbery. Discuss the situation and come to a decision regarding the outcome. Do you fire the employee, warn the employee, or commend his actions?

PRACTICE BEING A MANAGER

Observing History Today

The topic of management history may sound like old news, but many of the issues and problems addressed by Max Weber, Chester Barnard, and other management theorists still challenge managers today. *How can we structure an organization for maximum efficiency and just treatment of individuals? What is the basis for, and limits to, authority in organizations?* It is rather amazing that these thinkers of the late 19th and early 20th centuries generated such a wealth of theory that still influences our discussion of management and leadership challenges in the 21st century. This exercise will give you the opportunity to draw upon some ideas that trace their roots back to the pioneers of management thinking.

Preparing in Advance for Class Discussion

Step 1: Find an observation point. Identify a place where you can unobtrusively observe a group of people as they go about their work. You might select a coffee shop, bookstore, or restaurant.

Step 2: Settle in and observe. Go to your selected workplace and observe the people working there for at least 20 minutes. You should take along something like a notebook or PDA so that you can jot down a few notes. It is a good idea to go during a busy time, so long as it is not so crowded that you will be unable to easily observe the workers.

Step 3: Observe employees at work. Observe the process of work, and the interaction among the employees. Consider some of the following issues:

- Identify the steps that employees follow in completing a work cycle (for example, from taking an order to delivering a product). Can you see improvements that might be made, particularly steps that might be eliminated or streamlined?
- Observe the interaction and mood of the workers. Are they stressed? Or are they more relaxed? Does it seem to you that these workers like working with each other?
- Listen for signs of conflict. If you see signs of conflict, is the conflict resolved? If so, how did the workers resolve their conflict? If not, do you think that these workers suppress (bottle up) conflict?
- Can you tell who is in charge here? If so, how do the other workers respond to this person's directions? If not, how does the work group sort out who should be doing each task, and in what order?

Step 4: Consider what you saw. Immediately after your observation session, look through this chapter on management history for connections to your observations. For example, do you see any signs of the "Hawthorne effect"? Would Fredrick Taylor approve of the work process you observed, or might he have suggested improvements? What might Chester Barnard's theory have to say about how the workers you observed responded to instructions from their "boss"? Write a one-page paper of bullet-point notes describing possible connections between your observations and the thinking of management pioneers such as Mary Parker Follett.

Class Discussion:

Step 5: Share your findings as a class. Discuss the various points of connection that you found pioneering management thinkers and your own observations of people at work. Are some of the issues of management "timeless"? If so, what do you see as timeless issues of management? What are some ways in which work and management *have changed* since the days of the management pioneers?

DEVELOP YOUR CAREER POTENTIAL

Know Where Management Is Going

As you read in the chapter, management theories are dynamic. In other words, they change over time, sometimes very rapidly. In addition, management theories have often been cumulative, meaning that later theorists tend to build on theories previously advanced by other scholars. Thus, a new theory becomes the starting point for yet another theory that can either refine or refute the management thinking of the day.

One way to prepare for your career as a manager is by becoming aware of management trends today. The best (and easiest) way to do that is by regularly combing through business newspapers and periodicals. You will always find at least one article that relates to management concepts, and as you scan the business press over time, you will see which theories are influencing current management thinking the most. By understanding management history and management today, you will be better able to anticipate changes to management ideas in the future. This exercise is designed to introduce you to the business press and to help you make the connection between the concepts you learn in the classroom and real-world management activities. Done regularly, it will provide you with invaluable insights into business activities at all types of organizations around the world.

Activities

1. Find a current article of substance in the business press (for example, the *Wall Street Journal*, the *Financial Times, Fortune, BusinessWeek, Inc.*) that discusses topics covered in this course. Although this is only Chapter 2, you will be surprised by the amount of terminology you have already learned. If you are having trouble finding an article, read through the table of contents on pages iv–viii to familiarize yourself with the names of concepts that will be presented later in the term. Read your article carefully, making notes about relevant content.
2. Write a one-paragraph summary of the key points in your article. List the terms or concepts critical to understanding the article, and provide definitions of those terms. If you are unfamiliar with a term or concept that is central to the article, do some research in your textbook or see your professor during office hours. Relate these key points to the concepts in your text by citing page numbers.
3. How does your article relate to the management theories covered in this chapter? Explain the situation detailed in your article in terms of the history of management.

REEL TO REAL

BIZ FLIX

In Good Company

In Good Company is a 2004 film featuring Dennis Quaid in the role of Dan Foreman, an advertising sales executive at a top publication. After a corporate takeover, Dan is placed under a supervisor half his age named Carter Duryea (Topher Grace). Matters are made worse when Carter becomes romantically involved with Dan's daughter Alex (Scarlett Johansson), a college student. The film's working title was *Synergy*, and in this clip you will see Carter Duryea explaining how that concept works to the benefit of the company and its clients.

What to Watch for and Ask Yourself

1. Does Carter Duryea's explanation of synergy reflect the discussion of synergy in Section 5.3?
2. What potential downside with Carter's plan does Dan identify during the meeting? Do you agree with Dan or Carter?
3. What kind of system is Carter Duryea describing in the clip? Explain.

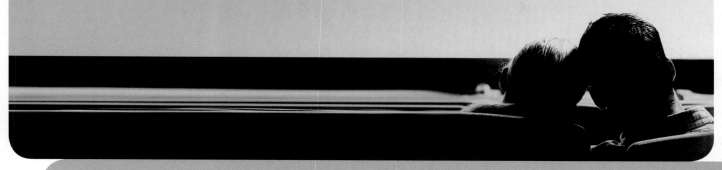

MANAGEMENT WORKPLACE

Original Penguin

Ideas about managing people and their work have changed over the past 125 years. At Original Penguin, Chris Kolbe has used a nontraditional, hands-on management style to transform a clothing icon that had its heyday over 30 years ago into a popular brand for today. Instead of ordering his employees around, Chris works with them to achieve a shared vision. His personal style motivates others to take pride in their work and to see themselves as part of an exciting project.

What to Watch for and Ask Yourself

1. Where does Chris Kolbe's authority come from? How do his ideas about authority compare to those of Mary Parker Follett?
2. Kolbe likes to use one-on-one communication with his employees. Is this a good idea? Why or why not?
3. Chester Barnard claimed that managers need to encourage workers' willing cooperation through incentives. How does Kolbe do this?

CHAPTER 3

Organizational Environments and Cultures

© ETHAN MILLER/GETTY IMAGES

Learning Outcomes:

1 Discuss how changing environments affect organizations.
2 Describe the four components of the general environment.
3 Explain the five components of the specific environment.
4 Describe the process that companies use to make sense of their changing environments.
5 Explain how organizational cultures are created and how they can help companies be successful.

In This Chapter:

WHAT WOULD YOU DO?

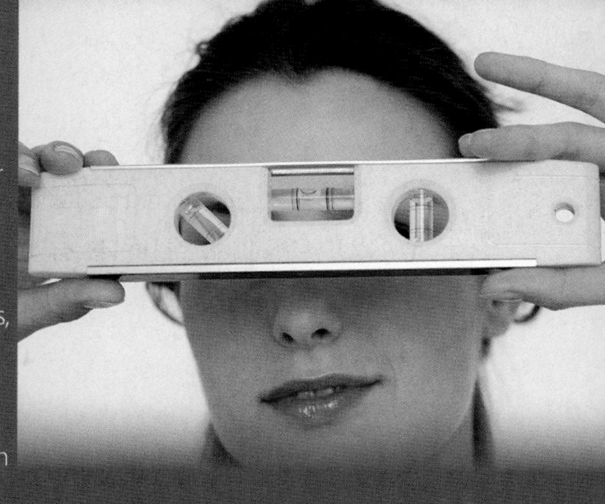

XM Satellite Radio Holdings, Inc, Washington, D.C.[1] As the new director of marketing for XM Satellite Radio, you're starting to wonder if you've joined the crew of a sinking ship. Despite years of hopeful forecasts, XM and its main competitor in the satellite radio industry, Sirius, recently reported a combined annual loss in excess of $1.5 billion. XM's shares are now trading for less than 30 percent of their initial offering price, and the company's net subscriber increase (the number of new subscribers minus defecting ones) has slowed considerably.

When the company was formed in the late 1980s, there were no iPods or MP3s, so a music lover away from home had no choice but to tote around cassette tapes or compact discs. In March 1997, American Mobile received the first Satellite digital audio radio license and contracted with Hughes Space (now Boeing Space Systems) to build and launch two satellites. Over the next four years, the company sold shares of stock to the public, signed licensing agreements with media providers to provide content for each channel, and prepared for the launch of its first satellite (Rock) followed in May by its second satellite (Roll). XM started with almost 200 channels of mostly commercial-free content. Its competitor Sirius Satellite Radio was founded in as CD Radio. Sirius launched their service, which was very similar to XM, and the two have competed fiercely for customers ever since. In the original charter agreements granting each the satellite frequencies, congress specifically forbade any merger between the two companies.

The stakes were raised to almost astronomical levels when shock jock Howard Stern moved from CBS Radio to Sirius under a contract that paid him $500 million over five years. XM countered by announcing deals for Major League Baseball ($650 million over 11 years), the National Hockey League, and Oprah Winfrey; Sirius announced deals with the National Basketball Association, the National Football League ($220 million over seven years) and the English Premier League. These deals have coincided with almost ritualistic restatements lowering subscriber forecasts. These forecasts (their prediction about how many subscribers they will retain and attain each quarter) are crucial to their stockholders because that information provides insights into the potential success of the company.

According to the *Wall Street Journal*, "many people are simply having iPod adapters installed in their cars and skipping satellite altogether." Indeed, XM and Sirius compete with established ground-based stations and personal music devices as well as each other in a bid for listeners' attention. Both companies have offered free trial subscriptions, reduced rate radios that can be installed in your car, pre-installed radios on new vehicles, and cut-rate programs that provide up to a year of free service.

To separate itself from Sirius and standard AM/FM radio, XM introduced NavTraffic, a system that compiles ground-based traffic information into recommended travel routes for cars equipped with navigation systems. The new XM2go devices that allow the customer to take their radio with them when they leave the car have received rave market feedback. Unfortunately, the record industry is not pleased with a new system that can capture digital songs and sued XM *(Atlantic Recordings Corp. v. XM Satellite Radio, Inc.)*. On another front, the Federal Communications Commission began investigating these new receivers as their powerful signal interferes with radios in nearby automobiles.

XM is facing competition from areas they never anticipated when they spend hundreds of millions to launch a satellite service. They have a large physical and contractual commitment to provide continuous satellite radio and yet they must find a way to evaluate the new environment in which they are working. How would you evaluate their current situation? XM needs to find a way to be unique relative to their new competitors (including the iPod). What should XM do if they want to be successful? **If you were the director of marketing, what would you do?**

ACTIVITIES + VIDEOS

CengageNOW Audio study guide, electronic flashcards, author FAQ videos, On the Job and Biz Flix videos, concept tutorial, and concept exercise

Web (academic.cengage.com/management/williams) Quiz, PowerPoint slides, and glossary terms for this chapter

Study Tip

Create your own diagram of the business environment and compare it with the example in the chapter. Read several articles in the business press and list the environmental factors at play in each of the articles.

"What's New" Companies

XM Satellite Radio

Natural Ovens

EA Sports

Napster

Apple Computer

Novartis

Dinner by Design

Goodyear

Hoover

Dyson

And others . . .

Wherever XM's top managers look, they see changes and forces outside the company that threaten their ability to continue to make XM a successful business. Their direct competitor spent hundreds of millions of dollars to acquire the type of content that listeners would prefer and previously unknown technologies have threatened to make their business obsolete.

This chapter examines the internal and external forces that affect business. We begin by explaining how the changes in external organizational environments affect the decisions and performance of a company. Next, we examine the two types of external organizational environments: the general environment that affects all organizations and the specific environment unique to each company. Then, we learn how managers make sense of their changing general and specific environments. The chapter finishes with a discussion of internal organizational environments by focusing on organizational culture.

EXTERNAL ENVIRONMENTS

External environments are the forces and events outside a company that have the potential to influence or affect it. Ask adults what their favorite after-school snack was, and they're likely to tell you "milk and cookies." But that's not true today, as overall cookie sales, including those of Oreos and Chips Ahoy, have dropped over 8 percent in the past five years.[2] Several trends in cookie companies' external environments are behind this decline. As part of the fight against obesity, parents and school systems are replacing cookies with healthier alternatives, such as fruits and vegetables. Consequently, the Vista, California, school district stopped buying 28,000 chocolate-chip cookies *per month* for its students. Also, thanks to microwaves, nobody bakes any more. Fifteen minutes to bake a batch of cookies seems an eternity. Quaker Oats' annual baking contest attracts only half the entries it did a decade ago. Trying to reverse the decline, Kraft Foods has developed the Vanilla Oreo, which has no unhealthy trans fats, and small, prewrapped 100-calorie packages of Oreos and Chips Ahoy "thin crisps." Can the "cookie" be saved? Mike Senackerib of Kraft says, "I absolutely think we can revive the category." It's not a positive sign, however, that for the last nine years, Elmo, and not the Cookie Monster, has been the most popular character on the children's show *Sesame Street*.[3]

After reading the next four sections, you should be able to

1. *discuss how changing environments affect organizations.*
2. *describe the four components of the general environment.*
3. *explain the five components of the specific environment.*
4. *describe the process that companies use to make sense of their changing environments.*

1 Changing Environments

Let's examine the three basic characteristics of changing external environments: ***1.1 environmental change, 1.2 environmental complexity, 1.3 resource scarcity,*** *and* ***1.4 the uncertainty that environmental change, complexity, and resource scarcity can create for organizational managers.***

external environments all events outside a company that have the potential to influence or affect it

1.1 Environmental Change

Environmental change is the rate at which a company's general and specific environments change. In **stable environments**, the rate of environmental change is slow. For instance, except for more efficient ovens, bread is baked, wrapped, and delivered fresh to stores each day much as it was decades ago. And although some new breads have become popular, the white and wheat breads that customers bought 20 years ago are still today's best sellers. So after two decades of consistent double-digit growth, **NATURAL OVENS**, which makes preservative-free breads, spent $10 million to build a second baking facility. Soon after it was built, however, sales unexpectedly dropped. According to owner Paul Stitt, "We couldn't figure out what was going on because we have been accustomed, on average, to having a 15 percent sales growth in each of the last 25 years." What happened? The Atkins plan. The popularity of the diet, which advocates restricting carbohydrates, caused nationwide bread sales to drop for the first time in decades. Fortunately, the company adjusted to the first major change in its business in years by developing a very-difficult-to-bake low-carb bread, whose sales have increased from 1,200 to 60,000 loaves a week. Ironically, says Stitt, "We have a higher profit margin on our low-carb breads than on most of our other breads."[4]

> Although you might think that a company's external environment would be *either* stable *or* dynamic, research suggests that companies often experience both.

In contrast to Natural Ovens, which is in a stable environment, **EA SPORTS** competes in an extremely dynamic external environment—video games. In **dynamic environments**, the rate of environmental change is fast. EA Sports' best-selling products are sports games like *Madden NFL* (football), *NBA Live* (basketball), *NHL* (hockey), *Tiger Woods PGA Tour* (golf), and *FIFA* (soccer). EA Sports' business environment is dynamic primarily because gaming technology changes so quickly. The company's first product was designed for the Atari 800, one of the earliest computers designed to play computer games. The Atari 800 was soon replaced by the more powerful Commodore 64, which was then replaced by the Commodore Amiga, followed by the 8-bit Nintendo, the 16-bit Sega Genesis, the 32-bit and 64-bit Segas, Nintendos, Sony PlayStations, desktop computers, and now the Sony PlayStation3, Nintendo's Gamecube and Wii, and Microsoft's Xbox 360. With development costs exceeding $10 million per game and marketing costs running as high as $15 million for some games, if EA Sports guesses wrong and develops games that prove to be unpopular or quickly become obsolete, it could join the dozens of game companies that have already closed their doors.[5]

Although you might think that a company's external environment would be *either* stable *or* dynamic, research suggests that companies often experience both. According to **punctuated equilibrium theory**, companies go through long periods of stability (equilibrium) during which incremental changes occur, followed by short, complex periods of dynamic, fundamental change (revolutionary periods), finishing with a return to stability (new equilibrium).[6]

Exhibit 3.1 shows one example of punctuated equilibrium—the U.S. airline industry. Three times in the last 30 years, the U.S. airline industry has experienced revolutionary periods. The first, from mid-1979 to mid-1982, occurred immediately after airline deregulation in 1978. Prior to deregulation, the federal government

environmental change the rate at which a company's general and specific environments change

stable environment an environment in which the rate of change is slow

dynamic environment an environment in which the rate of change is fast

punctuated equilibrium theory the theory that companies go through long periods of stability (equilibrium), followed by short periods of dynamic, fundamental change (revolution), and finishing with a return to stability (new equilibrium)

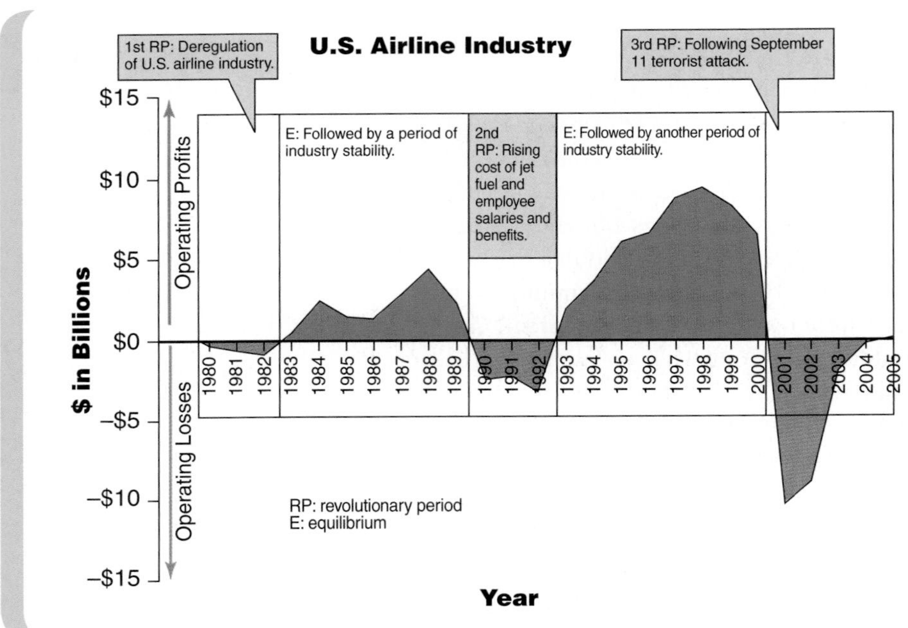

Exhibit 3.1

Punctuated Equilibrium: U.S. Airline Profits since 1979

Source: "Annual Revenues and Earnings: U.S. Airlines—All Services," Air Transport Association, available at http://www.airlines.org, January 2007.

controlled where airlines could fly, how much could be charged, when they could fly, and the number of flights they could have on a particular route. After deregulation, these choices were left to the airlines. The large financial losses during this period clearly indicate that the airlines had trouble adjusting to the intense competition that occurred after deregulation. By mid-1982, however, profits returned to the industry and held steady until mid-1989.

Then, after experiencing record growth and profits, U.S. airlines lost billions of dollars between 1989 and 1993 as the industry went through dramatic changes. Key expenses, including jet fuel and employee salaries, which had held steady for years, suddenly increased. Furthermore, revenues, which had grown steadily year after year, suddenly dropped because of dramatic changes in the airlines' customer base. Business travelers, who had typically paid full-price fares, comprised more than half of all passengers during the 1980s. However, by the late 1980s, the largest customer base had changed to leisure travelers, who wanted the cheapest flights they could get.[7] With expenses suddenly up and revenues suddenly down, the airlines responded to these changes in their business environment by laying off 5 to 10 percent of their workers, canceling orders for new planes, and eliminating unprofitable routes. Starting in 1993 and lasting till 1998, these changes helped the airline industry to achieve profits far in excess of their historical levels. The industry began to stabilize, if not flourish, just as punctuated equilibrium theory predicts.[8]

The third revolutionary period for the U.S. airline industry began with the terrorist attacks of September 11, 2001, in which planes were used as missiles to bring down the World Trade Center towers and damage the Pentagon. The immediate effect was a 20 percent drop in scheduled flights, a 40 percent drop in passengers, and losses so large that the U.S. government approved a $15 billion bailout to keep the airlines in business. Heightened airport security also affected airports, the airlines themselves, and airline customers. Five years after the 9/11 attacks, United Airlines, U.S. Airways, Delta, and American Airlines had reduced staffing by 169,000 full-time jobs to cut costs after losing a combined $42 billion.[9] Due to their financially weaker position, the airlines have now restructured operations to take advantage of the combined effect of increased passenger travel, a sharply reduced cost structure, and a 23 percent reduction in the fleet to move their businesses back to profitability.[10] As a result, the airlines may be moving back to a more stable period of equilibrium.

environmental complexity the number and the intensity of external factors in the environment that affect organizations

simple environment an environment with few environmental factors

complex environment an environment with many environmental factors

1.2 Environmental Complexity

Environmental complexity is the number and the intensity of external factors in the environment that affect organizations. **Simple environments** have few environmental factors, whereas **complex environments** have many environmental factors. The dairy industry is an excellent example of a relatively simple external environment.

Even accounting for decades-old advances in processing and automatic milking machines, milk is produced the same way today as it was 100 years ago. And while food manufacturers introduce dozens of new dairy-based products each year, U.S. milk production has grown a meager 1.25 percent per year over the last decade. In short, producing milk is a highly competitive but simple business that has experienced few changes.[11]

At the other end of the spectrum, few industries have dealt with more change in their environment than the recording industry. The first 12-inch-diameter records were released in the early 1900s and were virtually the only format for music delivery until the 1960s. In the next few decades came new formats including eight-track tapes, cassette tapes, and, in the early 1980s, the compact disc. The record labels balanced their shipments to handle the changing desires of their customers, and in 1988 CDs outsold the vinyl-record album format for the first time. The MP3 format was patented in Germany in 1989 and over the next 10 years became a standard format for compressing high-quality digital sound to CDs or other storage devices.

In 1999 a company called **Napster** created a peer-to-peer network that allowed (albeit illegally) users to share digital files with each other. Within a year, 30 percent of all PCs were running this software program, and the recording industry blamed illegal file sharing for the sharp declines in CD sales. In an effort to create a legal downloading mechanism that would support the rights of the recording industry, **Apple Computer** developed iTunes.com, where individual songs could be legally purchased and downloaded for 99 cents per song. Apple followed this up with the October 2001 release of the iPod, the now-ubiquitous MP3 player that uses an internal hard drive to hold up to thousands of songs. More than one billion songs have been downloaded from iTunes since the inception of the iTunes/iPod model, clearly changing the way the recording industry distributes and profits from music. In fact, previous nondigital formats have either all but disappeared or are in serious decline. Interestingly, sales from the digital media (which is dramatically cheaper for the producers) have more than made up for any decline in other formats.[12]

1.3 Resource Scarcity

The third characteristic of external environments is resource scarcity. **Resource scarcity** is the abundance or shortage of critical organizational resources in an organization's external environment.

For example, the primary reason that flat-screen LCD (liquid crystal display) televisions with lifelike pictures are six times more expensive per inch than regular TVs, two times more expensive than rear-projection TVs, and 25 percent more expensive than plasma TVs is that there aren't enough LCD screen factories to meet demand. As long as this condition persists, LCD TV prices will remain high. At $2 billion to $4 billion each, LCD factories are the scarce resource in this industry. LCD factories are expensive to build because, like computer chips, LCD flat screens must be made in superclean environments. Furthermore, the manufacturing process is complex and difficult to manage because the liquid crystal, which can be ruined by just one speck of dust, must be poured onto glass in a layer thinner than a sheet of paper. Each generation of factory has been focused on increasing the size of the glass panels from which the screens are cut. A seventh-generation factory (the latest) can produce a panel big enough to cut as many as twenty-four 23-inch LCD screens or as few as six 46-inch screens. The market is still growing at a torrid pace; despite recent predictions of manufacturing gluts, the demand for increasingly larger LCD panels has continued

resource scarcity the abundance or shortage of critical organizational resources in an organization's external environment to outpace production. The industry has also continued to advance its technical capability and can now successfully produce 100-inch LCD panels.[13]

1.4 Uncertainty

As Exhibit 3.2 shows, environmental change, environmental complexity, and resource scarcity affect environmental **uncertainty**, which is how well managers can understand or predict the external changes and trends affecting their businesses. Starting at the left side of the figure, environmental uncertainty is lowest when environmental change and environmental complexity are at low levels and resource scarcity is small (that is, resources are plentiful). In these environments, managers feel confident that they can understand, predict, and react to the external forces that affect their businesses. Because the AM/FM radio market had remained relatively unchanged from its founding (meaning that it was predictable), the founders of XM Radio saw an opportunity to change the industry. By contrast, the right side of the figure shows that environmental uncertainty is highest when environmental change and complexity are extensive and resource scarcity is a problem. In these environments, managers may not be confident that they can understand, predict, and handle the external forces affecting their businesses.

Review 1: Changing Environments

Environmental change, complexity, and resource scarcity are the basic components of external environments. Environmental change is the rate at which conditions or events affecting a business change. Environmental complexity is the number and intensity of external factors in an external environment. Resource scarcity is the scarcity or abundance of resources available in the external environment. The greater the degree of environmental change, environmental complexity, and resource scarcity, the less confident managers are that they can understand, predict, and effectively react to the trends affecting their businesses. According to punctuated equilibrium theory, companies experience periods of stability followed by short periods of dynamic, fundamental change, followed by a return to periods of stability.

uncertainty extent to which managers can understand or predict which environmental changes and trends will affect their businesses

Exhibit 3.2

Environmental Change, Environmental Complexity, and Resource Scarcity

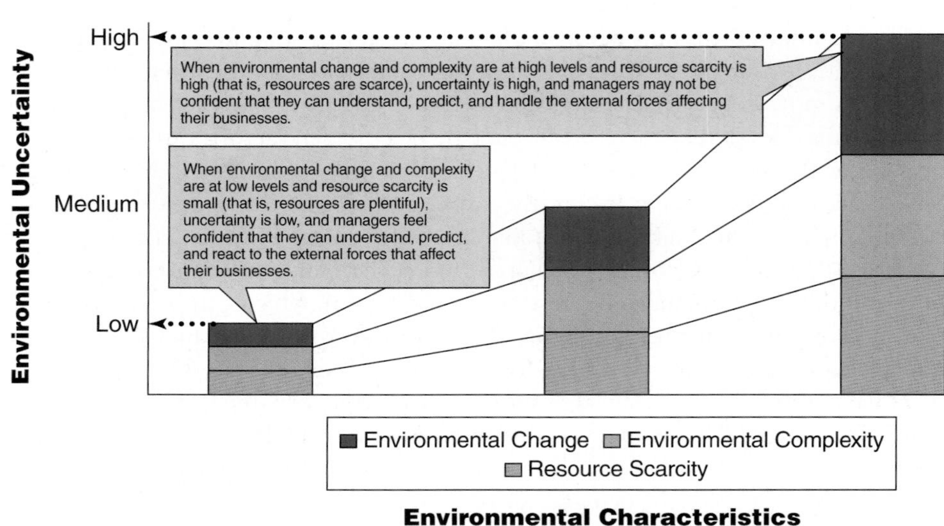
High
Medium
Low
Environmental Uncertainty
When environmental change and complexity are at high levels and resource scarcity is high (that is, resources are scarce), uncertainty is high, and managers may not be confident that they can understand, predict, and handle the external forces affecting their businesses.
When environmental change and complexity are at low levels and resource scarcity is small (that is, resources are plentiful), uncertainty is low, and managers feel confident that they can understand, predict, and react to the external forces that affect their businesses.
Environmental Change
Environmental Complexity
Resource Scarcity
Environmental Characteristics

2 General Environment

As Exhibit 3.3 shows, two kinds of external environments influence organizations: the general environment and the specific environment. The **general environment** consists of the economy and the technological, sociocultural, and political/legal trends that indirectly affect *all* organizations. Changes in any sector of the general environment eventually affect most organizations. For example, when the Federal Reserve lowers its prime lending rate, most businesses benefit because banks and credit card companies often lower the interest rates they charge for loans. Consumers, who can then borrow money more cheaply, might borrow more to buy homes, cars, refrigerators, and plasma or LCD large-screen TVs. By contrast, each organization also has a **specific environment** that is unique to that firm's industry and directly affects the way it conducts day-to-day business. For example, when the cost of coffee beans increased dramatically, Starbucks increased its prices, as did Kraft Foods, the maker of Maxwell House coffee.[14] But because that change came from the specific environment for this industry and not the general environment (which influences all businesses), only coffee-related businesses were affected. The specific environment, which will be discussed in detail in Section 3 of this chapter, includes customers, competitors, suppliers, industry regulation, and advocacy groups.

general environment the economic, technological, sociocultural, and political trends that indirectly affect all organizations

specific environment the customers, competitors, suppliers, industry regulations, and advocacy groups that are unique to an industry and directly affect how a company does business

Exhibit 3.3
General and Specific Environments

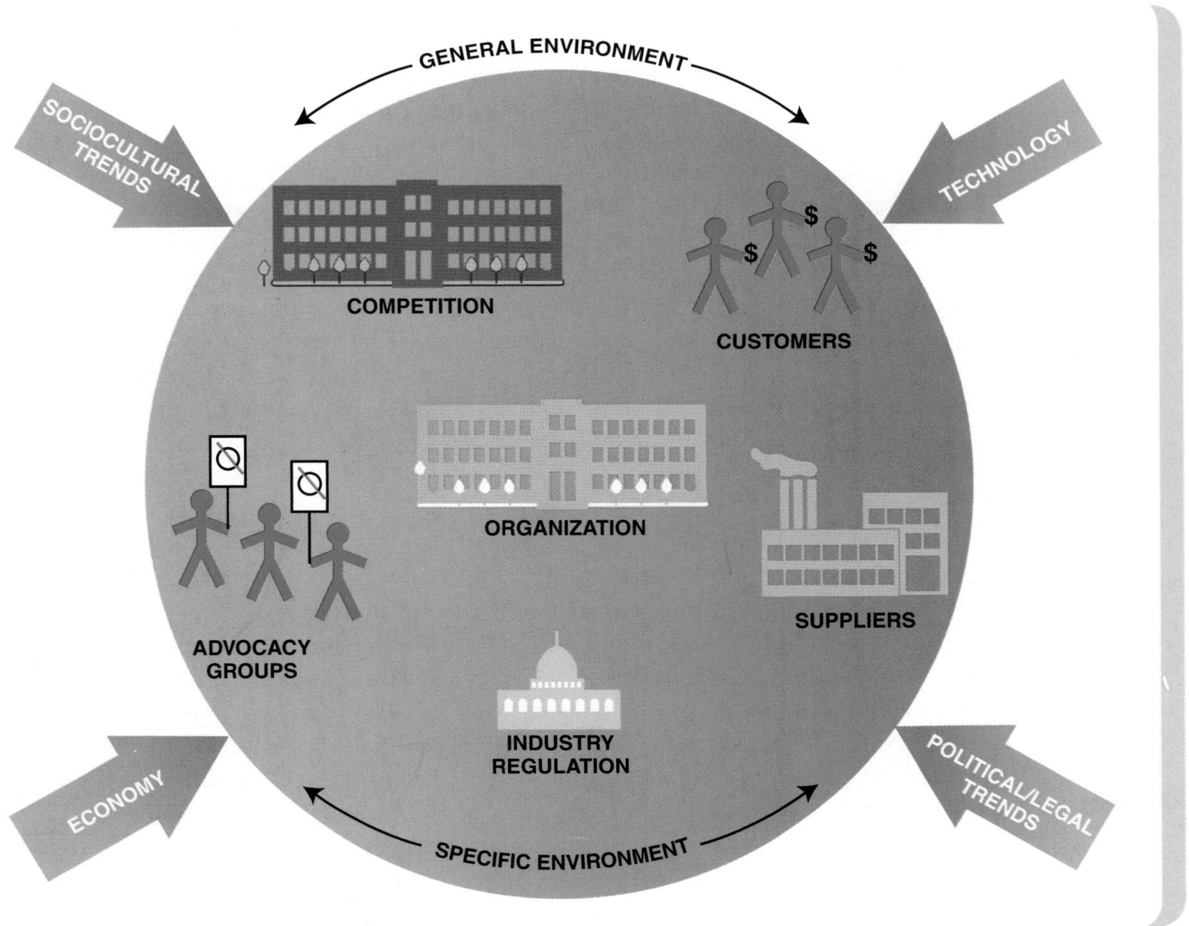

Let's take a closer look at the four components of the general environment: ***2.1 the economy****, and* ***2.2 the technological, 2.3 sociocultural****, and* ***2.4 political/ legal trends that indirectly affect all organizations****.*

2.1 Economy

The current state of a country's economy affects virtually every organization doing business there. In general, in a growing economy, more people are working and wages are growing, and therefore consumers have relatively more money to spend. More products are bought and sold in a growing economy than in a static or shrinking economy. Though an individual firm's sales will not necessarily increase, a growing economy does provide an environment favorable to business growth. In contrast, in a shrinking economy, consumers have less money to spend and relatively fewer products are bought and sold. Thus, a shrinking economy makes growth for individual businesses more difficult.

Because the economy influences basic business decisions, such as whether to hire more employees, expand production, or take out loans to purchase equipment, managers scan their economic environments for signs of significant change. Unfortunately, the economic statistics that managers rely on when making these decisions are notoriously poor predictors of *future* economic activity. A manager who decides to hire 10 more employees because economic data suggest future growth could very well have to lay off those newly hired workers when the economic growth does not occur. In fact, a famous economic study found that at the beginning of a business quarter (a period of only three months), even the best economic forecasters could not accurately predict whether economic activity would grow or shrink in that same quarter![15]

Because economic statistics can be poor predictors, some managers try to predict future economic activity by keeping track of business confidence. **Business confidence indices** show how confident actual managers are about future business growth. For example, the *Fortune* Business Confidence Index is a monthly survey of chief financial officers at large *Fortune* 1000 firms.[16] Another widely cited measure is the U.S. Chamber of Commerce Business Confidence Index, which asks 7,000 small business owners to express their optimism (or pessimism) about future business sales and prospects. Managers often prefer business confidence indices to economic statistics because they know that other managers make business decisions that are in line with their expectations concerning the economy's future. So if the *Fortune* or U.S. Chamber of Commerce business confidence indices are dropping, a manager might decide against hiring new employees, increasing production, or taking out additional loans to expand the business.

2.2 Technological Component

Technology is the knowledge, tools, and techniques used to transform inputs (raw materials, information, and so on) into outputs (products and services). For example, the inputs of authors, editors, and artists (knowledge) and the use of equipment like computers and printing presses (technology) transformed paper, ink, and glue (raw materials) into this book (the finished product). In the case of a service company such as an airline, the technology consists of equipment, including airplanes, repair tools, computers, as well as the knowledge of mechanics, ticketers, and flight crews. The output is the service of transporting people from one place to another.

Changes in technology can help companies provide better products or produce their products more efficiently. For example, advances in surgical techniques and imaging equipment have made open-heart surgery much faster and safer in recent years. While technological changes can benefit a business, they can also threaten

business confidence indices indices that show managers' level of confidence about future business growth

technology the knowledge, tools, and techniques used to transform input into output

it. Companies must embrace new technology and find effective ways to use it to improve their products and services or decrease costs. If they don't, they will lose out to those companies that do. For example, over-the-counter medications have traditionally been available in either pill or liquid form; now the new technology is edible film. Like those little, thin strips of breath freshener, medicinal edible film dissolves instantly on the tongue, allowing the medicine to enter the bloodstream more quickly. This new technology has applications in areas where administering oral medication can be challenging, such as to children and pets. **Novartis** has added edible film to many of its product lines, and its Triaminic line of cold medicines now sells multiple flavors of film in children's strength. The Triaminic franchise has grown from nothing to claim a 20 percent share of the pediatric cough and cold market. "Most of the growth has been driven by the Thin Strip [edible film]," says Brian McNamara, a vice-president at Novartis Consumer Health in Parsippany, New Jersey. Pet-care company Hartz Mountain Corp., which already produces breath-freshening strips for dogs, is investigating using edible film for delivering pet medication, an annual market valued at over $1 billion. Imagine: Instead of wrestling your pet to force pills down its throat, you'll simply place the edible medicine film on its tongue. Sales of edible film are estimated to increase from under $1 million to $350 million in the next few years.[17] Chapter 7, on organizational change and innovation, provides a more in-depth discussion of how technology affects a company's competitive advantage.

"Companies must embrace new technology and find effective ways to use it to improve their products and services or decrease costs."

"What's New" Company

2.3 Sociocultural Component

The sociocultural component of the general environment refers to the demographic characteristics, general behavior, attitudes, and beliefs of people in a particular society. Sociocultural changes and trends influence organizations in two important ways.

First, changes in demographic characteristics—such as the number of people with particular skills or the growth/decline in particular population segments (marital status, age, gender, ethnicity)—affect how companies staff their businesses. Exhibit 3.4 shows

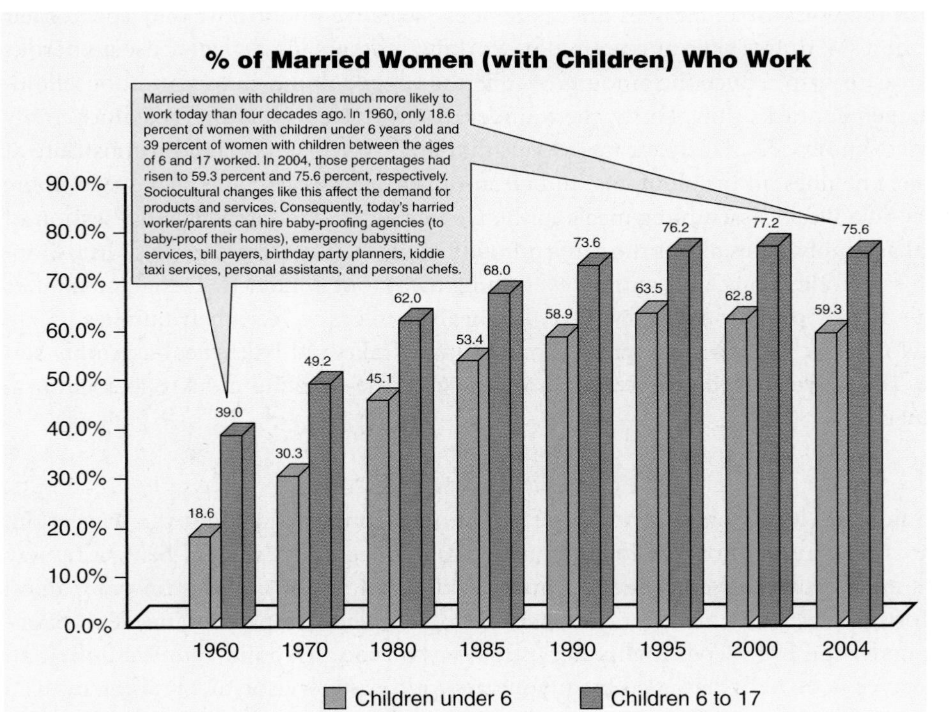

% of Married Women (with Children) Who Work
Married women with children are much more likely to work today than four decades ago. In 1960, only 18.6 percent of women with children under 6 years old and 39 percent of women with children between the ages of 6 and 17 worked. In 2004, those percentages had risen to 59.3 percent and 75.6 percent, respectively. Sociocultural changes like this affect the demand for products and services. Consequently, today's harried worker/parents can hire baby-proofing agencies (to baby-proof their homes), emergency babysitting services, bill payers, birthday party planners, kiddie taxi services, personal assistants, and personal chefs.
90.0%
80.0%
70.0%
60.0%
50.0%
40.0%
30.0%
20.0%
10.0%
0.0%
18.6
39.0
30.3
49.2
45.1
62.0
53.4
68.0
58.9
73.6
63.5
76.2
62.8
77.2
59.3
75.6
1960
1970
1980
1985
1990
1995
2000
2004
Children under 6
Children 6 to 17

Exhibit 3.4

Demographics: Percentage of Married Women (with Children) Who Work

Sources: U.S. Census Bureau, Statistical Abstract of the United States, 1999, 2001, and 2004–2005. (Washington, D.C.: U.S. Government Printing Office, 1999, 2001, and 2004), "Employment Status of Women by Marital Status and Presence and Age of Children: 1960 to 1998," Table No. 631; "Employment Status of Women by Marital Status and Presence and Age of Children: 1970 to 2004," Table No. 586.

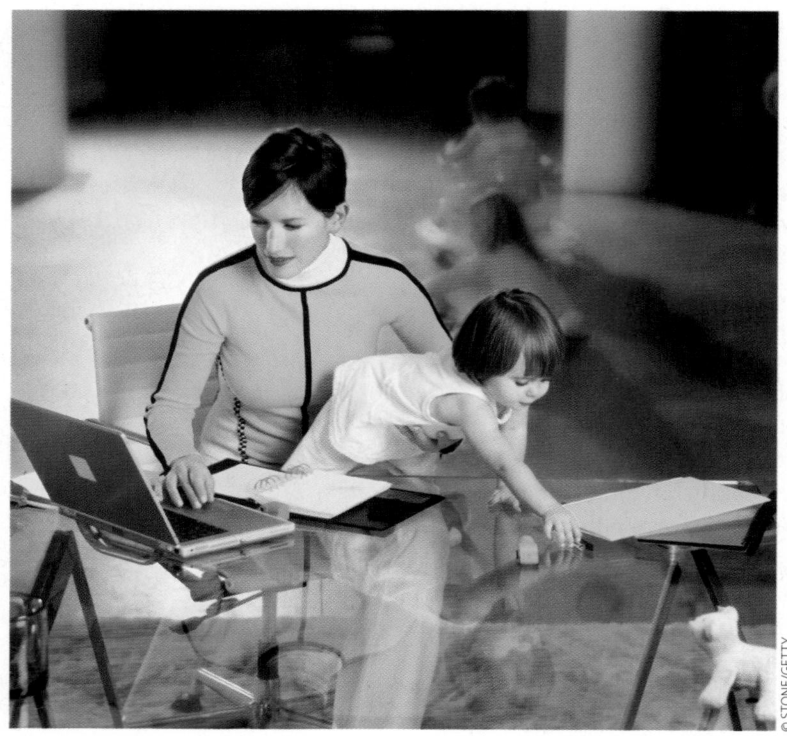
© STONE/GETTY

that married women with children are much more likely to work today than four decades ago. In 1960, only 18.6 percent of women with children under 6 years old and 39 percent of women with children between the ages of 6 and 17 worked. By 2004, those percentages had risen to 59.3 percent and 75.6 percent, respectively. Today, with traffic congestion creating longer commutes and both parents working longer hours, employees are much more likely to value products and services that allow them to recapture free time with their families. Priscilla La Barbera, a marketing professor at New York University, believes that there's been a "societal shift" in the way people view their free time. She says, "People are beginning to realize that their time has real value."[18] Companies such as CDW (Computer Discount Warehouse) in Vernon Hills, Illinois, help their employees by providing a service that picks up their dry cleaning at their desks.[19] At First Command Financial Planning in Fort Worth, Texas, employees can borrow movies for two nights of home viewing and drop off shoes for free shining as well as their cars for free washing.[20] Circles, an organization that provides employee concierge services, has more than 300 employees helping over 250,000 client employees find more free time by planning their vacations, finding pet sitters, or running their errands.[21]

Second, sociocultural changes in behavior, attitudes, and beliefs also affect the demand for a business's products and services. Because more women with children are in the workforce, families are deliberately selective about how they spend their free time. With free time at a premium, working mothers in particular use numerous services to help reduce the amount of time they spend doing chores and household-management tasks. Julie Duffy, the founder of **DINNER BY DESIGN**, a meal-assembly service, knows this. Duffy creates menus that are easy to prepare and reconstitute at home. She does all the shopping and clean-up for her clients, who spend two hours every two weeks assembling meals in the Dinner by Design kitchens. One session of meal assembly takes about the same amount of time as creating a grocery list, shopping for all the items, and putting everything away, but Dinner by Design customers don't do any of that. And they have full, healthy meals to feed their families for up to two weeks.[22] Duffy's company is one of many take-and-bake meal-assembly services that have started up recently in response to the working-mother sociocultural change.

2.4 Political/Legal Component

The political/legal component of the general environment includes the legislation, regulations, and court decisions that govern and regulate business behavior. New laws and regulations continue to impose additional responsibilities on companies. Unfortunately, many managers are unaware of these new responsibilities. For example, under the 1991 Civil Rights Act (**http://www.eeoc.gov/policy/cra91.html**), if an employee is sexually harassed by anyone at work (a supervisor, a coworker, or even a customer), the company—not just the harasser—is potentially liable for damages,

attorneys' fees, and back pay.[23] Under the Family and Medical Leave Act (**http://www.dol.gov/esa/whd/fmla**), employees who have been on the job one year are guaranteed 12 weeks of unpaid leave per year to tend to their own illnesses or to their elderly parents, a newborn baby, or a newly adopted child. Employees are guaranteed the same job, pay, and benefits when they return to work.[24]

Many managers are also unaware of the potential legal risks associated with traditional managerial decisions like recruiting, hiring, and firing employees. Increasingly, businesses and managers are being sued for negligent hiring and supervision, defamation, invasion of privacy, emotional distress, fraud, and misrepresentation during employee recruitment.[25] More than 24,000 suits for wrongful termination (unfairly firing employees) are filed each year.[26] In fact, wrongful termination lawsuits increased by 77 percent in the last decade and now account for 13 percent of all lawsuits against companies.[27] One in four employers will at some point be sued for wrongful termination. Employers lose 70 percent of these cases, and on average, the former employee is awarded $500,000 or more.[28]

Companies also face a variety of potential legal risks from customer-initiated lawsuits. For example, under product-liability law, manufacturers are liable for products made decades ago. Also, the law, as it is now written, does not consider whether manufactured products have been properly maintained and used by the customer. For instance, a Texas jury awarded $37 million in damages against **GOODYEAR TIRE AND RUBBER COMPANY** after concluding that one of its tires caused a traffic death. The tire in question was nine years old, twice the normal four- to five-year life span of most tires, and had been patched four times (once incorrectly).[29] Still, the jury required Goodyear to pay $37 million in damages. Why? Under product-liability law, plaintiffs only have to demonstrate that they were injured by the manufacturer's product. Under the concept of "strict liability," the burden of proof is shifted to the company, which must prove that the product was safe.[30] Thus, once injuries have been shown, the company is assumed guilty until it proves its innocence. Today, jury verdicts in product-liability cases cost companies an average of $6.8 million per case.[31]

Not everyone agrees that companies' legal risks are too severe. Indeed, many believe that the government should do more to regulate and restrict business behavior and that it should be easier for average citizens to sue dishonest or negligent corporations. From a managerial perspective, the best medicine against legal risk is prevention. As a manager, it is your responsibility to educate yourself about the laws, regulations, and potential lawsuits that could affect your business. Failure to do so may put you and your company at risk of sizable penalties, fines, or legal charges.

Review 2: General Environment

The general environment consists of economic, technological, sociocultural, and political/legal events and trends that affect all organizations. Because the economy influences basic business decisions, managers often use economic statistics and business confidence indices to predict future economic activity. Changes in technology, which transforms inputs into outputs, can be a benefit or a threat to a business. Sociocultural trends, like changing demographic characteristics, affect how companies run their businesses. Similarly, sociocultural changes in behavior, attitudes, and beliefs affect the demand for a business's products and services. Court decisions and new federal and state laws have imposed much greater political/legal responsibilities on companies. The best way to manage legal responsibilities is to educate managers and employees about laws and regulations and potential lawsuits that could affect a business.

mgmt: trends

States, Employers, and Health Care

Although health care is not a new issue, state-mandated employee coverage is. In 2006, Massachusetts began requiring businesses with more than 10 employees to provide health insurance or pay fines of $295 per employee per year. New York, Vermont, Washington, and Wisconsin quickly began examining the Massachusetts plan as a framework for crafting their own. Keep your eyes open for more states considering business-funded health-insurance requirements.

Source: Jane Zhang, "Massachusetts Law Encourages Others to Explore Initiatives on Universal Coverage," *Wall Street Journal*, May 27, 2006, A4.

© VEER

3 Specific Environment

As you just learned, changes in any sector of the general environment (economic, technological, sociocultural, and political/legal) eventually affect most organizations. By contrast, each organization also has a specific environment that is unique to that firm's industry and directly affects the way it conducts day-to-day business. For instance, if your customers decide to use another product, your main competitor cuts prices 10 percent, your best supplier can't deliver raw materials, federal regulators mandate reductions in pollutants in your industry, or environmental groups accuse your company of selling unsafe products, the impact from the specific environment on your business is immediate.

Let's examine how the ***3.1 customer, 3.2 competitor, 3.3 supplier, 3.4 industry regulation****, and* ***3.5 advocacy group components*** *of the specific environment affect businesses.*

3.1 Customer Component

Customers purchase products and services. Companies cannot exist without customer support. Therefore, monitoring customers' changing wants and needs is critical to business success. There are two basic strategies for monitoring customers: reactive and proactive.

Reactive customer monitoring is identifying and addressing customer trends and problems after they occur. One reactive strategy is to identify customer concerns by listening closely to customer complaints. This strategy involves not only listening to complaints but also responding to customer concerns. For example, companies that respond quickly to customer letters of complaint are viewed much more favorably than companies that are slow to respond or never respond.[32] In particular, studies have shown that when a company's follow-up letter thanks the customer for writing, offers a sincere, specific response to the complaint (not a form letter, but an explanation of how the problem will be handled), and contains a small gift, coupons, or a refund to make up for the problem, customers are much more likely to purchase products or services again from that company.[33] By contrast, companies that don't respond promptly to customer complaints are likely to find customer rants and tirades posted publicly on places like **http://www.planetfeedback.com**. Customers hope that posting complaints on these sites will force someone to address their problems. It worked for Lena West. The day after she posted a complaint against Budget Rent-a-Car, she received an e-mail containing an apology and a promise to resolve her problem.[34]

Proactive monitoring of customers means identifying and addressing customer needs, trends, and issues *before* they occur. For example, over the past few years more stores that sell toys have switched from selling gift certificates to selling electronic

gift cards that are preprogrammed with a dollar amount and are swiped like credit cards. With kids' bedrooms stuffed with toys, savvy retailers accurately predicted that parents and grandparents might rather give gift cards than worry about getting a wrong or duplicate item leading to a boon in the sales of these cards.[35] Another example of proactive monitoring is the fast-food industry's use of multibranding, in which two or more food chains share space under the same roof. Multibranding brings in more customers by giving them more choice. Customer research suggested that people dining together might like to eat at different places at the same time. Families were a particular target of Yum! Brands, which often pairs its subsidiaries Taco Bell and KFC in one building, finds that sales are one-third higher in multi-brand restaurants than in traditional single-brand restaurants.[36]

3.2 Competitor Component

competitors companies in the same industry that sell similar products or services to customers

competitive analysis a process for monitoring the competition that involves identifying competition, anticipating their moves, and determining their strengths and weaknesses

Competitors are companies in the same industry that sell similar products or services to customers. General Motors, Ford, Toyota, Honda, Nissan, Hyundai, Kia, and DaimlerChrysler all compete for automobile customers. NBC, ABC, CBS, and Fox (along with hundreds of cable channels) compete for TV viewers' attention. McDonald's, Burger King, Wendy's, Hardee's, Chick-fil-A, and a host of others compete for fast-food customers' dollars. Often the difference between business success and failure comes down to whether your company is doing a better job of satisfying customer wants and needs than the competition. Consequently, companies need to keep close track of what their competitors are doing. To do this, managers perform a **competitive analysis**, which involves deciding who your competitors are, anticipating competitors' moves, and determining competitors' strengths and weaknesses.

Surprisingly, managers often do a poor job of identifying potential competitors because they tend to focus on only two or three well-known competitors with similar goals and resources.[37] Historically Coke and Pepsi spent more time keeping track of each other than they spent on other competitors, but when they each started losing ground to start up energy drinks, bottled water, and fruit juices, both giants began to buy businesses to help them compete in these growing markets.[38] Likewise, **HOOVER**, Dirt Devil, and, more recently, Oreck competed fiercely in the market for vacuum cleaners. Because these companies produced relatively similar vacuum cleaners, they mostly competed on price. When **DYSON** entered the market with its radically different vacuum that developed and maintained significantly more suction power, the company garnered 20 percent market share within its first 12 months on the shelves.[39]

© GETTY IMAGES NEWS

Another mistake managers may make when analyzing the competition is to underestimate potential competitors' capabilities. When this happens, managers don't take the steps they should to continue to improve their products or services. The result can be significant decreases in both market share and profits. For nearly a decade, traditional phone companies ignored the threat to their business from VoIP (Voice over Internet Protocol). Early on, software products like Cool Talk, Internet Phone, and

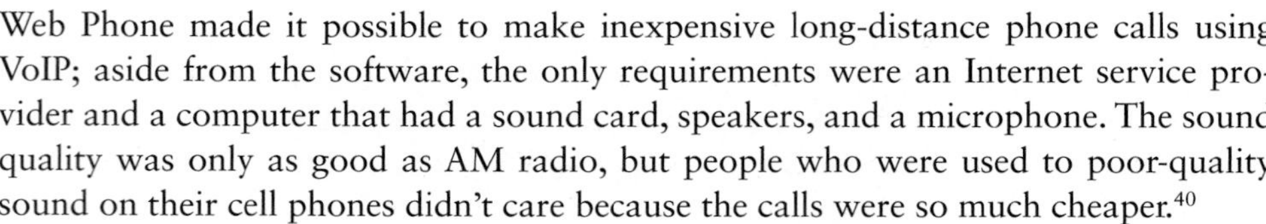

Web Phone made it possible to make inexpensive long-distance phone calls using VoIP; aside from the software, the only requirements were an Internet service provider and a computer that had a sound card, speakers, and a microphone. The sound quality was only as good as AM radio, but people who were used to poor-quality sound on their cell phones didn't care because the calls were so much cheaper.[40]

"What's New" Company

Primarily because phone companies were slow to adopt VoIP capabilities themselves, today they're facing a rash of new, unexpected VoIP competitors, all of which have slashed prices and taken market share using high-speed Internet service connections to people's homes. For example, **Comcast**, a cable-TV provider that also offers high-speed Internet service, plans to roll out Internet phone service to 40 million U.S. homes over the next two years.[41] In Hong Kong, City Telecom, which has built a fiber-optic network throughout the province, charges only $38 a month for phone service, high-speed Internet, *and* cable TV (delivered over fiber-optic cables).[42] Most U.S. consumers pay four to five times that much per month for the same services. Vonage, **http://www.vonage.com**, an Internet phone company, charges just $24.95 per month (maybe less by the time you read this) for unlimited calls in the United States, Canada, Puerto Rico, and Europe. Its non-European international long-distance charges start at six cents per minute. How much of a threat is Internet phone service to traditional phone companies today? Jeff Pulver, CEO of Pulver.com, which owns the Internet phone company Free World Dialup, says, "Within the next 10 years, it's quite possible that 50 percent or more of voice traffic will take the place of the traditional public telephone network and run on the Internet, wireless, or other systems."[43]

3.3 Supplier Component

Suppliers are companies that provide material, human, financial, and informational resources to other companies. U.S. Steel buys iron ore from suppliers to make steel products. When IBM sells a mainframe computer, it also provides support staff, engineers, and other technical consultants to the company that bought the computer. If you're shopping for desks, chairs, and office supplies, chances are Office Depot will be glad to help your business open a revolving charge account to pay for your purchases. When a clothing manufacturer has spent $100,000 to purchase new high-pressure "water drills" to cut shirt and pants patterns to precise sizes, the water drill manufacturer, as part of the purchase, will usually train the workers on the machinery.

A key factor influencing the impact and quality of the relationship between companies and their suppliers is how dependent they are on each other.[44] **Supplier dependence** is the degree to which a company relies on that supplier because of the importance of the supplier's product to the company and the difficulty of finding other sources for that product. Supplier dependence is very strong in the diamond business, given that **De Beers Consolidated Mines** provides 66 percent of the wholesale diamonds in the world. De Beers has dominated the diamond industry for more than a century, controlling the supply, price, and quality of the best diamonds on the market. The company's 125 customers, or "sightholders," as they're known in the industry, are summoned to De Beers's London office 10 times a year and given a shoebox of diamonds that they are required to buy. If they refuse, they lose the opportunity to purchase any more diamonds. De Beers initiated a Supplier of Choice (SoC) program that requires sightholders to pay more of the marketing, advertising, and branding costs for De Beers diamonds. SoC sightholders sign two-year contracts that spell out their responsibilities to develop marketing plans and advertising initiatives and to adhere to ethical guidelines. Just two-thirds of De Beers sightholders, however, qualified as SoCs. The one-third who didn't qualify as SoCs are no longer permitted to sell De Beers dia-

suppliers companies that provide material, human, financial, and informational resources to other companies

supplier dependence the degree to which a company relies on a supplier because of the importance of the supplier's product to the company and the difficulty of finding other sources of that product monds and must now get their diamonds from less prestigious diamond suppliers.[45] Sightholders agree to all this because they are dependent on their supplier De Beers.

Buyer dependence is the degree to which a supplier relies on a buyer because of the importance of that buyer to the supplier's sales and the difficulty of finding other buyers of its products. For example, **Superior Industries**, which makes car wheels, gets 85 percent of its $840 million in annual sales from Ford and General Motors. When the two automakers demanded that Superior match the low prices that Chinese wheel suppliers were offering, it had little choice. Superior's president, Steve Borick, says the ultimatum was presented very simply: "They said, 'This is the price we are getting [from Chinese suppliers] for this product. You either match that, or we'll take our business to them.' " He adds, "It's that black and white. Close the [cost] gap [of 20 to 40 percent] no matter how" you do it.[46]

As the De Beers and Superior Industries examples show, a high degree of buyer or seller dependence can lead to **opportunistic behavior**, in which one party benefits at the expense of the other. Though opportunistic behavior between buyers and suppliers will never be completely eliminated, many companies believe that both buyers and suppliers can benefit by improving the buyer-supplier relationship.[47] In contrast to opportunistic behavior, **relationship behavior** focuses on establishing a mutually beneficial, long-term relationship between buyers and suppliers.[48] **Toyota** is well known for developing positive long-term relationships with its key suppliers. Donald Esmond, who runs Toyota's U.S. division, says, "I think what they [suppliers] appreciate . . . is we don't go in and say, 'Reduce the costs by 6 percent; if you don't, somebody else is going to get the business.' We go in and say we want to come in and help you [figure out] where you can save costs so we can reduce our overall price. So it's a different approach."[49]

3.4 Industry Regulation Component

Whereas the political/legal component of the general environment affects all businesses, the **industry regulation** component consists of regulations and rules that govern the practices and procedures of specific industries, businesses, and professions. For example, if your neighbor decides to make a little extra money selling homemade baked goods and sells you two apple pies, your neighbor could be fined. In most states, it is illegal to sell food from your home. State regulations typically require a food business to obtain a license and a state certificate of inspection that indicates that the food is stored properly; insects have not infested the premises; ovens are state approved; electrical wiring, lighting, and smoke detectors are up to code; and so on.[50] Likewise, the auto industry is subject to CAFE (Corporate Average Fuel Economy) regulations that require cars and sport utility vehicles to average 27.5 and 22.5 miles, respectively, per gallon.[51]

Regulatory agencies affect businesses by creating and enforcing rules and regulations to protect consumers, workers, or society as a whole. For example, the U.S. Department of Agriculture and the Food and Drug Administration regulate the safety of seafood (as well as meat and poultry) through the science-based Hazard Analysis and Critical Control Points program. Seafood processors are required to identify hazards (toxins, chemicals, pesticides, and decomposition) that could cause the fish they process to be unsafe. They must also establish critical control points to control hazards both inside and outside their fish-processing plants and then establish monitoring, corrective action, and verification procedures to certify that the fish they process is safe to consume.[52]

The nearly 100 federal agencies and regulatory commissions can affect almost any kind of business. Exhibit 3.5 lists some of the most influential federal agencies

buyer dependence the degree to which a supplier relies on a buyer because of the importance of that buyer to the supplier and the difficulty of finding other buyers for its products

opportunistic behavior a transaction in which one party in the relationship benefits at the expense of the other

relationship behavior the establishment of mutually beneficial, long-term exchanges between buyers and suppliers

industry regulation regulations and rules that govern the business practices and procedures of specific industries, businesses, and professions

Federal Agency	Regulatory Responsibilities
Consumer Product Safety Commission **http://www.cpsc.gov**	Reduces risk of injuries and deaths associated with consumer products, sets product safety standards, enforces product recalls, and provides consumer education
Department of Labor **http://www.dol.gov**	Collects employment statistics and administers labor laws concerning safe working conditions, minimum hourly wages and overtime pay, employment discrimination, and unemployment insurance
Environmental Protection Agency **http://www.epa.gov**	Reduces and controls pollution through research, monitoring, standard setting, and enforcement activities
Equal Employment Opportunity Commission **http://www.eeoc.gov**	Promotes fair hiring and promotion practices
Federal Communications Commission **http://www.fcc.gov**	Regulates interstate and international communications by radio, television, wire, satellite, and cable
Federal Reserve System **http://www.federalreserve.gov**	As nation's central bank, controls interest rates and money supply, and monitors the U.S. banking system to produce a growing economy with stable prices
Federal Trade Commission **http://www.ftc.gov**	Restricts unfair methods of business competition and misleading advertising, and enforces consumer protection laws
Food and Drug Administration **http://www.fda.gov**	Protects nation's health by making sure food, drugs, and cosmetics are safe
National Labor Relations Board **http://www.nlrb.gov**	Monitors union elections and stops companies from engaging in unfair labor practices
Occupational Safety & Health Administration **http://www.osha.gov**	Issues and enforces standards to protect the lives and health of workers
Securities and Exchange Commission **http://www.sec.gov**	Protects investors in the bond and stock markets, guarantees access to information on publicly traded securities, and regulates firms that sell securities or give investment advice

Exhibit 3.5

Federal Regulatory Agencies and Commissions

and commissions, as well as their responsibilities and their websites. Overall, the number and cost of federal regulations has nearly tripled in the last 25 years. Today, for every $1 the federal government spends creating regulations, businesses spend $45 to comply with them.[53] In addition to federal regulations, businesses are also subject to state, county, and city regulations. Complying with all of these regulations costs businesses an estimated $189 billion per year or $1,700 per employee.[54] Surveys indicate that managers rank dealing with government regulation as one of the most demanding and frustrating parts of their jobs.[55]

3.5 Advocacy Groups

Advocacy groups are groups of concerned citizens who band together to try to influence the business practices of specific industries, businesses, and professions. The members of a group generally share the same point of view on a particular issue. For example, environmental advocacy groups might try to get manufacturers to reduce smokestack pollution emissions. Unlike the industry regulation component of the specific environment, advocacy groups cannot force organizations to change their practices. Nevertheless, they can use a number of techniques to try to influence companies, such as public communications, media advocacy, web pages, blogs, and product boycotts.

advocacy groups concerned citizens who band together to try to influence the business practices of specific industries, businesses, and professions

public communications an advocacy group tactic that relies on voluntary participation by the news media and the advertising industry to get the advocacy group's message out

The **public communications** approach relies on *voluntary* participation by the news media and the advertising industry to send out an advocacy group's message. For example, a public service campaign to encourage people to quit smoking ran the following ads in newspapers and magazines throughout Europe: a photo showing the foot of a young person with a toe tag (indicating the person was dead), with the caption "Smokers die younger"; a picture showing clean lungs next to brown- and black-stained lungs, with the caption "Smoking causes fatal lung cancer"; and, a photo of a baby in an intensive care unit hooked up to a respirator, with the caption "Smoking when pregnant harms your baby."[56]

Media advocacy is much more aggressive than the public communications approach. A **media advocacy** approach typically involves framing the group's concerns as public issues (affecting everyone); exposing questionable, exploitative, or unethical practices; and creating controversy that is likely to receive extensive news coverage. **PETA** (People for the Ethical Treatment of Animals), which has offices in the United States, England, Italy, and Germany, uses controversial publicity stunts and advertisements to try to change the behavior of large organizations, fashion designers, medical researchers, and anyone else it believes is hurting or mistreating animals. PETA cofounder and president Ingrid Newkirk says, "People now know that if they do something ghastly to an animal, they can't necessarily get away with it. When we started, nobody knew what animal rights meant. . . . Now, it's an issue." PETA protesters have stripped naked in front of the White House in front of a banner reading "I'd rather go naked than wear fur." From PETA's perspective, any animal-based product is bad. In one of its latest protests, PETA distributed 2,000 blood-covered, knife-holding, "evil Colonel Sanders" bobblehead dolls to news organizations and KFC restaurants. PETA spokesperson Joe Hinkle says, "We'd like them to stop breeding and drugging chickens so that they grow so big that they actually cripple under their own bulk." KFC issued this response: "PETA has disparaged our brand and misrepresented the truth about our responsible industry-leading animal welfare standards. KFC is committed to the humane treatment of chickens."[58]

doing the right thing

Dealing with Gifts and Suppliers

In hopes of getting a buyer's business or getting more business, suppliers sometimes offer buyers trips to exotic locations, dinners at expensive restaurants, or luxurious gifts. Excessive gift giving and receiving creates a conflict of interest between what's best for the company (purchasing items of the optimal quality and cost) and what's personally best for the buyer who receives the gifts. Follow these general guidelines to avoid conflicts of interest:

- **Remember that there is no such thing as a free lunch.**
- **Make sure that business meals and entertainment (parties, outings, sporting events) have a valid business purpose and that the buyer and the supplier take turns paying for or hosting them.**
- **Don't accept gifts worth more than $25. If you are offered a gift worth more than $25, ask your manager if the gift is appropriate.**
- **Never accept cash or cash equivalents, such as gift certificates.**
- **Don't accept discounts on goods and services, unless the discounts are generally available to others.**
- **Don't accept offers of stock in suppliers' companies.**
- **Don't allow personal friendships with suppliers to influence buying decisions.[57]**

media advocacy an advocacy group tactic that involves framing issues as public issues; exposing questionable, exploitative, or unethical practices; and forcing media coverage by buying media time or creating controversy that is likely to receive extensive news coverage

A **product boycott** is a tactic in which an advocacy group actively tries to persuade consumers not to purchase a company's product or service. One example of this is the **Rainforest Action Network** (RAN), whose members have chained themselves to wood piles at select Home Depot stores to get the company to stop selling old-growth lumber. Members also shadowed Citigroup's then-CEO Sandy Weill until he agreed to implement environmentally friendly lending policies. In 2006, the group targeted Ford Motor Company as the automobile manufacturer with the worst record of fuel efficiency. When Ford stated that RAN would have no impact upon the company, RAN's executive director Michael Brune responded, "Every company says we are not having an effect—straight up to the time they make their policy change."[59]

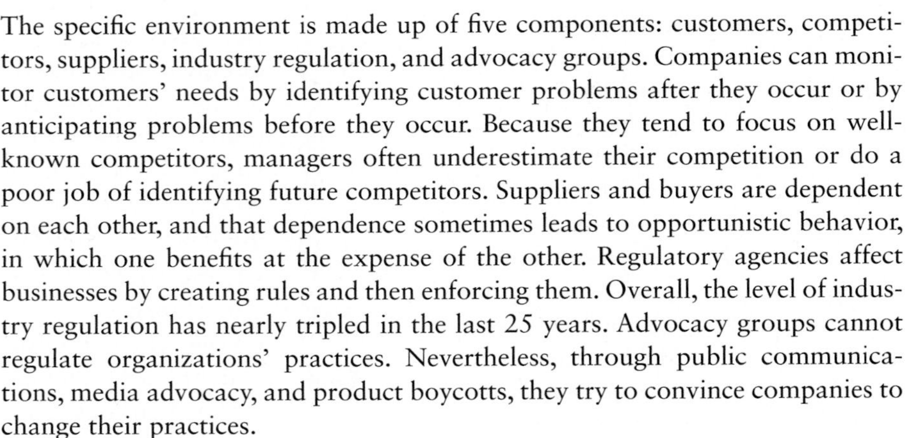

Review 3: Specific Environment

The specific environment is made up of five components: customers, competitors, suppliers, industry regulation, and advocacy groups. Companies can monitor customers' needs by identifying customer problems after they occur or by anticipating problems before they occur. Because they tend to focus on well-known competitors, managers often underestimate their competition or do a poor job of identifying future competitors. Suppliers and buyers are dependent on each other, and that dependence sometimes leads to opportunistic behavior, in which one benefits at the expense of the other. Regulatory agencies affect businesses by creating rules and then enforcing them. Overall, the level of industry regulation has nearly tripled in the last 25 years. Advocacy groups cannot regulate organizations' practices. Nevertheless, through public communications, media advocacy, and product boycotts, they try to convince companies to change their practices.

4 Making Sense of Changing Environments

In Chapter 1, you learned that managers are responsible for making sense of their business environments. As our discussions of the general and specific environments have indicated, however, making sense of business environments is not an easy task. Because external environments can be dynamic, confusing, and complex, managers use a three-step process to make sense of the changes in their external environments:

***4.1 environmental scanning*, *4.2 interpreting environmental factors*,** *and* ***4.3 acting on threats and opportunities*.**

4.1 Environmental Scanning

Environmental scanning is searching the environment for important events or issues that might affect an organization. Managers scan the environment to stay up-to-date on important factors in their industry. For example, with one out of every four new car buyers purchasing highly profitable sport utility vehicles (SUVs), auto executives hadn't paid much attention to environmental groups' complaints about SUVs' extremely poor gas mileage. Now, however, market research is showing that current SUV owners are unhappy with their vehicles' poor gas mileage. In addition, the rapid rise in retail gas prices and increasingly strong disapproval of SUVs by younger car buyers have resulted in large unsold inventories of SUVs. After gas prices rose, **General Motors** dealers had 125 days of inventory for the Chevrolet Tahoe, a

product boycott an advocacy group tactic that involves protesting a company's actions by persuading consumers not to purchase its product or service

environmental scanning searching the environment for important events or issues that might affect an organization full-size SUV. The optimal inventory for such a car is about half that.[60] James Schroer, DaimlerChrysler's executive vice president for sales and marketing, says that the increasingly negative view of SUVs is "a big deal, and it's real."[61]

Managers also scan their environments to reduce uncertainty. Faced with the responsibility of developing the marketing campaigns that sell their companies' most important products, the chief marketing officers (CMOs) of the world's best organizations willingly pay $50,000 a year to join the "Marketing 50," an exclusive group of CMOs who meet several times a year to exchange ideas and pick each others' brains. Richard Smith, founder of the group, says, "It's a noncompetitive group with just one executive from a particular industry, so they have a chance to get ideas they can use that their competitors may not know about and also try to figure out some of their common problems." Michael Linton, Best Buy's CMO, believes the "Marketing 50" is fantastic for finding out what other companies and CMOs are doing which helps him reduce uncertainty. He says, "It's impossible for any one company to know about every new tool, so hearing what is working for others helps."[62]

Organizational strategies also affect environmental scanning. In other words, managers pay close attention to trends and events that are directly related to their company's ability to compete in the marketplace.[63] **MICROSOFT** used to take software hackers to court to prosecute them for the damage caused by their efforts. However, since Chairman Bill Gates declared that security is Microsoft's top priority, the company is actively trying to engage the services of friendly hackers. Though companies like Microsoft long considered computer hackers to be the enemy, they are now a source of competitive advantage. One hacker who has seen his fortunes with respect to Microsoft improve is H.D. Moore, the director of security for BreakingPoint Systems in Austin, Texas, who was wined and dined by Microsoft employees during a hacker convention in Las Vegas. He says that Microsoft has "been on a hacker buying spree" as the company tries to convince so-called security researchers to work with it rather than against it. From Microsoft's perspective, teaming up with the hacker community to solve software problems prior to release simply makes good business sense. Microsoft security-program manager Steven Toulouse stated that with the "researchers" assistance, "we have discovered things during the development of these products that we might not have discovered otherwise."[64]

"What's New"
Company

Finally, environmental scanning is important because it contributes to organizational performance. Environmental scanning helps managers detect environmental changes and problems before they become organizational crises.[65] Furthermore, companies whose CEOs do more environmental scanning have higher profits.[66] CEOs in better-performing firms scan their firm's environments more frequently and scan more key factors in their environments in more depth and detail than do CEOs in poorer-performing firms.[67]

Environmental scanning helps managers detect environmental changes and problems before they become organizational crises.

4.2 Interpreting Environmental Factors

After scanning, managers determine what environmental events and issues mean to the organization. Typically, managers view environmental events and issues as either threats or opportunities. When managers interpret environmental events as threats, they take steps to protect the company from further harm. For example, now that Internet phone service (VoIP) has emerged as a threat, traditional phone companies have responded by announcing billion-dollar plans to expand their fiber-optic networks so that they can offer phone (using VoIP), Internet service, and TV packages, just like those the cable and satellite companies offer. However, the phone companies, such as Southwestern Bell, are finding that they are far behind the cable companies, which have already spent $65 billion over the last five years upgrading their digital networks. Industry analyst Glenn Greenberg says, "The telephone companies are way behind the curve."[68]

By contrast, when managers interpret environmental events as opportunities, they consider strategic alternatives for taking advantage of those events to improve company performance. Apple is known for recognizing opportunities and capitalizing on them. The market for high-end "smart" phones, full-featured mobile phones that also function as a handheld personal computer, is growing roughly 2 percent per year. These phones retail for between $500 and $20,000, generate high profit margins, and as luxury goods are insulated from fluctuations in consumer buying. To enter this attractive market (and so capitalize on an opportunity), Apple developed its own smart phone—the iPhone. CEO Steve Jobs announced the release more than six months in advance to generate hype, stimulate demand, and dampen sales of their competitors. The iPhone features a wider screen and a camera, the capability to use the new faster Wi-Fi networks so that users can use their e-mail, surf the Web, and communicate with Bluetooth-enabled devices—plus, of course, download and play iTunes music. Apple hopes to sell 10 million iPhones within the first 18 months on the market, which will account for only a modest 1 percent of global handset sales but roughly half the U.S. demand for smart phones.[69]

cognitive maps graphic depictions of how managers believe environmental factors relate to possible organizational actions

© ASSOCIATED PRESS

4.3 Acting on Threats and Opportunities

After scanning for information on environmental events and issues, and interpreting them as threats or opportunities, managers have to decide how to respond to these environmental factors. Deciding what to do under conditions of uncertainty is always difficult. Managers can never be completely confident that they have all the information they need or that they correctly understand the information they have.

Because it is impossible to comprehend all the factors and changes, managers often rely on simplified models of external environments called "cognitive maps." **Cognitive maps** summarize the perceived relationships between environmental factors and possible organizational actions. For example, the cognitive map shown in Exhibit 3.6 represents a small clothing-store owner's interpretation of her business environment. The map shows three kinds of variables. The first variables, shown as rectangles, are environmental factors, such as a Wal-Mart or a large mall 20 minutes away. The second variables, shown in ovals, are potential actions that the store owner might take, such as a low-cost strategy; a good-value, good-service strategy; or a "large selection of the latest fashions" strategy. The third variables, shown as trapezoids, are company strengths, such as low employee turnover, and weaknesses, such as small size.

The plus and minus signs on the map indicate whether the manager believes there is a positive or negative relationship between variables. For example, the manager believes that a low-cost strategy won't work because Wal-Mart and Target are nearby. Offering a large selection of the latest fashions would not work either—not with the small size of the store and that large nearby mall. However, the manager believes that a good-value, good-service strategy would lead to success and profits because of the store's low employee turnover, good knowledge of customers, reasonable selection of clothes at reasonable prices, and good location.

In the end, managers must complete all three steps—environmental scanning, interpreting environmental factors, and acting on threats and opportunities—to make sense of changing external environments. Environmental scanning helps managers more accurately interpret their environments and take actions that improve company performance. Through scanning, managers keep tabs on what competitors are doing, identify market trends, and stay alert to current events that affect their company's operations. Armed with the environmental information they have gathered, managers can then minimize the impact of threats and turn opportunities into increased profits.

Review 4: Making Sense of Changing Environments

Managers use a three-step process to make sense of external environments: environmental scanning, interpreting information, and acting on threats and opportunities. Managers scan their environments based on their organizational strategies, their need for up-to-date information, and their need to reduce uncertainty. When managers identify environmental events as threats, they take steps to protect the company from harm. When managers identify environmental events as opportunities, they formulate alternatives for taking advantage of them to improve company performance. Using cognitive maps can help managers visually summarize the relationships between environmental factors and the actions they might take to deal with them.

Exhibit 3.6
Cognitive Maps

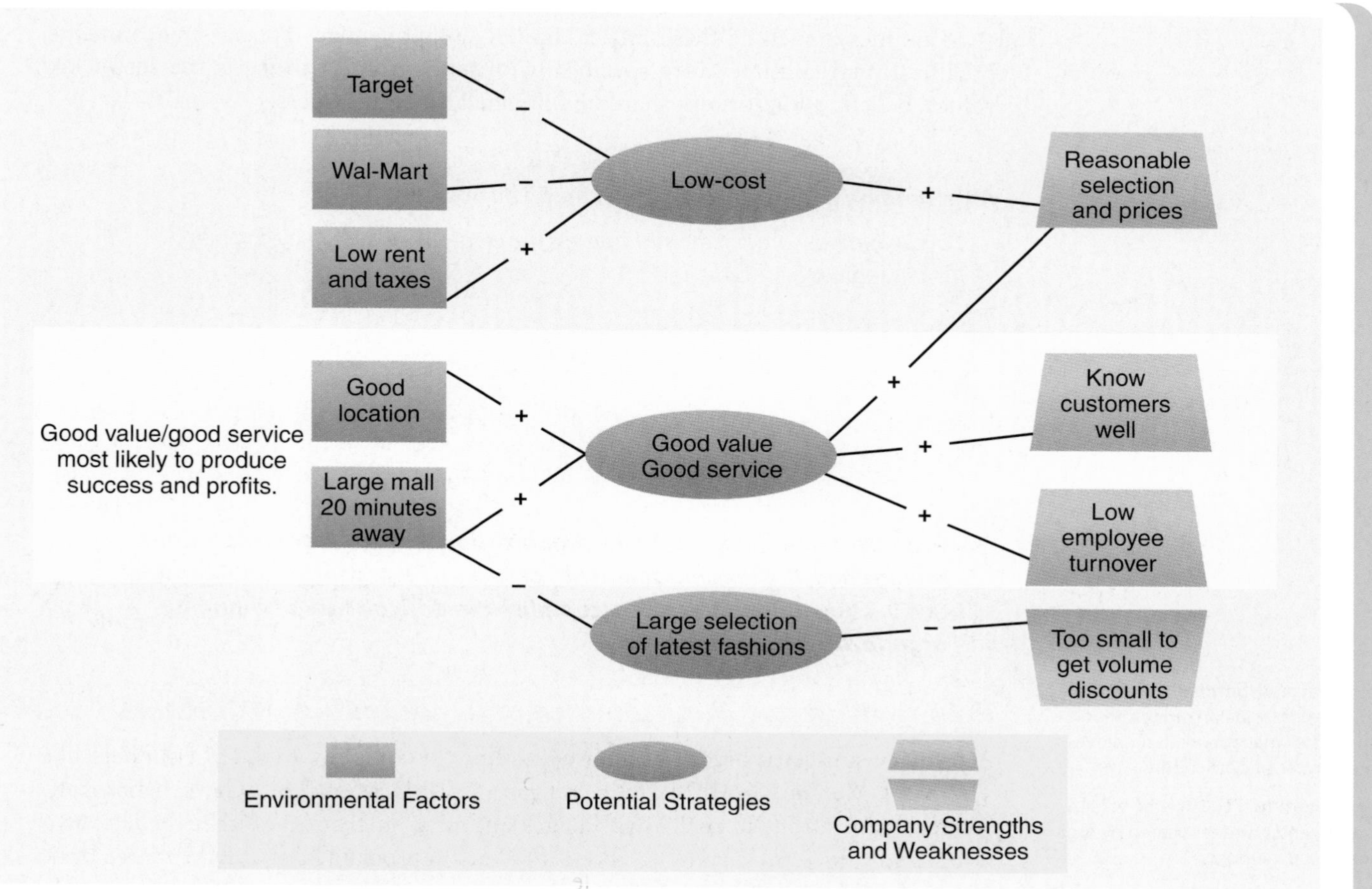

INTERNAL ENVIRONMENTS

External environments are *external* trends and events that have the potential to affect companies. By contrast, the **internal environment** consists of the trends and events *within* an organization that affect the management, employees, and organizational culture. The internal environment at **SAS**, the leading provider of statistical software, is unlike most software companies. Instead of expecting its employees to work 12- to 14-hour days, SAS has a seven-hour workday and closes its offices at 6 PM every evening. Employees receive unlimited sick days each year. To encourage employees to spend time with their families, there's an on-site day-care facility and the company cafeteria has plenty of highchairs and baby seats. Plus, every Wednesday, the company passes out M&M chocolate candies, plain and peanut, to all employees—a total of more than 22.5 tons of M&Ms per year. SAS senior vice president Jim Davis says, "We are firm believers that happy employees equal happy customers."[70]

Internal environments are important because they affect what people think, feel, and do at work. Given SAS's internal environment, it shouldn't surprise you to learn that almost no one quits. In a typical software company, 25 percent of the work force quits each year to take another job. At SAS, only 4 percent leave.[71] Jeff Chambers, SAS's vice president of human resources, says, "We have always had a commitment to investing in and cultivating meaningful, long-term relationships with our employees and clients. This has led to unusually low turnover in both populations and is at the core of our 28 years of sustained profitability and success."[72]

Comments such as these reflect the key component in internal environments, organizational culture. More specifically, **organizational culture** is the set of key values, beliefs, and attitudes shared by organizational members.

After reading the next section, you should be able to

5 explain how organizational cultures are created and how they can help companies be successful.

5 Organizational Cultures: Creation, Success, and Change

Let's take a closer look at ***5.1 how organizational cultures are created and maintained, 5.2 the characteristics of successful organizational cultures,*** *and* ***5.3 how companies can accomplish the difficult task of changing organizational cultures.***

5.1 Creation and Maintenance of Organizational Cultures

A primary source of organizational culture is the company founder. Founders like Thomas J. Watson, Sr. (IBM), Sam Walton (Wal-Mart), and Bill Gates (Microsoft) create organizations in their own images and imprint them with their beliefs, attitudes, and values. For example, Thomas J. Watson proclaimed that IBM's three basic

internal environment the events and trends inside an organization that affect management, employees, and organizational culture

organizational culture the values, beliefs, and attitudes shared by organizational members beliefs were the pursuit of excellence, customer service, and showing "respect for the individual," meaning company employees. Microsoft employees share founder Bill Gates's determination to stay ahead of software competitors. Says a Microsoft vice president, "No matter how good your product, you are only 18 months away from failure."[73]

Though company founders are instrumental in the creation of organizational cultures, eventually founders retire, die, or choose to leave their companies. When the founders are gone, how are their values, attitudes, and beliefs sustained in the organizational culture? Answer: stories and heroes.

> When the founders are gone, how are their values, attitudes, and beliefs sustained in the organizational culture?

Organizational members tell **organizational stories** to make sense of organizational events and changes and to emphasize culturally consistent assumptions, decisions, and actions.[74] At **WAL-MART**, stories abound about founder Sam Walton's thriftiness as he strove to make Wal-Mart the low-cost retailer that it is today.

> *In those days, we would go on buying trips with Sam, and we'd all stay, as much as we could, in one room or two. I remember one time in Chicago when we stayed eight of us to a room. And the room wasn't very big to begin with. You might say we were on a pretty restricted budget. (Gary Reinboth, one of Wal-Mart's first store managers)*[75]

Today, Sam Walton's thriftiness still permeates Wal-Mart. Everyone, including top executives and the CEO, flies coach rather than business or first class. When employees travel on business, it's still the norm to share rooms (though two to a room, not eight!) at inexpensive motels like Motel 6 and Super 8 instead of Holiday Inns. Likewise, for business travel, Wal-Mart will reimburse only up to $15 per meal, which is half to one-third the reimbursement rate at similar-sized companies (remember, Wal-Mart is one of the largest companies in the world). At one of its annual meetings, CEO Lee Scott reinforced Sam Walton's beliefs by exhorting Wal-Mart employees to bring back and use the free pencils and pens from their travels. Most people in the audience didn't think he was kidding, and he probably wasn't.[76]

A second way in which organizational culture is sustained is by recognizing and celebrating heroes. By definition, **organizational heroes** are organizational people admired for their qualities and achievements within the organization. **BOWA BUILDERS** is a full-service construction company in Virginia. When it was renovating a large auto dealership, its carpet subcontractor mistakenly scheduled the new carpet to be delivered two weeks *after* it was to be installed. Rather than allow construction to be delayed, a Bowa employee kept the project on schedule by immediately reordering the carpet, flying to the carpet manufacturer's factory, renting a truck, and then driving the carpet back to the auto dealership, all within 48 hours of learning about the problem. CEO and company cofounder Larry Weinberg says this story is told and retold within Bowa Builders as an example of heroic customer service. Moreover, the car dealership was so delighted with this extraordinary service that it has referred $10 million to $12 million in new business to Bowa Builders.[77]

organizational stories stories told by organizational members to make sense of organizational events and changes and to emphasize culturally consistent assumptions, decisions, and actions

organizational heroes people celebrated for their qualities and achievements within an organization

© JAY L. CLENDENIN

Bowa Builders has no shortage of organizational heroes, in part because management supports employees' efforts to go to extraordinary lengths to please customers. Every Friday, managers bring lunch to workers on the job site.

5.2 Successful Organizational Cultures

Preliminary research shows that organizational culture is related to organizational success. As shown in Exhibit 3.7, cultures based on adaptability, involvement, a clear vision, and consistency can help companies achieve higher sales growth, return on assets, profits, quality, and employee satisfaction.[78]

Adaptability is the ability to notice and respond to changes in the organization's environment. Cultures need to reinforce important values and behaviors, but a culture becomes dysfunctional if it prevents change, and one of the surest ways to do that is to discourage open discussion and disagreement. Organizational psychologist Kathleen Miller began working with a company that recognized the need to change its nonadaptive culture. However, she didn't realize how dysfunctional the culture was until she tried to start an honest discussion about the company's problems at one of her first meetings. The top managers simply would not speak up. They were so afraid to disagree with each other that they wrote their comments and questions anonymously on note cards and had them read aloud to the rest of the group.[79]

In cultures that promote higher levels of *employee involvement* in decision making, employees feel a greater sense of ownership and responsibility. Employee involvement has been a hallmark of **Genencor** since its creation as a joint venture between Genentech and Corning in 1982. Genencor designs its human resources programs by regularly polling employees about which benefits they enjoy and which they would like the company to offer. Most dramatically, when Genencor built its headquarters, it gave its employees a say in the design. Scientists requested that the labs be placed along the building's exterior so they could receive natural light. "I've worked in labs without windows," says staff scientist Fiona Harding, "and seeing the sun makes the time spent in the lab much more pleasant." For everyone else, the building features a "main street," where employees congregate to collaborate and interact throughout the day. CEO Jean-Jacques Bienaime believes that these employee-driven design features lead to a more stimulating workplace. "If you want employees to be productive, you have to create a nurturing environment and let them be creative," he says. Such a commitment to employee involvement in decision making is definitely paying off for the company. Its turnover rate was less than 4 percent (the national industry average is 18.5 percent), and its employees generate approximately $60,000 more revenue per employee than its largest competitor, Novozymes.[80]

company vision a company's purpose or reason for existing

Company vision is the business's purpose or reason for existing. In organizational cultures with a clear company vision, the organization's strategic purpose and direction are apparent to everyone in the company. When managers are uncertain about their business environments, the vision helps guide the discussions, decisions, and behavior of the people in the company. At F. H. Faulding & Company (a subsidiary of Mayne Group Limited), an Australia-based provider of health-care products and services doing business in 70 countries, the vision is "delivering innovative and valued solutions in health care."[81] This vision lets employees know why the company is in business (to deliver health-care solutions) and the values that really matter (innovative and valued solutions). To give its employees even more guidance, Faulding has clearly defined each of the key words in the vision statement. For example, "delivering" means targeting quality drugs, products, and services to the right place at the right time while concentrating on a global perspective. Likewise, "solutions" is defined as being focused, timely, and profitable by making quality products and services that satisfy customers' and partners' needs.

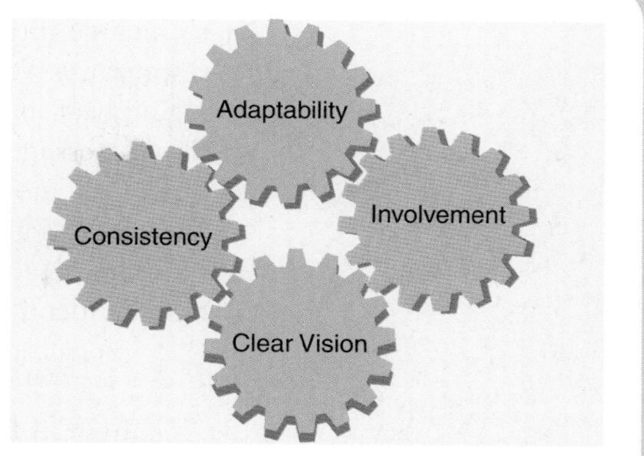

Source: D. R. Denison & A. K. Mishra, "Toward a Theory of Organizational Culture and Effectiveness," *Organization Science* 6 (1995): 204–223.

Exhibit 3.7

Successful Organizational Cultures

Specific vision statements strengthen organizational cultures by letting everyone know why the company is in business, what really matters (that is, the company's values), and how those values can be used to guide daily actions and behaviors.[82] Commenting on the value of Faulding's vision statement, Donna Martin, a former senior vice president of human resources, says, "A vision has to be more than a set of target revenue or profit numbers to meet. It has to be elevating, inspiring, with a strong emphasis on the future. A vision has to be a compelling and crystal-clear statement about where the organization is heading."[83] You will learn more about vision statements in Chapter 5 on planning and decision making.

Finally, in **consistent organizational cultures**, the company actively defines and teaches organizational values, beliefs, and attitudes. **McDonald's** helps preserve its history and culture by having its executives work in its restaurants one day each year, on founder Ray Kroc's birthday. According to Kroc, this is to remind McDonald's executives that "if it's below [their] dignity to mop floors, clean toilets, and roll up [their] sleeves, then [they] are not going to succeed: [Their] attitude is wrong." McDonald's also has an exhibit called "Talk to Ray," in which, thanks to messages videotaped before his death, anyone can "ask" Ray questions about McDonald's values and history.[84]

Consistent organizational cultures are also called *strong cultures* because the core beliefs are widely shared and strongly held. Indeed, everyone who has ever worked at McDonald's has been taught its four core values: quality, service, cleanliness, and value.[85] Studies show that companies with consistent or strong corporate cultures will outperform those with inconsistent or weak cultures most of the time.[86] Why? The reason is that when core beliefs are widely shared and strongly held, it is easy for everyone to figure out what to do or not do to achieve organizational goals.

Having a consistent or strong organizational culture doesn't guarantee good company performance. When core beliefs are widely shared and strongly held, it is very difficult to bring about needed change. Consequently, companies with strong cultures tend to perform poorly when they need to adapt to dramatic changes in their external environments. Their consistency sometimes prevents them from adapting to those changes.[87] Indeed, McDonald's saw its sales and profits decline in the late 1990s as customer eating patterns began changing. To rescue falling performance, the company introduced its "Plan to Win," which focuses on the five elements that drive its business: people, products, place, price, and promotion. McDonald's developed hospitality and multilingual computer-training programs and expanded its menu

consistent organizational culture
a company culture in which the company actively defines and teaches organizational values, beliefs, and attitudes

to include more healthful and snack-oriented selections. Over 5,000 McDonald's restaurants were remodeled in a three-year period and now feature warmer lighting, upbeat music, flat-screen TVs, and Wi-Fi networks. And the company's promotional message "I'm lovin' it" went from being derided by advertising executives to one of the most recognizable jingles in any market. Only a few years into the plan, McDonald's achieved 32 consecutive months of positive sales (its longest streak in 25 years), reached record annual revenues of more than $20 billion, and tripled the cash dividend paid to stockholders.[88]

5.3 Changing Organizational Cultures

As shown in Exhibit 3.8, organizational cultures exist on three levels.[89] First, on the surface level, are the reflections of an organization's culture that can be seen and observed, such as symbolic artifacts (such as dress codes and office layouts), and workers' and managers' behaviors. Next, just below the surface, are the values and beliefs expressed by people in the company. You can't see these values and beliefs, but they become clear if you listen carefully to what people say and to how decisions are made or explained. Finally, unconsciously held assumptions and beliefs about the company are buried deep below the surface. These are the unwritten views and rules that are so strongly held and so widely shared that they are rarely discussed or even thought about unless someone attempts to change them or unknowingly violates them. Changing such assumptions and beliefs can be very difficult. Instead, managers should focus on the parts of the organizational culture they can control; these include observable surface-level items, such as workers' behaviors and symbolic artifacts, and expressed values and beliefs, which can be influenced through employee selection. Let's see how these can be used to change organizational cultures.

behavioral addition the process of having managers and employees perform new behaviors that are central to and symbolic of the new organizational culture that a company wants to create

behavioral substitution the process of having managers and employees perform new behaviors central to the "new" organizational culture in place of behaviors that were central to the "old" organizational culture

One way of changing a corporate culture is to use behavioral addition or behavioral substitution to establish new patterns of behavior among managers and employees. **Behavioral addition** is the process of having managers and employees perform a new behavior, while **behavioral substitution** is having managers and employees perform a new behavior in place of another behavior. The key in both instances is to choose behaviors that are central to and symbolic of the "old" culture you're changing and the "new" culture that you want to create. When Mike Ullman became *JCPenney*'s CEO, he thought the company's culture was stuck in the nineteenth century, when it was started: Employees called each other Mr. and Mrs., casual attire was unacceptable (even on Fridays), and any elaborate decoration of office cubicles was reported to a team of "office police" charged with enforcing corporate décor guidelines. Ullman quickly determined that the company's stringent code of conduct was, among other things, keeping it from recruiting the talent it needed. Mike Theilmann, the human resources officer, drafted a list of what he called "quick hits," small changes that would have a big impact on the culture. The first of

Exhibit 3.8

Three Levels of Organizational Culture

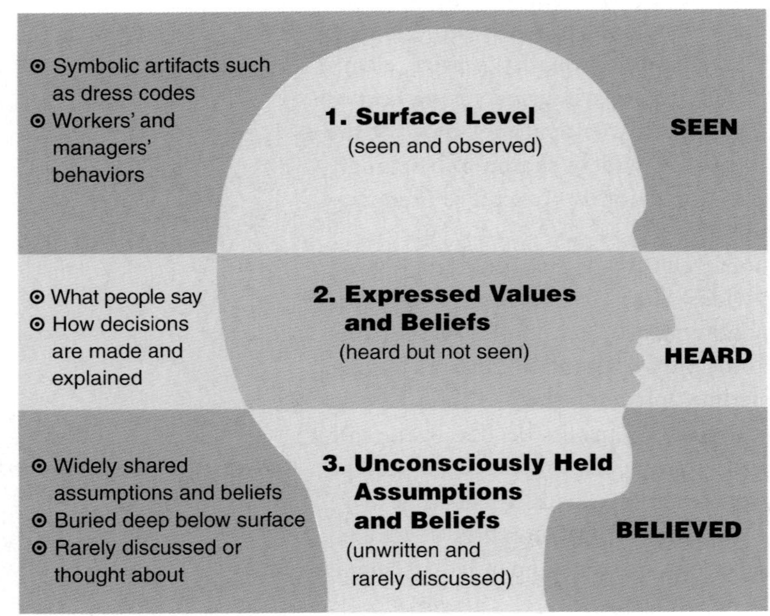

Theilmann's initiatives was a campaign titled "Just Call Me Mike," which he hoped would cure employees of the entrenched practice of calling executives and managers Mr. and Mrs. Three JCPenney officers are named Mike, along with nearly 400 other employees at headquarters. Theilmann created posters containing photos of the three executive Mikes along with a list of all the advantages of being on a first-name basis. Top of the list? "First names create a friendly place to shop and work."[90]

© ASSOCIATED PRESS; (INSET) © PHOTODISC/GETTY IMAGES

Another way in which managers can begin to change corporate culture is to change the **visible artifacts** of their old culture, such as the office design and layout, company dress code, and recipients (or nonrecipients) of company benefits and perks like stock options, personal parking spaces, or the private company dining room. To help anchor the internal culture change at JCPenney, Ullman issued all 150,000 JCPenney employees with new name badges. First names appear in large typeface; last names are printed much smaller. He also disbanded the office police, declared that suitable work attire was business casual, and sold or donated most of the 300 pieces in the company's art collection. (He replaced them with pictures of Penney's employees and other company-oriented art.) Most strikingly, Ullman updated founder James Cash Penney's code of conduct and replaced it with one that allows all employees—not just management—to receive the company's traditional Honor, Confidence, Service, Cooperation award for employee loyalty.[91]

Cultures can also be changed by hiring and selecting people with values and beliefs consistent with the company's desired culture. *Selection* is the process of gathering information about job applicants to decide who should be offered a job. As discussed in Chapter 11 on human resources, most selection instruments measure whether job applicants have the knowledge, skills, and abilities needed to succeed in their jobs. Today, however, companies are increasingly testing job applicants to determine how the fit with the company's desired culture (that is, values and beliefs). Management consultant Ram Charan says, "A poor job match is not only harmful to the individual but also to the company."[92] At **BRISTOL-MYERS SQUIBB**, people who didn't fit the culture tended to leave. According to Ben Dowell, who runs Bristol-Myers Squibb's Center for Leadership Development, "What came through was, those who left were uncomfortable in our culture or violated some core area of our value system."[93] The first step in hiring people who have values consistent with the desired culture is to define and describe that culture. Bristol-Myers Squibb hired an organizational psychologist who spent four months interviewing senior managers. He concluded that the company had a team-driven culture that focused on research and development, which meant that it valued self-motivated, intellectually curious people.

visible artifacts visible signs of an organization's culture, such as the office design and layout, company dress code, and company benefits and perks, like stock options, personal parking spaces, or the private company dining room

The second step is to ensure that applicants fit with the culture by using selection tests, instruments, and exercises to measure these values and beliefs in job applicants. (See Chapter 11 for a complete review of applicant and managerial selection.) At **Southwest Airlines**, humor and a good attitude are two of the most important requirements in its new hires. Chairman and former CEO Herb Kelleher says, "What's important is that a customer should get off the airplane feeling: 'I didn't just get from A to B. I had one of the most pleasant experiences I ever had and I'll be back for that reason.' "[94] For instance, on a flight from Houston to Dallas, a flight attendant addresses passengers over the speaker system, saying, "Could y'all lean in a little toward the center aisle, please?" Met with confused looks from passengers, he continues, "Just a bit, please. That's it. No, the other way, sir. Thanks. You see, the pilot has to pull out of this space here, and he needs to be able to check the rearview mirrors." On another Southwest plane, Yvonne Masters jokingly introduced her fellow flight attendants as her "former husband and his new girlfriend."[95] Southwest passenger Mark Rafferty said his favorite Southwest flight attendant joke was when "they told everyone on the plane's left side, toward the terminal, to put their faces in the window and smile so our competitors can see what a full flight looks like."[96] Corny, yes, but the humor is exactly what Southwest and its customers want, and the airline gets it by hiring people consistent with its hard-working, fun-loving culture. Says Kelleher, "We draft great attitudes. If you don't have a good attitude, we don't want you, no matter how skilled you are. We can change skill level through training. We can't change attitude."[97]

"We draft great attitudes. If you don't have a good attitude, we don't want you, no matter how skilled you are. We can change skill level through training. We can't change attitude."

HERB KELLEHER, CHAIRMAN AND FORMER CEO, SOUTHWEST AIRLINES

Corporate cultures are very difficult to change. Consequently, there is no guarantee that any one approach—changing visible cultural artifacts, using behavioral substitution, or hiring people with values consistent with a company's desired culture—will change a company's organizational culture. The best results are obtained by combining these methods. Together, these are some of the best tools managers have for changing culture because they send the clear message to managers and employees that "the accepted way of doing things" has changed.

Review 5: Organizational Cultures: Creation, Success, and Change

Organizational culture is the set of key values, beliefs, and attitudes shared by organizational members. Organizational cultures are often created by company founders and then sustained through the telling of organizational stories and the celebration of organizational heroes. Adaptable cultures that promote employee involvement, make clear the organization's strategic purpose and direction, and actively define and teach organizational values and beliefs can help companies achieve higher sales growth, return on assets, profits, quality,

and employee satisfaction. Organizational cultures exist on three levels: the surface level, where cultural artifacts and behaviors can be observed; just below the surface, where values and beliefs are expressed; and deep below the surface, where unconsciously held assumptions and beliefs exist. Managers can begin to change company cultures by focusing on the top two levels and by using behavioral substitution and behavioral addition, changing visible artifacts, and selecting job applicants with values and beliefs consistent with the desired company culture.

SELF ASSESSMENT

Check Your Tolerance for Ambiguity

Think of the difference between playing chess (where you can see all the pieces and anticipate attacks and plan counterattacks) and playing poker (where no one knows anyone else's hand, and you have to make guesses based on your interpretation of opponents' betting patterns). In chess, there is little ambiguity, whereas in poker there is tremendous ambiguity. Although many people liken business to a game of chess, probably because of the strategic aspects of the game, business is actually more like poker. The business environment is complex and uncertain, and managers never *really* know all the cards the opposition is holding. Managers must learn to adapt to environmental shifts and new developments—sometimes on a daily basis. For some managers, however, this can be a challenging task because everyone has a different comfort level when it comes to ambiguity. For some, not knowing all the details can be a source of significant stress, whereas for others uncertainty can be energizing.

As a manager, you will need to develop an appropriate tolerance for ambiguity. For example, being stressed out every time interest rates change can be counterproductive, but completely ignoring the economic environment can be detrimental to your company's performance.

Complete the following questionnaire to get a sense of your tolerance for ambiguity.[98] Indicate the extent to which you agree with the statements using the following scale:

1 Strongly disagree
2 Moderately disagree
3 Slightly disagree
4 Neutral
5 Slightly agree
6 Moderately agree
7 Strongly agree

1. I don't tolerate ambiguous situations well.
   1 2 3 4 5 6 7
2. I find it difficult to respond when faced with an unexpected event.
   1 2 3 4 5 6 7
3. I don't think new situations are any more threatening than familiar situations.
   1 2 3 4 5 6 7
4. I am drawn to situations which can be interpreted in more than one way.
   1 2 3 4 5 6 7
5. I would rather avoid solving problems that must be viewed from several different perspectives.
   1 2 3 4 5 6 7
6. I try to avoid situations which are ambiguous.
   1 2 3 4 5 6 7
7. I am good at managing unpredictable situations.
   1 2 3 4 5 6 7
8. I prefer familiar situations to new ones.
   1 2 3 4 5 6 7
9. Problems which cannot be considered from just one point of view are a little threatening.
   1 2 3 4 5 6 7
10. I avoid situations which are too complicated for me to easily understand.
    1 2 3 4 5 6 7
11. I am tolerant of ambiguous situations.
    1 2 3 4 5 6 7
12. I enjoy tackling problems which are complex enough to be ambiguous.
    1 2 3 4 5 6 7

KEY TERMS

13. I try to avoid problems which don't seem to have only one "best" solution.
    1 2 3 4 5 6 7
14. I often find myself looking for something new, rather than trying to hold things constant in my life.
    1 2 3 4 5 6 7
15. I generally prefer novelty over familiarity.
    1 2 3 4 5 6 7
16. I dislike ambiguous situations.
    1 2 3 4 5 6 7
17. Some problems are so complex that just trying to understand them is fun.
    1 2 3 4 5 6 7
18. I have little trouble coping with unexpected events.
    1 2 3 4 5 6 7
19. I pursue problem situations which are so complex some people call them "mind-boggling."
    1 2 3 4 5 6 7
20. I find it hard to make a choice when the outcome is uncertain.
    1 2 3 4 5 6 7
21. I enjoy an occasional surprise.
    1 2 3 4 5 6 7
22. I prefer a situation in which there is some ambiguity.
    1 2 3 4 5 6 7

Scoring

Determine your score by entering your response to each survey item below, as follows. In blanks that say *regular score,* simply enter your response for that item. If your response was a 6, place a 6 in the *regular score* blank. In blanks that say *reverse score,* subtract your response from 8 and enter the result. So if your response was a 6, place a 2 (8 – 6 = 2) in the *reverse score* blank. Add up your total score.

1. regular score ____
2. regular score ____
3. reverse score ____
4. reverse score ____
5. regular score ____
6. regular score ____
7. reverse score ____
8. regular score ____
9. regular score ____
10. regular score ____
11. regular score ____
12. reverse score ____
13. regular score ____
14. reverse score ____
15. reverse score ____
16. regular score ____
17. reverse score ____
18. reverse score ____
19. reverse score ____
20. regular score ____
21. reverse score ____
22. reverse score ____

TOTAL = ____

You can find the interpretation for your score on at: **academic.cengage.com/management/williams.**

Environmental Roller Coaster

It couldn't be a better day to be at Cedar Point amusement park. It's mid-September, sunny, and 75 degrees, and there's no one waiting in any of the lines. Passing by the Millennium Force roller coaster, you stop to get a slushee and then sit down at a nearby picnic table to start thinking about the annual environmental scan.

Since joining the management team of Cedar Point, a large regional amusement park located in Sandusky, Ohio, you've done this exercise 10 times. Each time, it is more difficult because the environment keeps changing, but doing the environmental assessment has kept Cedar Point viable. You think to yourself "We've just finished a tight season, but we managed to come out ahead. We are facing some big shifts, though both in the general business environment and in the amusement industry, so we need to build a plan to meet those environmental challenges."

Pausing for a moment, you stare at the coaster's 80-degree drop. Your mind dives just as steeply into a flurry of issues: shifts toward year-round schooling; trends in the insurance industry; new forms of entertainment; new competition; the effect of changing demographics on your attendance and your work force; higher gasoline prices; and the impact of the economy in general. You've been able to increase the price of admission year after year, but how long can you continue to do that? Your straw makes a loud noise as you finish your slushee. "I guess that means it's time to head back to the office and figure out what trends are going to affect the park and how."

Questions

1. Consider the issues that you as the Cedar Point manager are examining as part of this exercise. What other issues should you examine?
2. Create a list of issues addressing each of the environmental factors discussed in the chapter (economy, technology, political/legal, sociocultural, customer, competitor, supplier, industry regulation). For each item on your list, explain how Cedar Point will face the challenges posed by that factor in its environment.
3. Based on the solutions you generated in question 2, how uncertain is the amusement park industry? Why do you think as you do? (Think about the environmental change, complexity, and resources of the amusement park industry. You may wish to use Exhibit 3.2 as a guide.)

MANAGEMENT TEAM DECISION

Dog Day Blues

One of the reasons you accepted a management position at MicroTek several years ago was the company's laid-back culture.[99] A loose organizational structure enables employees to move freely between projects, and the open office space encourages informal encounters and generates a feeling of teamwork. And among the very generous corporate perks is a policy allowing employees to bring their pets to work. It is not uncommon to see a small animal sitting in an employee's in-box drinking from a hamster lick. Several employees bring their dogs, large and small, to the office.

As the company has grown, thanks in part to its informal culture, more and more people are taking advantage of the pet policy, and problems are arising. Food is swiped from desks, animals are rooting through trash bins, and dogs are marking territory on the partitions that surround their owners' desks. Visiting customers often try to mask startled (at best) or disapproving (at worst) looks when they tour your facility for the first time—and even the second and third times. During a recent breakfast meeting, when a board member refused to share her bagel with the CFO's dog, the dog relieved itself on her briefcase. At least one employee has complained of allergic reactions due to the high levels of pet dander in the office air, but rather than change the policy, you installed a high-power air cleaner.

Despite the challenges, you have resisted changing the pet policy because it symbolizes both the company's relaxed culture and MicroTek's commitment to its employees' work-life balance. This afternoon, however, you were notified by the federal Occupational Safety and Health Administration (OSHA) that your office does not meet the required indoor air quality standards. Apparently, the cleaner you installed can't handle all the pet dander. To meet the standards, you'll need an even more powerful air cleaner that costs between \$100,000 and \$200,000. That would be a significant investment in the pet policy! And who knows if it would solve the allergy problem. Is the policy worth the cost?

In 2003, only 5,000 offices participated in "Bring Your Pet to Work Day," but the number doubled the very next year. Companies bigger than MicroTek have figured out how to make pet policies work: IAMS Pet Food; Replacements Ltd., the world's largest supplier of old and new china; and Netscape, to name a few. A quarter of Burton Snowboards' 230 employees bring their dogs to work every day! Anecdotal evidence from those companies indicates that pets can spur creativity and lower occupational stress. You ask yourself, "How committed am I to the pet policy?" Is the pet policy just trendy (or avant-garde), or does it say something deeper about your company?

For this Management Team Decision, assemble three or four students to act as the management team for MicroTek. Include both pet owners and people without pets to avoid any bias. Before you begin the exercise, have each team member privately write down answers to each of the following questions. By sharing your individual responses, you may be able to have a more varied and rounded discussion.

Questions

1. Do you buy the expensive air cleaner, or eliminate the pet policy? Why?

2. If you choose to stop allowing animals at the office, what effect, if any, do you think the change will have on the company's culture?

3. Can you think of a way to allow people to bring pets to work without upgrading the air cleaner or running afoul of OSHA?

PRACTICE BEING A MANAGER

Navigating Different Organizational Cultures

Effective managers recognize that organizational culture is an important, often critical element of organizational health and performance. But recognizing and understanding culture, especially its less visible aspects, is often quite challenging. This exercise will give you some practice in recognizing cultural differences and the challenges and opportunities that managers face as they work with diverse cultures.

Suppose that major music recording company SonyBMG has announced plans to hire several college students to form a team that will invest in the "next big things in music." The selected students will be paid $50,000 per year for working part-time. SonyBMG will also allocate up to $10 million for hiring artists, producing records, and so on based on the team's recommendations.

The new team has been dubbed the Top Wave Team (TWT). If TWT's recommendations are fruitful, the company will sign each member of the team to $150,000 full-time contracts. The company also plans to keep the team together, and to give members bonuses and promotions based on their group performance.

Your class has been chosen as the representative college class. The music company is now asking you to form affinity groups by musical preferences in your class (for example, a Country Music group, an Urban/Hip-Hop group). Each group will nominate one of its members to receive the first $50,000 internship as a TWT team member at SonyBMG. The new TWT group will meet and discuss initial plans and investment recommendations, and then your class will discuss the process and outcomes.

Step 1: Choose your musical affinity. In the class session before this exercise, your professor will ask you to submit a survey form or sheet of paper with your name and your preferred musical genre/identity.

Identify yourself with one of the following musical genres based on (a) preference/affinity ("I prefer this music") and (b) knowledge/understanding ("Of all types of music, I know the most about ____ music/musicians"):

1. Rock
2. Country
3. Religious/Spiritual
4. Urban/Hip-Hop
5. Rap
6. Jazz/R&B
7. Pop/Mainstream
8. Classical
9. Folk/Bluegrass

Your professor will review your submitted preferences, and organize affinity groups for the next class session.

Step 2: Organize into groups. Your professor will organize you by musical affinity. If your class is heavily concentrated in one or a few of the musical genres, you may be asked to further divide into smaller groups by sub-categories (such as Rock—Heavy Metal and Rock—Popular/Hit).

Step 3: Prepare your recommendations. In groups, discuss what is important about your type of music, and what investments should be made by the TWT team. Keep in mind that the investments made by the TWT team could have a big impact on the future of your favorite music. Recommend a dollar amount or percentage of the $10 million that your representative ought to secure for investment in your genre.

Each group should then select one of its members to receive the internship from SonyBMG and represent the group on the TWT team.

Step 4: Discuss recommendations before the class. Nominees from the musical affinity groups should discuss their recommendations before the class. Those not on the TWT should observe the process and take notes on what happens in this meeting.

Step 5: Hold the team meeting. Your professor will allocate a short time for the initial meeting of the TWT. It may occur before or during the class meeting. After the TWT reaches agreement on how it might allocate its investments by genre (or by some alternative approach), reaches impasse, or reaches the time limit, your professor will call an end to the TWT meeting.

Step 6: Debrief and discuss. As a class, discuss the process and outcomes of this exercise. Consider the following questions and/or others posed by your professor.

- Did you sense some cultural affinity with others who shared your musical tastes? Why or why not?
- What expectations might be associated with choosing someone to "represent" a group on a team such as the TWT?
- What tensions and challenges might face each member of the TWT in a real-life setting of serving on a group that represents various cultures?

Dealing with the Press

In this age of 24-hour cable news channels, tabloid news shows, and aggressive local and national news reporters intent on exposing corporate wrongdoing, one of the most important skills for a manager to learn is how to deal effectively with the press.[100] Test your ability to deal effectively with the press by putting yourself in the following situations. To make the situation more realistic, read the scenario and then give yourself two minutes to write a response to each question.

Rats Take Over Manhattan Taco Bell

The release of Internet footage showed large rats running across the floors, over tables, and climbing onto countertops of a Manhattan Taco Bell. What is most surprising is that the day before the television crew filmed the rats through the restaurant window, New York City health inspectors had given the restaurant a passing grade! The broadcast prompted parent company Yum! Brands to temporarily close that and several other Taco Bell stores owned by franchisee ADF Companies. Based in New Jersey, ADF owns over 350 fast-food franchises in several states.

A TV reporter from Channel 5 has arrived with his camera crew at the Taco Bell you manage in Brooklyn. It's lunchtime, the restaurant is bustling, and the reporter walks right in with his crew and puts you on the spot, asking you if you would grant a short interview and let him ask questions of a few of your patrons. When you agree, he starts right in with these questions:

1. "Yesterday's filming of rats at an ADF-owned Taco Bell has caused consumers to question the cleanliness of the restaurants where they eat. This restaurant is also owned by ADF Companies. Do you also have problems with rodents?"
2. "Recent outbreaks of E. coli at other Taco Bells in the Northeast were finally attributed to contaminated lettuce, so Taco Bell changed suppliers." To the cameraman: "Get the camera in close here [camera zooms into the kitchen area, the slop sink, and the handwashing station] because I want our viewers to see the kitchen." Back to you: "How can consumers be sure that contamination occurred at the produce supplier and not inside filthy restaurants?"
3. "The health inspectors gave a passing grade to the rat-infested Taco Bell just a day before television crews filmed the rats running all over the restaurant. That doesn't instill our viewers with great confidence in the system. Would you be willing to let our camera crews accompany the health inspector during a full inspection of your restaurant so that viewers can see what an inspection entails?"

REEL TO REAL

BIZ FLIX
Brazil

Set somewhere in the twentieth century, the retro-futuristic world of *Brazil* is a gritty, urban cesspool patched over with cosmetic surgery and "designer ducts for your discriminating taste." Automation pervades every facet of life from toaster and coffee machine to doorways, but paperwork, inefficiency, and mechanical failures are the rule. *Brazil* stars Jonathan Pryce in the role of Sam, a low-level bureaucrat whose primary interests in life are his vivid dream fantasies to the tune of "Brazil," a 1940s big-band hit. In this scene, Sam is starting a new job and is being assigned an office and employee identification number.

What to Watch for and Ask Yourself

1. Describe the culture at Sam's new employer.
2. How easy would it be to change the culture at Sam's new company?
3. In which kind of business environment do you think the culture at Sam's employer is able to operate most successfully?

MANAGEMENT WORKPLACE
Lonely Planet's Travel Culture

When you think of corporate culture, the image of suits and ties, pantyhose and pumps often springs to mind. But at Lonely Planet, the values, beliefs, understandings, and norms of the firm are expressed by staff members and managers who wear T-shirts, khakis, soft skirts, and sandals or clogs to work. Lonely Planet is a publishing company based in Australia with offices in several other countries—including the United States—that produces travel books, guides, and language phrasebooks for people who want adventure.

Lonely Planet fosters an internal culture in which employees are free to be themselves—to exchange ideas and try new approaches to problems. Take a peek inside the management workplace of Lonely Planet.

What to Watch for and Ask Yourself

1. Create a list describing how each component of the general and specific external environment affects Lonely Planet. For example, under technology, you could write that the rise of the Internet has caused more people to research travel opportunities online rather than with guidebooks.
2. Which factors in the external environment could create uncertainty for Lonely Planet?
3. Give an example of Lonely Planet's corporate culture at each of the three levels identified in Exhibit 3.4.

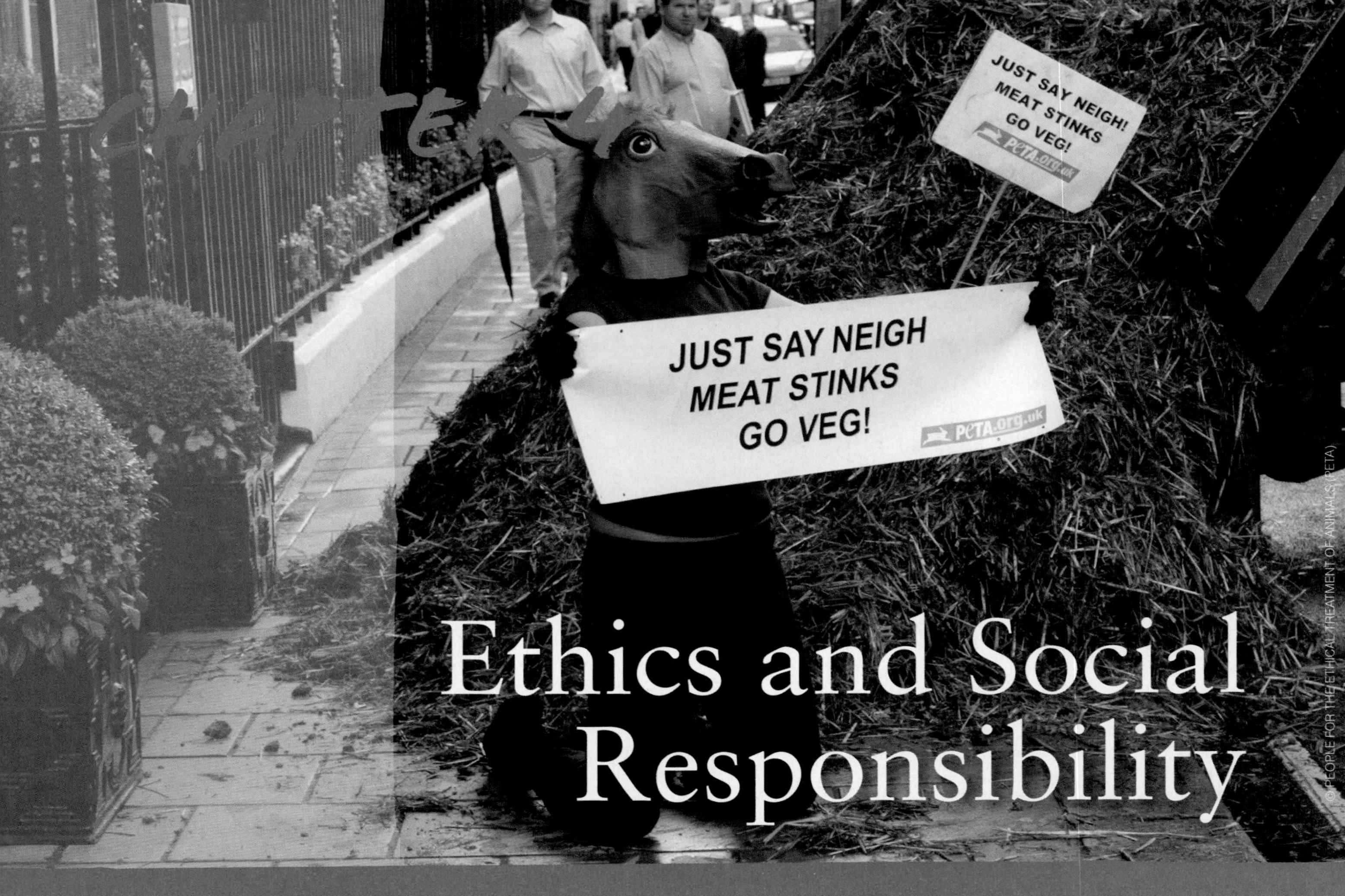

Ethics and Social Responsibility

Learning Outcomes:

1 Discuss how the nature of management jobs creates the possibility for ethical abuses.

2 Identify common kinds of workplace deviance.

3 Describe the U.S. Sentencing Commission Guidelines for Organizations and explain how they both encourage ethical behavior and punish unethical behavior by businesses.

4 Describe what influences ethical decision making.

5 Explain what practical steps managers can take to improve ethical decision making.

6 Explain to whom organizations are socially responsible.

7 Explain for what organizations are socially responsible.

8 Explain how organizations can choose to respond to societal demands for social responsibility.

9 Explain whether social responsibility hurts or helps an organization's economic performance.

In This Chapter:

WHAT WOULD YOU DO?

Procter & Gamble Headquarters, Cincinnati, Ohio.[1] "What's that?" you wonder as you look out your window. A small group of people are gathered on the sidewalk at the end of the wisteria gardens in front of the main headquarters of Procter & Gamble. If you squint, you can see they're holding signs, but the only text you can make out is the word "PETA" in big letters across the bottom. "Just great," you think to yourself.

People for the Ethical Treatment of Animals, the animal-rights group more commonly known as PETA, raises more than $25 million a year from its 1.6 million members and supporters. PETA not only campaigns for animal rights, but also funds lesser known animal-rights groups to engage in activism. PETA is extremely adept at organizing public campaigns and mobilizing the public to boycott companies. Its public-relations tactics include celebrity endorsements, traveling displays of animal abuse, and creative on-site demonstrations. Even large international companies like McDonald's, Burger King, and KFC have bowed to PETA's pressure, issuing strict guidelines for the humane treatment of animals, and then enforcing those standards with unannounced inspections of beef, pork, and chicken suppliers' production farms and processing plants.

PETA has been known to use aggressive tactics. In one instance, a viral ad featuring scantily clad women with cow udders instead of breasts was distributed in the UK as part of a campaign against milk drinking and production. PETA had hoped to air a television version of the ad on the ABC network in the United States during the Super Bowl, but was told that it "falls outside boundaries of good taste." Mimicking television shows like *Girls Gone Wild*, in which women are encouraged to disrobe for cameras, PETA's "Milk Gone Wild" ad shows models dancing in a bar, surrounded by men drinking glasses of milk. When the women tear off their tops, they expose cow udders. In another instance, PETA successfully launched a six-year campaign of intimidation against a farm that bred guinea pigs for scientific research. Their tactics, denounced as mob rule by some in the medical research community, included hate mail, malicious phone calls, death threats, fireworks, a pedophile smear campaign, car vandalism, arson attacks, and finally the theft of the remains of a relative of the farm owner from the churchyard cemetery.

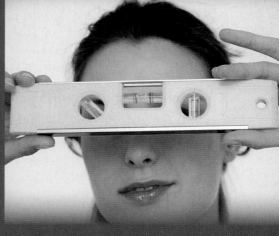

Procter & Gamble (P&G) does not use animals to test the safety of its cosmetics, shampoos, detergents, cleansers, and paper goods; it does, however, use animals to test the safety of new drugs, health-care products, and products intended for use on babies and children. Nonetheless, P&G still draws protests from PETA in the form of PETA's "Died" advertising campaign, based on P&G's best-selling laundry detergent Tide. The "Died" ad shows a woman holding a box of "Died" detergent with the words "Thousands of Animals Died for Your Laundry" boldly written on the box. PETA is urging consumers to boycott all P&G products until the company ends all forms of animal testing.

From P&G's perspective, testing is critical to producing safe products for its customers. P&G has to know, for example, that a product will not cause injury if children accidentally swallow it or get it into their eyes. Furthermore, in the event that a product liability lawsuit is filed against the company, its best legal defense would be the scientific testing it performs on rats and rabbits.

As the CEO of P&G should you, as PETA demands, eliminate all animal testing? Or, by minimizing but not eliminating animal testing, has P&G achieved a reasonable balance that still allows it to make sure its products are safe? The last thing you need are product liability lawsuits accusing P&G of selling unsafe products. On the other hand, PETA's protests have pressured other companies to change, but how do you appease PETA while not compromising customer safety? There's also the risk that if PETA launches new campaigns and boycotts, it could turn some customers against the company, which in turn could hurt revenue, and declining revenues could affect stockholders, and might even lead to downsizing affecting employees. PETA's aggressive tactics and history of misrepresentation of facts are cause for concern. With so many tradeoffs to consider, what is the most socially responsible thing to do? **If you were the CEO of Procter & Gamble, what would you do?**

ACTIVITIES + VIDEOS

CengageNOW Audio study guide, electronic flashcards, author FAQ videos, On the Job and Biz Flix videos, concept tutorial, and concept exercise

Web (academic.cengage.com/management/williams) Quiz, PowerPoint slides, and glossary terms for this chapter

Study Tip

Every chapter in this book contains diagrams and tables to illustrate the text material. One good way to study is to try to recreate the exhibit from scratch on your own. Draw a blank diagram, fill it in, then check your work by comparing your worksheet with the original exhibit in the chapter.

"What's New" Companies

Procter & Gamble
PETA
Chicago Sun-Times
DaimlerChrysler
Omega Engineering
Gillette
Caremark International
IBM
Nortel
And others . . .

The dilemma facing P&G's CEO is an example of the tough decisions involving ethics and social responsibility that managers face. Unfortunately, one of the "real-world" aspects of these decisions is that no matter what you decide, someone or some group will be unhappy with the outcome. Managers don't have the luxury of choosing theoretically optimal, win-win solutions that are obviously desirable to everyone involved. In practice, solutions to ethics and social responsibility problems aren't optimal. Often, managers must be satisfied with a solution that just "makes do" or "does the least harm." Crystal-clear rights and wrongs rarely reveal themselves to managers charged with "doing the right thing." The business world is much messier than that.

We begin this chapter by examining ethical behavior in the workplace and explaining how unethical behavior can expose a business to penalties under the U.S. Sentencing Commission Guidelines for Organizations. Second, we examine the influences on ethical decision making and review practical steps that managers can take to improve ethical decision making. We finish by considering to whom organizations are socially responsible, what organizations are socially responsible for, how they can respond to societal expectations for social responsibility, and whether social responsibility hurts or helps an organization's economic performance.

WHAT IS ETHICAL AND UNETHICAL WORKPLACE BEHAVIOR?

Ethics is the set of moral principles or values that defines right and wrong for a person or group. Unfortunately, numerous studies have consistently produced distressing results about the state of ethics in today's business world. According to an SHRM/CareerJournal.com survey, only 27 percent of employees felt that their organization's leadership was ethical.[2] In another study of 1,324 randomly selected workers, managers, and executives across multiple industries, 48 percent of the respondents admitted to actually committing an unethical or illegal act in the past year! These acts included cheating on an expense account, discriminating against coworkers, forging signatures, paying or accepting kickbacks, and "looking the other way" when environmental laws were broken.[3] Clearly, in an era with widely publicized corporate scandals at WorldCom, Tyco, and HealthSouth (where executives allegedly committed fraud by overstating company results by billions of dollars and used company funds for their personal gain), poor business ethics is a serious and widespread problem.[4]

The studies also contained good news, however. When people believe their work environment is ethical, they are six times more likely to stay with that company than if they believe they work in an unethical environment.[5] Furthermore, when 570 white-collar workers were asked which of 28 qualities were important in company leaders, honesty (24 percent) and integrity/morals/ethics (16 percent) ranked by far the highest (caring/compassion was third at 7 percent).[6] According to Dwight Reighard, the chief people officer at HomeBanc Mortgage Corp. in Atlanta, "people want to work for

ethics the set of moral principles or values that defines right and wrong for a person or group leaders they trust."[7] In short, much needs to be done to make workplaces more ethical, but—and this is very important—most managers and employees want this to happen.

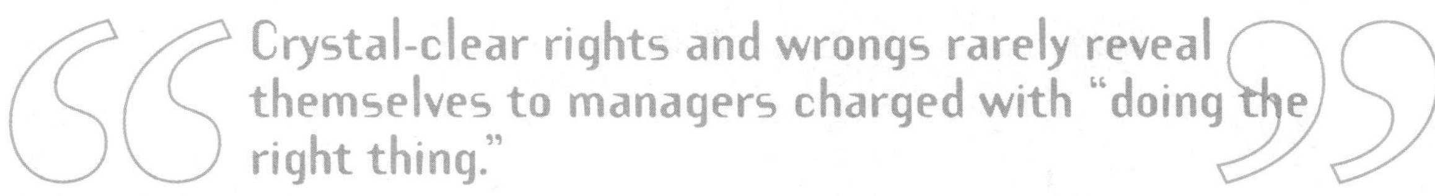
Crystal-clear rights and wrongs rarely reveal themselves to managers charged with "doing the right thing."

After reading the next three sections, you should be able to

1. *discuss how the nature of management jobs creates the possibility for ethical abuses.*
2. *identify common kinds of workplace deviance.*
3. *describe the U.S. Sentencing Commission Guidelines for Organizations and explain how they both encourage ethical behavior and punish unethical behavior by businesses.*

1 Ethics and the Nature of Management Jobs

Ethical behavior follows accepted principles of right and wrong. By contrast, unethical management behavior, such as lying about company profits or knowingly producing an unsafe product, occurs when managers personally violate accepted principles of right and wrong or encourage others to do so. Because of the nature of their jobs, managers can be tempted to engage in unethical managerial behavior in four areas: authority and power, handling information, influencing the behavior of others, and setting goals.

The *authority and power* inherent in some management positions can tempt managers to engage in unethical practices. Because managers often control company resources, there is a risk that some managers will cross the line from legitimate use of company resources to personal use. For example, treating a client to dinner is a common and legitimate business practice in many companies. But what about treating a client to a ski trip? Taking the company jet to attend a business meeting in San Diego is legitimate. But how about using the jet to come home to Chicago by way of Honolulu? Human resources can be misused as well. For example, unless it's in an employee's job description, using an employee to do personal chores, like picking up the manager's dry cleaning, is unethical behavior. Even worse, though, is using one's managerial authority and power for direct personal gain, as some managers have done by using corporate funds to pay for extravagant personal parties, lavish home decorating, jewelry, or expensive works of art.

Handling information is another area in which managers must be careful to behave ethically. Information is a key part of management work. Managers collect it, analyze it, act on it, and disseminate it. In doing so, they are expected to be truthful and, when necessary, to keep confidential information confidential. Leaking company secrets to competitors, "doctoring" the numbers, wrongfully withholding information, and lying are some of the ways managers may misuse information entrusted to them. After thousands of customers canceled subscriptions because their papers weren't delivered on time (thanks to chronic problems at a new printing facility) and a "horrendous drop" in advertising dollars severely lowered revenues,

ethical behavior behavior that conforms to a society's accepted principles of right and wrong

© AP PHOTO/NAM Y. HUH

When faced with plummeting subscription numbers, managers at the* Chicago Sun-Times *opted to continue selling advertising based on old, higher subscription numbers.

managers at the **Chicago Sun-Times** began inflating its daily sales numbers so that the newspaper could charge more for advertising and offset the declining revenues. By fraudulently padding the numbers by 50,000 papers per day, the *Sun-Times* tricked advertisers into paying much higher advertising rates. John Cruickshank, who became the paper's new publisher after the scandal was discovered, admitted, "Our appetite for fake numbers became greater and greater."[8]

Managers must also be careful to behave ethically in the way they *influence the behavior of others*, especially those they supervise. Managerial work gives managers significant power to influence others. If managers tell employees to perform unethical acts (or face punishment), such as "faking the numbers to get results," they are abusing their managerial power. This is sometimes called the "move it or lose it" syndrome. "Move it or lose it" managers tell employees, "Do it. You're paid to do it. If you can't do it, we'll find somebody who can."[9] A study of 400 managers found that the "move it or lose it" syndrome even affects top managers. Forty-seven percent of the corporate executives in this study said they would be willing to commit financial fraud by understating accounting write-offs that reduced company profits. Tulane University business professor Art Brief, who conducted the study, says, "People in subordinate roles will comply with their superiors even when that includes wrongdoing that goes against their individual moral code. I thought they would stick with their values, but most organizations are structured to produce obedience."[10]

Setting goals is another way that managers influence the behavior of their employees. If managers set unrealistic goals, the pressure to perform and achieve those goals can influence employees to engage in unethical business behaviors, especially if they are just short of meeting their goals or a deadline.[11] **DaimlerChrysler** dismissed several employees after an internal bribery probe found that key officials made "improper payments" in Africa, Asia, and Eastern Europe to meet revenue targets. The U.S. Justice Department conducted a criminal investigation into the bribery allegations and whether senior executives were aware of the practice. In response, the company established a "corporate compliance department" to make sure that business practices are in compliance with anticorruption laws and the company's ethics standards. It has also set up a "sales-practices hotline" that employees can call to report "questionable activities."[12]

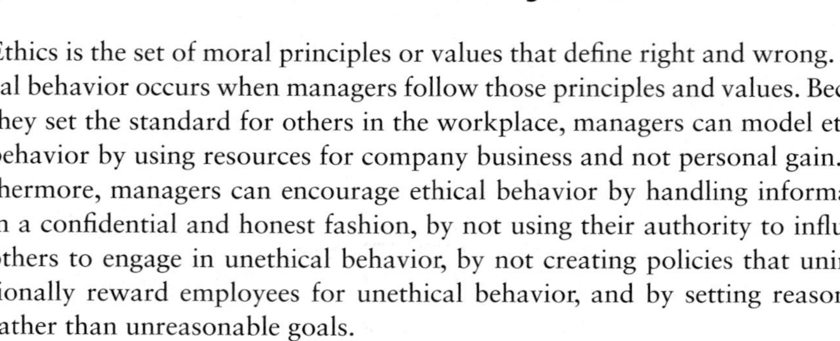

Review 1: Ethics and the Nature of Management Jobs

Ethics is the set of moral principles or values that define right and wrong. Ethical behavior occurs when managers follow those principles and values. Because they set the standard for others in the workplace, managers can model ethical behavior by using resources for company business and not personal gain. Furthermore, managers can encourage ethical behavior by handling information in a confidential and honest fashion, by not using their authority to influence others to engage in unethical behavior, by not creating policies that unintentionally reward employees for unethical behavior, and by setting reasonable rather than unreasonable goals.

2 Workplace Deviance

Depending on which study you look at, one-third to three-quarters of all employees admit that they have stolen from their employers, committed computer fraud, embezzled funds, vandalized company property, sabotaged company projects, faked injuries to receive workers' compensation benefits or insurance, or been "sick" from work when they weren't really sick. Experts estimate that unethical behaviors like these, which researchers call "workplace deviance" may cost companies as much as $660 billion a year, or roughly 6 percent of their revenues.[13]

More specifically, **workplace deviance** is unethical behavior that violates organizational norms about right and wrong. As Exhibit 4.1 shows, workplace deviance can be categorized by how deviant the behavior is, from minor to serious, and by the target of the deviant behavior, either the organization or particular people in the workplace.[14] One kind of workplace deviance, called **production deviance**, hurts the quality and quantity of work produced. Examples include leaving early, taking excessively long work breaks, intentionally working slower, or wasting resources.

Property deviance is unethical behavior aimed at company property or products. Examples include sabotaging, stealing, or damaging equipment or products, and overcharging for services and then pocketing the difference. For example, property deviance in the form of stealing was so bad at the telecommunications company where Bill Weiss worked that employees referred to the supply room as the "gift shop" where everything was available at "five-finger discount prices." Perforated boards, which were used to make prototypes for electronic devices, were taken by employees to finish the walls in their basements. Leather work gloves disappeared

workplace deviance unethical behavior that violates organizational norms about right and wrong

production deviance unethical behavior that hurts the quality and quantity of work produced

property deviance unethical behavior aimed at the organization's property or products

Exhibit 4.1

Types of Workplace Deviance

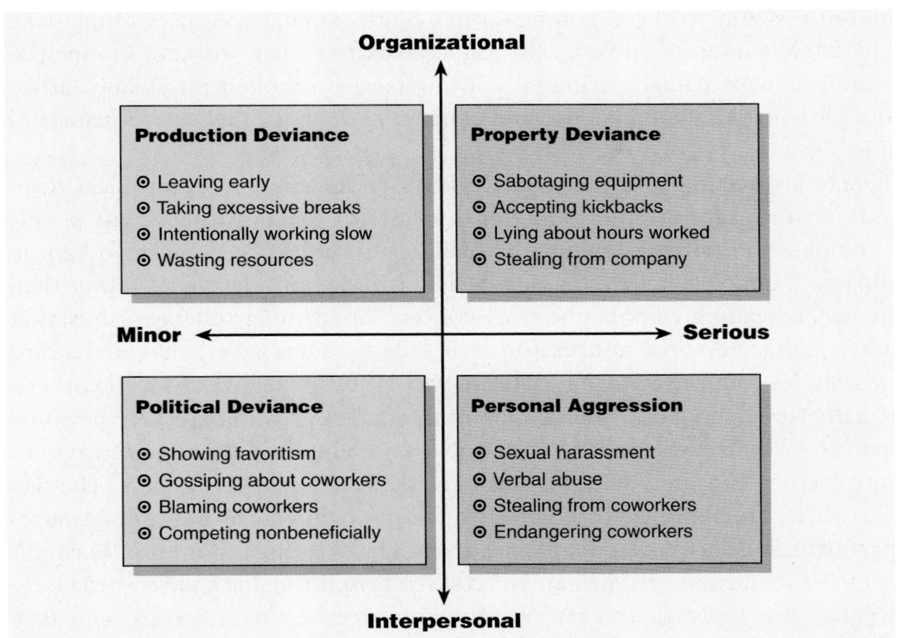

Source: Republished with permission of Academy of Management, P.O. Box 3020, Briar Cliff Manor, NY, 10510–8020. "A Typology of Deviant Workplace Behaviors," (Figure), S. L. Robinson & R. J. Bennett. *Academy of Management Journal*, 1995, Vol. 38. Reproduced by permission of the publisher via Copyright Clearance Center, Inc.

"What's New" Company

"What's New" Company

only to end up being used in employees' gardens. Says Weiss, "Every April, 4,000 pairs of these things used to disappear."[15] Fifty-eight percent of office workers acknowledge taking company property for personal use, according to a survey conducted for Lawyers.com.[16] Sometimes, property deviance involves the sabotage of company property. At **Omega Engineering**, an employee planted a software bomb in the centralized file server containing the company's key programs and data. The code destroyed the programs and data that ran the machines in Omega's manufacturing plant. The company lost $10 million as a result, including $2 million in reprogramming costs. Eighty employees had to be laid off because of lost business resulting from the incident.[17]

The theft of company merchandise by employees, called **employee shrinkage**, is another common form of property deviance. Employee shrinkage, which costs U.S. retailers more than $15.8 billion a year and typically reduces store profits by 2 to 3 percent, takes many forms.[18] "Sweethearting" occurs when employees discount or don't ring up merchandise their family or friends bring to the cash register. In "dumpster diving," employees unload trucks, stash merchandise in a dumpster, and then retrieve it after work.[19] To help grocery stores reduce employee shrinkage, which costs the typical store approximately $350,000 per year, companies such as Procter & Gamble and **Gillette**, its subsidiary, are inserting radio frequency antitheft tags (see Chapter 17 for further information), some as small as the head of a pin, in low-cost household products like Bounty paper towels and Gillette blades and razors. The antitheft tags have built-in antennas that transmit unique identification numbers that enable a store to track a product and determine whether it "disappears" off the loading truck, falls off the shelf, is properly purchased, or is stolen by employees when they leave for the day.[20]

Workers compensation fraud is another example of property deviance aimed at defrauding and hurting the company. According to the National Insurance Crime Bureau (NICB), about 10 percent of insurance claims are fraudulent, resulting in $5 billion in sham workers' compensation claims annually. Abuses range from people who fake an injury while on the job in order to collect workers' compensation insurance to "organized criminal conspiracies of crooked physicians, attorneys, and patients who submit false and exaggerated medical claims to insurance companies."[21]

Whereas production and property deviance harm companies, political deviance and personal aggression are unethical behaviors that hurt particular people within companies. **Political deviance** is using one's influence to harm others in the company. Examples include making decisions based on favoritism rather than performance, spreading rumors about coworkers, or blaming others for mistakes they didn't make. **Personal aggression** is hostile or aggressive behavior toward others. Examples include sexual harassment, verbal abuse, stealing from coworkers, or personally threatening coworkers. One of the fastest-growing kinds of personal aggression is workplace violence. A former Navistar employee forced his way into a Chicago factory and fired 30 shots from an AK-47, killing four people. The day after Christmas, an employee of Edgewater Technology walked into the accounting department and shot seven people dead. In the worst mass murder in Hawaii's history, a frustrated copier repairman killed seven people outside a parts warehouse in Honolulu.[22] The violence isn't reserved for employees. A client entered a law firm on the 38th floor of a downtown Chicago office building and shot three people dead before he was killed by a SWAT officer.[23]

More than 2 million Americans are victims of some form of workplace violence each year. In a survey of 7.4 million U.S. companies, employing more than

employee shrinkage employee theft of company merchandise

political deviance using one's influence to harm others in the company

personal aggression hostile or aggressive behavior toward others

128 million workers, the U.S. Bureau of Labor Statistics (BLS) found that 5.4 percent of all employees suffered an incident of workplace violence each year.[24] Between 650 and 1,000 people are actually killed at work each year.[25] Though many victims, as might be expected, are police officers, security guards, or taxi drivers, store owners and company managers are killed most often.[26] For more information on workplace violence, see the BLS website, **http://www.bls.gov/iif/osh_wpvs.html.**

Review 2: Workplace Deviance

Workplace deviance is behavior that violates important organizational norms about right and wrong and harms the organization or its workers. Production deviance and property deviance harm the company, whereas political deviance and personal aggression harm individuals within the company.

3 U.S. Sentencing Commission Guidelines for Organizations

A male supervisor is sexually harassing female coworkers. A sales representative offers a $10,000 kickback to persuade an indecisive customer to do business with his company. A company president secretly meets with the CEO of her biggest competitor, and they agree not to compete in markets where the other has already established customers. Each of these behaviors is clearly unethical (and, in these cases, also illegal). Historically, if management was unaware of such activities, the company could not be held responsible for an employee's unethical acts. Since 1991, however, when the U.S. Sentencing Commission Guidelines for Organizations were established, companies can be prosecuted and *punished even if management didn't know about the unethical behavior*. Moreover, penalties can be substantial, with maximum fines approaching a whopping $300 million.[27] An amendment made in 2004 outlines much stricter ethics training requirements and emphasizes creating a legal and ethical company culture.[28]

Let's examine ***3.1 to whom the guidelines apply and what they cover*** *and* ***3.2 how, according to the guidelines, an organization can be punished for the unethical behavior of its managers and employees.***

3.1 Who, What, and Why?

Nearly all businesses, nonprofits, partnerships, labor unions, unincorporated organizations and associations, incorporated organizations and even pension funds, trusts, and joint stock companies are covered by the U.S. Sentencing Commission's guidelines. If your organization can be characterized as a business (remember, nonprofits count, too), then it is subject to the guidelines.[29]

The guidelines cover offenses defined by federal laws, such as invasion of privacy, price fixing, fraud, customs violations, antitrust violations, civil rights violations, theft, money laundering, conflicts of interest, embezzlement, dealing in stolen goods, copyright infringements, extortion, and more. It's not enough merely to stay "within the law," however. The purpose of the guidelines is not just to punish companies *after* they or their employees break the law, but rather to encourage companies to take proactive steps that will discourage or prevent white-collar crime *before* it happens. The guidelines also give companies an incentive to cooperate with and disclose illegal

© COMSTOCK/JUPITER IMAGES

activities to federal authorities.[30] Today, companies are revamping their ethics training programs to focus on encouraging a culture committed to ethics and compliance in which ethics is part of almost every business discussion, says Dov Seidman, chairman and CEO of LRN, a legal and educational consultancy in Los Angeles.[31]

3.2 Determining the Punishment

The guidelines impose smaller fines on companies that take proactive steps to encourage ethical behavior or voluntarily disclose illegal activities to federal authorities. Essentially, the law uses a carrot-and-stick approach. The stick is the threat of heavy fines that can total millions of dollars. The carrot is a greatly reduced fine, but only if the company has started an effective compliance program (discussed below) to encourage ethical behavior *before* the illegal activity occurs.[32] The method used to determine a company's punishment illustrates the importance of establishing a compliance program.

The first step is to compute the *base fine* by determining what *level of offense* has occurred. The level of the offense (that is, its seriousness) varies depending on the kind of crime, the loss incurred by the victims, and how much planning went into the crime. For example, simple fraud is a level 6 offense (there are 38 levels in all). But if the victims of that fraud lost more than $5 million, that level 6 offense becomes a level 22 offense. Moreover, anything beyond minimal planning to commit the fraud results in an increase of two levels to a level 24 offense. How much difference would this make to the company? As Exhibit 4.2 shows, crimes at or below level 6 incur a base fine of $5,000, whereas the base fine for level 24 is $2.1 million. So the difference is $2.095 million! The base fine for level 38, the top-level offense, is a hefty $72.5 million.

After assessing a *base fine*, the judge computes a culpability score, which is a way of assigning blame to the company. The culpability score can range from a minimum of 0.05 to a maximum of 4.0. The greater the corporate responsibility in conducting, encouraging, or sanctioning illegal or unethical activity, the higher the culpability score. A company that already has a compliance program and voluntarily reports the offense to authorities will incur a culpability score of 0.05. By contrast, a company whose management secretly plans, approves, and participates in illegal or unethical activity will receive the maximum score of 4.0.

> The base fine for level 38, the top-level offense, is a hefty $72.5 million.

The culpability score is critical because the total fine is computed by multiplying the base fine by the culpability score. Going back to our level 24 fraud offense, the left point of the upper arrow in Exhibit 4.2 shows that a company with a compliance program that turns itself in will be fined only $105,000 ($2,100,000 × 0.05). In contrast, a company that secretly planned, approved, and participated in illegal activity will be fined $8.4 million ($2,100,0003 × 4.0), as shown by the right point of the upper arrow. The difference is even greater for level 38 offenses. As shown by the left point of the bottom arrow, a company with a compliance program and a 0.05 culpability score is fined only $3.625 million, whereas a company with the maximum 4.0 culpability score is fined a whopping $290 million, as indicated by the right point of the bottom arrow. These differences clearly show the importance

Offense Level	Base Fine	Culpability Score					
		0.05	0.5	1.0	2.0	3.0	4.0
6 or less	$ 5,000	$ 250	$ 2,500	$ 5,000	$ 10,000	$ 15,000	$ 20,000
7	7,500	375	3,750	7,500	15,000	22,500	30,000
8	10,000	500	5,000	10,000	20,000	30,000	40,000
9	15,000	750	7,500	15,000	30,000	45,000	60,000
10	20,000	1,000	10,000	20,000	40,000	60,000	80,000
11	30,000	1,500	15,000	30,000	60,000	90,000	120,000
12	40,000	2,000	20,000	40,000	80,000	120,000	160,000
13	60,000	3,000	30,000	60,000	120,000	180,000	240,000
14	85,000	4,250	42,500	85,000	170,000	255,000	340,000
15	125,000	6,250	62,500	125,000	250,000	375,000	500,000
16	175,000	8,750	87,500	175,000	350,000	525,000	700,000
17	250,000	12,500	125,000	250,000	500,000	750,000	1,000,000
18	350,000	17,500	175,000	350,000	700,000	1,050,000	1,400,000
19	500,000	25,000	250,000	500,000	1,000,000	1,500,000	2,000,000
20	650,000	32,500	325,000	650,000	1,300,000	1,950,000	2,600,000
21	910,000	45,500	455,000	910,000	1,820,000	2,730,000	3,640,000
22	1,200,000	60,000	600,000	1,200,000	2,400,000	3,600,000	4,800,000
23	1,600,000	80,000	800,000	1,600,000	3,200,000	4,800,000	6,400,000
24	2,100,000	105,000	1,050,000	2,100,000	4,200,000	6,300,000	8,400,000
25	2,800,000	140,000	1,400,000	2,800,000	5,600,000	8,400,000	11,200,000
26	3,700,000	185,000	1,850,000	3,700,000	7,400,000	11,100,000	14,800,000
27	4,800,000	240,000	2,400,000	4,800,000	9,600,000	14,400,000	19,200,000
28	6,300,000	315,000	3,150,000	6,300,000	12,600,000	18,900,000	25,200,000
29	8,100,000	405,000	4,050,000	8,100,000	16,200,000	24,300,000	32,400,000
30	10,500,000	525,000	5,250,000	10,500,000	21,000,000	31,500,000	42,000,000
31	13,500,000	675,000	6,750,000	13,500,000	27,000,000	40,500,000	54,000,000
32	17,500,000	875,000	8,750,000	17,500,000	35,000,000	52,500,000	70,000,000
34	28,500,000	1,425,000	14,250,000	28,500,000	57,000,000	85,500,000	114,000,000
35	36,000,000	1,800,000	18,000,000	36,000,000	72,000,000	108,000,000	144,000,000
36	45,500,000	2,275,000	22,750,000	45,500,000	91,000,000	136,500,000	182,000,000
37	57,500,000	2,875,000	28,750,000	57,500,000	115,000,000	172,500,000	230,000,000
38 or more	72,500,000	3,625,000	36,250,000	72,500,000	145,000,000	217,500,000	290,000,000

Source: "Chapter Eight—Part C—Fines," 2004 Federal Sentencing Guidelines, available at http://www.ussc.gov/2004guid/8c2_4.htm, 27 January 2005.

Exhibit 4.2

Offense Levels, Base Fines, Culpability Scores, and Possible Total Fines under the U.S. Sentencing Commission Guidelines for Organizations

of having a compliance program in place. Over the last decade, 1,494 companies have been charged under the U.S. Sentencing Guidelines. Seventy-six percent of those charged were fined, with the average fine exceeding $2 million. Company fines are on average 20 times larger now than before the implementation of the guidelines in 1991.[33]

Fortunately, for companies that want to avoid paying these stiff fines, the U.S. Sentencing Guidelines clearly spell out the seven necessary components of an effective compliance program.[34] Exhibit 4.3 lists those components. CAREMARK INTERNATIONAL, a managed-care service provider in Delaware, pleaded guilty to criminal charges related to its physician contracts and improper patient referrals. When it was then sued by shareholders for negligence and poor management, the Delaware court dismissed the case, ruling that the company's ethics compliance program, built on the components described in Exhibit 4.3, was a "good-faith attempt" to monitor employees and that the company did not knowingly allow illegal and unethical behavior to occur. The court went on to rule that a compliance program

based on the U.S. Sentencing Guidelines was enough to shield the company from liability.[35]

For more information, see "An Overview of the Organizational Sentencing Guidelines" at **http://www.ussc.gov/training/corpover.PDF** and "Sentencing Guidelines Educational Materials" at **http://www.ussc.gov/training/educat.htm.**

Review 3: U.S. Sentencing Commission Guidelines

Under the U.S. Sentencing Commission Guidelines, companies can be prosecuted and fined up to $300 million for employees' illegal actions. Fines are computed by multiplying the base fine by a culpability score, which ranges from 0.05 to 4.0. Companies that establish compliance programs to encourage ethical behavior can reduce their culpability scores and their fines. Companies without compliance programs can face much heavier fines than companies with established programs. Compliance programs must establish standards and procedures, be run by top managers, encourage hiring and promotion of honest and ethical people, encourage employees to report violations, educate employees about compliance, punish violators, and find ways to improve the program after violations occur.

Exhibit 4.3

Compliance Program Steps for the U.S. Sentencing Guidelines for Organizations

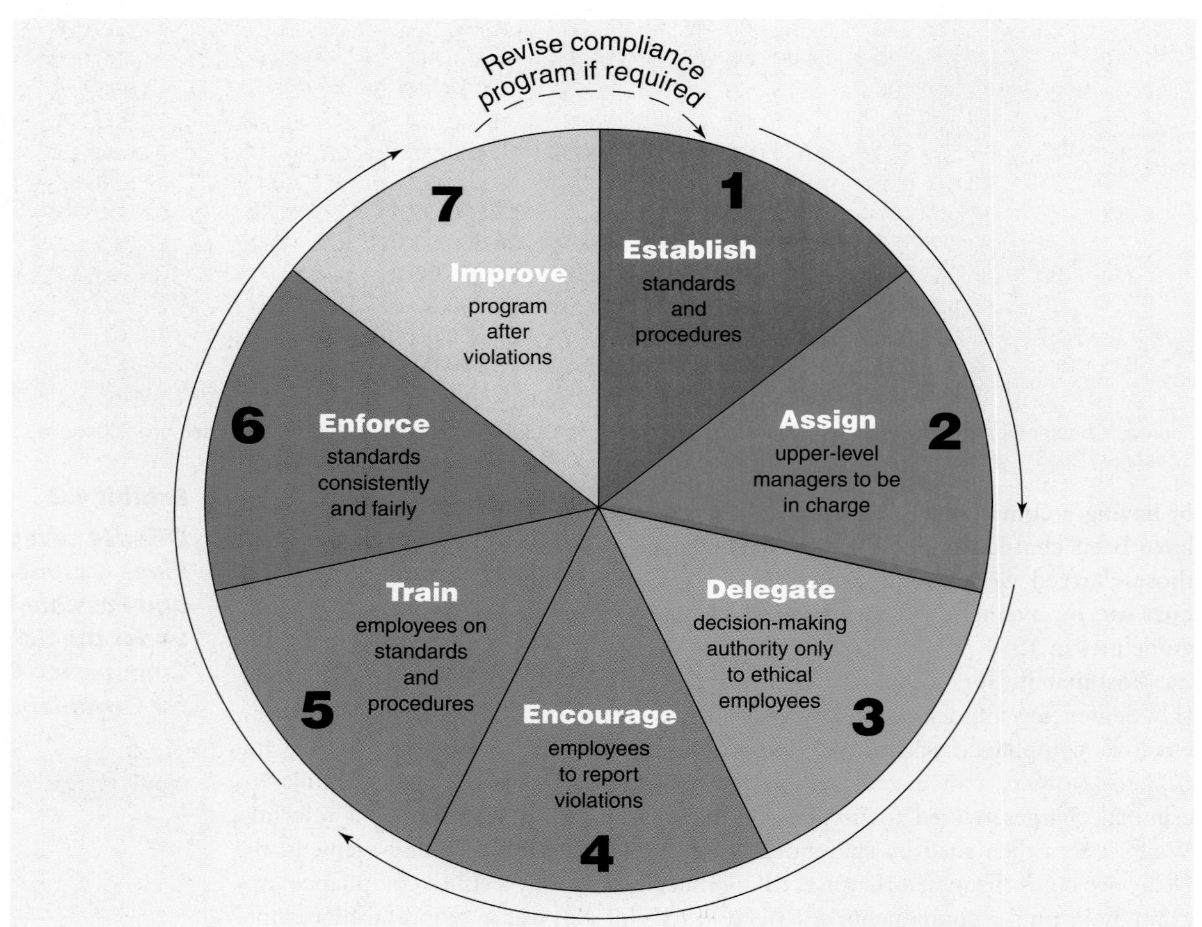

Source: D. R. Dalton, M. B. Metzger, & J. W. Hill, "The 'New' U.S. Sentencing Commission Guidelines: A Wake-up Call for Corporate America," *Academy of Management Executive* 8 (1994): 7–16.

HOW DO YOU MAKE ETHICAL DECISIONS?

On a cold morning in the midst of a winter storm, schools were closed and most people had decided to stay home from work. Nevertheless, Richard Addessi had already showered, shaved, and dressed for the office. He kissed his wife Joan goodbye, but before he could get to his car, he fell dead on the garage floor of a sudden heart attack. Addessi was four months short of his 30-year anniversary with the company. Having begun work at **IBM** at the age of 18, he was just 48 years old.[36]

You're the vice president in charge of benefits at IBM. Given that he was only four months short of full retirement, do you award full retirement benefits to Richard Addessi's wife and daughters? If the answer is yes, they will receive his full retirement benefits of $1,800 a month and free lifetime medical coverage. If you say no, his widow and two daughters will receive only $340 a month. They will also have to pay $473 a month just to continue their current medical coverage. As the VP in charge of benefits at IBM, what would be the ethical thing for you to do?

After reading the next two sections, you should be able to

4 describe what influences ethical decision making.
5 explain what practical steps managers can take to improve ethical decision making.

4 Influences on Ethical Decision Making

So, what did IBM decide to do? Since Richard Addessi had not completed 30 full years with the company, IBM officials felt they had no choice but to give Joan Addessi and her two daughters the smaller, partial retirement benefits. Do you think IBM's decision was ethical? Probably many of you don't. You wonder how the company could be so heartless as to deny Richard Addessi's family the full benefits to which you believe they were entitled. Yet others might argue that IBM did the ethical thing by strictly following the rules laid out in its pension benefit plan. After all, being fair means applying the rules to everyone. Although some ethical issues are easily solved, many do not have clearly right or wrong answers.

The ethical answers that managers choose depend on ***4.1 the ethical intensity of the decision, 4.2 the moral development of the manager,*** *and* ***4.3 the ethical principles used to solve the problem.***

4.1 Ethical Intensity of the Decision

Managers don't treat all ethical decisions the same. The manager who has to decide whether to deny or extend full benefits to Joan Addessi and her family is going to treat that decision much more seriously than the decision of how to deal with an assistant who has been taking computer paper home for personal use. These decisions differ in their **ethical intensity**, or the degree of concern people have about an ethical issue. When addressing an issue of high ethical intensity, managers are more aware of the

ethical intensity the degree of concern people have about an ethical issue impact their decision will have on others. They are more likely to view the decision as an ethical or moral decision rather than as an economic decision. They are also more likely to worry about doing the "right thing."

Ethical intensity depends on six factors:[37]

- magnitude of consequences
- social consensus
- probability of effect
- temporal immediacy
- proximity of effect
- concentration of effect.

Magnitude of consequences is the total harm or benefit derived from an ethical decision. The more people who are harmed or the greater the harm to those people, the larger the consequences. **Social consensus** is agreement on whether behavior is bad or good. **Probability of effect** is the chance that something will happen and then result in harm to others. If we combine these factors, we can see the effect they can have on ethical intensity. For example, if there is *clear agreement* (social consensus) that a managerial decision or action is *certain* (probability of effect) to have *large negative consequences* (magnitude of effect) in some way, then people will be highly concerned about that managerial decision or action, and ethical intensity will be high.

Temporal immediacy is the time between an act and the consequences the act produces. Temporal immediacy is stronger if a manager has to lay off workers next week as opposed to three months from now. **Proximity of effect** is the social, psychological, cultural, or physical distance of a decision maker from those affected by his or her decisions. Thus, proximity of effect is greater when a manager lays off employees he knows than when he lays off employees that he doesn't know. Finally, whereas the magnitude of consequences is the total effect across all people, **concentration of effect** is how much an act affects the average person. Temporarily laying off 100 employees for 10 months without pay is a greater concentration of effect than temporarily laying off 1,000 employees for 1 month.

Which of these six factors has the most impact? Studies indicate that managers are much more likely to view decisions as ethical decisions when the magnitude of consequences (total harm) is high and there is a social consensus (agreement) that a behavior or action is bad.[38]

Many people will likely feel IBM was wrong to deny full benefits to Joan Addessi. Why? In this situation, IBM's decision met five of the six characteristics of ethical intensity. The difference in benefits, more than $23,000 per year, was likely to have serious consequences for the family. The decision was certain to affect them and would do so immediately. We can closely identify with Joan Addessi and her daughters as opposed to IBM's faceless, nameless corporate identity. And the decision would have a concentrated effect on the family in terms of their monthly benefits ($1,800 and free medical coverage if full benefits were awarded versus $340 a month and medical care that costs $473 per month if they weren't).

The exception, as we will discuss below, is social consensus. Not everyone will agree that IBM's decision was unethical. The judgment also depends on your level of moral development and which ethical principles you use to decide.

magnitude of consequences the total harm or benefit derived from an ethical decision

social consensus agreement on whether behavior is bad or good

probability of effect the chance that something will happen and then harm others

temporal immediacy the time between an act and the consequences the act produces

proximity of effect the social, psychological, cultural, or physical distance between a decision maker and those affected by his or her decisions

concentration of effect the total harm or benefit that an act produces on the average person

4.2 Moral Development

A friend of yours has given you the latest version of Microsoft Office. She stuffed the software disks in your backpack with a note saying that you should install it on your computer and get it back to her in a couple of days. You're tempted. You have papers to write, notes to take, and presentations to plan. Besides, all of your friends have the same version of Microsoft Office. They didn't pay for it either. Copying the software to your hard drive without buying your own copy clearly violates copyright laws. But no one would find out. Even if someone does, Microsoft probably isn't going to come after you. Microsoft goes after the big fish—companies that illegally copy and distribute software to their workers. Your computer has booted up, and you've got your mouse in one hand and the installation disk in the other. What are you going to do?[39]

In part, according to psychologist Lawrence Kohlberg, your decision will be based on your level of moral development. Kohlberg identified three phases of moral development, with two stages in each phase (see Exhibit 4.4).[40] At the **preconventional level of moral development**, people decide based on selfish reasons. For example, if you are in Stage 1, the punishment and obedience stage, your primary concern will be to avoid trouble for yourself. So, you won't copy the software because you are afraid of being caught and punished. Yet, in Stage 2, the instrumental exchange stage, you worry less about punishment and more about doing things that directly advance your wants and needs. So, you copy the software.

People at the **conventional level of moral development** make decisions that conform to societal expectations. In other words, they look outside themselves to others for guidance on ethical issues. In Stage 3, the good boy, nice girl stage, you normally do what the other "good boys" and "nice girls" are doing. If everyone else is illegally copying software, you will, too. But if they aren't, you won't either. In the law and order stage, Stage 4, you again look for external guidance and do whatever the law permits, so you won't copy the software.

People at the **postconventional level of moral development** always use internalized ethical principles to solve ethical dilemmas. In Stage 5, the social contract stage, you will refuse to copy the software because, as a whole, society is better off when the rights of others—in this case, the rights of software authors and manufacturers—are not violated. In Stage 6, the universal principle stage, you might or might not copy the software, depending on your principles of right and wrong. Moreover, you will stick to your principles even if your decision conflicts with the law (Stage 4) or what others believe is best for society (Stage 5). For example, those with socialist or communist beliefs would probably choose to copy the software because they believe goods and services should be owned by society rather than by individuals and corporations. (For information about the dos, don'ts, and legal issues concerning software piracy, see the Software & Information Industry Association's website at **http://www.siia.net/piracy/default.asp**.)

Kohlberg believed that as people became more educated and mature, they would progress sequentially from earlier stages to later stages. But only 20 percent of adults ever reach the postconventional stage of moral development where internal principles guide their decisions. By contrast, most adults are in the conventional stage of moral development in which they look outside themselves to others for

preconventional level of moral development the first level of moral development, in which people make decisions based on selfish reasons

conventional level of moral development the second level of moral development, in which people make decisions that conform to societal expectations

postconventional level of moral development the third level of moral development, in which people make decisions based on internalized principles

Exhibit 4.4

Kohlberg's Stages of Moral Development

Stage 1	Stage 2	Stage 3	Stage 4	Stage 5	Stage 6
Punishment and Obedience	Instrumental Exchange	Good Boy, Nice Girl	Law and Order	Social Contract	Universal Principle
Preconventional		Conventional		Postconventional	
Selfish		Societal Expectations		Internalized Principles	

Source: W. Davidson III & D. Worrell, "Influencing Managers to Change Unpopular Corporate Behavior through Boycotts and Divestitures," *Business & Society* 34 (1995): 171–196.

guidance on ethical issues. This means that most people in the workplace look to and need leadership when it comes ethical decision making.[41]

4.3 Principles of Ethical Decision Making

Besides an issue's ethical intensity and a manager's level of moral maturity, the particular ethical principles that managers use will also affect how they solve ethical dilemmas. Unfortunately, there is no one "ideal principle" to use in making ethical business decisions.

According to professor LaRue Hosmer, a number of different ethical principles can be used to make business decisions: long-term self-interest, personal virtue, religious injunctions, government requirements, utilitarian benefits, individual rights, and distributive justice.[42] All of these ethical principles encourage managers and employees to take others' interests into account when making ethical decisions. At the same time, however, these principles can lead to very different ethical actions, as we can see by using these principles to decide whether to award full benefits to Joan Addessi and her children.

principle of long-term self-interest an ethical principle that holds that you should never take any action that is not in your or your organization's long-term self-interest

principle of personal virtue an ethical principle that holds that you should never do anything that is not honest, open, and truthful and that you would not be glad to see reported in the newspapers or on TV

principle of religious injunctions an ethical principle that holds that you should never take any action that is not kind and that does not build a sense of community

principle of government requirements an ethical principle that holds that you should never take any action that violates the law, for the law represents the minimal moral standard

principle of utilitarian benefits an ethical principle that holds that you should never take any action that does not result in greater good for society

According to the **principle of long-term self-interest**, you should never take any action that is not in your or your organization's long-term self-interest. Although this sounds as if the principle promotes selfishness, it doesn't. What we do to maximize our long-term interests (save more, spend less, exercise every day, watch what we eat) is often very different from what we do to maximize short-term interests (max out our credit cards, be couch potatoes, eat whatever we want). At any given time, IBM has nearly 1,000 employees who are just months away from retirement. Thus, because of the costs involved, it serves IBM's long-term interest to pay full benefits only after employees have put in their 30 years.

The **principle of personal virtue** holds that you should never do anything that is not honest, open, and truthful and that you would not be glad to see reported in the newspapers or on TV. Using the principle of personal virtue, IBM should have quietly awarded Joan Addessi her husband's full benefits. Had it done so, it could have avoided the publication of an embarrassing *Wall Street Journal* article on this topic.

The **principle of religious injunctions** holds that you should never take an action that is unkind or that harms a sense of community, such as the positive feelings that come from working together to accomplish a commonly accepted goal. Using this principle, IBM would have been concerned foremost with compassion and kindness. Thus, it would have awarded full benefits to Joan Addessi.

According to the **principle of government requirements**, the law represents the minimal moral standards of society, so you should never take any action that violates the law. Using this principle, IBM would deny full benefits to Joan Addessi because her husband did not work for the company for 30 years. Indeed, an IBM spokesperson stated that making exceptions would violate the federal Employee Retirement Income Security Act of 1974.

© REPORTAGE/GETTY IMAGES

The **principle of utilitarian benefits** states that you should never take an action that does not result in greater good for society. In short, you should do whatever creates the greatest good for the greatest number. At first, this principle seems to suggest that IBM should award full benefits to Joan Addessi. If IBM did this with any regularity, however, the costs would be enormous, profits would shrink, and IBM would have to cut its stock dividend, harming countless shareholders, many of whom rely on IBM dividends for retirement income. In this case, the principle does not lead to a clear choice.

The **principle of individual rights** holds that you should never take an action that infringes on others' agreed-upon rights. Using this principle, IBM would deny Joan Addessi full benefits. If it carefully followed the rules specified in its pension plan and granted Mrs. Addessi due process, meaning the right to appeal the decision, then IBM would not be violating her rights. In fact, it could be argued that providing full benefits to Mrs. Addessi would violate the rights of employees who had to wait 30 years to receive full benefits.

Finally, under the **principle of distributive justice**, you should never take any action that harms the least fortunate among us in some way. This principle is designed to protect the poor, the uneducated, and the unemployed. Although Joan Addessi could probably find a job, after 20 years as a stay-at-home mom it's unlikely that she could easily find one that would support her and her daughters in the manner to which they are accustomed. Using the principle of distributive justice, IBM would award her full benefits.

As mentioned at the beginning of this chapter, one of the "real-world" aspects of ethical decisions is that no matter *what* you decide, someone or some group will be unhappy. This corollary is also true: No matter *how* you decide, someone or some group will be unhappy. Consequently, although all of these ethical principles encourage managers to balance others' needs against their own, they can also lead to very different ethical actions. So even when managers strive to be ethical, there are often no clear answers when it comes to doing "the" right thing.

"Unfortunately, there is no one "ideal principle" to use in making ethical business decisions."

Review 4: Influences on Ethical Decision Making

Three factors influence ethical decisions: the ethical intensity of the decision, the moral development of the decision maker, and the ethical principles used to solve the problem. Ethical intensity is strong when decisions have large, certain, immediate consequences and when we are physically or psychologically close to those affected by the decision. There are three levels of moral maturity, each with two steps. At the preconventional level, decisions are made for selfish reasons. At the conventional level, decisions conform to societal expectations. At the postconventional level, internalized principles are used to make ethical decisions. Finally, managers can use a number of different principles when making ethical decisions: self-interest, personal virtue, religious injunctions, government requirements, utilitarian benefits, individual rights, and distributive justice.

5 Practical Steps to Ethical Decision Making

Managers can encourage more ethical decision making in their organizations by ***5.1 carefully selecting and hiring ethical employees, 5.2 establishing a specific code of ethics, 5.3 training employees to make ethical decisions****, and* ***5.4 creating an ethical climate****.*

5.1 Selecting and Hiring Ethical Employees

If you found a wallet containing $100, would you return it with the money? Informal studies typically show that 57 to 80 percent of people would, and that women and people in small towns are more likely to return the wallet with the money.[43]

principle of individual rights an ethical principle that holds that you should never take any action that infringes on others' agreed-upon rights

principle of distributive justice an ethical principle that holds that you should never take any action that harms the least fortunate among us: the poor, the uneducated, the unemployed

doing the right thing

If You Cheat in College, Will You Cheat in the Workplace?

Studies show that college students who cheat once are likely to cheat again. Students who cheat on exams are likely to cheat on assignments and projects. Furthermore, tolerance of cheating is widespread, as 70 percent of college students don't see cheating as a problem. Given these relaxed attitudes toward cheating, and with on-campus cheating at all-time highs, employers want to know whether someone who cheated in college will cheat in the workplace. Studies generally indicate that the answer is yes. The best predictor of cheating in medical school was cheating in high school or college. Likewise, students who cheated in school were much more likely to cheat on their taxes, in politics (by committing voter fraud or accepting illegal campaign contributions), in sports, and on the job. Why is this the case? Apparently, people who cheat and then cheat again come to see their behavior as normal and to rationalize it by telling themselves that cheating isn't wrong. In fact, 60 percent of the people who cheat their employers don't feel guilty about doing so. Cheating isn't situation-specific. Once you decide that cheating is acceptable, you're likely to cheat in most areas of your life.[48] Robert Hogan, a renowned personality psychologist, says there is an intrinsic link between cheating, embezzling, marital infidelity, public drunkenness, getting traffic tickets, fighting, vandalism, and so on. "All these things involve breaking the rules, and they're all motivated by hostility toward or disregard for authority."[49] If you want to do the right thing, don't cheat in college or tolerate cheating by others. Don't slide down the slippery slope of cheating.

As an employer, you can increase your chances of hiring the honest person who returns the wallet with the money if you give job applicants integrity tests. **Overt integrity tests** estimate job applicants' honesty by directly asking them what they think or feel about theft or about punishment of unethical behaviors.[44] For example, an employer might ask an applicant, "Would you ever consider buying something from somebody if you knew the person had stolen the item?" or "Don't most people steal from their companies?" Surprisingly, unethical people will usually answer "yes" to such questions, because they believe that the world is basically dishonest and that dishonest behavior is normal.[45]

Personality-based integrity tests indirectly estimate job applicants' honesty by measuring psychological traits such as dependability and conscientiousness. For example, prison inmates serving time for white-collar crimes (counterfeiting, embezzlement, and fraud) scored much lower than a comparison group of middle-level managers on scales measuring reliability, dependability, honesty, conscientiousness, and abiding by rules.[46] These results show that companies can selectively hire and promote people who will be more ethical.[47] For more on integrity testing, see the "What Really Works" feature in this chapter.

5.2 Codes of Ethics

Exhibit 4.5 displays the ethical code of conduct for Portland General Electric, a large electrical utility company in Oregon. The code urges employees to conduct themselves as "responsible and responsive corporate citizens," "respect the environment," "maintain high levels of legal and ethical conduct," and "deal honestly and fairly with customers."

Today, almost all large corporations have an ethics code in place. Still, two things must happen if those codes are to encourage ethical decision making and behavior.[50] First, a company must communicate its code to others both inside and outside the company. An excellent example of a well-communicated code of ethics can be found at Home Depot's website at **http://www.homedepot.com/governance/ethics**. With the click of a computer mouse, anyone inside or outside the company can obtain detailed information about the company's core values, specific ethical business practices, and much more. Second, executive sponsorship and involvement in ethics and compliance training is a must to create an ethical company culture.[51]

Second, in addition to having an ethics code with general guidelines like "do unto others as you would have others do unto you," management must also

One of the characteristics we value highly is the ability to make and keep commitments both to ourselves and to others. People who can make and keep commitments gain respect. They are known for their integrity, and it is the same with businesses.

Here is a list of commitments each of us needs to incorporate into our daily conduct of business:

- We will treat our fellow employees with honesty, respect, and dignity.
- We will strive to conduct our activities to protect the safety and health of our fellow employees.
- We will conduct ourselves as responsible and responsive corporate citizens in our communities.
- We will respect the environment and exercise good judgment concerning the impact of our activities on the environment.
- We will maintain high levels of legal and ethical conduct while pursuing our growth and earnings objectives.
- We will deal honestly and fairly with our customers and be responsive to their needs and requirements.
- We will strive to maintain the highest standards of excellence in the quality of the products and services we provide to our customers.
- We will strive to be the best customer we can be to our suppliers. We will emphasize fairness and integrity in all dealings with suppliers.
- We will respect and obey the law.

Source: "Law and Ethics: How We Do Business, A Compliance Guide for Portland General Electric Employees," Portland General Electric, available at http://www.portlandgeneral.com/about_pge/jobs/pdf/how_we_do_business.pdf, 20 March 2003.

Exhibit 4.5

Ethical Code of Conduct for Portland General Electric

develop practical ethical standards and procedures specific to the company's line of business. Visitors to NORTEL's website at **http://www.nortel.com/corporate/community/ethics/guide.html** can instantly access references to very specific ethical standards on topics ranging from bribes and kickbacks to expense vouchers and illegal copying of software. For example, most businesspeople believe that it is wrong to take bribes or other gifts from a company that wants your business. Therefore, one of Nortel's ethical guidelines is "We do not accept or offer any form of bribe, kickback, improper or illegal inducement—even where the practice is widely considered a way of doing business."[52] And just to be sure there's no confusion over what constitutes, say, a gift, the guidelines are even more specific: "When we do give or receive gifts, they should be modest. T-shirts, mugs, and pens that carry the company logo are examples of gifts we would normally give or receive. If you give a gift, you must accurately account for it in your expense claim or department records."[53]

Specific codes of ethics such as this make it much easier for employees to decide what to do when they want to do the "right thing."

5.3 Ethics Training

The first objective of ethics training is to develop employees' awareness of ethics.[54] This means helping employees recognize which issues are ethical issues and then avoid rationalizing unethical behavior by thinking, "This isn't really illegal or immoral" or "No one will ever find out." Several companies have created board

overt integrity test a written test that estimates job applicants' honesty by directly asking them what they think or feel about theft or about punishment of unethical behaviors

personality-based integrity test a written test that indirectly estimates job applicants' honesty by measuring psychological traits, such as dependability and conscientiousness

INTEGRITY TESTS

what *really* works:

Under the 1991 and 2004 U.S. Sentencing Commission Guidelines, unethical employee behavior can lead to multimillion-dollar fines for corporations and fraudulent behavior of executives can lead to criminal prosecution. Moreover, workplace deviance like stealing, fraud, and vandalism costs companies an estimated $660 billion a year. One way to reduce workplace deviance and the chances of a large fine for unethical employee behavior is to use overt and personality-based integrity tests to screen job applicants.

One hundred eighty-one studies, with a combined total of 576,460 study participants, have examined how well integrity tests can predict job performance and various kinds of workplace deviance. These studies show that not only can integrity tests help companies reduce workplace deviance, but they provide the added bonus of helping companies hire workers who are better performers in their jobs.

WORKPLACE DEVIANCE (COUNTERPRODUCTIVE BEHAVIORS)

Compared with job applicants who score poorly, there is an 82 percent chance that job applicants who score well on overt integrity tests will participate in less illegal activity, unethical behavior, drug abuse, or workplace violence.

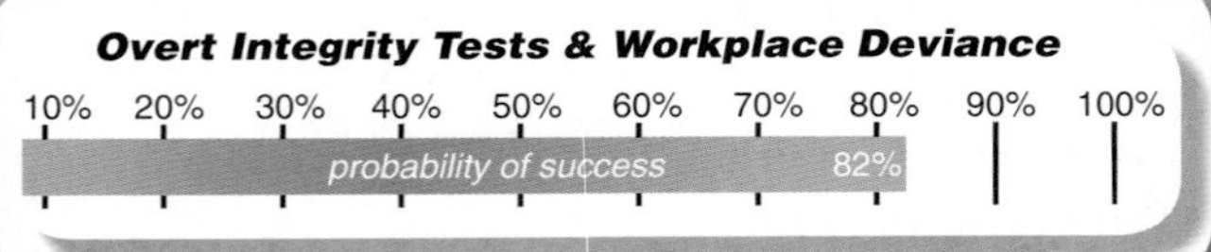

Personality-based integrity tests also do a good job of predicting who will engage in workplace deviance. Compared with job applicants who score poorly, there is a 68 percent chance that job applicants who score well on personality-based integrity tests will participate in less illegal activity, unethical behavior, excessive absences, drug abuse, or workplace violence.

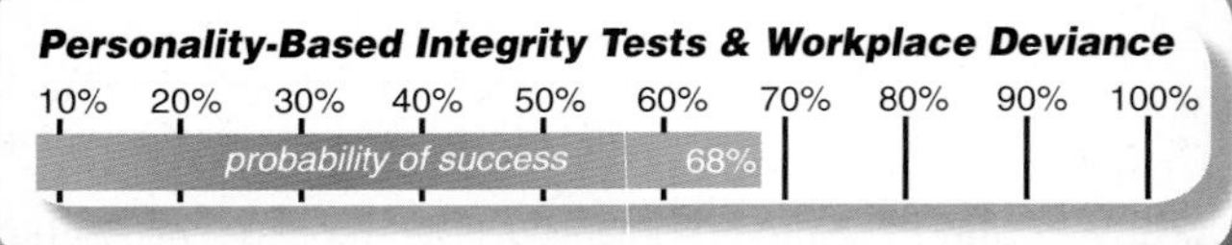

JOB PERFORMANCE

In addition to reducing unethical behavior and workplace deviance, integrity tests can help companies hire better performers. Compared with employees who score poorly, there is a 69 percent chance that employees who score well on overt integrity tests will be better performers.

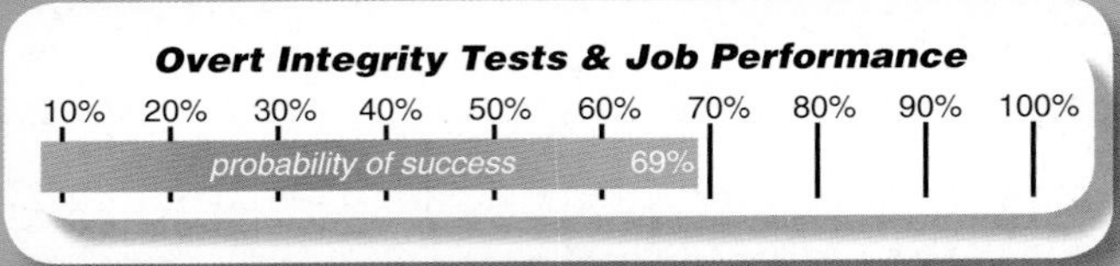

The figures are nearly identical for personality-based integrity tests. Compared with those who score poorly, there is a 70 percent chance that employees who score well on personality-based integrity tests will be better at their jobs.

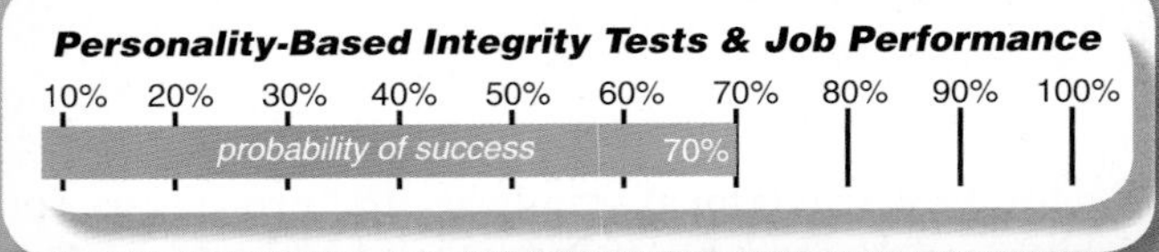

THEFT

Although integrity tests can help companies decrease most kinds of workplace deviance and increase employees' job performance, they have a smaller effect on a specific kind of workplace deviance: theft. Compared with employees who score poorly, there is a 57 percent chance that employees who score well on overt integrity tests will be less likely to steal. No theft data were available to assess personality-based integrity tests.

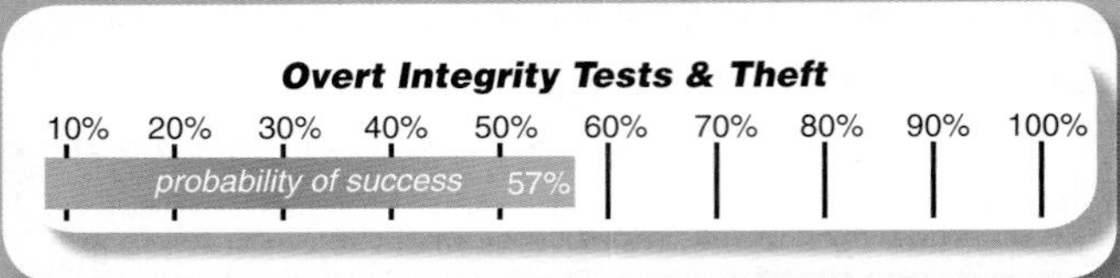

FAKING AND COACHING ON INTEGRITY TESTS

Although overt and personality-based integrity tests do a very good job of helping companies hire people of higher integrity, it is possible to improve scores on these tests through coaching and faking. In coaching, job applicants are taught the underlying rationale of an integrity test or given specific directions for improving their integrity scores. Faking occurs when applicants simply try to "beat the test" or try to fake a good impression. Unfortunately for the companies that use integrity tests, both strategies work. On average, coaching can improve scores on overt integrity tests by an astounding 1.5 standard deviations and on personality-based integrity tests by a meaningful .36 standard deviation. This would be the equivalent of increasing your total SAT score by 150 and 36 points, respectively (the SAT has a mean of 500 and a standard deviation of 100). Likewise, on average, faking can improve scores on overt integrity tests by an impressive 1.02 standard deviations and on personality-based integrity tests by a meaningful .59 standard deviation. Again, this would be the equivalent of increasing your SAT score by 102 and 59 points, respectively. Companies that want to avoid coaching and faking effects must maintain tight security over integrity tests so that applicants have little information regarding them, periodically check the validity of the tests to make sure they're accurately predicting workplace deviance and job performance, or periodically switch tests if they suspect that test security has been compromised.[55]

games to improve awareness of ethical issues.[56] Citigroup has a game called "The Work Ethic," in which players win or lose points depending on their answers to legal, regulatory, policy, and judgment questions. Defense contractor **Lockheed Martin** has created "The Ethics Challenge," which every employee, including the CEO, must play at least once a year. Lockheed workers sit around a table, roll dice, and then move their tokens ahead when they answer ethics questions correctly. Here's a sample question from the game:

A kickback may be in the form of:

A. Cash
B. Gift to a family member
C. Donation to a charity at your request
D. All of these (the correct answer)

The game has been very popular, except for one year when it was revised so that it did not indicate which answers were right. Brian Sears, an ethics officer for Lockheed's aeronautics division, comments that engineers, who are used to "correct answers," wanted more guidance. Says Sears, "They had a hard time with it," so the game was changed again to offer "preferred answers."[57]

The second objective for ethics training programs is to achieve credibility with employees. Not surprisingly, employees can be highly suspicious of management's reasons for offering ethics training. Some companies have hurt the credibility of their ethics programs by having outside instructors and consultants conduct the classes.[58] Employees often complain that outside instructors and consultants are teaching theory that has nothing to do with their jobs and the "real world." This is why Boeing has a vice president of ethics who employs 55 people to teach Boeing's 194,000 employees the difference between right and wrong in the aerospace industry.[59] And Boeing is not an exception. Almost every major corporation has a vice president of ethics and compliance. Ethics training becomes even more credible when top managers teach the initial ethics classes to their subordinates, who in turn teach their subordinates. In time, most managers will have both taken

In an effort to ensure that employees know how to act in an ethical manner, many companies have a code of ethics or ethical guidelines. Many companies use games to practice ethical decision making. There is even a game based on the popular cartoon character Dilbert.

and taught the ethics classes, thereby pushing ethics training and principles throughout the entire company.[60] Unfortunately, though, 25 percent of large companies don't require top managers to attend, much less teach, ethics training.[61] The good news is that this scenario is changing, thanks to the 2004 amendment to the Sentencing Guidelines. Indeed, a recent survey shows that board involvement in ethics and compliance programs jumped from 21 percent in 1987 to 96 percent in 2005.[62]

The third objective of ethics training is to teach employees a practical model of ethical decision making. A basic model should help them think about the consequences their choices will have on others and consider how they will choose between different solutions. Exhibit 4.6 presents a basic model of ethical decision making.

5.4 Ethical Climate

In study after study, when researchers ask, "What is the most important influence on your ethical behavior at work?" the answer comes back, "My manager." The first step in establishing an ethical climate is for managers, especially top managers, to act ethically themselves. The National Business Ethics Survey found that unethical misconduct occurred in just 15 percent of the organizations where top managers talked about the importance of ethics, kept their promises to others, and modeled ethical behavior themselves. By contrast, unethical misconduct occurred in 56 percent of the organizations in which top management only talked about the importance of ethics, but did nothing else.[63]

Exhibit 4.6

A Basic Model of Ethical Decision Making

1. **Identify the problem.** What makes it an ethical problem? Think in terms of rights, obligations, fairness, relationships, and integrity. How would you define the problem if you stood on the other side of the fence?
2. **Identify the constituents.** Who has been hurt? Who could be hurt? Who could be helped? Are they willing players, or are they victims? Can you negotiate with them?
3. **Diagnose the situation.** How did it happen in the first place? What could have prevented it? Is it going to get worse or better? Can the damage now be undone?
4. **Analyze your options.** Imagine the range of possibilities. Limit yourself to the two or three most manageable. What are the likely outcomes of each? What are the likely costs? Look to the company mission statement or code of ethics for guidance.
5. **Make your choice.** What is your intention in making this decision? How does it compare with the probable results? Can you discuss the problem with the affected parties before you act? Could you disclose without qualm your decision to your boss, the CEO, the board of directors, your family, or society as a whole?
6. **Act.** Do what you have to do. Don't be afraid to admit errors. Be as bold in confronting a problem as you were in causing it.

Source: L. A. Berger, "Train All Employees to Solve Ethical Dilemmas," *Best's Review—Life-Health Insurance Edition* 95 (1995): 70–80.

A second step in establishing an ethical climate is for top management to be active in and committed to the company ethics program.[64] Top managers who consistently talk about the importance of ethics and back up that talk by participating in their companies' ethics programs send the clear message that ethics matter. Business writer Dayton Fandray says, "You can have ethics offices and officers and training programs and reporting systems, but if the CEO doesn't seem to care, it's all just a sham. It's not surprising to find that the companies that really do care about ethics make a point of including senior management in all of their ethics and compliance programs."[65]

A third step is to put in place a reporting system that encourages managers and employees to report potential ethics violations. **Whistleblowing**, that is, reporting others' ethics violations, is a difficult step for most people to take.[66] Potential whistleblowers often fear that they, and not the ethics violators, will be punished.[67] Managers who have been interviewed about whistleblowing have said, "In every organization, someone's been screwed for standing up." "If anything, I figured that by taking a strong stand I might get myself in trouble. People might look at me as a goody two-shoes. Someone might try to force me out." This is exactly what happened to Sandy Baratta, who used to be a vice president at Oracle, which makes database software used by most large companies. Baratta was fired, she alleges, for complaining about Oracle's treatment of women and its unethical business practices. Under California's whistleblower protection laws, a jury awarded her $2.6 million in damages.[68]

Today, many federal and state laws protect the rights of whistleblowers (see **http://www.whistleblowers.org** for more information). In particular, the Sarbanes-Oxley Act of 2002 (see **http://www.aicpa.org/info/sarbanes_oxley_summary.htm**) made it a serious crime to retaliate in any way against corporate whistleblowers in publicly owned companies. Managers who punish whistleblowers can be imprisoned for up to 10 years.

Some companies, including defense contractor Northrop Grumman, have made it easier for whistleblowers to report possible violations by establishing anonymous, toll-free corporate ethics hot lines. Nortel, the telecommunications company, even publicizes which of its ethics hot lines don't have caller ID (so they can't identify the caller's phone number). The Sarbanes-Oxley Act also requires all publicly held companies to establish anonymous hot lines to encourage reporting of unethical and illegal behaviors, so it's not surprising that a recent survey found that 91 percent of companies have an anonymous reporting system whereby employees can report observed misconduct.[69] At HomeBanc, employees can call the "Associate Hotline" which goes directly to a voice mail in the CEO's office.

The factor that does the most to discourage whistleblowers from reporting problems, however, is lack of company action on their complaints.[70] Thus, the final step in developing an ethical climate is for management to fairly and consistently punish those who violate the company's code of ethics. For example, when an anonymous caller used hospital chain Columbia/HCA's toll-free ethics phone line to report that a supply clerk was stealing medical equipment and selling it online at eBay, the information was forwarded to company investigators who bid on and bought the equipment. Being a good eBay seller, the supply clerk quickly shipped the stolen goods directly from her home. When confronted with the stolen goods, she confessed and was immediately fired.[71] Amazingly, though, not all companies fire ethics violators. In fact, 8 percent of surveyed companies admit that they would promote top performers even if they violated ethical standards.[72]

whistleblowing reporting others' ethics violations to management or legal authorities

Review 5: Practical Steps to Ethical Decision Making

Employers can increase their chances of hiring ethical employees by administering overt integrity tests and personality-based integrity tests to all job applicants. Most large companies now have corporate codes of ethics. To affect ethical decision making, these codes must be known both inside and outside the organization. In addition to offering general rules, ethics codes must also provide specific, practical advice. Ethics training seeks to increase employees' awareness of ethical issues, make ethics a serious and credible factor in organizational decisions, and teach employees a practical model of ethical decision making. The most important factors in creating an ethical business climate are the personal examples set by company managers, involvement of management in the company ethics program, a reporting system that encourages whistleblowers to report potential ethics violations, and fair but consistent punishment of violators.

WHAT IS SOCIAL RESPONSIBILITY?

Social responsibility is a business's obligation to pursue policies, make decisions, and take actions that benefit society.[73] Unfortunately, because there are strong disagreements over to whom and for what in society organizations are responsible, it can be difficult for managers to know what is or will be perceived as socially responsible corporate behavior. In a recent McKinsey & Co. study of 1,144 top global executives, 79 percent predicted that at least some responsibility for dealing with future social and political issues would fall on corporations, but only 3 percent said they themselves do a good job of dealing with social pressures.[74] One thing is for sure: Corporate giving has increased 22 percent to $13.7 billion in cash and in-kind gifts. But checkbook philanthropy isn't enough, says Susan Puflea, senior vice president and director of GolinHarris Change.[75] Consider some examples. Former **Ford Motor Company** CEO William C. Ford Jr. has championed green causes for years. He spent $2 billion overhauling Ford's sprawling River Rouge complex, installing a 10-acre grass roof to capture rainwater. The company also donated $25 million to Conservation International for an environmental center. But it kept churning out popular gas-guzzling SUVs and pickups desired by its customers. Wal-Mart Stores, long assailed for its labor and global-outsourcing practices, has made a series of high-profile investments to slash energy use overall, from its stores to its vast trucking fleets, and has promised to purchase more electricity derived from renewable sources.[76] These two examples illustrate the difficulties of acting in a socially responsible manner—balancing the needs of different groups in the face of limited resources and/or constraints.

The opening vignette also captured the dilemma of how to balance the needs of different groups. Is P&G obligated to eliminate all animal testing, as PETA believes? Or, by minimizing but not eliminating animal testing, has P&G achieved a reasonable balance that still allows it to make sure its products are safe? In the end, are P&G's actions regarding animal testing socially responsible or irresponsible?

social responsibility a business's obligation to pursue policies, make decisions, and take actions that benefit society

> **After reading the next four sections, you should be able to explain**
> 6 *to whom organizations are socially responsible.*
> 7 *for what organizations are socially responsible.*
> 8 *how organizations can choose to respond to societal demands for social responsibility.*
> 9 *whether social responsibility hurts or helps an organization's economic performance.*

shareholder model a view of social responsibility that holds that an organization's overriding goal should be profit maximization for the benefit of shareholders

6 To Whom Are Organizations Socially Responsible?

There are two perspectives as to whom organizations are socially responsible: the shareholder model and the stakeholder model. According to the late Nobel Prize–winning economist Milton Friedman, the only social responsibility that organizations have is to satisfy their owners, that is, company shareholders. This view—called the **shareholder model**—holds that the only social responsibility that businesses have is to maximize profits. By maximizing profit, the firm maximizes shareholder wealth and satisfaction. More specifically, as profits rise, the company stock owned by shareholders generally increases in value.

Friedman argued that it is socially irresponsible for companies to divert time, money, and attention from maximizing profits to social causes and charitable organizations. The first problem, he believed, is that organizations cannot act effectively as moral agents for all company shareholders. Although shareholders are likely to agree on investment issues concerning a company, it's highly unlikely that they have common views on what social causes a company should or should not support. For example, corporate donations to the Boy Scouts dropped significantly after the U.S. Supreme Court ruled 5–4 that the Boy Scouts do not have to accept homosexual troop leaders. JPMorgan Chase, Levi-Strauss & Co., Textron, and Wells Fargo have all stopped donating to the Boy Scouts. Tom Unger of Wells Fargo explained, "The Boy Scouts are as American as apple pie, but this was an easy decision to make. We really have to, as a company, return to what our core vision and values are, and that's to not discriminate." Yet while corporate donations are down, overall donations to the Boy Scouts have risen.[77] Rather than act as moral agents, Friedman argued, companies should maximize profits for shareholders. Shareholders can then use their time and increased wealth to contribute to the social causes, charities, or institutions they want, rather than those that companies want.

The second major problem, Friedman said, is that the time, money, and attention diverted to social causes undermine market efficiency.[78] In competitive markets, companies compete for raw materials, talented workers, customers, and investment funds. A company that spends money on social causes will have less money to purchase quality materials or to hire talented workers who can produce a valuable product at a good price. If customers find the

© DAVID YOUNG-WOLFF/PHOTOEDIT, INC.

The U.S. Supreme Court ruled that the Boy Scouts of America do not have to accept homosexual troop leaders. As a result, corporate donations to the Boy Scouts dropped, while personal donations rose.

company's product less desirable, its sales and profits will fall. If profits fall, the company's stock price will decline, and the company will have difficulty attracting investment funds that could be used to fund long-term growth. In the end, Friedman argues, diverting the firm's money, time, and resources to social causes hurts customers, suppliers, employees, and shareholders. Russell Roberts, an economist at George Mason University, agrees with this viewpoint. He says, "Doesn't it make more sense to have companies do what they do best, make good products at fair prices, and then let consumers use the savings for the charity of their choice?"[79]

By contrast, under the **stakeholder model**, management's most important responsibility is the firm's long-term survival (not just maximizing profits), which is achieved by satisfying the interests of multiple corporate stakeholders (not just shareholders).[80] **Stakeholders** are persons or groups with a legitimate interest in a company.[81] Since stakeholders are interested in and affected by the organization's actions, they have a "stake" in what those actions are. Consequently, stakeholder groups may try to influence the firm to act in their own interests. Exhibit 4.7 shows the various stakeholder groups that the organization must satisfy to assure its long-term survival.

stakeholder model a theory of corporate responsibility that holds that management's most important responsibility, long-term survival, is achieved by satisfying the interests of multiple corporate stakeholders

stakeholders persons or groups with a "stake" or legitimate interest in a company's actions

primary stakeholder any group on which an organization relies for its long-term survival

Being responsible to multiple stakeholders raises two basic questions. First, how does a company identify organizational stakeholders? Second, how does a company balance the needs of different stakeholders? Distinguishing between primary and secondary stakeholders can help answer these questions.[82]

Some stakeholders are more important to the firm's survival than others. **Primary stakeholders** are groups on which the organization depends for its long-term sur-

Exhibit 4.7

Stakeholder Model of Corporate Social Responsibility

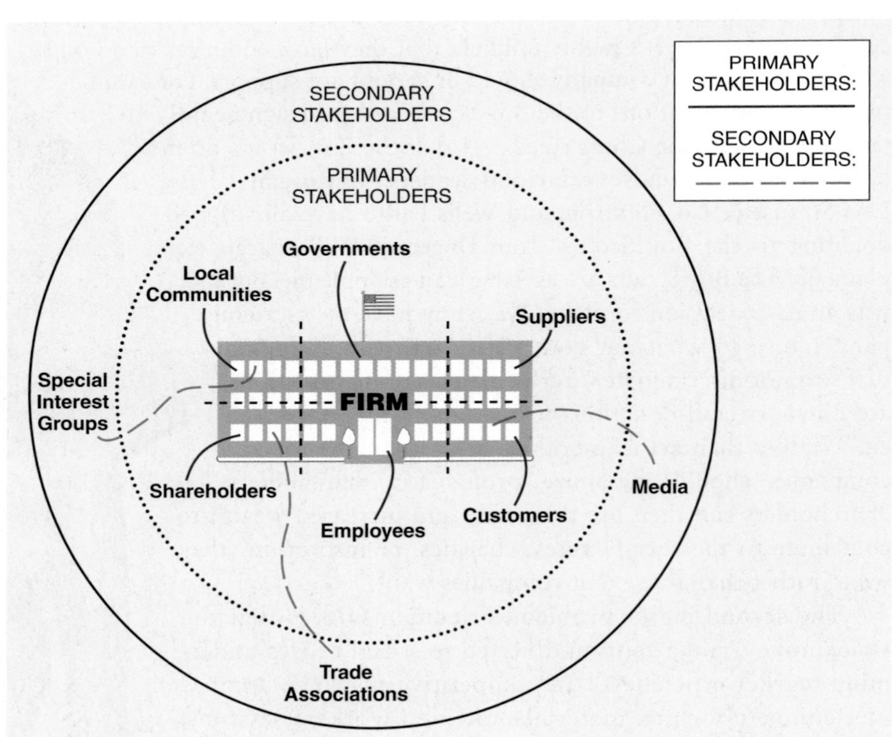

Source: Republished with permission of Academy of Management, P.O. Box 3020, Briar Cliff Manor, NY, 10510–8020. "The Stakeholder Theory of the Corporation: Concepts, Evidence and Implications" (Figure), T. Donaldson & L. E. Preston, *Academy of Management Review.* 1995, Vol. 20. Reproduced by permission of the publisher via Copyright Clearance Center, Inc.

vival; they include shareholders, employees, customers, suppliers, governments, and local communities. When managers are struggling to balance the needs of different stakeholders, the stakeholder model suggests that the needs of primary stakeholders take precedence over the needs of secondary stakeholders. But among primary stakeholders, are some more important than others? According to the life-cycle theory of organizations, the answer is yes. Which groups are primary at any given time depends on which life-cycle stage an organization is in. Organizations' needs change as they go through the life-cycle stages of formation/start-up, growth, maturity, and decline or transition. At each stage, different primary stakeholders will be critical to organizational well-being, and their concerns and issues will take precedence over those of other primary stakeholders.[83] In practice, though, CEOs typically give somewhat higher priority to shareholders, employees, and customers than to suppliers, governments, and local communities, no matter the life-cycle stage.[84] Exhibit 4.8 lists issues that organizations will probably have to address to keep their primary stakeholders satisfied.

Addressing the concerns of primary stakeholders is important because if a stakeholder group becomes dissatisfied and terminates its relationship with the company, the company could be seriously harmed or go out of business. With 4,300 drugstores, **WALGREENS** was one of **KODAK**'s key customers (and thus a stakeholder), selling two billion photo prints a year using Kodak paper and Kodak photo minilab machines. But with the growing popularity of digital photography, Kodak lost billions in sales because its film and film chemicals were no longer needed to make photos. Hoping to recapture lost sales, Kodak started Ofoto (**http://www.ofoto.com**), a website where customers can upload digital pictures to the Internet, view them, and then order prints directly from Kodak. Walgreens executives saw that Ofoto would cut them out of the print business. So even though it still had a $200 million agreement with Kodak, Walgreens installed 1,500 one-hour photo minilab machines (for traditional

Exhibit 4.8

Issues Important to Primary Stakeholders

Company	Company history, industry background, organization structure, economic performance, competitive environment, mission or purpose, corporate codes, and stakeholder and social issues management systems.
Employees	Benefits, compensation and rewards, training and development, career planning, employee assistance programs, health promotion, absenteeism and turnover, leaves of absence, relationships with unions, dismissal and appeal, termination, layoffs, retirement and termination counseling, employment equity and discrimination, women in management and on the board, day care and family accommodation, employee communication, occupational health and safety, and part-time, temporary, or contract employees.
Shareholders	Shareholder communications and complaints, shareholder advocacy, shareholder rights, and other shareholder issues.
Customers	Customer communications, product safety, customer complaints, special customer services, and other customer issues.
Suppliers	Relative power, general policy, and other supplier issues.
Public Stakeholders	Public health, safety, and protection, conservation of energy and materials, environmental assessment of capital projects, other environmental issues, public policy involvement, community relations, social investment and donations.

Source: M. B. E. Clarkson, "A Stakeholder Framework for Analyzing and Evaluating Corporate Social Performance," *Academy of Management Review* 20 (1995): 92–117.

After Kodak launched its own Ofoto.com website to sell photos directly to customers, Walgreens canceled its contracts with Kodak and began installing film processing kiosks from Fuji. Walgreens returned to Kodak after several months, however, because of quality problems with Fuji.

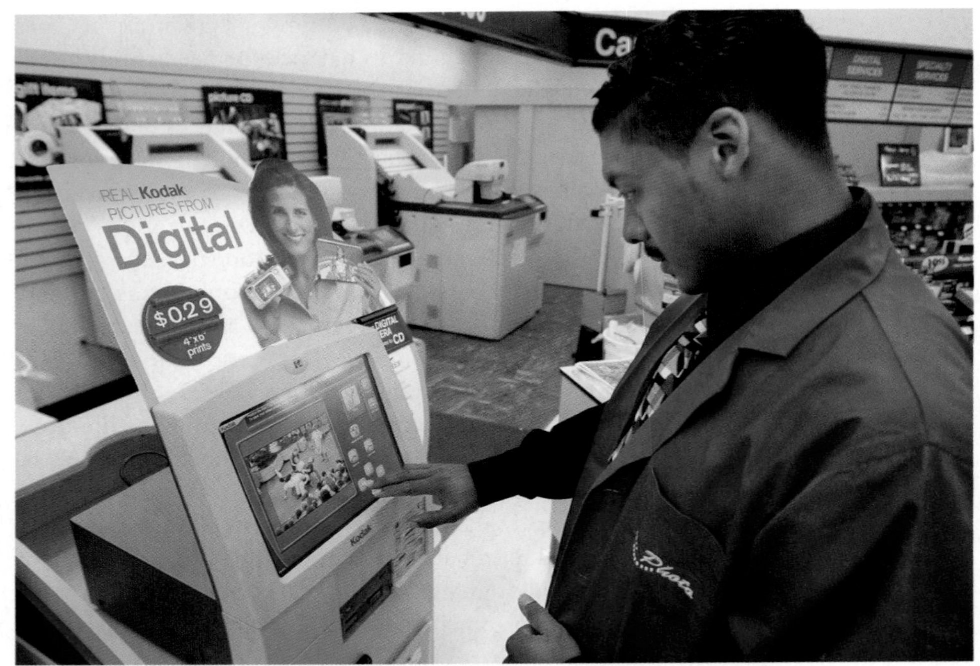

© JOHN FROSCHAUER/BLOOMBERG NEWS/LANDOV

film prints) and digital photo kiosks (for digital film prints) from Fuji, Kodak's main competitor. As Walgreens' Gordon Addington observed at the time, "You have to earn your way in, but you also have to earn your way out . . . Kodak did its best to earn its way out."[85] Walgreens' switch to Fuji cost Kodak $500 million a year in sales.

Secondary stakeholders, such as the media and special interest groups, can influence or be influenced by the company. Unlike the primary stakeholders, however, they do not engage in regular transactions with the company and are not critical to its long-term survival. Consequently, meeting the needs of primary stakeholders is usually more important than meeting the needs of secondary stakeholders. Nevertheless, secondary stakeholders are still important because they can affect public perceptions and opinions about socially responsible behavior. For instance, after hundreds of protests by animal-rights activists, including groups such as the People for the Ethical Treatment of Animals (PETA), **Smithfield Foods**, the nation's largest pork producer, announced that it would phase out "gestation crates" at all of its company-owned sow farms over the next decade. Gestation crates, 2 feet wide by 7 feet long, are used to confine female pigs during their 16-week gestation period. In this case, a secondary stakeholder, animal-rights activists, was able to mobilize public opinion and convince Smithfield Foods' primary stakeholders and large customers, such as McDonald's and Wal-Mart, to exert pressure on Smithfield to discontinue the practice. Smithfield is the first major pork producer to move to ban the crates, and others are sure to follow.[86]

So, to whom are organizations socially responsible? Many commentators, especially economists and financial analysts, continue to argue that organizations are responsible only to shareholders. Increasingly, however, top managers have come to believe that they and their companies must be socially responsible to their stakeholders. This view has gained adherents since the Great Depression, when General Electric first identified shareholders, employees, customers, and the general public as its stakeholders. In 1947, Johnson & Johnson listed customers, employees, managers, and shareholders as its stakeholders; and in 1950, Sears Roebuck announced that its most important stakeholders were "customers, employees, community, and stockholders."[87]

secondary stakeholder any group that can influence or be influenced by a company and can affect public perceptions about the company's socially responsible behavior

Today, surveys show that as many as 80 percent of top-level managers believe that it is unethical to focus just on shareholders. Twenty-nine states have changed their laws to allow company boards of directors to consider the needs of employees, creditors, suppliers, customers, and local communities, as well as those of shareholders.[88] So, although there is not complete agreement, a majority of opinion makers would argue that companies must be socially responsible to their stakeholders.

Review 6: To Whom Are Organizations Socially Responsible?

Social responsibility is a business's obligation to benefit society. To whom are organizations socially responsible? According to the shareholder model, the only social responsibility that organizations have is to maximize shareholder wealth by maximizing company profits. According to the stakeholder model, companies must satisfy the needs and interests of multiple corporate stakeholders, not just shareholders. However, the needs of primary stakeholders, on which the organization relies for its existence, take precedence over those of secondary stakeholders.

7 For What Are Organizations Socially Responsible?

If organizations are to be socially responsible to stakeholders, what are they to be socially responsible *for*? As Exhibit 4.9 illustrates, companies can best benefit their stakeholders by fulfilling their economic, legal, ethical, and discretionary responsibilities.[89] Exhibit 4.9 indicates that economic and legal responsibilities play a larger part in a company's social responsibility than do ethical and discretionary responsibilities. However, the relative importance of these various responsibilities depends on society's expectations of corporate social responsibility at a particular point in time.[90] A century ago, society expected businesses to meet their economic and legal responsibilities and little else. Today, when society judges whether businesses are socially responsible, ethical and discretionary responsibilities are considerably more important than they used to be.

Historically, **economic responsibility**, making a profit by producing a product or service valued by society, has been a business's most basic social responsibility. Organizations that don't meet their financial and economic expectations come under tremendous pressure. For example, company boards are very, very quick these days to fire CEOs. Typically, all it takes is two or three bad quarters in a row. Stagnant sales and declining profits led to Mary Forte's ouster as CEO of **ZALES**.[91] Kevin Rollins was relieved of his duties as CEO of Dell for a single bad quarter and for allowing arch-rival Hewlett-Packard to increase its lead over Dell.[92] Thomas Neff, who heads the executive recruiting firm Spencer Stuart, says, "It used to be a couple of years [and not two or three quarters]." William Rollnick, who became acting chairman of Mattel after the company fired its previous CEO, says, "There's zero forgiveness. You screw up and you're dead."[93] Indeed, in both Europe and the United States, nearly one-third of all CEOs are fired because of their inability to successfully change their companies.[94] In fact, CEOs are three times more likely to be fired today than two decades ago.

Legal responsibility is a company's social responsibility to obey society's laws and regulations as it tries to meet its economic responsibilities. For example, under

economic responsibility a company's social responsibility to make a profit by producing a valued product or service

legal responsibility a company's social responsibility to obey society's laws and regulations

Exhibit 4.9
Social Responsibilities

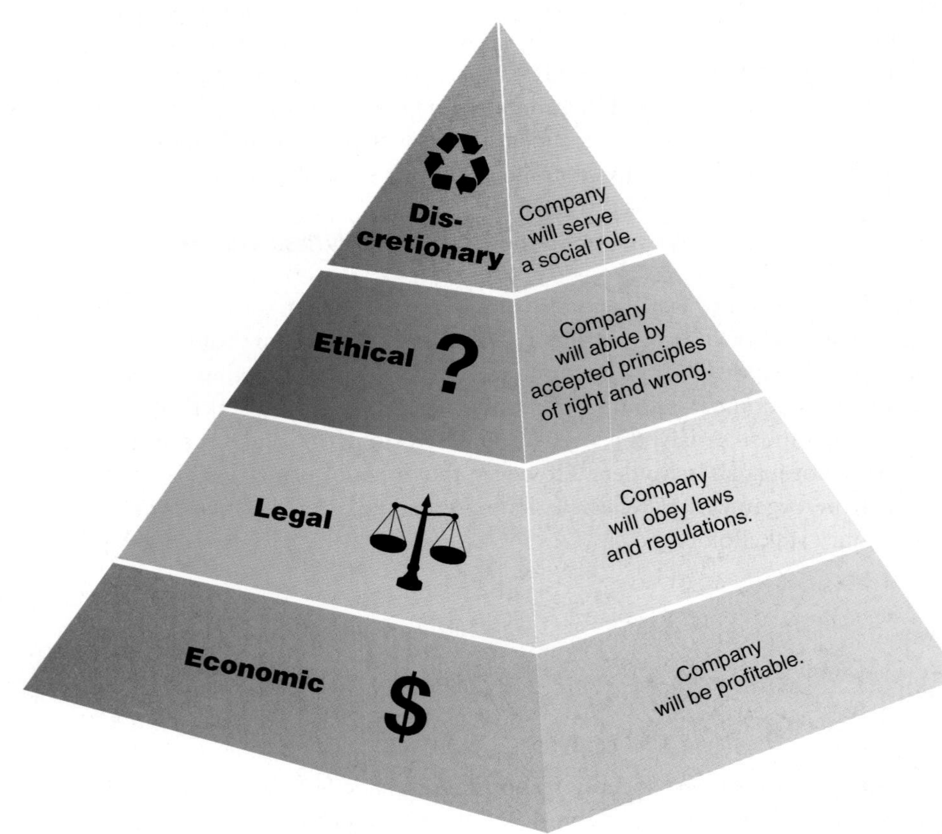

Source: Republished with permission of Academy of Management, P.O. Box 3020, Briar Cliff Manor, NY, 10510–8020. "A Three-Dimensional Conceptual Model of Corporate Performance." (Figure 3.3) A. B. Carroll, *Academy of Management Review,* 1979, Vol. 4. Reproduced by permission of the publisher via Copyright Clearance Center, Inc.

the 1990 Clean Air Act, the smell of fresh baked bread is now illegal. Actually, it's not the smell that is illegal, but the ethanol that is emitted when bread is baked.[95] Although ethanol itself is nontoxic, it contributes to pollution by promoting the formation of the harmful atmospheric compound ozone. Consequently, to meet the law, large bakery plants spent millions to purchase catalytic oxidizers that remove ethanol emissions.[96]

Ethical responsibility is a company's social responsibility not to violate accepted principles of right and wrong when conducting its business. For example, most people believe that ***KFC*** was wrong to run ads implying that its fried chicken was good for you and could help you lose weight. In one ad, one friend said to another, "Is that you? Man you look fantastic! What the heck you been doin'?" With his mouth full, the friend says, "Eatin' chicken." A voice-over then says, "So if you're watching carbs and going high protein, go KFC!" Pointing out that two fried chicken breasts contain 780 calories and 38 grams of fat, marketing consultant Marian Salzman says, "Marketers need to understand that you can't ask people to believe what isn't true."[97] Likewise, Michael Jacobsen, executive director of the Center for Science in the Public Interest, says, "These ads take the truth, dip it in batter and deep-fry it. Colonel Sanders himself would have a hard time swallowing this ad campaign."[98] After running the ads for a brief time, KFC quietly pulled them. Because different stakeholders may disagree about what is or is not ethical, meeting ethical responsibilities is more difficult than meeting economic or legal responsibilities.

ethical responsibility a company's social responsibility not to violate accepted principles of right and wrong when conducting its business

> Because different stakeholders may disagree about what is or is not ethical, meeting ethical responsibilities is more difficult than meeting economic or legal responsibilities.

Discretionary responsibilities pertain to the social roles that businesses play in society beyond their economic, legal, and ethical responsibilities. For example, dozens of companies support the fight against hunger at The Hunger Site, **http://www.thehungersite.com**. Each time someone clicks on the "donate free food" button (only one click per day per visitor), sponsors of The Hunger Site donate money to pay for food to be sent to Bosnia, Indonesia, Mozambique, or wherever people suffer from hunger. Thanks to the corporate sponsors and the clicks of 284 million visitors, nearly 49 million pounds of food have been distributed thus far.[99] Discretionary responsibilities such as these are voluntary. Companies are not considered unethical if they don't perform them. Today, however, corporate stakeholders expect companies to do much more than in the past to meet their discretionary responsibilities.

Review 7: For What Are Organizations Socially Responsible?

Companies can best benefit their stakeholders by fulfilling their economic, legal, ethical, and discretionary responsibilities. Being profitable, or meeting one's economic responsibility, is a business's most basic social responsibility. Legal responsibility consists of following a society's laws and regulations. Ethical responsibility means not violating accepted principles of right and wrong when doing business. Discretionary responsibilities are social responsibilities beyond basic economic, legal, and ethical responsibilities.

discretionary responsibilities the social roles that a company fulfills beyond its economic, legal, and ethical responsibilities

social responsiveness refers to a company's strategy to respond to stakeholders' economic, legal, ethical, or discretionary expectations concerning social responsibility

reactive strategy a social responsiveness strategy in which a company does less than society expects

Social responsiveness refers to a company's strategy to respond to stakeholders' economic, legal, ethical, or discretionary expectations concerning social responsibility. A social responsibility problem exists whenever company actions do not meet stakeholder expectations. One model of social responsiveness, shown in Exhibit 4.10, identifies four strategies for responding to social responsibility problems: reactive, defensive, accommodative, and proactive. These strategies differ in the extent to which the company is willing to act to meet or exceed society's expectations.

A company using a **reactive strategy** will do less than society expects. It may deny responsibility for a problem or fight any suggestions that the company should solve a problem. For example, in an attempt to treat all charitable institutions the same way, ***Target*** created a social responsibility problem by banning Salvation Army bell ringers with their red kettles from soliciting donations in front

Exhibit 4.10
Social Responsiveness

Reactive	Defensive	Accommodative	Proactive
Fight all the way	Do only what is required	Be progressive	Lead the industry

Withdrawal — Public Relations Approach — Legal Approach — Bargaining — Problem Solving

DO NOTHING ⟷ DO MUCH

SOURCE: A.B. CARROLL, "A THREE-DIMENSIONAL CONCEPTUAL MODEL OF CORPORATE PERFORMANCE," *ACADEMY OF MANAGEMENT REVIEW*, 1979, VOL 4 497-505.

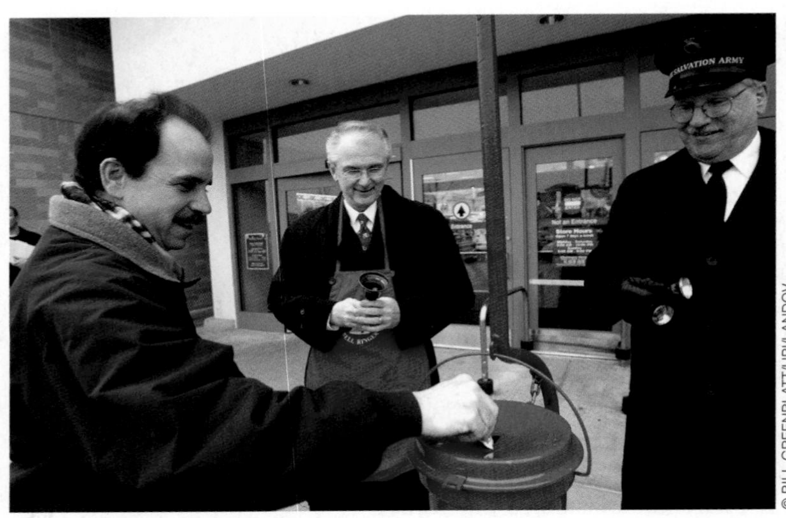
© BILL GREENBLATT/UPI/LANDOV

Even though Target maintains a policy against solicitation—even by the Salvation Army—Wal-Mart allows the holiday bell ringers to set up outside its stores and will match its customers' donations to the charity.

of its stores during the holiday season. A Target spokesperson says that because other nonprofit organizations made similar requests, "It's becoming increasingly difficult to have an exception to our policy, so we decided we would have no exceptions." Customer Phyllis McElaney spoke for many when she said this about Target's ban: "It's a disgrace. The bell ringers remind you of the meaning of Christmas, that it's about love, caring, and giving."[100] The ban also meant that the Salvation Army would have to find a way to replace the $9 million that Target customers typically donated each year. Wal-Mart, on the other hand, again welcomed the Salvation Army's bell ringers to its stores and pledged to match its customers' donations up to a total of $1 million.[101]

By contrast, a company using a **defensive strategy** would admit responsibility for a problem but would do the least required to meet societal expectations. **Second Chance Body Armor** makes bulletproof vests for police officers. According to company founder Richard Davis, tests indicated that the protective material in its vests deteriorated quickly under high temperatures and humidity, conditions under which they're typically used. As a result, Davis concluded that even vests that were only two years old were potentially unsafe. Nevertheless, he couldn't convince the company's executive committee to recall the vests (an accommodative strategy). Davis says he told the committee that it had three choices: recall the vests and stop selling them, do nothing and wait "until a customer is injured or killed," or wait until the problem becomes public and "be forced to make excuses as to why we didn't recognize and correct the problem."[102] After two vests were pierced by bullets, killing one police officer and wounding another, Second Chance announced that it would fix or replace 130,000 potentially defective vests. Although the company finally admitted responsibility for the problem, management decided to do only the minimum of what society expects (fix a defective product). Second Chance, therefore, used a defensive strategy.

A company using an **accommodative strategy** will accept responsibility for a problem and take a progressive approach by doing all that could be expected to solve the problem. For example, when an F4 tornado with winds of over 200 mph struck **Parsons Manufacturing** in Roanoke, Illinois, the metal-parts supplier's plant was completely destroyed. The owner, Bob Parsons, promised to rebuild. Workers continued to collect their paychecks as they helped with cleanup and reconstruction or with community service projects. A year later, the plant reopened and production was returned to 60 percent of its pre-tornado level. Dennis McCarthy, a director with the NOAA National Weather Service in Washington, D.C., presented Parsons with a Storm Ready Community Hero Award—only the second ever given. "It's important that we keep the Parsons story alive," McCarthy said. "I'm grateful. I'm humble," Bob Parsons said. "But I refuse to take all the credit for that. There were many other people involved." Parsons could have collected the insurance money and left, but he felt that workers were part of his extended family and the right thing to do was to rebuild.[103]

Finally, a company using a **proactive strategy** will anticipate responsibility for a problem before it occurs, do more than expected to address the problem, and lead the industry in its approach. Honda Motors announced that it will include side-curtain air

defensive strategy a social responsiveness strategy in which a company admits responsibility for a problem but does the least required to meet societal expectations

accommodative strategy a social responsiveness strategy in which a company accepts responsibility for a problem and does all that society expects to solve that problem

proactive strategy a social responsiveness strategy in which a company anticipates responsibility for a problem before it occurs and does more than society expects to address the problem bags (that drop from the roof and protect passengers' heads) and front-side air bags (that come out of the door to protect against side-impact collisions) as standard equipment on all of its cars. Although more expensive car brands, such as Lexus and Volvo, already included these safety features, Honda is the first to make them standard on all models. On most other cars, these features are optional, meaning that customers must pay extra for them. Brian O'Neill of the Insurance Institute for Highway Safety says, "This is a very positive development because we have been troubled by more and more manufacturers going the option route when it comes to safety equipment." Charlie Baker, Honda's vice president for U.S. research and development, says, "We are convinced this is the right direction and will save lives."[104]

Review 8: Responses to Demands for Social Responsibility

Social responsiveness is a company's response to stakeholders' demands for socially responsible behavior. There are four social responsiveness strategies. When a company uses a reactive strategy, it denies responsibility for a problem. When it uses a defensive strategy, it takes responsibility for a problem but does the minimum required to solve it. When a company uses an accommodative strategy, it accepts responsibility for problems and does all that society expects to solve them. Finally, when a company uses a proactive strategy, it does much more than expected to solve social responsibility problems.

9 Social Responsibility and Economic Performance

One question that managers often ask is, "Does it pay to be socially responsible?" Though understandable, asking whether social responsibility pays is a bit like asking if giving to your favorite charity will help you get a better-paying job. The obvious answer is no. There is not an inherent relationship between social responsibility and economic performance.[105] Nevertheless, this doesn't stop supporters of corporate social responsibility from claiming a positive relationship. For example, one study shows that the Domini 400 Social Index, which is a stock fund consisting of 400 socially responsible companies, has outperformed the Standard & Poor's 500 (an index of 500 stocks representative of the entire economy) by nearly 5 percent. At the same time, though, critics have plenty of facts to support their claim that social responsibility hurts economic performance. For example, another study of 42 socially responsible mutual funds found that they underperformed the Standard & Poor's 500 by 8 percent.[106]

When it comes to social responsibility and economic performance, the first reality is that being socially responsible can sometimes cost a company significantly. Boston-based **TIMBERLAND**, which makes an assortment of work and outdoor clothing and shoes, gives each of its employees a paid (yes, paid) week off each year to help local charities. For example, vice president Bonnie Monahan took four days off to organize a bike-a-thon that raised $50,000 to fight childhood cancer. Monahan, whose younger brother died from cancer, says, "Not too many companies will allow you to do this kind of stuff."[107] Each year, Timberland also gives four workers six months of paid leave so that they can work full-time for nonprofit organizations. Finally, Timberland closes the entire company for one day each year so that all of

its 5,400 workers can spend the day working on charitable projects sponsored by the company. This commitment to giving back doesn't come cheap. Indeed, closing down for one day costs Timberland $2 million. Furthermore, assuming that the average employee makes $50,000 a year, the cost of giving each employee a paid week off to do charitable work is at least $5 million. That's $7 million a year that doesn't go to Timberland's bottom line.

"What's New" Company

The second reality of social responsibility and economic performance is that sometimes it does pay to be socially responsible. The mission of **Worldwise**, which sells environmentally friendly consumer products, is "to make environmentally responsible products that work as well or better, look as good or finer, and cost the same or less as the competition." For example, its water bowls for pets are made out of 125 recycled bottle caps. Likewise, its ecoplanter, which looks like a heavy terra-cotta planter, is light, cheap, and made from 100 percent recycled plastic. In short, Worldwise doesn't think you should have to pay more for environmentally friendly products. In fact, its products are priced competitively enough to be sold in Wal-Mart, Target, and Home Depot. CEO Aaron Lamstein says, "Part of our concept is that we must have an incredibly focused mission that includes equally environmental and social issues and economic issues—that is, making sure that we have a really solid, healthy, financially secure business. You can't put one in front of the other. You can't be successful if you can't do both." The company, which is only 13 years old, has been profitable each of the last eight years.[108]

> Sometimes it does pay to be socially responsible.

The third reality of social responsibility and economic performance is that although socially responsible behavior may be "the right thing to do," it does not guarantee profitability. Socially responsible companies experience the same ups and downs in economic performance that traditional businesses do. A good example is **Ben & Jerry's**, the ice cream people. Ben & Jerry's started in 1978 when founders Ben Cohen and Jerry Greenfield sent away for a $5 course on how to make ice cream. Ben & Jerry's is as famous for its commitment to social responsibility as for its super premium ice cream. The company donates 7.5 percent of its pretax profits to support AIDS patients, homeless people, and the environment.[109] Moreover, customers buy Ben & Jerry's ice cream because it tastes great *and* because they want to support a socially responsible company. As Ben Cohen says, "We see ourselves as somewhat of a social service agency and somewhat of an ice cream company."[110] But—and this is a big but—despite its outstanding reputation as a socially responsible company, Ben & Jerry's consistently had financial troubles after going public (selling shares of stock to the public) a decade ago. In fact, its financial problems became so severe that Ben and Jerry sold the company to British-based Unilever.[111] Being socially responsible may be the "right thing to do," but it doesn't guarantee business success.

While Ben & Jerry's struggled, Seattle-based **Starbucks**, which also markets itself as a socially responsible company, grew from 11 to more than 8,836 gourmet coffee shops just in the United States, not to mention its stores in some three dozen other countries. Starbucks pays its coffee shop workers much more than minimum wage, provides full health insurance coverage to anyone who works at least 20 hours a week, and gives employees with six or more months at the company the opportunity to participate in its stock options program. Besides taking good care of its employees, Starbucks also makes an annual six-figure charitable contribution to CARE, an international relief agency, for feeding, clothing, and educating poor people in the coffee-growing regions where it gets its coffee beans.[112] Workers from its thousands of stores worldwide are paid to volunteer in community service programs, such as Earth Day cleanups, regional AIDS walks, and local literacy organizations. For example, Starbucks workers in its 19 New Zealand stores donate about

100 hours of volunteer work each week. Aasha Murthy, Starbucks' general manager in New Zealand, says, "Any company can write out a check to a worthy cause, send it off, and think nothing more of it, but that isn't what Starbucks is about. We've got an enormous amount of talent, energy, and passion in our business and that comes from our staff. So we decided to donate their skills. We want Starbucks New Zealand to be a successful organization, not just a profitable one, and there's more than one dimension to success. We want to reach out to the community we're part of."[113]

In the end, if company management chooses a proactive or accommodative strategy toward social responsibility (rather than a defensive or reactive strategy), it should do so because it wants to benefit society and its corporate stakeholders, not because it expects a better financial return.

Review 9: **Social Responsibility and Economic Performance**

Does it pay to be socially responsible? Sometimes it pays, and sometimes it costs. Overall, there is no clear relationship between social responsibility and economic performance. Consequently, managers should not expect an economic return from socially responsible corporate activities. If your company chooses to practice a proactive or accommodative social responsibility strategy, it should do so to better society and not to improve its financial performance.

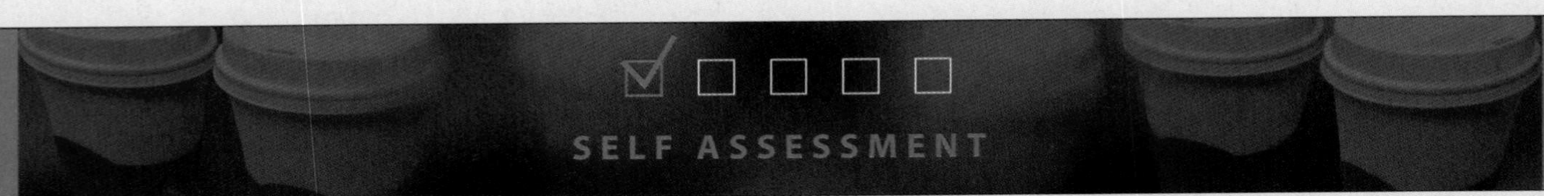

An Ethical Baseline

Most people think they are ethical, particularly when the right thing to do is seemingly obvious. But as you read in the chapter, 75 percent of the respondents in a nationwide survey indicated that they had witnessed unethical behavior at work. In another study across multiple industries, 48 percent of the respondents admitted to actually committing an unethical or illegal act in the past year! And recall that with so many ways to approach ethical decision making, ethical choices are not always cut and dried. To give you an idea of your ethical perspective, take this assessment.[114]

Answer each of the questions using the following scale:

1 Strongly agree
2 Agree
3 Not sure
4 Disagree
5 Strongly disagree

1. Did you ever think about taking money from where you worked, but didn't go through with it?
   1 2 3 4 5
2. Have you ever borrowed something from work without telling anyone?
   1 2 3 4 5
3. There are times I've been provoked into a fist fight.
   1 2 3 4 5
4. Is it okay to get around the law if you don't break it?
   1 2 3 4 5
5. I've had fellow employees show me how to take things from where I work.
   1 2 3 4 5
6. I will usually take someone up on a dare.
   1 2 3 4 5
7. I've always driven insured vehicles.
   1 2 3 4 5
8. If you were sent an extra item with an order, would you send it back?
   1 2 3 4 5
9. Would you say everyone is a little dishonest?
   1 2 3 4 5
10. Most supervisors treat their employees fairly.
    1 2 3 4 5
11. I worry about getting hurt at work.
    1 2 3 4 5
12. People say that I'm a workaholic.
    1 2 3 4 5
13. I like to plan things carefully ahead of time.
    1 2 3 4 5
14. Have you found a way a dishonest person in your job could take things from work?
    1 2 3 4 5
15. I often act quickly without stopping to think things through.
    1 2 3 4 5
16. It doesn't bother me what other people think.
    1 2 3 4 5
17. I have friends who are a little dishonest.
    1 2 3 4 5
18. I am not a thrill seeker.
    1 2 3 4 5
19. I have had my driver's license revoked.
    1 2 3 4 5
20. Are you too honest to steal?
    1 2 3 4 5
21. Do most employees take small items from work?
    1 2 3 4 5
22. Do most employees get along well with their supervisors?
    1 2 3 4 5
23. I'm lucky to avoid having accidents.
    1 2 3 4 5

KEY TERMS

accommodative strategy 142
concentration of effect 124
conventional level of moral development 125
defensive strategy 142
discretionary responsibilities 141
economic responsibility 139
employee shrinkage 118
ethical behavior 115
ethical intensity 124
ethical responsibility 140
ethics 114
legal responsibility 139
magnitude of consequences 124
overt integrity test 129
personal aggression 118
personality-based integrity test 129
political deviance 118
postconventional level of moral development 125
preconventional level of moral development 125
primary stakeholder 136
principle of distributive justice 127
principle of government requirements 126
principle of individual rights 127
principle of long-term self-interest 126
principle of personal virtue 126
principle of religious injunctions 126

24. I always finish what I start.
   1 2 3 4 5
25. I make sure everything is in its place before leaving home.
   1 2 3 4 5

Scoring

Determine your average score for each category by entering your response to each survey item below, as follows. In blanks that say *regular score*, simply enter your response for that item. If your response was a 4, place a 4 in the *regular score* blank. In blanks that say *reverse score*, subtract your response from 6 and enter the result. So if your response was a 4, place a 2 (6 − 4 = 2) in the *reverse score* blank. Total your scores then compute your average score for each section.

Antisocial Behavior

1. regular score	___	14. regular score	___
2. regular score	___	15. regular score	___
3. regular score	___	16. regular score	___
4. regular score	___	17. regular score	___
5. regular score	___	18. reverse score	___
6. regular score	___	19. regular score	___
7. reverse score	___	20. reverse score	___
8. reverse score	___		

TOTAL = ___ ÷ 15 = ___ (your average for Antisocial Behavior)

Orderliness/Diligence

12. regular score ___
13. regular score ___
24. regular score ___
25. regular score ___

TOTAL =
___ ÷ 4 = ___
(your average for Orderliness/Diligence)

Positive Outlook

9. reverse score ___
10. regular score ___
11. reverse score ___
21. reverse score ___
22. regular score ___
23. regular score ___

TOTAL =
___ ÷ 6 = ___
(your average for Positive Outlook)

You can find the interpretation for your scores at: **academic.cengage.com/management/williams.**

(continued)

Implementing Sustainability

Your heart is racing as you stand in front of the gathering of customers.[115] Though not usually at a loss for words, you are having trouble answering their questions about the dangers of the materials and processes used by your company, Interface, Inc., a manufacturer of commercial-grade carpet and flooring. What's more, when you hesitate, they doggedly persist. And none of the questions are about things you know, like discounts, lower prices, or inventory!

After you conclude the meeting, you race back to the office and convene a task force to respond to your customers' questions. But as soon as you assign the team its task, its members turn around and ask you to explain the company's environmental vision. "What vision?" you think to yourself. Desperately looking for inspiration, you happen upon a book by Paul Hawken entitled *The Ecology of Commerce: A Declaration of Sustainability*. You open it, hoping to glean some good ideas that you can repackage for your task force (and your customers).

Interface generates billions of dollars in revenue each year, but in the process, it extracts over 1 billion pounds of raw materials from the earth. The company is also a profligate water user, requiring millions of gallons a year for its manufacturing process—not to mention the petroleum-based materials consumed and the greenhouse gases emitted during the process. Furthermore, your product, carpet, is not recyclable. When people install new carpet, the old carpet is dumped in a landfill.

But Interface is not alone. The entire carpet industry works to the same standards. Competitors like Shaw Walker, J & J Industries, and C&A Floorcoverings use the same amount of materials, have essentially the same manufacturing processes, and generate the same amount of waste, all for products that can't be (or aren't) recycled.

After reading Hawken's book, you realize that Interface will have to change. The question is, how much? How much can Interface change its processes to be environmentally friendly without compromising the company's growth? Sustainability requires that products either be able to easily reenter nature without depositing toxins or be recyclable into new materials. For a manufacturing process to be sustainable, its net effect on the environment must be zero. That might mean using renewable resources, redesigning the process to eliminate all waste streams, or even creating a product that can be infinitely recycled. That's a lot to ask. Can you sustain the company if you adopt environmental sustainability as a vision?

Questions

1. Which level of social responsibility best describes your company's current operations?
2. What environmental vision do you communicate to your task force? In other words, what social responsiveness strategy will you adopt at Interface?
3. Can sustainability be economically viable for Interface? Defend your answer.

Sponsorship or Sellout

In the world of charitable organizations, the most grueling activity must certainly be fund-raising.[116] Although soliciting donations for popular causes can be easy, lesser-known nonprofits, which do very important work, may have difficulty consistently raising enough money to function. Sometimes, corporate sponsorship is necessary to obtain adequate funding. The obvious plus to corporate sponsorship is the cash, and perhaps greater visibility and legitimacy in the community (depending, of course, on the reputation of the sponsor). But corporate sponsorship can also have drawbacks. Potential donors may think that the charity no longer needs additional funding or withdraw support because they perceive that the charity has "sold out" to corporate financial inducements.

In considering a possible sponsorship, managers of charitable organizations can find themselves facing an ethical dilemma. Consider the following situation: A health-care foundation that is putting on a benefit concert to raise money to fund research on respiratory diseases signs up a popular regional band. Unable to cover the costs for the band, concert hall, decorations, and publicity, the foundation entertains an offer from operators of a new and controversial waste incineration plant, who are willing to put up $50,000 to become sponsors of the event.

Such situations are all too common in the world of nonprofit fund-raising, and getting these decisions right can often mean the difference between success and failure. To execute this management team decision, you will need to assemble a team of four to five students. Your management team will be working with the following scenario:

Women Against Violence (WAV) is a prominent local charity focused on providing victims of domestic violence with temporary housing, helping them cope with stress, and, in some cases, helping them begin a new life. During the 1990s, your management team was able to lift the fund-raising for WAV to all-time highs. Now, however, tight economic conditions have dried up donations. As WAV's management team is meeting to determine how and when to shut down operations, you receive a call from a local company, Famous Brewery and Bottling Company. Famous not only has its own brewery and specialty beers, but it also bottles and distributes beer for larger, nationally known beer brands. Famous is a progressive company with almost half its top management team comprised of women. But you also know that alcohol is involved in many domestic abuse situations.

You put the representative from Famous on speakerphone so the entire team can hear her. She proposes that Famous sponsor a spring festival to raise money for WAV. Famous will give WAV $40,000 to organize the festival (for advertising, tent and game rentals, concession stands, and so on), and WAV will receive all of the proceeds from the festival. In return, Famous wants to set up a booth at the festival and have its name and logo next to WAV's on any promotional materials, such as flyers, banners, and buttons. You thank the representative and turn off the phone. Turning to your team, you say, "So, do we take the money or not?"

You will be making a decision for or against corporate sponsorship for WAV by Famous Brewery and Bottling Company. Before beginning the exercise, review Exhibit 4.6.

Questions

1. Rank the ethical intensity of the decision. Consider assigning a numerical value to each of the six factors listed on page 124, on a scale of, say, 1 to 5. Add the six values together and assess the sum against a possible 30 points.
2. As a team, examine the situation through the lens of each of the principles of ethical decision making. What is your final decision?
3. What role did the ethical intensity of the decision play in your ultimate decision?

Discerning Unethical Behavior

Applying ethical judgment in an organizational setting can be challenging. This exercise offers you the opportunity to consider how you might approach such a situation as a manager in an investment firm.

Read the scenario and prepare your responses to the individual (homework) questions in advance of discussing this exercise in class.

Scenario

Imagine that you are a newly hired portfolio manager at Excalibur Funds. Although you're new to this job, you have eight years' experience in the mutual fund business. You left a larger and more established mutual fund company to join Excalibur because of its reputation as a bright, up-and-coming investment company, a place where someone like yourself could participate in building a new and dynamic investment company.

Your new fund, the Pioneer Fund, is a growth-oriented fund investing in small companies. Typically, the majority of the fund's stock investments is in high-technology companies. Pioneer is moving up fast in its peer group, and if the fund continues to perform well, you stand a good chance of being the manager recognized when it breaks into the top tier of performance.

One of the features that attracted you to this job is the opportunity to work with a seasoned group of traders, analysts, and staff professionals. The Pioneer Fund staff has averaged 10 percent turnover over the past five years, unusual in an industry where turnover commonly reaches 60 to 80 percent. After a month of working with your new team, however, you have noticed some troubling patterns. First, you felt that some of your staff were delaying or stonewalling you on several occasions when you requested more detailed information on particular trades. It took too long to get the information, and when you did receive it, the information looked a little *too* neat and well-organized. Second, the analysts have seemed guarded regarding their interaction with some of the technology companies in which the Pioneer Fund invests. On more than one occasion you've noticed analysts quickly ending phone calls when you entered the office, or minimizing computer screens when you walk by their desks. Finally, the group just seems a bit too *nice* when you are around. The investment business is often hectic and stressful. Shouting matches over investment decisions are not uncommon in this business, and grumbling is a second language. But all you get are smiles and charm.

So here you are at your desk on a Saturday evening, finishing off the last of a pot of coffee and planning for Monday morning. One thing is clear—you must begin to scratch below the surface of the Pioneer Fund team. Your gut tells you that something is wrong here, perhaps very wrong. For all you know you may be sitting on the next big investment scandal. Your head tells you that you have no hard evidence of unethical or illegal behavior, and that you'd better tread carefully. If your gut is wrong and you run around making hasty accusations you may lose what appears to be a very talented investment team.

What steps should you take starting Monday morning?

Preparing for Class Discussion

Complete the following steps individually in preparation for class discussion. Write your responses to the questions in each step.

Step 1: Understand the situation and key considerations. What considerations would be important to you in developing a plan of action in this situation? What resources might you draw upon to determine whether or not particular actions are unethical and/or illegal?

Step 2: Develop a plan of action. What steps would you follow in this scenario? What factors should you consider in planning your timing of these steps?

Step 3: Anticipate response(s). How might the Pioneer Fund employees respond to your plan of action? Develop a few scenarios.

Small Group and Class Discussion

Your professor will assign you to a small discussion group. Your group should discuss the following questions and be prepared to share your thoughts with the class:

1. What are the most difficult aspects of responding to a murky situation—those situations in which you sense the presence of unethical and/or illegal behavior, but you haven't seen unequivocal proof of wrongdoing?
2. What are the risks of waiting for unequivocal proof before beginning to take action? What are the risks of acting decisively based on your "gut" sense of a situation?
3. What is different about acting ethically/responsibly within an organizational environment/culture like that of the Pioneer Fund, versus acting ethically/responsibly as an individual? What are the particular challenges and dynamics associated with ethical and responsible behavior in an organization?

Examining Nonprofits

It is only the farmer who faithfully plants seeds in the Spring, who reaps a harvest in the Autumn.

—B. C. Forbes, founder of *Forbes* magazine

These assignments will help develop your present and future capabilities as a manager. Since stakeholders increasingly expect companies to do more to fulfill their discretionary responsibilities, chances are you and your company will be expected to support your community in some significant way. To begin learning about community needs and corporate social responsibility, visit a local charity or nonprofit organization of your choosing, perhaps a hospital, the Red Cross, Goodwill, Planned Parenthood, a soup kitchen, or a homeless shelter. Talk to the people who work or volunteer there. Gather the information you need to answer the following questions.

Questions

1. What is the organization's mission?
2. Who does the organization serve, and how does it serve them?
3. What percentage of the organization's donations is used for administrative purposes? What percentage is used to directly benefit those served by the organization? What is the ratio of volunteers to paid workers?
4. What job or task does a typical volunteer perform for the organization? How much time does a typical volunteer give to the organization each week? For what types of jobs does the organization need more volunteers?
5. How does the business community support the organization?
6. Why are you interested in the activities of this organization?

REEL TO REAL

BIZ FLIX
Emperor's Club

William Hundert (Kevin Kline), a professor at Saint Benedict's preparatory school, believes in teaching his students about living a principled life as well as teaching them his beloved classical literature. Hundert's principled ways are challenged, however, by a new student, Sedgewick Bell (Emile Hirsch). Bell's behavior during the 73rd annual Julius Caesar competition causes Hundert to suspect that Bell leads a less than principled life.

Years later Hundert is the honored guest of his former student Sedgewick Bell (Joel Gretsch) at Bell's estate. Depaak Mehta (Rahul Khanna), Bell, and Louis Masoudi (Patrick Dempsey) compete in a reenactment of the Julius Caesar competition. Bell nearly wins the competition, but when Hundert notices that Bell is wearing an earpiece and is cheating with an assistant's help, he gives him a question he knows he cannot answer. Earlier in the film Hundert had suspected that the young Bell also cheated during the competition, but Headmaster Woodbridge (Edward Herrmann) had pressed him to ignore his suspicion.

This scene appears at the end of the film. It is an edited portion of the competition reenactment. Bell announced his candidacy for the U.S. Senate just before talking to Hundert in the bathroom. He carefully described his commitment to specific values that he would pursue if elected.

What to Watch for and Ask Yourself

1. Based on the clip, what ethical principles do you think most inform William Hundert's thinking?
2. Describe Sedgewick Bell's level of moral development.

MANAGEMENT WORKPLACE
Organic Valley—Socially Responsible Farming

Organic Valley Cooperative planted its seeds in the lands and barns of a half-dozen family farmers in Wisconsin nearly 20 years ago. And although U.S. family farms seem to be a dying breed—more than 6 million have failed during this time period—Organic Valley is growing. Driven by the belief that meat, produce, and dairy products should be free of pesticides, antibiotics, and synthetic hormones, the first group of Organic Valley farmers set up a cooperative with an office in tiny LaFarge, Wisconsin, whose population is still less than 800. More and more farmers are joining the cooperative—and as consumer demand for organic products is increasing, so are sales. As a result, Organic Valley is adding 30 to 50 organizational staff employees per year. Growth like that requires greater management, particularly in the highly risky business environment of agriculture.

What to Watch for and Ask Yourself

1. In addition to the farmers, who are Organic Valley's other stakeholders?
2. Does it pay for Organic Valley to be socially responsible?

two

PART 2
Planning

Chapter 5
Planning and Decision Making

This chapter examines the benefits and pitfalls of planning, making plans work, and the different plans used in organizations. You'll also learn the steps and limitations of rational decision making and review various group decision techniques.

Chapter 6
Organizational Strategy

This chapter examines how managers use strategies to obtain a sustainable competitive advantage. Then you learn the strategy-making process and how companies answer these questions: What business should we be in? How should we compete in this industry? How should we compete against a particular firm?

Chapter 7
Innovation and Change

This chapter reviews the issues associated with organizational innovation. The first part of this chapter shows you why innovation matters and how to manage innovation to create and sustain a competitive advantage. In the second part of the chapter, you will learn about organizational change and about the risk of not changing.

Chapter 8
Global Management

In this chapter, we examine the impact of global business on U.S. firms and review the basic rules and agreements that govern global trade. You'll learn how and when companies go global. And you'll read how companies decide where to expand globally and confront issues like business climates and cultural differences.

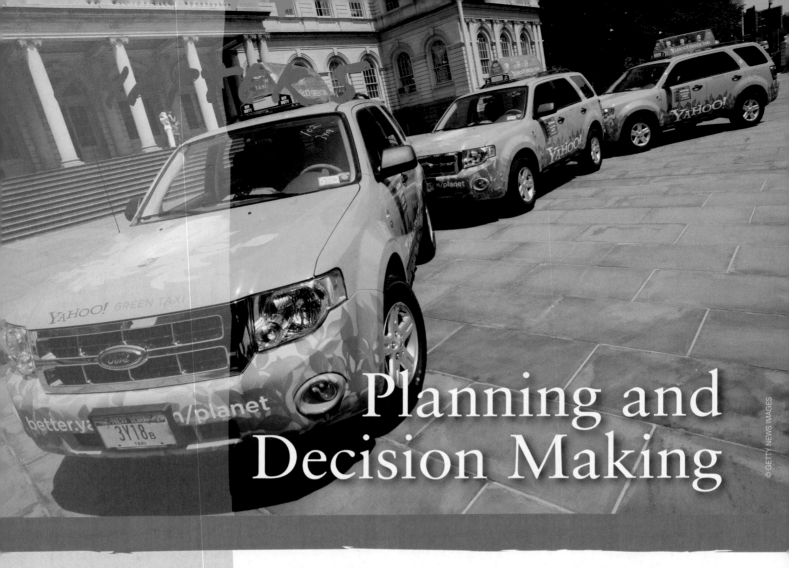

Planning and Decision Making

© GETTY NEWS IMAGES

Learning Outcomes:

1 Discuss the benefits and pitfalls of planning.
2 Describe how to make a plan that works.
3 Discuss how companies can use plans at all management levels, from top to bottom.
4 Explain the steps and limits to rational decision making.
5 Explain how group decisions and group decision-making techniques can improve decision making.

In This Chapter:

1 Benefits and Pitfalls of Planning

Are you one of those naturally organized people who always make a daily to-do list, write everything down so they won't forget, and never miss a deadline because they keep track of everything with their handy time management notebook or Palm PC? Or are you one of those flexible, creative, go-with-the-flow people who dislike planning and organizing because it restricts their freedom, energy, and performance? Some people are natural planners. They love it and can see only its benefits. Others dislike planning and can see only its disadvantages. It turns out that both views are have real value.

Planning has advantages and disadvantages. Let's learn about ***1.1 the benefits*** *and* ***1.2 the pitfalls of planning****.*

1.1 Benefits of Planning

Planning offers several important benefits: intensified effort, persistence, direction, and creation of task strategies.[5] First, as shown in Exhibit 5.1, managers and employees put forth greater effort when following a plan. Take two workers. Instruct one to "do your best" to increase production, and instruct the other to achieve a 2 percent increase in production each month. Research shows that the one with the specific plan will work harder.[6]

Second, planning leads to persistence, that is, working hard for long periods. In fact, planning encourages persistence even when there may be little chance of short-term success.[7] **McDonald's** founder Ray Kroc, a keen believer in the power of persistence, had this quotation from President Calvin Coolidge hung in all of his executives' offices: "Nothing in the world can take the place of persistence. Talent will not; nothing is more common than unsuccessful men with talent. Genius will not; unrewarded genius is almost a proverb. Education will not; the world is full of educated derelicts. Persistence and determination alone are omnipotent."[8]

The third benefit of planning is direction. Plans encourage managers and employees to direct their persistent efforts *toward* activities that help accomplish their goals and *away* from activities that don't.[9] For example, a large insurance company wanted to improve the performance evaluation feedback its managers gave employees. To help the managers improve, company trainers taught them 43 effective performance feedback behaviors, such as, "I will give my subordinate a clear understanding of the results I expect him or her to achieve" and "During the performance appraisal interview, I will be very supportive, stressing good points before discussing needed improvement." During the training, managers were instructed to choose just 12 behaviors (out of the 43) on which they wanted to make the most improvement. When subordinates rated their managers on the 43 behaviors, it became clear that no matter which 12 behaviors different managers chose to concentrate on, they improved only on those 12 behaviors. Thus, plans direct behavior toward activities that lead to goal accomplishment and away from those that don't.

The fourth benefit of planning is that it encourages the development of task strategies. In other words, planning not only encourages people to work hard for extended periods and to engage in behaviors directly related to goal accomplishment, it also encourages them to think of better ways to do their jobs.

Exhibit 5.1
Benefits of Planning

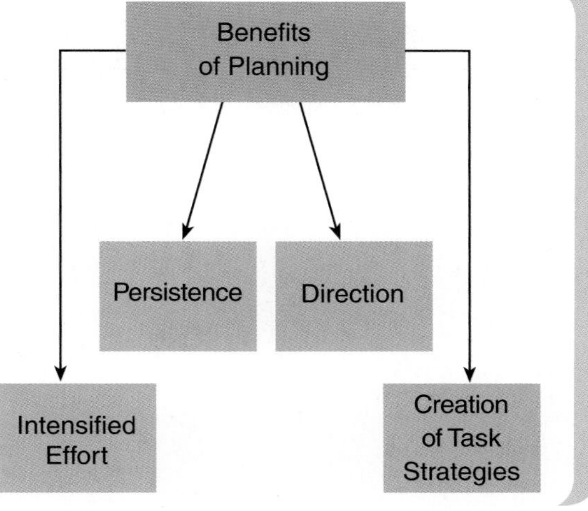

Despite the significant benefits associated with planning, planning is not a cure-all.

Finally, perhaps the most compelling benefit of planning is that it has been proved to work for both companies and individuals. On average, companies with plans have larger profits and grow much faster than companies that don't.[10] The same holds true for individual managers and employees: There is no better way to improve the performance of the people who work in a company than to have them set goals and develop strategies for achieving those goals.

1.2 Planning Pitfalls

Despite the significant benefits associated with planning, planning is not a cure-all. Plans won't fix all organizational problems. In fact, many management authors and consultants believe that planning can harm companies in several ways.[11]

As shown in Exhibit 5.2, the first pitfall of planning is that it can impede change and prevent or slow needed adaptation. Sometimes companies become so committed to achieving the goals set forth in their plans, or on following the strategies and tactics spelled out in them, that they fail to see that their plans aren't working or that their goals need to change. Ironically, **SONY**, one of the world's best known electronics innovators famous for its breakthrough Trinitron (picture tube) televisions, was one of the last major TV manufacturers to develop a line of flat-screen TVs. Sony's TV division was so committed to the old—and now outdated—Trinitron picture-tube technology that its engineers were reluctant to turn to Sony's audio, videogame, and computer monitor divisions for help and expertise in designing new flat-screen TVs. Makoto Kogure, who headed Sony's TV division, admits, "We did everything inside the TV group."[12]

The second pitfall is that planning can create a false sense of certainty. Planners sometimes feel that they know exactly what the future holds for their competitors, their suppliers, and their companies. However, all plans are based on assumptions. "The price of gasoline will increase by 4 percent per year." "Exports will continue to rise." For plans to work, the assumptions on which they are based must hold true. If the assumptions turn out to be false, then the plans based on them are likely to fail.

The third potential pitfall of planning is the detachment of planners. In theory, strategic planners and top-level managers are supposed to focus on the big picture and not concern themselves with the details of implementation, that is, carrying out the plan. According to management professor Henry Mintzberg, detachment leads planners to plan for things they don't understand.[13] Plans are meant to be guidelines for action, not abstract theories. Consequently, planners need to be familiar with the daily details of their businesses if they are to produce plans that can work.

Exhibit 5.2
Pitfalls of Planning

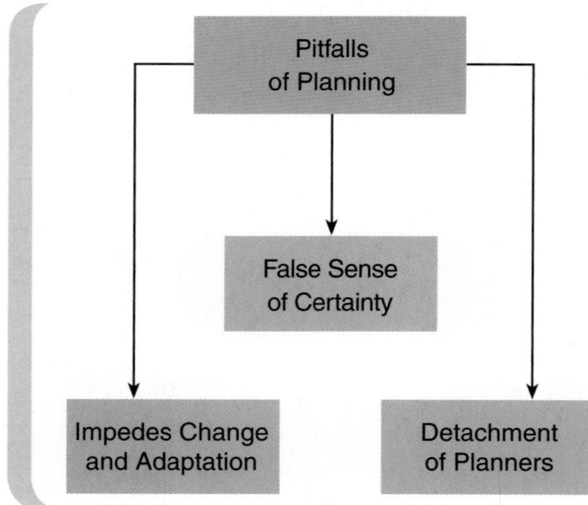

If you doubt that the "details" are important to good execution of a plan, imagine that you're about to have coronary bypass surgery to replace four clogged arteries. You can have either an experienced surgeon or a first-year medical intern perform your surgery. The intern is a fully qualified M.D. who clearly understands the theory and the plan behind bypass surgery, but has never performed such an operation. As you lie on the operating table, who is the last person you'd like to see as the anesthesia kicks in, the first-year intern who knows the plan but has never done a bypass or the experienced surgeon who has followed the plan hundreds of times? Planning works better when the people developing the plan are not detached from the process of executing the plan.

Review 1: Benefits and Pitfalls of Planning

Planning is choosing a goal and developing a method to achieve that goal. Planning is one of the best ways to improve organizational and individual performance. It encourages people to work harder (intensified effort), to work hard for extended periods (persistence), to engage in behaviors directly related to goal accomplishment (directed behavior), and to think of better ways to do their jobs (task strategies). Most importantly, companies that plan have larger profits and faster growth than companies that don't plan. However, planning also has three potential pitfalls. Companies that are overly committed to their plans may be slow to adapt to changes in their environment. Planning is based on assumptions about the future, and when those assumptions are wrong, the plans are likely to fail. Finally, planning can fail when planners are detached from the implementation of plans.

2 How to Make a Plan That Works

Planning is a double-edged sword. If done right, planning brings about tremendous increases in individual and organizational performance. If planning is done wrong, however, it can have just the opposite effect and harm individual and organizational performance.

In this section, you will learn how to make a plan that works. As depicted in Exhibit 5.3, planning consists of ***2.1 setting goals, 2.2 developing commitment to the goals, 2.3 developing effective action plans, 2.4 tracking progress toward goal achievement****, and* ***2.5 maintaining flexibility in planning****.*

2.1 Setting Goals

S.M.A.R.T. goals goals that are specific, measurable, attainable, realistic, and timely

Since planning involves choosing a goal and developing a method or strategy to achieve that goal, the first step in planning is to set goals. To direct behavior and increase effort, goals need to be specific and challenging.[14] For example, deciding to "increase sales this year" won't direct and energize workers as much as deciding to "increase North American sales by 4 percent in the next six months." Likewise, deciding to "drop a few pounds" won't motivate you as much as deciding to "lose 15 pounds." Specific, challenging goals provide a target for which to aim and a standard against which to measure success.

One way of writing effective goals for yourself, your job, or your company is to use the S.M.A.R.T. guidelines. **S.M.A.R.T. goals** are **S**pecific, **M**easurable, **A**ttainable, **R**ealistic, and **T**imely.[15] Let's see how a heating, ventilation, and air-conditioning (HVAC) company might use S.M.A.R.T. goals in its business.

Exhibit 5.3

How to Make a Plan That Works

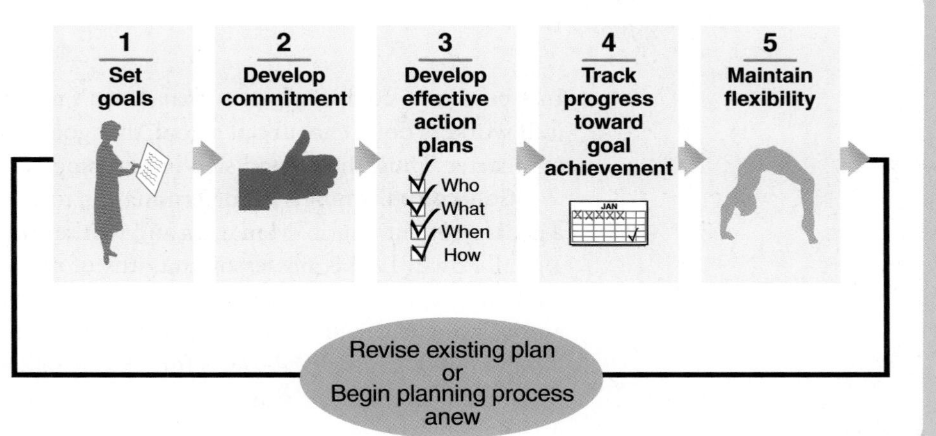

doing the right thing

Stretch Goals: Avoid the "15 Percent Delusion"

Stretch goals are extremely ambitious goals that you don't know how to reach. The purpose of stretch goals is to achieve extraordinary improvements in company performance. Stretch goals are so demanding that they force managers and workers to throw away old comfortable solutions and adopt radical, never-used solutions. Though stretch goals may encourage large improvements, they may also pressure people to do anything to meet "the numbers." The most common stretch goal CEOs set is "15 percent annual growth," the magical number that doubles corporate earnings every five years. But with earnings growth averaging just 8 percent over the last 40 years, the chances of achieving 15 percent growth every year are extremely low. So instead of promising generally unobtainable results, managers should set more realistic stretch goals. When Bob Eckert became CEO of Mattel, he dumped the company's stated goals of 15 percent annual earnings growth and 10 percent revenue growth. Says Eckert, "They were not realistic. We were not going to play that game anymore."[16]

The HVAC business is cyclical. It's extremely busy at the beginning of summer, when homeowners find that their air-conditioning isn't working, and at the beginning of winter, when furnaces and heat pumps need repair. During these times, most HVAC companies have more business than they can handle, while at other times of year their business can be very slow. So a *specific* goal would be to increase sales by 50 percent during the fall and spring, when business is slower. This goal could be *measured* by keeping track of the number of annual maintenance contracts sold to customers. This goal of increasing sales during the off-seasons is *attainable* because maintenance contracts typically include spring tune-ups (air-conditioning systems) and fall tune-ups (furnace or heating systems). Moreover, a 50 percent increase in sales during the slow seasons appears to be *realistic*. Because customers want their furnaces and air conditioners to work the first time it gets cold (or hot) each year, a well-designed pitch may make them very open to buying service contracts that ensure their equipment is in working order. Tune-up work can then be scheduled during the slow seasons, increasing sales at those times. Finally, this goal can be made *timely* by asking the staff to push sales of maintenance contracts before Labor Day, the traditional end of summer, when people start thinking about the cold days ahead, and in March, when winter-weary people start longing for hot days in air-conditioned comfort. The result should be more work during the slow fall and spring seasons.

2.2 Developing Commitment to Goals

Just because a company sets a goal doesn't mean that people will try to accomplish it. If workers don't care about a goal, that goal won't encourage them to work harder or smarter. Thus, the second step in planning is to develop commitment to goals.[17]

Goal commitment is the determination to achieve a goal. Commitment to achieve a goal is not automatic. Managers and workers must choose to commit themselves to a goal. Edwin Locke, professor emeritus of management at the University of Maryland and the foremost expert on how, why, and when goals work, tells a story about an overweight friend who finally lost 75 pounds. Locke says, "I asked him how he did it, knowing how hard it was for most people to lose so much weight." His friend responded, "Actually, it was quite simple. I simply decided that I *really wanted* to do it."[18] Put another way, goal commitment is really wanting to achieve a goal.

goal commitment the determination to achieve a goal

So how can managers bring about goal commitment? The most popular approach is to set goals participatively. Rather than assigning goals to workers ("Johnson, you've got till Tuesday of next week to redesign the flux capacitor so it gives us 10 percent more output"), managers and employees choose goals together. The goals are more likely to be realistic and attainable if employees participate in setting them.

Another technique for gaining commitment to a goal is to make the goal public. For example, college students who publicly communicated their semester grade goals ("This semester, I'm shooting for a 3.5") to significant others (usually a parent or sibling) were much more committed to achieving their grades. More important, those students earned grades that were nearly a half-grade higher than the grades of students who did not tell others about their grade goals. So, one way to increase commitment to goals is to "go public" by having individuals or work units tell others about their goals.

Another way to increase goal commitment is to obtain top management's support. Top management can show support for a plan or program by providing funds, speaking publicly about the plan, or participating in the plan itself.

"If workers don't care about a goal, that goal won't encourage them to work harder or smarter."

2.3 Developing Effective Action Plans

The third step in planning is to develop effective action plans. An **action plan** lists the specific steps (how), people (who), resources (what), and time period (when) for accomplishing a goal. Unlike most CEOs, Randy Papadellis has a unique goal that requires an extraordinary action plan. As the CEO of **OCEAN SPRAY**, Papadellis has to buy all of the cranberries that his farmers produce (Ocean Spray is a farmer cooperative) and buy the crop at the highest possible price. Then, it's Papadellis's job to figure out how to sell the entire crop of high-cost berries. He says, "Imagine if Pepsi had to maximize the aluminum it used, and at the highest price it could afford!" Under Papadellis's direction, Ocean Spray began looking for alternative uses for cranberries beyond the traditional juice and canned products. The company invented dried-fruit Craisins by reinfusing juice into husks that used to be thrown away. Craisins have grown into a $100 million product line. Ocean Spray also developed a set of light drinks that had just 40 calories, mock berries that could be infused with other flavors (such as blueberry and strawberry) and used in muffins and cereals, and was the first company to introduce juice boxes. Because these plans have worked to perfection, Ocean Spray has been able to increase the price it pays its farmers over 100 percent in the past three years.[19]

action plan the specific steps, people, and resources needed to accomplish a goal

proximal goals short-term goals or subgoals

distal goals long-term or primary goals

2.4 Tracking Progress

The fourth step in planning is to track progress toward goal achievement. There are two accepted methods of tracking progress. The first is to set proximal goals and distal goals. **Proximal goals** are short-term goals or subgoals, whereas **distal goals** are long-term or primary goals.[20] The idea behind setting proximal goals is that achieving them may be more motivating and rewarding than waiting to reach far-off distal goals. In a

© MATTHIEU BELANGER/REUTERS/LANDOV

Ocean Spray has been able to increase the price it pays its farmers over 100 percent in the past three years.

research study, Massachusetts Institute of Technology students were given a complex proofreading assignment; they were paid 10 cents for each error they found, but were penalized $1 a day for turning in their work late. One group of students was given a single deadline, that is, a distal goal, and told to turn in all of their work three weeks from the start of the study. A second group of students was given weekly deadlines, that is, proximal goals, and told to turn in one-third of their work each week. A third group of students was allowed to set their own deadlines; that is, they set their own proximal goals. The single-deadline students (those with no proximal goals, just a distal goal) were the worst performers: They turned in their work 12 days late and corrected only 70 errors. The students who were assigned weekly goals (proximal goals) were the best performers: They turned in their work only a half day late and corrected 136 errors. Next best were the students who set their own proximal goals: They turned in their work 6.5 days late and corrected 104 errors.[21] The lesson for managers is clear. If you want people to do a better job of tracking the quality and timeliness of their work, use proximal goals to set multiple deadlines.[22]

The second method of tracking progress is to gather and provide performance feedback. Regular, frequent performance feedback allows workers and managers to track their progress toward goal achievement and make adjustments in effort, direction, and strategies.[23] For example, Exhibit 5.4 shows the result of providing feedback on safety behavior to the makeup and wrapping workers in a large bakery company. The company had a worker safety record that was two-and-a-half

Exhibit 5.4

Effects of Goal Setting, Training, and Feedback on Safe Behavior in a Bread Factory

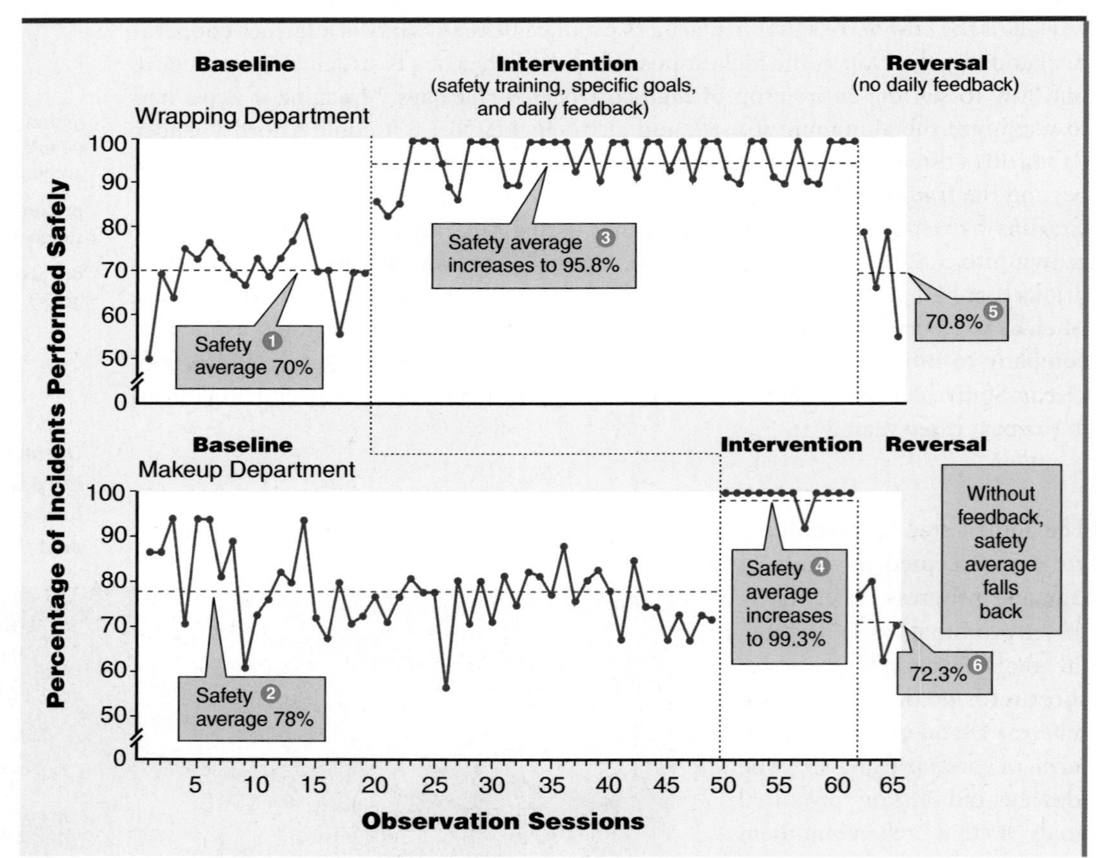

Source: © 1978 by the American Psychological Association. "A Behavioral Approach to Occupational Safety: Pinpointing and Reinforcing Safe Performance in a Food Manufacturing Plant." J. Komaki, K. D. Barwick, & L. R. Scott, *Journal of Applied Psychology*, 1978, V63. Reprinted with permission.

times worse than the industry average. During the baseline period, workers in the wrapping department, who measure and mix ingredients, roll the bread dough, and put it into baking pans, performed their jobs safely about 70 percent of the time (see ❶ in Exhibit 5.4). The baseline safety record for workers in the makeup department, who bag and seal baked bread and assemble, pack, and tape cardboard cartons for shipping, was somewhat better at 78 percent (see ❷). After the company gave workers 30 minutes of safety training, set a goal of 90 percent safe behavior, and then provided daily feedback (such as a chart similar to Exhibit 5.4), performance improved dramatically. During the intervention period, the percentage of safely performed behaviors rose to an average of 95.8 percent for wrapping workers (see ❸) and 99.3 percent for workers in the makeup department (see ❹), and never fell below 83 percent. Thus, the combination of training, a challenging goal, and feedback led to a dramatic increase in performance.

The importance of feedback alone can be seen in the reversal stage, when the company quit posting daily feedback on safe behavior. Without daily feedback, the percentage of safely performed behavior returned to baseline levels, 70.8 percent for the wrapping department (see ❺) and 72.3 percent for the makeup department (see ❻). For planning to be effective, workers need both a specific, challenging goal and regular feedback to track their progress. Indeed, additional research indicates that the effectiveness of goal setting can be doubled by the addition of feedback.[24]

2.5 Maintaining Flexibility

Because action plans are sometimes poorly conceived and goals sometimes turn out not to be achievable, the last step in developing an effective plan is to maintain flexibility. One method of maintaining flexibility while planning is to adopt an options-based approach.[25] The goal of **options-based planning** is to keep options open by making small, simultaneous investments in many options or plans. Then, when one or a few of these plans emerge as likely winners, you invest even more in these plans while discontinuing or reducing investment in the others. In part, options-based planning is the opposite of traditional planning. Whereas the purpose of an action plan is to commit people and resources to a particular course of action, the purpose of options-based planning is to leave those commitments open by maintaining **slack resources**, that is, a cushion of resources, such as extra time, people, money, or production capacity, that can be used to address and adapt to unanticipated changes, problems, or opportunities.[26] Holding options open gives you choices, and choices, combined with slack resources, gives you flexibility.

One example of options-based planning is **E.W. SCRIPPS**'s *Naples Daily News*, which has aggressively tried to counter the national trend in the newspaper industry of decreasing sales as the audience turns to the Internet for its news. Nationally, sales of daily newspapers are falling at rate of almost 3 percent a year. To increase readership, the *Naples Daily News* offers content via TV, radio, magazines, cell phones, PlayStations, and iPods. The newspaper posts a 15-minute video newscast on its website each day and offers services like calling readers at the end of each quarter in a football game to update the score. Publisher John Fish says profits are "a good bit higher than our print margins. It's just going to grow in the future. And if we don't provide the services, someone else will come up under us."[27]

Another method of maintaining flexibility while planning is to take a learning-based approach. In contrast to traditional planning, which assumes that initial action plans are correct and will lead to success, **learning-based planning** assumes that action plans need to be continually tested, changed, and improved as com-

options-based planning maintaining planning flexibility by making small, simultaneous investments in many alternative plans

slack resources a cushion of extra resources that can be used with options-based planning to adapt to unanticipated change, problems, or opportunities

learning-based planning learning better ways of achieving goals by continually testing, changing, and improving plans and strategies

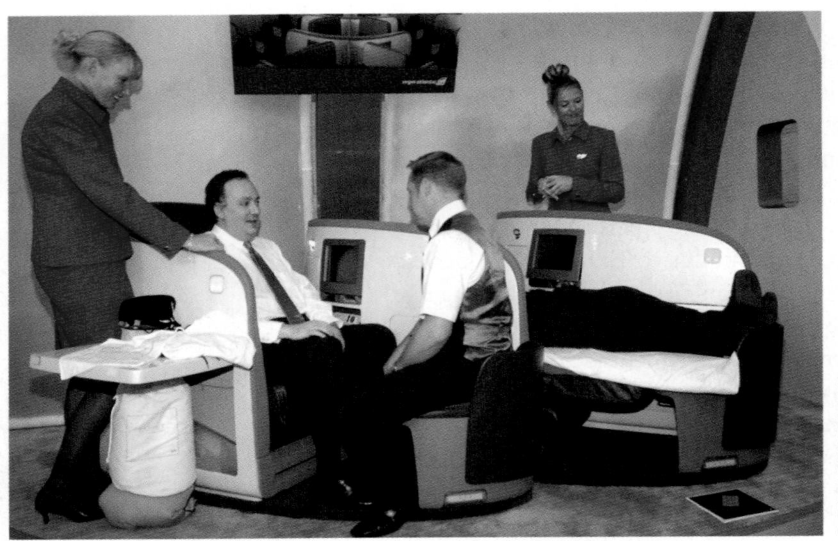

When a competitor came out with a better first-class seating option, Virgin Atlantic quickly changed its design plans and developed a first-class suite in advance of its original deadline.

panies learn better ways of achieving goals.[28] For example, Joe Ferry's design team at **Virgin Atlantic Airways** was charged with coming up with a new reclining sleeper seat for use in both the first- and business-class sections. Even though sleeper seats were common in first class, no one was using them in business class. Virgin hoped its plan to move the plush seats into business class would give it an edge against the competition. But the year Virgin started design and development, chief competitor British Airways launched a truly flat bed (not just a reclining seat) in business class, making Virgin's plan all but useless. Compounding Virgin's woes were customers complaining about sliding and discomfort when using the seat in the reclining position. Ferry describes the situation like this: "We were an also-ran, which didn't really sit well with us." So Virgin changed the plan and decided to focus on overhauling its first class seating well before it needed to be. This time, the airline asked Ferry's team to change from designing a seat to designing a suite and allocated $127 million to the project. Different from the first attempt, the seats in Virgin's so-called upper-class suite have been a hit with customers. That's because the new suite seats use two types of foam—one for sitting, one for sleeping—so that passengers are comfortable in both positions (no more sliding). Virgin expected the change in plan to increase market share by 1 percent, but only two years after launch, the new seats have allowed the company to exceed that goal.[29]

Review 2: How to Make a Plan That Works

There are five steps to making a plan that works: (1) Set S.M.A.R.T. goals—goals that are **S**pecific, **M**easurable, **A**ttainable, **R**ealistic, and **T**imely. (2) Develop commitment to the goals from the people who contribute to goal achievement. Managers can increase workers' goal commitment by encouraging worker participation in goal setting, making goals public, and getting top management to show support for workers' goals. (3) Develop action plans for goal accomplishment. (4) Track progress toward goal achievement by setting both proximal and distal goals and by providing workers with regular performance feedback. (5) Maintain flexibility. Keeping options open through options-based planning and seeking continuous improvement through learning-based planning help organizations maintain flexibility as they plan.

3 Planning from Top to Bottom

Planning works best when the goals and action plans at the bottom and middle of the organization support the goals and action plans at the top of the organization. In other words, planning works best when everybody pulls in the same direction. Exhibit 5.5 illustrates this planning continuity, beginning at the top with a clear

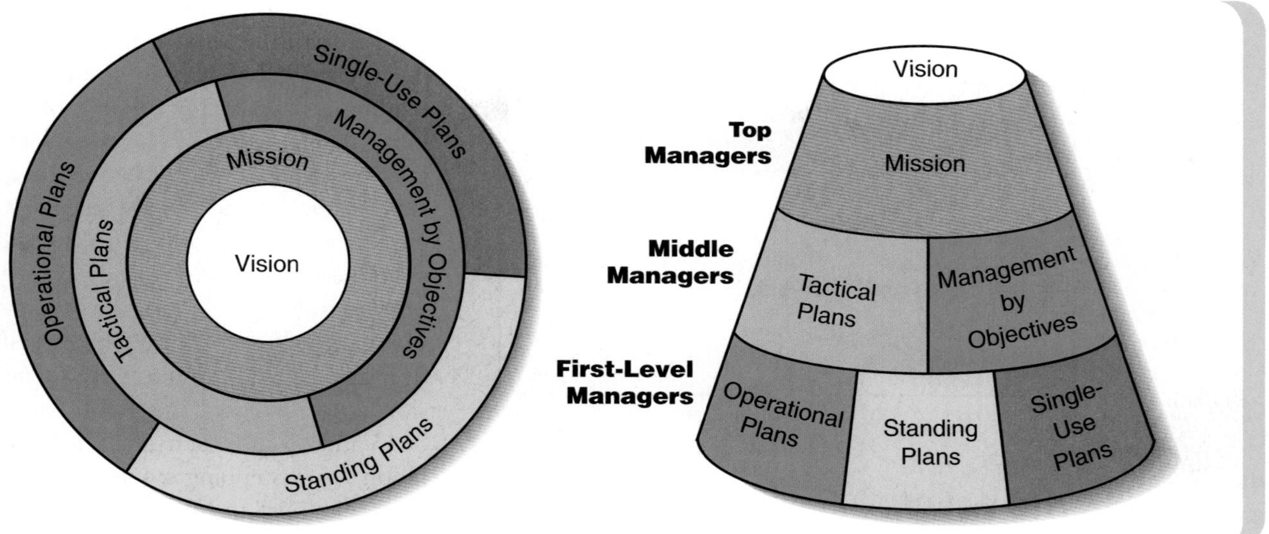

Exhibit 5.5

Planning from Top to Bottom

definition of the company vision and ending at the bottom with the execution of operational plans.

> *Let's see how **3.1 top managers create the organizational vision and mission, 3.2 middle managers develop tactical plans and use management by objectives to motivate employee efforts toward the overall vision and mission,** and **3.3 first-level managers use operational, single-use, and standing plans to implement the tactical plans.***

3.1 Starting at the Top

As shown in Exhibit 5.6, top management is responsible for developing long-term **strategic plans** that make clear how the company will serve customers and position itself against competitors in the next two to five years. (The strategic planning and management process is examined in its entirety in Chapter 6.) Strategic planning begins with the creation of an organizational vision and an organizational mission.

A **vision** is a statement of a company's purpose or reason for existing.[30] Vision statements should be brief—no more than two sentences. They should also be enduring, inspirational, clear, and consistent with widely shared company beliefs and values. An excellent example of a well-crafted vision statement is that of **AVON**, the cosmetics company, shown in Exhibit 5.7. It guides everyone in the organization and provides a focal point for the delivery of beauty products and services to the customer, women around the world. The vision is the same whether Avon is selling lipstick to women in India, shampoo packets to women in the Amazon, or jewelry to women in the United States. Understanding the needs of women—globally—does not change. Furthermore, Avon's vision is clear, inspirational, and consistent with Avon's company values and the principles that guide the company, also shown in Exhibit 5.7. Other examples of organizational visions that have been particularly effective include Walt Disney Company's "to make people happy" and Schlage Lock Company's "to make the world more secure."[31]

The **mission**, which flows from the vision, is a more specific goal that unifies company-wide efforts, stretches and challenges the organization, and possesses a finish line and a time frame. For example, in 1961, President John F. Kennedy

strategic plans overall company plans that clarify how the company will serve customers and position itself against competitors over the next two to five years

vision an inspirational statement of an organization's enduring purpose

mission a statement of a company's overall goal that unifies company-wide efforts toward its vision, stretches and challenges the organization, and possesses a finish line and a time frame

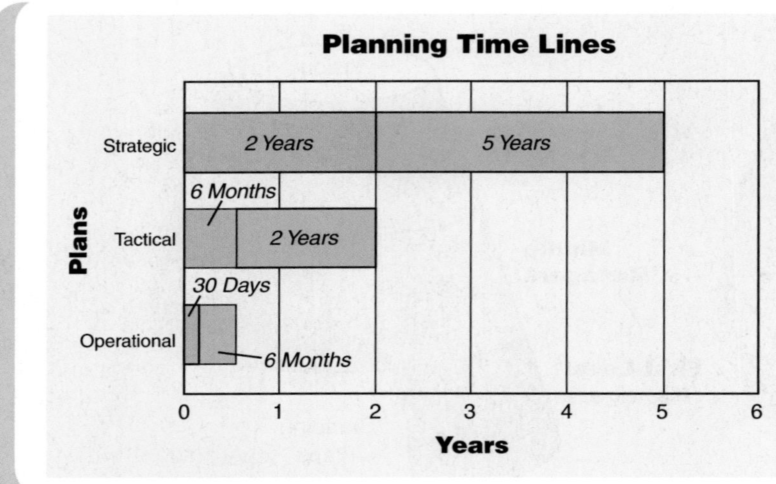

Exhibit 5.6

Time Lines for Strategic, Tactical, and Operational Plans

established an organizational mission for **NASA** with this simple statement: "Achieving the goal, before this decade is out, of landing a man on the moon and returning him safely to earth."[32] NASA achieved this goal on July 20, 1969, when astronaut Neil Armstrong walked on the moon. Once a mission has been accomplished, a new one should be chosen. Again, however, the new mission must grow out of the organization's vision, which does not change significantly over time. For example, NASA's new mission is to return to the moon "as early as 2015 and no later than 2020" and to use the moon "as a stepping stone for more ambitious missions" to Mars and beyond."[33]

3.2 Bending in the Middle

Middle management is responsible for developing and carrying out tactical plans to accomplish the organization's mission. **Tactical plans** specify how a company will use resources, budgets, and people to accomplish specific goals within its mission. Whereas strategic plans and objectives are used to focus company efforts over the next two to five years, tactical plans and objectives are used to direct behavior, efforts, and attention over the next six months to two years. For example, Craig Knouf, CEO of Associated Business Systems, a 110-person business that sells office equipment in Portland, Oregon, reviews his company's 30-page business plan monthly, semiannually, and annually to compare the company's actual performance with the goals set forth in the plan. When Knouf noticed that over a six-month period the company had sold more high-volume scanners than before, he changed his business plan to put more emphasis on scanners and scanning software. As a result, sales of scanning products, which will double this year over last, now account for one-third of all sales. Working without his business plan, says Knouf, "would be like driving a car with no steering wheel."[34]

tactical plans plans created and implemented by middle managers that specify how the company will use resources, budgets, and people over the next six months to two years to accomplish specific goals within its mission

management by objectives (MBO) a four-step process in which managers and employees discuss and select goals, develop tactical plans, and meet regularly to review progress toward goal accomplishment

Management by objectives is a management technique often used to develop and carry out tactical plans. **Management by objectives**, or MBO, is a four-step process in which managers and their employees (1) discuss possible goals; (2) participatively select goals that are challenging, attainable, and consistent with the company's overall goals; (3) jointly develop tactical plans that lead to the accomplishment of tactical goals and objectives; and (4) meet regularly to review progress toward accomplishment of those goals. Lee Iacocca, the CEO who brought the former Chrysler Corporation back from the verge of bankruptcy, credits MBO (though he called it a "quarterly review system") for his 30 years of extraordinary success as a manager. Iacocca says, "Over the years, I've regularly asked my key people—and I've had

Exhibit 5.7

Avon's Vision and Values

The Avon Vision	To be the company that best understands and satisfies the product, service and self-fulfillment needs of women—globally.
The Five Values of Avon	TRUST, RESPECT, BELIEF, HUMILITY, INTEGRITY.

Source: http://www.avoncompany.com/responsibility/values.html

MANAGEMENT BY OBJECTIVES

what really works.

For years, both managers and management researchers have wondered how much effect planning has on organizational performance, or indeed if it has any effect at all. While proponents argued that planning encourages workers to work hard, persist in their efforts, engage in behaviors directly related to goal accomplishment, and develop better strategies for achieving goals, opponents argued that planning impedes organizational change and adaptation, creates the illusion of managerial control, and artificially separates thinkers and doers.

Now, however, the results from 70 different organizations strongly support the effectiveness of management by objectives (that is, short-term planning).

MANAGEMENT BY OBJECTIVES (MBO)

Management by objectives is a process in which managers and subordinates at all levels in a company sit down together to jointly set goals, share information and discuss strategies that could lead to goal achievement, and regularly meet to review progress toward accomplishing those goals. Thus, MBO is based on goals, participation, and feedback. On average, companies that effectively use MBO outproduce those that don't use MBO by an incredible 44.6 percent. And in companies where top management is committed to MBO, that is, where objective setting begins at the top, the average increase in performance is an even more astounding 56.5 percent. By contrast, when top management does not participate in or support MBO, the average increase in productivity is only 6.1 percent. In all, there is a 97 percent chance that companies that use MBO will outperform those that don't! Thus, MBO can make a very big difference to the companies that use it.[35]

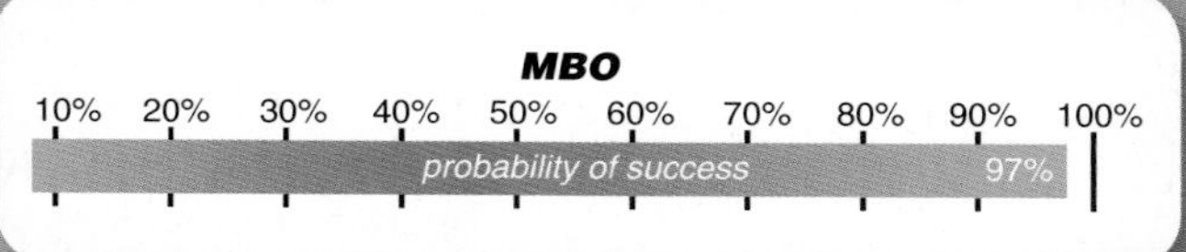

When done right, MBO is an extremely effective method of tactical planning. Still, MBO is not without disadvantages.[36] Some MBO programs involve excessive paperwork, requiring managers to file annual statements of plans and objectives, plus quarterly or semiannual written reviews assessing goal progress. Today, however, electronic and web-based management systems and software make it easier for managers and employees to set goals, link them to the organization's strategic direction, and continuously track and evaluate their progress.[37] Another difficulty is that managers are frequently reluctant to give employees feedback about their performance. A third disadvantage is that managers and employees sometimes have difficulty agreeing on goals. And when employees are forced to accept goals that they don't want, goal commitment and employee effort suffer. Last, because MBO focuses on quantitative, easily measured goals, employees may neglect important but unmeasured parts of their jobs. In other words, if your job performance is judged only by whether you reduce costs by 3 percent or raise revenues by 5 percent, then you are unlikely to give high priority to the unmeasured but still important parts of your job, such as mentoring new employees or sharing knowledge and skills with coworkers.

them ask *their* key people, and so on down the line—a few basic questions: 'What are your objectives for the next ninety days? What are your plans, your priorities, your hopes? And how do you intend to go about achieving them?'"[38]

> Working without his business plan, says Knouf, "would be like driving a car with no steering wheel."

3.3 Finishing at the Bottom

Lower-level managers are responsible for developing and carrying out **operational plans**, which are the day-to-day plans for producing or delivering the organization's products and services. Operational plans direct the behavior, efforts, and priorities of operative employees for periods ranging from 30 days to six months. There are three kinds of operational plans: single-use plans, standing plans, and budgets.

Single-use plans deal with unique, one-time-only events. For example, **PHILIP MORRIS** is relocating its headquarters and 682 employees from Park Avenue in New York City to Henrico County, Virginia. Although the move will cost $120 million, the company will save $60 million a year in operating costs. While stressing that this was a "difficult decision to make because of our company's long corporate history in New York City and the impact it will have on our employees," Philip Morris's chairman and CEO says, "This move will help to streamline our business operations, increase efficiencies, and deliver significant cost savings over the long run."[39]

Unlike single-use plans that are created, carried out, and then never used again, **standing plans** save managers time because once the plans are created, they can be used repeatedly to handle frequently recurring events. If you encounter a problem that you've seen before, someone in your company has probably written a standing plan that explains how to address it. There are three kinds of standing plans: policies, procedures, and rules and regulations.

Policies indicate the general course of action that company managers should take in response to a particular event or situation. A well-written policy will also specify why the policy exists and what outcome the policy is intended to produce. Because the average employee surfs the Internet 11.1 hours per week, many companies have policies of either monitoring or blocking access to non-work-related websites. After its monitoring policy failed, **CHAPARRAL ENERGY**, an oil and gas company, switched to software that blocks access to religious, political, or sexually oriented websites. Systems engineer Richard Underwood explains, "Out in the field offices [where oil and gas exploration occurs], there was an established rule that they weren't going by the [monitoring] rule. We wanted to make sure policies were followed."[40] Employee web surfing has now dropped from an hour to less than 15 minutes a day.

Procedures are more specific than policies because they indicate the series of steps that should be taken in response to a particular event. A manufacturer's procedure for handling defective products might include the following steps. Step 1: Rejected material is locked in a secure area with "reject" documentation attached. Step 2: Material Review Board (MRB) identifies the defect and how far outside the standard the rejected products are. Step 3: MRB determines the disposition of the defective product as either scrap or as rework. Step 4: Scrap is either discarded or recycled, and rework is sent back through the production line to be fixed. Step 5: If delays in delivery will result, MRB member notifies customer.[41]

Rules and regulations are even more specific than procedures because they specify what must happen or not happen. They describe precisely how a particular action should be performed. For instance, many companies have rules and regulations forbidding managers from writing job reference letters for employees who have worked at their firms because a negative reference may prompt a former employee to sue for defamation of character.[42]

Budgets are the third kind of operational plan. **Budgeting** is quantitative planning because it forces managers to decide how to allocate available money to best accomplish company goals. According to Jan King, author of *Business Plans to Game*

operational plans day-to-day plans, developed and implemented by lower-level managers, for producing or delivering the organization's products and services over a 30-day to six-month period

single-use plans plans that cover unique, one-time-only events

standing plans plans used repeatedly to handle frequently recurring events

policy a standing plan that indicates the general course of action that should be taken in response to a particular event or situation

procedure a standing plan that indicates the specific steps that should be taken in response to a particular event

rules and regulations standing plans that describe how a particular action should be performed, or what must happen or not happen in response to a particular event

budgeting quantitative planning through which managers decide how to allocate available money to best accomplish company goals

Plans, "Money sends a clear message about your priorities. Budgets act as a language for communicating your goals to others." For example, Exhibit 5.8 shows the operating budget outlays for the U.S. federal government. Together, social programs (Social Security and income security, or welfare) and health-care programs (Medicare and health) account for nearly 60 percent of the federal budget. Budgeting is a critical management task—one that most managers could do better. For more detailed information about budgeting, see *Essential Managers: Managing Budgets* by Stephen Brookson or *Budgeting Basics & Beyond: A Complete Step-by-Step Guide for Nonfinancial Managers* by Jae K. Shim and Joel G. Siegel. Both books are written for budget beginners.

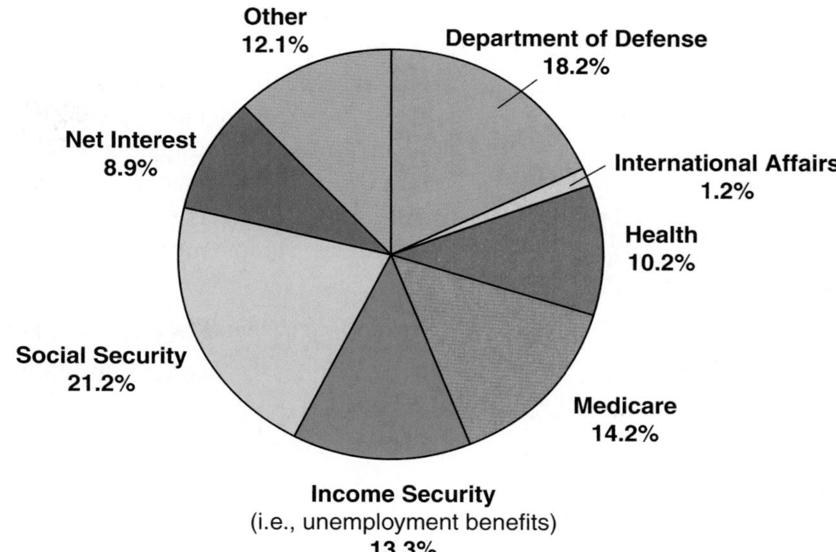

Source: "Table B-80. Federal Receipts and Outlays, by Major Category, and Surplus or Deficit, Fiscal Years 1940–2007," Economic Report of the President: 2006 Report Spreadsheet Tables, available at www.gpoaccess.gov/eop/2006/B80.xls.

Exhibit 5.8

2007 U.S. Federal Government Budget Outlays

Review 3: Planning from Top to Bottom

Proper planning requires that the goals at the bottom and middle of the organization support the objectives at the top of the organization. Top management develops strategic plans that indicate how a company will serve customers and position itself against competitors over a period of two to five years. Strategic planning starts with the creation of an organizational vision and mission. Middle managers use techniques like management by objectives to develop tactical plans that direct behavior, efforts, and priorities over the next six months to two years. Finally, lower-level managers develop operational plans that guide daily activities in producing or delivering an organization's products and services. Operational plans typically span periods ranging from 30 days to six months. There are three kinds of operational plans: single-use plans, standing plans (policies, procedures, and rules and regulations), and budgets.

WHAT IS RATIONAL DECISION MAKING?

Imagine that your boss asks you for a recommendation on outfitting the sales force, many of whom travel regularly, with new computers. She asks you to prepare a report that details the problems the sales team has been having with its computers and summarizes both current and future computer needs. You need to come up with at least five plans or options for getting computers to help members of the sales team do their job as efficiently as possible no matter where they are.

When your boss delegated this "computer problem," what she really wanted from you is a rational decision. **Decision making** is the process of choosing a solution from available alternatives.[43] **Rational decision making** is a systematic process in which managers define problems, evaluate alternatives, and choose optimal solutions that provide maximum benefits to their organizations. Thus, your boss expects you to define and analyze the computer problem and explore alternatives. Furthermore, your solution has to be "optimal," because the department is going to live with the computer equipment you recommend for the next three years.

After reading the next two sections, you should be able to

4 explain the steps and limits to rational decision making.

5 explain how group decisions and group decision-making techniques can improve decision making.

decision making the process of choosing a solution from available alternatives

rational decision making a systematic process of defining problems, evaluating alternatives, and choosing optimal solutions

problem a gap between a desired state and an existing state

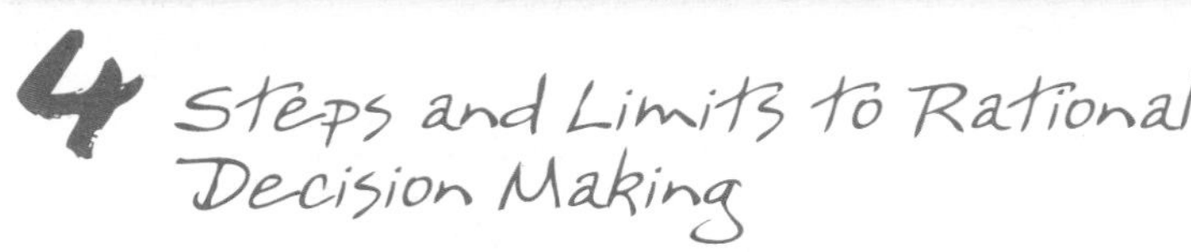

Exhibit 5.9 shows the six steps of the rational decision-making process. Let's learn more about each of these steps: ***4.1 define the problem, 4.2 identify decision criteria, 4.3 weight the criteria, 4.4 generate alternative courses of action, 4.5 evaluate each alternative****, and* ***4.6 compute the optimal decision****. Then we'll consider* ***4.7 limits to rational decision making****.*

4.1 Define the Problem

The first step in decision making is identifying and defining the problem. A **problem** exists when there is a gap between a desired state (what is wanted) and an existing state (the situation you are actually facing). Because it can hold 550 to 850 passengers, AIRBUS's new A380 super-jumbo jetliner could generate tremendous revenues for airlines. But with wings larger than a small passenger jet and wheels so large that it takes a crane to move them, the A380 was several tons too heavy. Randy Baseler of Boeing, Airbus's competitor, says, "If the plane's heavier, it consumes more fuel. That drives up landing and navigation fees, and also maintenance costs, especially for wheels, tires and brakes."[44] Fearing exorbitant costs, the airlines told Airbus they wouldn't buy the A380 unless it was substantially lighter.[45]

Exhibit 5.9

Steps of the Rational Decision-Making Process

1. Define the Problem
2. Identify Decision Criteria
3. Weight the Criteria
4. Generate Alternative Courses of Action
5. Evaluate Each Alternative
6. Compute the Optimal Decision

The existence of a gap between an existing state and a desired state is no guarantee that managers will make decisions to solve problems. Three things must occur for this to happen.[46] First, managers have to be aware of the gap. They have to know there is a problem before they can begin solving it. For example, after noticing that people were spending more money on their pets, a new dog food company created an expensive, high-quality dog food. To emphasize its quality, the dog food was sold in cans and bags with gold labels, red letters, and detailed information about its benefits and nutrients. Yet the product did not sell very well, and the company went out of business in less than a year. Its founders didn't understand why. When they asked a manager at a competing dog food company what their biggest mistake had been, the answer was, "Simple. You didn't have a picture of a dog on the package."[47] This problem would have been easy to solve, if management had only been aware of it.

The Airbus A380 is the largest passenger jet ever built. It's understandable that potential buyers of the two-story super-jumbo jet would be concerned about weight and fuel usage. Nose to tail, it's longer than this section of terminal where it's gated, and its 263-foot wingspan is nearly as long as a football field.

Being aware of the gap between a desired state and an existing state isn't enough to begin the decision-making process. Managers also have to be motivated to reduce the gap. For example, businesspeople have complained for years about unreasonable workplace regulation. Nevertheless, the ***U.S. Congress*** was not interested in solving this "problem" until the Congressional Accountability Act subjected Congress to the same laws as private businesses. Now, like any business, Congress must give overtime pay to anyone who works more than 40 hours a week. Legislative and office assistants, all of whom used to work 60 hours a week, are now limited by law to just 40. To limit hours and overtime pay, employees are not allowed to work during lunch (even if they want to). Computers are turned off. Phones go unanswered. Employees can't even watch C-Span while eating their sandwiches. At 6:00 PM, office managers walk through the offices, ringing loud bells and turning off lights to force employees who want to keep working to go home. Not surprisingly, these changes have motivated many in Congress to take a second look at the unintended effects that workplace laws and regulations have on businesses.[48]

Finally, it's not enough to be aware of a problem and be motivated to solve it. Managers must also have the knowledge, skills, abilities, and resources to fix the problem. So, how did Airbus reduce the weight of its A380 super-jumbo jet? Engineers achieved the biggest weight savings by substituting a light carbon-fiber composite material for heavier aluminum in the rear fuselage and the large structural ribs in the wings. Altogether, these changes and others reduced the A380's weight by four tons.[49]

4.2 Identify Decision Criteria

Decision criteria are the standards used to guide judgments and decisions. Typically, the more criteria a potential solution meets, the better that solution will be.

> The existence of a gap between an existing state and a desired state is no guarantee that managers will make decisions to solve problems.

Let's return to the employee who was given the responsibility for making a rational decision about the office computer setup. What general factors would be important when purchasing computers for the office? Reliability, price, warranty, on-site service, and compatibility with existing software, printers, and computers would all be important, but you must also consider the technical details. What specific factors would you want the office computers to have? Well, with technology changing so quickly, you'll probably want to buy computers with as much capability and flexibility as you can afford. Today, laptops account for over 25 percent of the market and their popularity is growing rapidly. They come in four distinct model types. There are budget models that are good for routine office work, but are usually saddled with a slower processor; workhorse models that are not lightweight, but have everything included; slim models for traveling but that usually require an external drive to read/write to a DVD/CD; and tablet models that include such items as handwriting-recognition software.[50] What will the users really need? Will they need to burn CDs and DVDs, or just read them? How much memory will the users need? How many files and programs will they need to store on their hard drive? What about Internet

decision criteria the standards used to guide judgments and decisions connectivity? Answering questions like these will help you identify the criteria that will guide the purchase of the new equipment.

4.3 Weight the Criteria

After identifying decision criteria, the next step is deciding which criteria are more or less important. Although there are numerous mathematical models for weighting decision criteria, all require the decision maker to provide an initial ranking of the criteria. Some use **absolute comparisons**, in which each criterion is compared with a standard or ranked on its own merits. For example, *Consumer Reports* uses this checklist when it rates and recommends new cars: predicted reliability, previous owners' satisfaction, predicted depreciation (the price you could expect if you sold the car), ability to avoid an accident, fuel economy, crash protection, acceleration, ride, and front seat comfort.[51]

Exhibit 5.10 shows the absolute weights that someone buying a car might use. Because these weights are absolute, each criterion is judged on its own importance, using a five-point scale, with "5" representing "critically important" and "1" representing "completely unimportant." In this instance, predicted reliability, fuel economy, and front seat comfort were rated most important, and acceleration and predicted depreciation were rated least important.

absolute comparisons a process in which each decision criterion is compared to a standard or ranked on its own merits

relative comparisons a process in which each decision criterion is compared directly with every other criterion

Another method uses **relative comparisons**, in which each criterion is compared directly with every other criterion.[52] For example, Exhibit 5.11 shows six criteria that someone might use when buying a house. Moving down the first column of Exhibit 5.11, we see that the time of the daily commute has been rated less important (−1) than school system quality; more important (+1) than having an inground pool, sun room, or a quiet street, and just as important as the house being brand new (0). Total weights, which are obtained by summing the scores in each column, indicate that the daily commute and school system quality are the most important factors to this home buyer, while an inground pool, sun room, and a quiet street are the least important. So with relative comparison, criteria are directly compared with each other.

Exhibit 5.10

Absolute Weighting of Decision Criteria for a Car Purchase

Highlighted numbers indicate how important the particular criterion is to a hypothetical car buyer. Your rankings might be very different.

5 critically important
4 important
3 somewhat important
2 not very important
1 completely unimportant

Criterion					
1. Predicted reliability	1	2	3	4	**5**
2. Owner satisfaction	1	**2**	3	4	5
3. Predicted depreciation	**1**	2	3	4	5
4. Avoiding accidents	1	2	3	**4**	5
5. Fuel economy	1	2	3	4	**5**
6. Crash protection	1	2	3	**4**	5
7. Acceleration	**1**	2	3	4	5
8. Ride	1	2	**3**	4	5
9. Front seat comfort	1	2	3	4	**5**

4.4 Generate Alternative Courses of Action

After identifying and weighting the criteria that will guide the decision-making process, the next step is to identify possible courses of action that could solve the problem. In general, at this step, the idea is to generate as many alternatives as possible. For instance, let's assume that you're trying to select a city in Europe to be the location of a major office. After meeting with your staff, you generate a list of possible alternatives: Amsterdam, the Netherlands; Barcelona or Madrid, Spain; Berlin or Frankfurt, Germany; Brussels, Belgium; London, England; Milan, Italy; Paris, France; and Zurich, Switzerland.

4.5 Evaluate Each Alternative

The next step is to systematically evaluate each alternative against each criterion. Because of the amount of information that must be collected, this step can take much longer and be much more expensive than other steps in the decision-making process. For example, in selecting a European city for your office, you could contact economic development offices in each city, systematically interview businesspeople or executives who operate there, retrieve and use published government data on each location, or rely on published studies such as Cushman & Wakefield Healy & Baker's *European Cities Monitor*, which conducts an annual survey of more than 500 senior European executives who rate 30 European cities on 12 business-related criteria.[53]

HOME CHARACTERISTICS	DC	SSQ	IP	SR	QS	NBH
Daily commute (DC)		+1	−1	−1	−1	0
School system quality (SSQ)	−1		−1	−1	−1	−1
Inground pool (IP)	+1	+1		0	0	+1
Sun room (SR)	+1	+1	0		0	0
Quiet street (QS)	+1	+1	0	0		0
Newly built house (NBH)	0	+1	−1	0	0	
Total weight	+2	+5	−3	−2	−2	0

Exhibit 5.11

Relative Comparison of Home Characteristics

No matter how you gather the information, once you have it, the key is to systematically use that information to evaluate each alternative against each criterion. For example, Exhibit 5.12 shows how each of the 10 cities on your staff's list fared on each of the 12 criteria (higher scores are better), from qualified staff to freedom from pollution. Although Paris has good access to markets and very good travel to and from the city, it has a poor business climate and relatively few different languages are spoken in its business community. On the other hand, Barcelona has the lowest costs for employing staff, but weak access to markets and poor ease of travel to and from the city.

4.6 Compute the Optimal Decision

The final step in the decision-making process is to compute the optimal decision by determining each alternative's optimal value. This is done by multiplying the rating for each criterion (Step 5) by the weight for that criterion (Step 3), and then summing those scores for each alternative course of action that you generated (Step 4). For example, the 500 executives participating in Cushman & Wakefield Healy & Baker's survey of the best European cities for business rated the 12 decision criteria in terms of importance as follows: qualified staff (57 percent felt this was important), access to major markets (60 percent), travel to and from the city (52 percent), good telecommunications (50 percent), positive business climate (32 percent), cost of staff (35 percent), cost and value of office space (31 percent), availability of office space (30 percent), travel within the city (22 percent), languages spoken in the business community (24 percent), quality of life (16 percent), and freedom from pollution (13 percent). Those weights are then multiplied by the ratings in each category. For example, Amsterdam's optimal value of 1.68 (that is, its weighted average) is determined by the following calculation:

$$(0.57 \times 0.35) + (0.60 \times 0.39) + (0.52 \times 0.66) + (0.50 \times 0.32) +$$
$$(0.32 \times 0.34) + (0.35 \times 0.16) + (0.31 \times 0.28) + (0.30 \times 0.26) +$$
$$(0.22 \times 0.34) + (0.24 \times 1.00) + (0.16 \times 0.30) + (0.13 \times 0.41) = 1.68$$

The weighted average (or optimal) scores in the next to last row of Exhibit 5.12 show that London clearly ranks as the best location for your company's new European office

	WEIGHTS	Amsterdam	Barcelona	Berlin	Brussels	Frankfurt	London	Madrid	Milan	Paris	Zurich
QUALIFIED STAFF	57%	.35	.30	.40	.44	.58	1.32	.30	.33	.78	.41
ACCESS TO MARKETS	60%	.39	.30	.28	.54	.71	1.36	.41	.38	1.18	.24
TRAVEL TO/ FROM CITY	52%	.66	.26	.19	.55	1.19	1.74	.30	.23	1.42	.27
TELECOMMU- NICATIONS	50%	.32	.21	.33	.40	.58	1.22	.24	.20	.80	.34
BUSINESS CLIMATE	32%	.34	.40	.36	.35	.11	.51	.52	.11	.20	.51
COST OF STAFF	35%	.16	.73	.27	.19	.05	.15	.60	.21	.11	.07
COST & VALUE OF OFFICE SPACE	31%	.28	.57	.52	.44	.26	.18	.48	.17	.20	.18
AVAILABLE OFFICE SPACE	30%	.26	.46	.63	.42	.45	.55	.58	.21	.39	.25
TRAVEL WITHIN CITY	22%	.34	.45	.53	.34	.41	1.09	.38	.19	1.19	.38
LANGUAGES SPOKEN	24%	1.00	.22	.34	1.13	.53	1.41	.21	.17	.50	.66
QUALITY OF LIFE	16%	.30	1.21	.24	.38	.14	.39	.61	.26	.67	.55
FREEDOM FROM POLLUTION	13%	.41	.44	.17	.18	.12	.06	.16	.03	.10	.94
WEIGHTED AVERAGE SCORE		1.68	1.69	1.48	1.93	2.20	4.17	1.63	.99	3.07	1.36
RANKING		6	5	8	4	3	1	7	11	2	10

Source: "European Cities Monitor," Cushman & Wakefield Healy & Baker, available at http://www.cushmanwakefield.com/cwglobal/docviewer/European%20Cities%20Monitor.pdf?id=ca1500006&repositoryKey=CoreRepository&itemDesc=document.

Exhibit 5.12

Criteria Ratings Used to Determine the Best Locations in Europe for a New Office

because of its large number of qualified staff; easy access to markets; outstanding ease of travel to, from, and within the city; excellent telecommunications; and top-notch business climate.

4.7 Limits to Rational Decision Making

In general, managers who diligently complete all six steps of the rational decision-making model will make better decisions than those who don't. So, when they can, managers should try to follow the steps in the rational decision-making model, especially for big decisions with long-range consequences.

It's highly doubtful, however, that rational decision making can always help managers choose *optimal* solutions that provide *maximum* benefits to their organizations.

The terms *optimal* and *maximum* suggest that rational decision making leads to perfect or near-perfect decisions. Of course, for managers to make perfect decisions, they have to operate in perfect worlds with no real-world constraints. For example, in an optimal world, the manager who asked you to develop a computer strategy for the sales team would be able to clearly define which salespeople needed budget laptops, slim laptops, workhorse laptops, or tablet laptops and simply ensure that all team members received exactly what they needed to do their jobs effectively. In developing your solutions, you would not have been constrained by price or time. Furthermore, without any constraints, the manager could identify and weight an extensive list of decision criteria, generate a complete list of possible solutions, and then test and evaluate each computer against each decision criterion. Finally, the manager would have the necessary experience and knowledge with computers to easily make sense of all these sophisticated tests and information.

Of course, it never works like that in the real world. Managers face time and money constraints. They often don't have time to make extensive lists of decision criteria. And they often don't have the resources to test all possible solutions against all possible criteria.

The rational decision-making model describes the way decisions *should* be made. In other words, decision makers wanting to make optimal decisions *should not* have to face time and cost constraints. They *should* have unlimited resources and time to generate and test all alternative solutions against all decision criteria. And they *should* be willing to recommend any decision that produces optimal benefits for the company, even if that decision would harm their own jobs or departments. Of course, very few managers actually make rational decisions the way they *should*. The way in which managers actually make decisions is more accurately described as bounded (or limited) rationality. **Bounded rationality** means that managers try to take a rational approach to decision making, but are restricted by real-world constraints, incomplete and imperfect information, and their own limited decision-making capabilities.

In theory, fully rational decision makers **maximize** decisions by choosing the optimal solution. In practice, however, limited resources, along with attention, memory, and expertise problems, make it nearly impossible for managers to maximize decisions. Consequently, most managers don't maximize—they "satisfice." Whereas maximizing is choosing the best alternative, **satisficing** is choosing a "good enough" alternative. With 24 decision criteria, 50 alternative computers to choose from, two computer labs with hundreds of thousands of dollars of equipment, and unlimited time and money, the manager could test all alternatives against all decision criteria and choose the "perfect PC." In reality, however, the manager's limited time, money, and expertise mean that only a few alternatives will be assessed against a few decision criteria. In practice, the manager will visit two or three computer or electronic stores, read a couple of recent computer reviews, and get bids from a few local computer stores that sell complete computer systems at competitive prices, as well as from Dell, Lenovo, Gateway, and Hewlett-Packard. The decision will be complete when the manager finds a "good enough" laptop computer that meets a few decision criteria.

© EMPICS/LANDOV

bounded rationality a decision-making process restricted in the real world by limited resources, incomplete and imperfect information, and managers' limited decision-making capabilities

maximizing choosing the best alternative

satisficing choosing a "good enough" alternative

doing the right thing

PLUS—A Process for Ethical Decision Making

People are often unsure how to include ethics in their decision-making processes. To help them, the Ethics Resource Center recommends using the following PLUS guidelines throughout the various steps of the rational decision-making model:

- **P is for policies. Is your decision consistent with your organization's policies, procedures, and guidelines?**
- **L is for legal. Is your decision acceptable under applicable laws and regulations?**
- **U is for universal. Is your decision consistent with your organization's values and principles?**
- **S is for self. Does your decision satisfy your personal sense of right, good, and fair?**

The PLUS guidelines can't guarantee ethical decisions, but they can help employees be more attentive to ethical issues as they define problems, evaluate alternatives, and choose solutions.[54]

Review 4: *Steps and Limits to Rational Decision Making*

Rational decision making is a six-step process in which managers define problems, evaluate alternatives, and compute optimal solutions. The first step is identifying and defining the problem. Problems exist where there is a gap between desired and existing states. Managers won't begin the decision-making process unless they are aware of the gap, motivated to reduce it, and possess the necessary resources to fix it. The second step is defining the decision criteria that are used when judging alternatives. In Step 3, an absolute or relative comparison process is used to rate the importance of the decision criteria. Step 4 involves generating as many alternative courses of action (that is, solutions) as possible. Potential solutions are assessed in Step 5 by systematically gathering information and evaluating each alternative against each criterion. In Step 6, criterion ratings and weights are used to compute the optimal value for each alternative course of action. Rational managers then choose the alternative with the highest optimal value.

The rational decision-making model describes how decisions should be made in an ideal world without limits. However, bounded rationality recognizes that in the real world, managers' limited resources, incomplete and imperfect information, and limited decision-making capabilities restrict their decision-making processes. These limitations often prevent managers from being rational decision makers.

According to a study reported in *Fortune* magazine, 91 percent of U.S. companies use teams and groups to solve specific problems (that is, make decisions).[55] Why so many? Because when done properly, group decision making can lead to much better decisions than decisions typically made by individuals. In fact, numerous studies show that groups consistently outperform individuals on complex tasks.

Let's explore the ***5.1 advantages and pitfalls of group decision making*** *and see how the following group decision-making methods—**5.2 structured conflict**, **5.3 the nominal group technique**, **5.4 the Delphi technique**, **5.5 the stepladder technique**, and **5.6 electronic brainstorming**—can be used to improve decision making.*

5.1 Advantages and Pitfalls of Group Decision Making

Groups can do a much better job than individuals in two important steps of the decision-making process: defining the problem and generating alternative solutions. Four reasons explain why.

First, because group members usually possess different knowledge, skills, abilities, and experiences, groups are able to view problems from multiple perspectives. Being able to view problems from different perspectives, in turn, can help groups perform better on complex tasks and make better decisions than individuals.[56]

Second, groups can find and access much more information than can individuals alone. At **1-800-Got-Junk?**, a national chain of over 200 locations that provides efficient, timely junk removal, applicants are not interviewed by one person at a time. Instead, each applicant is interviewed by a group of eight people with eight different areas of expertise, who, together, assess the candidate immediately following the interview. CEO Brian Scudamore believes there is wisdom in crowds, and relying on groups to conduct interviews has helped his company maintain a remarkably low employee turnover rate of only 1.4 percent.[57]

Third, the increased knowledge and information available to groups make it easier for them to generate more alternative solutions. Studies show that generating lots of alternative solutions is critical to improving the quality of decisions. Fourth, if groups are involved in the decision-making process, group members will be more committed to making chosen solutions work.

Although groups can do a better job of defining problems and generating alternative solutions, group decision making is subject to some pitfalls that can quickly erase these gains. One possible pitfall is groupthink. **Groupthink** occurs in highly cohesive groups when group members feel intense pressure to agree with each other so that the group can approve a proposed solution.[58] Because groupthink leads to consideration of a limited number of solutions and restricts discussion of any considered solutions, it usually results in poor decisions. Groupthink is most likely to occur under the following conditions:

- *The group is insulated from others with different perspectives.*
- *The group leader begins by expressing a strong preference for a particular decision.*
- *The group has no established procedure for systematically defining problems and exploring alternatives.*
- *Group members have similar backgrounds and experiences.*[59]

Groupthink may be one of the reasons that **Merck**'s prescription drug Vioxx stayed on the market for over five years despite fatal side effects. Merck, one of the largest drug makers in the world, viewed Vioxx as a miracle pain reliever, and over 100 million prescriptions for the drug were written in the five years it was on the market. The *New England Journal of Medicine*, however, had reported that Vioxx users suffered from significant heart problems almost from the beginning, and the drug was eventually withdrawn from the market. Court documents revealed that Merck's internal studies showed an association between Vioxx usage and an elevated incidence of heart attacks. Litigants allege that because the drug generated a substantial profit, managers chose to listen to positive feedback about how well the drug worked as a painkiller rather than act on the information about the drug's risky side effects. Merck disputes this, but the company is involved in nearly 50,000 Vioxx lawsuits.[60]

A second potential problem with group decision making is that it takes considerable time. Reconciling schedules so that group members can meet takes time.

groupthink a barrier to good decision making caused by pressure within the group for members to agree with each other

© ERIN LUBIN/BLOOMBERG NEWS/LANDOV

Google's Marissa Mayer uses six guidelines to keep the 70 meetings she holds each week on track.

Furthermore, it's a rare group that consistently holds productive task-oriented meetings to effectively work through the decision process. Some of the most common complaints about meetings (and thus decision making) are that the meeting's purpose is unclear, participants are unprepared, critical people are absent or late, conversation doesn't stay focused on the problem, and no one follows up on the decisions that were made. As Google's vice president of search products and user experience, Marissa Mayer holds over 70 meetings a week and is the last executive to hear a pitch before it is made to the cofounders. To keep meetings on track, Mayer has set down six guidelines. Meetings must (1) have a firm agenda and (2) an assigned note-taker. Meetings must occur (3) during established office hours, and (4) preferably in short, 10-minute micromeetings. Those running the meeting should (5) discourage office politics and rely on data, and above all, they should (6) stick to the clock. Mayer's guidelines help meetings stay focused and productive.[61]

A third possible pitfall to group decision making is that sometimes one or two people, perhaps the boss or a strong-willed, vocal group member, dominate group discussion, restricting consideration of different problem definitions and alternative solutions. Another potential problem is that, unlike with their own decisions and actions, group members may not feel accountable for the decisions made and actions taken by the group.

Although these pitfalls can lead to poor decision making, this doesn't mean that managers should avoid using groups to make decisions. When done properly, group decision making can lead to much better decisions. The pitfalls of group decision making are not inevitable. Managers can overcome most of them by using the various techniques described next.

5.2 Structured Conflict

Most people view conflict negatively. Yet the right kind of conflict can lead to much better group decision making. **C-type conflict**, or "cognitive conflict," focuses on problem- and issue-related differences of opinion.[62] In c-type conflict, group members disagree because their different experiences and expertise lead them to view the problem and its potential solutions differently. C-type conflict is also characterized by a willingness to examine, compare, and reconcile those differences to produce the best possible solution.

Alteon WebSystems, now a division of Nortel Networks, makes critical use of c-type conflict. Top manager Dominic Orr described Alteon's c-type conflict this way:

> *People arrive with a proposal or a solution—and with the facts to support it. After an idea is presented, we open the floor to objective, and often withering, critiques. And if the idea collapses under scrutiny, we move on to another: no hard feelings. We're judging the idea, not the person. At the same time, we don't really try to regulate emotions. Passionate conflict means that we're getting somewhere, not that the discussion is out of control. But one person does act as referee—by asking basic questions like "Is this good for the customer?" or "Does it keep our time-to-market advantage intact?" By focusing relentlessly on the facts, we're able to see the strengths and weaknesses of an idea clearly and quickly.*[63]

c-type conflict (cognitive conflict) disagreement that focuses on problem- and issue-related differences of opinion

By contrast, **a-type conflict**, meaning "affective conflict," refers to the emotional reactions that can occur when disagreements become personal rather than professional. A-type conflict often results in hostility, anger, resentment, distrust, cynicism, and apathy. Unlike c-type conflict, a-type conflict undermines team effectiveness by preventing teams from engaging in the activities characteristic of c-type conflict that are critical to team effectiveness. Examples of a-type conflict statements are "your idea," "our idea," "my department," "you don't know what you are talking about," or "you don't understand our situation." Rather than focusing on issues and ideas, these statements focus on individuals.[64]

> "The right kind of conflict can lead to much better group decision making."

Two methods of introducing structured c-type conflict into the group decision-making process are devil's advocacy and dialectical inquiry. **Devil's advocacy** creates c-type conflict by assigning an individual or a subgroup the role of critic. The following five steps establish a devil's advocacy program:

1. *Generate a potential solution.*
2. *Assign a devil's advocate to criticize and question the solution.*
3. *Present the critique of the potential solution to key decision makers.*
4. *Gather additional relevant information.*
5. *Decide whether to use, change, or not use the originally proposed solution.*[65]

Dialectical inquiry creates c-type conflict by forcing decision makers to state the assumptions of a proposed solution (a thesis) and then generate a solution that is the opposite (antithesis) of the proposed solution. The following are the five steps of the dialectical inquiry process:

1. *Generate a potential solution.*
2. *Identify the assumptions underlying the potential solution.*
3. *Generate a conflicting counterproposal based on the opposite assumptions.*
4. *Have advocates of each position present their arguments and engage in a debate in front of key decision makers.*
5. *Decide whether to use, change, or not use the originally proposed solution.*[66]

BMW uses dialectical inquiry in its design process, typically creating six internal design teams to compete against each other to design a new car. After a front-runner or leading design emerges from one of the teams, another team is assigned to design a car that is "diametrically opposed" to the leading design (Step 3 of the dialectical inquiry method).[67]

When properly used, both the devil's advocacy and dialectical inquiry approaches introduce c-type conflict into the decision-making process. Further, contrary to the common belief that conflict is bad, studies show that these methods lead to less a-type conflict, improved decision quality, and greater acceptance of decisions once they have been made.[68] See the "What Really Works" feature for more information on both techniques.

5.3 Nominal Group Technique

"Nominal" means "in name only." Accordingly, the **nominal group technique** received its name because it begins with "quiet time," in which group members independently write down as many problem definitions and alternative solutions as possible. In other words, the nominal group technique begins by having group members

a-type conflict (affective conflict) disagreement that focuses on individuals or personal issues

devil's advocacy a decision-making method in which an individual or a subgroup is assigned the role of a critic

dialectical inquiry a decision-making method in which decision makers state the assumptions of a proposed solution (a thesis) and generate a solution that is the opposite (antithesis) of that solution

nominal group technique a decision-making method that begins and ends by having group members quietly write down and evaluate ideas to be shared with the group act as individuals. After the "quiet time," the group leader asks each group member to share one idea at a time with the group. As they are read aloud, ideas are posted on flipcharts or wallboards for all to see. This step continues until all ideas have been shared. In the next step, the group discusses the advantages and disadvantages of the ideas. The nominal group technique closes with a second "quiet time," in which group members independently rank the ideas presented. Group members then read their rankings aloud, and the idea with the highest average rank is selected.[69]

The nominal group technique improves group decision making by decreasing a-type conflict. In doing so, however, it also restricts c-type conflict. Consequently, the nominal group technique typically produces poorer decisions than do the devil's advocacy and dialectical inquiry approaches. Nonetheless, more than 80 studies have found that nominal groups produce better ideas than those produced by traditional groups.[70]

5.4 Delphi Technique

In the **Delphi technique**, the members of a panel of experts respond to questions and to each other until reaching agreement on an issue. The first step is to assemble a panel of experts. Unlike other approaches to group decision making, however, it isn't necessary to bring the panel members together in one place. Because the Delphi technique does not require the experts to leave their offices or disrupt their schedules, they are more likely to participate. For example, a colleague and I were asked by a local government agency to use a Delphi-technique to assess the "10 most important steps for small businesses." The first step was to assemble a panel of local top-level managers and CEOs.

The second step is to create a questionnaire consisting of a series of open-ended questions for the experts. For example, we asked our panel to answer these questions: "What is the most common mistake made by small-business persons?" "Right now, what do you think is the biggest threat to the survival of most small businesses?" "If you had one piece of advice to give to the owner of a small business, what would it be?"

In Step 3, the panel members' written responses are analyzed, summarized, and fed back to the panel for reactions until the members reach agreement. In our Delphi study, it took about a month to get the panel members' written responses to the first three questions. Then we summarized their responses in a brief report (no more than two pages). We sent the summary to the panel members and asked them to explain why they agreed or disagreed with these conclusions from the first round of questions. Asking the members why they agree or disagree is important because it helps uncover their unstated assumptions and beliefs. Again, this process of summarizing panel feedback and obtaining reactions to that feedback continues until the panel members reach agreement. For our study, it took just one more round for the panel members' to reach a consensus. In all, it took approximately three and a half months to complete our Delphi study.

Delphi technique a decision-making method in which members of a panel of experts respond to questions and to each other until reaching agreement on an issue

stepladder technique a decision-making method in which group members are added to a group discussion one at a time (like a stepladder). The existing group members listen to each new member's thoughts, ideas, and recommendations; then the group shares the ideas and suggestions that it had already considered, discusses the new and old ideas, and makes a decision.

5.5 Stepladder Technique

The stepladder technique improves group decision making by ensuring that each member's contributions are independent, and are considered and discussed by the group. As shown in Exhibit 5.13, the **stepladder technique** begins with discussion between two group members who share their thoughts, ideas, and recommendations before jointly making a tentative decision. At each step, as other group members are added to the discussion one at a time, like a stepladder, the existing group members take the time to listen to each new member's thoughts, ideas, and

what *really* works:

DEVIL'S ADVOCACY, DIALECTICAL INQUIRY, AND CONSIDERING NEGATIVE CONSEQUENCES

Ninety percent of the decisions managers face are well-structured problems that recur frequently under conditions of certainty. For example, for most retailers, a customer's request for a refund on a returned item without a receipt is a well-structured problem. It happens every day (recurs frequently), and it's easy to determine if a customer has a receipt (condition of certainty).

Well-structured problems are solved with programmed decisions, in which a policy, procedure, or rule clearly specifies how to solve the problem. Thus, there's no mystery about what to do when someone shows up without a receipt: allow the item to be exchanged for one of similar value, but don't give a refund.

In some sense, programmed decisions really aren't decisions because anyone with experience knows what to do. No thought is required. What keeps managers up at night is the other 10 percent of problems. Ill-structured problems that are novel (no one's seen them before) and exist under conditions of uncertainty are solved with nonprogrammed decisions. Nonprogrammed decisions do not involve standard methods of resolution. Every time managers make a nonprogrammed decision, they have to figure out a new way of handling a new problem. That's what makes the decisions so tough.

Both the devil's advocacy and dialectical inquiry approaches to decision making, along with a related approach, considering negative consequences, can be used to improve nonprogrammed decision making. All three work because they force decision makers to identify and criticize the assumptions underlying the nonprogrammed decisions that they hope will solve ill-structured problems.

DEVIL'S ADVOCACY

There is a 58 percent chance that decision makers who use the devil's advocacy approach to criticize and question their solutions will produce decisions that are better than decisions based on the advice of experts.

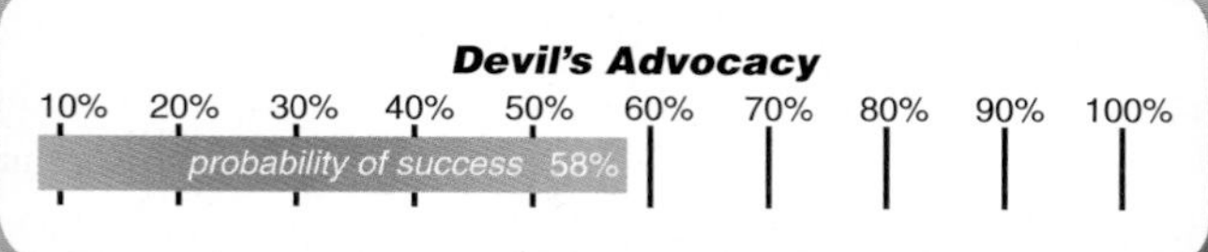

DIALECTICAL INQUIRY

There is a 55 percent chance that decision makers who use the dialectical inquiry approach to criticize and question their solutions will produce decisions that are better than decisions based on the advice of experts.

Note that each technique has been compared with decisions obtained by following experts' advice. So, although these probabilities of success, 55 percent and 58 percent, seem small, they very likely understate the effects of both techniques. In other words, the probabilities of better decisions would have been much larger if both techniques had been compared with unstructured decision-making processes.

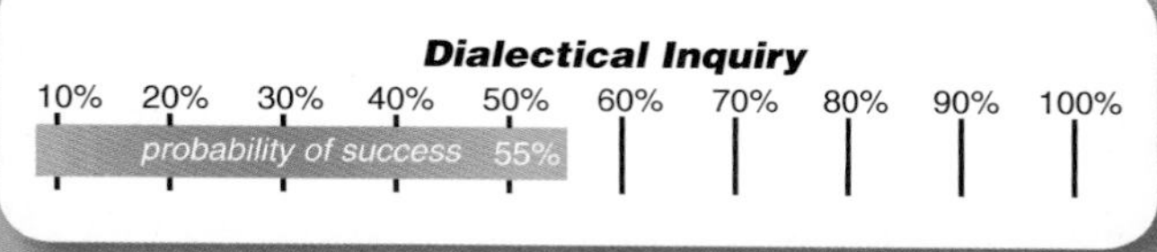

GROUP DECISION MAKING AND CONSIDERING NEGATIVE CONSEQUENCES

Considering negative consequences, such as with a devil's advocate or via critical inquiry, means pointing out the potential disadvantages of proposed solutions. There is an 86 percent chance that groups that consider negative consequences will produce better decisions than those that don't.[71]

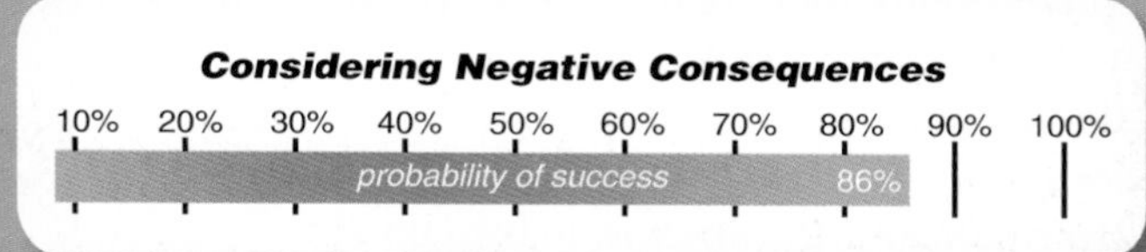

Managers should not use the Delphi technique for common decisions. Because it is a time-consuming, labor-intensive, and expensive process, the Delphi technique is best reserved for important long-term issues and problems. Nonetheless, the judgments and conclusions obtained from it are typically better than those you would get from one expert.

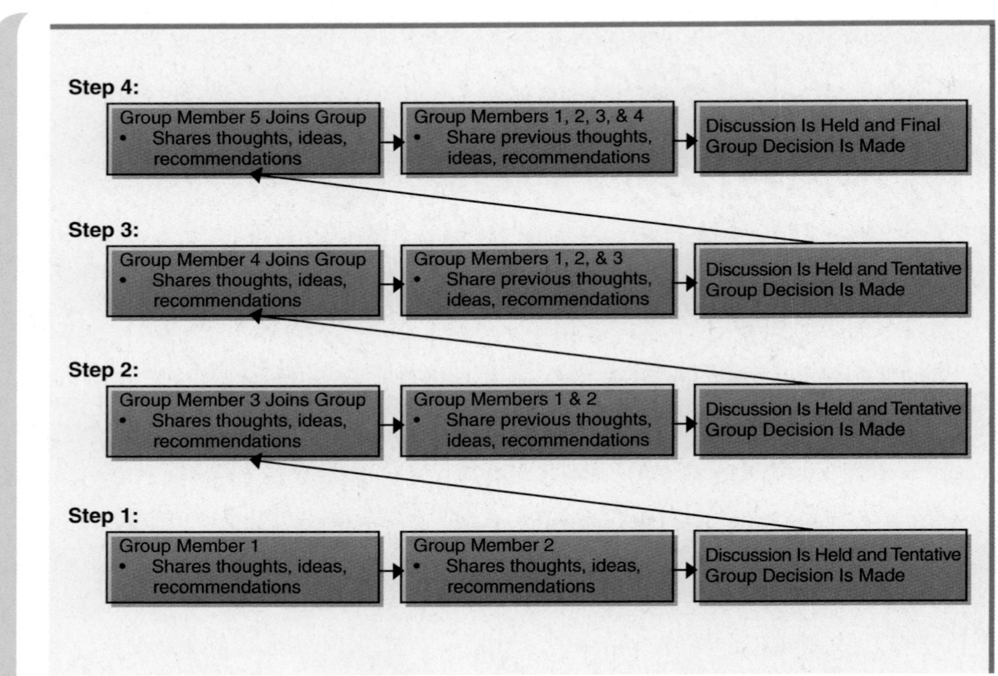

Exhibit 5.13

Stepladder Technique for Group Decision Making

recommendations. The existing members share the ideas and suggestions that they had already considered, and then the group discusses the new and old ideas and makes a tentative decision. This process (new member's ideas are heard, group shares previous ideas and suggestions, discussion is held, tentative group decision is made) continues until each group member's ideas have been discussed.

For the stepladder technique to work, group members must have enough time to consider the problem or decision on their own, to present their ideas to the group, and to thoroughly discuss all ideas and alternatives with the group at each step. Rushing through a step destroys the advantages of this technique. Also, groups must make sure that subsequent group members are completely unaware of previous discussions and suggestions. This will ensure that each member who joins the group brings truly independent thoughts and suggestions, thus greatly increasing the chances of making better decisions.

One study found that compared with traditional groups in which all group members are present for the entire discussion, groups using the stepladder technique produced significantly better decisions. Moreover, the stepladder groups performed better than the best individual member of their group 56 percent of the time, whereas traditional groups outperformed the best individual member of their group only 13 percent of the time.[72] Besides better performance, groups using the stepladder technique also generated more ideas and were more satisfied with the

mgmt: fact

Who First Thought of Brainstorming?

Alex Osborn, advertising executive and cofounder of the global advertising agency BBDO, is considered the father of brainstorming. His book *Your Creative Power*, published in 1948, introduced to America the idea generation technique BBDO had been using in-house for years. Osborn advocated having employees storm corporate problems "in commando fashion." Eventually, Osborn's career as a writer overtook his advertising career, and after more than 40 years at the helm, he retired from BBDO.

Sources: Jared Sandberg, "Brainstorming Works Best If People Scramble for Ideas on Their Own," *Wall Street Journal*, 13 June 2006, B1; "Alex Faickney Osborn," http://www.wikipedia.org, August 2006.

decision-making process. This technique also works particularly well with audio conferencing, in which geographically dispersed group members make decisions via a telephone conference call.[73]

5.6 Electronic Brainstorming

Brainstorming, in which group members build on others' ideas, is a technique for generating a large number of alternative solutions. Brainstorming has four rules:

1. *The more ideas, the better.*
2. *All ideas are acceptable, no matter how wild or crazy they might seem.*
3. *Other group members' ideas should be used to come up with even more ideas.*
4. *Criticism or evaluation of ideas is not allowed.*

Though brainstorming is great fun and can help managers generate a large number of alternative solutions, it does have a number of disadvantages. Fortunately, **electronic brainstorming**, in which group members use computers to communicate and generate alternative solutions, overcomes the disadvantages associated with face-to-face brainstorming.[74]

The first disadvantage that electronic brainstorming overcomes is **production blocking**, which occurs when you have an idea but have to wait to share it because someone else is already presenting an idea to the group. During this short delay, you may forget your idea or decide that it really wasn't worth sharing. With electronic brainstorming, production blocking doesn't happen. All group members are seated at computers, so everyone can type in ideas whenever they occur. There's no "waiting your turn" to be heard by the group.

The second disadvantage that electronic brainstorming overcomes is **evaluation apprehension**, that is, being afraid of what others will think of your ideas. With electronic brainstorming, all ideas are anonymous. When you type in an idea and hit the "Enter" key to share it with the group, group members see only the idea. Furthermore, many brainstorming software programs also protect anonymity by displaying ideas in random order. So if you laugh maniacally when you type "Cut top management's pay by 50 percent!" and then hit the "Enter" key, it won't show up immediately on everyone's screen. This makes it doubly difficult to determine who is responsible for which comments.

In the typical layout for electronic brainstorming, all participants sit in front of computers around a U-shaped table. This configuration allows them to see their computer screens, the other participants, a large main screen, and a meeting leader or facilitator. Exhibit 5.14 shows what the typical electronic brainstorming group member will see on his or her computer screen. The first step in electronic brainstorming is to anonymously generate as many ideas as possible. Groups commonly generate 100 ideas in a half-hour period. Step 2 is to edit the generated ideas, categorize them, and eliminate redundancies. Step 3 is to rank the categorized ideas in terms of quality. Step 4, the last step, has three parts: generate a series of action steps, decide the best order for accomplishing these steps, and identify who is responsible for each step. All four steps are accomplished with computers and electronic brainstorming software.[75]

Studies show that electronic brainstorming is much more productive than face-to-face brainstorming. Four-person electronic brainstorming groups produce 25 to 50 percent more ideas than four-person regular brainstorming groups, and 12-person electronic brainstorming groups produce 200 percent more ideas than regular groups of

brainstorming a decision-making method in which group members build on each others' ideas to generate as many alternative solutions as possible

electronic brainstorming a decision-making method in which group members use computers to build on each others' ideas and generate many alternative solutions

production blocking a disadvantage of face-to-face brainstorming in which a group member must wait to share an idea because another member is presenting an idea

evaluation apprehension fear of what others will think of your ideas

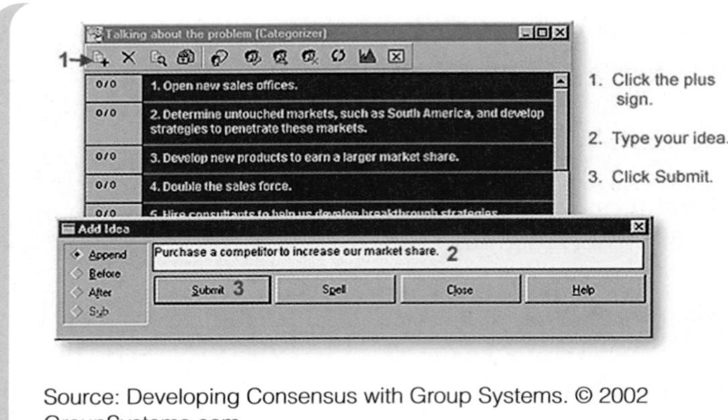

Source: Developing Consensus with Group Systems. © 2002 GroupSystems.com.

Exhibit 5.14

What You See on the Computer during Electronic Brainstorming

the same size! In fact, because production blocking (having to wait your turn) is not a problem for electronic brainstorming, the number and quality of ideas generally increase with group size.[76]

Even though it works much better than traditional brainstorming, electronic brainstorming has disadvantages, too. An obvious problem is the expense of computers, networks, software, and other equipment. As these costs continue to drop, however, electronic brainstorming will become cheaper.

Another problem is that the anonymity of ideas may bother people who are used to having their ideas accepted by virtue of their position (say, the boss). On the other hand, one CEO said, "Because the process is anonymous, the sky's the limit in terms of what you can say, and as a result it is more thought-provoking. As a CEO, you'll probably discover things you might not want to hear but need to be aware of."[77]

A third disadvantage is that outgoing individuals who are more comfortable expressing themselves verbally may find it difficult to express themselves in writing. Finally, the most obvious problem is that participants have to be able to type. Those who can't type, or who type slowly, may be easily frustrated and find themselves at a disadvantage to experienced typists. For example, one meeting facilitator was tipped off that an especially fast typist was pretending to be more than one person. Says the facilitator, "He'd type 'Oh, I agree' and then 'Ditto, ditto' or 'What a great idea,' all in quick succession, using different variations of uppercase and lowercase letters and punctuation. He tried to make it seem like a lot of people were concurring, but it was just him." Eventually, the person sitting next to him got suspicious and began watching his screen.[78]

Review 5: Using Groups to Improve Decision Making

When groups view problems from multiple perspectives, use more information, have a diversity of knowledge and experience, and become committed to solutions they help choose, they can produce better solutions than individual decision makers. However, group decisions can suffer from these disadvantages: groupthink, slowness, discussions dominated by just a few individuals, and unfelt responsibility for decisions. Group decisions work best when group members encourage c-type conflict. However, group decisions don't work as well when groups become mired in a-type conflict. The devil's advocacy and dialectical inquiry approaches improve group decisions because they bring structured c-type conflict into the decision-making process. By contrast, the nominal group technique and the Delphi technique both improve decision making by reducing a-type conflict through limited interactions between group members. The stepladder technique improves group decision making by adding each group member's independent contributions to the discussion one at a time. Finally, because it overcomes the problems of production blocking and evaluation apprehension, electronic brainstorming is a more effective method of generating alternatives than face-to-face brainstorming.

SELF ASSESSMENT

Self-Management

A key part of planning is setting goals and tracking progress toward their achievement. As a manager, you will be involved in some type of planning in an organization. But the planning process is also used in a personal context, where it is called self-management. Self-management involves setting goals for yourself, developing a method or strategy to achieve them, and then carrying it out. For some people, self-management comes naturally. Everyone seems to know someone who is highly organized, self-motivated, and disciplined. That someone may even be you. If that someone is not you, however, then you will need to develop your self-management skills as a means to becoming a better manager.

A part of planning, and therefore management, is setting goals and tracking progress toward goal achievement.[79] Answer each of the questions using the following scale:

1 Strongly disagree
2 Disagree
3 Not sure
4 Agree
5 Strongly Agree

1. I regularly set goals for myself.
1 2 3 4 5
2. I keep track of how well I've been doing.
1 2 3 4 5
3. I generally keep the resolutions that I make.
1 2 3 4 5
4. I often seek feedback about my performance.
1 2 3 4 5
5. I am able to focus on positive aspects of my work.
1 2 3 4 5
6. I'll sometimes deny myself something until I've set my goals.
1 2 3 4 5
7. I use a to-do list to plan my activities.
1 2 3 4 5
8. I have trouble working without supervision.
1 2 3 4 5
9. When I set my mind on some goal, I persevere until it's accomplished.
1 2 3 4 5
10. I'm a self-starter.
1 2 3 4 5
11. I make lists of things I need to do.
1 2 3 4 5
12. I'm good at time management.
1 2 3 4 5
13. I'm usually confident that I can reach my goals.
1 2 3 4 5
14. I am careful about how I manage my time.
1 2 3 4 5
15. I always plan my day.
1 2 3 4 5
16. I often find I spend my time on trivial things and put off doing what's really important.
1 2 3 4 5
17. Unless someone pushes me a bit, I have trouble getting motivated.
1 2 3 4 5
18. I reward myself when I meet my goals.
1 2 3 4 5
19. I tend to dwell on unpleasant aspects of the things I need to do.
1 2 3 4 5
20. I tend to deal with life as it comes rather than to try to plan things.
1 2 3 4 5
21. I generally try to find a place to work where I'll be free from interruptions.
1 2 3 4 5
22. I'm pretty disorganized.
1 2 3 4 5

KEY TERMS

absolute comparisons 172
action plan 161
a-type conflict (affective conflict) 179
bounded rationality 175
brainstorming 183
budgeting 168
c-type conflict (cognitive conflict) 178
decision criteria 171
decision making 170
Delphi technique 180
devil's advocacy 179
dialectical inquiry 179
distal goals 161
electronic brainstorming 183
evaluation apprehension 183
goal commitment 160
groupthink 177
learning-based planning 163
management by objectives (MBO) 166
maximizing 175
mission 165
nominal group technique179
operational plans 168
options-based planning 163
planning 156
policy 168
problem 170
procedure 168
production blocking 183
proximal goals 161
rational decision making 170
relative comparisons 172
rules and regulations 168
satisficing 175
single-use plans 168
slack resources 163
S.M.A.R.T. goals 159
standing plans 168
stepladder technique 180
strategic plans 165
tactical plans 166
vision 165

23. The goals I set are quite specific.
1 2 3 4 5

24. Distractions often interfere with my performance.
1 2 3 4 5

25. I sometimes give myself a treat if I've done something well.
1 2 3 4 5

26. I am able to focus on positive aspects of my activities.
1 2 3 4 5

27. I use notes or other prompts to remind myself of schedules and deadlines.
1 2 3 4 5

28. I seem to waste a lot of time.
1 2 3 4 5

29. I use a day planner or other aids to keep track of schedules and deadlines.
1 2 3 4 5

30. I often think about how I can improve my performance.
1 2 3 4 5

31. I tend to lose track of the goals I've set for myself.
1 2 3 4 5

32. I tend to set difficult goals for myself.
1 2 3 4 5

33. I plan things for weeks in advance.
1 2 3 4 5

34. I try to make a visible commitment to my goals.
1 2 3 4 5

35. I set aside blocks of time for important activities.
1 2 3 4 5

Scoring

Determine your score by entering your response to each survey item below, as follows. In blanks that say *regular score*, simply enter your response for that item. If your response was a 4, place a 4 in the *regular score* blank. In blanks that say *reverse score*, subtract your response from 6 and enter the result. So if your response was a 4, place a 2 (6 – 4 = 2) in the *reverse score* blank. Add up your total score.

1. regular score _____
2. regular score _____
3. regular score _____
4. regular score _____
5. regular score _____
6. regular score _____
7. regular score _____
8. reverse score _____
9. regular score _____
10. regular score _____
11. regular score _____
12. regular score _____
13. regular score _____
14. regular score _____
15. regular score _____
16. reverse score _____
17. reverse score _____
18. regular score _____
19. reverse score _____
20. reverse score _____
21. regular score _____
22. reverse score _____
23. regular score _____
24. reverse score _____
25. regular score _____
26. regular score _____
27. regular score _____
28. reverse score _____
29. regular score _____
30. regular score _____
31. reverse score _____
32. regular score _____
33. regular score _____
34. regular score _____
35. regular score _____

TOTAL = _____

You can find the interpretation for your score at: **academic.cengage.com/management/williams.**

MANAGEMENT DECISION

Drug Testing

The end of the week is always a relief, but this Friday, after everyone clocks out, you have a meeting with the company's frontline managers to discuss various problems that have been occurring in the warehouse. You've been bracing for the challenge since Monday.

Once all the managers are assembled, you begin to list the troubles that have been plaguing the warehouse. Petty theft and minor accidents have increased markedly in a relatively short period of time. Employees have run forklifts into walls and dropped pallets of boxes onto the floor as they were being moved. Items have disappeared from shipments being held by the company for its trucking customers. There have even been rumors that marijuana is being bought and sold on the premises. After you recite the laundry list of problems, you tell your managers that you don't think any single employee is the source of all these problems. Instead, you boldly state your suspicion: Drug use is probably the root of the problems in the warehouse.

A mumble circles the room, but no one wants to discuss the issue openly. Some managers look worried, others shocked, and the rest—you can't tell. So you begin slowly by saying, "I think we need to do drug testing. I'm sure we can't blame all our problems on drug use, but I'm convinced it's a contributing factor." You cite several successful companies that are committed to a drug-free workplace and some statistics on how much drug use costs U.S. businesses—$81 billion per year. Testing 100 employees over the course of a year will cost only about $5,000, but the average substance abuser costs his or her employer between $11,000 and $13,000 per year. Adding to the cost savings, the state gives a 5 percent rebate on workers' compensation insurance to certified drug-free workplaces. You conclude by saying, "I'll put together some materials for us to review next week."

Some of your managers nod perfunctorily, but others just raise an eyebrow. As they file out of the room in absolute silence, you murmur under your breath, "That went well," and let out a sigh. "I might as well get started now. Waiting is not going to make the task easier. But what do I really need to do? And how restrictive should I be?"[80]

Questions

1. What do you need to establish a drug-free workplace: a policy, a set of procedures, or rules and regulations—or maybe all three?
2. As the manager in question, draft the appropriate operational plan(s) for this situation. Think about issues like random versus regular testing, current employees versus future applicants only, all employees or only warehouse workers, the consequences of testing positive, and so forth.
3. Imagine that your drug-testing policy, whatever form it takes, has resulted in your company losing 40 percent of its work force. (That has actually happened to real companies.) What changes, if any, will you make as a result?

Selling to Wal-Mart

Because of your company's success, the end-of-the-year accounting review is usually an upbeat occasion, and this December is no different. Your company manufactures an innovative kickstand that reduces injuries by keeping a child's bike from falling all the way to the ground. After the device was written up in a parents' magazine recently, sales to specialty bike shops—your primary customers—have started to climb. Despite the increased demand, you can still make kickstands to order.

At a meeting with your management team, you remark that although sales are increasing at a slow but steady rate, the company still has a large amount of excess capacity. A colleague agrees and then enthusiastically announces, "I know how to take care of that. Let's sell to Wal-Mart!" A hush falls over the meeting. Becoming a Wal-Mart supplier would mean honing your current distribution process into a finely tuned, perfect delivery operation. The retailing behemoth gives suppliers a 30-second window to deliver their goods to Wal-Mart distribution centers;

you currently ship product via UPS ground. Wal-Mart requires severe price concessions from all its suppliers, a practice that has forced many American manufacturers to outsource production overseas in order to get their production costs low enough to meet Wal-Mart's pricing mandates. Master Lock, Carolina Mills, Levi's, and, a bit closer to home, Huffy Bicycle are a few examples. Your company uses local suppliers for metal, paint, plastics, and packaging, and it pays its 25 workers above-market wages. Thankfully, at the moment your company is the only manufacturer of the kickstand, so you have more freedom to set a competitive price on that item. If you begin selling through Wal-Mart, however, imitators will soon follow, and that would definitely affect your already modest margins. Not to mention that Wal-Mart uses historical price data about a company and its competitors to drive prices down across industries. Suppliers are rarely if ever granted a price increase; on the contrary, they are asked for regular price decreases!

In addition, if vendors want their products on Wal-Mart's shelves, they have to implement Wal-Mart's "customized business plans." Each year, the big retailer hands its suppliers detailed "strategic business planning packets." Wal-Mart grades its suppliers with weekly, quarterly, and annual report cards. And when it comes to discussion of price, there is no real negotiation even for household brands. Plus, Wal-Mart often requires its suppliers to underwrite the costs of the retailer's supply-chain productivity initiatives, like using radio-frequency identification (RFID) tags on their products for inventory tracking, a system that can cost between $13 million and $23 million to put in place. Trying to meet Wal-Mart's requirements has pushed many small- and medium-sized businesses into bankruptcy. Business that stay afloat have generally done so by outsourcing to China (in areas like shoes, housewares, and apparel, 80 to 90 percent of Wal-Mart's inventory comes from China).

But there are also benefits to selling to Wal-Mart. You have instant access to the world's largest global retailing network. Doing things the "Wal-Mart way" inevitably leads to more efficient operations. And the volume! You could sell exponentially more kickstands through Wal-Mart than through the small specialty retailers to whom you currently sell. If doing business with Wal-Mart is so bad, why do Unilever, P&G, and Dial sell 6, 17, and 28 percent of their goods, respectively, to the giant retailer? A former president of Huffy Bicycle once said that Wal-Mart gives you "a chance to compete. If you can't compete, that's your problem." You agree, to a point. Before you can voice any of the pros and cons, another manager expertly sums up the dilemma by saying, "The only thing worse than selling to Wal-Mart is not selling to Wal-Mart."[81]

Before you begin this Management Team Decision, each team member will probably need to do some preliminary research on Wal-Mart's business practices; go to the campus library to find articles on topics like productivity, inventory management, and even Wal-Mart's business practices. A visit to the Wal-Mart stores website (**http://www.walmartstores.com**) can give you a wealth of information on how the company manages its suppliers. You may also wish to visit the PBS show *Frontline*'s web page "Is Wal-Mart Good for America?" (**http://www.pbs.org/wgbh/pages/frontline/shows/walmart/secrets**).

Questions

1. As a team, use this exercise to practice one of the group decision-making techniques discussed in the chapter. Work together to decide which technique to use.
2. Do you apply to become a Wal-Mart supplier, with all that entails? Why or why not?
3. If you become a Wal-Mart supplier, what key areas of your operations will need to change and how?
4. Think about how the decision-making technique you chose affected the outcome of your decision. Do you think your collective decision would have been different if you had used, say, dialectical inquiry instead of the stepladder technique?

Effective planning and decision making are crucial to the success of organizations. Your success as a manager will be determined in large part by your planning and decision-making capabilities. This exercise highlights some well-tested tools for strengthening your planning and decision-making skills.

Individual Preparation

Step 1: Identify your "best company." Suppose that you are going to develop a plan that will result in your being hired to work for the single BEST COMPANY possible. "Best company" has not been defined for you, so you must determine what this might mean. Identify your "best company," and make your plan. You need to consider such aspects as building the right academic and work profile, marketing yourself to the company, and effectively interviewing. Carefully record both your plan, and the steps that you took to develop it. In class you will be asked to share this information with a small discussion group.

Small Group Discussion

Step 2: Discuss your plan. Taking turns, individually share your plan with the members of your discussion group. Members should listen carefully, ask questions, and make notes regarding the similarities and differences of individual plans.

Step 3: Create a brochure. Now suppose that your group has been asked to develop a brochure for distribution in college career centers. The brochure will be titled "Getting a Job with Your Dream Company."

Using what you have learned from sharing your individual plans, work as a group to develop a sketch/outline of this brochure.

Class Discussion

Step 4: As a class discuss the following questions:

- Did you follow the rational decision-making process in identifying your *best company* and creating your plan for landing a job with this company? Why, or why not?
- What role might bounded rationality have played in your individual and/or team decision-making process?
- Does planning increase the likelihood of success in being hired by a great company? Why, or why not?
- If you were an editor assigned the project of developing the brochure "Getting a Job with Your Dream Company," would you be more likely to give the assignment to: 1) a qualified individual; or 2) a qualified group? Considering your recent experiences in this exercise, what are the tradeoffs of each approach (individual versus group decision making)?

What Do You Want To Be When You Grow Up?

What do you want to be when you grow up?[82] Still not sure? Ask around. You're not alone. Chances are, your friends and relatives aren't certain either. Sure, they may have jobs and careers, but you're likely to find that, professionally, many of them don't want to be where they are today. Sometimes people's interests change, or they may burn out. And some people are unhappy with their current job or career because they weren't in the right one to begin with.

Getting the job and career you want is not easy. It takes time, effort, and persistence. And even though you will probably follow multiple career paths in your life, your career-planning process will be easier (and more effective) if you take the time to develop a personal career plan.

Begin by answering the following questions. (*Hint*: Treat this seriously. If you do it effectively, this plan could guide your career decisions for the next five to seven years.)

1. Describe your strengths and weaknesses. Don't just rely on your opinions of your abilities. Ask your parents, relatives, friends, and employers what they think, too. Encourage them to be honest and then be prepared to hear some things that you may not

want to hear. Remember, though, this information can help you pick the right job or career.

2. Write an advertisement for the job you want to have five years from now. Be specific. Describe the company, title, responsibilities, required education, and experience, salary, and benefits. Use employment ads in the Sunday job listings as inspiration.
3. Create a detailed plan to obtain this job. In the short term, what classes do you need to take? Should you change your major? Do you need a business major or minor or maybe a minor in a foreign language? What kind of summer work experience will move you closer to getting the job you want five years from now? What job do you need to get right out of college to obtain the work experience you need? Create a specific plan for each of the five years in your career plan, keeping in mind that the plans for later years are likely to change. The value in planning is that it forces you to think about what you want and the steps you can take now to help achieve those goals.
4. Decide when you will monitor and evaluate the progress you're making with your plan. Career experts suggest that every six months is about right. Pick two dates and write them in your schedule. Furthermore, right now, before you forget, set five specific, challenging goals that you need to accomplish in the next six months in order to achieve your career plans.

REEL TO REAL

BIZ FLIX

The Bourne Identity

Jason Bourne (Matt Damon) cannot remember who he is, but others believe he is an international assassin. Bourne tries to learn his identity with the help of his new friend and lover Marie (Franka Potente). Meanwhile, while CIA agents pursue him across Europe trying to kill him, Bourne slowly discovers that he is an extremely well-trained and lethal agent. The story is loosely based on Robert Ludlum's 1981 novel.

This scene is an edited version of the "Bourne's Game" sequence near the end of the film. Jason Bourne kills the hired assassin who tried to kill him the day after Jason and Marie arrived at the home of Eamon (Tim Dutton). Eamon is Marie's friend but is a stranger to Jason. Jason uses the dead man's cell phone after returning to his apartment in Paris, France. He presses the redial button, which connects him to Conklin (Chris Cooper), the CIA manager who is looking for him. Listen carefully to Jason's conversation with Conklin.

What to Watch for and Ask Yourself

1. Does Bourne describe a plan to Conklin? If he does, what are the plan's elements? What is Bourne's goal?
2. Does Bourne assess the plan's execution to determine if it conforms to his goal? If so, what does he do?
3. Was Bourne's plan successfully carried out? Why or why not? How does this scene relate to organizational strategic planning?

MANAGEMENT WORKPLACE

Timbuk2—Undemocratic Group Decision Making

Making decisions is a big part of any manager's job. Making the decisions that determine the direction a company will take is the job of a CEO. Mark Dwight, CEO of Timbuk2, is comfortable with this role, even though it means sometimes making unpopular decisions—or even making mistakes. Timbuk2's 45 workers tend to be young, so Dwight sees himself as the senior manager in more ways than one. "I'm the experienced executive here, and it's my charter to manage the company," he explains. "It's not a democracy. I ask the people that I think have a good perspective on [an] issue, who are affected by the issue, we discuss it, and I make a command decision based on those inputs. Hopefully, people think I make educated, informed decisions. That's my job."

What to Watch for and Ask Yourself

1. What problems does Dwight identify at the opening of the Tag Junkie planning meeting?
2. How does the team incorporate flexibility into its product plan?
3. Does what you see in the video qualify as group decision making? Why or why not?

© ROBIN NELSON/PHOTOEDIT, INC.

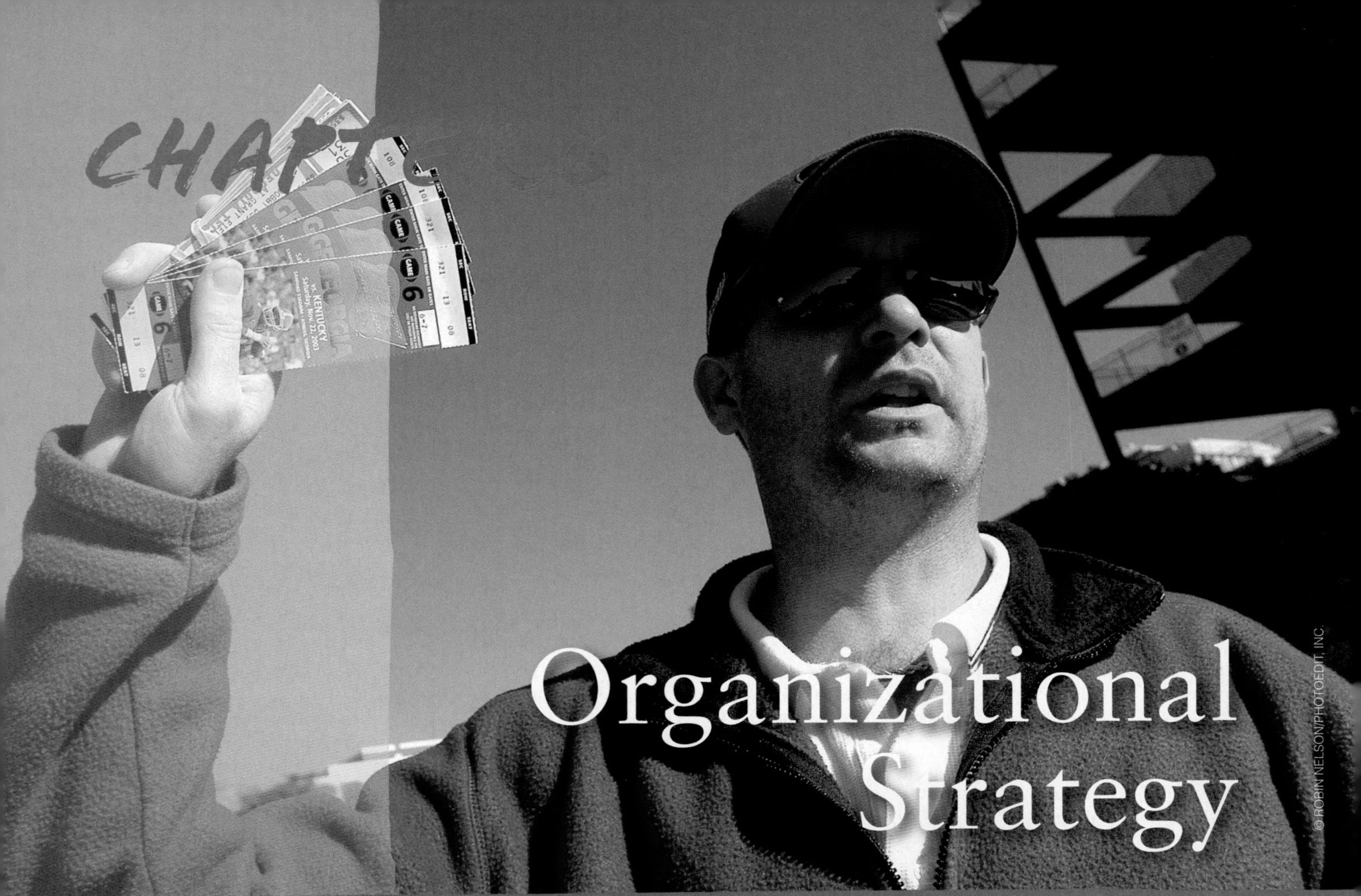

Organizational Strategy

Learning Outcomes:

1 Specify the components of sustainable competitive advantage and explain why it is important.
2 Describe the steps involved in the strategy-making process.
3 Explain the different kinds of corporate-level strategies.
4 Describe the different kinds of industry-level strategies.
5 Explain the components and kinds of firm-level strategies.

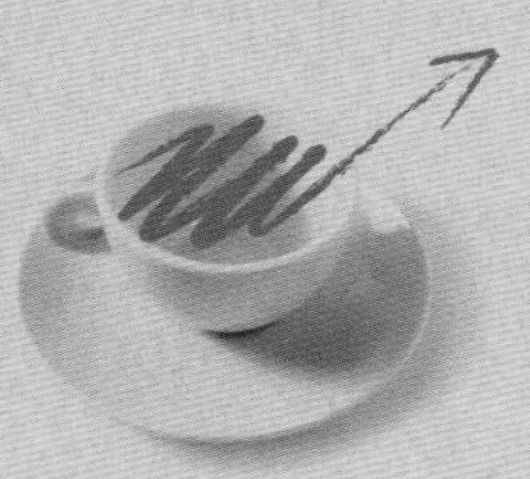

In This Chapter:

WHAT WOULD YOU DO?

StubHub, Inc., San Francisco, California.[1] Your management team at eBay just acquired rival upstart StubHub from its founders Jeff Fluhr and Eric Baker, who launched the company out of their Stanford dorm rooms. Fluhr and Baker wanted to use the Internet to replace scalping tickets at venue sites, so they developed a unique system comprised of ticket exchange, event information, and guaranteed delivery.

StubHub quickly signed contracts with Major League Baseball, the National Football League, National Hockey League, and National Basketball Association. Season-ticket holders used StubHub to safely sell their tickets for games they couldn't attend for whatever reason. To no one's surprise, StubHub acquired customers quickly and inexpensively, but once activity stabilized, the company became a slow-growth business—there are only so many season-ticket holders out there. That's when StubHub moved into direct consumer marketing.

StubHub started facilitating ticket sales between any two willing parties, a move that helped it become the second largest ticket resale auction site on the Internet. But as new companies entered (and filled) the market, companies like TicketsNow.com, RazorGator, eBay, and even Ticketmaster, StubHub watched its basic strategy and unique transaction capabilities begin to erode. And, industry powerhouse Ticketmaster launched a new lobbying effort to have states outlaw the reselling of tickets for more than their face value (the amount printed on the ticket).

Despite the competition, StubHub managed to attract 2.1 million unique visitors per month and generate over $100 million in annual revenue. Still, competition means lower prices means weakening revenues. You need a new strategy for growth and profit.

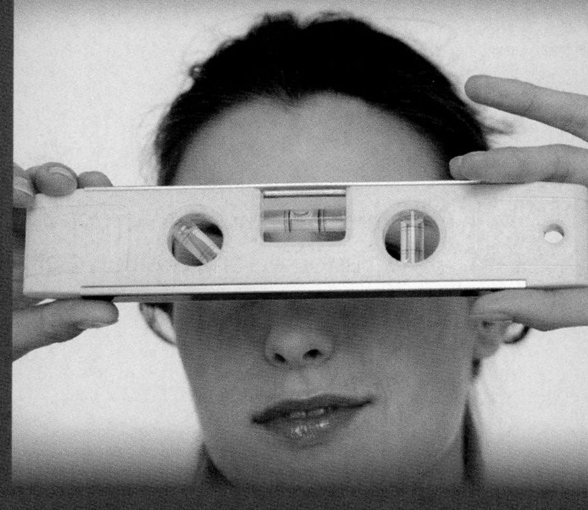

Could StubHub become an advertising medium for sporting and theatrical events? Huge revenues are possible, but advertisers are now regularly entering contracts with Google, YouTube, and Facebook. Should StubHub directly attack Ticketmaster's business of selling original tickets to concerts and sporting events? Finally, should you completely change the business model and actually buy tickets to resell on the open auction market? Buying the tickets would be costly and carry some risk, but if done well, you might end up with greater market power and the ability to maximize revenue. **If you had just bought StubHub and needed to spark additional growth, what would you do?**

ACTIVITIES + VIDEO

CengageNOW Audio study guide, electronic flashcards, author FAQ videos, On the Job and Biz Flix videos, concept tutorial, and concept exercise

Web (academic.cengage.com/management/williams) Quiz, PowerPoint slides, and glossary terms for this chapter

Study Tip

Fresh examples of management topics can be found every day in the business press. Pick up a copy of the *Wall Street Journal* and read several articles. List the strategy issues facing the companies you read about.

"WHAT'S NEW" COMPANIES

StubHub
Apple Computer
Sony
Microsoft
iTunes
Napster
Yahoo! Music
Kraft Foods
Warner Music Group
Memorial Hospital
IKEA
Home Depot
Lowe's
Ace Hardware
84 Lumber
Ciba-Geigy
Menards
And others . . .

In Chapter 5, you learned that *strategic plans* are overall company plans that clarify how a company intends to serve customers and position itself against competitors over the next two to five years. Although StubHub was the first online ticket reseller, it now faces challenges from numerous competitors and must develop a strategy to recapture its competitive advantage in this market. This chapter begins with an in-depth look at how managers create and use strategies to obtain a sustainable competitive advantage. Then you will learn the three steps of the strategy-making process. Next, you will learn about corporate-level strategies that help managers answer the question, What business or businesses should we be in? You will then examine the industry-level competitive strategies that help managers determine how to compete successfully within a particular line of business. The chapter finishes with a review of the firm-level strategies of direct competition and entrepreneurship.

BASICS OF ORGANIZATIONAL STRATEGY

"What's New" Company

Before October 2001, **APPLE COMPUTER** was not in the portable digital music business, but that month, the company released its iPod, which quickly set the standard for all other digital music devices. Designed around a 1.8-inch-diameter hard drive, the iPod boasted low battery consumption and enough memory to hold literally thousands of songs, all packaged in a case smaller than a deck of cards and fashioned with style unparalleled in the technology market. Because Apple used existing and readily available technology, competitors were able to move quickly and aggressively to copy Apple's innovation. Powerhouses like Sony, Samsung, and even Dell Computer soon released their own iPod-like devices.

As the market has matured over the past several years, competitors have increasingly tried to steal—or at least minimize—Apple's competitive advantage by adding unique features to the standard set of features on an MP3 player. **SONY**'s new Walkman includes software that examines the user's taste in music and, at the push of a button labeled "Artist Link," the device will suggest new artists the user might like. SanDisk, best known as a maker of basic flash drive memory, has entered the MP3 market with its Sansa e280, which has twice the storage of an iPod Nano yet sells at roughly the same price. Another significant new entrant to the digital music space is **MICROSOFT**. Its Zune player can store

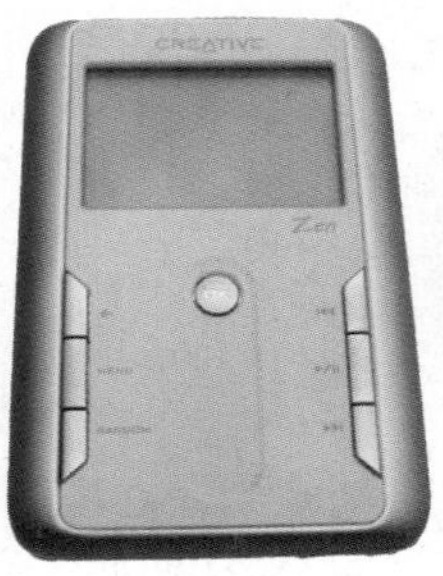

© CHAPEL HOUSE PHOTOGRAPHY [ALL]

the same number of songs as a video iPod, but Zune can also hold 100 hours of video (compared with the iPod's 40) and 25,000 pictures (same as an iPod). Plus the Zune allows users to wirelessly share music. Despite the creativity of the competition, however, Apple still holds a commanding 75 percent of the market for digital music players; SanDisk, its nearest competitor, has less than a 10 percent share.[2]

How can a company like Apple, which dominates a particular industry, maintain its competitive advantage as strong, well-financed competitors enter the market? What steps can Apple and other companies take to better manage their strategy-making process?

After reading the next two sections, you should be able to

1. *specify the components of sustainable competitive advantage and explain why it is important.*
2. *describe the steps involved in the strategy-making process.*

1 Sustainable Competitive Advantage

Resources are the assets, capabilities, processes, employee time, information, and knowledge that an organization controls. Firms use their resources to improve organizational effectiveness and efficiency. Resources are critical to organizational strategy because they can help companies create and sustain an advantage over competitors.[3]

Organizations can achieve a **competitive advantage** by using their resources to provide greater value for customers than competitors can. For example, *iTunes* and iPod created competitive advantage for Apple and value for its customers by combining elements of design, price, and capability in a unique way. But the most important advantage was being the first company to make it easy to legally download music to digital devices. (Prior to the iTunes store, the only means of acquiring digital music was file swapping, which was illegal.) Apple negotiated agreements with virtually all of the major record labels to distribute their songs from a central online library, and iTunes quickly became the premier platform for music downloading. The easy-to-understand site came with free downloadable software customers could use to organize and manage their digital music library.[4]

The goal of most organizational strategies is to create and then sustain a competitive advantage. A competitive advantage becomes a **sustainable competitive advantage** when other companies cannot duplicate the value a firm is providing to customers. Sustainable competitive advantage is *not* the same as a long-lasting competitive advantage, though companies obviously want a competitive advantage to last a long time. Instead, a competitive advantage is *sustained* if competitors have tried unsuccessfully to duplicate the advantage and have, for the moment, stopped trying to duplicate it. It's the corporate equivalent of your competitors saying, "We give up. You win. We can't do what you do, and we're not even going to try to do it any more." As Exhibit 6.1 shows, four conditions must be met if a firm's resources are to be used to achieve a sustainable competitive advantage. The resources must be valuable, rare, imperfectly imitable, *and* nonsubstitutable.

resources the assets, capabilities, processes, employee time, information, and knowledge that an organization uses to improve its effectiveness and efficiency, create and sustain competitive advantage, and fulfill a need or solve a problem

competitive advantage providing greater value for customers than competitors can

sustainable competitive advantage a competitive advantage that other companies have tried unsuccessfully to duplicate and have, for the moment, stopped trying to duplicate

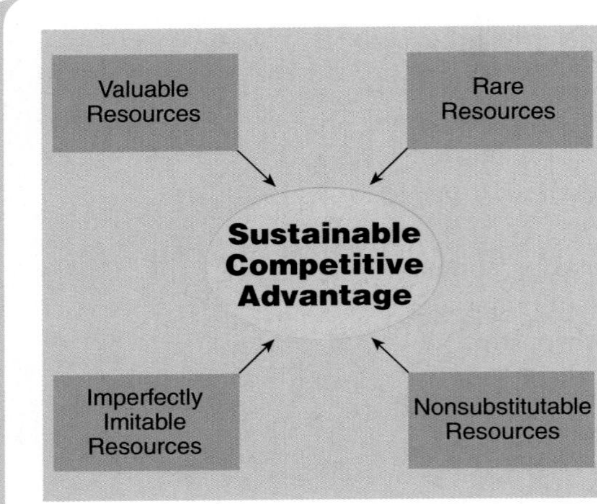

Exhibit 6.1

Four Requirements for Sustainable Competitive Advantage

Valuable resources allow companies to improve their efficiency and effectiveness. Unfortunately, changes in customer demand and preferences, competitors' actions, and technology can make once-valuable resources much less valuable. Throughout the 1980s, Sony controlled the portable music market with its ubiquitous Sony Walkman, which has sold over 230 million units worldwide since its introduction in 1979. For many years, Sony had the technology to produce a higher quality of music than any other portable format on the market. Sony leveraged the capabilities of its engineers and inventors (more resources) to make incremental changes to the Walkman that were unmatched by the competition—until the MP3 player came along. With the introduction of Apple's iPod to the market, Sony's previously valuable technology lost nearly all its value. Sony finally changed the Walkman to a portable digital device and created its own online music store (Connect), which does not match the iTunes store in either simplicity or availability of songs.[5]

For sustained competitive advantage, valuable resources must also be rare resources. Think about it: How can a company sustain a competitive advantage if all of its competitors have similar resources and capabilities? Consequently, **rare resources**, resources that are not controlled or possessed by many competing firms, are necessary to sustain a competitive advantage. When Apple introduced the iPod, no other portable music players on the market used existing hard-drive technology in their design. The iPod gained an immediate advantage over competitors because it was able to satisfy the desire of consumers to carry large numbers of songs in a portable device, something the newer MP3 systems and older individual CD players could not do. The technology that powered the iPod, however, was readily available, so competitors were able to quickly imitate iPod's basic storage capacity. As competitors began introducing their iPod look-alikes, Apple released a model with double the storage and replaced the original mechanical wheel with a solid-state touch wheel. Once again, Apple used its design talents (resources) to gain an advantage over the competition. One of Apple's truly rare resources is its ability to reconfigure existing technology into a package that is easy to use, elegantly designed, and therefore highly desired by customers.

As the example shows, valuable and rare resources can create temporary competitive advantage. For sustained competitive advantage, however, other firms must be unable to imitate or find substitutes for those valuable, rare resources. **Imperfectly imitable resources** are those resources that are impossible or extremely costly or difficult to duplicate. For example, despite numerous attempts by competitors to imitate it, iTunes has retained its competitive lock on the music download business. Capitalizing on Apple's reputation for developing customer-friendly software, and its library of music, movies, and podcasts, iTunes is still the market leader, although competition from Yahoo! Music and Zune is heating up. Because the company has developed a closed system for its iTunes and iPod, iPod owners cannot download music from sources other than Apple's iTunes store, but for many this is not a problem. Many devotees won't even consider another brand. Kelly Moore, a sales representative for a Texas software company, takes her pink iPod mini everywhere she goes and keeps it synchronized with her iBook laptop. She says, "Once I find something I like, I don't switch brands."[6] She's not alone: Since iTunes was launched, customers have downloaded over a billion songs. No other competitor comes close to those numbers.

valuable resource a resource that allows companies to improve efficiency and effectiveness

rare resource a resource that is not controlled or possessed by many competing firms

imperfectly imitable resource a resource that is impossible or extremely costly or difficult for other firms to duplicate

Valuable, rare, imperfectly imitable resources can produce sustainable competitive advantage only if they are also **nonsubstitutable resources**, meaning that no other resources can replace them and produce similar value or competitive advantage. To compete effectively against iTunes, competitors may need to change their business model. That is, competitors need to propose substitutes for iTunes that consumers will accept. For example, **NAPSTER** founders Shawn Fanning and Wayne Rosso have created a subscription-based service called Mashboxx that charges $15 a month for unlimited downloads. **YAHOO! MUSIC** uses a similar model but charges as little as $6 per month for complete access to its entire library of 2 million songs.[7] In addition to straight subscription models, some companies are experimenting with price. Where iTunes charges 99 cents per song, period, Amazon's online store will allow the record companies to charge different amounts for different songs based upon popularity. At Amie Street, a newly posted track can be downloaded for free, but as the number of downloads increases, so does the song's price, until it reaches the maximum of 98 cents.[8] In response to competitors' experimentation, Apple has stated that its one-flat-price model has been both effective and lucrative and has no plans to change. It will take years to find out whether these new means of purchase will constitute an effective substitute to iTunes.[9]

"WHAT'S NEW" COMPANY
"WHAT'S NEW" COMPANY

In summary, Apple has reaped the rewards of a first mover advantage from its interdependent iPod and iTunes. The company's history of developing customer-friendly software, the innovative capabilities of the iPod, the simple 99-cent-pay-as-you-go sales model of iTunes, and the unmatched list of music and movies available for download provide customers with a service that has been valuable, rare, relatively nonsubstitutable, and, in the past, imperfectly imitable. Past success is, however, no guarantee of future success: Apple needs to continually change and develop its offerings or risk being unseated by a more nimble competitor whose products are more relevant and have higher perceived value to the consumer.

Review 1: Sustainable Competitive Advantage

Firms can use their resources to create and sustain a competitive advantage, that is, to provide greater value for customers than competitors can. A competitive advantage becomes sustainable when other companies cannot duplicate the benefits it provides and have, for now, stopped trying. To provide a sustainable competitive advantage, the firm's resources must be valuable (capable of improving efficiency and effectiveness), rare (not possessed by many competing firms), imperfectly imitable (extremely costly or difficult to duplicate), and nonsubstitutable (competitors cannot substitute other resources to produce similar value).

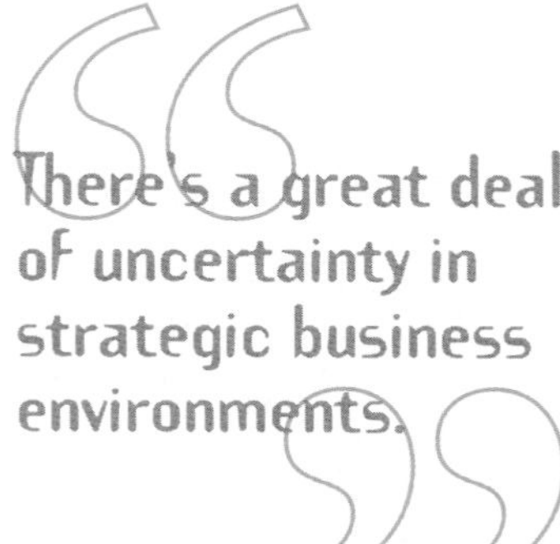
There's a great deal of uncertainty in strategic business environments.

2 Strategy-Making Process

*Companies use a strategy-making process to create strategies that produce sustainable competitive advantage.[10] Exhibit 6.2 displays the three steps of the strategy-making process: **2.1 assess the need for strategic change, 2.2 conduct a situational analysis**, and then **2.3 choose strategic alternatives**. Let's examine each of these steps in more detail.*

nonsubstitutable resource a resource that produces value or competitive advantage and has no equivalent substitutes or replacements

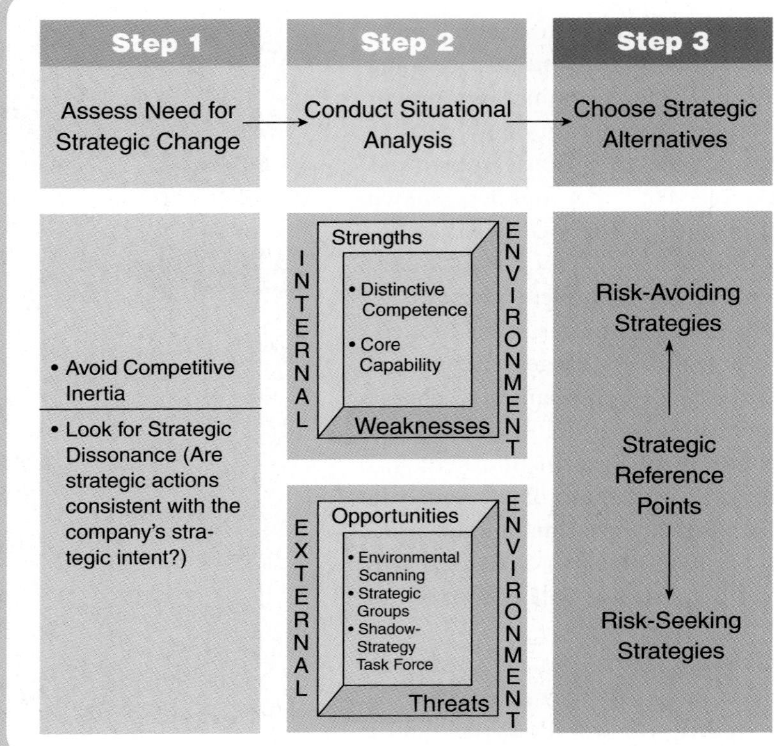

Exhibit 6.2

Three Steps of the Strategy-Making Process

2.1 Assessing the Need for Strategic Change

The external business environment is much more turbulent than it used to be. With customers' needs constantly growing and changing, and with competitors working harder, faster, and smarter to meet those needs, the first step in strategy making is determining the need for strategic change. In other words, the company should determine whether it needs to change its strategy to sustain a competitive advantage.[11]

Determining the need for strategic change might seem easy to do, but in reality, it's not. There's a great deal of uncertainty in strategic business environments. Furthermore, top-level managers are often slow to recognize the need for strategic change, especially at successful companies that have created and sustained competitive advantages. Because they are acutely aware of the strategies that made their companies successful, they continue to rely on those strategies, even as the competition changes. In other words, success often leads to **competitive inertia**—a reluctance to change strategies or competitive practices that have been successful in the past.

For example, **Kraft Foods** makes some of the best-selling food brands around, such as Oreo cookies, Lunchables (prepackaged lunches for children), and Velveeta cheese. But Kraft hasn't introduced a successful new brand since it began selling DiGiorno frozen pizza in the mid-1990s. Instead, Kraft has focused on brand extensions, developing "new and improved" versions of its best-selling brands, such as mini Oreos, Chocolate Cream Oreos, Fudge Mint Oreos, Mint and Crème Oreos, and Uh-Oh Oreos.[12] Kraft now has 14 different varieties of the original Oreo cookie, the newest of which is the Thin Crisp, packaged in 100-calorie servings, and eight other Oreo-branded products such as ice-cream cones, Jello, and cereal.[13] And Kraft's competitive inertia—its reliance on extending already established brands and its reluctance to develop new ones—has hurt its performance. According to the *Wall Street Journal*, "years of failing to develop new categories and products has given Kraft a lineup that seems stuck in a time warp."[14] Indeed, former customer Jennifer Stoll, who used to buy Kraft's food brands, says, "My perception of Kraft is that they are the more expensive version of processed food 'junk.'"[15]

Besides being aware of the dangers of competitive inertia, what can managers do to improve the speed and accuracy with which they determine the need for strategic change? One method is to actively look for signs of strategic dissonance. **Strategic dissonance** is a discrepancy between a company's intended strategy and the strategic actions managers take when actually implementing that strategy.[16]

competitive inertia a reluctance to change strategies or competitive practices that have been successful in the past

strategic dissonance a discrepancy between a company's intended strategy and the strategic actions managers take when implementing that strategy

For example, when Edgar Bronfman, Jr., bought the struggling **Warner Music Group**, his strategy was to cut costs and change a company culture where excessive spending—not uncommon in the entertainment industry—was the norm. Accordingly, he hoped to send a strong message with his first move, laying off 1,200 employees to save $250 million. Then, to drive the point home, he cut remaining salaries by as much as 50 percent. Bronfman justified the cuts by saying that managers, lawyers, accountants, and salespeople shouldn't be earning double or triple their normal salaries just because they worked for a music company. A few weeks later, however, he contradicted his new cost-cutting strategy. First, he signed off on a $13,000 bill to charter a private jet to fly top company managers and the agents of the company's best-selling artists to the Grammy awards in Los Angeles. Then, despite his insistence that music industry professionals shouldn't be paid more than their counterparts in other industries, Bronfman quietly restored the salary cuts he had made after top executives complained.[17]

Finally, while strategic dissonance can indicate that managers are not doing what they should to carry out company strategy, it can also mean that the intended strategy is out of date and needs to be changed.

doing the right thing

Is Ethics an Overlooked Source of Competitive Advantage?

Volvo's reputation for selling safe cars has been a source of competitive advantage for years. You didn't buy a boxy Volvo for its looks; you bought it because your family would be well protected in an accident. If safety can be a source of competitive advantage, could ethics be one, too? Though competitive advantage usually comes from physical capital (plant, equipment, finances), organizational capital (structure, planning, systems), and human capital (skills, judgment, adaptability of your work force), Johnson & Johnson is still widely admired, two decades afterward, for its response when several people died after someone put cyanide in Tylenol capsules. The company quickly pulled Tylenol from store shelves and introduced tamper-proof packaging. The move cost Johnson & Johnson half a billion dollars, but protected consumers from further harm. The company's market share was back to #1 within a year of the reintroduction. Should ethics be your first source of competitive advantage? Probably not. It makes more sense to start with low costs, good service, or unique product capabilities. But when you're looking for another way to create or sustain a competitive advantage, consider that a reputation as an ethical corporation may be an additional way to differentiate your company from the competition.[19]

2.2 Situational Analysis

A situational analysis can also help managers determine the need for strategic change. A **situational analysis**, also called a **SWOT analysis** for *strengths*, *weaknesses*, *opportunities*, and *threats*, is an assessment of the strengths and weaknesses in an organization's internal environment and the opportunities and threats in its external environment.[18] Ideally, as shown in Step 2 of Exhibit 6.2, a SWOT analysis helps a company determine how to increase internal strengths and minimize internal weaknesses while maximizing external opportunities and minimizing external threats.

When **Memorial Hospital** of Fremont, Ohio, decided that the process it used to order all the necessary medical and administrative supplies was out of control, managers asked all the departments to work together to conduct a SWOT analysis. The process helped the hospital identify its strengths, such as the experience of the materials management group, and its weaknesses, which included allowing anyone in the organization to order anything he or she wanted from any vendor. The departments outlined opportunities to dramatically improve the quality and flow of supplies while controlling the related costs, and participants determined that one of the biggest threats was expired supplies. Using the SWOT analysis as a map, the hospital began requiring all vendors to register when they entered the building, wear a visitor's badge while on hospital premises, and process all orders through the central purchasing department. Soon, the hospital staff developed the right mix of products

situational (SWOT) analysis an assessment of the strengths and weaknesses in an organization's internal environment and the opportunities and threats in its external environment

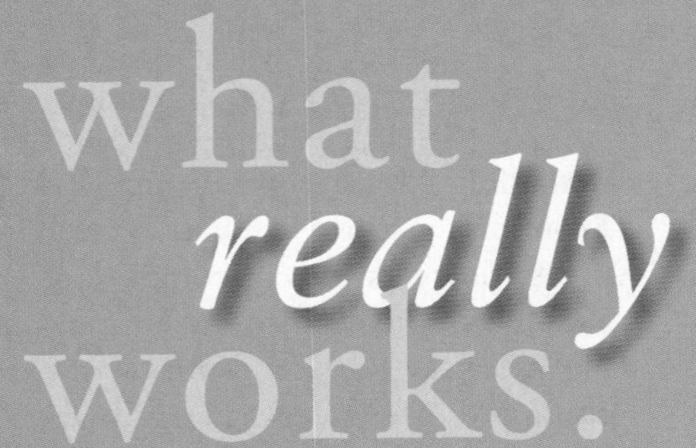

STRATEGY MAKING FOR FIRMS, BIG AND SMALL

Companies create strategies that produce sustainable competitive advantage by using the strategy-making process (assessing the need for strategic change, conducting a situational analysis, and choosing strategic alternatives). For years, it had been thought that strategy making was something that only large firms could do well. It was believed that small firms did not have the time, knowledge, or staff to do a good job of strategy making. However, two meta-analyses indicate that strategy making can improve the profits, sales growth, and return on investment of both big *and* small firms.

STRATEGY MAKING FOR BIG FIRMS

There is a 72 percent chance that big companies that engage in the strategy-making process will be more profitable than big companies that don't. Not only does strategy making improve profits, but it also helps companies grow. Specifically, there is a 75 percent chance that big companies that engage in the strategy-making process will have greater sales and earnings growth than big companies that don't. Thus, in practical terms, the strategy-making process can make a significant difference in a big company's profits and growth.

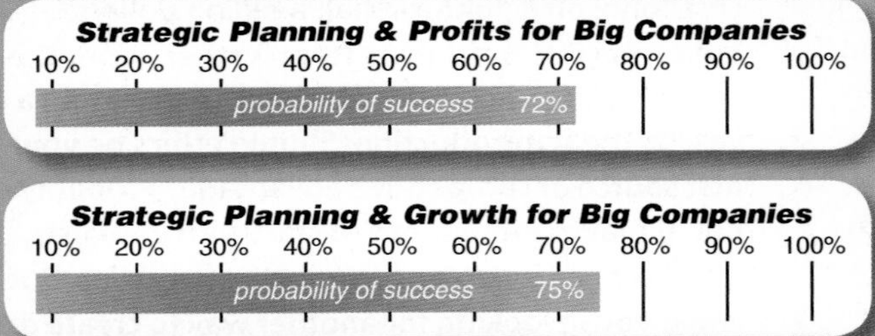

STRATEGY MAKING FOR SMALL FIRMS

Strategy making can also improve the performance of small firms. There is a 61 percent chance that small firms that engage in the strategy-making process will have more sales growth than small firms that don't. Likewise, there is a 62 percent chance that small firms that engage in the strategy-making process will have a larger return on investment than small companies that don't. Thus, in practical terms, the strategy-making process can make a significant difference in a small company's profits and growth, too.

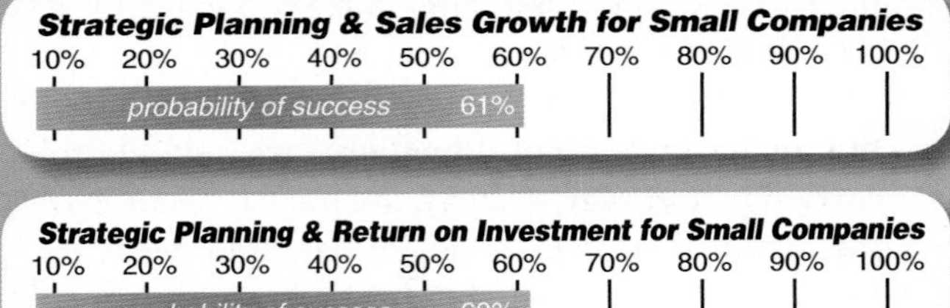

EXTERNAL GROWTH THROUGH ACQUISITIONS

One way to grow a company is through external growth, or buying other companies (see Section 3.1 on portfolio strategy). However, researchers have long debated whether buying other companies actually adds value to the acquiring company. A meta-analysis based on 103 studies and a sample of 25,205 companies indicates that, on average, acquiring other companies actually *hurts* the value of the acquiring firm. In other words, there is only a 45 percent chance that growing a company through external acquisitions will work![20]

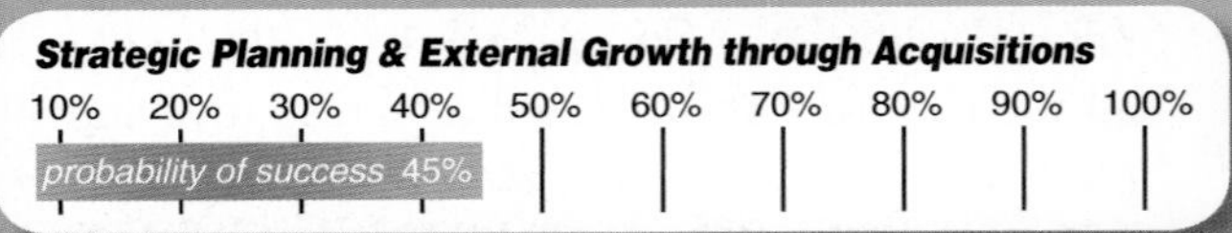

and product inventories required for each area of the hospital and, at the same time, dramatically reduced the number of staff involved in purchasing and stocking supplies. Over the next two years the hospital saved more than $1 million, and administrators won praise from hospital departments for their ability to improve services.[21]

As this example illustrates, SWOT can be used to evaluate entire companies or individual operations within an organization. All companies will find that their competitive advantages can erode over time if internal strengths eventually become weaknesses. Consequently, an analysis of an organization's internal environment, that is, a company's strengths and weaknesses, often begins with an assessment of its distinctive competencies and core capabilities. A **distinctive competence** is something that a company can make, do, or perform better than its competitors. For example, *Consumer Reports* magazine consistently ranks Toyota cars number one in quality and reliability.[22] Similarly, for 13 of the last 15 years, *PC Magazine* readers have ranked Dell's desktop computers best in terms of service and reliability.[23]

Whereas distinctive competencies are tangible—for example, a product or service is faster, cheaper, or better—the core capabilities that produce distinctive competencies are not. **Core capabilities** are the less visible, internal decision-making routines, problem-solving processes, and organizational cultures that determine how efficiently inputs can be turned into outputs. Distinctive competencies cannot be sustained for long without superior core capabilities. ***IKEA***'s core capability is the way it works with 1,800 suppliers in 55 countries that make products exclusively for IKEA. IKEA employees in 43 local trading offices work closely with these suppliers to improve quality, cut costs, and improve worker safety. When IKEA develops a new product, such as a $650 small kitchen, the trading offices, with the help of their suppliers, compete to earn the right to produce that product. IKEA uses the same approach for product design, encouraging its nine in-house designers and 80 freelance designers to compete to come up with the best design. This ability to work with so many suppliers and designers, to get them to compete to achieve the best design and the lowest-cost manufactured product, and to keep suppliers happy by guaranteeing them a high volume of work is the core capability that generates IKEA's distinctive competence, selling good-value, low-cost furniture, which it does better than anyone else in the world.[24]

> "Distinctive competencies cannot be sustained for long without superior core capabilities."

"What's New" Company

distinctive competence what a company can make, do, or perform better than its competitors

core capabilities the internal decision-making routines, problem-solving processes, and organizational cultures that determine how efficiently inputs can be turned into outputs

strategic group a group of companies within an industry that top managers choose to compare, evaluate, and benchmark strategic threats and opportunities

After examining internal strengths and weaknesses, the second part of a situational analysis is to look outside the company and assess the opportunities and threats in the external environment. In Chapter 3, you learned that *environmental scanning* involves searching the environment for important events or issues that might affect the organization. Managers use environmental scanning to stay up-to-date on important factors in their environment, such as pricing trends and technology changes in the industry. In a situational analysis, however, managers use environmental scanning to identify specific opportunities and threats that can either improve or harm the company's ability to sustain its competitive advantage. Identification of strategic groups and formation of shadow-strategy task forces are two ways to do this.

Strategic groups are not actual groups; they are companies, usually competitors, that managers closely follow. More specifically, a **strategic group** is a group of other companies within an industry that top managers choose for comparing, evaluating, and benchmarking their company's strategic threats and opportunities.[25] (*Benchmarking* involves identifying outstanding practices, processes, and standards at other companies and adapting them to your own company.) Typically, managers include companies as part of their strategic group if they compete directly with those companies for customers or if those companies use strategies similar to theirs. The U.S. home improvement industry has annual sales in excess of

IKEA's core capabilities help it keep its stores stocked with the merchandise customers want to buy.

© SUSAN VAN ETTEN

	# of Stores	# of States	Countries	Size of Modern Store (Sq. Feet)
Home Depot	2,079	50	3	130,000
Lowe's	1,325	49	2	117,000
Ace Hardware	4,700	50	70	17,000
84 Lumber	500	40	1	33,000

Exhibit 6.3

Strategic Groups for Home Depot

$300 billion. It's likely that the managers at **HOME DEPOT**, the largest U.S. home improvement supply store operation with $12 billion in revenue, assess strategic threats and opportunities by comparing their company with a strategic group consisting of the other major home improvement supply companies. To assist in these comparisons, Exhibit 6.3 shows the number of stores, the size of the typical new store, and the overall geographic distribution (states, countries) of Home Depot stores compared with **LOWE'S**, 84 Lumber, and Ace Hardware.

In fact, when scanning the environment for strategic threats and opportunities, managers tend to categorize the different companies in their industries as core, secondary, and transient firms.[26] **Core firms** are the central companies in a strategic group. Home Depot operates 2,079 stores covering all 50 states, Puerto Rico, the U.S. Virgin Islands, Mexico, and all 10 provinces of Canada. The company has more than 350,000 employees and annual revenue of over $85 billion, Lowe's has more than 1,325 stores in 49 states, stocks more than 40,000 products in each store, and has annual revenues of more than $43 billion.[27] Clearly, Lowe's is the closest competitor to Home Depot and would probably be classified as the core firm in Home Depot's strategic group. And even though **ACE HARDWARE** has more stores than Home Depot and appears to be a bigger multinational player, Ace's franchise structure and small, individualized stores (each store is laid out differently and has a different mix of products) keeps it from being a core firm in Home Depot's strategic group.[28] Likewise, Home Depot's management probably doesn't concern itself much with Aubuchon Hardware. Aubuchon is a fine operation that has been family owned and operated for more than 100 years, but with only 140 stores in New England and upstate New York, Aubuchon would probably not be included in Home Depot's core strategic group.[29] When most managers scan their environments for strategic threats and opportunities, they concentrate on the strategic actions of core firms, not unrelated firms like Aubuchon.

Where does a firm like Ace Hardware fit in? The company has made significant efforts to position itself as a more helpful version of Home Depot. Ace's Vision 21 strategic plan aims to make franchisees the leaders in Ace's unique convenient-store approach to selling hardware. Ace operates stores in over 70 countries and has moved aggressively over the past decade to improve its supply chain operation.[30] Nonetheless, because of its small size—annual sales of less than $4 billion—Home Depot's managers might not classify it as a core firm.

Secondary firms are firms that use strategies related to but somewhat different from those of core firms. **84 LUMBER** has over 500 stores in 40 states, but the company focuses on supplying professional contractors. Stores are open to the public, but without the wide variety of products on the shelves or any assistance available to the average consumer, people without expertise in building or remodeling probably don't find 84 Lumber stores very navigable. In fact, the company sells more than 95 percent of its products to professional contractors. Home Depot would most likely classify 84 Lumber as a secondary firm in its strategic group analysis.[31] Managers are aware of the potential threats and opportunities posed by secondary firms, but they spend more time assessing the threats and opportunities associated with core firms.

Transient firms are companies whose strategies are changing from one strategic position to another. Ace Hardware is moving directly toward Home Depot's primary

core firms the central companies in a strategic group

secondary firms the firms in a strategic group that follow strategies related to but somewhat different from those of the core firms

transient firms the firms in a strategic group whose strategies are changing from one strategic position to another market. To compete more effectively with Home Depot and Lowe's, Ace recently increased the capacity of its warehouse operations, which now carries more than 65,000 products and makes them available to all Ace stores.[32] In other words, Ace Hardware is trying to become one of Home Depot's core competitors. Likewise, True Value Hardware has expanded to 6,200 stores in 54 countries. But rather than compete on the basis of assortment, True Value is attempting to compete with Home Depot and Lowe's on price and fast delivery.[33] Note, however, that because the strategies of transient firms are changing, managers may not know what to think about these firms. Consequently, managers may overlook or misjudge the potential threats and opportunities posed by transient firms.

Because top managers tend to limit their attention to the core firms in their strategic group, some companies have started using shadow-strategy task forces to more aggressively scan their environments for strategic threats and opportunities. A **shadow-strategy task force** actively seeks out its own company's weaknesses and then, thinking like a competitor, determines how other companies could exploit them for competitive advantage.[34] Furthermore, to make sure that the task force challenges conventional thinking, its members should be independent-minded, come from a variety of company functions and levels, and have the access and authority to question the company's current strategic actions and intent. For example, **CIBA-GEIGY**'s Industrial Dye division makes color dyes used in carpet manufacturing. One of the difficulties in this business is ensuring color consistency, that is, making sure that the dark gray carpet manufactured next week will be the same dark gray color as the carpet manufactured today. Ciba-Geigy's shadow-strategy task force determined that if its competitors could find ways to consistently, precisely, and cheaply match color carpet dyes (so that carpet colors looked the same regardless of when and where they were manufactured), Ciba-Geigy would be at a considerable competitive disadvantage. After the shadow-strategy task force challenged top management with its conclusions, the company went about developing distinctive competencies in dye research and manufacturing, which allowed it to make dyes with scientific preciseness.[35]

In short, a situational analysis has two basic parts. The first is to examine internal strengths and weaknesses by focusing on distinctive competencies and core capabilities. The second is to examine external opportunities and threats by focusing on environmental scanning, strategic groups, and shadow-strategy task forces.

2.3 Choosing Strategic Alternatives

After determining the need for strategic change and conducting a situational analysis, the last step in the strategy-making process is to choose strategic alternatives that will help the company create or maintain a sustainable competitive advantage. According to strategic reference point theory, managers choose between two basic alternative strategies. They can choose a conservative, *risk-avoiding strategy* that aims to protect an existing competitive advantage. Or they can choose an aggressive, *risk-seeking strategy* that aims to extend or create a sustainable competitive advantage. For example, **MENARDS** is a hardware store chain with 170 locations throughout the Midwest.[36] When hardware giant Home Depot entered the Midwest, Menards faced a basic choice: Avoid risk by continuing with the strategy it had in place before Home Depot's arrival or seek risk by trying to further its competitive advantage against Home Depot, which is six times its size. Some of its competitors decided to fold. Kmart closed all of its Builders Square hardware stores when Home Depot came to Minneapolis. Handy Andy liquidated its 74 stores when Home Depot came to the Midwest. But Menards decided to fight, spending millions to open 35 new stores at the same time that Home Depot was opening 44 of its own.[37]

shadow-strategy task force a committee within a company that analyzes the company's own weaknesses to determine how competitors could exploit them for competitive advantage

PHOTO COURTESY OF LA CROSSE TRIBUNE, WISCONSIN

When Home Depot came to Chicago, Menards implemented an aggressive strategy to expand its presence in the region. It opened more stores and stocked them with as much inventory as the national chain. Because Menards stores are built to resemble a grocery store more than a warehouse, however, the merchandise seems more accessible, and that has translated into greater sales per square foot than its rival.

The choice to seek risk or avoid risk typically depends on whether top management views the company as falling above or below strategic reference points. **Strategic reference points** are the targets that managers use to measure whether their firm has developed the core competencies that it needs to achieve a sustainable competitive advantage. For example, if a hotel chain decides to compete by providing superior quality and service, then top management will track the success of this strategy through customer surveys or published hotel ratings, such as those provided by the prestigious *Mobil Travel Guide*. If a hotel chain decides to compete on price, it will regularly conduct market surveys to check the prices of other hotels. The competitors' prices are the hotel managers' strategic reference points against which to compare their own pricing strategy. If competitors can consistently underprice them, then the managers need to determine whether their staff and resources have the core competencies to compete on price.

As shown in Exhibit 6.4, when a company is performing above or better than its strategic reference points, top management will typically be satisfied with the company's strategy. Ironically, this satisfaction tends to make top management conservative and risk-averse. After all, since the company already has a sustainable competitive advantage, the worst thing that could happen would be to lose it. Consequently, new issues or changes in the company's external environments are viewed as threats. In contrast, when a company is performing below or worse than its strategic reference points, top management will typically be dissatisfied with the company's strategy. In this instance, managers are much more likely to choose a daring, risk-taking strategy. After all, if the current strategy is producing substandard results, the company has nothing to lose by switching to risky new strategies in the hopes that it can create a sustainable competitive advantage. Consequently, managers of companies in this situation view new issues or changes in external environments as opportunities for potential gain.

Strategic reference point theory is not deterministic, however. Managers are not predestined to choose risk-averse or risk-seeking strategies for their companies. Indeed, one of the most important elements of the theory is that managers *can* influence the strategies chosen by their company by *actively changing and adjusting* the strategic reference points they use to judge strategic performance. To illustrate, if a company has become complacent after consistently surpassing its strategic reference points, then top management can change from a risk-averse to a risk-taking orientation by raising the standards of performance (that is, the strategic reference points). Indeed, this is what happened at Menards.

Instead of being satisfied with just protecting its existing stores (a risk-averse strategy), founder John Menard changed the strategic reference points the company had been using to assess strategic performance. To encourage a daring, offensive-minded strategy that would allow the company to open nearly as many new stores as Home Depot, he determined that Menards would have to beat Home Depot on not one or two, but four strategic reference points: price, products, sales per square foot, and "friendly accessibility." The strategy appears to be succeeding. In terms of price, market research indicates that a 100-item shopping cart of goods is consistently cheaper at Menards.[38] In terms of products, Menards sells 50,000 products per store, the same as Home Depot. In terms of sales per square foot, Menards

strategic reference points the strategic targets managers use to measure whether a firm has developed the core competencies it needs to achieve a sustainable competitive advantage

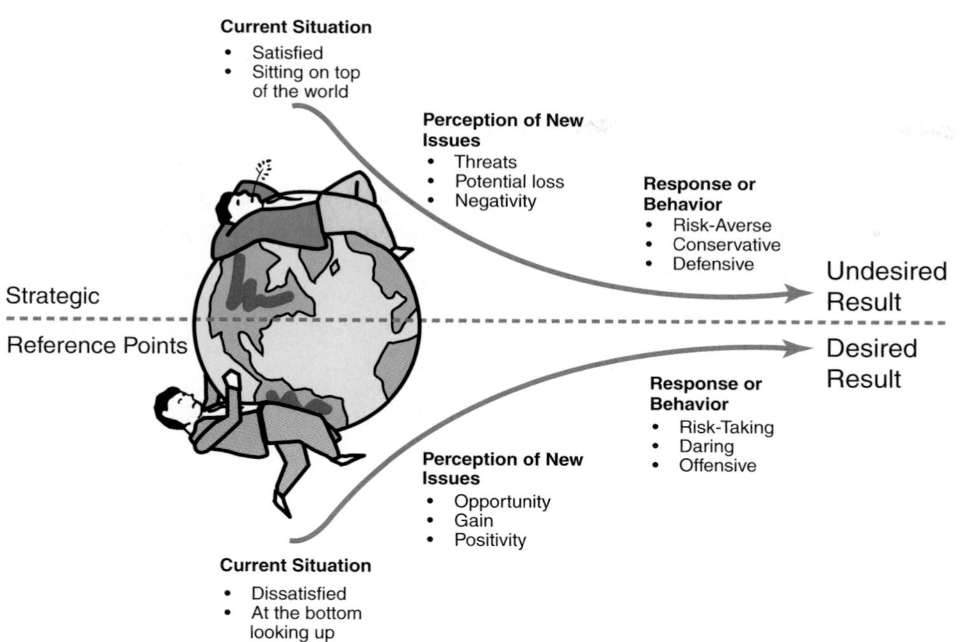

Source: A. Fiegenbaum, S. Hart, & D. Schendel, "Strategic Reference Point Theory," *Strategic Management Journal* 17 (1996): 219–235.

Exhibit 6.4
Strategic Reference Points

($407 per square foot) outsells Home Depot ($371 per square foot).[39] Finally, unlike Home Depot's warehouselike stores, Menards' stores are built to resemble grocery stores. Shiny tiled floors, wide aisles, and easy-to-reach products all make Menards a "friendlier" place for shoppers.[40] And now with Lowe's, the second-largest hardware store chain in the nation, also entering its markets, Menards has added a fifth strategic reference point, store size. At 225,000 square feet, most new Menards stores are more than double the size of Home Depot's stores and 75,000 square feet larger than Lowe's.[41] John Caulfield, who wrote a book about Home Depot and the hardware business, says, "Menards is clearly throwing the gauntlet down at Lowe's. They're saying, 'If you come into Chicago, here is what you're going to face.'"[42]

So even when (perhaps *especially* when) companies have achieved a sustainable competitive advantage, top managers must adjust or change strategic reference points to challenge themselves and their employees to develop new core competencies for the future. In the long run, effective organizations will frequently revise their strategic reference points to better focus managers' attention on the new challenges and opportunities that occur in their ever-changing business environments.

Review 2: Strategy-Making Process

The first step in strategy making is determining whether a strategy needs to be changed to sustain a competitive advantage. Because uncertainty and competitive inertia make this difficult to determine, managers can improve the speed and accuracy of this step by looking for differences between top management's intended strategy and the strategy actually implemented by lower-level managers (that is, looking for strategic dissonance). The second step is to conduct a situational analysis that examines internal strengths and weaknesses (distinctive competencies and core capabilities), as well as external threats and opportunities (environmental scanning, strategic groups, and shadow-strategy task forces). In the third step of strategy making, strategic reference point theory suggests that when companies are performing better than their strategic reference points, top management will typically choose a risk-averse strategy. When performance is below strategic reference points, risk-seeking strategies are more likely to be chosen. Importantly, however, managers can influence the choice of strategic alternatives by actively changing and adjusting the strategic reference points they use to judge strategic performance.

Corporate-, Industry-, and Firm-Level Strategies

To formulate effective strategies, companies must be able to answer these three basic questions:

- *What business are we in?*
- *How should we compete in this industry?*
- *Who are our competitors, and how should we respond to them?*

These simple but powerful questions are at the heart of corporate-, industry-, and firm-level strategies.

After reading the next three sections, you should be able to

3 explain the different kinds of corporate-level strategies.
4 describe the different kinds of industry-level strategies.
5 explain the components and kinds of firm-level strategies.

3 Corporate-Level Strategies

Corporate-level strategy is the overall organizational strategy that addresses the question "What business or businesses are we in or should we be in?" Garry Ridge, CEO of **WD-40** Corporation, explains how he changed its corporate-level strategy from a "Johnny one-note" business selling only WD-40 lubricant to an "innovation marketing and distribution company . . . [focused on] the squeak, smell, and dirt business."

In the U.S., WD-40 had reached what I named "fortress status" as a brand. Back then, more people used WD-40 every day than used dental floss. We decided to turn up the volume on that opportunity to grow. And also, to position ourselves not just to be a marketing company (which we were back then) but what we are now, which is an innovation marketing and distribution company. We decided we were going to be in the squeak, smell, and dirt business. I listened to what Warren Buffet had said. He said you have to be in businesses that are going to be [around] in the future. I felt that

corporate-level strategy the overall organizational strategy that addresses the question "What business or businesses are we in or should we be in?"

there would always be squeaks. There will always be smells. And there would always be dirt. That was the strategy as we started looking for brands that we could acquire. We then formed a team called Team Tomorrow, which focused only on revenues of the future. Team Tomorrow has a goal of being able to generate $100 million worth of annual revenue from products developed and launched in the previous three-year period. We are doing $35 million now from zero dollars in 2002.[43]

Exhibit 6.5 shows the two major approaches to corporate-level strategy that companies use to decide which businesses they should be in: ***3.1 portfolio strategy***[44] *and* ***3.2 grand strategies****.*

PORTFOLIO STRATEGY	GRAND STRATEGIES
• Acquisitions, unrelated diversification, related diversification, single businesses	• Growth
• Boston Consulting Group matrix	• Stability
• Stars	• Retrenchment/recovery
• Question marks	
• Cash cows	
• Dogs	

Exhibit 6.5
Corporate-Level Strategies

Corporate-level strategy is the overall organizational strategy that addresses the question "What business or businesses are we in or should we be in?"

3.1 Portfolio Strategy

One of the standard strategies for stock market investors is **diversification**: owning stocks in a variety of companies in different industries. The purpose of this strategy is to reduce risk in the overall stock portfolio (the entire collection of stocks). The basic idea is simple: If you invest in 10 companies in 10 different industries, you won't lose your entire investment if one company performs poorly. Furthermore, because they're in different industries, one company's losses are likely to be offset by another company's gains. Portfolio strategy is based on these same ideas. We'll start by taking a look at the theory and ideas behind portfolio strategy and then proceed with a critical review that suggests that some of the key ideas behind portfolio strategy are *not* supported.

Portfolio strategy is a corporate-level strategy that minimizes risk by diversifying investment among various businesses or product lines. Just as a diversification strategy guides an investor who invests in a variety of stocks, portfolio strategy guides the strategic decisions of corporations that compete in a variety of businesses. For example, portfolio strategy could be used to guide the strategy of a company like ***3M***, which makes 55,000 products for seven different business sectors: consumers and offices (Post-its, Scotch tape); display and graphics (for computers, cell phones, PDAs, TVs); electronics and communications (flexible circuits used in printers and electronic displays); health care (medical, surgical, dental, and personal care products); industrial (tapes, adhesives, supply chain software); safety, security, and protection services (glass safety, fire protection, respiratory products); and transportation (products and components for the manufacture, repair, and maintenance of autos, aircraft, boats, and other vehicles).[45] Similarly, portfolio strategy could be used by Johnson & Johnson, which has 200 divisions making health-care products for the pharmaceutical, diagnostic, consumer, and health-care-professionals markets.[46] Furthermore, just as investors consider the mix of stocks in their stock portfolio when deciding which stocks to buy or sell, managers following portfolio strategy try to acquire companies that fit well with the rest of their corporate portfolio and to sell

diversification a strategy for reducing risk by buying a variety of items (stocks or, in the case of a corporation, types of businesses) so that the failure of one stock or one business does not doom the entire portfolio

portfolio strategy a corporate-level strategy that minimizes risk by diversifying investment among various businesses or product lines

those that don't. For example, when **SARA LEE CORPORATION** decided to revise its strategy to become a premier maker and distributor of food, beverage, household, and body care products, the company sold off multiple divisions that no longer fit with the new strategy, like Hanes, Champion, Playtex, Wonderbra, and other apparel companies.[47] Portfolio strategy provides the following guidelines to help companies make these difficult decisions.

First, according to portfolio strategy, the more businesses in which a corporation competes, the smaller its overall chances of failing. Think of a corporation as a stool and its businesses as the legs of the stool. The more legs or businesses added to the stool, the less likely it is to tip over. Using this analogy, portfolio strategy reduces 3M's risk of failing because the corporation's survival depends on essentially seven different business sectors. Because the emphasis is on adding "legs to the stool," managers who use portfolio strategy are often on the lookout for **acquisitions**, that is, other companies to buy.

"WHAT'S NEW" COMPANY

Second, beyond adding new businesses to the corporate portfolio, portfolio strategy predicts that companies can reduce risk even more through **unrelated diversification**—creating or acquiring companies in completely unrelated businesses (more on the accuracy of this prediction later). According to portfolio strategy, when businesses are unrelated, losses in one business or industry should have minimal effect on the performance of other companies in the corporate portfolio. One of the best examples of unrelated diversification is **SAMSUNG** of Korea. Samsung has businesses in electronics (computer memory chips, computer and telecommunication equipment, color TV picture tubes, glass bulbs); machinery and heavy industries (shipbuilding, construction, airplane engine manufacturing, fiber optics, semiconductors); chemicals (engineering plastics, and specialty chemicals); financial services (life and accident insurance, credit cards, and financial securities and trusts); and other areas ranging from automobiles to hotels and entertainment.[48] Because most internally grown businesses tend to be related to existing products or services, portfolio strategy suggests that acquiring new businesses is the preferred method of unrelated diversification.

Third, investing the profits and cash flows from mature, slow-growth businesses into newer, faster-growing businesses can reduce long-term risk. The best-known portfolio strategy for guiding investment in a corporation's businesses is the **BOSTON CONSULTING GROUP** (BCG) matrix. The **BCG matrix** is a portfolio strategy that managers use to categorize their corporation's businesses by growth rate and relative market share, helping them decide how to invest corporate funds. The matrix, shown in Exhibit 6.6, separates businesses into four categories based on how fast the market is growing (high-growth or low-growth) and the size of the business's share of that market (small or large). **Stars** are companies that have a large share of a fast-growing market. To take advantage of a star's fast-growing market and its strength in that market (large share), the corporation must invest substantially in it. The investment is usually worthwhile, however, because many stars produce sizable future profits. **Question marks** are companies that have a small share of a fast-growing market. If the corporation invests in these companies, they may eventually become stars, but their relative weakness in the market (small share) makes investing in question marks more risky than investing in stars. **Cash cows** are companies that have a large share of a slow-growing market. Companies in this situation are often highly profitable, hence the name "cash cow." Finally, **dogs** are companies that have a small share of a slow-growing market. As the name "dogs" suggests, having a small share of a slow-growth market is often not profitable.

acquisition the purchase of a company by another company

unrelated diversification creating or acquiring companies in completely unrelated businesses

BCG matrix a portfolio strategy, developed by the Boston Consulting Group, that categorizes a corporation's businesses by growth rate and relative market share, and helps managers decide how to invest corporate funds

star a company with a large share of a fast-growing market

question mark a company with a small share of a fast-growing market

cash cow a company with a large share of a slow-growing market

dog a company with a small share of a slow-growing market

Since the idea is to redirect investment from slow-growing to fast-growing companies, the BCG matrix starts by recommending that while the substantial cash flows from cash cows last, they should be reinvested in stars (see ① in Exhibit 6.6) to help them grow even faster and obtain even more market share. Using this strategy, current profits help produce future profits. Over time, as their market growth slows, some stars may turn into cash cows (see ②). Cash flows should also be directed to some question marks (see ③). Though riskier than stars, question marks have great potential because of their fast-growing market. Managers must decide which question marks are most likely to turn into stars, and therefore warrant further investment, and which ones are too risky and should be sold. Over time, hopefully some question marks will become stars as their small markets become large ones (see ④). Finally, because dogs lose money, the corporation should "find them new owners" or "take them to the pound." In other words, dogs should either be sold to other companies or be closed down and liquidated for their assets (see ⑤).

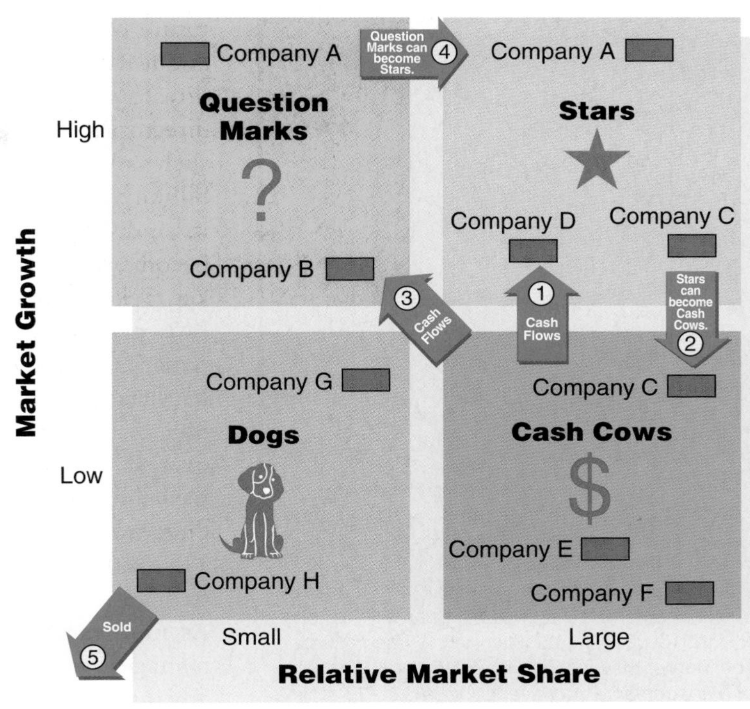

Exhibit 6.6
Boston Consulting Group Matrix

Although the BCG matrix and other forms of portfolio strategy are relatively popular among managers, portfolio strategy has some drawbacks. The most significant is that contrary to the predictions of portfolio strategy, the evidence does *not* support the usefulness of acquiring unrelated businesses. As shown in Exhibit 6.7, there is a U-shaped relationship between diversification and risk. The left side of the curve shows that single businesses with no diversification are extremely risky (if the single business fails, the entire business fails). So, in part, the portfolio strategy of diversifying is correct—competing in a variety of different businesses can lower risk. However, portfolio strategy is partly wrong, too—the right side of the curve shows that conglomerates composed of completely unrelated businesses are even riskier than single, undiversified businesses.

A second set of problems with portfolio strategy has to do with the dysfunctional consequences that occur when companies are categorized as stars, cash cows, question marks, or dogs. Contrary to expectations, the BCG matrix often yields incorrect judgments about a company's potential. This is because it relies on past performance (previous market share and previous market growth), which is a notoriously poor predictor of

BCG—A History

In 1963, the Boston Safe Deposit and Trust Company assigned employee Bruce Henderson to create a consulting business for the company, which ultimately became the Boston Consulting Group (BCG). In 1966, Henderson's group outlined the now-ubiquitous concept of the experience curve (costs go down as experience increases). In 1968, BCG introduced the growth-share matrix, which is now known simply as the BCG matrix and is depicted in Exhibit 6.6. By 2005, Boston Consulting Group had nearly 3,000 consultants in 61 offices in 37 countries and generated annual revenue of $1.5 billion (the company's first month of billings totaled $500).[49]

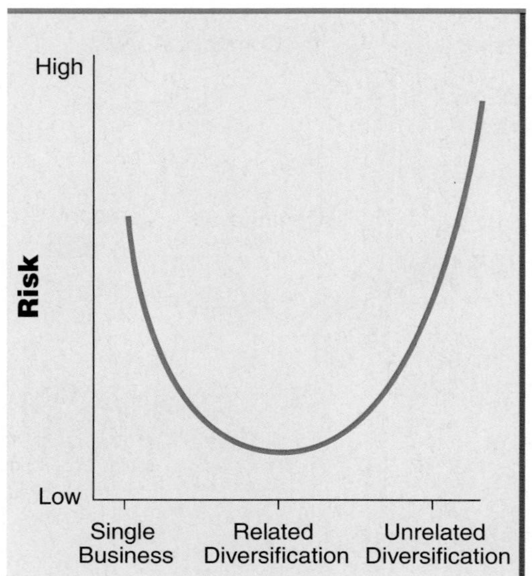

Source: Republished with permission of Academy of Management, P.O. Box 3020, Briar Cliff Manor, NY, 10510–8020. M. Lubatkin & P. J. Lane, "Psst . . . The Merger Mavens Still Have It Wrong!" *Academy of Management Executive* 10 (1996): 21–39. Reproduced with permission of the publisher via Copyright Clearance Center, Inc.

Exhibit 6.7

U-Shaped Relationship between Diversification and Risk

future company performance. For example, from 1930 until about 10 years ago, Yellow Book, the yellow pages phone-directory publisher, was a tiny publisher of community phone directories in Long Island, New York. With phone companies such as Verizon and SBC accounting for 96 percent of the $14 billion yellow pages business, there was no reason, based on its undistinguished past, to expect Yellow Book to suddenly become successful. With only a sliver of a slow-growing market, Yellow Book was undoubtedly a "dog" according to the BCG matrix. In the last decade, however, Yellow Book has had remarkable growth. By aggressively cutting prices (in some markets, charging 40 percent to 50 percent less than Verizon's SuperPages), it increased its annual sales from $46 million to over $1 billion. Yellow Book now has a 10 percent share of the yellow pages directory market and sells 500+ yellow pages directories that are used by 72 million people in 42 states.[50]

Furthermore, using the BCG matrix can also weaken the strongest performer in the corporate portfolio, the cash cow. As funds are redirected from cash cows to stars, corporate managers essentially take away the resources needed to take advantage of the cash cow's new business opportunities. As a result, the cash cow becomes less aggressive in seeking new business or in defending its present business. For example, **PROCTER & GAMBLE**'s Tide, the laundry detergent that P&G brought to market in 1946, is clearly a cash cow, accounting for billions in worldwide revenues. A few years ago, however, in a bid to bring new products to market—P&G hadn't introduced a top-selling new product since Pampers in 1961—the company was diverting up to half a billion dollars from cash cows like Tide to promote potential product blockbusters (that is, stars) such as Febreze, a spray that eliminates odors; Dryel, which dry-cleans clothes at home; Fit, a spray that kills bacteria on fruits and vegetables; and Impress, a high-tech plastic wrap.[51] Finally, labeling a top performer as a cash cow can harm employee morale. Cash-cow employees realize that they have inferior status and that instead of working for themselves, they are now working to fund the growth of stars and question marks. P&G ultimately reversed the diversion of funds as CEO A. G. Lafley refocused the company on its biggest brands (its cash cows).[52]

So, what kind of portfolio strategy does the best job of helping managers decide which companies to buy or sell? The U-shaped curve in Exhibit 6.7 indicates that, contrary to the predictions of portfolio strategy, the best approach is probably **related diversification**, in which the different business units share similar products, manufacturing, marketing, technology, or cultures. The key to related diversification is to acquire or create new companies with core capabilities that complement the core capabilities of businesses already in the corporate portfolio. We began this section with the example of 3M and its 55,000 products sold in over seven different business sectors. While seemingly different, most of 3M's product divisions are based in some fashion on its distinctive competencies in adhesives and tape (such as wet or dry sandpaper, Post-it notes, Scotchgard fabric protector, transdermal skin patches, and reflective material used in traffic signs). Furthermore, all of 3M's divisions share its strong corporate culture that promotes and encourages risk taking and innovation. In sum, in contrast to a single, undiversified business or unrelated diversification, related diversification reduces risk because

related diversification creating or acquiring companies that share similar products, manufacturing, marketing, technology, or cultures the different businesses can work as a team, relying on each other for needed experience, expertise, and support.

Exhibit 6.8 details the problems associated with portfolio strategy and recommends ways that managers can increase their chances of success through related diversification.

3.2 Grand Strategies

A **grand strategy** is a broad strategic plan used to help an organization achieve its strategic goals.[53] Grand strategies guide the strategic alternatives that managers of individual businesses or subunits may use in deciding what businesses they should be in. There are three kinds of grand strategies: growth, stability, and retrenchment/recovery.

grand strategy a broad corporate-level strategic plan used to achieve strategic goals and guide the strategic alternatives that managers of individual businesses or subunits may use

growth strategy a strategy that focuses on increasing profits, revenues, market share, or the number of places in which the company does business

The purpose of a **growth strategy** is to increase profits, revenues, market share, or the number of places (stores, offices, locations) in which the company does business. Companies can grow in several ways. They can grow externally by merging with or acquiring other companies in the same or different businesses. Some of the largest mergers and acquisitions of recent years include Procter & Gamble acquiring Gillette (consumer products), Kmart acquiring Sears (retailing), Alcatel acquiring Lucent Technologies (telecommunications), Hewlett-Packard acquiring Compaq (computers), and McClatchy acquiring Tribune (publishing).[54]

Another way to grow is internally, directly expanding the company's existing business or creating and growing new businesses. For example, over the last decade, **WALGREENS**, one of the largest pharmacy chains in the United States, opened approximately 100 stores a year. With baby boomers aging and the

Exhibit 6.8

Portfolio Strategy: Problems and Recommendations

Problems with Portfolio Strategy	Recommendations for Making Portfolio Strategy Work
Unrelated diversification does not reduce risk.	Don't be so quick to sell dogs or question marks. Instead, management should commit to the markets in which it competes by strengthening core capabilities.
Present performance is used to predict future performance.	Put your "eggs in similar (not different) baskets" by acquiring companies in related businesses.
Assessments of a business's growth potential are often inaccurate	Acquire companies with complementary core capabilities.
Cash cows fail to aggressively pursue opportunities and defend themselves from threats.	Encourage collaboration and cooperation between related firms and businesses within the company.
Being labeled a "cash cow" can hurt employee morale.	"Date before you marry." Work with a business before deciding to acquire it.
Companies often overpay to acquire stars.	When in doubt, don't acquire new businesses. Mergers and acquisitions are inherently risky and difficult to make work. Only acquire firms that can help create or extend a sustainable competitive advantage.
Acquiring firms often treat acquired stars as "conquered foes." Key stars' managers, who once controlled their own destiny, often leave because they are now treated as relatively unimportant middle managers.	

Sources: M. Lubatkin, "Value-Creating Mergers: Fact or Folklore?" *Academy of Management Executive* 2 (1988): 295–302; M. Lubatkin & S. Chatterjee, "Extending Modern Portfolio Theory into the Domain of Corporate Diversification: Does It Apply?" *Academy of Management Journal* 37 (1994): 109–136. M. H. Lubatkin & P. J. Lane, "Psst . . . The Merger Mavens Still Have It Wrong!" *Academy of Management Executive* 10 (1996): 21–39.

need for more pharmacies to sell prescription drugs growing rapidly, Walgreens opened 425 new stores last year and will shoot for 500 this year. In fact, with 4,582 stores in 44 states, it hopes to have 7,000 stores by 2010.[55] Walgreens chairman David Bernauer says, "Growth is a huge challenge, but it's the right thing to do. And this is absolutely the right time in our history to do it." Because Walgreens stores tend to draw customers from only a one- to two-mile radius, each additional store should add significant revenues and profits without cannibalizing existing stores' sales.[56]

"What's New" Company

The purpose of a **stability strategy** is to continue doing what the company has been doing, but just do it better. Consequently, companies following a stability strategy try to improve the way in which they sell the same products or services to the same customers. For example, **Subaru** has been making four-wheel-drive station wagons for 30 years. Over the last decade, it strengthened this focus by manufacturing only all-wheel-drive vehicles, like the Subaru Legacy and Outback (both come in four-door sedans or two-door coupes), which are popular in snowy and mountainous regions. Subaru's extremely loyal customers have rewarded the company with an average 7 percent annual increase in sales (extremely high for the auto industry) over the last 10 years.[57] Companies often choose a stability strategy when their external environment doesn't change much or after they have struggled with periods of explosive growth.

The purpose of a **retrenchment strategy** is to turn around very poor company performance by shrinking the size or scope of the business or, if a company is in multiple businesses, by closing or shutting down different lines of the business. The first step of a typical retrenchment strategy might include making significant cost reductions; laying off employees; closing poorly performing stores, offices, or manufacturing plants; or closing or selling entire lines of products or services.[58] For example, each time Home Depot, Menards, Lowe's, or Wal-Mart opened stores near Dave Umber's three Ace Hardware stores, the number of customers in his stores dropped by 10 percent. So, after losing $110,000 over two years, Umber began cutting. He says, "I had to walk up to people who've been employees of mine for years and say, 'I've got to let you go. You're a great person, but I can't afford to pay you anymore.' It was hard." He also reduced health benefits, eliminated bonuses, chopped his advertising budget by $20,000, saved $500 a month by using efficient fluorescent light bulbs, and made sure prices were within 10 percent of his competitors. Says Umber, "If it's the difference between $1.09 and $1.29, customers don't care, particularly if it saves them from having to run across town to Home Depot. But if something is $10 more, they will."[59]

After cutting costs and reducing a business's size or scope, the second step in a retrenchment strategy is recovery. **Recovery** consists of the strategic actions that a company takes to return to a growth strategy. This two-step process of cutting and recovery is analogous to pruning roses. Prior to each growing season, roses should be cut back to two-thirds their normal size. Pruning doesn't damage the roses; it makes them stronger and more likely to produce beautiful, fragrant flowers. The retrenchment-and-recovery process is similar. Cost reductions, layoffs, and plant closings are sometimes necessary to restore companies to "good health." But like pruning, those cuts are intended to allow companies to eventually return to growth strategies (that is, recovery). So, when company performance drops significantly, a strategy of retrenchment and recovery may help the company return to a successful growth strategy.

stability strategy a strategy that focuses on improving the way in which the company sells the same products or services to the same customers

retrenchment strategy a strategy that focuses on turning around very poor company performance by shrinking the size or scope of the business

recovery the strategic actions taken after retrenchment to return to a growth strategy

Review 3: Corporate-Level Strategies

Corporate-level strategies, such as portfolio strategy and grand strategies, help managers determine what businesses they should be in. Portfolio strategy focuses on lowering business risk by being in multiple, unrelated businesses and by investing the cash flows from slow-growth businesses into faster-growing businesses. One portfolio strategy, the BCG matrix, suggests that cash flows from cash cows should be reinvested in stars and in carefully chosen question marks. Dogs should be sold or liquidated. Portfolio strategy has several problems, however. Acquiring unrelated businesses actually increases risk rather than lowering it. The BCG matrix is often wrong when predicting companies' futures (as dogs or cash cows, for example). And redirecting cash flows can seriously weaken cash cows. The most successful way to use the portfolio approach to corporate strategy is to reduce risk through related diversification.

The three kinds of grand strategies are growth, stability, and retrenchment/recovery. Companies can grow externally by merging with or acquiring other companies, or they can grow internally through direct expansion or creating new businesses. Companies choose a stability strategy—selling the same products or services to the same customers—when their external environment changes very little or after they have dealt with periods of explosive growth. Retrenchment strategy, shrinking the size or scope of a business, is used to turn around poor performance. If retrenchment works, it is often followed by a recovery strategy that focuses on growing the business again.

Industry-level strategy addresses the question "How should we compete in this industry?"

> "Industry-level strategy addresses the question "How should we compete in this industry?""

Let's find out more about industry-level strategies, shown in Exhibit 6.9, by discussing ***4.1 the five industry forces that determine overall levels of competition in an industry*** *and* ***4.2 the positioning strategies*** *and* ***4.3 adaptive strategies that companies can use to achieve sustained competitive advantage and above-average profits.***

4.1 Five Industry Forces

According to Harvard professor Michael Porter, five industry forces—character of the rivalry, threat of new entrants, threat of substitute products or services, bargaining power of suppliers, and bargaining power of buyers—determine an industry's

industry-level strategy a corporate strategy that addresses the question "How should we compete in this industry?"

Five Industry Forces	Positioning Strategies	Adaptive Strategies
Character of the rivalry	Cost leadership	Defenders
Threat of new entrants	Differentiation	Prospectors
Threat of substitute products or services	Focus	Analyzers
Bargaining power of suppliers		Reactors
Bargaining power of buyers		

Exhibit 6.9
Industry-Level Strategies

overall attractiveness and potential for long-term profitability. The stronger these forces, the less attractive the industry becomes to corporate investors because it is more difficult for companies to be profitable. Porter's industry forces are illustrated in Exhibit 6.10. Let's examine how these industry forces are bringing changes to several kinds of industries.

Character of the rivalry is a measure of the intensity of competitive behavior between companies in an industry. Is the competition among firms aggressive and cutthroat, or do competitors focus more on serving customers than on attacking each other? Both industry attractiveness and profitability decrease when rivalry is cutthroat. For example, selling cars is a highly competitive business. Pick up a local newspaper on Friday, Saturday, or Sunday morning, and you'll find dozens of pages of car advertising ("Anniversary Sale-A-Bration," "Ford March Savings!" and "$99 Down, You Choose!"). In fact, competition in new car sales is so intense that if it weren't for used-car sales, repair work, and replacement parts, many auto dealers would actually lose money.

character of the rivalry a measure of the intensity of competitive behavior between companies in an industry

threat of new entrants a measure of the degree to which barriers to entry make it easy or difficult for new companies to get started in an industry

threat of substitute products or services a measure of the ease with which customers can find substitutes for an industry's products or services

The **threat of new entrants** is a measure of the degree to which barriers to entry make it easy or difficult for new companies to get started in an industry. If new companies can easily enter the industry, then competition will increase, and prices and profits will fall. However, if there are sufficient barriers to entry, such as large capital requirements to buy expensive equipment or plant facilities or the need for specialized knowledge, then competition will be weaker, and prices and profits will generally be higher. For instance, high costs and intense competition make it very difficult to enter the video-game business. With today's average video game taking 12 to 36 months to create, $5 million to $10 million to develop, and teams of high-paid creative workers that have the skills to develop realistic graphics, captivating story lines, and innovative game capabilities while also being disciplined enough to meet budgets and very strict deadlines and still produce efficient, reliable, bug-free code, the barriers to entry for this business are obviously extremely high. And with already dominant firms like **EA Sports** chalking up $3 billion in sales, 60 percent profit margins, 254 percent annual growth over the last three years, $2.4 billion in cash, and no debt, it will be extremely difficult to enter the video-game industry and be successful.[60]

Exhibit 6.10

Porter's Five Industry Forces

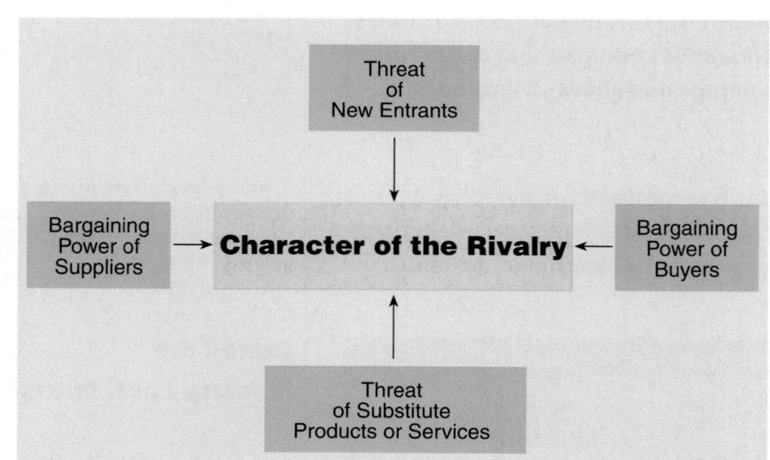

Source: Adapted with permission of The Free Press, a Division of Simon & Schuster, Inc. M. E. Porter, *Competitive Strategy: Techniques for Analyzing Industries and Competitors* (New York: Free Press, 1980). © 1980 by the Free Press.

The **threat of substitute products or services** is a measure of the ease with which customers can find substitutes for an industry's products or services. If customers can easily find substitute products or services, the competition will be greater, and profits will be lower. If there are few or no substitutes, competition will be weaker, and profits will be higher. Generic medicines are some of the best-known examples of substitute products. Under U.S. patent law, a company that develops a drug has exclusive rights to produce and market that drug for 20 years. During this time, if the drug sells well, prices and profits are generally high. After 20 years, however, the patent will expire, and any pharmaceutical company can manufacture and sell the same drug. When this happens, drug prices drop substantially, and the company that developed the drug typically sees its revenues drop sharply. For example, Prozac, a medication that fights depression, cost $30 a pill and returned $2.7 billion in sales revenues to **Eli Lilly & Co.** the last year it was under patent. In contrast, fluoxetine, a generic version of Prozac made by Merck-Medco that became available the day the patent for Prozac expired, costs only $5 per pill. As a result, Eli Lilly lost 90% of its Prozac business within one year. It faced a similar loss of revenue when patent protection ended for Zyprexa, its even more successful schizophrenia drug.[61]

© SUSAN VAN ETTEN

Bargaining power of suppliers is a measure of the influence that suppliers of parts, materials, and services to firms in an industry have on the prices of these inputs. When companies can buy parts, materials, and services from numerous suppliers, the companies will be able to bargain with the suppliers to keep prices low. On the other hand, if there are few suppliers, or if a company is dependent on a supplier with specialized skills and knowledge, then the suppliers will have the bargaining power to dictate price levels. Today, there are so many suppliers of inexpensive, standardized parts, computer chips, and video screens that dozens of new companies are beginning to manufacture flat-screen TVs. One of those companies is **Xoceco** (ZO-say-co), a Chinese company that has made inexpensive, low-quality TVs for two decades. But with dozens of companies able to supply the high-tech parts it needs, Xoceco was able to enter the flat-screen TV market without having to spend millions of dollars on research and development. Instead, it is simply buying the parts and software it needs directly from suppliers, assembling the TVs in its Chinese factories, and then undercutting the prices of now-struggling market leaders like Sony.[62]

Bargaining power of buyers is a measure of the influence that customers have on the firm's prices. If a company sells a popular product or service to multiple buyers, then the company has more power to set prices. By contrast, if a company is dependent on just a few high-volume buyers, those buyers will typically have enough bargaining power to dictate prices. For example, with more than 6,200 stores and 176 million weekly shoppers, **Wal-Mart** is the largest single buyer in the history of retailing.[63] Wal-Mart buys 30 percent of all toothpaste, shampoo, and paper towels made by retail suppliers; 15 to 20 percent of all CDs, videos, and DVDs; 15 percent of all magazines; 14 percent of all groceries; and 20 percent of all toys. And, of course, Wal-Mart uses its purchasing power as a buyer to push down prices. Wal-Mart's Gary Meyers, a vice president of global procurement, admits that "as things get more competitive [in the retail industry], the pressure that comes along with that, yeah, we try to take advantage of it."[64]

bargaining power of suppliers a measure of the influence that suppliers of parts, materials, and services to firms in an industry have on the prices of these inputs

bargaining power of buyers a measure of the influence that customers have on a firm's prices

cost leadership the positioning strategy of producing a product or service of acceptable quality at consistently lower production costs than competitors can, so that the firm can offer the product or service at the lowest price in the industry

4.2 Positioning Strategies

After analyzing industry forces, the next step in industry-level strategy is to protect your company from the negative effects of industry-wide competition and to create a sustainable competitive advantage. According to Michael Porter, there are three positioning strategies: cost leadership, differentiation, and focus.

Cost leadership means producing a product or service of acceptable quality at consistently lower production costs than competitors so that the firm can offer the product or service at the lowest price in the industry. Cost leadership protects companies from industry forces by deterring new entrants, who will have to match low costs and prices. Cost leadership also forces down the prices of substitute products and services, attracts bargain-seeking buyers, and increases bargaining power with suppliers, who have to keep their prices low if they want to do business with the cost leader. For example, although it sells the occasional $106,000 diamond ring or $11,000 Lalique crystal vase, thousands of $1,500 42-inch plasma televisions, and too many cases of $90 Dom Perignon champagne to count, **COSTCO**, the second-largest warehouse chain (behind Sam's), has a simple strategy—ultra-low costs. At Costco, nothing, not even the $106,000 diamond ring, is marked up more than 14 percent over the wholesale price. By contrast, low-priced Wal-Mart uses an average 33 percent markup. "This is not a tricky business. We just try to sell high-quality merchandise at a cost lower than everybody else," says Costco CEO Jim Sinegal, who, to keep overhead costs low, still answers his own phone and eats lunch at the same desk he had when he started the company two decades ago.[65]

Differentiation means making your product or service sufficiently different from competitors' offerings so that customers are willing to pay a premium price for the extra value or performance that it provides. Differentiation protects companies from industry forces by reducing the threat of substitute products. It also protects companies by making it easier to retain customers and more difficult for new entrants trying to attract new customers. For example, why would anyone pay $2,300 for **WHIRLPOOL**'s Duet, a deluxe washer-dryer combination, when they could purchase a regular washer-dryer combination for $700 or less? The answer is that the Duet washer does huge loads, almost twice what normal washers hold, with just 16 gallons of water, compared with 40 gallons for conventional washers. So it's incredibly efficient in terms of water and energy. But most importantly, the Duet saves time. Whirlpool brand manager Ali Evans says, "By doing larger loads, women can do fewer loads, and the chore of doing laundry is minimized tremendously. It's giving them back some freedom and time."[66] And, according to Evans, customers love the Duet. She says, "We've been surprised by the passion women have when they talk about it. They call it their 'buddy' or their 'baby.' They invite people over to see it and use it. People say it's changing their lives."[67]

With a **focus strategy**, a company uses either cost leadership or differentiation to produce a specialized product or service for a limited, specially targeted group of customers in a particular geographic region or market segment. Focus strategies typically work in market niches that competitors have overlooked or have difficulty serving. With 38 stores nationwide, the **CONTAINER STORE** sells products to reorganize and rebuild your closets, sort out your kitchen drawers and cabinets, or add shelves, hooks, and storage anywhere in your home, office, or dorm room.[68] But, unlike Wal-Mart or Target, that's all it does. President Kip Tindell says, "The fact is, we don't sell Bounty paper towels or Coca-Cola Classic. We sell complicated stuff like those Elfa storage systems [for closets or garages]. . . . But selling stuff that's hard to sell is a key business strategy for us. It ends up giving us incredible differentiation from other retailers, because they just can't seem to sell the hard stuff. That's why we give our first-year employees 235 hours of training, as opposed to the industry average of 7 hours."[69]

"WHAT'S NEW" COMPANY

differentiation the positioning strategy of providing a product or service that is sufficiently different from competitors' offerings that customers are willing to pay a premium price for it

focus strategy the positioning strategy of using cost leadership or differentiation to produce a specialized product or service for a limited, specially targeted group of customers in a particular geographic region or market segment

4.3 Adaptive Strategies

Adaptive strategies are another set of industry-level strategies. Whereas the aim of positioning strategies is to minimize the effects of industry competition and build a sustainable competitive advantage, the purpose of adaptive strategies is to choose an industry-level strategy that is best suited to changes in the organization's external environment. There are four kinds of adaptive strategies: defenders, prospectors, analyzers, and reactors.[70]

Defenders seek moderate, steady growth by offering a limited range of products and services to a well-defined set of customers. In other words, defenders aggressively "defend" their current strategic position by doing the best job they can to hold on to customers in a particular market segment. At Manoj Patel's small grocery in India, laundry detergent sales soared when Procter & Gamble drastically cut prices. Patel says, "It's so inexpensive now, my customers are buying more." Market leader Hindustan Lever responded by matching P&G's detergent price cuts and by cutting its shampoo prices, too. It also introduced a detergent that needs only half as much water to clean clothes, a considerable advantage since most Indians don't have running water. M.S. Banga, the company's chairman, says, "We have a very strong position that was built up over years. We are determined not just to defend it, but to strengthen our market share."[71] Despite P&G's price cuts, the strategy is working: Hindustan Lever's market share has increased from 27.8 to 29.5 percent in laundry detergent, and from 48.9 to 52.5 percent in shampoo.[72]

Prospectors seek fast growth by searching for new market opportunities, encouraging risk taking, and being the first to bring innovative new products to market. Prospectors are analogous to gold miners who "prospect" for gold nuggets (new products) in hopes that the nuggets will lead them to a rich deposit of gold (fast growth). 3M has long been known for its innovative products, particularly in the areas of adhesives. Since 1904, it has invented sandpaper; masking, cellophane, electrical, and scotch tapes; the first commercially available audio and video tapes; and its most famous invention, Post-It notes. Lately, 3M has invented a film that increases the brightness of LCD displays on laptop computers, developed a digital system for construction companies to detect underground telecommunication, gas, water, sewer, or electrical lines without digging, and created a pheromone spray that, by preventing harmful insects from mating, will protect apple, walnut, tomato, cranberry, and grape crops. For more on 3M's innovative products, see the 3M innovation archive (**http://solutions.3m.com/wps/portal/_l/en_US/_s.155/123515**).[73]

Analyzers are a blend of the defender and prospector strategies. Analyzers seek moderate, steady growth *and* limited opportunities for fast growth. Analyzers are rarely first to market with new products or services. Instead, they try to simultaneously minimize risk and maximize profits by following or imitating the proven successes of prospectors. India-based **Ranbaxy Pharmaceuticals** follows an analyzer strategy by making low-priced generic copies of already popular patented drugs, such as GlaxoSmithKline's antibiotic Ceftin and Eli Lilly and Company's Ceclor. With $80 billion of patented drugs losing their patent protection in the next four years, Ranbaxy plans to file applications with the U.S. Food and Drug Administration to make 20 more generic drugs.[74] Says Brian Tempest, president of Ranbaxy's pharmaceuticals division, "Our [drug] pipeline is getting stronger."[75] Since Ranbaxy spends very little on research and marketing, and its costs in India are one-fifth those of U.S. pharmaceutical firms, its profit margins are 16 percent, very close to the 20 percent margins of companies like Eli Lilly that have the high risk approach of researching and developing new drugs. Finally, unlike defenders, prospectors, or analyzers, **reactors** do not follow a consistent strategy. Rather than anticipating and preparing for external opportunities and threats, reactors tend to "react" to changes in their external environment after they occur. Not

defenders companies using an adaptive strategy aimed at defending strategic positions by seeking moderate, steady growth and by offering a limited range of high-quality products and services to a well-defined set of customers

prospectors companies using an adaptive strategy that seeks fast growth by searching for new market opportunities, encouraging risk taking, and being the first to bring innovative new products to market

analyzers companies using an adaptive strategy that seeks to minimize risk and maximize profits by following or imitating the proven successes of prospectors

reactors companies using an adaptive strategy of not following a consistent strategy, but instead reacting to changes in the external environment after they occur surprisingly, reactors tend to be poorer performers than defenders, prospectors, or analyzers. A reactor approach is inherently unstable, and firms that fall into this mode of operation must change their approach or face almost certain failure.

"What's New" Company

FIAT, the Italian automaker, the largest automaker in Europe just 15 years ago, fell into a reactor strategy with predictably bad results.[76] Protected from competition by quotas that kept high-quality foreign cars out of Italy until 10 years ago, and repeatedly bailed out of financial crises by Italian banks and the Italian government, Fiat underinvested in research and design and didn't begin serious efforts to improve quality or bring out new models until quotas had expired and Japanese and German companies had exported dozens of stylish, higher-quality cars to Italy. As a result of this reactive strategy, Fiat's share of the Italian market alone dropped from 44 percent to 32 percent. Recently Fiat has attempted to become more competitive and adopt a different posture with some limited success. Despite its efforts, Fiat remains not only the weakest competitor in the industry, but also the one with the lowest profit margins.[77]

Review 4: Industry-Level Strategies

Industry-level strategies focus on how companies choose to compete in their industry. Five industry forces determine an industry's overall attractiveness to corporate investors and its potential for long-term profitability. Together, a high level of new entrants, substitute products or services, bargaining power of suppliers, bargaining power of buyers, and rivalry between competitors combine to increase competition and decrease profits. Three positioning strategies can help companies protect themselves from the negative effects of industry-wide competition. Under a cost leadership strategy, firms try to keep production costs low so that they can sell products at prices lower than competitors'. Differentiation is a strategy aimed at making a product or service sufficiently different from competitors' that it can command a premium price. Using a focus strategy, firms seek to produce a specialized product or service for a limited, specially targeted group of customers. The four adaptive strategies help companies adapt to changes in the external environment. Defenders want to "defend" their current strategic positions. Prospectors look for new market opportunities by bringing innovative new products to market. Analyzers minimize risk by following the proven successes of prospectors. Reactors do not follow a consistent strategy, but instead react to changes in their external environment after they occur.

Firm-level strategy addresses the question "How should we compete against a particular firm?"

5 Firm-Level Strategies

5 Firm-Level Strategies

Microsoft brings out its Xbox 360 video-game console; Sony counters with its PlayStation 3. Sprint Nextel drops prices and increases monthly cell phone minutes; Verizon strikes back with better reception and even lower prices and more minutes. FedEx, the overnight delivery company, buys Kinko's copying and printing stores and turns them into FedEx Kinko's Office and Print Centers to provide a convenient place for businesspeople to drop off and pick up packages; UPS buys Mail Boxes, Etc. and turns its outlets into UPS Stores for exactly the same purpose. Starbucks Coffee opens a store, and nearby locally run coffeehouses respond by improving service, increasing portions, and holding the line on prices. Attack and respond, respond and attack. **Firm-level strategy** addresses the question "How should we compete against a particular firm?"

*Let's find out more about the firm-level strategies (direct competition between companies) shown in Exhibit 6.11 by reading about **5.1 the basics of direct competition, 5.2 the strategic moves involved in direct competition between companies,** and **5.3 entrepreneurship and intrapreneurship**.*

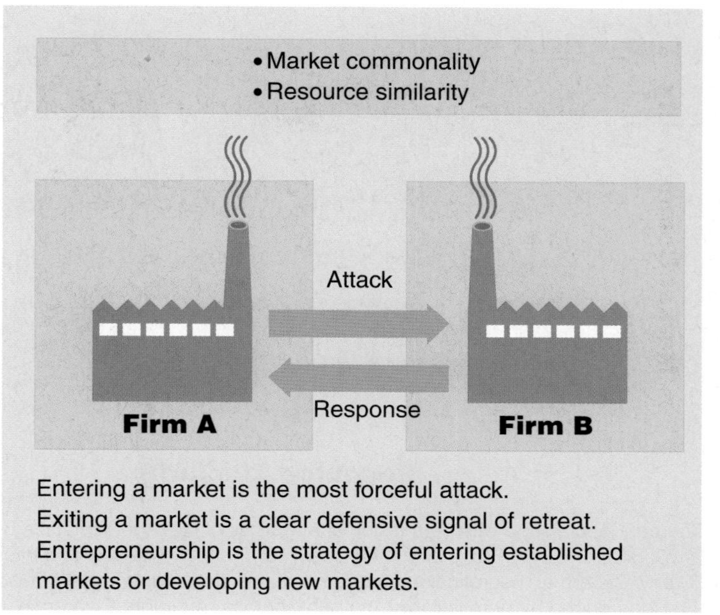

• Market commonality
• Resource similarity
Attack
Response
Firm A
Firm B
Entering a market is the most forceful attack.
Exiting a market is a clear defensive signal of retreat.
Entrepreneurship is the strategy of entering established markets or developing new markets.

Exhibit 6.11

Firm-Level Strategies (Direct Competition)

5.1 Direct Competition

Although Porter's five industry forces indicate the overall level of competition in an industry, most companies do not compete directly with all the firms in their industry. For example, McDonald's and Red Lobster are both in the restaurant business, but no one would characterize them as competitors. McDonald's offers low-cost, convenient fast food in a "seat yourself" restaurant, while Red Lobster offers mid-priced, sit-down seafood dinners complete with servers and a bar.

"What's New" Company

Instead of "competing" with the industry, most firms compete directly with just a few companies. **Direct competition** is the rivalry between two companies offering similar products and services that acknowledge each other as rivals and take offensive and defensive positions as they act and react to each other's strategic actions.[78] Two factors determine the extent to which firms will be in direct competition with each other: market commonality and resource similarity. **Market commonality** is the degree to which two companies have overlapping products, services, or customers in multiple markets. The more markets in which there is product, service, or customer overlap, the more intense the direct competition between the two companies. **Resource similarity** is the extent to which a competitor has similar amounts and kinds of resources, that is, similar assets, capabilities, processes, information, and knowledge used to create and sustain an advantage over competitors. From a competitive standpoint, resource similarity means that your direct competitors can probably match the strategic actions that your company takes.

Exhibit 6.12 shows how market commonality and resource similarity interact to determine when and where companies are in direct competition.[79] The overlapping area in each quadrant (between the triangle and the rectangle, or between the differently colored rectangles) depicts market commonality. The larger the overlap, the greater the market commonality. Shapes depict resource similarity, with rectangles representing one set of competitive resources and triangles representing another. Quadrant I shows two companies in direct competition because they have similar resources at their disposal and a high degree of market commonality. These companies try to sell similar products and services to similar customers. McDonald's and Burger King would clearly fit here as direct competitors.

"What's New" Company

firm-level strategy a corporate strategy that addresses the question "How should we compete against a particular firm?"

direct competition the rivalry between two companies that offer similar products and services, acknowledge each other as rivals, and act and react to each other's strategic actions

market commonality the degree to which two companies have overlapping products, services, or customers in multiple markets

resource similarity the extent to which a competitor has similar amounts and kinds of resources

In Quadrant II, the overlapping parts of the triangle and rectangle show two companies going after similar customers with some similar products or services,

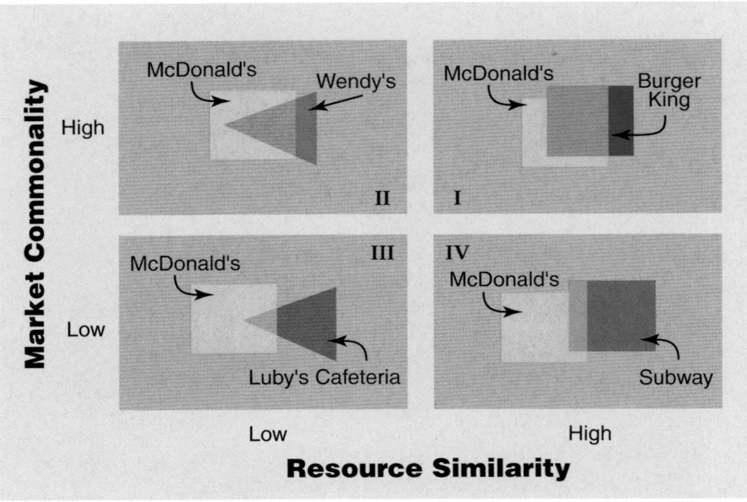

Source: Republished with permission of Academy of Management, P.O. Box 3020, Briar Cliff, NY, 10510–8020. M. Chen, "Competitor Analysis and Interfirm Rivalry: Toward a Theoretical Integration," *Academy of Management Review* 21. Reproduced by permission of the publisher via Copyright Clearance Center, Inc.

Exhibit 6.12

A Framework of Direct Competition

but doing so with different competitive resources. McDonald's and Wendy's restaurants would fit here. Wendy's is after the same lunchtime and dinner crowds that McDonald's is. Nevertheless, with its more expensive hamburgers, fries, shakes, and salads, Wendy's is less of a direct competitor to McDonald's than Burger King is. For example, Wendy's Garden Sensation salads (using fancy lettuce varieties, grape tomatoes, and mandarin oranges) bring in customers who would have eaten at more expensive casual dining restaurants like Applebee's.[80] A representative from Wendy's says, "We believe you win customers by consistently offering a better product at a strong, everyday value."[81]

In Quadrant III, the very small overlap shows two companies with different competitive resources and little market commonality. McDonald's and Luby's cafeterias fit here. Although both are in the fast-food business, there's almost no overlap in terms of products and customers. For example, Luby's sells baked chicken, turkey, roasts, meat loaf, and vegetables, none of which are available at McDonald's. Furthermore, Luby's customers aren't likely to eat at McDonald's. In fact, Luby's is not really competing with other fast-food restaurants, but with eating at home. Company surveys show that close to half of its customers would have eaten at home, not at another restaurant, if they hadn't come to Luby's.[82]

Finally, in Quadrant IV, the small overlap between the two rectangles shows that McDonald's and Subway compete with similar resources but with little market commonality. In terms of resources, McDonald's sales are much larger, but Subway, with its 27,270 stores worldwide, much faster growth, and plans to have 30,000 stores worldwide by 2010, will soon approach McDonald's 31,129 stores worldwide (just 13,000 in the United States).[83] Though Subway and McDonald's compete, they aren't direct competitors in terms of market commonality in the way that McDonald's and Burger King are, because Subway, unlike McDonald's, sells itself as a provider of healthy fast food. Thus, the overlap is much smaller in Quadrant IV than in Quadrant I. With its advertising featuring "Jared," who lost 245 pounds eating at Subway, the detailed nutritional information available in its stores, and its close relationship with the American Heart Association, Subway's goal "is to emphasize that the Subway brand represents all that is good about health and well-being."[84] And while fast-food customers tend to eat at both restaurants, Subway's customers are twice as loyal as McDonald's customers, most likely because of Subway's healthier food.[85]

5.2 Strategic Moves of Direct Competition

While corporate-level strategies help managers decide what business to be in and industry-level strategies help them determine how to compete within an industry, firm-level strategies help managers determine when, where, and what strategic actions should be taken against a direct competitor. Firms in direct competition can make two basic strategic moves: attacks and responses. These moves occur all the time in virtually every industry, but they are most noticeable in industries where multiple large competitors are pursuing customers in the same market space.

An **attack** is a competitive move designed to reduce a rival's market share or profits. For example, hoping to increase its market share at Burger King's expense, McDonald's began a brutal price war by putting eight items on a new $1 value menu, including two sandwiches, the Big N' Tasty quarter-pounder and the McChicken sandwich, that usually sold for $1.99.[86] Sales of those sandwiches doubled within weeks. The attack worked very well at first, as Robert Doughty, a Burger King spokesperson, complained: "They've created a senseless price war. That has put a lot of competitive pressure on us and others, too."[87] By contrast, a **response** is a countermove, prompted by a rival's attack, that is designed to defend or improve a company's market share or profit. There are two kinds of responses.[88] The first is to match or mirror your competitor's move. This is what Burger King did to McDonald's by selling 11 menu items at 99 cents each, including its popular double cheeseburgers. The second kind of response, however, is to respond along a different dimension from your competitor's move or attack. For example, instead of cutting prices, Burger King could have introduced a new menu item to attract customers away from McDonald's.

Market commonality and resource similarity determine the likelihood of an attack or response, that is, whether a company is likely to attack a direct competitor or to strike back with a strong response when attacked. When market commonality is strong and companies have overlapping products, services, or customers in multiple markets, there is less motivation to attack and more motivation to respond to an attack. The reason for this is straightforward: When firms are direct competitors in a large number of markets, they have a great deal at stake. So when McDonald's launched an aggressive price war with its value menu, Burger King had no choice but to respond by cutting its own prices.

Whereas market commonality affects the likelihood of an attack or a response to an attack, resource similarity largely affects response capability, that is, how quickly and forcefully a company can respond to an attack. When resource similarity is strong, the responding firm will generally be able to match the strategic moves of the attacking firm. Consequently, a firm is less likely to attack firms with similar levels of resources because it is unlikely to gain any sustained advantage when the responding firms strike back. On the other hand, if one firm is substantially stronger than another (that is, there is low resource similarity), then a competitive attack is more likely to produce sustained competitive advantage. With over 30,000 stores to Burger King's 11,000 stores and much greater financial resources, McDonald's hoped its price war would inflict serious financial damage on Burger King while suffering minimal financial damage itself. This strategy worked to some extent. Although Burger King already sold 11 menu items for 99 cents, it wasn't willing or able to cut the price of its best-selling Whopper sandwiches to 99 cents (from $1.99). Basically admitting that it couldn't afford to match McDonald's price cuts on more expensive sandwiches, a Burger King spokesperson insisted, "McDonald's can't sell those sandwiches at $1 without losing money. It isn't sustainable." Thanks to its much larger financial resources, McDonald's had the funds to outlast Burger King in the price war. As often happens, though, the price war ended up hurting both companies' profits.[89]

attack a competitive move designed to reduce a rival's market share or profits

response a competitive countermove, prompted by a rival's attack, to defend or improve a company's market share or profit

> Entering a market is perhaps the most forceful attack or response.

"What's New" Company

McDonald's ended the price war when it became clear that lower prices didn't draw more customers to its restaurants.

In general, the more moves (attacks) a company initiates against direct competitors, and the greater a company's tendency to respond when attacked, the better its performance. More specifically, attackers and early responders (companies that are quick to launch a retaliatory attack) tend to gain market share and profits at the expense of late responders. This is not to suggest that a "full attack" strategy always works best. In fact, attacks can provoke harsh retaliatory responses. When **Kimberly-Clark** cut the price of Huggies diapers below $10 a box (by reducing the number of diapers), Procter & Gamble, maker of Pampers diapers, retaliated by cutting prices 15 percent and printing "Compare" on Pampers boxes to point out that it had *not* reduced the number of diapers, only the price. In the end, Kimberly-Clark had to undo its price cut and increase the number of diapers per box. The price war was so damaging that profits declined, leading to a 12 percent drop in Kimberly-Clark's stock price.[90] Consequently, when deciding when, where, and what strategic actions to take against a direct competitor, managers should always consider the possibility of retaliation.

5.3 Entrepreneurship and Intrapreneurship: Entering New Markets

As the McDonald's–Burger King and Huggies-Pampers examples illustrate, attacks and responses can include smaller, more tactical moves, like price cuts, specially advertised sales or promotions, or improvements in service. On a larger scale, they can also involve resource-intensive strategic moves, such as expanding service and production facilities, introducing new products or services within the firm's existing business, or entering a completely new line of business for the first time.

entrepreneurship the process of entering new or established markets with new goods or services

Of these, *market entries* and *market exits* are probably the most important kinds of attacks and responses. Entering a market is perhaps the most forceful attack or response because it sends the clear signal that the company is committed to gaining or defending market share and profits at a direct competitor's expense. By contrast, exiting a market is an equally clear defensive signal that your company is retreating.[91]

Since **entrepreneurship** is the process of entering new or established markets with new goods or services, entrepreneurship is also a firm-level strategy. In fact, the basic strategic act of entrepreneurship is new entry—creating a new business from a brand-new startup firm. For example, Scott Griffith created a new rental car company called **Zipcar** to compete with such established companies as Enterprise, Hertz, and Avis. Zipcar is able to do this by offering more and doing it cheaply. After reserving a Zipcar (for an hour, day, or longer) online or via a toll-free phone number, Zipcar members simply go to a Zipcar location and use their access card to unlock their reserved car—but the wireless access system allows entry only during the time period that the car is reserved. That way, no one else can use the car during that time. When finished, the renter simply returns the car to its original location. Gas and insurance are included in the price (about $60 a day, or $8.50 to $12 an hour), so the car doesn't have to be filled up before it is returned. And all of this is done without filling out forms, dealing with people at a rental counter, and

Using entrepreneurial strategies, Zipcar entered an established market with a competitive product. Shown here is a member holding her membership card, which acts as an electronic car key.

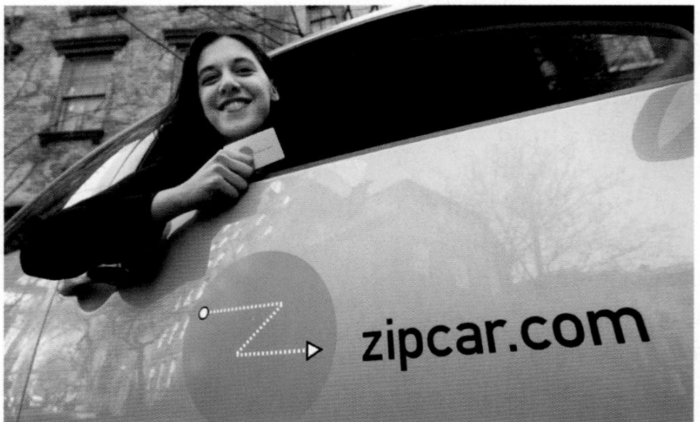

GETTY IMAGES

having the paperwork and car inspected by security personnel before leaving the rental car lot.[92]

Established firms can be entrepreneurial, too, by entering new or established markets with new goods or services. When existing companies are entrepreneurial, it's called **intrapreneurship**.[93] Think "coffee," and chances are you'll end up at a **DUNKIN' DONUTS**, which sells more regular coffee than anybody else. Think "latte," and you'll end up at Starbucks Coffee instead. Dunkin' Donuts, however, is branching out from its regular coffee and donuts and entering a new market. It wants to sell you a tall, medium, or large latte for 25 percent less than Starbucks. Rather than hire and train new staff to be coffee baristas, Dunkin' Donuts had a Swiss company produce an $8,000 automated, "idiot-proof" machine that consistently makes a good cappuccino or latte in less than 60 seconds. Boston lawyer Kathleen Brown, who has switched from Starbucks to Dunkin' Donuts, says, "I can order a plain medium caramel latte and not deal with all that fancy stuff."[94] Customer Leslie Bello agrees: "Both are good, but Starbucks takes too long."[95] With sales surging, Dunkin' Donuts plans to triple its stores to 15,000 over the next decade. As an executive at Dunkin' Donuts points out, "Espresso has become mainstream in America. And who does mainstream better than Dunkin' Donuts?" Accordingly, Dunkin' Donuts advertising proclaims, "Latte for Every Tom, Dick, and Lucciano."[96]

Whereas the goal of an intrapreneurial strategy is new entry, the process of carrying out an intrapreneurial strategy depends on the ability of the company's founders or existing managers to foster an entrepreneurial orientation (remember, intrapreneurship is entrepreneurship in an existing organization). An **entrepreneurial orientation** is the set of processes, practices, and decision-making activities that lead to new entry. Five key dimensions characterize an entrepreneurial orientation:[97]

- *Risk taking.* Entrepreneurial firms are willing to take some risks by making large resource commitments that may result in costly failure. Another way to conceptualize risk taking is to think of it as a managerial preference for bold rather than cautious acts.
- *Autonomy.* If a firm wants to successfully develop new products or services to enter new markets, it must foster creativity among employees. To be creative, employees need the freedom and control to develop a new idea into a new product or service opportunity without interference from others. In other words, they need autonomy.
- *Innovativeness.* Entrepreneurial firms also foster innovativeness by supporting new ideas, experimentation, and creative processes that might produce new products, services, or technological processes.
- *Proactiveness.* Entrepreneurial firms have the ability to anticipate future problems, needs, or changes by developing new products or services that may not be related to their current business, by introducing new products or services before the competition does, and by dropping products or services that are declining (and likely to be replaced by new products or services).[98]
- *Competitive aggressiveness.* Because new entrants are more likely to fail than existing firms are, they must be aggressive if they want to succeed. A new firm often must be willing to use unconventional methods to directly challenge competitors for their customers and market share.

Without these five key characteristics, an entrepreneurial orientation is unlikely to be created, and an intrapreneurial strategy is unlikely to succeed.

intrapreneurship entrepreneurship within an existing organization

entrepreneurial orientation the set of processes, practices, and decision-making activities that lead to new entry, characterized by five dimensions: risk taking, autonomy, innovativeness, proactiveness, and competitive aggressiveness

Review 5: Firm-Level Strategies

Firm-level strategies are concerned with direct competition between firms. Market commonality and resource similarity determine whether firms are in direct competition and thus likely to attack each other or respond to each other's attacks. In general, the more markets in which there is product, service, or customer overlap, and the greater the resource similarity between two firms, the more intense the direct competition between them. When firms are direct competitors in a large number of markets, attacks are less likely because responding firms are highly motivated to quickly and forcefully defend their profits and market share. By contrast, resource similarity affects response capability, meaning how quickly and forcefully a company responds to an attack. When resource similarity is strong, attacks are much less likely to produce a sustained advantage because the responding firm is capable of striking back with equal force.

Market entries and exits are the most important kinds of attacks and responses. Entering a new market is a clear offensive signal, while exiting a market is a clear signal that a company is retreating. Market entry is perhaps the most forceful attack or response because it sends the clear signal that the company is committed to gaining or defending market share and profits at a direct competitor's expense. In general, attackers and early responders gain market share and profits at the expense of late responders. Attacks must be carefully planned and carried out, however, because they can provoke harsh retaliatory responses.

Finally, the basic strategic act of entrepreneurship is new entry. To carry out an entrepreneurial strategy, a company must create an entrepreneurial orientation by encouraging risk taking, autonomy, innovativeness, proactiveness, and competitive aggressiveness.

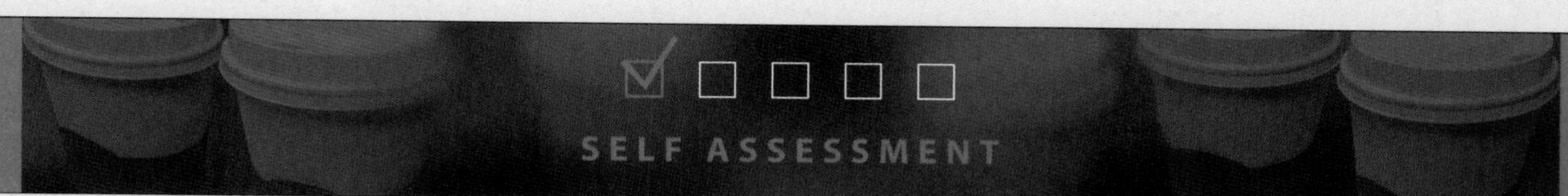

Strategy Questionnaire

Generally speaking, a strategy is a plan of action that is designed to help you achieve a goal. Strategies are not limited to grand plans that help you accomplish grand goals. You probably use strategies every day in simple ways. For example, think of a route you regularly drive. Do you know how fast (or slow) you need to go to catch all the lights on green? Or where to swerve to avoid a pothole? Or even when to take a side street to shave a few minutes off your commute? Speeding up for one block in order to catch the green lights at the next five intersections is a strategy. Strategy, then, involves thinking about how you are going to accomplish what you set out (that is, have planned) to do.

This assessment will provide some baseline information on attitudes you might have that will relate to your management skills.[99] Answer each of the questions either true or false. Try not to spend too much time on any one item, and be sure to answer all the questions.

1. I get satisfaction from competing with others.
2. It's usually not important to me to be the best.
3. Competition destroys friendships.
4. Games with no clear-cut winners are boring.
5. I am a competitive individual.
6. I will do almost anything to avoid an argument.
7. I try to avoid competing with others.
8. I would like to be on a debating team.
9. I often remain quiet rather than risk hurting another person.
10. I find competitive situations unpleasant.
11. I try to avoid arguments.
12. In general, I will go along with the group rather than create conflict.
13. I don't like competing against other people.
14. I don't like games that are winner-take-all.
15. I dread competing against other people.
16. I enjoy competing against an opponent.
17. When I play a game, I like to keep score.
18. I often try to outperform others.
19. I like competition.
20. I don't enjoy challenging others even when I think they are wrong.

To determine your score, count the number of responses marked "True" and enter it here _____. You can find the interpretation for your score at: academic.cengage.com/management/williams.

KEY TERMS

acquisition 208
analyzers 217
attack 221
bargaining power of buyers 215
bargaining power of suppliers 215
BCG matrix 208
cash cow 208
character of the rivalry 214
competitive advantage 195
competitive inertia 198
core capabilities 201
core firms 202
corporate-level strategy 206
cost leadership 215
defenders 217
differentiation 216
direct competition 219
distinctive competence 201
diversification 207
dog 208
entrepreneurial orientation 223
entrepreneurship 222
firm-level strategy 218
focus strategy 216
grand strategy 211
growth strategy 211
imperfectly imitable resource 196
industry-level strategy 213
intrapreneurship 223
market commonality 219
nonsubstitutable resources 198
portfolio strategy 207
prospectors 217
question mark 208
rare resources 196
reactors 217
recovery 212
related diversification 210
resource similarity 219
resources 195

MANAGEMENT DECISION

(continued)

How Does Your Garden (Company) Grow?

The Scotts Company is older than dirt. Well, almost. O.M. Scott founded the company in 1868 as a premium seed company for U.S. farmers, who, to his mind, needed and should have clean, weed-free fields.[100] The company began selling grass seed in 1907 and launched a dedicated research division in 1947. Throughout the 20th century and still today, Scotts has been associated with the Turf Builder line of consumer grass seed, professional turf seed (think golf courses and football fields), and numerous fertilizer products.

In 1995, the $100 million plant-food company Miracle-Gro, started by your grandfather, merged with Scotts to form Scotts Miracle-Gro. Since the merger was finalized, you've seen Scotts Miracle-Gro buy companies that make everything from fertilizer to insecticides. When conglomerate ITT, which primarily makes electronics and fluid controls and equipment, bought Burpee, the seed company, ITT asked Scotts to manage it. In addition, Scotts introduced a line of fertilizer spreaders under its own name, solidified relationships with big-box retail stores like Lowe's and Home Depot, and began selling products in the United Kingdom countries, known for their love of and knack for gardening.

Over the years Scotts Miracle-Gro has bought dozens of companies, and as a result, Scotts Miracle-Gro is huge. Now with $2.5 billion in annual sales, Scotts dominates lawn care like Budweiser dominates beer. (Your grandfather would never have imagined this.) So now that you're on top, how do you keep growing? Or *should* you keep growing? The lawn and garden market is a $35 billion annual market, so there could be plenty of upside, but drawing from your weed-killing technology, you know it's possible to grow a plant to death.

Questions

1. What strategic alternative—risk seeking or risk avoiding—do you think Scotts Miracle-Gro should pursue? Answer in terms of strategic reference point theory.
2. Using portfolio theory, map out a diversification plan that would help Scotts grow without straying too far from its distinctive competencies in turf, seed, and fertilizer.
3. Do you continue following a growth strategy, or do you shift to a stability strategy? Explain.

MANAGEMENT TEAM DECISION

Playing the Game

When you first started in the business of inventing video-game systems, it was fresh and exhilarating.[101] Nintendo had revolutionized the home video-game industry by making arcade-quality graphics available on home game consoles. By the mid 1990s, the company's Super Nintendo Entertainment System was a market leader, selling 49 million units, and your Sega Genesis system was no slacker, selling 30 million units globally. Today, however, video games and consoles have little in common with Nintendo's groundbreaking Mario Brothers and Donkey Kong games, let alone Atari's Pong.

The video-game industry is a $17 billion industry and consoles sell hundreds of millions of units. Sony's first PlayStation sold 102.5 million units worldwide, and its PlayStation 2, which was so powerful the Japanese government feared it could be used to make advanced weaponry, has sold 111.3 million units since its launch. Microsoft's first-generation Xbox sold roughly 25 million units and used chip technology that made it more powerful than Sony's market leader. Then Microsoft upped the ante with the Xbox 360, whose new-generation microchip transmits data 3.5 times faster than the original Xbox. Then Sony trumped Microsoft by making its PlayStation 3 even more powerful; it contains a chip able to perform 218 billion calculations per second—speed on par with a supercomputer!

All this one-upmanship comes at a heavy price that pushes smaller players out of the market. For example, Sony spent $1.8 billion just to develop the microchip that powers its PlayStation 3 console, which retails for approximately $500. Even at that price, though, Sony is selling the PlayStation hardware at a loss and counting on making up the money on the sale of related video games, which it expects will take three years! The same is true of Microsoft, whose Xbox console retails for nearly $300 but hadn't earned Microsoft a single penny after six years on the market.

You wonder if all these big investments make sense. After all, despite the general increase in the number of consoles sold, the same folks tend to buy the consoles year after year. Game playing in Japan is declining about 10 percent a year, and in the United States game consoles have been in the same percentage of households (36 percent, to be exact) for years. That means competitors are all vying for the same customers, those 18-to-34-year-old men who get a rush from the screamingly fast action of complex games. That is, until Nintendo came out with Wii, a simple console designed to play simple games and priced at a relatively reasonable $250. Wii was designed to attract new customers to video-gaming, like women and older consumers. As for handheld video games, Nintendo's DS is simpler than the Sony equivalent PSP3 and has sold more units. The cost to develop a game for DS is one tenth the cost to develop games for other platforms, which means Nintendo recoups its investments more quickly.

In the end, the industry is still exhilarating—not so much from the excitement of creating something new, but in a swimming-with-sharks kind of way. Sega hasn't been a serious force in the industry for over 20 years. If you're going to get back into the game, so to speak, how should you do it?

Assemble a team of four to five students to play the management team at Sega trying to reestablish itself in the gamer market.

Questions

1. Using Porter's Five Industry Forces, map the video-game industry.
2. What are the risks and opportunities of the strategies followed by Sony and Xbox? Of Nintendo?
3. Do you try to reestablish Sega by participating in the attack-and-respond dynamic of escalating technology, or do you try to follow Nintendo's go-simple path out of the video arms race? Explain.

PRACTICE BEING A MANAGER

Organizational strategy is aimed at achieving sustainable competitive advantage over rivals in a particular market. This exercise will offer you the opportunity to consider how companies in the restaurant industry might develop a strategy and attempt to gain sustainable competitive advantage.

For purposes of this exercise, your professor will organize your class into small teams. Each team will be competing for the title of "Most Likely to Succeed." One team will be designated as judges for this competition.

Step 1 (15 minutes): Develop a concept for a new restaurant business. You may choose to develop your concept as a local, regional, or national company—but in all cases, you must plan to open a restaurant in your local area. Your concept should include the following: (a) name of your restaurant/chain; (b) description of your menu, layout, and any other distinguishing features; and (c) likely direct competitors of your new concept. Prepare an informal presentation of not more than two minutes.

Step 2 (20 minutes): Present the concepts. Each team will make an informal two-minute presentation of the restaurant concepts.

Step 3 (5 minutes): Judge the presentations. Judges will confer and reach a decision regarding the top concepts on the basis of "Most Likely to Succeed." Judges should apply the Sustainable Competitive Advantage concept/factors in making their selections. While the judges are conferring, each team should discuss and evaluate the concepts presented by the competing teams. Teams should apply the tools and concepts in this chapter in evaluating these concepts.

Step 4: Discuss as a class.

- What are the challenges of achieving sustainable competitive advantage in the restaurant business? Consider cases of failure and success in your local market—what factors seemed to play a role in determining success or failure?

- What *strategic groups*, or clusters of direct competitors (for example, fast-food burger), were identified in the team presentations? Which strategic groups might be tougher to enter in your local area? Which might be easier to enter?
- Do major restaurant chains have a built-in sustainable competitive advantage over local competition in your area? If you think so, what is the source of this advantage, and is it more pronounced in some strategic groups than in others (for example, greater in tacos than in fine dining)? If not, what strategies have the "locals" used to successfully compete with larger restaurant chains?

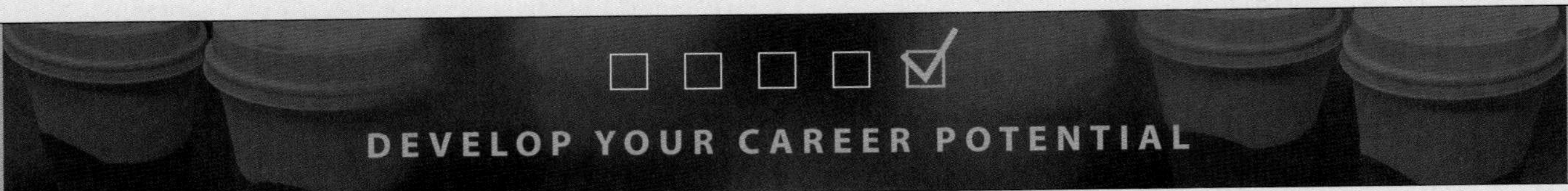

An Individual SWOT Analysis

In order to maintain and sustain a competitive advantage, companies continue to analyze their overall strategy in light of their current situation.[102] In doing so, they often use a SWOT analysis, which focuses on the strengths and weaknesses in the firm's internal environment and the opportunities and threats present in the firm's external environment. One way to gain experience in conducting a SWOT analysis is to perform one on yourself—in other words, conduct a personal SWOT analysis.

Assume you have just completed your college education and are ready to apply for a job as a manager of a small- to medium-sized facility. Perform a personal SWOT analysis to determine if your current situation matches your overall strategy. Identifying your strengths will probably be the easiest step in the analysis. They will most likely be the skills, abilities, experience, and knowledge that help differentiate you from your competitors. Take care to be realistic and honest in analyzing your strengths and weaknesses.

One way to identify both strengths and weaknesses is to look at previous job evaluation comments and talk to former and present employers and coworkers. Their comments will typically focus on objective strengths and weaknesses that you have exhibited on the job. You may also gather information about your strengths and weaknesses by analyzing your personal interests and learning more about your personality type. Most college placement offices have software to help students identify their interests and personality types and then match that information to certain career paths. This type of assessment can help ensure that you do not choose a career path that is incongruent with your personality and interests.

Probably the hardest portion of the personal SWOT analysis will be the identification of your weaknesses. As humans, we are often reluctant to focus on our deficiencies; nonetheless, being aware of potential weaknesses can help us reduce them or improve upon them. Since you are preparing for a career in management, you should research what skills, abilities, knowledge, and experience are needed to be a successful manager. Comparing your personal strengths against those needed as a manager can help you identify potential weaknesses. Once you identify weaknesses, develop a plan to overcome them. Remember that most annual evaluations will include both strengths and weaknesses, so don't forget to include them in your analysis.

You can identify opportunities now by looking at employment possibilities for entry-level managers. In this part of the analysis, it helps to match your personal strengths with opportunities. For example, if you have experience in manufacturing, you may initially choose to apply only to manufacturing-type businesses.

The last step of the analysis involves identifying potential threats. Threats are barriers that can prevent you from obtaining your goals. Threats may include events such as an economic recession that reduces the number of job openings for entry-level managers. By knowing what the barriers are and by assembling proactive plans to help deal with them, you can reduce the possibility of your strategy becoming ineffective.

Focusing on a personal SWOT analysis can be a practical way to prepare for an actual company analysis, and it also allows you to learn more about yourself and your long-term plans.

Questions

1. In light of the SWOT analysis, what plans might you propose for yourself that will help you maximize your strengths, exploit your opportunities, and minimize your weaknesses and threats? Write three S.M.A.R.T. goals (remember Chapter 5) that will help you implement your plans.
2. How might this assignment prepare you for both your academic and your professional career?

REEL TO REAL

BIZ FLIX

Seabiscuit

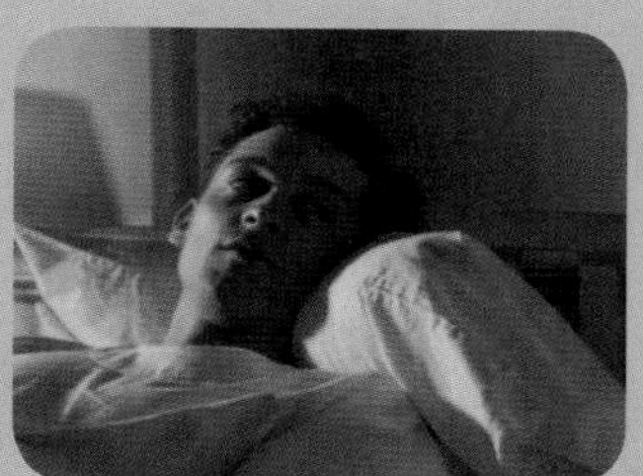

Seabiscuit is a 2003 American drama film based on the best-selling book *Seabiscuit: An American Legend*, by Laura Hillenbrand. The film stars Tobey Maguire as Red Pollard, the jockey for Seabiscuit, an undersized and overlooked Thoroughbred race horse whose unexpected successes made him a popular sensation in the United States near the end of the Great Depression. In this scene, a hospitalized Pollard is unable to ride during the final leg of the Triple Crown, so he tries to communicate to his friend and replacement jockey Charley Kurtsinger (played by Chris McCarron) what he needs to do to win the race.

What to Watch for and Ask Yourself

1. What aspects of strategic planning can you identify in the clip?
2. Which strategic alternative (risk seeking or risk avoiding) does Red Pollard advocate that his friend use during the race? Explain.

MANAGEMENT WORKPLACE

Timbuk2—Setting a New Course

"We want to make the *Swirl* as famous as the *Swoosh*," says Timbuk2's CEO Mark Dwight with a chuckle. While he may be joking by comparing his firm's logo to the Nike *Swoosh*, Dwight isn't kidding. When Dwight took over as head of Timbuk2 a few years ago, the company was on a downward slide, losing money because it had only one product to offer to a narrow market—a bag for bicycle messengers. Granted, the bag came in several sizes and colors, but Dwight realized that Timbuk2 couldn't survive, let alone grow, on the strength of one messenger bag. So Dwight and his managers developed corporate- and firm-level strategies to achieve the goal of turning the company around and then achieving growth: increasing and broadening the product line to reach into new markets, developing the brand while remaining true to the company's heritage, finding new distribution channels, creating alliances with other firms, and outsourcing some production to maintain quality but reduce costs.

Watch how Dwight transformed Timbuk2's management workplace with a strong strategy.

What to Watch for and Ask Yourself

1. In which category would you place Timbuk2's grand strategy? Why?
2. How would you define Timbuk2's core competency?
3. Identify one strength, weakness, opportunity, and threat for Timbuk2.

CHAPTER 7

Innovation and Change

© SUSAN VAN ETTEN

Learning Outcomes:

1 Explain why innovation matters to companies.
2 Discuss the different methods that managers can use to effectively manage innovation in their organizations.
3 Discuss why *not* changing can lead to organizational decline.
4 Discuss the different methods that managers can use to better manage change as it occurs.

In This Chapter:

WHAT WOULD YOU DO?

Whirlpool Headquarters, Benton Harbor, Michigan. Standing in the showroom of a local appliance store, you realize the problem almost immediately. Virtually all of the washers, dryers, refrigerators, freezers, and dishwashers are white. It is tough to tell one company's product from another, and the biggest signs in the place announce the low prices on this versus that model. This is why Whirlpool's senior management team developed the "Brand-Focused Value Creation" strategy: to create innovative, branded solutions that consumers will find appealing, that will generate brand loyalty, and, most important, that will command a premium price. During its 95-year history, Whirlpool has become an expert in manufacturing excellence. Its machines are among the most reliable in the industry, and its products have been in almost every household in the United States at one time or another. Periodically its products have gotten a facelift or a small improvement in performance or function, but no more than that.

How can you make a company like Whirlpool innovative? How can you teach your people to be creative and innovative, especially when your core capability is manufacturing reliable products? Corporate director Nancy Snyder said, "Over the years people have used many nice adjectives to describe Whirlpool. But 'innovative' has rarely been among them." Worse yet, J.C. Anderson, your VP of group manufacturing, proclaimed, "It's cost reduction that has made Whirlpool great."

Nonetheless, you can see that without significant innovation, Whirlpool will be mired in a never-ending price-cutting battle. Generic-looking products are compared on price, and your cost-cutting measures will only take the company so far. The first effort at

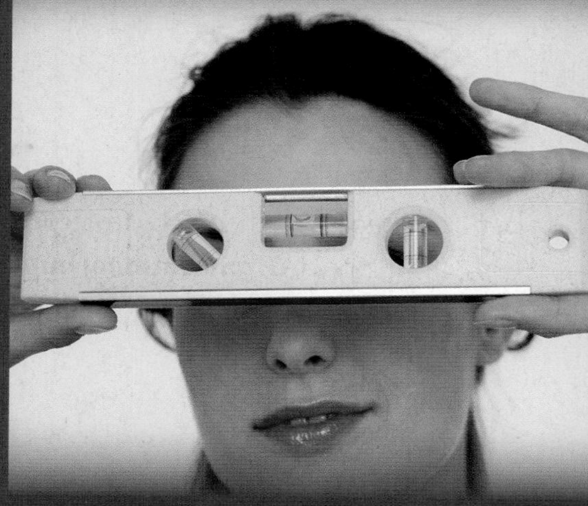

innovation within the company produced some new product lines, but expenses far exceeded the positive results of those innovations. During that effort, the former CEO pushed all 61,000 employees to unleash their creativity for the future of the company. Most employees saw the effort as a waste of time and employee morale dipped severely, making the next effort all the more difficult for you.

There is no real financial crisis at Whirlpool. The company is performing well for now, but future success will be limited if it can't differentiate its products from the pack. How can you develop a culture of innovation at Whirlpool? If the company produces a commodity item such as a standard, white clothes washer, how can that be changed so that it produces a premium-priced product? With manufacturing as Whirlpool's core strength, how will you develop a customer focus?

As you stand in the appliance store, you realize that these questions need to be addressed and need to be addressed quickly. You can't afford to have another failure in this effort at the company. Beyond managing for innovation, how might you implant innovation as a standard of your business? What role should the company's leaders play in this effort? **If you were in charge at Whirlpool, what would you do?**

ACTIVITIES + VIDEOS

CengageNOW Audio study guide, electronic flashcards, author FAQ videos, On the Job and Biz Flix videos, concept tutorial, and concept exercise

Web (academic.cengage.com/management/williams) Quiz, PowerPoint slides, and glossary terms for this chapter

Study Tip

On a separate sheet, write the titles of the exhibits in this chapter. Then, with your book closed, try to reproduce the diagrams exactly as they are in the text. Write a short description of what each diagram depicts; then open your book to check your work.

"What's New" Companies

Whirlpool
Intel
Eastman Kodak
Microsoft
Tractor Supply Company
Royal Philips Electronics
Best Buy
Avery Dennison
InnoCentive
Ford Motor Company
Nintendo
Sony
Bombardier Aerospace
FastCar
Incredible Universe
General Motors
Barneys New York
And others . . .

We begin this chapter by reviewing the issues associated with organizational innovation, the problem facing Whirlpool. **Organizational innovation** is the successful implementation of creative ideas in an organization.[2] **Creativity**, which is a form of organizational innovation, is the production of novel and useful ideas.[3] In the first part of this chapter, you will learn why innovation matters and how to manage innovation to create and sustain a competitive advantage.

In the second half of this chapter, you will learn about organizational change. **Organizational change** is a difference in the form, quality, or condition of an organization over time.[4] You will also learn about the risk of not changing and the ways in which companies can manage change.

ORGANIZATIONAL INNOVATION

"When you're done, be sure to turn off the lights and lock the doors. We don't want anyone breaking into the tent." The tent? Because of their low cost and interesting architectural features, organizations are increasingly using tents as buildings. A church in Colorado Springs spent $1.6 million to erect a 20,000-square-foot tent with tiled bathrooms, a second-floor mezzanine, and 32 aluminum arches for its chapel and youth facility. The facility has heavy vinyl walls and ceilings instead of canvas, huge metal frames instead of tent poles, windows and doors that lock instead of zippered openings, central heating and air-conditioning instead of campfires, and wood floors and carpeting instead of hard, uneven ground, leading architect Todd Dalland, who has designed tents for 30 years, to ask, "At what point is it a tent? At what point is it a building?"[5] Nine years ago, Trump Hotel & Casino Resorts put up a two-story, 80,000-square-foot "hospitality and entertainment center" at its Buffington Harbor riverboat casino in Gary, Indiana. From the inside, viewing its crystal chandeliers, marble walls and floors, elevator, numerous restaurants, and high-tech water display, you wouldn't know you were in a tent.

Organizational innovation is the successful implementation of creative ideas, like using tents for buildings, in an organization.[6]

After reading the next two sections on organizational innovation, you should be able to

1. *explain why innovation matters to companies.*
2. *discuss the different methods that managers can use to effectively manage innovation in their organizations.*

organizational innovation the successful implementation of creative ideas in organizations

creativity the production of novel and useful ideas

organizational change a difference in the form, quality, or condition of an organization over time

1 Why Innovation Matters

When was the last time you used a record player to listen to music, tuned up your car, baked cookies from scratch, or manually changed the channel on your TV? Because of product innovations and advances in technology, it's hard to remember, isn't it? In fact, since compact discs began replacing vinyl record albums more than a decade ago, many of you may *never* have played a record album. Lots of people used to tune up their own cars because doing a tune-up was easy, quick, and cheap. Change the points, spark plugs, and distributor cap, and your car was good for another six months or 12,000 miles. Today, with advanced technology and computerized components, tuning up a car is far too complex for most people. Hardly anybody makes cookies from scratch anymore, either. Millions of kids think that baking cookies means adding water to a powdered mix or getting premade cookie dough out of the refrigerator. As for manually changing the channels on your TV, you may have done that recently, but only because you couldn't find the remote.

We can only guess what changes technological innovations will bring in the next 20 years. Maybe we'll be listening to compact chips instead of compact discs. (Come to think of it, with iPods, we already do.) Maybe cars won't need tune-ups. Maybe we'll use the Internet to have cookies delivered hot to our homes like pizza. And maybe TVs will be voice activated, so it won't matter if you lose the remote (just don't lose your voice). Who knows? The only thing we do know about the next 20 years is that innovation will continue to change our lives. For a fuller appreciation of how technological innovation has changed our lives, see Exhibit 7.1.

Let's begin our discussion of innovation by learning about ***1.1 technology cycles*** *and* ***1.2 innovation streams****.*

1.1 Technology Cycles

In Chapter 3, you learned that technology is the knowledge, tools, and techniques used to transform inputs (such as raw materials and information) into outputs (products and services). A **technology cycle** begins with the "birth" of a new technology and ends when that technology reaches its limits and "dies" as it is replaced by a newer, substantially better technology.[7] For example, technology cycles occurred when air-conditioning supplanted fans, when Henry Ford's Model T replaced horse-drawn carriages, when planes replaced trains as a means of cross-country travel, when vaccines that prevented diseases replaced medicines designed to treat them, and when battery-powered wristwatches replaced mechanically powered, stem-wound wristwatches.

From Gutenberg's invention of the printing press in the 1400s to the rapid advance of the Internet, studies of hundreds of technological innovations have shown that nearly all technology cycles follow the typical **S-curve pattern of innovation** shown in Exhibit 7.2.[8] Early in a technology cycle, there is still much to learn, so progress is slow, as depicted by point A on the S-curve. The flat slope indicates that increased effort (in terms of money or research and development) brings only small improvements in technological performance. INTEL's technology cycles have followed this pattern. Intel spends billions to develop new computer chips and to build new production facilities to produce them. Intel has found that the technology cycle for its integrated circuits is about three years. In each three-year cycle, Intel introduces a new chip, improves the chip by making it a little bit faster each year, and then replaces that chip at the end of the cycle with a brand new, different chip that is substantially faster than the old chip. At first, though, the billions Intel spends typically produce only small improvements in performance. For instance, as shown in Exhibit 7.3, Intel's first 60 megahertz (MHz) Pentium processors ran at a speed of 51 based on the iComp Index.[9] (The iComp Index is a benchmark test for measuring relative computer speed. For example, a computer with an iComp score of 200 is twice as fast as a computer with an iComp score of 100.) Yet, six months later, Intel's new 75 MHz Pentium was only slightly faster, with an iComp speed of 67.

technology cycle a cycle that begins with the "birth" of a new technology and ends when that technology reaches its limits and is replaced by a newer, substantially better technology

S-curve pattern of innovation a pattern of technological innovation characterized by slow initial progress, then rapid progress, and then slow progress again as a technology matures and reaches its limits

Exhibit 7.1

Technological Innovation since 1900

There's no better way to understand how technology has repeatedly and deeply changed modern life than to read a decade-by-decade list of innovations since 1900. The first time through the list, simply appreciate the amount of change that has occurred. The second time through, look at each invention and ask yourself two questions: What brand new business or industry was created by this innovation? And what old business or industry was made obsolete by this innovation?

1900–1910
- electric typewriter
- air conditioner
- airplane
- reinforced concrete skyscraper
- vacuum tube
- plastic
- chemotherapy
- electric washing machine

1911–1920
- artificial kidney
- mammography
- 35mm camera
- zipper
- sonar
- tank
- Band-Aid
- submachine gun

1921–1930
- self-winding watch
- TB vaccine
- frozen food
- commercial fax service
- talking movies
- black and white television
- penicillin
- jet engine
- supermarket

1931–1940
- defibrillator
- radar
- Kodachrome film
- helicopter
- nylon
- ballpoint pen
- first working computer
- fluorescent lighting
- color television

1941–1950
- aerosol can
- nuclear reactor
- atomic bomb
- first modern herbicide
- microwave oven
- bikini
- disposable diaper
- ENIAC computer
- mobile phone
- transistor
- credit card

1951–1960
- Salk's polio vaccine
- DNA's structure deciphered
- oral contraceptive
- solar power
- Tylenol
- Sputnik
- integrated circuit
- breast implants

1961–1970
- measles vaccine
- navigation satellite
- miniskirt
- video recorder
- soft contact lenses
- coronary bypass
- handheld calculator
- computer mouse
- Arpanet (prototype Internet)
- bar-code scanner
- lunar landing

1971–1980
- compact disc
- Pong (first computer game)
- word processor
- gene splicing
- Post-it note
- Ethernet (computer network)
- laser printer
- personal computer
- VHS video recording
- fiber optics
- linked ATMs
- magnetic resonance imaging

1981–1990
- MS-DOS
- space shuttle
- clone of IBM personal computer
- cell phone network
- computer virus
- camcorder
- human embryo transfer
- CD-ROM
- Windows software
- 3-D video game
- disposable contact lenses
- Doppler radar
- RU-486 (abortion pill)
- global positioning system (GPS) by satellite
- stealth bomber
- World Wide Web

1991–2000
- baboon-human liver transplant
- Taxol (cancer drug)
- mapping of the male chromosome
- Pentium processor
- Channel tunnel opens
- HIV protease inhibitor
- gene for obesity discovered
- Java (computer language)
- MP3s
- cloning of an adult mammal

2001–Today
- mapping of human genome
- first cloning of human embryo
- inexpensive global positioning tracking/mapping/guidance systems
- Abiocor artificial heart

Source: T. Gideonse, "Decade by Decade: A Rich Century of Better Mousetraps," *Newsweek Special Issue: The Power of Invention,* Winter 1997–1998, 12–15.

Fortunately, as the new technology matures, researchers figure out how to get better performance from it. This is represented by point B of the S-curve in Exhibit 7.2. The steeper slope indicates that small amounts of effort will result in significant increases in performance. Again, Intel's technology cycles have followed this pattern. In fact, after six months to a year with a new chip design, Intel's engineering and production people typically figure out how to make the new chips much faster than they were initially. For example, as shown in Exhibit 7.3, Intel soon rolled out 100 MHz, 120 MHz, 133 MHz, 150 MHz, and 166 MHz Pentium chips that, based on their iComp scores, were 76 percent, 96 percent, 117 percent, 124 percent, and 149 percent faster than the original 60 MHz speed.

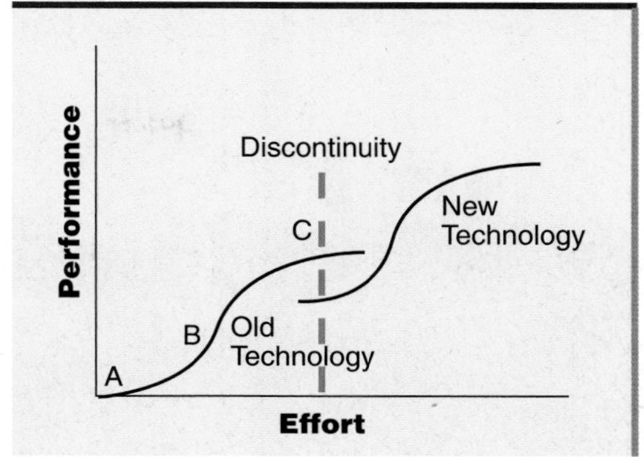

Source: R. N. Foster, *Innovation: The Attacker's Advantage* (New York: Summit, 1986).

Exhibit 7.2

S-Curves and Technological Innovation

At point C in Exhibit 7.2, the flat slope again indicates that further efforts to develop this particular technology will result in only small increases in performance. More importantly, however, point C indicates that the performance limits of that particular technology are being reached. In other words, additional significant improvements in performance are highly unlikely. For example, Exhibit 7.3 shows that with iComp speeds of 127 and 142, Intel's 166 MHz and 200 MHz Pentiums were 2.49 and 2.78 times as fast as its original 60 MHz Pentiums. Yet, despite these impressive gains in performance, Intel was unable to make its Pentium chips run any faster because the basic Pentium design had reached its limits.

Exhibit 7.3

iComp Index 2.0 Comparing the Relative Performance of Different Intel Microprocessors

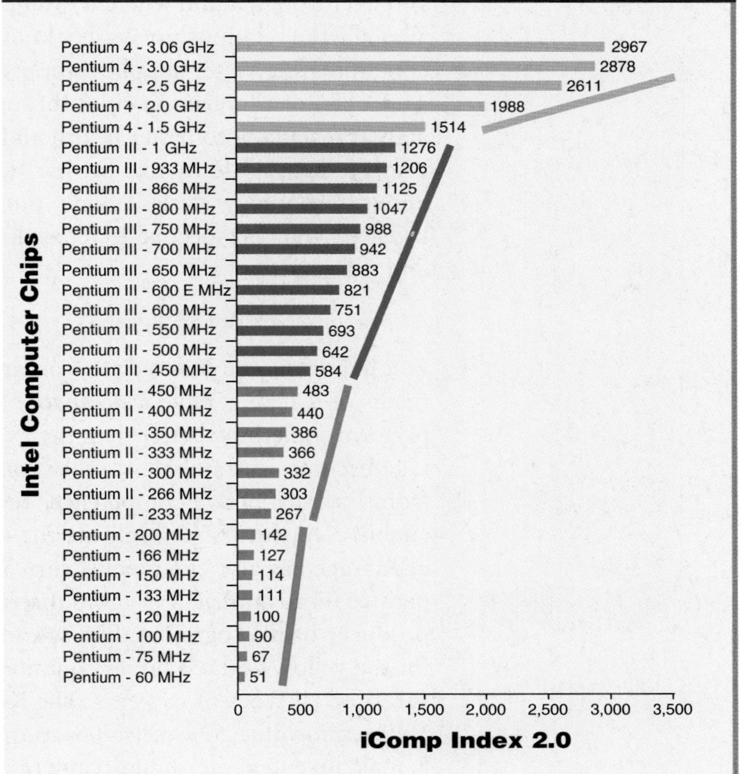

Sources: "Intel iComp (Full List)," Ideas International, available at http://www.ideasinternational.com, 16 May 2002; "Benchmark Resources: iComp Index3.0," Intel, available at http://developer.intel.com, 13 October 2001, "PC CPU Benchmarks, News, Prices and Reviews," *CPU Scorecard*, available at http://www.cpuscorecard.com, 17 March 2003.

After a technology has reached its limits at the top of the S-curve, significant improvements in performance usually come from radical new designs or new performance-enhancing materials. In Exhibit 7.2, that new technology is represented by the second S-curve. The changeover or discontinuity between the old and new technologies is represented by the dotted line. At first, the old and new technologies will likely coexist. Eventually, however, the new technology will replace the old technology. When that happens, the old technology cycle will be complete, and a new one will have started. The changeover between Intel's Pentium processors, the old technology, and its Pentium II processors, the new technology (despite their similar names, these chips used significantly different technologies), took approximately one year. Exhibit 7.3 shows this changeover or discontinuity between the two technologies. With an iComp speed of 267, the first Pentium II (233 MHz) was 88 percent faster than the last and fastest 200 MHz Pentium processor. And because their design and performance were significantly different from (and faster than) Pentium II chips, Intel's Pentium III chips represented the beginning

© GETTY IMAGES EDITORIAL

Technological change doesn't just mean computers. Building sewer lines to carry waste away from London represented a tremendous technological breakthrough. Pictured here is Joseph Bazalgette, father of the London sewer system, surveying work on the project.

of yet another S-curve technology cycle in integrated circuits. A 450 MHz Pentium III chip was 21 percent faster than a 450 MHz Pentium II chip. Over time, improving existing technology (tweaking the performance of the current technology cycle), combined with replacing old technology with new technology cycles (the Pentium 4 replacing the Pentium III replacing the Pentium II replacing the Pentium), has increased the speed of Pentium computer processors by a factor of 58 in just 17 years and all computer processors by a factor of 300!

Though the evolution of Intel's Pentium chips has been used to illustrate S-curves and technology cycles, it's important to note that technology cycles and technological innovation don't necessarily mean "high technology." Remember, *technology* is simply the knowledge, tools, and techniques used to transform inputs into outputs. So a technology cycle occurs whenever there are major advances or changes in the *knowledge, tools*, and *techniques* of a field or discipline. For example, one of the most important technology cycles in the history of civilization occurred in 1859, when 1,300 miles of central sewer line were constructed throughout London to carry human waste to the sea more than 11 miles away. This extensive sewer system replaced the widespread practice of dumping raw sewage directly into streets, where people walked through it and where it drained into public wells that supplied drinking water. Though the relationship wasn't known at the time, preventing waste runoff from contaminating water supplies stopped the spread of cholera that had killed millions of people for centuries in cities throughout the world.[10] Safe water supplies immediately translated into better health and longer life expectancies. Indeed, the water you drink today is safe thanks to this "technology" breakthrough. So, when you think about technology cycles, don't automatically think "high technology." Instead, broaden your perspective by considering advances or changes in knowledge, tools, and techniques.

1.2 Innovation Streams

In Chapter 6, you learned that organizations can create *competitive advantage* for themselves if they have a *distinctive competence* that allows them to make, do, or perform something better than their competitors. Furthermore, a competitive advantage becomes sustainable if other companies cannot duplicate the benefits obtained from that distinctive competence. Technological innovation, however, not only can enable competitors to duplicate the benefits obtained from a company's distinctive advantage but also can quickly turn a company's competitive advantage into a competitive disadvantage. For more than 110 years, **EASTMAN KODAK** was the dominant producer of photographic film worldwide. Retailers often dedicated an entire aisle for the yellow and red boxes containing Kodak film in a variety of speeds and exposures for all types of cameras. The Kodak brand was associated with quality, availability, and value, and consumers purchased rolls of film by the billions. That is, until Kodak invented the digital camera (patent number 4,131,919). But Kodak itself was unprepared for the rapid acceptance of its new technology by the market, and managers watched film quickly become obsolete for the majority of camera users. Technological innovation turned Kodak's competitive advantage into a competitive disadvantage. This technology shift has had a significant impact on Kodak, which

is in the process of reducing its film operation to a quarter of its former size by laying off over 27,000 employees. To adjust to the new marketplace, Kodak has been bolstering investments in its digital camera division and in the chemicals, paper, and kiosks used for picture printing.[11]

As the Kodak example shows, companies that want to sustain a competitive advantage must understand and protect themselves from the strategic threats of innovation. Over the long run, the best way for a company to do that is to create a stream of its own innovative ideas and products year after year. Consequently, we define **innovation streams** as patterns of innovation over time that can create sustainable competitive advantage.[12] Exhibit 7.4 shows a typical innovation consisting of a series of technology cycles. Recall that a technology cycle begins with a new technology and ends when that technology is replaced by a newer, substantially better technology. The innovation stream in Exhibit 7.4 shows three such technology cycles.

innovation streams patterns of innovation over time that can create sustainable competitive advantage

technological discontinuity the phase of an innovation stream in which a scientific advance or unique combination of existing technologies creates a significant breakthrough in performance or function

discontinuous change the phase of a technology cycle characterized by technological substitution and design competition

technological substitution the purchase of new technologies to replace older ones

An innovation stream begins with a **technological discontinuity**, in which a scientific advance or a unique combination of existing technologies creates a significant breakthrough in performance or function. For example, minimally invasive techniques are revolutionizing brain surgery. When Douglas Baptist had a golf ball–sized tumor, his surgeon cut a tiny opening through his eyebrow, removed the tumor, and sewed up the opening, leaving practically no trace of the operation. Previously, his skull would have been sawed open. Dr. John Mangiardi, who did the procedure, says, "We used to have to shave off half the head. We don't do that anymore."[13] Today, surgeons use endoscopes (tiny cameras with lights attached to minisurgical tools) and MRI and CT scans (which create 3-D maps of the brain) to remove brain tumors with precision and little physical trauma. As a result, the cost and length of hospital stays associated with these surgeries have been cut in half.

Technological discontinuities are followed by a **discontinuous change**, which is characterized by technological substitution and design competition. **Technological substitution** occurs when customers purchase new technologies to replace older technologies. For example, in the first half of the 1800s, letters, messages, and news traveled by boat, train, or horseback, such as the famous Pony Express, which, using a large number of fresh riders and fresh horses, could deliver mail from St. Joseph, Missouri, to Sacramento, California, in 10 days.[14] Between 1840 and 1860, however, many businesses began using the telegraph, which could transmit messages and news cross-country (or even around the world) in minutes rather than days, weeks, or months.[15] Indeed, telegraph companies were so successful that the Pony Express went out of business almost immediately

Exhibit 7.4

Innovation Streams: Technology Cycles over Time

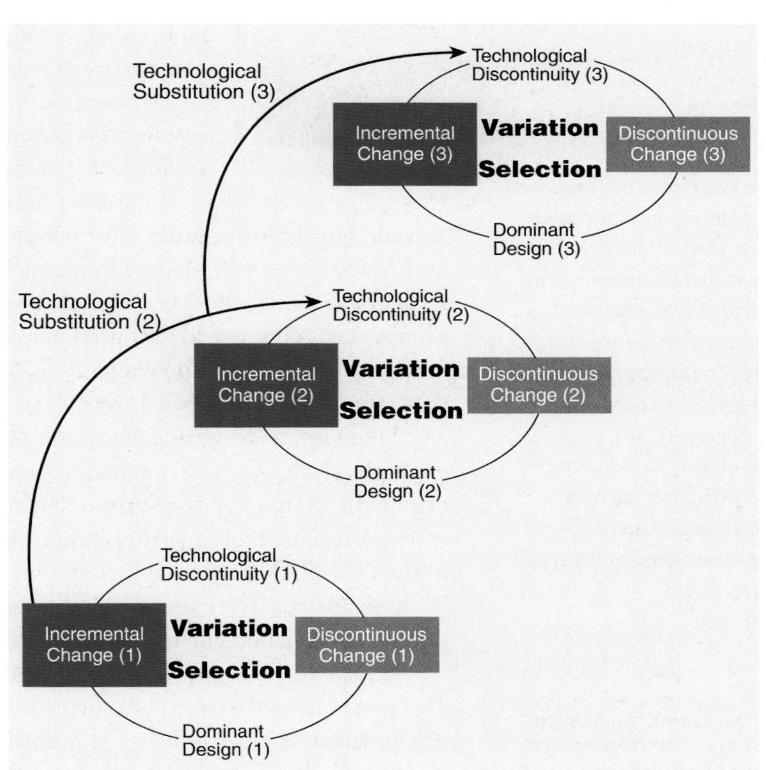

Source: Adapted from M. L. Tushman, P. C. Anderson, & C. O'Reilly, "Technology Cycles, Innovation Streams, and Ambidextrous Organizations," in *Managing Strategic Innovation and Change*, ed. M. L. Tushman & P. Anderson (1997), 3–23. © 1997 by Oxford University Press, Inc. Used by permission of Oxford University Press, Inc.

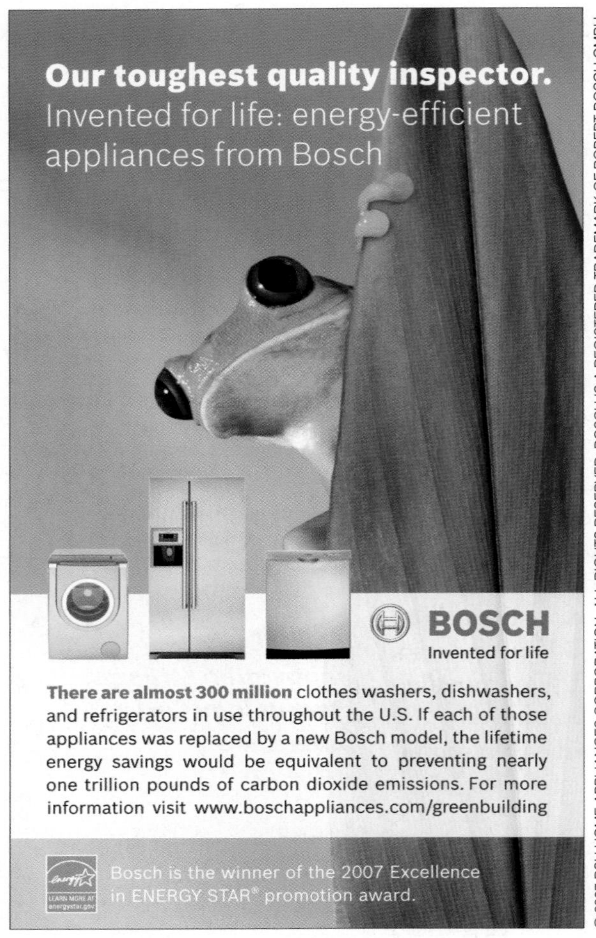

Whereas Whirlpool has begun a process of innovation focusing on design, competitor Bosch—whose products already had an aesthetically appealing look—has innovated on energy usage. Appliances requiring significantly less energy to function, like those invented by Bosch, are becoming increasingly popular and may ultimately displace current dominant designs for appliances that consume significantly more energy resources.

after the completion of the transcontinental telegraph, which linked telegraph systems from coast to coast.

Discontinuous change is also characterized by **design competition**, in which the old technology and several different new technologies compete to establish a new technological standard or dominant design. Because of large investments in old technology, and because the new and old technologies are often incompatible with each other, companies and consumers are reluctant to switch to a different technology during a design competition. Indeed, the telegraph was so widely used as a means of communication in the late 1800s that at first almost no one understood why telephones would be a better way to communicate. As Edwin Schlossberg explains in his book *Interactive Excellence*: "People could not imagine why they would want or need to talk immediately to someone who was across town or, even more absurdly, in another town. Although people could write letters to one another, and some could send telegraph messages, the idea of sending one's voice to another place and then instantly hearing another voice in return was simply not a model that existed in people's experience. They also did not think it was worth the money to accelerate sending or hearing a message."[16] In addition, during design competition, the older technology usually improves significantly in response to the competitive threat from the new technologies; this response also slows the changeover from older to newer technologies.

Discontinuous change is followed by the emergence of a **dominant design**, which becomes the new accepted market standard for technology.[17] Dominant designs emerge in several ways. One is critical mass, meaning that a particular technology can become the dominant design simply because most people use it. For example, even though Apple's AAC and MICROSOFT's WMA digital music file formats are arguably better (better sound, smaller file sizes), the MP3 digital file format became dominant because millions of people across the world first used Napster to exchange MP3 digital music files.[18] As a result, today, nearly all new digital file formats are compatible with the MP3 format. If they weren't, digital music lovers wouldn't use them.

Likewise, a design can become dominant if it solves a practical problem. For example, the QWERTY keyboard (named for the top left line of letters) became the dominant design for typewriters because it slowed typists who, by typing too fast, caused mechanical typewriter keys to jam. Though computers can easily be switched to the DVORAK keyboard layout, which doubles typing speed and cuts typing errors by half, QWERTY lives on as the standard keyboard. Thus, the best technology doesn't always become the dominant design.

Dominant designs can also emerge through independent standards bodies. The International Telecommunication Union (**http://www.itu.ch**) is an independent organization that establishes standards for the communications industry. The ITU was founded in Paris in 1865 because European countries all had different telegraph systems that could not communicate with each other. Messages crossing borders had to be transcribed from one country's system before they could be coded and delivered on another. After three months of negotiations, 20 countries signed the International Telegraph Convention, which standardized equipment and instructions, enabling

design competition competition between old and new technologies to establish a new technological standard or dominant design

dominant design a new technological design or process that becomes the accepted market standard telegraph messages to flow seamlessly from country to country. Today, as in 1865, various standards are proposed, discussed, negotiated, and changed until agreement is reached on a final set of standards that communication industries (Internet, telephony, satellites, radio) will follow worldwide. For example, within a few years, multibeam, or spot-beam, technology should double or triple the speed and capacity with which satellites deliver data streams to users on Earth.[19] Likewise, China has developed a new standard for third-generation (3G) mobile phone networks that is fast enough for graphics, video, and other high-speed Internet functions.[20] Eventually, the ITU will choose an official standard from several competing standards for both of those technologies.[21]

> A design can become dominant if it solves a practical problem.

No matter how it happens, the emergence of a dominant design is a key event in an innovation stream. First, the emergence of a dominant design indicates that there are winners and losers. Technological innovation is both competence enhancing and competence destroying. Companies that bet on the now-dominant design usually prosper. In contrast, when companies bet on the wrong design or the old technology, they may experience **technological lockout**, which occurs when a new dominant design (that is, a significantly better technology) prevents a company from competitively selling its products or makes it difficult to do so.[22] In fact, more companies are likely to go out of business in a time of discontinuous change and changing standards than in an economic recession or slowdown. Second, the emergence of a dominant design signals a shift from design experimentation and competition to **incremental change**, a phase in which companies innovate by lowering the cost and improving the functioning and performance of the dominant design. For example, during a technology cycle, manufacturing efficiencies enable Intel to cut the cost of its chips by one-half to two-thirds, while doubling or tripling their speed. This focus on improving the dominant design continues until the next technological discontinuity occurs.

Review 1: Why Innovation Matters

Technology cycles typically follow an S-curve pattern of innovation. Early in the cycle, technological progress is slow, and improvements in technological performance are small. As a technology matures, however, performance improves quickly. Finally, as the limits of a technology are reached, only small improvements occur. At this point, significant improvements in performance must come from new technologies. The best way to protect a competitive advantage is to create a stream of innovative ideas and products. Innovation streams begin with technological discontinuities that create significant breakthroughs in performance or function. Technological discontinuities are followed by discontinuous change, in which customers purchase new technologies (technological substitution) and companies compete to establish the new dominant design (design competition). Dominant designs emerge because of critical mass, because they solve a practical problem, or because of the negotiations of independent standards bodies. Because technological innovation is both competence enhancing and competence destroying, companies that bet on the wrong design often struggle (technological lockout), while companies that bet on the eventual dominant design usually prosper. Emergence of a dominant design leads to a focus on incremental change, lowering costs and making small, but steady improvements in the dominant design. This focus continues until the next technological discontinuity occurs.

technological lockout the inability of a company to competitively sell its products because it relied on old technology or a nondominant design

incremental change the phase of a technology cycle in which companies innovate by lowering costs and improving the functioning and performance of the dominant technological design

2 Managing Innovation

As the discussion of technology cycles and innovation streams showed, managers must be equally good at managing innovation in two very different circumstances. First, during discontinuous change, companies must find a way to anticipate and survive the technological changes that can suddenly transform industry leaders into losers and industry unknowns into powerhouses. Companies that can't manage innovation following technological discontinuities risk quick organizational decline and dissolution. Second, after a new dominant design emerges following discontinuous change, companies must manage the very different process of incremental improvement and innovation. Companies that can't manage incremental innovation slowly deteriorate as they fall farther behind industry leaders.

Unfortunately, what works well when managing innovation during discontinuous change doesn't work well when managing innovation during periods of incremental change (and vice versa).

Consequently, to successfully manage innovation streams, companies need to be good at three things: ***2.1 managing sources of innovation, 2.2 managing innovation during discontinuous change****, and* ***2.3 managing innovation during incremental change****.*

2.1 Managing Sources of Innovation

Innovation comes from great ideas. So a starting point for managing innovation is to manage the sources of innovation, that is, where new ideas come from. One place that new ideas originate is with brilliant inventors. For example, do you know who invented the telephone, the light bulb, a way to collect and store electricity, air-conditioning, radio, television, automobiles, the jet engine, computers, and the Internet? Respectively, these innovations were created by Alexander Graham Bell, Thomas Edison, Pieter van Musschenbroek, Willis Carrier, Guglielmo Marconi, John Baird and Philo T. Farnsworth, Gottlieb Daimler and Wilhelm Maybach, Sir Frank Whittle, Charles Babbage, and Vint Cerf and Robert Kahn. These innovators and their innovations forever changed the course of modern life. Only a few companies, however, have the likes of an Edison, Marconi, or Graham Bell working for them. Given that great thinkers and inventors are in short supply, what might companies do to ensure a steady flow of good ideas?

Well, when we say that innovation begins with great ideas, we're really saying that innovation begins with creativity. Creativity is the production of novel and useful ideas.[23] Although companies can't command employees to be creative ("You will be more creative!"), they can jump-start innovation by building **creative work environments**, in which workers perceive that creative thoughts and ideas are welcomed and valued. As Exhibit 7.5 shows, creative work environments have six components that encourage creativity: challenging work, organizational encouragement, supervisory encouragement, work group encouragement, freedom, and a lack of organizational impediments.[24]

Work is *challenging* when it requires effort, demands attention and focus, and is perceived as important to others in the organization. According to researcher Mihaly Csikszentmihalyi (pronounced ME-high-ee CHICK-sent-me-high-ee), challenging work promotes creativity because it creates a rewarding psychological experience known as "flow." **Flow** is a psychological state of effortlessness, in which you

creative work environments workplace cultures in which workers perceive that new ideas are welcomed, valued, and encouraged

flow a psychological state of effortlessness, in which you become completely absorbed in what you're doing and time seems to pass quickly become completely absorbed in what you're doing and time seems to fly. When flow occurs, who you are and what you're doing become one. Csikszentmihalyi first encountered flow when studying artists: "What struck me by looking at artists at work was their tremendous focus on the work, this enormous involvement, this forgetting of time and body. It wasn't justified by expectation of rewards, like, 'Aha, I'm going to sell this painting.'"[25] Csikszentmihalyi has found that chess players, rock climbers, dancers, surgeons, and athletes regularly experience flow, too. A key part of creating flow experiences, and thus creative work environments, is to achieve a balance between skills and task challenge. When workers can do more than is required of them, they become bored, and when their skills aren't sufficient to accomplish a task, they become anxious. When skills and task challenge are balanced, however, flow and creativity can occur.

Organizational Encouragement
Challenging Work
Supervisory Encouragement
Creative Work Environments
Lack of Organizational Impediments
Work Group Encouragement
Freedom

Sources: T. M. Amabile, R. Conti, H. Coon, J. Lazenby, & M. Herron, "Assessing the Work Environment for Creativity," *Academy of Management Journal* 39 (1996): 1154–1184.

Exhibit 7.5

Components of Creative Work Environments

> "When skills and task challenge are balanced, however, flow and creativity can occur."

A creative work environment requires three kinds of encouragement: organizational, supervisory, and work group encouragement. *Organizational encouragement* of creativity occurs when management encourages risk taking and new ideas, supports and fairly evaluates new ideas, rewards and recognizes creativity, and encourages the sharing of new ideas throughout different parts of the company. *Supervisory encouragement* of creativity occurs when supervisors provide clear goals, encourage open interaction with subordinates, and actively support development teams' work and ideas. *Work group encouragement* occurs when group members have diverse experience, education, and backgrounds and the group fosters mutual openness to ideas, positive, constructive challenge to ideas, and shared commitment to ideas. For further discussion of these ideas, see Chapter 10 on managing teams,.

An example of organizational and supervisory encouragement can be found at **Tractor Supply Company**, which sells farm supplies, equipment, and tools. Tractor Supply encourages employees to take calculated risks, and it doesn't punish them if those risks don't work out. Chairman Joe Scarlett explains what happened after a company buyer took a gamble on a new line of "Iron Smith" power tools for its stores: "It was well put together as a program. But we imported the product and it was junk. We could have fired the buyer. But he did a wonderful job conceptually. We took our punch in the mouth and our financial losses. Today, that buyer is our VP of marketing. The only reason the line didn't work was because the outside people we relied on for a piece of the execution didn't work out. Most people who take risks are not doing crazy things. We just tell them to fix the problem. Nobody gets chewed out."[26]

Freedom means having autonomy over one's day-to-day work and a sense of ownership and control over one's ideas. Numerous studies have indicated that creative ideas thrive under conditions of freedom. **Royal Philips Electronics** (Philips) embraced this freedom in its drive to both simplify its products and make everything sensible. All groups within the company have been given complete freedom to rethink every product with the goal of making it simpler for the end user to install and use. Says Andrea Ragnetti, chief marketing officer for Philips, "In the past, companies just

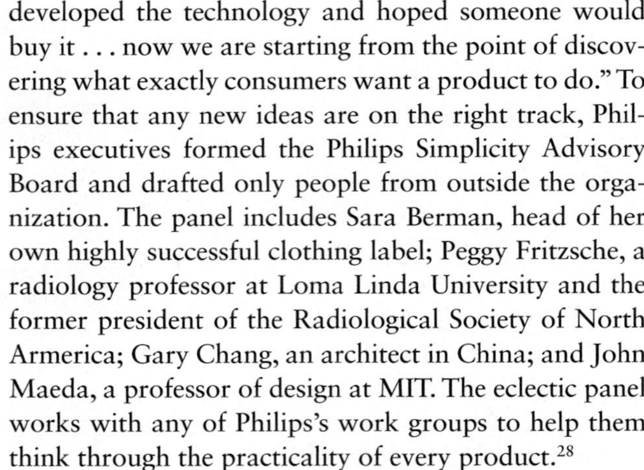

developed the technology and hoped someone would buy it . . . now we are starting from the point of discovering what exactly consumers want a product to do." To ensure that any new ideas are on the right track, Philips executives formed the Philips Simplicity Advisory Board and drafted only people from outside the organization. The panel includes Sara Berman, head of her own highly successful clothing label; Peggy Fritzsche, a radiology professor at Loma Linda University and the former president of the Radiological Society of North Armerica; Gary Chang, an architect in China; and John Maeda, a professor of design at MIT. The eclectic panel works with any of Philips's work groups to help them think through the practicality of every product.[28]

To foster creativity, companies may also have to *remove impediments* to creativity from their work environments. Internal conflict and power struggles, rigid management structures, and a conservative bias toward the status quo can all discourage creativity. They create the perception that others in the organization will decide which ideas are acceptable and deserve support. **Best Buy** developed a unique, somewhat risky program called ROWE (results-only work environment). All of the 4,000 employees at the company's headquarters in Minneapolis work on their own schedule. There are no office hours, no set meetings, and no need to come into the office at all—provided you get your work done. Employees are strictly evaluated on output measures that are determined by the management of the company. Since its inception, productivity has risen 35 percent, turnover has dropped dramatically, and employee satisfaction has skyrocketed. As pointed out by *BusinessWeek*, "the most innovative new product may be the structure of the workplace itself."[29]

doing the right thing

Give Credit, Don't Take It

You came up with a great idea and ran it by your boss, who loved it. Next thing you know, the office is buzzing about this "great new idea." But instead of giving you the credit, your boss shamelessly sold the idea as his own. Not only is stealing others' ideas wrong, but nothing kills a creative work environment faster than not giving people credit for their ideas. If you're the boss, no matter who comes up with "the" idea, give that person credit. Spread the recognition and acknowledgment around so that their coworkers and your boss's boss know about your employees' great ideas. Do the right thing. Give credit where it's due. You'll be rewarded with more great ideas.[27]

2.2 Experiential Approach: Managing Innovation during Discontinuous Change

experiential approach to innovation an approach to innovation that assumes a highly uncertain environment and uses intuition, flexible options, and hands-on experience to reduce uncertainty and accelerate learning and understanding

design iteration a cycle of repetition in which a company tests a prototype of a new product or service, improves on that design, and then builds and tests the improved prototype

product prototype a full-scale working model that is being tested for design, function, and reliability

testing the systematic comparison of different product designs or design iterations

A study of 72 product-development projects (that is, innovation) in 36 computer companies across the United States, Europe, and Asia found that companies that succeeded in periods of discontinuous change (characterized by technological substitution and design competition, as described earlier) typically followed an experiential approach to innovation.[30] The **experiential approach to innovation** assumes that innovation is occurring within a highly uncertain environment and that the key to fast product innovation is to use intuition, flexible options, and hands-on experience to reduce uncertainty and accelerate learning and understanding. As Exhibit 7.6 shows, the experiential approach to innovation has five aspects: design iterations, testing, milestones, multifunctional teams, and powerful leaders.[31]

An "iteration" is a repetition. So a **design iteration** is a cycle of repetition in which a company tests a prototype of a new product or service, improves on the design, and then builds and tests the improved product or service prototype. A **product prototype** is a full-scale working model that is being tested for design, function, and reliability. **Testing** is a systematic comparison of different product

	Experiential Approach to Innovation: Managing Innovation During Discontinuous Change	Compression Approach to Innovation: Managing Innovation during Incremental Change
Environment	Highly uncertain discontinuous change—technological substitution and design competition	Certain incremental change—established technology (i.e., dominant design)
Goals	Speed Significant improvements in performance Establishment of new dominant design	Speed Lower costs Incremental improvements in performance of dominant design
Approach	Build something new, different, and substantially better	Compress time and steps needed to bring about small improvements
Steps	Design iterations Testing Milestones Multifunctional teams Powerful leaders	Planning Supplier involvement Shortening the time of individual steps Overlapping steps Multifunctional teams

Exhibit 7.6

Comparing the Experiential and Compression Approaches to Managing Innovation

designs or design iterations. Companies that want to create a new dominant design following a technological discontinuity quickly build, test, improve, and retest a series of different product prototypes. When AVERY DENNISON decided to build a new label printer for offices, focus groups complained about paper cuts, the difficulty of peeling labels, the ends of labels sticking together, and labels that got dirty or wrinkled with handling. Office worker Heather Wilson said, "If all you had to do is just grab a label off and stick it on, it would save a lot of time."[32] Accordingly, Avery designed a prototype printer that prints and then partially peels each label. When Avery tested the prototype in offices, workers said that it was too heavy to move, its large electrical plug wouldn't fit a standard surge protector strip, and it was too loud. After numerous design iterations, Avery's Quick Peel Automatic Label Peeler is quiet, weighs just seven pounds, and can print 500 labels in just 30 minutes, as opposed to 54 minutes for earlier printers.

By trying a number of very different designs, or by making successive improvements and changes in the same design, frequent design iterations reduce uncertainty and improve understanding. Simply put, the more prototypes you build, the more likely you are to learn what works and what doesn't. Also, when designers and engineers build a number of prototypes, they are less likely to "fall in love" with a particular prototype. Instead, they'll be more concerned with improving the product or technology as much as they can. Testing speeds up and improves the innovation process, too. When two very different design prototypes are tested against each other, or the new design iteration is tested against the previous iteration, product design strengths and weaknesses quickly become apparent. Likewise, testing uncovers errors early in the design process when they are easiest to correct. Finally, testing accelerates learning and understanding by forcing engineers and product designers to examine hard data about product performance. When there's hard evidence that prototypes are testing well, the confidence of the design team grows. Also, personal conflict between design team members is less likely when testing focuses on hard measurements and facts rather than personal hunches and preferences.

mgmt: trends

A 90,000-Member Idea Machine

In an effort to tap unaffiliated scientific talent and expertise, companies are turning to the likes of INNOCENTIVE. Funded and launched by Eli Lilly in 2001, InnoCentive now boasts an army of 90,000 scientists willing to tackle problems posted to its website by companies (called "Seekers") like Procter & Gamble, DuPont, and Boeing. Seekers pay Solvers anywhere from $10,000 to $100,000 per solution. The purpose of the site is to spur innovation in chemistry, biology, biochemistry, and materials science. As of 2006, more than 30 percent of the problems posted on the site had been solved. Keep your eyes on the trend of using financial awards to spur innovative thinking.[34]

Milestones are formal project review points used to assess progress and performance. For example, a company that has put itself on a 12-month schedule to complete a project might schedule milestones at the 3-month, 6-month, and 9-month points on the schedule. By making people regularly assess what they're doing, how well they're performing, and whether they need to take corrective action, milestones provide structure to the general chaos that follows technological discontinuities. Milestones also shorten the innovation process by creating a sense of urgency that keeps everyone on task. For example, when Florida Power & Light was building its first nuclear power facility, the company's construction manager passed out 2,000 desk calendars to company employees, construction contractors, vendors, and suppliers to ensure that everyone involved in the project was aware of the construction timeline. Contractors that regularly missed deadlines were replaced.[33] Finally, milestones are beneficial for innovation because meeting regular milestones builds momentum by giving people a sense of accomplishment.

Multifunctional teams are work teams composed of people from different departments. Multifunctional teams accelerate learning and understanding by mixing and integrating technical, marketing, and manufacturing activities. By involving all key departments in development from the start, multifunctional teams speed innovation through early identification of new ideas or problems that would typically not have been generated or addressed until much later. FORD MOTOR COMPANY relied on multifunctional teams to design its hybrid sport utility vehicle (SUV) that runs on gas and battery power. The hybrid version of the Ford Escape is powerful enough to tow a boat, but still gets 36 miles per gallon. At Ford, researchers, who dream up and test ideas, and product engineers, who find ways to get them to work, usually work in separate buildings. But to design the hybrid Escape, they worked side by side in cubicles for over three years. Team member Tom Gee says, "Before, it might have been a half mile apart, but even one building away is a barrier compared with what we have now. It makes a huge difference."[35] Working side by side was critical to figuring out how to prevent the battery from being damaged by overcharging in cold weather. Ford's researchers and engineers solved the problem by designing sensors and software that monitor the energy sent to the battery (when the gas engine is being used) 50,000 times per second, making sure that the energy is sufficient to recharge the battery but not enough to damage it.

Powerful leaders provide the vision, discipline, and motivation to keep the innovation process focused, on time, and on target. Powerful leaders are able to get resources when they are needed, are typically more experienced, have high status in the company, and are held directly responsible for the products' success or failure. On average, powerful leaders can get innovation-related projects done nine months faster than leaders with little power or influence. One such powerful leader was Phil Martens, the former head of Ford's product development. With a year to go before introduction and Ford's hybrid Escape months behind schedule, he told the team, "We are going to deliver on time. . . . Anything you need you'll get."[36] Martens said, "You could have heard a pin drop." But he

milestones formal project review points used to assess progress and performance

multifunctional teams work teams composed of people from different departments followed this declaration by strongly supporting the team. Despite daily inquiries "from above," he promised no interruptions or interference from anyone—even top management. When the team members needed something, they got it without waiting. When language differences created problems with the Japanese company that made the hybrid's batteries, "a Ford battery expert fluent in Japanese was dispatched to Japan within 24 hours."[37] Martens said, "I allowed them to be entrepreneurial, and they doubled their productivity." Mary Ann Wright, the launch manager charged with making sure the project stayed on schedule, said, "The same people who had been coming into my office saying, 'I don't know how we're going to get there,' were saying within weeks and months, 'My God, we can get there.'"[38]

> I allowed them to be entrepreneurial, and they doubled their productivity.
>
> **PHIL MARTENS,** FORMER HEAD OF PRODUCT DEVELOPMENT, FORD

2.3 Compression Approach: Managing Innovation during Incremental Change

As Exhibit 7.6 shows, whereas the experiential approach is used to manage innovation in highly uncertain environments during periods of discontinuous change, the compression approach is used to manage innovation in more certain environments during periods of incremental change. Whereas the goals of the experiential approach are significant improvements in performance and the establishment of a *new* dominant design, the goals of the compression approach are lower costs and incremental improvements in the performance and function of the *existing* dominant design.

The general strategies in each approach are different, too. With the experiential approach, the general strategy is to build something new, different, and substantially better. Because there's so much uncertainty—no one knows which technology will become the market leader—companies adopt a winner-take-all approach by trying to create the market-leading, dominant design. With the compression approach, the general strategy is to compress the time and steps needed to bring about small, consistent improvements in performance and functionality. Because a dominant technology design already exists, the general strategy is to continue improving the existing technology as rapidly as possible.

In short, a **compression approach to innovation** assumes that innovation is a predictable process, that incremental innovation can be planned using a series of steps, and that compressing the time it takes to complete those steps can speed up innovation. As Exhibit 7.6 shows, the compression approach to innovation has five aspects: planning, supplier involvement, shortening the time of individual steps, overlapping steps, and multifunctional teams.[39]

In Chapter 5, *planning* was defined as choosing a goal and a method or strategy to achieve that goal. When *planning for incremental innovation*, the goal is to squeeze or compress development time as much as possible, and the general strategy is to create a series of planned steps to accomplish that goal. Planning for incremental innovation helps avoid unnecessary steps and enables developers to sequence steps in the right order to avoid wasted time and delays between steps. Planning also reduces misunderstandings and improves coordination.

compression approach to innovation an approach to innovation that assumes that incremental innovation can be planned using a series of steps and that compressing those steps can speed innovation

generational change change based on incremental improvements to a dominant technological design such that the improved technology is fully backward compatible with the older technology

Most planning for incremental innovation is based on the idea of generational change. **Generational change** occurs when incremental improvements are made to a dominant technological design such that the improved version of the technology is fully backward compatible with the older version.[40] Software is backward compatible if a new version of the software will work with files created by older versions. One of the expected and important features of gaming machines, like PlayStation 3, Xbox 360 and the **NINTENDO** Wii, is their ability to play games purchased for

"WHAT'S NEW" COMPANY

earlier machines. In fact, the latest Game Boy can play games released more than 20 years ago.[41] Backward compatibility is an important component to ensuring the success of new technology. When developing its PlayStation 3 (PS3), **SONY** decided to reduce the game machine's backward compatibility with its predecessor, the PlayStation 2 (PS2) because of production costs. Making the PS3 units fully compatible would have required including a high-end technology chip for PS2 games and one for PS3 games, which would have significantly added to the costs of the new unit. Designers opted instead to load software into the PS3 chip that would allow the new system to play older games. But not all PS2 games worked with the software, and often when PS2 games were played on the PS3 machines, the screens would freeze or the system would lock up. Adding to that frustration, dedicated PS3 games were not rolled out as quickly as expected. As you can imagine, Sony paid the price in reduced sales and angry consumers.[42]

"WHAT'S NEW" COMPANY

Because the compression approach assumes that innovation can follow a series of preplanned steps, one of the ways to shorten development time is *supplier involvement*. Delegating some of the preplanned steps in the innovation process to outside suppliers reduces the amount of work that internal development teams must do. Plus, suppliers provide an alternative source of ideas and expertise that can lead to better designs. When **BOMBARDIER AEROSPACE** designed its new Continental business jet, it relied heavily on 30 suppliers to design and test new parts and share in the $500 million development cost. In today's jets, it is essential that the various electronic components, most of which are computer controlled, do not interfere with each other (this is why you're asked to turn off all electrical devices before takeoff and touchdown). Instead of handling this itself, Bombardier relied on supplier Rockwell Collins, which built an electronics integration testing unit to ensure that the electronic controls for the throttles, wings and rudders, radar, and other components were compatible.[43] In general, the earlier suppliers are involved, the quicker they catch and prevent future problems, such as unrealistic designs or mismatched product specifications.

"WHAT'S NEW" COMPANY

Another way to shorten development time is simply to *shorten the time of individual steps* in the innovation process. A common way to do that is through computer-aided design (CAD). CAD speeds up the design process by allowing designers and engineers to make and test design changes using computer models rather than physically testing expensive prototypes. CAD also speeds innovation by making it easy to see how design changes affect engineering, purchasing, and production. Karenann Terrell, director of e-business strategy at DaimlerChrysler, explains how the company's CAD system, **FASTCAR**, works:

> *FastCar takes a virtual CAD/CAM design and teams it with all the other information that we already have on hand about the part or vehicle. So, no longer do we change a part and then ask: "How much do those new components cost? What are the quality implications?" As we make changes, all that information is integrated into the new designs. Think of the side of a sedan where the hood and fender come together . . . when we brought them together in a digital mock-up, there was a bigger gap than we wanted. Using FastCar technology, we were able to work out the effects of a proposed design change before it was made. In this case, we notified the engineers of the fender and hood, as well as the supplier of a plastic attachment in the wheel well. That vendor said: "If you make that change, I need to cut a new tool, which will cost you lots of money. Why don't I just move my fastening point? Then you don't have a gap." So we didn't have to make a design change. In the old world, it would have been four or five weeks before we knew about the supplier's tool change.*[44]

In a sequential design process, each step must be completed before the next step begins. But sometimes multiple development steps can be performed at the same time. *Overlapping steps* shorten the development process by reducing delays or waiting time between steps. For example, Warner Bros. is using overlapping steps to reduce the time it will take to make the entire series of seven Harry Potter films—one for each of the seven books in J.K. Rowling's series chronicling the seven years the title character is at Hogwarts School of Witchcraft and Wizardry. Unfortunately, it was taking Warner Bros. more than two years to write, shoot, and produce each movie. All the actors were aging, and the core cast of young actors would soon resemble adults more than high school students. So Warner Bros. decided to use new directors and new production teams for each of the movies in the *Harry Potter* series. That way, the company could begin shooting the next film while the previous one was in postproduction and the one prior to that was in the theaters. Without this effort, young Harry Potter might be in his early 30s by the time of the seventh and final movie.[45]

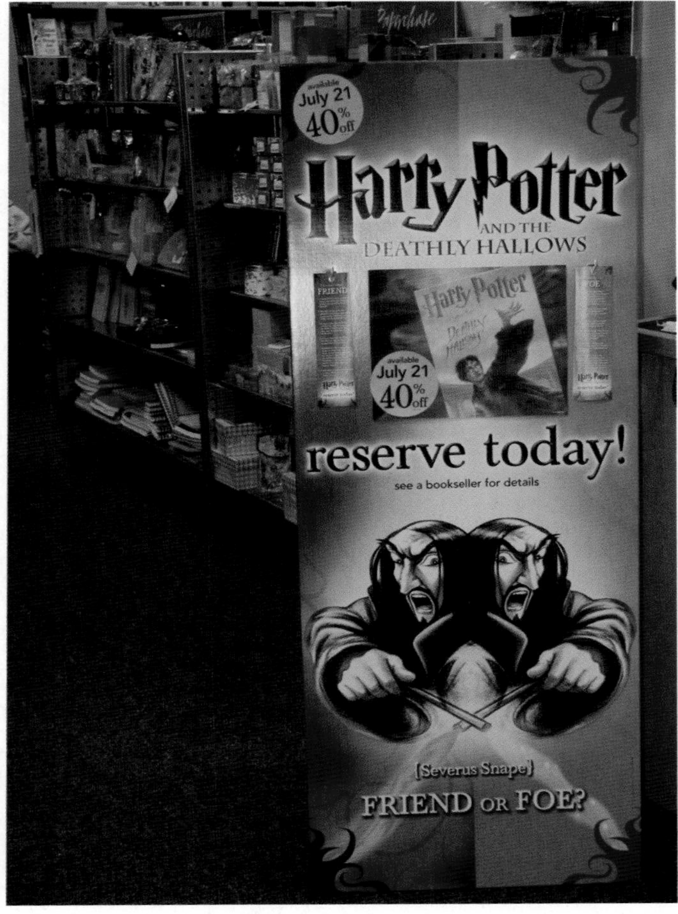

© SUSAN VAN ETTEN

Review 2: Managing Innovation

To successfully manage innovation streams, companies must manage the sources of innovation and learn to manage innovation during both discontinuous and incremental change. Since innovation begins with creativity, companies can manage the sources of innovation by supporting a creative work environment in which creative thoughts and ideas are welcomed, valued, and encouraged. Creative work environments provide challenging work; offer organizational, supervisory, and work group encouragement; allow significant freedom; and remove organizational impediments to creativity.

Companies that succeed in periods of discontinuous change typically follow an experiential approach to innovation. The experiential approach assumes that intuition, flexible options, and hands-on experience can reduce uncertainty and accelerate learning and understanding. This approach involves frequent design iterations, frequent testing, regular milestones, creation of multifunctional teams, and use of powerful leaders to guide the innovation process.

A compression approach to innovation works best during periods of incremental change. This approach assumes that innovation can be planned using a series of steps and that compressing the time it takes to complete those steps can speed up innovation. The five aspects of the compression approach are planning (generational change), supplier involvement, shortening the time of individual steps (computer-aided design), overlapping steps, and multifunctional teams.

ORGANIZATIONAL CHANGE

"WHAT'S NEW" COMPANY

The idea was simple. Build a series of electronics superstores and watch the customers and profits pour in. For a while, it seemed to work. Sales at **INCREDIBLE UNIVERSE** grew to $725 million in less than four years as the company grew to 17 stores, each of which stocked an average of 85,000 products in a 185,000-square-foot building. That's more than four times the size of rival Circuit City stores. Incredible Universe stores had a carnival atmosphere that featured laser shows, karaoke contests, and door prizes. Because of the size, inventory, and extras, the breakeven point for each store was $70 million in sales per year, so despite rapid growth, the company was losing money at record rates. Managers were unable to change the store concept quickly enough to reverse the situation, so the parent company, Tandy Corporation, closed Incredible Universe just four years after its founding. All told, the stores lost over $230 million and completely wiped out Tandy's profits for the year.

The company's collapse wasn't a surprise. Incredible Universe and everyone else in the industry knew it was hemorrhaging cash. Yet the company was unable to change its business quickly enough to stop the bleeding. That inability to change, to figure out ways to bring in more customers for higher end appliances and electronics, eventually led to its demise.[46]

After reading the next two sections on organizational change, you should be able to

3 *discuss why* not *changing can lead to organizational decline.*

4 *discuss the different methods that managers can use to better manage change as it occurs.*

Businesses operate in a constantly changing environment. Recognizing and adapting to internal and external changes can mean the difference between continued success and going out of business. Companies that fail to change run the risk of organizational decline.[47]

Organizational decline occurs when companies don't anticipate, recognize, neutralize, or adapt to the internal or external pressures that threaten their survival.[48] In other words, decline occurs when organizations don't recognize the need for change. **GENERAL MOTORS**' loss of market share in the automobile industry (from 50 percent to 25 percent) is an example of organizational decline. There are five stages of organizational decline: blinded, inaction, faulty action, crisis, and dissolution.[49]

In the *blinded stage*, decline begins because key managers fail to recognize the internal or external changes that will harm their organizations. This "blindness" may be due to a simple lack of awareness about changes or an inability to understand their significance. It may also come from the overconfidence that can develop when a company has been successful. For example, **BARNEYS NEW YORK** started as a tiny men's discount clothing store in New York City and grew into an international phenomenon with stores in Beverly Hills, Chicago, London, Tokyo, and a dozen other cities. Barneys sold some of the most expensive and fashionable designer clothes in the world until the overconfidence of the founder's grandsons, Gene and Bob Pressman, eventually led to the company's demise.[50] In his book *The Rise and Fall of the House of Barneys: A Family Tale of Chutzpah, Glory, and Greed*, Joshua Levine of

organizational decline a large decrease in organizational performance that occurs when companies don't anticipate, recognize, neutralize, or adapt to the internal or external pressures that threaten their survival

Forbes magazine described how overconfidence led the Pressmans to spend more time working out at the gym than running the company.[51] Sure of their success, the Pressmans blindly overspent and overbuilt the company. Indeed, just three years after opening a luxurious $270 million store on Madison Avenue in New York City, complete with marble floors, silver-plated windows, and an extravagantly priced restaurant, espresso bar, beauty salon, and health club, Barneys filed for bankruptcy.

In the *inaction stage*, as organizational performance problems become more visible, management may recognize the need to change but still take no action. The managers may be waiting to see if the problems will correct themselves. Or, they may find it difficult to change the practices and policies that previously led to success. Possibly, too, they wrongly assume that they can easily correct the problems, so they don't feel the situation is urgent. For example, when Barneys expanded from men's into women's clothing, management budgeted $12 million to buy and convert a building into a 70,000-square-foot women's clothing store. When the store ended up costing $25 million, more than double the estimate—a prospect that would have worried most managers—one of Barneys' top managers exclaimed, "What's money?"[52]

In the *faulty action stage*, faced with rising costs and decreasing profits and market share, management will announce "belt-tightening" plans designed to cut costs, increase efficiency, and restore profits. In other words, rather than recognizing the need for fundamental changes, managers assume that if they just run a "tighter ship," company performance will return to previous levels. Barneys fit this pattern, too. Rather than reexamine the basic need for change, Barneys' management focused on cost cutting. Company managers and staff were no longer allowed to spend hundreds of thousands of dollars a year on perks such as cell phones, cars, clothing allowances, and entertainment.[53] Unfortunately for Barneys, this belt-tightening move was too little too late.

In the *crisis stage*, bankruptcy or dissolution (breaking up the company and selling its parts) is likely to occur unless the company completely reorganizes the way it does business. At this point, however, companies typically lack the resources to fully change how they run their businesses. Cutbacks and layoffs will have reduced the level of talent among employees. Furthermore, talented managers who were savvy enough to see the crisis coming will have found jobs with other companies (often with competitors). Because of rising costs and lower sales, cash is tight. And lenders and suppliers are unlikely to extend further loans or credit to ease the cash crunch. For example, after lending Barneys more than $180 million, its bankers refused to extend the company any more credit.

In the *dissolution stage*, after failing to make the changes needed to sustain the organization, the company is dissolved through bankruptcy proceedings or by selling assets in order to pay suppliers, banks, and creditors. At this point, a new CEO may be brought in to oversee the closing of stores, offices, and manufacturing facilities, the final layoff of managers and employees, and the sale of assets. After filing for bankruptcy, Barneys closed four stores, including the original location.[54] Three years later, Barneys was sold to two investment companies that brought in new management to rebuild the company.[55]

When key managers fail to recognize the internal or external changes that will harm their organizations, decline is sure to follow. Sure of their success, the Pressmans blindly overspent and overbuilt Barneys, only to have to file for bankruptcy three years into their extravagant corporate spending spree.

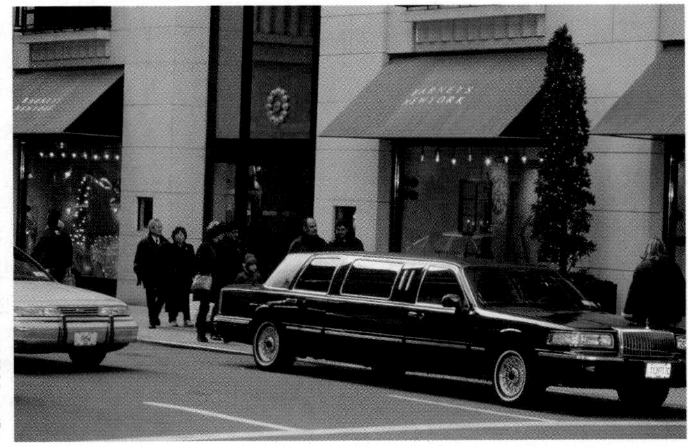

© LYNN GOLDSMITH/CORBIS

Finally, note that because decline is reversible at each of the first four stages, not all companies in decline reach final dissolution as Barneys did. For example, GM is trying to aggressively cut costs, stabilize its shrinking market share, and use innovative production techniques in an effort to reverse a decline that has lasted nearly a decade and resulted in all-time-low stock prices.

"Decline is reversible at each of the first four stages."

Review 3: Organizational Decline: The Risk of Not Changing

The five-stage process of organizational decline begins when organizations don't recognize the need for change. In the blinded stage, managers fail to recognize the changes that threaten their organization's survival. In the inaction stage, management recognizes the need to change, but doesn't act, hoping that the problems will correct themselves. In the faulty action stage, management focuses on cost cutting and efficiency rather than facing up to the fundamental changes needed to ensure survival. In the crisis stage, failure is likely unless fundamental reorganization occurs. Finally, in the dissolution stage, the company is dissolved through bankruptcy proceedings, by selling assets to pay creditors, or through the closing of stores, offices, and facilities. If companies recognize the need to change early enough, however, dissolution may be avoided.

According to social psychologist Kurt Lewin, change is a function of the forces that promote change and the opposing forces that slow or resist change.[56] **Change forces** lead to differences in the form, quality, or condition of an organization over time.

By contrast, **resistance forces** support the status quo, that is, the existing conditions in organizations. Change is difficult under any circumstances. Indeed, in a study of heart bypass patients, doctors told participants straightforwardly to change their eating and health habits or they would die. Unbelievably, a full 90 percent of participants did *not* change their habits at all![57] This fierce resistance to change also applies to organizations. A few years ago, **Xerox** was facing certain bankruptcy if it didn't change the method it used to sell its products and services. So, the senior management changed Xerox's sales system from a transaction-based model, which focused on the quantity of sales made, to a relationship-based model, which focused on partnering with clients to determine how Xerox could help them be more efficient and successful. James Firestone, president of Xerox North America, says succinctly, "Their whole careers, salespeople had done one thing. They would knock on doors, look at copiers, see how old they were, and sell a refresh." But under the new system, salespeople were expected to build relationships with clients and spend considerable time understanding their business. That meant it would take longer to get a sale. The salespeople resisted the changes, complaining that it took months to schedule training in the new approach. They also complained that the compensation system still rewarded salespeople for the number and value of sales made (transactions); they would be making less money because they were going to be spending more time making each sale (building relationships). It took the company more than two years to realign the incentive pay system to match the new relationship-based sales approach, and once the entire transformation was complete—four years later—Xerox returned to profitability. To prevent any tendency toward stagnation, Xerox now runs regular "alignment workshops" to outline ways its existing systems might inhibit change in the future.[58]

change forces forces that produce differences in the form, quality, or condition of an organization over time

resistance forces forces that support the existing state of conditions in organizations

resistance to change opposition to change resulting from self-interest, misunderstanding and distrust, or a general intolerance for change

Resistance to change, like that shown by the Xerox employees, is caused by self-interest, misunderstanding and distrust, and a general intolerance for change.[59] People resist change out of *self-interest* because they fear that change will cost or deprive them of something they value. For example, resistance might stem from a fear that the changes will result in a loss of pay, power, responsibility, or even perhaps one's job. People also resist change because of *misunderstanding and distrust*; they don't understand the change or the reasons for it, or they distrust the people, typically management, behind the change. Resistance isn't always visible at first, however. In fact, some of the strongest resisters may initially support the changes in public, nodding and smiling their agreement, but then ignore the changes in private and do their jobs as they always have. Management consultant Michael Hammer calls this deadly form of resistance the "Kiss of Yes."[60]

Resistance may also come from a generally low tolerance for change. Some people are simply less capable of handling change than others. People with a *low tolerance for change* feel threatened by the uncertainty associated with change and worry that they won't be able to learn the new skills and behaviors needed to successfully negotiate change in their companies.

*Because resistance to change is inevitable, successful change efforts require careful management. In this section you will learn about: **4.1 managing resistance to change, 4.2 what not to do when leading organizational change**, and **4.3 different change tools and techniques**.*

4.1 Managing Resistance to Change

According to Kurt Lewin, managing organizational change is a basic process of unfreezing, change intervention, and refreezing. **Unfreezing** is getting the people affected by change to believe that change is needed. During the **change intervention** itself, workers and managers change their behavior and work practices. **Refreezing** is supporting and reinforcing the new changes so that they "stick."

Resistance to change, as shown by Xerox's salespeople, is an example of frozen behavior. Given the choice between changing and not changing, most people would rather not change. Because resistance to change is natural and inevitable, managers need to unfreeze resistance to change to create successful change programs. The following methods can be used to manage resistance to change: education and communication, participation, negotiation, top management support, and coercion.[61]

When resistance to change is based on insufficient, incorrect, or misleading information, managers should *educate* employees about the need for change and *communicate* change-related information to them. Managers must also supply the information and funding or other support employees need to make changes. For example, resistance to change can be particularly strong when one company buys another company. Jeff Boyd, who worked for a large Canadian company that was acquired, describes the first meeting between his department and the same department from the acquiring company: "It wasn't a friendly meeting. It wasn't hostile or anything like that, but everybody was on their guard a little bit. Right now, everybody's wondering if they'll be able to get along with the other employees, because there's a big difference in both companies' cultures and in the way both companies operate." Boyd concludes, "There's a lot of tension down at the employee level. We're still being kept in the dark about certain things. Everything seems to be up in the air right now."[62] By contrast, **New York–Presbyterian Healthcare System** reduced resistance to change by designating mentors to coach individuals, groups, and departments in newly acquired companies about its procedures and practices. New York–Presbyterian's Diane Iorfida said at the time, "Keeping employees informed every step of the way is so important. It's also important to tell the truth, whatever you do. If you don't know, say you don't know."[63]

unfreezing getting the people affected by change to believe that change is needed

change intervention the process used to get workers and managers to change their behavior and work practices

refreezing supporting and reinforcing new changes so that they "stick"

"What's New" Company

Another way to reduce resistance to change is to have those affected by the change *participate in planning and implementing the change process*. Employees who participate have a better understanding of the change and the need for it. Furthermore, employee concerns about change can be addressed as they occur if employees participate in the planning and implementation process. As you learned in Chapter 6, CEO A. G. Lafley turned around **Procter & Gamble** by refocusing the company on its billion-dollar brands (Tide and Pantene, among others). Martin Nuechtern, then chief of global hair care, said, "A. G. made things very clear: Make sure you focus on Pantene."[64] While Lafley clearly shifted the focus to P&G's best brands, the strategies to reenergize those brands were generated through employee participation. At an informal luncheon with midlevel managers, Lafley said, "I don't have a speech planned. I thought we could talk. I'm searching for meaty issues. Give me some meaty issues."[65] Then, he listened to their ideas. Vice president Chris Start said, "You can tell him bad news or things you'd be afraid to tell other bosses."[66] As a result, there was little resistance to Lafley's sweeping changes at P&G.

Employees are also less likely to resist change if they are allowed *to discuss and agree on who will do what* after change occurs. The **Chugach School District** in Anchorage, Alaska, had some of the lowest test scores in the state. For superintendent Richard DeLorenzo, that was a clear sign that change was needed. After designing a system that would allow each student to advance at his or her own learning pace, DeLorenzo turned to teacher compensation. But rather than make wholesale changes himself, he went to the teacher's union for input. Together, DeLorenzo and the union developed a program that based teachers' pay on the average improvement of the entire district's students, rather than seniority. Four years later, after enthusiastic support from teachers and students, the district's standardized test scores improved from the 28th to the 71st percentile in the state.[67]

Resistance to change also decreases when change efforts receive *significant managerial support*. Managers must do more than talk about the importance of change, though. They must provide the training, resources, and autonomy needed to make change happen. For example, with a distinguished 70-year history of hand-drawing Hollywood's most successful animated films (*Snow White, Bambi, The Little Mermaid, Beauty and the Beast*), animators at **Walt Disney Company** naturally resisted the move to computer-generated (CG) animation. David Stainton, chief of animation, says his animators "fundamentally worry that, 20 years from now, nobody will know how to draw. They're afraid they won't be able to express their skill to the same level."[68] Animator Glen Keane worried that "I would have to go backwards from what I do by hand."[69] So Stainton told his animators, "Your talent really lies in . . . your ability to bring characters to life," and that can be done through drawing or computers.[70] Disney supported the difficult change by putting all of its animators through a six-month "CG Boot Camp," where they learned how to "draw" animated characters with computers.

Finally, resistance to change can be managed through **coercion**, or the use of formal power and authority to force others to change. Because of the intense negative reactions it can create (for example, fear, stress, resentment, sabotage of company products), coercion should be used only when a crisis exists or when all other attempts to reduce resistance to change have failed. Exhibit 7.7 summarizes some additional suggestions for what managers can do when employees resist change.

4.2 What Not to Do When Leading Change

So far, you've learned about the basic change process (unfreezing, change, refreezing) and managing resistance to change. However, Harvard Business School

coercion the use of formal power and authority to force others to change

UNFREEZING	
• Share reasons	Share the reasons for change with employees.
• Empathize	Be empathetic to the difficulties that change will create for managers and employees.
• Communicate	Communicate the details simply, clearly, extensively, verbally, and in writing.
CHANGE	
• Explain benefits	Explain the benefits, "what's in it for them."
• Champion	Identify a highly respected manager to manage the change effort.
• Seek input	Allow the people who will be affected by change to express their needs and offer their input.
• Choose timing	Don't begin change at a bad time, for example, during the busiest part of the year or month.
• Maintain security	If possible, maintain employees' job security to minimize fear of change.
• Offer training	Offer training to ensure that employees are both confident and competent to handle new requirements.
• Pace yourself	Change at a manageable pace. Don't rush.

Source: G. J. Iskat & J. Liebowitz, "What to Do When Employees Resist Change," *Supervision*, 1 August 1996.

Exhibit 7.7

What to Do When Employees Resist Change

professor John Kotter argues that knowing what *not* to do is just as important as knowing what to do when it comes to achieving successful organizational change.[71]

Exhibit 7.8 shows the most common errors that managers make when they lead change. The first two errors occur during the unfreezing phase, when managers try to get the people affected by change to believe that change is really needed. The first and potentially most serious error is *not establishing a great enough sense of urgency*. Indeed, Kotter estimates that more than half of all change efforts fail because the people affected are not convinced that change is necessary. People will feel a greater sense of urgency if a leader in the company makes a public, candid assessment of the company's problems and weaknesses. For example, KMART stores had (and maybe still have) a reputation for being dingy. After the company merged with Sears, *Chain Store Age* conducted an online survey to find out what its readership of retail professionals thought about the prospects of the combined company. Many thought that postmerger, Sears stores would become as dumpy as Kmarts. The company acknowledged its bad image when Sears's new CEO, Aylwin Lewis, told the managers of the recently acquired Kmart chain, "Our worst stores are dungeons! Well, who wants to work in a dungeon? Who wants to shop in a dungeon? Who wants to walk into an environment that is so dull and lifeless that it is sucking the air out of your body?" At the end of his speech there was a spontaneous standing ovation. They got it.[72]

Exhibit 7.8

Errors Managers Make When Leading Change

UNFREEZING
1. Not establishing a great enough sense of urgency.
2. Not creating a powerful enough guiding coalition.
CHANGE
3. Lacking a vision.
4. Undercommunicating the vision by a factor of 10.
5. Not removing obstacles to the new vision.
6. Not systematically planning for and creating short-term wins.
REFREEZING
7. Declaring victory too soon.
8. Not anchoring changes in the corporation's culture.

Source: J. P. Kotter, "Leading Change: Why Transformation Efforts Fail," *Harvard Business Review* 73, no. 2 (March–April 1995): 59.

> More than half of all change efforts fail because the people affected are not convinced that change is necessary.

The second mistake that occurs in the unfreezing process is *not creating a powerful enough coalition*. Change often starts with one or two people, but to build enough momentum to change an entire department, division, or company, change has to be supported by a critical and growing group of people. Besides top management, Kotter recommends that key employees, managers, board members, customers, and even union leaders be members of a *core change coalition*, which guides and supports organizational change. Procter & Gamble's CEO A. G. Lafley says, "I put together the guiding coalition—the leaders who would go with me. If you are going to make a significant change, you have to declare where are we going and why are we going there. Then you have to put together this guiding coalition. You have to put the true disciples together—the prophets who believe in it as passionately as you do. And they help you to carry the organization, because you can't carry a 100,000-person organization spread across 80 to 100 countries by yourself."[73] Furthermore, it's important to strengthen this group's resolve by periodically bringing its members together for off-site retreats.

The next four errors that managers make occur during the change phase, when a change intervention is used to try to get workers and managers to change their behavior and work practices. *Lacking a vision* for change is a significant error at this point. As you learned in Chapter 5, a *vision* is a statement of a company's purpose or reason for existing. A vision for change makes clear where a company or department is headed and why the change is occurring. Change efforts that lack vision tend to be confused, chaotic, and contradictory. By contrast, change efforts guided by visions are clear and easy to understand and can be effectively explained in five minutes or less. At Sears, rather than use the industry standards of market share and sales volume, CEO Aylwin Lewis focuses on profitability and giving "our customers reasons to shop our stores more frequently."[74] In the first year after the merger, Sears Holdings' profit rose over 230 percent.[75]

During his weekly store visits, Sears CEO Aylwin Lewis questions managers about their knowledge of the profit margins for various products. He asks them how they would run their stores better and pushes them to be financially literate. This is one way he's anchoring the changes he's making.

© ASSOCIATED PRESS

Undercommunicating the vision by a factor of 10 is another mistake in the change phase. According to Kotter, companies mistakenly hold just one meeting to announce the vision. Or, if the new vision receives heavy emphasis in executive speeches or company newsletters, senior management then undercuts the vision by behaving in ways contrary to it. Successful communication of the vision requires that top managers link everything the company does to the new vision and that they "walk the talk" by behaving in ways consistent with the vision.

Furthermore, even companies that begin change with a clear vision sometimes make the mistake of *not removing obstacles to the new vision*. They leave formidable barriers to change in place by failing to redesign jobs, pay plans, and technology to support the new way of doing things. One way CEO Lewis removed obstacles to Sears's new vision was by reorganizing how the work of store employees gets done so that they could spend less time with inventory in the back of the store and more time with customers in the front. Many employees at headquarters had never worked at a Sears store, so Lewis began requiring all 3,800 staff members at company headquarters to spend a day each year working in a store. Lewis himself spends every Thursday through Saturday visiting company stores. Without these store visits, management would be isolated from customers and less able to understand how customers perceive and use the store. Store visits help connect the staff at headquarters to the store employees and reinforce the sense that they are all working toward the same strategic goals.[76]

Another error in the change phase is *not systematically planning for and creating short-term wins*. Most people don't have the discipline and patience to wait two years to see if the new change effort works. Change is threatening and uncomfortable, so people need to see an immediate payoff if they are to continue to support it. Kotter recommends that managers create short-term wins by actively picking people and projects that are likely to work extremely well early in the change process. Even though Ford Motor Company posted a $12.7 billion loss in 2006, CEO Alan Mulally announced that he would award blue-collar employees year-end bonuses ranging from $300 to $800. Admitting that the company did not meet profit or market share goals for the year, Mulally acknowledged that workers did improve quality levels and reduce costs, and that those improvements are an important part of turning things around at what used to be America's second largest automaker (it has been surpassed by Toyota). "These awards underscore the importance of working together as a unified team," Mulally said in an e-mail. "That's the only way we'll make more progress down the road."[77]

The last two errors that managers make occur during the refreezing phase, when attempts are made to support and reinforce changes so that they "stick." *Declaring victory too soon* is a tempting mistake in the refreezing phase. Managers typically declare victory right after the first large-scale success in the change process. For instance, it would have been easy for Sears to declare victory the first time that it posted an increase in profits. Declaring success too early has the same effect as draining the gasoline out of a car: It stops change efforts dead in their tracks. With success declared, supporters of the change process stop pushing to make change happen. After all, why push when success has been achieved? Rather than declaring victory, managers should use the momentum from short-term wins to push for even bigger or faster changes. This maintains urgency and prevents change supporters from slacking off before the changes are frozen into the company's culture. During his weekly store visits, Sears CEO Lewis questions managers about their knowledge of the profit margins for various products. He asks them how they would run their stores better and pushes them to be financially literate. At today's Sears, one of the highest complements is to be called "commercial," meaning that the employee understands how to make money.[78]

The last mistake that managers make is *not anchoring changes in the corporation's culture*. An *organization's culture* is the set of key values, beliefs, and attitudes shared by organizational members that determines the "accepted way of doing things" in a company. As you learned in Chapter 3, changing cultures is extremely difficult and slow. According to Kotter, two things help anchor changes in a corporation's culture. The first is directly showing people that the changes have actually improved performance. At Sears, this was easily demonstrated by the company's ability to drastically increase profits despite declining sales. The year after Lewis became CEO and Sears began seriously focusing on cost-cutting and profitability, the company tripled its annual profits. The second is to make sure that the people who get promoted fit the new culture. If they don't, it's a clear sign that the changes were only temporary. To anchor its budding customer focus, Sears created a new executive position, chief customer officer, and hired the former head of Best Buy's online division, John Walden, to fill the position. He is in charge of customer strategies and new business development.[79] Lewis is also anchoring cultural change by identifying 500 future leaders at Sears who will attend his day-long course called "Sowing the Seeds of Our Culture." When they come for the class, Lewis tells them, "Make no mistake, we have to change" and either they can "drink the Kool-Aid" or leave.[80]

4.3 Change Tools and Techniques

Imagine that your boss came to you and said, "All right, genius, you wanted it. You're in charge of turning around the division." How would you start? Where would you begin? How would you encourage change-resistant managers to change? What would you do to include others in the change process? How would you get the change process off to a quick start? Finally, what long-term approach would you use to promote long-term effectiveness and performance? Results-driven change, the **General Electric** workout, transition management teams, and organizational development are different change tools and techniques that can be used to address these issues.

One of the reasons that organizational change efforts fail is that they are activity oriented rather than results oriented, meaning that they focus primarily on changing company procedures, management philosophy, or employee behavior. Typically, there is much buildup and preparation as consultants are brought in, presentations are made, books are read, and employees and managers are trained. There's a tremendous emphasis on "doing things the new way." But, with all the focus on activities, on "doing," almost no attention is paid to results, to seeing if all this activity has actually made a difference.

By contrast, **results-driven change** supplants the emphasis on activity with a laserlike focus on quickly measuring and improving results.[81] For example, top managers at **Hyundai** knew that if they were to compete successfully against the likes of Honda and Toyota, they would have to substantially improve the quality of their cars. So top managers guided the company's results-driven change process by first increasing the number of quality teams from 100 to 865. Then, all employees were required to attend seminars on quality improvement and use the results of industry quality studies, like those published annually by **J. D. Power and Associates**, as their benchmark. Hyundai then measured the effects of the focus on quality. Before the change, a new Hyundai averaged 23.4 initial quality problems; after the results-driven change efforts, that number dropped to 9.6.[82]

Another advantage of results-driven change is that managers introduce changes in procedures, philosophy, or behavior only if they are likely to improve measured performance. In other words, managers and workers actually test to see if changes make a difference. Consistent with this approach, Chairman Chung invested $30 million in a test center where cars could be subjected to a sequence of extremely harsh conditions for as long as they could withstand, allowing engineers to pinpoint defects and fix the problems.[83] A third advantage of results-driven change is that quick, visible improvements motivate employees to continue to make additional changes to improve measured performance. A few years into Hyundai's change process, DaimlerChrysler and Mitsubishi

results-driven change change created quickly by focusing on the measurement and improvement of results

Motors announced that they would use Hyundai-designed four-cylinder engines in their small and midsized cars, reinforcing that all the changes Hyundai had made to the way it measured and improved car quality had been worth the effort.[84] As at Hyundai, the quick successes associated with results-driven change can be particularly effective at reducing resistance to change. Exhibit 7.9 describes the basic steps of results-driven change.

- Management should create measurable, short-term goals to improve performance.
- Management should use action steps only if they are likely to improve measured performance.
- Management should stress the importance of immediate improvements.
- Consultants and staffers should help managers and employees achieve quick improvements in performance.
- Managers and employees should test action steps to see if they actually yield improvements. Action steps that don't should be discarded.
- It takes few resources to get results-driven change started.

Source: R. H. Schaffer & H. A. Thomson, J.D, "Successful Change Programs Begin with Results," *Harvard Business Review on Change* (Boston: Harvard Business School Press, 1998), 189–213.

Exhibit 7.9

Results-Driven Change Programs

The **General Electric workout** is a special kind of results-driven change. It is a three-day meeting that brings together managers and employees from different levels and parts of an organization to quickly generate and act on solutions to specific business problems.[85] On the first morning of a workout, the boss discusses the agenda and targets specific business problems that the group is to try to solve. Then, the boss leaves, and an outside facilitator breaks the group, typically 30 to 40 people, into five or six teams and helps them spend the next day and a half discussing and debating solutions. On day three, in what GE calls a "town meeting," the teams present specific solutions to their boss, who has been gone since day one. As each team's spokesperson makes specific suggestions, the boss has only three options: agree on the spot, say no, or ask for more information so that a decision can be made by a specific, agreed-on date. GE boss Armand Lauzon sweated his way through a town meeting. To encourage him to say yes, his workers set up the meeting room so that Lauzon couldn't make eye contact with his boss. He says, "I was wringing wet within half an hour. They had 108 proposals, I had about a minute to say yes or no to each one, and I couldn't make eye contact with my boss without turning around, which would show everyone in the room that I was chicken."[86] In the end, Lauzon agreed to all but eight suggestions. Furthermore, once those decisions were made, no one at GE was allowed to overrule them.

While the GE workout clearly speeds up change, it may also fragment change, if different managers approve conflicting suggestions in separate town meetings across a company. By contrast, a transition management team provides a way to coordinate change throughout an organization. A **transition management team (TMT)** is a team of 8 to 12 people whose full-time job is to manage and coordinate a company's change process.[87] One member of the TMT is assigned to anticipate and manage the emotions and behaviors related to resistance to change. Despite their importance, many companies overlook the impact that negative emotions and resistant behaviors can have on the change process. TMT members report to the CEO every day, decide which change projects are approved and funded, select and evaluate the people in charge of different change projects, and make sure that different change projects complement one another.

General Electric workout a three-day meeting in which managers and employees from different levels and parts of an organization quickly generate and act on solutions to specific business problems

transition management team (TMT) a team of 8 to 12 people whose full-time job is to manage and coordinate a company's change process

For example, when FleetBoston Financial merged with **BANK OF AMERICA** (BoA), a TMT was used to quickly implement Six Sigma quality programs (see Chapter 18 for an explanation) throughout the entire merged organization. Six Sigma programs, which eliminate mistakes and improve quality, had already saved BoA $2 billion by cutting the time required to open a new branch from 500 to 350 days, reducing the number of ATM and deposit errors by 88 percent, and cutting the response time on individual retirement accounts from three days to 10 minutes. Since BoA had been

© GETTY IMAGES

Transition management teams helped Bank of America better integrate Six Sigma practices at its acquisition of Fleet Boston. TMTs helped the company save money by cutting the number of days it takes to open a new branch from 500 to 350 days.

using Six Sigma for four years and FleetBoston for just two, the goal of the TMT was to ensure that the Six Sigma programs for FleetBoston's half of the merged company would catch up as quickly as possible. The team accomplished this by assigning a Six Sigma expert from BoA to each of FleetBoston's key lines of business. Jim Buchanan, who is in charge of the team, says, "We expect that within two years Fleet will be caught up."[88]

It is also important to say what a TMT is not. A TMT is not an extra layer of management further separating upper management from lower managers and employees. A TMT is not a steering committee that creates plans for others to carry out. Instead, the members of the TMT are fully involved with making change happen on a daily basis. Furthermore, it's not the TMT's job to determine how and why the company will change. That responsibility belongs to the CEO and upper management. Finally, a TMT is not permanent. Once the company has successfully changed, the TMT is disbanded. Indeed, Bank of America won't need a TMT anymore once everyone in the merged companies has been trained in Six Sigma practices. Exhibit 7.10 lists the primary responsibilities of TMTs.

organizational development a philosophy and collection of planned change interventions designed to improve an organization's long-term health and performance

change agent the person formally in charge of guiding a change effort

Organizational development is a philosophy and collection of planned change interventions designed to improve an organization's long-term health and performance. Organizational development takes a long-range approach to change; assumes that top management support is necessary for change to succeed; creates change by educating workers and managers to change ideas, beliefs, and behaviors so that problems can be solved in new ways; and emphasizes employee participation in diagnosing, solving, and evaluating problems.[89] As shown in Exhibit 7.11, organizational development interventions begin with the recognition of a problem. Then, the company designates a **change agent** to be formally in charge of guiding the change effort. This person can be someone from the company or a professional consultant. The change agent clarifies the problem, gathers information, works with decision makers to create and implement an action plan, helps to evaluate the plan's effectiveness, implements the plan throughout the company, and then leaves (if from outside the company) after making sure the change intervention will continue to work.

For example, change agent Hajime Oba is one of the key reasons that Toyota cars are tops in quality and reliability. Oba's job is to work closely with Toyota suppliers, showing them how to increase quality and decrease costs. For example, Michigan Summit Polymers installed a $280,000 paint system with robots and a paint oven to bake paint onto the dashboard vents that went into Toyota cars, but Oba showed that a $12 hair dryer did the job better and faster (3 minutes versus 90 minutes for the robots and paint oven). Because of Oba's demonstration, Summit replaced the robots with simple but effective $150 spray guns and the paint oven with intense light bulbs. Overall, Oba has helped Summit cut its defects from 3,000 parts

Exhibit 7.10

Primary Responsibilities of Transition Management Teams

1.	Establish a context for change and provide guidance.
2.	Stimulate conversation.
3.	Provide appropriate resources.
4.	Coordinate and align projects.
5.	Ensure congruence of messages, activities, policies, and behaviors.
6.	Provide opportunities for joint creation.
7.	Anticipate, identify, and address people problems.
8.	Prepare the critical mass.

Source: J. D. Duck, "Managing Change: The Art of Balancing," *Harvard Business Review on Change* (Boston: Harvard Business School Press, 1998), 55–81.

1. **Entry**	A problem is discovered and the need for change becomes apparent. A search begins for someone to deal with the problem and facilitate change.
2. **Startup**	A change agent enters the picture and works to clarify the problem and gain commitment to a change effort.
3. **Assessment & feedback**	The change agent gathers information about the problem and provides feedback about it to decision makers and those affected by it.
4. **Action planning**	The change agent works with decision makers to develop an action plan.
5. **Intervention**	The action plan, or organizational development intervention, is carried out.
6. **Evaluation**	The change agent helps decision makers assess the effectiveness of the intervention.
7. **Adoption**	Organizational members accept ownership and responsibility for the change, which is then carried out through the entire organization.
8. **Separation**	The change agent leaves the organization after first ensuring that the change intervention will continue to work.

Source: W. J. Rothwell, R. Sullivan, & G. M. McLean, *Practicing Organizational Development: A Guide for Consultants* (San Diego: Pfeiffer & Co., 1995).

Exhibit 7.11

General Steps for Organizational Development Interventions

per million to less than 60 parts per million.[90] Oba's efforts as a change agent have significantly improved the quality of parts at Toyota's other suppliers as well. That, in turn, has helped Toyota reach the top of the quality rankings issued by J. D. Power and Associates and *Consumer Reports* magazine.[91]

Organizational development interventions are aimed at changing large systems, small groups, or people.[92] More specifically, the purpose of *large system interventions* is to change the character and performance of an organization, business unit, or department. *Small group intervention* focuses on assessing how a group functions and helping it work more effectively to accomplish its goals. *Person-focused intervention* is intended to increase interpersonal effectiveness by helping people become aware of their attitudes and behaviors and acquire new skills and knowledge. Exhibit 7.12 describes the most frequently used organizational development interventions for large systems, small groups, and people. For additional information about changing systems, groups, and people, see the "What Really Works" feature.

Exhibit 7.12

Different Kinds of Organizational Development Interventions

LARGE SYSTEM INTERVENTIONS	
Sociotechnical systems	An intervention designed to improve how well employees use and adjust to the work technology used in an organization.
Survey feedback	An intervention that uses surveys to collect information from the members, reports the results of that survey to the members, and then uses those results to develop action plans for improvement.
SMALL GROUP INTERVENTIONS	
Team building	An intervention designed to increase the cohesion and cooperation of work group members.
Unit goal setting	An intervention designed to help a work group establish short- and long-term goals.
PERSON-FOCUSED INTERVENTIONS	
Counseling/coaching	An intervention designed so that a formal helper or coach listens to managers or employees and advises them on how to deal with work or interpersonal problems.
Training	An intervention designed to provide individuals with the knowledge, skills, or attitudes they need to become more effective at their jobs.

Source: W. J. Rothwell, R. Sullivan, & G. M. McLean, *Practicing Organizational Development: A Guide for Consultants* (San Diego: Pfeiffer & Co., 1995).

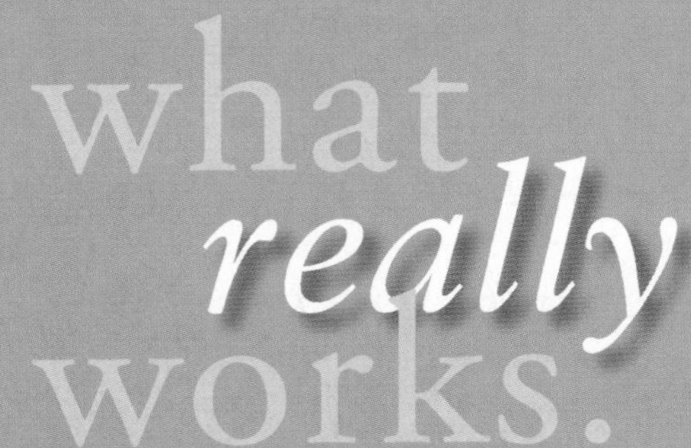

CHANGE THE WORK SETTING OR CHANGE THE PEOPLE? DO BOTH!

Let's assume that you believe that your company needs to change. Congratulations! Just recognizing the need for change puts you ahead of 80 percent of the companies in your industry. But now that you've recognized the need for change, how do you make change happen? Should you focus on changing the work setting or the behavior of the people who work in that setting? It's a classic chicken-or-egg type of question. Which would you do?

A recent meta-analysis based on 52 studies and a combined total of 29,611 study participants indicated that it's probably best to do both!

CHANGING THE WORK SETTING

An organizational work setting has four parts: organizing arrangements (control and reward systems, organizational structure), social factors (people, culture, patterns of interaction), technology (how inputs are transformed into outputs), and the physical setting (the actual physical space in which people work). Overall, there is a 55 percent chance that organizational change efforts will successfully bring changes to a company's work setting. Although the odds are 55–45 in your favor, this is a much lower probability of success than you've seen with the management techniques discussed in other chapters. This simply reflects how strong resistance to change is in most companies.

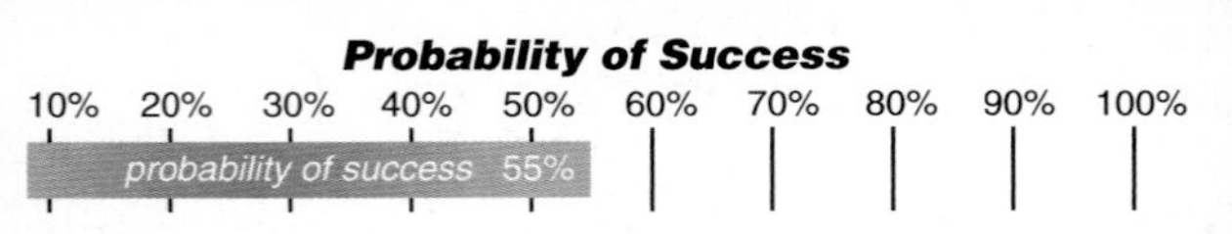

CHANGING THE PEOPLE

Changing people means changing individual work behavior. The idea is powerful. Change the decisions people make. Change the activities they perform. Change the information they share with others. And change the initiatives they take on their own. Change these individual behaviors and collectively you change the entire company. Overall, there is a 57 percent chance that organizational change efforts will successfully change people's individual work behavior. If you're wondering why the odds aren't higher, consider how difficult it is to change personal behavior. It's incredibly difficult to quit smoking, change your diet, or maintain a daily exercise program. Not surprisingly, changing personal behavior at work is also difficult. Viewed in this context, a 57 percent chance of success is a notable achievement.

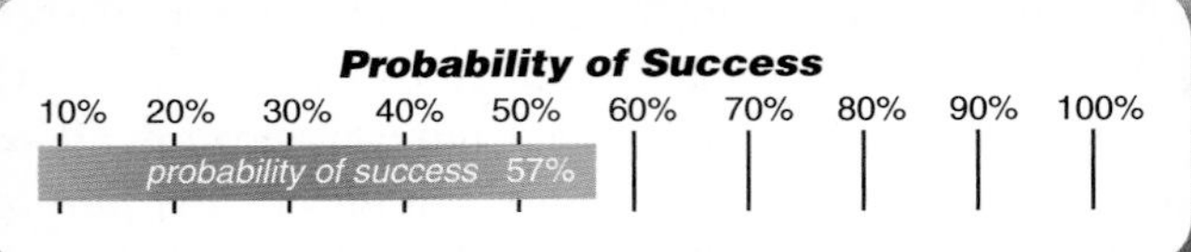

CHANGING INDIVIDUAL BEHAVIOR AND ORGANIZATIONAL PERFORMANCE

The point of changing individual behavior is to improve organizational performance (increase profits, market share, and productivity, and lower costs). Overall, there is a 76 percent chance that changes in individual behavior will produce changes in organizational outcomes. So, if you want to improve your company's profits, market share, or productivity, focus on changing the way that your people behave at work.[93]

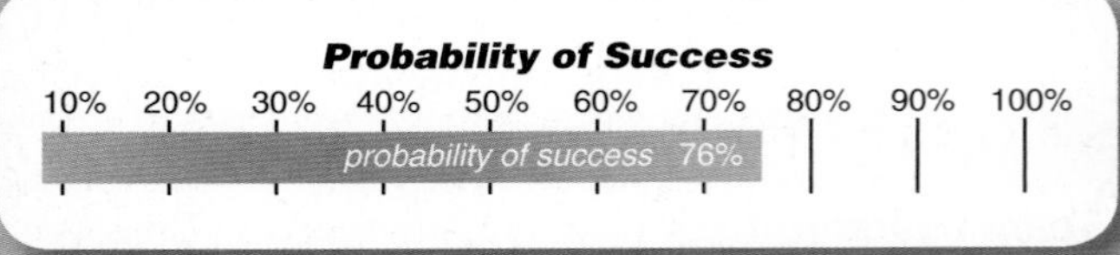

Review 4: Managing Change

The basic change process is unfreezing, change, and refreezing. Resistance to change, which stems from self-interest, misunderstanding and distrust, and a general intolerance for change, can be managed through education and communication, participation, negotiation, top management support, and coercion. Knowing what not to do is as important as knowing what to do to achieve successful change. Managers should avoid these errors when leading change: not establishing urgency, not creating a guiding coalition, lacking a vision, undercommunicating the vision, not removing obstacles to the vision, not creating short-term wins, declaring victory too soon, and not anchoring changes in the corporation's culture.

Finally, managers can use a number of change techniques. Results-driven change and the GE workout reduce resistance to change by getting change efforts off to a fast start. Transition management teams, which manage a company's change process, coordinate change efforts throughout an organization. Organizational development is a collection of planned change interventions (large system, small group, person-focused), guided by a change agent, that are designed to improve an organization's long-term health and performance.

SELF ASSESSMENT

KEY TERMS

Mind-Benders

Innovation is a key to corporate success. Companies that innovate and embrace the changes in their business environment tend to outperform those that stand still. Even so, innovative companies don't simply rely on the creativity of their own workforce. They often contract with outside providers to generate new ideas for everything from operations to new products. In other words, innovative companies fill gaps in their own creativity by looking outside the organization.

As a manager, you will benefit from understanding how you are creative (not *if* you are creative). And just as important as your own creativity is your attitude toward creative endeavors.

This assessment will provide some baseline information you can use as you develop your managerial skills.[94] Indicate the extent to which each of the following statements is true of either your actual behavior or your intentions at work. That is, describe the way you are or the way you intend to be on the job. Use this scale for your responses:

1 Almost never true
2 Seldom true
3 Not applicable
4 Often true
5 Almost always true

1. I openly discuss with my supervisor how to get ahead.
   1 2 3 4 5
2. I try new ideas and approaches to problems.
   1 2 3 4 5
3. I take things or situations apart to find out how they work.
   1 2 3 4 5
4. I welcome uncertainty and unusual circumstances related to my tasks.
   1 2 3 4 5
5. I negotiate my salary openly with my supervisor.
   1 2 3 4 5
6. I can be counted on to find a new use for existing methods or equipment.
   1 2 3 4 5
7. Among my colleagues and coworkers, I will be the first or nearly the first to try out a new idea or method.
   1 2 3 4 5
8. I take the opportunity to translate communications from other departments for my work group.
   1 2 3 4 5
9. I demonstrate originality.
   1 2 3 4 5
10. I will work on a problem that has caused others great difficulty.
    1 2 3 4 5
11. I provide critical input toward a new solution.
    1 2 3 4 5
12. I provide written evaluations of proposed ideas.
    1 2 3 4 5
13. I develop contacts with experts outside my firm.
    1 2 3 4 5
14. I use personal contacts to maneuver into choice work assignments.
    1 2 3 4 5
15. I make time to pursue my own pet ideas or projects.
    1 2 3 4 5
16. I set aside resources for the pursuit of a risky project.
    1 2 3 4 5
17. I tolerate people who depart from organizational routine.
    1 2 3 4 5

18. I speak out in staff meetings.
    1 2 3 4 5
19. I work in teams to try to solve complex problems.
    1 2 3 4 5
20. If my coworkers are asked, they will say I am a wit.
    1 2 3 4 5

=TOTAL

You can find an interpretation of your score at: **academic .cengage.com/management/williams**.

Change Costs More than Pennies

As you wipe your feet, you can't help but notice how messy the carpet is. "Well, that's what it's for," you think. "This is a factory, not a bookstore." But seeing all those metal chips in the rug makes you think about the plant floor. You turn back around and survey the shop. Everywhere you look, parts are stacked in metal bins on wooden palettes, next to the palettes, on tables by machines, encroaching into the aisles—which are marked off with vibrant yellow striping to remind workers to keep them clear. It looks like there is much more work than the roughly $500,000 worth of parts that are actually in process.

Slowly, you begin to wend your way through the machines. Your plant uses five basic types of machines to make hundreds of thousands of different parts for everything from motorcycles to hospital beds to nail guns to industrial water purifiers. You make the mechanism that fills Downy bottles at Procter & Gamble and the tumblers that spit the movie tickets out from under the counter at theaters across the country. Machines are organized by type, so as a job moves through the plant, it will hit any number of machines in a particular order. A job with multiple operations might get moved around the plant from area to area up to seven times. Even though things are always moving, many areas of the plant seem crowded, as jobs line up waiting for their turn on the next machine. Red tickets in pans scattered around the shop and in a designated area are a reminder that there's still quite a bit of scrap (or bad) work being run. Twenty-five percent of jobs going through the shop have to be fixed or rerun because the parts are the wrong size, if only by 0.001 inch. When you make it to the scheduling area, colored Post-it notes show how many jobs are rush, how many are late, and how many haven't even been started. The on-time delivery rate is only 70 percent. For a precision machine shop that can cut metal to measurements in the ten-thousandths of an inch, the overall operations aren't so precise.

Everywhere you look, you see disorder. Maybe those consultants were right: To be competitive, really to survive, you need to approach your operations in a more systematic fashion. A large percentage of companies with your capabilities have gone out of business, but even though there is less competition, there are fewer customers. The types of parts you manufacture are either being designed out of products or are being outsourced to China and Mexico. Without significant change, you're not going to be able to survive the decade, let alone double your size in two years (which is your secret stretch goal).

Last week, a local manufacturing consultancy sent a few members to your shop to present a preliminary proposal on how they could help you run a more efficient operation. The company would assign a team to help your workers learn new, leaner processes of doing work; promises of increased productivity, profitability, and morale were made, with references galore. The consultants even invited you and your management team to take a plant tour of one (or more) of their most recent clients. Ultimately, the consultants would provide materials, workshops, and follow-up support to your shop employees every day all day for several days over a period of six months—for approximately $200,000. Right out of the gate, they would send two consultants to your shop for five consecutive weeks. But at $250 per hour per consultant, that's a quick $100,000 to spend on teaching communication skills and showing workers how to identify waste issues that prevent them from doing their jobs effectively and efficiently.

With only $8 million in revenue in a business where labor and the costs of goods sold are high, your profits are slim. Spending money on the outsiders could very well mean finishing the year in the red instead of the black. Maybe you could hire someone to do the job full-time for half that amount. For $100,000, you could hire someone to do the same job full-time for a year. That might be better than having some consultants come, give their workshops, and leave the rest up to you after they head home. And will telling your employees that "things are going to change around here" be the best way to get things in order? Maybe it would be better if change initiatives started from the bottom. The majority of your 65 workers have been with you for over 20 years (turnover is not one of your problems), but with tenure comes intractability. In general, your employees are set in their ways. Still, they want the company to succeed, so maybe that concern will be a strong enough motivator.

Questions

1. Consider the above situation. What are the benefits to hiring outsiders to manage your change efforts?
2. Do you pay the $200,000 for the consultancy, do you hire a dedicated change agent, or do you try to marshal internal teams to spearhead a change effort?

Brushing Up at Colgate

Ever since Procter & Gamble merged with Gillette, your phone has been ringing off the hook from investment bankers wanting your company, Colgate, to make a deal with Alberto-Culver, S.C. Johnson, Reckitt Benckiser, or Clorox, and today is no exception.[95] Your management team has assembled to listen to yet another set of bankers outline some grandiose proposal. You've got another plan for Colgate, however, and it doesn't involve a big acquisition. Quite the opposite, in fact. For the first time in nearly a decade, Colgate's earnings shrank last quarter (by 10 percent), and you are planning to cut 4,400 jobs, restructure the company, and save $300 million in the process.

Colgate's problems are no secret. In a decades-long tug-of-war, P&G has regained the edge thanks to its innovation machine. In the last five years, P&G has aggressively expanded in the oral care markets where it competes most heavily with Colgate. New flavors of Crest whitening toothpastes, Crest Whitestrips, SpinBrush, and a licensing arrangement with W.L. Gore for Glide floss have all helped Crest reemerge as the leader in the markets it serves. Colgate's most recent innovations—Colgate Total, Motion and Actibrush electric toothbrushes, and Simply White tooth whitener—are now either fading memories or also-rans. And even though Colgate has a strong reputation as a reliable brand, it has been slow to develop new products for developing and existing markets. Perhaps it's just gun-shy. The company's most aggressive innovation was the tooth-whitening system Simply White. Regardless of the product's quality, the bottle and applicator looked like Liquid Paper and proved no match for P&G's Crest Whitestrips. After that near debacle, Colgate managers apparently decided that going for big hits wasn't a workable strategy. The company now seems to be playing catch-up to P&G and GlaxoSmithKline, a new competitor in the oral care market. In fact, in a recent year, P&G spent $229 million on its toothpaste and tooth-whitening products; Colgate spent only $80 million.

Innovation isn't the only area where Colgate has failed to invest. The company's annual ad budget of $1 billion pales in comparison with the $5 billion P&G spends each year to promote its consumer products. Heavy spending has helped P&G capture 51 percent of unit sales and 70 percent of dollar sales in the tooth-whitening segment. Colgate weighs in with 21 percent and 10 percent, respectively. P&G's innovative approach to advertising has helped catapult its products to the forefront of consumers' minds. For example, advertising and sales for Whitestrips began on the web, where the demand was overwhelming. Once the product was rolled out on the market, the day after Colgate's Simply White, P&G had a blockbuster. Simply White hit the shelves and stayed there.

After hanging up from yet another conference call with investment bankers urging your management team to consider a merger, you lean back in your chair and look around the table. "I think we all know what we're *not* going to do," you begin cautiously. "The real question is what we *are* going to do. Now that we have announced measures to conserve resources, we need to decide how to invest what we save."

For this exercise, assemble a team of four to five students to play the role of the management team at Colgate.

Questions

1. Is innovation really necessary at Colgate? In other words, in a market saturated with innovation, is there something to be said for the "keep it simple" approach? Explain.
2. Do you use the $300 million saved from operational cuts to fund innovation, or do you use the money to better market current products?

3. Where do you suggest Colgate look for sources of innovation?
4. As Colgate begins implementing a new innovation strategy, do you recommend that the company follow a compression approach to innovation or an experiential approach? Why?

Successfully managing innovation is challenging. Companies must find ways to support creativity and invention, while at the same time screening their investments in support of innovation. This exercise will give you an opportunity to experience a bit of the organizational dynamic regarding innovation and investment.

Step 1: Assign roles. Your professor will assign you to a pair or small group, and give your team a role as either "Inventors" or "Investors."

Regardless of role, assume that you work for a large clothing and accessories company that targets college students. Your company makes some traditional clothing and gear (such as backpacks and folios), but also prides itself on developing new and innovative products. And recently there has been some interest in considering new services that the company might offer to the college market, things like event or trip planning.

Step 2: Work with your partner(s) on the following tasks depending upon your assigned role.

Inventors: Brainstorm and work to develop a new product or service concept. Be prepared to explain your concept to those inside the company who screen ideas and recommend investments.

Investors: Discuss and agree upon some criteria that your company should use to screen new product and service concepts and to identify which ones to recommend to senior management. Be prepared to listen to one or more concept presentations, ask questions, and then to use your criteria to evaluate the concept(s).

Step 3: Pair up. As instructed by your professor, Inventor and Investor groups should pair up. Inventors will now present their new concept, and investors will ask questions and then use their criteria to rate the concept.

Step 4: Change roles. As time allows, your professor will rotate Inventor and Investor pairings through a few rounds of concept presentation and investor evaluation.

Step 5: Debrief. Return to your original Inventor or Investor pair/group, and discuss your experiences in this role play. What are some of the challenges of playing this role? What was it like to interact with the "other side" of the presentation/evaluation process?

Step 6: Discuss challenges. As a class, discuss the challenges likely faced by companies as they try to successfully manage innovation. Some items for discussion might include:

1. What is the impact of an "evaluation/rating" on the creative process?
2. Do you think that "inventor units" (such as product development and R&D) and "investor units" (finance) often clash over new-product investment decisions? Why or why not?
3. What role might organizational culture (and subculture) play in the innovation and investment processes?
4. How might managers support healthy innovation and wise investment?

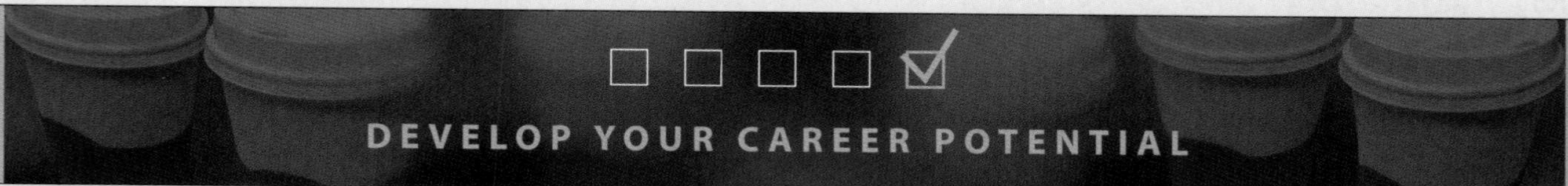

Spark Your Own Creativity

Creativity is a vital part of every organization—and not just the whiz-bang, multimillion-dollar type of creativity.[96] Even banal tasks can benefit from a new approach: an office assistant may think creatively about how to manage the company's filing system or figure out a simple way to keep track of who is in and out of the office. A Chicago company called Inventables has developed innovation kits—boxes containing disparate items to spark creativity—which it sells to clients like Procter & Gamble and Motorola four times a year. The idea is that designers and engineers will be inspired by tinkering with the contents of the kits.

You don't need Inventables to become inspired, however. Nor do you have to wait for your company to develop a creative work environment before you can become creative. You can spark your own creativity and think "outside the box" on your own. Eureka! Ranch, a Cincinnati-based innovation consultancy company, uses toys to help adults remember how to be imaginative, and its long client list of *Fortune* 500 companies is a testament to founder Doug Hall's methods. Another company, Mindware, specializes in educational activities and toys that can help adults regain access to their imaginations. Just looking through its catalog of erector sets, science sets, puzzle books, strategy games, and tangrams may be enough to get your juices flowing.

Activities

1. Visit **http://www.eurekaranch.com** and search for the audio clip of what the company does and how it does it. Listen to the clip. What do you think of the three dimensions of creativity?
2. At the Eureka Ranch website, find the page on Brain Brew. What is Brain Brew Radio? Is it available in your area? If it is, consider listening to it once a month to hear the creative ideas that people across the country are working on.
3. Visit **http://www.mindwareonline.com** and peruse some of the products the company sells. Which products do you find most appealing? If it's in your budget, order one of the items as a tool to help you develop and refine your creative side.

REEL TO REAL

BIZ FLIX

October Sky

The movie *October Sky* is based on the autobiographical book *Rocket Boys* by Homer Hickam. The talented cast is led by Jake Gyllenhaal, who plays Homer Hickam. As a teenager, Homer is facing a dreary future as a coal miner until he sees the Soviet satellite *Sputnik* pass over his small mining town of Coalwood, West Virginia. A new interest in rockets infects Homer, who begins to experiment with model rockets in the summer of 1957. Soon, Homer has convinced several of his friends to join him in designing a rocket to enter in the National Science Fair, where they hope to win college scholarships as a result.

What to Watch for and Ask Yourself

1. Are Homer and his friends working toward discontinuous change or incremental change? Explain.
2. Which approach to innovation best describes what the "Rocket Boys" are doing? Identify the elements of the approach you choose that are evident in the clip.

MANAGEMENT WORKPLACE

Original Penguin—Innovating a 50-Year-Old Brand

Original Penguin was a 1950s icon—the penguin logo appeared on Munsingwear Penguin knit sport shirts for men, mostly golfers. Eventually, its popularity faded, and Perry Ellis International later acquired the brand. Chris Kolbe was working in merchandising at retailer Urban Outfitters when he conceived the idea of rejuvenating the penguin—but with a new twist and for a new market. Starting with a few new shirts, which sold out almost immediately, the "new" Original Penguin began to grow. Watch the video to see how Kolbe has created a completely new management workplace for a 50-year-old brand.

What to Watch for and Ask Yourself

1. How can you apply the concept of innovation streams to the fashion industry?
2. Based on the tour of the store, what kind of work environment would you expect to find at Original Penguin?
3. What role does Kolbe play in the Perry Ellis organization?

Global Management

Learning Outcomes:

1 Discuss the impact of global business and the trade rules and agreements that govern it.
2 Explain why companies choose to standardize or adapt their business procedures.
3 Explain the different ways that companies can organize to do business globally.
4 Explain how to find a favorable business climate.
5 Discuss the importance of identifying and adapting to cultural differences.
6 Explain how to successfully prepare workers for international assignments.

In This Chapter:

What Would You Do?

Tommy Hilfiger Headquarters, New York, New York.[1] Over the last five years, Tommy Hilfiger's fashion, cosmetics, and accessories business has struggled. U.S. revenues, which peaked at $1.9 billion in 2000, fell to $1.1 billion in 2003, and now stand at a comparatively paltry $260 million. Thirty Tommy Hilfiger stores had to be closed in the United States. The company's children's wear and Tommy Jeans divisions, both based in the United States were shut down. At corporate headquarters, 230 people were let go. Business reporters began referring to the company as a "fading and mature brand."

There are a number of reasons that things changed so quickly. To start, U.S. clothing sales, which accounted for most of the company's sales, have grown less than 5 percent per year. But that's not enough to explain Tommy Hilfiger Inc.'s astounding 86 percent drop in U.S. revenues. A more damaging factor has been consolidation in U.S. retail stores. A decade ago, Tommy Hilfiger products were sold in hundreds of different department stores and discount stores in the United States. Today, many of those stores have either closed or been purchased by large department store chains. Macy's and Kohl's, which account for more than a third of U.S. clothing sales, sell their own private-label brands to increase profits, thus squeezing out opportunities for companies like Tommy Hilfiger."

The result, as one of your top managers says, is, "You become vulnerable if you are going to operate just in the U.S. marketplace." So growth in Europe and Asia is critical for future success, but the company has a poor track record over seas. At the height of its U.S. popularity, Hilfiger opened a large store on Bond Street in London, filling it with too much merchandise originally destined for U.S. stores. The Bond Street store closed a year later because Europeans have different fashion tastes from Americans.

If Tommy Hilfiger is to reduce its dependence on the U.S. market, it must grow in Europe and Asia. But how? How much should Tommy Hilfiger, which was unable to push its U.S. products overseas, adapt its products to different cultures in Europe and Asia? Can it have a standard set of products or should they be different in each market and culture? Similarly, who should make key decisions for the company? Should managers at headquarters make these decisions, or should managers in different countries make them? Should Tommy Hilfiger run its business around the world the same way it runs its business in the United States? Finally, *how* should Hilfiger expand internationally? Should it license its brands to local businesses, form strategic alliances with key foreign business partners, or bear the risk itself and wholly own and control each Tommy Hilfiger operation throughout the world? **If you were in charge at Tommy Hilfiger, what would you do?**

Activities + Video

CengageNOW Audio study guide, electronic flashcards, author FAQ videos, On the Job and Biz Flix videos, concept tutorial, and concept exercise

Web (academic.cengage.com/management/williams) Quiz, PowerPoint slides, and glossary terms for this chapter

Review your class notes. Do they give you enough information? Do they give you the right information? If not, visit your campus study center to learn how to take good notes.

"What's New" Companies

- Tommy Hilfiger
- Wal-Mart
- Infosys
- MTV
- FremantleMedia (American Idol)
- Cadbury Schweppes
- McDonald's
- Yum! Brands
- Fuji Xerox
- Powerex
- Venyon
- Shanghai Automotive
- Honda Motors of America
- Ford Motor Company
- Vodafone
- Vista Print
- Coca-Cola
- And others . . .

Tommy Hilfiger's struggle with international expansion is an example of the key issue in global business: How can you be sure that the way you run your business in one country is the right way to run that business in another? This chapter discusses how organizations make those decisions. We start by examining global business in two ways: first by exploring its impact on U.S. businesses, and then by reviewing the basic rules and agreements that govern global trade. Next, we examine how and when companies go global by examining the tradeoff between consistency and adaptation and by discussing how to organize a global company. Finally, we look at how companies decide where to expand globally. Here, we examine how to find the best business climate, how to adapt to cultural differences, and how to better prepare employees for international assignments.

WHAT IS GLOBAL BUSINESS?

"WHAT'S NEW" COMPANY

Business is the buying and selling of goods or services. Buying this textbook was a business transaction. So was selling your first car. So was getting paid for babysitting or for mowing lawns. **Global business** is the buying and selling of goods and services by people from different countries. The Timex watch on my wrist as I write this chapter was purchased at a **WAL-MART** in Texas. But since it was made in the Philippines, I participated in global business when I wrote Wal-Mart a check. Wal-Mart, for its part, had already paid Timex, which had paid the company that employs the Filipino managers and workers who made my watch.

Of course, there is more to global business than buying imported products at Wal-Mart. After reading the next section, you should be able to

1. *discuss the impact of global business and the trade rules and agreements that govern it.*

1 Global Business, Trade Rules, and Trade Agreements

If you want a simple demonstration of the impact of global business, look at the tag on your shirt, the inside of your shoes, and the inside of your cell phone (take your battery out). Chances are, all of these items were made in different places around the world. As I write this, my shirt, shoes, and cell phone were made in Thailand, China, and Korea. Where were yours made?

Let's learn more about ***1.1 the impact of global business, 1.2 how tariff and non-tariff trade barriers have historically restricted global business, 1.3 how today global and regional trade agreements are reducing those trade barriers worldwide,*** *and* ***1.4 how consumers are responding to those changes in trade rules and agreements****.*

global business the buying and selling of goods and services by people from different countries

1.1 The Impact of Global Business

Thomas Friedman, author and *New York Times* columnist, observed global business in action when he visited **INFOSYS**, a consulting and information technology company, in India:

> *I guess the eureka moment came on a visit to the campus of Infosys Technologies, one of the crown jewels of the Indian outsourcing and software industry. Nandan Nilekani, the Infosys CEO, was showing me his global videoconference room, pointing with pride to a wall-size flat-screen TV, which he said was the biggest in Asia. Infosys, he explained, could hold a virtual meeting of the key players from its entire global supply chain for any project at any time on that supersize screen. So its American designers could be on the screen speaking with their Indian software writers and their Asian manufacturers all at once. That's what globalization is all about today, Nilekani said. Above the screen there were eight clocks that pretty well summed up the Infosys workday: 24/7/365. The clocks were labeled United States West, United States East, G.M.T., India, Singapore, Hong Kong, Japan, Australia.*[2]

"Today, there are 77,175 multinational corporations, nearly 11.25 times as many as in 1970."

Infosys does global business by selling products and services worldwide with managers and employees from different continents working together as seamlessly as if they were next door to each other. But Infosys isn't unique. There are thousands of other multinational companies just like it.

multinational corporation a corporation that owns businesses in two or more countries

direct foreign investment a method of investment in which a company builds a new business or buys an existing business in a foreign country

Multinational corporations are corporations that own businesses in two or more countries. In 1970, more than half of the world's 7,000 multinational corporations were headquartered in just two countries: the United States and the United Kingdom. Today, there are 77,175 multinational corporations, nearly 11.25 times as many as in 1970, and only 2,418, or 2.8 percent, are based in the United States.[3] Today, 53,072 multinationals, or 68.8 percent, are based in other developed countries (such as Germany, Italy, Canada, and Japan), while 20,238, or 26.2 percent, are based in developing countries (such as Colombia, South Africa, and Tunisia). So, today, multinational companies can be found by the thousands all over the world!

Another way to appreciate the impact of global business is by considering direct foreign investment. **Direct foreign investment** occurs when a company builds a new business or buys an existing business in a foreign country. Brazilian steelmaker Gerdau S.A. made a direct foreign investment when it began purchasing U.S. steel companies such as International Steel Group. Over the last five years, these U.S. acquisitions have made Gerdau SA the fourth-largest steelmaker in the United States and the 16th-largest in the world.[4] Of course, companies from many other countries also own businesses in the United States. As Exhibit 8.1 shows, companies from the United Kingdom, Japan, Germany, the Netherlands, Canada, France, Switzerland, and Luxembourg have the largest direct foreign investment in the United States. Overall, foreign companies invest more than $1.6 trillion a year to do business in the United States.

Exhibit 8.1

Direct Foreign Investment in the United States

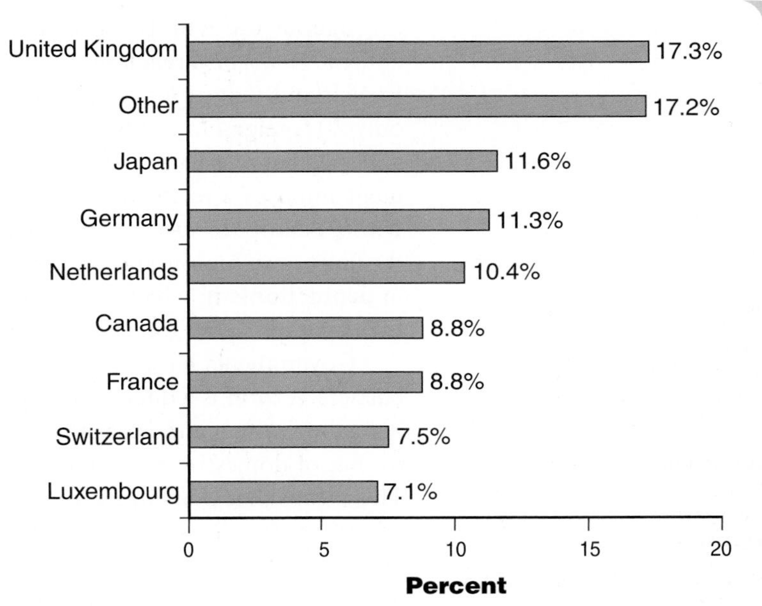

Source: J. Koncz & D. Yorgason, "Direct Investment Positions for 2005: Country and Industry Detail," available at http://www.bea.gov/bea/ARTICLES/2006/07July/0706_DIP_WEB.pdf, 7 February 2007.

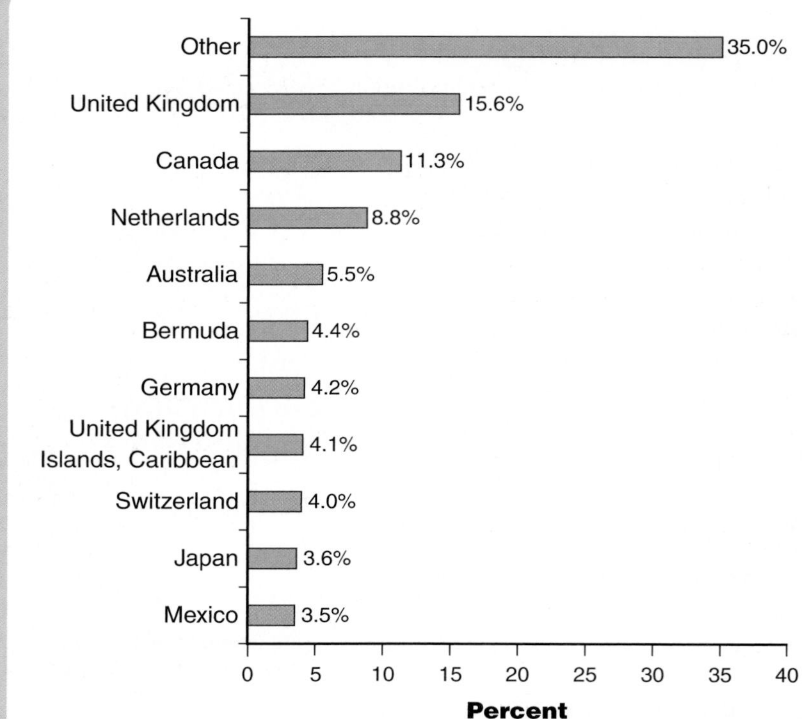

Source: J. Koncz & D. Yorgason, "Direct Investment Positions for 2005: Country and Industry Detail," available at http://www.bea.gov/bea/ARTICLES/2006/07July/0706_DIP_WEB.pdf, 7 February 2007.

Exhibit 8.2

U.S. Direct Foreign Investment Abroad

At the same time, direct foreign investment in the United States is just half the picture. U.S. companies also have made large direct foreign investments in countries throughout the world. For example, Anheuser-Busch, the brewer of Budweiser beer, paid $700 million to acquire Harbin Brewery Group, the fourth-largest beer company in China.[5] As Exhibit 8.2 shows, U.S. companies have made their largest direct foreign investments in the United Kingdom, Canada, the Netherlands, and Australia. Overall, U.S. companies invest more than $2 trillion a year to do business in other countries.

So, whether foreign companies invest in the United States or U.S. companies invest abroad, direct foreign investment is an increasingly important and common method of conducting global business.

1.2 Trade Barriers

Although today's consumers usually don't care where the products they buy come from (more on this in Section 1.4), national governments have traditionally preferred that consumers buy domestically made products in hopes that such purchases would increase the number of domestic businesses and workers. Indeed, governments have done much more than hope that you will buy from domestic companies. Historically, governments have actively used **trade barriers** to make it much more expensive or difficult (or sometimes impossible) for consumers to buy or consume imported goods. For example, countries throughout the world restrict the number and kind of imported television shows and movies. The French government requires that 40 percent of all TV shows be French and that at least 60 percent be European; the Chinese government permits only 20 foreign films to be imported each year.[6] Likewise, the European Union places a 34 percent tax on frozen strawberries imported from China.[7] And the U.S. government imposes a tariff of 54 cents a gallon on imported ethanol, which is blended with gasoline for use in automobiles.[8] By establishing these restrictions and taxes, the European Union and the French, Chinese, and U.S. governments are engaging in **protectionism**, which is the use of trade barriers to protect local companies and their workers from foreign competition.

Governments have used two general kinds of trade barriers: tariff and nontariff barriers. A **tariff** is a direct tax on imported goods. Like the U.S. government's 54-cent-per-gallon tax on imported ethanol, tariffs increase the cost of imported goods relative to that of domestic goods. For example, the U.S. import tax on trucks is 25 percent. This means that U.S. buyers must pay $25,000 for a $20,000 imported truck, with the $5,000 tariff going to the U.S. government. As a result, less than 10,000 pickup trucks are imported by the United States each year.[9] **Nontariff barriers** are nontax methods of increasing the cost or reducing the volume of imported goods. There are five types of nontariff barriers: quotas, voluntary export restraints, government import standards, government subsidies, and customs valuation/classification. Because there are so many

trade barriers government-imposed regulations that increase the cost and restrict the number of imported goods

protectionism a government's use of trade barriers to shield domestic companies and their workers from foreign competition

tariff a direct tax on imported goods

nontariff barriers nontax methods of increasing the cost or reducing the volume of imported goods different kinds of nontariff barriers, they can be an even more potent method of shielding domestic industries from foreign competition.

Quotas are specific limits on the number or volume of imported products. For example, because of strict import quotas, raw sugarcane imports into the United States are limited to approximately 1.2 million metric tons per year.[10] Since this is well below the demand for sugar in the United States, domestic U.S. sugar prices are twice as high as sugar prices in the rest of the world.[11] Like quotas, **voluntary export restraints** limit the amount of a product that can be imported annually. The difference is that the exporting country, rather than the importing country, imposes restraints. Usually, however, the "voluntary" offer to limit exports occurs because the importing country has implicitly threatened to impose quotas. For example, to protect South African textile manufacturers from cheap and plentiful Chinese textile products, the South African government convinced China to "voluntarily" restrict the textiles it exports to South Africa each year.[12] According to the World Trade Organization (see the discussion in Section 1.3), however, voluntary export restraints are illegal and should not be used to restrict imports.[13]

© SUSAN VAN ETTEN

France is only one of many countries that restrict the number of imported television shows and movies as a means of protecting its domestic entertainment industry.

In theory, **government import standards** are established to protect the health and safety of citizens. In reality, such standards are often used to restrict or ban imported goods. For example, Japan banned the importation of nearly all U.S. apples, which are one-third the cost of Japanese apples. Ostensibly, the ban was to prevent transmission of fire blight bacteria to Japanese apple orchards, but research conducted *jointly* by U.S. and Japanese scientists "does not support Japan's assertion that mature, symptomless apples can transmit" the fire blight bacteria.[14] The Japanese government was actually using this government import standard to protect the economic health of its apple farmers, rather than the biological health of its apple orchards. Only after the World Trade Organization ruled that there was no scientific basis for the ban did Japan allow U.S. apples to be imported without restrictions.[15]

Many nations also use **subsidies**, such as long-term, low-interest loans, cash grants, and tax deferments, to develop and protect companies in special industries. Not surprisingly, businesses complain about unfair trade practices when foreign companies receive government subsidies. Boeing, the U.S. jet manufacturer, protested when Airbus received $4.5 billion in "launch aid" from nine European countries to build its new A380 superjumbo jet. In a formal complaint to the World Trade Organization, the U.S. Trade Representative argued that "Airbus governments thus enable Airbus to launch aircraft at an otherwise unsustainable scale and pace, if it could have launched them at all. Thus they expand the range of the Airbus product family against which U.S. producers must compete, and lower the price at which Airbus is able to offer those products. . . . The subsidization of Airbus jeopardizes the durability of any recent improvement in Boeing's competitive situation."[16]

© INSIDE OUT/JUPITER IMAGES

quota a limit on the number or volume of imported products

voluntary export restraints voluntarily imposed limits on the number or volume of products exported to a particular country

government import standard a standard ostensibly established to protect the health and safety of citizens but, in reality, often used to restrict imports

subsidies government loans, grants, and tax deferments given to domestic companies to protect them from foreign competition

The last type of nontariff barrier is **customs classification**. As products are imported into a country, they are examined by customs agents, who must decide into which of nearly 9,000 categories they should classify a product (see the Official Harmonized Tariff Schedule of the United States at **http://www.usitc.gov/tata/hts/index.htm** for more information). Classification is important because the category assigned by customs agents can greatly affect the size of the tariff and whether the item is subject to import quotas. For example, the U.S. Customs Service has several customs classifications for imported shoes. Tariffs on imported leather or "nonrubber" shoes are about 8.5 percent, whereas tariffs on imported rubber shoes, such as athletic footwear or waterproof shoes, range from 20 to 67 percent.[17] The difference is large enough that some importers try to make their rubber shoes look like leather in hopes of receiving the nonrubber customs classification and lower tariff.

customs classification a classification assigned to imported products by government officials that affects the size of the tariff and imposition of import quotas

1.3 Trade Agreements

Thanks to the trade barriers described above, buying imported goods has often been much more expensive and difficult than buying domestic goods. During the 1990s, however, the regulations governing global trade were transformed. The most significant change was that 124 countries agreed to adopt the **General Agreement on Tariffs and Trade (GATT)**. Although GATT itself was replaced by the **World Trade Organization (WTO)** in 1995, the changes that it made continue to encourage international trade.

General Agreement on Tariffs and Trade (GATT) a worldwide trade agreement that reduced and eliminated tariffs, limited government subsidies, and established protections for intellectual property

World Trade Organization (WTO) the successor to GATT; the only international organization dealing with the global rules of trade between nations. Its main function is to ensure that trade flows as smoothly, predictably, and freely as possible.

Through tremendous decreases in tariff and nontariff barriers, GATT made it much easier and cheaper for consumers in all countries to buy foreign products. First, tariffs were cut 40 percent on average worldwide by 2005. Second, tariffs were eliminated in 10 specific industries: beer, alcohol, construction equipment, farm machinery, furniture, medical equipment, paper, pharmaceuticals, steel, and toys. Third, stricter limits were put on government subsidies. For example, GATT put limits on how much national governments can subsidize company research in electronic and high-technology industries (see the discussion of subsidies in Section 1.2). Fourth, GATT established protections for intellectual property, such as trademarks, patents, and copyrights. Protection of intellectual property has become an increasingly important issue in global trade because of widespread product piracy. For example, 90 percent of the computer software and 95 percent of the video games in China are illegal pirated copies.[18] Likewise, Chinese bootleggers regularly sell illegal DVD copies of movies, such as *Borat* or *The Da Vinci Code*, months before the movie studios release official copies to stores in the United States.[19] Product piracy like this costs movie companies $6 billion in lost revenue each year.[20] Finally, trade disputes between countries now are fully settled by arbitration panels from the WTO. In the past, countries could use their veto power to cancel a panel's decision.

Exhibit 8.3

World Trade Organization

FACT FILE

WORLD TRADE ORGANIZATION

Location: Geneva, Switzerland
Established: 1 January 1995
Created by: Uruguay Round negotiations (1986–1994)
Membership: 150 countries (as of 11 October 2007)
Budget: 175 million Swiss francs for 2006
Secretariat staff: 635
Head: Pascal Lamy (director-general)

Functions:

- Administering WTO trade agreements
- Forum for trade negotiations
- Handling trade disputes
- Monitoring national trade policies
- Technical assistance and training for developing countries
- Cooperation with other international organizations

Source: "WTO: About the Organization," World Trade Organization, available at http://www.wto.org/english/thewto_e/whatis_e/whatis_e.htm, 7 February 2007.

For instance, the French government routinely vetoed rulings that its large cash grants to French farmers constituted unfair subsidies. Now, however, countries that are members of the WTO (every country that agreed to GATT is a member) no longer have veto power. Thus, WTO rulings are complete and final. For more information about GATT and the WTO, go to the WTO's Web site at **http://www.wto.org.** Exhibit 8.3 provides a brief overview of the WTO and its functions.

The second major development that has reduced trade barriers has been the creation of **regional trading zones**, in which tariff and nontariff barriers are reduced or eliminated for countries within the trading zone. The largest and most important trading zones are in Europe (the Maastricht Treaty), North America (the North American Free Trade Agreement, or NAFTA), Central America (Central America Free Trade Agreement, or CAFTA-DR), South America (Mercosur, and the proposed South American Community of Nations, or SACN), and Asia (the Association of Southeast Asian Nations, or ASEAN, and Asia-Pacific Economic Cooperation, or APEC). The map in Exhibit 8.4 shows the extent to which free trade agreements govern global trade.

regional trading zones areas in which tariff and nontariff barriers on trade between countries are reduced or eliminated

Exhibit 8.4

Global Map of Regional Trade Agreements

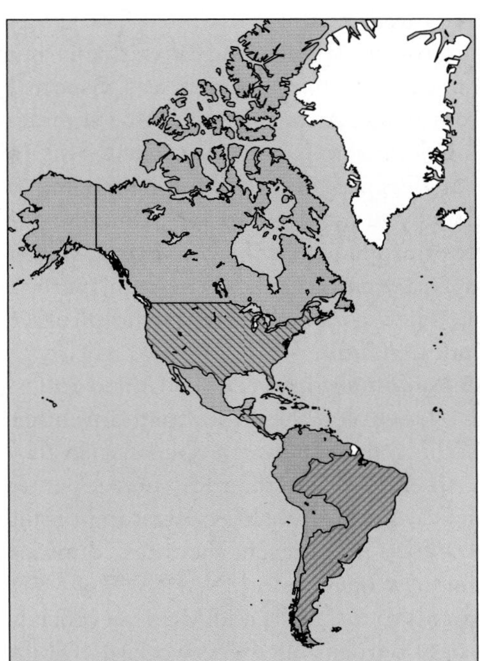

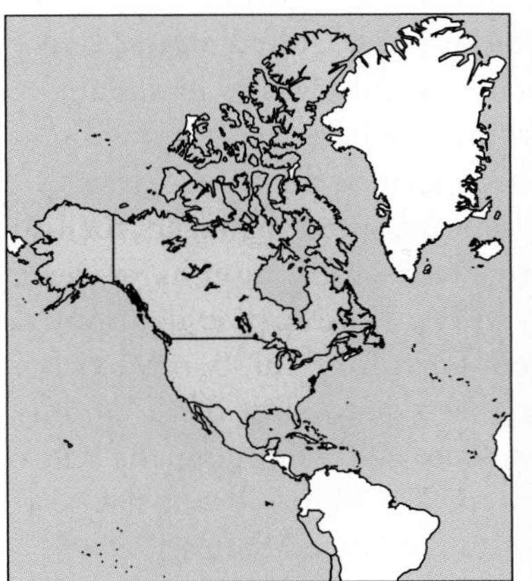

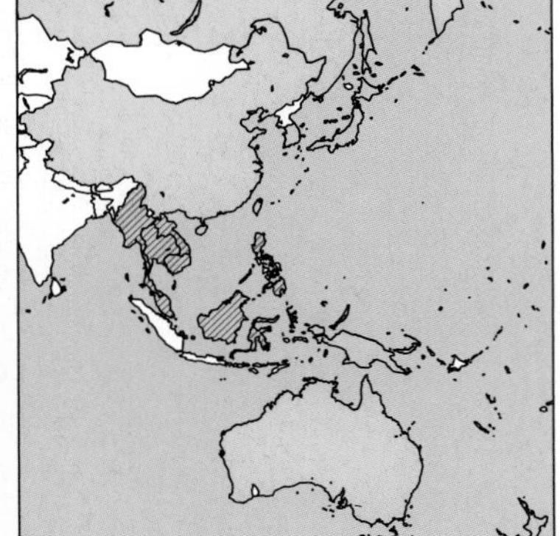

In 1992, Belgium, Denmark, France, Germany, Greece, Ireland, Italy, Luxembourg, the Netherlands, Portugal, Spain, and the United Kingdom implemented the **Maastricht Treaty of Europe**. The purpose of this treaty was to transform their 12 different economies and 12 currencies into one common economic market, called the European Union (EU), with one common currency. Austria, Finland, and Sweden joined the EU in 1995, followed by Cyprus, the Czech Republic, Estonia, Hungary, Latvia, Lithuania, Malta, Poland, Slovakia, and Slovenia in 2004, bringing the total membership to 25 countries.[21] Bulgaria and Romania joined in 2007; Croatia, Macedonia, and Turkey are now being considered for membership.[22] On 1 January 2002, a single common currency, the euro, went into circulation in 12 of the EU's members (Austria, Belgium, Finland, France, Germany, Greece, Ireland, Italy, Luxembourg, the Netherlands, Portugal, and Spain).

Prior to the treaty, trucks carrying products were stopped and inspected by customs agents at each border. Furthermore, since the required paperwork, tariffs, and government product specifications could be radically different in each country, companies often had to file 12 different sets of paperwork, pay 12 different tariffs, produce 12 different versions of their basic product to meet various government specifications, and exchange money in 12 different currencies. Likewise, open business travel from state to state, which we take for granted in the United States, was complicated by inspections at each border crossing. If you lived in Germany but worked in Luxembourg, your car was stopped and your passport was inspected twice every day, as you traveled to and from work. Also, every business transaction required a currency exchange, for example, from German deutsche marks to Italian lira, or from French francs to Dutch guilders. Imagine all of this happening to millions of trucks, cars, and businesspeople, and you can begin to appreciate the difficulty and cost of conducting business across Europe before the Maastricht Treaty. For more information about the Maastricht Treaty and the EU, go to **http://europa.eu.int/index-en.htm**. For more about Europe's new common currency, the euro, see **http://www.ecb.int/ecb/educational/html/index.en.html**.

NAFTA, the **North American Free Trade Agreement** between the United States, Canada, and Mexico, went into effect on 1 January 1994. More than any other regional trade agreement, NAFTA has liberalized trade between countries so that businesses can plan for one market, North America, rather than for three separate markets, the United States, Canada, and Mexico. One of NAFTA's most important achievements was to eliminate most product tariffs *and* prevent the three countries from increasing existing tariffs or introducing new ones. Before NAFTA, Wal-Mart used expensive intermediaries to distribute goods to its stores, and Mexican officials often pressured managers for bribes. Because of burdensome paperwork, deliveries sometimes took months to clear customs. This all changed with NAFTA. Before NAFTA, Wal-Mart sold a Sony flat-screen TV imported from Japan with a 23 percent tariff for $1,600 in Mexico. After NAFTA, Sony built a new factory in Mexico, enabling it to ship the TVs duty-free anywhere in the United States, Canada, or Mexico. With shipping costs now next to nothing and the 23 percent tariff eliminated, Wal-Mart sells the flat-screen TVs for $600 in Mexico, or about what they sell for in the United States.[23]

Overall, both Mexican and Canadian exports to the United States have doubled since NAFTA went into effect. U.S. exports to Mexico and Canada have doubled, too, growing twice as fast as U.S. exports to any other part of the world.[24] In fact, Mexico and Canada now account for 36 percent of all U.S. exports.[25] For more information about NAFTA, see the Office of NAFTA & Inter-American Affairs at **http://www.ustr.gov/Trade_Agreements/Regional/NAFTA/Section_Index.html**.

Maastricht Treaty of Europe a regional trade agreement between most European countries

North American Free Trade Agreement (NAFTA) a regional trade agreement between the United States, Canada, and Mexico

CAFTA-DR, the new **Central America Free Trade Agreement** between the United States, the Dominican Republic, and the Central American countries of Costa Rica, El Salvador, Guatemala, Honduras, and Nicaragua went into effect in August 2005. With a combined population of 347.6 million (302.3 million in the United States), the CAFTA-DR countries together are the 10th-largest U.S. export market in the world, and the second-largest U.S. export market in Latin America, after Mexico. U.S. companies export more than $16 billion in goods each year to the CAFTA-DR countries. Furthermore, U.S. exports to CAFTA-DR countries, which are increasing at 16 percent per year, are by far the fastest growing export market for U.S. companies.[26] For more information about CAFTA-DR, see **http://www.fas.usda.gov/itp/CAFTA/cafta.asp**.

One of the goals of the proposed SACN, the South American Community of Nations, is to establish a free trade zone throughout South America for the countries of Argentina, Bolivia, Brazil, Chile, Colombia, Ecuador, Guyana, Paraguay, Peru, Suriname, Uruguay, and Venezuela. If created, the SACA would likely supplant Mercosur, a free trade agreement between Brazil, Argentina, Uruguay, and Paraguay, which have been granted associate membership in SACN. For more information about Mercosur, see **http://www.sice.oas.org/agreemts/Mercin_e.asp#MERCOSUR**. If approved, SACN would become one of the largest trading zones in the world, encompassing 361 million people in 12 countries in South America with a combined gross domestic product of $1 trillion.[27] For more information about SACN, see **http://www.comunidadandina.org/ingles/sudamerican.htm**.

ASEAN, the **Association of Southeast Asian Nations**, and **APEC**, the **Asia-Pacific Economic Cooperation**, are the two largest and most important regional trading groups in Asia. ASEAN is a trade agreement between Brunei Darussalam, Cambodia, Indonesia, Lao PDR, Malaysia, Myanmar, the Philippines, Singapore, Thailand, and Vietnam, which form a market of more than 558 million people. U.S. trade with ASEAN countries exceeds $153 billion a year.[28] In fact, the United States is ASEAN's largest trading partner, and ASEAN'S member nations constitute the fifth-largest trading partner of the United States. ASEAN's members have agreed to create an ASEAN free trade area beginning in 2015 for the six original countries (Brunei Darussalam, Indonesia, Malaysia, the Philippines, Singapore, and Thailand) and in 2018 for the newer member countries (Cambodia, Lao PDR, Myanmar, and Vietnam).[29] For more information about ASEAN, see **http://www.aseansec.org**.

APEC is a broader agreement that includes Australia, Canada, Chile, the People's Republic of China, Hong Kong (China), Japan, Mexico, New Zealand, Papua New Guinea, Peru, Russia, South Korea, Taiwan, the United States, and all the members of ASEAN except Cambodia, Lao PDR, and Myanmar.[30] APEC's 21 member countries contain 2.6 billion people, account for 47 percent of all global trade, and have a combined gross domestic product of over $19 trillion.[31]APEC countries began reducing trade barriers in 2000, though all the reductions will not be completely phased in until 2020. For more information about APEC, see **http://www.apecsec.org.sg**.

1.4 Consumers, Trade Barriers, and Trade Agreements

In Tokyo, a Coke costs $1.33.[32] In Geneva, Switzerland, a small cup of regular coffee costs $1.70. In the United States, each of these items costs about a dollar. A McDonald's Big Mac sandwich costs an average of $3.22 in the United States, $3.90 in the United Kingdom, and $5.05 in Switzerland.[33] Although not all products are more expensive in other countries (in some, they are cheaper; for example, a Big Mac costs $1.41 in China and $2.66 in Mexico), international studies find

Central America Free Trade Agreement (CAFTA-DR) a regional trade agreement between Costa Rica, the Dominican Republic, El Salvador, Guatemala, Honduras, Nicaragua, and the United States

Association of Southeast Asian Nations (ASEAN) a regional trade agreement between Brunei Darussalam, Cambodia, Indonesia, Laos, Malaysia, Myanmar, the Philippines, Singapore, Thailand, and Vietnam

Asia-Pacific Economic Cooperation (APEC) a regional trade agreement between Australia, Canada, Chile, the People's Republic of China, Hong Kong, Japan, Mexico, New Zealand, Papua New Guinea, Peru, Russia, South Korea, Taiwan, the United States, and all the members of ASEAN, except Cambodia, Laos, and Myanmar

© ERIKO SUGITA/REUTERS/LANDOV

***One of the most widely known methods of comparing the purchasing power of nations is the Big Mac Index assembled yearly by* The Economist.**
In China, a Big Mac costs the equivalent of a mere $1.41.

that American consumers get much more for their money than most other consumers in the world. For example, the average worker earns nearly $54,930 a year in Switzerland, $59,590 in Norway, $38,980 in Japan, and $43,749 in America.[34] Yet, after adjusting these incomes for how much they can buy, the Swiss income is equivalent to just $37,080, the Norwegian income to $40,420, and the Japanese income to $31,410![35] This is the same as saying that $1 of income can buy you only 68 cents worth of goods in Switzerland and Norway, and 81 cents worth in Japan. In other words, Americans can buy much more with their incomes than those in other countries can.

One reason that Americans get more for their money is that the U.S. marketplace has been one of the easiest for foreign companies to enter. Although some U.S. industries, such as textiles, have been heavily protected from foreign competition by trade barriers, for the most part, American consumers (and businesses) have had plentiful choices among American-made and foreign-made products. More important, the high level of competition between foreign and domestic companies that creates these choices helps to keep prices low in the United States. Furthermore, it is precisely the lack of choice and the low level of competition that keep prices higher in countries that have not been as open to foreign companies and products. For example, Japanese trade barriers are estimated to cost Japanese consumers more than $100 billion a year. In fact, Japanese trade barriers amount to a 51 percent tax on food for the average Japanese family.[36]

So why do trade barriers and free trade agreements matter to consumers? They're important because free trade agreements increase choices, competition, and purchasing power and thus decrease what people pay for food, clothing, necessities, and luxuries. Accordingly, today's consumers rarely care where their products and services come from. For example, Mark Sneed, president of Phillips Foods, which imports blue crab from its Asian processing factories at one-third the cost of crab caught and processed in the United States, says, "I've never once had a customer ask me if we served domestic or imported crabs, just like they never ask if we have foreign shrimp."[37] Peter Germano, a New York jeweler who sells diamonds, says people don't care where the diamonds are from; they "just want to know which is cheaper."[38] Finally, Luis de Anda, who visits one of Wal-Mart's Sam's Wholesale Clubs in Mexico once a month to purchase diapers and toilet paper in bulk for his family and friends, says, "Why should I care where they're from? With the money I save, I take my family to the movies."[39]

Free trade agreements increase choices, competition, and purchasing power and thus decrease what people pay for food, clothing, necessities, and luxuries.

And why do trade barriers and free trade agreements matter to managers? The reason, as you're about to read, is that while free trade agreements create new business opportunities, they also intensify competition, and addressing that competition is a manager's job.

Review 1: *Global Business, Trade Rules, and Trade Agreements*

Today, there are more than 77,175 multinational corporations worldwide; just 3.1 percent are based in the United States. Global business affects the United States in two ways: through direct foreign investment in the United States by foreign companies, and through U.S. companies' investment in business in other countries. U.S. direct foreign investment throughout the world typically amounts to about $2 trillion per year, whereas direct foreign investment by foreign companies in the United States amounts to $1.6 trillion per year. Historically, tariffs and nontariff trade barriers, such as quotas, voluntary export restraints, government import standards, government subsidies, and customs classifications, have made buying foreign goods much harder or more expensive than buying domestically produced products. In recent years, however, worldwide trade agreements, such as GATT, along with regional trading agreements, like the Maastricht Treaty of Europe, NAFTA, CAFTA-DR, Mercosur, SACN, ASEAN, and APEC, have substantially reduced tariff and nontariff barriers to international trade. Companies have responded by investing in growing markets in Asia, eastern Europe, and Latin America. Consumers have responded by purchasing products based on value, rather than geography.

HOW TO GO GLOBAL?

Once a company has decided that it *will* go global, it must decide *how* to go global. For example, if you decide to sell in Singapore, should you try to find a local business partner who speaks the language, knows the laws, and understands the customs and norms of Singapore's culture, or should you simply export your products from your home country? What do you do if you are also entering eastern Europe, perhaps starting in Hungary? Should you use the same approach in Hungary that you used in Singapore?

Although there is no magical formula for answering these questions, after reading the next two sections, you should be able to

2 explain why companies choose to standardize or adapt their business procedures.

3 explain the different ways that companies can organize to do business globally.

2 Consistency or Adaptation?

In this section, we return to a key issue: How can you be sure that the way you run your business in one country is the right way to run that business in another? In other words, how can you strike the right balance between global consistency and local adaptation?

Global consistency means that when a multinational company has offices, manufacturing plants, and distribution facilities in different countries, it will use the same rules, guidelines, policies, and procedures to run those offices, plants, and facilities. Managers at company headquarters value global consistency because it simplifies decisions. In contrast, a company with a **local adaptation** policy modifies its standard operating procedures to adapt to differences in foreign customers, governments, and

global consistency when a multinational company has offices, manufacturing plants, and distribution facilities in different countries and runs them all using the same rules, guidelines, policies, and procedures

local adaptation modifying rules, guidelines, policies, and procedures to adapt to differences in foreign customers, governments, and regulatory agencies regulatory agencies. Local adaptation is typically more important to local managers who are charged with making the international business successful in their countries.

"WHAT'S NEW" COMPANY

If companies lean too much toward global consistency, they run the risk of using management procedures poorly suited to particular countries' markets, cultures, and employees (that is, not enough local adaptation). **MTV** made this mistake when going global. According to Divya Gupta, president of Media Edge, which helps companies buy advertising in India, "MTV, when it first entered the country, made the mistake of coming in as MTV. No changes." So MTV quickly learned from this mistake and stopped showing Western videos in international locations and started featuring local music and shows. In Brazil, it developed *Mochilão*, a travel show hosted by a popular model who backpacks to famous sites.[40] In China, it developed *Mei Mei Sees MTV*, in which an animated, "virtual" video disc jockey introduces music videos.[41] And in India it developed *Silly Point*, a humor show that takes a lighthearted view of India's most popular sport, cricket.[42]

If companies focus too much on local adaptation, however, they run the risk of losing the cost efficiencies and productivity that result from using standardized rules and procedures throughout the world. A decade into its development, MTV International was profitable, but not by much. While it had access to huge markets—in fact, 80 percent of MTV viewers were outside the United States—access to those markets was slow to translate into large profits. Why? Because of the enormous cost of building new studios, acquiring new talent, and developing local content for so many different international markets.

Review 2: Consistency or Adaptation?

Global business requires a balance between global consistency and local adaptation. Global consistency means using the same rules, guidelines, policies, and procedures in each location. Managers at company headquarters like global consistency because it simplifies decisions. Local adaptation means adapting standard procedures to individual markets. Local managers prefer a policy of local adaptation because it gives them more control. Not all businesses need the same combinations of global consistency and local adaptation. Some thrive by emphasizing global consistency and ignoring local adaptation. Others succeed by ignoring global consistency and emphasizing local adaptation.

3 Forms for Global Business

Besides determining whether to adapt organizational policies and procedures, a company must also determine how to organize itself for successful entry into foreign markets.

*Historically, companies have generally followed the phase model of globalization, in which a company makes the transition from a domestic company to a global company in the following sequential phases: **3.1 exporting**, **3.2 cooperative contracts**, **3.3 strategic alliances**, and **3.4 wholly owned affiliates**. At each step, the company grows much larger, uses those resources to enter more global markets, is less dependent on home country sales, and is more committed in its orientation to global business. Some companies, however, do not follow the phase model of globalization.[43] Some skip phases on their way to becoming more global and less domestic. Others don't follow the phase model at all. These are known as **3.5 global new ventures**. This section reviews these forms of global business.[44]*

3.1 Exporting

When companies produce products in their home countries and sell those products to customers in foreign countries, they are **exporting**. For example, **FremantleMedia**, the London-based company that originally developed the *Pop Idol* TV show in Britain and then exported a nearly identical version to the United States as *American Idol*, now has exported similar versions of the show to 35 different countries.[45]

Exporting as a form of global business offers many advantages. It makes the company less dependent on sales in its home market and provides a greater degree of control over research, design, and production decisions. Sheldon Bailey is a "flying producer" who helps FremantleMedia set up *Idol* in different countries and cultures. Bailey allows for some adaptation to local cultures. In Germany, for example, the word *Idol* is associated with Hitler, so the show is called *Germany Seeks the Superstar*; likewise, since popular Arabic songs last eight or nine minutes, three times as long as in the rest of the world, contestants get three minutes to sing, compared with 90 seconds in other versions of *Idol*. For the most part, however, the show is basically the same worldwide—find undiscovered talents and turn them into major recording artists—and it's Bailey's job to ensure that consistency. When local Russian producers claimed that Russians want to see celebrities and pushed to have them on the show, Bailey refused: "We told them this is not about celebrities, it's about kids. They're your stars."

Though advantageous in a number of ways, exporting also has its disadvantages. The primary disadvantage is that many exported goods are subject to tariff and nontariff barriers that can substantially increase their final cost to consumers. A second disadvantage is that transportation costs can significantly increase the price of an exported product. For example, because of special safety requirements such as maintaining particular temperatures and pressures, the ships that transport liquefied natural gas can cost up to $350 million to build. Consequently, shipping costs account for as much as 20 to 30 percent of the total cost of liquefied natural gas.[46] Another disadvantage is that companies that export depend on foreign importers for product distribution. This means that if, for example, the foreign importer makes a

doing the right thing

Fair and Safe Working Conditions in Foreign Factories

Requiring workers to work 15-hour days or to work seven days a week with no overtime pay, beating them for arriving late, requiring them to apply toxic materials with their bare hands, charging them excessive fees for food and lodging—these are just a few of the workplace violations found in the overseas factories that make shoes, clothes, bicycles, and other goods for large U.S. and multinational companies. The Fair Labor Association, which inspects overseas factories for Adidas-Salomon, Levi Strauss, Liz Claiborne, Nike, Reebok, Polo Ralph Lauren, and others, recommends the following workplace standards for foreign factories.

- **Make sure there is no forced labor or child labor; no physical, sexual, psychological, or verbal abuse or harassment; and no discrimination.**
- **Provide a safe and healthy working environment to prevent accidents.**
- **Respect the right of employees to freedom of association and collective bargaining. Compensate employees fairly by paying the legally required minimum wage or the prevailing industry wage, whichever is higher.**
- **Provide legally required benefits. Employees should not be required to work more than 48 hours per week and 12 hours of overtime (for which they should receive additional pay), and they should have at least one day off per week.**

Do the right thing. Investigate and monitor the working conditions of overseas factories where the goods sold by your company are made. Insist that improvements be made. Find another supplier if they aren't.[47]

exporting selling domestically produced products to customers in foreign countries

ACHIM SCHEIDEMANN/EPA/LANDOV

Local adaptation is a necessary consideration of global business. For example, since Germans associate the word 'idol' with Hitler, producers exporting the popular* American Idol *television show opted to change the name to* Deutschland sucht den SuperStar *("Germany Seeks the Superstar").

mistake on the paperwork that accompanies a shipment of imported goods, those goods can be returned to the foreign manufacturer at the manufacturer's expense.

3.2 Cooperative Contracts

When an organization wants to expand its business globally without making a large financial commitment to do so, it may sign a **cooperative contract** with a foreign business owner, who pays the company a fee for the right to conduct that business in his or her country. There are two kinds of cooperative contracts: licensing and franchising.

Under a **licensing** agreement, a domestic company, the *licensor*, receives royalty payments for allowing another company, the *licensee*, to produce its product, sell its service, or use its brand name in a particular foreign market. For example, brands such as Peter Paul Mounds and Almond Joy, which consumers associate with American companies, are not really American products. A British company, CADBURY SCHWEPPES, licenses those candy bars to Hershey for U.S. production.

One of the most important advantages of licensing is that it allows companies to earn additional profits without investing more money. As foreign sales increase, the royalties paid to the licensor by the foreign licensee increase. Moreover, the licensee, not the licensor, invests in production equipment and facilities to produce the licensed product. Licensing also helps companies avoid tariff and nontariff barriers. Since the licensee manufactures the product within the foreign country, tariff and nontariff barriers don't apply. For example, Britvic Corona is licensed to bottle and distribute Pepsi-Cola within the United Kingdom. Because it bottles the soft drink in Britain, tariff and nontariff barriers do not apply.

The biggest disadvantage associated with licensing is that the licensor gives up control over the quality of the product or service sold by the foreign licensee. Unless the licensing agreement contains specific restrictions, the licensee controls the entire business, from production to marketing to final sales. Many licensors include inspection clauses in their license contracts, but closely monitoring product or service quality from thousands of miles away can be difficult. An additional disadvantage is that licensees can eventually become competitors, especially when a licensing agreement includes access to important technology or proprietary business knowledge.

A **franchise** is a collection of networked firms in which the manufacturer or marketer of a product or service, the *franchisor*, licenses the entire business to another person or organization, the *franchisee*. For the price of an initial franchise fee plus royalties, franchisors provide franchisees with training, assistance with marketing and advertising, and an exclusive right to conduct business in a particular location. Most franchise fees run between $5,000 and $35,000. Franchisees pay MCDONALD'S, one of the largest franchisors in the world, an initial franchise fee of $45,000. Another $610,750 to $1,210,000 is needed beyond that to pay for food inventory, kitchen equipment, construction, landscaping, and other expenses (the cost varies per country). While franchisees typically borrow part of this cost from a bank, McDonald's requires that they invest $200,000 of their own money into a new McDonald's restaurant.[48] Since typical royalties range from 2.0 to 12.5 percent of gross sales, franchisors are well rewarded for the help they provide to franchisees. More than 400 U.S. companies franchise their businesses to foreign franchise partners.

cooperative contract an agreement in which a foreign business owner pays a company a fee for the right to conduct that business in his or her country

licensing an agreement in which a domestic company, the licensor, receives royalty payments for allowing another company, the licensee, to produce the licensor's product, sell its service, or use its brand name in a specified foreign market

franchise a collection of networked firms in which the manufacturer or marketer of a product or service, the franchisor, licenses the entire business to another person or organization, the franchisee

Overall, franchising is a fast way to enter foreign markets. Over the last 20 years, U.S. franchisors have more than doubled their global franchises for a total of more than 100,000 global franchise units. Because it gives the franchisor additional cash flows from franchisee fees and royalties, franchising can be a good strategy when a company's domestic sales have slowed. For example, **Yum! Brands**, which owns and runs Pizza Hut, Taco Bell, KFC (formerly Kentucky Fried Chicken), A&W Restaurants, and Long John Silver's, is accepting very few new franchises in the United States because the U.S. market is saturated with fast-food outlets. McDonald's opens only 50 to 100 new restaurants a year in the United States.[49] Outside the United States, however, these restaurants are experiencing much stronger growth. In the last decade, McDonald's nearly doubled the number of its overseas restaurants and continues to add approximately 700 to 800 new international restaurants per year.[50] Between Pizza Hut, Taco Bell, KFC, A&W Restaurants, and Long John Silvers, Yum! Brands opens nearly 700 new international franchise restaurants a year.[51]

Despite franchising's many advantages, franchisors face a loss of control when they sell businesses to franchisees who are thousands of miles away. Franchising specialist Cheryl Scott says, "One franchisor I know was wondering why the royalties coming from India were so small when he knew the shop was always packed. It was because the franchisee wasn't putting all of the sales through the cash register."[52]

Although there are exceptions, franchising success may be somewhat culture-bound. Because most global franchisors begin by franchising their businesses in similar countries or regions (Canada is by far the first choice for American companies taking their first step into global franchising), and because 65 percent of franchisors make absolutely no change in their business for overseas franchisees, that success may not generalize to cultures with different lifestyles, values, preferences, and technological infrastructures. When Jim Bryant began opening Subway sandwich shops in China 10 years ago, Americans living there were elated (one kissed the floor), but Chinese customers didn't know how to order (he had to make signs explaining how) or how to eat a sandwich (they peeled it like a banana because they didn't want to physically touch their food). Likewise, because the tuna in the tuna salad didn't have a visible head or a tail, they didn't believe it was actually fish.[53] Management consultant Dennis Custage says, "The number one mistake companies make is trying to run everything the way it was in their home country, with a bunch of expatriates."[54] Furthermore, unlike McDonald's, which added a new spicy chicken burger, and KFC, which replaced coleslaw with shredded carrots, fungus, or bamboo shoots, Subway didn't change its menu for Chinese tastes. Luo Bing Ling, who runs a Subway store in Beijing, says, "Subway should have at least one item tailored to Chinese tastes to show they are respecting the local culture."[55]

3.3 Strategic Alliances

Companies forming **strategic alliances** combine key resources, costs, risks, technology, and people. The most common strategic alliance is a **joint venture**, which occurs when two existing companies collaborate to form a third company. The two founding companies remain intact and unchanged, except that together they now own the newly created joint venture.

One of the oldest and most successful global joint ventures is **Fuji Xerox**, which is a joint venture between Fuji Film of Japan and U.S.-based Xerox Corporation, which makes copiers and automated office systems. More than 45 years after its creation, Fuji Xerox employs nearly 37,000 employees and has close to $9.1 billion in revenues. Fuji Xerox is largely responsible for copier sales in Asia, whereas Xerox is responsible for North American sales. Rank Xerox, a Xerox subsidiary, is responsible for sales in Europe.[56]

strategic alliance an agreement in which companies combine key resources, costs, risk, technology, and people

joint venture a strategic alliance in which two existing companies collaborate to form a third, independent company

"What's New" Company

One of the advantages of global joint ventures is that, like licensing and franchising, they help companies avoid tariff and nontariff barriers to entry. Another advantage is that companies participating in a joint venture bear only part of the costs and the risks of that business. Many companies find this attractive because of the expense of entering foreign markets or developing new products. For example, General Electric and Mitsubishi Electric have formed **Powerex**, an international joint venture to share the high development costs of designing and making parts for hybrid cars that run on both gasoline and electric power. Powerex makes electronic parts that help convert brake heat into power that is stored in batteries; the batteries run the electric motor when the car starts and during acceleration. Once the car attains a stable speed, the gasoline engine takes over and recharges the batteries. Hybrid cars are capable of getting 70 percent more miles per gallon than standard cars in city driving.[57]

"What's New" Company

Global joint ventures can be especially advantageous to smaller local partners that link up with larger, more experienced foreign firms that can bring advanced management, resources, and business skills to the joint venture. For instance, **Venyon** is a global joint venture between Finland-based cell phone giant Nokia and Germany-based Giesecke & Devrient (G&D), which specializes in secure smart cards, telecommunications, electronic payments and identification, and IT security. Through their combined efforts in Venyon, Nokia and G&D will enable consumers to securely use their cell phones, Blackberrys, or personal digital assistants to buy airline, rail, or taxi service, or to make credit card purchases from retailers, banks, and providers of digital services and media.[58] In short, if you can purchase something via the Internet, you should, thanks to Venyon, be able to purchase it securely via your cell phone.

Global joint ventures are not without problems, though. Because companies share costs and risks with their joint venture partners, they must also share profits. At one time, sharing of profits created some tension at Fuji Film, Xerox, and their joint venture, Fuji Xerox. In fact, until Xerox's recent turnaround, the company struggled for so long that business experts joked that Fuji Xerox, which has been highly profitable, should purchase Xerox.

Managing global joint ventures can also be difficult because they represent a merging of four cultures: the country and the organizational cultures of the first partner, and the country and the organizational cultures of the second partner. Oftentimes, to be "fair" to all involved, each partner in the global joint venture will have equal ownership and power. But this can result in power struggles and a lack of leadership. Because of these problems, companies forming global joint ventures should carefully develop detailed contracts that specify the obligations of each party. Toshiba, which participated in its first global joint ventures in the early 1900s by making light bulb filaments with General Electric, treats joint ventures like a marriage of the two companies and views the contract as a prenuptial agreement. The joint venture contract specifies how much each company will invest, what its rights and responsibilities are, and what it is entitled to if the joint venture does not work out. These steps are important, because the rate of failure for global joint ventures is estimated to be as high as 50 percent.[59]

"What's New" Company

When companies involved in global joint ventures don't carefully specify the obligations of each party, difficulties can occur. **Shanghai Automotive**, an auto manufacturer owned by the Chinese government that has global joint ventures with General Motors and Volkswagen, builds hundreds of thousands of Buicks, Chevys, Santanas, and Passats each year for Chinese consumers. Now, however, Shanghai Automotive has announced that it will build its own cars to the Chinese market to compete directly with its partners. Michael Dunne, president of Automotive

Resources Asia, says, "The Chinese formed joint ventures for one purpose: to learn how to do it themselves one day. That day is here."[60]

3.4 Wholly Owned Affiliates (Build or Buy)

Approximately one-third of multinational companies enter foreign markets through wholly owned affiliates. Unlike licensing arrangements, franchises, or joint ventures, **wholly owned affiliates** are 100 percent owned by the parent company. For example, **HONDA MOTORS OF AMERICA** in Marysville, Ohio, is 100 percent owned by Honda Motors of Japan. Ford Motor of Germany in Cologne is 100 percent owned by the **FORD MOTOR COMPANY** in Detroit, Michigan.

The primary advantage of wholly owned businesses is that the parent company receives all of the profits and has complete control over the foreign facilities. The biggest disadvantage is the expense of building new operations or buying existing businesses. While the payoff can be enormous if wholly owned affiliates succeed, the losses can be immense if they fail because the parent company assumes all of the risk. Two years after **VODAFONE**, the world's largest cell phone company, paid $2.2 billion to acquire J-Phone, the third-largest Japanese cell phone company, annual revenues continue to fall, and the number of new subscribers has dropped by 87 percent—a bad sign for future sales. The problem is that Vodafone focuses on selling small, reliable phones that work anywhere in the world, but most Japanese customers don't care whether their phones work outside the country. They want stylish, flashy, high-tech G3 cell phones that can download music, games, videos, and e-mail. And because Vodafone wholly owns J-Phone, it is bearing all the risk. Darryl Green, president of Vodafone in Japan, says, "We're losing our share of heavy users," the most profitable customers in the cell phone business.[61]

3.5 Global New Ventures

Companies used to evolve slowly from small operations selling in their home markets to large businesses selling to foreign markets. Furthermore, as companies went global, they usually followed the phase model of globalization. Recently, however, three trends have combined to allow companies to skip the phase model when going global. First, quick, reliable air travel can transport people to nearly any point in the world within one day. Second, low-cost communication technologies, such as international e-mail, teleconferencing, phone conferencing, and the Internet, make it easier to communicate with global customers, suppliers, managers, and employees. Third, there is now a critical mass of businesspeople with extensive personal experience in all aspects of global business.[62] This combination of developments has made it possible to start companies that are global from inception. With sales, employees, and financing in different countries, **global new ventures** are companies that are founded with an active global strategy.[63]

Although there are several different kinds of global new ventures, all share two common factors. First, the company founders successfully develop and communicate the company's global vision from inception. Winphoria Networks, which specializes in wireless networks, was global the day it started. Company investor Promod Haque explains: "Sales and marketing and the CEO were in Boston," but "the center of gravity was outside the United States. By having our employees based in Madrid and Bangalore, we were bidding contracts in Europe and Asia" during a time when sales were slow in the United States.[64] Winphoria's global launch was so successful that Motorola bought it only a few years after the start-up.

wholly owned affiliates foreign offices, facilities, and manufacturing plants that are 100 percent owned by the parent company

global new ventures new companies that are founded with an active global strategy and have sales, employees, and financing in different countries

Second, rather than going global one country at a time, new global ventures bring a product or service to market in several foreign markets at the same time. While headquartered in Lexington, Massachusetts, **VISTAPRINT** receives 15,000 orders a day from customers in 120 different countries who design their business cards, brochures, and invitations online using 17 different VistaPrint websites, each representing a different language or location. Printing happens at two automated production facilities, one in the Netherlands and the other in Canada. Once printed, the products are cut and sized by robots, and then packaged and delivered just three days after ordering. Regarding VistaPrint's commitment to worldwide customers, founder Robert Keane says, "The United States is blessed and cursed with a huge domestic market. It's often hard for startups to find their way out of their home nation. But you have to—it's not that type of world anymore."[65]

Review 3: Forms for Global Business

The phase model of globalization says that as companies move from a domestic to a global orientation, they use these organizational forms in sequence: exporting, cooperative contracts (licensing and franchising), strategic alliances, and wholly owned affiliates. Yet not all companies follow the phase model. For example, global new ventures are global from their inception.

WHERE TO GO GLOBAL?

Deciding where to go global is just as important as deciding how your company will go global. After reading the next three sections, you should be able to

4 explain how to find a favorable business climate.

5 discuss the importance of identifying and adapting to cultural differences.

6 explain how to successfully prepare workers for international assignments.

4 Finding the Best Business Climate

When deciding where to go global, companies try to find countries or regions with promising business climates.

An attractive global business climate ***4.1 positions the company for easy access to growing markets****,* ***4.2 is an effective but cost-efficient place to build an office or manufacturing facility****, and* ***4.3 minimizes the political risk to the company****.*

4.1 Growing Markets

The most important factor in an attractive business climate is access to a growing market. For example, no product is known and purchased by as many people throughout the world as **COCA-COLA**. Yet, even Coke, which is available in over 200 countries, still has tremendous potential for further global growth. Currently, the Coca-Cola Company gets about 80 percent of its sales from its 16 largest markets.[66] The remaining 20 percent is spread across the other 200 countries in which Coke does business.

Two factors help companies determine the growth potential of foreign markets: purchasing power and foreign competitors. **Purchasing power** is measured by comparing the relative cost of a standard set of goods and services in different countries. Earlier in the chapter we noted that a Coke costs $1.33 in Tokyo. Because a Coke costs only about $1.00 in the United States, the average American would have more purchasing power than the average Japanese. Purchasing power is strong in countries like Mexico, India, and China, which have low average levels of income. This is because basic living expenses, such as food, shelter, and transportation, are very inexpensive in those countries, so consumers still have money to spend after paying for necessities. For example, Mexican newlyweds Lucia Jiminez, a clothing store clerk, and Benjamin Macias, an office worker for an eyeglass store, earn just $650 a month. But that modest income easily qualifies them for a 30-year mortgage because the cost of their brand-new two-bedroom house 30 minutes outside Mexico City is just $25,200.[67] Because basic living expenses are so low in China, Mexico, and India and incomes are rising, purchasing power is strong, and millions of Chinese, Mexican, and Indian consumers increasingly have extra money to spend on what they want, in addition to what they need.[68]

> The number of Cokes a person drinks per year rises directly with purchasing power.

Consequently, countries with high and growing levels of purchasing power are good choices for companies looking for attractive global markets. As Exhibit 8.5 shows, Coke has found that the per capita consumption of Coca-Cola, or the number of Cokes a person drinks per year, rises directly with purchasing power. For example, in China, Colombia, and Argentina, where the average person earns $7,600, $9,100, and $15,000 annually, the respective number of Coca-Cola soft drinks increases from 18 to 80 to 253. The more purchasing power people have, the more likely they are to purchase soft drinks.[69]

purchasing power the relative cost of a standard set of goods and services in different countries

The second part of assessing the growth potential of global markets involves analyzing the degree of global competition, which is determined by the number

Exhibit 8.5

How Consumption of Coca-Cola Varies with Purchasing Power around the World

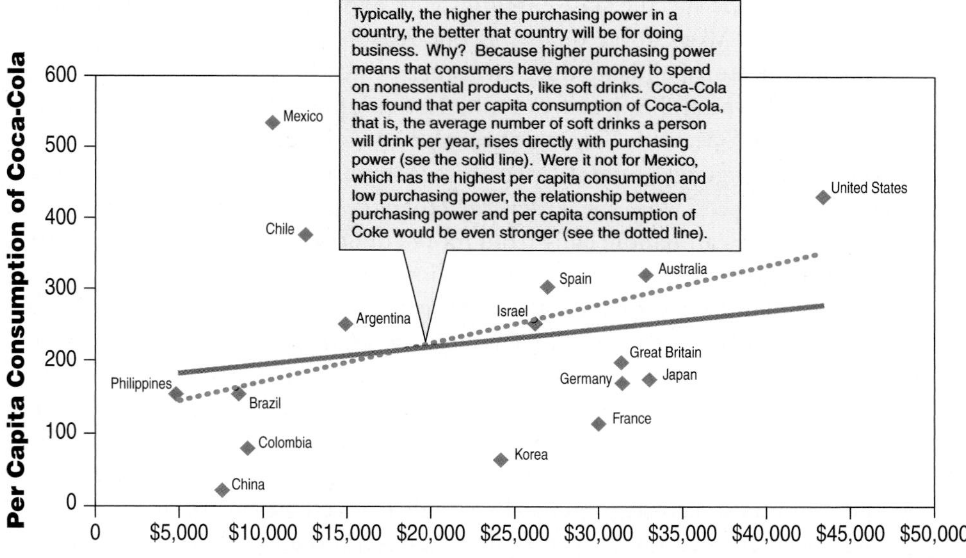

Sources: "Rank Order—GDP—Per Capita," *The World Factbook*, available at https://www.cia.gov/library/publications/the-world-factbook/rankorder/2004rank.html, 12 February 2007; "2005 Annual Per Capita Consumption of All Company Beverage Products," *The Coca-Cola Company 2005 Annual Review*, available at http://www.thecocacolacompany.com/investors/annualandotherreports/2005/companyToday_chart.html, 12 February 2007.

and quality of companies that already compete in a foreign market. Intel has been in China for 20 years not only because of the size of the potential market—China has 1.3 billion people and 95 percent of Chinese homes still don't have a computer—but also because there was almost no competition. But now that China is the third-largest computer chip market in the world, Intel faces competition from AMD, Intel's primary U.S. competitor, which entered China four years ago, and Shanghai Semiconductor Manufacturing International, a five-year-old Chinese company that manufactures low-end chips. Intel's 20-year head start, however, has given it a dominating 84 percent share of the Chinese market.[70]

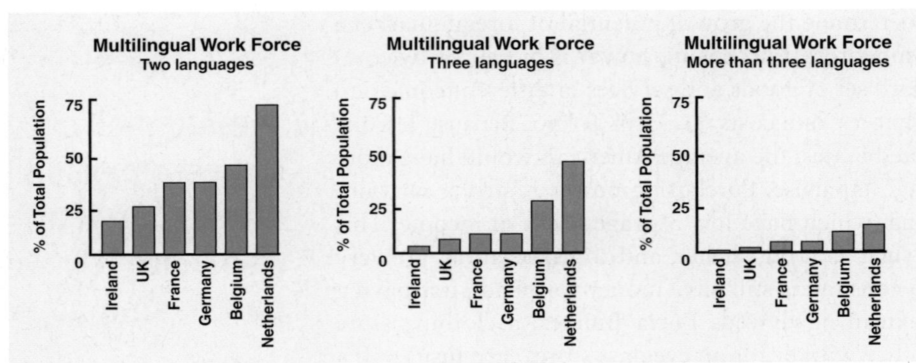

Sources: "Customer Care in the Netherlands," The Netherlands Foreign Investment Agency, available at http://www.nfia.com/solutions.php?pageid=11, 13 February 2007; "Customer Care Centers," *Netherlands Foreign Investment Agency Information Manual*, 13 February 2007, available at http://www.nfia.com/downloads/customercare.htm.

Exhibit 8.6

Quality of the Netherlands Work Force for Call Center Jobs

4.2 Choosing an Office/Manufacturing Location

Companies do not have to establish an office or manufacturing location in each country they enter. They can license, franchise, or export to foreign markets, or they can serve a larger region from one country. Thus, the criteria for choosing an office/manufacturing location are different from the criteria for entering a foreign market.

Rather than focusing on costs alone, companies should consider both qualitative and quantitative factors. Two key qualitative factors are work force quality and company strategy. Work force quality is important because it is often difficult to find workers with the specific skills, abilities, and experience that a company needs to run its business. Work force quality is one reason that many companies doing business in Europe locate their customer call centers in the Netherlands. As shown in Exhibit 8.6, workers in the Netherlands are the most linguistically gifted in Europe, with 73 percent speaking two languages, 44 percent speaking three languages, and 12 percent speaking more than three. Of course, with employees who speak several languages, call centers located in the Netherlands can handle calls from more countries and generally employ 30 to 50 percent fewer employees than those located in other parts of Europe. Another advantage of locating a call center in the Netherlands is that 60 percent of call center workers have university or advanced degrees in technology or management.[71]

A company's strategy is also important when choosing a location. For example, a company pursuing a low-cost strategy may need plentiful raw materials, low-cost transportation, and low-cost labor. A company pursuing a differentiation strategy (typically a higher-priced, better product or service) may need access to high-quality materials and a highly skilled and educated work force.

Quantitative factors, such as the kind of facility being built, tariff and non-tariff barriers, exchange rates, and transportation and labor costs, should also be considered when choosing an office/manufacturing location. Regarding the kind of facility being built, a real estate specialist in company location decisions

In today's environment, companies are not the only entities looking into global business. With the world's busiest airport and nonstop flights to 40 international destinations, the state of Georgia is positioning itself as an attractive gateway to doing "business with the world."

GEORGIA DEPARTMENT OF ECONOMIC DEVELOPMENT

explains: "If it's an assembly plant, a company might be inclined to look for incentives that would subsidize its hiring. With a distribution facility, an adequate transportation network will likely be critical. A corporate headquarters will need a good communications network, a multilingual labor force, and easy access by air. On the other hand, a research and development operation will require proximity to a high-tech infrastructure and access to good universities."[72]

Exhibit 8.7 shows the world's top cities for global business. This information is a good starting point if your company is trying to decide where to put an international office or manufacturing plant.

4.3 Minimizing Political Risk

When managers think about political risk in global business, they envision burning factories and riots in the streets. Although political events such as these receive dramatic and extended coverage from the media, the political risks that most companies face usually are not covered as breaking stories on Fox News and CNN. Nonetheless, the negative consequences of ordinary political risk can be just as devastating to companies that fail to identify and minimize that risk.[73]

political uncertainty the risk of major changes in political regimes that can result from war, revolution, death of political leaders, social unrest, or other influential events

When conducting global business, companies should attempt to identify two types of political risk: political uncertainty and policy uncertainty.[74] **Political uncertainty** is associated with the risk of major changes in political regimes that can result from

Exhibit 8.7
World's Best Cities for Business

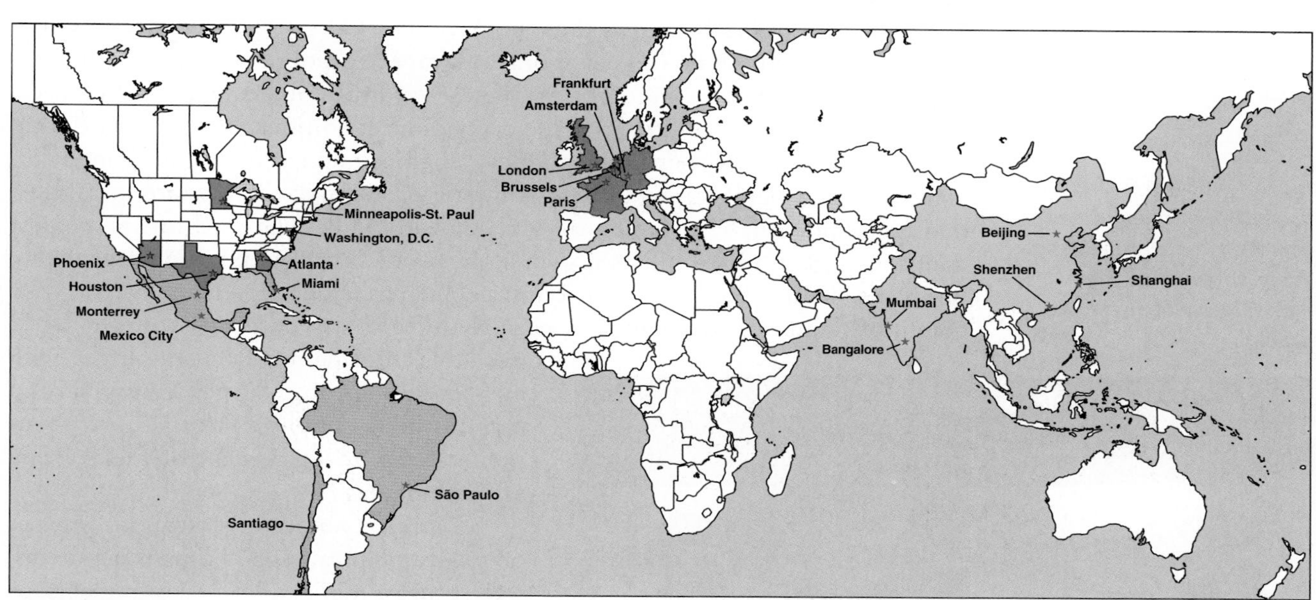

North America	Latin America	Europe	Asia Pacific
1. Washington, D.C.	1. Santiago	1. London	1. Shanghai
2. Atlanta	2. Miami	2. Paris	2. Beijing
3. Phoenix	3. São Paulo	3. Frankfurt	3. Shenzhen
4. Houston	4. Monterrey	4. Amsterdam	4. Bangalore
5. Minneapolis-St. Paul	5. Mexico City	5. Brussels	5. Mumbai

Sources: "European Cities Monitor 2006," *Cushman & Wakefield*, http://www.cushmanwakefield.com/cwglobal/jsp/publication.jsp?Country=EMEA&Language=EN, 13 February 2007. K. Badenhausen, "Best Places for Business and Careers," http://www.forbes.com/lists/2005/05/05/05bestplaces.html, 17 February 2007. "Shanghai, Beijing, Shenzhen Top 3 in Best City Survey," *Fortune China*, http://www.fortunechina.com/pdf/Best%20Cities%20Press%20Release%20(English)%202004.12.01.pdf, 13 February 2007. R. Sridharan, "Best Cities, Really?" *Business Today*, 13 August 2006, 62. "Miami Is the Best City for Doing Business in Latin America, According to AmericaEconomia Magazine," *PR Newswire*, 24 April 2003;

war, revolution, death of political leaders, social unrest, or other influential events. **Policy uncertainty** refers to the risk associated with changes in laws and government policies that directly affect the way foreign companies conduct business.

Policy uncertainty is the most common form of political risk in global business and perhaps the most frustrating, especially when changes in laws and government policies directly undercut sizable investments made by foreign companies. **ROYAL DUTCH SHELL** joined with Russia-based Gazprom, a state-owned company controlled by the Kremlin, to develop Sakhalin-2, one of the world's largest liquefied natural gas fields. Shell and its partners took the lead role with 55 percent ownership, and fronted a correspondingly larger amount of the estimated $20 billion in development costs. However, after years of development and billions in investment, the Russian government banned foreign companies from owning more than 49 percent of any energy development project. In the end, to avoid losing its investment, Royal Dutch Shell relinquished majority ownership to Gazprom in return for a $7.45 billion payment, well short of the $12 billion Shell had already invested. Furthermore, the deal significantly reduced Shell's access to develop and sell gas reserves in the Sakhalin-2 gas field and in the Zapolyarnoye gas field, which Shell had contracted to develop a year before.[75]

"WHAT'S NEW" COMPANY

Several strategies can be used to minimize or adapt to the political risk inherent in global business. An *avoidance strategy* is used when the political risks associated with a foreign country or region are viewed as too great. If firms are already invested in high-risk areas, they may divest or sell their businesses. If they have not yet invested, they will likely postpone their investment until the risk shrinks. Exhibit 8.8 shows the long-term political stability for various countries in the Middle East (higher scores indicate less political risk). The following factors, which were used to compile these ratings, indicate greater political risk: government instability, poor socioeconomic conditions, internal or external conflict, military involvement in politics, religious and ethnic tensions, high foreign debt as a percentage of gross domestic product, exchange rate instability, and high inflation.[76] An avoidance strategy would likely be used for the riskiest countries shown in Exhibit 8.8, such as Iran and Lebanon, but would probably not be needed for the least risky countries, such as Israel, Jordan, or Oman. Risk conditions and factors change, so be sure to make risk decisions with the latest available information from resources such as the PRS Group, **http://www.prsgroup.com**, which supplies information about political risk to 80 percent of the *Fortune* 500 companies.

policy uncertainty the risk associated with changes in laws and government policies that directly affect the way foreign companies conduct business

Ceding to political pressure, Royal Dutch Shell relinquished its majority ownership in Russia's Gazprom. Oil companies are facing similar problems in Venezuela.

© DENIS SINAKOV/REUTERS/LANDOV

Control is an active strategy to prevent or reduce political risks. Firms using a control strategy lobby foreign governments or international trade agencies to change laws, regulations, or trade barriers that hurt their business in that country.

Another method for dealing with political risk is *cooperation*, which involves using joint ventures and collaborative contracts, such as franchising and licensing. Although cooperation does not eliminate the political risk of doing business in a country, it can limit the risk associated with foreign ownership of

CROSS-CULTURAL TRAINING

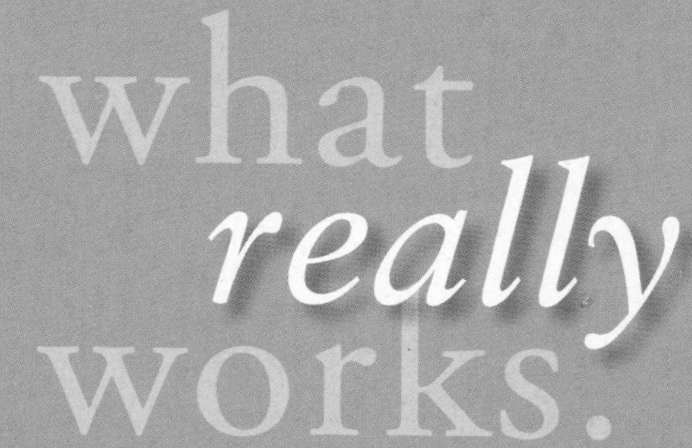

Most expatriates will tell you that cross-cultural training helped them adjust to foreign cultures. Such anecdotal data, however, are not as convincing as systematic studies. Twenty-one studies, with a combined total of 1,611 participants, have examined whether cross-cultural training affects the self-development, relationships, perceptions, adjustment, and job performance of expatriates. Overall, they show that cross-cultural training works extremely well in most instances.

SELF-DEVELOPMENT

When you first arrive in another country, you must learn how to make decisions that you took for granted in your home country: how to get to work, how to get to the grocery, how to pay your bills, and so on. If you've generally been confident about yourself and your abilities, an overseas assignment can challenge that sense of self. Cross-cultural training helps expatriates deal with these and other challenges. Expatriates who receive cross-cultural training are 79 percent more likely to report healthy psychological well-being and self-development than those who don't receive training.

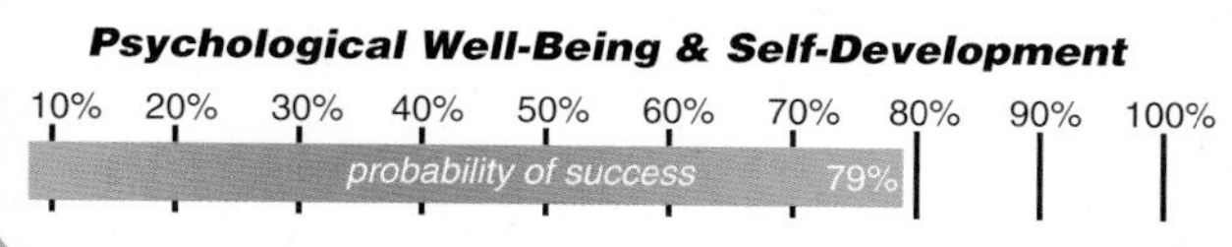

FOSTERING RELATIONSHIPS

One of the most important aspects of an overseas assignment is establishing and maintaining relationships with host nationals. If you're in Brazil, you need to make friends with Brazilians. Many expatriates, however, make the mistake of making friends only with other expatriates from their home country. In effect, they become social isolates in a foreign country. They work and live there, but as much as they can, they speak their native language, eat their native foods, and socialize with other expatriates from their home country. Cross-cultural training makes a big difference in whether expatriates establish relationships with host nationals. Expatriates who receive cross-cultural training are 74 percent more likely to establish such relationships.

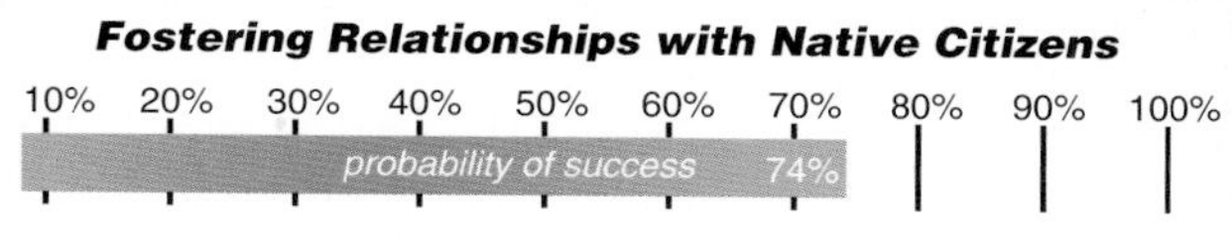

ACCURATE PERCEPTIONS OF CULTURE

Another characteristic of successful expatriates is that they understand the cultural norms and practices of the host country. For example, many Americans do not understand the famous pictures of Japanese troops turning their backs to American military commanders on V-J Day, when Japan surrendered to the United States at the end of World War II. Americans viewed this as a lack of respect, when, in fact, in Japan turning one's back in this way is a sign of respect. Cross-cultural training makes a big difference in the accuracy of perceptions concerning host country norms and practices. Expatriates who receive cross-cultural training are 74 percent more likely to have accurate perceptions.

RAPID ADJUSTMENT

New employees are most likely to quit in the first six months because this initial period requires the most adjustment: learning new names, new faces, new procedures, and new information. It's tough. Of course, expatriates have a much harder time adjusting to their new jobs because they are also learning new languages, new foods, new customs, and often new lifestyles. Expatriates who receive cross-cultural training are 74 percent more likely to make a rapid adjustment to a foreign country.

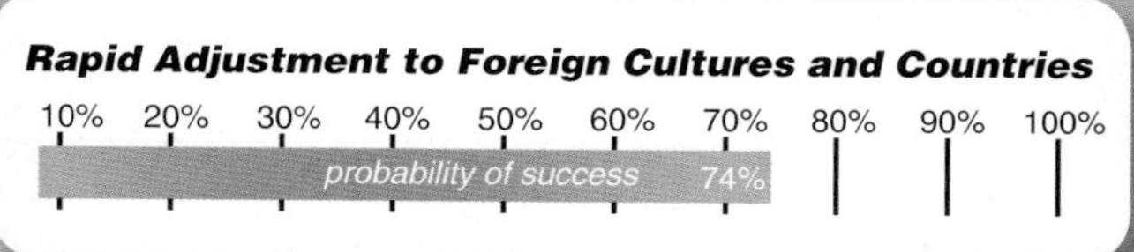

JOB PERFORMANCE

It's good that cross-cultural training improves self-development, fosters relationships, improves the accuracy of perceptions, and helps expatriates make rapid adjustments to foreign cultures. From an organizational standpoint, however, the ultimate test of cross-cultural training is whether it improves expatriates' job performance. The evidence shows that cross-cultural training makes a significant difference in expatriates' job performance, although the difference is not quite as large as for the other factors. Nonetheless, it is estimated that cross-cultural training for 100 managers could bring about $390,000 worth of benefits to a company, or nearly $4,000 per manager. This is an outstanding return on investment, especially when you consider the high rate of failure for expatriates. Expatriates who have received cross-cultural training are 71 percent more likely to have better on-the-job performance than those who did not receive cross-cultural training.[96]

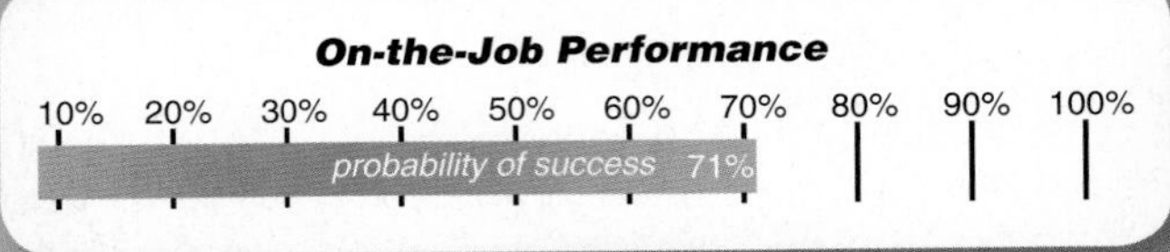

Only 40 percent of expatriates' families receive language and cross-cultural training, yet such training is just as important for the families of expatriates as for the expatriates themselves. In fact, it may be more important because, unlike expatriates, whose professional jobs often shield them from the full force of a country's culture, spouses and children are fully immersed in foreign neighborhoods and schools. Households must be run, shopping must be done, and bills must be paid. Unfortunately, expatriate spouse Laurel Larsen, despite two hours of Chinese lessons a week, hasn't learned enough of the language to communicate with the family's babysitter. She has to phone her husband, who became fluent in Chinese in his teens, to translate. Expatriates' children must deal with different cultural beliefs and practices, too. While the Larsens' three daughters love the private, international school that they attend, they still have had difficulty adapting to, from their perspective, the incredible differences in inner China. Six-year-old Emma taped this poem to her parents nightstand: "Amarica is my place! I love Amarica. It was fun. It was so fun. I miss it."[97] In addition to helping families prepare for the cultural differences they will encounter, language and cross-cultural training can help reduce uncertainty about how to act and decrease misunderstandings between expatriates and their families and locals.

> Training is just as important for the families of expatriates as for the expatriates themselves.

Review 6: Preparing for an International Assignment

Many expatriates return prematurely from international assignments because of poor performance. However, premature return is much less likely to happen if employees receive language and cross-cultural training, such as documentary training, cultural simulations, or field experiences, before going on assignment. Adjustment of expatriates' spouses and families, which is the most important determinant of success in international assignments, can be improved through adaptability screening and intercultural training.

SELF ASSESSMENT

Are You Nation-Minded or World-Minded?

Attitudes about global business are as varied as managers are numerous. It seems that the business press can always find someone who is for globalization and someone who is against it. But regardless of your opinion on the subject, managers will increasingly confront issues related to the globalization of the business environment. It is probable that, as a manager, you will need to develop global sensibilities (if you don't already have them). Understanding your own cultural perspective is the first step in doing so.

This assessment has three parts: Step 1, Complete the questionnaire shown below; Step 2, Determine your score; Step 3, Develop a plan to increase your global managerial potential.[98]

Step 1: Use the six-point rating scale to complete the 32-question inventory shown below.

Rating Scale

1 Strongly Disagree
2 Disagree
3 Mildly Disagree
4 Mildly Agree
5 Agree
6 Strongly Agree

1. Our country should have the right to prohibit certain racial and religious groups from entering it to live.
   1 2 3 4 5 6
2. Immigrants should not be permitted to come into our country if they compete with our own workers.
   1 2 3 4 5 6
3. It would set a dangerous precedent if every person in the world had equal rights that were guaranteed by an international charter.
   1 2 3 4 5 6
4. All prices for exported food and manufactured goods should be set by an international trade committee.
   1 2 3 4 5 6
5. Our country is probably no better than many others.
   1 2 3 4 5 6
6. Race prejudice may be a good thing for us because it keeps many undesirable foreigners from coming into this country.
   1 2 3 4 5 6
7. It would be a mistake for us to encourage certain racial groups to become well educated because they might use their knowledge against us.
   1 2 3 4 5 6
8. We should be willing to fight for our country without questioning whether it is right or wrong.
   1 2 3 4 5 6
9. Foreigners are particularly obnoxious because of their religious beliefs.
   1 2 3 4 5 6
10. Immigration should be controlled by a global organization rather than by each country on its own.
    1 2 3 4 5 6
11. We ought to have a world government to guarantee the welfare of all nations irrespective of the rights of any one.
    1 2 3 4 5 6
12. Our country should not cooperate in any global trade agreements that attempt to better world economic conditions at our expense.
    1 2 3 4 5 6
13. It would be better to be a citizen of the world than of any particular country.
    1 2 3 4 5 6

KEY TERMS

14. Our responsibility to people of other races ought to be as great as our responsibility to people of our own race.
1 2 3 4 5 6

15. A global committee on education should have full control over what is taught in all countries about history and politics.
1 2 3 4 5 6

16. Our country should refuse to cooperate in a total disarmament program even if some other nations agree to it.
1 2 3 4 5 6

17. It would be dangerous for our country to make international agreements with nations whose religious beliefs are antagonistic to ours.
1 2 3 4 5 6

18. Any healthy individual, regardless of race or religion, should be allowed to live wherever he or she wants to in the world.
1 2 3 4 5 6

19. Our country should not participate in any global organization that requires that we give up any of our national rights or freedom of action.
1 2 3 4 5 6

20. If necessary, we ought to be willing to lower our standard of living to cooperate with other countries in getting an equal standard for every person in the world.
1 2 3 4 5 6

21. We should strive for loyalty to our country before we can afford to consider world brotherhood.
1 2 3 4 5 6

22. Some races ought to be considered naturally less intelligent than ours.
1 2 3 4 5 6

23. Our schools should teach the history of the whole world rather than of our own country.
1 2 3 4 5 6

24. A global police force ought to be the only group in the world allowed to have armaments.
1 2 3 4 5 6

25. It would be dangerous for us to guarantee by international agreement that every person in the world should have complete religious freedom.
1 2 3 4 5 6

26. Our country should permit the immigration of foreign peoples, even if it lowers our standard of living.
1 2 3 4 5 6

27. All national governments ought to be abolished and replaced by one central world government.
1 2 3 4 5 6

28. It would not be wise for us to agree that working conditions in all countries should be subject to international control.
1 2 3 4 5 6

29. Patriotism should be a primary aim of education so that our children will believe our country is the best in the world.
1 2 3 4 5 6

30. It would be a good idea if all the races were to intermarry until there was only one race in the world.
1 2 3 4 5 6

31. We should teach our children to uphold the welfare of all people everywhere, even though it may be against the best interests of our own country.
1 2 3 4 5 6

32. War should never be justifiable, even if it is the only way to protect our national rights and honor.
1 2 3 4 5 6

Step 2: Determine your score by entering your response to each survey item below, as follows. In blanks that say *regular score*, simply enter your response for that item. If your response was a 4, place a 4 in the *regular score* blank. In blanks that say *reverse score*, subtract your response from 7 and enter the result. So if your response was a 4, place a 3 ($7 - 4 = 3$) in the *reverse score* blank.

1. reverse score _____
2. reverse score _____
3. reverse score _____
4. regular score _____
5. regular score _____
6. reverse score _____
7. reverse score _____
8. reverse score _____
9. reverse score _____
10. regular score _____
11. regular score _____
12. reverse score _____
13. regular score _____
14. regular score _____
15. regular score _____
16. reverse score _____
17. reverse score _____
18. regular score _____
19. reverse score _____
20. regular score _____
21. reverse score _____
22. reverse score _____

23. regular score _____
24. regular score _____
25. reverse score _____
26. regular score _____
27. regular score _____
28. reverse score _____
29. reverse score _____
30. regular score _____
31. regular score _____
32. regular score _____

Total your scores from items 1–16 _____
Total your scores from items 17–32 _____
Add together to compute TOTAL = _____
You can find an interpretation of your score at: **academic .cengage.com/management/williams.**

Forbidden Lattes?

There's no denying Starbucks is an international force.[99] The company had over 13,000 stores at the beginning of 2007, over 3,400 of them outside the United States, and is shooting for a long-term goal of 30,000 stores (international and domestic).

Starbucks opened its first overseas store in Tokyo in 1996. Asia was chosen as the point of entry because the company decided that the European coffee market was extremely mature and wasn't going to change much over the years. In contrast, the Asian market was still developing. Starbucks had the opportunity to position itself as the leader of a new industry. The table shows the operating regions for Starbucks retail stores and licenses as of October 2006.

ASIA-PACIFIC		EUROPE/MIDDLE EAST/AFRICA		AMERICAS	
Japan	650	United Kingdom	520	Canada	686
China	261	Germany	68	Mexico	101
Taiwan	175	Spain	55	Puerto Rico	17
South Korea	174	Turkey	51	Chile	16
Philippines	98	Greece	50	Peru	9
Thailand	85	Saudi Arabia	46	The Bahamas	5
Australia	83	United Arab Emirates	44		
Malaysia	71	Kuwait	36		
New Zealand	45	Switzerland	27		
Indonesia	45	France	26		
Singapore	37	Austria	11		
		Lebanon	11		
		Bahrain	8		
		Qatar	8		
		Cyprus	7		
		Jordan	5		
		Oman	4		
		Ireland	9		
TOTAL	**1,714**		**986**		**834**

Source: Starbucks Annual Report, 2006, 4–6.

Starbucks quickly jumped from Japan into other Asian countries, most notably China, where its presence has been nearly doubling on a yearly basis. But some troubles remain. In 2000, Starbucks opened a kiosk in Beijing's Forbidden City. Once home only to the emperor, his family, and his concubines, the Forbidden City is now a key tourist attraction in China's capital and still a symbol of Chinese heritage and culture. A Chinese newspaper criticized Starbucks for operating a kiosk there, so shortly after opening, Starbucks removed its hallmark signage from the outside of the building. A sign simply points to a "Coffee Bar."

Business as usual continued until 2007, when comments from a Chinese blogger reignited the debate about whether Starbucks should be allowed to continue operating inside the Forbidden City. About one third of the retailers that formerly operated inside the Forbidden City have closed as the museum plans a renovation, and Starbucks is only one of several retailers still open inside the museum site; the other retailers, however, are Chinese.

Popular opinion is divided. Some Chinese see the presence of Starbucks as against the spirit of the Forbidden City as emblematic of Chinese heritage. Others think having a Starbucks at the museum is a nice feature for tourists and support Starbucks' presence there as just another retailer. Still others consider the world to be global in nature and take a "Mi Starbucks, su Starbucks" attitude.

In South Korea, Starbucks opened up shop in the Insadong area of Seoul, famous for traditional Korean antiques and crafts. Even though the company sign is in Korean—not the standard board in English posted elsewhere around the world—owners of other shops in the district were upset. They posted signs of their own reading "Starbucks' invasion of Korea's pride, Insadong." Nonetheless, Starbucks doubled the number of stores in Korea and in China over a two-year period, and demand continues to rise.

Questions

1. Should Starbucks pursue areas near national historic sites and tourist attractions of foreign countries for placement of new international locations?
2. Using Hofstede's Cultural Dimensions and the information in Exhibit 8.9, outline an explanation for Starbucks's Forbidden City problems based on cultural differences between the United States and China.
3. If you were in charge, would you keep the Starbucks in Beijing's Forbidden City (and the Insadong district of Seoul, for that matter), or would you close those outlets and pursue growth elsewhere?

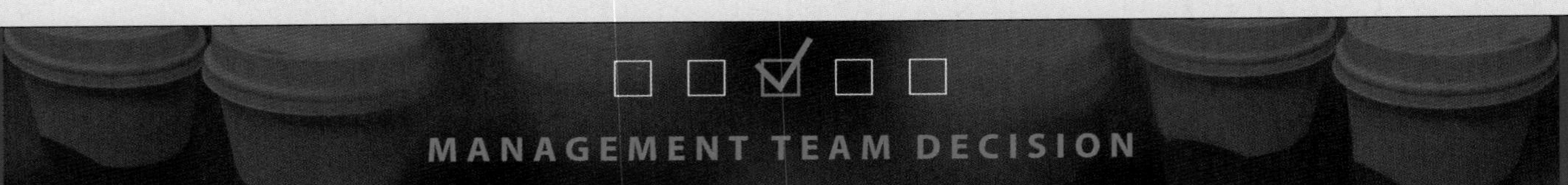

Men or Women, Who Goes Abroad?

As a member of the regional sales management team for a multinational corporation with offices located on almost every continent, you've made some tough decisions throughout your career.[100] Unfortunately, you feel that today's decision might possibly be the team's hardest yet. Sales in Asia have been dropping lately, and the team has been charged with choosing one of its salespersons to take over as the new regional manager for that area.

Two salespeople immediately come to mind. Laura, one of the potential candidates, has been a sales representative for the North American region for seven years. She has a master's degree in business administration and was a foreign exchange student in Hong Kong for two years during college. She is extremely competent, knowledgeable, and confident and has consistently been a top performer at the company since she was hired. Adam, the other possible candidate, has been with the North American region for only four years, but before that he served three and a half years as a sales representative for the European region of a well-known competitor. He too is qualified, with a master's degree in business and considerable experience in international assignments, but his performance has not been quite as stellar as Laura's. Neither candidate speaks any Asian languages.

Lingering in the back of your mind is a conversation you had with a colleague a few days ago. You and John, a fellow team member, were discussing international assignments, and the subject of sending women abroad came up. John said that in his experience, women do not make good expatriate candidates for several reasons. First, they are not as willing as men to take assignments in foreign countries due to family obligations and other personal reasons. Second, women are typically not as successful as men in foreign assignments because certain cultures tend to view women as inferior to men. (Including some Asian cultures, you think to yourself.) Last, John said that women are more likely to be subjected to discrimination or sexual harassment than men are. Although you initially agreed with John's perception, you later conclude that times have changed: after all, the world is much smaller and more culturally diverse today than it was when you went on your first international assignment.

You can't stop thinking about John's comments, though. You enter the meeting room weighing the pros and cons of each candidate and wondering if Laura would be accepted by her Asian counterparts.

To work this Management Team Decision, you will need to assemble a team of four to six students to represent the sales management team in the scenario.

Questions

1. Use either the stepladder technique or the nominal group technique (see Chapter 5) to decide which candidate the company should send abroad. Defend your decision.
2. Did the decision-making process change your mind? How so?
3. Determine what, if anything, the company should do to prepare the chosen candidate for the Asian assignment.

One of the major dilemmas in global management concerns the degree to which a multinational firm should adapt its business practices to particular locations and cultures versus the degree to which it should maintain consistency across all its operations. In general, firms prefer consistency because it streamlines operations and may result in global economies of scale. At the same time, multinational firms cannot gloss over differences without running the risk of losing a particular market to more responsive (local) competition. In this exercise, you will interpret your "hometown" culture for a large multinational company.

Suppose that a large multinational equipment company (based outside your country of origin) is planning to open a major production facility and retail dealership in your hometown. This company has hired you as a consultant to help them successfully establish operations in your hometown.

Step 1: Describe your hometown. Write a brief sketch (1–2 pages, using bullet points will suffice) in which you describe the important cultural features of your hometown, including such aspects as language, dress, courtesy/customs, and attitudes toward "foreignness" and newcomers. Try as much as possible to capture aspects of the location and culture of your hometown that would be important for newcomers to recognize and respect.

Step 2: Form a team. Your professor will assign you to small discussion groups of three to five students.

Step 3: Share your description. Take turns in your discussion groups introducing yourselves, identifying your hometown, and sharing the highlights of your brief sketch of your hometown. Listen for similarities and differences across your hometowns.

Step 4: Make recommendations. As a group, agree on some recommendations to the multinational company. Assume that the company is planning to enter all of your hometowns simultaneously. To what degree might the company use a consistent (same) approach in entering your hometowns? Is one or more of your hometowns likely to require a foreign multinational to make more particular adaptations?

Step 5: Share findings with class. Each group should share its list of hometowns and its recommendations with the class.

Step 6: Consider challenges. As a class discuss the challenges of entering global markets, particularly in regards to achieving the appropriate mix of consistency and adaptation.

Building Cultural Bridges inside American Business

All savvy managers seem to be familiar with the Japanese custom of exchanging business cards, the French custom of the two-hour lunch, and the South American custom of getting to know potential business partners on a personal level before discussing business.[101] But how many managers are aware of the cultural differences that exist within the United States? For example, how many Manhattanites know that in some parts of the country, businesses close down on the first day of hunting season?

Political rhetoric often refers to "two Americas" and the differences between the heartland and the coasts, but many other oppositional geographic pairings also represent different sets of cultural norms. Some other obvious examples are North–South, East–West, and the more general urban–rural. How many businesspeople know how to be effective in all these American cultures? Much has been made of the political and cultural implications of these divides, but not enough attention has been paid to what it means for business.

Cultural differences were addressed in Chapter 3 (Organizational Environments and Cultures) and will be again in Chapter 15 (Managing Communication). In the context of this chapter, however, it is important to note that many of the issues related to global management are applicable in any geographic context. Deciding whether to locate a firm in Alabama versus Oregon requires the same due diligence as deciding between Madrid and Madagascar. Managers need to assess the best business climate, identify and adapt to cultural differences, and prepare workers who will be transferred to the new location.

Activities

1. Think of yourself as a member of a particular geographical cultural group. (In the United States, we are conditioned to think of cultural groups based on ethnicity and race, but for this exercise, think in terms of location.) What are the characteristics of this group?
2. Once you have an outline of your geographic culture, try to identify the group most opposite to your own. For example, if you consider yourself a New Yorker, you may think of a Mississippian or a Californian.
3. Research regional and local periodicals to learn about the norms in the other culture. You might also talk with a friend who attends college in a different region or state to get a more personal understanding of norms in other parts of the country. List of some of the norms in the other location, and compare them with the norms in your area of the country.

REEL TO REAL

BIZ FLIX

Mr. Baseball

The New York Yankees trade aging baseball player Jack Elliot (Tom Selleck) to the Chunichi Dragons, a Japanese team. This lighthearted comedy traces Elliot's bungling entry into Japanese culture where he almost loses everything, including Hiroko Uchiyama (Aya Takanashi). As Elliot slowly begins to understand Japanese culture and Japanese baseball, he finally is accepted by his teammates. This film shows many examples of Japanese culture, especially the Japanese love for baseball.

Unknown to Hiroko's father, she and Jack develop an intimate relationship. Meanwhile, Jack does not know that Hiroko's father is "The Chief" (Ken Takakura), the manager of the Chunichi Dragons. This scene takes place after "The Chief" has removed Jack from a baseball game. The scene shows Jack dining with Hiroko and her grandmother (Mineko Yorozuyo), grandfather (Jun Hamamura), and father.

What to Watch for and Ask Yourself

1. Does Jack Elliot behave as if he had had cross-cultural training before arriving in Japan?
2. Is he culturally sensitive or insensitive?
3. What do you propose that Elliot do for the rest of his time in Japan?

MANAGEMENT WORKPLACE

Lonely Planet—Global from the Start

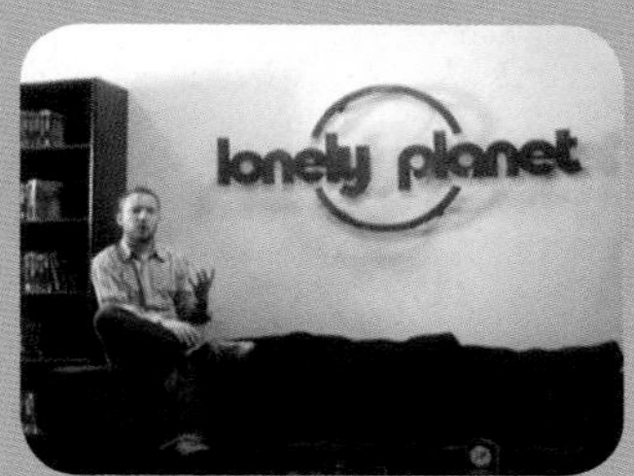

For a company such as Lonely Planet, the idea of a borderless world is nothing new. Founded in Australia by Tony and Maureen Wheeler so that they could fund their own travel dreams, the travel publisher now has offices in Australia, the United States, the United Kingdom, and France, with a total of about 450 employees. Its writers, photographers, and marketers span the globe on a regular basis in search of the best destinations for their customers to explore. However, despite the fact that the idea of globalization is built into the firm's culture, its managers still face international challenges every day. Watch the video to see how Lonely Planet grapples with global issues in its management workplace.

What to Watch for and Ask Yourself

1. To what extent does Lonely Planet practice global consistency versus adaptation?
2. How does the image being proposed for the global campaign illustrate the need to be aware of cultural differences?
3. Which of the forms for global business do you think Lonely Planet is using? Explain.

three

PART 3
Organizing

Chapter 9
Designing Adaptive Organizations

This chapter shows you the traditional organizational structure approach to organizational design (the vertical and horizontal configuration of departments, authority, and jobs within a company), as well as how contemporary organizations are redesigning their processes to better transform inputs into outputs.

Chapter 10
Managing Teams

Chapter 10 reviews the advantages and disadvantages of teams and explores when companies should use them. You'll also read about the different types of work teams and the characteristics common to all teams and learn practical steps to managing teams—team goals and priorities, and organizing, training, and compensating teams.

Chapter 11
Managing Human Resource Systems

This chapter covers the key aspects of human resource systems: determining your human resource needs; finding qualified employees; developing the knowledge, skills, and abilities of the work force; implementing effective compensation practices; and effectively managing separation.

Chapter 12
Managing Individuals and a Diverse Work Force

In this chapter, you'll learn what diversity is and why it matters. We'll go over surface-level diversity (how age, gender, race/ethnicity, and disabilities affect people at work) and deep-level diversity (how core personality differences influence behavior and attitudes). And you will learn how diversity can be managed.

CHAPTER 9

Designing Adaptive Organizations

© JEFF GREENBERG/PHOTOEDIT, INC

Learning Outcomes:

1 Describe the departmentalization approach to organizational structure.
2 Explain organizational authority.
3 Discuss the different methods for job design.
4 Explain the methods that companies are using to redesign internal organizational processes (that is, intraorganizational processes).
5 Describe the methods that companies are using to redesign external organizational processes (that is, interorganizational processes).

In This Chapter:

WHAT WOULD YOU DO?

Alcan Headquarters, Montreal, Canada.[1] On a beautiful spring morning that is unusually warm for this time of year, you find yourself once again contemplating whether your company is organized in the best manner possible. With almost 70,000 employees in 55 countries, Alcan has been one of the best performers in a slow-growth industry, aluminum. That said, aligning the organization for the best performance possible is an ongoing process, and having so many separate companies in so many different areas is a constant challenge.

The company was founded in 1902 as a producer of aluminum. Today, in addition to supplying basic metals, Alcan produces food and beauty product packaging and engineered products for the automobile and aerospace industries. The size and complexity of the organization has grown as the company has developed. Alcan currently has five corporate-wide staff operations (corporate development, external affairs, finance, human resources, and corporate headquarters), which work with all areas of the organization. The company also has four operating divisions: Bauxite and Alumina, Primary Metal, Engineered Products, and Packaging. Each of these divisions has its own staff operations, including such functions as finance, human resources, procurement, and information technology. And each division is also organized into sales groups; the Packaging division, for example, is grouped into Food Packaging—Europe, Food Packaging—Americas, Food Packaging—Asia, Global Pharmaceutical Packaging, Global Beauty Packaging, and Global Tobacco Packaging.

The company has made great strides to control its costs, divesting areas that it could not run profitably and moving into areas where it felt they had a competitive advantage. But beyond cost cutting, Alcan has found it difficult to raise net income as a percentage of sales. You realize that organizing the company to take advantage of growth opportunities and move it away from being a basic metals supplier is the key to the company's future. Would it make sense to organize the entire company geographically to focus on the needs of local markets? Or would an organizational structure geared toward new product development and marketing be more appropriate? The company could also organize exclusively around its customers and become experts in customer solutions. Other structuring options include a functional structure such that all of manufacturing is under one arm and all sales another; or a matrix structure that has employees reporting both functionally and geographically.

Another significant concern in an organization like Alcan that is seeking new areas of growth is how to manage creativity and communication within a company spread over 55 countries. What should you do about the informal organizational culture, part of which is critical to innovation and attracting and retaining topflight employees? **If you were in charge at Alcan, what would you do?**

ACTIVITIES + VIDEO

CengageNOW Audio study guide, electronic flashcards, author FAQ videos, On the Job and Biz Flix videos, concept tutorial, and concept exercise

Web (academic.cengage.com/management/williams) Quiz, PowerPoint slides, and glossary terms for this chapter

Think about your favorite company and imagine how you think it could be organized. Draw an organizational structure that you think makes sense for the business and the industry it's in. Try the exercise with a variety of company types and then see if the companies you used have organizational information on their websites. Practicing building organizational structures will help you better understand the different elements covered in the chapter.

"What's New" Companies

- Alcan
- Microsoft
- Sara Lee Corporation
- United Technologies
- Sprint Nextel
- Coca-Cola Enterprises
- Procter & Gamble
- Unilever
- Nike
- GlaxoSmithKline
- General Motors
- McDonald's
- AES
- IBM Credit
- Levi Strauss
- Wegmans
- Chipotle Mexican Grill
- And others . . .

No one builds a house without first looking at the design. Put a window there. Take out a wall here. Soon you've got the design you want. Only then do you start building. These days, the design of a company is just as important as the design of a house. As Alcan's case shows, even successful companies must constantly examine their organizational design.

This chapter begins by reviewing the traditional organizational structure approach to organizational design. **Organizational structure** is the vertical and horizontal configuration of departments, authority, and jobs within a company. As an example, Exhibit 9.1 shows MICROSOFT's organizational chart. From this chart, you can see the vertical dimensions of the company—who reports to whom, the number of management levels, who has authority over what, and so forth. Founder Bill Gates is the chairman and chief software architect. In this role, Gates focuses on Microsoft's product and technology strategies. CEO Steve Ballmer reports directly to him.[2] Three division presidents, each responsible for one of Microsoft's core businesses, report directly to Ballmer. In turn, each division has several group vice presidents who oversee a number of operations.[3] For instance, the group vice president for Information Worker works with managers and employees to develop and improve Microsoft's Office Suite (Word, Excel, PowerPoint, Outlook, and Access), Microsoft Publisher (for business publishing and marketing materials), Microsoft Visio (for drawing and diagramming business and technical concepts), Microsoft Project (project management software), and stand-alone desktop products.

organizational structure the vertical and horizontal configuration of departments, authority, and jobs within a company

Exhibit 9.1

Microsoft Corporation's Organizational Chart

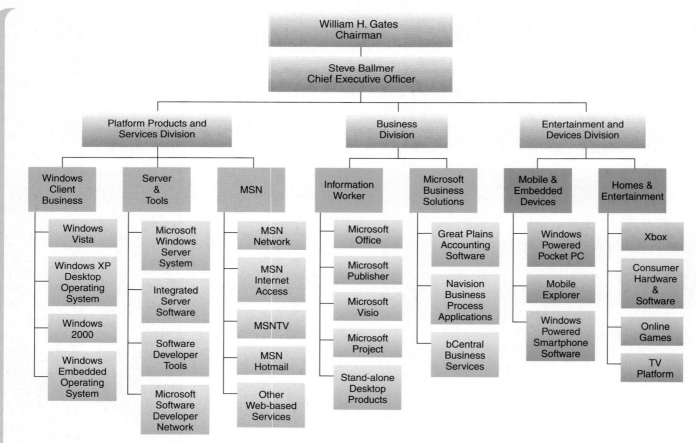

- William H. Gates, Chairman
  - Steve Ballmer, Chief Executive Officer
    - Platform Products and Services Division
      - Windows Client Business
        - Windows Vista
        - Windows XP Desktop Operating System
        - Windows 2000
        - Windows Embedded Operating System
      - Server & Tools
        - Microsoft Windows Server System
        - Integrated Server Software
        - Software Developer Tools
        - Microsoft Software Developer Network
      - MSN
        - MSN Network
        - MSN Internet Access
        - MSNTV
        - MSN Hotmail
        - Other Web-based Services
    - Business Division
      - Information Worker
        - Microsoft Office
        - Microsoft Publisher
        - Microsoft Visio
        - Microsoft Project
        - Stand-alone Desktop Products
      - Microsoft Business Solutions
        - Great Plains Accounting Software
        - Navision Business Process Applications
        - bCentral Business Services
    - Entertainment and Devices Division
      - Mobile & Embedded Devices
        - Windows Powered Pocket PC
        - Mobile Explorer
        - Windows Powered Smartphone Software
      - Homes & Entertainment
        - Xbox
        - Consumer Hardware & Software
        - Online Games
        - TV Platform

Source: "Our Commitment to Our Customers: The Business of Microsoft," Microsoft, available at http://www.microsoft.com/about/companyinformation/ourbusinesses/business.mspx.

The organizational chart also displays Microsoft's horizontal dimensions—who does what jobs, the number of different departments, and so forth. For instance, in addition to Information Worker, Microsoft's groups include Windows Client Business (where software such as Windows XP is written); Server and Tools (server software and development tools); MSN (the MSN online network, Internet access, TV, Hotmail e-mail services, and other web-based services); Microsoft Business Solutions (accounting and portals); Mobile and Embedded Devices (software for handheld computers and mobile phones); and Homes and Entertainment (Xbox game machine, consumer products, online games, and software for TVs). In the first half of the chapter, you will learn about the traditional vertical and horizontal approaches to organizational structure, including departmentalization, organizational authority, and job design.

In the second half of the chapter, you will learn how contemporary organizations are becoming more adaptive by redesigning their internal and external processes. An **organizational process** is the collection of activities that transform inputs into outputs that customers value.[4] For example, Microsoft uses basic internal and external processes to write computer software, shown in Exhibit 9.2. The process starts when Microsoft gets feedback from customers through Internet newsgroups, e-mail, phone calls, or letters. This information helps Microsoft understand customers' needs and problems and identify important software issues and needed changes and functions. Microsoft then rewrites the software, testing it internally at the company and then externally through its beta-testing process. In beta testing, early versions of software are distributed to beta testers (customers who volunteer or are selected by Microsoft), who give the company extensive feedback, which is then used to make improvements. The beta-testing process may take as long as a year and involve thousands of knowledgeable people. After "final" corrections are made to the software, the company distributes and sells it to customers, who start the process again by giving Microsoft more feedback.

organizational process the collection of activities that transform inputs into outputs that customers value

This process view of Microsoft, which focuses on how things get done, is very different from the hierarchical view of Microsoft (go back to Microsoft's organizational chart in Exhibit 9.1), which focuses on accountability, responsibility, and positions within the chain of command. In the second half of the chapter, you will learn how companies are using reengineering, empowerment, and behavioral informality to redesign their internal organizational processes. The chapter ends with a discussion about the ways in which companies are redesigning their external processes, that is, how they are changing to improve their interactions with those outside the company. In that discussion, you will explore the basics of modular and virtual organizations.

Exhibit 9.2

Process View of Microsoft's Organization

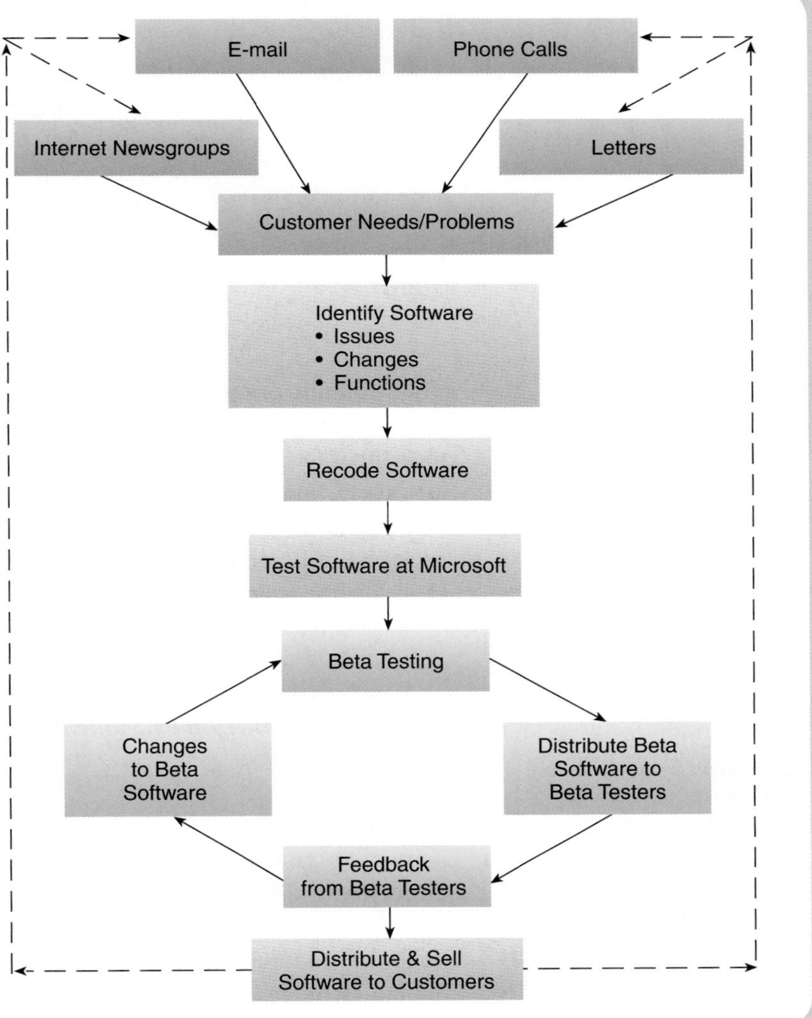

DESIGNING ORGANIZATIONAL STRUCTURES

With offices and operations in 58 countries, products in over 200, and more than 150,000 employees worldwide, **SARA LEE CORPORATION** owns some of the best-known brands (Sara Lee, Hillshire Farm, Ball Park, and Jimmy Dean) in the world. Nevertheless, in hopes of improving company performance, Sara Lee changed its organizational structure to focus on three key customer/geographic markets: North American retail (bakery, packaged meats, and Senseo coffee), North American food service (bakery goods, coffee, and meats sold to restaurants), and Sara Lee International (bakery and beverage businesses outside North America and global household products). Companies or divisions that didn't fit with the new structure, like the European meats division and the branded apparel businesses (including Hanes, Champion, and Playtex) were sold. As a result of the transformation plan, Sara Lee is now focused on its core businesses—food, beverage, and household and body care.[5]

Why would a large company like Sara Lee with 150,000 employees and $20 billion in annual revenues completely restructure its organizational design? What does it expect to gain from this change?

After reading the next three sections, you should be able to

1. *describe the departmentalization approach to organizational structure.*
2. *explain organizational authority.*
3. *discuss the different methods for job design.*

1 Departmentalization

Traditionally, organizational structures have been based on some form of departmentalization. **Departmentalization** is a method of subdividing work and workers into separate organizational units that take responsibility for completing particular tasks.[6] Sony, for example, has separate departments or divisions for electronics, music, movies, computer games and game consoles, and theaters.[7] Likewise, Bayer, a Germany-based company, has separate departments or divisions for health care, crop science, material science, and services.[8]

*Traditionally, organizational structures have been created by departmentalizing work according to five methods: **1.1 functional, 1.2 product, 1.3 customer, 1.4 geographic, and 1.5 matrix**.*

departmentalization subdividing work and workers into separate organizational units responsible for completing particular tasks

functional departmentalization organizing work and workers into separate units responsible for particular business functions or areas of expertise

1.1 Functional Departmentalization

The most common organizational structure is functional departmentalization. Companies tend to use this structure when they are small or just starting out. **Functional departmentalization** organizes work and workers into separate units responsible for particular business functions or areas of expertise. A common functional structure might have individuals organized into accounting, sales, marketing, production, and human resources departments.

Not all functionally departmentalized companies have the same functions, however. The insurance company and the advertising agency shown in Exhibit 9.3 both have sales, accounting, human resources, and information systems departments, as indicated by the orange boxes. The purple and red boxes indicate the functions that are different. As would be expected, the insurance company has separate departments for life, auto, home, and health insurance. The advertising agency has departments for artwork, creative work, print advertising, and Internet advertising. So the kind of functional departments in a functional structure depends, in part, on the business or industry a company is in.

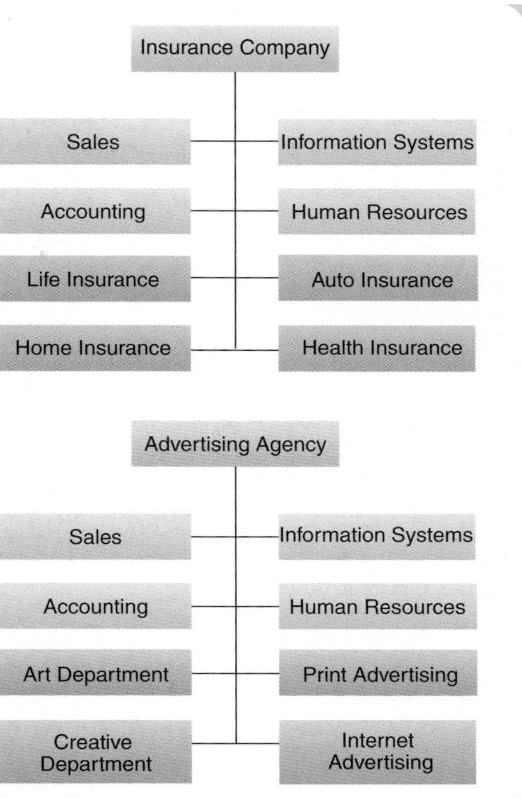

Exhibit 9.3
Functional Departmentalization

Functional departmentalization has some advantages. First, it allows work to be done by highly qualified specialists. While the accountants in the accounting department take responsibility for producing accurate revenue and expense figures, the engineers in research and development can focus their efforts on designing a product that is reliable and simple to manufacture. Second, it lowers costs by reducing duplication. When the engineers in research and development come up with that fantastic new product, they don't have to worry about creating an aggressive advertising campaign to sell it. That task belongs to the advertising experts and sales representatives in marketing. Third, with everyone in the same department having similar work experience or training, communication and coordination are less problematic for departmental managers.

At the same time, functional departmentalization has a number of disadvantages. To start, cross-department coordination can be difficult. Managers and employees are often more interested in doing what's right for their function than in doing what's right for the entire organization. A good example is the traditional conflict between marketing and manufacturing. Marketing typically pushes for spending more money to make more products with more accessories and capabilities to meet customer needs. By contrast, manufacturing pushes for fewer products with simpler designs so that manufacturing facilities can ship finished products on time and keep costs within expense budgets. As companies grow, functional departmentalization may also lead to slower decision making and produce managers and workers with narrow experience and expertise.

1.2 Product Departmentalization

Product departmentalization organizes work and workers into separate units responsible for producing particular products or services. Exhibit 9.4 shows the product departmentalization structure used by ***United Technologies***. United Technologies is organized along seven different product lines: Carrier (heating, ventilating, and air-conditioning); Chubb (security, monitoring, and fire protection systems); Hamilton Sundstrand (aircraft electrical power generation and distribution systems); Otis (design, manufacture, installation, maintenance, and servicing of elevators and escalators); Pratt & Whitney (commercial and military jet aircraft engines); Sikorsky (military and commercial helicopters); and UTC Power (heating, cooling, and power systems for commercial and industrial applications and fuel cell systems).[9]

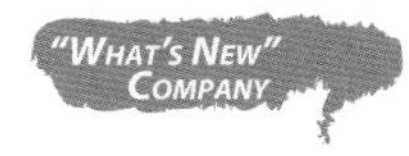

product departmentalization organizing work and workers into separate units responsible for producing particular products or services

One of the advantages of product departmentalization is that, like functional departmentalization, it allows managers and workers to specialize in one area of expertise. Unlike the narrow expertise and experiences in functional departmentalization,

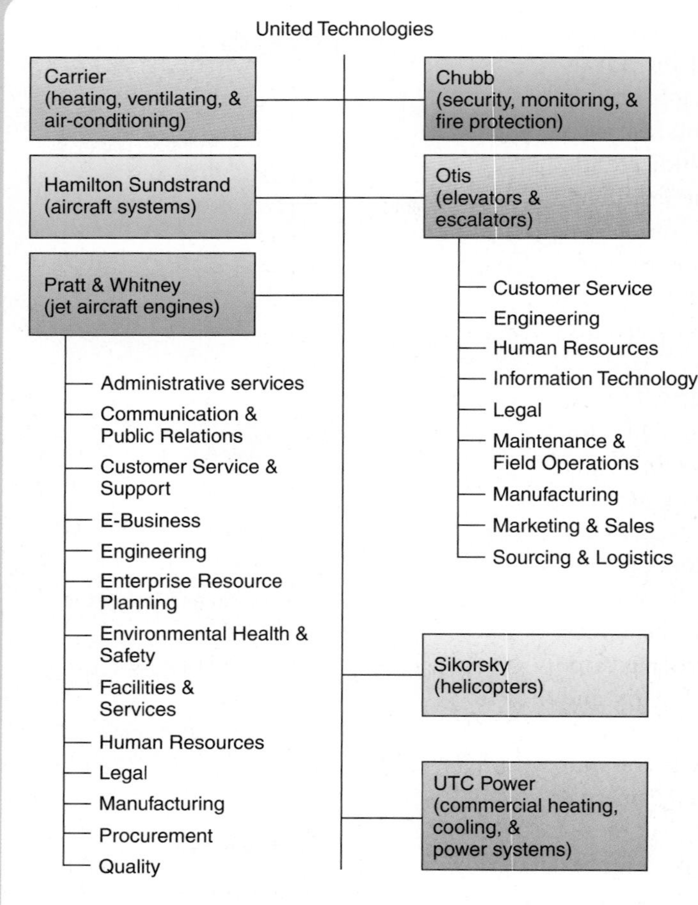

Source: *United Technologies Corporation 2004 Annual Report,* United Technologies, available at http://www.utc.com/annual_reports/2004/2004_ar.pdf, 1 May 2005.

Exhibit 9.4

Product Departmentalization: United Technologies

however, managers and workers develop a broader set of experiences and expertise related to an entire product line. Likewise, product departmentalization makes it easier for top managers to assess work-unit performance. Because of the clear separation of their seven different product divisions, United Technologies' top managers can easily compare the performance of, for example, its Otis elevators product division and its Pratt & Whitney aircraft engines division. The divisions had similar revenues— almost $8.99 billion for Otis and $8.3 billion for Pratt & Whitney—but Otis had a profit of $1.54 billion (a 17 percent profit margin) compared with just $1.1 billion (a 13 percent profit margin) for Pratt & Whitney. Finally, decision making should be faster because managers and workers are responsible for the entire product line rather than for separate functional departments, and thus there are fewer conflicts (compared to functional departmentalization).

The primary disadvantage of product departmentalization is duplication. You can see in Exhibit 9.4 that the Otis elevators and Pratt & Whitney divisions both have customer service, engineering, human resources, legal, manufacturing, and procurement (similar to sourcing and logistics) departments. Duplication like this often results in higher costs.

A second disadvantage is the challenge of coordinating across the different product departments. United Technologies would probably have difficulty standardizing its policies and procedures in product departments as different as the Carrier (heating, ventilating, and air-conditioning) and Sikorsky (military and commercial helicopters) divisions.

1.3 Customer Departmentalization

Customer departmentalization organizes work and workers into separate units responsible for particular kinds of customers. For example, as Exhibit 9.5 shows, the telecommunications company ***Sprint Nextel***, is organized into departments that cater to businesses (local, long-distance, and data and wireless services for U.S. and international businesses); consumers (local, long-distance, and wireless services for individuals, sold separately or bundled together); Mobile Broadband Operations (Network Design, Operations and Servicing); and product development.[11]

The primary advantage of customer departmentalization is that it focuses the organization on customer needs rather than on products or business functions. Furthermore, creating separate departments to serve specific kinds of customers allows companies to specialize and adapt their products and services to customer needs and problems.

The primary disadvantage of customer departmentalization is that, like product departmentalization, it leads to duplication of resources. Furthermore, as with product departmentalization, it can be difficult to achieve coordination across different customer departments. Finally, the emphasis on meeting customers' needs may lead workers to make decisions that please customers but hurt the business.

customer departmentalization organizing work and workers into separate units responsible for particular kinds of customers

1.4 Geographic Departmentalization

Geographic departmentalization organizes work and workers into separate units responsible for doing business in particular geographic areas. Exhibit 9.6 shows the geographic departmentalization used by COCA-COLA ENTERPRISES (CCE), the largest bottler and distributor of Coca-Cola products in the world. (The Coca-Cola Company develops and advertises soft drinks. CCE, which is a separate company with its own stock, buys the soft drink concentrate from the Coca-Cola Company, combines it with other ingredients, and then distributes the final product in cans, bottles, or fountain containers.) As shown in Exhibit 9.6, CCE has two regional groups: North America and Europe. As the table in the exhibit shows, each of these regions would be a sizable company by itself. The European Group alone serves a population of 146 million people in Belgium, Great Britain, France, Luxembourg, Monaco, and the Netherlands; sells one billion cases of soft drinks a year; employs 11,000 people; runs 32 bottling facilities; and has a customer base that drinks an average of 174 soft drinks per year per person.

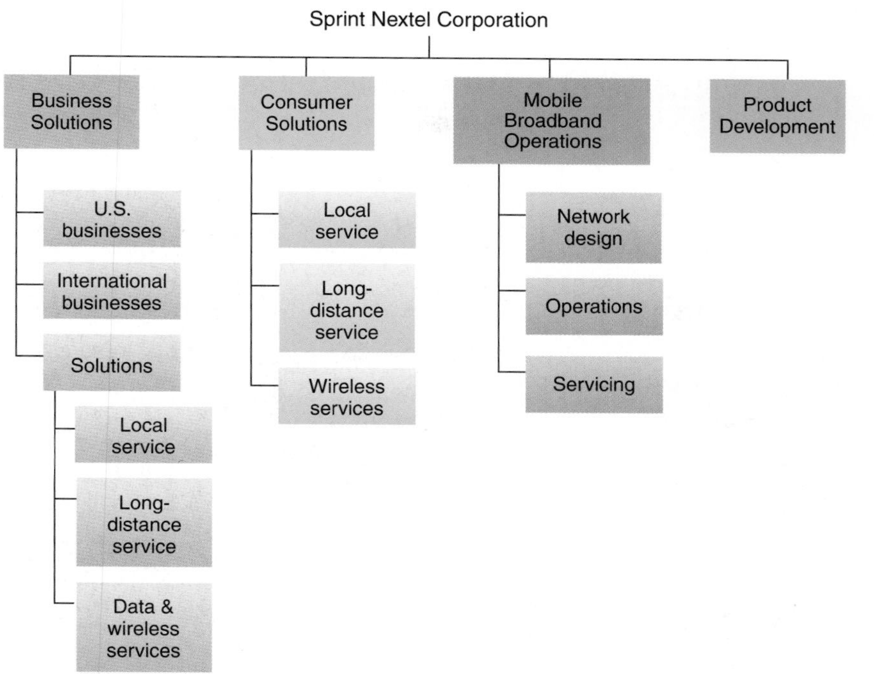

Source: "Overview," Sprint, available at http://www.sprint.com/sprint/fastfacts/overview/index.html, 1 May 2005.

Exhibit 9.5
Customer Departmentalization: Sprint Corporation

The primary advantage of geographic departmentalization is that it helps companies respond to the demands of different markets. This can be especially important when the company sells in different countries. For example, CCE's geographic divisions sell products suited to taste preferences in different countries. CCE bottles and distributes the following products in Europe but not in the United States: Aquarius, Bonaqua, and Burn, Coca-Cola Light (which is somewhat different from Diet Coke), Cresta flavors, Five Alive, Kia-Ora, Kinley, Lilt, Malvern, and Oasis.[12] Another advantage is that geographic departmentalization can reduce costs by locating unique organizational resources closer to customers. For instance, it is cheaper in the long run for CCE to build bottling plants in Belgium than to bottle Coke in England and then transport it across the English Channel to Belgium.

The primary disadvantage of geographic departmentalization is that it can lead to duplication of resources. For example, while it may be necessary to adapt products and marketing to different geographic locations, it's doubtful that CCE needs significantly different inventory tracking systems from location to location. Also, even more than with the other forms of departmentalization, it can be difficult to coordinate departments that are literally thousands of miles from each other and whose managers have very limited contact with each other.

geographic departmentalization organizing work and workers into separate units responsible for doing business in particular geographic areas

matrix departmentalization a hybrid organizational structure in which two or more forms of departmentalization, most often product and functional, are used together

1.5 Matrix Departmentalization

Matrix departmentalization is a hybrid structure in which two or more forms of departmentalization are used together. The most common matrix combines the product and functional forms of departmentalization, but other forms may also be used. Exhibit 9.7 shows the matrix structure used by **PROCTER & GAMBLE**, which has 98,000 employees working in 80 different countries. Across the top of Exhibit 9.7, you can see that the company uses a product unit structure with managers responsible for the global efforts of their branded products. The left side of the figure, however, shows that the company is also using a geographic structure. Geographic managers are responsible for taking P&G's globally positioned products and adapting them to fit the cultures of the countries where they are sold—more than 140 countries in all. P&G's roster of brands includes Pampers (diapers), Tide (laundry detergent), Always (feminine protection), Pantene (shampoo), Bounce (dryer sheets), Folgers (coffee), Pringles (snack food), Charmin (toilet paper), Downy (fabric softener), Iams (dog and cat food), Crest (toothpaste), Actonel (prescription drug) and Olay (body care).[13] The company also has two groups that cut across the entire matrix taking care of customer service and administration.

	POPULATION	PER CAPITA CONSUMPTION(1)	EMPLOYEES	FACILITIES(2)
North American Group	263 M	300	63,000	399
European Group	146 M	174	11,000	32
Total Company	409 M	255	74,000	431

(1) Number of 8-ounce servings consumed per person per year.
(2) Facilities include 18 production, 335 sales/distribution, and 46 combination sales and production plants in North America, and 3 production, 17 sales/distribution, and 12 combination plants in Europe.

Source: "Territories of Operation, 2004 Annual Report," Coca-Cola Enterprises, available at http://ir.cokecce.com/annuals.cfm, 1 May 2005.

Exhibit 9.6

Geographic Departmentalization: Coca-Cola Enterprises

The boxes in the figure represent the matrix structure, created by the combination of the geographic and product structures. For example, in the health-care business in Central-Eastern Europe, Middle East, and Africa, country managers in Hungary, United Arab Emirates, and Kenya are responsible for developing P&G's business in products such as Metamucil, Pepto-Bismol, Prilosec OTC, and Vicks. Likewise, in the snack and beverage business in Asia/India/Australia, country managers in China, Australia, and South Korea are responsible for developing P&G's business in products such as Folgers coffee, Millstone coffee, and Pringles potato chips in those countries.

Several things distinguish matrix departmentalization from the other traditional forms of departmentalization.[14] First, most employees report to two bosses, one from each core part of the matrix. For example, in Exhibit 9.7, the manager responsible for Charmin in France would report both to the president for Global Baby Care/Family Care and to the president for Western Europe. Second, by virtue of their hybrid design, matrix structures lead to much more cross-functional interaction than other forms of departmentalization. In fact, while matrix workers are typically members of only one functional department (based on their work experience and expertise), they are also commonly members of several ongoing project, product, or customer groups. Third, because of the high level of cross-functional interaction, matrix departmentalization requires significant coordination between managers in the different parts of the matrix. In particular, managers have the complex job of tracking and managing the multiple demands (project, product, customer, or functional) on employees' time.

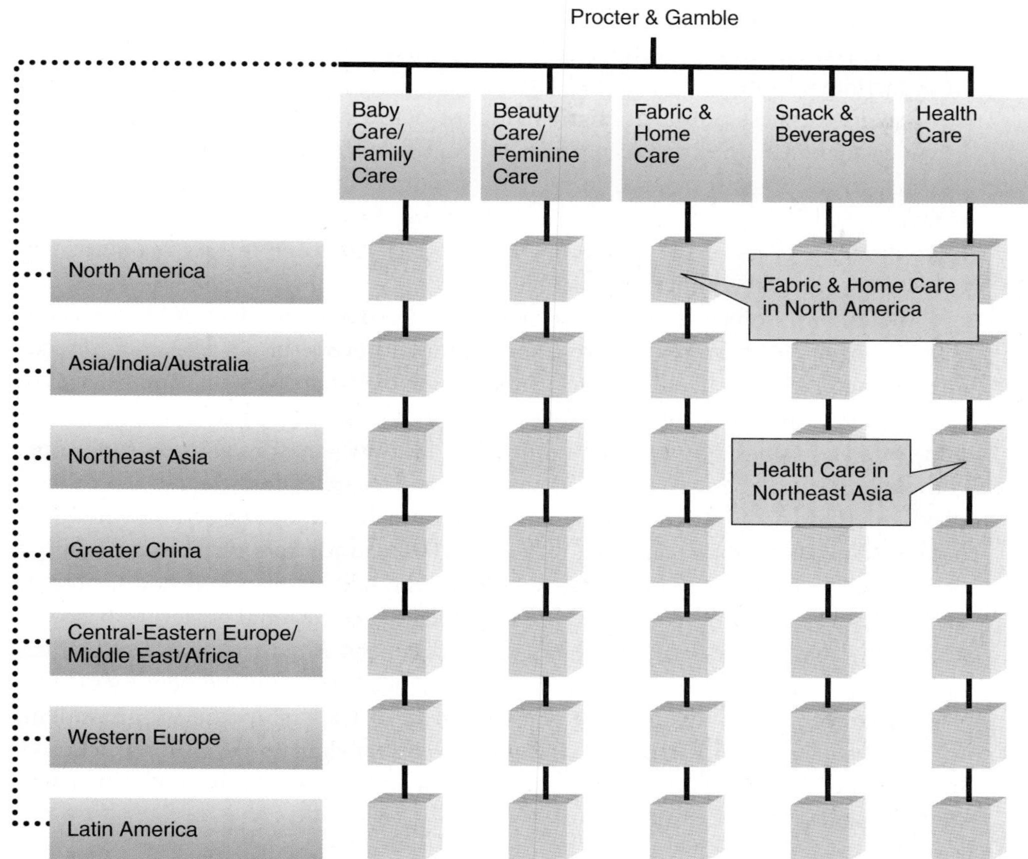

Source: "Corporate Info: Corporate Structure—Four Pillars," Procter & Gamble, http://www.pg.com/jobs/corporate_structure/four_pillars.jhtml; "P&G Management," Procter & Gamble, http://www.pg.com/news/management/bios_photos.jhtml.

Exhibit 9.7
Matrix Departmentalization: Procter & Gamble

The primary advantage of matrix departmentalization is that it allows companies to efficiently manage large, complex tasks like researching, developing, and marketing pharmaceuticals or carrying out complex global businesses. Efficiency comes from avoiding duplication. For example, rather than having an entire marketing function for each project, the company simply assigns and reassigns workers from the marketing department as they are needed at various stages of product completion. More specifically, an employee from a department may simultaneously be part of five different ongoing projects, but may be actively completing work on only a few projects at a time.

Another advantage is the pool of resources available to carry out large, complex tasks. Because of the ability to quickly pull in expert help from all the functional areas of the company, matrix project managers have a much more diverse set of expertise and experience at their disposal than do managers in the other forms of departmentalization.

The primary disadvantage of matrix departmentalization is the high level of coordination required to manage the complexity involved with running large, ongoing projects at various levels of completion. Matrix structures are notorious for confusion and conflict between project bosses in different parts of the matrix. At P&G, such confusion or conflict might occur between managers in the Global Fabric and Home Care division and the president of operations in Greater China. Disagreements or misunderstandings about schedules, budgets, available resources, and the availability of employees with particular functional expertise are common. Another disadvantage is that matrix structures require much more management skill than the other forms of departmentalization.

Because of these problems, many matrix structures evolve from a **simple matrix**, in which managers in different parts of the matrix negotiate conflicts and resources directly, to a **complex matrix**, in which specialized matrix managers and departments are added to the organizational structure. In a complex matrix, managers from different parts of the matrix might report to the same matrix manager, who helps them sort out conflicts and problems.

Sometimes, however, even these steps aren't enough to alleviate the problems that can occur in matrix structures. For example, Europe-based **Unilever**, maker and marketer of such well-known products as Dove soap, Vaseline Intensive Care lotions, Hellman's mayonnaise, I Can't Believe It's Not Butter, Lipton teas, Wishbone salad dressings, Skippy peanut butter, and Lawry's seasonings, was run using a complex matrix structure. The company even had dual headquarters in Rotterdam, the Netherlands, and London, England. The confusion and conflict associated with having two sets of management located in two headquarters were so great, however, that Unilever has now switched to just one CEO and one headquarters. In addition, the company has moved to a simpler organizational structure based on geography, with three regional chiefs (in Europe, the Americas, and Asia/Africa), plus two global divisions: foods and soaps.[15] Patrick Cescau, the new CEO, says, "We have recognized the need for greater clarity of leadership and we are moving to a simpler leadership structure that will provide a sharper operational focus."[16] In short, because everyone now reports to just one boss, "we have clarified who calls the shots," says Cescau.

Review 1: Departmentalization

The five traditional departmental structures are functional, product, customer, geographic, and matrix. Functional departmentalization is based on the different business functions or expertise used to run a business. Product departmentalization is organized according to the different products or services a company sells. Customer departmentalization focuses its divisions on the different kinds of customers a company has. Geographic departmentalization is based on the different geographic areas or markets in which the company does business. Matrix departmentalization is a hybrid form that combines two or more forms of departmentalization, the most common being the product and functional forms. There is no "best" departmental structure. Each structure has advantages and disadvantages.

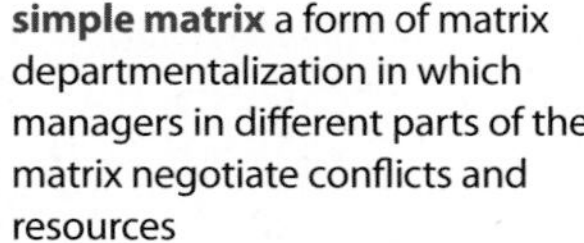

2 Organizational Authority

The second part of traditional organizational structures is authority. **Authority** is the right to give commands, take action, and make decisions to achieve organizational objectives.[17]

Traditionally, organizational authority has been characterized by the following dimensions: ***2.1 chain of command, 2.2 line versus staff authority, 2.3 delegation of authority,*** *and* ***2.4 degree of centralization.***

simple matrix a form of matrix departmentalization in which managers in different parts of the matrix negotiate conflicts and resources

complex matrix a form of matrix departmentalization in which managers in different parts of the matrix report to matrix managers, who help them sort out conflicts and problems

authority the right to give commands, take action, and make decisions to achieve organizational objectives

2.1 Chain of Command

Turn back a few pages to Microsoft's organizational chart in Exhibit 9.1. If you place your finger on any position in the chart, say, Central Business Services (under Business Division), you can trace a line upward to the company's CEO, Steve Ballmer. This line, which vertically connects every job in the company to higher levels of management, represents the chain of command. The **chain of command** is the vertical line of authority that clarifies who reports to whom throughout the organization. People higher in the chain of command have the right, *if they so choose*, to give commands, take action, and make decisions concerning activities occurring anywhere below them in the chain. In the following discussion about delegation and decentralization, you will learn that managers don't always choose to exercise their authority directly.[18]

One of the key assumptions underlying the chain of command is **unity of command**, which means that workers should report to just one boss.[19] In practical terms, this means that only one person can be in charge at a time. Matrix organizations, in which employees have two bosses, or—as in the Unilever example you just read about—two headquarters, automatically violate this principle. This is one of the primary reasons that matrix organizations are difficult to manage. The purpose of unity of command is to prevent the confusion that might arise when an employee receives conflicting commands from two different bosses. For example, when Bill Gates became chairman of Microsoft (after being CEO) and Steve Ballmer became CEO, there was confusion about the chain of command at Microsoft. In one meeting, Gates approved a budget increase for a project. Ballmer then denied the increase, shouting at Gates, "You put me in charge of the company. Let me run it."[20] With their different styles and approaches, with Gates not planning to leave active management until July 2008, and with managers and employees used to deferring to Gates over the 20 years that he was CEO, it's not surprising that the chain of command was unclear and that Gates and Ballmer had trouble adjusting to their new roles.

2.2 Line versus Staff Authority

A second dimension of authority is the distinction between line and staff authority. **Line authority** is the right to command immediate subordinates in the chain of command. For example, in the Microsoft organizational chart in Exhibit 9.1, CEO Steve Ballmer has line authority over the manager of the Business Division. Ballmer can issue orders to that division president and expect them to be carried out. In turn, the Business Division president can issue orders to the manager of the Information Worker group and expect them to be carried out.

Staff authority is the right to advise, but not command, others who are not subordinates in the chain of command. For example, at Microsoft, a manager in human resources might advise the vice president of MSN on a hiring decision but cannot order him or her to hire a certain applicant.

The terms *line* and *staff* are also used to describe different functions within the organization. A **line function** is an activity that contributes directly to creating or selling the company's products. So activities that take place within the manufacturing and marketing departments would be considered line functions. A **staff function**, such as accounting, human resources, or legal services, does not contribute directly to creating or selling the company's products, but instead supports line activities. For example, marketing managers might consult with the legal staff to make sure the wording of a particular advertisement is legal.

chain of command the vertical line of authority that clarifies who reports to whom throughout the organization

unity of command a management principle that workers should report to just one boss

line authority the right to command immediate subordinates in the chain of command

staff authority the right to advise, but not command, others who are not subordinates in the chain of command

line function an activity that contributes directly to creating or selling the company's products

staff function an activity that does not contribute directly to creating or selling the company's products, but instead supports line activities

2.3 Delegation of Authority

Managers can exercise their authority directly by completing the tasks themselves, or they can choose to pass on some of their authority to subordinates. **Delegation of authority** is the assignment of direct authority and responsibility to a subordinate to complete tasks for which the manager is normally responsible.

When a manager delegates work, three transfers occur, as illustrated in Exhibit 9.8. First, the manager transfers full responsibility for the assignment to the subordinate. Many managers find giving up full responsibility somewhat difficult. For example, Phil Knight, the charismatic founder of **NIKE**, has made three unsuccessful attempts at turning over the reigns of his multibillion-dollar corporation. According to former CEO William Perez, Knight's name belongs near the top of the list of CEO's who can't delegate. Perez says, "From virtually the day I arrived, Phil was as engaged in the company as he ever was. He was talking to my direct reports. It was confusing for the people and frustrating for me."[21]

Another problem is that managers often fear that the task won't be done as well as if they did it themselves. However, one CEO says, "If you can delegate a task to somebody who can do it 75 percent to 80 percent as well as you can today, you delegate it immediately." Why? The reason is that many tasks don't need to be done perfectly; they just need to be done. And delegating tasks that someone else can do frees managers to assume other important responsibilities.

Sometimes managers delegate only to later interfere with how the employee is performing the task. "Why are you doing it that way? That's not the way I do it." In contrast, delegating full responsibility means that the employee—not the manager—is now completely responsible for task completion.

delegation of authority the assignment of direct authority and responsibility to a subordinate to complete tasks for which the manager is normally responsible

The second transfer that occurs with delegation is that the manager gives the subordinate full authority over the budget, resources, and personnel needed to do the job. To do the job effectively, subordinates must have the same tools and information at their disposal that managers had when they were responsible for the same task. In other words, for delegation to work, delegated authority must be commensurate with delegated responsibility. Historically, pharmaceutical research at **GLAXOSMITHKLINE** followed a process common to nearly all drug companies: A panel of research and development chiefs far removed from the laboratory determined which drugs to develop and then decided how much money to invest in each. Research scientists in the labs had limited or no say in the drugs selected for research, and each scientist worked on only a single aspect of a drug, passing the resultant compounds onto the next researcher in line, who would do the next step. This assembly-line process led to fewer drugs in the pipeline and scientists who weren't particularly enthusiastic about their work. In order to improve the flow of new drugs as well as to retain the best talent, Glaxo began to delegate to its frontline researchers the ability to set research priorities and allocate the resources required to see a drug through development. Glaxo scientists are now organized into "pods" that focus on specific disease categories. Employees control their own budgets, decide which projects to pursue, and receive funding based on the number of useful compounds their labs have created. Delegating at Glaxo has worked. Not only has the number of drugs entering human trials tripled since the company began using "pods," Glaxo is now expanding into treatment areas where it previously had no presence.[22]

Exhibit 9.8
Delegation: Responsibility, Authority, and Accountability

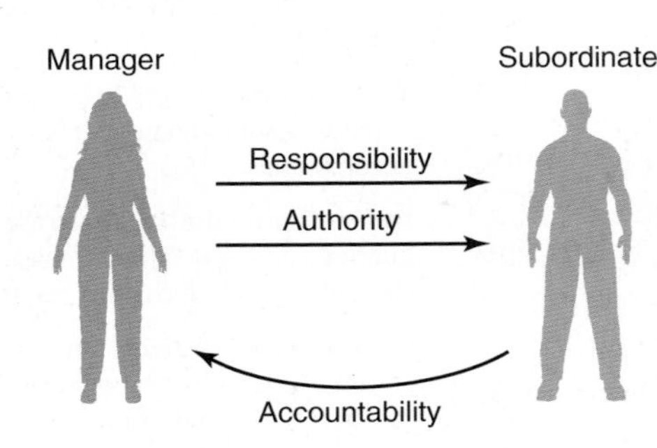

Source: C. D. Pringle, D. F. Jennings, & J. G. Longenecker, *Managing Organizations: Functions and Behaviors* © 1990. Adapted by permission of Pearson Education, Inc., Upper Saddle River, NJ.

The third transfer that occurs with delegation is the transfer of accountability. The subordinate now has the authority and responsibility to do the job and in return is accountable for getting the job done. In other words, managers delegate their managerial authority and responsibility to subordinates in exchange for results. *Forbes* magazine columnist John Rutledge calls delegation "MBB," Managing by Belly Button. He says, "The belly button is the person whose belly you point your finger at when you want to know how the work is proceeding, i.e., the person who will actually be accountable for each step. . . . The belly button is not a scapegoat—a person to blame later when things go wrong. He or she is the person who makes sure that things go right."[23] Exhibit 9.9 gives some tips on how to be an effective delegator.

> "The belly button is not a scapegoat—a person to blame later when things go wrong. He or she is the person who makes sure that things go right."
>
> JOHN RUTLEDGE, COLUMNIST, *FORBES* MAGAZINE

2.4 Degree of Centralization

centralization of authority the location of most authority at the upper levels of the organization

decentralization the location of a significant amount of authority in the lower levels of the organization

If you've ever called a company's toll-free number with a complaint or a special request and been told by the customer service representative, "I'll have to ask my manager," or "I'm not authorized to do that," you know that centralization of authority exists in that company. **Centralization of authority** is the location of most authority at the upper levels of the organization. In a centralized organization, managers make most decisions, even the relatively small ones. That's why the customer service representative you called couldn't make a decision without first asking the manager.

If you are lucky, however, you may have talked to a customer service representative at another company who said, "I can take care of that for you right now." In other words, the person was able to handle your problem without any input from or consultation with company management. **Decentralization** is the location of a significant amount of authority in the lower levels of the organization. An organization is decentralized if it has a high degree of delegation at all levels. In a decentralized organization, workers closest to problems are authorized to make the decisions necessary to solve the problems on their own.

Decentralization has a number of advantages. It develops employee capabilities throughout the company and leads to faster decision making and more satisfied customers and employees. Furthermore, a study of 1,000 large companies found that companies with a high degree of decentralization outperformed those with a low degree of decentralization in terms of return on assets (6.9 percent versus 4.7 percent), return on investment (14.6 percent

Exhibit 9.9

How to Be a More Effective Delegator

1. Trust your staff to do a good job. Recognize that others have the talent and ability to complete projects.
2. Avoid seeking perfection. Establish a standard of quality and provide a time frame for reaching it.
3. Give effective job instructions. Make sure employees have enough information to complete the job successfully.
4. Know your true interests. Delegation is difficult for some people who actually prefer doing the work themselves rather than managing it.
5. Follow up on progress. Build in checkpoints to help identify potential problems.
6. Praise the efforts of your staff.
7. Don't wait to the last minute to delegate. Avoid crisis management by routinely delegating work.
8. Ask questions, expect answers, and assist employees to help them complete the work assignments as expected.
9. Provide the resources you would expect if you were doing an assignment yourself.
10. Delegate to the lowest possible level to make the best possible use of organizational resources, energy, and knowledge.

Source: S. B. Wilson, "Are You an Effective Delegator?" *Female Executive*, 1 November 1994, 19.

versus 9.0 percent), return on equity (22.8 percent versus 16.6 percent), and return on sales (10.3 percent versus 6.3 percent). Surprisingly, the same study found that few large companies actually are decentralized. Specifically, only 31 percent of employees in these 1,000 companies were responsible for recommending improvements to management. Overall, just 10 percent of employees received the training and information needed to support a truly decentralized approach to management.[24]

With results like these, the key question is no longer whether companies should decentralize, but where they should decentralize. One rule of thumb is to stay centralized where standardization is important and to decentralize where standardization is unimportant. **Standardization** is solving problems by consistently applying the same rules, procedures, and processes. Each year, **General Motors** purchases roughly $85 billion worth of wheels, seats, bolts, and other automotive parts, many of which are only slight variations of the same thing. For instance, GM makes 26 different types of seat frames (the steel latticework that provides support for seat cushions), 20 different fuel pumps, and a dozen V6 engines. In contrast, highly profitable Toyota uses just two types of seat frames and a few models of V6 engines. One reason for GM's part redundancies is that the company used to have completely separate engineering groups for each of its cars and trucks. To become more competitive, however, GM has started standardizing the parts it uses across its product lines and wants to share as much technology and engineering across the company as possible. Today, GM uses only six types of fuel pump, and management wants to cut that number to five.[25]

"What's New" Company

Review 2: Organizational Authority

Organizational authority is determined by the chain of command, line versus staff authority, delegation, and the degree of centralization in a company. The chain of command vertically connects every job in the company to higher levels of management and makes clear who reports to whom. Managers have line authority to command employees below them in the chain of command, but have only staff, or advisory, authority over employees not below them in the chain of command. Managers delegate authority by transferring to subordinates the authority and responsibility needed to do a task; in exchange, subordinates become accountable for task completion. In centralized companies, most authority to make decisions lies with managers in the upper levels of the company. In decentralized companies, much of the authority is delegated to the workers closest to problems, who can then make the decisions necessary for solving the problems themselves. Centralization works best for tasks that require standardized decision making. When standardization isn't important, decentralization can lead to faster decisions, greater employee and customer satisfaction, and significantly better financial performance.

3 Job Design

Imagine that **McDonald's** decided to pay $50,000 a year to its drive-through window cashiers. That's $50,000 for saying, "Welcome to McDonald's. May I have your order please?" Would you take the job? Sure you would. Work a couple of years. Make a hundred grand. Why not? Let's assume, however, that to get this outrageous salary, you have to be a full-time McDonald's drive-through window cashier for the next 10 years. Would you still

standardization solving problems by consistently applying the same rules, procedures, and processes take the job? Just imagine, 40 to 60 times an hour, you repeat the same basic process:

1. *"Welcome to McDonald's. May I have your order please?"*
2. *Listen to the order. Repeat it for accuracy. State the total cost. "Please drive to the second window."*
3. *Take the money. Make change.*
4. *Give customers drinks, straws, and napkins.*
5. *Give customers food.*
6. *"Thank you for coming to McDonald's."*

BARRY SWEET/ EPA/ LANDOV

This two-window drive-thru in Monroe, Washington, is typical of McDonald's (and other fast-food restaurants) around the country. But even though this way of organizing the work is extremely efficient, it can be less than stimulating for employees.

Could you stand to do the same simple tasks an average of 50 times per hour, 400 times per day, 2,000 times per week, 8,000 times per month? Few can. Fast-food workers rarely stay on the job more than six months. Indeed, McDonald's and other fast-food restaurants have well over 100 percent employee turnover each year.[26]

In this next section, you will learn about ***job design****—the number, kind, and variety of tasks that individual workers perform in doing their jobs. You will learn* ***3.1 why companies continue to use specialized jobs like the McDonald's drive-through job*** *and* ***3.2 how job rotation, job enlargement, job enrichment****, and* ***3.3 the job characteristics model are being used to overcome the problems associated with job specialization****.*

3.1 Job Specialization

Job specialization occurs when a job is composed of a small part of a larger task or process. Specialized jobs are characterized by simple, easy-to-learn steps, low variety, and high repetition, like the McDonald's drive-through window job just described. One of the clear disadvantages of specialized jobs is that, being so easy to learn, they quickly become boring. This, in turn, can lead to low job satisfaction and high absenteeism and employee turnover, all of which are very costly to organizations.

Why, then, do companies continue to create and use specialized jobs? The primary reason is that specialized jobs are very economical. Once a job has been specialized, it takes little time to learn and master. Consequently, when experienced workers quit or are absent, the company can replace them with new employees and lose little productivity. For example, next time you're at McDonald's, notice the pictures of the food on the cash registers. These pictures make it easy for McDonald's trainees to quickly learn to take orders. Likewise, to simplify and speed operations, the drink dispensers behind the counter are set to automatically fill drink cups. Put a medium cup below the dispenser. Punch the medium drink button. The soft drink machine then fills the cup to within a half-inch of the top, while that same worker goes to get your fries. At McDonald's, every task has been simplified in this way. Because the work is designed to be simple, wages can remain low since it isn't necessary to pay high salaries to attract highly experienced, educated, or trained workers.

3.2 Job Rotation, Enlargement, and Enrichment

Because of the efficiency of specialized jobs, companies are often reluctant to eliminate them. Consequently, job redesign efforts have focused on modifying jobs to keep the benefits of specialized jobs, while reducing their obvious costs and disadvantages.

job design the number, kind, and variety of tasks that individual workers perform in doing their jobs

job specialization a job composed of a small part of a larger task or process

The more you increase individual responsibility, the better the chances for incremental improvements in operations.

DENNIS BAKKE, CEO, AES

Three methods—job rotation, job enlargement, and job enrichment—have been used to try to improve specialized jobs.[27]

In factory work or even some office jobs, many workers perform the same task all day long. For example, if you attach side mirrors in an auto factory, you probably complete this task 45 to 60 times an hour. If you work as the cashier at a grocery store, you check out a different customer every two to three minutes. And if you work as an office receptionist, you may answer and direct phone calls up to 200 times an hour.

Job rotation attempts to overcome the disadvantages of job specialization by periodically moving workers from one specialized job to another to give them more variety and the opportunity to use different skills. For example, the office receptionist who does nothing but answer phones could be systematically rotated to a different job, such as typing, filing, or data entry, every day or two. Likewise, the "mirror attacher" in the automobile plant might attach mirrors in the first half of the day's work shift and then install bumpers during the second half. Because employees simply switch from one specialized job to another, job rotation allows companies to retain the economic benefits of specialized work. At the same time, the greater variety of tasks makes the work less boring and more satisfying for workers.

Another way to counter the disadvantages of specialization is to enlarge the job. **Job enlargement** increases the number of different tasks that a worker performs within one particular job. Instead of being assigned just one task, workers with enlarged jobs are given several tasks to perform. For example, an enlarged "mirror attacher" job might include attaching the mirror, checking to see that the mirror's power adjustment controls work, and then cleaning the mirror's surface. Though job enlargement increases variety, many workers report feeling more stress when their jobs are enlarged. Consequently, many workers view enlarged jobs as simply "more work," especially if they are not given additional time to complete the additional tasks.

Job enrichment attempts to overcome the deficiencies in specialized work by increasing the number of tasks *and* by giving workers the authority and control to make meaningful decisions about their work.[28]

At ***AES***, an independent power company that sells electricity to public utilities and steam (for power) to industrial organizations, workers have been given an extraordinary level of authority and control. For example, with his hands still blackened after unloading coal from a barge, employee Jeff Hatch calls a broker to determine which Treasury bills the company should buy to maximize the short-term return on its available cash. Hatch asks his broker, "What kind of rate can you give me for $10 million at 30 days?" When the broker tells him, "6.09 percent," he responds, "But I just got a 6.13 percent quote from Chase."[29] Indeed, at AES, ordinary plant technicians are given budgets worth several million dollars and are trusted to purchase everything from mops to gas turbines. In most companies, such tasks would be entrusted only to managers, but CEO Dennis Bakke says, "The more you increase individual responsibility, the better the chances for incremental improvements in operations." Paul Burdick, an engineer entrusted with the ability to purchase billions of dollars of coal, agrees, adding, "You're given a lot of leeway and a lot of rope. You can use it to climb or you can hang yourself."[30]

job rotation periodically moving workers from one specialized job to another to give them more variety and the opportunity to use different skills

job enlargement increasing the number of different tasks that a worker performs within one particular job

job enrichment increasing the number of tasks in a particular job and giving workers the authority and control to make meaningful decisions about their work

job characteristics model (JCM) an approach to job redesign that seeks to formulate jobs in ways that motivate workers and lead to positive work outcomes

3.3 Job Characteristics Model

In contrast to job rotation, job enlargement, and job enrichment, which focus on providing variety in job tasks, the **job characteristics model (JCM)** is an approach to job redesign that seeks to formulate jobs in ways that motivate workers and lead to positive work outcomes.[31] As shown in Exhibit 9.10, the primary goal of the model is to create jobs that result in positive personal and work outcomes such as internal work motivation, satisfaction with one's job, and work effectiveness. Of these, the central concern of the JCM is internal motivation. **Internal motivation** is motivation that comes from the job itself rather than from outside rewards, such as a raise or praise from the boss. If workers feel that performing the job well is itself rewarding, then the job has internal motivation. Statements such as "I get a nice sense of accomplishment" or "I feel good about myself and what I'm producing" are examples of internal motivation.

Moving to the left in Exhibit 9.10, you can see that the JCM specifies three critical psychological states that must occur for work to be internally motivating. First, workers must *experience the work as meaningful*; that is, they must view their job as being important. Second, they must *experience responsibility for work outcomes*—they must feel personally responsible for the work being done well. Third, workers must have *knowledge of results*; that is, they must know how well they are performing their jobs. All three critical psychological states must occur for work to be internally motivating.

For example, let's return to our grocery store cashier. Cashiers usually have knowledge of results. When you're slow, your checkout line grows long. If you make a mistake, customers point it out: "No, I think that's on sale for $2.99, not $3.99." Likewise, cashiers experience responsibility for work outcomes. At the end of the day, the register is totaled and the money is counted. Ideally, the money matches the total sales in the register. If the money in the till is less than what's recorded in the register, most stores make the cashier pay the difference. Consequently, most cashiers are very careful to avoid being caught short at the end of the day. Nonetheless, despite knowing the results and experiencing responsibility for work outcomes, most grocery store cashiers (at least where I shop) aren't internally motivated because they don't experience the work as meaningful. With scanners, it takes little skill to learn or do the job. Anyone can do it. In addition, cashiers have few decisions to make, and the job is highly repetitive.

internal motivation motivation that comes from the job itself rather than from outside rewards

Exhibit 9.10

Job Characteristics Model

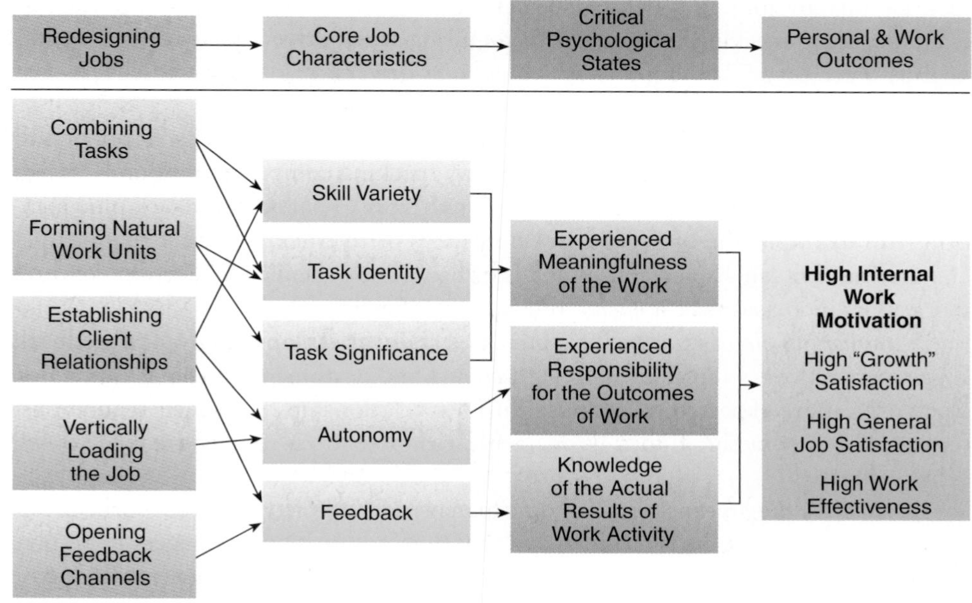

Source: J. R. Hackman & G. R. Oldham, *Work Redesign* (Reading, MA: Addison-Wesley, 1980). Reprinted by permission of Addison-Wesley Longman.

Of course, this raises the question: What kinds of jobs produce the three critical psychological states? Moving another step to the left in Exhibit 9.10, you can see that these psychological states arise from jobs that are strong on five core job characteristics: skill variety, task identity, task significance, autonomy, and feedback. **Skill variety** is the number of different activities performed in a job. **Task identity** is the degree to which a job, from beginning to end, requires completion of a whole and identifiable piece of work. **Task significance** is the degree to which a job is perceived to have a substantial impact on others inside or outside the organization. **Autonomy** is the degree to which a job gives workers the discretion, freedom, and independence to decide how and when to accomplish the work. Finally, **feedback** is the amount of information the job provides to workers about their work performance.

To illustrate how the core job characteristics work together, let's use them to more thoroughly assess why the McDonald's drive-through window job is not particularly satisfying or motivating. To start, skill variety is low. Except for the size of an order or special requests ("no onions"), the process is the same for each customer. At best, task identity is moderate. Although you take the order, handle the money, and deliver the food, others are responsible for a larger part of the process—preparing the food. Task identity will be even lower if the McDonald's has two drive-through windows because each drive-through window worker will have an even more specialized task. The first is limited to taking the order and making change, while the second just delivers the food. Task significance, the impact you have on others, is probably low. Autonomy is also very low: McDonald's has strict rules about dress, cleanliness, and procedures. But the job does provide immediate feedback, such as positive and negative customer comments, car horns honking, the amount of time it takes to process orders, and the number of cars in the drive-through. With the exception of feedback, the low levels of the core job characteristics show why the drive-through window job is not internally motivating for many workers.

What can managers do when jobs aren't internally motivating? The far left column of Exhibit 9.10 lists five job redesign techniques that managers can use to strengthen a job's core characteristics. *Combining tasks* increases skill variety and task identity by joining separate, specialized tasks into larger work modules. For example, some trucking firms are now requiring truck drivers to load their rigs as well as drive them. The hope is that involving drivers in loading will ensure that trucks are properly loaded, thus reducing damage claims.

Work can be formed into *natural work units* by arranging tasks according to logical or meaningful groups. Although many trucking companies randomly assign drivers to trucks, some have begun assigning drivers to particular geographic locations (for example, the Northeast or Southwest) or to truckloads that require special driving skill (such as oversized loads or hazardous chemicals). Forming natural work units increases task identity and task significance.

Establishing client relationships increases skill variety, autonomy, and feedback by giving employees direct contact with clients and customers. In some companies, truck drivers are expected to establish business relationships with their regular customers. When something goes wrong with a shipment, customers are told to call drivers directly.

Vertical loading means pushing some managerial authority down to workers. For truck drivers, this means that they have the same authority as managers to resolve customer problems. In some companies, if a late shipment causes problems for a customer, the driver has the authority to fully refund the cost of that shipment (without first obtaining management's approval).

skill variety the number of different activities performed in a job

task identity the degree to which a job, from beginning to end, requires the completion of a whole and identifiable piece of work

task significance the degree to which a job is perceived to have a substantial impact on others inside or outside the organization

autonomy the degree to which a job gives workers the discretion, freedom, and independence to decide how and when to accomplish the job

feedback the amount of information the job provides to workers about their work performance

The last job redesign technique offered by the model, *opening feedback channels*, means finding additional ways to give employees direct, frequent feedback about their job performance. For example, with advances in electronics, many truck drivers get instantaneous data as to whether they're on schedule and driving their rigs in a fuel-efficient manner. Likewise, the increased contact with customers also means that many drivers now receive monthly data on customer satisfaction. For additional information on the JCM, see this chapter's "What Really Works" feature.

© DIGITAL VISION/GETTY IMAGES

By allowing truck drivers to interact with customers and resolve customers' complaints, driving a truck can become more internally motivating.

Review 3: **Job Design**

Companies use specialized jobs because they are economical and easy to learn and don't require highly paid workers. However, specialized jobs aren't motivating or particularly satisfying for employees. Companies have used job rotation, job enlargement, job enrichment, and the job characteristics model to make specialized jobs more interesting and motivating. With job rotation, workers move from one specialized job to another. Job enlargement simply increases the number of different tasks within a particular job. Job enrichment increases the number of tasks in a job and gives workers authority and control over their work. The goal of the job characteristics model is to make jobs intrinsically motivating. For this to happen, jobs must be strong on five core job characteristics (skill variety, task identity, task significance, autonomy, and feedback), and workers must experience three critical psychological states (knowledge of results, responsibility for work outcomes, and meaningful work). If jobs aren't internally motivating, they can be redesigned by combining tasks, forming natural work units, establishing client relationships, vertical loading, and opening feedback channels.

DESIGNING ORGANIZATIONAL PROCESSES

More than 40 years ago, Tom Burns and G. M. Stalker described how two kinds of organizational designs, mechanistic and organic, are appropriate for different kinds of organizational environments.[32] **Mechanistic organizations** are characterized by specialized jobs and responsibilities; precisely defined, unchanging roles; and a rigid chain of command based on centralized authority and vertical communication. This type of organization works best in stable, unchanging business environments. By contrast, **organic organizations** are characterized by broadly defined jobs and responsibility; loosely defined, frequently changing roles; and decentralized authority and horizontal communication based on task knowledge. This type of organization works best in dynamic, changing business environments.

mechanistic organization an organization characterized by specialized jobs and responsibilities; precisely defined, unchanging roles; and a rigid chain of command based on centralized authority and vertical communication

organic organization an organization characterized by broadly defined jobs and responsibility; loosely defined, frequently changing roles; and decentralized authority and horizontal communication based on task knowledge

what really works.

THE JOB CHARACTERISTICS MODEL: MAKING JOBS MORE INTERESTING AND MOTIVATING

Think of the worst job you ever had. Was it factory work where you repeated the same task every few minutes? Was it an office job requiring a lot of meaningless paperwork? Or was it a job so specialized that it took no effort or thinking whatsoever to do?

The job characteristics model reviewed in this chapter suggests that workers will be more motivated or satisfied with their work if their jobs have greater task identity, task significance, skill variety, autonomy, and feedback. Eighty-four studies, with a combined total of 22,472 participants, found that, on average, these core job characteristics make jobs more satisfying for most workers. In addition, jobs rich with the five core job characteristics are especially satisfying for workers who possess an individual characteristic called *growth need strength*. Read on to see how well the JCM really increases job satisfaction and reduces workplace absenteeism.

JOB SATISFACTION

There is a 66 percent chance that workers will be more satisfied with their work when their jobs have task identity, the chance to complete an entire job from beginning to end, than when they don't.

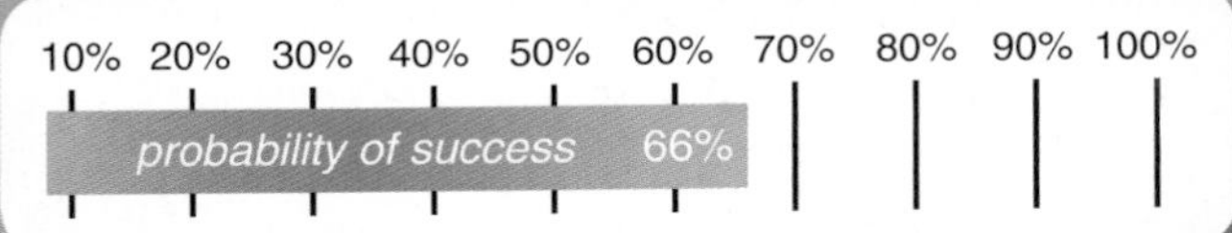

On average, there is a 69 percent chance that workers will be more satisfied with their work when their jobs have task significance—a substantial impact on others—than when they don't.

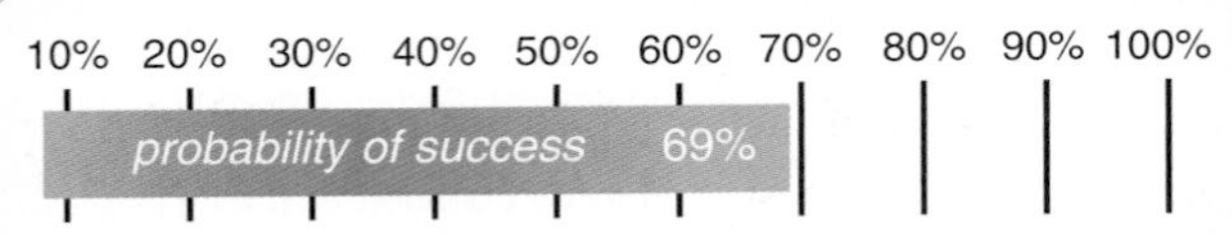

On average, there is a 70 percent chance that workers will be more satisfied with their work when their jobs have skill variety—a variety of activities, skills, and talents—than when they don't.

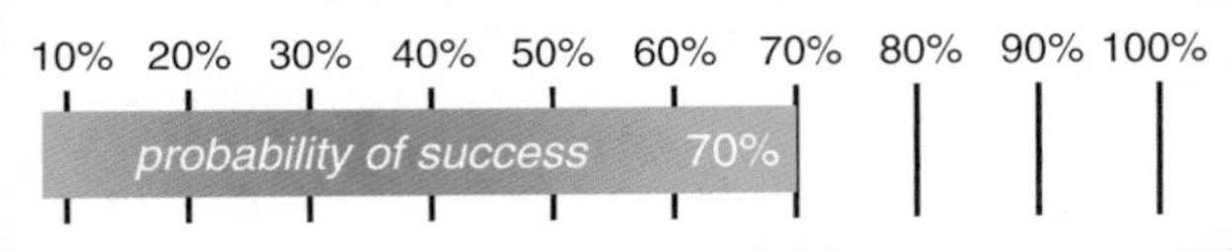

On average, there is a 73 percent chance that workers will be more satisfied with their work when their jobs have autonomy—the discretion to decide how and when to accomplish the work—than when they don't.

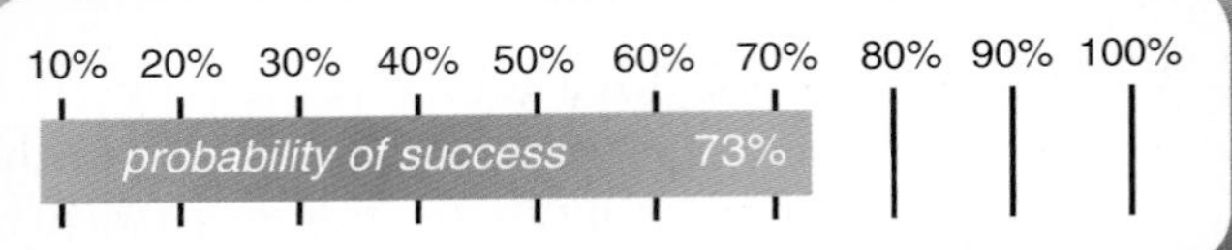

On average, there is a 70 percent chance that workers will be more satisfied with their work when their jobs provide feedback—information about their work performance—than when they don't.

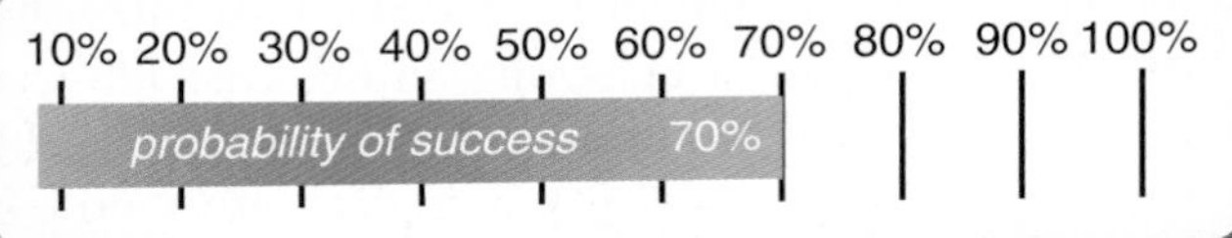

These statistics indicate that, on average, the JCM has at worst a 66 percent chance of improving workers' job satisfaction. In all, this is impressive evidence that the model works. In general, you can expect these results when redesigning jobs based on the model.

We can be more accurate about the effects of the JCM, however, if we split workers into two groups: those with high growth need strength and those with low growth need strength. *Growth need strength* is the need or desire to achieve personal growth and development through one's job. Workers high in growth need strength respond well to jobs designed according to the JCM because they enjoy work that challenges them and allows them to learn new skills and knowledge. In fact, there is an 84 percent chance that workers with high growth need strength will be more satisfied with their work when their jobs are redesigned according to the JCM.

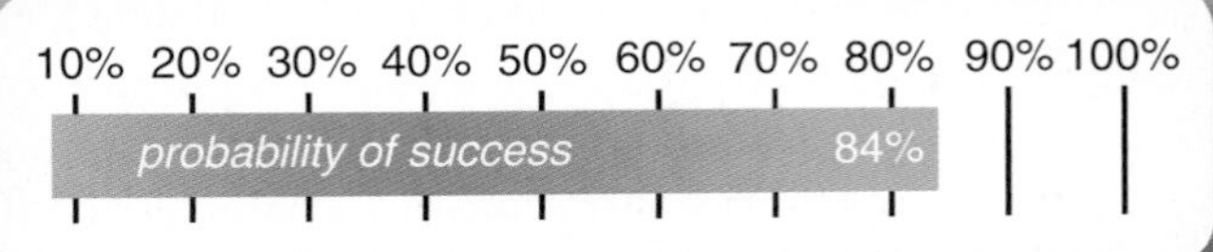

By comparison, because they aren't as interested in being challenged or learning new things at work, there is only a 69 percent chance that workers low in growth need strength will be satisfied with jobs that have been redesigned according to the principles of the JCM. This is still a favorable percentage, but it is weaker than the 84 percent chance of job satisfaction that occurs for workers high in growth need strength.

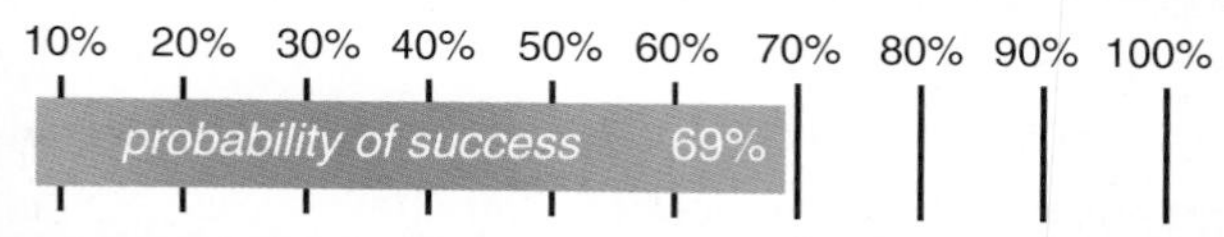

WORKPLACE ABSENTEEISM

Although not shown in the job characteristics model displayed in Exhibit 9.10, workplace absenteeism is an important personal or work outcome affected by a job's core job characteristics. In general, the "richer" your job is with task identity, task significance, skill variety, autonomy, and feedback, the more likely you are to show up for work every day.

Workers are 63 percent more likely to attend work when their jobs have task identity than when they don't.

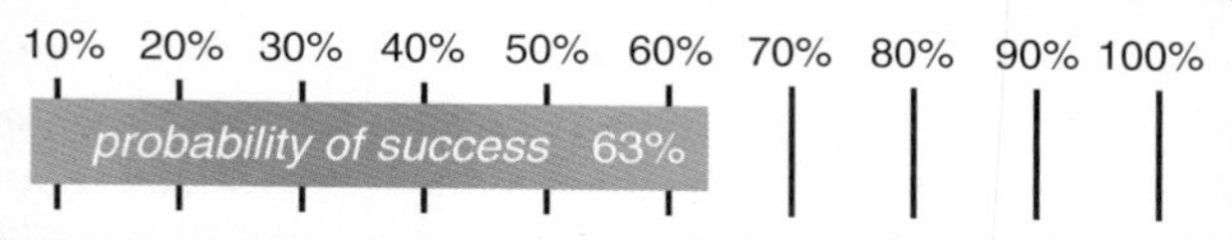

Workers are 68 percent more likely to attend work when their jobs have task significance than when they don't.

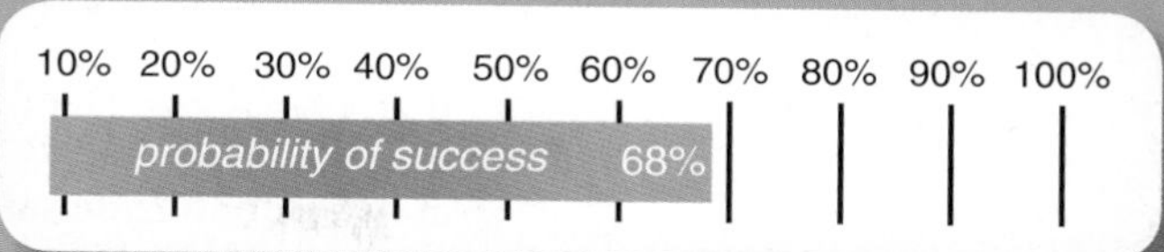

Workers are 72 percent more likely to attend work when their jobs have skill variety than when they don't.

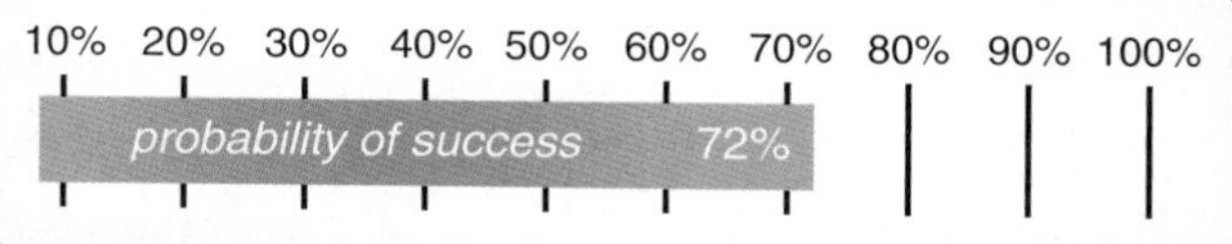

Workers are 74 percent more likely to attend work when their jobs have autonomy than when they don't.

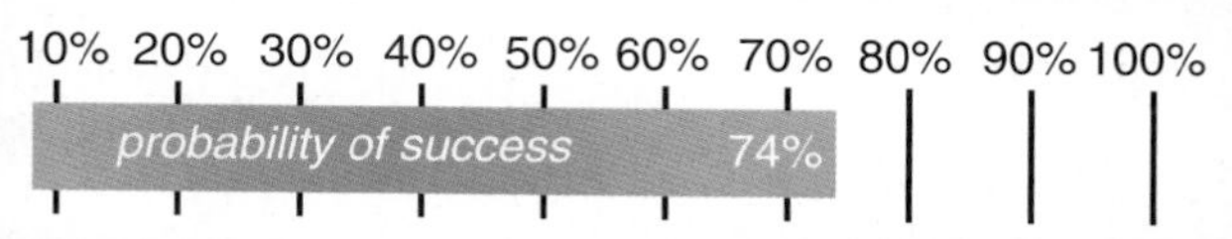

Workers are 72 percent more likely to attend work when their jobs provide feedback than when they don't.[33]

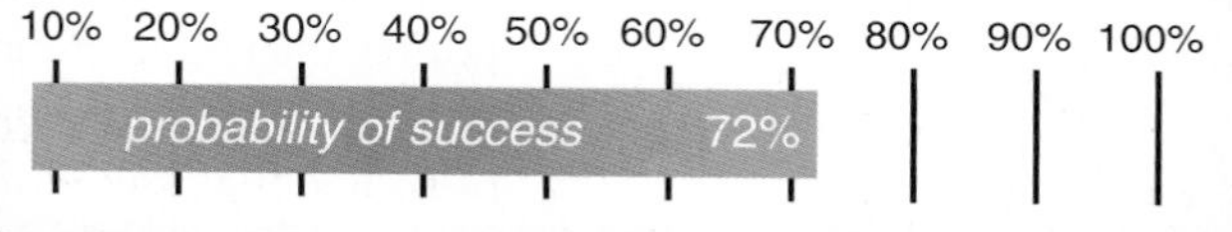

The organizational design techniques described in the first half of this chapter—departmentalization, authority, and job design—are better suited for mechanistic organizations and the stable business environments that were more prevalent before 1980. In contrast, the organizational design techniques discussed next, in the second part of the chapter, are more appropriate for organic organizations and the increasingly dynamic environments in which today's businesses compete.

The key difference between these approaches is that whereas mechanistic organizational designs focus on organizational structure, organic organizational designs are concerned with organizational process, the collection of activities that transform inputs into outputs valued by customers. After reading the next two sections, you should be able to

4 explain the methods that companies are using to redesign internal organizational processes (that is, intraorganizational processes).

5 describe the methods that companies are using to redesign external organizational processes (that is, interorganizational processes).

4 Intraorganizational Processes

An **intraorganizational process** is the collection of activities that take place within an organization to transform inputs into outputs that customers value. The steps involved in an automobile insurance claim are a good example of an intraorganizational process:

1. *Document the loss (the accident).*
2. *Assign an appraiser to determine the dollar amount of damage.*
3. *Make an appointment to inspect the vehicle.*
4. *Inspect the vehicle.*
5. *Write an appraisal and get the repair shop to agree to the damage estimate.*
6. *Pay for the repair work.*
7. *Return the repaired car to the customer.*

*Let's take a look at how companies are using **4.1 reengineering, 4.2 empowerment,** and **4.3 behavioral informality** to redesign intraorganizational processes like these.*

4.1 Reengineering

In their best-selling book *Reengineering the Corporation*, Michael Hammer and James Champy define **reengineering** as "the *fundamental* rethinking and *radical* redesign of business *processes* to achieve *dramatic* improvements in critical, contemporary measures of performance, such as cost, quality, service and speed."[34] Hammer and Champy further explained the four key words shown in italics in this definition. The first key word is *fundamental*. When reengineering organizational designs, managers must ask themselves, "Why do we do what we do?" and "Why do we do it the way we do?" The usual answer is, "Because that's the way we've always done it." The second key word is *radical*. Reengineering is about significant change, about starting over by throwing out the old ways of getting work done. The third key word is *processes*. Hammer and Champy noted that "most business people are not process oriented; they are focused on tasks, on jobs, on people, on structures, but not on processes." The fourth key word is *dramatic*. Reengineering is about achieving "quantum" improvements in company performance.

"I wasn't smart enough about that [the people issues]. I was reflecting my engineering background and was insufficiently appreciative of the human dimension. I've [now] learned that's critical."

MICHAEL HAMMER, CO-AUTHOR, *REENGINEERING THE CORPORATION*

intraorganizational process the collection of activities that take place within an organization to transform inputs into outputs that customers value

reengineering fundamental rethinking and radical redesign of business processes to achieve dramatic improvements in critical measures of performance, such as cost, quality, service, and speed

An example from **IBM Credit**'s operation illustrates how work can be reengineered.[35] IBM Credit lends businesses money to buy IBM computers. Previously, the loan process began when an IBM salesperson called the home office to obtain credit approval for a customer's purchase. The first department involved in the process took the credit information over the phone from the salesperson and recorded it on the credit form. The credit form was sent to the credit checking department, then to the pricing department (where the interest rate was determined), and on through a total of five departments. In all, it took the five departments six days to approve or deny the customer's loan. Of course, this delay cost IBM business. Some customers got their loans elsewhere. Others, frustrated by the wait, simply canceled their orders.

Finally, two IBM managers decided to walk a loan straight through each of the departments involved in the process. At each step, they asked the workers to stop what they were doing and immediately process their loan application. They were shocked by what they found. From start to finish, the entire process took just 90 minutes! The six-day turnaround time was almost entirely due to delays in handing off the work from one department to another. The solution: IBM redesigned the process so that one person, not five people in five separate departments, now handles the entire loan approval process without any handoffs. The results were indeed "dramatic." Reengineering the credit process reduced approval time from six days to four hours and allowed IBM Credit to increase the number of loans it handled by a factor of 100!

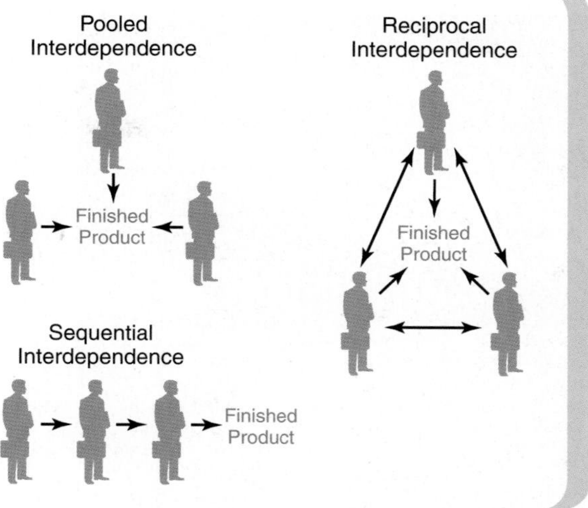

Exhibit 9.11

Reengineering and Task Interdependence

Reengineering changes an organization's orientation from vertical to horizontal. Instead of "taking orders" from upper management, lower- and middle-level managers and workers "take orders" from a customer who is at the beginning and end of each process. Instead of running independent functional departments, managers and workers in different departments take ownership of cross-functional processes. Instead of simplifying work so that it becomes increasingly specialized, reengineering complicates work by giving workers increased autonomy and responsibility for complete processes.

In essence, reengineering changes work by changing **task interdependence**, the extent to which collective action is required to complete an entire piece of work. As shown in Exhibit 9.11, there are three kinds of task interdependence.[36] In **pooled interdependence**, each job or department independently contributes to the whole. In **sequential interdependence**, work must be performed in succession, as one group's or job's outputs become the inputs for the next group or job. Finally, in **reciprocal interdependence**, different jobs or groups work together in a back-and-forth manner to complete the process. By reducing the handoffs between different jobs or groups, reengineering decreases sequential interdependence. Likewise, reengineering decreases pooled interdependence by redesigning work so that formerly independent jobs or departments now work together to complete processes. Finally, reengineering increases reciprocal interdependence by making groups or individuals responsible for larger, more complete processes in which several steps may be accomplished at the same time.

task interdependence the extent to which collective action is required to complete an entire piece of work

pooled interdependence work completed by having each job or department independently contribute to the whole

sequential interdependence work completed in succession, with one group's or job's outputs becoming the inputs for the next group or job

reciprocal interdependence work completed by different jobs or groups working together in a back-and-forth manner

As an organizational design tool, reengineering promises big rewards, but it has also come under severe criticism. The most serious complaint is that because it allows a few workers to do the work formerly done by many, reengineering is simply a corporate code word for cost cutting and worker layoffs.[37] Likewise, for that reason, detractors claim that reengineering hurts morale and performance. For example, even though ordering times were reduced from three weeks to three days, **Levi Strauss** ended an $850 million reengineering project because of the fear and turmoil it created in the company's work force. One low point occurred when Levi management, encouraged by its reengineering consultants, told 4,000 workers that they would have to "reapply for their jobs" as the company shifted from its traditional vertical structure to a process-based form of

© DANIEL ACKER/BLOOMBERG NEWS/LANDOV

As managers at Levi Strauss discovered, reengineering must make sense for the kind of work being done.

organizing. Thomas Kasten, Levi Strauss's vice president for reengineering and customer service, says, "We felt the pressure building up [over reengineering efforts], and we were worried about the business."[38] Today, even reengineering gurus Hammer and Champy admit that roughly 70 percent of all reengineering projects fail because of the effects on people in the workplace. Says Hammer, "I wasn't smart enough about that [the people issues]. I was reflecting my engineering background and was insufficiently appreciative of the human dimension. I've [now] learned that's critical."[39]

4.2 Empowerment

Another way of redesigning interorganizational processes is through empowerment. **Empowering workers** means permanently passing decision-making authority and responsibility from managers to workers. For workers to be fully empowered, companies must give them the information and resources they need to make and carry out good decisions, and then reward them for taking individual initiative.[40] Unfortunately, this doesn't happen often enough. As Michael Schrage, author and MIT researcher, wrote:

> *A warehouse employee can see on the intranet that a shipment is late but has no authority to accelerate its delivery. A project manager knows—and can mathematically demonstrate—that a seemingly minor spec change will bust both her budget and her schedule. The spec must be changed anyway. An airline reservations agent tells the Executive Platinum Premier frequent flier that first class appears wide open for an upgrade. However, the airline's yield management software won't permit any upgrades until just four hours before the flight, frequent fliers (and reservations) be damned. In all these cases, the employee has access to valuable information. Each one possesses the "knowledge" to do the job better. But the knowledge and information are irrelevant and useless. Knowledge isn't power; the ability to act on knowledge is power.*[41]

When workers are given the proper information and resources and are allowed to make good decisions, they experience strong feelings of empowerment. **Empowerment** is a feeling of intrinsic motivation, in which workers perceive their work to have meaning and perceive themselves to be competent, having an impact, and capable of self-determination.[42] Work has meaning when it is consistent with personal standards and beliefs. Workers feel competent when they believe they can perform an activity with skill. The belief that they are having an impact comes from a feeling that they can affect work outcomes. A feeling of self-determination arises from workers' belief that they have the autonomy to choose how best to do their work.

Empowerment can lead to changes in organizational processes because meaning, competence, impact, and self-determination produce empowered employees who take active, rather than passive, roles in their work. **WEGMANS** Food Market Inc., a perennial top company on the *Fortune* ranking of the best businesses to work for is a classic example of employee empowerment. Wegmans has 69 stores in New York, Pennsylvania, New Jersey and Virginia. Employees are encouraged to do just about anything to keep customers loyal to the organization and to do so on the spot, without consulting a higher-up. One day it could mean sending a chef to a customer's home to clear up a botched food order or it could mean cooking a family's Thanksgiving turkey in the store because the one bought was too big for the customer's oven. This approach leads to what operations chief Jack DePeters jokingly says is a "$3 billion company run by 16-year-old cashiers."[43]

empowering workers permanently passing decision-making authority and responsibility from managers to workers by giving them the information and resources they need to make and carry out good decisions

empowerment feelings of intrinsic motivation, in which workers perceive their work to have impact and meaning and perceive themselves to be competent and capable of self-determination

	FORMAL	INFORMAL
LANGUAGE USAGE	Fully articulated speech ("What are you doing?") Grammatically complete phrasing ("Would you like some coffee?") Use of formal word choices ("Would you care to dine?") Use of honorifics ("Ms.," "Sir," "Dr.") Elimination of "I" and "you" ("It is requested that...")	Phonological slurring ("Whatcha doin'?") Use of elliptical expressions ("Coffee?") Use of colloquial and slang expressions ("Wanna grab a bite to eat?") Use of the vivid present ("So I come down the stairs, and she says...") First name, in-group names ("Mac," "Bud")
CONVERSATIONAL TURN TAKING AND TOPIC SELECTION	Turn taking well regulated Few interruptions or overlaps Few changes of topic Generally serious topics	Turn taking relatively unregulated Many interruptions or overlaps Many shifts of topic possible Joking or conversational levity possible
EMOTIONAL AND PROXEMIC GESTURES	Sober facial demeanor Much interpersonal distance No touching; postural attention	Greater latitude of emotional expression Small interpersonal distance Touching, postural relaxation allowed
PHYSICAL AND CONTEXTUAL CUES	Formal clothing, shoes, etc. Central focus of attention Symmetric arrangement of chairs/furniture Artifacts related to official status Hushed atmosphere, little background noise	Informal clothing, shoes, etc. Decentralized, multiple centers of attention possible Asymmetric arrangement of chairs/furniture Informal trappings: flowers, art, food, soft furniture Background noise acceptable

Source: Republished with permission of Academy of Management, P.O. Box 3020, Briar Cliff Manor, NY, 10510–8020. D. A. Morland, "The Role of Behavioral Formality and Informality in the Enactment of Bureaucratic versus Organic Organizations," *Academy of Management Review* 20 (1995): 831–872. Reproduced by permission of the publisher via Copyright Clearance Center, Inc.

Exhibit 9.12

Differences between Formal and Informal Workplaces

4.3 Behavioral Informality

How would you describe the atmosphere in the office where you last worked? Was it a formal, by-the-book, follow-the-rules, address-each-other-by-last-names atmosphere? Or was it more informal, with an emphasis on results rather than rules, casual business dress rather than suits, and first names rather than last names and titles? Or was it somewhere in between?

Behavioral informality (or formality) is a third influence on intraorganizational processes. **Behavioral informality** refers to workplace atmospheres characterized by spontaneity, casualness, and interpersonal familiarity. By contrast, **behavioral formality** refers to workplace atmospheres characterized by routine and regimen, specific rules about how to behave, and impersonal detachment. As Exhibit 9.12 shows, behavioral formality and informality are characterized by four factors: language usage, conversational turn taking and topic selection, emotional and proxemic gestures, and physical and contextual cues. Let's examine each in more detail.[44]

behavioral informality a workplace atmosphere characterized by spontaneity, casualness, and interpersonal familiarity

behavioral formality a workplace atmosphere characterized by routine and regimen, specific rules about how to behave, and impersonal detachment

Compared with formal work atmospheres, the language in informal workplaces is often slurred ("Whatcha doin'?"), elliptical ("Coffee?" versus "Would you like some coffee?"), and filled with slang terms and vivid descriptions. People use first names and perhaps nicknames to address each other, rather than Mr., Ms., Dr., or formal titles. When it comes to conversations in informal workplaces, people jump right in when they have something to say (known as unregulated turn taking); conversations shift

Chipotle's unusual employee titles may be an extreme, but behavioral informality can help nearly any company unleash worker creativity.

from topic to topic, many of which are unrelated to business; and joking and laughter are common. From joy to disappointment, people show much more emotion in informal workplaces. Relaxed behavior, such as putting your feet on your desk or congregating in hallways for impromptu discussions, is more common, too. In terms of physical and contextual cues, informal workplaces de-emphasize differences in hierarchical status or rank to encourage more frequent interaction between organizational members. Consequently, to make their organizations feel less formal, many companies have eliminated such management perks as executive dining rooms, reserved parking spaces, and large corner offices separated from most workers by virtue of their location on a higher floor of the company building (the higher the floor, the greater one's status). **CHIPOTLE MEXICAN GRILL** de-emphasizes differences in hierarchical rank through an innovative employee title system that speaks volumes about the company's informal culture. The "Manager of Duct Tape and Plungers" is in charge of customer service. The "Director of Hoopla, Hype, and Ballyhoo" is the company's spokesman, and the leader of the creative services department is the "Head of Special Weapons and Tactics." Even though the title system has never received an official corporate blessing, the offbeat titles are still sanctioned: They are used on business cards and in formal business correspondence, reinforcing how seriously Chipotle takes behavioral informality.[45]

Casual dress policies and open office systems are two of the most popular methods for increasing behavioral informality. In fact, a survey conducted by the Society for Human Resource Management indicates that casual dress policies (no suits, ties, jackets, dresses, or formal clothing required) are extremely popular.[46] Today, 86 percent of companies have some form of casual dress code, up from 63 percent seven years ago and 24 percent 12 years ago.[47] Similarly, 42 percent of all companies permit casual dress at least one day a week, compared with 17 percent five years ago. Moreover, 33 percent of companies permit casual dress every day of the week, up from 20 percent seven years ago.

Although sales of formal business wear, such as men's suits, increased last year for the first time in eight years and some companies, such as retailer Target Corporation, have instituted formal dress codes that ban "business casual," "no study shows that productivity goes up with better dress," says John Challenger, chief executive of Challenger, Gray & Christmas, a Chicago-based outplacement company.[48] Indeed, casual dress appears to improve employee attitudes. For example, Colin Stanbridge, the chief executive of London's Chamber of Commerce, says, "People tend to work at their best when they feel most comfortable. And today I think the vast majority of people feel at their most comfortable when wearing casual dress."[49] In fact, 85 percent of human resources directors believe that casual dress can improve office morale, and 79 percent say that employees are very satisfied with casual dress codes.[50] Moreover, nearly two-thirds of the human resources directors believe that casual dress policies are an important tool for attracting qualified employees in tight labor markets. Michael Losey, president of the Society for Human Resource Management, concludes that "for the majority of corporations and industries, allowing casual dress can have clear advantages at virtually no cost."[51]

open office systems offices in which the physical barriers that separate workers have been removed in order to increase communication and interaction

While casual dress increases behavioral informality by having managers and workers at all levels dress in a more relaxed manner, open office systems increase behavioral informality by significantly increasing the level of communication and interaction among employees. By definition, **open office systems** try to increase interaction by removing physical barriers that separate workers. One characteristic of open office systems is that they have much more shared space than private space. **Shared spaces** are areas used by and open to all employees. Cubicles with low-to-the-ground partitions (used by 75 percent of office workers), offices with no doors or with glass walls, collections of comfortable furniture that encourage people to congregate, and common areas with tables and chairs that encourage people to meet, work, or eat together are examples of shared space.[52] In contrast, **private spaces**, such as private offices with doors, are used by and open to just one employee.

DIGITAL VISION

Open-offices encourage communication and interaction throughout an organization, but they have their drawbacks as well. In fact, sales of taller cube walls, like those shown here, are increasing, while sales of traditional four-foot walls are decreasing.

The advantage of an open office with extensive shared space is that it dramatically increases the amount of unplanned, spontaneous, and chance communication between employees.[53] People are much more likely to plan meetings and work together when numerous "collaboration spaces" with conference tables, white boards, and computers are readily available. With no office walls, inviting common areas, and different departments mixed together in large open spaces, spontaneous communication occurs more often. After RADIO SHACK moved from two traditional, 19-story office towers into a new headquarters with open offices, cubicles, and immense amounts of shared space, the volume of corporate e-mail dropped by 37 percent because people were much more likely to run into and actually talk to each other. Senior vice president Laura Moore says, "For somebody to stick his or her head over your workplace [cubicle] is accepted protocol. That has made executives much more approachable."[54] Also, open office systems increase chance encounters by making it much more likely that people from different departments or areas will run into each other. When SIGMA-ALDRICH, a biotechnology firm, built a new office with a three-story, open staircase at the center of the building, the main goal, according to Keld Sorensen, director of research and development, was increasing "interaction."[55] In fact, the open staircase, which is complemented by benches and expansive landings on each story (so people would sit and talk) has led to 156 percent more chance encounters than at the old building, which had elevators and an enclosed stairwell. Indeed, soon after the move to the new office, two scientists from opposite sides of the building ran into each other on the stairs, stopped to talk, and ended up generating a significant new reagent for scientific testing.

Not everyone is enthusiastic about open offices, however. For example, Ingrid Tischer, who sits in a cubicle next to the kitchen in her office, says she can't help being distracted by others' conversations and frequently joins in. Because of the location of her cubicle, "I know things about my colleagues' lives, and they know things about mine."[56] In fact, cubicle dwellers are interrupted by "noise, visual distractions, and chatty visitors" up to 21 times a day. And, since it takes about three minutes each time to refocus on what they were doing, cubicle workers can lose an hour a day to these interruptions.[57] Attorney Phillip Fisher says, "I honestly don't know how people can concentrate in a cubicle."[58] For this reason, SUN MICROSYSTEMS and Microsoft give their employees private offices. William Agnello, Sun's vice president of real estate and the workplace, says, "We have researched the heck out of this. Our studies show that, for our engineers, there are just too many distractions and interruptions."[59] Microsoft's John Pinette agrees: "Private offices allow our employees to concentrate on their work and to avoid unnecessary distractions—[which is] obviously critical when you're doing something that requires as much focus as developing software does."[60]

Indeed, because there is so much shared space and so little private space, companies with open systems have to take steps to give employees privacy when they need to concentrate on individual work. One step is simply to use taller cubicles. Indeed, Herman

shared spaces spaces used by and open to all employees

private spaces spaces used by and open to just one employee

> I honestly don't know how people can concentrate in a cubicle.
>
> PHILLIP FISHER, ATTORNEY

Miller, a manufacturer of office furniture and systems, has seen sales of its 62-inch-high cubicle panels increase by 18 percent while sales of its 46-inch-high panels have dropped by 19 percent. Another approach is to install white-noise machines to prevent voices and other noises from disrupting others.[62] At Procter & Gamble's headquarters in Cincinnati, white noise from two interior waterfalls provides a constant background sound that mutes other noises. Yet another approach is to make conference rooms available. In contrast to traditional offices, where such rooms are used for meetings, many employees in open systems reserve conference rooms when they need private time to work. Another possibility is to turn a cubicle into a more private space. When Mark Saunders, of GlaxoSmithKline Consumer Healthcare, moved from a private office to a cubicle at the end of a busy hallway, he "felt sensory overload." To make it easier for him to concentrate, the company's office design team created a nylon screen that can be placed around his cubicle to block out visual distractions.[63] If your office doesn't provide such screens, you can always fork out $39.95 for the Cube-a-Door, a free-standing cardboard partition stamped with the words "Work in Progress. Do Not Disturb," that will serve as a "door" to your cubicle when you need to screen out interruptions.

doing the right thing

Don't Scavenge That Office if Somebody Is Still in It

It's like roadkill in the animal kingdom. As soon as the word gets out that someone is leaving the company, coworkers start scheming to scavenge the office leftovers—chairs, computer monitors, filing cabinets, even staplers. "This issue is practically everywhere," says Mary Wong, president of a human resources consulting company. "Professionals—anyone you and I would normally consider to be very adult—turn into children" over the prospect of picking an empty office clean of its "goodies." Sometimes—and this is where it gets disrespectful—office scavengers move in even before the employee, who's often been laid off, has left. Ethics consultant Steve Lawler tells the story of a laid-off manager who, just hours after hearing the bad news, was already getting requests for the expensive Herman Miller Aeron chair in which he was still sitting. Office scavenging is a strange and predictable aspect of office life. It happens everywhere. But if you're going to scavenge, and you probably will, do the right thing by maintaining the dignity of departing coworkers: Wait until the office is empty before you strike.[61]

Review 4: Intraorganizational Processes

Today, companies are using reengineering, empowerment, and behavioral informality to change their intraorganizational processes. Through fundamental rethinking and radical redesign of business processes, reengineering changes an organization's orientation from vertical to horizontal. Reengineering changes work processes by decreasing sequential and pooled interdependence and by increasing reciprocal interdependence. Reengineering promises dramatic increases in productivity and customer satisfaction, but it has been criticized as simply an excuse to cut costs and lay off workers. Empowering workers means taking decision-making authority and responsibility from managers and giving it to workers. Empowered workers develop feelings of competence and self-determination and believe that their work has meaning and impact. Workplaces characterized by behavioral informality are spontaneous and casual. The formality or informality of a workplace depends on four factors: language usage, conversational turn taking and topic selection, emotional and proxemic gestures, and physical and contextual cues. Casual dress policies and open office systems are two of the most popular methods for increasing behavioral informality.

5 Interorganizational Processes

An **interorganizational process** is a collection of activities that occur *among companies* to transform inputs into outputs that customers value. In other words, many companies work together to create a product or service that keeps customers happy. For example, when you purchase a Liz Claiborne outfit, you're not just buying from **LIZ CLAIBORNE**; you're also buying from a network of 250 suppliers in 35 countries from Saipan, to Mexico, to Cambodia, to China that make those clothes for Liz Claiborne. After Liz Claiborne's New York–based designers come up with a concept, it is shipped to a "sourcing" team in Hong Kong, which changes the design as needed to keep costs low and then finds companies that can produce the right fabrics and the entire line of clothing. Those companies then manufacture the first product prototypes and send them back to the New York designers for final inspection and possibly last-minute changes.[64]

In this section, you'll explore interorganizational processes by learning about ***5.1 modular organizations*** *and* ***5.2 virtual organizations.***[65]

interorganizational process a collection of activities that take place among companies to transform inputs into outputs that customers value

modular organization an organization that outsources noncore business activities to outside companies, suppliers, specialists, or consultants

5.1 Modular Organizations

Stephen Roach, chief economist for investment bank Morgan Stanley, says that companies increasingly want to take "functions that aren't central to their core competency," and outsource them.[66] Except for the core business activities that they can perform better, faster, and cheaper than others, **modular organizations** outsource all remaining business activities to outside companies, suppliers, specialists, or consultants. The term *modular* is used because the business activities purchased from outside companies can be added and dropped as needed, much like adding pieces to a three-dimensional puzzle. Exhibit 9.13 depicts a modular organization in which the company has chosen to keep training, human resources, sales, product design, manufacturing, customer service, research and development, and information technology as core business activities, but it has outsourced the noncore activities of product distribution, web page design, advertising, payroll, accounting, and packaging.

Modular organizations have several advantages. First, because modular organizations pay for outsourced labor, expertise, or manufacturing capabilities only when needed, they can cost significantly less to run than traditional organizations. For example, when **APPLE** came up with its iPod digital music player, it outsourced the audio chip design and manufacture to SigmaTel in Austin, Texas, and final assembly to Asutek Computers in Taiwan. Doing so not only reduced costs and sped up production (beating Sony's Network Walkman to market), but also allowed Apple to do what it does best—design innovative products with easy-to-use software.[67] Furthermore, after other companies imitated Apple by producing their own digital music

Exhibit 9.13
Modular Organization

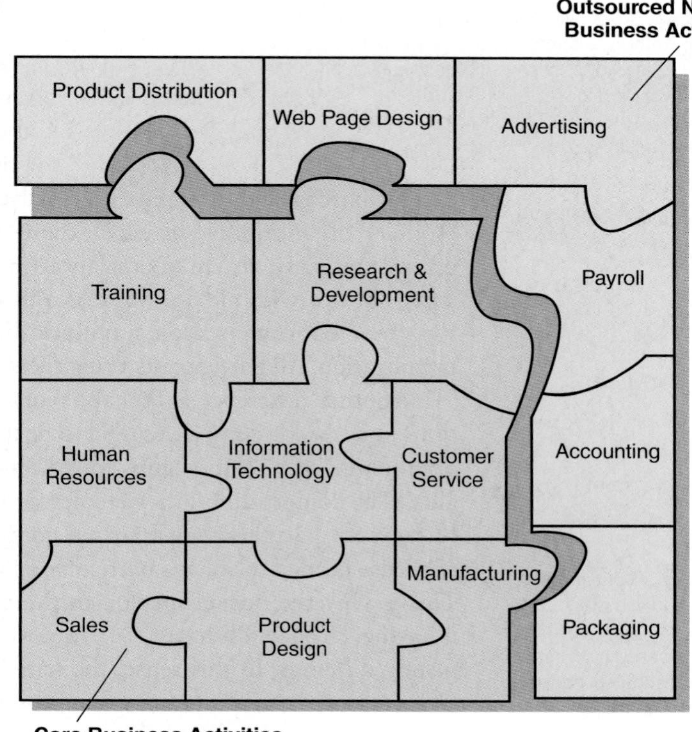

Trivia: What was the original Mechanical Turk? *See page 344 for the answer.*

mgmt: trend

Crowdsourcing

Companies are tapping into an army of people willing to work for literally pennies. At AMAZON's Mechanical Turk, companies or individuals (called "requesters") post repetitive tasks that can be completed only by human intelligence, such as identifying the best of a set of photos, writing product descriptions, and color-coding clothing sold by online retailers. Most of these jobs take only a few minutes and pay just a few cents. But requesters can also post tasks that are more involved. One manager originally paid a consultant $2,000 for a flow chart of his company's repair process. When the company needed additional work, however, it enlisted a "Turker." The second flow chart cost $5. Keep your eye on the trend of crowdsourcing.

Sources: Jeff Howe, "The Rise of Crowdsourcing," *Wired*, June 2006, 176; Katherine Mieszkowski, "I Make $1.45 a Week, and I Love It!," http://www.salon.com, August 2006; http://www.wikipedia.org, August 2006.

players, Apple was able to take advantage of its lower costs by aggressively cutting prices.[68] To obtain these advantages, however, modular organizations need reliable partners—vendors and suppliers that they can work closely with and can trust.

Modular organizations have disadvantages, too. The primary disadvantage is the loss of control that occurs when key business activities are outsourced to other companies. Also, companies may reduce their competitive advantage in two ways if they mistakenly outsource a core business activity. First, as a result of competitive and technological change, the noncore business activities a company has outsourced may suddenly become the basis for competitive advantage. Second, related to that point, suppliers to whom work is outsourced can sometimes become competitors.

5.2 Virtual Organizations

In contrast to modular organizations in which the interorganizational process revolves around a central company, a **virtual organization** is part of a network in which many companies share skills, costs, capabilities, markets, and customers with each other. Exhibit 9.14 shows a virtual organization in which, for "today," the parts of a virtual company consist of product design, purchasing, manufacturing, advertising, and information technology. Unlike modular organizations, in which the outside organizations are tightly linked to one central company, virtual organizations work with some companies in the network alliance, but not with all. So, whereas a puzzle with various pieces is a fitting metaphor for a modular organization, a potluck dinner is an appropriate metaphor for a virtual organization. All participants bring their finest food dish, but eat only what they want.

Another difference is that the working relationships between modular organizations and outside companies tend to be more stable and longer lasting than the shorter, often temporary relationships found among the virtual companies in a network alliance. The composition of a virtual organization is always changing. The combination of network partners that a virtual corporation has at any one time depends on the expertise needed to solve a particular problem or provide a specific product or service. This is why the businessperson in the network organization shown in Exhibit 9.14 is saying, "Today, I'll have. . . ." Tomorrow, the business could want something completely different. In this sense, the term *virtual organization* means the organization that exists "at the moment." For example, 19 small companies in Pennsylvania have formed a network of virtual organizations that they call the AGILE WEB.[69] Together,

virtual organization an organization that is part of a network in which many companies share skills, costs, capabilities, markets, and customers to collectively solve customer problems or provide specific products or services the companies have expertise in product development and design, machining, metal fabrication, die casting, plastic-injection molding, finishing and coating, and the design and manufacture of electronic components. Tony Nickel, who coordinates business opportunities for the 19 Agile Web members, says, "We do have multiple machine shops and multiple sheet-metal shops. If only one is needed, I make the decision based on the nature of the [customer's] request and the areas of specialization of the member firms." He adds, "We've already had one occasion where, while negotiating with a customer, we discovered that we really didn't have the right Web member for a particular part—so we changed members."[70]

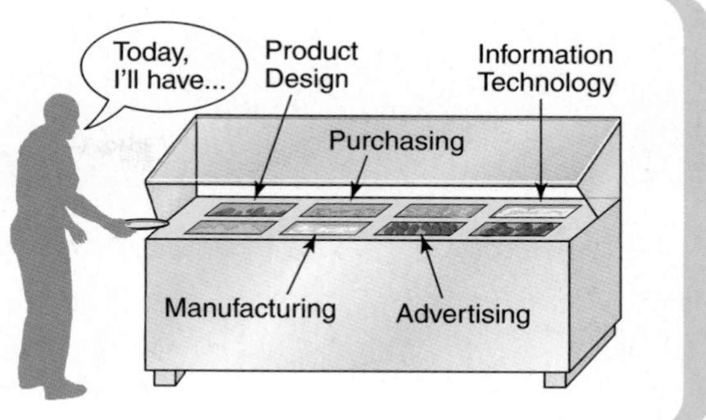

Exhibit 9.14
Virtual Organization

Virtual organizations have a number of advantages. They let companies share costs. And, because members can quickly combine their efforts to meet customers' needs, they are fast and flexible. For example, Tony Nickel of the Agile Web says, "Where we think we really can have rapid response is when a customer wants help in the design and building of an assembly or system. Then I can bring members of the Web to the table—or to the customer's facility—right away; the next day, if required. We are able to assemble a team from the Web within 24 hours if that is what the customer wants."[71] Finally, because each member of the network alliance is the "best" at what it does, virtual organizations should in theory provide better products and services in all respects.

As with modular organizations, a disadvantage of virtual organizations is that once work has been outsourced, it can be difficult to control the quality of work done by network partners. The greatest disadvantage, however, is that tremendous managerial skills are required to make a network of independent organizations work well together, especially since their relationships tend to be short and based on a single task or project. Virtual organizations are using two methods to solve this problem. The first is to use a *broker*, like Tony Nickel. In traditional, hierarchical organizations, managers plan, organize, and control. But with the horizontal, interorganizational processes that characterize virtual organizations, the job of a broker is to create and assemble the knowledge, skills, and resources from different companies for outside parties, such as customers.[72] The second way to make networks of virtual organizations more manageable is to use a *virtual organization agreement* that, somewhat like a contract, specifies the schedules, responsibilities, costs, payouts, and liabilities for participating organizations.[73] The AgileWeb has operationalized its virtual organization agreement on a day-to-day basis through web-based software that is used by all 19 companies to schedule work, share design specifications, and provide anything else they need to complete their work for particular customers.[74] For more information on how a virtual organization works, see **http://www.g5technologies.com/agileweb/overview/index.html.**

Review 5: Interorganizational Processes

Organizations are using modular and virtual organizations to change interorganizational processes. Because modular organizations outsource all noncore activities to other businesses, they are less expensive to run than traditional companies. However, modular organizations require extremely close relationships with suppliers, may result in a loss of control, and could create new competitors if the wrong business activities are outsourced. Virtual organizations participate in a network in which they share skills, costs, capabilities, markets, and customers. As customer problems, products, or services change, the combination of virtual organizations that work together changes. Virtual organizations can reduce costs, respond quickly, and, if they can successfully coordinate their efforts, produce outstanding products and service.

SELF ASSESSMENT

Flexibility and Structure

Every organization needs some degree of flexibility and standardization. In other words, companies need to have enough flexibility in their organizations to respond to changes in their business environment, but firms also must have certain structures in place to ensure smooth operations. For example, if someone gets hurt on company property, clear procedures about what to do in the case of an accident help managers respond quickly and confidently. But being overly committed to following rules can hamstring an organization and keep it from growing. As a manager, you will probably encounter both types of situations, and to respond appropriately you will need to have an idea of how comfortable you are in a formal environment versus a more loosely structured workplace. Every organization needs some degree of flexibility to adapt to new situations, and some degree of standardization to make routine tasks and decisions as efficient and effective as possible.[75] In this assessment, indicate the extent to which you agree or disagree with the following statements. Use this scale for your responses:

1	Strongly disagree
2	Disagree
3	Slightly disagree
4	Neutral
5	Slightly agree
6	Agree
7	Strongly agree

1. If a written rule does not cover some situation, we make up informal rules for doing things as we go along.
   1 2 3 4 5 6 7
2. I feel that I am my own boss in most matters.
   1 2 3 4 5 6 7
3. There are many things in my business that are not covered by some formal procedure.
   1 2 3 4 5 6 7
4. A person can make his or her own decisions without checking with somebody else.
   1 2 3 4 5 6 7
5. Usually, my contact with my company and its representatives involves doing things "by the rule book."
   1 2 3 4 5 6 7
6. How things are done here is left up to the person doing the work.
   1 2 3 4 5 6 7
7. Contacts with my company and its representatives are on a formal, preplanned basis.
   1 2 3 4 5 6 7
8. People here are allowed to do almost anything as they please.
   1 2 3 4 5 6 7

KEY TERMS

authority 318
autonomy 326
behavioral formality 333
behavioral informality 333
centralization of authority 321
chain of command 319
complex matrix 318
customer departmentalization 314
decentralization 321
delegation of authority 320
departmentalization 312
empowering workers 332
empowerment 332
feedback 326
functional departmentalization 312
geographic departmentalization 315
internal motivation 325
interorganizational process 337
intraorganizational process 330
job characteristics model (JCM) 324
job design 323
job enlargement 324
job enrichment 324
job rotation 324
job specialization 323
line authority 319
line function 319
matrix departmentalization 315
mechanistic organization 327
modular organization 337
open office systems 334
organic organization 327
organizational process 311
organizational structure 310
pooled interdependence 331
private spaces 335

9. I ignore the rules and reach informal agreements to handle some situations.
   1 2 3 4 5 6 7
10. Most people here make their own rules on the job.
   1 2 3 4 5 6 7
11. When rules and procedures exist in my company, they are usually written agreements.
   1 2 3 4 5 6 7
12. The employees are constantly being checked on for rule violations.
   1 2 3 4 5 6 7
13. People here feel as though they are constantly being watched, to see that they obey all the rules
   1 2 3 4 5 6 7

Scoring

Determine your score by entering your response to each survey item below, as follows. In blanks that say *regular score*, simply enter your response for that item. If your response was a 6, place a 6 in the *regular* score blank. In blanks that say *reverse score*, subtract your response from 8 and enter the result. So if your response was a 6, place a 2 (8 – 6 = 2) in the *reverse score* blank.

1. reverse score _____
2. reverse score _____
3. reverse score _____
4. reverse score _____
5. regular score _____
6. reverse score _____
7. regular score _____
8. reverse score _____
9. reverse score _____
10. reverse score _____
11. regular score _____
12. regular score _____
13. regular score _____

TOTAL = _____

You can see where you fall on the formality continuum and find the interpretation of your score at: **academic .cengage.com/ management/williams.**

(continued)

MANAGEMENT DECISION

Garbage Jobs

Glancing at the newspaper machine in the lobby, you are happy to see the headline proclaiming the end of the garbage collectors' strike in a nearby city.[76] That kind of strike tends to have a ripple effect on neighboring areas, and as the manager of a private waste collection company in the region, you breathe a sigh of relief.

Nonetheless, as you walk to your office, you can't help thinking about the job of your garbage collectors. It's repetitive, hot (or cold, depending on the season), anonymous, and relatively thankless. Your employees work in pairs, so each truck has one driver and one "thrower"—not much variety for either worker. There's not much on-the-job interaction either, as the driver is in the cab and the thrower rides on the back of the truck. And with the company looking into purchasing newer trucks that automatically lift and dump the garbage cans, you may even go to one person per truck.

In addition, to minimize the time it takes to collect the trash, you assign each team to the same neighborhood week after week. That ensures maximum efficiency: drivers subconsciously time traffic lights, pace themselves for starts and stops, and know the route without needing to consult a map. Even when collectors know the route, the work can be grueling. Each route has to be finished each day; no one will tolerate garbage left on the curb after the assigned pickup day. So even if a traffic accident or construction brings traffic to a standstill, the garbage has to be collected each day according to schedule.

The more you think about it, the more the job sounds dull—and somewhat stressful. As you fire up your computer and begin to look at your favorite industry blog, you wonder if you can make the job more interesting for your employees. Scanning the screen, you link to an article about a region in Britain that is putting defibrillators in garbage trucks to complement the ambulance service in rural areas. Well, that's not quite what you had in mind for making garbage collecting interesting for your employees, but still, it's something.

Questions

1. Can you use the job characteristics model (JCM) to redesign the job of the trash collector to be internally motivating? How?
2. Assume that the trash collection job is not internally motivating. Identify areas where you can strengthen the job's core characteristics and give specific examples.
3. Is it possible to redesign the very specialized job of a garbage collector to make it more satisfying? Is a redesign feasible? In other words, do you redesign the job or keep it as is? Explain your reasoning.

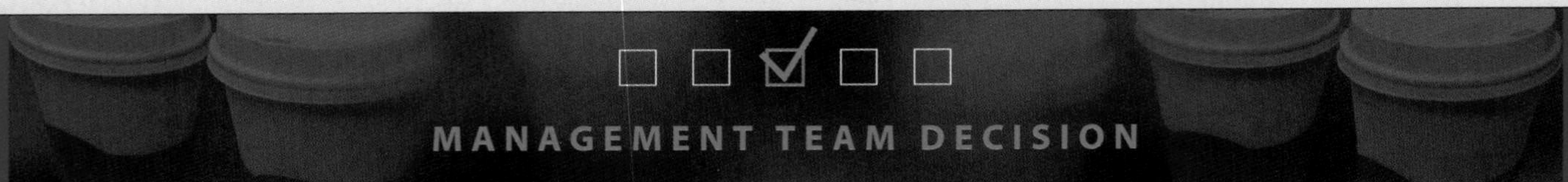

Letting Go at Lego

By definition, toys should be fun. Unfortunately for you, competing in today's toy industry is anything but.[77] Cutthroat competition and children's changing interests have pushed toymakers to consolidate, cut costs, and grow through licensing agreements with media giants like Disney and Nickelodeon, something many toymakers consider to be selling out.

No one needs to explain the crushing pressure to you—you're the new CEO of Lego, the first outsider in the company's history to run the family-owned business—because you were hired to save the company from sure decline. Last year, Lego had over $1 billion in sales. Its proprietary manufacturing operation pumps out 15 billion components a year—that's 1.7 million bricks, Lego people, and other elements per hour. By the numbers, Lego is the world's leading tire maker, producing 306 million tiny rubber tires a year for its sets. Lego's iconic bricks are so versatile that with a pack of only six bricks, a child can create 915,103,765 unique configurations. It's no wonder that Lego beat out Barbie and the teddy bear to be named Toy of the Century by *Fortune* magazine and by the British Toy Retailers Association.

Despite the volume of product being produced, the perennial accolades, and a reputation for nurturing creativity in children, Lego is losing money at an alarming rate. On last year's $1 billion in sales, the company lost a whopping $240 million. It also carries about $750 million in debt. That means you begin your stint as CEO squarely behind the eight ball. First on your list of things to do: change the company mission from "nurturing the child" to "I'm here to make money for the company."

Part of what's weighing Lego down is the fact that the company does it all. Lego uses its own designers to develop new products; other companies use a combination of in-house talent and innovation labs to come up with new product ideas. Lego manufactures its bricks (and other products) on extruding machines it developed itself at company-owned factories in Denmark and Switzerland, where labor costs are stratospheric; 70 percent of the world's toys are manufactured in China by contract manufacturers hired just to produce the toys and with labor that costs pennies on the kroner. Lego distributes all of its own products; other companies use third-party logistics companies like DHL and UPS to manage distribution. Lego even books $5.2 million in travel a year through an in-house travel agency that uses proprietary software; most companies use dedicated travel services, like American Express Travel.

To bring Lego back into the black, you've got to cut costs, and the fastest way to cut costs is outsourcing. The biggest savings would come from outsourcing your production, but that also carries the biggest risks. Controlling your manufacturing would be difficult. You'd have to share your machinery technology—what if a contractor started using your technology and specifications to make black-market Legos, something not at all inconceivable if you outsourced to China? And there's the fact that Legos are part of the fabric of Billund, the Danish town of 6,500 where the bricks were invented and where Lego's headquarters employs most of the company's 8,000 workers. Most of the people in Billund work for Lego. Still, savings from outsourcing manufacturing alone would bring the company to nearly break-even levels.

Controlling distribution helps you manage inventories and track sales trends, but should Lego really operate its own distribution network? So many companies specialize in this area that it's hard to equal their capabilities. Even something that is as seemingly easy to outsource as travel is not so easy. In-house travel agents know the ins and outs of Lego's travel policy; an outside provider is not always able to recognize a breach in the policy. Lego managers book 10,000 air tickets a year, and the head of the travel department says her team saves the company $325,000 in administrative costs alone over working with an outside company.

One thing is certain: You're not going to be able to make a decision on what to outsource (if anything) without consulting your management team. Form a team of four or five students to act as the management team for Lego. You may want to refer to Exhibit 9.13 as you work through the following questions.

Questions

1. What risks, if any, does outsourcing pose to Lego's corporate identity?
2. What do you think Lego's core and noncore business activities should be?
3. Do you outsource production, which will by itself achieve your cost-cutting goal, or do you outsource a smattering of other functions and keep Lego a "toymaker" rather than a "toy marketer"?

PRACTICE BEING A MANAGER

Effective organization is vital to the accomplishment of company objectives. Two critical aspects of effective organization are departmentalization and the design of jobs. In this role play exercise you will have the opportunity to experience some of the work dynamics surrounding the grouping of workers and the design of jobs.

Step 1: Form work groups. Your professor will form groups, and give you a role assignment.

Step 2: Review your role. Read your role assignment carefully and prepare to begin working per your role assignment.

Step 3 (10–20 minutes): Begin acting. When your professor directs you to begin you should start working as assigned by your role.

Step 4: Compile your results. Total your results by work group, and compare across the teams.

Step 5: Debrief as a class. Discuss the results as a class. What factors seemed to play a role in the efficiency and effectiveness of the work groups? What role did organization and job design play? If this were an actual organizational work group, what might you do to improve performance and worker satisfaction?

DEVELOP YOUR CAREER POTENTIAL

"Work" in Someone Else's Shoes

Why is learning to see things from someone else's perspective one of the most difficult things to do in today's workplace? Sometimes, the inability to see things as others see them has to do with the people involved. Inexperience, ignorance, and selfishness can all play a role. In most organizations, however, the inability to see things from someone else's perspective results from the jobs themselves, not the people who do them. Because jobs limit who we talk to, what we talk about, what we think about, and what we care about at work, it should not be a surprise that people who perform different jobs have very different views about each other and the workplace.

For example, at Southwest Airlines the pilots who fly the planes and the ground crews who unload, load, and refuel them had little appreciation for each other. The ground crews felt that the pilots treated them like second-class citizens. The pilots couldn't understand why the ground crews weren't doing more to get their planes out of the gates and in the air as fast as possible. To improve understanding and help them see things from each other's perspective, Southwest created a program called Cutting Edge, in which the captains and ground crews learned a lot about each other's jobs. For example, the pilots brought the ground crews into their cockpits and showed them the detailed processes they were required to follow to get planes ready for departure. The pilots, on the other hand, gained appreciation and understanding by actually working as members of Southwest's ground crews. After several days of demanding ground crew work, Southwest pilot Captain Mark Boyter said:

> *I remember one time when I was working the ramp [as a member of a ground crew] in Los Angeles. I was dead tired. I had flown that morning and had a couple of legs in, so I got out of my uniform and jumped into my ramp clothes. That afternoon was very hot. It was in the 80s—I can't imagine how they do it on a 120-degree day in Phoenix. I was tired and hungry and hadn't had a break. Then I saw this pilot sitting up there in the cockpit eating his frozen yogurt. I said to myself, "Man, I'd like to be up there now." Then I caught myself. I'm up there every day. Now, I know that pilot has been up since 3:00 in the morning. I know that he's been flying an airplane since 6:00* AM. *I know it's 3:00 in the afternoon and he hasn't had a chance to get off and have a meal yet today. I know all that, and yet, the yogurt still looks really good to me. Then I thought, "How can a ramp agent [on the ground crew] in Los Angeles who works his butt off for two or three years, working double shifts two or three times a week, understand this? It hit me that there's a big gap in understanding here."*[78]

The misunderstandings between Southwest's pilots and ground crews are not unique. All organizations experience them. Nurses and doctors, teachers and students, and managers and employees all have difficulty seeing things from each other's perspective. As Southwest's Cutting Edge program shows, however, you can minimize differences and build understanding by "working" in someone else's shoes.

Questions

1. Describe the job-related differences or tensions where you work. Who is involved? What jobs do they do? Explain why the job-related differences or tensions exist.
2. Since the best way to see things from someone else's perspective is to "work" in his or her shoes, see if you can spend a day, a morning, or even two hours performing one of these jobs. If that's not possible, spend some time carefully observing the jobs and then interview several people who perform them. Describe your boss's reaction to this request. Was he or she supportive? Why or why not?
3. Answer the following questions after you have worked the job or conducted your interviews. What most surprised you about this job? What was easiest? What was hardest? Explain. Now that you've had the chance to see things as others see them, what do you think would happen, good or bad, from letting other people in your organization work in someone else's shoes? Explain.

***Trivia answer: The original Mechanical Turk was an 18th-century chess playing automaton that purportedly could beat anyone at chess. The Turk was a mannequin, but the machine concealed a human chess master who would actuate the Turk with mechanical controls. The Turk beat many statesmen and luminaries, including Napoleon Bonaparte and Benjamin Franklin. Read more in Tom Standage's book* The Mechanical Turk.**

REEL TO REAL

BIZ FLIX

Reality Bites

Reality Bites is an American film starring Winona Ryder, Ethan Hawke, Ben Stiller, Steve Zahn, Janeane Garofalo, and David Spade. The plot follows the life of recent college graduate Lelaine Pierce (Ryder), who wants to make a documentary about her friends as a way to capture the strife and problems confronting her generation. In this scene, she is applying for a job at Wienerschnitzel, a fast-food restaurant managed by David Spade.

What to Watch for and Ask Yourself

1. Using the terms from the chapter, outline the job of cashier as Spade is describing it in the clip.
2. Is the cashier position a line or staff function?
3. Describe the atmosphere at the restaurant.

MANAGEMENT WORKPLACE

Lonely Planet's World Is Flat

When travelers Tony and Maureen Wheeler founded Lonely Planet in the early 1970s, they didn't intend to create a globe-spanning company. They didn't necessarily plan to start a publishing company. As newlyweds, they had just completed an overland trip from London through Asia, winding up in Australia. All they really wanted to do was finance their next trip—it never occurred to them to stop traveling around the world. So they wrote and published the first Lonely Planet guidebook, *Across Asia on the Cheap*; it was an instant bestseller among world wanderers.

With just two people, the Wheelers naturally didn't think about organization. They traveled, wrote, and published whatever they wanted. By the mid-1970s, they had completed *Nepal and Trekking in the Himalayas* and were working on a group of guides covering Australia, Europe, Africa, and New Zealand. In 1981, *Lonely Planet India* was published and became a travel best-seller. By then, Lonely Planet had a staff of 10. Watch the video to see how the Wheelers organized Lonely Planet's management workplace.

What to Watch for and Ask Yourself

1. In what ways is Lonely Planet decentralized? In what ways is it centralized?
2. What type of departmentalization does Lonely Planet use? Do you think another type of departmentalization would be as or more successful? Which one? Why?
3. How does Lonely Planet benefit from its flat organizational structure (limited hierarchy)? What does a flat structure indicate about the organization?

CHAPTER 10

Managing Teams

© ASSOCIATED PRESS

Learning Outcomes:

1 Explain the good and bad of using teams.
2 Recognize and understand the different kinds of teams.
3 Understand the general characteristics of work teams.
4 Explain how to enhance work team effectiveness.

In This Chapter:

WHAT WOULD YOU DO?

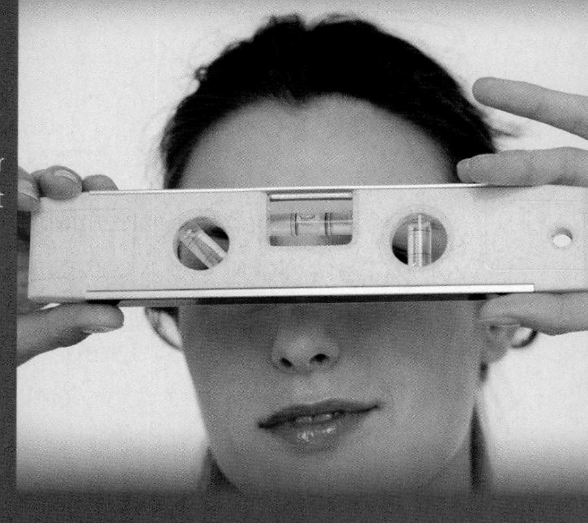

Kaiser Permanente, Oakland, California.[1] With 8.5 million health plan members in nine states and Washington, D.C., 148,884 employees, 12,879 physicians, 37 medical centers, 400 medical offices, and $31.1 billion in operating revenues, Kaiser Permanente is the largest not-for-profit managed care organization in the U.S. Overall, Kaiser has a solid reputation. Consumer Reports ranks Kaiser Permanente as an average or better hospital system. U.S. News and World Report ranks Kaiser Permanente Northern California 58th out of 257 health plans and Kaiser Permanente Southern California as 88th.

But lately Kaiser has come under intensive scrutiny for a series of management and patient care issues. For example, after Northern California Kaiser Permanente began an in-house program that required kidney transplant candidates to obtain medical treatment through their local Kaiser medical center, 56 people received kidney transplants, but twice that many died waiting for a kidney. In contrast, at other California transplant centers, more than twice as many people received kidneys than died during the same period. Another serious problem came to light when the California Office of Statewide Health Planning and Development determined that Kaiser had 5 of the 28 hospitals with the highest pneumonia death rates in the state. This was particularly troubling because pneumonia, the sixth-leading cause of death in the U.S., can be prevented with good care. "Timely diagnosis and treatment can greatly improve a patient's chances of surviving," said Mary Tran, a patient data analysis manager who helped with the study for the state agency. In other words, frequent pneumonia in your hospitals means that your medical control processes are breaking down. A well-run hospital system like Kaiser should not have problems treating pneumonia. Something is going wrong. But what?

You immediately pull your top managers together to analyze the problem and come up with potential solutions. One of your vice presidents mentioned that she had read that a number of hospitals use teams to improve patient care and service, maintain a clean and sanitary environment, manage costs, reduce patient mortality rate, and reduce medical errors. For instance, Baptist Memphis Hospital in Memphis, Tennessee, empowered Rapid Response Teams to call in the hospital's Medical Emergency Team to care for seriously ill patients whose condition was worsening. After doing so, the number of cardiac arrests dropped by 26 percent, and survival rates nearly doubled from 13 percent to 24 percent. Likewise, Stanford University Hospital uses Patient-Centered Care Teams, who are responsible for everything from admission to discharge, and Process-Centered Care Teams, who are charged with identifying hospital processes and making them effective and efficient.

Successful teams might help Kaiser reduce medical errors, increase quality of patient care, increase customer satisfaction, and could help reduce costs. And, you have to try new approaches, because not taking any action is no longer an option. You realize if you are going to use teams that you'll have to do your homework by answering these questions. First, does it make sense for Kaiser to use teams, and, if so, what kind of teams should it use and where? Second, how should people who work on teams be trained and paid? You have to find a way to encourage individual initiative, while at the same time encouraging people to work together on teams. Also, it's incredibly difficult to attract and retain nurses and highly trained medical personnel, so don't overlook that as you consider what to do. Third, who leads the teams, physicians, managers, or employees? And what roles should those leaders play? Finally, how large or small should the teams be and how do you build cohesion and make sure the team norms are functional and productive. **If you were in charge at Kaiser, what would you do?**

ACTIVITIES + VIDEO

CengageNOW Audio study guide, electronic flashcards, author FAQ videos, On the Job and Biz Flix videos, concept tutorial, and concept exercise

Web (academic.cengage.com/management/williams) Quiz, PowerPoint slides, and glossary terms for this chapter

Study Tip

Make up a crossword puzzle using the key terms in this chapter. Writing the clues will help you remember the definition and the context of each concept. Make photocopies for exam time and for your study group.

"What's New" Companies

- Three Counties
- Longaberger Company
- Whole Foods
- Industrial Light & Magic
- Ford Motor Company
- Orpheus Chamber Orchestra
- General Electric
- Eaton Corporation
- And others . . .

A growing number of organizations are significantly improving their effectiveness by establishing work teams. In fact, 91 percent of U.S. companies use teams and groups of one kind or another to solve specific problems.[2] Nonetheless, with the exception of early adopters such as Procter & Gamble and Cummins Engine, which began using teams in 1962 and 1973, respectively, many companies did not establish work teams until the mid to late 1980s. Boeing, Caterpillar, Champion International, Ford Motor Company, and General Electric, for example, set up their first teams in the 1980s.[3] So, most companies have been using teams for only 20 to 25 years, if that long. In other words, teams are a relatively new phenomenon in companies, and there's still much for organizations to learn about managing them.

We begin this chapter by reviewing the advantages and disadvantages of teams and exploring when companies should use them instead of more traditional approaches. Next, we discuss the different types of work teams and the characteristics common to all teams. The chapter ends by focusing on the practical steps to managing teams—team goals and priorities, and organizing, training, and compensating teams.

WHY WORK TEAMS?

Work teams consist of a small number of people with complementary skills who hold themselves mutually accountable for pursuing a common purpose, achieving performance goals, and improving interdependent work processes.[4] By this definition, computer programmers working on separate projects in the same department of a company would not be considered a team. To be a team, the programmers would have to be interdependent and share responsibility and accountability for the quality and amount of computer code they produced.[5] In many industries, teams are growing in importance because they help organizations respond to specific problems and challenges. Though work teams are not the answer for every situation or organization, if the right teams are used properly and in the right settings, teams can dramatically improve company performance over more traditional management approaches and instill a sense of vitality in the workplace that is otherwise difficult to achieve.

After reading the next two sections, you should be able to

1. *explain the good and bad of using teams.*
2. *recognize and understand the different kinds of teams.*

1 The Good and Bad of Using Teams

*Let's begin our discussion of teams by learning about **1.1 the advantages of teams**, **1.2 the disadvantages of teams**, and **1.3 when to use and not use teams**.*

work team a small number of people with complementary skills who hold themselves mutually accountable for pursuing a common purpose, achieving performance goals, and improving interdependent work processes

1.1 The Advantages of Teams

Companies are making greater use of teams because teams have been shown to improve customer satisfaction, product and service quality, speed and efficiency in product development, employee job satisfaction, and decision making.[6] For example, one survey indicated that 80 percent of companies with more than 100 employees use teams, and 90 percent of all U.S. employees work part of their day in a team.[7]

Teams help businesses increase *customer satisfaction* in several ways. One way is to create work teams that are trained to meet the needs of specific customers. Hewitt Associates, a consulting firm, manages benefits administration for hundreds of multinational client firms. To ensure customer satisfaction, Hewitt reengineered its customer service center and created specific teams to handle benefits-related questions posed by employees of specific client organizations.[8] Similarly, ***THREE COUNTIES***, a fund and portfolio management company, uses a team structure in which specific teams are responsible for specific groups of customers, thereby ensuring high quality service necessary for customer satisfaction.[9]

Businesses also create problem-solving teams and employee involvement teams to study ways to improve overall customer satisfaction and make recommendations for improvements. Teams like these typically meet on a weekly or monthly basis. Every day at the **LONGABERGER COMPANY**, 2,500 skilled weavers make over 40,000 high-quality baskets (which sell for $30 to $260). When productivity began to drop, management turned to an employee involvement group to solve the problem. After studying 40 basket makers for three weeks, the team found that the weavers often had the wrong materials. The team came up with a solution that makes sure each weaver has the proper kinds of wood veneers used to make the different baskets. Before the new system, workers ran out of the proper materials 53 times per day. Now, that happens only 9 times per day. And because the new system has also cut scrap (leftover, unusable materials) by 75 percent, the company is saving $3 million per year.[10]

Teams also help firms improve *product and service quality* in several ways.[11] In contrast to traditional organizational structures where management is responsible for organizational outcomes and performance, teams take direct responsibility for the quality of the products and service they produce. At ***WHOLE FOODS***, a supermarket chain that sells groceries and health foods, the 10 teams that manage each store are responsible for store quality and performance; they are also directly accountable because the size of their team bonus depends on the store's performance. Productive teams get an extra $1.50 to $2.00 per hour in every other paycheck. As a result, Whole Food teams don't want friends on their teams—they want talented, productive workers.[12] And making teams directly responsible for service and product quality pays off. At Whole Foods, comparable store sales, meaning a particular store's sales this year compared with its sales last year, are increasing between 7.7 and 10 percent per year on average! Likewise, a survey by *Industry Week* found that 42 percent of the companies that use teams report revenues of more than $250,000 per employee, compared with only 25 percent of the companies that don't use teams.[13]

A team-based structure is part of the reason for the resounding success of Whole Foods Market. Employee teams are responsible for all aspects of the store's operations. This Whole Foods team is in charge of preparing the seafood section for the opening of the New York City store.

GETTY IMAGES

As you learned in Chapter 7, companies that are slow to innovate or integrate new features and technologies into their products are at a competitive disadvantage. Therefore, a third reason that teams are increasingly popular is that they can increase *speed and efficiency when designing and manufacturing products*.[14] Traditional product design proceeds sequentially, meaning that one department, such as engineering or manufacturing, has to finish its work on the design before the next department, such as marketing, can start. Unfortunately, not only is sequential development slow, but it also encourages departments to work in isolation from one another.[15] A faster and better way to design products is to use *overlapping development phases*, which often requires the use of teams. With overlapping development phases, teams of employees, consisting of members from the different functional areas in a firm (such as engineering, manufacturing, and marketing), work on the product design at the same time. Because all of the different functional areas are involved in the design process from the start, the company can avoid most of the delays and frustration associated with sequential development.

"What's New" Company

Industrial Light & Magic (ILM), founded by George Lucas, the originator and producer of *Star Wars*, has won 19 Academy Awards for visual effects and technical achievement. ILM uses overlapping development phases to quickly produce specialized computer effects for movies. Teams of artists and animators work simultaneously on different scenes, such as the opening and closing of a movie, to speed up production. Visual-effects producer Jacqui Lopez says, "When we get down to the wire, our artists need every second they can get in front of their computers."[16] Oftentimes, she says, "Being late is not an option. The publicity is already locked in, and the studios have schedules to keep. We can't be late."[17] And ILM has *never* been late. Indeed, whether the movie is *Harry Potter* or *Pirates of the Caribbean*, when film studios and directors fall behind, they regularly come to ILM to avoid missing deadlines.

> Being late is not an option. The publicity is already locked in, and the studios have schedules to keep. We can't be late.
>
> JACQUI LOPEZ, VISUAL-EFFECTS PRODUCER, INDUSTRIAL LIGHT & MAGIC

Another reason for using teams is that teamwork often leads to increased *job satisfaction*.[18] One reason that teamwork can be more satisfying than traditional work is that it gives workers a chance to improve their skills. This is often accomplished through **cross-training**, in which team members are taught how to do all or most of the jobs performed by the other team members. Mary Keene used to stand in one spot for eight hours a day using a power chisel to chip cast iron from Ford automobile engines. She says, "You thought your arms would fall off. It was the worst job I had there." Today, thanks to cross-training, Mary and her Plant 2 coworkers at

Ford Motor Company's Brook Park, Ohio, manufacturing facility perform seven different jobs each shift, such as installing ignition coils, taking apart engines, restarting machinery after it breaks down, and contacting suppliers if engine parts are of subpar quality.[19] The advantage for the organization is that cross-training allows a team to function normally when one member is absent, quits, or is transferred. The advantage for workers is that cross-training broadens their skills and increases their capabilities while also making their work more varied and interesting. Indeed, Ford's Mary Keene says, "Plant 2 is the best we've ever had it." Huck Granakis, the United Auto Workers' building chairman and a member of Plant 2's operating committee, says, "They love it. I know of no one who has quit to go to another job."[20]

A second reason that teamwork is satisfying is that work teams often receive proprietary business information that is available only to managers at most companies. For example, at Whole Foods, the supermarket chain that sells groceries and health foods, team members are given full access to their store's financial information and everyone's salaries, including those of the store manager and the

cross-training training team members to do all or most of the jobs performed by the other team members

CEO.[21] Each day, next to the time clock, Whole Foods employees can see the previous day's sales for each team, as well as the sales on the same day from the previous year. Each week, team members can examine the same information, broken down by team, for all of the Whole Foods stores in their region. And each month, store managers review information on profitability, including sales, product costs, wages, and operating profits, with each team in the store. Since team members decide how much to spend, what to order, what things should cost, and how many team members should work each day, this information is critical to making teams work at Whole Foods.[22] Whole Foods creates an empowering work environment to honor one of its core values: "supporting team member excellence and happiness."[23]

Team members also gain job satisfaction from unique leadership responsibilities that typically are not available in traditional organizations. For example, in contrast to most orchestras, which are led by one conductor who is clearly in charge, at the award-winning, New York City–based **Orpheus Chamber Orchestra**, the concertmaster's role, as they call it, is rotated among different members of the orchestra. Flutist Susan Palma-Nidel says that assuming the concertmaster's role "has allowed me to discover strengths that I didn't know I had. Not only have I helped lead the group, but I've also been interviewed by the media—something I never thought I'd do. If I hadn't been forced to do those things, I'm not sure that I ever would have."[24] Furthermore, rotating leadership among team members can lead to more participation and cooperation in team decision making and improved team performance.[25]

Finally, teams share many of the advantages of group decision making discussed in Chapter 5. For instance, because team members possess different knowledge, skills, abilities, and experiences, a team is able to view problems from multiple perspectives. This diversity of viewpoints increases the odds that team decisions will solve the underlying causes of problems and not just address the symptoms. The increased knowledge and information available to teams also make it easier for them to generate more alternative solutions, which is a critical part of improving the quality of decisions. Because team members are involved in decision-making processes, they are also likely to be more committed to making those decisions work. In short, teams can do a much better job than individuals in two important steps of the decision-making process: defining the problem and generating alternative solutions. Exhibit 10.1 summarizes the advantages and disadvantages of teams (disadvantages are discussed in the next section).

Exhibit 10.1

Advantages and Disadvantages of Teams

ADVANTAGES	DISADVANTAGES
Customer satisfaction	Initially high employee turnover
Product and service quality	Social loafing
Speed and efficiency in product development	Disadvantages of group decision making (groupthink, inefficient meetings, domination by a minority, lack of accountability)
Employee job satisfaction	
Better decision making and problem solving (multiple perspectives, more alternative solutions, increased commitment to decisions)	

doing the right thing

Don't Be a Team Slacker—Do Your Share

Given the amount of teamwork required in business classes, most of you have encountered slackers in student groups. Perhaps you've even "slacked" yourself from time to time. From an ethical perspective, though, slacking is clearly wrong. In reality, it's no different from cheating on an exam. When you slack, you're relying on others to do your work. You benefit without putting forth effort. And "your" team's project, paper, or presentation hasn't benefited from your contributions. In fact, it's very likely that your slacking may have significantly hurt "your" team's performance. Furthermore, in the real world, the consequences of team slacking, such as lost sales, poorer decisions, lower-quality service or products, or lower productivity, are much larger. So, do the right thing. Whether it's in class or in business, don't be a slacker. Don't cheat your teammates. Pull your share of the "rope."

1.2 The Disadvantages of Teams

Although teams can significantly improve customer satisfaction, product and service quality, speed and efficiency in product development, employee job satisfaction, and decision making, using teams does not guarantee these positive outcomes. In fact, if you've ever participated in team projects in your classes, you're probably already aware of some of the problems inherent in work teams. Despite all of their promise, teams and teamwork are also prone to these significant disadvantages: initially high turnover, social loafing, and the problems associated with group decision making.

The first disadvantage of work teams is *initially high turnover*. Teams aren't for everyone, and some workers balk at the responsibility, effort, and learning required in team settings. When **GENERAL ELECTRIC**'s Salisbury plant switched to teams, the turnover rate jumped from near zero to 14 percent. Plant manager Roger Gasaway says of teams and teamwork, "It's not all wonderful stuff."[26] Other people may quit because they object to the way team members closely scrutinize each other's job performance, particularly when teams are small. Randy Savage, who works for **EATON CORPORATION**, a manufacturer of car and truck parts, said, "They say there are no bosses here, but if you screw up, you find one pretty fast." Beverly Reynolds, who quit Eaton's team-based system after nine months, says her coworkers "weren't standing watching me, but from afar, they were watching me." And even though her teammates were willing to help her improve her job performance, she concludes, "As it turns out, it just wasn't for me at all."[27]

Social loafing is another disadvantage of work teams. **Social loafing** occurs when workers withhold their efforts and fail to perform their share of the work.[28] A 19th-century French engineer named Maximilian Ringlemann first documented social loafing when he found that one person pulling on a rope alone exerted an average of 63 kilograms of force on the rope. In groups of three, the average force dropped to 53 kilograms per person. In groups of eight, the average dropped to just 31 kilograms per person. Ringlemann concluded that the larger the team, the smaller the individual effort. In fact, social loafing is more likely to occur in larger groups where identifying and monitoring the efforts of individual team members can be difficult.[29] In other words, social loafers count on being able to blend into the background, where their lack of effort isn't easily spotted. From team-based class projects, most students already know about social loafers or "slackers," who contribute poor, little, or no work whatsoever. Not surprisingly, a study of 250 student teams found that the most talented students are typically the least satisfied with teamwork because of having to carry "slackers" and do a disproportionate share of their team's work.[30] Perceptions of fairness are negatively related to the extent of social loafing within teams.[31]

social loafing behavior in which team members withhold their efforts and fail to perform their share of the work

How prevalent is social loafing on teams? One study found that when team activities were not mandatory, only 25 percent of manufacturing workers volunteered to

© DIGITAL VISION/GETTY IMAGES

join problem-solving teams, 70 percent were quiet, passive supporters (that is, they didn't put forth effort), and 5 percent were actively opposed to these activities.[32] Another study found that on management teams, 56 percent of the managers, or more than half, withheld their effort in one way or another. Exhibit 10.2 lists the factors that encourage people to withhold effort in teams.

Finally, teams share many of the *disadvantages of group decision making* discussed in Chapter 5, such as groupthink. In *groupthink*, members of highly cohesive groups feel intense pressure not to disagree with each other so that the group can approve a proposed solution. Because groupthink restricts discussion and leads to consideration of a limited number of alternative solutions, it usually results in poor decisions. Also, team decision making takes considerable time, and team meetings can often be unproductive and inefficient. Another possible pitfall is *minority domination*, where just one or two people dominate team discussions, thus restricting consideration of different problem definitions and alternative solutions. Finally, team members may not feel accountable for the decisions and actions taken by the "team."

1.3 When to Use Teams

As the two previous subsections made clear, teams have significant advantages *and* disadvantages. Therefore, the question is not whether to use teams, but when and where to use teams for maximum benefit and minimum cost. As Doug Johnson, associate director at the Center for Collaborative Organizations at the University of North Texas, puts it, "Teams are a means to an end, not an end in themselves. You have to ask yourself questions first. Does the work require interdependence? Will the team philosophy fit company strategy? Will management make a long-term commitment to this process?"[33] Exhibit 10.3 provides some additional guidelines on when to use or not use teams.[34]

Exhibit 10.2
Factors That Encourage People to Withhold Effort in Teams

1. **The presence of someone with expertise**. Team members will withhold effort when another team member is highly qualified to make a decision or comment on an issue.
2. **The presentation of a compelling argument**. Team members will withhold effort if the arguments for a course of action are very persuasive or similar to their own thinking.
3. **Lacking confidence in one's ability to contribute**. Team members will withhold effort if they are unsure about their ability to contribute to discussions, activities, or decisions. This is especially so for high-profile decisions.
4. **An unimportant or meaningless decision**. Team members will withhold effort by mentally withdrawing or adopting a "who cares" attitude if decisions don't affect them or their units, or if they don't see a connection between their efforts and their team's successes or failures.
5. **A dysfunctional decision-making climate**. Team members will withhold effort if other team members are frustrated or indifferent or if a team is floundering or disorganized.

Source: P. W. Mulvey, J. F. Veiga, & P. M. Elsass, "When Teammates Raise a White Flag," *Academy of Management Executive* 10, no. 1 (1996): 40–49.

USE TEAMS WHEN . . .	DON'T USE TEAMS WHEN . . .
✓ there is a clear, engaging reason or purpose.	X there isn't a clear, engaging reason or purpose.
✓ the job can't be done unless people work together.	X the job can be done by people working independently.
✓ rewards can be provided for teamwork and team performance.	X rewards are provided for individual effort and performance.
✓ ample resources are available.	X the necessary resources are not available.
✓ teams will have clear authority to manage and change how work gets done.	X management will continue to monitor and influence how work gets done.

Source: R. Wageman, "Critical Success Factors for Creating Superb Self-Managing Teams," *Organizational Dynamics* 26, no. 1 (1997): 49–61.

Exhibit 10.3

When to Use or Not Use Teams

First, teams should be used when there is a clear, engaging reason or purpose for using them. Too many companies use teams because they're popular or because the companies assume that teams can fix all problems. Teams are much more likely to succeed if they know why they exist and what they are supposed to accomplish, and more likely to fail if they don't. For example, at **CBS**, chief information officer Amy Berkowitz has split a sizable information technology staff into four different groups that support four kinds of company software—finance and administration, sales and traffic, programming and production, and interactive systems. Project managers oversee three to five dedicated work teams in each area. Berkowitz says, "The key is to make sure [the work teams] have a very focused purpose. And that they're very outcome-based."[35] Consequently, each support team is now measured on adaptability, speed, and innovation. Jon Katzenbach, coauthor of *The Wisdom of Teams*, supports Berkowitz's approach, saying, "If groups want to achieve team performance, the most important factor is not the leader of the team; it is the clarity around the performance purpose for that group. The more clear and compelling that is, the more naturally those people will function as a team."[36]

If groups want to achieve team performance, the most important factor is not the leader of the team; it is the clarity around the performance purpose for that group. The more clear and compelling that is, the more naturally those people will function as a team.

JON KATZENBACH, COAUTHOR, *THE WISDOM OF TEAMS*

Second, teams should be used when the job can't be done unless people work together. This typically means that teams are needed when tasks are complex, require multiple perspectives, or require repeated interaction with others to complete. For example, contrary to stories of legendary programmers who write software programs by themselves, **Microsoft** uses teams to write computer code because of the enormous complexity of today's software. Most software simply has too many options and features for one person (or even one team) to complete it all. Likewise, Microsoft uses teams because writing good software requires

repeated interaction with others. Microsoft ensures this interaction by having its teams "check in" their computer code every few days. The different pieces of code written by the different teams are then compiled to create an updated working build or prototype of the software. The next day, all the teams and team members begin testing and debugging the new build. Over and over again, the computer code is compiled, sent back to the teams to be tested and improved, and then compiled and tested again.[37]

If tasks are simple and don't require multiple perspectives or repeated interaction with others, however, teams should not be used.[38] For instance, production levels dropped by 23 percent when **LEVI STRAUSS** introduced teams in its factories. Levi Strauss's mistake was assuming that teams were appropriate for garment work, where workers perform single, specialized tasks, like sewing zippers or belt loops. Because this kind of work does not require interaction with others, Levi Strauss unwittingly pitted the faster workers against the slower workers on each team. Arguments, infighting, insults, and threats were common between faster workers and the slower workers who held back team performance. One seamstress even had to physically restrain an angry coworker who was about to throw a chair at a faster worker who constantly nagged her about her slow pace.[39]

Third, teams should be used when rewards can be provided for teamwork and team performance. Team rewards that depend on team performance, rather than individual performance, are the key to rewarding team behaviors and efforts. You'll read more about team rewards later in the chapter, but for now it's enough to know that if the level of rewards (individual versus team) is not matched to the level of performance (individual versus team), groups won't work. This was the case with Levi Strauss, where a team structure was superimposed on individual jobs that didn't require interaction between workers. After the switch to teams, faster workers placed tremendous pressure on slower workers to increase their production speed. And since pay was determined by team performance, top individual performers saw their pay drop by several dollars an hour, while slower workers saw their pay increase by several dollars an hour—all while overall productivity dropped in the plant.[40] Systems that reward individual performance but hope for high team-level performance are sure to fail.[41]

Review 1: The Good and Bad of Using Teams

In many industries, teams are growing in importance because they help organizations respond to specific problems and challenges. Teams have been shown to increase customer satisfaction (specific customer teams), product and service quality (direct responsibility), speed and efficiency in product development (overlapping development phases), and employee job satisfaction (cross-training, unique opportunities, and leadership responsibilities). Although teams can produce significant improvements in these areas, using teams does not guarantee these positive outcomes. Teams and teamwork have the disadvantages of initially high turnover and social loafing (especially in large groups). Teams also share many of the advantages (multiple perspectives, generation of more alternatives, and more commitment) and disadvantages (groupthink, time-consuming, poorly run meetings, domination by a few team members, and weak accountability) of group decision making. Finally, teams should be used for a clear purpose, when the work requires that people work together, when rewards can be provided for both teamwork and team performance, when ample resources can be provided, and when teams can be given clear authority over their work.

2 Kinds of Teams

Companies use different kinds of teams for different purposes. Google uses teams to innovate and develop new products and to tweak and improve its search algorithms and functions.[42] At Children's Hospital Boston, the use of teams and team-based rewards helped shorten the billing cycle by reducing the average number of days a bill spent in the accounts receivable department from 100 to just 65 days.[43]

Let's continue our discussion of teams by learning about the different kinds of teams that companies like Google and Maytag use to make themselves more competitive. We look first at ***2.1 how teams differ in terms of autonomy, which is the key dimension that makes one team different from another****, and then at* ***2.2 some special kinds of teams****.*

2.1 Autonomy, the Key Dimension

Teams can be classified in a number of ways, such as permanent or temporary, or functional or cross-functional. However, studies indicate that the key dimension that makes teams different from each another is the amount of autonomy possessed by a team.[44] *Autonomy* is the degree to which workers have the discretion, freedom, and independence to decide how and when to accomplish their jobs.

Exhibit 10.4 shows how five kinds of teams differ in terms of autonomy. Moving left to right across the autonomy continuum at the top of the exhibit, traditional work groups and employee involvement groups have the least autonomy, semi-autonomous work groups have more autonomy, and, finally, self-managing teams and self-designing teams have the most autonomy. Moving from bottom to top along the left side of the exhibit, note that the number of responsibilities given to each kind of team increases directly with its autonomy. Let's review each of these kinds of teams and their autonomy and responsibilities in more detail.

The smallest amount of autonomy is found in **traditional work groups**, where two or more people work together to achieve a shared goal. In these groups, workers are responsible for doing the work or "executing the task," but they do not have direct responsibility or control over their work. Workers report to managers, who are responsible for their performance and have the authority to hire and fire them, make job assignments, and control resources. For instance, suppose that an experienced worker blatantly refuses to do his share of the work, saying, "I've done my time. Let the younger employees do the work." In a team with high autonomy, the responsibility of getting this employee to put forth his fair share of effort would belong to his teammates. But in a traditional work group, that responsibility belongs to the boss or supervisor. The supervisor in this situation calmly confronted the employee and told him, "We need your talent, [and] your knowledge of these machines. But if you won't work, you'll have to go elsewhere." Within days, the employee's behavior improved.[45]

Employee involvement teams, which have somewhat more autonomy, meet on company time on a weekly or monthly basis to provide advice or make suggestions to management concerning specific issues, such as plant safety, customer relations, or product quality.[46] Though they offer advice and suggestions, they do not have the authority to make decisions. Membership on these teams is often voluntary, but members may be selected because of their expertise. The idea behind employee involvement teams is that the people closest to the problem or situation are best able to recommend solutions. When a large hospital found that it could

traditional work group a group composed of two or more people who work together to achieve a shared goal

employee involvement team team that provides advice or makes suggestions to management concerning specific issues

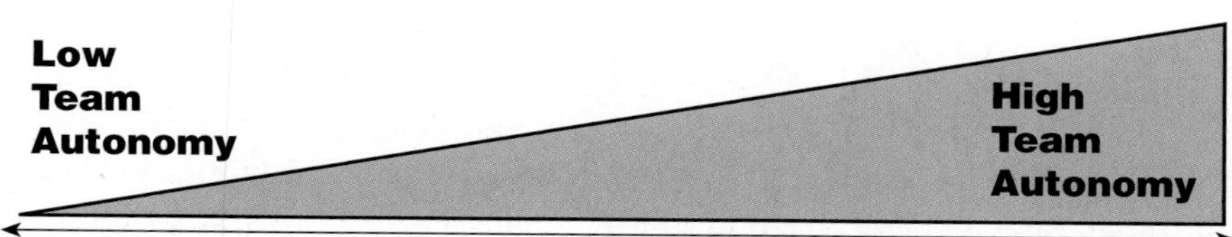

RESPONSIBILITIES	TRADITIONAL WORK GROUPS	EMPLOYEE INVOLVEMENT GROUPS	SEMI-AUTONOMOUS WORK GROUPS	SELF-MANAGING TEAMS	SELF-DESIGNING TEAMS
Control Design of					
Team					✓
Tasks					✓
Membership					✓
All Production/Service Tasks					
Make Decisions				✓	✓
Solve Problems				✓	✓
Major Production/Service Tasks					
Make Decisions			✓	✓	✓
Solve Problems			✓	✓	✓
Receive Information			✓	✓	✓
Give Advice/Make Suggestions		✓	✓	✓	✓
Execute Task	✓	✓	✓	✓	✓

Sources: R. D. Banker, J. M. Field, R. G. Schroeder, & K. K. Sinha, "Impact of Work Teams on Manufacturing Performance: A Longitudinal Field Study," *Academy of Management Journal* 39 (1996): 867–890; J. R. Hackman, "The Psychology of Self-Management in Organizations," in *Psychology and Work: Productivity, Change, and Employment*, ed. M. S. Pallak & R. Perlof (Washington, DC: American Psychological Association), 85–136.

Exhibit 10.4

Team Autonomy Continuum

no longer afford its expensive employee retirement plan, it turned to six employee involvement groups representing 3,000 workers for a solution. The groups analyzed the problem and then worked with retirement consultants (chosen by the groups) to generate new retirement options that were affordable, protected the retirement benefits that employees had already earned, and, in the end, were even better for employees.[47]

Semi-autonomous work groups not only provide advice and suggestions to management, but also have the authority to make decisions and solve problems related to the major tasks required to produce a product or service. Semi-autonomous groups regularly receive information about budgets, work quality and performance, and competitors' products. Furthermore, members of semi-autonomous work groups are typically cross-trained in a number of different skills and tasks. In short, semi-autonomous work groups give employees the authority to make decisions that are typically made by supervisors and managers.

semi-autonomous work group a group that has the authority to make decisions and solve problems related to the major tasks of producing a product or service

That authority is not complete, however. Managers still play a role, though much reduced compared with traditional work groups, in supporting the work of semi-autonomous work groups. The role a manager plays on a team usually evolves over time.

© THINKSTOCK/JUPITER IMAGES

"It may start with helping to transition problem-solving responsibilities to the team, filling miscellaneous requests for the team, and doing ad hoc tasks," says Steven Hitchcock, president of Axis Performance Advisors in Portland, Oregon. Later, the team may develop into a "mini-enterprise" and the former manager becomes externally focused—sort of an account manager for the customer. Managers have to adjust what they do based on the sophistication of the team, she explains.[48] A lot of what managers of semi-autonomous work groups do is ask good questions, provide resources, and facilitate performance of group goals.

Self-managing teams differ from semi-autonomous work groups in that team members manage and control *all* of the major tasks *directly related* to production of a product or service without first getting approval from management. This includes managing and controlling the acquisition of materials, making a product or providing a service, and ensuring timely delivery. At a CROWN CORK aluminum can factory in Texas, "The teams make and implement decisions regarding production, product quality, training, attendance, safety, maintenance, and certain types of discipline. The teams can stop production lines without management approval, stop delivery of cans that do not meet quality standards, decide which workers should receive training, decide whether to grant leave requests, and investigate and correct safety problems."[49] Seventy-two percent of *Fortune* 1,000 companies have at least one self-managing team, up from 28 percent in 1987.[50]

Self-designing teams have all the characteristics of self-managing teams, but they can also control and change the design of the teams themselves, the tasks they do and how and when they do them, and the membership of the teams. Two engineers, Roger Jellicoe and Gary Weiss, assembled a team of 20 for the "thin calm" project at MOTOROLA. Money and resources were no object, but secrecy and speed were. The team had complete control over all aspects of the project, and it delivered the Motorola RAZR V3. Since RAZR's launch in late 2004, it has sold almost as many units as Apple's iPod.[51]

2.2 Special Kinds of Teams

Companies are also increasingly using several other kinds of teams that can't easily be categorized in terms of autonomy: cross-functional teams, virtual teams, and project teams. Depending on how these teams are designed, they can be either low- or high-autonomy teams.

Cross-functional teams are intentionally composed of employees from different functional areas of the organization.[52] Because their members have different functional backgrounds, education, and experience, cross-functional teams usually attack problems from multiple perspectives and generate more ideas and alternative solutions, all of which are especially important when trying to innovate or do creative problem solving.[53] Cross-functional teams can be used almost anywhere in an organization and are often used in conjunction with matrix and product organizational structures (see Chapter 9). They can also be used either with part-time or temporary team assignments or with full-time, long-term teams.

CESSNA, which manufactures airplanes, created cross-functional teams for purchasing parts. With workers from purchasing, manufacturing engineering,

self-managing team a team that manages and controls all of the major tasks of producing a product or service

self-designing team a team that has the characteristics of self-managing teams but also controls team design, work tasks, and team membership

cross-functional team a team composed of employees from different functional areas of the organization quality engineering, product design engineering, reliability engineering, product support, and finance, each team addressed make-versus-buy decisions (make it themselves or buy from others), sourcing (who to buy from), internal plant and quality improvements, and the external training of suppliers to reduce costs and increase quality. The teams looked at every major parts category, from engines to wings to electronics. In the end, they came up with parts groups, such as sheet and plate aluminum, that could be completely outsourced to suppliers at lower cost and higher quality.[54]

Virtual teams are groups of geographically and/or organizationally dispersed coworkers who use a combination of telecommunications and information technologies to accomplish an organizational task.[55] Members of virtual teams rarely meet face-to-face; instead, they use e-mail, videoconferencing, and group communication software. For example, **pLotDevMultimedia Developers** is a website-development company of 12 people that does work for Sean Jean, P. Diddy's clothing label, among others. Yet the people in the company have never met. As Max Oshman, who started the company, describes it, "Some of them live in the U.K., two in Croatia, two in Sweden, and the rest are scattered around in southern California, New York, Texas, and Amsterdam." How do they communicate? Oshman says, "Mostly by e-mail. When we have a big project, we communicate via phone. We also have group talks using MSN Messenger."[56] Virtual teams can be employee involvement teams, self-managing teams, or nearly any kind of team discussed in this chapter. Virtual teams are often (but not necessarily) temporary teams that are set up to accomplish a specific task.[57]

The principal advantage of virtual teams is their flexibility. Employees can work with each other, regardless of physical location, time zone, or organizational affiliation.[58] Because the team members don't meet in a physical location, virtual teams also find it much easier to include other key stakeholders, such as suppliers and customers. Plus, virtual teams have certain efficiency advantages over traditional team structures. Because the teammates do not meet face-to-face, a virtual team typically requires a smaller time commitment than a traditional team does. Moreover, employees can fulfill the responsibilities of their virtual team membership from the comfort of their own offices, without the travel time or downtime typically required for face-to-face meetings.[59]

A drawback of virtual teams is that the team members must learn to express themselves in new contexts.[60] The give-and-take that naturally occurs in face-to-face meetings is more difficult to achieve through video conferencing or other methods of virtual teaming. For example, when an English-speaking member of a virtual, multinational website-development team e-mailed a Russian-speaking member that the website design she had developed was "awesome," the Russian-speaking member took offense and flamed an emotional e-mail back. At that point, other members of the team, all in different locations, started sending their own nasty e-mails. What caused the problem? The English-to-Russian website on which they relied incorrectly translated "awesome" as "awful." Chances are, this problem would not have occurred if the team members were working face-to-face.[61] Consistent with this example, several studies have shown that physical proximity enhances information processing.[62] Therefore, some companies bring virtual team members together on a regular basis to try to minimize these problems. Pat O'Day, who manages a five-person virtual team at accounting firm **KPMG** with members living in the states of Washington, Maryland, and Texas, says, "We communicate through e-mail and conference calls and meet in person four times a year."[63] Exhibit 10.5 provides a number of tips for successfully managing virtual teams.

virtual team a team composed of geographically and/or organizationally dispersed coworkers who use telecommunication and information technologies to accomplish an organizational task

- Select people who are self-starters and strong communicators.
- Keep the team focused by establishing clear, specific goals and by explaining the consequences and importance of meeting these goals.
- Provide frequent feedback so that team members can measure their progress.
- Keep team interactions upbeat and action-oriented by expressing appreciation for good work and completed tasks.
- "Personalize" the virtual team by periodically bringing team members together and by encouraging team members to share information with each other about their personal lives. This is especially important when the virtual team first forms.
- Improve communication through increased telephone calls, e-mails, and Internet messaging and video conference sessions.
- Periodically ask team members how well the team is working and what can be done to improve performance.
- Empower virtual teams so they have the discretion, freedom, and independence to decide how and when to accomplish their jobs.

Sources: W. F. Cascio, "Managing a Virtual Workplace," *Academy of Management Executive* 14 (2000): 81–90; B. Kirkman, B. Rosen, P. Tesluk, & C. Gibson, "The Impact of Team Empowerment on Virtual Team Performance: The Moderating Role of Face-to-Face Interaction," *Academy of Management Journal* 47 (2004): 175–192; S. Furst, M. Reeves, B. Rosen, & R. Blackburn, "Managing the Life Cycle of Virtual Teams," *Academy of Management Executive* (May 2004): 6–20; C. Solomon, "Managing Virtual Teams," *Workforce* 80 (June 2001), 60.

Exhibit 10.5

Tips for Managing Successful Virtual Teams

Project teams are created to complete specific, one-time projects or tasks within a limited time.[64] Project teams are often used to develop new products, significantly improve existing products, roll out new information systems, or build new factories or offices. The project team is typically led by a project manager, who has the overall responsibility for planning, staffing, and managing the team, which usually includes employees from different functional areas. Effective project teams demand both individual and collective responsibility.[65] One advantage of project teams is that drawing employees from different functional areas can reduce or eliminate communication barriers. In turn, as long as team members feel free to express their ideas, thoughts, and concerns, free-flowing communication encourages cooperation among separate departments and typically speeds up the design process.[66] For example, GXS, a supply chain management provider, used a cross-functional team to design its website so that it would have the same simple, intuitive feel in English, French, Spanish, German, and Italian. This website is equally effective across all of these languages and cultures because, according to GE employee Doug Irwin, the company used a "cross-functional, cross-geography tiger team" during development. Says Irwin, "Every Wednesday morning for an hour, we'd meet on a global conference call. There were 5 to 15 of us, from all areas of the business and from all across the globe."[67] Today, GXS uses its website (**http://www.gxs.com**) in 58 countries to operate one of the world's largest business-to-business e-commerce networks, with more than 100,000 trading partners.

Another advantage of project teams is their flexibility. When projects are finished, project team members either move on to the next project or return to their functional units. For example, publication of this book required designers, editors, page compositors, and web designers, among others. When the task was finished, these people applied their skills to other textbook projects. Because of this flexibility, project teams are often used with the matrix organizational designs discussed in Chapter 9.

project team a team created to complete specific, one-time projects or tasks within a limited time

Review 2: Kinds of Teams

Companies use different kinds of teams to make themselves more competitive. Autonomy is the key dimension that makes teams different. Traditional work groups (which execute tasks) and employee involvement groups (which make suggestions) have the lowest levels of autonomy. Semi-autonomous work groups (which control major direct tasks) have more autonomy, while self-managing teams (which control all direct tasks) and self-designing teams (which control membership and how tasks are done) have the highest levels of autonomy. Cross-functional, virtual, and project teams are common, but are not easily categorized in terms of autonomy. Cross-functional teams combine employees from different functional areas to help teams attack problems from multiple perspectives and generate more ideas and solutions. Virtual teams use telecommunications and information technologies to bring coworkers "together," regardless of physical location or time zone. Virtual teams reduce travel and work time, but communication may suffer since team members don't work face-to-face. Finally, project teams are used for specific, one-time projects or tasks that must be completed within a limited time. Project teams reduce communication barriers and promote flexibility; teams and team members are reassigned to their department or new projects as old projects are completed.

MANAGING WORK TEAMS

"Why did I ever let you talk me into teams? They're nothing but trouble."[68] Lots of managers have this reaction after making the move to teams. Many don't realize that this reaction is normal, both for them and for workers. In fact, such a reaction is characteristic of the *storming* stage of team development (discussed in Section 3.5). Managers who are familiar with these stages and with the other important characteristics of teams will be better prepared to manage the predictable changes that occur when companies make the switch to team-based structures.

After reading the next two sections, you should be able to

3 understand the general characteristics of work teams.

4 explain how to enhance work team effectiveness.

3 Work Team Characteristics

*Understanding the characteristics of work teams is essential for making teams an effective part of an organization. Therefore, in this section you'll learn about **3.1 team norms**, **3.2 team cohesiveness**, **3.3 team size**, **3.4 team conflict**, and **3.5 the stages of team development**.*

3.1 Team Norms

Over time, teams develop **norms**, informally agreed-on standards that regulate team behavior.[69] Norms are valuable because they let team members know what is expected of them. At Nucor Steel, work groups expect their members to get to work on time. To reinforce this norm, anyone who is late to work will not receive the team bonus

norms informally agreed-on standards that regulate team behavior

© THINKSTOCK/JUPITER IMAGES

for that day (assuming the team is productive). A worker who is more than 30 minutes late will not receive the team bonus for the entire week. At Nucor losing a bonus matters because work group bonuses can easily double the size of a worker's take-home pay.[70]

Studies indicate that norms are one of the most powerful influences on work behavior. Team norms are often associated with positive outcomes, such as stronger organizational commitment, more trust in management, and stronger job and organizational satisfaction.[71] In general, effective work teams develop norms about the quality and timeliness of job performance, absenteeism, safety, and honest expression of ideas and opinions. The power of norms also comes from the fact that they regulate the everyday behaviors that allow teams to function effectively. To encourage the development of team norms, trainer Tom Ruddy created a deck of 35 playing cards describing problems that **XEROX**'s customer service teams usually encounter. Ruddy has teams discuss each card/problem. When they agree what to do, they write their solution on the card along with the word *norm*. Everyone then gets a copy of the deck with the team's norms on them. When a team norm is broken, such as one teammate cutting off another's point, the card with the violated norm is played, in this case "everyone's opinion will be heard." It's a little corny at first, but, says Ruddy, "After a while, team members internalize the proper behavior. That's when the team really starts to click."[72]

Norms can also influence team behavior in negative ways. For example, most people would agree that damaging organizational property; saying or doing something to hurt someone at work; intentionally doing one's work badly, incorrectly, or slowly; griping about coworkers; deliberately bending or breaking rules; or doing something to harm the company or boss are negative behaviors. Nonetheless, a study of workers from 34 teams in 20 different organizations found that teams with negative norms strongly influenced their team members to engage in these negative behaviors. In fact, the longer individuals were members of a team with negative norms and the more frequently they interacted with their teammates, the more likely they were to perform negative behaviors. Since team norms typically develop early in the life of a team, these results indicate how important it is for teams to establish positive norms from the outset.[73]

> We were very comfortable working together, so we debated everything freely.
>
> JOYCE THOMAS, TEAM MEMBER, "PRICELESS" AD CAMPAIGNS, MASTERCARD

3.2 Team Cohesiveness

Cohesiveness is another important characteristic of work teams. **Cohesiveness** is the extent to which team members are attracted to a team and motivated to remain in it.[74] Burlington Northern Santa Fe Railway's intermodal team, which was charged with finding efficient ways to combine transportation through trucks and trains, was a particularly cohesive team. Dave Burns, a member of that team, says, "In my mind, the key word to this team was 'shared.' We shared everything. There was a complete openness among us. And the biggest thing that we shared was an objective and a strategy that we had put together jointly. That was our benchmark every day. Were we doing things in support of *our* plan?"[75] The same was true of the team that came up with **MASTERCARD**'s endearing "Priceless" ad campaigns. Each ad in the series features a list of ordinary transactions and the dollar amounts associated with those purchases. The final item in the series, however, is always pitched as "priceless." Joyce Thomas, one of the three-member team that conceived of and created those ads, says, "We were very comfortable working together, so we debated everything freely."[76]

cohesiveness the extent to which team members are attracted to a team and motivated to remain in it

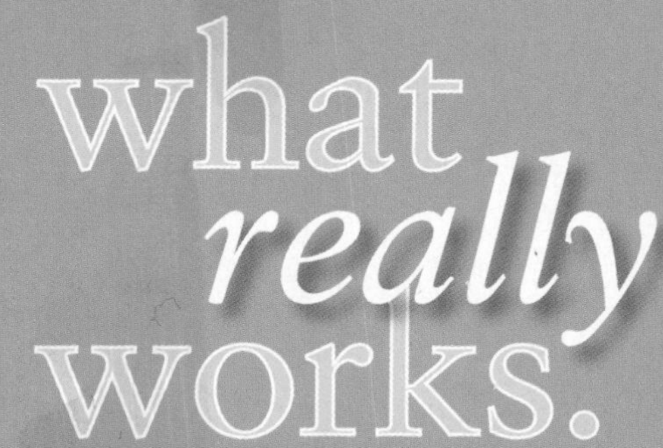

COHESION AND TEAM PERFORMANCE

Have you ever worked in a really cohesive group where everyone liked and enjoyed each other and was glad to be part of the group? It's great. By contrast, have you ever worked in a group where everyone really disliked each other and was unhappy to be part of the group? It's terrible. Anyone who has had either of these experiences can appreciate how important group cohesion is and the effect it can have on team performance. Indeed, 46 studies based on 1,279 groups confirm that cohesion does matter.

TEAM PERFORMANCE

On average, there is a 66 percent chance that cohesive teams will outperform less cohesive teams.

Probability of Success

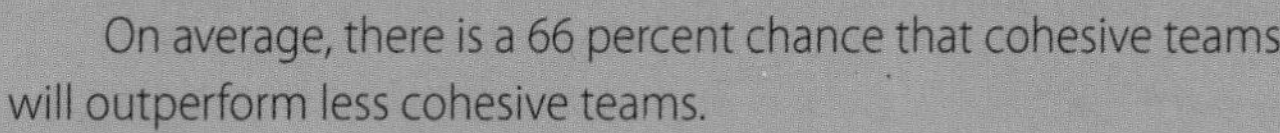

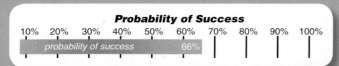

TEAM PERFORMANCE WITH INTERDEPENDENT TASKS

Teams work best for interdependent tasks that require people to work together to get the job done. When teams perform interdependent tasks, there is a 73 percent chance that cohesive teams will outperform less cohesive teams.

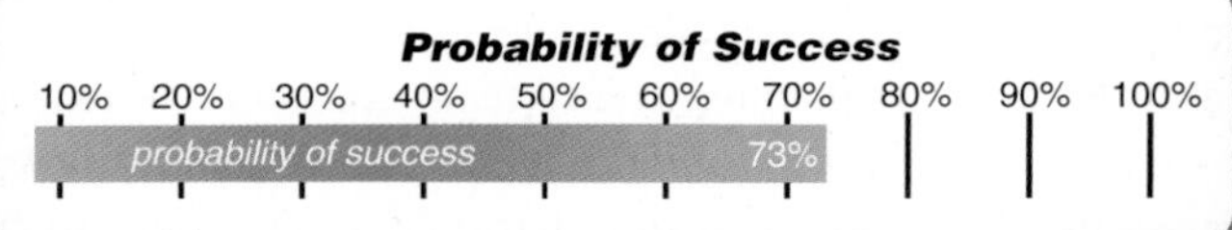

TEAM PERFORMANCE WITH INDEPENDENT TASKS

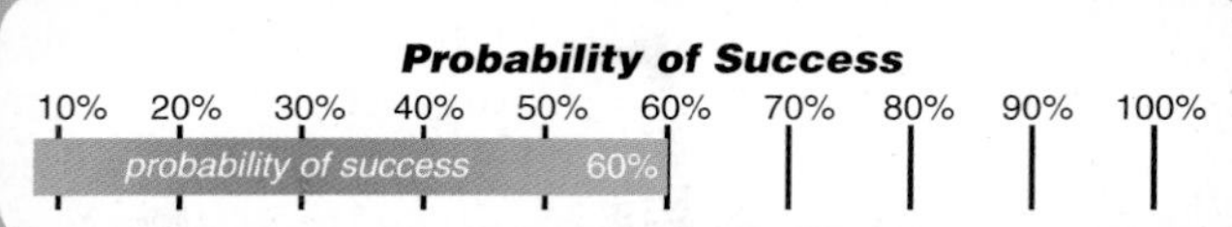

Teams generally are not suited for independent tasks that people can accomplish by themselves. When teams perform independent tasks, there is a only a 60 percent chance that cohesive teams will outperform less cohesive teams.

Some caution is warranted in interpreting these results. For example, there is always the possibility that a team could become so cohesive that its team goals become more important than organizational goals. Also, teams sometimes unite around negative goals and norms that are harmful rather than helpful to organizations. Nonetheless, there is also room for even more optimism about cohesive teams. Teams that are cohesive *and* committed to the goals they are asked to achieve should have an even higher probability of success than the numbers shown here.[77]

The level of cohesiveness in a group is important for several reasons. To start, cohesive groups have a better chance of retaining their members. As a result, cohesive groups typically experience lower turnover.[78] In addition, team cohesiveness promotes cooperative behavior, generosity, and a willingness on the part of team members to assist each other.[79] When team cohesiveness is high, team members are more motivated to contribute to the team because they want to gain the approval of other team members. For these reasons and others, studies have clearly established that cohesive teams consistently perform better.[80] Furthermore, cohesive teams quickly achieve high levels of performance. By contrast, teams low in cohesion take much longer to reach the same levels of performance.[81]

What can be done to promote team cohesiveness? First, make sure that all team members are present at team meetings and activities. Team cohesiveness suffers when members are allowed to withdraw from the team and miss team meetings and events.[82] Second, create additional opportunities for teammates to work together by rearranging work schedules and creating common workspaces. When task interdependence is high and team members have lots of chances to work together, team cohesiveness tends to increase.[83] Third, engaging in nonwork activities as a team can help build cohesion. At a company where teams put in extraordinarily long hours coding computer software, the software teams maintained cohesion by doing "fun stuff" together. Team leader Tammy Urban says, "We went on team outings at least once a week. We'd play darts, shoot pool. Teams work best when you get to know each other outside of work—what people's interests are, who they are. Personal connections go a long way when you're developing complex applications in our kind of time frames."[84] Finally, companies build team cohesiveness by making employees feel that they are part of a "special" organization. For example, all the new hires at Disney World in Orlando are required to take a course entitled "Traditions One," where they learn the traditions and history of the **WALT DISNEY COMPANY** (including the names of the seven dwarfs!). The purpose of Traditions One is to instill a sense of team pride in working for Disney.

3.3 Team Size

There appears to be a curvilinear relationship between team size and performance. Very small or very large teams may not perform as well as moderately sized teams. For most teams, the right size is somewhere between six and nine members.[85] This size is conducive to high team cohesion, which has a positive effect on team performance, as discussed above. A team of this size is small enough for the team members to get to know each other and for each member to have an opportunity to contribute in a meaningful way to the success of the team. At the same time, the team is also large enough to take advantage of team members' diverse skills, knowledge, and perspectives. It is also easier to instill a sense of responsibility and mutual accountability in teams of this size.[86]

By contrast, when teams get too large, team members find it difficult to get to know one another, and the team may splinter into smaller subgroups. When this occurs, subgroups sometimes argue and disagree, weakening overall team cohesion. As teams grow, there is also a greater chance of *minority domination*, where just a few team members dominate team discussions. Even if minority domination doesn't occur, larger groups may not have time for all team members to share their input. And when team members feel that their contributions are unimportant or not needed, the result is less involvement, effort, and accountability to the team.[87] Large teams also face logistical problems, such as finding an appropriate time or place to meet. Finally, the incidence of social loafing, discussed earlier in the chapter, is much higher in large teams.

Just as team performance can suffer when a team is too large, it can also be negatively affected when a team is too small. Teams with just a few people may lack the diversity of skills and knowledge found in larger teams. Also, teams that are too small are unlikely to gain the advantages of team decision making (multiple perspectives, generating more ideas and alternative solutions, and stronger commitment) found in larger teams.

What signs indicate that a team's size needs to be changed? If decisions are taking too long, if the team has difficulty making decisions or taking action, if a few members dominate the team, or if the commitment or efforts of team members are weak, chances are the team is too big. In contrast, if a team is having difficulty coming up with ideas or generating solutions, or if the team does not have the expertise to address a specific problem, chances are the team is too small.

3.4 Team Conflict

Conflict and disagreement are inevitable in most teams. But this shouldn't surprise anyone. From time to time, people who work together are going to disagree about what and how things get done. What causes conflict in teams? Although almost anything can lead to conflict—casual remarks that unintentionally offend a team member or fighting over scarce resources—the primary cause of team conflict is disagreement over team goals and priorities.[88] Other common causes of team conflict include disagreements over task-related issues, interpersonal incompatibilities, and simple fatigue.

Though most people view conflict negatively, the key to dealing with team conflict is not avoiding it, but rather making sure that the team experiences the right kind of conflict. In Chapter 5, you learned about *c-type conflict*, or *cognitive conflict*, which focuses on problem-related differences of opinion, and *a-type conflict*, or *affective conflict*, which refers to the emotional reactions that can occur when disagreements become personal rather than professional.[89] Cognitive conflict is strongly associated with improvements in team performance, whereas affective conflict is strongly associated with decreases in team performance.[90] Why does this happen? With cognitive conflict, team members disagree because their different experiences and expertise lead them to different views of the problem and solutions. Indeed, managers who participated on teams that emphasized cognitive conflict described their teammates as "smart," "team players," and "best in the business." They described their teams as "open," "fun," and "productive." One manager summed up the positive attitude that team members had about cognitive conflict by saying, "We scream a lot, then laugh, and then resolve the issue."[91] Thus, cognitive conflict is also characterized by a willingness to examine, compare, and reconcile differences to produce the best possible solution.

By contrast, affective conflict often results in hostility, anger, resentment, distrust, cynicism, and apathy. Managers who participated on teams that emphasized affective conflict described their teammates as "manipulative," "secretive," "burned out," and "political."[92] Not surprisingly, affective conflict can make people uncomfortable and cause them to withdraw and decrease their commitment to a team.[93] Affective conflict also lowers the satisfaction of team members, may lead to personal hostility between coworkers, and can decrease team cohesiveness.[94] So, unlike cognitive conflict, affective conflict undermines team performance by preventing teams from engaging in the kinds of activities that are critical to team effectiveness.

So, what can managers do to manage team conflict? First, managers need to realize that emphasizing cognitive conflict alone won't be enough. Studies show that cognitive and affective conflicts often occur together in the same teams! Therefore, sincere attempts to reach agreement on a difficult issue can quickly deteriorate from cognitive to affective conflict if the discussion turns personal and tempers and emotions flare. So, while cognitive conflict is clearly the better approach to take, efforts to engage in cognitive conflict should be approached with caution.

Can teams disagree and still get along? Fortunately, they can. In an attempt to study this issue, researchers examined team conflict in 12 high-tech companies. In four of the companies, work teams used cognitive conflict to address work problems but did so in a way that minimized the occurrence of affective conflict. Exhibit 10.6 shows the steps these teams took to be able to have a "good fight."[95]

First, work with more, rather than less, information. If data are plentiful, objective, and up-to-date, teams will focus on issues, not personalities. Second, develop multiple alternatives to enrich debate. Focusing on multiple solutions diffuses conflict by getting the team to keep searching for a better solution. Positions and opinions are naturally more flexible with five alternatives than with just two. Third, establish common goals. Remember, most team conflict arises from disagreements over team

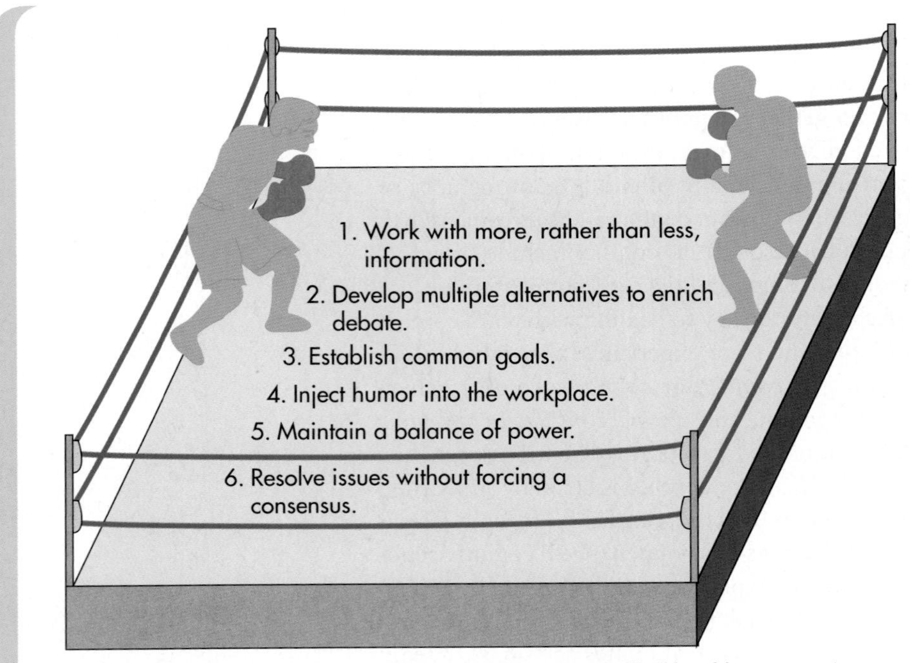
1. Work with more, rather than less, information.
2. Develop multiple alternatives to enrich debate.
3. Establish common goals.
4. Inject humor into the workplace.
5. Maintain a balance of power.
6. Resolve issues without forcing a consensus.

Source: K. M. Eisenhardt, J. L. Kahwajy, & L. J. Bourgeois III, "How Management Teams Can Have a Good Fight," *Harvard Business Review* 75, no. 4 (July–August 1997): 77–85.

Exhibit 10.6
How Teams Can Have a Good Fight

goals and priorities. Therefore, common goals encourage collaboration and minimize conflict over a team's purpose. Steve Jobs, CEO of **Apple**, explains it this way: "It's okay to spend a lot of time arguing about which route to take to San Francisco when everyone wants to end up there, but a lot of time gets wasted in such arguments if one person wants to go to San Francisco and another secretly wants to go to San Diego."[96] Fourth, inject humor into the workplace. Humor relieves tension, builds cohesion, and just makes being in teams fun. Fifth, maintain a balance of power by involving as many people as possible in the decision process. And sixth, resolve issues without forcing a consensus. Consensus means that everyone must agree before decisions are finalized. Effectively, requiring consensus gives everyone on the team veto power. Nothing gets done until everyone agrees, which, of course, is nearly impossible. As a result, insisting on consensus usually promotes affective rather than cognitive conflict. If team members can't agree after constructively discussing their options, it's better to have the team leader make the final choice. Most team members can accept the team leader's choice if they've been thoroughly involved in the decision process.

"What's New" Company

3.5 Stages of Team Development

As teams develop and grow, they pass through four stages of development. As shown in Exhibit 10.7, those stages are forming, storming, norming, and performing.[97] Although not every team passes through each of these stages, teams that do tend to be better performers.[98] This holds true even for teams composed of seasoned executives. After a period of time, however, if a team is not managed well, its performance may start to deteriorate as the team begins a process of decline and progresses through the stages of de-norming, de-storming, and de-forming.[99]

Forming is the initial stage of team development. This is the getting-acquainted stage, when team members first meet each other, form initial impressions, and try to get a sense of what it will be like to be part of the team. Some of the first team norms will be established during this stage, as team members begin to find out what behaviors will and won't be accepted by the team. During this stage, team leaders should allow time for team members to get to know each other, set early ground rules, and begin to set up a preliminary team structure.

forming the first stage of team development, in which team members meet each other, form initial impressions, and begin to establish team norms

storming the second stage of development, characterized by conflict and disagreement, in which team members disagree over what the team should do and how it should do it

Conflicts and disagreements often characterize the second stage of team development, **storming**. As team members begin working together, different personalities and work styles may clash. Team members become more assertive at this stage and more willing to state opinions. This is also the stage when team members jockey for position and try to establish a favorable role for themselves on the team. In addition, team members are likely to disagree about what the group should do and how it should do it. Team performance is still relatively low, given that team cohesion is weak and team members are still reluctant to support each other. Since teams that get stuck in the storming stage are almost always ineffective, it is important for team leaders to focus the team on team goals and on improving team performance. Team members need to be particularly patient and tolerant with each other in this stage.

During **norming**, the third stage of team development, team members begin to settle into their roles as team members. Positive team norms will have developed by this stage, and teammates should know what to expect from each other. Petty differences should have been resolved, friendships will have developed, and group cohesion will be relatively strong. At this point, team members will have accepted team goals, be operating as a unit, and, as indicated by the increase in performance, be working together effectively. This stage can be very short and is often characterized by someone on the team saying, "I think things are finally coming together." Note, however, that teams may also cycle back and forth between storming and norming several times before finally settling into norming.

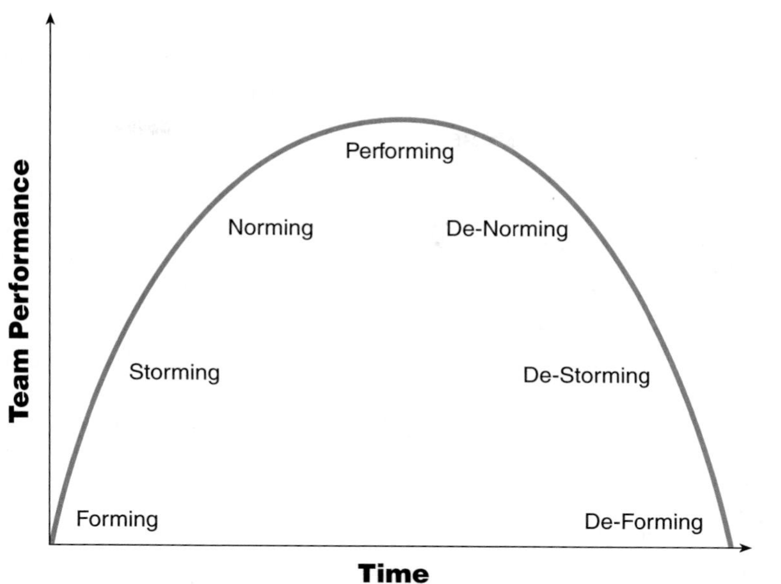

Sources: J. F. McGrew, J. G. Bilotta, & J. M. Deeney, "Software Team Formation and Decay: Extending the Standard Model for Small Groups," *Small Group Research* 30, no. 2 (1999): 209–234; B. W. Tuckman, "Development Sequence in Small Groups," *Psychological Bulletin* 63, no. 6 (1965): 384–399.

Exhibit 10.7

Stages of Team Development

In the last stage of team development, **performing**, performance improves because the team has finally matured into an effective, fully functioning team. At this point, members should be fully committed to the team and think of themselves as "members of a team" and not just "employees." Team members often become intensely loyal to one another at this stage and feel mutual accountability for team successes and failures. Trivial disagreements, which can take time and energy away from the work of the team, should be rare. At this stage, teams get a lot of work done, and it is fun to be a team member.

The team should not become complacent, however, because without effective management, its performance may begin to decline as the team passes through the stages of de-norming, de-storming, and de-forming.[100] Indeed, John Puckett, manufacturing vice president for circuit-board manufacturer ***XEL Communications***, says, "The books all say you start in this state of chaos and march through these various stages, and you end up in this state of ultimate self-direction, where everything is going just great. They never tell you it can go back in the other direction, sometimes just as quickly."[101]

In **de-norming**, which is a reversal of the norming stage, team performance begins to decline as the size, scope, goal, or members of the team change. With new members joining the group, older members may become defensive as established ways of doing things are questioned and challenged. Expression of ideas and opinions becomes less open. New members change team norms by actively rejecting or passively neglecting previously established team roles and behaviors.

In **de-storming**, which is a reversal of the storming phase, the team's comfort level decreases. Team cohesion weakens as more group members resist conforming to team norms and quit participating in team activities. Angry emotions flare as the group explodes in conflict and moves into the final stage of de-forming.

norming the third stage of team development, in which team members begin to settle into their roles, group cohesion grows, and positive team norms develop

performing the fourth and final stage of team development, in which performance improves because the team has matured into an effective, fully functioning team

de-norming a reversal of the norming stage, in which team performance begins to decline as the size, scope, goal, or members of the team change

de-storming a reversal of the storming phase, in which the team's comfort level decreases, team cohesion weakens, and angry emotions and conflict may flare

In **de-forming**, which is a reversal of the forming stage, team members position themselves to gain control of pieces of the team. Team members begin to avoid each other and isolate themselves from team leaders. Team performance rapidly declines as the members quit caring about even minimal requirements of team performance.

If teams are actively managed, decline is not inevitable. However, managers need to recognize that the forces at work in the de-norming, de-storming, and de-forming stages represent a powerful, disruptive, and real threat to teams that have finally made it to the performing stage. Getting to the performing stage is half the battle. Staying there is the second half.

Review 3: Work Team Characteristics

The most important characteristics of work teams are team norms, cohesiveness, size, conflict, and development. Norms let team members know what is expected of them and can influence team behavior in positive and negative ways. Positive team norms are associated with organizational commitment, trust, and job satisfaction. Team cohesiveness helps teams retain members, promotes cooperative behavior, increases motivation, and facilitates team performance. Attending team meetings and activities, creating opportunities to work together, and engaging in nonwork activities can increase cohesiveness. Team size has a curvilinear relationship with team performance: Teams that are very small or very large do not perform as well as moderate-sized teams of six to nine members. Teams of this size are cohesive and small enough for team members to get to know each other and contribute in a meaningful way, but are large enough to take advantage of team members' diverse skills, knowledge, and perspectives. Conflict and disagreement are inevitable in most teams. The key to dealing with team conflict is to maximize cognitive conflict, which focuses on issue-related differences, and minimize affective conflict, the emotional reactions that occur when disagreements become personal rather than professional. As teams develop and grow, they pass through four stages of development: forming, storming, norming, and performing. After a period of time, however, if a team is not managed well, its performance may decline as the team regresses through the stages of de-norming, de-storming, and de-forming.

4 Enhancing Work Team Effectiveness

*Making teams work is a challenging and difficult process. Nonetheless, companies can increase the likelihood that teams will succeed by carefully managing **4.1 the setting of team goals and priorities** and **4.2 how work team members are selected, 4.3 trained**, and **4.4 compensated.***[102]

4.1 Setting Team Goals and Priorities

In Chapter 5, you learned that having specific, measurable, attainable, realistic, and timely (S.M.A.R.T.) goals is one of the most effective means for improving individual job performance. Fortunately, team goals also improve team performance. In fact, team goals lead to much higher team performance 93 percent of the time.[103] For example, Nucor Steel sets specific, challenging *hourly* goals for each of its production teams, which consist of first-line supervisors and production and maintenance workers. The average in the steel industry is 10 tons of steel per hour. Nucor production teams have an hourly goal of 8 tons per hour, but get a 5 percent

de-forming a reversal of the forming stage, in which team members position themselves to control pieces of the team, avoid each other, and isolate themselves from team leaders bonus for every ton over 8 tons that they produce. With no limit on the bonuses they can receive, Nucor's production teams produce an average of 35 to 40 tons of steel per hour![104]

Why is setting specific, challenging team goals so critical to team success? One reason is that increasing a team's performance is inherently more complex than just increasing one individual's job performance. For instance, consider that any team is likely to involve at least four different kinds of goals: each member's goal for the team, each member's goal for himself or herself on the team, the team's goal for each member, and the team's goal for itself.[105] In other words, without a specific, challenging goal for the team itself (the last of the four goals listed), team members may head off in all directions at once pursuing these other goals. Consequently, setting a specific, challenging goal *for the team* clarifies team priorities by providing a clear focus and purpose.

> We'd look out our office windows at the tracks and wonder, "Why aren't the cars moving?"
>
> PETER MILLS, FINANCE DIRECTOR, CSX

Specific, challenging team goals also affect how hard team members work. In particular, challenging team goals greatly reduce the incidence of social loafing. When faced with difficult goals, team members necessarily expect everyone to contribute. Consequently, they are much more likely to notice and complain if a teammate isn't doing his or her share. In fact, when teammates know each other well, when team goals are specific, when team communication is good, and when teams are rewarded for team performance (discussed below), there is only a 1 in 16 chance that teammates will be social loafers.[106]

What can companies and teams do to ensure that team goals lead to superior team performance? One increasingly popular approach is to give teams stretch goals. *Stretch goals* are extremely ambitious goals that workers don't know how to reach.[107] **SONY**'s hardware is unrivaled, as are its movies and music. The bridge between content and hardware is software, an area in which Sony is far behind its rivals. Consequently, Sir Howard Stringer, CEO of Sony, says the company's most important priority, or stretch goal, is the "conquest of software." But Sony is so far behind that Stringer anticipates it will take years to make Sony a world-class software company. "We will succeed," he concludes, "because we must."[108] The purpose of stretch goals is to achieve extraordinary improvements in performance by forcing managers and workers to throw away old, comfortable solutions and adopt radical, never-used-before solutions.[109]

By setting specific and challenging goals, CSX was able to ship the same amount of coal with 16 percent fewer rail cars.

© GRAPHISTOCK IMAGE/JUPITER IMAGES

Four things must occur for stretch goals to effectively motivate teams.[110] First, teams must have a high degree of autonomy or control over how they achieve their goals. At **CSX**'s railroad division, top management challenged the new management team at its Cumberland, Maryland, office to increase productivity by 16 percent. The goal was specific and challenging: Ship the same amount of coal each month, but do it with 4,200 railcars instead of 5,000 railcars. The local team, consisting of five new managers, quickly figured out that the trains were spending too much time sitting idly in the rail yards. Finance director Peter Mills says, "We'd look out our office windows at the tracks and wonder, 'Why aren't the cars moving?'" The problem? Headquarters wouldn't let the trains run until they had 160 full railcars to pull, but amassing that many cars could take nearly a week. Since the local management team had the autonomy to pay for the extra crews to run the trains more

mgmt: trends

Two Sheets and a Blanket

Arguably, the organization with some of the highest performing teams in the United States (maybe the world) is the U.S. MARINE CORPS. One of the many exercises the Marines use to get new arrivals at its Parris Island boot camp to perform as a team is called "two sheets and a blanket." An entire platoon (about 50 recruits) gets three minutes to make all the beds in the barracks—with hospital corners tight enough to bounce a quarter. If the entire platoon doesn't finish, the drill instructor orders the platoon to strip the beds and start over. So it goes—all day if necessary—until the recruits realize that they can finish in time and to specification only if they work together with the faster guys helping the slower guys.

Source: J. Vesterman, "From Wharton to War," *Fortune*, 12 June 2006, 105–108.

frequently, it started running trains with as few as 78 cars. Now, coal cars never wait more than a day to be transported to customers, and rail productivity has skyrocketed.[111]

Second, teams must be empowered with control resources, such as budgets, workspaces, computers, or whatever else they need to do their jobs. Steve Kerr, Goldman Sachs' chief learning officer, says, "We have a moral obligation to try to give people the tools to meet tough goals. I think it's totally wrong if you don't give employees the tools to succeed, then punish them when they fail."[112]

Third, teams need structural accommodation. **Structural accommodation** means giving teams the ability to change organizational structures, policies, and practices if doing so helps them meet their stretch goals. PFIZER CEO Jeffrey Kindler has established five stretch goals for his top management team, one of which is to reduce costs by $2 billion by the end of 2008, while—and here's where the goal really stretches—maintaining rich funding for research and development, business development, and cultivating emerging markets. Structural accommodation is one of the key mechanisms the team will use to facilitate the accomplishment of these stretch goals. The team intends to cut down on bureaucracy and reduce management layers, and eliminate unnecessary committees, policies, and procedures. Kindler acknowledges that this change won't happen overnight and notes that it will take time, discipline, and persistence.[113]

Finally, teams need bureaucratic immunity. **Bureaucratic immunity** means that teams no longer have to go through the frustratingly slow process of multilevel reviews and sign-offs to get management approval before making changes. Once granted bureaucratic immunity, teams are immune from the influence of various organizational groups and are accountable only to top management. Therefore, teams can act quickly and even experiment with little fear of failure. Motorola gave the "thin calm" project team that invented the sleek RAZR V3 bureaucratic immunity. The team violated most existing bureaucratic checks and balances within Motorola, and reported directly to top management. The team leaders were given complete control over recruiting new team members and structuring and running the team.[114]

4.2 Selecting People for Teamwork

University of Southern California management professor Edward Lawler says, "People are very naive about how easy it is to create a team. Teams are the Ferraris of work design. They're high performance but high maintenance and expensive."[115] It's almost impossible to have an effective work team without carefully selecting people who are suited for teamwork or for working on a particular team. A focus on teamwork (individualism-collectivism), team level, and team diversity can help companies choose the right team members.[116]

Are you more comfortable working alone or with others? If you strongly prefer to work alone, you may not be well suited for teamwork. Indeed, studies show that job satisfaction is higher in teams when team members prefer working with others.[117] An indirect way to measure someone's *preference for teamwork* is to assess the person's degree

structural accommodation the ability to change organizational structures, policies, and practices in order to meet stretch goals

bureaucratic immunity the ability to make changes without first getting approval from managers or other parts of an organization of individualism or collectivism. **Individualism-collectivism** is the degree to which a person believes that people should be self-sufficient and that loyalty to one's self is more important than loyalty to one's team or company.[118] *Individualists*, who put their own welfare and interests first, generally prefer independent tasks in which they work alone. In contrast, *collectivists*, who put group or team interests ahead of self-interests, generally prefer interdependent tasks in which they work with others. Collectivists would also rather cooperate than compete and are fearful of disappointing team members or of being ostracized from teams. Given these differences, it makes sense to select team members who are collectivists rather than individualists. Indeed, many companies use individualism-collectivism as an initial screening device for team members. For example, when selecting workers for its team-based approach to manufacturing single-engine planes, Cessna focuses exclusively on team skills. If tests indicate that you aren't a "team player" with an aptitude and willingness to take on responsibility and work with others, Cessna doesn't hire you.[119] If team diversity is desired, however, individualists may also be appropriate, as discussed below. To determine your preference for teamwork, take the Team Player Inventory shown in Exhibit 10.8.

© STEPHANIE SINCLAIR/CORBIS

For the U.S. Marine Corps, effective team work on the battlefield begins with effective team work in the barracks.

individualism-collectivism the degree to which a person believes that people should be self-sufficient and that loyalty to one's self is more important than loyalty to team or company

team level the average level of ability, experience, personality, or any other factor on a team

Team level is the average level of ability, experience, personality, or any other factor on a team. For example, a high level of team experience means that a team has particularly experienced team members. This does not mean that every member of the team has considerable experience, but that enough team members do to significantly raise the average level of experience on the team. Team level is used to guide selection of teammates when teams need a particular set of skills or capabilities to do their jobs well. For example, at GE's Aerospace Engines manufacturing plant in Durham, North Carolina, only applicants who have an FAA-certified mechanic's

Exhibit 10.8

The Team Player Inventory

	STRONGLY DISAGREE				STRONGLY AGREE
1. I enjoy working on team/group projects.	1	2	3	4	5
2. Team/group project work easily allows others to not pull their weight.	1	2	3	4	5
3. Work that is done as a team/group is better than the work done individually.	1	2	3	4	5
4. I do my best work alone rather than in a team/group.	1	2	3	4	5
5. Team/group work is overrated in terms of the actual results produced.	1	2	3	4	5
6. Working in a team/group gets me to think more creatively.	1	2	3	4	5
7. Teams/groups are used too often, when individual work would be more effective.	1	2	3	4	5
8. My own work is enhanced when I am in a team/group situation.	1	2	3	4	5
9. My experiences working in team/group situations have been primarily negative.	1	2	3	4	5
10. More soultions/ideas are generated when working in a team/group situation than when working alone.	1	2	3	4	5

Reverse-score items 2, 4, 5, 7, and 9. Then add the scores for items 1 to 10. Higher scores indicate a preference for teamwork, whereas lower total scores indicate a preference for individual work.

Source: T. J. B. Kline, "The Team Player Inventory: Reliability and Validity of a Measure of Predisposition Toward Organizational Team-Working Environments," *Journal for Specialists in Group Work* 24, no. 1 (1999): 102–112.

license are considered for hire. Following that, all applicants are tested in 11 different areas, only one of which involved those technical skills. Keith McKee, who works at the plant, says, "You have to be above the bar in all 11 of the areas: helping skills, team skills, communication skills, diversity, flexibility, coaching ability, work ethic, and so forth. Even if just one thing out of the 11 knocks you down, you don't come to work here."[120]

Whereas team level represents the average level or capability on a team, **team diversity** represents the variances or differences in ability, experience, personality, or any other factor on a team.[121] From a practical perspective, why is team diversity important? Professor John Hollenbeck explains, "Imagine if you put all the extroverts together. Everyone is talking, but nobody is listening. [By contrast,] with a team of [nothing but] introverts, you can hear the clock ticking on the wall."[122] Strong teams not only have talented members (that is, a high team level), but those talented members are also different in terms of ability, experience, or personality. For example, teams with strong team diversity on job experience have a mix of team members, ranging from seasoned veterans to people with three or four years of experience to rookies with little or no experience. When Cessna built a brand new manufacturing plant for its single-engine Skyhawk planes in a new location, none of the new workers it hired for its teams had any manufacturing experience whatsoever. Having passed Cessna's team skills tests, they were all great team players, but none had ever worked in a factory. Consequently, Cessna diversified the teams by bringing in 60 retirees who had built Skyhawks before. The mentors worked with the teams, teaching them basic manufacturing skills and instilling confidence.[123] As in this example, team diversity is used to guide the selection of team members when teams must complete a wide range of different tasks or when tasks are particularly complex.

Once the right team has been put together in terms of individualism-collectivism, team level, and team diversity, it's important to keep the team together as long as practically possible. Interesting research by the National Transportation Safety Board shows that 73 percent of the serious mistakes made by jet cockpit crews are made the very first day that a crew flies together as a team and that 44 percent of serious mistakes occur on their very first flight together (pilot teams fly two to three flights per day). Moreover, research has shown that fatigued pilot crews who have worked together before make significantly fewer errors than rested crews who have never worked together.[124] Their experience working together helps them overcome their fatigue and outperform new teams that have not worked together before. So, once you've created effective teams, keep them together as long as possible.

4.3 Team Training

After selecting the right people for teamwork, you need to train them. And, to be successful, teams need significant training, particularly in interpersonal skills, decision making and problem solving, conflict resolution, and technical training. Team leaders need training, too.

Organizations that create work teams *often underestimate the amount of training* required to make teams effective. This mistake occurs frequently in successful organizations, where managers assume that if employees can work effectively on their own, they can work effectively in teams. In reality, companies that successfully use teams provide thousands of hours of training to make sure that teams work. Stacy Myers, a consultant who helps companies implement teams, says, "When we help companies move to teams, we also require that employees take basic quality and business knowledge classes as well. Teams must know how their work affects the company, and how their success will be measured."[125]

team diversity the variances or differences in ability, experience, personality, or any other factor on a team

Most commonly, members of work teams receive training in interpersonal skills. **Interpersonal skills**, such as listening, communicating, questioning, and providing feedback, enable people to have effective working relationships with others.

Because of teams' autonomy and responsibility, many companies also give team members training in *decision-making and problem-solving skills* to help them do a better job of cutting costs and improving quality and customer service. At **GENERAL MOTORS**' automobile assembly plant in Lansing, Michigan, each employee working on the assembly line receives 250 classroom hours of training, most of it in problem solving. According to Tim Lee, the group director of manufacturing for GM's North American car group, "Problem solving is not an easy task. Typically, in a plant we treat the symptoms, not the problem."[126] Many organizations also teach teams *conflict resolution skills*. "Teams at Delta Faucet have specific protocols for addressing conflict. For example, if an employee's behavior is creating a problem within a team, the team is expected to work it out without involving the team leader. Two team members will meet with the 'problem' team member and work toward a resolution. If this is unsuccessful, the whole team meets and confronts the issue. If necessary, the team leader can be brought in to make a decision, but . . . it is a rare occurrence for a team to reach that stage."[127]

Firms must also provide team members with the *technical training* they need to do their jobs, particularly if they are being cross-trained to perform all of the different jobs on the team. Before teams were created at Milwaukee Mutual Insurance, separate employees performed the tasks of rating, underwriting, and processing insurance policies. After extensive cross-training, however, each team member can now do all three jobs.[128] Cross-training is less appropriate for teams of highly skilled workers. For instance, it is unlikely that a group of engineers, computer programmers, and systems analysts would be cross-trained for each other's jobs.

Finally, companies need to provide *training for team leaders*, who often feel unprepared for their new duties. Exhibit 10.9 shows the top 10 problems reported by new team leaders. These range from confusion about their new roles as team leaders (compared with their old jobs as managers or employees) to not knowing where to go for help when their teams have problems. The solution is extensive training for team leaders.

interpersonal skills skills, such as listening, communicating, questioning, and providing feedback, that enable people to have effective working relationships with others

4.4 Team Compensation and Recognition

Compensating teams correctly is very difficult. For instance, one survey found that only 37 percent of companies were satisfied with their team compensation plans and even fewer, just 10 percent, reported being "very positive."[129] One of the problems,

Exhibit 10.9 Top 10 Problems Reported by Team Leaders

1.	Confusion about their new roles and about what they should be doing differently.
2.	Feeling they've lost control.
3.	Not knowing what it means to coach or empower.
4.	Having personal doubts about whether the team concept will really work.
5.	Uncertainty about how to deal with employees' doubts about the team concept.
6.	Confusion about when a team is ready for more responsibility.
7.	Confusion about how to share responsibility and accountability with the team.
8.	Concern about promotional opportunities, especially about whether the "team leader" title carries any prestige.
9.	Uncertainty about the strategic aspects of the leader's role as the team matures.
10.	Not knowing where to turn for help with team problems, as few, if any, of their organization's leaders have led teams.

Source: B. Filipczak, M. Hequet, C. Lee, M. Picard, & D. Stamps, "More Trouble with Teams," *Training*, October 1996, 21.

according to Susan Mohrman of the Center for Effective Organizations at the University of Southern California, is that "there is a very strong set of beliefs in most organizations that people should be paid for how well they do. So when people first get put into team-based organizations, they really balk at being paid for how well the team does. It sounds illogical to them. It sounds like their individuality and their sense of self-worth are being threatened."[130] Consequently, companies need to carefully choose a team compensation plan and then fully explain how teams will be rewarded. One basic requirement for team compensation to work is that the level of rewards (individual versus team) must match the level of performance (individual versus team).

"What's New" Company

skill-based pay compensation system that pays employees for learning additional skills or knowledge

gainsharing a compensation system in which companies share the financial value of performance gains, such as productivity, cost savings, or quality, with their workers

Employees can be compensated for team participation and accomplishments in three ways: skill-based pay, gainsharing, and nonfinancial rewards. **Skill-based pay** programs pay employees for learning additional skills or knowledge.[131] These programs encourage employees to acquire the additional skills they will need to perform multiple jobs within a team and to share knowledge with others within their work groups.[132] For example, at XEL Communications, the circuit-board manufacturer, the number of skills each employee has mastered determines his or her individual pay. An employee who takes a class and on-the-job training in advanced soldering will earn 30 cents more per hour. Passing a written test or satisfactorily performing a skill or job for a supervisor or trainer certifies mastery of new skills and results in increased pay. Eastman Chemical uses a similar approach with its teams, but team members also have to demonstrate that they use their new skills at least 10 percent of the time. Otherwise, they lose their pay increase.[133]

In **gainsharing** programs, companies share the financial value of performance gains, such as productivity increases, cost savings, or quality improvements, with their workers.[134] Over the last 25 years, the **U.S. Postal Service** (USPS) has lost $9 billion. Recently, however, a gainsharing program for its 84,000 supervisors produced annual savings of $497 million for the USPS and average annual gainsharing payments of $3,100 for each supervisor. Thanks to cost-saving suggestions, improved productivity, and better management, on-time delivery of first class mail increased by 10 percent, the number of workdays lost to injury dropped significantly, and, most impressively of all, the USPS had five straight years of positive net income. Nonetheless, Congress killed the USPS gainsharing program by passing a law prohibiting payment of gainsharing savings to employees for any year that the USPS lost money (which it has done the last few years).[135]

The USPS used gainsharing with great success. Politics, however, impeded progress when Congress killed the gainsharing program that had produced positive results.

© MARY KAY DENNY/PHOTOEDIT, INC.

Nonfinancial rewards are another way to reward teams for their performance. These rewards, which can range from vacation trips to T-shirts, plaques, and coffee mugs, are especially effective when coupled with management recognition, such as awards, certificates, and praise.[136] Nonfinancial awards tend to be most effective when teams or team-based interventions, such as total quality management (see Chapter 18), are first introduced.[137]

Which team compensation plan should your company use? In general, skill-based pay is most effective for self-managing and self-directing teams performing complex tasks. In these situations, the more each team member knows and can do, the better the whole team performs. By contrast, gainsharing works best in relatively stable environments where employees can focus on improving the productivity, cost savings, or quality of their current work system.

Finally, given the level of dissatisfaction with most team compensation systems, what compensation plans would today's managers like to use with the teams in their companies? As shown in Exhibit 10.10,

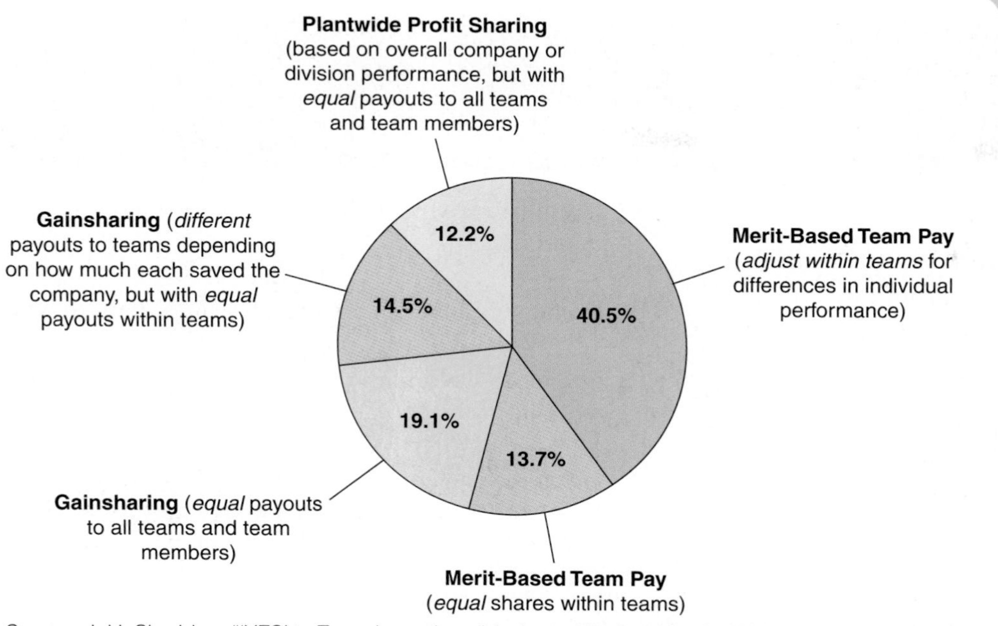

Source: J. H. Sheridan, "'YES' to Team Incentives," *Industry Week*, 4 March 1996, 63.

Exhibit 10.10
Managers' Preferences for Team-Based Pay

40.5 percent of managers would directly link merit-pay increases to team performance, but allow adjustments within teams for differences in individual performance. By contrast, 13.7 percent would also link merit-based increases directly to team performance but give each team member an equal share of the team's merit-based reward. Also, 19.1 percent would use gainsharing plans based on quality, delivery, productivity, or cost reduction and then provide equal payouts to all teams and team members. Another 14.5 percent would also use gainsharing, but they would vary the team gainsharing award, depending on how much money the team saved the company. Payouts would still be equally distributed within teams. Finally, 12.2 percent of managers would opt for plantwide profit-sharing plans tied to overall company or division performance.[138] In this case, there would be no payout distinctions between or within teams.

Review 4: **Enhancing Work Team Effectiveness**

Companies can make teams more effective by setting team goals and managing how team members are selected, trained, and compensated. Team goals provide a clear focus and purpose, reduce the incidence of social loafing, and lead to higher team performance 93 percent of the time. Extremely difficult stretch goals can be used to motivate teams as long as teams have autonomy, control over resources, structural accommodation, and bureaucratic immunity. Not everyone is suited for teamwork. When selecting team members, companies should select people who have a preference for teamwork (individualism-collectivism) and should consider team level (average ability on a team) and team diversity (different abilities on a team). Organizations that successfully use teams provide thousands of hours of training to make sure that teams work. The most common types of team training are for interpersonal skills, decision-making and problem-solving skills, conflict resolution, technical training to help team members learn multiple jobs (that is, cross-training), and training for team leaders. Employees can be compensated for team participation and accomplishments in three ways: skill-based pay, gainsharing, and nonfinancial rewards.

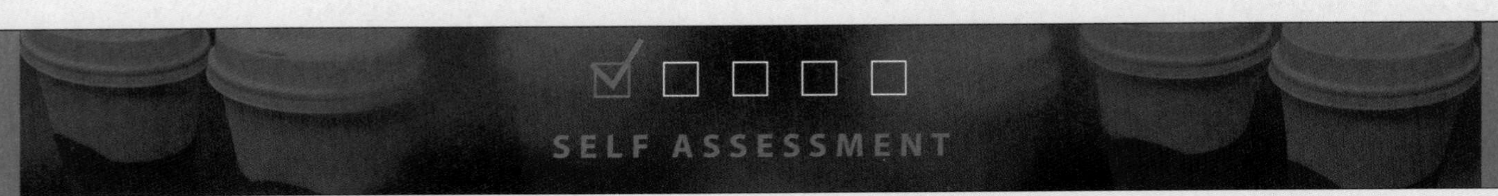

Working in Groups

From sports to school to work to civic involvement, working in teams is increasingly part of our experience. Even though teams are increasingly used to get work done, people still have widely varying opinions of their value. Think of your own situation. When a professor divides the class into groups to complete a project, do you respond with an inward smile or a heavy sigh? Do you enjoy team projects, or would you rather just do your own work? The following 20-question survey assesses your thoughts about working in teams.[139] Indicate the extent to which you agree with each of the following statements. Try not to spend too much time on any one item, and be sure to answer all the questions. Use this scale for your responses:

1 Strongly disagree
2 Disagree
3 Slightly disagree
4 Neutral
5 Slightly agree
6 Agree
7 Strongly agree

1. Only those who depend on themselves get ahead in life.
   1 2 3 4 5 6 7
2. To be superior, a person must stand alone.
   1 2 3 4 5 6 7
3. If you want something done right, you've got to do it yourself.
   1 2 3 4 5 6 7
4. What happens to me is my own doing.
   1 2 3 4 5 6 7
5. In the long run, the only person you can count on is yourself.
   1 2 3 4 5 6 7
6. Winning is everything.
   1 2 3 4 5 6 7
7. I feel that winning is important in both work and games.
   1 2 3 4 5 6 7
8. Success is the most important thing in life.
   1 2 3 4 5 6 7
9. It annoys me when other people perform better than I do.
   1 2 3 4 5 6 7
10. Doing your best isn't enough; it is important to win.
    1 2 3 4 5 6 7
11. I prefer to work with others in a group rather than working alone.
    1 2 3 4 5 6 7
12. Given the choice, I would rather do a job where I can work alone rather than doing a job where I have to work with others in a group.
    1 2 3 4
    5 6 7
13. Working with a group is better than working alone.
    1 2 3 4
    5 6 7
14. People should be made aware that if they are going to be part of a group, then they are sometimes going to have to do things they don't want to do.
    1 2 3 4
    5 6 7
15. People who belong to a group should realize that they're not always going to get what they personally want.
    1 2 3 4
    5 6 7
16. People in a group should realize that they sometimes are going to have to make sacrifices for the sake of the group as a whole.
    1 2 3 4
    5 6 7
17. People in a group should be willing to make sacrifices for the sake of the group's well-being.
    1 2 3 4
    5 6 7

KEY TERMS

18. A group is more productive when its members do what they want to do rather than what the group wants them to do.
    1 2 3 4 5 6 7
19. A group is most efficient when its members do what they think is best rather than doing what the group wants them to do.
    1 2 3 4 5 6 7
20. A group is more productive when its members follow their own interests and desires.
    1 2 3 4 5 6 7

Scoring

Determine your score by entering your response to each survey item below, as follows. In blanks that say *regular score*, simply enter your response for that item. If your response was a 3, place a 3 in the *regular score* blank. In blanks that say *reverse score*, subtract your response from 8 and enter the result. So if your response was a 3, place a 5 (8 – 3 = 5) in the *reverse score* blank.

1. reverse score _____
2. reverse score _____
3. reverse score _____
4. reverse score _____
5. reverse score _____
6. reverse score _____
7. reverse score _____
8. reverse score _____
9. reverse score _____
10. reverse score _____
11. regular score _____
12. reverse score _____
13. regular score _____
14. regular score _____
15. regular score _____
16. regular score _____
17. regular score _____
18. reverse score _____
19. reverse score _____
20. reverse score _____

TOTAL = _____

You can find the interpretation of your score at: **academic.cengage.com/management/williams.**

Do You Assemble a Team of Stars or Ordinary Players?

What criteria will you use to assemble a work team?[140] Is a team composed of all-stars better than one composed of ordinary players? Recall that the United States baseball team that included Roger Clemens, Derek Jeter, Alex Rodriguez and Johnny Damon lost to Mexico, South Korea, and Canada and failed to reach the semifinals of the World Baseball Classic. The 2004 U.S. Olympic basketball team consisting of NBA star players finished third and lost to Lithuania. How could a *Fortune* 500 company that was run by a brilliant former McKinsey consultant and that only hired graduates of America's elite business schools dissolve into fraud and bankruptcy? It happened at Enron. "Some of the worst teams I've ever seen have been those where everybody was a potential CEO," says David Nadler, chief of the Mercer Delta consulting firm, who has worked with executive teams for more than 30 years.

The most important lesson about team performance is that the basic theory of the dream team is wrong, says Geoffrey Colvin, senior editor at *Fortune*. Consider the 1980 U.S. hockey team that beat the Soviets at the Lake Placid Olympics; it was built entirely on anti-dream-team principles. Coach Herb Brooks based his picks on personal chemistry: "I'm not looking for the best players, I'm looking for the right players," he said at the time. CEO John McConnell of Worthington Industries, the Ohio-based steel processor, says, "Give us people who are dedicated to making the team work, as opposed to a bunch of talented people with big egos, and we'll win every time." That's the philosophy that powers teams such as the New England Patriots, which is only the second team in NFL history to win three Super Bowls in four years.

Questions

1. Briefly discuss the advantages and disadvantages of assembling a team composed of (a) star players, and (b) ordinary players.
2. If you were to include star players on your team, what should you do to make sure the team is not dysfunctional and is able to perform as well as expected? Explain.

MANAGEMENT TEAM DECISION

Taking a Chance on Teams at IBM

Evenings at home are the only time you can look over your management team's monthly reports without interruptions.[141] Tonight, you're quietly sipping coffee (decaf, naturally) as you review the reports in the comfort of your favorite chair. You are suddenly jarred, however, by a single line deep in one report, which might have gone unnoticed if you hadn't carved out this time away from the office. In discussing the prospects for a new opportunity, one of your managers wrote, "Pressures in the current quarter have forced us to cut costs by discontinuing efforts in this promising new area." Unbelievable! As you continue reading, you can't get this line out of your head. Why is the company abandoning "promising" avenues of growth and revenue because of external pressures? You finish reading the reports and resolve to discuss the issue with all of your managers—not just the one who wrote the report.

The next morning, you ask your senior vice president to investigate, and in short order, he discovers a pattern of nonconversion. In other words, even though your company, *IBM*, obtains thousands of patents each year, management seems to have tremendous difficulties turning its basic research into functioning businesses. The reason apparently stems from the company's focus on existing markets and short-term results. Rather than focusing on turning new ideas into new products and services, IBM's most talented and experienced executives are being rewarded based on how much revenue their divisions generate and the number of employees reporting to them. Not surprisingly, they're more concerned with growing existing products and services than they are with developing new products and services for the future. As a result, IBM has left many innovations on the table for outsiders to scoop up. For example, IBM invented the relational database and the router, but it was Oracle and Cisco that built huge companies around them.

You call your management team together and pose this problem: "How are we going to transform the work of our research scientists into new businesses? We need to figure out how to recognize and nurture these emerging business opportunities. IBM has hundreds of thousands of employees and billions of dollars in revenue. Surely, we have enough resources to commercialize our great ideas!"

In response, your VP for strategy says, "I wonder if we could do it with teams."

For this Management Team Decision, assemble five to six students to act as the management team at IBM.

Questions

1. Are teams a good idea for IBM's emerging business opportunities (EBOs) given the company's culture and well-defined organization? Why or why not?
2. If you do use teams, what kind of team would be best in the situation described? In other words, how much autonomy should teams working on EBOs have?
3. Who would you choose to lead the EBO teams—experienced executives who are successfully managing established divisions or less experienced managers who want to prove themselves? Explain your rationale. (You may want to review Chapter 1, Section 3, "Kinds of Managers.")
4. What will your management team need to do to help EBO teams be successful? Remember, the whole point of looking into EBOs is to increase IBM's revenue and reach.

PRACTICE BEING A MANAGER

Teamwork is vital to the success of organizations. And this makes creating high-performance teams an important management challenge. In this exercise, you will work with fellow students to brainstorm the creation of a high-performing team. Pay particular attention to the assumptions that you and your peers bring to this process regarding what works, and what doesn't work, in relation to creating a high-performance team. At the conclusion of the exercise, you will have an opportunity to discuss the theory and common assumptions regarding effective team building.

Step 1: Get into groups. Your professor will organize small groups.

Step 2: Review the situation. Assume that your group has been hand-picked by the president of your college or university to work for one semester as a "campus improvement" team. At the end of the year you will submit your recommendations to the president and the board of your institution. These leaders have assured you that they will make every effort to implement your recommendations.

Step 3: Develop a plan. Brainstorm and develop a plan for working as a team to achieve the objective of delivering a set of quality recommendations to the president and the board. You should consider the following in developing your plan:

- Working well together as a team
- Establishing criteria for "quality recommendations" (such as representing the various important constituencies and interests on campus)
- Outlining steps, areas and types of work, and assignments for each member that are most likely to take full advantage of the capabilities and resources in your team

Step 4: Discuss your plans as a class. Is this the sort of project that is well-suited to using a work team? Why, or why not? How might work team characteristics such as norms, cohesiveness, and team size play a role in this team effort? What conflicts might be likely down the road, and at what stage of the process are these conflicts most likely to occur?

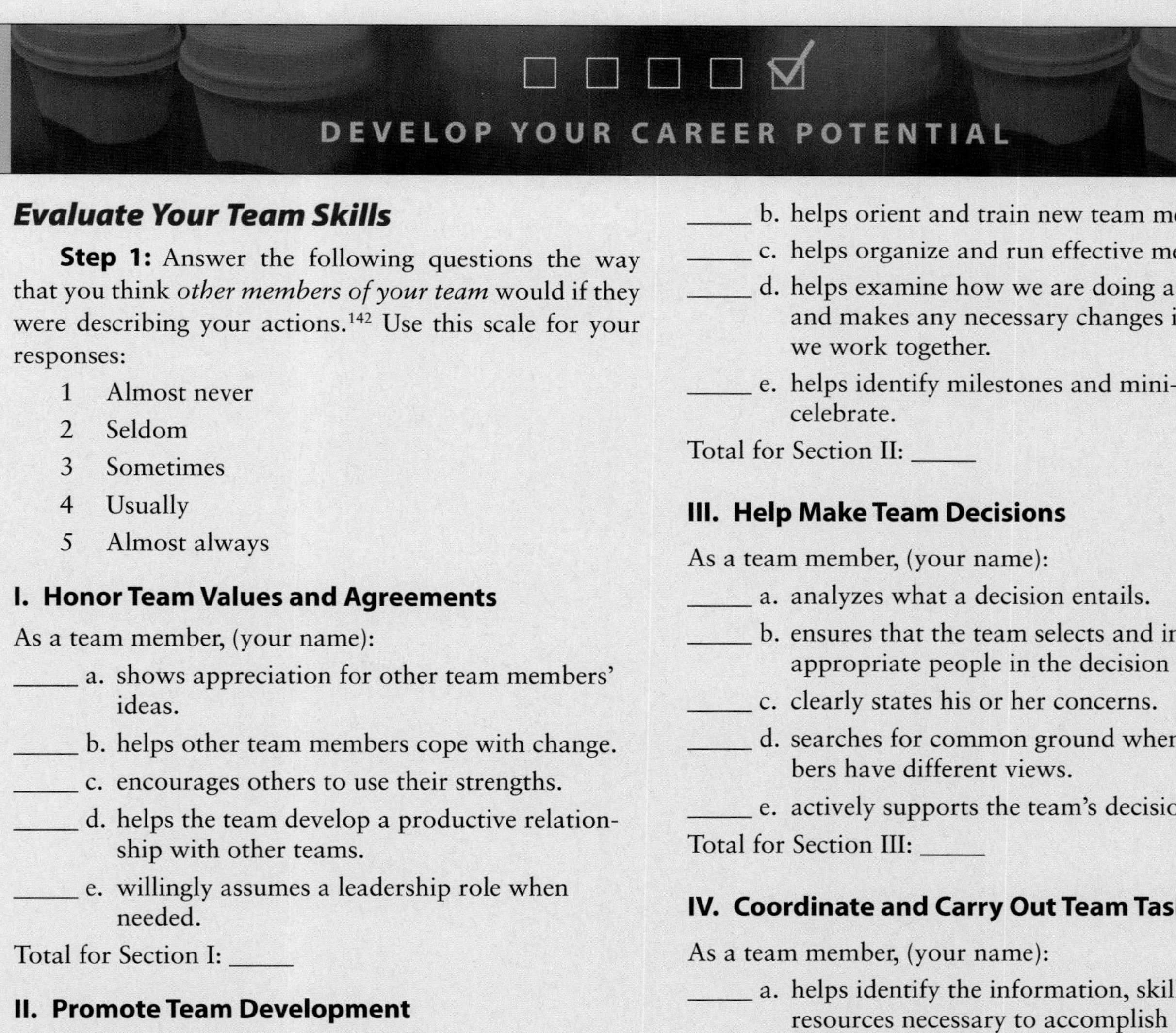

Evaluate Your Team Skills

Step 1: Answer the following questions the way that you think *other members of your team* would if they were describing your actions.[142] Use this scale for your responses:

1 Almost never
2 Seldom
3 Sometimes
4 Usually
5 Almost always

I. Honor Team Values and Agreements

As a team member, (your name):

_____ a. shows appreciation for other team members' ideas.

_____ b. helps other team members cope with change.

_____ c. encourages others to use their strengths.

_____ d. helps the team develop a productive relationship with other teams.

_____ e. willingly assumes a leadership role when needed.

Total for Section I: _____

II. Promote Team Development

As a team member, (your name):

_____ a. volunteers for all types of tasks, including the hard ones.

_____ b. helps orient and train new team members.

_____ c. helps organize and run effective meetings.

_____ d. helps examine how we are doing as a team and makes any necessary changes in the way we work together.

_____ e. helps identify milestones and mini-successes to celebrate.

Total for Section II: _____

III. Help Make Team Decisions

As a team member, (your name):

_____ a. analyzes what a decision entails.

_____ b. ensures that the team selects and includes the appropriate people in the decision process.

_____ c. clearly states his or her concerns.

_____ d. searches for common ground when team members have different views.

_____ e. actively supports the team's decisions.

Total for Section III: _____

IV. Coordinate and Carry Out Team Tasks

As a team member, (your name):

_____ a. helps identify the information, skills, and resources necessary to accomplish team tasks.

_____ b. helps formulate and agree on a plan to meet performance goals.

_____ c. stays abreast of what is happening in other parts of the organization and brings that information to the team.

_____ d. finds innovative ways to meet the needs of the team and of others in the organization.

_____ e. maintains a win-win outlook in all dealings with other teams.

Total for Section IV: _____

V. Handle Difficult Issues with the Team

As a team member, (your name):

_____ a. brings team issues and problems to the team's attention.

_____ b. encourages others on the team to state their views.

_____ c. helps build trust among team members by speaking openly about the team's problems.

_____ d. gives specific, constructive, and timely feedback to others.

_____ e. admits when he or she has made a mistake.

Total for Section V: _____

Step 2: Transfer the section totals to this table:

Category	Total Score
Honor team values and agreements.	_____
Promote team development.	_____
Help make team decisions.	_____
Coordinate and carry out team tasks.	_____
Handle difficult issues with the team.	_____

Interpreting Scores

- A score of 20 or above in any activity indicates an area of strength.
- A score of below 20 in any activity indicates an area that needs more attention.

Questions to Ask Yourself

Looking at your scores, what areas are strengths? How can you maintain these strengths? What areas are weaknesses? What steps can you take to turn these areas into strengths?

REEL TO REAL

BIZ FLIX

Apollo 13

This film re-creates the heroic efforts of astronaut Jim Lovell (Tom Hanks), his crew, NASA, and Mission Control to return the damaged Apollo spacecraft to earth. Examples of both problem solving and decision making occur in almost every scene.

This scene takes place during day 5 of the mission, about two-thirds of the way through the film. Early in Apollo 13's mission Jack Swigert (Kevin Bacon) stirred the oxygen tanks at the request of Mission Control. After this procedure, an explosion occurred, causing unknown damage to the command module. Before the scene takes place, the damage has forced the crew to move into the LEM (Lunar Exploration Module), which becomes their lifeboat for return to earth.

What to Watch for and Ask Yourself

1. What triggers the conflict in this scene?
2. Is this intergroup conflict or intragroup conflict? What effects can such conflict have on the group dynamics on board Apollo 13?
3. Does mission commander Jim Lovell successfully manage the group dynamics to return the group to a normal state?

MANAGEMENT WORKPLACE

NEADS—Unconventional Teams

All the teams you have encountered in this chapter have been teams of people. NEADS, the National Education for Assistance Dog Services, functions with teams of people as well. But another type of teamwork is central to the mission of NEADS: the team of human and dog. NEADS acquires, raises, trains, and matches service dogs to meet the needs of people with limited physical mobility or who are deaf. A typical service dog may be trained to respond to a blaring smoke alarm or ringing telephone, nudge a light switch on or off with its nose, or retrieve items for an owner. Since this partnership is intended to last a lifetime, it is important for the match to be perfect. Step into the management workplace of NEADS to find out how this unique organization implements teams—both human and canine.

What to Watch for and Ask Yourself

1. Describe the characteristics of a typical NEADS team, using the criteria discussed in the chapter.
2. What factors determine the cohesiveness of NEADS teams?
3. Describe a situation in which conflict might arise in a NEADS team.

Managing Human Resource Systems

Learning Outcomes:

1 Describe the basic steps involved in human resource planning.
2 Explain how different employment laws affect human resource practice.
3 Explain how companies use recruiting to find qualified job applicants.
4 Describe the selection techniques and procedures that companies use when deciding which applicants should receive job offers.
5 Describe how to determine training needs and select the appropriate training methods.
6 Discuss how to use performance appraisal to give meaningful performance feedback.
7 Describe basic compensation strategies and explain how they affect human resource practice.
8 Discuss the four kinds of employee separations: termination, downsizing, retirements, and turnover.

In This Chapter:

WHAT WOULD YOU DO?

RadioShack, Fort Worth, Texas.[1] "Radio Sacked," read the headline in the *Vancouver Sun*. "Read this E-Mail—Then Scram," wrote the *Los Angeles Times*. In an article published in the *Washington Post*, psychologist Ken Siegel said "To almost everyone who observes or reads about this, it represents a stupefying new low in the annals of management practice." These and other such headlines are referring to the manner in which layoffs were communicated to affected employees at RadioShack.

RadioShack needed to lay off over 400 employees, mostly at its corporate headquarters. It delivered the following e-mail to those selected for termination: *The work force reduction notification is currently in progress. Unfortunately your position is one that been eliminated.*

Workers who received the notification had 30 minutes to collect their thoughts and say their goodbyes before they went to meet with senior leaders. Workers who survived the layoff were shocked and demoralized.

This is not the first time RadioShack's reputation has taken a beating. Just a few months prior to this e-mail, CEO David J. Edmondson was fired after a newspaper investigation revealed that he had not, as he had claimed, earned degrees in theology and psychology from the Heartland Baptist Bible College; in fact, according to the school's records, he had completed only two semesters and had never even taken a single psychology class. What kind of message does that send to employees about the ethics of RadioShack's top executives?

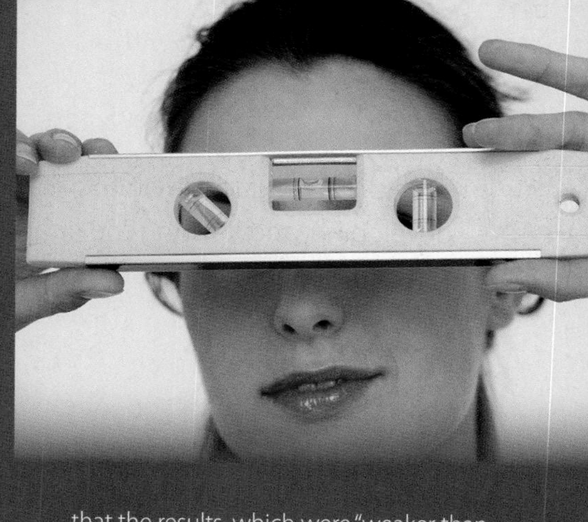

But RadioShack's human resource troubles don't stop there. The company also made the news for race discrimination in hiring practices and for its controversial "Fix 1500 Initiative." In that program, store managers were subjectively assessed relative to other store managers, and the bottom 1,500 were given 90 days to improve. As a result, in one six-month period, a total of 1,734 store managers were demoted to sales associates or fired. Executives also eliminated the stock purchase plan for employees but retained it for management, which did little to improve the company's image, especially among employees.

All the while, the company is struggling to compete with big-box retailers like Best Buy, Circuit City, Costco, and Wal-Mart. Total sales have fallen by 12 percent, 530 stores have been closed, and same-store sales fell 6.8 percent in one year. Credit Suisse analyst Gary Balter wrote in a report that the results, which were "weaker than the weak results we had expected, raise a number of questions, none of which we expect to get answers to from this company."

You knew this would be a tough job. But as the new Vice President of Human Resources you are committed to making things better at RadioShack; a lot of things. Should you focus on building trust and enhancing employee morale? What about recruiting and hiring processes? You wonder if RadioShack is hiring the right people. Background checks would be a good start, you think. But even if you hire good people, how are you going to tell if they're doing a good job? The performance-appraisal system of relative grading has got to go, but what should replace it? And there's surely going to be more restructuring, so you'll need to establish procedures to communicate layoffs, and guidelines for dealing with laid-off employees and survivors. Finally, what can you do about RadioShack's poor reputation? You know it will affect your ability to recruit high-quality applicants for management jobs. Human Resources can make a positive impact on Radio Shack's future and bottom line, but where do you start? **As the new VP of HR, what would you do?**

ACTIVITIES + VIDEO

CengageNOW Audio study guide, electronic flashcards, author FAQ videos, On the Job and Biz Flix videos, concept tutorial, and concept exercise

Web (academic.cengage.com/management/williams) Quiz, PowerPoint slides, and glossary terms for this chapter

Study Tip

Use the chapter outline on the preceding page as a study tool. After reading the whole chapter, return to the list and write a summary of each item. Check your work by reading the actual review paragraphs on pages 388, 393, 398, 408, 413, 417, 421, and 425.

"WHAT'S NEW" COMPANIES

RADIOSHACK
BEHLEN MANUFACTURING
CORNING GLASS
HOOTERS
MORGAN STANLEY
BRITISH PETROLEUM
COCA-COLA
BAKER & MCKENZIE
QUICK CHEK FOOD STORES
FUJISAWA PHARMACEUTICALS
AND OTHERS . . .

As the problems facing RadioShack show, **human resource management (HRM)**, or the process of finding, developing, and keeping the right people to form a qualified work force, is one of the most difficult and important of all management tasks. This chapter is organized around the four parts of the human resource management process shown in Exhibit 11.1: determining human resource needs and attracting, developing, and keeping a qualified work force.

Accordingly, the chapter begins by reviewing how human resource planning determines human resource needs, such as the kind and number of employees a company requires to meet its strategic plans and objectives. Next, we explore how companies use recruiting and selection techniques to attract and hire qualified employees to fulfill those needs. The third part of the chapter discusses how training and performance appraisal can develop the knowledge, skills, and abilities of the work force. The chapter concludes with a review of compensation and employee separation, that is, how companies can keep their best workers through effective compensation practices and how they can manage the separation process when employees leave the organization.

DETERMINING HUMAN RESOURCE NEEDS

Should we hire more workers? What should we pay our current employees to slow employee turnover? What kinds of training do our new employees need to be prepared to do a good job, and what's the best way to deliver that training? In other words, what are our human resource needs, and what's the best way to address them? The human resource management process, shown in Exhibit 11.1, can provide answers to these questions.

We can see how the HRM process works by examining what hospitals are doing to address the shortage of qualified nurses around the world. How acute is this shortage? Hospitals in London, England, find it so difficult to attract British nurses that they have sent managers all the way to Jamaica to recruit English-speaking nurses. But Jamaica has lost so many nurses to English hospitals that it now prevents the British government (which runs the health system in Britain) from hiring its nurses. And why do British hospitals have such a hard time finding nurses? Because Canadian nurses take higher-paying jobs in the United States, which forces Canadian hospitals to hire British nurses and British hospitals to hire nurses from Ghana (since they can no longer hire Jamaican nurses). The nursing shortage is so severe worldwide that even U.S. hospitals now recruit directly in many countries. In South Africa and the Philippines, nurses are encouraged to come to the United States by ads that say, "Nurses! Think of it as your seat in America. Gain invaluable experience, learn the latest medical techniques, and live a fuller life in a relaxed environment."[2] And, like all workers, nurses who work in poor conditions for poor pay are willing to move to other countries for better-paying jobs in good companies. So, for the hospitals around the world that struggle to hire nurses, the

human resource management (HRM) the process of finding, developing, and keeping the right people to form a qualified work force

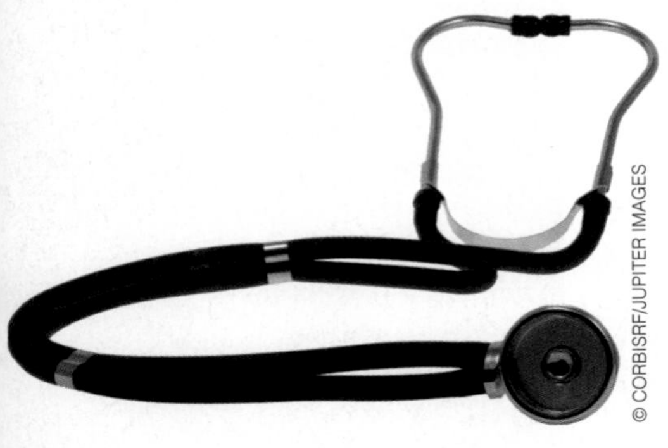

HRM process, as shown in Exhibit 11.1, comes full circle as attracting, developing, and then keeping qualified nurses affect their human resource needs.

After reading the next two sections, you should be able to

1. *describe the basic steps involved in human resource planning.*
2. *explain how different employment laws affect human resource practice.*

Determining Human Resource Needs — Human Resource Planning

Attracting Qualified Employees — Recruiting → Selection

Developing Qualified Employees — Training → Performance Appraisal

Keeping Qualified Employees — Compensation → Employee Separation → (back to Human Resource Planning)

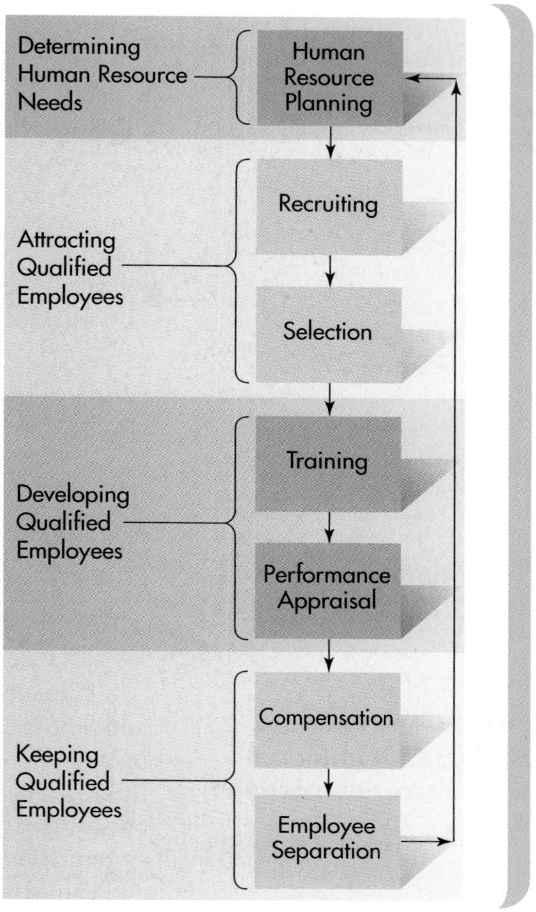

Exhibit 11.1

The Human Resource Management Process

1 Human Resource Planning

Human resource planning (HRP) is the process of using an organization's goals and strategy to forecast the organization's human resource needs in terms of attracting, developing, and keeping a qualified work force.[3] Importantly, companies that don't use HRP or that do it poorly may end up with either a surplus of employees that has to be corrected with layoffs or a shortage of employees that leads to increased overtime costs and an inability to meet demand for the company's product or service.

Let's explore human resource planning by examining how to ***1.1 forecast the demand and supply of human resources*** *and* ***1.2 use human resource information systems to improve those forecasts.***

1.1 Forecasting Demand and Supply

Work force forecasting is the process of predicting the number and kind of workers with specific skills and abilities that an organization will need in the future.[4] There are two kinds of work force forecasts, internal and external forecasts, and three kinds of forecasting methods—direct managerial input, best guess, and statistical/historical ratios.

Internal forecasts are projections about factors within the organization that affect the supply and demand for human resources. These factors include the financial performance of the organization, its productivity, its mission, changes in technology or the way the work is performed, and terminations, promotions, transfers, retirements, resignations, and deaths of current employees. For example, according to Mark Young, senior research associate for the Conference Board, Corning Glass focuses on trends over a period of three to four years, rather than a precise headcount and short-term plans. It then segments jobs based on how critical the jobs are to accomplishing its mission, and makes different levels of workforce investment in each segment.[5] Exhibit 11.2 provides a more complete list of factors that influence internal forecasts.

External forecasts are projections about factors outside the organization that affect the supply and demand for human resources. These factors include the labor supply for specific types of workers, the economy (unemployment rate), labor unions, demographics of the labor force (proportion of labor force in, for example, various age groups), geographic movement of the labor force, strength of competitors, and growth in particular businesses and markets.

human resource planning (HRP) using an organization's goals and strategy to forecast the organization's human resource needs in terms of attracting, developing, and keeping a qualified work force

work force forecasting the process of predicting the number and kind of workers with specific skills and abilities that an organization will need in the future

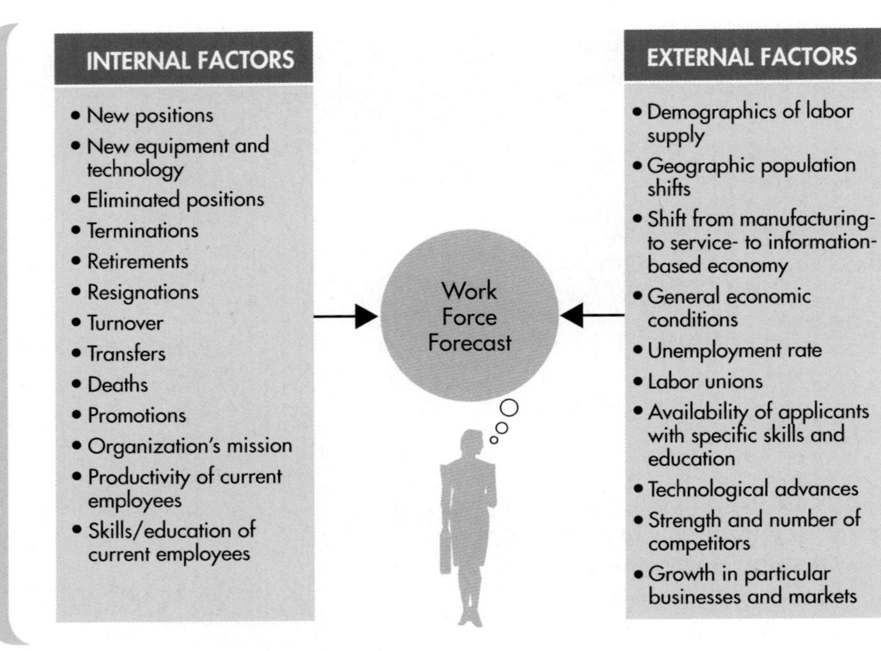

Exhibit 11.2

Internal and External Factors That Influence Work Force Forecasting

For example, when the economy slowed, **BEHLEN MANUFACTURING** switched its 400 factory workers from full-time to part-time work and cut the pay of its salaried workers by 10 percent. CEO Tony Raimondo said during the change, "This year, we've been reducing hours and telling people we believed it was short-term. We think we saved a lot of jobs by doing that."[6] When the economy strengthened and sales began increasing again, he quickly switched his factory workers back to full-time hours and removed the 10 percent pay cut. Exhibit 11.2 provides a more complete list of factors that influence external forecasts.

Three kinds of forecasting methods—direct managerial input, best guess, and statistical/historical ratios—are often used to predict the number and kind of workers with specific skills and abilities that an organization will need in the future.[7] The most common forecasting method, *direct managerial input*, is based on straightforward projections of cash flows, expenses, or financial measures, such as return on capital. Though financial indicators are relatively quick to calculate and can help managers determine how many workers might be needed, they don't help managers decide which critical skills new employees should possess.

The *best guess* forecasting method is based on managers' assessment of current head count, plus a best guess of how internal factors and external factors will affect that head count. A recent survey reported that managers typically overestimate future staffing levels needed to achieve business goals. The survey also found that organizations are more accurate when it comes to forecasting employment increases than when forecasting employment decreases.[8]

Finally, the *statistical/historical ratios* forecasting method uses statistical methods, such as multiple regression, in combination with historical data to predict the number and kind of workers a company should hire. For example, a manager might run a regression analysis using data from the last two years. In this analysis, the number of employees that need to be hired is the dependent (predicted) variable, and the number of items manufactured, number of clients, average increase in sales, and similar factors are the independent (predictor) variables. The regression analysis produces a simple equation that indicates how many more employees should be added for each increase in the independent variables, such as items manufactured or increased sales. This approach takes advantage of existing data and can be much more accurate than best guess predictions, but only if a company's internal and external environments have not changed significantly.

CORNING GLASS uses a variety of statistical tools to help predict its work force needs, a process it calls human capital planning. Corning uses human capital planning to improve its ability to identify human resource requirements of corporate strategy and reshape HR services to better support the business. "We've already realized considerable value from the human capital planning process," says Kurt Fischer, vice president of human resources at Corning.[9]

1.2 Human Resource Information Systems

Human resource information systems (HRISs) are computerized systems for gathering, analyzing, storing, and disseminating information related to attracting, developing, and keeping a qualified work force.[10] Exhibit 11.3 shows some of the data that are commonly used in HRISs, such as personal and educational data, company employment history, performance appraisal information, work history, and promotions.

Human resource information systems can be used for transaction processing, employee self-service, and decision support. For HRISs, *transaction processing* usually involves employee payroll checks, taxes, and benefit deductions. For example, when ER One, a Michigan-based company that provides physicians and other clinicians for hospital emergency rooms, was small, it used paper files and different computer spreadsheets and databases to keep track of compensation and benefits for its employees. But now that the company has 180 employees in seven different locations, it uses an HRIS to keep track of its employees. This system quickly provides accurate, up-to-date information about employee compensation and benefits and can be easily accessed from any of the seven locations, says Pat Brainard, the company's director of human resources.[11] HRISs can also reduce administrative costs by preparing certain routine reports, such as the EEOC (Equal Employment Opportunity Commission) or OSHA (Occupational Safety and Health Administration) reports that are required of many companies.

Though typically used to give managers and HR staffers access to human resource data, today's secure web-based HRISs also give employees immediate, 24-hour *self-service* access to personal data, such as benefits and retirement packages. By entering a user name and a password, employees can access and change their medical insurance plan, adjust the mix of investments in their 401(k) retirement plan, or check on the status of medical or child-care reimbursements. Hewitt Associates is a global HR consulting and benefits outsourcing firm that provides its customers with secure access to HR data and applications using web-services technology, 24/7. Customers, meaning, employees of client organizations, can access and change their current health care enrollment, check on their retirement benefits, and reallocate their 401(k) investments.[12]

In addition to gathering and storing information, HRISs also help managers by serving as decision support systems for critical HR decisions.[13] In Chapter 17, you will learn that *decision support systems (DSSs)* help managers understand problems and potential solutions by acquiring and analyzing information with sophisticated models and tools. For instance, an HRIS can help managers make HR decisions from the moment job applicants submit résumés to the company. Those résumés are scanned into the HRIS, where they are analyzed for the quality of the writing and for

"This year, we've been reducing hours and telling people we believed it was short-term. We think we saved a lot of jobs by doing that."

TONY RAIMONDO, CEO, BEHLEN MANUFACTURING

human resource information system (HRIS) a computerized system for gathering, analyzing, storing, and disseminating information related to the HRM process

Exhibit 11.3

Common Data Categories in Human Resource Information Systems

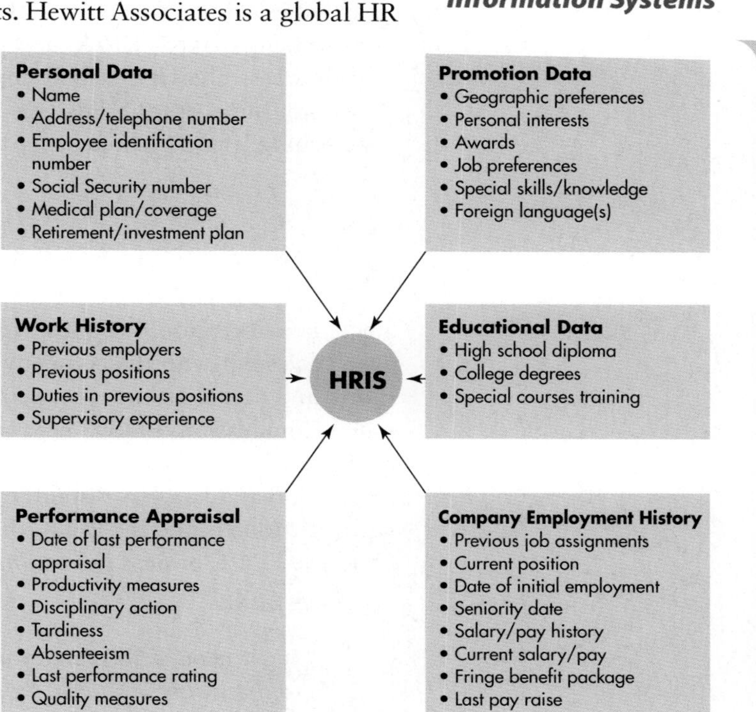

key words that match the organization's job database. For instance, to identify experienced tax preparers, tax preparation company H&R Block looks for key phrases like "certified financial planner" and "insurance license."[14]

An HRIS can even be used to do preemployment testing or background screening. At Sprint Nextel, when job applicants apply at **http://www.sprint.com/careers/index.html**, they are asked to answer screening questions, such as "Do you know C++ programming?" or "Have you sold to *Fortune* 500 companies?"[15] Sprint's HRIS then automatically ranks the applicants based on their responses. Recruiters then review the top 25 percent of applicants for job openings.

An HRIS can also be used effectively to screen *internal applicants* on particular qualifications, to match the qualifications of external applicants against those of internal applicants, to compare salaries within and between departments, and to review and change employees' salaries instantaneously without lengthy paperwork. In short, today's HRISs can help managers make any number of critical human resource decisions.

Review 1: **Human Resource Planning**

Human resource planning (HRP) uses organizational goals and strategies to determine what needs to be done to attract, develop, and keep a qualified work force. Work force forecasts are used to predict the number and kind of workers with specific skills and abilities that an organization needs. Work force forecasts consider both internal and external factors that affect the supply and demand for workers and can be formulated using three kinds of forecasting methods: direct managerial input, best guess, and statistical/historical ratios. Computerized human resource information systems improve HRP by gathering, analyzing, storing, and disseminating information (personal, educational, work history, performance, and promotions) related to human resource management activities. Human resource information systems can be used for transaction processing (payroll checks and routine reports), employee self-service (24-hour web access allowing instant changes to benefit and retirement packages), and decision support for human resource decisions (analyzing résumés, background screening, and preemployment testing).

2 Employment Legislation

Since their inception, **Hooters** restaurants have hired only female servers. Moreover, consistent with the company's marketing theme, the servers wear short nylon shorts and cutoff T-shirts that show their midriffs. The Equal Employment Opportunity Commission (EEOC) began an investigation of Hooters when a Chicago man filed a sex-based discrimination charge. The man alleged that he had applied for a server's job at a Hooters restaurant and was rejected because of his sex. The dispute between Hooters and the EEOC quickly gained national attention. One sarcastic letter to the EEOC printed in *Fortune* magazine read as follows:

Dear EEOC:

Hi! I just wanted to thank you for investigating those Hooters restaurants, where the waitresses wear those shorty shorts and midriffy T-shirts. I think it's a great idea that you have decided to make Hooters hire men as—how do you say it?—waitpersons. Gee, I never knew so many men wanted to be waitpersons at Hooters. No reason to let them sue on their own either. You're right, the government needs to take the lead on this one.[16]

This letter characterized public sentiment at the time. Given its backlog of 100,000 job discrimination cases, many wondered if the EEOC didn't have better things to do with its scarce resources.

Three years after the initial complaint, the EEOC ruled that Hooters had violated antidiscrimination laws and offered to settle the case if the company would agree to pay $22 million to the EEOC for distribution to male victims of the "Hooters Girl" hiring policy, establish a scholarship fund to enhance opportunities or education for men, and provide sensitivity training to teach Hooters' employees how to be more sensitive to men's needs. Hooters responded with a $1 million publicity campaign criticizing the EEOC's investigation. Billboards featuring "Vince," a man dressed in a Hooters Girl uniform and blond wig, sprang up all over the country. Hooters customers were given postcards to send complaints to the EEOC. Of course, Hooters paid the postage. As a result of the publicity campaign, restaurant sales increased by 10 percent. Soon thereafter, the EEOC announced that it would not pursue discriminatory hiring charges against Hooters.[17] Nonetheless, the company ended up paying $3.75 million to settle a class-action suit brought by seven men who claimed that their inability to get a job at Hooters violated federal law.[18] Under the settlement, Hooters maintained its women-only policy for server jobs, but had to create additional support jobs, such as hosts and bartenders, that would also be open to men.

As the Hooters example illustrates, the human resource planning process occurs in a very complicated legal environment. Let's explore employment legislation by reviewing ***2.1 the major federal employment laws that affect human resource practice, 2.2 how the concept of adverse impact is related to employment discrimination****, and* ***2.3 the laws regarding sexual harassment in the workplace****.*

2.1 Federal Employment Laws

Exhibit 11.4 lists the major federal employment laws and their websites, where you can find more detailed information. Except for the Family and Medical Leave Act and the Uniformed Services Employment and Reemployment Rights Act, which are administrated by the Department of Labor (**http://www.dol.gov**), all of these laws are administered by the EEOC (**http://www.eeoc.gov**). The general effect of this body of law, which is still evolving through court decisions, is that employers may not discriminate in employment decisions on the basis of sex, age, religion, color, national origin, race, or disability. The intent is to make these factors irrelevant in employment decisions. Stated another way, employment decisions should be based on factors that are "job related," "reasonably necessary," or a "business necessity" for successful job performance. The only time that sex, age, religion, and the like can be used to make employment decisions is when they are considered a bona fide occupational qualification.[19] Title VII of the 1964 Civil Rights Act says that it is not unlawful to hire and

Despite a favorable ruling, Hooters was still required to create more support jobs that would be open to men—even on its failed airline.

© TAMMY CHAPPELL/REUTERS/LANDOV

Equal Pay Act of 1963	http://www.eeoc.gov/policy/epa.html	Prohibits unequal pay for males and females doing substantially similar work.
Civil Rights Act of 1964	http://www.eeoc.gov/policy/vii.html	Prohibits discrimination on the basis of race, color, religion, sex, or national origin.
Age Discrimination in Employment Act of 1967	http://www.eeoc.gov/policy/adea.html	Prohibits discrimination in employment decisions against persons age 40 and over.
Pregnancy Discrimination Act of 1978	http://www.eeoc.gov/facts/fs-preg.html	Prohibits discrimination in employment against pregnant women.
Americans with Disabilities Act of 1990	http://www.eeoc.gov/policy/ada.html	Prohibits discrimination on the basis of physical or mental disabilities.
Civil Rights Act of 1991	http://www.eeoc.gov/policy/cra91.html	Strengthened the provisions of the Civil Rights Act of 1964 by providing for jury trials and punitive damages.
Family and Medical Leave Act of 1993	http://www.dol.gov/esa/whd/fmla//index.html	Permits workers to take up to 12 weeks of unpaid leave for pregnancy and/or birth of a new child, adoption or foster care of a new child, illness of an immediate family member, or personal medical leave.
Uniformed Services Employment and Reemployment Rights Act of 1994	http://www.osc.gov/userra.htm	Prohibits discrimination against those serving in the Armed Forces Reserve, the National Guard, or other uniformed services; guarantees that civilian employers will hold and then restore civilian jobs and benefits for those who have completed uniformed service.

Exhibit 11.4

Summary of Major Federal Employment Laws

employ someone on the basis of sex, religion, or national origin when there is a **bona fide occupational qualification (BFOQ)** that is "reasonably necessary to the normal operation of that particular business." For example, a Baptist church hiring a new minister can reasonably specify that being a Baptist rather than a Catholic or Presbyterian is a BFOQ for the position. However, it's unlikely that the church could specify race or national origin as a BFOQ. In general, the courts and the EEOC take a hard look when a business claims that sex, age, religion, color, national origin, race, or disability is a BFOQ. For instance, the EEOC disagreed with Hooters' claim that it was "in the business of providing vicarious sexual recreation" and that "female sexuality is a bona fide occupational qualification."[20]

It is important to understand, however, that these laws apply to the entire HRM process and not just to selection decisions (hiring or promotion). These laws also cover all training and development activities, performance appraisals, terminations, and compensation decisions. Employers who use sex, age, race, or religion to make employment-related decisions when those factors are unrelated to an applicant's or employee's ability to perform a job may face charges of discrimination from employee lawsuits or the EEOC. For example, Morgan Stanley, an investment bank, agreed to pay $54 million in damages after the EEOC filed a sex discrimination suit on behalf of 300 of the firm's female employees. The women were paid less and promoted less often than comparable male employees with whom they worked.[21] Boeing, the jet plane manufacturer, paid $72.5 million to settle a similar lawsuit brought by a group of its female employees.[22]

bona fide occupational qualification (BFOQ) an exception in employment law that permits sex, age, religion, and the like to be used when making employment decisions, but only if they are "reasonably necessary to the normal operation of that particular business." BFOQs are strictly monitored by the Equal Employment Opportunity Commission.

In addition to the laws presented in Exhibit 11.4, there are two other important sets of federal laws: labor laws and laws and regulations governing safety standards. Labor laws regulate the interaction between management and labor unions that represent groups of employees. These laws guarantee employees the right to form and join unions of their own choosing. For more information about labor laws, see the National Labor Relations Board at **http://www.nlrb.gov**. The Occupational Safety and Health Act (OSHA) requires that employers provide employees with a workplace that is "free from recognized hazards that are causing or are likely to cause death or serious physical harm." This law is administered by the Occupational Safety and Health Administration (which, like the act, is referred to as OSHA). OSHA sets safety and health standards for employers and conducts inspections to determine whether those standards are being met. Employers who do not meet OSHA standards may be fined.[23] For example, OSHA fined ***British Petroleum*** $23.8 million after a refinery explosion in Texas City, Texas, killed 15 workers and injured 180 employees.[24] OSHA announced the fine for "egregious, willful violations" of safety standards that led to the fatal explosion.[25] The U.S. Chemical Safety and Hazard Investigation Board, a government agency that investigates major workplace accidents, accused BP of knowing about "widespread safety problems" prior to the accident, which it said was the result of "drastic cost-cutting at the Texas refinery, where maintenance and infrastructure deteriorated over time, setting the stage for the disaster."[26] For more information about OSHA, see **http://www.osha.gov**.

2.2 Adverse Impact and Employment Discrimination

The EEOC has investigatory, enforcement, and informational responsibilities. Therefore, it investigates charges of discrimination, enforces the employment discrimination laws in federal court, and publishes guidelines that organizations can use to ensure they are in compliance with the law. One of the most important guidelines jointly issued by the EEOC, the Department of Labor, the U.S. Justice Department, and the federal Office of Personnel Management is the *Uniform Guidelines on Employee Selection Procedures*, which can be read in their entirety at **http://www.dol.gov/esa/regs/cfr/41cfr/toc_Chapt60/60_3_toc.htm**. These guidelines define two important criteria, disparate treatment and adverse impact, that are used in determining whether companies have engaged in discriminatory hiring and promotion practices.

disparate treatment intentional discrimination that occurs when people are purposely not given the same hiring, promotion, or membership opportunities because of their race, color, sex, age, ethnic group, national origin, or religious beliefs

adverse impact unintentional discrimination that occurs when members of a particular race, sex, or ethnic group are unintentionally harmed or disadvantaged because they are hired, promoted, or trained (or any other employment decision) at substantially lower rates than others

four-fifths (or 80 percent) rule a rule of thumb used by the courts and the EEOC to determine whether there is evidence of adverse impact. A violation of this rule occurs when the selection rate for a protected group is less than 80 percent or four-fifths of the selection rate for a nonprotected group.

Disparate treatment, which is *intentional* discrimination, occurs when people, despite being qualified, are *intentionally* not given the same hiring, promotion, or membership opportunities as other employees, because of their race, color, age, sex, ethnic group, national origin, or religious beliefs.[27] For example, ***Coca-Cola*** paid $192.5 million to settle a class-action disparate treatment lawsuit in which it was accused of purposely not giving African American employees equal opportunities in pay, promotions, and performance reviews.[28] Likewise, Rent-A-Center paid $12.3 million to settle a class-action disparate treatment lawsuit in which it was accused of not providing fair hiring and promotion opportunities to 4,600 female employees and job applicants.[29]

Legally, a key element of discrimination lawsuits is establishing motive, meaning that the employer intended to discriminate. If no motive can be established, then a claim of disparate treatment may actually be a case of adverse impact. **Adverse impact**, which is *unintentional* discrimination, occurs when members of a particular race, sex, or ethnic group are *unintentionally* harmed or disadvantaged because they are hired, promoted, or trained (or any other employment decision) at substantially lower rates than others. The courts and federal agencies use the **four-fifths (or 80 percent) rule** to determine if adverse impact has occurred. Adverse impact occurs if the decision rate for a protected group of people is less than four-fifths (or 80 percent) of the decision rate for a nonprotected group (usually white males). So, if 100 white applicants and 100 black applicants apply for entry-level jobs, and 60 white applicants are hired (60/100 = 60%), but only 20 black applicants are hired (20/100 = 20%), adverse impact has occurred (0.20/0.60 = 0.33). The criterion for the four-fifths rule in this situation is 0.48 (0.60 × 0.80 = 0.48). Since 0.33 is less than 0.48, the four-fifths rule has been violated.

Violation of the four-fifths rule is not an automatic indication of discrimination, however. If an employer can demonstrate that a selection procedure or test is valid, meaning that the test accurately predicts job performance or that the test is job related because it assesses applicants on specific tasks actually used in the job, then the organization may continue to use the test. If validity cannot be established, however, then a violation of the four-fifths rule may likely result in a lawsuit brought by employees, job applicants, or the EEOC itself.

2.3 Sexual Harassment

According to the EEOC, **sexual harassment** is a form of discrimination in which unwelcome sexual advances, requests for sexual favors, or other verbal or physical conduct of a sexual nature occurs. From a legal perspective, there are two kinds of sexual harassment, quid pro quo and hostile work environment.[30]

Quid pro quo sexual harassment occurs when employment outcomes, such as hiring, promotion, or simply keeping one's job, depend on whether an individual submits to being sexually harassed. For example, in a quid pro quo sexual harassment lawsuit against Costco, a female employee alleged that her boss groped her and bumped into her from behind to simulate sex. "He would tell her: 'You work with me and I'll work with you,' motioning to his private area."[31] The supervisor also allegedly told her that he would fire her if she reported his activities to upper management. In quid pro quo cases requests for sexual acts are linked to economic outcomes (such as keeping a job). A **hostile work environment** occurs when unwelcome and demeaning sexually related behavior creates an intimidating, hostile, and offensive work environment. In contrast to quid pro quo cases, a hostile work environment may not result in economic injury; however, it can lead to psychological injury. The world's largest law firm, BAKER & MCKENZIE, was fined $3.5 million for creating a sexually hostile work environment. Former secretary Rena Weeks accused partner Martin Greenstein of dropping candies in the pocket of her blouse, groping her breasts, pressing against her from behind, and pulling her arms back to "see which one is bigger." A number of women had already complained to supervisors that Greenstein harassed them, but the firm took no action against Greenstein in those cases. This fact, together with Greenstein's conduct toward Weeks, led the court to penalize the law firm.[32]

sexual harassment a form of discrimination in which unwelcome sexual advances, requests for sexual favors, or other verbal or physical conduct of a sexual nature occurs while performing one's job

quid pro quo sexual harassment a form of sexual harassment in which employment outcomes, such as hiring, promotion, or simply keeping one's job, depend on whether an individual submits to sexual harassment

hostile work environment a form of sexual harassment in which unwelcome and demeaning sexually related behavior creates an intimidating and offensive work environment

What common mistakes do managers make when it comes to sexual harassment laws?[33] First, many assume that the victim and harasser must be of opposite sexes. According to the courts, they do not. Sexual harassment can also occur between people of the same sex. Second, managers often assume that sexual harassment can occur only between coworkers or between supervisors and subordinates. Not so. Agents of employers, such as consultants, and even nonemployees can be sexual harassers. The key is not employee status but whether the harassment takes place while company business is being conducted. Third, it is often assumed that only people who have themselves been harassed can file complaints or lawsuits. In fact, especially in hostile work environments, anyone affected by offensive conduct can file a complaint or lawsuit.

Finally, what should companies do to make sure that sexual harassment laws are followed and not violated?[34] First, respond immediately when sexual harassment is reported. A quick response encourages victims of sexual harassment to report problems to management rather than to lawyers or the EEOC. Furthermore, a quick and fair investigation may serve as a deterrent to future harassment. A lawyer for the EEOC says, "Worse than having no sexual harassment policy is a policy that is not followed. It's merely window dressing. You wind up with destroyed morale when people who come forward are ignored, ridiculed, retaliated against, or nothing happens to the harasser."[35] Next, take the time to write a clear, understandable sexual harassment policy that is strongly worded, gives specific examples of what constitutes sexual harassment, spells outs sanctions and punishments, and is widely publicized within the company. This lets potential harassers and victims know what will not be tolerated and how the firm will deal with harassment should it occur.

Next, establish clear reporting procedures that indicate how, where, and to whom incidents of sexual harassment can be reported. The best procedures ensure that a complaint will receive a quick response, that impartial parties will handle the complaint, and that the privacy of the accused and accuser will be protected. At DuPont, Avon, and Texas Industries, employees can call a confidential hotline 24 hours a day, 365 days a year.[36]

> "Worse than having no sexual harassment policy is a policy that is not followed."
> EEOC LAWYER

Finally, managers should also be aware that most states and many cities or local governments have their own employment-related laws and enforcement agencies. So compliance with federal law is often not enough. In fact, organizations can be in full compliance with federal law and at the same time be in violation of state or local sexual harassment laws.

Review 2: Employment Legislation

Human resource management is subject to the following major federal employment laws: Equal Pay Act, Civil Rights Acts of 1964 and 1991, Age Discrimination in Employment Act, Pregnancy Discrimination Act, Americans with Disabilities Act, Family and Medical Leave Act, and Uniformed Services Employment and Reemployment Rights Act. Human resource management is also subject to review by these federal agencies: Equal Employment Opportunity Commission, Department of Labor, Occupational Safety and Health Administration, and National Labor Relations Board. In general, these laws state that sex, age, religion, color, national origin, race, disability, and pregnancy may not be considered in employment decisions unless these factors reasonably qualify as BFOQs. Two important criteria, disparate treatment (intentional discrimination) and adverse impact (unintentional discrimination), are used to decide whether companies have wrongly discriminated against someone. While motive is a key part of determining disparate treatment, the courts and federal enforcement agencies use the four-fifths rule to determine if adverse impact has occurred. The two kinds of sexual harassment are quid pro quo and hostile work environment. Managers often wrongly assume that the victim and harasser must be of the opposite sex, that sexual harassment can only occur between coworkers or between supervisors and their employees, and that only people who have themselves been harassed can file complaints or lawsuits. To ensure compliance with sexual harassment laws, companies should respond immediately when harassment is reported; write a clear, understandable sexual harassment policy; establish clear reporting procedures; and be aware of and follow city and state laws concerning sexual harassment.

FINDING QUALIFIED WORKERS

Technical Materials, which sells electroplating and metal-bonding processes to car manufacturers and high-tech industries, was enjoying record sales but could not find enough qualified employees to work in its factories. Its pool of prospective employees was so weak that one in six applicants failed its drug test; the usual failure rate was one in 25. Company president Al Lubrano made numerous strong job offers, added more pay and benefits to those offers when applicants asked for more, and still couldn't hire anybody. Finally, Lubrano says, "When it got ridiculous, we walked away."[37] Likewise, the nursing shortage mentioned at the beginning of the chapter is why Mary Viney, director of patient care services at Seton Northwest Hospital in Austin, Texas, found herself in Manila, trying to encourage Filipino nurses to work for her hospital in Austin, Texas. In Texas, says Viney, "it's a day-to-day, shift-to-shift challenge to get enough nurses."[38]

As these examples illustrate, finding qualified workers can be an increasingly difficult task. Finding qualified applicants is just the first step, however. Deciding which applicants to hire is the second. Gail Hyland-Savage, CEO of real estate and marketing firm Michaelson, Connor & Boul, says, "Staffing is absolutely critical to the success of every company. To be competitive in today's economy, companies need the best people to create ideas and execute them for the organization. Without a competent and talented workforce, organizations will stagnate and eventually perish. The right employees are the most important resources of companies today."[39]

After reading the next two sections, you should be able to

3 explain how companies use recruiting to find qualified job applicants.

4 describe the selection techniques and procedures that companies use when deciding which applicants should receive job offers.

3 Recruiting

Recruiting *is the process of developing a pool of qualified job applicants. Let's examine* ***3.1 what job analysis is and how it is used in recruiting*** *and* ***3.2 how companies use internal recruiting*** *and* ***3.3 external recruiting to find qualified job applicants***.

3.1 Job Analysis and Recruiting

Job analysis is a purposeful, systematic process for collecting information on the important work-related aspects of a job.[40] Typically, a job analysis collects four kinds of information:

- *Work activities, such as what workers do and how, when, and why they do it*
- *The tools and equipment used to do the job*
- *The context in which the job is performed, such as the actual working conditions or schedule*
- *The personnel requirements for performing the job, meaning the knowledge, skills, and abilities needed to do a job well*[41]

recruiting the process of developing a pool of qualified job applicants

job analysis a purposeful, systematic process for collecting information on the important work-related aspects of a job

Job analysis information can be collected by having job incumbents and/or supervisors complete questionnaires about their jobs, by direct observation, by interviews, or by filming employees as they perform their jobs.

Job descriptions and job specifications are two of the most important results of a job analysis. A **job description** is a written description of the basic tasks, duties, and responsibilities required of an employee holding a particular job. **Job specifications**, which are often included as a separate section of a job description, are a summary of the qualifications needed to successfully perform the job. Exhibit 11.5 shows a job description and the job specifications for a helicopter pilot for the city of Little Rock, Arkansas.

Because a job analysis specifies what a job entails, as well as the knowledge, skills, and abilities that are needed to do the job well, companies must complete a job analysis *before* beginning to recruit job applicants. Exhibit 11.6 shows that job analysis, job descriptions, and job specifications are the foundation on which all critical human resource activities are built. They are used during recruiting and selection to match applicant qualifications with the requirements of the job. They are used throughout the staffing process to ensure that selection devices and the decisions based on these devices are job related. For example, the questions asked in an interview should be based on the most important work activities identified by a job analysis. Likewise, during performance appraisals, employees should be evaluated in areas that a job analysis has identified as the most important in a job.

job description a written description of the basic tasks, duties, and responsibilities required of an employee holding a particular job

job specifications a written summary of the qualifications needed to successfully perform a particular job

Job analyses, job descriptions, and job specifications also help companies meet the legal requirement that their human resource decisions be job related. To be judged *job related*, recruitment, selection, training, performance appraisals, and employee separations must be valid and be directly related to the important aspects of the job, as identified by a careful job analysis. In fact, in *Griggs v. Duke Power Co.* and *Albemarle Paper Co. v. Moody*, the U.S. Supreme Court stated that companies should use job analyses to help establish the job relatedness of their human resource

Exhibit 11.5

Job Description and Job Specifications for a Helicopter Pilot for the City of Little Rock, Arkansas

DESCRIPTION FOR HELICOPTER PILOT
To provide assistance for air searches, river rescues, high-rise building rescues, and other assignments, by providing air survey and aviation response. Pilots a rotary-wing aircraft, serving as pilot or copilot, to assist in air searches, river rescues, high-rise building rescues, and other assignments. Ensures that aircraft is properly outfitted for each assignment (equipment, rigging tools, supplies, etc.). Performs preflight inspection of aircraft; checks rotors, fuel, lubricants, controls, etc. Prepares written reports on assignments; maintains flight logs. Obtains weather reports; determines to proceed with assignments given forecasted weather conditions. Operates a radio to maintain contact with and to report information to airport personnel and police department personnel.
JOB SPECIFICATIONS FOR HELICOPTER PILOT
Must possess a valid Commercial Pilot's License for rotary-wing aircraft before employment and maintain licensure for the duration of employment in this position. Must have considerable knowledge of Federal Aviation Administration (FAA) laws and regulations, rotary-wing aircraft operating procedures, air traffic safety, flying procedures and navigational techniques, and FAA and police radio operation and procedures. Must have some knowledge of preventive maintenance methods, repair practices, safety requirements, and inspection procedures. Must have skill in the operation of a rotary-wing aircraft and radio equipment and the ability to conduct safety inspections of aircraft, to maintain aircraft maintenance logs and prepare reports, to detect and identify aircraft malfunction symptoms, to detect and recognize ground conditions and characteristics (utility line breaks, river currents, etc.), to read maps and air navigation charts, and to communicate effectively, both orally and in writing. Must have completed high school; at least one thousand hours of flight time experience in piloting rotary-wing aircraft; OR any equivalent combination of experience and training that provides the required knowledge, skills, and abilities.

Source: "Job Description: Helicopter Pilot," City of Little Rock, Arkansas, http://www.littlerock.org, 31 May 2003.

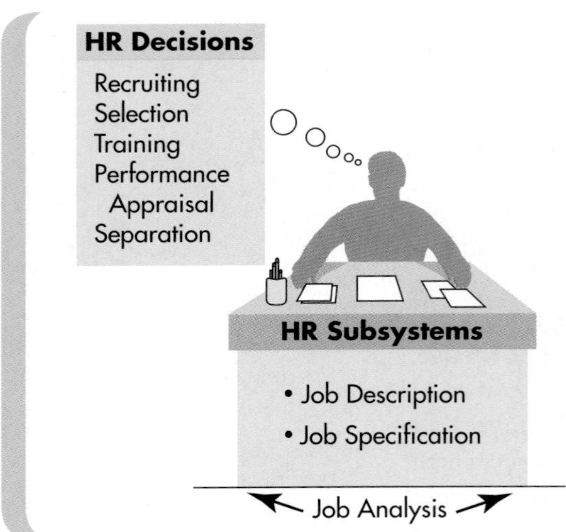

Exhibit 11.6

Importance of Job Analysis to Human Resource Management

procedures.[42] The EEOC's *Uniform Guidelines on Employee Selection Procedures* also recommend that companies base their human resource procedures on job analysis.

3.2 Internal Recruiting

Internal recruiting is the process of developing a pool of qualified job applicants from people who already work in the company. Internal recruiting, sometimes called "promotion from within," improves employee commitment, morale, and motivation. Recruiting current employees also reduces recruitment startup time and costs, and because employees are already familiar with the company's culture and procedures, they are more likely to succeed in new jobs. This is why, according to Bob Graczyk, director of human resources, that **QUICK CHEK FOOD STORES**' goal is to hire "100 percent" of its new store managers through internal recruiting. Graczyk says, "We try to find people whose personal values align with the company values."[43] And, of course, it's easier to do that when the applicants already work for the company. Job posting and career paths are two methods of internal recruiting.

Job posting is a procedure for advertising job openings within the company to existing employees. A job description and requirements are typically posted on a bulletin board, in a company newsletter, or in an internal computerized job bank that is accessible only to employees. For example, under Japan-based **FUJISAWA PHARMACEUTICALS**' "Job Challenge" policy, all Fujisawa departments and divisions recruit internally by posting job openings to the company's intranet for all employees to see.[44] Job posting helps organizations discover hidden talent, allows employees to take responsibility for career planning, and makes it easier for companies to retain talented workers who are dissatisfied in their current jobs and would otherwise leave the company.[45] Fujisawa Pharmaceuticals also has a "Free Agent" policy, which encourages employees who want to change jobs to post their résumés to the same intranet. When Fujisawa's departments and divisions have openings, the first place they look to fill the positions is the company intranet.[46]

A *career path* is a planned sequence of jobs through which employees may advance within an organization. For example, a person who starts as a sales representative may move up to sales manager and then to district or regional sales manager. Career paths help employees focus on long-term goals and development while also helping companies increase employee retention. **ECHOSTAR COMMUNICATIONS** developed a "career path" program designed to persuade call-center workers to stick around longer and cut the costs of hiring and training new workers. Employees who participate in training and meet required skill levels are eligible for rapid promotions and pay increases. EchoStar executives say the program is working—the average call-center agent now stays for 19 months, up from 9 months two years ago. Jessica Nicolo, an early participant in EchoStar's program, was promoted four times in two years and her pay is now 27 percent higher than when she started. Nicolo, a mother of two, says she doesn't expect to leave EchoStar for a long time because now she doesn't feel trapped in another dead-end job.[47]

internal recruiting the process of developing a pool of qualified job applicants from people who already work in the company

external recruiting the process of developing a pool of qualified job applicants from outside the company

3.3 External Recruiting

External recruiting is the process of developing a pool of qualified job applicants from outside the company. For example, as part of its strategic plan for long-term success, **ELECTRONIC ARTS**, the maker of top-selling video games such as *Madden NFL*, has put together a "top 40" list of the most talented managers in the industry (including senior executives, game directors and producers) that it hopes to eventually recruit to the company.[48] José Martin, head of human resources for EA's 13 game-production studios, says, "The challenge for companies now is not identifying talented people but persuading those people to join your company."[49]

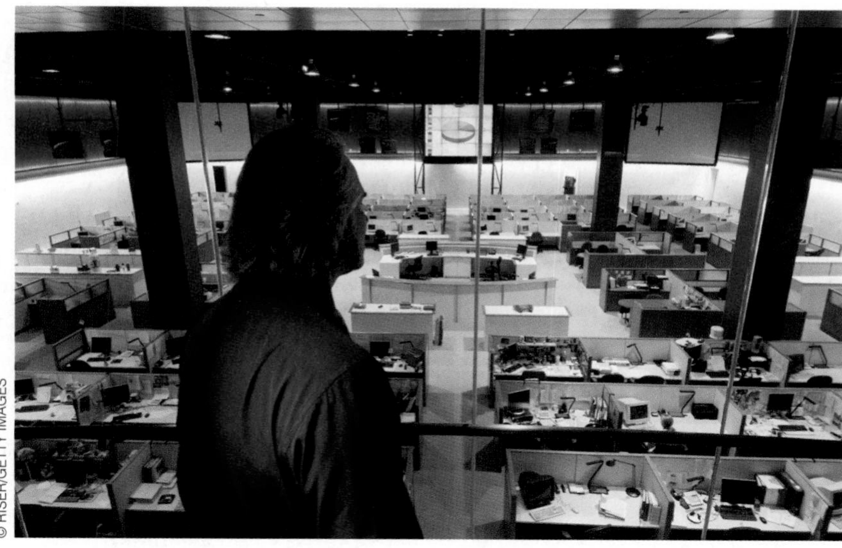

© RISER/GETTY IMAGES

Call centers are known to have high turnover rates. To reduce that churn, EchoStar developed career paths to help employees see how they could move up the corporate ladder. The result is that the average tenure of a call-center agent has more than doubled.

External recruitment methods include advertising (newspapers, magazines, direct mail, radio, or television), employee referrals (asking current employees to recommend possible job applicants), walk-ins (people who apply on their own), outside organizations (universities, technical/trade schools, professional societies), employment services (state or private employment agencies, temporary help agencies, and professional search firms), special events (career conferences or job fairs), and Internet job sites. Which external recruiting method should you use? Studies show that employee referrals, walk-ins, newspaper advertisements, and state employment agencies tend to be used most frequently for office/clerical and production/service employees. By contrast, newspaper advertisements and college/university recruiting are used most frequently for professional/technical employees. When recruiting managers, organizations tend to rely most heavily on newspaper advertisements, employee referrals, and search firms.[50]

In the last few years, the biggest changes in external recruiting has been the increased use of the Internet. Some companies now recruit applicants through Internet job sites such as **MONSTER.COM**, **HOTJOBS.COM**, Hire.com, and **CAREERBUILDER.COM**. Companies can post job openings for 30 days on one of these sites for about half of the cost of running an advertisement just once in a Sunday newspaper. Plus, Internet job listings generate nine times as many résumés as one ad in the Sunday newspaper.[51] And because these sites attract so many applicants and offer so many services, companies save by finding qualified applicants without having to use more expensive recruitment and search firms, which typically charge one-third of a new hire's salary.[52] Monica Albano, executive vice president of human resources for the Americas at Reuters, the news and information company, says, "Utilizing Hire.com, we're able to attract the best available talent, be specific about the data we retain on people, and utilize that data as openings become available. Overall, we saved in excess of $1.5 million worldwide."[53]

Despite their many benefits, job websites have a significant drawback: Companies may receive hundreds, if not thousands, of applications from *unqualified* applicants. The sheer volume increases the importance of proper screening and selection. For example, when IMLogic, which makes instant messaging software, advertised job openings on Monster.com and CareerBuilder.com, the company was flooded with 200 résumés the first hour the jobs were posted and nearly 750 résumés within two days. CEO Francis deSouza says, "We weren't ready for that."[54]

Therefore, assuming that the most qualified applicants will learn something about the company before applying, many organizations now advertise job openings directly on their websites. For example, Subway accepts applications for part-time work at its 27,868 restaurants in 86 countries at its website (**http://www.subway.com/applications/InStoreJobs/index.aspx**).[55] In fact, 60 percent of the people hired via the Internet have applied at a company website.

Today, between 82 percent and 92 percent of companies use the Internet to fill job openings. In fact, Internet recruiting is now second to newspaper advertising in terms of the number of applicants it generates.[56] And with the addition of the ".jobs" Internet top-level domain (for example, **http://www.dell.jobs** for jobs at Dell, Inc.), more and more companies will use their websites to attract, recruit, and screen job applicants.[57] That's because job seekers tend to first visit company websites before looking for a job through more general sites. In fact, 95 percent of *Fortune* 500 companies have career portals on their corporate websites.[58]

Review 3: **Recruiting**

Recruiting is the process of finding qualified job applicants. The first step in recruiting is to conduct a job analysis to collect information about the important work-related aspects of the job. The job analysis is then used to write a job description of basic tasks, duties, and responsibilities and to write job specifications indicating the knowledge, skills, and abilities needed to perform the job. Job analyses, descriptions, and specifications help companies meet the legal requirement that their human resource decisions be job related. Internal recruiting, or finding qualified job applicants from inside the company, can be done through job posting and career paths. External recruiting, or finding qualified job applicants from outside the company, is done through advertising, employee referrals, walk-ins, outside organizations, employment services, special events, and Internet job sites. The Internet is a particularly promising method of external recruiting because of its low cost, wide reach, and ability to communicate and receive unlimited information.

Selecting qualified applicants is especially critical for police departments. That's why in East Providence, Rhode Island, the police department uses the "rule of three."

© ASSOCIATED PRESS

4 Selection

Once the recruitment process has produced a pool of qualified applicants, the selection process is used to determine which applicants have the best chance of performing well on the job. When the **East Providence, Rhode Island Police Department** has job openings, it follows a "rule of three," meaning that no matter how many candidates it has for an opening, it looks at only the top three applicants, as determined by a standardized written test. Those top three applicants for every position must then pass a physical fitness test and a background check. Every applicant who makes it that far is then put on a list of official candidates for police jobs for two years. Only the best candidates on that list participate in group interviews with the city manager, police chief, deputy chief, a police captain, and the department's personnel director and affirmative action officer, each of whom privately ranks the candidates after each interview. Applicants with the highest rankings from the group interviews are offered positions in the Police Academy. The remaining applicants from the group interviews may be considered two more times before being rejected.[59]

As this example illustrates, **selection** is the process of gathering information about job applicants to decide who should be offered a job. To make sure that selection decisions are accurate and legally defendable, the EEOC's *Uniform Guidelines on Employee Selection Procedures* recommend that all selection procedures be validated. **Validation** is the process of determining how well a selection test or procedure predicts future job performance. The better or more accurate the prediction of future job performance, the more valid a test is said to be. See the "What Really Works" feature later in this chapter for more on the validity of common selection tests and procedures.

selection the process of gathering information about job applicants to decide who should be offered a job

validation the process of determining how well a selection test or procedure predicts future job performance. The better or more accurate the prediction of future job performance, the more valid a test is said to be.

Let's examine common selection procedures, such as ***4.1 application forms and résumés, 4.2 references and background checks, 4.3 selection tests,*** *and* ***4.4 interviews.***

4.1 Application Forms and Résumés

The first selection devices that most job applicants encounter when they seek a job are application forms and résumés. Both contain similar information about an applicant, such as name, address, job and educational history, and so forth. Though an organization's application form often asks for information already provided by the applicant's résumé, most organizations prefer to collect this information in their own format for entry into a human resource information system.

Employment laws apply to application forms, just as they do to all selection devices. Application forms may ask applicants for only valid, job-related information. Nonetheless, application forms commonly ask applicants for non-job-related information, such as marital status, maiden name, age, or date of high school graduation. Indeed, one study found that 73 percent of organizations had application forms that violated at least one federal or state law.[60] Exhibit 11.7 lists the kinds of information that companies may not request in application forms, during job interviews, or in any other part of the selection process. Courts will assume that

doing the right thing

Don't Embellish Your Résumé

Your résumé is supposed to help you get the interview that can get you a job. So where do you draw the line between making yourself look attractive to a potential employer and lying? Despite the strong temptation to improve your odds of getting a job, embellishing your résumé is wrong. Moreover, the information on your résumé is legally binding. If you misrepresent information or lie on your résumé—and many people do—you're breaking the law and can be fired. But where should you draw the line? In general, if what you put on your résumé feels wrong, don't do it. More specifically, don't embellish job titles, responsibilities, employment dates, college degrees, certifications, general qualifications, or previous experience in any way. Do the right thing: Tell the truth on your résumé.[61]

1. *Children.* Don't ask applicants if they have children, plan to have them, or have or need child care. Questions about children can unintentionally single out women.
2. *Age.* Because of the Age Discrimination in Employment Act, employers cannot ask job applicants their age during the hiring process. Since most people graduate high school at the age of 18, even asking for high school graduation dates could violate the law.
3. *Disabilities.* Don't ask if applicants have physical or mental disabilities. According to the Americans with Disabilities Act, disabilities (and reasonable accommodations for them) cannot be discussed until a job offer has been made.
4. *Physical characteristics.* Don't ask for information about height, weight, or other physical characteristics. Questions about weight could be construed as leading to discrimination toward overweight people, who studies show are less likely to be hired in general.
5. *Name.* Yes, you can ask an applicant's name, but you cannot ask a female applicant for her maiden name because it indicates marital status. Asking for a maiden name could also lead to charges that the organization was trying to establish a candidate's ethnic background.
6. *Citizenship.* Asking applicants about citizenship could lead to claims of discrimination on the basis of national origin. However, according to the Immigration Reform and Control Act, companies may ask applicants if they have a legal right to work in the United States.
7. *Lawsuits.* Applicants may not be asked if they have ever filed a lawsuit against an employer. Federal and state laws prevent this to protect whistleblowers from retaliation by future employers.
8. *Arrest records.* Applicants cannot be asked about their arrest records. Arrests don't have legal standing. However, applicants can be asked whether they have been convicted of a crime.
9. *Smoking.* Applicants cannot be asked if they smoke. Smokers might be able to claim that they weren't hired because of fears of higher absenteeism and medical costs. However, they can be asked if they are aware of company policies that restrict smoking at work.
10. *AIDS/HIV.* Applicants can't be asked about AIDS, HIV, or any other medical condition. Questions of this nature would violate the Americans with Disabilities Act, as well as federal and state civil rights laws.

Source: J. S. Pouliot, "Topics to Avoid with Applicants," *Nation's Business* 80, no. 7 (1992): 57.

Exhibit 11.7

Topics That Employers Should Avoid in Application Forms, Interviews, or Other Parts of the Selection Process

you consider all of the information you request of applicants, even if you don't. Be sure to ask only those questions that directly relate to the candidate's ability and motivation to perform the job.

Companies should also be aware that employment laws in other countries may differ from U.S. laws. For instance, in France, employers may ask applicants for non-job-related personal information such as their age or the number of children. And most French employers expect applicants to include a picture with their curriculum vitae (another term for résumé).[62] Consequently, companies should closely examine their application forms, interview questions, and other selection procedures for compliance with the law wherever they do business.

Résumés also pose problems for companies, but in a different way. Studies show that as many as one-third of job applicants intentionally falsify some information on their résumés and that 80 percent of the information on résumés may be misleading. A study of 200,000 job applicants found that 20 percent listed college degrees they hadn't earned, 30 percent changed the dates of their employment, 40 percent reported much higher salaries, 30 percent incorrectly described their previous jobs, 27 percent falsified their references, and 25 percent reported working at nonexistent or no longer existing companies, so the fact that they never worked there couldn't be discovered.[63]

Therefore, managers should verify the information collected via résumés and application forms by comparing it with additional information collected during interviews and other stages of the selection process, such as references and background checks, which are discussed next.

4.2 References and Background Checks

Nearly all companies ask an applicant to provide **employment references**, such as previous employers or coworkers, that they can contact to learn more about the candidate. **Background checks** are used to verify the truthfulness and accuracy of information that applicants provide about themselves and to uncover negative, job-related background information not provided by applicants. Background checks are conducted by contacting "educational institutions, prior employers, court records, police and governmental agencies, and other informational sources, either by telephone, mail, remote computer access, or through in-person investigations."[64]

Unfortunately, previous employers are increasingly reluctant to provide references or background check information for fear of being sued by previous employees for defamation. If former employers provide potential employers with unsubstantiated information that damages applicants' chances of being hired, applicants can (and do) sue for defamation. As a result, 54 percent of employers will not provide information about previous employees.[65] Many provide only dates of employment, positions held, and date of separation.

When previous employers decline to provide meaningful references or background information, they put other employers at risk of *negligent hiring* lawsuits, in which an employer is held liable for the actions of an employee who would not have been hired if the employer had conducted a thorough reference search and background check.[66] In Florida, the **Tallahassee Furniture Company** hired a worker to make home furniture deliveries but did not conduct a background check or even ask him to complete an application form. After being hired, he attacked a woman in her home with a knife. When she sued the company, it discovered that he had a history of drug use, violent assault, and mental illness. The courts awarded the woman $2.5 million in damages.[67]

With previous employers generally unwilling to give full, candid references and with negligent hiring lawsuits awaiting companies that don't get such references and background information, what can companies do? Conduct criminal record checks, especially if the job for which the person is applying involves money, drugs, control over valuable goods, or access to the elderly, people with disabilities, or people's homes.[68] According to the Society for Human Resource Management, 96 percent of companies conduct background checks and 80 percent of companies go further and conduct criminal record checks.[69]

Next, dig deeper for more information. Ask references to provide references. **Voca Corporation**, based in Columbus, Ohio, has 2,500 employees in six states who care for people with mental retardation and developmental disabilities. Hilary Franklin, director of human resources, says she not only checks references, but also asks the references to provide references and then asks those references for still others. She says, "As you get two or three times removed, you get more detailed, honest information."[70]

Next, ask applicants to sign a waiver that permits you to check references, run a background check, or contact anyone else with knowledge of their work performance or history. Likewise, ask applicants if there is anything they would like the company to know or if they expect you to hear anything "unusual" when contacting references.[71] This in itself is often enough to get applicants to share information that they typically withhold. When you've finished checking, keep the findings confidential to minimize the chances of a defamation charge.

employment references sources such as previous employers or coworkers who can provide job-related information about job candidates

background checks procedures used to verify the truthfulness and accuracy of information that applicants provide about themselves and to uncover negative, job-related background information not provided by applicants

© IMAGE SOURCE PINK/JUPITER IMAGES

Before hiring, make sure to conduct thorough background checks.

Always document all reference and background checks, noting who was called and what information was obtained. And to reduce the likelihood that negligent hiring lawsuits will succeed, it's particularly important to document which companies and people refused to share reference check and background information.

Finally, consider hiring private investigators to conduct background checks. They can often uncover surprising information not revealed by traditional background checks. When an American investment company was looking for a Japanese manager to run its Tokyo office, it quickly found a strong applicant who claimed to have experience with dozens of initial public offerings, or IPOs (the process of bringing privately held companies public so that shares of company stock can be sold in financial markets). In multiple interviews, this applicant clearly had detailed information about each IPO deal. However, a background check soon revealed that he was the Japanese translator and not the financier behind each deal.[72]

4.3 Selection Tests

We're all aware that some people do well in jobs while other people do poorly, but how do you determine into which category an applicant falls? Selection tests give organizational decision makers a chance to know who will likely do well in a job and who won't. The basic idea behind selection testing is to have applicants take a test that measures something directly or indirectly related to doing well on the job. The selection tests discussed here are specific ability tests, cognitive ability tests, biographical data, personality tests, work sample tests, and assessment centers.

specific ability tests (aptitude tests) tests that measure the extent to which an applicant possesses the particular kind of ability needed to do a job well

cognitive ability tests tests that measure the extent to which applicants have abilities in perceptual speed, verbal comprehension, numerical aptitude, general reasoning, and spatial aptitude

Specific ability tests measure the extent to which an applicant possesses the particular kind of ability needed to do a job well. Specific ability tests are also called **aptitude tests** because they measure aptitude for doing a particular task well. For example, if you took the SAT to get into college, then you've taken the aptly named Scholastic Aptitude Test, which is one of the best predictors of how well students will do in college (that is, their scholastic performance). Specific ability tests also exist for mechanical, clerical, sales, and physical work. For example, clerical workers have to be good at accurately reading and scanning numbers as they type or enter data. Exhibit 11.8 shows items similar to the Minnesota Clerical Test; applicants have only a short time to determine if the two columns of numbers and letters are identical. Applicants who are good at this are likely to do well as clerical or data-entry workers.

Cognitive ability tests measure the extent to which applicants have abilities in perceptual speed, verbal comprehension, numerical aptitude, general reasoning, and spatial aptitude. In other words, these tests indicate how quickly and how well people understand words, numbers, logic, and spatial dimensions. Whereas specific ability tests predict job performance in only particular types of jobs, cognitive ability tests accurately predict job performance in almost all kinds of jobs.[73] Why is this so? The reason is that people with strong cognitive or mental abilities are usually good at learning new things, processing complex information, solving problems, and making decisions, and these abilities are important in almost all jobs.[74] In fact, cognitive ability tests are almost always the best predictors of job performance. Consequently, if you were allowed to

Exhibit 11.8

Clerical Test Items Similar to Those Found on the Minnesota Clerical Test

	NUMBERS/LETTERS		SAME	
1.	3468251	3467251	Yes	No
2.	4681371	4681371	Yes	No
3.	7218510	7218520	Yes	No
4.	ZXYAZAB	ZXYAZAB	Yes	No
5.	ALZYXMN	ALZYXNM	Yes	No
6.	PRQZYMN	PRQZYMN	Yes	No

Source: N. W. Schmitt & R. J. Klimoski, *Research Methods in Human Resource Management* (Mason, OH: South-Western, 1991). Used with permission.

use just one selection test, cognitive ability tests would be the one to use.[75] (In practice, though, companies use a battery of different tests because doing so leads to much more accurate selection decisions.)

Biographical data, or **biodata**, are extensive surveys that ask applicants questions about their personal backgrounds and life experiences. The basic idea behind biodata is that past behavior (personal background and life experience) is the best predictor of future behavior. For example, during World War II, the ***U.S. Air Force*** had to quickly test tens of thousands of men without flying experience to determine who was likely to be a good pilot. Since flight training took several months and was very expensive, selecting the right people for training was important. After examining extensive biodata, it found that one of the best predictors of success in flight school was whether students had ever built model airplanes that actually flew. This one biodata item was almost as good a predictor as the entire set of selection tests that the Air Force was using at the time.[76]

Most biodata questionnaires have over 100 items that gather information about habits and attitudes, health, interpersonal relations, money, what it was like growing up in your family (parents, siblings, childhood years, teen years), personal habits, current home (spouse, children), hobbies, education and training, values, preferences, and work.[78] In general, biodata are very good predictors of future job performance, especially in entry-level jobs.

You may have noticed that some of the information requested in biodata surveys also appears in Exhibit 11.7 as topics employers should avoid in applications, interviews, or other parts of the selection process. This information can be requested in biodata questionnaires provided that the company can demonstrate that the information is job related (that is, valid) and does not result in adverse impact against protected groups of job applicants. Biodata surveys should be validated and tested for adverse impact before they are used to make selection decisions.[79]

Personality is the relatively stable set of behaviors, attitudes, and emotions displayed over time that makes people different from each other. **Personality tests** measure the extent to which applicants possess different kinds of job-related personality dimensions. In Chapter 12, you will learn that there are five major

doing the right thing

Don't Use Psychics, Lie Detectors, or Handwriting Analysis to Make HR Decisions

The Coronado Bay Resort in San Diego hired a psychic to work with its 18-member management team as a way of "moving the managers to the next step." Seventy-five percent of the organizations in France and Switzerland use handwriting analysis for hiring and promotion decisions. In the past, employers in the United States regularly used polygraphs (lie detectors) for preemployment screening. What do these methods have in common? Companies use them, but they don't work. For example, there is no scientific evidence that handwriting analysis works, yet managers continue to use it. Lie detectors are no more accurate than a coin flip in screening out unethical employees. Fortunately, the Employee Polygraph Protection Act now prevents organizations from using polygraphs for hiring and promotion decisions. As for psychics at work, well, enough said. So, when you're hiring and promoting people, do the right thing. Stay away from fads. Use the reliable, valid, scientifically proven selection and assessment procedures discussed here to hire the right workers and promote the right people into management.[77]

biographical data (biodata) extensive surveys that ask applicants questions about their personal backgrounds and life experiences

personality tests tests that measure the extent to which applicants possess different kinds of job-related personality dimensions personality dimensions (the Big Five)—extraversion, emotional stability, agreeableness, conscientiousness, and openness to experience—related to work behavior.[80] Of these, only conscientiousness, the degree to which someone is organized, hardworking, responsible, persevering, thorough, and achievement oriented, predicts job performance across a wide variety of jobs.[81] Conscientiousness works especially well in combination with cognitive ability tests, allowing companies to select applicants who are organized, hardworking, responsible, and smart!

work sample tests tests that require applicants to perform tasks that are actually done on the job

assessment centers a series of managerial simulations, graded by trained observers, that are used to determine applicants' capability for managerial work

Work sample tests, also called *performance tests*, require applicants to perform tasks that are actually done on the job. So, unlike specific ability, cognitive ability, biographical data, and personality tests, which are indirect predictors of job performance, work sample tests directly measure job applicants' capability to do the job. For example, a computer-based work sample test has applicants assume the role of a real estate agent who must decide how to interact with "virtual clients" in a gamelike scenario. And, as in real life, the clients can be frustrating, confusing, demanding, or indecisive. In one situation, the wife loves the "house" but the husband hates it. The applicants, just like actual real estate agents, must demonstrate what they would do in these realistic situations.[82] This work sample simulation gives real estate companies direct evidence of whether applicants can do the job if they are hired. Work sample tests are generally very good at predicting future job performance; however, they can be expensive to administer and can be used for only one kind of job. For example, an auto dealership could not use a work sample test for mechanics as a selection test for sales representatives.

Assessment centers use a series of job-specific simulations that are graded by multiple trained observers to determine applicants' ability to perform managerial work. Unlike the previously described selection tests that are commonly used for specific jobs or entry-level jobs, assessment centers are most often used to select applicants who have high potential to be good managers. Assessment centers often last two to five days and require participants to complete a number of tests and exercises that simulate managerial work.

Some of the more common assessment center exercises are in-basket exercises, role-plays, small-group presentations, and leaderless group discussions. An *in-basket exercise* is a paper-and-pencil test in which an applicant is given a manager's "in-basket" containing memos, phone messages, organizational policies, and other communications normally received by and available to managers. Applicants have a limited time to read through the in-basket, prioritize the items, and decide how to deal with each item. Experienced managers then score the applicants' decisions and recommendations. Exhibit 11.9 shows an item that could be used in an assessment center for evaluating applicants for a job as a store manager.

In a *leaderless group discussion*, another common assessment center exercise, a group of six applicants is given approximately two hours to solve a problem, but no one is put in charge (hence the name "leaderless" group discussion). Trained observers watch and score each participant on the extent to which he or she facilitates discussion, listens, leads, persuades, and works well with others.

Exhibit 11.9
In-Basket Item for an Assessment Center for Store Managers

February 28
Sam & Dave's Discount Warehouse
Orange, California

Dear Store Manager,

Last week, my children and I were shopping in your store. After doing our grocery shopping, we stopped in the electronics department and asked the clerk, whose name is Donald Block, to help usfind a copy of the latest version of the Madden NFL video game. Mr. Block was rude, unhelpful, and told us to find it for ourselves as he was busy.

I've been a loyal customer for over six years and expect you to immediately do something about Mr.Block's behavior. If you don't, I'll start doing my shopping somewhere else.

Sincerely,
Margaret Quinlan

Source: Adapted from N. W. Schmitt & R. J. Klimoski, *Research Methods in Human Resource Management* (Mason, OH: South-Western 1991).

Are tests perfect predictors of job performance? No, they aren't. Some people who do well on selection tests will do poorly in their jobs. Likewise, some people who do poorly on selection tests (and therefore weren't hired) would have been very good performers. Nonetheless, valid tests will minimize these selection errors (hiring people who should not have been hired, and not hiring people who should have been hired) while maximizing correct selection decisions (hiring people who should have been hired, and not hiring people who should not have been hired). In short, tests increase the chances that you'll hire the right person for the job, that is, someone who turns out to be a good performer. So, although tests aren't perfect, almost nothing predicts future job performance as well as the selection tests discussed here. For more on how well selection tests increase the odds of hiring the right person for the job, see the "What Really Works" feature.

4.4 Interviews

Sharon Ball, director of recruiting and administration for Epitec Group, has interviewed all kinds of mistake-prone job candidates: one with food on his sweater, another with breath that "smelled like bile," one who reeked of marijuana, and one who stopped the interview to talk on his cell phone for five minutes. Only the applicant with bad breath was hired. She says, "Nice guy. We had to pump him full of Tic Tacs."[83] In **interviews**, company representatives ask job applicants job-related questions to determine whether they are qualified for the job. Interviews are probably the most frequently used and relied on selection device. There are several basic kinds of interviews: unstructured, structured, and semistructured.

In **unstructured interviews**, interviewers are free to ask applicants anything they want, and studies show that they do. Because interviewers often disagree about which questions should be asked during interviews, different interviewers tend to ask applicants very different questions.[84] Furthermore, individual interviewers even seem to have a tough time asking the same questions from one interview to the next. This high level of inconsistency lowers the validity of unstructured interviews as a selection device because comparing applicant responses can be difficult. As a result, unstructured interviews are about half as accurate as structured interviews at predicting which job applicants should be hired.

By contrast, with **structured interviews**, standardized interview questions are prepared ahead of time so that all applicants are asked the same job-related questions.[85] Four kinds of questions are typically asked in structured interviews:

- Situational questions, *which ask applicants how they would respond in a hypothetical situation ("What would you do if . . . ?"). These questions are more appropriate for hiring new graduates, who are unlikely to have encountered real-work situations because of their limited work experience.*
- Behavioral questions, *which ask applicants what they did in previous jobs that were similar to the job for which they are applying ("In your previous jobs, tell me about . . ."). These questions are more appropriate for hiring experienced individuals.*
- Background questions, *which ask applicants about their work experience, education, and other qualifications ("Tell me about the training you received at . . .").*
- Job-knowledge questions, *which ask applicants to demonstrate their job knowledge (for example, nurses might be asked, "Give me an example of a time when one of your patients had a severe reaction to a medication. How did you handle it?")*[86]

The primary advantage of structured interviews is that comparing applicants is much easier because they are all asked the same questions. Structuring interviews also

interviews a selection tool in which company representatives ask job applicants job-related questions to determine whether they are qualified for the job

unstructured interviews interviews in which interviewers are free to ask the applicants anything they want

structured interviews interviews in which all applicants are asked the same set of standardized questions, usually including situational, behavioral, background, and job-knowledge questions

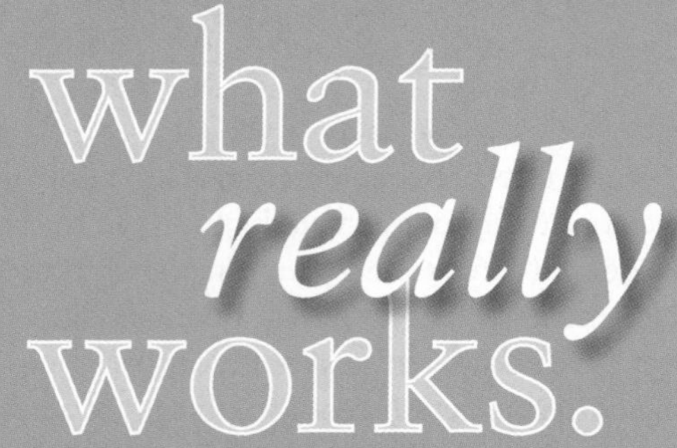

USING SELECTION TESTS TO HIRE GOOD WORKERS

Hiring new employees is always something of a gamble. When you say, "We'd like to offer you the job," you never know how it's going to turn out. Nonetheless, the selection tests discussed in this chapter can go a long way toward taking the gambling aspect out of the hiring process. Indeed, more than 1,000 studies based on over 100,000 study participants strongly indicate that selection tests can give employers a much better than average (50–50) chance of hiring the right workers. If you had odds like these working for you in Las Vegas, you'd make so much money the casinos wouldn't let you in the door.

COGNITIVE ABILITY TESTS

There is a 76 percent chance that applicants who do well on cognitive ability tests will be much better performers in their jobs than applicants who do not do well on such tests.

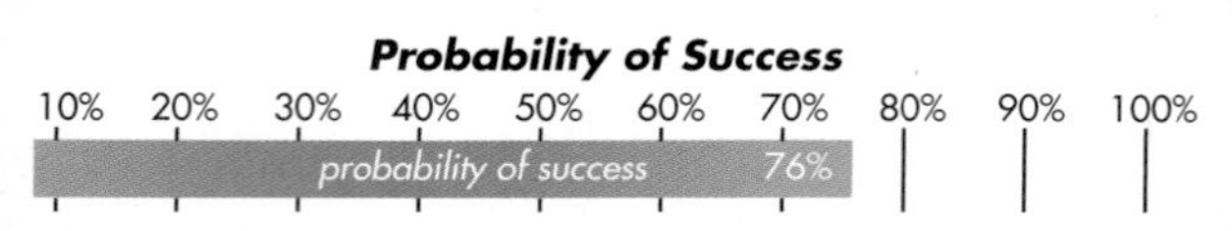

WORK SAMPLE TESTS

There is a 77 percent chance that applicants who do well on work sample tests will be much better performers in their jobs than applicants who do not do well on such tests.

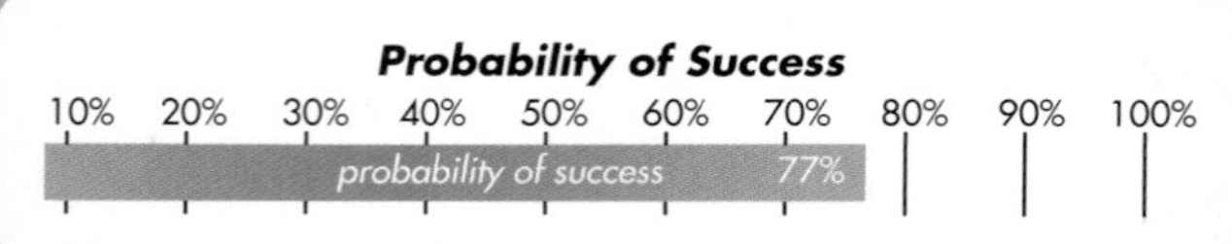

ASSESSMENT CENTERS

There is a 69 percent chance that applicants who do well on assessment center exercises will be much better managers than applicants who do not do well on such exercises.

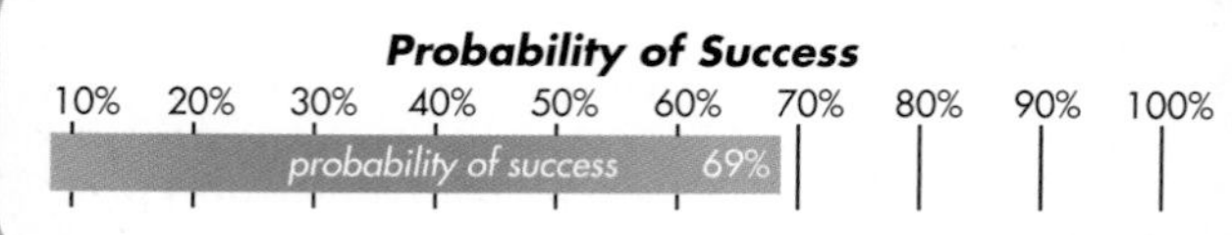

STRUCTURED INTERVIEWS

There is a 76 percent chance that applicants who do well in structured interviews will be much better performers in their jobs than applicants who do not do well in such interviews.

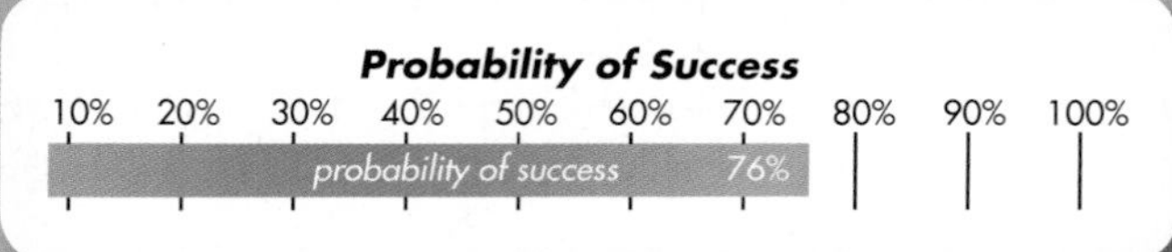

COGNITIVE ABILITY + WORK SAMPLE TESTS

When deciding whom to hire, most companies use a number of tests to make even more accurate selection decisions. There is an 82 percent chance that applicants who do well on a combination of cognitive ability tests and work sample tests will be much better performers in their jobs than applicants who do not do well on both tests.

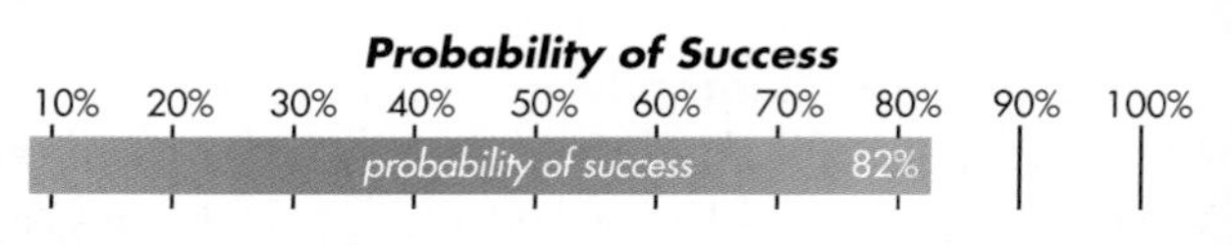

COGNITIVE ABILITY + INTEGRITY TESTS

There is an 83 percent chance that applicants who do well on a combination of cognitive ability tests and integrity tests (see Chapter 4 for a discussion of integrity tests) will be much better performers in their jobs than applicants who do not do well on both tests.

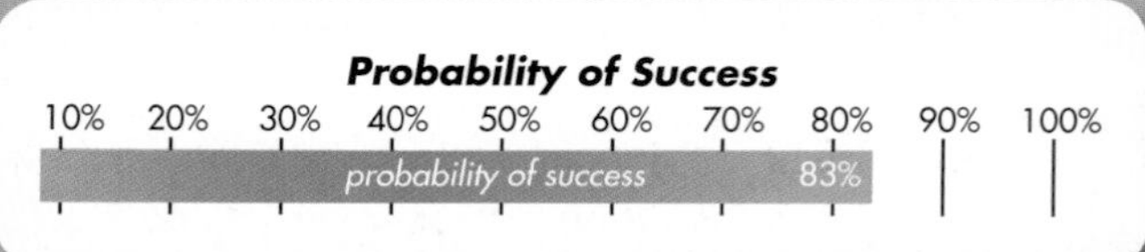

COGNITIVE ABILITY + STRUCTURED INTERVIEWS

There is an 82 percent chance that applicants who do well on a combination of cognitive ability tests and structured interviews will be much better performers in their jobs than applicants who do not do well on both tests.[87]

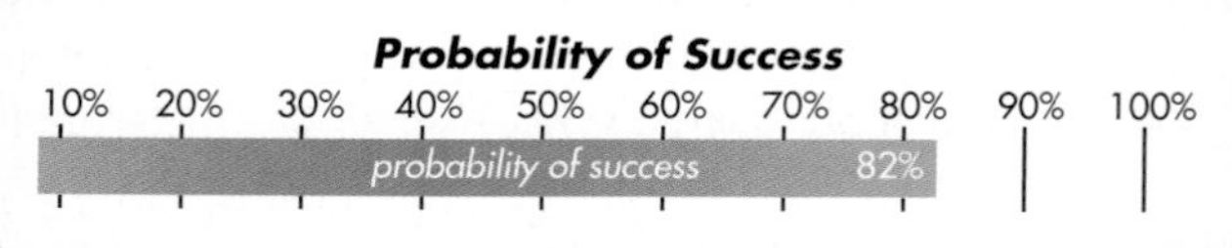

ensures that interviewers ask only for important, job-related information. Not only are the accuracy, usefulness, and validity of the interview improved, but the chances that interviewers will ask questions about topics that violate employment laws (go back to Exhibit 11.7 for a list of these topics) are reduced.

Semistructured interviews are in between structured and unstructured interviews. A major part of the semistructured interview (perhaps as much as 80 percent) is based on structured questions, but some time is set aside for unstructured interviewing to allow the interviewer to probe into ambiguous or missing information uncovered during the structured portion of the interview.

How well do interviews predict future job performance? Contrary to what you've probably heard, recent evidence indicates that even unstructured interviews do a fairly good job.[88] When conducted properly, however, structured interviews can lead to much more accurate hiring decisions than unstructured interviews. In some cases, the validity of structured interviews can rival that of cognitive ability tests. But even more important, because interviews are especially good at assessing applicants' interpersonal skills, they work particularly well with cognitive ability tests. Therefore, using structured interviews together with cognitive ability tests (that is, smart people who work well in conjunction with others) leads to even better selection decisions than using either alone.[89] Exhibit 11.10 provides a set of guidelines for conducting effective structured employment interviews.

Exhibit 11.10

Guidelines for Conducting Effective Structured Interviews

Interview Stage | **What to Do**

- Identify and define the knowledge, skills, abilities, and other (KSAO) characteristics needed for successful job performance.
- For each essential KSAO, develop key behavioral questions that will elicit examples of past accomplishments, activities, and performance.
- For each KSAO, develop a list of things to look for in the applicant's responses to key questions.

- Create a relaxed, nonstressful interview atmosphere.
- Review the applicant's application form, résumé, and other information.
- Allocate enough time to complete the interview without interruption.
- Put the applicant at ease; don't jump right into heavy questioning.
- Tell the applicant what to expect. Explain the interview process.
- Obtain job-related information from the applicant by asking those questions prepared for each KSAO.
- Describe the job and the organization to the applicant. Applicants need adequate information to make a selection decision about the organization.

- Immediately after the interview, review your notes and make sure they are complete.
- Evaluate the applicant on each essential KSAO.
- Determine each applicant's probability of success and make a hiring decision.

Source: B. M. Farrell, "The Art and Science of Employment Interviews," *Personnel Journal* 65 (1986): 91–94.

Review 4: Selection

Selection is the process of gathering information about job applicants to decide who should be offered a job. Accurate selection procedures are valid, are legally defendable, and improve organizational performance. Application forms and résumés are the most common selection devices. Because many application forms request illegal, non-job-related information, and as many as one-third of job applicants falsify information on résumés, these procedures are often of little value in making hiring decisions. References and background checks can also be problematic, given that previous employers are reluctant to provide such information for fear of being sued for defamation. Unfortunately, without this information, other employers are at risk of negligent hiring lawsuits. Selection tests generally do the best job of predicting applicants' future job performance. In general, cognitive ability tests, work sample tests, biographical data, and assessment centers are the most valid tests, followed by personality tests and specific ability tests, which are still good predictors. Selection tests aren't perfect predictors of job performance, but almost nothing predicts future job performance as well as selection tests. The three kinds of job interviews are unstructured, structured, and semistructured interviews. Of these, structured interviews work best because they ensure that all applicants are consistently asked the same situational, behavioral, background, or job-knowledge questions, in the same order.

DEVELOPING QUALIFIED WORKERS

According to a recent survey by Mercer Human Resource Consulting, 49 percent of companies are increasing their training budgets. For instance, Hewlett-Packard recently increased its training budget to a whopping $300 million.[90] What is driving the infusion of dollars into training and development budgets of companies? Companies like HP recognize that it is more cost-efficient and competitive to develop talent from within rather than compete for talent on the open market.[91] In addition, according to the American Society for Training and Development, a typical investment in training increases productivity by an average of 17 percent, reduces employee turnover, and makes companies more profitable.[92]

Giving employees the knowledge and skills they need to improve their performance is just the first step in developing employees, however. The second step, and not enough companies do this, is giving employees formal feedback about their actual job performance. A CEO of a large telecommunications company hired an outside consultant to assess and coach (provide feedback to) the company's top 50 managers. To the CEO's surprise, 75 percent of those managers indicated that the feedback they received from the consultant regarding their strengths and weaknesses was the only substantial feedback they had received about their performance in the last five years. On a more positive note, as a result of that feedback, two-thirds of the managers then took positive steps to improve their skills, knowledge, and job performance and expressed a clear desire for more feedback, especially from their boss, the CEO.[93] So, in today's competitive business environment, even top managers understand the importance of formal performance feedback to their growth and development.

After reading the next two sections, you should be able to

5 describe how to determine training needs and select the appropriate training methods.

6 discuss how to use performance appraisal to give meaningful performance feedback.

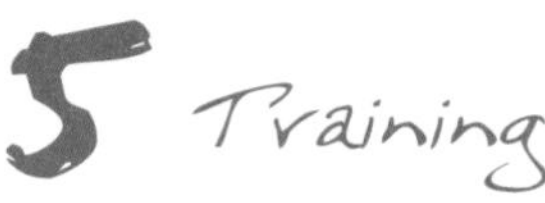

__Training__ means providing opportunities for employees to develop the job-specific skills, experience, and knowledge they need to do their jobs or improve their performance. American companies spend more than $60 billion a year on training. To make sure those training dollars are well spent, companies need to __5.1 determine specific training needs__, __5.2 select appropriate training methods__, and __5.3 evaluate training__.

5.1 Determining Training Needs

Needs assessment is the process of identifying and prioritizing the learning needs of employees. Needs assessments can be conducted by identifying performance deficiencies, listening to customer complaints, surveying employees and managers, or formally testing employees' skills and knowledge.

The Work Keys method created by American College Testing (maker of the ACT test used for college admissions) in Iowa City, Iowa, is a needs assessment tool used for 7,000 different jobs by more than 1,400 companies nationwide.[94] Work Keys is a series of tests that can be used to determine employees' knowledge and skill levels in communication (listening, reading for information, and writing), problem solving (applied mathematics, applied technology, locating information, and observation), and interpersonal skills (teamwork). As shown in Step 1 of Exhibit 11.11, a needs assessment using Work Keys begins with a job analysis (what ACT calls "job profiling") to determine the knowledge and skill levels required to perform a job successfully. Step 1 shows that a worker needs a skill level of 4 in reading for information, a 5 in applied mathematics, a 3 in applied technology, and a 4 in teamwork (skill levels range from 1 to 6) to do well in a manufacturing job. Following the job analysis, employees are tested to see how well their skills match those required for the job, as shown in Step 2 of Exhibit 11.11. Then, as shown in Step 3 of the exhibit, employees' skill levels are compared with the requirements for the job. The greater the difference between an employee's skill levels and those required, the greater the need for training. Based on the Work Keys needs assessment, this employee needs some training in reading for information, applied mathematics, and teamwork.

Note that training should never be conducted without first performing a needs assessment. Sometimes, training isn't needed at all or isn't needed for all employees. Since the needs assessment shown in Exhibit 11.11 indicates that the employee's applied technology skills match those required for the job, it would be a waste of time and money to send this employee for training in that area.

training developing the skills, experience, and knowledge employees need to perform their jobs or improve their performance

needs assessment the process of identifying and prioritizing the learning needs of employees

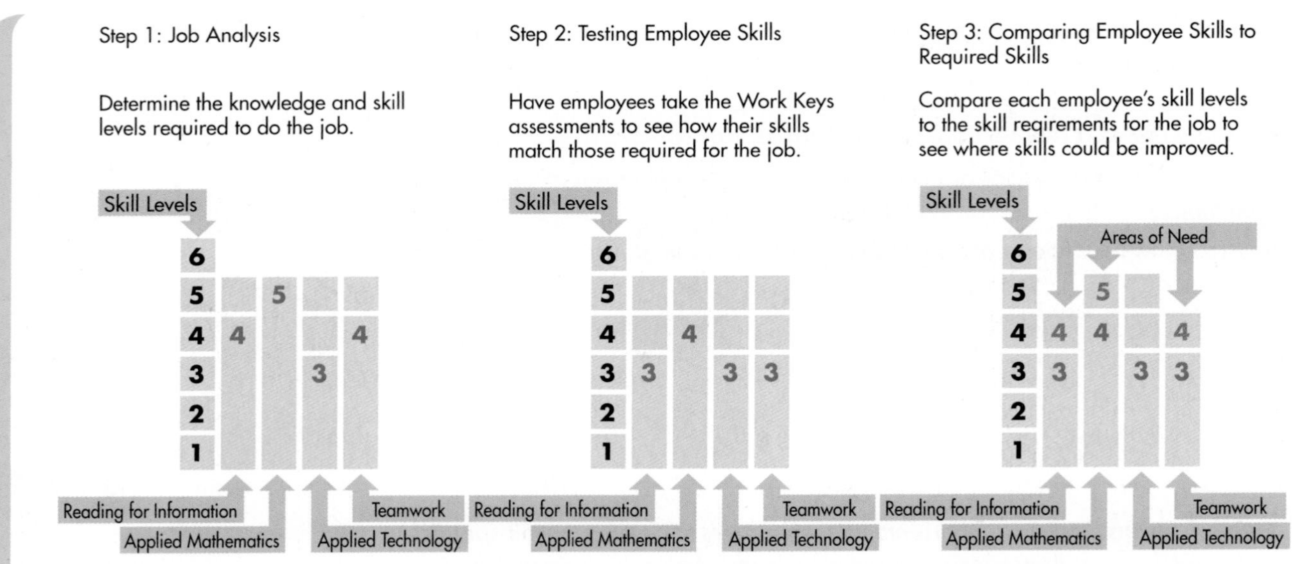
Step 1: Job Analysis
Determine the knowledge and skill levels required to do the job.
Step 2: Testing Employee Skills
Have employees take the Work Keys assessments to see how their skills match those required for the job.
Step 3: Comparing Employee Skills to Required Skills
Compare each employee's skill levels to the skill reqirements for the job to see where skills could be improved.
Skill Levels
Areas of Need
Reading for Information
Applied Mathematics
Applied Technology
Teamwork

Source: "Work Keys for Business: The System in Action," *ACT: Information for Life's Transitions*, available at http://www.act.org/workkeys/index.html/, 31 May 2003. Copyright 1999 by ACT. Inc.

Exhibit 11.11

Work Keys Needs Assessment for a Manufacturing Job

Unfortunately, however, many organizations simply require all employees to attend training, whether they need to or not. As a result, employees who are not interested or don't need the training may react negatively during or after training. Likewise, employees who should be sent for training but aren't may also react negatively. Consequently, a needs assessment is an important tool for deciding who should or should not attend training. In fact, employment law restricts employers from discriminating on the basis of age, sex, race, color, religion, national origin, or disability when selecting training participants. Just like hiring decisions, the selection of training participants should be based on job-related information.

5.2 Training Methods

Assume that you're a training director for a bank and that you're in charge of making sure that all bank employees know what to do in case of a robbery. Exhibit 11.12 lists a number of training methods you could use: films and videos, lectures, planned readings, case studies, coaching and mentoring, group discussions, on-the-job training, role-playing, simulations and games, vestibule training, and computer-based learning. Which method would be best?

To choose the best method, you should consider a number of factors, such as the number of people to be trained, the cost of training, and the objectives of the training. For instance, if the training objective is to impart information or knowledge to trainees, then you should use films and videos, lectures, and planned readings. In our robbery training example, trainees would hear, see, or read about what to do in case of a robbery.

If developing analytical and problem-solving skills is the objective, then use case studies, coaching and mentoring, and group discussions. In our example, trainees would read about a real robbery, talk to people who had been through robberies, and discuss what to do.

If practicing, learning, or changing job behaviors is the objective, then use on-the-job training, role-playing, simulations and games, and vestibule training. In our example, trainees would learn about robbery situations on the job, pretend that they were in a robbery situation, or participate in a highly realistic mock robbery.

TRAINING OBJECTIVE	TRAINING METHOD
Impart Information and Knowledge	• **Films and videos.** Films and videos share information, illustrate problems and solutions, and effectively hold trainees' attention.
	• **Lectures.** Trainees listen to instructors' oral presentations.
	• **Planned readings.** Trainees read about concepts or ideas before attending training.
Develop Analytical and Problem-Solving Skills	• **Case studies.** Cases are analyzed and discussed in small groups. The cases present a specific problem or decision, and trainees develop methods for solving the problem or making the decision.
	• **Coaching and mentoring.** Coaching and mentoring of trainees by managers involves informal advice, suggestions, and guidance. This method is helpful for reinforcing other kinds of training and for trainees who benefit from support and personal encouragement.
	• **Group discussions.** Small groups of trainees actively discuss specific topics. The instructor may perform the role of discussion leader.
Practice, Learn, or Change Job Behaviors	• **On-the-job training (OJT).** New employees are assigned to experienced employees. The trainee learns by watching the experienced employee perform the job and eventually by working alongside the experienced employee. Gradually, the trainee is left on his or her own to perform the job.
	• **Role-playing.** Trainees assume job-related roles and practice new behaviors by acting out what they would do in job-related situations.
	• **Simulations and games.** Experiential exercises place trainees in realistic job-related situations and give them the opportunity to experience a job-related condition in a relatively low-cost setting. The trainee benefits from "hands-on experience" before actually performing the job where mistakes may be more costly.
	• **Vestibule training.** Procedures and equipment similar to those used in the actual job are set up in a special area called a vestibule. The trainee is then taught how to perform the job at his or her own pace without disrupting the actual flow of work, making costly mistakes, or exposing the trainee and others to dangerous conditions.
Impart Information and Knowledge; Develop Analytical and Problem-Solving Skills; and Practice, Learn, or Change Job Behaviors	• **Computer-based learning.** Interactive videos, software, CD-ROMs, personal computers, teleconferencing, and the Internet may be combined to present multimedia-based training.

Source: A. Fowler, "How to Decide on Training Methods," *People Management* 25, no. 1 (1995): 36.

Exhibit 11.12

Training Objectives and Methods

If training is supposed to meet more than one of these objectives, then your best choice may be to combine one of the previous methods with computer-based training. **CDW** (Computer Discount Warehouse) now uses avatar-based training. An avatar is a computerized depiction of a person. If you've ever played a video game, you've encountered an avatar. When CDW account manager Danielle Paden took a sales course, the avatar first described a situation: an unhappy customer whose computer won't connect to her high-speed Internet hookup. Then, a picture of the customer appeared on the screen, accompanied by audio of the customer speaking. Finally, with help from the avatar when she needed it (just click on the avatar), Paden decided what to do and then received feedback from the avatar and another response from the customer. Paden describes the training as "the closest thing you can get to [actual] client interactions," because "the avatar went through almost every situation you will run across."[95]

> [Avatar training is] the closest thing you can get to [actual] client interactions [because] the avatar went through almost every situation you will run across.
>
> **DANIELLE PADEN**, ACCOUNT MANAGER, CDW

These days, many companies are adopting Internet training, or "e-learning." For instance, **Dow Chemical** now has the ability to provide electronic learning or training to all 40,000 employees in 70 countries using its **Learn@dow.now** web-based training system.[96] Likewise, Cisco Systems offers 4,500 e-learning courses to its managers and employees.[97] E-learning can offer several advantages. Because employees don't need to leave their jobs, travel costs are greatly reduced. Also, because employees can take training modules when it is convenient (in other words, they don't have to fall behind at their jobs to attend week-long training courses), workplace productivity should increase and employee stress should decrease. Finally, if the company's technology infrastructure can support it, e-learning can be much faster than traditional training methods. For example, British Telecom used an avatar-based course to train 4,500 salespeople in just over a month. Traditional classroom training would have cost twice as much and taken twice as long to deliver.[98]

There are, however, several disadvantages to e-learning. First, despite its increasing popularity, it's not always the appropriate training method. E-learning can be a good way to impart information, but it isn't always as effective for changing job behaviors or developing problem-solving and analytical skills. Second, e-learning requires a significant investment in computers and high-speed Internet and network connections for all employees. Finally, though e-learning can be faster, many employees find it so boring and unengaging that they may choose to do their jobs rather than complete e-learning courses when sitting alone at their desks. E-learning may become more interesting, however, as more companies incorporate gamelike features in training, such as avatars and competition, into their e-learning courses.

5.3 Evaluating Training

After selecting a training method and conducting the training, the last step is to evaluate the training. Training can be evaluated in four ways: on *reactions*, how satisfied trainees were with the program; on *learning*, how much employees improved their knowledge or skills; on *behavior*, how much employees actually changed their on-the-job behavior because of training; or on *results*, how much training improved job performance, such as increased sales or quality, or decreased costs.[99] In general, if done well, training provides meaningful benefits for most companies. For example, a study by the American Society for Training and Development shows that a training budget as small as $680 per employee can increase a company's total return on investment by 6 percent.[100]

Review 5: Training

Training is used to give employees the job-specific skills, experience, and knowledge they need to do their jobs or improve their job performance. To make sure training dollars are well spent, companies need to determine specific training needs, select appropriate training methods, and then evaluate the training. Needs assessments can be conducted by identifying performance deficiencies, listening to customer complaints, surveying employees and managers, or formally testing employees' skills and knowledge. Selection of an appropriate training method depends on a number of factors, such as the number of people to be trained, the cost of training, and the objectives of the training. If the objective is to impart information or knowledge, then films and videos, lectures, and planned readings should be used. If developing analytical and problem-solving skills is the objective, then case studies, coaching and mentoring, and group discussions should be used. If practicing, learning, or changing job behaviors is the objective, then on-the-job training, role-playing, simulations and games, and vestibule training should be used. If training is supposed to meet more than one of these objectives, then it may be best to combine one of the previous methods with computer-based training. Training can be evaluated on reactions, learning, behavior, or results.

6 Performance Appraisal

Performance appraisal is the process of assessing how well employees are doing their jobs. Most employees and managers intensely dislike the performance appraisal process. One manager says, "I hate annual performance reviews. I hated them when I used to get them, and I hate them now that I give them. If I had to choose between performance reviews and paper cuts, I'd take paper cuts every time. I'd even take razor burns and the sound of fingernails on a blackboard."[101] Unfortunately, attitudes like this are all too common. In fact, 70 percent of employees are dissatisfied with the performance appraisal process in their companies. Likewise, according to the Society for Human Resource Management, 90 percent of human resource managers are dissatisfied with the performance appraisal systems used by their companies.[102]

Performance appraisals are used for four broad purposes: making administrative decisions (such as pay increase, promotion, retention); providing feedback for employee development (such as performance feedback, developing career plans); evaluating Human Resource programs (such as validating selection systems); and for documentation purposes (such as documenting performance ratings and decisions based on those ratings).[103]

Let's explore how companies can avoid some of these problems with performance appraisals by ***6.1 accurately measuring job performance*** *and* ***6.2 effectively sharing performance feedback with employees****.*

6.1 Accurately Measuring Job Performance

Workers often have strong doubts about the accuracy of their performance appraisals—and they may be right. For example, it's widely known that assessors are prone to errors when rating worker performance. Three of the most common rating errors are central tendency, halo, and leniency. *Central tendency error* occurs when assessors rate all workers as average or in the middle of the scale. *Halo error* occurs when assessors rate all workers as performing at the same level (good, bad, or average) in all parts of their jobs. *Leniency error* occurs when assessors rate all workers as performing particularly well. One of the reasons that managers make these errors is that they often don't spend enough time gathering or reviewing performance data.

performance appraisal the process of assessing how well employees are doing their jobs

© IMAGE SOURCE PINK/JUPITER IMAGES

Winston Connor, the former vice president of human resources at Huntsman Chemical, says, "Most of the time, it's just a ritual that managers go through. They pull out last year's review, update it and do it quickly."[104]

What can be done to minimize rating errors and improve the accuracy with which job performance is measured? In general, two approaches have been used: improving performance appraisal measures themselves and training performance raters to be more accurate.

One of the ways companies try to improve performance appraisal measures is to use as many objective performance measures as possible. **Objective performance measures** are measures of performance that are easily and directly counted or quantified. Common objective performance measures include output, scrap, waste, sales, customer complaints, and rejection rates.

But when objective performance measures aren't available, and frequently they aren't, subjective performance measures have to be used instead. **Subjective performance measures** require that someone judge or assess a worker's performance. The most common kind of subjective performance measure is the Graphic Rating Scale (GRS) shown in Exhibit 11.13. Graphic rating scales are most widely used because they are easy to construct, but they are very susceptible to rating errors.

A popular alternative to graphic rating scales is the **Behavior Observation Scale (BOS)**. BOS requires raters to rate the frequency with which workers perform specific behaviors representative of the job dimensions that are critical to successful job performance. Exhibit 11.13 shows a BOS for two important job dimensions for a retail salesperson: customer service and money handling. Notice that each dimension lists several specific behaviors characteristic of a worker who excels in that dimension of job performance. (Normally, the scale would list 7 to 12 items per dimension, not 3, as in the exhibit.). Notice also, that the behaviors are good behaviors, meaning they indicate good performance, and the rater is asked to judge how frequently an employee engaged in those good behaviors. The logic behind the BOS is that better performers engage in good behaviors more often.

Not only do BOSs work well for rating critical dimensions of performance, but studies also show that managers strongly prefer BOSs for giving performance feedback; accurately differentiating between poor, average, and good workers; identifying training needs; and accurately measuring performance. And in response to the statement, "If I were defending a company, this rating format would be an asset to my case," attorneys strongly preferred BOSs over other kinds of subjective performance appraisal scales.[105]

The second approach to improving the measurement of workers' job performance is **rater training**. The most effective is frame-of-reference training, in which a group of trainees learn how to do performance appraisals by watching a videotape of an employee at work. Next, they evaluate the performance of the person in the videotape. A trainer (an expert in the subject matter) then shares his or her evaluations, and trainees' evaluations are compared with the expert's. The expert then explains the rationales behind his or her evaluations. This process is repeated until the difference in evaluations given by trainees and evaluations by the expert are minimized. The underlying logic behind the frame-of-reference training is that by adopting the frame of reference

objective performance measures measures of job performance that are easily and directly counted or quantified

subjective performance measures measures of job performance that require someone to judge or assess a worker's performance

behavior observation scales (BOSs) rating scales that indicate the frequency with which workers perform specific behaviors that are representative of the job dimensions critical to successful job performance

rater training training performance appraisal raters in how to avoid rating errors and increase rating accuracy used by an expert, trainees will be able to accurately observe, judge and use the scale to evaluate performance of others.[106]

6.2 Sharing Performance Feedback

After gathering accurate performance data, the next step is to share performance feedback with employees. Unfortunately, even when performance appraisal ratings are accurate, the appraisal process often breaks down at the feedback stage. Employees become defensive and dislike hearing any negative assessments of their work, no matter how small. Managers become defensive, too, and dislike giving appraisal feedback as much as employees dislike receiving it. One manager says, "I myself don't go as far as those who say performance reviews are inherently destructive and ought to be abolished, but I agree that the typical annual-review process does nothing but harm. It creates divisions. It undermines morale. It makes people angry, jealous, and cynical. It unleashes a whole lot of negative energy, and the organization gets nothing in return."[107]

What can be done to overcome the inherent difficulties in performance appraisal feedback sessions? Since performance appraisal ratings have traditionally been the judgments of just one person, the boss, one possibility is to use **360-degree feedback**. In this approach, feedback comes from four sources: the boss, subordinates, peers and coworkers, and the employees themselves. The data, which are obtained anonymously (except for the boss's), are compiled into a feedback report comparing the employee's self-ratings with those of the boss, subordinates, and peers and coworkers. Usually, a consultant or human resource specialist discusses the results with the employee. The advantage of 360-degree programs is that negative feedback ("You don't listen") is often more credible when it comes from several people. For example, one boss who received 360-degree feedback thought he was a great writer, so he regularly criticized and corrected his subordinates' reports. Though the subordinates had never discussed this among themselves, they all complained about it in the 360-degree feedback and asked that he stop rewriting their reports. After receiving the feedback, he apologized and stopped.[108]

Graphic Rating Scale

Example 1:	Very Poor	Poor	Average	Good	Very Good
1. Quality of work performed is........	1	2	3	4	5

Example 2:	Very Poor (20% errors)	Poor (15% errors)	Average (10% errors)	Good (5% errors)	Very Good (less than 5% errors)
2. Quality of work performed is........	1	2	3	4	5

Behavioral Observation Scale

Dimension: Customer Service	Almost Never				Almost Always
1. Greets customers with a smile and a "hello."........	1	2	3	4	5
2. Calls other stores to help customers find merchandise that is not in stock.	1	2	3	4	5
3. Promptly handles customer concerns and complaints........	1	2	3	4	5

Dimension: Money Handling	Almost Never				Almost Always
1. Accurately makes change from customer transactions.	1	2	3	4	5
2. Accounts balance at the end of the day, no shortages or surpluses.	1	2	3	4	5
3. Accurately records transactions in computer system.	1	2	3	4	5

Exhibit 11.13
Subjective Performance Appraisal Scales

360-degree feedback a performance appraisal process in which feedback is obtained from the boss, subordinates, peers and coworkers, and the employees themselves

A word of caution, though: About half of the companies using 360-degree feedback for performance appraisal now use the feedback only for developmental purposes. They found that sometimes when raises and promotions were on the line, peers and subordinates would give high ratings in order to get high ratings from others, and that they would also distort ratings to harm competitors or help people they liked. A senior manager at a New York City marketing company agrees, saying that 360-degree feedback "also allows people to vent their frustrations and anger on bosses and colleagues in an insensitive way."[109] On the other hand, studies clearly show that ratees prefer to receive feedback from multiple raters, so 360-degree feedback is likely to continue to grow in popularity.[110]

Herbert Meyer, who has been studying performance appraisal feedback for more than 30 years, recommends a list of topics for discussion in performance appraisal feedback sessions (see Exhibit 11.14)[111] First, managers should separate developmental feedback, which is designed to improve future performance, from administrative feedback, which is used as a reward for past performance, such as for raises. When managers give developmental feedback, they're acting as coaches, but when they give administrative feedback, they're acting as judges. These roles, coaches and judges, are clearly incompatible. As coaches, managers are encouraging, pointing out opportunities for growth and improvement, and employees are typically open and receptive to feedback. But as judges, managers are evaluative, and employees are typically defensive and closed to feedback.

Second, Meyer suggests that performance appraisal feedback sessions be based on self-appraisals, in which employees carefully assess their own strengths, weaknesses, successes, and failures in writing. Because employees play an active role in the review of their performance, managers can be coaches rather than judges. Also, because the focus is on future goals and development, both employees and managers are likely to be more satisfied with the process and more committed to future plans and changes. And, because the focus is on development and not administrative assessment, studies show that self-appraisals lead to more candid self-assessments than traditional supervisory reviews.[112] See Exhibit 11.14 for a list of topics that Meyer recommends for discussion in performance appraisal feedback sessions.

Exhibit 11.14

What to Discuss in a Performance Appraisal Feedback Session

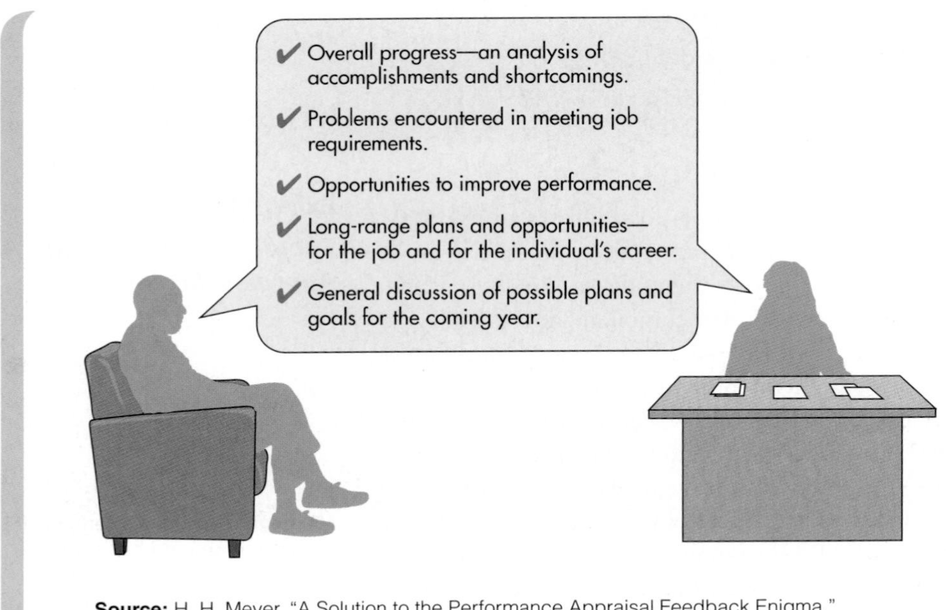
✔ Overall progress—an analysis of accomplishments and shortcomings.
✔ Problems encountered in meeting job requirements.
✔ Opportunities to improve performance.
✔ Long-range plans and opportunities—for the job and for the individual's career.
✔ General discussion of possible plans and goals for the coming year.

Source: H. H. Meyer, "A Solution to the Performance Appraisal Feedback Enigma," *Academy of Management Executive* 5, no. 1 (1991): 68–76.

Finally, what people do with the performance feedback they receive matters. A study of 1,361 senior managers found that managers who reviewed their 360-degree feedback with an executive coach (hired by the company) were more likely to set specific goals for improvement, ask their bosses for ways to improve, and subsequently improve their performance.[113] Also, a five-year study of 252 managers found that their performance improved dramatically if they met with their subordinates to discuss their 360-degree feedback ("You don't listen") and how they were going to address it ("I'll restate what others have said before stating my opinion"). Performance was dramatically lower for managers who never discussed their 360-degree feedback with subordinates and for managers who did not routinely do so (some managers did not review their 360-degree feedback with subordinates each year of the study). Why is discussing 360-degree feedback with subordinates so effective? These discussions help managers better understand their weaknesses, force them to develop a plan to improve, and demonstrate to the subordinates the managers' public commitment to improving.[114] In short, it helps to have people discuss their performance feedback with others, but it particularly helps to have them discuss their feedback with the people who provided it.

It is clear that organizations, and specifically managers, must take the task of providing feedback seriously. Recent studies have reported that employees' satisfaction with feedback they receive influences not only their job satisfaction but also their future performance.[115] An employee's satisfaction with feedback is influenced by his or her perceptions of how well the manager knows the employee's job, the extent to which evaluations were based on job-related factors, whether the feedback process included goal setting, and whether the manager provided insights on how to improve future performance.[116]

> "The typical annual-review process does nothing but harm. It creates divisions. It undermines morale. It makes people angry, jealous, and cynical. It unleashes a whole lot of negative energy, and the organization gets nothing in return."
>
> A MANAGER

Review 6: **Performance Appraisal**

Most employees and managers intensely dislike the performance appraisal process. Some of the problems associated with appraisals can be avoided, however, by accurately measuring job performance and effectively sharing performance feedback with employees. Organizations should develop good performance appraisal scales, preferably use behavior observation scales. They should train raters to accurately evaluate performance, perhaps by providing frame-of-reference training. They should impress upon managers the value of providing feedback in a clear, consistent, and fair manner, and of setting goals and monitoring progress toward those goals.

One way to overcome the inherent difficulties in performance appraisal feedback is to provide 360-degree feedback, in which feedback is obtained from four sources: the boss, subordinates, peers and coworkers, and the employees themselves. Feedback tends to be more credible if it is heard from several sources. Finally, especially for managers, it's helpful to have people discuss the feedback they received with executive coaches or the people who provided it.

KEEPING QUALIFIED WORKERS

China has a population of 1.3 billion people, but in the Pearl River delta there aren't enough workers to meet the skyrocketing demand for manufacturing workers. Consequently, companies such as **Chigo Air-Conditioning** are having to work hard to keep their employees. In the last five years, Chigo has raised salaries, started giving bonuses to workers who stay longer than three years, and built brand new housing with TV sets and swimming pools to entice workers to stay.[117] All this may not be enough, however, as Chinese economists estimate that companies will have to

pay wages 40 to 50 percent higher to keep the workers they have and to fill the two million job openings in this part of China.

Massey Energy, in Richmond, Virginia, faces similar problems keeping workers. With coal prices increasing 60 percent over the last two years, coal producers like Massey are running full out to meet demand. The rise in coal prices has been accompanied by a rise in demand for miners. Turnover is high as employees jump ship to work for Massey's competitors at better pay and benefits. As a result, Massey has given all of its production workers raises ranging from 3 to 15 percent over the last year. Furthermore, it offered a $3 an hour raise to electricians who already make $27 an hour and can earn $90,000 a year with overtime pay. And, like Chigo Air-Conditioning, Massey offers bonuses to workers who stay longer. Finally, Massey also gives its supervisors stock options to encourage them to stay.[118]

After reading the next two sections, you should be able to

7 *describe basic compensation strategies and explain how they affect human resource practice.*

8 *discuss the four kinds of employee separations: termination, downsizing, retirements, and turnover.*

7 Compensation

compensation the financial and nonfinancial rewards that organizations give employees in exchange for their work

job evaluation a process that determines the worth of each job in a company by evaluating the market value of the knowledge, skills, and requirements needed to perform it

Compensation *includes both the financial and the nonfinancial rewards that organizations give employees in exchange for their work. Let's learn more about compensation by examining the* ***7.1 compensation decisions that managers must make*** *and* ***7.2 the role that employment benefits play in compensating today's employees****.*

7.1 Compensation Decisions

As Exhibit 11.15 shows, there are four basic kinds of compensation decisions: pay level, pay variability, pay structure, and employment benefits. We'll discuss employment benefits in the next subsection.[119]

Pay-level decisions are decisions about whether to pay workers at a level that is below, above, or at current market wages. Companies use job evaluation to set their pay structures. **Job evaluation** determines the worth of each job by determining the market value of the knowledge, skills, and requirements needed to perform it. After conducting a job evaluation, most companies try to pay the "going rate," meaning the current market wage. There are always companies, however, whose financial situation causes them to pay considerably less than current market wages. The child-care industry, for example, has chronic difficulties filling jobs because it pays well below market wages. Also, because

Exhibit 11.15
Kinds of Compensation Decisions

Pay Level	Pay Variability	Pay Structure	Employment Benefits
• Job Evaluation	• Piecework • Commission • Profit Sharing • Employee Stock Ownership Plans • Stock Options	• Hierarchical • Compressed	• Cafeteria Plans • Flexible Plans • Payroll Deductions

wages are so low (an average of $7.86 an hour, or $16,350 a year), the applicants it attracts are increasingly less qualified.[120] Donna Krause, who runs Creative Learning and Child Care in Dundalk, Maryland, lost five child-care teachers one August when all were hired away by higher-paying public school systems. All of the teachers who left had college degrees, but none of their replacements did.[121]

Some companies choose to pay above-average wages to attract and keep employees. *Above-market wages* can attract a larger, more qualified pool of job applicants, increase the rate of job acceptance, decrease the time it takes to fill positions, and increase the time that employees stay.[122] For example, the severe nursing shortage discussed at the beginning of the chapter has begun to ease because, as Vanderbilt University nursing professor Peter Buerhaus explains, "Hospitals recognized that all their previous attempts weren't working so they had to raise wages."[123] Three years ago, 13 percent of the nursing positions at the Ochsner Clinic in New Orleans were open. After raising salaries substantially and giving nurses more flexible schedules (for example, $50,000+per year to work three 12-hour days per week), only 2.4 percent of its nursing positions were open, compared with a national average of 8.4 percent.

Pay-variability decisions concern the extent to which employees' pay varies with individual and organizational performance. Linking pay to performance is intended to increase employee motivation, effort, and job performance. Piecework, sales commissions, profit sharing, employee stock ownership plans, and stock options are common pay-variability options. For instance, under **piecework** pay plans, employees are paid a set rate for each item produced up to some standard (for example, 35 cents per item produced for output up to 100 units per day). Once productivity exceeds the standard, employees are paid a set amount for each unit of output over the standard (for example, 45 cents for each unit above 100 units). Under a sales **commission** plan, salespeople are paid a percentage of the purchase price of items they sell. The more they sell, the more they earn.

Because pay plans such as piecework and commissions are based on individual performance, they can reduce the incentive that people have to work together. Therefore, companies also use group incentives (discussed in Chapter 10) and organizational incentives, such as profit sharing, employee stock ownership plans, and stock options, to encourage teamwork and cooperation.

With **profit sharing**, employees receive a portion of the organization's profits over and above their regular compensation. The more profitable the company, the more profit is shared. Renault SAS, the French automaker, has a profit sharing agreement that distributes 6 percent of its net income to employees, with a minimum payout of 2,134 euros per employee.[124] **Employee stock ownership plans (ESOPs)** compensate employees by awarding them shares of the company stock in addition to their regular compensation. At **MCKAY NURSERY** in Waterloo, Wisconsin, Joe Hernandez, a 41-year-old migrant worker, makes $20,000 a year working from April to November. But Joe also gets an additional 20 to 25 percent in company stock. So far, he's accumulated more than $80,000 through the company ESOP.[125]

Stock options give employees the right to purchase shares of stock at a set price. Options work like this. Let's say that you are awarded the right (or option) to buy 100 shares of stock from the company for $5 a share. If the company's stock price rises to

piecework a compensation system in which employees are paid a set rate for each item they produce

commission a compensation system in which employees earn a percentage of each sale they make

profit sharing a compensation system in which a company pays a percentage of its profits to employees in addition to their regular compensation

employee stock ownership plan (ESOP) a compensation system that awards employees shares of company stock in addition to their regular compensation

stock options a compensation system that gives employees the right to purchase shares of stock at a set price, even if the value of the stock increases above that price

McKay Nursery includes company stock in its compensation program. The result is that employee ownership and commitment to the company grows.

$15 a share, you can exercise your options and make $1,000. When you exercise your options, you pay the company $500 (100 shares at $5 a share), but because the stock is selling for $15 in the stock market, you can sell your 100 shares for $1,500 and make $1,000. Of course, as the company's profits and share values increase, stock options become even more valuable to employees. Stock options have no value, however, if the company's stock falls below the option "grant price," the price at which the options have been issued to you. For instance, the options you have on 100 shares of stock with a grant price of $5 aren't going to do you a lot of good if the company's stock is worth $2.50. Why exercise your stock options and pay $5 a share for stock that sells for $2.50 a share in the stock market? (Stock options are said to be "underwater" when the grant price is lower than the market price.) Proponents of stock options argue that this gives employees and managers a strong incentive to work hard to make the company successful. If they do, the company's profits and stock price increase, and their stock options increase in value. If they don't, profits stagnate or turn into losses, and their stock options decrease in value or become worthless. To learn more about ESOPs and stock options, see the National Center for Employee Ownership (**http://www.nceo.org**).

Pay-structure decisions are concerned with internal pay distributions, meaning the extent to which people in the company receive very different levels of pay.[126] With *hierarchical pay structures*, there are big differences from one pay level to another. The highest pay levels are for people near the top of the pay distribution. The basic idea behind hierarchical pay structures is that large differences in pay between jobs or organizational levels should motivate people to work harder to obtain those higher-paying jobs. Many publicly owned companies have hierarchical pay structures by virtue of the huge amounts they pay their top managers and CEOs. For example, the average CEO now makes 289 times as much as the average worker, down from 475 times the pay of average workers just five years ago. But with CEO pay packages averaging $9.6 million per year and average workers earning just $33,176, the difference is still incredible.[127]

By contrast, *compressed pay structures* typically have fewer pay levels and smaller differences in pay between levels. Pay is less dispersed and more similar across jobs in the company. The basic idea behind compressed pay structures is that similar pay levels should lead to higher levels of cooperation, feelings of fairness and a common purpose, and better group and team performance.

So should companies choose hierarchical or compressed pay structures? The evidence isn't straightforward, but studies seem to indicate that there are significant problems with the hierarchical approach. The most damaging finding is that there appears to be little link between organizational performance and the pay of top managers.[128] Furthermore, studies of professional athletes indicate that hierarchical pay structures (for example, paying superstars 40 to 50 times as much as the lowest-paid athlete on the team) hurt the performance of teams and individual players.[129] Likewise, managers are twice as likely to quit their jobs when their companies have very strong hierarchical pay structures (that is, when they're paid dramatically less than the people above them).[130] For now, it seems that hierarchical pay structures work best for independent work, where it's easy to determine the contributions of individual performers and little coordination with others is needed to get the job done. In other words, hierarchical pay structures work best when clear links can be drawn between individual performance and individual rewards. By contrast, compressed pay structures, in which everyone receives similar pay, seem to work best for interdependent work, which requires employees to work together. Some companies are pursuing a middle ground: combining hierarchical and compressed pay structures by giving ordinary workers the chance to earn more through ESOPs, stock options, and profit sharing.

7.2 Employment Benefits

Employment benefits include virtually any kind of compensation other than direct wages paid to employees.[131] Three employee benefits are mandated by law: Social Security, workers' compensation insurance, and unemployment insurance. To attract and retain a good work force, however, most organizations offer a wide variety of benefits, including retirement plans and pensions, paid holidays, paid vacations, sick leave, health insurance, life insurance, dental care, eye care, day-care facilities, paid personal days, legal assistance, physical fitness facilities, educational assistance, and discounts on company products and services. Currently, benefits cost organizations about 29.3 percent of their payroll, with an average cost of $15,000 per employee for a basic benefit plan.[132]

Managers should understand that although benefits are unlikely to improve employee motivation and performance, they do affect job satisfaction, employee decisions about staying or leaving the company, and the company's attractiveness to job applicants.[133] One way that organizations make their benefit plans more attractive is by offering **cafeteria benefit plans** or **flexible benefit plans**, which allow employees to choose which benefits they receive, up to a certain dollar value.[134] Many cafeteria or flexible benefit plans start with a core of benefits, such as health insurance and life insurance, that are available to all employees. Then employees are allowed to select the other benefits that best fit their needs, up to a predetermined dollar amount. Some organizations allow employees to choose from several packages of benefits. The packages are of equivalent value, but offer a different mix of benefits. For example, older employees may prefer more benefit dollars spent on retirement plans, while younger employees may prefer additional vacation days.

Pretax payroll deductions, which enable employees to pay for expenses such as medical care, day care, and commuting out of pretax dollars, are one of the more popular benefits options because they provide significant tax savings for employees and organizations. Nevertheless, only 18 percent of eligible employees participate in their company's pretax payroll deduction plan. The problem, as employee Kate Morrison explained, has been that "by the time you filled out the paperwork and mailed it off and they processed it, it could take up to 45 days to get your money back [from your pretax account]."[135] Some companies have solved these problems by giving employees a debit card attached to their pretax spending accounts that they can use to pay expenses directly, thereby avoiding the paperwork and the wait for reimbursement.

The drawback to flexible benefit plans has been the high cost of administering them. With advances in information processing technology and HRISs, however, the cost has begun to drop in recent years.

Review 7: Compensation

Compensation includes both the financial and the nonfinancial rewards that organizations give employees in exchange for their work. There are four basic kinds of compensation decisions: pay level, pay variability, pay structure, and employment benefits. Pay-level decisions determine whether workers will receive wages below, above, or at current market levels. Pay-variability decisions concern the extent to which pay varies with individual and organizational performance. Piecework, sales commissions, profit sharing, employee stock ownership plans, and stock options are common pay-variability options. Pay-structure decisions concern the extent to which people in the company receive very different levels of pay. Hierarchical pay structures work best for independent work, while compressed pay structures work best for interdependent work.

employment benefits a method of rewarding employees that includes virtually any kind of compensation other than wages or salaries

cafeteria benefit plans (flexible benefit plans) plans that allow employees to choose which benefits they receive, up to a certain dollar value

Employee benefits include virtually any kind of compensation other than direct wages paid to employees. Flexible or cafeteria benefit plans offer employees a wide variety of benefits, improve job satisfaction, increase the chances that employees will stay with companies, and make organizations more attractive to job applicants. The cost of administering flexible benefit plans has begun to drop in recent years.

8 Employee Separations

Employee separation is a broad term covering the loss of an employee for any reason. *Involuntary separation* occurs when employers terminate or lay off employees. *Voluntary separation* occurs when employees quit or retire. Because employee separations affect recruiting, selection, training, and compensation, organizations should forecast the number of employees they expect to lose through terminations, layoffs, turnover, or retirements when doing human resource planning.

Let's explore employee separation by examining ***8.1 terminations, 8.2 downsizing, 8.3 retirements****, and* ***8.4 turnover****.*

8.1 Terminating Employees

Hopefully, the words "You're fired!" have never been directed at you. Lots of people hear them, however, as more than 400,000 people a year get fired from their jobs. Getting fired is a terrible thing, but many managers make it even worse by bungling the firing process, needlessly provoking the person who was fired and unintentionally inviting lawsuits. For example, one worker learned he had been fired only after a restaurant told him that his company credit card was no longer active. The top office manager for a professional sports team returned to the office to find his parking space taken by someone interviewing for his job. The CEO of a clothing store company gave all of his top managers a fruit basket one holiday season, except his top finance manager, who was soon fired.[136] A computer systems engineer was fired on "Take Your Daughter to Work Day," with his eight-year-old daughter sitting next to him in the human resource manager's office. He and his daughter were both escorted from the building.[137] Recall from the beginning of the chapter how 400 employees at the Fort Worth headquarters of RadioShack got the following e-mail message: "The work force reduction notification is currently in progress. Unfortunately your position is one that has been eliminated."[138] How would you feel if you had been fired in one of these ways? Though firing is never pleasant (and managers hate firings nearly as much as employees do), managers can do several things to minimize the problems inherent in firing employees.

First, in most situations, firing should not be the first option. Instead, employees should be given a chance to change their behavior. When problems arise, employees should have ample warning and must be specifically informed as to the nature and seriousness of the trouble they're in. After being notified, they should be given sufficient time to change. If the problems continue, the employees should again be counseled about their job performance, what could be done to improve it, and the possible consequences if things don't change (such as a written reprimand, suspension without pay, or firing). Sometimes this is enough to solve the problem. If the problem isn't corrected after several rounds of warnings and discussions, however, the employee may be terminated.[139]

Second, employees should be fired only for a good reason. Employers used to hire and fire employees under the legal principle of "employment at will," which allowed them to fire employees for a good reason, a bad reason, or no reason at all. (Employees could also quit for a good reason, a bad reason, or no reason whenever they desired.)

employee separation the voluntary or involuntary loss of an employee

As employees began contesting their firings in court, however, the principle of wrongful discharge emerged. **Wrongful discharge** is a legal doctrine that requires employers to have a job-related reason to terminate employees. In other words, like other major human resource decisions, termination decisions should be made on the basis of job-related factors, such as violating company rules or consistently poor performance. And with former employees winning 68 percent of wrongful discharge cases and the average wrongful termination award at $532,000 and climbing, managers should record the job-related reasons for the termination, document specific instances of rule violations or continued poor performance, and keep notes and documents from the counseling sessions held with employees.[140]

Finally, to reduce the chances of a wrongful discharge suit, employees should always be fired in private. State the reason for discharge, but don't go into detail or engage in a lengthy discussion with the employee. Make every attempt to be as kind and respectful as possible when informing someone that he or she is being fired. It is permissible, and sometimes a good idea, to have a witness present. This person should be from human resources or part of the employee's chain of command, such as the supervisor's boss. Company security may be nearby, but should not be in the room unless the employee has made direct threats toward others. Finally, managers should be careful not to publicly criticize the employee who has just been fired, as this can also lead to a wrongful discharge lawsuit. In general, unless someone has a "business reason to know" why an employee was fired, the reasons and details related to the firing should remain confidential.[141]

8.2 Downsizing

Downsizing is the planned elimination of jobs in a company. Whether it's because of cost cutting, declining market share, previous overaggressive hiring and growth, or outsourcing, companies typically eliminate 1 million to 1.9 million jobs a year.[142] Two-thirds of companies that downsize will downsize a second time within a year. For example, Eastman Kodak recently announced that it would be eliminating 21 percent of its work force—12,000 to 15,000 jobs—over the next two years. Previously, because of the long-term decline in its core photography business, Kodak had laid off 50,000 workers in an effort to cut costs.[143] **Ford Motor Company**'s "Way Forward" plan calls for shedding 25,000 to 30,000 jobs and closing 14 plants by 2012 to help return its North American automotive operations to profitability.[144] Does downsizing work? In theory, downsizing is supposed to lead to higher productivity and profits, better stock performance, and increased organizational flexibility. However, numerous studies demonstrate that it doesn't. For instance, a 15-year study of downsizing found that downsizing 10 percent of a company's work force produced only a 1.5 percent decrease in costs; that firms that downsized increased their stock price by only 4.7 percent over three years, compared with 34.3 percent for firms that didn't; and that profitability and productivity were generally not improved by downsizing.[145] These results make it clear that the best strategy is to conduct effective human resource planning and avoid downsizing altogether. Indeed, downsizing should always be a last resort.

If companies do find themselves in financial or strategic situations where downsizing is required for survival, however, they should train managers in how to break the news to downsized employees, have senior managers explain in detail why downsizing is necessary, and time the announcement so that employees hear it from the company and not from other sources, such as TV or newspaper reports.[146] Finally, companies should do everything they can to help downsized employees find other jobs. One of the best ways to do this is to use **outplacement services** that provide employment-counseling services for employees faced with downsizing. Outplacement services often include advice and training in preparing résumés, getting ready for job interviews, and even

wrongful discharge a legal doctrine that requires employers to have a job-related reason to terminate employees

downsizing the planned elimination of jobs in a company

outplacement services employment-counseling services offered to employees who are losing their jobs because of downsizing identifying job opportunities in other companies. Fifty-five percent of companies provide outplacement services for laid-off employees, 76 percent provide extended health coverage, and 45 percent offer extended access to employee assistance programs.[147] Exhibit 11.16 provides additional guidelines for conducting layoffs.

Companies also need to pay attention to the "survivors," the employees remaining after layoffs have occurred. University of Pennsylvania management professor Peter Cappelli says that survivors "may feel like they could just as easily be the next person laid off."[148] Management consultant Diane Durken agrees: "The people who are left behind start looking behind their backs and saying, 'Am I next?' They need to be rejuvenated, so they can refocus on the future. Honesty and integrity are the core of this."[149] The key to working with layoff survivors, according to Barry Nickerson, president of Dallas-based Marlow Industries, which downsized from 800 to 200 employees, is "Communicate. Communicate. Communicate." Nickerson says, "Every time we had a change we had a meeting to explain exactly what we were doing. We were very open with our employees about where we were financially. We would explain exactly the current status and where we were."[150]

8.3 Retirement

Early retirement incentive programs (ERIPs) offer financial benefits to employees to encourage them to retire early. Companies use ERIPs to reduce the number of employees in the organization, to lower costs by eliminating positions after employees retire, to lower costs by replacing high-paid retirees with lower-paid, less-experienced employees, or to create openings and job opportunities for people inside the company. For example, the state of Wyoming offered its employees a lump-sum bonus, additional insurance benefits, and increased monthly retirement payments to encourage early retirement. Its ERIP must have been fairly attractive, because 56 percent of the state employees eligible for early retirement accepted. Thirty percent of the 437 positions vacated by the early retirees remained empty, saving the state $23.2 million over the first 46 months of the program and a projected $65 million over eight years. After accounting for the costs of the increased early retirement benefits, the predicted savings came to more than $148,000 per retiree.[151]

early retirement incentive programs (ERIPs) programs that offer financial benefits to employees to encourage them to retire early

Although ERIPs can save companies money, they can pose a big problem for managers if they fail to accurately predict which employees—the good performers or the poor performers—and how many will retire early. Consultant Ron Nicol says, "The thing that doesn't work is just asking for volunteers. You get the wrong volunteers. Some of your best people will feel they can get a job anywhere. Or you have people who are close to retirement and are a real asset to the company."[152] When Ameritech Corporation (now part of AT&T) offered an ERIP, it carefully identified the number of employees near retirement age and estimated that 5,000 to 6,000 of its 48,000 employees would take advantage of the program. Instead, nearly 22,000 employees accepted the ERIP offer and applied for early retirement![153]

Exhibit 11.16

Guidelines for Conducting Layoffs

1. Provide clear reasons and explanations for the layoffs.
2. To avoid laying off employees with critical or irreplaceable skills, knowledge, and expertise, get input from human resources, the legal department, and several levels of management.
3. Train managers in how to tell employees that they are being laid off (stay calm; make the meeting short; explain why, but don't be personal; and provide information about immediate concerns, such as benefits, job search, and collecting personal goods).
4. Give employees the bad news early in the day, and try to avoid laying off employees just before holidays.
5. Provide outplacement services and counseling to help laid-off employees find new jobs.
6. Communicate with survivors to explain how the company and their jobs will change.

Source: M. Boyle, "The Not-So-Fine Art of the Layoff," *Fortune*, 19 March 2001, 209.

Because of the problems associated with ERIPs, many companies are now offering **phased retirement**, in which employees transition to retirement by working reduced hours over a period of time before completely retiring. The advantage for employees is that they have more free time, but continue to earn salaries and benefits without changing companies or careers. The advantage for companies is that it allows them to reduce salaries and hiring and training costs and retain experienced, valuable workers.[154]

8.4 Employee Turnover

Employee turnover is the loss of employees who voluntarily choose to leave the company. In general, most companies try to keep the rate of employee turnover low to reduce recruiting, hiring, training, and replacement costs. Not all kinds of employee turnover are bad for organizations, however. In fact, some turnover can actually be good. For instance, **functional turnover** is the loss of poor-performing employees who choose to leave the organization.[155] Functional turnover gives the organization a chance to replace poor performers with better workers. In fact, one study found that simply replacing poor-performing leavers with average workers would increase the revenues produced by retail salespeople in an upscale department store by $112,000 per person per year.[156] By contrast, **dysfunctional turnover**, the loss of high performers who choose to leave, is a costly loss to the organization.

Employee turnover should be carefully analyzed to determine whether good or poor performers are choosing to leave the organization. If the company is losing too many high performers, managers should determine the reasons and find ways to reduce the loss of valuable employees. The company may have to raise salary levels, offer enhanced benefits, or improve working conditions to retain skilled workers. One of the best ways to influence functional and dysfunctional turnover is to link pay directly to performance. A study of four sales forces found that when pay was strongly linked to performance via sales commissions and bonuses, poor performers were much more likely to leave (that is, functional turnover). By contrast, poor performers were much more likely to stay when paid large, guaranteed monthly salaries and small sales commissions and bonuses.[157]

Review 8: Employee Separations

Employee separation is the loss of an employee, which can occur voluntarily or involuntarily. Before firing or terminating employees, managers should give employees a chance to improve. If firing becomes necessary, it should be done because of job-related factors, such as violating company rules or consistently performing poorly. Downsizing is supposed to lead to higher productivity and profits, better stock performance, and increased organizational flexibility, but studies show that it doesn't. The best strategy is to downsize only as a last resort. Companies that do downsize should offer outplacement services to help employees find other jobs. Companies use early retirement incentive programs to reduce the number of employees in the organization, lower costs, and create openings and job opportunities for people inside the company. The biggest problem with ERIPs is accurately predicting who and how many will accept early retirement. Companies generally try to keep the rate of employee turnover low to reduce costs. Functional turnover can be good for organizations, however, because it offers the chance to replace poor performers with better workers. Managers should analyze employee turnover to determine who is resigning and take steps to reduce the loss of good performers.

phased retirement employees transition to retirement by working reduced hours over a period of time before completing retiring

employee turnover loss of employees who voluntarily choose to leave the company

functional turnover loss of poor-performing employees who voluntarily choose to leave a company

dysfunctional turnover loss of high-performing employees who voluntarily choose to leave a company

SELF ASSESSMENT

KEY TERMS

Interview Anxiety

How would you feel if you got a call to interview for your dream job? Excited? Nervous? Or downright panicked? It's not uncommon to get butterflies in your stomach at the prospect of a job interview, but some candidates have more than weak knees and sweaty palms. Complete the assessment below by indicating the extent to which you agree with each of the following statements.[158] Your score will be a baseline as you begin working on the skills you'll need during your job hunt. Try not to spend too much time on any one item, and be sure to answer all the questions. Use this scale for your responses:

1 Strongly disagree
2 Disagree
3 Neutral
4 Agree
5 Strongly agree

1. I become so apprehensive in job interviews that I am unable to express my thoughts clearly.
   1 2 3 4 5
2. I often feel uneasy about my appearance when I am being interviewed for a job.
   1 2 3 4 5
3. While taking a job interview, I become concerned that the interviewer will perceive me as socially awkward.
   1 2 3 4 5
4. In job interviews, I get very nervous about whether my performance is good enough.
   1 2 3 4 5
5. During job interviews, my hands shake.
   1 2 3 4 5
6. I get so anxious while taking job interviews that I have trouble answering questions that I know.
   1 2 3 4 5
7. Before a job interview I am so nervous that I spend an excessive amount of time on my appearance.
   1 2 3 4 5
8. I become very uptight about having to socially interact with a job interviewer.
   1 2 3 4 5
9. I am overwhelmed by thoughts of doing poorly when I am in job interview situations.
   1 2 3 4 5
10. My heartbeat is faster than usual during job interviews.
    1 2 3 4 5
11. During job interviews, I often can't think of a thing to say.
    1 2 3 4 5
12. In job interviews, I worry that the interviewer will focus on what I consider to be my least attractive physical features.
    1 2 3 4 5
13. I get afraid about what kind of personal impression I am making on job interviews.
    1 2 3 4 5
14. I worry that my job interview performance will be lower than that of other applicants.
    1 2 3 4 5
15. It is hard for me to avoid fidgeting during a job interview.
    1 2 3 4 5
16. I feel that my verbal communication skills are strong.
    1 2 3 4 5
17. If I do not look my absolute best in a job interview, I find it very hard to be relaxed.
    1 2 3 4 5
18. During a job interview, I worry that my actions will not be considered socially appropriate.
    1 2 3 4 5

19. During a job interview, I am so troubled by thoughts of failing that my performance is reduced.
1 2 3 4 5

20. Job interviews often make me perspire (e.g., sweaty palms and underarms).
1 2 3 4 5

21. During job interviews, I find it hard to understand what the interviewer is asking me.
1 2 3 4 5

22. I feel uneasy if my hair is not perfect when I walk into a job interview.
1 2 3 4 5

23. I worry about whether job interviewers will like me as a person.
1 2 3 4 5

24. During a job interview, I worry about what will happen if I don't get the job.
1 2 3 4 5

25. My mouth gets very dry during job interviews.
1 2 3 4 5

26. I find it easy to communicate my personal accomplishments during a job interview.
1 2 3 4 5

27. During a job interview, I worry about whether I have dressed appropriately.
1 2 3 4 5

28. When meeting a job interviewer, I worry that my handshake will not be correct.
1 2 3 4 5

29. While taking a job interview, I worry about whether I am a good candidate for the job.
1 2 3 4 5

30. I often feel sick to my stomach when I am interviewed for a job.
1 2 3 4 5

Scoring

Reverse your score on items 16 and 26. That is, if you wrote in a "5," change it to a "1" and vice versa; if you wrote in a "4," change it to a "2" and vice versa.
TOTAL = _____
You can find the interpretation of your score at: **academic.cengage.com/management/williams.**

(continued)

MANAGEMENT DECISION

Open for Abuse

This isn't the first time you've had an employee who wanted to take leave under the Family and Medical Leave Act (FMLA). The act has been in place for over a decade, and you've had employees take leave for childbirth, for elder care, and to recover from surgery or injuries. In general, most people have used the FMLA as it was intended and have been relieved that they didn't have to choose between their job and caring for a family member. As with most things, however, there are always abuses, and you have occasionally had to grapple with a request for time off that you considered questionable. Today, you've received one of those requests.

You operate two upscale restaurants, one in the financial district and one in the entertainment district. Last week, you had to tell Cal, one of your experienced bartenders in the financial district location, that he would be moving from the happy hour to the lunch hour because you needed his experience there. Although Cal would now be the team leader on the day shift, he was angry about the change, insisting that it amounted to a pay reduction because no one has three-martini lunches anymore. He said he'd only be serving soda and coffee, and tips on those drinks weren't going to pay his rent. Even without drinks, lunchtime checks generally average $75 per table, so you assure Cal that once the five waitresses tip out (give a portion of their tips to the bartenders and table clearers), his pay should be the same. You reiterate that you really need him on days because the new crew is having trouble keeping up, even though they are just serving soda and coffee. But Cal announced his resignation. Before leaving at the end of his shift, however, he told you he had changed his mind. Today he came in late, with a doctor's note saying he required a 12-week leave for stress!

Under the FMLA, stress is considered a serious health condition, so you have to grant Cal's request and continue his health coverage. Legally, you can ask that he get a second opinion, but you can't question a doctor's recommendation for time off. Cal has requested the maximum time allowed—12 weeks of unpaid leave per year—and if he decides to come back after that, you have to keep his job for him. You are convinced, however, that he intends to quit when the 12 weeks are up.

What are you going to do? Asking other employees to pick up the slack will create morale problems for both the day and evening shifts (they get testy enough when someone is on leave for a legitimate situation), but hiring a temporary replacement may not solve your problem. If you do hire a temp, you might find a great new employee whom you'd have to let go in 12 weeks if Cal does come back. Maybe you should just be thankful that Cal requested the leave in one block, instead of taking it in daily or hourly increments, which, according to the law, he could have done.

Questions

1. How do you handle Cal's three-month absence with the least disruption?
2. Do you have a frank discussion with Cal and ask him if he plans to return after his leave, or do you just plan around him?
3. How can businesses mitigate the unintended impact of the FMLA?

Hire or Holdout?

When your systems engineer left to have a baby, you had no idea how hard it would be to replace her.[159] You'd heard the labor market for engineers was tight, but you thought it wouldn't be too tough to find a new hire for a company as well known as Raytheon. That was six months ago.

Today, your team is sitting down again with another crop of 200 résumés to compare against the job specifications: Ph.D in science or computer engineering; experience in manufacturing; knowledge of the manufacturing software you use and with Pro/Engineer Wildfire, a computer-aided design (CAD) software package; able to get top-secret government security clearance; willingness to relocate to Waltham, Massachusetts, where Raytheon is headquartered; and more technical competency requirements. Really, when you look over the list, you don't think the requirements are that stringent, particularly when you consider that Raytheon designs and manufactures aircraft, missile systems, and intelligence and information systems for the U.S. Department of Defense.

And your pool of applicants is nowhere near that of some other companies. Microsoft receives 60,000 résumés a month, but it has only 2,000 openings for software-development jobs. Of the 100,000 résumés it received from graduating students last year, it screened only 15,000, interviewed 3,500, and hired 1,000. Come to think of it, though, your chances of getting hired at Microsoft are better than your chances of filling your systems engineer opening.

As you sit down with your team and begin to sift through the 200 résumés, you see right away that 100 don't have a Ph.D. Of the remaining 100 candidates, 40 wouldn't be able to get security clearance, 23 are overqualified, and 18 don't have manufacturing experience, and 10 only have experience on 2001i, an earlier version CAD software. So out of your 200 applicants, only 9 are left, and you haven't even broached the question about relocating.

You've gone through seven similar piles of résumés in the past six months. The whole point of specifying the exact qualifications you want in an applicant was to save time getting the person up and running at the company. Maybe you'd have been better off loosening up the requirements and developing appropriate training programs. What if none of the applicants left standing after this round wants to relocate? Then you'll be starting with another pile next month—or sooner.

Form a team of four to five students to play the role of the hiring team at Raytheon and work through the following questions to come to a decision.

Questions

1. What are the risks to keeping the job requirements tightly structured?
2. What are the risks to loosening up the job specifications?
3. How would loosening up the job specifications affect your training needs?

4. Do you hire an applicant who meets a good number of the job requirements and is generally compatible with the corporate culture; or do you wait for the perfect candidate, even if that means another six months of interviewing?

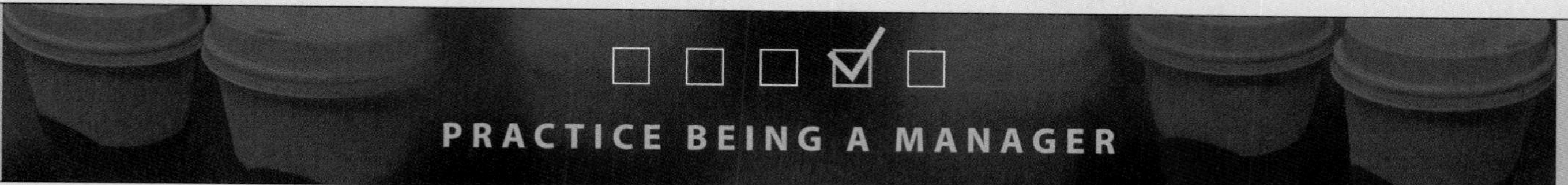

PRACTICE BEING A MANAGER

Managing human resources in today's complex business and legal environment is not easy. Not only must companies hire the creative and hard-working employees that will fuel growth and competitive advantage, but they must be careful to do so legally and ethically. Unfair discrimination in any HR process will result in poor placement, turnover, and legal woes. This exercise will give you some practice in navigating the challenges of legal and effective recruitment and selection of employees.

Step 1: Get into groups. Your professor will assign you to groups of four or five students. One student will be given the role of HR attorney for the applicants, two students the role of nursing shift (day/night) managers at Montclair Hospital, and the remaining student(s) will be assigned the role of senior hospital administrator at Montclair Hospital.

Scenario: Montclair Hospital needs to hire new nurses. In fact, the hospital is in a bit of a crisis. Three nurses were recently fired for using drugs while on duty. In the ensuing publicity, a journalist uncovered that two of these nurses were convicted felons. As if these problems were not enough, nurse turnover is up 20 percent this year over last, and productivity of the remaining staff is substandard. Absences are also up lately, particularly those related to child-care or elder-care issues.

Both the day and the night nursing shift managers need to hire some quality nurses—and fast. Hospital administrators have made it abundantly clear that they do not want a repeat of the headline "Felons and Drug Users among Montclair Nursing Staff." Your compensation and benefits are competitive, and, with the exception of the recent news coverage, your hospital enjoys a strong reputation. The nursing labor market is tight (there are fewer nurses than openings), and most new hires are recent nursing school graduates.

Nursing shift managers need to work together to develop a plan to achieve the following:

1. Hire top-flight nurses to fill vacancies left by recent firings and resignations.
2. Stem the turnover of quality nurses already employed by Montclair.
3. Reduce absenteeism, especially unplanned "emergency" absences that wreak havoc with planning the work of an upcoming shift.

Step 2a: Outline a plan. The day and the night nursing shift managers should work together to sketch out a plan for making progress on the three concerns of Montclair Hospital administration (hiring, turnover, absenteeism). Some elements of this plan might include

- Where and how to recruit top nursing candidates
- Screening applicants to reduce risks of turnover, criminal/behavioral problems, and disruptive absenteeism
- Dealing with the turnover, absenteeism, and productivity problems of existing nursing staff

Step 2b: Review the plan. Students in the roles of hospital administrator and HR attorney should listen to the nursing managers as they sketch out their plans. Do not offer comments unless one of the managers asks you for your input. Take careful notes regarding what you hear, with particular attention to concerns and questions. Those in the HR attorney role should consider what you hear from the perspective of both potential applicants (and litigants) and Montclair Hospital (defense of HR practices).

Are the nursing managers developing a plan likely to successfully address the three concerns related to hiring, turnover, and absenteeism? Why, or why not? Do you hear anything that might raise a legal concern (such as inappropriate interview question, possible discrimination)?

Step 3: Debrief as a class. Students should open with comments from each perspective: (1) HR attorneys, (2) hospital administrators, and (3) nursing shift managers. What are some of the particular concerns or questions that arose in your mind as you played your particular role? What are some of the tensions that face the managers and administrators in this situation? How might the HR system of a hospital be improved? Why might nurses represent a particularly challenging set of HR concerns?

DEVELOP YOUR CAREER POTENTIAL

360-Degree Feedback

Whereas most performance appraisal ratings have traditionally come from just one person, the boss, 360-degree feedback is obtained from four sources: the boss, subordinates, peers and coworkers, and the employees themselves. In this assignment, you will be gathering 360-degree feedback from people that you work with or from a team or group that you're a member of for a class.

Here are some guidelines for obtaining your 360-degree feedback:

- *Carefully select respondents*. One of the keys to good 360-degree feedback is getting feedback from the right people. In general, the people you ask for feedback should interact with you on a regular basis and should have the chance to regularly observe your behavior. Also, be sure to get a representative sample of opinions from a similar number of coworkers and subordinates (assuming you have some).
- *Get a large enough number of responses*. In addition to your boss, you should have a minimum of three peers and three subordinates giving you feedback. Five or six respondents in each of those categories is even better.
- *Ensure confidentiality*. Respondents are much more likely to be honest if they know that their comments are confidential and anonymous. So, when you ask respondents for feedback, have them return their comments to someone other than yourself. This person, your "feedback facilitator," will remove the names and any other information that would identify who made particular comments.
- *Explain how the 360-degree feedback will be used.* In this case, explain that the feedback is for a class assignment, that the results will be used for your own personal growth and development, and that the feedback they give you will not affect your grade or formal assessment at work.
- *Ask respondents to make their feedback as specific as possible*. For instance, "bad attitude" isn't very good feedback. "Won't listen to others' suggestions" is much better because it would let you know how to improve your behavior. Have your respondents use the feedback form below to provide your feedback.

Here's what you need to turn in for this assignment:

1. The names and relationships (boss, peers, subordinates, classmates, teammates) of those whom you've asked for feedback.
2. The name of the person you've asked to be your feedback facilitator.
3. Copies of all written feedback that was returned to you.
4. A one-page summary of the written feedback.
5. A one-page description of your specific goals and action plans for responding to the feedback you received.

360-Degree Feedback Form

As part of a class assignment, I, ___________, am collecting feedback from you about my performance. What you say or write will not affect my grade. The purpose of this assignment is for me to receive honest feedback from the people I work with in order to identify the things I'm doing well and the things that I need to improve. So please be honest and direct in your evaluation.

When you have completed this feedback form, please return it to ___________. He or she has been selected as my feedback facilitator and is responsible for ensuring that your confidentiality and anonymity are maintained. After all feedback forms have been returned to ___________, he or she will make sure that your particular responses cannot be identified. Only then will the feedback be shared with me.

Please provide the following feedback.

Continue doing . . .

Describe three things that ___________ is doing that are a positive part of his or her performance and that you want him or her to continue doing.

1.

2.

3.

Start doing . . .

Describe three things that ___________ needs to start doing that would significantly improve his or her performance.

1.

2.

3.

Please make your feedback as specific and behavioral as possible. For instance, "needs to adjust attitude" isn't very good feedback. "Needs to begin listening to others' suggestions" is much better because the person now knows exactly how to change his or her behavior. So please be specific. Also, please write more than one sentence per comment. This will help the feedback recipient better understand your comments.

REEL TO REAL

BIZ FLIX

Bowfinger

This film, which brought Steve Martin and Eddie Murphy together for the first time, offers a funny look at Hollywood filmmaking. Bobby Bowfinger (Martin), perhaps the least successful director in films, wants to produce a low-budget film with top star Kit Ramsey (Murphy). Bowfinger's problem: recruit a crew and cast with almost no budget and trick Kit into appearing in his film. So he decides to hire a lookalike.

Bowfinger interviews several candidates for the Kit Ramsey lookalike role. He rejects everyone until Jifferson (Jiff) Ramsey (also played by Murphy) auditions. This scene is an edited version of the "The Lookalike" sequence early in the film. It includes Jiff's audition and interview, and a brief look at his first day at work.

What to Watch for and Ask Yourself

1. Does Bobbie Bowfinger have a set of valid selection criteria for filling the role of a Kit Ramsey lookalike? Does Bowfinger apply the criteria uniformly to each applicant?
2. Is there a good person-job fit of Jiff Ramsey in the screen role of Kit Ramsey?
3. Do you predict that Jiff Ramsey will be successful as a Kit Ramsey substitute?

MANAGEMENT WORKPLACE

PepsiCo—Employee Champions

Whether a company employs five or five thousand people, its greatest resource is those workers. Many of today's companies view their workforces as part of their overall competitive strategy—the best people producing the best products. Human resource managers at large firms such as PepsiCo may be viewed as strategic business partners. No longer do they simply sign paychecks, approve vacations, and process health benefit claims. At PepsiCo, HR managers play an integral role in the day-to-day success of the business.

Headquartered in Purchase, New York, PepsiCo is a global organization, with more than 143,000 employees worldwide. The company produces and markets such brands as PepsiCo beverages, Frito-Lay snacks, Gatorade and Tropicana drinks, and Quaker Foods. PepsiCo brand products are available in nearly 200 countries and territories. But recruiting, selecting, training, and managing more than 100,000 workers requires planning to meet the career needs of so many people. Let's look inside the management workplace at PepsiCo to see how the company does it.

Questions

1. What do you think the role of the employee champion is in terms of the human resource (HR) function discussed in the chapter?
2. Which areas of human resources are handled by PepsiCo's administrative experts?
3. What do you think is the advantage of dividing HR functions into four distinct quadrants?

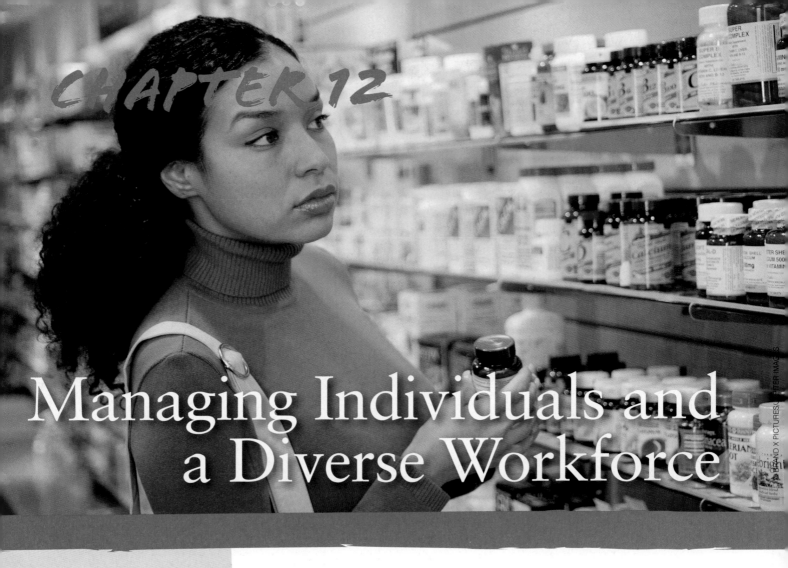

CHAPTER 12

Managing Individuals and a Diverse Workforce

© BRAND X PICTURES/JUPITER IMAGES

Learning Outcomes:

1 Describe diversity and explain why it matters.
2 Understand the special challenges that the dimensions of surface-level diversity pose for managers.
3 Explain how the dimensions of deep-level diversity affect individual behavior and interactions in the workplace.
4 Explain the basic principles and practices that can be used to manage diversity.

In This Chapter:

WHAT WOULD YOU DO?

Walgreens, Deerfield, Illinois. Walgreens is the nation's largest drugstore chain, with annual sales of $47.4 billion. It operates 5,584 stores in 47 states and Puerto Rico and plans to have 7,000 stores by 2010.[1]

The Equal Employment Opportunity Commission (EEOC) has filed an employment discrimination class-action lawsuit against Walgreens, alleging widespread racial bias against thousands of African American workers. The EEOC charges that company management assigns African American managers, management trainees, and pharmacists to low-performing stores in African American communities because of their race. Additionally, the EEOC asserts that Walgreens denies these managers and professionals promotional opportunities based on race—all in violation of federal law. The EEOC case started when a group of current and former African American managers filed a private lawsuit making similar allegations. Since then, more than 20 current and former employees have complained to the EEOC, alleging racial discrimination by Walgreens in employment decisions. An EEOC investigation offered enough evidence to file a class-action suit in federal court. With your guidance, the company issued a statement saying, "As a company with a history of commitment to fairness, diversity, and opportunity, we are saddened and disappointed by the EEOC's decision. Our commitment is to providing opportunity to all employees—not only because it is the right thing to do but because our business was built on this principle." The statement continued, "Fairness and equality always have been the cornerstone of our business. We're the nation's best represented retailer in urban areas, and managers of all backgrounds are promoted to senior levels from those locations." Obviously, data must suggest otherwise to file a class-action suit. "Black managers are assigned to stores in black neighborhoods more often than one would expect, and black employees are not being promoted to management and within management as often as similar white employees," said EEOC attorney Robert Johnson. Attorneys who filed the private lawsuit said that the employees not only "faced discrimination, but faced segregation. The segregation is a throwback that most of us thought was gone from American life."

The trial, the appeals that are sure to follow, and any final settlement may take years to resolve. The question now is, what do you do in the interim? Certainly, pressure is building to address these issues. Even stockholders are not happy, especially since the stock price dropped following the EEOC announcement.

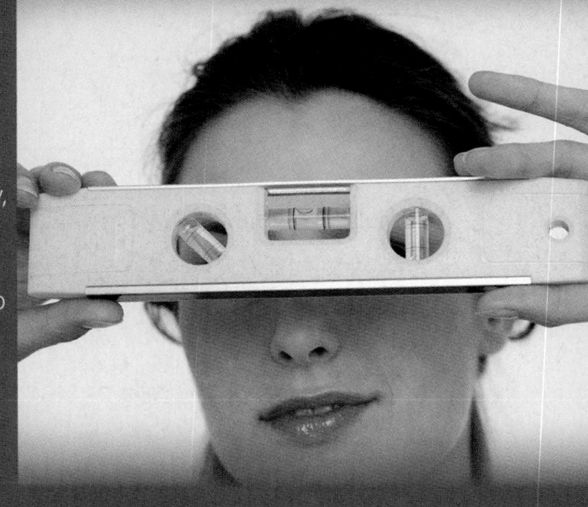

So, what should you do to address these issues as you wait for the case to wind its way through the court system? First, what should you do when it comes to placements, that is, assigning managers and pharmacists to stores? Should store location not be considered when making placement decisions? Should management make a conscious attempt to completely disregard race and other demographics when assigning people to stores? Second, what about promotion decisions? Should you reserve a percentage of promotions for minorities or base promotions strictly on performance with no regard to race? Some in the company argue that making changes now is tantamount to an admission of guilt and would weaken your court case. Others argue that both Walgreens' minority employees and the public perceive the promotion differences as real and problematic, and that something needs to be done regardless of the class-action suit. So, what, if anything, should you do? Finally, what changes does Walgreens need to make in its organizational structure and company leadership so that these issues aren't problems in the future? When all this started, Walgreens didn't have a senior vice president of diversity, a leadership position that many companies of Walgreens' size and revenue have. **If you were in charge of diversity at Walgreens, what would you do?**

ACTIVITIES + VIDEO

CengageNOW Audio study guide, electronic flashcards, author FAQ videos, On the Job and Biz Flix videos, concept tutorial, and concept exercise

Web (academic.cengage.com/management/williams) Quiz, PowerPoint slides, and glossary terms for this chapter

Study Tip

In the margin next to each paragraph or section in the chapter, write the question that the section answers. For example, "What is the difference between surface- and deep-level diversity?" could go on page 440. Once you have questions throughout the chapter, you can quiz yourself by using a blank piece of paper to cover the content. To check yourself, reveal each paragraph after you have answered the corresponding question.

"WHAT'S NEW" COMPANIES

WALGREENS
LONGO TOYOTA
DENNY'S
VERIZON
MCDONALD'S
COCA-COLA
PACIFIC ENTERPRISES
FRITO-LAY
HOECHST CELANESE
HABITAT INTERNATIONAL
AND OTHERS...

Workplace diversity as we know it today is changing. Exhibit 12.1 shows predictions from the U.S. Bureau of the Census of how the U.S. population will change over the next 65 years. The percentage of white, non-Hispanic Americans in the general population is expected to decline from 69.3 percent in 2005 to 46.8 percent by the year 2070. By contrast, the percentage of African Americans will increase (from 12.3 percent to 13.2 percent), as will the percentage of Asian Americans (from 4.3 percent to 10.6 percent). Meanwhile the proportion of Native Americans will hold steady (at 0.8 percent). The fastest-growing group by far, though, is Hispanics, who are expected to increase from 13.3 percent of the total population in 2005 to 28.6 percent by 2070.

Other significant changes have already occurred, as Walgreens' situation in the opening case illustrates. For example, today women hold half the jobs in the United States, up from 38.2 percent in 1970.[2] Furthermore, white males, who composed 63.9 percent of the work force in 1950, hold just 38.2 percent of today's jobs.[3]

These rather dramatic changes have taken place in a relatively short time. And, as these trends clearly show, the workforce of the near future will be increasingly Hispanic, Asian American, African American, and female. According to Hewitt Associates, by 2008, women and minorities will represent 70 percent of the new labor force entrants, and by 2010, 34 percent of the U.S. workforce will be non-Caucasian.[4] It will also be older, as the average baby boomer approaches the age of 60 around 2010. Since many boomers are likely to postpone retirement and work well into their 70s to offset predicted reductions in Social Security and Medicare benefits, the workforce may become even older than expected.[5] For instance, Hewitt Associates estimates that by 2010 the U.S. workforce will have a 29 percent increase in the 45–64 age group and a 14 percent increase in the 65+ age group, but a 1 percent decline in the 18–44 age group.[6] This chapter begins with a review of workforce diversity—what it is and why it matters. Next, you will learn about two basic dimensions of diversity: surface-level diversity, or how age, sex, race/ethnicity, and mental and physical disabilities affect people at

Exhibit 12.1

Predicted U.S. Population, Distributed by Race, 2005–2070

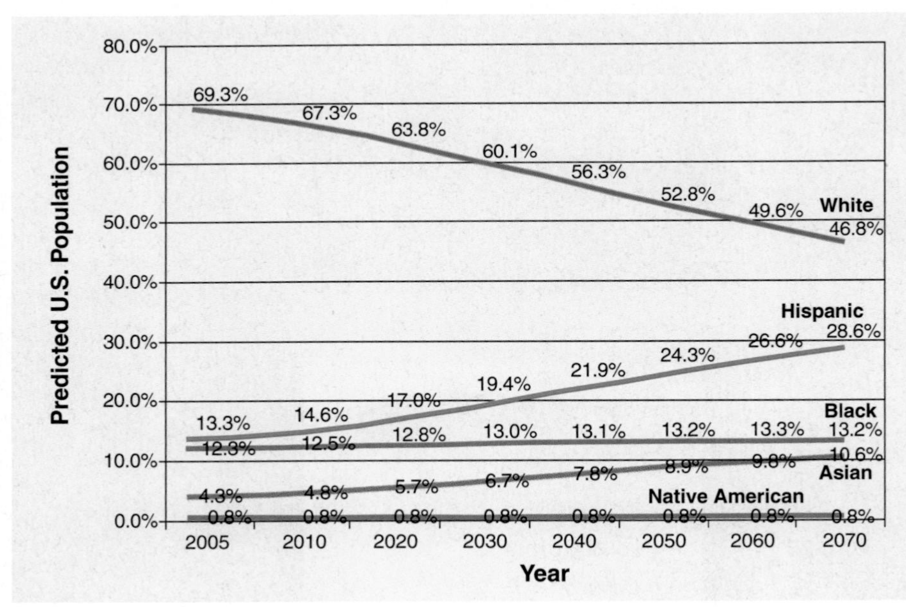

Sources: "Projections of the Resident Population by Race, Hispanic Origin, and Nativity: Middle Series, 2001–2005, 2006–2010, 2011–2015, 2016–2020, 2025–2045, 2050–2070," U.S. Census Bureau, available at http://www.census.gov/population/projections/nation/summary/np-t5-b.txt, http://www.census.gov/population/projections/nation/summary/np-t5-c.txt, http://www.census.gov/population/projections/nation/summary/np-t5-e.txt, http://www.census.gov/population/projections/nation/summary/np-t5-f.txt, http://www.census.gov/population/projections/nation/summary/np-t5-g.txt.

work; and deep-level diversity, or how core personality differences influence behavior and attitudes. In the last section, you will learn how diversity can be managed. Here, you'll read about diversity paradigms, principles, and practices that help managers strengthen the diversity *and* the competitiveness of their organizations.

DIVERSITY AND WHY IT MATTERS

Diversity means variety. Therefore, **diversity** exists in organizations when there is a variety of demographic, cultural, and personal differences among the people who work there and the customers who do business there. For example, step into **LONGO TOYOTA** in El Monte, California, one of Toyota's top-selling dealerships, and you'll find diversity in the form of salespeople who speak Spanish, Korean, Arabic, Vietnamese, Hebrew, and Mandarin Chinese. In fact, the 60 salespeople at Longo Toyota speak 30 different languages. Surprisingly, this level of diversity was achieved without a formal diversity plan in place.[7]

By contrast, some companies lack diversity, in their work force, their customers, or both. For example, **DENNY'S** restaurants paid $54.4 million to settle a class-action lawsuit alleging discriminatory treatment of black customers at its restaurants. Edison International, a California-based utility company, paid more than $11 million for wrongly rejecting job applicants on the basis of race. And phone company Bell Atlantic paid a whopping $500 million to African American employees who were unfairly passed over for promotions.[8] (Bell Atlantic and GTE have now merged and become **VERIZON** Communications.) In recent years, Tyson Foods, Coca-Cola, Los Alamos National Laboratory, and many other companies have settled class-action discrimination lawsuits.[9]

Today, however, Denny's, Edison International, Verizon, and Coca-Cola have made great improvements in their level of diversity. At Denny's, all of the company's charitable contributions now go to organizations that benefit minorities. Furthermore, minorities now constitute 29.1 percent, 28.6 percent, and 24.6 percent of managers at Denny's, Edison International, and Verizon, respectively, and 47.4 percent, 44.9 percent, and 32 percent, respectively, of their workers.[10] And Coca-Cola received a glowing report for its efforts to improve diversity.[11] In fact, these four companies have increased their diversity so much that they consistently make *Fortune* magazine's list of the 50 best companies for minorities.[12]

After reading the next section, you should be able to

1 *describe diversity and explain why it matters.*

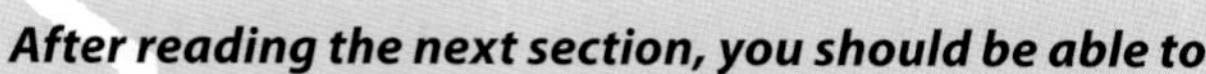

1 Diversity: Differences That Matter

You'll begin your exploration of diversity by learning ***1.1 that diversity is not affirmative action*** *and* ***1.2 how to build a business case for diversity****.*

diversity a variety of demographic, cultural, and personal differences among an organization's employees and customers

1.1 Diversity Is Not Affirmative Action

A common misconception is that workplace diversity and affirmative action are the same, yet these concepts differ in several critical ways. To start, **affirmative action** refers to purposeful steps taken by an organization to create employment opportunities for minorities and women.[13] By contrast, diversity exists in organizations when there is a variety of demographic, cultural, and personal differences among the people who work there and the customers who do business there. So one key difference is that affirmative action is more narrowly focused on demographics such as sex and race, while diversity has a broader focus that includes demographic, cultural, and personal differences. Furthermore, diversity can exist even if organizations don't take purposeful steps to create it. For example, as mentioned earlier, Longo Toyota achieved a high level of diversity without having a formal affirmative action program. Likewise, a local restaurant located near a university in a major city is likely to have a more diverse group of employees than one located in a small town. So, organizations can achieve diversity without affirmative action. Likewise, organizations that take affirmative action to create employment opportunities for women and minorities may not yet have diverse workforces.

Another important difference is that affirmative action is required by law for private employers with 15 or more employees, while diversity is not. Affirmative action originated with the 1964 Civil Rights Act, which bans discrimination in voting, public places, federal government programs, federally supported public education, and employment. Title VII of the Civil Rights Act (**http://www.eeoc.gov/policy/vii.html**) requires that workers have equal employment opportunities when being hired or promoted. More specifically, Title VII prohibits companies from discriminating on the basis of race, color, religion, sex, or national origin. Furthermore, Title VII created the Equal Employment Opportunity Commission, or EEOC (**http://www.eeoc.gov**), to administer these laws. By contrast, there is no federal law or agency to oversee diversity. Organizations that pursue diversity goals and programs do so voluntarily. "Until recently, the commitment many companies had to diversity was fundamentally based on moral, ethical and compliance reasons," says Rudy Mendez, vice president for diversity and inclusion at ***McDonald's***. "But now that we can add business impact, diversity executives are being given a much bigger role."[14]

> Until recently, the commitment many companies had to diversity was fundamentally based on moral, ethical and compliance reasons. But now that we can add business impact, diversity executives are being given a much bigger role.
>
> **RUDY MENDEZ**, VICE PRESIDENT FOR DIVERSITY AND INCLUSION, MCDONALD'S

affirmative action purposeful steps taken by an organization to create employment opportunities for minorities and women

Affirmative action programs and diversity programs also have different purposes. The purpose of affirmative action programs is to compensate for past discrimination, which was widespread when legislation was introduced in the 1960s; to prevent ongoing discrimination; and to provide equal opportunities to all, regardless of race, color, religion, sex, or national origin. Organizations that fail to uphold these laws may be required to

- *Hire, promote, or give back pay to those not hired or promoted*
- *Reinstate those who were wrongly terminated*
- *Pay attorneys' fees and court costs for those who bring charges against them*
- *Take other actions that make individuals whole by returning them to the condition or place they would have been had it not been for discrimination*[15]

Consequently, affirmative action is basically a punitive approach.[16] By contrast, as shown in Exhibit 12.2, the general purpose of diversity programs is to create a positive work environment where no one is advantaged or disadvantaged, where "we" is everyone, where everyone can do his or her best work, where differences are respected and not ignored, and where everyone feels comfortable.[17] So, unlike affirmative action, which punishes companies for not achieving specific sex and race ratios in their work forces, diversity programs seek to benefit both organizations and their employees by encouraging organizations to value all kinds of differences.

Despite affirmative action's overall success in making workplaces much fairer than they used to be,[18] many people argue that some affirmative action programs unconstitutionally offer preferential treatment to females and minorities at the expense of other employees—a view accepted by some courts.[19] In California, voters approved Proposition 209, which bans race- and sex-based affirmative action in college admissions, government hiring, and government contracting programs. Jake Weiss, a white worker in Jericho, New York, expressed a typical complaint when he said, "It used to be if you were white, you got everything in America and that wasn't right. But now [with affirmative action], all that's left for people like me are the crumbs."[20] And Christopher Katzenbach, an attorney in a San Francisco law firm, said, "I think people want to be evaluated on their merits, not their race or gender, and that is the driving force behind a lot of this [reverse discrimination] litigation."[21] Furthermore, research shows that people who have gotten a job or promotion as a result of affirmative action are frequently viewed as unqualified, even when clear evidence of their qualifications exists.[22] For example, one woman said, "I won a major prize [in my field], and some of the guys in my lab said it was because I was a woman. I'm certain they didn't choose me because I was a woman. But it gave some disgruntled guys who didn't get the prize a convenient excuse."[23] So, while affirmative action programs have created opportunities for minorities and women, those same minorities and women are frequently presumed to be unqualified when others believe they obtained their jobs as a result of affirmative action.

In summary, affirmative action and diversity are not the same thing. Not only are they fundamentally different, but they also differ in purpose, practice, and the reactions they produce.

1.2 Diversity Makes Good Business Sense

Those who support the idea of diversity in organizations often ignore its business aspects altogether, claiming instead that diversity is simply the "right thing to do." Yet diversity actually makes good business sense in several ways: cost savings, attracting and retaining talent, and driving business growth.[24]

Diversity helps companies with *cost savings* by reducing turnover, decreasing absenteeism, and avoiding expensive

Exhibit 12.2

General Purpose of Diversity Programs

To create a positive work environment where
• No one is advantaged or disadvantaged.
• "We" is everyone.
• Everyone can do his or her best work.
• Differences are respected and not ignored.
• Everyone feels comfortable.

Source: T. Roosevelt, "From Affirmative Action to Affirming Diversity," *Harvard Business Review* 68, no. 2 (1990): 107–117.

Affirmative action programs are substantially more controversial than diversity programs, but the former are finding some surprising proponents.

lawsuits.[25] Because of lost productivity and the cost of recruiting and selecting new workers, companies lose substantial amounts of money when employees quit their jobs. In fact, turnover costs typically amount to more than 90 percent of employees' salaries. By this estimate, if an executive who makes $200,000 leaves, the organization will have to spend approximately $180,000 to find a replacement, and even the lowest-paid hourly workers can cost the company as much as $10,000 when they quit. Since turnover rates for African Americans average 40 percent higher than for whites, and since women quit their jobs at twice the rate men do, companies that manage diverse workforces well can cut costs by reducing the turnover rates of these employees.[26] And, with women absent from work 60 percent more often than men, primarily because of family responsibilities, diversity programs that address the needs of female workers can also reduce the substantial costs of absenteeism.

Diversity programs also save companies money by helping them avoid discrimination lawsuits, which have increased by a factor of 20 since 1970 and quadrupled just since 1995. In one survey conducted by the Society of Human Resource Management, 78 percent of respondents reported that diversity efforts helped them avoid lawsuits and litigation costs.[27] Indeed, because companies lose two-thirds of all discrimination cases that go to trial, the best strategy from a business perspective is not to be sued for discrimination at all. When companies lose, the average individual settlement amounts to more than $600,000.[28] And settlement costs can be substantially higher in class-action lawsuits, in which individuals join together to sue a company as a group. For example, COCA-COLA paid $192.5 million to settle a class-action suit brought by 2,200 African American workers who were discriminated against in pay, promotions, and performance reviews; a similar lawsuit brought by 1,300 African American workers cost Texaco $176 million.[29] Boeing paid $72.5 million to settle a sex discrimination lawsuit with female employees who were paid less and not promoted because they were women.[30] And Dial Corporation, the soap manufacturer, paid $10 million to settle a sex discrimination lawsuit filed by 90 female employees at its manufacturing plants.[31] In fact, the average class-action lawsuit costs companies $58.9 million for racial discrimination and $24.9 million for sex discrimination.[32] According to the EEOC, companies paid $420 million in damages in 2004 for discrimination lawsuits.[33]

Diversity also makes business sense by helping companies *attract and retain talented workers*.[34] Indeed, diversity-friendly companies tend to attract better *and* more diverse job applicants. Very simply, diversity begets more diversity. Companies that make *Fortune* magazine's list of the 50 best companies for minorities already attract a diverse and talented pool of job applicants. But, after being recognized by *Fortune* for their efforts, they experience even bigger increases in both the quality and the diversity of people who apply for jobs. Indeed, research shows that companies with acclaimed diversity programs not only attract more talented workers, but also have higher stock market performance.[35]

Just as important, however, is that these companies also create opportunities that encourage workers to stay. For example, Anne Shen Smith, vice president of support services for **Pacific Enterprises**, a California-based utility holding company, said that the company created opportunities by replacing the "old-boy network," in which only bosses could nominate employees for promotions, with a program called "Readiness for Management," in which employees nominate themselves. Workers begin the process by taking a number of self-assessment tests to determine their strengths and weaknesses. Then they take training courses to improve their skills and knowledge. The Readiness for Management program works because it gives people who were previously overlooked a chance to move up and makes employees responsible for improving their skills and knowledge.[36] Employees who don't take that responsibility don't get promoted.

The third way that diversity makes business sense is by *driving business growth*. Diversity helps companies grow by improving their understanding of the marketplace. When companies have diverse workforces, they are better able to understand the needs of their increasingly diverse customer bases. For example, at **Frito Lay**, the Latino Employee Network proved invaluable during the development of Doritos' guacamole-flavored tortilla chips. Members of the network, called Adelante, provided feedback on the taste and packaging to help ensure that the product would be regarded as authentic in the Latino community. The Adelante members' insights helped make the guacamole-flavored Doritos one of the most successful new-product launches in the company's history, generating more than $100 million in sales in its first year alone.[37]

In the United States today there are 36 million African Americans, 41 million Hispanic Americans, and 12 million Asian Americans, who, together, represent 30 percent of U.S. consumers. Indeed, according to the U.S. Bureau of Labor Statistics, "America's population will increase 50 percent over the next 50 years, with almost 90 percent of that increase in the minority community."[38] By 2050, Hispanics will make up one-quarter of the population and will nearly triple in number to 97 million. Accordingly, the U.S. Department of Commerce expects minority purchasing power to grow fivefold to $6,080 billion.[39] In fact, a recent survey conducted by the Society for Human Resource Management found that tapping into "diverse customers and markets" was the number one reason managers gave for implementing diversity programs.[40] Diversity also helps companies grow through higher-quality problem solving. Though diverse groups initially have more difficulty working together than homogeneous groups, after several months diverse groups do a better job of identifying problems and generating alternative solutions, the two most important steps in problem solving.[41] Ernest Drew, former CEO of **Hoechst Celanese**, a chemical company, recalls a company conference in which the company's top 125 managers, mostly white males, were joined by 50 lower-level employees, mostly minorities and women. Problem-solving teams were formed to discuss how the company's corporate culture affected business and how it could be changed. Half the teams were composed of white males, while the other half were of mixed sex and race. Drew says, "It was so obvious that the diverse teams had the broader solutions. They had ideas I hadn't even thought of. For the first time, we realized that diversity is a strength as it relates to problem solving. Before, we just thought of diversity as the total number of minorities and women in the company, like affirmative action. Now we knew we needed diversity at every level of the company where decisions are made."[42]

> It was so obvious that the diverse teams had the broader solutions. They had ideas I hadn't even thought of.
>
> ERNEST DREW, FORMER CEO, HOECHST CELANESE

In short, "diversity is no longer about counting heads; it's about making heads counts," says Amy George, vice president of diversity and inclusion at Pepsico.[43]

Review 1: Diversity: Differences That Matter

Diversity exists in organizations when there is a variety of demographic, cultural, and personal differences among the people who work there and the customers who do business there. A common misconception is that workplace diversity and affirmative action are the same. However, affirmative action is more narrowly focused on demographics, is required by law, and is used to punish companies that discriminate on the basis of race, color, religion, sex, or national origin. By contrast, diversity is broader in focus (going beyond demographics), voluntary, more positive in that it encourages companies to value all kinds of differences, and, at the same time, substantially less controversial than affirmative action. Thus, affirmative action and diversity differ in purpose, practice, and the reactions they produce. Diversity also makes good business sense in terms of cost savings (reducing turnover, decreasing absenteeism, and avoiding lawsuits), attracting and retaining talent, and driving business growth (improving marketplace understanding and promoting higher-quality problem solving).

DIVERSITY AND INDIVIDUAL DIFFERENCES

A survey that asked managers, "What is meant by diversity to decision-makers in your organization?" found that they most frequently mentioned race, culture, sex, national origin, age, religion, and regional origin.[44] When managers describe workers this way, they are focusing on surface-level diversity. **Surface-level diversity**, as illustrated in Exhibit 12.3, consists of differences that are immediately observable, typically unchangeable, and easy to measure.[45] In other words, independent observers can usually agree on dimensions of surface-level diversity, such as another person's age, sex, race/ethnicity, or physical capabilities.

And while most people start by using easily observable characteristics, such as surface-level diversity, to categorize or stereotype other people, those initial, surface-level categorizations typically give way to deeper impressions formed from knowledge of others' behavior and psychological characteristics, such as personality and attitudes.[46] When you think of others this way, you are focusing on deep-level diversity. **Deep-level diversity** consists of differences that are communicated through verbal and nonverbal behaviors and are learned only through extended interaction with others.[47] Examples of deep-level diversity include personality differences, attitudes, beliefs, and values. In other words, as people in diverse

surface-level diversity differences such as age, sex, race/ethnicity, and physical disabilities that are observable, typically unchangeable, and easy to measure

deep-level diversity differences such as personality and attitudes that are communicated through verbal and nonverbal behaviors and are learned only through extended interaction with others workplaces get to know each other, the initial focus on surface-level differences such as age, race/ethnicity, sex, and physical capabilities is replaced by deeper, more accurate knowledge of coworkers.

If managed properly, the shift from surface- to deep-level diversity can accomplish two things.[48] First, coming to know and understand each other better can result in reduced prejudice and conflict. Second, it can lead to stronger social integration. **Social integration** is the degree to which group members are psychologically attracted to working with each other to accomplish a common objective, or, as one manager put it, "working together to get the job done."

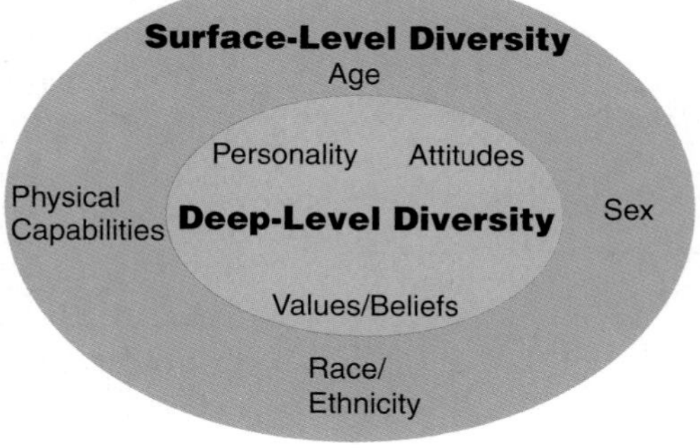

Exhibit 12.3

Surface- and Deep-Level Diversity

After reading the next two sections, you should be able to

2 understand the special challenges that the dimensions of surface-level diversity pose for managers.

3 explain how the dimensions of deep-level diversity affect individual behavior and interactions in the workplace.

2 Surface-Level Diversity

Because age, sex, race/ethnicity, and disabilities are usually immediately observable, many managers and workers use these dimensions of surface-level diversity to form initial impressions and categorizations of coworkers, bosses, customers, or job applicants. Whether intentionally or not, sometimes those initial categorizations and impressions lead to decisions or behaviors that discriminate. Consequently, these dimensions of surface-level diversity pose special challenges for managers who are trying to create positive work environments where everyone feels comfortable and no one is advantaged or disadvantaged.

Let's learn more about those challenges and the ways that ***2.1 age, 2.2 sex, 2.3 race/ethnicity****, and* ***2.4 mental or physical disabilities can affect decisions and behaviors in organizations****.*

2.1 Age

Age discrimination is treating people differently (e.g., in hiring and firing, promotion, and compensation decisions) because of their age. The victims of age discrimination are almost always "older" workers, based on the idea that "You can't teach an old dog new tricks." It's commonly believed that older workers can't learn how to use computers and technology, won't adapt to change, are sick more often, and, in general, are much more expensive to employ than younger workers. One manager explains his preference for younger workers over older workers this way: "The way I look at it, for $40,000 or $50,000, I can get a smart, raw kid right out of undergrad who's going to work seven days a week for me for the next two years. I'll train him the way I want him, he'll grow with me, and I'll pay him long-term options so I own him, for lack of a better word. He'll do exactly what I want—and if he doesn't, I'll fire him. . . . The alternative is to pay twice as much for some 40-year-old who does half the amount of work, has been trained improperly, and doesn't listen to what I say."[49]

social integration the degree to which group members are psychologically attracted to working with each other to accomplish a common objective

age discrimination treating people differently (e.g., in hiring and firing, promotion, and compensation decisions) because of their age

Unfortunately, attitudes like this are all too common.[50] According to the Society for Human Resource Management, 53 percent of 428 surveyed managers believed that older workers "didn't keep up with technology," and 28 percent said that older workers were "less flexible."[51] For example, when 57-year old Sam Horgan, a former chief financial officer, was interviewing for a job, he was asked by a 30-something job interviewer, "Would you have trouble working with young bright people?"[52] Not surprisingly, 80 percent of human resource managers surveyed by *Personnel Management* magazine said that age discrimination was a major problem in their organizations and that older employees were not receiving the same training and promotional opportunities as younger workers.[53] Likewise, two-thirds of 10,000 people surveyed by AARP (American Association of Retired Persons) felt that they had been wrongly discharged from a job because of their age. In fact, a study by the Society for Human Resource Management found that 20 percent of all companies had been sued for age discrimination in the preceding five years.[54] Normally, somewhere between 17,000 and 20,000 age discrimination cases are filed with the EEOC each year (**http://www.eeoc.gov/stats/adea.html**). And these numbers may increase, given a U.S. Supreme Court ruling that employees may sue for age discrimination even if the discrimination was not intentional (see Chapter 11's discussion of disparate treatment and adverse impact).[55] What's really sad is that it takes older workers not months, but years to find a suitable job.[56] Thankfully, in recent years, a number of companies have started specializing in recruiting and placing applicants who are 50 years and older.[57]

So, what's reality and what's myth? Do older employees actually cost more? In some ways, they do. The older people are and the longer they stay with a company, the more the company pays for salaries, pension plans, and vacation time. But older workers cost companies less, too, because they show better judgment, care more about the quality of their work, and are less likely to quit, show up late, or be absent, the cost of which can be substantial.[58] A survey by Chicago outplacement firm Challenger, Gray & Christmas found that only 3 percent of employees age 50 and over changed jobs in any given year, compared with 10 percent of the entire work force and 12 percent of workers ages 25 to 34. The study also found that while older workers make up about 14 percent of the work force, they suffer only 10 percent of all workplace injuries and use fewer healthcare benefits than younger workers with school-age children.[59] As for the widespread belief that job performance declines with age, the scientific evidence clearly refutes this stereotype. Performance does not decline with age, regardless of the type of job.[60]

What can companies do to reduce age discrimination?[61] To start, managers need to recognize that age discrimination is much more pervasive than they probably think. Whereas "old" used to mean mid-50s, in today's workplace, "old" is closer to 40. When 773 CEOs were asked, "At what age does a worker's productivity peak?" the average age they gave was 43. Thus, age discrimination may be affecting more workers because perceptions about age have changed. In addition, with the aging of the baby boomers, age discrimination is more likely to occur simply because there are millions more older workers than there used to be. And, because studies show that interviewers rate younger job candidates as more qualified (even when they aren't), companies need to train managers and recruiters to make hiring and promotion decisions on the basis of qualifications, not age. Companies also need to monitor the extent to which

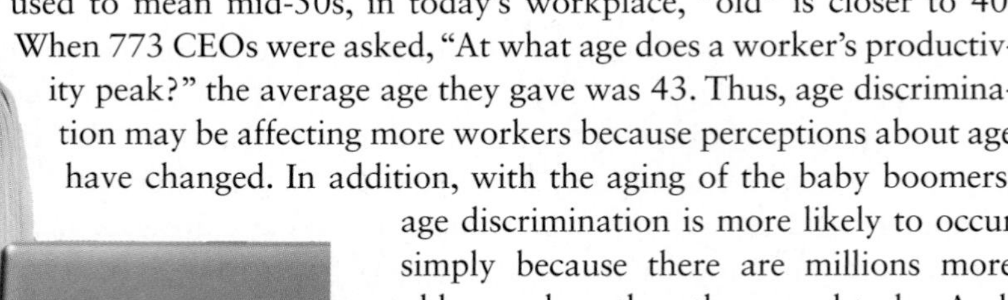

older workers receive training. The Bureau of Labor Statistics found that the number of training courses and number of hours spent in training drops dramatically after employees reach the age of 44.[62] Finally, companies need to ensure that younger and older workers interact with each other. One study found that younger workers generally hold positive views of older workers and that the more time they spent working with older coworkers, the more positive their attitudes became.[63]

2.2 Sex

Sex discrimination occurs when people are treated differently because of their sex. Sex discrimination and racial/ethnic discrimination (discussed in the next section) are often associated with the so-called **glass ceiling**, the invisible barrier that prevents women and minorities from advancing to the top jobs in organizations.

To what extent do women face sex discrimination in the workplace? Almost every year, the EEOC receives between 21,000 and 26,000 charges of sex-based discrimination (**http://www.eeoc.gov/stats/sex.html**). In some ways, there is much less sex discrimination than there used to be. For example, whereas women held only 17 percent of managerial jobs in 1972, today they now outnumber men with 50.6 percent of managerial jobs, a percentage that is nearly equal to their representation in the workforce.[64] Likewise, women own 47 percent of all U.S. businesses.[65] Whereas women owned 700,000 businesses in 1977 and 4.1 million businesses in 1987, today they own 9 million![66] Finally, though women still earn less than men on average, the differential is narrowing. As Exhibit 12.4 shows, women earned 79.5 percent of what men did in 2003, up from 63 percent in 1979.

Although progress is being made, sex discrimination continues to operate via the glass ceiling at higher levels in organizations. For instance, as shown in Exhibit 12.5, in 2002/2003 a woman had the highest salary (that is, was the top earner) in only 5.2 percent of *Fortune* 500 companies, and only 15.7 percent of corporate officers (top management) were women. Indeed, only 9 of the 500 largest companies in the United States have women CEOs.[67] Similarly, just 13.6 percent of the members of corporate boards of directors are women.[68]

sex discrimination treating people differently because of their sex

glass ceiling the invisible barrier that prevents women and minorities from advancing to the top jobs in organizations

Is sex discrimination the sole reason for the slow rate at which women have been promoted to middle and upper levels of management and corporate boards? Some studies indicate that it's not.[69] In some instances, the slow progress appears to be due to career and job choices. Whereas men's career and job choices are often driven by the search for higher pay and advancement, women are more likely to choose jobs or careers that also give them a greater sense of accomplishment, more control over their work schedules, and easier movement in and out of the workplace.[70] Furthermore, women are historically much more likely than men to prioritize family over work at some time in their careers. For example, 96 percent of 600 female Harvard MBAs held jobs while they were in their 20s. That dropped to 71 percent in their late 30s when they had children, but then increased to 82.5 percent in their late 40s as their children became older.[71]

Exhibit 12.4
Women's Earnings as a Percentage of Men's

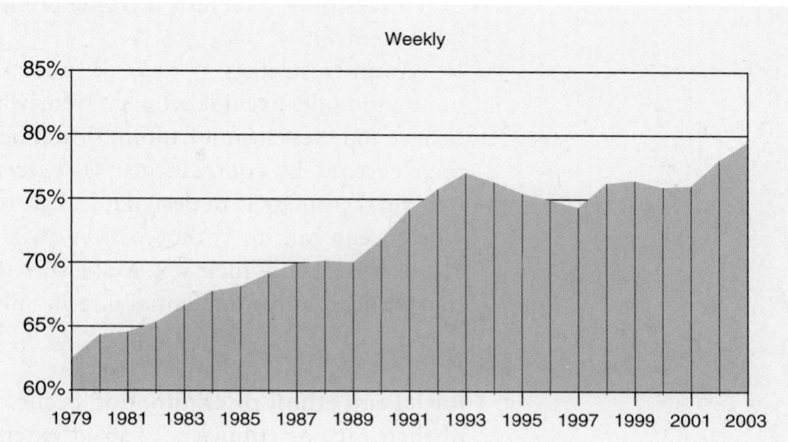

Sources: "Highlights of Women's Earnings in 2001, 2002, 2003," U.S. Department of Labor, Bureau of Labor Statistics, available at http://www.bls.gov/cps/cpswom2001.pdf and http://www.bls.gov/opub/ted/2004/oct/wk4/art01.htm, 25 May 2005.

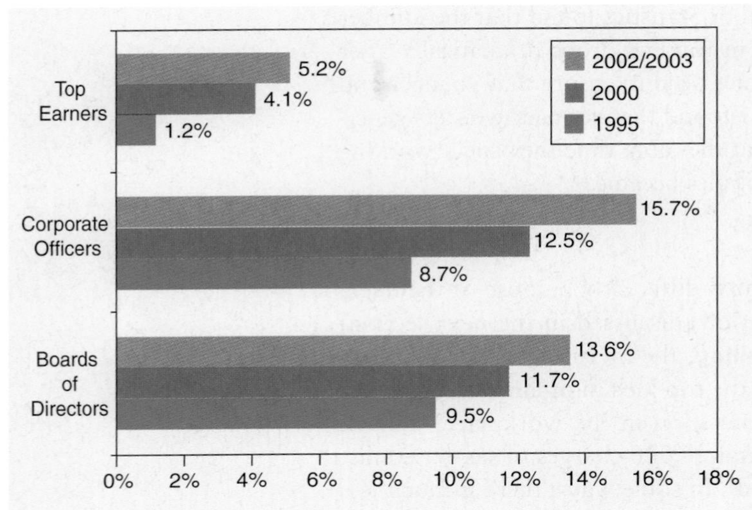

Sources: "Census of Women Corporate Officers and Top Earners" Catalyst, available at http://www.catalystwomen.org/knowledge/titles/title.php?page=cen_WOTE02, 26 May 2005; "2003 Catalyst Census of Women Board Directors of the *Fortune* 1000," Catalyst, available at http://www.catalystwomen.org/knowledge/titles/title.php?page=cen_WBD03, 26 May 2005.

Exhibit 12.5

Women at Fortune 500 and 1000 Companies

Beyond these reasons, however, it's likely that sex discrimination does play a role in women's slow progress into the higher levels of management. And even if you don't think so, many of the women you work with probably do. Indeed, one study found that more than 90 percent of executive women believed that the glass ceiling had hurt their careers.[72] In another study, 80 percent of women said they left their last organization because the glass ceiling had limited their chances for advancement.[73] A third study indicated that the glass ceiling is prompting more and more women to leave companies to start their own businesses.[74] Anita Borg, a senior researcher at a *Fortune* 500 company, sums up the frustrations of many professional women when she says, "You run into subtle sexism every day. It's like water torture. It wears you down."[75] Very few professional women achieve the same status as their male counterparts even in advanced economies, such as the United States, Canada, the United Kingdom, and Japan.[76]

In a Catalyst study of *Fortune* 1000 organizations, about two-thirds of the executives and half of the CEOs surveyed noted the failure of senior leadership to assume accountability for women's advancement to be the key barrier preventing professional women from progressing to senior executive positions.[77] So, what can companies do to make sure that women have the same opportunities for development and advancement as men? One strategy is mentoring, or pairing promising female executives with senior executives from whom they can seek advice and support. A vice president at a utility company says, "I think it's the single most critical piece to women advancing career-wise. In my experience you need somebody to help guide you and . . . go to bat for you."[78] In fact, 91 percent of female executives have a mentor at some point and feel their mentor was critical to their advancement.

Another strategy is to make sure that male-dominated social activities don't unintentionally exclude women. Nearly half (47 percent) of women in the workforce believe that "exclusion from informal networks" makes it more difficult to advance their careers. By contrast, just 18 percent of CEOs thought this was a problem.[79] One final strategy is to designate a "go-to person," other than their supervisors, that women can talk to if they believe that they are being held back or discriminated against because of their sex. Make sure this person has the knowledge and authority to conduct a fair, confidential internal investigation.[80]

2.3 Race/Ethnicity

Racial and ethnic discrimination occurs when people are treated differently because of their race or ethnicity. To what extent is racial and ethnic discrimination a factor in the workplace? Every year, the EEOC receives between 26,000 and 30,000 charges of race discrimination, which is more than any other type of charge of discrimination (**http://www.eeoc.gov/stats/race.html**). However, it is true that since

racial and ethnic discrimination treating people differently because of their race or ethnicity the passage of the 1964 Civil Rights Act and Title VII, there is much less racial and ethnic discrimination than there used to be. For example, 18 *Fortune* 500 firms had an African American or Hispanic CEO in 2005, whereas none did in 1988.[81] Nonetheless, strong racial and ethnic disparities still exist. For instance, whereas about 12 percent of Americans are black, only 5.9 percent of managers and 3.2 percent of top managers are black. Similarly, about 13 percent of Americans are Hispanic, but only 6.3 percent are managers and 3.7 percent are CEOs. By contrast, Asians, who constitute about 4 percent of the population, are better represented holding 4 percent of management jobs and 3.4 percent of CEO jobs.[82]

What accounts for the disparities between the percentages of minority groups in the general population and their smaller representation in management positions? Some studies have found that the disparities are due to preexisting differences in training, education, and skills; when African Americans, Hispanics, Asian Americans, and whites have similar skills, training, and education, they are much more likely to have similar jobs and salaries.[83]

Other studies, however, provide increasingly strong direct evidence of racial or ethnic discrimination in the workplace. For example, one study directly tested hiring discrimination by sending pairs of black and white males and pairs of Hispanic and non-Hispanic males to apply for the same jobs. Each pair had résumés with identical qualifications, and all were trained to present themselves in similar ways to minimize differences during interviews. The researchers found that the white males got three times as many job offers as the black males, and that the non-Hispanic males got three times as many offers as the Hispanic males.[84]

Another study, which used similar methods to test hiring procedures at 149 different companies, found that whites received 10 percent more interviews than blacks. Half of the whites interviewed received job offers, but only 11 percent of the blacks. And when job offers were made, blacks were much more likely to be offered lower-level positions, while whites were more likely to be offered jobs at higher levels than the jobs they had applied for.[85]

Critics of these studies point out that it's nearly impossible to train different applicants to give identical responses in job interviews and that differences in interviewing skills may have somehow accounted for the results. However, British researchers found similar kinds of discrimination just by sending letters of inquiry to prospective employers. As in the other studies, the letters were identical except for the applicant's race. Employers frequently responded to letters from Afro-Caribbean, Indian, or Pakistani "applicants" by

Pepsi's Diversity Culture

It's not surprising that when it came time for PepsiCo to choose a new CEO, the board picked the Indian-born female executive, Indra Nooyi. PepsiCo has a long history of diversity, stretching back to the end of World War II, when president Walter Mack hired Edward Boyd away from the National Urban League to head a team charged with launching a marketing program for African American consumers. In every area of the country where Boyd's team ran a marketing blitz, Pepsi sales increased, and soon Pepsi-Cola was able to overtake market leader Coca-Cola in cities like Cleveland and Chicago. One of the most successful campaigns was a series of print advertisements titled "Leaders in Their Fields," which profiled the accomplishments of professional and successful African Americans. Pepsi's print campaign was the first to shun the stereotypical images of African Americans used in advertising.

Source: S. Capparell, "How Pepsi Opened Door to Diversity," *Wall Street Journal*, 9 January 2007, B1.

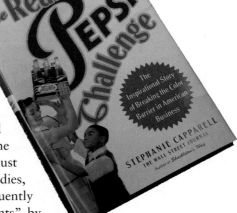

indicating that the positions had been filled. By contrast, they often responded to white, Anglo-Saxon "applicants" by inviting them to face-to-face interviews. Similar results were found with Vietnamese and Greek "applicants" in Australia.[86] In short, the evidence strongly indicates that there is strong and persistent racial and ethnic discrimination in the hiring processes of many organizations.

What can companies do to make sure that people of all racial and ethnic backgrounds have the same opportunities?[87] Start by looking at the numbers. Compare the hiring rates of whites with the hiring rates for racial and ethnic applicants. Do the same thing for promotions within the company. (Had Walgreens done this, it could have avoided the class-action suit filed by the EEOC.) See if nonwhite workers quit the company at higher rates than white workers. Also, survey employees to compare white and nonwhite employees' satisfaction with jobs, bosses, and the company, as well as their perceptions concerning equal treatment. Next, if the numbers indicate racial or ethnic disparities, consider employing a private firm to test your hiring system by having applicants of different races with identical qualifications apply for jobs in your company.[88] Although disparities aren't proof of discrimination, it's much better to investigate hiring and promotion disparities yourself than to have the EEOC or a plaintiff's lawyer do it for you.

Another step companies can take is to eliminate unclear selection and promotion criteria. Vague criteria allow decision makers to focus on non-job-related characteristics that may unintentionally lead to employment discrimination. Instead, selection and promotion criteria should spell out the specific knowledge, skills, abilities, education, and experience needed to perform a job well.

Finally, train managers and others who make hiring and promotion decisions. At Tower Records, the human resources staff assembles on a giant game board that covers a conference room floor. Tower store managers then answer questions about hiring situations. If they answer a question correctly, they move forward on the board. If they answer it incorrectly, they stay in place, and the group discusses what should have been done instead. The number of grievances about hiring procedures has dropped significantly since the training began.[89]

2.4 Mental or Physical Disabilities

Habitat International, a leading supplier of artificial-grass and indoor-outdoor carpet products for Home Depot, Lowe's, and other retailers, is also socially responsible business: It employs hard-to-place workers. In fact, 75 percent of Habitat's workers have a physical or mental disability, or both. Over the years the company has also employed recovering alcoholics, homeless people, non-English-speaking refugees, and others who, when given a chance, work hard to overcome the stereotypes about them. Launched by David Morris and his father Saul in 1981, the Chattanooga, Tennessee, company has become a role model for other businesses, disability advocates, and the general public. At Habitat, people matter most and its philosophy of love, kindness, and compassion honor the special diversity of the people who work at Habitat International (**http://www.habitatinc.com**).[90] According to the Americans with Disabilities Act (**http://www.ada.gov**), a **disability** is a mental or physical impairment that substantially limits one or more major life activities.[91] One in every five Americans, or more than 54 million people, has a disability.[92] **Disability discrimination** occurs when people are treated differently because of their disabilities.

disability a mental or physical impairment that substantially limits one or more major life activities

disability discrimination treating people differently because of their disabilities

To what extent is disability discrimination a factor in the workplace? According to the U.S. Census Bureau, 80 percent of able men have jobs, compared with only 60 percent of those with disabilities. For women, the statistic shows a similar pattern, with 67 percent of able women being employed versus only 51 percent of disabled women. More specifically, only 47 percent of those who have a sensory disability, 32 percent of those who have a physical disability, and 28 percent of those who have a mental disability have jobs.[93] Furthermore, people with disabilities are disproportionately employed in low-status or part-time jobs, have little chance for advancement, and, on average, are twice as likely to live in poverty as able people.[94] Numerous studies also indicate that managers and the general public believe that discrimination against people with disabilities is common and widespread.[95]

What accounts for the disparities between the employment and income levels of able people and people with disabilities? Contrary to popular opinion, it has nothing to do with the ability of people with disabilities to do their jobs well. Studies show that as long as companies make reasonable accommodations for disabilities (such as changing procedures or equipment), people with disabilities perform their jobs just as well as able people. Furthermore, they have better safety records and are not any more likely to be absent or quit their jobs.[96]

What can companies do to make sure that people with disabilities have the same opportunities as everyone else? Beyond educational efforts to address incorrect stereotypes and expectations, a good place to start is to commit to reasonable workplace accommodations such as changing work schedules, reassigning jobs, acquiring or modifying equipment, or providing assistance when needed. Accommodations for disabilities needn't be expensive. According to the Job Accommodation Network, 71 percent of accommodations cost employers $500 or less, and 20 percent of accommodations don't cost anything at all.[97] For example, rather than rebuild its offices, the U.S. Postal Service used inexpensive ramps to raise wheelchair-bound clerks to counter level so they could wait on customers. Other examples of low-cost accommodations include a telephone sound amplifier ($48) for a hearing-impaired factory worker; a card system with streets filed alphabetically with ZIP codes ($150) for a learning-impaired mail room worker who couldn't remember which streets had which ZIP codes; lateral filing cabinets ($450 each) for a clerk who couldn't reach the vertical filing cabinets from her wheelchair; and a personal paging device ($350) that vibrated to let a grocery store worker with Down syndrome who couldn't hear the public address system know when he was to go to the store office.[98] For further information about reasonable accommodations, visit the Job Accommodation Network (**http://janweb.icdi.wvu.edu**), which provides free help and has a database of 26,000 successful accommodations.[99] Exhibit 12.6 provides a list of common, inexpensive accommodations that companies can make for disabled workers.

Some of the accommodations just described involve *assistive technology* that gives workers with disabilities the tools they need to overcome their disabilities. Providing workers with assistive technology is also an effective strategy to

Exhibit 12.6
Reasonable Accommodations for Disabled Workers

- Physical changes, such as installing a ramp or modifying a workspace or restroom.
- A quieter workspace or other changes that reduce noisy distractions for someone with a mental disability.
- Training and other written materials in an accessible format, such as in Braille, on audio tape, or on computer disk.
- TTYs for use with telephones by people who are deaf, and hardware and software that make computers accessible to people who have vision impairments or who have difficulty using their hands.
- Time off for someone who needs treatment for a disability.

Source: "Americans with Disabilities Act: A Guide for People with Disabilities Seeking Employment," U.S. Department of Justice, available at http://www.usdoj.gov/crt/ada/workta.htm, 2 October 2003.

recruit, retain, and enhance productivity of people with disabilities. According to the National Council on Disability, 92 percent of workers with disabilities who use assistive technology report that it helps them work faster and better, 81 percent indicate that it helps them work longer hours, and 67 percent say that it is critical to getting a job.[100] To learn about assistive technologies that can help workers with disabilities, see Abledata (**http://www.abledata.com**), which lists 25,000 products from 3,000 organizations, or the National Rehabilitation Information Center (**http://www.naric.com**), which provides information for specific disabilities.

Finally, companies should actively recruit qualified workers with disabilities. Numerous organizations, such as Mainstream, Kidder Resources, the American Council of the Blind (**http://www.acb.org**), the National Federation of the Blind (**http://www.nfb.org**), the National Association of the Deaf (**http://www.nad.org**), the Epilepsy Foundation (**http://www.epilepsyfoundation.org**), and the National Amputation Foundation (**http://www.nationalamputation.org**), actively work with employers to find jobs for qualified people with disabilities. Companies can also place advertisements in publications, such as *Careers and the Disabled*, that specifically target workers with disabilities.[101]

Review 2: Surface-Level Diversity

Age, sex, race/ethnicity, and physical and mental disabilities are dimensions of surface-level diversity. Because those dimensions are (usually) easily observed, managers and workers tend to rely on them to form initial impressions and stereotypes. Sometimes this can lead to age, sex, racial/ethnic, or disability discrimination (that is, treating people differently) in the workplace. In general, older workers, women, people of color or different national origins, and people with disabilities are much less likely to be hired or promoted than white males. This disparity is often due to incorrect beliefs or stereotypes, such as "job performance declines with age," or "women aren't willing to travel on business," or "workers with disabilities aren't as competent as able workers." To reduce discrimination, companies can determine the hiring and promotion rates for different groups, train managers to make hiring and promotion decisions on the basis of specific criteria, and make sure that everyone has equal access to training, mentors, reasonable work accommodations, and assistive technology. Finally, companies need to designate a "go-to person" that employees can talk to if they believe they have suffered discrimination.

3 Deep-Level Diversity

Have you ever taken an instant dislike to someone—perhaps because of the way the person talked, acted, or treated you—only to decide, after spending some time working or interacting with this person, that your initial impressions were wrong and that he or she wasn't so bad after all?

If you've had this experience, then you understand the difference between surface- and deep-level diversity. As you just learned, people often use the dimensions of surface-level diversity to form initial impressions about others. Over time, however, as people have a chance to get to know each other, initial impressions based on age, sex, race/ethnicity, and mental or physical disabilities give way to deeper impressions based on behavior and psychological characteristics. When we think of others this way, we are focusing on deep-level diversity. *Deep-level diversity* represents differences that can be learned only through extended interaction with others. Examples of deep-level diversity include differences in personality, attitudes, beliefs, and values. In short, recognizing deep-level diversity requires getting to know and understand one another better. And that matters, because it can result in less prejudice, discrimination, and conflict in the workplace. These changes can then lead to better *social integration*, the degree to which organizational or group members are psychologically attracted to working with each other to accomplish a common objective.

Let's examine deep-level diversity by exploring ***3.1 the "Big Five" dimensions of personality*** *and* ***3.2 other significant work-related aspects of personality.***

3.1 Big Five Dimensions of Personality

Stop for a second and think about your boss (or the boss you had in your last job). What words would you use to describe him or her? Is your boss introverted or extraverted? Emotionally stable or unstable? Agreeable or disagreeable? Organized or disorganized? Open or closed to new experiences? When you describe your boss or others in this way, what you're really doing is describing dispositions and personality.

A **disposition** is the tendency to respond to situations and events in a predetermined manner. **Personality** is the relatively stable set of behaviors, attitudes, and emotions displayed over time that makes people different from each other.[102] For example, which of your aunts or uncles is a little offbeat, a little out of the ordinary? What was that aunt or uncle like when you were small? What is she or he like now? Chances are she or he is pretty much the same wacky person. In other words, the person's core personality hasn't changed. For years, personality researchers studied hundreds of different ways to describe people's personalities. In the last decade, however, personality research conducted in different cultures, different settings, and different languages has shown that five basic dimensions of personality account for most of the differences in peoples' behaviors, attitudes, and emotions (or for why your boss is the way he or she is!). The *Big Five Personality Dimensions* are extraversion, emotional stability, agreeableness, conscientiousness, and openness to experience.[103]

Extraversion is the degree to which someone is active, assertive, gregarious, sociable, talkative, and energized by others. In contrast to extraverts, introverts are less active, prefer to be alone, and are shy, quiet, and reserved. For the best results in the workplace, introverts and extraverts should be correctly matched to their jobs. Tim Burke, CEO of **Quest**, a technology consulting and management company based in Sacramento, California, has had trouble finding the right people for jobs. He says the biggest challenge is "when we've hired a person who has all the necessary skills but still is not right for the job." Now Quest uses personality assessment to match people to jobs, matching for instance, extraverts to outside sales jobs and introverts to technical jobs.[104]

Emotional stability is the degree to which someone is not angry, depressed, anxious, emotional, insecure, or excitable. People who are emotionally stable respond well to stress. In other words, they can maintain a calm, problem-solving attitude in even the toughest situations (such as conflict, hostility, dangerous conditions, or extreme time pressures). By contrast, under only moderately stressful situations, emotionally unstable people find it difficult to handle the most basic demands of their jobs and become distraught, tearful, self-doubting, and anxious. Emotional stability is particularly important for high-stress jobs, such as police work, fire fighting,

disposition the tendency to respond to situations and events in a predetermined manner

personality the relatively stable set of behaviors, attitudes, and emotions displayed over time that makes people different from each other

extraversion the degree to which someone is active, assertive, gregarious, sociable, talkative, and energized by others

emotional stability the degree to which someone is not angry, depressed, anxious, emotional, insecure, and excitable emergency medical treatment, piloting planes, or commanding rockets. The firing of astronaut Lisa Nowak by NASA illustrates the importance of emotional stability and the failure of employers to adequately screen potential employees for important characteristics. Nowak was charged with trying to kidnap a woman she regarded as her romantic rival for the affection of a space shuttle pilot. She allegedly pepper-sprayed the woman, and police found a BB gun, a steel mallet, a knife, and rubber tubing in her possession. The inability to handle stressful situations is a clear sign of emotional instability.[105] As you learned in Chapter 1, emotional stability is also important for managers. Indeed, the number one mistake managers make is intimidating, bullying, and being abrasive to the people who work for them.

agreeableness the degree to which someone is cooperative, polite, flexible, forgiving, good-natured, tolerant, and trusting

conscientiousness the degree to which someone is organized, hardworking, responsible, persevering, thorough, and achievement oriented

openness to experience the degree to which someone is curious, broad-minded, and open to new ideas, things, and experiences; is spontaneous; and has a high tolerance for ambiguity

People who are hardworking, responsible, persevering, and thorough are conscientious; this personality trait alone is a strong indicator of motivation and high performance.

Agreeableness is the degree to which someone is cooperative, polite, flexible, forgiving, good-natured, tolerant, and trusting. Basically, agreeable people are easy to work with and be around, whereas disagreeable people are distrusting and difficult to work with and be around. A number of companies have made general attitude or agreeableness the most important factor in their hiring decisions. Small-business owner Roger Cook says, "Hire nice people. I'm looking for personal—not professional—traits. I want a good or nice person. I can teach the skills. I call their references and ask, 'Is he or she a nice person?' I take a close look at how applicants answer questions and carry themselves. Why nice people? Because they're trustworthy; they get along with other crew members: they are good with customers and they are usually hard workers."[106]

Conscientiousness is the degree to which someone is organized, hardworking, responsible, persevering, thorough, and achievement oriented. One management consultant wrote about his experiences with a conscientious employee: "He arrived at our first meeting with a typed copy of his daily schedule, a sheet bearing his home and office phone numbers, addresses, and his e-mail address. At his request, we established a timetable for meetings for the next four months. He showed up on time every time, day planner in hand, and carefully listed tasks and due dates. He questioned me exhaustively if he didn't understand an assignment and returned on schedule with the completed work or with a clear explanation as to why it wasn't done."[107]

Openness to experience is the degree to which someone is curious, broad-minded, and open to new ideas, things, and experiences; is spontaneous; and has a high tolerance for ambiguity. Most companies need people who are strong in terms of openness to experience to fill certain positions, but for other positions, this dimension is less important. People in marketing, advertising, research, or other creative jobs need to be curious, open to new ideas, and spontaneous. By contrast, openness to experience is not particularly important to accountants, who need to consistently apply stringent rules and formulas to make sense out of complex financial information.

Which of the Big Five Personality Dimensions has the largest impact on behavior in organizations? The cumulative results indicate that conscientiousness is related to job performance across five different occupational groups (professionals, police, managers, sales, and skilled or semiskilled jobs).[108] In short, people who are dependable, persistent, goal directed, and organized tend to be higher performers on virtually any job; viewed negatively, those who are careless, irresponsible, low-achievement striving, and impulsive tend to

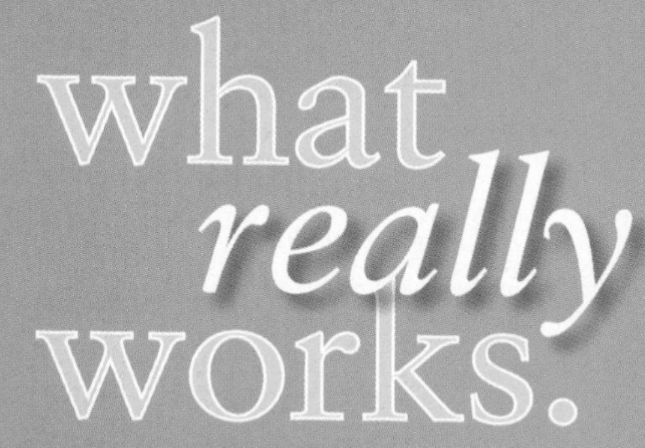

CONSCIENTIOUSNESS: THE ORGANIZED, HARDWORKING, RESPONSIBLE PERSONALITY

Conscientious people are organized, hardworking, responsible, persevering, thorough, and achievement oriented. Who wouldn't want to hire people with these personality traits? Indeed, 92 studies across five occupational groups (professionals, police, managers, sales, and skilled/semiskilled jobs) with a combined total of 12,893 study participants indicated that, on average, conscientious people are inherently more motivated and are better at their jobs.

MOTIVATIONAL EFFORT

There is a 71 percent chance that conscientious workers will be more motivated and will work harder than less conscientious workers.

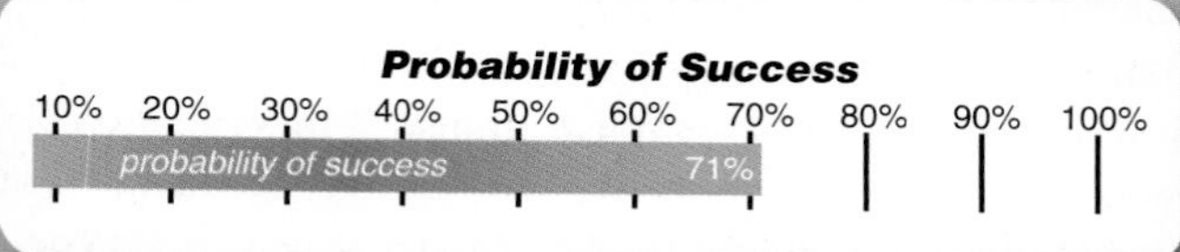

JOB PERFORMANCE

There is a 66 percent chance that conscientious workers will be better at their jobs than less conscientious workers.[109]

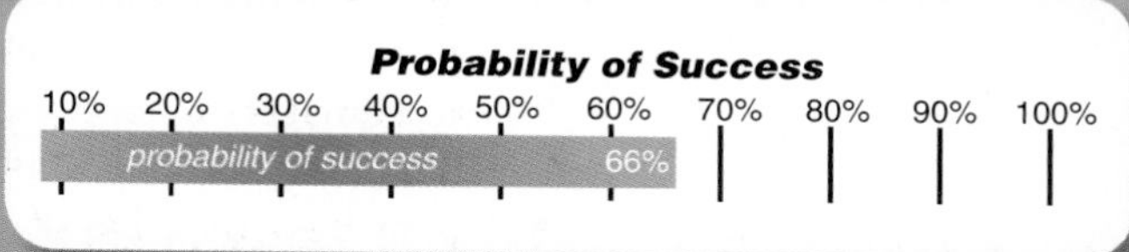

be lower performers on virtually any job.[110] See the "What Really Works" feature in this chapter for further explanation. The results also indicate that extraversion is related to performance in jobs that involve significant interaction with others, such as sales and management. In people-intensive jobs like these, it helps to be sociable, assertive, and talkative and to have energy and be able to energize others. Finally, people who are extraverted and open to experience seem to do much better in training. Being curious and open to new experiences, as well as sociable, assertive, talkative, and full of energy, helps people perform better in learning situations.[111]

3.2 Work-Related Personality Dimensions

Does the way you keep your desk reveal something about your personality? Lots of people think so. For example, people with ultra-neat desks tend to believe that a desk buried under mounds of paper, food wrappers, and old magazines is a sign that its owner is lazy, disorganized, undependable, and a dreamer. On the other hand, people with messy desks believe that a spotless desk with everything in its place is a sign that its owner is impatient, critical, controlling, analytical, and a perfectionist. Who knows, maybe if your desk is somewhere between operating-room clean and the aftermath of a tornado, it is a sign that you have a good-natured, flexible, and fun-loving personality.[112]

Although studies indicate that extraversion, emotional stability, agreeableness, conscientiousness, and openness to experience are the five basic dimensions of personality in any culture, setting, or language, research has also identified additional personality dimensions that directly affect workplace attitudes and behaviors. These additional personality dimensions are authoritarianism, Machiavellian tendencies, Type A/B personality, locus of control, and positive/negative affectivity.

Authoritarianism is the extent to which an individual believes there should be power and status differences within the organization.[113] Authoritarian employees are likely to prefer a direct leadership style, in which the boss tells them exactly what to do. While this sounds desirable, one disadvantage is that even when they know a better solution or are aware of problems, authoritarian employees may simply carry out their boss's orders without question. Also, authoritarian employees may not perform well on ambiguous tasks or for managers who encourage employees to use their own initiative and judgment.

Authoritarian leaders are highly demanding and expect employees to unquestioningly obey their orders. One such boss, a body builder who liked to show off his strength to managers by doing 25 pushups at the start of meetings, used to call the vice president of marketing at all hours to scream about things that had gone wrong. A second bully boss, the CEO of a semiconductor-network start-up, ridiculed employees publicly. "He'd pick up something I'd written and say, 'Who wrote this? A second grader? It's the stupidest thing I've ever read,'" says the firm's marketing vice president. Business executives who are too demanding or who ridicule and scream at employees undermine productivity, discourage innovation and may cause a talent drain at their companies, says James Clifton, CEO of the GALLUP ORGANIZATION.[114]

People with **Machiavellian** personalities believe that virtually any type of behavior is acceptable if it helps satisfy needs or accomplish goals.[115] In other words, people with Machiavellian personalities believe that the ends justify the means. For example, "high Machs" are generally more willing to use lies and deceit to get their way than are "low Machs," even in situations where the chances of being caught in a lie are high.[116] High Machs believe that most people are gullible and can be manipulated. High Machs are also more effective at persuading others than low Machs are and tend to be resistant to others' efforts to persuade them.[117] One reason high Machs are more effective at persuading others is that low Machs (meaning most people) may be distracted by emotions or issues unrelated to winning. By contrast, high Machs are difficult to persuade because they ignore emotions and secondary issues and focus only on the things that move them closer to their goals. Also, because they are out for themselves and no one else, high Machs don't do well in work teams. High Machs often cause conflicts within teams and sometimes cause teams to break up. The *Wall Street Journal* offers this vivid description of High Machs: "They tend to be narcissistic, arrogant, manipulative, and goal-oriented. They trust no one and refuse to collaborate. They lack a capacity for empathy but are skilled at politics. Though they purposely disregard how they're coming off to colleagues or subordinates, they're often very good at sweet-talking bosses, who remain oblivious to their dastardly ways."[118] One study found that employees stuck with such manipulative bosses experienced more exhaustion, job tension, nervousness, depressed mood, and mistrust.[119]

The **Type A/B personality dimension** is the extent to which people tend toward impatience, hurriedness, competitiveness, and hostility.[120] **Type A personalities** try to complete as many tasks as possible in the shortest possible time and are hard driving, competitive, impatient, perfectionistic, angry, and unable to relax.[121] Type As have a high need for achievement and are also likely to be aggressive, self-confident, dominant, and extraverted. In contrast, **Type B personalities** are easygoing, patient, and able to relax and engage in leisure activities. Unlike Type A personalities, they are neither highly competitive nor excessively driven to accomplishment.

authoritarianism the extent to which an individual believes there should be power and status differences within organizations

Machiavellian the extent to which individuals believe that virtually any type of behavior is acceptable in trying to satisfy their needs or meet their goals

Type A/B personality dimension the extent to which people tend toward impatience, hurriedness, competitiveness, and hostility

Type A personality a person who tries to complete as many tasks as possible in the shortest possible time and is hard driving, competitive, impatient, perfectionistic, angry, and unable to relax

Type B personality a person who is relaxed, easygoing, and able to engage in leisure activities without worrying about work

What do we know about the Type A/B personality dimension and the workplace? Contrary to what you'd expect, Type As don't always outperform Type Bs on the job. Type As tend to perform better on tasks that demand quick decisions made at a rapid work pace under time pressure, whereas Type Bs tend to perform better at tasks requiring well-thought-out decisions when there is little time pressure. And despite the characteristic Type A ambition to succeed, top managers are much more likely to have Type B personalities.[122] Ironically, the task complexity and psychological challenge inherent in management jobs actually work against many Type A managers by dramatically increasing their stress levels.[123] Type Bs, on the other hand, do a much better job of handling and responding to the stress of managerial jobs.

A recent study involving 6,148 people aged 14 to 102 conducted by a group of researchers and the U.S. National Institute of Aging found absolutely no connection between a hard-driving personality and heart disease, contrary to previous studies and conventional wisdom. This study clearly establishes that Type A personality in itself is not related to heart disease.[124] However, individuals who are Type A and also "hostile and angry," may be at risk of heart attack. For example, businessperson Matt Sicinski gets extremely hostile and angry when his coworkers miss deadlines or don't follow directions. Says Sicinski, "My feet get cold, and I get a throbbing in my head. I can feel every muscle in my body tense up." If he gets angry with someone on the phone, sometimes he presses the mute button so he can't be heard and begins "cursing somebody up one side and down the other."[125] How dangerous is angry, hostile behavior to your health? A long-term study at Duke University followed a group of lawyers for 25 years and found that those with higher hostility scores were 4.2 times as likely to have died over that period as those with low scores.[126] This does not bode well for Sicinski, who at age 30 already has dangerously high blood pressure, which he admits is not responding well to his blood pressure medications.

You do poorly on an exam. Quick: Who do you blame, yourself or the professor? The answer to that question may, to some extent, indicate whether you have an internal or external locus of control. **Locus of control** is the degree to which people believe that their actions influence what happens to them. **Internal locus of control** is the belief that what happens to you is largely under your control. Therefore, students with an internal locus of control are more likely to hold themselves accountable for their exam performance ("I studied the wrong material" or "I didn't study enough."). Besides believing that what happens to them is largely under their control, internals are also easier to motivate (especially when rewards are linked to performance), more difficult to lead, more independent, and better able to handle complex information and solve complex problems.[127] In contrast, an **external locus of control** is the belief that what happens to you is primarily due to factors beyond your control, such as luck, chance, or powerful people.[128] Therefore, students with an external locus of control are more likely to attribute their poor exam performance to luck ("If only it had been an essay exam instead of multiple choice"), chance ("I didn't get enough sleep"), or the professor (a powerful person). In general, externals are more compliant and conforming and therefore are easier to lead than internals. For example, internals may question directives from their managers, while externals are likely to quietly accept them. Finally, internals are likely to perform better on complex tasks that require initiative and independent decision making, whereas externals tend to perform better on simple, repetitive tasks that are well structured.

Affectivity is the stable tendency to experience positive or negative moods and to react to things in a generally positive or negative way.[129] People with **positive affectivity** consistently notice and focus on the positive aspects of themselves and

locus of control the degree to which individuals believe that their actions can influence what happens to them

internal locus of control the belief that what happens to you is largely the result of your own actions

external locus of control the belief that what happens to you is largely the result of factors beyond your control

affectivity the stable tendency to experience positive or negative moods and to react to things in a generally positive or negative way

positive affectivity a personality trait in which individuals tend to notice and focus on the positive aspects of themselves and their environments their environments. In other words, they seem to be in a good mood most of the time and are predisposed to being optimistic, cheerful, and cordial. By contrast, people with **negative affectivity** consistently notice and focus on the negative in themselves and their environments. They are frequently in bad moods, consistently expect the worst to happen, and are often irritated or pessimistic.

How stable are the positive or negative moods associated with positive/negative affectivity? A 10-year study by the National Institute of Aging found that even when people changed jobs or companies, the people who were the happiest at the beginning of the study were still the happiest at the end of the study 10 years later.[130] Likewise, a much longer study found that high school counselors' ratings of student cheerfulness predicted how satisfied these people were with their jobs 30 years later.[131] Since dispositions toward positive or negative affectivity are long lasting and very stable, some companies have begun measuring affectivity during the hiring process. Providing superior customer service is crucial to achieving a firm's goals, says Walter Timoshenko, chief marketing officer at the accounting firm Weiser LLP, adding that "people make the difference."[132] Indeed, a recent survey of 1,000 customers conducted by Accenture indicates that poor customer service drives nearly half of consumers to take their business elsewhere. Many experts agree that hiring people who are enthusiastic and have a positive outlook is important for providing world-class customer service.[133] Studies also show that employees with positive affectivity are absent less often, report feeling less stress, are less likely to be injured in workplace accidents, and are less likely to retaliate against management and the company when they believe that they have been treated unfairly.[134] Affectivity is also important because of **mood linkage**, a phenomenon in which one worker's negative affectivity and bad moods can spread to others. Studies of nurses and accountants show a strong relationship between individual workers' moods and the moods of their coworkers.[135] Finally, people with positive affectivity are better decision makers, are rated as having much higher managerial potential, and are more successful in sales jobs.[136] Indeed, numerous studies show that happy individuals are successful across multiple domains, including marriage, friendship, income, work performance and health.[137]

Review 3: Deep-Level Diversity

Deep-level diversity matters because it can reduce prejudice, discrimination, and conflict while increasing social integration. It consists of dispositional and personality differences that can be learned only through extended interaction with others. Research conducted in different cultures, settings, and languages indicates that there are five basic dimensions of personality: extraversion, emotional stability, agreeableness, conscientiousness, and openness to experience. Of these, conscientiousness is perhaps the most important to companies because conscientious workers tend to be better performers on virtually any job. Extraversion is also related to performance in jobs that require significant interaction with others. Studies also show that the personality dimensions of authoritarianism, Machiavellian tendencies, Type A/B personality, locus of control, and positive/negative affectivity are important in the workplace. These personality dimensions are related to honesty, trust, teamwork, persuasive abilities, job performance, decision making, stress, heart disease, adaptability, promotions, interpersonal skills, motivation, initiative, job satisfaction, absenteeism, accidents, retaliatory behavior, mood linkage, and management potential.

negative affectivity a personality trait in which individuals tend to notice and focus on the negative aspects of themselves and their environments

mood linkage a phenomenon in which one worker's negative affectivity and bad moods can spread to others

HOW CAN DIVERSITY BE MANAGED?

How much should companies change their standard business practices to accommodate the diversity of their workers? For example, at **Whirlpool**'s Lavergne, Tennessee, appliance factory, 10 percent of the work force is Muslim. Many Muslim men have long beards and wear skullcaps, while Muslim women traditionally wear flowing headscarves and modest, loose-fitting, form-hiding clothes. For safety reasons, long hair, hats of any kind, and loose clothing are prohibited on the factory floor. (Imagine any of these getting caught in moving machinery.) How should Whirlpool's managers deal with the obvious conflict between Muslim religious practices and the company's safety procedures that are designed to prevent injury? Furthermore, at noon on Fridays, observant Muslims attend 45- to 90-minute religious services at their mosques. With a typical Monday to Friday workweek and lunch breaks of just 30 minutes, how can Whirlpool's managers accommodate this Friday service without hurting the production schedule and without giving the Muslims special treatment (that may be resented by the 90 percent of workers who aren't Muslim)?[138]

Likewise, what do you do when a talented top executive has a drinking problem that only seems to affect his behavior at company business parties (for entertaining clients), where he has made inappropriate advances toward female employees? What do you do when, despite aggressive company policies against racial discrimination, employees continue to tell racial jokes and publicly post cartoons displaying racial humor? And, since many people confuse diversity with affirmative action, what do you do to make sure that your company's diversity practices and policies are viewed as benefiting all workers and not just some workers?

No doubt about it, questions like these make managing diversity one of the toughest challenges that managers face.[139] Nonetheless, there are steps companies can take to begin to address these issues.

After reading the next section, you should be able to

4 explain the basic principles and practices that can be used to manage diversity.

4 Managing Diversity

*As discussed earlier, diversity programs try to create a positive work environment where no one is advantaged or disadvantaged, where "we" is everyone, where everyone can do his or her best work, where differences are respected and not ignored, and where everyone feels comfortable. Let's begin to address those goals by learning about **4.1 different diversity paradigms**, **4.2 diversity principles**, and **4.3 diversity training and practices**.*

4.1 Diversity Paradigms

As shown in Exhibit 12.7, there are several different methods or paradigms for managing diversity: the discrimination and fairness paradigm, the access and legitimacy paradigm, and the learning and effectiveness paradigm.[140] The *discrimination and fairness paradigm*, which is the most common method of approaching

A MANAGER

diversity, focuses on equal opportunity, fair treatment, recruitment of minorities, and strict compliance with the equal employment opportunity laws. Under this approach, success is usually measured by how well companies achieve recruitment, promotion, and retention goals for women, people of different racial/ethnic backgrounds, or other underrepresented groups. According to a recent workplace diversity practices survey conducted by the Society of Human Resource Management, 66 percent to 91 percent of companies use specialized strategies to recruit, retain and promote talented women and minorities. The percentages increase with company size, with companies of more than 500 employees the most likely to use these strategies. And 77 percent of companies with more than 500 employees systematically collect measurements on diversity-related practices.[141] One manager says, "If you don't measure something, it doesn't count. You measure your market share. You measure your profitability. The same should be true for diversity. There has to be some way of measuring whether you did, in fact, cast your net widely, and whether the company is better off today in terms of the experience of people of color than it was a few years ago. I measure my market share and my profitability. Why not this?"[142] The primary benefit of the discrimination and fairness paradigm is that it generally brings about fairer treatment of employees and increases demographic diversity. The primary limitation is that the focus of diversity remains on the surface-level diversity dimensions of sex, race, and ethnicity.

Exhibit 12.7

Paradigms for Managing Diversity

DIVERSITY PARADIGM	FOCUS	SUCCESS MEASURED BY	BENEFITS	LIMITATIONS
Discrimination & Fairness	Equal opportunity Fair treatment Recruitment of minorities Strict compliance with laws	Recruitment, promotion, and retention goals for underrepresented groups	Fairer treatment Increased demographic diversity	Focus on surface-level diversity
Access & Legitimacy	Acceptance and celebration of differences	Diversity in company matches diversity of primary stakeholders	Establishes a clear business reason for diversity	Focus on surface-level diversity
Learning & Effectiveness	Integrating deep-level differences into organization	Valuing people on the basis of individual knowledge, skills, and abilities	Values common ground Distinction between individual and group differences Less conflict, backlash, and divisiveness Bringing different talents and perspectives together	Focus on deep-level diversity is more difficult to measure and quantify

The *access and legitimacy paradigm* focuses on the acceptance and celebration of differences to ensure that the diversity within the company matches the diversity found among primary stakeholders, such as customers, suppliers, and local communities. This is similar to the *business growth* advantage of diversity discussed earlier in the chapter. The basic idea behind this approach is to create a demographically diverse work force and gain access to different ethnic customer groups.[143] Consistent with this goal, Ed Adams, vice president of human resources for Enterprise Rent-a-Car, says, "We want people who speak the same language, literally and figuratively, as our customers. We don't set quotas. We say [to our managers], 'Reflect your local market.'"[144] The primary benefit of this approach is that it establishes a clear business reason for diversity. Like the discrimination and fairness paradigm, however, it focuses only on the surface-level diversity dimensions of sex, race, and ethnicity. Furthermore, employees who are assigned responsibility for customers and stakeholders on the basis of their sex, race, or ethnicity may eventually feel frustrated and exploited.

The most common method of managing diversity is the discrimination and fairness paradigm, which increases demographic diversity in even large companies.

While the discrimination and fairness paradigm focuses on assimilation (having a demographically representative workforce), and the access and legitimacy paradigm focuses on differentiation (having demographic differences inside the company match those of key customers and stakeholders), the *learning and effectiveness paradigm* focuses on integrating deep-level diversity differences, such as personality, attitudes, beliefs, and values, into the actual work of the organization. **AETNA**'s 28,000 employees are diverse not only in terms of sex, ethnicity and race, but also by age group, sexual orientation, work styles and levels, perspective, education, skills and other characteristics. Raymond Arroyo, head of diversity at Aetna, says, "Diversity at Aetna means treating individuals individually, leveraging everyone's best, and maximizing the powerful potential of our workforce." He adds, "Part of a top diversity executive's role in any organization is to integrate diversity into every aspect of a business, including the workforce, customers, suppliers, products, services and even into the community a business serves."[145] Exhibit 12.8 shows the necessary preconditions for creating a learning and effectiveness diversity paradigm within an organization.

"WHAT'S NEW" COMPANY

The learning and effectiveness paradigm is consistent with achieving organizational plurality. **Organizational plurality** is a work environment where (1) all members are empowered to contribute in a way that maximizes the benefits to the organization, customers, and themselves, and (2) the individuality of each member is respected by not segmenting or polarizing people on the basis of their membership in a particular group.[146]

organizational plurality a work environment where (1) all members are empowered to contribute in a way that maximizes the benefits to the organization, customers, and themselves, and (2) the individuality of each member is respected by not segmenting or polarizing people on the basis of their membership in a particular group

The learning and effectiveness diversity paradigm offers four benefits.[147] First, it values common ground. Dave Thomas of the Harvard Business School explains: "Like the fairness paradigm, it promotes equal opportunity for all individuals. And like the access paradigm, it acknowledges cultural differences among people and recognizes the value in those differences. Yet this new model for managing diversity lets the organization internalize differences among employees so that it learns

1. The leadership must understand that a diverse workforce will embody different perspectives and approaches to work, and must truly value variety of opinion and insight.
2. The leadership must recognize both the learning opportunities and the challenges that the expression of different perspectives presents for an organization.
3. The organizational culture must create an expectation of high standards of performance for everyone.
4. The organizational culture must stimulate personal development.
5. The organizational culture must encourage openness and a high tolerance for debate and support constructive conflict on work-related matters.
6. The culture must make workers feel valued.
7. The organization must have a well-articulated and widely understood mission. This keeps discussions about work differences from degenerating into debates about the validity of people's perspectives.
8. The organization must have a relatively egalitarian, nonbureaucratic structure.

Source: D. A. Thomas & R. J. Ely, "Making Differences Matter: A New Paradigm for Managing Diversity," *Harvard Business Review* 74 (September–October 1996): 79–90.

Exhibit 12.8

Creating a Learning and Effectiveness Diversity Paradigm in an Organization

and grows because of them. Indeed, with the model fully in place, members of the organization can say, 'We are all on the same team, with our differences—not despite them.'"[148]

Second, this paradigm makes a distinction between individual and group differences. When diversity focuses only on differences between groups, such as females versus males, large differences within groups are ignored.[149] For example, think of the women you know at work. Now, think for a second about what they have in common. After that, think about how they're different. If your situation is typical, the list of differences should be just as long as the list of commonalties, if not longer. In short, managers can achieve a greater understanding of diversity and their employees by treating them as individuals and by realizing that not all African Americans, Hispanics, women, or white males want the same things at work.[150]

Third, because the focus is on individual differences, the learning and effectiveness paradigm is less likely to encounter the conflict, backlash, and divisiveness sometimes associated with diversity programs that focus only on group differences. Taylor Cox, one of the leading management writers on diversity, says, "We are concerned here with these more destructive forms of conflict which may be present with diverse work forces due to language barriers, cultural clash, or resentment by majority-group members of what they may perceive as preferential and unwarranted treatment of minority-group members."[151] And Ray Haines, a consultant who has helped companies deal with the aftermath of diversity programs that became divisive, says, "There's a large amount of backlash related to diversity training. It stirs up a lot of hostility, anguish, and resentment but doesn't give people tools to deal with [the backlash]. You have people come in and talk about their specific ax to grind."[152] Certainly, not all diversity programs are divisive or lead to conflict. But, by focusing on individual rather than group differences, the learning and effectiveness paradigm helps to minimize these potential problems.

Finally, unlike the other diversity paradigms that simply focus on surface-level diversity, the learning and effectiveness paradigm focuses on bringing different talents and perspectives *together* (that is, deep-level diversity) to make the best organizational decisions and to produce innovative, competitive products and services.

4.2 Diversity Principles

While diversity paradigms represent general approaches or strategies for managing diversity, the diversity principles shown in Exhibit 12.9 will help managers do a better job of *managing company diversity programs*, no matter which diversity paradigm they choose.[153]

Begin by *carefully and faithfully following and enforcing federal and state laws regarding equal opportunity employment*. Diversity programs can't and won't succeed if the company is being sued for discriminatory actions and behavior. Faithfully following the law will also reduce the time and expense associated with EEOC investigations or lawsuits. Start by learning more at the EEOC website (**http://www.eeoc.gov**). Following the law also means strictly and fairly enforcing company policies.

1.	Carefully and faithfully follow and enforce federal and state laws regarding equal employment opportunity.
2.	Treat group differences as important, but not special.
3.	Find the common ground.
4.	Tailor opportunities to individuals, not groups.
5.	Reexamine, but maintain, high standards.
6.	Solicit negative as well as positive feedback.
7.	Set high but realistic goals.

Source: L. S. Gottfredson, "Dilemmas in Developing Diversity Programs," in *Diversity in the Workplace*, ed. S. E. Jackson & Associates (New York: Guildford Press, 1992).

Exhibit 12.9
Diversity Principles

Treat group differences as important, but not special. Surface-level diversity dimensions such as age, sex, and race/ethnicity should be respected, but should not be treated as more important than other kinds of differences (that is, deep-level diversity). Remember, the shift from surface- to deep-level diversity helps people know and understand each other better, reduces prejudice and conflict, and leads to stronger social integration with people wanting to work together and get the job done. Also, *find the common ground*. While respecting differences is important, it's just as important, especially with diverse workforces, to actively find ways for employees to see and share commonalties.

Tailor opportunities to individuals, not groups. Special programs for training, development, mentoring, or promotions should be based on individual strengths and weaknesses, not on group status. Instead of making mentoring available for just one group of workers, create mentoring opportunities for everyone who wants to be mentored. For example, at Pacific Enterprises, all programs, including Career Conversations forums, in which upper-level managers are publicly interviewed about themselves and how they got their jobs, are open to all employees.[154]

Reexamine, but maintain, high standards. Companies have a legal and moral obligation to make sure that their hiring and promotion procedures and standards are fair to all. At the same time, in today's competitive markets, companies should not lower standards to promote diversity. This not only hurts the organizations, but also feeds the stereotype that applicants who are hired or promoted in the name of affirmative action or diversity are less qualified. Monica Emerson, executive director

doing the right thing

Don't Break the Law in the Name of Diversity

As you learned in Chapter 11 on human resource management, the general effect of employment law, which is still evolving through court decisions, is that employers may not discriminate in employment decisions on the basis of sex, age, religion, color, national origin, race, or disability. Employment decisions should be based on factors that are "job related," "reasonably necessary," or a "business necessity" for successful job performance. With one exception (see Chapter 11 for further explanation), employers who use sex, age, race, or religion to make employment-related decisions when those factors are unrelated to an applicant's or employee's ability to perform a job may face charges of discrimination from employee lawsuits or the Equal Employment Opportunity Commission. So, do the right thing. Stay within the law as you build a diverse work force.

of diversity at **DAIMLERCHRYSLER**, says, "As a diversity executive, I not only have to have solid business capabilities, I need to be very knowledgeable of the different businesses in my organization to align diversity initiatives to support the needs of the businesses. Maintaining high standards when making employment decisions and involving the top-management and the board in diversity-initiatives is critical to the success of workplace diversity parctices."[155]

Solicit negative as well as positive feedback. Diversity is one of the most difficult management issues. No company or manager gets it right from the start. Consequently, companies should aggressively seek positive and negative feedback about their diversity programs. One way to do that is to use a series of measurements to see if progress is being made. **L'ORÉAL**, the cosmetics firm, has goals and measurements to track its progress in diversity with respect to recruitment, retention, and advancement, as well as the extent to which the company buys goods and services from minority- and women-owned suppliers.[156]

Set high but realistic goals. Just because diversity is difficult doesn't mean that organizations shouldn't try to accomplish as much as possible. The general purpose of diversity programs is to try to create a positive work environment where no one is advantaged or disadvantaged, where "we" is everyone, where everyone can do his or her best work, where differences are respected and not ignored, and where everyone feels comfortable. Even if progress is slow, companies should not shrink from these goals.

4.3 Diversity Training and Practices

Organizations use diversity training and several common diversity practices to manage diversity. There are two basic types of diversity training programs. **Awareness training** is designed to raise employees' awareness of diversity issues, such as the dimensions discussed in this chapter, and to get employees to challenge underlying assumptions or stereotypes they may have about others. As a starting point in awareness training, some companies have begun using the Implicit Association Test (IAT), which measures the extent to which people associate positive or negative thoughts (that is, underlying assumptions or stereotypes) with blacks or whites, men or women, homosexuals or heterosexuals, young or old, or other groups. For example, test takers are shown black or white faces that they must instantly pair with various words. Response times (shorter responses generally indicate stronger associations) and the pattern of associations indicates the extent to which people are biased. Most people are, and strongly so. For example, 88 percent of whites have a more positive mental association toward whites than toward blacks, but, surprisingly, so do blacks, 48 percent of whom show the same bias. Taking the IAT is a good way to increase awareness of diversity issues. To take the IAT and to learn more about the decade of research behind it, go to **https://implicit.harvard.edu**.[157] By contrast, **skills-based diversity training** teaches employees the practical skills they need for managing a diverse work force, such as flexibility and adaptability, negotiation, problem solving, and conflict resolution.[158]

awareness training training that is designed to raise employees' awareness of diversity issues and to challenge the underlying assumptions or stereotypes they may have about others

skills-based diversity training training that teaches employees the practical skills they need for managing a diverse work force, such as flexibility and adaptability, negotiation, problem solving, and conflict resolution

diversity audits formal assessments that measure employee and management attitudes, investigate the extent to which people are advantaged or disadvantaged with respect to hiring and promotions, and review companies' diversity-related policies and procedures

Companies also use diversity audits, diversity pairing, and minority experiences for top executives to better manage diversity. **Diversity audits** are formal assessments that measure employee and management attitudes, investigate the extent to which people are advantaged or disadvantaged with respect to hiring and promotions, and review companies' diversity-related policies and procedures. For example, the results of a formal diversity audit prompted BRW,

> The only way to break out of comfort zones is to be exposed to other people.
>
> CEO, HOECHST CELANESE

an architecture and engineering firm, to increase job advertising in minority publications, set up a diversity committee to make recommendations to upper management, provide diversity training for all employees, and rewrite the company handbook to make a stronger statement about the company's commitment to a diverse work force.[159]

"What's New" Company

Earlier in the chapter you learned that *mentoring*, pairing a junior employee with a senior employee, is a common strategy for creating learning and promotional opportunities for women. Diversity pairing is a special kind of mentoring. In **diversity pairing**, people of different cultural backgrounds, sexes, or races/ethnicities are paired for mentoring. The hope is that stereotypical beliefs and attitudes will change as people get to know each other as individuals.[160] Consultant Tom McGee, who has set up mentoring programs for numerous companies, supports diversity pairing, saying "the assumption that people participating in diversity mentoring programs are looking for someone of the same race or gender has been proved wrong in many cases."[161] Pat Carmichael, an African American female vice president at **JPMorgan Chase**, who was mentored early in her career by a white male, mentors men and women of all backgrounds. Regarding a current mentee, John Imperiale, a white assistant branch manager, she says, "My hope is that the exposure John has to me will give him insights when he's managing a diverse group of employees."[162]

diversity pairing a mentoring program in which people of different cultural backgrounds, sexes, or races/ethnicities are paired together to get to know each other and change stereotypical beliefs and attitudes

Finally, because top managers are still overwhelmingly white and male, a number of companies believe that it is worthwhile to *have top executives experience what it is like to be in the minority*. This can be done by having top managers go to places or events where nearly everyone else is of a different sex or racial/ethnic background. At Hoechst Celanese (which has now split into two companies), top managers would join two organizations in which they were a minority. For instance, the CEO, a white male, joined the board of Hampton University, a historically African American college, and Jobs for Progress, a Hispanic organization that helps people prepare for jobs. Commenting on his experiences, he said, "The only way to break out of comfort zones is to be exposed to other people. When we are, it becomes clear that all people are similar." A Hoechst vice president who joined three organizations in which he was in the minority said, "Joining these organizations has been more helpful to me than two weeks of diversity training."[163]

More and more companies are embracing diversity because it makes good business sense. As this ad for Cargill puts it, "no one has a monopoly on good ideas."

Good business is built on diversity.
Each day Cargill does business around the world in food, nutrition, agriculture, and supply chain management. Our work in diverse communities has made us very aware of the importance of diversity in our supply chain. We've learned that no one has a monopoly on good ideas and that they can come from anyone, anywhere. We're committed to supplier diversity because we know it's good business. It adds value to what we do for our customers, as well as promoting prosperity in communities where we live and work. For more information, visit www.cargill.com/about
©2005 Cargill, Incorporated

Cargill
Nourishing Ideas. Nourishing People.

Review 4: **Managing Diversity**

The three paradigms for managing diversity are the discrimination and fairness paradigm (equal opportunity, fair treatment, strict compliance with the law), the access and legitimacy paradigm (matching internal diversity to external diversity), and the learning and effectiveness paradigm (achieving organizational plurality by integrating deep-level diversity into the work of the organization). Unlike the other paradigms, which focus on surface-level differences, the learning and effectiveness program values common ground, distinguishes between individual and group differences, minimizes conflict and divisiveness, and focuses on bringing different talents and perspectives together. What principles can companies use when managing diversity? Follow and enforce federal and state laws regarding equal employment opportunity. Treat group differences as important, but not special. Find the common ground. Tailor opportunities to individuals, not groups. Reexamine, but maintain, high standards. Solicit negative as well as positive feedback. Set high but realistic goals. The two types of diversity training are awareness training and skills-based diversity training. Companies also manage diversity through diversity audits and diversity pairing and by having top executives experience what it is like to be in the minority.

SELF ASSESSMENT

Do You Know Your Mind?

Do you always speak your mind? Chances are that you probably don't—at least not always. In some cases, you may not even know your mind. Our conscious mind is not always aligned with our subconscious, and we may be motivated by deeply held beliefs that diverge from our image of who we are or want to be. Researchers at Harvard have developed a series of assessments to help you identify your implicit associations about a variety of topics, many related to the diversity issues you learned about in this chapter. Unlike the other assessments in this book, this one requires you to go online. Each Project Implicit test, which is also called an Implicit Association Test (IAT), takes about 10 minutes to complete. However, you'll find it worthwhile to complete all of the different IATs. The researchers ask that you complete the initial surveys so that they can further enrich their data, but you needn't worry about privacy issues. They are only interested in the raw data and not in who actually contributed it.

1. To begin, go to **https://implicit.harvard.edu** and click on **"Demonstration."**
2. You will then be given a brief description of the project and prompted to **"Go to the demonstration tests."** Click on that hot link.
3. The front page of the demonstration tests is a more detailed synopsis of the project and a disclaimer. Read the information and then click on **"I wish to proceed."**
4. You will then reach the list of all the tests: age, gender-science, race, presidents, sexuality, gender-career, Arab-Muslim, weight, religion, disability, Native, Asian, weapons, and skin-tone. The tests most closely related to Chapter 12's content on diversity are age, race, sexuality, gender-career, weight, disability, Native, Asian, and skin-tone. Each time you complete an IAT, return to the list to select the next relevant test for this course. We'll use the age IAT as the basis for these instructions. Once you get the hang of it, you will be able to move through the preliminaries on any of IATs. To begin, click on **"Age IAT."**
5. You will be directed to a page of technical information related to your computer settings. If you can see the green check mark, then click to begin. At the next page, click on **"Continue."**
6. A survey of general information will pop up. The survey for each IAT is slightly different, except for the main demographic information at the bottom (age, race, etc.). Once you complete the survey, click on **"Proceed."**
7. Read the instructions carefully. In essence, each time a certain word or image appears, you will need to either respond by typing an "e" or an "i." The words used are purposely set to be obviously good or bad. For example, few people would dispute that *evil* goes in the category labeled "bad," and *love* goes in the category labeled "good." Don't get caught up in semantics; just classify the terms as they are understood in the common language.
8. The test will ask you to classify the words and images several times, switching the words and images from the left hand to the right hand. That way, your right hand isn't always typing an "i" for good and your left an "e" for bad. Pay attention to the changes.
9. Once you have finished the IAT on a particular topic, you will receive a results page. Check with your professor if he or she wants you to print it out or keep track of results in any way. Your instructor may want to average class results.

After completing the IATs, think about your results. Do any surprise you, or were you aware that you were making the unconscious associations the software identified?

KEY TERMS

affectivity 455
affirmative action 438
age discrimination 443
agreeableness 452
authoritarianism 454
awareness training 462
conscientiousness 452
deep-level diversity 442
disability 448
disability discrimination 448
disposition 451
diversity 437
diversity audits 462
diversity pairing 463
emotional stability 451
external locus of control 455
extraversion 451
glass ceiling 445
internal locus of control 455
locus of control 455
Machiavellian 454
mood linkage 456
negative affectivity 456
openness to experience 452
organizational plurality 459
personality 451
positive affectivity 455
racial and ethnic discrimination 446
sex discrimination 445
skills-based diversity training 462
social integration 443
surface-level diversity 442
Type A personality 454
Type A/B personality dimension 454
Type B personality 454

Company of INTJs Seeks ESFP Employee

Every business magazine you've picked up recently has had some kind of article on personality testing in the workplace.[164] You've read about the Caliper, used by FedEx, the Chicago Cubs, and the WNBA's Phoenix Mercury. Anne Mariucci, part-owner of the Mercury, uses the test to evaluate potential draft picks and make coaching assignments. With the help of a consultant, venerable retailer Neiman Marcus designed a test to identify the characteristics needed to be a successful sales associate; as a result, it has increased sales per associate by 42 percent and reduced staff turnover by 18 percent. Today, you're reading about a personality test originally designed for Olympic teams and military units (small groups in high-pressure situations with a single, focused goal).

As you close your magazine, you can't help thinking about diversity. As the manager in a medium-sized candy company, you have always made sure that your work force was diverse with respect to minorities and women, but until now you've never considered managing based on personalities. Even though personality tests sound like a good idea (lots of reputable companies are using them), you wonder about the drawbacks. There must be some, in addition to the several hundred dollars it would cost to test each of your 75 employees, or you would have started testing a long time ago.

The stack of articles you've read, however, is prompting you to think that personality testing might be a good idea. It looks like the only way to ensure deep-level diversity. New wave of tests, like the NEO Personality Inventory (Neuroticism, Extroversion, and Openness) and the Occupational Personality Questionnaire, make less sweeping generalizations than their predecessors. By using narrower indicators, the NEO and OPQ can identify how people will behave in certain situations and, ultimately, how well an employee's personality is suited to the tasks his or her job requires.

Testing is already a $400 million industry in the United States, and it's growing at 8 percent a year. The amount spent on personality testing alone has increased 10 to 15 percent each of the last three years. Most *Fortune* 500 companies use the venerable Myers-Briggs test. A recent study found that poorly performing employees cost U.S. employers $100 billion a year, so perhaps it's time to jump on the bandwagon.

Questions

1. If you knew the personality profiles of your workers, how would you actually use the information to benefit the company? Can personality testing help you achieve the company's goal of becoming one of the largest candy makers in North America?
2. Does personality testing help cultivate deep-level diversity, or does it do the opposite, ensuring a company staffed with people who are the same? Is there another way to cultivate deep-level diversity besides personality testing?
3. Do you see any drawbacks to personality testing? In addition to a diverse work force, what benefits could a manager derive from personality testing?
4. Do you begin personality testing? Explain your answer.

Is Older Necessarily Wiser?

Two weeks ago, you were pleased to receive a fat envelope from the U.S. government awarding your aeronautics company several hefty contracts with the Department of Defense.[165] As a result of the contracts, you'll have to increase production, so you immediately placed ads in the local paper for four skilled mechanics.

Résumés have been flooding in, and to your surprise, the prospective applicants fall into one of two groups. In addition to the usual crop of inexperienced youngsters eager to start their careers, you have an equally large pool of retired mechanics, many of them older than 65. They've spent their entire lives building planes and now want to work only 15 to 20 hours a week.

Flipping through the second pile, you realize that you face a difficult decision. Younger hires would require more training and supervision, but they could eventually become productive full-timers with the potential to stay at the company for most (if not all) of their careers. On the other hand, older veterans would be able to jump in feet first, but they would work fewer hours and probably have much shorter careers with the company. Whereas the veterans will expect pay commensurate with their experience, the newbies will accept much lower starting salaries

Between 2000 and 2010, the number of Americans between the ages of 55 and 64 will jump 47 percent, compared with a scant 2.8 percent increase in the number of those aged 25 to 34. The group that makes up the bulk of most companies' management talent, those aged 35 to 45, will actually shrink by 13.7 percent! With the graying of the workforce, this may be the first time you have to decide whether to hire older or younger workers, but it certainly won't be the last.

For this exercise, assemble a team of three to four students to represent the senior management team at the aeronautics firm in the scenario. Try using the dialectical inquiry technique discussed in Chapter 5 (Planning and Decision Making) on page 179.

Questions

1. Do you hire older workers or younger workers? Explain your choice.
2. What challenges can you foresee in managing a multigenerational work force?

PRACTICE BEING A MANAGER

Diversity may contribute a richness of perspective and understanding to a work group or organization. But to unlock these riches, it is essential that we develop tools of understanding individuals and cultures different from our own. Not all college students have experienced crossing a cultural boundary to live in another country. But most have encountered subcultures in the context of their middle or high school years. Teen subcultures are often quite pronounced and diverse. This exercise will offer practice in recognizing and understanding diversity.

Step 1: Get into groups. Your professor will organize you in small groups of three or four students.

Step 2: Identify teen subcultures. Think back to your middle school or high school experiences and identify some of the major subcultures you observed (Athletes, Toughs, and so on). Share descriptions of these subcultures with the members of your group.

Step 3: Conduct diversity training. Take turns training each other on what it would be like to be a member of one of the subcultures which you knew well. It is not necessary that you belonged to this subculture, but only that you can recall it vividly. Teach your fellow group members what a young person would need to know to fit in with this subculture, including such dimensions as

- Clothing
- Manner of speech, common slang, or "code language"
- Music
- Value of the subculture to members; what it means to be "in" this group

Step 4: Discuss how teen subcultures are diverse. Discuss as a group the impact of teen subcultures on valuing diversity. In what ways do teen subcultures bond diverse people (athletes of different races, for example) together, and help them to understand one another better? In what ways do teen subcultures separate people into "cliques" or foster stereotyping ("us" vs. "them")?

Step 5: Debrief as a class. Based on your group discussions, what are the challenges for organizations who are seriously attempting to value diversity? What are the benefits to these organizations? How do organizations train people about cultural (and subcultural) differences without falling into stereotyping?

DEVELOP YOUR CAREER POTENTIAL

From Majority to Minority and Back Again

Do you know what it feels like to walk into a room where, because of your sex, race/ethnicity, religion, language, or some other dimension, you are intensely aware of being different from everyone else?[166] Some of you do. Most of you probably don't. And, since most managers are white and male, it's a good bet that they don't know either. The experience can be unsettling, especially the first time it happens.

Some companies have begun broadening perspectives and understanding by having their managers join groups or attend events where they are different from everyone else. As you read in Section 4.3, at Hoechst Celanese, the CEO, a white male, joined the board of Hampton University, a historically African American college, and Jobs for Progress, a Hispanic organization that helps people prepare for jobs.

For more than 30 years, UPS has required its top managers to participate in community service programs in inner cities or poor rural areas. James Casey, UPS's founder, started the program in 1968 to expose his white male managers to diverse experiences, people, and communities. Casey also hoped that the experience would increase empathy, break down stereotypes, and encourage volunteer and community service. Today, managers with 10 to 30 years of experience are assigned to community service tasks in inner cities or rural areas. Don Wofford, who directs the program, says, "We choose managers on the fast track, people who'll be positioned to influence their work force and the community for years to come." The managers spend two weeks doing community service, followed by a weekend at home and then two more weeks of community service. Wofford says, "This format gives them a chance to digest the experience—they tend to come back renewed after the break, with a new focus, sometimes even more bewildered, but still ready to go for it."

Your assignment is to attend an event, meeting, or activity where you are different from almost everyone else in terms of your sex, race/ethnicity, religion, language, or some other dimension. You can choose a church service, local community group, volunteer organization, or student group on campus. Ask your professor for ideas. You should probably contact the group beforehand to arrange your visit. Answer the following questions after your visit.

Questions

1. Describe the event, meeting, activity, or organization you visited.
2. How were you different from others in attendance? Describe what it was like to be different from everyone else.
3. In what ways was this experience actually similar to previous experiences that you've had? In other words, while question 2 focuses on differences, this question focuses on similarities and commonalties.
4. What did you learn from this experience?

REEL TO REAL

BIZ FLIX

In Good Company

In Good Company, a 2004 film, stars Dennis Quaid as Dan Foreman, a seasoned advertising sales executive at the magazine *Sports America*. A corporate takeover results in Dan having a new supervisor named Carter Duryea. On his first day on the job, Carter confesses to a young woman he meets on the elevator that he doesn't know what he's doing. In this scene, Dan and Carter meet for the first time.

What to Watch for and Ask Yourself

1. How does this scene relate to diversity?
2. Review the Chapter 2 clip from the same movie. How diverse is the advertising department at *Sports America*? Explain.
3. Consider the two clips together and think about deep-level diversity. Why do you think *Sports America* hired Carter Duryea?

MANAGEMENT WORKPLACE

PepsiCo

Imagine trying to manage and accommodate the needs of more than 140,000 people at once. Imagine a variety of voices, languages, cultures, ethnic backgrounds, families, lifestyles, ages, and geographies all vying for attention, all bearing the name PepsiCo. That's the challenge of managers throughout PepsiCo. From the top down, PepsiCo embraces diversity and inclusion in its worldwide workforce. Top executives, including former CEO Steve Reinemund, believe that nurturing diversity in the organization is not only a matter of responsible ethics but also good business. Because PepsiCo offers products to such a diverse array of customers, it makes sense for the PepsiCo workforce to mirror the market. In addition, a facility's workforce will likely reflect the local population. However, embracing a philosophy of diversity is entirely different from implementing it. Watch the video to see how PepsiCo takes on this global task.

What to Watch for and Ask Yourself

1. Why is it important for upper-level managers at PepsiCo to receive diversity and inclusion training?
2. Do you think that PepsiCo's encouragement of employee networks actually works against diversity and formation of multicultural teams? Why or why not?

four

PART 4
Leading

Chapter 13
Motivation

This chapter covers the basics of motivation—effort, needs, and intrinsic and extrinsic rewards. As we progress through the chapter, we build on that basic model of motivation by adding concepts of equity, expectancy, reinforcement, and goal-setting theories. There's also a summary of practical, theory-based actions that managers can take to motivate their workers.

Chapter 14
Leadership

This chapter discusses what leadership is, what characteristics are common of leaders, and what leaders do that makes them different from people who aren't leaders. We examine major contingency theories of leadership and review strategic leadership issues, such as charismatic and transformational leadership.

Chapter 15
Managing Communication

This chapter examines perception in communication, the communication process, and the kinds of organizational communication. You'll also learn about effective one-on-one communication as well as techniques for organization-wide communication.

Learning Outcomes:

1 Explain the basics of motivation.
2 Use equity theory to explain how employees' perceptions of fairness affect motivation.
3 Use expectancy theory to describe how workers' expectations about rewards, effort, and the link between rewards and performance influence motivation.
4 Explain how reinforcement theory works and how it can be used to motivate.
5 Describe the components of goal-setting theory and how managers can use them to motivate workers.
6 Discuss how the entire motivation model can be used to motivate workers.

In This Chapter:

WHAT WOULD YOU DO?

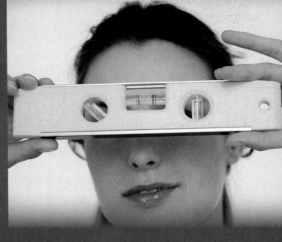

Nucor Corporation, Charlotte, North Carolina.[1] You love working for Nucor Corporation, whose mission is to "Take Care of Our Customers" by being the safest, highest-quality, lowest-cost, most productive, and most profitable steel and steel products company in the world. Nucor operates with one of the leanest corporate staffs in the nation. A typical *Fortune* 500 company has a triple-digit corporate staff. By contrast, Nucor's staff is just 65 corporate employees, which means that the staff serves the operating managers and employees, and not the other way around. Likewise, Nucor's streamlined chain of command, with just five levels of management (president and CEO, executive vice president, general manager, department manager, and supervisory/professional), allows general managers like you to operate your steel plant like an independent business. Since the day-to-day decisions are made at the steel plants, and not headquarters, you can quickly respond to suppliers, customers, and employees without waiting for a decision from the corporate office.

Operating employees also love working at Nucor because the company makes few distinctions between management and hourly employees. Another reason that hourly employees love Nucor is that the company is committed to not laying off employees. Indeed, since its entry into the steelmaking business, Nucor has not laid off a single worker. The result is a committed team of Nucor employees.

One of the things that has made it easier for you to be a general manager at Nucor is its aggressive use of bonuses to motivate employees. Employees involved directly in manufacturing are paid weekly bonuses based on the production of their work groups. Bonuses typically average 80–170 percent of the base wage, but can go higher as there is no limit. If productivity and production increase, bonuses will continue to rise. Department managers earn annual incentive bonuses based primarily on the return on investment of their facility. These bonuses can be as much as 100 percent of base salary. Professional and staff employees, such as accountants, engineers, clerks, and receptionists, can earn bonuses up to 28 percent of salary. As for manufacturing employees, their base pay is actually well below industry average, but their productivity bonuses make them among the highest-paid steel workers in the world. And Nucor's employees have responded positively to Nucor's production incentives, and produce high-quality products at the lowest possible cost. In short, Nucor has established itself as one of the best-run steel companies in the United States.

Part of that success, however, is due to the unprecedented domestic and international demand for steel, particularly in China. Now, though, China has become self-sufficient and not only produces enough steel to meet local demand but also is emerging as a major exporter of steel. As this chapter is being written, Chinese steelmakers are negotiating with Indian steel companies to start joint ventures to produce high-quality steel. Worldwide supply of steel is catching with demand, and current inventories are higher than industry analysts consider appropriate.

With increased competition, Nucor's sales could slow, which would mean that bonuses would decrease and total compensation (base pay plus bonus) could fall below the industry average. If sales and bonuses drop, how will you motivate your workforce? Are there any non-monetary steps you could take? What if the demand for steel decreases so much that Nucor is forced to revoke its "no layoff" policy? If you had to conduct layoffs for the first time in company history, what steps would you take to treat employees fairly and with dignity? Finally, what might you do to avoid layoffs or to postpone them as long as possible? You've got to come up with a plan. **If you were a general manager at Nucor, what would you do?**

ACTIVITIES + VIDEOS

CengageNOW Audio study guide, electronic flashcards, author FAQ videos, On the Job and Biz Flix videos, concept tutorial, and concept exercise

Web (academic.cengage.com/management/williams) Quiz, PowerPoint slides, and glossary terms for this chapter

Study Tip

One way to make sure you understand the concepts in the chapter is to recreate the chapter outline from scratch. After you read Chapter 13, write down as many concepts and terms as you can remember from your reading. You'll see right away where you have gaps in your understanding!.

"What's New" Companies

Nucor
Regent Square Tavern
Jamaican bobsled team
Checkers Drive-In Restaurants
Zillow
Boeing
Wal-Mart
CDW
Technology Professionals Corp.
And others . . .

What makes people happiest and most productive at work? Is it money, benefits, opportunities for growth, interesting work, or something else altogether? And if people desire different things, how can a company keep everyone motivated? It takes insight and hard work to motivate workers to join the company, perform well, and then stay with the company. Indeed, when asked to name their biggest management challenge, nearly one-third of executives polled by Creative Group, a specialized staffing service in Menlo Park, California, cited "motivating employees."[2]

This chapter begins by reviewing the basics of motivation—effort, needs, and intrinsic and extrinsic rewards. We will start with a basic model of motivation and add to it as we progress through each section in the chapter. Next, we will explore how employees' equity perceptions and reward expectations affect their motivation. If you're familiar with the phrase "perception is reality," you're off to a good start in understanding the importance of perceptions and expectations in motivation. The third part of the chapter reviews the role that rewards and goals play in motivating employees. You'll see that finding the right combination of goals and rewards is much harder in practice than it looks. The chapter finishes with a summary of practical, theory-based actions that managers can take to motivate their workers.

WHAT IS MOTIVATION?

Motivation is the set of forces that initiates, directs, and makes people persist in their efforts to accomplish a goal.[3] In terms of this definition, *initiation of effort* is concerned with the choices that people make about how much effort to put forth in their jobs. ("Do I really knock myself out for these performance appraisals or just do a decent job?") *Direction of effort* is concerned with the choices that people make in deciding where to put forth effort in their jobs. ("I should be spending time with my high-dollar accounts instead of learning this new computer system!") *Persistence of effort* is concerned with the choices that people make about how long they will put forth effort in their jobs before reducing or eliminating those efforts. ("I'm only halfway through the project, and I'm exhausted. Do I plow through to the end, or just call it quits?") As Exhibit 13.1 shows, initiation, direction, and persistence are at the heart of motivation.

motivation the set of forces that initiates, directs, and makes people persist in their efforts to accomplish a goal

Exhibit 13.1

The Components of Motivation

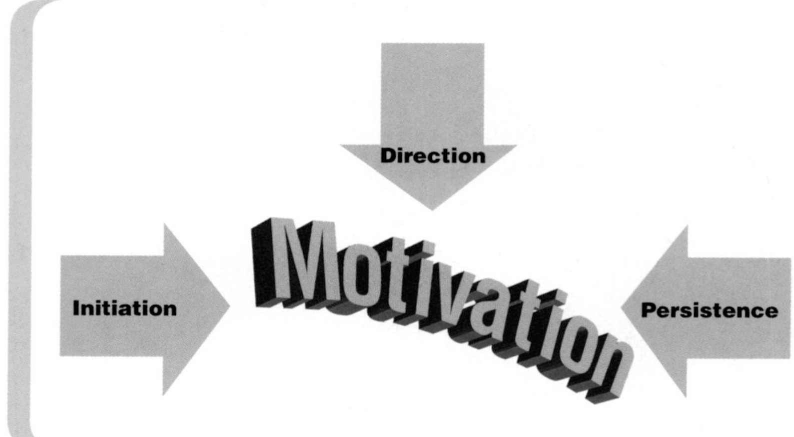

After reading the next section, you should be able to

1 explain the basics of motivation.

1 Basics of Motivation

Take your right hand and point the palm toward your face. Keep your thumb and pinky finger straight and bend the three middle fingers so the tips are touching your palm. Now rotate your wrist back and forth. If you were in the **REGENT SQUARE TAVERN** in Pittsburgh, Pennsylvania, that hand signal would tell waitress Marjorie Landale that you wanted a Yuengling beer. Marjorie, who isn't deaf, would not have understood that sign a few years ago. But with a state school for the deaf nearby, the tavern always has its share of deaf customers, so she decided on her own to take classes to learn how to sign. At first, deaf customers would signal for a pen and paper to write out their orders. But after Marjorie signaled that she was learning to sign, "their eyes [would] light up, and they [would] finger-spell their order." Word quickly spread as the students started bringing in their friends, classmates, teachers, and hearing friends as well. Says Marjorie, "The deaf customers are patient with my amateur signing. They appreciate the effort."[4]

What would motivate an employee like Marjorie to voluntarily learn a new language like American Sign Language? (Sign language is every bit as much a language as French or Spanish.) She wasn't paid to take classes in her free time. She chose to do it on her own. And while she undoubtedly makes more tip money with a full bar than with an empty one, it's highly unlikely that she began her classes with the objective of making more money. Just what is it that motivates employees like Marjorie Landale?

Let's learn more about motivation by building a basic model of motivation out of ***1.1 effort and performance****,* ***1.2 need satisfaction****, and* ***1.3 extrinsic and intrinsic rewards*** *and then discussing* ***1.4 how to motivate people with this basic model of motivation****.*

1.1 Effort and Performance

When most people think of work motivation, they think that working hard (effort) should lead to a good job (performance). Exhibit 13.2 shows a basic model of work motivation and performance, displaying this process.

The first thing to notice about Exhibit 13.2 is that this is a basic model of work motivation *and* performance. In practice, it's almost impossible to talk about one without mentioning the other. Not surprisingly, managers often assume motivation to be the only determinant of performance, saying things such as "Your performance was really terrible last quarter. What's the matter? Aren't you as motivated as you used to be?" In fact, motivation is just one of three primary determinants of job performance. In industrial psychology, job performance is frequently represented by this equation:

Job Performance = Motivation × Ability × Situational Constraints

In this formula, *job performance* is how well someone performs the requirements of the job. *Motivation*, as defined above, is effort, the degree to which someone works hard to do the job well. *Ability* is the degree to which workers possess the knowledge, skills, and talent needed to do a job well. And *situational constraints* are factors beyond the control of

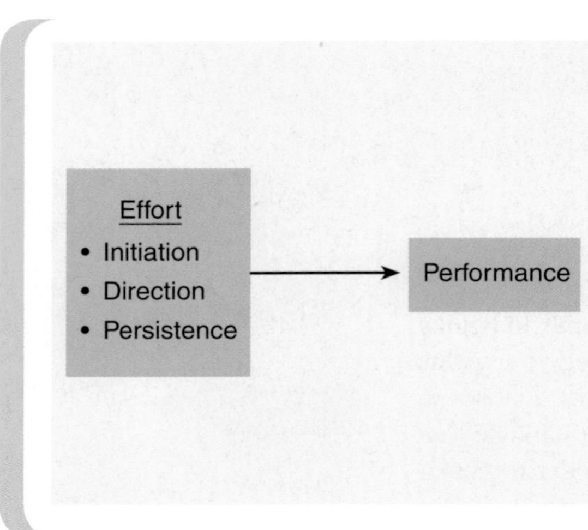

Exhibit 13.2

A Basic Model of Work Motivation and Performance

individual employees, such as tools, policies, and resources that have an effect on job performance.

Since job performance is a multiplicative function of motivation times ability times situational constraints, job performance will suffer if any one of these components is weak. For example, in 1988, the East German bobsled team was fully funded by the East German government and had state-of-the-art coaching and equipment (no situational constraints). The team members were recruited and selected from a large pool of talented athletes (ability) who had trained year-round for most of their lives (motivation) for a chance to make the highly prestigious team. By contrast, consider the ***JAMAICAN BOBSLED TEAM*** that Disney made famous in the movie *Cool Runnings*. In 1988 at its first Winter Olympics, the team had limited funding, a coach with bobsledding experience (a five-time U.S. champion) but no coaching experience, and an old bobsled that couldn't compete with the world-class equipment used by the best teams (high situational constraints). Furthermore, its members had been raised in tropical Jamaica and had almost no bobsledding or winter sports experience (very little ability). Nonetheless, they dreamed of competing in the Olympics and did what they could to train for several months, considering their limited circumstances (strong motivation).

It's not hard to guess which team did better, is it? With ample motivation, ability, and almost no situational constraints, you'd expect the East Germans to be competitive, and they were—finishing second and third in the two-man competition and second in the four-man competition.[5] By contrast, with strong motivation, little ability, and extremely high situational constraints, the Jamaican two-man team finished in 35th place, while the four-man team crashed spectacularly and had to push the bobsled across the line to complete the final run on the course.

Does this mean that motivation doesn't matter? No, not at all. It just means that all the motivation in the world won't translate into high performance when you have little ability and high situational constraints. In fact, prior to the 1996 Winter Olympics, the Jamaican team spent six weeks working with Sam Bock, who also worked with the elite Canadian team. Bock put the Jamaicans through their paces at a special bobsled training center in Oberhof, Germany. After training for four to eight hours a day in world-class conditions under world-class tutelage, the Jamaican four-man team finished in 14th place, ahead of the Americans, French, Russians, and one of the two Swiss and Italian teams. The two-man team did even better, finishing 10th.[6]

1.2 Need Satisfaction

In Exhibit 13.2, we started with a very basic model of motivation in which effort leads to job performance. However, managers want to know, "What leads to effort?" And they will try almost anything they can to find the answer. For example, ***CHECKERS DRIVE-IN RESTAURANTS*** pays highly competitive salaries and has a great benefits package, but it also offers out-of-this world rewards for outstanding performance, including cars, cruises, and consumer electronics. One year, Checkers took the top general managers, area managers, top-performing corporate employees, *and* their spouses on a week-long cruise.[7] At Seattle-based ***ZILLOW***, the online real-estate valuation service, teams have had to work overtime to add new features to the company's website. So, the company added foosball, ping pong, and air-hockey tables and free all-you-can-drink soft drinks, juice, and milk to its downtown offices.[8] Envision Technology, a Seattle software company, offers a variety of health-oriented perks, including on-site massages and "Business Boxes" of fresh fruit and healthy snacks.[9] At Parker LePla, a Seattle marketing and branding company, the employees regularly spend an afternoon playing WhirlyBall, lawn bowling, or kayaking on Lake Union.[10] As you can see, employers will do almost anything to motivate employees to put forth extra effort into their jobs.

Needs are the physical or psychological requirements that must be met to ensure survival and well-being.[11] As shown on the left side of Exhibit 13.3, a person's unmet need creates an uncomfortable, internal state of tension that must be resolved. For example, if you normally skip breakfast, but then have to work through lunch, chances are you'll be so hungry by late afternoon that the only thing you'll be motivated to do is find something to eat. So, according to needs theories, people are motivated by unmet needs. But once a need is met, it no longer motivates. When this occurs, people become satisfied, as shown on the right side of Exhibit 13.3.

Note: Throughout the chapter, as we build on this basic model, the parts of the model that we've already discussed will appear shaded in color. For example, since we've already discussed the effort → performance part of the model, those components are shown with a colored background. When we add new parts to the model, they will have a white background. For instance, since we're adding need satisfaction to the model at this step, the need-satisfaction components of unsatisfied need, tension, energized to take action, and satisfaction are shown with a white background. This shading convention should make it easier to understand the work motivation model as we add to it in each section of the chapter.

doing the right thing

Faking It, Not Making It

With technological assistance, you may be tempted to engage in "impression management" to try to convince your boss and coworkers that you're working hard when you're really not. For instance, a tech support worker who enjoyed three-hour lunches used a program on his Palm personal computer to remotely control his office computer. He would open, close, and move files so it would look as if he had just stepped away from his desk. Other employees write e-mails before they go home and then "send" them after midnight (we won't tell you how this is done) to make it look as though they are still at work. Some people leave early and, on their way home, send e-mails via their Blackberry device so it will appear they are still at the office. You may be thinking that these ruses are harmless, but 59 percent of human resource managers and 53 percent of supervisors have caught employees lying about the hours they work. Furthermore, if you're using technology to fake it, you're usually leaving high-tech tracks and footprints along the way. That tech worker who controlled his office computer with his Palm PC at lunch was fired for habitual lateness. Motivation is all about effort. So, do the right thing. Work hard for your company, your customers, and yourself.[15]

Since people are motivated by unmet needs, managers must learn what those unmet needs are and address them. This is not always a straightforward task, however, because different needs theories suggest different needs categories. Exhibit 13.4 shows needs from three well-known needs theories. Maslow's Hierarchy of Needs suggests that people are motivated by *physiological* (food and water), *safety* (physical and economic), *belongingness* (friendship, love, social interaction), *esteem* (achievement and recognition), and *self-actualization* (realizing your full potential) needs.[12] Alderfer's ERG Theory collapses Maslow's five needs into three: *existence* (safety and physiological needs), *relatedness* (belongingness), and *growth* (esteem and self-actualization).[13] McClelland's Learned Needs Theory suggests that people are motivated by the need for *affiliation* (to be liked and accepted), the need for *achievement* (to accomplish challenging goals), or the need for *power* (to influence others).[14]

needs the physical or psychological requirements that must be met to ensure survival and well-being

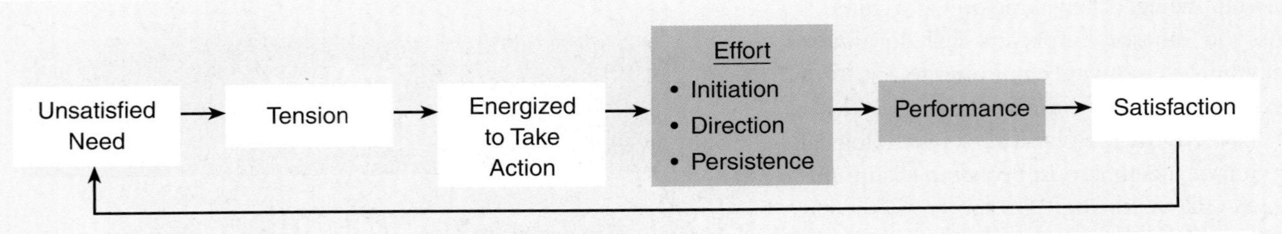

As shown on the left side of this exhibit, a person's unsatisfied need creates an uncomfortable, internal state of tension that must be resolved. So, according to needs theories, people are motivated by unmet needs. But once a need is met, it no longer motivates. When this occurs, people become satisfied, as shown on the right side of the exhibit.

Exhibit 13.3

Adding Need Satisfaction to the Model

Things become even more complicated when we consider the different predictions made by these theories. According to Maslow, needs are arranged in a hierarchy from low (physiological) to high (self-actualization). Within this hierarchy, people are motivated by their lowest unsatisfied need. As each need is met, they work their way up the hierarchy from physiological to self-actualization needs. By contrast, Alderfer says that people can be motivated by more than one need at a time. Furthermore, he suggests that people are just as likely to move down the needs hierarchy as up, particularly when they are unable to achieve satisfaction at the next higher need level. McClelland argues that the degree to which particular needs motivate varies tremendously from person to person, with some people being motivated primarily by achievement and others by power or affiliation. Moreover, McClelland says that needs are learned, not innate. For instance, studies show that children whose parents own a small business or hold a managerial position are much more likely to have a high need for achievement.[16]

So, with three different sets of needs and three very different ideas about how needs motivate, how do we provide a practical answer to managers who just want to know "What leads to effort?" Fortunately, the research evidence simplifies things a bit. To start, studies indicate that there are two basic kinds of needs categories.[17] As shown in Exhibit 13.4, *lower-order needs* are concerned with safety and with physiological and existence requirements, whereas *higher-order needs* are concerned with relationships (belongingness, relatedness, and affiliation); challenges and accomplishments (esteem, self-actualization, growth, and achievement); and influence (power). Studies generally show that higher-order needs will not motivate people as long as lower-order needs remain unsatisfied.[18]

For example, imagine that you graduated from college six months ago and are still looking for your first job. With money running short (you're probably living on your credit cards) and the possibility of having to move back in with your parents looming (if this doesn't motivate you, what will?), your basic needs for food, shelter, and security drive your thoughts, behavior, and choices at this point. But once you land that job, find a great place (of your own!) to live, and put some money in the bank, these basic needs should decrease in importance as you begin to think about making new friends and taking on challenging work assignments. In fact, once lower-order needs are satisfied, it's difficult for

Exhibit 13.4

Needs Classification of Different Theories

	MASLOW'S HIERARCHY	ALDERFER'S ERG	McCLELLAND'S LEARNED NEEDS
Higher-Order Needs	Self-Actualization Esteem Belongingness	Growth Relatedness	Power Achievement Affiliation
Lower-Order Needs	Safety Physiological	Existence	

managers to predict which higher-order needs will motivate behavior.[19] Some people will be motivated by affiliation, while others will be motivated by growth or esteem. Also, the relative importance of the various needs may change over time, but not necessarily in any predictable pattern. So, what leads to effort? In part, needs do. After we discuss rewards in Subsection 1.3, in Subsection 1.4 we discuss how managers can use what we know from need-satisfaction theories to motivate workers.

1.3 Extrinsic and Intrinsic Rewards

No discussion of motivation would be complete without considering rewards. Let's add two kinds of rewards, extrinsic and intrinsic, to the model, as shown in Exhibit 13.5.[20]

Extrinsic rewards are tangible and visible to others and are given to employees contingent on the performance of specific tasks or behaviors.[21] External agents (managers, for example) determine and control the distribution, frequency, and amount of extrinsic rewards, such as pay, company stock, benefits, and promotions. For example, 80 percent of 1,000 large and medium-sized U.S. companies surveyed by Hewitt Associates, a consulting company based in Lincolnshire, Illinois, offer incentives or bonuses to reward employees.[22] The payout from **BOEING**'s employee incentive plan is determined by how well Boeing meets financial targets. One year, the incentive plan paid $439 million to about 109,000 workers companywide.[23] Likewise, **WAL-MART** paid $529.8 million in bonuses to 813,759 hourly U.S. employees at Wal-Mart and Sam's Club stores. Lois Honeycutt, a 46-year old customer service manager at Wal-Mart in Altamonte Springs, Florida, says the bonus program will help increase employee performance and boost employee spirits and morale.[24] As described in the chapter-opening "What Would You Do?," manufacturing employees at Nucor Corporation can earn bonuses of up to 170 percent of base pay.[25]

Why do companies need extrinsic rewards? To get people to do things they wouldn't otherwise do. Companies use extrinsic rewards to motivate people to perform four basic behaviors: join the organization, regularly attend their jobs, perform their jobs well, and stay with the organization.[26] Think about it. Would you show up to work every day to do the best possible job that you could just out of the goodness of your heart? Very few people would. This is why **CDW** (Computer Discount Warehouse) rewards its employees for staying with the company. CDW found that new employees are only one-third as productive as employees who have at least three years of experience with the company. Accordingly, CDW has an "old-timers" program that rewards employees who have been with the company at least three years with a four-day trip for themselves and their families anywhere in the continental United States. There is one catch: The company has to meet its sales goals. But if it does, the company pays for the airline tickets and hotel costs associated with those trips. And CDW pays for such trips every year that employees stay with the company beyond three years.[27] At CDW's expense, account manager Brigid Brindley has taken her family to California and Washington, D.C., and is planning a trip to Seattle. Brindley says this about CDW: "They recognize that there are other things in life that you do besides just work." CDW's approach makes sense in light of a Maritz Incentives poll of 1,002 full-time employees, which concluded that employees who feel their value is recognized are seven times more likely to stay with their present company than employees who don't feel valued.[28]

extrinsic reward a reward that is tangible, visible to others, and given to employees contingent on the performance of specific tasks or behaviors

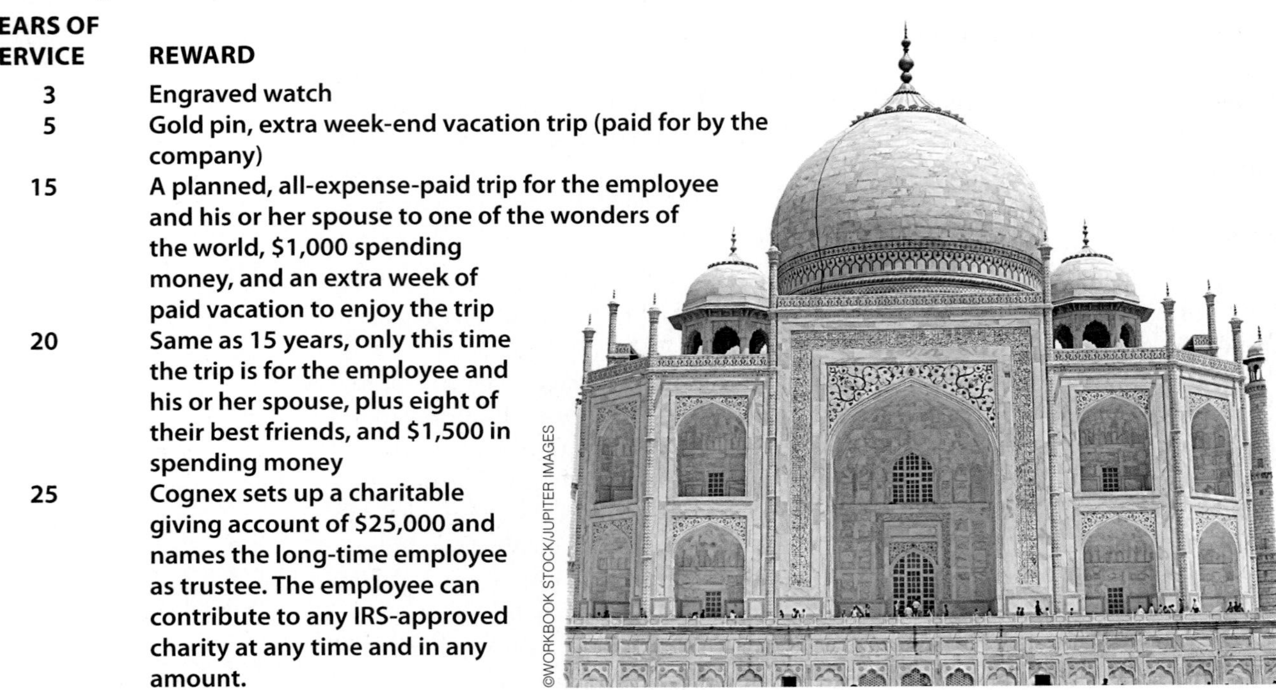

Join Cognex—and Stay—and Travel the World

YEARS OF SERVICE	REWARD
3	Engraved watch
5	Gold pin, extra week-end vacation trip (paid for by the company)
15	A planned, all-expense-paid trip for the employee and his or her spouse to one of the wonders of the world, $1,000 spending money, and an extra week of paid vacation to enjoy the trip
20	Same as 15 years, only this time the trip is for the employee and his or her spouse, plus eight of their best friends, and $1,500 in spending money
25	Cognex sets up a charitable giving account of $25,000 and names the long-time employee as trustee. The employee can contribute to any IRS-approved charity at any time and in any amount.

SOURCE: J. S. LUBLIN, "CREATIVE COMPENSATION: A CEO TALKS ABOUT HIS COMPANY'S INNOVATIVE PAY IDEAS. FREE ICE CREAM, ANYONE?" *WALL STREET JOURNAL,* 10 APRIL 2006, R6.

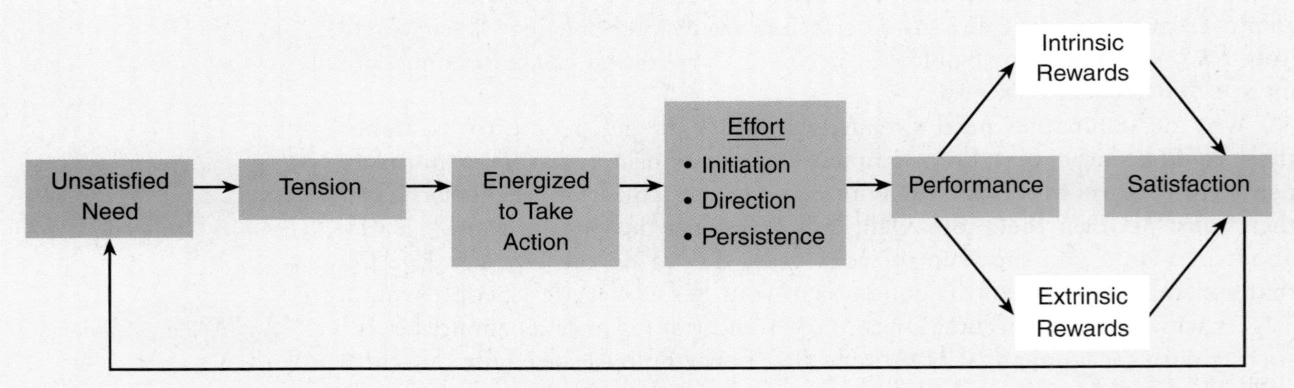

Performing a job well can be rewarding intrinsically (the job itself is fun, challenging, or interesting) or extrinsically (as you receive better pay or promotions, etc.). Intrinsic and extrinsic rewards lead to satisfaction of various needs.

Exhibit 13.5

Adding Rewards to the Model

By contrast, **intrinsic rewards** are the natural rewards associated with performing a task or activity for its own sake. For example, aside from the external rewards management offers for doing something well, employees often find the activities or tasks they perform interesting and enjoyable. Examples of intrinsic rewards include a sense of accomplishment or achievement, a feeling of responsibility, the chance to learn something new or interact with others, or simply the fun that comes from performing an interesting, challenging, and engaging task. For instance, researcher Mark Rise works for Medtronic, a leading medical technology company. Rise, one of Medtronic's most creative inventors, could have a more prestigious job at a university or make more money starting his own company, but he doesn't want to test theory or develop

intrinsic reward a natural reward associated with performing a task or activity for its own sake marketing plans or raise venture capital. What matters most to him is developing products that make a difference in people's lives. Says Rise, "That's what keeps me tied to what I'm doing now." Indeed, Rise thrives on the intrinsic aspects of his work such as being able to work with physicians, medical researchers, software developers, and engineers to identify new treatments and design and manufacture new products.[29]

Which types of rewards are most important to workers in general? A number of surveys suggest that both extrinsic and intrinsic rewards are important. One survey found that the most important rewards were good benefits and health insurance, job security, a week or more of vacation (all extrinsic rewards), interesting work, the opportunity to learn new skills, and independent work situations (all intrinsic rewards). And employee preferences for intrinsic and extrinsic rewards appear to be relatively stable. Studies conducted over the last three decades have consistently found that employees are twice as likely to indicate that "important and meaningful work" matters more to them than what they are paid.[30]

1.4 Motivating with the Basics

So, given the basic model of work motivation in Exhibit 13.5, what practical steps can managers take to motivate employees to increase their effort?

As shown in Exhibit 13.6, *start by asking people what their needs are*. If managers don't know what workers' needs are, they won't be able to provide them the opportunities and rewards that can satisfy those needs. Linda Connor, vice president of corporate culture at **Technology Professionals Corp.** (TPC) in Grand Rapids, Michigan, keeps careful notes about TPC employees' needs. She says, "I sit down at employees' 30-day reviews and ask specific questions about hobbies and interests for each member of their families."[31] For instance, her notes about top performer Phil Mayrose indicated that he loves college football, oldies music, and, more than anything else, golf. Armed with this information, Connor and TPC rewarded Mayrose with a weekend vacation at a dude ranch with a great golf course. Connor's notes also include ideas for helping employees deal with stress.[32] So, if you want to meet employees' needs, do what Linda Connor does and just ask.

Next, *satisfy lower-order needs first*. Since higher-order needs will not motivate people as long as lower-order needs remain unsatisfied, companies should satisfy lower-order needs first. In practice, this means providing the equipment, training, and knowledge to create a safe workplace free of physical risks, paying employees well enough to provide financial security, and offering a benefits package that will protect employees and their families through good medical coverage and health and disability insurance. Indeed, a survey based on a representative sample of Americans found that when people choose jobs or organizations, three of the four most important factors—starting pay/salary (62 percent), employee benefits (57 percent), and job security (47 percent)—are lower-order needs.[33]

Third, managers should *expect people's needs to change*. As some needs are satisfied or situations change, what motivated people before may not motivate them now. Likewise, what motivates people to accept a job may not necessarily motivate them once they have the job. For instance, David Stum, president of the Loyalty Institute, says, "The [attractive] power of pay and benefits is only [strong] during the recruitment stage. After employees take the job, pay and benefits become entitlements to them. They think: 'Now that I work here, you owe me that.'"[34] Managers should also expect needs to change as people mature.[35]

Exhibit 13.6
Motivating to Increase Effort

- Start by asking people what their needs are.
- Satisfy lower-order needs first.
- Expect people's needs to change.
- As needs change and lower-order needs are satisfied, create opportunities for employees to satisfy higher-order needs.

For older employees benefits are as important as pay, which is always ranked as more important by younger employees. Also, older employees rank job security as more important than personal and family time, which is more important to younger employees.[36]

Finally, *as needs change and lower-order needs are satisfied, create opportunities for employees to satisfy higher-order needs*. Recall that intrinsic rewards, such as accomplishment, achievement, learning something new, and interacting with others, are the natural rewards associated with performing a task or activity for its own sake. And, with the exception of influence (power), intrinsic rewards correspond very closely to higher-order needs that are concerned with relationships (belongingness, relatedness, and affiliation) and challenges and accomplishments (esteem, self-actualization, growth, and achievement). Therefore, one way for managers to meet employees' higher-order needs is to create opportunities for employees to experience intrinsic rewards by providing challenging work, encouraging employees to take greater responsibility for their work, and giving employees the freedom to pursue tasks and projects they find naturally interesting. For example, we began this section by asking what would motivate an employee like Marjorie Landale to voluntarily learn American Sign Language. Marjorie wasn't paid to do this. In fact, she even spent her own money and free time to learn how to sign. The reason that Marjorie learned to sign is that doing so met her higher-order needs. It gave her a sense of accomplishment, and it allowed her to interact with deaf customers with whom she had previously been unable to interact. And Marjorie's boss was smart enough to encourage her to pursue a project that she found naturally interesting.

mgmt: trend

Motivating the Multigenerational Work Force

Now that Generation Y (also known as millennials) is entering the work force, managers must juggle four generations of workers with distinctly different work styles, ambitions, and values. Gen Y-ers have grown up immersed in technology and have largely been insulated from negative feedback by overinvolved boomer parents. These workers tend to be fearless and blunt, believe that old-school ways don't necessarily generate the best results, and are more committed to work-life balance than previous generations. Today's managers need to adapt if they want to attract, retain, and motivate Gen Y-ers, who will conceivably dominate the work force for the next 70 years. What motivated older generations is probably not going to work as well with Gen Y.

Sources: Danielle Sacks, "Scenes from the Culture Clash: Companies Are Now Waking Up to the Havoc That the Newest Generation of Workers Is Causing in Their Offices," *Fast Company*, January–February 2006, 73–77; Claire Raines, "Managing Millennials," *Connecting Generations: The Sourcebook for the Workplace* (Menlo Park, CA: Crisp Publications, 2003).

Review 1: **Basics of Motivation**

Motivation is the set of forces that initiates, directs, and makes people persist in their efforts over time to accomplish a goal. Managers often assume motivation to be the only determinant of performance, but job performance is a multiplicative function of motivation times ability times situational constraints. If any one of these components is weak, job performance will suffer. Needs are the physical or psychological requirements that must be met to ensure survival and well-being. When needs are not met, people experience an internal state of tension. But once a particular need is met, it no longer motivates. When this occurs, people become satisfied and are then motivated by other unmet needs. Different motivational theories, such as Maslow's Hierarchy of Needs (physiological, safety, belongingness, esteem, and self-actualization), Alderfer's ERG Theory (existence, relatedness, and growth), and McClelland's Learned Needs Theory (affiliation, achievement, and power), specify a number of different needs. However, studies show that there are only two general kinds of needs, lower-order needs and higher-order needs, and that higher-order needs will not motivate people as long as lower-order needs remain unsatisfied. Both extrinsic and intrinsic rewards motivate people. Extrinsic rewards, which include pay, company stock, benefits, and promotions, are used to motivate people to join organizations and attend and perform their jobs. The basic model of motivation suggests that managers can motivate employees by asking them what their needs are, satisfying lower-order needs first, expecting people's needs to change, and satisfying higher-order needs through intrinsic rewards.

© BANANA STOCK/JUPITER IMAGES

Managing the multiple styles of multigenerational workforces is proving to be a delicate balancing act for managers.

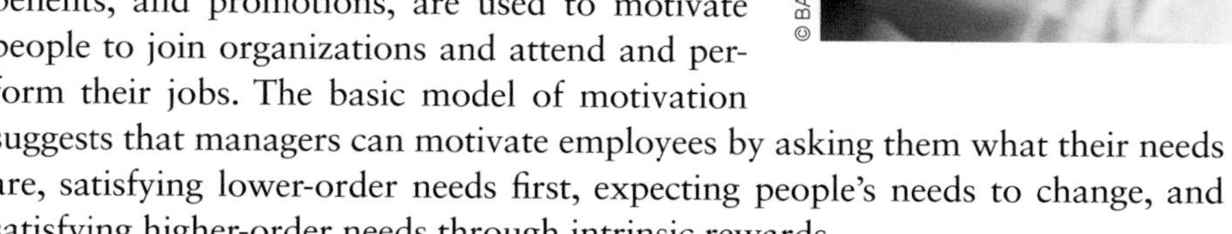

"The [attractive] power of pay and benefits is only [strong] during the recruitment stage. After employees take the job, pay and benefits become entitlements to them. They think: "Now that I work here, you owe me that.""

DAVID STUM, PRESIDENT, LOYALTY INSTITUTE

HOW PERCEPTIONS AND EXPECTATIONS AFFECT MOTIVATION

When employees perceive that they will be unable to perform at a level necessary to obtain rewards, whether extrinsic or intrinsic, they are likely to be *de-motivated*. Reward systems at many organizations are geared toward top performers and ignore the mid-level performers. Most banks, for instance, reward the top 10 percent of the sales force; other sales representatives, who don't believe they can generate enough sales to end up in the top category, simply give up. Stephen O'Malley, an independent consultant, says that one way to avoid this scenario is to create an open-ended incentive program that keeps the top-performer programs intact while offering awards for mid-level performers who surpass their annual sales goals by 10 percent. This system implemented at a large U.S.-based financial services institution was successful in influencing perceptions and expectations of mid-level performers and resulted in better performance from all employees and increased revenue for the company. Specifically, two-thirds of the company's mid-level performers qualified for rewards by collectively contributing almost 80 percent of the total sales growth and creating $14 million in incremental profit. The contributions of these mid-level performers as a group outpaced the growth of top performers by 16 percent. By influencing perceptions and expectations of the entire sales force, the company was able to achieve a 47 percent overall increase in sales growth, three times the industry average.[37]

After reading the next two sections, you should be able to

2 use equity theory to explain how employees' perceptions of fairness affect motivation.

3 use expectancy theory to describe how workers' expectations about rewards, effort, and the link between rewards and performance influence motivation.

2 Equity Theory

equity theory a theory that states that people will be motivated when they perceive that they are being treated fairly

Finnish businessman Jaako Rytsola was out driving in his car one evening. "The road was wide and I was feeling good. It was nice to be driving when there was no one in sight." Unfortunately for Rytsola, he wasn't really alone. A police officer pulled him over and issued him a speeding ticket for driving 43 miles per hour in a 25 mph zone. The cost of the ticket: $71,400! Janne Rajala, a college student, was also pulled over for driving 18 mph over the speed limit. However, Rajala's ticket cost him only $106. The $71,294 difference occurred because Finland bases traffic fines on the severity of the offense, which was identical in this case, *and* the income of the driver, which clearly wasn't.

Is Finland's method of determining speeding fines fair or unfair? Most Americans would argue that Finland's approach is unfair, that fairness requires that fines be proportional to the offense and that everyone who breaks the law to the same degree should pay the same fine. By contrast, most Finns believe that fines proportional to income are fair. Erkki Wuouma of Finland's Ministry of the Interior says, "This is a Nordic tradition. We have progressive taxation and progressive punishments. So the more you earn, the more you pay." Rytsola pays more because he is a high-earning Internet entrepreneur. Rajala pays less because he's a low-earning college student.[38]

© AP PHOTO/SARI GUSTAFSSON/LEHTIKUVA

Equity theory is not an absolute. It is dependent on many factors, including culture. Jaako Rytsola, pictured here with his Lamborghini, was fined $71,400 for speeding because in Finland traffic fines are based on a person's income. People of other cultures may not have the same view of equity as the Finns!

Fairness, or what people perceive to be fair, is also a critical issue in organizations. **Equity theory** says that people will be motivated at work when they *perceive* that they are being treated fairly. In particular, equity theory stresses the importance of perceptions. So, regardless of the actual level of rewards people receive, they must also perceive that, relative to others, they are being treated fairly. For example, you learned in Chapter 11 that the average CEO now makes 289 times more than the average worker.[39] On average, CEOs of the 500 largest U.S. companies make $10.9 million,[40] CEOs of the Standard & Poor's 500 make $13.51 million.[41] And many CEOs make in the $200 million range. For instance, Terry Semel, former CEO of Yahoo made $230.6 million one year.[42] Many people believe that CEO pay is obscenely high and unfair. Others believe that CEO pay is fair because the supply and demand for executive talent largely determine what CEOs are paid. They argue that if it were easier to find good CEOs, then CEOs would be paid much less.

As explained below, equity theory doesn't focus on objective equity (that is, that CEOs make 289 times more than blue-collar workers). Instead, equity theory says that equity, like beauty, is in the eye of the beholder.

Let's learn more about equity theory by examining ***2.1 the components of equity theory, 2.2 how people react to perceived inequities,*** *and* ***2.3 how to motivate people using equity theory.***

2.1 Components of Equity Theory

The basic components of equity theory are inputs, outcomes, and referents. **Inputs** are the contributions employees make to the organization. Inputs include education and training, intelligence, experience, effort, number of hours worked, and ability. **Outcomes** are what employees receive in exchange for their contributions to the organization. Outcomes include pay, fringe benefits, status symbols, and job titles and assignments. And, since perceptions of equity depend on comparisons, **referents** are others with whom people compare themselves to determine if they have been treated fairly. The referent can be a single person (comparing yourself with a coworker), or a generalized other (comparing yourself with "students in general," for example), or could be yourself over time ("I was better off last year than I am this year"). Usually, people choose to compare themselves with referents who hold the same or similar jobs or who are otherwise similar in gender, race, age, tenure, or other characteristics.[43] For instance, by any objective measure, it's hard to argue that the best professional athletes, who make as much as $30 million a year (and no doubt more by the time you read this), are treated unfairly, given that the typical American earns $43,318 a year.[44] Nonetheless, most top athletes' contracts include escalator clauses specifying that if another top player at the same position (that is, their referent) receives a larger contract, then their contract will automatically be increased to that amount.

According to the equity theory process shown in Exhibit 13.7, employees compare their outcomes, the rewards they receive from the organization, with their inputs, their contributions to the organization. This comparison of outcomes with inputs is called the **outcome/input (O/I) ratio**. After an internal comparison in which they compare their outcomes with their inputs, employees then make an external comparison in which they compare their O/I ratio with the O/I ratio of a referent.[45] When people perceive that their O/I ratio is equal to the referent's O/I ratio, they conclude that they are being treated fairly. But when people perceive that their O/I ratio is different from their referent's O/I ratio, they conclude that they have been treated inequitably or unfairly.

Inequity can take two forms, underreward and overreward. **Underreward** occurs when a referent's O/I ratio is better than your O/I ratio. In other words, you are getting fewer outcomes relative to your inputs than the referent you compare yourself with is getting. When people perceive that they have been underrewarded, they tend to experience anger or frustration. For example, when a manufacturing company received notice that some important contracts had been canceled, management cut employees' pay by 15 percent in one plant but not in another. Just as equity theory predicts, theft doubled in the plant that received the pay cut. Likewise, employee turnover increased from 5 percent to 23 percent.[46]

inputs in equity theory, the contributions employees make to the organization

outcomes in equity theory, the rewards employees receive for their contributions to the organization

referents in equity theory, others with whom people compare themselves to determine if they have been treated fairly

outcome/input (O/I) ratio in equity theory, an employee's perception of how the rewards received from an organization compare with the employee's contributions to that organization

underreward a form of inequity in which you are getting fewer outcomes relative to inputs than your referent is getting

Exhibit 13.7
Outcome/Input Ratios

$$\frac{\text{OUTCOMES}_{\text{SELF}}}{\text{INPUTS}_{\text{SELF}}} = \frac{\text{OUTCOMES}_{\text{REFERENT}}}{\text{INPUTS}_{\text{REFERENT}}}$$

By contrast, **overreward** occurs when a referent's O/I ratio is worse than your O/I ratio. In this case, you are getting more outcomes relative to your inputs than your referent is. In theory, when people perceive that they have been overrewarded, they experience guilt. But, not surprisingly, people have a very high tolerance for overreward. It takes a tremendous amount of overpayment before people decide that their pay or benefits are more than they deserve.

2.2 How People React to Perceived Inequity

overreward a form of inequity in which you are getting more outcomes relative to inputs than your referent

As a child do you ever remember calling for a do-over? Even as children, we have a strong desire for fairness, for being treated equitably. When this need isn't met, we are strongly motivated to find a way to restore equity and be fair, hence the "do-over." Not surprisingly, equity is just as important at the office as it is on the playground.

So what happens when people perceive that they have been treated inequitably at work? Exhibit 13.8 shows that perceived inequity affects satisfaction. In the case of underreward, this usually translates into frustration or anger; with overreward, the reaction is guilt. These reactions lead to tension and a strong need to take action to restore equity in some way. At first, a slight inequity may not be strong enough to motivate an employee to take immediate action. If the inequity continues or there are multiple inequities, however, tension may build over time until a point of intolerance is reached, and the person is energized to take action.[47] For example, when **The Accident Group**, an insurance company, laid off 2,500 employees in Manchester, Birmingham, and Liverpool, England,

Exhibit 13.8

Adding Equity Theory to the Model

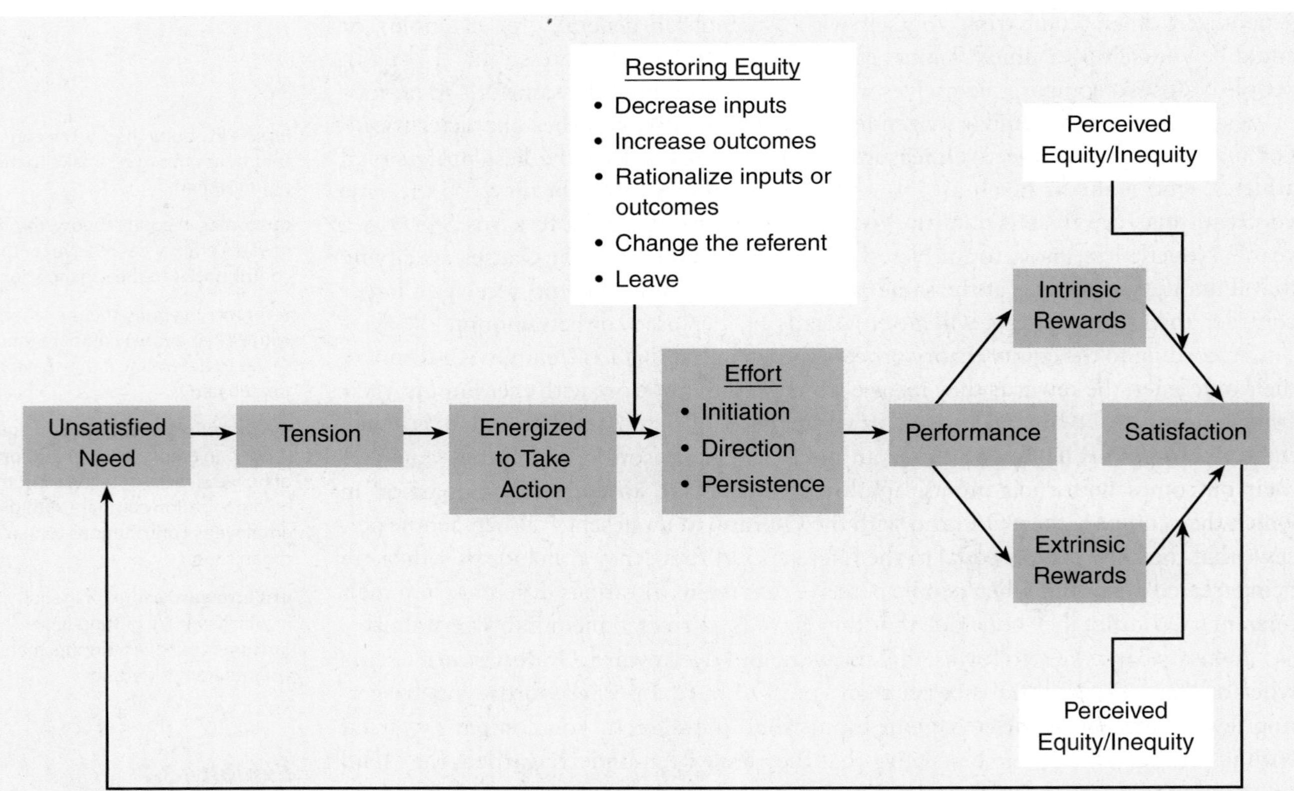

When people perceive that they have been treated inequitably at work because of the intrinsic or extrinsic rewards they receive relative to their efforts, they are dissatisfied (or frustrated or angry), because their needs aren't met. Those reactions lead to tension and a strong need to take action to restore equity in some way (as explained in the "Restoring Equity" box).

it made the announcement in an impersonal, insensitive way. Employees received text messages on their cell phones telling them to not go into work, that their final paychecks could not be issued, and that a more thorough explanation would be provided by e-mail. In addition, this message was left on everyone's office voice mail: "All staff who are being retained will be contacted today. If you have not been spoken to, you are therefore being made redundant [laid off] with immediate effect." Angry employees *and* managers ransacked offices, taking computers, phones, and anything else they could carry off. Claims assessor Andy Potton says, "I could hardly believe what I saw. There were people walking out of the office with computers. One chap quite high up in the company had loaded up his car with laptops and driven off."[48]

When people perceive that they have been treated unfairly, they may try to restore equity by reducing inputs, increasing outcomes, rationalizing inputs or outcomes, changing the referent, or simply leaving. We will discuss these possible responses in terms of the inequity associated with underreward, which is much more common than the inequity associated with overreward.

People who perceive that they have been underrewarded may try to restore equity by *decreasing or withholding their inputs (that is, effort)*. For example, when **IBERIA**, the Spanish airline, was near bankruptcy, it pressured its pilots to take substantial pay cuts. When Iberia's finances improved, the pilots requested that the pay cuts, which had cost them $140 million, be reversed. They also asked for annual pay increases substantially higher than the rate of inflation. When Iberia management refused, the pilots staged a work slowdown at the peak of the busy summer tourism season. Over the course of 10 separate days throughout the summer, 30 to 40 percent of Iberia's pilots called in sick, disrupting the airline's flight schedule, customers, and profits.[49]

Increasing outcomes is another way people try to restore equity. This might include asking for a raise or pointing out the inequity to the boss and hoping that he or she takes care of it. Sometimes, however, employees may go to external organizations, such as labor unions, federal agencies, or the courts for help in increasing outcomes to restore equity. For instance, the U.S. Department of Labor estimates that 10 percent of workers are not getting the extra overtime pay they deserve when they work more than 40 hours a week.[50] In fact, more than 30,000 such cases are brought each year, and employees win two-thirds of them.[51] For example, the managers of Waffle House restaurants sued the company because they were working an average of 89 hours a week without any overtime pay (managers at Radio Shack and Wal-Mart have sued their companies for similar reasons).[52] The company contended that as managers they were exempt from the Fair Labor Standards Act (FLSA), which mandates that workers be paid time and a half for any work beyond 40 hours a week. But because Waffle House managers were required to perform and be proficient in the duties of hourly workers in addition to their managerial responsibilities, the courts ruled that Waffle House managers were really employees who deserved overtime pay. As a result, they were awarded $2,868,841.50 in back overtime pay.[53]

Another method of restoring equity is to *rationalize or distort inputs or outcomes*. Instead of decreasing inputs or increasing outcomes, employees restore equity by making mental or emotional "adjustments" in their O/I ratios or the O/I ratios of their referents. For example, suppose that a company downsizes 10 percent of its work force. It's likely that the survivors, the people who still have jobs, will be angry or frustrated with company management because of the layoffs. If alternative jobs are difficult to find, however, these survivors may rationalize or distort their O/I ratios and conclude, "Well, things could be worse. At least I still have my job." Rationalizing or distorting outcomes may be used when other ways to restore equity aren't available.

Changing the referent is another way of restoring equity. In this case, people compare themselves with someone other than the referent they had been using for previous O/I ratio comparisons. Since people usually choose to compare themselves with others who hold the same or similar jobs or who are otherwise similar (such as friends, family members, neighbors who work at other companies), they may change referents to restore equity when their personal situations change, such as a decrease in job status or pay.[54]

Finally, when none of these methods—reducing inputs, increasing outcomes, rationalizing inputs or outcomes, or changing referents—are possible or restore equity, *employees may leave* by quitting their jobs, transferring, or increasing absenteeism.[55] For example, attorneys and accountants at the Securities and Exchange Commission (SEC) quit their jobs at twice the rate of employees in other federal agencies. Why? One reason is that the SEC's attorneys and accountants are paid 40 percent less than their counterparts at other government agencies. Furthermore, they can get jobs in the private sector that pay $180,000 to $250,000 per year.[56]

2.3 Motivating with Equity Theory

What practical steps can managers take to use equity theory to motivate employees? As Exhibit 13.9 shows, they can *start by looking for and correcting major inequities*. Among other things, equity theory makes us aware that an employee's sense of fairness is based on subjective perceptions. What one employee considers grossly unfair may not affect another employee's perceptions of equity at all. Although these different perceptions make it difficult for managers to create conditions that satisfy all employees, it's critical that they do their best to take care of major inequities that can energize employees to take disruptive, costly, or harmful actions, such as decreasing inputs or leaving. So, whenever possible, managers should look for and correct major inequities. Junior accountant Monica DiCenso supervised three auditors and regularly put in 80-hour weeks certifying the financial statements of **PriceWaterhouseCoopers**' corporate clients. After receiving a $2,000 annual bonus (effectively paying her $2.86 an hour for overtime work), DiCenso quit, as did 20 of the 35 accountants who started when she did. DiCenso says, "I could have made more working at a fast-food restaurant."[57] With turnover up significantly, the Big Four accounting firms have begun addressing those inequities by paying bigger bonuses and giving junior accountants more vacation time. To help with the long hours, the firms are offering concierge services, which pick up and drop off dry cleaning and take care of other daytime tasks that workers don't have time to do. Frequent "town hall" meetings also give junior accountants a chance to gripe to senior partners about the difficulties in their jobs.

Second, managers can *reduce employees' inputs*. Increasing outcomes is often the first and only strategy that companies use to restore equity, yet reducing employee inputs is just as viable a strategy. In fact, with dual-career couples working 50-hour weeks, more and more employees are looking for ways to reduce stress and restore a balance between work and family. Consequently, it may make sense to ask employees to do less, not more; to have them identify and eliminate the 20 percent of their jobs that doesn't increase productivity or add value for customers; and to eliminate company-imposed requirements that really aren't critical to the performance of managers, employees, or the company (for example, unnecessary meetings and reports). In addition to higher pay, more vacation time, concierge services, and town hall sessions, the Big Four accounting firms are trying to make the jobs of junior accountants more equitable by reducing the hours (that is, inputs) they must work. To shrink the workload, the firms are hiring more accountants, adding staff from other departments to help, and even actually turning away business that they lack the staff to handle. Bob Moritz, a senior partner at PriceWaterhouseCoopers, says,

Exhibit 13.9
Motivating with Equity Theory

- Look for and correct major inequities.
- Reduce employees' inputs.
- Make sure decision-making processes are fair.

"The profession has recognized that we have a lot of stress in the system, and we're doing a lot of things [to fix it]."[58]

Finally, managers should *make sure decision-making processes are fair*. Equity theory focuses **distributive justice**, the degree to which outcomes and rewards are fairly distributed or allocated. However, **procedural justice**, the fairness of the procedures used to make reward allocation decisions, is just as important.[59] Procedural justice matters because even when employees are unhappy with their outcomes (that is, low pay), they're much less likely to be unhappy with company management if they believe that the procedures used to allocate outcomes were fair. For example, employees who are laid off tend to be hostile toward their employer when they perceive that the procedures leading to the layoffs were unfair. By contrast, employees who perceive layoff procedures to be fair tend to continue to support and trust their employers.[60] Also, if employees perceive that their outcomes are unfair (that is, distributive injustice), but that the decisions and procedures leading to those outcomes were fair (that is, procedural justice), they are much more likely to seek constructive ways of restoring equity, such as discussing these matters with their manager. In contrast, if employees perceive both distributive and procedural injustice, they may resort to more destructive tactics, such as withholding effort, absenteeism, tardiness, or even sabotage and theft.[61] *Interactional justice* refers to the fairness of interpersonal treatment that individuals receive during the enactment of organizational procedures. Two elements central to perceptions of interactional justice are (1) whether the reasons underlying the resource allocation decisions are clearly, truthfully, and adequately explained to affected parties, and (2) whether those responsible for implementing the decision treat the affected individuals with dignity and respect.[62] Recent studies indicate that interactional justice perceptions are at least as important as perceptions of procedural justice and distributive justice.[63] In addition, most managers are likely to have more control over interactional justice perceptions than, for example, fairness of organizational procedures or reward allocations in organizations.

Review 2: Equity Theory

The basic components of equity theory are inputs, outcomes, and referents. After an internal comparison in which employees compare their outcomes with their inputs, they then make an external comparison in which they compare their O/I ratio with the O/I ratio of a referent, a person who works in a similar job or is otherwise similar. When their O/I ratio is equal to the referent's O/I ratio, employees perceive that they are being treated fairly. But when their O/I ratio is different from their referent's O/I ratio, they perceive that they have been treated inequitably or unfairly. There are two kinds of inequity, underreward and overreward. Underreward, which occurs when a referent's O/I ratio is better than the employee's O/I ratio, leads to anger or frustration. Overreward, which occurs when a referent's O/I ratio is worse than the employee's O/I ratio, can lead to guilt, but only when the level of overreward is extreme. When employees perceive that they

distributive justice the perceived degree to which outcomes and rewards are fairly distributed or allocated

procedural justice the perceived fairness of the process used to make reward allocation decisions have been treated inequitably (underrewarded), they may try to restore equity by reducing inputs, increasing outcomes, rationalizing inputs or outcomes, changing the referent, or simply leaving. Managers can use equity theory to motivate workers by looking for and correcting major inequities, reducing employees' inputs, and emphasizing procedural as well as distributive justice. Most importantly, they should treat workers in an interpersonally sensitive manner and work to make sure that organizational procedures are fair and are applied in a consistent manner.

3 Expectancy Theory

How attractive do you find each of the following rewards? A company concierge service that will pick up your car from the mechanic and send someone to be at your house when the cable guy or repair person shows up. A "7 to 7" travel policy stipulating that no one has to leave home for business travel before 7 AM on Mondays and that everyone should be home from business travel by 7 PM on Fridays. The opportunity to telecommute so that you can feed your kids breakfast, pick them up after school, and tuck them into bed at night.[64]

If you have kids, you might love the chance to telecommute; but if you don't, you may not be interested. If you don't travel much on business, you won't be interested in the "7 to 7" travel policy; but if you do, you'll probably love it. One of the hardest things about motivating people is that rewards that are attractive to some employees are unattractive to others. **Expectancy theory** says that people will be motivated to the extent to which they believe that their efforts will lead to good performance, that good performance will be rewarded, and that they will be offered attractive rewards.[65]

*Let's learn more about expectancy theory by examining **3.1 the components of expectancy theory** and **3.2 how to use expectancy theory as a motivational tool**.*

3.1 Components of Expectancy Theory

Expectancy theory holds that people make conscious choices about their motivation. The three factors that affect those choices are valence, expectancy, and instrumentality.

Valence is simply the attractiveness or desirability of various rewards or outcomes. Expectancy theory recognizes that the same reward or outcome, say, a promotion, will be highly attractive to some people, will be highly disliked by others, and will not make much difference one way or the other to still others. Accordingly, when people are deciding how much effort to put forth, expectancy theory says that they will consider the valence of all possible rewards and outcomes that they can receive from their jobs. The greater the sum of those valences, each of which can be positive, negative, or neutral, the more effort people will choose to put forth on the job.

Expectancy is the perceived relationship between effort and performance. When expectancies are strong, employees believe that their hard work and efforts will result in good performance, so they work harder. By contrast, when expectancies are weak, employees figure that no matter what they do or how hard they work, they won't be able to perform their jobs successfully, so they don't work as hard.

Instrumentality is the perceived relationship between performance and rewards. When instrumentality is strong, employees believe that improved performance will lead to better and more rewards, so they choose to work harder. When instrumentality is weak, employees don't believe that better performance will result in more or better rewards, so they choose not to work as hard.

expectancy theory the theory that people will be motivated to the extent to which they believe that their efforts will lead to good performance, that good performance will be rewarded, and that they will be offered attractive rewards

valence the attractiveness or desirability of a reward or outcome

expectancy the perceived relationship between effort and performance

instrumentality the perceived relationship between performance and rewards

Expectancy theory holds that for people to be highly motivated, all three variables—valence, expectancy, and instrumentality—must be high. Thus, expectancy theory can be represented by the following simple equation:

$$\text{Motivation} = \text{Valence} \times \text{Expectancy} \times \text{Instrumentality}$$

If any one of these variables (valence, expectancy, or instrumentality) declines, overall motivation will decline, too.

Exhibit 13.10 incorporates the expectancy theory variables into our motivation model. Valence and instrumentality combine to affect employees' willingness to put forth effort (that is, the degree to which they are energized to take action), while expectancy transforms intended effort ("I'm really going to work hard in this job") into actual effort. If you're offered rewards that you desire and you believe that you will in fact receive these rewards for good performance, you're highly likely to be energized to take action. However, you're not likely to actually exert effort unless you also believe that you can do the job (that is, that your efforts will lead to successful performance).

Kimberly-Clark, known for its brand name products such as Kleenex, Scott, Huggies, and Cottonelle, revamped its performance management system to integrate valence, expectancy, and instrumentality into its employee motivation program. First, Kimberly-Clark offers a wide variety of rewards, including international assignments, employee recognition programs, incentives, bonuses, and stock options, so that all of its employees can receive highly valent rewards that they desire. The company manages expectancies through rigorous selection, orientation, and placement

Exhibit 13.10

Adding Expectancy Theory to the Model

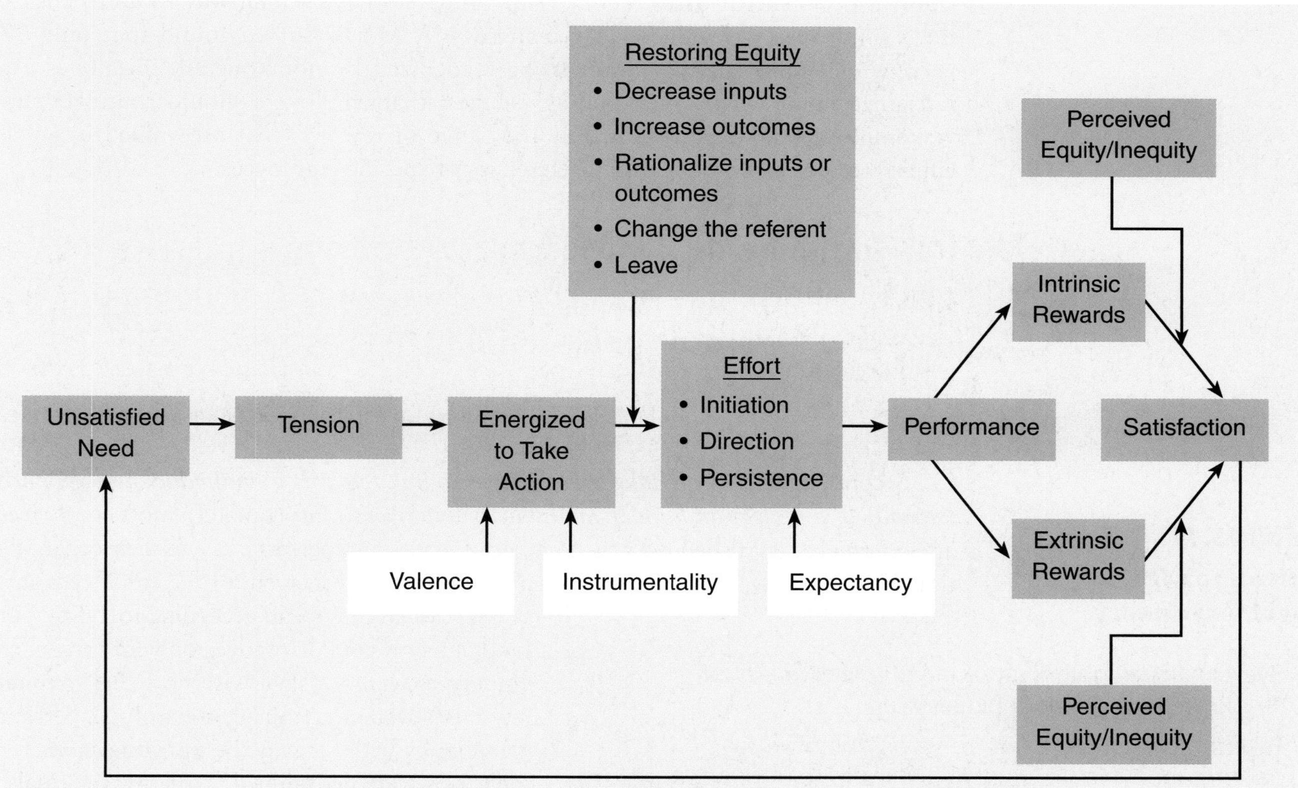

If rewards are attractive (valence) and linked to performance (instrumentality), then people are energized to take action. In other words, good performance gets them rewards that they want. Intended effort (i.e., energized to take action) turns into actual effort when people believe that their hard work and efforts will result in good performance. After all, why work hard if that hard work is wasted?

for new employees and through training and development opportunities for continuing employees. Finally, Kimberly-Clark manages instrumentality by linking rewards to the specific results, behaviors, and values it wants to reward. One of the primary goals of the new system was to treat the determination of compensation as "fully integrated business process, as opposed to an HR process," notes Liz Gottung, Kimberly-Clark's chief human resources officer. Employees know that base pay as well as consideration for stock options and variable pay are tied to performance, which is tied to the objectives, which are tied to the business plan.[66]

3.2 Motivating with Expectancy Theory

What practical steps can managers take to use expectancy theory to motivate employees? First, as Exhibit 13.11 shows, they can *systematically gather information to find out what employees want from their jobs*. In addition to individual managers directly asking employees what they want from their jobs (see Subsection 1.4 "Motivating with the Basics"), companies need to survey their employees regularly to determine their wants, needs, and dissatisfactions. Since people consider the valence of all the possible rewards and outcomes that they can receive from their jobs, regular identification of wants, needs, and dissatisfactions gives companies the chance to turn negatively valent rewards and outcomes into positively valent rewards and outcomes, thus raising overall motivation and effort. Mark Peterman, vice president of client solutions at **MARITZ INCENTIVES**, says that individual employees are motivated in vastly different ways; for example, he says, "For some, being honored in front of one's peers is a great award, but for others, the thought of being put on display in front of peers embarrasses them." And companies have a long way to go to ensure their employees feel valued, Peterman says. A Maritz survey found that only 27 percent of employees who want to be recognized by nonmonetary incentives are recognized that way.[67] Such findings suggest that employers should routinely survey employees to identify not only the range of rewards that are valued by most employees but also understand preferences of specific employees.

> For some, being honored in front of one's peers is a great award, but for others, the thought of being put on display in front of peers embarrasses them.
>
> MARK PETERMAN, VICE PRESIDENT OF CLIENT SOLUTIONS, MARITZ INCENTIVES

Second, managers can *take specific steps to link rewards to individual performance in a way that is clear and understandable to employees*. Unfortunately, most employees are extremely dissatisfied with the link between pay and performance in their organizations. In one study, based on a representative sample, 80 percent of the employees surveyed wanted to be paid according to a different kind of pay system! Moreover, only 32 percent of employees were satisfied with how their annual pay raises were determined, and only 22 percent were happy with the way the starting salaries for their jobs were determined.[68] One way to make sure that employees see the connection between pay and performance (see Chapter 11 for a discussion of compensation strategies) is for managers to publicize the way in which pay decisions

Exhibit 13.11
Motivating with Expectancy Theory

- Systematically gather information to find out what employees want from their jobs.
- Take specific steps to link rewards to individual performance in a way that is clear and understandable to employees.
- Empower employees to make decisions if management really wants them to believe that their hard work and effort will lead to good performance.

are made. This is especially important given that only 41 percent of employees know how their pay increases are determined.[69] Kerry Solomon, an HR executive, faced this challenge when she joined SecureWorks, an Atlanta-based Internet security services provider. She gathered accurate, comparable salary information and launched an aggressive educational enlightenment program to show employees how pay rates and increases are determined and how their pay compares with pay at other comparable firms. She believes that such information sharing is important because it allows employees to gain an accurate sense of where they stand—and to appreciate their employer's generosity.[70] Employees at Nucor Corporation know exactly how bonuses are computed and are able to calculate their bonus accurately, to the nearest dollar.

Finally, managers should *empower employees to make decisions if management really wants them to believe that their hard work and effort will lead to good performance.* If valent rewards are linked to good performance, people should be energized to take action. However, this works only if they also believe that their efforts will lead to good performance. One of the ways that managers destroy the expectancy that hard work and effort will lead to good performance is by restricting what employees can do or by ignoring employees' ideas. In Chapter 9, you learned that *empowerment* is a feeling of intrinsic motivation, in which workers perceive their work to have meaning and perceive themselves to be competent, to have an impact, and to be capable of self-determination.[71] So, if managers want workers to have strong expectancies, they should empower them to make decisions. Doing so will motivate employees to take active rather than passive roles in their work.

Review 3: **Expectancy Theory**

Expectancy theory holds that three factors affect the conscious choices people make about their motivation: valence, expectancy, and instrumentality. Valence is simply the attractiveness or desirability of various rewards or outcomes. Expectancy is the perceived relationship between effort and performance. Instrumentality is the perceived relationship between performance and rewards. Expectancy theory holds that for people to be highly motivated, all three factors must be high. If any one of these factors declines, overall motivation will decline, too. Managers can use expectancy theory to motivate workers by systematically gathering information to find out what employees want from their jobs, by linking rewards to individual performance in a way that is clear and understandable to employees, and by empowering employees to make decisions, which will increase their expectancies that hard work and effort will lead to good performance.

HOW REWARDS AND GOALS AFFECT MOTIVATION

When used properly, rewards motivate and energize employees. But when used incorrectly, they can demotivate, baffle, and even anger them. For example, consider the dot-com company that gave *every* employee a plaque for "outstanding performance." Then it compounded that mistake (how can every employee be "outstanding?") by firing one of those "outstanding" employees, James Finkel, two weeks after awarding him his plaque. Says Finkel, "My reward for outstanding performance was getting canned. I left the plaque sitting on my desk."[72]

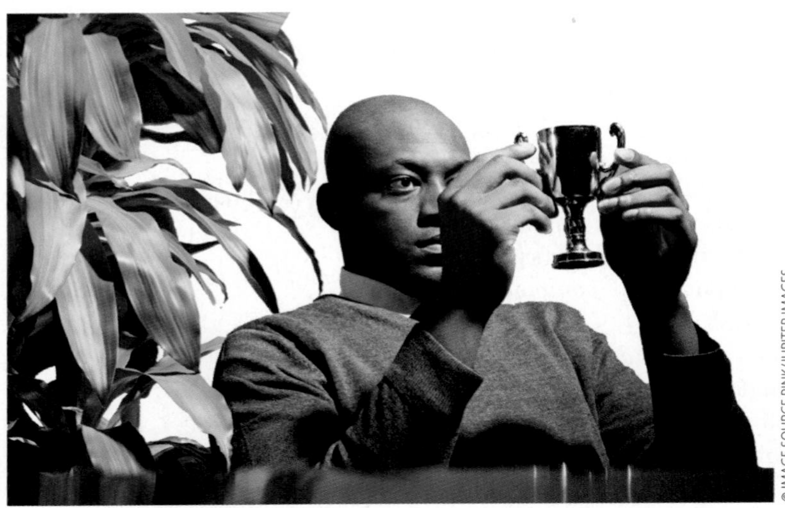

© IMAGE SOURCE PINK/JUPITER IMAGES

Sometimes rewards aren't as motivating as managers hope, and in fact, can work opposite to what managers intend.

Goals are also supposed to motivate employees. But leaders who focus blindly on meeting goals at all costs often find that they destroy motivation. For instance, a president of a technology company calls his vice president of sales *daily* and asks, "Did you make your numbers *today*?" Consultant Richard Hapburg, who works with the vice president who receives these daily calls, says that the VP should be focusing on long-term solutions that increase sales, but "he's under enormous pressure to meet certain sales and profit targets on a *daily basis* now." The clear danger to using goals in this way, says Hapburg, is "that it's hard to capture employees' hearts, and best efforts, with numbers alone."[73]

After reading the next three sections, you should be able to

4 explain how reinforcement theory works and how it can be used to motivate.

5 describe the components of goal-setting theory and how managers can use them to motivate workers.

6 discuss how the entire motivation model can be used to motivate workers.

4 Reinforcement Theory

Reinforcement theory says that behavior is a function of its consequences, that behaviors followed by positive consequences (that is, reinforced) will occur more frequently, and that behaviors followed by negative consequences, or not followed by positive consequences, will occur less frequently.[74] Therefore, to improve its safety record, Monsanto decided to reinforce safe behaviors. Chuck Davis, a safety consultant, says, "It's better to recognize a guy for success than beat him up for failure. It's amazing how little reward a guy needs so he doesn't stick his arm in a machine."[75] More specifically, **reinforcement** is the process of changing behavior by changing the consequences that follow behavior.[76]

Reinforcement has two parts: reinforcement contingencies and schedules of reinforcement. **Reinforcement contingencies** are the cause-and-effect relationships between the performance of specific behaviors and specific consequences. For example, if you get docked an hour's pay for being late to work, then a reinforcement contingency exists between a behavior, being late to work, and a consequence, losing an hour's pay. A **schedule of reinforcement** is the set of rules regarding reinforcement contingencies, such as which behaviors will be reinforced, which consequences will follow those behaviors, and the schedule by which those consequences will be delivered.[77]

Exhibit 13.12 incorporates reinforcement contingencies and reinforcement schedules into our motivation model. First, notice that extrinsic rewards and the schedules of reinforcement used to deliver them are the primary method for creating reinforcement contingencies in organizations. In turn, those reinforcement contingencies directly affect valences (the attractiveness of rewards), instrumentality (the perceived link between rewards and performance), and effort (how hard employees will work).

reinforcement theory the theory that behavior is a function of its consequences, that behaviors followed by positive consequences will occur more frequently, and that behaviors followed by negative consequences, or not followed by positive consequences, will occur less frequently

reinforcement the process of changing behavior by changing the consequences that follow behavior

reinforcement contingencies cause-and-effect relationships between the performance of specific behaviors and specific consequences

schedule of reinforcement rules that specify which behaviors will be reinforced, which consequences will follow those behaviors, and the schedule by which those consequences will be delivered

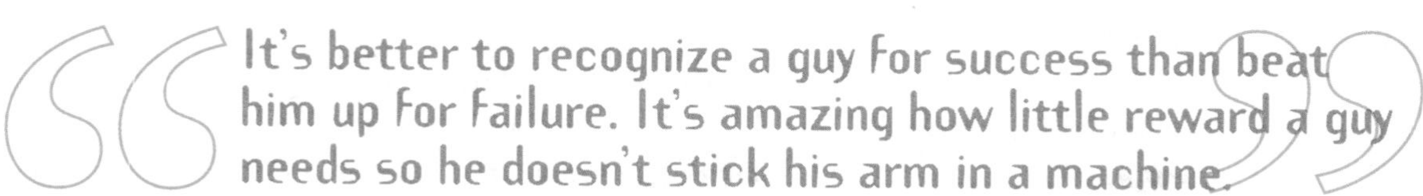

CHUCK DAVIS, SAFETY CONSULTANT

Let's learn more about reinforcement theory by examining ***4.1 the components of reinforcement theory, 4.2 the different schedules for delivering reinforcement,*** *and* ***4.3 how to motivate with reinforcement theory.***

4.1 Components of Reinforcement Theory

As just described, *reinforcement contingencies* are the cause-and-effect relationships between the performance of specific behaviors and specific consequences. There are four kinds of reinforcement contingencies: positive reinforcement, negative reinforcement, punishment, and extinction.

Positive reinforcement strengthens behavior (that is, increases its frequency) by following behaviors with desirable consequences. Harry Kraemer, the CEO of

positive reinforcement reinforcement that strengthens behavior by following behaviors with desirable consequences

Exhibit 13.12
Adding Reinforcement Theory to the Model

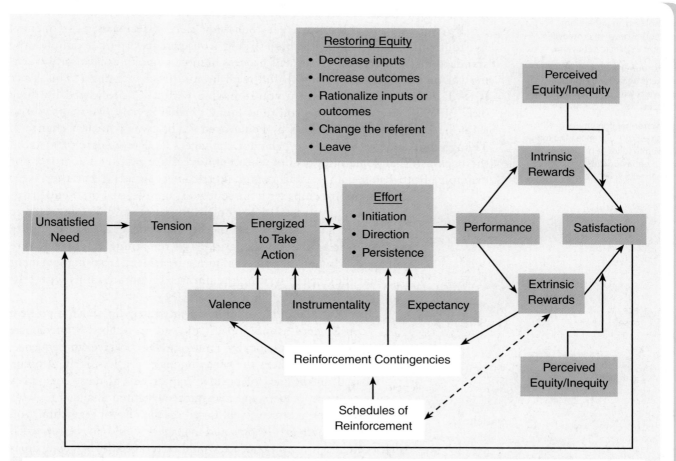

Restoring Equity
- Decrease inputs
- Increase outcomes
- Rationalize inputs or outcomes
- Change the referent
- Leave

Perceived Equity/Inequity

Intrinsic Rewards

Unsatisfied Need

Tension

Energized to Take Action

Effort
- Initiation
- Direction
- Persistence

Performance

Satisfaction

Extrinsic Rewards

Valence

Instrumentality

Expectancy

Reinforcement Contingencies

Perceived Equity/Inequity

Schedules of Reinforcement

Extrinsic rewards and the schedules of reinforcement used to deliver them are the primary method for creating reinforcement contingencies in organizations. In turn, those reinforcement contingencies directly affect valences (the attractiveness of rewards), instrumentality (the perceived link between rewards and performance), and effort (how hard employees will work).

BAXTER INTERNATIONAL, a pharmaceutical firm, included this story about his four-year-old son in Baxter's company newsletter to illustrate the power of incentives and positive reinforcement:

> *He had got a hold of his sister's bead set and he somehow got one of them stuck up his nose. He tried to get it out, and the thing kept getting higher up his nose. I got him in the car to take him to the emergency room, and right as I was getting ready to park I said to him, "Andrew, Daddy loves you a lot. We've got to get this thing out. If we go to the emergency room, this is going to cost Dad about $150. But here's the deal: If you can figure out a way to blow that out of your nose [the goal], first, we'll go to Blockbuster and you can buy any tape you want. And second, we'll go to Bakers Square, and you and I will split a French silk pie [the positive rewards]." Well, he blew the thing out, and it almost cracked my windshield.*[78]

negative reinforcement reinforcement that strengthens behavior by withholding an unpleasant consequence when employees perform a specific behavior

punishment reinforcement that weakens behavior by following behaviors with undesirable consequences

extinction reinforcement in which a positive consequence is no longer allowed to follow a previously reinforced behavior, thus weakening the behavior

Negative reinforcement strengthens behavior by withholding an unpleasant consequence when employees perform a specific behavior. Negative reinforcement is also called *avoidance learning* because workers perform a behavior to *avoid* a negative consequence. For example, at the Florist Network, a small business in Buffalo, New York, company management instituted a policy of requiring good attendance for employees to receive their annual bonuses. Employee attendance has improved significantly now that excessive absenteeism can result in the loss of $1,500 or more.[79]

By contrast, **punishment** weakens behavior (that is, decreases its frequency) by following behaviors with undesirable consequences. For example, the standard disciplinary or punishment process in most companies is an oral warning ("Don't ever do that again"), followed by a written warning ("This letter is to discuss the serious problem you're having with . . ."), followed by three days off without pay ("While you're at home not being paid, we want you to think hard about . . ."), followed by being fired ("That was your last chance"). Though punishment can weaken behavior, managers have to be careful to avoid the backlash that sometimes occurs when employees are punished at work. For example, Frito-Lay began getting complaints from customers that they were finding potato chips with obscene messages written on them. Frito-Lay eventually traced the problem to a potato chip plant where supervisors had fired 58 out of the 210 workers for disciplinary reasons over a nine-month period. The remaining employees were so angry over what they saw as unfair treatment from management that they began writing the phrases on potato chips with felt-tipped pens.[80]

Extinction is a reinforcement strategy in which a positive consequence is no longer allowed to follow a previously reinforced behavior. By removing the positive consequence, extinction weakens the behavior, making it less likely to occur. Based on the idea of positive reinforcement, most companies give company leaders and managers substantial financial rewards when the company performs well. Based on the idea of extinction, you would then expect that leaders and managers would not be rewarded (that is, the positive consequence would be removed) when companies perform poorly. If companies really want pay to reinforce the right kinds of behaviors, then rewards have to be removed when company management doesn't produce successful performance. For example, with a $1 billion loss, sales down 28 percent, and the stock price down

35 percent, **Agilent**'s board of directors cut CEO Ned Barnholt's base pay by 10 percent and didn't award him a cash or stock bonus. Says Barnholt, "I don't expect anything different. If the company doesn't perform, I shouldn't be getting any rewards."[81] By contrast, even though the **Walt Disney Company**'s income dropped from $1.9 billion to $1.4 billion in four years, Disney rewarded then-CEO Michael Eisner with a large increase in salary, options for 2 million shares of stock worth $37.7 million, a $5 million restricted stock bonus, and an $11.5 million cash bonus.[82]

4.2 Schedules for Delivering Reinforcement

As mentioned earlier, a *schedule of reinforcement* is the set of rules regarding reinforcement contingencies, such as which behaviors will be reinforced, which consequences will follow those behaviors, and the schedule by which those consequences will be delivered. There are two categories of reinforcement schedules: continuous and intermittent.

continuous reinforcement schedule a schedule that requires a consequence to be administered following every instance of a behavior

intermittent reinforcement schedule a schedule in which consequences are delivered after a specified or average time has elapsed or after a specified or average number of behaviors has occurred

fixed interval reinforcement schedule an intermittent schedule in which consequences follow a behavior only after a fixed time has elapsed

variable interval reinforcement schedule an intermittent schedule in which the time between a behavior and the following consequences varies around a specified average

fixed ratio reinforcement schedule an intermittent schedule in which consequences are delivered following a specific number of behaviors

variable ratio reinforcement schedule an intermittent schedule in which consequences are delivered following a different number of behaviors, sometimes more and sometimes less, that vary around a specified average number of behaviors

With **continuous reinforcement schedules**, a consequence follows every instance of a behavior. For example, employees working on a piece-rate pay system earn money (consequence) for every part they manufacture (behavior). The more they produce, the more they earn. By contrast, with **intermittent reinforcement schedules**, consequences are delivered after a specified or average time has elapsed or after a specified or average number of behaviors has occurred. As Exhibit 13.13 shows, there are four types of intermittent reinforcement schedules. Two of these are based on time and are called *interval reinforcement schedules*, while the other two, known as *ratio schedules*, are based on behaviors.

With **fixed interval reinforcement schedules**, consequences follow a behavior only after a fixed time has elapsed. For example, most people receive their paychecks on a fixed interval schedule (for example, once or twice per month). As long as they work (behavior) during a specified pay period (interval), they get a paycheck (consequence). With **variable interval reinforcement schedules**, consequences follow a behavior after different times, some shorter and some longer, that vary around a specified average time. On a 90-day variable interval reinforcement schedule, you might receive a bonus after 80 days or perhaps after 100 days, but the average interval between performing your job well (behavior) and receiving your bonus (consequence) would be 90 days.

With **fixed ratio reinforcement schedules**, consequences are delivered following a specific number of behaviors. For example, a car salesperson might receive a $1,000 bonus after every 10 sales. Therefore, a salesperson with only 9 sales would not receive the bonus until he or she finally sold a 10th car.

With **variable ratio reinforcement schedules**, consequences are delivered following a different number of behaviors, sometimes more and sometimes less, that vary around a specified average number of behaviors. With a 10-car variable ratio

Exhibit 13.13
Intermittent Reinforcement Schedules

INTERMITTENT REINFORCEMENT SCHEDULES		
	FIXED	VARIABLE
INTERVAL (TIME)	Consequences follow behavior after a fixed time has elapsed.	Consequences follow behavior after different times, some shorter and some longer, that vary around a specific average time.
RATIO (BEHAVIOR)	Consequences follow a specific number of behaviors.	Consequences follow a different number of behaviors, sometimes more and sometimes less, that vary around a specified average number of behaviors.

reinforcement schedule, a salesperson might receive the bonus after 7 car sales, or after 12, 11, or 9 sales, but the average number of cars sold before receiving the bonus would be 10 cars.

Students often have trouble envisioning how these schedules can actually be used in work settings, so a couple of examples will help. In a study designed to increase employee attendance, employees who came to work participated in an innovative variable ratio schedule in which they drew a card from a deck of playing cards every day they came to work. At the end of each week, the employee with the best poker hand from those cards received a $20 bonus.[83] In another variable reinforcement system, **ELECTRIC BOAT**, which builds nuclear submarines, uses a lottery that gives workers with good attendance a chance to win sizable rewards. Eligibility for the various rewards depends on the level of attendance. For example, 933 workers with two years of perfect attendance were placed in a lottery in which 20 of them would win $2,500. Likewise, 1,400 workers with a year of perfect attendance were placed in a lottery where 75 would win $1,000, 50 would win $500, 25 would win prime parking spaces, and all would win a $25 gift certificate for the company store. Greg Angelini, who won a $1,000 prize, says, "I'm not a gambler, but it sure was nice to get that check right before Christmas. And it was just as nice that the powers that be noticed that I've had perfect attendance."[84] Electric Boat's lottery system is so rewarding that on average an amazing 41 percent of its workers have perfect attendance.

Which reinforcement schedules work best? In the past, the standard advice was to use continuous reinforcement when employees were learning new behaviors because reinforcement after each success leads to faster learning. Likewise, the standard advice was to use intermittent reinforcement schedules to maintain behavior after it is learned because intermittent rewards are supposed to make behavior much less subject to extinction.[85] Research shows, however, that except for interval-based systems, which usually produce weak results, the effectiveness of continuous reinforcement, fixed ratio, and variable ratio schedules differs very little.[86] In organizational settings, all three produce consistently large increases over noncontingent reward schedules. So managers should choose whichever of these three is easiest to use in their companies.

4.3 Motivating with Reinforcement Theory

What practical steps can managers take to use reinforcement theory to motivate employees? University of Nebraska business professor Fred Luthans, who has been studying the effects of reinforcement theory in organizations for more than a quarter of a century, says that there are five steps to motivating workers with reinforcement theory: *identify*, *measure*, *analyze*, *intervene*, and *evaluate* critical performance-related behaviors.[87]

Identify means identifying critical, observable, performance-related behaviors. These are the behaviors that are most important to successful job performance. In addition, they must also be easily observed so that they can be accurately measured. *Measure* means measuring the baseline frequencies of these behaviors. In other words, find out how often workers perform them. *Analyze* means analyzing the causes and consequences of these behaviors. Analyzing the causes helps managers create the conditions that produce these critical behaviors, and analyzing the consequences helps them determine if these behaviors produce the results that they want. *Intervene* means changing the organization by using positive and negative reinforcement to increase the frequency of these critical behaviors. *Evaluate* means evaluating the extent to which the intervention actually changed workers' behavior. This is done by comparing behavior after the intervention to the original baseline of behavior before the intervention. For more on the effectiveness of reinforcement theory, see the "What Really Works?" feature in this chapter.

In addition to these five steps, Exhibit 13.14 lists three other things that managers should remember when motivating with reinforcement theory. *Don't reinforce the wrong behaviors*. Although reinforcement theory sounds simple, it's actually very difficult to put into practice. One of the most common mistakes is accidentally reinforcing the wrong behaviors. In fact, sometimes managers reinforce behaviors that they don't want! If you want to become a merit-based company, stop rewarding behavior that is not exceptional, says Dave Anderson, a management consultant. According to him, "the average car salesperson in the United States sells 10 cars per month, but many pay plans begin to pay bonuses at 7, 8, 9, or 10 cars. Under a typical plan, an employee who sells 8 cars gets a $200 bonus, another $250 for selling 2 additional cars, and $300 for selling 2 more cars. The total bonus for selling 12 cars in a month is $750." Anderson notes, "Based on national averages, such a pay plan financially rewards average and below-average results." Many of his clients have revised their system and only pay an $800 bonus to an employee *after* he or she has sold 12 cars, thus ending bonus payments for employees who sell fewer than the target amount of cars.[88] In this system, you pay more for better performance but don't fall into the trap of rewarding and endorsing the wrong things, rewarding below average performance.

Managers should also *correctly administer punishment at the appropriate time*. Many managers believe that punishment can change workers' behavior and help them improve their job performance. Furthermore, managers believe that fairly punishing workers also lets other workers know what is or isn't acceptable.[89] A danger of using punishment is that it can produce a backlash against managers and companies, but if administered properly, punishment can weaken the frequency of undesirable behaviors without creating a backlash.[90] To be effective, the punishment must be strong enough to stop the undesired behavior and must be administered objectively (same rules applied to everyone), impersonally (without emotion or anger), consistently and contingently (each time improper behavior occurs), and quickly (as soon as possible following the undesirable behavior). In addition, managers should clearly explain what the appropriate behavior is and why the employee is being punished. Employees typically respond well when punishment is administered this way.[91]

Finally, managers should *choose the simplest and most effective schedule of reinforcement*. When choosing a schedule of reinforcement, managers need to balance effectiveness against simplicity. In fact, the more complex the schedule of reinforcement, the more likely it is to be misunderstood and resisted by managers and employees. For example, a forestry and logging company experimented with a unique variable ratio schedule. When tree-planters finished planting a bag of seedlings (about 1,000 seedlings per bag), they got to flip a coin. If they called the coin flip correctly (heads or tails), they were paid $4, double the regular rate of $2 per bag. If they called the coin flip incorrectly, they got nothing. The company began having problems when several workers and a manager, who was a part-time minister, claimed that the coin flip was a form of gambling. Then, another worker found that the company was taking out too much money for taxes from workers' paychecks. Since the workers didn't really understand

Exhibit 13.14

Motivating with Reinforcement Theory

- Identify, measure, analyze, intervene, and evaluate critical performance-related behaviors.
- Don't reinforce the wrong behaviors.
- Correctly administer punishment at the appropriate time.
- Choose the simplest and most effective schedule of reinforcement.

FINANCIAL, NONFINANCIAL, AND SOCIAL REWARDS

what really works.

Throughout this chapter, we have been making the point that there is more to motivating people than money. But we haven't yet examined how well financial (money or prizes), nonfinancial (performance feedback), and social (recognition and attention) rewards motivate workers by themselves or in combination. However, the results of two meta-analyses, one with 19 studies based on more than 2,800 people (study 1) and another based on 72 studies and 13,301 people (study 2), clearly indicate that rewarding and reinforcing employees greatly improve motivation and performance, especially when combined.

FINANCIAL REWARDS

On average, there is a 68 percent chance that employees whose behavior is reinforced with financial rewards will outperform employees whose behavior is not reinforced. This increases to 84 percent in manufacturing organizations but drops to 61 percent in service organizations.

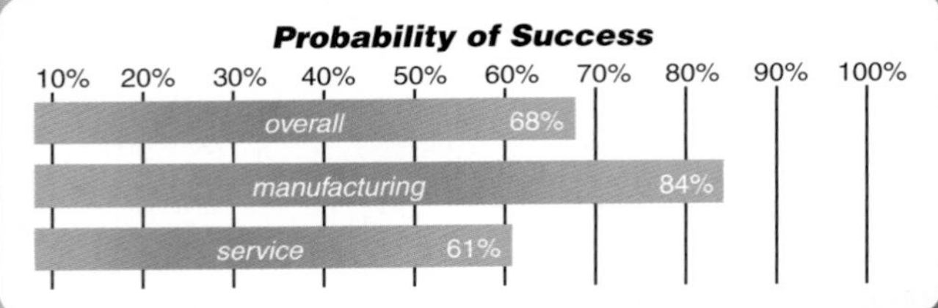

NONFINANCIAL REWARDS

On average, there is a 58 percent chance that employees whose behavior is reinforced with nonfinancial rewards will outperform employees whose behavior is not reinforced. This increases to 87 percent in manufacturing organizations but drops to 54 percent in service organizations.

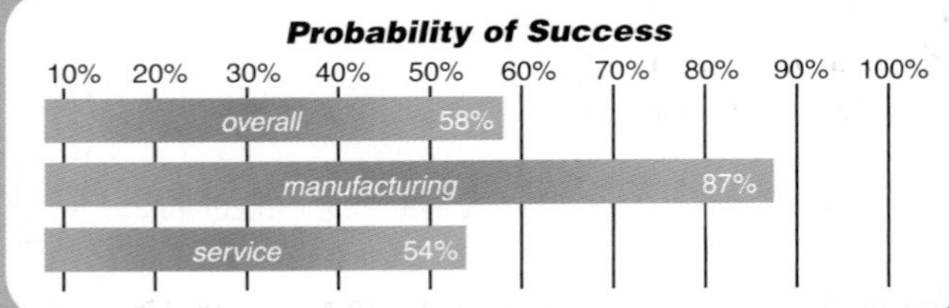

SOCIAL REWARDS

On average, there is a 63 percent chance that employees whose behavior is reinforced with social rewards will outperform employees whose behavior is not reinforced.

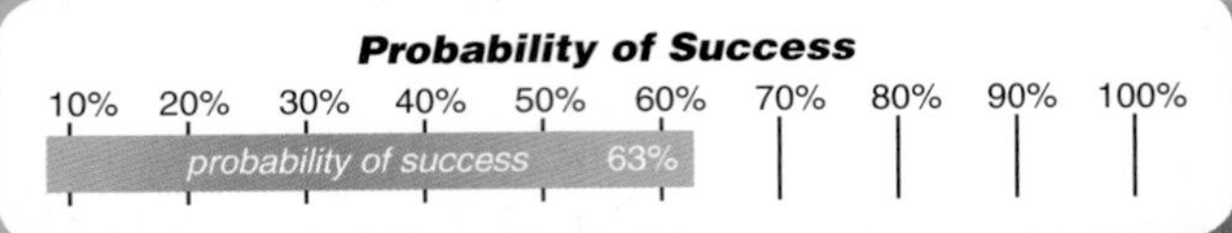

FINANCIAL AND NONFINANCIAL REWARDS

On average, there is a 62 percent chance that employees whose behavior is reinforced with a combination of financial and nonfinancial rewards will outperform employees whose behavior is not reinforced.

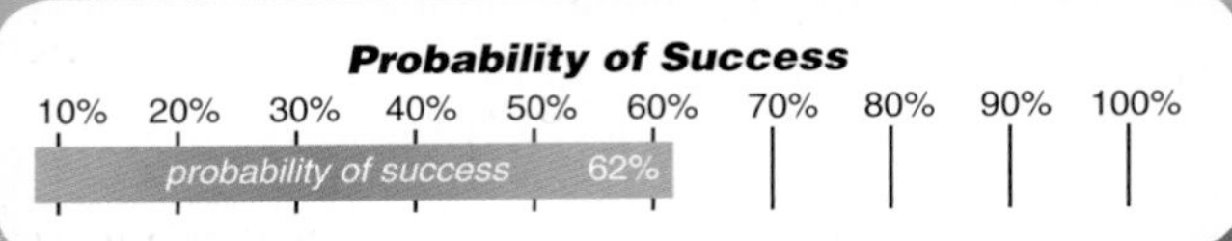

FINANCIAL AND SOCIAL REWARDS

On average, there is only a 52 percent chance that employees whose behavior is reinforced with a combination of financial and social rewards will outperform employees whose behavior is not reinforced.

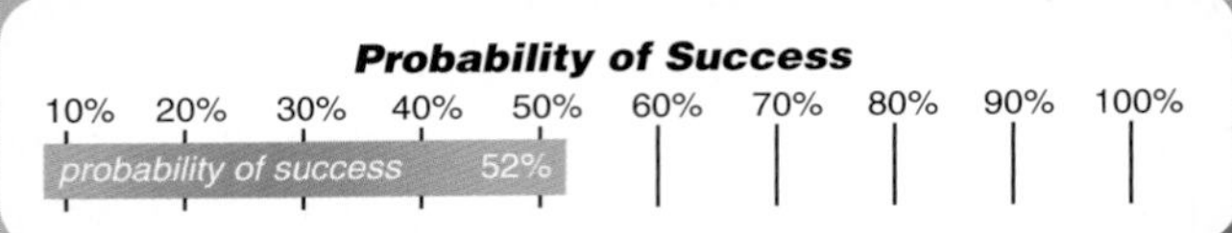

NONFINANCIAL AND SOCIAL REWARDS

On average, there is a 61 percent chance that employees whose behavior is reinforced with a combination of nonfinancial and social rewards will outperform employees whose behavior is not reinforced.

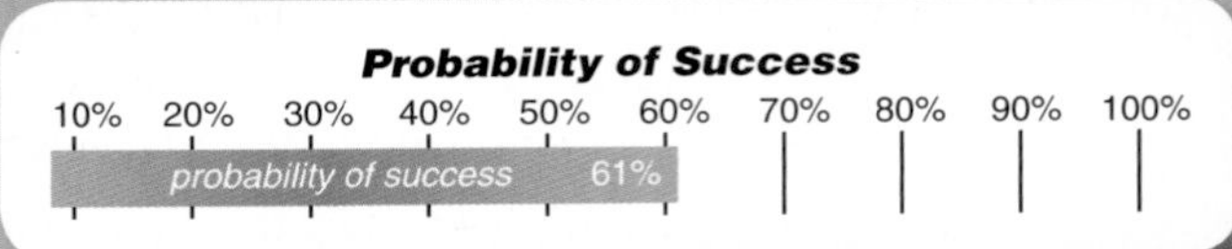

FINANCIAL, NONFINANCIAL, AND SOCIAL REWARDS

On average, there is a 90 percent chance that employees whose behavior is reinforced with a combination of financial, nonfinancial, and social rewards will outperform employees whose behavior is not reinforced.[92]

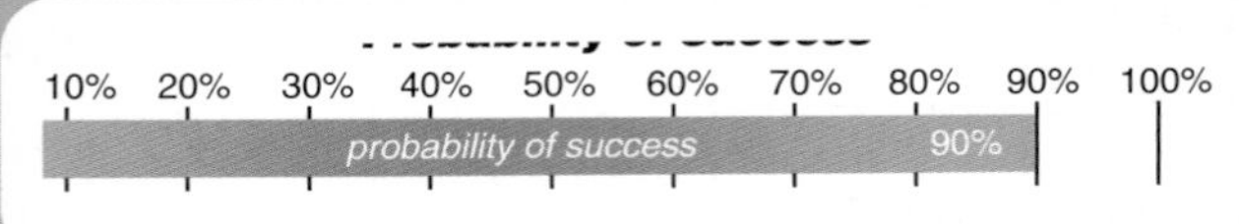

the reinforcement schedule, they blamed the payment plan associated with it and accused the company of trying to cheat them out of their money. After all of these problems, the researchers who implemented the variable ratio schedule concluded that "the results of this study may not be so much an indication of the relative effectiveness of different schedules of reinforcement as they are an indication of the types of problems that one encounters when applying these concepts in an industrial setting."[93] In short, choose the simplest, most effective schedule of reinforcement. Since continuous reinforcement, fixed ratio, and variable ratio schedules are about equally effective, continuous reinforcement schedules may be the best choice in many instances by virtue of their simplicity.

Review 4: **Reinforcement Theory**

Reinforcement theory says that behavior is a function of its consequences. Reinforcement has two parts: reinforcement contingencies and schedules of reinforcement. The four kinds of reinforcement contingencies are positive reinforcement and negative reinforcement, which strengthen behavior, and punishment and extinction, which weaken behavior. There are two kinds of reinforcement schedules, continuous and intermittent; intermittent schedules, in turn, can be divided into fixed and variable interval schedules and fixed and variable ratio schedules. Managers can use reinforcement theory to motivate workers by following five steps (identify, measure, analyze, intervene, and evaluate critical performance-related behaviors); not reinforcing the wrong behaviors; correctly administering punishment at the appropriate time; and choosing a reinforcement schedule, such as continuous reinforcement, that balances simplicity and effectiveness.

5 Goal-Setting Theory

The basic model of motivation with which we began this chapter showed that individuals feel tension after becoming aware of an unfulfilled need. Once they experience tension, they search for and select courses of action that they believe will eliminate this tension. In other words, they direct their behavior toward something. This something is a goal. A **goal** is a target, objective, or result that someone tries to accomplish. For example, one of the goals of discount airline **JETBLUE** is that all the baggage on a plane be delivered to the baggage pickup area no later than 20 minutes after the plane reaches the gate. Why? Because, as JetBlue CEO Dave Barger explains, "The 45 minutes you wait for your bags is your last impression," and a strongly negative one at that.[94] JetBlue also has specific goals for completion rate (the percentage of flights that aren't canceled) and on-time arrivals. Last year, JetBlue was first in the industry in completion rate and second in on-time arrivals.

goal a target, objective, or result that someone tries to accomplish

goal-setting theory the theory that people will be motivated to the extent to which they accept specific, challenging goals and receive feedback that indicates their progress toward goal achievement

Goal-setting theory *says that people will be motivated to the extent to which they accept specific, challenging goals and receive feedback that indicates their progress toward goal achievement. Let's learn more about goal setting by examining* ***5.1 the components of goal-setting theory*** *and* ***5.2 how to motivate with goal-setting theory.***

5.1 Components of Goal-Setting Theory

The basic components of goal-setting theory are goal specificity, goal difficulty, goal acceptance, and performance feedback.[95] **Goal specificity** is the extent to which goals are detailed, exact, and unambiguous. Specific goals, such as "I'm going to have a 3.0 average this semester," are more motivating than general goals, such as "I'm going to get better grades this semester."

Goal difficulty is the extent to which a goal is hard or challenging to accomplish. Difficult goals, such as "I'm going to have a 3.5 average and make the Dean's List this semester," are more motivating than easy goals, such as "I'm going to have a 2.0 average this semester."

Goal acceptance, which is similar to the idea of goal commitment discussed in Chapter 5, is the extent to which people consciously understand and agree to goals. Accepted goals, such as "I really want to get a 3.5 average this semester to show my parents how much I've improved," are more motivating than unaccepted goals, such as "My parents really want me to get a 3.5 average this semester, but there's so much more I'd rather do on campus than study!"

Performance feedback is information about the quality or quantity of past performance and indicates whether progress is being made toward the accomplishment of a goal. Performance feedback, such as "My prof said I need a 92 on the final to get an 'A' in that class," is more motivating than no feedback, "I have no idea what my grade is in that class." In short, goal-setting theory says that people will be motivated to the extent to which they accept specific, challenging goals and receive feedback that indicates their progress toward goal achievement.

How does goal setting work? To start, challenging goals focus employees' attention (that is, direction of effort) on the critical aspects of their jobs and away from unimportant areas. Goals also energize behavior. When faced with unaccomplished goals, employees typically develop plans and strategies to reach those goals. Goals also create tension between the goal, which is the desired future state of affairs, and where the employee or company is now, meaning the current state of affairs. This tension can be satisfied only by achieving or abandoning the goal. Finally, goals influence persistence. Since goals only "go away" when they are accomplished, employees are more likely to persist in their efforts in the presence of goals. Exhibit 13.15 incorporates goals into the motivation model by showing how goals directly affect tension, effort, and the extent to which employees are energized to take action.

5.2 Motivating with Goal-Setting Theory

What practical steps can managers take to use goal-setting theory to motivate employees? Exhibit 13.16 lists three suggestions beginning with *assign specific, challenging goals*. One of the simplest, most effective ways to motivate workers is to give them specific, challenging goals.

For example, although CDW (Computer Discount Warehouse) offers fantastic benefits and rewards, senior publicist Gary Ross says, "It's not a cushy place to work." According to vice president Art Friedson, CDW sets company-wide "Big Hairy Aggressive Goals," such as "A Million for a Billion," in which everyone in the company would split $1 million in bonuses (about $500 per employee at the time) when CDW booked $1 billion in annual sales.[96] With that accomplished, the next BHAG was $3 billion in annual sales with a payout of $5 million in bonuses (about $2,500 per employee at the time). And with that accomplished, the BHAG is now $10 billion in annual sales (sales were $6.8 billion last year). For more information on assigning specific, challenging goals, see the discussion in Chapter 5 on S.M.A.R.T. goals.

goal specificity the extent to which goals are detailed, exact, and unambiguous

goal difficulty the extent to which a goal is hard or challenging to accomplish

goal acceptance the extent to which people consciously understand and agree to goals

performance feedback information about the quality or quantity of past performance that indicates whether progress is being made toward the accomplishment of a goal

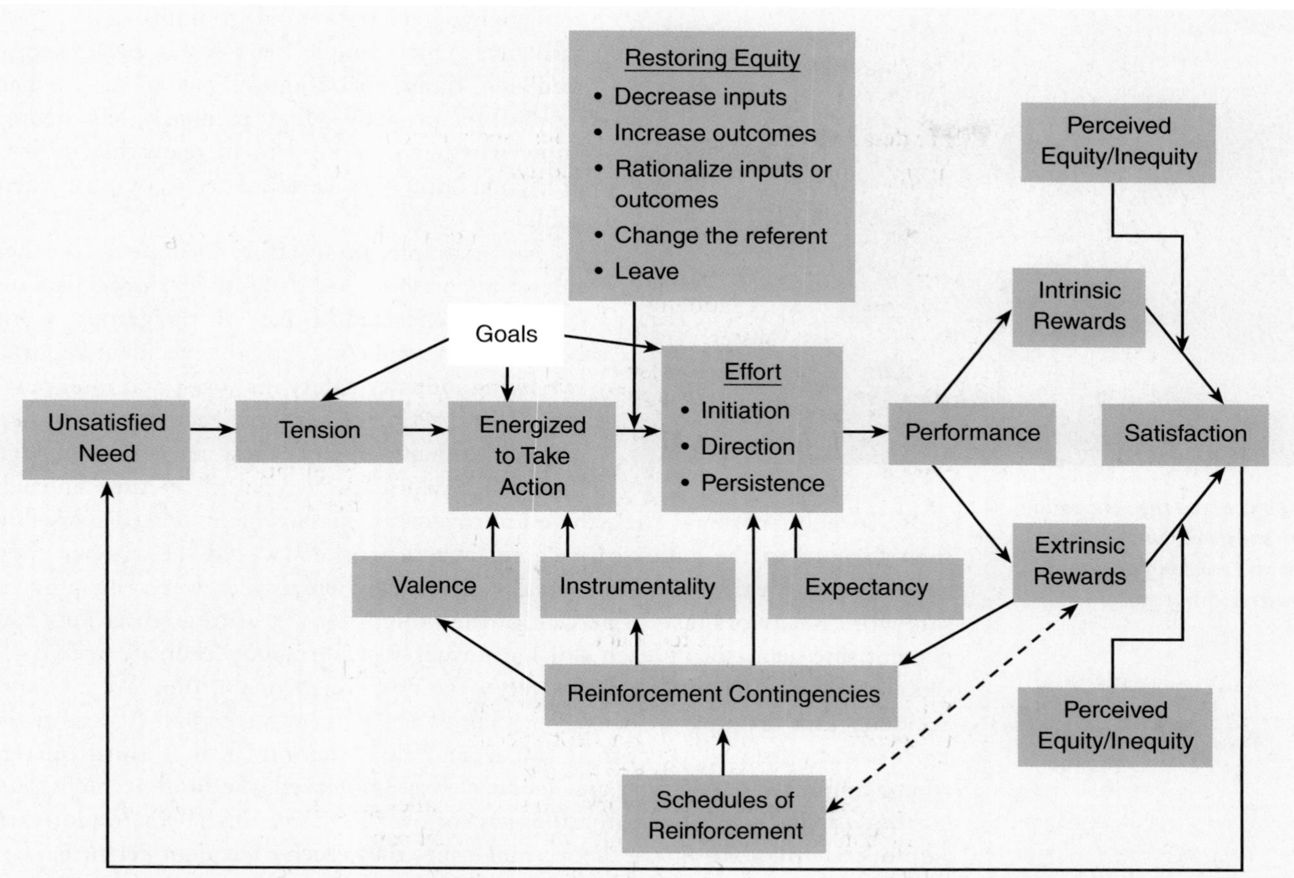

Goals create tension between the goal, which is the desired future state of affairs, and where the employee or company is now, meaning the current state of affairs. This tension can be satisfied only by achieving or abandoning the goal. Goals also energize behavior. When faced with unaccomplished goals, employees typically develop plans and strategies to reach those goals. Finally, goals influence persistence.

Exhibit 13.15
Adding Goal-Setting Theory to the Model

Second, managers should *make sure workers truly accept organizational goals*. Specific, challenging goals won't motivate workers unless they really accept, understand, and agree to the organization's goals. For this to occur, people must see the goals as fair and reasonable. Plus, they must trust management and believe that managers are using goals to clarify what is expected from them rather than to exploit or threaten them ("If you don't achieve these goals . . . "). Participative goal setting, in which managers and employees generate goals together, can help increase trust and understanding and thus acceptance of goals. Furthermore, providing workers with training can help increase goal acceptance, particularly when workers don't believe they are capable of reaching the organization's goals.[97]

Finally, managers should *provide frequent, specific, performance-related feedback*. Once employees have accepted specific, challenging goals, they should receive frequent performance-related feedback so that they can track their progress toward goal completion. Feedback leads to stronger motivation and effort in three ways.[98] Receiving specific feedback that indicates how well they're performing can encourage employees who don't have specific,

Exhibit 13.16
Motivating with Goal-Setting Theory

- Assign specific, challenging goals.
- Make sure workers truly accept organizational goals.
- Provide frequent, specific, performance-related feedback.

© STOCK CONNECTION/JUPITER IMAGES

What increased the safe behavior on the oil rig was setting goals and tracking progress toward reaching them.

challenging goals to set goals to improve their performance. Once people meet goals, performance feedback often encourages them to set higher, more difficult goals. And feedback lets people know whether they need to increase their efforts or change strategies in order to accomplish their goals.

For example, in an effort to improve worker safety on offshore oil-drilling platforms, an oil company generated a list of dangerous work behaviors by analyzing previous accident reports, reviewing industry safety manuals, and interviewing and observing workers. Following detailed safety training, each work crew set goals to engage in safe behaviors 100 percent of the time on each shift. To help workers track their improvement, management posted a weekly safety record in the galley of each rig, where workers would see it when they gathered for meals and coffee breaks. Previously, employees were engaging in safe work behaviors just 76 percent of the time. After a year of goal setting (100 percent safe behavior on each shift) and weekly performance feedback at two oil rigs, however, workers behaved safely over 90 percent of the time. As a result, accident rates dropped from 21.1 percent to 6.1 percent at the first rig and from 14.2 percent to 12.1 percent at the second rig. By contrast, at a third oil rig, where training, goal setting, and feedback were not used, the total accident rate *increased* from 11.6 percent to 20.3 percent over the same time.[99] So, to motivate employees with goal-setting theory, make sure they receive frequent performance-related feedback so that they can track their progress toward goal completion.

Review 5: **Goal-Setting Theory**

A goal is a target, objective, or result that someone tries to accomplish. Goal-setting theory says that people will be motivated to the extent to which they accept specific, challenging goals and receive feedback that indicates their progress toward goal achievement. The basic components of goal-setting theory are goal specificity, goal difficulty, goal acceptance, and performance feedback. Goal specificity is the extent to which goals are detailed, exact, and unambiguous. Goal difficulty is the extent to which a goal is hard or challenging to accomplish. Goal acceptance is the extent to which people consciously understand and agree to goals. Performance feedback is information about the quality or quantity of past performance and indicates whether progress is being made toward the accomplishment of a goal. Managers can use goal-setting theory to motivate workers by assigning specific, challenging goals, making sure workers truly accept organizational goals, and providing frequent, specific, performance-related feedback.

We began this chapter by defining motivation as the set of forces that initiates, directs, and makes people persist in their efforts to accomplish a goal. We also asked the basic question that managers ask when they try to figure out how to

MOTIVATING WITH	MANAGERS SHOULD...
THE BASICS	• Ask people what their needs are. • Satisfy lower-order needs first. • Expect people's needs to change. • As needs change and lower-order needs are satisfied, create opportunities for employees to satisfy higher-order needs.
EQUITY THEORY	• Look for and correct major inequities. • Reduce employees' inputs. • Make sure decision-making processes are fair.
EXPECTANCY THEORY	• Systematically gather information to find out what employees want from their jobs. • Take specific steps to link rewards to individual performance in a way that is clear and understandable to employees. • Empower employees to make decisions if management really wants them to believe that their hard work and efforts will lead to good performance.
REINFORCEMENT THEORY	• Identify, measure, analyze, intervene, and evaluate critical performance-related behaviors. • Don't reinforce the wrong behaviors. • Correctly administer punishment at the appropriate time. • Choose the simplest and most effective schedule of reinforcement.
GOAL-SETTING THEORY	• Assign specific, challenging goals. • Make sure workers truly accept organizational goals. • Provide frequent, specific, performance-related feedback.

Exhibit 13.17

Motivating with the Integrated Model

motivate their workers: "What leads to effort?" Though the answer to that question is likely to be somewhat different for each employee, Exhibit 13.17 helps you begin to answer it by consolidating the practical advice from the theories reviewed in this chapter in one convenient location. So, if you're having difficulty figuring out why people aren't motivated where you work, Exhibit 13.17 provides a useful, theory-based starting point.

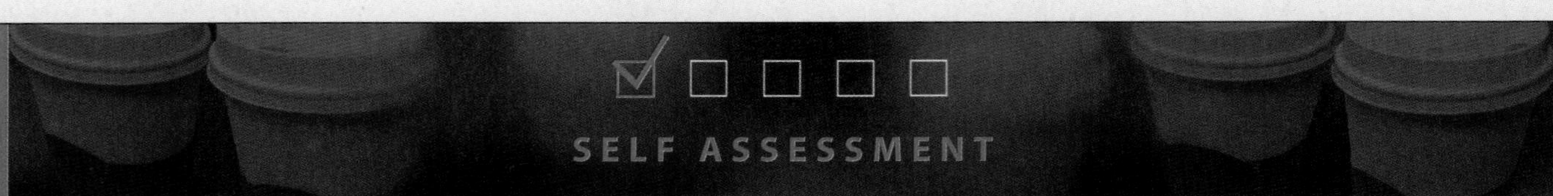

What Do You Need?

What people want out of their jobs is as varied as the jobs themselves.[100] And as you would expect, need theories show why not everyone wants to be CEO. Take the example of the woman who is extremely organized and efficient in her job as an assistant. She is so effective that she is offered a promotion to management, but she turns it down flatly, saying that she has no interest in moving up the ladder, that she is happy doing what she does. What she needs from work clearly differs from the needs of the person who jumps at every opportunity to move up the corporate hierarchy. Not everyone needs or wants the same things from their jobs.[101] Indicate the extent to which you agree with each of the following statements. Try not to spend too much time on any one item, and be sure to answer all the questions. Use this scale for your responses:

1 Strongly disagree
2 Disagree
3 Slightly disagree
4 Neutral
5 Slightly agree
6 Agree
7 Strongly agree

1. I get enough money from my job to live comfortably.
   1 2 3 4 5 6 7
2. Our benefits cover many of the areas they should.
   1 2 3 4 5 6 7
3. My boss encourages people to make suggestions.
   1 2 3 4 5 6 7
4. I can count on my coworkers to give me a hand when I need it.
   1 2 3 4 5 6 7
5. I always get the feeling of learning new things from my work.
   1 2 3 4 5 6 7
6. I often think about how to improve my job performance.
   1 2 3 4 5 6 7
7. My pay is adequate to provide for the basic things in life.
   1 2 3 4 5 6 7
8. The benefit program here gives nearly all the security I want.
   1 2 3 4 5 6 7
9. My boss takes account of my wishes and desires.
   1 2 3 4 5 6 7
10. My coworkers will speak out in my favor if justified.
    1 2 3 4 5 6 7
11. My job requires that a person use a wide range of abilities.
    1 2 3 4 5 6 7
12. I will actively try to improve my job performance in the future.
    1 2 3 4 5 6 7
13. Considering the work required, the pay is what it should be.
    1 2 3 4 5 6 7
14. Compared to other places, our benefits are excellent.
    1 2 3 4 5 6 7
15. My boss keeps me informed about what is happening in the company.
    1 2 3 4 5 6 7
16. I can tell my coworkers how I honestly feel.
    1 2 3 4 5 6 7
17. My job requires making one (or more) important decision(s) every day.
    1 2 3 4 5 6 7
18. I intend to do a lot more at work in the future.
    1 2 3 4 5 6 7

KEY TERMS

19. Compared to the rates for similar work, here, my pay is good.
    1 2 3 4 5 6 7
20. The benefit program here is adequate.
    1 2 3 4 5 6 7
21. My boss lets me know when I could improve my performance.
    1 2 3 4 5 6 7
22. My coworkers welcome opinions different from their own.
    1 2 3 4 5 6 7
23. I have the opportunity to do challenging things at work.
    1 2 3 4 5 6 7
24. I will probably do my best to perform well on the job in the future.
    1 2 3 4 5 6 7

Scoring

(A) Add together your scores for items 1, 2, 7, 8, 13, 14, 19, and 20: ____

(B) Add together your scores for items 3, 4, 9, 10, 15, 16, 21, and 22: ____

(C) Add together your scores for items 5, 6, 11, 12, 17, 18, 23, and 24: ____

You can find the interpretation for your score at: **academic.cengage.com/management/williams.**

(continued)

schedule of reinforcement 492
underreward 483
valence 488
variable interval reinforcement schedule 495
variable ratio reinforcement schedule 495

Motivating an "A" Who's Getting "Fs"

You have definitely reached a low point. Frustrated by an employee who is uncooperative, unmotivated, and sloppy about his work, you have resorted to writing a "Dear Abby" style letter to a columnist in a popular business magazine. Letting out a heavy sigh, you scroll back to the top of your screen to review your work:

Dear Business Guru,

A few months ago, I was promoted into my first management job at the greeting card company where I work. I inherited a whiz-bang team, full of talent and energy, with the exception of one person—Let's call him David. Unlike the others on our team, he is uncooperative and unmotivated, and his work is sloppy, even though I know he can do better! Several veteran employees have told me David used to be the crown jewel in the team, working hard, collaborating, and generating great ideas. But now he's altogether different. I'm reluctant to fire him for two reasons: from a technical standpoint, he would be difficult to replace; and our division is under an indefinite hiring freeze. But his attitude and performance are having a negative impact on the rest of the team. What can I do to pull this guy out of a slump? Evidently, he was quite the employee—and I need him to be that star employee again.

Pausing for a moment before hitting "send," your eyes fall on an old management book in your overhead. Grabbing it, you say to yourself, "There's got to be something in there to help me." But as you flip through the pages, you can't help thinking of all the time you've already spent on this guy. Maybe you should just fire him and be done.

Questions

1. Which motivational theory discussed in the chapter do you think would be most successful in helping David rekindle his spark? Why?
2. Which motivational theory will be most helpful in refocusing the efforts of your entire team? Explain.
3. Do you fire David or keep him on your team?

Mining Human Capital

Labor is probably the single largest expense of any business.[102] According to some estimates, labor costs average about 60 percent of sales. In addition to salaries, labor costs include health insurance, paid time off, child-care benefits, tuition reimbursements, and any number of other programs designed to extrinsically motivate the work force. Many companies offer the same types of benefits across their organizations without knowing whether the benefits really motivate employees at all. In other words, companies often don't know what return they are getting on their labor investment. The same is true where you work.

As you head back to your desk from a meeting on cafeteria-style benefit plans, your boss intercepts you and says she wants to talk with you about cutting labor costs. As she plops into your side chair, she is already describing a new type of software that applies data-mining technology to employee information to determine what is the best motivator. "We can get rid of one-size-fits-all benefit programs and tailor the benefits to each employee. This software lets you slice and dice employee data, like age, seniority, education, commute time, residential ZIP code, even the age and condition of the person's office," she says. "We could find out if we could pay someone, say, 20 percent less if we gave a three-month sabbatical every couple of years. Or we could predict the reaction of certain employees if we cut our 401(k) match. Maybe that's not as important to everyone as we think. We could find out who would quit if we did that and who couldn't care less. Basically, we could find out what incentives would spike productivity the most with each employee, and that way we could cut costs without sabotaging morale. It would reduce the guesswork of rewarding our employees. Here is some literature on the various programs. I'd like your team to draft a recommendation to top management by next Monday. I'm really excited about this." She leaves a small stack of brochures on your desk corner and leaves your office.

All you can do is wonder, "What will the employees think of this idea?"

Assemble a team of three to four students to review the issue of mining human resource data for information to help you customize incentives.

Questions

1. Which motivational theory provides the biggest justification for employee data mining? Explain.
2. Does employee data mining violate any of the motivational theories? If so, which ones and how?
3. Will your team recommend mining employee data or, despite your boss's enthusiasm, will you present reasons not to begin mining employee data? Explain your choice, using the motivational theories in the chapter as support for your recommendation.

Motivation is an invisible and powerful force. Strong motivation can drive individuals and organizations to remarkable heights of achievement. A loss of motivation can leave us dispirited and ineffective. One of the fundamental responsibilities of managers is to support healthy worker motivation. This exercise will allow you to practice designing support for worker motivation.

Step 1: Divide intro groups. Your professor will organize you in pairs or groups of three.

Step 2: Prepare interviews. Between this class session and the target date set by your professor, you and your partner(s) will each interview two individuals about motivation at work. You should brainstorm about possible types of work, interesting individuals, and so on, and then agree on each partner's list of interviewees/jobholders.

Some considerations for brainstorming include jobs or types of work that you consider particularly interesting, appealing, or mysterious; jobs or types of work that you consider particularly uninteresting, dull, or monotonous (how does a person do that work day after day?); and self-employed or creative work (how do such workers manage their own motivation without a boss or supervisor?)

Step 3: Conduct interviews. Outside of class each student should complete their assigned interviews. Inform the potential interviewee that you are interested in talking about workplace motivation. Set a time that is convenient and ensure that you arrive on time and prepared. Make the interview brief, with 15–20 minutes a good target. Go beyond 20 minutes only if the interviewee gives permission and the discussion is lively. Be sure to thank the interviewee for taking the time to visit with you.

Your instructor may give additional instructions for these interviews, and you should carefully follow these guidelines in conducting the interview.

Interview questions might include the following:

1. How would you describe your work? What are some of the things that you particularly like about your work?
2. We are currently studying the topic of motivation in one of my classes. What boosts your motivation at work? If you have ever experienced a period of low motivation, can you identify things that might have contributed to your losing steam in your work?
3. What kinds of rewards or incentives work best to motivate individuals and/or teams who do your type of work? What kinds of rewards or incentives don't work so well?

Step 4: Summarize your findings. Write a one-page paper summarizing your interview findings. Be prepared to compare notes with your partners, and to contribute to class discussion.

Step 5: Debrief as a class. Pairs/small groups report their findings and discuss as a class. What did you learn from your interviews? Did you notice common themes or issues across the interviews you conducted? Did you notice any striking differences across individuals or types of work? What are some possible implications of these interview findings for managers who are responsible for cultivating healthy motivation in a particular work setting?

Cut Your Costs, Not Your Morale

Management textbooks abound with discussions of the importance of honest and open communication when disseminating negative information to employees.[103] One study suggests that the best way to ruin morale and motivation is to spring bad news on employees without explaining the reasoning or rationale. Yet, despite the need to maintain a high level of motivation and morale during a receding economy, many companies cut perks without communicating the need to their employees. During the high-tech boom at the end of the 20th century, many companies implemented programs to increase productivity, motivation, and job satisfaction. Some of the perks provided were minor, such as free soft drinks, catered lunches, snacks, and tickets to events such as a baseball game or the opera. Other free perks were more extravagant, such as concierge services to run errands for employees, service their vehicles, and pick up their laundry. Some firms even provided their employees with in-house massages and annual Caribbean cruises. Obviously, cutting these non-value-added expenses can save tremendous money for a struggling firm. In fact, many firms cut out both the extravagant perks and the basics as a way to conserve much-needed cash. Cutting perks, however, doesn't have to be forever. Perks can be powerful motivational tools that companies can reintegrate into their performance reward systems.

For this assignment, consider your own budget and expenses in terms of revenue and perks. Imagine that like so many companies, you experience a cash crunch. Your revenue (income) shrinks 25 percent, so you must trim some fat from your budget.

Exercises

1. First, you will need to review your expenditures. What "perks" have you built into your budget as a student? (Think pizza and beer.) Make a list of all your non-value-added expenses. This includes anything not directly related to your studies (like books, tuition, enrollment fees, pens, paper) or your fixed expenses (like rent, car payments, insurance).
2. If you experienced a 25 percent reduction in your income—as numerous firms did after the tech bubble burst—which perks would you eliminate? In addition, are there items that you previously considered necessities that you could cut out? An example would be selling your car (thereby

eliminating car payments and related insurance) and taking public transportation or catching a ride with a friend. What about getting a roommate, moving into the dorms, or living with your parents?

3. Often employees develop a sense of entitlement about perks, and when the perks are trimmed, great dissatisfaction can result. Companies even lose employees when perks are cut. In this exercise, let's consider that cutting out your non-value-added (that is, fun) expenditures may put a crimp in your social life. In fact, you may have trouble staying in the loop. What can you do to "retain" your social friends as you cut down on your personal perks? Do you think that "retention" will even be an issue for you? Why or why not?

4. Once you have taken the ax to your perks, how can you reincorporate them into your budget, this time as motivational tools? Which perks would motivate you to have perfect attendance in class? To make an A? Straight As? Be creative. The purpose is to see if you can modify your own behavior by using your perks.

REEL TO REAL

BIZ FLIX

For Love of the Game

Billy Chapel (Kevin Costner), a 20-year veteran pitcher with the Detroit Tigers, learns just before the season's last game that the team's new owners want to trade him. He also learns that his partner, Jane Aubrey (Kelly Preston), intends to leave him. Faced with these daunting blows, Chapel, who decides to retire, wants to pitch a perfect final game. Director Sam Raimi's love of baseball shines through in some striking visual effects.

This scene is a slightly edited version of the "Just Throw" sequence, which begins the film's exciting closing scenes in which Chapel pitches his last game. In this scene, the Tigers' catcher Gus Sinski (John C. Reilly) comes out to the pitching mound to talk to Billy.

What to Watch for and Ask Yourself

1. How would you describe Billy Chapel's esteem needs at this point in the game?
2. Do you expect Gus Sinski's talk to have any effect on Chapel? If it will, what will be the effect? Why?
3. What rewards potentially exist for Billy Chapel? Remember, this is the last baseball game of his career.

MANAGEMENT WORKPLACE

P. F. Chang's—Motivating Workers Who Already Like Their Jobs

What motivates you—money, prestige, fear, vacation, recognition, or something else altogether different? Not everyone is motivated by the same things. The same is true for workers everywhere, including P. F. Chang's bistros. It's easy to see what motivates managers and executives at P. F. Chang's: They want customers to love the food and atmosphere, they want their business to succeed and grow, and they want to earn a good living in return for their investment and hard work. "We are truly glad you are here," says P. F. Chang's motto, "and we will do everything possible to make you want to come back again." This is the biggest motivation of all—to have customers come back. But what motivates the employees at P. F. Chang's—the wait staff, bartenders, hosts, chefs and kitchen crew, bussers, and dishwashers?

Questions

1. P. F. Chang's offers a menu of extrinsic rewards to its workers. What are some of the intrinsic rewards?
2. In what ways might managers at P. F. Chang's use positive reinforcement for their kitchen crew or wait staff?
3. Do you think managers at P. F. Chang's would be successful using expectancy theory? Explain.

CHAPTER 14

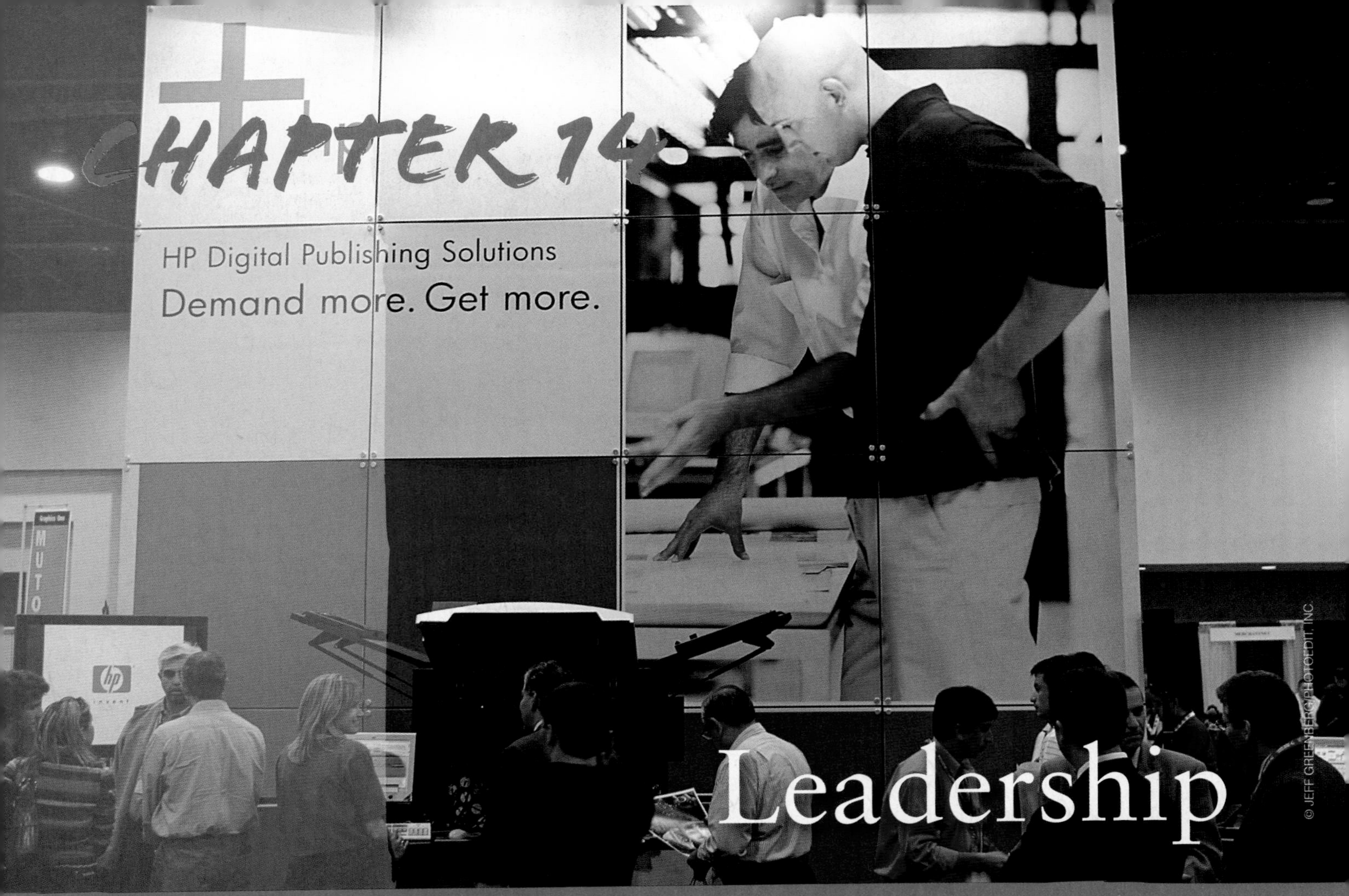

Leadership

© JEFF GREENBERG/PHOTOEDIT, INC.

Learning Outcomes:

1 Explain what leadership is.
2 Describe who leaders are and what effective leaders do.
3 Explain Fiedler's contingency theory.
4 Describe how path-goal theory works.
5 Discuss Hersey and Blanchard's Situational Leadership theory.
6 Explain the normative decision theory.
7 Explain how visionary leadership (that is, charismatic and transformational leadership) helps leaders achieve strategic leadership.

In This Chapter:

WHAT WOULD YOU DO?

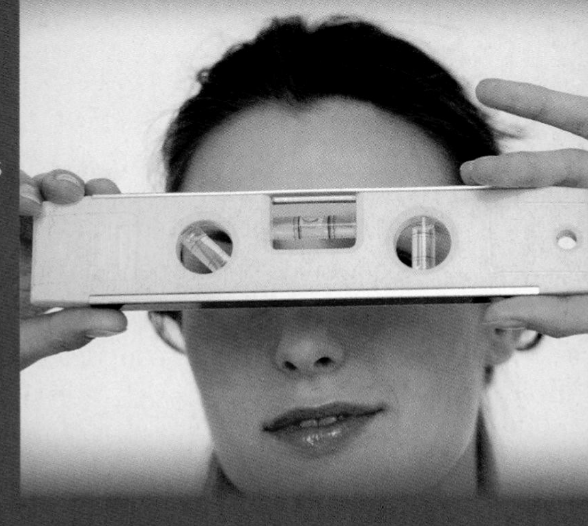

Hewlett-Packard Headquarters, Palo Alto, California.[1] As CEO at your previous company, you had to make plenty of tough decisions to turn things around. And not everyone was happy when you did. A laid-off employee tracked you down after hours on a basketball court, pushed you around, and later made repeated death threats against you and your family. Then, after another round of cost-cutting decisions, your and your top management team's car tires were slashed in the parking lot. But compared to the mess that you're in now as CEO of Hewlett-Packard, those were the good old days.

Since your predecessor, Carly Fiorina, was fired by the board, you expected to find a number of significant problems, the first of which was HP's strategic vision, which Fiorina had repeatedly described as "digital, virtual, mobile, personal." While this sounded good, no one was quite sure what it meant. But was it a bad strategy, or was HP just doing a poor job of executing it? This would take some time to figure out. Another problem was the confusing matrix structure, which blurred lines of accountability and slowed decision making. For example, HP's sales force was separate from the printing, computing, and corporate products divisions that were at the heart of the company. This meant that HP's salespeople sold everything from high-end corporate servers to low-end personal computers for consumers. Effectively, it also meant that instead of reporting to just one division, HP salespeople reported to people in four or more divisions, such as sales, printing, computing, and corporate. Carol Potts, one of your sales vice presidents in Chicago, complained, "We were very matrixed." A third problem was the reward system, which was so complex in its calculation that no one understood how their performance affected their bonuses. A fourth well-known problem was that HP was struggling financially. Under Fiorina's guidance, HP had paid $19 billion to acquire Compaq Computers, but then incurred, according to some estimates, more than $10 billion in expenses to integrate Compaq into HP. In short, expenses had risen too much, revenues and market share had risen too little, and HP was earning profits far below its competition.

But what worried you most of all was the deep sense of distrust that pervaded HP. The first sentence in the "HP Way," a set of corporate objectives written by founders Bill Hewlett and Dave Packard in 1957, says, "We have trust and respect for individuals." At HP, people were supposed to be as important as profits, but that was no longer the case. Some employees toasted Fiorina's departure with champagne, but the HP Way had been deteriorating long before she became CEO. Plus, top executives were leaving left and right and HP was unable to attract talented replacements. Finally, the board of directors was a dysfunctional soap opera. Patricia Dunn, the board chair, authorized an investigation to spy on board members' phone records to determine who was leaking confidential information to the press. When the leaker was confronted, another board member angrily resigned and contacted the press to air the story.

So, where do you start? Given HP's current problems, should you focus on what the company is doing or not doing, meaning its current strategy, or should you simply focus on doing what HP is doing, but doing it better Or should you follow your predecessor's strategy of HP being "digital, virtual, mobile, and personal"? Or do you reexamine the company's strategy and start anew? Finally, there are two key problems at HP: distrust, which is accompanied by poor morale; and poor company performance in terms of product innovation, market share, and profits. Which is more important and which should you fix first? **If you were in charge at HP, what would you do?**

ACTIVITIES + VIDEOS

CengageNOW Audio study guide, electronic flashcards, author FAQ videos, On the Job and Biz Flix videos, concept tutorial, and concept exercise

Web (academic.cengage.com/management/williams) Quiz, PowerPoint slides, and glossary terms for this chapter

Study Tip

Your professor and TA are the most valuable resources in your course. If you have questions on the fundamental concepts of leadership, visit them during office hours. Report back to your study partner or group.

"WHAT'S NEW" COMPANIES

Hewlett-Packard
Southwest Airlines
McDonald's
Citigroup
Home Depot
Hyperspace Communications
PepsiCo
Xerox
JPMorgan Chase
And others . . .

Do I have what it takes to lead? What are the most important things leaders do? How can I transform a poorly performing department, division, or company? Do I need to adjust my leadership depending on the situation and the employee? Why doesn't my leadership inspire people? If you've ever been "in charge," or even just thought about it, chances are you've considered similar questions. Well, you're not alone—millions of leaders in organizations across the world struggle with these fundamental leadership issues on a daily basis.

We begin this chapter by discussing what leadership is, who leaders are (meaning their traits and characteristics), and what leaders do that makes them different from people who aren't leaders. Next we examine four major contingency theories of leadership that specify which leaders are best suited for which situations or how leaders should change their behavior to lead different people in different circumstances. The chapter ends with a review of strategic leadership issues, such as charismatic and transformational leadership, which are concerned with working with others to meet long-term goals and with creating a viable future for an organization.

WHAT IS LEADERSHIP?

"WHAT'S NEW" COMPANY

SOUTHWEST AIRLINES flies two to three times as many passengers per employee as other airlines at a cost 25 to 40 percent below its competitors.[2] One of the keys to Southwest's performance is that it empties its planes; refills them with passengers, crews, fuel, and food (peanuts and soft drinks); and has them back on the runway in 20 minutes, one-third the time of most airlines. This allows Southwest to keep each of its planes filled with paying passengers about three more hours a day. Why is Southwest able to achieve such incredible results? It takes care of its employees. For instance, with most ticket sales moving to its website, Southwest closed reservation centers in Dallas, Little Rock, and Salt Lake City. But instead of laying off employees, it paid for them to commute or relocate to places it had jobs. Regarding layoffs, Colleen Barrett, Southwest's president, says, "We don't do those kind of things. That's what our competitors do. At Southwest, our employees come first."[3] The result, says Southwest spokesperson Paula Berg, is, "We work hard. I'll stay here until 10 PM, if necessary. . . . But we do it because the company takes care of us, so we want to take care of the company."[4] As Colleen Barrett and the rest of the managers at Southwest Airlines have discovered, **leadership** is the process of influencing others to achieve group or organizational goals.

After reading the next two sections, you should be able to

1 explain what leadership is.

2 describe who leaders are and what effective leaders do.

1 Leadership

leadership the process of influencing others to achieve group or organizational goals

In Chapter 1, we defined *management* as getting work done through others. In other words, managers don't do the work themselves. Managers help others do their jobs better. By contrast, *leadership* is the process of influencing others to achieve group or organizational goals. What then are the key differences between leaders and managers? Another question that goes to the nature of leadership is whether it's required in every situation. Does leadership always matter? Or are there situations when leadership isn't needed or may even make things worse?

Let's learn more about leadership by exploring ***1.1 the differences between leaders and managers*** *and* ***1.2 substitutes for leadership****.*

1.1 Leaders versus Managers

According to University of Southern California business professor Warren Bennis, the primary difference between leaders and managers, as shown in Exhibit 14.1, is that leaders are concerned with doing the right thing, while managers are concerned with doing things right.[5] In other words, leaders begin with the question, "What should we be doing?" while managers start with "How can we do what we're already doing better?" Leaders focus on vision, mission, goals, and objectives, while managers focus on productivity and efficiency. Managers see themselves as preservers of the status quo, while leaders see themselves as promoters of change and challengers of the status quo in that they encourage creativity and risk taking. Four years ago, **McDonald's** was losing money and closing down stores. Today, with faster, friendlier service, healthier, better-tasting food, and a focus on quality rather than growth, McDonald's stock is up 45 percent. Furthermore, 50 million customers walk into its restaurants each day, 3.5 million more per day than four years ago. Despite these successes, CEO Jim Skinner is not happy with the status quo. Says Skinner, "I worry about complacency. We're not satisfied. We have a lot [more] work to do."[6]

Another difference is that managers have a relatively short-term perspective, while leaders take a long-term view. After financial improprieties in investment banking, bond trading, consumer lending, and corporate financing led to investigations and penalties in Europe, Japan, and the United States, new **Citigroup** CEO Charles Prince replaced the company's focus on short-term goals, such as fast growth, acquisitions, and quarterly earnings gains, with longer-term goals to improve ethics and financial controls and to grow its international business and replace aging technology systems.[7] Says Prince, "You can never sacrifice your long-term growth, your long-term reputation, to the short term."[8] Managers are also more concerned with *means*, how to get things done, while leaders are more concerned with *ends*, what gets done. Managers are concerned with control and limiting the choices of others, while leaders are more concerned with expanding people's choices and options.[9] Finally, managers solve problems so that others can do their work, while leaders inspire and motivate others to find their own solutions.

Though leaders are different from managers, organizations need them both. Managers are critical to getting out the day-to-day work, and leaders are critical to inspiring employees and setting the organization's long-term direction. The key issue for any organization is the extent to which it is properly led and properly managed. As Warren Bennis said in summing up the difference between leaders and managers, "American organizations

Exhibit 14.1
Managers versus Leaders

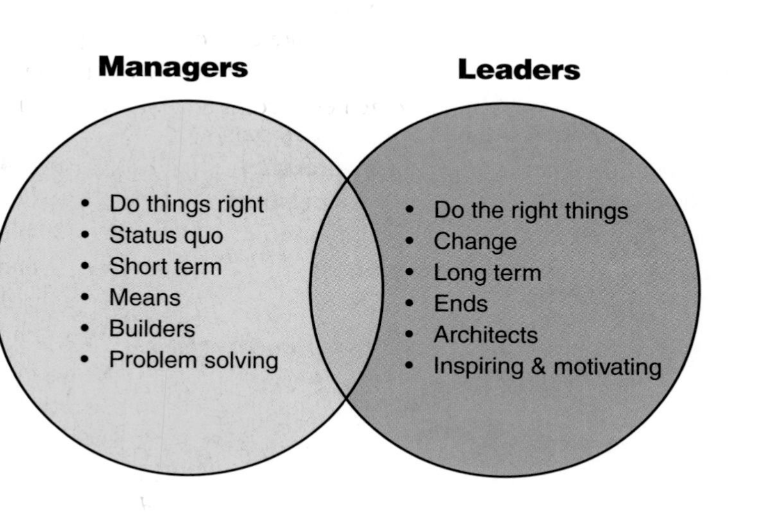

doing the right thing

The Three M's: Mission, Mentor, and Mirror

Doctors take the Hippocratic oath. Lawyers swear to protect and enforce the law. Leaders . . . well, there's no equivalent for business leaders. That's why Harvard professor Howard Gardner says that business leaders can develop personal ethics by focusing on their mission, a mentor, and the mirror.

First, leaders need to develop a personal mission statement by asking themselves these questions: *Why am I doing what I'm doing? What do I want from work? What are my personal goals?* Let your personal mission statement, and not the company's, guide your ethical behavior.

Second, take care in choosing a mentor. An interesting study compared 20 business leaders selected at random with 20 "good" business leaders nominated by businesspeople, business school professors, and deans. The randomly selected business leaders focused on short-term goals exclusively, worrying only about next quarter's results. By contrast, 18 of the 20 "good" executives focused on the long term, on doing what was right for the company in the long run. So, if you want to be a good leader, choose a "good" mentor.

Third, periodically stand in front of the mirror to assess your ethical performance as a business leader. Are you proud or ashamed of what you accomplished and how you accomplished it? Are you proud or ashamed of your company? What needs to change to make you proud?

So, do the right thing. Develop a personal mission statement. Choose the right mentor. And look hard at yourself in the mirror.[11]

(and probably those in much of the rest of the industrialized world) are under led and over managed. They do not pay enough attention to doing the right thing, while they pay too much attention to doing things right."[10]

1.2 Substitutes for Leadership: Do Leaders Always Matter?

One of the basic assumptions about leadership is that leaders always matter. According to this thinking, without sound leadership, organizations are sure to fail. In fact, when companies struggle, their leaders are almost always blamed for their poor performance. When **HOME DEPOT** fired CEO Robert Nardelli, *BusinessWeek* wrote:

> *Nardelli's "numbers were quite good," says Matthew J. Fassler, an analyst at Goldman Sachs Group Inc. But "the fact is that this retail organization never really embraced his leadership style." The CEO's reputation also suffered because of Wall Street's affection for Home Depot's smaller archrival, Lowe's Companies, whose stock price has soared more than 200 percent since 2000, while Home Depot's shares declined 6 percent. . . . "He's not a very humble guy. He seems to have enormous energy but needs to be front and center, and that can wear on the board and the employees after a while," says Edward E. Lawler, director of the Center for Effective Organizations at the University of Southern California's Marshall School of Business. . . .*
>
> *. . . [T]he Nardelli departure was already brightening the mood at some company stores. "It's amazing the reaction of people on my floor. People are openly ecstatic. High-fiving," said an Atlanta store operations manager only hours after the Jan. 3 announcement.*[12]

In some situations and circumstances, however, leadership isn't necessary, is unlikely to make much of a difference, or isn't to blame for poor performance. These are known as leadership substitutes and leadership neutralizers.[13] Exhibit 14.2 lists a number of subordinate, task, or organizational characteristics that can act as leadership substitutes or neutralizers (some can act as both) for either people-related or task-related leader behaviors. Leaders' people-related behaviors, such as being

approachable, supportive, or showing concern for employees, affect how satisfied people are with their jobs. Leaders' task-related behaviors, such as setting goals, giving directions, and providing resources, affect the extent to which people are able to perform their jobs well.

American organizations (and probably those in much of the rest of the industrialized world) are under led and over managed.

WARREN BENNIS, BUSINESS PROFESSOR, UNIVERSITY OF SOUTHERN CALIFORNIA

Leadership substitutes are subordinate, task, or organizational characteristics that make leaders redundant or unnecessary. For instance, when subordinates have ability, experience, training, and knowledge about their jobs (see subordinate characteristics in Exhibit 14.2), task-related leader behavior that specifies goals, task assignments, and how to do the job is unlikely to improve a subordinate's work performance. Think about it. Workers already have the capability to do their jobs. And the job itself provides enough information to let them know how well they're doing or what they might do to correct performance problems. In situations like this, where leadership substitutes are strong, leaders don't need to tell workers what to do or how to do their jobs.

Leadership neutralizers are subordinate, task, or organizational characteristics that can interfere with a leader's actions or make it impossible for a leader

leadership substitutes subordinate, task, or organizational characteristics that make leaders redundant or unnecessary

leadership neutralizers subordinate, task, or organizational characteristics that can interfere with a leader's actions or make it impossible for a leader to influence followers' performance

Exhibit 14.2

Leadership Substitutes and Neutralizers

Characteristics	People-Related Leadership Behaviors	Task-Related Leadership Behaviors
SUBORDINATE		
• Ability, experience, training, knowledge	Neutralize	Substitute, Neutralize
• Need for independence	Neutralize	Neutralize
• Professional orientation	Substitute, Neutralize	Substitute, Neutralize
• Indifference toward organizational rewards	Neutralize	Neutralize
TASK		
• Unambiguous and routine tasks	No effect	Substitute, Neutralize
• Performance feedback provided by the work itself	No effect	Substitute, Neutralize
• Intrinsically satisfying work	Substitute, Neutralize	Neutralize
ORGANIZATIONAL		
• Formalization, meaning specific plans, goals, and areas of responsibility	No effect	Neutralize
• Inflexibility, meaning rigid, unbending rules and procedures	No effect	Neutralize
• Highly specified staff functions	No effect	Neutralize
• Cohesive work groups	Substitute, Neutralize	Substitute, Neutralize
• Organizational rewards beyond a leader's	Neutralize	Neutralize control
• Spatial distance between supervisors and subordinates	Neutralize	Neutralize

Source: S. Kerr & J. M. Jermier, "Substitutes for Leadership: Their Meaning and Measurement," *Organizational Behavior and Human Performance* 22 (1978): 375–403.

to influence followers' performance. Unlike substitutes, which simply take the place of leaders, leadership neutralizers create an "influence vacuum." In other words, leadership neutralizers actually create a need for leadership by preventing leadership from working. For example, when subordinates are indifferent toward organizational rewards (see subordinate characteristics in Exhibit 14.2), there may be nothing that a leader can do to reward them for good performance. Likewise, inflexible rules and procedures (see organizational characteristics in Exhibit 14.2), such as union contracts that specify that all employees be paid the same, organizational policies that reward employees by seniority, and salary and raise processes that don't give leaders enough money to substantially reward good performers, effectively neutralize the ability of leaders to reward workers.

Spatial distance (see organizational characteristics in Exhibit 14.2) can also neutralize leadership. Spatial distance arises when supervisors and subordinates don't work in the same place, as occurs with telecommuters or people working thousands of miles away in overseas offices. Spatial distance typically results in infrequent feedback, little or no face-to-face contact, and being "out of sight and out of mind," all of which make it very difficult for leaders to lead. Because of those problems, John Yeros, founder and CEO of software company **HYPERSPACE COMMUNICATIONS**, lets only one of his employees, a programmer, work from home. Yeros says that when everyone is at the office, it's easier to "keep on the same page." Plus, it's easier for him as a leader. "I like to see them, feel them, touch them, and have them around," he says.[14] In fact, some companies find telecommuting to be so disruptive to leadership processes that they require their telecommuters to come into the office at least once or twice a week.

So do leaders *always* matter? Leadership substitutes and neutralizers indicate that sometimes they don't. This doesn't mean that leaders never matter, though. Quite the opposite. Leaders do matter, but they're not superhuman. They can't do it all by themselves. And they can't fix every situation. In short, leadership is very important. But poor leadership isn't the cause of every organizational crisis, and changing leaders isn't the solution to every company problem.

Review 1: **Leadership**

Leadership is the process of influencing others to achieve group or organizational goals. Leaders are different from managers. The primary difference is that leaders are concerned with doing the right thing, while managers are concerned with doing things right. Furthermore, managers have a short-term focus and are concerned with the status quo, with means rather than ends, and with solving others' problems. By contrast, leaders have a long-term focus and are concerned with change, with ends rather than means, and with inspiring and motivating others to solve their own problems. Organizations need both managers and leaders. But in general, companies are overmanaged and underled. While leadership is important, leadership substitutes and neutralizers create situations in which leadership isn't necessary or is unlikely to make much of a difference. Leadership substitutes are subordinate, task, or organizational characteristics that make leaders redundant or unnecessary. By contrast, leadership neutralizers are subordinate, task, or organizational characteristics that interfere with a leader's actions or make it impossible for a leader to influence followers' performance.

2 Who Leaders Are and What Leaders Do

"WHAT'S NEW" COMPANY

Indra Nooyi, **PEPSICO**'s new CEO, talks straight, has a sharp sense of humor, and sings in the hallways wherever she is. She's commonly described as a "force." By contrast, J.C. Penney's CEO, Mike Ullman, is soft-spoken and easy to approach.[15] Nooyi is an extrovert. Ullman is an introvert. Which one is likely to be successful as a CEO? According to a survey of 1,542 senior managers, it's the extrovert. Forty-seven percent of those 1,542 senior managers felt that extroverts make better CEOs, while 65 percent said that being an introvert hurts a CEO's chances of success.[16] So clearly senior managers believe that extroverted CEOs are better leaders. But are they? Not necessarily. In fact, a relatively high percentage of CEOs, 40 percent, are introverts. Sara Lee CEO Brenda Barnes says, "I've always been shy. . . . People wouldn't call me that [an introvert], but I am."[17] Indeed, Barnes turns down all speaking requests and rarely gives interviews.

So, what makes a good leader? Does leadership success depend on who leaders are, such as introverts or extroverts, or on what leaders do and how they behave? Let's learn more about who leaders are by investigating ***2.1 leadership traits*** *and* ***2.2 leadership behaviors****.*

2.1 Leadership Traits

Trait theory is one way to describe who leaders are. **Trait theory** says that effective leaders possess a similar set of traits or characteristics. **Traits** are relatively stable characteristics, such as abilities, psychological motives, or consistent patterns of behavior. For example, according to trait theory, leaders are taller and more confident and have greater physical stamina (that is, higher energy levels) than nonleaders. Indeed, while just 14.5 percent of men are six feet tall, 58 percent of Fortune 500 CEOs are six foot or taller.[18] Author Malcolm Gladwell says, "We have this sense of what a leader is supposed to look like. And that stereotype is so powerful that when someone fits it, we simply become blind to other considerations."[19] Trait theory is also known as the "great person" theory because early versions of the theory stated that leaders are born, not made. In other words, you either have the "right stuff" to be a leader, or you don't. And if you don't, there is no way to get "it."

trait theory a leadership theory that holds that effective leaders possess a similar set of traits or characteristics

traits relatively stable characteristics, such as abilities, psychological motives, or consistent patterns of behavior

Because we think we know what a leader should look like, we become blind to other considerations.

© DIGITAL VISION/GETTY

For some time, it was thought that trait theory was wrong and that there are no consistent trait differences between leaders and nonleaders, or between effective and ineffective leaders. However, more recent evidence shows that "successful leaders are not like other people," that successful leaders are indeed different from the rest of us.[20] More specifically, as shown in Exhibit 14.3, leaders are different from nonleaders in the following traits: drive, the desire to lead, honesty/integrity, self-confidence, emotional stability, cognitive ability, and knowledge of the business.[21]

Drive refers to high levels of effort and is characterized by achievement, motivation, initiative, energy, and tenacity. In terms of achievement and ambition, leaders always try

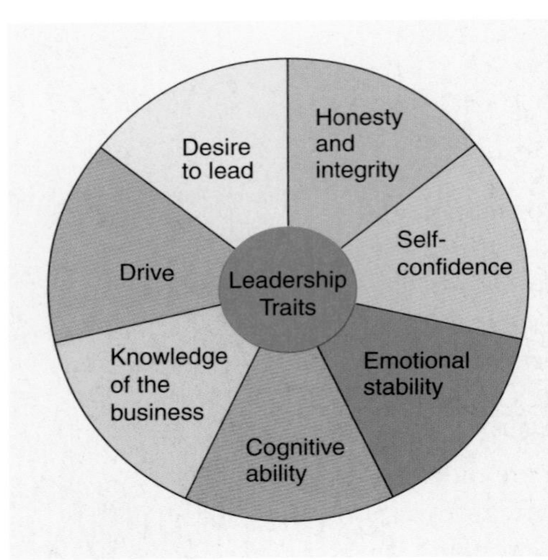

Exhibit 14.3
Leadership Traits

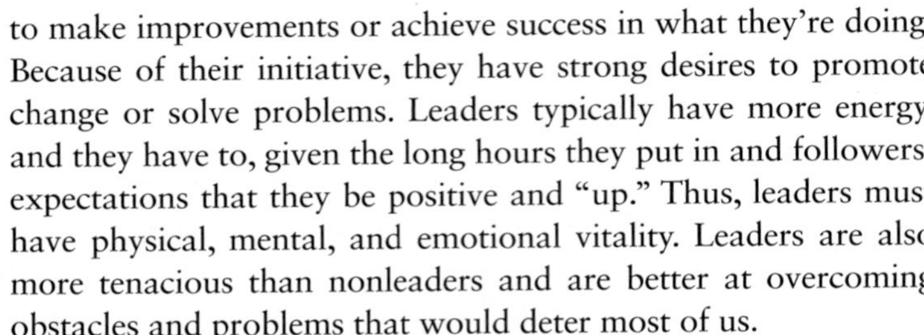

to make improvements or achieve success in what they're doing. Because of their initiative, they have strong desires to promote change or solve problems. Leaders typically have more energy, and they have to, given the long hours they put in and followers' expectations that they be positive and "up." Thus, leaders must have physical, mental, and emotional vitality. Leaders are also more tenacious than nonleaders and are better at overcoming obstacles and problems that would deter most of us.

Successful leaders also have a stronger *desire to lead*. They want to be in charge and think about ways to influence or convince others about what should or shouldn't be done. *Honesty/integrity* is also important to leaders. *Honesty*, being truthful with others, is a cornerstone of leadership. Without honesty, leaders won't be trusted. When leaders have it, subordinates are willing to overlook other flaws. For example, one follower said this about the leadership qualities of his manager: "I don't like a lot of the things he does, but he's basically honest. He's a genuine article, and you'll forgive a lot of things because of that. That goes a long way in how much I trust him."[22] *Integrity* is the extent to which leaders do what they said they would do. Leaders may be honest and have good intentions, but if they don't consistently deliver on what they promise, they won't be trusted.

Self-confidence, believing in one's abilities, also distinguishes leaders from nonleaders. Self-confident leaders are more decisive and assertive and are more likely to gain others' confidence. Moreover, self-confident leaders will admit mistakes because they view them as learning opportunities rather than a refutation of their leadership capabilities. This also means that leaders have *emotional stability*. Even when things go wrong, they remain even-tempered and consistent in their outlook and in the way they treat others. Leaders who can't control their emotions, who anger quickly or attack and blame others for mistakes, are unlikely to be trusted.

Leaders are also smart. Leaders typically have strong *cognitive abilities*. This doesn't mean that leaders are geniuses, far from it. But it does mean that leaders have the capacity to analyze large amounts of seemingly unrelated, complex information and see patterns, opportunities, or threats where others might not see them. Finally, leaders also "know their stuff," which means they have superior technical knowledge about the businesses they run. Leaders who have a good *knowledge of the business* understand the key technological decisions and concerns facing their companies. More often than not, studies indicate that effective leaders have long, extensive experience in their industries.

How does Anne Mulcahy, the CEO who turned around **Xerox**, measure up on these traits? In general, quite well. *Fortune* magazine said this about her: "She is straightforward, hard-working, disciplined. She is fiercely loyal to Xerox—the company, the brand, the people. She has the integrity of the Catholic schoolgirl she was for 16 years. Her coworkers describe her as both compassionate and tough. She is not afraid of bad news. . . . Her willingness to work shoulder to shoulder with subordinates gives her unusual credibility and the ability to galvanize her team."[23]

Initially, however, Mulcahy had a clear weakness: Because her experience was limited to sales, she lacked knowledge of the entire business. And since Xerox was $14.1 billion in debt and had only $154 million in cash on hand, she had to learn fast. So she asked Joe Mancini, Jr., the director of corporate financial analysis, to give her a course in "Balance Sheet 101." Mulcahy says, "It was an unusual situation for me—tutoring the CEO. But there wasn't a lot of time for false pride."[24] Every night she took home binders full of information to study, and eventually she transformed her knowledge of the financial side of the business from a weakness into a strength.

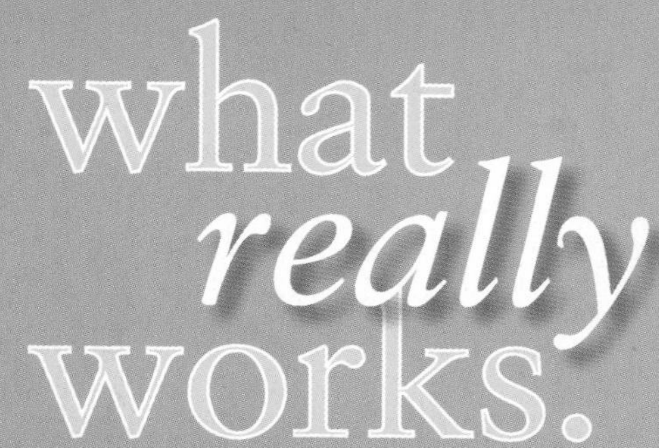

LEADERSHIP TRAITS DO MAKE A DIFFERENCE

For decades, researchers assumed that leadership traits, such as drive, emotional stability, cognitive ability, and charisma were *not* related to effective leadership. More recent evidence, however, shows that there are reliable trait differences between leaders and nonleaders. In fact, 54 studies based on more than 6,000 people clearly indicate that in terms of leadership traits, "successful leaders are not like other people."

TRAITS AND PERCEPTIONS OF LEADERSHIP EFFECTIVENESS

Several leadership models argue that in order to be successful, leaders must be viewed as good leaders by their followers. (This is completely different from determining whether leaders actually improve organizational performance.) Consequently, one test of trait theory is whether leaders with particular traits are viewed as more or less effective leaders by their followers.

Intelligence. On average, there is a 75 percent chance that intelligent leaders will be seen as better leaders than less intelligent leaders.

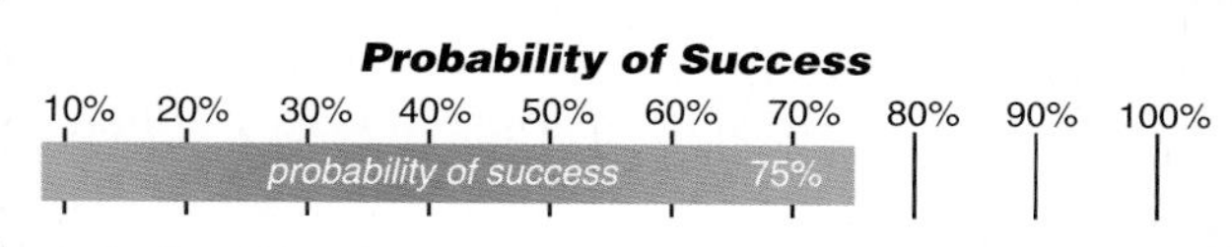

Dominance. On average, there is only a 57 percent chance that leaders with highly dominant personalities will be seen as better leaders than those with less dominant personalities.

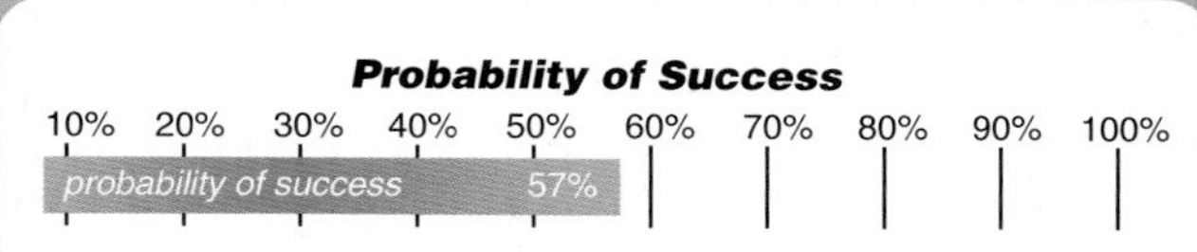

Extroversion. On average, there is a 63 percent chance that extroverts will be seen as better leaders than introverts.

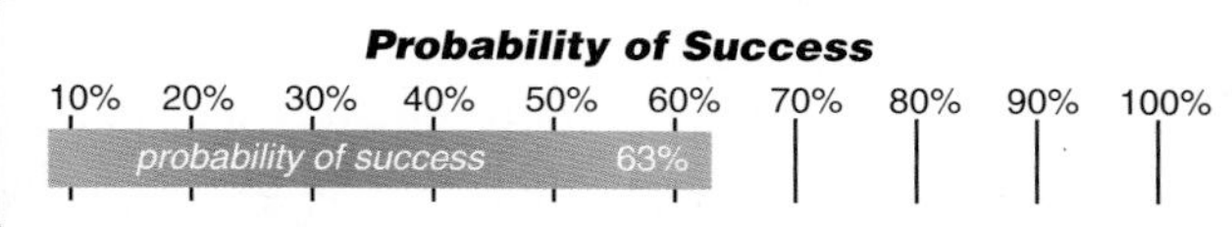

CHARISMA AND LEADERSHIP EFFECTIVENESS

As discussed at the end of the chapter, *charismatic leadership* is the set of behavioral tendencies and personal characteristics of leaders that creates an exceptionally strong relationship between leaders and their followers. More specifically, charismatic leaders articulate a clear vision for the future that is based on strongly held values or morals; model those values by acting in a way consistent with the company's vision; communicate high performance expectations to followers; and display confidence in followers' abilities to achieve the vision.

Charisma and Performance. On average, there is a 72 percent chance that charismatic leaders will have better-performing followers and organizations than less charismatic leaders.

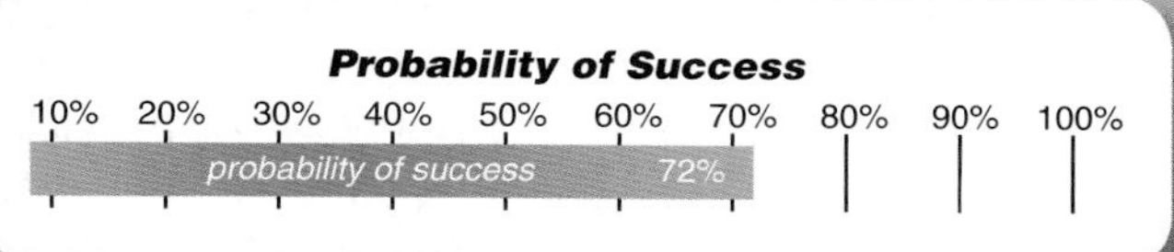

Charisma and Perceived Leader Effectiveness. On average, there is an 89 percent chance that charismatic leaders will be perceived as more effective leaders than less charismatic leaders.

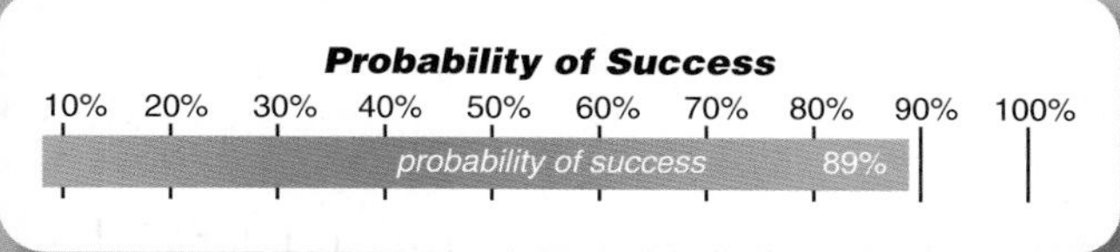

Charisma and Leader Satisfaction. On average, there is a 90 percent chance that the followers of charismatic leaders will be more satisfied with their leaders than the followers of less charismatic leaders.[25]

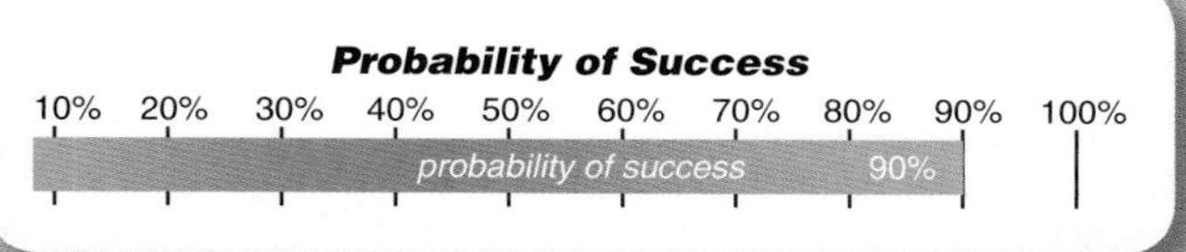

2.2 Leadership Behaviors

Thus far, you've read about who leaders *are*. Traits alone are not enough to make a successful leader, however, though they are a precondition for success. After all, it's hard to imagine a truly successful leader who lacks all of these qualities. Leaders who have these traits (or many of them) must then take actions that encourage people to achieve group or organizational goals.[26] Accordingly, we now examine what leaders *do*, meaning the behaviors they perform or the actions they take to influence others to achieve group or organizational goals.

Researchers at the University of Michigan, Ohio State University, and the University of Texas examined the specific behaviors that leaders use to improve subordinate satisfaction and performance. Hundreds of studies were conducted and hundreds of leader behaviors were examined. At all three universities, two basic leader behaviors emerged as central to successful leadership: initiating structure (called *job-centered leadership* at the University of Michigan and *concern for production* at the University of Texas) and considerate leader behavior (called *employee-centered leadership* at the University of Michigan and *concern for people* at the University of Texas).[27] These two leader behaviors form the basis for many of the leadership theories discussed in this chapter.

Initiating structure is the degree to which a leader structures the roles of followers by setting goals, giving directions, setting deadlines, and assigning tasks. A leader's ability to initiate structure primarily affects subordinates' job performance. When Jamie Dimon became CEO of **JPMorgan Chase**, the financial services company had four different computer systems from previously acquired companies. Branch bankers couldn't access checking histories, or determine whether customers qualified for credit cards or mortgages. Dimon initiated structure by telling his executives to put one system in place, and, "If you don't do it in six weeks, I'll make all the choices myself."[28] The deadline was met. Now, with just one software system, the annual cost of processing credit card statements has dropped from $80 to $52 a customer. Furthermore, with a new system that calculates which credit card deals are best for particular customers, Morgan has increased its open credit card accounts by 55 percent.

"What's New" Company

Consideration is the extent to which a leader is friendly, approachable, and supportive and shows concern for employees. Consideration primarily affects subordinates' job satisfaction. Specific leader consideration behaviors include listening to employees' problems and concerns, consulting with employees before making decisions, and treating employees as equals. Twenty-five years ago **Wal-Mart**'s CEO, Lee Scott, received a lesson in the importance of consideration from founder Sam Walton. Scott, who was then in charge of a transportation unit, was known for his tough management style and for sending "blistering memos." When "Mr. Sam" called him into his office, Scott found nine of his truck drivers there waiting for him. The drivers, who were taking advantage of Wal-Mart's open-door policy, had complained to Walton about the way Scott treated them and asked that he be fired. According to Scott, "They just wanted to do their work and be appreciated for it. So Mr. Walton asked me, with them there, if I could do it differently."[29] After agreeing that he could, Scott said that Walton "had me stand at the door as they were leaving and thank each one for having the courage to use the open door, which is one of the very basic principles of Wal-Mart."[30] That office is now Scott's, and Wal-Mart has the same open door through which any Wal-Mart employee can walk to talk with the CEO.

Although researchers at all three universities generally agreed that initiating structure and consideration were basic leader behaviors, they differed on the interaction and effectiveness of these behaviors. The University of Michigan studies

initiating structure the degree to which a leader structures the roles of followers by setting goals, giving directions, setting deadlines, and assigning tasks

consideration the extent to which a leader is friendly, approachable, and supportive and shows concern for employees indicated that initiating structure and consideration were mutually exclusive behaviors on opposite ends of the same continuum. In other words, leaders who wanted to be more considerate would have to do less initiating of structure (and vice versa). The University of Michigan studies also indicated that only considerate leader behaviors (that is, employee-centered behaviors) were associated with successful leadership. By contrast, researchers at Ohio State University and the University of Texas found that initiating structure and consideration were independent behaviors, meaning that leaders can be considerate and initiate structure at the same time. Additional evidence confirms this finding.[31] The same researchers also concluded that the most effective leaders were strong on both initiating structure and considerate leader behaviors.

This "high-high" approach can be seen in the upper right corner of the Blake/Mouton leadership grid, shown in Exhibit 14.4. Blake and Mouton used two leadership behaviors, concern for people (that is, consideration) and concern for production (that is, initiating structure), to categorize five different leadership styles. Both behaviors are rated on a 9-point scale with 1 representing "low" and 9 representing "high." Blake and Mouton suggest that a "high-high" or 9,9 leadership style is the best. They call this style *team management* because leaders who use it display a high concern for people (9) and a high concern for production (9).

By contrast, leaders use a 9,1 *authority-compliance* leadership style when they have a high concern for production and a low concern for people. A 1,9 *country*

Exhibit 14.4

Blake/Mouton Leadership Grid

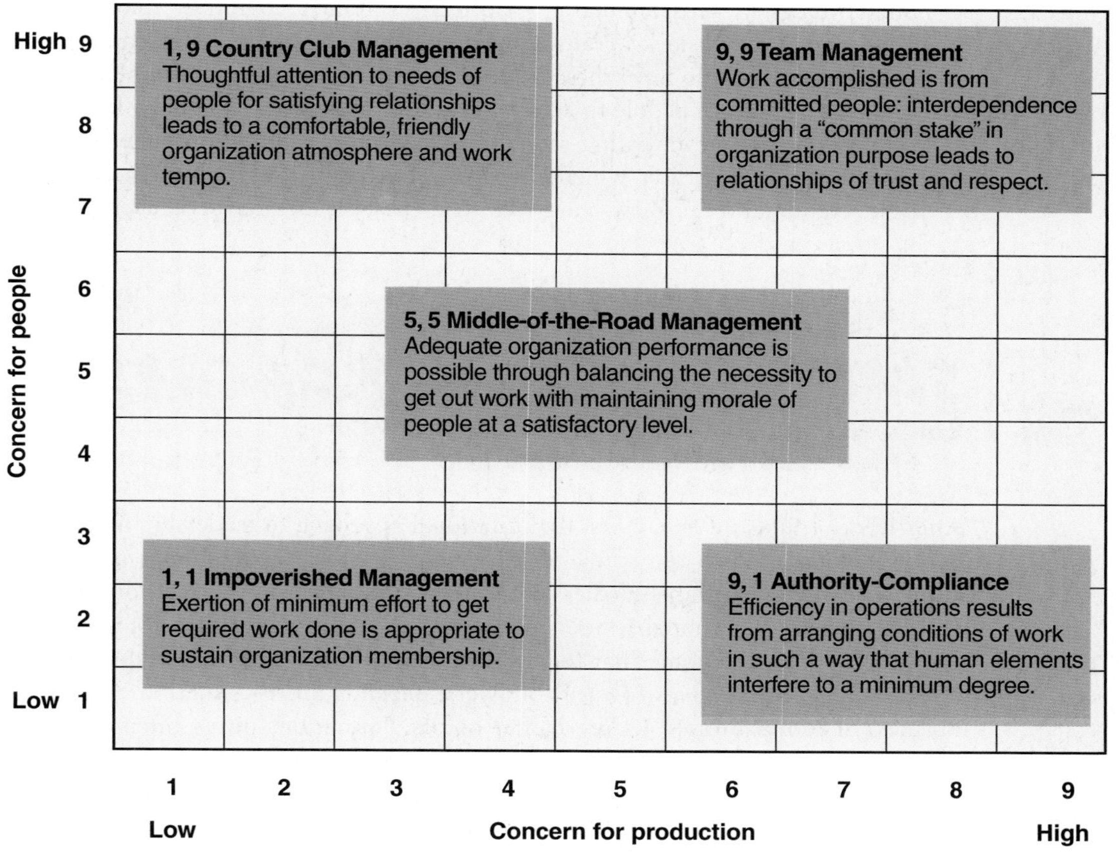

Source: R. R. Blake & A. A. McCanse, "The Leadership Grid®," *Leadership Dilemmas—Grid Solutions* (Houston: Gulf Publishing Company), 21. Copyright © 1991, by Scientific Methods, Inc. Reproduced by permission of the owners.

A fun work environment where little attention is paid to production or performance is a country club style.

club style occurs when leaders care about having a friendly enjoyable work environment but don't really pay much attention to production or performance. The worst leadership style, according to the grid, is the 1,1 *impoverished* leader, who shows little concern for people or production and does the bare minimum needed to keep his or her job. Finally, the 5,5 *middle-of-the-road* style occurs when leaders show a moderate amount of concern for both people and production.

Is the team management style, with a high concern for production and a high concern for people, the "best" leadership style? Logically, it would seem so. Why wouldn't you want to show high concern for both people and production? Nonetheless, nearly 50 years of research indicates that there isn't one "best" leadership style. The "best" leadership style depends on the situation. In other words, no one leadership behavior by itself and no one combination of leadership behaviors works well across all situations and employees.

Review 2: **Who Leaders Are and What Leaders Do**

Trait theory says that effective leaders possess traits or characteristics that differentiate them from nonleaders. Those traits are drive, the desire to lead, honesty/integrity, self-confidence, emotional stability, cognitive ability, and knowledge of the business. Traits alone aren't enough for successful leadership, however; leaders who have these traits (or many of them) must also behave in ways that encourage people to achieve group or organizational goals. Two key leader behaviors are initiating structure, which improves subordinate performance, and consideration, which improves subordinate satisfaction. There is no "best" combination of these behaviors. The "best" leadership style depends on the situation.

SITUATIONAL APPROACHES TO LEADERSHIP

After leader traits and behaviors, the situational approach to leadership is the third major method used in the study of leadership. There are four major situational approaches to leadership—Fiedler's contingency theory, path-goal theory, Hersey and Blanchard's Situational Leadership theory, and Vroom and Yetton's normative decision model. All assume that the effectiveness of any **leadership style**, the way a leader generally behaves toward followers, depends on the situation.[32] Stanford Business School professor Jeffrey Pfeffer agrees: "Situations differ, often wildly, in the extent to which one individual can make a difference and in the set of attributes required to be successful. . . . But utopia is impossible, which is why management consultants and authors should stop talking so much about how to find an ideal leader and instead focus on placing people into jobs that play to their strengths—and where their flaws won't be fatal."[33]

leadership style the way a leader generally behaves toward followers

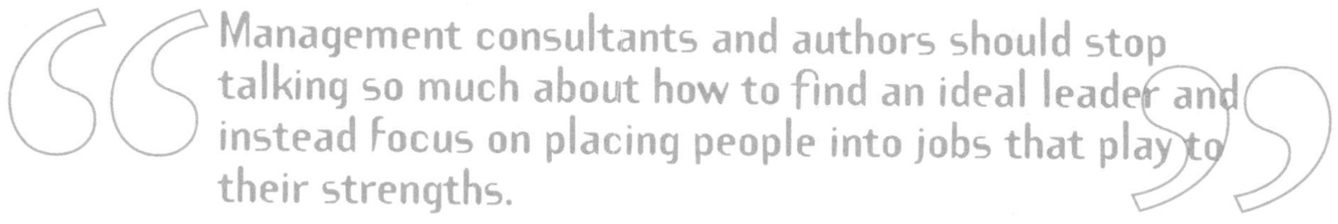
Management consultants and authors should stop talking so much about how to find an ideal leader and instead focus on placing people into jobs that play to their strengths.

JEFFREY PFEFFER, PROFESSOR, STANFORD BUSINESS SCHOOL

According to situational leadership theories, there is no one "best" leadership style. But, one of these situational theories differs from the other three in one significant way. Fiedler's contingency theory assumes that leadership styles are consistent and difficult to change. Therefore, leaders must be placed in or "matched" to a situation that fits their leadership style. In contrast, the other three situational theories all assume that leaders are capable of adapting and adjusting their leadership styles to fit the demands of different situations.

After reading the next four sections, you should be able to

3 explain Fiedler's contingency theory.
4 describe how path-goal theory works.
5 discuss Hersey and Blanchard's Situational Leadership theory.
6 explain the normative decision theory.

3 Putting Leaders in the Right Situation: Fiedler's Contingency Theory

Fiedler's **contingency theory** states that in order to maximize work group performance, leaders must be matched to the right leadership situation.[34] More specifically, as shown in Exhibit 14.5, the first basic assumption of Fiedler's theory is that leaders are effective when the work groups they lead perform well. So, instead of judging leaders' effectiveness by what the leaders do (initiating structure and consideration) or who they are (trait theory), Fiedler assesses leaders by the conduct and performance of the people they supervise. Second, Fiedler assumes that leaders are generally unable to change their leadership styles and that they will be more effective when their styles are matched to the proper situation. Third, Fiedler assumes that the favorableness of a situation for a leader depends on the degree to which the situation permits the leader to influence the behavior of group members. Thus, Fiedler's third assumption is consistent with our definition of leadership, which is the process of influencing others to achieve group or organizational goals.

contingency theory a leadership theory that states that in order to maximize work group performance, leaders must be matched to the situation that best fits their leadership style

Exhibit 14.5
Fiedler's Contingency Theory

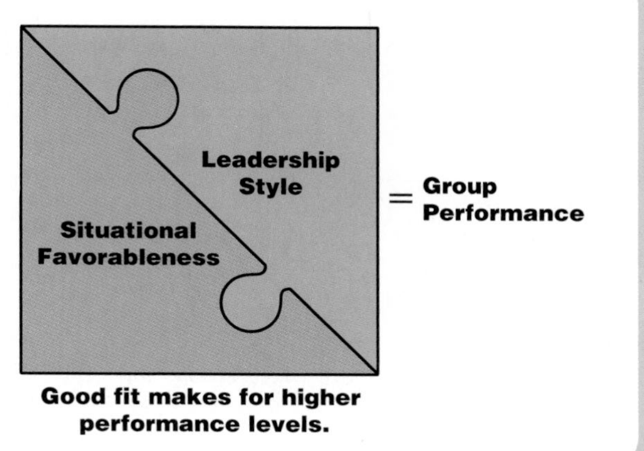
Leadership Style
Situational Favorableness
= Group Performance
Good fit makes for higher performance levels.

Let's learn more about Fiedler's contingency theory by examining ***3.1 the least preferred coworker and leadership styles, 3.2 situational favorableness****, and* ***3.3 how to match leadership styles to situations****.*

3.1 Leadership Style: Least Preferred Coworker

When Fiedler refers to *leadership style*, he means the way that leaders generally behave toward their followers. Do the leaders yell and scream and blame others when things go wrong? Or do they correct mistakes by listening and then quietly but directly make their point? Do they take credit for others' work when things go right? Or do they make sure that those who did the work receive the credit they rightfully deserve? Do they let others make their own decisions and hold them accountable for the results? Or do they microman-age, insisting that all decisions be approved first by them? Fiedler also assumes that leadership styles are tied to leaders' underlying needs and personalities. And since personality and needs are relatively stable, he assumes that leaders are generally incapable of changing their leadership styles. In other words, the way that leaders treat people now is probably the way they've always treated others. So, according to Fiedler, if your boss's first instinct is to yell and scream and blame others, chances are he or she has always done that.

Fiedler uses a questionnaire called the Least Preferred Coworker (LPC) scale to measure leadership style (sample shown in Exhibit 14.6). When completing the LPC scale, people are instructed to consider all of the people with whom they have ever worked and then to choose the one person with whom they have worked *least* well. Fiedler explains, "This does not have to be the person you liked least well, but should be the one person with whom you have the most trouble getting the job done."[35]

Would you describe your LPC as pleasant, friendly, supportive, interesting, cheer-ful, and sincere? Or would you describe the person as unpleasant, unfriendly, hostile, boring, gloomy, and insincere? (The Self-Assessment at the end of this chapter con-tains the full LPC scale.) People who describe their LPC in a positive way (scoring 64 and above) have *relationship-oriented* leadership styles. After all, if they can still be positive about their least preferred coworker, they must be people oriented. By con-trast, people who describe their LPC in a negative way (scoring 57 or below) have *task-oriented* leadership styles. Given a choice, they'll focus first on getting the job done and second on making sure everyone gets along. Finally, those with moderate scores (from 58 to 63) have a more flexible leadership style and can be somewhat relationship oriented or somewhat task oriented.

situational favorableness the degree to which a particular situation either permits or denies a leader the chance to influence the behavior of group members

3.2 Situational Favorableness

Fiedler assumes that leaders will be more effective when their leadership styles are matched to the proper situation. Specifically, Fiedler defines **situational favorableness**

Exhibit 14.6

Sample from Fiedler's Least Preferred Coworker Scale

Pleasant	____ 8	____ 7	____ 6	____ 5	____ 4	____ 3	____ 2	____ 1	**Unpleasant**
Friendly	____ 8	____ 7	____ 6	____ 5	____ 4	____ 3	____ 2	____ 1	**Unfriendly**
Supportive	____ 8	____ 7	____ 6	____ 5	____ 4	____ 3	____ 2	____ 1	**Hostile**
Boring	____ 1	____ 2	____ 3	____ 4	____ 5	____ 6	____ 7	____ 8	**Interesting**
Gloomy	____ 1	____ 2	____ 3	____ 4	____ 5	____ 6	____ 7	____ 8	**Cheerful**
Insincere	____ 1	____ 2	____ 3	____ 4	____ 5	____ 6	____ 7	____ 8	**Sincere**

Source: F. E. Fiedler & M. M. Chemers, *Improving Leadership Effectiveness: The Leader Match Concept,* 2nd ed. (New York: Wiley, 1984). Available at http://depts.washington.edu/psych/faculty/*cv/fiedler_cv.pdf, 23 March 2002. Reprinted by permission of the authors.

as the degree to which a particular situation either permits or denies a leader the chance to influence the behavior of group members.[36] In highly favorable situations, leaders find that their actions influence followers, but in highly unfavorable situations, leaders have little or no success influencing the people they are trying to lead.

Three situational factors determine the favorability of a situation: leader-member relations, task structure, and position power. The most important situational factor is **leader-member relations**, which refers to how well followers respect, trust, and like their leaders. When leader-member relations are good, followers trust the leader and there is a friendly work atmosphere. Such was the case under Gordon Bethune, CEO of **CONTINENTAL AIRLINES** for 10 years. Joe Caudle, a Continental employee, says, "I've worked under a lot of presidents and CEOs. When the others came around, the employees would be ducking out. But with him, it's 'Hey, Bethune's upstairs!' They start smiling and want to shake his hand."[37] **Task structure** is the degree to which the requirements of a subordinate's tasks are clearly specified. With highly structured tasks, employees have clear job responsibilities, goals, and procedures. **Position power** is the degree to which leaders are able to hire, fire, reward, and punish workers. The more influence leaders have over hiring, firing, rewards, and punishments, the greater their power.

Exhibit 14.7 shows how leader-member relations, task structure, and position power can be combined into eight situations that differ in their favorability to leaders. In general, Situation I, on the left side of Exhibit 14.7, is the most favorable leader situation. Followers like and trust their leaders and know what to do because their tasks are highly structured. Also, the leaders have the formal power to influence workers through hiring, firing, rewarding, and punishing them. Therefore, in Situation I, it's relatively easy for a leader to influence followers. By contrast, Situation VIII, on the right side of Exhibit 14.7, is the least favorable situation for leaders. Followers don't like or trust their leaders. Plus, followers are not sure what they're supposed to be doing, given that their tasks or jobs are highly unstructured. Finally, leaders find it difficult to influence followers because they don't have the ability to hire, fire, reward, or punish the people who work for them. In short, it's very difficult to influence followers given the conditions found in Situation VIII.

3.3 Matching Leadership Styles to Situations

After studying thousands of leaders and followers in hundreds of different situations, Fiedler found that the performance of relationship- and task-oriented leaders followed the pattern displayed in Exhibit 14.8.

Relationship-oriented leaders with high LPC scores were better leaders (that is, their groups performed more effectively) under moderately favorable situations. In moderately favorable situations, the leader may be liked somewhat, tasks may be somewhat structured, and the leader may have some position power. In this situation, a relationship-oriented leader improves leader-member relations, which is the most

leader-member relations the degree to which followers respect, trust, and like their leaders

task structure the degree to which the requirements of a subordinate's tasks are clearly specified

position power the degree to which leaders are able to hire, fire, reward, and punish workers

Exhibit 14.7
Situational Favorableness

Leader-Member Relations	Good	Good	Good	Good	Poor	Poor	Poor	Poor
Task Structure	High	High	Low	Low	High	High	Low	Low
Position Power	Strong	Weak	Strong	Weak	Strong	Weak	Strong	Weak
Situation	I	II	III	IV	V	VI	VII	VIII
	Favorable			**Moderately Favorable**			**Unfavorable**	

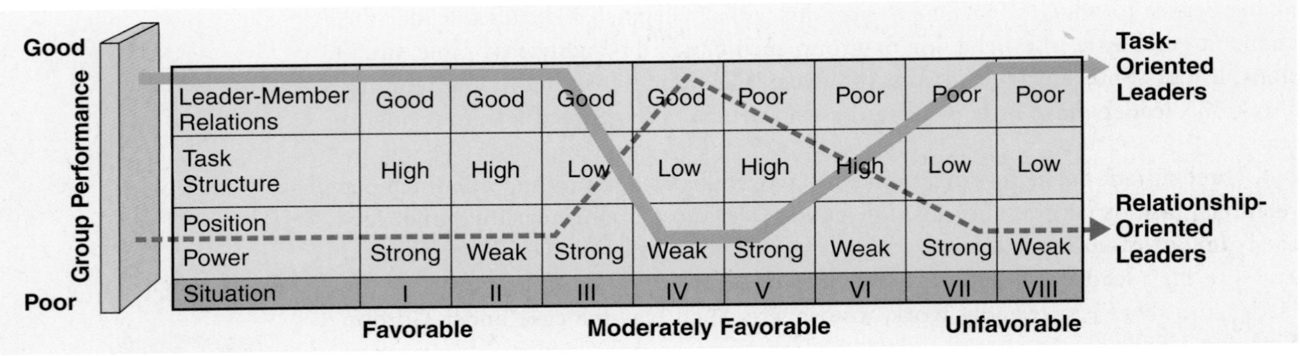

Exhibit 14.8

Matching Leadership Styles to Situations

important of the three situational factors. In turn, morale and performance improve. How did Gordon Bethune turn around Continental Airlines and its previously poisonous labor-management relations? Bethune explains it this way: "When I was a mechanic, I knew how much faster I could fix an airplane when I wanted to fix it than when I didn't. I've tried to make it so our guys want to do it."[38] By contrast, as Exhibit 14.8 shows, task-oriented leaders with low LPC scores are better leaders in highly favorable and unfavorable situations. Task-oriented leaders do well in favorable situations where leaders are liked, tasks are structured, and the leader has the power to hire, fire, reward, and punish. In these favorable situations, task-oriented leaders effectively step on the gas of a well-tuned car that's in perfect running condition. Their focus on performance sets the goal for the group, which then charges forward to meet it. But task-oriented leaders also do well in unfavorable situations where leaders are disliked, tasks are unstructured, and the leader doesn't have the power to hire, fire, reward, and punish. In these unfavorable situations, the task-oriented leader sets goals, which focus attention on performance, and clarifies what needs to be done, thus overcoming low task structure. This is enough to jump-start performance, even if workers don't like or trust the leader. Finally, though not shown in Exhibit 14.8, people with moderate LPC scores, who can be somewhat relationship oriented or somewhat task oriented, tend to do fairly well in all situations because they can adapt their behavior. Typically, though, they don't perform quite as well as relationship-oriented or task-oriented leaders whose leadership styles are well matched to the situation.

Recall, however, that Fiedler assumes that leaders are incapable of changing their leadership styles. Accordingly, the key to applying Fiedler's contingency theory in the workplace is to accurately measure and match leaders to situations or to teach leaders how to change situational favorableness by changing leader-member relations, task structure, or position power. Though matching or placing leaders in appropriate situations works particularly well, practicing managers have had little luck with "reengineering situations" to fit their leadership styles. The primary problem, as you've no doubt realized, is the complexity of the theory. In a study designed to teach leaders how to reengineer their situations to fit their leadership styles, Fiedler found that most of the leaders simply did not understand what they were supposed to do to change their leadership situations. Furthermore, if they didn't like their LPC profile (perhaps they felt they were more relationship oriented than their scores indicated), they arbitrarily changed it to better suit their view of themselves. Of course, the theory won't work as well if leaders are attempting to change situational factors to fit their perceived leadership style and not their real leadership style.[39]

Review 3: Putting Leaders in the Right Situation: Fiedler's Contingency Theory

Fiedler's theory assumes that leaders are effective when their work groups perform well, that leaders are unable to change their leadership styles, that leadership styles must be matched to the proper situation, and that favorable situations permit leaders to influence group members. According to the Least Preferred Coworker (LPC) scale, there are two basic leadership styles. People who describe their LPC in a positive way have relationship-oriented leadership styles. By contrast, people who describe their LPC in a negative way have task-oriented leadership styles. Situational favorableness, which occurs when leaders can influence followers is determined by leader-member relations, task structure, and position power. In general, relationship-oriented leaders with high LPC scores are better leaders under moderately favorable situations, while task-oriented leaders with low LPC scores are better leaders in highly favorable and unfavorable situations. Since Fiedler assumes that leaders are incapable of changing their leadership styles, the key is to accurately measure and match leaders to situations or to teach leaders how to change situational factors. Though matching or placing leaders in appropriate situations works well, "reengineering situations" to fit leadership styles doesn't because of the complexity of the model, which makes it difficult for people to understand.

Just as its name suggests, **path-goal theory** states that leaders can increase subordinate satisfaction and performance by clarifying and clearing the paths to goals and by increasing the number and kinds of rewards available for goal attainment. Said another way, leaders need to clarify how followers can achieve organizational goals, take care of problems that prevent followers from achieving goals, and then find more and varied rewards to motivate followers to achieve those goals.[40]

path-goal theory a leadership theory that states that leaders can increase subordinate satisfaction and performance by clarifying and clearing the paths to goals and by increasing the number and kinds of rewards available for goal attainment

For path clarification, path clearing, and rewards to increase followers' motivation and effort, however, leaders must meet two conditions. First, leader behavior must be a source of immediate or future satisfaction for followers. Therefore, the things you do as a leader must please your followers today or lead to activities or rewards that will satisfy them in the future. For example, Carla Jones, who works in marketing for **Edward Jones**, the St. Louis–based investment company that has been near the top of *Fortune*'s list of the top 100 companies to work for, hasn't looked outside the company for career opportunities since she joined the company 14 years ago. Indeed, Edward Jones' management does such a good job of satisfying its workers that a phenomenal 83 percent of its associates plan to work there until they retire.[41]

Exhibit 14.9

Basic Assumptions of Path-Goal Theory

- Clarify paths to goals.
- Clear paths to goals by solving problems and removing roadblocks.
- Increase the number and kinds of rewards available for goal attainment.
- Do things that satisfy followers today or will lead to future rewards or satisfaction.
- Offer followers something unique and valuable beyond what they're experiencing or can already do for themselves.

Source: R. J. House & T. R. Mitchell, "Path-Goal Theory of Leadership," *Journal of Contemporary Business* 3 (1974): 81–97.

Second, while providing the coaching, guidance, support, and rewards necessary for effective work performance, leader behaviors must complement and not duplicate the characteristics of followers' work environments. Thus, leader behaviors must offer something unique and valuable to followers beyond what they're already experiencing as they do their jobs or what they can already do for themselves. Exhibit 14.9 summarizes these basic assumptions of path-goal theory.

In contrast to Fiedler's contingency theory, path-goal theory assumes that leaders can change and adapt their leadership styles. Exhibit 14.10 illustrates this process, showing that leaders change and adapt their leadership styles contingent on their subordinates or the environment in which those subordinates work.

*Let's learn more about path-goal theory by examining **4.1 the four kinds of leadership styles that leaders use, 4.2 the subordinate and environmental contingency factors that determine when different leader styles are effective,** and **4.3 the outcomes of path-goal theory in improving employee satisfaction and performance.***

4.1 Leadership Styles

directive leadership a leadership style in which the leader lets employees know precisely what is expected of them, gives them specific guidelines for performing tasks, schedules work, sets standards of performance, and makes sure that people follow standard rules and regulations

supportive leadership a leadership style in which the leader is friendly to and approachable, shows concern for employees and their welfare, treats them as equals, and creates a friendly climate

As illustrated in Exhibit 14.10, the four leadership styles in path-goal theory are directive, supportive, participative, and achievement oriented.[42] **Directive leadership** involves letting employees know precisely what is expected of them, giving them specific guidelines for performing tasks, scheduling work, setting standards of performance, and making sure that people follow standard rules and regulations. For example, "each month, **Audi**'s compulsive chief executive, Martin Winterkorn, rolls up his sleeves and leads a trouble-shooting session with managers and engineers at the company's electronics center, zeroing in on faulty systems and problem parts. Winterkorn's rules: no shifting the blame to anyone else, such as suppliers. No phone calls to subordinates—the brains to remedy the defects better be in the room. And no one leaves until a fix is found."[43] Why is Winterkorn so demanding (that is, directive)? As he explains, "We want [Audi] to be the No. 1 premium [car] brand," and you don't achieve that goal easily when you're competing with Lexus, Mercedes, BMW, and Acura.

Supportive leadership involves being friendly to and approachable by employees, showing concern for them and their welfare, treating them as equals, and creating a friendly climate. Supportive leadership is very similar to considerate leader behavior. Supportive leadership often results in employee satisfaction with the job and with leaders. This leadership style may also result in improved performance when it increases employee confidence, lowers employee job stress, or improves relations and trust between employees and leaders.[44] For example, husband and wife Shane and Allison Alexander both work for Wal-Mart in Madisonville, Kentucky. Over the years, the Wal-Mart managers in their store have shown concern for them in a number of important ways. For example, since the Alexanders had only one car, Wal-Mart managers scheduled them for alternating shifts, which also allowed them to care for their baby without outside help, and made sure the couple had some Saturdays off to spend time as a family.[45]

Exhibit 14.10

Path-Goal Theory

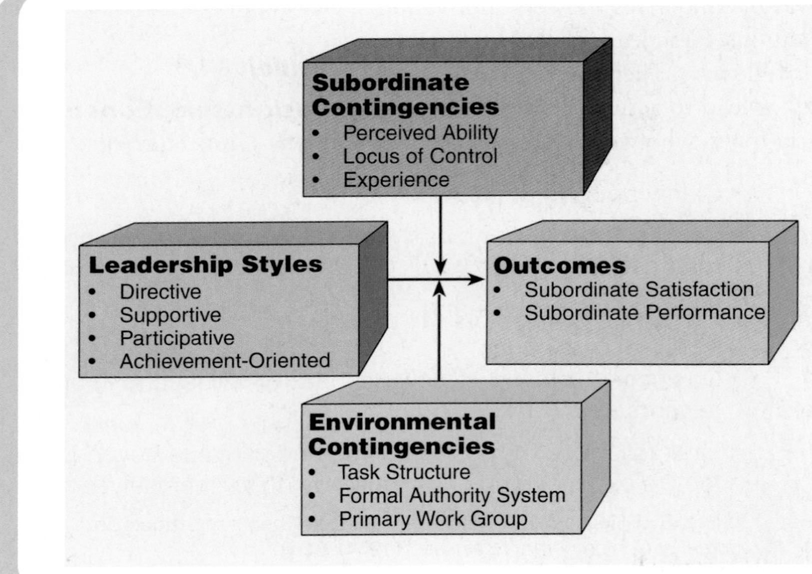

Participative leadership involves consulting employees for their suggestions and input before making decisions. Participation in decision making should help followers understand which goals are most important and clarify the paths to accomplishing them. Furthermore, when people participate in decisions, they become more committed to making them work. At the customer call center at United Kingdom–based Kwik-Fit Financial Services, managers were overly aggressive, employees were not consulted about anything, and annual employee turnover was 52 percent. When Kwik-Fit changed to a highly participative approach, managers met with all 650 employees in small groups and asked them what it would take to make the call center a good place to work. After those initial discussions, seven project groups, which included people from across the company, began addressing problems in facilities, incentives, pay, management style, management processes, and customer service. Today, because of those project groups, Kwik-Fit has an improved flexible benefits plan; flextime work scheduling; a "chillout" room with a TV, video game machine, pool table, and air hockey table; a concierge to take care of employees' nonwork tasks (dry cleaning, running to the bank); and new phone/customer software for doing their jobs. As a result of these employee-suggested changes, employee turnover has fallen to 35 percent, 66 percent of employees (up from 40 percent) recommend Kwik-Fit as a place to work, customer complaints are down 50 percent, customer satisfaction has risen from 90 to 94 percent, and profits are up by 50 percent.[46]

In addition to being a directive leader, Audi president Martin Winterkorn has deep technical knowledge in his field, which gives him credibility when he assigns work and sets goals and procedures. Winterkorn is shown here giving a lecture on car design concepts at the Budapest Technical University.

Achievement-oriented leadership means setting challenging goals, having high expectations of employees, and displaying confidence that employees will assume responsibility and put forth extraordinary effort. Simon Cooper, president and COO of the **RITZ-CARLTON** luxury hotel chain, uses the phrase "He who says it, does" to describe achievement-oriented leadership, Cooper explains, "I use this phrase whenever someone convinces me that they can achieve something I consider to be unachievable. In the past I've been known to add focus to a goal by making a bet to see if they can make it—sometimes with amusing consequences. I remember being at a mountain resort in Canada and proposing an incredible goal for the season. The team convinced me that they could achieve it, and I offered to jump into the lake if they did. It's a long story, but they made it. There's a great scene of a hole being cut in the ice and an ambulance on standby while I gave a whole new meaning to the term 'dunking.' The cognac [afterwards] was very welcome."[47]

4.2 Subordinate and Environmental Contingencies

As shown in Exhibit 14.10, path-goal theory specifies that leader behaviors should be fitted to subordinate characteristics. The theory identifies three kinds of subordinate contingencies: perceived ability, experience, and locus of control. *Perceived ability* is simply how much ability subordinates believe they have for doing their jobs well. Subordinates who perceive that they have a great deal of ability will be dissatisfied with directive leader behaviors. Experienced employees are likely to react in a similar way. Since they already know how to do their jobs (or perceive that they do), they don't need or want close supervision. By contrast, subordinates with little experience or little perceived ability will welcome directive leadership.

Locus of control is a personality measure that indicates the extent to which people believe that they have control over what happens to them in life. *Internals* believe

participative leadership a leadership style in which the leader consults employees for their suggestions and input before making decisions

achievement-oriented leadership a leadership style in which the leader sets challenging goals, has high expectations of employees, and displays confidence that employees will assume responsibility and put forth extraordinary effort that what happens to them, good or bad, is largely a result of their choices and actions. *Externals*, on the other hand, believe that what happens to them is caused by external forces beyond their control. Accordingly, externals are much more comfortable with a directive leadership style, while internals greatly prefer a participative leadership style because they like to have a say in what goes on at work.

> In the past I've been known to add focus to a goal by making a bet to see if they can make it—sometimes with amusing consequences.
>
> SIMON COOPER, PRESIDENT AND COO, RITZ-CARLTON

Path-goal theory specifies that leader behaviors should complement rather than duplicate the characteristics of followers' work environments. There are three kinds of environmental contingencies: task structure, the formal authority system, and the primary work group. As in Fiedler's contingency theory, *task structure* is the degree to which the requirements of a subordinate's tasks are clearly specified. When task structure is low and tasks are unclear, directive leadership should be used because it complements the work environment. When task structure is high and tasks are clear, however, directive leadership is not needed because it duplicates what task structure provides. Alternatively, when tasks are stressful, frustrating, or dissatisfying, leaders should respond with supportive leadership.

The *formal authority system* is an organization's set of procedures, rules, and policies. When the formal authority system is unclear, directive leadership complements the situation by reducing uncertainty and increasing clarity. But when the formal authority system is clear, directive leadership is redundant and should not be used.

Primary work group refers to the amount of work-oriented participation or emotional support that is provided by an employee's immediate work group. Participative leadership should be used when tasks are complex and there is little existing work-oriented participation in the primary work group. When tasks are stressful, frustrating, or repetitive, supportive leadership is called for.

Finally, since keeping track of all of these subordinate and environmental contingencies can get a bit confusing, Exhibit 14.11 provides a summary of when directive, supportive, participative, and achievement-oriented leadership styles should be used.

Exhibit 14.11

Path-Goal Theory: When to Use Directive, Supportive, Participative, or Achievement-Oriented Leadership

DIRECTIVE LEADERSHIP	SUPPORTIVE LEADERSHIP	PARTICIPATIVE LEADERSHIP	ACHIEVEMENT-ORIENTED LEADERSHIP
Unstructured tasks	Structured, simple, repetitive tasks	Experienced workers	Unchallenging tasks
Inexperienced workers	Stressful, frustrating tasks	Workers with high perceived ability	
Workers with low perceived ability	When workers lack confidence	Workers with internal locus of control	
Workers with external locus of control	Clear formal authority system	Workers not satisfied with rewards	
Unclear formal authority system		Complex tasks	

4.3 Outcomes

Does following path-goal theory improve subordinate satisfaction and performance? Preliminary evidence suggests that it does.[48] In particular, people who work for supportive leaders are much more satisfied with their jobs and their bosses. Likewise, people who work for directive leaders are more satisfied with their jobs and bosses (but not quite as much as when their bosses are supportive) and perform their jobs better, too. Does adapting one's leadership style to subordinate and environmental characteristics improve subordinate satisfaction and performance? At this point, because of the difficulty of completely testing this complex theory, it's too early to tell.[49] However, since the data clearly show that it makes sense for leaders to be both supportive *and* directive, it also makes sense that leaders could improve subordinate satisfaction and performance by adding participative and achievement-oriented leadership styles to their capabilities as leaders.

Executive Turnover

In 2005, 1,322 CEOs changed at U.S. companies, for an average of five exits per business day. The first half of 2006 proved just as robust, with 728 CEOs leaving (or losing) their positions—an average of six per day. The health-care industry alone accounted for 124 of those exits.

Source: Telis Demos, "Leading Indicators," *Fortune*, August 7, 2006, 15.

Review 4: Adapting Leader Behavior: Path-Goal Theory

Path-goal theory states that leaders can increase subordinate satisfaction and performance by clarifying and clearing the paths to goals and by increasing the number and kinds of rewards available for goal attainment. For this to work, however, leader behavior must be a source of immediate or future satisfaction for followers and must complement and not duplicate the characteristics of followers' work environments. In contrast to Fiedler's contingency theory, path-goal theory assumes that leaders can and do change and adapt their leadership styles (directive, supportive, participative, and achievement oriented), depending on their subordinates (experience, perceived ability, internal or external) or the environment in which those subordinates work (task structure, formal authority system, or primary work group).

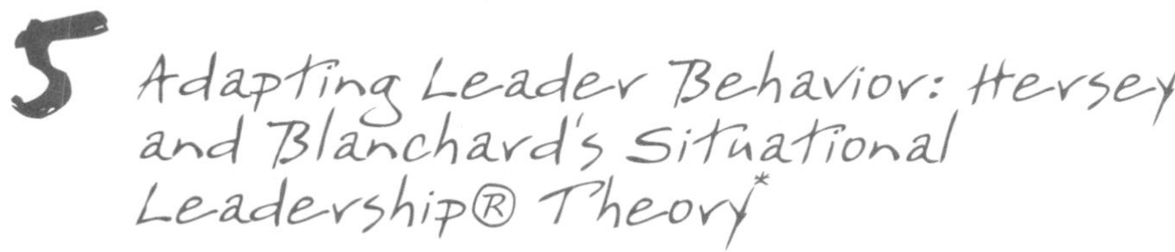

5 Adapting Leader Behavior: Hersey and Blanchard's Situational Leadership® Theory*

Have you ever had a new job that you didn't know how to do and your boss was not around to help you learn it? Conversely, have you ever known exactly how to do your job but your boss kept treating you as though you didn't? Hersey and Blanchard's Situational Leadership theory is based on the idea of follower readiness. Hersey and Blanchard argue that employees have different levels of readiness for handling different jobs, responsibilities, and work assignments. Accordingly, Hersey

* Situational Leadership® is a registered trademark of the Center for Leadership Studies.

and Blanchard's **situational theory** states that leaders need to adjust their leadership styles to match followers' readiness.[50]

*Let's learn more about Hersey and Blanchard's situational theory by examining **5.1 worker readiness** and **5.2 different leadership styles**.*

5.1 Worker Readiness

Worker readiness is the ability and willingness to take responsibility for directing one's behavior at work. Readiness is composed of two components. *Job readiness* consists of the amount of knowledge, skill, ability, and experience people have to perform their jobs. As you would expect, people with greater skill, ability, and experience do a better job of supervising their own work. *Psychological readiness*, on the other hand, is a feeling of self-confidence or self-respect. Likewise, confident people are better at guiding their own work than insecure people are. Job readiness and psychological readiness are combined to produce four different levels of readiness in Hersey and Blanchard's Situational Leadership theory. The lowest level, R1, represents insecure people who are neither willing nor able to take responsibility for guiding their own work. R2 represents people who are confident and willing but not able to take responsibility for guiding their own work. R3 represents people who are insecure and able but not willing to take responsibility for guiding their own work. And R4 represents people who are confident and willing and able to take responsibility for guiding their own work. It's important to note that a follower's readiness is usually task specific. For example, you may be highly confident and capable when it comes to personal computers, but know nothing about setting up budgets for planning purposes. Thus, you would possess readiness (R4) with respect to computers but not with respect to budgets.

5.2 Leadership Styles

Similar to Blake and Mouton's managerial grid, situational theory defines leadership styles in terms of task behavior (that is, concern for production) and relationship behavior (that is, concern for people). These two behaviors can be combined to form four different leadership styles: telling, selling, participating, and delegating. Leaders choose one of these styles depending on the readiness a follower has for a specific task.

A *telling* leadership style (high task behavior and low relationship behavior) is based on one-way communication, in which followers are told what, how, when, and where to do particular tasks. Telling is used when people are at the R1 stage. For instance, someone using a telling leadership style would identify all the steps in a project and give explicit instructions on exactly how to execute each one.

A *selling* leadership style (high task behavior and high relationship behavior) involves two-way communication and psychological support to encourage followers to "own" or "buy into" particular ways of doing things. Selling is used most appropriately at the R2 stage. For instance, someone using a selling leadership style might say, "We're going to start a company newsletter. I really think that's a great idea, don't you? We're going to need some cost estimates from printers and some comments from each manager. But that's pretty straightforward. Oh, don't forget that we need the CEO's comments, too. She's expecting you to call. I know that you'll do a great job on this. We'll meet next Tuesday to see if you have any questions once you've dug into this. By the way, we need to have this done by next Friday."

A *participating* style (low task behavior and high relationship behavior) is based on two-way communication and shared decision making. Participating is used with

situational theory a leadership theory that states that leaders need to adjust their leadership styles to match their followers' readiness

worker readiness the ability and willingness to take responsibility for directing one's behavior at work employees at R3. Since the problem is with motivation and not ability, someone using a participating leadership style might solicit ideas from a subordinate about a project, let the subordinate get started, but ask to review progress along the way.

A *delegating* style (low task behavior and low relationship behavior) is used when leaders basically let workers "run their own show" and make their own decisions. Delegating is used for people at R4. For instance, someone using a delegating leadership style might say, "We're going to start a company newsletter. You've got 10 days to do it. Run with it. Let me know when you've got it done. I'll e-mail you a couple of ideas, but other than that, do what you think is best. Thanks."

In general, as people become more "ready," and thus more willing and able to guide their own behavior, leaders should become less task oriented and more relationship oriented. Then, as people become even more "ready," leaders should become both less task oriented and less relationship oriented until people eventually manage their own work with little input from their leaders.

How well does Hersey and Blanchard's situational theory work? Despite its intuitive appeal (managers and consultants tend to prefer it over Fiedler's contingency theory because of its underlying logic and simplicity), most studies don't support situational theory.[51] While managers generally do a good job of judging followers' readiness levels, the theory doesn't seem to work well, except at lower levels, where a telling style is recommended for people who are insecure and neither willing nor able to take responsibility for guiding their own work.[52]

Review 5: **Adapting Leader Behavior: Hersey and Blanchard's Situational Leadership Theory**

According to situational theory, leaders need to adjust their leadership styles to match their followers' readiness, which is the ability (job readiness) and willingness (psychological readiness) to take responsibility for directing one's work. Job readiness and psychological readiness combine to produce four different levels of readiness (R1–R4), which vary based on people's confidence, ability, and willingness to guide their own work. Situational theory combines task and relationship behavior to create four leadership styles—telling (R1), selling (R2), participating (R3), and delegating (R4)—that are used with employees at different readiness levels.

6 Adapting Leader Behavior: Normative Decision Theory

For years, your company has insisted on formal business attire for men and women. Now, however, you want to make a change to casual wear. Do you make the decision yourself and announce it, or do you consult your employees before making the decision?

To keep up with the exponential growth in one of your sales regions, you're going to cut the region in half, add staff, and effectively reduce the earnings of its sales representatives and managers. Do you make the decision yourself, announce it, and then live with the backlash? Do you consult all of your regional managers before making this decision? Or do you go straight to the salespeople in the region to let them know about your concerns?

Many people believe that making tough decisions is at the heart of leadership. Yet experienced leaders will tell you that deciding how to make decisions is just as important. The **normative decision theory** (also known as the *Vroom-Yetton-Jago model*) helps leaders decide how much employee participation (from none to letting employees make the entire decision) should be used when making decisions.[53]

*Let's learn more about normative decision theory by investigating **6.1 decision styles** and **6.2 decision quality and acceptance**.*

6.1 Decision Styles

Unlike nearly all of the other leadership theories discussed in this chapter, which have specified leadership styles, that is, the way a leader generally behaves toward followers, the normative decision theory specifies five different decision styles, or ways of making decisions. (See Chapter 5 for a more complete review of decision making in organizations.) As shown in Exhibit 14.12, those styles vary from *autocratic decisions* (AI or AII) on the left, in which leaders make the decisions by themselves, to *consultative decisions* (CI or CII), in which leaders share problems with subordinates but still make the decisions themselves, to *group decisions* (GII) on the right, in which leaders share the problems with subordinates and then have the group make the decisions. **GE Aircraft Engines** in Durham, North Carolina, uses a similar approach when making decisions. According to *Fast Company* magazine, "At GE/Durham, every decision is either an 'A' decision, a 'B' decision, or a 'C' decision. An 'A' decision is one that the plant manager makes herself, without consulting anyone."[54] Plant manager Paula Sims says, "I don't make very many of those, and when I do make one, everyone at the plant knows it. I make maybe 10 or 12 a year."[55] "B" decisions are also made by the plant manager, but with input from the people affected. "C" decisions, the most common type, are made by consensus, by the people directly involved, with plenty of discussion. With "C" decisions, the view of the plant manager doesn't necessarily carry more weight than the views of those affected."[56]

normative decision theory a theory that suggests how leaders can determine an appropriate amount of employee participation when making decisions

Exhibit 14.12

Decision Styles and Levels of Employee Participation

Leader solves the problem or makes the decision				Leader is willing to accept any decision supported by the entire group
AI	**AII**	**CI**	**CII**	**GII**
Using information available at the time, the leader solves the problem or makes the decision.	The leader obtains necessary information from employees, and then selects a solution to the problem. When asked to share information, employees may or may not be told what the problem is.	The leader shares the problem and gets ideas and suggestions from relevant employees on an individual basis. Individuals are not brought together as a group. Then the leader makes the decision, which may or may not reflect their input.	The leader shares the problem with employees as a group, obtains their ideas and suggestions, and then makes the decision, which may or may not reflect their input.	The leader shares the problem with employees as a group. Together, the leader and employees generate and evaluate alternatives and try to reach an agreement on a solution. The leader acts as a facilitator and does not try to influence the group. The leader is willing to accept and implement any solution that has the support of the entire group.

Source: Adapted from V. H. Vroom & P. W. Yetton, *Leadership and Decision Making* (Pittsburgh: University of Pittsburgh Press, 1973),

6.2 Decision Quality and Acceptance

According to the normative decision theory, using the right degree of employee participation improves the quality of decisions and the extent to which employees accept and are committed to decisions. Exhibit 14.13 lists the decision rules that normative decision theory uses to increase decision quality and employee acceptance and commitment. The quality, leader information, subordinate information, goal congruence, and problem structure rules are used to increase decision quality. For example, the leader information rule states that if a leader doesn't have enough information to make a decision on his or her own, then the leader should not use an autocratic decision style.

The commitment probability, subordinate conflict, and commitment requirement rules shown in Exhibit 14.13 are used to increase employee acceptance and commitment to decisions. For example, the commitment requirement rule says that if decision acceptance and commitment are important, and the subordinates share the organization's goals, then you shouldn't use an autocratic or consultative style. In other words, if followers want to do what's best for the company and you need their acceptance and commitment to make a decision work, then use a group decision style and let them make the decision.

As you can see, these decision rules help leaders improve decision quality and follower acceptance and commitment by eliminating decision styles that don't fit the decision or situation they're facing. Normative decision theory then operationalizes these decision rules in the form of yes/no questions, which are shown in the decision tree displayed in Exhibit 14.14. You start at the left side of the model and answer the first question, "How important is the technical quality of this decision?" by choosing "high" or "low." Then you continue by answering each question as you proceed along the decision tree until you get to a recommended decision style.

Exhibit 14.13
Normative Theory Decision Rules

DECISION RULES TO INCREASE DECISION QUALITY
Quality Rule. If the quality of the decision is important, then don't use an autocratic decision style.
Leader Information Rule. If the quality of the decision is important, and if the leader doesn't have enough information to make the decision on his or her own, then don't use an autocratic decision style.
Subordinate Information Rule. If the quality of the decision is important, and if the subordinates don't have enough information to make the decision themselves, then don't use a group decision style.
Goal Congruence Rule. If the quality of the decision is important, and subordinates' goals are different from the organization's goals, then don't use a group decision style.
Problem Structure Rule. If the quality of the decision is important, the leader doesn't have enough information to make the decision on his or her own, and the problem is unstructured, then don't use an autocratic decision style.
DECISION RULES TO INCREASE DECISION ACCEPTANCE
Commitment Probability Rule. If having subordinates accept and commit to the decision is important, then don't use an autocratic decision style.
Subordinate Conflict Rule. If having subordinates accept the decision is important and critical to successful implementation and subordinates are likely to disagree or end up in conflict over the decision, then don't use an autocratic or consultative decision style.
Commitment Requirement Rule. If having subordinates accept the decision is absolutely required for successful implementation and subordinates share the organization's goals, then don't use an autocratic or consultative style.

Sources: Adapted from V. H. Vroom, "Leadership," in *Handbook of Industrial and Organizational Psychology*, ed. M. D. Dunnette (Chicago: Rand McNally, 1976); V. H. Vroom & A. G. Jago, *The New Leadership: Managing Participation in Organizations* (Englewood Cliffs, NJ: Prentice Hall, 1988).

Exhibit 14.14

Normative Decision Theory Tree for Determining the Level of Participation in Decision Making

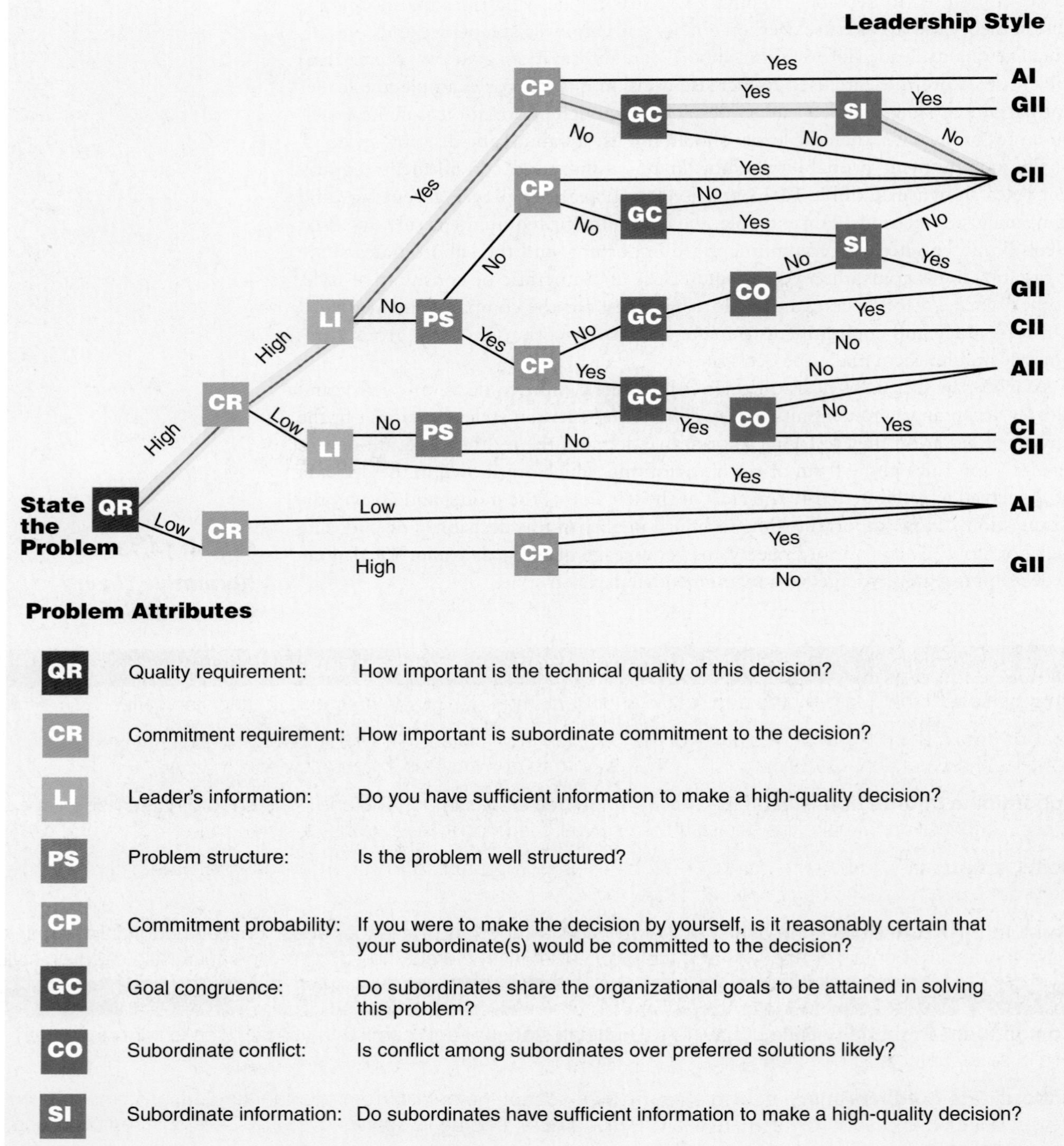
Leadership Style
State the Problem
QR
High
Low
CR
High
Low
LI
PS
CP
GC
SI
CO
Yes
No
AI
GII
CII
AII
CI
Problem Attributes
QR Quality requirement: How important is the technical quality of this decision?
CR Commitment requirement: How important is subordinate commitment to the decision?
LI Leader's information: Do you have sufficient information to make a high-quality decision?
PS Problem structure: Is the problem well structured?
CP Commitment probability: If you were to make the decision by yourself, is it reasonably certain that your subordinate(s) would be committed to the decision?
GC Goal congruence: Do subordinates share the organizational goals to be attained in solving this problem?
CO Subordinate conflict: Is conflict among subordinates over preferred solutions likely?
SI Subordinate information: Do subordinates have sufficient information to make a high-quality decision?

Source: V. H. Vroom & P. W. Yetton, *Leadership and Decision Making* (Pittsburgh: University of Pittsburgh Press, 1973). Adapted and reprinted by permission of University of Pittsburgh Press.

Let's use the model to make the decision of whether to change from a formal business attire policy to a casual wear policy. The problem sounds simple, but it is actually more complex than you might think. Follow the yellow line in Exhibit 14.14 as we work through the decision in the discussion below.

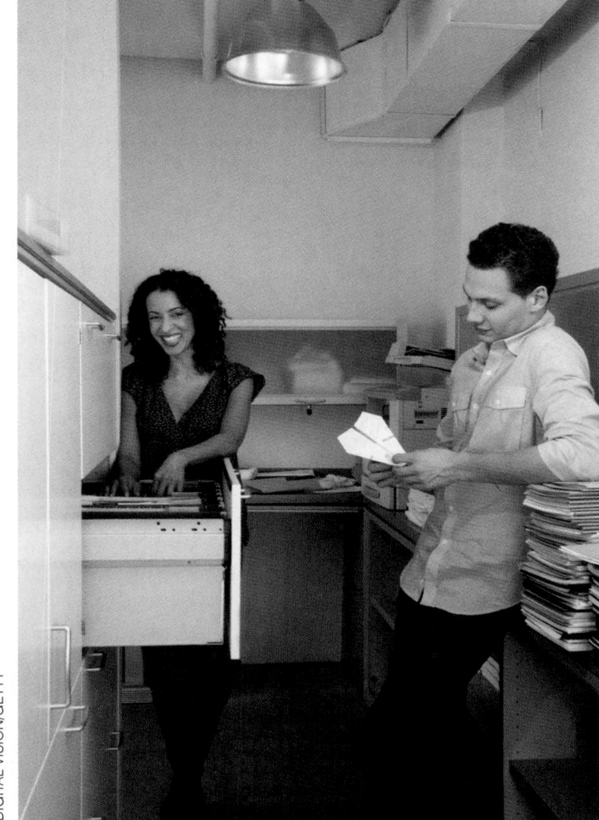
© DIGITAL VISION/GETTY

How much involvement should employees have in creating the company dress code? Use Exhibit 14.14 as you think through the issue.

Problem: Change to Casual Wear?

1. *Quality requirement: How important is the technical quality of this decision?* High. This question has to do with whether there are quality differences in the alternatives and whether those quality differences matter. Although most people would assume that quality isn't an issue here, it really is, given the overall positive changes that generally accompany changes to casual wear.
2. *Commitment requirement: How important is subordinate commitment to the decision?* High. Changes in culture, like dress codes, require subordinate commitment or they fail.
3. *Leader's information: Do you have sufficient information to make a high-quality decision?* Yes. Let's assume that you've done your homework. Much has been written about casual wear, from how to make the change to the effects it has in companies (almost all positive).
4. *Commitment probability: If you were to make the decision by yourself, is it reasonably certain that your subordinate(s) would be committed to the decision?* No. Studies of casual wear find that employees' reactions are almost uniformly positive. Nonetheless, employees are likely to be angry if you change something as personal as clothing policies without consulting them.
5. *Goal congruence: Do subordinates share the organizational goals to be attained in solving this problem?* Yes. The goals that usually accompany a change to casual dress policies are a more informal culture, better communication, and less money spent on business attire.
6. *Subordinate information: Do subordinates have sufficient information to make a high-quality decision?* No. Most employees know little about casual wear policies or even what constitutes casual wear in most companies. Consequently, most companies have to educate employees about casual wear practices and policies before making a decision.
7. *CII is the answer:* With a CII, or consultative decision process, the leader shares the problem with employees as a group, obtains their ideas and suggestions, and then makes the decision, which may or may not reflect their input. So, given the answers to these questions (remember, different managers won't necessarily answer these questions the same way), the normative decision theory recommends that leaders consult with their subordinates before deciding whether to change to a casual wear policy.

How well does the normative decision theory work? A prominent leadership scholar has described it as the best supported of all leadership theories.[57] In general, the more managers violate the decision rules in Exhibit 14.13, the less effective their decisions are, especially with respect to subordinate acceptance and commitment.[58]

Review 6: Adapting Leader Behavior: Normative Decision Theory

The normative decision theory helps leaders decide how much employee participation should be used when making decisions. Using the right degree of employee participation improves the quality of decisions and the extent to which employees accept and are committed to decisions. The theory specifies five different decision styles or ways of making decisions: autocratic decisions (AI or AII), consultative decisions (CI or CII), and group decisions (GII). The theory improves decision quality via the quality, leader information, subordinate information, goal congruence, and unstructured problem decision rules. The theory improves employee commitment and acceptance via the commitment probability, subordinate conflict, and commitment requirement decision rules. These decision rules help leaders improve decision quality and follower acceptance and commitment by eliminating decision styles that don't fit the decision or situation they're facing. Normative decision theory then operationalizes these decision rules in the form of yes/no questions, as shown in the decision tree displayed in Exhibit 14.14.

STRATEGIC LEADERSHIP

Thus far, you have read about three major leadership ideas: traits, behaviors, and situational theories. Leader *traits* are relatively stable characteristics, such as abilities or psychological motives. Traits capture who effective leaders are. Leader *behaviors* are the actions leaders take to influence others to achieve group or organizational goals. Behaviors capture what effective leaders do (that is, initiate structure and consideration). And *situational theories* indicate that the effectiveness of a leadership style, the way a leader generally behaves toward followers, depends on the situation. Situational theories capture what leaders need to do or not do in particular situations or circumstances. This final part of the chapter introduces a fourth major leadership idea—strategic leadership—and its components: visionary, charismatic, and transformational leadership.

"WHAT'S NEW" COMPANY

Strategic leadership is the ability to anticipate, envision, maintain flexibility, think strategically, and work with others to initiate changes that will create a positive future for an organization.[59] **GENERAL ELECTRIC** is one of the best run and most profitable companies in the world. Yet since taking charge seven years ago, CEO Jeffrey Immelt has led GE through a series of strategic changes that have made the company more global, more customer-oriented, and more focused on developing new technology for new markets.[60] Immelt explains his strategic leadership this way, "In my case, I was taking over a well-known company that had been led by a famous and excellent CEO [Jack Welch]. But I never wanted to run *that* company, and I never wanted to be *that* CEO. [But] I knew the company had to change. I would say most of us were trained to have a pretty healthy disrespect for history. We respect performance, respect integrity, but everybody was trained to have a look-forward attitude instead of look-backward. I inherited a company that had great strengths for a long time—good risk management, good cost control, good productivity—and I viewed the mission for my generation as not to lose those things but to build capability around growth, which we didn't have."[61] Thus, strategic leadership captures how leaders inspire their companies to change and their followers to give extraordinary effort to accomplish organizational goals.

strategic leadership the ability to anticipate, envision, maintain flexibility, think strategically, and work with others to initiate changes that will create a positive future for an organization

After reading the next section, you should be able to

7 explain how visionary leadership (that is, charismatic and transformational leadership) helps leaders achieve strategic leadership.

In Chapter 5, we defined *vision* as a statement of a company's purpose or reason for existing. Similarly, **visionary leadership** creates a positive image of the future that motivates organizational members and provides direction for future planning and goal setting.[62]

Two kinds of visionary leadership are ***7.1 charismatic leadership*** *and* ***7.2 transformational leadership****.*

7.1 Charismatic Leadership

Charisma is a Greek word meaning "divine gift." The ancient Greeks saw people with charisma as inspired by the gods and capable of incredible accomplishments. German sociologist Max Weber viewed charisma as a special bond between leaders and followers.[63] Weber wrote that the special qualities of charismatic leaders enable them to strongly influence followers. For example, Richard Scrushy, a founder and the former CEO of HealthSouth, a worldwide provider of health care (outpatient surgery, diagnostic imaging, and rehabilitation), was undoubtedly a charismatic leader. Scrushy, who had a magnetic personality, personally recruited many of HealthSouth's employees and top managers. Says one employee, "When he was talking, you could be hypnotized by him."[64] Dean Thomas Ratcliffe of Troy State University's business school says, "Heck, I [got] goosebumps listening to him."[65] Weber also noted that charismatic leaders tend to emerge in times of crisis and that the radical solutions they propose enhance the admiration that followers feel for them. Indeed, charismatic leaders tend to have incredible influence over their followers, who may be inspired by their leaders and become fanatically devoted to them. From this perspective, charismatic leaders are often seen as larger-than-life or uniquely special.

Charismatic leaders have strong, confident, dynamic personalities that attract followers and enable the leaders to create strong bonds with their followers. Followers trust charismatic leaders, are loyal to them, and are inspired to work toward the accomplishment of the leader's vision. Followers who become devoted to charismatic leaders may go to extraordinary lengths to please them. Therefore, we can define **charismatic leadership** as the behavioral tendencies and personal characteristics of leaders that create an exceptionally strong relationship between them and their followers. Charismatic leaders also

- *Articulate a clear vision for the future that is based on strongly held values or morals*
- *Model those values by acting in a way consistent with the vision*
- *Communicate high performance expectations to followers*
- *Display confidence in followers' abilities to achieve the vision*[66]

Does charismatic leadership work? Studies indicate that it often does. In general, the followers of charismatic leaders are more committed and satisfied, are better performers, are more likely to trust their leaders, and simply work harder.[67] Nonetheless, charismatic leadership also has risks that are at least as large as its benefits. The problems are likely to occur with ego-driven charismatic leaders who take advantage of fanatical followers.

In general, there are two kinds of charismatic leaders, ethical charismatics and unethical charismatics.[68] **Ethical charismatics** provide developmental opportunities for followers, are open to positive and negative feedback, recognize others' contributions, share information, and have moral standards that emphasize the larger interests of the group, organization, or society. Jim McNerney, **BOEING**'s CEO, believes that providing development opportunities for followers should be a leader's highest priority. Says

visionary leadership leadership that creates a positive image of the future that motivates organizational members and provides direction for future planning and goal setting

charismatic leadership the behavioral tendencies and personal characteristics of leaders that create an exceptionally strong relationship between them and their followers

ethical charismatics charismatic leaders who provide developmental opportunities for followers, are open to positive and negative feedback, recognize others' contributions, share information, and have moral standards that emphasize the larger interests of the group, organization, or society

> We're worshipful of top executives who seem charismatic, visionary, and tough.
>
> FAST COMPANY MAGAZINE

McNerney, "I don't start with the company's strategy or products. I start with people's growth because I believe that if the people who are running and participating in a company grow, then the company's growth will in many respects take care of itself. I have this idea in my mind—all of us get 15 percent better every year. . . . Usually that means your ability to lead, and that's all about your ability to chart the course for [your employees], to inspire them to reach for performance—the values you bring to the job, with a focus on the courage to do the right thing. I tend to think about this in terms of helping others get better."[69] As you would expect, ethical charismatics produce stronger commitment, higher satisfaction, more effort, better performance, and greater trust.

By contrast, **unethical charismatics** control and manipulate followers, do what is best for themselves instead of their organizations, want to hear only positive feedback, share only information that is beneficial to themselves, and have moral standards that put their interests before everyone else's. Because followers can become just as committed to unethical charismatics as to ethical characteristics, unethical characteristics pose a tremendous risk for companies. Why? According to *Fast Company*, "We're worshipful of top executives who seem charismatic, visionary, and tough. So long as they're lifting profits and stock prices, we're willing to overlook that they can also be callous, cunning, manipulative, deceitful, verbally and psychologically abusive, remorseless, exploitative, self-delusional, irresponsible, and megalomaniacal."[70]

unethical charismatics charismatic leaders who control and manipulate followers, do what is best for themselves instead of their organizations, want to hear only positive feedback, share only information that is beneficial to themselves, and have moral standards that put their interests before everyone else's

John Thompson, a management consultant, warns, "Often what begins as a mission becomes an obsession. Leaders can cut corners on values and become driven by self-interest. Then they may abuse anyone who makes a mistake."[71] In terms of cutting corners and self-interest, it's hard to top the unethical charismatic behavior of former ENRON chief financial officer Andrew Fastow, whom *Fast Company* described as follows: "He pressured his bosses for a promotion to CFO even though he had a shaky grasp of the position's basic responsibilities, such as accounting and treasury operations. Suffering delusions of grandeur after just a little time on the job, Fastow ordered Enron's PR people to lobby *CFO* magazine to make him its CFO of the Year. But Fastow's master manipulation was a scheme to loot Enron. He set up separate partnerships, secretly run by himself, to engage in deals with Enron. The deals quickly made tens of millions of dollars for Fastow—and prettified Enron's financials in the short run by taking unwanted assets off its books. But they left Enron with time bombs that would ultimately cause the company's total implosion—and lose shareholders billions. When Enron's scandals were exposed, Fastow pleaded guilty to securities fraud and agreed to pay back nearly $24 million and serve 10 years in prison."[72]

"WHAT'S NEW" COMPANY

Exhibit 14.15 shows the stark differences between ethical and unethical charismatics on several leader behaviors: exercising power, creating the vision, communicating with followers, accepting feedback, stimulating followers intellectually, developing followers, and living by moral standards. For example, in terms of creating a vision, ethical charismatics include followers' concerns and wishes by having them participate in the development of the company vision. By contrast, unethical charismatics develop a vision by themselves solely to meet their personal agendas. One unethical charismatic said, "The key thing is that it is my idea; and I am going to win with it at all costs."[73]

Six CEOs a day leave their position.

© POLKA DOT IMAGES/JUPITER IMAGES

So, what can companies do to reduce the risks associated with unethical charismatics?[74] To start, they need a clearly written code of conduct that is fairly and consistently enforced for all managers. Next, companies should recruit, select, and promote managers with high ethical standards. Also, companies need to train leaders to value, seek, and use diverse points of view. Leaders and subordinates also need training regarding

CHARISMATIC LEADER BEHAVIORS	ETHICAL CHARISMATICS	UNETHICAL CHARISMATICS
Exercising power	Power is used to serve others.	Power is used to dominate or manipulate others for personal gain.
Creating the vision	Followers help develop the vision.	Vision comes solely from leader and serves his or her personal agenda.
Communicating with followers	Two-way communication: Seek out viewpoints on critical issues.	One-way communication: Not open to input and suggestions from others.
Accepting feedback	Open to feedback. Willing to learn from criticism.	Inflated ego thrives on attention and admiration of sycophants. Avoid or punish candid feedback.
Stimulating followers	Want followers to think and question status quo as well as leader's views.	Don't want followers to think. Want uncritical, intellectually unquestioning acceptance of leader's ideas.
Developing followers	Focus on developing people with whom they interact. Express confidence in them and share recognition with others.	Insensitive and unresponsive to followers' needs and aspirations.
Living by moral standards	Follow self-guided principles that may go against popular opinion. Have three virtues: courage, a sense of fairness or justice, and integrity.	Follow standards only if they satisfy immediate self-interests. Manipulate impressions so that others think they are "doing the right thing." Use communication skills to manipulate others to support their personal agenda.

Source: J. M. Howell & B. J. Avolio, "The Ethics of Charismatic Leadership: Submission or Liberation?" *Academy of Management Executive* 6, no. 2 (1992): 43–54.

Exhibit 14.15

Ethical and Unethical Charismatics

ethical leader behaviors so that abuses can be recognized and corrected. Finally, companies should celebrate and reward people who exhibit ethical behaviors, especially ethical leader behaviors.[75]

7.2 Transformational Leadership

While charismatic leaders are able to articulate a clear vision, model values consistent with that vision, communicate high performance expectations, and establish very strong relationships with their followers, **transformational leadership** goes further by generating awareness and acceptance of a group's purpose and mission and by getting employees to see beyond their own needs and self-interest for the good of the group.[76] Like charismatic leaders, transformational leaders are visionary, but they transform their organizations by getting their followers to accomplish more than they intended and even more than they thought possible.

Transformational leaders are able to make their followers feel that they are a vital part of the organization and help them see how their jobs fit with the organization's vision. By linking individual and organizational interests, transformational leaders encourage followers to make sacrifices for the organization because they know that they will prosper when the organization prospers. As Exhibit 14.16 shows, transformational leadership has four components: charismatic leadership or idealized influence, inspirational motivation, intellectual stimulation, and individualized consideration.[77]

Charismatic leadership or idealized influence means that transformational leaders act as role models for their followers. Because transformational leaders put others' needs

transformational leadership leadership that generates awareness and acceptance of a group's purpose and mission and gets employees to see beyond their own needs and self-interests for the good of the group

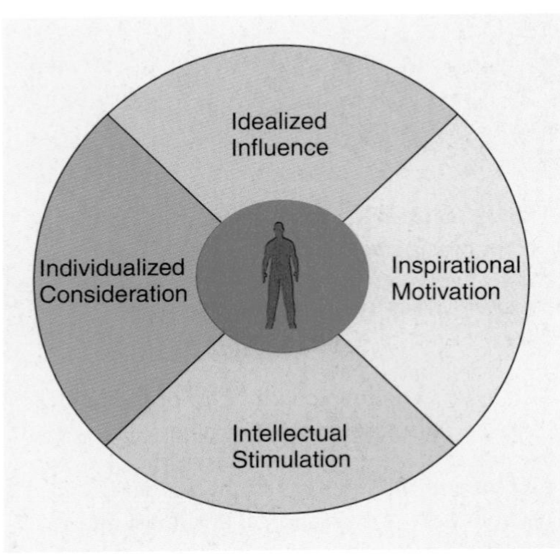

Exhibit 14.16

Components of Transformational Leadership

ahead of their own and share risks with their followers, they are admired, respected, and trusted, and followers want to emulate them. Thus, in contrast to purely charismatic leaders (especially unethical charismatics), transformational leaders can be counted on to do the right thing and maintain high standards for ethical and personal conduct. After Jim McNerney became Boeing's third CEO in three years, he pushed company lawyers to settle ethics violations that occurred under his predecessors. Under the settlement with the U.S. Justice Department, Boeing agreed to pay a $615 million penalty. But for McNerney, that wasn't enough. He apologized before a Senate committee and refused to take a $200 million tax deduction to which Boeing was entitled for its costs in obtaining the settlement. Critics charge that McNerney's decision to not take the tax deduction wrongly cost Boeing shareholders $200 million. McNerney, who was responsible for restoring the company's commitment to ethical behavior, said, "I thought it was the right thing to do."[78] McNerney also instituted a new organization-wide ethics program and has linked bonuses and promotion to ethical behavior.

Inspirational motivation means that transformational leaders motivate and inspire followers by providing meaning and challenge to their work. By clearly communicating expectations and demonstrating commitment to goals, transformational leaders help followers envision future states, such as the organizational vision or mission. In turn, this leads to greater enthusiasm and optimism about the future. MEDTRONIC's mission is "To contribute to human welfare by application of biomedical engineering in the research, design, manufacture, and sale of instruments or appliances that *alleviate pain, restore health, and extend life*."[79] Because Medtronic designs and makes life-altering products, it has an opportunity to inspire the managers and workers who work there. Every December for the holiday party, Medtronic flies in six patients to demonstrate that the company is accomplishing its mission to "alleviate pain, restore health, and extend life." The patients give testimonials describing the difference that Medtronic's products have made to them and their loved ones. Production supervisor Karen McFadzen says, "We have patients who come in who would be dead if it wasn't for us. I mean, they sit right up there and they tell us what their lives are like. You don't walk away from them not feeling anything." *Fortune* magazine described the annual event this way: "It's a teary, communal reminder that what goes on here day after day is not the same as making VCRs."[80]

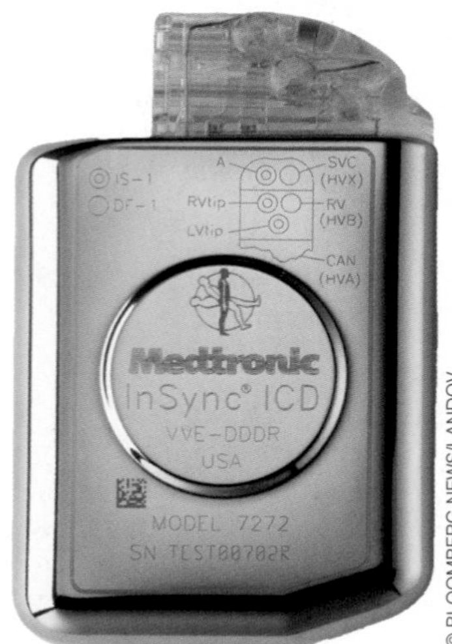

© BLOOMBERG NEWS/LANDOV

Intellectual stimulation means that transformational leaders encourage followers to be creative and innovative, to question assumptions, and to look at problems and situations in new ways, even if their ideas are different from the leader's. CEO Anne Mulcahy encourages a questioning approach by regularly meeting with Xerox's 500 top managers in groups of 80 managers at a time. Mulcahy says that the meetings, which last for several days, are "designed to be critical," to encourage honest, unfiltered discussions, and to realistically face up to problems that need solving. She asks the managers to tell her what Xerox's weaknesses are and what their major concerns are. In general, says Mulcahy, "They worry about growth, and whether our strategy is sufficient to deliver growth, especially with the economy we're in."[81] In return, Mulcahy uses these meetings to be brutally candid with her managers regarding their performance and where Xerox stands. Says one manager, "Part of her DNA is to tell you the good, the bad, and the ugly."[82]

Individualized consideration means that transformational leaders pay special attention to followers' individual needs by creating learning opportunities, accepting and tolerating individual differences, encouraging two-way communication, and being good listeners. Roy Pelaez, who supervises 426 **Aramark** employees who clean airplanes, believes in attending to employees' needs. He says, "Managers are not supposed to get involved with the personal problems of their employees, but I take the opposite view."[83] With morale low and turnover high, he hired a tutor to improve his employees' English skills. To keep absences low, he found government programs that provided certified babysitters for his low-paid employees. And he set up three computers so that employees could teach each other to use word processors and spreadsheets. Says Pelaez, "All of these things are important, because we want employees who really feel connected to the company." Clearly, they do. Turnover, once almost 100 percent per year, dropped to 12 percent after Pelaez began paying attention to his employees' needs.

Finally, a distinction needs to be drawn between transformational leadership and transactional leadership. While transformational leaders use visionary and inspirational appeals to influence followers, **transactional leadership** is based on an exchange process, in which followers are rewarded for good performance and punished for poor performance. When leaders administer rewards fairly and offer followers the rewards that they want, followers will often reciprocate with effort. A problem, however, is that transactional leaders often rely too heavily on discipline or threats to bring performance up to standards. Though this may work in the short run, it's much less effective in the long run. Also, as discussed in Chapters 11 and 13, many leaders and organizations have difficulty successfully linking pay practices to individual performance. As a result, studies consistently show that transformational leadership is much more effective on average than transactional leadership. In the United States, Canada, Japan, and India, and at all organizational levels, from first-level supervisors to upper-level executives, followers view transformational leaders as much better leaders and are much more satisfied when working for them. Furthermore, companies with transformational leaders have significantly better financial performance.[84]

Review 7: Visionary Leadership

Strategic leadership requires visionary, charismatic, and transformational leadership. Visionary leadership creates a positive image of the future that motivates organizational members and provides direction for future planning and goal setting. Charismatic leaders have strong, confident, dynamic personalities that attract followers, enable the leader to create strong bonds, and inspire followers to accomplish the leader's vision. Followers of ethical charismatic leaders work harder, are more committed and satisfied, are better performers, and are more likely to trust their leaders. Followers can be just as supportive and committed to unethical charismatics, but these leaders can pose a tremendous risk for companies. Unethical charismatics control and manipulate followers and do what is best for themselves instead of their organizations. To reduce the risks associated with unethical charismatics, companies need to enforce a clearly written code of conduct; recruit, select, and promote managers with high ethical standards; train leaders to value, seek, and use diverse points of view; teach everyone in the company to recognize unethical leader behaviors; and celebrate and reward people who exhibit ethical behaviors. Transformational leadership goes beyond charismatic leadership by generating awareness and acceptance of a group's purpose and mission and by getting employees to see beyond their own needs and self-interest for the good of the group. The four components of transformational leadership are charisma or idealized influence, inspirational motivation, intellectual stimulation, and individualized consideration.

transactional leadership leadership based on an exchange process, in which followers are rewarded for good performance and punished for poor performance

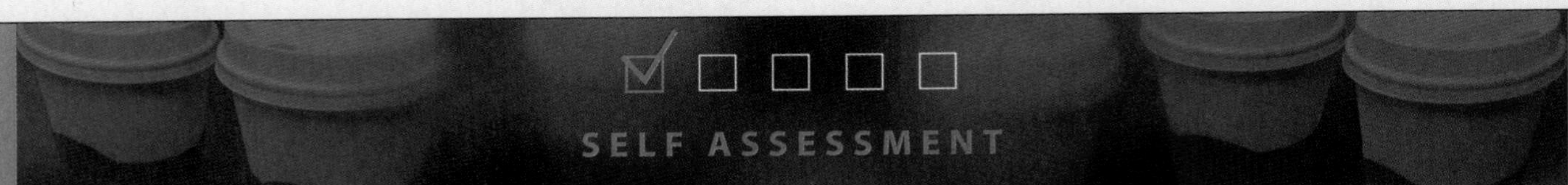

Leadership Orientation

Think of everyone you have ever worked with in jobs, clubs, volunteer positions, student projects—everything. Now that you have all those situations in mind, try to identify the one person with whom you least liked to work. Who was the most difficult person to work with to get a job done? For whatever reason, you had trouble working with this person. The person can be a peer, boss, or subordinate. Once you have that person in mind, think of how you would describe him or her to another person. The Least Preferred Coworker scale uses 18 oppositional adjective pairs to help you build your description.[85] For each pair, choose the number closest to the word that best describes your LPC.

Pleasant	8	7	6	5	4	3	2	1	Unpleasant
Friendly	8	7	6	5	4	3	2	1	Unfriendly
Rejecting	1	2	3	4	5	6	7	8	Accepting
Tense	1	2	3	4	5	6	7	8	Relaxed
Distant	1	2	3	4	5	6	7	8	Close
Cold	1	2	3	4	5	6	7	8	Warm
Supportive	8	7	6	5	4	3	2	1	Hostile
Boring	1	2	3	4	5	6	7	8	Interesting
Quarrelsome	1	2	3	4	5	6	7	8	Harmonious
Gloomy	1	2	3	4	5	6	7	8	Cheerful
Open	8	7	6	5	4	3	2	1	Guarded
Backbiting	1	2	3	4	5	6	7	8	Loyal
Untrustworthy	1	2	3	4	5	6	7	8	Trustworthy
Considerate	8	7	6	5	4	3	2	1	Inconsiderate
Nasty	1	2	3	4	5	6	7	8	Nice
Agreeable	8	7	6	5	4	3	2	1	Disagreeable
Insincere	1	2	3	4	5	6	7	8	Sincere
Kind	8	7	6	5	4	3	2	1	Unkind
TOTAL = _____									

Scoring

Determine your leadership style by totaling all the numbers you selected into a single sum. Your score will fall between 18 and 96.

You can find the interpretation for your score at: **academic.cengage.com/management/williams.**

KEY TERMS

achievement-oriented leadership 529
charismatic leadership 539
consideration 520
contingency theory 523
directive leadership 528
ethical charismatics 539
initiating structure 520
leader-member relations 525
leadership 512
leadership neutralizers 515
leadership style 522
leadership substitutes 515
normative decision theory 534
participative leadership 529
path-goal theory 527
position power 525
situational favorableness 524
situational theory 532
strategic leadership 538
supportive leadership 528
task structure 525
trait theory 517
traits 517
transactional leadership 543
transformational leadership 541
unethical charismatics 540
visionary leadership 539
worker readiness 532

MANAGEMENT DECISION

Are New Offices Necessary?

Everyone says that when business is good, you're supposed to be able to relax a little. Whoever said that never set foot in the office of your magazine.[86]

When you launched the magazine, the staff consisted of you (editor and publisher), an advertising salesperson (who also handled distribution), an art director, a page designer, and a production director. All writing was by freelancers. As circulation has grown, so has the number of pages in the magazine and the frequency with which you publish issues. That core of six people has quadrupled, causing the space all of you occupy to become cramped. At 6,000 square feet, the office is comfortably full with 25 people. Your problem is that you have more work than your 25 employees can comfortably handle, and you need to hire about five more people. Where will you put them?

The way you see it, you have a couple of options. First, you could move. Pack everyone's desk up, all the equipment, and find a space that will accommodate a larger and growing workforce. Moving, though, would be costly. Companies typically charge upwards of $50 per hour per mover, plus you'd have to get insurance to cover the move. The Better Business Bureau received complaints about companies in over 1,000 industries; the moving industry received over 5,000 complaints, putting them 11th on that list. Finding a reputable, high-quality moving company could take time away from magazine work. And managing the logistics could be a nightmare. You can't just shut down, turn off the phones, and move in peace. You'd still have to conduct business, sell ads, edit copy, handle subscriptions, lay out pages, shoot photos, and do dozens of other day-to-day activities. Plus, the sheer volume of paper archives related to five years of magazine publishing, not to mention all the technology hardware, would make packing and unpacking a big endeavor for each of your workers.

The second option: Stay put and let workers telecommute. Although you'd avoid the headache of a move, you'd trade the management of a one-time event (moving offices) for regular management of everyone's on-site and off-site schedules. Telecommuting is on the verge of being a widely accepted form of scheduling despite the very real danger of work and home life blending into one big pot of time. Already 40 percent of Americans work evenings, weekends, or on rotating shifts, and the numbers of full-time workers who work from home at least one day a month rose 30 percent in a single year, proving the trend is toward working from home. People tend to romanticize working from home, however, and forget that there are real challenges (like not having access to convenient photocopying or shipping, lack of quiet space, not enough space, and, yes, no social interaction).

You're primarily concerned about a drop in creativity as fewer people are on site to collaborate and give feedback on article ideas, layouts, and other decisions that come up nearly every hour. Statistically, 14 percent of U.S. workers who could telecommute if they wanted still prefer to work in an office. That means you could be left with only four people in the office! But offering telecommuting would let you tap into a larger talent pool and help you retain workers who are looking for flexibility with their schedules and work locations. If your employees could work from home, you wouldn't lose as much time during inclement weather either—no more snow days.

Even though your choice is between two options—move or offer telecommuting—you also need to consider how involved your employees should be in the decision. Telecommuting affects their work and home lives, but the expense and the responsibility for managing the project will be yours.

Questions

1. How involved should your employees be in making the decision? (Hint: Consider using the decision tree in Exhibit 14.14 to determine the appropriate level of employee participation in this decision.)
2. Because everyone has worked closely in the same open office, you've been able to use an achievement-oriented leadership style. Would a shift to telecommuting require a change in style? Explain.
3. How do you manage space issues as your business grows?

MANAGEMENT TEAM DECISION

Transition at Habitat for Humanity

With 500 full-time employees, roughly 500,000 unpaid volunteers, 2,303 affiliates worldwide, and upwards of $160 million in annual donations, Habitat for Humanity International (HFHI) is the 19th largest nonprofit organization in the United States.[87] Since it was founded in 1976 by Millard and Linda Fuller, HFHI has built some 175,000 houses around the world, more than 20,000 of them in a single year. Clearly, what started as a straightforward, ecumenical Christian ministry has grown into a global force for housing the poor and one of the world's most renowned nonprofit organizations. And that success is due in large part to the efforts of Millard Fuller, an avid fund-raiser, prolific author (he has written nine books), sought-after public speaker, and an all-around passionate spokesperson for the cause.

When Fuller's tenure as president was set to end after 28 years at the helm of HFHI, he and the board of directors had serious disagreements about the transition of leadership. Fuller feared that the board was moving toward a culture of "bean-counting" and away from a strong Christian commitment. He charged that many board members were not spiritually grounded. The board defended its Christian focus, but recognized that the organization's mission had become much larger than the influence of a single individual.

After 11 months of wrangling, Fuller, who was approaching 70 years of age, agreed to step down as CEO and hire an interim CEO. Fuller took a new position with the title Founder/President and became the chief spokesperson for Habitat. Taking the CEO position was Paul Leonard, who couldn't have been more different from his predecessor. Leonard, a retired real estate and construction industry executive, had expertise in organizational development and a deep knowledge of the construction industry. He accepted the position and with it responsibility for the overall management of HFHI for a period of two years.

Only three months after naming Leonard as CEO, however, the HFHI board of directors fired Fuller altogether for a pattern of "divisive and disruptive" public comments and went so far as to lock him out of the HFHI building. In the face of soaring land costs and growing housing regulations, Leonard will have to contend with a changing external environment that requires more careful planning. At the same time, HFHI's five-year plan calls for the organization to seek exponential annual growth, rather than the 5 to 10 percent annual growth it has been experiencing in recent years.

As a member of the board, you face significant challenges as well. Even though Leonard was a solid choice for interim CEO, the board is conducting an executive search to fill the permanent position. Should the permanent CEO be more like Fuller, a passionate and charismatic evangelist not afraid of setting tremendous stretch goals (like eradicating substandard housing in 20 years), or like Leonard, a methodical executive who can manage and grow Habitat's sprawling, decentralized organization? Or should the permanent CEO fit an altogether different profile?

Assemble a team of four to five students to act as the board of directors of Habitat for Humanity International. As a group, discuss each of the following questions to identify the chief characteristics the new CEO of HFHI will need to possess.

Questions

1. Does Habitat for Humanity need a leader or a seasoned manager? In other words, do you look to fill the CEO position with a visionary leader (like Fuller) or a seasoned manager (like Leonard) whose strengths lie more in organizational development than charismatic passion?
2. The new CEO will need to work with both the employees of HFHI and its hundreds of thousands of volunteers and donors. What leadership style will you look for in prospective candidates to meet the needs of those two constituencies?

PRACTICE BEING A MANAGER

Leadership is a highly prized process and capability. Organizations invest billions of dollars each year in recruiting and developing leadership talent. As more companies compete primarily on the basis of how well they employ their human capabilities, the importance of leadership continues to grow. This exercise will provide you with an opportunity to play coach to a leader entering a challenging situation.

Step 1: Get into groups. Your professor will assign you to pairs or small groups.

Scenario: The opening "What would you do?" segment in this chapter focused on the challenges facing the new CEO of Hewlett-Packard (HP). HP is a company with a remarkable tradition of product and management innovations, including a much-admired business philosophy known as the "HP Way." But as the opening segment makes clear, over the past several years HP seems to have lost its way. As the new CEO scans the situation, it is difficult to know how to prioritize. Where to begin?

Assume that the members of your small team are a group of consultants working with HP's new CEO. Your job is behind the scenes—you are simply helping the CEO to brainstorm and think carefully about how to lead this company, improve performance, and restore the once-vibrant HP culture.

Step 2: Outline leadership criteria. Work as a team to develop a set of leadership recommendations that are well-matched to the HP situation. What do you think employees need most from their new leader? Should the CEO help employees to look back and learn from the company's past, or should the CEO encourage employees to move on and focus on the future? What are the tradeoffs of each approach? The opening segment highlights some key areas of concern: (a) structural issues (for example, problems with the matrix structure); (b) unclear vision; (c) declining financial and marketing performance; (d) distrust and low morale. So how would you recommend that the CEO prioritize these issues? Are there creative possibilities for tackling some of these concerns simultaneously?

Step 3: Determine a coaching plan. Prepare to coach the CEO during the process of transforming HP. How might path-goal thinking help the CEO guide HP employees through the transition? What should the CEO keep in mind regarding such situational factors as worker readiness, situation favorableness, and environmental contingencies? Assuming the CEO possesses charismatic capabilities, would you recommend relying upon a charismatic leadership style in this situation? Why, or why not?

Step 4: Debrief as a class. Share some of the highlights of your recommendations, and discuss what leadership consultants/coaches need to know to effectively advise their clients.

The Role of Humility in Leadership

Everybody makes mistakes; today's media-saturated culture makes everyone's mistakes everyone else's news.[88] This is particularly true of leaders, who are less able (perhaps simply unable) to hide from the media microscope than in times past. We want our leaders to have an unshakable integrity, so when their mistakes turn into front-page news, it provides a unique look at the mettle of those who lead our governments, institutions, and businesses. One of the functions of leadership is to assume responsibility for company actions, even when those actions are dubious at best or downright shameful at worst. But how can leaders—who are supposed to always take the high road—work through mistakes that they or their organizations have made?

The answer is simple: a sincere apology. Okay, so the answer is not so simple. Everyone knows that apologizing is not so easy, as proved by the associated lump-in-the-throat and the awful feeling that comes from knowing that something you did caused someone else pain, embarrassment, loss, or hardship. But as you read in the chapter, a critical element of what leaders do and how leaders succeed is consideration, which is akin to empathy, the engine of a sincere apology.

How do *you* apologize for mistakes? Do you use the word "sorry" so often that it is devoid of meaning? Or do you apologize profusely, which comes to the same effect? Do you wait until you have time to think things over, or do you apologize immediately if briefly? The biggest mistake that leaders make when apologizing is passing the buck and using the word "regret" instead of "apologize." Leaders take responsibility for actions and should assume blame even if it is not their own. Making an unqualified assumption of responsibility helps demonstrate that your apology is sincere, as does going beyond a basic "I'm sorry." According to Karen Friedman, a communication coach, " 'I'm sorry' doesn't cut it.... It's empty, hollow, and quite frankly, pathetic: 'I'm sorry I cooked the books.' 'I'm sorry I beat my wife. I won't do it again.' You have to say, 'I made a terrible mistake. I offended people. I lied. I was stupid.'"[89] So, one of the marks of a true leader is not hubris, but humility. In other words, the best way to *appear* sincere is to *be* sincere.

Questions

1. Describe a time when something you did or said had a profound negative impact on a person, group, or situation.
2. Did you take responsibility for your actions, or did you try to blame circumstances or other people?
3. Did you apologize? How do you think the person who was receiving the apology took it?
4. What was the most difficult thing about apologizing?
5. Think about some high-profile blunders in recent news, whether in the world of sports, business, or entertainment. How do you think the company or individual involved did at delivering a public apology? Explain why you thought it was—or was not—sincere.

REEL TO REAL

BIZ FLIX

U-571

This action-packed thriller deals with a U.S. submarine crew's efforts to retrieve an Enigma encryption device from a disabled German submarine during World War II. After the crew gets the device, the U.S. submarine sinks, and they must use the German submarine to escape from enemy destroyers. The film's nonstop action and extraordinary special effects powerfully illustrate the challenges facing the leadership on board the submarine.

This scene is an edited composite of scenes that appear early in the film. The S33, an older U.S. submarine, is embarking on a secret mission. Before departure, the S33's officers receive a briefing on their mission from Office of Naval Intelligence representatives on board. Executive officer Lt. Andrew Tyler (Matthew McConaughey) reports on the submarine's status to Lt. Commander Mike Dahlgren (Bill Paxton). The film continues with the S33 finding the disabled German submarine.

What to Watch for and Ask Yourself

1. What aspects of leadership does Dahlgren say are important for a submarine commander?
2. Which leadership behaviors or traits does he emphasize?
3. Are these traits or behaviors right for this situation? Why or why not?

MANAGEMENT WORKPLACE

P. F. Chang's—Leading by Involvement

How do you manage 97 bistros and 33 diners at once? This isn't a riddle. It is actually the daily challenge of Rick Federico, CEO of P. F. Chang's, which owns and operates a chain of Asian-style restaurants across the country. During the time he has been head of the company, Federico has taken on the huge tasks of taking the company public and launching Pei Wei, the firm's chain of diners. In addition, he has developed management teams and laid out clear expectations for his employees. He has earned the respect of his managers, his workers, his customers, and even his competitors. He has won accolades and leadership awards. "Rick has done a great job of building a strong team culture and has built an organization that is based upon quality of execution," notes one colleague. Watch the video to see Federico's leadership style in action at P. F. Chang's.

What to Watch for and Ask Yourself

1. Describe some of Rick Federico's personal leadership traits.
2. What leadership style does he use with his chefs? Why do you think so?
3. Would you characterize Rick Federico as a charismatic or a transformational leader? Why?

CHAPTER 15

Managing Communication

© GETTY NEWS IMAGES

Learning Outcomes:

1 Explain the role that perception plays in communication and communication problems.

2 Describe the communication process and the various kinds of communication in organizations.

3 Explain how managers can manage effective one-on-one communication.

4 Describe how managers can manage effective organization-wide communication.

In This Chapter:

What Would You Do?

Sony Headquarters, Tokyo, Japan.[1] Since becoming Sony's CEO, you've spent 10 days a month in Tokyo, 10 days a month at Sony's New York City office, and 10 days a month at home in London. So after yet another long international flight, you return exhausted to your Tokyo hotel room. When the travel wears you down, you sometimes question why you took this job. You didn't actively campaign for the position. However, the board and the previous CEO picked you because they felt an "outsider" was needed to shake Sony out of it funk. As head of Sony's U.S. operations, you restored profitability by cutting $700 million in costs and laying off one-third of the employees. More importantly, though, you were able to get Sony's entertainment, electronics, and games units to work together. So why are you an outsider if you turned around a Sony Division? Well, it's simple. Unlike Sony's previous CEOs, you're not Japanese and you're not an engineer.

Sony was in terrible shape when you took over, posting its first loss in more than a decade after a series of embarrassing business mistakes, including Sony BMG's music copy protection software (which installed itself on computers when music was played and unintentionally made computers vulnerable to hackers), and flawed laptop batteries (which overheated and occasionally caught fire). The most visible and expensive mistake, though, was the long delay in introducing Sony's new PlayStation 3 videogame console. By the time the PlayStation 3 came out, Microsoft had already sold 10 million of its competing Xbox 360 game stations, cutting significantly into Sony's market share. And, with the Xbox 360 priced at a relatively cheap $400, Sony's $700 price for the PlayStation 3 will barely cover costs. So, not only was the PS3 late, it won't be adding the $2 billion in annual profits to the bottom line that it was supposed to.

Some of Sony's problems lie in its competitive corporate culture, which celebrates the success of maverick innovators who did what was needed, including going around their bosses, to bring new, innovative products to market. Consequently, working independently, not communicating, and not collaborating became the norm. That worked when Sony was a smaller and primarily Japanese company, but it no longer works given Sony's size and global scale (just 25 percent of Sony's revenues come from Japan). With over 1,000 products, one

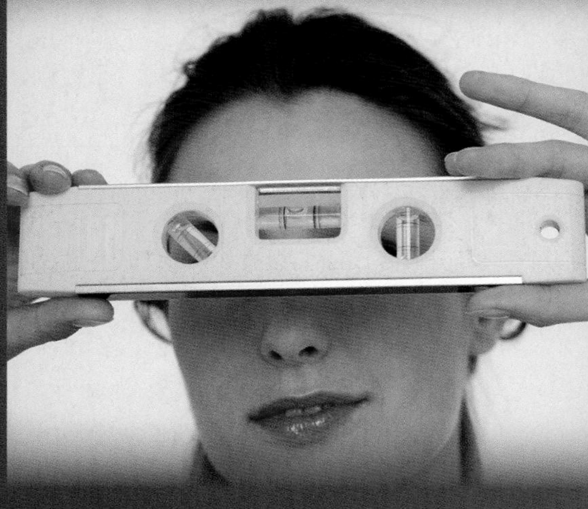

manager put it best when he said, "Sony's gotten so big that things don't connect any more." One of your top executives explained the problem this way: "I have 35 Sony devices at home. I have 35 battery chargers. That's all you need to know." Other signs of the poor communication and collaboration included actively discouraging designers and engineers from listening to customers; the Walkman and PC groups—without consultation—simultaneously bringing new MP3 players to market; and the head of Sony's videogames division going over his budget by hundreds of millions of dollars without telling the then CEO.

None of those problems are going to get solved unless you can convince your Japanese managers and employees, who criticize you for spending too little time in Tokyo, to follow your lead. Despite your success at Sony's U.S. division, you're seen as an outsider because you don't speak Japanese. So what can you do to improve cross-cultural communication? Beyond that, how do you get Sony's different divisions to talk to each other and work together? Sony will fail if these groups ignore each other. Finally, how do you change the culture of organizational silence that encourages Sony's independent managers and employees to not keep their bosses informed about problems? Problems are opportunities, but only if you know about them. **If you were in charge at Sony, what would you do?**

Activities + Videos

CengageNOW Audio study guide, electronic flashcards, author FAQ videos, On the Job and Biz Flix videos, concept tutorial, and concept exercise

Web (academic.cengage.com/managment/williams) Quiz, PowerPoint slides, and glossary terms for this chapter

Study Tip

Close your book and write a list of the key concepts in this chapter. Or create flashcards for key concepts (concept on one side, explanation and example on the other). Flashcards are great portable study aids that you can use over and over, in a group, with a partner, or on your own.

"What's New" Companies

- Sony
- National Football League
- General Motors
- Agilent
- Cisco Systems
- Kaiser Permanente
- University of Texas Medical Branch
- General Electric
- And others . . .

It's estimated that managers spend over 80 percent of their day communicating with others.[2] Indeed, much of the basic management process—planning, organizing, leading, and controlling—cannot be performed without effective communication. If this weren't reason enough to study communication, consider that effective oral communication, such as listening, following instructions, conversing, and giving feedback, is the most important skill for college graduates who are entering the work force.[3] Furthermore, across all industries, poor communication skills rank as the single most important reason that people do not advance in their careers.[4] Finally, communication is especially important for top managers like Sony's CEO. As Mark DeMichele, former CEO of Arizona Public Service Company, puts it, "Communication is the key to success. CEOs can have good ideas, a vision, and a plan. But they also have to be able to communicate those plans to people who work for them."[5]

This chapter begins by examining the role of perception in communication and how perception can make it difficult for managers to achieve effective communication. Next, you'll read about the communication process and the various kinds of communication found in most organizations. In the last half of the chapter, the focus is on improving communication in organizations. You'll learn about one-on-one communication and then about how to communicate and listen to others effectively organization-wide.

WHAT IS COMMUNICATION?

Whenever Kristy Keith's boss said, "Today is a good day for change," she knew that bad news, such as layoffs or a lost client, was sure to follow. Keith says, "It was comforting to some people who didn't know better," but the experienced employees went "back to their offices and huddled" to discuss what her boss's announcement really meant (and it usually wasn't good).[6] Many bosses try to make bad news sound good with phrases like "rightsizing" for layoffs, "merger of equals" for another company has acquired ours, "pursuing other interests" for employees who were fired, and "cost efficiencies" for your job is being outsourced to India. Why do managers sugarcoat bad news when communicating? Because, says Dartmouth management professor Paul Argenti, they think "they'll get less flak."

Communication is the process of transmitting information from one person or place to another. While some bosses sugarcoat bad news, smart managers understand that in the end effective, straightforward communication between managers and employees is essential for success.

After reading the next two sections, you should be able to

1 explain the role that perception plays in communication and communication problems.

2 describe the communication process and the various kinds of communication in organizations.

communication the process of transmitting information from one person or place to another

1 Perception and Communication Problems

One study found that when *employees* were asked whether their supervisor gave recognition for good work, only 13 percent said their supervisor gave a pat on the back, and a mere 14 percent said their supervisor gave sincere and thorough praise. But when the *supervisors* of these employees were asked if they gave recognition for good work, 82 percent said they gave pats on the back, while 80 percent said that they gave sincere and thorough praise.[7] Given that these managers and employees worked closely together, how could they have had such different perceptions of something as simple as praise?

Let's learn more about perception and communication problems by examining ***1.1 the basic perception process, 1.2 perception problems, 1.3 how we perceive others****, and* ***1.4 how we perceive ourselves****. We'll also consider how all of these factors make it difficult for managers to achieve effective communication.*

perception the process by which individuals attend to, organize, interpret, and retain information from their environments

perceptual filters the personality-, psychology-, or experience-based differences that influence people to ignore or pay attention to particular stimuli

1.1 Basic Perception Process

As shown in Exhibit 15.1, **perception** is the process by which individuals attend to, organize, interpret, and retain information from their environments. And since communication is the process of transmitting information from one person or place to another, perception is obviously a key part of communication. Yet, perception can also be a key obstacle to communication.

As people perform their jobs, they are exposed to a wide variety of informational stimuli, such as e-mails, direct conversations with the boss or coworkers, rumors heard over lunch, stories about the company in the press, or a video broadcast of a speech from the CEO to all employees. Just being exposed to an informational stimulus, however, is no guarantee that an individual will pay attention or attend to that stimulus. People experience stimuli through their own **perceptual filters**—the personality-, psychology-, or experience-based differences that influence them to ignore or pay attention to particular stimuli. Because of filtering, people exposed to the same information will often disagree about what they saw or heard. For example, every major stadium in the **National Football League** has a huge TV monitor on which fans can watch replays. As the slow motion video is replayed on the monitor, you can often hear cheers *and* boos, as fans of both teams perceive the same replay in completely different ways. This happens because the fans' perceptual filters predispose them to attend to stimuli that support their team and not their opponents.

And the same perceptual filters that affect whether we believe our favorite team was "robbed" by the referees also affect communication, that is, the transmitting of information from one person or place to another. As shown in Exhibit 15.1, perceptual filters affect each part of the *perception process*: attention, organization, interpretation, and retention.

Attention is the process of noticing or becoming aware of particular stimuli. Because of perceptual filters, we attend to some stimuli and not others. *Organization* is the process of incorporating new information (from the stimuli that you notice) into your existing knowledge. Because of perceptual filters, we are more likely

Exhibit 15.1
Basic Perception Process

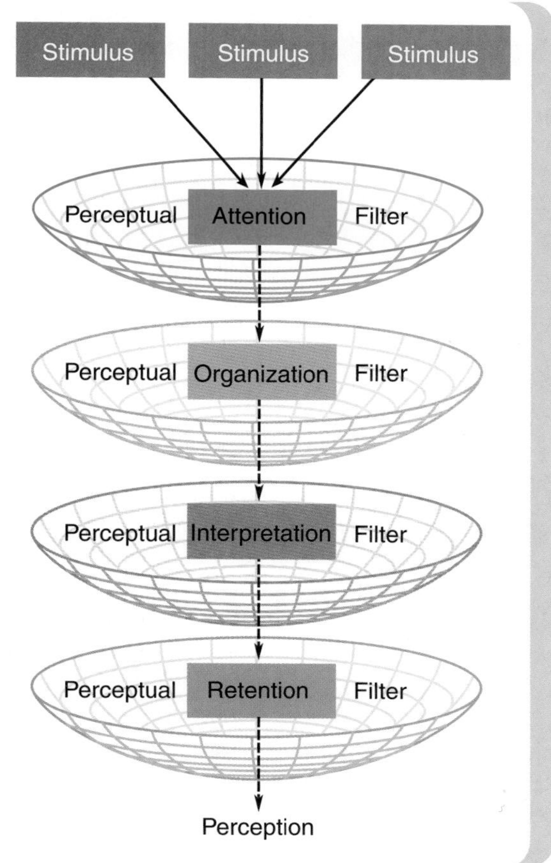

This play probably elicited both cheers and boos. The same perceptual filters that affect whether we think our team was "robbed" also affect management communication.

to incorporate new knowledge that is consistent with what we already know or believe. *Interpretation* is the process of attaching meaning to new knowledge. Because of perceptual filters, our preferences and beliefs strongly influence the meaning we attach to new information ("This must mean that top management supports our project."). Finally, *retention* is the process of remembering interpreted information. In other words, retention is what we recall and commit to memory after we have perceived something. Of course, perceptual filters also affect retention, that is, what we're likely to remember in the end.

For instance, imagine that you miss the first 10 minutes of a TV show and turn on your TV to see two people talking to each other in a living room. As they talk, they walk around the room, picking up and putting down various items; some items, such as a ring, watch, and credit card, appear to be valuable, and others appear to be drug related, such as a water pipe for smoking marijuana. In fact, this situation was depicted on videotape in a well-known study that manipulated people's perceptual filters.[8] Before watching the video, one-third of the study participants were told that the people were there to rob the apartment. Another third of the participants were told that police were on their way to conduct a drug raid and that the people in the apartment were getting rid of incriminating evidence. The remaining third of the participants were told that the people were simply waiting for a friend.

After watching the video, participants were asked to list all of the objects from the video that they could remember. Not surprisingly, the different perceptual filters (theft, drug raid, and waiting for a friend) affected what the participants attended to, how they organized the information, how they interpreted it, and ultimately which objects they remembered. Participants who thought a theft was in progress were more likely to remember the valuable objects in the video. Those who thought a drug raid was imminent were more likely to remember the drug-related objects. There was no discernible pattern to the items remembered by those who thought that the people in the video were simply waiting for a friend.

In short, because of perception and perceptual filters, people are likely to pay attention to different things, organize and interpret what they pay attention to differently, and, finally, remember things differently. Consequently, even when people are exposed to the same communications (for example, organizational memos, discussions with managers or customers), they can end up with very different perceptions and understandings. This is why communication can be so difficult and frustrating for managers. Let's review some of the communication problems created by perception and perceptual filters.

1.2 Perception Problems

Perception creates communication problems for organizations because people exposed to the same communication and information can end up with completely different ideas and understandings. Two of the most common perception problems in organizations are selective perception and closure.

At work, we are constantly bombarded with sensory stimuli—phones ringing, people talking in the background, computers dinging as new e-mail arrives, people calling our names, and so forth. As limited processors of information, we cannot possibly notice, receive, and interpret all of this information. As a result, we attend to and accept some stimuli but screen out and reject others. This isn't a random process, however. **Selective perception** is the tendency to notice and accept objects and information consistent with our values, beliefs, and expectations, while ignoring or screening out inconsistent information. For example, when Jack Smith, the former CEO of **General Motors**, was a junior-level executive, he traveled to Japan to learn why Toyota's cars were so reliable and why Toyota was so productive. When he learned that Toyota could build a car with half as many people as GM, he wrote a report and shared his findings with GM's all-powerful executive committee. But no one on the committee believed what he told them. The executives just couldn't accept that a Japanese company was so much more effective than GM. Says Smith, "Never in my life have I been so quickly and unceremoniously blown out of the water."[9]

Once we have initial information about a person, event, or process, **closure** is the tendency to fill in the gaps where information is missing, that is, to assume that what we don't know is consistent with what we already know. If employees are told that budgets must be cut by 10 percent, they may automatically assume that 10 percent of employees will lose their jobs, too, even if that isn't the case. Not surprisingly, when closure occurs, people sometimes "fill in the gaps" with inaccurate information, and this can create problems for organizations.

For example, one of the first decisions faced by a new CEO was whether to approve a marketing campaign to launch a new product. Promotional materials, advertising, and a sales and distribution plan had all been completed. The only thing missing was the CEO's approval. Though he liked the campaign, he wanted to send a strong message that the company needed to change. So he killed the campaign, which demoralized the marketing manager and team that had spent a year developing it. Because they didn't know why the CEO canceled the marketing campaign, his top managers assumed (that is, closure) that the CEO didn't have confidence in any of them either. Fearing that their decisions would be overturned, too, they began seeking the CEO's approval on everything from capital expenditures to personnel decisions to lower-level issues such as where, when, and whether to hold a conference for customers. After the marketing manager quit to take a job at another company, the CEO called his top managers together, assured them they had his confidence, told them he probably should have approved the marketing campaign, and said that he wouldn't repeat his mistake by doing anything to undermine their confidence or their authority.[10]

1.3 Perceptions of Others

Attribution theory says that we all have a basic need to understand and explain the causes of other people's behavior.[11] In other words, we need to know why people do what they do. According to attribution theory, we use two general reasons or attributions to explain people's behavior: an *internal attribution*, in which behavior is thought to be voluntary or under the control of the individual, and an *external attribution*, in which behavior is thought to be involuntary and outside of the control of the individual.

For example, have you ever seen someone changing a flat tire on the side of the road and thought to yourself, "What rotten luck—somebody's having a bad day"? If you did, you perceived the person through an external attribution known as the defensive bias. The **defensive bias** is the tendency for people to perceive themselves as personally and situationally similar to someone who is having difficulty or trouble.[12] And, when we identify with the person in a situation, we tend to use external attributions (the situation) to explain the person's behavior. For instance,

selective perception the tendency to notice and accept objects and information consistent with our values, beliefs, and expectations, while ignoring or screening out or not accepting inconsistent information

closure the tendency to fill in gaps of missing information by assuming that what we don't know is consistent with what we already know

attribution theory the theory that we all have a basic need to understand and explain the causes of other people's behavior

defensive bias the tendency for people to perceive themselves as personally and situationally similar to someone who is having difficulty or trouble since flat tires are common, it's easy to perceive ourselves in that same situation and put the blame on external causes, such as running over a nail.

Now, let's assume a different situation, this time in the workplace:

> *A utility company worker puts a ladder on a utility pole and then climbs up to do his work. As he's doing his work, he falls from the ladder and seriously injures himself.*[13]

Answer this question: Who or what caused the accident? If you thought, "It's not the worker's fault. Anybody could fall from a tall ladder," then you're still operating from a defensive bias in which you see yourself as personally and situationally similar to someone who is having difficulty or trouble. In other words, you made an external attribution by attributing the accident to an external cause, meaning the situation.

In reality, however, most accident investigations initially blame the worker (an internal attribution) and not the situation (an external attribution). Typically, 60 to 80 percent of workplace accidents each year are blamed on "operator error," that is, the employees themselves. More complete investigations, however, usually show that workers are responsible for only 30 to 40 percent of all workplace accidents.[14] Why are accident investigators so quick to blame workers? The reason is that they are committing the **fundamental attribution error**, which is the tendency to ignore external causes of behavior and to attribute other people's actions to internal causes.[15] In other words, when investigators examine the possible causes of an accident, they're much more likely to assume that the accident is a function of the person and not the situation.

fundamental attribution error the tendency to ignore external causes of behavior and to attribute other people's actions to internal causes

Which attribution, the defensive bias or the fundamental attribution error, are workers likely to make when something goes wrong? In general, as shown in Exhibit 15.2, employees and coworkers are more likely to perceive events and explain behavior from a defensive bias. Because they do the work themselves and see themselves as similar to others who make mistakes, have accidents, or are otherwise held responsible for things that go wrong at work, employees and coworkers are likely

Exhibit 15.2

Defensive Bias and Fundamental Attribution Error

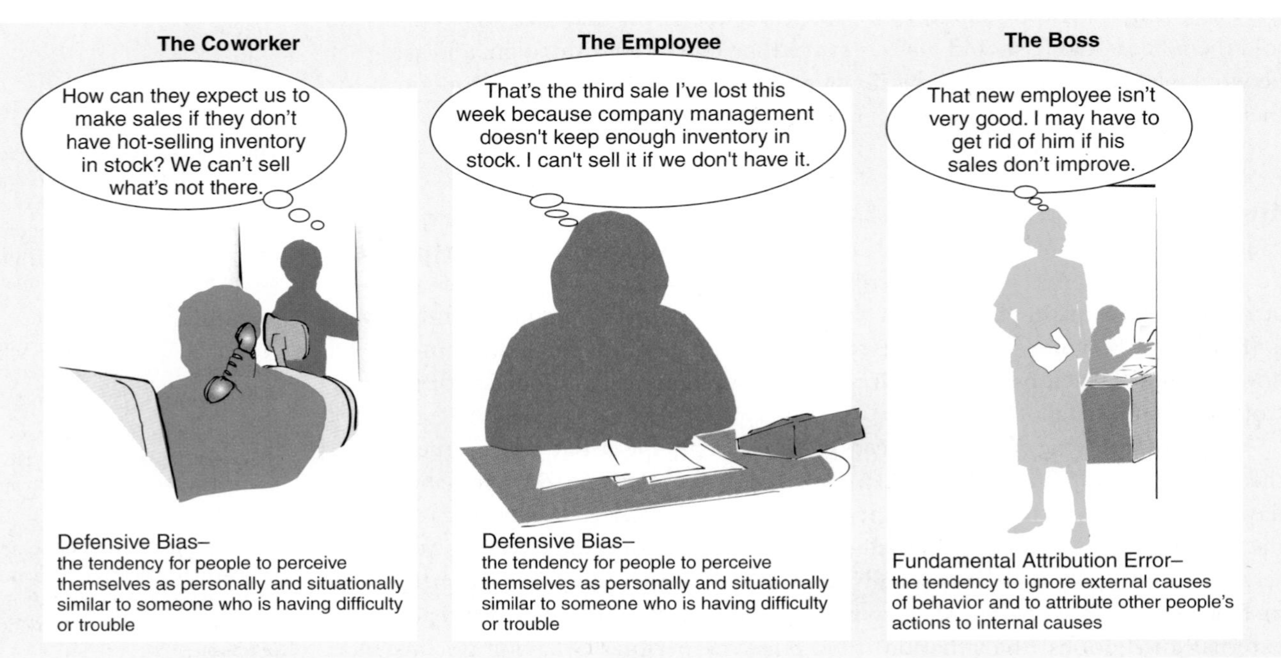

to attribute problems to external causes, such as failed machinery, poor support, or inadequate training. By contrast, because they are typically observers (who don't do the work themselves) and see themselves as situationally and personally different from workers, managers (that is, the boss) tend to commit the fundamental attribution error and blame mistakes, accidents, and other things that go wrong on workers (an internal attribution).

Consequently, in most workplaces, when things go wrong, workers and managers can be expected to take opposite views. Therefore, together, the defensive bias, which is typically used by workers, and the fundamental attribution error, which is typically made by managers, present a significant challenge to effective communication and understanding in organizations.

1.4 Self-Perception

Cindy Pruit is a professional development and recruiting manager at the law firm of Womble Carlyle Sandridge & Rice. Pruitt works frequently with the firm's summer associates, law school students who are interning with the company during summer break. Pruitt was surprised when one of the summer associates broke down in tears after being told that the writing structure on a memo he had written was "a little too loose." Says Pruitt, "They're simply stunned when they get any kind of negative feedback. I practically had to walk him off the ledge."[16]

> "They're simply stunned when they get any kind of negative feedback. I practically had to walk him off the ledge."
>
> CINDY PRUIT, PROFESSIONAL DEVELOPMENT AND RECRUITING MANAGER, WOMBLE CARLYLE SANDRIDGE & RICE

The **self-serving bias** is the tendency to overestimate our value by attributing successes to ourselves (internal causes) and attributing failures to others or the environment (external causes).[17] As the example with the upset summer law associate illustrates, the self-serving bias can make it especially difficult for managers to talk to employees about performance problems. In general, people have a need to maintain a positive self-image. This need is so strong that when people seek feedback at work, they typically want verification of their worth (rather than information about performance deficiencies) or assurance that mistakes or problems weren't their fault.[18] And, when managerial communication threatens people's positive self-image, they can become defensive and emotional. They quit listening, and communication becomes ineffective. In the second half of the chapter, which focuses on improving communication, we'll explain ways in which managers can minimize this self-serving bias and improve effective one-on-one communication with employees.

self-serving bias the tendency to overestimate our value by attributing successes to ourselves (internal causes) and attributing failures to others or the environment (external causes)

Review 1: Perception and Communication Problems

Perception is the process by which people attend to, organize, interpret, and retain information from their environments. Perception is not a straightforward process, however. Because of perceptual filters, such as selective perception and closure, people exposed to the same information stimuli often end up with very different perceptions and understandings. Perception-based differences can also lead to differences in the attributions (internal or external) that managers and workers make when explaining workplace behavior. In general, workers are more likely to explain behavior from a defensive bias, in which they attribute problems to external causes (the situation). Managers, on the other hand, tend to commit the fundamental attribution error, attributing problems to internal causes (the worker associated with a mistake or error). Consequently, when things go wrong, it's common for managers to blame workers and for workers to blame the situation or context in which they do their jobs. Finally, this problem is compounded by a self-serving bias that leads people to attribute successes to internal causes and failures to external causes. So, when workers receive negative feedback from managers, they may become defensive and emotional and not hear what their managers have to say. In short, perceptions and attributions represent a significant challenge to effective communication and understanding in organizations.

2 Kinds of Communication

Each year, on the anniversary of your hiring date, you receive a written assessment of your performance from your boss. This year, after receiving your performance appraisal, you gripe about it to your best friend, a coworker in a cubicle down the hall. Despite your griping, however, you appreciate that your boss cut you some slack, allowing you extra days off when you went through a divorce earlier this year. How did your boss know you were having personal problems? He knew something was wrong from your nonverbal communication—your rounded shoulders, the bags under your eyes, and your overall lack of energy. There are many kinds of communication—formal, informal, coaching/counseling, and nonverbal—but they all follow the same fundamental process.

Let's learn more about the different kinds of communication by examining ***2.1 the communication process, 2.2 formal communication channels, 2.3 informal communication channels, 2.4 coaching and counseling, or one-on-one communication,*** *and* ***2.5 nonverbal communication.***

2.1 The Communication Process

Earlier in the chapter, we defined *communication* as the process of transmitting information from one person or place to another. Exhibit 15.3 displays a model of the communication process and its major components: the sender (message to be conveyed, encoding the message, transmitting the message); the receiver (receiving message, decoding message, and the message that was understood); and noise, which interferes with the communication process.

encoding putting a message into a written, verbal, or symbolic form that can be recognized and understood by the receiver

The communication process begins when a *sender* thinks of a message he or she wants to convey to another person. For example, a few years ago, the CEO of a phone company turned a corner near his house, saw a pay phone booth sitting there, and thought, "That's an odd location for a phone booth. I wonder how much money it earns us."[19] The next step is to encode the message. **Encoding** means putting a message into a written, verbal, or symbolic form that can be recognized and understood by the receiver. The sender then *transmits the message* via *communication channels*. In the case of the CEO and the phone booth, the CEO ran into a midlevel employee the next day and said, "I'm curious. How much do we make on that phone booth near my house? It's not a big deal. Don't spend a lot of time on it. Just send me a note."[20] With some communication channels such as the telephone and face-to-face communication, the sender

Exhibit 15.3

The Interpersonal Communication Process

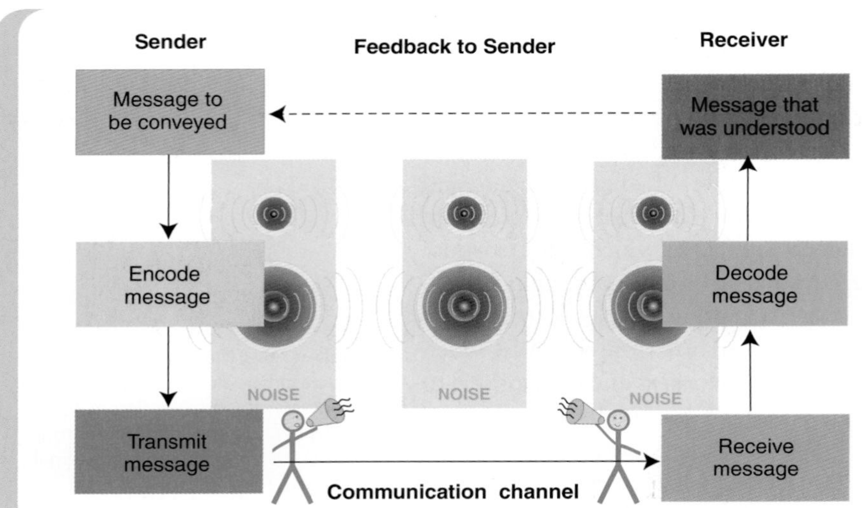

receives immediate feedback, whereas with others such as e-mail (text messages and file attachments), fax, beepers, voice mail, memos, and letters, the sender must wait for the receiver to respond.

© CREATAS/JUPITER IMAGES

Unfortunately, because of technical difficulties (for example, fax down, dead battery on the mobile phone, inability to read e-mail attachments) or people-based transmission problems (for example, forgetting to pass on the message), messages aren't always transmitted. If the message is transmitted and received, however, the next step is for the receiver to decode it. **Decoding** is the process by which the receiver translates the written, verbal, or symbolic form of the message into an understood message. However, the message, as understood by the receiver, isn't always the same message that was intended by the sender. Because of different experiences or perceptual filters, receivers may attach a completely different meaning to a message than was intended. With respect to the phone booth, the midlevel employee was writing that quick note that the CEO wanted when his manager walked up and asked, "What are you doing?" The employee explained, "Oh, this is for the CEO. He stopped by and wanted to know how much we make on that phone booth near his house." At this point the manager said—and this is where the message is improperly decoded—"You can't send him a little note. There's no comparison between that phone booth and other booths in the area."

The last step of the communication process occurs when the receiver gives the sender feedback. **Feedback to sender** is a return message to the sender that indicates the receiver's understanding of the message (of what the receiver was supposed to know, to do, or to not do). Feedback makes senders aware of possible miscommunications and enables them to continue communicating until the receiver understands the intended message. Unfortunately, feedback doesn't always occur in the communication process. In the case of the CEO and the phone booth, two months after his inquiry about the phone booth near his house, the midlevel employee to whom he posed the question and that employee's executive vice president walked into his office. When they presented the CEO with a three-ring binder containing a report and detailed analysis and charts regarding the phone booth near his house, he looked at them and said, "I have no idea what you're talking about."[21]

Complacency and overconfidence about the ease and simplicity of communication can lead senders and receivers to simply assume that they share a common understanding of the message and to not use feedback to improve the effectiveness of their communication. This is a serious mistake, especially since messages and feedback are always transmitted with and against a background of noise. **Noise** is anything that interferes with the transmission of the intended message. Noise can occur in any of the following situations:

1. *The sender isn't sure what message to communicate.*
2. *The message is not clearly encoded.*
3. *The wrong communication channel is chosen.*
4. *The message is not received or decoded properly.*
5. *The receiver doesn't have the experience or time to understand the message.*

Any idea what "rightsizing," "delayering," "unsiloing," and "knowledge acquisition" mean? Rightsizing means laying off workers. Delayering means firing managers, or getting rid of layers of management. Unsiloing means getting workers in different parts of the company (that is, different vertical silos) to work with others outside their own areas. Knowledge acquisition means teaching workers new knowledge or

decoding the process by which the receiver translates the written, verbal, or symbolic form of a message into an understood message

feedback to sender in the communication process, a return message to the sender that indicates the receiver's understanding of the message

noise anything that interferes with the transmission of the intended message skills. **Jargon**, which is vocabulary particular to a profession or group, is another form of noise that interferes with communication in the workplace. Unfortunately, the business world is rife with jargon. Carol Hymowitz of the *Wall Street Journal* points out, "A new crop of buzzwords usually sprouts every three to five years, or about the same length of time many top executives have to prove themselves. Some can be useful in swiftly communicating, and spreading, new business concepts. Others are less useful, even devious."[22]

A new crop of buzzwords usually sprouts every three to five years, or about the same length of time many top executives have to prove themselves.

CAROL HYMOWITZ, *WALL STREET JOURNAL*

When managers wrongly assume that communication is easy, they reduce communication to something called the "conduit metaphor."[23] Strictly speaking, a conduit is a pipe or tube that protects electrical wire. The **conduit metaphor** refers to the mistaken assumption that senders can pipe their intended messages directly into the heads of receivers with perfect clarity and without noise or perceptual filters interfering with the receivers' understanding of the message. However, this just isn't possible. Even if managers could telepathically direct their thoughts straight into receivers' heads, misunderstandings and communication problems would still occur because words and symbols typically have multiple meanings, depending on how they're used. For example, Exhibit 15.4 shows several meanings of an extremely common word, *fine*. Depending on how you use it, *fine* can mean a penalty; a good job; that something is delicate, small, pure, or flimsy; or that something is okay.

In summary, the conduit metaphor causes problems in communication by making managers too complacent and confident in their ability to easily and accurately transfer messages to receivers. Managers who want to be effective communicators need to carefully choose words and symbols that will help receivers derive the intended meaning of a message. Furthermore, they need to be aware of all steps of the communication process, beginning with the sender (message to be conveyed, encoding the message, transmitting the message) and ending with the receiver (receiving message, decoding message, understanding the message, and using feedback to communicate what was understood).

jargon vocabulary particular to a profession or group that interferes with communication in the workplace

conduit metaphor the mistaken assumption that senders can pipe their intended messages directly into the heads of receivers with perfect clarity and without noise or perceptual filters interfering with the receivers' understanding of the message

formal communication channel the system of official channels that carry organizationally approved messages and information

Exhibit 15.4
Meanings of the Word **Fine**

1. If you exceed the 55 mph speed limit, you may have to pay a *fine* (penalty).
2. During the playoffs, Shaquille O'Neal turned in a *fine* performance (excellent).
3. The machine has to run at a slow speed because the tolerance is extremely *fine* (tight).
4. Putting this puzzle together is difficult because many of the pieces are so *fine* (small).
5. Recently, experiments have been conducted on manufacturing certain drugs in space. It is hoped that these drugs, as compared with those manufactured on Earth, will be extremely *fine* (pure).
6. Be careful when you handle that antique book. Its pages are extremely *fine* (flimsy).
7. That's *fine* with me (okay).

2.2 Formal Communication Channels

An organization's **formal communication channel** is the system of official channels that carry organizationally approved messages and information. Organizational objectives, rules, policies, procedures, instructions, commands, and requests for information are all transmitted via the formal communication system or "channel." There are three formal communication channels: downward communication, upward communication, and horizontal communication.[24]

Downward communication flows from higher to lower levels in an organization. Downward communication is used to issue orders down the organizational hierarchy, to give organizational members job-related information, to give managers and workers performance reviews from upper managers, and to clarify organizational objectives and goals.[25] When an economic downturn quickly caused a significant drop in sales at **Agilent**, a technology company, then-CEO Ned Barnholt summoned his top managers. Together, they decided that their first strategy would be to freeze hiring, cut expenses, and cut temporary workers. Then, through e-mails, the twice-weekly company newsletter, and a speech played over the public-address system at all Agilent facilities, Barnholt explained why the cuts were necessary and how they would help the company; then he encouraged the troops to cut costs any way they could. Agilent managers reinforced the message at "coffee talks," the regular brainstorming meetings that they hold with their employees. Employees responded by using websites to house data electronically (to avoid printing costs), staying with friends and family when on company travel (to avoid hotel charges), and bringing bags of potato chips to company recruiting events (to avoid costly catering charges). Within months, thanks to effective downward communicating, Agilent's travel expenses had dropped by 50 percent, and the company's purchases of personal computers had dropped by 70 percent.[26]

Upward communication flows from lower levels to higher levels in an organization. Upward communication is used to give higher-level managers feedback about operations, issues, and problems; to help higher-level managers assess organizational performance and effectiveness; to encourage lower-level managers and employees to participate in organizational decision making; and to give those at lower levels the chance to share their concerns with higher-level authorities. At **Cisco Systems**, the manufacturer of the switches, routers, and computer equipment that form the backbone of the Internet and company computer networks, CEO John Chambers uses monthly birthday breakfasts to create upward communication. Says Chambers, "As for how I hear from employees, I host a monthly birthday breakfast. Anybody who has a birthday in that month gets to come and quiz me for an hour and 15 minutes. No directors or VPs in the room. It's how I keep my finger on the pulse of what's working and what's not. It's brutal, but it's my most enjoyable session."[27]

Horizontal communication flows among managers and workers who are at the same organizational level, such as when a day shift nurse comes in at 7:30 AM for a half-hour discussion with the midnight nurse supervisor who leaves at 8:00 AM. Horizontal communication helps facilitate coordination and cooperation between different parts of a company and allows coworkers to share relevant information. It also helps people at the same level resolve conflicts and solve problems without involving high levels of management. Studies show that communication breakdowns, which occur most often during horizontal communication, such as when patients are handed over from one nurse or doctor to another, are the largest source of medical errors in hospitals. Different communication styles, time pressures, and a general lack of standardized procedures for sharing information during patient handoffs are the likely causes. Medical organizations like **Kaiser Permanente**, which has 30 patient care facilities, are changing that by requiring all of its doctors and nurses to communicate SBAR information (situation, background, assessment, and recommendation) about each patient in 60 seconds. Since its adoption at Kaiser's St. Joseph Medical Center in Bloomington, Illinois, the number of unexpected medical problems fell

downward communication communication that flows from higher to lower levels in an organization

upward communication communication that flows from lower to higher levels in an organization

horizontal communication communication that flows among managers and workers who are at the same organizational level from 89.9 per 1,000 patient days to 39.6 per 1,000 patient days. Using the SBAR protocol significantly reduces the horizontal communication problems associated with patient handoffs.[28]

In general, what can managers do to improve formal communication? First, decrease reliance on downward communication. Second, increase chances for upward communication by increasing personal contact with lower-level managers and workers. Third, as at Kaiser Permanente, encourage much better use of horizontal communication. Finally, be aware of the problems associated with downward, upward, and horizontal communication, some of which are listed in Exhibit 15.5.

2.3 Informal Communication Channels

An organization's **informal communication channel**, sometimes called the **grapevine**, is the transmission of messages from employee to employee outside of formal communication channels. The grapevine arises out of curiosity, that is, the need to know what is going on in an organization and how it might affect you or others. To satisfy this curiosity, employees need a consistent supply of relevant, accurate, in-depth information about "who is doing what and what changes are occurring within the organization."[29] Employee Paul Haze agrees, saying, "If employees don't have a definite explanation from management, they tend to interpret for themselves."[30]

informal communication channel ("grapevine") the transmission of messages from employee to employee outside of formal communication channels

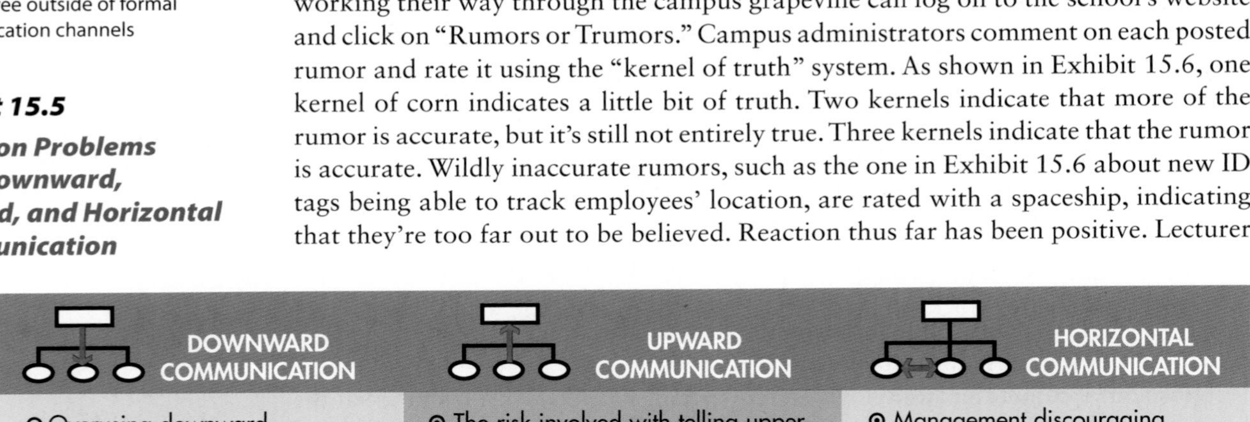

For example, at the *University of Texas Medical Branch* (part of the UT system), any of the 13,000 employees wanting to know the truth about rumors working their way through the campus grapevine can log on to the school's website and click on "Rumors or Trumors." Campus administrators comment on each posted rumor and rate it using the "kernel of truth" system. As shown in Exhibit 15.6, one kernel of corn indicates a little bit of truth. Two kernels indicate that more of the rumor is accurate, but it's still not entirely true. Three kernels indicate that the rumor is accurate. Wildly inaccurate rumors, such as the one in Exhibit 15.6 about new ID tags being able to track employees' location, are rated with a spaceship, indicating that they're too far out to be believed. Reaction thus far has been positive. Lecturer

Exhibit 15.5

Common Problems with Downward, Upward, and Horizontal Communication

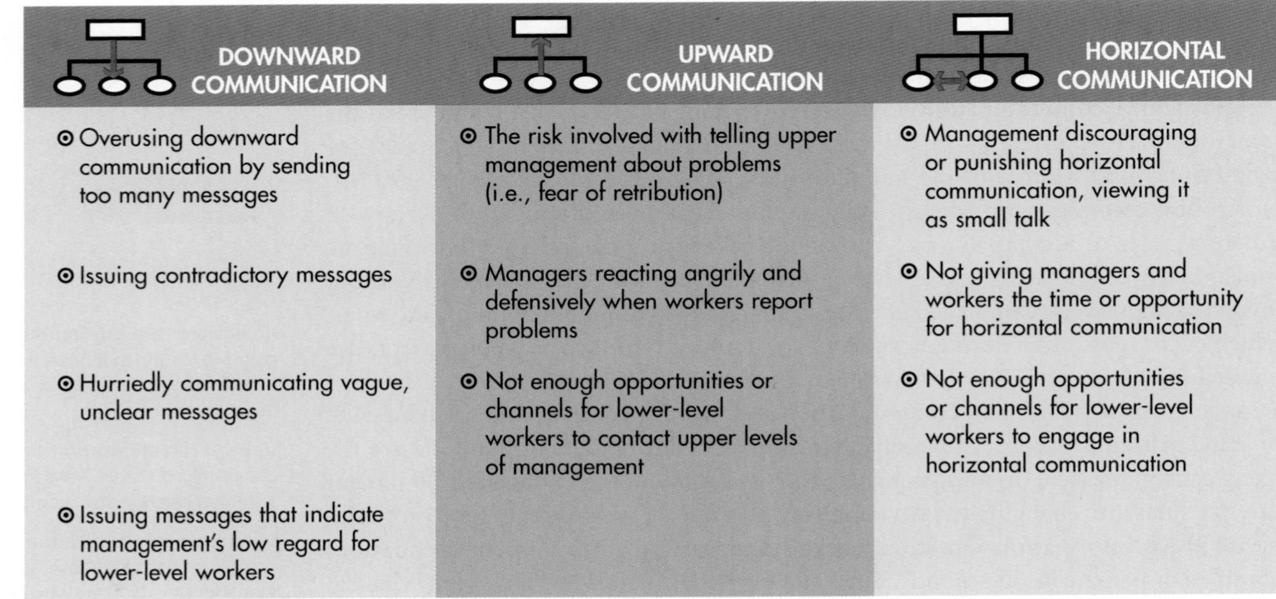

DOWNWARD COMMUNICATION	UPWARD COMMUNICATION	HORIZONTAL COMMUNICATION
Overusing downward communication by sending too many messages	The risk involved with telling upper management about problems (i.e., fear of retribution)	Management discouraging or punishing horizontal communication, viewing it as small talk
Issuing contradictory messages	Managers reacting angrily and defensively when workers report problems	Not giving managers and workers the time or opportunity for horizontal communication
Hurriedly communicating vague, unclear messages	Not enough opportunities or channels for lower-level workers to contact upper levels of management	Not enough opportunities or channels for lower-level workers to engage in horizontal communication
Issuing messages that indicate management's low regard for lower-level workers		

Source: G. L. Kreps, *Organizational Communication: Theory and Practice* (New York: Longman, 1990).

Sheryl Prather says, "It looks sincere. I've found that everything thus far has been pretty factual. It at least shows that somebody's listening to some of the talk that goes on around here and [is] putting it down on the computer where we can all see it."[31]

Grapevines arise out of informal communication networks, such as the gossip or cluster chains shown in Exhibit 15.7. In a *gossip chain*, one "highly connected" individual shares information with many other managers and workers. By contrast, in a *cluster chain*, numerous people simply tell a few of their friends. The result in both cases is that information flows freely and quickly through the organization. Some believe that grapevines are a waste of employees' time, that they promote gossip and rumors that fuel political speculation, and that they are sources of highly unreliable, inaccurate information. Yet studies clearly show that grapevines are highly accurate sources of information for a number of reasons.[32] First, because grapevines typically carry "juicy" information that is interesting and timely, information spreads rapidly. At Meghan De Goyler Hauser's former company, the word on the grapevine was that her boss drank on the job, the company accountant was stealing the company blind, and that one of her coworkers was a nude model. She says, "The rumors all turned out to be true."[33] Second, since information is typically spread by face-to-face conversation, receivers can send feedback to make sure they understand the message that is being communicated. This reduces misunderstandings and increases accuracy. Third, since most of the information in a company moves along the grapevine, as opposed to formal communication channels, people can usually verify the accuracy of information by "checking it out" with others.

What can managers do to "manage" organizational grapevines? The very worst thing managers can do is withhold information or try to punish those who share information with others. The grapevine abhors a vacuum, and in the absence of information from company management, rumors and anxiety will flourish. Why does this occur? According to workplace psychologist Nicholas DiFonzo, "The main focus of rumor is to figure out the truth. It's the group trying to make sense of something that's important to them."[34] A better strategy is to embrace the grapevine and keep employees informed about possible changes and strategies. Failure to do so will just make things work.

Exhibit 15.6

"Rumors or Trumors" at the University of Texas Medical Branch

Rumor: I heard that the new "smart" ID badges will store all kinds of my private information, and worse, they can be used to track where I am at UTMB. True?

Rating:

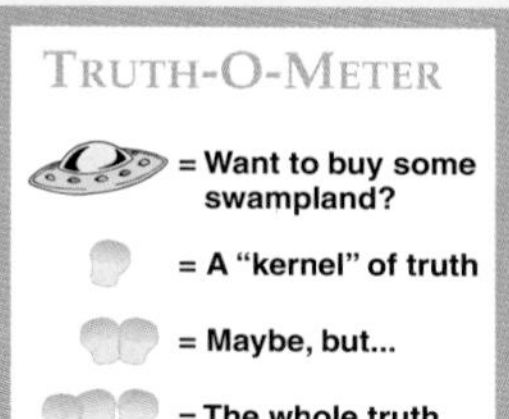

Response: No, the cards will not contain anything but the most basic information, much as ID cards do today. No personal data, no employment history, no critical financial info or medical records. The cards will primarily verify identity (your photo and name help do that) and access, the same way magnetic strips and keys do now. In the future, they will also enable a user, at his/her discretion, to use them as a debit card for campus purchases, like a pre-paid phone card, and will help manage access to computer resources.

The cards can't track your location. The proximity readers are designed with a narrow sensitivity field (you wouldn't want doors unexpectedly unlocking because someone with access is walking in a nearby hallway). However, the system does register when you are in or out of a restricted area. This is no different than is currently the case with the magnetic key cards, and is an important aspect of maintaining security in sensitive research, clinical, and business areas.

Source: "Rumors or Trumors," *The University of Texas Medical Branch*, available at http://www.utmb.edu/impact/rumors/default.htm, 1 March 2007.

Exhibit 15.7

Grapevine Communication Networks

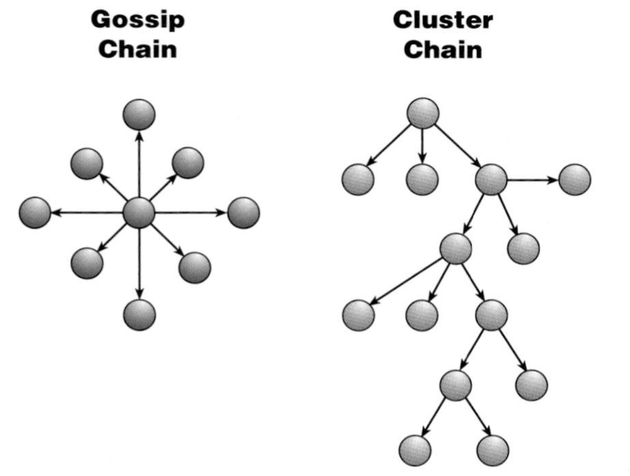

Source: K. Davis & J. W. Newstrom, *Human Behavior at Work: Organizational Behavior*, 8th ed. (New York: McGraw-Hill, 1989).

An employee who works in a company where management maintains a "culture of silence" says, "They [management] think that not communicating the tough stuff will keep employees unaware of it. Of course, it doesn't work. It just fuels the grapevine. . . ."[35]

Finally, in addition to using the grapevine to communicate with others, managers should not overlook the grapevine as a tremendous source of valuable information and feedback. In fact, information flowing through organizational grapevines is estimated to be 75 to 95 percent accurate.[36] For this reason, managers should gather their courage and be willing to read the anonymous comments that angry, frustrated employees post on Internet "gripe sites" like untied.com (about United Airlines) or stainedapron.com (for griping restaurant workers), where employees post gripes about hundreds of different companies. Bob Rosner, who runs a gripe site called workingwounded.com, suggests managers look for themes rather than responding to any particular message. And Jeff Jarvis, author of *The Blog BuzzMachine*, says, "There should be someone at every company whose job is to put into Google and blog search engines the name of the company or the brand, followed by the word 'sucks,' just to see what customers [and employees] are saying."[37]

Exhibit 15.8 lists other strategies that today's managers can use in dealing with gripe sites and blogs, the newest forms of the traditional organizational grapevine. See Section 4.2 for more on how managers can use blogs to do a better job of hearing what employees and customers feel and think about their companies.

2.4 Coaching and Counseling: One-on-One Communication

When the Wyatt Company surveyed 531 U.S. companies undergoing major changes and restructuring, it asked their CEOs, "If you could go back and change one thing, what would it be?" The answer? "The way we communicated with our employees." The CEOs said that instead of flashy videos, printed materials, or formal meetings, they would make greater use of one-on-one communication, especially with employees' immediate supervisors instead of with higher-level executives that employees didn't know.[38]

coaching communicating with someone for the direct purpose of improving the person's on-the-job performance or behavior

Coaching and counseling are two kinds of one-on-one communication. **Coaching** is communicating with someone for the direct purpose of improving the person's on-the-job performance or behavior.[39] Managers tend to make several mistakes when coaching employees, however. First, they wait for a problem before coaching. Jim Concelman, who is manager for leadership development at Development Dimensions International, says, "Of course, a boss has to coach an employee if a mistake has been made, but they shouldn't be waiting for the error. While it is a lot easier to see a mistake and correct it, people learn more through success than through failure, so bosses should ensure that employees are experiencing as many successes as possible. Successful employees lead to a more successful organization."[40] Second, when mistakes *are* made, managers wait much too long before talking to the

Exhibit 15.8

Organizational Grapevines: Dealing with Internet Gripe Sites

1. Correct misinformation. Put an end to false rumors and set the record straight. Don't be defensive.
2. Don't take angry comments personally.
3. Give your name and contact number to show employees that you're concerned and that they can contact you directly.
4. Hold a town meeting to discuss the issues raised on the gripe site.
5. Set up anonymous internal discussion forums on the company server. Then encourage employees to gripe anonymously on the company intranet, rather than on the Web.

Source: J. Simons, "Stop Moaning about Gripe Sites and Log On," *Fortune*, 2 April 2001, 181.

employee about the problem. Management professor Ray Hilgert says, "A manager must respond as soon as possible after an incident of poor performance. Don't bury your head. . . . When employees are told nothing, they assume everything is okay."[41] When Jay Whitehead, now president of Outsourcing Today, was a manager at a previous company, one of his employees accidentally copied an e-mail to a customer that insulted the customer. Whitehead immediately talked to the employee, who offered to quit. Whitehead told him, "No, instead you're going to do something much harder. You're going to apologize." He did, and, according to White, "all was forgiven."[42] The key to this successful result was that Whitehead acted immediately to coach the employee on his mistake. In Section 3, you'll learn a number of specific steps for effective one-on-one communication and coaching.

By contrast, **counseling** is communicating with someone about non-job-related issues that may be affecting or interfering with the person's performance. However, counseling does not mean that managers should try to be clinicians, even though an estimated 20 percent of employees are dealing with personal problems at any one time. Dana Kiel, who works for **CIGNA Behavioral Health**, says, "We call it the quicksand. If you're a good supervisor, you do care about your employees, but it's not your job to be a therapist."[43] Instead, managers should discuss specific performance problems, listen if the employee chooses to share personal issues, and then recommend that the employee call the company's *Employee Assistance Program (EAP)*. EAPs are typically free when provided as part of a company's benefit package. In emergencies or times of crisis, EAPs can offer immediate counseling and support; they can also provide referrals to organizations and professionals that can help employees and their family members address personal issues. Exhibit 15.9 lists the standard services provided by EAPs.

"What's New" Company

counseling communicating with someone about non-job-related issues that may be affecting or interfering with the person's performance

nonverbal communication any communication that doesn't involve words

2.5 Nonverbal Communication

When people talk, they send both verbal and nonverbal messages. Verbal messages are sent and received through the words we speak. "That was a great presentation." By contrast, nonverbal messages are sent through body language, facial expressions, or tone of voice. For instance, hearing "*That* was a *great* presentation!" is very different from hearing "ahem [clearing throat], that was, ahem, ahem, a great presentation."

More specifically, **nonverbal communication** is any communication that doesn't involve words. Nonverbal communication and messages almost always accompany verbal communication and may support and reinforce the verbal message or contradict it. The importance of nonverbal communication is well established. Researchers have estimated that as much as 93 percent of any message is transmitted nonverbally, with 55 percent coming from body language and facial expressions and 38 percent coming from the tone and pitch of the voice.[44] Since many nonverbal cues are unintentional, receivers often consider nonverbal communication to be a more accurate representation of what senders are

mgmt: trends

Hey Coach!

Management coaching has grown into an estimated $1 billion business and is no longer just for the likes of General Electric's Jeffrey Immelt and eBay's Meg Whitman, both of whom have sought tips on being better leaders. Many companies use coaching as a means to help overachievers (that is, task-oriented managers) develop their people skills. Yahoo, Inc., and Genentech enlist coaching services to groom internal candidates for future executive positions within the company.

Source: Phred Dvorak, "Construction Firm Rebuilds Managers to Make Them Softer," *Wall Street Journal*, May 16, 2006, A1.

PROBLEM OR NEED	SERVICE PROVIDED
Stress, depression, relationships, substance abuse	Counseling
Pregnancy, adoption, day care, nutrition, fertility	Child care
Health and nutrition, care options, Alzheimer's disease	Senior care
Wills, leases, estate plans, adoptions	Legal services
Referrals and discounts on chiropractic care, acupuncture, massage therapy, vitamins	Health/lifestyle assistance
Pet-sitting resources, obedience training, veterinarians	Pet care
Retirement planning, debt consolidation, budgeting	Financial services

Source: "You Can Do It. We Can Help," CIGNA Behavioral Health, available at http://www.hr.tcu.edu/eappages/core/html/default.html, 30 March 2002.

Exhibit 15.9

Services Provided by Employee Assistance Programs (EAPs)

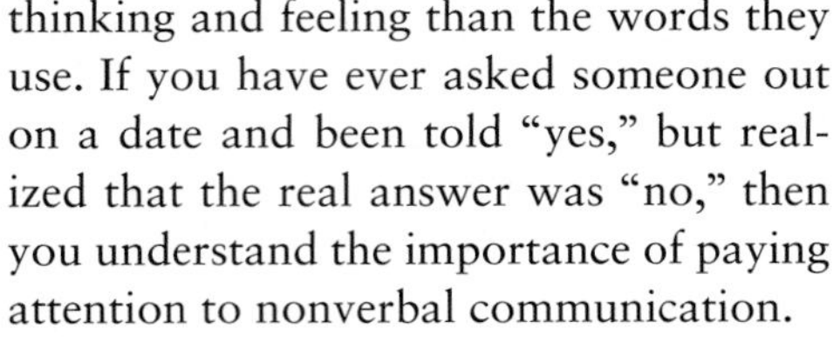

thinking and feeling than the words they use. If you have ever asked someone out on a date and been told "yes," but realized that the real answer was "no," then you understand the importance of paying attention to nonverbal communication.

Kinesics and paralanguage are two kinds of nonverbal communication.[45] **Kinesics** (from the Greek word *kinesis*, meaning "movement") are movements of the body and face.[46] These movements include arm and hand gestures, facial expressions, eye contact, folding arms, crossing legs, and leaning toward or away from another person. For example, people tend to avoid eye contact when they are embarrassed or unsure of the message they are sending. Crossed arms or legs usually indicate defensiveness or that the person is not receptive to the message or the sender. Also, people tend to smile frequently when they are seeking someone's approval.

kinesics movements of the body and face

paralanguage the pitch, rate, tone, volume, and speaking pattern (i.e., use of silences, pauses, or hesitations) of one's voice

It turns out that kinesics play an incredibly important role in communication. Studies of married couples' kinesic interactions can predict whether they will stay married with 93 percent accuracy.[47] The key is the ratio of positive to negative kinesic interactions that husbands and wives make as they communicate. Negative kinesic expressions such as eye rolling suggest contempt, whereas positive kinetic expressions such as maintaining eye contact and nodding suggest listening and caring. When the ratio of positive to negative interactions drops below 5 to 1, the chances for divorce quickly increase. Kinesics operate similarly in the workplace, providing clues about people's true feelings, over and beyond what they say (or don't say). For instance, Louis Giuliano, former CEO of *ITT*, which makes heavy use of teams, says, "When you get a team together and say to them we're going to change a process, you always have people who say, 'No, we're not.'" They usually don't say it out loud, but "the body language is there," making it clear that their real answer is "no."[48]

Paralanguage includes the pitch, rate, tone, volume, and speaking pattern (use of silences, pauses, or hesitations) of one's voice. For example, when people are unsure what to say, they tend to decrease their communication effectiveness by speaking softly. When people are nervous, they tend to talk faster and louder. These characteristics have a tremendous influence on whether listeners are receptive to what speakers are saying. For example, Vinya Lynch believes that her "timid and sing-songy" voice is why others don't take her seriously and cut her off when she makes presentations. Lynch says, "When I listen to myself, it doesn't sound intelligent." She began working with a speech coach ($2,250 for 10 sessions) because, as she says, "I want my voice to be charismatic and confident all at the same time."[49]

Body language can be one of the most telling methods of communicating, particularly when the message is "I'm not listening."

© IMAGE SOURCE BLACK/JUPITER IMAGES

In short, because nonverbal communication is so informative, especially when it contradicts verbal communication, managers need to learn how to monitor and control their nonverbal behavior.

Review 2: Kinds of Communication

Organizational communication depends on the communication process, formal and informal communication channels, one-on-one communication, and nonverbal communication. The major components of the communication process are the sender, the receiver, noise, and feedback. The conduit metaphor refers to the mistaken assumption that senders can pipe their intended messages directly into receivers' heads with perfect clarity. With noise, perceptual filters, and little feedback, however, this just isn't possible. Formal communication channels, such as downward, upward, and horizontal communication, carry organizationally approved messages and information. By contrast, the informal communication channel, called the grapevine, arises out of curiosity and is carried out through gossip or cluster chains. Managers should use the grapevine to keep employees informed and to obtain better, clearer information for themselves. There are two kinds of one-on-one communication. Coaching is used to improve on-the-job performance while counseling is used to communicate about non-job-related issues affecting job performance. Nonverbal communication, such as kinesics and paralanguage, accounts for as much as 93 percent of a message's content and understanding. Since nonverbal communication is so informative, managers need to learn how to monitor and control their nonverbal behavior.

doing the right thing

Protect Personal, Confidential Information

By virtue of their jobs, managers are privy to information that others aren't. Although much of that information will be about the company, some of it will be personal and confidential information about employees. As a manager, you have a moral and legal obligation to protect employees' privacy. Moreover, sharing others' personal, confidential information may dissuade employees from confiding in managers or seeking help from a company's employee assistance program. Does this mean that if employees confide in you that you can't tell anyone else? No, if you're a manager, sometimes you may have to inform your boss or human resources about a situation. But inform only those who have a need to know and who are also obligated to protect employee privacy. Furthermore, not all information that employees disclose to you should be protected. Information about discrimination, sexual harassment, potential workplace violence, or conflicts of interest between employees and the company may need to be shared with upper management to protect the rights and well-being of others. So, when employees disclose personal, confidential information, do the right thing. Don't discuss it with others unless it falls into one of the exceptions discussed here.[50]

How to Improve Communication

An employee comes in late every day, takes long lunches, and leaves early. His coworkers resent his tardiness and having to do his share of the work. Another employee makes as many as 10 personal phone calls a day on company time. Still another employee's job performance has dropped significantly in the last three months. How do you communicate with these employees to begin solving these problems? Or suppose that you supervise a division of 50, 100, or even 1,000 people. How can you communicate effectively with everyone in that division? Moreover, how can top managers communicate effectively with everyone in the company when employees work in different offices, states, countries, and time zones? Turning that around, how can managers make themselves accessible so that they can hear what employees feel and think throughout the organization?

When it comes to improving communication, managers face two primary tasks, managing one-on-one communication and managing organization-wide communication.

After reading the next two sections, you should be able to

3 explain how managers can manage effective one-on-one communication.

4 describe how managers can manage effective organization-wide communication.

3 Managing One-on-One Communication

In Chapter 1, you learned that, on average, first-line managers spend 57 percent of their time with people, middle managers spend 63 percent of their time directly with people, and top managers spend as much as 78 percent of their time dealing with people.[51] These numbers make it clear that managers spend a great deal of time in one-on-one communication with others.

Learn more about managing one-on-one communication by reading how to ***3.1 choose the right communication medium, 3.2 be a good listener, 3.3 give effective feedback**, and **3.4 improve cross-cultural communication**.*

3.1 Choosing the Right Communication Medium

Sometimes messages are poorly communicated simply because they are delivered using the wrong **communication medium**, which is the method used to deliver a message. For example, the wrong communication medium is being used when an employee returns from lunch, picks up the note left on her office chair, and learns she has been fired. The wrong communication medium is also being used when an employee pops into your office every 10 minutes with a simple request. (An e-mail would be better.)

There are two general kinds of communication media: oral and written communication. *Oral communication* includes face-to-face and group meetings through telephone calls, videoconferencing, or any other means of sending and receiving spoken messages. Studies show that managers generally prefer oral communication over written because it provides the opportunity to ask questions about parts of the message that they don't understand. Oral communication is also a rich communication medium because it allows managers to receive and assess the nonverbal communication that accompanies spoken messages (body language, facial expressions, and the voice characteristics associated with paralanguage).

Furthermore, you don't need a personal computer and an Internet connection to conduct oral communication. Simply schedule an appointment, track someone down in the hall, or catch someone on the phone. In fact, **WALL STREET JOURNAL** columnist Jason Fry worries that with voice mail and e-mail, managers are not as willing to engage in meaningful, face-to-face oral communication as they once were. In fact, 67 percent of managers admit to using e-mail as a substitute for face-to-face conversations.[52] While there are advantages to e-mail—it creates a record of what's been said—it's often better to talk to people instead of just e-mailing them. Jason Fry writes, "If you're close enough that the person you're e-mailing uses the plonk of your return key as a cue to look for the little Outlook envelope, [it's] best [to]

communication medium the method used to deliver an oral or written message think carefully about whether you should be typing instead of talking."[53] Oral communication should not be used for all communication, however. In general, when the message is simple, such as a quick request or a presentation of straightforward information, a memo or e-mail is often the better communication medium.

Written communication includes letters, e-mail, and memos. Although most managers still like and use oral communication, e-mail in particular is changing how they communicate with workers, customers, and each other. E-mail is the fastest-growing form of communication in organizations primarily because of its convenience and speed. For instance, because people read six times faster than they can listen, they usually can read 30 e-mail messages in 10 to 15 minutes.[54] By contrast, dealing with voice messages can take a considerable amount of time. Fred DeLuca, founder of the **SUBWAY** sandwich shop franchise, says, "I get about 60 messages a day from employees and franchisees, and I listen to all of them. For my sanity, I set a time limit of 75 seconds, because people can be long-winded when they're excited. When I hear, 'You have 30 messages,' I know right away that I'll spend 60 minutes on voice mail. I take two minutes per message, listening and returning or forwarding."[55]

Written communication, such as e-mail, is well suited for delivering straightforward messages and information. Furthermore, with e-mail accessible at the office, at home, and on the road (by laptop computer, cell phone, or web-based e-mail), managers can use e-mail to stay in touch from anywhere at almost any time. And since e-mail and other written communications don't have to be sent and received simultaneously, messages can be sent and stored for reading at any time. Consequently, managers can send and receive many more messages using e-mail than using oral communication, which requires people to get together in person or by phone or video conference.

Although written communication is well suited for delivering straightforward messages and information, it is not well suited to complex, ambiguous, or emotionally laden messages, which are better delivered through oral communication. Neal Patterson, CEO of **CERNER CORPORATION**, which develops health-care software, learned this lesson when he sent the following e-mail to 400 company managers:

> *We are getting less than 40 hours of work from a large number of our KC-based EMPLOYEES.... The parking lot is sparsely used at 8 AM, likewise at 5 PM. As managers—you either do not know what your EMPLOYEES are doing or YOU do not CARE. You have created expectations on the work effort which allowed this to happen inside Cerner, creating a very unhealthy environment. In either case, you have a problem and you will fix it or I will replace you.*
>
> *NEVER in my career have I allowed a team which worked for me to think they had a 40-hour job. I have allowed YOU to create a culture which is permitting this. NO LONGER.*[56]

Patterson continued: "We passed a Stock Purchase Program, allowing for the EMPLOYEE to purchase Cerner stock at a 15 percent discount, at Friday's BOD [board of directors] meeting. Hell will freeze over before this CEO implements ANOTHER EMPLOYEE benefit in this Culture."[57] He concluded by saying, "I will hold you accountable. You have allowed this to get to this state. You have two weeks. Tick, tock."[58]

Reaction to the message was so strong that, in just over a week, the e-mail had been leaked to the entire company. And then someone, nobody knows who, posted the e-mail on a Yahoo.com discussion board about Cerner. As word spread about the negative e-mail, Cerner's stock price dropped from $44 to $31 per share in just three days. By the end of the week, Patterson issued another e-mail, offering an apology.

Not surprisingly, that e-mail began, "Please treat this memo with the utmost confidentiality. It is for internal dissemination only. Do not copy or e-mail to anyone else."[59]

3.2 Listening

Are you a good listener? You probably think so. But in fact most people, including managers, are terrible listeners, retaining only about 25 percent of what they hear.[60] You qualify as a poor listener if you frequently interrupt others, jump to conclusions about what people will say before they've said it, hurry the speaker to finish his or her point, are a passive listener (not actively working at your listening), or simply don't pay attention to what people are saying.[61] On this last point, attentiveness, college students were periodically asked to record their thoughts during a psychology course. On average, 20 percent of the students were paying attention (only 12 percent were actively working at being good listeners), 20 percent were thinking about sex, 20 percent were thinking about things they had done before, and the remaining 40 percent were thinking about other things unrelated to the class (for example, worries, religion, lunch, daydreaming).[62]

How important is it to be a good listener? In general, about 45 percent of the total time you spend communicating with others is spent listening. Furthermore, listening is important for managerial and business success, even for those at the top of an organization. According to *Fortune* magazine, listening is one of the reasons that CEO A. G. Lafley has been able to turn around Procter & Gamble so quickly: "He's a listener, not a storyteller. He's likable but not awe inspiring. He's the type of guy who gets excited in the mop aisle of a grocery store. His plan to fix P&G isn't anything groundbreaking, but rather a straightforward, back-to-basics tack. And so far it's worked. He has rallied his troops not with big speeches and dazzling promises, but by *hearing them out* (practically) one at a time."[63]

"What's New" Company

hearing the act or process of perceiving sounds

listening making a conscious effort to hear

active listening assuming half the responsibility for successful communication by actively giving the speaker nonjudgmental feedback that shows you've accurately heard what he or she said

As Feargal Quinn, CEO of Irish grocery chain **Superquinn's**, points out, "Listening is not an activity you can delegate—no matter who you are."[64] In fact, managers with better listening skills are rated as better managers by their employees and are much more likely to be promoted.[65]

So, what can you do to improve your listening ability? First, understand the difference between hearing and listening. According to *Webster's New World Dictionary*, **hearing** is the "act or process of perceiving sounds," whereas **listening** is "making a conscious effort to hear." In other words, we react to sounds, such as bottles breaking or music being played too loud, because hearing is an involuntary physiological process. By contrast, listening is a voluntary behavior. So, if you want to be a good listener, you have to choose to be a good listener. Typically, that means choosing to be an active, empathetic listener.[66]

Part of what makes A.G. Lafley so successful as Procter & Gamble's CEO is his ability to listen intently.

© RICHARD DREW/ASSOCIATED PRESS

Active listening means assuming half the responsibility for successful communication by actively giving the speaker nonjudgmental feedback that shows you've accurately heard what he or she said. Active listeners make it clear from their behavior that they are listening carefully to what the speaker has to say. Active listeners put the speaker at ease, maintain eye contact, and show the speaker that they are attentively listening by nodding and making short statements.

Several specific strategies can help you be a better active listener. First, *clarify responses* by asking the speaker to explain confusing or ambiguous statements.

Second, when there are natural breaks in the speaker's delivery, use this time to paraphrase or summarize what has been said. *Paraphrasing* is restating what has been said in your own words. *Summarizing* is reviewing the speaker's main points or emotions. Paraphrasing and summarizing give the speaker the chance to correct the message if the active listener has attached the wrong meaning to it. Paraphrasing and summarizing also show the speaker that the active listener is interested in the speaker's message. Exhibit 15.10 lists specific statements that listeners can use to clarify responses, paraphrase, or summarize what has been said.

> [CEO A. G. Lafley's] plan to fix P&G isn't anything groundbreaking, but rather a straightforward, back-to-basics tack. And so far it's worked. He has rallied his troops not with big speeches and dazzling promises, but by *hearing them out* (practically) one at a time.
>
> *FORTUNE* MAGAZINE

Active listeners also avoid evaluating the message or being critical until the message is complete. They recognize that their only responsibility during the transmission of a message is to receive it accurately and derive the intended meaning from it. Evaluation and criticism can take place after the message is accurately received. Finally, active listeners also recognize that a large portion of any message is transmitted nonverbally and thus pay very careful attention to the nonverbal cues transmitted by the speaker.

Empathetic listening means understanding the speaker's perspective and personal frame of reference and giving feedback that conveys that understanding to the speaker. Empathetic listening goes beyond active listening because it depends on our ability to set aside our own attitudes or relationships to be able to see and understand things through someone else's eyes. Empathetic listening is just as important as active listening, especially for managers, because it helps build rapport and trust with others.

empathetic listening understanding the speaker's perspective and personal frame of reference and giving feedback that conveys that understanding to the speaker

The key to being a more empathetic listener is to show your desire to understand and to reflect people's feelings. You can *show your desire to understand* by listening, that is, asking people to talk about what's most important to them and then by giving them sufficient time to talk before responding or interrupting. Altera Corp., which makes computer chips, uses empathetic listening as the key sales tool for its salesforce. When salesperson Mike Dionne first met with an information technology manager from a medical company, he told him he was there to find out how Altera could expand its business in the medical field. During the 90-minute meeting, Dionne

Exhibit 15.10
Clarifying, Paraphrasing, and Summarizing Responses for Active Listeners

CLARIFYING RESPONSES	PARAPHRASING RESPONSES	SUMMARIZING RESPONSES
Could you explain that again?	What you're really saying is . . .	Let me summarize . . .
I don't understand what you mean.	If I understand you correctly . . .	Okay, your main concerns are . . .
I'm not sure how . . .	In other words . . .	To recap what you've said . . .
I'm confused. Would you run through that again?	So your perspective is that . . .	Thus far, you've discussed . . .
	Tell me if I'm wrong, but what you're saying is . . .	

Source: E. Atwater, *I Hear You*, revised ed. (New York: Walker, 1992).

rarely spoke and never said that Altera wanted to sell him computer chips. Instead, Dionne listened quietly and didn't interrupt as the manager described the kinds of technology (using computer chips) that his company wanted to buy. Dionne says, "You could tell [he] was jazzed. He was comfortable, leaning back in his chair and talking freely."[67]

Reflecting feelings is also an important part of empathetic listening because it demonstrates that you understand the speaker's emotions. Unlike active listening, in which you restate or summarize the informational content of what has been said, the focus is on the affective part of the message. As an empathetic listener, you can use the following statements to reflect the speaker's emotions:

- *So, right now it sounds like you're feeling. . . .*
- *You seem as if you're. . . .*
- *Do you feel a bit. . .?*
- *I could be wrong, but I'm sensing that you're feeling. . . .*

In the end, says management consultant Terry Pearce, empathetic listening can be boiled down to these three steps. First, wait 10 seconds before you answer or respond. It will seem an eternity, but waiting prevents you from interrupting others and rushing your response. Second, to be sure you understand what the speaker wants, ask questions to clarify the speaker's intent. Third, only then should you respond first with feelings and then facts (notice that facts *follow* feelings).[68]

3.3 Giving Feedback

In Chapter 11, you learned that performance appraisal feedback (that is, judging) should be separated from developmental feedback (that is, coaching).[69] At this point, we now focus on the steps needed to communicate feedback one-on-one to employees.

To start, managers need to recognize that feedback can be constructive or destructive. **Destructive feedback** is disapproving without any intention of being helpful and almost always causes a negative or defensive reaction in the recipient. When business reporter Margaret Heffernan worked in television, her boss Tim frequently gave destructive feedback. Says Heffernan, "Standard procedure required that all films be seen in an early rough cut by the program editor. These viewings filled me with dread. Not only was I revealing my carefully nurtured work to the outside world for the first time; I also happened to work for a screamer. Tim almost never liked the first cut of anything, and his displeasure took the form of tantrums: yelling, screaming, throwing phones against the wall, occasionally dragging in other producers to see what a miserable piece of dumb garbage I'd wasted his budget on. The only (very slight) compensation was knowing that he treated everyone this way."[70] Heffernan eventually quit her job because of her boss's behavior. Some employees, however, will push back when their bosses behave this way. In fact, one study found that 98 percent of employees responded to destructive feedback from their bosses with either verbal aggression (two-thirds) or physical aggression (one-third).[71]

By contrast, **constructive feedback** is intended to be helpful, corrective, and/or encouraging. It is aimed at correcting performance deficiencies and motivating employees. When providing constructive feedback, Jenet Noriega Schwind, vice president and chief people officer of Zantaz, an e-business archiving company, tells employees, "What I'm going to tell you may be upsetting to you—but it's important to your success." She says, "When you are telling people things they don't necessarily want to hear, you have to deliver your message in a way that gets their attention and acceptance."[72]

destructive feedback feedback that disapproves without any intention of being helpful and almost always causes a negative or defensive reaction in the recipient

constructive feedback feedback intended to be helpful, corrective, and/or encouraging

For feedback to be constructive rather than destructive, it must be immediate, focused on specific behaviors, and problem oriented. *Immediate feedback* is much more effective than delayed feedback because manager and worker can recall the mistake or incident more accurately and discuss it in detail. For example, if a worker is rude to a customer and the customer immediately reports the incident to management, and the manager, in turn, immediately discusses the incident with the employee, there should be little disagreement over what was said or done. By contrast, if the manager waits several weeks to discuss the incident, it's unlikely that either the manager or the worker will be able to accurately remember the specifics of what occurred. When that happens, it's usually too late to have a meaningful conversation.

Specific feedback focuses on particular acts or incidents that are clearly under the control of the employee. For instance, instead of telling an employee that he or she is "always late for work," it's much more constructive to say, "In the last three weeks, you have been 30 minutes late on four occasions and more than an hour late on two others." Furthermore, specific feedback isn't very helpful unless employees have control over the problems that the feedback addresses. Indeed, giving negative feedback about behaviors beyond someone's control is likely to be seen as unfair. Similarly, giving positive feedback about behaviors beyond someone's control may be viewed as insincere.

Last, *problem-oriented feedback* focuses on the problems or incidents associated with the poor performance rather than on the worker or the worker's personality. Giving feedback does not give managers the right to personally attack workers. Though managers may be frustrated by a worker's poor performance, the point of problem-oriented feedback is to draw attention to the problem in a nonjudgmental way so that the employee has enough information to correct it. For example, if an employee has body odor, a surprisingly common workplace problem, don't leave deodorant, soap, or shampoo on the person's desk (for all to see) or say, "You stink." *HR Magazine* advises handling the problem this way: "Because this is a sensitive issue and the employee will likely be uncomfortable and embarrassed in discussing it, keep the meeting private and confidential. Be compassionate but direct. Treat it as you would handle any other job-related performance issue. Explain the problem and the need to correct it. Be specific about expectations....If the employer has a dress and grooming policy, refer to the policy and provide the employee with a copy."[73]

3.4 Improving Cross-Cultural Communication

As you know by now, effective communication is very difficult to accomplish. **Cross-cultural communication**, which involves transmitting information from a person in one country or culture to a person from another country or culture, is even more difficult. For example, when a French company bought a U.S. company, it found that the American managers would not implement the new strategy that it recommended. As tensions grew worse, the American managers challenged their new French boss's strategy and explained why they hadn't followed it. Meanwhile, the French, who now owned the company, couldn't understand why the American managers, who, after all, worked for them, didn't just do as they were told.[74] Exhibit 15.11, which shows the rather different views that French and American workers have about work, gives us some insight into the difficulty of cross-cultural communication in this situation. Overall, the French are much more likely to believe that managers need to have precise answers to subordinates' questions (53 percent versus 18 percent), that organizations would be better off without conflict (24 percent versus 5 percent), and that managers are more motivated by power than by achieving objectives (56 percent

cross-cultural communication transmitting information from a person in one country or culture to a person from another country or culture

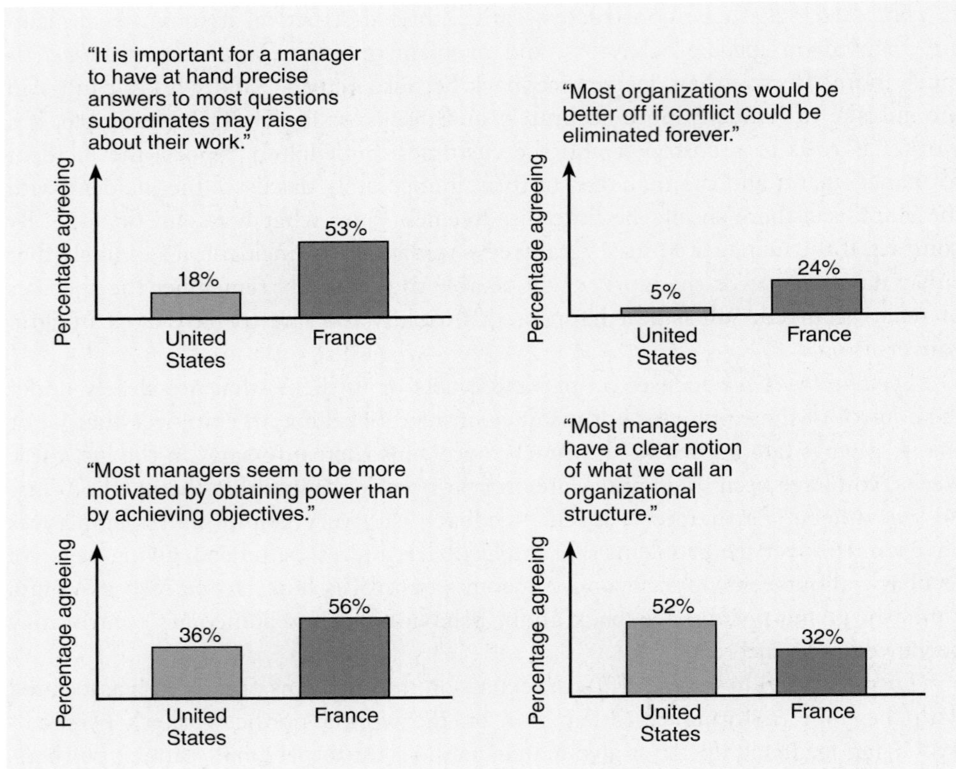
"It is important for a manager to have at hand precise answers to most questions subordinates may raise about their work."
Percentage agreeing
18%
53%
United States
France
"Most organizations would be better off if conflict could be eliminated forever."
Percentage agreeing
5%
24%
United States
France
"Most managers seem to be more motivated by obtaining power than by achieving objectives."
Percentage agreeing
36%
56%
United States
France
"Most managers have a clear notion of what we call an organizational structure."
Percentage agreeing
52%
32%
United States
France

Exhibit 15.11

A Comparison of French and American Views of Work

Source: From N. J. Adler, *From Boston to Beijing: Managing with a World View* (Cincinnati, OH: South-Western, 2002), based on A. Laurent, "The Cultural Diversity of Western Conceptions of Management," in *International Studies of Management and Organization*, vol. 13, no. 1–2 (Spring–Summer 1983): 75–96.

versus 36 percent).[75] With such different views on these basic topics, no wonder there were communication difficulties.

You can do a number of things to increase your chances for successful cross-cultural communication: familiarize yourself with a culture's general work norms; determine whether a culture is emotionally affective or neutral; develop respect for other cultures; and understand how address terms and attitudes toward time (polychronic versus monochronic time, and appointment, schedule, discussion, and acquaintance time) differ from culture to culture.

In Chapter 8, you learned that expatriates who receive predeparture language and cross-cultural training make faster adjustments to foreign cultures and perform better on their international assignments.[76] Therefore, the first step for successful cross-cultural communication is *familiarizing yourself with a culture's general work norms*, that is, the shared values, beliefs, and perceptions toward work and how it should be done. (See Chapter 8 for a more complete discussion of international cultures.) And don't assume that it will be easy. British engineer Mike Cantelo says, "In Europe, people are neighbors and they kind of look the same and it's not far to travel and 'I have been there on vacation and so it's no big deal.' But working in a culture is a hugely different thing."[77] Yet, no matter how difficult, you should work hard to learn different cultures and languages. When New Yorker Donald Dowling was working in his law firm's Paris office, his boss came up to him at a Christmas party hugged him, and declared, "I love this guy because he speaks French." Dowling says, "It took me a minute to figure out he wasn't making fun of me. I think he just appreciated that I tried, unlike one American stationed in that office for two years who managed to pick up a total of three words."[78]

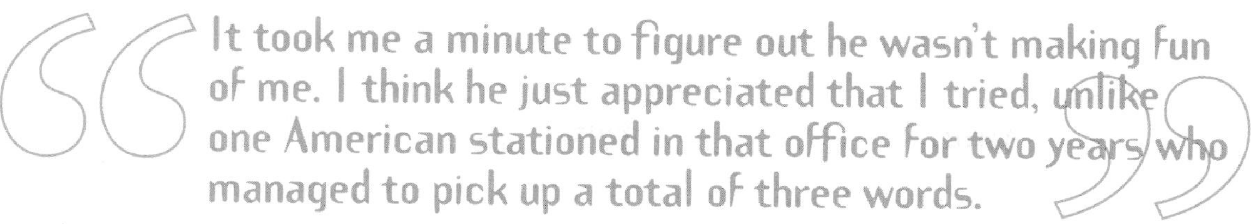
It took me a minute to figure out he wasn't making fun of me. I think he just appreciated that I tried, unlike one American stationed in that office for two years who managed to pick up a total of three words.

DONALD DOWLING, NEW YORKER WORKING IN PARIS

Fortunately, books such as *Kiss, Bow, or Shake Hands: How to Do Business in 60 Countries* (by Terri Morrison, Wayne Conaway, George Borden, and Hans Koehler), *Do's and Taboos Around the World* (by Roger E. Axtell), and *Dun & Bradstreet's Guide to Doing Business Around the World (* by Terri Morrison, Wayne Conaway, and Joseph Douress) and websites such as BusinessCulture.com and ExecutivePlanet.com provide a wealth of information about countries, their cultures, and their work and communication norms.

Determining whether a culture is emotionally affective or neutral is also important to cross-cultural communication. People in **affective cultures** tend to display their emotions and feelings openly when communicating, whereas people in **neutral cultures** do not.[79] For example, while Italians are prone to strong bursts of emotion (positive and negative), Chinese don't show strong emotions because doing so is thought to disrupt harmony and lead to conflict. Likewise, a smiling American is displaying happiness, but a smiling Japanese may be trying to hide another emotion or avoid answering a question.[80] The mistake most managers make is misunderstanding the differences between affective and neutral cultures. People from neutral cultures aren't by definition cold and unfeeling. They just don't show their emotions in the same way or with the same intensity as people from affective cultures. The key is to recognize the differences and then make sure your judgments are not based on the lack or presence of emotional reactions. Exhibit 15.12 provides a more detailed explanation of the differences between affective and neutral cultures.

affective cultures cultures in which people display emotions and feelings when communicating

neutral cultures cultures in which people do not display emotions and feelings when communicating

Respecting other cultures is also an important part of improving cross-cultural communication. Because we use our own culture as the standard of comparison,

Exhibit 15.12

Affective and Neutral Cultures

IN AFFECTIVE CULTURES, PEOPLE	IN NEUTRAL CULTURES, PEOPLE
1. Reveal thoughts and feelings through verbal and nonverbal communication	1. Don't reveal what they are thinking or feeling
2. Express and show feelings of tension	2. Hide tension and only show it accidentally in face or posture
3. Let their emotions flow easily, intensely, and without inhibition	3. Suppress emotions, leading to occasional "explosions"
4. Admire heated, animated, and intense expression of emotion	4. Admire remaining cool, calm, and relaxed
5. Are used to touching, gesturing, and showing strong emotions through facial expressions (all are common)	5. Resist touching, gesturing, and showing strong emotions through facial expressions
6. Make statements with emotion	6. Often make statements in an unexpressive manner

Source: F. Trompenaars, *Riding the Waves of Culture: Understanding Diversity in Global Business* (London: Economist Books, 1994).

it's very easy to make the common mistake of assuming that "different" means "inferior."[81] Take this example:

> *A Swiss executive waits more than an hour past the appointed time for his Spanish colleague to arrive and to sign a major supply contract. In his impatience he concludes that the Spaniard must be lazy and totally unconcerned about business.*[82]

According to Professor Nancy J. Adler,

> *The Swiss executive has misevaluated his colleague by negatively comparing the colleague's behavior to his own culture's standard for business punctuality. Implicitly, he has labeled his own culture's behavior as good ("The Swiss arrive on time, especially for important meetings, and that is good.") and the other culture's behavior as bad ("The Spanish do not arrive on time and that is bad.").*[83]

According to Adler, "Evaluating others' behavior rarely helps in trying to understand, communicate with, or conduct business with people from another culture."[84] The key, she says, is taking a step back and realizing that you don't know or understand everything that is going on and that your assumptions and interpretations of others' behavior and motives may be wrong. So, instead of judging or evaluating your international business colleagues, observe what they do. Also, delay your judgments until you have more experience with your colleagues and their culture. Lastly, treat any judgments or conclusions you do make as guesses, and then double-check those judgments or conclusions with others.[85] The more patient you are in forming opinions and drawing conclusions, the better you'll be at cross-cultural communication.

Next, you can improve cross-cultural communication by *knowing the address terms* that different cultures use to address each other in the workplace.[86] **Address terms** are the cultural norms that establish whether you address businesspeople by their first names, family names, or titles. When meeting for the first time, Americans and Australians tend to be informal and address each other by first names, even nicknames. Such immediate informality is not accepted in many cultures, however.

For instance, an American manager working in one of his company's British subsidiaries introduced himself as "Chuck" to his British employees and coworkers. Nonetheless, even after six months on the job, his British counterparts still referred to him as "Charles." And the more he insisted they call him "Chuck," the more they seemed to dig in their heels and call him "Charles."[87] So, to decrease defensiveness, know your address terms before addressing your international business counterparts.

Understanding different cultural attitudes toward time is another major consideration for effective cross-cultural communication. Cultures tend to be either monochronic or polychronic in their orientation toward time.[88] In **monochronic cultures**, people tend to do one thing at a time and view time as linear, meaning that time is the passage of sequential events. You may have heard the saying, "There are three stages in people's lives: when they believe in Santa Claus, when they don't believe in Santa Claus, and when they are Santa Claus." The progression from childhood, to young adulthood, to parenthood (when they are Santa Claus) reflects a linear view of time. Schedules are important in monochronic cultures because you schedule time to get a particular thing done. Professor Frons Trompenaars, a noted researcher on international cultures and business, gives these examples of monochronic cultures:

> *In London I once saw a long queue of people waiting for a bus when it started pouring rain. They all stood stolidly, getting soaked even though cover was*

address terms cultural norms that establish whether you should address business-people by their first names, family names, or titles

monochronic cultures cultures in which people tend to do one thing at a time and view time as linear *close by, lest they lose their sequential order. They preferred to do things right rather than do the right thing. In the Netherlands, you could be the queen, but if you are in a butcher's shop with number 46 and you step up for service when number 12 is called, you are still in deep trouble. Nor does it matter if you have an emergency; order is order.*[89]

By contrast, in **polychronic cultures**, people tend to do more than one thing at a time and view time as circular, meaning that time is a combination of the past, present, and future. Consider the following example from a polychronic culture:

> *In the Bahamas, bus service is managed similarly to many taxi systems. Drivers own their own buses and collect passenger fares for their income. There is no set schedule nor set time when buses will run or arrive at a particular location. Everything depends on the driver.*
>
> *Bus drivers in the Bahamas are present-oriented; what they feel like doing on a particular day at a particular hour dictates what they will actually do. If the bus driver feels hungry, for example, the driver will go home to eat lunch without waiting for a preset lunch hour. Drivers see no need to repeat yesterday's actions today, nor to set tomorrow's schedule according to the needs and patterns of yesterday.*[90]

As you can easily imagine, businesspeople from monochronic cultures are driven to distraction by what they perceive as the laxness of polychronic cultures, while people from polychronic cultures chafe under what they perceive as the strict regimentation of monochronic cultures. Conflicts between these two views of time occur rather easily. Let's go back to Trompenaars's butcher shop for an example:

> *At my local butcher shop in Amsterdam, the butcher calls a number, unwraps, cuts, rewraps each item the customer wants, and then calls the next number. Once I ventured a suggestion, "While you have the salami out, cut a pound for me, too." Customers and staff went into shock. The system may be inefficient, but they were not about to let some wise guy change it.*

Researchers Edward and Mildred Hall summed up the conflicts between these different views of time by saying, "It is impossible to know how many millions of dollars have been lost in international business because monochronic and polychronic people do not understand each other or even realize that two such different time systems exist."[91] Exhibit 15.13 provides a more detailed explanation of the differences between monochronic and polychronic cultures.

Differences in monochronic and polychronic time show up in four important temporal concepts that affect cross-cultural communication: appointment time, schedule time, discussion time, and acquaintance time.[92] **Appointment time** refers to how punctual you must be when showing up for scheduled appointments or meetings. In the United States, you are considered "late" if you arrive more than five minutes after the appointed time. Swedes don't even allow five minutes, expecting others to arrive "on the dot." By contrast, in Latin countries people can arrive 20 to 30 minutes after a scheduled appointment and still not be considered late.

Schedule time is the time by which scheduled projects or jobs should actually be completed. In the United States and other Anglo cultures, a premium is placed on completing things on time. By contrast, more relaxed attitudes toward schedule time can be found throughout Asia and Latin America.

Discussion time concerns how much time should be spent in discussion with others. In the United States, we carefully manage discussion time to avoid "wasting"

polychronic cultures cultures in which people tend to do more than one thing at a time and view times as circular

appointment time a cultural norm for how punctual you must be when showing up for scheduled appointments or meetings

schedule time a cultural norm for the time by which scheduled projects or jobs should actually be completed

discussion time a cultural norm for how much time should be spent in discussion with others

PEOPLE IN MONOCHRONIC CULTURES	PEOPLE IN POLYCHRONIC CULTURES
• Do one thing at a time	• Do many things at once
• Concentrate on the job	• Are highly distractible and subject to interruptions
• Take time commitments (deadlines, schedules) seriously	• Meet time commitments only if possible without extreme measures
• Are committed to the job	• Are committed to people
• Adhere scrupulously to plans	• Change plans easily and often
• Are concerned about not disturbing others (privacy is to be respected)	• Are more concerned with relationships (family, friends, business associates) than with privacy
• Show respect for private property (rarely lend or borrow things)	• Frequently borrow and lend things
• Emphasize promptness	• Vary their promptness by the relationship
• Are accustomed to short-term relationships	• Tend to build lifetime relationships

Source: E. T. Hall & M. R. Hall, *Understanding Cultural Differences* (Yarmouth, ME: Intercultural Press, 1990).

Exhibit 15.13

Monochronic versus Polychronic Cultures

time on nonbusiness topics. In Brazil, though, because of the emphasis on building relationships, as much as two hours of general discussion on nonbusiness topics can take place before moving on to business issues.

Finally, **acquaintance time** is how much time you must spend getting to know someone before the person is prepared to do business with you. Again, in the United States, people quickly get down to business and are willing to strike a deal on the same day if the terms are good and initial impressions are positive. In the Middle East, however, it may take two or three weeks of meetings before reaching this comfort level. The French also have a different attitude toward acquaintance time. Polly Platt, author of *French or Foe*, a book that explains French culture and people for travelers and businesspeople, says, "Know that things are going to take longer and don't resent it. Realize that the time system is different. Time is not a quantity for them. We save time, we spend time, we waste time; all this comes from money. The French don't. They pass time. It's a totally different concept."[93]

Review 3: Managing One-on-One Communication

One-on-one communication can be managed by choosing the right communication medium, being a good listener, giving effective feedback, and understanding cross-cultural communication. Managers generally prefer oral communication because it provides the opportunity to ask questions and assess nonverbal communication. Oral communication is best suited to complex, ambiguous, or emotionally laden topics. Written communication is best suited for delivering straightforward messages and information. Listening is important for managerial success, but most people are terrible listeners. To improve your listening skills, choose to be an active listener (clarify responses, paraphrase, and summarize) and an empathetic listener (show your desire to understand, reflect feelings). Feedback can be constructive or destructive. To be constructive, feedback must be immediate, focused on specific behaviors, and problem oriented. Finally, to increase the chances for successful cross-cultural communication, familiarize yourself with a culture's general work norms, determine whether a culture is emotionally affective or neutral, develop respect for other cultures, and understand how address terms and attitudes toward time (polychronic versus monochronic time, and appointment, schedule, discussion, and acquaintance time) differ from culture to culture.

acquaintance time a cultural norm for how much time you must spend getting to know someone before the person is prepared to do business with you

4 Managing Organization-Wide Communication

Although managing one-on-one communication is important, managers must also know how to communicate effectively with a larger number of people throughout an organization. When Bill Zollars became CEO of **Yellow Corporation**, a trucking company, he decided that he needed to communicate directly with all 25,000 of the company's employees, most of whom did not work at company headquarters in Overland Park, Kansas. For a year and a half, he traveled across the country conducting small, "town hall" meetings. Zollars says, "When I first got to Yellow, we were in a bad state. So I spent 85 percent of my time on the road talking to people one-on-one or in small groups. I would start off in the morning with the sales force, then talk to drivers, and then the people on the docks. At the end of the day I would have a customer dinner. I would say the same thing to every group and repeat it ad nauseam. The people traveling with me were ready to shoot me. But you have to be relentless in terms of your message."[94] Effective leaders, however, don't just communicate to others; they also make themselves accessible so that they can hear what employees throughout their organizations are feeling and thinking.

*Learn more about organization-wide communication by reading the following sections about **4.1 improving transmission by getting the message out** and **4.2 improving reception by finding ways to hear what others feel and think**.*

4.1 Improving Transmission: Getting the Message Out

Several methods of electronic communication—e-mail, online discussion forums, televised/videotaped speeches and conferences, corporate talk shows, and broadcast voice mail—now make it easier for managers to communicate with people throughout the organization and "get the message out."

Although we normally think of *e-mail*, the transmission of messages via computers, as a means of one-on-one communication, it also plays an important role in organization-wide communication. With the click of a button, managers can send e-mail to everyone in the company via e-mail distribution lists. Many CEOs now use this capability regularly to keep employees up-to-date on changes and developments. On his first day as CEO of **Diebold**, which makes ATM machines, Thomas Swidarski e-mailed Diebold's 14,500 employees a message about improving customer loyalty, increasing the speed with which products were manufactured and delivered, and "providing quality products and outstanding service." Swidarski concluded his e-mail by writing that leading Diebold, "does not rest with one person—it rests with each and every one of us."[95]

Many CEOs and top executives make their e-mail addresses public and encourage employees to contact them directly. On his first day as the new CEO of Quest Communications, Richard Notebaert sent this simple e-mail to his 50,000 employees, "I'm here. Talk to me." Since then he has received 200,000 e-mails, most of which he has "reacted to" by taking some action.[96]

Discussion forums are another means of electronically promoting organization-wide communication. **Online discussion forums** are the in-house equivalent of Internet newsgroups; by using web- or software-based discussion tools that are available across the company, employees can easily ask questions and share knowledge with each other. The point is to share expertise and not duplicate solutions

online discussion forums the in-house equivalent of Internet newsgroups. By using Web- or software-based discussion tools that are available across the company, employees can easily ask questions and share knowledge with each other.

already "discovered" by others in the company. Furthermore, because online discussion forums remain online, they provide a historical database for people who are dealing with particular problems for the first time.

"What's New" Company

Online discussion forums are typically organized by topic. For example, at **Ernst & Young**, a major accounting firm, accountants who have questions about multinational tax analysis can simply log on to the E&Y tax forum (one of dozens of forums). They can either post new questions and wait for others to respond with answers or read previously posted questions and answers to see if the information they need has already been discussed. If both of these options fail, they will at least learn the names of people in the organization that they can contact for help.[97]

Exhibit 15.14 lists the steps companies need to take to establish successful online discussion forums. First, pinpoint your company's top intellectual assets through a knowledge audit; then spread that knowledge throughout the organization. Second, create an online directory detailing the expertise of individual workers and make it available to all employees. Third, set up discussion groups on the intranet so that managers and workers can collaborate on problem solving. Finally, reward information sharing by making the online sharing of knowledge a key part of performance ratings.

Televised/videotaped speeches and meetings are a third electronic method of organization-wide communication. **Televised/videotaped speeches and meetings** are simply speeches and meetings originally made to a smaller audience that are either simultaneously broadcast to other locations in the company or videotaped for subsequent distribution and viewing. Cisco's John Chambers describes how, over his 15 years as CEO, he's added televised messages to his communication strategies:

> *I started off with classic communication methods when I got here 15 years ago. I'd walk around and talk to small groups and larger groups. I'd see who was here in the evening. To this day I can tell you whose car is out in the parking lot. Then e-mail became very effective, because it gave me the ability to send a message to the whole group. But I'm a voice person. I communicate with emotion that way. I like to listen to emotion too. It's a lot easier to listen to a key customer if I hear how they're describing a problem to me. I'll leave 40 or 50 voice mails a day. I do them on the way to work and coming back from work. The newest thing for me is video on demand, which is my primary communication vehicle today. We have a small studio downstairs. We probably tape 10 to 15 videos a quarter. That way employees, and customers, can watch them when they want.*[98]

televised/videotaped speeches and meetings speeches and meetings originally made to a smaller audience that are either simultaneously broadcast to other locations in the company or videotaped for subsequent distribution and viewing

corporate talk shows televised company meetings that allow remote audiences (employees) to pose questions to the show's host and guests

Corporate talk shows are a variant on televised/videotaped speeches and meetings. But instead of simply being watched, **corporate talk shows** allow remote audience members, all of whom are typically workers or managers, to pose questions to the show's host and guests. For example, once a month, Emma Carrasco, vice president of marketing and communication, and Dan Hunt, president of Caribbean and Latin American operations, host the Virtual Leadership Academy, which is a corporate talk show for **Nortel Networks**. Typically, 2,000 employees in 46 countries watch the live broadcast and can call in with questions about Nortel and its competitors. Why a corporate talk show? Carrasco says, "We're always looking for ways to break down barriers in the company, and people are comfortable with the talk-show format. People watch talk shows in every country in the region, and they've learned that it's okay to say what's on their mind. In fact, it's expected."[99]

Exhibit 15.14

Establishing Online Discussion Forums

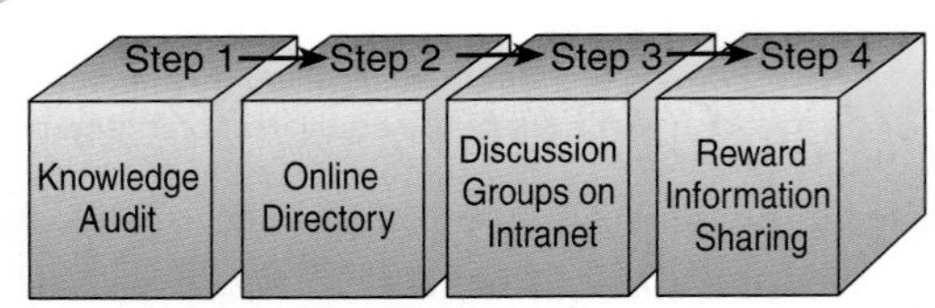

Source: Based on G. McWilliams & M. Stepanek, "Knowledge Management: Taming the Info Monster," *BusinessWeek*, 22 June 1998, 170.

Voice messaging, or voice mail, is a telephone answering system that records audio messages. In one survey, 89 percent of respondents said that voice messaging is critical to business communication,

78 percent said that it improves productivity, and 58 percent said they would rather leave a message on a voice messaging system than with a receptionist.[100] Nonetheless, most people are unfamiliar with the ability to *broadcast voice mail* by sending a recorded message to everyone in the company. Broadcast voice mail gives top managers a quick, convenient way to address their work forces via oral communication. Harry Kraemer, CEO of pharmaceutical giant **Baxter International**, describes Baxter's broadcast voice mail system: "We have more than 30,000 Baxter team members hooked onto the same voice-mail system. That includes everybody but the folks on the factory line. This is hooked up in over 50 countries."[101] At Ernst & Young, the company-wide broadcast voice mails of chairman Phil Laskawy were so well known and well liked that E & Y employees called them "Travels with Phil." No matter where he was traveling on business for the company—and he traveled all over the world—Phil would begin his voice mails, most of which lasted 5 to 10 minutes, with a weather report, a couple of bad jokes, and an update on his beloved New York Yankees baseball team; then came the core part of his message.[102]

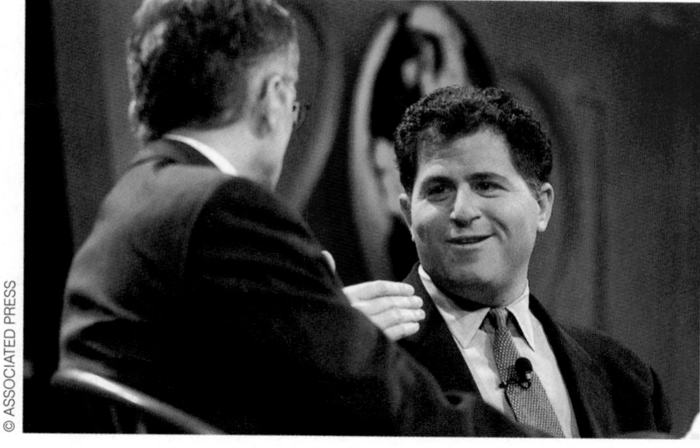

© ASSOCIATED PRESS

Corporate talk shows are an increasingly popular — and effective — way to get the word out about and to hear what people throughout the company are thinking.

4.2 Improving Reception: Hearing What Others Feel and Think

"What's New" Company

When people think of "organization-wide" communication, they think of the CEO and top managers getting their message out to people in the company. But organization-wide communication also means finding ways to hear what people throughout the organization are feeling and thinking. This is important because most employees and managers are reluctant to share their thoughts and feelings with top managers. Surveys indicate that only 29 percent of first-level managers feel that their companies encourage employees to express their opinions openly. Another study of 22 companies found that 70 percent of the people surveyed were afraid to speak up about problems they knew existed at work.

Withholding information about organizational problems or issues is called **organizational silence**. Organizational silence occurs when employees believe that telling management about problems won't make a difference or that they'll be punished or hurt in some way for sharing such information.[103] For example, the norm in most operating rooms is that the surgeon is clearly in charge. At first look, there doesn't seem to be anything wrong with that. After all, if the surgeon wasn't in charge, who would be? However, at 20 hospitals, 60 percent of the operating room staffers—nurses, technicians, and other doctors—agreed with this statement, "In the ORs here, it is difficult to speak up if I perceive a problem with patient care."[104] And when nurses and other operating room staffers don't speak up (organizational silence), serious mistakes can occur. **VHA** Inc., which helps 2,400 hospitals coordinate best practices, has a new program called "Transformation of the Operating Room," in which operating teams use "safety pauses" and "time-outs." The surgical team pauses for a moment, is asked if anyone has concerns or comments, and then addresses them if need be. Studies show that programs such as this are not only changing the norms in operating rooms but also reducing mistakes, such as operating on the wrong leg or noticing that key surgical instruments are missing prior to beginning surgery.

"What's New" Company

organizational silence when employees withhold information about organizational problems or issues

Company hotlines, survey feedback, frequent informal meetings, surprise visits, and blogs are additional ways of overcoming organizational silence. **Company hotlines** are phone numbers that anyone in the company can call anonymously to leave information for upper management. For example, **Deloitte Touche Tohmatsu** has a toll-free

company hotlines phone numbers that anyone in the company can call anonymously to leave information for upper management hotline for employees to call to report any kind of problem or issue within the company. Hotlines are particularly important because 44 percent of employees will not report misconduct. Why not? The reason is twofold: They don't believe anything will be done, *and* they "fear that the report will not be kept confidential."[105] David Childers, CEO of **EthicsPoint**, which runs hotlines for corporations, says that companies can expect 1 to 1.5 percent of their employees to call their hotlines and that 10 to 15 percent of the calls will involve serious problems that require immediate company action.[106]

"What's New" Company

Survey feedback is information that is collected by survey from organization members and then compiled, disseminated, and used to develop action plans for improvement. Many organizations make use of survey feedback by surveying their managers and employees several times a year. **FedEx**, for example, runs its own Survey Feedback Action program. The survey, which is administered online and is completely anonymous, includes sections for employees to evaluate their managers and the overall environment at FedEx, including benefits, incentives, and working conditions. After the surveys are completed, the results are compiled and then fed back to each FedEx work group. Each group then uses the results to decide where changes and improvements need to be made and to develop specific action plans to address those problems. The final step is to look for improvements in subsequent employee surveys to see if those plans worked. John Allison, vice president of HR for FedEx Asia Pacific, says, "It's a means of engaging all of our employees so that they can participate in expressing concerns about issues and at the same time participate in solving any problems that might arise."[107]

"What's New" Company

> There is no "they" here. It's "we" and "us." We succeed together or we fail together.
>
> **AL SPAIN,** SENIOR VICE PRESIDENT OF OPERATIONS, JETBLUE

Frequent, *informal meetings* between top managers and lower-level employees are one of the best ways for top managers to hear what others feel and think. Many people assume that top managers are at the center of everything that goes on in organizations, but top managers commonly feel isolated from most of their lower-level managers and employees. Consequently, more and more top managers are scheduling frequent, informal meetings with people throughout their companies. At **JetBlue**, founder and chairman David Neeleman uses informal meetings to listen to customers and employees. On an almost daily basis, Neeleman can be found on a JetBlue flight talking to customers. Neeleman listens, writing thoughts and customer comments on airplane napkins that he stuffs in his pockets to be turned into organizational to-do's once the flight is over. However, Neeleman also flies to work with and listen to his company's flight crews. Says Neeleman, "I want them to know that I value what they do. I value it so much that I'm not too good to do it. I fly with 8 to 12 crew-members a week, but the other 1,200 flight attendants know about it."[108] Al Spain, senior vice president of operations, emphasizes how important these visits are, saying, "There is no 'they' here. It's 'we' and 'us.' We succeed together or we fail together."[109]

"What's New" Company

Have you ever been around when a supervisor learns that upper management is going to be paying a visit? First, there's shock. Next, there's anxiety. And then there's panic, as everyone is told to drop what he or she is doing to polish, shine, and spruce up the workplace so that it looks perfect for the visit. Of course, when visits are conducted under these conditions, top managers don't get a realistic look at what's going on in the company. Consequently, one of the ways to get an accurate picture is to pay *surprise visits* to various parts of the organization. These visits should not just be surprise inspections, but should also be used as an opportunity to encourage meaningful upward communication from those who normally don't get a chance to communicate with upper management. Such surprise visits are now part of the culture at the **Royal Mail**, the United Kingdom's postal service. Chairman Allan Leighton frequently shows up announced at Royal Mail delivery offices. Leighton says the initial reaction is always the same, "Oh s***, it's the chairman." However, Leighton isn't there to catch his employees doing something wrong. He's there to find out, right or wrong, what's really going on. Says Leighton, "Those

"What's New" Company

survey feedback information that is collected by surveys from organizational members and then compiled, disseminated, and used to develop action plans for improvement visits at half past five in the morning [with employees] are the most important part" of turning around the Royal Mail, which was once losing 1.5 million pounds a day.[110] Today, thanks in part to his communication with employees, the Royal Mail delivers 95 percent of first-class mail in one day, better than any other postal service in the world, and now earns a profit of 1.5 million pounds per day.

Blogs are another way to hear what people are thinking and saying, both inside and outside the organization. A **blog** is a personal website that provides personal opinions or recommendations, news summaries, and reader comments. At Google, which owns the blog-hosting service Blogger, hundreds of employees are writing *internal blogs*. One employee even wrote a blog for posting all the notes from the brainstorming sessions used to redesign the search page used by millions each day. Staffer Marissa Mayer says, "Our legal department loves the blogs, because it basically is a written-down, backed-up, permanent time-stamped version of the scientist's notebook. When you want to file a patent, you can now show in blogs where this idea happened."[111]

© MARTIN PARR/MAGNUM

External blogs, written by people outside the company, can be a good way to find out what others are saying or thinking about your organization or its products or actions. Tim Holmes, Ford's executive director of public affairs, believes that companies have to pay attention to what is being said about them online. Says Holmes, "Like most big companies, we monitor the press, but the problem with that is it's always retrospective, everything's a few weeks old. The real value of searching the net, including blogs, is that you get a live picture of what people are thinking about certain issues. It means that you can predict if there is going to be an issue that's going to grow and become something you need to respond to before it gets to the mainstream press."[112] Some companies have created the new position of chief blogging officer to manage internal company blogs and to monitor what it said about the company and its products on external blogs.[113]

PROCTER & GAMBLE is also turning to the Internet to do a better job of hearing what people outside the company are feeling and thinking. P&G is working with PlanetFeedback to find out what consumers are saying about P&G's two biggest brands, Tide detergent and Pampers diapers. PlanetFeedback collects consumer comments on its website about various companies and their products. It will also search online message boards, discussion websites, Usenet user groups, and blogs to find out what people are saying about P&G's brands.[114]

Review 4: Managing Organization-Wide Communication

Managers need methods for managing organization-wide communication and for making themselves accessible so that they can hear what employees throughout their organizations are feeling and thinking. E-mail, online discussion forums, televised/videotaped speeches and conferences, corporate talk shows, and broadcast voice mail make it much easier for managers to improve message transmission and "get the message out." By contrast, anonymous company hotlines, survey feedback, frequent informal meetings, and surprise visits help managers avoid organizational silence and improve reception by hearing what others in the organization feel and think. Monitoring internal and external blogs is another way to find out what people are saying and thinking about your organization.

blog a personal Web site that provides personal opinions or recommendations, news summaries, and reader comments

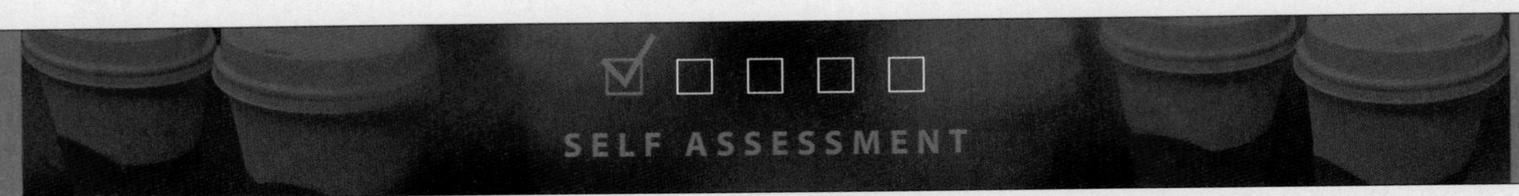

KEY TERMS

acquaintance time 578
active listening 570
address terms 576
affective cultures 575
appointment time 577
attribution theory 555
blog 583
closure 555
coaching 564
communication 552
communication medium 568
company hotlines 581
conduit metaphor 560
constructive feedback 572
corporate talk shows 580
counseling 565
cross-cultural communication 573
decoding 559
defensive bias 555
destructive feedback 572
discussion time 577
downward communication 561
empathetic listening 571
encoding 558
feedback to sender 559
formal communication channel 560
fundamental attribution error 556
hearing 570
horizontal communication 561
informal communication channel ("grapevine") 562
jargon 560
kinesics 566
listening 570
monochronic cultures 576
neutral cultures 575
noise 559
nonverbal communication 565

How Do You Listen?

Have you ever been eager to tell someone a funny story, only to have that person interrupt you repeatedly to ask for details or clarification? And have you ever said in exasperation, "Will you just listen?" Some people prefer an inquisitive listening style, whereas others prefer a contemplative listening style. What listening style best describes you? This listening styles inventory will help you establish a baseline to use as a foundation for developing your listening skills.

The following items relate to listening style.[115] Circle the appropriate responses. Please be candid.

	Almost always	Often	Sometimes	Seldom	Almost never
1. I want to listen to what others have to say when they are talking.	5	4	3	2	1
2. I do not listen at my capacity when others are talking.	1	2	3	4	5
3. By listening, I can guess a speaker's intent or purpose without being told.	5	4	3	2	1
4. I have a purpose for listening when others are talking.	5	4	3	2	1
5. I keep control of my biases and attitudes when listening to others speak so that these factors won't affect my interpretation of the message.	5	4	3	2	1
6. I analyze my listening errors so as not to make them again.	5	4	3	2	1
7. I listen to the complete message before making judgments about what the speaker has said.	5	4	3	2	1
8. I cannot tell when a speaker's biases or attitudes are affecting his or her message.	1	2	3	4	5
9. I ask questions when I don't fully understand a speaker's message.	5	4	3	2	1
10. I am aware of whether or not a speaker's meaning of words and concepts is the same as mine.	5	4	3	2	1

SUBTOTAL = ____ + ____ + ____ + ____+ ____ =

GRAND TOTAL =____

You can find the interpretation of your score at: **academic.cengage.com/management/williams.**

MANAGEMENT DECISION

To Blog or Not to Blog

Just this month, your company, AeroPrecision, a manufacturer of aircraft engine components, completed the upgrade of its computer system—the first upgrade in nearly 15 years.[116] Everyone cheered when the DOS-based operating software was replaced with the newest Windows-based version. Now, for the first time data are being electronically collected directly from the factory floor, and the engineering, tooling, and maintenance departments are connected. You and the other top managers expect to reap terrific gains in productivity—and profitability—as a result of the upgrade. As the operations manager, you were ultimately responsible for revamping the entire system, and the process has left you motivated to adopt even more technological advances.

Over the course of the upgrade, you came across several short articles and references to *blogs*, which you learned was short for "Web logs." Not too savvy about these things at the time, you turned to asked your IT consultant, and she told you that blogs are web pages that serve as publicly accessible journals. That didn't help you much, so she directed you to a variety of blogs to find out what they were all about. After only a few visits you started thinking about creating a blog for AeroPrecision.

Some managers use blogs to communicate with employees, and others use them as marketing tools to "get the message out" about their companies. The question for you is how AeroPrecision would use blogs. Only 30 of AeroPrecision's 100 employees have computers at their desks (only 30 have desks). The rest of the employees are shop-floor workers who use the 20 terminals located on stands throughout the factory to record their personal production information. Shop-floor terminals don't have Internet access. Could you justify connecting the 20 factory terminals to the Internet? And do you really want employees standing around the shop-floor terminals reading a company blog? But then you wonder, "Would that be any different from them hovering around the bulletin board by the time clock reading the company's biweekly newsletter? And with a blog, the information would be more timely."

Or would it? You pause to think about the time required to maintain a blog. And what would you link out to? A public blog would need to be an authoritative voice on, well, what? You could hook up to links about aerodynamics, metal prices, and travel statistics. If you could leverage AeroPrecision's technical expertise, you would be able to position the company as a premier provider of component parts for aircraft engines. You may even be able to convert the research you do for the blog into new customers or products for new industries. If you put your mind to it, you are confident that you can brainstorm enough valuable resources for a blog, but you come back to the issue of time. Would the time spent be worth it?

Questions

1. Does it make sense for AeroPrecision to create a company blog for employees only? In other words, is a blog the best medium to get the company's message out to employees and to hear what they feel and think? Explain.
2. Brainstorm possible items for inclusion on an AeroPrecision blog destined for public viewing. Can you think of any topics that you would want to avoid linking to?
3. How could a blog play a role in designing a company's strategy? (Recall the issues discussed in Chapter 6, Organizational Strategy.)
4. Do you create a public blog for AeroPrecision? Why or why not?

MANAGEMENT TEAM DECISION

Communication Dilemmas and Decisions

As you watch the falling snow, you can't help thinking about the way the fax machine coughs out legal missives into a collection bin. You are a partner at Shaw Walker Theobald, a law firm with offices across the United States, and your office sits right next to the constantly humming fax machine. You're at your wit's end from the incessant buzzing. Documents of all lengths and levels of importance come through the fax; sometimes, a lawyer on one floor will write a question on a cover letter, send it by fax to a lawyer on another floor at your firm, and then request the answer by fax! While you pack your briefcase before heading home, you think, "What a drain on productivity! And the client ends up footing the bill. There has to be a more efficient way to communicate."

After you finish dinner, you open your work, and are again distracted—not by a fax, but by the pinging of your teenager's instant messaging on the computer in the den. Immediately, you think you've hit on a solution for the office. If the firm used instant messaging, you could save the energy used by the fax, eliminate all the paper, and have answers in an instant. Communication would reach terminal speed! Unfortunately, you can't just implement your idea when you walk in tomorrow morning. You're only one of many partners, and they all have to approve anything that affects the management of the firm. How are you going to persuade a team of people trained to object? Instead of pulling a brief out of your bag, you flip to a clean sheet on your legal pad and begin drafting a convincing memo.

Getting Started

This exercise will give you practice in writing memos and giving verbal feedback. You will begin by writing a memo on your own based on the scenario you just read. Then assemble a team of five to six students. Make enough copies of your memo so that each team member can have one. The job of the team is to review and critique all the memos. You will want to review Section 3.3 on giving feedback before convening the team to evaluate the memos. Choose one team member to be the moderator. The moderator will be in charge of keeping the discussion on track and ensuring that it doesn't disintegrate into subjective attacks.

Activities

1. Write a memo to your colleagues proposing the use of instant messaging to speed communication.
2. Convene the team and critique the members' memos. Try to use descriptive terms to give feedback about the memos. Avoid words like "good" and "bad"—they don't give the writer any real information about the effectiveness of the memo. Here are some adjectives that you might find useful as a starting point:
   - Convincing
   - Persuasive
   - Condescending
   - Concise
   - Wordy
   - Informative
   - Detailed
   - Sparse
   - Neat
   - Hard to follow
   - Clear
   - Sloppy
   - Off-putting
   - Effective
   - Inappropriate
   - Unprofessional

   Don't limit your comment to a negative adjective, either. If you say a memo is hard to follow, explain *why*. What makes it hard to follow? If you say a memo is wordy, explain how it is wordy. And be specific: point out which phrases are redundant, unnecessary, or repetitive.
3. Assume that your individual proposal was accepted, and the partners (your team) have asked you to announce the new capabilities and outline the rules for their use. Determine the best way to communicate the instant messaging plan to the junior partners, associates, paralegals, and office staff. Using whatever medium you think is best, write out your communication. For example, if you think e-mail is best, draft a relevant e-mail. If you think a memo would be appropriate, then draft one. If you think oral communication would be a better choice, draft the speech you will give. Regardless of your medium, you will need to remember your audience.
4. If you have time, repeat the group critique session with the second communication. You may also wish to discuss as a team which medium would be the best for telling everyone at the firm about the new instant messaging initiative.

PRACTICE BEING A MANAGER

When problems occur in organizations, they are frequently attributed to a breakdown in communication. The communication process may get more than its share of the blame for some breakdowns that result from organizational or leadership problems. But there is some truth to the common perception that communication is problematic. In this exercise you will have the opportunity to consider how you might improve your own communication from two sides of the table—coaching/disciplining an employee; and receiving coaching/disciplining from a manager.

Step 1: Get into groups and read the scenario. Your professor will organize you in small groups of three or four students.

Scenario: Chalet is a fine dining restaurant in a ski resort setting. The restaurant is well known for its gourmet cuisine, fine wine selection, and outstanding service. Dinner for two at Chalet would typically cost $100 or more. A key management responsibility at Chalet is the training and development of wait staff. Service quality is carefully monitored and standards rigorously maintained. In exchange for meeting these demanding standards, Chalet wait staff are well-compensated and enjoy good benefits. As time permits, you should complete conversations in which you play each of the following roles: Dennis/Denise (new wait staff member with three months of experience at Chalet); Christy/Chris (service manager); and D.J./R.J. (communication consultant to Chalet).

Here are some basic facts of the situation:

- The service manager has not directly observed any problems with Dennis/Denise interacting with customers of the restaurant.
- Over this past busy weekend three tables of customers reported problems with the service they received from Dennis/Denise. Only one other table received any negative feedback at all during the weekend, and that concerned the quality of a particular dessert item.
- The reports about Dennis/Denise were rather vague—"server seemed distant, unresponsive" and "acted aloof, like we were a bother."
- Christy/Chris, the service manager, did catch the tail end of what seemed like an argument between Dennis/Denise and one of the cooks on Friday night. When the cook was asked about the incident, she said, "It was nothing...usual cook versus server stuff."
- Dennis/Denise needs this job to pay for college, and is taking a full load of classes.

The role play should involve a brief conversation (five to seven minutes) initiated by Christy/Chris on Monday afternoon prior to opening. The focus of this conversation should be to coach and/or discipline regarding the concerns of the previous weekend. Those playing the role of communication consultant should take notes and provide feedback on the communication in this conversation (strengths and areas for improvement). As time allows, rotate roles after completing a conversation and hearing consultant feedback.

Step 2: Do the role play. Complete a role play conversation with one person playing the role of the service manager (Christy/Chris) and another person playing the role of the wait staffer (Dennis/Denise). Communication consultant(s) should listen and take notes in order to provide feedback to the two individuals who are role-playing the coaching/discipline conversation.

Step 3: Give feedback. Communication consultant(s) should give feedback to the role players at the conclusion of the conversation, considering key aspects of communication discussed in this chapter.

Step 4: Switch roles. Switch roles and repeat the role-play conversation and post-conversation feedback as time allows.

Step 5: Debrief as a class. What challenges face the communicators in this scenario? Which role was most difficult for you, and why? Why is it important for managers to do coach and discipline effectively? Why might managers avoid (or underutilize) this form of communication?

DEVELOP YOUR CAREER POTENTIAL

I Don't Agree, but I'm Listening

Being a good listener is a critical part of effective communication. Without it, you're unlikely to be a good manager. Therefore, the purpose of this assignment is to help you develop your listening skills. And there's no better way to do that than to talk to someone whose views are quite different from yours. In the best of situations, being a good listener is difficult. Because of perceptual filters, distractions, or daydreams, we retain only about 25 percent of what we hear. When we're talking with people who have very different views and opinions, it can be almost impossible to be good listeners. We tend to interrupt, jump to conclusions about what they'll say, and hurry them to finish their points (which we don't want to listen to anyway) so that we can "correct" their thinking with our own opinions.

To complete this assignment, you'll have to find someone who has different views or opinions on some topic (handgun control, abortion, capital punishment, and euthanasia are just some of the topics on which you can always find someone with a different viewpoint). Once you've found someone, conduct a 10-minute listening session, following this simple rule: Before stating your opinion, you must first accurately reflect or paraphrase the statement that your listening partner just made (be sure to reread Subsection 3.2 on listening). For example, suppose that your listening partner says, "Women shouldn't have to ask anyone for permission for what they do to their bodies. If they decide they want an abortion, they should go ahead and have it." Before making your point or disagreeing with your partner's, you will have to accurately paraphrase that statement in your own words. If you don't paraphrase it correctly, your listening partner will tell you. If you or your partner has difficulty accurately paraphrasing a statement, ask the other person to repeat the statement, and try again. Also, don't parrot the statement by repeating it word for word. Good listening isn't mimicry. It's capturing the essence of what others have said in your own words. And before your listening partner responds, he or she, too, has to accurately paraphrase what you say. Continue this listening-based discussion for 10 minutes.

Questions

1. Was this discussion different from the way you normally discuss contentious topics with other people? Why or why not?
2. Was it difficult to reflect or paraphrase your listening partner's perspectives? Explain and give an example.
3. Did active listening techniques or empathetic listening techniques lead to more effective listening for you? Explain.

REEL TO REAL

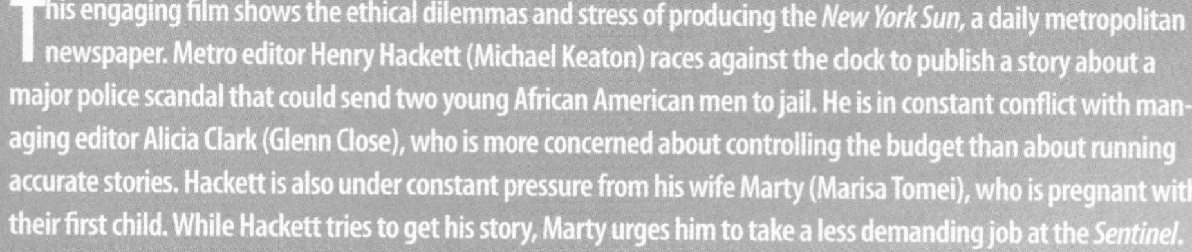

BIZFLIX

The Paper

This engaging film shows the ethical dilemmas and stress of producing the *New York Sun,* a daily metropolitan newspaper. Metro editor Henry Hackett (Michael Keaton) races against the clock to publish a story about a major police scandal that could send two young African American men to jail. He is in constant conflict with managing editor Alicia Clark (Glenn Close), who is more concerned about controlling the budget than about running accurate stories. Hackett is also under constant pressure from his wife Marty (Marisa Tomei), who is pregnant with their first child. While Hackett tries to get his story, Marty urges him to take a less demanding job at the *Sentinel.*

This scene occurs early in *The Paper.* It shows a staff meeting that takes place the day after the *Sun* missed a story about a murder and other shootings with racial overtones. Instead, the *Sun* ran a front-page story about parking problems. At the meeting, senior editor Bernie White (Robert Duvall) discusses his preferences in front-page stories.

What to Watch for and Ask Yourself

1. Use the model of the communication process to diagram what is occurring in the clip.
2. What types of communication do you see in the video?
3. Discuss the paralanguage used in the clip. What mood or attitude does it convey?

MANAGEMENT WORKPLACE

NEADS—Communicating with and without Voice

Suppose you woke up one day and couldn't see. Or perhaps you couldn't hear, couldn't speak, or couldn't walk. How would you communicate and interact with the world around you? Today's technology provides solutions to some of these challenges, but there is a live solution as well: assistance dogs. National Education for Assistance Dog Services (NEADS) acquires, trains, and matches dogs with people who need assistance. Founded in 1976 as a nonprofit organization, NEADS is based in the rural community of Princeton, Massachusetts, where it adopts and trains dogs to serve their new owners. Watch the video to see why communication is a central part of success at this unique management workplace.

What to Watch for and Ask Yourself

1. How does perception affect the communication process at NEADS?
2. What role does nonverbal communication play at NEADS?
3. Why are listening skills so important at NEADS?

five

PART 5 Controlling

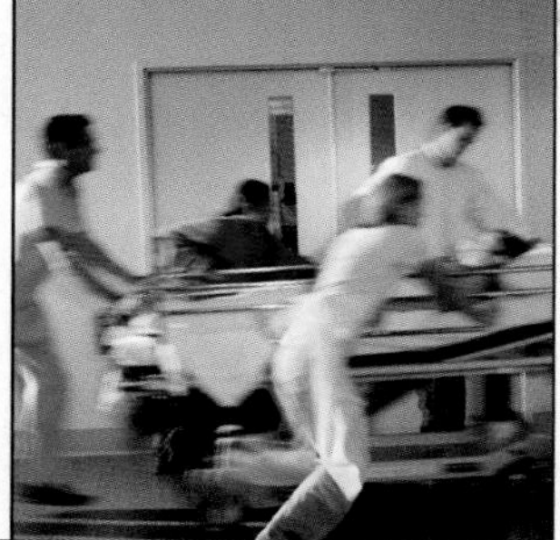

Chapter 16
Control

This chapter examines the basic and in-depth methods that companies use to achieve control, as well as those things that companies choose to control (finances, customer retention, and product quality, among others).

Chapter 17
Managing Information

This chapter explains why information matters, the value of strategic information to companies, and the cost and characteristics of good information. We investigate how companies capture, process, and protect information, and how information, knowledge, and expertise are shared.

Chapter 18
Managing Service and Manufacturing Operations

This chapter discusses the daily production of goods and services, starting with the basics of productivity and quality. Next, you will read about managing service and manufacturing operations, and the measures, costs, and methods for managing inventory.

CHAPTER 16

Control

Learning Outcomes:

1 Describe the basic control process.

2 Discuss the various methods that managers can use to maintain control.

3 Describe the behaviors, processes, and outcomes that today's managers are choosing to control in their organizations.

In This Chapter:

WHAT WOULD YOU DO?

Gap Headquarters, San Francisco, CA[1]—Standing outside one of Gap's mall stores, you realize how difficult it will be to turn around this venerable chain. The company consists of more than 3,200 locations worldwide, and same-store sales have been flat or declining in 29 of the past 31 months. Furthermore, same-store sales have dropped 9 percent each of the last two years. You have been hired to change the pattern and bring glory back to the operation.

Donald and Doris Fisher opened the first Gap store in 1969 in San Francisco. Over the next few decades they grew the business into America's largest fashion retailer. In 1983 they took over Banana Republic and in 1994 they launched Old Navy. Old Navy became the first fashion retailer to reach $1 billion in annual sales in less than four years from their founding. Mickey Drexler, the brilliant CEO who grew the business for two decades, was known as a fashion icon who let the financial part of the business slip as he focused on the fashion side. All of this was fine while the business grew at astronomical rates. However, the wheels came off the machine when sales slumped across the board as the company's efforts to attract teenagers alienated their main group of customers (people in their 20s and 30s). Frustrated with out-of-control costs and a burgeoning inventory, the Fishers fired Drexler and brought in Paul Pressler, who had a long history of strict organizational control at Disney. Pressler rapidly closed underperforming stores, reduced inventory, and cleaned up the finances of the organization. Unfortunately, the fashion side of the business had no real direction and although the organization was carefully managing its finances, foot traffic fell in its stores. (Pressler was ultimately replaced.)

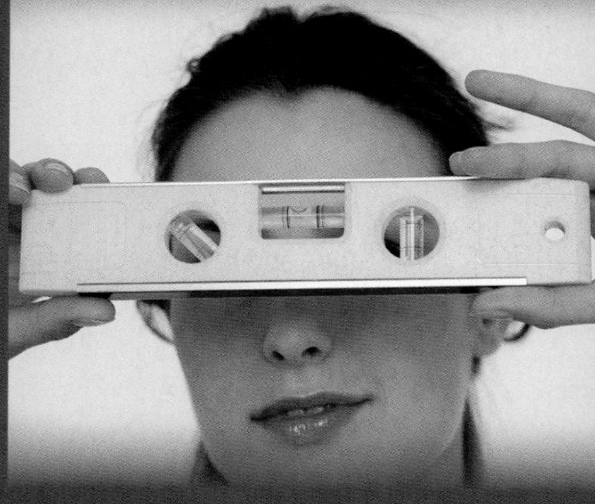

You knew when you took over that fashion is a difficult business. Consistently attracting profitable customers is your goal, but how can the Gap do that? Financial controls and efficient operations are crucial, but so is presenting desirable fashions, because numerous competitors do the same thing extraordinarily well. Abercrombie & Fitch, which made a significant turnaround after being spun off from Limited Brands, is now one of the hottest stores in the teen market. Even old-line retailer JCPenney turned its clothing line into a strength again behind the fashion expertise of merchandiser Vanessa Castagna.

The top companies in any industry benchmark the best practices of their competitors, effectively understand and manage their financial and human resources, and consistently deliver innovative products that attract customers. So what companies should Gap benchmark in order to turn around its operations and increase customer traffic? With these things in mind, should Gap hire a fashion head to focus on the products in its stores, or should it hire someone who will focus on controlling the organization's costs, schedules, and operations? How much control and what types of controls should be in place? How do you achieve a balance between control and creativity? What techniques might help you achieve this balance? **If you were in charge at Gap, what would you do?**

ACTIVITIES + VIDEOS

CengageNOW Audio study guide, electronic flashcards, author FAQ videos, On the Job and Biz Flix videos, concept tutorial, and concept exercise

Web (academic.cengage.com/management/williams) Quiz, PowerPoint slides, and glossary terms for this chapter

Study Tip

The list of key terms on page 621 can be a valuable study aid. Write down the definition of each term on a separate piece of paper without consulting the margin terms in the chapter. Cement your understanding by also writing an example if possible.

"What's New" Companies

- Gap
- Coventry Mall
- iRobot
- Cadillac
- Google
- Microsoft
- Kmart
- Wal-Mart
- Nike
- Apple
- Phones4U
- State of California
- Motorola
- Smithfield Foods
- Nordstrom
- Nucor
- Duke Children's Hospital
- And others . . .

As Gap's situation shows, past success is no guarantee of future success. Even successful companies fall short, face challenges, and have to make changes. **Control** is a regulatory process of establishing standards to achieve organizational goals, comparing actual performance against the standards, and taking corrective action when necessary, as at Gap, to restore performance to those standards. Control is achieved when behavior and work procedures conform to standards and company goals are accomplished.[2] Control is not just an after-the-fact process, however. Preventive measures are also a form of control.

We begin this chapter by examining the basic control process used in organizations. In the second part of the chapter, we go beyond the basics to an in-depth examination of the different methods that companies use to achieve control. We conclude the chapter by looking at the things that companies choose to control (finances, customer retention, and product quality, among others).

BASICS OF CONTROL

"WHAT'S NEW" COMPANY

With many empty stores and a dated look, **COVENTRY MALL** in Pottstown, Pennsylvania, just 22 miles from the gigantic King of Prussia Mall, *was* dying, but mall manager Rene Daniel has it on the mend. The first step was fixing the food. With the mall down to just six food vendors (for example, Hot Dogs & More and Egg Roll Hut), he convinced McDonald's, Subway, and Saladworks to open restaurants. When the lease expired on the "Everything 99 Cent" store, he convinced Gap to lease the adjacent space, knock out the wall, and replace the aging blue Formica with blond wood and modern glass. Changes like this have increased mall sales by a third, and they are now above the national average. Nevertheless, despite the changes, Vickey Sihler, who started shopping at the Coventry Mall again because of Gap and the new Children's Place store, still sees room for improvement. "This place really needs to be fixed up," she says.[3] So, by working the control process (standards, comparison to standards, and corrective action), Rene Daniel is slowly but surely fixing Coventry Mall.

After reading the next section, you should be able to

1 describe the basic control process.

1 The Control Process

The basic control process ***1.1 begins with the establishment of clear standards of performance, 1.2 involves a comparison of performance to those standards, 1.3 takes corrective action, if needed, to repair performance deficiencies, 1.4 is a dynamic, cybernetic process****, and* ***1.5 consists of three basic methods: feedback control, concurrent control, and feedforward control****. However, as much as managers would like,* ***1.6 control isn't always worthwhile or possible****.*

control a regulatory process of establishing standards to achieve organizational goals, comparing actual performance against the standards, and taking corrective action, when necessary

1.1 Standards

The control process begins when managers set goals, such as satisfying 90 percent of customers or increasing sales by 5 percent. Companies then specify the performance standards that must be met to accomplish those goals. **Standards** are a basis of comparison for measuring the extent to which organizational performance is satisfactory or unsatisfactory. For example, many pizzerias use 30–40 minutes as the standard for delivery times. Since anything longer is viewed as unsatisfactory, they'll typically reduce the price if they can't deliver a hot pizza to you within that time period.

So how do managers set standards? How do they decide which levels of performance are satisfactory and which are unsatisfactory? The first criterion for a good standard is that it must enable goal achievement. If you're meeting the standard, but still not achieving company goals, then the standard may have to be changed. For example, hospital patients are typically billed a month or two after treatment. But with the amount of unreimbursed care totaling $22.3 billion nationwide, many hospitals are changing payment standards by asking that insurance copayments be paid before the patient leaves the hospital. Anyone who can't afford the entire copayment at once is asked to at least make a down payment (those who do are much more likely to pay their entire bill). Karen Dostart, at Marshall Medical Center in Placerville, California, says, "My goal is to reduce elective services that go to bad debt by 50 percent within a year."[4]

> "My goal is to reduce elective services that go to bad debt by 50 percent within a year."
>
> **KAREN DOSTART,** MARSHALL MEDICAL CENTER, PLACERVILLE, CALIFORNIA

Companies also determine standards by listening to customers or observing competitors. After hearing from consumers that they were interested in machines that would automate routine household tasks, **iRobot**, a manufacturer of industrial and government (military) robots, created the Scooba, a robot that washes floors. Founder Colin Angle says, "People just hated to mop, so we saw a real opportunity."[5] The Scooba vacuums up dirt and debris, sprays a bleach cleaning solution, and then squeegees and sucks up the dirty water from the floor. At about $250, the Scooba can mop a typical kitchen in 45 minutes.

Standards can also be determined by benchmarking other companies. **Benchmarking** is the process of determining how well other companies (though not just competitors) perform business functions or tasks. In other words, benchmarking is the process of determining other companies' standards.

standards a basis of comparison for measuring the extent to which various kinds of organizational performance are satisfactory or unsatisfactory

benchmarking the process of identifying outstanding practices, processes, and standards in other companies and adapting them to your company

When setting standards by benchmarking, the first step is to determine what to benchmark. Companies can benchmark anything, from cycle time (how fast) to quality (how well) to price (how much). The next step is to identify the companies against which to benchmark your standards. The last step is to collect data to determine other companies' performance standards. **Cadillac** sales dropped for three straight decades because car buyers saw Cadillacs as big, bloated, poor-quality, luxury cars. Then, several years ago, after losing most of its luxury car market share, Cadillac began systematically benchmarking its quality and driving performance against Mercedes, BMW, Audi, and Lexus cars. Because of the changes made as a result of that benchmarking, Cadillac's STS sedan is now giving those luxury automakers' cars a run for their money. The *Wall Street Journal* concluded, "We'd have been impressed if the STS had matched these European cars' performance, but what surprised us was that in some ways it was better. The STS felt more nimble and fun to drive than heavier-feeling models including the Mercedes E-Class or Audi A6. It kept us feeling connected to the road, while a Lexus LS430 left us feeling isolated. And up against BMW's 5 Series,

© GETTY IMAGES NEWS

considered the benchmark in the class? We'd call it a draw."[6] Cadillac now consistently sells more cars than Mercedes in the all-important luxury car market.[7]

1.2 Comparison to Standards

The next step in the control process is to compare actual performance against performance standards. Although this sounds straightforward, the quality of the comparison largely depends on the measurement and information systems a company uses to keep track of performance. The better the system, the easier it is for companies to track their progress and identify problems that need to be fixed. One way for retailers to verify that performance standards are being met is to use "secret shoppers." Retail stores spend $600 million a year to hire these consultants, who visit the stores pretending to be customers, to determine whether employees provide helpful customer service. The "secret shoppers" make detailed observations of the service provided (or not). Secret shopper Cliff Fill recalls the fast-food restaurant where the workers discussed their dating plans as he stood in front of them ready to order. After ignoring him for 90 seconds (secret shoppers often carry timers with them), they turned to him and said, "We'll be done with our conversation in a minute and be with you."[8] Mystery shoppers also note great service. Mike Bare, cofounder of the Mystery Shopping Providers Association, says, "It used to be about catching people doing something wrong. But, more and more, it's validating people who do things right."[9] Indeed, Intrawest, a ski resort, gives $100 bills to employees praised in its secret shopper reports.

1.3 Corrective Action

The next step in the control process is to identify performance deviations, analyze those deviations, and then develop and implement programs to correct them. This is similar to the planning process discussed in Chapter 5: regular, frequent performance feedback allows workers and managers to track their performance and make adjustments in effort, direction, and strategies.

Beta versions of software programs are a classic tool that developers use to monitor deviations from the standard and take corrective action—before the product is released on the market. **GOOGLE** used a beta version of its Google Groups software for close to a decade as managers mined users' comments to improve the product.[10] Likewise, **MICROSOFT** has an internal program called Software Quality Metrics (SQM) that company software developers use when creating new software releases. SQM helps the developers determine how each change in the software code will affect the functionality of the program and uses a system of comparison charts to show how the changes will affect users of new software.[11]

1.4 Dynamic, Cybernetic Process

As shown in Exhibit 16.1, control is a continuous, dynamic, cybernetic process. Control begins by setting standards, measuring performance, and then comparing performance to the standards. If the performance deviates from the standards, then managers and employees analyze the deviations and develop and implement corrective programs that (hopefully) achieve the desired performance by meeting the standards. Managers must repeat the entire process again and again in an endless feedback loop (a continuous process). Thus, control is not a onetime achievement or result. It continues over time (that is, it is dynamic) and requires daily, weekly, and monthly attention from managers to maintain performance levels at the standard (that is, it is cybernetic). **Cybernetic** derives from the Greek word *kubernetes*, meaning "steersman," that is, one who steers or keeps on course.[12] Therefore, the

cybernetic the process of steering or keeping on course

control process shown in Exhibit 16.1 is cybernetic because of the feedback loop in which actual performance is compared against standards so that deviations from those standards can be minimized or corrected.

Keeping control of business expenses is an example of a continuous, dynamic, cybernetic process. A company that doesn't closely monitor expenses usually finds that they quickly get out of control, even for the smallest things. For example, when Eddie Lampert became chairman of **KMART**, everywhere he looked, he saw expenses that could be cut. He demanded that everyone stop looking at sales and instead focus on profitability. He told all of his store managers that he was willing to spend money, but only when they could assure the company of a big return. He didn't allow a proposal to improve lighting in stores that would have cost more than $2 million; declaring, "It doesn't matter what Target and Wal-Mart do," he wanted to know the positive value of every investment. He quickly eliminated what he referred to as "crazy promotions" that were designed to clear out inventory. Kmart stopped pricing DVDs at **WAL-MART** levels (that is, heavily discounted) and began selling DVDs only at full price. Lampert knew the stores would sell less in terms of volume but make more profit on each sale. Lampert says, "For the first year or so, we had declining same-store sales, but more stores made a profit. To some people, it looked like a plane that was going from 40,000 feet to 20,000 feet, and in five minutes from now, it's going to hit the ground. We said, 'We're going to land this plane' and we did."[13]

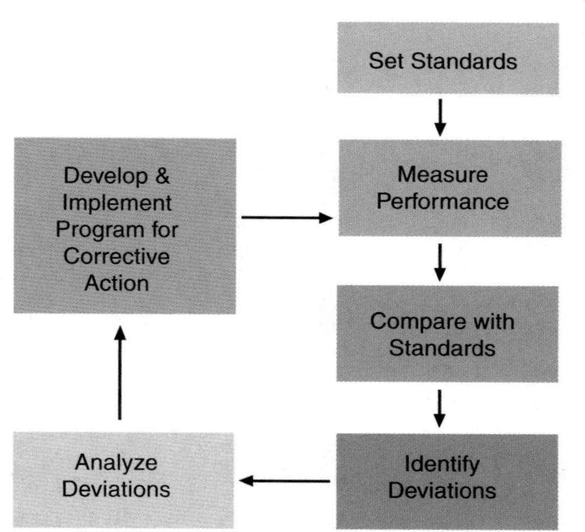

Source: H. Koontz & R. W. Bradspies, "Managing through Feedforward Control: A Future-Directed View," *Business Horizons*, June 1972, 25–36. Reprinted with permission from *Business Horizons*, © 1972 by the Trustees at Indiana University, Kelley School of Business.

Exhibit 16.1

Cybernetic Control Process

Sure, it's a cliché, but it's just as true in business as in sports: If you take your eye off the ball, you're going to strike out. Control is an ongoing, dynamic, cybernetic process.

1.5 Feedback, Concurrent, and Feedforward Control

The three basic control methods are feedback control, concurrent control, and feedforward control.[12] **Feedback control** is a mechanism for gathering information about performance deficiencies *after* they occur. This information is then used to correct or prevent performance deficiencies. Study after study has clearly shown that feedback improves both individual and organizational performance. In most instances, any feedback is better than no feedback.

If there is a downside to feedback, however, it is that it is always after the fact. Wal-Mart instituted a new feedback system when it began building more stores closer to urban areas. The company engaged the services of business analysts whose job it is to roam Wal-Mart stores and competitors' stores looking for opportunities to increase sales. This new feedback system is designed to help Wal-Mart managers and merchandisers tailor store floor plans to produce maximum sales per square foot, a standard metric in retailing. One business analyst noticed that a Wal-Mart in a mostly Hispanic neighborhood was out of women's shoes in size 5½ and concluded that the buyers at headquarters were not "aware of the store's large base of Hispanic women, who tend to have small feet—an insight that could aid buying decisions." Wal-Mart's feedback system helps it identify problems on the floor with merchandise locations and displays, as well as opportunities to sell products the analysts discover in other stores. Still, the feedback is always lagging the actual opportunity.[14]

Concurrent control is a mechanism for gathering information about performance deficiencies *as* they occur. Thus, it is an improvement over feedback because

feedback control a mechanism for gathering information about performance deficiencies after they occur

concurrent control a mechanism for gathering information about performance deficiencies as they occur, thereby eliminating or shortening the delay between performance and feedback

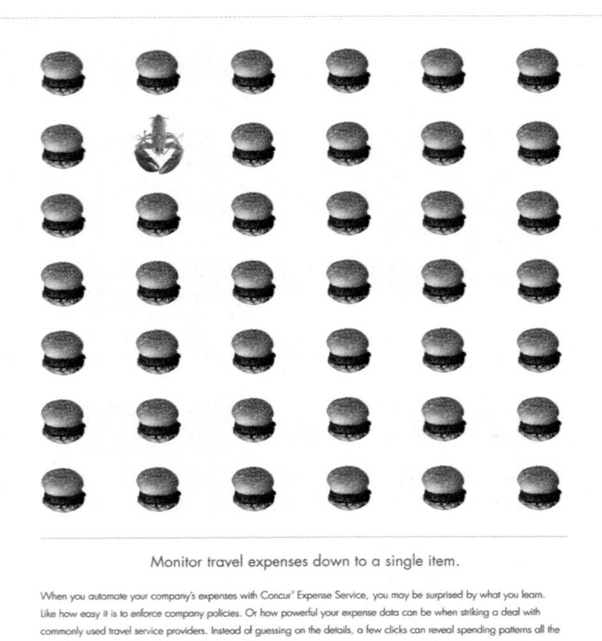

Monitor travel expenses down to a single item.
When you automate your company's expenses with Concur® Expense Service, you may be surprised by what you learn. Like how easy it is to enforce company policies. Or how powerful your expense data can be when striking a deal with commonly used travel service providers. Instead of guessing on the details, a few clicks can reveal spending patterns all the way down to a specific employee. Which streamlines the process, eliminates paperwork, and most important, saves you a whole lot of money. Call 888.800.4883 or visit www.ExpenseTour.com to take a free Concur Expense Service tour.
concur®
TECHNOLOGIES

Concur Technologies has developed software to help companies automate their expenses and keep track of expenditures and all the spending patterns way down to a specific employee. Without controls for business expenses (like travel), companies would soon be unwittingly paying for luxuries (like lobster) rather than basic business necessities (like meals). Imagine the costs associated with 41 lobsters and 1 hamburger!

it attempts to eliminate or shorten the delay between performance and feedback about the performance. Apple and NIKE teamed up to create a real-time exercise feedback system called Nike + iPod. After a runner installs the system in her shoes, it transmits concurrent information to her iPod. The system measures time, distance, calories burned, and pace. Runners can actually track their efforts every moment of their run and make changes on the fly. Greg Joswiak, APPLE's vice president of worldwide iPod marketing, says, "We've enabled people to have a much better running experience than ever before."[15]

Feedforward control is a mechanism for gathering information about performance deficiencies *before* they occur. In contrast to feedback and concurrent control, which provide feedback on the basis of outcomes and results, feedforward control provides information about performance deficiencies by monitoring inputs, not outputs. Thus, feedforward control seeks to prevent or minimize performance deficiencies *before* they happen. Microsoft uses feedforward controls to try to prevent software problems before they occur. For example, when developing the latest version of its Windows Server software (for network and Internet computer servers), Microsoft taught 8,500 experienced programmers new methods for writing more reliable software code *before* asking them to develop new features for Windows Server software. Microsoft has also developed new software testing tools that let the programmers thoroughly test the code they've written (that is, input) before passing the code on to others to be used in beta testing and then in final products.[16] Exhibit 16.2 lists guidelines that companies can follow to get the most out of feedforward control.

1.6 Control Isn't Always Worthwhile or Possible

Control is achieved when behavior and work procedures conform to standards and goals are accomplished. By contrast, **control loss** occurs when behavior and work procedures do not conform to standards.[17] John Caudwell, owner of PHONES4U, one of the United Kingdom's largest mobile phone chains, felt that his company had control loss with respect to e-mail. Managers and employees were averaging three hours per day on e-mail and, according to Caudwell, not spending enough time with customers. So he completely banned e-mail. "The policy came from me. The staff was initially slightly shocked that I should make such a revolutionary move," said Caudwell. "We have email paralysis. If you have a cancer, you have to cut it out. That's what I've done."[18]

"WHAT'S NEW" x 3
COMPANY

Maintaining control is important because control loss prevents goal achievement (in the Phones4U example, not spending enough time with customers). When control loss occurs managers need to find out what, if anything, they could have done to prevent it. Usually, as discussed above, that means identifying deviations from standard performance, analyzing the causes of those deviations, and taking corrective action. Implementing controls, however, isn't always worthwhile or possible. For example, it's debatable whether, in the long run, Phones4U's e-mail ban is a net plus for the company. Indeed, Tanno Massar, director of media relations at TPG, a logistics company, said "It would be a serious setback for the company if we could

feedforward control a mechanism for monitoring performance inputs rather than outputs to prevent or minimize performance deficiencies before they occur

control loss the situation in which behavior and work procedures do not conform to standards no longer use e-mail, and we are not considering it."[19] Let's look at regulation costs and cybernetic feasibility to see why implementing controls isn't always worthwhile or possible.

To determine whether control is worthwhile, managers need to carefully assess **regulation costs**, that is, whether the costs and both the intended and unintended consequences of control exceed its benefits. Initially enacted with the very best of intentions, the corporate average fuel economy (CAFE) standards have not been increased since 1985. The standards require that the entire fleet of a particular automaker achieve an average miles per gallon standard. That standard has been 27.5 mpg highway with a reduced requirement of 22.2 mpg for light trucks. With the dramatic increases in gasoline over the past few years there has been added pressure to increase the CAFE standards. In his 2007 State of the Union address, President George Bush proposed an increase of 4 percent per year through 2017 as a means of increasing U.S. independence and providing a boost to the ecology of the country. Later that year the Senate passed a new fleetwide standard of 35 mpg. The impact on the automakers is extreme. A recent estimate is that the new standards will cost the automakers more than $114 billion over the next ten years. The automakers feel that the market is not demanding sufficient numbers of high-mileage cars and the CAFE standards are a distortion and detriment to their business model. Ford Motor Chief Executive Alan Mulally called CAFE the most "market-distorting" policy he had ever come across. This all comes at a time when the big Detroit-based automakers are suffering through enormous financial losses and are in the process of radically working their business models to remain competitive.[20]

1. Thorough planning and analysis are required.
2. Careful discrimination must be applied in selecting input variables.
3. The feedforward system must be kept dynamic.
4. A model of the control system should be developed.
5. Data on input variables must be regularly collected.
6. Data on input variables must be regularly assessed.
7. Feedforward control requires action.

Source: H. Koontz & R. W. Bradspies, "Managing through Feedforward Control: A Future Directed View," *Business Horizons*, June 1972, 25–36. Reprinted with permission from *Business Horizons*, © 1972 by the Trustees at Indiana University, Kelley School of Business.

Exhibit 16.2
Guidelines for Using Feedforward Control

> We have email paralysis. If you have a cancer, you have to cut it out. That's what I've done.
>
> JOHN CAUDWELL, OWNER, PHONES4U

An often-overlooked factor in determining the cost of control is that *unintended consequences* sometimes accompany increased control. Control systems help companies, managers, and workers accomplish their goals, but at the same time that control systems help solve some problems, they can create others. For example, Six Sigma is a quality control system originally developed by **MOTOROLA**, that manufacturers use to achieve the goal of producing only 3.4 defective or nonstandard parts per million parts made. Clearly, manufacturers who reach Six Sigma consistently produce extremely high-quality products. But aligning the very constrictive process needed to attain Six Sigma with the need for out-of-the box thinking and innovation can be a feat. For example, Motorola's focus on achieving near-perfect production (99.9997 percent error-free) was stifling the company's creativity and innovation, both of which are critical for organizations to grow. In the late 1990s, Motorola lost its lead in mobile phones to Nokia, in part because tight manufacturing control systems were crushing efforts to develop new products. To mitigate the unintended consequences of Six Sigma, Motorola designers are now given a free hand to design, but the process engineers are always on hand to help ensure that even the coolest

regulation costs the costs associated with implementing or maintaining control

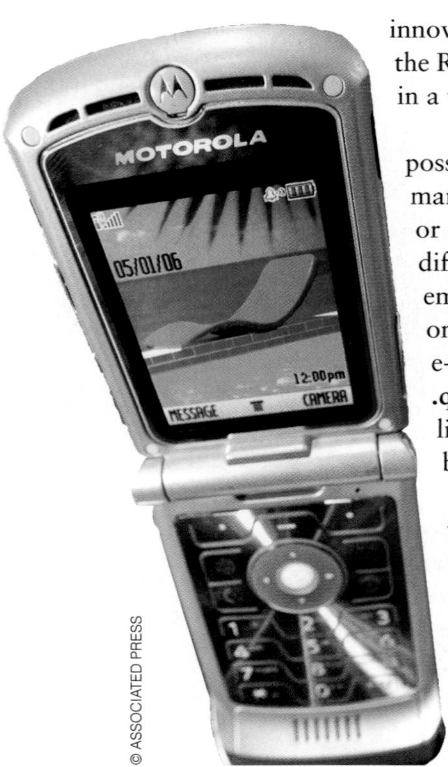

© ASSOCIATED PRESS

innovation—like the RAZR—can actually be manufactured to perfection. In fact, the RAZR helped Motorola climb from a 15.4 percent market share to 22.4 percent in a two-year period.[21]

Another factor to consider is **cybernetic feasibility**, the extent to which it is possible to implement each step in the control process: clear standards of performance, comparison of performance against standards, and corrective action. If one or more steps cannot be implemented, then maintaining effective control may be difficult or impossible. For example, many retail companies provide significant employee discounts, which can be used by entering special codes at the company's online store. However, those codes, meant for employee use, have leaked out via e-mail to nonemployees and are also published at websites such as **http://www.quicktoclick.com**. Amy Krasuna doesn't work for Old Navy or Banana Republic, but she has the employee codes for each company. Says Krasuna, "I'm being bombarded with them."[22]

Is it possible to control these discounts so that only employees can use them? Yes, with sufficient money, technical expertise, and the proper software tools (the costs of control), online retailers can create unique online discount codes that work only once and e-mail them to employees. A spokesperson for Gap, which uses such codes, says, "We want to make sure we're protecting the integrity of the [sales] event. We really consider it a benefit to our employees." However, at Banana Republic, which is owned by Gap, a spokesperson said that "technological challenges" prevented the company from using unique onetime codes. As a result, Banana Republic's 25 percent employee discount was being widely used by people who aren't employees, like Amy Krasuna.

Review 1: The Control Process

The control process begins by setting standards, measuring performance, and then comparing performance against the standards. The better a company's information and measurement systems, the easier it is to make these comparisons. The control process continues by identifying and analyzing performance deviations, and then developing and implementing programs for corrective action. However, control is a continuous, dynamic, cybernetic process, not a onetime achievement or result. Control requires frequent managerial attention. The three basic control methods are feedback control (after-the-fact performance information), concurrent control (simultaneous performance information), and feedforward control (preventive performance information). Control, however, has regulation costs and unanticipated consequences and therefore isn't always worthwhile or possible.

HOW AND WHAT TO CONTROL

At about 10 percent of Sam's Club and Wal-Mart stores, the doors are locked on midnight-shift employees to keep out robbers and, some say, also to prevent employee theft. According to Mona Williams, Wal-Mart's vice president for communications, "Wal-Mart secures these stores just as any other business does that has employees working overnight. Doors are locked to protect associates and the store from intruders."[23] But many employees dislike the policy. When Michael Rodriguez

cybernetic feasibility the extent to which it is possible to implement each step in the control process injured his ankle at 3 AM, he had to wait an hour for a store manager to show up to unlock the doors. Says Rodriguez, "Being locked in in an emergency like that, that's not right."[24] Wal-Mart's Mona Williams responds, "Fire doors are always accessible [and unlocked from the inside] for safety, and there will always be at least one manager in the store with a set of keys to unlock the doors."[25]

If you managed a Wal-Mart store, would you lock in your midnight employees? Would doing so jeopardize or improve their safety? Kmart, Sears, Home Depot, and Costco don't lock in their employees, so is Wal-Mart being overly restrictive? Or is this policy a reasonable response to employee theft, which can often exceed a store's profits? Former Sam's Club manager Tom Lewis says of the lock-in practice, "They're concerned about the bottom line, and the bottom line is affected by shrinkage in the store."[26] If you were a Wal-Mart or Sam's Club store manager, what would you do?

After reading the next two sections, you should be able to

2 discuss the various methods that managers can use to maintain control.

3 describe the behaviors, processes, and outcomes that today's managers are choosing to control in their organizations.

2 Control Methods

Managers can use five different methods to achieve control in their organizations: ***2.1 bureaucratic, 2.2 objective, 2.3 normative, 2.4 concertive****, and* ***2.5 self-control****.*

2.1 Bureaucratic Control

When most people think of managerial control, what they have in mind is bureaucratic control. **Bureaucratic control** is top-down control, in which managers try to influence employee behavior by rewarding or punishing employees for compliance or noncompliance with organizational policies, rules, and procedures. Most employees, however, would argue that bureaucratic managers emphasize punishment for noncompliance much more than rewards for compliance. For instance, when visiting the company's regional offices and managers, the president of a training company, who was known for his temper and for micromanaging others, would get some toilet paper from the restrooms and aggressively ask, "What's this?" When the managers answered, "Toilet paper," the president would scream that it was two-ply toilet paper that the company couldn't afford. When told of a cracked toilet seat in one of the women's restrooms, he said, "If you don't like sitting on that seat, you can stand up like I do!"[27]

Ironically, bureaucratic management and control were created to prevent just this type of managerial behavior. By encouraging managers to apply well-thought-out rules, policies, and procedures in an impartial, consistent manner to everyone in the organization, bureaucratic control is supposed to make companies more efficient, effective, and fair. Perversely, it frequently has just the opposite effect. Managers who use bureaucratic control often emphasize following the rules above all else. When an employee collapsed from chest pains, her boss, fearing a heart attack, helped carry her to an ambulance. Yet when the employee was diagnosed with indigestion and not a heart attack and returned to work several hours later, her boss filed a disciplinary action accusing her of an unexcused absence. Employees complained to the company

bureaucratic control the use of hierarchical authority to influence employee behavior by rewarding or punishing employees for compliance or noncompliance with organizational policies, rules, and procedures

CEO, who then took steps to correct the situation. The boss subsequently apologized to the employee and to his entire 25-person staff, explaining that he was wrong for taking the company's absence policy "too literally."[28]

Another characteristic of bureaucratically controlled companies is that due to their rule- and policy-driven decision making, they are highly resistant to change and slow to respond to customers and competitors. Recall from Chapter 2 that even Max Weber, the German philosopher who is largely credited with popularizing bureaucratic ideals in the late 19th century, referred to bureaucracy as the "iron cage." He said, "Once fully established, bureaucracy is among those social structures which are the hardest to destroy."[29] Of course, the national government, with hundreds of bureaus, agencies, and departments, is typically the largest bureaucracy in most countries. In the United States, because of the thousands of career bureaucrats who staff the offices of the federal government, even presidents and Congress have difficulty making changes. When General Dwight Eisenhower became president, his predecessor, Harry Truman, quipped, "Poor Ike. It won't be a bit like the army. He'll sit here and he'll say, 'Do this, do that,' and nothing will happen."[30]

> Poor Ike. It won't be a bit like the army. He'll sit here and he'll say, "Do this, do that," and nothing will happen.
>
> HARRY TRUMAN

2.2 Objective Control

In many companies, bureaucratic control has evolved into **objective control**, which is the use of observable measures of employee behavior or output to assess performance and influence behavior. Whereas bureaucratic control focuses on whether policies and rules are followed, objective control focuses on the observation or measurement of worker behavior or output. Three employees at Kwik Trip Convenience stores were fired for postings they made about the company on the social networking website Facebook. Because the employees' postings were complaints about rude customers and their jobs in general, the company determined that their behavior was not appropriate, especially given that an employee can be let go for treating customers badly in the store.[31] There are two kinds of objective control: behavior control and output control.

Behavior control is regulating behaviors and actions that workers perform on the job. The basic assumption of behavior control is that if you do the right things (that is, the right behaviors) every day, then those things should lead to goal achievement. Behavior control is still management-based, however, which means that managers are responsible for monitoring and rewarding or punishing workers for exhibiting desired or undesired behaviors. Companies that use global positioning satellite (GPS) technology to track where workers are and what they're doing are using behavior control. For example, after getting complaints that his Clinton Township, New Jersey, police officers weren't always on the job, Sergeant John Kuczynski quietly put GPS tracking devices in his officers' cars. Contrary to the officers' reports indicating that they were patrolling streets or using radar to catch speeding drivers, the GPS tracking software soon showed that five officers were sitting for long periods in parking lots or taking long breaks for meals. All five are now barred from law enforcement jobs.[32] Likewise, some organizations, worried that employees are wasting time on nonproductive behaviors, are removing Solitaire and Mine Sweeper games from employees' computers. The reason? Researchers at the Internal Revenue Service have found that half the time IRS employees are using computers they're playing games, gambling, or shopping on the Internet.[33]

Instead of measuring what managers and workers do, **output control** measures the results of their efforts. Whereas behavior control regulates, guides, and measures how workers behave on the job, output control gives managers and workers the freedom to behave as they see fit as long as they accomplish prespecified, measurable

objective control the use of observable measures of worker behavior or outputs to assess performance and influence behavior

behavior control the regulation of the behaviors and actions that workers perform on the job

output control the regulation of workers' results or outputs through rewards and incentives

results. Output control is often coupled with rewards and incentives.

Three things must occur for output control and rewards to lead to improved business results. First, output control measures must be reliable, fair, and accurate. Second, employees and managers must believe that they can produce the desired results. If they don't, then the output controls won't affect their behavior. Third, the rewards or incentives tied to outcome control measures must truly be dependent on achieving established standards of performance. For example, **Smithfield Foods** CEO Joseph Luter doesn't earn a bonus unless pretax profits exceed $100 million. Ray Goldberg, chairman of the company's compensation committee, says that the performance requirements shouldn't "be so low that you get a bonus no matter what you do."[35] Goldberg explains, "We were trying to make sure [Luter's] rewards are based on the ups and downs of the company."[36] So, with pretax profits of $227.1 million, Luter's bonus, based on 2 percent of earnings between $100 million and $300 million, and 3 percent of profits over $300 million, would total just over $2.5 million. For output control to work with rewards, the rewards must truly be at risk if performance doesn't measure up.

doing the right thing

Don't Cheat on Travel Expense Reports

Workers are often tempted to pad their travel expense reports. As one puts it, "After a while you feel that they owe it to ya, so the hell with 'em. I'm going to expense it." Frank Navran of the Ethics Resource Center says that people justify this by telling themselves, "I'm not really stealing from the company—I'm just getting back what I feel I'm entitled to." However, Joel Richards, executive vice president and chief administrative officer of El Paso Corporation, says, "You learn a lot about people from their expense reports. If you can't trust an employee to be truthful on an expense report, if you can't trust them with small dollars, how can you trust them with making decisions involving millions of dollars?" So, do the right thing: Don't cheat on your travel expense reports.[34]

2.3 Normative Control

Rather than monitoring rules, behavior, or output, another way to control what goes on in organizations is to use normative control to shape the beliefs and values of the people who work there. With **normative controls**, a company's widely shared values and beliefs guide workers' behavior and decisions. For example, at **Nordstrom**, a Seattle-based department store chain, one value permeates the entire work force from top to bottom: extraordinary customer service. On the first day of work at Nordstrom, trainees begin their transformation to the "Nordstrom way" by reading the employee handbook. Sounds boring, doesn't it? But Nordstrom's handbook is printed on one side of a 3-by-5-inch note card. In its entirety, it reads:

> *Welcome to Nordstrom's. We're glad to have you with our company. Our Number One goal is to provide outstanding customer service. Set both your personal and professional goals high. We have great confidence in your ability to achieve them. Nordstrom Rules: Rule #1: Use your good judgment in all situations. There will be no additional rules. Please feel free to ask your department manager, store manager, or division general manager any question at any time.*[37]

That's it. No lengthy rules. No specifics about what behavior is or is not appropriate. Use your judgment.[38]

Normative controls are created in two ways. First, companies that use normative controls are very careful about whom they hire. While many companies screen potential applicants on the basis of their abilities, normatively controlled companies

normative control the regulation of workers' behavior and decisions through widely shared organizational values and beliefs

Nordstrom sets the retailing industry's benchmark for customer service by using normative control. Here an employee is helping customers in Nordstrom's Costa Mesa, California, store.

are just as likely to screen potential applicants based on their attitudes and values. For example, before building stores in a new city, Nordstrom sends its human resource team into town to interview prospective applicants. In a few cities, the company canceled its expansion plans when it could not find enough qualified applicants who embodied the service attitudes and values for which Nordstrom is known. Nordstrom would rather give up potential sales in lucrative markets than do business using people who cannot provide Nordstrom's level of service.[39]

Second, with normative controls, managers and employees learn what they should and should not do by observing experienced employees and by listening to the stories they tell about the company. At Nordstrom, many of these stories, which employees call "heroics," have been inspired by the company motto, "Respond to Unreasonable Customer Requests!"[40] "Nordies," as Nordstrom employees call themselves, like to tell the story about a customer who just had to have a pair of burgundy Donna Karan slacks that had gone on sale, but she could not find her size. The sales associate who was helping her contacted five nearby Nordstrom stores, but none had the customer's size. So rather than leave the customer dissatisfied with her shopping experience, the sales associate went to her manager for petty cash and then went across the street and paid full price for the slacks at a competitor's store. She then resold them to the customer at Nordstrom's lower sale price.[41] Obviously, Nordstrom would quickly go out of business if this were the norm. Nevertheless, this story makes clear the attitude that drives employee performance at Nordstrom in ways that rules, behavioral guidelines, or output controls could not.

2.4 Concertive Control

Whereas normative controls are based on beliefs that are strongly held and widely shared throughout a company, **concertive controls** are based on beliefs that are shaped and negotiated by work groups.[42] Whereas normative controls are driven by strong organizational cultures, concertive controls usually arise when companies give autonomous work groups complete autonomy and responsibility for task completion (see Chapter 10, Managing Teams, for a complete discussion of the role of autonomy in teams and groups). The most autonomous groups operate without managers and are completely responsible for controlling work group processes, outputs, and behavior. Such groups do their own hiring, firing, worker discipline, work schedules, materials ordering, budget making and meeting, and decision making.

Concertive control is not established overnight. Highly autonomous work groups evolve through two phases as they develop concertive control. In phase one, group members learn to work with each other, supervise each other's work, and develop the values and beliefs that will guide and control their behavior. And because they develop these values and beliefs themselves, work group members feel strongly about following them.

concertive control the regulation of workers' behavior and decisions through work group values and beliefs

In the steel industry, **Nucor** was long considered an upstart compared with the "biggies" U.S. Steel and Bethlehem Steel. Today, however, not only has Nucor managed to outlast many other mills, the company has bought out 13 other mills in the past five years. But Nucor has a unique culture that gives real power to employees on the line and fosters teamwork throughout the organization. This type of teamwork can be a difficult thing for a newly acquired group of employees to get used to. For example, at Nucor's first big acquisition in Auburn, New York, David Hutchins is a frontline supervisor or "lead man" in the rolling mill, where steel from the furnace is spread thin enough to be cut into sheets. When the plant was under the previous ownership, if the guys doing the cutting got backed up, the guys doing the rolling—including Hutchins—would just take a break. He says, "We'd sit back, have a cup of coffee, and complain: 'Those guys stink.' " It took six months to convince the employees at the Auburn plant that the Nucor teamwork way was better than the old way. Now, Hutchins says, "At Nucor, we're not 'you guys' and 'us guys.' It's all of us guys. Wherever the bottleneck is, we go there, and everyone works on it."[43]

> At Nucor, we're not "you guys" and "us guys." It's all of us guys. Wherever the bottleneck is, we go there, and everyone works on it.
>
> **DAVID HUTCHINS**, FRONTLINE SUPERVISOR, NUCOR

The second phase in the development of concertive control is the emergence and formalization of objective rules to guide and control behavior. The beliefs and values developed in phase one usually develop into more objective rules as new members join teams. The clearer those rules, the easier it becomes for new members to figure out how and how not to behave.

Before Nucor finalizes an acquisition, it sends a team of long-time employees to the new plant. People at all levels, from managers to steelworkers, visit with their counterparts at the mill being acquired and tell them about the "Nucor way." Getting new employees on board quickly helps preserve everyone's bonus and performance-based pay. By following the "program" of working together and increasing output, Dave Hutchins saw his annual pay of $53,000 rise to $67,000 the year after Nucor acquired his plant, then to $92,000 only four years after that.[44] Again, the key difference in concertive control is that the teams—and not management—enforce these rules, but a system based upon team equality permeates the best companies.

Ironically, concertive control may lead to even more stress for workers to conform to expectations than bureaucratic control. Under bureaucratic control, most workers only have to worry about pleasing the boss. But with concertive control, their behavior has to satisfy the rest of their team members. For example, one team member says, "I don't have to sit there and look for the boss to be around; and if the boss is not around, I can sit there and talk to my neighbor or do what I want. Now the whole team is around me and the whole team is observing what I'm doing."[45] Plus, with concertive control, team members have a second, much more stressful role to perform—that of making sure that their team members adhere to team values and rules.

2.5 Self-Control

Self-control, also known as **self-management**, is a control system in which managers and workers control their own behavior.[46] Self-control does not result in anarchy in which everyone gets to do whatever he or she wants. In self-control or self-management, leaders and managers provide workers with clear boundaries within which they may guide and control their own goals and behaviors.[47] Leaders and managers also contribute to self-control by teaching others the skills they need to maximize and monitor their own work effectiveness. In turn, individuals who manage and lead themselves establish self-control by setting their own goals, monitoring their own progress, rewarding or punishing themselves for achieving or for not achieving

self-control (self-management) a control system in which managers and workers control their own behavior by setting their own goals, monitoring their own progress, and rewarding themselves for goal achievement their self-set goals, and constructing positive thought patterns that remind them of the importance of their goals and their ability to accomplish them.[48]

For example, let's assume you need to do a better job of praising and recognizing the good work that your staff does for you. You can use goal setting, self-observation, and self-reward to self-manage this behavior. For self-observation, write "praise/recognition" on a 3-by-5-inch card. Put the card in your pocket. Put a check on the card each time you praise or recognize someone (wait until the person has left before you do this). Keep track for a week. This serves as your baseline or starting point. Simply keeping track will probably increase how often you do this. After a week, assess your baseline or starting point, and then set a specific goal. For instance, if your baseline was twice a day, you might set a specific goal to praise or recognize others' work five times a day. Continue monitoring your performance with your cards. Once you've achieved your goal every day for a week, give yourself a reward (perhaps a CD, a movie, lunch with a friend at a new restaurant) for achieving your goal.[49]

As you can see, the components of self-management, self-set goals, self-observation, and self-reward have their roots in the motivation theories you read about in Chapter 13. The key difference, though, is that the goals, feedback, and rewards originate from employees themselves and not from their managers or organizations.

Review 2: **Control Methods**

The five methods of control are bureaucratic, objective, normative, concertive, and self-control (self-management). Bureaucratic and objective controls are top-down, management-based, and measurement-based. Normative and concertive controls represent shared forms of control because they evolve from company-wide or team-based beliefs and values. Self-control, or self-management, is a control system in which managers turn much, but not all, control over to the individuals themselves.

Bureaucratic control is based on organizational policies, rules, and procedures. Objective controls are based on reliable measures of behavior or outputs. Normative control is based on strong corporate beliefs and careful hiring practices. Concertive control is based on the development of values, beliefs, and rules in autonomous work groups. Self-control is based on individuals' setting their own goals, monitoring themselves, and rewarding or punishing themselves with respect to goal achievement.

We end this section by noting that each of these control methods may be more or less appropriate depending on the circumstances. Examine Exhibit 16.3 to find out when each of these five control methods should be used.

3 What to Control?

In the first section of this chapter, we discussed the basics of the control process and that control isn't always worthwhile or possible. In the second section, we looked at the various ways in which control can be obtained. In this third and final section, we address an equally important issue, "What should managers control?" The way managers answer this question has critical implications for most businesses. In the midst of an economic slowdown, a medium-sized financial company created a huge upheaval when it tried to cut costs by eliminating company-paid-for cell phones. Salespeople were furious, claiming, "No other group in the company had their cell phone use restricted." Lynda Ford, a consultant who was working with the

BUREAUCRATIC CONTROL	• When it is necessary to standardize operating procedures • When it is necessary to establish limits
BEHAVIOR CONTROL	• When it is easier to measure what workers do on the job than what they accomplish on the job • When "cause-effect" relationships are clear, that is, when companies know which behaviors will lead to success and which won't • When good measures of worker behavior can be created
OUTPUT CONTROL	• When it is easier to measure what workers accomplish on the job than what they do on the job • When good measures of worker output can be created • When it is possible to set clear goals and standards for worker output • When "cause-effect" relationships are unclear
NORMATIVE CONTROL	• When organizational culture, values, and beliefs are strong • When it is difficult to create good measures of worker behavior • When it is difficult to create good measures of worker output
CONCERTIVE CONTROL	• When responsibility for task accomplishment is given to autonomous work groups • When management wants workers to take "ownership" of their behavior and outputs • When management desires a strong form of worker-based control
SELF-CONTROL	• When workers are intrinsically motivated to do their jobs well • When it is difficult to create good measures of worker behavior • When it is difficult to create good measures of worker output • When workers have or are taught self-control and self-leadership skills

Sources: L. J. Kirsch, "The Management of Complex Tasks in Organizations: Controlling the Systems Development Process," *Organization Science* 7 (1996): 1–21; S. A. Snell, "Control Theory in Strategic Human Resource Management: The Mediating Effect of Administrative Information," *Academy of Management Journal* 35 (1992): 292–327.

Exhibit 16.3

When to Use Different Methods of Control

company at the time, says that canceling cell phones "became the straw that broke the camel's back." As a result, salespeople started quitting and productivity dropped significantly. Several months later, realizing the policy was wrong, the company reinstated company cell phones.[50]

This financial company lost salespeople and productivity because it worried about (that is, controlled) only one thing—reducing costs. Companies need to have a clear vision. They can't be everything to everybody. Most companies successfully carry out their visions and missions by finding a balance that comes from doing a multitude of small things right, like managing costs, providing value, and keeping customers and employees satisfied.

After reading this section, you should be able to explain ***3.1 the balanced scorecard approach to control*** *and how companies can achieve balanced control of company performance by choosing to control* ***3.2 budgets, cash flows, and economic value added, 3.3 customer defections, 3.4 quality****, and* ***3.5 waste and pollution****.*

3.1 The Balanced Scorecard

Most companies measure performance using standard financial and accounting measures such as return on capital, return on assets, return on investments, cash flow, net income, and net margins. The **balanced scorecard** encourages managers to look beyond traditional financial measures to four different perspectives on company performance. How do customers see us (the customer perspective)? At what must we excel (the internal perspective)? Can we continue to improve and create value (the innovation and learning perspective)? How do we look to shareholders (the financial perspective)?[51]

The balanced scorecard has several advantages over traditional control processes that rely solely on financial measures. First, it forces managers at each level of the company to set specific goals and measure performance in each of the four areas. For example, Exhibit 16.4 shows that Southwest Airlines uses nine different measures in its balanced scorecard. Of those, only three, market value, seat revenue, and plane lease costs (at various compounded annual growth rates, or CAGR), are standard financial measures of performance. In addition, Southwest measures its Federal Aviation Administration (FAA) on-time arrival rating and the cost of its airfares compared with competitors (customer perspective); how much time each plane spends on the ground after landing and the percentage of planes that depart on time (internal business perspective); and the percentage of its ground crew workers, such as mechanics and luggage handlers, who own company stock and have received job training (learning perspective).

balanced scorecard measurement of organizational performance in four equally important areas: finances, customers, internal operations, and innovation and learning

suboptimization performance improvement in one part of an organization but only at the expense of decreased performance in another part

The second major advantage of the balanced scorecard approach to control is that it minimizes the chances of **suboptimization**, which occurs when performance improves in one area, but at the expense of decreased performance in others. Jon Meliones, chief medical director at **Duke Children's Hospital**, says, "We explained the [balanced scorecard] theory to clinicians and administrators like this.... if you sacrifice too much in one quadrant to satisfy another, your organization as a whole is thrown out of balance. We could, for example, cut costs to improve the financial quadrant by firing half the staff, but that would hurt quality of service, and the customer quadrant would fall out of balance. Or we could increase productivity in the internal business quadrant by assigning more patients to a nurse, but doing so would raise the likelihood of errors—an unacceptable trade-off."[52]

Exhibit 16.4

Southwest Airlines' Balanced Scorecard

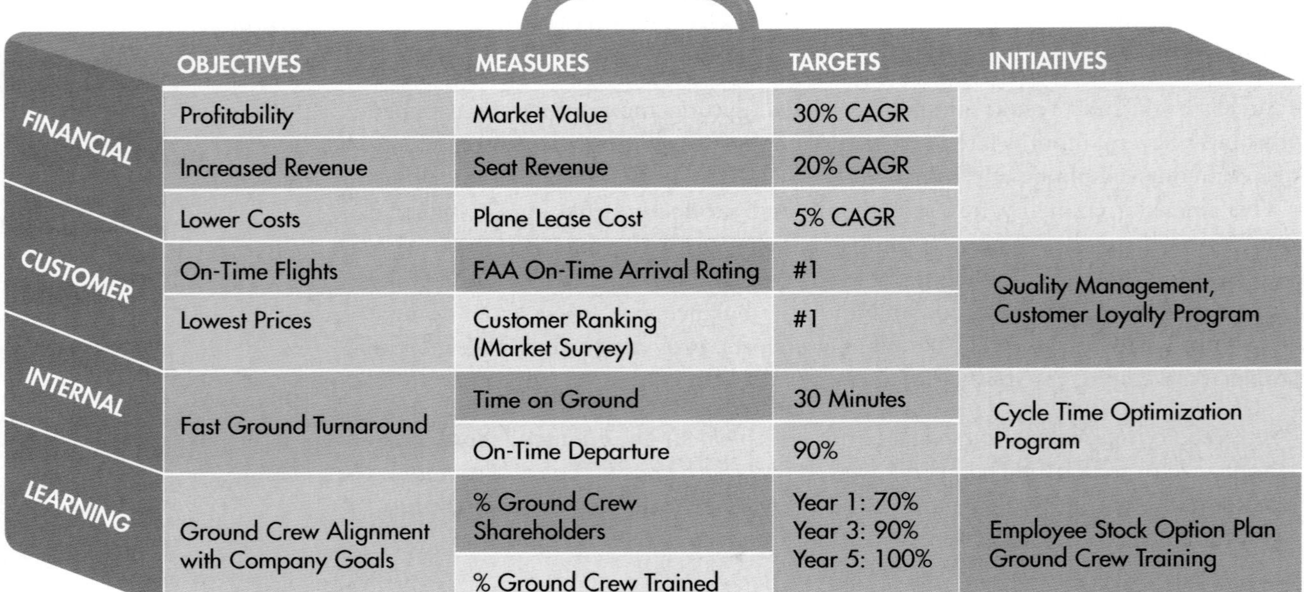

	OBJECTIVES	MEASURES	TARGETS	INITIATIVES
FINANCIAL	Profitability	Market Value	30% CAGR	
	Increased Revenue	Seat Revenue	20% CAGR	
	Lower Costs	Plane Lease Cost	5% CAGR	
CUSTOMER	On-Time Flights	FAA On-Time Arrival Rating	#1	Quality Management, Customer Loyalty Program
	Lowest Prices	Customer Ranking (Market Survey)	#1	
INTERNAL	Fast Ground Turnaround	Time on Ground	30 Minutes	Cycle Time Optimization Program
		On-Time Departure	90%	
LEARNING	Ground Crew Alignment with Company Goals	% Ground Crew Shareholders	Year 1: 70% Year 3: 90% Year 5: 100%	Employee Stock Option Plan Ground Crew Training
		% Ground Crew Trained		

Sources: G. Anthes, "ROI Guide: Balanced Scorecard," *Computer World* available at http://www.computerworld.com/managementtopics/roi/story/0,10801,78512,00.html, 5 May 2003.

Let's examine some of the ways in which companies are controlling the four basic parts of the balanced scorecard: the financial perspective (budgets, cash flows, and economic value added), the customer perspective (customer defections), the internal perspective (total quality management), and the innovation and learning perspective (waste and pollution).

cash flow analysis a type of analysis that predicts how changes in a business will affect its ability to take in more cash than it pays out

balance sheets accounting statements that provide a snapshot of a company's financial position at a particular time

income statements accounting statements, also called "profit and loss statements," that show what has happened to an organization's income, expenses, and net profit over a period of time

financial ratios calculations typically used to track a business's liquidity (cash), efficiency, and profitability over time compared to other businesses in its industry

budgets quantitative plans through which managers decide how to allocate available money to best accomplish company goals

3.2 The Financial Perspective: Controlling Budgets, Cash Flows, and Economic Value Added

The traditional approach to controlling financial performance focuses on accounting tools, such as cash flow analysis, balance sheets, income statements, financial ratios, and budgets. **Cash flow analysis** predicts how changes in a business will affect its ability to take in more cash than it pays out. **Balance sheets** provide a snapshot of a company's financial position at a particular time (but not the future). **Income statements**, also called profit and loss statements, show what has happened to an organization's income, expenses, and net profit (income less expenses) over a period of time. Exhibit 16.5 shows the basic steps or parts for cash flow analyses, balance sheets, and income statements. **Financial ratios** are typically used to track a business's liquidity (cash), efficiency, and profitability over time compared with other businesses in its industry. Exhibit 16.6 lists a few of the most common financial ratios and explains how they are calculated, what they mean, and when to use them. Finally, **budgets** are used to project costs and revenues, prioritize and control spending, and ensure that expenses don't exceed available funds and revenues. Exhibit 16.7 reviews the different kinds of budgets managers can use to track and control company finances.

By themselves, none of these tools—cash flow analyses, balance sheets, income statements, financial ratios, or budgets—tell the whole financial story of a business. They must be used together when assessing a company's financial performance. Since these tools are reviewed in detail in your accounting and finance classes, only a brief overview is provided here. Still, these are necessary tools for controlling organizational finances and expenses, and they should be part of your business toolbox. Unfortunately, most managers don't (but should) have a good understanding of these accounting tools.[53] When **Boeing**'s new chief financial officer attended her first company retreat with other Boeing executives, she assumed that her discussion of financial ratios, like those shown in Exhibit 16.6, would be a boring review for everyone present. Afterwards, she was shocked when dozens of the 280 executives attending the retreat told her that for the very first time they finally understood what the formulas meant.[54]

So if, like those experienced executives, you struggle to understand how financial ratios can be used where you work, you might find help in the following books: *Accounting the Easy Way*, by Peter J. Eisen; *Accounting for Dummies* and *How to Read a Financial Report: Wringing Vital Signs Out of the Numbers*, both by John A. Tracy; *Schaum's Quick Guide to Business Formulas: 201 Decision-Making Tools for Business, Finance, and Accounting Students*, by Joel G. Siegel, Jae K. Shim, and Stephen W. Hartman; *The Vest-Pocket Guide to Business Ratios*, by Michael R. Tyran; *Essential Managers: Managing Budgets*, by Stephen Brookson; or *Forecasting Budgets: 25 Keys to Successful Planning (The New York Times Pocket MBA Series)*, by Norman Moore and Grover Gardner.

Though no one would dispute the importance of cash flow analyses, balance sheets, income statements, financial ratios, or budgets for

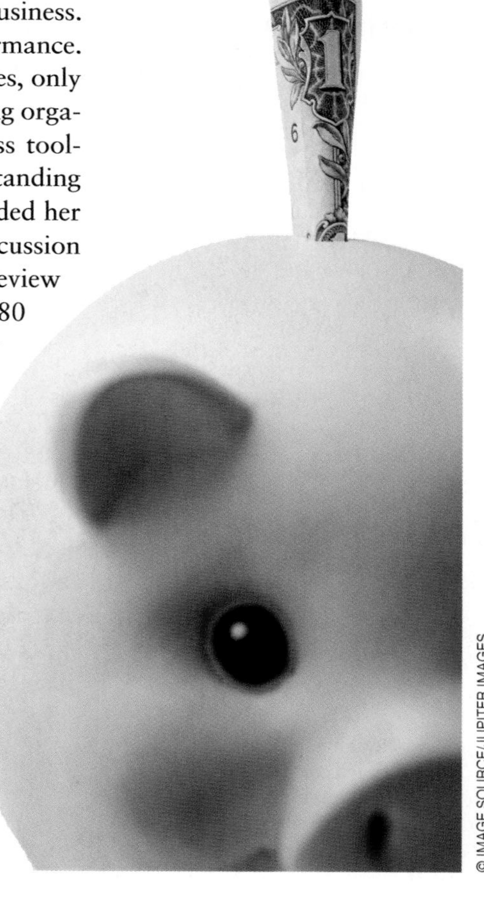

STEPS FOR A BASIC CASH FLOW ANALYSIS
1. Forecast sales (steady, up, or down).
2. Project changes in anticipated cash inflows (as a result of changes).
3. Project anticipated cash outflows (as a result of changes).
4. Project net cash flows by combining anticipated cash inflows and outflows.
PARTS OF A BASIC BALANCE SHEET (ASSETS = LIABILITIES + OWNER'S EQUITY)
1. Assets a. Current Assets (cash, short-term investment, marketable securities, accounts receivable, etc.) b. Fixed Assets (land, buildings, machinery, equipment, etc.)
2. Liabilities a. Current Liabilities (accounts payable, notes payable, taxes payable, etc.) b. Long-Term Liabilities (long-term debt, deferred income taxes, etc.)
3. Owner's Equity a. Preferred stock and common stock b. Additional paid-in capital c. Retained earnings
BASIC INCOME STATEMENT
SALES REVENUE
– sales returns and allowances
+ other income
= NET REVENUE
– cost of goods sold (beginning inventory, costs of goods purchased, ending inventory)
= GROSS PROFIT
– total operating expenses (selling, general, and administrative expenses)
= INCOME FROM OPERATIONS
– interest expense
= PRETAX INCOME
– income taxes
= NET INCOME

Exhibit 16.5

Basic Accounting Tools for Controlling Financial Performance

determining the financial health of a business, accounting research also indicates that the complexity and sheer amount of information contained in these accounting tools can shut down the brain and glaze over the eyes of even the most experienced manager.[55] Sometimes, there's simply too much information to make sense of. The balanced scorecard simplifies things by focusing on one simple question when it comes to finances: How do we look to shareholders? One way to answer that question is through something called economic value added.

Conceptually, **economic value added (EVA)** is not the same thing as profits. It is the amount by which profits exceed the cost of capital in a given year. It is based on the simple idea that capital is necessary to run a business and that capital comes at a cost. Although most people think of capital as cash, capital, once invested (that is, spent), is more likely to be found in a business in the form of computers, manufacturing plants, employees, raw materials, and so forth. And just like the interest that a homeowner pays on a mortgage or that a college student pays on a student loan, there is a cost to that capital.

The most common costs of capital are the interest paid on long-term bank loans used to buy all those resources, the interest paid to bondholders (who lend organizations their money), and the dividends (cash payments) and growth in stock value that accrue to shareholders. EVA is positive when company profits (revenues minus expenses minus taxes) exceed the cost of capital in a given year. In other words, if a business is to truly grow, its revenues must be large enough to cover both short-term costs (annual expenses and taxes) and long-term costs (the cost of borrowing capital from bondholders and shareholders). If you're a bit confused, the late Roberto Goizueta, the former CEO of Coca-Cola, explained it this way: "You borrow money at a certain rate and invest it at a higher rate and pocket the difference. It is simple. It is the essence of banking."[56]

economic value added (EVA) the amount by which company profits (revenues, minus expenses, minus taxes) exceed the cost of capital in a given year

RATIOS	FORMULA	WHAT IT MEANS	WHEN TO USE
LIQUIDITY RATIOS			
Current Ratio	Current Assets / Current Liabilities	• Whether you have enough assets on hand to pay for short-term bills and obligations. • Higher is better. • Recommended level is two times as many current assets as current liabilities.	• Track monthly and quarterly. • Basic measure of your company's health.
Quick (Acid Test) Ratio	(Current Assets–Inventories) / Current Liabilities	• Stricter than current ratio • Whether you have enough (i.e., cash) to pay short-term bills and obligations. • Higher is better. • Recommended level is one or higher.	• Track monthly. • Also calculate quick ratio with potential customers to evaluate whether they're likely to pay you in a timely manner.
LEVERAGE RATIOS			
Debt to Equity	Total Liabilities / Total Equity	• Indicates how much the company is leveraged (in debt) by comparing what is owed (liabilities) with what is owned (equity). • Lower is better. A high debt-to-equity ratio could indicate that the company has too much debt. • Recommended level depends on industry.	• Track monthly. • Lenders often use this to determine the creditworthiness of a business (i.e., whether to approve additional loans).
Debt Coverage	(Net Profit + Noncash Expense) / Debt	• Indicates how well cash flow covers debt payments. • Higher is better.	• Track monthly. • Lenders look at this ratio to determine if there is adequate cash to make loan payments.
EFFICIENCY RATIOS			
Inventory Turnover	Cost of Goods Sold / Average Value of Inventory	• Whether you're making efficient use of inventory. • Higher is better, indicating that inventory (dollars) isn't purchased (spent) until needed. • Recommended level depends on industry.	• Track monthly by using a 12-month rolling average.
Average Collections Period	Accounts Receivable / (Annual Net Credit Sales Divided by 365)	• Shows on average how quickly your customers are paying their bills. • Lower is better. • Recommended level is no more than 15 days longer than credit terms. If credit is net 30 days, then average should not be longer than 45 days.	• Track monthly. • Use to determine how long company's money is being tied up in customer credit.
PROFITABILITY RATIOS			
Gross Profit Margin	Gross Profit / Total Sales	• Shows how efficiently a business is using its materials and labor in the production process. • Higher is better, indicating that a profit can be made if fixed costs are controlled.	• Track monthly. • Analyze when unsure about product or service pricing. • Low margin compared with competitors means you're underpricing.
Return on Equity	Net Income / Owner's Equity	• Shows what was earned on your investment in the business during a particular period. Often called "return on investment." • Higher is better.	• Track quarterly and annually. • Use to compare what you might have earned on the stock market, bonds, or government Treasury bills during the same period.

Exhibit 16.6

Common Financial Ratios

Type of budget	Key points
Revenue Budgets—used to project or forecast future sales.	• Accuracy of projection depends on economy, competitors, sales force estimates, etc. • Determined by estimating future sales volume and sales prices for all products and services
Expense Budgets—used within departments and divisions to determine how much will be spent on various supplies, projects, or activities.	• One of the first places that companies look for cuts when trying to lower expenses
Profit Budgets—used by profit centers, which have "profit and loss" responsibility.	• Profit budgets combine revenue and expense budgets into one budget • Typically used in large businesses with multiple plants and divisions
Cash Budgets—used to forecast how much cash a company will have on hand to meet expenses.	• Similar to cash flow analyses • Used to identify cash shortfalls, which must be covered to pay bills, or cash excesses, which should be invested for a higher return
Capital Expenditure Budgets—used to forecast large, long-lasting investments in equipment, buildings, and property.	• Help managers identify funding that will be needed to pay for future expansion or strategic moves designed to increase competitive advantage
Variable Budgets—used to project costs across varying levels of sales and revenues.	• Important because it is difficult to accurately predict sales revenue and volume • Lead to more accurate budgeting with respect to labor, materials, and administrative expenses, which vary with sales volume and revenues • Build flexibility into the budgeting process

Exhibit 16.7

Common Kinds of Budgets

Exhibit 16.8 shows how to calculate EVA. First, starting with a company's income statement, you calculate the net operating profit after taxes (NOPAT) by subtracting taxes owed from income from operations (see Exhibit 16.5 for a review of an income statement). The NOPAT shown in Exhibit 16.8 is $3,500,000. Second, identify how much capital the company has invested (that is, spent). Total liabilities (what the company owes) less accounts payable and less accrued expenses, neither of which you pay interest on, provides a rough approximation of this amount. In Exhibit 16.8, total capital invested is $16,800,000. Third, calculate the cost (that is, rate) paid for capital by determining the interest paid to bondholders (who lend organizations their money), which is usually somewhere between 5 and 8 percent, and the return that stockholders want in terms of dividends and stock price appreciation, which is historically about 13 percent. Take a weighted average of the two to determine the overall cost of capital. In Exhibit 16.8, the cost of capital is 10 percent. Fourth, multiply the total capital ($16,800,000) from Step 2 by the cost of capital (10 percent) from Step 3. In Exhibit 16.8, this amount is $1,680,000. Fifth, subtract the total dollar cost of capital in Step 4 from the NOPAT in Step 1. In Exhibit 16.8, this value is $1,820,000, which means that our example company has created economic value or wealth this year. If our EVA number had been negative, meaning that the company didn't make enough profit to cover the cost of capital from bondholders and shareholders, then the company would have destroyed economic value or wealth by taking in more money than it returned.[57]

But why is EVA so important? First and most importantly, because it includes the cost of capital, it shows whether a business, division, department, profit center, or product is really paying for itself. The key is to make sure that managers and employees can see how their choices and behavior affect the company's EVA.

1. Calculate net operating profit after tax (NOPAT).	$3,500,000
2. Identify how much capital the company has invested (i.e., spent).	$16,800,000
3. Determine the cost (i.e., rate) paid for capital (usually between 5 percent and 13 percent).	10 percent
4. Multiply capital used (Step 2) times cost of capital (Step 3).	(10% × $16,800,000) = $1,680,000
5. Subtract the total dollar cost of capital from net profit after taxes.	$3,500,000 NOPAT –$1,680,000 Total cost of capital $1,820,000 Economic value added

Exhibit 16.8

Calculating Economic Value Added (EVA)

For example, because of EVA training and information systems, factory workers at Herman Miller, a leading office furniture manufacturer, understand that using more efficient materials, such as less expensive wood-dust board instead of real wood sheeting, contributes an extra dollar of EVA from each desk the company makes.[58]

Second, because EVA can easily be determined for subsets of a company, such as divisions, regional offices, manufacturing plants, and sometimes even departments, it makes managers and workers at all levels pay much closer attention to their segment of the business. When company offices were being refurbished at Genesco, a shoe company, a worker who had EVA training handed CEO Ben Harris $4,000 in cash. The worker explained that he now understood the effect his job had on the company's ability to survive and prosper. And since the company was struggling, he had sold the old doors that had been removed during remodeling so that the company could have the cash.[59] In other words, EVA motivates managers and workers to think like small-business owners who must scramble to contain costs and generate enough business to meet their bills each month. And, unlike many kinds of financial controls, EVA doesn't specify what should or should not be done to improve performance. Thus, it encourages managers and workers to be creative in looking for ways to improve EVA performance.

Exhibit 16.9 shows the top 10 U.S. companies in terms of EVA and market value added (MVA), as measured by the Stern Stewart Performance 1000 index. Remember that EVA is the amount by which profits exceed the cost of capital in a given year. So the more that EVA exceeds the total dollar cost of capital, the better a company has used investors' money that year. MVA is simply the cumulative EVA created by a company over time. Thus, MVA indicates how much value or wealth a company has

Exhibit 16.9

Leading Companies by Market Value Added and Economic Value Added

MVA RANKING IN 2004	MVA RANKING IN 2003	COMPANY	MARKET VALUE ADDED ($ MILLIONS)	ECONOMIC VALUE ADDED/(LOST) ($ MILLIONS)
1	1	General Electric	$299,810	$5,288
2	9	ExxonMobil	197,782	14,456
3	3	Microsoft	178,032	6,426
4	2	Wal-Mart	161,693	4,972
5	10	Johnson & Johnson	138,199	5,655
6	15	United Health Group	112,755	1,897
7	7	Procter & Gamble	105,858	3,951
8	4	CitiGroup	99,485	4,536
9	5	Intel	97,468	1,720
10	13	Dell	88,086	1,891

Source: R. Grizzetti, "U.S. Performance 1000," Stern Stewart & Co, available by request, http://www.sternstewart.com, 20 June 2005.

created or destroyed in total during its existence. As indicated by the MVA figures in Exhibit 16.9, over time the top 10 companies have created considerable wealth, ranging from almost $88 billion at Dell to $300 billion at General Electric; thus, they have returned substantially more than they took in. All of the top 10 in MVA had positive EVAs in the most recent year. However, this doesn't always happen. Good businesses sometimes have years with negative EVAs.

3.3 The Customer Perspective: Controlling Customer Defections

The second aspect of organizational performance that the balanced scorecard helps managers monitor is customers. It does so by forcing managers to address the question, "How do customers see us?" Unfortunately, most companies try to answer this question through customer satisfaction surveys, but these are often misleadingly positive. Most customers are reluctant to talk about their problems because they don't know who to complain to or think that complaining will not do any good. Indeed, a study by the federal Office of Consumer Affairs found that 96 percent of unhappy customers never complain to anyone in the company.[60]

One reason that customer satisfaction surveys can be misleading is that sometimes even very satisfied customers will leave to do business with competitors. Another challenge is getting effective feedback when there is a problem. Jon Piot, co-founder of **Impact Innovations Group**, an IT solutions provider, sent a team of 20 employees to work with a client at the client's facility. He thought everything was going well: All of the feedback from the client's CIO (chief information officer) was positive. So Piot was shocked when the client did not renew Impact's contract. As it turned out, the rest of the client's organization was very dissatisfied with the performance of Impact's employees. Piot says, "This was pretty painful for us; we had a pretty big team there, and it was a prestigious client."[61]

customer defections a performance assessment in which companies identify which customers are leaving and measure the rate at which they are leaving

Rather than pouring over customer satisfaction surveys from current customers, studies indicate that companies may do a better job of answering the question "How do customers see us?" by closely monitoring **customer defections**, that is, by identifying which customers are leaving the company and measuring the rate at which they are leaving. Unlike the results of customer satisfaction surveys, customer defections and retention do have a great effect on profits.

For example, very few managers realize that obtaining a new customer costs five times as much as keeping a current one. In fact, the cost of replacing old customers with new ones is so great that most companies could double their profits by increasing the rate of customer retention by just 5 to 10 percent per year.[62] And if a company can keep a customer for life, the benefits are even larger. According to Stew Leonard, owner of the Connecticut-based **Stew Leonard's** grocery store chain, "The lifetime value of a customer in a supermarket is about $246,000. Every time a customer comes through our front door I see, stamped on their forehead in big red numbers, '$246,000.' I'm never going to make that person unhappy with me. Or lose her to the competition."[63]

Customer retention is critical for the grocery industry. Margins are razor thin and incapable of underwriting the expense involved with finding new customers, which can be tremendous.

Beyond the clear benefits to the bottom line, the second reason to study customer defections is that customers who have left are much more likely than current customers to tell you what you are doing wrong. Perhaps the best way to tap into this source of good feedback is to have top-level managers from various departments talk directly to customers who have left. It's also worthwhile to have top managers talk to dissatisfied customers who are still with the company. Every day, John Chambers, CEO of **Cisco Systems**, has 15 to 20 voice mails from dissatisfied Cisco customers forwarded to his phone. Chambers says, "E-mail would be more efficient, but I want to hear the emotion, I want to hear the frustration, I want to hear the caller's level of comfort with the strategy we're employing. I can't get that through e-mail." Likewise, at Vanguard, a leading investment fund company, CEO Jack Brennan visits the customer call center and, working alongside call representatives, answers customer questions and addresses customer complaints.[64] Some might argue that it's a waste of valuable executive time to have upper-level managers make or listen to these calls, but there's no faster way for the people in charge to learn what needs to be done than to hear it directly from customers who are unhappy with the company's performance.

> Every time a customer comes through our front door I see, stamped on their forehead in big red numbers, "$246,000."
>
> **STEW LEONARD**, OWNER, STEW LEONARD'S GROCERY STORE CHAIN

Finally, companies that understand why customers leave can not only take steps to fix ongoing problems, but can also identify which customers are likely to leave and make changes to prevent them from leaving.

3.4 The Internal Perspective: Controlling Quality

The third part of the balanced scorecard, the internal perspective, consists of the processes, decisions, and actions that managers and workers make within the organization. In contrast to the financial perspective of EVA and the outward-looking customer perspective, the internal perspective asks the question "At what must we excel?" For McDonald's, the answer would be consistent, quick, low-cost food. For Toyota, the answer would be reliability—when you turn on your car it starts, no matter whether the car has 20,000 or 200,000 miles on it. Yet no matter what area a company chooses, the key is to excel in that area. Consequently, the internal perspective of the balanced scorecard usually leads managers to a focus on quality.

Quality is typically defined and measured in three ways: excellence, value, and conformance to expectations.[65] When the company defines its quality goal as *excellence*, then managers must try to produce a product or service of unsurpassed performance and features. For example, by almost any standard, **SINGAPORE AIRLINES** is the best airline in the world. It has been named "best" 18 years in a row by readers of *Conde Nast Traveler* magazine.[66] It has also received various "best airline" awards from the *Asian Wall Street Journal, Business Traveler International, Germany Business Traveler, Travel and Leisure*, and *Fortune*.[67] Whereas many airlines try to cram passengers into every available inch on a plane, Singapore Airlines delivers creature comforts to encourage repeat business and customers willing to pay premium prices. On its newer planes, the first-class cabin is divided into

mgmt: trends

An Old Standby Is a Hot Trend

Vertical integration is making a comeback. In an effort to better control resources—namely, raw materials—some companies are buying suppliers who furnish critical components for important product lines. In 2006, Armor Holdings bought the North Carolina textile manufacturer that supplied the super-strong fibers used in its armored cars. Toyota took control of a key battery supplier for hybrid gasoline-electric engines, and Bridgestone Tire bought a rubber plantation in Indonesia. Watch the business press for articles on companies expanding vertically rather than horizontally.

Source: Timothy Aeppel, "A Hot Commodities Market Spurs Buying Spree by Manufacturers," *Wall Street Journal*, August 14, 2006, A1, A7.

© AFP/GETTY

Singapore Airlines excels at providing high-quality amenities for its customers. By incorporating many elements of private air travel into a regular plane ride, the airline offers its passengers a luxurious travel experience.

eight private mini-rooms, each with an unusually wide leather seat that folds down flat for sleeping, a 23-inch LCD TV that doubles as a computer monitor, and an adjustable table. These amenities and services are common for private jets but truly unique in the commercial airline industry.[68] Singapore Airlines was the first airline, in the 1970s, to introduce a choice of meals, complimentary drinks, and earphones in coach class. It was the first to introduce worldwide video, news, telephone, and fax services, and the first to feature personal video monitors for movies, news, documentaries, and games. Singapore Airlines has had AC power for laptop computers for some time, and recently it became the first airline to introduce on-board, high-speed Internet access.[69]

value customer perception that the product quality is excellent for the price offered

Value is the customer perception that the product quality is excellent for the price offered. At a higher price, for example, customers may perceive the product to be less of a value. When a company emphasizes value as its quality goal, managers must simultaneously control excellence, price, durability, or other features of a product or service that customers strongly associate with value. ***Aldi***, a grocery store company with 7,500 stores worldwide, operates on the single principle of bringing maximum value to customers. Aldi stocks only 3 percent of the products that a typical grocery store carries, and most of its products are store brands. Customers bring their own bags and pick products off pallets rather than store shelves. Yet Aldi's store brands have consistently beaten the name-brand rivals in taste and quality, and in Germany, Aldi was voted the most trusted name in the grocery business.[70]

When a company defines its quality goal as conformance to specifications, employees must base decisions and actions on whether services and products measure up to standard specifications. In contrast to excellence and value-based definitions of quality that can be somewhat ambiguous, measuring whether products and services are "in spec" is relatively easy. Furthermore, while conformance to specifications (that is, precise tolerances for a part's weight or thickness) is usually associated with manufacturing, it can be used equally well to control quality in nonmanufacturing jobs. Exhibit 16.10 shows a checklist that a cook or restaurant owner would use to ensure quality when buying fresh fish.

Exhibit 16.10

Conformance to Specifications Checklist for Buying Fresh Fish

QUALITY CHECKLIST FOR BUYING FRESH FISH		
FRESH WHOLE FISH	**ACCEPTABLE**	**NOT ACCEPTABLE**
Gills	✓ bright red; free of slime; clear mucus	X brown to grayish; thick, yellow mucus
Eyes	✓ clear, bright, bulging, black pupils	X dull, sunken, cloudy, gray pupils
Smell	✓ inoffensive, slight ocean smell	X ammonia or putrid smell
Skin	✓ opalescent sheen; scales adhere tightly to skin	X dull or faded color; scales missing or easily removed
Flesh	✓ firm and elastic to touch, tight to the bone	X soft and flabby, separating from the bone
Belly cavity	✓ no viscera or blood visible; lining intact; no bone protruding	X incomplete evisceration; cuts or protruding bones; off-odor

Sources: "A Closer Look: Buy It Fresh, Keep It Fresh," *Consumer Reports Online*, available at http://www.seagrant.sunysb.edu/SeafoodTechnology/SeafoodMedia/CR02-2001/CR-SeafoodII020101.htm, 20 June 2005; National Fisheries Institute, "How to Purchase: Buying Fish," http://www.aboutseafood.com, 20 June 2005.

QUALITY MEASURE	ADVANTAGES	DISADVANTAGES
Excellence	Promotes clear organizational vision.	Provides little practical guidance for managers.
	Being/providing the "best" motivates and inspires managers and employees.	Excellence is ambiguous. What is it? Who defines it?
	Appeals to customers, who "know excellence when they see it."	Difficult to measure and control.
Value	Customers recognize differences in value.	Can be difficult to determine what factors influence whether a product/service is seen as having value.
	Easier to measure and compare whether products/services differ in value.	Controlling the balance between excellence and cost (i.e., affordable excellence) can be difficult.
Conformance to Specifications	If specifications can be written, conformance to specifications is usually measurable.	Many products/services cannot be easily evaluated in terms of conformance to specifications.
	Should lead to increased efficiency.	Promotes standardization, so may hurt performance when adapting to changes is more important.
	Promotes consistency in quality.	May be less appropriate for services, which are dependent on a high degree of human contact.

Source: Republished with permission of Academy of Management, PO Box 3020, Briar Cliff Manor, NY, 10510–8020. C. A. Reeves & D. A. Bednar, "Defining Quality: Alternatives and Implications," *Academy of Management Review* 19 (1994): 419–445. Reproduced by permission of the publisher via Copyright Clearance Center, Inc.

Exhibit 16.11

Advantages and Disadvantages of Different Measures of Quality

The way in which a company defines quality affects the methods and measures that workers use to control quality. Accordingly, Exhibit 16.11 shows the advantages and disadvantages associated with the excellence, value, and conformance to specification definitions of quality.

3.5 The Innovation and Learning Perspective: Controlling Waste and Pollution

The last part of the balance scorecard, the innovation and learning perspective, addresses the question "Can we continue to improve and create value?" Thus, the innovation and learning perspective involves continuous improvement in ongoing products and services (discussed in Chapter 18), as well as relearning and redesigning the processes by which products and services are created (discussed in Chapter 7). Since these are discussed in more detail elsewhere in the text, this section reviews an increasingly important topic, waste and pollution minimization. Exhibit 16.12 shows the four levels of waste minimization, from waste disposal, which produces the smallest minimization of waste, to waste prevention and reduction, which produces the greatest minimization.[71] The goals of the top level, *waste prevention and reduction*, are to prevent waste and pollution before they occur, or to reduce them when they do occur. There are three strategies for waste prevention and reduction.

1. *Good housekeeping*—performing regularly scheduled preventive maintenance for offices, plants, and equipment. Quickly fixing leaky valves and making sure machines are running properly so that they don't use more fuel than necessary are examples of good housekeeping. For example, Doug Goulding, a maintenance

supervisor at **Canada Cordage**, a producer of synthetic and natural fiber ropes, reduced the water bills at the company's factory in Kitchener, Canada, from $1,200 to $200 per month by systematically plugging leaks in machines and pipes and installing water-saving devices.[72]

2. *Material/product substitution*—replacing toxic or hazardous materials with less harmful materials. As part of its Pollution Prevention Pays program over the last 30 years, **3M** eliminated 2.2 billion pounds of pollutants and saved $1 billion by using benign substitutes for toxic solvents in its manufacturing processes.[73]

3. *Process modification*—changing steps or procedures to eliminate or reduce waste. **Terracycle** is a manufacturer of plant food made from the castings (that is, the droppings) of red worms that have feasted on various types of organic waste. But rather than package the plant food in new bottles, Terracycle packages its product in used beverage containers and ships the bottles in recycled boxes to the retailers. The company's entire process operation is 100 percent geared toward reducing or eliminating waste.[74]

At the second level of waste minimization, *recycle and reuse*, wastes are reduced by reusing materials as long as possible or by collecting materials for on- or off-site recycling. **Recycline** recycles more than 50,000 pounds of plastic each year and provides recycled material to business customers and recyclable products to consumers. The company recycles all manner of plastic waste, including its own products, into new toothbrushes, plastic dinnerware, razors, and toothpicks. In addition to the waste plastic the company receives from other manufacturers and garbage collectors, Recycline receives about 15 percent of its own products back each year for recycling, which it heats to over 400 degrees to thoroughly sterilize. Partners like Stonyfield Farm, a maker of yogurt, donate their plastic cups to Recycline and give Recycline advertising space on their lids.[75]

A growing trend in recycling is *design for disassembly*, where products are designed from the start for easy disassembly, recycling, and reuse once they are no longer usable. For example, the European Union (EU) is moving toward prohibiting companies from selling products unless most of the product and its packaging can be recycled.[76] Since companies, not consumers, will be held responsible for recycling the products they manufacture, they must design their products from the start with recycling in mind.[77] At reclamation centers throughout Europe, companies will have to be able to recover and recycle 80 percent of the parts that go into their original products.[78] Already, under the EU's end-of-life vehicle program, all cars built in Europe since June 2002 are subject to the 80 percent requirement, which rose to 85 percent in 2006 and will be 95 percent by 2015 for autos. Moreover, effective in 2007, the EU requires auto manufacturers to pay to recycle all the cars they made

Exhibit 16.12

Four Levels of Waste Minimization

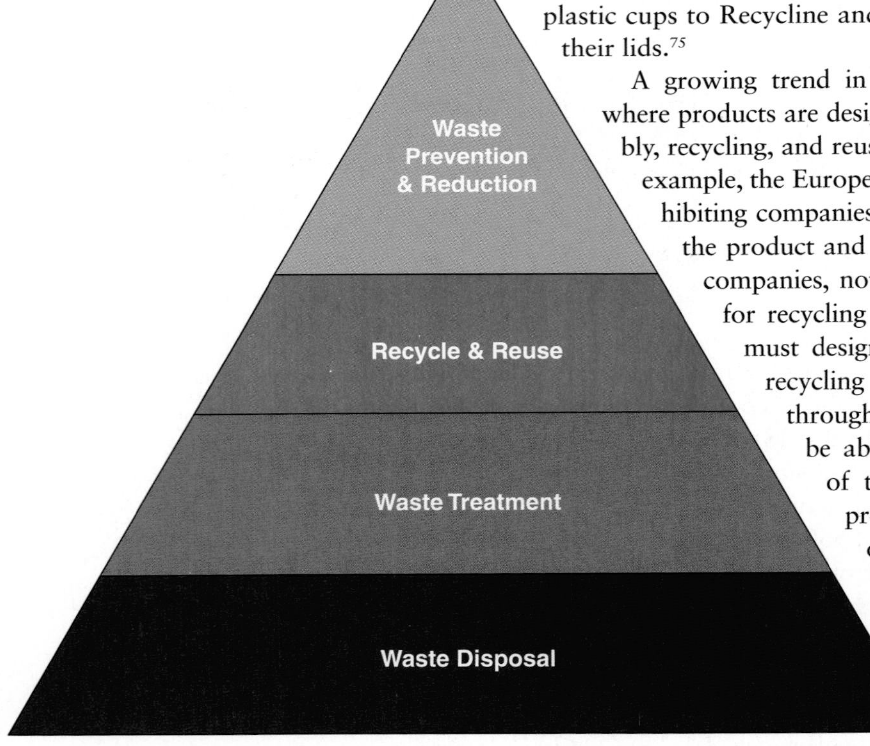

Source: D. R. May & B. L. Flannery, "Cutting Waste with Employee Involvement Teams," *Business Horizons*, September–October 1995, 28–38. Reprinted with permission from *Business Horizons*, © 1995 by the Trustees at Indiana University, Kelley School of Business.

between 1989 and 2002.[79] Roughly 160 million cars in Europe are covered by these strict end-of-life regulations, and although rising prices for recycled steel have made the regulations less burdensome than they might have been otherwise, the high level of composite plastics that make up today's lighter, more environmentally friendly cars are more difficult to recycle. One critic calls the 95 percent threshold "utopian," but others are more optimistic. DaimlerChrysler, for example, has begun to replace fiberglass in some of its car exterior panels with a type of banana-plant fiber.[80]

At the third level of waste minimization, *waste treatment*, companies use biological, chemical, or other processes to turn potentially harmful waste into harmless compounds or useful by-products. For example, during "pickling," a process in the manufacture of steel sheets, the steel is bathed in an acid solution to clean impurities and oxides (which would rust) from its surface. Getting rid of the "pickle juice" has always been a problem. Not only is the juice an acid, but it also contains ferric chloride and other metals, so steelmakers can't dump it into local water supplies. Fortunately, **MAGNETICS INTERNATIONAL** has found a safe, profitable way to treat the pickle juice. It sprays the juice into a 100-foot-high chamber at 1,200 degrees Fahrenheit. The iron chloride in the juice reacts with oxygen at that temperature to form pure iron oxide, which can be transformed into a useful magnetic powder. Inland Steel is now using this process to transform pickle juice into 25,000 tons of magnetic powder that can be reused in electric motors, stereo speakers, and refrigerator gaskets.[81]

The fourth and lowest level of waste minimization is *waste disposal*. Wastes that cannot be prevented, reduced, recycled, reused, or treated should be safely disposed of in processing plants or in environmentally secure landfills that prevent leakage and contamination of soil and underground water supplies. Contrary to common belief, all businesses, not just manufacturing firms, have waste disposal problems. For example, with the average computer lasting just three years, approximately 60 million computers come out of service each year, creating disposal problems for offices all over the world.[82] But with lead-containing cathode ray tubes in the monitors, toxic metals in the circuit boards, paint-coated plastic, and metal coatings that can contaminate ground water, organizations can't just throw old computers away.[83] Many companies give old computers and computer equipment to local computer recycling centers that distribute usable computers to nonprofit organizations or safely dispose of lead and other toxic materials. **HEWLETT-PACKARD** has started a unique computer disposal program that allows individual computer users to recycle PCs and electronic equipment.. The service is available at **http://www.hp.com/hpinfo/globalcitizenship/environment/recycle/index.html**. With three clicks and a credit card number (prices range from $13 to $34 per item), the old PC equipment will be picked up and properly disposed of.[84] HP makes no profit from this service.

Review 3: What to Control?

Deciding what to control is just as important as deciding whether to control or how to control. In most companies, performance is measured using financial measures alone. However, the balanced scorecard encourages managers to measure and control company performance from four perspectives: financial, customers, internal operations, and innovation and learning. Traditionally, financial control has been achieved through cash flow analysis, balance sheets, income statements, financial ratios, and budgets. Another way to measure and control financial performance is through economic value added (EVA). Unlike

traditional financial measures, EVA helps managers assess whether they are performing well enough to pay the cost of the capital needed to run the business. Instead of using customer satisfaction surveys to measure performance, companies should pay attention to customer defectors, who are more likely to speak up about what the company is doing wrong. Performance of internal operations is often measured in terms of quality, which is defined in three ways: excellence, value, and conformance to expectations.[85] Minimization of waste has become an important part of innovation and learning in companies. The four levels of waste minimization are waste prevention and reduction, recycling and reuse, waste treatment, and waste disposal.

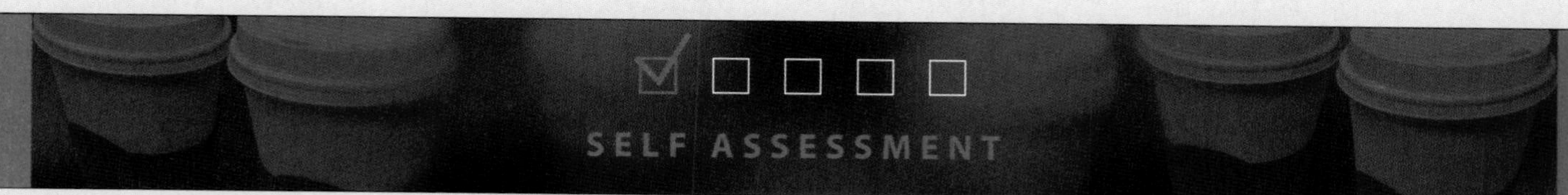

Too Much Information?

Imagine that your professor handed back term papers, and the only mark on yours was the grade. Would you be content, or would you feel gypped? People have different comfort about receiving feedback: Some thrive on it; others are ambivalent. What about you? Would you rather see comments in the margins of your term paper or not? This Self Assessment will give you insights into your perceptions of feedback. Understanding your preferences in this area will help you develop the skills you'll need as a manager.[86]

As you complete this feedback inventory, be candid as you circle the appropriate responses.

		Extremely Untrue					Extremely True
1.	It is important for me to obtain useful information about my performance.	1	2	3	4	5	6
2.	If I receive negative feedback, I would have a negative attitude towards myself, so I try to avoid criticism.	1	2	3	4	5	6
3.	I am not really worried about what people will think of me if I ask for feedback about my performance.	1	2	3	4	5	6
4.	I like people to hear about my good performance at work (or at college).	1	2	3	4	5	6
5.	Receiving feedback about my performance helps me to improve my skills.	1	2	3	4	5	6
6.	Negative feedback doesn't really lower my self worth, so I don't go out of my way to avoid it.	1	2	3	4	5	6
7.	I'm concerned about what people would think of me if I were to ask for feedback.	1	2	3	4	5	6
8.	Seeking feedback from my supervisor (instructor) is one way to show that I want to improve my performance.	1	2	3	4	5	6
9.	I would like to obtain more information to let me know how I am performing.	1	2	3	4	5	6
10.	Receiving negative feedback wouldn't really change the way I feel about myself.	1	2	3	4	5	6
11.	I am worried about the impression I would make if I were to ask for feedback.	1	2	3	4	5	6
12.	I want people to know when I ask for feedback so I can show my responsible nature.	1	2	3	4	5	6
13.	I would like to receive more useful information about my performance.	1	2	3	4	5	6
14.	It's hard to feel good about myself when I receive negative feedback.	1	2	3	4	5	6
15	I don't really worry about what others would think of me if I asked for feedback.	1	2	3	4	5	6

KEY TERMS

		Extremely Untrue					Extremely True
16.	I don't really care if people hear the good feedback that is given to me.	1	2	3	4	5	6
17.	I'm not really concerned about whether I receive useful information about my performance.	1	2	3	4	5	6
18.	I don't really worry about getting negative feedback because I still feel I am a person of worth.	1	2	3	4	5	6
19.	I don't really care if people know the type of feedback I get.	1	2	3	4	5	6
20.	When I receive praise, I don't really want others to hear it.	1	2	3	4	5	6
21.	Feedback is not really useful to help me improve my performance.	1	2	3	4	5	6
22.	I try to avoid negative feedback because it makes me feel bad about myself.	1	2	3	4	5	6
23.	If I sought feedback about my performance, I wouldn't want other people to know what type of feedback I received.	1	2	3	4	5	6
24.	I don't care either way if people see me asking my supervisor (instructor) for feedback.	1	2	3	4	5	6
25.	Obtaining useful feedback information is not very important to me.	1	2	3	4	5	6
26.	I worry about receiving feedback that is likely to be negative because it hurts to be criticized.	1	2	3	4	5	6
27.	I am usually concerned about other people hearing the content of the individual feedback I receive.	1	2	3	4	5	6
28.	I hope positive feedback about my performance will make a good impression on others.	1	2	3	4	5	6
29.	I don't really require more feedback to let me know how I am performing.	1	2	3	4	5	6
30.	Negative feedback doesn't really worry me because I still have a positive attitude towards myself.	1	2	3	4	5	6
31.	It doesn't worry me if people know how I've performed at something.	1	2	3	4	5	6
32.	I don't really need to impress others by letting them know about the positive feedback I receive regarding my performance.	1	2	3	4	5	6

Scoring

Determine your average score for each category by entering your response to each survey item below, as follows. In blanks that say *regular score*, simply enter your response for that item. If your response was a 4, place a 4 in the *regular score* blank. In blanks that say *reverse score*, subtract your response from 7 and enter the result. So if your response was a 4, place a 3 (7 − 4 = 3) in the *reverse score* blank. Total your scores, then compute each average score.

Desire for Useful Information		Ego Defense		Defensive Impression Management		Assertive Impression Management	
1. regular score	_____	2. regular score	_____	3. reverse score	_____	4. reverse score	_____
5. regular score	_____	6. reverse score	_____	7. reverse score	_____	8. reverse score	_____
9. regular score	_____	10. regular score	_____	11. reverse score	_____	12. reverse score	_____
13. reverse score	_____	14. regular score	_____	15. reverse score	_____	16. reverse score	_____
17. reverse score	_____	18. reverse score	_____	19. reverse score	_____	20. reverse score	_____
21. reverse score	_____	22. reverse score	_____	23. reverse score	_____	24. reverse score	_____
25. reverse score	_____	26. regular score	_____	27. reverse score	_____	28. reverse score	_____
29. reverse score	_____	30. regular score	_____	31. reverse score	_____	32. reverse score	_____
TOTAL =	_____	TOTAL =	_____	TOTAL =	_____	TOTAL =	_____

You can find the interpretation for your score at: **academic.cengage.com/management/williams.**

Too Many Machines

You've just looked at your company's total spending and it's way too high, particularly in the areas of energy and supplies.[87] Top managers have ordered you to cut costs, so you sit down to assess the situation. The main culprits are the nearly 3,000 printers, copiers, scanners, and fax machines crowding your 200 office sites. A recent inventory shows that you have one machine for every four employees.

Running so many machines racks up huge operating costs for your company (buying supplies like ink and paper, electricity, and renting enough office space to contain them). Machine breakdowns, a frequent occurrence because of the sheer number of machines, eat up even more time and money with maintenance and repairs. Mechanical breakdowns are also mucking up your organization's chain-of-command, since no one knows who is responsible for which machines.

Even when the machines themselves are running efficiently, they generate confusion. Employees are printing too many documents and making too many copies—so many, in fact, that people are loosing track of them. Every office you visit is filled with humming machines and flurries of paper. This makes it hard to find paper files when they are needed. Even worse, you're in danger of accidentally leaking confidential information. Still, having such a high machine-employee ratio means that employees don't spend a lot of time collecting copies (and collecting coffee and conversation on the way).

Clearly, your company's printing is out of control. But how to get it back into control? You can reduce the number of machines and save on costs, or you can implement more controls on employees in the way of policies and procedures.

Questions

1. Can you control employees' printing and copying habits?
2. What control measures can you implement that relate only to controlling the machines?
3. What control measures can you implement that relate only to controlling employee behavior?
4. How do you get your printing problem under control: controlling machines, controlling employees, or both?

Is H & R Block Taxed to Its Limits?

When you first came to H & R Block four years ago, you had a vision: increase the scope of the company and transform it from a simple tax preparation service to a full-service financial services provider.[88] And why not? Block has roughly 17 million customers, and converting only a fraction of them to financial services clients would mean substantial growth for the 60-year-old company. Couple that with the company's recent expansion into mortgage financing, and Block could become a financial services powerhouse.

Eagerly you set about mapping the company's growth. You bought Olde Financial, a discount-brokerage business, and quickly found yourself with around $50 billion in assets under management. You hired financial advisers, and then to get them more clients, you instructed tax preparers to refer new financial prospects to them. Another way you planned to fuel growth was by aggressively opening new tax preparation outlets. Today, Block has more U.S. storefronts (over 11,000) than Barnes & Noble (2,356), Gap (3,051), and even growth-happy Starbucks (6,409)! Over 1,000 outlets were added just this year to expand coverage during tax-filing season.

Despite all the good ideas, H & R Block is not producing the results you expected. In fact, it is struggling. Assets under management in the financial services division have declined by more than 30 percent since the division was acquired, and its advisers are leaving faster than they can be replaced. Outwardly, you say that the economic upswing is creating more demand for junior advisers, the largest percentage of your financial managers, but you also know that even new advisers are going to follow the money. And the money seems to be flowing out of Block.

Mortgage refinancing, which at its peak contributed an incredible 70 percent of pretax income, now contributes only 28 percent per year, or $112 million. Mortgage activity has dropped since the Federal Reserve began increasing interest rates, and competitive pricing among lenders has not subsided as you expected it would.

On the tax front, the company faces serious competition from smaller upstarts like Jackson Hewitt and Liberty Tax Service, which are both experiencing increases in the number of returns prepared at Block's expense. This tax season Jackson Hewitt handled nearly 6 percent more returns than last year. Compare that with Block, which has lost over one million customers in the past three years. Aggressive cost cutting is minimizing damage to the bottom line, but it is also having some adverse effects, including waits as long as two to three hours for some customers. Digitally, Block is being surpassed by Intuit's TurboTax software. Even though Intuit's TurboTax costs 50 percent more than Block's competing TaxCut software, Intuit has three times the market share of TaxCut, and is growing by double digits each tax season. All this trouble has caused Block's revenues to slide over 5 percent from last year.

As you hang up the phone from yet another apologetic conference call with Wall Street analysts, during which you revised your expectations for earnings per share sharply downward, you sigh and sink back into your chair. You are getting tired of announcing quarterly losses. Plans should be flexible enough to change if expected results don't materialize, but you really believe in the growth strategy. One analyst even said, "It seems like a smart strategy, and they seem to have the right infrastructure, but for some reason it's just not happening." You think to yourself, "There's got to be a way to get things back on track!"

Form a team of four students to answer the following questions.

Questions

1. As a team, identify where more control is needed at H & R Block. Is control in these areas possible? Explain.
2. Build a balanced scorecard for H & R Block that proposes objectives and measures for each the four quadrants of the card (financial, customer, internal, and learning).

PRACTICE BEING A MANAGER

Control is one of the most controversial aspects of management. Exercising too much control can foster employee resentment and bureaucratic delays. Exercising too little control can raise employee stress and breed organizational chaos. And not only must managers work to achieve a healthy *level* of control, but they must also strive to set controls around the *right targets*. The control process is about more than charts and feedback loops—it is about focusing personal and organizational efforts toward desired outcomes. This exercise will allow you an opportunity to try your hand at developing a control system that is tailored to a particular company and type of work.

Step 1: Get into groups. Your professor will organize your class into teams of three or four students per team. One team will be designated as Company Leadership.

Scenario: Razor's Edge (RE) is a young and growing company that serves the needs of those who engage in extreme sports, adventure/exploration, and guiding services. Some examples of RE's core market include expert/professional mountain climbers, white-water rafting guides, and polar explorers. The founders of RE are the husband and wife team of Dan and Alice Connors, world-famous mountain climbers and explorers. Dan and Alice have both reached the summit of Mount Everest and each is well-respected in the rather small and close-knit community of adventurers and explorers. RE is an eclectic company of employees who, like Dan and Alice, share a passion for adventure and extreme sports. The company not only designs and sells its own lines of specialized products such as mountain-climbing shoes and ropes, but also develops software designed to support expedition planning, communication and navigation, and simulation and scenario response (that is, training tools for guides and newer expedition members). For the first five years of its development, RE did not worry too much about organizational policies or controls. Employees were encouraged to climb, trek, and guide, and attendance issues were addressed on a case-by-case basis. Although officially all employees were given two weeks of paid vacation, many employees were allowed to take up to two months off at half-pay so that they could complete an expedition. Sick days were jokingly referred to as "mountain flu" days, and it was not unusual for the small company to be thinly staffed on Mondays and Fridays.

But in the past three years RE has grown from 25 employees to 85. The company is too big, and the jobs too diverse, for Dan and Alice to deal with each employee request for "expedition time" away from work. And the "mountain flu" has occasionally weakened the company's response to customers. Dan and Alice have also become victims of their own success as they attracted other climbers to join their company—most climbers want time off in the peak climbing seasons. But this also happens to be a peak time for RE orders and service requests.

The company has organized all employees into teams and announced a contest. Each team should come up with an approach for controlling staffing levels to meet or exceed customer expectations for responsiveness, while at the same time preserving RE's tradition as a company of active adventurers and explorers. The company has announced that each member of the employee team that develops the winning solution will receive $2,500 worth of RE gear of their choice.

Step 2: Determine staffing levels. You are a team of workers at RE. Design an approach to controlling daily staffing levels so that RE is able to meet customer or exceed customer expectations for responsiveness without sacrificing its own identity as a company of adventurers and explorers. Keep in mind that RE is somewhat unusual in that even its accounting staff members (five full-time employees) are experienced adventurers and explorers, and are expected to answer customer questions and handle their service needs. You should consider the following elements:

- Paid vacation
- Expedition time
- Sick days and "mountain flu" (Monday/Friday absences)
- Dealing with peak times, and/or most desirable times for vacation or expedition
- Knowing whether customers are pleased with RE's responsiveness to their needs

Step 3: Outline a proposal. Submit a one-page handwritten outline of your proposal to the Company Leadership team.

Step 4: Present the proposal. Each team will briefly present their proposal to the Company Leadership team, and members of the Company Leadership team may ask questions.

Step 5: Vote. The Company Leadership will confer, vote, and announce the winning proposal.

Step 6: Debrief as a class. What tensions confronted you as you worked to design an approach to staffing control for Razor's Edge? What tradeoffs and challenges might you anticipate for the company when it implements the winning proposal? In what ways is control related to employee motivation? In what ways is control related to organizational culture? Do you think that the winning RE proposal would be well-suited for use by a major outdoor and casual clothing company such as Lands' End? Why, or why not?

Learning from Failure

There is the greatest practical benefit of making a few failures early in life.

—T. H. Huxley

No one wants to fail.[89] Everyone wants to succeed. Nevertheless, some businesspeople believe that failure can have enormous value. At Microsoft, founder and chairman Bill Gates encourages his managers to hire people who have made mistakes in their jobs or careers. A Microsoft vice president says, "We look for somebody who learns, adapts, and is active in the process of learning from mistakes. We always ask, what was a major failure you had? What did you learn from it?" Another reason that failure is viewed positively is that it is often a sign of risk taking and experimentation, both of which are in short supply in many companies. Harvard Business School professor John Kotter says, "I can imagine a group of executives 20 years ago discussing a candidate for a top job and saying, 'This guy had a big failure when he was 32.' Everyone else would say, 'Yep, yep, that's a bad sign.' I can imagine that same group considering a candidate today and saying, 'What worries me about this guy is that he's never failed.'" Jack Matson, who teaches a class at the University of Michigan called Failure 101, says, "If you are doing something innovative, you are going to trip and fumble. So the more failing you do faster, the quicker you can get to success."

One of the most common mistakes that occurs after failure is the *attribution error*. To *attribute* is to assign blame or credit. When we succeed, we take credit for the success by claiming it was due to our strategies, how we behaved, and how hard we worked. When we fail, however, we ignore our strategies, how we behaved, and how hard we worked (or didn't). Instead, when we fail, we assign the blame to other people, or to the circumstances, or to bad luck. In other words, the basic attribution error is that success is our fault but failure isn't. The disappointment we feel when we fail often prevents us from learning from our failures.

This means that attribution errors disrupt the control process. The three basic steps of control are to set goals and performance standards, to compare actual performance against the performance standards, and to identify and correct performance deviations. When we put all of the blame on external forces rather than our own actions, we stop ourselves from identifying and correcting performance deviations.

Furthermore, by not learning from our mistakes, we make it even more likely that we will fail again. Your task in this exercise is to begin the process of learning from failure. This is not an easy thing to do. When *Fortune* magazine writer Patricia Sellers wrote an article called "So You Fail," she found that most of the people she contacted were reluctant to talk about their failures. She wrote:

> *Compiling this story required months of pleading and letter writing to dozens of people who failed and came back. "If it weren't for the 'F' word, I'd talk," lamented one senior executive who got fired twice, reformed his know-it-all management style, and considered bragging about his current hot streak. Others cringed at hearing the word "failure" in the same breath as "your career."*

Questions

1. Identify and describe a point in your life when you failed. Don't write about simple or silly mistakes. The difference between a failure and a mistake is how bad you felt afterwards. A real failure still makes you cringe when you think about it years later. What was the situation? What were your goals? And how did it turn out?
2. Describe your initial reaction to the failure. Were you shocked, surprised, angry, or depressed? Initially, who or what did you blame for the failure? Explain.
3. One purpose of control is to identify and correct performance deviations. With that in mind, describe three mistakes that you made that contributed to your failure. Now that you've had time to think about it, what could you have done differently to prevent these mistakes? Finally, summarize what you learned from your mistakes that will increase your chances of success the next time around.

REEL TO REAL

BIZ FLIX

Brazil

Brazil takes place in a retro-futuristic world in which automation pervades every facet of life, but paperwork, inefficiency, and mechanical failures are the rule. *Brazil* stars Jonathan Pryce in the role of Sam, a low-level bureaucrat. In this scene, Sam inadvertently gets wrapped up in an intrigue surrounding the so-called terrorist Harry Tuttle (played by Robert DeNiro), who is actually a renegade heating technician for whom the Ministry of Central Services has issued an arrest order. The clip moves quickly, so you may need to review it several times to grasp all the nuances in the conversation.

What to Watch for and Ask Yourself

1. What kind of control is being used by Central Services?
2. Tuttle describes a paradox of control. What is it?
3. What kind of control does Tuttle seem to prefer? Explain.

MANAGEMENT WORKPLACE

Peapod—Controlling the Process to Ensure the Outcome

The grocery industry is a like a food fight without the mess. It is so competitive that only the strongest survive. Now imagine trying to survive in the online grocery industry, where customers can't see, smell, or touch the goods, and they expect their orders to be accurate and arrive on time. Finally, picture being one of the few companies to ride out the original dot-com storm. Those are daunting challenges for any firm. But Peapod, the online grocery service founded in 1989 by brothers Andrew and Thomas Parkinson, is succeeding on all three fronts.

Peapod introduced a new concept 15 years ago: the convenience of shopping for groceries online. Plenty of skeptics said the idea wouldn't fly, but some consumers and businesses were intrigued and began to order their groceries online. When many dot-coms of the era began to fail, Peapod hung on. Step into the management workplace at Peapod to see how the company maintained control during such challenging and turbulent times.

What to Watch for and Ask Yourself

1. What types of feedforward controls might Peapod use in the next few years?
2. Using the feedback control model, identify at least two standards that Peapod might establish.
3. What elements would you expect to be in each quadrant of Peapod's balanced scorecard?

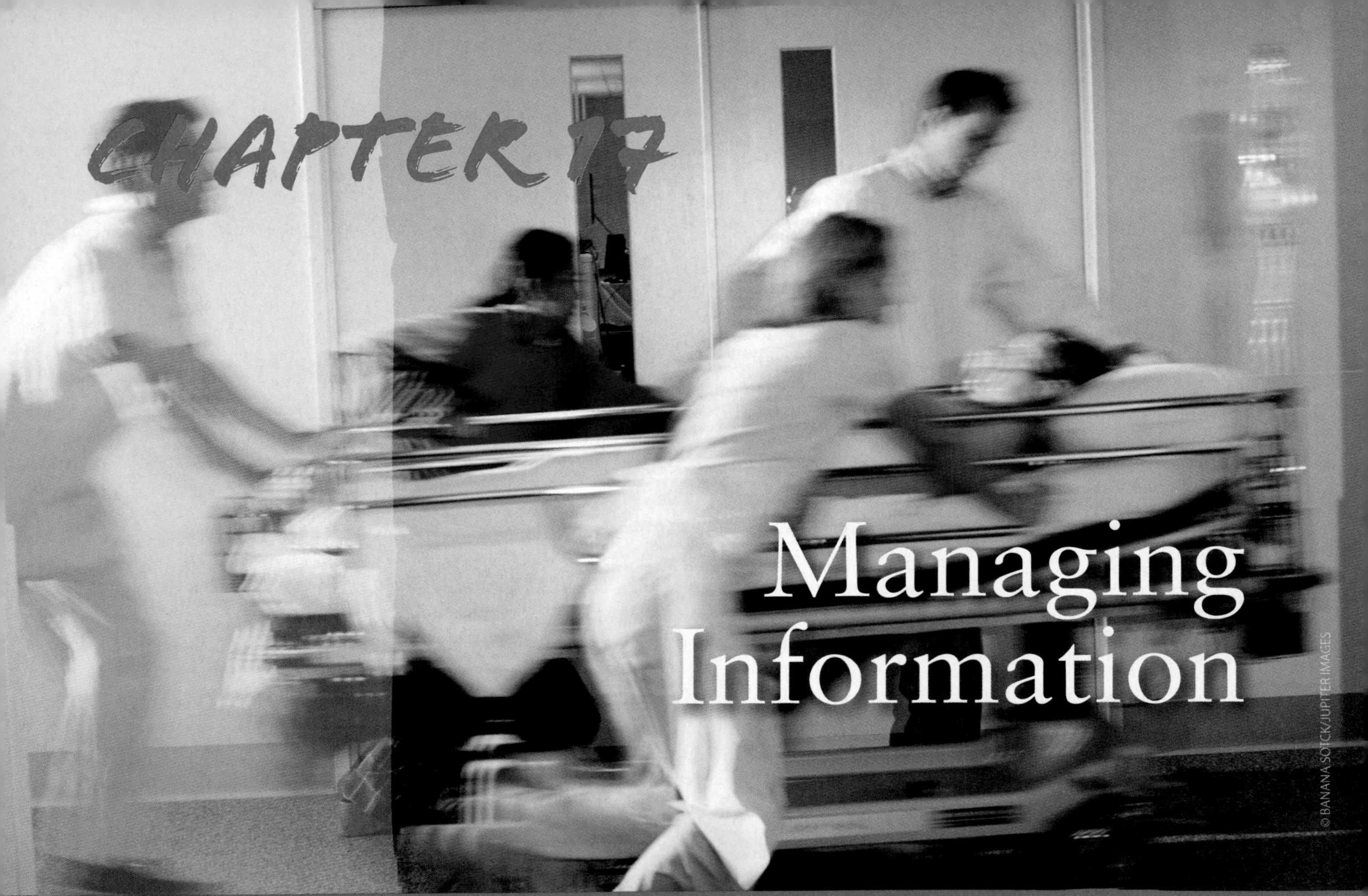

CHAPTER 17

Managing Information

© BANANA SOTCK/JUPITER IMAGES

Learning Outcomes:

1 Explain the strategic importance of information.

2 Describe the characteristics of useful information (that is, its value and costs).

3 Explain the basics of capturing, processing, and protecting information.

4 Describe how companies can access and share information and knowledge.

In This Chapter:

WHAT WOULD YOU DO?

University of Pittsburgh Medical Center, Pittsburgh, Pennsylvania.[1] The University of Pittsburgh Medical Center, which has a $5 billion annual budget, includes 19 hospitals with 3,340 beds, 4,500 physicians spread across 400 offices, 50 outpatient facilities, and 43,000 employees. Each year, it handles 167,000 inpatient admissions, three million outpatient visits, 400,000 emergency visits, 130,000 surgeries, and one million home care visits.

You've been chief information officer (CIO) for 18 months now, but with so many problems it seems like 18 years. To start, the hospital's databases contain information on over four million patients whose data are spread across 162 Unix servers, 624 Windows/Intel servers, and 40 storage systems, which are often incapable of sharing data or "talking to each other." That means that doctors, nurses, therapists, and patients frequently don't have the right information when they need it. For example, a doctor in one of the suburban offices who sends a patient to the downtown UPMC hospital for an MRI scan will be frustrated when the results are not received in time for the patient's next appointment. This is unfortunately the norm and not the exception.

Another problem, this one assigned to you by the CEO, is that departments regularly overspend their budgets. Normally, this would be the chief financial officer's problem, but at UPMC, purchasing procedures, which rely on carbon copy forms straight out of the 1960s, make it difficult to get up-to-date budget information. Since no one is sure what's been ordered or whether they're over or under their budgets, it's your problem. Furthermore, UPMC's employees use the carbon copy forms to make "rogue" purchases, bypassing UPMC's 70-member purchasing staff, which is supposed to approve or deny all purchase requests. Says one manager, "Unfortunately, anybody can file a form, call a supplier, and get whatever they want delivered."

Another significant issue is medication errors, many of which are created by illegible prescription orders. In hospitals, the average patient is exposed to a medication error every day, though most mistakes are caught by staff, the patient, or a family member before any harm is done. Nationwide each year, however, medication errors harm 1.5 million patients and cause 9,000 deaths. Fixing medication errors with additional medical treatments, and settling related legal settlements, costs hospitals an estimated $2 billion to $3.5 billion per year. Illegible handwritten prescriptions and medical orders are a significant problem at UPMC, too. There's no doubt in your mind that electronic medical records and a computer physician order entry (CPOE) system, in which doctors

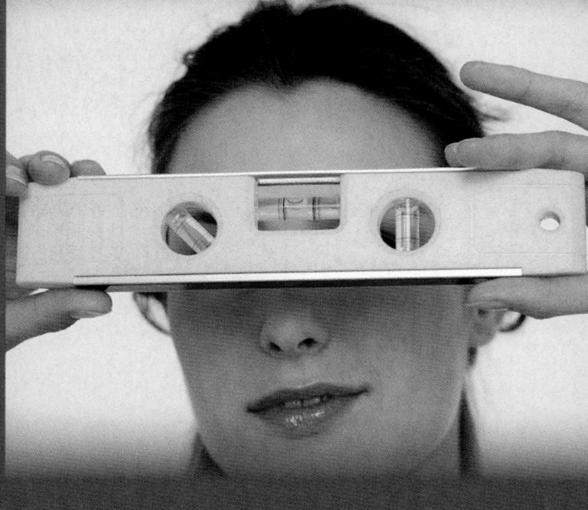

electronically record their orders, treatment, and prescriptions, will solve these problems. Doctors and nurses would be able to quickly access patients' medical records any time from any location. And doctors' orders would be typed and thus legible.

Creating electronic patient records and a CPOE from scratch won't be easy. Doctors are incredibly resistant to change, especially if they don't see how it benefits them. So, the most important question you face is how to create an electronic system that doctors will use. You could have the most advanced computerized system in the world, but if the doctors don't buy in, it won't work. Next, what steps do you need to take to consolidate those 162 Unix servers, 624 Windows/Intel servers, and 40 storage systems? While it's tempting to centralize everything into one large system managed by your IT staff, doctors, nurses, and other caregivers want to easily process, store, retrieve, and communicate their patients' medical information. How can you do that while shrinking the number of servers and storage systems? Finally, how will you fix the budgeting problems and get rid of those 1960s carbon copy order forms? With the cost of medical services increasing 8 to 10 percent per year, and the employers and HMOs who pay those bills pressuring you to keep costs down, what's the best way to fix this? **If you were the Chief Information Officer of the University of Pittsburgh Medical Center, what would you do?**

ACTIVITIES + VIDEO

CengageNOW Audio study guide, electronic flashcards, author FAQ videos, On the Job and Biz Flix videos, concept tutorial, and concept exercise

Web (academic.cengage.com/management/williams) Quiz, PowerPoint slides, and glossary terms for this chapter

Study Tip ***Imagine you are the professor, and make up your own test for Chapter 17.*** What are the main topics and key concepts that students should know? If you work with a study group, exchange practice tests. Work them individually, then "grade" them collectively. This way you can discuss trouble spots and answer each other's questions.

"What's New" Companies

University of Pittsburgh Medical Center

Crate and Barrel

Pier 1

Wal-Mart

Portsmouth Traffic Systems Group

Avero

Con-way

Health Decisions

And others . . .

A generation ago, computer hardware and software had little to do with managing business information. Rather than storing information on hard drives, managers stored it in filing cabinets. Instead of uploading daily sales and inventory levels by satellite to corporate headquarters, they mailed hard-copy summaries to headquarters at the end of each month. Instead of word processing, reports were typed on an electric typewriter. Instead of spreadsheets, calculations were made on adding machines. Managers communicated by sticky notes, not e-mail. Phone messages were written down by assistants and coworkers, not left on voice mail. Workers did not use desktop or laptop computers as a daily tool to get work done; they scheduled limited access time to run batch jobs on the mainframe computer (and prayed that the batch job computer code they wrote would work).

Today, a generation later, computer hardware and software are an integral part of managing business information. In large part, this is due to something called **Moore's law**. Gordon Moore is one of the founders of Intel Corporation, which makes 75 percent of the integrated processors used in personal computers. In 1965, Moore predicted that about every two years, computer-processing power would double and its cost would drop by 50 percent.[2] As Exhibit 17.1 shows, Moore was right. Every few years, computer power, as measured by the number of transistors per computer chip, *has* more than doubled. Consequently, the computer sitting in your lap or your desk is not only smaller, but also much cheaper and more powerful than the large mainframe computers used by *Fortune* 500 companies 15 years ago. In fact, if car manufacturers had achieved the same power increases and cost decreases attained by computer manufacturers, a fully outfitted Lexus or Mercedes sedan would cost less than $1,000!

We begin this chapter by explaining why information matters. In particular, you will learn the value of strategic information to companies, as well as the cost and characteristics of good information. Next, you will investigate how companies capture, process, and protect information. Finally, you'll learn how information is accessed and shared with those within and outside the company, and how knowledge and expertise (not just information or data) are shared, too.

WHY INFORMATION MATTERS

Moore's law the prediction that about every two years, computer-processing power would double and its cost would drop by 50 percent

raw data facts and figures

information useful data that can influence people's choices and behavior

Raw data are facts and figures. For example, 11, $452, 4, and 26,100 are some data that I used the day I wrote this section of the chapter. However, facts and figures aren't particularly useful unless they have meaning. For example, you probably can't guess what these four pieces of raw data represent, can you? And if you can't, these data are useless. That's why researchers make the distinction between raw data and information. Whereas raw data consist of facts and figures, **information** is useful data

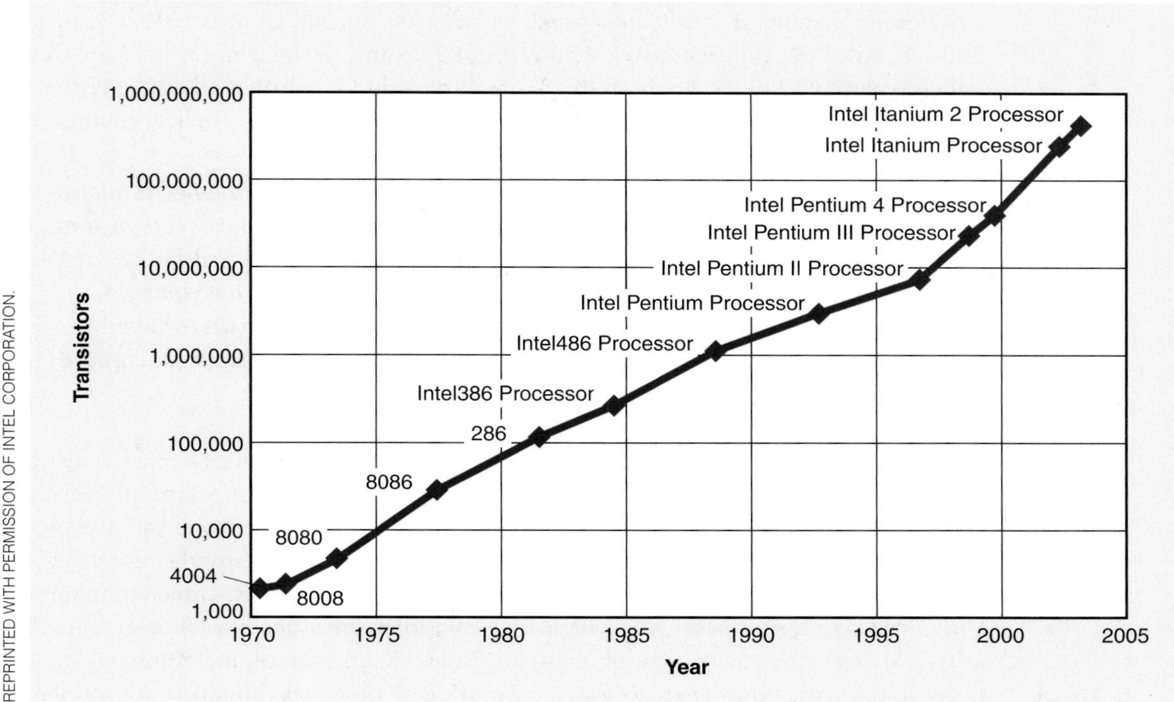

Source: "Moore's Law: Overviews," © Intel Corporation, available at http://www.intel.com/technology/mooreslaw, 27 June 2005.

Exhibit 17.1
Moore's Law

that can influence someone's choices and behavior. So what did those four pieces of data mean to me? Well, 11 stands for Channel 11, the local CBS affiliate on which I watched part of the men's PGA golf tournament; $452 is how much it would cost me to rent a minivan for a week if I go skiing over spring break; 4 is for the 4-gigabyte storage card that I want to add to my digital camera (prices are low, so I'll probably buy it); and 26,100 means that it's time to get the oil changed in my car.

After reading the next two sections, you should be able to

1 explain the strategic importance of information.
2 describe the characteristics of useful information (that is, its value and costs).

1 Strategic Importance of Information

Each year 15,000 customers file formal complaints over late, bungled deliveries of their furniture. If it was promised to be delivered in a month, it actually shows up in eight weeks, but with only three of the four pieces you ordered. Then, on the day the furniture is finally scheduled for delivery, the furniture truck shows up late or doesn't show at all, leaving furious customers who were required to be home from 9 AM to 5 PM to receive delivery. The strategic use of technology, however, is beginning to address these problems. **CRATE AND BARREL** and **PIER 1** now use their websites to give customers instant access to estimated completion dates using inventory tracking programs that follow the construction of furniture through the factory. This way customers don't have to guess when their furniture will be ready. Sophisticated route-tracking software, which determines the fastest and most efficient

combination of directions and deliveries for each furniture truck, joined with global positioning systems that track each truck's progress and location is reducing costs and scheduled delivery windows. As a result, Crate and Barrel charges only $69 for delivery within 50 miles, no matter how much furniture you order. Likewise, Pottery Barn requires furniture customers to be home for just a two-hour delivery window instead of all day.[3]

In today's hypercompetitive business environments, information, whether it's about furniture delivery, product inventory, pricing, or costs, is as important as capital (that is, money) for business success. It takes money to get businesses started, but businesses can't survive and grow without the right information. Information has strategic importance for organizations because it can be used to ***1.1 obtain first-mover advantage*** *and* ***1.2 sustain a competitive advantage once it has been created****.*

1.1 First-Mover Advantage

First-mover advantage is the strategic advantage that companies earn by being the first in an industry to use new information technology to substantially lower costs or to differentiate a product or service from that of competitors. By investing $90 billion over the last decade to replace copper coaxial lines with digital lines that fed high-speed cable modems and digital TV cable channels, cable companies convinced two out of every three high-speed Internet subscribers to choose "cable" over DSL service provided by phone companies.[4] While the phone companies are beginning to catch up—they now sign up more new high-speed Internet subscribers than cable providers—does that mean that cable companies' first-mover advantage is slipping away? Well, not yet, as 57 percent of high-speed Internet subscribers still choose cable.[5] And with a growing subscriber base for residential phone service, the cable companies are now going after the phone companies' business customers, offering them high-speed Internet and business phone service.[7]

In all, first-mover advantages, like those established by high-speed Internet cable companies, can be sizable. On average, first movers earn a 30 percent market share, compared with 19 percent for the companies that follow.[8] Likewise, over 70 percent of market leaders started as first movers.[9]

1.2 Sustaining a Competitive Advantage

As described above, companies that use information technology to establish first-mover advantage usually have higher market shares and profits. According to the resource-based view of information technology shown in Exhibit 17.2, companies need to address three critical issues in order to sustain a competitive advantage through information technology. First, does the information technology create value for the firm by lowering costs or providing a better product or service? If an information technology doesn't add value, then investing in it would put the firm at a competitive disadvantage to companies that choose information technologies that do add value.

Second, is the information technology the same or different across competing firms? If all the firms have access to the same information technology and use it in the same way, then no firm has an advantage over another (there is competitive parity).

Third, is it difficult for another company to create or buy the information technology used by the firm? If so, then the firm has established a sustainable competitive advantage over competitors through information technology. If not, then the competitive advantage is just temporary, and competitors should eventually be able to duplicate the advantages the leading firm has gained from information technology. For more about sustainable competitive advantage and its sources, see Chapter 6 on organizational strategy.

first-mover advantage the strategic advantage that companies earn by being the first to use new information technology to substantially lower costs or to make a product or service different from that of competitors

In short, the key to sustaining a competitive advantage is not faster computers, more memory, and larger hard drives. The key is using information technology to continuously improve and support the core functions of a business. Ron Ireland, a former **WAL-MART** manager, says, "Wal-Mart has always considered information technology as a competitive advantage, never as a business expense."[10] Thanks to innovative use of information technology and the largest private satellite network and database system in the world, Wal-Mart's costs are 10 percent lower than its competitors'.[11] Wal-Mart was one of the first retailers to use computers and bar codes to track sales and inventory data and then share those data with suppliers. Today, Wal-Mart's $4 billion supplier network, Retail Link, allows vendors like Ted Haedicke of Coca-Cola to "look at how much [and what kind of] Coke [has] sold ... and at what prices at any store in the Wal-Mart system." He went on to say, "You can't do that with any other retailer today."[12]

Companies like Wal-Mart that achieve first-mover advantage with information technology and then sustain it with continued investment create a moving target that competitors have difficulty hitting.

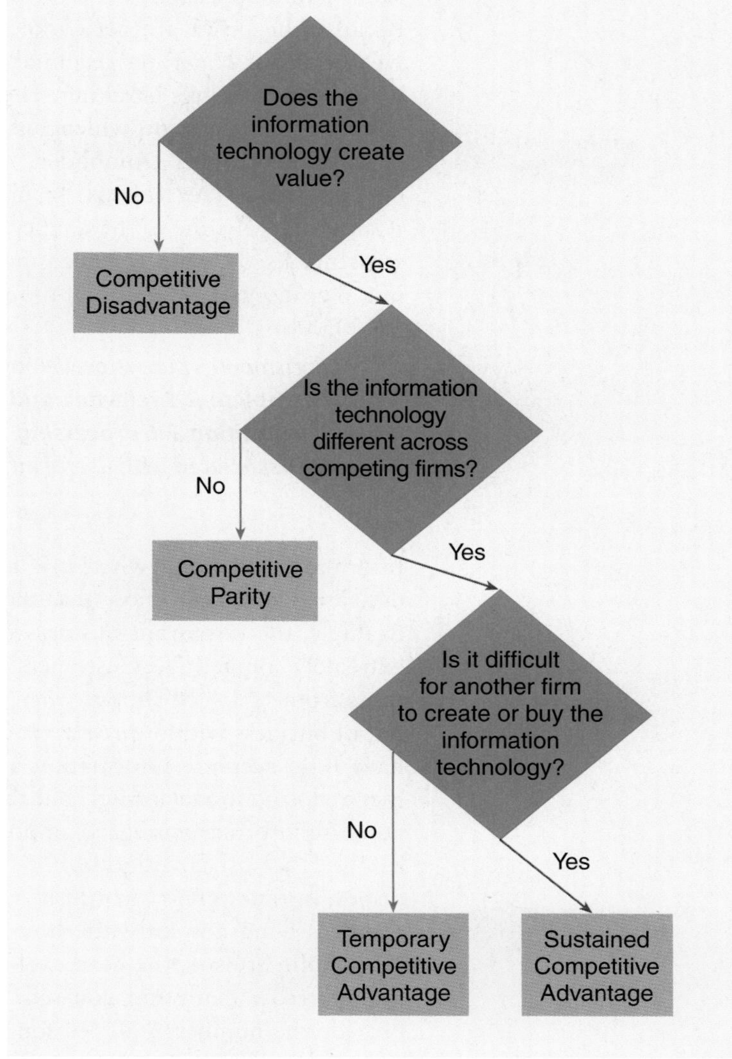

Source: Adapted from F. J. Mata, W. L. Fuerst, & J. B. Barney, "Information Technology and Sustained Competitive Advantage: A Resource-Based Analysis," *MIS Quarterly* 19, no. 4, December 1995, 487–505. Reprinted by special permission by the Society for Information Management and the Management Information Systems Research Center at the University of Minnesota.

Exhibit 17.2

Using Information Technology to Sustain a Competitive Advantage

Review 1: Strategic Importance of Information

The first company to use new information technology to substantially lower costs or differentiate products or services often gains first-mover advantage, which can lead to higher profits and larger market share. Creating a first-mover advantage can be difficult, expensive, and risky, however. According to the resource-based view of information technology, sustainable competitive advantage occurs when information technology adds value, is different across firms, and is difficult to create or acquire.

2 Characteristics and Costs of Useful Information

Portsmouth, a scenic city of 190,000 on the southern coast of England, attracts 6.5 million visitors a year, primarily because of its historic role as the home of the British Royal Navy. To handle the crush of visitors, Portsmouth relies on 320 buses, all equipped with computers and QDMA (quad-division multiple access)

radio communication, which works reliably at speeds up to 250 miles per hour. Because the buses are networked, passengers waiting at bus stops can access a weatherproof computer terminal to find out when the next bus will arrive and what route that bus is taking. They can also check their e-mail, use trip planning software to determine which bus routes to take, or swipe a credit card to purchase tickets. John Domblides, who works for Portmouth's **TRAFFIC SYSTEMS GROUP**, says, "The response from the public using the new facilities has been very positive, largely due to the quality of both the information displayed and the infrastructure used—stainless-steel and glass bus shelters with bright displays."[13] The initial cost was £3.2 million (about $6.4 million), and the annual cost is £200,000 ($400,000).

As Portsmouth's bus system demonstrates, information is useful when it is ***2.1 accurate, 2.2 complete, 2.3 relevant, and 2.4 timely****. However, there can be significant* ***2.5 acquisition, 2.6 processing, 2.7 storage, 2.8 retrieval****, and* ***2.9 communication costs associated with useful information****.*

2.1 Accurate Information

Information is useful when it is accurate. Before relying on information to make decisions, you must know that the information is correct. But what if it isn't? For example, the restaurant business is notoriously difficult for two reasons. First, it's extremely competitive. Customers in any location typically have hundreds of restaurants from which to choose when dining out. Second, 60 percent of restaurants go out of business within three years. Why? Restaurant owners and managers typically have little accurate information about their businesses. Sure, they know whether they're losing money or not, but they don't know why. Most restaurants don't have accurate information regarding how much alcohol they sell, for example, wine versus beer versus hard liquor, nor do they have information regarding which food dishes, lobster versus swordfish, sell more or are more expensive to prepare. With **AVERO**'s Slingshot software, however, restaurants can track this information and more. John Stinson, the head chef at Antonio's in Las Vegas, says, "My bosses keep asking, 'How many did you sell? How many did you sell?' I constantly need to provide the numbers." So Stinson uses Slingshot to examine the data and plan his menus accordingly. For instance, he found out that sea bass sold 196 times in one month, whereas ahi tuna sold 89 times. Since they both cost the same and sell for $29, Stinson reduced costs and eliminated unsold food by cutting his ahi tuna orders from suppliers in half.[14]

> My bosses keep asking, "How many did you sell? How many did you sell?" I constantly need to provide the numbers.
>
> JOHN STINSON, HEAD CHEF, ANTONIO'S, LAS VEGAS

2.2 Complete Information

Information is useful when it is complete. Incomplete or missing information makes it difficult to recognize problems and identify potential solutions. For example, dispatchers at **CON-WAY**, a freight transportation company, are responsible for choosing truck routes that maximize trailer loads, minimize expenses (time, miles, and fuel), and get drivers home as soon as possible. On a typical day, Con-way's dispatchers must consider the number of trucks (2,100) and available

drivers (varies), locations (200 across 25 states), shipments (typically 50,000), and the tonnage and trailer capacity for that day. Though Con-way's dispatchers do extremely well, they typically have only 85 percent of the information they need. Because they lack information about last-minute changes in orders, weather, accidents, driver no-shows, and breakdowns, they end up assigning longer, less efficient truck routes with less than full trucks that ultimately increase costs by $5 million per year.[15]

2.3 Relevant Information

You can have accurate, complete information, but if it doesn't pertain to the problems you're facing, then it's irrelevant and not very useful. Con-way dispatchers not only lacked complete information, they also lacked relevant information about their problems. To address these issues, the company spent $3 million over five years to build a computerized truck route optimization system. This system tracks all customer shipment requests (which can be made as late as 5:15 PM each day for the next day's delivery) and communicates by satellite with each truck to monitor truck availability, loads, miles, fuel, weather, and accidents. Then, armed with all of this relevant information, it cranks out optimal truck routes in just seven minutes. On an average day, this system allows Con-way to use 111 fewer trucks and 68 fewer drivers, drive 26,000 fewer miles, and increase the load in each truck by 370 revenue-generating pounds. Route optimization analyst Marty Robinson says, "It saves us a lot of time each night, which we use to make sure we've got accurate order information, look into problems and handle changes."[16]

2.4 Timely Information

Finally, information is useful when it is timely. To be timely, the information must be available when needed to define a problem or to begin to identify possible solutions. If you've ever thought, "I wish I had known that earlier," then you understand the importance of timely information and the opportunity cost of not having it. For instance, **Health Decisions** is a company that designs and runs clinical drug-testing trials for pharmaceutical companies. To provide timely access to study results, it records data using specially designed bubble forms (like multiple-choice test Scantrons). By scanning a form every second, the company can read up to 8,000 per day—entering the same amount of data by hand would take months. This allows medical clinics and labs to verify and correct their data just four days after sending the data to Health Decisions. By contrast, the industry average is 122 days. How much does this matter? A Health Decisions study of a potential Alzheimer's drug based on 450,000 pages of data was completed in three and a half years rather than seven. Although the Food and Drug Administration did not approve the drug, completing the research so quickly saved the pharmaceutical company three and a half years and $32 million in additional expenses that it was able to put toward the development of another drug.[17]

One of the key criteria for useful information is that it be timely. This humorous ad for Pitney-Bowes conveys that fact with a simple tag line, "The British Were Here!"

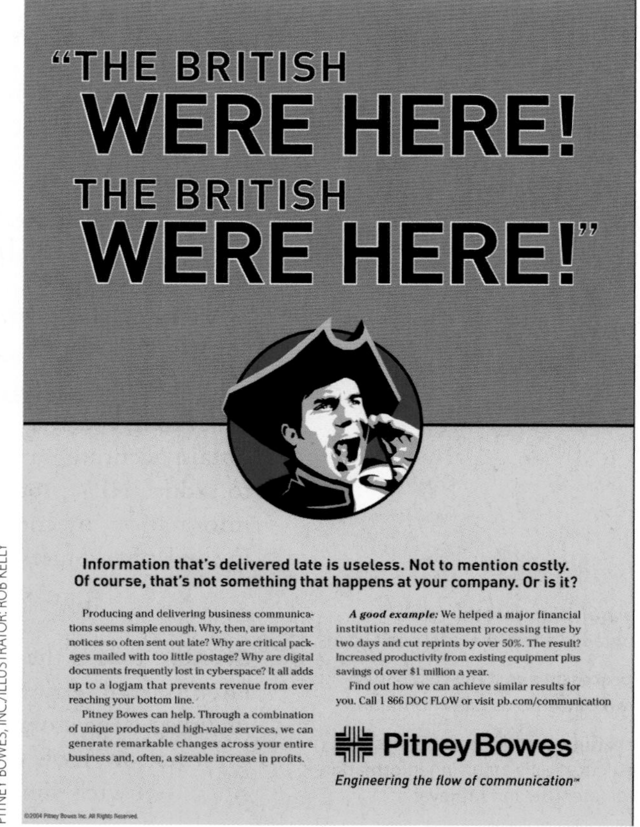

PITNEY BOWES, INC./ILLUSTRATOR: ROB KELLY

doing the right thing

Recycling and Disposing of Computer Equipment

With most companies replacing computers every four years, an estimated 250 million computers will be discarded over the next five years. Computers and computer monitors contain hazardous materials, however, so you can't just toss them in the trash. Doing that is not just wrong—it's against the law. Instead, contact your state's department of environmental protection for help in finding a recycling company. Or donate your old computers to deserving individuals or charitable organizations. Or sell the computers at a steep discount to your employees. And when you buy your new corporate computers, bargain with the vendor to make it responsible for recycling those computers the next time around.[19]

2.5 Acquisition Costs

Acquisition cost is the cost of obtaining data that you don't have. For example, among other things, ACXIOM, a billion-dollar company, gathers and processes data for direct-mail marketing companies. If you've received an unsolicited, "preapproved" credit card application recently (and who hasn't?), chances are Acxiom helped the credit card company gather information about you. Where does Acxiom get that information? The first place it turns is to companies that sell consumer credit reports at a wholesale cost of $1 each. Acxiom also obtains information from retailers. Each time you use your credit card, retailers' checkout scanners gather information about your spending habits and product preferences. Many retailers sell this information to companies like Acxiom that use it for market research. So why pay for this information? The reason is that acquiring it can help credit card companies do a better job of identifying who will mail back a signed credit card application and who will rip the credit card application in half and toss it in the trash.[18]

2.6 Processing Costs

Companies often have massive amounts of data, but not in the form or combination they need. Consequently, **processing cost** is the cost of turning raw data into usable information. For example, HEWLETT-PACKARD, which sells everything from handheld personal digital assistants to personal computers to large computer servers to high definition TVs, has 150,000 employees world wide. HP also has 85 different data centers in 29 countries, many of which can't "talk" to each other or share data. Why is this so? HP's chief information officer, Randy Mott explains, "Think about all of the steps involved from actually taking the order to having that order arrive on time, at all of the right locations, with all of the right components included and then promptly follow[ing]-up with accurate line-item billing, taxes, shipping costs, etc." Consequently, because of high processing costs, it's difficult for HP executives located throughout the world to obtain accurate, up-to-date information. It's Mott's job over the next three years to reduce HP's processing costs (that is, the cost of turning raw data into usable information) by consolidating those 85 data centers into just six data warehouses in the United States.[20]

2.7 Storage Costs

Storage cost is the cost of physically or electronically archiving information for later use and retrieval. For instance, Google and YAHOO! and Microsoft Live have incurred large storage costs to make it easy and fast for you to retrieve archived information. How costly can the storage for a simple web search be? Well, consider that each time you conduct a web search at Yahoo, 7,000 computers are

acquisition cost the cost of obtaining data that you don't have

processing cost the cost of turning raw data into usable information

storage cost the cost of physically or electronically archiving information for later use and retrieval activated to return the results of your search to you in less than 18/100 of a second.[21] And with the need for data storage doubling every 14 months, Yahoo, Google, Microsoft, and other *Fortune* 500 companies are building server farms, large collections of networked computer servers in 750,000-square-foot buildings (seven times the size of a Costco), to keep up with demand. Google's new server farm, located on 30 acres in Oregon where hydroelectric plants produce some of the cheapest electricity in the United States, will handle up to 2.7 billion online searches a month.

2.8 Retrieval Costs

Retrieval cost is the cost of accessing already-stored and processed information. One of the most common misunderstandings about information is that it is easy and cheap to retrieve once the company has it. Not so. First, you have to find the information. Then, you've got to convince whoever has it to share it with you. Then the information has to be processed into a form that is useful for you. By the time you get the information you need, it may not be timely anymore. Before the University of Illinois at Chicago Medical Center switched to the computer physician order entry (CPOE) system described in "What Would You Do?," doctors resisted the change, fearing that the new system would slow them down (that is, would have high retrieval costs). Dr. Patrick Tranmer says, "I have a maximum of 20 minutes to do everything when I see a patient. I have to find out what's wrong, get their history, do a physical exam, make a phone call, write a prescription, instruct the patient, make a follow-up appointment and then educate a student doctor about what I've just done."[22] The doctors were pleasantly surprised to find that the new system actually reduced retrieval costs. Before the new system, doctors and nurses used to waste time tracking down patient information. Now, when X-rays and lab reports are completed, they are immediately available for review at any computer in the hospital. When doctors noticed that it took nurses only one minute (rather than 10) to obtain these medical records, they started retrieving the X-rays and lab reports themselves, freeing nurses to spend more time attending to patients.[23] Overall, the new system saves physicians at the medical center 130,000 hours a year.

2.9 Communication Costs

Communication cost is the cost of transmitting information from one place to another. For example, the most important information that an electric utility company collects each month is the information from the electric meter attached to the side of your house. Traditionally, electric companies employed meter readers to walk from house to house to gather information that would then be entered into company computers. Now, however, meter readers are losing their jobs to water, gas, and electric meters built with radio frequency (RF) transmitters (see Section 3.1 for more on this technology). The transmitters turn on when a meter reader drives by the house in a utility company van that has a laptop computer specially equipped to receive the RF signals. Such a van, traveling at legal speeds, can read 12,000 to 13,000 meters in an eight-hour day. By contrast, a meter reader on foot would record data from 500 meters per day.[24] The Niagara Mohawk utility company in New York is spending $100 million over three years to install two million meters with RF transmitters, but expects to save $15 to $20 million a year in communication costs once they're installed.

retrieval cost the cost of accessing already-stored and processed information

communication cost the cost of transmitting information from one place to another

Review 2: **Characteristics and Costs of Useful Information**

Raw data are facts and figures. Raw data do not become information until they are in a form that can affect decisions and behavior. For information to be useful, it has to be reliable and valid (accurate), of sufficient quantity (complete), pertinent to the problems you're facing (relevant), and available when you need it (timely). Useful information does not come cheaply. The five costs of obtaining good information are the costs of acquiring, processing, storing, retrieving, and communicating information.

GETTING AND SHARING INFORMATION

In 1907, **METROPOLITAN LIFE INSURANCE** built a huge office building in New York City for its brand new, state-of-the-art information technology system. What was this great breakthrough in information management? Card files. That's right, the same card file system that every library in America used before computers. Metropolitan Life's information "technology" consisted of 20,000 separate file drawers that sat in hundreds of file cabinets more than 15 feet tall. This filing system held 20 million insurance applications, 700,000 accounting books, and 500,000 death certificates. Metropolitan Life employed 61 workers who did nothing but sort, file, and climb ladders to pull files as needed.[25]

A century later, the cost, inefficiency, and ineffectiveness of using this formerly state-of-the-art system would put an insurance company out of business within months. Today, if storms, fire, or accidents damage policyholders' property, insurance companies write checks on the spot to cover the losses. When policyholders buy a car, they call their insurance agent from the dealership to activate their insurance before driving off in their new car. And now, insurance companies are marketing their products and services to customers directly from the Internet.

From card files to Internet files in just under a century, the rate of change in information technology is spectacular. After reading the next two sections, you should be able to

3 explain the basics of capturing, processing, and protecting information.
4 describe how companies can access and share information and knowledge.

3 Capturing, Processing, and Protecting Information

"What's New" Company

When you go to your local **RITE AID** pharmacy to pick up a prescription, the pharmacist reviews an electronic file that shows all of the medications you're taking. That same system automatically checks to make sure that your new prescription won't create adverse side effects by interacting with your other medications. When you pay for your prescription, Rite Aid's point-of-sale information system determines whether you've written any bad checks lately (to Rite Aid or other stores), records your payment, and then checks with the computer of the pharmaceutical company that makes your prescription drugs to see if it's time to reorder. Throughout the process, Rite Aid protects your information to make sure that your data are readily available only to you, your physician, and your pharmacist.

*In this section, you will learn about the information technologies that companies like Rite Aid use to **3.1 capture, 3.2 process,** and **3.3 protect information**.*

3.1 Capturing Information

There are two basic methods of capturing information: manual and electronic. Manual capture of information is a labor-intensive process, which entails recording and entering data by hand into a data storage device. For example, when you applied for a driver's license, you probably recorded personal information about yourself by filling out a form. Then, after you passed your driver's test, someone typed your handwritten information into the department of motor vehicles' computer database so that local and state police could access it from their patrol cars when they pulled you over for speeding. (Isn't information great?) The problem with manual capture of information is that it is slow, expensive, and often inaccurate.

Consequently, companies are relying more on electronic capture, in which data are electronically recorded and entered into electronic storage devices. Bar codes, radio frequency identification tags, and document scanners are methods of electronically capturing data. **Bar codes** represent numerical data by varying the thickness and pattern of vertical bars. The primary advantage that bar codes offer is that the data they represent can be read and recorded in an instant with a handheld or pen-type scanner. One pass of the scanner (okay, sometimes several) and "beep!" The information has been captured. Bar codes cut checkout times in half, reduce data entry errors by 75 percent, and save stores money because stockers don't have to go through the labor-intensive process of putting a price tag on each item in the store.[26]

bar code a visual pattern that represents numerical data by varying the thickness and pattern of vertical bars

radio frequency identification (RFID) tags tags containing minuscule microchips that transmit information via radio waves and can be used to track the number and location of the objects into which the tags have been inserted

Radio frequency identification (RFID) tags contain minuscule microchips and antennas that transmit information via radio waves.[27] Unlike bar codes, which require direct line-of-sight scanning, RFID tags are read by turning on an RFID reader that, like a radio, tunes into a specific frequency to determine the number *and* location of products, parts, or anything else to which the RFID tags are attached. Turn on an RFID reader, and every RFID tag within the reader's range (from several hundred to several thousand feet) is accounted for. Each year, airlines mishandle or lose four million of the 700 million luggage bags checked by U.S. airline passengers. The annual cost to deliver late bags or to reimburse passengers for lost bags is approximately $400 million. Las Vegas's **MCCARRAN INTERNATIONAL AIRPORT** is reducing those costs by attaching luggage tags with embedded RFID chips. RFID readers accurately read 99 percent of RFID-tagged bags, compared with 80 to 90 percent of bar-coded tags read by optical scanners. That means that of the 70,000 outbound bags that are handled each day at McCarran, only 700 (1%) have to be sorted by hand now that RFID chips are used, much fewer than the 7,000 to 14,000 (10%–20%) that would have to be hand-sorted if bar-coded tags were used.

RFID technology greatly increases the efficiency of getting the right luggage to the right person, something that baggage handlers and travelers can appreciate.

Now that the price of RFID luggage tags has dropped dramatically from $5 just a few years ago to only 15 cents each, more airports will be using RFID tags to reduce their luggage handling costs.[28]

Because they are inexpensive and easy to use, **electronic scanners**, which convert printed text and pictures into digital images, have become an increasingly popular method of electronically capturing data. The first requirement for a good scanner is a *document feeder* that automatically feeds document pages into the scanner or turns the pages (often with a puff of air) when scanning books or bound documents.[29] Text that has been digitized cannot be searched or edited like the regular text in your word processing software, however, so the second requirement for a good scanner is **optical character recognition** software to scan and convert original or digitized documents into ASCII text (American Standard Code for Information Interchange) or Adobe PDF documents. ASCII text can be searched, read, and edited with standard word processing, e-mail, desktop publishing, database management, and spreadsheet software, and PDF documents can be searched and edited with Adobe's Acrobat software. Sloans Lake Managed Care, a Colorado health-care organization, uses scanners and optical character recognition software to read the medical claims forms submitted by the 450,000 people covered by its health plan. Sloans Lake can scan 450 to 500 characters per form with 98 percent accuracy. As a result, the company now automatically scans and processes over 5,000 claims forms per day and has lowered the time for processing claims by an average of 65 percent.[30]

3.2 Processing Information

Processing information means transforming raw data into meaningful information that can be applied to business decision making. Evaluating sales data to determine the best- and worst-selling products, examining repair records to determine product reliability, and monitoring the cost of long-distance phone calls are all examples of processing raw data into meaningful information. And with automated, electronic capture of data, increased processing power, and cheaper and more plentiful ways to store data, managers no longer worry about getting data. Instead, they scratch their heads about how to use the overwhelming amount of data that pours into their businesses every day. Furthermore, most managers know little about statistics and have neither the time nor the inclination to learn how to use them to analyze data.

One promising tool to help managers dig out from under the avalanche of data is data mining. **Data mining** is the process of discovering patterns and relationships in large amounts of data.[31] Data mining works by using complex algorithms such as neural networks, rule induction, and decision trees. If you don't know what those are, that's okay. With data mining, you don't have to. Most managers only need to know that data mining looks for patterns that are already in the data but are too complex for them to spot on their own. For example, when Yahoo decided to redesign its front page at Yahoo.com, it was faced with analyzing 10 terabytes (a terabyte is the same as 500 million pages of single-spaced text) of data per day generated by users clicks! Since there was no way to make sense of that much data, Yahoo bought DMX Group, a company that provides simple data mining tools to employees who pose simple questions such as "Are users more likely to click on an ad placed in the middle of the page or at the top of the page?" Bassel Ojjeh, vice president of DMX, which Yahoo has renamed the department of Strategic Data Solutions, says that Yahoo is now using data and not wild guesses to make changes to its websites. Says Ojjeh, "We say: Use data to make decisions. Don't make decisions based on a fad or what your competitors are doing."[32]

Data mining typically splits a data set in half, finds patterns in one half, and then tests the validity of those patterns by trying to find them again in the second

electronic scanner an electronic device that converts printed text and pictures into digital images

optical character recognition the ability of software to convert digitized documents into ASCII text (American Standard Code for Information Interchange) that can be searched, read, and edited by word processing and other kinds of software

processing information transforming raw data into meaningful information

data mining the process of discovering unknown patterns and relationships in large amounts of data half of the data set. The data typically come from a **data warehouse** that stores huge amounts of data that have been prepared for data mining analysis by being cleaned of errors and redundancy. The data in a data warehouse can then be analyzed using two kinds of data mining. **Supervised data mining** usually begins with the user telling the data mining software to look and test for specific patterns and relationships in a data set. Typically, this is done through a series of "what if?" questions or statements. For instance, a grocery store manager might instruct the data mining software to determine if coupons placed in the Sunday paper increase or decrease sales. By contrast, with **unsupervised data mining**, the user simply tells the data mining software to uncover whatever patterns and relationships it can find in a data set. For example, STATE FARM INSURANCE used to have three pricing categories for car insurance, depending on your driving record: preferred for the best drivers, standard for typical drivers, and nonstandard for the worst drivers. Now, however, it has moved to "tiered pricing" based on the 300 different kinds of driving records that its data mining software was able to discover. This allows State Farm to be much more precise in matching 300 different price levels to 300 different kinds of driving records.[33]

data warehouse stores huge amounts of data that have been prepared for data mining analysis by being cleaned of errors and redundancy

supervised data mining the process when the user tells the data mining software to look and test for specific patterns and relationships in a data set

unsupervised data mining the process when the user simply tells the data mining software to uncover whatever patterns and relationships it can find in a data set

association or affinity patterns when two or more database elements tend to occur together in a significant way

sequence patterns when two or more database elements occur together in a significant pattern, but one of the elements precedes the other

Data mining can uncover some astounding patterns—like the fact that new dads tend to buy beer and diapers at the same time, at least at Osco.

Unsupervised data mining is particularly good at identifying association or affinity patterns, sequence patterns, and predictive patterns. It can also identify what data mining "techies" call data clusters.[34] **Association or affinity patterns** occur when two or more database elements tend to occur together in a significant way. Surprisingly, OSCO DRUGS, based in Chicago, found that beer and diapers tended to be bought together between 5 and 7 PM. The question, of course, was "why?" The answer, on further review, was fairly straightforward: fathers, who were told by their wives to buy some diapers on their way home, decided to pick up a six-pack for themselves, too.[35] Likewise, because Wal-Mart's data mining indicated that people tend to buy bananas and cereal at the same time, Wal-Mart now places bananas near the cereal aisle, in addition to the fruits and vegetables aisle.[36]

Sequence patterns occur when two or more database elements occur together in a significant pattern, but with one of the elements preceding the other. StratBridge provides data mining capability to professional sports teams, like basketball's BOSTON CELTICS, to analyze their ticket sales in real time. One of its products is a "live" color-coded graphic of the Celtics stadium seating chart. Prior to a game, colors will change every few seconds to show whether a seat has been sold, at what price, and whether the seat was bought as part of a group purchase or an individual purchase. One season, after the Celtics had been eliminated from playoff eligibility, StratBridge's data mining software connected demographic data, sales data, seat location, and the timing of the seats to indicate that families typically bought tickets behind the basket just a few hours before tipoff. When the Celtics noticed that sales were lagging for those seats, they bundled those seats together in a family four-pack, dropped the prices, added food coupons, and then e-mailed a list of local families who had previously purchased tickets to the game. As a result, all of those unsold seats sold. Says Shawn Sullivan, a vice-president for the team, "If we'd done our usual newspaper ad [for those seats], there'd have been no return at all."[37]

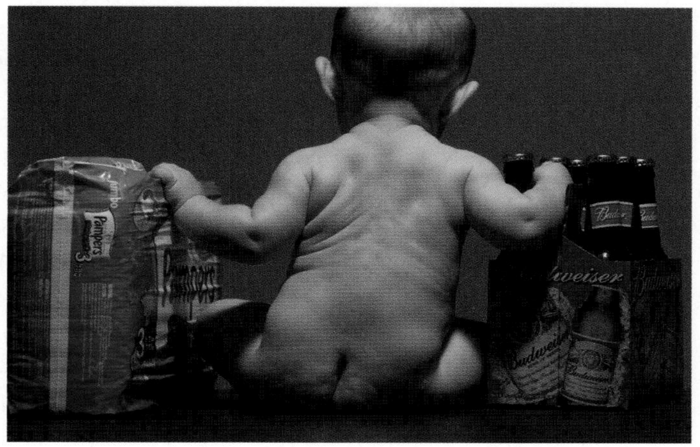

Predictive patterns are just the opposite of association or affinity patterns. Whereas association or affinity patterns look for database elements that seem to go

together, **predictive patterns** help identify database elements that are different. On the day after Thanksgiving, typically the busiest shopping day of the year, Wal-Mart's data mining indicated that sales were unexpectedly slow for a boxed computer and printer combination that was offered at an extremely good price. Sales were slow everywhere, except one Wal-Mart store where sales greatly exceeded expectations. After noting the difference, headquarters called the store manager who said that the products were displayed in an open box that made it clear to customers that the low price was for the computer *and* the printer. Sales took off at all stores after headquarters relayed this simple message, "Open the box."[38]

> If we'd done our usual newspaper ad [for those seats], there'd have been no return at all.
>
> SHAWN SULLIVAN, VICE-PRESIDENT, BOSTON CELTICS

Data clusters are the last kind of pattern found by data mining. **Data clusters** occur when three or more database elements occur together (that is, cluster) in a significant way. For example, after analyzing several years worth of repair and warranty claims, **Ford Motor Company** might find that, compared with cars built in its Chicago plant, the cars it builds in Atlanta (first element) are more likely to have problems with overtightened fan belts (second element) that break (third element) and result in overheated engines (fourth element), ruined radiators (fifth element), and payments for tow trucks (sixth element), which are paid for by Ford's three-year, 36,000 mile warranty.

Traditionally, data mining has been very expensive and very complex. Today, however, data mining services and analysis are much more affordable and within reach of most companies' budgets. And, if it follows the path of most technologies, it will become even easier and cheaper to use in the future.

3.3 Protecting Information

Protecting information is the process of ensuring that data are reliably and consistently retrievable in a usable format for authorized users, but no one else. For instance, when customers purchase prescription medicine at **Drugstore.com**, an online drugstore and health-aid retailer, they want to be confident that their medical and credit card information is available only to them, the pharmacists at Drugstore .com, and their doctors. In fact, Drugstore.com has an extensive privacy policy (click "Privacy Policy" at **http://www.drugstore.com**) to make sure this is the case.

Companies like Drugstore.com find it necessary to protect information because of the numerous security threats to data and data security listed in Exhibit 17.3. People inside and outside companies can steal or destroy company data in various ways including denial-of-service web server attacks that can bring down some of the busiest and best-run sites on the Internet; viruses and spyware/adware that spread quickly and can result in data loss and business disruption; keystroke monitoring in which every mouse click and keystroke you make is monitored, stored, and sent to unauthorized users; password cracking software that steals supposedly secure passwords; and phishing, where fake but real-looking e-mails and websites trick users into sharing personal information (user names, passwords, account numbers) that leads to unauthorized account access. Indeed, on average, 19 percent of computers are infected with viruses, 80 percent have spyware, and only one-third are running behind a protected firewall (discussed shortly). Studies show that the threats listed in Exhibit 17.3 are so widespread that automatic attacks will begin on an unprotected computer just 15 seconds after it connects to the Internet.[39]

As shown in the right-hand column of Exhibit 17.3, numerous steps can be taken to secure data and data networks. Some of the most important are authentication and authorization, firewalls, antivirus software for PCs and e-mail servers, data encryption, and virtual private networks.[40] We will review those steps and then finish this section with a brief review of the dangers of wireless networks, which are exploding in popularity.

predictive patterns patterns that help identify database elements that are different

data clusters when three or more database elements occur together (i.e., cluster) in a significant way

protecting information the process of ensuring that data are reliably and consistently retrievable in a usable format for authorized users, but no one else

Exhibit 17.3

Security Threats to Data and Data Networks

SECURITY PROBLEM	SOURCE	AFFECTS	SEVERITY	THE THREAT	THE SOLUTION
Denial of service, web server attacks, and corporate network attacks	Internet hackers	All servers	High	Loss of data, disruption of service, and theft of service.	Implement firewall, password control, serverside review, threat monitoring, and bug fixes, and turn PCs off when not in use.
Password cracking software and unauthorized access to PCs	Local area network, Internet	All users, especially digital subscriber line and cable Internet users	High	Hackers take over PCs. Privacy can be invaded. Corporate users' systems are exposed to other machines on the network.	Close ports and firewalls, disable file and print sharing, and use strong passwords.
Viruses, worms, Trojan horses, and rootkits	E-mail, downloaded and distributed software	All users	Moderate to high	Monitor activities and cause data loss and file deletion: compromise security by sometimes concealing their presence.	Use antivirus software and firewalls, and control Internet access.
Spyware, adware, malicious scripts, and applets	Rogue web pages	All users	Moderate to high	Invade privacy, intercept passwords, and damage files or file system.	Disable browser script support, and use security, blocking, and spyware/ adware software.
E-mail snooping	Hackers on your network and the Internet	All users	Moderate to high	People read your e-mail from intermediate servers or packets, or they physically access your machine.	Encrypt message, ensure strong password protection, and limit physical access to machines.
Keystroke monitoring	Trojan horses, people with direct access to PCs	All users	High	Records everything typed at the keyboard and intercepts keystrokes before password masking or encryption occurs.	Use antivirus software to catch Trojan horses, control Internet access to transmission, and implement system monitoring and physical access control.

(continued)

Exhibit 17.3 (Continued)

Security Threats to Data and Data Networks

SECURITY PROBLEM	SOURCE	AFFECTS	SEVERITY	THE THREAT	THE SOLUTION
Phishing	Hackers on your network and the Internet	All users, including customers	High	Fake but real-looking e-mails and websites that trick users into sharing personal information on what they wrongly thought was the company's website. This leads to unauthorized account access.	Educate and warn users and customers about the dangers. Encourage both not to click on potentially fake URLs, which might take them to phishing websites. Instead, have them type your company's URL into the web browser.
Spam	E-mail	All users and corporations	Mild to high	Clogs and overloads e-mail servers and inboxes with junk mail. HTML-based spam may be used for profiling and identifying users.	Filter known spam sources and senders on e-mail servers, and have users create further lists of approved and unapproved senders on their personal computers.
Cookies	Websites you visit	Individual users	Mild to moderate	Trace web usage and permit the creation of personalized web pages that track behavior and interest profiles.	Use cookie managers to control and edit cookies, and use ad blockers.

Sources: K. Bannan, "Look Out: Watching You, Watching Me," *PC Magazine*, July 2002, 99; A. Dragoon, "Fighting Phish, Fakes, and Frauds," CIO, 1 September 2004, 33; B. Glass, "Are You Being Watched?" *PC Magazine*, 23 April 2002, 54; K. Karagiannis, "DDoS: Are You Next?" *PC Magazine*, January 2003, 79; B. Machrone, "Protect & Defend," *PC Magazine*, 27 June 2000, 168–181.

Two critical steps are required to make sure that data can be accessed by authorized users and no one else. One is **authentication**, that is, making sure users are who they claim to be.[41] The other is **authorization**, that is, granting authenticated users approved access to data, software, and systems.[42] For example, when an ATM prompts you to enter your personal identification number (PIN), the bank is authenticating that you are you. Once you've been authenticated, you are authorized to access your funds and no one else's. Of course, as anyone who has lost a PIN or password or had one stolen knows, user authentication systems are not foolproof. In particular, users create security risks by not changing their default account passwords (such as birth dates) or by using weak passwords such as names ("Larry") or complete words ("football") that are quickly guessed by password cracker software.[43] (See "Doing the Right Thing" on password do's and don'ts to learn how to prevent this.)

authentication making sure potential users are who they claim to be

authorization granting authenticated users approved access to data, software, and systems

two-factor authentication authentication based on what users know, such as a password and what they have in their possession, such as a secure ID card or key

This is why many companies are now turning to **two-factor authentication**, which is based on what users know, such as a password, and what they have, such as a secure ID card. For example, to log onto their computer accounts, employees

at ***Bloomberg***, a global provider of business news, data, and analysis, must enter a password, such as a four-digit personal identification number, plus a secure number that changes every 60 seconds and is displayed on the tiny screen of the secure electronic ID (about the size of a pack of gum) they carry. For these same reasons, some companies are turning to biometrics for authentication. With **biometrics** such as fingerprint recognition or iris scanning, users are identified by unique, measurable body features.[44] Troy Appling, vice president of The Bankers Bank, says, "With fingerprint biometrics, we can reduce the risk of unauthorized people making millions of dollars off fraudulent transfers. And we don't have to spend up to 60 percent of our IT [information technology] time resolving lost or forgotten passwords."[45] Of course, since some fingerprint scanners can be fooled by fingerprint molds, some companies take security measures even further by requiring users to simultaneously scan their fingerprint *and* insert a secure, smart card containing a digital file of their fingerprint. This is another form of two-factor authentication.

> With fingerprint biometrics, we can reduce the risk of unauthorized people making millions of dollars off fraudulent transfers. And we don't have to spend up to 60 percent of our IT [information technology] time resolving lost or forgotten passwords.
>
> **TROY APPLING**, VICE PRESIDENT, THE BANKERS BANK

Unfortunately, stolen or cracked passwords are not the only way for hackers and electronic thieves to gain access to an organization's computer resources. Unless special safeguards are put in place, every time corporate users are online there's literally nothing between their personal computers and the Internet (home users with high-speed DSL or cable Internet access face the same risks). Hackers can access files, run programs, and control key parts of computers if precautions aren't taken. To reduce these risks, companies use **firewalls**, hardware or software devices that sit between the computers in an internal organizational network and outside networks, such as the Internet. Firewalls filter and check incoming and outgoing data. They prevent company insiders from accessing unauthorized sites or from sending confidential company information to people outside the company. Firewalls also prevent outsiders from identifying and gaining access to company computers and data. Indeed, if a firewall is working properly, the computers behind the company firewall literally cannot be seen or accessed by outsiders.

A **virus** is a program or piece of code that, without your knowledge, attaches itself to other programs on your computer and can trigger anything from a harmless flashing message to the reformatting of your hard drive to a systemwide network shutdown. You used to have to do or run something to get a virus, such as double-clicking an infected e-mail attachment. Today's viruses are much more threatening. In fact, with some viruses, just being connected to a network can infect your computer. *Antivirus software for personal computers* scans e-mail, downloaded files, and computer hard drives, disk drives, and memory to detect and stop computer viruses from doing damage. However, this software is effective only to the extent that users of individual computers have and use up-to-date versions. With new viruses appearing all the time, users should update their antivirus software weekly or, even better, configure their virus software to automatically check for, download, and install updates. By contrast, *corporate antivirus software* automatically scans e-mail attachments, such as Microsoft Word documents,

biometrics identifying users by unique, measurable body features, such as fingerprint recognition or iris scanning

firewall a protective hardware or software device that sits between the computers in an internal organizational network and outside networks, such as the Internet

virus a program or piece of code that, without your knowledge, attaches itself to other programs on your computer and can trigger anything from a harmless flashing message to the reformatting of your hard drive to a systemwide network shutdown

doing the right thing

Password Do's and Don'ts

Anyone with access to sensitive personal (personnel or medical files), customer (credit cards), or corporate data (costs) has a clear responsibility to protect those data from unauthorized access. Use the following dos and don'ts to maintain a "strong" password system and protect your data.

- **Don't use any public information such as part of your name, address, or birth date to create a password.**
- **Don't use complete words, English or foreign, that are easily guessed by password software using "dictionary attacks."**
- **Use eight or more characters and include some unique characters such as !@#$ to create passwords like "cow@#boy."**
- **The longer the password and the more unique characters, the more difficult it is to guess.**
- **Consider using "passphrases," such as "My European vacation starts July 8th," instead of shorter passwords. The longer password, including upper- and lowercase letters, spaces, and numbers, is easy to remember and much, much more difficult to guess using password cracking software.**
- **Remember your password and don't write it down on a sticky note attached to your computer.**
- **Change your password every six weeks. Better yet, specify that your computer system force all users to change their passwords this often.**
- **Don't reuse old passwords.**

Together, these basic steps can make it much more difficult to gain unauthorized access to sensitive data.[47]

graphics, or text files, as they come across the company e-mail server. It also monitors and scans all file downloads across company databases and network servers. So, while antivirus software for personal computers prevents individual computers from being infected, corporate antivirus software for e-mail servers, databases, and network servers adds another layer of protection by preventing infected files from multiplying and being sent to others.

Another way of protecting information is to encrypt sensitive data. **Data encryption** transforms data into complex, scrambled digital codes that can be unencrypted only by authorized users who possess unique decryption keys. One method of data encryption is to use products by PGP (Pretty Good Privacy) (**http://www.pgp.com**) to encrypt the files stored on personal computers or network servers and databases. This is especially important with laptop computers, which are easily stolen. After a Boeing employee's laptop PC was stolen from his hotel room, the company implemented a training program that requires managers and employees to have data encryption software installed on their laptops and become certified in using it. Those not following the encryption procedures can be reprimanded and even fired.[46]

And, with people increasingly gaining unauthorized access to e-mail messages—e-mail snooping—it's also important to encrypt sensitive e-mail messages and file attachments. You can use a system called "public key encryption" to do so. First, give copies of your "public key" to anyone who sends you files or e-mail. Have the sender use the public key, which is actually a piece of software, to encrypt files before sending them to you. The only way to decrypt the files is with a companion "private key" that you keep to yourself.

Although firewalls can protect personal computers and network servers connected to the corporate network, people away from their offices (for example, salespeople, business travelers, telecommuters who work at home) who interact with their company networks via the Internet face a security risk. Because Internet data are not encrypted, packet sniffer software easily allows hackers to read everything sent or received, except files that have been encrypted before sending. Previously, the only practical solution was to have employees dial in to secure company phone lines for direct access to the company network. Of course, with international and long-distance phone calls, the costs quickly added up. Now, **virtual private networks (VPNs)** have solved this problem by using software to encrypt all Internet data at both ends of the transmission process. Instead of making long-distance calls, employees connect to the Internet. But, unlike typical Internet connections in which Internet data packets are unencrypted, the VPN encrypts the data sent by employees outside the company computer network, decrypts the data when they arrive within the company network, and does the same when data are sent back to the computer outside the network.

Alternatively, many companies are now adopting web-based **secure sockets layer (SSL) encryption** to provide secure off-site access to data and programs. If you've ever entered your credit card in a web browser to make an online purchase, you've used SSL technology to encrypt and protect that information. SSL encryption is being used if a gold lock (Internet Explorer) or a gold key (Netscape) appears along the bottom of your web browser. SSL encryption works the same way in the workplace. Managers and employees who aren't at the office simply connect to the Internet, open a web browser, and then enter a user name and password to gain access to SSL encrypted data and programs. For example, the Catholic Health System of Buffalo, New York, uses an SSL system to allow radiologists to access and review medical images like X-rays from their homes. Likewise, lawyers at Sonnenschein, Nath & Rosenthal, a Chicago law firm, use the Internet and their SSL encrypted system to securely access case records from anywhere in the world.[48] SSL encryption is cheaper than VPNs, but it typically provides only limited access to data and files. By contrast, VPN connections, though more expensive, provide complete, secure access to everything on a company's network.

Finally, many companies now have wireless networks, which make it possible for anybody with a laptop and a wireless card to access the company network from anywhere in the office. Though wireless networks come equipped with security and encryption capabilities that, in theory, permit only authorized users to access the wireless network, those capabilities are easily bypassed with the right tools. Furthermore, for ease of installation, many wireless networks are shipped with their security and encryption capabilities turned off.[49] Plus, although it's better to have it turned on than off, be wary of the WEP (Wired Equivalent Privacy) security protocol, which is easily compromised. See the Wi-Fi Alliance site at **http://www.wi-fi.org** for the latest information on wireless security and encryption protocols that provide much stronger protection for your company's wireless network.

data encryption the transformation of data into complex, scrambled digital codes that can be unencrypted only by authorized users who possess unique decryption keys

virtual private network (VPN) software that securely encrypts data sent by employees outside the company network, decrypts the data when they arrive within the company computer network, and does the same when data are sent back to employees outside the network

secure sockets layer (SSL) encryption Internet browser–based encryption that provides secure off-site web access to some data and programs

Seconds after connecting to the Internet, a computer starts being attacked by viruses and malicious scripts. This ad from Stay Safe Online underscores the importance of protecting information from outside threats.

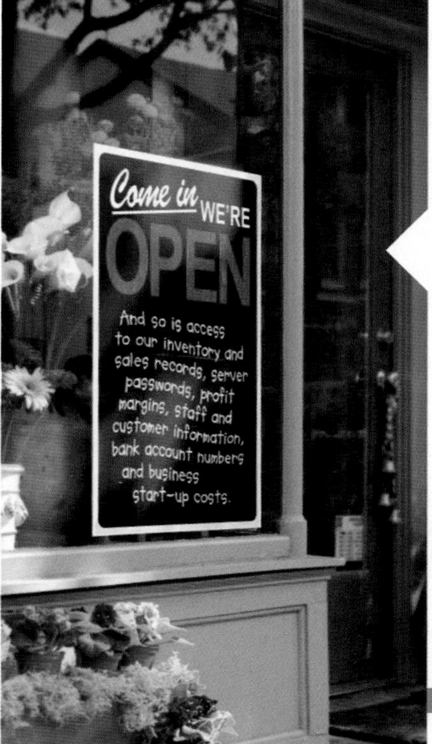
Come in WE'RE OPEN
And so is access to our inventory and sales records, server passwords, profit margins, staff and customer information, bank account numbers and business start-up costs.
Is your business everybody's business?
You wouldn't leave the door to your business unlocked after hours. So why would you make it easy for hackers and thieves to steal your business records, or even take control of your computer to attack others? Protect yourself, your employees and your customers. Get in the habit of keeping your cyber security up to date.
To learn how, visit
STAYSAFEONLINE.org
Make it a habit.
NATIONAL CYBER SECURITY ALLIANCE

Review 3: Capturing, Processing, and Protecting Information

Electronic data capture (bar codes, radio frequency identification [RFID] tags, scanners, and optical character recognition) is much faster, easier, and cheaper than manual data capture. Processing information means transforming raw data into meaningful information that can be applied to business decision making. Data mining helps managers with this transformation by discovering unknown patterns and relationships in data. Supervised data mining looks for patterns specified by managers, while unsupervised data mining looks for four general kinds of data patterns: association/affinity patterns, sequence patterns, predictive patterns, and data clusters. Protecting information ensures that data are reliably and consistently retrievable in a usable format by authorized users, but no one else. Authentication and authorization, firewalls, antivirus software for PCs and corporate e-mail and network servers, data encryption, virtual private networks, and web-based secure sockets layer (SSL) encryption are some of the best ways to protect information. Be careful with wireless networks, which are easily compromised even when security and encryption protocols are in place.

Simplest-Shop.com sells a multitude of books, cameras, computers, DVDs, electronics, games, music, software, toys, and videos. Clicking on "DVD" brings up the 10 best-selling titles and the option of searching for 3,000 others. The page for each DVD (and every other product) lists customer advice, such as "recommended by 80 percent of our customers"; shares specific customer comments, such as "*Charlie and the Chocolate Factory* is a quirky but fun adaptation of Roald Dahl's classic children's tale"; and typically lists two or three different prices and places from which to order. Amazingly, with tens of thousands of products, this entire website and business is run by just one person, Calin Uioreanu, a software engineer from Munich, Germany. How can Uioreanu run this business by himself? He uses web services, a growing Internet technology that allows him to tie directly into Amazon.com's back-office resources. All of the product descriptions, pictures, and customer comments and feedback ratings on Simplest-Shop.com come straight from Amazon.com, which also verifies credit cards and arranges for shipping. Uioreanu uses web services software to connect his Simplest-Shop.com server to Amazon's servers for continuous information updates. The advantage for Amazon.com is that it has another website for selling its goods. The advantage for consumers is that they can buy many items directly from either Simplest-Shop.com or Amazon.com, whichever is cheaper. The advantage for Calin Uioreanu is that he can run a huge web business that sells over 50,000 products all by himself. According to Uioreanu, without web services and the ability to share information with Amazon.com, "it would have been 10 times more difficult to do."[50]

Today, information technologies are letting companies communicate data, share data, and provide data access to workers, managers, suppliers, and customers in ways that were unthinkable just a few years ago. After reading this section, you should be able to explain how companies use information technology to improve ***4.1 internal access and sharing of information, 4.2 external access and sharing of information,*** *and* ***4.3 the sharing of knowledge and expertise****.*

4.1 Internal Access and Sharing

executive information system (EIS) a data processing system that uses internal and external data sources to provide the information needed to monitor and analyze organizational performance

Executives, managers, and workers inside the company use three kinds of information technology to access and share information: executive information systems, intranets, and portals. An **executive information system (EIS)** uses internal and external sources of data to provide managers and executives the information they need to monitor and analyze organizational performance.[51] The goal of an EIS is to provide accurate, complete, relevant, and timely information to managers.

Managers at **Lands' End**, the web/mail-order company, use their EIS, which they call their "dashboard," to see how well the company is running. With just a few mouse clicks and basic commands such as *find, compare*, and *show*, the EIS displays costs, sales revenues, and other kinds of data in color-coded charts and graphs. Managers can drill down to view and compare data by region, state, time period, and product. Frank Giannantonio, Lands' End's CIO, says, "Our dashboards include an early alert system that utilizes key performance metrics to target items selling faster than expected and gives our managers the ability to adjust product levels far earlier than they were able to do in the past."[52] Exhibit 17.4 describes the capabilities of two of the best-selling products that companies use for EIS programs.

Intranets are private company networks that allow employees to easily access, share, and publish information using Internet software. Intranet websites are just like external websites, but the firewall separating the internal company network from the Internet permits only authorized internal access.[53] Companies typically use intranets to share information (for example, about benefits) and to replace paper forms with online forms. At IBM, however, the company intranet is used for electronic meetings, instant messaging, online libraries of policies and procedures, distance learning and training, online reimbursement of travel expenses, and travel schedules and

intranets private company networks that allow employees to easily access, share, and publish information using Internet software

Exhibit 17.4

Characteristics of Best-Selling Executive Information Systems

EASE OF USE	Few commands to learn.	Simply drag-and-drop or point-and-click to create charts and tables or get the information you need.
	Important views saved.	Need to see weekly sales by store every Monday? Save that "view" of the data, and it will automatically be updated with new data every week.
	3-D charts to display data.	Column, square, pie, ring, line, area, scatter, bar, cube, etc.
	Geographic dimensions.	Different geographic areas are automatically color-coded for easy understanding.
ANALYSIS OF INFORMATION	Sales tracking.	Track sales performance by product, region, account, and channel.
	Easy-to-understand displays.	Information is displayed in tabular and graphical charts.
	Time periods.	Data can be analyzed by current year, prior year, year to date, quarter to date, and month to date.
IDENTIFICATION OF PROBLEMS AND EXCEPTIONS	Compare with standards.	Compares actual company performance (actual expenses versus planned expenses, or actual sales by sales quotas).
	Trigger exceptions.	Allows users to set triggers (5 percent over budget, 3 percent under sales quota), which then highlight negative exceptions in red and positive exceptions in green.
	Drill down.	Once exceptions have been identified, users can drill down for more information to determine why the exception is occurring.
	Detect & alert newspaper.	When things go wrong, the EIS delivers a "newspaper" via e-mail to alert managers to problems. The newspaper offers an intuitive interface for easily navigating and further analyzing the alert content.
	Detect & alert robots.	Detect & alert robots keep an extra "eye" out for events and problems. Want to keep an eye out for news about one of your competitors? Use a news robot to track stories on Dow Jones News Retrieval. Robots can also be used to track stock quotes, internal databases, and e-mail messages.

Sources: "Business Intelligence: Overview: Enterprise Services from Pilot Software," Accrue Software, http://www.pilotsw.com, 9 February 2002; Comshare home page, http://www.comshare.com, February 2002.

- Intranets are inexpensive.
- Intranets increase efficiencies and reduce costs.
- Intranets are intuitive and easy to use and web-based.
- Intranets work across all computer systems and platforms (web-based).
- Intranets can be built on top of an existing computer network.
- Intranets work with software programs that easily convert electronic documents to HTML files for intranet use.
- Much of the software required to set up an intranet is either freeware (no cost) or shareware (try before you buy, usually less expensive than commercial software).

Exhibit 17.5
Why Companies Use Intranets

reservations. As a result, 4,800 electronic meetings are held each month, one million instant message discussions are held each day, and 40 percent of company training is done online.[54] With 300,000 employees in 164 countries, the company's travel savings from online training have been huge. IBM's Jeanette Barlow says, "We saved between $4 million and $5 million a month not paying for travel."[55] Exhibit 17.5 further explains why companies use intranets.

Finally, corporate portals are a hybrid of executive information systems and intranets. While an EIS provides managers and executives with the information they need to monitor and analyze organizational performance, and intranets help companies distribute and publish information and forms within the company, **corporate portals** allow company managers and employees to access customized information *and* complete specialized transactions using a web browser. **HILLMAN GROUP** is the company that sells the nuts, bolts, fasteners, keys, and key cutting machines that you find in Home Depot, Lowes, Ace, and nearly every other hardware store. Hillman's 1,800 employees produce products for 25,000 customers. Two years ago, Hillman hired a new CIO, Jim Honerkamp, to improve the quality of information that Hillman's managers and employees used to make decisions. Says Honerkamp, "Our executives were trying to piecemeal information together to make business decisions on spreadsheets." So the first thing he did was to create a corporate portal that contained a real time revenue report for every product that updated sales and production numbers on a continuous basis. The portal and the report were so useful that CEO Mick Hillman began using them on a daily basis. Says Honerkamp, "The first thing he [Hillman] does when he arrives at 6:30 AM is to get on the portal and start looking at reports. He picks up the phone and starts calling my peers, the SVP of operations or the VP of distribution or the CFO and starts asking questions based on what he's seeing."[56] Today, Hillman's portal contains 75 specialized reports that are accessed by 800 managers and employees.

4.2 External Access and Sharing

Historically, companies have been unable or reluctant to let outside groups have access to corporate information. Now, however, a number of information technologies— electronic data interchange, extranets, web services, and the Internet—are making it easier to share company data with external groups like suppliers and customers. They're also reducing costs, increasing productivity by eliminating manual information processing (70 percent of the data output from one company, such as a purchase order, ends up as data input at another company, such as a sales invoice or shipping order), reducing data entry errors, improving customer service, and speeding communications. As a result, managers are scrambling to adopt these technologies.

corporate portal a hybrid of executive information systems and intranets that allows managers and employees to use a web browser to gain access to customized company information and to complete specialized transactions

> Our executives were trying to piecemeal information together to make business decisions on spreadsheets.
>
> **JIM HONERKAMP**, CIO, HILLMAN GROUP

With **electronic data interchange**, or **EDI**, two companies convert purchase and ordering information to a standardized format to enable direct electronic transmission of that information from one company's computer system to the other company's system. For example, when a Wal-Mart checkout clerk drags a CD across the checkout scanner, Wal-Mart's computerized inventory system automatically reorders another copy of that CD through the direct EDI connection that its computer has with the manufacturing and shipping computer at the company that publishes the CD, say, Atlantic Records. No one at Wal-Mart or Atlantic Records fills out paperwork. No one makes phone calls. There are no delays to wait to find out whether Atlantic has the CD in stock. The transaction takes place instantly and automatically because the data from both companies were translated into a standardized, shareable, compatible format.

Web services, as mentioned above in the Simplest Shop example, are another way for companies to directly and automatically transmit purchase and ordering information from one company's computer systems to another company's computer systems. **Web services** use standardized protocols to describe and transfer data from one company in such a way that those data can automatically be read, understood, transcribed, and processed by different computer systems in another company.[57] For instance, **ROUTE ONE**, which helps automobile processes auto loans for car buyers, was started by the financing companies of DaimlerChrysler, Ford, General Motors, and Toyota. Not surprisingly, each auto company had a different computer system with different operating systems, different programs, and different data structures. Route One relies on web services to connect these different computer systems to the wide variety of different databases and software used by various auto dealers, credit bureaus, banks, and other auto financing companies. Without web services, there's no way these different companies and systems could share information.[58]

Now, what's the difference between web services and EDI? For EDI to work, the data in different companies' computer, database, and network systems must adhere to a particular set of standards for data structure and processing. For example, company X, which has a 7-digit parts numbering system, and company Y, which has an 8-digit parts numbering system, would agree to convert their internal parts numbering systems to identical 10-digit parts numbers when their computer systems talk to each other. By contrast, the tools underlying web services, such as extensible markup language, or XML (don't worry if you don't how this works, just appreciate what it does), automatically do the describing and transcribing so that data with different structures can be shared across very different computer systems in different companies. As a result, web services allow organizations to communicate data without special knowledge of each other's computer information systems by automatically handling those differences.

In EDI and web services, the different purchasing and ordering applications in each company interact automatically without any human input. No one has to lift a finger to click a mouse, enter data, or hit the "return" key. An **extranet**, by contrast, allows companies to exchange information and conduct transactions by purposely providing outsiders with direct, web browser–based access to authorized parts of a company's intranet or information system. Typically, user names and passwords are required to access an extranet.[59] For example, to make sure that its distribution trucks don't waste money by running half empty (or make late deliveries to customers because it waited to ship until the trucks were full), **GENERAL MILLS** uses an extranet to provide web-based access to its

electronic data interchange (EDI) when two companies convert their purchase and ordering information to a standardized format to enable the direct electronic transmission of that information from one company's computer system to the other company's computer system

web services using standardized protocols to describe data from one company in such a way that those data can automatically be read, understood, transcribed, and processed by different computer systems in another company

extranets networks that allow companies to exchange information and conduct transactions with outsiders by providing them direct, web-based access to authorized parts of a company's intranet or information system trucking database to 20 other companies that ship their products over similar distribution routes. When other companies are ready to ship products, they log on to General Mills' trucking database, check the availability, and then enter the shipping load, place, and pickup time. Thus, by sharing shipping capacity on its trucks, General Mills can run its trucks fully loaded all the time. In several test areas, General Mills saved 7 percent on shipping costs, or nearly $2 million in the first year. Expanding the program company-wide is producing even larger cost savings.[60]

Finally, similar to the way in which extranets are used to handle transactions with suppliers and distributors, companies are reducing paperwork and manual information processing by using the Internet to electronically automate transactions with customers. For example, most airlines have automated the ticketing process by eliminating paper tickets altogether. Simply buy an e-ticket via the Internet, and then check yourself in online by printing your boarding pass from your personal computer or from a kiosk at the airport. Together, Internet purchases, ticketless travel, and automated check-ins have fully automated the purchase of airline tickets. Self-service kiosk uses are expanding, too. For example, **ALAMO RENT-A-CAR** has introduced kiosks that print rental agreements, permit upgrades to nicer cars, and allow customers to add additional drivers or buy rental insurance. Jerry Dow, Alamo's chief marketing officer, says, "Customers are already comfortable using the check-in kiosk for flights. Using a self-service kiosk for car rental is a natural progression."[61] Alamo has found that kiosks reduce check-in times by 50 percent.

In the long run, the goal is to link customer Internet sites with company intranets (or EDI) and extranets so that everyone—all the employees and managers within a company, and the suppliers and distributors outside the company—who is involved in providing a service or making a product for a customer is automatically notified when a purchase is made. Companies that use EDI, web services, extranets, and the Internet to share data with customers and suppliers achieve increases in productivity 2.7 times larger than those that don't.[62]

4.3 Sharing Knowledge and Expertise

At the beginning of the chapter, we distinguished between raw data, which consist of facts and figures, and information, which consists of useful data that influence someone's choices and behavior. One more important distinction needs to be made, namely, that data and information are not the same as knowledge. **Knowledge** is the understanding that one gains from information. Importantly, knowledge does not reside in information. Knowledge resides in people. That's why companies hire consultants and why family doctors refer patients to specialists. Unfortunately, it can be quite expensive to employ consultants, specialists, and experts. So companies have begun using two information technologies, decision support systems and expert systems, to capture and share the knowledge of consultants, specialists, and experts with other managers and workers.

Whereas an executive information system speeds up and simplifies the acquisition of information, a **decision support system (DSS)** helps managers understand problems and potential solutions by acquiring and analyzing information with sophisticated models and tools.[63] Furthermore, whereas EIS programs are broad in scope and permit managers to retrieve all kinds of information about a company, DSS programs are usually narrow in scope and targeted toward helping managers solve specific kinds of problems. DSS programs have been developed to help managers pick the shortest and most efficient routes for delivery trucks, select the best combination of stocks for investors, and schedule the flow of inventory through complex manufacturing facilities.

knowledge the understanding that one gains from information

decision support system (DSS) an information system that helps managers understand specific kinds of problems and potential solutions and analyze the impact of different decision options using "what if" scenarios

It's important to understand that DSS programs don't replace managerial decision making; they improve it by furthering managers' and workers' understanding of the problems they face and the solutions that might work. Though used by just 2 percent of physicians, medical DSS programs hold the promise of helping doctors make more accurate patient diagnoses. A British study of 88 cases misdiagnosed or initially misdiagnosed (to be correctly diagnosed much later) found that a medical DSS made the right diagnosis 69 percent of the time.[64] With a medical DSS, doctors enter patient data, such as age, gender, weight, and medical symptoms. The medical DSS then produces a list of diseases and conditions, ranked by probability, low or high, or by medical specialty, such as cardiology or oncology. For instance, when emergency room physician Dr. Harold Cross treated a 10-year old boy who had been ill with nausea and dizziness for two weeks, he wasn't sure what was wrong, given that the boy had a healthy appetite, no abdominal pain, and just one brief headache. However, when the medical DSS that Dr. Cross used suggested a possible problem in the back of the boy's brain, he ordered an MRI scan that revealed a tumor, which was successfully removed two days later. Says Dr. Cross, "My personal knowledge of the literature and physical findings would not have prompted me to suspect a brain tumor."[65]

Expert systems are created by capturing the specialized knowledge and decision rules used by experts and experienced decision makers. They permit nonexpert employees to draw on this expert knowledge base to make decisions. Most expert systems work by using a collection of "if–then" rules to sort through information and recommend a course of action. For example, let's say that you're using your **American Express** card to help your spouse celebrate a promotion. After dinner and a movie, the two of you stroll by a travel office with a Las Vegas poster in its window. Thirty minutes later, caught up in the moment, you find yourselves at the airport ticket counter trying to purchase last-minute tickets to Vegas. But there's just one problem. American Express didn't approve your purchase. In fact, the ticket counter agent is now on the phone with an American Express customer service agent.

expert system an information system that contains the specialized knowledge and decision rules used by experts and experienced decision makers so that nonexperts can draw on this knowledge base to make decisions

So what put a temporary halt to your weekend escape to Vegas? An expert system that American Express calls "Authorizer's Assistant."[66] The first "if–then" rule that prevented your purchase was the rule "*if* a purchase is much larger than the cardholder's regular spending habits, *then* deny approval of the purchase." This if–then rule, just one of 3,000, is built into American Express's transaction-processing system that handles thousands of purchase requests per second. Now that the American Express customer service agent is on the line, he or she is prompted by the Authorizer's Assistant to ask the ticket counter agent to examine your identification. You hand over your driver's license and another credit card to prove you're you. Then the ticket agent asks for your address, phone number, Social Security number, and your mother's maiden name and relays the information to American Express. Finally, your ticket purchase is approved. Why? Because you met the last series of "if–then" rules. *If* the purchaser can provide proof of identity and *if* the purchaser can provide personal information that isn't common knowledge, *then* approve the purchase.

Expert systems like American Express's Authorizer's Assistant make available the knowledge of experienced decision makers to employees throughout the company—which is good if you're trying to buy tickets on the spur of the moment.

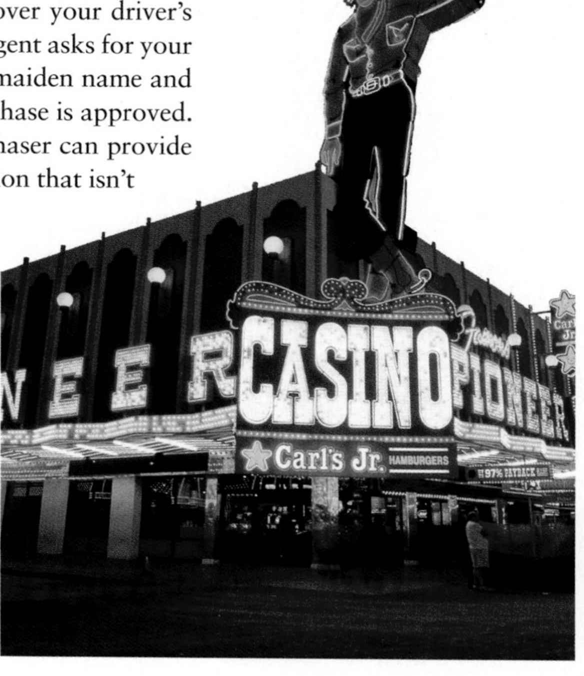

Review 4: Accessing and Sharing Information and Knowledge

Executive information systems, intranets, and corporate portals facilitate internal sharing and access to company information and transactions. Electronic data interchange, web services, and the Internet allow external groups, like suppliers and customers, to easily access company information. All three decrease costs by reducing or eliminating data entry, data errors, and paperwork, and by speeding up communication. Organizations use decision support systems and expert systems to capture and share specialized knowledge with nonexpert employees.

SELF ASSESSMENT

Computer Comfort

Computers are ubiquitous in modern society, but that does not mean that everyone embraces them. As with any innovation, some people are reluctant to adopt computer technology for whatever reason. How comfortable are you with computer technology?[67] Be candid as you complete the assessment by circling the appropriate responses.

	Strongly disagree				Strongly agree
1. I hesitate to use a computer for fear of making mistakes that I cannot correct.	1	2	3	4	5
2. The challenge of learning about computers is exciting.	1	2	3	4	5
3. I feel apprehensive about using computers.	1	2	3	4	5
4. I am confident that I can learn computer skills.	1	2	3	4	5
5. I feel insecure about my ability to interpret a computer printout.	1	2	3	4	5
6. I look forward to using a computer on my job.	1	2	3	4	5
7. I have avoided computers because they are unfamiliar and somewhat intimidating to me.	1	2	3	4	5
8. Learning to operate computers is like learning any new skill—the more you practice, the better you become.	1	2	3	4	5
9. It scares me to think that I could cause the computer to destroy a large amount of information by hitting the wrong key.	1	2	3	4	5
10. If given the opportunity, I would like to learn about and use computers.	1	2	3	4	5
11. I have difficulty in understanding the technical aspects of computers.	1	2	3	4	5
12. I am sure that with time and practice, I will be as comfortable working with computers as I am working with a typewriter.	1	2	3	4	5
13. You have to be a genius to understand all the special keys contained on most computer terminals.	1	2	3	4	5
14. Anyone can learn to use a computer if they are patient and motivated.	1	2	3	4	5
15. I do not think I would be able to learn a computer programming language.	1	2	3	4	5
16. I feel computers are necessary tools in both educational and work settings.	1	2	3	4	5
17. I dislike working with machines that are smarter than I am.	1	2	3	4	5

KEY TERMS

acquisition cost 636
association/affinity patterns 641
authentication 644
authorization 644
bar code 639
biometrics 645
communication cost 637
corporate portals 650
data clusters 642
data encryption 647
data mining 640
data warehouse 641
decision support system (DSS) 652
electronic data interchange (EDI) 651
electronic scanner 640
executive information system (EIS) 648
expert system 653
extranet 651
firewall 645
first-mover advantage 632
information 630
intranets 649
knowledge 652
Moore's law 630
optical character recognition 640
predictive patterns 642
processing cost 636
processing information 640
protecting information 642
radio frequency identification (RFID) tags 639
raw data 630
retrieval cost 637
secure sockets layer (SSL) encryption 647

18. I feel that I will be able to keep up with the advances happening in the computer field.	1	2	3	4	5
19. I am afraid that if I begin using computers, I will become dependent upon them and lose some of my reasoning skills.	1	2	3	4	5

TOTAL = ________

Scoring

Reverse scores on even-numbered items. Reverse means, for instance, a 1 becomes a 5; a 4 becomes a 2, and so on. Using the reversed scores and the remaining scores, compute your score for the 19 items by adding up the scores.

You can find the interpretation for your score at: **academic.cengage.com/management/williams.**

(continued)

sequence patterns 641
storage cost 636
supervised data mining 641
two-factor authentication 644
unsupervised data mining 641
virtual private network (VPN) 647
virus 645
web services 651

MANAGEMENT DECISION

Can You See It Now?

After a long weekend working with your information technology team, you are confident that the company's server is thoroughly protected from outside attacks.[68] You and your team spent months planning and four days working around the clock to update the IT system, install, firewalls, and load SSL into the company's e-commerce tools, just to name a few of the security measures you upgraded. Now your company's information is protected with the latest and greatest.

When you stumble back to work on Wednesday, you follow your familiar route through the marketing department. Turning a corner, you overhear a junior marketing employee talking on her cell phone. She's saying, "I'm sooooooo far behind. No, really, I am. Check it out." Then she lifts her cell phone in the air and begins taking pictures of her desk.

Suddenly, you've lost your mission-accomplished swagger. Your team just spent thousands of labor hours protecting the company's digital assets, but anybody with a camera phone can take pictures of printouts, office layouts, client lists, accounting reports, marketing strategies, trade secrets—anything. A cell phone is the telecommunication version of a Swiss army knife: a versatile tool with potentially dangerous capabilities. Most cell phones have large memories for storing images, and what's more, they have GPRS technology, which enables them to connect them wirelessly to the Internet. Someone could take a picture of sensitive information, and in seconds, it could travel around the world and land on a competitor's computer (or cell phone, for that matter).

Camera-equipped cell phones are quickly becoming the norm. The market for the hybrid phones grew 200 percent in 2004, and researchers estimate that by 2008, 68 percent of all cell phones will be equipped with cameras and video capabilities—and the memory necessary to drive them.

Your pace quickens. You stop at your office to ditch your briefcase and then head straight to the CEO. Halfway there, however, you realize you need to be more composed before sounding alarm bells. Returning to your office, you fire up your computer and begin working on a memo.

Questions

1. What areas of a company are most likely to be compromised by the presence of camera phones?
2. Besides cell phones, can you think of other personal items that represent threats to a company's information, digital or otherwise? What are they? Should companies be able to restrict such items in the work place?
3. How could camera phones *improve* the collection and dissemination of information in a company?
4. Do you recommend banning camera phones in the workplace? Why or why not? Write a brief memo to the CEO explaining your position.

Brain Drain

The whistle blows signaling the end of the work day, and you automatically cringe. These days, that whistle seems like a warning bell for the mass exodus of employees you'll soon experience. You're a top manager at a nuclear power generator that employs thousands of engineers—for now, anyway. Very soon, though, you'll start loosing baby boomer workers to retirement. And you're not the only one. Within one decade, 43 percent of the workforce will be eligible to retire. United States businesses expect a 10 million worker shortage by 2010.

As you wait the arrival of your management team, you start to review the topic of your after-hours meeting. Your company will be hit hard by a double loss. Not only will you lose people (hard to replace), you'll lose their know-how (nearly impossible to replace). Skilled engineers have spent years acquiring the 'tricks-of-the-trade' and developing strategies for dealing with specific problems, so when they retire, a huge knowledge base will walk with them out the door.

A recent survey found that 63 percent of companies worry that the retirement of talented workers will create a "brain drain." Like many companies, yours has put off dealing with its aging workforce. Even though there's a plan for retaining some of your older workers on a part time basis, it's only a temporary measure. What you really need is a way to transmit knowledge from one group of employees to another—and to identify who has the knowledge you need to transmit.

Many companies in similar situations have developed knowledge management projects. Bruce Power—another nuclear power generator—uses a knowledge management system called Kana IQ that helps engineers document their solutions to certain problems so that future workers can search previous employees' notes using decision trees and other algorithms. Technology isn't the only way to stem the knowledge hemorrhage, however. Some companies are implementing mentoring programs to educate their next generation of skilled employees. At Tennessee Valley Authority power plants, younger engineers are assigned to shadow older engineers to facilitate the transfer of impossible-to-document skills.

So what will you do? Operating a nuclear power plant with less experienced workers is a dangerous proposition. Profitability and efficiency aren't the only concerns: safety is also paramount. You can't delay much longer or you'll be in a crisis when the retirements start in large number. When you open your door to see what on earth is keeping your management team you see them standing on your threshold mid-knock. It's time to get down to the hard business of creating a process for transmitting the wisdom of your older employees to your next generation of workers.

Questions

1. How can you find out which employees are about to retire? And how do you determine whose knowledge is most critical? Develop a strategy for identifying soon-to-retire workers and ranking the importance of their knowledge.
2. What are the pros and cons of developing a knowledge management database? What could you do to keep your engineers from becoming overly dependent upon a database? What steps might you take to ensure that your knowledge management project stays inclusive and accessible?
3. What if you developed a mentoring program? What would be the pros and cons of that?
4. Will you invest in a knowledge management project or a mentoring program? Explain your decision.

Information is the lifeblood of organizations and one of the keys to sustaining a competitive advantage. The tools for processing and sharing information have improved and proliferated rapidly over the past few decades. But growing sophistication has also meant growing challenges in maintaining quality and security across far flung corporate information systems. And managers increasingly feel deluged by the rising flow of e-mail, text messages, and near-instantaneous reports. To thrive in the information rich environment of modern business, managers must effectively utilize the various tools available. This exercise will give you an opportunity to consider which tools might work best for a given need.

Step 1: Get into groups and read the scenario. Your professor will organize you into pairs or groups of three.

Scenario: Suppose that you and your partner(s) are going into business together. Brainstorm about some new ventures that might interest you. Select one of these ideas that seem appealing, and then talk about how you might build a sustainable competitive advantage for your new business. (*Hint*: You may want to review the first few sections of the chapter.) With this initial sketch of your business plan in mind, discuss how you might use information systems and tools to accomplish the following tasks:

- Researching the likely competition that you will face
- Finding out what steps will be required to get the necessary permits, licenses, and/or regulatory approvals to open and maintain your business
- Determining what price you should charge for your product(s) or service(s)
- Deciding what computer and communication equipment you will need to buy to support your new venture
- Recruiting and hiring the best people for available jobs in your new company

Step 2: Discuss the issues. Discuss how you might develop the information system that your company needs to successfully launch and grow. Be sure to include security issues/concerns in your discussion.

Step 3: Debrief as a class. What are the major challenges in creating and maintaining a sustainable competitive advantage? What role does information and information technology play in successfully competing with other companies in a given market? Is it possible to secure sensitive information and at the same share information with employees and/or other key stakeholders (suppliers, customers)?

Learn to Talk Tech

Most people are intimidated by technology. But like many things, technology becomes easier if you familiarize yourself with the basics. One way to learn to "speak a geek" is to subscribe to *PC Magazine*, the premier magazine about personal computing. Depending on your budget, it may be more feasible (and possibly more productive) if you spend a set amount of time each week perusing the periodical section of the library and flipping through a selection of magazines dedicated to technology. The important thing is to be patient, however. After several issues, you should begin to understand what they're talking about. After that, it's easy to stay current. Subscribe at **http://pcmag.com**. You can also sign up for the "Term of the Day" e-mail newsletter at **http://webopedia.com.** Each day, Webopedia will e-mail you a new technology term and its definition. Either way, you'll soon be able to talk tech.

Why is talking tech so important? Information technology (IT) is an integral part of nearly every business, whether it's simple e-mail applications or more complex networking, e-commerce, and operations software. Very few companies are able to get by without using IT regularly. This being the case, managers need to understand this critical component of their companies' operations. That's not to say that managers (other than IT managers, of course) need to know every last technical detail, but as a manager, you will need—and want—to know what your tech staff is talking about when they bring problems, concerns, or suggestions for improvement to your office.

Computers are becoming an integral part of all kinds of work, so you need to do more than just understand the terminology, however. You also need to be able to use technology effectively. The reason is that people with basic computer skills earn 15 to 30 percent higher lifetime incomes than those without them. What should you do to learn about computers? Subscribe to *PC Magazine, PC World*, or *Macworld*. Buy a book about Microsoft Office and then take tests to be Microsoft Office User certified (see the Microsoft website for more information) in Word, Excel, PowerPoint, or Access. Take more than the required computer classes for your degree. Unless you want less job security and earning power, start learning more about computers today.

Activities

1. If you are completely new to IT, you might be more comfortable reading about it in the context of your favorite business publication. Walter Mossberg has a regular technology column in the *Wall Street Journal*, and Peter Lewis has a column titled "Gadgets," which can always be found in the so-called First section of *Fortune* magazine. Articles in both publications are on the shorter side, so take an hour and read through a few weeks' worth of each.
2. The U.S. government operates a technology website at **http://www.technology.gov/reports.htm.** Go there to download a report, "Education and Training for the Information Technology Workforce," published in June 2003 on technology training opportunities (there may even be a more recent one). The table of contents alone will give you a wealth of ideas about where and what kind of IT training you may want to pursue in conjunction with your business degree.

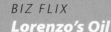

REEL TO REAL

BIZ FLIX

Lorenzo's Oil

This film tells the true story of young Lorenzo Odone, who suffers from adrenoleukodystrophy (ALD), an incurable degenerative brain disorder. (Six actors and actresses play Lorenzo throughout the film.) Physicians and medical scientists offer little help to Lorenzo's desperate parents, Michaela (Susan Sarandon) and Augusto (Nick Nolte). They use their resources to learn about ALD to try to save their son. Director George Miller cowrote the script, which benefited from his medical training as a physician.

Six months after Lorenzo's ALD diagnosis, his condition fails to improve with a restricted diet. Michaela and Augusto continue their research at the National Institutes of Health library in Bethesda, Maryland. Michaela finds a report of a critical Polish experiment that showed positive effects of fatty acid manipulation in rats. Convinced that a panel of experts could systematically focus on their problem, they help organize the First International ALD Symposium. This scene is an edited version of the symposium sequence that appears about midway through the film. The film continues with the Odones' efforts to save their son.

What to Watch for and Ask Yourself

1. Do the scientists present data or information during the symposium?
2. If it is information, who transformed the data into information? Speculate about how such data become information.
3. What do you predict will be the next course of action for the Odones?

MANAGEMENT WORKPLACE

Peapod—Data Management at Its Best

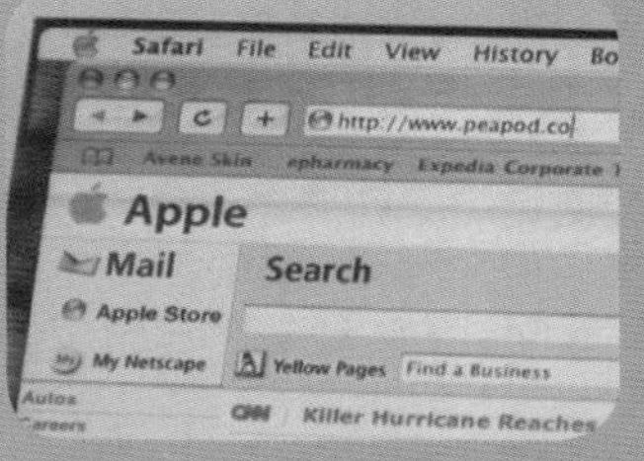

It's hard to imagine a time before e-commerce. The dot-com boom and bust seems to be ancient history, particularly because so many start-up firms didn't survive. But a few of them did, and one that not only survived but thrived is a company with the unlikely name of Peapod. Peapod was founded by brothers Andrew and Thomas Parkinson in 1989, several years before the dot-com boom began. Both brothers stayed with the firm after its sale to Royal Ahold.

Thomas Parkinson remains with the company today as its chief technology officer (CTO) and vice president. Peapod offers consumers a relatively simple service—online grocery shopping with delivery—but its success depends on a great deal more. Peapod wouldn't exist without Internet technology, the vehicle for e-commerce. Let's see how technology makes Peapod's management workplace so successful.

What to Watch for and Ask Yourself

1. Describe how Peapod uses data mining to process information.
2. How does Peapod share information both internally and externally?
3. In what ways might Peapod use a customer relationship management system to maintain its competitive advantage in the marketplace?

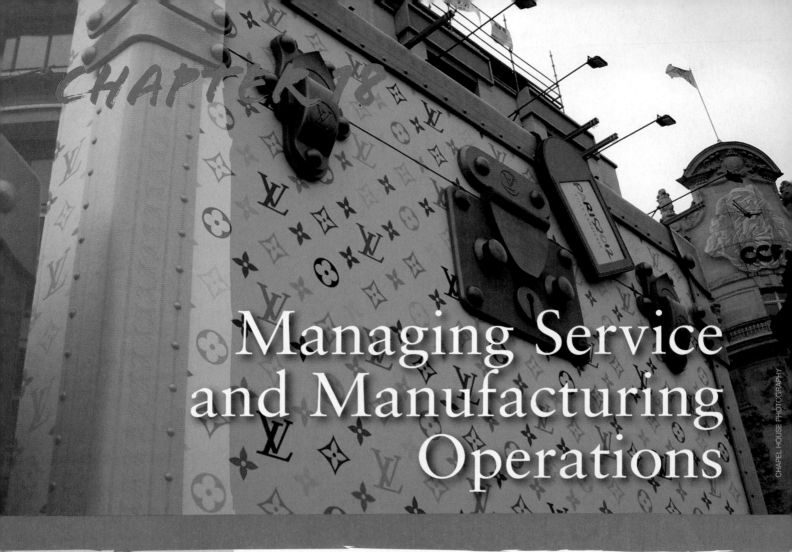

CHAPTER 18

Managing Service and Manufacturing Operations

CHAPEL HOUSE PHOTOGRAPHY

Learning Outcomes:

1 Discuss the kinds of productivity and their importance in managing operations.
2 Explain the role that quality plays in managing operations.
3 Explain the essentials of managing a service business.
4 Describe the different kinds of manufacturing operations.
5 Explain why and how companies should manage inventory levels.

In This Chapter:

WHAT WOULD YOU DO?

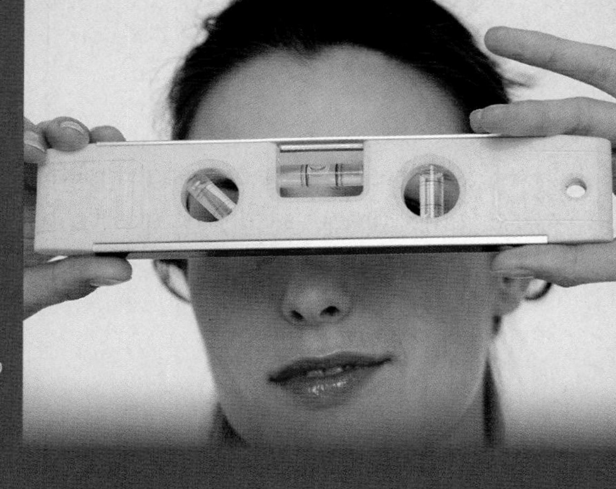

Louis Vuitton Manufacturing Plant, Asnières, France. Today as you walked out of the Louis Vuitton boutique on the Avenue Montaigne in downtown Paris, you found yourself at the center of Paris' high-end luxury fashion sector. With competition from less-expensive brands pushing into traditional upscale shopping districts, many high-end designers have relocated here. Similar movements have been occurring from New York to Tokyo and forced luxury fashion companies to regroup, a shift indicative of changing trends within the fashion world.

Louis Vuitton was founded in 1854 and opened its first workshop in 1860 in the Paris suburb of Asnières. Work at Asnières is still done by hand, and many current models are closely based on the original designs that made Vuitton a fashion icon. Workers specialize in making certain types of bags, and 20 to 30 craftsmen can take up to 8 days to complete one tote! That level of precision and care has been encouraged to maintain the traditional appeal of the brand.

As a fashion icon, Vuitton's reputation for high-quality handcrafted products is critical to its success. Over 150 years after its founding, Vuitton still considers make-to-order custom pieces as a central part of its production, and depending on their complexity, special requests can take as long as 8 months to complete. All work is done by craftsmen using hand tools (handsaws, hammers, pincers, cutters, brushes, punchers, sanders, and even stones).

Maintaining that caché involves creating high demand, frequent use of limited-edition products, and suppressing supply levels on their standard product lines. Vuitton sells its luggage at prices from roughly $2,000 to $4,000 per piece and has never put its products on sale. In the 1970s, the single factory in Asnières could not meet the increased demands of globalization, so Vuitton began adding new factories every other year. As a result of major pushes in marketing, store-opening, and expansion into the U.S. and Japan, Vuitton experienced annual sales increases from $760 million in 1990 to $3.7 billion in 2000.

That increase in volume is stressing your production system. Demand for new models is so high that at times people are on waiting lists for months. (You don't know how many sales you're losing because people are impatient.) As it is, manufacturing can't keep up with the new seasonal design schedule—it can take as long as a year for a new model to get from the design studio to the store shelves. What's worse, when an item becomes hot, your team is unable to quickly change its production to capitalize on the trend. If Vuitton wants to continue to grow, sales volume needs to increase, and the current limitations on your production process are preventing this.

So what is the best way to deal with the pressure toward increased revenue? Many competing brands are starting to make moves to increase sales and reduce customer waiting lists. That means increasing production volume and maybe even creating inventory. How do you accomplish this while maintaining your reputation for high-quality luxury? After all, that's what keeps customers loyal and made you successful in the first place! Finally, when items do become hot, how can you capitalize on the immediate demand? Not only do you need to make more, you need to make more and more quickly. **If you were the COO at Louis Vuitton, what would you do?**

ACTIVITIES + VIDEO

CengageNOW Audio study guide, electronic flashcards, author FAQ videos, On the Job and Biz Flix videos, concept tutorial, and concept exercise

Web (academic.cengage.com/management/williams) Quiz, PowerPoint slides, and glossary terms for this chapter

Study Tip

Studying for comprehensive exams doesn't have to be a chore. Form a study group. Photocopy the glossary at the end of this text, and cut the copies into strips, one term per strip. Put all strips into a large bowl. Divide into two teams and have one team at a time draw out a strip. Quiz the opposing team and then read the correct answer. You can do the same with the chapter outlines at the beginning of each chapter. You can tabulate points, but you'll all win!

"What's New" Companies

Louis Vuitton Manufacturing Plant

Ryanair

McDonald's

Toyota

Dell

Quantum Corporation

Reva

Physio-Control

EMC

Eastman Chemical

Enterprise Rent-A-Car

Freudenberg-NOK

And others . . .

As you read in the opening vignette, Louis Vuitton Manufacturing Plant is trying to increase production volume without sacrificing quality. In this chapter, you will learn about **operations management**—managing the daily production of goods and services. You will begin by learning about the basics of operations management: productivity and quality. Next, you will read about managing operations, beginning with service operations, turning next to manufacturing operations, and finishing with an examination of the types, measures, costs, and methods for managing inventory.

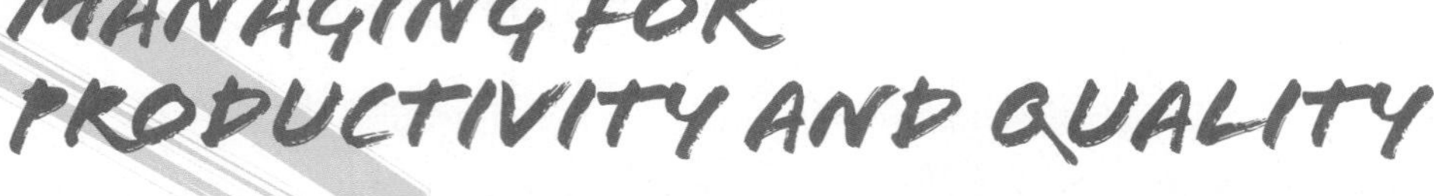

MANAGING FOR PRODUCTIVITY AND QUALITY

You're "crossing the pond" in September to visit your company's European offices and suppliers. Because business is down, your boss has given you a limited budget of $1,600 for airfare. Your round-trip ticket from Chicago to London costs $990 on American Airlines, but that leaves only $610 for airfare in Europe. The total cost of flying from London to Dublin (via British Airways), Dublin to Brussels (via Aer Lingus), Brussels to Venice (via Lufthansa), and Venice to London (via Alitalia) is $1,191—$581 more than your remaining budget and $201 more than your flight from the United States. At lunch, you're griping about the cost of European air travel when the company intern tells you to check out RYANAIR, which she flew when she backpacked in Europe last summer. So, after lunch, you surf to **http://www.ryanair.com** and find that the total cost to travel to the same cities on the same dates and times is an amazing $84, or just 7.5 percent of the cost of flying the other major European airlines!

Modeled after U.S.-based Southwest Airlines, Ryanair achieves dramatically lower prices through aggressive price cutting, much higher productivity, and quality customer service. Want a frequent-flier plan? You won't find one at Ryanair. It's too expensive. Want a meal on your flight? Pack a lunch. Ryanair doesn't even serve peanuts because it takes too much time (and thus expense) to get them out of the seat cushions. Passengers enter and exit the planes using old-fashioned rolling stairs because they're quicker and cheaper than extendable boarding gates. As a result of such cost-cutting moves, Ryanair does more with less and thus has higher productivity. For example, most airlines break even on their flights when they're 75 percent full, but even with its incredibly low prices, Ryanair's productivity allows it to break even when its planes are only half full. And with this low breakeven point, Ryanair attracts plenty of customers, who enable it to fill most of its seats (84 percent) and earn 20 percent net profit margins. Finally, because of its extremely low prices (and its competitors' extremely high prices), Ryanair has increased passenger traffic and profits for 17 straight years.[2]

After reading the next two sections, you should be able to

1 discuss the kinds of productivity and their importance in managing operations.

2 explain the role that quality plays in managing operations.

operations management
managing the daily production of goods and services

1 Productivity

At their core, organizations are production systems. Companies combine inputs, such as labor, raw materials, capital, and knowledge, to produce outputs in the form of finished products or services. **Productivity** is a measure of performance that indicates how many inputs it takes to produce or create an output.

$$\text{Productivity} = \frac{\text{Outputs}}{\text{Inputs}}$$

The fewer inputs it takes to create an output (or the greater the output from one input), the higher the productivity. For example, a car's gas mileage is a common measure of productivity. A car that gets 35 miles (output) per gallon (input) is more productive and fuel efficient than a car that gets 18 miles per gallon.

Let's examine ***1.1 why productivity matters*** *and* ***1.2 the different kinds of productivity****.*

1.1 Why Productivity Matters

Why does productivity matter? For companies, higher productivity, that is, doing more with less, results in lower costs. In turn, doing more with less can lead to lower prices, faster service, higher market share, and higher profits. For example, at fast-food restaurants, every second saved in the drive-through lane increases sales by 1 percent. Furthermore, increasing the efficiency of drive-through service by 10 percent adds nearly 10 percent to a fast-food restaurant's sales. And with 65 percent of all fast-food restaurant sales coming from the drive-through window, it's no wonder that Wendy's (average drive-through time of 124.7 seconds), McDONALD'S (average time of 152.5 seconds), and Burger King (average time of 173.2 seconds) continue to look for ways to shorten the time it takes to process a drive-through order.[3] Productivity matters so much at the drive-through that McDonald's is experimenting with outsourcing its drive-through window operations to remote call centers. When you drive through at roughly 50 McDonald's franchises around the country, your order is taken by someone at a California call center. An operator takes orders from customers at restaurants in Honolulu one minute, and from Gulfport, Mississippi, the next. Although it seems counterintuitive, initial results show the system has improved order-taking accuracy and improved productivity. During the 10 seconds it takes for a car to pull away from the microphone at the drive through, a call center operator can take the order of a different customer who has pulled up to the microphone at another restaurant, even if it's thousands of miles away. According to Jon Anton, cofounder of Bronco Communications, which operates the call center for McDonald's, the goal is "saving seconds to make millions," because more efficient service can lead to more sales and lower labor costs.[4]

For countries, productivity matters because it results in a higher standard of living. One way productivity leads to a higher standard of living is through increased wages. When companies can do more with less, they can raise employee wages without increasing prices or sacrificing normal profits. For instance, when I wrote this chapter, recent government economic data indicated that companies were paying workers 3.5 percent more than in the previous year. But since workers were producing 5.1 percent more than they had the year before, real labor costs had actually decreased by 1.6 percent.[5] How much difference can productivity increases make to wages and standards of living? If productivity grows just 1 percent a year, it will

productivity a measure of performance that indicates how many inputs it takes to produce or create an output

In terms of real purchasing power, productivity gains have actually made today's $29,400 car of today cheaper than that $2,000 car in 1960.

take 70 years to double the standard of living. But if productivity grows 2 percent per year, the standard of living will double in just 35 years. One way to demonstrate this is to examine the effect that productivity has on wages. For example, the average American family earned approximately $56,914 in 2005. If productivity grows 1 percent a year, that family's income will increase to $71,351 in 2030. But if productivity grows 2 percent a year, their annual income in 2030 will be $90,384, more than $18,000 higher, and that's without working longer hours.[6] Thanks to long-term increases in business productivity, the average American family today earns 33 percent more than the average family in 1980 and 223 percent more than the average family in 1953—and that's after accounting for inflation.[7]

Rising income stemming from increased productivity creates numerous other benefits as well. For example, with productivity increases exceeding 3.8 percent per year from 1999 to 2005 the U.S. economy created three million new jobs.[8] In 2005 alone, the economy added two million jobs.[9] And when more people have jobs that pay more, they give more to charity. For example, in 2005 Americans donated over $260 billion to charities, 6.1 percent more than they gave in 2004.[10] Did Americans become more thoughtful, caring, conscientious, and giving? Probably not. Yet, because of strong increases in productivity during that time, the average American family saw its income increase by 15 percent. Because more people earned more money, they were able to share their good fortune with others by giving more to charity.[11]

partial productivity a measure of performance that indicates how much of a particular kind of input it takes to produce an output

Another benefit of productivity is that it makes products more affordable or better. For example, while inflation has pushed the average cost of a car to about $29,400 (after incentives and discounts), increases in productivity have actually made cars cheaper.[12] In 1960, the average family needed 26 weeks of income to pay for the average car. Today, the average family needs only 23.6 weeks of income—and today's car is loaded with accessories that weren't even available in 1960, including air bags, power steering and brakes, power windows, cruise control, stereo/CD/DVD players, seat warmers, air-conditioning, and satellite navigation.[13] So, in terms of real purchasing power, productivity gains have actually made today's $29,400 car of today cheaper than that $2,000 car in 1960.[14]

One of the largest drivers of manufacturing productivity has been the increased use of robotic technology. Using robotics, manufacturing facilities can keep producing through breaks, lunch, and the night to create a 24/7 manufacturing schedule.

COURTESY OF FANUC ROBOTICS AMERICA, INC.

1.2 Kinds of Productivity

Two common measures of productivity are partial productivity and multifactor productivity. **Partial productivity** indicates how much of a particular kind of input it takes to produce an output.

$$\text{Partial Productivity} = \frac{\text{Outputs}}{\text{Single Kind of Input}}$$

Labor is one kind of input that is frequently used when determining partial productivity. *Labor productivity* typically indicates the cost or number of hours of labor it takes to produce an output. In other words, the lower the cost of the labor to produce a unit of output, or the less time it takes to produce a unit of output, the higher the labor productivity. For example, the automobile industry often measures labor productivity by determining the average number of hours of labor needed to completely assemble a car. The three most productive auto manufacturers can assemble a car with 32 or fewer hours of labor. **Toyota** assembles a car in only 27.9 hours of labor, Nissan does it in 29.4 hours, and Honda in 32 hours. These manufacturers have higher labor productivity than General Motors, which needs 34.3 hours of labor to assemble a car, DaimlerChrysler, which needs 35.8 hours, and Ford, which needs 36.9 hours.[15] These lower labor costs give Nissan, Honda, and Toyota an average cost advantage of $350 to $500 per car.[16]

Partial productivity assesses how efficiently companies use only one input, such as labor, when creating outputs. Multifactor productivity is an overall measure of productivity that assesses how efficiently companies use all the inputs it takes to make outputs. More specifically, **multifactor productivity** indicates how much labor, capital, materials, and energy it takes to produce an output.[17]

$$\text{Multifactor Productivity} = \frac{\text{Outputs}}{(\text{Labor} + \text{Capital} + \text{Materials} + \text{Energy})}$$

Exhibit 18.1 shows the trends in multifactor productivity across a number of U.S. industries since 1987. With a 78 percent increase between 1997 (scaled at 100) and 2001 (when it reached a level of 178) and nearly a sixfold increase since 1987, the growth in multifactor productivity in the computers and electronic products industry far exceeded the productivity growth in retail stores, auto manufacturing, mining, utilities, finance and insurance, and air transportation as well as most other industries tracked by the U.S. government.

Of course, the surge in productivity in the computer and electronics industry isn't a surprise. Each round of technology advances brings significantly smaller and cheaper, yet much more powerful electronic devices. Significantly less labor, capital, materials, and energy are needed to produce computers and electronic products (including cell phones, MP3 players, and computer game devices such as the PlayStation 3) today than in the past. An examination of some of the components of multifactor productivity shows how firms in the computer and electronics industry, such as **DELL,** have achieved such large increases in productivity.

multifactor productivity an overall measure of performance that indicates how much labor, capital, materials, and energy it takes to produce an output

First, with respect to labor, every time Dell opens a new factory, it increases productivity by producing more computers with fewer factory workers. John Egan, who directs manufacturing and distribution for one of Dell's most popular computer

Exhibit 18.1

Multifactor Productivity Growth across Industries

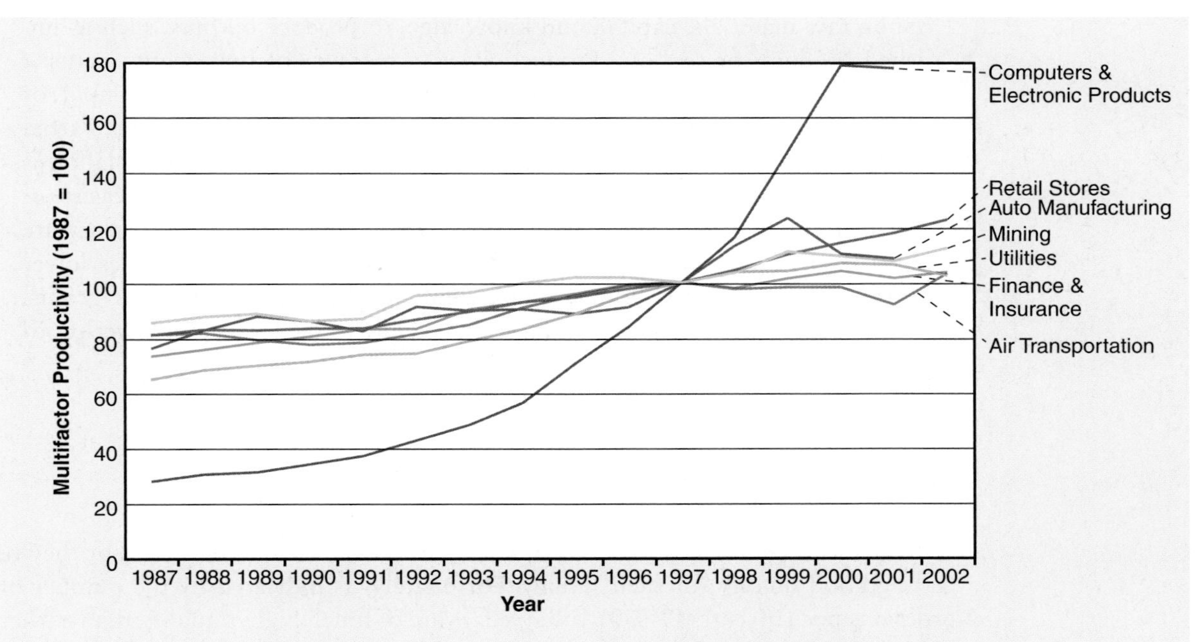

Source: "Productivity and Costs," Bureau of Labor Statistics, available at http://data.bls.gov/cgi-bin/surveymost?ip, 1 July 2005.

lines, says, "Every time [we open a new plant,] we get more and more efficient."[18] In fact, Dell's plant in Austin, Texas, is twice as productive as the plant it replaced. Likewise, Dell saves on labor costs because 95 percent of the orders processed by this plant are handled automatically when customers place their orders on the Internet.

Second, with respect to capital, multifactor productivity assesses how efficiently a company uses the money it spends on equipment, facilities (offices and operating plants), inventories, and land. Dell has greatly increased the productivity of its assembly plants by aggressively cutting costs and by building plants twice as fast as its competitors. For instance, Dell built its new assembly plant in Lebanon, Tennessee, in only 62 days. Dell cut two weeks out of the construction process by picking the architectural firm one morning and then working with the architects from noon until midnight on that same day to put together a construction schedule and budget.[19]

Finally, in terms of materials, that is, the components used to manufacture computers, Dell's new factories have almost no parts or finished product inventory. Computer parts are ordered when customers place their orders. And, according to Sharon Boyle, who manages Dell's Austin plant, "More than 95 percent of the orders received are shipped within eight hours." In fact, when the plant was designed, the company completely eliminated space that would normally hold parts and finished goods.[20]

Should managers use multiple or partial productivity measures? In general, they should use both. Multifactor productivity indicates a company's overall level of productivity relative to its competitors. In the end, that's what counts most. However, multifactor productivity measures don't indicate the specific contributions that labor, capital, materials, or energy make to overall productivity. To analyze the contributions of these individual components, managers need to use partial productivity measures.

Review 1: **Productivity**

At their core, companies are production systems that combine inputs, such as labor, raw materials, capital, and knowledge, to produce outputs, such as finished products or services. Productivity is a measure of how many inputs it takes to produce or create an output. The greater the output from one input, or the fewer inputs it takes to create an output, the higher the productivity. Partial productivity measures how much of a single kind of input, such as labor, is needed to produce an output. Multifactor productivity is an overall measure of productivity that indicates how much labor, capital, materials, and energy are needed to produce an output. Increased productivity helps companies lower costs, which can lead to lower prices, higher market share, and higher profits. Increased productivity helps countries by leading to higher wages, lower product prices, and a higher standard of living.

2 Quality

With the average car costing $29,400, car buyers want to make sure that they're getting good quality for their money. Fortunately, as indicated by the number of problems per 100 cars (PP100), today's cars are of much higher quality than earlier models. In 1981, Japanese cars averaged 240 PP100. General Motors' cars averaged

670, Ford's averaged 740, and Chrysler's averaged 870 PP100! In other words, as measured by PP100, the quality of American cars was two to three times worse than Japanese cars. By 1992, however, U.S. carmakers had made great strides, significantly reducing the number of problems to an average of 155 PP100. Japanese vehicles had improved, too, averaging just 125 PP100. Exhibit 18.2 shows the results of the 2006 J. D. Power and Associates survey of initial car quality. Porsche, with just 91 PP100, had the best quality, followed by Lexus at 93 PP100 and Hyundai at 102 PP100; at the bottom of the list were Isuzu, with 191 PPM, and Land Rover, with 204 PP100, had the worst.[21]

The American Society for Quality gives two meanings for **quality**. It can mean a product or service free of deficiencies, such as the number of problems per 100 cars, or it can mean the characteristics of a product or service that satisfy customer needs.[22] In this sense, today's cars with their additional standard features (power brakes and steering, stereo/CD player, power windows and locks, air bags, cruise control) are of higher quality than those produced 20 years ago.

In this part of the chapter, you will learn about ***2.1 quality-related characteristics for products and services, 2.2 ISO 9000 and 14000, 2.3 the Baldrige National Quality Award****, and* ***2.4 total quality management****.*

2.1 Quality-Related Characteristics for Products and Services

As shown in Exhibit 18.3, quality products usually possess three characteristics: reliability, serviceability, and durability.[23] A breakdown occurs when a product

quality a product or service free of deficiencies, or the characteristics of a product or service that satisfy customer needs

Exhibit 18.2

J. D. Power and Associates Survey of Initial Car Quality

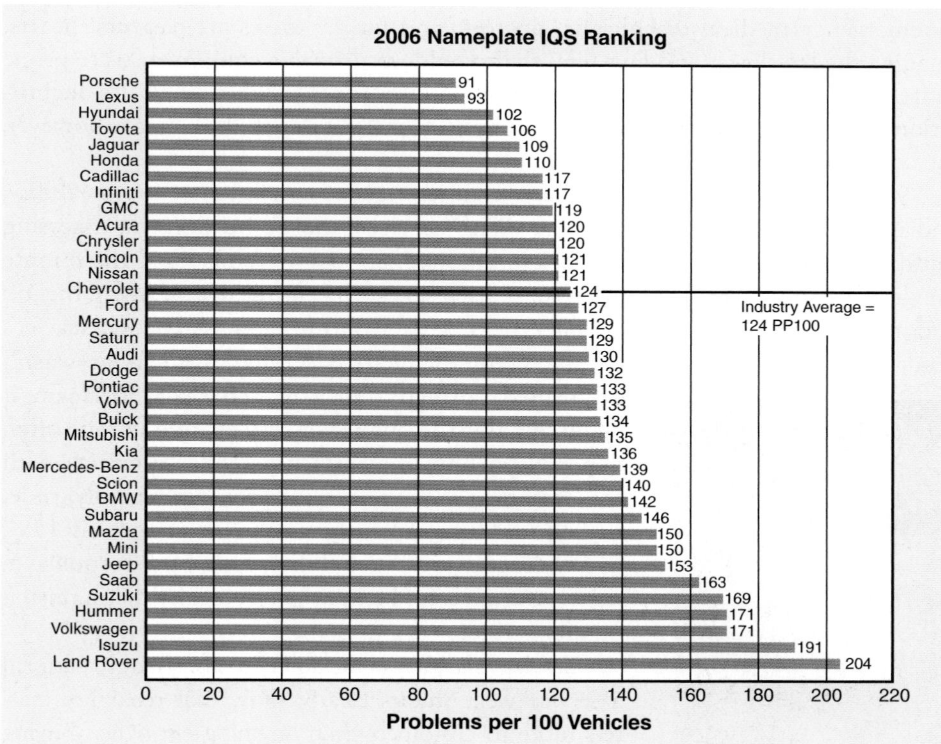

NOTE: Due to changes in study methodology, 2006 IQS scores are not comparable to previous years' scores. Scores are based on rounded figures for problems per 100 vehicles.

Source: "J. D. Power and Associates 2006 Initial Quality Study (IQS)," J. D. Power and Associates, http://www.jdpower.com/auots/quality-ratings, 10 March 2007.

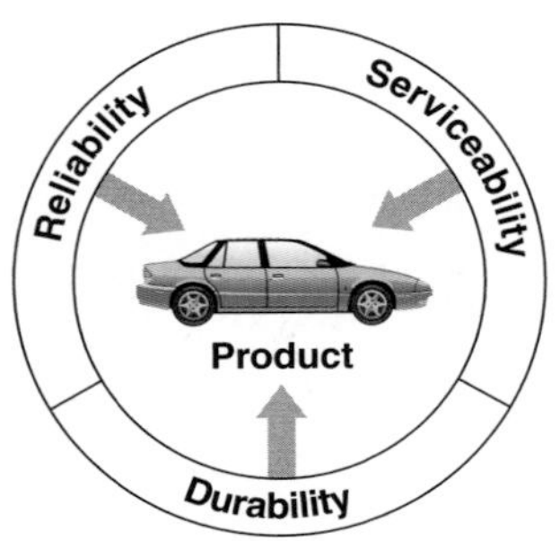

Exhibit 18.3
Characteristics of Product Quality

quits working or doesn't do what it was designed to do. The longer it takes for a product to break down, or the longer the time between breakdowns, the more reliable the product. Consequently, many companies define *product reliability* in terms of the average time between breakdowns. For example, **QUANTUM CORPORATION** sells the SDLT 600, a computer tape drive that customers can use to back up 600 gigabytes of data. The SDLT 600 is so reliable that the estimated mean time between breakdowns is 250,000 hours, or more than 28.5 years![24] Of course, this is just an average. Some SDLT 600 tape drives will break down much sooner, but others will last even longer than 28.5 years.

Serviceability refers to how easy or difficult it is to fix a product. The easier it is to maintain a working product or fix a broken product, the more serviceable that product is. The **REVA** is an electric two-seater car, built in India, for city use. It goes 50 miles on a single battery charge (a recharge takes just five hours), and its operating costs per mile are one-third that of a typical gasoline-powered car. The Reva has high serviceability by virtue of a computerized diagnostic system that plugs into a portable electronic tool (PET) about the size of a personal digital assistant that assesses how well the car is running. Because the PET can be linked to a phone, customers can easily transmit their Reva's operational history to instantly find out if their car needs work and, if so, what kind. In many instances, a simple computer change downloaded to the PET and then to the Reva will fix the problem.[25]

A product breakdown assumes that a product can be repaired. However, some products don't break down—they fail. *Product failure* means products can't be repaired. They can only be replaced. Thus, durability is a quality characteristic that applies to products that can't be repaired. *Durability* is defined as the mean time to failure. Durability is crucial for products such as the defibrillation equipment used by emergency medical technicians, doctors, and nurses to restart patients' hearts. Imagine the lost lives (and lawsuits) that would occur if this equipment were prone to frequent failure. The mean time between failures for **PHYSIO-CONTROL**'s defibrillation units is 55.6 to 69.4 years.[26] If a Physio-Control Lifepak does break, however, the company replaces it within 24 hours.

While high-quality products are characterized by reliability, serviceability, and durability, services are different. With services, there's no point in assessing durability. Unlike products, services don't last. Services are consumed the minute they're performed. For example, once a lawn service has mowed your lawn, the job is done until the mowers come back next week to do it again. Likewise, services don't have serviceability. You can't maintain or fix a service. If a service wasn't performed correctly, all you can do is perform it again. Finally, the quality of service interactions often depends on how the service provider interacts with the customer. Was the service provider friendly, rude, or helpful? Consequently, as shown in Exhibit 18.4, five characteristics—reliability, tangibles, responsiveness, assurance, and empathy—typically distinguish a quality service.[27]

An electric Reva automobile drives along a city street during Bangalore's celebration of World Environment Day. Reva uses a computer diagnostic system that can sync to the owner's cell phone and indicate the type of service the vehicle needs.

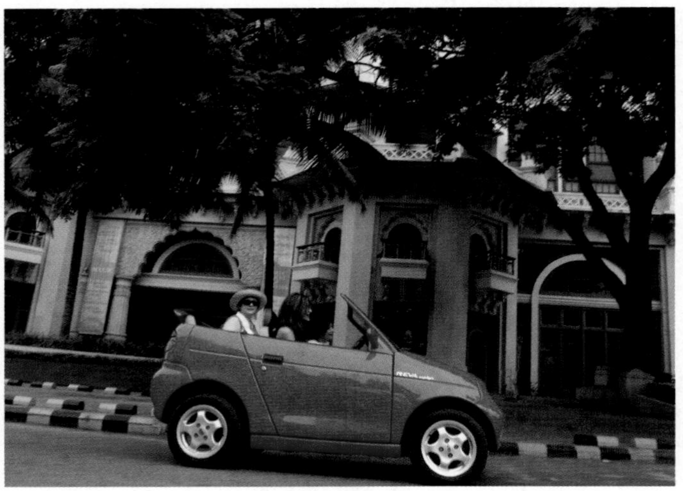

AFP/GETTY IMAGES

Service reliability is the ability to consistently perform a service well. Studies clearly show that reliability matters more to customers than anything else when buying services. Also, although services themselves are not tangible (you can't see or touch them), services are provided in tangible places. Thus, *tangibles* refer to the appearance of the offices, equipment, and personnel involved with the delivery of a service. *Responsiveness* is the promptness and willingness with which service providers give good service. *Assurance* is the confidence that service providers are knowledgeable, courteous, and trustworthy. *Empathy* is the extent to which service providers give individual attention and care to customers' concerns and problems.

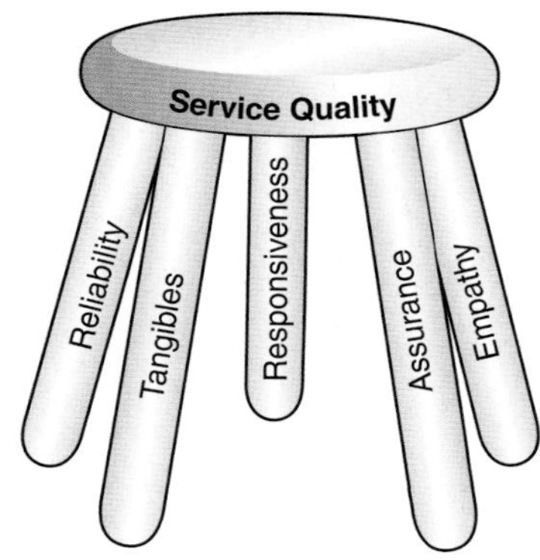

Exhibit 18.4
Characteristics of Service Quality

EMC Corporation makes highly reliable computers that are used by some of the largest companies in the world (including banks, phone companies, and auto manufacturers). If EMC's equipment goes down for even a few minutes, its customers can lose millions from vanished sales. While its equipment is incredibly reliable, what distinguishes EMC from its competition is the level of service it provides when problems occur. In other words, EMC is a standout performer in *service reliability*, the ability to consistently perform a service well. Because of its excellent service, EMC retains an amazing 99 percent of its customers from year to year. When Carl Howe of Forrester Research, a marketing research firm, asked 50 *Fortune* 500 companies about the technology companies they worked with, "EMC came out looking like God." Howe says EMC "had the best customer-service reviews we have ever seen, in any industry."[28]

EMC also excels in *responsiveness*, the promptness and willingness with which service providers give good service. When a Wisconsin bank lost access to all its data (no account numbers, no deposits, no withdrawals, nada!), which were stored on an EMC machine, EMC service engineers were on the problem within minutes (EMC's computers "call home" automatically whenever a problem arises). In four hours EMC had created a setup identical to the bank's in a $1 billion facility designed for such purposes, where EMC engineers identified the problem and put together a software patch that had the bank up and running by the end of the day.[29]

EMC provides quality service by virtue of clear *assurance* that it can be trusted. Every customer knows that the company follows a disciplined procedure for addressing customer problems. First, every EMC system does a self-check every two hours to make sure it is running the way it's supposed to. If even the slightest thing is wrong, the system "phones home" to tell EMC's engineers what's happening. EMC gets 3,500 such "calls" from its machines and systems every day. Second, if a problem isn't fixed within four hours, Leo Colborne, the vice president of global technical support, is notified. After six hours, Colborne's boss, the senior vice president of global customer services, is contacted. After eight hours, the company's CEO and chairman are notified. In most cases, the CEO will leave immediately to visit the customer, apologize for the problem, reassure the customer that everything is being done to solve the problem, and begin working with the customer to implement procedures or solutions to prevent the problem from recurring in the future.[30]

Finally, EMC provides quality service because of the *empathy* it has for its customers' problems. Indeed, early in the company's history, its customers' businesses were suffering because EMC could not figure out why one of its best-selling systems had unexpectedly become unreliable. With key information systems frozen up, business ground to a halt for major customers. Rather than make excuses or empty promises, EMC gave its customers the choice between a brand new EMC computer system or a similar system, made by EMC's competitor, IBM. At the height of its problems, EMC installed more of IBM's machines than its own. But the company benefited in the long run as customers realized that EMC would do almost anything to solve their problems. And once EMC solved the problems with that machine, customers trusted the company enough to begin ordering again. EMC's then-CEO said, "What that proved to me, to all of us, was that when a customer believes in you, and you go to great lengths to preserve that relationship, they'll stick with you almost no matter what. It opened our eyes to the power of customer service."[31]

2.2 ISO 9000 and 14000

ISO, pronounced *ice-o*, comes from the Greek word *isos*, meaning *equal*, *similar*, *alike*, or *identical*. **ISO 9000** is a series of five international standards, from ISO 9000 to ISO 9004, for achieving consistency in quality management and quality assurance in companies throughout the world. **ISO 14000** is a series of international standards for managing, monitoring, and minimizing an organization's harmful effects on the environment.[32] (For more on environmental quality and issues, see Section 3.5 on controlling waste and pollution in Chapter 16.) The ISO 9000 and 14000 standards were created by the International Organization for Standardization, an international agency that helps set standards for 157 countries. The purpose of this agency is to develop and publish standards that facilitate the international exchange of goods and services.[33]

The ISO 9000 standards publications, which are available from the American National Standards Institute (see the end of this section), are general and can be used for manufacturing any kind of product or delivering any kind of service. Importantly, the ISO 9000 standards don't describe how to make a better-quality car, computer, or widget. Instead, they describe how companies can extensively document (and thus standardize) the steps they take to create and improve the quality of their products. Why should companies go to the trouble to achieve ISO 9000 certification? The reason is that, increasingly, their customers want them to. In fact, studies show that customers clearly prefer to buy from companies that are ISO 9000 certified. Companies, in turn, believe that being ISO 9000 certified helps them keep customers who might otherwise switch to an ISO 9000 certified competitor.[34]

Typically, "getting" ISO 9000 means having your company certified for ISO 9000 registration by an accredited third party. ISO 9000 certification is similar to having a certified public accountant indicate that a company's financial accounts are up-to-date and accurate. Like an accountant's audit, the certification process can take months. But in this case, the certification is for quality, not accounting procedures. To become certified, a company must show that it is following its own procedures for improving production, updating design plans and specifications, keeping machinery in top condition, educating and training workers, and satisfactorily dealing with customer complaints.[35]

Once a company has been certified as ISO 9000 compliant, the accredited third party will issue an ISO 9000 certificate that the company can use in its advertising and publications. This is the quality equivalent of the Good Housekeeping Seal of Approval. Continued ISO 9000 certification is not guaranteed, however. Accredited third parties typically conduct periodic audits to make sure the company is still following quality procedures. If it is not, its certification is suspended or canceled.

It's estimated that more than half of mid-sized U.S. manufacturers have achieved ISO 9000 certification. Two-thirds of the certified companies say they wanted certification because it increases customer satisfaction. Accordingly, most advertise their ISO certification in their promotional materials and mention or even post it on their website. For example, Midmark Medical Equipment, a maker of examination tables, sterilizers, electrocardiograms, and the like, has posted its certificate at **http://www.midmark.com/iso9000.asp** and states, "Midmark is proud to have the distinction of receiving the ISO 9001 certification for quality." See the American National Standards Institute (**http://www.ansi.org**; the ISO 9000 and ISO 14000 standards publications are available here for about $600 and $100, respectively), the American Society for Quality (**http://www.asq.org**), and the International Organization for Standardization (**http://www.iso.ch**) for additional information on ISO 9000 guidelines and procedures.

ISO 9000 a series of five international standards, from ISO 9000 to ISO 9004, for achieving consistency in quality management and quality assurance in companies throughout the world

ISO 14000 a series of international standards for managing, monitoring, and minimizing an organization's harmful effects on the environment

2.3 Baldrige National Quality Award

The Baldrige National Quality Award, which is administered by the U.S. government's National Institute for Standards and Technology, is given "to recognize U.S. companies for their achievements in quality and business performance and to raise awareness about the importance of quality and performance excellence as a competitive edge."[36] Each year, up to three awards may be given in these categories: manufacturing, service, small business, education, and healthcare (the latter two categories were added in 1999). Exhibit 18.5 lists the latest Baldrige Award winners.

The cost of applying for the Baldrige Award is $5,000 for manufacturing and service companies and $2,000 for small businesses.[37] At a minimum, each company that applies receives an extensive report based on 300 hours of assessment from at least eight business and quality experts. At $6.67 an hour for small businesses and about $16.67 an hour for manufacturing and service businesses, the *Journal for Quality and Participation* called the Baldrige feedback report "the best bargain in consulting in America."[38] Arnold Weimerskirch, former chair of the Baldrige Award panel of judges and vice president of quality at Honeywell, says, "The application and review process for the Baldrige Award is the best, most cost-effective and comprehensive business health audit you can get."[39]

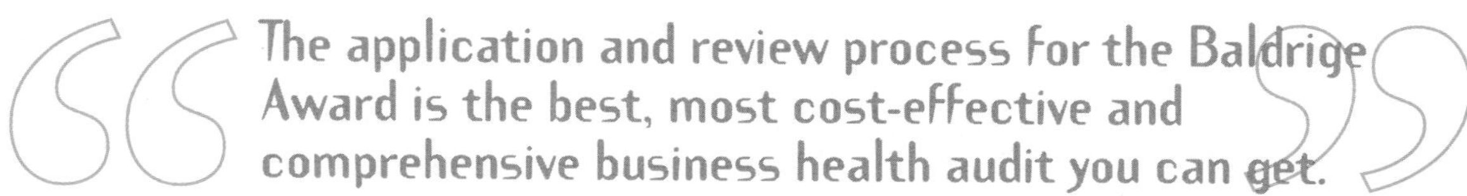
The application and review process for the Baldrige Award is the best, most cost-effective and comprehensive business health audit you can get.

ARNOLD WEIMERSKIRCH, FORMER CHAIR, BALDRIGE AWARD PANEL OF JUDGES, AND VICE PRESIDENT OF QUALITY, HONEYWELL

The criteria for the Baldrige Award are different for business, education, and health-care organizations. As shown in Exhibit 18.6, businesses that apply for the Baldrige Award are judged on a 1,000-point scale based on seven criteria: leadership; strategic planning; customer and market focus; measurement, analysis, and knowledge management; workforce focus; process management; and results.[40] With 450 out of 1,000 points, "results" are clearly the most important. In other words, in addition to the six other criteria, companies must show that they have achieved superior quality when it comes to products and services, customers, financial performance and market share, treatment of employees, organizational effectiveness, and leadership and social responsibility. This emphasis on "results" is what differentiates the Baldrige Award from the ISO 9000 standards. The Baldrige Award indicates the

Exhibit 18.5

Latest Baldrige National Quality Award Recipients

Sector	2005	2006
Manufacturing	Sunny Fresh Foods, Inc.	——
Education	Jenks Public Schools	——
	Richland College	
Health care	Bronson Methodist Hospital	North Mississippi Medical Center
Service	DynMcDermott Petroleum Operations Co.	Premier, Inc.
Small business	Park Place Lexus	MESA Products, Inc.

Source: "1988–2006 Award Recipients' Contacts and Profiles," National Institute of Standards and Technology, http://www.quality.nist.gov/Contacts_Profiles.htm, 7 April 2007.

	2007 Categories and Items	Point Values
1	**Leadership**	**120**
1.1	Senior Leadership	70
1.2	Governance and Social Responsibilities	50
2	**Strategic Planning**	**85**
2.1	Strategy Development	40
2.2	Strategy Deployment	45
3	**Customer and Market Focus**	**85**
3.1	Customer and Market Knowledge	40
3.2	Customer Relationships and Satisfaction	45
4	**Measurement, Analysis, and Knowledge Management**	**90**
4.1	Measurement, Analysis, and Improvement of Organizational Performance	45
4.2	Management of Information, Information Technology, and Knowledge	45
5	**Workforce Focus**	**85**
5.1	Workforce Engagement	45
5.2	Workforce Environment	40
6	**Process Management**	**85**
6.1	Work Systems Design	35
6.2	Work Process Management and Improvement	50
7	**Results**	**450**
7.1	Product and Service Outcomes	100
7.2	Customer-Focused Outcomes	70
7.3	Financial and Market Outcomes	70
7.4	Workforce-Focused Outcomes	70
7.5	Process Effectiveness Outcomes	70
7.6	Leadership Outcomes	70
	TOTAL POINTS	**1,000**

Source: "Criteria for Performance Excellence," Baldrige National Quality Program 2007, available at http://www.quality.nist.gov/PDF_files/2007_Business_Nonprofit_Criteria.pdf, 7 April 2007.

Exhibit 18.6

Criteria for the Baldrige National Quality Award

extent to which companies have actually achieved world-class quality. The ISO 9000 standards simply indicate whether a company is following the management system it put in place to improve quality. In fact, ISO 9000 certification covers less than 10 percent of the requirements for the Baldrige Award.[41]

Why should companies go to the trouble of applying for the Baldrige Award? Earnest Deavenport, CEO of **Eastman Chemical**, explains, "Eastman, like other Baldrige Award winners, didn't apply the concepts of total quality management to win an award. We did it to win customers. We did it to grow. We did it to prosper and to remain competitive in a world marketplace."[42] Furthermore, the companies that have won the Baldrige Award have achieved superior financial returns. Since 1988, an investment in Baldrige Award winners would have outperformed the Standard & Poor's 500 stock index 80 percent of the time.[43] For additional information about the Baldrige Award, see the National Institute of Standards and Technology website at **http://www.quality.nist.gov.**

2.4 Total Quality Management

Total quality management (TQM) is an integrated organization-wide strategy for improving product and service quality.[44] TQM is not a specific tool or technique. Rather, TQM is a philosophy or overall approach to management that is characterized by three principles: customer focus and satisfaction, continuous improvement, and teamwork.[45]

Contrary to most economists, accountants, and financiers who argue that companies exist to earn profits for shareholders, TQM suggests that customer focus and customer satisfaction should be a company's primary goals. **Customer focus** means that the entire organization, from top to bottom, should be focused on meeting customers' needs. The result of that customer focus should be **customer satisfaction**, which occurs when the company's products or services meet or exceed customers' expectations. At companies where TQM is taken seriously, such as **ENTERPRISE RENT-A-CAR**, paychecks and promotions depend on keeping customers satisfied.[46] For example, Enterprise Rent-a-Car measures customer satisfaction with a detailed survey called the Enterprise Service Quality index. Enterprise not only ranks each branch office by operating profits and customer satisfaction, but it also makes promotions to higher-paying jobs contingent on above-average customer satisfaction scores. According to Andy Taylor, Enterprise's CEO, "Once we showed we were serious—a couple of star performers who had achieved good growth and profit numbers but had generated below-average satisfaction scores were passed over for promotions—all doubt about the importance of the scores vanished."[47] Not surprisingly, this emphasis on quality increased the number of completely satisfied Enterprise Rent-a-Car customers from the high 60 percent range to the high 70 percent range in just five years. As a result, Enterprise customers are three times more likely to rent an Enterprise car again than are customers of other car rental companies.

total quality management (TQM) an integrated, principle-based, organization-wide strategy for improving product and service quality

customer focus an organizational goal to concentrate on meeting customers' needs at all levels of the organization

customer satisfaction an organizational goal to provide products or services that meet or exceed customers' expectations

continuous improvement an organization's ongoing commitment to constantly assess and improve the processes and procedures used to create products and services

variation a deviation in the form, condition, or appearance of a product from the quality standard for that product

Continuous improvement is an ongoing commitment to increase product and service quality by constantly assessing and improving the processes and procedures used to create those products and services. How do companies know whether they're achieving continuous improvement? Besides higher customer satisfaction, continuous improvement is usually associated with a reduction in variation. **Variation** is a deviation in the form, condition, or appearance of a product from the quality standard for that product. The less a product varies from the quality standard, or the more consistently a company's products meet a quality standard, the higher the quality. At **FREUDENBERG-NOK**, a manufacturer of seals and gaskets for the automotive industry, continuous improvement means shooting for a goal of "Six Sigma" quality, meaning just 3.4 defective or nonstandard parts per million (PPM). Achieving this goal would eliminate almost all product variation. In a recent year, Freudenberg-NOK made over 200 million seals and gaskets with a defect rate of 9 PPM.[48] As Exhibit 18.7 shows, this almost puts Freudenberg-NOK at Six Sigma, or 3.4 defective PPM. Furthermore, this represents a significant improvement from seven years ago when Freudenberg-NOK was averaging 650 defective PPM. General manager Gary VanWambeke says, "The whole goal is variation reduction," so Freudenberg-NOK expects the quality of its products to continue to improve.[49]

Exhibit 18.7

Number of Defects per Million with Six Sigma Quality

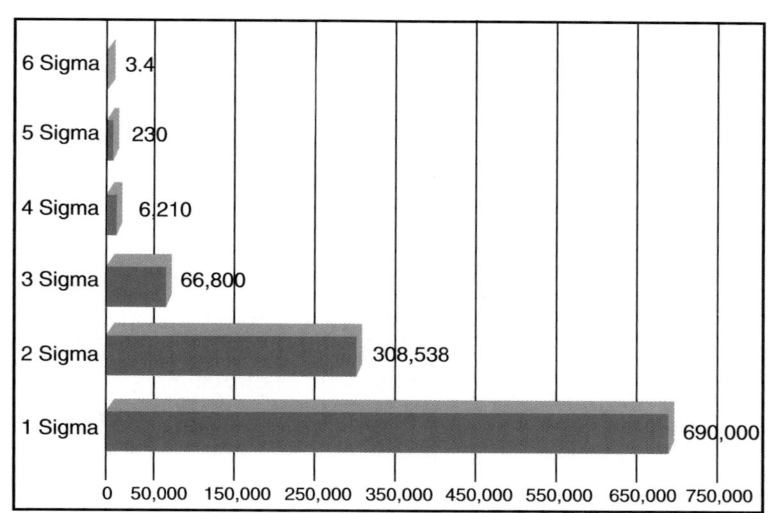

© IMAGE100/JUPITER IMAGES

Reduction in variation is typically associated with even (and higher) quality. The pinnacle is achieving only 3.4 nonconforming parts per million which indicates attainment of Six Sigma.

The third principle of TQM is teamwork. **Teamwork** means collaboration between managers and nonmanagers, across business functions, and between the company and its customers and suppliers. In short, quality improves when everyone in the company is given the incentive to work together and the responsibility and authority to make improvements and solve problems. At Valassis, a printing company long famous for its use of teams, management turned to employees for additional suggestions when business fell during a recession. Teams offered so many ideas to cut costs and raise quality that the company was able to avoid layoffs.[50]

Together, customer focus and satisfaction, continuous improvement, and teamwork mutually reinforce each other to improve quality throughout a company. Customer-focused continuous improvement is necessary to increase customer satisfaction. At the same time, continuous improvement depends on teamwork from different functional and hierarchical parts of the company.

Review 2: Quality

Quality can mean a product or service free of deficiencies or the characteristics of a product or service that satisfy customer needs. Quality products usually possess three characteristics: reliability, serviceability, and durability. Quality service means reliability, tangibles, responsiveness, assurance, and empathy. ISO 9000 is a series of five international standards for achieving consistency in quality management and quality assurance, while ISO 14000 is a set of standards for minimizing an organization's harmful effects on the environment. The ISO 9000 standards can be used for any product or service because they ensure that companies carefully document the steps they take to create and improve quality. ISO 9000 certification is awarded following a quality audit from an accredited third party. The Baldrige National Quality Award recognizes U.S. companies for their achievements in quality and business performance. Each year, up to three Baldrige Awards may be given for manufacturing, service, small business, education, and health care. Companies that apply for the Baldrige Award are judged on a 1,000-point scale based on leadership; strategic planning; customer and market focus; measurement, analysis, and knowledge management; workforce focus; process management; and results. Total quality management (TQM) is an integrated organization-wide strategy for improving product and service quality. TQM is based on three mutually reinforcing principles: customer focus and satisfaction, continuous improvement, and teamwork.

MANAGING OPERATIONS

At the start of this chapter, you learned that operations management means managing the daily production of goods and services. Then you learned that to manage production, you must oversee the factors that affect productivity and quality. In this half of the chapter, you will learn about managing operations in service and manufacturing businesses. The chapter ends with a discussion of inventory management, a key factor in a company's profitability.

teamwork collaboration between managers and nonmanagers, across business functions, and between companies, customers, and suppliers

After reading the next three sections, you should be able to

3 *explain the essentials of managing a service business.*
4 *describe the different kinds of manufacturing operations.*
5 *explain why and how companies should manage inventory levels.*

3 Service Operations

Imagine that your trusty VCR breaks down as you try to record your favorite TV show. (You're still saving your money for a TiVo.) You've got two choices. You can run to Wal-Mart and spend $45 to $75 to purchase a new VCR, or you can spend about the same amount (you hope) to have it fixed at a repair shop. Either way you end up with the same thing, a working VCR. However, the first choice, getting a new VCR, involves buying a physical product (a "good"), while the second, dealing with a repair shop, involves buying a service.

Services differ from goods in several ways. First, goods are produced or made, but services are performed. In other words, services are almost always labor-intensive: Someone typically has to perform the service for you. A repair shop could give you the parts needed to repair your old VCR, but without the technician to perform the repairs, you're still going to have a broken VCR. Second, goods are tangible, but services are intangible. You can touch and see that new VCR, but you can't touch or see the service provided by the technician who fixed your old VCR. All you can "see" is that the VCR works. Third, services are perishable and unstorable. If you don't use them when they're available, they're wasted. For example, if your VCR repair shop is backlogged on repair jobs, then you'll just have to wait until next week to get your VCR repaired. You can't store an unused service and use it when you like. By contrast, you can purchase a good, such as motor oil, and store it until you're ready to use it. Finally, services account for 59.1 percent of gross national product whereas manufacturing accounts for only 30.9 percent.[51] So any review of operations management would be incomplete without an examination of how to manage service operations.

Because services are different from goods, managing a service operation is different from managing a manufacturing or production operation. Let's look at ***3.1 the service-profit chain*** *and* ***3.2 service recovery and empowerment****.*

3.1 The Service-Profit Chain

One of the key assumptions in the service business is that success depends on how well employees, that is, service providers, deliver their services to customers. However, the concept of the service-profit chain, depicted in Exhibit 18.8, suggests that in service businesses, success begins with how well management treats service employees.[52]

The first step in the service-profit chain is *internal service quality*, meaning the quality of treatment that employees receive from a company's internal service providers, such as management, payroll and benefits, human resources, and so forth. For example, **SOUTHWEST AIRLINES**, which has the cheapest fares in the airline industry,

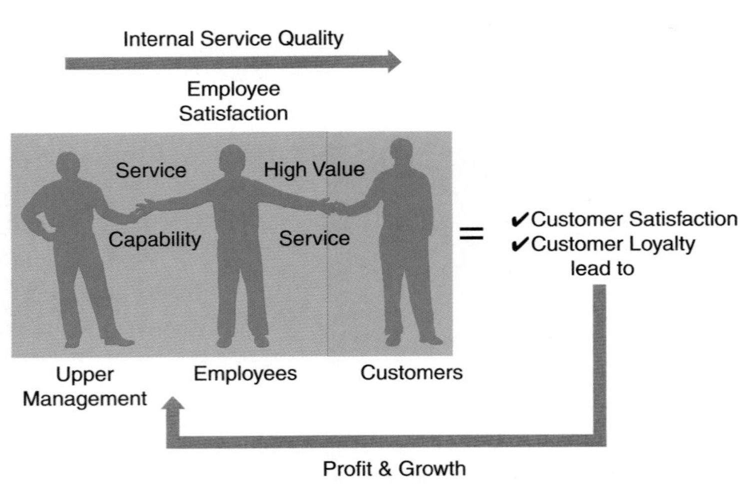

Sources: R. Hallowell, L. A. Schlesinger, & J. Zornitsky, "Internal Service Quality, Customer and Job Satisfaction: Linkages and Implications for Management," *Human Resource Planning* 19 (1996): 20–31; J. L. Heskett, T. O. Jones, G. W. Loveman, W. E. Sasser, Jr., & L. A. Schlesinger, "Putting the Service-Profit Chain to Work," *Harvard Business Review*, March–April 1994, 164–174.

Exhibit 18.8

Service-Profit Chain

is legendary for its excellent treatment of employees and, to the surprise of many, its great customer service. Southwest's chairman Herb Kelleher says, "In the old days, my mother told me that in business school they'd say, 'This is a real conundrum: Who comes first, your employees, your shareholders, or your customers?' My mother taught me that your employees come first. If you treat them well, then they treat the customers well, and that means your customers come back and your shareholders are happy."[53]

Exhibit 18.9 defines the elements that constitute good internal service quality. For employees to do a good job serving customers, management must implement policies and procedures that support good customer service; provide workers the tools and training they need to do their jobs; reward, recognize, and support good customer service; facilitate communication; and encourage people and departments to work together as teams to accomplish company goals with respect to internal service quality and customer service. For example, at **CVS**, a large drugstore chain, the first step was to reward good customer service. CEO Tom Ryan says, "My bonus, the store manager's bonus, the assistant manager's bonus, the guys in information systems . . . a significant amount is based on customer service. We are 100 percent focused on it, and we are passionate about it." As the second step, CVS developed a special monthly scorecard to measure and reward internal service quality for 19 different areas in the company. Executive vice president Deborah Ellinger explains, "The [internal] service ethic is something that we think is important throughout the company. We can't expect our stores to be good at [customer] service if we don't provide them with good [internal] service."[54] Since CVS instituted the monthly scorecard, internal service quality ratings are up by 30 percent.[55]

Exhibit 18.9

Components of Internal Service Quality

Policies and Procedures	Do policies and procedures facilitate serving customers?
Tools	Has the organization provided service employees the tools they need to serve customers?
Effective Training	Is effective, useful, job-specific training made available in a timely fashion?
Rewards and Recognition	Are individuals rewarded and/or recognized for good performance?
Communication	Does necessary communication occur both vertically and horizontally throughout the organization?
Management Support	Does management aid (versus hinder) employees' ability to serve customers?
Goal Alignment	Are the goals of senior management aligned with the goals of frontline service employees?
Teamwork	Do individuals and departments engage in teamwork when necessary?

Source: R. Hallowell, L. A. Schlesinger, & J. Zornitsky, "Internal Service Quality, Customer and Job Satisfaction: Linkages and Implications for Management," *Human Resource Planning* 19 (1996):20–31.

As depicted in Exhibit 18.8, good internal service leads to employee satisfaction and service capability. *Employee satisfaction* occurs when companies treat employees in a way that meets or exceeds their expectations. In other words, the better employees are treated, the more satisfied they are, and the more likely they are to give high-value service that satisfies customers.

Service capability is an employee's perception of his or

her ability to serve customers well. When an organization serves its employees in ways that help them to do their jobs well, employees, in turn, are more likely to believe that they can and ought to provide high-value service to customers. Again, Southwest Airlines not only treats its employees well, but also takes a number of direct steps to strengthen their service capability. Chairman Herb Kelleher says, "I can't anticipate all of the situations that will arise at the stations [airport terminals] across our system. So what we tell our people is, 'Hey, we can't anticipate all of these things; *you* handle them the best way possible. *You* make a judgment and use *your* discretion; we trust you'll do the right thing. If we think you've done something erroneous, we'll let you know—without criticism, without backbiting.'"[56]

Finally, according to the service-profit chain shown in Exhibit 18.8, *high-value service* leads to *customer satisfaction* and *customer loyalty*, which, in turn, lead to *long-term profits and growth*. What's the link between customer satisfaction and loyalty and profits? To start, the average business keeps only 70 to 90 percent of its existing customers each year. No big deal, you say? Just replace leaving customers with new customers. Well, there's one significant problem with that solution. It costs 5 times as much to find a new customer as it does to keep an existing customer. Also, new customers typically buy only 20 percent as much as established customers. In fact, keeping existing customers is so cost-effective that most businesses could double their profits by simply keeping 5 percent more customers per year![57]

One service company that understands the relationship between high-value service, customer loyalty, and profits is **USAA**, a Texas-based finance/insurance company. USAA sends booklets on how to save for a college education to its customers who have young children. When its customers near the age of 50, the company contacts them about retirement and estate planning. And when USAA issues credit cards to college students, it takes the time to teach them how to manage their credit and avoid excessive credit card debt. Says USAA vice president Phyllis Stahle, "We build loyalty by convincing [customers] we're loyal to them."[58] Indeed, USAA has a 97 percent customer retention rate!

3.2 Service Recovery and Empowerment

When mistakes are made, when problems occur, and when customers become dissatisfied with the service they've received, service businesses must switch from the process of service delivery to the process of **service recovery**, that is, restoring customer satisfaction to strongly dissatisfied customers.[59] Sometimes, service recovery requires service employees to not only fix whatever mistake was made, but also perform heroic service acts that delight highly dissatisfied customers by far surpassing their expectations of fair treatment. When accountant Tom Taylor checked into his room at a **Hampton Inn** in Greenville, South Carolina, he wasn't happy. The company website had given him incorrect directions. The lights in his room weren't plugged in. The shower controls were backwards—"hot" was cold and "cold" was hot. And the air-conditioning was malfunctioning, so his room was freezing cold. When he complained, the employee at the front desk immediately offered him two free nights of lodging. Taylor was delighted by the offer, but since he thought it was excessive, he took just one free night.[60]

Unfortunately, when mistakes occur, service employees often don't have the discretion to resolve customer complaints. Customers who want service employees to correct or make up for poor service are frequently told, "I'm not allowed to do that," "I'm just following company rules," or "I'm sorry, only managers are allowed to make changes of any kind." In other words, company rules prevent them from engaging in acts of service recovery meant to turn dissatisfied customers back into

service recovery restoring customer satisfaction to strongly dissatisfied customers

doing the right thing

Protect Your Frontline Staff: The Customer Isn't Always Right

In 1909, Harry Gordon Selfridge, an American who founded London's famous Selfridge's department store, coined the phrase "The customer is always right." Though managers and employees should do what they can to provide great service and make up for mistakes with great service recovery, the customer isn't always right. Companies should fire customers who use foul language, make threats against employees or other customers, lie, demand unethical or illegal service, try to bully frontline employees into granting special favors, or are just generally belligerent. Management consultant John Curtis says, "If you don't [fire these customers], you're telling your employees and your other customers that you care more about money than the safety of the people in the business." So, do the right thing. Protect your frontline staff by telling bad customers that you won't tolerate these kinds of behavior. Ask them to leave. Close their accounts. Inform them that they'll need to go elsewhere.[61]

satisfied customers. The result is frustration for customers and service employees and lost customers for the company.

Now, however, many companies are empowering their service employees.[62] In Chapter 9, you learned that *empowering workers* means permanently passing decision-making authority and responsibility from managers to workers. With respect to service recovery, empowering workers means giving service employees the authority and responsibility to make decisions that immediately solve customer problems.[63] At Hampton Inn, all employees are empowered to solve customer problems. Senior vice president Phil Cordell says, "You don't have to call an 800 number. Just mention it at the front desk or to any employee—a housekeeper, maintenance person or breakfast hostess—and, on the spot, your stay is free."[64]

In short, the purpose of empowering service employees is zero customer defections, that is, to turn dissatisfied customers back into satisfied customers who continue to do business with the company.

Empowering service workers does entail some costs, although they are usually less than the company's savings from retaining customers. For example, over a typical year, Hampton Inn will give back 0.5 percent of its room rental charges to dissatisfied customers. But according to Cordell, service recovery pays off because every dollar refunded to disgruntled customers results in a $7 payoff as those formerly dissatisfied customers return to Hampton Inn or recommend Hampton Inn to their friends.[65] Exhibit 18.10 describes some costs and benefits of empowering service workers to act in ways that they believe will accomplish service recovery.

Review 3: **Service Operations**

Services are different from goods. Goods are produced, tangible, and storable. Services are performed, intangible, and perishable. Likewise, managing service operations is different from managing production operations. The service-profit chain indicates that success begins with internal service quality, meaning how well management treats service employees. Internal service quality leads to employee satisfaction and service capability, which, in turn, lead to high-value service to customers, customer satisfaction, customer loyalty, and long-term profits and growth. Keeping existing customers is far more cost-effective than finding new ones. Consequently, to prevent disgruntled customers from leaving, some companies are empowering service employees to perform service recovery—restoring customer satisfaction to strongly dissatisfied customers—by giving them the authority and responsibility to immediately solve customer problems. The hope is that empowered service recovery will prevent customer defections.

COSTS
1. Finding service workers who are capable of solving problems and dealing with upset customers increases selection costs.
2. Training service workers to solve different kinds of problems entails increased costs.
3. Higher wages are needed to attract and keep talented service workers.
4. A focus on service recovery may lead to less emphasis on service reliability, doing it right the first time. Ultimately, this could lead to slower delivery of services.
5. In their quest to please customers, empowered service workers may cost the company money by being too eager to provide "giveaways" to make up for poor or slow service.
6. Empowered service workers may unintentionally treat customers unfairly by occasionally being overly generous to make up for poor or slow service.
BENEFITS
1. Responses to customer complaints and problems are quicker.
2. Employees feel better about their jobs and themselves.
3. Employee interaction with customers will be warm and enthusiastic.
4. Employees are more likely to offer ideas for improving service or preventing problems.
5. Empowered employees who provide service recovery lead to great word-of-mouth advertising and customer retention.
6. Satisfied employees who take good care of customers are more likely to stay with the company.

Sources: D. E. Bowen & E. E. Lawler III, "The Empowerment of Service Workers: What, Why, How, and When," *Sloan Management Review* 33 (Spring 1992): 31–39; S. Kundu & J. Vora, "Creating a Talented Workforce for Delivering Service Quality," *Human Resource Planning* 27 (1 January 2004): 40.

Exhibit 18.10

Costs and Benefits of Empowering Service Workers for Service Recovery

DaimlerChrysler makes cars; Dell makes computers. Shell produces gasoline; Sherwin-Williams makes paint. Boeing makes jet planes; Budweiser makes beer. Maxtor makes hard drives; Maytag makes appliances. The manufacturing operations of these companies all produce physical goods. But not all manufacturing operations, especially these, are the same. Let's learn how various manufacturing operations differ in terms of ***4.1 the amount of processing that is done to produce and assemble a product*** *and* ***4.2 the flexibility to change the number, kind, and characteristics of products that are produced.***

4.1 Amount of Processing in Manufacturing Operations

As Exhibit 18.11 shows, manufacturing operations can be classified according to the amount of processing or assembly that occurs after a customer order is received. The highest degree of processing occurs in **make-to-order operations**. A make-to-order operation does not start processing or assembling products until it receives a customer order. In fact, some make-to-order operations may not even order parts until a customer order is received. Not surprisingly, make-to-order operations produce or assemble highly specialized or customized products for customers.

For example, Dell has one of the most advanced make-to-order operations in the computer business. Dell has no finished goods inventory—it does not build a computer until someone buys it. Because Dell doesn't order parts from suppliers until machines are purchased, its computers always have the latest, most advanced components. No one who buys a Dell computer gets stuck with old technology. Also, because prices of computer components tend to fall, Dell's make-to-order operation can pass on price cuts to customers. Plus, Dell can customize all of its orders, big and small. So whether you're ordering 5,000 personal computers for your company or just one personal computer for your home, Dell doesn't make the computers until you order them.

make-to-order operation a manufacturing operation that does not start processing or assembling products until a customer order is received

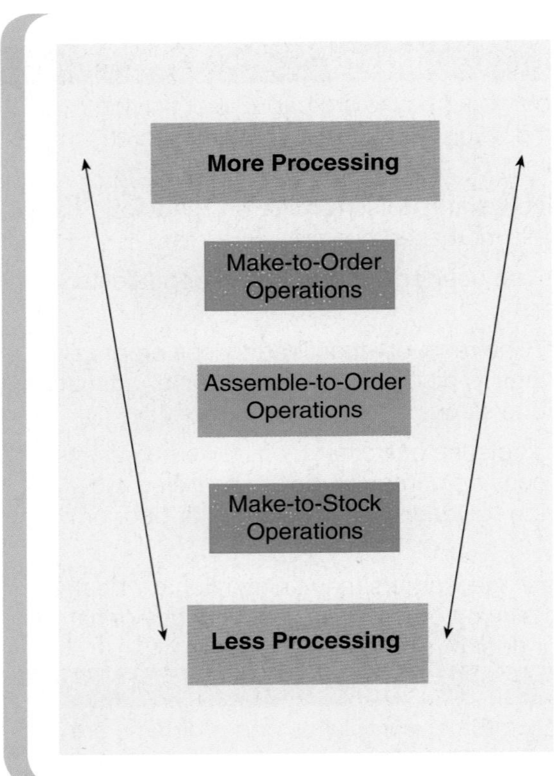

Exhibit 18.11

Processing in Manufacturing Operations

A moderate degree of processing occurs in **assemble-to-order operations**. A company using an assemble-to-order operation divides its manufacturing or assembly process into separate parts or modules. The company orders parts and assembles modules ahead of customer orders. Then, based on actual customer orders or on research forecasting what customers will want, those modules are combined to create semicustomized products. For example, when a customer orders a new car, General Motors may have already ordered the basic parts or modules it needs from suppliers. In other words, based on sales forecasts, GM may already have ordered enough tires, air-conditioning compressors, brake systems, and seats from suppliers to accommodate nearly all customer orders on a particular day. Special orders from customers and car dealers are then used to determine the final assembly checklist for particular cars as they move down the assembly line.

The lowest degree of processing occurs in **make-to-stock operations** (also called build-to-stock). Because the products are standardized, meaning each product is exactly the same as the next, a company using a make-to-stock operation starts ordering parts and assembling finished products before receiving customer orders. Customers then purchase these standardized products, such as Rubbermaid storage containers, microwave ovens, and vacuum cleaners, at retail stores or directly from the manufacturer. Because parts are ordered and products are assembled before customers order the products, make-to-stock operations are highly dependent on the accuracy of sales forecasts. If sales forecasts are incorrect, make-to-stock operations may end up building too many or too few products, or they may make products with the wrong features or without the features that customers want.

These disadvantages are leading many companies to move from make-to-stock to build-to-order systems. Mark Simons, a vice president at Toshiba, says, "Toshiba is expanding beyond make-to-stock systems and offering a quick and easy way to customize a notebook to fit the individual needs of our customers. We've listened to our customers' feedback and are answering their call to have direct access to Toshiba mobile technology on various levels and at all times."[66]

4.2 Flexibility of Manufacturing Operations

A second way to categorize manufacturing operations is by **manufacturing flexibility**, meaning the degree to which manufacturing operations can easily and quickly change the number, kind, and characteristics of products they produce. Flexibility allows companies to respond quickly to changes in the marketplace (that is, respond to competitors and customers) and to reduce the lead time between ordering and final delivery of products. There is often a tradeoff between flexibility and cost, however, with the most flexible manufacturing operations frequently having higher costs per unit and the least flexible operations having lower costs per unit.[67] Exhibit 18.12 shows different types of manufacturing operations arranged in order from the least flexible to the most flexible: continuous-flow production, line-flow production, batch production, job shops, and project manufacturing.

Most production processes generate finished products at a discrete rate. A product is completed, and then, perhaps a few seconds, minutes, or hours later, another is completed, and so on. For instance, if you stood at the end of an automobile assembly line, nothing much would seem to be happening for 55 seconds of every minute. In that last

assemble-to-order operation a manufacturing operation that divides manufacturing processes into separate parts or modules that are combined to create semicustomized products

make-to-stock operation a manufacturing operation that orders parts and assembles standardized products before receiving customer orders

manufacturing flexibility the degree to which manufacturing operations can easily and quickly change the number, kind, and characteristics of products they produce

5 seconds, however, a new car would be started and driven off the assembly line, ready for its new owner. By contrast, in **continuous-flow production**, products are produced continuously, rather than at a discrete rate. Like a water hose that is never turned off and just keeps on flowing, production of the final product never stops. Liquid chemicals and petroleum products are examples of continuous-flow production. If you're still struggling with this concept, think of Play-Doh. Continuous-flow production is similar to squeezing Play-Doh into a toy press and watching the various shapes ooze out of the Play-Doh "machine." With continuous-flow production, the Play-Doh machine would never stop oozing or producing rectangle- or triangle-shaped Play-Doh. Because of their complexity, continuous-flow production processes are the most standardized and least flexible manufacturing operations.

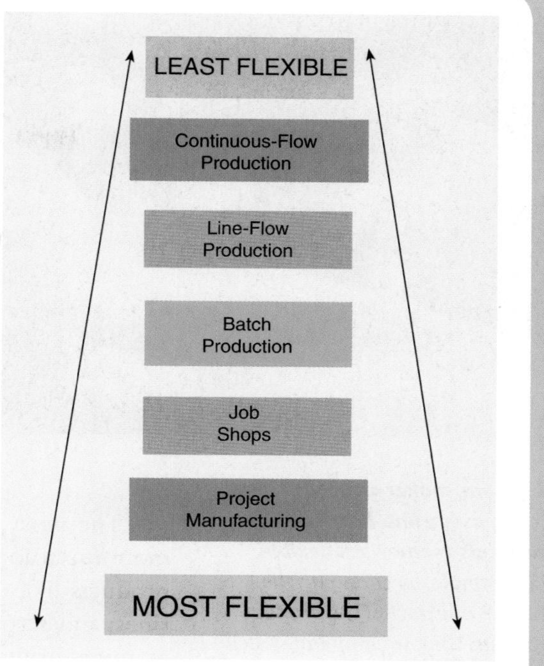

Exhibit 18.12

Flexibility of Manufacturing Operations

Line-flow production processes are preestablished, occur in a serial or linear manner, and are dedicated to making one type of product. In this way, the 10 different steps required to make product X can be completed in a separate manufacturing process (with separate machines, parts, treatments, locations, and workers) from the 12 different steps required to make product Y. Line-flow production processes are inflexible because they are typically dedicated to manufacturing one kind of product. For example, nearly every city has a local bottling plant for soft drinks or beer. The processes or steps in bottling plants are serial, meaning they must occur in a particular order. For example, after empty bottles are sterilized, they are filled with soft drinks or beer using a special dispenser that distributes the liquid down the inside walls of the bottle. This fills the bottle from the bottom up and displaces the air that was in the bottle. The bottles are then crowned or capped, checked for underfilling and missing caps, labeled, inspected a final time for fill levels and missing labels, and then placed in cases that are shrink-wrapped on pallets and put on trucks for delivery.[68]

The next most flexible manufacturing operation is **batch production**, which involves the manufacture of large batches of different products in standard lot sizes. Consequently, a worker in a batch production operation will perform the same manufacturing process on 100 copies of product X, followed by 200 copies of product Y, and then 50 copies of product Z. Furthermore, these "batches" move through each manufacturing department or process in identical order. So, if the paint department follows chemical treatment, and chemical treatment is now processing a batch of 50 copies of product Z, then the paint department's next task will be to paint 50 copies of product Z. Batch production is finding increasing use among restaurant chains. To ensure consistency in the taste and quality of their products, many restaurant chains have central kitchens, or commissaries, that produce batches of food, such as mashed potatoes, stuffing, macaroni and cheese, rice, quiche filling, and chili, in volumes ranging from 10 to 200 gallons. These batches are then delivered to the individual restaurant locations, which serve the food to customers.

Next in terms of flexibility is the job shop. **Job shops** are typically small manufacturing operations that handle special manufacturing processes or jobs. In contrast to batch production, which handles large batches of different products, job shops typically handle very small batches, some as small as one product or process per "batch." Basically, each "job" in a job shop is different, and once a job is done, the job shop moves on to a completely different job or manufacturing process for, most likely, a different customer. For example, **LEGGETT & PLATT MACHINE PRODUCTS** in Carthage, Missouri, is a job shop that makes coil springs, innerspring units, welded metal grids,

continuous-flow production a manufacturing operation that produces goods at a continuous, rather than a discrete, rate

line-flow production manufacturing processes that are preestablished, occur in a serial or linear manner, and are dedicated to making one type of product

batch production a manufacturing operation that produces goods in large batches in standard lot sizes

job shops manufacturing operations that handle custom orders or small batch jobs

Just Born, maker of Marshmallow Peeps, uses a line-flow system that is also somewhat flexible. For example, by changing the mold in one part of the production line, the company can switch from making its hallmark Peep Chicks and Bunnies to making new shapes, like the pumpkins shown here.

and various other parts for mattress manufacturers around the world. Since its inception, its 225 employees have made over 25,000 *different* parts; in other words, they have completed 25,000 different jobs for customers.[69] Another example of a job shop is **HEIL TRAILER INTERNATIONAL** in Athens, Tennessee. Heil specializes in the production of custom truck trailers that carry petroleum or dry bulk. Heil also makes intermodal trailers that can be pulled by trucks and transported by trains. Steve Slaughter, Heil's general manager, says, "Even when we get orders for multiple trailers, the trailers normally aren't the same. The shape of the tank itself doesn't really change that much. But with all the different weight laws and customer preferences, it's unusual to see two identical trailers going down the same assembly line."[70]

The most flexible manufacturing operation is project manufacturing. **Project manufacturing** is an operation designed to produce large, expensive, specialized products like custom homes; military systems such as aircraft carriers and submarines; and aerospace products such as passenger planes and the space shuttle. Project manufacturing is highly flexible because each project is usually significantly different from the one before it, even if the projects involve the same general type of product, such as a submarine. Because of each project's size, expense, and high degree of customization, project manufacturing can take an extremely long time to complete. For instance, General Dynamics uses project manufacturing when making new submarines. The U.S. Navy's Virginia class subs, which are its newest and most advanced attack submarines, are 377 feet long and able to attain speeds greater than 25 knots (28 miles per hour/46.3 kilometers per hour). Therefore, they will be significantly quieter and faster than the Los Angeles class submarines that they replace.[71] Project manufacturing is required for submarine construction because of the tremendous cost (budgeted cost of $1.6 billion each), the complexity of the subs, and the length of time it takes to complete a new submarine (six years). Because of these enormous challenges, only one new Virginia class submarine is being completed each year.

Review 4: Manufacturing Operations

Manufacturing operations produce physical goods. Manufacturing operations can be classified according to the amount of processing or assembly that occurs after receiving an order from customers. Make-to-order operations, in which assembly doesn't begin until products are ordered, involve the most processing. The next-highest degree of processing occurs in assemble-to-order operations, in which preassembled modules are combined after orders are received to produce semicustomized products. The least processing occurs in make-to-stock operations, in which standard parts are ordered, on the basis of sales forecasts, and assembled before orders are received.

Manufacturing operations can also be classified in terms of flexibility, the degree to which the number, kind, and characteristics of products can easily and quickly be changed. Flexibility allows companies to respond quickly to competitors and customers and to reduce order lead times, but it can also lead to higher unit costs. Manufacturing operations can be arranged in order from the least to the most flexible as follows: continuous-flow production, line-flow production, batch production, job shops, and project manufacturing.

project manufacturing
manufacturing operations designed to produce large, expensive, specialized products

5 Inventory

With SUVs and pickup trucks accounting for nearly 80 percent of its sales, **Chrysler** was reluctant to stop making them—even when consumer demand dried up. Unfortunately, though, the automaker built SUVs and pickups that people didn't want, and it ended up with nearly a three-month supply of inventory. In addition to what was already on dealer lots, the automaker had 50,000 vehicles sitting on random storage lots around the midwestern United States. Ultimately, Chrysler significantly reduced production for six months to sell off its unsold vehicles.[72]

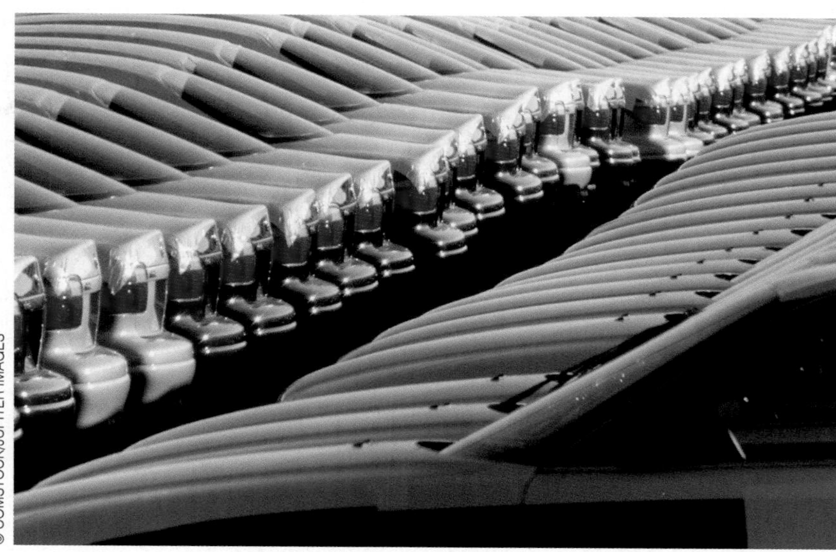

Chrysler's SUV inventory was recently nearly three times that of Toyota. The costs for maintaining such a robust inventory can be quite high and, ultimately, crippling to the organization if the products being inventoried sit too long on the shelf (or the lot).

***Inventory** is the amount and number of raw materials, parts, and finished products that a company has in its possession. Industry experts estimate Chrysler has more SUV inventory (82 days) than GM (77) and Ford (74) and almost three times as much as Toyota (28).[73] In this section, you will learn about **5.1 the different types of inventory, 5.2 how to measure inventory levels, 5.3 the costs of maintaining an inventory,** and **5.4 the different systems for managing inventory**.*

5.1 Types of Inventory

Exhibit 18.13 shows the four kinds of inventory a manufacturer stores: raw materials, component parts, work-in-process, and finished goods. The flow of inventory through a manufacturing plant begins when the purchasing department buys raw materials from vendors. **Raw material inventories** are the basic inputs in the manufacturing process. For example, to begin making a car, automobile manufacturers purchase raw materials like steel, iron, aluminum, copper, rubber, and unprocessed plastic.

Next, raw materials are fabricated or processed into **component parts inventories,** meaning the basic parts used in manufacturing a product. For example, in an automobile plant, steel is fabricated or processed into a car's body panels, and steel and iron are melted and shaped into engine parts like pistons or engine blocks. Some component parts are purchased from vendors rather than fabricated in-house.

The component parts are then assembled to make unfinished **work-in-process inventories**, which are also known as partially finished goods. This process is also called *initial assembly*. For example, steel body panels are welded to each other and to the frame of the car to make a "unibody," which comprises the unpainted interior frame and exterior structure of the car. Likewise, pistons, camshafts, and other engine parts are inserted into the engine block to create a working engine.

Next, all the work-in-process inventories are assembled to create **finished goods inventories**, which are the final outputs of the manufacturing process. This process is also called *final assembly*. For a car, the engine, wheels, brake system, suspension, interior, and electrical system are assembled into a car's painted unibody to make the working automobile, which is the factory's finished product. In the last step in the process, the finished goods are sent to field warehouses, distribution centers, or wholesalers, and then to retailers for final sale to customers.

inventory the amount and number of raw materials, parts, and finished products that a company has in its possession

raw material inventories the basic inputs in a manufacturing process

component parts inventories the basic parts used in manufacturing that are fabricated from raw materials

work-in-process inventories partially finished goods consisting of assembled component parts

finished goods inventories the final outputs of manufacturing operations

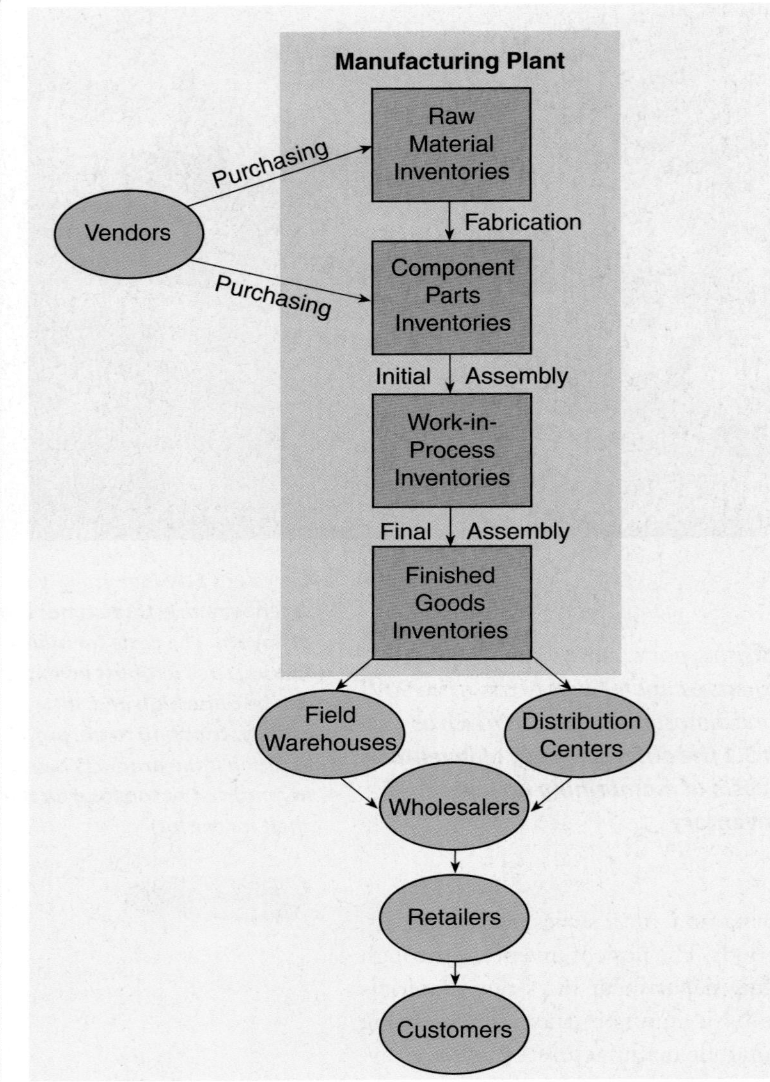

Source: R. E. Markland, S. K. Vickery, & R. A. Davis, *Operations Management*, 2nd ed. (Mason, OH: South-Western, 1998). Reprinted with permission.

Exhibit 18.13
Types of Inventory

5.2 Measuring Inventory

As you'll learn below, uncontrolled inventory can lead to huge costs for a manufacturing operation. Consequently, managers need good measures of inventory to prevent inventory costs from becoming too large. Three basic measures of inventory are average aggregate inventory, weeks of supply, and inventory turnover.

If you've ever worked in a retail store and had to "take inventory," you probably weren't too excited about the process of counting every item in the store and storeroom. It's an extensive task. Fortunately, "taking inventory" is somewhat easier today because of bar codes that mark items and computers that can count and track them. Nonetheless, inventories still differ from day to day. For example, an inventory count taken at the beginning of the month will likely be different from a count taken at the end of the month. Similarly, an inventory count taken on a Friday will differ from a count taken on a Monday. Because of such differences, companies often measure **average aggregate inventory**, which is the average overall inventory during a particular time period. Average aggregate inventory for a month can be determined by simply averaging the inventory counts at the end of each business day for that month. One way companies know whether they're carrying too much or too little inventory is to compare their average aggregate inventory with the industry average for aggregate inventory. For example, 72 days of inventory is the average for the automobile industry.

While the automobile industry records inventory in terms of days of supply, most other industries measure inventory in terms of *weeks of supply*, meaning the number of weeks it would take for a company to run out of its current supply of inventory. In general, there is an acceptable number of weeks of inventory for a particular kind of business. Too few weeks of inventory on hand, and a company risks a **stockout**—running out of inventory. During a recent holiday season, the busiest shopping time of the year, retail and online stores ran out of ***Apple Computer***'s fast-selling iPods. Industry analyst Stephen Baker says, "Given how strong demand has been all year you would have thought [Apple] would have gotten every last one they could into stores."[74] Apple issued a statement saying, "To try to meet the high demand, we're making and shipping iPods as fast as we can. So, if one store has run out, you may find iPods in another authorized iPod reseller."[75] Nevertheless, iPods were in such short supply that the iPod mini was selling for $380 on eBay, $130 over the suggested retail price. On the other hand, a business that has too many weeks of

average aggregate inventory average overall inventory during a particular time period

stockout the point when a company runs out of finished product inventory on hand incurs high costs (discussed below). For example, companies that make the linerboard used for corrugated cardboard boxes typically have too much inventory when they have more than six weeks' supply on hand; the right amount is about four weeks' supply.[76] Anything more than that results in excess inventory, which can be reduced only by cutting prices or temporarily stopping production.

Another common inventory measure, **inventory turnover**, is the number of times per year that a company sells or "turns over" its average inventory. For example, if a company keeps an average of 100 finished widgets in inventory each month, and it sold 1,000 widgets this year, then it "turned" its inventory 10 times this year.

In general, the higher the number of inventory "turns," the better. In practice, a high turnover means that a company can continue its daily operations with just a small amount of inventory on hand. For example, let's take two companies, A and B, which, over the course of a year, have identical inventory levels (520,000 widget parts and raw materials). If company A turns its inventories 26 times a year, it will completely replenish its inventory every two weeks and have an average inventory of 20,000 widget parts and raw materials. By contrast, if company B turns its inventories only two times a year, it will completely replenish its inventory every 26 weeks and have an average inventory of 260,000 widget parts and raw materials. So, by turning its inventory more often, company A has 92 percent less inventory on hand at any one time than company B.

Across all kinds of manufacturing plants, the average number of inventory turns is approximately eight per year, as shown in Exhibit 18.14, although the average can be higher or lower for different industries.[77] The exhibit also shows the inventory turn rates for some of the best companies in each industry (that is, the 75th percentile). For example, whereas the average auto company turns its entire inventory 13 times per year, some of the best auto companies more than double that rate, turning their inventory 27.8 times per year, or once every two weeks.[78] For an auto company, turning inventory more frequently than the industry average can cut costs by several hundred million dollars per year. Finally, it should be pointed out that even make-to-order companies like Dell turn their inventory. In theory, make-to-order companies have no inventory. In fact, they've got inventory, but you have to measure it in hours.

inventory turnover the number of times per year that a company sells or "turns over" its average inventory

Exhibit 18.14

Inventory Turn Rates across Industries

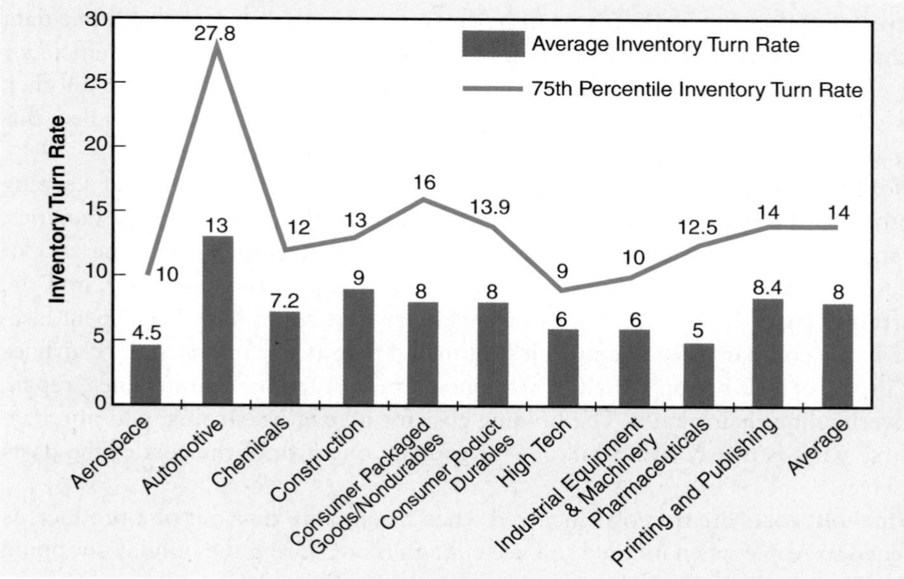

Source: D. Drickhamer, "Zeroing in on World-Class," *Industry Week*, November 2001, 36.

For example, in its factories, Dell turns its inventory 500 times a year, which means that on average it has 17 hours—that's hours and not days—of inventory on hand in its factories.[79]

5.3 Costs of Maintaining an Inventory

Maintaining an inventory incurs four kinds of costs: ordering, setup, holding, and stockout. **Ordering cost** is not the cost of the inventory itself, but the costs associated with ordering the inventory. It includes the costs of completing paperwork, manually entering data into a computer, making phone calls, getting competing bids, correcting mistakes, and simply determining when and how much new inventory should be reordered. For example, ordering costs are relatively high in the restaurant business because 80 percent of food service orders (in which restaurants reorder food supplies) are processed manually. It's estimated that the food industry could save $6.6 billion if all restaurants converted to electronic data interchange (see Chapter 17), in which purchase and ordering information from one company's computer system is automatically relayed to another company's computer system. In fact, a number of restaurants and food service trade groups have formed an interest group called Efficient Foodservice Response to encourage restaurants and food suppliers to use EDI and other methods of electronic commerce.[80]

Setup cost is the cost of changing or adjusting a machine so that it can produce a different kind of inventory.[81] For example, 3M uses the same production machinery to make several kinds of industrial tape, but it must adjust the machines whenever it switches from one kind of tape to another. There are two kinds of setup costs, downtime and lost efficiency. *Downtime* occurs whenever a machine is not being used to process inventory. So, if it takes five hours to switch a machine from processing one kind of inventory to another, then five hours of downtime have occurred. Downtime is costly because companies earn an economic return only when machines are actively turning raw materials into parts or parts into finished products. The second setup cost is *lost efficiency*. Typically, after a switchover, it takes some time to recalibrate a machine to its optimal settings. It may take several days of fine-tuning before a machine finally produces the number of high-quality parts that it is supposed to. Exhibit 18.15 illustrates the tradeoff between setup costs, meaning downtime and lost efficiency, and manufacturing flexibility, that is, the number of *different* products (or inventory) that can be processed or assembled on a particular machine. The data in Exhibit 18.15 assume that four hours of downtime and 3 percent lost efficiency occur each time a machine's setup has to be changed from one product to another. So, as shown in the exhibit, each time a machine has to be changed to handle a different kind of inventory, setup costs (downtime and lost efficiency) rise.

Holding cost, also known as *carrying* or *storage cost*, is the cost of keeping inventory until it is used or sold. Holding cost includes the cost of storage facilities, insurance to protect inventory from damage or theft, inventory taxes, the cost of obsolescence (holding inventory that is no longer useful to the company), and the opportunity cost of spending money on inventory that could have been spent elsewhere in the company. For example, it's estimated that at any one time, U.S. airlines have a total of $60 billion worth of airplane parts in stock for maintenance, repair, and overhauling their planes. The holding cost for managing, storing, and purchasing these parts is nearly $12.5 billion—or roughly one-fifth of the cost of the parts themselves.[82]

Stockout costs are the costs incurred when a company runs out of a product, as happened to Apple when it failed to have enough iPods during the holiday shopping season. There are two basic kinds of stockout costs. First, the company incurs the

ordering cost the costs associated with ordering inventory, including the cost of data entry, phone calls, obtaining bids, correcting mistakes, and determining when and how much inventory to order

setup cost the costs of downtime and lost efficiency that occur when a machine is changed or adjusted to produce a different kind of inventory

holding cost the cost of keeping inventory until it is used or sold, including storage, insurance, taxes, obsolescence, and opportunity costs

stockout costs the costs incurred when a company runs out of a product, including transaction costs to replace inventory and the loss of customers' goodwill transaction costs of overtime work, shipping, and the like in trying to quickly replace out-of-stock inventories with new inventories. The second and perhaps more damaging cost is the loss of customers' goodwill when a company cannot deliver the products that it promised. Stockouts occur more often than you might think. In the United States, the supermarket industry's average out-of-stock rate (the percentage of items that are unavailable at a given time) is 7.9 percent, according to research firm Market6. Highly promoted items have, as would be expected, a higher average out-of-stock rate of 13.1 percent. How costly is it for stores to run out of stock? For a grocery store, research firm Market6 estimates that running out of stock on the 25 best-selling product categories reduces store revenue by an average of $200,000 per year, per store.[83] In general, retailers can increase sales 4 percent if they never run out of stock.

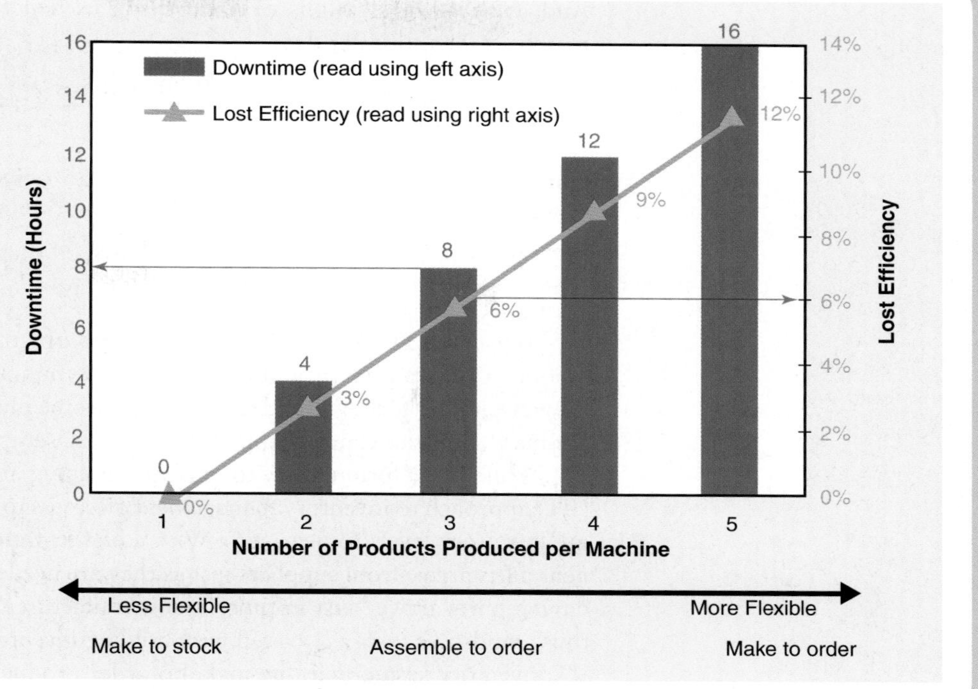

Exhibit 18.15

Tradeoff between Setup Costs and Manufacturing Flexibility

5.4 Managing Inventory

Inventory management has two basic goals. The first is to avoid running out of stock and thus angering and dissatisfying customers. Consequently, this goal seeks to increase inventory levels to a "safe" level that won't risk stockouts. The second is to efficiently reduce inventory levels and costs as much as possible without impairing daily operations. Thus, this goal seeks a minimum level of inventory. The following inventory management techniques—economic order quantity (EOQ), just-in-time inventory (JIT), and materials requirement planning (MRP)—are different ways of balancing these competing goals.

Economic order quantity (EOQ) is a system of formulas that helps determine how much and how often inventory should be ordered. EOQ takes into account the overall demand (D) for a product while trying to minimize ordering costs (O) and holding costs (H). The formula for EOQ is

$$\text{EOQ} = \sqrt{\frac{2DO}{4}}$$

For example, if a factory uses 40,000 gallons of paint a year (D), ordering costs (O) are $75 per order, and holding costs (H) are $4 per gallon, then the optimal quantity to order is 1,225 gallons:

$$\text{EOQ} = \sqrt{\frac{2(40{,}000)(75)}{4}} = 1{,}225$$

economic order quantity (EOQ) a system of formulas that minimizes ordering and holding costs and helps determine how much and how often inventory should be ordered

And, with 40,000 gallons of paint being used per year, the factory uses approximately 110 gallons per day:

$$\frac{40{,}000 \text{ gallons}}{365 \text{ days}} = 110$$

Consequently, the factory would order 1,225 new gallons of paint approximately every 11 days:

$$\frac{1{,}225 \text{ gallons}}{110 \text{ gallons per day}} = 11.1 \text{ days}$$

In general, EOQ formulas do a good job of letting managers know what size or amount of inventory they should reorder to minimize ordering and holding costs. However, EOQ formulas and models can become much more complex as adjustments are made for price changes, quantity discounts, setup costs, and many other factors.[84]

While EOQ formulas try to minimize holding and ordering costs, the just-in-time (JIT) approach to inventory management attempts to eliminate holding costs by reducing inventory levels to near zero. With a **just-in-time (JIT) inventory** system, component parts arrive from suppliers just as they are needed at each stage of production. By having parts arrive "just in time," the manufacturer has little inventory on hand and thus avoids the costs associated with holding inventory. For example, by combining a JIT inventory system with its make-to-order production system, Dell turns its inventory more than 500 times a year, as mentioned above. Regarding Dell's JIT inventory system, John Egan, who heads Dell's inventory fulfillment center in Austin, Texas, says "We used to measure our factory inventory in days; but now we manage it in hours. Our suppliers see demand changes every two hours. We try to achieve a perfect balance" between the parts that are needed and what's already in the factory.[85]

> We used to measure our factory inventory in days; but now we manage it in hours.
>
> **JOHN EGAN**, HEAD OF DELL'S INVENTORY FULFILLMENT CENTER

To have just the right amount of inventory arrive at just the right time requires a tremendous amount of coordination between manufacturing operations and suppliers. One way to promote tight coordination under JIT is close proximity. Most parts suppliers for Toyota's JIT system at its Georgetown, Kentucky, plant are located within 200 miles of the plant. Furthermore, parts are picked up from suppliers and delivered to Toyota as often as 16 times a day.[86]

A second way to promote close coordination under JIT is to have a shared information system that allows a manufacturer and its suppliers to know the quantity and kinds of parts inventory the other has in stock. Generally, factories and suppliers facilitate information sharing by using the same part numbers and names. Ford's seat supplier accomplishes this by sticking a bar code on each seat, which Ford then uses to route the seat through its factory.

just-in-time (JIT) inventory system an inventory system in which component parts arrive from suppliers just as they are needed at each stage of production

kanban a ticket-based JIT system that indicates when to reorder inventory

Manufacturing operations and their parts suppliers can also facilitate close coordination by using the system of kanban. **Kanban**, which is Japanese for "sign," is a simple ticket-based system that indicates when it is time to reorder inventory. Suppliers attach kanban cards to batches of parts. Then, when an assembly-line worker uses the first part out of a batch, the kanban card is removed. The cards are then collected, sorted, and quickly returned to the supplier, who begins resupplying the factory with parts that match the order information on the kanban cards. Glenn

Uminger, manager of production control and logistics at Toyota's Georgetown, Kentucky, plant, says, "We are placing orders for new parts as the first part is used out of a box." And, because prices and batch sizes are typically agreed to ahead of time, kanban tickets greatly reduce paperwork and ordering costs.[87]

A third method for managing inventory is **materials requirement planning (MRP)**. MRP is a production and inventory system that, from beginning to end, precisely determines the production schedule, production batch sizes, and inventories needed to complete final products. The three key parts of MRP systems are the master production schedule, the bill of materials, and inventory records. The *master production schedule* is a detailed schedule that indicates the quantity of each item to be produced, the planned delivery dates for those items, and the time by which each step of the production process must be completed in order to meet those delivery dates. Based on the quantity and kind of products set forth in the master production schedule, the *bill of materials* identifies all the necessary parts and inventory, the quantity or volume of inventory to be ordered, and the order in which the parts and inventory should be assembled. *Inventory records* indicate the kind, quantity, and location of inventory that is on hand or that has been ordered. When inventory records are combined with the bill of materials, the resulting report indicates what to buy, when to buy it, and what it will cost to order. Today, nearly all MRP systems are available in the form of powerful, flexible computer software.[88]

Which inventory management system should you use? Economic order quantity (EOQ) formulas are intended for use with **independent demand systems**, in which the level of one kind of inventory does not depend on another. For example, because inventory levels for automobile tires are unrelated to the inventory levels of women's dresses, Sears could use EOQ formulas to calculate separate optimal order quantities for dresses and tires. By contrast, JIT and MRP are used with **dependent demand systems**, in which the level of inventory depends on the number of finished units to be produced. For example, if Yamaha makes 1,000 motorcycles a day, then it will need 1,000 seats, 1,000 gas tanks, and 2,000 wheels and tires each day. So, when optimal inventory levels depend on the number of products to be produced, use a JIT or MRP management system.

Review 5: Inventory

There are four kinds of inventory: raw materials, component parts, work-in-process, and finished goods. Because companies incur ordering, setup, holding, and stockout costs when handling inventory, inventory costs can be enormous. To control those costs, companies measure and track inventory in three ways: average aggregate inventory, weeks of supply, and turnover. Companies meet the basic goals of inventory management (avoiding stockouts and reducing inventory without hurting daily operations) through economic order quantity (EOQ) formulas, just-in-time (JIT) inventory systems, and materials requirement planning (MRP). EOQ formulas minimize holding and ordering costs by determining how much and how often inventory should be ordered. By having parts arrive just when they are needed at each stage of production, JIT systems attempt to minimize inventory levels and holding costs. JIT systems often depend on proximity, shared information, and the system of kanban made popular by Japanese manufacturers. MRP precisely determines the production schedule, production batch sizes, and the ordering of inventories needed to complete final products. The three key parts of MRP systems are the master production schedule, the bill of materials, and inventory records. Use EOQ formulas when inventory levels are independent, and use JIT and MRP when inventory levels are dependent on the number of products to be produced.

materials requirement planning (MRP) a production and inventory system that determines the production schedule, production batch sizes, and inventory needed to complete final products

independent demand system an inventory system in which the level of one kind of inventory does not depend on another

dependent demand system an inventory system in which the level of inventory depends on the number of finished units to be produced

SELF ASSESSMENT

KEY TERMS

assemble-to-order operation 680
average aggregate inventory 684
batch production 681
component parts inventories 683
continuous-flow production 681
continuous improvement 673
customer focus 673
customer satisfaction 673
dependent demand systems 689
economic order quantity (EOQ) 687
finished goods inventories 683
holding cost 686
independent demand system 689
inventory 683
inventory turnover 685
ISO 9000 670
ISO 14000 670
job shops 681
just-in-time (JIT) inventory system 688
kanban 688
line-flow production 681
make-to-order operation 679
make-to-stock operation 680
manufacturing flexibility 680
materials requirement planning (MRP) 689
multifactor productivity 665
operations management 662
ordering cost 686
partial productivity 664
productivity 663
project manufacturing 682
quality 667
raw material inventories 683

How to Handle Disgruntled Customers

How a company manages its customers is an important indicator of its future success. But managing customers can be as difficult as it is critical. For example, one customer may like to be greeted by an employee and immediately helped upon entering the store. Another might find this approach a bit aggressive. What is your style? If you were responsible for interacting with customers, which approach would you use? The following assessment will evaluate your perspectives on the relationship a company has with its customers. Be candid as you respond to the questions using a scale from 1 to 9 in which 1 means you strongly disagree, 5 means you are neutral, and 9 means you strongly agree (other numbers indicate varying degrees of agreement or disagreement).[89]

1. I try to bring a customer with a problem together with a product/service that helps solve that problem.
2. I keep alert for weaknesses in a customer's personality so I can use them to put pressure on them to agree with me.
3. I try to influence a customer by information rather than pressure.
4. It is necessary to stretch the truth in describing a product to a customer.
5. I decide what product/service to offer on the basis of what I can convince customers to accept, not on the basis of what will satisfy them in the long run.
6. I paint too rosy a picture of my product/service to make them sound as good as possible.
7. I try to find out what kind of products/services will be most helpful to a customer.
8. I try to sell a customer all I can convince them to buy, even if I think it is more than a wise customer would buy.
9. I begin talking about the product/service before exploring a customer's need with him or her.
10. I try to help a customer achieve their goals.
11. I try to figure out what a customer's needs are.
12. A good employee has to have the customer's best interest in mind.
13. I try to sell as much as I can rather than to satisfy a customer.
14. I try to give customers an accurate expectation of what our product/service will do for them.
15. I imply to a customer that something is beyond my control when it is not.
16. I try to achieve my goals by satisfying customers.
17. If I am not sure if our product/service is right for a customer, I will still apply pressure to get him or her to buy.
18. I answer a customer's question about product/services as correctly as I can.
19. I offer the product/service that is best suited to the customer's problem.
20. I treat a customer as a rival.
21. I spend more time trying to persuade a customer to buy than I do trying to discover his or her needs.
22. I am willing to disagree with a customer in order to help him or her make a better decision.
23. I try to get the customer to discuss their needs with me.
24. I pretend to agree with a customer to please them.

Scoring

Determine your score by entering your response to each survey item below, as follows. Total each column to derive two scores.

Customer Orientation		**Selling Orientation**	
1. regular score	_____	2. regular score	_____
3. regular score	_____	4. regular score	_____
7. regular score	_____	5. regular score	_____
10. regular score	_____	6. regular score	_____
11. regular score	_____	8. regular score	_____
12. regular score	_____	9. regular score	_____
14. regular score	_____	13. regular score	_____
16. regular score	_____	15. regular score	_____
18. regular score	_____	17. regular score	_____
19. regular score	_____	20. regular score	_____
22. regular score	_____	21. regular score	_____
23. regular score	_____	24. regular score	_____
TOTAL =	_____	TOTAL =	_____

You can find the interpretation for your score at: **academic.cengage.com/management/williams.**

(continued)

MANAGEMENT DECISION

Moving to a Make-to-Order Operation

You've never been so energized by a sales pitch in your entire career.[90] Consultants from a highly reputable software developer have just given a presentation to your management team on how to integrate your supply chain, which is no mean feat. Your company, Nike, sells multiple variations of 120,000 products in four sales cycles throughout the year. Anything that can help you get this process under control is welcome. The only problem with the consultants' presentation is their underlying assumption: Nike should move from a make-to-stock operation to a make-to-order operation. That is, the consultant wants Nike to begin making shoes only after a retailer sends in an order.

In the $16 billion U.S. running-shoe market, Nike commands a full 39 percent market share, much larger than that of any other athletic shoe company. Your closest competitor, Reebok, is at a significantly lower 14 percent. Nike grew to that stature by creating a supply chain for the fragmented running shoe market of the 1970s. Nike guaranteed delivery and an inflation-proof discount in return for getting orders six months in advance. Retailers went along happily because runners typically didn't care if the shoes were the latest fashion as long as they were technically advanced. Because Nike shoes functioned impeccably, they became the standard.

After over two decades of astronomical growth, however, Nike is suffering from its own fragmentation. The company has 27 order management systems around the globe and uses tens of millions of product numbers (think number of models times available sizes). Even though the sales cycle is three months, the design and production cycle is nine months, so to meet sales deadlines, the company is building and holding a small fortune in inventory (think number of models times available sizes times cost per pair). Furthermore, today's customers want style, not just technically sophisticated shoes, and style changes a lot faster now than it did in the 1970s. Nike's extensive inventory, which was previously a strength, is becoming a weakness, as the risks of finished inventories becoming outdated are increasing sharply.

That's why you welcomed the consultants' initial recommendations to switch to make-to-order system. But you don't want to rush headlong into such a major change based only on the recommendation of outside consultants. After all, they're trying to sell you $400 million in software, and you have an $11 billion business on the line.

Questions

1. What issues do you need to consider as you make this decision? If you are overwhelmed thinking of a mammoth company like Nike, keep in mind that much smaller companies wrestle with this basic operations dilemma as well.

2. Do you invest in the $400 million software and commit to changing your manufacturing process from a make-to-stock to a make-to-order operation? (At this point, you are only considering make-to-order processing for retailers. That is, Nike wouldn't begin making shoes until a retailer, like FootLocker, actually ordered them.) Explain your rationale.
3. How would changing to make-to-order processing for retailers affect how Nike manages its inventory? Address all aspects of managing inventory.
4. The more you reflect on the sales proposal, the more you wonder why Nike would stop at make-to-order processing for retailers. Why not go all the way and do a make-to-order system for the consumer? Is that even feasible? Explain.
5. Think about the price of athletic shoes. If Nike began manufacturing customized products for consumers, how would you expect the changes in manufacturing operations, manufacturing flexibility, and inventory to affect the cost and final price of a pair of Nikes? Why?

Recovery Plan

As you read in Chapter 5, crisis management planning is an important component of business planning and corporate communication.[91] Typically, when you hear "crisis management," you think of a company responding to catastrophic publicity, but companies also need to think about managing smaller negative encounters because those encounters play a large role in customer retention. The retention rate for customers whose complaints or problems are resolved satisfactorily is 70 percent; when complaints are resolved quickly as well—typically on the spot—the retention rate soars to 95 percent. But when complaints are not resolved to the customer's satisfaction, customer retention falls to 46 percent. And research shows that for major purchases (defined as being over $100), customers whose complaints are unresolved stay with the company only 19 percent of the time. So, companies should have a plan for responding to customers' complaints and problems. Putting service recovery plans in place enables companies to respond quickly, the biggest factor in reversing the damage from negative customer experiences.

In the spa industry, customer service and satisfaction are paramount. Not only do customers have high expectations for spa and salon services such as massage, skin treatments, nail treatments, and hair coloring and cutting, but spa service tabs can quickly surpass that $100 threshold defining major purchases. And what would upset a customer more than a horrendous haircut, botched fingernails, or losing half an eyebrow during a wax!

For this exercise, assemble four to five students to act as the management team for a local salon and day spa that is getting ready to expand into several new neighborhoods by adding four local salons. Your salon has always had a high reputation for service, but as you expand, your experienced staff will be spread thin. In the next month, your team plans to hire and train 25 new cosmetologists and estheticians (skin-care providers). To ensure that the new stores are successful, your team has decided to map out very clear service recovery procedures. After all, during the training periods and the first few months the new stores are open, mistakes are bound to happen. How you respond to them will mean the difference between a successful expansion and possible bankruptcy.

Questions

1. As a team, brainstorm a list of service failures that could occur in a salon and day spa. (The examples of a bad haircut, damaged nails, and losing half an eyebrow during a wax job were mentioned above, but there are many more possibilities.) Then identify ways that you can resolve each problem on the list quickly and to the customer's satisfaction.
2. There are bound to be situations that you haven't planned for. How will you instruct your employees to handle unanticipated problems?
3. How can a complaint-response system be considered part of delivering quality service?
4. What kind of metric(s) can you create to measure the quality of your service delivery? Manufacturing companies typically measure things like on-time delivery, defects per million, production rate (how many pieces per hour), and so forth. What can a spa measure to keep its service operation in control?

PRACTICE BEING A MANAGER

Success in service and manufacturing operations requires managers to maintain high levels of both productivity and quality. High productivity ensures that the company is cost competitive with rivals; and high quality helps the company to attract customers and grow revenues and profits. Because productivity and quality are basic drivers of company success, managers must be adept at measuring and improving both. This exercise will give you some practice in developing productivity and quality measures.

Step 1: Your professor will organize your class into small groups of three or four students.

Scenario: Your group is a management team working to improve productivity and quality in a pharmaceutical company. You have been assigned two units of this company as the focus of your improvement efforts. The first is a pill-packaging unit, and the second is a research and development (R&D) laboratory.

Workers in the packaging unit are responsible for checking to ensure that the pills in the box match the packaging and labeling; placing the appropriate labels and packaging information on each box; and then certifying with a stamp that the box of pills is ready for shipping to wholesale customers, for example, chains like Walgreens and Costco. Mistakes in packaging, if undetected by pharmacists, could have serious, even fatal, outcomes. These manufacturing workers are skilled and highly trained. If they detect a problem, they have the authority to halt production.

Workers in the R&D unit are responsible for developing new drugs and for testing their effectiveness and safety. The company relies for its success upon a steady pipeline of promising new products. At the same time, some basic research (for example, study of progression of a particular type of cancer) is necessary in order to develop new drugs. These workers are mostly Ph.D.s and highly skilled laboratory technicians.

Step 2: Develop metrics. Working as a team, develop some productivity and quality measures for (a) packaging unit workers and (b) R&D unit workers. Be sure to consider whether productivity and quality should be measured on an individual or unit basis, and why.

Step 3: Analyze the metrics. Critically examine your team's measures for each unit. What unintended consequences might develop as workers in each unit strive to improve on the measures you have designed? Are you more confident of your measures in one unit versus the other? Why or why not?

Step 4: Debrief as a class. What are some of the challenges of measuring productivity and quality? Are these challenges greater for particular types of work? Which level of measurement and accountability—individual or unit—is most likely to generate positive results? Why? What impact do productivity and quality systems of measurement and improvement have on workers? How can firms ensure productivity and quality without overloading workers and/or fostering unhealthy levels of stress?

DEVELOP YOUR CAREER POTENTIAL

Take a Factory Tour

Imagine that you arrive back at your dorm room one afternoon to find your roommate watching a *Mister Rogers* rerun. When asked why, your roommate replies, "Management homework." That may not be as crazy as it sounds. The late Fred Rogers, host of PBS's *Mr. Rogers' Neighborhood*, may well hold the record for factory tours. During his long career, he broadcast footage to millions of children showing how Cheerios, plastic drinking straws, raincoats, pasta, blue jeans, spoons, and a host of other products are made. He was even at Crayola when the one-billionth crayon rolled off the production line. (He also broadcast footage of how Crayola crayons are made and packaged.)

Today, John Ratzenberger (known for his role as Cliff Clavin on *Cheers* and as a regular voice in Pixar animated feature movies (most recently Mustafa the waiter in *Ratatouille*), hosts a cable television program titled *Made in America* that features nothing but factory tours around the United States. The Food Network also broadcasts a program that describes how all kinds of food products are manufactured. Beyond the world of television, however, each year thousands of people visit corporate facilities like these:

- The Boeing Everett Tour Center outside Seattle introduces visitors to how Boeing makes its 747, 767, and 777 passenger jets.
- Steinway & Sons in Queens, New York, offers a two-and-a-half-hour tour that is like a master class. Each Steinway piano takes about a year to build, so you will be able to see pianos at every stage of the production process.
- Ben & Jerry's in Waterbury, Vermont, offers tours accompanied with a scoop of whatever flavor ice cream was made that day.
- Tabasco Factory on Avery Island, Louisiana, is part factory tour, part nature preserve. You can see how the pepper sauce is aged in oak barrels and then step outside to see Bird City, a special structure devised by E. A. McIlhenny to provide a sanctuary for snowy egrets.
- Mack Truck has an assembly plant in Macungie, Pennsylvania. The production line is a mile and a half long, so wear comfortable shoes!
- Yuengling Brewery (which you read about at the beginning of Chapter 5) in Pottsville, Pennsylvania, also offers tours, which include a trip to the cave where the nation's oldest brewery used to age its beer.
- Louisville Slugger in Louisville, Kentucky (where else?), offers a factory tour at the end of which you receive a miniature Slugger bat to take home.
- Harley-Davidson plants in Milwaukee, Kansas City, and York, Pennsylvania, offer factory tours for teens and adults.
- Carousel Magic in Mansfield, Ohio, is one of the few remaining carousel horse manufacturers and restorers.

Many companies no longer open their factories for tours. Kellogg's in Battle Creek, Michigan, ceased giving factory tours in 1986, but now the company operates a museum/activity center called Cereal City. Other companies say they offer factory tours, but in reality the tour is just a marketing device. Budweiser in St. Louis has an enormous visitor center for its tours, but you won't be able to see any of the actual production—just videos and the various outbuildings on the Anheuser-Busch campus. Still other companies offer virtual tours of their operations. Just Born, maker of Marshmallow Peeps, Mike & Ikes, and Hot Tamales, offers a static tour of the Peep production line at **http://www.marshmallowpeeps.com**. Hershey Foods also has an online tour at **http://www.hersheys.com/kidztown/factorytour.shtml**.[92]

Your assignment is to take a factory tour. Use the Internet or other resources to locate a factory tour near you. The site Factory Tours USA (**http://www.factorytoursusa.com**) organizes tours by state, so locating something interesting is easy.

Questions

1. What steps or procedures does the company take to ensure the quality of its products?
2. How does the company measure productivity, and how does its productivity compare with others in the industry?
3. Using the vocabulary from the chapter, describe the basic steps used to make the finished products in this factory.
4. What did you find most impressive about this company or its manufacturing processes? Based on what you read in the chapter, describe one thing the company could do differently to improve quality, increase productivity, or reduce inventory.

REEL TO REAL

BIZ FLIX

Casino

Martin Scorsese's lengthy, complex, and beautifully filmed *Casino* offers a close look at the gambling casinos of Las Vegas and their organized crime connections in the 1970s. It completes his trilogy that began with *Mean Streets* (1973) and continued with *Goodfellas* (1990). In *Casino*, ambition, greed, drugs, and sex ultimately destroy the mob's gambling empire. The film includes strong performances by Robert De Niro, Joe Pesci, and Sharon Stone. The violence and expletive-filled dialogue give *Casino* an R rating.

This scene, which comes from the beginning of "The Truth about Las Vegas" sequence, opens the film and establishes important background about casino operations. Listen carefully to Sam Rothstein's (De Niro) voice-over. He quickly describes the casino's operation and explains how it tries to reach its goals.

What to Watch for and Ask Yourself

1. What type of operations management does this scene show—manufacturing operations management or service operations management?
2. Are the customers directly involved in this operation? If they are, in what way? What likely effects does their involvement have on the casino's operation and its management?
3. Does the casino have independent or interdependent demand systems?

MANAGEMENT WORKPLACE

Peapod—Blurring the Line between Product and Service

From the company's beginning, Peapod cofounder Thomas Parkinson insisted that his firm's website be inviting—packed with images of bright carrots, fresh-baked bread, deep red tomatoes, flavorful beef. But none of these images would have credibility if the food delivered to customers who shopped online at Peapod didn't live up to expectations. All it would take to turn a customer away from placing a second order would be one overripe banana, one slightly gray piece of meat, or a carton of ice cream with freezer burn. To get it right the first time and every time, Peapod relies on an operation that mixes elements of both manufacturing and service businesses. Watch the video to find out how managers at Peapod handle operations at this hybrid management workplace.

Questions

1. What systems and tools has Peapod implemented to insure the highest possible level of productivity?
2. Explain how quality affects the product and service aspects of Peapod's business.
3. Describe the inventory issues Peapod must manage.

ENDNOTES

Chapter 1

1. Factiva, "Q&A with Nortel's Mike Zafirovski," *BusinessWeek Online*, 8 November 2006; E. Gubbins, "Fired Nortel CEO Finds Work," *Prism Insight*, 8 January 2007; M. Heinzl, "Nortel's Plan for Recovery—CEO Is Cutting Costs, Adding Products; Analysts See Hurdles," *Wall Street Journal Asia*, 23 November 2006, 30; M. Heinzl, "Nortel's CEO Details Recovery Plan—Costs Will Be Cut to Save about $1.5 Billion a Year; New Products Part of Mix," *Wall Street Journal*, 24 November 2006, B2; B. Hill, "Nortel Inc. CEO Mike Zafirovski Has Initiated a Host of Changes to Try to Turn Canada's Telecom Giant around, But He Knows There's a Long Way to Go," *Ottawa Citizen*, 29 December 2006, E1; J. Lublin, "How a Rookie CEO Is Testing His Limits," *Wall Street Journal*, 2 January 2007, A1.
2. K. Voigt, "Top Dogs," *Wall Street Journal*, 15 March 2002, W1.
3. A. Horowitz, D. Jacobson, M. Lasswell & O. Thomas, "101 Dumbest Moments in Business," *Business 2.0*, 1 January 2006, 98.
4. M. Herper & R. Langreth, "Dangerous Devices," *Forbes*, 27 November 2006, 94.
5. N. Byrnes & J. Merritt, "Professional Services: The Help Needs Help," *Business Week*, 13 January 2003, 129.
6. T. Peters, "The Leadership Alliance" (Pat Carrigan excerpt), *In Search of Excellence* (Northbrook, IL: Video Arts distributor, 1985), videocassette.
7. K. Hickey, "Faster, Better, More," *Traffic World*, 6 October 2003, 24.
8. K. Jaher, "Wal-Mart Seeks New Flexibility in Worker Shifts," *Wall Street Journal*, 3 January 2007, A1.
9. D. A. Wren, A. G. Bedeian, & J. D. Breeze, "The Foundations of Henri Fayol's Administrative Theory," *Management Decision* 40 (2002): 906–918.
10. H. Fayol, *General and Industrial Management* (London: Pittman & Sons, 1949).
11. R. Stagner, "Corporate Decision Making," *Journal of Applied Psychology* 53 (1969): 1–13.
12. D. W. Bray, R. J. Campbell, & D. L. Grant, *Formative Years in Business: A Long-Term AT&T Study of Managerial Lives* (New York: Wiley, 1993).
13. N. Schwartzreporter & P. Neering, "The Biggest Company in America . . . Is Also a Big Target," *Fortune*, 17 April 2006, 77.
14. A. Lashinsky, "Search and Enjoy," *Fortune*, 22 January 2007, 70.
15. "Yahoo! Re-Aligns Organization to More Effectively Focus on Key Customer Segments and Capture Future Growth Opportunities," Yahoo!, http://yhoo.client .shareholder. com/ press/ReleaseDetail .cfm?ReleaseID = 220987, 5 December 2006.
16. R. J. Grisson, "Probability of the Superior Outcome of One Treatment over Another," *Journal of Applied Psychology* 79 (1994): 314–316; J. E. Hunter & F. L. Schmidt, *Methods of Meta-Analysis: Correcting Error and Bias in Research Findings* (Beverly Hills, CA: Sage, 1990).
17. B. Morris, "The Accidental CEO," *Fortune*, 28 June 2003, 58.
18. Ibid.
19. "Xerox's Chief Copies Good Practice, Not Past Mistakes," *Irish Times*, 21 March 2003, 62.
20. "Xerox's 3Q Profits Jump on Product Sales," *eWeek*, 21 October 2004.
21. A. Warren, "The Small Stuff: It's the Little Things That Add Up—and Often Annoy," *Wall Street Journal*, 10 May 2004, R9.
22. "Why Corporate Boardrooms Are in Turmoil," *Wall Street Journal*, 16 September 2006, A7.
23. "Why Corporate Boardrooms Are in Turmoil," *Wall Street Journal*, 16 September 2006, A7.
24. M. Arndt, "Creativity Overflowing," *BusinessWeek*, 8 May 2006, 50.
25. H. S. Jonas III, R. E. Fry, & S. Srivastva, "The Office of the CEO: Understanding the Executive Experience," *Academy of Management Executive* 4 (1990): 36–47.
26. M. Porter, J. Lorsch, & N. Nohria, "Seven Surprises for New CEOS," *Harvard Business Review*, October 2004, 62.
27. M. Murray, "As Huge Firms Keep Growing, CEOs Struggle to Keep Pace," *Wall Street Journal*, 8 February 2001, A1.
28. Ibid.
29. Q. Huy, "In Praise of Middle Managers," *Harvard Business Review*, September 2001, 72–79.
30. C. Hymowitz, "CEOs Work Hard to Maintain the Faith in the Corner Office," *Wall Street Journal*, 9 July 2002, B1; L. Mitchell, "How to Do the Right Thing," *Optimize*, February 2002, http://www.optimizemag .com, 1 February 2003.
31. C. Hymowitz, "Middle Managers Are Unsung Heroes on Corporate Stage," *Wall Street Journal*, 19 September 2005, B1.
32. "Management & Professional: Regional Manager," *Pharmacy Today*, 18 October 2006, 27.
33. T. Seideman, "Harnessing the Giant," *World Trade* 15 (2002): 28–29.

34. G. Will, "Waging War on Wal-Mart," *Newsweek*, 5 July 2004, 64.

35. S. Warren, "The Transient Workers," *Wall Street Journal*, 28 October 2002, R4.

36. J. Adamy, "A Menu of Options: Restaurants Have a Host of Ways to Motivate Employees to Provide Good Service," *Wall Street Journal*, 30 October 2006, R1, R6.

37. C. Hymowitz, "Today's Bosses Find Mentoring Isn't Worth the Time and Risks," *Wall Street Journal*, 13 March 2006, B1.

38. S. Tully, "What Team Leaders Need to Know," *Fortune*, 20 February 1995, 93.

39. B. Francella, "In a Day's Work," *Convenience Store News*, 25 September 2001, 7.

40. L. Liu & A. McMurray, "Frontline Leaders: The Entry Point for Leadership Development in the Manufacturing Industry," *Journal of European Industrial Training* 28, issue 2–4 (2004): 339–352.

41. Tully, "What Team Leaders Need to Know."

42. Ibid.

43. "What Makes Teams Work?" *Fast Company*, 1 November 2000, 109.

44. K. Hultman, "The 10 Commandments of Team Leadership," *Training & Development*, 1 February 1998, 12–13.

45. N. Steckler & N. Fondas, "Building Team Leader Effectiveness: A Diagnostic Tool," *Organizational Dynamics*, Winter 1995, 20–34.

46. L. Landro, "The Informed Patient: Bringing Surgeons Down to Earth—New Programs Aim to Curb Fear that Prevents Nurses from Flagging Problems," *Wall Street Journal*, 16 November 2005, D1.

47. Ibid.

48. H. Mintzberg, *The Nature of Managerial Work* (New York: Harper & Row, 1973).

49. C. P. Hales, "What Do Managers Do? A Critical Review of the Evidence," *Journal of Management Studies* 23, no. 1 (1986): 88–115.

50. "Grand Opening of Kikkoman Foods Europe," Kikkoman Corporation, http://www.kikkoman.com/news/news15.html, 26 January 2003.

51. "CDW Named One of the Best Companies to Work for in America for Fourth Consecutive Year," CDW Corporation, http://www.cdw.com, 26 January 2003.

52. J. Boorstin, "J. M. Smucker," *Fortune*, 12 January 2004, 58.

53. R. Levering & M. Moskowitz, "The 100 Best Companies to Work For," *Fortune*, 12 January 2004, 56.

54. B. Einhorn & M. Kripalani, "India 3.0: Bangalore Wants to Move Beyond Simple Code," *BusinessWeek*, 26 February 2001, 16.

55. Francella, "In a Day's Work."

56. "Industry Specific: News Segmented by Major Industries," *Business Wire*, http://www.businesswire.com, 27 January 2003.

57. "Media Monitoring," *CyberAlert*, http://www.cyberalert.com, 27 January 2003.

58. "What Is FNS News Clips Online?" *FNS NewsClips*, http://www.news-clips.com, 27 January 2003.

59. "Cultural Practices of the Best Companies," *Great Place to Work Institute*, 4 January 2005, http://www.greatplacetoworkcom/great/culture.php.

60. Murray, "As Huge Firms Keep Growing."

61. R. Guth, J. Delaney, & D. Clark, "Microsoft to Launch Challenge to Google, Yahoo," *Wall Street Journal*, 10 November 2004, A3.

62. C. Arnst, "The Best Medical Care in the U.S.: How Veterans Affairs Transformed Itself," *BusinessWeek*, 17 July 2006, 50.

63. M. Langley, "Changing Gears," *Wall Street Journal*, 22 December 2006, A1.

64. M. Rieker, "E-Trade Raises Banking Sights for '07," *American Banker*, 8 January 2007, 1.

65. D. Welch & G. Khermouch, "Can GM Save an Icon?" *BusinessWeek*, 8 April 2002, 60.

66. A. Sharma, "Poor Reception: After Sprint and Nextel Merge, Customers and Executives Leave," *Wall Street Journal*, 11 October 2006, A1.

67. L. A. Hill, *Becoming a Manager: Mastery of a New Identity* (Boston: Harvard Business School Press, 1992).

68. R. L. Katz, "Skills of an Effective Administrator," *Harvard Business Review*, September–October 1974, 90–102.

69. C. A. Bartlett & S. Ghoshal, "Changing the Role of Top Management: Beyond Systems to People," *Harvard Business Review*, May–June 1995, 132–142.

70. F. L. Schmidt & J. E. Hunter, "Development of a Causal Model of Process Determining Job Performance," *Current Directions in Psychological Science* 1 (1992): 89–92.

71. J. B. Miner, "Sentence Completion Measures in Personnel Research: The Development and Validation of the Miner Sentence Completion Scales," in *Personality Assessment in Organizations*, ed. H. J. Bernardin & D. A. Bownas (New York: Praeger, 1986), 147–146.

72. M. W. McCall, Jr. & M. M. Lombardo, "What Makes a Top Executive?" *Psychology Today*, February 1983, 26–31; E. van Velsor & J. Brittain, "Why Executives Derail: Perspectives across Time and Cultures," *Academy of Management Executive*, November 1995, 62–72.

73. McCall, Jr. & Lombardo, "What Makes a Top Executive?"

74. A. K. Naj, "Corporate Therapy: The Latest Addition to Executive Suite Is Psychologist's Couch," *Wall Street Journal*, 29 August 1994, A1.

75. Ibid.

76. P. Wallington, "Management2 Toxic!" *Financial Mail*, 28 July 2006, 48.

77. J. Sandberg, "Overcontrolling Bosses Aren't Just Annoying; They're Also Inefficient," *Wall Street Journal*, 30 March 2005, B1.

78. J. Pfeffer, *The Human Equation: Building Profits by Putting People First* (Boston: Harvard Business School Press, 1996); *Competitive Advantage through People: Unleashing the Power of the Work Force* (Boston: Harvard Business School Press, 1994).

79. D. McDonald & A. Smith, "A Proven Connection: Performance Management and Business Results," *Compensation & Benefits Review* 27, no. 6 (1 January 1995): 59.

80. I. Fulmer, B. Gerhart, & K. Scott, "Are the 100 Best Better? An Empirical Investigation of the Relationship between Being a 'Great Place to Work' and Firm Performance," *Personnel Psychology* (Winter 2003): 965–993.

81. B. Schneider & D. E. Bowen, "Employee and Customer Perceptions of Service in Banks: Replication and Extension," *Journal of Applied Psychology* 70 (1985): 423–433; B. Schneider, J. J. Parkington, & V. M. Buxton, "Employee and Customer Perceptions of Service in Banks," *Administrative Science Quarterly* 25 (1980): 252–267.

82. P. L. Hunsaker, *Management: A Skills Approach* (Upper Saddle River, New Jersey: Pearson Prentice Hall, 2005) 24–25.

83. N. Brodsky, "Pennies from Heaven," *Inc.*, 1 December 2004, 54.

84. S. McCartney, "A New Way to Prevent Lost Luggage," *Wall Street Journal*, 27 February 2007, D1; S. McCartney, "Why Airlines Keep Losing Your Luggage," *Wall Street Journal*, 16 January 2007, D1; S. McCartney, "Travelers Blast Airlines for Lost Bags," *Wall Street Journal*, 16 January 2007, online; J. Ogando, "It's the Luggage that Flies at Siemens' Mock Airport," *Design News*, 8 January 2007, 30; R. Grantham, "Heightened Security Leads to 40% Increase in Checked Baggage," *Atlanta Journal-Constitution*, 18 August 2006, online; K. Tagami, "Atlanta Airport's Finances Rated High," *Atlanta Journal-Constitution*, 16 July 2004, online; K. Tagami, "Airline Bankruptcies Blow Hole in Atlanta Airport Budget as Hangar Leases Flag," *Atlanta Journal-Constitution*, 26 January 2006, online; http://www.atlanta-airport.com/sublevels/airport_info/pdfs/Traffic/200701.pdf.

85. Hill, *Becoming a Manager*.

Chapter 2

1. J. Hough & M. White, "Using Stories to Create Change: The Object Lesson of Frederick Taylor's 'Pig-Tale,'" *Journal of Management* 27 (2001): 585–601; E. Locke, "The Ideas of Frederick W. Taylor: An Evaluation," *Academy of Management Review* 7 (1982): 14–24; F. W. Taylor, *The Principles of Scientific Management* (New York: Harper, 1911); C. Wrege & R. Hodgetts, "Frederick W. Taylor's 1899 Pig Iron Observations: Examining Fact, Fiction, and Lessons for the New Millennium," *Academy of Management Journal* 43 (2000): 1283–1291; D. Wren, *The History of Management Thought*, 5th ed. (New York: Wiley, 2005).

2. G. Glotz, *Ancient Greece at Work* (New York: Alfred A. Knopf, 1926).

3. C. S. George, Jr., *The History of Management Thought* (Englewood Cliffs, NJ: Prentice-Hall, 1972).

4. "Sumerian Language," *Britannica Online 2003*, http:// www.eb.com, 16 September 2003.

5. A. Erman, *Life in Ancient Egypt* (London: Macmillan & Co., 1984).

6. J. Burke, *The Day the Universe Changed* (Boston: Little, Brown, 1985).

7. "History of the Organization of Work: Organization of Work in Preindustrial Times: Medieval Industry," *Britannica Online*, http://www.eb.com, 15 January 1999.

8. "History of the Organization of Work: Organization of Work in Preindustrial Times: The Ancient World," *Britannica Online*, http://www.eb.com, 15 January 1999.

9. "History of the Organization of Work: Organization of Work in Preindustrial Times: From the 16th to the 18th Century," *Britannica Online*, http://www.eb.com, 15 January 1999.

10. J. B. White, "The Line Starts Here: Mass-Production Techniques Changed the Way People Work and Live throughout the World," *Wall Street Journal*, 11 January 1999, R25.

11. R. B. Reich, *The Next American Frontier* (New York: Times Books, 1983).

12. J. Mickelwait & A. Wooldridge, *The Company: A Short History of a Revolutionary Idea* (New York: Modern Library, 2003).

13. "How Business Schools Began," *BusinessWeek*, 12 October 1963, 114–116.

14. *Industrial Management: The Engineering Magazine* 61 (1921): 232.

15. H. Kendall, "Unsystematized, Systematized, and Scientific Management," in *Scientific Management: A Collection of the More Significant Articles Describing the Taylor System of Management*, ed. C. Thompson (Easton, PA: Hive Publishing, 1972), 103–131.

16. United States Congress, House, Special Committee, *Hearings to Investigate the Taylor and Other Systems of Shop Management*, vol. 3. (Washington, D.C.: Government Printing Office, 1912).

17. Ibid.

18. Ibid.

19. Taylor, *The Principles of Scientific Management*.

20. A. Derickson, "Physiological Science and Scientific Management in the Progressive Era: Frederic S. Lee and the Committee on Industrial Fatigue," *Business History Review* 68 (1994): 483–514.

21. United States Congress, House, Special Committee, 1912.

22. Taylor, *The Principles of Scientific Management*.

23. Ibid.

24. Wrege & Hodgetts, "Frederick W. Taylor's 1899 Pig Iron Observations"; Hough & White, "Using Stories to Create Change."

25. Locke, "The Ideas of Frederick W. Taylor."

26. George, Jr., *The History of Management Thought*.

27. F. Gilbreth & L. Gilbreth, "Applied Motion Study," in *The Writings of the Gilbreths*, ed. W. R. Spriegel & C. E. Myers (1917; rpr. Homewood, IL: Irwin, 1953), 207–274.

28. D. Ferguson, "Don't Call It 'Time and Motion Study,'" *IIE Solutions* 29, no. 5 (1997): 22–23.

29. Ibid.

30. "Frank and Lillian Gilbreth: Motion Study Pioneers," *Thinkers*, December 2000.

31. J. Gotcher, "Assisting the Handicapped: The Pioneering Efforts of Frank and Lillian Gilbreth," *Journal of Management* 18 (1992): 5–14.

32. F. Gilbreth & L. Gilbreth, "Motion Study for the Crippled Soldier," *American Society of Mechanical Engineers Journal* 37 (1915): 669–673.

33. H. Gantt, "A Bonus System for Rewarding Labor," *Transactions of the American Society of Mechanical Engineers* 23 (1901): 373.

34. P. Peterson, "Training and Development: The View of Henry L. Gantt (1861–1919)," *SAM Advanced Management Journal*, Winter 1987, 20–23.

35. H. Gantt, "Industrial Efficiency," *National Civic Federation Report of the 11th Annual Meeting*, New York, 12 January 1991, 103.

36. Ibid.

37. M. Weber, *The Theory of Economic and Social Organization*, trans. by A. Henderson & T. Parsons (New York: Free Press, 1947).

38. M. Weber, *The Protestant Ethic and the Spirit of Capitalism* (New York: Scribner's, 1958).

39. George, Jr., *The History of Management Thought*.

40. D. Wren, "Henri Fayol As Strategist: A Nineteenth Century Corporate Turnaround," *Management Decision* 39 (2001): 475–487.

41. D. Reid, "Fayol: From Experience to Theory," *Journal of Management History* 3 (1995): 21–36.

42. H. Fayol, "Observations et expériences personnelles," *Archives Fayol*, no date, 4–11.

43. Wren, "Henri Fayol As Strategist"; Reid, "Fayol: From Experience to Theory."

44. Wren, "Henri Fayol As Strategist."

45. Ibid.

46. Ibid.

47. Ibid.

48. F. Blancpain, "Les cahiers inédits d'Henri Fayol," trans. D. Wren, *Extrait du bulletin de l'institut international d'administration publique* 28–9 (1974): 1–48.

49. H. Verney, "Un grand ingénieur: Henri Fayol," *La fondateur de la doctrine administrative: Henri Fayol* (Paris: Dunod, 1925), as cited in Wren, "Henri Fayol As Strategist."

50. D. A. Wren, A. G. Bedeian, & J. D. Breeze, "The Foundations of Henri Fayol's Administrative Theory," *Management Decision* 40 (2002): 906–918.

51. H. Fayol, *General and Industrial Management* (London: Pittman & Sons, 1949).

52. M. P. Follett, *Mary Parker Follett—Prophet of Management: A Celebration of Writings from the 1920s*, ed. P. Graham (Boston: Harvard Business School Press, 1995).

53. Ibid.

54. D. Linden, "The Mother of Them All," *Forbes*, 16 January 1995, 75.

55. E. O'Connor, "The Politics of Management Thought: A Case Study of the Harvard Business School and the Human Relations School," *Academy of Management Review* 24 (1999): 117–131.

56. M. Losey, "HR Comes of Age," *HRMagazine* 43, no. 3 (1998): 40–53.

57. J. H. Smith, "The Enduring Legacy of Elton Mayo," *Human Relations* 51, no. 3 (1998): 221–249.

58. E. Mayo, *The Human Problems of an Industrial Civilization* (New York: Macmillan, 1933).

59. Ibid.

60. "Hawthorne Revisited: The Legend and the Legacy," *Organizational Dynamics* (Winter 1975): 66–80.

61. E. Mayo, *The Social Problems of an Industrial Civilization* (Boston: Harvard Graduate School of Business Administration, 1945).

62. Mayo, *The Social Problems of an Industrial Civilization*, 65–67.

63. "Hawthorne Revisited: The Legend and the Legacy."

64. Mayo, *The Social Problems of an Industrial Civilization*, 45.

65. George, Jr., *The History of Management Thought*.

66. C. I. Barnard, *The Functions of the Executive* (Cambridge, MA: Harvard University Press, 1938), 4.

67. C. I. Barnard, *The Functions of the Executive: 30th Anniversary Edition* (Cambridge, MA: Harvard University Press, 1968), 5.

68. S. Parayitam, M. White, & J. Hough, "Juxtaposition of Chester I. Barnard and Frederick W. Taylor: Forerunners of Management," *Management Decision* 40 (2002): 1003–1012.

69. J. Dunkelberg & D. Jessup, "So Then Why Did You Do It?" *Journal of Business Ethics* 29 (2001): 422–426.

70. J. Fuller & A. Mansour, "Operations Management and Operations Research: A Historical and Relational Perspective," *Management Decision* 41 (2003): 422–426.

71. "Monge, Gaspard, comte de Péluse," *Britannica Online*, http://www.eb.com, 9 January 2005.

72. D. Ashmos & G. Huber, "The Systems Paradigm in Organization Theory: Correcting the Record and Suggesting the Future," *Academy of Management Review* 12 (1987): 607–621; F. Kast & J. Rosenzweig, "General Systems Theory: Applications for Organizations and Management," *Academy of Management Journal* 15 (1972): 447–465; D. Katz & R. Kahn, *The Social Psychology of Organizations* (New York: Wiley, 1966).

73. R. Mockler, "The Systems Approach to Business Organization and Decision Making," *California Management Review* 11, issue 2 (1968): 53–58.

74. F. Luthans & T. Stewart, "A General Contingency Theory of Management," *Academy of Management Review* 2, issue 2 (1977): 181–195.

75. C.K.W. de Dreu, A. Evers, B. Beersma, E.S. Kluwer, & A. Nauta, "A Theory-Based Measure of Conflict Management Strategies in the Workplace," *Journal of Organizational Behavior* 22 (2001) 645–668.

76. A. Scharf, "Scripted Talk: From 'Welcome to McDonald's' to 'Paper or Plastic?' Employers Control the Speech of Service Workers," *Dollars & Sense*, September–October 2003, 35; C. McCann, "Have a Nice Day and an Icy Stare," *Marketing Week*, 2 September 2004, 27; G. Garfinkel Weiss, "Improving Collections: To Collect at the Time of Service and Overcome Patient Excuses for Nonpayment, Tell Staffers to Stick to the Script," *Medical Economics*, 9 July 2004, 70.

Chapter 3

1. "Until Recently Full of Promise, Satellite Radio Runs Into Static," *Wall Street Journal*, 15 August 2006, A1.; S. Finlay, "XM Radio Ventures Beyond Audio Services," *Ward's Dealer Business*, July 2005, 39(7): 8; S. Finlay "XM Radio Looks Beyond Audio," *Ward's Auto World*, June 2005, 41(6): 18; N. Bussey, "Can Satellite Radio Become a Serious Medium?," *Campaign (UK)*, 27 January 2006, (4):17; T. Lowry & P. Lehman, "Grudge Match," *BusinessWeek*, 21–28 August 2006, 86–87; C. Edwards, "Taking XM Out for a Stroll," 14 August 2006, 18; "Record Companies Sue XM Radio for Copyright Infringement," *Computer & Internet Lawyer*, September 2006, 23(9): 38; S. Wildstrom, "Copyrights and Wrongs," *BusinessWeek*, 3 July 2006, 24; http://www.xmradio.com; http://www.sirius.com; "Two Upstarts Vie for Dominance in Satellite Radio," *Wall Street Journal*, 30, March 2005, A1–A9.

2. L. Heller, "Health Could Boost Declining US Cookie Sales: Report," www.foodnavigator.com, 18 August 2006. http://www.foodnavigator-usa.com/news/ng.asp?id=69965-cookies-whole-grains-healthy-eating.

3. "A Nation of Snackers Snubs Old Favorite," *Wall Street Journal*, 16 June 2004, A1.

4. D. Alexander, "Bread Makers Feel the Diet Pinch," *Chicago Tribune*, 30 December 2003, Business 1.

5. R. Guth, "Videogame Giant Links with Sony, Snubbing Microsoft," *Wall Street Journal*, 12 May 2003, A1; "Cost of Making Games Set to Soar," *BBC News*, 17, November 2005, http://news.bbc.co.uk/1/hi/technology/4442346.stm

6. E. Romanelli & M. L. Tushman, "Organizational Transformation as Punctuated Equilibrium: An Empirical Test," *Academy of Management Journal* 37 (1994): 1141–1166.

7. H. Banks, "A Sixties Industry in a Nineties Economy," *Forbes*, 9 May 1994, 107–112.

8. L. Cowan, "Cheap Fuel Should Carry Many Airlines to More Record Profits for 1st Quarter," *Wall Street Journal*, 4 April 1998, B17A.

9. "Annual Revenues and Earnings: U.S. Airlines—All Services," Air Transport Association, http://www.airlines.org, 15 January 2005; S. Carey, "Carrier Makes Deeper Cuts As It Seeks Federal

Backing Needed to Exit Chapter 11," *Wall Street Journal*, 27 November 2002, A3; S. Carey, "UAL Will Lay Off 1,500 Workers As Part of Cost-Cutting Strategy," *Wall Street Journal*, 6 January 2003, A3; D. Carty, "Oral Testimony of Mr. Donald J. Carty, Chairman and CEO, American Airlines: United States Senate, Committee on Commerce, Science, and Transportation," http://www.amrcorp.com 9 January 2003; S. McCartney, M. Trottman, & S. Carey, "Northwest, Continental, America West Post Losses As Delta Cuts Jobs," *Wall Street Journal*, 18 November 2002, B4.

10. "Airlines Still in Upheaval, 5 Years after 9/11," *CNNMoney.com*, 8 September 2006, http://money.cnn.com/2006/09/08/news/companies/ airlines_sept11/?postversion = 2006090812.

11. "New Product Review," *Dairy Foods*, http://www.dairyfoods.com, 15 January 2005; B. Jones, "The Changing Dairy Industry," Department of Agricultural & Applied Economics & Center for Dairy Profitability, http://www.aae.wisc.edu/jones/Presentations/Wisc&TotalDairyTrends.pdf, 15 January 2003.

12. S. Ghosemajumder, "Digital Music Distribution," *MIT Sloan School of Management*, http://shumans.com/digital-music/?p=1&p2=1.html; "30 Products for 30 Years," *MacWorld*, June 2006, 15–16; T. Mennecke, "CD Sales, Shipments Down in 2005," *Slyck News*, 31 March 2006, http://www. slyck.com/news.php?story=1143; P. Burrows, "Microsoft Singing Its Own iTune," *BusinessWeek Online*, 11 July 2006, 20; "Apple Presents iPod," 23 October 2001, http://www.apple.com/pr/library/2001/oct/23ipod.html; http://www.wikipedia.com.

13. "Samsung Invests $2.1B in LCD Line," *Electronic News*, 7 March 2005; "L. G. Philips LCD Develops 100-Inch LCD Panel, the Largest in the World," L. G. Philips, www.lgphilips-lcd.com/homeContain/jsp/eng/inv/inv101_j_e.jsp?BOARD_IDX=1054&languageSec=E; "Samsung, L. G. Philips start new LCD Production," *CyberMedia India Online*, www.ciol.com/content/news/2006/106010202.asp; "Samsung Develops World's Largest (82") Full HDTV TFT-LCD," Samsung, http://www.samsung.com/Products/TFTLCD/News/category_TFTLCD_20050307_0000101494.htm, "Samsung and L. G. Philips start new LCD Production," *Boston.com*, 1 January 2006, http://www.boston.com/business/articles/2006/01/01/samsung_and_lgphilips_start_new_lcd_production; E. Ramstad, "I Want My Flat TV Now!" *Wall Street Journal*, 27 May 2004, B1.

14. "Consumer Products Brief—Kraft Foods Inc.: Price of Maxwell House Coffee to Rise 14% As Costs Increase," *Wall Street Journal*, 15 December 2004, A16.

15. R. Norton, "Where Is This Economy Really Heading?" *Fortune*, 7 August 1995, 54–56.

16. "First, by the Numbers, the CFO Poll," *Fortune*, 17 February 2003, 30.

17. A. Weintraub, "It's on the Tip of Your Tongue," *BusinessWeek*, 31 July 2006, 32.

18. J. Fletcher, "Extreme Nesting," *Wall Street Journal*, 7 January 2000, W1.

19. "CDW Ranks on Best Places to Work List for Fifth Straight Year," *PR Newswire*, 7 January 2003.

20. M. Perotin, "Dallas-Based Baylor Health Care Offers Concierge Perk to Employees," *Fort Worth Star-Telegram*, 8 December 2002.

21. R. Sharpe, "Nannies on Speed Dial: There Is Growing Army of Domestic Help Out There, and More and More Families Are Picking Up the Phone," *BusinessWeek*, 18 September 2000, 108; N. Powell, "Going Above and Beyond," *The Hamilton Spectator*, 25 July 2006, http://www.circles.com/news/news_Jul06_article_Above_and_Beyond.htm.

22 C. R. Gentry & M. Wilson, "Living Made Easy: Service-Oriented Concepts Cater to Time-Starved Consumers," *Chain Store Age*, October 2006, 39–41.

23. The Civil Rights Act of 1991, available at U.S. Equal Employment Opportunity Commission, http://www.eeoc.gov/policy/cra91.html, 16 January 2005.

24. Compliance Assistance—Family and Medical Leave Act (FMLA), U.S. Department of Labor: Employment Standards Administration Wage and Hour Division, http://www.dol.gov/esa/whd/fmla, 16 January 2005.

25. R. J. Bies & T. R. Tyler, "The Litigation Mentality in Organizations: A Test of Alternative Psychological Explanations," *Organization Science* 4 (1993): 352–366.

26. D. Jones, "Fired Workers Fight Back ... and Win," *USA Today*, 2 April 1998, B1.

27. S. Gardner, G. Gomes, & J. Morgan, "Wrongful Termination and the Expanding Public Policy Exception: Implications and Advice," *SAM Advanced Management Journal* 65 (2000): 38.

28. Jones, "Fired Workers Fight Back."

29. T. Gerdel, "Liability Suits Have Lasting Effect on Transportation Companies," *Cleveland Plain Dealer*, 13 August 2002, C5.

30. "Products Liability Law: An Overview," Legal Information Institute, http://www.law.cornell.edu/wex/index.php/Products_liability, 8 February 2003.

31. Gerdel, "Liability Suits."

32. R. Johnston & S. Mehra, "Best-Practice Complaint Management," *Academy of Management Experience* 16 (November 2002): 145–154.

33. D. Smart & C. Martin, "Manufacturer Responsiveness to Consumer Correspondence: An Empirical Investigation of Consumer Perceptions," *Journal of Consumer Affairs* 26 (1992): 104.

34. H. Appelman, "I Scream, You Scream: Consumers Vent over the Net," *New York Times*, 4 March 2001.

35. J. Pereira, "Trends (A Special Report)—It's a Whole New Game," *Wall Street Journal*, 22 November 2004, R9; http://www.kbtoys.com/help/giftcard.html; http://www4.toysrus.com/corpgiftcard.

36. S. Gray, "Trends (A Special Report)—On the Menu: Speed and Variety," *Wall Street Journal*, 22 November 2004, R4.

37. S. A. Zahra & S. S. Chaples, "Blind Spots in Competitive Analysis," *Academy of Management Executive* 7 (1993): 7–28.

38. "The Cola Wars: Over a Century of Cola Slogans, Commercials, Blunders, and Coups," http://www.geocities.com/colacentury/.

39. M. Frazier, "You Suck: Dyson, Hoover and Oreck Trade Accusations in Court, on TV as Brit Upstart Leaves Rivals in Dust," *Advertising Age*, 25 July 2005, 1.

40. J. M. Moran, "Getting Closer Together—Videophones Don't Deliver TV Quality Sound, Visuals, but They're

Improving," *Seattle Times*, 15 March 1998.

41. P. Grant, "Comcast Plans Major Rollout of Phone Service over Cable," *Wall Street Journal*, 10 January 2005, B1.
42. R. Buckman, "Telecom Price Wars Get Brutal in Hong Kong," *Wall Street Journal*, 28 October 2004, B4.
43. A. Squeo, "FCC Is Poised to Clarify Future of Internet Phone Calls," *Wall Street Journal*, 22 January 2004, B1.
44. K. G. Provan, "Embeddedness, Interdependence, and Opportunism in Organizational Supplier-Buyer Networks," *Journal of Management* 19 (1993): 841–856.
45. C. Unninayar & N. P. Sindt, "Diamonds' an Industry in Transition: Sometimes the Speed of Change Is Alarming," *Couture International Jeweler*, August–Sept 2003, 68–75. N. Gaouette, "Israel's Diamond Dealers Tremble: Diamond Colossus De Beers Today Launches Fundamental Changes to $56 Billion Retail Market," *Christian Science Monitor*, 1 June 2001, online.
46. N. Shirouzu, "Chain Reaction—Big Three's Outsourcing Plan: Make Parts Suppliers Do It," *Wall Street Journal*, 10 June 2004, A1.
47. D. Birch, "Staying on Good Terms," *Supply Management*, 12 April 2001, 36.
48. S. Parker & C. Axtell, "Seeing Another Viewpoint: Antecedents and Outcomes of Employee Perspective Taking," *Academy of Management Journal* 44 (2001): 1085–1100; B. K. Pilling, L. A. Crosby, & D. W. Jackson, "Relational Bonds in Industrial Exchange: An Experimental Test of the Transaction Cost Economic Framework," *Journal of Business Research* 30 (1994): 237–251.
49. "Carmakers Eye Economy with Unease," *USA Today*, 24 May 2004, B.06.
50. Title 25 Health Services Part 1: Texas Department of Health Chapter 229, Food and Drug Subchapter U, Permitting Retail Food Establishments," Texas Department of Health, http://www.tdh.state.tx.us/bfds/retail/permittingrules.html, 11 February 2003.
51. M. Horn, "Sinning in an SUV," *U.S. News & World Report*, 16 December 2002, 10; http://www.nhtsa.dot.gov/cars/rules/cafe/overview.htm
52. "Seafood HACCP," U.S. Food and Drug Administration Center for Food Safety & Applied Nutrition, http://www.cfsan.fda.gov/~comm/haccpsea.html, 11 February 2003.
53. S. Dudley, "The Coming Shift in Regulation," *Regulation*, 1 October 2002.
54. S. Dudley, "Regulation and Small Business Competitive," *Federal Document Clearing House*, Congressional Testimony, Prepared Remarks for the House Committee on Small Business Subcommittee on Regulatory Reform and Oversight, 20 May 2004.
55. H. Morley, "Bush Orders Cut in Regulations—Change Will Cut Red Tape for Small Businesses," *Knight-Ridder Tribune*, 17 August 2002.
56. "EU's Aggressive Anti-Smoking Campaign," *Creative Bits*, http://creativebits.org/eus_agressive_anti-smoking_campaign, 17 January 2005.
57. "Ethical Dangers Multiply," *Purchasing*, 17 October 1996; J. Dubinsky, "How to Foster Ethical Conduct: Companies Have a Clear Role in Preventing Conflicts of Interest," *Supplier Selection & Management*, 1 June 2001; "Amerinet Joins Groups Issuing Compliance Documents Based on Code of Conduct," *Hospital Materials Management*, 1 January 2003, 6; M. Lawson, "The Ethical Dilemma of Corporate Generosity," *Australian Financial Review*, 5 December 2002, 16.
58. M. Hudson, "PETA Doll Ruffles KFC's Feathers," *Roanoke Times*, http://www.roanoke.com/extra%5C16581.html, 8 January 2005.
59. "Another Ford Trial: Steering around Activists," *Wall Street Journal*, 26 July 2006, A2.
60. N. E. Boudette & J. A. White, "At GM, Curbing Inventories Calls for Juggling Act," *Wall Street Journal*, 8 January 2007, A1.
61. J. Ball, "Detroit Fears Some Consumers May Be Souring on Big SUVs," *Wall Street Journal Online*, http://online.wsj.com/article/B1041979477724000464.html, 8 January 2003.
62. C. Hymowitz, "Top Marketing Officers Find Getting Together Helps Them Do the Job," *Wall Street Journal*, 11 January 2005, B1.
63. D. F. Jennings & J. R. Lumpkin, "Insights between Environmental Scanning Activities and Porter's Generic Strategies: An Empirical Analysis," *Journal of Management* 4 (1992): 791–803.
64. V. Vara, "Software Giants Seek Friends among Hackers," *Wall Street Journal*, 3 August 2006, B1.
65. S. E. Jackson & J. E. Dutton, "Discerning Threats and Opportunities," *Administrative Science Quarterly* 33 (1988): 370–387.
66. B. Thomas, S. M. Clark, & D. A. Gioia, "Strategic Sensemaking and Organizational Performance: Linkages among Scanning, Interpretation, Action, and Outcomes," *Academy of Management Journal* 36 (1993): 239–270.
67. R. Daft, J. Sormunen, & D. Parks, "Chief Executive Scanning, Environmental Characteristics, and Company Performance: An Empirical Study," *Strategic Management Journal* 9 (1988): 123–139; V. Garg, B. Walters, & R. Priem, "Chief Executive Scanning Emphases, Environmental Dynamism, and Manufacturing Firm Performance," *Strategic Management Journal* 24 (2003): 725–744; D. Miller & P. H. Friesen, "Strategy-Making and Environment: The Third Link," *Strategic Management Journal* 4 (1983): 221–235.
68. P. Grant, "Comcast Plans Major Rollout of Phone Service over Cable."
69. L. Yuan & C. Bryan-Low, "iPhone Hinges On the Likes of Mr. Digate: In High-End Realm, Handset Must Court the Affluent Tech-Set," *Wall Street Journal*, 11 January 2007, B4.
70. K. Maney, "SAS Workers Won When Greed Lost," *USA Today*, 22 April 2004, B.01.
71. A. Harrington, N. Hira, & C. Tkaczyk, "Hall of Fame: If Making the 100 Best List Is an Enormous Accomplishment, Consider How Tough It Is to Repeat the Feat Every Single Year," *Fortune*, 24 January 2005, 94.
72. "SAS Makes the *Fortune* 'Hall of Fame,'" SAS, http://www.sas.com/news/feature/16jan05/fortune.html, 20 January 2005.
73. P. Elmer-DeWitt, "Mine, All Mine; Bill Gates Wants a Piece of Everybody's Action, but Can He Get It?" *Time*, 5 June 1995.
74. D. M. Boje, "The Storytelling Organization: A Study of Story Performance in an Office-Supply Firm," *Administrative Science Quarterly* 36 (1991): 106–126.

75. S. Walton & J. Huey, *Sam Walton: Made in America* (New York: Doubleday, 1992).

76. D. Rushe, "Wal-Martians," *Sunday Times–London*, 10 June 2001, 5.

77. M. Hayes, "Bowa Builders: NRS Excellence in Class, 50—Plus," *HousingZone.com*, http://www.housingzone.com/topics/pr/nrs/pr03ia009.asp, 19 January 2005.

78. D. R. Denison & A. K. Mishra, "Toward a Theory of Organizational Culture and Effectiveness," *Organization Science* 6 (1995): 204–223.

79. D. Jones, "When You're Smiling, Are You Seething Inside? Passive-Aggressive Culture Hurts Companies, Workers," *USA Today*, 12 April 2004, B.01.

80. F. Haley, "Mutual Benefit: How Does Genencor Maintain Its Incredibly Loyal Workforce? By Involving Its Employees in Almost Everything," *Fast Company*, October 2004, 98–100.

81. "Company Profile," F. H. Faulding & Company, http://www.faulding.com.au/home/comp_profile/mission/mission.html, 21 June 2001.

82. S. Yearout, G. Miles, & R. Koonce, "Multi-Level Visioning," *Training & Development*, 1 March 2001, 31.

83. T. Brown, "A Vision from Scratch," *Across the Board*, 1 May 2001, 77.

84. M. A. Salva-Ramirez, "McDonald's: A Prime Example of Corporate Culture," *Public Relations Quarterly*, Winter 1995, 30–32.

85. "Hamburger University," McDonald's Media Site, http://www.mcdonalds.com/corp/career/hamburger_university.html, 18 January 2005.

86. J. Sorenson, "The Strength of Corporate Culture and the Reliability of Firm Performance," *Administrative Science Quarterly* 47 (2002): 70–91.

87. A. Zuckerman, "Strong Corporate Cultures and Firm Performance: Are There Tradeoffs?" *Academy of Management Executive*, November 2002, 158–160.

88. *McDonald's Summary Annual Report 2005*, 2–4; D. Stires, "McDonald's Keeps Right on Cooking," *Fortune*, 17 May 2004, 102.

89. E. Schein, *Organizational Culture and Leadership*, 2d ed. (San Francisco: Jossey-Bass, 1992).

90. E. Byron, "'Call Me Mike!'—To Attract and Keep Talent, JCPenney CEO Loosens Up Once-Formal Workplace," *Wall Street Journal*, 27 March 2006, B1.

91. Ibid.

92. C. Daniels, "Does This Man Need a Shrink? Companies Are Using Psychological Testing to Screen Candidates for Top Jobs," *Fortune*, 5 February 2001, 205.

93. Ibid.

94. S. Chakravarty, "Hit 'Em Hardest with the Mostest (Southwest Airlines' Management)," *Forbes*, 16 September 1991, 48.

95. R. Suskind, "Humor Has Returned to Southwest Airlines after 9/11 Hiatus," *Wall Street Journal*, 13 January 2003, A1.

96. Ibid.

97. K. Godsey, "Slow Climb to New Heights; Combine Strict Discipline with Goofy Antics and Make Billions," *Success*, 1 October 1996, 20.

98. D.L. McCain, "The MSTAT-I: A New Measure of an Individual's Tolerance for Ambiguity," *Educational and Psychological Measurement*, 53 (1993): 183–190.

99. K. Maher, "For Some Co-Workers, Bringing Fido to Office Has Become Pet Peeve," *Wall Street Journal*, 12 January 2005, B1; "Making the Office Pet Friendly," *Plant Sites & Parks*, February 2001, 11; S. Linstedt, "Pets at Work Is Gnawing Subject for Many Buffalo, N.Y., Firms," *Buffalo News*, 30 September 2002; M. M. Perotin, "Some Fort Worth, Texas–Area Employers Allow Pets at Work," *Fort Worth Star-Telegram*, 12 August 2002; P. Lopes Harris, "Firms Begin to Ban Pets at Work," *San Jose Mercury News*, 2 January 2001; J. Saranow, "Anybody Want to Take a Nap? Fun Perks Didn't End with the Dot-Com Bust—They Just Changed," *Wall Street Journal*, 25 January 2005, R5.

100. "Yum Brands Temporarily Closes Restaurants after Rat Incident," *Wall Street Journal*, March 1, 2007, online; "Lettuce Most Likely Cause of Taco Bell E. coli," *Wall Street Journal*," December 14, 2006, B11; P. Flanagan, "Ten Public Relations Pitfalls," *Management Review*, October 1995, 45–48.

Chapter 4

1. "PETA Adopts Crude Tactics to Attack Milk Production," *Marketing Week*, 2 February 2006, 12; C. Roselli & J. Newman, "Responding to PETA," *The National Post* (Canada), 29 January 2007, A14; A. Enright, "PETA's PR Has Claws," *Marketing News*, 1 October 2005, 13–24; H. Harviliciz, "P& G Stops Most Animal Tests Victory Claimed by PETA," *Chemical Marker Reporter*, 5 July 1999, 25; G. Poste, "Animal Testing a Necessary Research Tool, for Now," *Arizona Republic*, 14 March 2007; A. Zuber, "BK Enacts Penalties, Surprise Inspection in Wake of PETA Boycott," *Nation's Restaurant News*, 9 July 2001, 6; A. Garber, "Fur Flies as PETA Sues KFC," *Nation's Restaurant News* 21 July 2003, 1; "Targeted Guinea Pig Farm Closes—A Farm that Has Been Breeding Guinea Pigs for Medical Research for More than 30 Years Is to Stop after Intimidation by Animal Rights Activist," available at http://findarticles.com/p/articles/mi_m3190/is_29_37/ai_106114301; D. Ward "'We Give Up,' Says Family Besieged by Activists," *The Guardian*, 24 August 2005; "Boycott Procter & Gamble," available at http://www.uncaged.co.uk/pg.htm; A. Kershaw, "Rise of World's Biggest Animal Rights Group," *The Press Association Newsfile*, 19 September 2006.

2. J. Schramm, "Perceptions on Ethics," *HR Magazine*, November 2004, available at http://www.shrm.org.

3. M. Jackson (Associated Press), "Workplace Cheating Rampant, Half of Employees Surveyed Admit They Take Unethical Actions," *Peoria Journal Star*, 5 April 1997.

4. M.A. Cohen, "Prosecutors of Corporate Scandals Share Insights," *The Legal Ledger* 16 November 2006; "Corporate Ethics," *Washington Post*, http://www.washingtonpost.com/wp-dyn/business/specials/corporateethics, 27 January 2005.

5. C. Smith, "The Ethical Workplace," *Association Management* 52 (2000): 70–73.

6. D. Jones, "More Workers Do Now Than Before Recent Big Scandals," *USA Today*, 12 February 2003, B7.

7. K. Tyler, "Do the Right Thing: Ethics Training Programs Help Employees Deal with Ethical Dilemmas," *HR Magazine*, February 2005, available at http://www.shrm.org/hrmagazine/articles/0205/0205tyler.asp.

8. F. Ahrens (*Washington Post*), "How Papers Faked Sales Figures," *Wall Street Journal Europe*, 1 December 2004, A5.

9. M. Bordwin, "Don't Ask Employees to Do Your

Dirty Work," *Management Review*, 1 October 1995.

10. C. Hymowitz, "Managers Must Respond to Employee Concerns about Honest Business," *Wall Street Journal*, 19 February 2002, B1.

11. M. Schweitzer, L. Ordonez, & B. Douma, "Goal Setting As a Motivator of Unethical Behavior," *Academy of Management Journal* 47 (2004): 422–432.

12. S. Power & C. Rauwald, "Daimler Audit Sparks Scrutiny as Executives Are Suspended: Disclosures about Bus Unit Prompt New Questions Tied to Internal Controls," *Wall Street Journal*, 14 November 2006, A17.

13. "2004 Report to the Nation on Occupational Fraud and Abuse," Association of Certified Fraud Examiners," http://www.acfe.com/documents/2004RttN.pdf; K. Gibson, "Excuses, Excuses: Moral Slippage in the Workplace," *Business Horizons* 43, no. 6 (2000): 65; S. L. Robinson & R. J. Bennett, "A Typology of Deviant Workplace Behaviors: A Multidimensional Scaling Study," *Academy of Management Journal* 38 (1995): 555–572.

14. Ibid.

15. J. Sandberg, "Office Sticky Fingers Can Turn the Rest of Us into Joe Fridays," *Wall Street Journal*, 19 November 2003, B1.

16. J. Norman, "Cultivating a Culture of Honesty," *The Orange County Register* (Santa Ana, CA), 23 October 2006.

17. S. Gaudin, "Computer Sabotage Case Back in Court," *Network World Fusion*, 19 April 2001, 12.

18. R. Hollinger & J. Davis, "2005 National Retail Security Final Report," Center for Studies in Criminology and Law, University of Florida, http://web.crim.ufl.edu/research/srp/srp.html, 15 June 2007.

19. M. Pressler, "Cost and Robbers; Shoplifting and Employee Thievery Add Dollars to Price Tag," *Washington Post*, 16 February 2003, H05.

20. G. Gatlin, "New, Improved! Way to Fight Theft Nears," *Boston Herald*, 17 June 2002, 21.

21. S. Miller, "Despite Workers' Comp Relief, Fraud Still Costly," available at http://www.shrm.org

22. M. France & M. Arndt, "After the Shooting Stops: When Employees Are Murdered on the Job, the Trauma Can Last for Years," *BusinessWeek*, 12 March 2001, 98.

23. D. Babwin, "Downtown Chicago Office Shooting Leaves 4 Dead, Including Gunman," *Associated Press State and Local Wire*, 9 December 2006, Saturday, 12:48 PM GMT.

24. Lehr Middlebrooks & Vreeland, P.C. (byline), "Many U.S. Employers Aren't Doing Enough to Address Workplace Violence," *Alabama Employment Law Letter*, December 2006.

25. J. Merchant & J. Lundell, "Workplace Violence: A Report to the Nation," University of Iowa Injury Prevention Center, http://www.public-health.uiowa.edu/iprc/nation.pdf, 15 June 2007.

26. M. P. Coco, Jr., "The New War Zone: The Workplace," *SAM Advanced Management Journal* 63, no. 1 (1998): 15; M. G. Harvey & R. A. Cosier, "Homicides in the Workplace: Crisis or False Alarm?" *Business Horizons* 38, no. 10 (1995): 11.

27. D. Palmer & A. Zakhem, "Bridging the Gap between Theory and Practice: Using the 1991 Federal Sentencing Guidelines as a Paradigm for Ethics Training," *Journal of Business Ethics* 29, no. 1/2 (2001): 77–84.

28. K. Tyler, "Do the Right Thing: Ethics Training Programs Help Employees Deal with Ethical Dilemmas."

29. D. R. Dalton, M. B. Metzger, & J. W. Hill, "The 'New' U.S. Sentencing Commission Guidelines: A Wake-Up Call for Corporate America," *Academy of Management Executive* 8 (1994): 7–16.

30. B. Ettore, "Crime and Punishment: A Hard Look at White-Collar Crime," *Management Review* 83 (1994): 10–16.

31. K. Tyler, "Do the Right Thing: Ethics Training Programs Help Employees Deal with Ethical Dilemmas."

32. F. Robinson & C. C. Pauze, "What Is a Board's Liability for Not Adopting a Compliance Program?" *Healthcare Financial Management* 51, no. 9 (1997): 64.

33. D. Murphy, "The Federal Sentencing Guidelines for Organizations: A Decade of Promoting Compliance and Ethics," *Iowa Law Review* 87 (2002): 697–719.

34. Robinson & Pauze, "What Is a Board's Liability?"

35. B. Schwartz, "The Nuts and Bolts of an Effective Compliance Program," *HR Focus* 74, no. 8 (1997): 13(2).

36. L. A. Hays, "A Matter of Time: Widow Sues IBM over Death Benefits," *Wall Street Journal*, 6 July 1995.

37. T. M. Jones, "Ethical Decision Making by Individuals in Organizations: An Issue-Contingent Model," *Academy of Management Review* 16 (1991): 366–395.

38. S. Morris & R. McDonald, "The Role of Moral Intensity in Moral Judgments: An Empirical Investigation," *Journal of Business Ethics* 14 (1995): 715–726; B. Flannery & D. May, "Environmental Ethical Decision Making in the U.S. Metal-Finishing Industry," *Academy of Management Journal* 43 (2000): 642–662.

39. S. Sparks, "Federal Agents Seize Computers in 27 Cities As Part of Crackdown on Software Piracy," *Wall Street Journal*, 12 December 2001, B4.

40. L. Kohlberg, "Stage and Sequence: The Cognitive-Developmental Approach to Socialization," in *Handbook of Socialization Theory and Research*, ed. D. A. Goslin (Chicago: Rand McNally, 1969); L. Trevino, "Moral Reasoning and Business Ethics: Implications for Research, Education, and Management," *Journal of Business Ethics* 11 (1992): 445–459.

41. L. Trevino & M. Brown, "Managing to be Ethical: Debunking Five Business Ethics Myths," *Academy of Management Executive* 18 (May 2004): 69–81.

42. L. T. Hosmer, "Trust: The Connecting Link between Organizational Theory and Philosophical Ethics," *Academy of Management Review* 20 (1995): 379–403.

43. R. K. Bennett, "How Honest Are We?" *Reader's Digest*, December 1995, 49–55; L. Callaway, "On the Wallet Watch—Honesty's Not Big Apple's Policy," *New York Post*, 31 July 2000, 41; A. Golab, "Results of Honesty Test: Mostly 'Finders, Keepers,' " *Chicago Sun-Times*, 12 March 1999, 3.

44. M. R. Cunningham, D. T. Wong, & A. P. Barbee, "Self-Presentation Dynamics on Overt Integrity Tests: Experimental Studies of the Reid Report," *Journal of Applied Psychology* 79 (1994): 643–658; J. Wanek, P. Sackett & D. Ones, "Toward an Understanding of Integrity Test Similarities and Differences: An Item-Level Analysis of Seven Tests," *Personnel Psychology* 56 (Winter 2003): 873–894.

45. H. J. Bernardin, "Validity of an Honesty Test in Predicting Theft among Convenience Store Employees," *Academy of Management Journal* 36 (1993): 1097–1108.

46. J. M. Collins & F. L. Schmidt, "Personality, Integrity, and White Collar Crime: A Construct Validity Study," *Personnel Psychology* (1993): 295–311.

47. W. C. Borman, M. A. Hanson, & J. W. Hedge, "Personnel Selection," *Annual Review of Psychology* 48 (1997).

48. S. Nonis & C. Swift, "An Examination of the Relationship between Academic Dishonesty and Workplace Dishonesty: A Multicampus Investigation," *Journal of Education for Business* (November 2001): 69–77.

49. L.W. Andrews, "The Nexus of Ethics," *HR Magazine*, August 2005, available at http://www.shrm.org.

50. P. E. Murphy, "Corporate Ethics Statements: Current Status and Future Prospects," *Journal of Business Ethics* 14 (1995): 727–740.

51. "More Corporate Boards Involved in Ethics Programs; Ethics Training Becoming Standard Practice," *PR Newswire*, 16 October 2006, http://www.prnewswire.com.

52. "Integrity Means . . ." Nortel Networks, http://www.nortel.com/corporate/community/ethics/collateral/code_of_conduct_nolinks.pdf, 15 June 2007.

53. Ibid.

54. S. J. Harrington, "What Corporate America Is Teaching about Ethics," *Academy of Management Executive* 5 (1991): 21–30.

55. G. Alliger & S. Dwight, "A Meta-Analytic Investigation of the Susceptibility of Integrity Tests to Faking and Coaching," *Educational and Psychological Measurement* 60 (2000): 59–72; D. S. Ones, C. Viswesvaran, & F. L. Schmidt, "Comprehensive Meta-Analysis of Integrity Test Validities: Findings and Implications for Personnel Selection and Theories of Job Performance," *Journal of Applied Psychology* 78 (1993): 679–703; "2004 Report to the Nation on Occupational Fraud and Abuse."

56. L. A. Berger, "Train All Employees to Solve Ethical Dilemmas," *Best's Review—Life-Health Insurance Edition* 95 (1995): 70–80.

57. M. McCarthy, "How One Firm Tracks Ethics Electronically," *Wall Street Journal*, 21 October 1999, B1.

58. L. Trevino, G. Weaver, D. Gibson, & B. Toffler, "Managing Ethics and Legal Compliance: What Works and What Hurts," *California Management Review* 41, no. 2 (1999): 131–151.

59. "Business Ethics Training: Teaching Right from Wrong," *Salt Lake Tribune*, 11 June 2000, E5.

60. Trevino, Weaver, Gibson, & Toffler, "Managing Ethics."

61. A. Countryman, "Leadership Key Ingredient in Ethics Recipe, Experts Say," *Chicago Tribune*, 1 December 2002, Business 1.

62. "More Corporate Boards Involved in Ethics Programs; Ethics Training Becoming Standard Practice," *PR Newswire*, 16 October 2006, http://www.prnewswire.com.

63. Executive Summary, "2003 National Business Ethics Survey," Ethics Resource Center Research Department, http://www.ethics.org/ research/2003-executive-summary.asp.

64. G. Weaver & L. Trevino, "Integrated and Decoupled Corporate Social Performance: Management Commitments, External Pressures, and Corporate Ethics Practices," *Academy of Management Journal* 42 (1999): 539–552; Weaver, Trevino, & Cochran, "Corporate Ethics Programs as Control Systems."

65. J. Salopek, "Do the Right Thing," *Training & Development* 55 (July 2001): 38–44.

66. M. Gundlach, S. Douglas, & M. Martinko, "The Decision to Blow the Whistle: A Social Information Processing Framework," *Academy of Management Executive* 17 (2003): 107–123.

67. M. Schwartz, "Business Ethics: Time to Blow the Whistle?" *Globe & Mail*, 5 March 1998, B2.

68. M. Jacobs, "The Legal Option: Employees Dreamed of Getting Rich from Stock Options; Now They're Heading to Court to Make Sure Those Dreams Come True," *Wall Street Journal*, 12 April 2001, R9.

69. "More Corporate Boards Involved in Ethics Programs; Ethics Training Becoming Standard Practice," *PR Newswire*, 16 October 2006, http://www.prnewswire.com.

70. M. P. Miceli & J. P. Near, "Whistleblowing: Reaping the Benefits," *Academy of Management Executive* 8 (1994): 65–72.

71. N. Weinberg, "Healing Thyself; Reformed Corporate Convict HCA Walks the Straight and Narrow—Very Slowly," *Forbes*, 17 March 2003, 64.

72. M. Master & E. Heresniak. "The Disconnect in Ethics Training," *Across the Board* 39 (September 2002): 51–52.

73. H. R. Bower, *Social Responsibilities of the Businessman* (New York: Harper & Row, 1953).

74. "Beyond the Green Corporation," *BusinessWeek*, 29 January 2007.

75. Z. Zuno, "Americans Send the Message: Get Down to Business on Corporate Citizenship: Ben & Jerry's, Target, Patagonia, SC Johnson and Gerber Top the 4th GolinHarris Corporate Citizenship Index in Rating of 152 Brands by 5,000 Americans," *Business Wire*, 6 December 2006, http://www.businesswire.com.

76. J. Nocera, "The Paradoxes of Business as Do-Gooders," *New York Times*, C1.

77. J. Chipman, "U.S. Boy Scouts Pay Price for Anti-Gay Policy: High-Profile Corporations Cut Ties, Withdraw Donations," *National Post*, 29 December 2000, A16; Associated Press, "Justices Let Boy Scouts Ruling Stand: Move Upholds State's Right to Drop Group from Charity Program," *St. Louis Post-Dispatch*, 9 March 2004, A5.

78. S. L. Wartick & P. L. Cochran, "The Evolution of the Corporate Social Performance Model," *Academy of Management Review* 10 (1985): 758–769.

79. J. Nocera, "The Paradox of Businesses as Do-Gooders."

80. S. Waddock, C. Bodwell, & S. Graves. "Responsibility: The New Business Imperative," *Academy of Management Executive* 16 (2002): 132–148.

81. T. Donaldson & L. E. Preston, "The Stakeholder Theory of the Corporation: Concepts, Evidence, and Implications," *Academy of Management Review* 20 (1995): 65–91.

82. M. B. E. Clarkson, "A Stakeholder Framework for Analyzing and Evaluating Corporate Social Performance," *Academy of Management Review* 20 (1995): 92–117.

83. I. M. Jawahar & G. McLaughlin, "Toward a Descriptive Stakeholder Theory: An Organizational Life Cycle Approach," *Academy of Management Review* 26 (2001: 397–414).

84. B. Agle, R. Mitchell, & J. Sonnenfeld, "Who Matters to CEOs? An Investigation of Stakeholder Attributes and Salience, Corporate

Performance, and CEO Values," *Academy of Management Journal* 42 (1999): 507–525.

85. J. Bandler, "Losing Focus: As Kodak Eyes Digital Future, a Big Partner Starts to Fade," *Wall Street Journal*, 23 January 2004, A1.

86. L. Etter, "Smithfield to Phase Out Crates: Big Pork Producer Yields to Activists, Customers on Animal-Welfare Issue," *Wall Street Journal*, 25 January 2007, A14.

87. L. E. Preston, "Stakeholder Management and Corporate Performance," *Journal of Behavioral Economics* 19 (1990): 361–375.

88. E. W. Orts, "Beyond Shareholders: Interpreting Corporate Constituency Statutes," *George Washington Law Review* 61 (1992): 14–135.

89. A. B. Carroll, "A Three-Dimensional Conceptual Model of Corporate Performance," *Academy of Management Review* 4 (1979): 497–505.

90. Ibid.

91. R. Bates, "Zale Names New President and CEO," *JCK-Jewelers Circular Keystone*, 1 September 2006, 41.

92. C. Lawton & J. Lublin, "Dell's Founder Returns as CEO as Rollins Quits—Computer Firm Expects to Miss Earnings Mark: Stock Rises after Hours," *Wall Street Journal*, 1 February 2007, C1.

93. J. Lublin & M. Murrary, "CEOs Leave Faster Than Ever Before as Boards, Investors Lose Patience," *Wall Street Journal Interactive*, 27 October 2000.

94. D. Woodruff, "Europe Shows More CEOs the Door," *Wall Street Journal*, 1 July 2002.

95. C. Bowman, "Success of Capital Area's War on Smog Challenged," *Sacramento Bee*, 7 February 1998, A1.

96. "Air Guide 31: Implementation of Part 201 and Part 212 Permitting and Reasonably Available Control Technology Requirements for Bakeries," New York State Department of Environmental Conservation, http://www.dec.ny.gov/regulations/25211.html, 5 February 2005.

97. T. Howard, "Low-Carb Message Not Popular, but Sales Are Up," *USA Today*, 8 December 2003, 10B.

98. Ibid.

99. "Results: How You're Helping," The Hunger Site, http://www.thehungersite.com, 5 February 2005.

100. N. Aoki, "Retailer Discord Rings over Charity's Bells," *Boston Globe*, 17 November 2004, A1.

101. M. Tierney, "Target Incurs Wrath for Salvation Army Ban," *Atlanta Journal-Constitution*, 18 December 2004, 1F.

102. K. Scannell, "Witness Says Police-Vest Maker Ignored Safety Concerns," *Wall Street Journal*, 15 November 2004, C1.

103. S. Richardson, "No Time to Stop—Parsons Plant Gives Thanks," *The Pantagraph*, 14 July 2005, 1.

104. J. White, "Move by Honda Ups the Ante on Car Safety," *Wall Street Journal*, 30 October 2003, D1.

105. A. McWilliams & D. Siegel, "Corporate Social Responsibility: A Theory of the Firm Perspective," *Academy of Management Review* 26, no.1 (2001): 117–127.

106. H. Haines, "Noah Joins Ranks of Socially Responsible Funds," *Dow Jones News Service*, 13 October 1995. A meta-analysis of 41 different studies also found no relationship between corporate social responsibility and profitability. Though not reported in the meta-analysis, when confidence intervals are placed around its average sample-weighted correlation of .06, the lower confidence interval includes zero, leading to the conclusion that there is no relationship between corporate social responsibility and profitability. See M. Orlitzky, "Does Firm Size Confound the Relationship between Corporate Social Responsibility and Firm Performance?" *Journal of Business Ethics* 33 (2001): 167–180.

107. J. Pereira, "Doing Good and Doing Well at Timberland," *Wall Street Journal*, 9 September 2003, B1.

108. T. Singer, "Can Business Still Save the World?" *Inc.*, 1 April 2001, 58.

109. D. Kadlec & B. Van Voorst, "The New World of Giving: Companies Are Doing More Good, and Demanding More Back," *Time*, 5 May 1997, 62.

110. P. Carlin, "Will Rapid Growth Stunt Corporate Do-Gooders?" *Business & Society Review*, Spring 1995, 36–43.

111. K. Brown, "Chilling at Ben & Jerry's: Cleaner, Greener," *Wall Street Journal*, 15 April 2004, B1.

112. "Starbucks Timeline & History," Starbucks, http://www.starbucks.com/aboutus/timeline.asp.

113. M. Alexander, "Charity Begins at the Coffee Cup," *Sunday Star-Times*, 17 June 2001, E4.

114. J. E. Wanek, P. R. Sackett, & D. S. Ones, "Towards an Understanding of Integrity Test Similarities and Differences: An Item-Level Analysis of Seven Tests," *Personnel Psychology* 56 (2003): 873–894.

115. R. Anderson, "Sustainability Drives Innovation," *Environmental Design & Construction*, December 2004, 38; M. Conlin, "From Plunderer to Protector: In a New Documentary, Interface's Ray Anderson Discusses His Green Epiphany," *BusinessWeek*, July 19, 2004, 60; L. Stevens, "It's Hip to Make Squares: Carpet Company Charts New Course," *Fort Worth Star-Telegram*, March 10, 2005; "Recyling Commercial Carpet Has Become Easier with INVISTA Carpet Reclamation Center's Announcement That It Will Accept Carpet," *Buildings*, March 2005, 7; K. Weeks, "A Walk in the Garden: Taking Carpet Sustainability to a New Level, Shaw and William McDonough Focus on a Cradle-to-Cradle Lifecycle to Develop a New Collection of Commercial Carpet Tile," *Contract*. April 2004, 36–38.

116. D. H. Dean, "Associating the Corporation with a Charitable Event through Sponsorship: Measuring the Effects on Corporate Community Relations," *Journal of Advertising*, Winter 2002, 77; D. Nelson, "Sponsorship or Selling Out?" *Fund Raising Management*, June 1998, 32; A. Taylor, "Poverty: Lack of Income Kills Off Low-Pay Unit," *Community Care*, February 20, 2003, 9.

Chapter 5

1. A. Ohnsman, "Ford Market Share Targets Suggest Toyota Soon No. 2," *Bloomberg.com*, http://www.bloomberg.com/apps/news?pid=20601101&sid=aAEsMChx_agU, 15 September 2006; C. Tierney, "Toyota Sets Big Goal for Tundra," *Detroit News*, http://www.detnews.com, 15 September 2006; J. McCracken & J. Stoll, "Ford Unveils Plan for Sweeping Cuts in '06

Production," *Wall Street Journal*, 18 August 2006, A1; A. Chozick, "Toyota Net Rises 39% as Auto Maker Deals with Growth Challenges," *Wall Street Journal*, 5 August 2006, A3.

2. L. A. Hill, *Becoming a Manager: Master a New Identity* (Boston: Harvard Business School Press, 1992).

3. N. Shirouzu, "Low-Key Chief of Toyota's U.S. Unit Discloses Bold Goals," *Wall Street Journal*, 17 March 2004.

4. A. Chozick, "Toyota Net Rises 39% As Auto Maker Deals with Growth Challenges," *Wall Street Journal*, 5 August 2006, A3.

5. E. A. Locke & G. P. Latham, *A Theory of Goal Setting & Task Performance* (Englewood Cliffs, NJ: Prentice Hall, 1990).

6. M. E. Tubbs, "Goal-Setting: A Meta-Analytic Examination of the Empirical Evidence," *Journal of Applied Psychology* 71 (1986): 474–483.

7. J. Bavelas & E. S. Lee, "Effect of Goal Level on Performance: A Trade-Off of Quantity and Quality," *Canadian Journal of Psychology* 32 (1978): 219–240.

8. D. Turner, "Ability, Aspirations Fine, but Persistence Is What Gets Results," *Seattle Times*, http://archives.seattletimes.nwsource.com/cgi-bin/texis.cgi/web/vortex/display?slug=dale15m&date=20030215, 13 February 2005.

9. Harvard Management Update, "Learn by 'Failing Forward,'" *Globe & Mail*, 31 October 2000, B17.

10. C. C. Miller, "Strategic Planning and Firm Performance: A Synthesis of More Than Two Decades of Research," *Academy of Management Performance* 37 (1994): 1649–1665.

11. H. Mintzberg, "Rethinking Strategic Planning: Part I: Pitfalls and Fallacies," *Long Range Planning* 27 (1994): 12–21, and "Part II: New Roles for Planners," 22–30; H. Mintzberg, "The Pitfalls of Strategic Planning," *California Management Review* 36 (1993): 32–47.

12. P. Dvorak, "Sony TVs Take Sibling Tips—Latest Machines Borrow from Videogame and Audio Technology," *Wall Street Journal*, 20 August 2004, B3.

13. Mintzberg, "The Pitfalls of Strategic Planning."

14. Locke & Latham, *A Theory of Goal Setting & Task Performance*.

15. A. King, B. Oliver, B. Sloop, & K. Vaverek, *Planning & Goal Setting for Improved Performance: Participant's Guide* (Cincinnati, OH: Thomson Executive Press, 1995).

16. C. Loomis, J. Schlosser, J. Sung, M. Boyle, & P. Neering, "The 15% Delusion: Brash Predictions about Earnings Growth Often Lead to Missed Targets, Battered Stock, and Creative Accounting—And That's When Times Are Good," *Fortune*, 5 February 2001, 102; H. Paster, "Manager's Journal: Be Prepared," *Wall Street Journal*, 24 September 2001, A24; P. Sellers, "The New Breed: The Latest Crop of CEOs Is Disciplined, Deferential, Even a Bit Dull," *Fortune*, 18 November 2002, 66. H. Klein & M. Wesson, "Goal and Commitment and the Goal-Setting Process: Conceptual Clarification and Empirical Synthesis," *Journal of Applied Psychology* 84 (1999): 885–896.

17. H. Klein & M. Wesson, "Goal and Commitment and the Goal-Setting Process: Conceptual Clarification and Empirical Synthesis," *Journal of Applied Psychology* 84 (1999): 885–886

18. Locke & Latham, *A Theory of Goal Setting & Task Performance*.

19. A. Pressman, "Ocean Spray's Creative Juices," *Business Week*, 15 May 2006, 88–90.

20. A. Bandura & D. H. Schunk, "Cultivating Competence, Self-Efficacy, and Intrinsic Interest through Proximal Self-Motivation," *Journal of Personality & Social Psycho-logy* 41 (1981): 586–598.

21. D. Ariely & K. Wertenboch, "Procrastination, Deadlines, and Performance: Self-Control by Precommitment," *Psychological Science* 13 (2002): 219–224.

22. N. Carr, "Curbing the Procrastination Instinct," *Harvard Business Review* (October 2001): 26.

23. Locke & Latham, *A Theory of Goal Setting & Task Performance*.

24. M. J. Neubert, "The Value of Feedback and Goal Setting over Goal Setting Alone and Potential Moderators of This Effect: A Meta-Analysis," *Human Performance* 11 (1998): 321–335.

25. E. H. Bowman & D. Hurry, "Strategy through the Option Lens: An Integrated View of Resource Investments and the Incremental-Choice Process," *Academy of Management Review* 18 (1993): 760–782.

26. M. Lawson, "In Praise of Slack: Time Is of the Essence," *Academy of Management Executive* 15 (2000): 125–135.

27. D. Lieberman, "Papers Take a Leap Forward, Opening Up to New Ideas," *USA Today*, 30 January 2006, http://www.usatoday.com/tech/news/techinnovations/2006-01-30-newspapers-change_x.htm.

28. N. A. Wishart, J. J. Elam, & D. Robey, "Redrawing the Portrait of a Learning Organization: Inside Knight-Ridder, Inc.," *Academy of Management Executive* 10 (1996): 7–20.

29. J. McGregor et al., "How Failure Breeds Success: Everyone Fears Failure. But Breakthroughs Depend on It. The Best Companies Embrace Their Mistakes and Learn from Them," *BusinessWeek*, 10 July 2006, 42.

30. J. C. Collins & J. I. Porras, "Organizational Vision and Visionary Organizations," *California Management Review* (Fall 1991): 30–52.

31. Ibid.

32. Ibid.

33. "President Bush Announces New Vision for Space Exploration Program," The White House, http://www.whitehouse.gov, 17 April 2005.

34. N. Gull, "Plan B (and C and D and ...)," *Inc.*, March 2004, 40.

35. R. Rodgers & J. E. Hunter, "Impact of Management by Objectives on Organizational Productivity," *Journal of Applied Psychology* 76 (1991): 322–336.

36. E. Marlow & R. Schilhavy, "Expectation Issues in Management by Objectives Programs," *Industrial Management* 33, no. 4 (1991): 29.

37. "Web MBO Teams with Deloitte & Touche to Deliver Innovative Web-Based 'Management-by-Objectives and Performance Management' Solutions," *PR Newswire*, 19 June 2001.

38. L. Iacocca, with W. Novak, *Iacocca* (New York: Bantam, 1984).

39. J. Lyne, "Philip Morris Relocating NYC Headquarters to Native Virginia Area," *Site Selection*, http://www.conway.com/ssinsider/bbdeal/bd030324.htm, 17 February 2005.

40. R. Richmond, "It's 10 A.M. Do You Know Where Your Workers Are?" *Wall Street Journal*, 12 January 2004, R1.

41. Adapted from quality procedure at G & G Manufacturing, Cincinnati, Ohio.

42. N. Humphrey, "References a Tricky Issue for Both Sides," *Nashville Business Journal* 11 (8 May 1995): 1A.

43. K. R. MacCrimmon, R. N. Taylor, & E. A. Locke, "Decision Making and Problem Solving," in *Handbook of Industrial & Organizational Psychology*, ed. M. D. Dunnette (Chicago: Rand McNally, 1976), 1397–1453.

44. "Airbus's 'Big Baby,' the A380 Airliner, Fights a Weight Problem," *JEC Composites*, http://www.jeccomposites.com/composites-news/1095/Airbuss-%60big-baby.html, 19 February 2005.

45. D. Michaels, "Jumbo Bet: At Airbus, Picturing Huge Jet Was Easy; Building It Is Hard," *Wall Street Journal*, 27 May 2004, A1.

46. MacCrimmon, Taylor, & Locke, "Decision Making and Problem Solving."

47. G. Kress, "The Role of Interpretation in the Decision Process," *Industrial Management* 37 (1995): 10–14.

48. D. Milbrank, "We Feel Your Pain, Congress Is Saying, with Real Empathy," *Wall Street Journal*, 1 April 1996; S. Nelson, "Shays, Moran: Defend CAA," *Roll Call*, 30 September 2002.

49. Michaels, "Jumbo Bet: At Airbus, Picturing Huge Jet Was Easy."

50. *Consumer Reports Buying Guide 2006*, 129–131.

51. "New-Vehicle Ratings Comparison by Car Category," ConsumerReports.org, http://www.consumerreports.org/cro/cars/index.htm, 19 February 2005.

52. P. Djang, "Selecting Personal Computers," *Journal of Research on Computing in Education* 25 (1993): 327.

53. "European Cities Monitor," Cushman & Wakefield Healy & Baker, 2005. available at http://www.cushmanwakefield.com/cwglobal/docviewer/European%20Cities%20Monitor.pdf?id=ca1500006&repositoryKey=CoreRepository&itemDesc=document.

54. "The PLUS Decision Making Model," Ethics Resource Center, http://www.ethics.org/resources/decision-making-model.asp, 19 February 2005.

55. B. Dumaine, "The Trouble with Teams," *Fortune*, 5 September 1994, 86–92.

56. L. Pelled, K. Eisenhardt, & K. Xin, "Exploring the Black Box: An Analysis of Work Group Diversity, Conflict, and Performance," *Administrative Science Quarterly* 44, no. 1 (March 1, 1999): 1.

57. B. Scudamore, "Gather Round! For a Group Interview," *Inc.*, August 2006, 94.

58. I. L. Janis, *Groupthink* (Boston: Houghton Mifflin, 1983).

59. C. P. Neck & C. C. Manz, "From Groupthink to Teamthink: Toward the Creation of Constructive Thought Patterns in Self-Managing Work Teams," *Human Relations* 47 (1994): 929–952; J. Schwartz & M. L. Wald, "'Groupthink' Is 30 Years Old, and Still Going Strong," *New York Times*, 9 March 2003, 5.

60. M. Bazerman & D. Chugh, "Decisions without Blinders," *Harvard Business Review*, January 2006, 84(1): 88–97.

61. C. Gallo, "How to Run a Meeting Like Google," *BusinessWeek Online*, 8 September 2006, 15.

62. A. Mason, W. A. Hochwarter, & K. R. Thompson, "Conflict: An Important Dimension in Successful Management Teams," *Organizational Dynamics* 24 (1995): 20.

63. C. Olofson, "So Many Decisions, So Little Time: What's Your Problem?" *Fast Company*, 1 October 1999, 62.

64. Ibid.

65. R. Cosier & C. R. Schwenk, "Agreement and Thinking Alike: Ingredients for Poor Decisions," *Academy of Management Executive* 4 (1990): 69–74.

66. Ibid.

67. B. Breen, "BMW: Driven by Design," *Fast Company*, 1 September 2002, 123.

68. K. Jenn & E. Mannix, "The Dynamic Nature of Conflict: A Longitudinal Study of Intragroup Conflict and Group Performance," *Academy of Management Journal* 44, no. 2 (2001): 238–251; R. L. Priem, D. A. Harrison, & N. K. Muir, "Structured Conflict and Consensus Outcomes in Group Decision Making," *Journal of Management* 21 (1995): 691–710.

69. A. Van De Ven & A. L. Delbecq, "Nominal versus Interacting Group Processes for Committee Decision Making Effectiveness," *Academy of Management Journal* 14 (1971): 203–212.

70. A. R. Dennis & J. S. Valicich, "Group, Sub-Group, and Nominal Group Idea Generation: New Rules for a New Media?" *Journal of Management* 20 (1994): 723–736.

71. C. R. Schwenk, "Effects of Devil's Advocacy and Dialectical Inquiry on Decision Making: A Meta-Analysis," *Organizational Behavior & Human Decision Performance* 47 (1990): 161–176; M. Orlitzky & R. Hirokawa, "To Err Is Human, to Correct for It Divine: A Meta-Analysis of Research Testing the Functional Theory of Group Decision-Making Effectiveness," *Small Group Research* 32, no. 3 (June 2001): 313–341.

72. S. G. Rogelberg, J. L. Barnes-Farrell, & C. A. Lowe, "The Stepladder Technique: An Alternative Group Structure Facilitating Effective Group Decision Making," *Journal of Applied Psychology* 77 (1992): 730–737; S. G. Rogelberg & M. S. O'Connor, "Extending the Stepladder Technique: An Examination of the Self-Paced Stepladder Groups," *Group Dynamics: Theory, Research, & Practice* 2 (1998): 82–91.

73. S. Rogelberg, M. O'Connor, & M. Sedergurg, "Using the Stepladder Technique to Facilitate the Performance of Audioconferencing Groups," *Journal of Applied Psychology* 87 (2002): 994–1000.

74. R. B. Gallupe, W. H. Cooper, M. L. Grise, & L. M. Bastianutti, "Blocking Electronic Brainstorms," *Journal of Applied Psychology* 79 (1994): 77–86.

75. R. B. Gallupe & W. H. Cooper, "Brainstorming Electronically," *Sloan Management Review*, Fall 1993, 27–36.

76. Ibid.

77. G. Kay, "Effective Meetings through Electronic Brainstorming," *Management Quarterly* 35 (1995): 15.

78. A. LaPlante, "90s Style Brainstorming," *Forbes ASAP*, 25 October 1993, 44.

79. R.J. Aldag & L. W. Kuzuhara, *Mastering Management Skills: A Manager's Toolkit* (Mason, OH: Thomson South-Western, 2005) 172–173.

80. N. Brodsky, "Just Say Yes: How a Policy That Sounds Tough Can Turn into a Lifeline for Some," *Inc.*, November 2004, 67; S. Smith, "What Every Employer Should Know

about Drug Testing in the Workplace: Think You Don't Have a Problem with Drugs in the Workplace? Think Again," *Occupational Hazards*, August 2004, 45; "Small Firms More Likely to See Drug Problems, Labor Department Study Reports," *Pueblo Chieftain*, 3 August 2004; D. Willoughby, "Drugs, Workplaces Don't Mix; Employers Take Steps to Prevent Substance Abuse," *Montgomery Advertiser*, 4 May 2004.

81. C. Fishman, "The Wal-Mart You Don't Know," *Fast Company*, December 2003, 68–80; M. Boyle, "Wal-Mart Keeps the Change," *Fortune*, 10 November 2003, 46; C. Y. Chen, "Wal-Mart Drives a New Tech Boom," *Fortune*, May 2004; "Is Wal-Mart Good for America?," *Frontline*, http://www.pbs.org/wgbh/pages/frontline/shows/walmart.

82. "20 Hot Job Tracks," *U.S. News & World Report*, 30 October 1995, 98–104; C. Boivie, "Planning for the Future ... Your Future," *Journal of Systems Management* 44 (1993): 25–27; J. Connelly, "How to Choose Your Next Career," *Fortune*, 6 February 1995, 145–146; P. Sherrid, "A 12-Hour Test of My Personality," *U.S. News & World Report*, 31 October 1994, 109.

Chapter 6

1. S. Lacy, "The Hot Ticket Isn't Ticketmaster," *BusinessWeek*, 4 September 2006, 36; S. Stecklow, "StubHub's Ticket to Ride," *Wall Street Journal*, 17 January 2006, B1-B2; "Jeff Fleur, 32," *Entrepreneur*, October 2006, 94.; "StubHub(A): January 2004," *Stanford Graduate School of Business Case*, 15 March 2005, Case SM-132A; V. Vara, D. Berman, & R. Adams, "EBay-StubHub Deal a Boon to Start-Ups," *Wall Street Journal*, 11 January 2007, B4; http://www.stubhub.com.

2. L. Kahney, "Inside Look at the Birth of the iPod," *Wired*, 21 July 2004, http://www.wired.com/news/culture/0,64286-0.html; http://www.apple-history.com/?page=gallery&model=ipod; K. Hall, "Sony's iPod Assault Is No Threat to Apple," *BusinessWeek*, 13 March 2006, 53; N. Wingfield, "SanDisk Raises Music-Player Stakes," *Wall Street Journal*, 21 August 2006, B4; "Growing Louder: Microsoft Plods after iPod Like a Giant—Powerful, Determined, Untiring," *Winston-Salem Journal*, 15 November 2006, D1–D2; A. Athavaley & R. A. Guth, "How the Zune Is Faring So Far with Consumers," *Wall Street Journal*, 12 December 2006, D1, D7.

3. J. Barney, "Firm Resources and Sustained Competitive Advantage," *Journal of Management* 17 (1991): 99–120; J. Barney, "Looking Inside for Competitive Advantage," *Academy of Management Executive* 9 (1995): 49–61.

4. J. Snell, "Apple's Home Run," *Macworld*, November 2006, 7.

5. J. D'Arcy, & T. Davies, "The Walkman at 20," *Maclean's*, 30 August 1999, 10; K. Hall, "Sony's iPod Assault Is no Threat to Apple," *BusinessWeek*, 13 March 2006, 53.

6. A. Athavaley & R.A. Guth, "How the Zune Is Faring So Far with Consumers," D7.

7. http://music.yahoo.com

8. J. Warren, "At New Web Store, Many Songs Sell for a Few Cents," *Wall Street Journal*, 14 October 2006, P2.

9. R. Levine, "Napster's Ghost Rises," *Fortune*, 6 March 2006, 30; "30 Products for 30 Years," *MacWorld*, June 2006, 15–16.

10. S. Hart & C. Banbury, "How Strategy-Making Processes Can Make a Difference," *Strategic Management Journal* 15 (1994): 251–269.

11. R. A. Burgelman, "Fading Memories: A Process Theory of Strategic Business Exit in Dynamic Environments," *Administrative Science Quarterly* 39 (1994): 24–56; R. A. Burgelman & A. S. Grove, "Strategic Dissonance," *California Management Review* 38 (1996): 8–28.

12. S. Ellison, "Kraft's Stale Strategy—Endless Extensions of Oreos, Chips Ahoy and Jell-O Brands Created a New-Product Void," *Wall Street Journal*, 18 December 2003, B1.

13. J. Barrett, "The 100-Calorie Snack Attack," *Newsweek*, 14 August 2006, 34; http://www.oreo.com.

14. S. Ellison, "Kraft's Stale Strategy."

15. Ibid.

16. R. Burgelman & A. Grove, "Strategic Dissonance," *California Management Review* (Winter 1996): 8–28.

17. E. Smith & M. Peers, "Cost Cutting Is an Uphill Fight at Warner Music," *Wall Street Journal*, 24 May 2004, B1.

18. A. Fiegenbaum, S. Hart, & D. Schendel, "Strategic Reference Point Theory," *Strategic Management Journal* 17 (1996): 219–235.

19. P. Buller & G. McEvoy, "Creating and Sustaining Ethical Capability in the Multi-National Corporation," *Journal of World Business* 34 (1999): 326–343.

20. Hart & Banbury, "How Strategy-Making Processes Can Make a Difference"; C. C. Miller & L. B. Cardinal, "Strategic Planning and Firm Performance: A Synthesis of More Than Two Decades of Research," *Academy of Management Journal* 37 (1994): 1649–1665; D. King, D. Dalton, C. Daily, & J. Covin, "Meta-Analyses of Post-Acquisition Performance: Indications of Unidentified Moderators," *Strategic Management Journal* 25 (2004): 187–200; C. R. Schwenk, "Effects of Formal Strategic Planning on Financial Performance in Small Firms: A Meta-Analysis," *Entrepreneurship Theory & Practice*, Spring 1993, 53–64.

21. D. Carpenter, "SWOT Team Solves Supply Chain Issues," *Materials Management in Health Care*, April 2006, 40–42.

22. "Reliability Histories: Detailed Histories for 1997 to 2004 Models," *Consumer Reports*, http://www.consumerreports.org, 5 March 2005.

23. C. Metz, "19th Annual Reader Satisfaction Survey," *PC Magazine*, 21 August 2006, http://www.pcmag.com/article2/0,1895,2006502,00.asp.

24. L. Margonelli, "How Ikea Designs Its Sexy Price Tags," *Business 2.0*, http://www.money.cnn.com, 1 October 2002.

25. A. Fiegenbaum & H. Thomas, "Strategic Groups as Reference Groups: Theory, Modeling and Empirical Examination of Industry and Competitive Strategy," *Strategic Management Journal* 16 (1995): 461–476.

26. R. K. Reger & A. S. Huff, "Strategic Groups: A Cognitive Perspective," *Strategic Management Journal* 14 (1993): 103–124.

27. http://homedepot.com; M. Hogan, "Big Box Battle: Home Depot vs. Lowe's," *BusinessWeek Online*, 22 August 2006, 7; F. Miller, "Growing Pains," *Kitchen & Bath Business*, September 2006, 53.

28. http://ourcompany.acehardware.com/download/pdf_word/FACTFILE.PDF

29. http://www.hardwarestore.com/about-aubuchon-hardware.aspx

30. http://ourcompany.acehardware.com/

download/pdf_word/ FACTFILE.PDF.

31. http://84lumber.com/ About84/about.asp.

32. http://ourcompany .acehardware.com/ download/pdf_word/ FACTFILE.PDF

33. http://www .truevaluecompany.com/ overview/annualreport.asp

34. W. B. Werther, Jr. & J. L. Kerr, "The Shifting Sands of Competitive Advantage," *Business Horizons*, May–June 1995, 11–17.

35. Ibid.

36. "Menard, Inc.," *Hoover's Company Profiles*, 8 May 2003.

37. J. Samuelson, "Tough Guy Billionaire," *Forbes*, 24 February 1997, 64–66.

38. "Menards vs. Home Depot," WCCO Channel 4000, http://www. channel4000.com, 25 September 2001.

39. S. Bucksot, C. Jensen, & D. Tratensek, "Where Are We Headed?" *2005 Market Measure: The Industry's Annual Report*, http://www.nrha.org/ MM2004.pdf, 6 March 2005.

40. Ibid.

41. H. Murphy, "Menard's Tool in Retail Battle: Gigantic Stores," *Crain's Chicago Business*, 12 August 2002, 3.

42. Ibid.

43. G. Bounds, "More than Squeaking By," *Wall Street Journal*, 23 May 2006, B1; www.wd40.com; www.wikipedia.com; http://www.octanecreative .com/WD40/; http://home .howstuffworks.com/ question155.htm.

44. M. Lubatkin, "Value-Creating Mergers: Fact or Folklore?" *Academy of Management Executive* 2 (1988): 295–302; M. Lubatkin & S. Chatterjee, "Extending Modern Portfolio Theory into the Domain of Corporate Diversification: Does It Apply?" *Academy of Management Journal* 37 (1994): 109–136; M. H. Lubatkin & P. J. Lane, "Psst . . . The Merger Mavens Still Have It Wrong!" *Academy of Management Executive* 10 (1996): 21–39.

45. "Who We Are," 3M, http://www.3m.com, 6 March 2005.

46. "Our Company," Johnson & Johnson, http://www .jnj.com/our_company/ index.htm, 6 March 2005.

47. http://www.saralee.com.

48. "About Samsung," Samsung, http:// www.samsung.com/ AboutSAMSUNG/index .htm, 6 March 2005.

49. http://www.bcg.com/ this_is_BCG/bcg_history/ bcg_history_2005.html; http:www.wikipedia.org.

50. "Phonebook Company Yellow Book Enters into Lynchburg, Va.-Area Market," *Lynchburg (VA) News & Advance*, 16 January 2005; "Leading Independents Project Double-Digit Gains in 2004; Plan Aggressive Expansion," *Yellow Pages & Directory Report*, 27 August 2004; G. David, "The Good Book/Unmellow Yellow: A Battle among Business Directories Could Cut Your Ad Costs," *FSB*, 1 November 2003, 85.

51. K. Brooker, "Plugging the Leaks at P&G: A First-Year Report Card for CEO Durk Jager," *Fortune*, 21 February 2000, 44; "R&D's Formula for Success," Procter & Gamble, http:// www.pg.com/science/rd_ formula_success.jhtml, 14 May 2003.

52. P. Sellers, "P&G: Teaching an Old Dog New Tricks," *Fortune*, 31 May 2004, 166.

53. J. A. Pearce II, "Selecting among Alternative Grand Strategies," *California Management Review* (Spring 1982): 23–31.

54. N. Deogun, C. Forelle, D. Berman, & E. Nelson, "Razor's Edge: P&G to Buy Gillette for $54 Billion," *Wall Street Journal*, 28 January 2005, A1; A. Latour, "Closing Bell: After a Year of Frenzied Deals, Two Telecom Giants Emerge," *Wall Street Journal*, 15 February 2005, A1; G. Zuckerman, "What to Do Amid All the Big Deals?" *Wall Street Journal Sunday*, 6 February 2005, 1; V. Tong, "Acquisitions Made in 2006 Set Records," 21 November, 2006, CBS News, http://www.cbsnews .com/stories/2006/11/21/ap/ business/mainD8LH4UM00 .shtml.

55. "Financial and Other Numbers: Store Growth," Walgreens.com, http:// www.walgreens.com/ about/press/facts/fact1 .jhtml,8 May 2005; A. Tsao, "Why CVS May Be the Pick of the Pack: While Walgreen Is Considered the Drugstore Sector's Blue Chip, CVS Has a Much Cheaper P-E and Plenty of Upside Potential," *BusinessWeek Online*, http://www .businessweek.com/ bwdaily/dnflash/may2003/ nf20030512_9097_db014 .htm, 13 May 2003.

56. S. Chandler, "Walgreens Adding 500 Stores, Posts Record Profit," *Chicago Tribune*, 3 January 2001, 2.

57. "Subaru Archives Homepage," Cars101 .com, http://www.cars101 .com/subaru_archives .html, 8 March 2005.

58. J. A. Pearce II, "Retrenchment Remains the Foundation of Business Turnaround," *Strategic Management Journal* 15 (1994): 407–417.

59. J. Hyatt, J. Sloane, E. Welles, & M. Overfelt, "Beat the Beast," *Fortune Small Business*, 1 September 2004, 42.

60. A. Lustgarden & R. Oliver, "Seven Stocks to Bet On," *Fortune*, 6 September 2004, 137.

61. M. Maiello, "Prozac Hangover," *Forbes*, 10 May 2004, 116.

62. E. Ramstad & P. Dvorak, "Off-the-Shelf Parts Create New Order in TVs, Electronics," *Wall Street Journal*, 16 December 2003, A1.

63. http://www.walmartfacts. com/FactSheets/8252006_ Merchandising.pdf, http://www.walmartfacts .com/content/default .aspx?id = 3.

64. P. Wonacott, "Wal-Mart, Others Demand Lowest Prices, Managers Scramble to Slash Costs," *Wall Street Journal*, 13 November 2003, A1.

65. M. Veverka, "Bigger and Better: Costco's Costly Expansion Is About to Pay Off—For Shoppers and Shareholders," *Barron's*, 12 May 2003, 28.

66. L. Tischler, "The Price Is Right," *Fast Company*, 1 November 2003, 83.

67. Ibid.

68. http://www.containerstore .com

69. B. Breen, "What's Selling in America: The Lamest Question in Retails Is 'Can I Help You,'" *Fast Company*, January 2003, 82.

70. R. E. Miles & C. C. Snow, *Organizational Strategy, Structure, & Process* (New York: McGraw Hill, 1978); S. Zahra & J. A. Pearce, "Research Evidence on the Miles-Snow Typology," *Journal of Management* 16 (1990): 751–768; W. L. James & K. J. Hatten, "Further Evidence on the Validity of the Self Typing Paragraph Approach: Miles and Snow Strategic Archetypes in Banking," *Strategic Management Journal* 16 (1995): 161–168.

71. E. Bellman & D. Ball, "Unilever, P&G Wage Price War for Edge in India," *Wall Street Journal*, 11 August 2004, B1.

72. E. Bellman, "Hindustan Lever Posts 27% Drop In Quarterly Net—India's Competitive Market for Consumer Goods Forces Company to Slash Prices," *Wall Street Journal*, 29 October 2004, A2.

73. "A Century of Innovation," *3M*. Available at http://

solutions.3m.com/wps/portal/_l/en_US/_s.155/123515, 10 March 2005.

74. G. Harris & J. Slater, "Bitter Pills: Drug Makers See 'Branded Generics' Eating into Profits," *Wall Street Journal*, 17 April 2003, A1.

75. B. Einhorn, M. Kripalani, & K. Capell, "The Little Drugmakers That Could: India's Scrappy Industry Is Making Big Western Outfits Sweat," *BusinessWeek*, 3 March 2003, 20.

76. C. Emsden, "Fiat Set to Make Comeback Bid on Bumpy Road," *Wall Street Journal*, 27 October 2004, B2E.

77. G. Kahn & S. Power, "Fiat's CEO Grabs Wheel at Auto Unit—Surprise Firing of Demel by Marchionne May Augur Shifts in Turnaround Plan," *Wall Street Journal Europe*, 18 February 2005, A1; K. Maxwell, "Fiat Auto Unit Drives Sales Drive," *Wall Street Journal*, 27 October 2006, http://online.wsj.com/article/SB116187138996104636-search.html?KEYWORDS=fiat&COLLECTION=sjie/6month.

78. M. Chen, "Competitor Analysis and Interfirm Rivalry: Toward a Theoretical Integration," *Academy of Management Review* 21 (1996): 100–134; J. C. Baum & H. J. Korn, "Competitive Dynamics of Interfirm Rivalry," *Academy of Management Journal* 39 (1996): 255–291.

79. Ibid.

80. S. Leung, "Wendy's Sees Green in Salad Offerings—More Sophistication, Ethnic Flavors Appeal to Women, Crucial to Building Market Share," *Wall Street Journal*, 24 April 2003, B2.

81. M. Stopa, "Wendy's New-Fashioned Growth: Buy Hardee's," *Crain's Detroit Business*, 21 October 1996.

82. L. Lavelle, "The Chickens Come Home to Roost, and Boston Market Is Prepared to Expand," *The Record*, 6 October 1996.

83. "International Subway Locations," Subway, http://www.subway.com, 1 March 2007; "Investor Fact Sheet January 2004," McDonald's Corporation Annual Report 2005; N. Torres, "View from the Top: Subway Takes the Title of the #1 Franchise for the 13th Time," Entrepreneur.com, http://www.entrepreneur.com, 11 March 2005.

84. "Frequently Asked Questions," Subway Restaurants, http://www.subway.com/subwayroot/AboutSubway/subwayFaqs.aspx, 11 March 2005.

85. S. Leung, "Fast-Food Firms' Big Budgets Don't Buy Consumer Loyalty," *Wall Street Journal*, 24 July 2003, B4.

86. G. Marcial, "How Wendy's Stayed Out of the Fire," *BusinessWeek*, 9 December 2002, 138.

87. S. Kilman, "Leading the News: Diageo Says Industry Price War Is Crimping Its Burger King Sale," *Wall Street Journal*, 8 November 2002, A3.

88. D. Ketchen, Jr., C. Snow, & V. Street, "Improving Firm Performance by Matching Strategic Decision-Making Processes to Competitive Dynamics," *Academy of Management Executive* 18 (2004): 29–43.

89. S. Matthews, "Financial: Salads Help McD Post First U.S. Sales Gain in 14 Months," *Chicago Sun-Times*, 14 May 2003, 69.

90. S. Ellison, "In Lean Times, Big Companies Make a Grab for Market Share," *Wall Street Journal*, 5 September 2003, A1.

91. J. C. Baum & H. J. Korn, "Competitive Dynamics of Interfirm Rivalry," *Academy of Management Journal* 39 (1996): 255–291.

92. S. Kirsner, "They May Not Be CNBC Regulars, but This Fab Four Represent What's Needed Today: CEOs with Vision Who Also Aren't Afraid to Get Their Hands Dirty," *Fast Company*, 1 February 2005, 68.

93. B. Antoncic & R. D. Hisrich, "Intrapreneurship: Construct Refinement and Cross-Cultural Validation," *Journal of Business Venturing* 16 (2001): 495–527.

94. D. Ball & S. Leung, "Latte versus Latte—Starbucks, Dunkin' Donuts Seek Growth by Capturing Each Other's Customers," *Wall Street Journal*, 10 February 2004, B1.

95. W. Symonds, D. Kiley, & S. Holmes, "A Java Jolt for Dunkin' Donuts," *BusinessWeek*, 20 December 2004, 61.

96. Ball & Leung, "Latte versus Latte."

97. G. T. Lumpkin & G. G. Dess, "Clarifying the Entrepreneurial Orientation Construct and Linking It to Performance," *Academy of Management Review* 21 (1996): 135–172.

98. N. Venkatraman, "Strategic Orientation of Business Enterprises: The Construct, Dimensionality, and Measurement," *Management Science* 35 (1989): 942–962.

99. J. M. Houston & R. D. Smither, "The Nature of Competitiveness: The Development and Validation of the Competitiveness Index," *Educational and Psychological Measurement* 52 (1992): 407–418.

100. I. Brat, "GreenThumb's Profits Grow," *Wall Street Journal*, 17 April 2006, B5; http://www.scotts.com.

101. Y. I. Kane & N. Wingfield, "Out of the Box: Amid Videogame Arms Race, Nintendo Slows Things Down," *Wall Street Journal*, 2 November 2006, A1; J. Alabaster, "Nintendo's 9-Month Net Beats Full-Year Target," *Wall Street Journal*, 26 January 2007, B4; Y. Kim, "In War of Game Consoles, Chip Makers Are Winners," *Wall Street Journal*, 1 March 2007, online; R. Guth, "IPod Envy: Microsoft's Xbox Whiz Drives Strategic Shift," *Wall Street Journal*, 5 January 2007, A1.

102. P. Buhler, "Managing Your Career: No Longer Your Company's Responsibility," *Supervision*, May 1997.

Chapter 7

1. M. Arndt, "Creativity Overflowing," *Business Week*, 8 May 2006, 50–53; C. Salter, "Whirlpool Finds Its Cool," *Fast Company*, June 2005, 72–75; J. Rivkin, D. Leonard, & G. Hamel, "Change at Whirlpool Corporation (A)," *Harvard Business School*, 20 September 2005, Case 9, 705–762; http://www.whirlpoolcorp.com/about/corpfactsheet/default.asp.

2. T. M. Amabile, R. Conti, H. Coon, J. Lazenby, & M. Herron, "Assessing the Work Environment for Creativity," *Academy of Management Journal* 39 (1996): 1154–1184.

3. Ibid.

4. A. H. Van de Ven & M. S. Poole, "Explaining Development and Change in Organizations," *Academy of Management Review* 20 (1995): 510–540.

5. J. Adamy, "Pitching Tents That Go Up for Good: Chandeliers and Elevators," *Wall Street Journal*, 10 May 2004, A1.

6. Amabile, et al., "Assessing the Work Environment for Creativity."

7. P. Anderson & M. L. Tushman, "Managing through Cycles of Technological Change," *Research/Technology Management*, May–June 1991, 26–31.

8. R. N. Foster, *Innovation: The Attacker's Advantage* (New York: Summit, 1986).

9. "iComp Index 2.0," Intel, http://www.intel.com, 5 December 1997.

10. J. Burke, *The Day the Universe Changed* (Boston: Little, Brown, 1985).

11. http://www.kodak.com; "Industry Snapshot," *Time*, 5 December 2005, 110; W. Symonds, "Kodak: Is This the Darkest Hour?" *BusinessWeek Online*, 8 August 2006, 3.

12. M. L. Tushman, P. C. Anderson, & C. O'Reilly, "Technology Cycles, Innovation Streams, and Ambidextrous Organizations: Organization Renewal through Innovation Streams and Strategic Change," in *Managing Strategic Innovation and Change*, ed. M. L. Tushman & P. Anderson (New York: Oxford Press, 1997), 3–23.

13. P. Landers, "Brain Surgery Made Simple—New Less-Invasive Procedures Reduce Pain, Recovery Time; Sending in the Tiny Robots," *Wall Street Journal*, 31 October 2002, D1.

14. "Pony Express," *Encyclopedia Britannica Online*, http://www.eb.com, 6 March 1999.

15. J. R. Aldern, "The Victorian Internet: The Remarkable Story of the Telegraph and the Nineteenth Century's On-Line Pioneers (Review)," *Smithsonian*, 1 January 1999.

16. E. Schlossberg, *Interactive Excellence: Defining and Developing New Standards for the Twenty-First Century* (New York: Ballantine, 1998).

17. W. Abernathy & J. Utterback, "Patterns of Industrial Innovation," *Technology Review* 2 (1978): 40–47.

18. "Glossary," MP3.com, http://www.mp3.com, 18 March 2005; B. Chaffin, "The Back Page: Music Format Wars," *Mac Observer*, http://www.macobserver.com/columns/thebackpage/2004/20040203.shtml, 18 March 2005; C. Goodwin, "Technology Insights: Online Music Stores," *Ticker*, http://www.ticker.com, 18 March 2005.

19. J. Bosma, "Satellites Must Look to Earth for Success," *Satellite News*, 5 August 2002.

20. D. Young, "Foreign Mobile Telcos Look at Chinese 3G Standard," *Reuters News*, 15 March 2005.

21. Y. Utsumi, "Harmonizing Global Standards: The Future of 3G," International Telecommunication Union: 3G Mobile 2003, http://www.itu.int/osg/sg/speeches/2003/01143GMobile.html, 14 January 2003.

22. M. Schilling, "Technological Lockout: An Integrative Model of the Economic and Strategic Factors Driving Technology Success and Failure," *Academy of Management Review* 23 (1998): 267–284; M. Schilling, "Technology Success and Failure in Winner-Take-All Markets: The Impact of Learning Orientation, Timing, and Network Externalities," *Academy of Management Journal* 45 (2002): 387–398.

23. Amabile, et al., "Assessing the Work Environment for Creativity."

24. Ibid.

25. M. Csikszentmihalyi, *Flow: The Psychology of Optimal Experience* (New York: Harper & Row, 1990).

26. D. Garbato, "On the Beaten Track: Tractor Supply Co. Embraces Change but Stays Focused in All Areas of Its Business," *Retail Merchandiser*, January 2005, 30–31.

27. D. Murphy, "Ways That Managers Can Help Workers—Or Hinder Them," *San Francisco Chronicle*, 26 November 2000, J1; M. Schrage, "Your Idea Is Brilliant; Glad I Thought of It," *Fortune*, 16 October 2000, 412.

28. K. Capell, "Thinking Simple at Philips," 11 December 2006, 50.

29. M. Conlin, "Smashing the Clock," 11 December 2006, 60–68.

30. K. M. Eisenhardt, "Accelerating Adaptive Processes: Product Innovation in the Global Computer Industry," *Administrative Science Quarterly* 40 (1995): 84–110.

31. Ibid.

32. G. Bounds, "Sticky Fingers? How Avery Found an Office Problem to Solve," *Wall Street Journal*, 13 July 2004, B1.

33. R. Winslow, "Atomic Speed: Utility Cuts Red Tape, Builds Nuclear Plant Almost on Schedule," *Wall Street Journal Interactive*, 22 February 1984.

34. Jeff Howe, "The Rise of Crowdsourcing," *Wired*, June 2006, 176; http://www.innocentive.com.

35. C. Salter, "Ford's Escape Route," *Fast Company*, 1 October 2004, 106.

36. Ibid.

37. Ibid.

38. Ibid.

39. L. Kraar, "25 Who Help the U.S. Win: Innovators Everywhere Are Generating Ideas to Make America a Stronger Competitor. They Range from a Boss Who Demands the Impossible to a Mathematician with a Mop," *Fortune*, 22 March 1991.

40. M. W. Lawless & P. C. Anderson, "Generational Technological Change: Effects of Innovation and Local Rivalry on Performance," *Academy of Management Journal* 39 (1996): 1185–1217.

41. http://micro.gameboy.com.

42. "Sony Cuts Backward Compatibility for PlayStation 3 in Europe," *Wall Street Journal*, 27 February 2007, http://online.wsj.com.

43. P. Siekman, "The Snap-Together Business Jet," *Fortune*, 21 January 2002, 104[A].

44. J. Muller, "Chrysler Redesigns the Way It Designs: Karenann Terrell's High-Tech Quest for Change," *BusinessWeek*, 2 September 2002, 26B.

45. http://movies.about.com/cs/upcomingreleases/a/harrypotter4dir.htm, http://www.wizardnews.com/, http://www.cinematical.com/2006/11/03/latest-harry-potter-director-michael-who/; K. Kelly, "Older Harry Rates a PG-13: The Awkward, Lovelorn Hero of 'Goblet of Fire' May Lose Kids, Gain Broader Audience," *Wall Street Journal*, 16 November 2005, B1.

46. B. Baumohl & W. Cole "The Perils of Having Way More than Enough," *Time*, 13 January 1997, 58; S. Forest, "Incredible Universe: Lost in Space," *BusinessWeek*, 4 March 1996, http://www.businessweek.com/1996/10/b346580.htm.

47. P. Strebel, "Choosing the Right Change Path," *California Management Review*, Winter 1994, 29–51.

48. W. Weitzel & E. Jonsson, "Reversing the Downward Spiral: Lessons from W. T. Grant and Sears Roebuck," *Academy of Management Executive* 5 (1991): 7–22.

49. J. Peters, "Ford and GM Suffer as Buyers Shun SUVs," *New York Times*, 4 May 2005, C1.

50. T. Agins, L. Bird, & L. Jereski, "Overdoing It: A Thirst for Glitter and a Pliant Partner Got Barney's in a Bind," *Wall Street Journal Interactive*, 19 January 1996.

51. "The Rise and Fall of the House of Barneys: A Family Tale of Chutzpah, Glory, and Greed (Review)," *Publishers Weekly*, 22 February 1999, 73.

52. Ibid.

53. D. Moin, V. M. Young, & A. Friedman, "Dickson

Pool Sees Barney's IPO," *Women's Wear Daily*, 5 August 1997.

54. L. Bird, "Barney's to Close Original Store and Three Others," *Asian Wall Street Journal Interactive*, 19 June 1997.

55. D. Moin, "Barney's New Owners Plan to Retain Company, Grow Business: Strategy Calls for Boosting Sales, Increasing Cash Flow This Year," *Daily News Record*, 15 February 1999.

56. K. Lewin, *Field Theory in Social Science: Selected Theoretical Papers* (New York: Harper & Brothers, 1951).

57. A. Deutschman, "Making Change: Why Is It So Darn Hard to Change Our Ways?" *Fast Company*, May 2005, 52–62.

58. C. Taylor, "Changing Gears," *Sales & Marketing Management*, October 2005, 1.

59. K. Lewin, *Field Theory in Social Science*.

60. A. B. Fisher, "Making Change Stick," *Fortune*, 17 April 1995, 121.

61. J. P. Kotter & L. A. Schlesinger, "Choosing Strategies for Change," *Harvard Business Review*, March–April 1979, 106–114.

62. M. Johne, "The Human Factor: Integrating People and Cultures after a Merger," *CMA Management*, 1 April 2000, 30.

63. Ibid.

64. K. Booker & J. Schlosser, "The Un-CEO," *Fortune*, 16 September 2002, 88.

65. Ibid.

66. Ibid.

67. S. LaFee, "Professional Learning Communities: A Story of Five Superintendents Trying to Transform the Organizational Culture," *School Administrator*, 1 May 2003, 6.

68. B. Orwall, "Disney Decides It Must Draw Artists into Computer Age," *Wall Street Journal*, 23 October 2003, A1.

69. Ibid.

70. Ibid.

71. J. P. Kotter, "Leading Change: Why Transformation Efforts Fail," *Harvard Business Review* 73, no. 2 (March–April 1995): 59.

72. "The New Sears Holdings: Where America Speculates," *Chain Store Age*, 15 December 2004, 1; R. Berner, "At Sears, a Great Communicator," *BusinessWeek*, 31 October 2005, 50–52.

73. Booker & Schlosser, "The Un-CEO."

74. "Sears Results Mixed," *MMR*, 18 September 2006, 5.

75. "Sears Sees the Softer Side of Sales," *BusinessWeek Online*, 17 November 2006, 3.

76. R. Berner, "At Sears, a Great Communicator: New CEO Lewis Will Need His People Skills to Overhaul the Giant's Hidebound Culture," *BusinessWeek*, 31 October 2005, 50–52.

77. J. McCrackent & T. Kosdrosky, "Ford Plans to Offer Bonuses to Blue-Collar, Salaried Workers," *Wall Street Journal*, 9 March 2007, A10.

78. Berner, "At Sears, a Great Communicator."

79. "Sears Selects New Chief for Strategy: Former Best Buy Executive to Sharpen Focus on Customers," *Chicago Tribune*, 18 January 2007, online.

80. Ibid.

81. S. Cramm, "A Change of Hearts," *CIO*, 1 April 2003, http://www.cio.com/archive/040103/hs_leadership.html, 20 May 2003.

82. M. Ihlwan, L. Armstrong, & M. Eidam, "Hyundai: Kissing Clunkers Goodbye," *BusinessWeek*, 17 May 2004, 46.

83. Ibid.

84. Ibid.

85. R. N. Ashkenas & T. D. Jick, "From Dialogue to Action in GE WorkOut: Developmental Learning in a Change Process," in *Research in Organizational Change and Development*, vol. 6, ed. W. A. Pasmore & R. W. Woodman (Greenwich, CT: JAI Press, 1992), 267–287.

86. T. Stewart, "GE Keeps Those Ideas Coming," *Fortune*, 12 August 1991, 40.

87. J. D. Duck, "Managing Change: The Art of Balancing," *Harvard Business Review on Change* (Boston: Harvard Business School Press, 1998), 55–81.

88. C. Costanzo, "B of A's Six Sigma Teams Begin Work on Integration with Fleet," *American Banker*, 10 March 2004, 1.

89. W. J. Rothwell, R. Sullivan, & G. M. McLean, *Practicing Organizational Development: A Guide for Consultants* (San Diego, CA: Pfeiffer & Co., 1995).

90. N. Shirouzu, "Gadget Inspector: Why Toyota Wins Such High Marks on Quality Surveys—Hajime Oba Is a Key Coach as Japanese Auto Maker Steps Up U.S. Production—Striving to Reach Heijunka," *Wall Street Journal*, 15 March 2001, A1.

91. Ibid.

92. Rothwell, Sullivan, & McLean, *Practicing Organizational Development*.

93. P. J. Robertson, D. R. Roberts, & J. I. Porras, "Dynamics of Planned Organizational Change: Assessing Empirical Support for a Theoretical Model," *Academy of Management Journal* 36 (1993): 619–634.

94. J. E. Ettlie and R. D. O'Keefe, "Innovative Attitudes, Values, and Intentions in Organizations," *Journal of Management Studies* 19 (1982): 163–182.

95. "Can Colgate Brush Off the Competition?" *Marketing Week*, 27 January 2005, 23; Seth Mendelson, "The War of the Roses: Colgate and Crest Have Fought for Decades for Supremacy in the Toothpaste Category. Suddenly, One Has Gained an Edge and the Other Is Challenged to Change Its Strategy," *Grocery Headquarters*, January 2005, 64; David Kiley, "Reuben Mark: Profit and Floss," *BusinessWeek*, 20 December 2004, 46; Pallavi Gogoi, "Colgate's Big Bid to Freshen Up Profits," *BusinessWeek Online*, 8 December 2004; "Colgate: Brushing Mergers Aside," *BusinessWeek Online*, 4 February 2005; Eric Dash, "Colgate to Cut Jobs and Use Savings to Spur Sales," *New York Times*, 8 December 2004, C1; "Squeezed: Colgate-Palmolive Shuts Factories to Save $300 Million," *Sunday Business (London)*, 12 December 2004.

96. Julie Schlosser, "Inside-the-Box Thinking," *Fortune*, 1 November 2004, 54; http://www.mindwareonline.com; http://www.eurekaranch.com.

Chapter 8

1. "Business Brief—Tommy Hilfiger Corp. Revenue Drop of 6.4% Expected Amid Declines in U.S. Business," *Wall Street Journal*, 10 November 2005; T. Agins, "By A Thread: A Hot Designer Can Generate Buzz But Not Profits," *Wall Street Journal*, 16 September 2005, A1; T. Agins, "For U.S. Fashion Firms, A Global Makeover—Tommy Hilfiger Finds Assimilating in Europe Requires a New Look," *Wall Street Journal*, 2 February 2007; T. Agins & C. Rohwedder, "Hilfiger Tries on Lagerfeld Designs," *Wall Street Journal*, 14 December 2004, B6; D. Berman & T. Agins, "Apax Nears Deal To Buy Hilfiger For $1.5 Billion," *Wall Street Journal*, 23 December 2005, B2; A. Caroll, "Brand Barrage: When the Murjani Group, in a Joint Venture with Arvind . . . ," *Business Standard*, 13 February

2007, 11; S. Conti, "Hilfiger Signs French Soccer Star—Tommy to Design Capsule Line Inspired by Thierry Henry, Who will also Appear in Formal and Underwear Ads," *DNR*, 11 December 2006, 12; J. Greenberg, "Tommy Seeks to Revive Brand in U.S.," *Women's Wear Daily*, 12 July 2006, 6; P. Ho, "Li & Fung Surges on Hilfiger Buy," *The Standard*, 13 February 2007; R. Jana, "Bridging the Fashion Culture Gap; Apparel Company Murjani Group Is Leading the Charge, Bringing Western Labels such as Tommy Hilfiger and Calvin Klein to Indian Shoppers," *Business Week Online*, 5 February 2007.

2. T. Friedman, "It's a Flat World, After All," *New York Times*, 3 April 2005, 33.
3. World Investment Report, 2006," United Nations Conference on Trade & Development, http://www.unctad.org/en/docs/wir2006annexes_en.pdf, 30 January 2007.
4. G. Samor, "Steelmaker Girds for Growth—Gerdau of Brazil Looks to Bulk Up Further in United States Market," *Wall Street Journal*, 5 April 2005, B2.
5. C. Rong, "Chinese Assets Are Looking Pricey—How Much Is Too Much to Pay for Market Share? A Slew of Big-Profile Deals," *Wall Street Journal Europe*, 4 February 2005, M4.
6. C. Baughn & M. Buchanan, "Cultural Protectionism," *Business Horizons*, 1 November 2001, 5; "Senior US Trade Official Raises Limits on Hollywood Movies in Beijing," *AFX News Limited*, 27 May 2004.
7. J. Miller, "China's Low Fruit Prices Highlight EU's Vulnerabilities Over Trade," *Wall Street Journal*, 26 December 2006, A4.
8. L. Etter, "Can Ethanol Get a Ticket to Ride?" *Wall Street Journal*, 1 February 2007, B1.
9. G. Williams, III, "News on the Road Column," *San Antonio Express–News*, 3 March 2006.
10. "Determination of Total Amounts and Quota Period for Tariff-Rate Quotas for Raw Cane Sugar and Certain Imported Sugars, Syrups, and Molasses," *Federal Register*, 15 April 2002, 18162.
11. J. Sparshott, "U.S. Sugar Growers Fear Losses from Free-Trade Push," *Washington Times*, 24 March 2005, C07.
12. R. Geldenhuys, "China Import Quotas Illegal under WTO Law?" Floor, Inc. Attorneys, http://www.tradelaw.co.za/news/article.asp?newsID=101, 18 September 2006.
13. "The Agreements: Anti-Dumping, Subsidies, Safeguards, Contingencies, etc.," World Trade Organization, http://www.wto.org/english/thewto_e/whatis_e/tif_e/agrm8_e. htm, 22 April 2005.
14. C. Hale, "HortFACT—Why Fireblight Shouldn't Be a Market Access Problem," Hortnet, http://www.hortnet.co.nz/publications/hortfacts/hf205010.htm, 9 May 2003; "USTR Lists Barriers to U.S. Trade, Focusing on Agriculture—Annual Report Also Emphasizes Intellectual Property, Transparency," U.S. Department Press Releases & Documents, 7 February 2007.
15. J. Morgan, "Building Seeds of Case against OZ Apple Ban," *Dominion Post*, 18 January 2007, 7.
16. "USA Claims Airbus Drove out Rivals," *Flight International*, 23 January 2007.
17. "Rocky Receives Customs Clarification on Imported Boots," *FN*, 31 March 2003.
18. H. Blodget, "How to Solve China's Piracy Problem: A Dozen Ideas. Maybe One Will Work," *Slate*, 12 April 2005, http://www.slate.com/id/2116629.
19. G. Fowler, "Estimates of Copyright Piracy Losses Vary Widely," *Wall Street Journal*, 2 June 2006, A13.
20. Ibid.
21. "The History of the European Union," *Europa—The European Union Online*, 7 February 2007, http://europa.eu.int/abc/history/index_en.htm.
22. "The History of the European Union," *Europa—The European Union Online*, 22 April 2005, http://europa.eu.int/abc/history/index_en.htm.
23. D. Luhnow, "Crossover Success: How NAFTA Helped Wal-Mart Reshape the Mexican Market," *Wall Street Journal*, 31 August 2001, A1.
24. "Testimony of Under Secretary of Commerce for International Trade Grant D. Aldona: The Impact of NAFTA on the United States Economy," Senate Foreign Relations Committee, Subcommittee on International Economic Policy, Export & Trade Promotion, 7 February 2007.
25. Office of Industry Trade Policy, "NAFTA: 10 Years Later," U.S. Department of Commerce, International Trade Administration, http://ita.doc.gov/td/industry/otea/nafta/CoverPage.pdf, 7 February 2007.
26. Office of the United States Trade Representative, "The Case for CAFTA: Growth, Opportunity, and Democracy in our Neighborhood," United States Department of Agriculture: Foreign Agricultural Service, http://www.ustr.gov/assets/Trade_Agreements/Bilateral/CAFTA/Briefing_Book/asset_upload_file235_7178.pdf, 10 February 2007.
27. "South American Community of Nations," Andean Community, http://www.comunidadandina.org/ingles/sudamerican.htm, 10 February 2007.
28. "Selected Basic ASEAN Indicators, 2005," Association of Southeast Nations, http://www.aseansec.org/stat/Table1.pdf, 10 February 2007. "Top Ten ASEAN Trade Partner Countries/Regions, 2005," Association of Southeast Nations, http://www.aseansec.org/Stat/Table20.pdf, 10 February 2007.
29. "ASEAN Free Trade Area (Afta): An Update," Association of Southeast Nations, http://www.aseansec.org, 10 September 2001.
30. "Member Economies' Websites," Asia-Pacific Economic Cooperation, http://www.apecsec.org.sg/apec/member_economies/key_websites.html, 10 September 2001.
31. "Frequently Asked Questions (FAQs): How much of the world's trade takes place in the APEC Region?" *Asia-Pacific Economic Cooperation*, http://www.apecsec.org.sg/apec/tools/faqs.html, 10 February 2007.
32. "An Unofficial Price List of Everyday Items in Tokyo," *PriceCheckTokyo*, 10 February 2007, http://www.pricechecktokyo.com.
33. "The Big Mac Index," *Economist*, http://www.economist.com/markets/indicators/displaystory.cfm?story_id=8649005, 10 February 2007.
34. Ibid.
35. Ibid.
36. "Freer Trade Cuts the Cost of Living," World Trade Organization, http://www.wto.org/english/thewto_e/whatis_e/10ben_e/10b04_e.htm, 10 February 2007.
37. B. Thevenot, "Clawing for Survival, Louisiana's Crab Processors Are Being Pinched by Low Prices and Foreign Competition," *New Orleans Times-Picayune*, 6 October 1999, A1.
38. L. Grant, "More United States Diamond Buyers Turn to Canada: Gem Seekers Want to Avoid Stones at Center of

Conflicts," *USA Today*, 17 July 2001, B2.

39. Luhnow, "Crossover Success."

40. MTV Brasil, http://mtv.uol.com.br, 30 January 2007.

41. MTV China, http://mtvchina.com, 30 January 2007.

42. MTV India, http://www.mtvindia.com/sillypoint/sourav.php, 30 January 2007.

43. A. Sundaram & J. S. Black, "The Environment and Internal-Organization of Multinational Enterprises," *Academy of Management Review* 17 (1992): 729–757.

44. H. S. James, Jr., & M. Weidenbaum, *When Businesses Cross International Borders: Strategic Alliances & Their Alternatives* (Westport, CT: Praeger Publishers, 1993).

45. "Our Programmes: Idols," *Fremantle Media*, http://www.fremantlemedia.com/our-programmes/view/Global+Hit+Formats/viewprogramme/Idols, 10 February 2007.

46. "LNG Imports Needed to Meet Growing US Gas Supply Deficit," *Oil & Gas Journal*, 2 October 2001, 28.

47. "Workplace Code of Conduct," Fair Labor Association, http://www.fairlabor.org/all/code/index.html, 12 May 2003; A. Bernstein, M. Shari, & E. Malkin, "A World of Sweatshops," *BusinessWeek*, 6 November 2000, 84.

48. "New Restaurants," McDonald's, http://www.mcdonalds.com/corp/franchise/purchasingYourFranchise/newRestaurants.html, 10 February 2007.

49. "McDonald's FAQ," McDonald's, 23 April 2005, http://www.mcdonalds.com/corp/about/mcd_faq.html.

50. M. Arndt, "McDonald's 24/7," *BusinessWeek*, 5 February 2007, 64.

51. "Yum! Restaurants International," *Yum!*, http://www.yum.com/about/yri.asp, 10 February 2007.

52. K. Le Mesurier, "Overseas and Overwhelmed," *BRW*, 25 January 2007, 51.

53. C. Adler, "How China Eats a Sandwich: Opening Subway Franchises in the People's Republic," *Fortune*, 21 March 2005, F310 [B].

54. D. Hemlock, "World Wise: Strategies That Work around the Corner Don't Always Work in Locales Abroad, Office Depot's Chief Executive Says," *South Florida Sun*, 18 December 2000, 16.

55. Ibid.

56. "Company Profile," Fuji Xerox, http://www.fujixerox.co.jp/eng/company/profile.html, 12 February 2007;

57. P. Huber & M. Mills, "A Power Portfolio," *Forbes*, 11 April 2005, 76.

58. "Joint Venture Foundation of Giesecke & Devrient and Nokia Completed," Hugin Press Release, 20 December 2006.

59. B. R. Schlender, "How Toshiba Makes Alliances Work," *Fortune*, 4 October 1993, 116–120.

60. G. Fairclough, "GM's Partner in China Plans Competing Car," *Wall Street Journal*, 5 April 2006, B1.

61. G. Parker, "Going Global Can Hit Snags, Vodafone Finds," *Wall Street Journal*, 16 June 2004, B1.

62. M. W. Hordes, J. A. Clancy, & J. Baddaley, "A Primer for Global Start-Ups." *Academy of Management Executive*, May 1995, 7–11.

63. D. Pavlos, J. Johnson, J. Slow, & S. Young, "Micromultinationals: New Types of Firms for the Global Competitive Landscape," *European Management Journal* 21, issue 2 (April 2003): 164; B. M. Oviatt & P. P. McDougall, "Toward a Theory of International New Ventures," *Journal of International Business Studies*, Spring 1994, 45–64; S. Zahra, "A Theory of International New Ventures: A Decade of Research," *Journal of International Business Studies*, January 2005, 20–28.

64. A. Grimes, "Venture Firms Seek Start-Ups That Outsource," *Wall Street Journal*, 2 April 2004, B1.

65. M. Copeland, "The Mighty Micro-Multinational," *Business 2.0*, 1 July 2006, 106.

66. "Operations Review: Selected Market Results: Estimated 2002 Volume by Operating Segment," The Coca-Cola Company 2002 Annual Report.

67. G. Smith, "Mexico: Piggybanks Full of Pesos," *BusinessWeek*, 13 March 2006, 51.

68. D. Lynch, "Developing Nations Poised to Challenge USA as King of the Hill," *USA Today*, 8 February 2007, B.1. N. Srinivas, "Of Carats & Calories," *Economic Times*, 29 December 2006.

69. "Operations Review: Selected Market Results: Estimated 2002 Volume by Operating Segment," The Coca-Cola Company 2002 Annual Report.

70. F. Vogelstein, "How Intel Got Inside," *Fortune*, 4 October 2004, 127.

71. "Customer Care in the Netherlands," The Netherlands Foreign Investment Agency, available at http://www.nfia.com/solutions.php?pageid=11, 13 February 2007; "Customer Care Centers," Netherlands Foreign Investment Agency Information Manual, 13 February 2007, available at http://www.nfia.com/downloads/customercare.htm.

72. A. Snyder, "European Expansion: How to Shop Around," *Management Review*,1 November 1993, 16.

73. J. Oetzel, R. Bettis, & M. Zenner, "How Risky Are They?" *Journal of World Business* 36, no. 2 (Summer 2001): 128–145.

74. K. D. Miller, "A Framework for Integrated Risk Management in International Business," *Journal of International Business Studies*, 2nd Quarter 1992, 311.

75. J. Schuman, "The Morning Brief: Shell, Partners Give in to Kremlin Oil Game . . . ," *Wall Street Journal*, 22 December 2006.

76. Chapter 1: Political Outlook," *UAE Business Forecast Report*, 2007 1st Quarter, 5–10.

77. "Foreign Corrupt Business Practices Act," U.S. Department of Justice, http://www.usdoj.gov/criminal/fraud/fcpa, 10 May 2003.

78. G. Fowler, "In China's Offices, Foreign Colleagues Might Get an Earful," *Wall Street Journal*, 13 February 2007, B1.

79. Ibid.

80. G. Hofstede, "The Cultural Relativity of the Quality of Life Concept," *Academy of Management Review* 9 (1984): 389–398; G. Hofstede, "The Cultural Relativity of Organizational Practices and Theories," *Journal of International Business Studies*, Fall 1983, 75–89; G. Hofstede, "The Interaction between National and Organizational Value Systems," *Journal of Management Studies*, July 1985, 347–357; M. Hoppe, "An Interview with Geert Hofstede," *Academy of Management Executive*, February 2004, 75–79.

81. R. Hodgetts, "A Conversation with Geert Hofstede," *Organizational Dynamics*, Spring 1993, 53–61.

82. T. Lenartowicz & K. Roth, "Does Subculture within a Country Matter?

A Cross-Cultural Study of Motivational Domains and Business Performance in Brazil," *Journal of International Business Studies* 32 (2001): 305–325.

83. M. Janssens, J. M. Brett, & F. J. Smith, "Confirmatory Cross-Cultural Research: Testing the Viability of a Corporation-Wide Safety Policy," *Academy of Management Journal* 38 (1995): 364–382.

84. R. G. Linowes, "The Japanese Manager's Traumatic Entry into the United States: Understanding the American-Japanese Cultural Divide," *Academy of Management Executive* 7 (1993): 21–40.

85. J. S. Black, M. Mendenhall, & G. Oddou, "Toward a Comprehensive Model of International Adjustment: An Integration of Multiple Theoretical Perspectives," *Academy of Management Review* 16 (1991): 291–317; R. L. Tung, "American Expatriates Abroad: From Neophytes to Cosmopolitans," *Columbia Journal of World Business*, 22 June 1998, 125; A. Harzing, "The Persistent Myth of High Expatriate Failure Rates," *International Journal of Human Resource Management* 6 (1995): 457–475; A. Harzing, "Are Our Referencing Errors Undermining Our Scholarship and Credibility? The Case of Expatriate Failure Rates," *Journal of Organizational Behavior* 23 (2002): 127–148; N. Forster, "The Persistent Myth of High Expatriate Failure Rates: A Reappraisal," *International Journal of Human Resource Management* 8 (1997): 414–433.

86. J. Black, "The Right Way to Manage Expats," *Harvard Business Review* 77 (March–April 1999): 52; C. Joinson, "No Returns," *HR Magazine*, 1 November 2002, 70.

87. C. Joinson, "No Returns," *HR Magazine*, November 2002, 70.

88. J. S. Black & M. Mendenhall, "Cross-Cultural Training Effectiveness: A Review and Theoretical Framework for Future Research," *Academy of Management Review* 15 (1990): 113–136.

89. K. Essick, "Executive Education: Transferees Prep for Life, Work in Far-Flung Lands," *Wall Street Journal*, 12 November 2004, A6.

90. Ibid.

91. P. W. Tam, "Culture Course—'Awareness Training' Helps U.S. Workers Better Know Their Counterparts in India," *Wall Street Journal*, 25 May 2004, B1.

92. J. Areddy, "Deep Inside China, American Family Struggles to Cope," *Wall Street Journal*, 2 August 2005, A1.

93. W. Arthur, Jr., & W. Bennett, Jr., "The International Assignee: The Relative Importance of Factors Perceived to Contribute to Success," *Personnel Psychology* 48 (1995): 99–114; B. Cheng, "Home Truths about Foreign Postings; To Make an Overseas Assignment Work, Employers Need More Than an Eager Exec with a Suitcase. They Must Also Motivate the Staffer's Spouse," *BusinessWeek Online*, http://www.businessweek.com/careers/content/jul2002/ca20020715_9110.htm, 16 July 2002.

94. M. Netz, "It's Not Judging— It's Assessing: The Truth about Candidate Assessments," *NRRE Magazine*, March 2004, http://www.rismedia.com.

95. R. Donkin, "Recruitment: Overseas Gravy Train May Be Running Out of Steam—Preparing Expatriate Packages Is Challenging the Expertise of Human Resource Management," *Financial Times*, 30 November 1994, 10.

96. S. P. Deshpande & C. Viswesvaran, "Is Cross-Cultural Training of Expatriate Managers Effective? A Meta-Analysis," *International Journal of Intercultural Relations* 16, no. 3 (1992): 295–310.

97. J. Areddy, "Deep Inside China, American Family Struggles to Cope."

98. R. W. Boatler, "Study Abroad: Impact on Student Worldmindedness," *Journal of Teaching in International Business* 2, no. 2 (1990): 13–17; R. W. Boatler, "Worldminded Attitude Change in a Study Abroad Program: Contact and Content Issues," *Journal of Teaching in International Business* 3, no. 4 (1992): 59–68; H. Lancaster, "Learning to Manage in a Global Workplace (You're on Your Own)," The *Wall Street Journal*, 2 June 1998, B1; D. L. Sampson & H. P. Smith, "A Scale to Measure Worldminded Attitudes," *Journal of Social Psychology* 45 (1957): 99–106.

99. Starbucks Annual Report, 2006, Form 10-K / A; "Lattes in the Forbidden City," *Wall Street Journal*, 7 March 2007, online video in partnership with Reuters online at www.wsj.com; G. Fowler, "It's Called the Forbidden City for a Reason," *Wall Street Journal*, 19 January 2007, B1; "Question Authority: Starbucks—The Next Generation," *Fortune*, 4 April 2005, 30; C. Mee-young, "Starbucks Likely to Expand Asia Plan," *Reuters English News Service*, 23 August 2001, available online; "An American (Coffee) in Paris—and Rome," *United States News & World Report*, 19 February 2001, 47.

100. L. Stroh, "Why Are Women Left at Home? Are They Unwilling to Go on International Assignments?" *Journal of World Business*, Fall 2000.

101. A. Hanft, "Passport to America," *Inc.*, October 2004, 14.

Chapter 9

1. "About Alcan," Alcan, http://www.alcan.com /web/publishing.nsf/Content/About+Alcan+-+Company+Structure; R. Barker, "Novelis: All Set to Gain Speed," *BusinessWeek*, 14 November 2005, 32.

2. B. Schlender, "Microsoft: The Beast Is Back," *Fortune*, 11 June 2001, 75.

3. Y. Noguchi, "Microsoft Remakes Corporate Structure," *Washington Post*, 21 September 2005, D5; "Microsoft Announces Plans for July 2008 Transition for Bill Gates," Microsoft, http://www.microsoft.com/presspass/press/2006/jun06/06-15CorpNewsPR.mspx.

4. M. Hammer & J. Champy, *Reengineering the Corporation: A Manifesto for Business Revolution* (New York: Harper & Row, 1993).

5. "Sara Lee Announces Transformation Plan; Brenda C. Barnes Appointed the Company's CEO, Effective Immediately," *Retail Merchandiser*, 10 February 2005; "Our Timeline," Sara Lee Corporation, http://www.saralee.com/AboutSaraLee/OurTimeline.aspx.

6. J. G. March & H. A. Simon, *Organizations* (New York: John Wiley & Sons, 1958).

7. "Bayer Group: Profile and Organization," Bayer AG, http://www.bayer.com/bayer-group/profile-and-organization/page2351.htm.

8. "Outline of Principle Operations," Sony Corporation, http://www.sony.com/SCA/outline.shtml.

9. "Our Companies," United Technologies 2004 Annual Report, United Technologies, http://www.utc.com/annual_reports/2004/html/page5.htm.

10. "Form 10-K, United Technologies Corporation: Segment Review," United States Securities and Exchange Commission, http://investors.utc.com.

11. "Company Info: Executive Team," Sprint Nextel, http://www2.sprint.com/mr/exListPrev.do?Span=20.

12. "Our Company: The Best Brands in the World," Coca-Cola Enterprises, http://www.cokecce.com/pages/allContent.asp?page_id=85.

13. "Corporate Info: Corporate Structure—Four Pillars," Procter & Gamble, http://www.pg.com/jobs/corporate_structure/four_pillars.jhtml; "P&G Management," Procter & Gamble, http://www.pg.com/news/management/bios_photos.jhtml.

14. L. R. Burns, "Adoption and Abandonment of Matrix Management Programs: Effects of Organizational Characteristics and Interorganizational Networks," *Academy of Management Journal* 36 (1993): 106–138.

15. D. Ball, "Unilever Shakes Up Its Management to Spur Growth," *Wall Street Journal*, 11 February 2005, A2.

16. "Unilever Streamlines Its Leadership Structure," Unilever, http://www.unilever.com/ourcompany/newsandmedia/pressreleases/2005/Unileverstreamlinesitsleadershipstructure.asp.

17. H. Fayol, *General and Industrial Management*, trans. Constance Storrs (London: Pitman Publishing, 1949).

18. M. Weber, *The Theory of Social and Economic Organization*, trans. and ed. A. M. Henderson & T. Parsons (New York: Free Press, 1947).

19. Fayol, *General and Industrial Management.*

20. J. Greene, S. Hamm, & J. Kerstetter, "How CEO Steve Ballmer Is Remaking the Company That Bill Gates Built," *BusinessWeek*, 17 June 2002, 66.

21. S. Holmes, "Inside the Coup at Nike," *BusinessWeek Online*, 26 January 2006, http://www.businessweek.com/bwdaily/dnflash/jan2006/nf20060126_9724_db016.htm?chan=search; S. Holmes, "Nike CEO Gets the Boot," *BusinessWeek Online*, 24 January 2006, http://www.businessweek.com/bwdaily/dnflash/jan2006/nf20060124_6652_db016.htm?chan=search.

22. J. Whalen, "Bureaucracy Buster? Glaxo Lets Scientists Choose Its New Drugs," *Wall Street Journal*, 27 March 2006, B1.

23. J. Rutledge, "Management by Belly Button," *Forbes*, 4 November 1996, 64.

24. E. E. Lawler, S. A. Mohrman, & G. E. Ledford, *Creating High Performance Organizations: Practices and Results of Employee Involvement and Quality Management in Fortune 1000 Companies* (San Francisco: Jossey-Bass, 1995).

25. D. Welch, "Renault-Nissan: Say Hello to Bo," *BusinessWeek*, 31 July 2006, 56–57.

26. S. Curry, "Retention Getters," *Incentive*, 1 April 2005.

27. R. W. Griffin, *Task Design* (Glenview, IL: Scott, Foresman, 1982).

28. F. Herzberg, *Work and the Nature of Man* (Cleveland, OH: World Press, 1966).

29. A. Markels, "Team Approach: A Power Producer Is Intent on Giving Power to Its People—Groups of AES Employees Do Complex Tasks Ranging from Hiring to Investing—Making Sure Work Is 'Fun,'" *Wall Street Journal*, 3 July 1995, A1.

30. Ibid.

31. J. R. Hackman & G. R. Oldham, *Work Redesign* (Reading, MA: Addison-Wesley, 1980).

32. T. Burns & G. M. Stalker, *The Management of Innovation* (London: Tavistock, 1961).

33. Y. Fried & G. R. Ferris, "The Validity of the Job Characteristics Model: A Review and Meta-Analysis," *Personnel Psychology* 40 (1987): 287–322; B. T. Loher, R. A. Noe, N. L. Moeller, & M. P. Fitzgerald, "A Meta-Analysis of the Relation of Job Characteristics to Job Satisfaction," *Journal of Applied Psychology* 70 (1985): 280–289.

34. M. Hammer & J. Champy, *Reengineering the Corporation.*

35. Ibid.

36. J. D. Thompson, *Organizations in Action* (New York: McGraw-Hill, 1967).

37. D. Pink, "Who Has the Next Big Idea?" *Fast Company*, 1 September 2001, 108.

38. J. B. White, "'Next Big Thing': Re-Engineering Gurus Take Steps to Remodel Their Stalling Vehicles," *Wall Street Journal Interactive*, 26 November 1996.

39. Ibid.

40. G. M. Spreitzer, "Individual Empowerment in the Workplace: Dimensions, Measurement, and Validation," *Academy of Management Journal* 38 (1995): 1442–1465.

41. M. Schrage, "I Know What You Mean. And I Can't Do Anything about It," *Fortune*, 2 April 2001, 186.

42. K. W. Thomas & B. A. Velthouse, "Cognitive Elements of Empowerment," *Academy of Management Review* 15 (1990): 666–681.

43. "Wegmans: History," Wegmans, http://www.wegmans.com/about/history/index.asp; M. Boyle & E. Kratz, "The Wegmans Way," *Fortune*, 24 January 2005, 62–68.

44. D. A. Morand, "The Role of Behavioral Formality and Informality in the Enactment of Bureaucratic versus Organic Organizations," *Academy of Management Review* 20 (1995): 831–872.

45. "Hot Tamale," *Wall Street Journal*, January 28–29, 2006, B3.

46. L. Munoz, "The Suit Is Back—Or Is It? As Dot-Coms Die, So Should Business Casual. But the Numbers Don't Lie," *Fortune*, 25 June 2001, 202; F. Swoboda, "Casual Dress Becomes the Rule," *Las Vegas Review-Journal*, 3 March 1996.

47. A. Merrick, "Tailors Spin a Yarn: Men's Suit Is Back! But Story Unravels—Stores Say 'Serious' Is In, Sales Keep Slacking Off; An Overstretched Theory," *Wall Street Journal*, 27 December 2002, A1; Munoz, "The Suit Is Back."

48. "Casual Office Attire Going, Going ..." *USA Today*, 1 January 2005, 8; J. Fassnacht, "Pendulum Swings Away from Casual Attire in the Workplace," *Reading (PA) Eagle*, 18 October 2004.

49. "Suits Lose Appeal As Casual Dress Rules in London Offices," *Evening Standard* (London), 19 October 2004.

50. "SHRM Online Poll Results," Society for Human Resource Management, http://www.shrm.org/poll/results.asp?Question=89, 21 May 2003.

51. K. McCullough, "Analysis: More Companies Allowing Employees to Dress Down, Which Makes Productivity Go Up," *Money Club*, 26 March 1996.

52. W. Bounds, "Phone Calls Are Public Affairs for Open-Plan Office

Dwellers," *Wall Street Journal*, 10 July 2002, B1.

53. "Designing the Ever-Changing Workplace," *Architectural Record*, September 1995, 32–37.

54. H. Landy, "All Moved in at Radio Shack," *Fort Worth Star-Telegram*, 3 March 2005, 1C.

55. A. Frangos, "Property Report: See You on the Way Up! Office Stairs Get 'Aspirational,'" *Wall Street Journal*, 19 May 2004, B1.

56. J. Sandberg, "Cookies, Gossip, Cubes: It's a Wonder Any Work Gets Done at the Office," *Wall Street Journal*, 28 April 2004, B1.

57. Ibid.

58. Ibid.

59. L. Gallagher, "At Work: Get Out of My Face: Open Offices Were Hailed as the Answer to Hierarchical, Rigid Organizations. Employees Would Rather Have Privacy," *Forbes*, 18 October 1999, 105.

60. K. A. Edelman, "Take Down the Walls!" *Across the Board*, 1 March 1997.

61. S. Hwang, "Cubicle Culture: Office Vultures Circle Still-Warm Desks Left Empty by Layoffs," *Wall Street Journal*, 14 August 2002, B1.

62. M. Rich, "Shut Up So We Can Do Our Jobs!—Fed Up Workers Try to Muffle Chitchat, Conference Calls and Other Opens-Office Din," *Wall Street Journal*, 29 August 2001, B1.

63. J. Gannon, "GlaxoSmithKline, Alcoa, Marconi, PNC Open Up Office Environments," *Pittsburgh Post-Gazette*, 9 February 2003.

64. G. Kahn, "Making Labels for Less—Supply-Chain City Transforms Far-Flung Apparel Industry; Help for 'The Button Guy,'" *Wall Street Journal*, 13 August 2004, B1.

65. G. G. Dess, A. M. A. Rasheed, K. J. McLaughlin, & R. L. Priem, "The New Corporate Architecture," *Academy of Management Executive* 9 (1995): 7–18.

66. W. Bulkeley, "New IBM Jobs Can Mean Fewer Jobs Elsewhere," *Wall Street Journal*, 8 March 2004, B1.

67. G. McWilliams, "Apple Uses Software, Outsourcing to Gain Share As Sony Struggles to Grow," *Wall Street Journal*, 10 March 2005, A1.

68. P. Cohen & J. Dalrymple, "Apple Updates iPod Line, Cuts Prices," *Computer World*, 23 February 2005, available at http://www.computerworld.com/softwaretopics/os/macos/story/0,10801,99956,00.html.

69. "Overview: Collaborative Business Network Solutions," *G5 Technologies: Agile Web*, http://www.g5technologies.com/agileweb/overview/index.html.

70. J. H. Sheridan, "The Agile Web: A Model for the Future?" *Industry Week*, 4 March 1996, 31.

71. Ibid.

72. C. C. Snow, R. E. Miles, & H. J. Coleman, Jr., "Managing 21st Century Network Organizations," *Organizational Dynamics*, Winter 1992, 5–20.

73. Sheridan, "The Agile Web: A Model for the Future?"

74. "Virtual Corporation Management System (VCMS) Solution," *G5 Technologies: Agile Web*, http://www.g5technologies.com/VCMS.htm.

75. Bruner, James, Hensel, *Marketing Scales Handbook*, 931–934.

76. "Britain Mulls Life-Saving Garbage Men," *UPI News Track*, 13 January 2005; J. K. Borchardt, "Hey, It's a Dirty Job … But Garbage Collectors, Prison Guards, and Morticians Are Doing It—and Often Finding Fulfillment," *Christian Science Monitor*, 9 August 2004, 14; T. Barry, "Ogden, Utah, Garbage Collector Takes Pride in Job," *Ogden (UT) Standard-Examiner*, 25 May 2001; P. Paul, F. M. Kuijer, et al., "Effect of Job Rotation on Work Demands, Workload, and Recovery of Refuse Truck Drivers and Collectors," *Human Factors*, Fall 2004, 437–449.

77. A. Cohen, "Lego Builds Self-Booking Tool," *Business Travel News*, 19 June 2006, 10; Q. Hardy, "Son of Lego," *Forbes*, 4 September 2006, 108; M. Defosse, "Toy Industry's Essential Block: Outsourcing. Few Markets Have Been More Speedily Outsourced to Low-Wage Lands than the Ones for Toys and Sporting Goods. Lego's Recent Announcement Is a Prime Example," *Modern Plastics Worldwide*, August 2006, 20–22; "Outsourcing Move by Lego," *New York Times*, 21 June 2006, C11; "What's NXT? Lego Embraces Third-Party Development," *PR Newswire*, 15 September 2006; J. Pisani, "The Making of a Lego. The Bricks Are so Versatile that Just Six of Them Can Be Arranged in 915,103,765 Ways. No Wonder Lego Has Been Named 'Toy of the Century'—Twice," *BusinessWeek Online*, 29 November 2006; "Picking Up the Pieces: Lego's Turnaround," *Economist*, 28 October 2006, 76; "LEGO Group Outsources Logistics to DHL," *M2Presswire*, 27 October 2005; N. Schwartz, "One Brick at a Time," *Fortune*, 8 June 2006, 45.

78. K. Freiberg & J. Freiberg, *Nuts! Southwest Airlines' Crazy Recipe for Business and Personal Success* (Austin, TX: Bard, 1996).

Chapter 10

1. Catherine Larkin (16 October 2006), Gap grows between best, worst care," *The Denver Post*, retrieved from http://www.denverpost.com/business/ci_4500867 on 11 April 2007; Kaiser Permanente. *Wikipedia, the free encyclopedia*, retrieved from http:// en.wikipedia.org/wiki/kaiser_Permanente 10 April 2007; "Building Rapid Response Teams," *Institute of Healthcare Improvement*, http://www.ihi.org/IHI/Topics/ReducingMortality/Reducing Mortality General/Improvement, 11 April 2007; "The Kaiser Papers," *California News Stories about Kaiser Permanente*, http://www.kaiserpapers.info/californianews.html, on 11 April 2007; M. Marquez, "Trend: 'Dumping' Homeless on L.A.'s Skid Row," *ABC News, Good Morning America*, 24 March 2006, http://www.abcnews.go.com/GMA/print?id=1761873; S. Hollander, L. Gunderson & J. Mechanic, "Process Improvements Boost Patient Satisfaction and Quality of Care at Stanford University Hospital," *Shaw Resources Online*, http://www.shawresource.com/artstanford.htm; F. Vara-Orta, "State Lists Worst Hospitals for Care of Pneumonia: Five Kaiser Facilities Have among the Highest Mortality Rates," *Los Angeles Times Online*, 27 February 2007, http://www.latimescom/news/local/la-me-hospitals 27feb27,1, 3287281.story?coll=laheadline.

2. B. Dumaine, "The Trouble with Teams," *Fortune*, 5 September 1994, 86–92.

3. J. Hoerr, "The Payoff from Teamwork—The Gains in Quality Are Substantial—So Why Isn't It Spreading Faster?" *BusinessWeek*, 10 July 1989, 56.

4. J. R. Katzenbach & D. K. Smith, *The Wisdom of Teams* (Boston: Harvard Business School Press, 1993).

5. S. G. Cohen & D. E. Bailey, "What Makes Teams Work: Group Effectiveness Research

from the Shop Floor to the Executive Suite," *Journal of Management* 23, no. 3 (1997): 239–290.

6. S. E. Gross, *Compensation for Teams* (New York: American Management Association, 1995); B. L. Kirkman & B. Rosen, "Beyond Self-Management: Antecedents and Consequences of Team Empowerment," *Academy of Management Journal* 42 (1999): 58–74; G. Stalk & T. M. Hout, *Competing against Time: How Time-Based Competition Is Reshaping Global Markets* (New York: Free Press, 1990); S. C. Wheelwright & K. B. Clark, *Revolutionizing New Product Development* (New York: Free Press, 1992).

7. D. A. Harrison, S. Mohamed, J. E. McGrath, A. T. Florey & S. W. Vanderstoep, "Time Matters in Team Performance: Effects of Member Familiarity, Entrainment, and Task Discontinuity on Speed and Quality," *Personnel Psychology* 56(3) (2003, August): 633–669.

8. J. Marquez, "Hewitt-BP Split May Signal End of "Lift and Shift" Deals," *Workforce Management*, 29 December 2006: 3.

9. Anonymous, "Tailored Service Alters with Needs of Clients," *The Journal* (Newcastle, UK), 20 October 2006, 38.

10. D. Kiley, "Crafty Basket Makers Cut Downtime, Waste. So Far, Changes Saving $3 Million a Year," *USA Today*, 10 May 2001, B3.

11. R. D. Banker, J. M. Field, R. G. Schroeder, & K. K. Sinha, "Impact of Work Teams on Manufacturing Performance: A Longitudinal Field Study," *Academy of Management Journal* 39 (1996): 867–890.

12. C. Fishman, "The Anarchist's Cookbook: John Mackey's Approach to Management Is Equal Parts Star Trek and 1970s Flashback," *Fast Company*, 1 July 2004, 70.

13. "Beating the Joneses (Learning What the Competition Is Doing)," *Industry Week* 1 (7 December 1998): 27.

14. Stalk & Hout, *Competing against Time*.

15. H. K. Bowen, K. B. Clark, C. A. Holloway, & S. C. Wheelwright, *The Perpetual Enterprise Machine* (New York: Oxford Press, 1994).

16. C. Dahle, "Xtreme Teams," *Fast Company*, 1 November 1999, 310.

17. Ibid.

18. J. L. Cordery, W. S. Mueller, & L. M. Smith, "Attitudinal and Behavioral Effects of Autonomous Group Working: A Longitudinal Field Study," *Academy of Management Journal* 34 (1991): 464–476; T. D. Wall, N. J. Kemp, P. R. Jackson, & C. W. Clegg, "Outcomes of Autonomous Workgroups: A Long-Term Field Experiment," *Academy of Management Journal* 29 (1986): 280–304.

19. M. Vanac, "Working the Line: U.S. Businesses Retool Modes of Production and Ratchet Up Morale," *Cleveland Plain Dealer*, 2 September 2001, H1.

20. Ibid.

21. "Declaration of Interdependence," Whole Foods Market, http://www.wholefoodsmarket.com/company/declaration.html.

22. Fishman, "The Anarchist's Cookbook."

23. "Whole Foods Market Soars to Number 5 Spot on *Fortune*'s '100 Best Companies to Work For' List," Whole Foods, http://www.wholefoodsmarket.com/company/pr_01-09-07.html.

24. R. Lieber, "Leadership Ensemble: How Do the Musicians of Orpheus Get to Carnegie Hall? They Practice—Not Just Their Music, but a Radical Approach to Leadership That Has Become a Compelling Metaphor for Business," *Fast Company*, 1 May 2000, 286.

25. A. Erez, J. Lepine, & H. Elms, "Effects of Rotated Leadership and Peer Evaluation on the Functioning and Effectiveness of Self-Managed Teams: A Quasi-Experiment," *Personnel Psychology* 55, issue 4 (2002): 929.

26. Hoerr, "The Payoff from Teamwork."

27. T. Aeppel, "Missing the Boss: Not All Workers Find Idea of Empowerment As Neat As It Sounds—Some Hate Fixing Machines, Apologizing for Errors, Disciplining Teammates—Rah-Rah Types Do the Best," *Wall Street Journal*, 8 September 1997, A1.

28. R. Liden, S. Wayne, R. Jaworski, & N. Bennett, "Social Loafing: A Field Investigation," *Journal of Management* 30 (2004): 285–304.

29. J. George, "Extrinsic and Intrinsic Origins of Perceived Social Loafing in Organizations," *Academy of Management Journal* 35 (1992): 191–202.

30. T. T. Baldwin, M. D. Bedell, & J. L. Johnson, "The Social Fabric of a Team-Based M.B.A. Program: Network Effects on Student Satisfaction and Performance," *Academy of Management Journal* 40 (1997): 1369–1397.

31. K. H. Price, D. A. Harrison & J. H. Gavin, "Withholding Inputs in Team Contexts: Member Composition, Interaction Processes, Evaluation Structure and Social Loafing," *Journal of Applied Psychology* 91(6) (2006): 1375–1384.

32. Hoerr, "The Payoff from Teamwork."

33. C. Joinson, "Teams at Work," *HR Magazine*, 1 May 1999, 30.

34. R. Wageman, "Critical Success Factors for Creating Superb Self-Managing Teams," *Organizational Dynamics* 26, no. 1 (1997): 49–61.

35. A. Dragoon, "Small Teams, Big Returns," *CIO*, 1 December 2003, http://bpubs.tradepub.com/free/cio.

36. Ibid.

37. M. A. Cusumano, "How Microsoft Makes Large Teams Work Like Small Teams," *Sloan Management Review* 39, no 1 (Fall 1997): 9–20.

38. D. A. Harrison, S. Mohammed, J. E. McGrath, A. T. Florey & S. W. Vanderstoep, "Time Matters in Team Performance: Effects of Member Familiarity, Entrainment, and Task Discontinuity on Speed and Quality," *Personnel Psychology* 56(3) (2003, August): 633–669.

39. R. T. King, Jr., "Jeans Therapy: Levi's Factory Workers Are Assigned to Teams, and Morale Takes a Hit—Infighting Rises, Productivity Falls as Employees Miss the Piecework System," *Wall Street Journal*, 20 May 1998, A1.

40. Ibid.

41. M. Bolch, "Rewarding the Team: Make Sure Team-Oriented Compensation Plans Are Designed Carefully," *HR Magazine*, February 2007, 52(2).

42. K. Hammonds, "How Google Grows . . . and Grows . . . and Grows," *Fast Company*, 1 April 2003, 74.

43. G. Bylinsky, "Heroes of U.S. Manufacturing," *Fortune*, 19 March 2001, 177; D. Cadrain, "Put Success in Sight," *HR Magazine*, May 2003, 48(5).

44. Kirkman & Rosen, "Beyond Self-Management: Antecedents and Consequences of Team Empowerment."

45. K. Kelly, "Managing Workers Is Tough Enough in Theory. When Human Nature Enters the Picture, It's Worse," *BusinessWeek*, 21 October 1996, 32.

46. S. Easton & G. Porter, "Selecting the Right Team Structure to Work in Your Organization," in *Handbook of Best Practices for Teams*, vol. 1, ed. G. M. Parker (Amherst, MA: Irwin, 1996).

47. S. Metz & G. Walter, "From Skeptic to Believer: Involving Employees in Retirement and Benefits Planning," *Workspan*, 1 November 2004, 36.

48. R. M. Yandrick, "A Team Effort: The Promise of Teams Isn't Achieved without Attention to Skills and Training," *HR Magazine*, June 2001, 46(6).

49. Labor-Employee Participation Committees Receive NLRB's Approval," *Personnel Manager's Legal Letter*, 1 October 2001.

50. R. M. Yandrick, "A Team Effort: The Promise of Teams Isn't Achieved without Attention to Skills and Training."

51. A. Lashinsky, "RAZR's Edge: How a Team of Engineers and Designers Defied Motorola's Own Rules to Create the Cellphone that Revived Their Company," *Fortune*, 12 June 2006, 124–132.

52. R. J. Recardo, D. Wade, C. A. Mention, & J. Jolly, *Teams* (Houston: Gulf Publishing Co., 1996).

53. D. R. Denison, S. L. Hart, & J. A. Kahn, "From Chimneys to Cross-Functional Teams: Developing and Validating a Diagnostic Model," *Academy of Management Journal* 39, no. 4 (1996): 1005–1023.

54. J. Morgan, "Cessna Aims to Drive SCM to Its Very Core: Here Are 21 Steps and Tools It's Using to Make This Happen," *Purchasing*, 6 June 2002, 31.

55. A. M. Townsend, S. M. DeMarie, & A. R. Hendrickson, "Virtual Teams: Technology and the Workplace of the Future," *Academy of Management Executive* 13, no. 3 (1998): 17–29.

56. R. Karlgaard, "Flash Kid; Rich Karlgaard Meets a Teen Titan," *Forbes*, 17 March 2003, 39.

57. A. M. Townsend, S. M. DeMarie, & A. R. Hendrickson, "Are You Ready for Virtual Teams?" *HR Magazine* 41, no. 9 (1996): 122–126.

58. Wellins, Byham, & Dixon, *Inside Teams*.

59. Townsend, DeMarie, & Hendrickson, "Virtual Teams."

60. W. F. Cascio, "Managing a Virtual Workplace," *Academy of Management Executive* 14 (2000): 81–90.

61. S. Prashad, "Building Trust Tricky for 'Virtual' Teams," *Toronto Star*, 23 October 2003, K06.

62. R. Katz, "The Effects of Group Longevity on Project Communication and Performance," *Administrative Science Quarterly* 27 (1982): 245–282.

63. C. Kleiman, "Virtual Teams Make Loyalty More Realistic," *Chicago Tribune*, 23 January 2001, Business 1.

64. D. Mankin, S. G. Cohen, & T. K. Bikson, *Teams and Technology: Fulfilling the Promise of the New Organization* (Boston: Harvard Business School Press, 1996).

65. A. P. Ammeter & J. M. Dukerich, "Leadership, Team Building, and Team Member Characteristics in High Performance Project Teams," *Engineering Management* 14 (4) (2002, December): 3–11.

66. K. Lovelace, D. Shapiro, & L. Weingart, "Maximizing Cross-Functional New Product Teams' Innovativeness and Constraint Adherence: A Conflict Communications Perspective," *Academy of Management Journal* 44 (2001): 779–793.

67. G. Anthes, "Think Globally, Act Locally: Running Global IT Operations Effectively Often Means Creating Standard Systems and Processes That Have to Be Tweaked to Meet Local Requirements," *Computer World*, 28 May 2001, 36.

68. L. Holpp & H. P. Phillips, "When Is a Team Its Own Worst Enemy?" *Training*, 1 September 1995, 71.

69. S. Asche, "Opinions and Social Pressure," *Scientific American* 193 (1995): 31–35.

70. G. Smith, "How Nucor Steel Rewards Performance and Productivity," *Business Know How*, 26 May 2003, http://www.businessknowhow.com/manage/nucor.htm.

71. S. G. Cohen, G. E. Ledford, & G. M. Spreitzer, "A Predictive Model of Self-Managing Work Team Effectiveness," *Human Relations* 49, no. 5 (1996): 643–676.

72. M. Fischetti, "'Team Doctors, Report To ER': Is Your Team Headed for Intensive Care? Our Specialists Offer Prescriptions for the Five Illnesses That Can Afflict Even the Best Teams," *Fast Company*, 1 February 1998, 170.

73. K. Bettenhausen & J. K. Murnighan, "The Emergence of Norms in Competitive Decision-Making Groups," *Administrative Science Quarterly* 30 (1985): 350–372.

74. M. E. Shaw, *Group Dynamics* (New York: McGraw Hill, 1981).

75. Katzenback & Smith, *The Wisdom of Teams*.

76. E. Levenson, "The Power of an Idea," *Fortune*, 12 June 2006, 131.

77. S. M. Gully, D. S. Devine, & D. J. Whitney, "A Meta-Analysis of Cohesion and Performance: Effects of Level of Analysis and Task Interdependence," *Small Group Research* 26, no. 4 (1995): 497–520.

78. S. E. Jackson, "The Consequences of Diversity in Multidisciplinary Work Teams," in *Handbook of Work Group Psychology*, ed. M. A. West (Chichester, UK: Wiley, 1996).

79. A. M. Isen & R. A. Baron, "Positive Affect as a Factor in Organizational Behavior," in *Research in Organizational Behavior* 13, ed. L. L. Cummings & B. M. Staw (Greenwich, CT: JAI Press, 1991): 1–53.

80. C. R. Evans & K. L. Dion, "Group Cohesion and Performance: A Meta Analysis," *Small Group Research* 22, no. 2 (1991): 175–186.

81. R. Stankiewicsz, "The Effectiveness of Research Groups in Six Countries," in *Scientific Productivity*, ed. F. M. Andrews (Cambridge: Cambridge University Press, 1979), 191–221.

82. F. Rees, *Teamwork from Start to Finish* (San Francisco: Jossey-Bass, 1997).

83. Gully, Devine, & Whitney, "A Meta-Analysis of Cohesion and Performance."

84. E. Matson, "Four Rules for Fast Teams," *Fast Company*, August 1996, 87.

85. F. Tschan & M. V. Cranach, "Group Task Structure, Processes and Outcomes," in *Handbook of Work Group Psychology*, ed. M. A. West (Chichester, UK: Wiley, 1996).

86. D. E. Yeatts & C. Hyten, *High Performance Self Managed Teams* (Thousand Oaks, CA: Sage Publications, 1998); H. M. Guttman & R. S. Hawkes, "New Rules for Strategic Development," *Journal of Business Strategy* 25 (1) (2004): 34–39.

87. Ibid; J. Colquitt, R. Noe, & C. Jackson, "Justice in Teams: Antecedents and Consequences of Procedural Justice Climate," *Personnel Psychology*, 1 April 2002, 83.

88. D. S. Kezsbom, "Re-Opening Pandora's Box: Sources of Project Team Conflict in the '90s," *Industrial Engineering* 24, no. 5 (1992): 54–59.

89. A. C. Amason, W. A. Hochwarter, & K. R. Thompson, "Conflict: An Important Dimension in Successful Management Teams," *Organizational Dynamics* 24 (1995): 20.

90. A. C. Amason, "Distinguishing the Effects of Functional and Dysfunctional Conflict on Strategic Decision Making: Resolving a Paradox for Top Management Teams," *Academy of Management Journal* 39, no. 1 (1996): 123–148.

91. K. M. Eisenhardt, J. L. Kahwajy, & L. J. Bourgeois III, "How Management Teams Can Have a Good Fight," *Harvard Business Review* 75, no. 4 (July–August 1997): 77–85.

92. Ibid.

93. C. Nemeth & P. Owens, "Making Work Groups More Effective: The Value of Minority Dissent," in *Handbook of Work Group Psychology*, ed. M. A. West (Chichester, UK: Wiley, 1996).

94. J. M. Levin & R. L. Moreland, "Progress in Small Group Research," *Annual Review of Psychology* 9 (1990): 72–78; S. E. Jackson, "Team Composition in Organizational Settings: Issues in Managing a Diverse Work Force," in *Group Processes and Productivity*, ed. S. Worchel, W. Wood, & J. Simpson (Beverly Hills, CA: Sage, 1992).

95. Eisenhardt, Kahwajy, & Bourgeois, "How Management Teams Can Have a Good Fight."

96. Ibid.

97. B. W. Tuckman, "Development Sequence in Small Groups," *Psychological Bulletin* 63, no. 6 (1965): 384–399.

98. Gross, *Compensation for Teams*.

99. J. F. McGrew, J. G. Bilotta, & J. M. Deeney, "Software Team Formation and Decay: Extending the Standard Model for Small Groups," *Small Group Research* 30, no. 2 (1999): 209–234.

100. Ibid.

101 J. Case, "What the Experts Forgot to Mention: Management Teams Create New Difficulties, but Succeed for XEL Communication," *Inc.*, 1 September 1993, 66.

102. J. R. Hackman, "The Psychology of Self-Management in Organizations," in *Psychology and Work: Productivity, Change, and Employment*, ed. M. S. Pallak & R. Perloff (Washington, DC: American Psychological Association, 1986), 85–136.

103. A. O 'Leary-Kelly, J. J. Martocchio, & D. D. Frink, "A Review of the Influence of Group Goals on Group Performance," *Academy of Management Journal* 37, no. 5 (1994): 1285–1301.

104. Smith, "How Nucor Steel Rewards Performance and Productivity."

105. A. Zander, "The Origins and Consequences of Group Goals," in *Retrospections on Social Psychology*, ed. L. Festinger (New York: Oxford University Press, 1980), 205–235.

106. M. Erez & A. Somech, "Is Group Productivity Loss the Rule or the Exception? Effects of Culture and Group-Based Motivation," *Academy of Management Journal* 39, no. 6 (1996): 1513–1537.

107. S. Sherman, "Stretch Goals: The Dark Side of Asking for Miracles," *Fortune*, 13 November 1995.

108. M. Gunther, "The Welshman, the Walkman, and the Salarymen."

109. S. Kerr & S. Landauer, "Using Stretch Goals to Promote Organizational Effectiveness and Personal Growth: General Electric and Goldman Sachs," *Academy of Management Executive* (November 2004): 134–138.

110. K. R. Thompson, W. A. Hochwarter, & N. J. Mathys, "Stretch Targets: What Makes Them Effective?" *Academy of Management Executive* 11, no. 3 (1997): 48–60.

111. S. Tully, "Why to Go for Stretch Targets," *Fortune*, 14 November 1994, 145.

112. Sherman, "Stretch Goals."

113. "Pfizer's Press Release," *Wall Street Journal*.

114. A. Lashinsky, "RAZR's Edge."

115. Dumaine, "The Trouble with Teams."

116. G. A. Neuman, S. H. Wagner, & N. D. Christiansen, "The Relationship between Work-Team Personality Composition and the Job Performance of Teams," *Group & Organization Management* 24, no. 1 (1999): 28–45.

117. M. A. Campion, G. J. Medsker, & A. C. Higgs, "Relations between Work Group Characteristics and Effectiveness: Implications for Designing Effective Work Groups," *Personnel Psychology* 46, no. 4 (1993): 823–850.

118. B. L. Kirkman & D. L. Shapiro, "The Impact of Cultural Values on Employee Resistance to Teams: Toward a Model of Globalized Self-Managing Work Team Effectiveness," *Academy of Management Review* 22, no. 3 (1997): 730–757.

119. P. Siekman, "Cessna Tackles Lean Manufacturing," *Fortune*, 1 May 2000, I222.

120. C. Fishman, "Engines of Democracy: The General Electric Plant in Durham, North Carolina Builds Some of the World's Most Powerful Jet Engines. But the Plant's Real Power Lies in the Lessons That It Teaches about the Future of Work and about Workplace Democracy," *Fast Company*, 1 October 1999, 174.

121. J. Bunderson & K. Sutcliffe, "Comparing Alternative Conceptualizations of Functional Diversity in Management Teams: Process and Performance Effects," *Academy of Management Journal* 45 (2002): 875–893.

122. J. Barbian, "Getting to Know You," *Training*, June 2001, 60–63.

123. Siekman, "Cessna Tackles Lean Manufacturing."

124. J. Hackman, "New Rules for Team Building—The Times Are Changing—And So Are the Guidelines for Maximizing Team Performance," *Optimize*, 1 July 2002, 50.

125. Joinson, "Teams at Work."

126. D. Zoia, "GM Manufacturing: Brand Spanking New," *Ward's Auto World*, March 2000, http://waw.wardsauto.com.

127. K. Mollica, "Stay Above the Fray: Protect Your Time—and Your Sanity—by Coaching Employees to Deal with Interpersonal Conflicts on Their Own," *HR Magazine*, April 2005, 111.

128. Wellins, Byham, & Dixon, *Inside Teams*.

129. S. Caudron, "Tie Individual Pay to Team Success," *Personnel Journal* 73, no. 10 (October 1994): 40.

130. Ibid.

131. Gross, *Compensation for Teams*.

132. G. Ledford, "Three Case Studies on Skill-Based Pay: An Overview," *Compensation & Benefits Review* 23, no.2 (1991): 11–24.

133. Wellins, Byham, & Dixon, *Inside Teams*.

134. J. R. Schuster & P. K. Zingheim, *The New Pay: Linking Employee and Organizational Performance* (New York: Lexington Books, 1992).

135. G. Shives & K. Scott, "Gainsharing and EVA: The U.S. Postal Service Experience," *WorldatWork Journal*, 1 January 2003, 21.

136. Cohen & Bailey, "What Makes Teams Work."

137. R. Allen & R. Kilmann, "Aligning Reward

Practices in Support of Total Quality Management," *Business Horizons* 44 (May 2001): 77–85.

138. J. H. Sheridan, "'Yes' to Team Incentives," *Industry Week*, 4 March 1996, 63.

139. J.A. Wagner, "Studies of Individualism-Collectivism: Effects on Cooperation in Groups," *Academy of Management Journal* 38, no. 1 (1995): 152–172.

140. G. Colvin, "Dream Teams Fail: It May Be Tempting to Recruit All-Stars and Let 'Em Rip. Don't Do It," *Fortune*, 12 June 2006, 87–92.

141. Alan Deutschman, "Building a Better Skunk Works," *Fast Company*, March 2005, 69–73.

142. M. A. West, ed., *Handbook of Work Group Psychology* (Chichester, UK: Wiley, 1996).

Chapter 11

1. R. Berner, "Weak Signals from RadioShack: The Electronics Retailer Can't Seem to Shake the Blues. It May Take Some Magic for New CEO Julian Day to Overcome Its Stalled Biz," *BusinessWeek Online*, 15 September 2006, http://web.lexis-nexis.com/universe/document?_m=4187417de)f92335dbeee2e110993a (accessed 9 February 2007); Greenebaum Doll & McDonald PLLC, "Employee's Race Claim against RadioShack Doesn't Compute," *Kentucky Employment Law Letter*, January 2007, http://web.lexis-nexis.com/universe/document?_m=1b6391082eb29c36ef09c6739830498b9 (accessed 9 February 2007); H. Landy, "Bad News Grows for RadioShack," *Fort Worth Star-Telegram*, 26 October 2006, http://web.lexis-nexis.com/universe/document?_m=e4ec5f178619a63122d825a4a9f3801d (accessed February 9 2007); "RadioShack," Wikipedia, http://www.en.wikipedia.org/wiki/RadioShack (accessed 9 February 2007); "RadioShack Uses E-mail to Fire Employees," *Associated Press Online*, 30 August 2006, http://web.lexis-nexis.com/universe/document?_m=705b09259308bc83c24a18520db60132 (accessed 9 February 2007); M. Schnurman, "Mitchell Shnurman Column," *Fort Worth Star-Telegram*, 13 September 2006, http://web.lexis-nexis.com/ universe/document?_m=db97b0109306ec21f9ac4adf9205b710 (accessed 9 February 2007); R. Strauss, "When the Resume Is Not to Be Believed," *New York Times*, 12 September 2006, G2.

2. "Facts on the Nursing Shortage in North America," Sigma Theta Tau International: Honor Society of Nursing, http://www.nursingsociety.org/media/facts_nursingshortage.html; C. Prystay, "U.S. Solution Is Philippine Dilemma—As Recruiters Snap Up More Nurses, Hospitals in Manila Are Scrambling," *Wall Street Journal*, 18 July 2002, A8; G. Zachary, "Shortage of Nurses Hits Hardest Where They Are Needed the Most," *Wall Street Journal*, 24 January 2001, A1.

3. B. Schneider & N. Schmitt, *Staffing Organizations*, 2d ed. (Glenview, IL: Scott, Foresman & Co., 1986).

4. D. M. Atwater, "Workforce Forecasting," *Human Resource Planning* 18, no. 4 (1995): 50.

5. "More Companies Turn to Workplace Planning to Boost Productivity and Efficiency, The Conference Board Reports in New Study," *PR Newswire*, 7 August 2006, http://web.lexis-nexis.com/universe/document?_m=2c3b0f8b6a240b2e39edabd16f4292c9 (accessed 9 February 2007); C. Donaldson, "Workforce Planning Comes of Age." *Human Resources*, 22 August 2006, available through http://www.lexis-nexis.com.

6. J. Eig, "Do Part-Time Workers Hold Key to When the Recession Breaks?" *Wall Street Journal*, 3 January 2002, A1.

7. Atwater, "Workforce Forecasting"; D. Ward, "Workforce Demand Forecasting Techniques," *Human Resource Planning* 19, no. 1 (1996): 54.

8. S. M. Director & J. Schramm, "Staffing Research: Estimating Future Staffing Levels: Implications for HR Strategy," Society for Human Resource Management, http://www.shrm.org / research/staffresearch_published.

9. M. Brush & D. H. Ruse, "Driving Strategic Success through Human Capital Planning: How Corning Links Business and HR Strategy to Improve the Value and Impact of Its HR Function," *Human Resource Planning*, 2005, 49–60.

10. A. J. Walker, "The Analytical Element Is Important to an HRIS," *Personnel Administrator* 28 (1983): 33–35, 85.

11. L. Thornburg, "Case Study: HRIS Implementation: ER-One Chooses HROffice," Society for Human Resource Management, http://www.shrm.org.

12. C. Allen, "Enabling Faster HRIS Integration," Society for Human Resource Management, http://www.shrm.org.

13. T. Jolls, "Technology Continues to Redefine HR's Role," *Personnel Journal* 76, no. 7 (July 1997): 46.

14. S. Greengard, "Smarter Screening Takes Technology and HR Savvy," *Workforce*, 1 June 2002, 56–60.

15. S. Forster, "Technology (A Special Report)—The Best Way to Recruit New Workers," *Wall Street Journal*, 15 September 2003, R8.

16. S. Bing, "The Feds Make a Pass at Hooters," *Fortune*, 15 January 1996, 82.

17. J. Helyar, "Hooters: A Case Study," *Fortune*, 1 September 2003, 140.

18. A. Samuels, "Pushing Hot Buttons and Wings," *St. Petersburg (FL) Times*, 10 March 2003, 1A.

19. P. S. Greenlaw & J. P. Kohl, "Employer 'Business' and 'Job' Defenses in Civil Rights Actions," *Public Personnel Management* 23, no. 4 (1994): 573.

20. Associated Press, "Hooters Settles Suit, Won't Hire Waiters," *Denver Post*, 1 October 1997, A11.

21. D. Lewis, "EEOC: Damage Awards Reach $420m in 2004," *Boston Globe*, 20 February 2005, D2.

22. B. Morris, K. Bonamici, S. Kaufman, & P. Neering, "How Corporate America Is Betraying Women," *Fortune*, 10 January 2005, 64.

23. J. L. Ledvinka, *Federal Regulation of Personnel and Human Resource Management* (Boston: Kent Publishing Co., 1982), 137–198.

24. C. Cummins. "BP's Accident Put Its Celebrated CEO on the Hot Seat," *Wall Street Journal*, 16 June 2006, B1.

25. N. Adams, "Marketplace Report: BP Oil Fined for Lax Safety," National Pubic Radio, 23 September 2005, http://www.npr.org/templates/story/story.php?storyId=4860782.

26. A. Smith, "BP Faces Disaster Report from Baker Panel," CNNMoney.com, 17 January 2007, http://money.cnn.com/2007/01/15/news/companies/bp/index.htm.

27. Greenlaw & Kohl, "Employer 'Business' and 'Job' Defenses in Civil Rights Actions."

28. "Judge Approves Settlement of Coca-Cola Bias Lawsuit," *Wall Street Journal*, 30 May 2001, B7.

29. "Rent-A-Center Settles Gender-Bias Lawsuit, Will Pay $12.3 Million,"

Wall Street Journal, 2 November 2001, http://online.wsj.com.

30. W. Peirce, C. A. Smolinski, & B. Rosen, "Why Sexual Harassment Complaints Fall on Deaf Ears," *Academy of Management Executive* 12, no. 3 (1998): 41–54.
31. B. Mims, "Suit Claims Costco Forced Woman to Quit After She Complained of Harassment," *Salt Lake Tribune*, 24 February 2005, C14.
32. "The Baker & McKenzie Sexual Discrimination Case," Georgia Trial Lawyers Association, http://www.gtla.org?public/cases/baker.html; "Examples of Actual Judgments and Settlements," Employers Publications, http://www.sexualharassmentpolicy.com/judge.html.
33. "Facts about Sexual Harassment." U.S. Equal Employment Opportunity Commission, http://www.eeoc.gov/facts/fs-sex.html.
34. Peirce, Smolinski, & Rosen, "Why Sexual Harassment Complaints Fall on Deaf Ears."
35. Ibid.
36. E. Larson, "The Economic Costs of Sexual Harassment," http://www.hospitalitycampus.com/investors/facts.asp (accessed 16 July 2007).
37. K. Dunham & G. Ip, "Slow Economy Takes Unusually Heavy Toll on White-Collar Jobs," *Wall Street Journal*, 5 November 2001, A1.
38. Prystay, "U.S. Solution Is Philippine Dilemma."
39. G. Hyland-Savage, "General Management Perspective on Staffing: The Staffing Commandments," in N. C. Bukholder, P. J. Edwards, Jr., & L. Sartain (Eds.), *On Staffing* (Hoboken, NJ: Wiley, 2004), 280.
40. R. D. Gatewood & H. S. Field, *Human Resource Selection* (Fort Worth, TX: Dryden Press, 1998).
41. Ibid.
42. *Griggs v. Duke Power Co.*, 401 U.S. 424, 436 (1971); *Albemarle Paper Co. v. Moody*, 422 U.S. 405 (1975).
43. A. Embrey, "A Good Manager Is Hard to Find," *Convenience Store News*, 10 January 2005, http://www.csnews.com.
44. "Fujisawa Launches 'Jobs Challenge' Policy," *Market Letter*, 17 September 2001, http://www.marketletter.com/.
45. J. A. Breaugh, *Recruitment: Science and Practice* (Boston: PWS-Kent, 1992).
46. "Fujisawa Launches 'Jobs Challenge' Policy."
47. J. Badal, "Career Path Programs Help Retain Workers," *Wall Street Journal*, 24 July 2006, http://online.wsj.com.
48. A. Muoio, "Man with a (Talent) Plan," *Fast Company*, 1 January 2001, 83.
49. Ibid.
50. J. Breaugh & M. Starke, "Research on Employee Recruitment: So Many Studies, So Many Remaining Questions," *Journal of Management* 26 (2000): 405–434.
51. S. Gale, "Internet Recruiting: Better, Cheaper, Faster," *Personnel Journal*, 1 December 2000, 74.
52. K. Maher, "Corporations Cut Middlemen and Do Their Own Recruiting," *Wall Street Journal*, 14 January 2003, B10.
53. "Hire.com Customers Save Millions in Costs While Increasing Quality of Recruits," *Business Wire*, 9 March 2004, 08:00.
54. S. Forster, "Technology (A Special Report)—The Best Way To . . . Recruit New Workers," *Wall Street Journal*, 15 September 2003, R8.
55. "Job Opportunities," Subway Restaurants, http://www.subway.com/applications/InStoreJobs/index.aspx.
56. "Research Demonstrates the Success of Internet Recruiting," *HR Focus*, April 2003, 7.
57. "New Jobs Suffix Approved for Worldwide Recruiting/Hiring," *Human Resource Department Management Report*, May 2005, 9.
58. E. Agnvall, "Recruiting by Ones and Zeros," Society for Human Resource Management, http://www.shrm.org; D. Robb, "Career Portals Boost Online Recruiting," *HR Magazine*, April 2004, Society for Human Resource Management, http://www.shrm.org.
59. A. Milkovits, "Survey Shows Methods Vary for Selecting Police Recruits," *Providence Journal*, 19 May 2003, B-01.
60. C. Camden & B. Wallace, "Job Application Forms: A Hazardous Employment Practice," *Personnel Administrator* 28 (1983): 31–32.
61. K. Maher, "Career Journal: The Jungle," *Wall Street Journal*, 6 May 2003, B8.
62. J. Kennedy, "Europeans Expect Different Type of Résumé," *Chicago Sun-Times*, 3 June 1999, 73.
63. J. Tamen, "Job Applicants' Résumés Are Often Riddled with Misinformation," *South Florida Sun-Sentinel*, 24 February 2003, available at http://www.sun-sentinel.com/.
64. S. Adler, "Verifying a Job Candidate's Background: The State of Practice in a Vital Human Resources Activity," *Review of Business* 15, no. 2 (1993/1994): 3–8.
65. "More Than 70 Percent of HR Professionals Say Reference Checking Is Effective in Identifying Poor Performers," Society for Human Resource Management, http://www.shrm.org.
66. P. Babcock, "Spotting Lies: The High Cost of Careless Hiring," *HR Magazine*, October 2003, Society for Human Resource Management, http://www.shrm.org.
67. T. Thiesen, "Prisoners of the Past: Workers with Criminal Records Have Tough Time," *Orlando Sentinel*, 3 October 2001, G1.
68. M. Le, T. Nguyen, & B. Kleiner, "Legal Counsel: Don't Be Sued for Negligent Hiring," *Nonprofit World*, 1 May 2003, 14–15.
69. "Why It's Critical to Set a Policy on Background Checks for New Hires," *Managing Accounts Payable*, September 2004, 6; J. Schramm, "Future Focus: Background Checking," *HR Magazine*, January 2005, Society for Human Resource Management, http://www .shrm.org.
70. M. P. Cronin, "This Is a Test," *Inc.*, August 1993, 64–69.
71. C. Cohen, "Reference Checks," *CA Magazine*, November 2004, 41.
72. S. Marshall, "Spot Inflated Résumés with Simple Sleuthing," *Asian Wall Street Journal*, 7 April 2000, P3.
73. J. Hunter, "Cognitive Ability, Cognitive Aptitudes, Job Knowledge, and Job Performance," *Journal of Vocational Behavior* 29 (1986): 340–362.
74. F. L. Schmidt, "The Role of General Cognitive Ability and Job Performance: Why There Cannot be a Debate," *Human Performance* 15 (2002): 187–210.
75. K. Murphy, "Can Conflicting Perspectives on the Role of *g* in Personnel Selection Be Resolved?" *Human Performance* 15 (2002): 173–186.
76. E. E. Cureton, "Comment," in E. R. Henry, *Research Conference on the Use of Autobiographical Data as Psychological Predictors* (Greensboro, NC: The Richardson Foundation, 1965), 13.
77. G. Dean, "The Bottom Line: Effect Size," in *The Write Stuff: Evaluations of Graphology—The Study of Handwriting Analysis*,

ed. B. Beyerstein & D. Beyerstein (Buffalo, NY: Prometheus Books, 1992); K. Dunham, "Career Journal: The Jungle, Seeing the Future," *Wall Street Journal*, 15 May 2001, B12; J. Kurtz & W. Wells, "The Employee Polygraph Protection Act: The End of Lie Detector Use in Employment Decisions?" *Journal of Small Business Management* 27, no. 4 (1989): 76–80; B. Leonard, "Reading Employees," *HRMagazine*, April 1999, 67; S. Lilienfeld, J. Wood, & H. Garb, "The Scientific Status of Projective Techniques," *Psychological Science in the Public Interest* 1 (2000): 27–66; E. Neter & G. Ben-Shakhar, "The Predictive Validity of Graphological Inferences: A Meta-Analytic Approach," *Personality & Individual Differences* 10 (1989): 737–745.

78. J. R. Glennon, L. E. Albright, & W. A. Owens, *A Catalog of Life History Items* (Greensboro, NC: The Richardson Foundation, 1966).

79. Gatewood & Field, *Human Resource Selection*.

80. J. M. Digman, "Personality Structure: Emergence of the Five-Factor Model," *Annual Review of Psychology* 41 (1990): 417–440; M. R. Barrick & M. K. Mount, "The Big Five Personality Dimensions and Job Performance: A Meta-Analysis," *Personnel Psychology* 44 (1991): 1–26.

81. N. Schmitt, "Beyond the Big Five: Increases in Understanding and Practical Utility," *Human Performance* 17 (2004): 347–357.

82. I. Kotlyar & K. Ades, "HR Technology: Assessment Technology Can Help Match the Best Applicant to the Right Job," *HR Magazine*, 1 May 2002, 97.

83. K. Maher, "The Jungle: Focus on Recruitment, Pay and Getting Ahead," *Wall Street Journal*, 19 November 2002, B8.

85. M. S. Taylor & J. A. Sniezek, "The College Recruitment Interview: Topical Content and Applicant Reactions," *Journal of Occupational Psychology* 57 (1984): 157–168.

86. R. Burnett, C. Fan, S. J. Motowidlo, & T. DeGroot, "Interview Notes and Validity," *Personnel Psychology* 51, no. X (1998): 375–396; M. A. Campion, D. K. Palmer, & J. E. Campion, "A Review of Structure in the Selection Interview," *Personnel Psychology* 50, no. 3 (1997): 655–702.

86. Campion, et al., "A Review of Structure in the Selection Interview."

87. J. Cortina, N. Goldstein, S. Payne, K. Davison, & S. Gilliland, "The Incremental Validity of Interview Scores Over and Above Cognitive Ability and Conscientiousness Scores," *Personnel Psychology* 53, issue 2 (2000): 325–351; F. L. Schmidt & J. E. Hunter, "The Validity and Utility of Selection Methods in Personnel Psychology: Practical and Theoretical Implications of 85 Years of Research Findings," *Psychological Bulletin* 124, no. 2 (1998): 262–274.

88. T. Judge, "The Employment Interview: A Review of Recent Research and Recommendations for Future Research," *Human Resource Management Review* 10, issue 4 (2000): 383–406.

89. Cortina, Goldstein, Payne, Davison, & Gilliland, "The Incremental Validity of Interview Scores."

90. K. Tyler, "Training Revs Up," *HR Magazine*, April 2005, Society for Human Resource Management, http://www.shrm.org.

91. Ibid.

92. S. Livingston, T. W. Gerdel, M. Hill, B. Yerak, C. Melvin, & B. Lubinger, "Ohio's Strongest Companies All Agree That Training Is Vital to Their Success," *Cleveland Plain Dealer*, 21 May 1997, 30S.

93. G. Kesler, "Why the Leadership Bench Never Gets Deeper: Ten Insights about Executive Talent Development," *Human Resource Planning*, 1 January 2002, 32.

94. "Frequently Asked Questions," WorkKeys, http://www.act.org/workkeys/overview/faq.html#skills.

95. J. Borzo, "Almost Human: Using Avatars for Corporate Training, Advocates Say, Can Combine the Best Parts of Face-to-Face Interaction and Computer-Based Learning," *Wall Street Journal*, 24 May 2004, R4.

96. S. Overby, "The World's Biggest Classroom," *CIO*, 1 February 2002, www.cio.com/archive/020102/dow.html.

97. M. Totty, "Better Training through Gaming," *Wall Street Journal*, 25 April 2005, R6.

98. Borzo, "Almost Human: Using Avatars for Corporate Training."

99. D. L. Kirkpatrick, "Four Steps to Measuring Training Effectiveness," *Personnel Administrator* 28 (1983): 19–25.

100. L. Bassi, J. Ludwig, D. McMurrer, & M. Van Buren, "Profiting from Learning: Do Firms' Investments in Education and Training Pay Off?" American Society for Training and Development, http://www.astd.org/NR/rdonlyres/15C0E2AB-B16D-4E3C-A081–4205B865DA3F/0/PFLWhitePaper.pdf.

101. J. Stack, "The Curse of the Annual Performance Review," *Inc.*, 1 March 1997, 39.

102. D. Murphy, "Are Performance Appraisals Worse Than a Waste of Time? Book Derides Unintended Consequences," *San Francisco Chronicle*, 9 September 2001, W1.

103. K. R. Murphy & J. N. Cleveland, *Understanding Performance Appraisal: Social, Organizational and Goal-Based Perspectives*, (Thousand Oaks, CA: Sage, 1995).

104. T. D. Schellhardt, "Annual Agony: It's Time to Evaluate Your Work, and All Involved Are Groaning" *Wall Street Journal*, 19 November 1996, A1.

105. U. J. Wiersma & G. P. Latham, "The Practicality of Behavioral Observation Scales, Behavioral Expectation Scales, and Trait Scales," *Personnel Psychology* 39 (1986): 619–628; U. J. Wiersma, P. T. Van Den Berg, & G. P. Latham, "Dutch Reactions to Behavioral Observation, Behavioral Expectation, and Trait Scales," *Group & Organization Management* 20 (1995): 297–309.

106. D. J. Schleicher, D. V. Day, B. T. Mayes, R. E. Riggio, "A New Frame for Frame-of-Reference Training: Enhancing the Construct Validity of Assessment Centers," *Journal of Applied Psychology*, August 2002, 735–746.

107. Stack, "The Curse of the Annual Performance Review."

108. B. O'Reilly, "360-Degree Feedback Can Change Your Life," *Fortune*, 17 October 1994, 93.

109. C. Hymowitz, "Do '360' Job Reviews by Colleagues Promote Honesty or Insults?" *Wall Street Journal*, 12 December 2000, B1.

110. D. A. Waldman, L. E. Atwater, & D. Antonioni, "Has 360 Feedback Gone Amok?" *Academy of Management Executive* 12, no. 2 (1998): 86–94.

111. H. H. Meyer, "A Solution to the Performance Appraisal Feedback Enigma," *Academy of Management Executive* 5, no. 1 (1991): 68–76; G. C. Thornton, "Psychometric Properties of Self-Appraisals of Job Performance," *Personnel Psychology* 33 (1980): 263–271.

112. G. C. Thornton, "Psychometric Properties of Self-Appraisals of Job Performance," *Personnel Psychology* 33 (1980): 263–271.

113. J. Smither, M. London, R. Flautt, Y. Vargas, & I. Kucine, "Can Working with an Executive Coach Improve Multisource Feedback Ratings over Time? A Quasi-Experimental Field Study," *Personnel Psychology* (Spring 2003): 21–43.

114. A. Walker & J. Smither, "A Five-Year Study of Upward Feedback: What Managers Do with Their Results Matters," *Personnel Psychology* (Summer 1999): 393–422.

115. I. M. Jawahar, "Correlates of Satisfaction with Performance Appraisal Feedback," *Journal of Labor Research* 26 (2006): 213–236.

116. Ibid.

117. M. Fong, "Chinese Puzzle—Surprising Shortage of Workers Forces Factories to Add Perks; Pressure on Pay—and Prices," *Wall Street Journal*, 16 August 2004, B1.

118. K. Maher, "Coal Companies Are Slowed by Severe Shortage of Workers—Mines Can't Boost Output, So Utilities' Low Stockpiles May Lift Electricity Prices," *Wall Street Journal*, 5 May 2005, A2.

119. G. T. Milkovich & J. M. Newman, *Compensation*, 4th ed. (Homewood, IL: Irwin, 1993).

120. E. Rasmusson, "Ten Things Your Child Care Provider Won't Tell You," *SmartMoney*, 1 May 2003, 69.

121. S. Shellenbarger, "Tight Labor Market Is Putting Squeeze on Quality Day Care," *Wall Street Journal*, 21 October 1998, B1.

122. M. L. Williams & G. F. Dreher, "Compensation System Attributes and Applicant Pool Characteristics," *Academy of Management Journal* 35, no. 3 (1992): 571–595.

123. C. Windham, "Nursing Shortage Eases with Higher Pay and a Weak Labor Market," *Wall Street Journal*, 17 November 2004, D5.

124. "Renault SAS to Pay EUR174.2M in Profit Sharing for 2006," *Dow Jones Newswires*, 8 February 2007, http://online.wsj.com.

125. J. Kaufman, "Sharing the Wealth: At McKay Nursery, Migrant Workers Get a Chance to Own Part of the Company," *Wall Street Journal*, 9 April 1998, R10.

126. M. Bloom, "The Performance Effects of Pay Dispersion on Individuals and Organizations," *Academy of Management Journal* 42, no. 1 (1999): 25–40.

127. L. Lavelle, F. Jespersen, S. Ante, & J. Kerstetter, "Executive Pay: The Days of the Fantasyland CEO Pay Package Appear to Be in the Past. A 33% Decline in Compensation Has Returned America's Bosses to the Year 1996," *BusinessWeek*, 21 April 2003, 86; L. Lavelle, "A Payday for Performance; Compensation Is Less Outrageous This Year, Except for CEOs Who Delivered," *BusinessWeek*, 18 April 2005, 78.

128. W. Grossman & R. E. Hoskisson, "CEO Pay at the Crossroads of Wall Street and Main: Toward the Strategic Design of Executive Compensation," *Academy of Management Executive* 12, no. 1 (1998): 43–57.

129. Bloom, "The Performance Effects of Pay Dispersion on Individuals and Organizations."

130. M. Bloom & J. Michel, "The Relationships among Organizational Context, Pay Dispersion, and Managerial Turnover," *Academy of Management Journal* 45 (2002): 33–42.

131. J. S. Rosenbloom, "The Environment of Employee Benefit Plans," in *The Handbook of Employee Benefits*, ed. J. S. Rosenbloom (Chicago: Irwin, 1996), 3–13.

132. "Employer Costs for Employee Compensation Summary," Bureau of Labor Statistics, http://www.bls.gov/news.release/ecec.nr0.htm.

133. A. E. Barber, R. B. Dunham, & R. A. Formisano, "The Impact of Flexible Benefits on Employee Satisfaction: A Field Study," *Personnel Psychology* 45 (1992): 55–75; B. Heshizer, "The Impact of Flexible Benefits on Job Satisfaction and Turnover Intentions," *Benefits Quarterly* 4 (1994): 84–90; D. M. Cable & T. A. Judge, "Pay Preferences and Job Search Decisions: A Person-Organization Fit Perspective," *Personnel Psychology* 47 (1994): 317–348.

134. B. T. Beam & J. J. McFadden, *Employee Benefits* (Chicago: Dearborn Financial Publishing, 1996).

135. R. Lieber, "Employers Offer New Pretax Perk: Debit Cards Allow Instant Access to Accounts for Medical Fees and Commuting Expenses," *Wall Street Journal*, 2 September 2003, D1.

136. J. Lublin, "Left Out of a Meeting? Parking Space Taken? Worry about Your Job," *Wall Street Journal*, 3 April 2001, B1.

137. A. Rupe, "Horrors from the Bad-Firing File," *Workforce Management*, November 2003, 16.

138. "400 at RadioShack Are Told by E-Mail: You're Outta Here," Associated Press, 31 August 2006, available at http://seattletimes.nwsource.com/html/businesstechnology/2003236874_radioshack31.html.

139. P. Michal-Johnson, *Saying Good-Bye: A Manager's Guide to Employee Dismissal* (Glenview, IL: Scott, Foresman & Co., 1985).

140. M. Bordwin, "Employment Law: Beware of Time Bombs and Shark-Infested Waters," *HR Focus*, 1 April 1995, 19; D. Jones, "Fired Workers Fight Back . . . and Win; Laws, Juries Shift Protection to Terminated Employees," *USA Today*, 2 April 1998, 01B.

141. T. Bland, "Fire at Will, Repent at Leisure," *Security Management* 44 (May 2000), 64.

142. "Planned Layoffs May Top 1 Million for Fourth Year in a Row," U.S. Steel Workers of America, http://www.uswa.org.

143. J. Bandler, "Kodak to Cut Staff up to 21%, Amid Digital Push—As Film Business Shrinks, Company Retools for Future," *Wall Street Journal*, 22 January 2004, A1.

144. "Ford CEO Says It Must Change the Way It Does Business," *Wall Street Journal*, 3 September 2006, http://online.wsj.com.

145. J. R. Morris, W. F. Cascio, & C. E. Young, "Downsizing after All These Years: Questions and Answers about Who Did It, How Many Did It, and Who Benefited from It," *Organizational Dynamics* 27, no. 3 (1999): 78–87.

146. K. E. Mishra, G. M. Spreitzer, & A. K. Mishra, "Preserving Employee Morale during Downsizing," *Sloan Management Review* 39, no. 2 (1998): 83–95.

147. K. Frieswick, "Until We Meet Again?" *CFO*, 1 October 2001, 41.

148. J. Hilsenrath, "Adventures in Cost Cutting," *Wall Street Journal*, 10 May 2004, R1.

149. J. Ackerman, "Helping Layoff Survivors Cope: Companies Strive to Keep Morale High," *Boston Globe*, 30 December 2001, H1.

150. Ibid.

151. D. Ferrari, "Designing and Evaluating Early Retirement Programs: The State of Wyoming Experience," *Government Finance Review* 15, no. 1 (1999): 29–31.

152. Hilsenrath, "Adventures in Cost Cutting."

153. R. Mullins, "Early Retirement Programs Can End Up Being Costly," *Business Journal–Milwaukee*, 20 January 1996, Section 1, 25.

154. M. Willett, "Early Retirement and Phased Retirement Programs for the Public Sector," *Benefits & Compensation Digest*, April 2005, 31.

155. D. R. Dalton, W. D. Todor, & D. M. Krackhardt, "Turnover Overstated: The Functional Taxonomy," *Academy of Management Review* 7 (1982): 117–123.

156. J. R. Hollenbeck & C. R. Williams, "Turnover Functionality versus Turnover Frequency: A Note on Work Attitudes and Organizational Effectiveness," *Journal of Applied Psychology* 71 (1986): 606–611.

157. C. R. Williams, "Reward Contingency, Unemployment, and Functional Turnover," *Human Resource Management Review* 9 (1999): 549–576.

158. J. McCarthy & R. Goffin, "Measuring Job Interview Anxiety: Beyond Weak Knees and Sweaty Palms," *Personnel Psychology* 54, no. 3 (2004): 31.

159. S. Begley, "Behind 'Shortage' of Engineers, Employers Grow More Choosy," *Wall Street Journal*, 16 November 2005, A1, A12.

Chapter 12

1. C. Wittenauer, "Walgreens Is the Target of U.S. Racial-Bias Lawsuit," *Philadelphia Inquirer*, 8 March 2007, http://www.philly.com/inquirer; Walgreens press release, http://www.walgreensclass.com; M. Albright, "Walgreens Suit Cites Racial Bias," *St. Petersburg Times*, 21 June 2005, http://www.sptimes.ru; N. J. C. Pistor, "Federal Government Targets Walgreens in Discrimination Lawsuit," *St. Louis Post-Dispatch*, 8 March 2007, http://www.stltoday.com; "Walgreens Sued for Job Bias against Blacks," Equal Employment Opportunity Commission, http://www.eeoc.gov/press/3-7-07.html; "EEOC Files Class-Action Racial Bias Suit against Walgreens," *Financial Times*, 8 March 2007, https://www.financialtimes.net.

2. J. H. Boyett & J. T. Boyett, *Beyond Workforce 2000* (New York: Dutton, 1995).

3. Ibid.

4. "Preparing the Workforce of Tomorrow," Hewitt Associates, February 2004, http://www.hewitt.com.

5. R. Stodghill, "The Coming Job Bottleneck," *BusinessWeek*, 24 March 1997, 183–185.

6. "Preparing the Workforce of Tomorrow."

7. K. Wallsten, "Diversity Pays Off in Big Sales for Toyota Dealership," *Workforce*, September 1998, 91–92.

8. R. S. Johnson, "The 50 Best Companies for Asians, Blacks, & Hispanics: Talent Comes in All Colors," *Fortune*, 3 August 1999, 94.

9. D. D. Stanford, "Coke's Diversity Case Closed: Report Says Progress Made," *Atlanta Journal-Constitution*, 2 December 2006, 1C; "Racism Lawsuit against New York Manufacturer Settled for $1.25 Million," Associated Press Financial Wire, 28 December 2006, available at http://www.ap.org; "Payouts Delayed in Lawsuit Settlement with Los Alamos Lab," Associated Press State & Local Wire, 27 November 2006, available at http://www.ap.org; "Tyson Settles Discrimination Lawsuit for $871,000," *Financial Times*, 7 November 2006, http://www.financialtimes.net.

10. "Best Companies for Minorities: Diversity Leaders," *Fortune*, http://www.fortune.com.

11. D. D. Stanford, "Coke's Diversity Case Closed: Report Says Progress Made."

12. J. Hickman, "50 Best Companies for Minorities," *Fortune*, 28 June 2004, 136.

13. Affirmative action, available at http://www.dol.gov/dol/topic/hiring/affirmativeact.htm.

14. R. Rodriguez, "Diversity Finds Its Place: More Organizations Are Dedicating Senior-Level Executives to Drive Diversity Initiatives for Bottom-Line Effect," *HR Magazine*, August 2006, Society for Human Resource Management, http://www.shrm.org.

15. "Federal Laws Prohibiting Job Discrimination: Questions and Answers," Equal Employment Opportunity Commission, http://www.eeoc.gov/facts/qanda.html.

16. A. P. Carnevale & S. C. Stone, *The American Mosaic: An In-Depth Report on the Future of Diversity at Work* (New York: McGraw-Hill, 1995).

17. T. Roosevelt, "From Affirmative Action to Affirming Diversity," *Harvard Business Review* 68, no. 2 (1990): 107–117.

18. A. M. Konrad & F. Linnehan, "Formalized HRM Structures: Coordinating Equal Employment Opportunity or Concealing Organizational Practices?" *Academy of Management Journal* 38, no. 3 (1995): 787–820.

19. See, e.g., *Hopwood v. Texas*, 78 F.3d 932 (5th Cir., 18 March 1996). The U.S. Supreme Court has upheld the principle of affirmative action but has struck down some specific programs.

20. J. Madore, "Losing Historical Advantages: White Males Say They're Hurt, Too," *Newsday*, 9 April 2000, A45.

21. Ibid.

22. M. E. Heilman, C. J. Block, & P. Stathatos, "The Affirmative Action Stigma of Incompetence: Effects of Performance Information Ambiguity," *Academy of Management Journal* 40, no. 3 (1997): 603–625.

23. K. C. Cole, "Jury Out on Whether Affirmative Action Beneficiaries Face Stigma: Research Studies Arrive at Conflicting Conclusions," *Los Angeles Times*, 1 May 1995, 18.

24. E. Orenstein, "The Business Case for Diversity," *Financial Executive*, May 2005, 22–25; G. Robinson & K. Dechant, "Building a Business Case for Diversity," *Academy of Management Executive* 11, no. 3 (1997): 21–31.

25. E. Esen, "2005 Workplace Diversity Practices: Survey Report," Survey conducted by the Society for Human Resource Management. SHRM Research Department, Alexandria, Virginia (http://www.shrm.org/research), October 2005.

26. E. Orenstein, "The Business Case for Diversity."

27. E. Esen, "2005 Workplace Diversity Practices: Survey Report."

28. E. Orenstein, "The Business Case for Diversity."

29. "Judge Approves Settlement of Coca-Cola Bias Lawsuit," *Wall Street Journal*, 30 May 2001, B7; A. Reifenberg, "Texaco Settlement in Racial-Bias Case Endorsed by Judge," *Wall Street Journal*, 26 March 1997, B15.

30. B. Morris, K. Bonamici, S. Kaufman, & P. Neering, "How Corporate America Is Betraying Women,"

Fortune, 10 January 2005, 64.

31. S. Ellison & J. Lublin, "Dial to Pay $10 Million to Settle a Sexual-Harassment Lawsuit," *Wall Street Journal*, 30 April 2003, B4.

32. M. Selmi, "The Price of Discrimination: The Nature of Class Action Employment Discrimination Litigation and Its Effects," *Texas Law Review*, 1 April 2003, 1249.

33. D. Lewis, "EEOC: Damage Awards; Reach $420m in 2004," *Boston Globe*, 20 February 2005, D2.

34. P. Wright & S. P. Ferris, "Competitiveness through Management of Diversity: Effects on Stock Price Valuation," *Academy of Management Journal* 38 (1995): 272–285.

35. Ibid.

36. R. B. Lieber & L. Urresta, "Pacific Enterprises Keeping Talent: After Being Encouraged to Explore Jobs Elsewhere, Most Employees Stay Put," *Fortune*, 3 August 1998, 96.

37. R. Rodriguez, "Diversity Finds Its Place: More Organizations Are Dedicating Senior-Level Executives to Drive Diversity Initiatives for Bottom-Line Effect."

38. W. He & F. Hobbs, "Minority Purchasing Power: 2000 to 2045," Minority Business Development Agency, U.S. Department of Commerce, September 2000.

39. "The Emerging Minority Marketplace: Minority Purchasing Power 2000 to 2045," U.S. Department of Commerce, Minority Business Development Agency, http://www.mbda.gov/documents/purchasing_power.pdf.

40. E. Esen, "2005 Workplace Diversity Practices: Survey Report."; L. E. Wynter, "Business & Race: Advocates Try to Tie Diversity to Profit," *Wall Street Journal*, 7 February 1996, B1.

41. W. W. Watson, K. Kumar, & L. K. Michaelsen, "Cultural Diversity's Impact on Interaction Process and Performance: Comparing Homogeneous and Diverse Task Groups," *Academy of Management Journal* 36 (1993): 590–602; K. A. Jehn, G. B. Northcraft, & M. A. Neale, "Why Differences Make a Difference: A Field Study of Diversity, Conflict, and Performance in Workgroups," *Administrative Science Quarterly* 44 (1999): 741–763.

42. F. Rice, "How to Make Diversity Pay," *Fortune*, 8 August 1994, 78.

43. R. Rodriguez, "Diversity Finds Its Place: More Organizations Are Dedicating Senior-Level Executives to Drive Diversity Initiatives for Bottom-Line Effect."

44. M. R. Carrell & E. E. Mann, "Defining Workplace Diversity Programs and Practices in Organizations," *Labor Law Journal* 44 (1993): 743–764.

45. D. A. Harrison, K. H. Price, & M. P. Bell, "Beyond Relational Demography: Time and the Effects of Surface- and Deep-Level Diversity on Work Group Cohesion," *Academy of Management Journal* 41 (1998): 96–107.

46. D. Harrison, K. Price, J. Gavin, & A. Florey, "Time, Teams, and Task Performance: Changing Effects of Surface-and Deep-Level Diversity on Group Functioning," *Academy of Management Journal* 45 (2002): 1029–1045.

47. Harrison, Price, & Bell, "Beyond Relational Demography."

48. Ibid.

49. N. Munk, "Finished at Forty: In the New Economy, the Skills That Come with Age Count for Less and Less," *Fortune*, 1 February 1999, 50.

50. K. Wrenn & T. Maurer, "Beliefs about Older Workers' Learning and Development Behavior in Relation to Beliefs about Malleability of Skills, Age-Related Decline, and Control," *Journal of Applied Social Psychology* 34 (February 2004): 223–242.

51. J. Helyar & B. Cherry, "50 and Fired," *Fortune*, 16 May 2005, 78.

52. Ibid.

53. S. E. Sullivan & E. A. Duplaga, "Recruiting and Retaining Older Workers for the Millennium," *Business Horizons* 40 (12 November 1997): 65.

54. Munk, "Finished at Forty."

55. J. Bravin, "Court Expands Age Bias Claims for Work Force," *Wall Street Journal*, 31 March 2005, B1.

56. J. Helyar & B. Cherry, "50 and Fired."

57. Hampshire & Isle of Wight. Useful websites for older workers, available at http://www.link2learn.co.uk/content/default.asp?PageId=372

58. S. R. Rhodes, "Age-Related Differences in Work Attitudes and Behavior," *Psychological Bulletin* 92 (1983): 328–367.

59. A. Fisher, "Wanted: Aging Baby-Boomers," *Fortune*, 30 September 1996, 204.

60. G. M. McEvoy & W. F. Cascio, "Cumulative Evidence of the Relationship between Employee Age and Job Performance," *Journal of Applied Psychology* 74 (1989): 11–17.

61. Sullivan & Duplaga, "Recruiting and Retaining Older Workers for the Millennium."

62. T. Maurer & N. Rafuse, "Learning, Not Litigating: Managing Employee Development and Avoiding Claims of Age Discrimination," *Academy of Management Executive* 15, issue 4 (2001): 110–121.

63. B. L. Hassell & P. L. Perrewe, "An Examination of Beliefs about Older Workers: Do Stereotypes Still Exist?" *Journal of Organizational Behavior* 16 (1995): 457–468.

64. "Women in the Labor Force: A Databook (Updated and Available on the Internet)," Bureau of Labor Statistics, http://www.bls.gov/bls/databooknews2005.pdf.

65. "Top Facts about Women-Owned Businesses," Center for Women's Business Research, http://www.cfwbr.org/facts/index.php.

66. "Women Own 9 Million U.S. Businesses," U.S. Small Business Administration, http://www.sba.gov/advo/press/01–09.html.

67. "The 2005 *Fortune* 500: Women CEOs," *Fortune*, http://www.fortune.com.

68. "2003 Catalyst Census of Women Board Directors of the *Fortune* 1000," http://www.catalystwomen.org.

69. M. Bertrand & K. Hallock, "The Gender Gap in Top Corporate Jobs," *Industrial & Labor Relations Review* 55 (2001): 3–21.

70. J. R. Hollenbeck, D. R. Ilgen, C. Ostroff, & J. B. Vancouver, "Sex Differences in Occupational Choice, Pay, and Worth: A Supply-Side Approach to Understanding the Male-Female Wage Gap," *Personnel Psychology* 40 (1987): 715–744.

71. A. Chaker & H. Stout, "Second Chances: After Years Off, Women Struggle to Revive Careers," *Wall Street Journal*, 6 May 2004, A1.

72. Korn-Ferry International, 1993.

73. Department of Industry, Labor and Human Relations, *Report of the Governor's Task Force on the Glass Ceiling Commission* (Madison, WI: State of Wisconsin, 1993).

74. M. Fix, G. C. Galster, & R. J. Struyk, "An Overview of Auditing for Discrimination," in *Clear and Convincing Evidence: Measurement of Discrimination in America*, ed. Michael Fix & Raymond Struyk (Washington, DC: Urban Institute Press, 1993), 1–68.

75. S. Hamm, "Why Are Women So Invisible?" *BusinessWeek*, 25 August 1997, 136.

76. D. Chenevert, & M. Tremblay, "Managerial Career Success in Canadian Organizations: Is Gender a Determinant?" *International Journal of Human Resource Management* (2002: 13) 920–941; F. Neathey, S. Dench, & L. Thomas, "Monitoring Progress toward Pay Equality," Institute for Employment Studies report on behalf of the Equal Opportunities Commission 2003, available at http://www.eoc.org.uk; S. Wellington, M. B. Kropf, & P. R. Gerkovich, "What's Holding Women Back?" *Harvard Business Review* (2003: 81) 82–111.

77. S. Wellington et al., "What's Holding Women Back?"

78. B. R. Ragins, B. Townsend, & M. Mattis, "Gender Gap in the Executive Suite: CEOs and Female Executives Report on Breaking the Glass Ceiling," *Academy of Management Executive* 12 (1998): 28–42.

79. N. Lockwood, "The Glass Ceiling: Domestic and International Perspectives," *HRMagazine* (2004 Research Quarterly): 2–10.

80. T. B. Foley, "Discrimination Lawsuits Are a Small-Business Nightmare: A Guide to Minimizing the Potential Damage," *Wall Street Journal*, 28 September 1998, 15.

81. J. Johnson, "Black CEOs Gaining in Corporate America," *San Francisco Chronicle*, 10 February 2005, http://www.sfgate.com/cgi-bin/article.cgi?file=/chronicle/archive/2005/02/10/BUGDRB8K781.DTL&type=business.

82. "Household Data: Annual Averages, Table 11. Employed Persons by Detailed Occupation, Sex, Race, and Hispanic or Latino Ethnicity," Bureau of Labor Statistics, ftp://ftp.bls.gov/pub/special.requests/lf/aat11.txt.

83. D. A. Neal & W. R. Johnson, "The Role of Premarket Factors in Black-White Wage Differences," *Journal of Political Economy* 104, no. 5 (1996): 869–895.

84. Fix, Galster, & Struyk, "An Overview of Auditing for Discrimination."

85. M. Bendick, Jr., C. W. Jackson, & V. A. Reinoso, "Measuring Employment Discrimination through Controlled Experiments," in *African-Americans and Post-Industrial Labor Markets*, ed. James B. Stewart (New Brunswick, NJ: Transaction Publishers, 1997), 77–100.

86. P. B. Riach & J. Rich, "Measuring Discrimination by Direct Experimental Methods: Seeking Gunsmoke," *Journal of PostKeynesian Economics* 14, no. 2 (Winter 1991–1992): 143–50.

87. A. P. Brief, R. T. Buttram, R. M. Reizenstein, & S. D. Pugh, "Beyond Good Intentions: The Next Steps toward Racial Equality in the American Workplace," *Academy of Management Executive* 11 (1997): 59–72.

88. L. E. Wynter, "Business & Race: Federal Agencies, Spurred on by Nonprofit Groups, Are Increasingly Embracing the Use of Undercover Investigators to Identify Discrimination in the Marketplace," *Wall Street Journal*, 1 July 1998, B1.

89. S. J. Well, "When the Bias Is in the Hiring," *Journal Record* (Oklahoma City), 26 March 1998, 1.

90. D. Morris, "The Next Great Hiring Frontier," *Wall Street Journal*, 13 September 2005, B2.

91. "The Americans with Disabilities Act: Questions and Answers," U.S. Department of Justice, September 1992, http://www.usdoj.gov/crt/ada/ada.html.

92. "Frequently Asked Questions," *Disability Statistics: Online Resource for U.S. Disability Statistics*, Cornell University School of Industrial and Labor Relations, http://www.ilr.cornell.edu/edi/disabilitystatistics.

93. "Census Brief: Disabilities Affect One-Fifth of All Americans," U.S. Bureau of the Census, December 1997, http://www.census.gov/prod/3/97pubs/cenbr975.pdf.

94. F. Bowe, "Adults with Disabilities: A Portrait," *President's Committee on Employment of People with Disabilities* (Washington, DC: GPO, 1992); D. Braddock & L. Bachelder, *The Glass Ceiling and Persons with Disabilities*, Glass Ceiling Commission, U.S. Department of Labor (Washington, DC: GPO, 1994). "Disability Status 2000," *Census Brief 2000*, March 2003, 11, available at http://www.census.gov/prod/2003pubs/c2kbr-17.pdf.

95. Louis Harris & Associates, Inc., *Public Attitudes toward People with Disabilities* (Washington, DC: National Organization on Disability, 1991); Louis Harris & Associates, Inc., *The ICD Survey II: Employing Disabled Americans* (New York: 1987).

96. R. Greenwood & V. A. Johnson, "Employer Perspectives on Workers with Disabilities," *Journal of Rehabilitation* 53 (1987): 37–45.

97. "Low Cost Accommodation Solutions," Office of Disability Employment Policy, http://www.jan.wvu.edu/media/LowCostSolutions.html.

98. Ibid.

99. "Job Accommodation Network," Office of Disability Employment Policy, http://janweb.icdi.wvu.edu.

100. "Study on the Financing of Assistive Technology Devices and Services for Individuals with Disabilities: A Report to the President and the Congress of the United States," National Council on Disability, http://www.ncd.gov.

101. Ibid.

102. R. B. Cattell, "Personality Pinned Down," *Psychology Today* 7 (1973): 40–46; C. S. Carver & M. F. Scheier, *Perspectives on Personality* (Boston: Allyn & Bacon, 1992).

103. J. M. Digman, "Personality Structure: Emergence of the Five-Factor Model," *Annual Review of Psychology* 41 (1990): 417–440; M. R. Barrick & M. K. Mount, "The Big Five Personality Dimensions and Job Performance: A Meta-Analysis," *Personnel Psychology* 44 (1991): 1–26.

104. S. Bates, "Personality Counts: Psychological Tests Can Help Peg the Job Applicants Best Suited for Certain Job," *HR Magazine*, February 2002, http://www.shrm.org/hrmagazine/articles/0202/0202covstory.asp.

105. "NASA Fires Astronaut Nowak," CNN.com, 7 March 2007, http://www.cnn.com/2007/TECH/space/03/07/nasa.nowak/index.html.

106. R. Cook, "The Changing 'Face' of Your Business: Finding Good People . . . and Keeping Them Motivated," *PRO Magazine*, March 2005, 43.

107. O. Behling, "Employee Selection: Will Intelligence and Conscientiousness Do the Job?" *Academy of Management Executive* 12 (1998): 77–86.

108. Barrick & Mount, "The Big Five Personality

Dimensions and Job Performance."

109. Barrick & Mount, "The Big Five Personality Dimensions and Job Performance"; M. K. Mount & M. R. Barrick, "The Big Five Personality Dimensions: Implications for Research and Practice in Human Resource Management," *Research in Personnel & Human Resources Management* 13 (1995): 153–200; M. K. Mount & M. R. Barrick, "Five Reasons Why the 'Big Five' Article Has Been Frequently Cited," *Personnel Psychology* 51 (1998): 849–857; D. S. Ones, M. K. Mount, M. R. Barrick, & J. E. Hunter, "Personality and Job Performance: A Critique of the Tett, Jackson, and Rothstein (1991) Meta-Analysis," *Personnel Psychology* 47 (1994): 147–156.

110. Mount & Barrick, "Five Reasons Why the 'Big Five' Article Has Been Frequently Cited."

111. Ibid.

112. J. A. Lopez, "Talking Desks: Personality Types Revealed in State Workstations," *Arizona Republic*, 7 January 1996, Section D, 1.

113. T. W. Adorno, E. Frenkel-Brunswik, D. J. Levinson, & R. N. Stanford, *The Authoritarian Personality* (New York: Harper & Row, 1950).

114. C. Hymowitz, "In the Lead: Two Football Coaches Have a Lot to Teach Screaming Managers," *Wall Street Journal*, 29 January 2007, B1.

115. R. G. Vleeming, "Machiavellianism: A Preliminary Review," *Psychological Reports* 53 (1979): 295–310.

116. F. L. Geis & T. H. Moon, "Machiavellianism and Deception," *Journal of Personality & Social Psychology* 41 (1981): 766–775.

117. R. Christie & F. L. Geis, *Studies in Machiavellianism* (New York: Academic Press, 1970), 312.

118. J. Zaslow, "Why Jerks Get Ahead: Being Obnoxious Often Pays Off in the Workplace," *Wall Street Journal*, 29 March 2004, R6.

119. B. Kallestad, "Florida State Research Shows Bad Managers' Effect on Workers," Associated Press State & Local Wire, 1 January 2007, available at http://www.ap.org.

120. K. A. Matthews, "Psychological Perspectives on the Type A Behavior Pattern," *Psychological Bulletin* 91 (1982): 293–323.

121. M. Friedman & R. H. Rosenman, *Type A Behavior and Your Heart* (New York: Fawcett Crest, 1974).

122. M. Lee & R. Kanungo, *Management of Work and Personal Life* (New York: Praeger, 1984).

123. J. Schaubroeck, D. C. Ganster, & B. E. Kemmerer, "Job Complexity, 'Type A' Behavior, and Cardiovascular Disorders," *Academy of Management Journal* 37 (1994): 37.

124. "Cardiovascular Research: Type A Personality Is Not Linked to Heart Disease," *Science Letter*, 19 September 2006, 386.

125. R. Winslow, "Choose Your Neurosis: Some Type-A Traits Are Riskier Than Others," *Wall Street Journal*, 22 October 2003, D1.

126. J. E. Bishop, "Health: Hostility, Distrust May Put Type A's at Coronary Risk," *Wall Street Journal Interactive*, 17 January 1989.

127. P. E. Spector, "Behavior in Organizations as a Function of Employee's Locus of Control," *Psychological Bulletin* 91 (1982): 482–497.

128. J. B. Rotter, "Generalized Expectancies for Internal versus External Control of Reinforcement," *Psychological Monographs* 80 (1966): Whole No. 609; J. B. Rotter, "Some Problems and Misconceptions Related to the Construct of Internal versus External Control of Reinforcement," *Journal of Consulting & Clinical Psychology* 43 (1975): 56–67.

129. R. S. Lazarus, *Emotion and Adaptation* (New York: Oxford University Press, 1991).

130. "The Secrets of Happiness," *Psychology Today* 25 (July 1992): 38.

131. B. M. Staw, N. E. Bell, & J. A. Clausen, "The Dispositional Approach to Job Attitudes: A Lifetime Longitudinal Test," *Administrative Science Quarterly* 31 (1986): 56–77.

132. "Put Customer Service at the Heart of Marketing to Grow the Firm," Accounting Office Management & Administration Report, January 2007, http://www.ioma.com/issues/AOMAR/2007_1/1610735-1.html.

133. "Accenture Survey: Poor Customer Service Drives Nearly Half of U.S. Consumers to Take Their Business Elsewhere," *Wireless News*, 8 August 2006, available at M2 Communications, http://www.m2.com.

134. A. M. Isen & R. A. Baron, "Positive Affect and Organizational Behavior," in *Research in Organizational Behavior* 12, ed. B. M. Staw & L. L. Cummings (Greenwich, CT: JAI Press, 1990); J. M. George & A. P. Brief, "Feeling Good–Doing Good: A Conceptual Analysis of the Mood at Work—Organizational Spontaneity Relationships," *Psychological Bulletin* 112 (1992): 310–329; R. D. Iverson & P. J. Erwin, "Predicting Occupational Injury: The Role of Affectivity," *Journal of Occupational & Organizational Psychology* 70 (1997): 113–128; D. P. Skarlicki, R. Folger, & P. Tesluk, "Personality as a Moderator in the Relationship between Fairness and Retaliation," *Academy of Management Journal* 42 (1999): 100–108.

135. P. Totterdell, S. Kellett, K. Teuchmann, & R. B. Briner, "Evidence of Mood Linkage in Work Groups," *Journal of Personality & Social Psychology* 74 (1998): 1503–1515.

136. M. E. P. Seligman & S. Schulman, "Explanatory Style as a Predictor of Productivity and Quitting among Life Insurance Sales Agents," *Journal of Personality & Social Psychology* 50 (1986): 832–838.

137. Sonja, L., Laura, K., & E. Diener, "The Benefits of Frequent Positive Affect: Does Happiness Lead to Success?" *Psychological Bulletin*, November 2005, 803–855.

138. T. D. Schellhardt, "In a Tight Factory Schedule, Where Does Religion Fit In?" *Wall Street Journal Interactive*, 4 March 1999.

139. Staff, "The Diverse Work Force," *Inc.*, January 1993, 33.

140. D. A. Thomas & R. J. Ely, "Making Differences Matter: A New Paradigm for Managing Diversity," *Harvard Business Review* 74 (September–October 1996): 79–90.

141. E. Esen "2005 Workplace Diversity Practices: Survey Report."

142. D. A. Thomas & S. Wetlaufer, "A Question of Color: A Debate on Race in the U.S. Workplace," *Harvard Business Review* 75 (September–October 1997), 118–132.

143. Thomas & Ely, "Making Differences Matter."

144. A. Fisher, "How You Can Do Better on Diversity," *Fortune*, 15 November 2004, 60.

145. Aetna 2005 Diversity Annual Report (http://www.aetna.com), obtained from SHRM Research Department.

146. J. R. Norton & R. E. Fox, *The Change Equation: Capitalizing on Diversity for Effective Organizational Change* (Washington, DC: American Psychological Association, 1997).

147. Ibid.

148. Thomas & Ely, "Making Differences Matter."

149. R. R. Thomas, Jr., *Beyond Race and Gender: Unleashing the Power of Your Total Workforce by Managing Diversity* (New York: AMACOM, 1991).

150. Ibid.

151. T. Cox, Jr., "The Multicultural Organization," *Academy of Management Executive* 5 (1991): 34–47.

152. S. Lubove, "Damned If You Do, Damned If You Don't: Preference Programs Are on the Defensive in the Public Sector, but Plaintiffs' Attorneys and Bureaucrats Keep Diversity Inc. Thriving in Corporate America," *Forbes*, 15 December 1997, 122.

153. L. S. Gottfredson, "Dilemmas in Developing Diversity Programs," in *Diversity in the Workplace*, ed. S. E. Jackson & Associates (New York: Guildford Press, 1992).

154. Lieber & Urresta, "Pacific Enterprises Keeping Talent."

155. R. Rodriguez, "Diversity Finds Its Place."

156. "L'Oreal Receives Diversity Best Practices 2004 Global CEO Leadership Award," *PR Newswire*, 26 October 2004, 11:01.

157. A. Greenwald, B. Nosek, & M. Banaji, "Understanding and Using the Implicit Association Test: I. An Improved Scoring Algorithm," *Journal of Personality & Social Psychology* (August 2003): 197–206; S. Vedantam, "See No Bias; Many Americans Believe They Are Not Prejudiced," *Washington Post*, 23 January 2005, W12.

158. Carnevale & Stone, *The American Mosaic*.

159. D. Fenn, "Diversity: More Than Just Affirmative Action," *Inc.*, July 1995, 93.

160. J. R. Joplin & C. S. Daus, "Challenges of Leading a Diverse Workforce," *Academy of Management Executive* 11 (1997): 32–47.

161. A. Fisher, "Ask Annie: Should People Choose Their Own Mentors?" *Fortune*, 29 November 2004, 72.

162. Ibid.

163. Rice, "How to Make Diversity Pay."

164. T. Pepper, "Getting to Know You: Finding Out Which Job Candidate Would Make a Savvy Manager or a Level-Headed Cop Used to Be an Art, Now It's Cutting-Edge Science," *Newsweek International*, 17 January 2005, http://www.msnbc.msn.com/id/3037881/site/newsweek, 44; A. Overholt, "Personality Tests: Back with a Vengeance," *Fast Company*, November 2004, 115–117; A. Blantyre, "Testing, Testing: More Companies Are Giving Psychological Tests to Their Current Employees," *Inc.*, June 2004, 35–37; K. J. Sulkowicz, "The Corporate Shrink," *Fast Company*, October 2004, 48; A. Overholt, "Are You a Polyolefin Optimizer? Take This Quiz!" *Fast Company*, April 2004, 37; L. Gettler, "What You See Isn't Necessarily What You Get," *Australasian Business Intelligence*, November 23, 2004, available at http://www.highbeam.com/browse/Business-International-Australasian+Business+Intelligence; Douglas P. Shuit, "At 60, Myers-Briggs Is Still Sorting Out and Identifying People's Types," *Workforce Management*, December 2003, 72.

165. Donna Fenn, "Respect Your Elders," *Inc.*, September 2003, 29; Bureau of Labor Statistics, http://www.bls.gov.

166. M. Crowe, "UPS Managers Trained in the Real World to Deliver Results," *The Business Journal—San Jose*, 21 September 1998, 26; Rice, "How to Make Diversity Pay."

Chapter 13

1. Nucor 2006 Annual Report, http://www.nucor.com/indexinner.aspx?finpage=investorinfo; M. Polanco, "The Mill that Gives and Takes: Dedicated to the Job, Despite Heat, Dust and Danger," *Hartford Courant*, 29 January 2007, available at http://web.lexis-nexis.com; G. P. Smith, "How Nucor Steel Rewards Performance and Productivity," ManagerWise, available at http://www. managerwise.com; "The Nucor Story," http://www.nucor-fastener.com/nucor.html; C. Carpenter & M. Song, "Steel Is Beginning to Collect Rust in Stock Market," Bloomberg.com, 19 March 2007, http://www.bloomberg.com/apps/news?pid=20601109&refer=home&sid=avJsya9w6v84; L. Haoting, "China's Steel Sector Still Red Hot," China Daily, 9 May 2004, http://www.chinadaily.com. cn/english/doc/2004–05/ 09/content_329014. htm; D. Lague, "China's Demand for Steel Slows, but the Mills Keep Churning," *International Herald Tribune*, 20 July 2005, http://www.iht.com/articles/2005/07/19/business/steel.php.

2. T. Daniel & G. Metcalf, "The Science of Motivation," *SHRM White Paper*, Society for Human Resource Management, May 2005 http://www.shrm.org.

3. J. P. Campbell & R. D. Pritchard, "Motivation Theory in Industrial and Organizational Psychology," in *Handbook of Industrial and Organizational Psychology*, ed. M. D. Dunnette (Chicago: Rand McNally, 1976).

4. P. Thomas, "Waitress Makes the Difference in Bringing Deaf to Pittsburgh," *Wall Street Journal Interactive Edition*, 2 March 1999, available at http://online.wsj.com.

5. "Winter Olympics, Bobsled, Past Results," *ESPN*, 9 June 1999, http://espn.go.com.

6. "Jamaica Bobsleigh History," Team Jamaica.com, 9 June 1999, available at http://www.thereggaeboyz.com/bobsled.htm.

7. "Double-Drive-Thru Chain Awarded NRN's People and Performance Award for Excellence in Employee Recognition," Checkers press release, 14 October 2003, available at http://phx.corporate-ir.net/phoenix.zhtml?c=61892&p=irol-newsArticle_print&ID=458217.

8. S. Monson, "Feeling Perky," *Seattle Times*, 24 December 2006, G1.

9. Ibid.

10. Ibid.

11. E. A. Locke, "The Nature and Causes of Job Satisfaction," in *Handbook of Industrial and Organizational Psychology*, ed. M. D. Dunnette (Chicago: Rand McNally, 1976).

12. A. H. Maslow, "A Theory of Human Motivation," *Psychological Review* 50 (1943): 370–396.

13. C. P. Alderfer, *Existence, Relatedness, and Growth: Human Needs in Organizational Settings* (New York: Free Press, 1972).

14. D. C. McClelland, "Toward a Theory of Motive Acquisition," *American Psychologist* 20 (1965): 321–333; D. C. McClelland & D. H. Burnham, "Power Is the Great Motivator," *Harvard*

Business Review 54, no. 2 (1976): 100–110.

15. J. Spencer, "Shirk Ethic: How to Fake a Hard Day at the Office—White-Collar Slackers Get Help from New Gadgets: The Faux 4 A.M. E-Mail," *Wall Street Journal*, 15 May 2003, D1.
16. J. H. Turner, "Entrepreneurial Environments and the Emergence of Achievement Motivation in Adolescent Males," *Sociometry* 33 (1970): 147–165.
17. L. W. Porter, E. E. Lawler III, & J. R. Hackman, *Behavior in Organizations* (New York: McGraw-Hill, 1975).
18. C. Ajila, "Maslow's Hierarchy of Needs Theory: Applicability to the Nigerian Industrial Setting," *IFE Psychology* (1997): 162–174.
19. M. A. Wahba & L. B. Birdwell, "Maslow Reconsidered: A Review of Research on the Need Hierarchy Theory," *Organizational Behavior & Human Performance* 15 (1976): 212–240; J. Rauschenberger, N. Schmitt, & J. E. Hunter, "A Test of the Need Hierarchy Concept by a Markov Model of Change in Need Strength," *Administrative Science Quarterly* 25 (1980): 654–670.
20. E. E. Lawler III & L. W. Porter, "The Effect of Performance on Job Satisfaction," *Industrial Relations* 7 (1967): 20–28.
21. Porter, Lawler III, & Hackman, *Behavior in Organizations*.
22. E. White, "Employers Increasingly Favor Bonuses to Raises," *Wall Street Journal*, 28 August 2006, B3.
23. J. Wallace, "Many at Boeing Will Share Windfall 12 Days' Extra Pay for 45,000 in Area," *Seattle Post-Intelligencer*, 2 February 2007, C1.
24. K. Maher & K. Hudson, "Wal-Mart to Sweeten Bonus Plan for Staff," *Wall Street Journal*, 22 March 2007, A11.
25. S. Miller, "Countering the Employee Recognition Gap," SHRM Library, Society for Human Resource Management, February 2006, http://www.shrm.org.
26. Porter, Lawler III, & Hackman, *Behavior in Organizations*.
27. B. Coffee, "Motivating a Big Company in Small Ways," Forum for People Management and Measurement, 31 May 2005, http://www.performanceforum.org.
28. S. Miller, "Countering the Employee Recognition Gap."
29. D. Whitford, "A Human Place to Work," *Fortune*, 8 January 2001, 108.
30. C. Caggiano, "What Do Workers Want?" *Inc.*, November 1992, 101–104; "National Study of the Changing Workforce," Families & Work Institute, http://www.familiesandwork.org/summary/nscw.pdf.
31. L. Buchanan, "Managing One-to-One," *Inc.*, 1 October 2001, 82.
32. Ibid.
33. "America@Work: A Focus on Benefits and Compensation," Aon Consulting, http://www.aon.com/pdf/america/awork2.pdf.
34. J. Laabs, "Satisfy Them with More Than Money," *Personnel Journal* 77, no. 11 (1998): 40.
35. R. Kanfer & P. Ackerman, "Aging, Adult Development, and Work Motivation," *Academy of Management Review* (2004): 440–458.
36. "Staying Ahead of the Curve: The AARP Work and Career Study," AARP, http://assets.aarp.org/rgcenter/econ/d17772_multiwork.pdf.
37. S. J. O'Malley, "Motivate the Middle: How Mid-Level Performance Can Bring Top Growth to the Bottom Line," *Bank Investment Consultant*, February 2007, 39.
38. S. Stecklow, "Fast Finns' Fines Fit Their Finances—Traffic Penalties Are Assessed According to Driver Income," *Wall Street Journal*, 2 January 2001, A1.
39. L. Lavelle, "A Payday for Performance; Compensation Is Less Outrageous This Year, except for CEO Who Delivered," *BusinessWeek*, 18 April 2005, 78.
40. S. DeCarlo, "Special Report: CEO Compensation," *Forbes Magazine*, 20 April 2006, http://www.forbes.com/2006/04/17/06ceo_ceo-compensation_land.html.
41. "Executive Paywatch," AFL-CIO, 16 March 2007, http://www.aflcio.org/corporatewatch/paywatch.
42. S. DeCarlo, "Special Report."
43. C. T. Kulik & M. L. Ambrose, "Personal and Situational Determinants of Referent Choice," *Academy of Management Review* 17 (1992): 212–237.
44. C. DeNavas-Walt, B. Proctor, & R. Mills, "Income, Poverty, and Health Insurance Coverage in the United States: 2003," U.S. Census Bureau, http://www.census.gov/prod/2004pubs/p60-226.pdf.
45. J. S. Adams, "Toward an Understanding of Inequity," *Journal of Abnormal Social Psychology* 67 (1963): 422–436.
46. J. Greenberg, "Employee Theft as a Reaction to Underpayment Inequity: The Hidden Costs of Pay Cuts," *Journal of Applied Psychology* 75 (1990): 561–568.
47. R. A. Cosier & D. R. Dalton, "Equity Theory and Time: A Reformulation," *Academy of Management Review* 8 (1983): 311–319; M. R. Carrell & J. E. Dittrich, "Equity Theory: The Recent Literature, Methodological Considerations, and New Directions," *Academy of Management Review* 3 (1978): 202–209.
48. M. Patterson, "2,500 Staff Sacked by Text Message," *Daily Telegraph*, 31 May 2003, http://www.telegraph.co.uk/news/main.jhtml?xml=/news/2003/05/31/nsack31.xml.
49. "Iberia Pilots' Strike Causes Cancellation of 30% of Flights—Airline Plans to Ask Union to Pay for Earlier Slowdown," *Wall Street Journal Europe*, 20 June 2001, 5; C. Vitzthum, "Chairman Voices Optimism after Airline Weathers Difficult Year—Spanish Carrier Overcomes Labor Strife, Industry Woes to Post Small Profit," *Wall Street Journal Europe*, 28 January 2002, 5.
50. J. Bendich, "When Is a Temp Not a Temp?" *Trial Magazine*, 1 October 2001, 42.
51. "2002 Statistics Fact Sheet: Back Wages for Fair Labor Standards Act Violations Increased by 29%," U.S. Department of Labor, http://www.dol.gov/esa/whd/statistics/200212.htm; M. Orey, "Lawsuits Abound from Workers Seeking Overtime Pay," *Wall Street Journal*, 30 May 2002, B1.
52. A. Zimmerman, "Big Retailers Face Overtime Suits as Bosses Do More 'Hourly' Work," *Wall Street Journal*, 26 May 2004, A1.
53. J. Pollack, "Exemption under the Fair Labor Standards Act: The Cost of Misclassifying Employees," *Cornell Hotel & Restaurant Administration Quarterly* 42 (2001): 16.
54. C. Chen, J. Choi, & S. Chi, "Making Justice Sense of Local-Expatriate Compensation Disparity: Mitigation by Local Referents, Ideological Explanations, and Interpersonal Sensitivity in China-Foreign Joint Ventures," *Academy of*

Management Journal (2002): 807–817.

55. K. Aquino, R. W. Griffeth, D. G. Allen, & P. W. Hom, "Integrating Justice Constructs into the Turnover Process: A Test of a Referent Cognitions Model," *Academy of Management Journal* 40, no. 5 (1997): 1208–1227.

56. S. Barr, "While the SEC Watches the Markets, the Job Market Is Draining the SEC," *Washington Post*, 10 March 2002, C3.

57. D. Gullapalli, "Take This Job and . . . File It—Burdened by Extra Work Created by the Sarbanes-Oxley Act, CPAs Leave the Big Four for Better Life," *Wall Street Journal*, 4 May 2005, C1.

58. Ibid.

59. R. Folger & M. A. Konovsky, "Effects of Procedural and Distributive Justice on Reactions to Pay Raise Decisions," *Academy of Management Journal* 32 (1989): 115–130; M. A. Konovsky, "Understanding Procedural Justice and Its Impact on Business Organizations," *Journal of Management* 26 (2000): 489–512.

60. E. Barret-Howard & T. R. Tyler, "Procedural Justice as a Criterion in Allocation Decisions," *Journal of Personality & Social Psychology* 50 (1986): 296–305; Folger & Konovsky, "Effects of Procedural and Distributive Justice on Reactions to Pay Raise Decisions."

61. R. Folger & J. Greenberg, "Procedural Justice: An Interpretive Analysis of Personnel Systems," in *Research in Personnel and Human Resources Management*, Vol. 3, ed. K. Rowland & G. Ferris (Greenwich, CT: JAI, 1985); R. Folger, D. Rosenfield, J. Grove, & L. Corkran, "Effects of 'Voice' and Peer Opinions on Responses to Inequity," *Journal of Personality & Social Psychology* 37 (1979): 2253–2261; E. A. Lind & T. R. Tyler, *The Social Psychology of Procedural Justice* (New York: Plenum, 1988); Konovsky, "Understanding Procedural Justice and Its Impact on Business Organizations."

62. R. J. Bies & J. S. Moag, "Interactional Justice: Communication Criteria for Fairness," in R. J. Lewicki, B. H. Sheppard, & M. Bazerman (Eds.), *Research on Negotiation in Organizations* (Greenwich, CT: JAI, 1986), 43–55.

63. J. A. Colquitt, "On the Dimensionality of Organizational Justice: A Construct Validation of a Measure," *Journal of Applied Psychology* (2001: 86), 386–400; J. A. Colquitt, D. E. Conlon, M. J. Wesson, C. Porter & K. Yee Ng, "Justice at the Millennium: A Meta-Analytic Review of 25 Years of Organizational Justice Research," *Journal of Applied Psychology*, 86, 425–445.

64. K. A. Dolan, "When Money Isn't Enough," *Forbes*, 18 November 1996, 164–170.

65. V. H. Vroom, *Work and Motivation* (New York: John Wiley & Sons, 1964); L. W. Porter & E. E. Lawler III, *Managerial Attitudes and Performance* (Homewood, IL: Dorsey & Richard D. Irwin, 1968).

66. S. Miller, "Strategic HR Leadership Award," *HR Magazine*, November 2006, http://www.shrm.org.

67. S. Miller, "Countering the Employee Recognition Gap," SHRM Library, Society for Human Resource Management, February 2006, http://www.shrm.org.

68. P. V. LeBlanc & P. W. Mulvey, "How American Workers See the Rewards of Work," *Compensation & Benefits Review* 30 (February 1998): 24–28.

69. A. Fox, "Companies Can Benefit When They Disclose Pay Processes to Employees," *HR Magazine*, July 2002, 25.

70. S. Wellner, "Spoiled Brats—Your HR Policies May Be Contributing to a Sense of Employee Entitlement," *HR Magazine*, November 2004, http://www.shrm.org.

71. K. W. Thomas & B. A. Velthouse, "Cognitive Elements of Empowerment," *Academy of Management Review* 15 (1990): 666–681.

72. J. Sandberg, "Been Here 25 Years and All I Got Was This Lousy T-Shirt," *Wall Street Journal*, 28 January 2004, B1.

73. C. Hymowitz, "When Meeting Targets Becomes the Strategy, CEO Is on Wrong Path," *Wall Street Journal*, 8 March 2005, A8.

74. E. L. Thorndike, *Animal Intelligence* (New York: Macmillan, 1911).

75. D. Milbank, "Workplace: Companies Turn to Peer Pressure to Cut Injuries as Psychologists Join the Battle," *Wall Street Journal*, 29 March 1991, B1.

76. B. F. Skinner, *Science and Human Behavior* (New York: Macmillan, 1954); B. F. Skinner, *Beyond Freedom and Dignity* (New York: Bantam, 1971); B. F. Skinner, *A Matter of Consequences* (New York: New York University Press, 1984).

77. A. M. Dickinson & A. D. Poling, "Schedules of Monetary Reinforcement in Organizational Behavior Management: Latham and Huber Revisited," *Journal of Organizational Behavior Management* 16, no. 1 (1992): 71–91.

78. D. Harbrecht, "CEO Q&A: Baxter's Harry Kraemer: 'I Don't Golf,'" *BusinessWeek Online*, 28 March 2003, http://www.businessweek.com/bwdaily/dnflash/mar2002/nf20020328_0720.htm.

79. R. Ho, "Attending to Attendance," *Wall Street Journal Interactive*, 7 December 1998, available at http://online.wsj.com.

80. D. Grote, "Manager's Journal: Discipline without Punishment," *Wall Street Journal*, 23 May 1994, A14.

81. L. Lavelle, F. Jespersen, S. Ante, & J. Kerstetter, "Special Report: Executive Pay," *BusinessWeek*, 21 April 2003, 86.

82. L. Lavelle & F. Jespersen, "While the CEO Gravy Train May Be Slowing Down, It Hasn't Jumped the Rails," *BusinessWeek*, 16 April 2001, 76; B. Orwall, "Disney Awards Bonuses to Top Brass," *Wall Street Journal*, 29 January 2003, B5.

83. E. Pedalino & V. U. Gamboa, "Behavior Modification and Absenteeism: Intervention in One Industrial Setting," *Journal of Applied Psychology* 59 (1974): 694–698.

84. C. Cole, "Retooling Absentee Programs Bolsters Profits," *Workforce Management*, September 2002, http://www.workforce.com/section/09/feature/23/31/64.

85. J. B. Miner, *Theories of Organizational Behavior* (Hinsdale, IL: Dryden, 1980).

86. Dickinson & Poling, "Schedules of Monetary Reinforcement in Organizational Behavior Management."

87. F. Luthans & A. D. Stajkovic, "Reinforce for Performance: The Need to Go beyond Pay and Even Rewards," *Academy of Management Executive* 13, no. 2 (1999): 49–57.

88. D. Anderson, *Up Your Business! 7 Steps to Fix, Build or Stretch Your Organization* (New York: Wiley, 2003).

89. K. D. Butterfield, L. K. Trevino, & G. A. Ball, "Punishment from the Manager's Perspective: A Grounded Investigation and Inductive Model," *Academy of Management*

Journal 39 (1996): 1479–1512.

90. R. D. Arvey & J. M. Ivancevich, "Punishment in Organizations: A Review, Propositions, and Research Suggestions," *Academy of Management Review* 5 (1980): 123–132.

91. R. D. Arvey, G. A. Davis, & S. M. Nelson, "Use of Discipline in an Organization: A Field Study," *Journal of Applied Psychology* 69 (1984): 448–460; M. E. Schnake, "Vicarious Punishment in a Work Setting," *Journal of Applied Psychology* 71 (1986): 343–345.

92. A. D. Stajkovic & F. Luthans, "A Meta-Analysis of the Effects of Organizational Behavior Modification on Task Performance, 1975–95," *Academy of Management Journal* 40, no. 5 (1997): 1122–1149; A. D. Stajkovic & F. Luthans, "Behavioral Management and Task Performance in Organizations: Conceptual Background, Meta-Analysis, and Test of Alternative Models," *Personnel Psychology* 56, issue 1 (2003): 155–194.

93. G. A. Yukl & G. P. Latham, "Consequences of Reinforcement Schedules and Incentive Magnitudes for Employee Performance: Problems Encountered in a Field Setting," *Journal of Applied Psychology* 60 (1975): 294–298.

94. C. Salter, "Can JetBlue Make the Leap from Popular (and Profitable) Niche Airline to Major Player—without Losing Its Soul?" *Fast Company*, 1 May 2004, 67.

95. E. A. Locke & G. P. Latham, *Goal Setting: A Motivational Technique That Works* (Englewood Cliffs, NJ: Prentice Hall, 1984); E. A. Locke & G. P. Latham, *A Theory of Goal Setting and Task Performance* (Englewood Cliffs, NJ: Prentice Hall, 1990).

96. P. Valade, "CDW's Formula for Success: Vernon Hills Company Says Happy Coworkers Can Create Culture for Even Happier Customers," *Chicago Daily Herald*, 5 June 2002, 1.

97. G. P. Latham & E. A. Locke, "Goal Setting—A Motivational Technique That Works," *Organizational Dynamics* 8, no. 2 (1979): 68.

98. Ibid.

99. Z. Zhiwei, J. A. Wallin, & R. A. Reber, "Safety Improvements: An Application of Behaviour Modification Techniques," *Journal of Applied Management Studies* 15 (2000): 135–140.

100. C. A. Arnolds & C. Boshoff, "Compensation, Esteem Valence, and Job Performance: An Empirical Assessment of Alderfer's ERG Theory," *International Journal of Human Resource Management* 13, no. 4 (2002): 697–719.

101. Maslow, "A Theory of Human Motivation," *Psychological Review*.

102. M. Conlin, "Compensation Is Getting Personal: Companies Are Mining Employee Data to Identify the Perks That Spur Productivity," *BusinessWeek Online*, 6 December 2002, available at http://businessweek.com.

103. M. Boyle, "How to Cut Perks without Killing Morale," *Fortune* 19 February 2001; T. Pollock, " Managing for Better Morale, " *Automotive Manufacturing & Production*, February 2001, available at http://www.autofieldguide.com.

Chapter 14

1. G. Anders & A. Murray, "Behind H-P Chairman's fall, Clash with a Powerful Director," *Wall Street Journal*, 9 October 2006, A1; P. Burrows, "HP Says Goodbye to Drama," *BusinessWeek*, 12 September 2005, 83; P. Burrows, "What Would Hewlett and Packard Say?" *BusinessWeek*, 18 September 2006, 35; P. Burrows, L. Lee, R. Hof, & A. Carter, "Controlling the Damage at HP," *BusinessWeek*, 9 October 2006, 36; G. Colvin, "A Growth Plan for HP's CEO," *Fortune*, 16 October 2006, 70; J. Hopkins & J. Swartz, "HP Chief Tackles Boardroom Scandal Head On," *USA Today*, 25 September 2006, A10; M. Kessler, "HP Restructuring Will Cut 14,500 Jobs," *USA Today*, 20 July 2005, B1; M. Kessler, "Strong PC Sales help Drive up HP's Earnings," *USA Today*, 21 February 2007, B2; M. Kessler & J. Swartz, "HP Leader Hurd Expected to Apologize at Hearing," *USA Today*, B1; M. Kessler, J. Swartz, & S. Kirchhoff, "HP Execs on Spying: It Wasn't Me," *USA Today*, 29 September 2006, B1; A. Lashinsky, "Coffee with Mark Hurd," *Fortune*, 16 October 2006, 44; A. Lashinsky, D. Burke, & S. Kaufman, "The Hurd Way: How a Sales-Obsessed CEO Rebooted HP," *Fortune*, 17 April 2006, 92; H. Maurer, "HP Settles," *BusinessWeek*, 25 December 2006, 33; A. Murray, "H-P Board Clash over Leaks Triggers Angry Resignation," *Wall Street Journal*, 6 September 2006, A1; Staff, "'I Should Have Figured It Out," *BusinessWeek*, 9 October 2006, 44.

2. S. Warren, "Remembrances: Lamar Muse (1920–2007) Steered Southwest Airlines' Take Off On Booze to Fliers and a Razor to Costs," *Wall Street Journal*, 10 February 2007, A4.

3. B. Gimbel, "Southwest's New Flight Plan," *Fortune*, 16 May 2005, 93.

4. J. Stancavage, "Southwest Has Fun, Profit," *Tulsa World*, 2 July 2006.

5. W. Bennis, "Why Leaders Can't Lead," *Training & Development Journal* 43, no. 4 (1989).

6. J. Adamy, "How Jim Skinner Flipped McDonald's," *Wall Street Journal*, 5 January 2007, B1.

7. M. Langley, C. Riley, & R. Sidel, "Tightening the Belt: In Citigroup Ouster, a Battle Over Expenses," *Wall Street Journal*, 24 January 2007, A1.

8. M. Langley, "Behind Citigroup Departures: A Culture Shift by CEO Prince," *Wall Street Journal*, 24 August 2005, A1.

9. A. Zaleznik, "Managers and Leaders: Are They Different?" *Harvard Business Review* 55 (1977): 76–78; A. Zaleznik, "The Leadership Gap," *Washington Quarterly* 6 (1983): 32–39.

10. Bennis, "Why Leaders Can't Lead."

11. K. Voigt, "Enron, Andersen Scandals Offer Ethical Lessons—Businesspeople Can Strive to Avoid Common Pitfalls through the 'Three Ms,'" *Wall Street Journal Europe*, 3 September 2002, A12.

12. B. Grow, D. Foust, E. Thornton, R. Farzad, J. McGregor, S. Zegel, & E. Javers, "Out at Home Depot behind the Flameout of Controversial CEO Bob Nardelli," *BusinessWeek*, 15 January 2007, http://www.businessweek.com/magazine/content/07_03/b4017001.htm.

13. J. P. Howell, D. E. Bowen, P. W. Dorfman, S. Kerr, & P. M. Podsakoff, "Substitutes for Leadership: Effective Alternatives to Ineffective Leadership," *Organizational Dynamics*, 22 June 1990, 20; S. Kerr & J. M. Jermier, "Substitutes for Leadership: Their Meaning and Measurement," *Organizational Behavior & Human Performance* 22 (1978): 375–403.

14. L. Black, "Telecommuting Offers Work Alternative for Some," *Rocky Mountain News*, 10 November 2003, 7B.

15. S. Berfield, "The Best of 2006: Leaders," *BusinessWeek*, 18 December 2006, 58.

16. D. Jones, "Not all Successful CEOs are Extroverts," *USA Today*, 7 June 2006, B.1.

17. Ibid.

18. M. Gladwell, "Why Do We Love Tall Men?" Gladwell Dot Com, http://www.gladwell.com/blink/blink_excerpt2.html.

19. D. Sacks, "The Accidental Guru," *Fast Company*, 1 January 2005, 64.

20. R. J. House & R. M Aditya, "The Social Scientific Study of Leadership: Quo Vadis?" *Journal of Management* 23 (1997): 409–473; T. Judge, R. Illies, J. Bono, & M. Gerhardt, "Personality and Leadership: A Qualitative and Quantitative Review," *Journal of Applied Psychology* (August 2002): 765–782; S. A. Kirkpatrick & E. A. Locke, "Leadership: Do Traits Matter?" *Academy of Management Executive* 5, no. 2 (1991): 48–60.

21. House & Aditya, "The Social Scientific Study of Leadership"; Kirkpatrick & Locke, "Leadership: Do Traits Matter?"

22. J. J. Gabarro, *The Dynamics of Taking Charge* (Boston: Harvard Business School Press, 1987).

23. B. Morris, "The Accidental CEO," *Fortune*, 28 June 2003, 58.

24. J. B. Fuller, C. E. P. Patterson, K. Hester, & D. Stringer, "A Quantitative Review of Research on Charismatic Leadership," *Psychological Reports* 78 (1996): 271–287; R. G. Lord, C. L. De Vader, & G. M. Alliger, "A Meta-Analysis of the Relation between Personality Traits and Leadership Perceptions: An Application of Validity Generalization Procedures," *Journal of Applied Psychology* 71, no. 3 (1986): 402–410.

25. Ibid.

26. Kirkpatrick & Locke, "Leadership: Do Traits Matter?"

27. E. A. Fleishman, "The Description of Supervisory Behavior," *Journal of Applied Psychology* 37 (1953): 1–6; L. R. Katz, *New Patterns of Management* (New York: McGraw-Hill, 1961).

28. S. Tully & E. Levenson, "In This Corner! The Contender—Jamie Dimon—The New CEO of J.P. Morgan Chase," *Fortune*, 3 April 2006, 54.

29. L. Grant, "Retail Giant Wal-Mart Faces Challenges on Many Fronts; Protests, Allegations Are Price of Success, CEO Says," *USA Today*, 11 November 2003, B1.

30. Ibid.

31. P. Weissenberg & M. H. Kavanagh, "The Independence of Initiating Structure and Consideration: A Review of the Evidence," *Personnel Psychology* 25 (1972): 119–130.

32. R. J. House & T. R. Mitchell, "Path-Goal Theory of Leadership," *Journal of Contemporary Business* 3 (1974): 81–97; F. E. Fiedler, "A Contingency Model of Leadership Effectiveness," in *Advances in Experimental Social Psychology*, ed. L. Berkowitz (New York: Academic Press, 1964); V. H. Vroom & P. W. Yetton, *Leadership and Decision Making* (Pittsburgh: University of Pittsburgh Press, 1973); P. Hersey & K. H. Blanchard, The *Management of Organizational Behavior*, 4th ed. (Englewood Cliffs, NJ: Prentice Hall, 1984); Kerr & Jermier, "Substitutes for Leadership."

33. J. Pfeffer, "In Defense of the Boss from Hell," *Business 2.0*, 1 March 2007, 70.

34. F. E. Fiedler & M. M. Chemers, *Leadership and Effective Management* (Glenview, IL: Scott, Foresman, 1974); F. E. Fiedler & M. M. Chemers, *Improving Leadership Effectiveness: The Leader Match Concept*, 2d ed. (New York: Wiley, 1984).

35. Fiedler & Chemers, *Improving Leadership Effectiveness*.

36. F. E. Fiedler, "The Effects of Leadership Training and Experience: A Contingency Model Interpretation," *Administrative Science Quarterly* 17, no. 4 (1972): 455; F. E. Fiedler, *A Theory of Leadership Effectiveness* (New York: McGraw-Hill, 1967).

37. J. Helyar, "Why Is This Man Smiling?" *Fortune*, 18 October 2004, 130.

38. Ibid.

39. L. S. Csoka & F. E. Fiedler, "The Effect of Military Leadership Training: A Test of the Contingency Model," *Organizational Behavior & Human Performance* 8 (1972): 395–407.

40. House & Mitchell, "Path-Goal Theory of Leadership."

41. B. Andelman, "Keep 'em Happy," *Corporate Meetings & Incentives*, 1 May 2003, 24.

42. House & Mitchell, "Path-Goal Theory of Leadership."

43. G. Edmondson, K. Kerwin, & K. Anhalt, "Hot Audi: It's Finally Blasting into the Luxury-Car Pack. Can It Stay There?" *BusinessWeek*, 14 March 2005, 24.

44. B. M. Fisher & J. E. Edwards, "Consideration and Initiating Structure and Their Relationships with Leader Effectiveness: A Meta-Analysis," *Proceedings of the Academy of Management*, August 1988, 201–205.

45. M. Gimein, "Wal-Mart's Founder Made a Pact with Employees: He Would Be Fair to Them, and They Would Work Hard for Him. It Was a Good Deal, but Can It Survive in the 24-Hour Service Economy?" *Fortune*, 18 March 2002, 120.

46. K. Edwards, "Utilizing Employee Innovation at Kwik-Fit Financial Services," *Strategic HR Review*, November–December 2004, 12–13.

47. M. Copeland, K. Crawford, J. Davis, S. Hamner, C. Hawn, R. Howe, P. Kaihla, M. Maier, O. Malik, D. McDonald, C. Null, E. Schonfeld, O. Thomas, & G. Zachary, "My Golden Rule," *Business 2.0*, 1 December 2005, 108.

48. J. C. Wofford & L. Z. Liska, "Path-Goal Theories of Leadership: A Meta-Analysis," *Journal of Management* 19 (1993): 857–876.

49. House & Aditya, "The Social Scientific Study of Leadership."

50. P. Hersey & K. Blanchard, *Management of Organizational Behavior: Leading Human Resources*, 8th ed. (Escondido, CA: Center for Leadership Studies, 2001).

51. W. Blank, J. R. Weitzel, & S. G. Green, "A Test of the Situational Leadership Theory," *Personnel Psychology* 43, no. 3 (1990): 579–597; W. R. Norris & R. P. Vecchio, "Situational Leadership Theory: A Replication," *Group & Organization Management* 17, no. 3 (1992): 331–342.

52. Ibid.

53. V. H. Vroom & A. G. Jago, *The New Leadership: Managing Participation in Organizations* (Englewood Cliffs, NJ: Prentice Hall, 1988).

54. C. Fishman, "How Teamwork Took Flight: This Team Built a Commercial Engine—and Self-Managing GE Plant—from Scratch," *Fast Company*, 1 October 1999, 188.

55. Ibid.

56. Ibid.

57. G. A. Yukl, *Leadership in Organizations*, 3d ed. (Englewood Cliffs, NJ: Prentice Hall, 1995).

58. B. M. Bass, *Bass & Stogdill's Handbook of Leadership: Theory, Research, and Managerial Applications* (New York: Free Press, 1990).

59. R. D. Ireland & M. A. Hitt, "Achieving and Maintaining Strategic Competitiveness in the 21st Century: The Role of Strategic Leadership," *Academy of Management Executive* 13, no. 1 (1999): 43–57.

60. K. Kranhold, "The Immelt Era, Five Years Old, Transforms GE," *Wall Street Journal*, 11 September 2006, B1.

61. G. Colvin, "Lafley and Immelt: Q & A," *Fortune*, 11 December 2006, 75.

62. P. Thoms & D. B. Greenberger, "Training Business Leaders to Create Positive Organizational Visions of the Future: Is It Successful?" *Academy of Management Journal* [Best Papers & Proceedings], 1995, 212–216.

63. M. Weber, *The Theory of Social and Economic Organizations*, trans. R. A. Henderson & T. Parsons (New York: Free Press, 1947).

64. C. Terhune, C. Mollenkamp, & A. Carrns, "Inside Alleged Fraud at HealthSouth, A 'Family' Plot—CEO Scrushy Cultivated Loyalties as Staffers Fixed Books, Played in His Band," *Wall Street Journal*, 3 April 2003, A1.

65. Ibid.

66. D. A. Waldman & F. J. Yammarino, "CEO Charismatic Leadership: Levels-of-Management and Levels-of-Analysis Effects," *Academy of Management Review* 24, no. 2 (1999): 266–285.

67. K. B. Lowe, K. G. Kroeck, & N. Sivasubramaniam, "Effectiveness Correlates of Transformational and Transactional Leadership: A Meta-Analytic Review of the MLQ Literature," *Leadership Quarterly* 7 (1996): 385–425.

68. J. M. Howell & B. J. Avolio, "The Ethics of Charismatic Leadership: Submission or Liberation?" Academy of *Management Executive* 6, no. 2 (1992): 43–54.

69. G. Colvin, "Lafley and Immelt: Q & A."

70. A. Deutschman, "Is Your Boss a Psychopath?" *Fast Company*, July 2005, 44.

71. P. Sellers, "What Exactly Is Charisma?" *Fortune*, 15 January 1996, 68.

72. Deutschman, "Is Your Boss a Psychopath?"

73. Howell & Avolio, "The Ethics of Charismatic Leadership."

74. Ibid.

75. J. M. Burns, *Leadership* (New York: Harper & Row, 1978); B. M. Bass, "From Transactional to Transformational Leadership: Learning to Share the Vision," *Organizational Dynamics* 18 (1990): 19–36.

76. Bass, "From Transactional to Transformational Leadership."

77. B. M. Bass, *A New Paradigm of Leadership: An Inquiry into Transformational Leadership* (Alexandra, VA: U.S. Army Research Institute for the Behavioral and Social Sciences, 1996).

78. M. Adams, "Boeing Bounces Back against Odds," *USA Today*, 11 January 2007, B1.

79. "Read the Medtronic Mission Statement to Learn about the Company Goals at Medtronic.com," Medtronic, http://www.medtronic.com/corporate/mission.html, 12 June 2003.

80. D. Whitford, "A Human Place to Work: A Company Can't Be Everything to All People, but It Can Try. Here's the Tale of Medtronic's Effort," *Fortune*, 8 January 2001, 108.

81. Sellers, "The New Breed."

82. Morris, "The Accidental CEO."

83. Byrne, "How to Lead Now."

84. Bass, "From Transactional to Transformational Leadership."

85. F. E. Fiedler and M. M. Chemers, *Improving Leadership Effectiveness: The Leader Match Concept* (New York: Wiley, 1984).

86. T. Rivas, "Atypical Workdays Becoming Routine," *Wall Street Journal*, 4 April 2006, A19; S. Shellenbarger, "When Working at Home Doesn't Work: How Companies Comfort Telecommuters," *Wall Street Journal*, 24 August 2006, B1; "Real Estate Exchange," U.S. Department of Transportation, Federal Highway Administration, http://knowledge.fhwa.dot. gov/cops/rex.nsf/discussion Display?Open&id=EF35631CF1E86D918525709200504C4E&Group=Relocation%20Forum&tab=DISCUSSION; M.-Y. Lee, "Don't Fall into the Trap of Paying Extra Moving Costs," BuyerZone.com, 15 May 2001, www.buyerzone.com/features/savvy_shopper/ss051501.html.

87. J. Jewell, "New Times, New Leaders: Firing of Millard Fuller the Result of Longstanding Tensions," *Christianity Today*, April 2005, 24; L. D. Maloney, "No House of Cards: Leadership Changes Stirred a Cauldron of Emotions at Habitat for Humanity, but the Foundation of the World's Premier 'Sweat Equity' Housing Group Remains Strong," *Builder*, April 2005, 120; J. F. Krentz, "Davidson Man to Lead Habitat for Humanity," *Charlotte Observer*, 5 February 2005; "New CEO Takes Helm at Habitat for Humanity International; Millard Fuller to Continue as Founder President of House-Building Ministry," *PR Newswire*, 11 October 2004, http://www.prnewswire.com; J. Pierce, "Habitat Founder and Board Disagree on His Retirement Date," *Christian Century*, 5 October 2004, 15.

88. J. Zaslow, "Mistakes Were Made: What to Take Away from the High-Profile Blunders of 2006," *Wall Street Journal*, 26 December 2006, D1; J. Brodkin, "Corporate Apologies Don't Mean Much: Data Breaches Force Company Executives to Apologize, But a Bad Apology Can Make Things Worse," *Network World*, 14 March 2007, 1; L. Smith, "How Your Corporate Clients Can and Sometimes Must Apologize for Their Mistakes," *Of Counsel*, October 2005, 11–13.

89. J. Zaslow, "Mistakes Were Made."

Chapter 15

1. K. Belson & M. Richtel, "Sony Shifts Duties of the Leader of the PlayStation Unit," *New York Times*, 1 December 2006, Section 3, 1; P. Dvorak, "Out of Tune: At Sony, Rivalries Were Encouraged," *Wall Street Journal*, 29 June 2005, A1; P. Dvorak, "Culture Clash Crimps Sony CEO," *Wall Street Journal*, 24 September 2005, A6; P. Dvorak, "Stringer Faces First Big Test as Sony's Chief," *Wall Street Journal*, 19 September 2005, B1; M. Gunther & P. Lewis, "The Welshman, the Walkman, and the Salary Men," *Fortune*, 12 June 2006, 70; K. Hall, "Sony Walkman Finally Gets the Picture," *BusinessWeek Online*, 9 March 2007; Y. Kane & P. Dvorak, "Howard Stringer, Japanese CEO," *Wall Street Journal*, 3 March 2007, A1; Y. Kane & A. Morse, "Sony's Videogame Unit Names U.S. Marketing Star as President," *Wall Street Journal*, 1 December 2006, B7; L. Lewis,

"Sony Gains Ground on Margins," *Financial Times*, 30 January 2007, http://www.ft.com; W. Mossberg, "Boss Talk: Shaking up Sony," *Wall Street Journal*, 6 June 2006, B1; B. Schlender, "Inside the Shakeup at Sony," *Fortune*, 4 April 2005, 94; R. Siklos & M. Fackler, "Sony's Road Warrior," *New York Times*, 28 May 2006, Section 3, 1.

2. E. E. Lawler III, L. W. Porter, & A. Tannenbaum, "Manager's Attitudes toward Interaction Episodes," *Journal of Applied Psychology* 52 (1968): 423–439; H. Mintzberg, *The Nature of Managerial Work* (New York: Harper & Row, 1973).
3. J. D. Maes, T. G. Weldy, & M. L. Icenogle, "A Managerial Perspective: Oral Communication Competency Is Most Important for Business Students in the Workplace," *Journal of Business Communication* 34 (1997): 67–80.
4. R. Lepsinger & A. D. Lucia, *The Art and Science of 360 Degree Feedback* (San Francisco: Pfeiffer, 1997).
5. I. M. Botero, "Good Communication Skills Needed Today," *Business Journal: Serving Phoenix and the Valley of the Sun*, 21 October 1996.
6. J. Sandberg, "Bosses Often Sugarcoat Their Worst News, but Staffers Don't Bite," *Wall Street Journal*, 21 April 2004, B1.
7. E. E. Jones & K. E. Davis, "From Acts to Dispositions: The Attribution Process in Person Perception," in *Advances in Experimental and Social Psychology*, vol. 2, ed. L. Berkowitz (New York: Academic Press, 1965), 219–266; R. G. Lord & J. E. Smith, "Theoretical, Information-Processing, and Situational Factors Affecting Attribution Theory Models of Organizational Behavior," *Academy of Management Review* 8 (1983): 50–60.
8. J. Zadney & H. B. Gerard, "Attributed Intentions and Informational Selectivity," *Journal of Experimental Social Psychology* 10 (1974): 34–52.
9. A. Taylor, "GM Gets Its Act Together. Finally," *Fortune*, 5 April 2004, 136.
10. M. Porter, J. Lorsch, & N. Nohria, "Seven Surprises for New CEOs," *Harvard Business Review* (October 2004): 62.
11. H. H. Kelly, *Attribution in Social Interaction* (Morristown, NJ: General Learning Press, 1971).
12. J. M. Burger, "Motivational Biases in the Attribution of Responsibility for an Accident: A Meta-Analysis of the Defensive-Attribution Hypothesis," *Psychological Bulletin* 90 (1981): 496–512.
13. D. A. Hofmann & A. Stetzer, "The Role of Safety Climate and Communication in Accident Interpretation: Implications for Learning from Negative Events," *Academy of Management Journal* 41, no. 6 (1998): 644–657.
14. C. Perrow, *Normal Accidents: Living with High-Risk Technologies* (New York: Basic Books, 1984).
15. A. G. Miller & T. Lawson, "The Effect of an Informational Opinion on the Fundamental Attribution Error," *Journal of Personality & Social Psychology* 47 (1989): 873–896; J. M. Burger, "Changes in Attribution Errors over Time: The Ephemeral Fundamental Attribution Error," *Social Cognition* 9 (1991): 182–193.
16. D. Sacks, "Scenes from the Culture Clash," *Fast Company*, 1 January 2006, 72.
17. F. Heider, *The Psychology of Interpersonal Relations* (New York: Wiley, 1958); D. T. Miller & M. Ross, "Self-Serving Biases in Attribution of Causality: Fact or Fiction?" *Psychological Bulletin* 82 (1975): 213–225.
18. J. R. Larson, Jr., "The Dynamic Interplay between Employees' Feedback-Seeking Strategies and Supervisors' Delivery of Performance Feedback," *Academy of Management Review* 14, no. 3 (1989): 408–422.
19. Porter, Lorsch, & Nohria, "Seven Surprises for New CEOs."
20. Ibid.
21. Ibid.
22. C. Hymowitz, "Mind Your Language: To Do Business Today, Consider Delayering," *Wall Street Journal*, 27 March 2006, B1.
23. M. Reddy, "The Conduit Metaphor—A Case of Frame Conflict in Our Language about Our Language," in *Metaphor and Thought*, ed. A. Ortony (Cambridge: Cambridge University Press, 1979), 284–324.
24. G. L. Kreps, *Organizational Communication: Theory and Practice* (New York: Longman, 1990).
25. Ibid.
26. D. Roth, "How to Cut Pay, Lay Off 8,000 People, and Still Have Workers Who Love You," *Fortune*, 4 February 2002, 62.
27. K. Voight, "Office Intelligence," *Asian Wall Street Journal*, 21 January 2005, P1.
28. L. Landro, "The Informed Patient: Hospitals Combat Errors at the 'Hand-Off,'" *Wall Street Journal*, 28 June 2006, D1.
29. Kreps, *Organizational Communication: Theory and Practice.*
30. J. Sandberg, "Ruthless Rumors and the Managers Who Enable Them," *Wall Street Journal*, 29 October 2003, B1.
31. K. Moran, "Web Used to Answer Rumors: UT Medical Staff Gets Truth Quickly," *Houston Chronicle*, 18 April 1999, 35.
32. W. Davis & J. R. O'Connor, "Serial Transmission of Information: A Study of the Grapevine," *Journal of Applied Communication Research* 5 (1977): 61–72.
33. Sandberg, "Ruthless Rumors and the Managers Who Enable Them."
34. K. Voight, "Office Intelligence," *Asian Wall Street Journal*, 21 January 2005, P1.
35. G. Hoover, "Maintaining Employee Engagement when Communicating Difficult Issues," *Communication World*, 1 November 2005, 25.
36. Davis & O'Connor, "Serial Transmission of Information: A Study of the Grapevine"; Hymowitz, "Managing: Spread the Word, Gossip Is Good."
37. D. Kirkpatrick & D. Roth, "Why There's No Escaping the Blog," *Fortune (Europe)*, 24 January 2005, 64.
38. W. C. Redding, *Communication within the Organization: An Interpretive View of Theory and Research* (New York: Industrial Communication Council, 1972).
39. D. T. Hall, K. L. Otazo, & G. P. Hollenbeck, "Behind Closed Doors: What Really Happens in Executive Coaching," *Organizational Dynamics* 27, no. 3 (1999): 39–53.
40. J. Kelly, "Blowing the Whistle on the Boss," *PR Newswire*, 15 November 2004, http://www.prnewswire.com.
41. R. McGarvey, "Lords of Discipline," *Entrepreneur Magazine*, 1 January 2000.
42. S. Needleman, "Career Journal: Tips for Managers on Handling Their Workers' Personal Problems," *Wall Street Journal*, 25 April 2006, B9.
43. C. Hirschman, "Firm Ground: EAP Training for HR and Managers Improves Supervisor-Employee Communication

and Helps Organizations Avoid Legal Quagmires," *Employee Benefit News*, 13 June 2005, http://www.benefitnews.com.

44. A. Mehrabian, "Communication without Words," *Psychology Today* 3 (1968): 53; A. Mehrabian, *Silent Messages* (Belmont, CA: Wadsworth, 1971); R. Harrison, *Beyond Words: An Introduction to Nonverbal Communication* (Upper Saddle River, NJ: Prentice Hall, 1974); A. Mehrabian, *Non-Verbal Communication* (Chicago: Aldine, 1972).

45. M. L. Knapp, *Nonverbal Communication in Human Interaction*, 2d ed. (New York: Holt, Rinehart & Winston, 1978).

46. H. M. Rosenfeld, "Instrumental Affiliative Functions of Facial and Gestural Expressions," *Journal of Personality & Social Psychology* 24 (1966): 65–72; P. Ekman, "Differential Communication of Affect by Head and Body Cues," *Journal of Personality & Social Psychology* 23 (1965): 726–735; A. Mehrabian, "Significance of Posture and Position in the Communication of Attitude and Status Relationships," *Psychological Bulletin* 71 (1969): 359–372.

47. J. Gottman & R. Levenson, "The Timing of Divorce: Predicting When a Couple Will Divorce over a 14-Year Period," *Journal of Marriage & the Family* 62 (August 2000): 737–745; J. Gottman, R. Levenson, & E. Woodin, "Facial Expressions during Marital Conflict," *Journal of Family Communication* 1, issue 1 (2001): 37–57.

48. T. Aeppel, "Career Journal: Nicknamed 'Nag,' She's Just Doing Her Job," *Wall Street Journal*, 14 May 2002, B1.

49. J. Saranow, "A Personal Trainer for Your Voice," *Wall Street Journal*, 3 February 2004, D1.

50. A. Joyce, "Confidentiality as a Valued Benefit; Loose Lips Can Defeat the Purpose of an Employee Assistance Program," *Washington Post*, 11 May 2003, F05.

51. C. A. Bartlett & S. Ghoshal, "Changing the Role of Top Management: Beyond Systems to People," *Harvard Business Review*, May–June 1995, 132–142.

52. E. Spragins, "Sending the Wrong Message," *Fortune Small Business*, 1 July 2003, 32.

53. J. Fry, "When Talk Isn't Cheap: Is Emailing Colleagues Who Sit Feet Away a Sign of Office Dysfunction, or a Wise Move?" *Wall Street Journal*, 28 November 2005, http://online.wsj.com.

54. T. Andrews, "E-Mail Empowers, Voice-Mail Enslaves," *PC Week*, 10 April 1995, E11.

55. "The Joys of Voice Mail," *Inc.*, November 1995, 102.

56. E. Wong, "A Stinging Office Memo Boomerangs; Chief Executive Is Criticized after Upbraiding Workers by E-Mail," *New York Times*, 5 April 2001, C1.

57. Ibid.

58. Ibid.

59. Ibid.

60. R. G. Nichols, "Do We Know How to Listen? Practical Helps in a Modern Age," in *Communication Concepts and Processes*, ed. J. DeVitor (Englewood Cliffs, NJ: Prentice Hall, 1971); P. V. Lewis, *Organizational Communication: The Essence of Effective Management* (Columbus, OH: Grid Publishing Company, 1975).

61. E. Atwater, *I Hear You*, rev. ed. (New York: Walker, 1992).

62. R. Adler & N. Towne, *Looking Out/Looking In* (San Francisco: Rinehart, 1975).

63. K. Brooker & J. Schlosser, "The Un-CEO; A. G. Lafley Doesn't Overpromise. He Doesn't Believe in the Vision Thing. All He's Done Is Turn Around P&G in 27 Months," *Fortune*, 16 September 2002, 88.

64. P. LaBaree, "Feargal Quinn: Ireland's 'Pope of Customer Service' Dominates His Market—and Continues to Beat Bigger and Better-Financed Rivals—with a Leadership Philosophy That Is at Once Folksy and Radical," *Fast Company*, 1 November 2001, 88.

65. B. D. Seyber, R. N. Bostrom, & J. H. Seibert, "Listening, Communication Abilities, and Success at Work," *Journal of Business Communication* 26 (1989): 293–303.

66. Atwater, *I Hear You*.

67. C. Edwards, "Death of A Pushy Salesman," *BusinessWeek*, 3 July 2006, 108.

68. P. Sellers, A. Diba, & E. Florian, "Get over Yourself—Your Ego Is out of Control. You're Screwing up Your Career," *Fortune*, 30 April 2001, 76.

69. H. H. Meyer, "A Solution to the Performance Appraisal Feedback Enigma," *Academy of Management Executive* 5, no. 1 (1991): 68–76.

70. M. Heffernan, "The Wrong Stuff." *Fast Company*, 12 April 2004, http://www.fastcompany.com/resources/columnists/mh/041204.html.

71. T. D. Schellhardt, "Annual Agony: It's Time to Evaluate Your Work, and All Involved Are Groaning," *Wall Street Journal*, 19 November 1996, A1.

72. C. Hymowitz, "How to Tell Employees All the Things They Don't Want to Hear," *Wall Street Journal*, 22 August 2000, B1.

73. L. Anguish, N. Cossack, & A. Maingault, "Payroll Cuts, Personal Hygiene, Extra Leave," *HR Magazine*, 1 June 2003, 41.

74. G. Gitelson, J. Bing, & L. Laroche, "How the Cultural Trap Deepens in Cross-Border Deals," *Dealmakers*, 1 December 2001.

75. From N. J. Adler, *From Boston to Beijing: Managing with a World View* (Cincinnati, OH: South-Western, 2002), based on A. Laurent, "The Cultural Diversity of Western Conceptions of Management," in *International Studies of Management and Organization* 13, no. 1–2 (Spring–Summer 1983): 75–96.

76. J. S. Black & M. Mendenhall, "Cross-Cultural Training Effectiveness: A Review and Theoretical Framework for Future Research," *Academy of Management Review* 15 (1990): 113–136.

77. C. Timberlake, "The Ladder: Even Inside Europe, Cultures Can Collide in the Workplace," *Wall Street Journal Europe*, 16 October 2001, 25.

78. P. Garfinkel, "On Keeping Your Foot Safely out of Your Mouth," *New York Times*, 13 July 2004, 8.

79. F. Trompenaars, *Riding the Waves of Culture: Understanding Diversity in Global Business* (London: Economist Books, 1994).

80. N. Forster, "Expatriates and the Impact of Cross-Cultural Training," *Human Resource Management* 10 (2000): 63–78.

81. Adler, *From Boston to Beijing: Managing with a World View*.

82. Ibid.

83. Ibid.

84. Ibid.

85. Ibid.

86. R. Mead, *Cross-Cultural Management* (New York: Wiley, 1990).

87 Ibid.

88. Edward T. Hall, *The Dance of Life* (New York: Doubleday, 1983).

89. Trompenaars, *Riding the Waves of Culture.*

90. Adler, *From Boston to Beijing: Managing with a World View.*

91. E. T. Hall & M. R. Hall, *Understanding Cultural Differences* (Yarmouth, ME: Intercultural Press, 1990).

92. E. T. Hall & W. F. Whyte, "Intercultural Communication: A Guide to Men of Action," *Human Organization* 19, no. 1 (1961): 5–12.

93. N. Libman, "French Tip: Just Walk the Walk and Talk the Talk, but Not Too Loud," *Chicago Tribune Online*, 17 March 1996.

94. C. Tkaczyk & M. Boyle, "Follow These Leaders," *Fortune*, 12 December 2005, 125.

95. C. Hymowitz, "Diebold's New Chief Shows How to Lead after a Sudden Rise," *Wall Street Journal*, 8 May 2006, B1.

96. J. Lublin, "The 'Open Inbox'—Some CEOs Stay Up Late Reading Employee Emails; Replies Can Be Brief: 'Thanks,'" *Wall Street Journal*, 10 October 2005, B1.

97. Ernst & Young Online: "Collaborate," Ernst & Young, http://www.ey.com/global.

98. A. Lashinsky, "Lights! Camera! Cue the CEO!" *Fortune*, 21 August 2006, 27.

99. C. Olofson, Global Reach, "Virtual Leadership," *Fast Company*, August 1999, http://www.fastcompany.com/online/27/minm.html.

100. M. Campanelli & N. Friedman, "Welcome to Voice Mail Hell: The New Technology Has Become a Barrier between Salespeople and Customers," *Sales & Marketing Management* 147 (May 1995): 98–101.

101. D. Harbrecht, "CEO Q&A: Baxter's Harry Kraemer: 'I Don't Golf,'" *BusinessWeek Online*, 28 March 2003, http://www.businessweek.com/bwdaily/dnflash/mar2002/nf20020328_0720.htm.

102. E. Florian & W. Henderson, "Class of '01: Ellen Florian Spotlights Four Retirees—Their Legacies, Their Plans, and What They've Learned That Can Help You Work Better," *Fortune*, 13 August 2001, 185.

103. E. W. Morrison, "Organizational Silence: A Barrier to Change and Development in a Pluralistic World," *Academy of Management Review* 25 (2000): 706–725.

104. L. Landro, "The Informed Patient: Bringing Surgeons Down to Earth—New Programs Aim to Curb Fear That Prevents Nurses from Flagging Problems," *Wall Street Journal*, November 16, 2005, D1.

105. K. Maher, "Global Companies Face Reality of Instituting Ethics Programs," *Wall Street Journal*, 9 November 2004, B8.

106. Ibid.

107. HR, "Anytime, Anywhere," *Human Resources*, 16 May 2006, http://www.humanresourcesmagazine.com.au/articles/83/0C03FC83.asp?Type=60&Category=875.

108. C. Salter, "And Now the Hard Part: Can JetBlue Make the Leap from Popular (and profitable) Niche Airline to Major Player—without Losing Its Soul?" *Fast Company*, 1 May 2004, 67.

109. Ibid.

110. J. Bevan, "Leadership, Clarity, and a Very Thick Skin," *Spectator*, 14 October 2006, 32.

111. Kirkpatrick & Roth, "Why There's No Escaping the Blog."

112. S. Hargrave, "The Blog Busters," *Guardian*, 9 August 2004, http://www.guardian.co.uk.

113. W. Ross, Jr., "What Every Human Resource Manager Should Know about Web Logs," *SAM Advanced Management Journal*, 1 July 2005, 4.

114. J. Neff, "P&G Inks Deal with PlanetFeedback for Pampers and Tide," *Advertising Age*, 15 July 2002, 11.

115. C. G. Pearce, I. W. Johnson, & R. T. Barker, "Assessment of the Listening Styles Inventory: Progress in Establishing Reliability and Validity," *Journal of Business and Technical Communication* 17, no. 1 (2003): 84–113.

116. D. Kirkpatrick, "It's Hard to Manage if You Don't Blog," *Fortune*, 24 October, 2004, 46; L. Tiffany, "Easy Read: Build Business Relationships with a Company Blog," *Entrepreneur*, December 2003, 25.

Chapter 16

1. K. Dell, "Why the Gap Keeps Getting Crushed," *Time*, 5 February 2007, 50–51; A. Merrick, "Gap Will Fashion Its Future without Pressler," *Wall Street Journal*, 23 January 2007, B1; "Fashion Victim," *Economist*, 20 January 2007, 74; S. Ryst, "Sales Gap at the Gap," *BusinessWeek Online*, 5 January 2007, 6; J. Boorstin, "Fashion Victim," *Fortune*, 17 April 2006, 160–166; A Merrick & J. Lublin, "Gap Needs a CEO and Many Qualify; Will Any Apply?" *Wall Street Journal*, 24 January 2007, B1; Gap home page, http://www.gap.com.

2. R. Leifer & P. K. Mills, "An Information Processing Approach for Deciding upon Control Strategies and Reducing Control Loss in Emerging Organizations," *Journal of Management* 22 (1996): 113–137.

3. D. Starkman, "Making 'Sick' Malls Better—Specialists Advise Landlords on Redesigns, Ejecting Stores; Step One: Fix the Food," *Wall Street Journal*, 21 January 2004, B1.

4. R. Rundle & P. Davies, "Hospitals Start to Seek Payment Upfront," *Wall Street Journal*, 2 June 2004, D1.

5. W. Mossberg & K. Swisher, "Using a Computer to Clean Up Spilled Milk," *Wall Street Journal*, 24 May 2005, D5.

6. J. Welsh, "Drive Buys—Cadillac STS. Caddy Shock—U.S. Maker Matches Europeans with a Sharp, Sporty Sedan; Our Surprise Drive of the Year," *Wall Street Journal*, 31 December 2004, W1.

7. J. LaReau, "Absent New Cars, Cadillac Hopes for Modest Gain," *Automotive News*, 28 August 2006, 42; J. Henry, "Luxury Imports Roll Out Dec. Deals," *Automotive News*, 18 December 2006, 6,41.

8. B. Whitaker, "Yes, There Is a Job That Pays You to Shop," *New York Times*, 13 March 2005, 8.

9. J. Caplan, "Secret Travelers: That Fussy Tourist on Your Next Trip May Be Working for the Resort," *Time*, 6 June 2005, W14.

10. D. Bradbury, "Beta Test Numbers Skyrocket," *Computing Canada*, 3 March 2006, 1, 8.

11. M. Foley, "Blame Vista Delay on Quality?" *eWeek*, 3 April 2006, 33.

12. N. Wiener, *Cybernetics; Or Control and Communication in the Animal and the Machine* (New York: Wiley, 1948).

13. P. Sellers, J. Boorstin, J. Levinstein, "The Best Investor of His Generation (So What Is He Doing with Sears?)," *Fortune*, 20 February 2006, 90–104.

14. R. Berner, "Fashion Emergency at Wal-Mart," *BusinessWeek*, 31 July 2006, 67.

15. J. Dalrymple & M. Honan, "Nike to Add iPod Integration," *MacWorld*, August 2006, 22–23.

16. R. Guth, "The To-Do List: Make Software More Reliable," *Wall Street Journal*, 17 November 2003, R4.

17. Leifer & Mills, "An Information Processing Approach for Deciding upon Control Strategies and Reducing Control Loss in Emerging Organizations."

18. B. Warner, "Deluged Telecoms Boss Bans Staff E-Mails," Yahoo News (Reuters), 19 September 2003, http://story.news.yahoo.com.

19. Ibid.

20. J. Welsh, "Why Your Car Has Lousy Gas Mileage," *Wall Street Journal*, 31 May 2007, D1; M. Spector, "Car Dealers to Lobby on Fuel Economy," *Wall Street Journal*, 12 July 2007, wsj.com; C. Conkey & M. Spector, "Behind the Wheel for Auto Makers," *Wall Street Journal*, 31 July 2007, A4.

21. R. Crockett & J. McGregor, "Six Sigma Still Pays Off at Motorola," *BusinessWeek*, 4 December 2006, 50.

22. M. Higgins, "The Discounts You Aren't Meant to Have," *Wall Street Journal*, 3 December 2003, D1.

23. S. Greenhouse, "Workers Assail Night Lock-Ins by Wal-Mart," *New York Times*, 18 January 2004, 1.

24. Ibid.

25. Ibid.

26. Ibid.

27. S. Shellenbarger, "Is the Awful Behavior of Some Bad Bosses Rooted in Their Past?" *Wall Street Journal*, 17 May 2000, B1.

28. S. Shellenbarger, "Workers, Emboldened by Tight Job Market, Take on Their Bosses," *Wall Street Journal*, 17 May 2000, B1.

29. M. Weber, *The Protestant Ethic and the Spirit of Capitalism* (New York: Scribner's, 1958).

30. L. Criner, "Politicians Come and Go, Bureaucracies Stay and Grow," *Washington Times*, 11 March 1996, 33.

31. "Kwik Trip Fires Three over Online Postings," *Convenience Store News*, 15 January 2007, 10.

32. C. Forelle, "On the Road Again, but Now the Boss Is Sitting beside You," *Wall Street Journal*, 14 May 2004, A1.

33. P. Jonsson, "That a Spreadsheet on Your Screen, or Solitaire?" *Seattle Times*, 12 June 2005, F3.

34. M. Boyle, "Expensing It: Guilty As Charged—When Times Are Tough, Employees Become Even More Devoted to Mastering the Art of Self-Perking," *Fortune*, 9 July 2001, 179; R. Grugal, "Be Honest and Dependable: Integrity—The Must-Have," *Investor's Business Daily*, 11 April 2003, A03.

35. J. Lublin, "CEO Compensation Survey (A Special Report)—Goodbye to Pay for No Performance," *Wall Street Journal*, 11 April 2005, R1.

36. J. Lublin, "CEO Bonuses Rose 46.4% at 100 Big Firms in 2004," *Wall Street Journal*, 25 February 2005, A1.

37. S. Williford, "Nordstrom Sets the Standard for Customer Service," *Memphis Business Journal*, 1 July 1996, 21.

38. A. DeFelice, "A Century of Customer Love: Nordstrom Is the Gold Standard for Customer Service Excellence," *CRM Magazine*, 1 June 2005, 42.

39. R. T. Pascale, "Nordstrom: Respond to Unreasonable Customer Requests!" *Planning Review* 2 (May–June 1994): 17.

40. Ibid.

41. Ibid.

42. J. R. Barker, "Tightening the Iron Cage: Concertive Control in Self-Managing Teams," *Administrative Science Quarterly* 38 (1993): 408–437.

43. N, Byrnes, "The Art of Motivation," *BusinessWeek*, 1 May 2006, 56–62.

44. Ibid.

45. J. R. Barker, "Tightening the Iron Cage."

46. C. Manz & H. Sims, "Leading Workers to Lead Themselves: The External Leadership of Self-Managed Work Teams," *Administrative Science Quarterly* 32 (1987): 106–128.

47. J. Slocum & H. A. Sims, "Typology for Integrating Technology, Organization and Job Design," *Human Relations* 33 (1980): 193–212.

48. C. C. Manz & H. P. Sims, Jr., "Self-Management as a Substitute for Leadership: A Social Learning Perspective," *Academy of Management Review* 5 (1980): 361–367.

49. C. Manz & C. Neck, *Mastering Self-Leadership*, 3rd ed. (Upper Saddle River, NJ: Pearson, Prentice Hall, 2004).

50. J. Lublin, "More Big Companies End Perks; Critics Say Cutbacks Sap Morale," *Wall Street Journal*, 4 January 2001, B1.

51. R. S. Kaplan & D. P. Norton, "Using the Balanced Scorecard as a Strategic Management System," *Harvard Business Review*, January–February 1996, 75–85; R. S. Kaplan & D. P. Norton, "The Balanced Scorecard: Measures That Drive Performance," *Harvard Business Review*, January–February 1992, 71–79.

52. J. Meliones, "Saving Money, Saving Lives," *Harvard Business Review*, November–December 2000, 57–65.

53. S. L. Fawcett, "Fear of Accounts: Improving Managers' Competence and Confidence through Simulation Exercises," *Journal of European Industrial Training*, February 1996, 17.

54. J. Cole, "New Boeing CFO's Assignment: Signal a Turnaround Quickly," *Wall Street Journal*, 26 January 1999, B1.

55. M. H. Stocks & A. Harrell, "The Impact of an Increase in Accounting Information Level on the Judgment Quality of Individuals and Groups," *Accounting, Organizations & Society*, October–November 1995, 685–700.

56. B. Morris, "Roberto Goizueta and Jack Welch: The Wealth Builders," *Fortune*, 11 December 1995, 80–94.

57. G. Colvin, "America's Best & Worst Wealth Creators: The Real Champions Aren't Always Who You Think. Here's an Eye-Opening Look at Which Companies Produce and Destroy the Most Money for Investors—Plus a New Tool for Spotting Future Winners," *Fortune*, 18 December 2000, 207.

58. B. Birchard, "Metrics for the Masses," *CFO*, 1 May 1999, http://www.cfo.com/article.cfm/2989821?f=search.

59. E. Varon, "Implementation Is Not for the Meek," *CIO*, 15 November 2002, http://www.cio.com/article/31510.

60. "Welcome Complaints," Office of Consumer and Business Affairs, Government of South Australia, http://www.ocba.sa.gov.au/businessadvice/customers/complaints.html#Welcome_complaints.

61. C. Bielaszka-DuVernay, "How to Get the Bad News You Need," *Harvard Management Update*, January 2007, 3–5.

62. C. B. Furlong, "12 Rules for Customer Retention," *Bank Marketing* 5 (January 1993): 14.

63. M. Raphel, "Vanished Customers Are Valuable Customers," *Art Business News*, June 2002, 46.

64. F. F. Reichheld, "Lead for Loyalty," *Harvard Business Review* 79 (July–August 2001): 76.

65. C. A. Reeves & D. A. Bednar, "Defining Quality: Alternatives and Implications," *Academy of Management Review* 19 (1994): 419–445.

66. "The 2002 Readers' Choice Awards: Top Travel Services, Condé Nast Traveler," Concierge.com, http://www.concierge.com.

67. "Singapore Airlines Presents Our Awards & Accolades," Singapore Airlines, http://www.singaporeair.com/saa/en_UK/content/company_info/news/achievements.jsp

68. S. Holmes, "Creature Comforts at 30,000 Feet," *BusinessWeek*, 18 December 2006, 138.

69. "ATW Daily News," *ATW*, 8 March 2005, http://www.atwonline.com/news/story.html?storyID=186.

70. K. Nirmalya, " Strategies to Fight Low-Cost Rivals," *Harvard Business Review* 84 (December 2006): 104–112.

71. D. R. May & B. L. Flannery, "Cutting Waste with Employee Involvement Teams," *Business Horizons*, September–October 1995, 28–38.

72. F. Etherington, "Leak in City's Water Valve Angers Kitchener Man," *Kitchener-Waterloo (Ontario) Record*, 1 August 2002, B4.

73. "Pollution Prevention Pays (3P)," 3M, http://www.3m.com.

74. B. Burlingham, "The Coolest Little Start-up in America," *Inc.*, July 2006, 78–85.

75. M. Baer, A. Bluestein, M. Chafkin, J. Gill, B. Gossage, R. McCarthy, K. Mieszkowski, K. Wehrum, & A. Wellner, "The Recyclers," *Inc.*, November 2006, 100–103.

76. M. Conlin & P. Raeburn, "Industrial Evolution: Bill McDonough Has the Wild Idea He Can Eliminate Waste. Surprise! Business Is Listening," *BusinessWeek*, 8 April 2002, 70.

77. Ibid.

78. J. Sprovieri, "Environmental Management Affects Manufacturing Bottom Line," *Assembly*, 1 July 2001, 24.

79. B. Byrne, "EU Says Makers Must Destroy Their Own Brand End-of-Life Cars," *Irish Times*, 23 April 2003, 52.

80. S. Power, "Take It Back: Where Do Cars Go When They Die? In Europe, They Have Little Choice," *Wall Street Journal*, 17 April 2006, R6.

81. J. Szekely & G. Trapaga, "From Villain to Hero (Materials Industry's Waste Recovery Efforts)," *Technology Review*, 1 January 1995, 30.

83. "The End of the Road: Schools and Computer Recycling," Intel, http://www.intel.com/education/recycling_computers/recycling.htm.

84. B. Rose, "Where Old Computers Go: While Too Many Are Dumped Illegally, Sr. Center Salvages Thousands," *Santa Rosa (CA) Press Democrat*, 18 June 2001, D1.

85. "Hardware Recycling Services—US," Hewlett-Packard, https://warp1.external.hp.com/recycle.

85. Reeves & Bednar, "Defining Quality."

86. M. Tuckey, N. Brewer, P. Williamson, "The Influence of Motives and Goal Orientation on Feedback Seeking," *Journal of Occupational and Organizational Psychology* 75, no. 2 (2002): 195.

87. E. Shein, "Multifunction Junction," *CFO*, May 2007, 31.

88. G. Meyer, "H & R Block Sees Jump in Revenue," *Kansas City Star*, 18 March 2005; F. P. Gabriel, Jr., "Block Still Falling Short in Investment Services—Despite Aggressive Campaign, It Can't Retain Advisers," *Investment News*, 6 December 2004, 1; D. Stires, "Taxing Times at H & R Block," *Fortune*, 21 March 2005, 181–184; G. Meyer, "H & R Block to Add 1,000 Outlets to Bolster 2005 Tax Office Traffic," *Kansas City Star*, 19 September 2004.

89. S. Caulkin, "If You Want to Stay a Winner, Learn from Your Mistakes," *The Observer*, 3 March 1996, 7; J. Hyatt, "Failure 101," *Inc.*, January 1989, 18; B. McMenamin, "The Virtue of Making Mistakes," *Forbes*, 9 May 1994, 192–194; P. Sellers, "So You Fail," *Fortune*, 1 May 1995, 48–66; P. Sellers, "Where Failures Get Fixed," *Fortune*, 1 May 1995, 64; B. Weiner, I. Freize, A. Kukla, L. Reed, S. Rest, & R.M. Rosenbaum, "Perceiving the Causes of Success and Failure," in *Attribution: Perceiving the Causes of Behavior*, eds. E. Jones, D. Kanouse, H. Kelley, R. Nesbitt, S. Valins, and B. Weiner (Morristown, NJ: General Learning Press, 1971), 45–61.

Chapter 17

1. University of Pittsburgh Medical Center, http://www.upmc.com. "UPMC Reports Higher First-Half Revenue, Significant Investments for the Future," *Business Wire*, 14 February 2007; C. Becker, "Recent Health IT Security Breaches Are Unlikely to Improve the Public's Perception about the Safety of Personal Data," *Modern Healthcare*, 20 February 2006, 6; J. Ericson, "Trinity Health Harnesses Technology to Improve Care and Efficiency across 30 Hospitals," Business Intelligence Review, 1 December 2006, 20; J. Fahy, "1.5 Million Hurt by Med Errors," *Pittsburgh Post-Gazette*, 21 July 2006, A1; A. Gilbert, "High-Tech Hospitals Better at Keeping Patients Alive?" *CNet*, 12 July 2005, http://www.cnet.com; M. McGee, "Chief of the Year—Can Technology Transform Health Care?"; C. Shropshire, "Stat UPMC Throws out the Paper in Favor of Computerized System for Buying Medical Supplies," *Pittsburgh Post-Gazette*, 27 December 2006, E1; B. Schuerenberg, "Taking an Aggressive Approach to Technology Development," *Health Data Management*, 1 March 2007, 12.

2. R. Lenzner, "The Reluctant Entrepreneur," *Forbes*, 11 September 1995, 162–166.

3. S. Munoz, "How to Get a New Couch Delivered On Time," *Wall Street Journal*, 6 April 2006, D1.

4. M. Totty, "Who's Going to Win the Living-Room Wars? The Battle to Control Home Entertainment Is Heating Up," *Wall Street Journal*, 25 April 2005, R1.

5. P. Grant & A. Schatz, "For Cable Giants, AT&T Deal Is One More Reason to Worry," *Wall Street Journal*, 7 March 2006, A1.

6. J. Angwin & A Pasztor, "Satellite TV Growth Is Losing Altitude As Cable Takes Off," *Wall Street Journal*, 5 August 2006, A1.

7. P. Grant, "Cable Firms Woo Business in Fight for Telecom Turf," *Wall Street Journal*, 17 January 2007, A1.

8. R. D. Buzzell & B. T. Gale, *The PIMS Principles: Linking Strategy to Performance* (New York: Free Press, 1987); M. Lambkin, "Order of Entry and Performance in New Markets," *Strategic Management Journal* 9 (1988): 127–140.

9. G. L. Urban, T. Carter, S. Gaskin, & Z. Mucha, "Market Share Rewards to Pioneering Brands: An Empirical Analysis and Strategic Implications," *Management Science* 32 (1986): 645–659.

10. M. Garry & S. Mulholland, "Master of Its Supply Chain: To Keep Its Inventory Costs

Low and Its Shelves Fully Stocked, Wal-Mart Has Always Invested Extensively—and First—in Technology for the Supply Chain," *Supermarket News*, 2 December 2002, 55.

11. N. Buckley & S. Voyle, "Can Wal-Mart Conquer Markets outside the US?" *Financial Times*, 8 January 2003.
12. Garry & Mulholland, "Master of Its Supply Chain."
13. S. Rupley, "A Moveable Mesh," *PC Magazine*, 21 September 2004, 94.
14. L. Tischler, "Tech for Toques," *Fast Company*, 1 May 2006, 68.
15. R. Pastore, "Cruise Control," *CIO*, 1 February 2003, 60–66.
16. Ibid.
17. B. Worthen, "The Little Company That Could," *CIO*, 1 February 2003, 68–72.
18. C. Quintanilla & L. Claman, "Acxiom Corporation—Chmn. & Pres. Interview," *CNBC/Dow Jones Business Video*, 21 November 2002.
19. M. Santosus, "Technology Recycling: Rising Costs of High-Tech Garbage," *CIO*, 15 April 2003, 36.
20. P. Tam, "The Chief Information Officer's Job Isn't What It Used to Be; Just Ask Hewlett-Packard's Randy Mott," *Wall Street Journal*, 16 April 2007, R5.
21. S. Mehta, "Behold the Server Farm!" *Fortune*, 7 August 2006, 68.
22. C. Koch, "Off the Charts," *CIO*, 1 February 2003, 46.
23. Ibid.
24. T. Knauss, "Niagara Mohawk Meters to Send Readings by Radio; $100 Million Project Will Eventually Eliminate Need for Door-to-Door Readers," *Post-Standard Syracuse*, 17 September 2002, A1.
25. S. Lubar, *Infoculture: The Smithsonian Book of Information Age Inventions* (Boston: Houghton Mifflin, 1993).
26. Ibid.
27. B. Worthen, "Bar Codes on Steroids," *CIO*, 15 December 2002, 53.
28. S. McCartney, "A New Way to Prevent Lost Luggage," *Wall Street Journal*, 27 February 2007, D1.
29. M. Stone, "Scanning for Business," *PC Magazine*, 10 May 2005, 117.
30. "Check It Out: Efficient, Accurate Claims," *Health Management Technology*, 1 April 2003.
31. N. Rubenking, "Hidden Messages," *PC Magazine*, 22 May 2001, 86.
32. J. Hibbard, "How Yahoo! Gave Itself a Face-Lift," *BusinessWeek*, 9 October 2006, 74.
33. A. Carter & D. Beucke, "A Good Neighbor Gets Better," *BusinessWeek*, 20 June 2005, 16.
34. Rubenking, "Hidden Messages."
35. G. Saitz, "Naked Truth—Data Miners, Who Taught Retailers to Stock Beer Near Diapers, Find Hidden Sales Trends, a Science That's Becoming Big Business," *Newark (NJ) Star-Ledger*, 1 August 2002, 041.
36. E. Nelson, "Retailing: Why Wal-Mart Sings, 'Yes, We Have Bananas!'" *Wall Street Journal*, 6 October 1998, B1.
37. M. Overfelt, "A Better Way to Sell Tickets," *Fortune Small Business*, 1 December 2006, 76.
38. B. Saporita, W. Boston, N. Gough, & R. Healy, "Can Wal-Mart Get Any Bigger? (Yes, a Lot Bigger ... Here's How)," *Time*, 19 January 2003, 38.
39. B. Gottesman & K. Karagiannis, "A False Sense of Security," *PC Magazine*, 22 February 2005, 72.
40. F. J. Derfler, Jr., "Secure Your Network," *PC Magazine*, 27 June 2000, 183–200.
41. "Authentication," Webopedia, http://www.webopedia.com/TERM/a/authentication.html.
42. "Authorization," Webopedia, http://www.webopedia.com/TERM/a/authorization.html.
43. L. Seltzer, "Password Crackers," *PC Magazine*, 12 February 2002, 68.
44. B. Grimes, "Biometric Security," *PC Magazine*, 22 April 2003, 74.
45. Ibid.
46. M. McQueen, "Laptop Lockdown," *Wall Street Journal*, 28 June 2006, D1.
47. K. Karagiannis, "Security Watch: Don't Make It Easy," *PC Magazine*, 8 April 2003, 72; M. Steinhart, "Password Dos and Don'ts," *PC Magazine*, 12 February 2002, 69; L. Seltzer, "Are Pa55.W0rd5 Dead?" *PC Magazine*, 28 December 2004, 86.
48. S. Patton, "Simply Secure Communications," *CIO*, 15 January 2003, 100.
49. C. Metz, "Total Security," *PC Magazine*, 1 October 2003, 83.
50. P. Loftus, "Web Services—Smooth Talk: New Software Allows Different Computer Systems to Communicate with Each Other Seamlessly," *Wall Street Journal*, 31 March 2003, R9.
51. J. van den Hoven, "Executive Support Systems & Decision Making," *Journal of Systems Management* 47, no. 8 (March–April 1996): 48.
52. "Business Objects Customers Take Off with Performance Management; Management Dashboards Help Organizations Gain Insight and Optimize Performance," *Business Wire*, 4 April 2005.
53. "Intranet," Webopedia, http://www.webopedia.com/TERM/i/intranet.html.
54. "IBM Dynamic Workplaces for Air," IBM, http://www.ibm.com.
55. V. Ganesan, "IBM Product Enables Firms to See Returns within One Year," *Business Times (Malaysia)*, 10 February 2003, 4.
56. J. Ericson, "The Hillman Group Leverages Consolidated Reporting, Geographic Analysis to Support its Hardware Manufacturing/distribution Leadership," *Business Intelligence Review*, 1 March 2007, 12.
57. "Web Services," Webopedia, http://www.webopedia.com/TERM/W/Web_Services.html.
58. S. Overby, "This Could Be the Start of Something Small," *CIO*, 15 February 2003, 54.
59. "Extranet," Webopedia, http://www.webopedia.com/TERM/E/extranet.html.
60. S. Hamm, D. Welch, W. Zellner, F. Keenan, & F. Engardio, "Down but Hardly Out: Downturn Be Damned, Companies Are Still Anxious to Expand Online," *BusinessWeek*, 26 March 2001, 126.
61. S. Nassauer, "Travel Watch: Eliminating the Human Element," *Wall Street Journal*, 14 November 2006, D7.
62. Hamm, Welch, Zellner, Keenan, & Engardio, "Down but Hardly Out."
63. K. C. Laudon & J. P. Laudon, *Management Information Systems: Organization and Technology* (Upper Saddle River, NJ: Prentice Hall, 1996).
64. J. Borzo, "Software for Symptoms," *Wall Street Journal*, 23 May 2005, R10.
65. Ibid.
66. R. Hernandez, "American Express Authorizer's Assistant," *Business Rules Journal*, August 2001,

http://bizrules.info/page/art_amexaa.htm.

67. Heinssen, Jr., R., Glass, C., & Knight, L. "Assessing Computer Anxiety: Development and Validation of the Computer Anxiety Rating Scale," *Computers in Human Behavior* (1987) 49–59.

68. A. Fisher, "Ask Annie: Can My Employer Really Ban Camera Phones?" *Fortune*, 9 August 2004, 54; C. Rhoads, "Cellphones Become 'Swiss Army Knives' as Technology Blurs," *Wall Street Journal*, 4 January 2005, B1; "In-STAT/MDR Reports 200% Growth in Shipments of Camera Phones," *AsiaPulse*, 15 December 2004; D. Takahashi, "Video Camera Phones Start to Pack Megapixel Punch," *San Jose Mercury News*, 25 October 2004; M. Thiruvengadam, "Popularity of Camera Phones Opens New Windows on Privacy Rights," *San Antonio Express-News*, 4 August 2004; K. Yatish Rajawat, "Camera Phones' Large Memories Pose Hidden Risk to India Business Security," *Economic Times*, 23 December 2004.

69. A. Fisher, "Retain Your Brains," *Fortune*, 24 July 2006, 49; A.Y.K. Chua, "The Curse of Success," *Wall Street Journal*, 28 April 2007, R8; S. Earley, "To Keep KM Current, Pay Attention to Context Changes," *Information Outlook*, April 2006, 31; E. Schwartz, "Reality Check: Filling the Void Left by Baby-Boomer Techies," *InfoWorld*, 6 March 2006, 22; "Putting It Off Until Tomorrow," *PR Newswire*, 26 January 2006.

Chapter 18

1. C. Passariello, "Louis Vuitton Tries Modern Methods on Factory Lines," *Wall Street Journal*, 9 October 2006, A1; "Blending New Technologies with Trustworthy Tradition and Creativity at Louis Vuitton," *i2 for Retail*, i2 Success Story #265, www.i2.com; C. Passariello, "A New Lease on Luxury," *Wall Street Journal*, 7 October 2006, wsj.com; R. Murphy, "LVMH, PPR Thriving and Bullish," *WWD*, 27 July 2007, 9; V. Vienne, "Luxe Luggage," *Town & Country*, January 2001, 140; C. Matlack, "The Vuitton Money Machine," *BusinessWeek*, 22 March 2004, businessweek.com; M. Socha, "Extras: Shoe-Licious," *WWD*, 7 August 2006, 38.

2. "Ryanair Celebrates 20 Years of Operations," Ryanair, http://www.ryanair.com/site/about/invest/docs/2005/q4_2005.pdf.

3. L. Tutor, "The Best Drive-Through in America, '04: Average Service Time Ranking," *Quick Service Restaurant*, http://www.qsrmagazine.com.

4. M. Richtel, "The Long-Distance Journey of a Fast-Food Order," *New York Times*, 11 April 2006, http://www.nytimes.com/2006/04/11/technology/11fast.html?ei=5090&en=fba08317788e24.

5. "Employment Cost Index News Release Text," Bureau of Labor Statistics, 1 July 2005, http://www.bls.gov/news.release/eci.nr0.htm; "Productivity and Costs, First Quarter 2005, Revised," Bureau of Labor Statistics, 1 July 2005, http://www.bls.gov/news.release/prod2.nr0.htm.

6. "HINC-03. People in Households—Households, by Total Money Income in 2003, Age, Race, and Hispanic Origin of Householder," U.S. Census Bureau, http://pubdb3.census.gov/macro/032004/hhinc/new03_001.htm.

7. "Historical Income Tables—Families," U.S. Census Bureau; "Table H-6. Regions—All Races by Median and Mean Income: 1975 to 2005," U.S. Census Bureau, http://www.census.gov/hhes/www/income/histinc/h06ar.html, 20 August 2007.

8. "Productivity and Costs, First Quarter 2005, Revised," Bureau of Labor Statistics, ftp://ftp.bls.gov/pub/news.release/History/prod2.06022005.news; "Employment, Hours, and Earnings from the Current Employment Statistics Survey (National)," Bureau of Labor Statistics, http://data.bls.gov/cgi-bin/surveymost?ce; "Productivity and Costs, First Quarter 200, Revised," Bureau of Labor Statistics, http://www.bls.gov/news.release/prod2.nr0.htm; "Employment, Hours, and Earnings from the Current Employment Statistics Survey (National)," Bureau of Labor Statistics, http://data.bls.gov/cgi-bin/surveymost?ce.

9. M. Ferguson, "It's the Right Time to Look for a New Job," *US News and World Report*, 9 April 2007, http://www.newsalerts.com/news/article/it-s-the-right-time-to-look-for-a-new-job.html:us2:926598.

10. Joanne Fritz, "Giving USA Releases Report on Charitable Giving for 2005," About.com, http://www.nonprofit.about.com/od/trendsissuesstatistics/a/givingusa.htm.

11. "Philanthropy in the American Economy," Council of Economic Advisers, 19 February 2002, http://clinton4.nara.gov/media/pdf/philanthropy.pdf.

12. "Cars' Affordability: Cheapest Since 1980," *CNN Money*, 13 November 2006, http://money.cnn.com/2006/11/13/autos/affordability/index.htm; "Auto Affordability Shows a Record Deterioration; Comerica Bank Chief Economist Reports," Auto Channel, 12 February 2007, http://www.theautochannel.com/news/2007/02/12/036903.html.

13. "Auto Affordability Slipped a Notch in Summer," Comerica, http://www.comerica.com.

14. "Cars' Affordability: Cheapest Since 1980."

15. B. Clanton, "Asians Outpace Big Three in Factory Efficiency," *Detroit News*, 3 June 2005, http://www.detnews.com/2005/autosinsider/0506/07/A01–202894.htm.

16. Ibid.

17. "Multifactor Productivity," Bureau of Labor Statistics, 31 January 2007, http://stats.bls.gov/bls/productivity.htm.

18. J. Dodge, "Dell's Internet-Based Plant Keeps Production Efficient," *Wall Street Journal Interactive Edition*, 26 September 2000, http://online.wsj.com.

19. J. Pletz, "Dell Computer's Basic Building Blocks: Famous Model for Computers Translates Well to Construction," *Austin American-Statesman*, 10 April 2000, D1.

20. J. Teresko, "The Value of Velocity," *Industry Week*, 1 October 2001, 43.

21. M. Rechtin "Porsche, Hyundai Score Big Gains in J. D. Power Quality Survey," *Auto Week*, 7 June 2006, http://www.autoweek.com/apps/pbcs.dll/article?AID=/20060608/FREE/60607007/1041&te.

22. "ASQ Glossary," American Society for Quality, http://www.asq.org/glossary/q.html.

23. R. E. Markland, S. K. Vickery, & R. A. Davis, "Managing Quality," ch. 7 in *Operations Management: Concepts in Manufacturing and Services* (Cincinnati, OH: South-Western College Publishing, 1998).

24. "SDLT 600 Tape Drive Product Specification," Quantum Corporation, http://www.quantum.com/ServiceandSupport/Softwareand Documentation Downloads/SDLT600/Index.aspx#Specifications.

25. G. Rao, "Computers to Be at the Heart of a Car," *Economic Times*, 12 February 2004, http://economictimes.indiatimes.com/.

26. "The 'R' Word: Product Reliability Is Measured at Physio-Control," *InSync*, http://www.medtronic-ers.com/insync/archives/istfal97.htm.

27. L. L. Berry & A. Parasuraman, *Marketing Services* (New York: Free Press, 1991).

28. P. Judge, "When a Customer Believes in You…They'll Stick with You Almost No Matter What," *Fast Company* 47 (June 2001): 138.

29. Ibid.

30. Ibid.

31. Ibid.

32. "ISO 9000 and ISO 14000 in Plain Language," International Organization for Standardization, http://www.iso.org/iso/en/iso9000–14000/understand/basics/general/basics_4.html.

33. "FAQs—General," International Organization for Standardization, http://www.iso.org/iso/en/faqs/faq-general.html.

34. J. Briscoe, S. Fawcett, & R. Todd, "The Implementation and Impact of ISO 9000 among Small Manufacturing Enterprises," *Journal of Small Business Management* 43 (1 July 2005): 309.

35. R. Henkoff, "The Hot New Seal of Quality (ISO 9000 Standard of Quality Management)," *Fortune*, 28 June 1993, 116.

36. "Frequently Asked Questions about the Malcolm Baldrige National Quality Award," National Institute of Standards & Technology, http://www.nist.gov/public_affairs/factsheet/baldfaqs.htm.

37. "Baldrige Award Application Forms," National Institute of Standards & Technology, http://www.baldrige.nist.gov/PDF_files/2005_Award_Application_Forms.pdf.

38. "Frequently Asked Questions and Answers about the Malcolm Baldrige National Quality Award."

39. Ibid.

40. "Criteria for Performance Excellence," Baldrige National Quality Program 2003, http://www.quality.nist.gov/PDF_files/2005_Business_Criteria.pdf.

41. Ibid.

42. Ibid.

43. "NIST Stock Studies Show Quality Pays (Baldrige National Quality Award)," National Institute of Standards & Technology, http://www.quality.nist.gov/Stock_Studies.htm.

44. J. W. Dean, Jr., & J. Evans, *Total Quality: Management, Organization, and Strategy* (St. Paul, MN: West, 1994).

45. J. W. Dean, Jr., & D. E. Bowen, "Management Theory and Total Quality: Improving Research and Practice through Theory Development," *Academy of Management Review* 19 (1994): 392–418.

46. R. Allen & R. Kilmann, "Aligning Reward Practices in Support of Total Quality Management," *Business Horizons*, 1 May 2001, 77.

47. A. Taylor, "Driving Customer Satisfaction," *Harvard Business Review*, July 2002, 24.

48. R. Carter, "Best Practices: Freudenberg-NOK/Cleveland, GA: Continuous Kaizens," *Industrial Maintenance & Plant Operations*, 1 June 2004, 10.

49. Ibid.

50. R. Levering, M. Moskowitz, L. Munoz, & P. Hjelt, "The 100 Best Companies to Work for," *Fortune*, 4 February 2002, 72.

51. "News Release: Gross Domestic Product and Corporate Profits," Bureau of Economic Analysis, U.S. Department of Commerce, http://www.bea.gov http://www.bea.gov/newsreleases/national/gdp/2007/gdp107a.htm.

52. R. Hallowell, L. A. Schlesinger, & J. Zornitsky, http://economictimes.indiatimes.com/ "Internal Service Quality, Customer and Job Satisfaction: Linkages and Implications for Management," *Human Resource Planning* 19 (1996): 20–31; J. L. Heskett, T. O. Jones, G. W. Loveman, W. E. Sasser, Jr., & L. A. Schlesinger, "Putting the Service-Profit Chain to Work," *Harvard Business Review*, March–April 1994, 164–174.

53. J. Huey, G. Bethune, & H. Kelleher, "Two Texas Mavericks Rant about the Wreckage of the U.S. Aviation Industry—And Reveal How They've Managed to Keep Their Companies above the Miserable Average," *Fortune*, 13 November 2000, 237.

54. R. Eder, "Customer-Easy Doesn't Come Easy," *Drug Store News*, 21 October 2002, 52.

55. "CVS Gears 'Service-Profit Chain' to the Customer" (Company Profile), *Chain Drug Review*, 11 December 2000, 44.

56. K. L. Freiberg & J. A. Freiberg, *NUTS! Southwest Airlines' Crazy Recipe for Business and Personal Success* (Austin, TX: Bard, 1996), 289.

57. G. Brewer, "The Ultimate Guide to Winning Customers: The Customer Stops Here," *Sales & Marketing Management* 150 (March 1998): 30; F. F. Reichheld, "The Loyalty Effect: The Hidden Force behind Growth, Profits, and Lasting Value," (Cambridge, MA: Harvard Business School Press, 2001).

58. Ibid.

59. L. L. Berry & A. Parasuraman, "Listening to the Customer—The Concept of a Service-Quality Information System," *Sloan Management Review* 38, no. 3 (Spring 1997): 65; C. W. L. Hart, J. L. Heskett, & W. E. Sasser, Jr., "The Profitable Art of Service Recovery," *Harvard Business Review*, July–August 1990, 148–156.

60. G. Stoller, "Companies Give Front-Line Employees More Power," *USA Today*, 27 June 2005, A.1.

61. S. Hale, "The Customer Is Always Right—Usually—Some Are Just Annoying, but Others Deserve the Boot," *Orlando Sentinel*, 15 April 2002, 54.

62. D. E. Bowen & E. E. Lawler III, "The Empowerment of Service Workers: What, Why, How, and When," *Sloan Management Review* 33 (Spring 1992): 31–39; D. E. Bowen & E. E. Lawler III, "Empowering Service Employees," *Sloan Management Review* 36 (Summer 1995): 73–84.

63. Bowen & Lawler III, "The Empowerment of Service Workers: What, Why, How, and When."

64. Stoller, "Companies Give Front-Line Employees More Power."

65. Ibid.

66. "Toshiba Offers Build-to-Order Option on Notebook Products for Customers Purchasing On-Line," EDP Weekly's IT Monitor, 7 April 2003 (available at http://findarticles.com/p/articles/mi_m0GZQ/is_14_44/ai_99824254).

67. G. V. Frazier & M. T. Spiggs, "Achieving Competitive Advantage through Group Technology," *Business Horizons* 39 (1996): 83–88.

68. "The Top 100 Beverage Companies: The List," *Beverage Industry*, July 2001, 30.

69. E. Gruber, "Cutting Time," *Modern Machine Shop*, March 2001, 102.

70. B. Sauer, "Heil 'Automated Job Shop' Produces Custom Trailers on Assembly Lines," Trailer/Body Builders, 1 December 1998, http://trailer-bodybuilders.com/mag/trucks_heil_automated_job.

71. "Attack Submarines—SSN," United States Navy Fact File, http://www.navy.mil/navydata/fact_display.asp?cid=4100&tid=100&ct=4.

72. S. Silke Carty, "Chrysler Wrestles with High Levels of Inventory as Unsold Vehicles Sit on Lots," *USA Today*, 2 November 2006, http://www.usatoday.com/money/autos/2006-11-02-chrysler-high-inventory_x.htm; J. D. Stoll, "Chrysler Maintains Plan to Cut Production as Inventory Rises," *Wall Street Journal*, 24 August 2006, http://www.wsj.com.

73. Ibid.

74. N. Wingfield, "Out of Tune: iPod Shortage Rocks Apple," *Wall Street Journal*, 16 December 2004, B1.

75. Ibid.

76. C. Marshall, "Linerboard: Market Recovery Will Continue; Price Hikes Predicted for 1998," *Pulp & Paper*, 1 January 1998, 13.

77. D. Drickhamer, "Reality Check," *Industry Week*, November 2001, 29.

78. D. Drickhamer, "Zeroing In on World-Class," *Industry Week*, November 2001, 36.

79. J. Zeiler, "The Need for Speed," *Operations & Fulfillment*, 1 April 2004, 38.

80. "About EFR," Efficient Foodservice Response, http://www.efr-central.com/aboutefr.html.

81. J. R. Henry, "Minimized Setup Will Make Your Packaging Line S.M.I.L.E.," *Packaging Technology & Engineering*, 1 February 1998, 24.

82. J. Donoghue, "The Future Is Now," *Air Transport World*, 1 April 2001, 78.

83. K. Clark, "An Eagle Eye for Inventory," *Chain Store Age*, May 2005, Supplement, 8A.

84. E. Powell, Jr., & F. Sahin, "Economic Production Lot Sizing with Periodic Costs and Overtime," *Decision Sciences* 32 (2001): 423–452.

85. J. Bonasia, "Just-in-Time Cuts Costs, but Has Risks," *Investor's Business Daily*, 3 October 2002, 4.

86. N. Shirouzu, "Why Toyota Wins Such High Marks on Quality Surveys," *Wall Street Journal*, 15 March 2001, A1.

87. Ibid.

88. G. Gruman, "Supply on Demand; Manufacturers Need to Know What's Selling before They Can Produce and Deliver Their Wares in the Right Quantities," *Info World*, 18 April 2005, http://www.infoworld.com/.

89. J. A. Perriat, S. LeMay, S. Chakrabarty, "The Selling Orientation—Customer Orientation (SOCO) Scale: Cross-Validation of the Revised Version," *Journal of Personal Selling & Sales Management* 24, no. 1 (2004): 49–54.

90. C. Koch, "Nike Rebounds," *CIO*, 15 June 2004, 57–62; J. Schlosser, "Just Do It," *Fortune*, 13 December 2004, 25; T. Wilson, "Nike Just Doesn't Do It," *Internet Week*, 28 December 2001, available at http://www.theopensourcecollective.com/press/InternetWeek/Internet_Week.htm; S. Holmes, "Nike," *BusinessWeek*, 24 November 2003, 98.

91. R. A. Donnelley, Jr., "Managing the Moment of Truth for a Service Organization," *Supervision*, December 2004, 3; M. De Paula, "Dispensing with the Data Dump to Achieve Customer Loyalty," *Banking Wire*, 11 February 2005, 24.

92. J. Craddock, ed., *VideoHound's Golden Movie Retriever* (Farmington Hills, MI: Gale Group, 2000); "John Ratzenberger," wikipedia.org, 6 September 2007; Grainger David, "Day Trippers," *Fortune*, 4 April 2005, 108–118; www.marshmallowpeeps.com; www.tabasco.com; www.factorytoursusa.com.

GLOSSARY

A

a-type conflict (affective conflict) disagreement that focuses on individuals or personal issues

absolute comparisons a process in which each decision criterion is compared to a standard or ranked on its own merits

accommodative strategy a social responsiveness strategy in which a company accepts responsibility for a problem and does all that society expects to solve that problem

achievement-oriented leadership a leadership style in which the leader sets challenging goals, has high expectations of employees, and displays confidence that employees will assume responsibility and put forth extraordinary effort

acquaintance time a cultural norm for how much time you must spend getting to know someone before the person is prepared to do business with you

acquisition the purchase of a company by another company

acquisition cost the cost of obtaining data that you don't have

action plan the specific steps, people, and resources needed to accomplish a goal

active listening assuming half the responsibility for successful communication by actively giving the speaker nonjudgmental feedback that shows you've accurately heard what he or she said

address terms cultural norms that establish whether you should address businesspeople by their first names, family names, or titles

adverse impact unintentional discrimination that occurs when members of a particular race, sex, or ethnic group are unintentionally harmed or disadvantaged because they are hired, promoted, or trained (or any other employment decision) at substantially lower rates than others

advocacy groups groups of concerned citizens who band together to try to influence the business practices of specific industries, businesses, and professions

affective cultures cultures in which people display emotions and feelings when communicating

affectivity the stable tendency to experience positive or negative moods and to react to things in a generally positive or negative way

affirmative action purposeful steps taken by an organization to create employment opportunities for minorities and women

age discrimination treating people differently (e.g., in hiring and firing, promotion, and compensation decisions) because of their age

agreeableness the degree to which someone is cooperative, polite, flexible, forgiving, good-natured, tolerant, and trusting

analyzers companies using an adaptive strategy that seeks to minimize risk and maximize profits by following or imitating the proven successes of prospectors

appointment time a cultural norm for how punctual you must be when showing up for scheduled appointments or meetings

Asia-Pacific Economic Cooperation (APEC) a regional trade agreement between Australia, Canada, Chile, the People's Republic of China, Hong Kong, Japan, Mexico, New Zealand, Papua New Guinea, Peru, Russia, South Korea, Taiwan, the United States, and all the members of ASEAN, except Cambodia, Laos, and Myanmar

assemble-to-order operation a manufacturing operation that divides manufacturing processes into separate parts or modules that are combined to create semicustomized products

assessment centers a series of managerial simulations, graded by trained observers, that are used to determine applicants' capability for managerial work

Association of Southeast Asian Nations (ASEAN) a regional trade agreement between Brunei Darussalam, Cambodia, Indonesia, Laos, Malaysia, Myanmar, the Philippines, Singapore, Thailand, and Vietnam

association or affinity patterns when two or more database elements tend to occur together in a significant way

attack a competitive move designed to reduce a rival's market share or profits

attribution theory the theory that we all have a basic need to understand and explain the causes of other people's behavior

authentication making sure potential users are who they claim to be

authoritarianism the extent to which an individual believes there should be power and status differences within organizations

authority the right to give commands, take action, and make decisions to achieve organizational objectives

authorization granting authenticated users approved access to data, software, and systems

autonomy the degree to which a job gives workers the discretion, freedom, and independence to decide how and when to accomplish the job

average aggregate inventory average overall inventory during a particular time period

awareness training training that is designed to raise employees' awareness of diversity issues and to challenge the underlying assumptions or stereotypes they may have about others

B

BCG matrix a portfolio strategy, developed by the Boston Consulting Group, that categorizes a corporation's businesses by growth rate and relative market share, and helps managers decide how to invest corporate funds

background checks procedures used to verify the truthfulness and accuracy of information that applicants provide about themselves and to uncover negative, job-related background information not provided by applicants

balance sheets accounting statements that provide a snapshot of a company's financial position at a particular time

balanced scorecard measurement of organizational performance in four equally important areas: finances, customers, internal operations, and innovation and learning

bar code a visual pattern that represents numerical data by varying the thickness and pattern of vertical bars

bargaining power of buyers a measure of the influence that customers have on a firm's prices

bargaining power of suppliers a measure of the influence that suppliers of parts, materials, and services to firms in an industry have on the prices of these inputs

batch production a manufacturing operation that produces goods in large batches in standard lot sizes

behavior control the regulation of the behaviors and actions that workers perform on the job

behavioral addition the process of having managers and employees perform new behaviors that are central to and symbolic of the new organizational culture that a company wants to create

behavioral formality a workplace atmosphere characterized by routine and regimen, specific rules about how to behave, and impersonal detachment

behavioral informality a workplace atmosphere characterized by spontaneity, casualness, and interpersonal familiarity

behavior observation scales (BOSs) rating scales that indicate the frequency with which workers perform specific behaviors that are representative of the job dimensions critical to successful job performance

behavioral substitution the process of having managers and employees perform new behaviors central to the "new" organizational culture in place of behaviors that were central to the "old" organizational culture

benchmarking the process of identifying outstanding practices, processes, and standards in other companies and adapting them to your company

biographical data (biodata) extensive surveys that ask applicants questions about their personal backgrounds and life experiences

biometrics identifying users by unique, measurable body features, such as fingerprint recognition or iris scanning

blog a personal website that provides personal opinions or recommendations, news summaries, and reader comments

bona fide occupational qualification (BFOQ) an exception in employment law that permits sex, age, religion, and the like to be used when making employment decisions, but only if they are "reasonably necessary to the normal operation of that particular business." BFOQs are strictly monitored by the Equal Employment Opportunity Commission.

bounded rationality a decision-making process restricted in the real world by limited resources, incomplete and imperfect information, and managers' limited decision-making capabilities

brainstorming a decision-making method in which group members build on each others' ideas to generate as many alternative solutions as possible

budgeting quantitative planning through which managers decide how to allocate available money to best accomplish company goals

budgets quantitative plans through which managers decide how to allocate available money to best accomplish company goals

bureaucracy the exercise of control on the basis of knowledge, expertise, or experience

bureaucratic control the use of hierarchical authority to influence employee behavior by rewarding or punishing employees for compliance or noncompliance with organizational policies, rules, and procedures

bureaucratic immunity the ability to make changes without first getting approval from managers or other parts of an organization

business confidence indices indices that show managers' level of confidence about future business growth

buyer dependence the degree to which a supplier relies on a buyer because of the importance of that buyer to the supplier and the difficulty of finding other buyers for its products

C

c-type conflict (cognitive conflict) disagreement that focuses on problem- and issue-related differences of opinion

cafeteria benefit plans (flexible benefit plans) plans that allow employees to choose which benefits they receive, up to a certain dollar value

cash cow a company with a large share of a slow-growing market

cash flow analysis a type of analysis that predicts how changes in a business will affect its ability to take in more cash than it pays out

Central America Free Trade Agreement (CAFTA-DR) a regional trade agreement between Costa Rica, the Dominican Republic, El Salvador, Guatemala, Honduras, Nicaragua, and the United States

centralization of authority the location of most authority at the upper levels of the organization

chain of command the vertical line of authority that clarifies who reports to whom throughout the organization

change agent the person formally in charge of guiding a change effort

change forces forces that produce differences in the form, quality, or condition of an organization over time

change intervention the process used to get workers and managers to change their behavior and work practices

character of the rivalry a measure of the intensity of competitive behavior between companies in an industry

charismatic leadership the behavioral tendencies and personal characteristics of leaders that create an exceptionally strong relationship between them and their followers

closed systems systems that can sustain themselves without interacting with their environments

closure the tendency to fill in gaps of missing information by assuming that what we don't know is consistent with what we already know

coaching communicating with someone for the direct purpose of improving the person's on-the-job performance or behavior

coercion the use of formal power and authority to force others to change

cognitive ability tests tests that measure the extent to which applicants have abilities in perceptual speed, verbal comprehension, numerical aptitude, general reasoning, and spatial aptitude

cognitive maps graphic depictions of how managers believe environmental factors relate to possible organizational actions

cohesiveness the extent to which team members are attracted to a team and motivated to remain in it

commission a compensation system in which employees earn a percentage of each sale they make

communication the process of transmitting information from one person or place to another

communication cost the cost of transmitting information from one place to another

communication medium the method used to deliver an oral or written message

company hotlines phone numbers that anyone in the company can call anonymously to leave information for upper management

company vision a company's purpose or reason for existing

compensation the financial and nonfinancial rewards that organizations give employees in exchange for their work

competitive advantage providing greater value for customers than competitors can

competitive analysis a process for monitoring the competition that involves identifying competition, anticipating their moves, and determining their strengths and weaknesses

competitive inertia a reluctance to change strategies or competitive practices that have been successful in the past

competitors companies in the same industry that sell similar products or services to customers

complex environment an environment with many environmental factors

complex matrix a form of matrix departmentalization in which managers in different parts of the matrix report to matrix managers, who help them sort out conflicts and problems

component parts inventories the basic parts used in manufacturing that are fabricated from raw materials

compression approach to innovation an approach to innovation that assumes that incremental innovation can be planned using a series of steps and that compressing those steps can speed innovation

compromise an approach to dealing with conflict in which both parties give up some of what they want in order to reach agreement on a plan to reduce or settle the conflict

concentration of effect the total harm or benefit that an act produces on the average person

conceptual skills the ability to see the organization as a whole, understand how the different parts affect each other, and recognize how the company fits into or is affected by its environment

concertive control the regulation of workers' behavior and decisions through work group values and beliefs

concurrent control a mechanism for gathering information about performance deficiencies as they occur, thereby eliminating or shortening the delay between performance and feedback

conduit metaphor the mistaken assumption that senders can pipe their intended messages directly into the heads of receivers with perfect clarity and without noise or perceptual filters interfering with the receivers' understanding of the message

conscientiousness the degree to which someone is organized, hardworking, responsible, persevering, thorough, and achievement oriented

consideration the extent to which a leader is friendly, approachable, and supportive and shows concern for employees

consistent organizational culture a company culture in which the company actively defines and teaches organizational values, beliefs, and attitudes

constructive feedback feedback intended to be helpful, corrective, and/or encouraging

contingency approach holds that there are no universal management theories and that the most effective management theory or idea depends on the kinds of problems or situations that managers are facing at a particular time and place

contingency theory a leadership theory that states that in order to maximize work group performance, leaders must be matched to the situation that best fits their leadership style

continuous-flow production a manufacturing operation that produces goods at a continuous, rather than a discrete, rate

continuous improvement an organization's ongoing commitment to constantly assess and improve the processes and procedures used to create products and services

continuous reinforcement schedule a schedule that requires a consequence to be administered following every instance of a behavior

control a regulatory process of establishing standards to achieve organizational goals, comparing actual performance against the standards, and taking corrective action, when necessary

control loss the situation in which behavior and work procedures do not conform to standards

controlling monitoring progress toward goal achievement and taking corrective action when needed

conventional level of moral development the second level of moral development in which people make decisions that conform to societal expectations

cooperative contract an agreement in which a foreign business owner pays a company a fee for the right to conduct that business in his or her country

core capabilities the internal decision-making routines, problem-solving processes, and organizational cultures that determine how efficiently inputs can be turned into outputs

core firms the central companies in a strategic group

corporate portal a hybrid of executive information systems and intranets that allows managers and employees to use a web browser to gain access to customized company information and to complete specialized transactions

corporate talk shows televised company meetings that allow remote audiences (employees) to pose questions to the show's host and guests

corporate-level strategy the overall organizational strategy that addresses the question "What business or businesses are we in or should we be in?"

cost leadership the positioning strategy of producing a product or service of acceptable quality at consistently lower production costs than competitors can, so that the firm can offer the product or service at the lowest price in the industry

counseling communicating with someone about non-job-related issues that may be affecting or interfering with the person's performance

creative work environments workplace cultures in which workers perceive that new ideas are welcomed, valued, and encouraged

creativity the production of novel and useful ideas

cross-cultural communication transmitting information from a person in one country or culture to a person from another country or culture

cross-functional team a team composed of employees from different functional areas of the organization

cross-training training team members to do all or most of the jobs performed by the other team members

customer defections a performance assessment in which companies identify which customers are leaving and measure the rate at which they are leaving

customer departmentalization organizing work and workers into separate units responsible for particular kinds of customers

customer focus an organizational goal to concentrate on meeting customers' needs at all levels of the organization

customer satisfaction an organizational goal to provide products or services that meet or exceed customers' expectations

customs classification a classification assigned to imported products by government officials that affects the size of the tariff and imposition of import quotas

cybernetic the process of steering or keeping on course

cybernetic feasibility the extent to which it is possible to implement each step in the control process

D

data clusters when three or more database elements occur together (i.e., cluster) in a significant way

data encryption the transformation of data into complex, scrambled digital codes that can be unencrypted only by authorized users who possess unique decryption keys

data mining the process of discovering unknown patterns and relationships in large amounts of data

data warehouse stores huge amounts of data that have been prepared for data mining analysis by being cleaned of errors and redundancy

decentralization the location of a significant amount of authority in the lower levels of the organization

decision criteria the standards used to guide judgments and decisions

decision making the process of choosing a solution from available alternatives

decision support system (DSS) an information system that helps managers understand specific kinds of problems and potential solutions and analyze the impact of different decision options using "what if" scenarios

decoding the process by which the receiver translates the written, verbal, or symbolic form of a message into an understood message

deep-level diversity differences such as personality and attitudes that are communicated through verbal and nonverbal behaviors and are learned only through extended interaction with others

defenders companies using an adaptive strategy aimed at defending strategic positions by seeking moderate, steady growth and by offering a limited range of high-quality products and services to a well-defined set of customers

defensive bias the tendency for people to perceive themselves as personally and situationally similar to someone who is having difficulty or trouble

defensive strategy a social responsiveness strategy in which a company admits responsibility for a problem but does the least required to meet societal expectations

de-forming a reversal of the forming stage, in which team members position themselves to control pieces of the team, avoid each other, and isolate themselves from team leaders

delegation of authority the assignment of direct authority and responsibility to a subordinate to complete tasks for which the manager is normally responsible

Delphi technique a decision-making method in which members of a panel of experts respond to questions and to each other until reaching agreement on an issue

de-norming a reversal of the norming stage, in which team performance begins to decline as the size, scope, goal, or members of the team change

departmentalization subdividing work and workers into separate organizational units responsible for completing particular tasks

dependent demand system an inventory system in which the level of inventory depends on the number of finished units to be produced

design competition competition between old and new technologies to establish a new technological standard or dominant design

design iteration a cycle of repetition in which a company tests a prototype of a new product or service, improves on that design, and then builds and tests the improved prototype

de-storming a reversal of the storming phase, in which the team's comfort level decreases, team cohesion weakens, and angry emotions and conflict may flare

destructive feedback feedback that disapproves without any intention of being helpful and almost always causes a negative or defensive reaction in the recipient

devil's advocacy a decision-making method in which an individual or a subgroup is assigned the role of a critic

dialectical inquiry a decision-making method in which decision makers state the assumptions of a proposed solution (a thesis) and generate a solution that is the opposite (antithesis) of that solution

differentiation the positioning strategy of providing a product or service that is sufficiently different from competitors' offerings that customers are willing to pay a premium price for it

direct competition the rivalry between two companies that offer similar products and services, acknowledge each other as rivals, and act and react to each other's strategic actions

direct foreign investment a method of investment in which a company builds a new business or buys an existing business in a foreign country

directive leadership a leadership style in which the leader lets employees know precisely what is expected of them, gives them specific guidelines for performing tasks, schedules work, sets standards of performance, and makes sure that people follow standard rules and regulations

disability a mental or physical impairment that substantially limits one or more major life activities

disability discrimination treating people differently because of their disabilities

discontinuous change the phase of a technology cycle characterized by technological substitution and design competition

discretionary responsibilities the expectation that a company will voluntarily serve a social role beyond its economic, legal, and ethical responsibilities

discussion time a cultural norm for how much time should be spent in discussion with others

disparate treatment intentional discrimination that occurs when people are purposely not given the same hiring, promotion, or membership opportunities because of their race, color, sex, age, ethnic group, national origin, or religious beliefs

disposition the tendency to respond to situations and events in a predetermined manner

disseminator role the informational role managers play when they share information with others in their departments or companies

distal goals long-term or primary goals

distinctive competence what a company can make, do, or perform better than its competitors

distributive justice the perceived degree to which outcomes and rewards are fairly distributed or allocated

disturbance handler role the decisional role managers play when they respond to severe problems that demand immediate action

diversification a strategy for reducing risk by buying a variety of items (stocks or, in the case of a corporation, types of businesses) so that the failure of one stock or one business does not hurt the performance of the entire portfolio

diversity a variety of demographic, cultural, and personal differences among an organization's employees and customers

diversity audits formal assessments that measure employee and management attitudes, investigate the extent to which people are advantaged or disadvantaged with respect to hiring and promotions, and review companies' diversity-related policies and procedures

diversity pairing a mentoring program in which people of different cultural backgrounds, sexes, or races/ethnicities are paired together to get to know each other and change stereotypical beliefs and attitudes

dog a company with a small share of a slow-growing market

dominant design a new technological design or process that becomes the accepted market standard

domination an approach to dealing with conflict in which one party satisfies its desires and objectives at the expense of the other party's desires and objectives

downsizing the planned elimination of jobs in a company

downward communication communication that flows from higher to lower levels in an organization

dynamic environment an environment in which the rate of change is fast

dysfunctional turnover loss of high-performing employees who voluntarily choose to leave a company

E

early retirement incentive programs (ERIPs) programs that offer financial benefits to employees to encourage them to retire early

economic order quantity (EOQ) a system of formulas that minimizes ordering and holding costs and helps determine how much and how often inventory should be ordered

economic responsibility the expectation that a company will make a profit by producing a valued product or service

economic value added (EVA) the amount by which company profits (revenues, minus expenses, minus taxes) exceed the cost of capital in a given year

efficiency getting work done with a minimum of effort, expense, or waste

effectiveness accomplishing tasks that help fulfill organizational objectives

electronic brainstorming a decision-making method in which group members use computers to build on each others' ideas and generate many alternative solutions

electronic data interchange (EDI) when two companies convert their purchase and ordering information to a standardized format to enable the direct electronic transmission of that information from one company's computer system to the other company's computer system

electronic scanner an electronic device that converts printed text and pictures into digital images

emotional stability the degree to which someone is not angry, depressed, anxious, emotional, insecure, and excitable

empathetic listening understanding the speaker's perspective and personal frame of reference and giving feedback that conveys that understanding to the speaker

employee involvement team team that provides advice or makes suggestions to management concerning specific issues

employee separation the voluntary or involuntary loss of an employee

employee shrinkage employee theft of company merchandise

employee stock ownership plan (ESOP) a compensation system that awards employees shares of company stock in addition to their regular compensation

employee turnover loss of employees who voluntarily choose to leave the company

employment benefits a method of rewarding employees that includes virtually any kind of compensation other than wages or salaries

employment references sources such as previous employers or coworkers who can provide job-related information about job candidates

empowering workers permanently passing decision-making authority and responsibility from managers to workers by giving them the information and resources they need to make and carry out good decisions

empowerment feelings of intrinsic motivation, in which workers perceive their work to have impact and meaning and perceive themselves to be competent and capable of self-determination

encoding putting a message into a written, verbal, or symbolic form that can be recognized and understood by the receiver

entrepreneur role the decisional role managers play when they adapt themselves, their subordinates, and their units to change

entrepreneurial orientation the set of processes, practices, and decision-making activities that lead to new entry, characterized by five dimensions: risk taking, autonomy, innovativeness, proactiveness, and competitive aggressiveness

entrepreneurship the process of entering new or established markets with new goods or services

entropy the inevitable and steady deterioration of a system

environmental change the change in a company's general and specific environments

environmental complexity the number and the intensity of external factors in the environment that affect organizations

environmental scanning searching the environment for important events or issues that might affect an organization

equity theory a theory that states that people will be motivated when they perceive that they are being treated fairly

ethical behavior behavior that conforms to a society's accepted principles of right and wrong

ethical charismatics charismatic leaders who provide developmental opportunities for followers, are open to positive and negative feedback, recognize others' contributions, share information, and have moral standards that emphasize the larger interests of the group, organization, or society

ethical intensity the degree of concern people have about an ethical issue

ethical responsibility the expectation that a company will not violate accepted principles of right and wrong when conducting its business

ethics the set of moral principles or values that defines right and wrong for a person or group

evaluation apprehension fear of what others will think of your ideas

executive information system (EIS) a data processing system that uses internal and external data sources to provide the information needed to monitor and analyze organizational performance

expatriate someone who lives and works outside his or her native country

expectancy the perceived relationship between effort and performance

expectancy theory the theory that people will be motivated to the extent to which they believe that their efforts will lead to good performance, that good performance will be rewarded, and that they will be offered attractive rewards

experiential approach to innovation an approach to innovation that assumes a highly uncertain environment and uses intuition, flexible options, and hands-on experience to reduce uncertainty and accelerate learning and understanding

expert system an information system that contains the specialized knowledge and decision rules used by experts and experienced decision makers so that nonexperts can draw on this knowledge base to make decisions

exporting selling domestically produced products to customers in foreign countries

external environments all events outside a company that have the potential to influence or affect it

external locus of control the belief that what happens to you is largely the result of factors beyond your control

external recruiting the process of developing a pool of qualified job applicants from outside the company

extinction reinforcement in which a positive consequence is no longer allowed to follow a previously reinforced behavior, thus weakening the behavior

extranets networks that allow companies to exchange information and conduct transactions with outsiders by providing them direct, web-based access to authorized parts of a company's intranet or information system

extraversion the degree to which someone is active, assertive, gregarious, sociable, talkative, and energized by others

extrinsic reward a reward that is tangible, visible to others, and given to employees contingent on the performance of specific tasks or behaviors

F

feedback the amount of information the job provides to workers about their work performance

feedback control a mechanism for gathering information about performance deficiencies after they occur

feedback to sender in the communication process, a return message to the sender that indicates the receiver's understanding of the message

feedforward control a mechanism for monitoring performance inputs rather than outputs to prevent or minimize performance deficiencies before they occur

figurehead role the interpersonal role managers play when they perform ceremonial duties

financial ratios calculations typically used to track a business's liquidity (cash), efficiency, and profitability over time compared with other businesses in its industry

finished goods inventories the final outputs of manufacturing operations

firewall a protective hardware or software device that sits between the computers in an internal organizational network and outside networks, such as the Internet

firm-level strategy a corporate strategy that addresses the question "How should we compete against a particular firm?"

first-line managers managers who train and supervise the performance of nonmanagerial employees who are directly responsible for producing the company's products or services

first-mover advantage the strategic advantage that companies earn by being the first to use new information technology to substantially lower costs or to make a product or service different from that of competitors

fixed interval reinforcement schedule an intermittent schedule in which consequences follow a behavior only after a fixed time has elapsed

fixed ratio reinforcement schedule an intermittent schedule in which consequences are delivered following a specific number of behaviors

flow a psychological state of effortlessness, in which you become completely absorbed in what you're doing and time seems to pass quickly

focus strategy the positioning strategy of using cost leadership or differentiation to produce a specialized product or service for a limited, specially targeted group of customers in a particular geographic region or market segment

formal communication channel the system of official channels that carry organizationally approved messages and information

forming the first stage of team development, in which team members meet each other, form initial impressions, and begin to establish team norms

four-fifths (or 80 percent) rule a rule of thumb used by the courts and the EEOC to determine whether there is evidence of adverse impact. A violation of this rule occurs when the selection rate for a protected group is less than 80 percent or four-fifths of the selection rate for a nonprotected group.

franchise a collection of networked firms in which the manufacturer or marketer of a product or service, the franchisor, licenses the entire business to another person or organization, the franchisee

functional departmentalization organizing work and workers into separate units responsible for particular business functions or areas of expertise

functional turnover loss of poor-performing employees who voluntarily choose to leave a company

fundamental attribution error the tendency to ignore external causes of behavior and to attribute other people's actions to internal causes

G

gainsharing a compensation system in which companies share the financial value of performance gains, such as productivity, cost savings, or quality, with their workers

Gantt chart a graphical chart that shows which tasks must be completed at which times in order to complete a project or task

General Agreement on Tariffs and Trade (GATT) a worldwide trade agreement that reduced and eliminated tariffs, limited government subsidies, and established protections for intellectual property

General Electric workout a three-day meeting in which managers and employees from different levels and parts of an organization quickly generate and act on solutions to specific business problems

general environment the economic, technological, sociocultural, and political trends that indirectly affect all organizations

generational change change based on incremental improvements to a dominant technological design such that the improved technology is fully backward compatible with the older technology

geographic departmentalization organizing work and workers into separate units responsible for doing business in particular geographic areas

glass ceiling the invisible barrier that prevents women and minorities from advancing to the top jobs in organizations

global business the buying and selling of goods and services by people from different countries

global consistency for a multinational company, using the same rules, guidelines, policies, and procedures for offices, manufacturing plants, and distribution facilities in different countries

global new ventures new companies that are founded with an active global strategy and have sales, employees, and financing in different countries

goal a target, objective, or result that someone tries to accomplish

goal acceptance the extent to which people consciously understand and agree to goals

goal commitment the determination to achieve a goal

goal difficulty the extent to which a goal is hard or challenging to accomplish

goal-setting theory the theory that people will be motivated to the extent to which they accept specific, challenging goals and receive feedback that indicates their progress toward goal achievement

goal specificity the extent to which goals are detailed, exact, and unambiguous

government import standard a standard ostensibly established to protect the health and safety of citizens but, in reality, often used to restrict imports

grand strategy a broad corporate-level strategic plan used to achieve strategic goals and guide the strategic alternatives that managers of individual businesses or subunits may use

groupthink a barrier to good decision making caused by pressure within the group for members to agree with each other

growth strategy a strategy that focuses on increasing profits, revenues, market share, or the number of places in which the company does business

H

hearing the act or process of perceiving sounds

holding cost the cost of keeping inventory until it is used or sold, including storage, insurance, taxes, obsolescence, and opportunity costs

horizontal communication communication that flows among managers and workers who are at the same organizational level

hostile work environment a form of sexual harassment in which unwelcome and demeaning sexually related behavior creates an intimidating and offensive work environment

human resource information system (HRIS) a computerized system for gathering, analyzing, storing, and disseminating information related to the HRM process

human resource management (HRM) the process of finding, developing, and keeping the right people to form a qualified work force

human resource planning (HRP) using an organization's goals and strategy to forecast the organization's human resource needs in terms of attracting, developing, and keeping a qualified work force

human skills the ability to work well with others

I

ISO 9000 a series of five international standards, from ISO 9000 to ISO 9004, for achieving consistency in quality management and quality assurance in companies throughout the world

ISO 14000 a series of international standards for managing, monitoring, and minimizing an organization's harmful effects on the environment

imperfectly imitable resource a resource that is impossible or extremely costly or difficult for other firms to duplicate

income statements accounting statements, also called "profit and loss statements," that show what has happened to an organization's income, expenses, and net profit over a period of time

incremental change the phase of a technology cycle in which companies innovate by lowering costs and improving the functioning and performance of the dominant technological design

independent demand system an inventory system in which the level of one kind of inventory does not depend on another

individualism-collectivism the degree to which a person believes that people should be self-sufficient and that loyalty to one's self is more important than loyalty to team or company

industry regulation regulations and rules that govern the business practices and procedures of specific industries, businesses, and professions

industry-level strategy a corporate strategy that addresses the question "How should we compete in this industry?"

informal communication channel ("grapevine") the transmission of messages from employee to employee outside of formal communication channels

information useful data that can influence people's choices and behavior

initiating structure the degree to which a leader structures the roles of followers by setting goals, giving directions, setting deadlines, and assigning tasks

innovation streams patterns of innovation over time that can create sustainable competitive advantage

inputs in equity theory, the contributions employees make to the organization

instrumentality the perceived relationship between performance and rewards

integrative conflict resolution an approach to dealing with conflict in which both parties indicate their preferences and then work together to find an alternative the meets the needs of both

intermittent reinforcement schedule a schedule in which consequences are delivered after a specified or average time has elapsed or after a specified or average number of behaviors has occurred

internal environment the events and trends inside an organization that affect management, employees, and organizational culture

internal locus of control the belief that what happens to you is largely the result of your own actions

internal motivation motivation that comes from the job itself rather than from outside rewards

internal recruiting the process of developing a pool of qualified job applicants from people who already work in the company

interorganizational process a collection of activities that take place among companies to transform inputs into outputs that customers value

interpersonal skills skills, such as listening, communicating, questioning, and providing feedback, that enable people to have effective working relationships with others

interviews a selection tool in which company representatives ask job applicants job-related questions to determine whether they are qualified for the job

intranets private company networks that allow employees to easily access, share, and publish information using Internet software

intraorganizational process the collection of activities that take place within an organization to transform inputs into outputs that customers value

intrapreneurship entrepreneurship within an existing organization

intrinsic reward a natural reward associated with performing a task or activity for its own sake

inventory the amount and number of raw materials, parts, and finished products that a company has in its possession

inventory turnover the number of times per year that a company sells or "turns over" its average inventory

J

jargon vocabulary particular to a profession or group that interferes with communication in the workplace

job analysis a purposeful, systematic process for collecting information on the important work-related aspects of a job

job characteristics model (JCM) an approach to job redesign that seeks to formulate jobs in ways that motivate workers and lead to positive work outcomes

job description a written description of the basic tasks, duties, and responsibilities required of an employee holding a particular job

job design the number, kind, and variety of tasks that individual workers perform in doing their jobs

job enlargement increasing the number of different tasks that a worker performs within one particular job

job enrichment increasing the number of tasks in a particular job and giving workers the authority and control to make meaningful decisions about their work

job evaluation a process that determines the worth of each job in a company by evaluating the market value of the knowledge, skills, and requirements needed to perform it

job rotation periodically moving workers from one specialized job to another to give them more variety and the opportunity to use different skills

job shops manufacturing operations that handle custom orders or small batch jobs

job specialization a job composed of a small part of a larger task or process

job specifications a written summary of the qualifications needed to successfully perform a particular job

joint venture a strategic alliance in which two existing companies collaborate to form a third, independent company

just-in-time (JIT) inventory system an inventory system in which component parts arrive from suppliers just as they are needed at each stage of production

K

kanban a ticket-based JIT system that indicates when to reorder inventory

kinesics movements of the body and face

knowledge the understanding that one gains from information

L

leader role the interpersonal role managers play when they motivate and encourage workers to accomplish organizational objectives

leader-member relations the degree to which followers respect, trust, and like their leaders

leadership the process of influencing others to achieve group or organizational goals

leadership neutralizers subordinate, task, or organizational characteristics that can interfere with a leader's actions or make it impossible for a leader to influence followers' performance

leadership style the way a leader generally behaves toward followers

leadership substitutes subordinate, task, or organizational characteristics that make leaders redundant or unnecessary

leading inspiring and motivating workers to work hard to achieve organizational goals

learning-based planning learning better ways of achieving goals by continually testing, changing, and improving plans and strategies

legal responsibility the expectation that a company will obey society's laws and regulations

liaison role the interpersonal role managers play when they deal with people outside their units

licensing an agreement in which a domestic company, the licensor, receives royalty payments for allowing another company, the licensee, to produce the licensor's product, sell its service, or use its brand name in a specified foreign market

line authority the right to command immediate subordinates in the chain of command

line function an activity that contributes directly to creating or selling the company's products

line-flow production manufacturing processes that are preestablished, occur in a serial or linear manner, and are dedicated to making one type of product

listening making a conscious effort to hear

local adaptation modifying rules, guidelines, policies, and procedures to adapt to differences in foreign customers, governments, and regulatory agencies

locus of control the degree to which individuals believe that their actions can influence what happens to them

M

Maastricht Treaty of Europe a regional trade agreement between most European countries

Machiavellian the extent to which individuals believe that virtually any type of behavior is acceptable in trying to satisfy their needs or meet their goals

magnitude of consequences the total harm or benefit derived from an ethical decision

make-to-order operation a manufacturing operation that does not start processing or assembling products until a customer order is received

make-to-stock operation a manufacturing operation that orders parts and assembles standardized products before receiving customer orders

management getting work done through others

management by objectives (MBO) a four-step process in which managers and employees discuss and select goals, develop tactical plans, and meet regularly to review progress toward goal accomplishment

manufacturing flexibility the degree to which manufacturing operations can easily and quickly change the number, kind, and characteristics of products they produce

market commonality the degree to which two companies have overlapping products, services, or customers in multiple markets

materials requirement planning (MRP) a production and inventory system that determines the production schedule, production batch sizes, and inventory needed to complete final products

matrix departmentalization a hybrid organizational structure in which two or more forms of departmentalization, most often product and functional, are used together

maximizing choosing the best alternative

mechanistic organization an organization characterized by specialized jobs and responsibilities, precisely defined, unchanging roles, and a rigid chain of command based on centralized authority and vertical communication

media advocacy an advocacy group tactic that involves framing issues as public issues; exposing questionable, exploitative, or unethical practices; and forcing media coverage by buying media time or creating controversy that is likely to receive extensive news coverage

meta-analysis a study of studies, a statistical approach that provides one of the best scientific estimates of how well management theories and practices work

middle managers managers responsible for setting objectives consistent with top management's goals and for planning and implementing subunit strategies for achieving these objectives

milestones formal project review points used to assess progress and performance

mission a statement of a company's overall goal that unifies company-wide efforts toward its vision, stretches and challenges the organization, and possesses a finish line and a time frame

modular organization an organization that outsources noncore business activities to outside companies, suppliers, specialists, or consultants

monitor role the informational role managers play when they scan their environment for information

monochronic cultures cultures in which people tend to do one thing at a time and view time as linear

mood linkage a phenomenon in which one worker's negative affectivity and bad moods can spread to others

Moore's law the prediction that about every two years, computer-processing power would double and its cost would drop by 50 percent

motion study breaking each task or job into its separate motions and then eliminating those that are unnecessary or repetitive

motivation the set of forces that initiates, directs, and makes people persist in their efforts to accomplish a goal

motivation to manage an assessment of how enthusiastic employees are about managing the work of others

multifactor productivity an overall measure of performance that indicates how much labor, capital, materials, and energy it takes to produce an output

multifunctional teams work teams composed of people from different departments

multinational corporation a corporation that owns businesses in two or more countries

N

national culture the set of shared values and beliefs that affects the perceptions, decisions, and behavior of the people from a particular country

needs the physical or psychological requirements that must be met to ensure survival and well-being

needs assessment the process of identifying and prioritizing the learning needs of employees

negative affectivity a personality trait in which individuals tend to notice and focus on the negative aspects of themselves and their environments

negative reinforcement reinforcement that strengthens behavior by withholding an unpleasant consequence when employees perform a specific behavior

negotiator role the decisional role managers play when they negotiate schedules, projects, goals, outcomes, resources, and employee raises

neutral cultures cultures in which people do not display emotions and feelings when communicating

noise anything that interferes with the transmission of the intended message

nominal group technique a decision-making method that begins and ends by having group members quietly write down and evaluate ideas to be shared with the group

nonsubstitutable resource a resource that produces value or competitive advantage and has no equivalent substitutes or replacements

nontariff barriers nontax methods of increasing the cost or reducing the volume of imported goods

nonverbal communication any communication that doesn't involve words

normative control the regulation of workers' behavior and decisions through widely shared organizational values and beliefs

normative decision theory a theory that suggests how leaders can determine an appropriate amount of employee participation when making decisions

norming the third stage of team development, in which team members begin to settle into their roles, group cohesion grows, and positive team norms develop

norms informally agreed-on standards that regulate team behavior

North American Free Trade Agreement (NAFTA) a regional trade agreement between the United States, Canada, and Mexico

O

objective control the use of observable measures of worker behavior or outputs to assess performance and influence behavior

objective performance measures measures of job performance that are easily and directly counted or quantified

online discussion forums the in-house equivalent of Internet newsgroups. By using web- or software-based discussion tools that are available across the company, employees can easily ask questions and share knowledge with each other.

open office systems offices in which the physical barriers that separate workers have been removed in order to increase communication and interaction

open systems systems that can sustain themselves only by interacting with their environments, on which they depend for their survival

openness to experience the degree to which someone is curious, broad-minded, and open to new ideas, things, and experiences; is spontaneous; and has a high tolerance for ambiguity

operational plans day-to-day plans, developed and implemented by lower-level managers, for producing or delivering the organization's products and services over a 30-day to six-month period

operations management managing the daily production of goods and services

opportunistic behavior a transaction in which one party in the relationship benefits at the expense of the other

optical character recognition the ability of software to convert digitized documents into ASCII text (American Standard Code for Information Interchange) that can be searched, read, and edited by word processing and other kinds of software

options-based planning maintaining planning flexibility by making small, simultaneous investments in many alternative plans

ordering cost the costs associated with ordering inventory, including the cost of data entry, phone calls, obtaining bids, correcting mistakes, and determining when and how much inventory to order

organic organization an organization characterized by broadly defined jobs and responsibility, loosely defined, frequently changing roles, and decentralized authority and horizontal communication based on task knowledge

organization a system of consciously coordinated activities or forces created by two or more people

organizational change a difference in the form, quality, or condition of an organization over time

organizational culture the values, beliefs, and attitudes shared by organizational members

organizational decline a large decrease in organizational performance that occurs when companies don't anticipate, recognize, neutralize, or adapt to the internal or external pressures that threaten their survival

organizational development a philosophy and collection of planned change interventions designed to improve an organization's long-term health and performance

organizational heroes people celebrated for their qualities and achievements within an organization

organizational innovation the successful implementation of creative ideas in organizations

organizational plurality a work environment where (1) all members are empowered to contribute in a way that maximizes the benefits to the organization, customers, and themselves, and (2) the individuality of each member is respected by not segmenting or polarizing people on the basis of their membership in a particular group

organizational process the collection of activities that transform inputs into outputs that customers value

organizational silence when employees withhold information about organizational problems or issues

organizational stories stories told by organizational members to make sense of organizational events and changes and to emphasize culturally consistent assumptions, decisions, and actions

organizational structure the vertical and horizontal configuration of departments, authority, and jobs within a company

organizing deciding where decisions will be made, who will do what jobs and tasks, and who will work for whom

outcome/input (O/I) ratio in equity theory, an employee's perception of how the rewards received from an organization compare with the employee's contributions to that organization

outcomes in equity theory, the rewards employees receive for their contributions to the organization

outplacement services employment-counseling services offered to employees who are losing their jobs because of downsizing

output control the regulation of workers' results or outputs through rewards and incentives

overreward a form of inequity in which you are getting more outcomes relative to inputs than your referent

overt integrity test a written test that estimates job applicants' honesty by directly asking them what they think or feel about theft or about punishment of unethical behaviors

P

paralanguage the pitch, rate, tone, volume, and speaking pattern (i.e., use of silences, pauses, or hesitations) of one's voice

partial productivity a measure of performance that indicates how much of a particular kind of input it takes to produce an output

participative leadership a leadership style in which the leader consults employees for their suggestions and input before making decisions

path-goal theory a leadership theory that states that leaders can increase subordinate satisfaction and performance by clarifying and clearing the paths to goals and by increasing the number and kinds of rewards available for goal attainment

perception the process by which individuals attend to, organize, interpret, and retain information from their environments

perceptual filters the personality-, psychology-, or experience-based differences that influence people to ignore or pay attention to particular stimuli

performance appraisal the process of assessing how well employees are doing their jobs

performance feedback information about the quality or quantity of past performance that indicates whether progress is being made toward the accomplishment of a goal

performing the fourth and final stage of team development, in which performance improves because the team has matured into an effective, fully functioning team

personal aggression hostile or aggressive behavior toward others

personality the relatively stable set of behaviors, attitudes, and emotions displayed over time that makes people different from each other

personality-based integrity test a written test that indirectly estimates job applicants' honesty by measuring psychological traits, such as dependability and conscientiousness

personality tests tests that measure the extent to which applicants possess different kinds of job-related personality dimensions

phased retirement employees transition to retirement by working reduced hours over a period of time before completing retiring

piecework a compensation system in which employees are paid a set rate for each item they produce

planning (management functions) determining organizational goals and a means for achieving them

planning choosing a goal and developing a strategy to achieve that goal

policy a standing plan that indicates the general course of action that should be taken in response to a particular event or situation

policy uncertainty the risk associated with changes in laws and government policies that directly affect the way foreign companies conduct business

political deviance using one's influence to harm others in the company

political uncertainty the risk of major changes in political regimes that can result from war, revolution, death of political leaders, social unrest, or other influential events

polychronic cultures cultures in which people tend to do more than one thing at a time and view times as circular

pooled interdependence work completed by having each job or department independently contribute to the whole

portfolio strategy a corporate-level strategy that minimizes risk by diversifying investment among various businesses or product lines

position power the degree to which leaders are able to hire, fire, reward, and punish workers

positive affectivity a personality trait in which individuals tend to notice and focus on the positive aspects of themselves and their environments

positive reinforcement reinforcement that strengthens behavior by following behaviors with desirable consequences

postconventional level of moral development the third level of moral development in which people make decisions based on internalized principles

preconventional level of moral development the first level of moral development in which people make decisions based on selfish reasons

predictive patterns patterns that help identify database elements that are different

primary stakeholder any group on which an organization relies for its long-term survival

principle of distributive justice an ethical principle that holds that you should never take any action that harms the least among us: the poor, the uneducated, the unemployed

principle of government requirements an ethical principle that holds that you should never take any action that violates the law, for the law represents the minimal moral standard

principle of individual rights an ethical principle that holds that you should never take any action that infringes on others' agreed-upon rights

principle of long-term self-interest an ethical principle that holds that you should never take any action that is not in your or your organization's long-term self-interest

principle of personal virtue an ethical principle that holds that you should never do anything that is not honest, open, and truthful and that you would not be glad to see reported in the newspapers or on TV

principle of religious injunctions an ethical principle that holds that you should never take any action that is not kind and that does not build a sense of community

principle of utilitarian benefits an ethical principle that holds that you should never take any action that does not result in greater good for society

private spaces spaces used by and open to just one employee

proactive strategy a social responsiveness strategy in which a company anticipates responsibility for a problem before it occurs and does more than society expects to address the problem

probability of effect the chance that something will happen and then harm others

problem a gap between a desired state and an existing state

procedural justice the perceived fairness of the process used to make reward allocation decisions

procedure a standing plan that indicates the specific steps that should be taken in response to a particular event

processing cost the cost of turning raw data into usable information

processing information transforming raw data into meaningful information

product boycott an advocacy group tactic that involves protesting a company's actions by persuading consumers not to purchase its product or service

product departmentalization organizing work and workers into separate units responsible for producing particular products or services

product prototype a full-scale working model that is being tested for design, function, and reliability

production blocking a disadvantage of face-to-face brainstorming in which a group member must wait to share an idea because another member is presenting an idea

production deviance unethical behavior that hurts the quality and quantity of work produced

productivity a measure of performance that indicates how many inputs it takes to produce or create an output

profit sharing a compensation system in which a company pays a percentage of its profits to employees in addition to their regular compensation

project team a team created to complete specific, one-time projects or tasks within a limited time

project manufacturing manufacturing operations designed to produce large, expensive, specialized products

property deviance unethical behavior aimed at the organization's property or products

prospectors companies using an adaptive strategy that seeks fast growth by searching for new market opportunities, encouraging risk taking, and being the first to bring innovative new products to market

protecting information the process of ensuring that data are reliably and consistently retrievable in a usable format for authorized users, but no one else

protectionism a government's use of trade barriers to shield domestic companies and their workers from foreign competition

proximal goals short-term goals or subgoals

proximity of effect the social, psychological, cultural, or physical distance between a decision maker and those affected by his or her decisions

public communications an advocacy group tactic that relies on voluntary participation by the news media and the advertising industry to get the advocacy group's message out

punctuated equilibrium theory the theory that companies go through long periods of stability (equilibrium), followed by short periods of dynamic, fundamental change (revolution), and finishing with a return to stability (new equilibrium)

punishment reinforcement that weakens behavior by following behaviors with undesirable consequences

purchasing power the relative cost of a standard set of goods and services in different countries

Q

quality a product or service free of deficiencies, or the characteristics of a product or service that satisfy customer needs

question mark a company with a small share of a fast-growing market

quid pro quo sexual harassment a form of sexual harassment in which employment outcomes, such as hiring, promotion, or simply keeping one's job, depend on whether an individual submits to sexual harassment

quota a limit on the number or volume of imported products

R

racial and ethnic discrimination treating people differently because of their race or ethnicity

radio frequency identification (RFID) tags tags containing minuscule microchips that transmit information via radio waves and can be used to track the number and location of the objects into which the tags have been inserted

rare resource a resource that is not controlled or possessed by many competing firms

rate buster a group member whose work pace is significantly faster than the normal pace in his or her group

rater training training performance appraisal raters in how to avoid rating errors and increase rating accuracy

rational decision making a systematic process of defining problems, evaluating alternatives, and choosing optimal solutions

raw data facts and figures

raw material inventories the basic inputs in a manufacturing process

reactive strategy a social responsiveness strategy in which a company does less than society expects

reactors companies using an adaptive strategy of not following a consistent strategy, but instead reacting to changes in the external environment after they occur

reciprocal interdependence work completed by different jobs or groups working together in a back-and-forth manner

recovery the strategic actions taken after retrenchment to return to a growth strategy

recruiting the process of developing a pool of qualified job applicants

reengineering fundamental rethinking and radical redesign of business processes to achieve dramatic improvements in critical measures of performance, such as cost, quality, service, and speed

referents in equity theory, others with whom people compare themselves to determine if they have been treated fairly

refreezing supporting and reinforcing new changes so that they "stick"

regional trading zones areas in which tariff and nontariff barriers on trade between countries are reduced or eliminated

regulation costs the costs associated with implementing or maintaining control

reinforcement the process of changing behavior by changing the consequences that follow behavior

reinforcement contingencies cause-and-effect relationships between the performance of specific behaviors and specific consequences

reinforcement theory the theory that behavior is a function of its consequences, that behaviors followed by positive consequences will occur more frequently, and that behaviors followed by negative consequences, or not followed by positive consequences, will occur less frequently

related diversification creating or acquiring companies that share similar products, manufacturing, marketing, technology, or cultures

relationship behavior the establishment of mutually beneficial, long-term exchanges between buyers and suppliers

relative comparisons a process in which each decision criterion is compared directly with every other criterion

resistance forces forces that support the existing state of conditions in organizations

resistance to change opposition to change resulting from self-interest, misunderstanding and distrust, or a general intolerance for change

resource allocator role the decisional role managers play when they decide who gets what resources

resource scarcity the abundance or shortage of critical organizational resources in an organization's external environment

resource similarity the extent to which a competitor has similar amounts and kinds of resources

resources the assets, capabilities, processes, employee time, information, and knowledge that an organization uses to improve its effectiveness and efficiency, create and sustain competitive advantage, and fulfill a need or solve a problem

response a competitive countermove, prompted by a rival's attack, to defend or improve a company's market share or profit

results-driven change change created quickly by focusing on the measurement and improvement of results

retrenchment strategy a strategy that focuses on turning around very poor company performance by shrinking the size or scope of the business

retrieval cost the cost of accessing already-stored and processed information

rules and regulations standing plans that describe how a particular action should be performed, or what must happen or not happen in response to a particular event

S

S.M.A.R.T. goals goals that are specific, measurable, attainable, realistic, and timely

satisficing choosing a "good enough" alternative

schedule of reinforcement rules that specify which behaviors will be reinforced, which consequences will follow those behaviors, and the schedule by which those consequences will be delivered

schedule time a cultural norm for the time by which scheduled projects or jobs should actually be completed

scientific management thoroughly studying and testing different work methods to identify the best, most efficient way to complete a job

S-curve pattern of innovation a pattern of technological innovation characterized by slow initial progress, then rapid progress, and then slow progress again as a technology matures and reaches its limits

secondary firms the firms in a strategic group that follow strategies related to but somewhat different from those of the core firms

secondary stakeholder any group that can influence or be influenced by a company and can affect public perceptions about its socially responsible behavior

secure sockets layer (SSL) encryption Internet browser–based encryption that provides secure off-site web access to some data and programs

selection the process of gathering information about job applicants to decide who should be offered a job

selective perception the tendency to notice and accept objects and information consistent with our values, beliefs, and expectations, while ignoring or screening out or not accepting inconsistent information

self-control (self-management) a control system in which managers and workers control their own behavior by setting their own goals, monitoring their own progress, and rewarding themselves for goal achievement

self-designing team a team that has the characteristics of self-managing teams but also controls team design, work tasks, and team membership

self-managing team a team that manages and controls all of the major tasks of producing a product or service

self-serving bias the tendency to overestimate our value by attributing successes to ourselves (internal causes) and attributing failures to others or the environment (external causes)

semi-autonomous work group a group that has the authority to make decisions and solve problems related to the major tasks of producing a product or service

sequence patterns when two or more database elements occur together in a significant pattern, but one of the elements precedes the other

sequential interdependence work completed in succession, with one group's or job's outputs becoming the inputs for the next group or job

service recovery restoring customer satisfaction to strongly dissatisfied customers

setup cost the costs of downtime and lost efficiency that occur when a machine is changed or adjusted to produce a different kind of inventory

sex discrimination treating people differently because of their sex

sexual harassment a form of discrimination in which unwelcome sexual advances, requests for sexual favors, or other verbal or physical conduct of a sexual nature occurs while performing one's job

shadow-strategy task force a committee within a company that analyzes the company's own weaknesses to determine how competitors could exploit them for competitive advantage

shared spaces spaces used by and open to all employees

shareholder model a view of social responsibility that holds that an organization's overriding goal should be profit maximization for the benefit of shareholders

simple environment an environment with few environmental factors

simple matrix a form of matrix departmentalization in which managers in different parts of the matrix negotiate conflicts and resources

single-use plans plans that cover unique, one-time-only events

situational (SWOT) analysis an assessment of the strengths and weaknesses in an organization's internal environment and the opportunities and threats in its external environment

situational favorableness the degree to which a particular situation either permits or denies a leader the chance to influence the behavior of group members

situational theory a leadership theory that states that leaders need to adjust their leadership styles to match their followers' readiness

skill-based pay compensation system that pays employees for learning additional skills or knowledge

skills-based diversity training training that teaches employees the practical skills they need for managing a diverse work force, such as flexibility and adaptability, negotiation, problem solving, and conflict resolution

skill variety the number of different activities performed in a job

slack resources a cushion of extra resources that can be used with options-based planning to adapt to unanticipated change, problems, or opportunities

social consensus agreement on whether behavior is bad or good

social integration the degree to which group members are psychologically attracted to working with each other to accomplish a common objective

social loafing behavior in which team members withhold their efforts and fail to perform their share of the work

social responsibility a business's obligation to pursue policies, make decisions, and take actions that benefit society

social responsiveness the strategy chosen by a company to respond to stakeholders' economic, legal, ethical, or discretionary expectations concerning social responsibility

soldiering when workers deliberately slow their pace or restrict their work outputs

specific ability tests (aptitude tests) tests that measure the extent to which an applicant possesses the particular kind of ability needed to do a job well

specific environment the customers, competitors, suppliers, industry regulations, and advocacy groups that are unique to an industry and directly affect how a company does business

spokesperson role the informational role managers play when they share information with people outside their departments or companies

stability strategy a strategy that focuses on improving the way in which the company sells the same products or services to the same customers

stable environment an environment in which the rate of change is slow

staff authority the right to advise, but not command, others who are not subordinates in the chain of command

staff function an activity that does not contribute directly to creating or selling the company's products, but instead supports line activities

stakeholder model a theory of corporate responsibility that holds that management's most important responsibility, long-term survival, is achieved by satisfying the interests of multiple corporate stakeholders

stakeholders persons or groups with a "stake" or legitimate interest in a company's actions

standardization solving problems by consistently applying the same rules, procedures, and processes

standards a basis of comparison for measuring the extent to which various kinds of organizational performance are satisfactory or unsatisfactory

standing plans plans used repeatedly to handle frequently recurring events

star a company with a large share of a fast-growing market

stepladder technique a decision-making method in which group members are added to a group discussion one at a time (i.e., like a stepladder). The existing group members listen to each new member's thoughts, ideas, and recommendations; then the group shares the ideas and suggestions that it had already considered, discusses the new and old ideas, and makes a decision.

stock options a compensation system that gives employees the right to purchase shares of stock at a set price, even if the value of the stock increases above that price

stockout the point when a company runs out of finished product

stockout costs the costs incurred when a company runs out of a product, including transaction costs to replace inventory and the loss of customers' goodwill

storage cost the cost of physically or electronically archiving information for later use and retrieval

storming the second stage of development, characterized by conflict and disagreement, in which team members disagree over what the team should do and how it should do it

strategic alliance an agreement in which companies combine key resources, costs, risk, technology, and people

strategic dissonance a discrepancy between a company's intended strategy and the strategic actions managers take when implementing that strategy

strategic group a group of companies within an industry that top managers choose to compare, evaluate, and benchmark strategic threats and opportunities

strategic leadership the ability to anticipate, envision, maintain flexibility, think strategically, and work with others to initiate changes that will create a positive future for an organization

strategic plans overall company plans that clarify how the company will serve customers and position itself against competitors over the next two to five years

strategic reference points the strategic targets managers use to measure whether a firm has developed the core competencies it needs to achieve a sustainable competitive advantage

stretch goals extremely ambitious goals that employees initially don't know how to accomplish

structural accommodation the ability to change organizational structures, policies, and practices in order to meet stretch goals

structured interviews interviews in which all applicants are asked the same set of standardized questions, usually including situational, behavioral, background, and job-knowledge questions

subjective performance measures measures of job performance that require someone to judge or assess a worker's performance

suboptimization performance improvement in one part of an organization but only at the expense of decreased performance in another part

subsidies government loans, grants, and tax deferments given to domestic companies to protect them from foreign competition

subsystems smaller systems that operate within the context of a larger system

supervised data mining the process when the user tells the data mining software to look and test for specific patterns and relationships in a data set

supplier dependence the degree to which a company relies on a supplier because of the importance of the supplier's product to the company and the difficulty of finding other sources of that product

suppliers companies that provide material, human, financial, and informational resources to other companies

supportive leadership a leadership style in which the leader is friendly to and approachable, shows concern for employees and their welfare, treats them as equals, and creates a friendly climate

surface-level diversity differences such as age, sex, race/ethnicity, and physical disabilities that are observable, typically unchangeable, and easy to measure

survey feedback information that is collected by surveys from organizational members and then compiled, disseminated, and used to develop action plans for improvement

sustainable competitive advantage a competitive advantage that other companies have tried unsuccessfully to duplicate and have, for the moment, stopped trying to duplicate

synergy when two or more subsystems working together can produce more than they can working apart

system a set of interrelated elements or parts that function as a whole

T

tactical plans plans created and implemented by middle managers that specify how the company will use resources, budgets, and people over the next six months to two years to accomplish specific goals within its mission

tariff a direct tax on imported goods

task identity the degree to which a job, from beginning to end, requires the completion of a whole and identifiable piece of work

task interdependence the extent to which collective action is required to complete an entire piece of work

task significance the degree to which a job is perceived to have a substantial impact on others inside or outside the organization

task structure the degree to which the requirements of a subordinate's tasks are clearly specified

team diversity the variances or differences in ability, experience, personality, or any other factor on a team

team leaders managers responsible for facilitating team activities toward goal accomplishment

team level the average level of ability, experience, personality, or any other factor on a team

teamwork collaboration between managers and nonmanagers, across business functions, and between companies, customers, and suppliers

technical skills the ability to apply the specialized procedures, techniques, and knowledge required to get the job done

technological discontinuity the phase of an innovation stream in which a scientific advance or unique combination of existing technologies creates a significant breakthrough in performance or function

technological lockout the inability of a company to competitively sell its products because it relied on old technology or a nondominant design

technological substitution the purchase of new technologies to replace older ones

technology the knowledge, tools, and techniques used to transform input into output

technology cycle a cycle that begins with the "birth" of a new technology and ends when that technology reaches its limits and is replaced by a newer, substantially better technology

televised/videotaped speeches and meetings speeches and meetings originally made to a smaller audience that are either simultaneously broadcast to other locations in the company or videotaped for subsequent distribution and viewing

temporal immediacy the time between an act and the consequences the act produces

testing the systematic comparison of different product designs or design iterations

threat of new entrants a measure of the degree to which barriers to entry make it easy or difficult for new companies to get started in an industry

threat of substitute products or services a measure of the ease with which customers can find substitutes for an industry's products or services

360-degree feedback a performance appraisal process in which feedback is obtained from the boss, subordinates, peers and coworkers, and the employees themselves

time study timing how long it takes good workers to complete each part of their jobs

top managers executives responsible for the overall direction of the organization

total quality management (TQM) an integrated, principle-based, organization-wide strategy for improving product and service quality

trade barriers government-imposed regulations that increase the cost and restrict the number of imported goods

traditional work group a group composed of two or more people who work together to achieve a shared goal

training developing the skills, experience, and knowledge employees need to perform their jobs or improve their performance

trait theory a leadership theory that holds that effective leaders possess a similar set of traits or characteristics

traits relatively stable characteristics, such as abilities, psychological motives, or consistent patterns of behavior

transactional leadership leadership based on an exchange process, in which followers are rewarded for good performance and punished for poor performance

transformational leadership leadership that generates awareness and acceptance of a group's purpose and mission and gets employees to see beyond their own needs and self-interests for the good of the group

transient firms the firms in a strategic group whose strategies are changing from one strategic position to another

transition management team (TMT) a team of 8 to 12 people whose full-time job is to manage and coordinate a company's change process

two-factor authentication authentication based on what users know, such as a password and what they have in their possession, such as a secure ID card or key

Type A personality a person who tries to complete as many tasks as possible in the shortest possible time and is hard driving, competitive, impatient, perfectionistic, angry, and unable to relax

Type A/B personality dimension the extent to which people tend toward impatience, hurriedness, competitiveness, and hostility

Type B personality a person who is relaxed, easygoing, and able to engage in leisure activities without worrying about work

U

uncertainty extent to which managers can understand or predict which environmental changes and trends will affect their businesses

underreward a form of inequity in which you are getting fewer outcomes relative to inputs than your referent

unethical charismatics charismatic leaders who control and manipulate followers, do what is best for themselves instead of their organizations, want to hear only positive feedback, share only information that is beneficial to themselves, and have moral standards that put their interests before everyone else's

unfreezing getting the people affected by change to believe that change is needed

unity of command a management principle that workers should report to just one boss

unrelated diversification creating or acquiring companies in completely unrelated businesses

unstructured interviews interviews in which interviewers are free to ask the applicants anything they want

unsupervised data mining the process when the user simply tells the data mining software to uncover whatever patterns and relationships it can find in a data set

upward communication communication that flows from lower to higher levels in an organization

V

valence the attractiveness or desirability of a reward or outcome

validation the process of determining how well a selection test or procedure predicts future job performance. The better or more accurate the prediction of future job performance, the more valid a test is said to be.

valuable resource a resource that allows companies to improve efficiency and effectiveness

value customer perception that the product quality is excellent for the price offered

variable interval reinforcement schedule an intermittent schedule in which the time between a behavior and the following consequences varies around a specified average

variable ratio reinforcement schedule an intermittent schedule in which consequences are delivered following a different number of behaviors, sometimes more and sometimes less, that vary around a specified average number of behaviors

variation a deviation in the form, condition, or appearance of a product from the quality standard for that product

virtual organization an organization that is part of a network in which many companies share skills, costs, capabilities, markets, and customers to collectively solve customer problems or provide specific products or services

virtual private network (VPN) software that securely encrypts data sent by employees outside the company network, decrypts the data when they arrive within the company computer network, and does the same when data are sent back to employees outside the network

virtual team a team composed of geographically and/or organizationally dispersed coworkers who use telecommunication and information technologies to accomplish an organizational task

virus a program or piece of code that, without your knowledge, attaches itself to other programs on your computer and can trigger anything from a harmless flashing message to the reformatting of your hard drive to a systemwide network shutdown

visible artifacts visible signs of an organization's culture, such as the office design and layout, company dress code, and company benefits and perks, like stock options, personal parking spaces, or the private company dining room

vision an inspirational statement of an organization's enduring purpose

visionary leadership leadership that creates a positive image of the future that motivates organizational members and provides direction for future planning and goal setting

voluntary export restraints voluntarily imposed limits on the number or volume of products exported to a particular country

web services using standardized protocols to describe data from one company in such a way that those data can automatically be read, understood, transcribed, and processed by different computer systems in another company

whistleblowing reporting others' ethics violations to management or legal authorities

wholly owned affiliates foreign offices, facilities, and manufacturing plants that are 100 percent owned by the parent company

work force forecasting the process of predicting the number and kind of workers with specific skills and abilities that an organization will need in the future

work sample tests tests that require applicants to perform tasks that are actually done on the job

work team a small number of people with complementary skills who hold themselves mutually accountable for pursuing a common purpose, achieving performance goals, and improving interdependent work processes

worker readiness the ability and willingness to take responsibility for directing one's behavior at work

workplace deviance unethical behavior that violates organizational norms about right and wrong

work-in-process inventories partially finished goods consisting of assembled component parts

World Trade Organization (WTO) as the successor to GATT, the only international organization dealing with the global rules of trade between nations. Its main function is to ensure that trade flows as smoothly, predictably, and freely as possible.

wrongful discharge a legal doctrine that requires employers to have a job-related reason to terminate employees

NAME INDEX

C

D

E

F

G

H

I

T

U

V

W

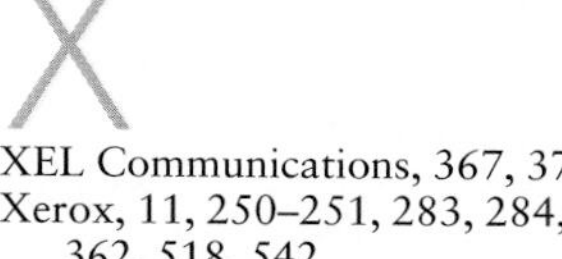

Y

Z

SUBJECT INDEX

D

E

F

G

H

I

J

K

L

M

Q

R

S

T

U

"What's New" Companies

A

Ace Hardware
Acxiom
AES
Aetna
Agile Web
Agilent
Airbus
Alamo Rent-a-Car
Alcan
Aldi
Alteon WebSystems
Amazon
American Express
Apple
Aramark
AT&T
Audi
Avero
Avery Dennison
Avon
Axcelis Technologies

B

Baker & McKenzie
Bank of America
Barneys New York
Baxter International
BBDO
Behlen Manufacturing
Ben & Jerry's
Beretta
Best Buy
Bloomberg
BMW
Boeing
Bombardier Aerospace
Boston Celtics
Boston Consulting Group
Bowa Builders
Bristol-Myers Squibb
British Petroleum
Burger King

C

Cadbury Schweppes
Cadillac
Canada Cordage
CareerBuilder.com
Caremark International
CBS
CDW
Cerner Corporation
Cessna
Chaparral Energy
Checkers Drive-In Restaurants
Chicago Harvester
Chicago Sun-Times
Chigo Air-Conditioning
Chipotle Mexican Grill
Chrysler
Chugach School District
Ciba-Geigy
CIGNA Behavioral Health
Cisco Systems
Citigroup
Coca-Cola
Coca-Cola Enterprises Three Counties
Comambault
Comcast
Container Store
Continental Airlines
Con-way
Corning Glass
Costco
Coventry Mall
Crate and Barrel
Crown Cork
CSX
CVS

D

DaimlerChrysler
De Beers Consolidated Mines
Dell
Deloitte Touche Tohmatsu
Denny's
Diebold
Dinner by Design
Dow Chemical
Drugstore.com
Duke Children's Hospital
Dunkin' Donuts
Dyson

E

E.W. Scripps
EA Sports
East Providence, Rhode Island Police Department
Eastman Chemical
Eastman Kodak
Eaton Corporation
EchoStar Communications
Edward Jones
84 Lumber
Electric Boat
Electronic Arts
Eli Lilly & Co.
EMC
Enron
Enterprise Rent-a-Car
Ernst & Young
EthicsPoint
ExxonMobil

F

FastCar
FedEx
Fiat
Ford Motor Company
FremantleMedia (American Idol)
Freudenberg-NOK
Frito-Lay
Fuji Xerox
Fujisawa Pharmaceuticals

G

Gallup Organization
GE Aircraft Engines Gap
Genencor
General Electric
General Mills
General Motors
Gillette
GlaxoSmithKline
Goodyear
Google

H

Habitat International
Hampton Inn
Health Decisions
Heil Trailer International
Hewlett-Packard
Hillman Group
Hoechst Celanese
Home Depot
Honda Motors of America
Hooters
Hoover
HotJobs.com
Hyperspace Communications
Hyundai

I

Iberia
IBM
IBM Credit
IKEA
Impact Innovations Group
Incredible Universe
Industrial Light & Magic
Infosys
InnoCentive
Intel
iRobot
ISG Steelton
ITT
iTunes

J

J. D. Power and Associates
J.M. Smucker
Jamaican Bobsled Team
JCPenney
JetBlue
JPMorgan Chase

K

Kaiser Permanente
KFC
Kikkoman
Kimberly-Clark
Kmart

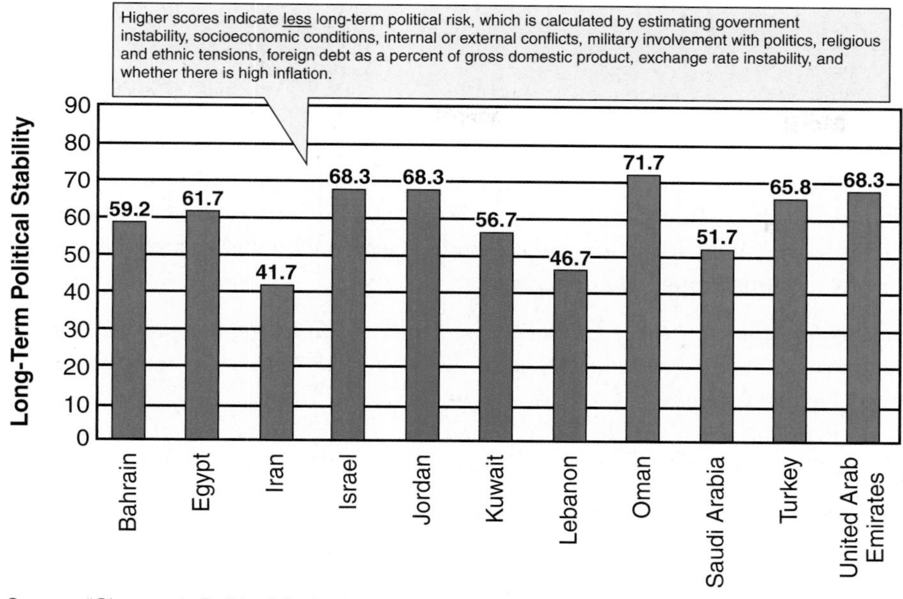

Source: "Chapter 1: Political Outlook," *UAE Business Forecast Report*, 2007 1st Quarter, 5–10.

Exhibit 8.8

Long-Term Political Stability in the Middle East

a business. For example, a German company forming a joint venture with a Chinese company to do business in China may structure the joint venture contract so that the Chinese company owns 51 percent or more of the joint venture. Doing so qualifies the joint venture as a Chinese company and exempts it from Chinese laws that apply to foreign-owned businesses. However, as we saw with Shell and Gazprom, the state-controlled Russian oil company, cooperation cannot always protect against *policy risk* if a foreign government changes its laws and policies to directly affect the way foreign companies conduct business.

Review 4: Finding the Best Business Climate

The first step in deciding where to take your company global is finding an attractive business climate. Look for a growing market where consumers have strong purchasing power and foreign competitors are weak. When locating an office or manufacturing facility, consider both qualitative and quantitative factors. In assessing political risk, be sure to examine political uncertainty and policy uncertainty. If the location you choose has considerable political risk, you can avoid it, try to control the risk, or use a cooperation strategy.

doing the right thing

Foreign Corrupt Business Practices Act

The Foreign Corrupt Business Practices Act (FCPA) prohibits company managers, employees, or agents from offering money or anything else of value to bribe officials of foreign governments or political parties to use their influence to help that firm acquire new business or keep existing business in that country. Individuals violating the FCPA can be fined up to $100,000 and imprisoned for up to 10 years. Companies that violate the FCPA can be fined up to $2 million, suspended from government contracts, denied export licensing privileges, and investigated by the Securities and Exchange Commission. U.S. businesspeople often worry that the FCPA puts them at a disadvantage because other countries have permitted bribes to be deducted as business expenses. Recently, however, 33 major trading partners of the United States agreed to enact laws similar to the FCPA.[77]

5 Becoming Aware of Cultural Differences

Some of the more interesting and amusing aspects of global business are the unexpected confrontations that people have with cultural differences, "the way they do things over there." *Wall Street Journal* columnist Geoffrey Fowler relates the following story from Hong Kong, where he works:

> *I was riding the elevator a few weeks ago with a Chinese colleague here in the* Journal's *Asian headquarters. I smiled and said, "Hi." She responded, "You've gained weight."*
>
> *I might have been appalled, but at least three other Chinese coworkers also have told me I'm fat. I probably should cut back on the pork dumplings.*[78]

Uttered in the United States, such comments would be considered rude. Fowler indicates that in China, where people openly talk about people's weight, body shapes, and salaries, such comments are probably just friendliness. Likewise, the Chinese colleagues of American Jennifer Gallo, who works in Beijing, have commented on her clothing ("very nice, could be European"), her muscle tone ("flabby"), and her likeliness to bear children ("certain to have many boys").[79] So what does Fowler say when his friendly Chinese colleagues tell him he's fat? "There's so much good food here."

National culture is the set of shared values and beliefs that affects the perceptions, decisions, and behavior of the people from a particular country. The first step in dealing with culture is to recognize that there are meaningful differences in national cultures. Professor Geert Hofstede spent 20 years studying cultural differences in 53 different countries. His research shows that there are five consistent cultural dimensions across countries: power distance, individualism, masculinity, uncertainty avoidance, and short-term versus long-term orientation.[80]

> "The first step in dealing with culture is to recognize that there are meaningful differences in national cultures."

Power distance is the extent to which people in a country accept that power is distributed unequally in society and organizations. In countries where power distance is weak, such as Denmark and Sweden, employees don't like their organization or their boss to have power over them or tell them what to do. They want to have a say in decisions that affect them. As Exhibit 8.9 shows, Russia and China, with scores of 95 and 80 respectively, are much stronger in power distance than Germany (35), the Netherlands (38), and the United States (40).

Individualism is the degree to which societies believe that individuals should be self-sufficient. In individualistic societies, employees put loyalty to themselves first and loyalty to their company and work group second. In Exhibit 8.9, the United States (91), the Netherlands (80), France (71), and Germany (67) are the strongest in individualism, while Indonesia (14), West Africa (20), and China (20) are the weakest.

Masculinity and *femininity* capture the difference between highly assertive and highly nurturing cultures. Masculine cultures emphasize assertiveness, competition, material success, and achievement, whereas feminine cultures emphasize the importance of relationships, modesty, caring for the weak, and quality of life. In Exhibit 8.9, Japan (95), Germany (66), and the United States (62) have the most masculine orientations, while the Netherlands (14) has the most feminine orientation.

national culture the set of shared values and beliefs that affects the perceptions, decisions, and behavior of the people from a particular country

The cultural difference of *uncertainty avoidance* is the degree to which people in a country are uncomfortable with unstructured, ambiguous, unpredictable situations. In countries with strong uncertainty avoidance, like Greece and Portugal, people tend to be aggressive and emotional and seek security (rather than uncertainty). In Exhibit 8.9,

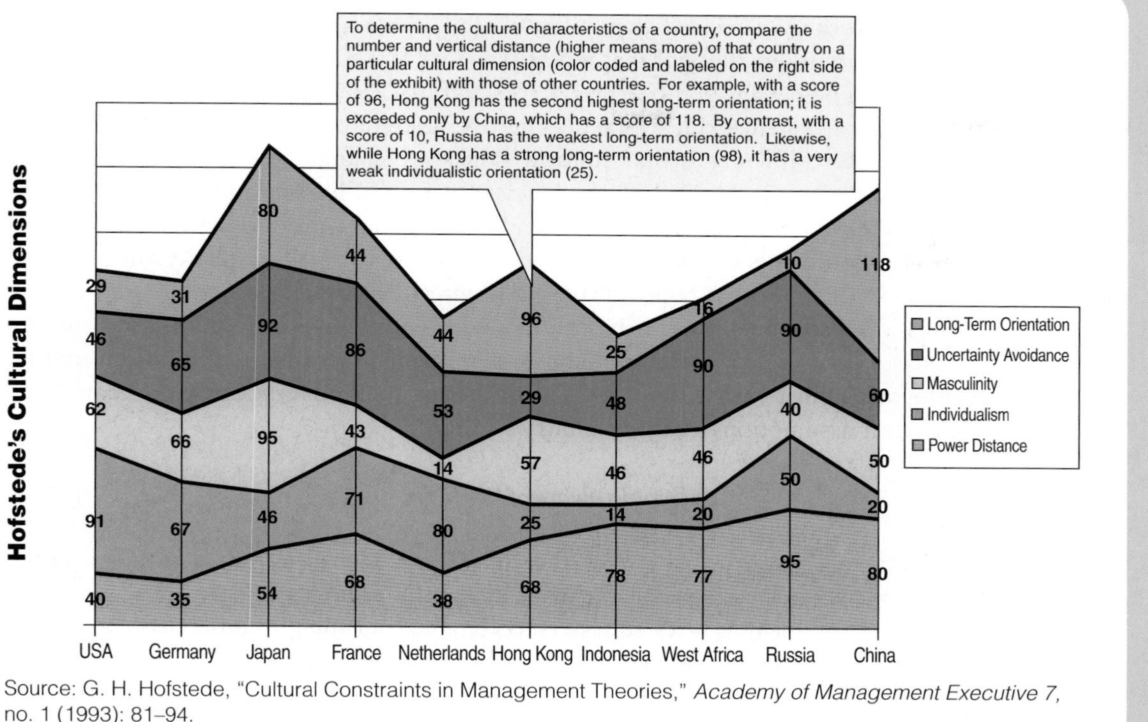

Source: G. H. Hofstede, "Cultural Constraints in Management Theories," *Academy of Management Executive 7*, no. 1 (1993): 81–94.

Exhibit 8.9

Hofstede's Five Cultural Dimensions

Japan (92), France (86), West Africa (90), and Russia (90) are strongest in uncertainty avoidance, while Hong Kong (29) is the weakest.

Short-term/long-term orientation addresses whether cultures are oriented to the present and seek immediate gratification, or to the future and defer gratification. Not surprisingly, countries with short-term orientations are consumer driven, whereas countries with long-term orientations are savings driven. In Exhibit 8.9, China (118) and Hong Kong (96) have very strong long-term orientations, while Russia (10), West Africa (16), Indonesia (25), the United States (29), and Germany (31) have very strong short-term orientations. To generate a graphical comparison of two different country's cultures, go to **http://www.geert-hofstede.com/hofstede_dimensions.php.** Select a "home culture." Then select a "host culture." A graph comparing the countries on each of Hofstede's five cultural differences will automatically be generated.

Cultural differences affect perceptions, understanding, and behavior. Recognizing cultural differences is critical to succeeding in global business. Nevertheless, as Hofstede pointed out, descriptions of cultural differences are based on averages—the average level of uncertainty avoidance in Portugal, the average level of power distance in Argentina, and so forth. Accordingly, says Hofstede, "If you are going to spend time with a Japanese colleague, you shouldn't assume that overall cultural statements about Japanese society automatically apply to this person."[81] Similarly, cultural beliefs may differ significantly from one part of a country to another.[82]

After becoming aware of cultural differences, the second step is deciding how to adapt your company to those differences. Unfortunately, studies investigating the effects of cultural differences on management practice point more to difficulties than to easy solutions. One problem is that different cultures will probably perceive management policies and practices differently. For example, blue-collar workers in France and Argentina, all of whom performed the same factory jobs for the same multinational company, perceived its company-wide safety policy differently.[83]

French workers perceived that safety wasn't very important to the company, but Argentine workers thought that it was. The fact that something as simple as a safety policy can be perceived differently across cultures shows just how difficult it can be to standardize management practices across different countries and cultures.

Another difficulty is that cultural values are changing, albeit slowly, in many parts of the world. The fall of communism in eastern Europe and the former Soviet Union and the broad economic reforms in China have produced sweeping changes on two continents in the last decade. Thanks to increased global trade resulting from GATT and other regional free trade agreements, major economic transformations are also under way in India, Mexico, Central America, and South America. Consequently, when trying to adapt management practices to cultural differences, companies must ensure that they are not basing their adaptations on outdated and incorrect assumptions about a country's culture.

Review 5: Becoming Aware of Cultural Differences

National culture is the set of shared values and beliefs that affects the perceptions, decisions, and behavior of the people from a particular country. The first step in dealing with culture is to recognize meaningful differences, such as power distance, individualism, masculinity, uncertainty avoidance, and short-term/long-term orientation. Cultural differences should be carefully interpreted because they are based on averages, not individuals. Adapting managerial practices to cultural differences is difficult because policies and practices can be perceived differently in different cultures. Another difficulty is that cultural values may be changing in many parts of the world. Consequently, when companies try to adapt management practices to cultural differences, they need to be sure that they are not using outdated assumptions about a country's culture.

6 Preparing for an International Assignment

Around a conference table in a large U.S. office tower, three American executives sat with their new boss, Akiro Kusumoto, the newly appointed head of a Japanese firm's American subsidiary, and two of his Japanese lieutenants. The meeting was called to discuss ideas for reducing operating costs. Kusumoto began by outlining his company's aspirations for its long-term U.S. presence. He then turned to the budgetary matter. One Japanese manager politely offered one suggestion, and an American then proposed another. After gingerly discussing the alternatives for quite some time, the exasperated American blurted out: "Look, that idea is just not going to have much impact. Look at the numbers!" In the face of such bluntness, uncommon and unacceptable in Japan, Kusumoto fell silent. He leaned back, drew air between his teeth, and felt a deep longing to return home.

mgmt: fact

Bilingualism—A Growing Trend

Over 50 million people in the United States speak more than one language. This number is double what it was just 20 years ago, and it continues to grow. In Europe even more value is placed on the ability to speak multiple languages; more Europeans are multilingual, speaking three or more languages, than are just bilingual. Being able to communicate in multiple languages is an important asset in any business and can help give a company the edge it needs to succeed in a competitive market.

Source: "Two Languages Spoken Here," Talaris Research Institute, April 2006, http://www.talaris.org/spotlight_bilingual.htm.

He realized his life in this country would be filled with many such jarring encounters and lamented his posting to a land of such rudeness.[84]

Akiro Kusumoto is a Japanese **expatriate**, someone who lives and works outside his or her native country. The cultural shock that he was experiencing is common. The difficulty of adjusting to language, cultural, and social differences is the primary reason for expatriate failure in overseas assignments. For example, although there have recently been disagreements among researchers about these numbers, it is probably safe to say that 5 to 20 percent of American expatriates sent abroad by their companies will return to the United States before they have successfully completed their assignments.[85] Of those who do complete their international assignments, about one-third are judged by their companies to be no better than marginally effective.[86]

Since the average cost of sending an employee on a three-year international assignment is $1 million, failure in those assignments can be extraordinarily expensive.[87]

© SUSAN VAN ETTEN

*The chances for a successful international assignment can be increased through **6.1 language and cross-cultural training** and **6.2 consideration of spouse, family, and dual-career issues**.*

6.1 Language and Cross-Cultural Training

Predeparture language and cross-cultural training can reduce the uncertainty that expatriates feel, the misunderstandings that take place between expatriates and natives, and the inappropriate behaviors that expatriates unknowingly commit when they travel to a foreign country. Indeed, simple things like using a phone, locating a public toilet, asking for directions, finding out how much things cost, exchanging greetings, or understanding what people want can become tremendously complex when expatriates don't know a foreign language or a country's customs and cultures. In his book *Blunders in International Business*, David Ricks tells the story of an American manager working in the South Pacific who, by hiring too many local workers from one native group, unknowingly upset the balance of power in the island's traditional status system. The islanders met on their own and quickly worked out a solution to the problem. After concluding their meeting at 3 AM, they calmly went to the manager's home to discuss their solution with him (time was not important in their culture). But since the American didn't speak their language and didn't understand why they had shown up en masse outside his home at 3 AM, he called in the Marines, who were stationed nearby, to disperse what he thought was a riot.

Expatriates who receive predeparture language and cross-cultural training make faster adjustments to foreign cultures and perform better on their international assignments.[88] Unfortunately, only a third of the managers who go on international assignments are offered any kind of predeparture training, and only half of those actually participate in the training![89] Suzanne Bernard, director of international mobility at **Bombardier Aerospace** in Canada, says, "We always offer cross-cultural training, but it's very seldom used by executives leaving in a rush at the last minute."[90] This is somewhat surprising given the failure rates for expatriates and the high cost of those failures. Furthermore, with the exception of some language courses, predeparture training is not particularly expensive or difficult to provide. Three methods can be used to prepare workers for international assignments: documentary training, cultural simulations, and field experiences.

Documentary training focuses on identifying specific critical differences between cultures. For example, when 60 workers at **Axcelis Technologies** in Beverly, Massachusetts, were preparing to do business in India, they learned that while

expatriate someone who lives and works outside his or her native country

Americans make eye contact and shake hands firmly when greeting others, Indians, as a sign of respect, do just the opposite, avoiding eye contact and shaking hands limply.[91]

After learning specific critical differences through documentary training, trainees can then participate in *cultural simulations*, in which they practice adapting to cultural differences. After the workers at Axcelis Technologies learned about key differences between their culture and India's, they practiced adapting to those differences by role playing: Some Axcelis workers would take the roles of Indian workers, while other Axcelis workers would play themselves and try to behave in a way consistent with Indian culture. As they role-played, Indian music played loudly in the background, and they were coached on what to do or not do by Bidhan Chandra, an international consultant. Chandra says, "When people understand these differences, they're less likely to make mistakes with each other." Axcelis human resources director Randy Longo says, "At first, I was skeptical and wondered what I'd get out of the class. But it was enlightening for me. Not everyone operates like we do in America."

Finally, *field simulation* training, a technique made popular by the **U.S. Peace Corps**, places trainees in an ethnic neighborhood for three to four hours to talk to residents about cultural differences. For example, a U.S. electronics manufacturer prepared workers for assignments in South Korea by having trainees explore a nearby South Korean neighborhood and talk to shopkeepers and people on the street about South Korean politics, family orientation, and day-to-day living practices.

6.2 Spouse, Family, and Dual-Career Issues

When Ford Motor Company manager John Larsen moved his wife, Laurel, and their children, ages 2, 4, and 6, to Chongqing, China, his children became a "crowd-stopping spectacle" as local people, who had never seen Westerners, much less their children, stopped to gawk. Laurel Larsen says, "It's not very fun and my kids hate it. . . . When we go home [to the 19th-floor Hilton hotel suite in which they live] and close the door, we feel like we are back in America.[92]

Not all international assignments are as difficult for expatriates and their families, but the evidence clearly shows that how well an expatriate's spouse and family adjust to the foreign culture is the most important factor in determining the success or failure of an international assignment.[93] Barry Kozloff of Selection Research International says, "The cost of sending a family on a foreign assignment is around $1 million and their failure to adjust is an enormous loss."[94] Unfortunately, despite its importance, there has been little systematic research on what does and does not help expatriates' families successfully adapt. A number of companies, however, have found that adaptability screening and intercultural training for families can lead to more successful overseas adjustment.

Adaptability screening is used to assess how well managers and their families are likely to adjust to foreign cultures. For example, **Prudential Relocation Management**'s international division has developed an "Overseas Assignment Inventory" to assess a spouse and family's open-mindedness, respect for others' beliefs, sense of humor, and marital communication. Likewise, Pennsylvania-based AMP, a worldwide producer of electrical connectors, conducts extensive psychological screening on expatriates and their spouses when making international assignments. But adaptability screening does not just involve a company assessing an employee; it can also involve an employee screening international assignments for desirability. Since more employees are becoming aware of the costs of international assignments (spouses having to give up or change jobs, children having to change schools, everyone having to learn a new language), some companies are willing to pay for a preassignment trip so the employee and his or her spouse can investigate the country *before* accepting the international assignment.[95]

MARK SHANAHAN
106 ROXBURY St.
KEENE, N.H.
03431

357-7661

MICROPROCESSORS AND INTERFACING
Programming and Hardware

Douglas V. Hall

GLENCOE
Macmillan/McGraw-Hill
Lake Forest, Illinois   Columbus, Ohio
Mission Hills, California   Peoria, Illinois

Sponsoring Editor: Paul Berk
Editing Supervisor: James Fields
Design and Art Supervisor/Cover Designer: Frances Conte Saracco
Production Supervisor: Priscilla Taguer
Text Designer: Susan Brorein

Library of Congress Cataloging-in-Publication Data

Hall, Douglas V., date.
Microprocessors and interfacing.

Includes index.
1. Microprocessors—Programming. 2. Microprocessors. 3. Computer interfaces. I. Title.
QA76.6.H2994 1986 005.26 86-156
ISBN 0-07-025526-1

The manuscript for this book was prepared electronically.

Microprocessors and Interfacing:
Programming and Hardware
Imprint 1991

6 7 8 9 10 11 12 13 14 15 SEM 00 99 98 97 96 95 94 93 92 91

ISBN 0-07-025526-1

CONTENTS

PREFACE

For the most part, *Microprocessors and Interfacing: Programming and Hardware* is based on a three-quarter series of microprocessor courses that my colleagues and I teach. The book is intended for students in electrical engineering programs, students in electronic engineering technician training programs, and people working in industry who want to upgrade their knowledge of microprocessors.

Before reading this book, you should have some basic knowledge of diodes, transistors, and digital circuitry. One of its aims is to teach you how to decipher and use manufacturer's literature; accordingly, many relevant parts of data sheets are shown. Because of the large number of actual devices discussed here, it was impossible to put the complete data sheets for all these devices in the appendixes. Therefore, I strongly suggest that you acquire or gain access to the latest edition of the Intel *Microsystem Components Handbook* so that, as you work your way through this book, you can refer to it if you need further information about a particular device. The bibliography lists other materials I have found useful.

I have chosen here to teach the programming, system connections, and interfacing of 16-bit microprocessors, which function as the "brains" of microcomputers such as the IBM PC. My experience as an engineer and as a teacher indicates that it is more productive to learn one microprocessor family very thoroughly, and from that strong base learn other families as needed. Therefore, this book concentrates on the Intel 8086/8088/80186/80188/80286/80386 family of microprocessors, rather than superficially covering the microprocessor families of several manufacturers.

I came into the world of electronics through the route of vacuum tubes. Therefore, my first tendency was to approach microprocessors from a hardware orientation. However, the more I designed with microprocessors and taught microprocessor classes, the more I became aware that the real essence of a microprocessor is what you can program it to do. For this reason the book begins with just a brief overview of the hardware of a computer. The next five chapters show how a microprocessor-based microcomputer can be programmed to do some real tasks.

The emphasis throughout is on writing assembly language programs in a top-down structured manner. The idea is to make programs easy to write, test, and debug. Experience has shown that the most successful approach to writing a program is to solve the problem first, and then simply implement the solution in the desired programming language.

The 8086 instructions are introduced in Chapters 2 through 5, as they are needed to solve simple programming problems. Chapter 6 contains a dictionary of all the 8086 and 80186 instructions. You can refer to this chapter to find further details about an instruction you want to use to do a particular operation in a program.

Chapter 7 discusses the hardware signals, timing, and system connections of a simple microcomputer. Chapter 7 also teaches a systematic approach to troubleshooting a malfunctioning 8086-based system. The remaining chapters show how the hardware and the programs work together. Troubleshooting a microprocessor-based system, for example, usually requires knowledge of both its hardware and programming, so I discuss here how diagnostic routines are written and used to find a problem.

Chapter 8 discusses how the 8086 responds to interrupts and how interrupt service procedures are written and used. Chapters 9 through 13 describe in detail how a microcomputer is interfaced with a wide variety of devices and systems. Also these chapters describe how the hardware and programs for microprocessor-based products are developed. Finally, Chapter 14 discusses operating system programs, and the 80286 and 80386 microprocessors that are designed to be used as the brains of multiuser microcomputer systems.

Program development for 16-bit microprocessors is somewhat tedious on hex-keypad-type development boards such as we used for 8-bit processors. Furthermore, industry does not usually develop microprocessor-based products in this manner. Therefore, for working with 16-bit processors I recommend a systems approach. A microprocessor development system, an IBM PC, or IBM PC-compatible computer, can be used to edit, assemble, link/locate, run, and debug 8086 assembly language programs. For programs that require external hardware, the object code for these programs can be downloaded to some prototype hardware such as an Intel SDK-86 development board. Chapter 13 contains a program that allows you to download object code programs from an IBM or IBM-compatible computer to an SDK-86 board. An available laboratory manual, written to accompany this book, shows you how to use the SDK-86 board and an IBM PC-compatible computer for assembly language programming and interfacing.

In the interfacing sections of this book I have tried to show as many circuits as possible that you can build, add to your microcomputer, and experiment with. Building and experimenting with real circuits will help you become fluent with microprocessors. The circuits in this book are intended just as starters. Hopefully you will grow far beyond what is shown here. If you have suggestions for improving this book or ideas that might clarify a point for someone else, please communicate with me.

I wish to express my profound thanks to the people who helped make this book a reality. Thanks to Pat Hunter, without whose cheerful encouragement I might not have made it through the book. She proofread and coded the manuscript, worked out the answers to the end-of-chapter problems to verify that they are solvable, and made many suggestions and contributions too numerous to mention. Thanks to Lee Campbell of Spokane Community College in Spokane, Washington, who meticulously worked his way through the manuscript and made many valuable suggestions. Thanks to Wayne J. Vyrostek of Westark College in Fort Smith, Arkansas, who reviewed the manuscript and contributed several valuable suggestions. Thanks to Intel Corporation for letting me use many drawings from their data books, so that this book could lead readers into the material they can use to continue their learning. Finally, thanks to my family and friends for their patience and support during the long effort of writing this book.

Douglas V. Hall

DEDICATION

To my students — Who grow beyond what I give and return to pull me into the future with them.

CHAPTER

1 Computer Number Systems, Codes, and Digital Devices

Before starting our discussion of microprocessors and microcomputers we need to make sure that some key concepts of the number systems, codes, and digital devices used in microcomputers are fresh in your mind. If the short summaries of these concepts in this chapter are not enough to refresh your memory, then it is a good idea to review them in a current digital text before going on in this book.

OBJECTIVES

At the conclusion of this chapter you should be able to:

1. Convert numbers between the following codes: binary, octal, hexadecimal, and BCD.
2. Define the terms bit, nibble, byte, word, most significant bit, and least significant bit.
3. Use a table to find the ASCII or EBCDIC code for a given alphanumeric character.
4. Perform addition and subtraction of binary, octal, hexadecimal, and BCD numbers.
5. Describe the operation of gates, flip-flops, latches, registers, ROMs, dynamic RAMs, static RAMs, and buses.
6. Describe how an arithemtic logic unit can be instructed to perform arithmetic or logical operations on binary words.

COMPUTER NUMBER SYSTEMS AND CODES

Review of Decimal System

To understand the structure of the binary number system, the first step is to review the familiar decimal or base-10 number system. Figure 1-1*a* shows a decimal number with the value of each place holder or digit expressed as a power of 10. The digits in the decimal number 5346.72 then tell you that you have 5 thousands, 3 hundreds, 4 tens, 6 ones, 7 tenths, and 2 hundredths.

The number of symbols needed in any base number system is equal to the base number. In the decimal number system then, there are 10 symbols, 0 through 9. When the count in any digit position passes that of the highest value symbol, a carry of 1 is added to the next digit position and the other digit rolls back to zero. A car odometer is a good example of this.

A number system can be built using powers of any number as place holders or digits, but some bases are more useful than others. It is difficult to build electronic circuits which can store and manipulate 10 different voltage levels but relatively easy to build circuits which can handle two levels. Therefore, a *binary* or *base-2* number system is used.

The Binary Number System

Figure 1-1*b* shows the value of each digit in a binary number. Each binary digit represents a power of 2. A binary digit is often called a *bit*. Note that digits to the right of the *binary point* represent fractions used for numbers less than one. The binary system uses only two symbols, zero (0) and one (1). Therefore, in binary you count as follows: 0, 1, 10, 11, 100, 101, 110, 111, 1000, etc.

Binary numbers are often called *binary words* or just *words*. Binary words of certain numbers of bits have also acquired special names. A 4-bit binary word is

5 3 4 6 . 7 2

10^3 10^2 10^1 10^0 10^{-1} 10^{-2}

(*a*)

1 0 1 1 0 . 1 1

2^7 2^6 2^5 2^4 2^3 2^2 2^1 2^0 2^{-1} 2^{-2}

128 64 32 16 8 4 2 1 $\frac{1}{2}$ $\frac{1}{4}$

(*b*)

FIGURE 1-1 Digit values in decimal and binary. *(a)* Decimal. *(b)* Binary.

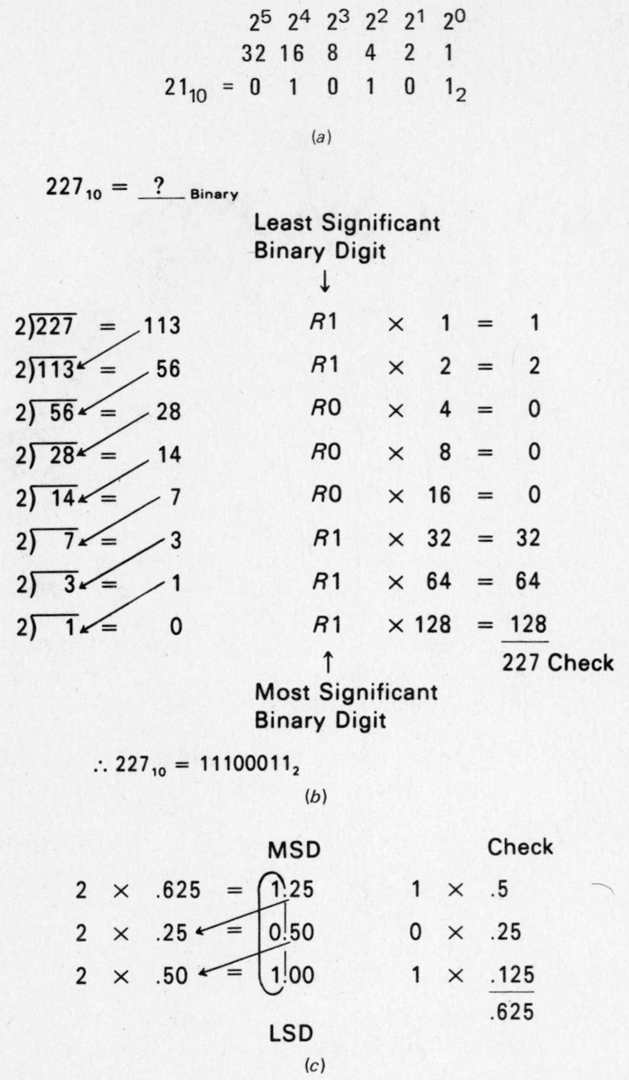

$$\begin{array}{rcccccc} & 2^5 & 2^4 & 2^3 & 2^2 & 2^1 & 2^0 \\ & 32 & 16 & 8 & 4 & 2 & 1 \\ 21_{10} = & 0 & 1 & 0 & 1 & 0 & 1_2 \end{array}$$

(a)

$227_{10} = \underline{\ ?\ }_{\text{Binary}}$

Least Significant Binary Digit ↓

Division		Quotient	Remainder		Weight		Value
2)227	=	113	R1	×	1	=	1
2)113	=	56	R1	×	2	=	2
2)56	=	28	R0	×	4	=	0
2)28	=	14	R0	×	8	=	0
2)14	=	7	R0	×	16	=	0
2)7	=	3	R1	×	32	=	32
2)3	=	1	R1	×	64	=	64
2)1	=	0	R1	×	128	=	128
							227 Check

↑ Most Significant Binary Digit

$\therefore 227_{10} = 11100011_2$

(b)

MSD

				Check
2 × .625	=	1.25		1 × .5
2 × .25	=	0.50		0 × .25
2 × .50	=	1.00		1 × .125
				.625

LSD

(c)

FIGURE 1-2 Converting decimal to binary. *(a)* Digit value method. *(b)* Divide by 2 method. *(c)* Decimal fraction conversion.

called a *nibble*, and an 8-bit binary word is called a *byte*. A 16-bit binary word is often referred to just as a *word*, and a 32-bit binary word is referred to as a *doubleword*. The rightmost or *least-significant bit* of a binary word is usually referred to as the LSB. The leftmost or *most-significant bit* of a binary word is usually called the MSB.

To convert a binary number to its equivalent decimal number multiply each digit times the decimal value of the digit and just add these up. The binary number 101, for example, represents: $(1 \times 2^2) + (0 \times 2^1) + (1 \times 2^0)$ or $4 + 0 + 1 =$ decimal 5. For the binary number 10110.11 you have:

$$\begin{aligned} &(1 \times 2^4) + (0 \times 2^3) + (1 \times 2^2) + (1 \times 2^1) \\ &+ (0 \times 2^0) + (1 \times 2^{-1}) + (1 \times 2^{-2}) \\ &= 16 + 0 + 4 + 2 + 0 + 0.5 + 0.25 \\ &= \text{decimal } 22.75 \end{aligned}$$

To convert a decimal number to binary there are two common methods. The first (Figure 1-2*a*) is simply a reverse of the binary-to-decimal method above. For example, to convert the decimal number 21 (sometimes written as 21_{10}) to binary, first subtract the largest power of 2 that will fit in the number. For 21_{10} the largest power of 2 that will fit is 16 or 2^4. Subtracting 16 from 21 gives a remainder of 5. Put a one in the 2^4 digit position and see if the next lower power of 2 will fit in the remainder. Since 2^3 is 8 and 8 will not fit in the remainder of 5, put a zero in the 2^3 digit position. Then try the next lower power of 2. In this case the next is 2^2 or 4, which will fit in the remainder of 5. A 1 is, therefore, put in the 2^2 digit position. When 2^2 or 4 is subtracted from the old remainder of 5 a new remainder of 1 is left. Since 2^1 or 2 will not fit into this remainder, a zero is put in that position. A 1 is put in the 2^0 position because 2^0 is equal to 1 and this fits exactly into the remainder of 1. The result shows that 21_{10} is equal to 10101 in binary. The conversion process is somewhat messy to describe, but easy to do. Try converting 46_{10} to binary. You should get 101110.

Another method of converting a decimal number to binary is shown in Figure 1-2*b*. Divide the decimal number by 2 and write the quotient and remainder as shown. Divide this quotient and following quotients by 2 until the quotient reaches zero. The column of remainders will be the binary equivalent of the given decimal number. Note that the MSD is on the bottom of the column and the LSD is on the top of the column if you perform the divisions in order from the top to the bottom of the page. You can demonstrate that the binary number is correct by reconverting from binary to decimal as shown in the right-hand side of Figure 1-2*b*.

You can convert decimal numbers less than 1 to binary by successive multiplication by 2, and recording carries until the quantity to the right of the decimal point becomes zero, as shown in Figure 1-2*c*. The carries represent the binary equivalent of the decimal number, with the *most-significant bit* at the top of the column. Decimal 0.625 equals 0.101 in binary. For decimal values that do not convert exactly the way this one did (quantity to the right of the decimal never becomes zero), you can continue the conversion process until you get the number of binary digits desired.

At this point it is interesting to compare the number of digits required to express numbers in decimal with the number required to express them in binary. In decimal, one digit can represent 10^1 numbers, 0–9; two digits can represent 10^2 or 100 numbers, 0–99; and three digits can represent 10^3 or 1000 numbers, 0–999. In binary, a similar pattern exists. One binary digit can represent two numbers, 0–1; two binary digits can represent 2^2 or 4 numbers, 0–11; and three binary digits can represent 2^3 or 8 numbers. The pattern then is that N decimal digits can represent 10^N numbers and N binary digits can represent 2^N numbers. Eight binary digits can represent the 2^8 or 256 numbers, 0–255.

Octal

Binary is not a very compact code. This means that it requires many more digits to express a number than does, for example, decimal. Twelve binary digits can only

$$\begin{array}{ccccccccc} 4096 & 512 & 64 & 8 & 1 & . & \frac{1}{8} & \frac{1}{64} & \frac{1}{512} \\ 8^4 & 8^3 & 8^2 & 8^1 & 8^0 & . & 8^{-1} & 8^{-2} & 8^{-3} \end{array}$$

(a)

$327_{\text{Decimal}} = \underline{\ ?\ }_{\text{Octal}} \qquad 327_D = 507_8$

			LSD		
8)327	= 40	R	7	× 1	= 7
8) 40	= 5	R	0	× 8	= 0
8) 5	= 0	R	5	× 64	= 320
			MSD		327

(b)

Binary 101 011 111 .
Octal 5 3 7 ↑ Binary Point

(c)

FIGURE 1-3 Octal numbers. *(a)* Value of place holders. *(b)* Conversion of decimal to octal. *(c)* Conversion of binary to octal.

describe a number up to 4095_{10}. Computers require binary data, but people working with computers have trouble remembering the long binary words produced by the noncompact code. One solution to the problem is to use the *octal* or *base-8* code. As you can see in Figure 1-3*a*, the digits in this code represent powers of 8. The symbols then are 0 through 7. You can convert a decimal number to the octal equivalent number with the same trick you used to convert decimal to binary. Figure 1-3*b* shows the technique for decimal-to-octal conversion. Decimal 327 is equal to 507_8. Verification of this is shown by reconverting the octal to decimal in the second half of Figure 1-3*b*.

Since 8 is an integral power of 2, conversions from binary to octal, and octal to binary, are quite simple. If you have a binary number such as 101011111, then, starting from the binary point and moving to the left, mark off the binary digits in groups of three, as shown in Figure 1-3*c*. Each group of three binary digits is equal to one octal digit. For the example above, 111 is a 7, 011 is a 3, and 101 is a 5. Therefore, 101011111 binary is equal to 537_8.

You convert from octal to binary by replacing each octal digit with its 3-bit binary equivalent.

Hexadecimal

Some once-popular minicomputers, such as the PDP-8, have 12 parallel data lines. Four octal digits are an easy way to represent the binary data word on these 12 parallel lines. For example, 100001010111 binary is easily remembered or written as 4127 octal. Most microprocessors have 4-bit, 8-bit, 16-bit, or 32-bit data words. For these microprocessors, it is more logical to use a code which groups the binary digits in groups of four rather than three. *Hexadecimal* or base-16 code does this. Figure 1-4*a* shows the digit values for hexadecimal, which is often just called *hex*. Since hex is base-16, you have to have 16 possible symbols for each digit. The table of Figure 1-4*b* shows the symbols for hex code. After the decimal symbols 0 through 9 are used up, you use the letters A through F for values 10 through 15.

As mentioned above, each hex digit is equal to four binary digits. To convert the binary number 11010110

$$\begin{array}{ccccccccc} 16^3 & 16^2 & 16^1 & 16^0 & . & 16^{-1} & 16^{-2} & 16^{-3} \\ 4096 & 256 & 16 & 1 & & \frac{1}{16} & \frac{1}{256} & \frac{1}{4096} \end{array}$$

(a)

Dec		Hex
0	=	0
1	=	1
2	=	2
3	=	3
4	=	4
5	=	5
6	=	6
7	=	7
8	=	8
9	=	9
10	=	A
11	=	B
12	=	C
13	=	D
14	=	E
15	=	F

(b)

$1101 \quad 0110_2$
D 6 HEX

(c)

$227_{10} = \underline{\ ?\ }_{\text{Hex}}$

16)227	= 14	R3	× 1	= 3
16) 14	= 0	RE	× 16	= 224
				227

$227_{10} = E3_{16}$

(d)

FIGURE 1-4 Hexadecimal numbers. *(a)* Value of place holders. *(b)* Symbols. *(c)* Binary to hexadecimal conversion. *(d)* Decimal to hexadecimal conversion.

TABLE 1-1
COMMON NUMBER CODES

DECIMAL SYSTEM	BINARY	OCTAL	HEXA-DECIMAL	DECIMAL CODES				REFLECTED GRAY CODE	SEVEN-SEGMENT DISPLAY (1 = ON)							
				8421 BCD	2421	5421	EXCESS-3		*A*	*B*	*C*	*D*	*E*	*F*	*G*	DISPLAY
0	0000	0	0	0000	0000	0000	0011 0011	0000	1	1	1	1	1	1	0	0
1	0001	1	1	0001	0001	0001	0011 0100	0001	0	1	1	0	0	0	0	1
2	0010	2	2	0010	0010	0010	0011 0101	0011	1	1	0	1	1	0	1	2
3	0011	3	3	0011	0011	0011	0011 0110	0010	1	1	1	1	0	0	1	3
4	0100	4	4	0100	0100	0100	0011 0111	0110	0	1	1	0	0	1	1	4
5	0101	5	5	0101	1011	1000	0011 1000	0111	1	0	1	1	0	1	1	5
6	0110	6	6	0110	1100	1001	0011 1001	0101	1	0	1	1	1	1	1	6
7	0111	7	7	0111	1101	1010	0011 1010	0100	1	1	1	0	0	0	0	7
8	1000	10	8	1000	1110	1011	0011 1011	1100	1	1	1	1	1	1	1	8
9	1001	11	9	1001	1111	1100	0011 1100	1101	1	1	1	0	0	1	1	9
10	1010	12	A	0001 0000	0001 0000	0001 0000	0100 0011	1111	1	1	1	1	1	0	1	A
11	1011	13	B	0001 0001	0001 0001	0001 0001	0100 0100	1110	0	0	1	1	1	1	1	B
12	1100	14	C	0001 0010	0001 0010	0001 0010	0100 0101	1010	0	0	0	1	1	0	1	C
13	1101	15	D	0001 0011	0001 0011	0001 0011	0100 0110	1011	0	1	1	1	1	0	1	D
14	1110	16	E	0001 0100	0001 0100	0001 0100	0100 0111	1001	1	1	0	1	1	1	1	E
15	1111	17	F	0001 0101	0001 1011	0001 1000	0100 1000	1000	1	0	0	0	1	1	1	F

to hex, mark off groups of four, moving to the left from the binary point, as shown in Figure 1-4*c*. Then write the hex symbol for the value of each group of four. The 0110 group is equal to 6 and the 1101 group is equal to 13. Since 13 is D in hex, 11010110 binary is equal to D6 in hex. "H" is usually used after a number to indicate that it is a hexadecimal number. For example, D6 hex is usually written D6H. Eight bits require only two hex digits to represent them.

If you want to convert from decimal to hexadecimal, Figure 1-4*d* shows a familiar trick to do this. The result shows that 227_{10} is equal to E3H. As you can see, hex is an even more compact code than decimal. Two hexadecimal digits can indicate a number up to 255. Only four hex digits are needed to represent a 16-bit binary number.

To illustrate how hexadecimal numbers are used in digital logic, a service manual tells you that the 8-bit-wide data bus of an 8088A microprocessor should contain 3FH during a certain operation. Converting 3FH to binary gives the pattern of 1's and 0's (0011 1111) you would expect to find with your oscilloscope or logic analyzer on the parallel lines. The 3FH is simply a shorthand which is easier to remember and less prone to errors.

To convert from octal code to hex code, the easiest way is to write the binary equivalent of the octal and then convert the binary digits, four at a time, into the appropriate hex digits. Reverse the procedure to get from hex to octal.

BCD Codes

STANDARD BCD

In applications such as frequency counters, digital voltmeters, or calculators, where the output is a decimal display, a binary-coded decimal or BCD code is often used. The advantage of BCD for these applications is that information for each decimal digit is contained in a separate 4-bit binary word. As you can see in Table 1-1, the simplest BCD code uses the first 10 numbers of standard binary code for the BCD number 0 through 9. The hex codes A through F are invalid BCD codes. Each decimal digit then is individually represented by its 4-bit binary equivalent. Figure 1-5 illustrates this.

GRAY CODE

Gray code is another important binary code which is often used for encoding shaft position data from machines such as computer-controlled lathes. This code has the same possible combinations as standard binary, but as you can see in the 4-bit example in Table 1-1, they are arranged in a different order. Notice that only one binary digit changes at a time as you count up in this code.

5	2	9	Decimal
0101	0010	1001	BCD

FIGURE 1-5 Decimal to BCD conversion.

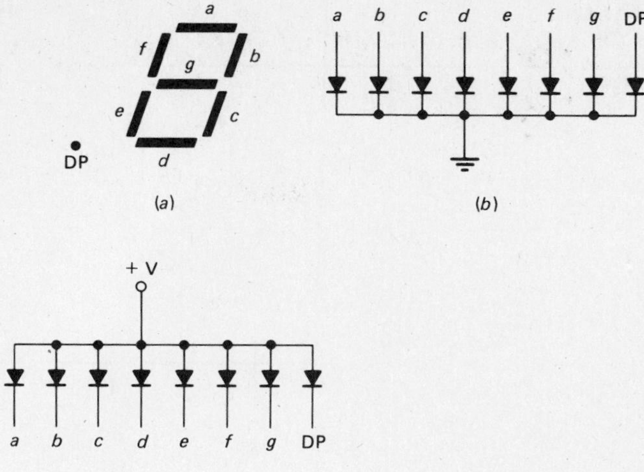

FIGURE 1-6 Seven-segment LED display. *(a)* Segment labels. *(b)* Schematic of common-cathode type. *(c)* Schematic of common-anode type.

If you need to construct a Gray-code table larger than that in Table 1-1, a handy way to do so is to observe the pattern of 1's and 0's and just extend it. The least-significant digit column starts with one 0 and then has alternating groups of two 1's and two 0's as you go down the column. The second-most-significant digit column starts with two 0's and then has alternating groups of four 1's and four 0's. The third column starts with four 0's, then has alternating groups of eight 1's and eight 0's. By now you should see the pattern. Try to figure out the Gray code for the decimal number 16. You should get 11000.

Seven-Segment Display Code

Since seven-segment displays such as that shown in Figure 1-6 are now so common in everything from calculators to gasoline pumps, the segment code for these has been included in Table 1-1. Some single seven-segment displays will display the last six numbers (10–15) of this code as the hexadecimal digits A–F. In Table 1-1, a 1 indicates that the segment is lit, which is true for displays such as the common-cathode light-emitting diode (LED) display in Figure 1-6*b*. For some displays, such as the common-anode LED display shown in Figure 1-6*c*, a low actually lights the segment, so you have to invert all the values.

Alphanumeric Codes

When communicating with or between computers you need a binary-based code which can represent letters of the alphabet as well as numbers. Common codes used for this have from 5 to 12 bits per word and are referred to as *alphanumeric codes*. To detect possible errors in

TABLE 1-2
COMMON ALPHANUMERIC CODES

ASCII SYMBOL	HEX CODE FOR 7-BIT ASCII	BCDIC SYMBOL	HEX CODE FOR EP BCDIC	EBCDIC SYMBOL	HEX CODE FOR EBCDIC	SELEC-TRIC SYMBOL	HEX CODE FOR SELEC-TRIC	HOL-LERITH SYMBOL	HOLES PUNCHED CODE FOR HOLLERITH
N U L	0 0			N U L	0 0			N U L	12 0 9 8 1
S 0 H	0 1			S 0 H	0 1			S C H	12 9 1
S T X	0 2			S T X	0 2			S T X	12 9 2
E T X	0 3			E T X	0 3			E T X	12 9 3
E 0 T	0 4			E 0 T	3 7			E C T	9 7
E N Q	0 5			E N Q	2 D			E N Q	0 9 8 5
A C K	0 6			A C K	2 E			A C K	0 9 8 6
B E L	0 7			B E L	2 F			B E L	0 9 8 7
B S	0 8			B S	1 6			B S	11 9 6
H T	0 9			H T	0 5			H T	12 9 5
L F	0 A			L F	2 5			L F	0 9 5
V T	0 B	‡	9 A	V T	0 B			V T	12 9 8 3
F F	0 C			F F	0 C			F F	12 9 8 4
C R	0 D	ǂ	F F	C R	0 D			C R	12 9 8 5
S 0	0 E			S 0	0 E			S 0	12 9 8 6
S 1	0 F			S 1	0 F			S 1	12 9 8 7
D L E	1 0			D L E	1 0			D L E	12 11 9 8 1
D C 1	1 1			D C 1	1 1			D C 1	11 9 1
D C 2	1 2			D C 2	1 2			D C 2	11 9 2
D C 3	1 3			D C 3	1 3			D C 3	11 9 3
D C 4	1 4			D C 4	3 5			D C 4	9 8 4
N A K	1 5			N A K	3 D			N A K	9 8 5
S Y N	1 6			S Y N	3 2			S Y N	9 2
E T B	1 7			E 0 B	2 6			E T B	0 9 6
C A N	1 8			C A N	1 8			C A N	11 9 8
E M	1 9			E M	1 9			E M	11 9 8 1
S U B	1 A			S U B	3 F			S U B	9 8 7
E S C	1 B			B Y P	2 4			E S C	0 9 7
F S	1 C			F L S	1 C			F S	11 9 8 4
G S	1 D			G S	1 D			G S	11 9 8 5
R S	1 E			R D S	1 E			R S	11 9 8 6
U S	1 F			U S	1 F			U S	11 9 8 7
S P	2 0	S P	0 0	S P	4 0			S P	NO PNCH
!	2 1	!	6 A	!	5 A	½!	2 7	!	12 8 7
″	2 2	⧻	5 F	″	7 F	″	2 D	″	8 7
#	2 3	#	4 B	#	7 B	#	7 E	#	8 3
$	2 4	$	2 B	$	5 B	$	7 9	$	11 8 3
%	2 5	%	5 C	%	6 C	%	3 D	%	0 8 4
&	2 6	&	3 0	&	5 0	&	7 D		12
′	2 7	V	1 D	′	7 D	′	2 5		8 5
(	2 8	Blank	5 0	(	4 D	(	3 8	(	12 8 5
)	2 9	△	6 F	)	5 D	)	3 9	)	11 8 5
*	2 A	*	6 C	*	5 C	*	7 C	*	11 8 4

(continued)

TABLE 1-2
COMMON ALPHANUMERIC CODES (*CONTINUED*)

ASCII SYMBOL	HEX CODE FOR 7-BIT ASCII	BCDIC SYMBOL	HEX CODE FOR EP BCDIC	EBCDIC SYMBOL	HEX CODE FOR EBCDIC	SELEC-TRIC SYMBOL	HEX CODE FOR SELEC-TRIC	HOL-LERITH SYMBOL	HOLES PUNCHED CODE FOR HOLLERITH
+	2 B			+	4 E	+	0 E	+	12 8 6
,	2 C	,	1 B	,	6 B	,	4 4	,	0 8 3
–	2 D			–	6 0	–	0 0	–	11
.	2 E	.	7 B	.	4 B	.	2 6	.	12 8 3
/	2 F	/	1 1	/	6 1	/	4 1	/	0 1
0	3 0	0	0 A	0	F 0	0	3 1	0	0
1	3 1	1	4 1	1	F 1	1	7 7	1	1
2	3 2	2	4 2	2	F 2	2	3 6	2	2
3	3 3	3	0 3	3	F 3	3	7 6	3	3
4	3 4	4	4 4	4	F 4	4	7 1	4	4
5	3 5	5	0 5	5	F 5	5	3 5	5	5
6	3 6	6	0 6	6	F 6	6	3 4	6	6
7	3 7	7	4 7	7	F 7	7	7 5	7	7
8	3 8	8	4 8	8	F 8	8	7 4	8	8
9	3 9	9	0 9	9	F 9	9	3 0	9	9
:	3 A	:	4 D	:	7 A	:	4 D	:	8 2
;	3 B	;	2 E	;	5 E	;	4 5	;	11 8 6
<	3 C	≤	7 E	<	4 C			<	12 8 4
=	3 D	√‾	0 F	=	7 E	=	0 6	=	8 6
>	3 E	>	4 E	>	6 E			>	0 8 6
?	3 F	?	3 A	?	6 F	?	4 9	?	0 8 7
@	4 0	@	0 C	@	7 C	@	3 E	@	8 4
A	4 1	A	7 1	A	C 1	A	6 C	A	12 1
B	4 2	B	7 2	B	C 2	B	1 8	B	12 2
C	4 3	C	3 3	C	C 3	C	5 C	C	12 3
D	4 4	D	7 4	D	C 4	D	5 D	D	12 4
E	4 5	E	3 5	E	C 5	E	1 D	E	12 5
F	4 6	F	3 6	F	C 6	F	4 E	F	12 6
G	4 7	G	7 7	G	C 7	G	4 F	G	12 7
H	4 8	H	7 8	H	C 8	H	1 9	H	12 8
I	4 9	I	3 9	I	C 9	I	2 C	I	12 9
J	4 A	J	2 1	J	D 1	J	0 7	J	11 1
K	4 B	K	2 2	K	D 2	K	1 C	K	11 2
L	4 C	L	6 3	L	D 3	L	5 9	L	11 3
M	4 D	M	2 4	M	D 4	M	6 F	M	11 4
N	4 E	N	6 5	N	D 5	N	1 E	N	11 5
O	4 F	O	6 6	O	D 6	O	6 9	O	11 6
P	5 0	P	2 7	P	D 7	P	0 D	P	11 7
Q	5 1	Q	2 8	Q	D 8	Q	0 C	Q	11 8
R	5 2	R	6 9	R	D 9	R	6 D	R	11 9
S	5 3	S	1 2	S	E 2	S	2 9	S	0 2
T	5 4	T	5 3	T	E 3	T	1 F	T	0 3

(*continued*)

TABLE 1-2
COMMON ALPHANUMERIC CODES (*CONTINUED*)

ASCII SYMBOL	HEX CODE FOR 7-BIT ASCII	BCDIC SYMBOL	HEX CODE FOR EP BCDIC	EBCDIC SYMBOL	HEX CODE FOR EBCDIC	SELEC-TRIC SYMBOL	HEX CODE FOR SELEC-TRIC	HOL-LERITH SYMBOL	HOLES PUNCHED CODE FOR HOLLERITH
U	55	U	14	U	E4	U	5E	U	0 4
V	56	V	55	V	E5	V	6E	V	0 5
W	57	W	56	W	E6	W	28	W	0 6
X	58	X	17	X	E7	X	5F	X	0 7
Y	59	Y	18	Y	E8	Y	09	Y	0 8
Z	5A	Z	59	Z	E9	Z	3F	Z	0 9
[	5B	[	7D	[	AD	[	7F	[	12 8 2
\	5C	\	1E	NL	15			\	0 8 2
]	5D	]	2D	]	DD			]	11 8 2
^	5E	□	3C	¬	5F			^	11 8 7
—	5F	—	60	—	6D	—	08	—	0 8 5
`	60			RES	14			`	8 1
a	61			a	81	a	64	a	12 0 1
b	62			b	82	b	10	b	12 0 2
c	63			c	83	c	54	c	12 0 3
d	64			d	84	d	55	d	12 0 4
e	65			e	85	e	15	e	12 0 5
f	66			f	86	f	46	f	12 0 6
g	67			g	87	g	47	g	12 0 7
h	68			h	88	h	11	h	12 0 8
i	69			i	89	i	24	i	12 0 9
j	6A			j	91	j	07	j	12 11 1
k	6B			k	92	k	14	k	12 11 2
l	6C			l	93	l	51	l	12 11 3
m	6D			m	94	m	67	m	12 11 4
n	6E			n	95	n	16	n	12 11 5
o	6F			o	96	o	61	o	12 11 6
p	70			p	97	p	05	p	12 11 7
q	71			q	98	q	04	9	12 11 8
r	72			r	99	r	65	r	12 11 9
s	73			s	A2	s	21	s	11 0 2
t	74			t	A3	t	17	t	11 0 3
u	75			u	A4	u	56	u	11 0 4
v	76			v	A5	v	66	v	11 0 5
w	77			w	A6	w	20	w	11 0 6
x	78			x	A7	x	57	x	11 0 7
y	79			y	A8	y	01	y	11 0 8
z	7A			z	A9	z	37	z	11 0 9
{	7B			{	8B			{	12 0
|	7C			|	4F			|	12 11
}	7D			}	9B			}	11 0
~	7E			¢	4A			~	11 0 1
DEL	7F			DEL	07			DEL	12 9 7

BCDIC: HEX DIGIT (PCBA) HEX DIGIT ($2^3 2^2 2^1 2^0$)

SELECTRIC: $R_5 T_1 T_2$ (HEX DIGIT) $SR_{2_A} R_2 R_1$ (HEX DIGIT) these codes, an additional bit, called a *parity bit*, is often added as the most-significant bit.

Parity is a term used to identify whether a data word has an odd or even number of 1's. If a data word contains an odd number of 1's, the word is said to have *odd parity*. The binary word 0110111 with five 1's has odd parity. The binary word 0110000 has an even number of 1's (two) so it has *even parity*.

In practice the parity bit may function as follows. The system that is sending a data word checks the parity of the word. If the parity of the data word is odd, the system will set the parity bit to a 1. This makes the parity of the data word plus parity bit even. If the parity of the data word is even, the sending system will reset the parity bit to a 0. This again makes the parity of the data word plus parity even. The receiving system checks the parity of the data word plus parity bit that it receives. If the receiving system detects odd parity in the received data word plus parity, it can assume an error occurred and tells the sending system to send the data again. The system is then said to be using even parity. The system could have been set up to use (maintain) odd parity in a similar manner.

The difficulty with this method of detecting errors introduced during transmission is that two errors introduced into a data word may keep the correct parity and, therefore, the parity checker won't indicate an error. Other, more complex methods, such as CRC and "Hamming codes" can be used to detect multiple errors in transmitted data, and even to correct errors. Some of these will be described in Chapters 12 and 13.

ASCII

Table 1-2 shows several alphanumeric codes. The first of these is *ASCII*, or American Standard Code for Information Interchange. This is shown in the table as a 7-bit code. With seven bits you can code up to 128 characters, which is enough for the full upper- and lower-case alphabet, numbers, punctuation marks, and control characters. The code is arranged so that if only upper-case letters, numbers, and a few control characters are needed, the lower six bits are all that is required. If a parity check is wanted, a parity bit is added to the basic 7-bit code in the MSB position. The binary word 1100 0100, for example, is the ASCII code for upper-case D with odd parity. Table 1-3 gives the meanings of the control character symbols used in the ASCII code table.

BCDIC

BCDIC code is the Binary Coded Decimal Interchange Code used with some computers. It uses seven bits plus a parity bit. The lower four bits are referred to as the *numeric bits*. The upper four bits contain a parity bit and three *zone bits*. The arrangement of these bits is shown at the bottom of Table 1-2. To save space in Table 1-2, the hex equivalent of the binary digits is used for the BCDIC code expressed with even parity.

EBCDIC

Another alphanumeric code commonly encountered in IBM equipment is the Extended Binary Coded Decimal Interchange Code or *EBCDIC*. This is an 8-bit code without parity. A ninth bit can be added for parity. To save space in Table 1-2, the eight binary digits of EBCDIC are represented with their 2-digit hex equivalent.

TABLE 1-3
DEFINITIONS OF CONTROL CHARACTERS

NUL	NULL	**DC2**	DIRECT CONTROL 2
SOH	START OF HEADING	**DC3**	DIRECT CONTROL 3
STX	START TEXT	**DC4**	DIRECT CONTROL 4
ETX	END TEXT	**NAK**	NEGATIVE ACKNOWLEDGE
EOT	END OF TRANSMISSION	**SYN**	SYNCHRONOUS IDLE
ENQ	ENQUIRY	**ETB**	END TRANSMISSION BLOCK
ACK	ACKNOWLEDGE	**CAN**	CANCEL
BEL	BELL	**EM**	END OF MEDIUM
BS	BACKSPACE	**SUB**	SUBSTITUTE
HT	HORIZONTAL TAB	**ESC**	ESCAPE
LF	LINE FEED	**FS**	FORM SEPARATOR
VT	VERTICAL TAB	**GS**	GROUP SEPARATOR
FF	FORM FEED	**RS**	RECORD SEPARATOR
CR	CARRIAGE RETURN	**US**	UNIT SEPARATOR
SO	SHIFT OUT		
SI	SHIFT IN		
DLE	DATA LINK ESCAPE		
DC1	DIRECT CONTROL 1		

SELECTRIC

Selectric is a 7-bit code used in the familiar IBM spinning ball typewriters and printers. Table 1-2 shows this code for reference also. Each bit position in the code controls an operation of the spinning ball.

From most-significant to least-significant bit, the meaning of the seven bits are: ROTATE 5, TILT 1, TILT 2, SHIFT, ROTATE 2A, ROTATE 2, and ROTATE 1. In addition to this 7-bit code, Selectrics have separate machine commands for space, return, backspace, tabs, bell, and index.

HOLLERITH

Hollerith is a 12-bit code used to encode data from those computer cards which threaten you with a fate worse than death if you "fold, spindle, or mutilate" them. Figure 1-7*b* shows a standard 12-row by 80-column card. The 12 data rows are referenced as, starting from the top, 12, 11, 0, 1, 2, 3, 4, 5, 6, 7, 8, 9. The top three rows are called *zone punches* and the bottom 10 rows are called *digit punches*. Note that the zero row is included in both categories. A punched hole represents a 1 and a data word is described by the 12 bits in a vertical column. The card in Figure 1-7*b* shows the Hollerith code for the numbers and letters printed across the top of the card. Table 1-3 shows the entire code and the punched-hole equivalent for each character. Since Hollerith code uses very few of the possible combinations for 12 bits, it is not very efficient. Therefore, it is usually converted to ASCII or EBCDIC for use.

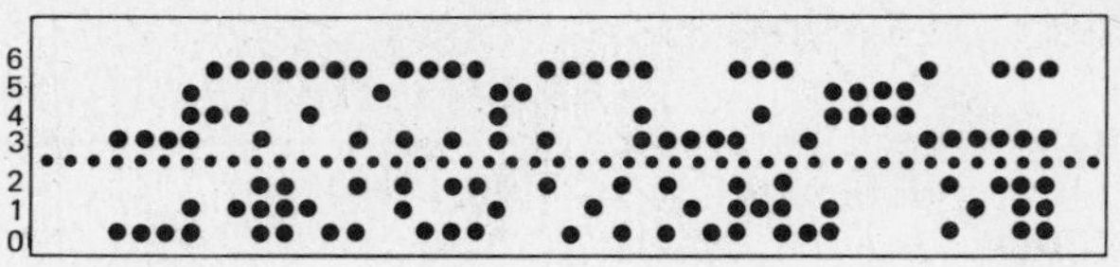

(a)

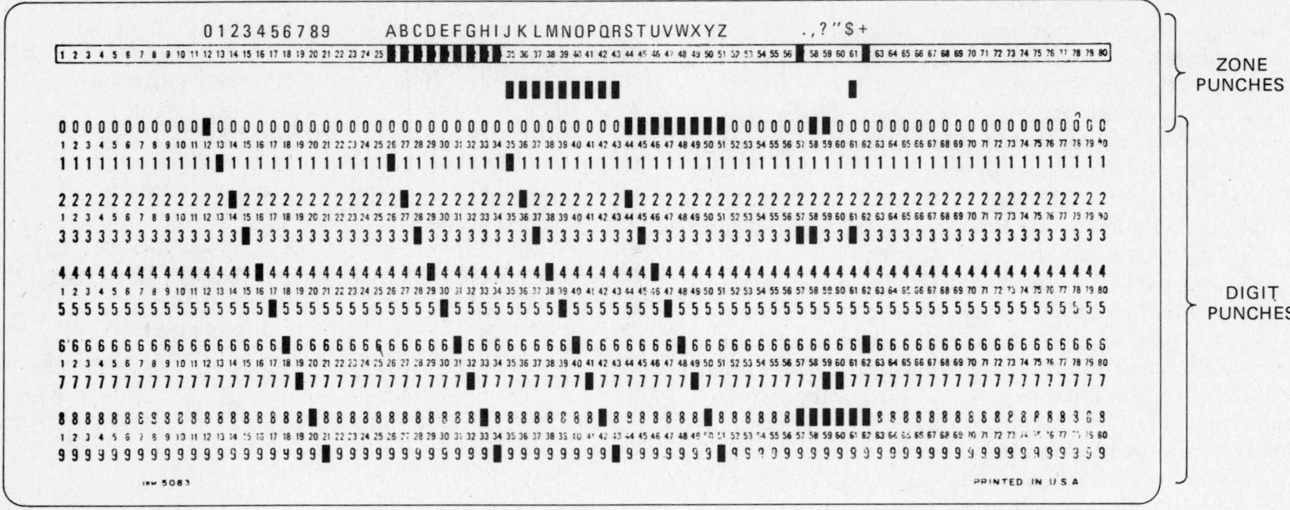

(b)

FIGURE 1-7 *(a)* ASCII punched paper tape; *(b)* Hollerith punched card.

ADDING AND SUBTRACTING BINARY, OCTAL, HEX, AND BCD NUMBERS

The previous section of this chapter reviewed common number systems and codes used with computers. This section reviews how to do computations in the previously described number systems.

Binary

ADDITION

Figure 1-8*a* shows the truth table for addition of two binary digits and carry in (C_{IN}) from addition of previous digits. Figure 1-8*b* shows the result of adding two 8-bit binary numbers together using these rules. Assuming that $C_{IN} = 1$, $1 + 0 + C_{IN}$ = a sum of 0 and a carry into the next digit, and $1 + 1 + C_{IN}$ = a sum of 1 and a carry into the next digit because the result in any digit position can only be a one or a zero.

2's COMPLEMENT BINARY

2's complement binary is a way of representing negative numbers in binary. When you handwrite a number which represents some physical quantity such as temperature, you can simply put a + sign in front of the number when you wish to indicate that the number is positive. You can write a − sign when you wish to indicate that the number is negative. If however, you want to store values such as temperatures, which can be positive or negative in a computer memory, there is a problem. Since the computer memory can only store 1's or

INPUTS			OUTPUTS	
A	B	C_{IN}	S	C_{OUT}
0	0	0	0	0
0	0	1	1	0
0	1	0	1	0
0	1	1	0	1
1	0	0	1	0
1	0	1	0	1
1	1	0	0	1
1	1	1	1	1

$S = A \oplus B \oplus C_{IN}$

$C_{OUT} = A \cdot B + C_{IN}(A \oplus B)$

(a)

```
    10011010
  + 11011100
  ----------
 [1] 01110110
  ↑
  └─ Carry
```

(b)

FIGURE 1-8 Binary addition. *(a)* Truth table for 2 bits plus carry. *(b)* Addition of two 8-bit words.

0's, some way must be established to represent the sign of the number with a 1 or a 0.

The way to do this is to reserve the most significant bit of the data word as a *sign bit* and to use the rest of the bits of the data word to represent the size (magnitude) of the quantity. A computer that works with 8-bit words will use the MSB (bit 7) as the sign bit and the lower seven bits to represent the magnitude for the numbers. The usual convention is to represent a positive number with a 0 sign bit and a negative number with a 1 sign bit.

To make computations with signed numbers easier, the magnitude of negative numbers is represented in a special form called *2's complement*. The 2's complement of a binary number is formed by inverting each bit of the data word and adding one to the result. Some examples should help clarify all of this.

The number $+7_{10}$ is represented in 8-bit sign-and-magnitude form as 0000 0111. The sign bit is zero, which indicates a positive number. The magnitude of positive numbers is represented in straight binary, so 0000 0111 in the least-significant bits represents 7_{10}.

To represent -7_{10} in 8-bit 2's complement sign-and-magnitude form, start with the 8-bit code for +7, 0000 0111. Invert each bit to get 1111 1000. Then add 1 to get 1111 1001. This result is the correct representation of -7_{10}. Figure 1-9 shows some more examples of positive and negative numbers expressed in 8-bit sign-and-magnitude form. For practice, try generating each of these yourself to see if you get the same result as shown.

To reverse the above procedure and find the magnitude of a number expressed in sign-and-magnitude form, proceed as follows. If the number is positive, as indicated by the sign bit being a 0, then the least-significant 7 bits represent the magnitude directly in binary. If the number is negative, as indicated by the sign bit being a 1, then the magnitude is expressed in 2's complement. To get the magnitude of this negative number expressed in standard binary, invert each bit of the data word, including the sign bit and add one to the result. For example, given the word 1110 1011, invert each bit to get 0001 0100. Then add 1 to get 0001 0101. This equals 21_{10} so you know that the original numbers represent -21_{10}. Again, try reconverting a few of the numbers in Figure 1-9 for practice.

	Sign bit		
+ 7	0	0000111	
+ 46	0	0101110	
+105	0	1101001	
− 12	1	1110100	Sign and two's complement of magnitude
− 54	1	1001010	
−117	1	0001011	
− 46	1	1010010	

FIGURE 1-9 Positive and negative numbers represented with a sign bit and 2's complement.

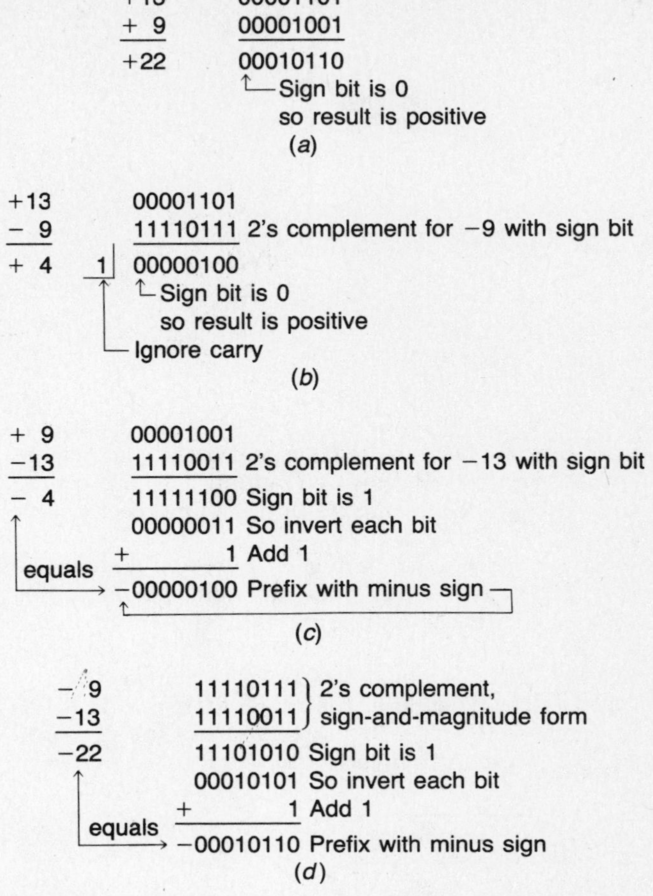

FIGURE 1-10 Addition of signed binary numbers. (*a*) +9 and +13. (*b*) −9 and +13. (*c*) +9 and −13. (*d*) −9 and −13.

Figure 1-10 shows some examples of addition of signed binary numbers of this type. Sign bits are added together just as the other bits are. Figure 1-10*a* shows the results of adding two positive numbers. The sign bit of the result is zero, so the result is positive. The second example, in Figure 1-10*b*, adds a −9 to a +13 or, in effect, subtracts 9 from 13. As indicated by the zero sign bit, the result of this, 4, is positive and in true binary form.

Figure 1-10*c* shows the result of adding a −13 to a smaller positive number, +9. The sign bit of the result is a 1. This indicates that the result is negative and the magnitude is in 2's complement form. To reconvert a 2's complement result to a signed number in true binary form:

1. Invert each bit, to produce 1's complement.
2. Add one.
3. Put a minus sign in front to indicate that the result is negative.

The final example in Figure 1-10*d* shows the results of adding two negative numbers. The sign bit of the result

```
01111111    +127
   •
   •
   •
00000001    +1
00000000    ZERO
11111111    −1
   •
   •
   •
10000001    −127
10000000    −128
```

FIGURE 1-11 Range of signed numbers that can be represented with 8 binary bits.

is a 1, and the result is negative and in 2's complement form. Again, inverting each bit, adding 1, and prefixing a minus sign will put the result in a more recognizable form.

Now let's consider the range of numbers that can be represented with eight bits in sign-and-magnitude form. Eight bits can represent a maximum of 2^8 or 256 numbers. Since we are representing both positive and negative numbers, half of this range will be positive and half negative. Therefore, the range then is 0 to +127 and from −1 to −128. Figure 1-11 shows the sign-and-magnitude binary representations for these values. If you like number patterns, you might notice that this scheme shifts the normal codes for 128 to 255 downward to represent −128 to −1.

If a computer is storing signed numbers as 16-bit words, then a much larger range of numbers can be represented. Since 16 bits gives 2^{16} or 65,536 possible values, the range for 16-bit sign-and-magnitude numbers is −32,768 to +32,767. Operations with 16-bit sign-and-magnitude numbers are done the same as was demonstrated above for 8-bit sign-and-magnitude numbers.

BINARY SUBTRACTION

There are two common methods for doing binary subtraction. These are the pencil method and the 2's complement add method. Figure 1-12*a* shows the truth table for binary subtraction of two binary digits A and B. Also included in the truth table is the effect of a borrow in, B_{IN}, from subtracting previous digits. Figure 1-12*b* shows an example of the "pencil" method of subtracting two 8-bit numbers. Using the truth table, this method is done the same way that you do decimal subtraction.

A second method of performing binary subtraction is by adding the 2's complement representation of the bottom number (subtrahend) to the top number (minuend). Figure 1-12*c* shows how this is done. First represent the top number in sign-and-magnitude form. Then form the 2's complement sign-and-magnitude represen-

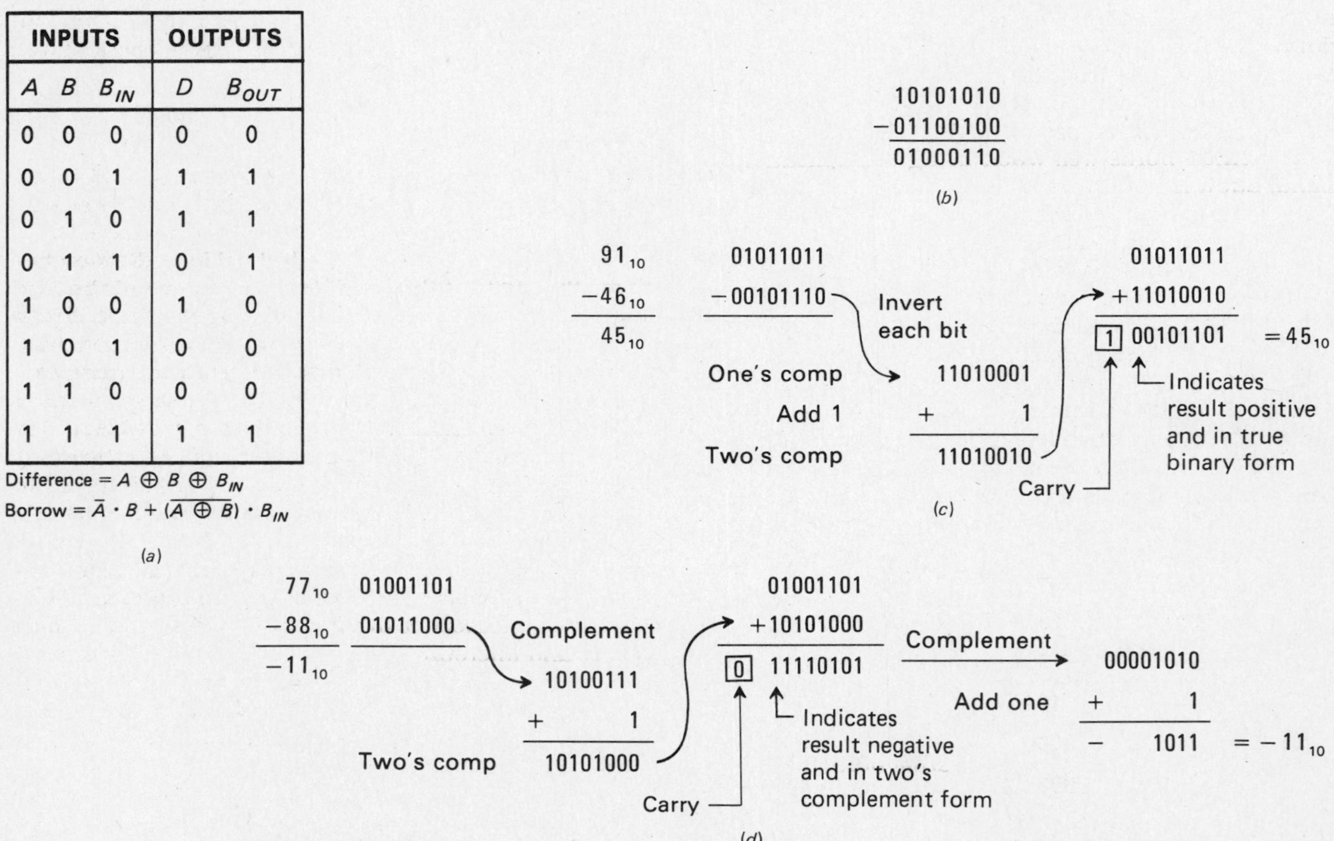

INPUTS			OUTPUTS	
A	B	B_{IN}	D	B_{OUT}
0	0	0	0	0
0	0	1	1	1
0	1	0	1	1
0	1	1	0	1
1	0	0	1	0
1	0	1	0	0
1	1	0	0	0
1	1	1	1	1

Difference = $A \oplus B \oplus B_{IN}$

Borrow = $\bar{A} \cdot B + (\overline{A \oplus B}) \cdot B_{IN}$

(*a*)

FIGURE 1-12 Binary subtraction. *(a)* Truth table for 2 bits and borrow. *(b)* Pencil method. *(c)* 2's complement positive result. *(d)* 2's complement negative result.

tation for the negative of the bottom number. Finally, add the two parts formed. For the example in Figure 1-12*c*, the sign of the result is a zero which indicates the result is positive and in true form. The final carry produced by the addition can be ignored. Figure 1-12*d* shows another example of this method of subtraction. In this case the bottom number is larger than the top number. Again, represent the top number in sign-and-magnitude form, produce the 2's complement sign-and-magnitude form for the negative of the bottom number, and add the two together. The sign bit of the result is a 1 for this example. This indicates that the result is negative and its magnitude is represented in 2's complement form. To get the result into a form that is more recognizable to you, invert each bit of the result, add 1 to it, and put a minus sign in front of it as shown in Figure 1-12*d*.

The examples shown use eight bits, but the process works for any number of bits. This method may seem awkward, but it is easy to do in a computer or microprocessor because it requires only the simple operations of inverting and adding.

```
                 01100   Quotient
Divisor   110) 1001000   Dividend          12
               -110                      6)72
               ----
                 110
                -110
                ----
                   0
                       (a)

           110.01                   6.25
  100)   11001.00                4)25.00
        -100
        ----
          100
         -100
         ----
            01 00
                       (b)
```

FIGURE 1-14 Binary division.

BINARY MULTIPLICATION

There are several methods of doing binary multiplication. Figure 1-13 shows what is called the pencil method because it is the same as the way you learned to multiply decimal numbers. The top number or multiplicand is multiplied by the least-significant digit of the bottom number or multiplier. The partial product is written down. The top number is multiplied by the next digit of the multiplier. The resultant partial product is written down under the last, but shifted one place to the left. Adding all the partial products gives the total product. This method works well when doing multiplication by hand, but it is not practical for a computer because the type of shifts required make it awkward to implement.

One of the multiplication methods used by computers is repeated addition. To multiply 7 × 55, for example, the computer can just add up seven 55's. For large numbers, however, this method is slow. To multiply 786 × 253, for example, requires 252 add operations.

Most computers use an add-and-shift-right method. This method takes advantage of the fact that, for binary multiplication, the partial product can only be either the top number exactly if the multiplier digit is a 1, or a 0 if the multiplier digit is a 0. The method does the same thing as the pencil method except that the partial products are added as they are produced and the sum of the partial products is shifted right rather than each partial product being shifted left.

```
  11          1011    Multiplicand
 × 9       ×  1001    Multiplier
 ---       -------
  99          1011  }
             0000   }
            0000    }  Partial products
           1011     }
          -------
          1100011     Product
```

FIGURE 1-13 Binary multiplication.

A point to note about multiplying numbers is the number of bits the product requires. For example, multiplying two 4-bit numbers can give a product with as many as 8 bits, and two 8-bit numbers can give a 16-bit product.

BINARY DIVISION

Binary division can also be performed in several ways. Figure 1-14 shows two examples of the pencil method. This is the same process as decimal long division. However, it is much simpler than decimal long division because the digits of the result (quotient) can only be 0 or 1. A division is attempted on part of the dividend. If this is not possible because the divisor is larger than that part of the dividend, a 0 is entered into the quotient. Another attempt is then made to divide using one more digit of the dividend. When a division is possible, a 1 is entered in the quotient. The divisor is then subtracted from the portion of the dividend used. The process is continued as with standard long division until all the dividend is used. As shown in Figure 1-14*b*, 0's can be added to the right of the binary point and division continued to convert a remainder to a binary equivalent.

Another method of division that is easier for computers and microprocessors to perform uses successive subtractions. The divisor is subtracted from the dividend and from each successive remainder until a borrow is produced. The desired quotient is 1 less than the number of subtractions needed to produce a borrow. This method is simple, but for large numbers it is slow.

For faster division of large numbers, computers use a subtract-and-shift-left method that is essentially the same process you go through with a pencil long division.

$$\begin{array}{r} 47_8 \\ +36_8 \\ \hline \end{array} \qquad \begin{array}{r} 100\ 111 \\ +\ \ 011\ 110 \\ \hline 1\ 000\ 101 \\ 1\ \ 0\ \ \ 5_8 \end{array} \qquad \begin{array}{r} \text{Carry} \\ \downarrow \\ {}^{1}47_8 \\ +\ 36_8 \\ \hline 8_{10}\ 13_{10} \\ 1\ 0\ 5_8 \end{array}$$

(a) (b)

FIGURE 1-15 Octal addition. *(a)* Adding binary equivalents. *(b)* Direct octal addition.

Octal and Hexadecimal Addition and Subtraction

People working with computers or microprocessors often use octal or hexadecimal as a shorthand way of representing long binary numbers such as memory addresses. It is therefore useful to be able to add and subtract octal and hexadecimal numbers.

OCTAL ADDITION

Figure 1-15 shows two ways of adding the octal numbers 47 and 36. The first way is to convert both numbers to their binary equivalents. Remember, each octal digit represents three binary digits. These binary numbers are then added using the rules for binary addition from Figure 1-8*a*. The resultant binary sum is then converted back to octal.

The second method works directly with the octal form: 7 added to 6 gives 13, which is a carry to the next digit and a remainder of 5. The 5 is written down and the carry added to the next digit column. Then 4 plus 3 plus a carry gives 8, which is a carry with no remainder. The 0 is written down and the carry is added to the next digit column. This is the same process you use for decimal addition but a carry is produced any time the sum is 8 or greater, rather than 10.

HEXADECIMAL ADDITION

As shown in Figure 1-16 the same approaches can be used to add two hexadecimal numbers. For converting to binary, remember that each hex digit represents four binary digits. The binary numbers are added and the result is converted back to hexadecimal.

The second method works directly with the hex numbers. With hex addition, a carry is produced whenever the sum is 16 or greater. An A in hex is a 10 in decimal and an F is 15 in decimal. These add to give 25, which is a carry with a remainder of 9. The 9 is written down and the carry is added to the next digit column. Then 7 plus 3 plus a carry gives a decimal 11, or B in hex.

You may use whichever method seems easier to you and gives you consistently right answers. If you are doing a great deal of octal or hexadecimal arithmetic you might buy an electronic calculator specifically designed to do decimal, octal, and hexadecimal arithmetic.

$$\begin{array}{r} 7A \\ +3F \\ \hline B9 \end{array} \qquad \begin{array}{r} 0111\ \ 1010 \\ +0011\ \ 1111 \\ \hline 1011\ \ 1001 \end{array} \qquad \begin{array}{r} \text{Carry} \\ \downarrow \\ 7\ {}^{1}\ A_{16} \\ +\ 3\ \ \ F_{16} \\ \hline 11_{10}\ \ 25_{10} \\ B_{16}\ \ \ 9_{16} \end{array}$$

(a) (b)

FIGURE 1-16 Hexadecimal addition.

OCTAL SUBTRACTION

Octal subtraction is shown in Figure 1-17. Since the least-significant digit of the top number is smaller than the least-significant digit of the bottom number, a borrow must be done. In octal subtraction, 8 is borrowed from the next digit position and added to the top number. The bottom number is then subtracted and the remainder written down. The process is continued until all digits are subtracted. If you are uncomfortable "borrowing 8's," you can just convert the number to decimal, subtract, and convert the result back to octal.

$$\begin{array}{r} 34_8 \\ -17_8 \\ \hline 15_8 \end{array} \qquad \begin{array}{r} 28_{10} \\ -15_{10} \\ \hline 13_{10} \end{array}$$

FIGURE 1-17 Octal subtraction.

HEXADECIMAL SUBTRACTION

Hexadecimal subtraction is similar to octal subtraction except that, when a borrow is needed, 16 is borrowed from the next-most-significant digit. Figure 1-18 shows this. It may help you to follow the example if you do partial conversions to decimal in your head. For example, 7 plus a borrowed 16 is 23. Subtracting B or 11 leaves 12 or C in hexadecimal. Then 3 from the 6 left after a borrow leaves 3, so the result is 3CH.

$$\begin{array}{r} 77_{16} \\ -3B_{16} \\ \hline 3C_{16} \end{array} \quad \begin{array}{c} = \\ = \\ \\ \end{array} \quad \begin{array}{r} 119_{10} \\ -\ 59_{10} \\ \hline 60_{10} \end{array}$$

FIGURE 1-18 Hexadecimal subtraction.

BCD Addition and Subtraction

In systems where the final result of a calculation is to be displayed, such as a calculator, it may be easier to work with numbers in a BCD format. These codes, as shown in Table 1-1, represent each decimal digit, 0 through 9, with a 4-bit binary word. The BCD words are the same as the binary equivalents for 0 through 9.

BCD ADDITION

BCD can have no digit-word with a value greater than 9. Therefore, a carry must be generated if the result of a

BCD addition is greater than 1001 or 9. Figure 1-19 shows three examples of BCD addition. The first, in Figure 1-19*a*, is very straightforward because the sum is less than 9. The result is the same as it would be for standard binary.

For the second example, in Figure 1-19*b*, adding BCD 7 to BCD 5 produces 1100. This is a correct binary result of 12 but it is an illegal BCD code. To convert the result to BCD format, a correction factor of 6 is added. The result of adding 6 is 0001 0010, which is the legal BCD code for 12.

Figure 1-19*c* shows another case where a correction factor must be added. The initial addition of 9 and 8 produces 0001 0001. Even though the lower four digits are less than 9, this is an incorrect BCD result because a carry out of bit 3 of the BCD digit-word was produced. This carry out of bit 3 is often called an *auxiliary carry*. Adding the correction factor of 6 gives the correct BCD result of 0001 0111 or 17.

To summarize, a correction factor of 6 must be added to the result if the result in the lower 4 bits is greater than 9 or if the initial addition produces a carry out of bit 3 of any BCD digit-word. This correction is sometimes called a *decimal adjust operation*.

The reason for the correction factor of 6 is that in BCD we want a carry into the next digit after 1001 or 9, but in binary a carry out of the lower four bits does not occur until after 1111 or 15, which is 6 more than 9.

	BCD
35	0011 0101
+23	+0010 0011
58	0101 1000

(*a*)

	BCD	
7	0111	
+ 5	+ 0101	
12	1100	Incorrect BCD
	+ 110	Add 6
	00010010	Correct BCD 12

(*b*)

	BCD	
9	1001	
+ 8	+ 1000	
17	00010001	Incorrect BCD
	110	Add 6
	00010111	Correct BCD 17

(*c*)

FIGURE 1-19 BCD addition. *(a)* No correction needed. *(b)* Correction needed because of illegal BCD result. *(c)* Correction needed because of carry out of BCD digit.

17	1 0111	
− 9	0 1001	
8	0 1110	Illegal BCD
	− 110	Subtract 6
	1000	$= 8_{10}$

FIGURE 1-20 BCD subtraction.

BCD SUBTRACTION

Figure 1-20 shows a subtraction of BCD 17 (0001 0111) minus BCD 9 (0000 1001). The initial result, 0000 1110, is not a legal BCD number. Whenever this occurs in BCD subtraction, 6 must be *subtracted* from the initial result to produce the correct BCD result. For the example shown in Figure 1-20, subtracting 6 gives a correct BCD result of 0000 1000 or 8.

The correction factor of 6 must be subtracted from any BCD digit-word if that digit-word is greater than 1001, or if a borrow from the next higher digit occurred during the subtraction.

BASIC LOGIC GATES

Microcomputers such as those we discuss throughout this book often contain basic logic gates as "glue" between LSI (large scale integration) devices. For troubleshooting these systems it is important to be able to predict logic levels at any point directly from the schematic, rather than having to work your way through a truth table for each gate. This section should help refresh your memory of basic logic functions and help you remember how to quickly analyze logic gate circuits.

Inverting and Non-inverting Buffers

Figure 1-21 shows the schematic symbols and truth tables for simple buffers and logic gates. The first thing to remember about these symbols is that the shape of the symbol indicates the logic function performed by the device. The second thing to remember about these symbols is that a bubble or no bubble indicates the *assertion* level for an input or output signal. Let's review how modern logic designers use these symbols.

The first symbol for a *buffer* in Figure 1-21*a* has no bubbles on the input or output. Therefore, the input is active high and the output is active high. We read this symbol as follows. If the input, A, is asserted high, then the output, Y, will be asserted high. The rest of the truth table is covered by the assumption that if the A input is not asserted high, then the Y output will not be asserted high.

The next two symbols for a buffer each contain a bubble. The bubble on the output of the first of these indicates that the output is active low. The input has no bubble so it is active high. You can read the function of the device directly from the schematic symbol as follows. If the A input is asserted high, then the Y output will be

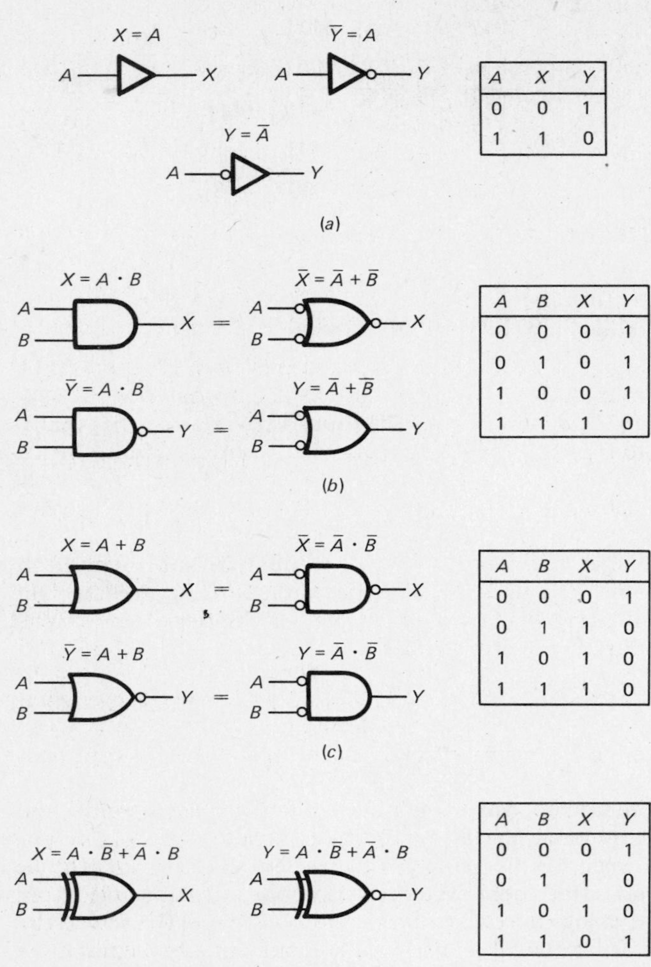

A	X	Y
0	0	1
1	1	0

A	B	X	Y
0	0	0	1
0	1	0	1
1	0	0	1
1	1	1	0

A	B	X	Y
0	0	0	1
0	1	1	0
1	0	1	0
1	1	1	0

A	B	X	Y
0	0	0	1
0	1	1	0
1	0	1	0
1	1	0	1

FIGURE 1-21 Buffers and logic gates. *(a)* Buffers. *(b)* AND—NAND. *(c)* OR—NOR. *(d)* Exclusive OR.

asserted low. This device then simply changes the assertion level of a signal. The output, Y, will always have a logic state which is the complement or inverse of that on the input, so the device is usually referred to as an *inverter*.

The second schematic symbol for an inverter in Figure 1-21*a* has the bubble on the input. We draw the symbol this way when we want to indicate that we are using the device to change an asserted-low signal to an asserted-high signal. For example, if we pass the signal $\overline{\text{CS}}$ through this device it becomes CS. The symbol tells you directly that if the input is asserted low, then the output will be asserted high. Now let's review how you express the functions of logic gates using this approach.

Logic Gates

Figure 1-21*b* shows the symbols and truth tables for simple logic gates. A symbol with a flat back and a round front indicates that the device performs the logical *AND* function. This means that the output will be asserted if the A input is asserted AND the B input is asserted. Again bubbles or no bubbles are used to indicate the assertion level of each input and output. The first AND symbol in Figure 1-21*b* has no bubbles so the inputs and the output are active high. The output then will be asserted high if the A input is asserted high AND the B input is asserted high. The bubble on the output of the second AND symbol in Figure 1-21*b* indicates that this device, commonly called a *NAND* gate, has an active low output. If the A input is asserted high and the B input is asserted high, then the Y output will be asserted low. Look at the truth table in Figure 1-21*b* to see if you agree with this.

Figure 1-21*c* shows the other two possible cases for the AND symbol. The first of these has bubbles on the inputs and on the outputs. If you see this symbol in a schematic, you should immediately see that the output will be asserted low if the A input is asserted low AND the B input is asserted low. The second AND symbol in Figure 1-21*c* has no bubble on the output, so the output will be asserted high if the A AND B inputs are both asserted low.

A logic symbol with a curved back indicates that the output of the device will be asserted if the A input is asserted OR the B input of the device is asserted. Again bubbles or no bubbles are used to indicate the assertion level for inputs and outputs. Note in Figure 1-21*b* and Figure 1-21*c* that each of the AND symbol forms has an equivalent OR symbol form. An AND symbol with active high inputs and an active high output, for example, represents the same device (a 74LS08 perhaps) as an OR symbol with active low inputs and an active low output. Use the truth table in Figure 1-21*b* to convince yourself of this. The bubbled-OR representation tells you that if one input is asserted low, the output will be low, regardless of the state on the other input. As we will show later in this chapter, this is often a useful way to think of the operation of an AND gate.

Figure 1-21*d* shows the symbol and truth table for an *exclusive* OR gate. The output of this device will be asserted if the A input is asserted OR if the B input is asserted, but the output will not be asserted if both A AND B are asserted.

You need to be able to read all of these symbols, because most logic designers will use the symbol that best describes the function they want a device to perform in a particular circuit.

Latches, Flip-flops, Registers, and Counters

THE D LATCH

A *latch* is a digital device that stores a one or a zero on its output. Figure 1-22*a* shows the schematic symbol and truth table for a D latch. The device functions as follows. If the *enable* input, E, is low, any data present on the D input will have no effect on the Q or $\overline{\text{Q}}$ outputs. This is indicated in the truth table by an *X* in the *D* column. If the enable input is high, a high or a low on the D input will be passed to the Q output. In other words, the Q output will follow the D input as long as the enable input is high. The $\overline{\text{Q}}$ output will contain the complement of the logic state on Q. When the enable input is made low again, the state on Q at that time will be latched there. Any changes on D will have no effect on Q until the enable input is made high again. When the enable input goes low, then, the state present on D just before the enable goes low will be stored on the Q output. Keep this operation in mind as you read about the D flip-flop in the next section.

THE D FLIP-FLOP

The first type of *flip-flop* to review is the D type. Figure 1-22*b* shows the schematic symbol and the truth table for a typical D flip-flop. Note that this device has a *clock* input, CK, in place of the enable input on the D latch. Also note the up arrows in the clock column of the truth table. These arrows are used to indicate that a one or zero on the D input will be copied to the Q output at the instant the clock input goes from low to high. In other words, the D flip-flop takes a snapshot of whatever state is on the D input when the clock goes high, and displays the photo on the Q output. If the clock input is low, a change on D will have no effect on the output. Likewise, if the clock input is high, a change on D will have no effect on the Q output. Contrast this operation with that of the D latch to make sure you understand the difference between the two devices.

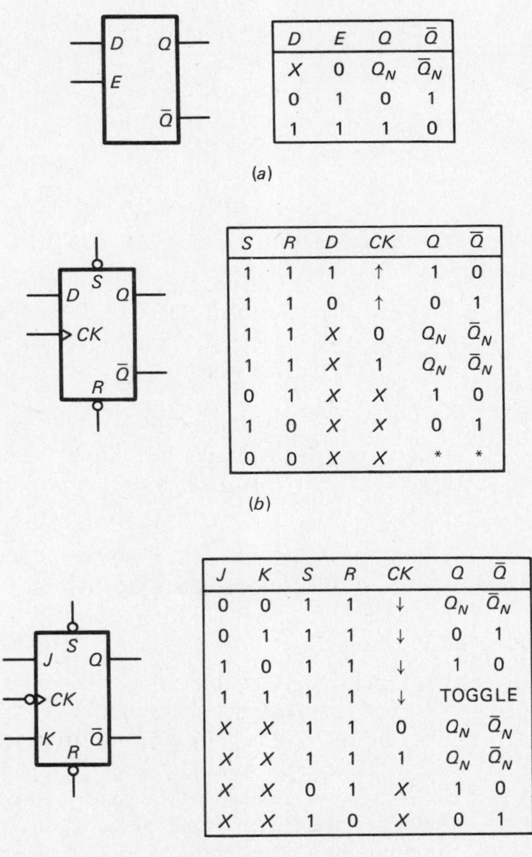

D	E	Q	$\bar{Q}$
X	0	Q_N	$\bar{Q}_N$
0	1	0	1
1	1	1	0

(*a*)

S	R	D	CK	Q	$\bar{Q}$
1	1	1	↑	1	0
1	1	0	↑	0	1
1	1	X	0	Q_N	$\bar{Q}_N$
1	1	X	1	Q_N	$\bar{Q}_N$
0	1	X	X	1	0
1	0	X	X	0	1
0	0	X	X	*	*

(*b*)

J	K	S	R	CK	Q	$\bar{Q}$
0	0	1	1	↓	Q_N	$\bar{Q}_N$
0	1	1	1	↓	0	1
1	0	1	1	↓	1	0
1	1	1	1	↓	TOGGLE	
X	X	1	1	0	Q_N	$\bar{Q}_N$
X	X	1	1	1	Q_N	$\bar{Q}_N$
X	X	0	1	X	1	0
X	X	1	0	X	0	1

(*c*)

FIGURE 1-22 Latches and flip-flops. *(a)* **D** latch. *(b)* **D** flip-flop. *(c)* **J-K** flip-flop.

The D flip-flop in Figure 1-22*b* also has direct *set* (S) and *reset* (R) inputs. A flip-flop is considered *set* if its Q output is a one. It is *reset* if its Q output is a zero. The bubbles on the set and reset inputs tell you that these inputs are active low. The truth table for the D flip-flop in Figure 1-22*b* indicates that the set and reset inputs are *asynchonous*. This means that if the set input is asserted low, the output will be set, regardless of the state on the D and the clock inputs. Likewise, if the reset input is asserted low, the Q output will be reset, regardless of the state of the D and clock inputs. The *X*s in the *D* and *CK* columns of the truth table remind you that these inputs are "don't cares" if set or reset is asserted. The condition indicated by the asterisks (*) is a nonstable condition; that is, it will not persist when reset or clear inputs return to their inactive (high) level.

THE JK FLIP-FLOP

Figure 1-22*c* shows the schematic symbol and the truth table for a common JK flip-flop such as the 74LS76. The two data inputs, J and K make this device more versatile than a D flip-flop. The bubble on the clock input of the symbol and the downward arrows in the truth table indicate that the Q and $\bar{Q}$ outputs will only change when the clock input goes from a high to a low. Changes on J or K will have no effect on the output if the clock input is low or if the clock input is high.

If J and K are both low when the CK input goes low, the outputs will remain the same as they were before the clock edge. This is indicated by Q_N and $\bar{Q}_N$ in the truth table. If J is low and K is high at the time of the clock edge, Q will become a zero. If J is high and K is low at the time of the clock edge, Q will become a one. If J and K are both high at the time of the clock edge, the Q output will *toggle*. This means that it will change to the opposite state of what it was before the clock edge. The JK flip-flop also has asynchronous set and reset inputs which function the same as those of the D flip-flop described previously.

REGISTERS

Flip-flops can be used individually or in groups to store binary data. A *register* is a group of D flip-flops connected in parallel as shown in Figure 1-23*a*. A binary word applied to the data inputs of this register will be transferred to the Q outputs when the clock input is made high. The binary word will remain stored on the Q outputs until a new binary word is applied to the D inputs and a low-to-high signal applied to the clock input. Other circuitry can read the stored binary word from the Q outputs at any time without changing its value.

If the Q output of each flip-flop in the register is connected to the D input of the next as shown in Figure 1-23*b*, then the register will function as a *shift register*. A one applied to the first D input will be shifted to the first Q output by a clock pulse. The next clock pulse will shift this one to the output of the second flip-flop. Each additional clock pulse will shift the one to the next flip-flop in the register. Some shift registers allow you to load a binary word into the register and shift the loaded

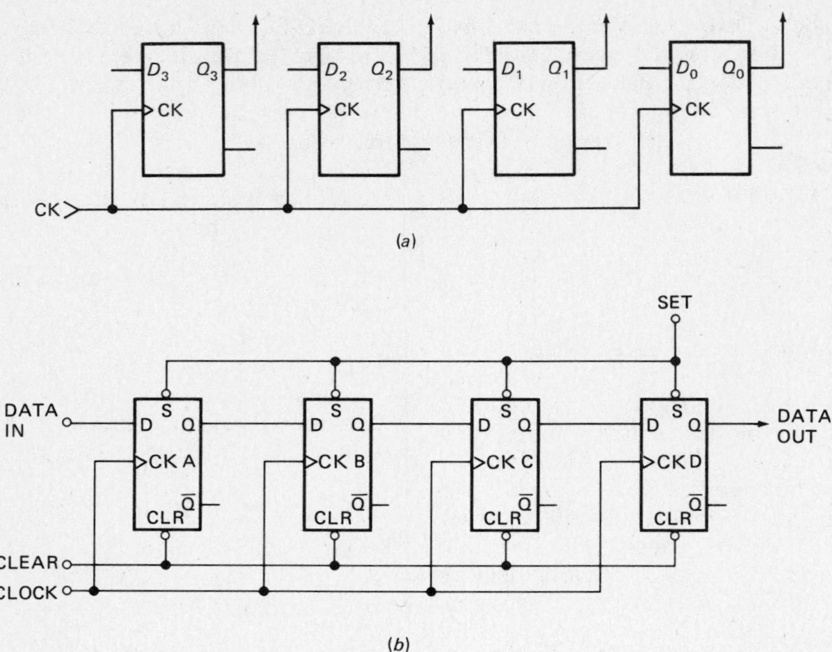

FIGURE 1-23 Registers. *(a)* Simple data storage. *(b)* Shift register.

word left or right when the register is clocked. As we will show later in this chapter, the ability to shift binary numbers is very useful.

COUNTERS

Flip-flops can also be connected in parallel to make *counters*. Figure 1-24 shows a schematic symbol and count sequence for a presettable 4-bit binary counter. The main point we want to review here is how a presettable counter functions, so there is no need to go into the internal circuitry of the device. If the reset input is asserted, the Q outputs will all be made zeros. After the reset signal is unasserted, each clock pulse will cause the binary count on the outputs to be incremented by one. As shown in Figure 1-24*b*, the count sequence will go from 0000 to 1111. If the outputs are at 1111, then the next clock pulse will cause the outputs to "roll over" to 0000 and a carry pulse to be sent out the carry output. This carry pulse can be used as the clock input for another counter.

Now, suppose that we want the counter to start counting from some number other than 0000. We can do this by applying the desired number to the four data inputs and asserting the load input. For example if we apply a binary 6, 0110, to the data inputs and assert the load input, this value will be transferred to the Q outputs. After the load signal is unasserted, the next clock signal will increment the Q outputs to 0111 or 7. Counters such as this can be connected in series (cascaded) to produce counters of any desired number of bits.

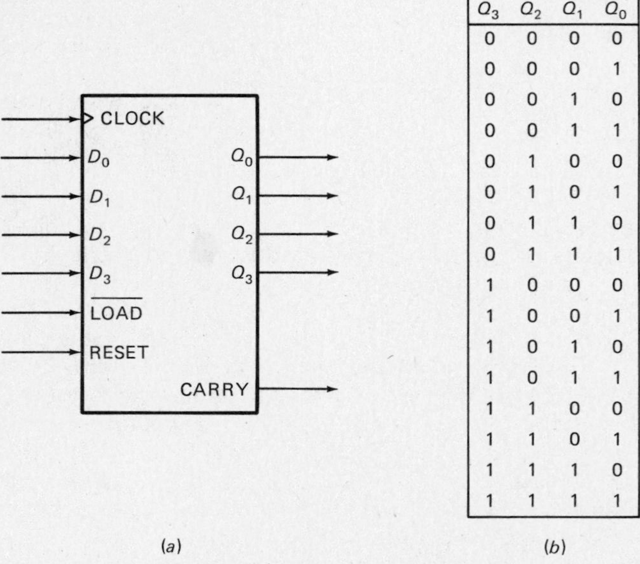

Q_3	Q_2	Q_1	Q_0
0	0	0	0
0	0	0	1
0	0	1	0
0	0	1	1
0	1	0	0
0	1	0	1
0	1	1	0
0	1	1	1
1	0	0	0
1	0	0	1
1	0	1	0
1	0	1	1
1	1	0	0
1	1	0	1
1	1	1	0
1	1	1	1

FIGURE 1-24 Four-bit, presettable binary counter. *(a)* Schematic symbol. *(b)* Count sequence.

ROMs, RAMs, and Buses

The next topics we need to review are the devices which store large numbers of binary words and how combinations of these devices can be connected together.

ROMs

The term ROM stands for *read-only memory*. There are several types of ROM that can be written to, read, erased, and written to with new data, but the main feature of ROMs is that they are *nonvolatile*. This means

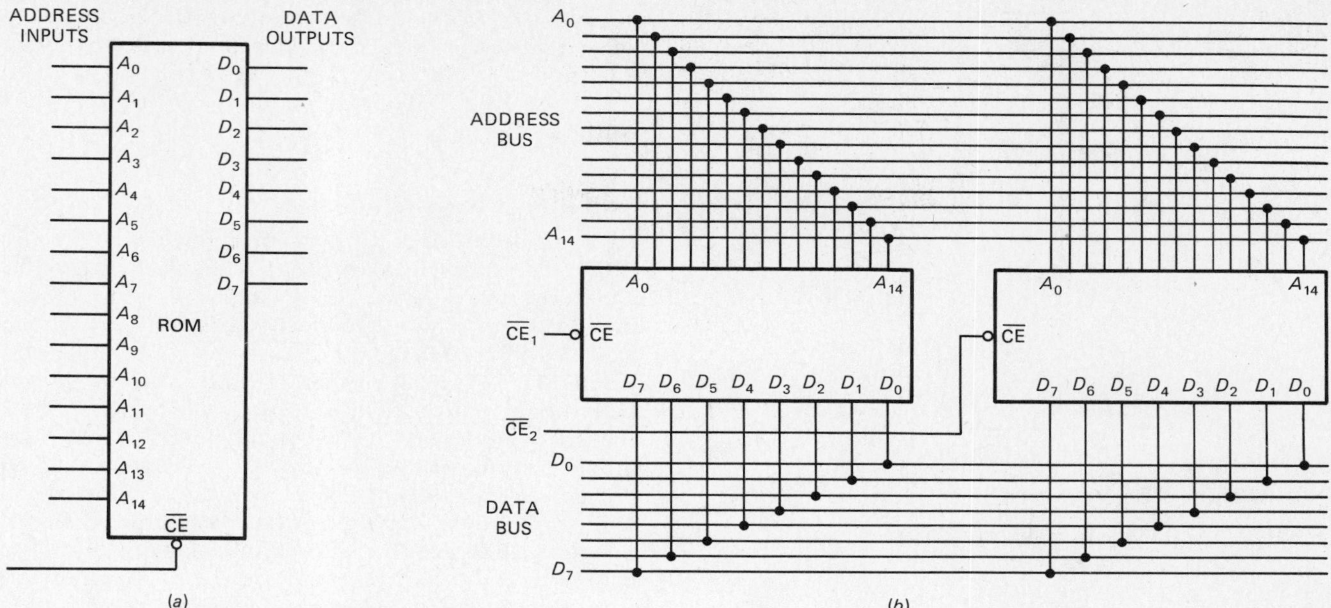

FIGURE 1-25 ROMs. *(a)* Schematic symbol. *(b)* Connection in parallel.

that the information stored in them is not lost when the power is removed from them.

Figure 1-25*a* shows the schematic symbol of a common ROM. As indicated by the eight *data* outputs, D0–D7, this ROM stores 8-bit data words. The data outputs are *three-state* outputs. This means that each output can be at a logic low state, a logic high state, or a high-impedance, floating state. In the high-impedance state an output is essentially disconnected from anything connected to it. If the $\overline{CE}$ input of the ROM is not asserted, then all of the outputs will be in the high-impedance state. Also, most ROMs switch to a lower-power-consumption condition if $\overline{CE}$ is not asserted. If the $\overline{CE}$ input is asserted, the device will be powered up, and the output buffers will be enabled. Therefore, the outputs will be at a normal logic low or logic high state. You will soon see why this is important if you don't happen to remember.

You can think of the binary words stored in the ROM as being in a long, numbered list. The number that corresponds to each stored word is called its *address*. In order to get a particular word onto the outputs of the ROM you have to do two things. You have to apply the address of that word to the address inputs, A0–A14, and you have to assert the $\overline{CE}$ input to turn on the outputs. Incidentally, you can tell the number of binary words stored in the ROM by the number of address inputs. The number of words is equal to 2^N where N is the number of address lines. The device in Figure 1-25*a* has 15 address lines, A0–A14, so the number of words is 2^{15} or 32,768. In a data sheet this device would be referred to as a 32K × 8 ROM. This means 32K addresses by 8 bits per address.

Now, let's see why we want three-state outputs on this ROM. Suppose that we want to store more than 32K data words. We can do this by connecting two or more ROMs in parallel as shown in Figure 1-25*b*. The address lines connect to each device to allow us to address one of the 32,768 words in each. A set of parallel lines used to send addresses or data to several devices in this way is called a *bus*. The data outputs of the ROMs are likewise connected in parallel so that any one of the ROMs can output data on the common data bus. If these ROMs had standard two state outputs, a serious problem would occur because each device would be trying to output an addressed word onto the data bus. The resulting argument between data outputs would probably destroy some of the outputs and give meaningless information on the data bus. Since the ROMs have three-state outputs, however, we can use external circuitry to make sure that only one ROM at a time has its outputs enabled. The very important principle here is that whenever several outputs are connected on a bus, the outputs should all be three-state, and only one set of outputs should be enabled at a time.

At the beginning of this section we mentioned that some ROMs can be erased and rewritten or reprogrammed with new data. Here's a summary of the different types of ROM.

Mask-programmed ROM—Programmed during manufacture; cannot be altered.

PROM—User programs by blowing fuses; cannot be altered except to blow additional fuses.

EPROM—Electrically programmable by user; erased by shining ultraviolet light on quartz window in package.

EEPROM—Electrically programmable by user; erased with electrical signals instead of ultraviolet light.

STATIC AND DYNAMIC RAMs

The name RAM stands for *random-access memory*, but since ROMs are also random access, the name probably

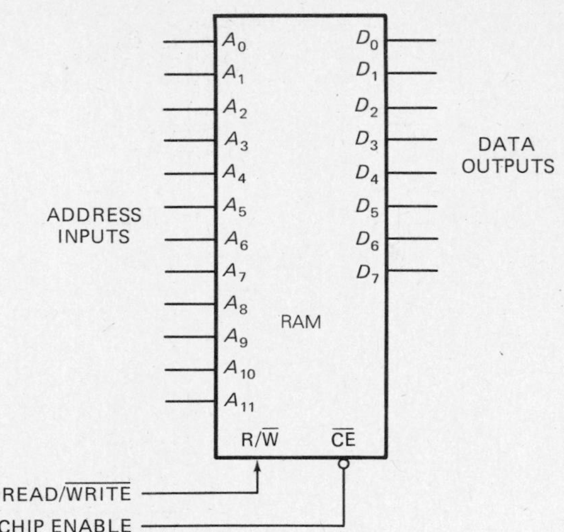

FIGURE 1-26 RAM schematic symbol.

should be read-write memory. RAMs are also used to store binary words. A *static* RAM is essentially a matrix of flip-flops. Therefore, we can write a new data word in a RAM location at any time by applying the word to the flip-flop data inputs and clocking the flip-flops. The stored data word will remain on the flip-flop outputs as long as the power is left on. This type of memory is *volatile* because data is lost when the power is turned off.

Figure 1-26 shows the schematic symbol for a common RAM. This RAM has 12 address lines, A0–A11, so it stores 2^{12} (4096) binary words. The eight data lines tell you that the RAM stores 8-bit words. When we are reading a word from the RAM these lines function as outputs. When we are writing a word to the RAM, these lines function as inputs. The *chip enable* input, $\overline{CE}$, is used to enable the device for a read or for a write. The R/$\overline{W}$ input will be asserted high if we want to read from the RAM or it will be asserted low if we want to write a word to the RAM. Here's how all these lines work for reading from and writing to the device.

To write to the RAM we apply the desired address to the address inputs, assert the $\overline{CE}$ input low to turn on the device, and assert the R/$\overline{W}$ input low to tell the RAM we want to write to it. We then apply the data word we want to store to the data lines of the RAM for a specified time. To read a word from the RAM we address the desired word, assert $\overline{CE}$ low to turn on the device, and assert R/$\overline{W}$ high to tell the RAM we want to read from it. For a read operation the output buffers on the data lines will be enabled and the addressed data word will be present on the outputs.

The static RAMs we have just reviewed store binary words in a matrix of flip-flops. In *dynamic* RAMs (DRAMs), binary 1's and 0's are stored as an electrical charge or no charge on a tiny capacitor. Since these tiny capacitors take up less space on a chip than a flip-flop would, a dynamic RAM chip can store many more bits than the same size static RAM chip. The disadvantage of dynamic RAMs is that the charge leaks off the tiny capacitors. The logic state stored in each capacitor must be *refreshed* every two milliseconds or so. A device called a *dynamic RAM refresh controller* can be used to refresh a large number of dynamic RAMs in a system. Some newer dynamic RAM devices contain built-in refresh circuitry so they appear static to external circuitry.

Arithmetic Logic Units

Previous sections of this chapter reviewed ANDing, ORing, exclusive ORing, adding, and subtracting of binary numbers. A device which can perform any of these functions and others on binary words is an *arithmetic logic* unit or ALU. Figure 1-27*a* shows a block diagram for the 74LS181 which is a 4-bit ALU. This device can perform any one of 16 logic functions or any one of 16 arithmetic functions on two 4-bit binary words. The function performed on the two words is determined by the logic level applied to the mode input, M, and by the 4-bit binary code applied to the select inputs, S0–S3.

Figure 1-27*b* shows the truth table for the 74LS181. In this truth table *A* represents the 4-bit binary word applied to the A0–A3 inputs and *B* represents the 4-bit binary word applied to the B0–B3 inputs. *F* represents the 4-bit binary word that will be produced on the F0–F3 outputs. If the mode input, M, is high, the device will perform one of 16 logic functions on the two words applied to the A and B inputs. For example, if M is high and we make S3 high, S2 low, S1 high, and S0 high, the 4-bit word on the A inputs will be ANDed with the 4-bit word on the B inputs. The result of this ANDing will appear on the F outputs. Each bit of the A word is ANDed with the corresponding bit of the B word to produce the result on F. Figure 1-27*c* shows an example of ANDing two words with this device. As you can see in this example, an output bit is high only if the corresponding bit is high in both the A word AND in the B word.

For another example of the operation of the 74LS181, suppose that the M input is high, S3 is high, S2 is high, S2 is high, and S0 is low. According to the truth table the device will now OR each bit in the A word with the corresponding bit in the B word and give the result on the corresponding F output. Figure 1-27*c* shows the result that will be produced by ORing two 4-bit words. Figure 1-27*c* also shows for your reference the result that would be produced by exclusive ORing these two 4-bit words together.

If the M input of the 74LS181 is low, then the device will perform one of 16 arithmetic functions on the A and B words. Again the result of the operation will be put on the F outputs. Several 74LS181s can be cascaded to operate on words longer than 4 bits. The ripple-carry input, $\overline{C}_n$, allows a carry from an operation on previous words to be included in the current operation. If the $\overline{C}_n$ input is asserted low, then a carry will be added to the results of the operation on A and B. For example if the M input is low, S3 is high, S2 is low, S1 is low, S0 is high, and $\overline{C}_n$ is low, the F outputs will have the sum of A plus B plus a carry.

The real importance of an ALU such as the 74LS181 is that it can be programmed with a binary instruction applied to its mode and select inputs to perform many different functions on two binary words applied to its

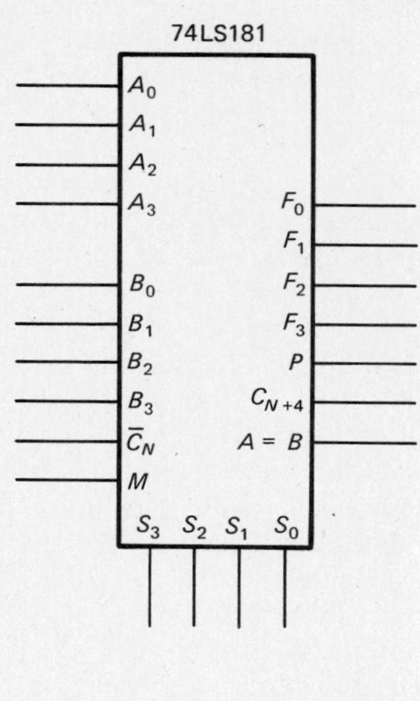

(*a*)

SELECTION				ACTIVE-HIGH DATA		
				$M = H$ LOGIC FUNCTIONS	$M - L$; ARITHMETIC OPERATIONS	
S3	S2	S1	S0		$\overline{C}_N = H$ (no carry)	$\overline{C}_N = L$ (with carry)
L	L	L	L	$F = \overline{A}$	$F = A$	$F = A$ PLUS 1
L	L	L	H	$F = \overline{A + B}$	$F = A + B$	$F = (A + B)$ PLUS 1
L	L	H	L	$F = \overline{A}B$	$F = A + \overline{B}$	$F = (A + \overline{B})$ PLUS 1
L	L	H	H	$F = 0$	$F =$ MINUS 1 (2's COMPL)	$F =$ ZERO
L	H	L	L	$F = \overline{AB}$	$F = A$ PLUS $A\overline{B}$	$F = A$ PLUS $A\overline{B}$ PLUS 1
L	H	L	H	$F = \overline{B}$	$F = (A + B)$ PLUS $A\overline{B}$	$F = (A + B)$ PLUS $A\overline{B}$ PLUS 1
L	H	H	L	$F = A \oplus B$	$F = A$ MINUS B MINUS 1	$F = A$ MINUS B
L	H	H	H	$F = A\overline{B}$	$F = A\overline{B}$ MINUS 1	$F = A\overline{B}$
H	L	L	L	$F = \overline{A} + B$	$F = A$ PLUS AB	$F = A$ PLUS AB PLUS 1
H	L	L	H	$F = \overline{A \oplus B}$	$F = A$ PLUS B	$F = A$ PLUS B PLUS 1
H	L	H	L	$F = B$	$F = (A + \overline{B})$ PLUS AB	$F = (A + \overline{B})$ PLUS AB PLUS 1
H	L	H	H	$F = AB$	$F = AB$ MINUS 1	$F = AB$
H	H	L	L	$F = 1$	$F = A$ PLUS A	$F = A$ PLUS A PLUS 1
H	H	L	H	$F = A + \overline{B}$	$F = (A + B)$ PLUS A	$F = (A + B)$ PLUS A PLUS 1
H	H	H	L	$F = A + B$	$F = (A + \overline{B})$ PLUS A	$F = (A + \overline{B})$ PLUS A PLUS 1
H	H	H	H	$F = A$	$F = A$ MINUS 1	$F = A$

(*b*)

	A_3	A_2	A_1	A_0
A	1	0	1	0
	B_3	B_2	B_1	B_0
B	0	1	1	0
	F_3	F_2	F_1	F_0
$A \cdot B$	0	0	1	0
	F_3	F_2	F_1	F_0
$A + B$	1	1	1	0
	F_3	F_2	F_1	F_0
$A \oplus B$	1	1	0	0

(*c*)

FIGURE 1-27 Arithmetic logic unit (ALU). *(a)* Schematic symbol. *(b)* Truth table. *(c)* Sample AND, OR, XOR operations.

data inputs. In other words, instead of having to build a different circuit to perform each of these functions, we have one programmable device. We can perform any of the operations that we want in a computer with a sequence of simple operations such as those of the 74LS181. Therefore, an ALU is a very important part of the microprocessors and microcomputers which we discuss in the next chapter.

CHECKLIST OF IMPORTANT TERMS AND CONCEPTS IN THIS CHAPTER

If you do not remember any of the terms or concepts in this list, use the index to find them in the chapter.

Binary, bit, nibble, byte, word, double word

LSB, MSB, LSD, MSD

Octal, hexadecimal, standard BCD, Gray code

Seven-segment display code

Alphanumeric codes: ASCII, BCDIC, EBCDIC, Selectric, Hollerith

Parity bit, odd parity, even parity

Converting between binary, octal, hexadecimal, BCD

Arithmetic with binary, octal, hexadecimal, BCD

BCD decimal adjust operation

Signed numbers, sign bit

2's complement sign-and-magnitude form

Signal assertion level

Inverting and noninverting buffers

Symbols and truth tables for AND, NAND, OR, NOR, XOR logic gates.

D latch, D flip-flop, JK flip-flop

Register, shift register, binary counter

ROM: address lines, data lines, bus lines
- nonvolatile
- three-state
- cascaded outputs
- enable input

PROM, EPROM, EEPROM

RAM: static, dynamic
- volatile
- READ/WRITE input

ALU

REVIEW QUESTIONS AND PROBLEMS

1. Convert the following decimal numbers to binary:
- *a.* 22
- *b.* 76
- *c.* 500

2. Convert the following binary numbers to decimal:
- *a.* 1011
- *b.* 11010001
- *c.* 1110111001011001

3. Convert to following numbers to octal:
- *a.* 110101001 binary
- *b.* 11 decimal
- *c.* 111011101100 binary

4. Convert the following octal numbers to decimal:
- *a.* 314
- *b.* 74
- *c.* 43

5. Convert to hexadecimal:
- *a.* 53 decimal
- *b.* 756 decimal
- *c.* 0110110010 binary
- *d.* 1100010111 binary

6. Convert to decimal:
- *a.* D3H
- *b.* 3FEH
- *c.* 44H

7. Convert the following decimal numbers to BCD:
- *a.* 86
- *b.* 62
- *c.* 33

8. The L key is depressed on an ASCII-encoded keyboard. What pattern of 1's and 0's would you expect to find on the seven parallel data lines coming from the keyboard? What pattern would a carriage return, CR, give?

9. Define parity and describe how it is used to detect an error in transmitted data.

10. Show addition of:
- *a.* 10011_2 and 1011_2 in binary
- *b.* 37_{10} and 25_{10} in BCD
- *c.* 37_8 and 25_8 in octal
- *d.* 4AH and 77H

11. Express the following decimal numbers in 8-bit sign-and-magnitude form:
- *a.* +26
- *b.* −7
- *c.* −26
- *d.* −125

12. Show the subtraction, in binary, of the following decimal numbers using both the pencil method and the 2's complement addition method:
- *a.* 7 − 4
- *b.* 37 − 26
- *c.* 125 − 93

13. Show the multiplication of 1001 and 011 by the pencil method. Do the same for 11010 and 101.

14. Show the division of 1100100 by 1010 using the pencil method.

15. Perform the indicated operations on the following numbers:
- *a.* The octal numbers 27 + 16
- *b.* The octal numbers 132 − 45
- *c.* 3AH + 94H
- *d.* 17AH − 4CH
- *e.*
  0101 1001 BCD
  + 0100 0010 BCD
- *f.*
  0111 1001 BCD
  + 0100 1001 BCD
- *g.*
  0101 1001 BCD
  − 0010 0110 BCD
- *h.*
  0110 0111 BCD
  − 0011 1001 BCD

16. For the circuit in Figure 1-28
- *a.* Is the Y output active high or active low?
- *b.* Is the C signal active high or active low?
- *c.* What input conditions on A, B, and C will cause the Y output to be asserted?

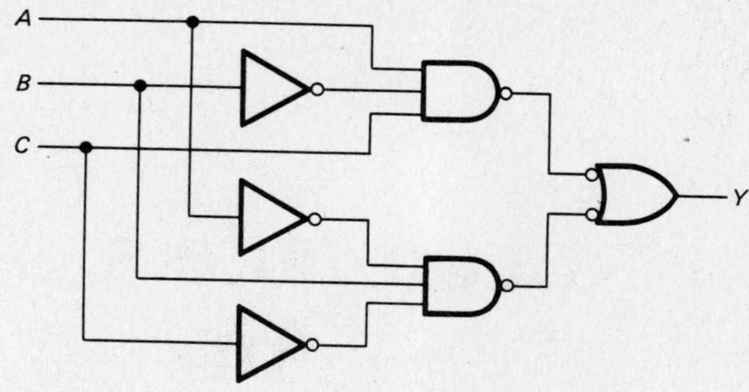

FIGURE 1-28 Circuit for Problem 1-16.

17. What is the main difference between a D latch and a D flip-flop?

18. The National Semiconductor INS8298 is a 65,536-bit ROM organized as 8192 words or bytes of 8 bits. How many address lines are required to address one of the 8192 bytes?

19. Why do most ROMs and RAMs have three-state outputs?

20. Using Figure 1-27, show the programming of the select and mode inputs the 74181 requires to perform the following arithmetic functions:
    a. A + B
    b. A MINUS B MINUS 1
    c. A PLUS B

21. Show the output word produced when the following binary words are ANDed with each other and when they are ORed with each other:
    a. 1010 and 0111
    b. 1011 and 1100
    c. 11010111 and 111000
    d. ANDing an 8-bit binary number with 1111 0000 is sometimes referred to as "masking" the lower 4 bits. Why?

CHAPTER

2 Computers, Microcomputers, and Microprocessors—An Introduction

We live in a computer oriented society and we are constantly bombarded with a multitude of terms relating to computers. Before getting started with the main flow of the book we will try to clarify some of these terms and to give an overview of computers and computer systems.

OBJECTIVES

At the conclusion of this chapter you should be able to:

1. Define the terms: microcomputer, microprocessor, hardware, software, firmware, time share, multitasking, distributed processing, and multiprocessing.
2. Describe how a microcomputer fetches and executes an instruction.
3. List the registers and other parts in the 8086/8088 execution unit and bus interface unit.
4. Describe the function of the 8086/8088 queue.
5. Demonstrate the way in which the 8086/8088 calculates memory addresses.

COMPUTERS

What is a Computer?

Figure 2-1 shows a block diagram for a simple computer. The major parts are the *central processing unit* or CPU, *memory*, and the *input and output* circuitry or I/O. Connecting these parts together are three sets of parallel lines called buses. The three buses are the *address bus*, the *data bus*, and the *control bus*.

MEMORY

The *memory* section usually consists of a mixture of RAM and ROM. It may also have magnetic floppy disks, magnetic hard disks, or laser optical disks. Memory has two purposes. The first purpose is to store the binary codes for the sequence of instructions you want the computer to carry out. When you write a computer program, what you are really doing is just writing a sequential list of instructions for the computer. The second purpose of the memory is to store the binary-coded data with which the computer is going to be working. This data might be the inventory records of a supermarket, for example.

INPUT/OUTPUT

The *input/output* or I/O section allows the computer to take in data from the outside world or send data to the outside world. Peripherals such as keyboards, video display terminals, printers, and modems are connected to the I/O section. These allow the user and the computer to communicate with each other. The actual physical devices used to interface the computer buses to external systems are often called *ports*. Ports in a computer function just as shipping ports do for a country. An *input port* allows data from a keyboard, an analog-to-digital (A/D) converter, or some other source to be read into the computer under control of the CPU. An *output port* is used to send data from the computer to some peripheral

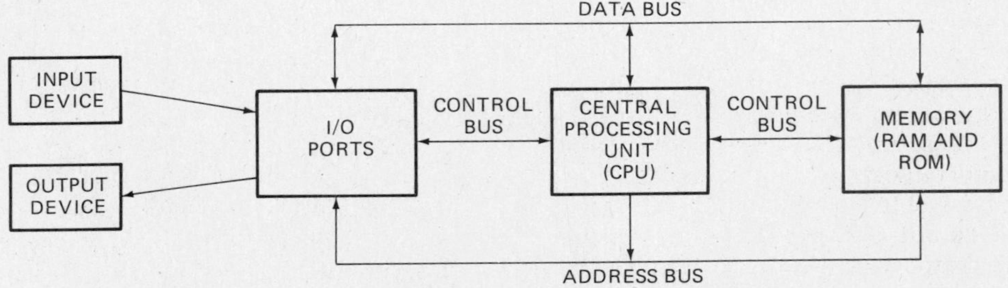

FIGURE 2-1 Block diagrams of a simple computer or microcomputer.

such as a video display terminal, a printer, or a digital-to-analog (D/A) converter. Physically, an input or output port is often just a set of parallel D flip-flops which let data pass through when they are enabled or clocked by a control signal from the CPU.

CENTRAL PROCESSING UNIT

The *central processing unit* or CPU controls the operation of the computer. It fetches binary-coded instructions from memory, decodes the instructions into a series of simple actions, and carries out these actions. The CPU contains an *arithmetic logic unit*, or ALU, which can perform add, subtract, OR, AND, invert, or exclusive-OR operations on binary words when instructed to do so. The CPU also contains an *address counter* which is used to hold the address of the next instruction or data to be fetched from memory, general-purpose registers which are used for temporary storage of binary data, and circuitry which generates the control bus signals.

ADDRESS BUS

The *address bus* consists of 16, 20, 24, or more parallel signal lines. On these lines the CPU sends out the address of the memory location that is to be written to or read from. The number of memory locations that the CPU can address is determined by the number of address lines. If the CPU has *N* address lines then it can directly address 2 to the *N* power memory locations. For example, a CPU with 16 address lines can address 2^{16} or 65,536 memory locations, a CPU with 20 address lines can address 2^{20} or 1,048,576 locations, and a CPU with 24 address lines can address 2^{24} or 16,777,216 locations. When the CPU reads data from or writes data to a port, the port address is also sent out on the address bus.

DATA BUS

The *data bus* consists of 8, 16, 32 or more parallel signal lines. As indicated by the double-ended arrows on the data bus line in Figure 2-1, the data bus lines are *bidirectional*. This means that the CPU can read data in on these lines from memory or from a port as well as send data out on these lines to a memory location or to a port. Many devices in a system will have their outputs connected to the data bus, but the outputs of only one device at a time will be enabled. Any device outputs connected on the data bus must be three-state so that they can be floated when the device is not in use.

CONTROL BUS

The *control bus* consists of 4–10 parallel signal lines. The CPU sends out signals on the control bus to enable the outputs of addressed memory devices or port devices. Typical control bus signals are *memory read*, *memory write*, *I/O read*, and *I/O write*. To read a byte of data from a memory location, for example, the CPU sends out the address of the desired byte on the address bus and then sends out a memory read signal on the control bus. The memory read signal enables the addressed memory device to output the byte of data onto the data bus where it is read by the CPU.

HARDWARE, SOFTWARE, AND FIRMWARE

When working around computers you hear the terms hardware, software, and firmware almost constantly. *Hardware* is the name given to the physical devices and circuitry of the computer. *Software* refers to the programs written for the computer. *Firmware* is the term given to programs stored in ROMs or in other devices which keep their stored information when the power is turned off.

Execution of a Three-Instruction Program

EXECUTION SEQUENCE

To give you a better idea of how the parts of a computer function together, we will now describe the actions a simple computer might go through to carry out (*execute*) a simple program. The three instructions of the program are:

1. Input a value from a keyboard connected to the port at address 05H.
2. Add 7 to the value read in.
3. Output the result to a display connected to the port at address 02H.

Figure 2-2*a* shows in diagram form the actions that the computer will perform to execute these three instructions.

For this example assume that the CPU fetches instructions and data from memory one byte at a time. Also assume that the binary codes for the instructions are in sequential memory locations starting at address 00100H. Figure 2-2*b* shows the binary codes that would be required in successive memory locations to execute this program on an 8086- or 8088-based microcomputer.

The first action a computer will do is to fetch the first instruction byte from memory. To do this the CPU sends out the address of the first instruction byte, in this case 00100H, to memory. This action is represented by line *1A* in Figure 2-2*a*. The CPU then sends out a memory read signal on the control bus (line *1B* in the figure). This causes the memory to output the first instruction byte (E4H) on the data bus as represented by line *1C*. The CPU reads in the byte from the data bus and *decodes* it. By decode we mean that the CPU determines from the binary code read in what actions it is supposed to take. In this case the CPU determines that the code read in represents an input instruction. Also from decoding this instruction byte, the CPU determines that it needs more information before it can carry out the instruction. The CPU must fetch from memory the input port address. To do this the CPU sends out the next sequential address (00101H) to memory as indicated by line *2A* in the figure. The CPU also sends out another memory read signal on the control bus (line *2B*). This enables the memory to put the addressed byte on the data bus (line *2C*). When the CPU reads in this second byte, 05H in this case, it has all the information it needs to execute the instruction.

FIGURE 2-2 *(a)* Execution of a three-step computer program. *(b)* Memory addresses and memory contents for a three-step program.

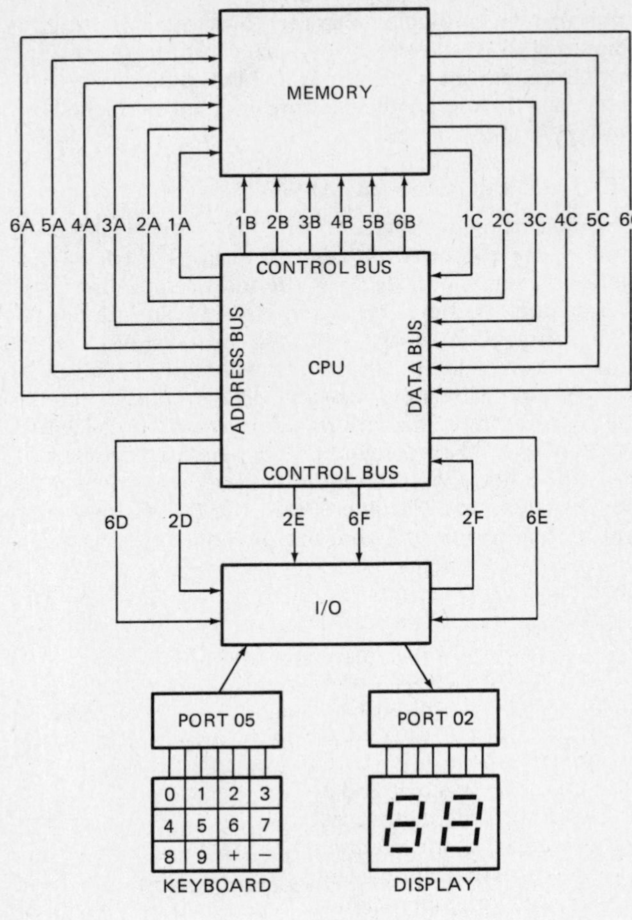

(a)

PROGRAM

1. Input a value from port 05.
2. Add 7 to this value.
3. Output the result to port 02.

SEQUENCE

1A CPU sends out address of first instruction to memory.
1B CPU sends out memory read control signal to enable memory.
1C Instruction byte sent from memory to CPU on data bus.
2A Address next memory location to get rest of instruction.
2B Send memory read control signal to enable memory.
2C Port address byte sent from memory to CPU on data bus.
2D CPU sends out port address on address bus.
2E CPU sends out input read control signal to enable port.
2F Data from port sent to CPU on data bus.
3A CPU sends address of next instruction to memory.
3B CPU sends memory read control signal to enable memory.
3C Instruction byte from memory sent to CPU on data bus.
4A CPU sends next address to memory to get rest of instruction.
4B CPU sends memory read control signal to enable memory.
4C Number 07H sent from memory to CPU on data bus.
5A CPU sends address of next instruction to memory.
5B CPU sends memory read control signal to enable memory.
5C Instruction byte from memory sent to CPU on data bus.
6A CPU sends out next address to get rest of instruction.
6B CPU sends out memory read control signal to enable memory.
6C Port address byte sent from memory to CPU on data bus.
6D CPU sends out port address on address bus.
6E CPU sends out data to port on data bus.
6F CPU sends out output write signal to enable port.

MEMORY ADDRESS	CONTENTS (BINARY)	CONTENTS (HEX)	OPERATION
00100H	11100100	E4	INPUT FROM
00101H	00000101	05	PORT 05H
00102H	00000100	04	ADD
00103H	00000111	07	07H
00104H	11100110	E6	OUTPUT TO
00105H	00000010	02	PORT 02

(*b*)

To execute the input instruction the CPU sends out the port address (05H) on the address bus (line *2D*) and sends out an I/O read signal on the control bus (line *2E*). The addressed port device then puts a byte of data on the data bus (line *2F*). The CPU reads in the byte of data and stores it in an internal register called the *accumulator*. This completes the first instruction.

Having completed the first instruction, the CPU must now fetch its next instruction from memory. To do this it sends out the next sequential address (00102H) on the address bus (line *3A*). The CPU then sends out a memory read signal on the control bus (line *3B*). This allows the memory to put the addressed byte (04H) on the data bus (line *3C*). The CPU reads in the instruction byte from the data bus and decodes it. From the instruction byte the CPU determines that it is supposed to add some number to the number stored in the accumulator. The CPU also determines from this instruction byte that it must go to memory again to get the number that it is supposed to add. To get the required byte, the CPU will send out the next sequential address (00103H) on the address bus (line *4A*) and a memory read signal on the control bus (line *4B*). The memory will then put the contents of the addressed byte (in this case the number 07H) on the data bus (line *4C*). The CPU will read in the byte on the data bus and add it to the contents of the accumulator as instructed. Assume the result of the addition is left in the accumulator. This completes the second instruction.

The CPU must now fetch its next instruction. To do this it sends out the next sequential address (00104H) on the address bus (line *5A*), sends out a memory read signal on the control bus (line *5B*), and reads in the addressed byte (E6H) from the data bus (line *5C*). From this byte the CPU determines that it is now supposed to do an output operation to a port. The CPU also determines that it must go to memory again to get the address of the port that it is supposed to output to. To do this it sends out the next sequential address (00105H) on the address bus (line *6A*), sends out a memory read signal on the control bus (line *6B*), and reads in the byte (02H) put on the data bus by the memory (line *6C*). The CPU now has all the information that it needs to execute the instruction. To output a data byte to a port, the CPU first sends out the address of the desired port on the address bus (line *6D*). Next it puts the data byte from the accumulator onto the data bus (line *6E*). The CPU then sends out an I/O write signal on the control bus (line *6F*). This signal enables the addressed output port device so the data from the data bus lines can pass through it. When the CPU removes the I/O write signal to proceed with the next instruction, the data output will remain latched on the output pins of the port device. Therefore, the computer does not have to keep outputting a value in order for it to remain there.

All of the steps described above may seem like a great deal of work just to input a value from a keyboard, add 7 to it, and output the result to a display. Even a simple computer, however, can run through all these steps in a few microseconds.

SUMMARY OF SIMPLE COMPUTER OPERATION

1. A simple computer CPU fetches instructions or reads data from memory (reads memory) by sending out an address on the address bus and a memory read signal on the control bus. The addressed instruction or data is sent from memory to the CPU on the data bus.
2. The CPU can write data in RAM by sending out an address on the address bus, sending out the data to be written on the data bus, and sending out a memory write signal on the control bus.
3. To read data from a port, the CPU sends the port address out on the address bus and sends an I/O read signal on the control bus. Data from the port comes into the CPU on the data bus.
4. To write data to a port, the CPU sends out the port address on the address bus, sends the data to be written to the port out on the data bus, and sends an I/O write signal out on the control bus.
5. A microcomputer fetches each program instruction in sequence, decodes the instruction, and executes it.

Types of Computers

MAINFRAMES

Computers come in a wide variety of sizes and capabilities. The largest and most powerful are often called *mainframes*. Mainframe computers may fill an entire room. They are designed to work at very high speeds with large data words, typically 64 bits or greater, and they have massive amounts of memory. Computers of this type are used for military defense control, business

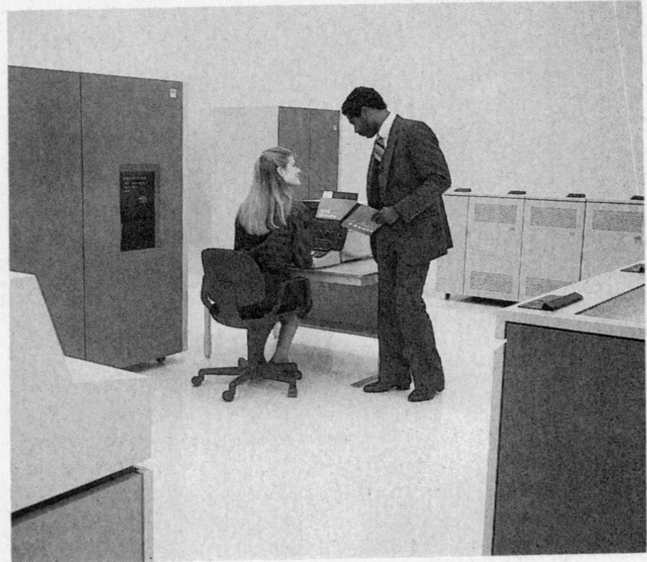

(a)

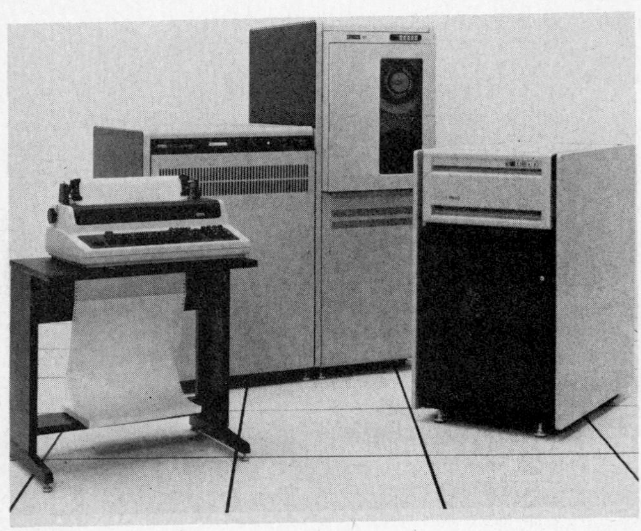

(b)

FIGURE 2-3 *(a)* Photograph of IBM mainframe computer. *(IBM Corp.) (b)* Photograph of DEC minicomputer. *(Digital Equipment Corp.)*

data processing (an insurance company, for example), and for creating computer graphics displays for science fiction movies. Examples of this type of computer are the IBM 4381, the Honeywell DPS8, and the CRAY X-MP/48. Figure 2-3*a* shows a photograph of an IBM 4381 mainframe.

MINICOMPUTERS

Scaled-down versions of mainframe computers are often called *minicomputers*. The main unit of a minicomputer usually fits in a single rack or box. A minicomputer runs more slowly, works directly with smaller data words (often 32-bit words), and does not have as much memory as a mainframe. Computers of this type are used for business data processing, industrial control (an oil refinery, for example), and scientific research. Examples of this type of computer are the Digital Equipment Corp. VAX 11/730 and the Data General MV/8000II. Figure 2-3*b* shows a photograph of a Digital Equipment Corp. VAX 11/730 minicomputer.

MICROCOMPUTERS

As the name implies, *microcomputers* are small computers. They range from small controllers that work directly with 4-bit words and can address a few thousand bytes of memory to larger units that work directly with 32-bit words and can address millions or billions of bytes of memory. Some of the more powerful microcomputers have all or most of the features of earlier minicomputers. Therefore, it has become very hard to draw a sharp line between these two types. One distinguishing feature of a microcomputer is that the CPU is usually a single integrated circuit called a *microprocessor*. Older books often used the terms microprocessor and microcomputer interchangeably, but actually the microprocessor is the CPU to which you add ROM, RAM, and ports to make a microcomputer. A later section in this chapter discusses the evolution of different types of microprocessors. Microcomputers are used in everything from smart sewing machines to computer-aided design systems. Examples of microcomputers are the Intel 8051 single-chip controller; the SDK-86, a single-board computer design kit; the IBM Personal Computer (PC); and the Apple Macintosh computer. Figure 2-4*a* shows a block diagram of the Intel 8051 single-chip microcontroller, Figure 2-4*b* shows the SDK-86 board, and Figure 2-4*c* shows the IBM PC. The purpose of this book is to teach you how microprocessors are connected with other components to build microcomputers, how the microcomputers are interfaced with peripheral components to build microcomputer systems, and how these systems are programmed. We use the IBM PC and the SDK-86 as example systems throughout this book. An available laboratory manual, written to accompany this book, shows you how to get started using the SDK-86 board and the IBM PC for assembly language programming.

SUMMARY OF IMPORTANT POINTS SO FAR

1. A computer or microcomputer consists of memory, a CPU, and some input/output circuitry.
2. These three parts are connected together by the address bus, the data bus, and the control bus.
3. The sequence of instructions, or program, for a computer is stored as binary numbers in successive memory locations.
4. The CPU fetches an instruction from memory, decodes the instruction to determine what actions must be done for the instruction, and carries out these actions.
5. Three types of computer are mainframes, minicomputers, and microcomputers.
6. The CPU in a microcomputer is called a microprocessor.

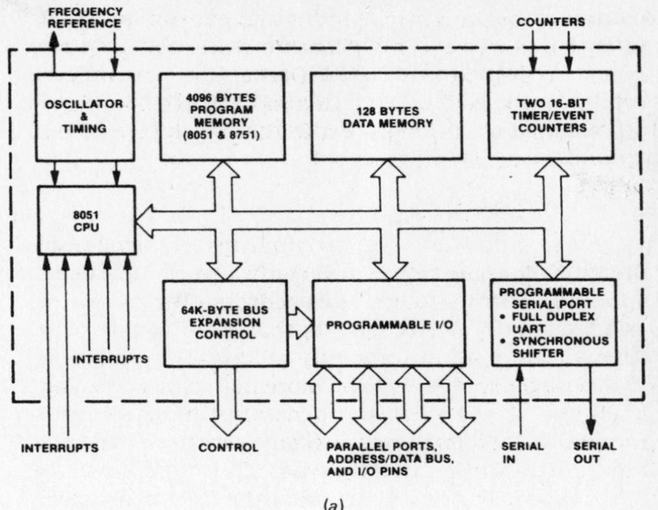

(a)

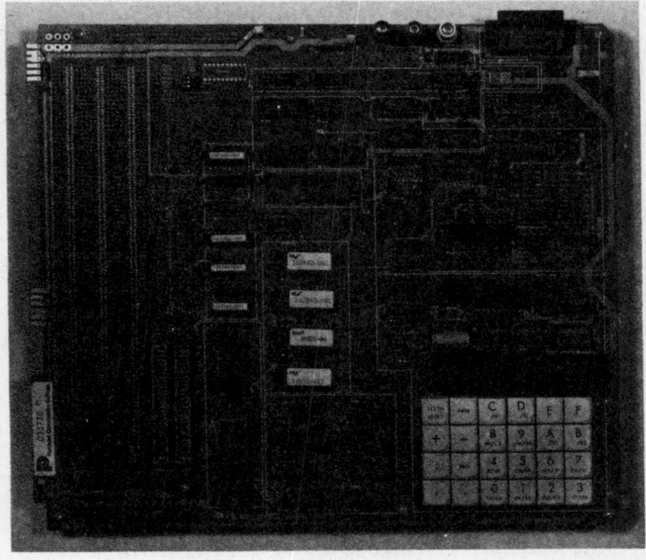

(b)

(c)

FIGURE 2-4 *(a)* Block diagram of Intel 8051 single chip microcomputer. *(Intel Corp.)* *(b)* Photograph of Intel SDK-86 board. *(Intel Corp.)* *(c)* Photograph of IBM PC. *(IBM Corp.)*

How Computers and Microcomputers are Used—An Example

The following sections are intended to give you an overview of how computers are interfaced with users to do useful work. These sections should help you understand many of the features designed into current microprocessors and where this book is heading.

COMPUTERIZING AN ELECTRONICS FACTORY—PROBLEM

Now, suppose that we want to "computerize" an electronics company. By this we mean that we want to make computer use available to as many people in the company as possible as cheaply as possible. We want the engineers to have access to a computer which can help them design circuits. People in the drafting department should have access to a computer which can be used for computer-aided drafting. The accounting department should have access to a computer for doing all of the financial bookkeeping. The warehouse should have access to a computer to help with inventory control. The manufacturing department should have access to a computer for controlling machines and testing finished products. The president, vice presidents, and supervisors should have access to a computer to help them with long range planning. Secretaries should have access to a computer for word processing. Sales people should have access to a computer to help them keep track of current pricing, product availability, and commissions. There are several ways to provide all the needed computer power. The next sections discuss some of the ways that are used to give people access to a computer.

BATCH PROCESSING

In the 1960s the available computers were very large and were kept in separate air-conditioned rooms. When programmers wanted to run their programs, they brought them to the computer room. Usually the program was in the form of a batch of punched cards. A computer operator would then run the program. A new programming job could not be started until the last one finished. Therefore, if a large job was being run, there might be a considerable wait before a programmer could get his or her job run. Also, if an error was found when the program ran, the programmer had to punch new cards, and either bribe the computer operator or put the corrected program cards on the bottom of the jobs-to-be-done pile. Needless to say, a system of this sort is not acceptable for computerizing our electronics company, because it only serves one user at a time and does not allow easy back-and-forth interaction between the computer and the user.

MULTIPROGRAMMING

An improvement over the basic batch system is a *multiprogramming* system. In this type of system several programs are put in the computer's memory at the same time. The computer runs one programming job until it reaches a point where it needs access to some slow peripheral device such as a printer. If the printer is not busy, the computer will print out the produced results. If the printer is busy, the data to be printed is stored on a magnetic disk. The computer can then start another programming job while it waits for the printer to become available. When the printer becomes available, the computer can print out the results from the first program, and then return to the second program. To further reduce the burden on the computer, some computers have separate circuitry that takes care of copying output data from magnetic disks to the printer. Multiprogramming improves the efficiency of the computer by keeping it busy more of the time, but it still does not allow the user to easily interact with the computer.

TIME-SHARE AND MULTITASKING SYSTEMS

A further improvement in computer access is *time-sharing*. Figure 2-5 shows a block diagram of one type of time-share system. Several video terminals are connected to the computer through direct wires or through telephone lines. The terminal can be on the user's desk or even in the user's home. The rate at which a user usually enters data is very slow as compared to the rate that a computer can process the data. Therefore, the computer can serve many users by dividing its time among them in small increments. In other words, the computer works on user #1's program for perhaps 20 milliseconds, works on user #2's program for 20 milliseconds, then works on user #3's program for 20 milliseconds, and so on until all all the users have had a turn. In a few milliseconds the computer will get back to user #1 again and repeat the cycle. To each user it will appear as if he or she has exclusive use of the computer because the computer processes data as fast as the user enters it. A time-share system such as this allows several users to interact with the computer at the same time. Each user can get information from or store information in the large memory attached to the computer. Each user can have an inexpensive printer attached to the terminal or can direct program or data output to a high-speed printer attached directly to the computer.

An airline ticket reservation computer might use a time-share system such as this to allow users from all over the country to access flight information and make reservations. A time-multiplexed or time-sliced system such as this can also allow a computer to control many machines or processes in a factory. A computer is much faster than the machines or processes. Therefore, it can check and adjust many pressures, temperatures, motor speeds, etc. before it needs to get back and recheck the first one. A system such as this is often called a *multitasking system* because it appears to be doing many tasks at the same time.

Now let's take another look at our problem of computerizing the electronics company. A time-share system seems to be a better idea than a batch system or even a multiprogramming system. We could put a powerful computer in some central location and run wires from it to video display terminals on users' desks. Each user could then run the program needed to do a particular task. The accountant can run a ledger program, the secretary can run a word processor program, etc. Each user can access the computer's large data memory. Incidentally, a large collection of data stored in a computer's

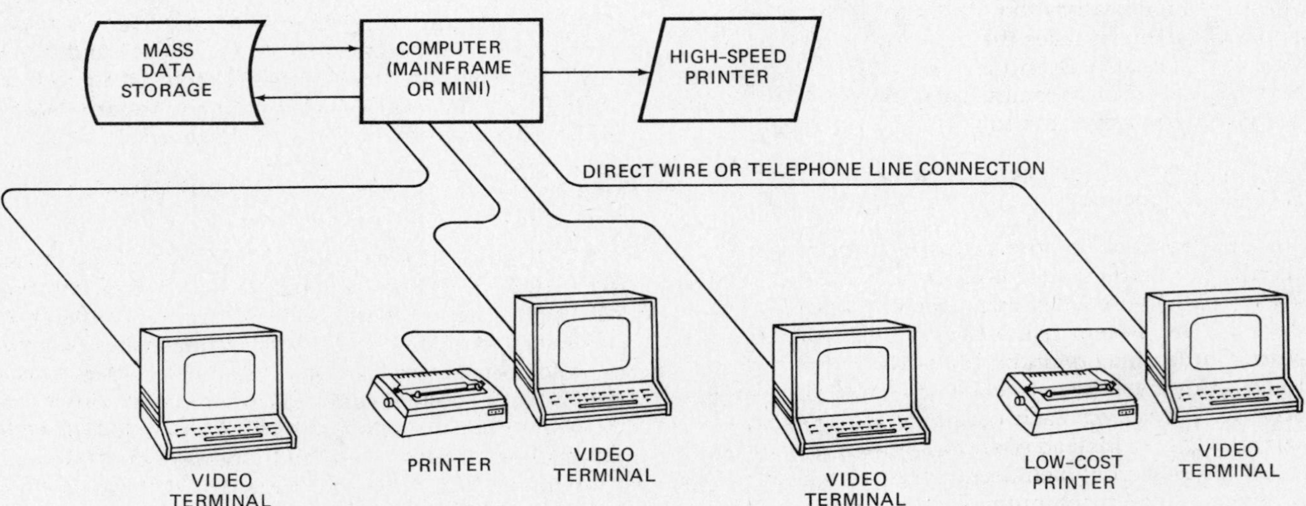

FIGURE 2-5 Block diagram of a computer time-share system.

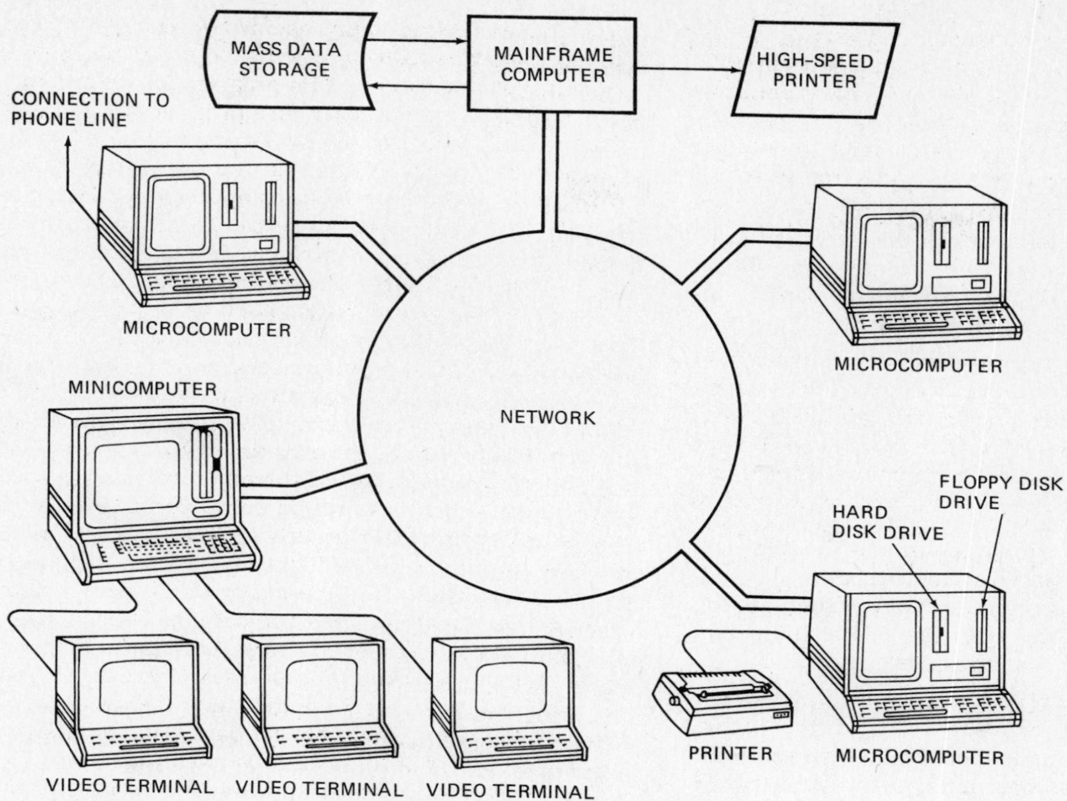

FIGURE 2-6 Block diagram of distributed processing computer system.

memory is often referred to as a *data base*. For a small company a system such as this might be adequate. However, there are at least two potential problems.

The first potential problem is "What happens if the computer is not working?" The answer to this question is that everything grinds to a halt. In a situation where people have become dependent upon the computer, not much gets done until the computer is up and running again. The old saying about putting all your eggs in one basket comes to mind here.

The second potential problem of the simple time share system is saturation. As the number of users increases, the time it takes the computer to do each user's task increases also. Eventually the computer's response time to each user becomes unreasonably long. People get very upset about the time they have to wait.

DISTRIBUTED PROCESSING OR MULTIPROCESSING

A partial solution for the two potential problems of a simple time-share system is to use a *distributed processor* system. Figure 2-6 shows a block diagram for such a system. The system has a powerful central computer with a large memory and a high-speed printer as does the simple time-share system decribed previously. However, in this system each user or group of users has a microcomputer instead of simply a video display terminal. In other words, each user station is an independent functioning microcomputer with a CPU, ROM, RAM, and probably magnetic or optical disk memory. This means that a person can do many tasks locally on the microcomputer without having to use the large computer at all. Since the microcomputers are connected to the large computer with a network, however, a user can access the computing power, memory, or other resources of the large computer when needed.

Distributing the processing around to multiple computers or processors in a system has several advantages. First, if the large computer goes down, the local microcomputers can continue working until they need to access the large computer for something. Second, the burden on the large computer is reduced greatly, because much of the computing is done by the local microcomputers. Finally, the distributed processor approach allows the system designer to use a local microcomputer best suited to the task it has to do.

COMPUTERIZED ELECTRONICS COMPANY OVERVIEW

Distributed processing seems to be the best way to go about computerizing our electronics factory. Engineers can each have a personal computer on their desk. With this they can use available programs to design and test circuits. They can access the large computer if they need data from its memory. Through the telephone lines, the engineer with a personal computer can access data in the memory of other computers all over the world. The drafting people can have personal computers for simple work, or large computer-aided design systems for more complex work. Completed work can be stored in the large computer memory. The accounting department can use personal computers with spread sheet programs to work with financial data kept in the memory of the large computer. The warehouse supervisor can likewise use a personal computer with an inventory program to keep personal records and those in the large computer's memory updated. Corporate officers can have personal computers tied into the network. They then can interact with any of the other systems on the network. Sales people can have portable personal computers that they can carry with them in the field. They can communicate with the main computer over the telephone lines using a modem. Secretaries doing word processing can use individual word processing units or personal computers. Since word processing is not a high intensity use for a computer, several video display terminals for word processing can be connected to a local microcomputer, and this local microcomputer can be connected to the large computer through the network. Users can also send messages to each other over the network. The specifics of a computer system such as this will obviously depend on the needs of the individual company for which the system is designed.

SUMMARY AND DIRECTION FROM HERE

The main concepts that you should take with you from this section are multiprogramming, time-sharing or multitasking, and distributed processing or multiprocessing. As you work your way through the rest of this book, keep an overview of the computerized electronics company in the back of your mind. The goal of this book is to teach you how all the parts of a system such as this work, how the parts are connected together, and how the system is programmed at different levels.

The first step toward this goal will be a quick look at the different types of microprocessors available. We then discuss a specific microprocessor, the Intel 8086, and the programming of a microcomputer built around a member of this microprocessor family, the IBM PC. Next we discuss the hardware connections and timing of this microcomputer. From there we show how the microcomputer is interfaced to a wide variety of peripheral devices. And finally we cycle back to our computerized electronics company, the networks it uses, and the system programs it requires.

Common Microprocessor Types

MICROPROCESSOR EVOLUTION

A common way of categorizing microprocessors is by the number of bits that their ALU can work with at a time. In other words, a microprocessor with a 4-bit ALU will be referred to as a 4-bit microprocessor, regardless of the number of address lines or the number of data bus lines that it has. The first microprocessor was the Intel 4004 produced in 1971. It contained 2300 PMOS transistors. The 4004 was a 4-bit device intended to be used with some other devices in making a calculator. Some logic designers, however, saw that this device could be used to replace PC boards full of combinational and sequential logic devices. Also, the ability to change the function of a system by just changing the programming, rather than redesigning the hardware, is very appealing. It was these factors that pushed the evolution of microprocessors.

In 1972 Intel came out with the 8008 which was capable of working with 8-bit words. The 8008, however, required 20 or more additional devices to form a functional CPU. In 1974 Intel announced the 8080, which had a much larger instruction set than the 8008 and only required two additional devices to form a functional CPU. Also, the 8080 used NMOS transistors, so it operated much faster than the 8008. The 8080 is referred to as a second-generation microprocessor.

Soon after Intel produced the 8080, Motorola came out with the MC6800, another 8-bit general-purpose CPU. The 6800 had the advantage that it required only a +5 V supply rather than the −5 V, +5 V, and +12 V supplies required by the 8080. For several years the 8080 and the 6800 were the top-selling 8-bit microprocessors. Some of their competitors were the MOS Technology 6502 used as the CPU in the Apple II microcomputer, and the Zilog Z80 used as the CPU in the Radio Shack TRS-80 microcomputer.

As designers found more and more applications for microprocessors, they pressured microprocessor manufacturers to develop devices with architectures and features optimized for doing certain types of tasks. In response to the expressed needs, microprocessors have evolved in three major directions during the last 10 years.

DEDICATED CONTROLLERS

One direction has been *dedicated controllers*. These devices are used to control "smart" machines such as microwave ovens, clothes washers, sewing machines, auto ignition systems, and metal lathes. Texas Instruments produced millions of their TMS-1000 family of 4-bit microprocessors for this type of application. In 1976 Intel introduced the 8048, which contains an 8-bit CPU, RAM, ROM, and some I/O ports all in one 40-pin package. Other manufacturers have followed with similar products. These devices are often referred to as *microcontrollers*. Some currently available devices in this category, the Intel 8051 and the Motorola MC6801, for example, contain programmable counters, a serial port (UART) as well as a CPU, ROM, RAM, and parallel I/O ports. A more recently introduced single-chip microcontroller, the Intel 8096, contains a 16-bit CPU, ROM, RAM, a UART, ports, timers, and a 10-bit analog-to-digital converter.

BIT-SLICE PROCESSORS

A second direction of microprocessor evolution has been bit-slice processors. For some applications general-purpose CPUs such as the 8080 and 6800 are not fast enough or their instruction sets are not suitable. For these applications several manufacturers produce devices which can be used to build a custom CPU. An example is the Advanced Micro Devices 2900 family of devices. This family includes 4-bit ALUs, multiplexers, sequencers, and other parts needed for custom-building a CPU. The term *slice* comes from the fact that these parts can be connected in parallel to work with 8-bit words, 16-bit words, or 32-bit words. In other words, a designer can add as many slices as needed for a particular application. The designer not only custom-designs the hardware of the CPU, but also custom-makes the instruction set for it using "microcode."

GENERAL-PURPOSE CPUs

The third major direction of microprocessor evolution has been toward general-purpose CPUs which give a microcomputer most or all of the computing power of earlier minicomputers. After Motorola came out with the MC6800, Intel produced the 8085, an upgrade of the 8080 requiring only a +5 V supply. Motorola then produced the MC6809 which has a few 16-bit instructions, but is still basically an 8-bit processor. In 1978 Intel came out with the 8086 which is a full 16-bit processor. Some 16-bit microprocessors, such as the National PACE and the Texas Instruments 9900 family of devices, were available previously, but the market apparently wasn't ready. Soon after Intel came out with the 8086, Motorola came out with the 16-bit MC68000, and the 16-bit race was off and running. The 8086 and the 68000 work directly with 16-bit words instead of with 8-bit words, they can address a million or more bytes of memory instead of the 64 Kbytes addressable by the 8-bit processors, and they execute instructions much faster than the 8-bit processors. Also these 16-bit processors have single instructions for functions that required a lengthy sequence of instructions on the 8-bit processors.

The evolution along this last path has continued on to 32-bit processors that work with giga (10^9) bytes or tera (10^{12}) bytes of memory. Examples of these devices are the Intel 80386, the Motorola MC68020, and the National 32032.

Since we could not possibly describe in this book the operation and programming of even a few of the available processors, we confine our discussions to primarily one group of related microprocessors. The family we have chosen is the Intel 8086, 8088, 80186, 80188, 80286 family. Members of this family are very widely used in personal computers, business computer systems, and industrial control systems. Our experience has shown that learning the programming and operation of one family of microcomputers very thoroughly is much more useful than looking at many processors superficially. If you learn one processor family well, you will most likely find it quite easy to learn another when you have to.

THE 8086, 8088, 80186, 80188, AND 80286 MICROPROCESSORS—INTRODUCTION

The Intel 8086 is a 16-bit microprocessor intended to be used as the CPU in a microcomputer. The term "16-bit" means that its arithmetic logic unit, internal registers, and most of its instructions are designed to work with 16-bit binary words. The 8086 has a 16-bit data bus, so it can read data from or write data to memory and ports either 16 bits or 8 bits at a time. The 8086 has a 20-bit address bus, so it can address any one of 2^{20} or 1,048,576 memory locations. Each of the 1,048,576 memory addresses of the 8086 represents a byte-wide location. Words will be stored in two consecutive memory locations. If the first byte of a word is at an even address, the 8086 can read the entire word in one operation. If the first byte of the word is at an odd address, the 8086 will read the first byte in one operation, and the second byte in another operation. Later we will discuss this in detail. The main point here is that if the first byte of a 16-bit word is at an even address, the 8086 can read the word in one operation.

The Intel 8088 has the same arithmetic logic unit, the same registers, and the same instruction set as the 8086. The 8088 also has a 20-bit address bus so it can address any one of 1,048,576 bytes in memory. The 8088, however, has an 8-bit data bus so it can only read data from or write data to memory and ports 8 bits at a time. The 8086, remember, can read or write either 8 or 16 bits at a time. To read a 16-bit word from two successive memory locations, the 8088 will always have to do two read operations. Since the 8086 and the 8088 are almost identical, any reference we make to the 8086 in the rest of the book will also pertain to the 8088 unless we specifically indicate otherwise. This is done to make reading easier. The Intel 8088, incidentally, is used as the CPU in the IBM Personal Computer and several compatible personal computers.

The Intel 80186 is an improved version of the 8086, and the 80188 is an improved version of the 8088. In addition to a 16-bit CPU the 80186 and 80188 each have programmable peripheral devices integrated in the same package. In a later chapter we will discuss these integrated peripherals. The instruction set of the 80186 and the 80188 is a *superset* of the instruction set of the 8086. The term superset means that all of the 8086 and 8088 instructions will execute properly on an 80186 or on an 80188, but the 80186 and the 80188 have a few additional instructions. In other words, a program written for an 8086 or for an 8088 is *upward-compatible* to an 80186 or to an 80188, but a program written for an 80186 or for an 80188 may not execute correctly on an 8086 or an 8088. In the instruction set descriptions in Chapter 6, we specifically indicate which instructions only work with the 80186 or 80188. The 80186 is used as the CPU in several personal computers.

The Intel 80286 is an advanced version of the 8086 specifically designed for use as the CPU in a multiuser or multitasking microcomputer. Programs written for an 8086 can be run on an 80286 operating in its *real address mode*. We discuss in Chapter 14 the operation and use of the 80286. The 80286 is the CPU used in the IBM PC/AT personal computer.

8086 INTERNAL ARCHITECTURE

The three-instruction program section of this chapter describes how a CPU sends out addresses, sends out

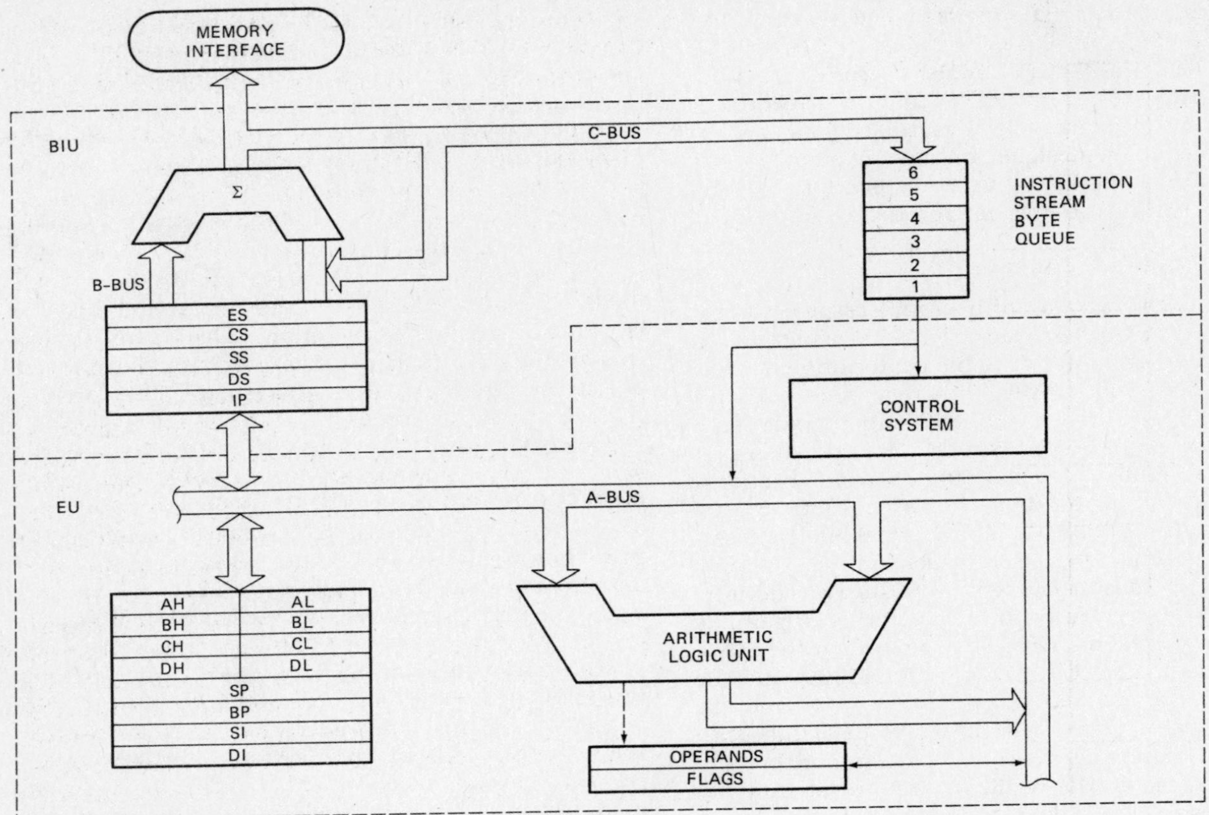

FIGURE 2-7 8086 internal block diagram. *(Intel Corp.)*

control signals, reads in instructions and data to internal registers, and sends out data to ports or memory. Before we can talk about how to write programs for the 8086, we need to discuss its specific internal features such as registers, instruction byte queue, and flags.

As shown by the block diagram in Figure 2-7, the 8086 CPU is divided into two independent functional parts, the *bus interface unit* or BIU, and the *execution unit* or EU. Dividing the work between these two units speeds up processing.

The Bus Interface Unit

The BIU sends out addresses, fetches instructions from memory, reads data from ports and memory, and writes data to ports and memory. In other words the BIU handles all transfers of data and addresses on the buses for the execution unit. The following sections describe the functional parts of the BIU.

THE QUEUE

To speed up program execution, the BIU fetches as many as six instruction bytes ahead of time from memory. The prefetched instruction bytes are held for the EU in a first-in-first-out group of registers called a *queue*. The BIU can be fetching instruction bytes while the EU is decoding an instruction or executing an instruction which does not require use of the buses. When the EU is ready for its next instruction, it simply reads the instruction from the queue in the BIU. This is much faster than sending out an address to the system memory and waiting for memory to send back the next instruction byte or bytes. The process is analogous to the way a bricklayer's assistant fetches bricks ahead of time and keeps a queue of bricks lined up so that the bricklayer can just reach out and grab a brick when necessary. Except in the cases of JUMP and CALL instructions where the queue must be dumped and then reloaded starting from a new address, this prefetch-and-queue scheme greatly speeds up processing. Fetching the next instruction while the current instruction executes is called *pipelining*.

SEGMENT REGISTERS

The BIU contains four 16-bit *segment registers*. They are: the *code segment* (CS) register, the *stack segment* (SS) register, the *extra segment* (ES) register, and the *data segment* (DS) register. These segment registers are used to hold the upper 16 bits of the starting addresses of four memory segments that the 8086 is working with at a particular time. The 8086 BIU sends out 20-bit addresses, so it can address any of 2^{20} or 1,048,576 bytes in memory. However, at any given time the 8086 only works with four, 65,536-byte (64 Kbyte) segments within this 1,048,576-byte (1 Mbyte) range. Figure 2-8

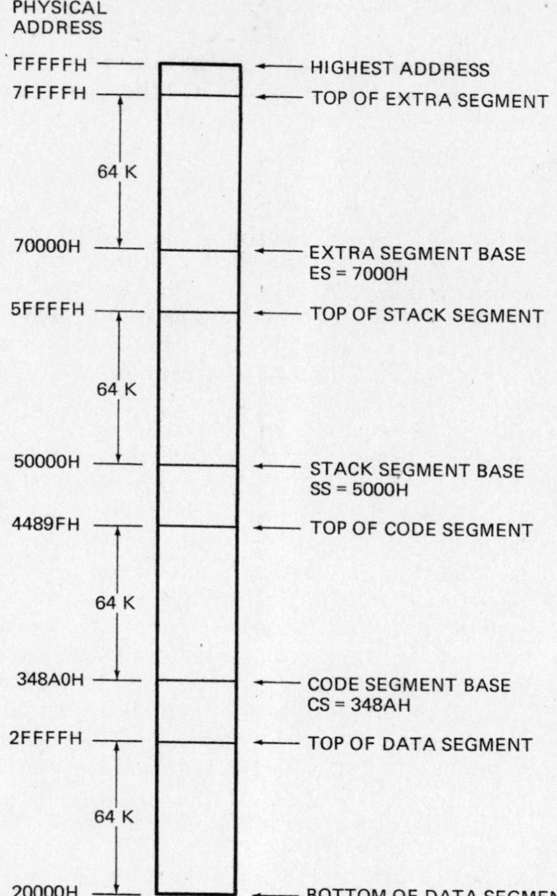

FIGURE 2-8 One way that four 64 Kbyte segments might be positioned within 1 Mbyte address space of 8086.

shows how these four segments might be positioned in memory at a given time. The four segments can be separated as shown, or, for small programs which do not need all 64 Kbytes in each segment, they can overlap. A minimum system, for example, might start all four segments at address 00000H.

To repeat then, a segment register is used to hold the upper 16 bits of the starting address for each of the segments. The code segment register, for example, holds the upper 16 bits of the starting address for the segment from which the BIU is currently fetching instruction code bytes. The BIU always inserts zeros for the lowest four bits (nibble) of the 20-bit starting address for a segment. If the code segment register contains 348AH, for example, then the code segment will start at address 348A0H. In other words, a 64 Kbyte segment can be located anywhere within the 1 Mbyte address space, but the segment will always start at an address with zeros in the lowest 4 bits. This constraint was put on the location of segments so that it is only necessary to store and manipulate 16-bit numbers when working with the starting address of a segment. The part of a segment starting address stored in a segment register is often called the *segment base*.

A *stack* is a section of memory set aside to store addresses and data while a *subprogram* executes. The stack segment register is used for the upper 16 bits of the starting address for the program stack. We will discuss the use and operation of a stack in detail later.

The extra segment register and the data segment register are used to hold the upper 16 bits of the starting addresses of two memory segments that are used for data.

INSTRUCTION POINTER

The next feature to look at in the BIU is the *instruction pointer* (IP) register. As discussed previously, the code segment register holds the upper 16 bits of the starting address of the segment from which the BIU is fetching instruction code bytes. The instruction pointer register holds the 16-bit address of the next code byte *within* this code segment. The value contained in the IP is often referred to as an *offset*, because this value must be offset from (added to) the segment base address in CS to produce the required 20-bit physical address. Figure 2-9*a* shows in diagram form how this works. The CS register points to the *base* or start of the current code segment. The IP contains the distance or offset from this base address to the next instruction byte to be fetched. Figure 2-9*b* shows how the 16-bit offset in IP is added to the 16-bit segment base address in CS to produce the 20-bit *physical* address. Notice that the two 16-bit numbers are not added directly in line. One way to describe this process is to say that the contents of the CS register are shifted left four bit positions before the contents of the IP are added to it. CS contains 348AH. When shifted left by four bit positions this produces 348A0H as the starting address of the code segment. The offset of 4214H in the IP is added to this base to give a 20-bit physical address of 38AB4H.

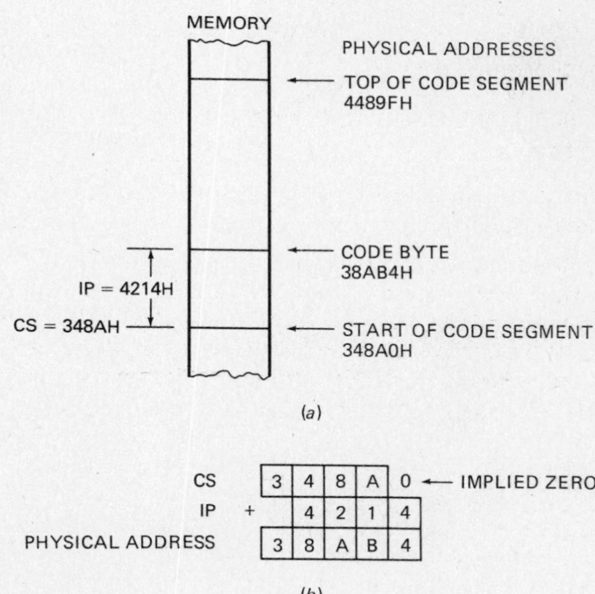

FIGURE 2-9 Addition of IP to CS to produce physical address of code byte. *(a)* Diagram. *(b)* Computation.

The 8086 20-bit physical addresses are often represented in a *segment base:offset form* rather than in the single number form. For the address of a code byte the alternative form will be CS:IP. For example, the address constructed in the preceding paragraph, 38AB4H, can also be represented as 348A:4214.

To summarize, then, the CS register contains the upper 16 bits of the starting address of the code segment in the 1 Mbyte address range of the 8086. The instruction pointer register contains a 16-bit offset which tells where in that 64 Kbyte code segment the next instruction byte will be fetched from. The actual physical address sent to memory is produced by shifting the contents of the CS register four bit positions left and adding the offset contained in IP.

As you will see in later sections, any time the 8086 accesses memory, the BIU produces the required 20-bit physical address by shifting the contents of one of the segment registers left four bit positions and adding to it a displacement or offset.

The Execution Unit

The execution unit of the 8086 tells the BIU where to fetch instructions or data from, decodes instructions, and executes instructions. The following sections describe the functional parts of the execution unit.

CONTROL CIRCUITRY, INSTRUCTION DECODER, AND ALU

Now take another look at the 8086 block diagram in Figure 2-7 to see what is contained in the execution unit. The EU contains *control circuitry* which directs internal operations. A *decoder* in the EU translates instructions fetched from memory into a series of actions which the EU carries out. The EU has a 16-bit *arithmetic logic unit* which can add, subtract, AND, OR, XOR, increment, decrement, complement, or shift binary numbers.

FLAG REGISTER

A *flag* is a flip-flop which indicates some condition produced by the execution of an instruction, or controls certain operations of the EU. A 16-bit *flag register* in the EU contains nine active flags. Figure 2-10 shows the location of the nine flags in the flag register. Six of the nine flags are used to indicate some *condition* produced by an instruction. For example, a flip-flop called the carry flag will be set to a one if the addition of two 16-bit binary numbers produces a carry out of the most significant bit position. If no carry out of the MSB is produced by the addition, then the carry flag will be a zero. The EU then effectively runs up a "flag" to tell you that a carry was produced.

The six conditional flags in this group are: the *carry flag* (CF), the *parity flag* (PF), the *auxiliary carry flag* (AF), the *zero flag* (ZF), the *sign flag* (SF), and the *overflow flag* (OF). The names of these flags should give you hints as to what conditions affect them. Certain 8086 instructions check these flags to determine which of two alternative actions should be done in executing the instruction.

The three remaining flags in the flag register are used to *control* certain operations of the processor. These flags are different from the six conditional flags described above in the way they get set or reset. The six conditional flags are set or reset by the EU on the basis of the results of some arithmetic or logic operation. The *control flags* are deliberately set or reset with specific instructions you put in the program. The three control flags are the *trap flag* (TF), which is used for single stepping through a program; the *interrupt flag* (IF), which is used to allow/prohibit the interruption of a program, and the *direction flag* (DF), which is used with string instructions.

Later we will discuss in detail the operation and use of the nine flags.

GENERAL-PURPOSE REGISTERS

Observe in Figure 2-7 that the EU has eight *general purpose registers* labeled AH, AL, BH, BL, CH, CL, DH, and DL. These registers can be used individually for temporary storage of 8-bit data. The AL register is also called the *accumulator*. It has some features that the other general-purpose registers do not have.

Certain pairs of these general-purpose registers can be used together to store 16-bit data words. The acceptable register pairs are AH and AL, BH and BL, CH and CL, and DH and DL. The AH-AL pair is referred to as the *AX register*, the BH-BL pair is referred to as the *BX register*, the CH-CL pair is referred to as the *CX register*,

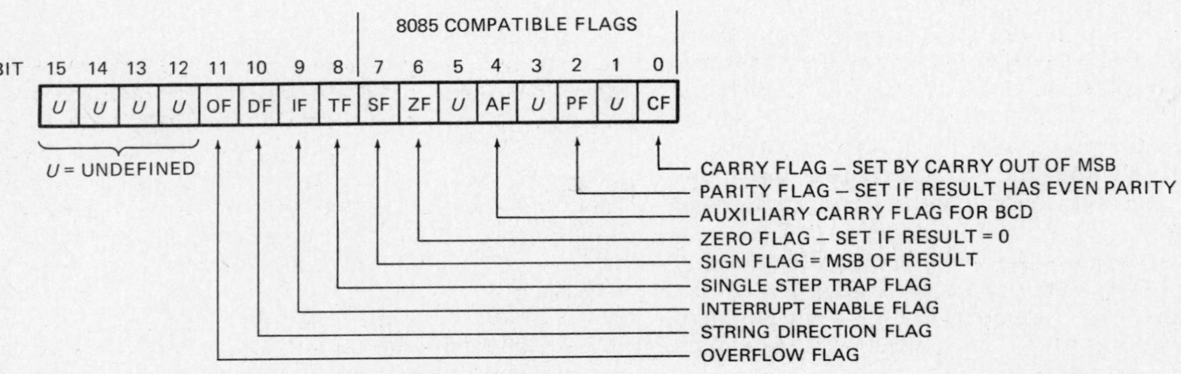

FIGURE 2-10 8086 flag register format. *(Intel Corp.)*

and the DH-DL pair is referred to as the *DX register*. For 16-bit operations, AX is called the accumulator.

The 8086 register set is very similar to those of the earlier generation 8080 and 8085 microprocessors. It was designed this way so that the many programs written for the 8080 and 8085 could easily be translated to run on the 8086 or the 8088. The advantage of using internal registers for the temporary storage of data is that, since the data is already in the EU, it can be accessed much more quickly than it could be accessed in external memory.

STACK POINTER REGISTER

A stack, remember, is a section of memory set aside to store addresses and data while a subprogram is executing. The 8086 allows you to set aside an entire 64 Kbyte segment as a stack. The upper 16 bits of the starting address for this segment is kept in the stack segment register. The *stack pointer* (SP) register contains the 16-bit offset from the start of the segment to the memory location where a word was most recently stored on the stack. The memory location where a word was most recently stored is called the *top of stack*. Figure 2-11*a* shows this in diagram form.

The physical address for a stack read or for a stack write is produced by adding the contents of the stack pointer register to the segment base address in SS. To do this the contents of the stack segment register are shifted four bit positions left and the contents of SP are added to the shifted result. Figure 2-11*b* shows an example. The 5000H in SS is shifted left four bit positions to give 50000H. When FFE0H in the SP is added to this, the resultant physical address for the top of the stack will be 5FFE0H. The physical address can be represented either as a single number, 5FFE0H, or it can be represented in SS:SP form as 5000:FFE0H.

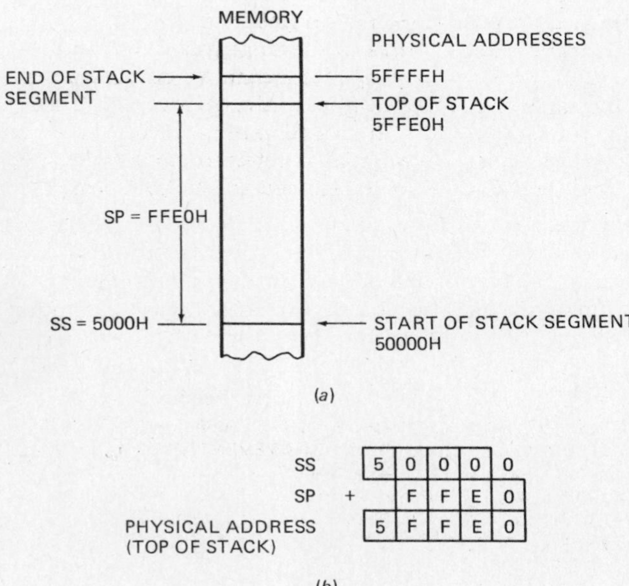

FIGURE 2-11 Addition of SS and SP to produce physical address of top of stack. *(a)* Diagram. *(b)* Computation.

The operation and use of the stack will be discussed in detail later as need arises.

OTHER POINTER AND INDEX REGISTERS

In addition to the stack pointer register, SP, the EU contains a 16-bit *base pointer* (BP) register. It also contains a 16-bit *source index* (SI) register and a 16-bit *destination index* (DI) register. These three registers can be used for temporary storage of data just as the general-purpose registers described above. However, their main use is to hold the 16-bit offset of a data word in one of the segments. SI, for example, can be used to hold the offset of a data word in the data segment. The physical address of the data in memory will be generated in this case by shifting the contents of the data segment register four bit positions to the left and adding the contents of SI to the result. A later section on addressing modes will discuss and show many examples of the use of these base and index registers.

INTRODUCTION TO PROGRAMMING THE 8086

Programming Languages

Now that you have an overview of the 8086 CPU, it is time to start you thinking about how it is programmed. To run a program, a microcomputer must have the program stored in binary form in successive memory locations. There are three language levels that can be used to write a program for a microcomputer.

MACHINE LANGUAGE

You can write programs as simply a sequence of the binary codes for the instructions you want the microcomputer to execute. The three-instruction program in Figure 2-2*b* is an example. This binary form of the program is referred to as *machine language* because it is the form required by the machine. However, it is difficult, if not impossible, for a programmer to memorize the thousands of binary instruction codes for a CPU such as the 8086. Also, it is very easy for an error to occur when working with long series of 1's and 0's. Using hexadecimal representation for the binary codes might help some, but there are still thousands of instruction codes to cope with.

ASSEMBLY LANGUAGE

To make programming easier many programmers write programs in *assembly language*. They then translate the assembly language program to machine language so it can be loaded into memory and run. Assembly language uses two-, three-, or four-letter *mnemonics* to represent each instruction type. A mnemonic is just a device to help you remember something. The letters in an assembly language mnemonic are usually initials or a shortened form of the English word(s) for the operation performed by the instruction. For example, the mnemonic for subtract is SUB, the mnemonic for exclusive OR is XOR, and the mnemonic for the instruction to copy data from one location to another is MOV.

LABEL FIELD	OP CODE FIELD	OPERAND FIELD	COMMENT FIELD
NEXT:	ADD	AL, 07H	; ADD CORRECTION FACTOR

FIGURE 2-12 Assembly language program statement format.

Assembly language statements are usually written in a standard form having four *fields*. Figure 2-12 shows an assembly language statement with the four fields indicated. The first field in an assembly language statement is the *label field*. A *label* is a symbol or group of symbols used to represent an address which is not specifically known at the time the statement is written. Labels are usually followed by a colon. Labels are not required in a statement, they are just inserted where they are needed. We will show later many uses of labels.

The *opcode field* of the instruction contains the mnemonic for the instruction to be performed. Instruction mnemonics are sometimes called *operation codes* or *opcodes*. The ADD mnemonic in the example statement in Figure 2-12 indicates that we want the instruction to do an addition. Chapter 6 describes the function of each 8086 instruction type and gives the opcodes for each.

The *operand field* of the statement contains the data, the memory address, the port address, or the name of the register on which the instruction is to be performed. *Operand* is just another name for the data item(s) acted on by an instruction. In the example instruction in Figure 2-12 there are two operands, AL and 07H, specified in the operand field. AL represents the AL register, and 07H represents the number 07H. This assembly language statement then says add the number 07H to the contents of the AL register. By Intel convention the result of the addition will be put in the register or the memory location specified *before* the comma in the operand field. For the example statement in Figure 2-12 then, the result will be left in the AL register. As another example, the assembly language statement, ADD BH, AL, when converted to machine language and run, will add the contents of the AL register to the contents of the BH register. The results will be left in the BH register.

Looking back at the example assembly language statement in Figure 2-12, observe the *comment field* which starts with a semicolon. This field is very important. Comments do not become part of the machine language program. You write *comments* in a program to remind you of the function that this instruction or group of instructions performs in the program.

To summarize why we use assembly language, let's look a little more closely at the assembly language ADD statement. The general format of the 8086 ADD instruction is:

ADD destination, source

The *source* can be a number written in the instruction, the contents of a specified register, or the contents of a memory location. The *destination* can be a specified register or a specified memory location. The source and the destination, however, cannot both be memory locations in an instruction.

A later section on 8086 addressing modes will show all of the ways in which the source of an operand and the destination of the result can be specified. The point here is that the single mnemonic, ADD, together with a specified source and a specified destination can represent a great many 8086 instructions in an easily understandable form.

The question that may occur to you at this point is, "If I write a program in assembly language, how do I get it translated into machine language which can be loaded into the microcomputer and executed?" There are two answers to this question. The first method of doing the translation is by working out the binary code for each instruction a bit at a time using the templates given in the manufacturer's data books. We will show you how to do this in the next chapter. It is a tedious and error-prone task. The second method of doing the translation is with an *assembler*. An assembler is a program which can be run on a personal computer or *microcomputer development system*. It reads the assembly language instructions and generates the correct binary code for each. For developing all but the simplest assembly language programs, an assembler and other program development tools are essential. We will introduce you to these program development tools in the next chapter and describe their use throughout the rest of this book.

HIGH LEVEL LANGUAGES

Another way of writing a program for a microcomputer is with a *high level language* such as BASIC, FORTRAN, or Pascal. These languages use program statements which are even more English-like than those of assembly language. Each high level statement may represent many machine code instructions. An *interpreter program* or a *compiler program* is used to translate higher level language statements to machine codes which can be loaded into memory and executed. Programs can usually be written faster in high level languages than in assembly language because the high level language works with bigger building blocks. However, programs written in a high level language and interpreted or compiled execute slower than the same programs written in assembly language. Programs that involve a lot of hardware control, such as robots and factory control systems, or programs that must run as quickly as possible are usually best written in assembly language. Programs that manipulate massive amounts of data, such as insurance company records, are usually best written in a high level language. The decision of which language to use has recently been made more difficult by the fact that current assemblers allow the use of many high level language features, and the fact that some current high level languages provide assembly language features.

OUR CHOICE

Throughout this book we will use mostly assembly language because we will be working very closely with hardware interfacing. Before we start teaching you assembly language programming in the next chapter, however, we want to give you an introduction to how the 8086 accesses data.

How the 8086 Accesses Immediate and Register Data

In a previous discussion of the 8086 BIU we described how the 8086 accesses code bytes using CS and IP. We also described how the 8086 accesses the stack using SS and SP. Before we can teach you assembly language programming techniques, we need to discuss some of the different ways that an 8086 can access the data that it operates on. The different ways that a processor can access data are referred to as its *addressing modes*. In assembly language statements the addressing mode is indicated in the instruction. We will use the 8086 MOV instruction to illustrate some of the 8086 addressing modes.

The MOV instruction has the format:

MOV destination, source

When executed, this instruction copies a word or a byte from the specified source location to the specified destination location. The source can be a number written directly in the instruction, a specified register, or a memory location specified in one of 24 different ways. The destination can be a specified register or a memory location specified in any one of 24 different ways. The source and the destination cannot both be memory locations in an instruction.

IMMEDIATE ADDRESSING MODE

Suppose that in a program you need to put the number 437BH in the CX register. The MOV CX, 437BH instruction can be used to do this. When it executes, this instruction will put the *immediate* hexadecimal number 437BH in the 16-bit CX register. This is referred to as *immediate addressing mode* because the number to be loaded into the CX register will be put in two memory locations immediately following the code for the MOV instruction. This is similar to the way the port address was put in memory immediately after the code for the input instruction in the three-instruction program in Figure 2-2*b*.

A similar instruction, MOV CL, 48H could be used to load the 8-bit immediate number 48H into the 8-bit CL register. You can also write instructions to load an 8-bit immediate number into an 8-bit memory location or to load a 16-bit number into two consecutive memory locations, but we are not yet ready to show you how to specify these.

REGISTER ADDRESSING MODE

Register addressing mode means that a register is the source of an operand for an instruction. The instruction MOV CX, AX, for example, copies the contents of the 16-bit AX register into the 16-bit CX register. Remember that the destination location is specified in the instruction before the source. Also note that the contents of AX are just *copied* to CX, not actually moved. In other words, the previous contents of CX are written over, but the contents of AX are not changed. For example, if CX contains 2A84H and AX contains 4971H before the MOV CX, AX instruction executes, then after the instruction executes CX will contain 4971H and AX will still contain 4971H. You can MOV any 16-bit register to any 16-bit register, or you can MOV any 8-bit register to any 8-bit register. However, you cannot use an instruction such as MOV CX, AL because this is an attempt to copy a *byte-type* operand (AL) into a *word-type* destination (CX). The byte in AL would fit in CX, but the 8086 would not know which half of CX to put it in. If you try to write an instruction like this and you are using a good assembler, the assembler will tell you that the instruction contains a *type error*. To copy the byte from AL to the high byte of CX you can use the instruction MOV CH, AL. The instruction MOV CL, AL will copy the byte from AL to CL, the low byte of CX.

How the 8086 Accesses Data in Memory

OVERVIEW OF MEMORY ADDRESSING MODES

The addressing modes described in the following sections are used to specify the location of an operand in memory. A previous section described how the 8086 produces the physical address for instruction codes by adding an offset in the instruction pointer to the code segment base in the CS register. Remember that the contents of CS are shifted four bit positions left before the contents of IP are added. Another previous section described how the 8086 accesses stack locations by adding an offset in the stack pointer register to the stack segment base in the stack segment register. Here again the contents of the stack segment register are shifted four bit positions left before the contents of the stack pointer are added.

To access data in memory the 8086 must also produce a 20-bit physical address. It does this by adding a 16-bit value called the *effective address* to one of the four segment bases. The effective address (EA) represents the *displacement* or *offset* of the desired operand from the segment base. In most cases, any of the segment bases can be specified, but the data segment is the one most often used. Figure 2-13*a* shows in graphic form how the EA is added to the data segment base to point to an operand in memory. Figure 2-13*b* shows how the 20-bit physical address is generated by the BIU. The starting address for the data segment in Figure 2-13*b* is 20000H so the data segment register will contain 2000H. The BIU shifts the 2000H four bit positions left and adds the effective address, 437AH, to the result. The 20-bit physical address sent out to memory by the BIU will then be 2437AH. The physical address can be represented either as a single number, 2437AH, or in the segment base: offset form as 2000:437AH.

The execution unit calculates the effective address for an operand using information you specify in the in-

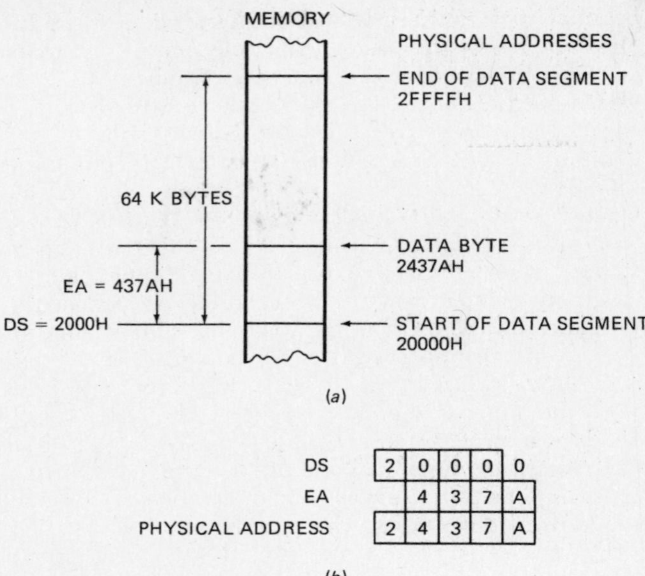

FIGURE 2-13 Addition of data segment register and effective address to produce physical address of data byte. *(a)* Diagram. *(b)* Computation.

struction. You can tell the EU to use a number in the instruction as the effective address, to use the contents of a specified register as the effective address, or to compute the effective address by adding a number in the instruction to the contents of one or two specified registers. The following section describes one way you can tell the execution unit to calculate an effective address. In later chapters we show other ways of specifying the effective address. We also show how the addressing modes this provides are used to solve some common programming problems.

DIRECT ADDRESSING MODE

For the simplest memory addressing mode the effective address is just an 8- or 16-bit number written directly in the instruction. The instruction MOV CL, [437AH] is an example. The square brackets around the 437AH are shorthand for "the contents of the memory location(s) at a displacement from the segment base of." When executed, this instruction will copy the contents of the memory location, at a displacement of 437AH from the data segment base, into the CL register. The actual 20-bit physical memory address will be produced by shifting the data segment base in DS four bits left and adding the effective address 437AH to the result. Figure 2-13*b* shows how the operation is done. This addressing mode is called *direct* because the displacement of the operand from the segment base is specified directly in the instruction. The displacement in the instruction will be added to the data segment base in DS unless you use a *segment override prefix* to tell the BIU to add it to some other segment base. We will discuss the segment overide prefix later.

Another example of this addressing mode is the instruction MOV BX, [437AH]. When executed, this instruction copies a word from memory into the BX register. Since each memory address of the 8086 represents a byte of storage, the word must come from two memory locations. The byte at a displacement of 437AH from the data segment base will be copied into BL. The contents of the next higher address, displacement 437BH, will be copied into the BH register. The 8086 will automatically access the required number of bytes in memory for a given instruction.

The previous two examples showed how the direct addressing mode can be used to specify the source of an operand. It can also be used to specify the destination of an operand. The instruction MOV [437AH], BX, for example, will copy the contents of the BX register to two memory locations in the data segment. The contents of BL will be copied to the memory location at a displacement of 437AH. The contents of BH will be copied to the memory location at a displacement of 437BH.

NOTE: When you are *hand-coding* progams using direct addressing of the form shown above, make sure to put in the square brackets to remind you how to code the instruction. If you leave the brackets out of an instruction such as **MOV CX, [437AH]**, you will code it as if it were the instruction **MOV CX, 437AH.** This will load the immediate number 437AH into CX, rather than load a word from memory at a displacement of 437AH. Also note that if you are writing an instruction using direct addressing such as this for an *assembler*, you must use a form such as **MOV BL, DS:BYTE PTR[437AH]** to give the assembler all the information it needs. As will be shown in the next chapter, when using an assembler, we usually use a name to represent the direct address rather than the actual numerical offset.

A FEW WORDS ABOUT SEGMENTATION

At this point you may be wondering why Intel designed the 8086 family devices to use *memory segmentation*. At least two reasons come to mind. First, by working with only 64 Kbyte segments of memory at a time, the 8086 only has to work with 16-bit effective addresses to access any location in the segment. In other words, because of the segmentation scheme the 8086 only has to manipulate and store 16-bit address components. The second reason has to do with the type of microcomputer in which an 8086 family CPU is likely to be used. A previous section of this chapter described briefly the operation of a time-share microcomputer system. In a time-share system several users share a CPU. The CPU works on one user's program for perhaps 20 milliseconds, then works on the next user's program for 20 milliseconds. After working 20 milliseconds for each of the other users, the CPU comes back to working on the first user's program again. Each time the CPU switches from one user's program to the next it must access a new section of code and new sections of data. Segmentation makes this switching quite easy. Each user's program can be assigned a separate set of logical segments for its code and data. The user's program will contain offsets or displacements from these segment bases. To change from one user's program to a second user's program all that has to be done is to reload the four segment registers with the segment base addresses assigned to the second user's program. In other words, segmentation makes it easy to keep users' programs and data separate from each other, and segmentation makes it easy to switch from one user's program to another user's program.

IMPORTANT TERMS AND CONCEPTS FROM THIS CHAPTER

If you do not remember any of the terms or concepts in the following list, use the index to find them in the chapter.

Microcomputer, microprocessor

Hardware, software, firmware

Time-share

Multitasking computer system

Distributed processing system

Multiprocessing

CPU

Memory, RAM, ROM

I/O ports

Address, data, and control buses

Control bus signals

ALU

Segmentation

BIU
  Instruction byte queue, pipelining
  ES, CS, SS, DS registers, IP register

EU
  AX, BX, CX, DX registers, flag register
  ALU, SP, BP, SI, DI registers

Machine language

Assembly language
  Mnemonic, opcode, operand, label, comment,

Assembler

High level language

Compiler

Immediate address mode, register address mode, direct address mode

Effective address

REVIEW QUESTIONS AND PROBLEMS

1. Describe the sequence of signals that occurs on the address bus, the control bus, and the data bus when a computer fetches an instruction.

2. Describe the main advantages of a distributed processing computer system over a simple time-share system.

3. What determines whether a microprocessor is considered an 8-bit, 16-bit, or 32-bit device?

4. *a.* How many address lines does an 8086 have?
b. How many memory addresses does this number of address lines allow the 8086 to access directly?
c. At any given time, the 8086 works with four segments in this address space. How many bytes are contained in each segment?
d. Why was the 8086 designed with this segmentation of the address space?

5. What is the main difference between the 8086 and the 8088?

6. *a.* Describe the function of the 8086 queue.
b. How does the queue speed up process operation?

7. *a.* If the code segment for an 8086 program starts at address 70400H, what number will be in the CS register?
b. Assuming this same code segment base, what physical address will a code byte be fetched from if the instruction pointer contains 539CH?

8. What physical address is represented by:
a. 4370:561EH
b. 7A32:0028H

9. What is the advantage of using a CPU register for temporary data storage over using a memory location?

10. If the stack segment register contains 3000H and the stack pointer register contains 8434H, what is the physical address of the top of the stack?

11. *a.* What is the advantage of using assembly language instead of writing a program directly in machine language?
b. Describe the operation an 8086 will perform when it executes ADD AX, BX.

12. What types of programs are usually written in assembly language?

13. Describe the operation that an 8086 will perform when it executes each of the following instructions:
a. MOV BX, 03FFH
b. MOV AL, 0DBH
c. MOV DH, CL
d. MOV BX, AX

14. Write the 8086 assembly language statement which will perform the following operations:
   a. Load the number 7986H into the BP register.
   b. Copy the BP register contents to the SP register.
   c. Copy the contents of the AX register to the DS register.
   d. Load the number F3H into the AL register.

15. If the 8086 execution unit calculates an effective address of 14A3H and DS contains 7000H, what physical address will the BIU produce?

16. If the data segment register, DS, contains 4000H, what physical address will the instruction MOV AL, [234BH] read?

17. If the 8086 data segment register contains 7000H, write the instruction that will copy the contents of DL to address 74B2CH.

18. Describe the difference between the instructions MOV AX, 2437H and MOV AX, [2437H].

CHAPTER

3 8086 Family Assembly Language Programming—Introduction

The last chapter showed you the format for 8086 assembly language programs and introduced you to a few 8086 instructions. Developing a program, however, requires more than just writing down a series of instructions. When you want to build a house, it is a good idea to first develop a complete set of plans for the house. With the plans you can see if the house has the rooms you need, if the rooms are efficiently placed, and if the house is structured so that you can easily add on to it if you have more kids. We have all probably seen examples of what happens when someone attempts to build a house by just putting pieces together without a plan.

Likewise, when you write computer programs it is a good idea to start by developing a detailed plan or outline. A good outline helps you to break a large and seemingly overwhelming programming job down into small modules which can easily be written, tested, and debugged. The more time you spend organizing your programs the less time it will take you to write and debug them. You should *never* start writing an assembly language program by just writing down instructions! In this chapter we show you how to develop assembly language programs in a systematic way.

OBJECTIVES

At the conclusion of this chapter you should be able to:

1. Write a task list, flowchart, or pseudocode for a simple programming problem.
2. Write, code or assemble, and run a very simple assembly language program.
3. Describe the use of program development tools such as editors, assemblers, linkers, locators, debuggers, and emulators.
4. Properly document assembly language programs.

PROGRAM DEVELOPMENT STEPS

Defining the Problem

The first step in writing a program is to think very carefully about the problem that you want the program to solve. In other words, ask yourself many times, "What do I really want this program to do?" If you don't do this, you may write a great program that works, but does not do what you need it to do. As you think about the problem it is a good idea to write down exactly what you want the program to do and the order in which you want the program to do it. At this point you do not write down program statements, you just write the operations you want in general terms. An example for a simple programming problem might be:

1. Read temperature from sensor
2. Add correction factor of +7
3. Save result in a memory location

For a program as simple as this, the three actions desired are very close to the eventual assembly language statements. For more complex problems, however, we develop a more extensive outline before writing the assembly language statements. The next section shows you some of the common ways of representing program operations in a program outline.

Representing Program Operations

The formula or sequence of operations used to solve a programming problem is often called the *algorithm* of the program. The following sections show you several ways of representing the algorithm for a program or program segment.

SEQUENTIAL TASK LISTS

Some programmers use just a *sequential list of the tasks* such as that in the preceding section to show the algorithm for their programs. To give you a better idea of this form, we will show another slightly different example. Suppose that, instead of taking in one data sample from the temperature sensor, we want to take in a data sample every hour for 24 hours, add 7 to each sample, and put each corrected value in a memory location. We could write a task list for this problem as:

1. Read data sample from temperature sensor.

2. Add 7 to value read in.

3. Store corrected value in memory location.

4. Wait one hour.

5. Read next sample from temperature sensor.

6. Add 7 to value read in.

7. Store corrected value in next memory location.

.
.
.
.
.

97. Read last data sample from temperature sensor.

98. Add 7 to value read in.

99. Store corrected value in next memory location.

As you can see, this direct form is not a very compact or efficient way of representing the operation of the program. A more efficient way of writing the sequential task list for this program is:

Read a data sample from temperature sensor.

Add 7 to the value read in.

Store corrected value in memory location.

Wait one hour.

24 samples yet?
  No, read next sample and process.
  Yes, done.

The last three lines indicate that we want the program to do the read, add, store, and wait operations 24 times. Carefully written sequential task lists are often quite close to the assembly language statements that will implement them, so you may find them useful. As you determine hardware details, such as port addresses for the system on which the program is to run, you can add this information to the appropriate task statement. The next section shows you a more graphic way of representing the algorithm of a program or program segment.

FLOWCHARTS

If you have done any previous programming in BASIC or in FORTRAN, you are probably familiar with *flowcharts*. Flowcharts use graphic shapes to represent different types of program operations. The specific operation desired is written in the graphic symbol. Figure 3-1 shows some of the common flowchart symbols. Plastic templates are available to help you draw these symbols if you decide to use them for your programs.

Figure 3-2 shows a flowchart for a program to read in 24 data samples from a temperature sensor at 1-hour intervals, add 7 to each, and store each result in a memory location. A *racetrack-shaped* symbol labeled START is used to indicate the *beginning* of the program. A *parallelogram* is used to represent *input* or *output operations*. In the example we use it to indicate reading data from the temperature sensor. A *rectangular box symbol* is used to represent *simple operations* other than input and output operations. The box containing "add 7" in Figure 3-2 is an example.

A *rectangular box with double lines at each end* is often used to represent a *subroutine* or *procedure* that will be written separately from the main program. When a set of operations must be done several times throughout a program, it is usually more efficient to write the series of operations once as a separate *subprogram* and then just use or "call" this subprogram as it is needed. For example, suppose that there are several times in a program where you need to compute the square root of a number. Instead of writing the series of instructions for computing a square root each time you need it in the program, you can write the instruction sequence once as a subprogram and set it aside in some location in memory. You can then call this subprogram each time you need to compute a square root. In the flowchart in Figure 3-2 we use the double-ended box to indicate that the "wait 1 hour" operation will be programmed as a subroutine. Incidentally, the terms *subprogram*, *subroutine*, and *procedure* all have the same meaning. Chapter 5 shows how procedures are written and used.

A *diamond-shaped* box is used in flowcharts to represent a *decision* point or crossroad. Usually it indicates that some condition is to be checked at this point in the program and, if the condition is found to be *true*, one set

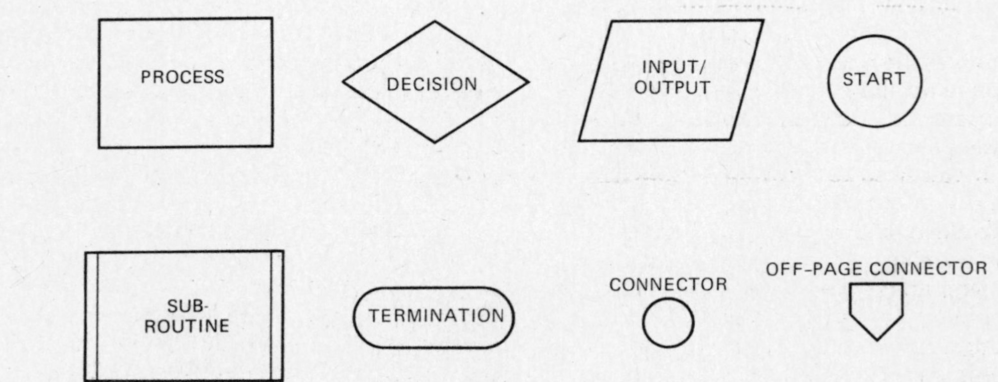

FIGURE 3-1 Flowchart symbols.

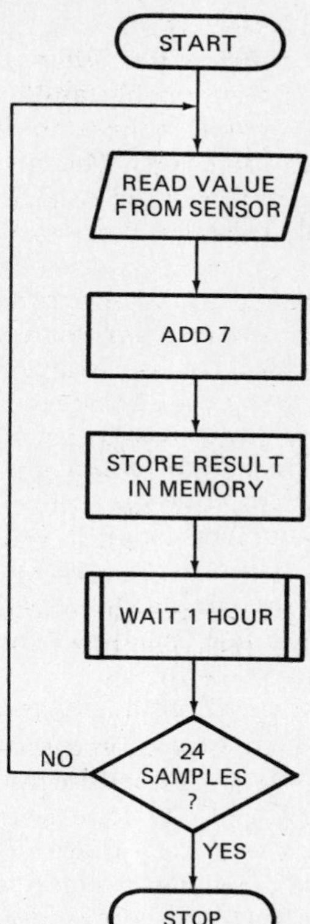

FIGURE 3-2 Flowchart for program to read in 24 data samples from a port, correct each value, and store each in a memory location.

of actions is to be done. If the condition is found to be *false*, then another set of actions is to be done. In the example flowchart in Figure 3-2 the condition to be checked is whether 24 samples have been read in and processed. If 24 samples have not been read in and processed, the arrow labeled NO in the flowchart indicates that we want the computer to jump back and execute the read, add, store, and wait steps again. If 24 samples have been read in, the arrow labeled YES in the flowchart of Figure 3-2 indicates that all the desired operations have been done. The *racetrack-shaped* symbol at the bottom of the flowchart indicates the *end* of the program.

The two additional flowchart symbols in Figure 3-1 are *connectors*. If a flowchart column gets to the bottom of the paper, but all of the program has not been represented, you can put a small circle with a letter in it at the bottom of the column. You then start the next column at the top of the same paper with a small circle containing the same letter. If you need to continue a flowchart to another page, you can end the flowchart on the first page with the five-sided off-page connector symbol containing a letter or number. You then start the flowchart on the next page with an off-page connector symbol containing the same letter or number.

For simple programs and program sections, flowcharts are a graphic way of showing the operational flow of the program. We will show flowcharts for many of the program examples throughout this book. Flowcharts, however, have several disadvantages. First, you can't write much information in the little boxes. Second, flowcharts do not present information in a very compact form. For more complex problems, flowcharts tend to become spread out over many pages. They are very hard to follow back and forth between pages. Third, and most important, with flowcharts the overall structure of the program tends to get lost in the details. The following section describes a more clearly *structured* and *compact* method of representing the algorithm of a program or program segment.

STRUCTURED PROGRAMMING AND PSEUDOCODE OVERVIEW

In the early days of computers a single brilliant person might write even a large program single-handedly. The main concerns in this case were, "Does the program work?" and "What do we do if this person leaves the company?" As the number of computers increased and the complexity of the programs being written increased, large programming jobs were usually turned over to a team of programmers. In this case the compatibility of parts written by different programmers became an important concern. During the 1970s it became obvious to many professional programmers that, in order for team programming to work, a systematic approach and standardized tools were absolutely necessary.

One suggested systematic approach is called *top-down design*. In this approach a large programming problem is first broken down into major *modules*. The top level of the outline shows the relationship and function of these modules. This top level then presents a one-page overview of the entire program. Each of the major modules is broken down into still smaller modules on following pages. The division is continued until the steps in each module are clearly understandable. Each programmer can then be assigned a module or set of modules to write for the program. Also, those who want to learn about the program later can start with the overview and work their way down to the level of detail they need. This approach is the same as drawing the complete plans for a house before starting to build it.

The opposite of top-down design is *bottom-up design*. In this approach each programmer starts writing low-level modules and hopes that all the pieces will eventually fit together. When completed, the result should be similar to that produced by the top-down design. Many modern programming teams use a combination of the two techniques. They do the top-down design and then build, test, and link modules starting from the smallest and working upward.

The development of standard programming tools was helped by the discovery that any desired program operation could be represented by three basic types of operation. The first type of operation is *sequence* which means simply doing a series of actions. The second basic type of operation is *decision* or *selection*, which means choosing between two alternative actions. The third basic type of operation is *repetition or iteration*, which means repeating a series of actions until some condition is or is not present.

On the basis of this observation, the suggestion was made that all programmers use a set of three to seven standard *structures* to represent all of the operations in their programs. Actually, only three structures, SEQUENCE, IF–THEN–ELSE, and WHILE–DO, are required to represent any desired program action, but three or four more structures derived from these often make programs clearer. If you have previously written programs in a structured language such as Pascal, then these structures are probably already familiar to you. Figure 3-3 uses flowchart symbols to represent the commonly used structures so you can more easily visualize their operations. In actual program documentation, however, English-like statements called *pseudocode* are used rather than the space-consuming flowchart symbols. Figure 3-3 also shows the pseudocode format and an example for each structure.

Each structure has only *one entry point* and *one exit point*. The output of one structure is connected to the input of the next structure. Program execution then proceeds through a series of these structures.

Any structure can be used within another. An IF–THEN–ELSE structure, for example, can contain a sequence of statements. Any place that the term *statement(s)* appears in Figure 3-3, one of the other structures could be substituted for it. The term "statement(s)" can also represent a subprogram or procedure that is called to do a series of actions.

STANDARD PROGRAMMING STRUCTURES

The structure shown in Figure 3-3*a* is an example of a simple sequence. In this structure the actions are simply written down in the desired order. An example is:

Read temperature from sensor.

Add correction factor of +7.

Store corrected value in memory.

Figure 3-3*b* shows an IF–THEN–ELSE example of the decision operation. This structure is used to direct operation to one of two different actions based on some condition. An example is:

```
IF temperature less than 70 degrees THEN
  Turn on heater
ELSE
  Turn off heater
```

The example says that if the temperature is below the thermostat setting, we want to turn the heater on. If the temperature is equal to or above the thermostat setting, we want to turn the heater off.

The IF–THEN structure shown in Figure 3-3*c* is the same as the IF–THEN–ELSE except that one of the paths contains no action. An example of this is:

```
IF hungry THEN
  Get food.
```

The assumption for this example is that if you are not hungry, you will just continue on with your next task.

The WHILE–DO structure in Figure 3-3*d* is one form of repetition. It is used to indicate that you want to do some action or sequence of actions as long as some condition is present. This structure represents a *program loop*. The example in Figure 3-3*d* is:

```
WHILE money lasts DO
  Eat supper out.
  Go to movie.
  Take a taxi home.
```

This example shows a sequence of actions you might do each evening until you ran out of money. Note that, in this structure, the condition is checked *before* the action is done the first time. You certainly would want to check how much money you have before eating out.

Another useful structure, derived from the WHILE–DO structure, is the REPEAT–UNTIL structure shown in Figure 3-3*e*. You use this structure to indicate that you want the program to repeat some action or series of actions until some condition is present. A good example of the use of this structure is the programming problem we used in the discussion of flowcharts. The example is:

```
REPEAT
  Get data sample from sensor.
  Add correction of +7.
  Store result in a memory location.
  Wait one hour.
UNTIL 24 samples taken.
```

Compare the space required by the pseudocode representation for the desired action with the space required by the flowchart representation shown in Figure 3-2. The space advantage of pseudocode should be obvious.

As indicated previously, the REPEAT–UNTIL structure is derived from the WHILE–DO. In other words, any problem that can be represented by a REPEAT–UNTIL can also be represented by a properly written WHILE–DO. The example in Figure 3-3*e* could be written as:

```
WHILE NOT 24 samples DO
  Read data sample from temperature sensor.
  Add correction factor of +7.
  Store result in memory location.
  Wait one hour.
```

Note that the REPEAT–UNTIL structure indicates that the condition is first checked *after* the statement(s) is performed. In other words, a REPEAT–UNTIL structure indicates that the action or series of actions will always be done at least once. If you don't want this to happen, then use the WHILE–DO which indicates that the condition is checked before any action is taken. As we will show later, the structure you use makes a difference in the actual assembly language program you write to implement it.

The WHILE–DO and REPEAT–UNTIL structures contain a simple IF–THEN–ELSE decision operation. However, since this decision is an *implied* part of these two structures, we don't indicate the decision separately in them.

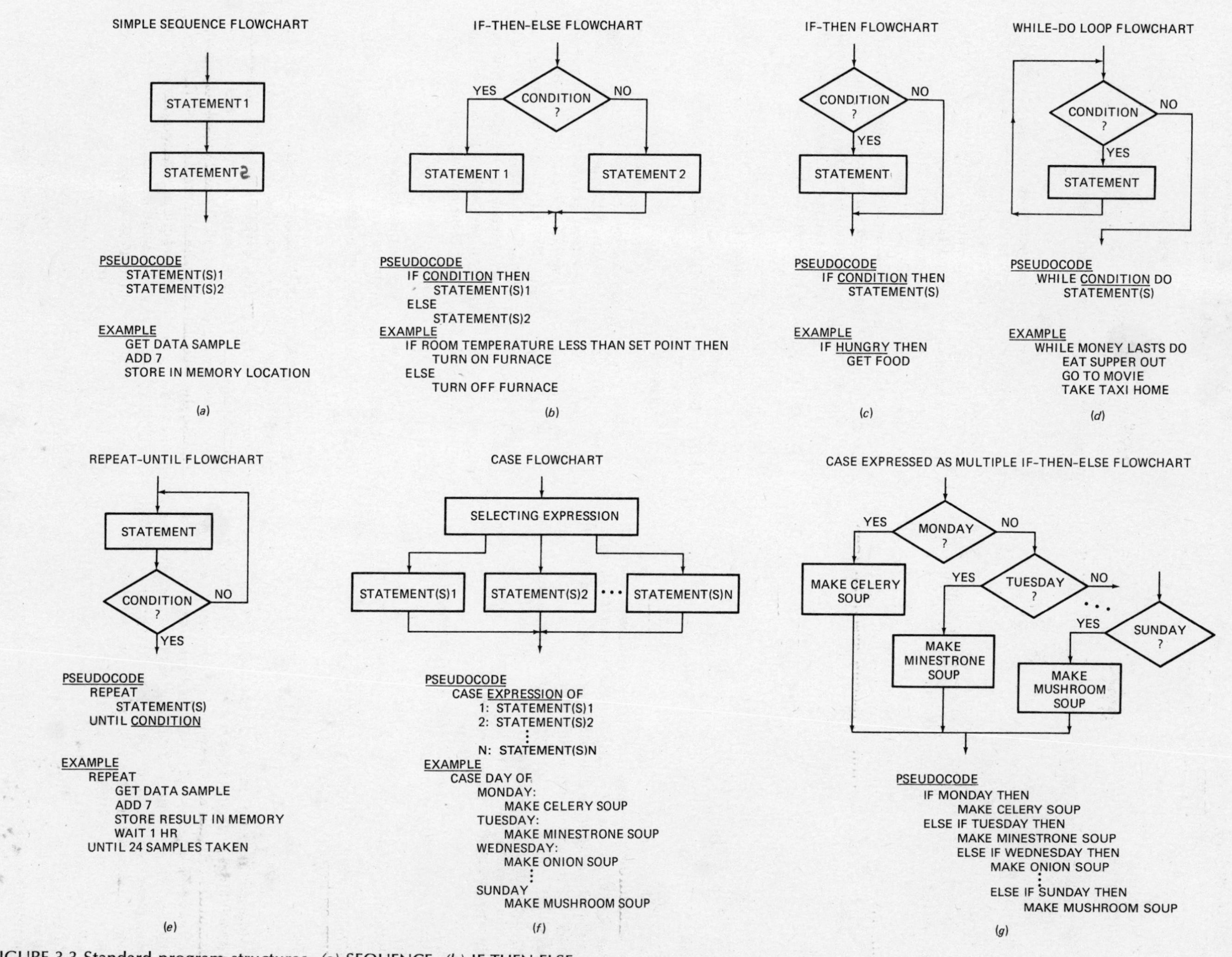
SIMPLE SEQUENCE FLOWCHART
STATEMENT 1
STATEMENT 2
PSEUDOCODE
STATEMENT(S)1
STATEMENT(S)2
EXAMPLE
GET DATA SAMPLE
ADD 7
STORE IN MEMORY LOCATION
(a)
IF-THEN-ELSE FLOWCHART
CONDITION ?
YES
NO
STATEMENT 1
STATEMENT 2
PSEUDOCODE
IF CONDITION THEN
STATEMENT(S)1
ELSE
STATEMENT(S)2
EXAMPLE
IF ROOM TEMPERATURE LESS THAN SET POINT THEN
TURN ON FURNACE
ELSE
TURN OFF FURNACE
(b)
IF-THEN FLOWCHART
CONDITION ?
NO
YES
STATEMENT
PSEUDOCODE
IF CONDITION THEN
STATEMENT(S)
EXAMPLE
IF HUNGRY THEN
GET FOOD
(c)
WHILE-DO LOOP FLOWCHART
CONDITION ?
NO
YES
STATEMENT
PSEUDOCODE
WHILE CONDITION DO
STATEMENT(S)
EXAMPLE
WHILE MONEY LASTS DO
EAT SUPPER OUT
GO TO MOVIE
TAKE TAXI HOME
(d)
REPEAT-UNTIL FLOWCHART
STATEMENT
CONDITION ?
NO
YES
PSEUDOCODE
REPEAT
STATEMENT(S)
UNTIL CONDITION
EXAMPLE
REPEAT
GET DATA SAMPLE
ADD 7
STORE RESULT IN MEMORY
WAIT 1 HR
UNTIL 24 SAMPLES TAKEN
(e)
CASE FLOWCHART
SELECTING EXPRESSION
STATEMENT(S)1
STATEMENT(S)2
STATEMENT(S)N
PSEUDOCODE
CASE EXPRESSION OF
1: STATEMENT(S)1
2: STATEMENT(S)2
N: STATEMENT(S)N
EXAMPLE
CASE DAY OF
MONDAY:
MAKE CELERY SOUP
TUESDAY:
MAKE MINESTRONE SOUP
WEDNESDAY:
MAKE ONION SOUP
SUNDAY
MAKE MUSHROOM SOUP
(f)
CASE EXPRESSED AS MULTIPLE IF-THEN-ELSE FLOWCHART
YES
MONDAY ?
NO
MAKE CELERY SOUP
YES
TUESDAY ?
NO
YES
SUNDAY ?
MAKE MINESTRONE SOUP
MAKE MUSHROOM SOUP
PSEUDOCODE
IF MONDAY THEN
MAKE CELERY SOUP
ELSE IF TUESDAY THEN
MAKE MINESTRONE SOUP
ELSE IF WEDNESDAY THEN
MAKE ONION SOUP
ELSE IF SUNDAY THEN
MAKE MUSHROOM SOUP
(g)

FIGURE 3-3 Standard program structures. *(a)* SEQUENCE. *(b)* IF-THEN-ELSE. *(c)* IF-THEN. *(d)* WHILE-DO. *(e)* REPEAT-UNTIL. *(f)* CASE. *(g)* CASE expressed as multiple IF-THEN-ELSE.

Another form of the repetition operation that you might see in high level language programs is the FOR–DO loop. This structure has the form:

```
FOR count = 1 TO n DO
   statement
   statement
```

In assembly language we usually implement this type of operation with a REPEAT–UNTIL structure, so we have not included a sample of it.

The CASE structure shown in Figure 3-3*f* is a compact way of representing a choice among several alternative actions. The choice is determined by testing some quantity. The example in Figure 3-3*f* best shows how this is used. This everyday example describes the desired actions for a cook in a restaurant. The pseudocode is just a summary of the thinking the cook might go through. The cook or the computer checks the value of the variable called "day" and selects the appropriate actions for that day. Each of the indicated actions, such as "Make celery soup," is itself a sequence of actions which could be represented by the structures we have described.

The CASE structure is really just a compact way to represent a complex IF–THEN–ELSE structure. To illustrate this, Figure 3-3*g* also shows how the soup cook example can be represented as a series of IF–THEN–ELSE structures. Note that, in this example, the last IF–THEN has no ELSE after it because all of the possible days have been checked. You can, if you want, add the final ELSE to the IF–THEN–ELSE chain to send an error message if the data does not match any of the choices. The CASE structure does contain the final ELSE, however. The CASE form is more compact for documentation purposes and some high-level languages such as Pascal allow you to implement it directly. However, the IF–THEN–ELSE structure gives you a much better idea of how you write an assembly language program section to choose between several alternative actions.

Throughout the rest of this book we show you how to use these structures to represent program actions and how to implement these structures in assembly language.

SUMMARY OF PROGRAM STRUCTURE REPRESENTATION FORMS

Writing a successful program does not consist of just writing down a series of instructions. You must first think carefully about what you want the program to do and how you want the program to do it. Then you must represent the structure of the program in some way that is very clear to you and to anyone else who might have to work on the program. If the structure is well developed, it is usually not a difficult step to write the actual programming language statements that implement it.

One way of representing program operations is with a sequential task list. For initial thinking and simple programming problems this technique works well. For more complex programming problems, a sequential list may become very messy because it has little real structure or standardization. Another way of representing program operations is with flowcharts. Flowcharts are a very graphic representation, and they are useful for short program segments, especially those that deal directly with hardware. However, flowcharts use a great deal of space. Consequently, the flowchart for even a moderately complex program may take up several pages. It often becomes difficult to follow program flow back and forth between pages. Also, since there are no agreed-upon structures, a poor programmer can write a flowchart which jumps all over the place and is even more difficult to follow. The term "logical spaghetti" comes to mind here.

A third way of representing the operations you want in a program is with a top-down design approach and standard program structures. The overall program problem is first broken down into major functional modules. Each of these modules is broken down into smaller and smaller modules until the steps in each module are obvious. The algorithms for the whole program and for each module are each expressed with a standard structure. Only three basic structures, SEQUENCE, IF–THEN–ELSE, and WHILE–DO, are needed to represent any needed program action or series of actions. However, other useful structures such as IF–THEN, REPEAT–UNTIL, FOR–DO, and CASE can be derived from these basic three. A structure can contain another structure of the same type or one of the other types. Each structure has only one entry point and one exit point. These programing structures may seem restrictive, but using them usually results in program representations which are easy to understand and for which it is easy to write the programs. A program written in a structured manner is easier to debug and much more understandable to someone else who has to work on it. Furthermore, a program representation developed with structured programming techniques can be implemented easily in assembly language or in a high-level language such as Modula II or C.

Finding the Right Instruction

After you get the structure of a program worked out and written down, the next step is to determine the instruction statements required to do each part of the program. Since the examples in this book are based on the 8086 family of microprocessors, now is a good time to give you an overview of the instructions the 8086 has for you to use.

You do not usually learn a new language by studying its dictionary from cover to cover. It is more productive to first learn a few very useful words and learn how to put together simple sentences. You can then learn more words as you need them to express more complex thoughts. Chapter 6 contains a dictionary of all of the 8086 instructions with detailed descriptions and examples for each. You can use this as a reference as you write programs. Here we simply list the 8086 instructions in *functional* groups with single-sentence descriptions so that you can see the types of instructions that are available to you. As you read through this section, do not expect to understand all of the instructions. When you start writing programs, you will probably use this section to determine the type of instruction and Chapter 6 to get the instruction details as you need them. After you have written a few programs, you will remember most of the basic instruction types and will be able to just look up an instruction in Chapter 6 to get any additional details you need. Chapter 4 shows you in detail how to use the *move*, *arithmetic*, *logical*, *jump*, and *string* instructions. Chapter 5 shows how to use the *call* instructions and the *stack*.

As you skim through the following overview of the 8086 instructions, see if you can find the instructions needed to do the "read temperature sensor value from a port, add +7, and store result in memory" example program.

DATA TRANSFER INSTRUCTIONS

General-purpose byte or word transfer instructions:

MNEMONIC	DESCRIPTION
MOV	Copy byte or word from specified source to specified destination.
PUSH	Copy specified word to top of stack.
POP	Copy word from top of stack to specified location.
PUSHA	(80186/80188 ONLY) Copy all registers to stack.
POPA	(80186/80188 ONLY) Copy words from stack to all registers.
XCHG	Exchange bytes or exchange words.
XLAT	Translate a byte in AL using a table in memory.

Simple input and output port transfer instructions:

IN	Copy a byte or word from specified port to accumulator.
OUT	Copy a byte or word from accumulator to specified port.

Special address transfer instructions:

LEA	Load effective address of operand into specified register.
LDS	Load DS register and other specified register from memory.
LES	Load ES register and other specified register from memory.

Flag transfer instructions:

LAHF	Load (copy to) AH with the low byte of the flag register.
SAHF	Store (copy) AH register to low byte of flag register.
PUSHF	Copy flag register to top of stack.
POPF	Copy word at top of stack to flag register.

ARITHMETIC INSTRUCTIONS

Addition instructions:

ADD	Add specified byte to byte, or specified word to word.
ADC	Add byte + byte + carry flag or word + word + carry flag.
INC	Increment specified byte or specified word by one.
AAA	ASCII adjust after addition.
DAA	Decimal (BCD) adjust after addition.

Subtraction instructions:

SUB	Subtract byte from byte, or word from word.
SBB	Subtract byte and carry flag from byte, or word and carry flag from word.
DEC	Decrement specified byte or specified word by one.
NEG	Negate—invert each bit of a specified byte or word and add 1 (form 2's complement).
CMP	Compare two specified bytes or two specified words.
AAS	ASCII adjust after subtraction.
DAS	Decimal (BCD) adjust after subtraction.

Multiplication instructions:

MUL	Multiply unsigned byte by byte or unsigned word by word.
IMUL	Multiply signed byte by byte or signed word by word.
AAM	ASCII adjust after multiply.

Division instructions:

DIV	Divide unsigned word by byte, or unsigned double word by word.
IDIV	Divide signed word by byte, or signed double word by word.
AAD	ASCII adjust before division.
CBW	Fill upper byte of word with copies of sign bit of lower byte.
CWD	Fill upper word of double word with sign bit of lower word.

BIT MANIPULATION INSTRUCTIONS

Logical instructions:

NOT	Invert each bit of a byte or word.
AND	AND each bit in byte or word with the corresponding bit in another byte or word.
OR	OR each bit in a byte or word with the corresponding bit in another byte or word.
XOR	Exclusive OR each bit in a byte or word with the corresponding bit in another byte or word.
TEST	AND operands to update flags, but don't change operands.

Shift instructions:

SHL/SAL	Shift bits of word or byte left, put zero(s) in LSB(s).
SHR	Shift bits of word or byte right, put zero(s) in MSB(s).
SAR	Shift bits of word or byte right, copy old MSB into new MSB.

Rotate instructions:

ROL	Rotate bits of byte or word left, MSB to LSB and to CF.
ROR	Rotate bits of byte or word right, LSB to MSB and to CF.
RCL	Rotate bits of byte or word left, MSB to CF and CF to LSB.
RCR	Rotate bits of byte or word right, LSB to CF and CF to MSB.

STRING INSTRUCTIONS

NOTES A *string* is a series of bytes or a series of words in sequential memory locations. A string often consists of ASCII character codes. In the list a "/" is used to separate different mnemonics for the same instruction. Use the mnemonic which most clearly describes the function of the instruction in a specific application. A "B" in a mnemonic is used to specifically indicate that a string of bytes is to be acted upon. A "W" in the mnemonic is used to indicate that a string of words is to be acted upon.

REP	An instruction prefix. Repeat following instruction until CX = 0.
REPE/REPZ	An instruction prefix. Repeat instruction until CX = 0 or ZF ≠ 1.
REPNE/REPNZ	An instruction prefix. Repeat until CX = 0 or ZF = 1.
MOVS/MOVSB/MOVSW	Move byte or word from one string to another.
COMPS/COMPSB/COMPSW	Compare two string bytes or two string words.
INS/INSB/INSW	(80186/80188) Input string byte or word from port.
OUTS/OUTSB/OUTSW	(80186/80188) Output string byte or word to port.
SCAS/SCASB/SCASW	Scan a string. Compare a string byte with byte in AL or a string word with word in AX.
LODS/LODSB/LODSW	Load string byte into AL or string word into AX.
STOS/STOSB/STOSW	Store byte from AL or word from AX into string.

PROGRAM EXECUTION TRANSFER INSTRUCTIONS

These instructions are used to tell the 8086 to start fetching instructions from some new address, rather than continuing in sequence.

Unconditional transfer instructions:

CALL	Call a procedure (subprogram), save return address on stack.
RET	Return from procedure to calling program.
JMP	Go to specified address to get next instruction.

Conditional transfer instructions:

NOTE A "/" is used to separate two mnemonics which represent the same instruction. Use the mnemonic which most clearly describes the decision condition in a specific program. These instructions are often used after a compare instruction. The terms *below* and *above* refer to unsigned binary numbers. Above means larger in magnitude. The terms *greater than* or *less than* refer to signed binary numbers. Greater than means more positive.

JA/JNBE	Jump if above/Jump if not below nor equal.
JAE/JNB	Jump if above or equal/Jump if not below.
JB/JNAE	Jump if below/Jump if not above nor equal.

JBE/JNA Jump if below or equal/Jump if not above.

JC Jump if carry flag (CF) = 1.

JE/JZ Jump if equal/Jump if zero flag (ZF) = 1.

JG/JNLE Jump if greater/Jump if not less than nor equal.

JGE/JNL Jump if greater than or equal/Jump if not less than.

JL/JNGE Jump if less than/Jump if not greater than nor equal.

JLE/JNG Jump if less than or equal/Jump if not greater than.

JNC Jump if no carry (Jump if carry flag = 0).

JNE/JNZ Jump if not equal/Jump if not zero (zero flag = 0).

JNO Jump if no overflow (Jump if overflow flag = 0).

JNP/JPO Jump if not parity/Jump if parity odd (PF = 0).

JNS Jump if not sign (Jump if sign flag = 0).

JO Jump if overflow flag = 1.

JP/JPE Jump if parity/Jump if parity even (PF = 1).

JS Jump if sign flag = 1.

Iteration control instructions:

These instructions can be used to execute a series of instructions some number of times. Here mnemonics separated by a "/" represent the same instruction. Use the one that best fits the specific application.

LOOP Loop through a sequence of instructions until CX = 0.

LOOPE/LOOPZ Loop through a sequence of instructions while zero flag = 1 and CX ≠ 0.

LOOPNE/LOOPNZ Loop through a sequence of instructions while zero flag = 0 and CX ≠ 0.

JCXZ Jump to specified address if CX = 0.

If you aren't tired of instructions, continue skimming through the rest of the list. Don't worry if the explanation is not clear to you because we will explain these instructions in detail in later chapters.

Interrupt instructions:

INT Interrupt program execution, call service procedure.

INTO Interrupt program execution if overflow flag = 1.

IRET Return from interrupt service procedure to main program.

High-level language interface instructions:

ENTER (80186/80188 ONLY) Enter procedure.

LEAVE (80186/80188 ONLY) Leave procedure.

BOUND (80186/80188 ONLY) Check if effective address within specified array bounds.

PROCESSOR CONTROL INSTRUCTIONS

Flag set/clear instructions:

STC Set carry flag (CF) to 1.

CLC Clear carry flag (CF) to 0.

CMC Complement the state of the carry flag (CF).

STD Set direction flag (DF) to 1 (decrement string pointers).

CLD Clear direction flag (DF) to 0.

STI Set interrupt enable flag to 1 (enable INTR input).

CLI Clear interrupt enable flag to 0 (disable INTR input).

External hardware synchronization instructions:

HLT Halt (do nothing) until interrupt or reset.

WAIT Wait (do nothing) until signal on the TEST pin is low.

ESC Escape to external coprocessor such as 8087 or 8089.

LOCK An instruction prefix. Prevents another processor from taking bus while the adjacent instruction executes.

No operation instruction:

NOP No action except fetch and decode.

Now that you have glanced through an overview of the 8086 instruction set, let's see if you found the instructions needed to implement the "read sensor, add +7, and store result in memory" example program. The IN instruction can be used to read the temperature value from an A/D converter connected to a port. The ADD instruction can be used to add the correction factor of +7 to the value read in. Finally, the MOV instruction can be used to copy the result of the addition to a memory location. A major point here is that breaking the programming problem down into a sequence of steps makes it easy to find the instruction or small group of instructions that will perform each step. The next section shows you how to write the actual program using these instructions.

Writing a Program

INITIALIZATION INSTRUCTIONS

After finding the instructions needed to do the main part of your program, there are a few additional instructions you need to determine before you actually write your program. The purpose of these additional instructions is to *initialize* various parts of the system such as segment registers, flags, and programmable port devices. Segment registers, for example, must be loaded with the upper 16 bits of the address in memory where you want the segment to begin. For our "read temperature sensor, add +7, and store result in memory" example program, the only part we need to initialize is the data segment register. The data segment register must be initialized so that we can copy the result of the addition to a location in memory. If, for example, we want to store data in memory starting at address 00100H, then we want the data segment register to contain the upper 16 bits of this address, 0010H. The 8086 does not have an instruction to move a number directly into a segment register. Therefore, we move the desired number into one of the 16-bit general-purpose registers, and then copy it to the desired segment register. Two MOV instructions will do this.

If you are using the stack in your program, then you must include an instruction to load the stack pointer register with the offset of the top of the stack. Most microcomputer systems contain several programmable peripheral devices such as ports, timers, and controllers. You must include instructions which send control words to these devices to tell them the function you want them to perform. Also, you usually want to include instructions which set or clear the control flags such as the interrupt enable flag and the direction flag.

The best way to approach the initialization task is to make a checklist of all the registers, programmable devices, and flags in the system you are working on. Then you can mark the ones you need for a specific program and determine the instructions needed to initialize each part. An initialization list for an 8086-based system, such as the SDK-86 prototyping board, might look like the following.

INITIALIZATION LIST

Data segment register ✓

Stack segment register

Extra segment register

Stack pointer register

Base pointer register

Source index register

Destination index register ✓

8255 programmable ports ✓

8259A priority interrupt controller

8254 programmable counter ✓

8251A programmable serial port

Initialize data variables ✓

Reset/clear direction flag and interrupt enable flag

As you can see, the list can become quite lengthy even though we have not included all of the devices a system might commonly have. Note that initializing the code segment register is absent from this list. The code segment register gets loaded with the correct starting value by the system command you use to run the program. Now let's see how you put all of these parts together to make a program.

A STANDARD PROGRAM FORMAT

In this section we show you the form your programs should have if you are going to construct the machine codes for each instruction by *hand*. A later section of this chapter will show you the additional parts you need to add to the program if you are going to use an *assembler* to produce the binary codes for the instructions.

To help you format your programs, *assembly language coding sheets* such as that shown in Figure 3-4 are available. The *address* column is used for the address or the offset of a code byte or data byte. The actual code bytes or data bytes are put in the *data/code* column. A *label* is a name which represents an address referred to in a jump or call instruction. A label is put in the *label* column. It is followed by a colon (:) if it is used by a jump or call instruction in the same code segment. The *opcode* column contains the mnemonics for the instructions. The *operand* column contains the registers, memory locations, or data acted upon by the instructions. A *comment* column gives you space to describe the function of the instruction for future reference.

Figure 3-4 shows how the instructions for the "read temperature, add +7, store result in memory" program can be written in sequence on a coding sheet. We will discuss here the operation of these instructions to the extent needed. If you want more information about any of these, detailed descriptions of the *syntax* (assembly language grammar) and operation of each of these instructions can be found in Chapter 6.

The first line at the top of coding form in Figure 3-4 does not represent an instruction. It simply indicates that we want to set aside a memory location to store the result. This location must be in available RAM so that we can write to it. Address 00100H is an available RAM location on an SDK-86 prototyping board, for example. Next, we decide where in memory we want to start putting the code bytes for the instructions of the program. Again, on an SDK-86 prototyping board, address 00200H and above is available RAM, so we chose to start the program at address 00200H.

The first operation we want to do in the program is to initialize the data segment register. As discussed previously, two MOV instructions are used to do this. The MOV AX, 0010H instruction, when executed, will load

PROGRAMMER	D. V. HALL	SHEET 1	OF 1
PROGRAM TITLE	READ TEMPERATURE & CORRECT	DATE:	1/1/86

ABSTRACT: This program reads in a temperature value from a sensor connected to port 05H, adds a correction factor of +7 to the value read in, and then stores the result in a reserved memory location.
PROCEDURES: None called.
REGISTERS USED: Ax
FLAGS AFFECTED: All conditional
PORTS: Uses 05 as input port
MEMORY: 00100H–DATA; 00200H–0020CH, CODE

ADDRESS	DATA or CODE	LABELS	MNEM.	OPERAND(S)	COMMENTS
00100	XX				Reserve memory location to store
00101					result. This location will be loaded
00102					with a data byte as read in
00103					& corrected by the program.
00104					XX means "don't care" about
00105					contents of location.
00106					
00107					
00108					
00109					
0010A					
0010B					
0010C					
0010D					
0010E					Code starts here
0010F					Note break in address
200	B8		MOV	AX, 0010H	Initialize DS to point to start of
01	10				memory set aside for storing data
02	00				
03	8E		MOV	DS, AX	
04	D8				
05	E4		IN	AL, 05H	Read temperature from
06	05				port 05H
07	04		ADD	AL, 07H	Add correction factor
08	07				of +07
09	A2		MOV	[0000], AL	Store result in reserved
0A	00				memory
0B	00				
0C	CC		INT	3	Stop, wait for command
0D					from user
0E					
0F					

FIGURE 3-4 Assembly language program on standard coding form.

the upper 16 bits of the address we chose for data storage into the AX register. The MOV DS, AX instruction will copy this number from the AX register to the data segment register. Now we get to the instructions that do what we started out to do. The IN AL, 05H instruction will copy a data byte from port 05H to the AL register. The ADD AL, 07 instruction will add 07H to the AL register and leave the result in the AL register. The MOV [0000], AL instruction will copy the byte in AL to a memory location at a displacement of 0000H from the data segment base. In other words, AL will be copied to a physical address computed by shifting the data segment base in DS, 0010H, four bit positions left and adding the displacement, 0000H, contained in the instruction. The data will then be copied to physical address 00100H in memory. This is an example of the direct addressing mode described near the end of the previous chapter.

The INT 3 instruction at the end of the program functions as a *breakpoint*. In most 8086 systems, when the 8086 executes this instruction it will cause the 8086 to stop executing the instructions of your program and return control to the *monitor* or *system program*. You can then use *system commands* to look at the contents of registers and memory locations, or run another program. Without an instruction such as this at the end of the program, the 8086 would fetch and execute the code bytes for your program, and then it would go on fetching meaningless bytes from memory and trying to execute them as if they were code bytes.

The next major section of this chapter will show you how to construct the binary codes for these and other 8086 instructions so that you can assemble and run the programs on a development board such as the SDK-86. First, however, we want to use Figure 3-4 to make an important point about writing assembly language programs.

DOCUMENTATION

In a previous section of this chapter we stressed the point that you should do a lot of thinking and carefully write down the algorithm for a program before you start writing instruction statements. You should also document the program itself so that its operation is clear to you and to anyone else who needs to understand it.

Each page of the program should contain the name of the program, the page number, the name of the programmer, and perhaps a version number. Each program or procedure should have a heading block which contains an *abstract* describing what the program is supposed to do, which procedures it calls, which registers it uses, which ports it uses, which flags it affects, the memory used, and any other information which will make it easier for another programmer to interface with the program.

Comments should be used generously to describe the specific function of an instruction or group of instructions. Not every statement needs an individual comment. Comments should not just repeat the instruction mnemonic.

We cannot overemphasize the importance of clear, concise documentation in your programs. Experience has shown that even a short program that you wrote a month ago and forgot to put comments on may not be at all understandable to you now.

CONSTRUCTING THE MACHINE CODES FOR 8086 INSTRUCTIONS

This section shows you how to construct the binary codes for 8086 instructions. Most of the time you will probably use an assembler do this for you, but it is useful to understand how the codes are constructed. If you have an 8086-based prototyping board such as the Intel SDK-86 available, knowing how to hand-code instructions will enable you to code, enter, and run simple programs as you work your way through the 8086 instruction set examples in the next chapters.

Instruction Templates

To code the instructions for 8-bit processors such as the 8085, all you have to do is look up the hexadecimal code for each instruction on a one-page chart. For the 8086 the process is not quite as simple. Here's why. There are 32 ways to specify the source of the operand in an instruction such as MOV CX, source. The source of the operand can be any one of eight 16-bit registers, or a memory location specified by any one of 24 memory addressing modes. Each of the 32 possible instructions requires a different binary code. If CX is made the source rather than the destination then there are 32 ways of specifying the destination. Each of these 32 possible instructions requires a different binary code. There are then 64 different codes for MOV instructions using CX as a source or as a destination. Likewise, another 64 codes are required to specify all of the possible MOVs using CL as a source or a destination, and 64 more are required to specify all of the possible MOVs using CH as a source or a destination. The point here is that, because there is such a large number of possible codes for the 8086 instructions, it is impractical to list them all in a simple table. Instead, we use a *template* for each basic instruction type and fill in bits within this template to indicate the desired addressing mode, data type, etc. In other words, we build up the instruction codes on a bit-by-bit basis.

Different Intel literature shows the code templates for the 8086 instructions in two slightly different formats. One format is shown at the end of the 8086 data sheet in Appendix A. The second format is shown along with the 8086 instruction timings in Appendix B. We will start by showing you how to use the templates shown in the 8086 data sheet. As a first example of how to use these templates we will build the code for the IN AL, 05H instruction from our example program. Figure 3-5*a* shows the template for this instruction. Note that two bytes are required for the instruction. The upper 7 bits of the first byte tell the 8086 that this is an "input from a fixed port" instruction. The bit labeled W in the template is used to tell the 8086 whether you want to input a byte or input a word. If you want the 8086 to input a byte from

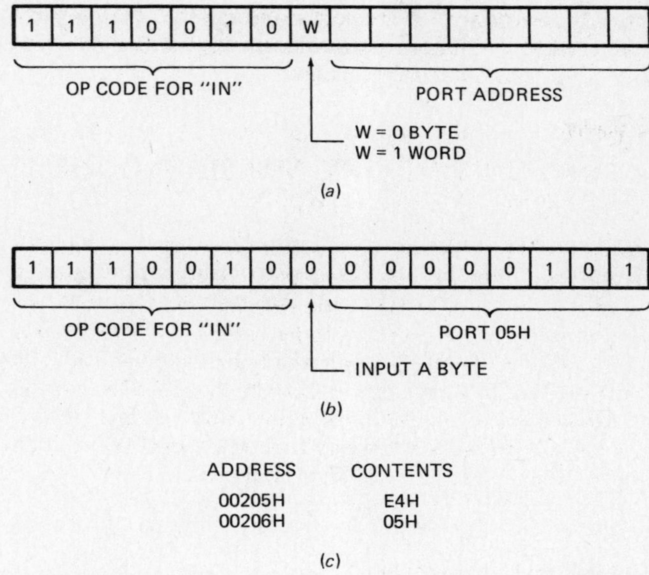

FIGURE 3-5 Coding template for 8086 IN (fixed-port) instruction. *(a)* Template. *(b)* Example. *(c)* Hex codes in sequential memory locations.

an 8-bit port to AL, then make the W bit a 0. If you want the 8086 to input a word from a 16-bit port to the AX register, then make the W bit a 1. The 8-bit port address, 05H or 00000101 binary, is put in the second byte of the instruction. When the program is loaded into memory to be run, the first instruction byte will be put in one memory location and the second instruction byte will be put in the next. Figure 3-5*c* shows this in hexadecimal form as E4H, 05H.

To further illustrate how these templates are used, we will show here several examples with the simple MOV instruction. We will then construct the codes for the example program in Figure 3-4. Other examples will be shown as needed in the following chapters. Figure 3-6 shows the coding template or format for 8086 instructions which MOV data from a register to a register, from a register to a memory location, or from a memory location to a register. Note that at least two code bytes are required for the instruction.

The upper 6 bits of the first byte are an opcode which indicates the general type of instruction. Look in the table in Appendix A to find the 6-bit opcode for this MOV register/memory to /from register instruction. You should find it to be 100010. The W bit in the first word is used to indicate whether a byte or a word is being moved. If you are moving a byte, make this bit a 0. If you are moving a word, make this bit a 1. In this instruction, one operand must always be a register, so 3 bits in the second byte are used to indicate which register is involved. The 3-bit codes for each register are shown at the end of the table in Appendix A and in Figure 3-7*a*. Look in one of these places to find the code for the CL register. You should get 001. The D bit in the first byte of the instruction code is used to indicate whether the data is being moved *to* the register identified in the REG field of the second byte or *from* that register. If you are moving data *to* the register identified in the REG field, make the D bit a 1. If you are moving data *from* that register, make the D bit a 0.

Now remember that in this instruction one operand must be a register. The 2-bit field labeled MOD and the 3-bit field labeled R/M in the second byte of the instruction code are used to specify the desired addressing mode for the other operand. Figure 3-8 shows the MOD and R/M bit patterns for each of the 32 possible addressing modes.

If the other operand in the instruction is also one of the eight registers, then put in 11 for the MOD bits in the code template. Put the 3-bit code for that register in the R/M bits in the code template.

For the case where the other operand is a memory location there are 24 ways of specifying how the execution unit should compute the effective address of the operand in memory. Remember from Chapter 2 that the effective address can be specified directly in the instruction, it can be contained in a register, or it can be the sum of one or two registers and a displacement. Figure 3-8 shows the MOD and R/M codes for each of the 24 ways of specifying an effective address. The MOD code indicates whether the address specification in the in-

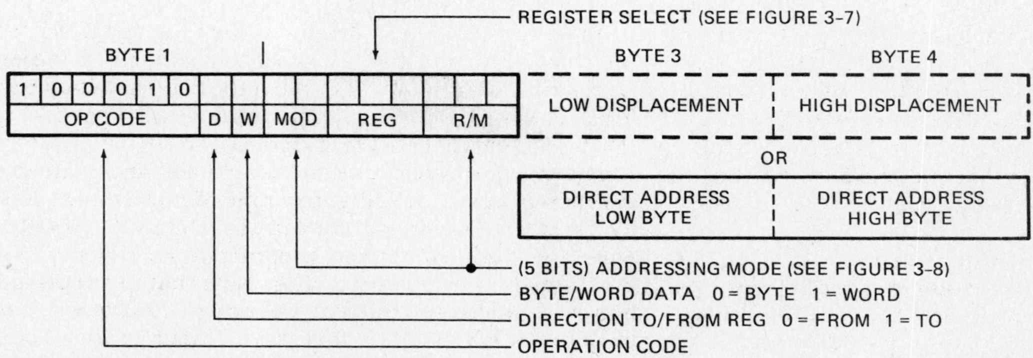

FIGURE 3-6 Coding template for 8086 instructions which MOV data between registers or between a register and a memory location.

```
REG FIELD BIT ASSIGNMENTS
IF W = 1   16-BIT REGISTER

   REGISTER CODE

      AX    ØØØ
      CX    ØØ1
      DX    Ø1Ø
      BX    Ø11
      SP    1ØØ
      BP    1Ø1
      SI    11Ø
      DI    111

IF W = Ø    8-BIT REGISTER

   REGISTER CODE

      AL    ØØØ
      CL    ØØ1
      DL    Ø1Ø
      BL    Ø11
      AH    1ØØ
      CH    1Ø1
      DH    11Ø
      BH    111
```

(a)

```
   SEGREG    CODE

      ES       ØØ
      CS       Ø1
      SS       1Ø
      DS       11
```

(b)

FIGURE 3-7 Instruction codes for 8086 registers. *(a)* General purpose, pointers, and index. *(b)* Segment registers.

struction contains a displacement. The R/M code indicates which register(s) contain part(s) of the effective address. Here's how it works:

1. If the specified effective address contains no displacement as in the instruction MOV CX, [BX] or in the instruction MOV [BX][SI], DX, then make the MOD bits 00, and chose the R/M bits which correspond to the register(s) containing the effective address. For example, if an instruction contains [BX], the 3-bit R/M code is 111. For an instruction which contains [BX][SI], the R/M code is 000. Note that for direct addressing where the displacement of the operand from the segment base is specified directly in the instruction, MOD is 00 and R/M is 110. For an instruction using direct addressing the low byte of the direct address is put in as a third instruction code byte of the instruction, and the high byte of the direct address is put in as a fourth instruction code byte.
2. If the effective address specified in the instruction contains a displacement less than 256 along with a reference to the contents of a register, as in the instruction MOV CX, 43H[BX], then code in MOD as 01, and chose the R/M bits which correspond to the register(s) which contain the part(s) for the effective address. For the instruction MOV CX, 43H[BX], MOD will be 01 and R/M will be 111. Put the 8-bit value of the displacement in as the third byte of the instruction.
3. If the expression for the effective address contains a displacement which is too large to fit in 8 bits, as in the instruction MOV DX, 4527H[BX], then put in 10 for MOD, and chose the R/M bits which correspond to the register(s) which contain the part(s) for the effective address. For the instruction MOV DX, 4527H[BX] the R/M bits are 111. The low byte of the displacement is put in as a third byte of the instruction. The high byte of the displacement is put in as a fourth byte of the instruction. The examples which follow should help clarify all of this for you.

MOV Instruction Coding Examples

All of the examples in this section use the MOV instruction template in Figure 3-6. As you read through these examples, it is a good idea to keep track of the bit-by-bit development on a separate paper for practice.

CODING MOV SP, BX

This instruction will copy a word from the BX register to the SP register. Consulting the table in Appendix A, you find that the 6-bit opcode for this instruction is 100010. Make the W bit a 1 because you are moving a word. The D bit for this instruction may be somewhat confusing, however. Since two registers are involved, you can think of the move as *to* SP, or *from* BX. Actually, it does not matter which you assume as long as you are consistent in coding the rest of the instruction. If you think of the instruction as moving a word *to* SP, then make the D bit

R/M \ MOD	00	01	10	11 W = 0	11 W = 1
000	[BX] + [SI]	[BX] + [SI] + d8	[BX] + [SI] + d16	AL	AX
001	[BX] + [DI]	[BX] + [DI] + d8	[BX] + [DI] + d16	CL	CX
010	[BP] + [SI]	[BP] + [SI] + d8	[BP] + [SI] + d16	DL	DX
011	[BP] + [DI]	[BP] + [DI] + d8	[BP] + [DI] + d16	BL	BX
100	[SI]	[SI] + d8	[SI] + d16	AH	SP
101	[DI]	[DI] + d8	[DI] + d16	CH	BP
110	d16 (direct address)	[BP] + d8	[BP] + d16	DH	SI
111	[BX]	[BX] + d8	[BX] + d16	BH	DI
	MEMORY MODE			REGISTER MODE	

d8 = 8-bit displacement d16 = 16-bit displacement

FIGURE 3-8 MOD and R/M bit patterns for 8086 instructions. The effective address (EA) produced by these addressing modes will be added to the data-segment base to form the physical address except for those cases where BP is used as part of the EA. In that case the EA will be added to the stack-segment base to form the physical address. You can use a segment-override prefix to indicate that you want the EA to be added to some other segment base.

a 1, and put 100 in the REG field to represent SP. The MOD field will be 11 to represent register addressing mode. Make the R/M field 011 to represent the other register, BX. The resultant code for the instruction MOV SP,BX will be 10001011 11100011. Figure 3-9*a* shows the meaning of all of these bits.

If you change the D bit to a 0 and swap the codes in the REG and R/M fields, you will get 10001001 11011100, which is another equally valid code for the instruction. Figure 3-9*b* shows the meaning of the bits in this form. This second form, incidentally, is the form that the Intel 8086 Macroassembler produces.

CODING MOV CL, [BX]

This instruction will copy a byte to CL from the memory location whose effective address is contained in BX. The effective address will be added to the data segment base in DS to produce the physical address.

To find the 6-bit opcode for byte one of the instruction, consult the table in Appendix A. You should find that this code is 100010. Make the D bit a 1 because data is being moved *to* register CL. Make the W bit a 0 because the instruction is moving a byte into CL. Next you need to put the 3-bit code which represents register CL in the REG field of the second byte of the instruction code. The codes for each register are shown in Figure 3-7. In this figure you should find that the code for CL is 001. Now, all you need to determine is the bit patterns for the MOD and R/M fields. Again use the table in Figure 3-8 to do this. To use the table, first find the box containing the desired addressing mode. The box containing [BX], for example, is in the lower left corner of the table. Read the required MOD-bit pattern from the top of the column. In this case, MOD is 00. Then read the required R/M-bit pattern at the left of the box. For this instruction you should find R/M to be 111. Assembling all of these bits together should give you 10001010 00001111 as the binary code for the instruction MOV CL, [BX]. Figure 3-9*c* summarizes the meaning of all the bits in this result.

MOV 43H[SI], DH

This instruction will copy a byte from the DH register to a memory location. The effective address of the memory location will be computed by adding the indicated displacement of 43H to the contents of the SI register. The actual physical address will be produced by shifting the contents of the data segment base in DS 4 bits left and adding this effective address to the result.

The 6-bit opcode for this instruction is again 100010. Make the D bit a 0 because you are moving *from* a register. Make the W bit a 0 because you are moving a byte. Put 110 in the REG field to represent the DH register. The R/M field will be 100 because SI contains part of the effective address. Make the MOD field 01 because the displacement contained in the instruction, 43H, will fit in one byte. If the specified displacement had been a number larger than FFH, then MOD would have been 10. Putting all these pieces together gives 10001000 01110100 for the first two bytes of the instruction code. The specified displacement, 43H or 01000011 binary is put after these two as a third instruction byte. Figure 3-9*d* shows this. If an instruction specifies a 16-bit displacement, then the low byte of the displacement is put

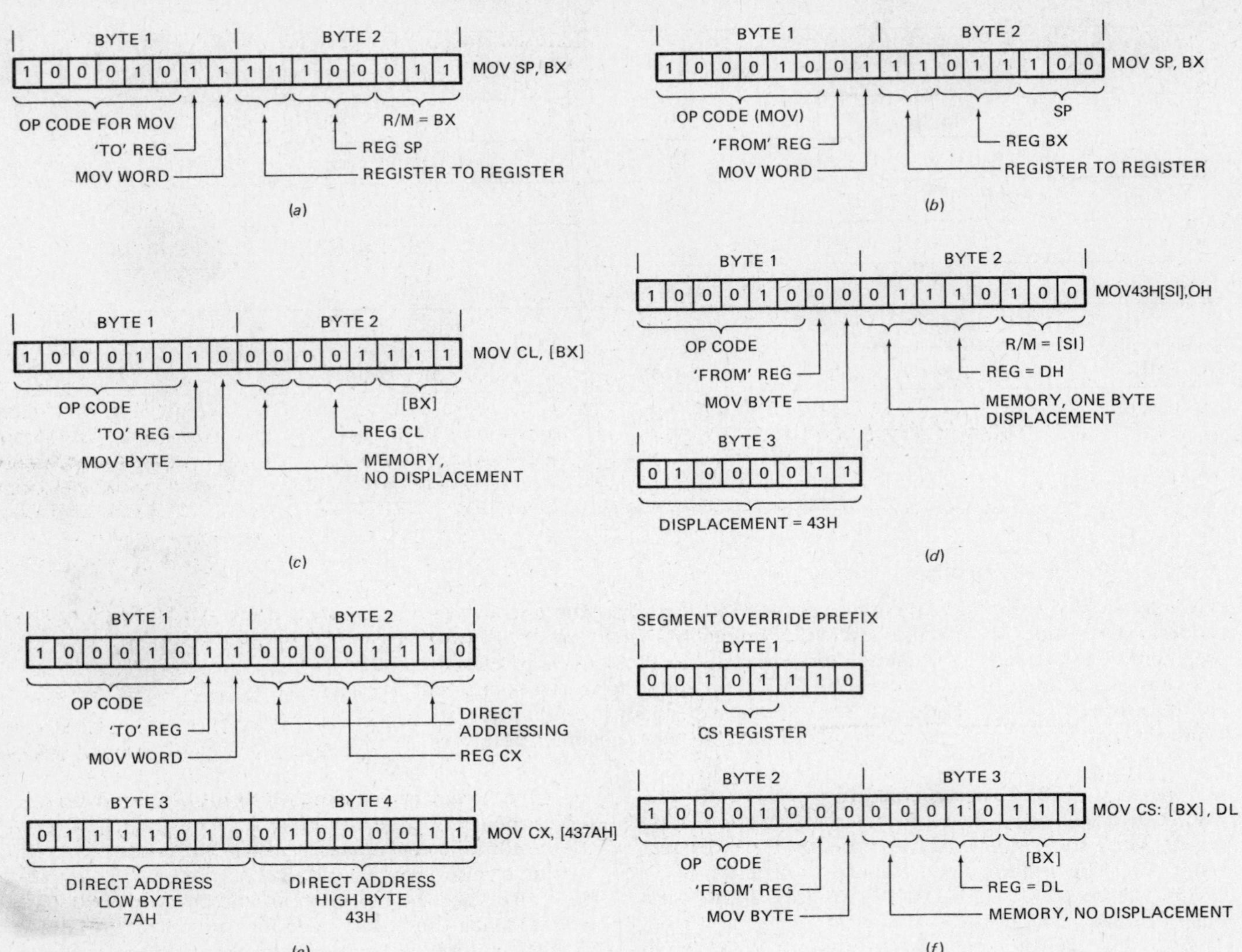

FIGURE 3-9 MOV instruction coding examples. *(a)* MOV SP, BX. *(b)* MOV SP, BX alternative. *(c)* MOV CL, [BX]. *(d)* MOV 43H [SI], DH. *(e)* MOV CX, [437AH]. *(f)* MOV CS:[BX], DL.

in as byte three of the instruction code, and the high byte of the displacement is put in as byte four of the instruction code.

CODING MOV CX, [437AH]

This instruction copies the contents of two memory locations into CX. The direct address or displacement of the first memory location from the start of the data segment is 437AH. The physical memory address will be produced by shifting the contents of the data segment register, DS, 4 bit positions left and adding this direct address to the result.

The 6-bit opcode for this instruction is again 100010. Make the D bit a 1 and the W bit a 1 because you are moving a word to CX. Put 001 in the REG field to represent the CX register, and then consult Figure 3-8 to find the MOD and R/M codes. In the first column of the figure you should find a box labeled "direct addressing," which is the mode specified by this instruction. For direct addressing you should find MOD to be 00 and R/M to be 110. The first two code bytes for the instruction then are 10001011 00001110. These two bytes will be followed by the low byte of the direct address, 7AH (01111010 binary). The high byte of the direct address 43H (01000011 binary) will be put after that. The instruction will be coded into four successive memory addresses as 8BH, 0EH, 7AH, and 43H. Figure 3-9*e* spells this out in detail.

CODING MOV CS:[BX], DL

This instruction copies a byte from the DL register to a memory location. The effective address for the memory location is contained in the BX register. Normally an effective address in BX will be added to the data segment base in DS to produce the physical memory address. In this instruction, CS: indicates that we want the BIU to add the effective address to the code segment base in CS to produce the physical address. The CS: is called a *segment override prefix*.

When an instruction containing a segment override prefix is coded, an 8-bit code for the segment override prefix is put in memory before the code for the rest of the instruction. The code byte for the segment override prefix has the format 001XX110. You insert a 2-bit code in place of the X's to indicate which segment base you want the effective address to be added to. The codes for these 2 bits are as follows: 00 = ES, 01 = CS, 10 = SS, and 11 = DS. The segment override prefix byte for CS then is 00101110. For practice, code out the rest of this instruction. Figure 3-9*f* shows the result you should get and how the code for the segment override prefix is put before the other code bytes for the instruction.

Coding the Example Program

Again, as you read through this section follow the bit-by-bit development of the instruction codes on a separate paper for practice.

MOV AX, 0010H

This instruction will move the immediate word 0010H into the AX accumulator. The simplest code template to use for this instruction is listed in the table in Appendix A under the MOV "immediate to register" heading. The format for it is 1011 W REG, data byte low, data byte high. Make the W bit a 1 because you want to move a word. Consult Figure 3-7 to find the code for the AX register. You should find this to be 000. Put this 3-bit code in the REG field of the instruction code. The completed instruction code byte is 10111000. Put the low byte of the immediate number, 10H, in as the second code byte. Then put the high byte of the immediate data, 00H, in as the third code byte.

MOV DS, AX

This instruction copies the contents of the AX register into the data segment register. The template to use for coding this instruction is found in the table in Appendix A under the heading "Register/memory to segment register." The format for this template is 10001110 MOD 0 segreg R/M . Segreg represents the 2-bit code for the desired segment register. These codes are also found in the table at the end of Appendix A. The segreg code for the DS register is 11. Since the other operand is a register, MOD should be 11. Put the 3-bit code for the AX register, 000, in the R/M field. The resultant codes for the two code bytes should then be 10001110 11011000.

IN AL, 05H

This instruction copies a byte of data from port 05H to the AL register. The coding for this instruction was described in a previous section. The code for the instruction is 11100100 00000101.

ADD AL, 07H

This instruction adds the immediate number 07H to the AL register and puts the result in the AL register. The simplest template to use for coding this instruction is found in the table in Appendix A under the heading "ADD—Immediate to accumulator." The format is 0000010W, data byte, data byte. Since we are adding a byte, the W bit should be a 0. The immediate data byte we are adding will be put in the second code byte. The third code byte will not be needed because we are only adding a byte. The code then will be 00000100 00000111.

MOV [0000], AL

This instruction copies the contents of the AL register to a memory location. The direct address or displacement of the memory location from the start of the data segment is 0000H. The code template for this instruction is found in the table in Appendix A under the heading "MOV—Accumulator to memory." The format for the instruction is 1010001W, address low byte, address high byte. Since the instruction moves a byte, the W bit should be a 0. The low byte of the direct address is written in as the second instruction code byte, and the high byte of the direct address is written in as the third instruction code byte. The codes for these 3 bytes then will be 10100010 00000000 00000000.

INT 3

In most 8086 systems this instruction causes the 8086 to stop executing instructions and do nothing but wait for the user to tell it what to do next. According to the format table in the appendix, the code for this instruction is the single byte 11001100 or CCH.

SUMMARY OF HAND CODING THE EXAMPLE PROGRAM

Figure 3-4 shows the example program with all the instruction codes in sequential order as you would write them so that you could load the program into memory and run it. Codes are in HEX to save space.

A Look at Another Coding Template Format

As we mentioned previously, Intel literature shows the 8086 instruction coding templates in two different forms. The preceeding sections have shown you how to use the templates found in the 8086 data sheet in Appendix A. Now let's take a brief look at the second form shown along with the instruction clock cycles in Appendix B.

The only difference between the second form for the templates and the form we discussed previously is that the D and W bits are not individually identified. Instead, the complete opcode bytes are shown for each version of an instruction. For example, in Appendix B the opcode byte for the MOV memory, register 8 instruction is shown as 88H, and the opcode byte for the MOV memory, register 16 instruction is shown as 89H. The only difference between the two codes is that the W bit is a 0 for the 8-bit move and the W bit is a 1 for the 16-bit move. One important point to make about using the templates in Appendix B is that for operations which involve two registers, the 3-bit code for the source register is put in the REG field of the MOD/RM instruction byte. The 3-bit code for the destination register is put in the R/M field of the MOD/RM instruction byte. The instruction MOV BX, CX, for example, is coded out as 10001001 11001011, or 89H CBH. You can use whichever set of templates you find easier to use.

A Few Words About Hand Coding

If you have to hand-code 8086 assembly language programs, here are a few tips to make your life easier. First, check your algorithm very carefully to make sure that it really does what it is supposed to do. Second, initially write down just the assembly language statements and comments for your program. You can check the table in the appendix to determine how many bytes each instruction takes so you know how many blank lines to leave between instruction statements. You may find it helpful to insert three or four NOP instructions after every nine or ten instructions. The NOP instruction doesn't do anything but kill time. However, if you accidentally leave out an instruction in your program, you can replace the NOPs with the needed instruction. This way you don't have to rewrite the entire program after the missing instruction.

After you have written down the instruction statements, recheck very carefully to make sure you have the right instructions to implement your algorithm. Then, work out the binary codes for each instruction and write them in the appropriate places on the coding form.

Hand coding is laborious for long programs. When writing long programs, it is much more efficient to use an assembler. The next section of this chapter shows you how to write your programs so you can use an assembler to produce the machine codes for the instructions.

WRITING PROGRAMS FOR USE WITH AN ASSEMBLER

If you have an 8086 assembler available, you should learn to use it as soon as possible. Besides doing the tedious task of producing the binary codes for your instruction statements, an assembler also allows you to refer to data items by name rather than by numerical addresses. As you should soon see, this greatly reduces the work you have to do and makes your programs much more readable. In this section we show you how to write your programs so that you can use an assembler on them. The assemblers used for the programs in this book were the Intel 8086/8088/80186/80188 Macro Assembler and the Microsoft Macro Assembler for the IBM Personal Computer. If you are using another assembler, some features may be slightly different so consult the manual for it.

Program Format

The best way to approach this section seems to be to show you a simple, but complete, program written for an assembler and explain the function of the various parts. By now you are probably tired of the "read temperature, add +7, and store result in memory" program, so we will use another example.

Figure 3-10 shows an 8086 assembly language program which multiplies two 16-bit binary numbers to give a 32-bit binary result. If you have a development system or a computer with an 8086 assembler to work on, this is a good program for you to key in, assemble, and run to become familiar with the operation of your system. If you are working on a prototyping board such as the SDK-86, you can construct the binary codes for each of the instructions, load the program into the on-board RAM, and run it. In any case, you can use the structure of this example program as a model for your own programs.

In addition to program instructions, the example program in Figure 3-10 contains directions to the assembler. These directions to the assembler are commonly called *assembler directives* or *pseudo operations*. A section at the end of Chapter 6 lists and describes for your reference a large number of the available assembler directives. Here we will discuss the basic assembler directives you need to get started writing programs. We will introduce more of these directives as we need them in the next two chapters.

SEGMENT and ENDS Directives

The SEGMENT and ENDS directives are used to identify a group of data items or a group of instructions that you want to be put together in a particular segment. These directives are used in the same way that parentheses are used to group like terms in algebra. A group of data statements or a group of instruction statements contained between SEGMENT and ENDS directives is called a *logical segment*. When you set up a logical segment, you give it a name of your choosing. In the example program the statements DATA_HERE SEGMENT and DATA_HERE ENDS set up a logical segment named DATA_HERE. There is nothing sacred about the name DATA_HERE. We simply chose this name to help us remember that this logical segment contains data statements. The statements CODE_HERE SEGMENT and CODE_HERE ENDS in the example program set up a logical segment named CODE_HERE which contains instruction statements. The Intel and the IBM 8086 macro assemblers, incidentally, allow you to use names and labels of up to 31 characters. You can't use spaces in a name, but you can use an underscore as shown to separate words in a name. Also, you can't use instruction mnemonics as segment names or labels. Throughout the rest of the program you will refer to a logical segment by the name that you give it when you define it.

```
PAGE ,132              ; Makes listing file lines 132 characters wide
;8086 program
;ABSTRACT              : This program multiplies the two 16-bit words in
                       ; the memory locations called MULTIPLICAND and
                       ; MULTIPLIER. The result is stored in the memory
                       ; location called PRODUCT
;PORTS USED            : None
;PROCEDURES USED: None
;REGISTERS USED : CS, DS, DX and AX

DATA_HERE        SEGMENT

MULTIPLICAND     DW      204AH                ; first word here
MULTIPLIER       DW      3B2AH                ; second word here
PRODUCT          DW      2 DUP(0)             ; result here

DATA_HERE        ENDS


CODE_HERE        SEGMENT
                 ASSUME CS : CODE_HERE, DS : DATA_HERE

                 MOV AX, DATA_HERE            ; initialize DS register
                 MOV DS,AX

                 MOV AX, MULTIPLICAND         ; get one word
                 MUL MULTIPLIER               ; multiply by second word
                 MOV PRODUCT, AX              ; store low word of result
                 MOV PRODUCT+2, DX            ; store high word of result
                 INT 3                        ; wait for command from user

CODE_HERE        ENDS
                 END
```

FIGURE 3-10 Assembly language source program to multiply two 16-bit binary numbers to give a 32-bit result.

A logical segment is not usually given a physical starting address when it is declared. After the program is assembled, and perhaps linked with other assembled program modules, it is then assigned the physical address where it will be loaded in memory to be run.

Data and Addresses Naming Directives—EQU, DB, DW, and DD

Programs work with three general categories of data: constants, variables, and addresses. The value of a constant does not change during the execution of the program. The number 7 is an example of a constant you might use in a program. A variable is the name given to a data item which can change during the execution of a program. The current temperature of an oven is an example of a variable. Addresses are referred to in many instructions. You may, for example, load an address into a register or jump to an address.

Constants, variables, and addresses used in your programs can be given names. This allows you to refer to them by name rather than having to remember or calculate their value each time you refer to them in an instruction. In other words, if you give names to constants, variables, and addresses the assembler can use these names to find the desired data item or address when you refer to it in an instruction. Specific directives are used to give names to constants and variables in your programs. Labels are used to give names to addresses in your programs.

THE EQU DIRECTIVE

The EQU or *equate* directive is used to assign a name to constants used in your programs. The statement CORRECTION_FACTOR EQU 07H, in a program such as our previous example, would tell the assembler to insert the value 07H every time that it finds the name CORRECTION_FACTOR in a program statement. In other words, when the assembler reads the statement ADD AL, CORRECTION_FACTOR, it will automatically code the instruction as if you had written it ADD AL, 07H. Here's the advantage of using an EQU directive to declare constants at the start of your program. Suppose that you use the correction factor of +07H 23 times in your program. Now the company you work for changes brands of temperature sensor and the new correction factor is +09H. If you used the number 07H in the 23 instructions which contain this correction factor, then you have to go through the entire program, find each instruction that uses the correction factor, and update the value. Murphy's law being what it is, you are likely to miss one or two of these, and the program won't work correctly. If you used an EQU at the start of your program and then referred to CORRECTION_FACTOR by name in the 23 instructions, then all you do is change the value in the EQU statement from 07H to 09H and reassemble the program. The assembler automatically inserts the new value of 09H in all 23 instructions.

NOTE In large programs consisting of modules assembled separately, constants must be declared in each module. The assembler has no way to remember an EQU value from one module when it assembles another module.

DB, DW, AND DD DIRECTIVES

The DB, DW, and DD directives are used to assign names to variables in your programs. The DB directive after a name specifies that the data is of *type byte*. The program statement OVEN_TEMPERATURE DB 27, for example declares a variable of type byte and gives it the name OVEN_TEMPERATURE. DW is used to specify that the data is of *type word* (16 bits), and DD is used to specify that the data is of *type double word* (32 bits). If a number is written after the DB, DW, or DD, the data item will be *initialized* with that value when the program is loaded from disk into RAM. The statement CONVERSION_FACTORS DB 27H,48H,32H,69H will declare a data item of 4 bytes and initialize the 4 bytes with the specified 4 values. If we don't care what a data item is initialized to then we can indicate this with a "?", as in the statement TARE_WEIGHT DW ?. Note that data variables which are changed during the operation of a program should also be initialized with program instructions so that the program can be rerun from the start without reloading it to initialize the variables. Figure 3-10 shows three more examples of naming and initializing data items.

The first example, MULTIPLICAND DW 204AH, declares a data word named MULTIPLICAND, and initializes that data word with the value 204AH. What this means is that the assembler will set aside two successive memory locations and assign the name MULTIPLICAND to the first location. As you will see, this allows us to access the data in these memory locations by name. The MULTIPLICAND DW 204AH statement also indicates that when the final program is loaded into memory to be run, these memory locations will be loaded with (initialized to) 204AH. Actually, since this is an Intel microprocessor, the first address in memory will contain the low byte of the word, 4AH, and the second memory address will contain the high byte of the word, 20H.

The second data declaration example in Figure 3-10, MULTIPLIER DW 3B2AH, sets aside storage for a word in memory and gives the starting address of this word

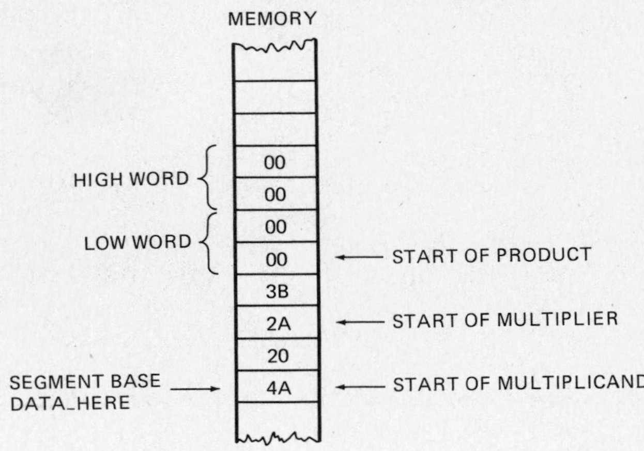

FIGURE 3-11 Data arrangement in memory for multiply program.

the name MULTIPLIER. When the program is loaded, the first memory address will be initialized with 2AH, and the second memory location with 3BH.

The third data declaration example in Figure 3-10, PRODUCT DW 2 DUP(0), sets aside storage for two words in memory and gives the starting address of the first word the name PRODUCT. The DUP(0) part of the statement tells the assembler to initialize the two words to all zeros. When we multiply two 16-bit binary numbers, the product can be as large as 32 bits. Therefore, we must set aside this much space to store the product. We could have used the DD directive to declare PRODUCT as a double word, but, since in the program we move the result to PRODUCT one word at a time, it is more convenient to declare PRODUCT as 2 words.

Figure 3-11 shows how the data for MULTIPLICAND, MULTIPLIER, and PRODUCT will actually be arranged in memory starting from the base of the DATA_HERE segment. The first byte of MULTIPLICAND, 4AH, will be at a displacement of zero from the segment base, because MULTIPLICAND is the first data item declared in the logical segment DATA_HERE. The displacement of the second byte of MULTIPLICAND is 0001. The displacement of the first byte of MULTIPLIER from the segment base is 0002H, and the displacement of the second byte of MULTIPLIER is 0003H. These are the displacements that we would have to figure out for each data item if we were not using names to refer to them.

If the logical segment DATA_HERE is eventually put in ROM or EPROM, then MULTIPLICAND will function as a constant, because it cannot be changed during program execution. However, if DATA_HERE is eventually put in RAM then MULTIPLICAND can function as a variable because a new value could be written in those memory locations during program execution.

Types of Numbers Used in Data Statements

All of the previous examples of DB, DW, and DD declarations use hexadecimal numbers as indicated by an "H" after the number. You can, however, put in a number in any one of several other forms. For each form you must tell the assembler which form you are using.

BINARY

For example, when you use a binary number in a statement, you put a B after the string of 1's and 0's to let the assembler know that you want the number to be treated as a binary number. The statement TEMP_MAX DB 01111001B is an example. If you want to put in a negative binary number, write the number in its 2's complement sign-and-magnitude form.

OCTAL

To indicate that you want a number to be evaluated as base-8 or octal, put a Q after the string of octal digits. The statement OLD_COMPUTER DW 7341Q is an example.

DECIMAL

The assembler treats a number with no identifying letter after it as a decimal number. In other words, if you forget to put an H after a number that you want the assembler to treat as hexadecimal, the assembler will treat it as a decimal number. The assembler automatically converts a decimal number in a statement to binary so the value can be loaded into memory. The statement TEMPERATURE_MAX DB 49 is an example. If you indicate a negative number in a data declaration statement, the assembler will convert the number to its 2's complement sign-and-magnitude form. For example, given the statement TEMP_MIN DB −20, the assembler will insert the value 11101100, which is the 2's complement representation for −20 decimal.

NOTE You can put a D after decimal values if you want to more clearly indicate that the value is decimal.

HEXADECIMAL

As shown in several previous examples, a hexadecimal number is indicated by an H after the hexadecimal digits. The statement MULTIPLIER DW 3B2AH is an example.

ASCII

ASCII characters can be put in data declaration statements by enclosing them in single quotation marks. The statement BOY_1 DB 'ALBERT', for example, tells the assembler to set aside six memory locations named BOY_1. It also tells the assembler to put the ASCII code for A in the first memory location, the ASCII code for L in the second, the ASCII code for B in the third, etc. The assembler will automatically determine the ASCII codes for the letters or numbers within the quotes.

NOTE ASCII can only be used with the DB directive.

DECIMAL REAL AND HEXADECIMAL REAL

These two types are used to represent noninteger numbers such as 3.14159. We will discuss how these are used in Chapter 11.

Accessing Named Data with Program Instructions

Now that we have shown you how the data structure is set up, let's look at how program instructions access this data. Temporarily skipping over the first two instructions in the CODE_HERE section of the program in Figure 3-10, find the instruction MOV AX, MULTIPLICAND. This instruction, when executed, will copy a word from memory to the AX register. When the assembler reads through this program the first time, it will automatically calculate the displacement of each of the named data items from the segment base DATA_HERE. Referring to Figure 3-11 you can see that the displacement of MULTIPLICAND from the segment base is 0000. This is because MULTIPLICAND is the first data item declared in the segment. The assembler, then, will find that the displacement of MULTIPLICAND is 0000H. When the assembler reads the program the second time to produce the binary codes for the instructions, it will insert this displacement as part of the binary code for the instruction MOV AX, MULTIPLICAND. Since we know that the displacement of MULTIPLICAND is 0000, we could have written the instruction as MOV AX, [0000]. However, there would be a problem if we later changed the program by adding another data item before MULTIPLICAND in DATA_HERE. The displacement of MULTIPLICAND would be changed. Therefore, we would have to remember to go through the entire program and correct the displacement in all instructions that access MULTIPLICAND. If you use a name to refer to each data item as shown, the assembler will automatically calculate the correct displacement of that data item for you and insert this displacement each time you refer to it in an instruction.

To summarize how this works, then, the instruction MOV AX, MULTIPLICAND is an example of direct addressing where the direct address or displacement within a segment is represented by a name. For instructions such as this, the assembler will automatically calculate the displacement of the named data item from the start of the segment and insert this value as part of the binary code for the instruction. When the instruction executes, the BIU will add the displacement contained in the instruction to the data segment base in DS. (Remember, the contents of DS are shifted 4 bit positions left before the displacement is added.) This addition produces the 20-bit physical address needed to address the data named MULTIPLICAND in memory.

The next instruction in the program in Figure 3-10 is another example of direct addressing using a named data item. The instruction MUL MULTIPLIER multiplies the word named MULTIPLIER in DATA_HERE times the word in the AX register. The low word of the result is left in the AX register, and the high word of the result is left in the DX register. When the assembler reads through this program the first time, it will find the displacement of MULTIPLIER in DATA_HERE is 0002H. When it reads through the program the second time it inserts this displacement as part of the binary code for the MUL instruction. When the MUL MULTIPLIER instruction executes, the BIU will add the displacement contained in the instruction to the data segment base in DS to address MULTIPLIER in memory.

The next instruction, MOV PRODUCT, AX, in the program in Figure 3-10 copies the low word of the result from AX to memory. The low byte of AX will be copied to a memory location named PRODUCT. The high byte of

AX will be copied to the next higher address which we can refer to as PRODUCT + 1.

The following instruction in the program, MOV PRODUCT + 2, DX, copies the high word of the multiplication result from DX to memory. When the assembler reads this instruction, it will add the indicated "2" to the displacement it calculated for PRODUCT and insert the result as part of the binary code for the instruction. Therefore, when the instruction executes, the low byte of DX will be copied to memory at a displacement of PRODUCT + 2. The high byte of DX will be copied to a memory location which we can refer to as PRODUCT + 3. Figure 3-11 shows how the two words of the product are put in memory. Note that the lower byte of a word is always put in the lower memory address.

This example program should show you that if you are using an assembler, names are a very convenient way of specifying the direct address of data in memory.

Naming Addresses—Labels

Names representing addresses are called *labels*. They are written in the label field of an instruction statement or a directive statement. One major use of labels is to represent the destination for jump and call instructions. Suppose, for example, we want the 8086 to jump back to some previous instruction over and over. Instead of computing the numerical address that we want to jump to, we put a label in front of the instruction we want to jump to and write the jump instruction as JMP label. Here is a specific example.

```
NEXT: IN   AL, 05H ; Get data sample form port 05H
      .            ; Process data value read in.
      .
      JMP NEXT     ; Get next data value and process
```

If you use a label to represent an address as shown in this example, the assembler will automatically calculate the address that needs to be put in the code for the jump instruction. The next two chapters show many examples of the use of labels with jump and call instructions.

Another example of using a name to represent an address is in the SEGMENT directive statement. The name DATA_HERE in the statement DATA_HERE SEGMENT, for example, represents the starting address of a segment named DATA_HERE. Later we show you how we use this name to initialize the data segment register. We will now discuss some other parts of the example program that you will need to use in your programs.

The ASSUME Directive

An 8086 program may have several logical segments which contain code, several that contain data, and several that can serve as a stack. However, at any given time the 8086 works directly with only four physical segments; a *code segment*, a *data segment*, a *stack segment*, and an *extra segment*. The ASSUME directive tells the assembler which logical segment to use for each of these physical segments at a given time.

In Figure 3-10, for example, the statement ASSUME CS:CODE_HERE, DS:DATA_HERE tells the assembler that the logical segment CODE_HERE contains the instruction statements for the program and should be treated as a code segment. It also tells the assembler that it should treat the logical segment DATA_HERE as the data segment for this program. In other words, the DS:DATA_HERE part of the statement tells the assembler that, for any instruction which refers to data in the data segment, that data will be found in the logical segment DATA_HERE. The ASSUME . . . DS:DATA_HERE, for example, tells the assembler that a named data item such as MULTIPLICAND is contained in the logical segment called DATA_HERE. Given this information, the assembler can construct the binary codes for the instruction. The displacement of MULTIPLICAND from the start of DATA_HERE will be inserted as part of the instruction by the assembler.

If you are using an assembler, you must use an ASSUME statement in your program. Also, if you are using the stack segment and the extra segment in your program, you must include terms in the statement to tell the assembler the name of the logical segment to use for the stack and the name of the logical segment to use for the extra segment. These additional terms might look like: SS:STACK_HERE, ES:EXTRA_HERE. As we will show later, you can put another ASSUME directive later in the program to tell the assembler to use different logical segments from that point on.

If the ASSUME directive is not completely clear to you at this point, don't worry. We show many more examples of its use thoroughout the rest of the book. We introduced the ASSUME directive here because you need to put it in your programs for most 8086 assemblers. You can use the assume statement in Figure 3-10 as a model of how to write this directive for your programs.

Initializing Segment Registers

The ASSUME directive tells the assembler the names of the logical segments to use as code segment, data segment, stack segment, and extra segment. The assembler uses displacements from the start of the specified logical segment to code out instructions. When the instructions are executed, the displacements in the instructions will be added to segment registers to produce the actual physical addresses. The assembler, however, cannot directly load the segment registers with the starting physical addresses of the segments.

The segment registers, other than the code segment register, must be initialized by program instructions before they are used to access data. The first two instructions of the example program in Figure 3-10 show how this is done for the data segment register. DATA_HERE in the first instruction represents the upper 16 bits of the starting address you give the segment DATA_HERE. Since the 8086 does not allow us to move this immediate number directly into the data segment register, we must first load it into one of the general-purpose registers and then copy it into the data segment register. MOV AX, DATA_HERE loads the upper 16 bits of the segment starting address into the AX register. MOV DS, AX copies this value from AX to the data segment register. This is the same operation we described for hand coding the example program in Figure 3-4, except that here we use the segment name instead of a number to refer to the segment base address. In this example we used the AX register to pass the value, but any 16-bit register other than a segment register can be used. If you are hand coding your programs, you can just insert the upper 16 bits of the 20-bit segment starting address in place of DATA_HERE in the instruction. For example, if in your particular system you decide to locate DATA_HERE at address 00300H, DS should be loaded with 0030H. If you are using an assembler, you can use the segment name to refer to its base address as shown in the example.

If you use the stack segment and the extra segment in a program, the stack segment register and the extra segment register must also be initialized by program instructions in the same way.

When the assembler reads through your assembly language program, it calculates the displacement of each named variable from the start of the logical segment that contains it. The assembler also keeps track of the displacement of each instruction code byte from the start of a logical segment. The CS:CODE_HERE part of the ASSUME statement in Figure 3-10 tells the assembler to calculate the displacements of the following instructions from the start of the logical segment CODE_HERE. In other words, it tells the assembler that, when this program is run, the code segment register will contain the upper 16-bits of the address where the logical segment CODE_HERE was located in memory. The instruction byte displacements that the assembler is keeping track of are the values that the 8086 will put in the instruction pointer, IP, to fetch each instruction byte.

There are several ways that the CS register can be loaded with the code segment base address and the instruction pointer can be loaded with the displacement of the instruction byte to be fetched next. The first way is with the command you give your system to execute a program starting at a given address. A typical command of this sort is G = 0010:0000 <CR>. (<CR> means "press the return key.") This command will load CS with 0010 and load IP with 0000. The 8086 will then fetch and execute instructions starting from address 00100, the address produced when the BIU shifts CS and adds IP. The other ways of loading CS and IP will be discussed in later sections.

The END Directive

The END directive, as the name implies, tells the assembler to stop reading. Any instructions or statements that you write after an END directive will be ignored.

ASSEMBLY LANGUAGE PROGRAM DEVELOPMENT TOOLS

Introduction

For all but the very simplest assembly language programs you will probably want to use some type of *microcomputer development system* and *program development tools* to make your work easier. These systems usually contain several hundred Kbytes of RAM, a keyboard and video display, floppy and/or hard disk drives, a printer, and an emulator. Figure 3-12 shows an Applied Microsystems ES 1800 16-bit emulator which can be added to an IBM PC/AT or compatible computer to produce a complete 8086/80186/80286 development system. The following sections give you an introduction to several common program development tools which you use with these systems. Most of these tools are programs which you run to perform some function on the program you are writing. You will have to consult the manuals for your system to get the specific details for it, but this section should give you an overview of the steps involved in developing an assembly language microcomputer program using a system. An accompanying lab manual steps you through the use of all these tools with the SDK-86 board and the IBM Personal Computer.

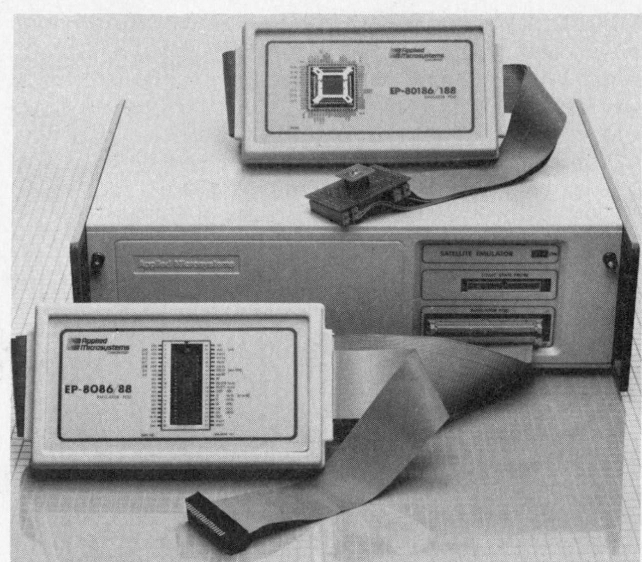

FIGURE 3-12 Applied Microsystems ES 1800 16-bit emulator. *(Applied Microsystems Corp.)*

Editor

An editor is a program which, when run on a system, lets you type in the assembly language statements for your program. Examples of editors are ALTER which runs on Intel systems, EDLIN which runs on IBM PCs, and Wordstar which runs on most systems. The main function of an editor is to help you construct your assembly language program in just the right format so that the assembler will translate it correctly to machine language. Figure 3-10 shows an example of the format you should use when typing in your program. This form of your program is called the *source program*. The actual position of each field on a line is not important, but you must put the fields of each statement in the correct order, and you must leave at least one blank between fields. Whenever possible, we like to line the fields up in columns so that it is easier to read the program.

As you type in your program, the editor stores the ASCII codes for the letters and numbers in successive

RAM locations. If you make a typing error the editor will let you back up and correct it. If you leave out a program statement, the editor will let you move everything down and insert the line. This is much easier than working with pencil and paper, even if you type as slowly as I do.

When you have typed in all of your program, you then copy it from memory to a file on a floppy or hard magnetic disk. This file, such as the one in Figure 3-10, is called a *source file*. If you later find that your program contains errors, you can use the editor to load the source file back into RAM and make the needed corrections in the source program.

Assembler

An *assembler* program is used to translate assembly language mnemonics to the correct binary code for each instruction. The assembler will read the source file of your program from the disk where you saved it after editing. An assembler usually reads your source file more than once. On the first pass through the source program, the assembler finds everything. It determines the displacement of named data items and the offset of labels, and puts this information in a *symbol table*. On a second pass through the source program, the assembler produces the binary code for each instruction and assigns addresses to each.

The assembler generates two files on the floppy or hard disk. The first file is called the *object file*. The object file contains the binary codes for the instructions and information about the addresses of the instructions. This file contains the information that will eventually be loaded into memory and executed. The second file generated by the assembler is called the *assembler list file*. Figure 3-13 shows the assembler list file for the source program in Figure 3-10. This file contains the assembly language statements, the binary codes for each instruction, and the offset for each instruction. You usually send this file to a printer so that you will have a printout of the entire program to work with when you are testing and troubleshooting the program. The assembler listing will also indicate any typing or syntax (assembly language grammar) errors you made in typing in your source program.

NOTE The assembler will not tell you if you made a programming error. You usually have to run the program to find these. To correct the errors indicated on the listing, you use the editor to reedit your source program and save the corrected source program on disk. You then reassemble the corrected source program. It may take several times through the edit-assemble loop before you get all of the syntax errors out of your source program.

Now let's take a look at some of the information given on the assembler listing. The left-most column in the listing gives the offsets of data items from the start of the data segment and the offsets of code bytes from the start of the code segment. Note that the assembler does not generate absolute physical addresses. A linker or locator will do this later. Also note that the MOV AX, DATA_HERE statement is assembled with some blanks after the basic instruction code because the start of DS is not known at the time the program is assembled.

The trailer section of the listing in Figure 3-13 gives some additional information about the segments and names used in the program. The statement CODE_HERE 0014 PARA NONE, for example, tells you that the segment CODE_HERE is 14H bytes long and will be located at a physical address whose lower 4 bits are 0000. The statement MULTIPLIER . . . . L WORD 0002 DATA_HERE tells you that MULTIPLIER is a variable of type word and that it is located at an offset of 0002 in the segment DATA_HERE.

Linker

A *linker* is a program used to join together several object files into one large object file. When writing large programs it is usually much more efficient to divide the large program into smaller *modules*. Each module can be individually written, tested, and debugged. When all of the modules work they can be linked together to form a large functioning program. Also, the object modules for useful programs, a square root program, for example, can be kept in a *library file* and linked into other programs as needed.

The linker produces a *link file* which contains the binary codes for all the combined modules. The linker also produces a *link map* file which contains the address information about the linked files. The linker, however, does not assign absolute addresses to the program, it only assigns relative addresses starting from zero. This form of the program is said to be *relocatable*, because it can be put anywhere in memory to be run. If you are going to run your program on a system such as the IBM PC, you can just load the link file into memory and run it. If you are going to run your program on a system such as the Intel Series IV, then you must use a *locator program* to assign absolute addresses to the linker file.

Locator

A *locator* is a program used to assign the specific addresses of where the object code is to be loaded into memory. A locator program that comes with the IBM PC Disk Operating System (DOS) is called EXE2BIN. Here's how you proceed if you want to produce a program with absolute addresses that you can download to an SDK-86 from an IBM PC. First build a source (.ASM) file using  the EDLIN or perhaps the WORDSTAR editor. Assemble the source file with the IBM PC Macroassembler (MASM)  to produce the .OBJ file. Use the LINK program to produce a relocatable .EXE file. Then use the EXE2BIN program to give your program an absolute starting address such as 0010:0000H. Finally, use the SDKDMP program from Chapter 13 to download the .BIN file produced by EXE2BIN and run it. In some systems a single program performs both the link and the locate functions.

Debugger

If your program requires no external hardware or requires only hardware accessible directly from your system, then you can use a *debugger* to run and debug your program. A debugger is a program which allows you to load your object code program into system mem-

```
The IBM Personal Computer MACRO Assembler 03-06-85      PAGE    1-1
                                 PAGE ,132        ; Makes listing file lines 132 characters wide
                                 ;8086 program
                                 ;ABSTRACT        : This program multiplies the two 16-bit words in
                                                  ; the memory locations called MULTIPLICAND and
                                                  ; MULTIPLIER. The result is stored in the memory
                                                  ; location called PRODUCT
                                 ;PORTS USED      : None
                                 ;PROCEDURES USED: None
                                 ;REGISTERS USED : CS, DS, DX and AX

0000                             DATA_HERE        SEGMENT

0000  204A                       MULTIPLICAND     DW      204AH           ; first word here
0002  3B2A                       MULTIPLIER       DW      3B2AH           ; second word here
0004     02 [                    PRODUCT          DW      2 DUP(0)        ; result here
               0000
                        ]

0008                             DATA_HERE        ENDS

0000                             CODE_HERE        SEGMENT
                                                  ASSUME CS : CODE_HERE, DS : DATA_HERE

0000  B8  ---- R                                  MOV AX, DATA_HERE       ; initialize DS register
0003  8E D8                                       MOV DS,AX

0005  A1 0000 R                                   MOV AX, MULTIPLICAND    ; get one word
0008  F7 26 0002 R                                MUL MULTIPLIER          ; multiply by second word
000C  A3 0004 R                                   MOV PRODUCT, AX         ; store low word of result
000F  89 16 0006 R                                MOV PRODUCT+2, DX       ; store high word of result
0013  CC                                          INT 3                   ; wait for command from user

0014                             CODE_HERE        ENDS
                                                  END

The IBM Personal Computer MACRO Assembler 03-06-85      PAGE    Symbols-1

Segments and groups:

            N a m e                    Size    align   combine class

CODE_HERE. . . . . . . . . . . .       0014    PARA    NONE
DATA_HERE. . . . . . . . . . . .       0008    PARA    NONE

Symbols:
            N a m e                    Type    Value   Attr

MULTIPLICAND . . . . . . . . . .       L WORD  0000    DATA_HERE
MULTIPLIER . . . . . . . . . . .       L WORD  0002    DATA_HERE
PRODUCT. . . . . . . . . . . . .       L WORD  0004    DATA_HERE       Length =0002

Warning Severe
Errors  Errors
0       0
```

FIGURE 3-13 Assembler listing for example program in Figure 3-10.

ory, execute the program, and troubleshoot or "debug" it. The debugger allows you to look at the contents of registers and memory locations after your program runs. It allows you to change the contents of registers and memory locations and rerun the program. Some debuggers allow you stop execution after each instruction so you can check or alter memory and register contents. A debugger also allows you to set a *breakpoint* at any point in your program. When you run the program the system will execute instructions up to this breakpoint and stop. You can then examine register and memory contents to see if the results are correct at that point. If the results are correct, you can move the breakpoint to a later point in the program. If the results are not correct, you can check the program up to that point to find out why they are not correct. The debugger tools can help you isolate a problem in your program. Once you find the problem, you can then cycle back and correct the algorithm if necessary. You then use the editor to correct your source program, reassemble the corrected source program, relink, and run the program again.

Microprocessor prototyping boards such as the SDK-86 contain a debugger program in ROM. On boards such as this the debugger is commonly called a *monitor program* because it lets you monitor program activity. The SDK-86 monitor program, for example, lets you enter and run programs, single step through programs, examine register and memory contents, and insert breakpoints. The DEBUG program, used with the IBM PC, allows you to do the same functions and also has a trace function which shows you the contents of all the registers after each instruction executes.

Emulator

Another way to run your program is with an *emulator*. An emulator is a mixture of hardware and software. It is usually used to test and debug the hardware and software of an external system such as the prototype of a microprocessor-based instrument. Part of the hardware of an emulator is a multiwire cable which connects the host system to the system being developed. A plug at the end of the cable is plugged into the prototype in place of its microprocessor. Through this connection the software of the emulator allows you to download your object-code program into RAM in the system being tested and run it. As with a debugger, an emulator allows you to load and run programs, examine and change the contents of registers, examine and change the contents of memory locations, and insert breakpoints in the program. The emulator also takes a "snapshot" of the contents of registers, activity on the address and data bus, and the state of the flags as each instruction executes. The emulator stores this *trace data*, as it is called, in a large RAM. You can do a printout of the trace data to see the results that your program produced on a step-by-step basis.

Another powerful feature of an emulator is the ability to use either system memory or the memory on the prototype for the program you are debugging. In a later chapter we discuss in detail the use of an emulator in developing a microprocessor-based product.

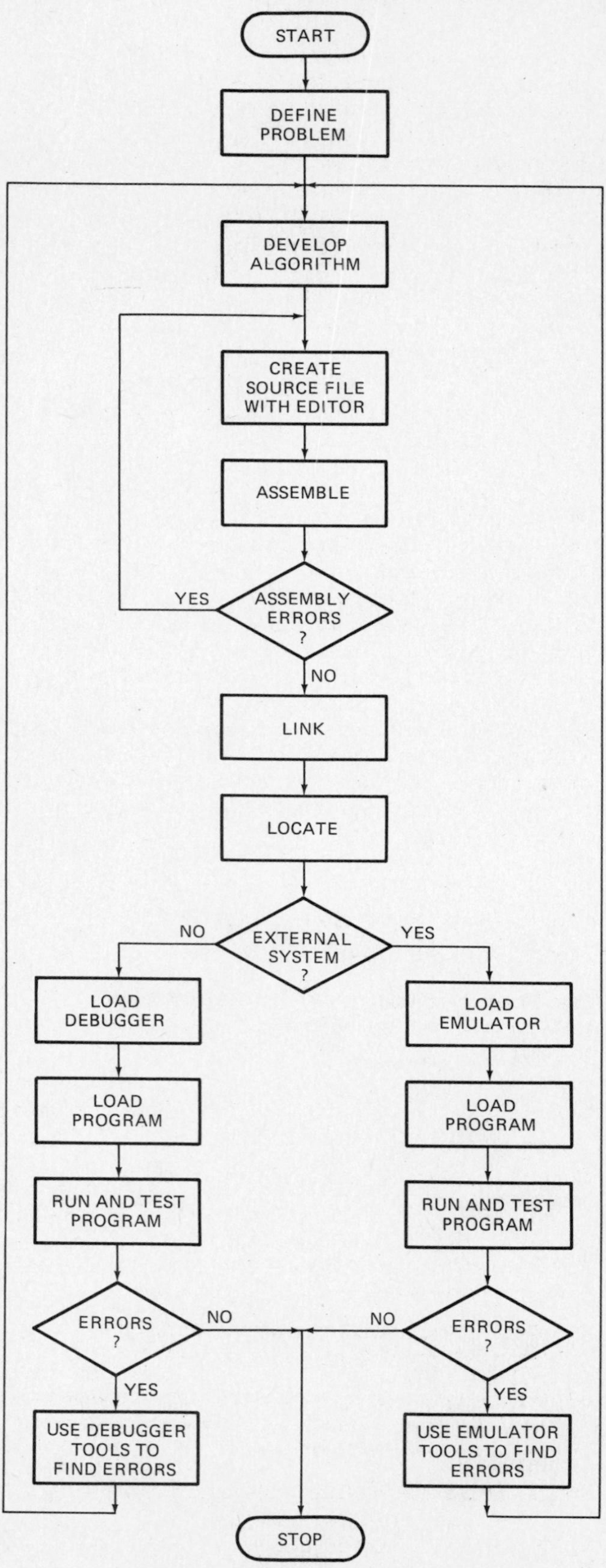

FIGURE 3-14 Program development algorithm.

Summary of the Use of Program Development Tools

Figure 3-14 shows in diagram form the order in which you will use the program development tools we have described. The first and most important step is to think out very carefully what you want the program to do and how you want the program to do it. Next, use an editor to create the source file for your program. Assemble the source file with the assembler. If the assembler list file indicates any errors in your program, use the editor to correct these errors. Cycle through the edit-assemble loop until the assembler tells you on the listing that it found no errors. If your program consists of several modules, then use the linker to join their object modules together into one large object module.

NOTE On some systems such as the IBM PC you must use the linker even if your program has only one module.

Now, if your system requires it, use the locate program to specify where in memory you want your program to be put. Your program is now ready to be loaded into memory and run. If your program does not interact with any external hardware other than that connected directly to the system, then you can use the system debugger to run and debug your program. If your program is intended to work with external hardware such as the prototype of a microprocessor-based instrument, then you will probably use an emulator to run and debug your program. We will be discussing and showing the use of these program development tools throughout the rest of this book, but this section should give you an overview.

CHECKLIST OF IMPORTANT TERMS AND CONCEPTS IN THIS CHAPTER

If you do not remember any of the terms or concepts in the following list, use the index to find them in the chapter.

Algorithm

Sequential task list

Flowcharts and flowchart symbols

Structured programming

Pseudocode

Top-down and bottom-up design

Sequence, repetition, and decision operations

IF—THEN—ELSE, IF—THEN, WHILE—DO, REPEAT—UNTIL, and CASE structures

8086 instruction types

Mnemonics

Initialization list

Standard program format

Documentation

Instruction template: W-bit, MOD, R/M, D-bit

Segment-override prefix

Assembler

Assembler directives: SEGMENT, ENDS, END, DB, DW, DD, EQU, ASSUME

Named data items

Development tools

Editor

Linker: library file, link files, link map, relocatable

Locator

Debugger, monitor program

Emulator, trace data

REVIEW QUESTIONS AND PROBLEMS

1. List the major steps in developing an assembly language program.

2. What is the main advantage of a top-down design approach to solving a programming problem?

3. Why is it necessary to develop a detailed algorithm for a program before writing down any assembly language instructions?

4. *a.* What are the three basic structure types used when writing programs?
b. What is the advantage of using only these structures when writing the algorithm for a program?

5. A program is like a recipe. Use a flowchart or pseudocode to show the algorithm for the following recipe. The operations in it are sequence and repetition. Instead of implementing the resulting algorithm in assembly language, implement it in your microwave and use the result to help you get through the rest of the book.

Peanut Brittle:

1	cup sugar	1 teaspoon butter
0.5	cup white corn syrup	1 teaspoon vanilla
1	cup unsalted peanuts	1 teaspoon baking soda

i. Put sugar and syrup in 1.5 quart casserole (with handle) and stir until thoroughly mixed.

ii. Microwave at HIGH setting for 4 minutes.
iii. Add peanuts and stir until thoroughly mixed.
iv. Microwave at HIGH setting for 4 minutes. Add butter and vanilla, stir until well mixed and microwave at HIGH setting for 2 more minutes.
v. Add baking soda and gently stir until light and foamy. Pour mixture onto nonstick cookie sheet and let cool for 1 hour. When cool, break into pieces. Makes 1 pound.

6. Use a flowchart or pseudocode to show the algorithm for a program which gets a number from a memory location, subtracts 20H from it, and outputs 01H to port 3AH if the result of the subtraction is greater than 25H.

7. Given the register contents in Figure 3-15, answer the following questions:
a. What physical address will the next instruction be fetched from?
b. What is the physical address for the top of the stack?

8. Describe the operation and results of each of the following instructions, given the register contents shown in Figure 3-15. Include in your answer the physical address or register that each instruction will get its operands from and the physical address or register that each instruction will put the result. Use the instruction descriptions in Chapter 6 to help you. Assume that the instructions below are independent, not sequential unless listed together under a letter.

a. MOV AX, BX
b. MOV CL, 37H
c. INC BX
d. MOV CX, [246BH]
e. MOV CX, 246BH
f. ADD AL, DH
g. MUL BX
h. DEC BP
i. DIV BL
j. SUB AX, DX
k. OR CL, BL
l. NOT AH
m. ROL BX, 1
n. AND AL, CH
o. MOV DS, AX
p. ROR BX, CL
q. AND AL, 0FH
r. MOV AX, [BX]
s. MOV [BX][SI], CL

9. See if you can spot the grammatical (SYNTAX) errors in the following instructions (use Chapter 6 to help you):

a. MOV BH, AX
b. MOV DX, CL
c. ADD AL, 2073H
d. MOV 7632H, CX
e. IN BL, 04H

10. Show the results that will be in the affected registers or memory locations after each of the following groups of instructions execute. Assume that each group of instructions starts with the register and memory contents shown in Figure 3-15. (Use Chapter 6.)

a. ADD BL, AL
MOV [0004], BL
b. MOV CL, 04
ROR DI. CL
c. MOV BX, 000AH
MOV AL, [BX]
SUB AL, CL
INC BX
MOV [BX], AL
d. ADD AL, BH
DAA

ES	6000	
CS	4000	
SS	7000	
DS	5000	
IP	43E8	
	AH	AL
AX	42	35
	BH	BL
BX	07	5A
	CH	CL
CX	00	04
	DH	DL
DX	33	02
SP	0000	
BP	2468	
SI	4C00	
DI	7D00	

DATA SEGMENT	
5000CH	D7
5000BH	9A
5000AH	7C
50009H	DB
50008H	C3
50007H	B2
50006H	49
50005H	21
50004H	89
50003H	71
50002H	22
50001H	4A
50000H	3B

FIGURE 3-15 8086 register and memory contents for Problems 7, 8, and 10.

11. Write the 8086 instruction which will perform the indicated operation. Use the instruction overview in this chapter and the detailed descriptions in Chapter 6 to help you.

a. Copies AL to BL
b. Loads 43H into CL
c. Increments the contents of CX by one
d. Copies SP to BP
e. Adds 07H to DL
f. Multiplies AL times BL
g. Copies AX to a memory location at offset 245AH in the data segment
h. Decrements SP by one
i. Rotates the most significant bit of AL into the least-significant bit position
j. Copies DL to a memory location whose offset is in BX
k. Masks the lower 4 bits of BL
l. Sets the most significant bit of AX to a one but does not affect the other bits
m. Inverts the lower 4 bits of BL but does not affect the other bits.

12. Construct the binary code for each of the following 8086 instructions.

a. MOV BL, AL
b. MOV [BX], CX
c. ADD BX, 59H[DI]
d. SUB [2048], DH
e. XCHG CH, ES:[BX]
f. ROR AX, 1
g. OUT DX, AL
h. AND AL, 0FH
i. NOP
j. IN AL, DX

13. Describe the function of each assembler directive and instruction statement in the short program shown below these review problems.

14. Describe how an assembly language program is developed and debugged using system tools such as editors, assemblers, linkers, locators, emulators, and debuggers.

15. Write the pseudocode representation for the flowchart in Figure 3-14.

```
;     pressure read program
DATA_HERE SEGMENT
       PRESSURE  DB    0          ;storage for pressure
DATA_HERE ENDS
PRESSURE_PORT  EQU  04H           ;pressure sensor connected
                                  ;to port 04H
CORRECTION_FACTOR   EQU  07H  ;current correction factor, 07
CODE_HERE SEGMENT
     ASSUME     CS:CODE_HERE, DS:DATA_HERE
     MOV  AX, DATA_HERE
     MOV  DS, AX
     IN   AL, PRESSURE_PORT
     ADD  AL, CORRECTION_FACTOR
     MOV  PRESSURE, AL
CODE_HERE ENDS
          END
```

CHAPTER

4 8086 Assembly Language Programming Techniques—Part 1

The purposes of this chapter are to show you how some of the standard program structures described in the last chapter are implemented in 8086 assembly language, how these structures are used to solve some common programming problems, and how some of the 8086 instructions work.

OBJECTIVES

At the conclusion of this chapter you should be able to:

1. Write flowcharts or pseudocode for simple programming problems.
2. Implement WHILE—DO and REPEAT—UNTIL program structures in 8086 assembly language.
3. Describe the operation of selected data transfer, arithmetic, logical, jump, loop, and string instructions.
4. Use based and indexed addressing modes to access data in your programs.
5. Describe a systematic approach to debugging a simple assembly language program using debugger, monitor, or emulator tools.

MORE PRACTICE WITH SIMPLE SEQUENCE PROGRAMS

Finding the Average of Two Numbers

DEFINING THE PROBLEM AND WRITING THE ALGORITHM

A common need in programming is to find the average of two numbers. Suppose, for example, we know the maximum temperature of a day and the minimum temperature of a day, and we want to determine the average temperature. The sequence of steps we go through to do this might look something like the following.

Add maximum temperature and minimum temperature.

Divide sum by two to get average temperature.

This sequence doesn't look much like an assembly language program and it shouldn't. The algorithm at this point should be general enough that it could be implemented in any programming language, or on any machine. Once you are reasonably sure of your algorithm, then you can start thinking about the architecture and instructions of the specific microcomputer on which you plan to run the program. Now let's show you how we get from the algorithm to the assembly language program for it.

SETTING UP THE DATA STRUCTURE

One of the first things for you to think about in this process is the data that the program will be working with. You need to ask yourself questions such as:

1. Will the data be in memory or in registers?
2. Is the data of type byte, type word, or perhaps type doubleword?
3. How many data items are there?
4. Does the data represent only positive numbers, or does it represent positive and negative (signed) numbers?
5. For more complex problems you might ask how the data is structured. For example, is the data in an array or in a record?

Let's assume for this example that the data is all in memory, the data is of type byte, and that the data represents only positive numbers in the range 0 to 0FFH. The top part of Figure 4-1, between the DATA_HERE SEGMENT and the DATA_HERE ENDS directives, shows how you might set up the data structure for this program. It is very similar to the data structure for the multiply example in the last chapter. In the logical segment called

```
;8086 PROGRAM
;ABSTRACT        : this program averages two temperatures
;                  named  HI_TEMP and LO_TEMP and puts the
;                  result in the memory location AV_TEMP.
;REGISTERS USED: DS, CS, AX, BX
;PORTS USED      : None used
;PROCEDURES      : None used

DATA_HERE       SEGMENT

HI_TEMP         DB      92H         ; max temp storage
LO_TEMP         DB      52H         ; low temp storage
AV_TEMP         DB      ?           ; put average here

DATA_HERE       ENDS

CODE_HERE       SEGMENT
                ASSUME CS : CODE_HERE, DS : DATA_HERE

        MOV     AX, DATA_HERE       ; initialize data segment
        MOV     DS, AX
        MOV     AL, HI_TEMP         ; get first temperature
        ADD     AL, LO_TEMP         ; add second to it
        MOV     AH, 00H             ; clear all of AH register
        ADC     AH, 00H             ; put carry in LSB of AH
        MOV     BL, 02H             ; load divisor in BL register
        DIV     BL                  ; divide AX by BL
                                    ; quotient in AL,
                                    ; remainder in AH
        MOV     AV_TEMP, AL         ; copy result to memory

CODE_HERE       ENDS
                END
```

FIGURE 4-1 8086 program to average two temperatures.

DATA_HERE, HI_TEMP is declared as a variable of type byte and initialized with a value of 92H. In an actual application, the value in HI_TEMP would probably be put there by another program which reads the output from a temperature sensor. The statement LO_TEMP DB 52H declares a variable of type byte and initializes it with the value 52H. The statement AV_TEMP DB ? sets aside a byte location to store the average temperature, but does not initialize the location to any value. When the program executes, it will write a value to this location.

INITIALIZATION CHECKLIST

Now that you have the data structure set up, let's start thinking about the instructions that we can use to perform the actions we want on this data. Although it does not show in the algorithm, we know from a discussion in Chapter 3 that we should start the program with a list of initialization instructions. Start by putting this checklist at the top of the paper. At this point you may not know exactly which parts on the checklist will have to be initialized, but the presence of the list will remind you that it has to be done. For this example program the only part you have to initialize is the data segment register.

CHOOSING INSTRUCTIONS

Next look at the major actions that you want the program to perform other than moving data from one place to another. You want the program to add two byte-type numbers together, so scan through the instruction groups in Chapter 3 to determine which 8086 instruction will do this for you. The ADD instruction is the obvious choice in this case. Now find and read the detailed discussion of this instruction in Chapter 6. From this discussion you can determine how the instruction works and see if it will do the necessary job. From the discussion of the ADD instruction you should find that the ADD instruction has the format ADD destination, source. A byte from the specified source is added to a byte in the specified destination, or a word from the specified source is added to a word in the specified destination. (Note that you cannot directly add a byte to a word.) The result in either case is put in the specified destination. The source can be an immediate number, a register, or a memory location. The destination can be a register or a memory location. The source and the destination cannot both be memory locations in an instruction. This means that you have to move one of the operands from memory to a register before you can do the ADD. Another point to consider here is that if you add two 8-bit numbers, the sum can be larger than 8 bits. Adding F0H and 40H, for example, gives 130H. The 8-bit destination will contain 30H, and the carry will be held in the carry flag. What this means is that you must collect the parts of the result in a location large enough to hold all 9 bits. A 16-bit register is a good choice. To summarize then, you need to move one of the numbers you want to add into a register such as AL, add the other number from memory to it, and move any carry produced by the addition to the upper half of the 16-bit register containing the result (which is in AL).

Now let's see how you can do this with program instructions. Take a look now at the first six instruction statements of the example program in Figure 4-1. As explained in the last chapter, the first two instructions, MOV AX, DATA_HERE and MOV DS, AX, are required to initialize the data segment register. These instructions load the DS register with the upper 16 bits of the starting address for the data segment. If you are using an assembler, you can use the name DATA_HERE in the instruction to refer to this address. If you are not using an assembler, then just put the hex for the upper 16 bits of the address in the MOV AX, DATA_HERE instruction in place of the name.

The next instruction in the example program in Figure 4-1, MOV AL, HI_TEMP, copies one of the temperatures from a memory location to the AL register. The name HI_TEMP in the instruction represents the direct address or displacement of the variable in the logical segment DATA_HERE. The ADD AL, LO_TEMP instruction adds a byte from memory to the contents of the AL register. The result of the addition (sum) is left in the AL register.

Now that we have done the addition, the next thing to do is get the carry bit where we want it. We would like to get the contents of the carry flag into the least significant bit of the AH register. The MOV AH, 00H instruction clears all of the bits of AH to 0's. The ADC AH, 00H instruction adds the immediate number 00H plus the contents of the carry flag to the contents of the AH register. The result will be left in the AH register. Since we cleared AH to all 0's before the add, what we are really adding is 00H + 00H + CF. The result of all this is that the carry bit ends up in the least-significant bit of AH, which is what we set out to do.

The next major action in our algorithm is to divide the sum of the two temperatures by two. Look at the instruction groups in the last chapter to see if the 8086 has a divide instruction. You should find that it has two divide instructions, DIV and IDIV. DIV is for dividing unsigned numbers, and IDIV is used for dividing signed binary numbers. Since in this example we are dividing unsigned binary numbers, look up the DIV instruction in Chapter 6 to find out how it works. The DIV instruction can be used to divide a 16-bit number in AX by a specified byte in a register or in a memory location. After the division an 8-bit quotient is left in the AL register and an 8-bit remainder is left in the AH register. The DIV instruction can also be used to divide a 32-bit number in the DX and AX registers by a 16-bit number from a specified register or memory location. In this case a 16-bit quotient is left in the AX register, and a 16-bit remainder is left in the DX register. In either case there is a problem if the quotient is too large to fit in the indicated destination. In a later chapter we discuss what to do about this problem. Fortunately, for the example here the data is such that the problem will not arise.

As you can see, we already have the sum of the two temperatures already positioned in the AX register, ready for the DIV operation. Before we can do the DIV operation, however, we have to get the divisor, 02H, into a register or memory location to satisfy the requirements of the DIV instruction. A simple way to do this is with the MOV BL, 02H instruction, which loads the immediate number 02H into the BL register. Now we can do the divide operation with the instruction DIV BL. The 8-bit quotient from the division will be left in the AL register. All we have left to do is to copy the quotient to the memory location we set aside for the average temperature. The instruction MOV AV_TEMP, AL will copy AL to this memory location. Take another look at Figure 4-1 to see how these instructions are added on to the previous instructions.

NOTE: We could have used the remainder in AH to round off the average temperature, but that would have made the program more complex than desired for this example.

SUMMARY OF CONVERTING AN ALGORITHM TO ASSEMBLY LANGUAGE

A first step in converting an algorithm to assembly language is to set up and declare the data structure that the algorithm will be working with. Then write down the instructions required for initialization at the start of the code section. Next determine the instructions required to implement the major actions in the algorithm, and decide how the data must be positioned for these instructions. Finally, insert the MOV or other instructions required to get the data in the correct position.

A Few Comments about the 8086 Arithmetic Instructions

The 8086 has instructions to add, subtract, multiply, and divide. It can operate on signed or unsigned binary numbers, BCD numbers, or numbers represented in ASCII. Rather than put a lot of arithmetic examples at this point in the book, we show arithmetic examples with each arithmetic instruction description in Chapter 6. The description of the MUL instruction in Chapter 6, for example, shows how unsigned binary numbers are multiplied. Also we show other arithmetic examples as needed throughout the rest of the book. If you need to do some arithmetic operations on the 8086 there are a few instructions in addition to the basic add, subtract, multiply, and divide instructions that you need to look up in Chapter 6.

If you are adding BCD numbers, you need to also look up the Decimal Adjust for Addition (DAA) instruction. If you are subtracting BCD numbers, then you need to look up the Decimal Adjust for Subtraction (DAS) instruction. If you are working with ASCII numbers, then you need to look up the ASCII Adjust after Addition (AAA) instruction, the ASCII Adjust after Subtraction (AAS) instruction, the ASCII Adjust after Multiply (AAM) instruction, and the ASCII Adjust before Division (AAD) instruction.

Converting Two ASCII Number Codes to Packed BCD

DEFINING THE PROBLEM AND WRITING THE ALGORITHM

If you type a 9 on an ASCII-encoded computer terminal keyboard, the 8-bit ASCII code sent to the computer will be 00111001 binary, or 39H. If you type a 5 on the keyboard, the code sent to the computer will be 00110101 binary or 35H, the ASCII code for 5. The ASCII codes for the numbers 0 through 9 are 30H through 39H. As you can see, the lower nibble of the ASCII codes contains the 4-bit BCD code for the number represented by the ASCII code. For many applications we want to convert the ASCII code coming in from the terminal to its simple BCD equivalent. We can do this by simply replacing the 3 in the upper nibble of the byte with four 0's. For example, suppose we read in 00111001 binary or 39H, the ASCII code for 9. If we replace the upper 4 bits with 0's, we are left with 00001001 binary or 09H. The lower 4 bits contain 1001 binary, the BCD code for 9. Numbers represented as one BCD digit per byte are referred to as *unpacked BCD*. If two BCD digits are put in a byte, this form is referred to as *packed BCD*. Figure 4-2 shows examples of ASCII, unpacked BCD, and packed BCD. When we want to store BCD numbers in memory the packed form is obviously more efficient because it has two BCD digits in each byte memory location. The problem we are going to work on here is how to convert two numbers from ASCII code form to unpacked BCD and then pack the two BCD digits into one byte. Figure 4-2 shows the steps in numerical form.

The algorithm for this problem can be stated simply as:

Convert first ASCII number to unpacked BCD.

Convert second ASCII number to unpacked BCD.

Move first BCD nibble to upper nibble position in byte.

Pack two BCD nibbles in one byte.

Now let's see how you can implement this algorithm in 8086 assembly language.

THE DATA STRUCTURE AND INITIALIZATION LIST

For this example program let's assume that the first ASCII code entered is in the BL register, and the second ASCII code entered is in the AL register. Since we are not using memory for data in this program, we do not need to declare a data segment. Also then we do not need to initialize the data segment register. In a real application this program would probably be a procedure or a part of a larger program.

MASKING WITH THE AND INSTRUCTION

The first operation in the algorithm is to convert a number in ASCII form to its unpacked BCD equivalent. This is done by replacing the upper 4 bits of the ASCII byte with four 0's. The 8086 AND instruction can be used to do this operation. Remember from basic logic or from the review in Chapter 1 that, when a 1 or a 0 is ANDed with a 0, the result is always a zero. ANDing a bit with a 0 is called *masking* that bit, because the previous state of the bit is hidden or masked. To mask 4 bits in a word, then, all you do is AND each bit you want to mask with a 0. A bit ANDed with a 1, remember, is not changed.

```
ASCII                     5     0011 0101  =   35H
ASCII                     9     0011 1001  =   39H

UNPACKED BCD              5     0000 0101  =   05H
UNPACKED BCD              9     0000 1001  =   09H

UNPACKED BCD              5     0101 0000  =   50H
moved to upper nibble
PACKED BCD                59    0101 1001  =   59H
```

FIGURE 4-2 ASCII, UNPACKED BCD, and PACKED BCD examples.

ASCII 5	0 0 1 1	0 1 0 1
MASK	0 0 0 0	1 1 1 1
RESULT	0 0 0 0	0 1 0 1

FIGURE 4-3 Effects of ANDing with 1's and 0's.

According to the description of the AND instruction in Chapter 6, the instruction has the format AND destination, source. The instruction ANDs each bit of the specified source with the corresponding bit of the specified destination and puts the result in the specified destination. The source can be an immediate number, a register, or a memory location specified in one of those 24 different ways. The destination can be a register or a memory location. The source and the destination must both be bytes, or they must both be words. The source and the destination cannot both be memory locations in an instruction.

For this example the first ASCII number is in the BL register, so we can just AND an immediate number with this register to mask the desired bits. The upper 4 bits of the immediate number should be 0's because these correspond to the bits we want to mask in BL. The lower 4 bits of the immediate number should be 1's because we want to leave these bits unchanged. The immediate number then should be 00001111 binary or 0FH. The instruction to convert the first ASCII number is AND BL, 0FH. When this instruction executes, it will leave the desired unpacked BCD in BL. Figure 4-3 shows how this will work for an ASCII number of 35H initially in BL.

For the next action in the algorithm we want to perform the same operation on a second ASCII number in the AL register. The instruction AND AL, 0FH will do this for us. After this instruction executes AL will contain the unpacked BCD for the second ASCII number.

MOVING A NIBBLE WITH THE ROTATE INSTRUCTION

The next action in the algorithm is to move the 4 BCD bits in the first unpacked BCD byte to the upper nibble position in the byte. We need to do this so that the 4 BCD bits are in the correct position for packing with the second BCD nibble. Take another look at Figure 4-2 to help you visualize this. What we are effectively doing here is swapping or exchanging the top nibble with the bottom nibble of the byte. If you check the instruction groups in Chapter 3 you will find that the 8086 has an exchange instruction, XCHG, which can be used to swap two bytes or to swap two words. The 8086 does not have a specific instruction to swap the nibbles in a byte. However, if you think of the operation that we need to do as shifting or rotating the BCD bits four bit positions to the left, this will give you a good idea which instruction will do the job for you. The 8086 has a wide variety of rotate and shift instructions. For now let's look at the rotate instructions. There are two instructions, ROL and RCL, which rotate the bits of a specified operand to the left. Figure 4-4 shows in diagram form how these two work. For ROL each bit in the specified register or memory location is rotated one bit position to the left. The bit that was the MSB is rotated around into the LSB position. The old MSB is also copied to the carry flag. For the RCL instruction each bit of the specified register or memory location is also rotated one bit position to the left. However, the bit that was in the MSB position is moved to the carry flag, and the bit that was in the carry flag is moved into the LSB position. As indicated by the C in the middle of the mnemonic, the carry flag is in the rotated loop when the RCL instruction executes.

In the example program we really don't want the contents of the carry flag rotated into our operand, so the ROL instruction seems to be the one we want. If you consult the ROL instruction description in Chapter 6, you will find that the instruction has the format ROL destination, count. The destination can be a register or a memory location. It can be a byte location or a word location. The count can be the immediate number 1 specified directly in the instruction, or the count can be a number previously loaded into the CL register. The instruction ROL AL,1 for example will rotate the contents of AL one bit position to the left. We could repeat this instruction four times to produce the shift of four bit positions we need for our BCD packing problem. However, there is an easier way to do it. We first load the CL register with the number of times we want to rotate AL. The instruction MOV CL, 04H will do this. Then we use the instruction ROL BL, CL to do the rotation. When it executes, this instruction will automatically rotate BL the number of bit positions loaded into CL. Note that for the 80186 you can write the single instruction ROL BL, 04H to do this job.

Now that we have determined the instructions needed to mask the upper nibbles and the instructions necessary to move the first BCD digit into position, the only thing left is to pack the upper nibble in BL and the lower nibble in AL into the same byte.

COMBINING BYTES OR WORDS WITH THE ADD OR THE OR INSTRUCTION

You can't use a standard MOV instruction to combine two bytes into one as we need to do here. The reason is that the MOV instruction copies an operand from a specified source to a specified destination. The previous

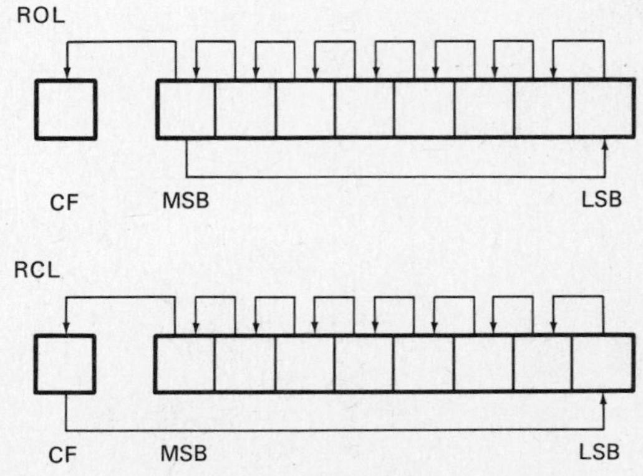

FIGURE 4-4 ROL instruction and RCL instruction operations for byte operands.

contents of the destination are lost. You can, however, use an ADD or an OR instruction to pack the two BCD nibbles.

As described in the previous program example, the ADD instruction adds the contents of a specified source to the contents of a specified destination and leaves the result in the specified destination. For the example program here, the instruction ADD AL, BL can be used to combine the two BCD nibbles. Take a look at Figure 4-2 to help you visualize this addition.

If you look up the OR instruction in Chapter 6, you will find that it has the format OR destination, source. This instruction ORs each bit in the specified source with the corresponding bit in the specified destination. The result of the ORing is left in the specified destination. Remember from basic logic or the review in Chapter 1 that ORing a bit with a 1 always produces a result of 1. ORing a bit with a 0 leaves the bit unchanged. To set a bit in a word to a 1 then, all you have to do is OR that bit with a word which has a 1 in that bit position and 0's in all the other bit positions. This is similar to the way the AND instruction is used to clear bits in a word to 0's. See the OR instruction description in Chapter 6 for examples of this.

For the example program here we use the instruction OR AL, BL to pack the two BCD nibbles. Bits ORed with 0's will not be changed. Bits ORed with 1's will become or stay 1's. Again look at Figure 4-2 to help you visualize this operation.

SUMMARY OF BCD PACKING PROGRAM

Figure 4-5 shows the complete program to produce a packed BCD byte from two ASCII bytes. Work your way through this to make sure you understand how each part works. In this program we use the AND instruction to zero (mask) unwanted bits in the ASCII bytes. Any bit ANDed with a 0 will become or remain a zero. Any bit ANDed with a 1 will remain the same. We use the ROL instruction to rotate a nibble from the lower nibble position to the higher nibble position. In this case the ROR instruction would also accomplish the same result. Finally, we use the OR instruction to combine the two BCD nibbles in one byte. Any bit ORed with a 1 will become or remain a 1. Any bit ORed with a 0 will remain the same.

FLAGS, JUMPS, AND WHILE—DO IMPLEMENTATION

Introduction

The real power of a computer comes from its ability to repeat a sequence of instructions *as long as* some condition exists, repeat a sequence of instructions *until* some condition exists, or choose between two or more sequences of actions based on some condition. *Flags* indicate whether some condition is present or not. *Jump* instructions are used to tell the computer what sequence of actions to take based on the condition indicated by the flags. In this section we first discuss the 8086 conditional flags and the 8086 jump instructions. Then we show with examples how the WHILE—DO structure is implemented and used.

The 8086 Conditional Flags

The 8086 has six *conditional flags*. They are the *carry* flag, the *parity* flag, the *auxiliary carry* flag, the *zero*

```
;8086 PROGRAM
;ABSTRACT        : Program to produce a packed BCD byte from
;                  two ASCII-encoded digits.
;                  The first ASCII digit (5) is located in AL
;                  The second ASCII digit (9)is located in BL
;                  The result (packed BCD) to be left in AL
;REGISTERS USED: CS, AL, BL, CL
;PORTS USED      : None
;PROCEDURES      : None used

CODE_HERE         SEGMENT
                  ASSUME CS : CODE_HERE
         MOV      AL, '5'          ; load first ASCII digit into AL
         MOV      BL, '9'          ; load second ASCII digit into BL
         AND      AL, 0FH          ; mask upper 4 bits of first digit
         AND      BL, 0FH          ; mask upper 4 bits of second digit
         MOV      CL, 04H          ; load CL for 4 rotates required
         ROL      AL, CL           ; rotate AL 4 bit positions
         OR       AL, BL           ; combine nibbles, result in AL

CODE_HERE         ENDS
                  END
```

FIGURE 4-5 8086 assembly language program to produce packed BCD from two ASCII characters.

flag, the *sign* flag, and the *overflow* flag. Chapter 1 shows numerical examples of the conditions indicated by these flags. Here we review these conditions and show how some of the important 8086 instructions affect these flags.

THE CARRY FLAG WITH ADD, SUBTRACT, AND COMPARE INSTRUCTIONS

If the addition of two 8-bit numbers produces a sum greater than 8 bits, the carry flag will be set to a 1 to indicate a carry into the next bit position. Likewise, if the addition of two 16-bit numbers produces a sum greater than 16 bits then the carry flag will be set to a 1 to indicate that a final carry was produced by the addition.

During subtraction the carry flag functions as a borrow flag. If the bottom number in a subtraction is larger than the top number, then the carry/borrow flag will be set to indicate that a borrow was needed to perform the subtraction.

The 8086 compare instruction has the format CMP destination, source. The source can be an immediate number, a register, or a memory location. The destination can be a register or a memory location. The comparison is done by subtracting the contents of the specified source from the contents of the specified destination. Flags are updated to reflect the result of the comparison, but neither the source nor the destination is changed. If the source operand is greater than the specified destination operand, then the carry/borrow flag will be set to indicate that a borrow was needed to do the comparison (subtraction). If the source operand is the same size as or smaller than the specified destination operand, then the carry/borrow flag will not be set after the compare. If the two operands are equal, the zero flag will be set to a 1 to indicate that the result of the compare (subtraction) was all 0's. Here's an example and summary of this for your reference.

CMP BX, CX

condition	CF	ZF
CX > BX	1	0
CX < BX	0	0
CX = BX	0	1

The compare instruction is very important because it allows you to easily determine whether one operand is greater than, less than, or the same size as another operand.

THE PARITY FLAG

Parity is a term used to indicate whether a binary word has an even number of 1's or an odd number of 1's. A binary number with an even number of 1's is said to have even parity. The 8086 parity flag will be set to a 1 after an instruction if the lower 8 bits of the destination operand has an even number of 1's. Probably the most common use of the parity flag is to determine if ASCII data sent to a computer over phone lines or some other communications link contains any errors. A later chapter will describe this use of parity.

THE AUXILIARY CARRY FLAG

This flag has significance in BCD addition or BCD subtraction. If a carry is produced when the least-significant nibbles of 2 bytes are added, the auxiliary carry flag will be set. In other words, a carry out of bit 3 sets the auxiliary carry flag. Likewise, if the subtraction of the least-significant nibbles requires a borrow, the auxiliary carry/borrow flag will be set. The auxiliary carry/borrow flag is only used by the DAA and the DAS instructions. Consult the DAA and the DAS instruction descriptions in Chapter 6 and the BCD operation examples section of Chapter 1 for further discussion of BCD operations.

THE ZERO FLAG WITH INCREMENT, DECREMENT, AND COMPARE INSTRUCTIONS

As the name implies, this flag will be set to a 1 if the result of an arithmetic or logic operation is zero. For example, if you subtract two numbers which are equal, the zero flag will be set to indicate that the result of the subtraction was zero. If you AND two words together and the result contains no 1's, the zero flag will be set to indicate that the result was all 0's.

Besides the more obvious arithmetic and logic instructions which affect the zero flag, there are a few other very useful instructions which also do. One of these is the compare instruction, CMP, which we discussed with the carry flag previously. As shown there, the zero flag will be set to a 1 if the two operands compared are equal.

Another important instruction which affects the zero flag is the decrement instruction, DEC. This instruction will decrement or, in other words, subtract one from, a number in a specified register or memory location. If, after decrementing, the contents of the register or memory location are zero, the zero flag will be set. Here's a preview of how this is used. Suppose that we want to repeat a sequence of actions nine times. To do this we first load a register with the number 09H, and execute the sequence of actions. We then decrement the register and look at the zero flag to see if the register is down to zero yet. If the zero flag is not set, then we know that the register is not yet down to zero, so we tell the 8086, with a jump instruction, to go back and execute the sequence of instructions again. The following sections will show many specific examples of how this is done.

The increment instruction, INC destination, also affects the zero flag. If an 8-bit destination containing FFH or a 16-bit destination containing FFFFH is incremented, the result in the destination will be all 0's. The zero flag will be set to indicate this.

THE SIGN FLAG—POSITIVE AND NEGATIVE NUMBERS

When you need to represent both positive and negative numbers for an 8086, you use 2's complement sign-and-magnitude form as described in Chapter 1. In this form the most significant bit of the byte or word is used as a sign bit. A 0 in this bit indicates that the number is positive. A 1 in this bit indicates that the number is negative. The remaining 7 bits of a byte or the remaining 15 bits of a word are used to represent the magnitude of the number. For a positive number the magnitude will be in standard binary form. For a negative number the magnitude will be in 2's complement form. After an arithmetic or logic instruction executes, the sign flag will be a copy of the most significant bit of the destination byte or the destination word. In addition to its use with signed arithmetic operations, the sign flag can be used to determine if an operand has been decremented beyond zero. Decrementing 00H, for example, will give FFH. Since the MSB of FFH is a 1, the sign flag will be set.

THE OVERFLOW FLAG

This flag will be set if the result of a signed operation is too large to fit in the number of bits available to represent it. To remind you of what overflow means, here is an example. Suppose you add the 8-bit signed number 01110101 (+117 decimal) and the 8-bit signed number 00110111 (+55 decimal). The result will be 10101100 (+172 decimal) which is the correct binary result in this case, but is too large to fit in the 7 bits allowed for the magnitude in an 8-bit signed number. For an 8-bit signed number, a 1 in the most significant bit indicates a negative number. The overflow flag will be set after this operation to indicate that the result of the addition has overflowed into the sign bit.

The 8086 Unconditional Jump Instruction

INTRODUCTION

Jump instructions can be used to tell the 8086 to start fetching its instructions from some new location. Figure 4-6 shows in diagram form how a jump instruction affects the program execution flow. The 8086 remember, computes the physical address to fetch the next code byte from by adding the offset in the instruction pointer to the code segment base in CS. Jump instructions change the number in the instruction pointer register, and in some cases they also load a new number into the code segment register. The 8086 JMP instruction always causes a jump to occur. This is referred to as an *unconditional* jump. The 8086 also has a large collection of conditional jump instructions which cause a jump based on whether some condition is present or not. In this section we discuss how the unconditional jump instruction operates. In a later section we discuss the operation of the conditional jump instructions.

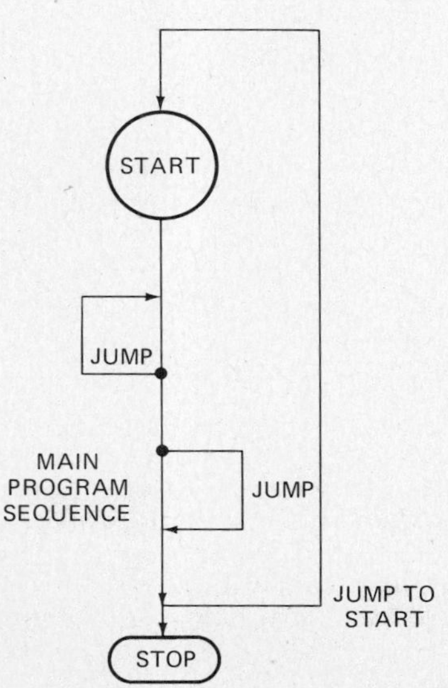

FIGURE 4-6 Change in program flow that can be caused by jump instructions.

UNCONDITIONAL JUMP INSTRUCTION TYPES—OVERVIEW

The 8086 unconditional jump instruction, JMP, has five different types. Figure 4-7 shows the names and instruction coding templates for these five types. We will first summarize how these five work to give you an overview, and then we will describe in detail the two types you need for your programs at this point. The JMP instruction description in Chapter 6 shows examples of each of the five types.

JMP = Jump

Within segment or group, IP relative—near and short

Opcode	DispL	DispH

Opcode	Clocks	Operation
E9	15	IP ← IP + Disp16
EB	15	IP ← IP + Disp8 (Disp8 sign-extended)

Within segment or group, Indirect

Opcode	mod 100 r/m	mem-low	mem-high

Opcode	Clocks	Operation
FF	11	IP ← Reg16
FF	18+EA	IP ← Mem16

Inter-segment or group, Direct

Opcode	offset-low	offset-high	seg-low	seg-high

Opcode	Clocks	Operation
EA	15	CS ← segbase IP ← offset

Inter-segment or group, Indirect

Opcode	mod 101 r/m		

Opcode	Clocks	Operation
FF	24+EA	CS ← segbase IP ← offset

FIGURE 4-7 8086 unconditional JMP instructions *(Intel Corp.)*.

THE DIRECT WITHIN-SEGMENT NEAR JMP INSTRUCTION

This instruction can cause the next instruction to be fetched from anywhere in the current code segment. A jump to an address in the same segment as the jump instruction is commonly called an *intrasegment* or a *near* jump. To produce the new instruction fetch address this instruction adds a 16-bit signed displacement contained in the instruction to the contents of the instruction pointer register. A signed 16-bit displacement means that the jump can be to a location anywhere from +32,767 to −32,768 bytes from the current instruction pointer location. A positive displacement usually means you are jumping ahead in the program, and a negative displacement usually means you are jumping "backward" in the program.

THE DIRECT WITHIN-SEGMENT SHORT-TYPE JMP INSTRUCTION

This instruction is a special case of a near jump. This JMP instruction produces the new instruction fetch address by adding a signed 8-bit displacement, contained in the instruction, to the contents of the instruction pointer register. With an 8-bit signed displacement the jump can be to a location anywhere from +127 to −128 bytes from the current instruction pointer location.

THE INDIRECT WITHIN-SEGMENT JMP INSTRUCTION

This instruction replaces the contents of the instruction pointer register with the contents of a specified 16-bit register or the contents of a specified memory location. The MOD—R/M byte in the second byte position of the coding template for this instruction indicates that the register or memory location can be specified in any of the 32 register and memory addressing modes shown in Figure 3-8. Since this type JMP is to an address in the same code segment as the JMP instruction, it is another example of a near jump.

THE DIRECT INTERSEGMENT-TYPE JMP

This instruction causes a jump to another code segment. A jump to another code segment is often referred to as an *intersegment* or *far jump*. In order to get to another segment, you have to change the contents of both the instruction pointer and the code segment registers. As shown in Figure 4-7, for this type instruction the new value for the instruction pointer is written in as bytes 2 and 3 of the instruction code. The new value for the code segment register is written in as bytes 4 and 5 of the instruction code. Note that in each case, the low byte is written before the high byte.

THE INDIRECT INTERSEGMENT JMP

This instruction also causes a far (to another code segment) JMP. Therefore, both the instruction pointer register and the code segment register contents have to be changed. For this type instruction the new values are taken from four memory locations. The new value for IP will be written in the first two memory locations, low byte first, and the new value for CS will be written in the next two memory locations, low byte first. Again, the MOD—R/M byte in the second byte position of the instruction code template indicates that the first memory address can be specified in any one of the 24 memory addressing modes shown in Figure 3-8.

DIRECT WITHIN-SEGMENT NEAR AND DIRECT WITHIN-SEGMENT SHORT JMP EXAMPLES

Suppose that in a program you want to keep executing an instruction or group of instructions over and over again. Figure 4-8 shows how the JMP instruction can be used to do this. In this program the label BACK followed by a colon is used to give a name to the address we want to jump back to. When the assembler reads this label it will make an entry in its symbol table as to where it found the label. Then when the assembler reads the JMP instruction and finds the name BACK, it will be able to calculate the displacement from the jump instruction to the label. This displacement will be part of the code for the instruction. Even if you are not using an assembler, you should use labels to indicate jump destinations so that you can easily see them. The NOP instruction used in the program in Figure 4-8 does nothing except fill space. We used it in this example to represent the instructions that we want to loop through over and over. We also use it to represent the instructions after the JMP—BACK loop. Actually, the way this program is written the 8086 will never get to the instructions after the JMP instruction. Can you see why? The answer is that once the 8086 gets into the JMP—BACK loop, the only ways it can get out are if the power is turned off, an interrupt occurs, or the system is reset. In most programs one of the instructions we have represented with a NOP would be a conditional jump instruction which would get execution out of the loop when the specified condition occurred.

Now let's see how the binary code for the JMP instruction in Figure 4-8 is constructed. The jump is to a label in the same segment so this narrows our choices down to the first three types of JMP instruction shown in Figure 4-7. For several reasons it is best to use the direct-type JMP instruction whenever possible. This narrows our choices down to the first two types in Figure 4-7. The choice between these two is determined by whether you need a 1-byte displacement to reach the JMP destination address, or whether you need a 2-byte displacement to reach the JMP destination. Since for our example program the destination address is within the range of −128 to +127 bytes from the instruction after the JMP instruction, we can use the direct within-segment short type of JMP. According to Figure 4-7 the instruction template for this instruction is 11101011 (EBH) followed by some displacement. Here's how you calculate the displacement to put in the instruction.

NOTE: An assembler automatically does this for you, but you should still learn how it is done to help you in troubleshooting.

The numbers in the left column of Figure 4-8 represent the offset of each code byte from the code segment

```
The IBM Personal Computer MACRO Assembler 10-17-84      PAGE    1-1

                                   page,132
                                   ;8086 program
                                   ;ABSTRACT       : This program illustrates a "backwards" jump
                                   ;REGISTERS USED: CS, AL
                                   ;PORTS USED     : None
                                   ;PROCEDURES     : None used

0000                               CODE_HERE       SEGMENT
                                                   ASSUME  CS : CODE_HERE

0000  04 03                        BACK:   ADD     AL, 03H          ; add 3 to total
0002  90                                   NOP                      ; dummy instructions
0003  90                                   NOP                      ; to represent those
0004  90                                   NOP                      ; instructions jumped
0005  90                                   NOP                      ; back over
0006  EB F8                                JMP     BACK             ; loop back through
                                                                    ; series of instructions
0008  90                                   NOP                      ; dummy instructions to
0009  90                                   NOP                      ; represent continuation
                                                                    ; after loop
000A                               CODE_HERE       ENDS
                                                   END
```

FIGURE 4-8 Program demonstrating "backward" JMP.

base. These are the numbers that will be in the instruction pointer as the program executes. After the 8086 fetches an instruction byte it automatically increments the instruction pointer to point to the next instruction byte. The displacement in the instruction then will be added to the offset of the next in-line instruction after the JMP instruction. For the example program in Figure 4-8 the displacement in the JMP instruction will be added to offset 0008H, which is in the instruction pointer after the JMP instruction executes. What this means is that when you are counting the number of bytes of displacement, you always start counting from the address of the instruction immediately after the JMP instruction. For the example program we want to jump from offset 0008H back to offset 0000H. This is a displacement of −8H.

You can't, however, write the displacement in the instruction as −8H. Negative displacements must be expressed in 2's complement, sign-and-magnitude form. We showed how to do this in Chapter 1. First, write the number as an 8-bit positive binary number. In this case that is 00001000. Then, invert each bit of this, including the sign bit, to give 11110111. Finally, add 1 to that result to give 11111000 binary or F8H which is the correct 2's complement representation for −8H. As shown in the assembler listing for the program in Figure 4-8, the two code bytes for this JMP instruction then are EBH and F8H.

To summarize this example then, a label is used to give a name to the destination address for the jump. This name is used to refer to the destination address in the JMP instruction. Since the destination in this example is within the range of −128 to +127 bytes from the address after the JMP instruction, the instruction can be coded as a direct within-segment short-type JMP. The displacement is calculated by counting the number of bytes from the next address after the JMP instruction to the destination. If the displacement is negative (backward in the program), then it must be expressed in 2's complement form before it can be written in the instruction code template.

Now let's look at another simple example program, in Figure 4-9, to see how you can jump ahead over a group of instructions in a program. Here again we use a label to give a name to the address that we want to JMP to. We also use NOP instructions to represent the instructions that we want to skip over and the instructions that continue after the JMP. Now let's see how this JMP instruction is coded.

When the assembler reads through the source file for this program it will find the label "THERE" after the JMP mnemonic. At this point the assembler has no way of knowing whether it will need 1 byte or 2 bytes to represent the displacement to the destination address. The assembler plays it safe by reserving 2 bytes for the displacement. Then the assembler reads on through the rest of the program. When the assembler finds the specified label, it calculates the displacement from the instruction after the JMP instruction to the label. If the assembler finds the displacement to be outside the range of −128 bytes to +127 bytes, then it will code the instruction as a direct within-segment near JMP with 2 bytes of displacement. If the assembler finds the displacement to be within the −128 to +127 byte range,

```
The IBM Personal Computer MACRO Assembler 10-17-84      PAGE    1-1

                                        page,132
                                        ;8086 program
                                        ;ABSTRACT       : This program illustrates a "forwards" jump
                                        ;REGISTERS USED : CS, AX
                                        ;PORTS USED     : None
                                        ;PROCEDURES USED: None

 0000                                   CODE_HERE       SEGMENT
                                                        ASSUME  CS : CODE_HERE

 0000  EB 05 90                                 JMP     THERE           ; skip over a series
                                                                        ; of instructions
 0003  90                                       NOP                     ; dummy instructions
 0004  90                                       NOP                     ; to represent those
 0005  90                                       NOP                     ; instructions skipped
 0006  90                                       NOP                     ; over
 0007  B8 0000                          THERE:  MOV     AX, 0000H       ; zero accumulator before addition
 000A  90                                       NOP                     ; dummy instructions to
 000B  90                                       NOP                     ; represent continuation
                                                                        ; of execution
 000C                                   CODE_HERE       ENDS
                                                        END
```

FIGURE 4-9 Program demonstrating "forward" JMP.

then it will code the instruction as a direct within-segment short-type JMP with a 1-byte displacement. In the latter case the assembler will put the code for a NOP instruction, 90H, in the third byte it had reserved for the JMP instruction. The instruction codes for the JMP THERE instruction in Figure 4-9 demonstrate this. As shown in the instruction template in Figure 4-7, EBH is the basic opcode for the direct within-segment short JMP. The 05H represents the displacement to the JMP destination. Since we are jumping forward in this case, the displacement is a positive number. The 90H in the next memory byte is the code for a NOP instruction. The displacement is calculated from the offset of this instruction, 0002H, to the offset of the destination label, 0007H. The difference of 05 between these two is the displacement you see coded in the instruction.

If you are hand coding a program such as this, you will probably know how far it is to the label and you can leave just 1 byte for the displacement if that is enough. If you are using an assembler and you don't want to waste the byte of memory or the time it takes to fetch the extra NOP instruction, you can write the instruction as JMP SHORT label. The SHORT operator is a promise to the assembler that the destination will not be outside the range of −128 to +127 bytes. Trusting your promise, the assembler then only reserves 1 byte for the displacement.

SUMMARY OF UNCONDITIONAL JMPS

The 8086 has five types of unconditional JMP instructions. The types you will probably use most often in your programs are the direct within-segment near and the direct within-segment short. A label followed by a colon is used to give the destination address a name for both of these JMP types. For the direct within-segment near type, a 16-bit displacement contained in the instruction is added to the contents of the instruction pointer to produce the destination address. This type of jump can be to an address in the range of −32,768 bytes to +32,767 bytes from the current IP contents. The direct within-segment short JMP instruction adds an 8-bit displacement contained in the instruction to the IP to produce the destination address. For this type JMP the destination can be in the range of −128 bytes to +127 bytes from the current instruction pointer contents. The displacement for both of these JMP types is counted from the address of the instruction after the JMP instruction to the address of the destination instruction. A jump ahead in the program is usually represented by a positive displacement. A jump backward in the program is usually represented by a negative displacement which is coded in the instruction in its 2's complement sign-and-magnitude form. Note that if you are making a JMP from an address near the start of a 64 Kbyte segment to an address near the end of the segment, you may not be able to get there with a jump of +32,767. The way you get there is to JMP backwards around to the desired destination address. An assembler will automatically do this for you.

One advantage of the direct near- and short-type JMPs is that the destination address is specified *relative* to the address of the instruction after the JMP instruction.

Since the JMP instruction in this case does not contain an absolute address or offset, the program can be loaded anywhere in memory and it will still run correctly. A program which can be loaded anywhere in memory to be run is said to be *relocatable*. You should try to write your programs so that they are relocatable.

The indirect within-segment type of JMP instruction replaces the contents of the instruction pointer with a 16-bit value from a register or memory location specified in the instruction. The direct intersegment far-type JMP loads IP with a new value contained in bytes 2 and 3 of the instruction code, and it loads CS with a new value from bytes 4 and 5 of the instruction code. The intersegment indirect far-type JMP loads IP and CS with new values read from a memory location specified in the instruction.

The 8086 Conditional Jump Instructions

As we stated previously, much of the real power of a computer comes from its ability to choose between two courses of action depending on whether some condition is present or not. In the 8086 the six conditional flags indicate the conditions that are present after an instruction. The 8086 conditional jump instructions look at the state of a specified flag(s) to determine whether a jump should be made or not. Figure 4-10 shows the mnemonics for the 8086 conditional jump instructions. Next to each mnemonic is a brief explanation of the mnemonic. Note that the terms "above" and "below" are used when you are working with unsigned binary numbers. The 8-bit unsigned number 11000110 is above the 8-bit unsigned number 00111001, for example. The terms "greater" and "less" are used when you are working with signed binary numbers. The 8-bit signed number 00111001 is greater (more positive) than the 8-bit signed number 11000110 which represents a negative number. Also shown in Figure 4-10 is an indication of the flag conditions that will cause the 8086 to do the jump. If the specified flag conditions are not present, the 8086 will just continue on to the next instruction in sequence. In other words, if the jump condition is not met, the conditional jump instruction will effectively function as a NOP. Suppose, for example, we have the instruction JC SAVE, where SAVE is the label at the destination address. If the carry flag is set, this instruction will cause the 8086 to jump to the instruction at the SAVE: label. If the carry flag is not set, the instruction will have no effect other than taking up a little processor time.

All conditional jumps are *short-type* jumps. This means that the destination label must be in the same code segment as the jump instruction. Also, the destination address must be in the range of −128 bytes to +127 bytes from the address of the instruction after the jump instruction. As we show in later examples, this limit on the range of unconditional jumps is important to be aware of as you write your programs.

The conditional jump instructions are usually used after arithmetic or logic instructions. Very commonly they are used after compare instructions. For this case the compare instruction syntax and the conditional jump instruction syntax are such that a little trick makes it very easy to see what will cause a jump to occur. Here's the trick. Suppose that you see the instruction sequence

MNEMONIC	CONDITION TESTED	"JUMP IF . . ."
JA/JNBE	(CF or ZF)=0	above/not below nor equal
JAE/JNB	CF=0	above or equal/not below
JB/JNAE	CF=1	below/not above nor equal
JBE/JNA	(CF or ZF)=1	below or equal/not above
JC	CF=1	carry
JE/JZ	ZF=1	equal/zero
JG/JNLE	((SF xor OF) or ZF)=0	greater/not less nor equal
JGE/JNL	(SF xor OF)=0	greater or equal/not less
JL/JNGE	(SF xor OF)=1	less/not greater nor equal
JLE/JNG	((SF xor OF) or ZF)=1	less or equal/not greater
JNC	CF=0	not carry
JNE/JNZ	ZF=0	not equal/not zero
JNO	OF=0	not overflow
JNP/JPO	PF=0	not parity/parity odd
JNS	SF=0	not sign
JO	OF=1	overflow
JP/JPE	PF=1	parity/parity equal
JS	SF=1	sign

Note: "above" and "below" refer to the relationship of two unsigned values;
"greater" and "less" refer to the relationship of two signed values.

FIGURE 4-10 8086 conditional JMP instructions *(Intel Corp.)*.

CMP BL, DH

JAE HEATER_OFF

in a program, and you want to determine what these instructions do. The CMP instruction compares the byte in the DH register with the byte in the BL register and sets flags according to the result. A previous section showed you how the carry and zero flags are affected by a compare instruction. According to Figure 4-10 the JAE instruction says "Jump if above or equal" to the label HEATER_OFF. The question now is, will it jump if BL is above DH, or will it jump if DH is above BL. You could determine how the flags will be affected by the comparison and use Figure 4-10 to answer the question. However, an easier way is to mentally read parts of the compare instruction between parts of the jump instruction. If you read the example sequence as "Jump if BL is above or equal to DH," the meaning of the sequence is immediately clear. As you write your own programs, thinking of a conditional sequence in this way should help you to choose the right conditional jump instruction. The next sections show you how we use conditional and unconditional jump instructions to implement some of the standard program structures and solve some common programming problems.

WHILE—DO Implementation and Example

Remember from the discussion in Chapter 3 that the WHILE—DO structure has the form:

WHILE some condition is present DO
  Action
  Action

An important point about this structure is that the condition is checked *before* any action is done. In industrial control applications of microprocessors there are many cases where we want to do this. The following very simple example will show you how to implement this structure in 8086 assembly language.

DEFINING THE PROBLEM AND WRITING THE ALGORITHM

Suppose that in controlling a chemical process we want to bring the temperature of a solution up to 100°C before going on to the next step in the process. If the solution temperature is below 100°, we want to turn on a heater and wait for the temperature to reach 100°. If the solution temperature is at or above 100°, then we want to go on with the next step in the process. The WHILE—DO structure fits this problem because we want to check the condition (temperature) before we turn on the heater. We don't want to turn on the heater if the temperature is already high enough because we might overheat the solution.

Figure 4-11 shows a flowchart and the pseudocode of an algorithm for this problem. The first step in the algorithm is to read in the temperature from a sensor connected to a port. The temperature read in is then compared with 100°. These two parts represent the condition-checking part of the structure. If the temperature is at or above 100°, execution will exit the structure and do the next mainline action, turn off the heater. If the heater is already off, it will not do any harm to turn it off again. If the temperature is less than 100°, the heater is turned on and the temperature rechecked. Execution will stay in this loop while the temperature is below 100°. Incidentally, it will not do any harm to turn the heater on if it is already on. When the temperature reaches 100°, execution will exit the structure and go on to the next mainline action, turn off the heater.

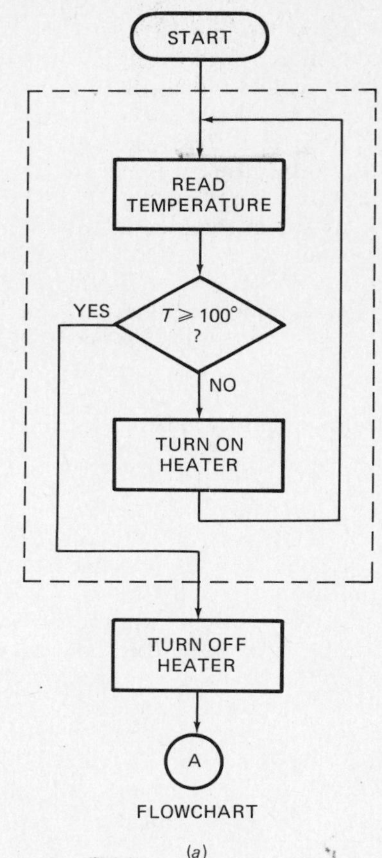

FLOWCHART

(*a*)

READ TEMPERATURE
WHILE TEMPERATURE < 100° DO
  TURN HEATER ON
TURN HEATER OFF

PSEUDOCODE

(*b*)

FIGURE 4-11 Flowchart and pseudocode for heater control problem.

IMPLEMENTING THE ALGORITHM IN ASSEMBLY LANGUAGE

Figure 4-12 shows one way to write the assembly language for this example. We have assumed for this example that the temperature sensor inputs an 8-bit binary value for the Celsius temperature to port FFF8H. We have also assumed that the heater control output is connected to the most significant bit of port FFFAH. (Incidentally, these port addresses are two of the available

```
The IBM Personal Computer MACRO Assembler 02-16-85      PAGE    1-1

                              page, 132
                              ;8086 program
                              ;ABSTRACT       : program turns heater off if temperature equals
                              ;                 100 degrees or more, and to turn the heater on
                              ;                 if the temperature is below 100 degrees.
                              ;REGISTERS USED: CS, DX, AL
                              ;PORTS USED     : FFF8H - for temperature data input
                              ;                 FFFAH - MSB for heater control output
                              ;PROCEDURES     : None used

 0000                         CODE_HERE       SEGMENT
                                              ASSUME  CS : CODE_HERE

                                                                  ; initialize port FFFA as an output port
 0000  BA FFFE                                MOV     DX, 0FFFEH  ; point DX to port contol register
 0003  B0 99                                  MOV     AL, 99H     ; control word to set up port FFFA as an output
 0005  EE                                     OUT     DX, AL      ; send control word to port

 0006  BA FFF8                TEMP_IN:        MOV     DX, 0FFF8H  ; read in temperature data
 0009  EC                                     IN      AL, DX
 000A  3C 64                                  CMP     AL, 100     ; if temp >= 100
 000C  73 08                                  JAE     HEATER_OFF  ; go turn heater off

 000E  B0 80                                  MOV     AL, 80H     ; load code for heater on
 0010  BA FFFA                                MOV     DX, 0FFFAH  ; point DX to output port
 0013  EE                                     OUT     DX, AL      ; turn heater on
 0014  EB F0                                  JMP     TEMP_IN     ; go & read temp again
 0016  B0 00                  HEATER_OFF:     MOV     AL, 00      ; load code for heater off
 0018  BA FFFA                                MOV     DX, 0FFFAH  ; point DX to output port
 001B  EE                                     OUT     DX, AL      ; turn heater off

 001C                         CODE_HERE       ENDS
                                              END
```

(a)

```
The IBM Personal Computer MACRO Assembler 02-16-85      PAGE    1-1

                              page, 132
                              ;8086 PROGRAM
                              ;ABSTRACT       : program to turn heater off if temperature
                              ;                 equals 100 degrees or more, and to turn the
                              ;                 heater on if the temperature is below 100 degrees.
                              ;REGISTERS USED: CS, DX, AL
                              ;PORTS USED     : FFF8H - for temperature data input
                              ;                 FFFAH _ MSB for heater control output
                              ;PROCEDURES     : None used

 0000                         CODE_HERE       SEGMENT
                                              ASSUME  CS : CODE_HERE
```

FIGURE 4-12 Assembly language program for heater control problem. *(a)* First approach. *(b)* Improved version.

```
                                                        ; initialize port FFFA as an output port
0000  BA FFFE                      MOV    DX, 0FFFEH    ; point DX to port contol register
0003  B0 99                        MOV    AL, 99H       ; control word to set up port FFFA as an output
0005  EE                           OUT    DX, AL        ; send control word to port

0006  BA FFF8         TEMP_IN:     MOV    DX, 0FFF8H    ; point DX at input port
0009  EC                           IN     AL, DX        ; read in temperature data
000A  3C 64                        CMP    AL, 100
000C  72 03                        JB     HEATER_ON     ; if temp < 100 go
                                                        ; turn heater ON
000E  EB 09 90                     JMP    HEATER_OFF    ; temp >= 100 go
                                                        ; turn heater OFF
0011  B0 80           HEATER_ON:   MOV    AL, 80H       ; load code for heater ON
0013  BA FFFA                      MOV    DX, 0FFFAH    ; point DX at output port
0016  EE                           OUT    DX, AL        ; turn heater ON
0017  EB ED                        JMP    TEMP_IN       ; read temp again

0019  B0 00           HEATER_OFF:  MOV    AL,  00       ; load code for heater OFF
001B  BA FFFA                      MOV    DX, 0FFFAH    ; point DX at output port
001E  EE                           OUT    DX, AL        ; turn heater OFF

001F                  CODE_HERE    ENDS
                                   END
```

(*b*)

FIGURE 4-12 *(continued)*.

ports, P2A and P2B, on an SDK-86 board.) A 1 sent to the MSB of port FFFAH turns the heater on.

The 8086 has two types of input instruction, *fixed* port and *variable* port. The fixed port instruction has the format IN AL, port or IN AX, port. The term "port" in these represents an 8-bit port address to be put directly in the instruction. The instruction IN AX, 07H, for example, will copy a word from port 07H to the AX register. With an 8-bit port address you can address any one of 256 possible ports. The port address is fixed, however. The program cannot change the port address as it executes.

For the variable-port input instruction, the address of the desired port is put in the DX register. The input instruction for this type then has the format IN AL, DX or IN AX, DX. If you load DX with FFF8H and then do an IN AL, DX as in Figure 4-12*a*, the 8086 will copy a byte of data from port FFF8H to the AL register. The variable-port type instruction has two major advantages. First, up to 65,536 different ports can be specified with the 16-bit port address in DX. Second, the port address can be changed as a program executes by simply putting a different number in DX. This is handy in a case where you want the computer to be able to input from 15 different terminals, for example. Instead of writing 15 different input programs, you can write one input program which changes the contents of DX to input from different terminals.

The 8086 also has a fixed-port output instruction and a variable-port output instruction. The fixed-port output instruction has the form OUT port, AL or OUT port, AX. Here again the term *port* represents an 8-bit port address written in the instruction. OUT 05, AL, for example, will copy the contents of the AL register to port 05H. For the variable port output instruction the 16-bit port address is put in the DX register. The output instruction format for this type is OUT DX, AL or OUT DX, AX. If you load DX with FFFAH and then do an OUT DX, AL instruction as in Figure 4-12*a*, the 8086 will copy the contents of the AL register to port FFFAH.

Most common devices used as ports for microcomputers can be used for input or output. When the power is first applied to these devices they are in the input mode. If you want to use any of these devices as output ports, you must send the device a control word which switches the device to output mode. Chapter 9 and later chapters will describe in detail how you initialize programmable port devices, but to give you an introduction we show you here how to initialize one of the ports in an 8255 device on an SDK-86 microcomputer for use as an output port. To specify the function of one of these programmable devices you send a control word to a register inside the device. You can find the control word format for each type of device in the manufacturer's data book. For one of the 8255s on an SDK-86 board, the address of the control register in the device is FFFEH. The instruction MOV DX, 0FFFEH points DX at this address. The control word needed to make port P2B of this 8255 an output, and P2A and P2C inputs, is 99H. (In Chapter 9 we show how we determined this control word.) We load this control word into AL with MOV AL, 99H and send it to the 8255 control register with OUT DX, AL. Now we can output a byte to port P2B of this device any time we need to in the program. The actual address of this port P2B on the SDK-86 board is FFFAH. It is to this address that we will output a byte to turn the heater on or off.

After we input the data from the temperature sensor in Figure 4-12*a* we compare the value read with 100

(64H). The JAE instruction after the compare can be read as "jump to the label HEATER_OFF if AL is above or equal to 100." Note that we used the Jump if Above or Equal instruction rather than a Jump if Equal instruction. Can you see why? To see the answer, visualize what would happen if we had used a JE instruction and the temperature of the solution were 101°. On the first check the temperature would not be equal to 100° so the 8086 would turn on the heater. The heater would not get turned off until meltdown.

If the heater temperature is below 100°, we turn on the heater by loading a 1 in the most significant bit of AL and outputting this value to the most significant bit of port FFFAH. We then do an unconditional JMP back to check the temperature again.

When the temperature is at or above 100°, we load a 0 in the most significant bit of AL and output this to port FFFAH to turn off the heater. Note that the action of turning off the heater is outside the basic WHILE—DO structure. The WHILE-DO structure is shown by the dotted box in the flowchart in Figure 4-11*a* and by the indentation in the pseudocode in Figure 4-11*b*.

SOLVING A POTENTIAL PROBLEM OF CONDITIONAL JUMP INSTRUCTIONS

In the example program in Figure 4-12*a* we used the conditional jump instruction JAE to help implement the WHILE—DO structure. Conditional jump instructions have a potential problem which you should become aware of at this point. *All the conditional jump instructions are short-type jumps*. This means that a conditional jump can only be to a location within the range of −128 to +127 bytes from the instruction after the conditional jump instruction. This limit on the range of the jump posed no problem for the example program in Figure 4-12*a* because we were only jumping to a location 8 bytes ahead in the program. Suppose, however, that the instructions for turning on the heater required 220 bytes of memory. The HEATER_OFF label would then be outside the range of the JAE instruction.

Figure 4-12*b* shows how you can change the instructions slightly to solve the problem without changing the basic WHILE—DO overall structure. In this example we read the temperature in as before and compare it to 100 (64H). We then use the Jump if Below instruction to jump to the program section which turns on the heater. This instruction, together with the CMP instruction, says jump to the label HEATER_ON if AL is below 100. If the temperature is at or above 100, the JB instruction will act like a NOP, and the 8086 will go on to the JMP HEATER_OFF instruction. Changing the conditional jump instruction and writing the program in this way means that the destination for the conditional jump instruction is always just two instructions away. Therefore, you know that the destination will always be reachable. Except for very time-critical program sections, you should always write conditional jump instruction sequences in this way so that you don't have to worry about the potential problem. The disadvantages of this approach are the time and memory space required by the extra JMP instruction.

REPEAT—UNTIL IMPLEMENTATION AND EXAMPLES

Remember from the discussion in Chapter 3 that the REPEAT—UNTIL structure has the form

```
REPEAT
  Action
  Action
  .
  .
UNTIL some condition is present
```

An important point about this structure is that the action or series of actions is done once before the condition is checked. Compare this with the WHILE—DO structure.

The following examples will show you how you can implement the REPEAT—UNTIL with 8086 assembly language and introduce you to some more assembly language programming techniques.

Waiting for a Strobe Signal

DEFINING THE PROBLEM AND WRITING THE ALGORITHM

Many systems that interface with a microcomputer output data on parallel-signal lines and then output a separate signal to indicate that valid data is on the parallel lines. The data-ready signal is often called a *strobe*. An example of a strobed data system such as this is an ASCII-encoded computer-type keyboard. Figure 4-13 shows how the parallel data lines and the strobe line from such a keyboard are connected to ports of a micro-

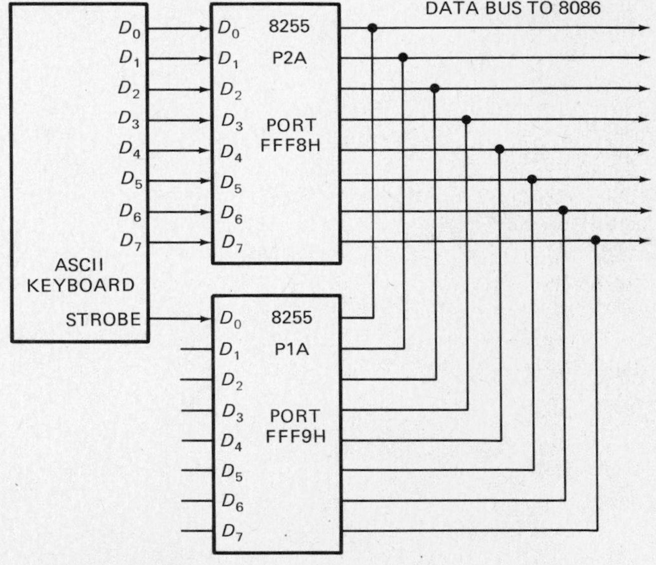

FIGURE 4-13 ASCII encoded keyboard with strobe connected to microcomputer ports.

computer. When a key is pressed on the keyboard, circuitry in the keyboard detects which key is pressed and sends the ASCII code for that key out on the eight data lines connected to port FFF8H. After the data has had time to settle on these lines, the circuitry in the keyboard sends out a key-pressed strobe which lets you know that the data on the eight lines is valid. We have connected this strobe line to the least-significant bit of port FFF9H. A strobe can be an active high signal or an active low signal. For the example here, assume that the strobe signal goes high when a valid ASCII code is on the parallel data lines.

If we want to read the data from this keyboard, we can't do it at just any time. We must wait for the strobe to go high so that we know that the data we read will be valid. Basically what we have to do is look at the strobe signal and test it over and over until it goes high. Figure 4-14*a* shows how we can represent this operation with a flowchart, and Figure 4-14*b* shows the pseudocode. We want to repeat the read-strobe-and-test loop until the strobe is found to be high. Then we want to exit the loop and read in the ASCII code byte. The basic REPEAT-UNTIL structure is shown by the indentation in the pseudocode. Note that the read ASCII data action is not part of this structure and is therefore not indented.

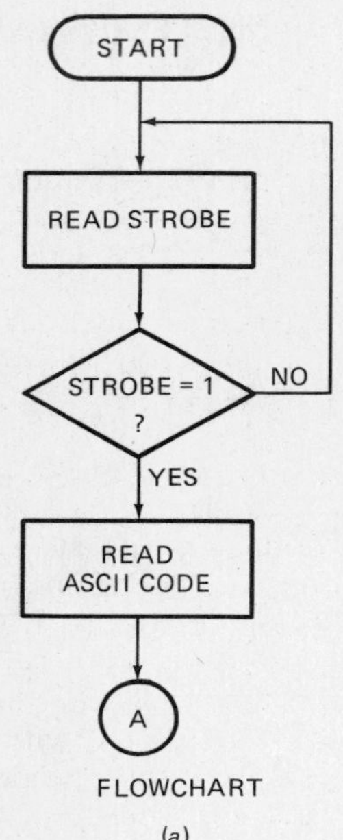

FLOWCHART

(*a*)

```
REPEAT
    READ KEYPRESSED STROBE
UNTIL STROBE = 1
READ ASCII CODE FOR KEY PRESSED
```

PSEUDOCODE

(*b*)

```
The IBM Personal Computer MACRO Assembler 02-18-85        PAGE    1-1

                                  page, 132
                                  ;8086 PROGRAM
                                  ;ABSTRACT      : program to read ASCII code when a strobe
                                  ;                 signal is sent from a keyboard
                                  ;REGISTERS USED: CS, DX, AL
                                  ;PORTS USED    : FFF9H - strobe signal input port
                                  ;              : FFF8H - ASCII data input port
                                  ;PROCEDURES    : None used

0000                              CODE_HERE    SEGMENT
                                               ASSUME  CS : CODE_HERE

0000  BA FFF9                                  MOV     DX, 0FFF9H      ; point DX at strobe port
0003  EC                          LOOK_AGAIN:  IN      AL, DX          ; read keyboard strobe
0004  24 01                                    AND     AL, 01          ; mask extra bits and
                                                                       ; set flags
0006  74 FB                                    JZ      LOOK_AGAIN      ; strobe low, keep looking
0008  BA FFF8                                  MOV     DX, 0FFF8H      ; point DX at data port
000B  EC                                       IN      AL, DX          ; read in ASCII code

000C                              CODE_HERE    ENDS
                                               END
```

(*c*)

FIGURE 4-14 Flowchart, pseudocode, and assembly language for reading ASCII code when a strobe is present. *(a)* Flowchart. *(b)* Pseudocode. *(c)* Assembly language program.

IMPLEMENTING THE ALGORITHM WITH ASSEMBLY LANGUAGE

Figure 4-14*c* shows the 8086 assembly language to implement this algorithm. To read in the key-pressed strobe signal, we first load the address of the port to which it is connected into the DX register. Then we use the variable port input instruction, IN AL, DX, to read the strobe data to AL. This input instruction copies a byte of data from port FFF9H to the AL register. However, we only care about the least-significant bit of the byte, because that is the one the strobe is connected to. We would like to find out if this bit is a 1. We will show you three ways to do it.

The first way, shown in Figure 4-14*c*, is to AND the byte in AL with the immediate number 01H. Remember that a bit ANDed with a 0 becomes a 0 (is masked). A bit ANDed with a 1 is not changed. If the least-significant bit is a 0, then the result of the ANDing will be all 0's. The zero flag, ZF, will be set to a 1 to indicate this. If the least-significant bit is a 1, the zero flag will not be set to a 1 because the result of the ANDing will still have a 1 in the least-significant bit. The Jump if Zero instruction, JZ, will check the state of the zero flag and, if it finds the zero flag set, will jump to the label LOOK_AGAIN. If the JZ instruction finds the zero flag not set (indicating that the LSB was a one), it passes execution on to the instructions which read in the ASCII data.

Another way to check the least-significant bit of the strobe word is with the TEST instruction instead of the AND instruction. The 8086 TEST instruction has the format TEST destination, source. The TEST instruction ANDs the contents of the specified source with the contents of the specified destination and sets flags according to the result. However, the TEST instruction does not change the contents of either the source or the destination. The AND instruction, remember, puts the result of the ANDing in the specified destination. The TEST instruction is useful if you want to set flags without changing the operands. In the example program in Figure 4-14*c* the AND AL, 01H instruction could be replaced with the TEST AL, 01H instruction.

Still another way to check the least-significant bit of the strobe byte is with a rotate instruction. If we rotate the least-significant bit into the carry flag, we can use a Jump if Carry or Jump if Not Carry instruction to control the loop. For this example program we can use either the ROR instruction or the RCR instruction. Assuming that we choose the ROR instruction, the check and jump instruction sequence would look like this:

```
LOOK_AGAIN: IN AL, DX
            ROR AL,1          ; Rotate LSB into
                              ; carry
            JNC LOOK_AGAIN;   ; If LSB = 0, keep
                              ; looking
```

For your programs you can use the way of checking a bit that seems easiest in a particular situation.

To read the ASCII data we first have to load the port address, FFF8H, into the DX register. We then use the variable port input instruction IN AL, DX to copy the ASCII data byte from the port to the AL register.

The main purpose of the preceding section was to show you how you can use a conditional jump instruction to make the 8086 REPEAT a series of actions UNTIL the flags indicate that some condition is present. The following section shows another example of implementing the REPEAT—UNTIL structure. This example also shows you how a register-based addressing mode is used to access data in memory.

Operating on a Series of Data Items in Memory

In many programming situations we want to perform some operation on a series of data items stored in successive memory locations. We might, for example, want to read in a series of data values from a port and put the values in successive memory locations. A series of data values of the *same type* stored in successive memory locations is often called an *array*. Each value in the array is referred to as an *element* of the array. For our example program here we want to add an inflation factor of 03H to each price in an 8-element array of prices. Each price is stored in a byte location as packed BCD (two BCD digits per byte). The prices then are in the range of 1 cent to 99 cents. Figure 4-15*a* and *b* shows a flowchart and the pseudocode for the operations that we want to perform. Follow through whichever form you feel more comfortable with.

We read one of the BCD prices from memory, add the inflation factor to it, and adjust the result to keep it in BCD format. The new value is then copied back to the array, replacing the old value. After that, a check is made to see if all of the prices have been operated on. If they haven't, then we loop back and operate on the next price. The two questions that may occur to you at this point are, "How are we going to indicate in the program which price we want to operate on, and how are we going to know when we have operated on all of the prices?" To indicate which price we are operating on at a particular time, we use a register as a pointer. To keep track of how many prices we have operated on we use another register as a counter. The example program in Figure 4-15*c* shows one way in which our algorithm for this problem can be implemented in assembly language.

The example program in Figure 4-15*c* uses several assembler directives. Let's review the function of these before describing the operation of the program instructions. The ARRAYS_HERE SEGMENT and the ARRAYS_HERE ENDS directives are used to set up a logical segment containing the data definitions. The CODE_HERE SEGMENT and the CODE_HERE ENDS directives are used to set up a logical segment which contains the program instructions. The ASSUME CS:CODE_HERE, DS:ARRAYS_HERE directive tells the assembler to use CODE_HERE as the code segment and use ARRAYS_HERE for all references to the data segment. The END directive lets the assembler know that it has reached the end of the program. Now let's discuss the data structure for the program.

The statement, COST DB 20H,28H,15H,26H,19H, 27H,16H,29H, in the program tells the assembler to set aside successive memory locations for an 8-element array of bytes. The array is given the name COST. When the assembled program is loaded into memory to be run, the eight memory locations will be loaded with the eight

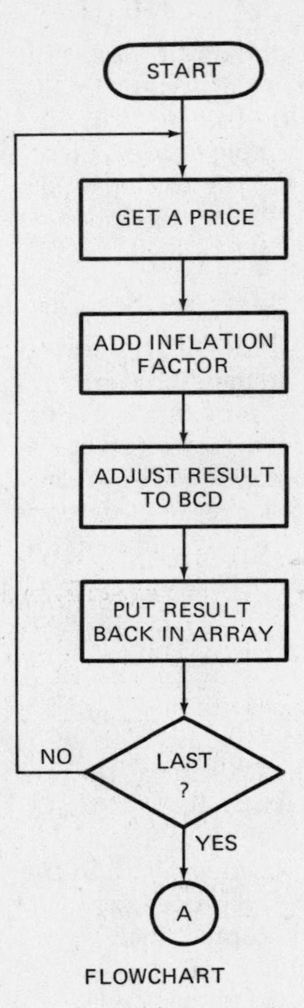

FLOWCHART

(*a*)

FIGURE 4-15 Adding a constant to a series of values in memory. *(a)* Flowchart. *(b)* Pseudocode. *(c)* Assembly language program. *(d)* Example program showing array indexing.

```
REPEAT
     GET A PRICE FROM ARRAY
     ADD INFLATION FACTOR
     ADJUST RESULT TO CORRECT BCD
     PUT RESULT BACK IN ARRAY
UNTIL ALL PRICES ARE INFLATED
```

PSEUDOCODE

(*b*)

```
page, 132
;8086 PROGRAM
;ABSTRACT        : program adds an inflation factor to a series
;                  of prices in memory. It copies the new price
;                  over the old price
;REGISTERS USED: DS, CS, AX, BX, CX
;PORTS USED      : None
;PROCEDURES      : None used
ARRAYS_HERE      SEGMENT
                 COST     DB  20H, 28H, 15H, 26H, 19H, 27H, 16H, 29H
                 PRICES   DB  36H, 55H, 27H, 42H, 38H, 41H, 29H, 59H
ARRAYS_HERE      ENDS
CODE_HERE        SEGMENT
                 ASSUME CS : CODE_HERE, DS : ARRAYS_HERE
                 MOV     AX, ARRAYS_HERE
                 MOV     DS, AX              ; initialize data segment
                 LEA     BX, PRICES          ; initialize pointer
                 MOV     CX, 0008H           ; initialize counter
DO_NEXT:         MOV     AL, [BX]            ; copy a price to AL
                 ADD     AL, 03H             ; add inflation factor
                 DAA                         ; make sure result is BCD
                 MOV     [BX], AL            ; copy result back to memory
                 INC     BX                  ; point to next price
                 DEC     CX                  ; decrement counter
                 JNZ     DO_NEXT             ; if not last, go get next
CODE_HERE        ENDS
                 END
```

(*c*)

```
page ,132
;8086 PROGRAM
;ABSTRACT          : Program adds a profit factor to each element in
;                  : a COST array and puts the result in an array
;                  : called PRICES
;REGISTERS USED : DS, CS, AX, BX, CX
;PORTS USED        : None
;PROCEDURES        : None used
ARRAYS_HERE        SEGMENT
                   COST    DB  20H, 28H, 15H, 26H, 19H, 27H, 16H, 29H
                   PRICES  DB  8 DUP(0)
ARRAYS_HERE        ENDS
PROFIT             EQU      15H                  ; profit = 15 cents
CODE_HERE          SEGMENT
                   ASSUME  CS:CODE_HERE, DS:ARRAYS_HERE
                   MOV  AX, ARRAYS_HERE          ; initialize data segment
                   MOV  DS, AX
                   MOV  CX, 0008H                ; initialize counter
                   MOV  BX, 0000H                ; initialize pointer
DO_NEXT:           MOV  AL, COST[BX]             ; point to element in COST
                   ADD  AL, PROFIT               ; add the profit to COST
                   DAA                           ; decimal adjust result
                   MOV  PRICES[BX], AL           ; store result in PRICES
                   INC  BX                       ; point to next element
                                                 ; in the arrays
                   DEC  CX                       ; decrement the counter
                   JNZ  DO_NEXT                  ; if not last, do again
CODE_HERE          ENDS
                   END
```

(d)

FIGURE 4-15 *(continued)*.

values specified in the DB statement. The statement, PRICES DB 36H,55H,27H,42H,38H,41H,29H,59H, sets up another 8-element array of bytes and gives it the name PRICES. The eight memory locations will be loaded with the specified values when the assembled program is loaded into memory. Figure 4-16 shows how these two arrays will be arranged in memory. Note that the name of the array represents the displacement or offset of the first element of the array from the start of the data segment.

The first two instructions, MOV AX, ARRAYS_HERE and MOV DS, AX initialize the data segment register as was described for the example program in Figure 3-10. The LEA mnemonic in the next instruction stands for load effective address. An effective address, remember, is the number of bytes from the start of a segment to the desired data item. The instruction LEA BX, PRICES loads the displacement of the first element of PRICES into the BX register. A displacement contained in a register is usually referred to as an offset. If you take another look at the data structure for this program in Figure 4-16 you should see that the offset of PRICES is 0008H. Therefore, the LEA BX, PRICES instruction will load BX with

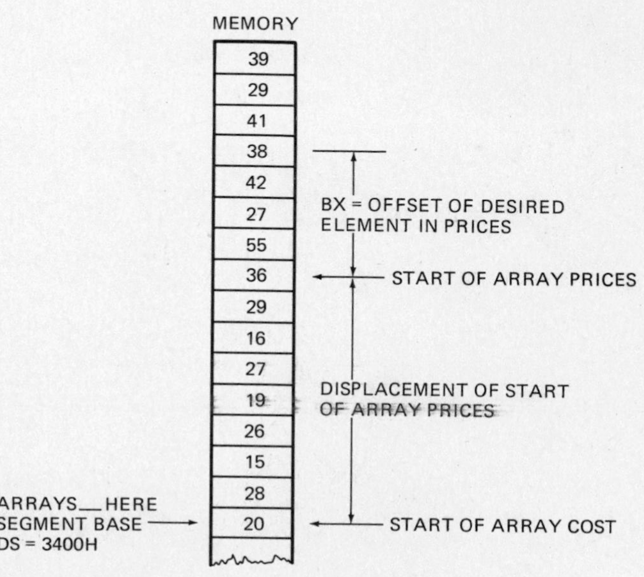

FIGURE 4-16 Data arrangement in memory for "inflate prices" program.

0008H. We say that BX is a *pointer* to an element in PRICES. We will soon show you how this pointer is used to indicate which price we want to operate on at a given time in the program. The next instruction, MOV CX, 0008H, loads the CX register with the number of prices in the array. We use this register as a counter to keep track of how many prices we have operated on. After we operate on each price, we decrement the counter by one. When the counter reaches zero, we know that we have operated on all of the prices.

The MOV AL, [BX] instruction copies one of the prices from memory to the AL register. Remember, the 8086 produces the physical address for accessing data in memory by shifting the contents of a segment register four bit positions left and adding an effective address, EA, to the result. A section in Chapter 3 showed you how the effective address could be specified directly in the instruction with either a name or a number. The instructions MOV AX, MULTIPLICAND and MOV AX, DS:WORD PTR [0000H] are examples of this addressing mode. For the instruction MOV AL, [BX] the effective address is contained in the BX register where we put it with the LEA instruction above. The first time this instruction executes, BX will contain 0008H, the effective address or offset of the first price in the array. Therefore, the first price will be copied into AL. To produce the physical memory address the 8086 will shift the contents of the data segment register four bit positions left and add this 0008H to the result.

The next instruction ADD AL, 03H adds the immediate number 03H to the contents of the AL register. The binary result of the addition will be left in AL. We want the prices in the array to be in BCD form, so we have to make sure the result is adjusted to be a legal BCD number. For example, if we add 03 to 29 the result in AL will be 2C. Most people would not understand this as a price so we have to adjust the result to the desired BCD number. The Decimal Adjust after Addition instruction DAA will automatically make this adjustment for us. DAA will adjust the 2CH by adding six to the lower nibble and the carry produced to the upper nibble. The result of this in AL will be 32H which is the result we want from adding 03 to 29. The DAA instruction only works on the AL register. For further examples of DAA operation, consult the DAA instruction description in Chapter 6.

The INC BX instruction adds 1 to the number in BX. BX now contains the effective address or offset of the next price in the array. We like to say that BX now points to the next element in the array. The DEC CX instruction decrements the count we set up in the CX register by 1. If CX contains 0 after this decrement, the zero flag will be set to a 1. The JNZ DO_NEXT checks the zero flag. If it finds the zero flag set, it just passes execution out of the structure to the next mainline instruction. If it finds the zero flag not set, the JNZ instruction will cause a jump to the label DO_NEXT. Execution will repeat the sequence of instructions between the label and the JNZ instruction until CX is counted down to zero. Each time through the loop, BX will be incremented to point to the next price in the array.

Using a pointer to access data items in memory is a powerful technique that you will want to use in your programs. Figure 4-15*d* shows another example. Here we want to add a profit of 15 cents to each element of an array called COST and put the result in the corresponding element of an array called PRICES. We first initialize BX as a pointer to the first element of each array with MOV BX, 000H. The instruction MOV AL, COST[BX] will copy the first cost value into AL. The effective address for this instruction will be produced by adding the displacement represented by the name COST to the contents of BX. Likewise, the instruction MOV PRICES[BX], AL copies the result of the addition to the first element of PRICES. When BX is incremented, COST[BX] and PRICES[BX] will each access the next element in the array. A programmer familiar with higher level lan-

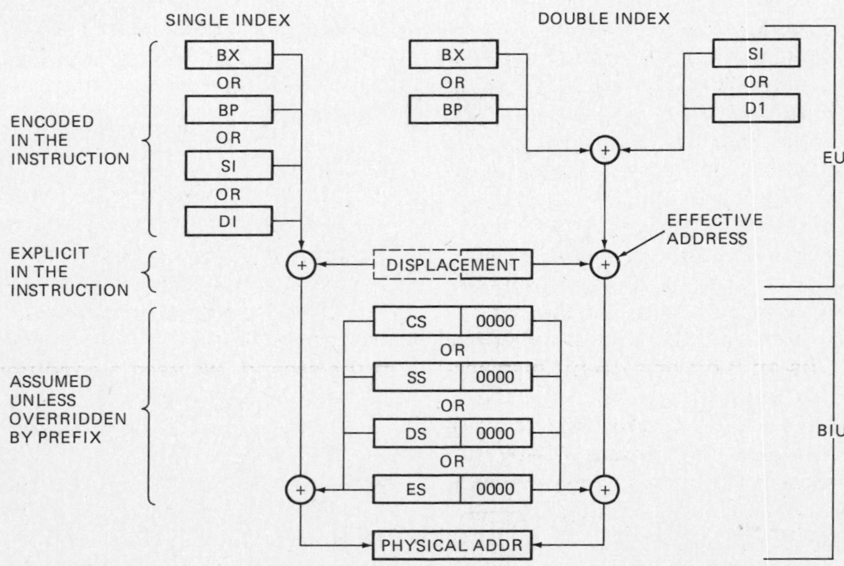

FIGURE 4-17 Summary of 8086 addressing modes.

```
SEGMENT BASE
        .
        .                Name PATIENTS represents displacement of
        .                start of array of records from segment base

PATIENTS                    ; array of patient records starts here

                                  RECORD 1
                                  TV N. BEER
                                  1324 Down Street
                                  Portland, OR 97219
                                  2/15/45
                                  247 lb
                                  $327.56

BX holds offset of ---------> RECORD 2
desired record in array       IM A. RUNNER
                                  13733 S.W. Knaus Rd
                                  Lake Oswego, OR 97304
                                  6/30/41
                                  145 lb
SI holds offset of ---------> $0.00
desired field in record

                                  RECORD 3
```

FIGURE 4-18 Use of double indexed addressing mode.

guages would probably say that BX is being used as an array index. The 8086 has several registers which can be used to index or to point to data in memory.

Figure 4-17 summarizes all the ways you can tell the 8086 to calculate an effective address and a physical address for accessing data in memory. In all cases the physical address is generated by adding an effective address to one of the segment bases, CS, SS, DS, or ES. The effective address can be a direct displacement specified directly in the instruction as, for example, MOV AX, MULTIPLIER. The effective address or offset can be specified to be in a register, as in the instruction MOV AL, [BX]. Also the effective address can be specified to be the contents of a register plus a displacement in the instruction. The instruction MOV AX, PRICES[BX] is an example. For this example, PRICES represents the displacement of the start of the array from the segment base and BX represents the number of the element in the array that we want to access. The effective address of the desired element then is the sum of these two.

For working with more complex data structures such as records, you can tell the 8086 to compute an effective address by adding the contents of BX or BP plus the contents of SI or DI plus an 8-bit or a 16-bit displacement contained in the instruction. The instruction MOV AL, PATIENTS [BX][SI] is an example of this addressing mode. Figure 4-18 shows an example of why you might want an addressing mode such as this to access the balance due field in some medical records in memory. We will illustrate the use of some of these more complex addressing modes in later chapters.

When BX, SI, or DI is used to contain all or part of the effective address, the physical address will be produced by adding the effective address to the data segment base in DS. When BP is used to contain all or part of the effective address, the physical address will be produced by adding the effective address to the stack segment base in SS. For any of these four, you can use a segment override prefix to tell the 8086 to add the effective address to some other segment base. The instruction MOV AL, CS:[BX] tells the 8086 to produce a physical memory address by adding the offset in BX to the code segment base instead of to the data segment base. An exception to this is that with a special group of instructions called *string instructions* an offset in DI will always be added to the extra segment base in ES to produce the physical address.

Summary of REPEAT—UNTIL Implementation

The preceding sections have shown two examples of implementing the REPEAT—UNTIL structure. In the first example we repeated a series of actions until a condition was found to be present. Specifically, we kept looking and testing until we found a strobe signal high. In the second. We used a conditional jump instruction to check the condition of a flag and make the decision whether to repeat the series of actions or not.

In the second REPEAT—UNTIL example we introduced the concept of using a register as a pointer to a data element in an array. We also showed in this example how to make a program repeat a sequence of instructions a specific number of times. To do this we load the desired number of repeats in a register or memory location. Each time we execute the series of instructions, we decrement this counter by one. When the count in the register is decremented to zero, the zero flag will be set. Again we use a conditional jump instruction to check this flag and to decide whether to repeat the instruction sequence in the loop again.

The need for performing a sequence of actions a specified number of times in a program is so common that some programming languages use a specific structure to express it. This structure, derived from the basic WHILE—DO, is called the FOR—DO. It has the form

FOR count = 1 to count = *n* DO
  Action
  Action

where *n* is the number of times we want to do the sequence of actions. In assembly language you will usually implement this by loading *n* into a register and counting it down as shown in Figure 4-15*c*.

The common need to repeat a sequence of actions a specified number of times also led the designers of the 8086 to give it a group of instructions which make this easier for you. These instructions are the LOOP instructions which we discuss in the next section.

The 8086 LOOP Instructions

INSTRUCTION OPERATION AND EXAMPLES

The LOOP instructions have the format LOOP label. These instructions combine two operations in each instruction. The first operation is to decrement the CX register by one. The second operation is to check the CX register and, in some cases, also the zero flag to decide whether to do a jump to the specified label. As with the previously described conditional jump instructions, the LOOP instructions can only do short jumps. This means that the destination label must be in the range of −128 bytes to +127 bytes from the instruction after the LOOP instruction. Figure 4-19 summarizes the LOOP instructions. Instruction mnemonics separated by a "/" represent the same instruction. NE in the mnemonics stands for not equal, and NZ in the mnemonics stands for not zero. Also shown in the figure is the condition(s) checked by each instruction to decide if it should do the jump.

The basic LOOP-label instruction will decrement the CX register by 1 and jump to the specified label if the CX register is not 0. The instruction LOOP DO_NEXT, for example, could be used in place of the DEC CX and the JNZ DO_NEXT instructions in the program in Figure 4-15*c*.

The LOOP instructions decrement the CX register, but do not affect the zero flag. This leaves the zero flag available for other tests. The LOOPE/LOOPZ label instruction will decrement the CX register by one and jump to the specified label if CX is not equal to zero *and* if the zero flag is set to a one. In other words program execution will exit from the repeat loop if CX has been decremented down to zero *or* the zero flag is not set. This instruction might be used after a compare instruction, for example, to continue a sequence of operations for a specified number of times or until compared values were no longer equal.

LOOP	Loop until CX = 0
LOOPE/LOOPZ	Loop if zero flag set and CX < > 0
LOOPNE/LOOPNZ	Loop if zero flag not set and CX < > 0
JCXZ	Jump if CX = 0

FIGURE 4-19 8086 LOOP instructions.

The LOOPNE/LOOPNZ label instruction decrements the CX register by one. If CX is not zero *and* the zero flag is not set, this instruction will cause a jump to the specified label. In other words, execution will exit from the loop if CX is equal to zero *or* the zero flag is set. This instruction is useful when you want to execute a sequence of instructions a fixed number of times or until two values are equal. An example might be a program to read data from a disk. We typically write this type of program so that it attempts to read the data until the checksums are equal or until 10 unsuccessful attempts have been made to read the disk.

Another instruction often listed with the LOOP instructions is the JCXZ label instruction. This instruction does not affect the CX register. It simply does a short jump to the specified label if the CX register is zero. The JCXZ instruction checks the CX register directly, it does not check the zero flag.

In summary then, the LOOP instructions are useful for implementing the REPEAT—UNTIL structure for those special cases where we want to do a series of actions a fixed number of times *or* until the zero flag changes state. LOOP instructions incorporate two operations in each instruction; therefore, they are somewhat more efficient than single instructions to do the same job. The 8086 string instructions, which we discuss in a later section of this chapter, incorporate even more operations in single instructions. Some of the string instructions can implement an entire REPEAT—UNTIL structure with a single instruction. In the next section, we introduce you to instruction timing and show how the LOOP instruction can be used to produce a delay between the execution of instructions.

INSTRUCTION TIMING AND DELAY LOOPS

The rate at which 8086 instructions are executed is determined by a crystal-controlled clock with a frequency of a few megahertz. Each instruction takes a certain number of clock cycles to execute. The MOV register, register instruction, for example, requires 2 clock cycles to execute and the DAA instruction requires 4 clock cycles. The JNZ instruction requires 16 clock cycles if it does the jump and only 4 clock cycles if it doesn't do the jump. A table in Appendix B shows the number of clock cycles required by each instruction. Using the numbers in this table you can calculate how long it takes to execute an instruction or series of instructions. For example, if we are running an 8086 with a 5-MHz clock, then each clock cycle takes 1/5 MHz or 0.2 μs. An instruction which takes 4 clock cycles then will take 4 clock cycles x 0.2 μs/clock cycle or 0.8 μs to execute.

A common programming problem is the need to introduce a delay between the execution of two instructions. For example, we might want to read a data value from a port, wait 1 ms, and then read the port again. A later chapter will show how you can use interrupts to mark off time intervals. Here we show you how to use a program loop to do it.

The basic principle is to execute an instruction or series of instructions over and over until the desired time has elapsed. Figure 4-20*a* shows a program we might use to do this. The MOV CX, N instruction loads the CX register with the number of times we want to repeat the delay loop. Just ahead we show you how to calculate this number for a desired amount of delay. The NOP instructions next in the program are not required. The KILL_TIME label could be right in front of the LOOP instruction. In this case, only the LOOP instruction would be repeated. We put the NOPs in to show you how you can get more delay by extending the time it takes to execute the loop. The LOOP KILL_TIME instruction will decrement CX and, if it is not down to zero yet, do a jump to the label KILL_TIME. The program then will execute the two NOP instructions and the LOOP instruction over and over until CX is counted down to zero. The number in CX will determine how long this takes. Here's how you determine the value to put in CX for a given amount of delay.

First you calculate the number of clock cycles needed to produce the desired delay. If you are running your 8086 with a 5-MHz clock, then the time for each clock cycle then is 1/5 MHz or 0.2 μs. Now, suppose that you want to create a delay of 1 ms or 1000 μs with a delay loop. If you divide the 1000 μs desired by the 0.2 μs per clock cycle, you get the number of clock cycles required to produce the desired delay. For this example then you need a total of 5000 (1000/0.2) clock cycles to produce the desired delay.

The next step is to write the number of clock cycles required for each instruction next to that instruction as shown in Figure 4-20*a*. Then look at the program to determine which instructions get executed only once. The number of clock cycles for these instructions will only contribute to the total once. Instructions which only enter once in the calculation are often called *overhead*. We will represent the number of cycles of overhead with the symbol C_o. In Figure 4-20*a* the only instruction which executes just once is MOV CX, N, which takes 4 clock cycles. For this example then, C_o is 4.

Now determine how many clock cycles are required for the loop. The two NOPs in the loop require a total of 6 clock cycles. The LOOP instruction requires 17 clock cycles if it does the jump back to KILL_TIME, but it requires only 5 clock cycles when it exits the loop. The jump takes longer because the instruction byte queue has to be reloaded starting from the new address. For all but the very last time through the loop it will require 17 clock cycles for the LOOP instruction. Therefore, you can use 17 as the number of cycles for the LOOP instruction and compensate later for the fact that for the last time it uses 12 cycles less. For the example program the number of cycles per loop, C_L, is 6 + 17 or 23. The total number of clock cycles delayed by the loop is equal to the number of times the loop executes multiplied by

```
                                     Clock Cycles
            MOV   CX, N              4       = Co
KILL_TIME:  NOP                      3
            NOP                      3       = CL
            LOOP KILL_TIME           17/5
```

(a)

$$C_T = C_O + N(C_L) - 12$$

$$N = \frac{C_T - C_O + 12}{C_L} = \frac{5000 - 4 + 12}{23} = 218 = 0D9H$$

(b)

FIGURE 4-20 Delay loop program and calculations. *(a)* Program. *(b)* Calculations.

the time per loop. To be somewhat more accurate you can subtract the 12 cycles that were not used when the last LOOP instruction executed. The total number of clock cycles required for the example program to execute is $C_O + N(C_L) - 12$. Set this equal to the number of clock cycles of delay you want, 5000 for this example, and solve the result for *N*. Figure 4-20*b* shows how this is done. The resultant value for *N* is 218 decimal or 0D9H. This is the number of times you want the loop to repeat, so this is the value of *N* that you will load into CX before entering the loop.

With the simple relationship shown in Figure 4-20*b*, you can determine the value of *N* to put in a delay loop you write, or you can determine the time a delay loop written by someone else will take to execute.

If you can't get a long enough delay by counting down a single register or memory location, you can nest delay loops. An example of this nesting is:

```
                                 ;number of states
         MOV  BX,COUNT1          ;4
CNTDN1:  MOV  CX, COUNT2         ;4 x COUNT1
CNTDN2:  LOOP CNTDN2             ;((17xCOUNT2)-12)COUNT1
         DEC  BX                 ;2(COUNT1)
         JNZ  CNTDN1             ;16(COUNT1)-12
```

The principle here is to load CX with COUNT2 and count CX down COUNT1 times. To determine the number of states that this program section will take to execute, observe that the LOOP instruction will execute COUNT2 times for each time CX is loaded with COUNT1. The total number of states then is COUNT1 times the number of states for the last four instructions plus 4, for the MOV BX, COUNT1 instruction. The best way to approach getting values for the two unknowns, COUNT1 and COUNT2, is to choose a value such as FFFFH for COUNT2 and then solve for the value of COUNT1. A couple of tries should get reasonable values for both COUNT1 and COUNT2.

Delay loops are a very common use of the REPEAT—UNTIL structure. The next section describes the 8086 string instructions which are often used in REPEAT—UNTIL structures.

The 8086 String Instructions

INTRODUCTION AND OPERATION

A string is a series of bytes or words stored in successive memory locations. Often a string consists of a series of ASCII character codes. When you use a word processor or text-editor program, you are actually creating a string of this sort as you type in characters. One important feature of a word processor is the ability to move a sentence or group of sentences from one place in the text to another. Doing this involves moving a string of ASCII characters from one place in memory to another. The 8086 Move String instruction, MOVS, allows you to do this very easily. Another important feature of most word processors is the ability to search through the text looking for a given word or phrase. The 8086 Compare String instruction, CMPS, allows you to do this easily. Let's see how these string instructions work.

MOVING A STRING

Suppose that we have a string of ASCII characters in successive memory locations starting at offset 2000H in the data segment, and we want to move this string to an offset of 2400H in the data segment. Figure 4-21*a* shows the basic pseudocode for this operation. When we start thinking about how we can implement this algorithm in assembly language, several points come to mind. We need a pointer to the source string to keep track of which string element we are moving at a given time. This is the same reason we needed a pointer in the price-fixing program in Figure 4-15*c*. We use the source index register for this pointer. SI will hold the offset of the byte that we are moving at a given time. We also need a pointer to the location where we are moving string elements to. The destination index register DI is used to hold the offset of the location where a byte is being moved to at a given time. Another need is for a counter to keep track of how many string bytes have been moved so we can determine when we have moved all of the string. We use the CX register as a counter for string operations. Having these pieces in mind we can expand the pseudocode for the problem as shown in Figure 4-21*b*. We often describe an algorithm in general terms at first and then expand sections as needed to help us see how the algorithm is implemented in a specific language. In the expanded version in Figure 4-21*b*, you can see that we need to initialize the two pointers and the counter. The REPEAT—UNTIL loop consists of moving a byte, incrementing the pointers to point to the source and destination for the next byte, and decrementing the counter so we can see if all of the bytes have been moved.

As it turns out, the single 8086 string instruction, MOVSB, will perform all of the actions in the REPEAT—UNTIL loop. In other words the MOVSB instruction will copy a byte from the location pointed to by the SI register to a location pointed to by the DI register. It will then automatically increment SI to point to the next source location, increment DI to point to the next destination location. Actually, as we will show you soon, we can specify whether we want SI and DI to increment or decrement. If we add a special prefix called the *repeat* prefix in front of the MOVSB instruction, the MOVSB instruction will be repeated and CX decremented until CX is counted down to zero. In other words it will repeat the MOVSB instruction until the entire string is copied to the destination location.

Figure 4-21*c* shows the program instructions to move our string of bytes. The first three instructions in the program initialize the data segment register and the extra segment register. After that we load the SI register with 2000H so that it points to the start of the source string. We then load the DI register with 2400H so that it points to the first address of the desired destination. Actually, for string instructions, the offset in DI is added to the extra segment to produce the physical address.

However, if DS and ES are initialized with the same value as we did with the first three instructions in the program, then SI and DI will both be added to the same segment base. Next we load the CX register with the number of bytes in the string we are moving. CX will function as a counter to keep track of how many string bytes have been moved at any given time. Finally, we make the direction flag a 0 with the Clear Direction Flag instruction, CLD. This will cause both SI and DI to be automatically incremented after a string byte is moved. If the direction flag is set with the STD instruction, then SI and DI will be automatically decremented after each string byte is moved. Now when the Move String Byte instruction, MOVSB, executes, a byte pointed to by SI will be copied to the location pointed to by DI. SI and DI will be automatically incremented to point to the next source and to the next destination. The count register will be automatically decremented. The MOVSB instruction by itself will just copy one byte and update SI and DI. However, with the repeat prefix, REP, in front of the MOVSB instruction as shown, CX will be decremented and the instruction will execute over and over again until the CX register is counted down to zero. When the program is coded, the 8-bit code for the REP prefix, 11110010, is put in the memory location before the code for the MOVSB instruction, 10100100. After the MOVSB instruction is finished, SI will be pointing to the location after the last source string byte, DI will be pointing to the location after the last destination address, and CX will be zero.

The MOVSW instruction can be used to move a string of words. Depending on the state of the direction flag, SI and DI will automatically be incremented or decremented by two after each move. CX will be decremented by one after each word move with the REP prefix so CX should be initialized with the number of words in the string.

```
REPEAT
      MOVE BYTE FROM SOURCE STRING TO DESTINATION STRING
UNTIL ALL BYTES MOVED
```

(a)

```
INITIALIZE SOURCE POINTER, SI
INITIALIZE DESTINATION POINTER, DI
INITIALIZE COUNTER, CX

REPEAT
     COPY BYTE FROM SOURCE TO DESTINATION
     INCREMENT SOURCE POINTER, SI
     INCREMENT DESTINATION POINTER, DI
     DECREMENT COUNTER, CX
UNTIL CX = 0
```

(b)

```
CODE_HERE SEGMENT
          ASSUME    CS:CODE_HERE, DS:STRINGS_HERE, ES:STRINGS_HERE
          MOV  AX, 0000
          MOV  DS, AX               ; initialize DS
          MOV  ES, AX               ; initialize ES
          MOV  SI, 2000H            ; initialize SI
          MOV  DI, 2400H            ; initialize DI
          MOV  CX, 0080H            ; initialize counter -
                                    ; 128 bytes in string
          CLD                       ; increment SI & DI
REP       MOVSB                     ; move one byte
```

(c)

FIGURE 4-21 Program for moving a string from one location to another in memory. *(a)* First-version pseudocode. *(b)* Expanded-version pseudocode. *(c)* Assembly language.

STRING INSTRUCTIONS OVERVIEW

A section in Chapter 3 shows a list of the string instructions with short descriptions of their operations. Take a look at this list to give you an overview of this group of instructions, and then go on to the second string instruction example which follows. Consult the detailed descriptions of the individual instructions in Chapter 6 for further information and short program examples for each.

USING THE COMPARE STRING BYTE TO CHECK A PASSWORD

For this program example suppose that we want to compare a password entered by a person who wants to use the computer with the correct password stored in memory. If the passwords do not match, we want to sound an alarm. If the passwords match, we want to continue on with the mainline program. Figure 4-22 shows how we might represent the algorithm for this with a flowchart and with pseudocode. Note that we want to terminate the REPEAT—UNTIL when either the compared bytes do not match, or when we are at the end of the string. We then use an IF—THEN structure to sound the alarm if the compared strings were not equal at any point. If the strings match, the IF—THEN just directs execution on to the main program.

To implement this algorithm in assembly language, we probably would first expand the basic structures as we did for the previous string example in Figure 4-21. Figure 4-22*c* shows how we might do this expansion. The first action in the expanded algorithm is to initialize the port device for output. We need to have an output port because we will turn on the alarm by outputting a 1 to the alarm control circuit. You can see that we need a pointer to each string and a counter to keep track of how many string elements have been compared. If you use SI and DI for the pointers and CX for the counter, then the 8086 Compare String Bytes instruction, CMPSB, will implement all of the actions between REPEAT and UNTIL. If we put the correct repeat prefix in front of this instruction, the single instruction statement will implement the entire REPEAT—UNTIL structure.

Figure 4-23 reviews some old concepts, introduces a few new ones, and shows how this program can be done in assembly language. First let's look at the data structure for this program. The statement PASSWORD DB 'FAILSAFE' sets aside 8 bytes of memory and gives the first memory location the name PASSWORD. This statement also initializes the eight memory locations with the ASCII codes for the letters FAILSAFE. The single quotes around FAILSAFE tell the assembler to put the ASCII codes for the letters of this word in successive memory locations. For FAILSAFE the ASCII codes will be 46H, 41H, 49H, 4CH, 53H, 41H, 46H, 45H. The statement INPUT_WORD DB 8 DUP(?) will set aside eight memory locations and assign the name INPUT_WORD to the first location. The DUP(?) in the statement tells the assembler not to initialize these eight locations. We assume that another program section will load these locations with ASCII codes read from the keyboard.

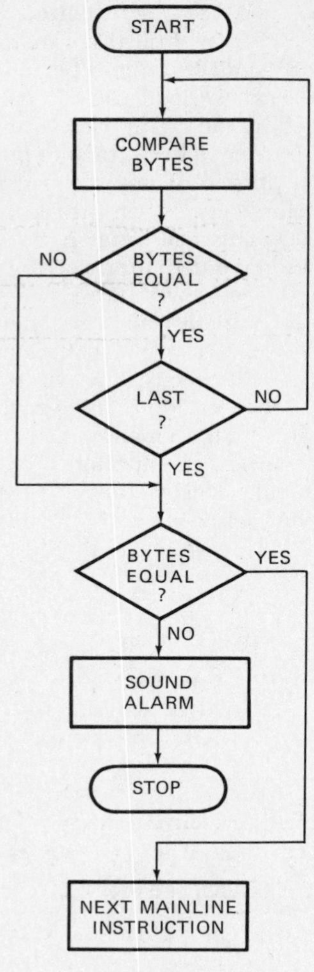

(*a*)

```
REPEAT
    COMPARE SOURCE BYTE WITH DESTINATION BYTE
UNTIL (BYTES NOT EQUAL) OR (END OF STRING)
IF BYTES NOT EQUAL THEN
    SOUND ALARM
    STOP
DO NEXT MAINLINE INSTRUCTION
```

(*b*)

```
INITIALIZE PORT DEVICE FOR OUTPUT
INITIALIZE SOURCE POINTER — SI
INITIALIZE DESTINATION POINTER — DI
INITIALIZE COUNTER — CX
REPEAT
    COMPARE SOURCE BYTE WITH DESTINATION BYTE
    INCREMENT SOURCE POINTER
    INCREMENT DESTINATION POINTER
    DECREMENT COUNTER
UNTIL (STRING BYTES NOT EQUAL) OR (CX = 0)
IF STRING BYTES NOT EQUAL THEN
    SOUND ALARM
    STOP
DO NEXT MAINLINE INSTRUCTION
```

(*c*)

FIGURE 4-22 Flowchart and pseudocode for comparing strings program. *(a)* Flowchart. *(b)* Initial pseudocode. *(c)* Expanded pseudocode.

Now let's look at the code segment section of the program. The ASSUME statement tells the assembler that the instructions will be in the segment CODE_HERE. It also tells the assembler that any references to the data segment or to the extra segment will mean the segment DATA_HERE. We have to tell the assembler what to assume about the extra segment, because with string instructions an offset in DI is added to the extra segment base to produce the physical address.

The next three MOV statements in the program initialize the data and extra segment registers. Since we initialize DS and ES with the same values, both SI and DI will point to locations in the segment DATA_HERE. The next three instructions initialize port P2B of an SDK-86 board as an output port.

LEA SI, PASSWORD loads the effective address or offset of the start of the FAILSAFE string into the SI register. Since PASSWORD is the first data item in the segment DATA_HERE, SI will be loaded with 0000H. LEA DI, INPUT_WORD loads the effective address or offset of the start of the INPUT_WORD string into the DI register. Since the offset of INPUT_WORD is 0008H, DI will be loaded with this value. The MOV CX, 08H statement initializes CX with the number of bytes in the string. The clear direction flag instruction tells the 8086 to automatically increment SI and DI after two string bytes are compared.

The CMPSB instruction will compare the byte pointed to by SI with the byte pointed to by DI and set the flags according to the result. It will also increment the pointers, SI and DI, to point to the next string elements, and decrement the counter, CX, to indicate that two string elements have been compared. The REPE prefix in front of this instruction tells the 8086 to repeat the CMPSB instruction if the compared bytes were equal *and* CX is not decremented down to zero yet. When the instruction is coded, the code for this prefix, 11110011, will be put in memory before the code for the CMPSB instruction, 10100110.

If the zero flag is not set when execution leaves the repeat loop then we know that the two strings are not equal. This means that the password entered was not valid so we want to sound an alarm. The JNE SOUND_ALARM will check the zero flag and, if it is not set, do a jump to the specified label. If the zero flag is set, indicating a valid password, then execution falls through to the JMP OK instruction. This JMP instruction simply jumps over the instructions which sound the alarm and stops the computer.

For this example we assume that the alarm control is connected to the least-significant bit of port FFFAH and that a 1 output to this bit turns on the alarm. The MOV AL, 01 instruction loads a 1 in the LSB of AL. The MOV DX, 0FFFAH instruction points DX at the port that the alarm is connected to and the OUT DX, AL instruction copies this byte to port FFFAH. Finally, the HLT instruction stops the computer. An interrupt or reset will be required to get it started again.

As the preceding examples show, the string instructions make it very easy to implement some commonly needed REPEAT—UNTIL algorithms. Some of the programming problems at the end of the chapter will give you practice with these. The next section here gives you some hints on how to debug the programs that you write.

DEBUGGING ASSEMBLY LANGUAGE PROGRAMS

So far in this book we have tried to show you the tools and techniques used to write assembly language programs. By now you should be writing some programs of your own, so we need to give you a few hints on how to debug your programs if they don't work correctly the first time you try to run them.

The first technique you use when you hit a difficult-to-find problem in either hardware or software is the *Five Minute Rule*. This rule says "You get 5 minutes to freak out and mumble about changing vocations, then you have to cope with the problem in a systematic manner." What this means is step back from the problem, collect your wits, and think out a systematic series of steps to find the solution. We have seen many technicians waste a lot of valuable time randomly poking and probing to try to find the cause of a problem. Here is a list of additional techniques you may find useful in writing and debugging your programs.

1. Very carefully define the problem you are trying to solve with the program and work out the best algorithm you can.

2. If the program consists of several parts, write, test and debug each part individually then add parts one at a time.

3. If a program or program section does not work, first recheck the algorithm to make sure it really does what you want it to. You might have someone else look at it also. Another person may quickly spot an error you have overlooked 17 times.

4. If the algorithm seems correct, check to make sure that you have used the correct instructions to implement the algorithm. It is very easy to accidentally switch the operands in an instruction. You might, for example, write down the instruction MOV AX, DX when the instruction you really want is MOV DX, AX. Sometimes it helps to work out on paper the effect that a series of instructions will have on some sample numbers. These predictions on paper can later be compared with the actual results produced when the program section runs.

5. If you are hand coding your programs, this is the next place to check. It is very easy to get a bit wrong when you construct the 8086 instruction codes. Also remember, when constructing instruction codes which contain addresses or displacements, that the low byte of the address or displacement is coded in before the high byte.

```
page, 132
;8086 PROGRAM
;ABSTRACT       : This program inputs a password and sounds an
;                 alarm if the password is incorrect
;REGISTERS USED: CS, DS, ES, AX, DX, CX, SI, DI
;PORTS USED     : FFFAH - alarm output port
;PROCEDURES     : None used

DATA_HERE       SEGMENT
        PASSWORD        DB   'FAILSAFE'
        INPUT_WORD      DB   8 DUP(?)     ; space for user input
DATA_HERE       ENDS

CODE_HERE       SEGMENT
                ASSUME CS:CODE_HERE, DS:DATA_HERE, ES:DATA_HERE

                MOV     AX, DATA_HERE     ; initialize data &
                MOV     DS, AX            ; extra segments
                MOV     ES, AX

                MOV     DX, OFFFEH        ; set up port
                MOV     AL, 99H           ; as an output port
                OUT     DX, AL

                LEA     SI, PASSWORD      ; load source pointer
                LEA     DI, INPUT_WORD    ; load destination pointer
                MOV     CX, 08H           ; counter = password length
                CLD                       ; increment DI & SI
REPE            CMPSB                     ; compare the two strings
                JNE     SOUND_ALARM       ; not equal, sound alarm
                JMP     OK                ; equal - continue
SOUND_ALARM:    MOV     AL, 01            ; to sound alarm, send
                MOV     DX, OFFFAH        ; a 1 to the output
                OUT     DX, AL            ; port whose address is
                HLT                       ; in DX and HALT.
OK:             NOP                       ; rest of program for user
                                          ; whose password = FAILSAFE
CODE_HERE       ENDS
                END
```

FIGURE 4-23 Assembly language program for comparing strings.

6. If you don't find a problem in the algorithm, instructions, or coding, now is the time to use debugger, monitor, or emulator tools to help you localize the problem. You could use these tools right from the start, but by doing this it is easy to get lost in chasing bits and not see the bigger picture of what is causing the program to fail. For short program sections, the debugger or monitor *trace* and *single-step* functions may help you determine where the program is not doing what you want it to do. The IBM PC Debugger Trace command displays the contents of the registers after each instruction executes. After you run to a breakpoint then you can use the dump memory command to examine the contents of the memory. The SDK-86 board's Single Step command executes one instruction and then stops execution. You can then use the Examine Register and Examine Memory commands to see if registers and memory contain the correct data at that point. If the results are correct at that point you can use the trace or single step command to execute the next instruction. Once you have localized the problem to one or two instructions, it is usually not too hard to find out what is wrong. See the accompanying laboratory manual instructions for using these functions.

7. For longer programs, the single-step approach can be somewhat tedious. Using breakpoints is often a faster technique to narrow the source of a problem down to a small region. Most debuggers, monitors,

and emulators allow you to specify both a starting address and an ending address in their "GO" command. The SDK-86 monitor GO command, for example, has the format: GO address, breakpoint address. The GO command for the IBM PC debugger has the format: G = address address. When you give these commands, execution will start at the address specified first in the command and stop when it reaches the address specified in the second position in the command. After the program runs to a breakpoint you can use the examine register and examine memory commands to check the results at that point. Here's how we use breakpoints.

Instead of running the entire program, specify a breakpoint so that execution stops some distance into the program. You can then check to see if the results are correct at this point. If they are, you can run the program again with the breakpoint at a later address and check the results at that point. If the results are not correct, you can move the breakpoint to an earlier point in the program, run it again, and check if the results in registers and memory are correct.

Suppose, for example, you write a program such as the price-fixing program in Figure 4-15*c* and it does not give the correct results. The first place to put a breakpoint might be at the address of the ADD AL, 03 instruction. Incidentally, the instruction at the address where you put the breakpoint does not get executed in most systems. After the program runs to this breakpoint, you check to see if the data segment register, pointer register and counter register were correctly initialized. You can also see if the first price got copied into AL. If the program works correctly to this point, you can run it again with the breakpoint at the address of the JNZ DO_NEXT instruction. After the program executes to this breakpoint you can check AL to see if the addition and decimal adjustment produced the results you predicted. If the 8086 is working at all it will almost always do operations such as this correctly, so recheck your predictions if you disagree with it. You can check the pointer in BX to see if it is pointing at the next price, and you can check the count in CX to see if it has been decremented as it should be. Also you can check to see if the adjusted price got put back in memory. If you have not found the problem by now, the problem may be in the JNZ DO_NEXT instruction. Perhaps you accidentally put the DO_NEXT label next to the ADD AL, 03H instruction instead of next to the MOV AL, [BX] instruction. Or, if you are hand coding, perhaps you calculated the displacement for the JNZ instruction incorrectly.

It helps your frustration level if you make a game of thinking where to put breakpoints to track down the little bug that is messing up your program. With a little practice you should soon develop an efficient debugging algorithm of your own using the specific tools available on your system.

CHECKLIST OF IMPORTANT TERMS AND CONCEPTS IN THIS CHAPTER

If you do not remember any of the terms or concepts in the following list, use the index to find them in the chapter.

Defining a problem

Setting up a data structure

Making an initialization checklist

Masking and moving nibbles using AND and OR instructions

Packed and unpacked BCD numbers

Conditional flags: CF, PF, AF, ZF, SF, OF

Jump instructions:
- Unconditional
- Direct and indirect within-segment near jumps
- Direct and indirect within-segment short jumps
- Direct and indirect intersegment jumps

Relocatable

Conditional jumps

Fixed- and variable-port input/output

Based and indexed addressing modes

Loop instruction

Delay loop clock cycles

String instructions

Debugging—breakpoints, trace, single step

REVIEW QUESTIONS AND PROBLEMS

1. Describe the operation and results of each of the following instructions, given the register contents shown in Figure 4-24. Include in your answer the physical address or register that each instruction will get its operands from and the physical address or register that each instruction will put the result in. Use the instruction descriptions in Chapter 6 to help you. Assume that the instructions below are independent, not sequential unless listed together under a letter.

a. ROL AX, CL

b. IN AL, DX

c. MOV CX, [BX]

d. ADD AX, [BX][SI]

e. JMP 023AH

f. JMP BX

g.
```
        MOV  AL, [BX]
NEXT:   ADD  AL, 02
        DEC  CL
        JNZ  NEXT
```

h.
```
             MOV  CX, 3FC2H
COUNT_DOWN:  LOOP COUNT_DOWN
```

i.
```
    MOV CX, 100 ;length of STRING_1
    MOV SI, OFFSET STRING_1
    MOV DI, OFFSET STRING_2
    CLD
REP MOVSB
```

2. Construct the binary codes for the instructions of Questions 1*a* through 1*f*.

3. Predict the state of the six 8086 conditional flags after each of the following instructions or group of instructions executes. Use the register contents shown in Figure 4-24. Assume all flags are reset before the instructions execute. Use the detailed instruction descriptions in Chapter 6 to help you.
   a. MOV AL, AH
   b. ADD BL, CL
   c. ADD CL, DH
   d. OR CX, BX

4. See if you can find any errors in the following instructions or groups of instructions.
   a.
   ```
   CNTDOWN: MOV BL, 72H
            DEC BL
            JNZ CNTDOWN
   ```
   b. REP ADD AL, 07
   c. JMP BL
   d. ADD CX, AL
   e. DIV AX, BX

5. *a.* Write an algorithm for a program which adds a byte number from one memory location to a byte from the next memory location, puts the sum in a third memory location, and saves the state of the carry flag in the least-significant bit of a fourth memory location. Mask the upper 7 bits of the memory location where the carry is stored.
   b. Write an 8086 assembly language program for this algorithm. *HINTS*: Set up data declarations similar to those in Figure 3-10. Use a rotate instruction to get the carry flag state into the LSB of a register or memory location.
   c. What additional instructions would you have to add to this program so that it correctly adds 2 BCD bytes?

For each of the following programming problems, draw a flowchart or write the pseudocode for an algorithm to solve the problem. Then write an 8086 assembly language program to implement the algorithm. If you have an 8086 system available, enter and assemble your source program, then load the object code for the program into memory so you can run and test it. If the program does not work correctly, use the approach described in the last section of this chapter to help you debug it.

6. Convert a packed BCD byte to two ASCII characters for the two BCD digits in the byte. For example, given a BCD byte containing 57H (01010111 binary), produce the two ASCII codes 35H and 37H.

7. Compute the average of 4 bytes stored in an array in memory.

8. Compute the average of any number of bytes in an array in memory. The number of bytes to be added is in the first byte of the array.

9. Add a 5-byte number in one array to a 5-byte number in another array. Put the sum in another array. Put the state of the carry flag in byte 6 of the array that contains the sum. The first value in each array is the least-significant byte of that number. *HINT*: See Figure 4-15*d*.

10. An 8086-based process control system outputs a measured Fahrenheit temperature to a display on its front panel. You need to write a short program which converts the Fahrenheit temperature to Celsius so that the system can be sold in Europe. The relationship between Fahrenheit and Celsius is: $C = (F - 32)5/9$. The Fahrenheit temperature will always be in the range of 50° to 250°. Round the Celsius value to the nearest degree.

11. An ASCII keyboard outputs parallel ASCII + parity to port FFF8H of an SDK-86 board. The keyboard also outputs a strobe to the least-significant bit (D0) of port FFFAH. (See Figure 4-13.) When you press a key, the keyboard outputs the ASCII code for the pressed key on the eight parallel lines and outputs a strobe pulse high for 1 ms. You want to poll the strobe over and over until you find it high. Then you want to read in the ASCII code, mask the parity bit (D7), and store the ASCII code in an array in memory. Next you want to poll the strobe over and over again until you find it low. When you find the strobe has gone low, check to see if you have read in 10 characters yet. If not, then go back and wait for the strobe to go high again. If 10 characters have been read in, stop.

12. *a.* Write a delay loop which produces a delay of 500 μs on an 8086 with an 8-MHz clock.

	AH	AL			BH	BL
AX	A4	07		BX	24	B3

	CH	CL			DH	DL
CX	00	02		DX	FF	FA

```
SP = FFFF        CS = 2000
BP = 0009        DS = 3000
SI = 4200        SS = 4000
DI = 4300        ES = 3000
```

FIGURE 4-24 Figure for Chapter 4 problems.

b. Write a short program which outputs a 1-kHz square wave on D0 of port FFFAH. The basic principle here is to output a high, wait 500 μs (0.5 ms), output a low, wait 500 μs and output a high, etc. Remember that, before you can output to a port device, you must first initialize it as in Figure 4-12*a*. If you connect a buffer such as that shown in Figure 8-22 and a speaker to D0 of the port, you will be able to hear the tone produced.

13. *a.* Move a string containing your name in the form "Charlie T. Tuna" from one string location in memory to a new string location named NEW_HOME which is just above the initial location.

b. Move the string containing your name up four addresses in memory. Consider whether the pointers should be incremented or decremented after each byte is moved in order to keep any needed byte from being written over. *HINT*: Initialize DI with the value of SI + 4.

14. Scan a string of 80 characters, looking for a carriage return (0DH). If a carriage return is found, put the length of the string up to the carriage return in AL. If no carriage return is found, put 50H (80 decimal) in AL.

15. Given a string containing your name in the form "Charlie T. Tuna", put the characters in a second string called LAST_FIRST in the order "Tuna Charlie T".

CHAPTER

5 IF—THEN—ELSE STRUCTURES, PROCEDURES, AND MACROS

The last chapter showed you how quite a few of the 8086 instructions work, and how jump instructions are used to implement WHILE—DO and REPEAT—UNTIL structures. A section of this chapter shows how IF—THEN—ELSE structures are also implemented with jump instructions. The major point of this chapter, however, is to show you how to write and use subprograms called *procedures*. A final section of the chapter shows you how to write and use assembler MACROs.

OBJECTIVES

At the conclusion of this chapter you should be able to:

1. Write 8086 assembly language programs to solve IF—THEN, IF—THEN—ELSE, and multiple IF—THEN—ELSE type programming problems.
2. Write an 8086 assembly language program which calls a near procedure.
3. Write an 8086 assembly language program which calls a far procedure.
4. Describe how a stack is initialized and used in 8086 assembly language programs which call procedures.
5. Write and use an assembler MACRO.

IF—THEN, IF—THEN—ELSE, AND MULTIPLE IF—THEN—ELSE PROGRAMS

IF—THEN Programs

Remember from Chapter 2 that the IF—THEN structure has the format:

```
IF condition THEN
  action
  action
```

This structure says that IF the stated condition is found to be true, the series of actions following THEN will be executed. If the condition is false, then execution will skip over the actions after the THEN and proceed on with the next mainline instruction.

The simple IF—THEN is implemented with a conditional jump instruction. In some cases an instruction to set flags is needed before the conditional jump instruction. Figure 5-1*a* shows, with a program fragment, one way to implement the simple IF—THEN structure. In this program we first compare BX with AX to set the required flags. If the zero flag is set after the comparison, indicating that AX is equal to BX, the JE instruction will cause execution to jump to the MOV CL, 07H instruction labeled THERE. If AX is not equal to BX, then the three NOP instructions after the JE instruction will be executed before the MOV CL, 07H instruction.

The implementation in Figure 5-1*a* will work well for a short sequence of instructions after the conditional jump instruction. However, if the sequence of instructions is lengthy, there is a potential problem. Remember from the discussion of conditional jumps in the last chapter that a conditional jump can only be to a location in the range of −128 bytes to +127 bytes from the address after the conditional jump instruction. A long sequence of instructions after the conditional jump instruction may put the label out of range of the conditional jump instruction. If you are absolutely sure that the destination label will not be out of range, then use the instruction sequence shown in Figure 5-1*a* to implement an IF—THEN structure. If you are not sure if the destination will be in range, Figure 5-1*b* shows an instruction sequence that will always work. In this sequence the conditional jump instruction only has to jump over the JMP instruction. The JMP instruction used to get to the label THERE can jump to anywhere in the code segment, or even to another code segment. Note that you have to change the conditional jump instruction from JE to JNE in this second version. The price

```
        CMP     AX, BX   ; compare to set flags
        JE      THERE    ; if equal then skip correction
        NOP
        NOP              ; NOPs represent correction
        NOP              ; instructions
THERE:  MOV     CL, 07H  ; load count
```

(a)

```
        CMP     AX, BX   ; compare to set flags
        JNE     FIX      ; if not equal do correction
        JMP     THERE
FIX:    NOP              ; NOPs represent correction
        NOP              ; instructions
        NOP
THERE:  MOV     CL, 07H  ; load count
```

(b)

FIGURE 5-1 IF—THEN implementations. *(a)* Conditional jump destinations closer than ±128 bytes. *(b)* Conditional jump destinations further than ±128 bytes.

you pay for not having to worry whether the destination is in range is an extra jump instruction.

By now you are probably thinking that this IF—THEN structure looks very familiar. It should, because a simple IF—THEN is part of the WHILE—DO and REPEAT—UNTIL structures. If you look back at the programs in the last chapter, you should see several examples of simple IF—THEN. One example is the instruction sequence in Figure 4-23 which turns on an alarm if two compared strings are not equal. We cycled through the simple IF—THEN again here as a lead-in to the IF—THEN—ELSE discussed next.

IF—THEN—ELSE Programs

The IF—THEN—ELSE structure is used to indicate a choice between two alternative courses of action. Figure 3-3*b* shows the flowchart and pseudocode for this structure. Basically the structure has the format:

IF condition THEN
  action
  action
ELSE
  action
  action
  action

This is a different situation than the simple IF—THEN, because here either one series of actions or another series of actions is done before the program goes on with the next mainline instruction. An example will show how we implement this structure.

Suppose that in the computerized factory we discussed in Chapter 2 we have an 8086 microcomputer which controls a printed-circuit-board-making machine. Part of the job of this 8086 is to check a temperature sensor and turn on a green lamp or a yellow lamp depending on the value of the temperature it reads in. If the temperature is below 30°C, we want to turn on a yellow lamp to tell the operator that the solution is not up to temperature. If the temperature is greater than or equal to 30°C, we want to light a green lamp. With a system such as this the operator can visually scan all the lamps on the control panel until all green lamps are lit. When all the lamps are green, the operator can push the GO button to start making boards. The reason that we have the yellow lamp is to let the operator know that this part of the machine is working, but that the temperature is not yet up to 30°C.

Figure 5-2 shows with flowcharts and with pseudocode two ways we can represent the algorithm for this problem. The difference between the two is simply a matter of whether we make the decision based on the temperature being below 30°C, or we make the decision based on the temperature being above or equal to 30°C. The two approaches are equally valid, but your choice determines which conditional jump instruction you choose. Figure 5-3*a* shows the 8086 assembly language implementation of the algorithm in Figure 5-2*a*.

For this program segment, assume that we read the temperature in from an analog-to-digital converter connected to input port FFF8H. Also assume that the control for the yellow lamp is connected to bit 0 of port FFFAH, and the control for the green lamp is connected to bit 1 of port FFFAH. A 1 sent to a bit position of port FFFAH turns on the lamp connected to that line. After we read the data in from the port, we compare it with our set point value of 30°C. If the input value is below 30°C, then we jump to the instructions which turn on the yellow lamp. If the temperature is above or equal to 30°C, we jump to the instructions which turn on the green lamp. Note that we have implemented this algorithm in such a way that the JB instruction will always be able to reach the label YELLOW.

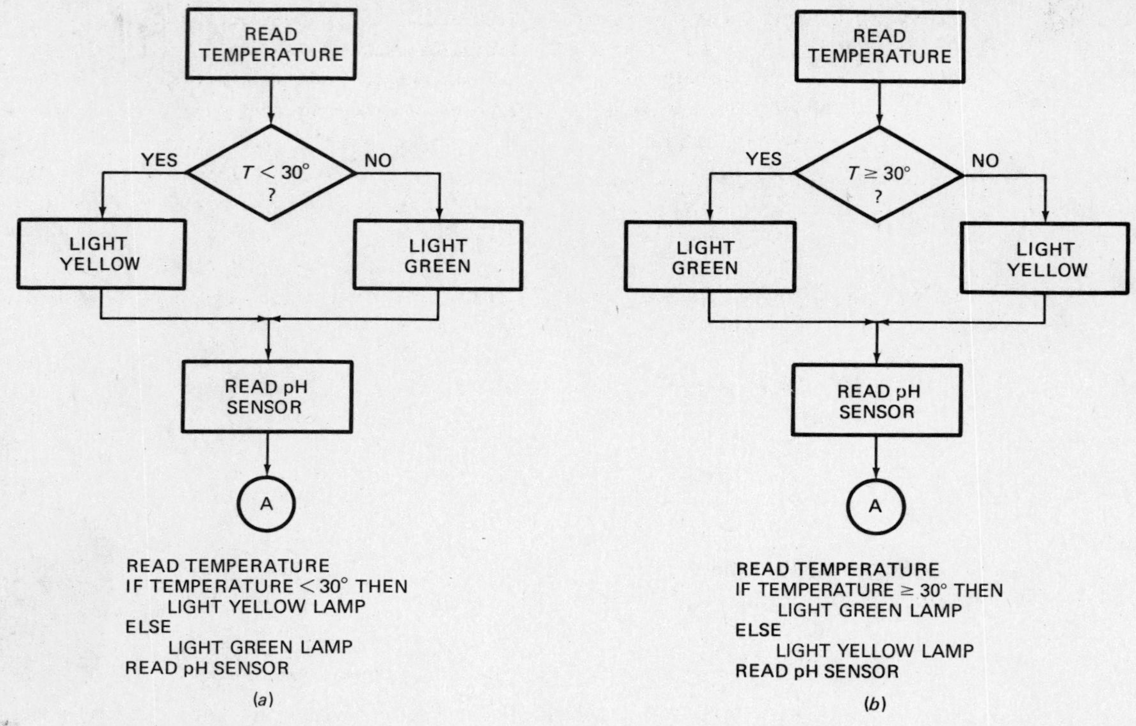

FIGURE 5-2 Flowcharts and pseudocode for two ways of expressing algorithm for printed-circuit-board-making machine. *(a)* Temperature below 30° test. *(b)* Temperature above 30° test.

```
The IBM Personal Computer MACRO Assembler 02-19-85      PAGE    1-1

                            PAGE ,132
                            ;8086 program section for PC board making machine
                            ;
                            ;ABSTRACT:      This program section reads the temperature of a cleaning
                            ;               bath solution and lights one of two lamps according to
                            ;               the temperature read. If the temp is below 30 degrees
                            ;               Celsius, a yellow lamp will be turned on. If the temp
                            ;               is above or equal to 30 degrees, a green lamp willbe
                            ;               turned on.
                            ;REGISTERS USED: CS, AL, DX
                            ;PORTS USED    : FFF8H as a temperature input
                            ;                FFFAH as lamp control output (yellow=bit 0, green=bit 1)
                            ;PROCEDURES    : None used

 0000                       CODE_HERE      SEGMENT
                                           ASSUME CS:CODE_HERE

                            ;intialize port FFFAH as an output port
 0000  BA FFFE                             MOV DX, 0FFFEH      ; Point DX to port control register
 0003  B0 99                               MOV AL, 99H         ; load control word to set up output port
 0005  EE                                  OUT DX, AL          ; send control word to control register
                            ;initialization complete

 0006  BA FFF8                             MOV DX, 0FFF8H      ; point DX at input port
 0009  EC                                  IN  AL, DX          ; read temp from sensor on input port
 000A  3C 1E                               CMP AL, 30          ; compare temp with 30 degrees C
```

FIGURE 5-3 Assembly language program segments for printed-circuit-board-making machine. *(a)* Below 30° version. *(b)* Above 30° version.

```
000C  72 03                              JB  YELLOW          ; if temp < 30 go light yellow lamp
000E  EB 0A 90                           JMP GREEN           ; else go light green lamp
0011  B0 01               YELLOW:        MOV AL, 01H         ; load code to light yellow lamp
0013  BA FFFA                            MOV DX, 0FFFAH      ; point DX at output port
0016  EE                                 OUT DX, AL          ; send code to light yellow lamp
0017  EB 07 90                           JMP EXIT            ; go to next mainline instruction
001A  B0 02               GREEN:         MOV AL, 02H         ; load code to light green lamp
001C  BA FFFA                            MOV DX, 0FFFAH      ; point DX at output port
001F  EE                                 OUT DX, AL          ; send code to light green lamp
0020  BA FFFC             EXIT:          MOV DX, 0FFFCH      ; next mainline instruction

0023                      CODE_HERE      ENDS
                                         END
```

(a)

```
IBM Personal Computer MACRO Assembler  Version 2.00  Page 1-1 11-07-85

                          PAGE ,132
                          ;8086 program section for PC board making machine
                          ;
                          ;ABSTRACT:      This program section reads the temperature of a cleaning
                          ;               bath solution and lights one of two lamps according to
                          ;               the temperature read. If the temp is below 30 degrees
                          ;               Celsius, a yellow lamp will be turned on. If the temp
                          ;               is above or equal to 30 degrees, a green lamp will be
                          ;               turned on.
                          ;REGISTERS USED: CS, AL, DX
                          ;PORTS USED    : FFF8H as a temperature input
                          ;                FFFAH as lamp control output (yellow=bit 0, green=bit 1)
                          ;PROCEDURES    : None used
0000                      CODE_HERE      SEGMENT
                                         ASSUME CS:CODE_HERE

                          ;intialize port FFFAH as an output port
0000  BA FFFE                            MOV DX, 0FFFEH       ; Point DX to port control register
0003  B0 99                              MOV AL, 99H          ; load control word to set up output port
0005  EE                                 OUT DX, AL           ; send control word to control register
                          ;initialization complete
0006  BA FFF8                            MOV DX, 0FFF8H       ; point DX at input port
0009  EC                                 IN  AL, DX           ; read temp from sensor on input port
000A  3C 1E                              CMP AL, 30           ; compare temp with 30 degrees C
000C  73 03                              JAE GREEN            ; if temp >= 30, go light green lamp
000E  EB 0A 90                           JMP YELLOW           ; else go light yellow lamp
0011  B0 02               GREEN:         MOV AL, 02H          ; load code to light green lamp
0013  BA FFFA                            MOV DX, 0FFFAH       ; point DX at output port
0016  EE                                 OUT DX, AL           ; send code to light green lamp
0017  EB 07 90                           JMP EXIT             ; go to next mainline instruction
001A  B0 01               YELLOW:        MOV AL, 01H          ; load code to light yellow lamp
001C  BA FFFA                            MOV DX, 0FFFAH       ; point DX at output port
001F  EE                                 OUT DX, AL           ; send code to light yellow lamp
0020  BA FFFC             EXIT:          MOV DX, 0FFFCH       ; next mainline instruction
0023                      CODE_HERE      ENDS
                                         END
```

(b)

FIGURE 5-3 (*continued*)

To actually turn on a lamp, we load a 1 in the appropriate bit of the AL register with a MOV instruction and send the byte to the lamp control port, FFFAH. For example, the instruction sequence MOV AL, 01H—OUT DX, AL will light the yellow lamp by sending a 1 to bit 0 of port FFFAH.

Figure 5-3*b* shows another equally valid assembly language program segment to solve our problem. This one uses a Jump if Above or Equal instruction, JAE, at the decision point and switches the order of the actions. This program more closely follows the second algorithm statement in Figure 5-2*b*. Perhaps you can see from these examples why two programmers may write very different programs to solve even very simple programming problems.

Multiple IF—THEN—ELSE Implementation

In the preceding section we showed how to implement and use the IF—THEN—ELSE structure which chooses between two alternative courses of action. In many situations we want a computer to choose one of several alternative actions based on the value of some variable read in or on a command code entered by a user. To choose one alternative from several we can *nest* IF—THEN—ELSE structures. The result has the form:

```
IF condition THEN
    action
    action
ELSE IF condition THEN
        action
        action
      ELSE
         action
         action
```

It is important to note in this structure that the last ELSE is part of the IF—THEN just before it. Figure 3-3*g* showed a flowchart and pseudocode for a "soup cook" example using this structure. The soup cook example, however, is too messy to implement here. Therefore, while the printed-circuit-board machine from the last section is still fresh in your mind, we will expand that example to show you how a multiple IF—THEN—ELSE is implemented.

Suppose that we want to have three lamps on our printed-circuit-board-making machine. We want a yellow lamp to indicate that the temperature is below 30°C, a green lamp to indicate that the temperature is above or equal to 30°C but below 40°C, and a red lamp to indicate that the temperature is at or above 40°C. Figure 5-4 shows three ways to indicate what we want to do here. The first way in Figure 5-4*a* simply indicates the desired action next to each temperature range. You may find this form very useful in visualizing problems where the alternatives are based on the range of a variable. Don't miss the ASCII-to-hexadecimal problem at the end of the chapter for some practice with this. Once you get the problem defined in this list form, you can easily convert it to a flowchart or pseudocode. When writing the flowchart or the pseudocode, it is best to start at one end of the overall range and work your way to the other. For example, in the flowchart in Figure 5-4*b* we start by checking if the temperature is below 30°. If the temperature is not below 30° then it must be above or equal to 30° and you do not have to do another test to determine this. You then check if the temperature is below 40°. If the temperature is above or equal to 30°, but below 40°, then you know that the temperature is in the green lamp range. If the temperature is not below 40°, then you know that the temperature must be above or equal to 40°. In other words, two carefully chosen tests will direct execution to one of the three alternatives.

Figure 5-5 shows how we can write a program for this algorithm in 8086 assembly language. In the program we first initialize port FFFAH as an output port. We then

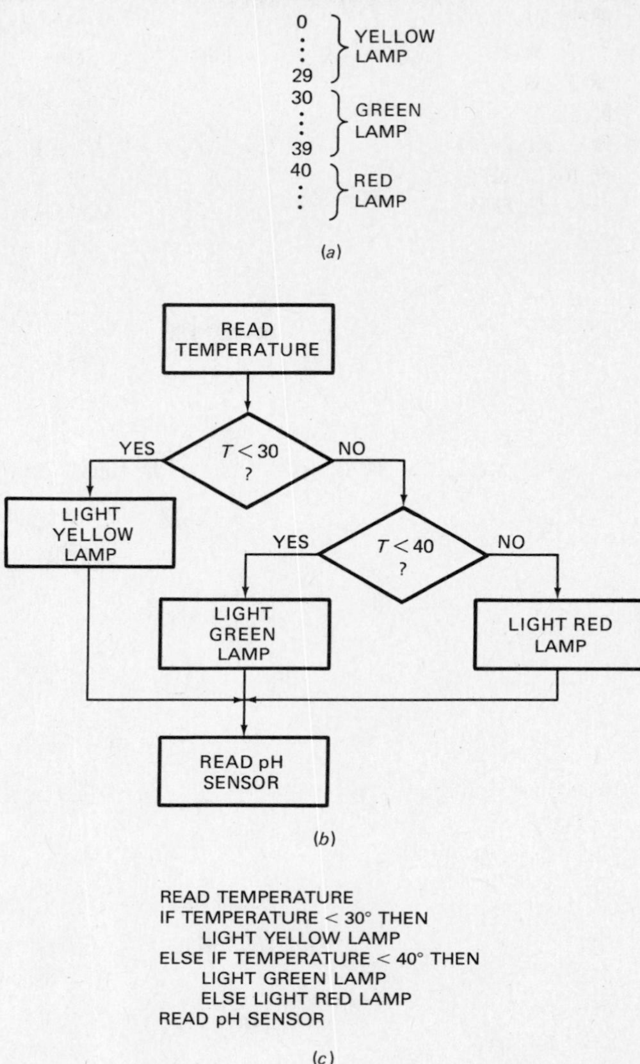

FIGURE 5-4 Algorithm for 3-lamp printed-circuit-board-making machine. *(a)* Condition list. *(b)* Flowchart. *(c)* Pseudocode.

```
                         PAGE ,132
                         ;8086 program section for PC board making machine
                         ;
                         ;ABSTRACT:     This program section reads the temperature of a cleaning
                         ;              bath solution and lights one of 3 lamps according to
                         ;              the temperature read. If the temp is below 30 degrees
                         ;              Celsius, a yellow lamp will be turned on. If the temp
                         ;              is >= 30 and < 40 degrees, a green lamp will be turned on
                         ;              Temps >= 40 degrees will turn on a red lamp.
                         ;REGISTERS USED: CS, AL, DX
                         ;PORTS USED    : FFF8H as a temperature input
                         ;                FFFAH as lamp control output (yellow = bit 0,
                         ;                               green = bit 1, red  = bit 2)
                         ;PROCEDURES    : None used

0000                     CODE_HERE     SEGMENT
                                       ASSUME CS:CODE_HERE

                         ;intialize port FFFAH as an output port
0000  BA FFFE                          MOV DX, 0FFFEH      ; Point DX to port control register
0003  B0 99                            MOV AL, 99H         ; load control word to set up output port
0005  EE                               OUT DX, AL          ; send control word to control register
                         ;initialization complete

0006  BA FFF8                          MOV DX, 0FFF8H      ; point DX at input port
0009  EC                               IN  AL, DX          ; read temp from sensor on input port
000A  BA FFFA                          MOV DX, 0FFFAH      ; point DX at output port
000D  3C 1E                            CMP AL, 1EH         ; compare temp with 30 degrees C
000F  72 0A                            JB  YELLOW          ; if temp < 30 go light yellow lamp
0011  3C 28                            CMP AL, 28H         ; compare with 40 degrees
0013  72 0C                            JB  GREEN           ; if temp < 40 go light green lamp
0015  B0 04              RED:          MOV AL, 04H         ; temp >= 40 so load code to light red lamp
0017  EE                               OUT DX, AL          ; send code to light red lamp
0018  EB 0A 90                         JMP EXIT            ; go to next mainline instruction
001B  B0 01              YELLOW:       MOV AL, 01H         ; load code to light yellow lamp
001D  EE                               OUT DX, AL          ; send code to light yellow lamp
001E  EB 04 90                         JMP EXIT            ; go to next mainline instruction
0021  B0 02              GREEN:        MOV AL, 02H         ; load code to light green lamp
0023  EE                               OUT DX, AL          ; send code to light green lamp
0024  BA FFFC            EXIT:         MOV DX, 0FFFCH      ; next mainline instruction
0027  EC                               IN  AL, DX          ; read ph sensor
0028                     CODE_HERE     ENDS
                                       END
```

FIGURE 5-5 Assembly language program for 3-lamp printed-circuit-board-making machine.

read in the temperature from an A/D converter connected to port FFF8H. We compare the temperature read in with the first set point value, 30° (1EH). If the temperature is below 30°, the jump if below, JB, instruction will cause a jump to the label YELLOW. If the jump is not taken, we know the temperature is above or equal to 30° so we go on to the CMP AL, 28H instruction to see if the temperature is below the second set point, 40° (28H). The JB GREEN instruction will cause a jump to the label GREEN, if the temperature is less than 40° (28H). If the jump is not taken, we know that the temperature must be at or above 40°C so we just go ahead and turn on the red lamp.

For this program we assume that the lines which control the three lamps are connected to port FFFAH. The yellow lamp is connected to bit 0, the green is connected to bit 1, and the red is connected to bit 2. We turn on a lamp by outputting a 1 to the the appropriate bit of port

FFFAH. The instruction sequence MOV AL, 02H—OUT DX, AL, for example, will turn on the green lamp by sending a 1 to bit 1 of port FFFAH.

SUMMARY OF IF—THEN—ELSE IMPLEMENTATION

Conditional jump instructions and instructions which set flags for them are used to implement IF—THEN—ELSE structures. A single IF—THEN—ELSE structure is used to choose one of two alternative series of actions. IF—THEN—ELSE structures can be linked to choose one of three or more alternative series of actions. As shown in Figure 3-3*g*, linked IF—THEN—ELSE structures are one way to implement the CASE structure. The algorithm for the printed-circuit-board machine lamps program in the preceding section example could have been expressed as:

```
CASE temperature OF
< 30              : light yellow lamp
≥ 30 and < 40     : light green lamp
≥ 40              : light red lamp
```

This CASE structure would be implemented in the same way as the program in Figure 5-5. However, expressing the algorithm for the problem as linked IF—THEN—ELSE structures makes it much easier to see how to implement the algorithm in assembly language. Later we show you another way to implement some CASE situations using a *jump table*.

In many programs where we want to choose between two or more alternative series of actions, each of the series of actions is quite lengthy. In this case we write each series of actions as a *subprogram* and CALL this subprogram when it is needed. The next major section of this chapter shows you how to write and use subprograms, or *procedures*, as they are often called.

WRITING AND USING PROCEDURES

Introduction

Whenever we have a series of instructions that we want to execute several times in a program, we write the series of instructions as a separate subprogram. We can then CALL this subprogram each time we want to execute that series of instructions. This saves us from having to write the series of instructions over and over each time we want it to execute in the program. This subprogram is usually called a *subroutine* or a *procedure*. To be consistent with the Intel literature we will use the term *procedure* when referring to called subprograms.

There is another major reason for using procedures in programs. Recall from Chapter 2 the *top-down design* approach to solving a programming problem. In this approach the problem is carefully defined, and then the overall job is broken down into modules. Each of these modules is broken down into smaller modules. The process is continued until the algorithm for each module is clearly obvious. Figure 5-6 shows how this hierarchy of modules can be represented in diagram form. A diagram such as this is often called a *hierarchial chart*. The point of all this is to break a large problem down into manageable-size pieces which can be individually written, tested, and debugged. The individual modules are usually written as procedures and called from a mainline program which implements the highest level of the hierarchy. This approach has the added advantage that a person can read the mainline program to get an overview of what the program does, and then work down into the procedures to see the amount of detail needed at a particular point. Now that you know what procedures are used for, we will give you an overview of how they work.

Figure 5-7*a* shows in diagram form how program execution goes from the mainline to a procedure and back to the mainline. A CALL instruction in the mainline loads the instruction pointer and in some cases also the code segment register with the starting address of the procedure. The next instruction fetched then will be the first instruction of the procedure. At the end of the procedure a return instruction, RET, sends execution back to the next instruction after the CALL in the mainline program. The RET instruction does this by loading the instruction pointer, and, if necessary, the code segment register with the address of the next instruction after the CALL instruction. As shown in Figure 5-7*b*, a procedure can call another procedure. This is called *nesting* procedures. Nested procedures are used to implement the hierarchy of modules we described in the preceding

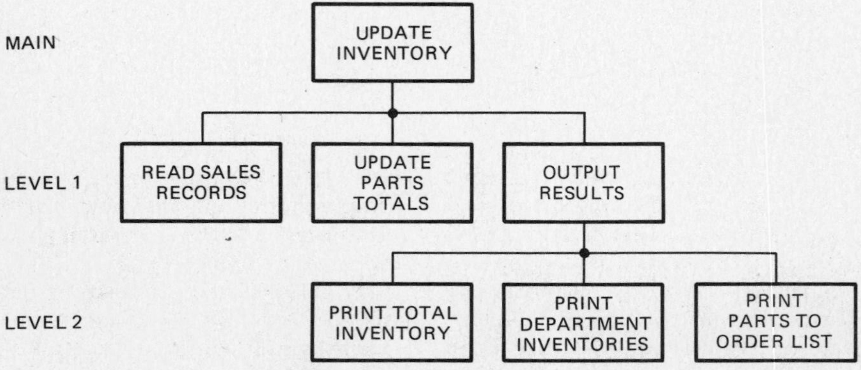

FIGURE 5-6 Hierarchical chart for inventory update program.

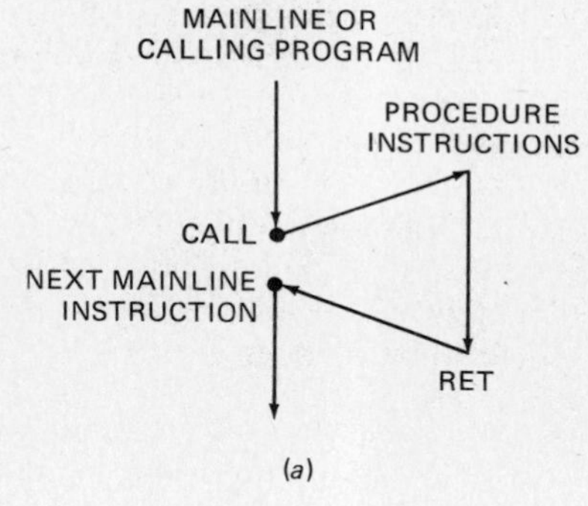

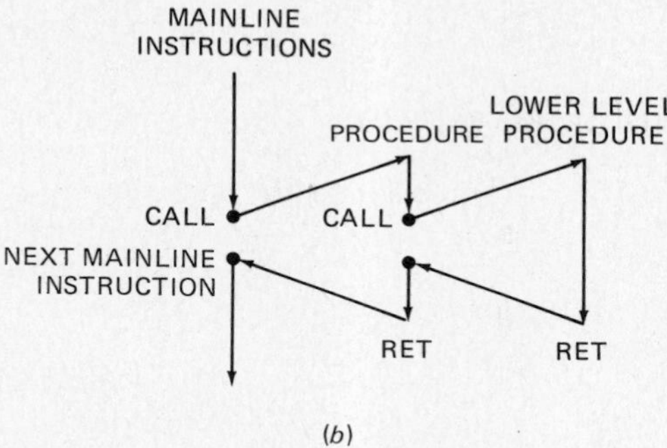

FIGURE 5-7 Program flow to and from procedures. *(a)* Single procedures. *(b)* Nested procedures.

paragraph. In the case of nested procedures, a RET instruction at the end of the lower level procedure returns execution to the higher level procedure. A second RET instruction at the end of the higher level procedure returns execution to the mainline program.

The question that may occur to you at this point is, "If a procedure can be called from anywhere in a program, how does the RET instruction know where to return execution to?" The answer to this question is that when a CALL instruction executes, it automatically stores the return address in a special section of memory called *the stack*. A later section will introduce you to how the 8086 stack works. For now let's take a closer look at the 8086 CALL and RET instructions.

The 8086 CALL and RET Instruction

THE CALL INSTRUCTION OVERVIEW

The 8086 CALL instruction performs two operations when it executes. First, it stores the address of the instruction after the CALL instruction on the stack. This address is called the *return* address because it is the address that execution will return to after the procedure executes. If the CALL is to a procedure in the same code segment, then only the instruction pointer contents will be saved on the stack. If the CALL is to a procedure in another code segment, both the instruction pointer and the code segment register contents will be saved on the stack.

The second operation of the CALL instruction is to change the contents of the instruction pointer and, in some cases, the code segment register to contain the starting address of the procedure. Figure 5-8*a* shows the coding formats for the four forms of the 8086 CALL instruction. The differences between these four forms are in the way they tell the 8086 to get the starting address for the procedure.

CALL = Call

Within segment or group, IP relative

Opcode	DispLow	DispHigh

Opcode	Clocks	Operation
E8	19	IP ← IP+Disp16—(SP) ← return link

Within segment or group, Indirect

Opcode	mod 010 r/m		

Opcode	Clocks	Operation
FF	16	IP ← Reg16—(SP) ← return link
FF	21+EA	IP ← Mem16—(SP) ← return link

Inter-segment or group, Direct

Opcode	offset-low	offset-high	seg-low	seg-high

Opcode	Clocks	Operation
9A	28	CS ← segbase IP ← offset

Inter-segment or group, Indirect

Opcode	mod 011 r/m	mem-low	mem-high

Opcode	Clocks	Operation
FF	37+EA	CS ← segbase IP ← offset

(a)

RET = Return from Subroutine

Opcode

Opcode	Clocks	Operation
C3	8	intra-segment return
CB	18	inter-segment return

Return and add constant to SP

Opcode	DataL	DataH

Opcode	Clocks	Operation
C2	12	intra-segment ret and add
CA	17	inter-segment ret and add

(b)

FIGURE 5-8 8086 CALL and RET instruction formats *(Intel Corp.)*. *(a)* CALL. *(b)* RET.

DIRECT WITHIN-SEGMENT NEAR CALLS

The first form, direct within-segment near call, tells the 8086 to produce the starting address of the procedure by adding a 16-bit signed displacement contained in the instruction to the contents of the instruction pointer. This is the same process as we described for the direct within-segment near JMP instruction in Chapter 4. With this instruction the starting address of the procedure can be anywhere in the range of −32,768 bytes to +32,767 bytes from the address of the instruction after the CALL. If you are hand coding a program, you calculate the displacement by counting from the address of the instruction after the CALL to the starting address of the procedure. If the procedure is in memory before the CALL instruction, then the displacement will be negative. In this case you represent the displacement in 16-bit, 2's complement sign-and-magnitude form just as you do for backward JMP instructions. If you are using an assembler, the assembler will automatically calculate the displacement from the instruction after the CALL to a label at the start of the procedure.

THE INDIRECT WITHIN-SEGMENT CALL

The indirect within-segment CALL instruction is also a near call. When this form of CALL executes, the instruction pointer is replaced with a 16-bit value from a specified register or memory location. As indicated by the MOD—R/M byte in the coding template, the source of the value can be any of the eight 16-bit registers or a memory location specified by any one of the 24 addressing modes shown in Figure 3-8. This form of CALL instruction can be used to choose one of several procedures based on a computed value. The instruction CALL BP, for example, will do a near call to the offset contained in BP. In other words the value in BP will be put in the instruction pointer. The instruction CALL WORD PTR [BX] will get the new value for the instruction pointer from a memory location pointed to by BX.

THE DIRECT INTERSEGMENT FAR CALL

The direct intersegment far CALL is used when the procedure is in another segment. If the procedure is in another segment, you have to change both the instruction pointer and the code segment register to get to it. For this form of the CALL instruction, the new value for the instruction pointer is written in as bytes 2 and 3 of the instruction code. Note that the low byte of the new IP value is written before the high byte. The new value for the code segment register is written in as bytes 4 and 5 of the instruction code. Again the low byte is written before the high byte. A program example later in this chapter shows you how to write your programs so that an assembler can find a procedure label in another segment.

THE INDIRECT INTERSEGMENT FAR CALL

This form of the CALL instruction replaces the instruction pointer and the code segment register contents with two 16-bit values from memory. Since two 16-bit values are needed, the values cannot come from a register. The MOD—R/M byte in the instruction is used to specify the addressing mode for the memory location where the 8086 goes to get the new values. The first word from memory is put in the instruction pointer, and the second word from memory is put in the code segment register. The instruction CALL DWORD PTR [BX] will compute a new value for IP from [BX] and [BX + 1] and a new value for CS from [BX + 2] and [BX + 3]. In other words it does a far call to an address contained in 4 bytes pointed to by BX in the data segment.

THE 8086 RET INSTRUCTION

As we described in the previous section, when the 8086 does a near CALL it saves the instruction pointer value for the instruction after the CALL on the stack. A return instruction, RET, at the end of the procedure copies this value from the stack back to the instruction pointer. This then returns execution to the mainline program.

When the 8086 does a far CALL it saves the contents of both the instruction pointer and the code segment register on the stack. An RET instruction at the end of the procedure copies these values from the stack back into the IP and CS registers to return execution to the mainline program. Obviously we need one form of the RET instruction to handle returns from near procedures, and another form of the instruction to handle returns from far procedures. Actually the 8086 has four forms of the RET instruction. Figure 5-8*b* shows the coding templates for these four.

The simple within-segment form of RET copies a word from the top of the stack to the instruction-pointer register. This is the instruction form you will usually use to return from a near procedure. The within-segment adding immediate to SP form is also used to return from a near procedure. When this form executes, however, it will copy the word at the top of the stack to the instruction pointer and also add an immediate number contained in the instruction to the contents of SP. Later, we will show you what this form is used for.

The intersegment form of the RET instruction is used to return from far procedures. When this form of the RET instruction executes, it will copy the word from the top of the stack to the instruction pointer. It will then increment the stack pointer by two and copy the next word from the stack to the code segment register. The intersegment adding immediate to SP form of the instruction also copies a new value for IP and a new value for CS from the stack. However, it also adds a 16-bit immediate number contained in the instruction code to SP.

Throughout the preceding discussions of the CALL and RET instructions we have talked about writing words to the stack and copying these words back to the instruction pointer and/or code segment register. Now we will show you how to set up a stack in your programs.

The 8086 Stack

The *stack* is a section of memory you set aside for storing return addresses. The stack is also used to save the contents of registers for the mainline program while a procedure executes. A third use of the stack is to hold data or addresses that will be acted upon by a procedure.

The 8086 lets you set aside up to an entire 64 Kbyte segment of memory as a stack. Remember from the block diagram in Figure 2-7 that the 8086 contains a stack segment register and a stack pointer register. The stack segment register is used to hold the upper 16 bits of the starting address you give to the stack segment. If you decide to start the stack segment at 70000H, for example, the stack segment register will contain 7000H. The stack pointer register is used to hold the offset of the last word written on the stack. The 8086 produces the physical address for a stack location by shifting the contents of the stack segment register four bit positions to the left and adding the contents of the stack pointer to the result. Figure 2-11 shows a numerical example of this.

If you are going to call procedures or use the stack in some other way in your program, then you need to initialize both the stack segment register and the stack pointer register. Figure 5-9 shows the pieces you need to add to your programs to declare a stack segment, and to initialize SS and SP. We have shown in Figure 5-9 how you should format all this for an assembler. If you are not using an assembler, then you should use the same format, but put the desired numbers in place of the names we have used.

The STACK_HERE SEGMENT STACK and STACK_HERE ENDS statements in Figure 5-9 are used to declare a logical segment that will be used for the stack. The STACK directive tells the assembler that this segment will be used as a last-in, first-out stack.

NOTE: If you are going to use the IBM program EXE2BIN on your programs so that you can download them to an SDK-86, omit the STACK directive here. The linker will then give you an error message, WARNING—NO STACK SEGMENT, which you can ignore.

We don't need all 64 Kbytes of the logical segment in our programs so we tell the assembler to set aside 40 decimal or 28H words of storage in this logical segment with the DW 40 DUP(0) statement. By limiting the stack to near the size actually needed, this segment can be overlapped with other logical segments to save on the amount of physical memory required for a program. In other words, there is no use having a larger stack set aside than you are going to need.

Now, when we store addresses or data in these stack locations, we start at the highest location and fill toward the bottom. This is opposite to the way you put instruction code bytes in memory. In the case of instruction codes you start at the lowest address in a code segment and fill toward the top. Since we start writing to the highest location in the stack first, we need a name attached to this location so we can access it by name. The statement STACK_TOP LABEL WORD in Figure 5-9 gives the name STACK_TOP to the next even address after the 40 words we set aside for the stack. We will explain later why we want the name at the address after the actual stack. The WORD in this statement indicates that writes to and reads from the stack will be done as words. Figure 5-10 shows in diagram form how this example stack would be arranged in memory.

We arbitrarily choose to start the stack segment at address 70000H for this example, and we set a stack length of 40 words with the DW 40 DUP(0) statement. Since each memory address represents a byte, these 40 words will occupy the 80 addresses 70000H to 7004FH as shown in Figure 5-10. The label STACK_TOP is associated with address 70050H, the next address after the stack.

The next program addition you need to look at is in the ASSUME statement. Note that we have added the term SS:STACK_HERE, to tell the assembler that any reference in the program to the stack means the segment STACK_HERE. This term tells the assembler that SS will contain the starting address of STACK_HERE, but

```
;8086 Program fragment showing the intialization of the stack
;      segment and the stack pointer

STACK_HERE       SEGMENT  STACK
        DW       40       DUP(0)
STACK_TOP        LABEL    WORD
STACK_HERE       ENDS

CODE_HERE        SEGMENT
                 ASSUME CS:CODE_HERE, SS:STACK_HERE

                 MOV      AX, STACK_HERE   ; initialize stack segment
                 MOV      SS, AX           ; register
                 LEA      SP, STACK_TOP    ; intialize stack pointer
                 :                         ; continue with program
                 :
CODE_HERE        ENDS
                 END
```

FIGURE 5-9 Required program additions when a stack is used.

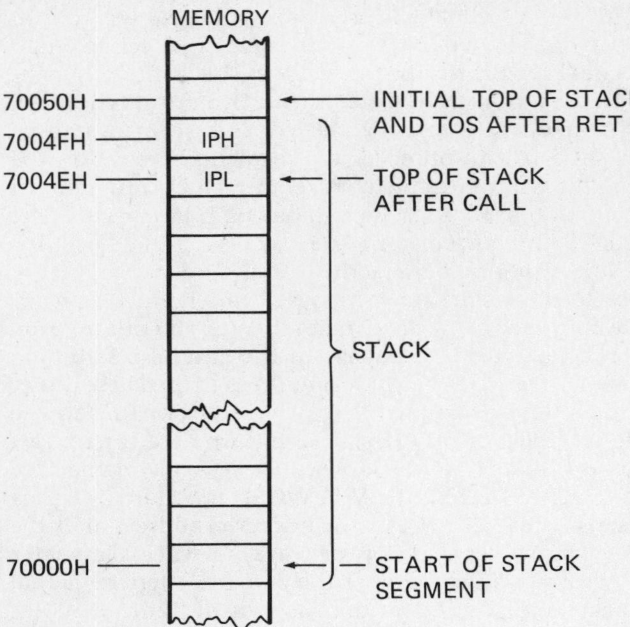

FIGURE 5-10 Stack diagram showing how the return address is pushed on the stack by CALL.

it does not load this value in the SS register. Loading the SS register must be done with program instructions, just as we do with the data segment register and the extra segment register. Again, we can't load an immediate number directly into a segment register, so we load the starting address of the segment into a register and then copy it into the stack segment register. The MOV AX, STACK_HERE and the MOV SS, AX instructions do this. Now all we have to do is initialize the stack pointer. We want to initialize SP so that the first word written to the stack goes to the highest location in the memory we set aside for the stack. All of the instructions which directly write a word to the stack decrement the stack pointer by two before writing the word. Therefore, we want the stack pointer to be initially loaded with the next even address above the actual stack. We gave this location the name STACK_TOP. Therefore, we can use the LEA SP, STACK_TOP instruction to initialize the stack pointer. We could also have used the instruction MOV SP, OFFSET STACK_TOP to initialize the stack pointer.

The next section shows how the pieces we have discussed are put in an example program which calls a near procedure. We also use this example to show you how the stack functions during a procedure call and return.

A Near Procedure Call and Return Example

Previous sections introduced you to the 8086 CALL and RET instructions and showed you how to set up a stack. Here we use a program example to show you how procedures are written and to dig more deeply into how the stack operates.

DEFINING THE PROBLEM AND WRITING THE ALGORITHM

Delay loops such as that shown in Figure 4-20 are often written as procedures so that they can be called from anywhere in a program. Suppose that we want to have a program which reads 100 data words from a port at 1-ms intervals, masks the upper 4 bits of each word, and puts each result in an array in memory. Before you read on, see if you can write a flowchart or pseudocode for this problem. Now compare your results with those in Figure 5-11*a* or *b*. Hopefully you recognized this problem as a REPEAT—UNTIL situation.

The next step is to expand the algorithm to take into account the specific architectural features of the 8086 that we will use to implement the algorithm. Figure 5-11*c* shows one way to do this expansion. We know that

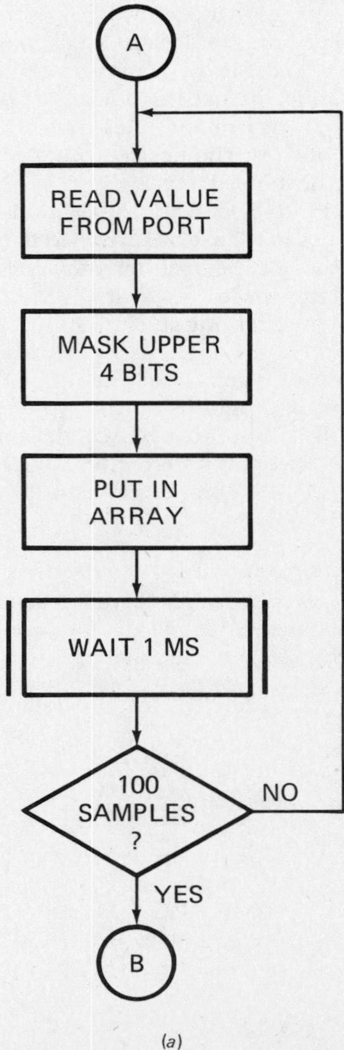

(*a*)

FIGURE 5-11 Algorithm for taking data samples at 1-ms intervals. *(a)* Flowchart. *(b)* Pseudocode. *(c)* Pseudocode expanded.

```
DATA SAMPLES PROGRAM
REPEAT
        GET DATA SAMPLE FROM PORT
        MASK UPPER 4 BITS
        PUT IN ARRAY
        WAIT 1 ms
UNTIL   100 samples taken
```

(b)

```
DATA SAMPLES PROGRAM

INITIALIZE POINTER TO ARRAY [SI]
INITIALIZE COUNTER, BX

REPEAT
        READ PORT
        MASK UPPER 4 BITS
        PUT IN ARRAY [SI]
        INCREMENT POINTER SI
        DECREMENT COUNTER BX
        WAIT_1MS PROCEDURE
UNTIL  COUNTER = 0

WAIT_1MS  PROC
          LOAD COUNT VALUE
          REPEAT
             DECREMENT COUNT VALUE
          UNTIL  COUNT = 0
```

(c)

FIGURE 5-11 (*continued*)

we need a pointer to the array and a counter to keep track of how many values we have put in the array. Therefore we initialize these at the start. After we read in each value and put it in the array, we increment the pointer so that it points to the next location in the array. We then decrement the counter to indicate that we have taken another sample, and call the WAIT_1MS procedure. Note that the algorithm for the procedure is done separately from that for the main program. As we discussed in the introduction to procedures, the flow of the mainline program is clearer if much of the detail is put in separate procedures. Upon returning from the delay procedure we repeat the series of instructions if our sample counter is not yet down to zero.

For the delay procedure we simply load a number in a register or memory location and decrement the number until it is down to zero. Note that even this expanded algorithm is general enough that it could be implemented on almost any microprocessor.

THE 8086 ASSEMBLY LANGUAGE PROGRAM

Figure 5-12 shows the assembly language program for our expanded algorithm. This program reviews some of the concepts from previous chapters and demonstrates some new ones from this chapter. The program is a little longer than our previous examples, but don't let this overwhelm you. A large part of the program is simply initializing everything. Read through this program and see how much of it you can remember and/or figure out before you read our explanations in the following paragraphs. Deciphering a program written by someone else is an important skill to develop.

At the start of the program we declare a logical segment for data with the DATA_HERE SEGMENT—DATA_HERE ENDS statements. The statement PRESSURES DW 100 DUP(0) in this segment sets aside 100 words of memory to store the values read in from a pressure sensor. This statement also initializes these 100 words to all 0's. It really doesn't matter what values are initially in these locations, because the program is going to write values in them. However, we like to initialize arrays such as this to all 0's so that during debugging we can tell if the program wrote any values to these locations.

Next we declare a logical segment to be used for the stack with the STACK_HERE SEGMENT STACK and the STACK_HERE ENDS statements. The statement DW 40 DUP(0) sets up a stack length of 40 words and initializes these words to all 0's. Again we really don't care what value these words have initially because we will be writing values there as we call procedures. The statement STACK_TOP LABEL WORD gives a name to the next even address after the highest address in the stack we have set up. As described in the previous section, we can then access this location by name when we initialize the stack pointer.

Now let's work our way through the main program and the procedure in the code segment. We have to tell the assembler which logical segments are being used for code, data, and stack in the program. The ASSUME CS:CODE_HERE, DS:DATA_HERE, SS:STACK_HERE statement does this. The ASSUME statement, however, does not actually initialize the segment registers. We have to do this with program instructions. The MOV AX,DATA_HERE and MOV DS,AX instructions initialize the data segment register. The MOV AX, STACK_HERE and MOV SS,AX instructions initialize the stack segment register. The stack pointer register must be initialized to point to the next even address after the memory space we set aside for the stack. The MOV SP, OFFSET STACK_TOP statement will do this. The OFFSET operator, remember, tells the assembler to calculate the distance from the start of a segment to the specified name and put this number in the specified register. We set aside 40 words for the stack so the offset of the label STACK_TOP will be 80 decimal or 0050H. This number is twice the number of words because each 8086 address represents a byte. The 0050H is the number that you would put in the instruction, if you were hand coding the program.

Up to this point most of what we have done is essentially housekeeping chores. Now we get started on the actual algorithm for our initially stated problem. The statement LEA SI, PRESSURES initializes the SI register as a pointer to the first location in the array PRESSURES. It loads the effective address or offset of the first

```
IBM Personal Computer MACRO Assembler  Version 2.00 Page 1-1 11-07-85
                                PAGE ,132
                                ;8086 Program
                                ;ABSTRACT:      This program takes in data samples from a port at 1 ms
                                ;               intervals, masks the upper 4 bits of each sample, and
                                ;               puts each masked sample in successive locations in an array.
                                ;REGISTERS USED:CS, SS, DS, AX, BX, CX, DX, SI, SP
                                ;PORTS USED:    0FFF8H - input port for data samples
                                ;PROCEDURES:    WAIT_1MS
 = FFF8                         PRESSURE_PORT   EQU  0FFF8H

 0000                           DATA_HERE       SEGMENT
 0000     64 [                  PRESSURES  DW  100  DUP(0)      ; set up array of 100 words
                0000
                      ]
 00C8                           DATA_HERE       ENDS

 0000                           STACK_HERE      SEGMENT STACK
 0000     28 [                             DW   40  DUP(0)      ; set stack length of 40 words
                0000
                      ]
 0050                           STACK_TOP       LABEL   WORD
 0050                           STACK_HERE      ENDS

 0000                           CODE_HERE       SEGMENT
                                                ASSUME  CS:CODE_HERE, DS:DATA_HERE, SS:STACK_HERE

 0000  B8 ---- R                START:     MOV AX, DATA_HERE            ; initialize data segment register
 0003  8E D8                               MOV DS, AX
 0005  B8 ---- R                           MOV AX, STACK_HERE           ; initialize stack segment register
 0008  8E D0                               MOV SS, AX
 000A  BC 0050 R                           MOV SP, OFFSET STACK_TOP     ; intialize stack pointer to top of stack

 000D  8D 36 0000 R                        LEA SI, PRESSURES            ; point SI to start of array
 0011  BB 0064                             MOV BX, 100                  ; load BX with number of samples
 0014  BA FFF8                             MOV DX, PRESSURE_PORT        ; Point DX at input port
 0017                           NEXT_VALUE:
 0017  ED                                  IN  AX, DX                   ; read data from port
 0018  25 0FFF                             AND AX, 0FFFH                ; mask upper 4 bits
 001B  89 04                               MOV [SI], AX                 ; store data word in array
 001D  E8 0026 R                           CALL WAIT_1MS                ; delay of 1 ms
 0020  46                                  INC SI                       ; point SI at next location in array
 0021  46                                  INC SI
 0022  4B                                  DEC BX                       ; decrement sample counter
 0023  75 F2                               JNZ NEXT_VALUE               ; repeat until 100 samples done
 0025  90                       STOP:      NOP

 0026                           WAIT_1MS   PROC NEAR
 0026  B9 23F2                             MOV CX, 23F2H                ; load delay constant into CX
 0029  E2 FE                    HERE:      LOOP HERE                    ; loop until CX = 0
 002B  C3                                  RET
 002C                           WAIT_1MS   ENDP
 002C                           CODE_HERE  ENDS
                                           END
```

FIGURE 5-12 Assembly language program to read in 100 samples of data at 1-ms intervals.

```
IBM Personal Computer MACRO Assembler  Version 2.00  Page Symbols-1 11-07-85


Segments and Groups:

                N a m e                 Size    Align   Combine Class

CODE_HERE. . . . . . . . . . . . .      002C    PARA    NONE
DATA_HERE. . . . . . . . . . . . .      00C8    PARA    NONE
STACK_HERE . . . . . . . . . . . .      0050    PARA    STACK

Symbols:

                N a m e                 Type    Value   Attr

HERE . . . . . . . . . . . . . . .      L NEAR  0029    CODE_HERE
NEXT_VALUE . . . . . . . . . . . .      L NEAR  0017    CODE_HERE
PRESSURES. . . . . . . . . . . . .      L WORD  0000    DATA_HERE       Length =0064
PRESSURE_PORT. . . . . . . . . . .      Number  FFF8
STACK_TOP. . . . . . . . . . . . .      L WORD  0050    STACK_HERE
START. . . . . . . . . . . . . . .      L NEAR  0000    CODE_HERE
STOP . . . . . . . . . . . . . . .      L NEAR  0025    CODE_HERE
WAIT_1MS . . . . . . . . . . . . .      N PROC  0026    CODE_HERE       Length =0006

50092 Bytes free

Warning Severe
Errors  Errors
0       0
```

FIGURE 5-12 (*continued*)

word in PRESSURES into SI. For our example here PRESSURES is the first data item in the segment so the value loaded into SI will be 0000H. We chose to use the BX register as a sample counter, so we use the statement MOV BX, 100 to initialize BX with the number of samples we want to take and store. Finally, we are going to get to some action.

As indicated by the PRESSURE_PORT EQU 0FFF8H statement at the top of the program, the pressure sensor is connected to port FFF8H. Since this port address is larger than FFH, we have to use the variable port input instruction. For this input instruction we first load the port address in the DX register with the MOV DX, PRESSURE_PORT instruction, and then read the data word in with the IN AX, DX instruction. Notice how much more understandable it makes a program when we use a name such as PRESSURE_PORT in an instruction rather than 0FFF8H, the numerical port address. If you are working with an assembler, use EQU statements to give names to constants in your program.

When we get the pressure value into AX, we mask out the upper 4 bits with the AND AX, 0FFFH instruction. The reason why we want to do this is that the analog-to-digital converter that the pressure sensor is connected to is a 12-bit unit. The upper 4 bits of the 16-bit port are not connected to anything and may pick up random-noise signals. To prevent noise signals on the upper 4 bits from getting put in memory with our data, we mask these bits out by ANDing them with 0's. The instruction MOV [SI], AX will copy the data word from the AX register to the memory location pointed to by SI in the data segment.

To produce the desired delay between samples we CALL the WAIT_1MS procedure. This is a direct within segment CALL because the procedure is contained in the same code segment as the CALL instruction.

We use the PROC and ENDP directives to "bracket" the assembly language statements of the procedure. Putting a name in front of these directives allows us to call the procedure by name. For the example in Figure 5-12 we gave the procedure the name WAIT_1MS to remind us of the function of the procedure. To produce the desired delay we load a number into the CX register with the MOV CX, 23F2H instruction and count the number down to 0 with the LOOP HERE instruction. The LOOP instruction, remember, decrements CX by 1 and jumps to the specified label if CX is not yet down to 0. Since we put the label on the LOOP instruction, the LOOP instruction will simply execute over and over until CX reaches 0. The RET instruction at the end of the procedure will return execution to the next instruction after the CALL in the mainline of the program. Since this procedure is in the same code segment as the mainline program, only the instruction pointer has to be changed to get back to the mainline. The CALL instruction copied the desired value for the instruction pointer to the stack before going to the procedure. The RET instruction will copy this value from the stack back to the instruction pointer. If you are hand coding a program such as this, make sure to use the correct form of the RET instruction. After we briefly discuss the rest of the mainline program, we will show you what happens to the stack and stack pointer as the return address is copied to and from the stack.

Now, back in the mainline we need to get ready for reading the next data value. First we want to get SI pointed to the location where we want to put the next data word. Since each address represents a byte, and we are storing words, we have to increment the pointer by two to point to the next storage location. Two INC SI instructions do this. You could use the single instruction ADD SI, 02H to do the same job. After updating the pointer we decrement the sample counter in BX with the DEC BX instruction. If BX is not yet counted down to 0, the JNZ NEXT_VALUE instruction will cause the 8086 to read in and process another value from the port. If BX is 0, indicating that all 100 samples have been taken, execution goes on to the next mainline instruction after JNZ. Now let's see what happens to the stack and the stack pointer during all of this.

More Stack Operation and Use

STACK OPERATION DURING A CALL AND RET

To show how the stack operates during a CALL and RET we will use some specific numbers with the example program in Figure 5-12. Suppose that for the program we start the stack at address 70000H. The stack segment register then will be initialized with 7000H. We set a stack length of 40 decimal or 28H words with the DW 40 DUP(0) statement. These 28H words will occupy the 50H memory locations from 70000H to 7004FH. Figure 5-13*a* shows this in diagram form. Now remember, when we write words to the stack, we put the first word at the highest address. For our example here the first word will be written at addresses 7004EH and 7004FH. As we write other words to the stack they are written at lower addresses. In other words the stack fills from the top down. We use the stack pointer to keep track of where the last word was written to the stack. The location pointed to by the stack pointer at any time is called the *top of the stack*. In the program we initialized the stack pointer to offset 0050H, the next even address above our actual stack, with the MOV SP, OFFSET TOP_STACK instruction.

After the 8086 fetches the CALL instruction from the instruction-byte queue in the BIU it automatically increments the instruction pointer to 0020H, the offset of the next instruction after the CALL. You can see this if you look at the first column of the program listing in Figure 5-12. The instruction pointer then contains the address we want execution to return to after the procedure is completed. When the near CALL instruction in our example program executes, the 8086 first decrements the stack pointer by two. Then it copies the return address

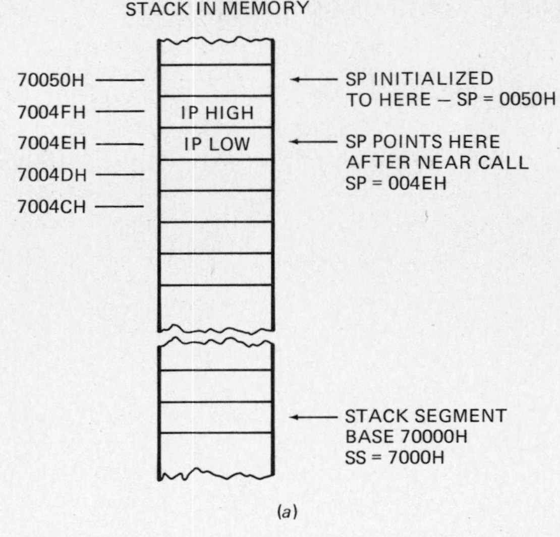

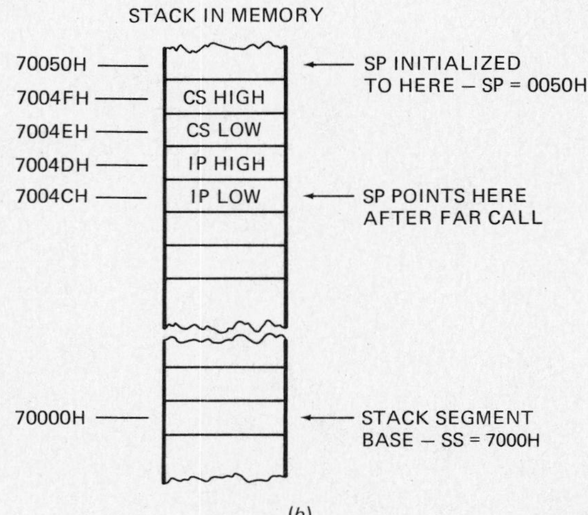

FIGURE 5-13 Stack diagram for program in Figure 5-10. *(a)* For near CALL. *(b)* For far CALL.

in the instruction pointer to the memory location now pointed to by the stack pointer. If the stack pointer contained 0050H before being decremented, then after being decremented by two it contains 004EH. The physical address pointed to by the stack pointer and the stack segment register will be 7004EH. The low byte of the instruction pointer will be copied to address 7004EH and the high byte of the instruction pointer will be copied to address 7004FH. This follows the Intel convention of putting the lower byte of a word at the lower address in memory. Figure 5-13*a* shows these two bytes labeled as IP LOW and IP HIGH. After the CALL instruction executes, the stack pointer is left pointing to offset 004EH. This location is now the top of the stack or TOS.

When the RET instruction at the end of the procedure in the example program executes, the 8086 copies the return address from the top of the stack to the instruction pointer. Since the top of the stack was at offset 004EH, the word from addresses 7004EH and 7004FH will be copied to the instruction pointer. After it copies the word from the top of the stack to the instruction pointer, the 8086 increments the stack pointer by two. For our example here it will increment the stack pointer from 004EH to 0050H. The stack pointer is now back where it was before the CALL instruction executed. Note that the return address is still present in memory because the RET instruction simply copied it to the instruction pointer and incremented the stack pointer over it.

When the 8086 executes a far CALL instruction it decrements the stack pointer by two and copies the contents of the code segment register to the stack. It then decrements the stack pointer by two again and copies the offset of the next mainline instruction from the instruction pointer to the stack. To help you visualize this Figure 5-13*b* shows how these would be written to the stack assuming the same stack starting addresses that we used for the previous example. As you can see from this figure, after a far CALL the top of the stack will be four addresses lower than it was before the CALL.

A far RET used at the end of a far procedure will copy a word from the top of the stack to the instruction pointer and increment the stack pointer by two. It will then copy the word from the new top of the stack to the code segment register and increment the stack pointer again by 2. The next instruction will then be fetched from the physical address after the far CALL instruction. The top of the stack will be back to where it was before the CALL and RET.

As we mentioned previously the stack is also used to save the contents of registers while a procedure executes and to hold data that the procedure is to act on. The next section shows you how we do this.

USING PUSH AND POP TO SAVE REGISTER CONTENTS

In the example program in Figure 5-12 we used the BX register to keep track of how many data samples we had taken in. After each data sample was taken in we decremented the BX register and used the JNZ instruction to determine whether to take another sample or to exit. We would like to have used the CX register to keep track of the number of samples taken so that we could have used a single LOOP instruction instead of the DEC BX and JNZ label instructions. The reason that we couldn't use CX for this in the program is because CX is used in the procedure. Any value we put in CX in the mainline program would be written over by the MOV CX, 23F2H instruction in the procedure. It is very common to want to use registers both in the mainline program and in a procedure without the two uses interfering with each other. The PUSH and POP instructions make this easy to do.

The PUSH register/memory instruction decrements the stack pointer by two and copies the contents of the specified 16-bit register or memory location to memory at the new top of stack location. The PUSH CX instruction, for example, will decrement the stack pointer by two and copy the contents of the CX register to the stack where the stack pointer now points. This instruction then can be used to save the contents of CX while a procedure executes. The next question is, how do we get the saved value back when we want it?

The POP register/memory instruction copies a word from the top of the stack to the specified 16-bit register or memory location and increments the stack pointer by two. The POP CX instruction, for example, will copy a word from the top of the stack to the CX register and increment the stack pointer by two. After a POP the stack pointer will point to the next word on the stack.

You can PUSH any of the 16-bit general purpose registers, AX, BX, CX, and DX; any of the base or pointer registers, BP, SP, SI, and DI; any of the segment registers, CS, DS, SS, and ES; or even a word from a memory location specified by one of those 24 memory addressing modes in Figure 3-8. A separate instruction, PUSHF, decrements the stack pointer by two and copies the flag word to the stack. The 80186 and 80188 PUSHA instruction copies AX, CX, DX, BX, SP, BP, SI and DI to the stack.

You can POP a word from the stack to any of the registers except CS, and you can POP a word from the stack to a memory location specified in any one of those 24 ways. The POPF instruction copies a word from the stack to the flag register and increments the stack pointer by two. The 80186 and 80188 POPA instruction copies words from the stack to the DI, SI, BP, BX, DX, CX, and AX registers. Note that the POPA instruction does not return a value to the SP register.

When you PUSH several registers on the stack you have to remember to POP them off in the reverse order that you pushed them on. This is because the stack functions in a *last-in—first-out* manner. An everyday example of this type of operation is the spring-loaded plate stacks seen in some restaurants. The last plate pushed on the stack is the first one popped off. Figure 5-14*a* should help you visualize how this works for the 8086. It shows a sequence of PUSH instructions you might use to save registers and flags at the start of a near procedure called MULTO. Figure 5-14*b* shows how the PUSH instructions will put the contents of these registers on the stack. The first entry in the stack is the copy of the instruction pointer put there by the CALL instruction that called the procedure. Following this are the flag word and the words from registers AX, BX, and CX. After all of these are pushed on the stack, the stack pointer is left pointing at the location in the stack where CX was pushed.

When we want to restore the saved values to the registers and flags at the end of the procedure we first POP CX because it was the last register pushed on the stack. After CX is popped the stack pointer will be left pointing at the location where BX is stored. Therefore, we POP BX next. We continue popping until all of the registers and the flags are restored. The RET instruction then copies the return address from the stack to the instruction pointer to return execution to the main program. It is very important to keep the number of pushes equal to the number of pops or in some other way keep the stack balanced so that the RET instruction finds the correct word to put in the instruction pointer.

Some programmers like to push and pop registers in the mainline or calling program rather than in the procedure as we did in Figure 5-14*a*. This approach has the advantage that you can push only those registers that

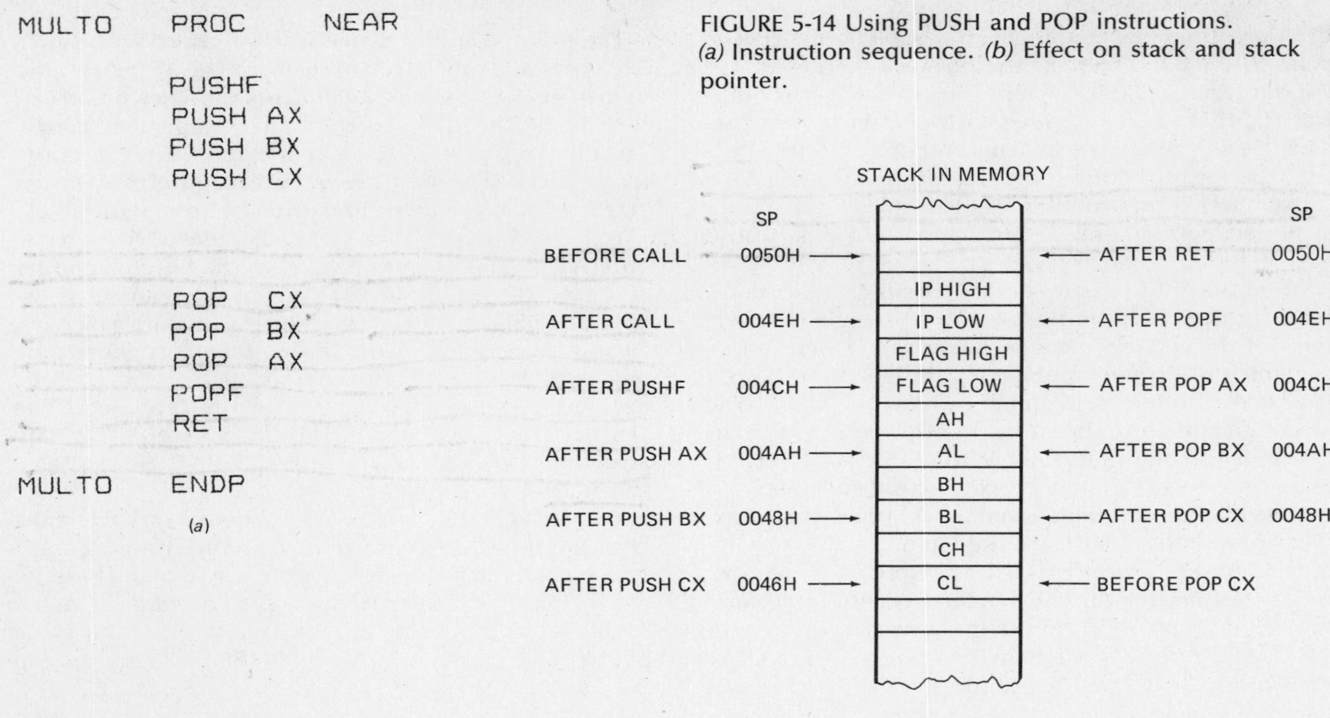

FIGURE 5-14 Using PUSH and POP instructions. *(a)* Instruction sequence. *(b)* Effect on stack and stack pointer.

you care about saving each time you call the procedure. The disadvantages of this approach are that the pushes and pops clutter up the mainline program, and you may decide to use another register at some point in the program and forget to add a push for it. We like to push the flags and any registers used in a procedure directly in the procedure. This way we always know that the procedure can be called from anywhere in the program without losing the contents of any registers. Another advantage of this approach is that you only have to write the pushes and pops once. A disadvantage is that in a situation where all the pushes are not needed, the procedure may take a little longer to run.

Passing Parameters to and from Procedures

Often when we call a procedure we want to make some data values or addresses available to the procedure. Likewise we often want a procedure to make some processed data values or addresses available to the main program. These address or data values passed back and forth between the mainline and the procedure are commonly called *parameters*. There are three major ways of passing parameters to and from a procedure. Parameters can be passed in *registers*, they can be passed in *dedicated memory locations*, or they can be passed in *stack locations*. In the following sections we use three versions of a simple program to show you how each of these methods work.

DEFINING THE PROGRAMMING PROBLEM

A common programming need is to convert a packed BCD number such as 4596 to its binary or hexadecimal equivalent. The hexadecimal equivalent of BCD 4596 is 11F4H, for example. There are several ways to do this conversion, but to us the easiest is based on using the

```
4596  =    (4 x 1000) + (5 x 100) + (9 x 10) + (6 x 1)

1000  = 03E8H   therefore      4000 = 4 x 3E8H  = 0FA0H
 100  = 0064H   therefore       500 = 5 x 064H  = 01F4H
  10  = 000AH   therefore        90 = 9 x 00AH  = 005AH
   1  = 00001H  therefore         6 = 6 x 001H  = 0006H

                                     4596  = 11F4H
```

FIGURE 5-15 BCD-to-HEX or -BINARY algorithm.

value of each placeholder in the BCD number. Figure 5-15 shows the names and values for each digit in a 4-digit BCD number such as 4596. When we write a number such as this it means that we have a total of 4 thousands + 5 hundreds + 9 tens + 6 units. To determine the value of this number in hexadecimal we just multiply the number in each digit position by the value of that digit position in hexadecimal and add up the results. The right-hand side of Figure 5-15 shows how this works. The units position has a value of 1 in hex so multiplying this by 6 units gives 0006H. The tens position has a value of 0AH. Multiplying this value by 9, the number of tens, gives 005AH. The hex value of the hundreds position is 64H. When we multiply this value by 5, the number of hundreds, we get 01F4H. When we multiply the hex value of the thousands position, 03E8H, by 4 (the number of thousands), we get 0FA0H. Adding up the results for the 4 digits gives 11F4H which is the hex equivalent of 4596 BCD. You can use this method to convert a BCD number with any number of digits to its binary equivalent, but to conserve space here we will do it for just a 2-digit BCD number.

The algorithm for this program then is the simple sequence of operations:

Separate nibbles

Save lower nibble (don't need to multiply by one)

Multiply upper nibble by 0AH

Add lower nibble to result of multiplication

We want to implement this program as a procedure which can be called from anywhere in a mainline program. For our first version we pass the BCD number to the procedure in a register.

PASSING PARAMETERS IN REGISTERS

Figure 5-16 shows our first version of a procedure to convert a 2-digit packed BCD number to its hex (binary) equivalent. The BCD number is passed to the procedure in the AL register and the hex equivalent is passed back to the calling program in the AL register. We start the procedure by pushing the flag register and the other registers we use in the procedure. Notice that we don't need to push and pop the AX register because we are using it to pass a value to the procedure and expecting the procedure to pass a different value back to the calling program in it.

Hopefully the function of the rest of the instructions in the procedure are reasonably clear from the comments with them. We first make a copy of the BCD in AL so we have two copies to work on. We then mask the upper nibble of one and save it in BL. Since multiplying this nibble by one would not change its value, we are done with it for now. We mask the lower nibble of the other copy of the BCD and rotate this nibble into the lower nibble position of the byte so we can multiply it correctly. When we multiply this nibble by the digit weight of 0AH, the result is left in the AX register. However, since the result can never be greater than 8 bits, we can disregard the contents of AH. Finally, we add the lower nibble we saved in BL to the result in AL to get the hex total. The desired result is left in AL. Before returning to the main program we pop the registers we pushed at the start of the procedure.

USING GENERAL MEMORY TO PASS PARAMETERS

For cases where we only have to pass a few parameters to and from a procedure, registers are a convenient way to do it. However, in cases where we need to pass a large number of parameters to a procedure or in cases where we don't want to use registers, we use memory. This memory may be a dedicated section of general memory or part of the stack. The following example shows a very simple case using dedicated memory locations.

Figure 5-17*a* shows a fragment of a program that uses another version of our BCD_TO_HEX procedure. In this version the number to be converted is stored in a dedicated memory location named BCD_INPUT and the hex result is returned from the procedure to a dedicated memory location called HEX_VALUE.

In the procedure we first push the flags and all of the registers used in the procedure. We then copy the BCD number into AL with the MOV AL, BCD_INPUT instruction. From here on the procedure is the same as the previous version until we reach the point where we want to pass the hex result back to the calling program. Here we use the MOV HEX_VALUE, AL instruction to copy the result to the dedicated memory location we set aside for it. To complete the procedure we pop the flags and registers, and return to the main program.

The approach used in Figure 5-17*a* works in this case, but it has a severe limitation. Can you see what it is? The limitation is that this procedure will always look to the memory location named BCD_INPUT to get its data and always put its result in the memory location called HEX_VALUE. In other words, the way it is written we can't easily use this procedure to convert a BCD number in some other memory location.

PASSING PARAMETERS USING POINTERS

A parameter passing method which overcomes the disadvantage of using data item names directly in a procedure is to pass the procedure a pointer to the desired data. Figure 5-17*b* shows one way to do this. In the main program before we call the procedure we use the MOV SI, OFFSET BCD_INPUT instruction to set up the SI register as a pointer to the memory location BCD_INPUT. We also use the MOV DI, OFFSET HEX_VALUE instruction to set up the DI register as a pointer to the memory location named HEX_VALUE. In the procedure the MOV AL, [SI] instruction will copy the byte pointed to by SI into AL. Likewise, the instruction MOV [DI], AL instruction later in the procedure will copy the byte from AL to the memory location pointed to by DI.

This second approach which actually uses a combination of registers and memory is more versatile because you can pass the procedure pointers to data anywhere in memory. You can pass pointers to individual values or pointers to arrays or strings. If you don't want to use

```
;8086 PROGRAM FRAGMENT BCD TO HEX CONVERSION
;ABSTRACT:        Program fragment that uses a procedure to convert
;                 BCD numbers to HEX (binary). It shows how to use
;                 AL register to pass parameters to the procedure
;Not shown  -     SS contains segment base for STACK_HERE
;Not shown  -     Initialization of segment registers
;PORTS USED       : none
;PROCEDURES USED: BCD_HEX

DATA_HERE       SEGMENT
                BCD_INPUT          DB ?        ; storage for BCD value
                HEX_VALUE          DB ?        ; storage for binary value
DATA_HERE       ENDS

CODE_HERE       SEGMENT WORD
                ASSUME CS:CODE_HERE, DS:DATA_HERE, SS:STACK_HERE
                :
                :
        MOV     AL, BCD_INPUT
        CALL    BCD_HEX
        MOV     HEX_VALUE, AL              ; store the result
                :


;PROCEDURE:     BCD_HEX
;               Converts BCD numbers to HEX (binary), uses
;               registers to pass parameters to the procedure
;SAVES:         All registers used except AH

BCD_HEX         PROC    NEAR
                PUSHF             ; save flags
                PUSH    BX        ; and registers
                PUSH    CX
;start conversion
                MOV     AH, AL    ; save copy of BCD in AH
                AND     AH, OFH   ; separate and save lower
                MOV     BL, AH    ; BCD digit
                AND     AL, OFOH  ; separate upper nibble
                MOV     CL, 04    ; move upper BCD digit to low
                ROR     AL, CL    ; nibble position for multiply
                MOV     BH, OAH   ; load conversion factor in BH
                MUL     BH        ; upper BCD digit in AL * OAH in BH
                                  ; result in AX
                ADD     AL, BL    ; add lower BCD to result of MUL
                                  ; final result in AL
;end conversion, restore registers
                POP     CX
                POP     BX
                POPF
                RET
BCD_HEX         ENDP
CODE_HERE       ENDS
                END
```

FIGURE 5-16 Example program passing parameters in registers.

```
;8086 PROGRAM FRAGMENT - BCD to HEX CONVERSION
;ABSTRACT:        Program fragment that uses a procedure to convert BCD
;                 numbers to HEX (binary). It shows how to use dedicated
;                 memory locations to pass parameters to a procedure.
;not shown -      SS contains segment base for STACK_HERE
;not shown -      Initialization of segment registers
;PORTS USED       : None
;PROCEDURES USED: BCD_HEX

DATA_HERE         SEGMENT
                  BCD_INPUT        DB ?   ; storage for BCD value
                  HEX_VALUE        DB ?   ; storage for binary value
DATA_HERE         ENDS
CODE_HERE         SEGMENT
                  ASSUME CS:CODE_HERE, DS:DATA_HERE, SS:STACK_HERE
                  :
                  :                             ; intitialization
                  CALL BCD_HEX
                  :

;PROCEDURE:       BCD_HEX
;ABSTRACT :       Converts BCD numbers to HEX, uses dedicated
;                 memory locations for data
;SAVES:           All registers used

BCD_HEX           PROC     NEAR
                  PUSH     AX
                  PUSHF                          ; save flags
                  PUSH     BX                    ; and registers
                  PUSH     CX
;get BCD value from named memory location
                  MOV      AL, BCD_INPUT
;do conversion
                  MOV      AH, AL     ; save copy of BCD in AH
                  AND      AH, OFH    ; separate and save lower
                  MOV      BL, AH     ; BCD digit
                  AND      AL, OFOH   ; separate upper nibble
                  MOV      CL, 04     ; move upper BCD digit to low
                  ROR      AL, CL     ; nibble position for multiply
                  MOV      BH, OAH    ; load conversion factor in BH
                  MUL      BH         ; upper BCD digit in AL * OAH in BH
                                      ; result in AX
                  ADD      AL, BL     ; add lower BCD to result of MUL
                                      ; final result in AL
;end of conversion now store Hex value in named memory location
                  MOV      HEX_VALUE, AL
                  POP      CX           ; restore flags and
                  POP      BX           ; registers
                  POPF
                  POP      AX
                  RET
BCD_HEX           ENDP
CODE_HERE         ENDS
                  END
```

(a)

FIGURE 5-17 Example program passing parameters in named memory locations. *(a)* Named memory location only. *(b)* More versatile approach using pointers to named memory locations.

```
;8086 PROGRAM FRAGMENT - BCD to HEX CONVERSION
;ABSTRACT:       Program fragment that uses a procedure to convert BCD
;                numbers to HEX (binary). It shows how to use pointers
;                to pass parameters to procedure.
;not shown -     SS contains segment base for STACK_HERE
;not shown -     Initialization of segment registers
;PORTS USED      : None
;PROCEDURES USED: BCD_HEX

DATA_HERE        SEGMENT
                 BCD_INPUT        DB ?   ; storage for BCD value
                 HEX_VALUE        DB ?   ; storage for binary value
DATA_HERE        ENDS
CODE_HERE        SEGMENT
                 ASSUME CS:CODE_HERE, DS:DATA_HERE, SS:STACK_HERE
                 :
                 :
;put pointer to BCD in SI and pointer to HEX storage in DI
                 MOV      SI, OFFSET BCD_INPUT
                 MOV      DI, OFFSET HEX_VALUE
                 CALL BCD_HEX
                 :

;PROCEDURE:      BCD_HEX
;ABSTRACT :      Converts BCD numbers to HEX. Uses pointers
;                to get data parameters
;SAVES:          All registers used
BCD_HEX          PROC     NEAR
                 PUSH     AX                   ; save registers and flags
                 PUSHF
                 PUSH     BX
                 PUSH     CX
;byte in DS pointed to by SI is moved to AL
                 MOV      AL, [SI]
;do conversion
                 MOV      AH, AL    ; save copy of BCD in AH
                 AND      AH, OFH   ; separate and save lower
                 MOV      BL, AH    ; BCD digit
                 AND      AL, OFOH  ; separate upper nibble
                 MOV      CL, 04    ; move upper BCD digit to low
                 ROR      AL, CL    ; nibble position for multiply
                 MOV      BH, OAH   ; load conversion factor in BH
                 MUL      BH        ; upper digit * OAH,result in AX
                 ADD      AL, BL    ; add lower BCD to result of MUL
                 MOV      [DI], AL  ; move HEX value result in AL
                                    ; to DS location pointed to by DI
                 POP      CX        ; restore registers and flags
                 POP      BX
                 POPF
                 POP      AX
                 RET
BCD_HEX          ENDP
CODE_HERE        ENDS
                 END
```

(*b*)

FIGURE 5-17 (*continued*)

registers to pass the pointers, you can use memory locations dedicated specifically to holding the pointers. In that case the procedure will first fetch the pointer and then use it to access the desired data.

For many of your programs you will probably use registers or a combination of registers and general memory to pass parameters to procedures. However, for more complex programs, such as those which allow several users to time-share a system, we often use the stack to pass parameters to and from procedures.

PASSING PARAMETERS USING THE STACK

To pass parameters to a procedure using the stack we push them on the stack somewhere in the mainline program before we call the procedure. Instructions in the procedure then read these parameters from the stack. Likewise, parameters to be passed back to the calling program are written to the stack by instructions in the procedure and read off the stack by instructions in the mainline. A simple example will best show you how this works.

Figure 5-18*a* shows a version of our BCD-to-hex procedure which uses the stack for passing the BCD number to the procedure and for passing the hex value back to the calling program. To save space here we assume that previous instructions in the mainline set up a stack segment, initialized the stack segment register, and initialized the stack pointer. We also assume that previous instructions in the mainline have left the BCD number in AL. Now in the mainline fragment in Figure 5-18*a* we copy AX to the stack with the PUSH AX instruction. In a more complex example the BCD number or a pointer to it would probably be put on the stack by a different mechanism, but the important point for now is that the parameter is on the stack for the procedure to access. The CALL instruction in the mainline decrements the stack pointer by two, copies the return address on the stack, and loads the instruction pointer with the starting address of the procedure. PUSH instructions at the start of the procedure save the flags and all of the registers used in the procedure on the stack. Before discussing any more instructions, let's take a look at the contents of the stack after these pushes.

Figure 5-18*b* shows how the values pushed on the stack will be arranged. Note that the BCD value is in the stack at a higher address than the return address. After the registers are pushed on the stack the stack pointer is left pointing to the stack location where BP is stored. Now, the question is, how can we easily access the parameter that seems buried in the stack? One way is to add 12 to the stack pointer with an ADD SP, 0CH instruction so the stack pointer points to the word we want from the stack. A POP AX instruction could then be used to copy the desired word from the stack to AX. However, for a variety of reasons which we will explain later, we would like to be able to access the parameter without changing the contents of the stack pointer.

The design of the 8086 makes it very easy to use the base pointer register to do this. Remember from Chapter 2 that an offset in the BP register will be added to the stack segment register to produce a physical memory address. In other words the BP register can act as a second pointer to a location in the stack. This is how we use it in our example program here. In the procedure we copy the contents of the stack pointer register to the BP register with the MOV BP, SP instruction. BP then points to the same location as the stack pointer. Now we use the MOV AX, [BP + 12] instruction to copy the desired word from the stack to AX. The 8086 will produce the effective address for this instruction by adding the displacement of 12, specified in the instruction, to the contents of the BP register. The 0042H in BP gives an effective address of 004EH. As you can see in Figure 5-18*b* the effective address produced will be that of the desired parameter. Note that this instruction does not change the contents of BP. BP can then be used to access other parameters on the stack by simply specifying a different displacement in the instruction used to access the parameter.

Once we have the BCD number copied from the stack into AL, the instructions which convert it to hex are the same as those in the previous versions. When we want to put the hex value back in the stack to return it to the calling program, we again use BP as a pointer to the stack. The instruction MOV [BP +12], AX will copy AX to a stack location 12 addresses higher than that where BP is pointing. This of course is the same location we used to pass the BCD number to the procedure. After we pop the registers and return to the calling program, the registers will all have the values they had before the CALL instruction executed. AX will contain the original BCD number and the stack pointer will be pointing to the hex value now at the top of the stack. In the mainline we can now pop this hex value into a register with an instruction such as POP CX.

Whenever you are using the stack to pass parameters it is very important to keep track of what you have pushed on the stack and where the stack pointer is at each point in a program. We have found that diagrams such as the one in Figure 5-18*b* are very helpful in doing this. One potential problem to watch for when using the stack to pass parameters is *stack overflow*. Stack overflow means that the stack fills up and overflows the memory space you set aside for it. To see how this can easily happen if you don't watch for it, consider the following. Suppose that we use the stack to pass four word parameters to a procedure, but that we only pass one word parameter back to the calling program on the stack. Figure 5-19 shows a stack diagram for this situation. Before a CALL instruction the four parameters to be passed to the procedure are pushed on the stack. During the procedure the parameter to be returned is put in the stack location previously occupied by the fourth input parameter. After the RET instruction at the end of the procedure executes, the stack pointer will be left pointing at this value. Now assume we pop this value into a register. The POP instruction will copy the value to a register and increment the stack pointer by two. The stack pointer now points to the third word we pushed to pass to the procedure. In other words the stack pointer is six addresses lower than it was when we started this process. Now suppose that we call this procedure many times in the course of the mainline pro-

```
;8086 PROGRAM
;ABSTRACT:         Program fragment that uses a procedure to convert
;                  BCD numbers to HEX (binary). It shows how to use
;                  the stack to pass parameters to procedure.
;not shown -       SS contains segment base for STACK_HERE
;not shown -       Initialization of segment registers
;PROCEDURES USED: BCD_HEX

DATA_HERE       SEGMENT
                BCD_INPUT         DB   ? ; storage for BCD value
                HEX_VALUE         DB   ? ; storage for binary value
DATA_HERE       ENDS
CODE_HERE       SEGMENT
                ASSUME CS:CODE_HERE, DS:DATA_HERE, SS:STACK_HERE
                :                          ; initialize segments
                MOV AL, BCD_INPUT          ; move BCD value into AL
                PUSH AX                    ; put BCD value on stack
                CALL BCD_HEX               ; convert to binary
;program continues here with result of conversion on the top of stack
                :
;PROCEDURE:     BCD_HEX
;ABSTRACT :     converts BCD numbers to HEX (binary).
;               Takes its parameters from stack
;SAVES:         All registers used and flags
BCD_HEX         PROC NEAR
                PUSH AX                ; save registers and flags
                PUSHF
                PUSH BX
                PUSH CX
                PUSH BP                ; save BP
                MOV  BP, SP            ; copy SP into BP
                MOV  AX, [BP+12]       ; copy BCD # from stack to AX
;do conversion
                MOV  AH, AL            ; save copy of BCD in AH
                AND  AH, OFH           ; separate and save lower
                MOV  BL, AH            ; BCD digit
                AND  AL, OFOH          ; separate upper nibble
                MOV  CL, 04            ; move upper BCD digit to low
                ROR  AL, CL            ; nibble position for multiply
                MOV  BH, OAH           ; load conversion factor in BH
                MUL  BH                ; upper digit*OAH,result in AX
                ADD  AL, BL            ; add lower BCD to result of MUL
                                       ; final result in AL
;end of conversion now move HEX value from AL to location onto the stack
                MOV  [BP+12], AX
                POP  BP                ; restore registers
                POP  CX                ; and flags and return
                POP  BX
                POPF
                POP       AX
                RET
BCD_HEX         ENDP
CODE_HERE       ENDS
                END
```

(*a*)

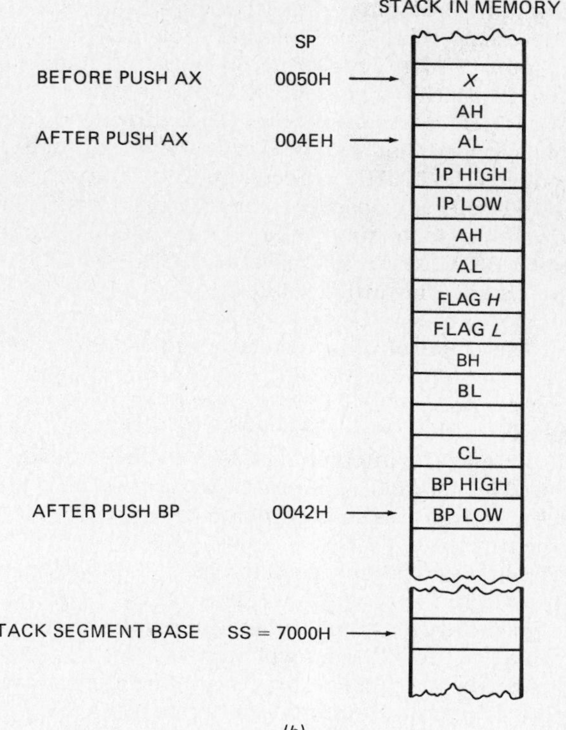

FIGURE 5-18 Example program passing parameters on the stack. *(a)* Assembly language program. *(b)* Stack diagram.

gram. Each time we push four words on the stack but only pop one word off, the stack pointer will be left six addresses lower than it was before the process. The top of the stack will keep getting moved downward. When the stack pointer gets down to 0000H, the next push will roll it around to FFFEH and write a word at the very top of the 64 Kbyte stack segment. If you overlapped segments as you usually do in a small system, the word may get written in a memory location that you are using for data or your program code and your data or code will be lost! This is what we mean by the term stack overflow.

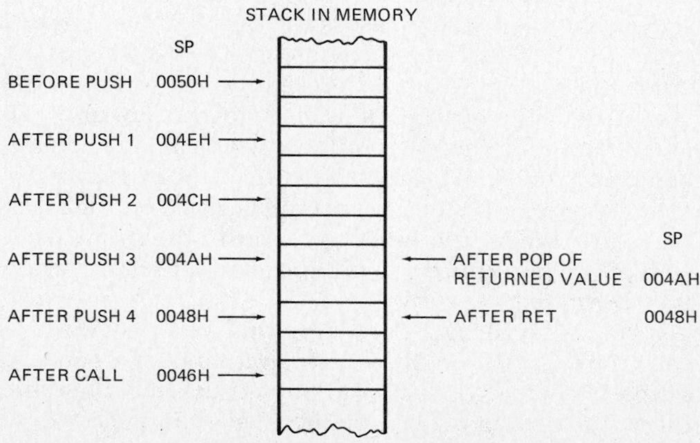

FIGURE 5-19 Stack diagram showing cause of stack overflow.

The cure for this potential problem is to use your stack diagrams to help you keep the stack balanced. You need to keep the number of pops equal to the number of pushes or in some other way make sure the stack pointer gets back to its initial location.

For this example we could use an ADD SP, 06H instruction after the POP instruction to get the stack pointer back up the additional six addresses to where it was before we pushed the four parameters on the stack.

For other cases such as this the 8086 RET instruction has two forms which help you to keep the stack balanced. Remember from a previous section of this chapter that the 8086 has four forms of the RET instruction. The regular near RET instruction copies the return address from the stack to the instruction pointer and increments the stack pointer by 2. The regular far RET instruction copies the return IP and CS values from the stack to IP and CS, and increments the stack pointer by 4. The other two RET instruction forms perform the same functions respectively, but they also add a number specified in the instruction to the stack pointer. The near RET 6 instruction, for example, will first copy a word from the stack to the instruction pointer and increment the stack pointer by 2. It will then add 6 more to the stack pointer. This is a quick way to skip the stack pointer up over some old parameters on the stack.

SUMMARY OF PASSING PARAMETERS TO AND FROM PROCEDURES

You can pass parameters between a calling program and a procedure using registers, dedicated memory locations, or the stack. The method you choose depends largely on the specific program. There are no hard rules, but here are a few guidelines. For simple programs with just a few parameters to pass, registers are usually the easiest to use. For passing arrays or other data structures to and from procedures you can use registers to pass pointers to the start of these data structures. As we explained previously, passing pointers to the procedure is a much more versatile method than having the procedure access the data structure directly by name.

For procedures in a multiuser-system program, procedures that will be called from a high level language program, or procedures that call themselves, parameters should be passed on the stack. When writing programs which pass parameters on the stack you should use stack diagrams such as the one in Figure 5-18*b* to help you keep track of where everything is in the stack at a particular time. The following section will give you some additional guidance as to when to use the stack to pass parameters, and it will give you some additional practice following the stack and stack pointer as a program executes.

Reentrant and Recursive Procedures

The terms *reentrant* and *recursive* are often used in microprocessor manufacturers' literature, but seldom illustrated with examples. Here we try to give these terms some meaning for you. You should make almost all of the procedures you write reentrant, so read that section carefully. You will seldom have to write a recursive procedure so the main points to look for in that section are the definition of the term and the operation of the stack as a recursive procedure operates.

REENTRANT PROCEDURES

The 8086 has a signal input which allows a signal from some external device to interrupt the normal program execution sequence and call a specified procedure. In our electronics factory, for example, a temperature sensor in a flow-solder machine could be connected to the interrupt input. If the temperature gets too high, the sensor sends an interrupting signal to the 8086. The 8086 will then stop whatever it is doing and go to a procedure which takes whatever steps are necessary to cool down the solder bath. This procedure is called an *interrupt service procedure*. Chapter 8 discusses 8086 interrupts and interrupt service procedures in great detail, but it is appropriate to introduce the concept here.

Now, suppose that the 8086 was in the middle of executing a multiply procedure when the interrupt signal occurred, and that we also need to use the multiply procedure in the interrupt service subroutine. Figure 5-20 shows the program execution flow we want for this situation. When the interrupt occurs, execution goes to the interrupt service procedure. The interrupt service procedure then calls the multiply procedure when it needs it. The RET instruction at the end of the multiply procedure returns execution to the interrupt service procedure. A special return instruction at the end of the interrupt service procedure returns execution to the multiply procedure where it was executing when the interrupt occurred. The multiply procedure must be written such that it can be interrupted, used, and "reentered" without losing or writing over anything. A procedure which can function in this way is said to be reentrant.

To be reentrant a procedure must first of all push the flags and all registers used in the procedure. Also, to be reentrant a program should use only registers or the

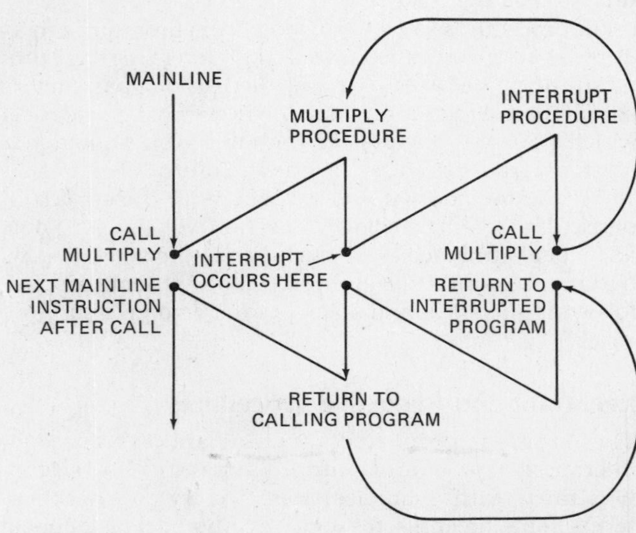

FIGURE 5-20 Program execution flow for reentrant procedure.

stack to hold parameters. To see why this second point is necessary, let's take another look at the program in Figure 5-17*a*. This program uses the named variables BCD_INPUT and HEX_VALUE. The procedure BCD_TO_HEX accesses these two directly by name. Now, suppose that the 8086 is in the middle of executing the BCD_TO_HEX procedure and an interrupt occurs. Further suppose that the interrupt service procedure loads some new value in the memory location named BCD_INPUT, and calls the BCD_TO_HEX procedure again. The initial value in BCD_INPUT has now been written over. If the interrupt occurred before the first execution of the procedure had a chance to read this value in, the value will be lost forever. When execution returns to BCD_TO_HEX after the interrupt service procedure, the value used for BCD_INPUT will be that put there by the interrupt service routine instead of the desired initial value. There are several ways we can handle the parameters so that the procedure BCD_TO_HEX is reentrant.

The first is to simply pass the parameters in registers as we did in the program in Figure 5-16. If this form of the procedure is called by an interrupt service procedure, all of the variables will be saved by push instructions at the start of the procedure and they will be restored by pop instructions before returning to complete the first execution.

A second method of making the BCD_TO_HEX procedure reentrant is to pass pointers to the data items in registers as we did in the program in Figure 5-17*b*. Again, anything in registers will be saved by push instructions and restored by pop instructions when the procedure is called by the interrupt service routine.

Usually at this point someone remembers that the 8086 allows you to push the contents of a memory location on the stack and asks, "Why can't I just save the contents of BCD_INPUT on the stack with a PUSH BCD_INPUT instruction?" You can do this, but if an interrupt occurs before this instruction occurs, you still have the problem.

The third way to make the BCD_TO_HEX procedure reentrant is by passing parameters on the stack as we did in the version in Figure 5-18. In this version the mainline pushes the BCD number on the stack and then calls the procedure. The procedure pushes registers on the stack and accesses the BCD number relative to where the stack pointer ends up. If an interrupt occurs, the interrupt service procedure will push on the stack the BCD number it wishes to convert and call BCD_TO_HEX. This BCD number will be pushed on the stack at a different location from the first BCD number that was pushed. Since everything is saved on the stack no matter where the interrupt occurs, the first execution of the procedure will produce correct results when it is reentered.

If you are writing a procedure that you may want to call from a program in a high-level language such as Pascal, PL/M, or C, then you should definitely use the stack for passing parameters because that is how these languages do it. Check the manual for the high-level language to determine the parameter passing conventions for that language.

RECURSIVE PROCEDURES

A recursive procedure is a procedure which calls itself. This seems simple enough, but the question you may be thinking is, "Why would we want a procedure to call itself?" The answer is that certain types of problems, such as choosing the next move in a computer chess program, can best be solved with a recursive procedure. Recursive procedures are used to work with complex data structures called *trees*. It is unlikely that you will have to write a recursive procedure because most of the programming problems that you are likely to encounter can be solved with a simple WHILE—DO or REPEAT—UNTIL approach. You should, however, know what the term means when you encounter it. For those of you who wish to know more about how a recursive procedure works, we have included an example in the following sections.

Most of the examples of recursive procedures that we could think of are too complex to show here. Therefore, to show you how recursion works, we have chosen a simple problem which could be solved without recursion.

RECURSIVE PROCEDURE EXAMPLE—ALGORITHM

The problem we have chosen to solve is to compute the factorial of a given number in the range of 1 to 9. The factorial of a number is the product of the number and all of the positive integers less than the number. For example, 5 factorial is equal to $5 \times 4 \times 3 \times 2 \times 1$. The word factorial is often represented with "!". You can therefore write 5 factorial as 5!.

What we want to do here is write a recursive procedure which will compute the factorial of a number, *N*, which we pass to it on the stack, and pass the factorial back to the calling program on the stack. The basic algorithm can be expressed very simply as: IF N = 1 THEN factorial = 1, ELSE factorial = N × (factorial of N − 1). This says that if the number we pass to the procedure is 1, the procedure should return the factorial of 1 which is 1. If the number we pass is not 1, then the procedure should multiply this number by the factorial of the number minus one. Now here's where the recursion comes in. Suppose we pass a 3 to the procedure. When the procedure is first called it has the value of 3 for *N*, but it does not have the value for the factorial of *N* − 1

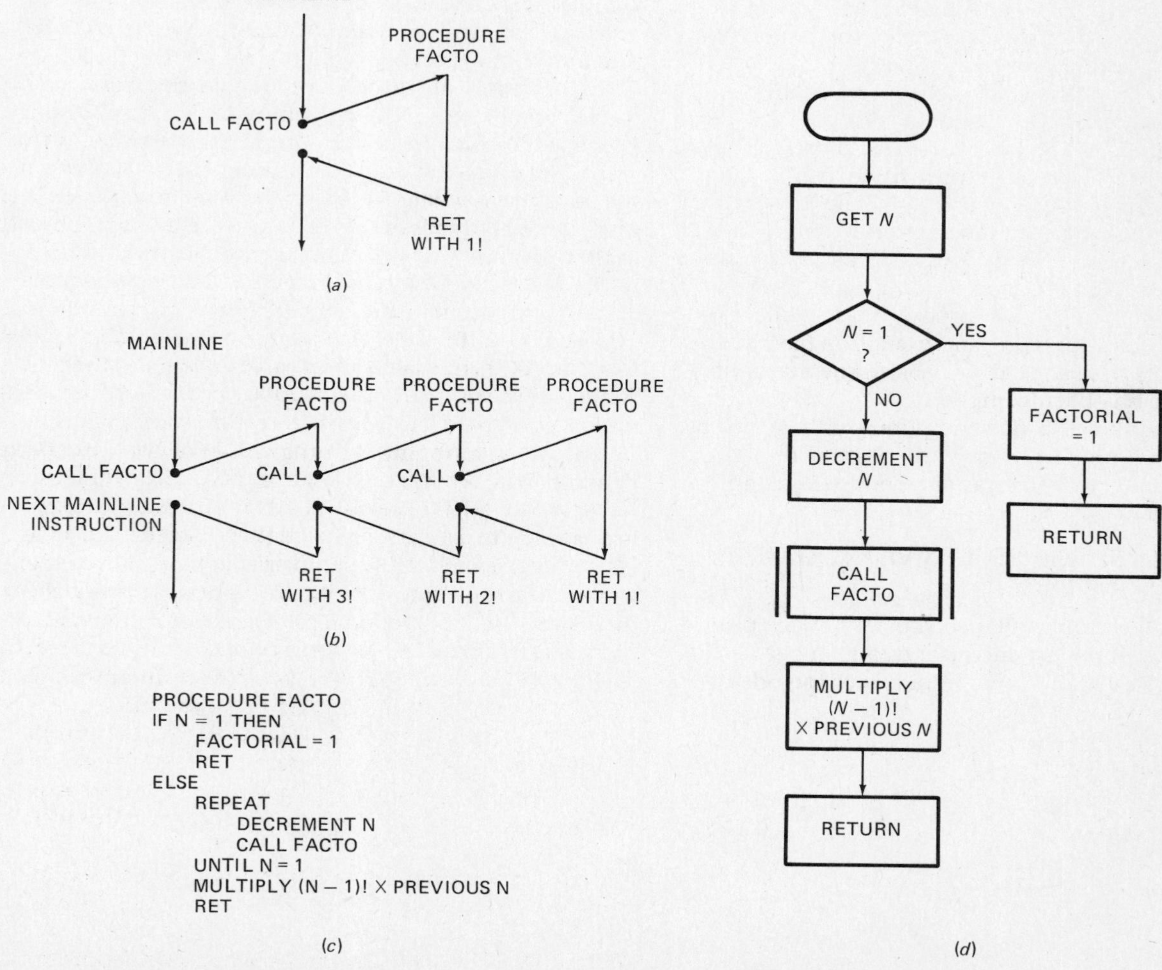

FIGURE 5-21 Algorithm for program to compute factorial for a number *N* between 1 and 9. *(a)* Flow diagram for *N* = 1. *(b)* Flow diagram for *N* = 3. *(c)* Pseudocode. *(d)* Flowchart.

that it needs to do the multiplication indicated in the algorithm. The procedure solves this problem by calling itself to compute the needed factorial of $N - 1$. It calls itself over and over until the factorial of $N - 1$ that it has to compute is the factorial of 1.

Figure 5-21 shows in several ways how we can represent this process. In the program flow diagram in Figure 5-21*a* you can see that if the value of *N* passed to the procedure is 1 then the procedure simply loads 1 in the stack location reserved for *N*! and returns to the calling program. Figure 5-21*b* shows the program flow that will occur when the number passed to the procedure is some number other than one. If we call the procedure with an *N* of 3, the procedure will call itself to compute $N - 1!$ or 2! It will then call itself again to compute the value of the next $N - 1$ factorial or 1!. Since 1! is 1 the procedure will return this value to the program that called it. In this case the program that called it was a previous execution of the same procedure that needed this value to compute 2! Given this value it will compute 2! and return the value to the program that called it. Here again the program that called it was a previous execution of the same procedure that needed 2! to compute the factorial of 3. Given the factorial of 2 this call of the procedure can now compute the factorial of 3 and return to the program that called it. For the example here the return now will be to the mainline program.

Figure 5-21*c* shows how we can represent this algorithm in slightly expanded pseudocode. Use the program flow diagram in Figure 5-21*b* to help you see how execution continues after the return when $N = 1$ and $N = 3$. Can you see that if *N* is initially 1 the first return will return execution to the instruction following CALL FACTO in the mainline? If the initial *N* was 3, for example, this return will return execution back to the instruction after the call in the procedure. Likewise, the return after the multiply can send execution back to the next instruction after the call or back to the mainline if the final result has been computed.

Figure 5-21*d* shows a flowchart for this algorithm. Note that the flowchart shows the same ambiguity about where the return operations send execution to.

ASSEMBLY LANGUAGE RECURSIVE FACTORIAL PROCEDURE

Figure 5-22*a* shows an 8086 assembly language procedure which computes the factorial of a number in the range of 1 to 9. To save space we have not included instructions to return an error message if the number passed to the procedure is out of this range. Figure 5-22*b* shows, with a stack diagram, how the stack will be affected if this procedure is called with an *N* of 3. When working your way through a recursive procedure or any procedure which uses the stack extensively, a stack diagram such as this is absolutely necessary to keep track of everything.

The first parts of the program are housekeeping chores we described in some previous examples. We start the mainline program by declaring a stack segment and setting aside a stack of 200 words with a label at the top of the stack. The first three instructions in the code segment of the mainline program initialize the stack segment register and the stack pointer register. The SUB SP,04 instruction after this will decrement the stack pointer register by 4. In other words we skip the stack pointer down over 2 words in the stack. These two word locations will be used to pass the computed factorial from the procedure back to the mainline program. Next we load the number whose factorial we want into AX and push the value on the stack where the procedure will access it. Now we are ready to call the procedure. We have given the procedure the name FACTO with the FACTO PROC NEAR and FACTO ENDP directives. The procedure is near because it is in the same code segment as the instruction which calls it.

At the start of the procedure we save the flags and all the registers used in the procedure on the stack. Take a look at Figure 5-22*b* to see what is on the stack at this point. Note that the value of *N* is buried 10 addresses up the stack from where the stack pointer was left after BP was pushed. To access this buried value we first copy SP to BP with the MOV BP, SP instruction so that BP points to the top of the stack. We can then use the expression [BP + 10] to refer to the address where *N* was pushed. The MOV AX, [BP + 10] instruction will copy *N* from the stack to AX. If the value of *N* read in is 1 then the factorial is 1. We want to put 00000001H in the stack locations we reserved for the result, restore the registers and return to the mainline program. Follow this path through the program in Figure 5-22*a*. Note how the MOV WORD PTR [BP + 12], 0001H instruction is used to load a value to a location buried in the stack. The WORD PTR directives tell the assembler that you want to move a word to the specified memory location. Without these directives the assembler will not know whether to code the instruction for moving a byte or for moving a word. The MOV WORD PTR [BP + 14], 0000H instruction is

```
;8086 PROGRAM
;ABSTRACT        : This program computes the factorial of a
;                  number between 1 and 9
;PORTS USED      : None
;PROCEDURES USED: FACTO

STACK_HERE       SEGMENT STACK
        DW       200 DUP(0)      ; set aside 200 words for stack
STACK_TOP        LABEL   WORD    ; assign name to word above stack top
STACK_HERE       ENDS
```

```
NUMBER   EQU      03
CODE_HERE         SEGMENT
                  ASSUME CS:CODE_HERE, SS:STACK_HERE
         MOV      AX, STACK_HERE  ; initialize stack segment register
         MOV      SS, AX
         MOV      SP, OFFSET STACK_TOP ; initialize stack pointer
         SUB      SP, 0004H           ; make space in stack for factorial
                                      ; to be returned
         MOV      AX, NUMBER          ; put number to be passed on stack
         PUSH     AX
         CALL     FACTO               ; compute factorial of number
         POP      AX                  ; get result
         NOP                          ; simulate next mainline instructions
         NOP
         NOP
;PROCEDURE: FACTO
;ABSTRACT : Recursive procedure that computes the factorial of
;           a number. It takes its parameter from the stack and
;           returns the result on the stack.
;SAVES    : all registers used
FACTO    PROC     NEAR
         PUSHF                        ; save flags and registers on stack
         PUSH     AX
         PUSH     DX
         PUSH     BP
         MOV      BP, SP              ; point BP at top of stack
         MOV      AX,[BP+10]          ; copy number from stack to AX
         CMP      AX, 0001H           ; if number not equal 1 then go on
         JNE      GO_ON               ;  and compute factorial
         MOV WORD PTR [BP+12], 0001H      ; else load factorial of one in
         MOV WORD PTR [BP+14], 0000H      ; stack and return to mainline
         JMP      EXIT
GO_ON:   SUB      SP, 0004H           ; make space in stack for preliminary
                                      ;  factorial
         DEC      AX                  ; decrement number now in AX
         PUSH     AX                  ; save number - 1 on stack
         CALL     FACTO               ; compute factorial of number - 1
         MOV      BP, SP              ; point BP at top of stack
         MOV      AX, [BP+2]          ; last (N-1)! from stack to AX
         MUL WORD PTR [BP+16]         ; multiply by previous N
         MOV      [BP+18], AX         ; copy new factorial to stack
         MOV      [BP+20], DX
         ADD      SP, 0006H           ; point stack pointer at pushed register
EXIT:    POP      BP                  ; restore registers
         POP DX
         POP AX
         POPF
         RET
FACTO    ENDP
CODE_HERE ENDS
         END
```

(a)

FIGURE 5-22 Recursive procedure to calculate factorial of number between 1 and 9. *(a)* Assembly language. *(b)* Stack diagram showing contents of stack for $N = 3$.

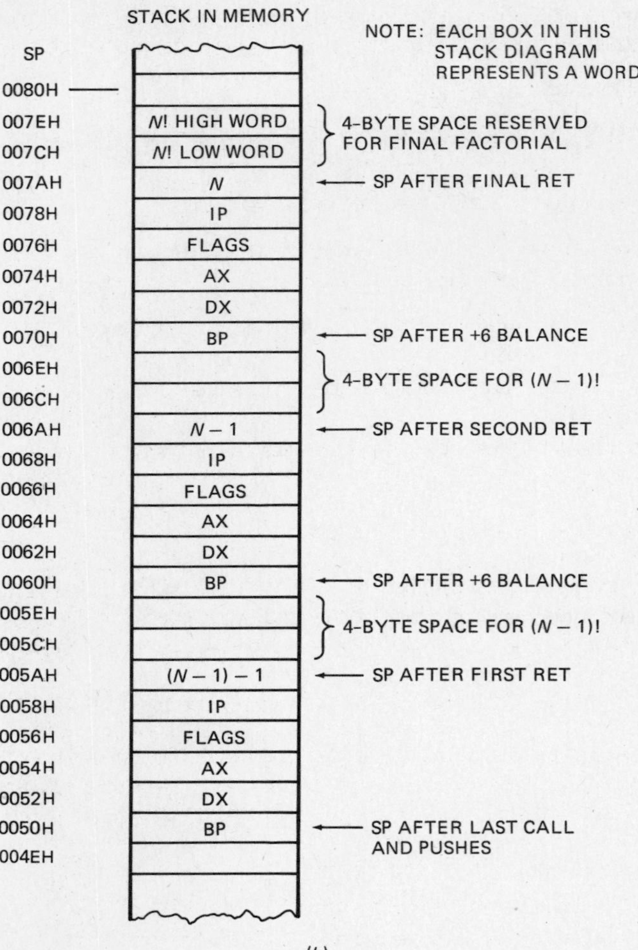

FIGURE 5-22*b* Stack diagram showing contents of stack for N = 3.

likewise used to move a word value to the other word location reserved in the stack for the factorial.

Now let's see what happens if the number passed to FACTO is a 3. The CMP AX, 0001H instruction and the JNE GO_ON instructions determine that N is not 1 and send execution to the SUB SP, 04H instruction. According to the algorithm we are going to find the value of $N!$ by multiplying N times the value of $(N - 1)!$. We will be calling FACTO again to find the value of $(N - 1)!$. The SUB SP, 04H instruction skips the stack pointer down over four addresses in the stack. The value of $(3 - 1)!$ will be returned in these locations. We then decrement N by one and push the value of $N - 1$ on the stack where FACTO will access it.

When we call FACTO now to compute the value of $(N - 1)!$ the registers and flags will again be pushed on the stack. Take another look at Figure 5-22*b* to see what is on the stack at this point. The value of $N - 1$ that we need is again buried 10 addresses up in the stack. This is no problem because the MOV BP, SP and MOV AX, [BP + 10] instructions will allow us to access the value. We started with $N = 3$ for this example, so the value of $N - 1$ that we read in at this point is equal to 2. Since this value is not 1 execution will again go to the label GO_ON. The SUB SP, 04 instruction will again skip the stack pointer down over four addresses to leave space for $(2 - 1)!$ to be returned by FACTO. We decrement N by 1 to get $N - 1$, which is now 1. We push this value on the stack and call FACTO to compute the factorial of 1.

After pushing all the registers on the stack FACTO reads this 1 from the stack with the MOV AX, [BP + 10] instruction. When the CMP AX, 0001H instruction in FACTO finds that the number passed to it is 1, FACTO loads a factorial value of 1 in the four memory locations we most recently set aside for a returned factorial. The MOV WORD PTR [BP + 12], 0001 and the MOV WORD PTR [BP + 14], 0000 instructions do this. Look at the stack diagram in Figure 5-22*b* to see where these four locations are in the stack. FACTO will then do a return to the next instruction after the CALL instruction that called it.

Now in this case FACTO was called from a previous execution of FACTO so the return will be to the MOV BP,SP instruction after CALL FACTO. The MOV BP, SP instruction points BP at the top of the stack so that we can access data on the stack without affecting the stack pointer. The MOV AX, [BP + 2] instruction after this copies the low word of the last computed $(N - 1)!$ from the stack to AX so that we can multiply it by N. We only need the lower word of the two we set aside for the factorial, because for an N of eight or less, only the lower word will contain data. Restricting the allowed range of N for this example means that we only have to do a 16-bit by 16-bit multiply. We could increase the allowed range of N by simply setting aside larger spaces in the stack for factorials and including instructions to multiply larger numbers. In this example the MUL WORD PTR [BP + 16] instruction multiplies the $(N - 1)!$ in AX by the previous N from the stack. The low word of the product is left in AX and the high word of the product is left in DX. The MOV [BP + 18], AX and the MOV [BP + 20], DX instructions copy these two words to the stack locations we reserved for the next factorial. Now take a look at the stack diagram in Figure 5-22*b* to see where these two words get put and where the stack pointer is at this time. The next operation we would like to do in the program is pop the registers and return. As you can see from Figure 5-22*b*, however, the stack pointer is now pointing at some old data on the stack, not at the first register we want to pop. To get the stack pointer pointing where we want it, we add six to it with the ADD SP,06H instruction. Then we pop the registers and return.

To see where we are returning to, take another look at Figure 5-22*b*. We are returning with 2! in the stack so we still have one more computation to produce the desired 3!. Therefore, the return is again to the MOV BP, SP instruction after CALL in FACTO. The instructions after this will multiply 2! times 3 to produce the desired 3!, and copy 3! to the stack as described in the preceding paragraph. The ADD SP,06H instruction will again adjust the stack pointer so that we can pop the registers and return. Since we have done all the required computations, this time the return will be to the mainline program. The desired result, 3!, will be in the memory locations we reserved for it in the stack. We can access this result with a BP addressing mode when we need the value in the mainline.

If you work your way through the flow of the stack and the stack pointer in this example program, you should have a good understanding of how the stack is used.

Writing and Calling FAR Procedures

INTRODUCTION AND OVERVIEW

A far procedure is one which is located in a different segment from the CALL instruction which calls it. To get to the starting address of a far procedure the 8086 must change the contents of both the code segment register and the contents of the instruction pointer. Therefore, if you are hand coding a program which calls a far procedure, make sure to use one of the intersegment forms of the CALL instruction to do this. You might, for example, use the direct intersegment CALL instruction. If you look at the coding template for this instruction you will see that the destination instruction pointer value is coded in as bytes 2 and 3 of the instruction, and the destination code segment register value is coded in as bytes 4 and 5 of the instruction. Likewise, at the end of a far procedure, both the contents of the code segment register and the contents of the instruction pointer must be popped off the stack to return to the calling program. Make sure to use one of the intersegment forms of the RET instruction to do this.

If you are using an assembler to assemble a program containing a far procedure, there are a few additional directives you have to give the assembler. The following sections show you how to put these needed additions in your programs. The first case we will describe is one where the procedure is in the same assembly module, but it is in a segment with a different name than the segment that contains the CALL instruction.

ACCESSING A PROCEDURE IN ANOTHER SEGMENT

Suppose that in a program we want to put all of the mainline in one logical segment and we want to put several procedures in another logical segment to keep them separate. Figure 5-23 shows some program fragments which illustrate this situation. For this example our mainline instructions are in a segment named CODE_HERE. A procedure called MULTIPLY_32 is in a segment named PROCEDURES_HERE. Since the procedure is in a different segment from the CALL instruction we must change the contents of the code segment register to access it. Therefore, the procedure is far.

We let the assembler know that the procedure is far by using the word FAR in the MULTIPLY_32 PROC FAR statement. When the assembler finds that the procedure is declared as far, it will automatically code the CALL instruction as an intersegment CALL.

Now the remaining thing we have to do, so that the program gets assembled correctly, is to make sure that the assembler uses the right code segment for each part of the program. We use the ASSUME statement to do this. At the start of the mainline we use the statement ASSUME CS:CODE_HERE to tell the assembler to compute the offsets of the following instructions from the segment base named CODE_HERE. At the start of the procedure we use the ASSUME CS:PROCEDURES_HERE

```
CODE_HERE SEGMENT
          ASSUME    CS:CODE_HERE, DS:DATA_HERE, SS:STACK_HERE
             :
          CALL MULTIPLY_32
CODE_HERE ENDS


PROCEDURES_HERE      SEGMENT
MULTIPLY_32     PROC FAR
          ASSUME    CS:PROCEDURES_HERE
             :
MULTIPLY_32          ENDP
PROCEDURES_HERE      ENDS
```

FIGURE 5-23 Program additions needed for a far procedure.

statement to tell the assembler to compute the offsets for the instructions in the procedure. The assembler will then compute these offsets starting from the segment base named PROCEDURES_HERE.

When the assembler finally codes out the CALL instruction, it will put the value of PROCEDURES_HERE in for CS in the instruction. It will put the offset of the first instruction of the procedure in PROCEDURES_HERE as the IP value in the instruction.

To summarize then, if a procedure is in another segment you must declare it far with the FAR directive. Also you must put an ASSUME statement in the procedure to tell the assembler what segment base to use for the instructions in the procedure.

ACCESSING A PROCEDURE AND DATA IN A SEPARATE ASSEMBLY MODULE

As we have discussed previously, the best way to write a large program is as a series of modules. Each module can be individually written, assembled, tested, and debugged. Working modules can then be linked together. The previous section showed you how to access a procedure in the same assembly module, but in a different segment from the CALL instruction. Here we show you how to write your programs so that they can access data or procedures in another assembly module.

In order for a linker to be able to access data or a procedure in another assembly module correctly, there are four major types of information that you must give the assembler. We will give you an overview of these four and then show with a program example how you actually write them.

In the assembly module which contains the calling program you must use the EXTRN directive to tell the assembler the names of any procedures or data items that are in other assembly modules. Also, in the module that contains the calling program you must use the PUBLIC directive to tell the assembler any labels or data items that will be accessed from another assembly module.

In the assembly module which contains the procedure you must likewise use the EXTRN directive to tell the assembler the names of any labels or data items that it must look for in another assembly module. Also in the assembly module that contains the procedure you must use the PUBLIC directive to tell the assembler that a label or data item will be accessed from another assembly module.

PROBLEM DEFINITION AND ALGORITHM DISCUSSION

The procedure in the following example program was written to solve a small problem we encountered when writing the program for a microprocessor-controlled medical instrument. Here's the problem.

In the program we add up a series of values read in from an A/D converter. The sum is an unsigned number of between 24 and 32 bits. We needed to scale this value by dividing it by 10. This seems easy because the 8086 DIV instruction will divide a 32-bit unsigned binary number by a 16-bit binary number. The quotient from the division, remember, is put in AX and the remainder is put in DX. However, if the quotient is larger than 16 bits as it will be for our scaling, the quotient will not fit in AX. In this case the 8086 will automatically respond in the same way that it would if you tried to divide a number by zero. We will discuss the details of this response in Chapter 8. For now it is enough to say that we don't want the 8086 to make this response. The simple solution we came up with is to do the division in two steps in such a way that we get a 32-bit quotient and a 16-bit remainder.

Our algorithm is a simple sequence of actions very similar to the way we were taught to do long division. We will first describe how this works with decimal numbers and then we will show how it works with 32-bit and 16-bit binary numbers. Figure 5-24*a* shows an example of long division of the decimal number 433 by the decimal number 9. The 9 won't divide into the 4, so we put a 0 or nothing in this digit position of the quotient. We then see if 9 divides into 43. It fits 4 times, so we put a 4 in this digit position of the quotient and subtract 4 × 9 from the 43. The remainder of 7 now becomes the high digit of the 73, the next number we try to divide the 9 into. After we find that the 9 fits 8 times and subtract 9 × 8 from the 73, we are left with a final remainder of 1. Now let's see how we do this with large binary numbers.

As shown in Figure 5-24*b* we first divide the 16-bit divisor into a 32-bit number made up of a word of all 0's and the high word of the dividend. This division gives us the high word of the quotient and a remainder. The remainder becomes the high word of the dividend for the next division, just as it did for the decimal division.

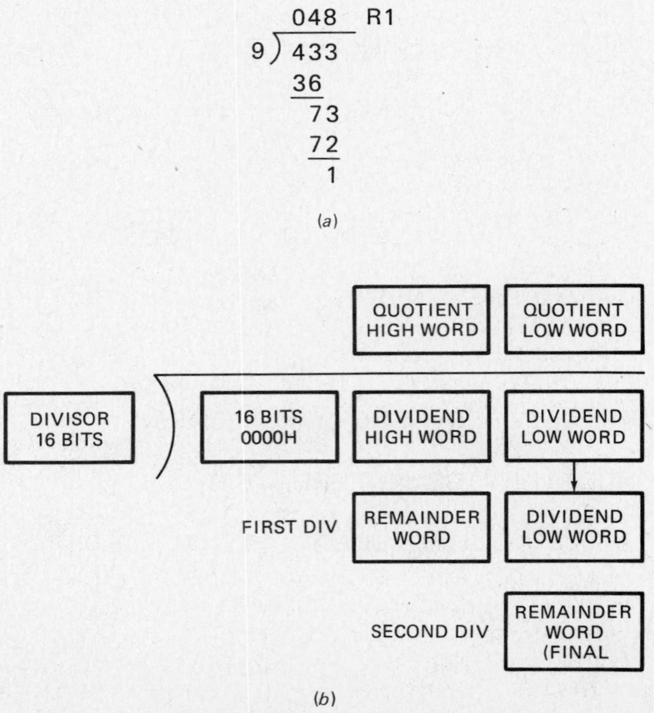

```
     048  R1
  9 ) 433
      36
       73
       72
        1
```

(*a*)

(*b*)

FIGURE 5-24 Algorithm for smart divide procedure. *(a)* Decimal analogy. *(b)* 8086 approach.

We move the low word of the original dividend in as the low word of this dividend and divide by the 16-bit divisor again. The 16-bit quotient from this division is the low word of the 32-bit quotient we want. The 16-bit final remainder can be used to round off the quotient or be discarded, depending on the application.

THE ASSEMBLY LANGUAGE PROGRAM

Figure 5-25*a* shows the mainline of a program which calls the procedure shown in Figure 5-25*b* which implements our division algorithm. We wrote these two as separate assembly modules so that we could show you what you need to add to each module in order for the modules to be linkable. Let's look closely at these added parts before we discuss the actual division procedure.

The first added part of the program to look at is in the statement DATA_HERE SEGMENT WORD PUBLIC. The word PUBLIC in this statement tells the assembler that the contents of this segment will be added to the contents of a segment with the same name in another assembly module when the two modules are linked. In other words, if two or more assembly modules have PUBLIC segments named DATA_HERE, their contents will be pulled together in successive memory locations when the program modules are linked. You should then declare a segment PUBLIC anytime you want it to be linked with other segments of the same name in other modules.

The next addition to look at is the statement PUBLIC DIVISOR in the mainline module in Figure 5-25*a*. This statement is necessary to tell the assembler that the data item named DIVISOR will be accessed from some other assembly module or modules. Essentially what we are doing here is telling the assembler to put the offset of DIVISOR in a special table where it can be accessed when the program modules are linked. Whenever you want a named data item or a label to be accessible from another assembly module you must declare it as PUBLIC. Note in the table at the end of the assembler listing that DIVISOR is global. This is the assembler's way of telling you that it can be accessed from other modules by the linker.

The other side of this coin is that, when you need to access a label or a named data item in another module, you must use the EXTRN directive to tell the assembler that the label or data item is not in the present module. In the example program the statement EXTRN SMART_DIVIDE:FAR tells the assembler that we will be accessing a label or procedure of type far in some other assembly module. For this example we will be accessing our procedure, SMART_DIVIDE. We enclose the EXTRN statement with the PROCEDURES_HERE PUBLIC and the PROCEDURES_HERE ENDS statements to tell the assembler that the procedure SMART_DIVIDE is located in the segment PROCEDURES_HERE. There are some cases where these statements are not needed, but we have found that bracketing the EXTRN statement with SEGMENT—ENDS directives in this way is the best way to make sure that the linker can find everything when it links modules. As you can see in the table at the end of the assembler listing in Figure 5-25*a*, SMART_DIVIDE is identified as an external label of type far, found in a segment named PROCEDURES_HERE.

Now let's see how we handle EXTRN and PUBLIC in the procedure module. The procedure accesses the data item named DIVISOR which is defined in the mainline module. Therefore, we must use the statement EXTRN DIVISOR:WORD to tell the assembler that DIVISOR, a data item of type word, will be found in some other module. Furthermore we enclose the EXTRN statement with the DATA_HERE SEGMENT PUBLIC and DATA_HERE ENDS statements to tell the assembler that DIVISOR will be found in a segment named DATA_HERE.

NOTE: If we had needed to also access DIVIDEND we could have written the EXTRN statement as EXTRN DIVISOR:WORD, DIVIDEND:WORD. To add more terms, just separate them with a comma.

The procedure SMART_DIVIDE must be accessible from other modules so we declare it public with the PUBLIC SMART_DIVIDE statement in the procedure module. If we needed to make other labels or data items public, we could have listed them separated by commas after PUBLIC SMART_DIVIDE. An example is PUBLIC SMART_DIVIDE, EXIT.

Now that we have explained the use of PUBLIC and EXTRN, let's work our way through the rest of the program. At the start of the mainline the ASSUME statement tells the assembler which logical segments to use as code, data, and stack. We then initialize the data segment, stack segment, and stack pointer registers as described in previous example programs. Now before calling the SMART_DIVIDE procedure we copy the dividend and divisor from memory to some registers. The dividend and the divisor are passed to the procedure in these registers. As we explained in a previous section, if we pass parameters to a procedure in registers, the procedure does not have to refer to specific named memory locations. The procedure is then more general and can more easily be called from any place in the mainline. However, in this example we referenced the named memory location, DIVISOR, from the procedure to show you how it can be done using the EXTRN and PUBLIC directives. The procedure is of type far so when we call it, both the code segment register and the instruction pointer contents will be changed.

In the procedure we first check to see if the divisor is zero with a CMP DIVISOR, 0 instruction. If the divisor is zero the JE instruction will send execution to the label ERROR_EXIT. There we set the carry flag with STC as an error indicator and return to the mainline program. If the divisor is not zero, then we go on with the division. To understand how we do the division, remember that the 8086 DIV instruction divides the 32-bit number in DX and AX by the 16-bit number in a specified register or memory location. It puts a 16-bit quotient in AX and a 16-bit remainder in DX. Now, according to our algorithm in Figure 5-24*b* we want to put 0000H in DX and the high word of the dividend in AX for our first DIV operation. MOV BX, AX saves a copy of the low word of the dividend for future reference. MOV AX, DX copies the high word of the dividend into AX where we want it, and MOV DX, 0000H puts all 0's in DX. After the first DIV

```
                              PAGE ,132
                              ;8086 Program
                              ;ABSTRACT:     This program divides a 32-bit number by a 16-bit number
                              ;              to give a 32-bit quotient and a 16-bit remainder.
                              ;REGISTERS USED:CS, DS, SS, AX, SP, BX, CX, DX
                              ;PROCEDURES:   Calls SMART_DIVIDE which is a far procedure
                              ;PORTS USED:   None

0000                          DATA_HERE      SEGMENT   WORD PUBLIC
0000  403B 8C72                   DIVIDEND DW   403BH, 8C72H    ; dividend 8C72403BH
0004  5692                        DIVISOR  DW   5692H           ; 16-bit divisor
0006                          DATA_HERE ENDS

0000                          MORE_DATA      SEGMENT   WORD
0000     02 [                     QUOTIENT  DW   2 DUP(0)
               0000
                    ]

0004  0000                        REMAINDER DW   0
0006                          MORE_DATA ENDS

0000                          STACK_HERE     SEGMENT   STACK
0000     64 [                              DW   100 DUP(0)      ; stack of 100 words
               0000
                    ]

00C8                              TOP_STACK LABEL    WORD       ; name pointer to top of stack
00C8                          STACK_HERE     ENDS

                              PUBLIC    DIVISOR

0000                          PROCEDURES_HERE SEGMENT PUBLIC     ; let assembler know that SMART_DIVIDE
                                  EXTRN     SMART_DIVIDE : FAR   ; is a label of type FAR and is located
0000                          PROCEDURES_HERE     ENDS           ; in the segment PROCEDURES_HERE

0000                          CODE_HERE SEGMENT WORD PUBLIC
                                        ASSUME CS:CODE_HERE, DS:DATA_HERE, SS:STACK_HERE

0000  B8  ---- R              START:    MOV  AX, DATA_HERE         ; initialize data segment
0003  8E D8                             MOV  DS, AX
0005  B8  ---- R                        MOV  AX, STACK_HERE        ; initialize stack segment
0008  8E D0                             MOV  SS, AX
000A  BC 00C8 R                         MOV  SP, OFFSET TOP_STACK  ; initialize stack pointer
                              ; load low word of dividend in AX, high word of dividend in DX, divisor in CX
000D  A1 0000 R                         MOV  AX, DIVIDEND          ; load low  word
0010  8B 16 0002 R                      MOV  DX, DIVIDEND + 2      ; load high word
0014  8B 0E 0004 R                      MOV  CX, DIVISOR           ; load divisor
0018  9A 0000 ---- E                    CALL SMART_DIVIDE
                              ; quotient returned in DX:AX, remainder returned in CX, carry set if result invalid
001D  73 03                             JNC  SAVE_ALL              ; carry = 0, result valid
001F  EB 13 90                          JMP  STOP                  ; carry set, don't save result
                                    ASSUME DS:MORE_DATA            ; change data segment
0022  1E                      SAVE_ALL: PUSH DS                    ; save old DS
```

FIGURE 5-25 Assembly language program to divide a 32-bit number by a 16-bit number and return a 32-bit quotient. *(a)* Mainline program module. *(b)* Procedure module.

```
The IBM Personal Computer MACRO Assembler 02-19-85       PAGE    1-2

 0023  BB  ---- R                       MOV    BX, MORE_DATA        ; load new data segment
 0026  8E DB                            MOV    DS, BX
 0028  A3 0000 R                        MOV    QUOTIENT, AX         ; store low  word of quotient
 002B  89 16 0002 R                     MOV    QUOTIENT + 2, DX     ; store high word of quotient
 002F  89 0E 0004 R                     MOV    REMAINDER, CX        ; store remainder
                                   ASSUME DS:DATA_HERE
 0033  1F                               POP    DS                   ; restore initial DS
 0034  90                     STOP:     NOP
 0035                         CODE_HERE ENDS
                                        END

Segments and groups:

            N a m e              Size   align   combine class

CODE_HERE. . . . . . . . . . . . .    0035   WORD    PUBLIC
DATA_HERE. . . . . . . . . . . . .    0006   WORD    PUBLIC
MORE_DATA. . . . . . . . . . . . .    0006   WORD    NONE
PROCEDURES_HERE. . . . . . . . . .    0000   PARA    PUBLIC
STACK_HERE . . . . . . . . . . . .    00C8   PARA    STACK

Symbols:

            N a m e              Type    Value   Attr

DIVIDEND . . . . . . . . . . . . .    L WORD  0000    DATA_HERE
DIVISOR. . . . . . . . . . . . . .    L WORD  0004    DATA_HERE        Global
QUOTIENT . . . . . . . . . . . . .    L WORD  0000    MORE_DATA        Length =0002
REMAINDER. . . . . . . . . . . . .    L WORD  0004    MORE_DATA
SAVE_ALL . . . . . . . . . . . . .    L NEAR  0022    CODE_HERE
SMART_DIVIDE . . . . . . . . . . .    L FAR   0000    PROCEDURES_HERE External
START. . . . . . . . . . . . . . .    L NEAR  0000    CODE_HERE
STOP . . . . . . . . . . . . . . .    L NEAR  0034    CODE_HERE
TOP_STACK. . . . . . . . . . . . .    L WORD  00C8    STACK_HERE

Warning Severe
Errors  Errors
0       0
```

(a)

```
The IBM Personal Computer MACRO Assembler 01-01-80       PAGE    1-1

                              PAGE ,132
                              ;8086 procedure called SMART_DIVIDE
                              ;ABSTRACT:      This procedure divides a 32-bit number by a 16-bit number
                              ;               to give a 32-bit quotient and a 16-bit remainder. The
                              ;               parameters are passed to and from the procedure in the
                              ;               following way:
                              ;               Dividend : low word in AX, high word in DX
                              ;               Divisor  : word in CX
                              ;               Quotient : low word in AX, high word in DX
                              ;               Remainder: in CX
                              ;               Carry    : carry set if try to divide by zero
                              ;USES:          AX, BX, CX, DX, BP, FLAGS
```

```
                              ;the following block tells the assembler that the divisor is a word
                              ;variable found in the external segment named DATA_HERE
0000                          DATA_HERE       SEGMENT PUBLIC
                                    EXTRN   DIVISOR:WORD
0000                          DATA_HERE       ENDS

                              ;the next statement makes SMART_DIVIDE available to other modules
                              PUBLIC          SMART_DIVIDE

0000                          PROCEDURES_HERE SEGMENT PUBLIC
0000                          SMART_DIVIDE    PROC    FAR
                                              ASSUME  CS:PROCEDURES_HERE, DS:DATA_HERE
0000  83 3E 0000 E 00                         CMP     DIVISOR, 0       ; check for illegal divide
0005  74 17                                   JE      ERROR_EXIT       ; divisor = 0 so exit
0007  8B D8                                   MOV     BX, AX           ; save low order of dividend
0009  8B C2                                   MOV     AX, DX           ; position high word for 1st divide
000B  BA 0000                                 MOV     DX, 0000H        ; zero DX
000E  F7 F1                                   DIV     CX               ; AX/CX, quotient in AX, remainder in DX
0010  8B E8                                   MOV     BP, AX           ; save high order of final result
0012  8B C3                                   MOV     AX, BX           ; get back low order of dividend
0014  F7 F1                                   DIV     CX               ; AX/CX, quotient in AX, remainder in DX
0016  8B CA                                   MOV     CX, DX           ; pass remainder back in CX
0018  8B D5                                   MOV     DX,BP            ; pass high order result back in DX
001A  F8                                      CLC                      ; clear carry to indicate valid result
001B  EB 02 90                                JMP     EXIT             ; finished
001E  F9                      ERROR_EXIT:     STC                      ; set carry to indicate divide by zero
001F  CB                      EXIT:           RET
0020                          SMART_DIVIDE    ENDP
0020                          PROCEDURES_HERE ENDS
                                              END


The IBM Personal Computer MACRO Assembler 01-01-80       PAGE    Symbols-1

Segments and groups:

                N a m e                 Size    align   combine class

DATA_HERE. . . . . . . . . . . . .      0000    PARA    PUBLIC
PROCEDURES_HERE. . . . . . . . .        0020    PARA    PUBLIC

Symbols:

                N a m e                 Type    Value   Attr

DIVISOR. . . . . . . . . . . . . .      V WORD  0000    DATA_HERE       External
ERROR_EXIT . . . . . . . . . . . .      L NEAR  001E    PROCEDURES_HERE
EXIT . . . . . . . . . . . . . . .      L NEAR  001F    PROCEDURES_HERE
SMART_DIVIDE . . . . . . . . . . .      F PROC  0000    PROCEDURES_HERE Global  Length =0020

Warning Severe
Errors  Errors
0       0
```

(*b*)

FIGURE 5-25 (*continued*)

instruction executes, AX will contain the high word of the 32-bit quotient we want as our final answer. We save this in BP with the MOV BP,AX instruction so that we can use AX for the second DIV operation.

The remainder from the first DIV operation was left in the DX register. As shown by the diagram in Figure 5-24*b*, this is right where we want it for the second DIV operation. All we have to do now, before we do the second DIV operation, is to get the low word of the original dividend back into AX with the MOV AX, BX instruction. After the second DIV instruction executes, the 16-bit quotient will be in AX. This word is the low word of our desired 32-bit quotient. We just leave this word in AX to be passed back to the mainline. The DX register was left with the final remainder. We copy this remainder to CX with the MOV CX, DX instruction to be passed back to the mainline program. After the first DIV operation we saved the high word of our 32-bit quotient in BP. We now use the MOV DX, BP instruction to copy this word back to DX where we want it to be when we return to the mainline. You really don't have to shuffle the results around the way we did with these last three instructions, but we like to pass parameters to and from procedures in as systematic a way as possible so that we can more easily keep track of everything. After the shuffling we clear the carry flag with CLC before returning.

Back in the mainline we check the carry flag with the JNC instruction. If the carry flag is set we know that the divisor was 0, no division was done, and there is no result to put in memory. If the carry flag is not set then we know that a valid 32-bit quotient was returned in DX and AX and a 16-bit remainder was returned in CX. We now want to copy this quotient and this remainder to some named memory locations we set aside for them. If you look at some earlier lines in the program, you will see that the memory locations called QUOTIENT and REMAINDER are in a segment called MORE_DATA. At the start of the mainline we tell the assembler to ASSUME that we will be using DATA_HERE as the data segment. Now, however, we want to access some data items in MORE_DATA using DS. To do this we have to do two things. First we have to tell the assembler to ASSUME DS:MORE_DATA. Second, we have to load the segment base of MORE_DATA into DS. In our program we save the old value of DS by pushing it on the stack. We do this so that we can easily reload DS with the base address of DATA_HERE later in the program. The MOV BX, MORE_DATA and MOV DS,BX instructions load the base address of MORE_DATA into DS. The three MOV instructions after this copy the quotient and the remainder into the named memory locations.

Finally in the program we point DS back at DATA_HERE so that later instructions can access data items in the DATA_HERE segment. To do this we first tell the assembler to ASSUME DS:DATA_HERE. We then POP the base address of DATA_HERE off the stack into DS. As you write more complex programs you will often want to access different segments at different times in the program. We wrote this example to show you how to do it. When you do change segments, make sure to change both the ASSUME and the actual contents of the segment register.

Writing and Debugging Programs Containing Procedures

The most important point in writing a program containing procedures is to approach the overall job very systematically. We carefully work out the overall structure of the program and break it down into modules which can easily be written as procedures. We then write the mainline program so that we know what each procedure has to do and how parameters can be most easily be passed to each procedure. To test this mainline we simulate each procedure with a few instructions which simply pass test values back to the mainline. Some programmers refer to these "dummy" procedures as *stubs*. If the structure of the mainline seems reasonable, we then develop each procedure and replace the dummy with it. The advantage of this approach is that you have a structure to hang the procedures on. If you write the procedures first, you have the messy problem of trying to write a mainline to connect all the pieces together.

Now, suppose that you have approached a program as we suggested, and the program doesn't work. After you have checked the algorithm and instructions, you should check that the number of PUSH and POP instructions are equal for each call and return operation. If none of the checks turns up anything, you can use the system debugging tools to track down the problem. Probably the best tools to help you localize a problem to a small area are breakpoints. Run the program to a breakpoint just before a CALL instruction to see if the correct parameters are being passed to the procedure. Put a breakpoint at the start of the procedure to see if execution ever gets to the procedure. Move the breakpoint to a later point in the procedure to determine if the procedure found the parameters passed from the mainline. Use a breakpoint just before the RET instruction to see if the procedure produced the correct results and put these results in the correct locations to pass them back to the mainline program. Inserting breakpoints at key points in your program is much more effective in locating a problem than random poking and experimenting.

WRITING AND USING ASSEMBLER MACROS

Macros and Procedures Compared

Whenever we need to use a group of instructions several times throughout a program there are two ways we can avoid having to write the group of instructions each time we want to use it. One way is to write the group of instructions as a separate procedure. We can then just CALL the procedure whenever we need to execute that group of instructions. A big advantage of using a procedure is that the machine codes for the group of instructions in the procedure only have to be put in memory once. Disadvantages of using a procedure are the need for a stack, and the overhead time required to call the procedure and return to the calling program.

When the repeated group of instructions is too short or not appropriate to be written as a procedure, we use a macro. A macro is a group of instructions we bracket and give a name to at the start of our program. Each time we "call" the macro in our program, the assembler will insert the defined group of instructions in place of the "call." In other words the macro call is like a shorthand expression which tells the assembler, "Every time you see a macro name in the program, replace it with the group of instructions defined as that macro at the start of the program." An important point here is that the assembler generates machine codes for the group of instructions each time the macro is called. Replacing the macro with the instructions it represents is commonly called "expanding" the macro. Since the generated machine codes are right *in-line* with the rest of the program, the processor does not have to go off to a procedure and return. Therefore, using a macro avoids the overhead time involved in calling and returning from a procedure. A disadvantage of generating in-line code each time a macro is called is that this may make the program take up more memory. The examples which follow should help you see how to define and call macros. For these examples we use the syntax of the IBM PC macro assembler, MASM, written by Microsoft Corporation. If you are developing your programs on some other machine, consult the assembly language programming manual for your machine to find the macro definition and calling formats for it.

Defining and Calling a Macro Without Parameters

For our first example suppose that we are writing an 8086 program which has many complex procedures. At the start of each procedure we want to save the flags and all of the registers by pushing them on the stack. At the end of each procedure we want to restore the flags and all of the registers by popping them off the stack. Each procedure would normally contain a long series of PUSH instructions at the start and a long series of POP instructions at the end. Typing in these lists of push and pop instructions is tedious and prone to errors. We could write a procedure to do the pushing and another procedure to do the popping. However, this adds more complexity to the program and is therefore not appropriate. Two simple macros will solve the problem for us.

Here's how we write a macro to save all the registers.

```
PUSH_ALL MACRO
  PUSHF
  PUSH AX
  PUSH BX
  PUSH CX
  PUSH DX
  PUSH BP
  PUSH SI
  PUSH DI
  PUSH DS
  PUSH ES
  PUSH SS
ENDM
```

The PUSH_ALL MACRO statement identifies the start of the macro and gives the macro a name. The ENDM identifies the end of the macro.

Now, to call the macro in one of our procedures we simply put in the name of the macro just as we would an instruction mnemonic. The start of a procedure which does this might look like this.

```
BREATH_RATE   PROC FAR
ASSUME CS:PROCEDURES_HERE, DS:PATIENT_PARAMETERS
PUSH_ALL                          ; macro call
MOV AX, PATIENT_PARAMETERS        ; Initialize data
                                  ; segment reg
MOV DS, AX
          .
          .
          .
```

When the assembler assembles this program section it will replace PUSH_ALL with the instructions that it represents and insert the machine codes for these instructions in the object code version of the program. The assembler listing tells you which lines were inserted by a macro call by putting a + in each program line inserted by a macro call. As you can see from the example here, using a macro makes the source program much more readable because the source program does not have the long series of push instructions cluttering it up.

The preceding example showed how a macro can be used as simple shorthand for a series of instructions. The real power of macros, however, comes from being able to pass parameters to them when you call them. The next section shows you how and why this is done.

Passing Parameters to Macros

Most of us have received computer printed letters of the form:

Dear MR. HALL,

We are pleased to inform you that you may have won up to $1,000,000 in the *Reader's Weekly* sweepstakes. To find out if you are a winner MR. HALL, return the gold card to *Reader's Weekly* in the enclosed envelope before OCTOBER 22, 1986. You can take advantage of our special offer of three years of *Reader's Weekly* for only $24.95 by putting an X in the YES box on the gold card. If you do not wish to take advantage of this offer, which is one third off the newstand price, mark the no box on the gold card.

Thank you,

A letter such as this is an everyday example of the macro with parameters concept. The basic letter "macro" is written with dummy words in place of the addressee's name, the reply date, and the cost of a three-year subscription. Each time the macro which prints the letter is called, new values for these parameters are passed to the macro. The result is a "personal" looking letter.

In assembly language programs we likewise can write a generalized macro with dummy parameters. Then when we call the macro we can pass it the actual parameters needed for the specific application.

Suppose, for example, we are writing a word processor program. A frequent need in a word processor program is to move strings of ASCII characters from one place in memory to another. The 8086 MOVS instruction is intended to do this. Remember from the discussion of the string instructions in Chapter 4, however, that in order for the MOVS instruction to work correctly, you first have to load SI with the offset of the source start, DI with the offset of the destination start, and CX with the number of bytes or words to be moved. We can define a macro to do all of this as follows.

```
    MOVE_ASCII MACRO NUMBER, SOURCE,
                                  DESTINATION
    MOV CX, NUMBER      ; Number of characters
                        ; to be moved in CX
    LEA SI, SOURCE      ; Point SI at ASCII source
    LEA DI, DESTINATION ; Point DI at ASCII
                        ; destination
REP MOVSB               ; Copy ASCII string to
                        ; new location
    ENDM
```

The words NUMBER, SOURCE, and DESTINATION in this macro are called dummy variables. When we call the macro, values from the calling statement will be put in the instructions in place of the dummies. If, for example, we call this macro with the statement: MOVE_ASCII 03DH, BLOCK_START, BLOCK_DEST, the assembler will expand the macro as follows.

```
    MOV CX, 03DH        ; Number of characters to be
                        ; moved in CX
    LEA SI, BLOCK_START ; Point SI at ASCII destination
    LEA DI, BLOCK_DEST  ; Point DI at ASCII destination
REP MOVSB               ; Copy ASCII string to new
                        ; location
```

We do not have space here to show you very much of what you can do with macros. Read through the assembly language programming manual for your system to find more details about working with macros.

Summary of Procedures vs. Macros

PROCEDURE

Accessed by CALL and RET mechanism during program execution.

Machine code for instructions only put in memory once.

Parameters passed in registers, memory locations, or stack.

MACRO

Accessed during assembly with name given to macro when defined.

Machine code generated for instructions each time called.

Parameters passed as part of statement which calls macro.

IMPORTANT TERMS AND CONCEPTS FROM THIS CHAPTER

If you do not remember any of the terms in the following list, use the index to help you find them in the chapter for review.

Procedure

Subprogram

CALL, RET

PUBLIC, EXTRN

Nested procedures

Direct intersegment far CALL

Indirect intersegment far CALL

Direct intersegment near CALL

Indirect intersegment near CALL

Stack: top of stack, stack pointer

PUSH, POP

Parameter, parameter passing

Near and far procedures

Stack overflow

Reentrant and recursive procedures

Interrupt

Interrupt service procedure

Separate assembly modules

Macro

REVIEW QUESTIONS AND PROBLEMS

1. In order to avoid hand keying programs into an SDK-86 board we wrote a program to send machine code programs from an IBM PC to an SDK-86 board through a serial link. As part of this program we had to convert each byte of the machine code program to ASCII codes for the two nibbles in the byte. In other words, a byte of 7AH has to be sent as 37H, the ASCII code for 7, and 41H, the ASCII code for A.

Once you separate the nibbles of the byte, this conversion is a simple IF—THEN—ELSE situation. Write an algorithm and assembly language program section which does the needed conversion.

2. A common problem when reading a series of ASCII characters from a keyboard is the need to filter out those codes which represent the hex digits 0–9 and A–F, and convert these ASCII codes to the hex digits they represent. For example, if we read in 34H, the ASCII code for 4, we want to mask the upper 4 bits to leave 04, the 8-bit hex code for 4. If we read in 42H, the ASCII code for B, we want to add 09 and mask the upper 4 bits to leave 0B, the 8-bit code for hex B. If we read in an ASCII code that is not in the range of 30H–39H or 41H–46H, then we want to load an error code of FFH instead of the hex value of the entered character. Figure 5-26 shows the desired action next to each range of ASCII values. Write an algorithm and an assembly language program which implements these actions. *HINT*: a nested IF—THEN—ELSE structure might be useful.

3. Show the 8086 instruction or group of instructions which will:
   a. Initialize the stack segment register to 4000H and the stack pointer register to 8000H.
   b. Call a near procedure named FIXIT.
   c. Save BX and BP at the start of a procedure and restore them at the end of the procedure.
   d. Return from a procedure and automatically increment the stack pointer by 8.

4. *a.* Use a stack map to show the effect of each of the following instructions on the stack pointer and on the contents of the stack.

```
        MOV  SP,4000H
        PUSH  AX
        CALL MULTO
        POP AX
MULTO   PROC NEAR
        PUSHF
        PUSH BX
          .
          .
          .
        POP  BX
        POPF
        RET
MULTO   ENDP
```

   b. What effect would it have on the execution of this program if the POPF instruction in the procedure was accidentally left out? Describe the steps you would take in tracking down this problem if you did not notice it in the program listing.

5. Show the binary codes for the following instructions.
   a. CALL BX
   b. CALL WORD PTR [BX]

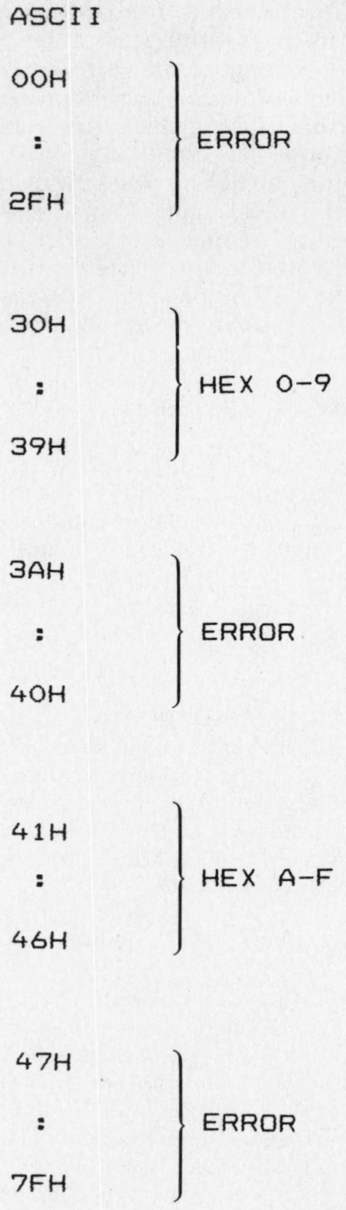

ASCII	
00H : 2FH	ERROR
30H : 39H	HEX 0–9
3AH : 40H	ERROR
41H : 46H	HEX A–F
47H : 7FH	ERROR

FIGURE 5-26 ASCII chart for Problem 5-2.

   c. The instruction which will call a procedure which is 97H addresses higher in memory than the instruction after a call instruction.
   d. An instruction which returns execution from a far procedure to a mainline program and increments the stack pointer by 4.

6. *a.* List three methods of passing parameters to a procedure. Give the advantage and disadvantage of each method.
   b. Define the term "reentrant" and explain how you must pass parameters to a procedure so that it is reentrant.

7. *a.* Write a procedure which produces a delay of

3.33 ms when run on an 8086 with a 5-MHz clock.

b. Write a mainline program which uses this procedure to output a square wave on bit D0 of port FFFAH.

8. Write a procedure which converts a 4-digit BCD number passed in AX to its binary equivalent. Use the algorithm in Figure 5-15.

9. The 8086 MUL instruction allows you to multiply a 16-bit number by a 16-bit binary number to give a 32-bit result. In some cases, however, you may need to multiply a 32-bit number by a 32-bit number to give a 64-bit result. With the MUL instruction and a little adding you can easily do this. Figure 5-27 shows in diagram form how to do it. Each letter in the diagram represents a 16-bit number. The principle is to use MUL to form partial products and add these partial products together as shown. Write an algorithm for this multiplication and then write the 8086 assembly language program for the algorithm.

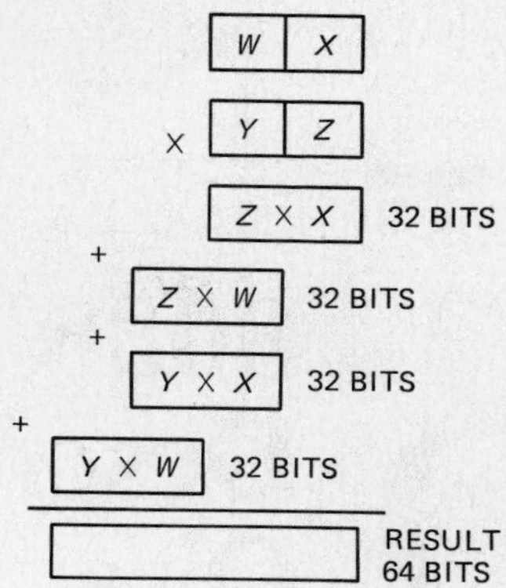

FIGURE 5-27 32-bit by 32-bit multiply method for Problem 5-9.

10. Calculating the factorial of a number which we did with a recursive procedure in Figure 5-22*a* can easily be done with a simple REPEAT UNTIL structure of the form:

```
IF N=1 THEN
    FACTORIAL = 1
ELSE
    FACTORIAL = 1
    REPEAT
        FACTORIAL = FACTORIAL × N
        DECREMENT N
    UNTIL N = 0
```

Write an 8086 procedure which implements this algorithm for an *N* between 1 and 8.

11. Write an assembler macro which will restore, in the correct order, the registers saved by the macro PUSH_ALL in this chapter.

12. *a.* Show how you would tell the assembler to make the label BINADD available to other assembly modules.

b. Show how you would tell the assembler to look for a byte type data item named CONVERSION_FACTOR in a segment named FIXUPS.

CHAPTER

6 8086 Instruction Descriptions and Assembler Directives

This chapter consists of two major sections. The first section is a dictionary of all of the 8086/8088/80186/80188 instructions. For each instruction we give a detailed description of its operation, the correct syntax for the instruction, and the flags affected by the instruction. Also, numerical examples are shown for those instructions where they are appropriate. The binary coding templates for the instructions are shown alphabetically in a table in the appendix. Putting the codes together in a table makes it easier to find codes if you are hand coding a program.

The second major section of this chapter is a dictionary of commonly used 8086 assembler directives. The directives described here are those defined for the Intel 8086 macro assembler and the IBM macro assembler, MASM. If you are using some other assembler, it probably has similar capabilities, but the names may be different.

You will probably use this chapter mostly as a reference to get the details of an instruction or directive as you write programs of your own or decipher someone else's programs. However, you should skim through the chapter at least once to give yourself an overview of the material contained here. You should not try to absorb all of this chapter at once. Most of the instructions described here are used and discussed in various example programs throughout the book. Therefore, we have included references to the appropriate sections in the instruction descriptions here.

INSTRUCTION DESCRIPTIONS

AAA INSTRUCTION—ASCII Adjust for Addition—AAA

Numerical data coming into a computer from a terminal is usually in ASCII code. In this code the numbers 0–9 are represented by the ASCII codes 30H–39H. The 8086 allows you to add the ASCII codes for two decimal digits without masking off the "3" in the upper nibble of each. The AAA instruction is then used to make sure the result is the correct unpacked BCD. A simple numerical example will show how this works.

EXAMPLE:

```
ADD AL, BL   ; AL = 00110101,   ASCII 5
             ; BL = 00111001,   ASCII 9
             ; AL = 01101110,
             ; 6EH - Incorrect Temporary Result
AAA          ; AL = 00000101.   Unpacked BCD for 4.
             ; Carry = 1 to indicate correct answer is
             ; 14 decimal.
```

NOTES: OR AL with 30H to get 34H, the ASCII code for 4, if you want to send the result back to a CRT terminal. The one in the carry can be rotated into the low nibble of a register, ORed with 30H to give the ASCII code for 1, and then sent to the terminal.
The AAA instruction only works on the AL register.
The AAA instruction correctly updates the AF and the CF, but the OF, PF, SF, and ZF are left undefined.

AAD INSTRUCTION—BCD-to-Binary Convert before Division—AAD

The mnemonic for this instruction might tempt you to call it ASCII Adjust for Division. However, the instruction actually works with unpacked BCD. You must mask out the 3 in the upper nibble of the ASCII codes for decimal digits before you can use AAD. AAD converts two unpacked BCD digits in AH and AL to the equivalent binary number in AL. This adjustment must be made before dividing the two unpacked BCD digits in AX by an unpacked BCD byte. After the division AL will then contain the unpacked BCD quotient and AH will contain the unpacked BCD remainder. The PF, SF, and ZF are updated. The AF, CF, and OF are undefined after AAD.

EXAMPLE:

```
         ; AX = 0607   unpacked BCD for 67 decimal
         ; CH = 09H
AAD      ; Adjust to binary before division
         ; AX = 0043 = 43H = 67 decimal
DIV CH   ; Divide AX by unpacked BCD in CH
         ; AL = quotient = 07 unpacked BCD
         ; AH = remainder = 04 unpacked BCD
         ; PF = 0 SF = 0 ZF = 0
```

NOTE: If an attempt is made to divide by 0, or if the quotient is greater than 09, the 8086 will do a type 0 interrupt. Interrupts are explained in Chapter 8.

AAM INSTRUCTION—BCD Adjust after Multiply—AAM

The mnemonic for this instruction may tempt you to call it ASCII Adjust for Multiply. In truth, however, the 8086 does not allow you to multiply the ASCII codes for decimal digits directly. Before you can multiply two ASCII digits, you must first mask the upper 4 bits of each. This leaves unpacked BCD (one BCD digit per byte) in each byte. After the two unpacked BCD digits are multiplied, the AAM instruction is used to adjust the product to two unpacked BCD digits in AX.

AAM only works after the multiplication of two unpacked BCD bytes. It only works on an operand in AL. The PF, SF, and ZF are updated by AAM. The AF, CF, and OF are undefined after AAM.

EXAMPLE:

```
               ; AL = 00000101 = unpacked BCD 5
               ; BH = 00001001 = unpacked BCD 9
MUL BH         ; AL × BH Result in AX
               ; AX = 00000000 00101101 = 002DH
AAM            ; AX = 00000100 00000101
               ; which is unpacked BCD for 45.
               ; If ASCII codes for the result are
               ; desired,
               ; use the next instruction.
OR AX,3030H    ; Put 3 in upper nibble of each byte.
               ; AX = 00110100 00110101 = ASCII
               ; codes for 45.
```

AAS INSTRUCTION—ASCII Adjust for Subtraction—AAS

Numerical data coming into a computer from a terminal is usually in ASCII code. In this code the numbers 0–9 are represented by the ASCII codes 30H–39H. The 8086 allows you to subtract the ASCII codes for two decimal digits without masking the "3" in the upper nibble of each. The AAS instruction is then used to make sure the result is the correct unpacked BCD. Some simple numerical examples will show how this works.

EXAMPLE:

```
               ;          (a)
               ; AL = 0011 1001 = ASCII 9
               ; BL = 0011 0101 = ASCII 5
SUB AL, BL     ; (9 – 5) Results:
               ; AL = 0000 0100 = BCD 04
               ; CF = 0
AAS            ; Results:
               ; AL = 0000 0100 = BCD 04
               ; CF = 0 no borrow required
```

```
               ;          (b)
               ; AL = 0011 0101 = ASCII 5
               ; BL = 0011 1001 = ASCII 9
SUB AL, BL     ; (5 – 9) Results:
               ; AL = 1111 1100 = –4
               ; in 2's complement
               ; CF = 1
AAS            ; Results;
               ; AL = 0000 0100 = BCD 04
               ; CF = 1 borrow needed
```

The AAS instruction leaves the correct unpacked BCD result in the low nibble of AL and resets the upper nibble of AL to all 0's. If you want to send the result back to a CRT terminal, you can OR AL with 30H to produce the correct ASCII code for the result. If multiple-digit numbers are being subtracted, the CF can be taken into account by using the SBB instruction when subtracting the next digits.

NOTES: The AAS instruction only works on the AL register. The AAS instruction correctly updates the AF and the CF, but the OF, PF, SF, and the ZF are left undefined.

ADC INSTRUCTION—Add with carry—ADC destination, source

ADD INSTRUCTION—Add—ADD destination, source

These instructions add a number from some source to a number from some destination and put the result in the specified destination. The add with carry instruction, ADC, also adds the status of the carry flag into the result. The source may be an immediate number, a register, or a memory location as specified by any of the 24 addressing modes shown in Figure 3-8. The destination may be a register or a memory location specified by any one of the 24 addressing modes in Figure 3-8. The source and the destination in an instruction cannot both be memory locations. The source and the destination must be of the same type. In other words, they must both be byte locations, or they must both be word locations. If you want to add a byte to a word, you must copy the byte to a word location and fill the upper byte of the word with zeroes before adding. Flags affected: AF, CF, OF, PF, SF, ZF.

EXAMPLES (CODING):

```
ADD AL, 74H      ; Add immediate number 74H
                 ; to contents of AL

ADC CL, BL       ; Add contents of BL plus
                 ; carry status to
                 ; contents of CL.
                 ; Result in CL.

ADD DX, BX       ; Add contents of BX to
                 ; contents of DX
```

```
ADD DX,[SI]            ; Add word from memory at
                       ; offset [SI] in DS
                       ; to contents of DX

ADC AL, PRICES[BX]     ; Add byte from Effective
                       ; Address PRICES[BX]
                       ; plus carry status to
                       ; contents of AL

ADD PRICES[BX], AL     ; Add contents of AL to
                       ; contents of memory
                       ; location at Effective
                       ; Address PRICES[BX]
```

EXAMPLES (NUMERICAL):

```
                       ; Addition of Unsigned
                       ; numbers
ADD CL, BL             ; CL = 01110011 = 115
                       ; decimal
                       ; + BL = 01001111 =
                       ; 79 decimal
                       ; Result in CL
                       ; CL = 11000010 = 194
                       ; decimal

ADD CL, BL             ; Addition of Signed numbers
                       ; CL = 01110011 = +115
                       ; decimal
                       ; + BL = 01001111 = + 79
                       ; decimal
                       ; Result in CL
                       ; CL = 11000010 = -62
                       ; decimal.
     ; Incorrect because result too large to fit in 7 bits.
```

FLAG RESULTS:

CF = 0 No carry out of bit 7

PF = 0 Result has odd parity

AF = 1 Carry was produced out of bit 3

ZF = 0 Result in destination was not zero

SF = 1 Copies most-significant bit of result; indicates negative result if you are adding signed numbers

OF = 1 Set to indicate that the result of the addition was too large to fit in the lower 7 bits of the destination used to represent the magnitude of a signed number. In other words the result was greater than +127 decimal so the result overflows into the sign bit position and incorrectly indicates that the result is negative. If you are adding two signed 16-bit values, the OF will be set if the magnitude of the result is too large to fit in the lower 15 bits of the destination.

NOTES: The PF is only meaningful for an 8-bit result. The AF is only set by a carry out of bit 3. Therefore, the DAA instruction cannot be used after word additions to convert the result to correct BCD.

AND INSTRUCTION—AND corresponding bits of two operands—AND destination, source

This instruction ANDs each bit in a source byte or word with the same number bit in a destination byte or word. The result is put in the specified destination. The contents of the specified source will not be changed. The result for each bit position will follow the truth table for a two-input AND gate. In other words, a bit in the specified destination will be a one only if that bit is a one in both the source and the destination operands. Therefore, a bit can be masked (reset) by ANDing it with 0.

The source operand can be an immediate number, the contents of a register, or the contents of a memory location specified by one of the 24 addressing modes shown in Figure 3-8. The destination can be a register or a memory location. The source and the destination cannot both be memory locations in the same instruction. The CF and OF are both 0 after AND. The PF, SF, and ZF are updated by AND. AF is undefined. Note that PF only has meaning for an 8-bit operand.

EXAMPLES (CODING):

```
AND BH, CL        ; AND byte in CL with byte in BH,
                  ; result in BH

AND BX, 00FFH     ; AND word in BX with immediate
                  ; 00FFH.
                  ; Mask upper byte, leave
                  ; lower unchanged.

AND CX, [SI]      ; AND word at offset [SI] in
                  ; data segment
                  ; with word in CX
                  ; register. Result in CX register.
```

EXAMPLE (NUMERICAL)

```
                  ; BX = 10110011 01011110
AND BX, 00FFH     ; Mask out upper 8 bits of BX.
                  ; Result BX = 00000000 01011110.
     ; CF = 0 OF = 0 PF = 0 SF = 0 ZF = 0
```

BOUND—80186/80188 ONLY—Check if Array Operation Out of Bounds

When performing some operation on an array of data in memory the BOUND instruction can be used to make sure that data values outside the array are not being operated on. To use this instruction the offset of the lowest element in the array (lower bound) is loaded in two memory addresses. The offset of the highest element in the array (upper bound) is loaded into the next two memory addresses. The offset of the array element currently being worked on is loaded into a general-purpose register such as BX. When the BOUND instruction executes, it will compare the value in BX with the lower and upper bounds in the two memory locations. If the offset in BX is less than the lower bound or greater than the upper bound, then the 80186/80188 will do a type 5 interrupt. Refer to Chapter 8 for a thorough discussion of interrupts. BOUND affects no flags.

EXAMPLE:

```
L_ARRAY1   EQU   15   ; Length of ARRAY1 = 15 bytes
MOV BOUND_STORE, OFFSET ARRAY1   ; Store offset
; of lowest element
; Now store offset of highest element of the array.
MOV BOUND_STORE+2, OFFSET ARRAY1+L_ARRAY1
; Assume BX contains offset of array element
; currently being operated upon and then
; generate type 5 interrupt if trying to
; operate on an element which is out of bounds
BOUND BX, BOUND_STORE
```

CALL INSTRUCTION—Call a procedure

The CALL instruction is used to transfer execution to a subprogram or procedure. There are two basic types of CALLs, *near* and *far*. A near CALL is a call to a procedure which is in the same code segment as the CALL instruction. When the 8086 executes a near CALL instruction it decrements the stack pointer by two and copies the offset of the next instruction after the CALL on the stack. This offset saved on the stack is referred to as the return address, because this is the address that execution will return to after the procedure executes. A near CALL instruction will also load the instruction pointer with the offset of the first instruction in the procedure. A RET instruction at the end of the procedure will return execution to the instruction after the CALL by copying the offset saved on the stack back to IP.

A far CALL is a call to a procedure which is in a different segment from that which contains the CALL instruction. When the 8086 executes a far CALL it decrements the stack pointer by two and copies the contents of the CS register to the stack. It then decrements the stack pointer by two again and copies the offset of the instruction after the CALL to the stack. Finally, it loads CS with the segment base of the segment which contains the procedure and IP with the offset of the first instruction of the procedure in that segment. A RET instruction at the end of the procedure will return execution to the next instruction after the CALL by restoring the saved values of CS and IP from the stack.

EXAMPLES

; Direct within-segment (near or intrasegment)

CALL MULTO   ; MULTO is the name of the procedure. The assembler determines displacement of MULTO from the instruction after the CALL and codes this displacement in as part of the instruction.

; Indirect within-segment near or intrasegment

CALL BX   ; BX contains the offset of the first instruction of the procedure. Replaces contents of IP with contents of register BX.

CALL WORD PTR [BX]   ; Offset of first instruction of procedure is in two memory addresses in DS. Replaces contents of IP with contents of word memory location in DS pointed to by BX.

; Direct to another segment-far or intersegment

CALL SMART_DIVIDE   ; SMART_DIVIDE is the name of the procedure. The procedure must be declared FAR with SMART_DIVIDE PROC FAR at its start (see section in Chapter 5). The assembler will determine the code segment base for the segment which contains the procedure and the offset of the start of the procedure in that segment. It will put these values in as part of the instruction code.

; Indirect to another segment-far or intersegment

CALL DWORD PTR[BX]   ; New values for CS and IP are fetched from four memory locations in DS. The new value for CS is fetched from [BX] and [BX + 1], the new IP is fetched from [BX + 2] and [BX + 3].

CBW INSTRUCTION—Convert signed Byte to signed Word—CBW

This instruction copies the sign of a byte in AL to all the bits in AH. AH is then said to be the sign extension of AL. The CBW operation must be done before a signed byte in AL can be divided by another signed byte with the IDIV instruction. CBW affects no flags.

EXAMPLE:

```
     ; AX = 00000000 10011011 = -155 decimal
CBW; Convert signed byte in AL to signed word in AX.
     ; Result in AX = 11111111 10011011
     ;               = -155 decimal.
```

For further examples of the use of CBW, see the IDIV instruction description.

CLC INSTRUCTION—Clear the carry flag, CF—CLC

This instruction resets the carry flag to zero. No other flags are affected.

EXAMPLE:

```
CLC   ; Clear carry flag
```

CLD INSTRUCTION—Clear direction flag—CLD

This instruction resets the direction flag to zero. No other flags are affected. If the direction flag is reset, SI and DI will automatically be incremented when one of the string instructions such as MOVS, CMPS, or SCAS executes. Consult the string instruction descriptions for examples of the use of the direction flag.

EXAMPLE:

```
CLD   ; Clear direction flag so that string pointers
      ; autoincrement
```

CLI INSTRUCTION—Clear interrupt flag—CLI

This instruction resets the interrupt flag to zero. No other flags are affected. If the interrupt flag is reset, the 8086 will not respond to an interrupt signal on its INTR input. The CLI instruction, however, has no effect on the nonmaskable interrupt input, NMI.

CMC INSTRUCTION—Complement the carry flag—CMC

If the carry flag, CF, is a zero before this instruction, it will be set to a one after the instruction. If the carry flag is one before this instruction, it will be reset to a zero after the instruction executes. CMC affects no other flags.

EXAMPLE:

```
CMC   ; Invert the carry flag
```

CMP INSTRUCTION—Compare byte or word—CMP destination, source

This instruction compares a byte from the specified source with a byte from the specified destination, or a word from a specified source with a word from a specified destination. The source can be an immediate number, a register, or a memory location specified by one of the 24 addressing modes shown in Figure 3-8. The destination can also be an immediate number, a register, or a memory location. However, the source and the destination cannot both be memory locations in the same instruction. The comparison is actually done by subtracting the source byte or word from the destination byte or word. The source and the destination are not changed, but the flags are set to indicate the results of the comparison. The AF, OF, SF, ZF, PF, and CF are updated by the CMP instruction. For the instruction CMP CX, BX the CF, ZF, and SF will be left as follows:

	CF	ZF	SF	
CX = BX	0	1	0	; Result of subtraction is 0
CX > BX	0	0	0	; No borrow required ; so CF = 0
CX < BX	1	0	1	; Subtraction required ; borrow so CF = 1

EXAMPLES:

```
CMP AL, 01H            ; Compare immediate number
                       ; 01H with byte in AL

CMP BH, CL             ; Compare byte in CL with
                       ; byte in BH

CMP CX, TEMP_MIN       ; Compare word at
                       ; displacement TEMP_MIN
                       ; in DS
                       ; with word in CX

CMP TEMP_MAX, CX       ; Compare CX with word at
                       ; displacement TEMP_MAX
                       ; in data segment

CMP PRICES[BX],49H     ; Compare immediate 49H
                       ; with byte at offset
                       ; [BX] in array PRICES
```

NOTE: The compare instructions are often used with the conditional jump instructions described in a later section. Having the compare instructions formatted the way they are makes this use very easy to understand. For example, given the instruction sequence:

```
CMP BX, CX
JAE TARGET
```

you can mentally read it as jump to target if BX is above or equal to CX. In other words, just mentally insert the first operand after the J for jump and the second operand after the condition.

CMPS/CMPSB/CMPSW—Compare string bytes or string words

A string is a series of the same type of data items in sequential memory locations. The CMPS instruction can be used to compare a byte in one string with a byte in another string or to compare a word in one string with a word in another string. SI is used to hold the offset of a byte or word in the source string and DI is used hold the offset of a byte or a word in the other string. The comparison is done by subtracting the byte or word pointed to by DI from the byte or word pointed to by SI. The AF, CF, OF, PF, SF, and ZF flags are affected by the comparison, but neither operand is affected. After the comparison SI and DI will automatically be incremented or decremented to point to the next elements in the two strings. If the direction flag has previously been set to a one with an STD instruction, then SI and DI will automatically be decremented by one for a byte string or by two for a word string. If the direction flag has been previously reset to a zero with a CLD instruction, then SI and DI will automatically be incremented after the compare. They will be incremented by one for byte strings and by two for word strings.

The string pointed to by DI must be in the extra segment. The string pointed to by SI is assumed to be in the data segment, but you can use a segment override prefix to tell the 8086 to add the offset in SI to CS, SS, or ES.

The CMPS instruction can be used with a REP, REPE, or REPNE prefix to compare all of the elements of a string. To see how this is done, read the discussion of strings in Chapter 4 and the example program in Figure 4-23.

EXAMPLES:

```
                    ; Point SI at source string
                    ; Point DI at destination string
MOV   SI, OFFSET FIRST_STRING
MOV   DI, OFFSET SECOND_STRING
CLD                 ; DF cleared so SI and DI will
                    ; autoincrement after compare
CMPS   FIRST_STRING, SECOND_STRING
; The assembler uses names to determine whether
; strings were declared as type byte or as type word.

   MOV CX, 100 ; Put number of string
               ; elements in CX
               ; Point SI at source of string
               ; and DI at destination of string
   MOV SI, OFFSET FIRST_STRING
   MOV DI, OFFSET SECOND_STRING
```

```
STD            ; DF set so SI and DI will auto-
               ; decrement after compare
REPE CMPSB     ; Repeat the comparison of string
               ; bytes until end
               ; of string or until compared
               ; bytes are not equal
```

NOTE: CX functions as a counter which the REPE prefix will cause to be decremented after each compare. The B attached to CMPS tells the assembler that the strings are of type byte. With this addition you don't have to put in the string names as we did in the previous example. If you want to tell the assembler that the strings are of type word, write the instruction as CMPSW.

CWD INSTRUCTION—Convert Signed Word to Signed Doubleword—CWD

CWD copies the sign bit of a word in AX to all the bits of the DX register. In other words it extends the sign of AX into all of DX. The CWD operation must be done before a signed word in AX can be divided by another signed word with the IDIV instruction. CWD affects no flags.

EXAMPLE:

```
      ; DX = 00000000 00000000
      ; AX = 11110000 11000111 = -3897 decimal
CWD   ; Convert signed word in AX to signed double
      ; word in DX:AX.
      ; Result DX = 11111111 11111111
      ; AX = 11110000 11000111 = -3897 decimal
```

For a further example of the use of CWD see the IDIV instruction description.

DAA INSTRUCTION—Decimal Adjust Accumulator—DAA

This instruction is used to make sure the result of adding two packed BCD numbers is adjusted to be a legal BCD number. DAA only works on AL. If the lower nibble in AL after an addition is greater than 9 or the AF was set by the addition, then the DAA instruction will add 6 to the lower nibble in AL. If the result in the upper nibble of AL is now greater than 9 or if the carry flag was set by the addition or correction, then the DAA instruction will add 60H to AL. A couple of simple examples should clarify how this works.

EXAMPLES:

```
                 (a)

             ; AL = 0101 1001 = 59 BCD
             ; BL = 0011 0101 = 35 BCD
ADD AL, BL   ; AL = 1000 1110 = 8EH
DAA
             ; add 0110 Because 1110 > 9
             ; AL = 1001 0100 = 94 BCD

                 (b)

             ; AL = 1000 1000 = 88 BCD
             ; BL = 0100 1001 = 49 BCD
ADD AL, BL   ; AL = 1101 0001, AF = 1
DAA
             ; add 0110 Because AF = 1
             ; AL = 1101 0111 = D7H
             ; 1101 > 9 so add 0110 0000
             ; AL = 0011 0111 = 37 BCD, CF = 1
```

NOTES: The DAA instruction updates the AF, CF, PF, and ZF. The OF is undefined after a DAA instruction.

A decimal UP counter can be implemented using the DAA instruction as follows:

```
MOV COUNT, 00H   ; Initialize count in memory
                 ; location to 0
  .
  .
MOV AL, COUNT    ; Bring count into AL to work on
ADD AL, 01H      ; Can also count up by 2, by 3, or
                 ; by some other number using the
                 ; ADD instruction
DAA              ; Decimal adjust the result
MOV COUNT, AL    ; Put decimal result back in
                 ; memory store
```

DAS INSTRUCTION—Decimal Adjust after Subtraction—DAS

This instruction is used after subtracting two packed BCD numbers to make sure the result is correct packed BCD. DAS only works on the AL register. If the lower nibble in AL after a subtraction is greater than 9 or the AF was set by the subtraction, then the DAS instruction will subtract 6 from the lower nibble of AL. If the result in the upper nibble is now greater than 9 or if the carry flag was set, the DAS instruction will subtract 60 from AL. A couple of simple examples should clarify how this works.

EXAMPLES:

```
             ;        (a)
             ; AL = 1000 0110 = 86 BCD
             ; BH = 0101 0111 = 57 BCD
SUB AL, BH   ; AL = 0010 1111 = 2FH, CF = 0
DAS          ; Subtract 0000 0110 (-06H).
             ; Because 1111 in low nibble > 9
             ; AL = 0010 1001 = 29 BCD

             ;        (b)
             ; AL = 0100 1001 = 49 BCD
             ; BH = 0111 0010 = 72 BCD
SUB AL, BH   ; AL = 1101 0111 = D7H CF = 1
DAS          ; Subtract 0110 0000 (-60H).
             ; Because 1101 in upper nibble > 9
             ; AL = 0111 0111 = 77 BCD CF = 1
             ; CF = 1 means borrow was needed
```

NOTES: The DAS instruction updates the AF, CF, SF, PF, and ZF. The OF is undefined after DAS.

A decimal down counter can be implemented using the DAS instruction as follows:

```
MOV AL, COUNT   ; Bring count into AL to work on
SUB AL, 01H     ; Decrement. Can also count down
                ; by 2, 3,
                ; etc. using SUB instruction.
DAS             ; Keep results in BCD format
MOV COUNT, AL   ; Put new count back in memory
```

DEC INSTRUCTION—Decrement destination register or memory—DEC destination

This instruction subtracts one from the destination word or byte. The destination can be a register or a memory location specified by any one of the 24 addressing modes shown in Figure 3-8. The AF, OF, PF, SF, and ZF are updated, but the CF is not affected. This means that if an 8-bit destination containing 00H or a 16-bit destination containing 0000H is decremented, the result will be FFH or FFFFH with no carry (borrow).

EXAMPLES:

DEC CL ; Subtract one from contents of CL register

DEC BP ; Subtract one from contents of BP register

DEC BYTE PTR [BX] ; Subtract one from byte at offset [BX] in DS. The BYTE PTR directive is necessary to tell the assembler to put in the correct code for decrementing a byte in memory, rather than decrementing a word. The instruction essentially says "Decrement the byte in memory pointed to by [BX]."

DEC WORD PTR [BP] ; Subtract one from a word at offset [BP] in SS. The WORD PTR directive tells the assembler to put in the code for decrementing a word pointed to by the contents of BP. An offset in BP will be added to the SS register contents to produce the physical address.

DEC TOMATO_CAN_COUNT ; Subtract one from byte or word named TOMATO_CAN_COUNT in DS. If TOMATO_CAN_COUNT was declared with a DB then the assembler will code this instruction to decrement a byte. If TOMATO_CAN_COUNT declared with DW, then the assembler will code this instruction to decrement a word.

DEC HERD_COUNT [BX] ; Decrement word or byte at offset [BX] in array HERD_COUNT. Array is in DS. This instruction will decrement a byte if HERD_COUNT was declared with a DB. It will decrement a word if HERD_COUNT was declared with a DW directive.

DIV INSTRUCTION—Unsigned divide—DIV source

This instruction is used to divide an unsigned word by a byte, or to divide an unsigned double word (32 bits) by a word.

When dividing a word by a byte, the word must be in the AX register. After the division AL will contain an 8-bit result (quotient) and AH will contain an 8-bit remainder. If an attempt is made to divide by 0 or the quotient is too large to fit in AL (greater than FFH), the 8086 will automatically do a type 0 interrupt. Interrupts are explained in Chapter 8.

When a double word is divided by a word, the most-significant word of the double word must be in DX and the least-significant word of the double word must be in AX. After the division AX will contain the 16-bit result (quotient), and DX will contain a 16-bit remainder. Again, if an attempt is made to divide by 0 or the quotient is too large to fit in AX (greater than FFFFH), the 8086 will do a type 0 interrupt.

For a DIV the dividend (numerator) must always be in AX or DX and AX, but the source of the divisor (denominator) can be a register or a memory location specified by any one of the 24 addressing modes shown in Figure 3-8. If the divisor does not divide an integral number of times into the dividend, the quotient is truncated, not rounded. The example below will illustrate this. All flags are undefined after a DIV instruction.

If you want to divide a byte by a byte, you must first put the dividend byte in AL and fill AH with all 0's. The SUB AH, AH instruction is a quick way to do this. Likewise, if you want to divide a word by a word, put the dividend word in AX, and fill DX with all 0's. The SUB DX, DX instruction does this quickly.

EXAMPLES (CODING):

```
DIV BL   ; Word in AX/byte in BL.
         ; Quotient in AL, remainder in AH.

DIV CX   ; Double word in DX and AX/word in CX.
         ; Quotient in AX, remainder in DX.
```

DIV SCALE[BX] ; AX/(byte at effective address SCALE[BX]) if SCALE[BX] is of type byte or (DX and AX)/(word at effective address SCALE[BX]) if SCALE[BX] is of type word.

EXAMPLE (NUMERICAL)

```
         ; AX = 37D7H = 14295 decimal
         ; BH = 97H = 151 decimal
DIV BH   ; AX/BH
         ; Quotient in AL = 5EH = 94 decimal.
         ; Remainder in AH = 65H = 101 decimal.
```

Since the remainder is greater than half of the divisor, the actual quotient is closer to 5FH than to the 5EH produced. However, as indicated above, the quotient is always truncated to the next lower integer rather than rounded to the closest integer. If you want to round the quotient, you can compare the remainder with (divisor/2), and then add one to the quotient if the remainder is greater than the (divisor/2).

ENTER—80186/80188 ONLY—Enter Procedure

This instruction is used at the start of an assembly language procedure which is intended to be called from a high-level language program such as those written in Pascal or C. Its main functions are to save space on the stack for variables used in the procedure, and to determine pointers to data areas in the stack used by lower-level procedures (subprocedures). Refer to the Intel literature for further explanation of this instruction if you need it.

ESC INSTRUCTION
Escape—ESC

This instruction is used to pass instructions to a coprocessor such as the 8087 math coprocessor which shares the address and data bus with an 8086. Instructions for the coprocessor are represented by a 6-bit code imbedded in the escape instruction. As the 8086 fetches instruction bytes, the coprocessor also catches these bytes from the data bus and puts them in its queue. However, the coprocessor treats all of the normal 8086 instructions as NOPs. When the 8086 fetches an ESC instruction, the coprocessor decodes the instruction and carries out the action specified by the 6-bit code specified in the instruction. In most cases the 8086 treats the ESC instruction as a NOP. In some cases the 8086 will access a data item in memory for the coprocessor. A section in Chapter 11 describes the operation and use of the ESC instruction.

HLT INSTRUCTION
Halt processing—HLT

The HLT instruction will cause the 8086 to stop fetching and executing instructions. The 8086 will enter a halt state. The only ways to get the processor out of the halt state are with an interrupt signal on the INTR pin, an interrupt signal on the NMI pin, or a reset signal on the RESET input. See Chapter 7 for further details about the halt state.

IDIV INSTRUCTION
Divide by signed byte or word—IDIV source

This instruction is used to divide a signed word by a signed byte, or to divide a signed double word (32 bits) by a signed word.

When dividing a signed word by a signed byte, the word must be in the AX register. After the division, AL will contain the signed result (quotient), and AH will contain the signed remainder. The sign of the remainder will be the same as the sign of the dividend. If an attempt is made to divide by 0, the quotient is greater than 127 (7FH), or the quotient is less than −127 (81H), the 8086 will automatically do a type 0 interrupt. Interrupts are discussed in Chapter 8. For the 80186 this range is −128 to +127.

NOTE: When dividing a signed double word by a signed word, the most-significant word of the dividend (numerator) must be in the DX register and the least-significant word of the dividend must be in the AX register. After the division AX will contain a signed 16-bit quotient and DX will contain a signed 16-bit remainder. The sign of the remainder will be the same as the sign of the dividend. Again, if an attempt is made to divide by 0, the quotient is greater than +32,767 (7FFFH), or the quotient is less than −32,767 (8001H), the 8086 will automatically do a type 0 interrupt.

NOTE: For the 80186 this range is −32,768 to +32,767.

The dividend for IDIV must always be in AX or DX and AX but the source of the divisor can be a register or a memory location specified by any one of the 24 addressing modes shown in Figure 3-8. If the divisor does not divide into the dividend the quotient will be truncated, not rounded. The example below will illustrate this. All flags are undefined after an IDIV.

If you want to divide a signed byte by a signed byte, you must first put the dividend byte in AL and fill AH with copies of the sign bit from AL. In other words, if AL is positive (sign bit = 0) then AH should be filled with 0's. If AL is negative (sign bit = 1), the AH should be filled with 1's. The 8086 Convert Byte to Word instruction, CBW, does this by copying the sign bit of AL to all the bits of AH. AH is then said to contain the "sign extension of AL." Likewise, if you want to divide a signed word by a signed word, you must put the dividend word in AX and extend the sign of AX to all the bits of DX. The 8086 Convert Word to Doubleword instruction, CWD, will copy the sign bit of AX to all the bits of DX.

EXAMPLES (CODING)

```
IDIV BL                ; Signed word in AX/signed byte
                       ; in BL

IDIV BP                ; Signed double word in DX and
                       ; AX/signed word in BP

IDIV BYTE PTR [BX]     ; AX/byte at offset [BX] in DS

MOV AL, DIVIDEND       ; Position byte dividend
CBW                    ; Extend sign of AL into AH
IDIV DIVISOR           ; Divide by byte divisor
```

EXAMPLES (NUMERICAL)

```
; Example showing a signed word divided by a signed
; byte
; AX = 00000011 10101011 = 03ABH = 939 decimal
; BL = 11010011 = D3H = -2DH = -45 decimal

IDIV BL   ; Quotient in AL = 11101100
          ; AL = ECH = -14H = -20 decimal
          ; Remainder in AH = 00100111
          ; AH = 27H = +39 decimal
```

NOTE: Quotient is negative because positive was divided by negative. Remainder has same sign as dividend (positive).

```
; Example showing a signed byte divided by a signed
; byte
          ; AL = 11001010 = -26H = -38 decimal
          ; CH = 00000011 = +3H = +3 decimal
CBW       ; Extend sign of AL through AH,
          ; AX = 11111111 11001010
IDIV CH   ; Divide AX by CH
          ; AL = 11110100 = -0CH = -12 decimal
          ; AH = 11111110 = -2H = -2 decimal
```

Although the quotient is actually closer to 13 (12.666667) than to 12, the 8086 truncates it to 12 rather than rounding it to 13. If you want to round the quotient, you can compare the magnitude of the remainder with the (dividend/2) and add one to the quotient if the remainder is greater than (dividend/2). Note that the sign of the remainder is the same as the sign of the dividend (negative). All flags are undefined after IDIV.

IMUL INSTRUCTION—Multiply signed number—IMUL source

This instruction multiplies a signed byte from some source times a signed byte in AL, or a signed word from some source times a signed word in AX. The source can be another register or a memory location specified by any one of the 24 addressing modes shown in Figure 3-8. When a byte from some source is multiplied by AL, the signed result (product) will be put in AX. A 16-bit destination is required because the result of multiplying two 8-bit numbers can be as large as 16 bits. When a word from some source is multiplied by AX, the result can be as large as 32 bits. The high-order (most-significant) word of the signed result is put in DX and the low-order (least-significant) word of the signed result is put in AX. If the magnitude of the product does not require all of the bits of the destination, the unused bits will be filled with copies of the sign bit. If the upper byte of a 16-bit result or the upper word of a 32-bit result contains only copies of the sign bit (all 0's or all 1's), then the CF and the OF will both be 0's. If the upper byte of a 16-bit result or the upper word of a 32-bit result contains part of the product, the CF and OF will both be 1's. You can use the status of these flags to determine whether the upper byte or word of the product needs to be kept. The AF, PF, SF, and ZF are undefined after IMUL.

If you want to multiply a signed byte by a signed word, you must first move the byte into a word location and fill the upper byte of the word with copies of the sign bit. If you move the byte into AL you can use the 8086 Convert Byte to Word instruction, CBW, to do this. CBW extends the sign bit from AL into all the bits of AH. Once you have converted the byte to a word, you can do word times word IMUL. The result will be in DX and AX.

EXAMPLES(CODING):

```
IMUL BH   ; Signed byte in AL times signed
          ; byte in BH, result in AX

IMUL AX   ; AX times AX, result in DX and AX

; Example showing a signed byte multiplied by a
; signed word

MOV CX, MULTIPLIER     ; Load signed word
                       ; multiplier in CX
MOV AL, MULTIPLICAND   ; Load byte multiplicand
                       ; into AL
CBW                    ; Extend sign of AL into AH
IMUL CX                ; Word multiply;
                       ; result in DX and AX
```

EXAMPLES(NUMERICAL):

```
         ;            (a)
         ; AL = 01000101 = 69 decimal
         ; BL = 00001110 = 14 decimal
IMUL BL  ; AX = +966 decimal
         ; AX = 00000011 11000110
         ; MSB = 0, positive result
         ; magnitude in true form.
         ; SF = 0, CF = 1, OF = 1

         ;            (b)
         ; AL = 11100100 = -28 decimal
         ; BL = 00111011 = +59 decimal
IMUL BL  ; AX = -1652 decimal
         ; AX = 11111001 10001100
         ; MSB = 1, negative result
         ; magnitude in 2's complement.
         ; SF = 1, CF = 1, OF = 1
```

IMUL—80186/80188 ONLY—Integer (signed) Multiply Immediate—IMUL destination register, source, immediate byte or word

This version of the IMUL instruction functions the same as the IMUL instruction described in the preceding section except that this version allows you to multiply an immediate byte or word by a byte or word in a specified register and put the result in a specified general-purpose register. If the immediate number is a byte, it will be automatically sign-extended to 16 bits. The source of the other operand for the multiplication can be a register or a memory location specified by any one of the addressing modes shown in Figure 3-8. Since the result is put in a 16-bit general-purpose register, only the lower 16 bits of the product are saved!

EXAMPLE:

```
IMUL CX, BX, 07H   ; Multiply contents of BX times
                   ; 07H and put

                   ; lower 16 bits of result in CX
```

IN INSTRUCTION—IN accumulator, port

The IN instruction will copy data from a port to the accumulator. If an 8-bit port is read, the data will go to AL. If a 16-bit port is read, the data read will go to AX. The IN instruction has two possible formats, fixed port and variable port.

For the fixed port type the 8-bit address of a port is specified directly in the instruction.

EXAMPLES:

```
IN AL, 0C8H      ; Input a byte from port 0C8H to AL

IN AX, 34H       ; Input a word from port 34H to AX

A_TO_D EQU 4AH
IN AX, A_TO_D    ; Input a word from port 4AH to AX
```

For the variable-port type IN instruction, the port address is contained in the DX register. Since DX is a 16-bit register, the port address can be any number between 0000H and FFFFH. Therefore, up to 65,536 ports are addressable in this mode. The DX register, however, must always be loaded with the port address before the IN instruction.

EXAMPLES:

```
MOV DX,0FF78H    ; Initialize DX to point to port
IN AL, DX        ; Input a byte from 8-bit port
                 ; 0FF78H to AL
IN AX, DX        ; Input a word from 16-bit port
                 ; 0FF78H to AX
```

The variable-port IN instruction has the advantage that the port address can be computed or dynamically determined in the program. Suppose, for example, that an 8086-based computer needs to input data from 10 terminals, each having its own port address. Instead of having separate routines to input data from each port, we can write one general input subroutine and simply pass the address of the desired port to the subroutine in DX. The IN instructions do not change any flags.

INC INSTRUCTION—INCREMENT destination

The INC instruction adds 1 to the indicated destination. The destination can be a register or memory location specified by any one of the 24 ways shown in Figure 3-8. The AF, OF, PF, SF, and ZF are affected (updated) by this instruction. Note that the carry flag, CF, is not affected. This means that if an 8-bit destination containing FFH or a 16-bit destination containing FFFFH is incremented, the result will be all 0's with no carry.

EXAMPLES:

INC BL ; Add 1 to contents of BL register

INC CX ; Add 1 to contents of CX register

INC BYTE PTR [BX] ; Increment byte at offset of BX in data segment. The BYTE PTR directive is necessary to tell the assembler to put in the right code to indicate that a byte in memory, rather than a word, is to be incremented. The instruction essentially says "increment the byte pointed to by the contents of BX."

INC WORD PTR [BX]; Increment the word at offset of [BX] and [BX + 1] in the data segment. In other words, increment the word in memory pointed to by BX.

INC MAX_TEMPERATURE ; Increment byte or word named MAX TEMPERATURE in data segment. Increment byte if MAX_TEMPERATURE declared with DB. Increment word if MAX_TEMPERATURE declared with DW.

INC PRICES [BX] ; Increment element [BX] in array PRICES. Increment a word if PRICES was defined as an array of words with a DW directive. Increment a byte if PRICES was defined as an array of bytes with a DB directive.

NOTE: The PTR operator is not needed in the last two examples because the assembler knows the type of the operand from the DB or DW used to declare the named data initially.

INS/INSB/INSW—80186/80188 ONLY—Input String from Port—INS destination string, DX

INS copies a byte or a word from a port to a memory location in the extra segment pointed to by DI. The address of the port to be copied from must be put in DX before this instruction executes. If the direction flag is cleared when this instruction executes, DI will automatically be incremented by one for a byte operation, and incremented by two for a word operation after the data is copied from the port. If the direction flag is set, DI will automatically be decremented by one for a byte operation and decremented by two for a word operation after data is copied from the port. When used with the REP prefix or as part of a loop, the INS instruction can input a block of data directly to a series of memory locations without having the data go through AL or AX as it does with the regular IN instruction.

When using the INS instruction you must in some way tell the assembler whether you want to input bytes or input words. There are two ways to do this. The first is to use the name of the destination string in the instruction statement as in the statement INS BUFFER, DX. The assembler will code the instruction for a byte input if BUFFER was declared with a DB and it will code the instruction for a word input if BUFFER was declared with a DW. The second way to tell the assembler whether to code the instruction for a byte or for a word input is to add a B or a W to the basic instruction mnemonic. For example, INSB DX, tells the assembler to code the instruction for copying a byte from a port pointed to by DX to a memory location pointed to by DI in the extra segment. INS affects no flags.

EXAMPLE:

```
CLD                  ; Clear direction flag to
                     ; autoincrement DI
MOV DI, OFFSET BUF   ; Point DI at input buffer
MOV DX, 0FFF8H       ; Load DX with
                     ; port address
MOV CX, LENGTH BUF   ; Load number of bytes
                     ; to be read in CX
REP INSB DX          ; Copy bytes from port
                     ; until buffer full
```

INT INSTRUCTION—Interrupt program execution—INT type

This instruction causes the 8086 to call a far procedure in a manner similar to the way in which the 8086 responds to an interrupt signal on its INTR or NMI inputs. Part of the response is to do an indirect far call to a procedure which responds to that particular interrupt. The term type in the instruction refers to a number between 0 and 255 which identifies the interrupt. When an 8086 executes an INT type instruction, it will:

1. Decrement the stack pointer by two and push the flags on the stack.
2. Decrement the stack pointer by two and push the contents of CS on the stack.
3. Decrement the stack pointer by two and push the offset of the next instruction after the INT number instruction on the stack.
4. Get a new value for IP from an absolute memory address of 4 times the type specified in the instruction. For an INT 8 instruction, for example, the new IP will be read from address 00020H.
5. Get a new value for CS from an absolute memory address of 4 times the type specified in the instruction plus 2. For an INT 8 instruction, for example, the new value of CS will be read from address 00022H.
6. Reset both the IF and the TF. Other flags are not affected.

Chapter 8 further describes the use of this instruction.

EXAMPLES:

INT 35 ; New IP from 0008CH, new CS from 0008EH

INT 3 ; This is a special form which has the single byte code of CCH. Many systems use this as a breakpoint instruction. New IP from 0000CH, new CS from 0000EH.

INTO INSTRUCTION—Interrupt on overflow

If the overflow flag, OF, is set, this instruction will cause the 8086 to do an indirect far call to a procedure you write to handle the overflow condition. Before doing the call the 8086 will:

1. Decrement the stack pointer by 2 and push the flags on the stack.
2. Decrement the stack pointer by 2 and push CS on the stack.
3. Decrement the stack pointer by 2 and push the offset of the next instruction after the INTO instruction on the stack
4. Reset the TF and the IF, other flags are not affected.

To do the call the 8086 will read a new value for IP from address 00010H and a new value of CS from address 00012H.

Chapter 8 further describes the 8086 interrupt system.

EXAMPLE:

INTO ; Call interrupt procedure if OF = 1

IRET INSTRUCTION—Interrupt return—IRET

When the 8086 responds to an interrupt signal or to an interrupt instruction, it pushes the flags, the current value of CS, and the current value of IP on the stack. It then loads CS and IP with the starting address of the procedure which you write for the response to that interrupt. The IRET instruction is used at the end of the interrupt service procedure to return execution to the interrupted program. To do this return the 8086 copies the saved value of IP from the stack to IP, the stored value of CS from the stack to CS, and the stored value of the flags back to the flag register. Flags will have the values they had before the interrupt, so any flag settings from the procedure will be lost unless they are specifically saved in some way.

NOTE: The RET instruction should not normally be used to return from interrupt procedures because it does not copy the flags from the stack back to the flag register. See Chapter 8 for further discussion of interrupts and the use of IRET.

EXAMPLE:

IRET

JA/JNBE INSTRUCTION—Jump if above/Jump if not below nor equal

These two mnemonics represent the same instruction. The terms "above" and "below" are used when referring to the magnitude of unsigned numbers. The number 0111 is above the number 0010. If, after a compare or some other instruction which affects flags, the zero flag and the carry flag are both 0, this instruction will cause execution to jump to a label given in the instruction. If CF and ZF are not both 0, the instruction will have no effect on program execution. The destination label for the jump must be in the range of −128 bytes to +127 bytes from the address of the instruction after the JA. JA/JNBE affects no flags. For further explanation of conditional jump instructions, see Chapter 4.

EXAMPLES:

```
CMP AX, 4371H        ; Compare by subtracting 4371H
                     ; from AX
JA RUN_PRESS         ; Jump to label RUN_PRESS if AX
                     ; above 4371H

CMP AX, 4371H        ; Compare by subtracting 4371H
                     ; from AX
JNBE RUN_PRESS       ; Jump to label RUN_PRESS if AX
                     ; not below nor
                     ; equal to 4371H
```

JAE/JNB/JNC INSTRUCTIONS
Jump if above or equal/Jump if not below/Jump if no carry

These three mnemonics represent the same instruction. The terms "above" and "below" are used when referring to the magnitude of unsigned numbers. The number 0111 is above the number 0010. If, after a compare or some other instruction which affects flags, the carry flag is 0, this instruction will cause execution to jump to a label given in the instruction. If CF is 1, the instruction will have no effect on program execution. The destination label for the jump must be in the range of −128 bytes to +127 bytes from the address of the instruction after the JA. JAE/JNB/JNC affects no flags. For further explanation of conditional jump instructions, see Chapter 4.

EXAMPLES:

```
CMP AX, 4371H      ; Compare by subtracting 4371H
                   ; from AX
JAE RUN_PRESS      ; Jump to label RUN_PRESS if AX
                   ; is above or equal to 4371H

CMP AX, 4371H      ; Compare by subtracting 4371H
                   ; from AX
JNB RUN_PRESS      ; Jump to label RUN_PRESS if AX
                   ; not below 4371H

ADD AL, BL         ; Add two bytes
JNC OK             ; Result within acceptable range,
                   ; continue
```

JB/JC/JNAE INSTRUCTIONS
Jump if below/Jump if carry/Jump if not above nor equal

These three mnemonics represent the same instruction. The terms "above" and "below" are used when referring to the magnitude of unsigned numbers. The number 0111 is above the number 0010. If, after a compare or some other instruction which affects flags, the carry flag is a 1, this instruction will cause execution to jump to a label given in the instruction. If CF is 0, the instruction will have no effect on program execution. The destination label for the jump must be in the range of −128 bytes to +127 bytes from the address of the instruction after the JB. JB/JC/JNAE affects no flags. For further explanation of conditional jump instructions, see Chapter 4.

EXAMPLES:

```
CMP AX, 4371H      ; Compare by subtracting 4371H
                   ; from AX
JB RUN_PRESS       ; Jump to label RUN_PRESS if
                   ; AX below 4371H

ADD BX, CX         ; Add two words
JC ERROR_FIX       ; Jump to label ERROR_FIX if
                   ; CF = 1

CMP AX, 4371H      ; Compare by subtracting 4371H
                   ; from AX
JNAE RUN_PRESS     ; Jump to label RUN_PRESS if
                   ; AX not above nor
                   ; equal to 4371H
```

JBE/JNA INSTRUCTIONS
Jump if below or equal/Jump if not above

These two mnemonics represent the same instruction. The terms "above" and "below" are used when referring to the magnitude of unsigned numbers. The number 0111 is above the number 0010. If, after a compare or some other instruction which affects flags, either the zero flag or the carry flag is 1, this instruction will cause execution to jump to a label given in the instruction. If CF and ZF are both 0, the instruction will have no effect on program execution. The destination label for the jump must be in the range of −128 bytes to +127 bytes from the address of the instruction after the JBE. JBE/JNA affects no flags. For further explanation of conditional jump instructions, see Chapter 4.

EXAMPLES:

```
CMP AX, 4371H      ; Compare by subtracting 4371H
                   ; from AX
JBE RUN_PRESS      ; Jump to label RUN_PRESS if AX
                   ; is below or equal to 4371H

CMP AX, 4371H      ; Compare by subtracting 4371H
                   ; from AX
JNA RUN_PRESS      ; Jump to label RUN_PRESS if AX
                   ; not above 4371H
```

JCXZ INSTRUCTION
Jump if the CX register is zero

This instruction will cause a jump to a label given in the instruction if the CX register contains all 0's. If CX does not contain all 0's, execution will simply proceed to the next instruction. Note that this instruction does not look at the zero flag when it decides whether to jump or not. The destination label for this instruction must be in the range of −128 to +127 bytes from the address of the instruction after the JCXZ instruction. JCXZ affects no flags.

EXAMPLE:

```
; If CX already 0 skip over the process

            JCXZ SKIP_LOOP
LOOP:       SUB [BX], 07H     ; Subtract 7 from
                              ; data value
            INC BX            ; point to
                              ; next value
            LOOP COUNT        ; Loop until CX = 0
SKIP_LOOP:                    ; next instruction
```

JE/JZ INSTRUCTIONS—Jump if equal/Jump if zero

These two mnemonics represent the same instruction. If the zero flag is set, then this instruction will cause execution to jump to a label given in the instruction. If the zero flag is not 1, then execution will simply go on to the next instruction after JE or JZ. The destination label for the JE/JZ instruction must be in the range of −128 to +127 bytes from the address of the instruction after the JE/JZ instruction. JE/JZ affects no flags.

EXAMPLES:

```
AGAIN: CMP BX, DX        ; Compare by subtracting DX
                         ; from BX
       JE DONE           ; Jump to label DONE
                         ; if BX = DX
       SUB BX, AX        ; Else subtract AX
       INC CX            ; Increment counter
       JMP AGAIN         ; Check again
DONE:  MOV AX, CX        ; Copy count to AX

IN AL, 8FH               ; Read data from port 8FH
SUB AL, 30H              ; Subtract minimum value
JZ START_MACHINE         ; Jump to label if result of
                         ; subtraction was 0
```

JG/JNLE INSTRUCTION—Jump if greater/Jump if not less than nor equal

These two mnemonics represent the same instruction. The terms "greater" and "less" are used to refer to the relationship of two signed numbers. Greater means more positive. The number 00000111 is greater than the number 11101010, because the second number is negative. This instruction is usually used after a compare instruction. The instruction will cause a jump to a label given in the instruction if the zero flag is 0 and the carry flag is the same as the overflow flag. The destination label must be in the range of −128 bytes to +127 bytes from the address of the instruction after the JG/JNLE instruction. If the jump is not taken, execution simply goes on to the next instruction after the JG or JNLE instruction. JG/JNLE affects no flags.

EXAMPLES:

```
CMP BL, 39H              ; Compare by subtracting 39H
                         ; from BL
JG SHORT_LABEL           ; Jump to label if BL more
                         ; positive than 39H

CMP BL, 39H              ; Compare by subtracting
                         ; 39H from BL
JNLE SHORT_LABEL         ; Jump to label if BL not less
                         ; than nor equal to 39H
```

JGE/JNL INSTRUCTION—Jump if greater than or equal/Jump if not less than

These two mnemonics represent the same instruction. The terms "greater" and "less" are used to refer to the relationship of two signed numbers. Greater means more positive. The number 00000111 is greater than the number 11101010, because the second number is negative. This instruction is usually used after a compare instruction. The instruction will cause a jump to a label given in the instruction if the sign flag is equal to the overflow flag. The destination label must be in the range of −128 bytes to +127 bytes from the address of the instruction after the JGE/JNL instruction. If the jump is not taken, execution simply goes on to the next instruction after the JGE or JNL instruction. JGE/JNL affects no flags.

EXAMPLES:

```
CMP BL, 39H              ; Compare by subtracting 39H
                         ; from BL
JGE SHORT_LABEL          ; Jump to label if BL more
                         ; positive than 39H
                         ; or equal to 39H

CMP BL, 39H              ; Compare by subtracting 39H
                         ; from BL
JNL SHORT_LABEL          ; Jump to label if BL not less
                         ; than 39H
```

JL/JNGE INSTRUCTION—Jump if less than/Jump if not greater than nor equal

These two mnemonics represent the same instruction. The terms "greater" and "less" are used to refer to the relationship of two signed numbers. Greater means more positive. The number 00000111 is greater than the number 11101010, because the second number is negative. This instruction is usually used after a compare instruction. The instruction will cause a jump to a label given in the instruction if the sign flag is not equal to the overflow flag. The destination label must be in the range of −128 bytes to +127 bytes from the address of the instruction after the JL/JNGE instruction. If the jump is not taken, execution simply goes on to the next instruction after the JL or JNGE instruction. JL/JNGE affects no flags.

EXAMPLES:

```
CMP BL, 39H              ; Compare by subtracting 39H
                         ; from BL
JL SHORT_LABEL           ; Jump to label if BL more
                         ; negative than 39H

CMP BL, 39H              ; Compare by subtracting 39H
                         ; from BL
JNGE SHORT_LABEL         ; Jump to label if BL not more
                         ; positive than 39H
                         ; or BL not equal to 39H
```

JLE/JNG INSTRUCTIONS—Jump if less than or equal/Jump if not greater

These two mnemonics represent the same instruction. The terms "greater" and "less" are used to refer to the relationship of two signed numbers. Greater means more positive. The number 00000111 is greater than the number 11101010, because the second number is negative. This instruction is usually used after a compare instruction. The instruction will cause a jump to a label given in the instruction if the zero flag is set, or if the sign flag is not equal to the overflow flag. The destination label must be in the range of −128 bytes to +127 bytes from the address of the instruction after the JLE/JNG instruction. If the jump is not taken, execution simply goes on to the next instruction after the JLE/JNG instruction. JLE/JNG affects no flags.

EXAMPLES:

```
CMP BL, 39H          ; Compare by subtracting 39H
                     ; from BL
JLE SHORT_LABEL      ; Jump to label if BL more
                     ; negative than 39H or
                     ; equal to 39H

CMP BL, 39H          ; Compare by subtracting 39H
                     ; from BL
JNG SHORT_LABEL      ; Jump to label if BL not more
                     ; positive than 39H
```

JMP INSTRUCTION—Unconditional jump to specified destination

This instruction will always cause the 8086 to fetch its next instruction from the location specified in the instruction rather than from the next location after the JMP instruction. If the destination is in the same code segment as the JMP instruction, then only the instruction pointer will be changed to get to the destination location. This is referred to as a near jump. If the destination for the jump instruction is in a segment with a name different from that containing the JMP instruction, then both the instruction pointer and the code segment register contents will be changed to get to the destination location. This is referred to as a far jump. The JMP instruction affects no flags. Refer to a section in Chapter 4 for a detailed discussion of the different forms of the unconditional JMP instruction.

EXAMPLES:

JMP CONTINUE ; Fetch next instruction from address at label CONTINUE. If label is in same segment, an offset coded as part of the instruction will be added to the instruction pointer to produce the new fetch address. If the label is in another segment then IP and CS will be replaced with values coded in as part of the instruction. This type of jump is referred to as direct because the displacement of the destination or the destination itself is specified directly in the instruction.

JMP BX ; Replace the contents of IP with the contents of BX. BX must first be loaded with the offset of the destination instruction in CS. This is a near jump. It is also referred to as an indirect jump because the new value for IP comes from a register rather than from the instruction itself as in a direct-type jump.

JMP WORD PTR [BX] ; Replace IP with a word from a memory location pointed to by BX in DS. This is an indirect near jump.

JMP DWORD PTR [SI] ; Replace IP with word pointed to by SI in DS. Replace CS with word pointed to by SI + 2 in DS. This is an indirect far jump.

JNA/JBE INSTRUCTION—Jump if not above/Jump if below or equal

Please refer to the discussion of this instruction under the heading JBE.

JNAE/JB INSTRUCTION—Jump if not above or equal/Jump if below

Please refer to the discussion of this instruction under the heading JB.

JNB/JNC/JAE INSTRUCTION—Jump if not below/Jump if no carry/Jump if above or equal

Please refer to the discussion of this instruction under the heading JAE.

JNBE/JA INSTRUCTION—Jump if not below or equal/Jump if above

Please refer to the discussion of this instruction under the heading JA.

JNC/JNB/JAE INSTRUCTION—Jump if not carry/Jump if not below/Jump if above or equal

Please refer to the discussion of this instruction under the heading JAE.

JNE/JNZ INSTRUCTION—Jump if not equal/Jump if not zero

These two mnemonics represent the same instruction. If the zero flag is 0, then this instruction will cause execution to jump to a label given in the instruction. If the zero flag is 1, then execution will simply go on to the next instruction after JNE or JNZ. The destination label for the JNE/JNZ instruction must be in the range of −128 to +127 bytes from the address of the instruction after the JNE/JNZ instruction. JNE/JNZ affects no flags.

EXAMPLES:

```
AGAIN:  IN AL, 0F8H      ; Read data value from port
        CMP AL, 72       ; Compare by subtracting
                         ; 72 from AL
        JNE AGAIN        ; Jump to label AGAIN if
                         ; AL not equal 72
        IN AL, 0F9H      ; Read next port when
                         ; AL = 72
        MOV BX, 2734H    ; Load BX as counter
```

```
NEXT 1: ADD AX, 0002H    ; Add count factor to AX
        DEC BX           ;
        JNZ NEXT 1:      ; Repeat until BX = 0
```

JNG/JLE INSTRUCTION—Jump if not greater/Jump if less than or equal

Please refer to the discussion of this instruction under the heading JLE.

JNGE/JL INSTRUCTION—Jump if not greater than nor equal/Jump if less than

Please refer to the discussion of this instruction under the heading JL.

JNL/JGE INSTRUCTION—Jump if not less than/Jump if greater than or equal

Please refer to the discussion of this instruction of this instruction under the heading JGE.

JNLE/JG INSTRUCTION—Jump if not less than nor equal to/Jump if greater than

Please refer to the discussion of this instruction under the heading JG.

JNO INSTRUCTION—Jump if no overflow

The overflow flag will be set if the result of some signed arithmetic operation is too large to fit in the destination register or memory location. The JNO instruction will cause the 8086 to jump to a destination given in the instruction if the overflow flag is not set. The destination must be in the range of −128 bytes to +127 bytes from the address of the instruction after the JNO instruction. If the overflow flag is set, execution will simply continue with the next instruction after JNO. JNO affects no flags.

EXAMPLE:

```
        ADD AL, BL    ; Add signed bytes in AL and BL
        JNO DONE      ; Process done if no overflow
        MOV AL, 00H   ; Else load error code in AL
DONE:   OUT 24H,AL    ; Send result to display
```

JNP/JPO INSTRUCTION—Jump if no parity/Jump if parity odd

If the number of 1's left in a data byte after an instruction which affects the parity flag is odd, then the parity flag will be 0. The JNP/JPO instruction will cause execution to jump to a specified destination address if the parity flag is 0. The destination address must be in the range of −128 bytes to +127 bytes from the address of the instruction after the JNP/JNO instruction. If the parity flag is set, execution will simply continue on to the instruction after the JNO/JPO instruction. The JNO/JPO instruction affects no flags.

EXAMPLE:

```
IN AL, 0F8H           ; Read ASCII character
                      ; from UART
OR AL, AL             ; Set flags
JPO ERR_MESSAGE       ; Even parity expected, send
                      ; error message if parity
                      ; found odd
```

JNS INSTRUCTION—Jump if not signed (Jump if positive)

This instruction will cause execution to jump to a specified destination if the sign flag is 0. Since a 0 in the sign flag indicates a positive signed number, you can think of this instruction as saying "jump if positive." If the sign flag is set, indicating a negative signed result, execution will simply go on to the next instruction after JNS. The destination for the jump must be in the range of −128 bytes to +127 bytes from the address of the instruction after the JNS. JNS affects no flags.

EXAMPLE:

```
DEC AL        ; Decrement counter
JNS REDO      ; Jump to label REDO if counter has not
              ; decremented to FFH
```

JNZ/JNE INSTRUCTION—Jump if not zero/Jump if not equal

Please refer to the discussion of this instruction under the heading JNE.

JO INSTRUCTION—Jump if overflow

The overflow flag will be set if the result of some signed arithmetic operation is too large to fit in the destination register or memory location. The JO instruction will cause the 8086 to jump to a destination given in the instruction if the overflow flag is set. The destination must be in the range of −128 bytes to +127 bytes from the address of the instruction after the JO instruction. If the overflow flag is not set, execution will simply continue with the next instruction after JO. JO affects no flags.

EXAMPLE:

```
ADD AL, BL       ; Add signed bytes in AL and BL
JO ERROR         ; Jump to label ERROR if overflow
                 ; from add
MOV SUM, AL      ; Else put result in memory location
                 ; named SUM
```

JP/JPE INSTRUCTION—Jump if parity/Jump if parity even

If the number of 1's left in a data word after an instruction which affects the parity flag is even, then the parity flag will be set. The JP/JPE instruction will cause execution to jump to a specified destination address if the parity flag is set. If the parity flag is 0, execution will simply continue on to the instruction after the JP/JPE instruction. The destination address must be in the range of −128 bytes to +127 bytes from the address of the instruction after the JP/JPE instruction. The JP/JPE instruction affects no flags.

EXAMPLE:

```
IN AL, 0F8H           ; Read ASCII character
                      ; from UART
OR AL, AL             ; Set flags
JPE ERR_MESSAGE       ; Odd parity expected, send
                      ; error message if parity
                      ; found even
```

JPE/JP INSTRUCTION—Jump if parity even/Jump if parity

Please refer to the discussion of this instruction under the heading JP.

JPO/JNP INSTRUCTION—Jump if parity odd/Jump if no parity

Please refer to the discussion of this instruction under the heading JNP.

JS INSTRUCTION—Jump if signed (Jump if negative)

This instruction will cause execution to jump to a specified destination if the sign flag is set. Since a 1 in the sign flag indicates a negative signed number, you can think of this instruction as saying "jump if negative" or "jump if minus." If the sign flag is 0, indicating a positive signed result, execution will simply go on to the next instruction after JS. The destination for the jump must be in the range of −128 bytes to +127 bytes from the address of the instruction after the JS. JS affects no flags.

EXAMPLE:

```
ADD BL, DH      ; Add signed byte in DH to signed
                ; byte in BL
JS TOO_COLD     ; Jump to label TOO_COLD if result
                ; of addition is negative number
```

JZ/JE INSTRUCTION—Jump if zero/Jump if equal

Please refer to the discussion of this instruction under the heading JE.

LAHF INSTRUCTION—Copy low byte of flag register to AH

The lower byte of the 8086 flag register is the same as the flag byte for the 8085. LAHF copies these 8085 equivalent flags to the AH register. They can then be pushed on the stack along with AL by a PUSH AX instruction. An LAHF instruction followed by a PUSH AX instruction has the same effect as the 8085 PUSH PSW instruction. The LAHF instruction was included in the 8086 instruction set so that the 8085 PUSH PSW instruction could easily be simulated on an 8086. LAHF changes no flags.

EXAMPLE: LAHF

LDS INSTRUCTION—Load register and DS with words from memory—LDS register, memory address of first word

This instruction copies a word from two memory locations into the register specified in the instruction. It then copies a word from the next two memory locations into the DS register. LDS is useful for pointing SI and DS at the start of a string before using one of the string instructions. LDS affects no flags.

EXAMPLES:

LDS BX, [4326]   ; Copy contents of memory at displacement 4326H in DS to BL, contents of 4327H to BH. Copy contents at displacement of 4328H and 4329H in DS to DS register.

LDS SI, STRING_POINTER   ; Copy contents of memory at displacements STRING_POINTER and STRING_POINTER+1 in DS to SI register. Copy contents of memory at displacements STRING_POINTER+2 and STRING_POINTER+3 in DS to DS register. DS:SI now points at start of desired string.

LEA INSTRUCTION—Load Effective Address—LEA register, source

This instruction determines the offset of the variable or memory location named as the source and puts this offset in the indicated 16-bit register. LEA changes no flags.

EXAMPLES:

```
LEA BX, PRICES           ; Load BX with offset of
                         ; PRICES in DS
LEA BP, SS:STACK_TOP     ; Load BP with offset of
                         ; STACK_TOP in SS
LEA CX, [BX][DI]         ; Load CX with
                         ; EA = (BX) + (DI)
```

A program example will better show the context in which this instruction is used. If you look at the program in Figure 4-15c you will see that PRICES is an array of bytes in a segment called ARRAYS_HERE. The program gets a byte from this array with the instruction LEA BX, PRICES. This will load the displacement of the first element of PRICES directly into BX. The instruction MOV AL, [BX] can then be used to bring an element from the array into AL. After one element in the array is processed, BX is incremented to point to the next element.

LEAVE—80186/80188 ONLY—Leave procedure

The LEAVE instruction is used at the end of an assembly language procedure which is intended to be called from a high level language program such as Pascal or C. An ENTER instruction at the start of such a procedure sets aside stack space for variables used in the procedure and in subprocedures. The main function of the LEAVE instruction is to increment SP and BP up over this reserved space so they have the values they had before the ENTER instruction. In other words, LEAVE restores SP and BP to the values they had at the start of the procedure. A RET instruction can then be used to return execution to the calling program. Leave affects no flags. Refer to the Intel literature for further explanation of this instruction if you need it.

LES INSTRUCTION—Load register and ES with words from memory—LES register, memory address of first word

This instruction loads new values into the specified register and into the ES register from four successive memory locations. The word from the first two memory locations is copied into the specified register, and the word from the next two memory locations is copied into the ES register. LES can be used to point DI and ES at the start of a string before a string instruction is executed. LES affects no flags.

EXAMPLES:

LES BX, [789AH] ; Contents of memory at displacements 789AH and 789BH in DS copied to BX. Contents of memory at displacements 789CH and 789DH in DS copied to ES register.

LES DI, [BX] ; Copy contents of memory at offset [BX] and offset [BX + 1] in DS to DI register copy contents of memory at offsets [BX + 2] and [BX + 3] to ES register.

LOCK INSTRUCTION—Assert bus lock signal

Many microcomputer systems contain several microprocessors. Each microprocesor has its own local buses and memory. The individual microprocessors are connected together by a system bus so that each can access system resources such as disk drives or memory. Each microprocessor only takes control of the system bus when it needs to access some system resource. The LOCK prefix allows a microprocessor to make sure that another processor does not take control of the system bus while it is in the middle of a critical instruction which uses the system bus. The LOCK prefix is put in front of the critical instruction. When an instruction with a LOCK prefix executes, the 8086 will assert its bus lock signal output. This signal is connected to an external bus controller device which then prevents any other processor from taking over the system bus. LOCK affects no flags.

EXAMPLE:

LOCK XCHG SEMAPHORE, AL ; The XCHG instruction requires two bus accesses. The LOCK prefix prevents another processor from taking control of the system bus between the two accesses.

LODS/LODSB/LODSW INSTRUCTION—Load string byte into AL or Load string word into AX

This instruction copies a byte from a string location pointed to by SI to AL, or a word from a string location pointed to by SI to AX. If the direction flag is cleared (0), SI will automatically be incremented to point to the next element of the string. For a string of bytes SI will be incremented by one. For a string of words SI will be incremented by two. If the direction flag, DF, is set (1), SI will be automatically decremented to point to the next string element. For a byte string SI will be decremented by one, and for a word string SI will be decremented by two. LODS affects no flags.

EXAMPLE:

```
CLD   ; Clear direction flag so SI is autoincremented
MOV SI, OFFSET SOURCE_STRING  ; Point SI at
                              ; string
LODS SOURCE_STRING
```

NOTE: Assembler uses name of string to determine whether string is of type byte or of type word. Instead of using the string name to do this, you can use the mnemonic LODSB to tell the assembler that the string is of type byte or the mnemonic LODSW to tell the assembler that the string is of type word.

LOOP INSTRUCTION—Loop to specified label until CX = 0

This instruction is used to repeat a series of instructions some number of times. The number of times the instruction sequence is to be repeated is loaded into the count register. Each time the LOOP instruction executes, CX is automatically decremented by one. If CX is not 0, execution will jump to a destination specified by a label in the instruction. If CX = 0 after the autodecrement, execution will simply go on to the next instruction after LOOP. The destination address for the jump must be in the range of −128 bytes to +127 bytes from the address of the instruction after the LOOP instruction. LOOP affects no flags. See Chapter 4 for further discussion and examples of the LOOP instruction.

EXAMPLE:

```
        MOV BX, OFFSET PRICES  ; Point BX at
                               ; first element in array
        MOV CX, 40             ; Load CX with number of
                               ; elements in array
NEXT:   MOV AL, [BX]           ; Get element from array
        ADD AL, 07H            ; Add correction factor
        DAA                    ; Decimal adjust result
        MOV [BX],AL            ; Put result back in array
        INC BX                 ; Repeat until all elements
        LOOP NEXT              ; adjusted
```

LOOPE/LOOPZ INSTRUCTION—Loop while CX not = 0 and ZF = 1

LOOPE and LOOPZ are two mnemonics for the same instruction. This instruction is used to repeat a group of instructions some number of times or until the zero flag becomes 0. The number of times the instruction sequence is to be repeated is loaded into the count register. Each time the LOOP instruction executes, CX is automatically decremented by one. If CX is not 0 and the zero flag is set, execution will jump to a destination specified by a label in the instruction. If CX is 0 after the autodecrement or if the zero flag is not set, execution will simply go on to the next instruction after LOOPE/LOOPZ. In other words, the two ways to exit the loop are CX = 0 or ZF = 0. The destination address for the jump must be in the range of −128 bytes to +127 bytes from the address of the instruction after the LOOPE/LOOPZ instruction. LOOPE/LOOPZ affects no flags. See Chapter 4 for further discussion and examples of the LOOPE/LOOPZ instruction.

EXAMPLE:

```
        MOV BX, OFFSET ARRAY   ; Point BX at start
        DEC BX                 ; of array
        MOV CX, 100            ; Put number of
                               ; array elements
                               ; in CX
NEXT:   INC BX                 ; Point to next
                               ; element in array
        CMP [BX], 0FFH         ; Compare array
                               ; element with
                               ; FFH
        LOOPE NEXT
```

NOTE: The next element is checked if the element equals FFH and the element was not the last one in the array. If CX = 0 and ZF = 1 on exit, all elements were equal to FFH. If CX is not equal to 0 on exit from loop, then BX points to next element after first byte that was not FFH.

LOOPNE/LOOPNZ INSTRUCTION—Loop while CX is not 0 and ZF = 0

LOOPNE and LOOPNZ are two mnemonics for the same instruction. This instruction is used to repeat a group of instructions some number of times or until the zero flag becomes a 1. The number of times the instruction sequence is to be repeated is loaded into the count register, CX. Each time the LOOPNE/LOOPNZ instruction executes, CX is automatically decremented by one. If CX is not 0 and the zero flag is not set, execution will jump to a destination specified by a label in the instruction. If CX is 1 after the autodecrement or if the zero flag is set, execution will simply go on to the next instruction after LOOPNE/LOOPNZ. In other words, the two ways to exit the loop are CX = 0 or ZF = 1. The destination address for the jump must be in the range of −128 bytes to +127 bytes from the address of the instruction after the LOOPNE/LOOPNZ instruction. LOOPNE/LOOPNZ affects no flags. See Chapter 4 for further discussion and examples of the LOOPNE/LOOPNZ instruction.

EXAMPLE:

```
        MOV BX, OFFSET ARRAY   ; Point BX at start
        DEC BX                 ; of array
        MOV CX, 100            ; Put number of
                               ; array elements
                               ; in CX
NEXT:   INC BX                 ; Point to next
                               ; element in array
        CMP [BX], 0DH          ; Compare array
        LOOPNE NEXT            ; element with
                               ; 0DH
```

NOTE: The next element in the array is checked if the element was not equal 0DH and the element was not the last one in array. If CX = 0 and ZF = 0 on exit, 0DH was not found in the array. If CX does not equal 0 on exit from loop, then BX points to next element after the first element containing 0DH.

LOOPNZ/LOOPNE INSTRUCTION—Loop while CX is not 0 and ZF = 0

Please see the discussion of this instruction under the heading LOOPNE.

LOOPZ/LOOPE INSTRUCTION—Loop while CX is not 0 and ZF = 1

Please see the discussion of this instruction under the heading LOOPE.

MOV INSTRUCTION—MOV destination, source

The MOV instructions transfer a word or byte of data from some source to a destination. The destination can be a register or a memory location. The source can be a register, a memory location, or an immediate number. The source and destination in an instruction cannot both be memory locations. The source and destination in a MOV instruction must both be of type byte, or they must both be of type word. MOV instructions do not affect any flags.

EXAMPLES:

```
MOV CX, 037AH      ; Put the immediate number
                   ; 037AH in CX

MOV BL, [437AH]    ; Copy byte from offset 437AH
                   ; in DS to BL

MOV AX, BX         ; Copy contents of register BX
                   ; to AX

MOV DL, [BX]       ; Copy byte from memory address
                   ; to DL

                   ; Offset of memory address
                   ; in DS is in BX

MOV DS, BX         ; Copy word from BX to data
                   ; segment register
```

MOV RESULTS [BP], AX ; Copy AX to two memory locations, AL to first location, AH to second. EA of first memory location is the sum of displacement represented by RESULTS and contents of BP. Physical address = EA + SS.

MOV CS:RESULTS [BP], AX ; Same as the above instruction, but Physical Address = EA + CS because of segment override prefix, CS.

MOVS/MOVSB/MOVSW INSTRUCTION—Move string byte or string word—MOVS destination, source

This instruction copies a byte or word from a location in the data segment to a location in the extra segment. The offset of the source byte or word in the data segment must be in the SI register. The offset of the destination in the extra segment must be contained in the DI register. For multiple byte or multiple word moves the number of elements to be moved is put in the CX register so that it can function as a counter. After the byte or word is moved SI and DI are automatically adjusted to point to the next source and the next destination. If the direction flag is 0, then SI and DI will be incremented by 1 after a byte move and they will be incremented by 2 after a word move. If the DF is a 1, then SI and DI will be decremented by 1 after a byte move and they will be decremented by 2 after a word move. MOVS affects no flags.

When using the MOVS instruction you must in some way tell the assembler whether you want to move a string as bytes or as words. There are two ways to do this. The first way is to indicate the names of the source and the destination strings in the instruction as, for example, MOVS STRING_DUMP, STRING_CREATE. The assembler will code the instruction for a byte move if STRING_DUMP and STRING_CREATE were declared with a DB. It will code the instruction for a word move if they were declared with a DW. Note that this reference to the source and destination strings does not load SI and DI. This must be done with separate instructions. The second way to tell the assembler whether to code the instruction for a byte or word move is to add a "B" or a "W" to the MOVS mnemonic. MOVSB, for example, says move a string as bytes. MOVSW says move a string as words.

EXAMPLE:

```
    CLD   ; Clear Direction Flag to autoincrement SI
          ; and DI
    MOV AX, 00H
    MOV DS, AX       ; Initialize data segment
                     ; register to 0

    MOV ES, AX       ; Initialize extra segment
                     ; register to 0

    MOV SI, 2000H    ; Load offset of start of source
                     ; string into SI

    MOV DI, 2400H    ; Load offset of start of
                     ; destination into DI

    MOV CX, 04H      ; Load length of string in CX
                     ; as counter

REP MOVSB            ; Decrement CX and
                     ; MOVSB until CX = 0
```

After move SI will be one greater than offset of last byte in source string. DI will be one greater than offset of last byte of destination string. CX will be 0.

MUL INSTRUCTION—Multiply unsigned bytes or words—MUL source

This instruction multiplies an unsigned byte from some source times an unsigned byte in the AL register, or an unsigned word from some source times an unsigned word in the AX register. The source can be a register or a memory location specified by any one of the 24 addressing modes shown in Figure 3-8. When a byte is multiplied by the contents of AL, the result (product) is put in AX. A 16-bit destination is required because the result of multiplying an 8-bit number by an 8-bit number can be as large as 16 bits. The most-significant byte of the result is put in AH and the least-significant byte of the result is put in AL. When a word is multiplied by the contents of AX, the product can be as large as 32 bits. The most-significant word of the result is put in the DX register, and the least-significant word of the result is put in the AX register. If the most-significant byte of a 16-bit result or the most-significant word of a 32-bit result is 0, the CF and the OF will both be 0's. Checking these flags then allows you to detect and perhaps discard unnecessary leading 0's in a result. The AF, PF, SF, and ZF are undefined after a MUL instruction.

If you want to multiply a byte by a word, you must first move the byte to a word location such as an extended register and fill the upper byte of the word with all 0's.

NOTE: You cannot use the 8086 Convert Byte to Word instruction, CBW, to do this. The CBW instruction fills the upper byte of AX with copies of the MSB of AL. If the number in AL is 80H or greater, CBW will fill the upper half of AX with 1's instead of with 0's. Once you get the byte converted correctly to a word with 0's in the upper byte, you can then do a word times word multiply. The 32-bit result will be in DX and AX.

EXAMPLES:

```
MUL BH    ; AL times BH, result in AX
MUL CX    ; AX times CX, result high word in DX,
          ; low word in AX
MUL BYTE PTR [BX]   ; AL times byte in DS pointed
                    ; to by [BX]
```

MUL CONVERSION_FACTOR [BX] ; Multiply AL times byte at effective address CONVERSION_FACTOR [BX] if it was declared as type byte with DB. Multiply AX times word at effective address CONVERSION_FACTOR [BX], if it was declared as type word with DW.

```
; Example showing a byte multiplied by a word
MOV AX, MULTIPLICAND_16     ; Load 16-bit
                            ; multiplicand in AX
MOV CL, MULTIPLIER_8        ; Load 8-bit multiplier
                            ; in CL
MOV CH, 00H                 ; Set upper byte of CX
                            ; to all 0's
MUL CX                      ; AX times CX, 32-bit
                            ; result in DX and AX
```

NEG INSTRUCTION—Form 2's complement—NEG destination

This instruction replaces the number in a destination with the 2's complement of that number. The destination can be a register or a memory location specified by any one of the addressing modes shown in Figure 3-8. This instruction forms the 2's complement by subtracting the original word or byte in the indicated destination from zero. You may want to try this with a couple of numbers to convince yourself that it gives the same result as the invert each bit and add one algorithm. As shown in some examples below, the NEG instruction is useful for changing the sign of a signed word or byte. An attempt to NEG a byte location containing −128 or a word location containing −32,768 will produce no change in the destination contents because the maximum positive signed number in 8 bits is +127 and the maximum positive signed number in 16 bits is +32,767. The OF will be set to indicate that the operation could not be done. The NEG instruction updates the AF, CF, SF, PF, ZF, and OF.

EXAMPLES (CODING)

```
NEG AL   ; Replace number in AL with its
         ; 2's complement
NEG BX   ; Replace word in BX with its
         ; 2's complement
NEG BYTE PTR [BX]   ; Replace byte at offset [BX] in
                    ; DS with its 2's complement
NEG WORD PTR [BP]   ; Replace word at offset [BP] in
                    ; SS with its 2's complement
```

Note that the BYTE PTR and WORD PTR directives are required in the last two examples to tell the assembler whether to code the instruction for a byte operation or a word operation. The [BP] reference by itself does not indicate the type of the operand.

NOP INSTRUCTION—Perform no operation

This instruction simply uses up three clock cycles and increments the instruction pointer to point to the next instruction. NOP affects no flags. The NOP instruction can be used to increase the delay of a delay loop as shown in Figure 4-20. It can also be used to hold a place in a program for instructions that will be added later.

NOT INSTRUCTION—Invert each bit of operand—NOT destination

The NOT instruction inverts each bit (forms the 1's complement of) the byte or word at the specified destination. The destination can be a register or a memory location specified by any one of the addressing modes shown in Figure 3-8. No flags are affected by the NOT instruction.

EXAMPLES:

```
NOT BX              ; Complement contents of BX
                    ; register
NOT BYTE PTR [BX]   ; Complement memory byte at
                    ; offset [BX] in
                    ; data segment
```

OR INSTRUCTION—Logically OR corresponding bits of two operands—OR destination, source

This instruction ORs each bit in a source byte or word with the corresponding bit in a destination byte or word. The result is put in the specified destination. The contents of the specified source will not be changed. The result for each bit will follow the truth table for a two-input OR gate. In other words, a bit in the destination will become a one if that bit is a one in the source operand OR that bit is a one in the original destination operand. Therefore, a bit in the destination operand can be set to a one by simply ORing that bit with a one in the same bit of the source operand. A bit ORed with zero is not changed.

The source operand can be an immediate number, the contents of a register, or the contents of a memory location specified by one of the 24 addressing modes shown in Figure 3-8. The destination can be a register or a memory location. The source and the destination cannot both be memory locations in the same instruction. The CF and OF are both zero after OR. The PF, SF, and ZF are updated by the OR instruction. AF is undefined after OR. Note that PF only has meaning for an 8-bit operand.

EXAMPLES (CODING):

```
OR AH, CL     ; CL ORed with AH, result in AH.
              ; CL not changed.

OR BP, SI     ; SI ORed with BP, result in BP.
              ; SI not changed.

OR SI, BP     ; BP ORed with SI, result in SI.
              ; BP not changed.

OR BL, 80H    ; BL ORed with immediate 80H.
              ; Set MSB of BL to a 1.
```

OR CX, TABLE[BX][SI] ; CX ORed with word from effective address TABLE[BX][SI] in data segment. Word in memory is not changed.

EXAMPLE (NUMERICAL):

```
                ; CX = 00111101 10100101
OR CX, 0FF00H   ; OR CX with immediate FF00H.
                ; Result in CX = 11111111 10100101
                ; note upper byte now all 1's
                ; CF = 0 OF = 0 ZF = 1 SF = 1
                ; PF UNDEFINED
```

OUT INSTRUCTION—Output a byte or word to a port—OUT port, accumulator AL or AX

The OUT instruction copies a byte from AL or a word from AX to the specified port. The OUT instruction has two possible forms, fixed-port and variable port.

For the fixed-port form the 8-bit port address is specified directly in the instruction. With this form any one of 256 possible ports can be addressed.

EXAMPLES:

```
OUT 3BH, AL   ; Copy the contents of AL to port 3BH
OUT 2CH, AX   ; Copy the contents of AX to port 2CH
```

For the variable port form of the OUT instruction, the contents of AL or AX will be copied to the port at an address contained in DX. Since DX is a 16 bit register, the port address contained there can be any number between 0000H and FFFFH. Therefore, up to 65,536 possible ports can be addressed in this mode. The DX register must always be loaded with the desired port address before this form of the OUT instruction is used. The advantage of the variable port form of addressing is described within the discussion of the IN instruction.

EXAMPLES:

```
MOV DX, 0FFF8H ; Load desired port address in DX
OUT DX, AL     ; Copy contents of AL to port FFF8H
OUT DX, AX     ; Copy contents of AX to port FFF8H
```

NOTE: The OUT instruction does not affect any flags.

OUTS/OUTSB/OUTSW—80186/80188 ONLY—Output String to Port—OUTS port, source string

OUTS copies a byte or a word from a string location pointed to by SI to a port whose address is contained in DX. The address of the port to be copied to must be put in DX before this instruction executes. If the direction flag is cleared when this instruction executes, SI will automatically be incremented by one for a byte operation, and incremented by two for a word operation after the data is copied to the port. If the direction flag is set, SI will automatically be decremented by one for a byte operation and decremented by two for a word operation after data is copied to the port. When used with the REP prefix or as part of a loop the OUTS instruction can output a block of data directly from a series of memory locations to a port without having the data go through AL or AX as it does with the regular OUT instruction.

When using the OUTS instruction you must in some way tell the assembler whether you want to output bytes or output words. There are two ways to do this. The first is to use the name of the source string in the instruction statement as in the statement OUTS DX, BUFFER. The assembler will code the instruction for a byte output if BUFFER was declared with a DB and it will code the instruction for a word output if BUFFER was declared with a DW. The second way to tell the assembler whether to code the instruction for a byte or for a word input is to add a B or a W to the basic instruction mnemonic. OUTSB DX, for example, tells the assembler to code the instruction for copying a byte from a string location pointed to by SI to a port whose address is in DX. SI normally points to a location in the data segment, but you can use a segment override prefix to point it to a location in some other segment. OUTS affects no flags.

EXAMPLE:

```
     CLD   ; Clear direction flag, autoincrement DI

     MOV DI, OFFSET BUFFER   ; Point DI at
                             ; output buffer

     MOV DX, 0FFF8H   ; Load DX with
                      ; port address

     MOV CX, 100      ; Load number of
                      ; bytes to be output in CX

REP OUTSB DX          ; Copy bytes to port
                      ; until buffer empty
```

POP INSTRUCTION—POP destination

The POP instruction copies a word from the stack location pointed to by the stack pointer to a destination specified in the instruction. The destination can be a general-purpose register, a segment register, or a memory location. The data in the stack is not changed. After the word is copied to the specified destination, the stack pointer is automatically incremented by 2 to point to the next word on the stack. No flags are affected by the POP instruction.

NOTE: POP CS is illegal.

EXAMPLES:

```
POP DX           ; Copy a word from top of stack to
                 ; DX, SP = SP + 2

POP DS           ; Copy a word from the top of the
                 ; stack to DS.
                 ; Increment SP by 2

POP TABLE [BX]   ; Copy a word from the top of the
                 ; stack to memory in DS
                 ; with EA = TABLE + [BX]
```

POPA INSTRUCTION—80186/80188 ONLY—Pop all Registers from Stack

POPA restores four pointer and index registers and four general-purpose registers that were saved on the stack with a PUSHA instruction. After the saved value is copied from the stack to the appropriate register, the stack pointer is incremented by two. Register contents are popped off the stack in the following order: DI, SI, BP, SP, BX, DX, CX, AX. POPA affects no flags.

POPF INSTRUCTION—Pop word from top of stack to flag register

This instruction copies a word from the two memory locations at the top of the stack to the flag register and increments the stack pointer by two. The stack segment register is not affected. All flags are affected.

PUSH INSTRUCTION—PUSH source

The PUSH instruction decrements the stack pointer by two and copies a word from some source to the location in the stack segment where the stack pointer then points. The source of the word can be a general-purpose register, a segment register, or memory. The stack segment register and the stack pointer must be initialized before this instruction can be used. PUSH can be used to save data on the stack so it will not be destroyed by a procedure. It can also be used to put data on the stack so that a procedure can access it there as needed. No flags are affected by this instruction. Refer to Chapter 5 for further discussion of the stack and the PUSH instruction.

EXAMPLES:

```
PUSH BX          ; Decrement SP by 2, copy BX to stack

PUSH DS          ; Decrement SP by 2, copy DS to stack

PUSH AL          ; Illegal, must push a word

PUSH TABLE [BX]  ; Decrement SP by 2, copy word
                 ; from memory
                 ; at EA = TABLE + [BX]
                 ; in DS to stack
```

PUSH INSTRUCTION—80186/80188 ONLY—PUSH Immediate

This version of the PUSH instruction allows you to store an immediate byte or word given in the instruction on the stack. If an immediate byte is specified, the byte will be sign-extended to a word before the PUSH is done, because all stack pushes are word operations. The stack pointer will be decremented by two before the word is pushed on the stack. PUSH affects no flags.

EXAMPLE:

```
PUSH 437AH   ; Decrement SP by 2 and write
             ; number 437AH on stack.
```

PUSHA INSTRUCTION—80186/80188 ONLY—Push all Registers on Stack

PUSHA copies the contents of the four general-purpose registers and the contents of four pointer and index registers to memory locations in the stack. The stack pointer is decremented by two before each register is pushed on the stack. The registers are pushed in the following order: AX, CX, DX, BX, SP, BP, SI, DI. The value pushed for SP is the value that SP had before AX was pushed. PUSHA affects no flags. PUSHA can be used at the start of a procedure to save the contents of these eight registers. A POPA instruction at the end of the procedure can be used to restore the original contents of the registers before returning to the program which called the procedure.

PUSHF INSTRUCTION—Push flag register on the stack

This instruction decrements the stack pointer by two and copies the word in the flag register to the memory location(s) pointed to by the stack pointer. The stack segment register is not affected. No flags are changed.

EXAMPLE: PUSHF

RCL INSTRUCTION—Rotate operand around to the left through CF—RCL destination, count

This instruction rotates all of the bits in a specified word or byte some number of bit positions to the left. The operation is circular because the MSB of the operand is rotated into the carry flag and the bit in the carry flag is rotated around into the LSB of the operand. See the diagram below.

The "C" in the middle of the mnemonic should help you remember that CF is in the rotated loop and it should help distinguish this instruction from the ROL instruction. For multibit rotates CF will contain the bit most recently rotated out of the MSB.

The destination operand can be in a register or in a memory location specified by any one of the 24 addressing modes shown in Figure 3-8. If you want to rotate the operand one bit position, you can specify this by putting a 1 in the count position of the instruction. To rotate more than one bit position, load the desired number in the CL register and put "CL" in the count position of the instruction.

NOTE: The 80186 and the 80188 allow you to specify a rotate of up to 32 bit positions with either an immediate number in the instruction or with a number in CL.

RCL affects only the CF and OF. After RCL the CF will contain the bit most recently rotated out of the MSB. The OF will be a 1 after a single bit RCL if the MSB was changed by the rotate. OF is undefined after a multibit rotate.

The RCL instruction is a handy way to move the CF into the LSB of a register or memory location to save it after addition.

EXAMPLES (CODING)

```
RCL DX, 1          ; Word in DX 1 bit left, MSB to CF
                   ; CF to LSB

MOV CL, 4          ; Load number of bit positions to
                   ; rotate in CL

RCL SUM[BX], CL    ; Rotate byte or word at effective
                   ; address SUM[BX] 4 bits left.
                   ; Original bit 4 now in CF,
                   ; original CF now in bit 3.
```

EXAMPLES (NUMERICAL)

```
               ; CF = 0 BH = 10110011
RCL BH, 1      ; Byte in BH 1 bit left. MSB to CF,
               ; CF to LSB.
               ; CF = 1 BH = 01100110
               ; OF = 1 because MSB changed

               ; CF = 1 AX =00011111 10101001
MOV CL, 2      ; Load CL for rotating two bit positions.
RCL AX, CL     ; Rotate AX two bit positions.
               ; CF = 0  AX = 01111110 10100110
               ; OF undefined
```

RCR INSTRUCTION—Rotate operand around to the right through CF—RCR destination, count

This instruction rotates all of the bits in a specified word or byte some number of bit positions to the right. The operation is circular because the LSB of the operand is rotated into the carry flag and the bit in the carry flag is rotated around into the MSB of the operand. See the diagram below.

The "C" in the middle of the mnemonic should help you remember that CF is in the rotated loop and it should help distinguish this instruction from the ROR instruction. For multibit rotates CF will contain the bit most recently rotated out of the LSB.

The destination operand can be in a register or in a memory location specified by any one of the 24 addressing modes shown in Figure 3-8. If you want to rotate the operand one bit position, you can specify this by putting a 1 in the count position of the instruction. To rotate more than one bit position, load the desired number in the CL register and put "CL" in the count position of the instruction.

NOTE: The 80186 and the 80188 allow you to specify a rotate of up to 32 bit positions with either an immediate number in the instruction or with a number in CL.

RCR affects only the CF and OF. After RCR the CF will contain the bit most recently rotated out of the MSB. The OF will be a 1 after a single bit RCR if the MSB was changed by the rotate. OF will be undefined after multibit rotates.

EXAMPLES (CODING)

```
RCR BX, 1            ; Word in BX right 1 bit.
                     ; CF to MSB, LSB to CF

MOV CL, 04H          ; Load CL for rotating four bit
                     ; positions

RCR BYTE PTR [BX]    ; Rotate byte at offset [BX] in
                     ; data segment four bit
                     ; positions right.
                     ; CF = original bit 3.
                     ; Bit 4 = original CF.
```

EXAMPLES (NUMERICAL)

```
               ; CF = 1 BL = 00111000
RCR BL, 1      ; Byte in BL one bit position right.
               ; LSB to CF.
               ; CF = 0,BL = 10011100
               ; OF = 1 because MSB changed to 1

               ; CF = 0
               ; WORD PTR [BX] = 01011110 00001111
MOV CL, 02H                ; Load CL for rotate two
                           ; bit positions
RCR WORD PTR [BX], CL      ; Rotate word at offset [BX]
                           ; in data segment 2
                           ; bits right.
                           ; CF = original bit 1.
                           ; Bit 14 = original CF
                           ; WORD PTR [BX] =
                           ; 10010111 10000011
```

REP/REPE/REPZ/REPNE/REPNZ—(Prefix) Repeat string instruction until specified conditions exist

REP is a prefix which is written before one of the string instructions. It will cause the CX register to be decremented and the string instruction to be repeated until CX = 0. The instruction REP MOVSB, for example, will continue to move string bytes until the length of the string which was loaded into CX is counted down to zero.

REPE and REPZ are two mnemonics for the same prefix. They stand for Repeat if Equal and Repeat if Zero, respectively. You can use whichever prefix makes the operation clearer to you in a given program. REPE or REPZ is often used with the Compare String instruction or with the Scan String instruction. REPE or REPZ will cause the string instruction to be repeated as long as the compared bytes or words are equal (ZF = 1), AND CX is not yet counted down to zero. In other words there are two conditions that will stop the repetition: CX = 0 or string bytes or words NOT equal.

EXAMPLE:

REPE CMPSB ; Compare string bytes until end of string or until string bytes not equal. See the discussion of the CMPS instruction for a more detailed example of the use of REPE.

REPNE and REPNZ are also two mnemonics for the same prefix. They stand for Repeat if Not Equal and Repeat if Not Zero, respectively. REPNE or REPNZ is often used with the Scan String instruction. REPNE or REPNZ will cause the string instruction to be repeated as long as the compared bytes or words are not equal (ZF = 0), or until CX = 0 (end of string).

EXAMPLE:

REPNE SCASW ; Scan a string of words until a word in the string matches the word in AX or until all of the string has been scanned. See the discussion of SCAS for a more detailed example of the use of this prefix.

The string instruction used with the prefix determines which flags are affected. See the individual instructions for this information. Also see Chapter 5 for further examples of the REP instruction with string instructions.

NOTE: Interrupts should be disabled when multiple prefixes are used, such as LOCK, segment override, and REP with string instructions on the 8086/8088. This is because, during an interrupt response, the 8086 can only remember the prefix just before the string instruction. The 80186/80188 will correctly remember all of the prefixes and start up correctly after an interrupt.

RET INSTRUCTION—Return execution from procedure to calling program

The RET instruction will return execution from a procedure to the next instruction after the CALL instruction in the calling program. If the procedure is a near procedure (in the same code segment as the CALL instruction), then the return will be done by replacing the instruction pointer with a word from the top of the stack. The word from the top of the stack is the offset of the next instruction after the CALL. This offset was pushed on the stack as part of the operation of the CALL instruction. The stack pointer will be incremented by two as the return address is popped off the stack.

If the procedure is a far procedure (in a different code segment from the CALL instruction which calls it), then the instruction pointer will be replaced by the word at the top of the stack. This word is the offset part of the return address put there by the CALL instruction. The stack pointer will then be incremented by two. The code segment register is then replaced with a word from the new top of the stack. This word is the segment part of the return address that was pushed on the stack by a far call operation. After the code segment word is popped off the stack the stack pointer is again incremented by two.

A RET instruction can be followed by a number, for example, RET 6. In this case the stack pointer will be incremented by an additional six addresses after the IP or the IP and CS are popped off the stack. This form is used to increment the stack pointer up over parameters passed to the procedure on the stack.

The RET instruction affects no flags.

Please refer to Chapter 5 for further discussion of the CALL and RET instructions.

ROL INSTRUCTION—Rotate all bits of operand left, MSB to LSB—ROL destination, count

This instruction rotates all the bits in a specified word or byte to the left some number of bit positions. The operation can be thought of as circular, because the data bit rotated out of the MSB is circled back into the LSB. The data bit rotated out of the MSB is also copied to the CF during ROL. In the case of multiple bit rotates, CF will contain a copy of the bit most recently moved out of the MSB. See the diagram below.

The destination operand can be in a register or in a memory location specified by any one of the 24 addressing modes shown in Figure 3-8. If you want to rotate the operand one bit position, you can specify this by putting a 1 in the count position of the instruction. To rotate more than one bit position, load the desired number in the CL register and put "CL" in the count position of the instruction.

NOTE: The 80186 and the 80188 allow you to specify a rotate of up to 32 bit positions with either an immediate number in the instruction or with a number in CL.

ROL affects only the CF and OF. After ROL the CF will contain the bit most recently rotated out of the MSB. The OF will be a 1 after ROL if the MSB was changed by the rotate.

The ROL instruction can be used to swap the nibbles in a byte or to swap the bytes in a word. It can also be used to rotate a bit into CF where it can be checked and acted upon by the conditional jump instructions, JC (Jump if Carry) or JNC (Jump if No Carry).

EXAMPLES (CODING)

```
ROL AX,1          ; Word in AX one bit position left,
                  ; MSB to LSB and CF

MOV CL, 04H       ; Load number of bits to rotate in CL
ROL BL, CL        ; Rotate BL four bit positions
                  ; (swap nibbles)

ROL FACTOR[BX], 1 ; MSB of word or byte at
                  ; effective address
                  ; FACTOR[BX]
                  ; in data segment one bit
                  ; position left into CF
JC ERROR          ; Jump if CF = 1 to error routine
```

EXAMPLES (NUMERICAL)

```
              ; CF = 0   BH = 10101110
ROL BH, 1     ; CF = 1   BH = 01011101   OF = 1

              ; CL = 8   Set for 8-bit rotate
              ; BX = 01011100 11010011
ROL BX, CL    ; Rotate BX 8 times left (swap bytes)
              ; CF = 0, BX = 11010011 01011100
              ; OF = ?
```

ROR INSTRUCTION—Rotate all bits of operand right, LSB to MSB—ROR destination, count

This instruction rotates all of the bits of the specified word or byte some number of bit positions to the right. The operation is described as a rotate rather than a shift because the bit moved out of the LSB is rotated around into the MSB. To help visualize the operation, think of the operand as a loop with the LSB connected around to the MSB. The data bit moved out of the LSB is also copied to the CF during ROR. See diagram below. In the case of multiple bit rotates the CF will contain a copy of the bit most recently moved out of the LSB.

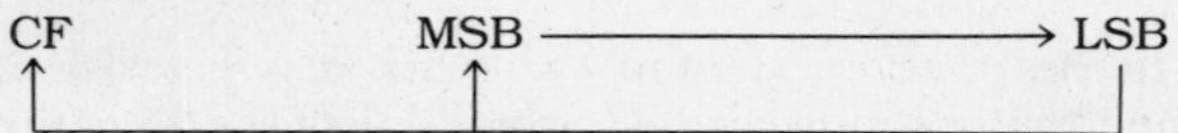

The destination operand can be in a register or in a memory location specified by any one of the 24 addressing modes shown in Figure 3-8. If you want to rotate the operand one bit position, you can specify this by putting a 1 in the count position of the instruction. To rotate more than one bit position, load the desired number in the CL register, and put "CL" in the count position of the instruction.

NOTE: The 80186 and the 80188 allow you to specify a rotate of up to 32 bit positions with either an immediate number or with a number in CL.

ROR affects only the CF and the AF. After ROR the CF will contain the bit most recently rotated out of the LSB. The OF will be a 1 after ROR if the MSB is changed by the rotate.

The ROR instruction can be used to swap the nibbles in a byte or to swap the bytes in a word. It can also be used to rotate a bit into the CF where it can be checked and acted upon by the conditional jump instructions, JC (Jump if Carry) or JNC (Jump if No Carry).

EXAMPLES (CODING)

```
ROR BL, 1             ; Rotate all bits in BL right one bit
                      ; position
                      ; LSB to MSB and to CF
MOV CL, 08H           ; Load number of bit positions to be
                      ; rotated in CL
ROR WORD PTR [BX], CL ; Rotate word at offset
                      ; [BX] in data segment eight bit
                      ; positions right (swaps bytes in word)
```

EXAMPLES (NUMERICAL)

```
              ; CF = 0, BX = 00111011 01110101
ROR BX,1      ; Rotate all bits of BX one bit
              ; position right
              ; CF = 1, BX = 10011101 10111010

              ; CF = 0, AL = 10110011 OF = 1
MOV CL, 04H   ; Load CL for rotate four bit positions
ROR AL, CL    ; Rotate all bits of AL around four
              ; bit positions right
              ; CF = 0   AL = 00111011   OF = ?
```

SAHF INSTRUCTION—Copy AH register to low byte of flag register

The lower byte of the 8086 flag register corresponds exactly to the 8085 flag byte. SAHF replaces this 8085 equivalent flag byte with a byte from the AH register. SAHF is used with the POP AX instruction to simulate the 8085 POP PSW instruction. As described under the heading LAHF, an 8085 PUSH PSW instruction will be translated to an LAHF—PUSH AX sequence to run on an 8086. An 8085 POP PSW instruction will be translated to a POP AX— SAHF sequence to run on an 8086. SAHF changes the flags in the lower byte of the flag register.

EXAMPLE: SAHF

SAL/SHL INSTRUCTION—Shift operand bits left, put zero in LSB(s)—SAL/SHL destination, count

SAL and SHL are two mnemonics for the same instruction. This instruction shifts each bit in the specified destination some number of bit positions to the left. As a bit is shifted out of the LSB position, a 0 is put in the LSB position. The MSB will be shifted into the CF. In the case of multiple bit shifts, CF will contain the bit most recently shifted in from the MSB. Bits shifted into CF previously will be lost. See diagram below.

CF ← MSB ←———————— LSB ← 0

The destination operand can be a byte or a word. It can be in a register or in a memory location specified by any one of the 24 addressing modes shown in Figure 3-8.

If the desired number of shifts is one, this can be specified by putting a 1 in the count position of the instruction. For shifts of more than 1 bit position the desired number of shifts is loaded into the CL register and CL is put in the count position of the instruction. The advantage of the CL way is that the number of shifts can be dynamically calculated as the program executes.

NOTE: The 80186 and the 80188 allow you to specify a shift of up to 32 bit positions with either an immediate number in the instruction or with a number in CL.

The flags are affected as follows: CF contains the bit most recently shifted in from MSB. For a count of one OF will be 1 if the CF and the current MSB are not the same. For multiple bit shifts, the OF is undefined. The SF and the ZF will be updated to reflect the condition of the destination. The PF will only have meaning if the destination is AL. AF is undefined.

The SAL or SHL instruction can also be used to multiply an unsigned binary number by a power of two. Shifting a binary number one bit position to the left and putting a 0 in the LSB multiplies the number by 2. Shifting the number two bit positions multiplies it by 4. Shifting the number three bit positions multiplies it by 8, etc. For this specific type of multiply the SAL method is faster than using MUL, but you must make sure that the result does not become too large for the destination.

EXAMPLES (CODING)

```
SAL BX, 1        ; Shift word in BX 1 bit position left,
                 ; 0 in LSB

MOV CL, 02H      ; Load desired number of shifts in CL
SAL BP, CL       ; Shift word in BP left (CL) bit
                 ; positions, 0's in
                 ; 2 least-significant bits

SAL BYTE PTR [BX], 1   ; Shift byte at offset [BX] in
                       ; data segment one bit
                       ; position left, 0 in LSB

; Example of SAL instruction's use to help pack BCD

IN AL, COUNTER_DIGIT   ; Unpacked BCD from
                       ; counter to AL

MOV CL, 04H   ; Set count for four bit positions

SAL AL, CL     ; Shift BCD to upper nibble, 0's in
; lower nibble. Ready to OR another BCD digit into
; lower nibble of AL.
```

EXAMPLE (NUMERICAL)

```
            ; CF = 0,   BX = 11100101 11010011
SAL BX,1    ; Shift BX register contents one bit left
            ; CF = 1, BX = 11001011 10100110
            ; OF = 0   PF = ?   SF = 1   ZF = 0
```

SAR INSTRUCTION—Shift operand bits right, new MSB = old MSB—SAR destination, count

This instruction shifts each bit in the specified destination some number of bit positions to the right. As a bit is shifted out of the MSB position, a copy of the old MSB is put in the MSB position. In other words the sign bit is copied into the MSB. The LSB will be shifted into CF. In the case of multiple bit shifts, CF will contain the bit most recently shifted in from the LSB. Bits shifted into CF previously will be lost. See diagram below.

MSB → MSB ————————————→ LSB → CF

The destination operand can be a byte or a word. It can be in a register or in a memory location specified by any one of the 24 addressing modes shown in Figure 3-8.

If the desired number of shifts is one, this can be specified by putting a 1 in the count position of the instruction. For shifts of more than one bit position the desired number of shifts is loaded into the CL register and CL is put in the count position of the instruction.

NOTE: The 80186 and the 80188 allow you to specify a shift of up to 32 bit positions with either an immediate number in the instruction or with a number in CL.

The flags are affected as follows: CF contains the bit most recently shifted in from the LSB. For a count of one the OF will be a 1 if the two MSBs are not the same. After a multibit SAR the OF will be 0. The SF and the ZF will be updated to show the condition of the destination. PF will only have meaning for an 8-bit destination. AF will be undefined after SAR.

The SAR instruction can be used to divide a signed byte or word by a power of two. Shifting a binary number right one bit position divides it by 2. Shifting a binary number right two bit positions divides it by 4. Shifting it three positions divides it by 8, etc. For unsigned numbers a 0 is put in the MSB after the old MSB is shifted right. (See discussion of SHR instruction.) For signed binary numbers the sign bit must be copied into the new MSB as the old sign bit is shifted right. This is necessary to retain the correct sign in the result. SAR shifts the operand right and copies the sign bit into the MSB as required for this operation. Using SAR to do a divide by 2, however, gives slightly different results than using the IDIV instruction to do the same job. IDIV always truncates a signed result toward zero. For example, an IDIV of 7 by 2 gives 3 and an IDIV of −7 by 2 gives −3. SAR always truncates a result in a downward direction. Using SAR to divide 7 by 2 gives 3, but using SAR to divide −7 by 2 gives −3.

EXAMPLES (CODING)

```
SAR DI, 1    ; Shift word in DI one bit position right,
             ; new MSB = old MSB

MOV CL, 02H   ; Load desired number of shifts in CL
SAR WORD PTR [BP], CL   ; Shift word at offset [BP]
; in stack segment right two bit positions. Two MSBs
; are now copies of original MSB.
```

EXAMPLES (NUMERICAL)

```
              ; AL = 00011101 = +29 decimal CF = 0
SAR AL, 1     ; Shift signed byte in AL right
              ; to divide by 2.
              ; AL = 00001110 = +14 decimal. CF = 1
              ; OF = 0  PF = 0  SF = 0  ZF = 0
              ; BH = 11110011 = -13 decimal
SAR BH, 1     ; Shift signed byte in BH right to
              ; divide by 2
              ; BH = 11111001 = -7 decimal CF = 1
              ; OF = 0  PF = 1  SF = 1  ZF = 0
```

SBB INSTRUCTION—Subtract with borrow—SBB destination, source

SUB INSTRUCTION—Subtract—SUB destination, source

These instructions subtract the number in the indicated source from the number in the indicated destination and put the result in the indicated destination. For subtraction the carry flag, CF, functions as a borrow flag. The carry flag will be set after a subtraction if the number in the specified source is larger than the number in the specified destination. In other words, the carry/borrow flag will be set if a borrow was required to do the subtraction. The Subtract instruction, SUB, subtracts just the contents of the specified source from the contents of the specified destination. The Subtract with Borrow instruction, SBB, subtracts the contents of the source and the contents of the CF from the indicated destination. The source may be an immediate number, a register, or a memory location specified by any of the 24 addressing modes shown in Figure 3-8. The destination may be a register or a memory location. The source and the destination cannot both be memory locations in the same instruction. The source and the destination must both be of type byte or they must both be of type word. If you want to subtract a byte from a word, you must first move the byte to a word location such as an extended register and fill the upper byte of the word with 0's. The AF, CF, OF, PF, SF, and ZF are updated by the SUB instruction.

EXAMPLES (CODING):

```
SUB CX, BX          ; Subtract contents of BX from
                    ; contents of CX Leave result in CX
SBB CH, AL          ; Subtract contents of AL and
                    ; contents of CF
                    ; from contents of CH. Result in CH.
SUB AX, 3427H       ; Subtract immediate number
                    ; 3427H from AX
SBB BX, [3427H]     ; Subtract word at displacement
                    ; 3427H in DS
                    ; and contents of CF from BX.
SUB PRICES [BX], 04H   ; Subtract 04 from byte at
effective address PRICES[BX] if PRICES declared with
DB. Subtract 04 from word at effective address
PRICES[BX] if PRICES declared with DW.
SBB CX, TABLE[BX]   ; Subtract word from effective
                    ; address TABLE[BX] and
                    ; status of CF from CX
SBB TABLE[BX], CX   ; Subtract CX and status of CF
                    ; from word in memory at
                    ; effective address TABLE[BX]
```

EXAMPLES(NUMERICAL):

```
; Example subtracting unsigned numbers
             ; CL = 10011100 = 156 decimal
             ; BH = 00110111 = 55 decimal
SUB CL, BH   ; Subtract BH from CL. Result:
             ; CL = 01100101 = 101 decimal
             ; CF = 0, AF = 0, PF = 1, OF = 0,
             ; SF = 0, ZF = 0

; Two examples subtracting Signed numbers
             ;          (a)
             ; CL = 00101110 =+46 decimal
             ; BH = 01001010 =+74 decimal
SUB CL, BH   ; Results:
             ; CL = 11100100 = -28 decimal
             ; CF = 1, borrow required
             ; AF = 0  PF = 1  ZF = 0
             ; SF = 1, result negative
             ; OF = 0, magnitude of result
             ; fits in 7 bits

             ;          (b)
             ; CL = 10100010 = -95 decimal
             ; BH = 01001100 = +76 decimal
SUB CL, BH   ; Results:
             ; CL = 01010101 = +85 decimal
             ; CF = 1, borrow required
             ; AF = 0  PF = 1  ZF = 0
             ; SF = 0, result positive !
             ; OF = 1, invalid result
```

The overflow flag being set indicates that the magnitude of the expected result, −171 decimal, is too large to fit in the 7 bits used for the magnitude in an 8-bit signed number. If the Interrupt on Overflow instruction, INTO, has been executed, this error will cause the 8086 to perform a software interrupt procedure. Part of this procedure is a user-written subroutine to handle the error.

NOTES: The SBB instruction allows you to subtract two multibyte numbers because any borrow produced by subtracting less-significant bytes is included in the result when the SBB instruction executes. Although the examples above were for 8-bit numbers to save space, the principles are the same for 16-bit numbers. For 16-bit signed numbers, however, the SF is a copy of bit 15, and the least-significant 15 bits of the number are used to represent the magnitude. Also, the PF and the AF only function for the lower 8 bits.

SCAS/SCASB/SCASW INSTRUCTION—Scan string byte or a string word

SCAS compares a string byte with a byte in AL or a string word with word in AX. The instruction affects the flags, but it does not change either the operand in AL(AX) or the operand in the string. The string to be scanned must be in the extra segment and DI must contain the offset of the byte or the word to be compared. After SCAS executes, DI will be automatically incremented or decremented to point to the next element in the string. For byte strings DI will be incremented or decremented by one, and for word strings DI will be incremented or decremented by two. If the direction flag is cleared (0), then DI will be incremented after SCAS. If the direction flag is set (1), then DI will be decremented after SCAS. SCAS affects the AF, CF, OF, PF, SF, and ZF. This instruction is often used with a repeat prefix to find the first occurrence of a specified byte or word in a string.

EXAMPLE:

```
; Scan a text string of 80 characters for a carriage
; return
          MOV AL, 0DH   ; Byte to be scanned for into AL
MOV DI, OFFSET TEXT_STRING   ; Offset of string
                             ; to DI

          MOV CX, 80   ; CX used as element counter
          CLD          ; Clear DF so DI autoincrements
REPNE SCAS TEXT_STRING   ; Compare byte in
                         ; string with byte in AL
```

NOTE: Scanning is repeated while the bytes are not equal and it is not end of the string. If a carriage return 0DH is found, ZF = 1 and DI will point at the next byte after the carriage return in string. If a carriage return is not found then CX = 0 and ZF = 0. The assembler uses the name of the string to determine whether the string is of type byte or type word. Instead of using the name you can tell the assembler directly the type of the string by using the mnemonic SCASB for a byte string and SCASW for a word string.

SHL/SAL INSTRUCTION—Shift operand bits left, put zero in LSB(s)—SHL/SAL destination, count

SAL and SHL are two mnemonics for the same instruction. Please refer to the discussions of this instruction under the heading SAL/SHL.

SHR INSTRUCTION—Shift operand bits right, put zero in MSB(s)—SHR destination, count

This instruction shifts each bit in the specified destination some number of bit positions to the right. As a bit is shifted right out of the MSB position, a 0 is put in its place. The bit shifted out of the LSB position goes to the CF. In the case of a multiple bit shift, CF will contain the bit most recently shifted in from the LSB. Bits shifted into CF previously will be lost. See diagram below.

0 → MSB ——————————→ LSB → CF

The destination operand can be a byte or a word. It can be in a register or in a memory location specified by any one of the 24 addressing modes shown in Figure 3-8.

If the desired number of shifts is one, this can be specified by putting a 1 in the count position of the instruction. For shifts of more than one bit position the desired number of shifts is loaded into the CL register, and CL is put in the count position of the instruction.

NOTE: The 80186 and 80188 allow you to specify a shift of up to 32 bit positions with either an immediate number in the instruction or a number in CL.

The flags are affected by SHR as follows: CF contains the bit most recently shifted in from the LSB. For a count of one, OF will be a 1 if the two MSBs are not both 0's. For multiple bit shifts, OF is meaningless. The SF and ZF will be updated to show the condition of the destination. PF will only have meaning for the lower eight bits of destination. AF is undefined.

The SHR instruction can be used to divide an unsigned binary number by a power of two. Shifting a binary number one bit position to the right and putting 0 in the MSB divides the number by two. Shifting the number two bit positions divides it by 4. Shifting it three bit positions divides it by 8, etc. When an odd number is divided with this method, the result will be truncated. In other words, dividing 7 by 2 will give a result of 3.

EXAMPLES (CODING)

```
SHR BP, 1   ; Shift word in BP one bit position right,
            ; 0 in MSB

MOV CL, 03H          ; Load desired number of shifts
                     ; into CL

SHR BYTE PTR [BX]    ; Shift byte at offset [BX] in
                     ; data segment
                     ; 3 bits right.
                     ; 0's in 3 MSBs.

; Example of SHR Used to Help Unpack Two BCD
; Digits in AL to BH and BL

MOV BL, AL     ; Copy packed BCD to BL
AND BL, 0FH    ; Mask out upper nibble. Low BCD
               ; digit now in BL.

MOV CL, 04H    ; Load count for shift in CL
SHR AL, CL     ; Shift AL four bit positions right and
               ; put 0's in upper 4 bits
MOV BH, AL     ; Copy upper BCD nibble to BH
```

EXAMPLES (NUMERICAL)

```
           ; SI = 10010011 10101101   CF = 0
SHR SI,1   ; Shift contents of SI register right one bit
           ; position, SI =  01001001 11010110

           ; CF = 1   OF = 1   PF = ?   SF = 0
           ; ZF = 0
```

STC INSTRUCTION—Set the carry flag to a one

STC does not affect any other flags.

STD INSTRUCTION—Set the direction flag to a one

STD is used to set the direction flag to a one so that SI and/or DI will automatically be decremented to point to the next string element when one of the string instructions executes. If the direction flag is set, SI and/or DI will be decremented by one for byte strings, and by two for word strings. STD affects no other flags. Please refer to Chapter 5 and the discussion of the REP prefix in this chapter for examples of the use of this instruction.

STI INSTRUCTION—Set interrupt flag (IF)

Setting the interrupt flag to a one enables the INTR interrupt of the 8086 after the next instruction after STI. An interrupt signal on this input will then cause the 8086 to interrupt program execution, push the return address and flags on the stack, and execute an interrupt service procedure. An IRET instruction at the end of the interrupt service procedure will restore the flags which were pushed on the stack, and return execution to the interrupted program. Because STI does not allow the INTR input to be enabled until the instruction after STI executes, the instruction sequence STI—IRET will return execution to the interrupted program before another interrupt will be recognized. This is important to keep the stack from filling up in systems which have many different interrupts. STI does not affect any other flags.

Please refer to Chapter 8 for a thorough discussion of interrupts.

EXAMPLE:

```
STI    ; Enable interrupts after next instruction
IRET   ; Return from interrupt service procedure.
       ; Interrupts enabled after return.
```

STOS/STOSB/STOSW INSTRUCTION—Store byte or word in string

The STOS instruction copies a byte from AL or a word from AX to a memory location in the extra segment. In effect it replaces a string element with a byte from AL or a word from AX. DI is used to hold the offset of the memory location in the extra segment. After the copy, DI is automatically incremented or decremented to point to the next string element in memory. If the direction flag, DF, is cleared, then DI will automatically be incremented by one for a byte string or incremented by two for a word string. If the direction flag is set, DI will be automatically decremented by one for a byte string or decremented by two for a word string. STOS does not affect any flags.

EXAMPLES:

```
MOV DI, OFFSET TARGET_STRING   ; Point DI at
                               ; destination string
STOS TARGET_STRING             ; Assembler uses string
```
name to determine whether string is of type byte or type word. If byte string, then string byte replaced with contents of AL. If word string, then string word replaced with contents of AX.

```
MOV DI, OFFSET TARGET_STRING   ; Point DI at
                               ; destination string
STOSB                          ; "B" added to STOS
```
mnemonic directly tells assembler to replace byte in string with byte from AL. STOSW would tell assembler directly to replace a word in the string with a word from AX.

SUB INSTRUCTION—Subtract—SUB destination, source

Please refer to the discussion of this instruction under the heading SBB.

TEST INSTRUCTION—AND operands to update flags—TEST destination, source

This instruction ANDs the contents of a source byte or word with the contents of the specified destination word. Flags are updated, but neither operand is changed. The TEST instruction is often used to set flags before a conditional jump instruction.

The source operand can be an immediate number, the contents of a register, or the contents of a memory location specified by one of the 24 addressing modes shown in Figure 3-8. The destination operand can be from a register or from a memory location. The source and the destination cannot both be memory locations in an instruction. The CF and OF are both 0's after TEST. The PF, SF, and ZF will be updated to show the results of the ANDing. AF will be undefined. PF only has meaning for the lower eight bits of the destination.

EXAMPLES (CODING)

```
TEST AL, BH          ; AND BH with AL, no result.
                     ; Update PF, SF, ZF.

TEST CX, 0001H       ; AND CX with immediate number
                     ; 0001H no result stored.
                     ; Update PF, SF, ZF.

TEST BP, [BX][DI]    ; AND word at offset [BX][DI] in
                     ; data segment with word in BP,
                     ; no results stored.
                     ; Update PF, SF, and ZF.

; Example of a Polling Sequence Using TEST

AGAIN: IN AL, 2AH         ; Read port with strobe
                          ; connected to LSB
       TEST AL, 01H       ; AND immediate 01H with AL
                          ; to test if LSB of AL is 1 or 0.
                          ; ZF = 1 if LSB of result is 0.
                          ; No result stored.
       JZ AGAIN           ; Read port again if LSB = 0
```

EXAMPLES (NUMERICAL)

```
                 ; AL = 01010001
TEST AL, 80H     ; AND immediate 80H with AL to test
                 ; if MSB of AL is 1 or 0.
                 ; ZF = 1 if MSB of AL =0.
```

```
; AL = 01010001 (Unchanged)
; PF = 0   SF = 0
; ZF = 1 because ANDing produced 00
```

WAIT INSTRUCTION—Wait for test signal or interrupt signal

When this instruction executes, the 8086 enters an idle condition where it is doing no processing. The 8086 will stay in this idle state until a signal is asserted on the 8086 TEST input pin, or until a valid interrupt signal is received on the INTR or the NMI interrupt input pins. If a valid interrupt occurs while the 8086 is in this idle state, the 8086 will return to the idle state after the interrupt service procedure executes. It returns to the idle state because the address of the WAIT instruction is the address pushed on the stack when the 8086 responds to the interrupt request. WAIT affects no flags. The WAIT instruction is used to synchronize the 8086 with external hardware such as the 8087 math coprocessor. In Chapter 11 we describe how this works.

XCHG INSTRUCTION—XCHG destination, source

The XCHG instruction exchanges the contents of a register with the contents of another register or the contents of a register with the contents of a memory location(s). The instruction cannot directly exchange the contents of two memory locations. A memory location can be specified as the source or as the destination by any of the 24 addressing modes summarized in Figure 3-8. The source and destination must both be words, or they must both be bytes. The segment registers cannot be used in this instruction. No flags are affected by this instruction.

EXAMPLES:

```
XCHG AX, DX            ; Exchange word in AX
                       ; with word in DX

XCHG BL, CH            ; Exchange byte in BL
                       ; with byte in CH

XCHG AL, PRICES [BX]   ; Exchange byte in AL with
                       ; byte in memory at
                       ; EA = PRICES [BX] in DS
```

XLAT/XLATB INSTRUCTION—Translate a byte in AL

The XLAT instruction replaces a byte in the AL register with a byte from a lookup table in memory. Before the XLAT instruction can be executed the lookup table containing the values for the new code must be put in memory, and the offset of the starting address of the lookup table must be loaded in BX. To point to the desired byte in the lookup table the XLAT instruction adds the byte in AL to the offset of the start of the table in BX. It then copies the byte from the address pointed to by (BX + AL) back into AL. XLAT changes no flags. The section "Converting One Keyboard Code to Another" in Chapter 9 should clarify the use of the XLAT instruction.

EXAMPLE:

```
; 8086 routine to convert ASCII code byte to EBCDIC
; equivalent
; ASCII code byte is in AL at start. EBCDIC code in
; AL at end.
    MOV BX, 2800H   ; Point BX at start of EBCDIC
                    ; table in DS

    XLAT            ; Replace ASCII in AL with
                    ; EBCDIC from table
```

The XLAT instruction can be used to convert any code of 8 bits or less to any other code of 8 bits or less.

XOR INSTRUCTION—Exclusive OR corresponding bits of two operands—XOR destination, source

This instruction exclusive ORs each bit in a source byte or word with the same number bit in a destination byte or word. The result replaces the contents of the specified destination. The contents of the specified source will not be changed. The result for each bit position will follow the truth table for a two-input exclusive OR gate. In other words, a bit in the destination will be set to a 1 if that bit in the source and that bit in the original destination were not the same. A bit exclusive-ORed with a 1 will be inverted. A bit exclusive-ORed with a 0 will not be changed. Because of this you can use the XOR instruction to selectively invert or not invert bits in an operand.

The source operand can be an immediate number, the contents of a register, or the contents of a memory location specified by any one of the addressing modes shown in Figure 3-8. The destination can be a register or a memory location. The source and destination cannot both be memory locations in the same instruction. The CF and OF are both 0 after XOR. The PF, SF, and ZF are updated. AF is undefined after XOR.

NOTE: PF only has meaning for an 8-bit operand.

EXAMPLES (CODING):

```
XOR CL, BH    ; Byte in BH exclusive ORed with byte
              ; in CL. Result in CL. BH not changed.

XOR BP, DI    ; Word in DI exclusive ORed with word
              ; in BP. Result in BP. DI not changed.

XOR WORD PTR [BX], 00FFH   ; Exclusive OR
              ; immediate number 00FFH
              ; with word at offset [BX] in data
              ; segment. Result in memory
              ; location [BX].
```

EXAMPLE (NUMERICAL)

```
              ; BX = 00111101 01101001
              ; CX = 00000000 11111111
```

```
XOR BX, CX   ; Exclusive OR CX with BX,
             ; result in BX
             ; BX = 00111101 10010110
             ; Note bits in lower byte are inverted
             ; CF = 0   OF = 0   PF = 1   SF = 0
             ; ZF = 0   AF = ?
```

ASSEMBLER DIRECTIVES

The words defined in this section are directions to the assembler, they are not instructions for the 8086. The assembler directives described here are those for the Intel 8086 macro assembler and the IBM macro assembler, MASM. If you are using some other assembler, consult the manual for it to find the corresponding directives.

ASSUME

The ASSUME directive is used to tell the assembler the name of the logical segment it should use for a specified segment. The statement ASSUME CS:CODE_HERE, for example tells the assembler that the instructions for a program are in a logical segment named CODE_HERE. The statement ASSUME DS:DATA_HERE, tells the assembler that for any program instruction which refers to the data segment it should use the logical segment called DATA_HERE. If, for example, the assembler reads the statement MOV AX, [BX] after it reads this ASSUME, it will know that the memory location referred to by [BX] is in the logical segment DATA_HERE. You must tell the assembler what to assume for any segment you use in a program. If you use a stack in your program you must tell the assembler the name of the logical segment you have set up as a stack with a statement such as ASSUME SS:STACK_HERE. For a program with string instructions which use DI, the assembler must be told what to assume for the extra segment with a statement such as ASSUME ES:STRING_DESTINATION. For further discussion of the ASSUME directive refer to the appropriate section of Chapter 3.

DB—Define Byte

The DB directive is used to define a byte-type variable, or to set aside one or more storage locations of type byte in memory. The statement CURRENT_TEMPERATURE DB 42H, for example, tells the assembler to reserve 1 byte of memory for a variable named CURRENT_TEMPERATURE and to put the value 42H in that memory location when the program is loaded into memory to be run. Refer to Chapter 3 for further discussion of the DB directive and to Chapter 4 for a discussion of how you can access variables named with a DB in your programs. Here are a few more examples of DB statements.

```
PRICES DB 49H, 98H, 29H   ; Declare array of 3
                          ; bytes named PRICES
                          ; and initialize 3 bytes
                          ; as shown

NAME_HERE DB 'THOMAS'     ; Declare array of
                          ; 6 bytes and initialize
                          ; with ASCII codes for
                          ; letters in THOMAS
```

TEMPERATURE_STORAGE DB 100 DUP(?) ; Set aside 100 bytes of storage in memory and give it the name TEMPERATURE_STORAGE, but leave the 100 bytes uninitialized. Program instructions will load values into these locations.

PRESSURE_STORAGE DB 20H DUP(0) ; Set aside 20H bytes of storage in memory, give it the name PRESSURE_STORAGE, and put 0 in all 20H locations.

DD—Define Doubleword

The DD directive is used to declare a variable of type doubleword or to reserve memory locations which can be accessed as type doubleword. The statement ARRAY_POINTER DD 25629261H, for example, will define a doubleword named ARRAY_POINTER, and initialize the doubleword with the specified value when the program is loaded into memory to be run. The low word, 9261H, will be put in memory at a lower address than the high word. A declaration of this type is often used with the LES or LDS instruction. The instruction LES DI, ARRAY_POINTER, for example, will copy the low word of this doubleword, 9261H, into the DI register, and the high word of the doubleword, 2562H, into the extra segment register.

DQ—Define Quadword

This directive is used to tell the assembler to declare a variable 4 words in length, or to reserve 4 words of storage in memory. The statement BIG_NUMBER DQ 243598740192A92BH, for example, will declare a variable named BIG_NUMBER, and initialize the 4 words set aside with the specified number when the program is loaded into memory to be run. The statement STORAGE DQ 100 DUP(0) reserves 100 quad words of storage and initializes them all to 0 when the program is loaded into memory to be run.

DT—Define Ten bytes

DT is used to tell the assembler to define a variable which is 10 bytes in length, or to reserve 10 bytes of storage in memory. The statement PACKED_BCD DT 1234567890 will declare an array named PACKED_BCD which is 10 bytes in length. It will initialize the 10 bytes with the values 1234567890 when the program is loaded into memory to be run. This directive is often used when declaring data arrays for the 8087 math coprocessor discussed in Chapter 11. The statement RESULTS DT 20H DUP(0) will declare an array of 20H blocks of 10 bytes each and initialize all 320 bytes to 00 when the program is loaded into memory to be run.

DW—Define Word

The DW directive is used to tell the assembler to define a variable of type word, or to reserve storage locations of type word in memory. The statement MULTIPLIER DW 437AH, for example, declares a variable of type word named MULTIPLIER. The statement also tells the assembler that the variable MULTIPLIER should be initialized with the value 437AH when the program is loaded into memory to be run. Refer to Chapter 3 for further discussion of the DW directive and how you can access variables named with a DW in your programs. Here are a few more examples of DW statements.

```
THREE_LITTLE_WORDS DW 1234H, 3456H,
5678H  ; Declare array of three words and initialize
with specified values

STORAGE DW 100 DUP(0)  ; Reserve an array of 100
words of memory and initialize all 100 words with
0000. Array is named STORAGE.

STORAGE DW 100 DUP(?)  ; Reserve 100 words of
storage in memory and give it the name STORAGE,
but leave the words uninitialized.
```

END—End Program

The END directive is put after the last statement of a program to tell the assembler that this is the end of the program module. The assembler will ignore any statements after an END directive, so you should make sure to only use one END directive at the very end of your program module. A carriage return is required after the END directive.

ENDP—End Procedure

This directive is used along with the name of the procedure to indicate the end of a procedure to the assembler. This directive, together with the procedure directive, PROC, is used to "bracket" a procedure. Here's an example.

```
SQUARE_ROOT PROC   ; Start of procedure
                   ; Procedure instruction
                   ; statements
SQUARE_ROOT ENDP   ; End of procedure
```

Chapter 5 shows more examples and describes how procedures are written and called.

ENDS—End Segment

This directive is used with the name of a segment to indicate the end of that logical segment. ENDS is used with the SEGMENT directive to "bracket" a logical segment containing instructions or data. Here's an example.

```
CODE_HERE SEGMENT   ; Start of logical segment
                    ; containing code
                    ; Instruction statements
CODE_HERE ENDS      ; End of segment named
                    ; CODE_HERE
```

EQU—Equate

EQU is used to give a name to some value or symbol. Each time the assembler finds the given name in the program it will replace the name with the value or symbol you equated with that name. Suppose, for example, you write the statement CORRECTION_FACTOR EQU 03H at the start of your program and later in the program you write the instruction statement ADD AL, CORRECTION_FACTOR. When it codes this instruction statement, the assembler will code it as if you had written the instruction ADD AL, 03H. The advantage of using EQU in this manner is that if CORRECTION_FACTOR is used 27 times in a program, and you want to change the value, all you have to do is change the EQU statement and reassemble the program. The assembler will automatically put in the new value each time it finds the name CORRECTION_FACTOR. If you had used 03H instead of the EQU approach, then you would have to try to find and change all 27 instructions yourself. Here are some more examples.

```
DECIMAL_ADJUST EQU DAA   ; Create clearer
                         ; mnemonic for DAA

STRING_START EQU [BX]    ; Give name to [BX]
```

EVEN—Align on Even Memory Address

As the assembler assembles a section of data declarations or instruction statements, it uses a location counter to keep track of how many bytes it is from the start of a segment at any time. The EVEN directive tells the assembler to increment the location counter to the next even address if it is not already at an even address. The 8086 can read a word from memory in one bus cycle if the word is at an even address. If the word starts on an odd address, the 8086 must do two bus cycles to get the 2 bytes of the word. Therefore, a series of words can be much more quickly read if they are on even addresses. When EVEN is used in a data segment, the location counter will simply be incremented to the next even address if necessary. When EVEN is used in a code segment, the location counter will be incremented to the next even address if necessary. A NOP instruction will be inserted in the location incremented over. Here's an example which shows why you might want to use EVEN in a data segment.

```
DATA_HERE SEGMENT
; Declare array of 9 bytes. Location
; counter will point to 0009 after
; assembler reads next statement.
SALES_AVERAGES DB 9 DUP(?)
EVEN  ; Increment location counter to 000AH
INVENTORY_RECORDS DW 100 DUP(0)
   ; Array of 100 words starting
   ; on even address for quicker read.
DATA_HERE ENDS
```

EXTRN

The EXTRN directive is used to tell the assembler that the names or labels following the directive are in some other assembly module. For example, if you want to call a procedure which is in a program module assembled at a different time from that which contains the CALL instruction, you must tell the assembler that the procedure is external. The assembler will then put information in the object code file so that the linker can connect the two modules together. For a reference to an external named variable you must specify the type of the variable as in the statement EXTRN DIVISOR:WORD. For a reference to a label you must specify whether the label is near (in a code segment with the same name), or far (in a code segment with a different name). The statement EXTRN SMART_DIVIDE:FAR tells the assembler that SMART_DIVIDE is a label of type far in another assembly module. Names or labels referred to as external in one module must be declared public with the PUBLIC directive in the module where they are defined.

EXTRN statements should usually be bracketed with SEGMENT—ENDS directives which identify the segment in which the external name or label will be found. Here's an example of how to do this.

```
PROCEDURES_HERE SEGMENT
    EXTRN SMART_DIVIDE:FAR   ; Found in segment
                             ; PROCEDURES_HERE
PROCEDURES_HERE ENDS
```

Refer to Chapter 5 for a thorough discussion of the use of the EXTRN and the PUBLIC directives.

GROUP—Group-Related Segments

The GROUP directive is used to tell the assembler to group the logical segments named after the directive into one logical group segment. This allows the contents of all of the segments to be accessed from the same group segment base. The assembler sends a message to the linker and/or locator telling it to link the segments so that the segments are physically in the same 64 Kbyte segment. Here's an example of the GROUP directive: SMALL_SYSTEM GROUP CODE_HERE, DATA_HERE, STACK_HERE
An appropriate ASSUME statement to follow this would be: ASSUME CS:SMALL_SYSTEM, DS:SMALL_SYSTEM, SS:SMALL_SYSTEM

LABEL

As the assembler assembles a section of data declarations or instruction statements, it uses a location counter to keep track of how many bytes it is from the start of a segment at any time. The LABEL directive is used to give a name to the current value in the location counter. The LABEL directive must be followed by a term which specifies the type you want associated with that name. If the label is going to be used as the destination for a jump or a call, then the label must be specified as type near or as type far. If the label is going to be used to reference a data item, then the label must be specified as type byte, type word, or type double word. Here's how we use the LABEL directive for a jump address.

```
ENTRY_POINT LABEL FAR   ; Can jump to here from
                        ; another segment
NEXT: MOV AL, BL        ; Cannot do a far jump
                        ; directly to a label
                        ; with a colon
```

Here's how we use the LABEL directive for a data reference.

```
STACK_HERE SEGMENT STACK
    DW 100 DUP(0)       ; Set aside 100 words
                        ; for stack
STACK_TOP LABEL WORD    ; Give name to next
                        ; location after last
                        ; word in stack
STACK_HERE ENDS
```

To initialize stack pointer then, MOV SP, OFFSET STACK_TOP.

LENGTH—Not implemented in IBM MASM

LENGTH is an operator which tells the assembler to determine the number of elements in some named data item such as a string or array. When the assembler reads the statement MOV CX, LENGTH STRING1, for example, it will determine the number of elements in STRING1 and code this number in as part of the instruction. When the instruction executes then, the length of the string will be loaded into CX. If the string was declared as a string of bytes, LENGTH will produce the number of bytes in the string. If the string was declared as a word string, LENGTH will produce the number of words in the string.

NAME

The NAME directive is used to give specific names to each assembly module when programs consisting of several modules are written. The statement NAME PC_BOARD, for example, might be used to name an assembly module which contains the instructions for controlling a printed-circuit-board-making machine.

OFFSET

OFFSET is an operator which tells the assembler to determine the offset or displacement of a named data item (variable) from the start of the segment which contains it. This operator is usually used to load the offset of a variable into a register so that the variable can be accessed with one of the indexed addressing modes. When the assembler reads the statement MOV BX, OFFSET PRICES, for example, it will determine the offset of the variable PRICES from the start of the segment in which PRICES is defined and code this displacement in as part of the instruction. When the instruction executes, this computed displacement will be loaded into BX. An instruction such as ADD AL, [BX] can then be used to add a value from PRICES to AL.

ORG—Originate

As the assembler assembles a section of data declarations or instruction statements, it uses a location counter to keep track of how many bytes it is from the start of a segment at any time. The location counter is automatically set to 0000 when the assembler starts reading a segment. The ORG directive allows you to set the location counter to a desired value at any point in the program. The statement ORG 2000H tells the assembler to set the location counter to 2000H, for example.

A "$" is often used to symbolically represent the current value of the location counter. The $ actually represents the next available byte location where the assembler can put a data or code byte. The $ is often used in ORG statements to tell the assembler to make some change in the location counter relative to its current value. The statement ORG $ + 100 tells the assembler to increment the value of the location counter by 100 from its current value. A statement such as this might be used in a data segment to leave 100 bytes of space for future use.

PROC—Procedure

The PROC directive is used to identify the start of a procedure. The PROC directive follows a name you give the procedure. After the PROC directive the term NEAR or the term FAR is used to specify the type of the procedure. The statement SMART_DIVIDE PROC FAR, for example, identifies the start of a procedure named SMART_DIVIDE and tells the assembler that the procedure is far (in a segment with a different name from that which contains the instruction which calls the procedure). The PROC directive is used with the ENDP directive to "bracket" a procedure. Refer to the ENDP discussion for an example of this. Also refer to Chapter 5 for a thorough discussion of how procedures are written and called.

PTR—Pointer

The PTR operator is used to assign a specific type to a variable or to a label. It is necessary to do this in any instruction where the type of the operand is not clear. When the assembler reads the instruction INC [BX], for example, it will not know whether to increment the byte pointed to by BX or increment the word pointed to by BX. We use the PRT operator to clarify how we want the assembler to code the instruction. The statement INC BYTE PRT [BX] tells the assembler that we want to increment the byte pointed to by BX. The statement INC WORD PTR [BX] tells the assembler that we want to increment the word pointed to by BX. The PTR operator assigns the type specified before PTR to the variable specified after PTR.

The PTR operator can be used to override the declared type of a variable. Suppose, for example, that we have declared an array of words with the statement WORDS DW 437AH, B972H, 7C41H. Normally we would access the elements in this array as words. However, if we want to access a byte in the array, we can do it with an instruction such as MOV AL, BYTE PTR WORDS.

We also use the PTR operator to clarify our intentions when we use indirect jump instructions. The statement JMP [BX], for example, does not tell the assembler whether to code the instruction for a near jump or for a far jump. If we want to do a near jump we write the instruction as JMP WORD PTR [BX]. If we want to do a far jump we write the instruction as JMP DWORD PTR [BX]. Please refer to Chapter 3 for further discussion of the 8086 jump instructions.

PUBLIC

Large programs are usually written as several separate modules. Each module is individually assembled, tested and debugged. When all the modules are working correctly, their object code files are linked together to form the complete program. In order for the modules to link together correctly, any variable name or label referred to in other modules must be declared public in the module where it is defined. The PUBLIC directive is used to tell the assembler that a specified name or label will be accessed from other modules. An example is the statement PUBLIC DIVISOR, DIVIDEND which makes the two variables, DIVISOR and DIVIDEND, available to other assembly modules.

If an instruction in a module refers to a variable or label in another assembly module, the assembler must be told that it is external with the EXTRN directive. Refer to the discussion of the EXTRN directive to see how this is done.

SEGMENT

The SEGMENT directive is used to indicate the start of a logical segment. Preceding the SEGMENT directive is the name you want to give the segment. The statement CODE_HERE SEGMENT, for example, indicates to the assembler the start of a logical segment called CODE_HERE. The SEGMENT and ENDS directives are used to "bracket" a logical segment containing code or data. Refer to the ENDS directive for an example of how this is done.

Additional terms are often added to a SEGMENT directive statement to indicate some special way in which we want the assembler to treat the segment. The statement CODE_HERE SEGMENT WORD tells the assembler that we want this segment located on the next available word address when the segments are located and given absolute addresses. Without this WORD addition the segment will be located on the next available paragraph (16-byte) address which might waste as much as 15 bytes of memory. The statement CODE_HERE SEGMENT

PUBLIC tells the assembler that this segment will be put together with other segments named CODE_HERE from other assembly modules when the modules are linked together.

SHORT

The SHORT operator is used to tell the assembler that only a 1-byte displacement is needed to code a jump instruction. If the jump destination is after the jump instruction in the program, the assembler will automatically reserve 2 bytes for the displacement. Using the short operator saves 1 byte of memory by telling the assembler that it only needs to reserve 1 byte for this particular jump. In order for this to work the destination must be in the range of −128 bytes to +127 bytes from the address of the instruction after the jump. The statement JMP SHORT NEARBY_LABEL is an example of the use of SHORT.

TYPE

The TYPE operator tells the assembler to determine the type of a specified variable. The assembler actually determines the number of bytes in the type of the variable. For a byte-type variable the assembler will give a value of 1. For a word-type variable the assembler will give a value of 2, and for a doubleword-type variable it will give a value of 4. The TYPE operator can be used in an instruction such as ADD BX, TYPE WORD_ARRAY, where we want to increment BX to point to the next word in an array of words.

CHAPTER

7 8086 System Connections, Timing, and Troubleshooting

In Chapter 2 we showed that a microcomputer consists of a CPU, memory, and ports. We also showed in Chapter 2 that these parts are connected together by three major buses: the address bus, the control bus, and the data bus. For Chapters 3 through 6, however, we made little mention of the hardware of a microcomputer because we were mostly concerned in these chapters with how a microcomputer is programmed. In this chapter we come back to take a closer look at the hardware of a microcomputer.

OBJECTIVES

At the conclusion of this chapter you should be able to:

1. Draw a diagram showing how RAMs, ROMs, and ports are added to an 8086 CPU to make a simple microcomputer.
2. Describe how addresses sent out on the 8086 data bus are demultiplexed.
3. Describe the signal sequence on the buses as a simple 8086-based microcomputer fetches and executes an instruction.
4. Describe how address decoding circuitry gives a specific address to each device in a system and makes sure only one device is enabled at a time.
5. Calculate the required access time for a memory device or port to work correctly in an 8086 microcomputer system.
6. List a series of steps you might take to troubleshoot a malfunctioning microcomputer system that once worked.

8086 HARDWARE OVERVIEW

In previous chapters we worked with what is often called the *programmer's model* of the 8086. This model shows features, such as internal registers, number of address lines, and number of data lines, that we need in order to be able to program the device. Now we will look at the hardware model of the 8086 so that we can show how a microcomputer system is built around it. We will also discuss in this chapter the hardware connections for an 8088. A later chapter will show the hardware connections for the 80186 and 80286 microprocessors.

To get started, let's take a look at the pin diagram for the 8086 in Figure 7-1. Don't be overwhelmed by all of those pins with strange mnemonics next to them. You don't need to learn the detailed functions of all of these at once. We describe and show the use of these different pins throughout the next few chapters as needed. When you later need to refresh your memory of the function of a particular pin, consult the index to find the section where that particular pin or signal is described in detail. For reference, the complete data sheet showing all of the pin descriptions is shown in the appendix.

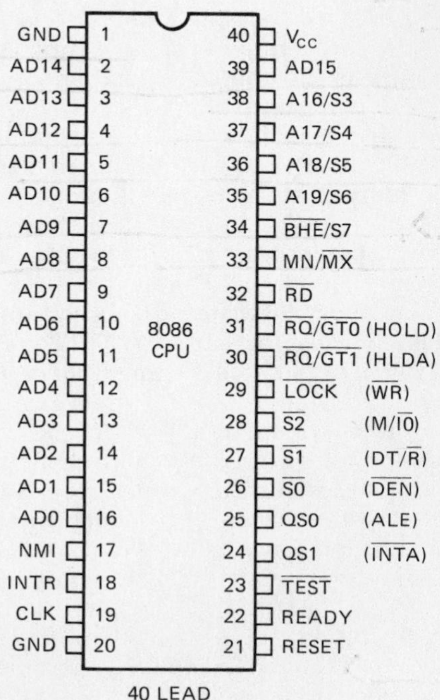

FIGURE 7-1 8086 pin diagram. *(Intel Corporation)*

Note first in Figure 7-1 that V_{cc} is on pin 40 and ground on pins 1 and 20. Next find the clock input labeled CLK on pin 19. An 8086 requires a clock signal from some external, crystal-controlled clock generator to synchronize internal operations in the processor. Different versions of the 8086 have maximum clock frequencies ranging from 5 MHz to 10 MHz.

Now look for the address and data bus lines. Remember from previous chapters that the 8086 has a 20-bit address bus and a 16-bit data bus. A look at Figure 7-1, however, does not immediately reveal these 36 lines. The reason is that the designers multiplexed the lower 16 address lines out on the data bus to minimize the number of pins needed. The 8086 could then be put in a 40-pin package. In other words, the data bus lines, labeled AD0 through AD15 in Figure 7-1, are used at the start of a machine cycle to send out addresses, and later in the machine cycle they are used to send or receive data. The 8086 sends out a signal called *address latch enable*, or ALE on pin 25 to let external circuitry know that an address is on the data bus. Later we will discuss in detail how this works. The upper 4 bits of an address are sent out on the lines labeled A16/S3 through A19/S6. The double mnemonic on these pins indicates that address bits A16 through A19 are sent out on these lines during the first part of a machine cyle and status information, which identifies the type of operation to be done in that cycle, is sent out on these lines during a later part of the cycle.

Having found the address bus and the data bus, now look for the control bus lines. Some of the control bus lines on a microprocessor usually have mnemonics such as $\overline{RD}$, $\overline{WR}$, and M/$\overline{IO}$. Pin 32 of the 8086 in Figure 7-1 is labeled $\overline{RD}$. This signal will be asserted low when the 8086 is reading data from memory or from a port. Pin 29 has a label $\overline{WR}$ next to it. However, pin 29 also has a label $\overline{LOCK}$ next to it, because this pin has two functions. The function of this pin and the functions of the other pins between 24 and 31 depend on the *mode* in which the 8086 is operating.

The operating mode of the 8086 is determined by the logic level applied to the MN/$\overline{MX}$ input, pin 33. If pin 33 is assserted high, then the 8086 will function in *minimum mode* and pins 24 through 31 will have the functions shown in parentheses next to the pins in Figure 7-1. Pin 29, for example, will function as $\overline{WR}$ which will go low any time the 8086 writes to a port or to a memory location. Pin 28 will function as M/$\overline{IO}$. The 8086 will assert this signal high if it is reading from or writing to a memory location, and it will assert this signal low if it is reading from or writing to a port. The $\overline{RD}$, $\overline{WR}$, and M/$\overline{IO}$ signals form the heart of the control bus for a minimum mode 8086 system. The 8086 is operated in minimum mode in systems where it is the only microprocessor on the system buses. Later in this chapter we discuss in detail the operation of a minimum mode system.

If the MN/$\overline{MX}$ pin is asserted low, then the 8086 is in *maximum mode*. In this mode pins 24 through 31 will have the functions described by the mnemonics next to the pins in Figure 7-1. In this mode the control bus signals ($\overline{S0}$, $\overline{S1}$, $\overline{S2}$) are sent out in encoded form on pins 26, 27, and 28. An external bus controller device decodes these signals to produce the control bus signals required for a system which has two or more microprocessors sharing the same buses. In Chapter 11 we discuss how a maximum mode 8086 system operates.

Here's a brief introduction to the functions of a few more of the 8086 pins. First note pin 21, the RESET input. If this input is made high, the 8086 will, no matter what it is doing, reset its DS, SS, ES, IP, and flag registers to all 0's. It will set its CS register to FFFFH. When the RESET signal is removed from pin 21, the 8086 will then fetch its next instruction from physical address FFFF0H. This address is produced in the 8086 Bus Interface Unit (BIU) by shifting the FFFFH in the CS register 4 bits left and adding the 0000H in the instruction pointer to it. The first instruction you want to execute after a reset is put at this address, FFFF0H. An example would be the first instruction of a monitor program such as the one on the SDK-86.

Next notice that the 8086 has two interrupt inputs, *nonmaskable interrupt* (NMI) input on pin 17 and the *interrupt* (INTR) input on 18. A signal can be applied to one of these inputs to cause the 8086 to interrupt the program it is executing and go execute a specified procedure. We might, for example, connect a temperature sensor from a steam boiler to an interrupt input on an 8086. If the boiler gets too hot, then it will assert the interrupt input. This will cause the 8086 to stop executing its current program and go execute a procedure to turn off the fuel supply to the boiler. At the end of the procedure we can return to executing the interrupted program. Chapter 8 describes in detail the operation and uses of interrupts.

Now that you have an overview of most of the major pins on an 8086, we will take a closer look at what is happening on the buses during a read operation and during a write operation.

Basic Signal Flow on 8086 Buses

Figure 7-2 shows, in timing diagram form, the activities on the 8086 buses during simple read and write operations. Don't be overwhelmed by all of the lines on this diagram. Their meaning should become clear to you as we work our way through the diagram.

8086 BUS ACTIVITIES DURING A READ MACHINE CYCLE

The first line to look at in Figure 7-2 is the *clock waveform* at the top. This represents the crystal-controlled clock signal sent to the 8086 from an external clock generator device as shown in the top left of Figure 7-3. One cycle of this clock is referred to as a *state*. A state is measured from the 50 percent point on the falling edge of one clock pulse to the 50 percent point on the falling edge of the next clock pulse. T1 in the figure is a state. Each basic bus operation such as reading a byte from memory or writing a word to a port requires some number of states. The group of states required for a basic bus operation is called a *machine cycle*. The total time it takes the 8086 to fetch and execute an instruction is

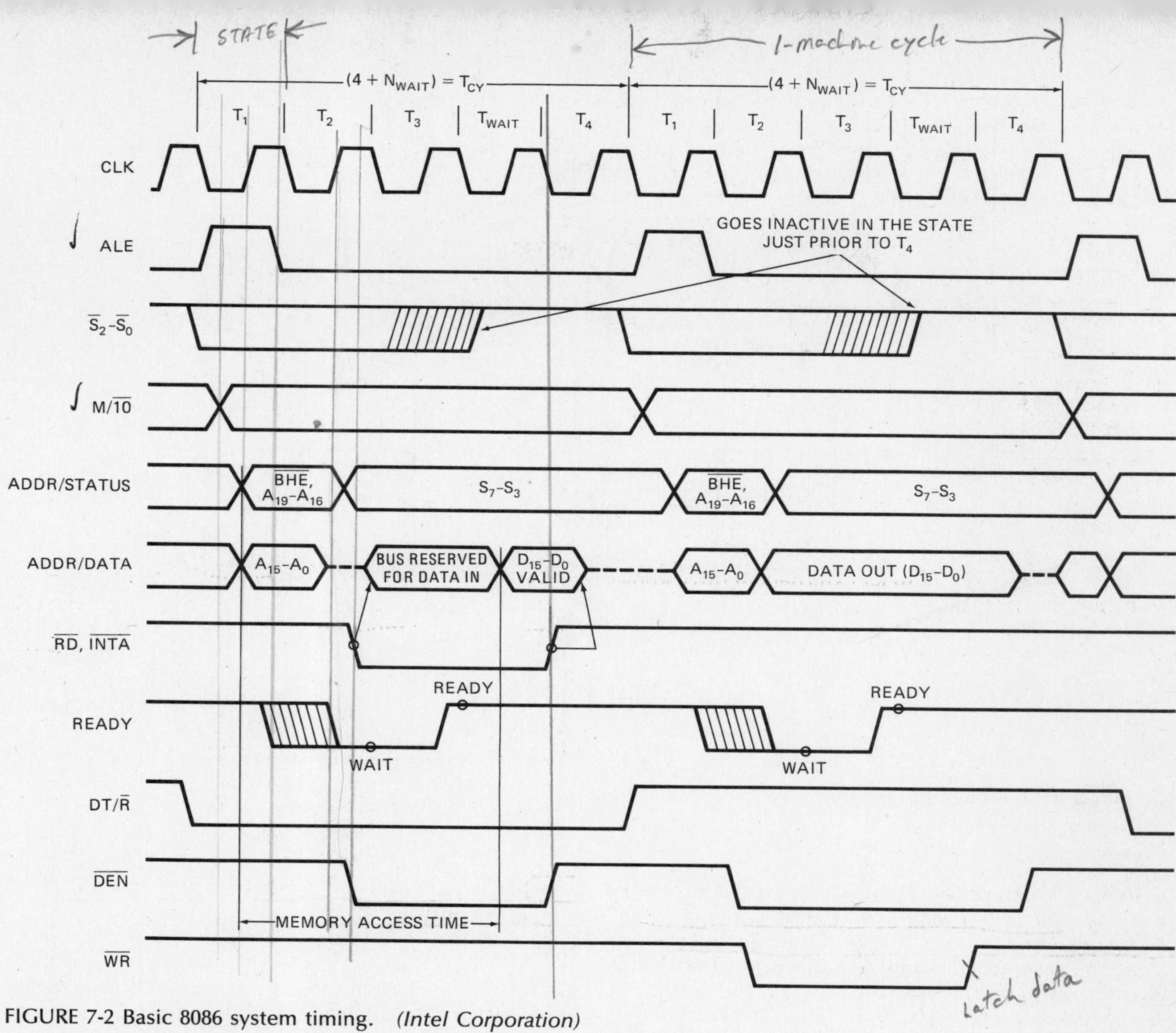

FIGURE 7-2 Basic 8086 system timing. *(Intel Corporation)*

called an *instruction cycle*. An instruction cycle consists of one or more machine cycles. To summarize this, then, an instruction cycle is made up of machine cycles, and a machine cycle is made up of states. What we are going to examine here are the activities that occur on the buses during a read machine cycle.

During T1 of a read machine cycle an 8086 first asserts the M/$\overline{\text{IO}}$ signal. It will assert this signal high if it is going to do a read from memory during this cycle, and it will assert M/$\overline{\text{IO}}$ low if it is going to do a read from a port during this cycle. The timing diagram in Figure 7-2 shows two waveforms for the M/$\overline{\text{IO}}$ signal, because the signal may be going low or going high for a read cycle. The point where the two waveforms cross indicates the time at which the signal becomes valid for this machine cycle. Likewise, in the rest of the timing diagram, crossed lines are used to represent the time when information on a line or group of lines is changed. Incidentally, the best way to analyze a timing diagram such as this one is to think of time as a vertical line moving from left to right across the diagram. With this technique you can easily see the sequence of activities on the signal lines as you move your imaginary time line across the waveforms.

After asserting M/$\overline{\text{IO}}$, the 8086 sends out a high on the *address latch enable signal*, ALE. This signal is connected to the enable input (STB) of the 8282 latches as shown in Figure 7-3. As you can also see in Figure 7-3, the data inputs of these latches are connected to the 8086 AD0–AD15, A16–A19, and $\overline{\text{BHE}}$ (*bus high enable*) lines. After the 8086 asserts ALE high, it sends out on these lines the address of the memory location that it wants to read. Since the latches are enabled by ALE being high, this address information passes through the latches to their outputs. The 8086 then makes the ALE output low. This disables the latches and holds the address information latched on the latch outputs. The address information on the latch outputs can now be used to select the desired memory or port location.

Observe in the timing diagram in Figure 7-2 how the activity on the ADDR/DATA lines is represented. The first point at which the two waveforms cross represents

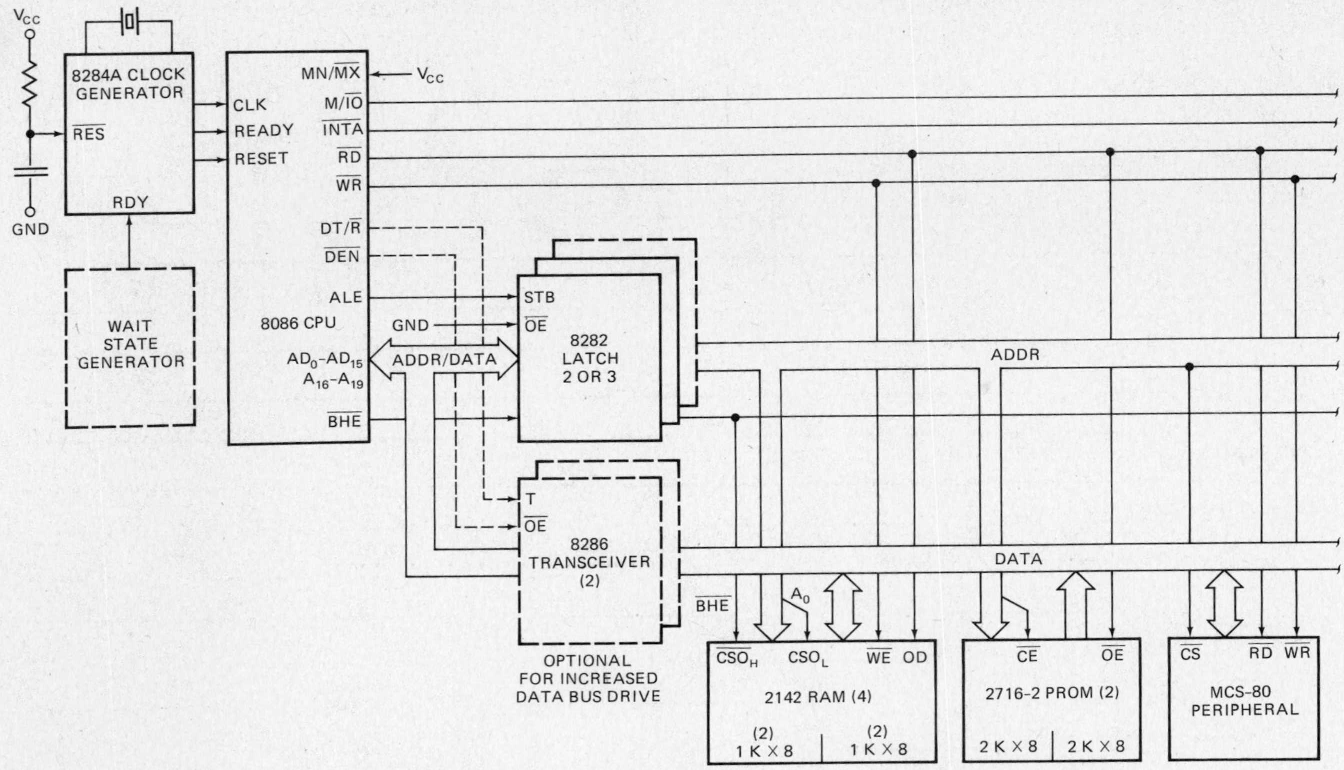

FIGURE 7-3 Basic 8086 minimum mode system. *(Intel Corporation)*

the time at which the 8086 has put a valid address on these lines. These two waveforms DO NOT indicate that all 16 lines are going high or going low at this point. Again, the crossed lines indicate the time at which a valid address is on the bus.

Since the address information is now held on the latches, the 8086 does not need to send it out anymore. Therefore, as shown by a dashed line in Figure 7-2, the 8086 floats the AD0–AD15 lines so that they can be used to input data from memory or from a port. At about the same time the 8086 also removes the $\overline{BHE}$ and A16–A19 information from the upper lines and sends out some status information on those lines.

The 8086 is now ready to read data from the addressed memory location or port, so near the end of state T2 the 8086 asserts its $\overline{RD}$ signal low. As you will see in a later section of the chapter, this signal is used to enable the addressed memory device or port device. When enabled the addressed device will put a byte or word of data on the data bus. In other words, asserting the $\overline{RD}$ signal low causes the addressed device to put data on the data bus. This cause-and-effect relationship is shown on the timing diagram in Figure 7-2 by an arrow going from the falling edge of RD to the "bus reserved for data in" section of the ADDR/DATA waveforms. The bubble on the tail of the arrow always is put on the signal transition or level that causes some action, and the point of the arrow always indicates the action caused. Arrows of this sort are only used to indicate the effect a signal from one device will have on another device. They are not usually used to indicate signal cause and effect within a device.

Now, referring to Figure 7-2 again, find the section of the AD0–AD15 waveform marked off as memory access time near the bottom of the diagram. The addressed memory location or port must put valid data on the data bus before the end of this indicated time interval. Suppose, for example, that we are addressing a ROM. ROMs typically have an access time of a few hundred nanoseconds. In other words, after we apply an address to a ROM, it will be a few hundred nanoseconds before we will see valid data on the outputs of the ROM. If the access time for a ROM in a system is longer than the maximum memory access time specified for the 8086, then the 8086 will not get valid data when it addresses that ROM. A later section of this chapter shows you how to calculate whether a particular ROM, RAM, or port device has a short enough access time to work properly in a given 8086 system. For now, however, we just need you to understand the concept so we can show you one way that an 8086 can accommodate a slow device.

If you look at the pin diagram for the 8086 in Figure 7-1, you should find an input labeled READY. If this pin is high the 8086 is "ready" and operates normally. If the READY input is made low at the right time in a machine cycle, the 8086 will insert one or more *WAIT* states between T3 and T4 in that machine cycle. The timing diagram in Figure 7-2 shows an example of this. An external hardware device is set up to pulse READY low before the rising edge of the clock in T2. After the 8086 finishes

T3 of the machine cycle, it enters a WAIT state. During a WAIT state the signals on the buses remain the same as they were at the start of the WAIT state. The address of the addressed memory location is held on the output of the latches so it does not change. As you can see from the timing diagram in Figure 7-2, the control bus signals, M/$\overline{IO}$ and $\overline{RD}$, also do not change during the WAIT state, Twait. If the READY input is made high again during T3 or during the WAIT state as shown in Figure 7-2, then after one WAIT state the 8086 will go on with the regular T4 of the machine cycle. What we have done by inserting the WAIT state is to freeze the action on the buses for one clock cycle. This gives the addressed device an extra clock cycle time to put out valid data. If, for example, we want to use a slower (cheaper) ROM in a system, we can add a simple circuit which pulses the READY input low each time that ROM is addressed. Note in Figure 7-3 that a READY input signal is usually passed through the 8284 clock generator IC so that the signal actually applied to the 8086 is synchronized with the system clock. Incidentally, a cross-hatched section on a waveform indicates that the signal may be changed at any time during that time interval.

If the 8086 READY input is still low at the end of a WAIT state, then the 8086 will insert another WAIT state. The 8086 will continue inserting WAIT states until the READY input is made high again. In later chapters we show more applications using the READY input to insert WAIT states in a machine cycle.

Another look now at Figure 7-2 will show you that there are still two waveforms we haven't discussed yet. These two are the $\overline{DEN}$ signal and the DT/$\overline{R}$ signal. The $\overline{DEN}$ signal is used to enable bidirectional buffers on the data bus. Figure 7-3 shows how buffers such as 8286s are connected on the data bus in a system. For a very small system these buffers are not needed, but as more devices are added to a system they become necessary. Here's why. Most of the devices such as ROMs and RAMs used around microprocessors have MOS inputs, so on a dc basis they don't require much current. However, each input or output added to the system data bus, for example, acts like a capacitor of a few picofarads connected to ground. In order to change the logic state on these inputs from low to high, all of this added capacitance must be charged. To change the logic state to a low, the capacitance must be discharged. If we add more than a few devices on the data bus lines, the 8086 outputs cannot supply enough current drive to charge and discharge the circuit capacitance rapidly. Therefore, we add high-current drive buffers to do the job.

We must be able to float the outputs of buffers used on the data bus so that they do not interfere with other activities on these lines. For example, we certainly don't want data bus buffer outputs enabled onto the data bus while the 8086 is putting out the lower 16 bits of an address on these lines. The *data enable signal*, $\overline{DEN}$, from the 8086 will enable the data bus buffers when it is asserted low. Buffers used on the data bus must also be bidirectional, because we both send data out on the data bus and read data in on the data bus. The *data transmit/receive signal*, DT/$\overline{R}$, from the 8086 is used to specify the direction in which the buffers are enabled. When DT/$\overline{R}$ is asserted high, the buffers will, if enabled by $\overline{DEN}$, transmit data from the 8086 to ROM, RAM, or ports. When DT/$\overline{R}$ is asserted low, the buffers, if enabled by $\overline{DEN}$, will allow data to come in from ROM, RAM, or ports to the 8086.

Now let's look back at Figure 7-2 to see how $\overline{DEN}$ and DT/$\overline{R}$ function during a read machine cycle. During T1 of the machine cycle the 8086 asserts DT/$\overline{R}$ low to put the data buffers in the receive mode. Then, after the 8086 finishes using the data bus to send out the lower 16 address bits, it asserts $\overline{DEN}$ low to enable the data bus buffers. The data put on the data bus by an addressed port or memory will then be able to come in through the buffer to the 8086.

We can summarize the activities on the buses during an 8086 read machine cycle as follows. The 8086 asserts M/$\overline{IO}$ high if the read is to be from memory and asserts M/$\overline{IO}$ low if the read is going to be from a port. At about the same time, the 8086 asserts ALE high to enable some external latches. It then sends out $\overline{BHE}$ and, on the lines AD0–A19, the desired address. The 8086 then pulls the ALE line low to latch the address information in the external latches. After the 8086 is through using lines AD0–AD15 for an address, it removes the address from these lines and puts the lines in the input mode (floats them). It then asserts its $\overline{RD}$ signal low. The $\overline{RD}$ signal going low turns on the addressed memory or port which then puts the desired data on the data bus. To complete the cycle the 8086 brings the $\overline{RD}$ line high again. This causes the addressed memory or port to turn off, thereby floating the bus again. If the 8086 READY input is made low before or during T2 of a machine cycle, the 8086 will insert WAIT states as long as the READY input is low. When READY is made high the 8086 will continue on with T4 of the machine cycle. WAIT states can be used to give slow devices additional time to put out valid data. If a system is large enough to need data bus buffers, then the 8086 $\overline{DEN}$ signal will be asserted low to enable the buffers, and the 8086 DT/$\overline{R}$ signal will be asserted high to set the buffers for output or asserted low to set the buffers for input.

8086 BUS ACTIVITIES DURING A WRITE MACHINE CYCLE

Now that we have analyzed the 8086 bus activities for a read machine cycle, let's take a look at the timing diagram for a write machine cycle in the right-hand half of Figure 7-2. Most of this diagram should look very familiar to you because it is very similar to the read cycle.

During T1 of a write machine cycle the 8086 asserts M/$\overline{IO}$ low if the write is going to be to a port and it asserts M/$\overline{IO}$ high if the write is going to be to memory. At about the same time the 8086 raises ALE high to enable the address latches. The 8086 then outputs $\overline{BHE}$ and the address that it will be writing to on AD0–A19. When reading from or writing to a port, lines A16–A19 will always be low, because the 8086 only sends out 16-bit port addresses. After this address has had time to pass through the latches, the 8086 brings ALE low again to latch the address on the outputs of the latches. In addition to holding the address, these latches also function as buffers for the address lines. After the address information is latched, the 8086 removes the address information from AD0–AD15 and puts the desired data on the data bus. It then asserts its $\overline{\text{WR}}$ signal low. The $\overline{\text{WR}}$ signal is used to turn on the memory or port where the data is to be written. After the addressed memory or port has had time to accept the data from the data bus, the 8086 raises the $\overline{\text{WR}}$ signal line high again and floats the data bus.

If the READY input is made low by external hardware before or during T2 of the machine cycle, the 8086 will insert a WAIT state after T3. If the READY input is made high before the end of the WAIT state, the 8086 will go on with state T4 as soon as it finishes the WAIT state. If the READY input is still low just before the end of the WAIT state, the 8086 will insert another WAIT state. It will continue to insert WAIT states until READY is made high. During a WAIT state the logic levels on the buses are held constant. Therefore, if we have a memory or port device which needs more time to absorb the data from the data bus, we can use some external hardware to pulse the READY line low each time this device is addressed. Pulling the READY line low will cause the 8086 to insert one or more WAIT states in the machine cycle, thus giving the addressed device more time to absorb the data.

If the system is large enough to need buffers on the data bus, then DT/$\overline{\text{R}}$ will be connected to the buffers. During a write cycle the 8086 asserts DT/$\overline{\text{R}}$ high to put the buffers in the transmit mode. When the 8086 asserts $\overline{\text{DEN}}$ low to enable the buffers, data output from the 8086 will pass through the buffers to the addressed port or memory location.

Work your way across the timing diagrams for the read and write machine cycles in Figure 7-2 until you feel that you understand the sequence of activities that occur. Understanding this well will make later sections easier to understand.

FIGURE 7-4 Intel SDK-86 microprocessor development board. *(Intel Corporation)*

Analyzing a Minimum-Mode System, the SDK-86

The previous sections showed how a clock generator, address latches, and data bus buffers are connected to an 8086 to form what we might call the minimum-mode CPU group. As shown in Figure 7-3 this group of ICs generates the address bus, data bus, and control bus signals needed for an 8086 minimum-mode system. In this major section of the chapter we discuss how this CPU group is connected with ROM, RAM, ports, and other devices to form a system. The system we use for this discussion is the *Intel SDK-86 system design kit*, a readily available 8086-based unit suitable for building the prototypes of small microcomputer-based instruments.

Figure 7-4 shows a photograph of an SDK-86 board. From the photograph you can see that, in addition to the microcomputer ICs, the board has a hexadecimal keypad, some seven-segment displays, and a large open area for adding more ROM, RAM, ports, or other circuitry. A monitor program in ROM on the board allows you to enter, execute, and debug machine code programs using the on-board hex keypad or an external CRT terminal connected to the serial port on the board. The board comes with 2 Kbytes of RAM and sockets where you can add another 2 Kbytes. The board also has six 8-bit parallel ports which you can program to be inputs or outputs. To get a better idea of the hardware functions on the board and the devices used to implement these functions, let's look at the detailed block diagram of the SDK-86 in Figure 7-5.

Whenever you are approaching a system that is new to you, it is a good idea to carefully study the detailed block diagram of the system before you start digging into the actual schematics. The schematics for even a small system such as this are often spread over many pages. Without the overview that the block diagram gives, it is very difficult for you to see how all of the schematic pieces fit together.

The first parts to look at in Figure 7-5 are the 8086 CPU and the 8284 *clock generator*. Note that the 8284 has a 14.7456-MHz crystal connected to it. According to the data sheet for the the 8284, the frequency of the crystal connected to the 8284 will be divided by three to produce the clock signal sent to the 8086. Therefore, the actual 8086 clock frequency for this board will be 4.915 MHz. Another clock signal called PCLK is also produced by the 8284. This signal is used as a general-purpose clock signal throughout the system. The hardware RST signal and the RDY signal are also passed through the 8284 to synchronize them with the clock signal before they are sent to the 8086. As you can see in Figure 7-5, considerable circuitry is connected to the RDY1 input so that several conditions can cause a WAIT state to be inserted in a machine cycle. The structure labeled W27 through W34 above the WAIT state generator in Figure

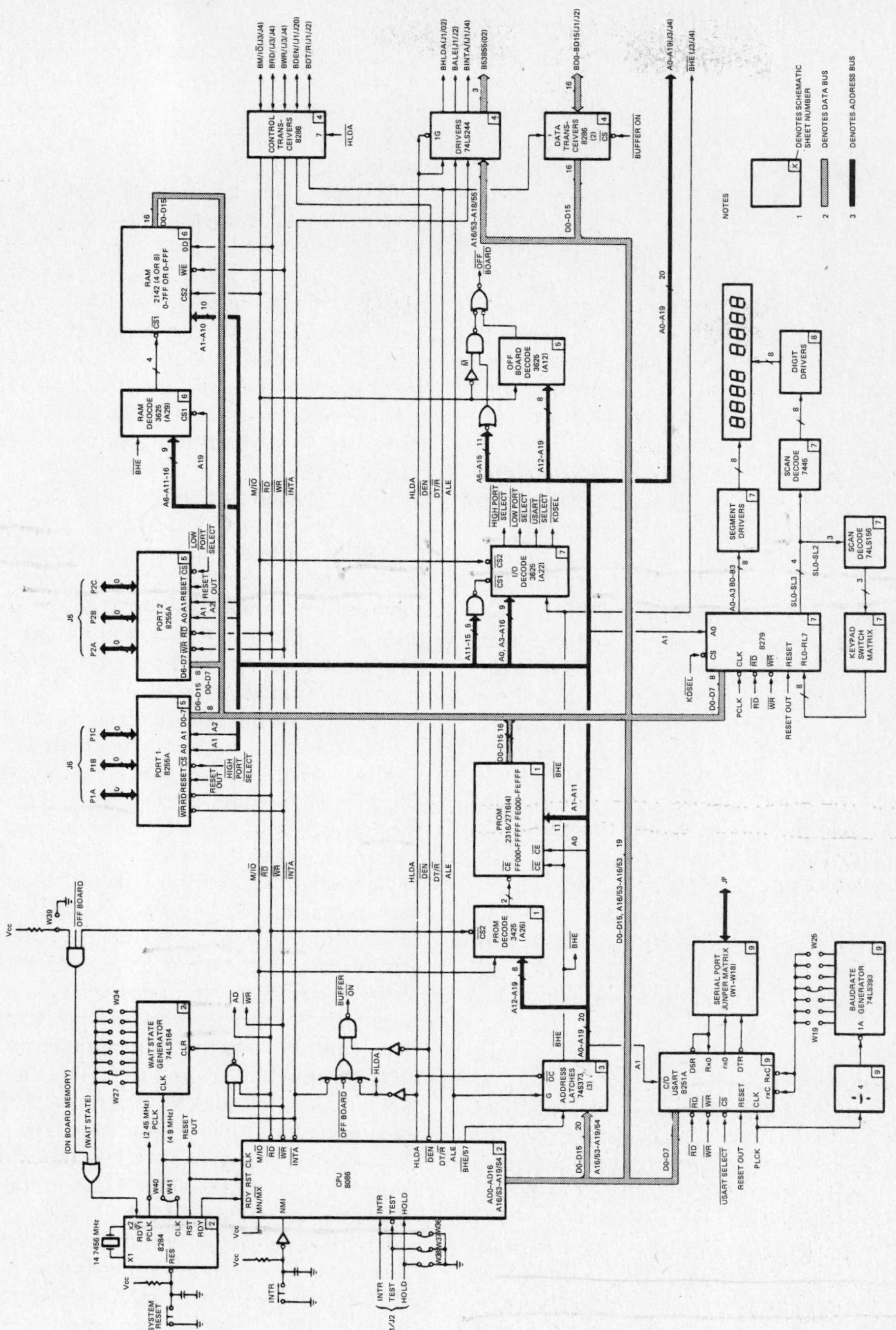

FIGURE 7-5 Detailed block diagram of SDK-86 board. *(Intel Corporation)*

7-5 represents wire wrap pins which can be jumpered to specify the number of WAIT states desired in a machine cycle. We will discuss this in detail later.

By this time you may have noticed that the symbols for the 8284, 8086, and WAIT state generator each have a small box containing a 2 in their lower right corner. This number tells you that the detailed schematic for these parts will be found on sheet number two of the set of schematics. Figure 7-6 shows the complete schematic set for the SDK-86 board, so you can check this out if you wish.

The next parts to look for in the block diagram of the SDK-86 are the *address latches* which you know are needed to grab address information during T1 of a machine cycle. The box just below the 8086 in the diagram indicates that three 74S373s are used for address latches. AD0–AD15, A16–A19, and $\overline{BHE}$ are connected to the inputs of these latches. As expected, ALE is used to enable the latches. The information held on the output of the latches after ALE goes low is A0–A19 and $\overline{BHE}$. The /20 after A0–A19 on the output of the latches indicates that there are 20 lines in this group. A heavy black line is used to distinguish the demultiplexed address bus from the data bus.

Next, follow the address lines to the right on the diagram to find the ROM in the system. The box labeled PROM indicates that four 2316 or 2716 devices are used for EPROM in the system. Each of these devices holds 2 Kbytes of memory. Also indicated in the PROM box in the diagram are the absolute addresses where these devices are located. Two of the EPROMs occupy the address space from FE000H–FEFFFH, and the other two occupy the address space from FF000H–FFFFFH. The 3625 PROM decoder connected to these EPROMs has two related purposes. The first is to produce a signal which turns on the desired EPROM when you send out an address in the range assigned to that device. The second purpose is to make sure that only one device is outputting onto the data bus at a time. We discuss in detail later how address decoders are connected to give a desired address to a particular device in a system. Note that the enable input, $\overline{CS2}$, of the decoder PROM is connected to the $\overline{RD}$ signal from the 8086. The result of this is that the PROM decoder will only be enabled if the 8086 is doing a read operation. Can you see why you would not want an EPROM to be turned on if you accidentally sent out an address in its range during a write operation? The answer is that attempting to write to the outputs of an EPROM can burn out both the ROM and buffer outputs. The "*A26*" in the PROM decoder box of the block diagram, incidentally, indicates that the 3625 IC will be numbered *XA26* on the schematic sheet where it is found.

Follow the address bus to the upper right corner of the block diagram in Figure 7-5 to find how RAM is implemented in this system. The board comes with 2 Kbytes of static RAM contained in four 2142s, but there are sockets for another four 2142s. The initial four devices occupy the address space from 00000H–007FFH. If four more 2142s are added, they will be in the address space 00800H–00FFFH. Another 3625 is used here as a RAM decoder. As with the PROM decoder, the purposes of this device are to turn on a memory device which corresponds to the address sent out on the address bus, and to make sure that only one device at a time is outputting data on a data bus line. The 8086 can read or write a byte, or it can read or write a word. Therefore, 16 data lines are connected to the RAM block.

Now let's find the *system ports* in the block diagram in Figure 7-5. Two 8255As at the top of the page give the system *programmable* parallel ports. The term programmable in this case means that as part of your program, you send the 8255A a *control byte*. The control byte tells the 8255A whether you want a particular group of lines on the device to function as outputs or as inputs. In Chapter 9 we show you how to make up and send these control words. The two 8255As in this system can be used individually to input or output parallel bytes. They can also be used together to input or output words. For byte input or output operations, only one of the devices will be turned on by asserting its $\overline{CS}$ input low. For word input or output operations, both 8255As will be turned on by asserting their $\overline{CS}$ inputs low. The high byte of a word to be output, for example, will then be sent to one of the ports in the PORT 1 device. The low byte of the word to be output will go to the corresponding port in the PORT 2 device. To be more specific, if the high byte of an output word goes to port P1A, then the low byte of that word will go to port P2A. In a later section on address decoding, we show how the addresses work out for these ports.

Most systems need a serial port so they can communicate with CRT terminals, modems, and other devices which require data to be sent and received in serial form. As shown in the lower left corner of Figure 7-5 the SDK-86 uses an 8251A as a *serial port*. The letters USART on this device stand for *universal synchronous/asynchronous receiver transmitter*, which is quite a mouthful. Chapter 13 discusses the initialization and use of the 8251A. For now, just think of this device as two back-to-back shift registers. One shift register accepts a parallel byte from the system data bus and shifts it out the TxD output in serial form. The other shift register shifts in serial data from the RxD input and converts it to parallel bytes which can be read by the 8086 on the system data bus. The 8251A has only eight data inputs, so data can only be written to or read from the 8251A a byte at a time. Therefore, only the lower 8 bits of the data bus are connected to it. Each of the shift registers in the 8251A requires a clock signal with a frequency of 16 or 64 times the rate at which you want to shift data bits in or out. The clock for the transmit shift register is called TxC and the clock for the receive shift register is called RxC on the block diagram. These are tied together because you usually want to send and receive data at the same rates. The clock for these inputs is produced by dividing down the 2.45-MHz PCLK signal from the 8284 clock generator. Wire wrap jumper pins, W19–W25, allow you to select the desired TxC and RxC frequency from a divider chain in the *74LS393 baud rate generator*. *Baud rate* is a way of specifying the rate at which data bits are shifted in or out of a serial device. Baud rate for a device such as the 8251A is defined as one over the time per bit. If the time per bit is 3.33 ms, for example, then the baud rate is 300 baud. Common baud rates for serial data transmission are 300, 600, 1200, 2400, 9600, and 19,200.

The final port to discuss here is the 8279 in the bottom center of the SDK-86 block diagram (Figure 7-5). The 8279 is a *specialized input/output device* which has two major functions. The first function is to scan the hex keypad, detect when a key is pressed, debounce the signal from a pressed key, and store the code for the pressed key in an internal RAM where it can be read by the 8086. The second major function of the 8279 is to refresh the multiplexed display on the eight 7-segment LED displays. Seven-segment codes for the digits to be displayed are sent to a RAM in the 8279. The 8279 then

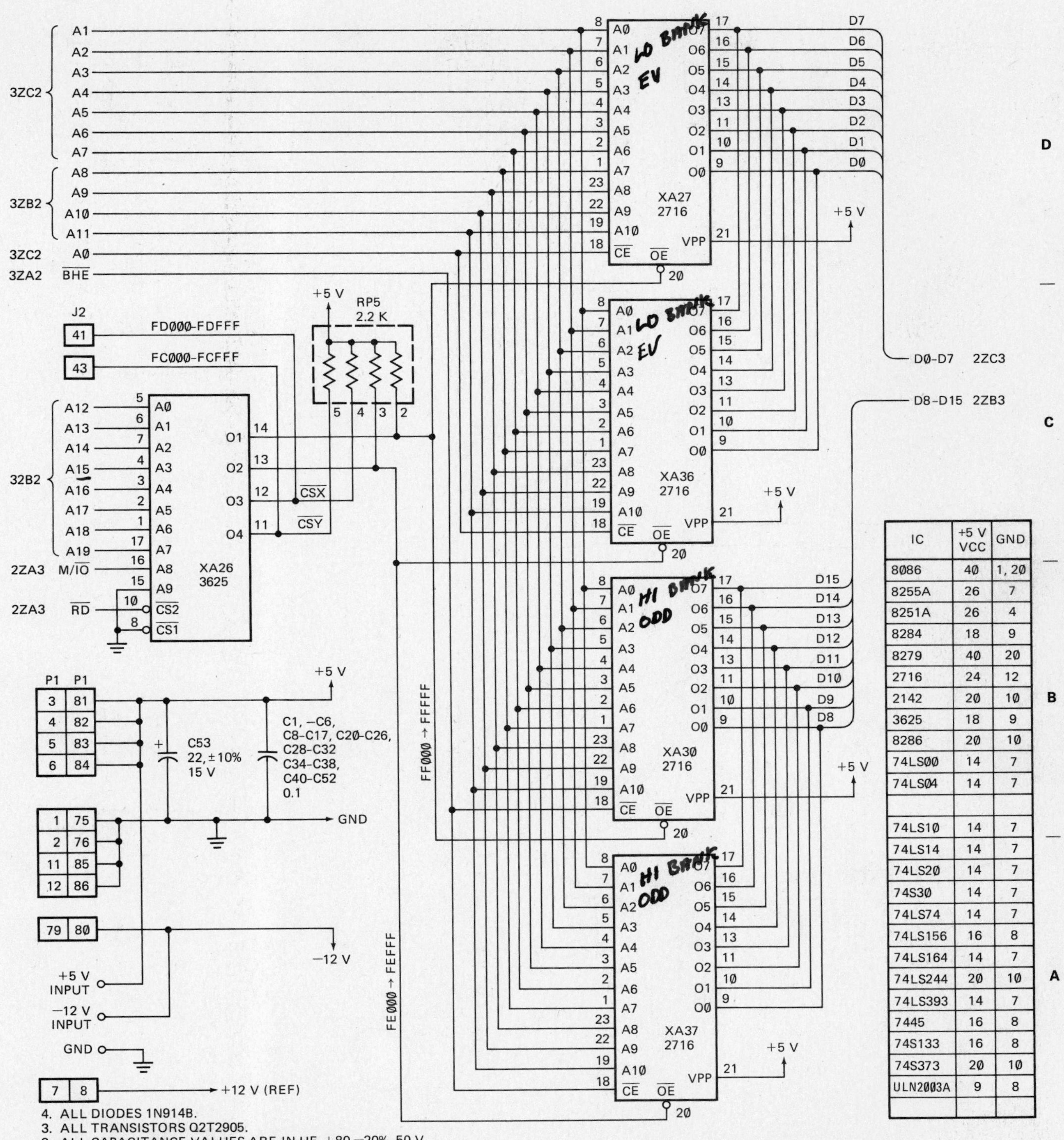

IC	+5 V VCC	GND
8086	40	1, 20
8255A	26	7
8251A	26	4
8284	18	9
8279	40	20
2716	24	12
2142	20	10
3625	18	9
8286	20	10
74LSØØ	14	7
74LSØ4	14	7
74LS1Ø	14	7
74LS14	14	7
74LS20	14	7
74S30	14	7
74LS74	14	7
74LS156	16	8
74LS164	14	7
74LS244	2Ø	10
74LS393	14	7
7445	16	8
74S133	16	8
74S373	2Ø	1Ø
ULN2ØØ3A	9	8

4. ALL DIODES 1N914B.
3. ALL TRANSISTORS Q2T2905.
2. ALL CAPACITANCE VALUES ARE IN UF, +80 –20%, 50 V.
1. ALL RESISTANCE VALUES ARE IN OHMS, ± 5%, 1/4 WATT.
NOTES: UNLESS OTHERWISE SPECIFIED,

FIGURE 7-6 SDK-86 complete schematics. (sheet 1 of 9) (*Intel Corporation*)

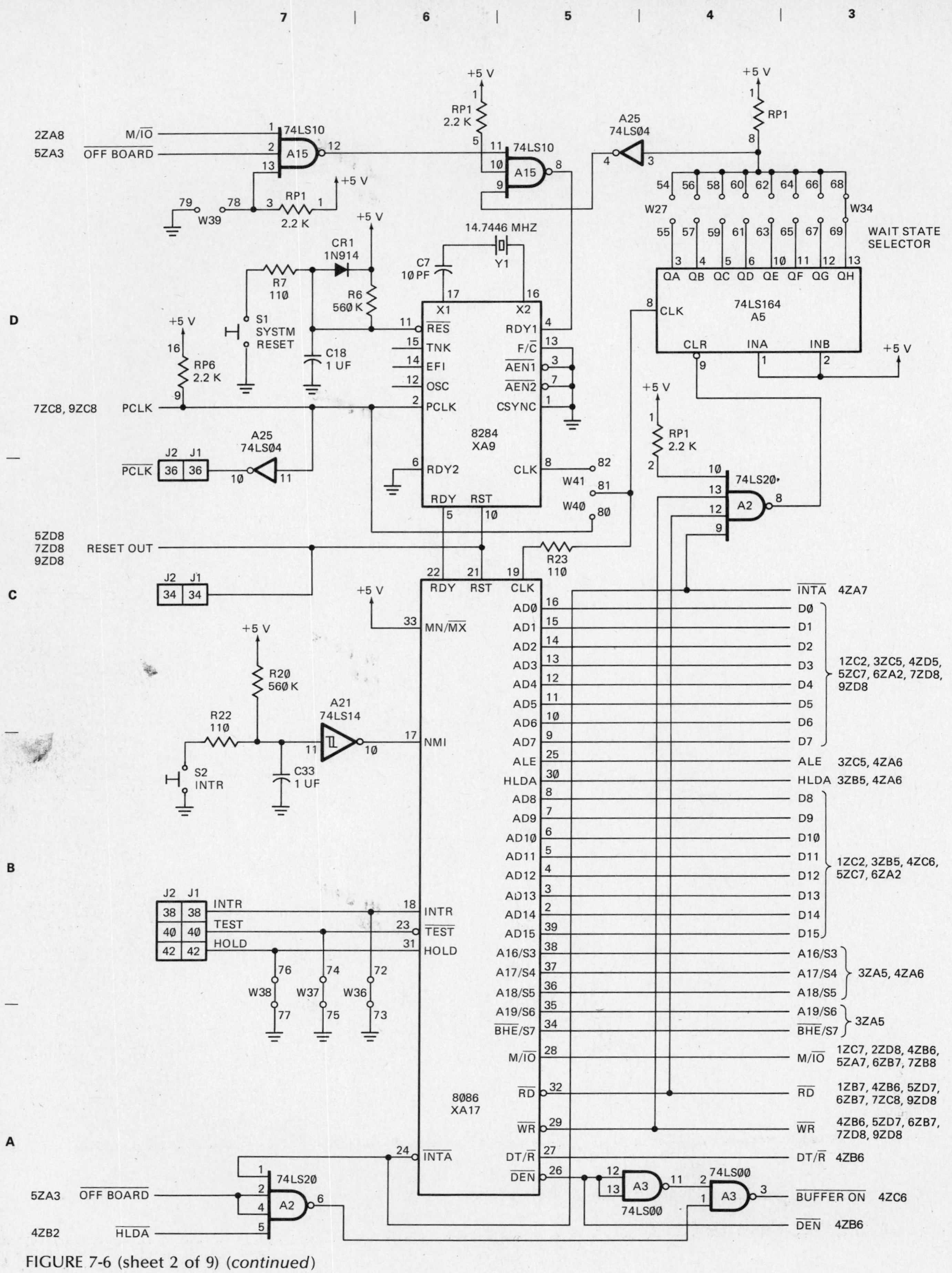

7 | 6 | 5 | 4 | 3

D

C

B

A

2ZA8 M/$\overline{IO}$
5ZA3 $\overline{OFF\ BOARD}$
74LS10 A15
RP1 2.2 K
W39
74LS10 A15
A25 74LS04
RP1
+5 V
14.7446 MHZ
Y1
C7 10 PF
CR1 1N914
R7 110
R6 560 K
S1 SYSTM RESET
RP6 2.2 K
C18 1 UF
7ZC8, 9ZC8 PCLK
J2 J1 36 36 $\overline{PCLK}$
A25 74LS04
8284 XA9
X1 X2 $\overline{RES}$ RDY1 TNK F/$\overline{C}$ EFI $\overline{AEN1}$ OSC $\overline{AEN2}$ PCLK CSYNC RDY2 CLK RDY RST
W41 W40
5ZD8 7ZD8 9ZD8 RESET OUT
J2 J1 34 34
W27 W34
WAIT STATE SELECTOR
QA QB QC QD QE QF QG QH
74LS164 A5
CLK CLR INA INB
RP1 2.2 K
74LS20 A2
R23 110
R20 560 K
R22 110
A21 74LS14
S2 INTR
C33 1 UF
MN/$\overline{MX}$ NMI
8086 XA17
$\overline{INTA}$ 4ZA7
D0–D7: 1ZC2, 3ZC5, 4ZD5, 5ZC7, 6ZA2, 7ZD8, 9ZD8
ALE 3ZC5, 4ZA6
HLDA 3ZB5, 4ZA6
D8–D15: 1ZC2, 3ZB5, 4ZC6, 5ZC7, 6ZA2
A16/S3, A17/S4, A18/S5: 3ZA5, 4ZA6
A19/S6, $\overline{BHE}$/S7: 3ZA5
M/$\overline{IO}$ 1ZC7, 2ZD8, 4ZB6, 5ZA7, 6ZB7, 7ZB8
$\overline{RD}$ 1ZB7, 4ZB6, 5ZD7, 6ZB7, 7ZC8, 9ZD8
$\overline{WR}$ 4ZB6, 5ZD7, 6ZB7, 7ZD8, 9ZD8
DT/$\overline{R}$ 4ZB6
$\overline{BUFFER\ ON}$ 4ZC6
$\overline{DEN}$ 4ZB6
J2 J1 38 38 INTR, 40 40 TEST, 42 42 HOLD
W38 W37 W36
$\overline{INTA}$ $\overline{TEST}$ HOLD
5ZA3 $\overline{OFF\ BOARD}$
4ZB2 $\overline{HLDA}$
74LS20 A2
74LS00 A3

FIGURE 7-6 (sheet 2 of 9) (*continued*)

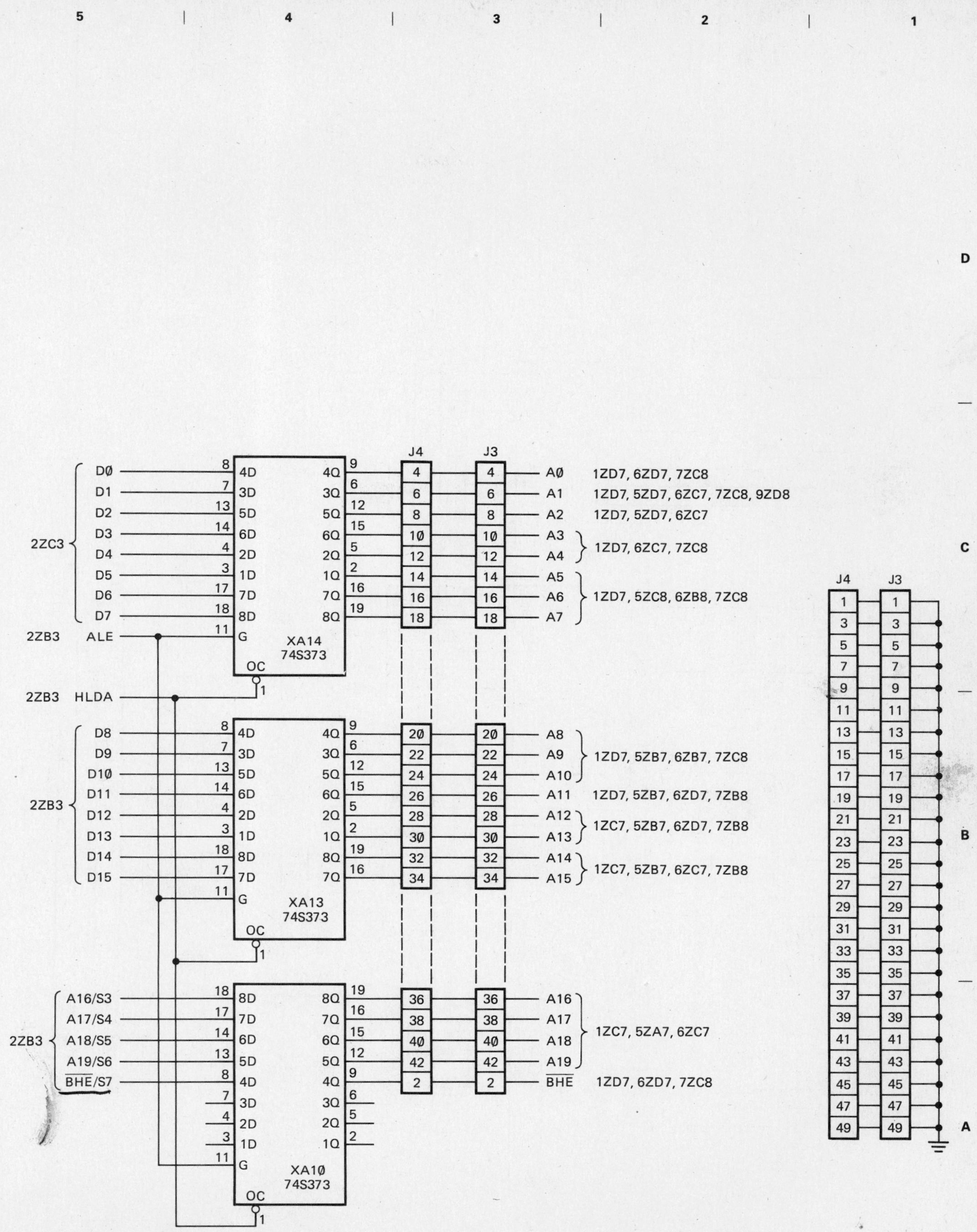

FIGURE 7-6 (sheet 3 of 9) (*continued*)

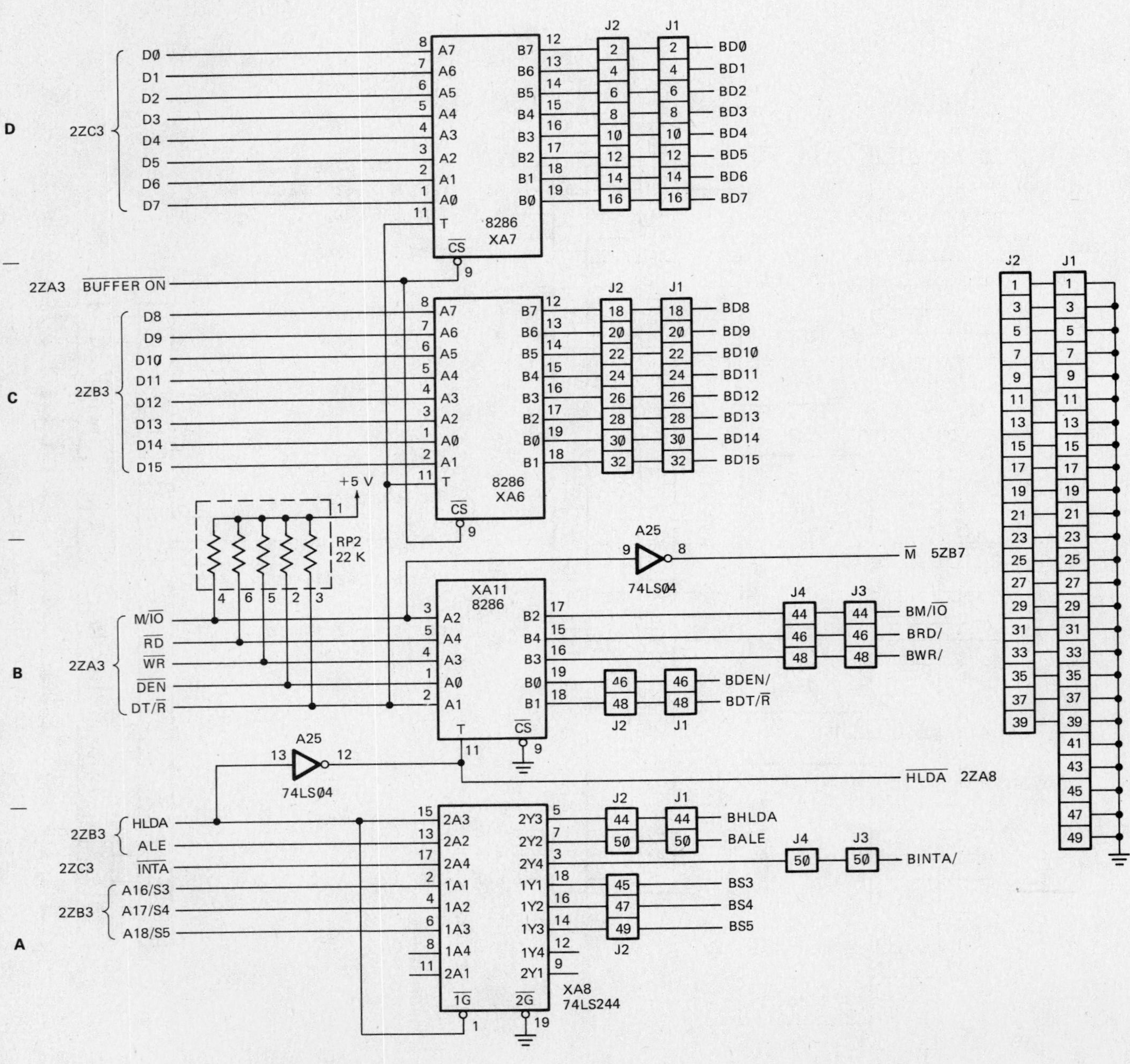

FIGURE 7-6 (sheet 4 of 9) (*continued*)

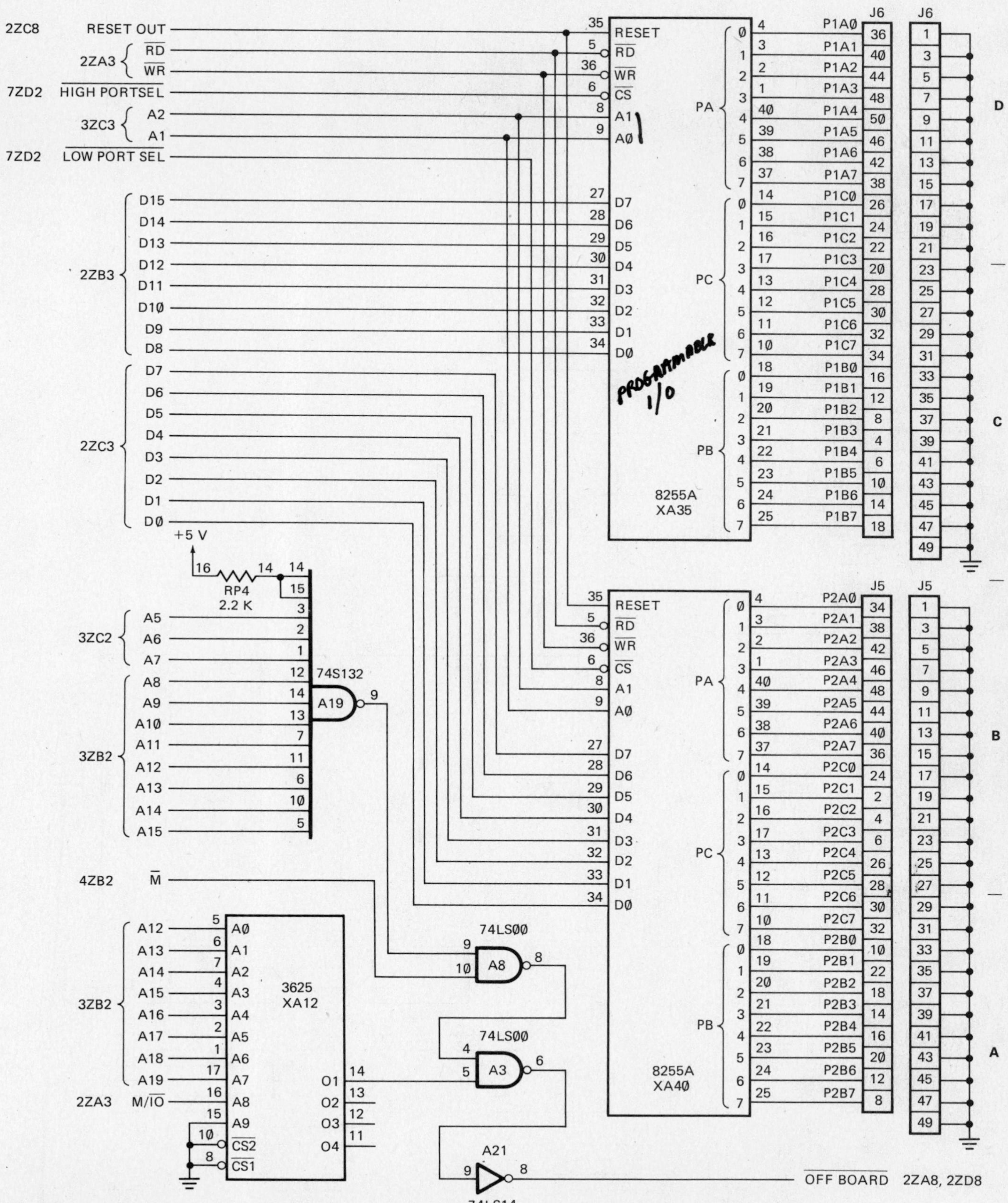

FIGURE 7-6 (sheet 5 of 9) (*continued*)

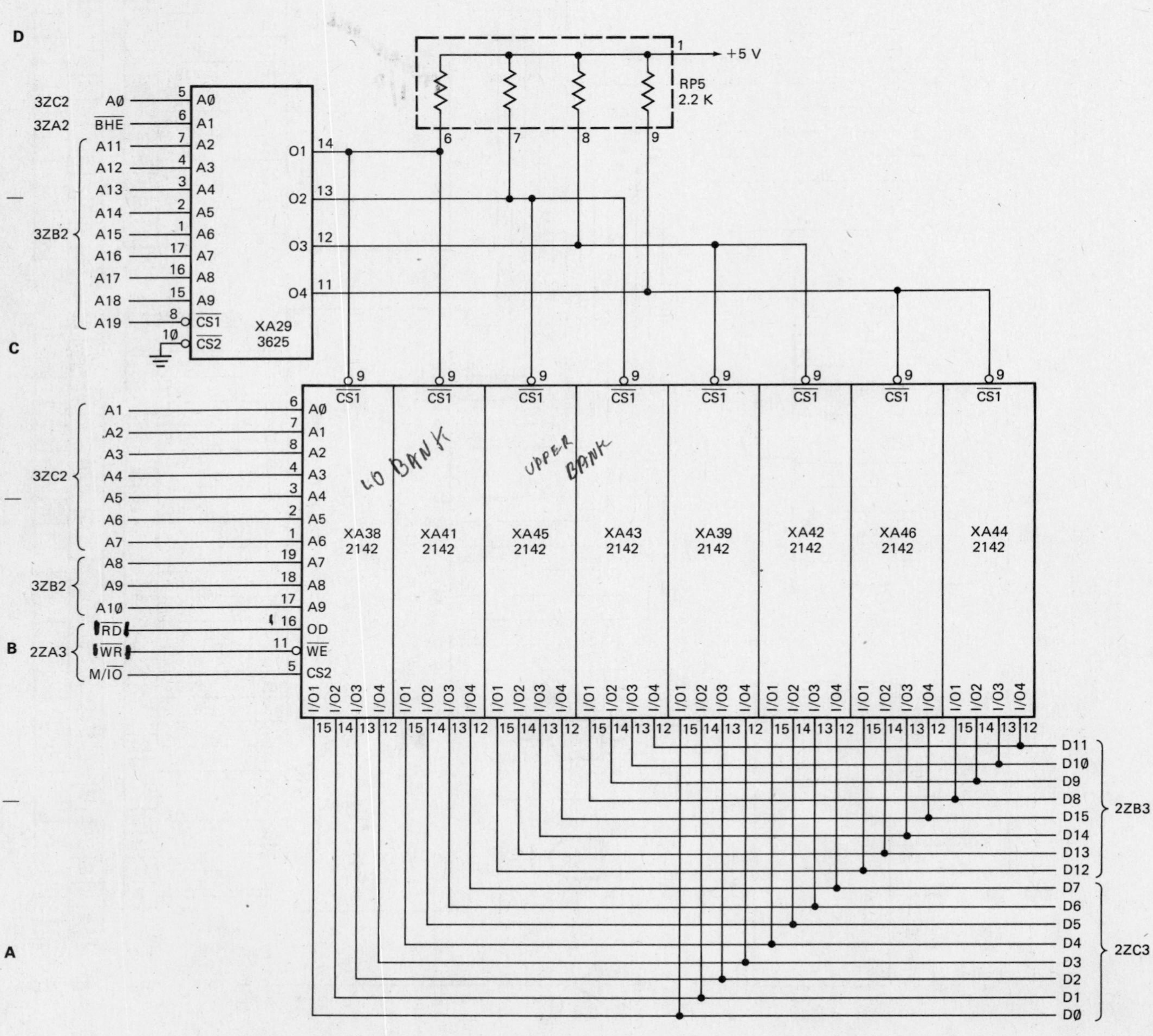

FIGURE 7-6 (sheet 6 of 9) *(continued)*

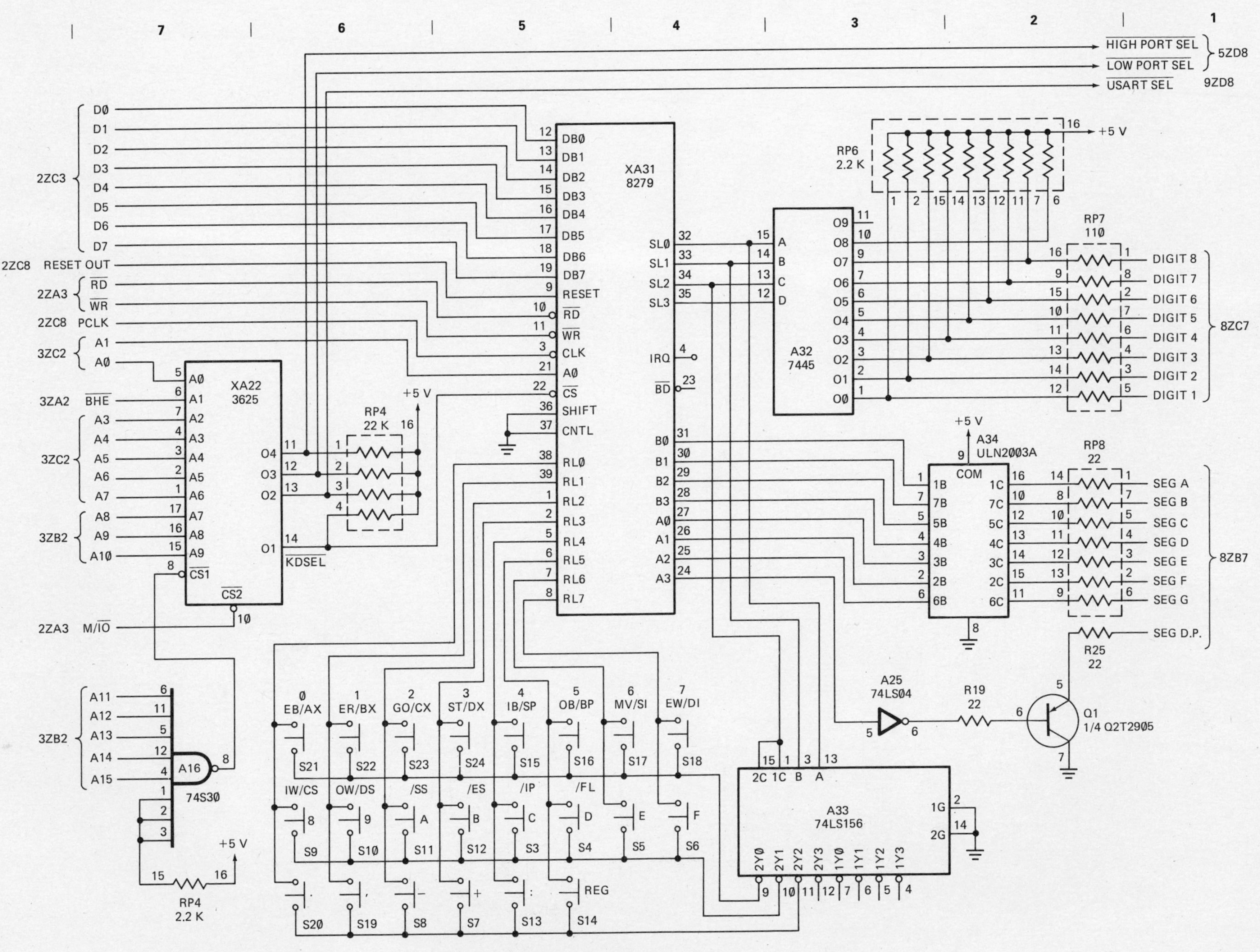

FIGURE 7-6 (sheet 7 of 9) (*continued*)

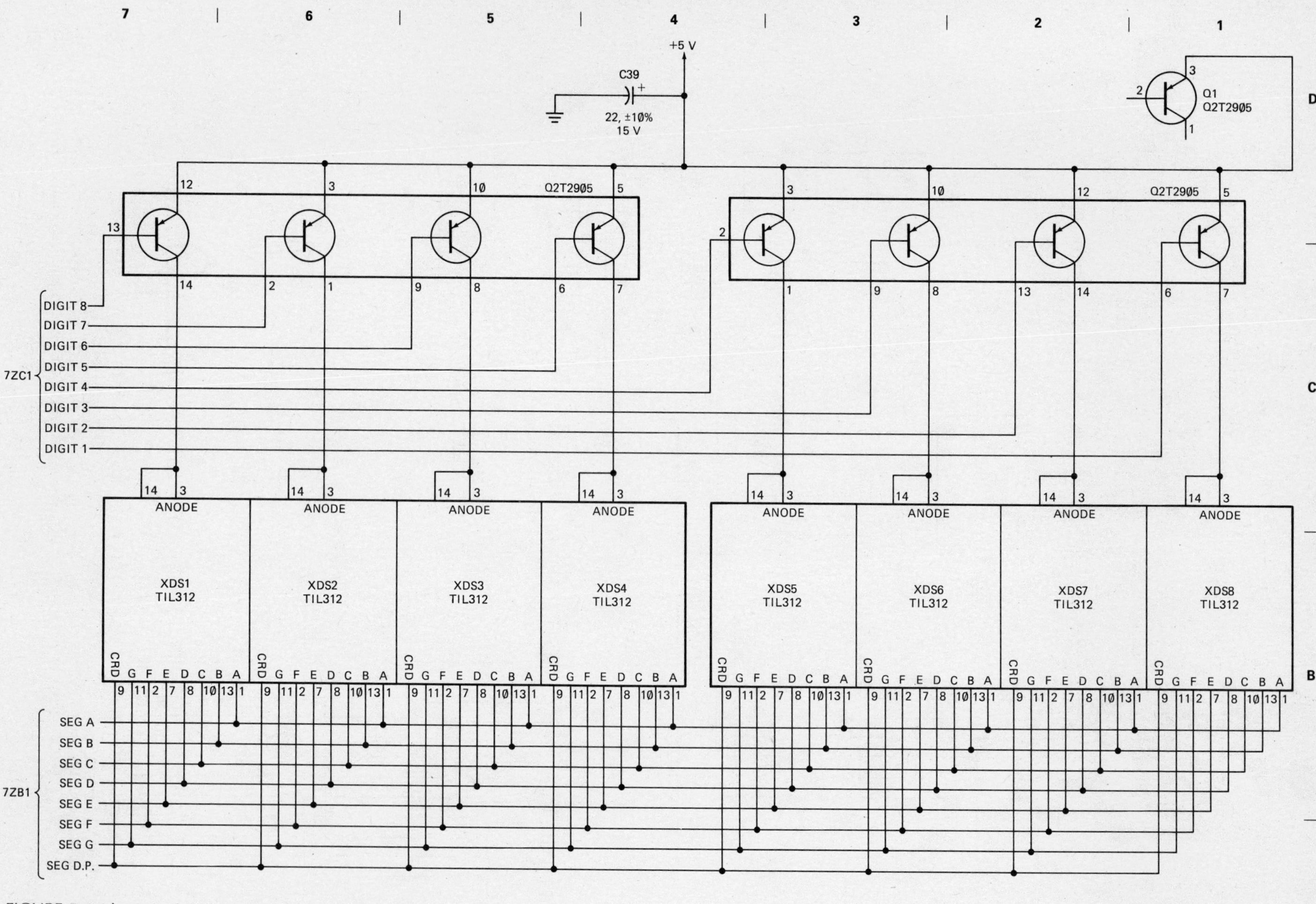

FIGURE 7-6 (sheet 8 of 9) *(continued)*

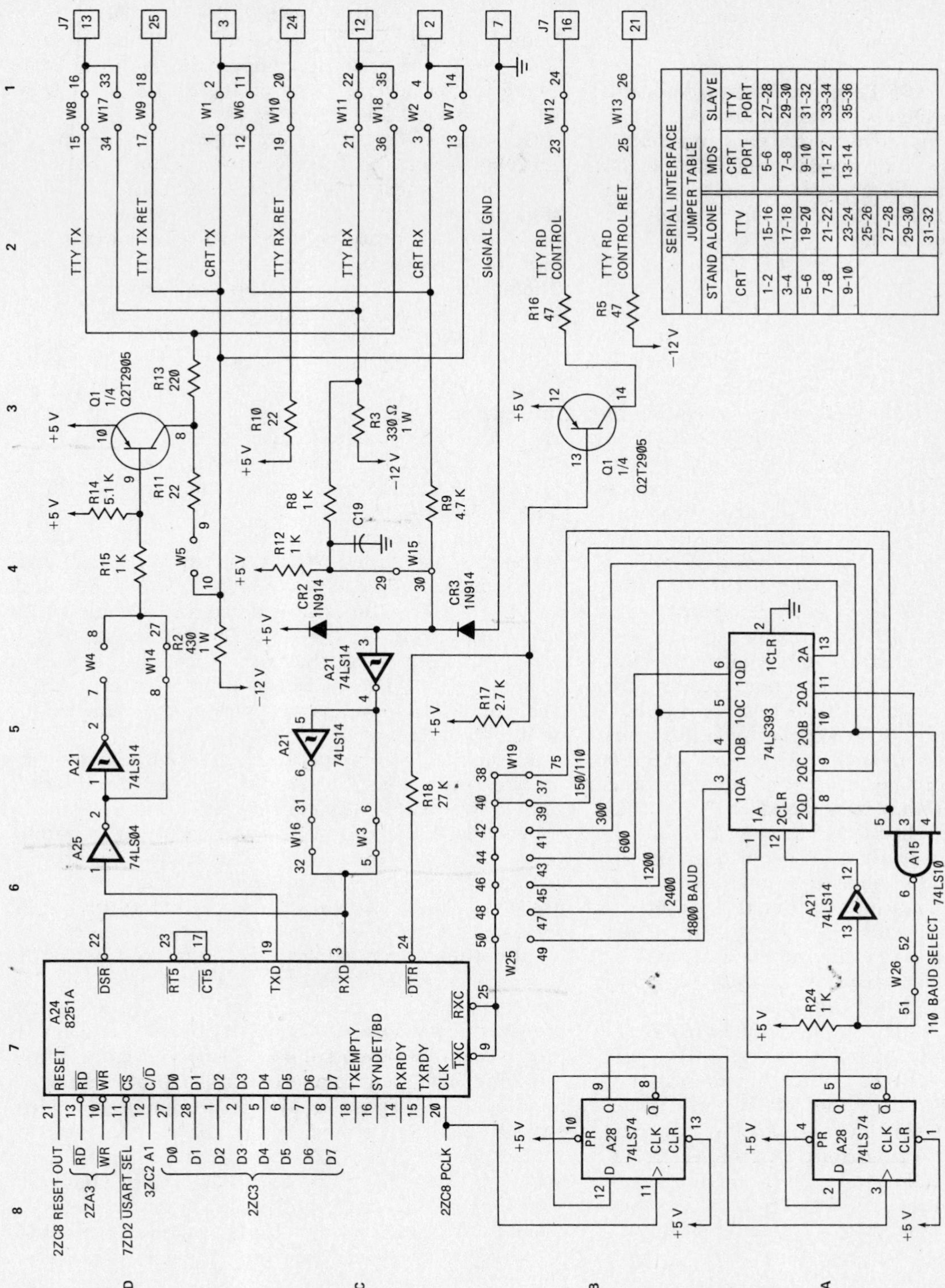

FIGURE 7-6 (sheet 9 of 9) *(continued)*

automatically sends out the code for one digit and turns on that digit. After a millisecond or so the 8279 sends out the seven-segment code for the next digit and turns on that digit. The process is continued until all digits have been lit, and then the 8279 cycles back to the first digit again. In Chapter 9 we discuss in detail how you use an 8279. The main point for now is that this device takes care of scanning a keyboard and refreshing a display so that you don't have to do these operations as part of your program.

Now that you have an overview of the ports in this system, see if you can find in the block diagram the decoder which selects an addressed port. You should find the 3625 labeled *A22* about in the center of the block diagram. We discuss later how this device produces the port select signals from a port address sent out by the 8086.

The final part of the SDK-86 block diagram to take a look at is the buffers along the right-hand edge. The purpose of these devices is to buffer the data and control bus lines so that they can drive additional ROM, RAM, or ports that you might add to the expansion area of the board. Note that the address lines are already buffered by the 74S373 address latches.

A First Look at the SDK-86 Schematics

Now that you have seen an overview of the SDK-86, the next step is to take a first look at Figure 7-6, which shows the actual schematics for the board. At first these many pages of schematics may seem overwhelming to you, but if you use the *5-minute freak-out rule* and then approach the schematics one part at a time, you should have no trouble understanding them. The schematics simply show greater detail for each of the parts of the block diagram that we discussed in the preceding sections of the chapter.

At this point we want to make clear that it is not the purpose of this chapter to make you an expert on the circuit connections of an SDK-86 board. We use parts of these schematics to demonstrate some major concepts such as address decoding and to show how the parts are connected together to form a small but real system. Even if you do not have an SDK-86 board, you can learn a great deal from these schematics about how an 8086 system functions. Multipage schematics such as these are typical for any microprocessor-based board or product, so you need to get used to working with them.

Before getting started on the next major concept, we will discuss some of the symbols used on most microprocessor system schematics. The first thing that we want to look at in the schematics are the numbers across the top and bottom of each and the letters along the sides of each. These are called *zone coordinates*. You use these coordinates to identify the location of a part or connection on the schematic just as you might use similar coordinates on a road map to help you locate Bowers Avenue. For example, on sheet 1 of the schematics find the lines labeled A1–A7 in the upper left corner. Next to these lines you should see *3ZC2*. This indicates that these address lines come from zone *C2* on sheet 3. To see what the lines actually connect to, first find schematic sheet 3. Then move across the row of the schematic labeled *C* until you come to the column labeled 2. This zone is small enough that you should easily be able to find where these lines come from. The zone coordinates next to these lines on sheet 3 indicate the other schematic sheets and zones that these lines go to. For practice, try finding where a few more lines connect from and to.

The next points to look at on the schematics are the numbers on the ICs. In addition to a part number such as 2716, each IC has a number of the form *XA*36. This second number is used to help locate the IC on the printed circuit board. The number is usually silk-screened on the board next to the corresponding IC. Usually IC numbers are sequential and start from the upper left corner of the component side of a board. There may be several 2716s on the board, but only one will be labeled *XA*36.

Other devices often found on microprocessor boards are *resistor packs*. You can find an example in zone *C5* of schematic sheet 1. As you can see from the schematic, this device contains four 2.2-kΩ resistors. Resistor packs may physically be thin, vertical, rectangular wafers, or they may be in packages similar to small ICs. The advantages of resistor packs are that they take up less printed circuit board space and that they are easier to install than individual resistors.

Some other symbols to look at in the schematics are the structures with labels such as J2 and P1. You can find examples of these in zones *C7* and *B7* of schematic sheet 1. These symbols are used to indicate *connectors*. The number in the rectangular box specifies the pin number on the connector that a signal goes to. The letter P stands for *plug*. A connector is considered a plug if it plugs into something else. In the case of the SDK-86, the connector labeled P1 is the printed circuit board edge connector. The letter J next to a connector stands for *jack*. A connector is considered a jack if something else plugs into it. On the SDK-86 board the jacks J1–J6 are 50-pin connectors that you can plug ribbon cable connectors into. These jacks allow the address bus, data bus, control bus, and parallel ports to be connected to additional circuitry.

One more point to notice on the SDK-86 schematics is the capacitors on the power supply inputs shown in zone *B6* of sheet 1. As you can see there, the schematic shows a large number of 0.1-μF capacitors in parallel with a 22-μF capacitor. Most systems have *filtering* such as this on their power lines. You may wonder what is the use of putting all of these small capacitors in parallel with one which is obviously many times larger. The point of this is that the large capacitor filters out or *bypasses* low-frequency noise on the power lines, and the small capacitors, spread around the board, bypass high-frequency noise on the power supply lines. Noise is produced on the power supply lines by devices switching from one logic state to another. If this noise is not filtered out with bypass capacitors, it may become large enough to disturb system operation.

Glance through the SDK-86 schematics to get an idea of where various parts are located and to see what additional information you can pick up from the notes on them. In the next section of this chapter we discuss how microcomputer systems address memory and ports. As part of the discussion we cycle back to these schematics to see how the SDK-86 does it.

ADDRESSING MEMORY AND PORTS IN MICROCOMPUTER SYSTEMS

Address Decoder Concept

While discussing the block diagram of the SDK-86 board earlier in this chapter, we mentioned that the 3625 devices on the board serve as *address decoders*. One function of an address decoder is to produce a signal which enables the ROM, RAM, or port device that you want enabled for a particular address. A second, related function of an address decoder is to make sure that only one device at a time is enabled to put data on the data bus lines.

It seems that every microcomputer system does address decoding in a different way from every other system. Therefore, instead of memorizing the method used in one particular system, it is important that you understand the concept of address decoding. You can then figure out any system you have to work on.

A SYSTEM ROM DECODER

To start, look at Figure 7-7. This figure shows how eight EPROMs can be connected in parallel on a common address bus and common data bus. From just looking at the schematic you can see that these EPROMs output bytes of data because each has eight outputs connected to the system data bus. The number of address lines connected to each device gives you an indication of how many bytes are stored in it. Each EPROM has 12 address lines (A0–A11) connected to it. Therefore, the number of bytes stored in the device is 2^{12} or 4096. If you have trouble with this, think of how many bits a counter has to have to count the 4096 states from 0 to 4095 decimal, or 0000H to 0FFFFH.

Note that each 2732 in Figure 7-7 has a Chip Select ($\overline{CS}$) input. When this input is asserted low the addressed byte in a device will be output on the data bus. To get meaningful data from the EPROMs we need to make sure that the $\overline{CS}$ input of only one device at a time is low. In the circuit in Figure 7-7 this is done by the 74LS138. If the 74LS138 is enabled by making its $\overline{G2A}$ and $\overline{G2B}$ inputs low and its G1 input high, then only one output of the device will be low at a time. The output that will be low is determined by the 3-bit address applied to the C, B, and A select inputs. For example, if CBA is 000, then the Y0 output will be low, and all the other outputs will be high. ROM 0 will be selected. If CBA is 001, the Y1 output will be low and the ROM 1 will be selected. If CBA is 111, then Y7 will be low, and only ROM 7 will be enabled. Now let's see what address range each of these ROMs will have in the system.

To determine the addresses of ROMs, RAMs, and ports in a system, a good approach in many cases is to use a worksheet such as that in Figure 7-8. To make one of these worksheets you start by writing the address bits and the binary weight of each address bit across the top of the paper as shown in the figure. To make it easier to convert binary addresses to hex, it helps if you mark off the address lines in groups of four as shown. Next, draw vertical lines which mark off the three address lines that connect to the decoder select inputs (C, B, and A). For the decoder in Figure 7-7 address lines A14, A13, and A12 are connected to the C, B, and A inputs of the decoder,

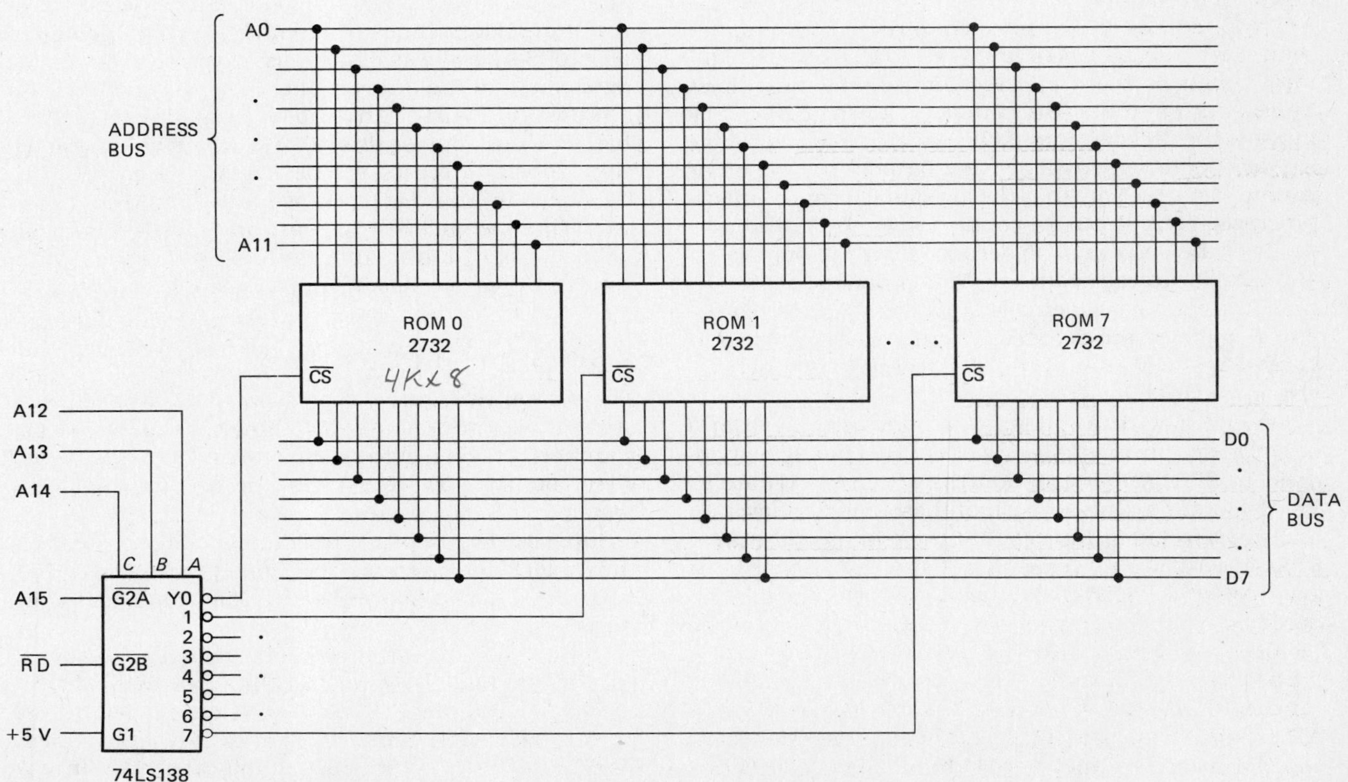

FIGURE 7-7 Parallel ROMs with decoder.

		HEX DIGIT				HEX DIGIT				HEX DIGIT				HEX DIGIT			HEX EQUIVALENT ADDRESS
	2^{15} A15	2^{14} A14	2^{13} A13	2^{12} A12	2^{11} A11	2^{10} A10	2^{9} A9	2^{8} A8	2^{7} A7	2^{6} A6	2^{5} A5	2^{4} A4	2^{3} A3	2^{2} A2	2^{1} A1	2^{0} A0	
BLOCK 1 START	0	0	0	0	0	0	0	0	0	0	0	0	0	0	0	0	= 0000
BLOCK 1 END	0	0	0	0	1	1	1	1	1	1	1	1	1	1	1	1	= 0FFF
BLOCK 2 START	0	0	0	1	0	0	0	0	0	0	0	0	0	0	0	0	= 1000
BLOCK 2 END	0	0	0	1	1	1	1	1	1	1	1	1	1	1	1	1	= 1FFF
BLOCK 3 START	0	0	1	0	0	0	0	0	0	0	0	0	0	0	0	0	= 2000
BLOCK 3 END	0	0	1	0	1	1	1	1	1	1	1	1	1	1	1	1	= 2FFF
BLOCK 4 START	0	0	1	1	0	0	0	0	0	0	0	0	0	0	0	0	= 3000
BLOCK 4 END	0	0	1	1	1	1	1	1	1	1	1	1	1	1	1	1	= 3FFF
BLOCK 5 START	0	1	0	0	0	0	0	0	0	0	0	0	0	0	0	0	= 4000
BLOCK 5 END	0	1	0	0	1	1	1	1	1	1	1	1	1	1	1	1	= 4FFF
BLOCK 6 START	0	1	0	1	0	0	0	0	0	0	0	0	0	0	0	0	= 5000
BLOCK 6 END	0	1	0	1	1	1	1	1	1	1	1	1	1	1	1	1	= 5FFF
BLOCK 7 START	0	1	1	0	0	0	0	0	0	0	0	0	0	0	0	0	= 6000
BLOCK 7 END	0	1	1	0	1	1	1	1	1	1	1	1	1	1	1	1	= 6FFF
BLOCK 8 START	0	1	1	1	0	0	0	0	0	0	0	0	0	0	0	0	= 7000
BLOCK 8 END	0	1	1	1	1	1	1	1	1	1	1	1	1	1	1	1	= 7FFF
		DECODER ADDRESS INPUTS (A14–A12)															

FIGURE 7-8 Address decoder worksheet showing address decoding for eight 2732s in Figure 7-7.

respectively. Then write under each address bit the logic level that must be on that line to address the first location in the first EPROM. To address the first location in any of the EPROMs, the A0 through A11 address lines must all be low, so put a 0 under each of these address bits on the worksheet. To enable EPROM 0, the select inputs of the decoder must be all 0's. Since address lines A14, A13, and A12 are connected to these select inputs, they must then all be 0's to enable EPROM 0. Write a 0 under each of these address bits on the worksheet. Since address line A15 is connected to the $\overline{G2A}$ enable input of the decoder, it must be asserted low in order for the decoder to work at all. Write a 0 under the A15 bit on your worksheet. Note that the $\overline{RD}$ signal from the microprocessor control bus is connected to the $\overline{G2B}$ enable input of the decoder. The decoder then will only be enabled during a read operation. This is done to make sure that data cannot accidentally be written to ROM. The G1 enable input of the decoder is permanently asserted by tying it to +5 V because we don't need it for anything else in this circuit.

You can now read the starting address of EPROM 0 directly from the worksheet as 0000H. The highest address in EPROM 0 is that address where A0–A11 are all 1's. If you put a 1 under each of these bits as shown on the worksheet, you can see that the ending address for EPROM 0 is 0FFFH. Remember that A12–A14 have to be low to select EPROM 0. A15 has to be low to enable the decoder. The address range of EPROM 0 is said to be 0000H to 0FFFH, a 4 Kbyte block.

Now let's use the worksheet to determine the address range for EPROM 1. EPROM 1 is enabled when A15 is 0, A14 is 0, A13 is 0, and A12 is 1. For the first address in EPROM 1 address lines A0–A11 must all be low. Therefore, the starting address of EPROM 1 is 1000H. Its ending address, when A0–A11 are all 1's, is 1FFFH. If you look at the worksheet in Figure 7-8 you should see that the address ranges for the other six EPROMs in the system are 2000H to 2FFFH, 3000H to 3FFFH, 4000H to 4FFFH, 5000H to 5FFFH, 6000H to 6FFFH, and 7000H to 7FFFH. In this system then we use address lines A14, A13, and A12 to select one of eight EPROMs in the overall address range of 0000H to 7FFFH. Some people like to think of address lines A14, A13, and A12 as "counting off" 4096-byte blocks of memory. If you think of the address lines as the outputs of a 16-bit counter, you can see how this works. The end address for each EPROM has all 1's in address bits A0–A11. When you increment the address to access the next byte in memory, these bits all go to 0, and a 1 rolls over into bits A14, A13, and A12. This increments the count in these 3 bits by one and enables the next highest 4096-byte EPROM. The count in these bits goes from binary 000 to 111.

A SYSTEM RAM DECODER

The system in Figure 7-7 contains only ROM. In most systems we want to have ROM, RAM, and ports. To give you more practice with basic address decoding we will show you now how we can add a decoder for RAM to the system.

Suppose that we want to add eight 2K × 8 RAMs to the system, and we want the first RAM to start at address 8000H, just above the EPROMs which end at address 7FFFH.

To start, make another worksheet such as the one in Figure 7-8. Addressing one of the 2048 bytes (2^{11}) in each RAM requires 11 address lines, A0–A10. These lines will be connected directly to each RAM, so draw a vertical line on the worksheet to indicate this. Since we want to select one of eight RAM devices, we can use another 74LS138 such as we used for the EPROMs. We

HEX DIGIT				HEX DIGIT				HEX DIGIT				HEX DIGIT				HEX EQUIVALENT ADDRESS	START OF BLOCK
A15	A14	A13	A12	A11	A10	A9	A8	A7	A6	A5	A4	A3	A2	A1	A0		
1	0	0	0	0	0	0	0	0	0	0	0	0	0	0	0	= 8000H	1
1	0	0	0	1	0	0	0	0	0	0	0	0	0	0	0	= 8800H	2
1	0	0	1	0	0	0	0	0	0	0	0	0	0	0	0	= 9000H	3
1	0	0	1	1	0	0	0	0	0	0	0	0	0	0	0	= 9800H	4
1	0	1	0	0	0	0	0	0	0	0	0	0	0	0	0	= A000H	5
1	0	1	0	1	0	0	0	0	0	0	0	0	0	0	0	= A800H	6
1	0	1	1	0	0	0	0	0	0	0	0	0	0	0	0	= B000H	7
1	0	1	1	1	0	0	0	0	0	0	0	0	0	0	0	= B800H	8

DECODER ADDRESS INPUTS (A13, A12, A11)

FIGURE 7-9 Address decoder worksheet for eight 2 Kbyte RAMs starting at address 8000H.

want to select 2048-byte blocks of memory, so address line A11 will be connected to the A input of the decoder, A12 will be connected to the B input of the decoder, and A13 will be connected to the C input of the decoder. Under these 3 address bits on the worksheet list the 3-bit binary count sequence from 000 to 111 as we did in Figure 7-8. All we have left to decide is what to connect to the enable inputs of the decoder. We want the block of RAM selected by the outputs of this decoder to start at address 8000H. For this, address A15 is high and A14 is low. The G1 enable input of the decoder is active high so we connect it to the A15 address line. This input will then be asserted when A15 is high. We connect A14 to $\overline{\text{G2A}}$ of the decoder so that this input will be asserted when A14 is low. Because we don't need to use it in this circuit, we simply tie the $\overline{\text{G2B}}$ input of the decoder to ground so that it will be asserted all the time. Note that we don't connect the $\overline{\text{RD}}$ signal to an enable input on a RAM decoder, because we want to enable the RAMs for both read and write operations. Figure 7-9 shows the address decoder worksheet for the 74LS138 connections that we have just described.

Now, if you put a 1 under A15 on your worksheet and a 0 under A14, you will be able to quickly determine the address range for each of the RAMs. The first RAM will start at address 8000H. The ending address for this RAM will be at the address where bits A0–A10 are all 1's. If you put 1's under these bits on your worksheet, you should see that the ending address for the first RAM is 87FFH. For practice, work out the hexadecimal addresses for each of the other seven RAMs. When you finish, compare your results with those in Figure 7-9. The eight RAMs occupy the address space from 8000H to BFFFH.

A SYSTEM PORT DECODER

Figure 7-10*a* shows how another 74LS138 can be connected in our system to produce chip select signals for some port devices. Make another address decoder worksheet and see if you can figure out the system address that corresponds to each of these decoder outputs. Check your results with those in Figure 7-10*b*. First note that A15 and A14 must be high to enable the decoder, and write 1's under these bits on your worksheet. Then notice that A13 and A12 must be low to enable the

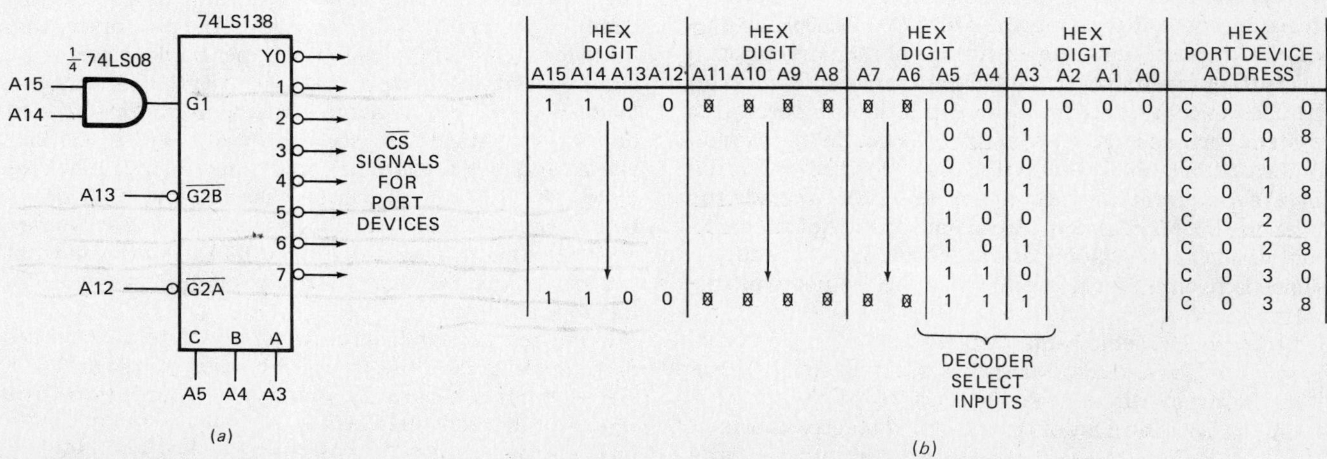

A15	A14	A13	A12	A11	A10	A9	A8	A7	A6	A5	A4	A3	A2	A1	A0	HEX PORT DEVICE ADDRESS
1	1	0	0	X	X	X	X	X	X	0	0	0	0	0	0	C 0 0 0
										0	0	1				C 0 0 8
										0	1	0				C 0 1 0
										0	1	1				C 0 1 8
										1	0	0				C 0 2 0
										1	0	1				C 0 2 8
										1	1	0				C 0 3 0
1	1	0	0	X	X	X	X	X	X	1	1	1				C 0 3 8

FIGURE 7-10 Adding a port device decoder. *(a)* Schematic for 74LS138 connections. *(b)* Address decoder worksheet.

decoder, and write a 0 under each of these bits on your worksheet. Finally determine which three address lines are connected to the select inputs of the decoder, and write the binary count sequence from 000 to 111 under these bits. For this port decoder, address lines A3, A4, and A5 will be connected to the decoder select inputs. Address lines A0, A1, and A2 will be connected directly to the port devices to address individual ports and control registers in the devices. This is the same idea as connecting the lower address lines directly to a ROM so that we can address one of the bytes stored there.

Address lines A6–A11 are not connected to the port devices or to the decoder, so they have no effect on selecting a port. We don't care then whether these bits are 1's or 0's. As you will see, these "don't care" bits mean that there are many addresses which will turn on one of the port devices. To give the simplest address for each device, however, we assume that each of these don't care bits is 0. Write 0's under each of these bits on your worksheet. You should now see that the address C000H will cause the Y0 output of the decoder to be asserted. The address C008H will cause the Y1 output of the decoder to be asserted. Using address lines A3, A4, and A5 on the decoder select inputs then leaves eight address spaces for each port device.

To see that any one of several different addresses can select one of these port devices, replace the 0 you put under A6 on the first line of your worksheet with a 1. This represents a system address of C040H. A15 and A14 are 1's and A13, A12, A5, A4, and A3 are 0's, for this address. Therefore, this address will also cause the Y0 output of the decoder to be asserted. You can try other combinations of 1's and 0's on A6–A11 if you need to further convince yourself that these bits don't matter when addressing ports. Again, we usually use 0's for these bits to give the simplest address.

Using a decoder which translates memory addresses to chip select signals for port devices is called *memory-mapped I/O*. In this system a port will be written to or read from in the same way as any other memory location. In other words, if this were an 8088 system, you would use an instruction such as MOV AL, DS:BYTE PTR 0C000H to read a byte of data from the first port to the AL register, instead of using the MOV DX, 0C000H and IN AL, DX instructions. The advantage of memory-mapped I/O is that any instruction which references memory can be used to input data from or output data to ports. In a system such as this, for example, the single instruction ADD AL, DS:BYTE PTR [0C000H] could be used to input a byte of data from the port at address C000H and add the byte to the AL register. The disadvantage of memory-mapped I/O is that some of the system memory address space is used up for ports and is therefore not available for memory.

You can use memory-mapped I/O with any microprocessor, but some microprocessors such as those of the 8086 family allow you to set up separate address spaces 'or input ports and for output ports. You access ports in hese separate address spaces directly with the IN and JT instructions. Having separate address spaces for ut and output ports is called *direct I/O*. The advantage of direct I/O is that none of the system memory space is used for ports. The disadvantage is that only the specialized IN and OUT instructions can be used to input or output data.

In a later section of this chapter we show how direct I/O is done with the 8086, but first we will discuss how the 8086 addresses memory.

8086 and 8088 Addressing and Address Decoding

8086 MEMORY BANKS

The 8086 has a 20-bit address bus, so it can address 2^{20} or 1,048,576 addresses. Each address represents a stored byte. As you know from previous chapters, when you write a word to memory with an instruction such as MOV DS:WORD PTR[437AH], BX, the word is actually written into two consecutive memory addresses. Assuming that DS contains 0000, the low byte of the word is written into the specified memory address, 0437AH, and the high byte of the word is written into the next higher address, 0437BH. To make it possible to read or write a word with one machine cycle, the memory for an 8086 is set up as two "banks" of up to 524,288 bytes each. Figure 7-11*a* shows this in diagram form.

One memory bank contains all the bytes which have even addresses such as 00000, 00002, and 00004. The data lines of this bank are connected to the lower eight data lines, D0–D7, of the 8086. The other memory bank contains all of the bytes which have odd addresses such as 00001, 00003, and 00005. The data lines of this bank are connected to the upper eight data lines, D8–D15, of the 8086. Address line A0 is used as part of the enabling for memory devices in the lower bank. An addressed memory device in this bank will be enabled when address line A0 is low, as it will be for any even address. Address lines A1–A19 are used to select the desired memory device in the bank and to address the desired byte in that device.

Address lines A1–A19 are also used to select a desired memory device in the upper bank and to address the desired byte in that bank. An additional part of the enabling for memory devices in the upper bank is a separate signal called *bus high enable*, or $\overline{BHE}$. $\overline{BHE}$ is sent out from the 8086 at the same time as an address is sent out. An external latch, strobed by ALE, grabs the $\overline{BHE}$ signal and holds it stable for the rest of the machine cycle. The $\overline{BHE}$ signal will be asserted low if a *byte* is being accessed at an odd address, or if a *word* at an even address is being accessed. Figure 7-11*b* shows you what will be on the $\overline{BHE}$ and A0 lines for different types of memory accesses.

If you read a byte from or write a byte to an even address such as 00000H, A0 will be asserted low and $\overline{BHE}$ will be high. The lower bank will be enabled and the upper bank will be disabled. A byte will be transferred to or from the addressed location in the low bank on D0–D7. For an instruction such as MOV AH, DS:BYTE PTR [0000], the 8086 will automatically transfer the byte of

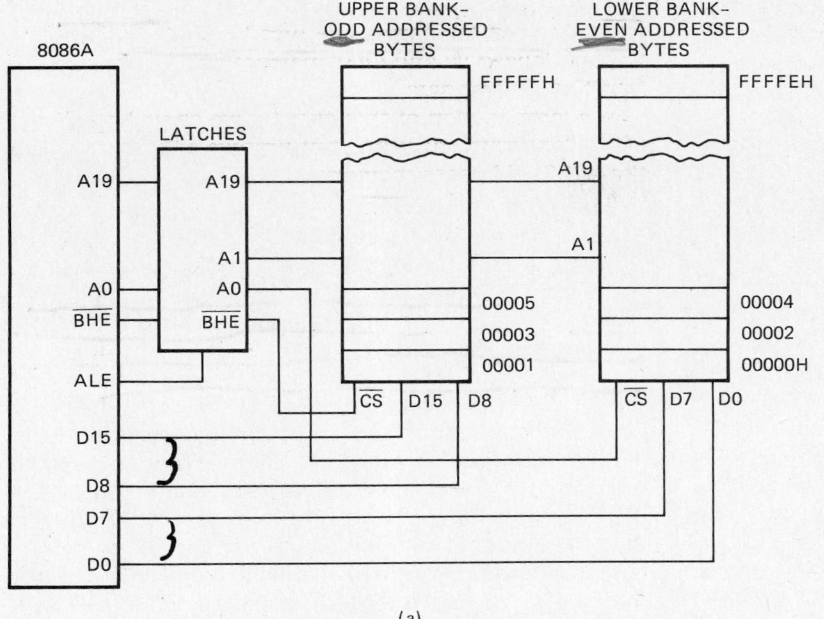

ADDRESS	DATA TYPE	$\overline{BHE}$	A0	BUS CYCLES
0000	BYTE	1	0	ONE
0000	WORD	0	0	ONE
0001	BYTE	0	1	ONE
0001	WORD	0	1	FIRST
		1	0	SECOND

(b)

FIGURE 7-11 8086 memory banks. *(a)* Block diagram. *(b)* Signals for byte and word operations.

data from the lower data bus lines to AH, the upper byte of the AX register. You just write the instruction and the 8086 takes care of getting the data in the right place.

Now, if the DS register contains 0000H and you use an instruction such as MOV AX, DS:WORD PTR [0000] to read a word from memory into AX, both A0 and $\overline{BHE}$ will be asserted low. Therefore, both banks will be enabled. The low byte of the word will be transferred from address 00000H to the 8086 on D0–D7. The high byte of the word will be transferred from address 00001H to the 8086 on D8–D15. The 8086 memory, remember, is set up in banks so that words, which have their low byte at an even address, can be transferred to or from the 8086 in one bus cycle. When programming an 8086, then, it is important to start an array of words on an even address for most efficient operation. If you are using an assembler, the EVEN directive is used to do this.

When you use an instruction such as MOV AL, DS:BYTE PTR [0001] to access just a byte at an odd address, A0 will be high and $\overline{BHE}$ will be asserted low. Therefore, the low bank will be disabled, and the high bank will be enabled. The byte will be transferred from memory address 00001H in the high bank to the 8086 on lines D8–D15. The 8086 will automatically transfer the byte of data from the higher eight data lines to AL, the low byte of the AX register. Note that address 00001H is actually the first location in the upper bank.

The final case in Figure 7-11*b* is that where you want to read a word from or write a word to an odd address. The instruction MOV AX, DS:WORD PTR [0001H] copies the low byte of a word from address 00001 to AL and the high byte from address 00002H to AH. In this case the 8086 requires two machine cycles to copy the two bytes from memory. During the first machine cycle the 8086 will output address 00001H and assert $\overline{BHE}$ low. A0 will be high. The byte from address 00001H will be read into the 8086 on lines D8–D15 and put in AL. During the second machine cycle the 8086 will send out address 00002H. A0 will be low, but $\overline{BHE}$ will be high. The second byte will be read into the 8086 on lines D0–D7 and put in AH. Note that the 8086 automatically takes care of getting a byte to the correct register regardless of which data lines the byte comes in on. 

The main reason that the A0 and $\overline{BHE}$ signals function the way they do is to prevent the writing of an unwanted byte into an adjacent memory location when the 8086 writes a byte. To understand this, think what would happen if both memory banks were turned on for all write operations, and you wrote a byte to address 00002 with the instruction MOV DS:BYTE PTR [0002], AL. The data from AL would be written to address 00002 as desired. However, since the upper bank is also enabled, the random data on D8–D15 would be written into address 00003. The 8086 then is designed so that $\overline{BHE}$ is high during this byte write. This disables the upper bank of memory and prevents the random data on D8–D15 from being written to address 00003.

Now that you have an overview of address decoding and of the 8086 memory banks, let's look at some examples of how all of this is put together in a small system.

ROM ADDRESS DECODING ON THE SDK-86

Sheet 1 of the SDK-86 schematics in Figure 7-6 shows the circuit connections for the EPROMs and EPROM decoder. The 2716 EPROMs there are 2K × 8 devices.

Two of the EPROMs have their eight data outputs connected in parallel to system data lines D0–D7. These two EPROMs then give 4 Kbytes of storage in the lower memory bank. The other two EPROMs have their data outputs connected in parallel on system data lines D8–D15 to give 4 Kbytes of storage in the upper bank of ROM. Eleven address lines are needed to address the 2 Kbytes in each device. Therefore, system address lines A1–A11 are connected to each EPROM. Remember that we can't use A0 for this because, as we described in the last section, it is used in enabling the lower bank.

A 2716 has two enable inputs, $\overline{CE}$ and $\overline{OE}$. In order for the 2716 to output an addressed byte, both of these enable inputs must be asserted low. The $\overline{CE}$ inputs of the two devices in the lower bank are connected to system address line A0, so the $\overline{CE}$ inputs of these devices will be asserted if A0 is a 0. The $\overline{CE}$ inputs of the two 2716s in the upper bank are connected to the $\overline{BHE}$ line. The $\overline{CE}$ inputs of these devices then will be asserted whenever $\overline{BHE}$ is asserted low. To summarize, then, the two devices labeled *XA*27 and *XA*36 form the lower bank of EPROM and the two devices labeled *XA*30 and *XA*37 form the upper bank of EPROM in this system. To see how the $\overline{OE}$ enable input of each of these devices gets asserted and to determine the address that each device will have in the system you need to look next at the 3625 address decoder labeled *XA*26.

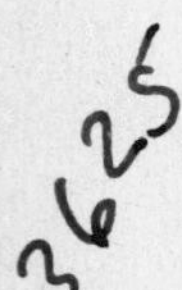

A 3625 is a 1K × 4 bipolar PROM which performs the same function that a 74LS138 performs in Figures 7-7 and 7-10. Since a 3625 has open collector outputs, a pull-up resistor to +5 V is required on each output. The dotted box around the four resistors on the schematic indicates the four are all contained in one package, resistor pack 5 (*RP*5). The 3625 translates an address to a signal which is used as part of the enabling of the desired device. Using a PROM as an address decoder, however, is for several reasons much more powerful than using a simple decoder such as the 74LS138. In the first place, the 3625 is programmable, which means that you can move the memory devices to new addresses in memory by simply programming a new PROM. Secondly, the large number of inputs on the PROM allow you to select a specific area of memory without using external gates. If, for example, you wanted the G2A input of a 74LS138 to be asserted if A11–A15 were all high, you would have to use an external NAND gate to detect this condition. With a PROM you can just make this condition part of the truth table you use to burn the PROM.

Now, to analyze any decoder circuit, first determine what signals are required to enable the decoder. The $\overline{CS1}$ enable input of the 3625 EPROM decoder is tied to ground so it is permanently enabled. The $\overline{CS2}$ enable input is tied to the $\overline{RD}$ signal from the 8086, so that the decoder will only be enabled if the 8086 is doing a read operation. As explained previously, you don't want to accidentally enable a ROM if you send out a wrong address during a write operation.

The next step in analyzing a decoder circuit using a PROM is to consult the manufacturer's manual for the system. You need to do this because, for a PROM, the relationship between the inputs and the outputs cannot be determined directly from the schematic.

Figure 7-12 shows the truth table for the PROM from the SDK-86 manual. This truth table is very similar to the address decoder worksheet that we used in previous sections of the chapter. From the truth table you can see that in order for the O1 output to be asserted low, M/$\overline{IO}$ has to be high. This is reasonable since this decoder is enabling memory devices. Address lines A12–A19 also have to be high in order for the O1 output of the PROM to be asserted low. Since the upper eight address bits must all be 1's for the O1 output to be asserted, the lowest address which will cause this is FF000H. Refer to sheet 1 of the SDK-86 schematics in Figure 7-6 to see that the O1 output of the decoder PROM connects to the $\overline{OE}$ enable inputs of two of the 2716 EPROMs, *XA*27 and *XA*30. Note also on the schematic, or remember from a previous discussion, that the other enable input of *XA*27, $\overline{CE}$, is connected to system address line A0. The *XA*27 EPROM then will be enabled whenever the 8086 does a memory read from an even address (A0 = 0) in the range FF000H to FFFFFH. Now let's look at the *XA*30 EPROM.

The $\overline{CE}$ enable input of *XA*30 is connected to the system $\overline{BHE}$ line. As shown in Figure 7-11, $\overline{BHE}$ will be asserted low whenever the 8086 accesses a byte at an odd address or a word at an even address. The *XA*30 EPROM then will be enabled when the 8086 reads a byte from an odd address in the range FF000H to FFFFFH. *XA*30 will also be enabled when the 8086 asserts both A0 and $\overline{BHE}$ low to read a word that starts on an even address in the range FF000H to FFFFFH.

These EPROMs are put at this high address in memory on the SDK-86 board because, after a RESET, the 8086 goes to address FFFF0H to get its first instruction. Since we want the SDK-86 to execute its monitor program after we press the RESET button, we locate the

PROM INPUTS				PROM OUTPUTS				PROM ADDRESS BLOCK SELECTED
M/$\overline{IO}$	A14–A19	A13	A12	O4	O3	O2	O1	
1	1	1	1	1	1	1	0	FF000H–FFFFFH
1	1	1	0	1	1	0	1	FE000H–FEFFFH
1	1	0	1	1	0	1	1	FD000H–FDFFFH ($\overline{CSX}$)
1	1	0	0	0	1	1	1	FC000H–FCFFFH ($\overline{CSY}$)
ALL OTHER STATES				1	1	1	1	NONE

12 Truth table for an SDK-86 (A26) ROM decoder PROM.

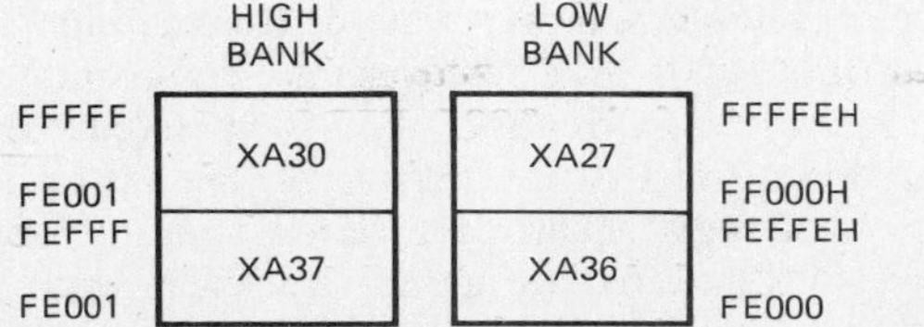

FIGURE 7-13 ROM memory map for SDK-86 board.

EPROM containing the monitor program such that this address is in it. The four SDK-86 EPROMs actually contain two monitor programs. One monitor in devices *XA*27 and *XA*30 allows you to use the hex keypad for entering and running programs. The other monitor in devices *XA*36 and *XA*37 allows you to use an external CRT terminal to enter and run programs. Using sheet 1 of the schematic and the PROM truth table in Figure 7-12, see if you can determine the address range for the *XA*36 and *XA*37 EPROMS.

The $\overline{OE}$ enable inputs of the *XA*36 and *XA*37 devices are connected to the O2 output of the address decoder PROM. According to the truth table for the PROM, the O2 output will be asserted low if M/$\overline{IO}$ is high, A14–A19 are high, A13 is high, and A12 is low. The lowest address that will assert the O2 output of the PROM then is FE000H, and the highest address that will assert the O2 output low is FEFFFH. Therefore the address range for *XA*36 and *XA*37 is FE000H—FEFFFH. Since A0 must also be low to enable the *XA*36 EPROM, this device contains the even-addressed bytes in this range. Since $\overline{BHE}$ must also be low to enable the *XA*37 EPROM, this device contains the odd-addressed bytes in the range FE000H—FEFFFH. A memory map such as the one in Figure 7-13 is a convenient way to summarize where each device is located in the system address space. Note that the 3625 ROM decoder has two unused outputs which can be used as part of the enabling for EPROMs you add to the prototyping section of the board.

RAM ADDRESS DECODING ON THE SDK-86

To give you another example of memory address decoding in a real system, we now discuss the RAM decoding of the SDK-86 board. Sheet 6 of the SDK-86 schematics in Figure 7-6 shows the circuit for the system RAM and RAM decoder. Let's look at this schematic to see what we can learn from it.

First take a look at the input and output lines on the 2142 static RAM devices. From the fact that each device has four data I/O lines you can conclude that the devices store 4-bit words. The fact that each device has 10 address inputs, A0–A9, indicates that each one stores 2^{10} or 1024 of these 4-bit words. To store bytes, two 2142s are enabled in parallel. Devices *A*38 and *A*41, for example, are enabled together to store bytes from the lower eight data lines,and devices *A*43 and *A*45 are enabled together to store bytes from the upper eight data lines. Note next that the control bus signals $\overline{RD}$, $\overline{WR}$, and M/$\overline{IO}$ are connected to all of the 2142s. $\overline{RD}$ is connected to the *output disable* (OD) pin on the 2142s. When the $\overline{RD}$ signal is high or when the device is not enabled, the output buffers will be disabled. During a read operation the RD signal is asserted low. If a 2142 is enabled and its OD input is low, the output buffers will be turned on so that an addressed word is output onto the data bus.

$\overline{WR}$ from the 8086 is connected to the *write enable*, ($\overline{WE}$) input of the 2142s. If a 2142 is enabled, data on the data bus will be written into the addressed location in the RAM when the 8086 asserts $\overline{WR}$ low.

The 2142s have two *enable* inputs, $\overline{CS1}$ and CS2. The M/$\overline{IO}$ signal from the 8086 is connected to the CS2 input of all of the 2142s. Since the CS2 input is active high, it will be asserted whenever the 8086 is doing a memory operation. The $\overline{CS1}$ inputs of the 2142s are connected in pairs to the outputs of a 3625 PROM which functions as an address decoder.

In order to assert any of its outputs and enable some RAM, the 3625 must itself be enabled. Since the CS2 enable input of the PROM is tied to ground, it is permanently enabled. The $\overline{CS1}$ enable input will be asserted when system address line A19 is low. To determine any more information about this PROM you need to look at the truth table for the device. Before we go on to that, however, note that A0 and $\overline{BHE}$ are connected to two of the address inputs on the 3625 PROM. Knowing what you do about 8086 memory banks, why do you think we want A0 and $\overline{BHE}$ to be part of what determines the outputs for this decoder? If you don't have the answer to this question, a look at the truth table for the device in Figure 7-14 should help you.

According to the third line of the truth table/address decoder worksheet in Figure 7-14, the O1 output of the PROM will be asserted low if A12–A18 are low, A11 is low, $\overline{BHE}$ is high, and A0 is low. The O1 output then will be

PROM INPUTS				PROM OUTPUTS				BYTE(S) SELECTED (ADDRESS BLOCK)
A12–A18	A11	$\overline{BHE}$	A0	O4	O3	O2	O1	
0	0	0	0	1	1	0	0	BOTH BYTES (0H–07FFH)
0	0	0	1	1	1	0	1	HIGH BYTE (0H–07FFH)
0	0	1	0	1	1	1	0	LOW BYTE (0H–07FFH)
0	1	0	0	0	0	1	1	BOTH BYTES (0800H–0FFFH)
0	1	0	1	0	1	1	1	HIGH BYTE (0800H–0FFFH)
0	1	1	0	1	0	1	1	LOW BYTE (0800H–0FFFH)
ALL OTHER STATES				1	1	1	1	NONE

FIGURE 7-14 Truth table for an SDK-86 (A29) RAM decoder PROM.

asserted for even system addresses starting with 00000H. A low on the O1 output will enable the *A*38 and *A*41 RAMs which are connected to the lower half of the data bus. These two devices are part of the lower bank of RAM.

Next look at the second line of the PROM truth table in Figure 7-14. From this line you should see that the O2 output of the PROM will be asserted low if A12–A18 are low, A11 is low, $\overline{\text{BHE}}$ is low, and A0 is high. The O2 output will then be asserted for odd system addresses starting with 0001H. A low on the O2 output will enable the *A*43 and *A*45 RAMs which are connected on the upper half of the data bus. These two devices are part of the upper bank of RAM.

Now, suppose we want to write a 16-bit word to RAM at an even address. To do this we want both O1 and O2 to be asserted low so that both the lower bank RAMs and the upper bank RAMs are enabled. According to the first line of the PROM truth table in Figure 7-14, O1 and O2 will both be asserted low if $\overline{\text{BHE}}$ and A0 are both low. Remember from Figure 7-11 that $\overline{\text{BHE}}$ and A0 will both be low whenever you write a word to an even address or read a word from an even address. This last case gives the answer to the question we asked earlier about why A0 and $\overline{\text{BHE}}$ are connected to the address decoder PROM inputs. The two inputs are required to tell the PROM decoder to assert both O1 and O2 for a word read or write operation.

The address range for the *XA*38, *XA*41, *XA*43, and *XA*45 RAMs is 00000H to 007FFH. Another look at the PROM truth table in Figure 7-14 should show you that RAMS *XA*39, *XA*42, *XA*44, and *XA*46 contain 2K more bytes in the range 00800H to 00FFFH. Again, both banks of this additional RAM will be enabled if A0 and $\overline{\text{BHE}}$ are both low, as they are for reading or writing a word to an even address.

SDK-86 PORT ADDRESSING AND PORT DECODING

In a previous section of this chapter we described *memory-mapped input/output*. In a system with memory-mapped I/O, port devices are addressed and selected by decoders as if they were memory devices. The main advantage of memory-mapped I/O is that any instruction which refers to memory can theoretically be used to read from or write to a port. The single instruction ADD BH, DS:BYTE PTR [437AH] could be used to read a byte from a port and add the byte read in to the BH register. The disadvantage of memory-mapped I/O is that the ports occupy part of the system memory space. This space is then not available for storing data or instructions.

To avoid having to use part of the system memory ...e for ports, the 8086 family microprocessors have a ...rate address space for ports. Having a separate ad... space for ports is called *direct I/O*, because this ...e address space is accessed directly with the IN ... OUT instructions.

...ber from previous chapters that the 8086 IN ... instructions each have two forms, *fixed port* ...*le port*. For fixed-port instructions an 8-bit port address is written as part of the instruction. The instruction IN AL, 38H, for example, copies a byte from port 38H to the AL register. For variable-port input or output operations, the 16-bit port address is first loaded into the DX register with an instruction such as MOV DX, 0FFF8H. The instruction IN AL, DX is then used to copy a byte from port FFF8H to the AL register. MOV DX, 0038H followed by IN AL, DX has the same effect as IN AL, 38H.

Whenever the 8086 uses the IN or OUT instructions to access a port, the port address is sent out directly from the 8086 on lines AD0–AD15. None of the segment registers has any effect on the address for an IN or OUT instruction. The 8086 always outputs 0's on lines A16–A19 during an IN or OUT instruction. Since the 8086 outputs a 16-bit address for direct I/O operations, it can address any one of 2^{16} or 65,536 input ports, and any one of 65,536 output ports. An 8086 system which uses direct I/O is designed so that the separate address space for ports is enabled when the M/$\overline{\text{IO}}$ signal from the 8086 is low. Remember that the M/$\overline{\text{IO}}$ signal being high was one of the enabling conditions for the SDK-86 ROM and RAM decoders we discussed in previous sections. The M/$\overline{\text{IO}}$ signal will be low during any direct input or output operation. The $\overline{\text{RD}}$ signal from the 8086 will also be low during an IN operation, so this signal is used to enable an addressed port device for input. The $\overline{\text{WR}}$ signal from the 8086 will be low along with M/$\overline{\text{IO}}$ during an OUT operation, so this signal is used to enable an addressed port for output.

For an example of how direct I/O ports are addressed and selected in a real system, we will again look at the SDK-86 schematics in Figure 7-6, sheet 7. Here another 3625 PROM (*XA*22) is used to produce the chip select signals for four I/O devices. The O1 output of the PROM is used to enable the 8279 keyboard/display interface device. A section of Chapter 9 discusses in detail the operation of this device. The O2 output of the PROM is used to enable the 8251A USART shown on sheet 9 of the schematics. The 8251A allows communication with other systems in serial form. A section in Chapter 13 discusses the operation of this device. The O3 and O4 outputs are connected to two 8255A parallel port devices shown on sheet 5 of the schematics. These devices can be enabled individually to input or output bytes. They can also be enabled together to input or output words. A section in Chapter 9 shows you how to tell each port in these devices whether you want it to be an input or an output.

Take a look now at the 3625 decoder PROM to see if you can determine what conditions enable it. You should find that the $\overline{\text{CS2}}$ enable input of the PROM will be asserted when M/$\overline{\text{IO}}$ is low as it is during an input or output operation. Furthermore, you should see that the $\overline{\text{CS1}}$ input will be asserted when A11–A15 are all high. Now, to see what addresses cause each of the PROM outputs to be asserted, refer to the address decoder worksheet for the PROM in Figure 7-15*a*. From this figure you can see that to assert the O1 output low, A5–A15 have to be high, A4 has to be low, and A3 has to be high and A0 has to be low. $\overline{\text{BHE}}$ can be either a high or a low. Note, however, that only the lower eight data lines, D0–

PROM INPUTS						PROM OUTPUTS*			
A11–A15	A5–A10	A4	A3	$\overline{BHE}$	A0	$\overline{O4}$ HIGH PORT SELECT	$\overline{O3}$ LOW PORT SELECT	$\overline{O2}$ USART SELECT	$\overline{O1}$ KDSEL
1	1	0	1	0	0	1	1	1	0
1	1	0	1	1	0	1	1	1	0
1	1	1	0	0	0	1	1	0	1
1	1	1	0	1	0	1	1	0	1
1	1	1	1	0	0	0	0	1	1
1	1	1	1	0	1	0	1	1	1
1	1	1	1	1	0	1	0	1	1
ALL OTHER STATES						1	1	1	1

(*a*)

PORT ADDRESS	PORT FUNCTION
0000 to FFDF	OPEN
FFE8	READ/WRITE 8279 DISPLAY RAM OR READ 8279 FIFO
E9	
EA	READ 8279 STATUS OR WRITE 8279 COMMAND
EB	
EC	RESERVED
ED	
EE	RESERVED
FFEF	
FFF0	READ/WRITE 8251A DATA
F1	
F2	READ 8251A STATUS OR WRITE 8251A CONTROL
F3	
F4	RESERVED
F5	
F6	RESERVED
FFF7	
FFF8	READ/WRITE 8255A PORT P2A
F9	READ/WRITE 8255A PORT P1A
FA	READ/WRITE 8255A PORT P2B
FB	READ/WRITE 8255A PORT P1B
FC	READ/WRITE 8255A PORT P2C
FD	READ/WRITE 8255A PORT P1C
FE	WRITE 8255A P2 CONTROL
FFFF	WRITE 8255A P1 CONTROL

(*b*)

FIGURE 7-15 Truth table and map for SDK-86 port decoder. *(a)* Truth table. *(b)* Map.

D7, are connected to the 8279. Therefore, data must be sent to or read from the 8279 at an even byte address. In other words data must be sent as a byte to an even address or as the lower byte of a word to an even address.

The system base address for this device then is FFE8H. System address line A1 is connected to the 8279 to select one of two internal addresses in the device. A1 low selects one internal address and A1 high selects the other internal address. A1 low gives system address FFE8H, and A1 high gives system address FFEAH. These are then the two addresses for the 8279 in this system.

According to the worksheet in Figure 7-15*a*, the O2 output of the decoder PROM will be asserted low when A4–A15 are high, and A3 and A0 are low. $\overline{BHE}$ can be either a low or a high, but, since only the lower eight data lines are connected to the 8251A USART, data must be sent to or read from the device as bytes at an even address. Again system address line A1 is used to select one of two internal addresses in the 8251A (Figure 7-6, sheet 9). A1 low selects one internal address and A1 high selects the other internal address. The two system addresses for this device then are FFF0H and FFF2H.

Now, before discussing the O3 and O4 outputs of the decoder PROM, we will take a brief look at the two 8255 parallel port devices they enable. These devices are shown on sheet 5 of the schematics in Figure 7-6. Each of these devices contains three 8-bit parallel ports and a control register. System address lines A1 and A2 are used to address the desired port or register in the device just as lower address lines are used to address the desired internal location in a memory device. Note that the lower eight data lines, D0–D7, are connected to the *XA*40 device, and the upper eight data lines are connected to the *XA*35 device. This is done so that you have several input or output possibilities. You can read a byte from or write a byte to an even-addressed port in device

*XA*40. You can read a byte from or write a byte to an odd-addressed port in device *XA*35. You can read a word from or write a word to a 16-bit port made up from an 8-bit port from device *XA*40 and an 8-bit port from device *XA*35. To input or output a word both devices have to be enabled. Now let's look at the decoder truth table to determine what addresses enable the various ports in these devices.

The *XA*40 device will be enabled by the O3 output of the decoder PROM if address lines A3–A15 are high and A0 is low. A1 and A2 are used to select internal ports of the 8255A. Let's assume that these two bits are 0 for the first address in the device. To select the A port in the *XA*40 8255A, address lines A1 and A2 have to be low. The system address that will enable this device and select the A port within it is FFF8H. Other values of A2 and A1 will select one of the other ports or the control register in this device. Figure 7-15*b* shows the system addresses for the ports and control register in this 8255. Note that the ports in this device (*XA*40) are identified as port 2A, port 2B, and port 2C. These all have even addresses because A0 must be low for this device to be selected.

The *XA*35 8255A which contains port 1A, port 1B, and port 1C will be enabled by the O4 output of the decoder PROM if A3–A15 are high and the $\overline{\text{BHE}}$ line is low. If this 8255A is being enabled for a byte read or write, then the A0 line will also be high. A2 and A1 are again used to address one of the ports or the control register within the 8255A. A2 = 0 and A1 = 1 will select port 1A in this 8255A. As shown in Figure 7-15*b*, then, the system address for port 1A is FFF9H. Port 1B will be accessed with a system address of FFFBH, port 1C will be accessed with a system address of FFFDH, and the internal control register will be accessed with a system address of FFFFH.

Note in the truth table in Figure 7-15*a* that the 3625 PROM decoder will enable a port device only when the specific address assigned to that device is sent out by the 8086. This is sometimes called *complete decoding* because all of the address lines play a part in selecting a device and one of its internal ports or registers. As we show in a later section, adding another decoder to produce enable signals for more port devices is very easy in a system which uses this complete decoding.

THE SDK-86 "OFF-BOARD" DECODER

Before we show you how another port decoder can be added to the SDK-86, we need to briefly discuss the operation of the *off-board circuitry* on sheet 5 of the SDK-86 schematics. The purpose of this circuitry is to produce the signal $\overline{\text{OFF BOARD}}$ whenever the 8086 sends out a memory or port address which does not correspond to a device decoded on the board. The $\overline{\text{OFF BOARD}}$ signal will be asserted low if pin 4 of the A3 NAND gate is low or if pin 5 of the *A*3 NAND gate is low. According to the truth table for the *XA*12 PROM in Figure 7-16, the O1 output will be low if the the 8086 is doing a memory operation and the address sent out is not in one of the ranges decoded for the on-board RAM or ROM.

In order for pin 4 of the *A*3 NAND gate to be low, both pin 9 and pin 10 of the *A*3 NAND gate must be high. Pin 10 will be high if the 8086 is doing an input or output operation (IO/$\overline{\text{M}}$ from the 8286 inverting buffer equals 1). Pin 9 of the *A*3 NAND gate will be high if any one of the *A*19 NAND gate inputs is low. Since system address lines A5–A15 are connected to the inputs of the 74LS133 NAND gate, the signal to pin 9 of *A*3 will be high for any address less than FFE0H. In other words, pin 4 of the *A*3 NAND gate will be asserted low for any I/O operation in an address range not selected by the *XA*22 port decoder.

The $\overline{\text{OFF BOARD}}$ signal produced by the previously discussed PROM and logic gates is connected to an input of a NAND gate labeled *A*2 on sheet 2 of the schematics. If $\overline{\text{OFF BOARD}}$ is asserted low, or $\overline{\text{INTA}}$ is asserted low, or HLDA is asserted low, the output of this gate will be high. For now all we are interested in is the fact that if $\overline{\text{OFF BOARD}}$ is asserted low, a high will be applied to pin 1 of the *A*3 NAND gate in zone *A4* of the schematic. If the $\overline{\text{DEN}}$ signal from the 8086 is also asserted low, the signal labeled $\overline{\text{BUFFER ON}}$ will be asserted low. The $\overline{\text{DEN}}$ signal from the 8086 will be asserted whenever the 8086 reads in data from a memory location or a port, or when it writes data to a memory location or port. The $\overline{\text{BUFFER ON}}$ signal produced here is used to enable the 8286 data bus buffers (*XA*6 and *XA*7) shown on sheet 4 of the schematics. Now here's the point of all this.

In the next chapter we show you how to add another I/O decoder and some other devices to the prototyping area of an SDK-86 board. To drive these additional devices, the address, data and control buses must all be buffered. The address bus on the SDK-86 board is buffered by the 74S373 address latches shown on sheet 3 of the schematics. Data bus and control bus buffers are not needed to drive the ROM, RAM, and port devices that come with the SDK-86 board. To read data from or write data to external devices, however, the data bus is buffered by two 8286s shown as *XA*7 and *XA*6 on sheet 4 of the SDK-86 schematics. These two buffers are turned

PROM INPUTS									PROM OUTPUT (O1)	CORRESPONDING ADDRESS BLOCK
M/$\overline{\text{IO}}$	A19	A18	A17	A16	A15	A14	A13	A12		
1	0	0	0	0	0	0	0	0	1 (INACTIVE)	0H–0FFFH (ON-BOARD RAM)
1	1	1	1	1	1	1	1	0	1 (INACTIVE)	FE000H–FEFFFH (ON-BOARD PROM)
1	1	1	1	1	1	1	1	1	1 (INACTIVE)	FF000H–FFFFFH (ON-BOARD PROM)
ALL OTHER STATES									0 (ACTIVE)	01000H–FDFFFH (OFF-BOARD)

FIGURE 7-16 SDK-86 "off-board" decoder PROM truth table.

on when the $\overline{\text{BUFFER ON}}$ signal, described in the preceding paragraph, is asserted low. The 8286 buffers are bidirectional. When these buffers are enabled, the Data Transmit/Receive signal, DT/$\overline{\text{R}}$, from the 8086 will determine in which direction the buffers are pointed. If DT/$\overline{\text{R}}$ is high, the buffers will be enabled to write data to some external device. If DT/$\overline{\text{R}}$ is low, the buffers will be enabled to read data in from some external device.

The control bus signals are buffered by an 8286 labeled *XA*11 and a 74LS244 labeled *XA*8 on sheet 4 of the SDK-86 schematics. These buffers are permanently enabled to send out the control bus signals except during a HOLD state which we will explain later.

THE SDK-86 WAIT STATE GENERATOR CIRCUITRY

Now that you know how the $\overline{\text{OFF BOARD}}$ signal is produced on the SDK-86 board, we can explain the operation of the *WAIT state generator circuitry* shown on sheet 2 of the schematics.

In a previous section of the chapter we mentioned that if the RDY input of the 8086 is asserted low, the 8086 will insert one or more WAIT states in the machine cycle it is currently executing. Figure 7-2 shows how a WAIT state is inserted in an 8086 machine cycle. During a WAIT state the information on the buses is held constant. Whatever was on the buses at the start of the WAIT state remains throughout the WAIT state. The main purpose of inserting one or more WAIT states in a machine cycle is to give an addressed memory device or I/O device more time to accept or output data. In the next major section of the chapter we show you how to determine whether a WAIT state is needed for a given device with a given 8086 clock frequency. For now, however, let's just see how the circuitry on the SDK-86 board causes the 8086 to insert a selected number of WAIT states.

WAIT states are inserted by pulling the RDY1 input of the 8284 clock generator IC low (Figure 7-6, sheet 2, zone *C6*). The 8284 internally synchronizes the RDY1 input signal with the clock signal and sends the resultant signal to the RDY input of the 8086. For the SDK-86 the RDY1 input will be asserted low if all three inputs of the *A*15 NAND gate shown in zone *D5* of the schematic are high. Pin 10 of this device is tied to +5 V, so it is permanently high. Pin 11 of *A*15 will be high if any of the inputs of the NAND gate in zone *D7* are asserted low. Pin 1 of this gate will be low whenever the 8086 does an input or output operation. Pin 2 of this gate will be low whenever the 8086 accesses a port or memory location which is not decoded on the board. In other words, with these connections the selected number of WAIT states will be inserted in each machine cycle when the 8086 does a read from or a write to an on-board I/O device, or when the 8086 does a read from or a write to any device not decoded on the board. If jumper W39 is installed on pin 13 of *A*15, pin 11 of *A*15 will always be high. The selected number of WAIT states selected by the W27–W34 jumpers will be inserted for all read and write operations.

The desired number of wait states to be inserted is selected by putting a jumper between two pins in the W27–W34 matrix shown in zone *D3* (sheet 2) of the schematic. If a jumper is installed in the W27 position, for example, no WAIT states will be inserted. If a jumper is installed in the W28 position, one WAIT state will be inserted. The pattern continues to jumper W34 which will cause seven WAIT states to be inserted in each machine cycle. Here's how the WAIT state generator itself works.

The 74LS164 WAIT state generator is an 8-bit shift register. At the start of a machine cycle the $\overline{\text{RD}}$, $\overline{\text{WR}}$, and $\overline{\text{INTA}}$ signals from the 8086 are all high. These three signals being high will cause the NAND gate in zone *C4* to assert the clear input, CLR, of the shift register. The outputs of the shift register will then all be low. One of these lows will be coupled through a jumper and an inverter to pin 9 of the *A*15 NAND gate we discussed previously. This high on pin 9 together with a high on pin 11 will cause the RDY1 input of the 8284 to be pulled low. However, wait states will not be inserted unless RDY1 remains low long enough. Now, when $\overline{\text{RD}}$, $\overline{\text{WR}}$, or $\overline{\text{INTA}}$ goes low in the machine cycle, the $\overline{\text{CLR}}$ input of the 74LS164 shift register will go high, and the shift register will function normally. The highs on the INA and INB inputs will be loaded onto the QA output on the next positive edge of the clock. If the wait state jumper is in the W27 position, then this high on the QA output will, through the inverter and NAND gate, cause the RDY1 input of the 8284 to go high again. For this case the RDY1 input goes high soon enough that no WAIT states are inserted.

The high loaded into the 74LS164 shift register is shifted one stage to the right by each successive clock pulse. When the high reaches the jumper connected to the *A*25 inverter, it will cause the RDY1 input of the 8284 to go high. The 8086 will then exit from a WAIT state on the next clock pulse. The number of WAIT states inserted in a machine cycle is determined by how many stages the high has to be shifted before it reaches the installed jumper.

To summarize all of this, the 8086 will insert the selected number of WAIT states in any machine cycle which accesses any device not addressed on the board, or any I/O device on the board. If jumper W39 is inserted, the selected number of WAIT states will be inserted for any on-board or off-board access. The purpose of inserting wait states is to give the addressed device more time to accept or output data.

How the 8088 Microprocessor Accesses Memory and Ports

Now that we have shown in detail how the 8086 accesses memory and port devices, we can show you how the 8088 does it.

In Chapter 2 we mentioned that the 8088 is the CPU used in the IBM PC and the IBM PC/XT. The instruction set of the 8088 is identical to that of the 8086, and the registers of the two are the same. There are two major differences between the two devices. First, the 8088 instruction byte queue is only 4 bytes long instead of 6. Second, and more important, the 8088 memory is not divided into two banks as the 8086 memory is. The 8088 only has an 8-bit data bus, AD0–AD7. All of the memory devices and ports in an 8088 system are con-

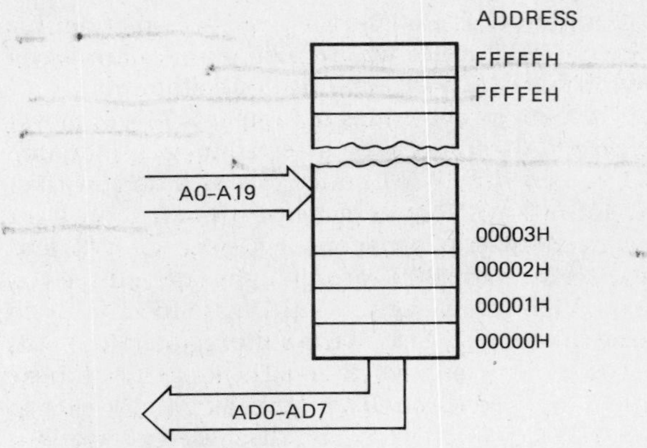

FIGURE 7-17 8088 memory structure.

nected onto these eight lines. The 8088 memory then functions as a single bank of up to 1,048,576 bytes. Figure 7-17 shows this structure. This single bank structure means that an 8088 cannot read a word from or write a word to memory in one machine cycle as the 8086 can. The 8088 can only read or write bytes, so the 8088 must always do 2 machine cycles to read or write a word. Address lines A0–A19 are used with some decoders to select a desired byte in memory. The 8088 does not produce the $\overline{BHE}$ signal, because it is not needed.

Most of the available memory devices and I/O devices were designed for 8-bit microprocessors which have 8-bit data buses. The 8088 was designed with an 8-bit data bus so that it would interface more easily with 8-bit memory devices and I/O devices. For example, in an 8088 system a simple 74LS138 can be used for a port device decoder as we showed in Figure 7-10*a*. An 8086 system requires a more complex decoder such as the 3625 PROM in Figure 7-6 (sheet 7), because the decoder has to take into account the states of A0 and $\overline{BHE}$.

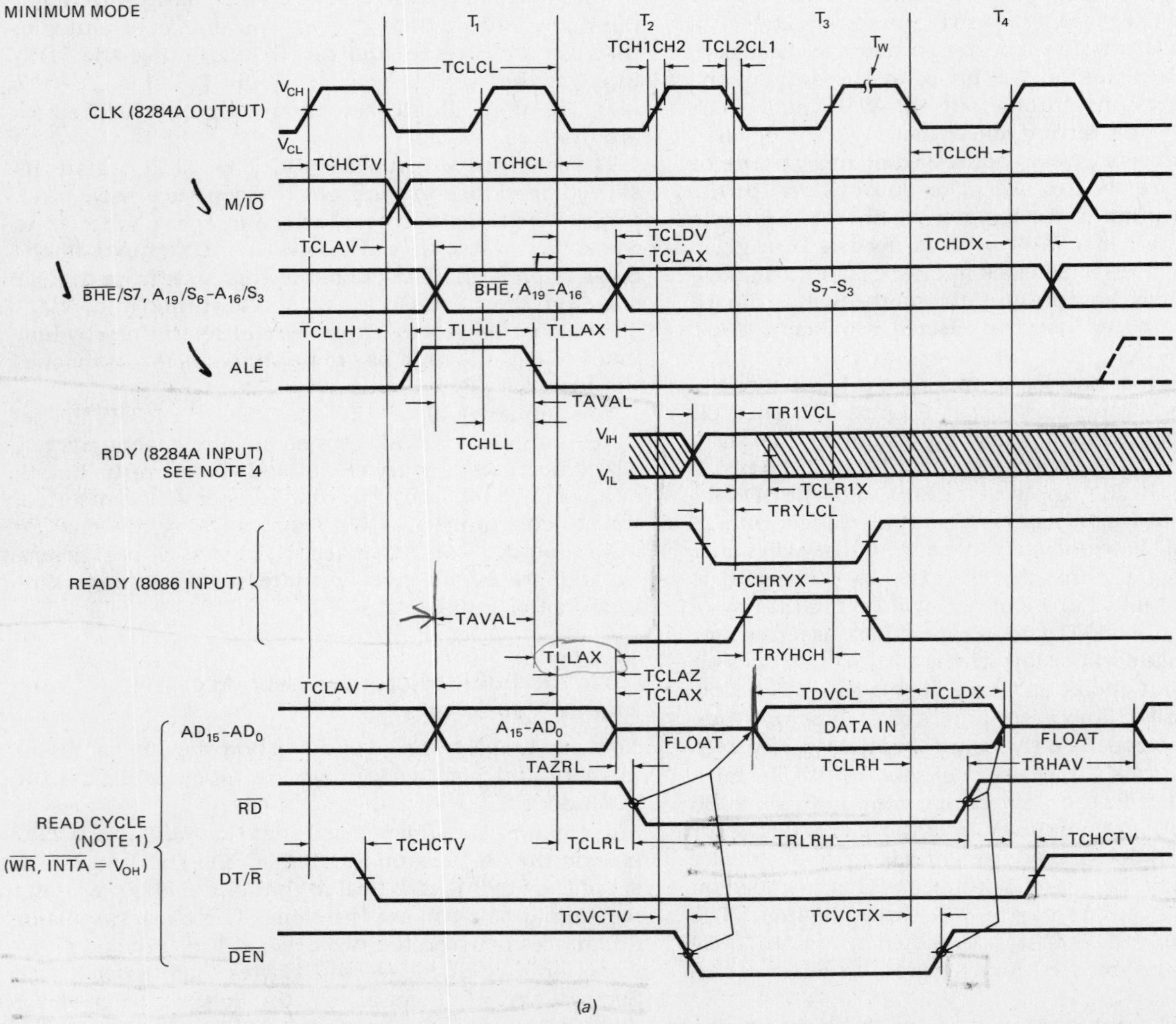

(*a*)

FIGURE 7-18 8086 minimum-mode timing waveforms and parameters. *(a)* Read waveforms. *(b)* Simplified read waveforms. *(c)* Timing parameters. *(Intel Corporation)*

8086 TIMING PARAMETERS

In previous sections of this chapter we used generalized timing waveforms such as that in Figure 7-2. These diagrams are sufficient to show the sequence of activities on the 8086 buses. However, they are not detailed enough to determine, for example, whether a memory device is fast enough to work in a given 8086 system. To allow you to make precise timing calculations, manufacturer's data books give detailed timing waveforms and lists of timing parameters for each microprocessor. Complete timing information for the 8086 is contained in the data sheet in the appendix. Figure 7-18 shows some of these for the 8086 operating in minimum mode.

As you look at Figure 7-18 remember the *5-minute freak-out rule*. Most of the time there are only a very few of these parameters that you need to worry about. In most systems, for example, you don't need to worry about the clock signal parameters, because an 8284 clock generator and a crystal will be used to produce the clock signal. The frequency of the clock signal from an 8284 is always one-third the resonant frequency of the crystal connected to it. The 8284 is designed to guarantee the correct clock period, clock time low, clock time high, etc. as long as the correct suffix number part is used. The 8284A, for example, can be used in an 8-MHz system, but a faster part, the 8284A-1 must be used for a system where a 10-MHz clock is desired.

The edges of the clock signal cause operations in the 8086 to occur; therefore, as you can see in Figure 7-18*a*, the clock waveform is used as a reference for other times. The timing values for when the 8086 puts out M/$\overline{IO}$, addresses, ALE, and control signals, for example, are all specified with reference to an appropriate clock edge.

As we mentioned earlier, one of the main things you use these diagrams and parameters for is to find out whether a particular memory or port device is fast enough to work in a system with a given clock frequency. Here's an example of how you do this.

If you look in zone *C5* of sheet 2 of the SDK-86 schematics, you will see that if jumper W41 is installed, the 8086 will receive a 4.9-MHz clock signal from the 8284. If jumper W40 is installed, the 8086 will receive the 2.45-MHz PCLK signal from the 8284. Now, suppose that you want to determine whether the 2716 EPROMs on the SDK-86 board will work correctly with no WAIT states if you install jumper W41 to run the 8086 with the 4.9-MHz clock.

First you look up the access times for the 2716

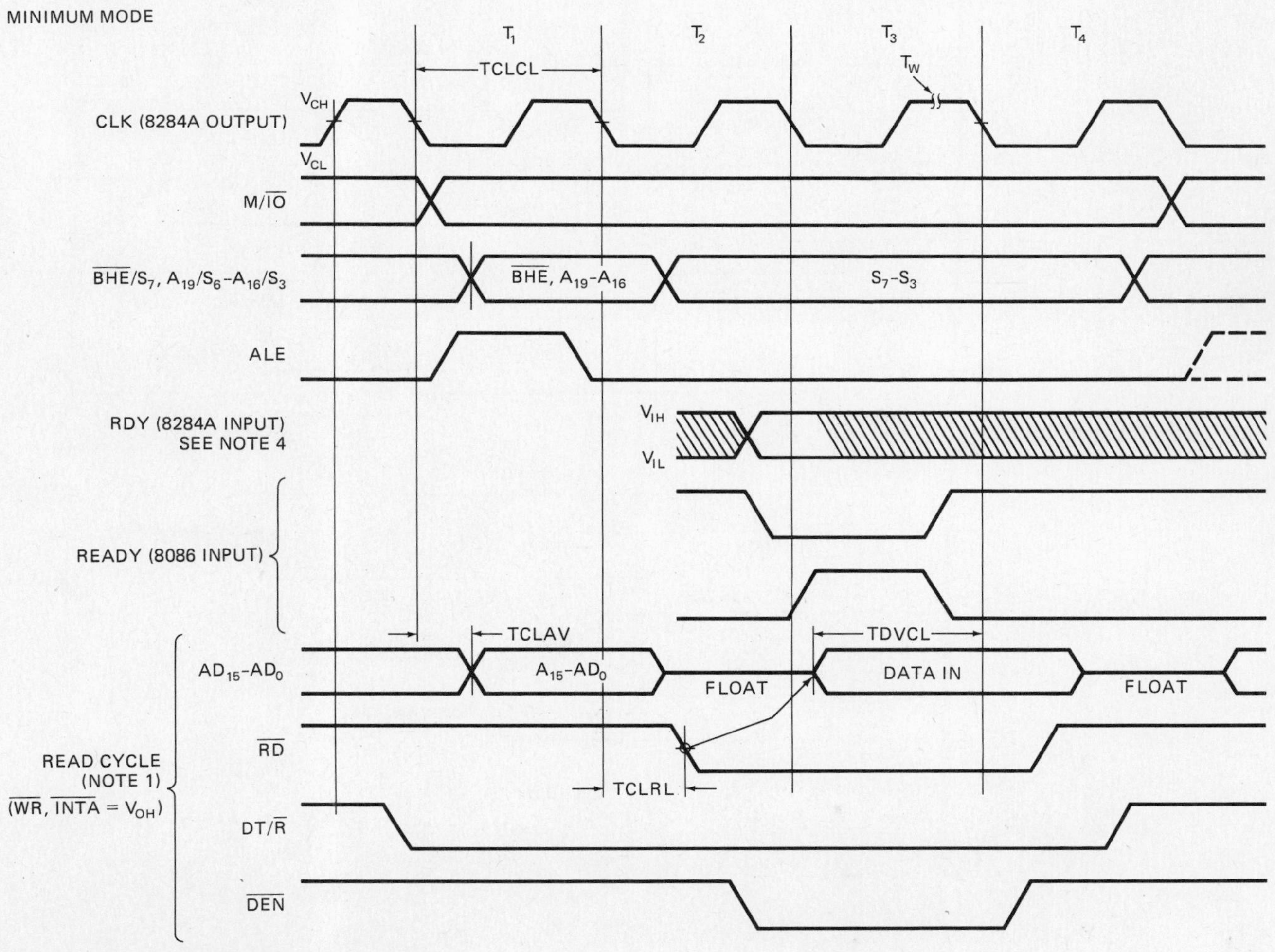

FIGURE 7-18 (*continued*)

EPROM in the appropriate data book. According to an Intel data book, the 2716 has a maximum address to output access time, t_{ACC}, of 450 ns. This means that if the 2716 is already enabled and its output buffers turned on, it will put valid data on its outputs no more than 450 ns after an address is applied to the address inputs. The 2716 data sheet also gives a chip enable to output access time, t_{CE}, of 450 ns. This means that if an address is already present on the address inputs of the 2716, and the output buffers are already enabled, the 2716 will put valid data on its outputs no later than 450 ns after the $\overline{CE}$ input is asserted low. A third parameter given for the 2716 in the data book is an output enable to output time, t_{OE}, of 120 ns maximum. This means that if the device already has an address on its address inputs, and its $\overline{CE}$ input is already asserted, valid data

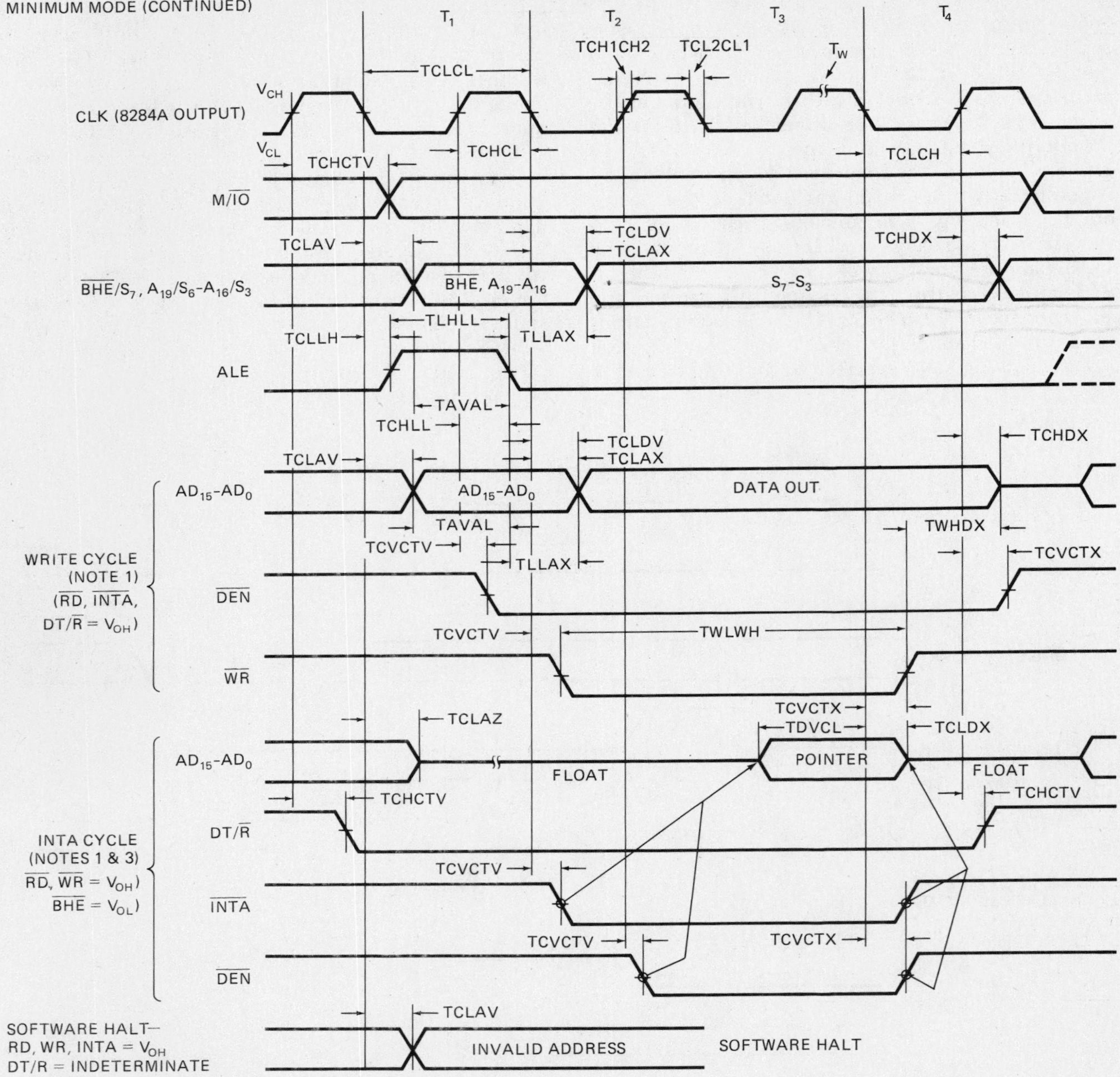

NOTES:

1. All signals switch between V_{OH} and V_{OL} unless otherwise specified.
2. RDY is sampled near the end of T_2, T_3, T_W to determine if T_W machines states are to be inserted.
3. Two INTA cycles run back-to-back. The 8086 LOCAL ADDR/DATA BUS is floating during both INTA cycles. Control signals shown for second INTA cycle.
4. Signals at 8284A are shown for reference only.
5. All timing measurements are made at 1.5 V unless otherwise noted.

(*b*)

FIGURE 7-18 (*continued*)

MINIMUM COMPLEXITY SYSTEM TIMING REQUIREMENTS

SYMBOL	PARAMETER	8086		8086-1 (Preliminary)		8086-2		UNITS	TEST CONDITIONS
		MIN.	MAX.	MIN.	MAX.	MIN.	MAX.		
TCLCL	CLK Cycle Period	200	500	100	500	125	500	ns	
TCLCH	CLK Low Time	118		53		68		ns	
TCHCL	CLK High Time	69		39		44		ns	
TCH1CH2	CLK Rise Time		10		10		10	ns	From 1.0 V to 3.5 V
TCL2CL1	CLK Fall Time		10		10		10	ns	From 3.5 V to 1.0 V
TDVCL	Data in Setup Time	30		5		20		ns	
TCLDX	Data in Hold Time	10		10		10		ns	
TR1VCL	RDY Setup Time into 8284A (See Notes 1, 2)	35		35		35		ns	
TCLR1X	RDY Hold Time into 8284A (See Notes 1, 2)	0		0		0		ns	
TRYHCH	READY Setup Time into 8086	118		53		68		ns	
TCHRYX	READY Hold Time into 8086	30		20		20		ns	
TRYLCL	READY Inactive to CLK (See Note 3)	–8		–10		–8		ns	
THVCH	HOLD Setup Time	35		20		20		ns	
TINVCH	INTR, NMI, $\overline{\text{TEST}}$ Setup Time (See Note 2)	30		15		15		ns	
TILIH	Input Rise Time (Except CLK)		20		20		20	ns	From 0.8 V to 2.0 V
TIHIL	Input Fall Time (Except CLK)		12		12		12	ns	From 2.0 V to 0.8 V
TCLAV	Address Valid Delay	10	110	10	50	10	60	ns	
TCLAX	Address Hold Time	10		10		10		ns	
TCLAZ	Address Float Delay	TCLAX	80	10	40	TCLAX	50	ns	
TLHLL	ALE Width	TCLCH-20		TCLCH-10		TCLCH-10		ns	
TCLLH	ALE Active Delay		80		40		50	ns	
TCHLL	ALE Inactive Delay		85		45		55	ns	
TLLAX	Address Hold Time to ALE Inactive	TCHCL-10		TCHCL-10		TCHCL-10		ns	
TCLDV	Data Valid Delay	10	110	10	50	10	60	ns	
TCHDX	Data Hold Time	10		10		10		ns	
TWHDX	Data Hold Time After WR	TCLCH-30		TCLCH-25		TCLCH-30		ns	
TCVCTV	Control Active Delay 1	10	110	10	50	10	70	ns	*C_L = 20 – 100 pF for all 8086 Outputs (In addition to 8086 selfload)
TCHCTV	Control Active Delay 2	10	110	10	45	10	60	ns	
TCVCTX	Control Inactive Delay	10	110	10	50	10	70	ns	
TAZRL	Address Float to READ Active	0		0		0		ns	
TCLRL	$\overline{\text{RD}}$ Active Delay	10	165	10	70	10	100	ns	
TCLRH	$\overline{\text{RD}}$ Inactive Delay	10	150	10	60	10	80	ns	
TRHAV	$\overline{\text{RD}}$ Inactive to Next Address Active	TCLCL-45		TCLCL-35		TCLCL-40		ns	
TCLHAV	HLDA Valid Delay	10	160	10	60	10	100	ns	
TRLRH	$\overline{\text{RD}}$ Width	2TCLCL-75		2TCLCL-40		2TCLCL-50		ns	
TWLWH	$\overline{\text{WR}}$ Width	2TCLCL-60		2TCLCL-35		2TCLCL-40		ns	
TAVAL	Address Valid to ALE Low	TCLCH-60		TCLCH-35		TCLCH-40		ns	
TOLOH	Output Rise Time		20		20		20	ns	From 0.8 V to 2.0 V
TOHOL	Output Fall Time		12		12		12	ns	From 2.0 V to 0.8 V

NOTES:
1. Signal at 8284A shown for reference only.
2. Setup requirement for asynchronous signal only to guarantee recognition at next CLK.
3. Applies only to T2 state. (8 ns into T3).

(*c*)

FIGURE 7-18 (*continued*)

will appear on the output pins at most 120 ns after the $\overline{OE}$ pin is asserted low.

Now that you have these three parameters for the 2716, the next step is to check if each one of these times is short enough for the device to work with a 4.9-MHz 8086. In other words, does the 2716 put out valid data soon enough after it is addressed and enabled to satisfy the requirements of the 8086? To determine this you need to look at both the 8086 timing parameters and how the 2716 is addressed and enabled on the SDK-86 board.

To make it easier for you to find the important parameters for these calculation, we show in Figure 7-18*b* a simplified version of the timing diagram in Figure 7-18*a*. You should try to mentally do this simplification whenever you are faced with a timing diagram. As shown by the timing diagram in Figure 7-18*b* the 8086 sends out M/$\overline{IO}$, $\overline{BHE}$, and an address during T1 of the machine cycle. Note on the AD15–AD0 line of the timing diagram that the 8086 outputs this information within a time labeled TCLAV after the falling edge of the clock at the start of T1. TCLAV stands for *time from clock low to address valid*. According to the data sheet shown in Figure 7-18*c* in the 8086 column, the maximum value of this time is 110 ns. Now look further to the right on the AD15–AD0 lines. You should see that valid data must arrive at the 8086 from memory a time TDVCL before the falling edge of the clock at the end of T3. TDVCL stands for *time data must be valid before clock goes low*. The data sheet gives a value of 30 ns for this parameter.

The time between the end of the TCLAV interval (time clock low to address valid) and the start of the TDVCL interval is the time available for getting the address to the memory, and for the t_{ACC} of the memory device. You can determine this time by subtracting TCLAV and TDVCL from the time for 3 clock cycles. With a 4.9-MHz clock each clock cycle will be 204 ns. Three clock cycles then total 612 ns. Subtracting a TCLAV of 110 ns and a TDVCL of 30 ns leaves 472 ns available for getting the address to the 2716 and for its t_{ACC}. To help you visualize these times, Figure 7-19*a* shows this operation in simplified diagram form.

If you look at sheets 1 and 3 of the SDK-86 schematics you should see that the $\overline{BHE}$ signal and the A0–A11 address information goes from the 8086 through the 74S373 latches to get to the 2716s. The propagation delay of the 74S373s then must be subtracted from the 472 ns to determine how much time is actually available for the t_{ACC} of the 2716. The maximum delay of a 74S373 is 12 ns. As shown in Figure 7-19*a*, subtracting this from the 472 ns leaves 460 ns for the t_{ACC} of the 2716. Now, as we told you in a previous paragraph, the 2716 has a maximum t_{ACC} of 450 ns. Since this 450 ns is less than the 460 ns available, you know that the t_{ACC} of the 2716 is acceptable for the SDK-86 operating with a 4.9-MHz clock. You still, however, must check if the values of t_{CE} and t_{OE} for the 2716 are acceptable.

If you look at sheet 1 of the SDK-86 schematics, you should see that the $\overline{CE}$ inputs of the 2716s are connected to either A0 or to $\overline{BHE}$. The timing for these signals is the same as that for the addresses in the preceding section. As shown in Figure 7-19*a* the time available for t_{CE} of the 2716 will be 460 ns. Since the maximum t_{CE} of the 2716 is 450 ns, you know that this parameter is also acceptable for an SDK-86 operating with a 4.9-MHz clock.

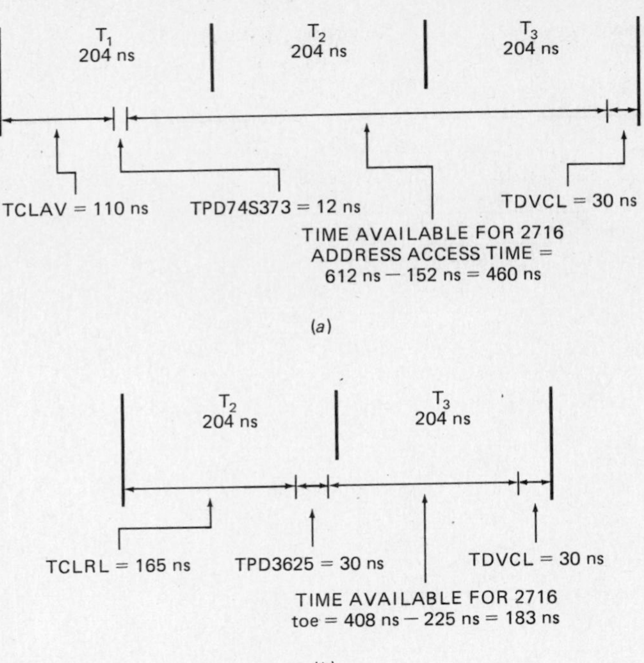

FIGURE 7-19 Calculations of 8086 times available for 2716 EPROM access. *(a)* Time for t_{ACC} and t_{RD}. *(b)* Time for t_{OE}.

The final parameter to check is t_{OE} of the 2716. According to sheet 1 of the SDK-86 schematics, the $\overline{OE}$ signals for the 2716s are produced by the 3625 decoder. The signals coming to this decoder are A12–A19, M/$\overline{IO}$, and $\overline{RD}$. Look at the 8086 timing diagram in Figure 7-18*b* to see if you can determine which of these signals arrives last at the 3625. You should find that addresses and M/$\overline{IO}$ are sent out during T1, but $\overline{RD}$ is not sent out until T2. As indicated by the arrow from the falling edge of the $\overline{RD}$ signal, $\overline{RD}$ going low causes the address decoder to send an $\overline{OE}$ signal to the 2716 EROMs. Since $\overline{RD}$ is sent out so much later than addresses, it will be the limiting factor for timing. $\overline{RD}$ going low and the EPROM returning valid data must occur within the time of states T2 and T3. Now, according to the timing diagram, $\overline{RD}$ is sent out from the 8086 within a time TCLRL after the falling edge of the clock at the start of T2. From the data sheet the maximum value of TCLRL is 165 ns. As we discussed before, the 8086 requires that valid data arrive on AD0–AD15 from memory a time TDVCL before the falling edge of the clock at the end of T3. The minimum value of TDVCL from the data sheet is 30 ns. The time between the end of the TCLRL interval and the start of the TDVCL interval is the time available for the $\overline{OE}$ signal to get produced and for the $\overline{OE}$ signal to turn on the memory. To determine the actual time available for these operations, first compute the time for states T2 and T3. For a 4.9-MHz clock each clock cycle or state will be 204 ns, so the two together total 408 ns. Then subtract the TCLRL of 165 ns and the TDVCL of 30 ns. As shown by the simple diagram in Figure 7-19*b*, this leaves 213 ns available for the decoder delay and the t_{OE} of the 2716. Checking a data sheet for the 3625 would show you that it has a maximum $\overline{CS2}$ to output delay of 30 ns. Subtract this from the available 213 ns to see how much time is left for the t_{OE} of the 2716. The result of this subtraction is 183 ns. As we indicated in a previous paragraph, the 2716 has a maximum t_{OE} of 120 ns. Since this time is considerably less than the 183 ns available, the 2716 has an acceptable t_{OE} value for operating on the SDK-86 board with a 4.9-MHz clock.

You have now checked all three 2716 parameters and found that all three are acceptable for an SDK-86 operating on a 4.9-MHz clock. No wait states need to be inserted when these devices are accessed, so jumper W39 in zone *D7* on sheet 2 of the schematics can be left out. As discussed in a previous section, installing jumper W39 will cause the selected number of WAIT states to be inserted for all memory or I/O operations.

Here's a final point about calculating the time available for t_{ACC}, t_{CE}, and t_{OE} of some device in a system. Suppose that you want to add another pair of 2716 EPROMs in the prototyping area of the SDK-86 board, and you want to enable the outputs of these added devices with the O3 output of the 3625 ROM decoder on sheet 1 of the schematics. The timing for these added devices will be the same as for the previously discussed 2716s except that the data from the added devices must come back through the 8286 buffers shown on sheet 4 of the SDK-86 schematics. According to an 8286 data sheet, these buffers have a maximum delay of 30 ns. This 30 ns must be subtracted from the times available for t_{ACC}, t_{CE}, and t_{OE}. If you look back at our calculations of the time available for t_{ACC} in Figure 7-19*a*, for example, you will see that we ended up with 460 ns available for t_{ACC}. Subtracting the 30 ns of buffer delay from this leaves only 430 ns, which is considerably less than the maximum t_{ACC} of 450 ns for the 2716. This tells you that, because of the buffer delay, the added 2716's are not fast enough to operate on an SDK-86 board with a 4.9-MHz clock and no WAIT states. To take care of this problem, the SDK-86 is designed so that any access to a memory or I/O device "off board" will cause the selected number of WAIT states to be inserted in the machine cycle. For our example here, selecting one WAIT state with jumper W28 on sheet 2 will give another 204 ns for the data to get from the 2716s to the 8086. This is more than enough time to compensate for the buffer delay, so the added 2716s will work correctly.

TROUBLESHOOTING A SIMPLE 8086-BASED MICROCOMPUTER

Now that you have some knowledge of the software and the hardware of a microcomputer system, we can start teaching you how to troubleshoot a simple microcomputer system such as an SDK-86 board. For this section assume that the microcomputer or microprocessor-based instrument previously worked. Later sections of this book will describe how the prototype of a microprocessor-based instrument is developed.

The following sections describe a series of steps that we have found effective in troubleshooting various microcomputer systems. The first point to impress on your mind about troubleshooting a microcomputer is that a systematic approach is almost always more effective than random poking, probing, and hoping. You don't, for example, want to spend 2 hours troubleshooting a system and finally find that the only problem is that the power supply is putting out only 3 V instead of 5 V. Use the list of steps below or a list of your own each time you have to troubleshoot a microcomputer.

1. Identifying the Symptoms

Make a list of the symptoms that you find or those that a customer describes to you. Find out, for example, whether the symptom is present immediately or whether the system must operate for a while before it shows up. If someone else describes the symptoms to you, check them yourself, or have that person demonstrate the symptoms to you. This allows you to check if the problem is with the machine or with how the person is attempting to use the machine.

2. Making a Careful Visual and Tactile Inspection

This step is good for preventive maintenance as well for finding a current problem. Check for components that have been or are excesively hot. When touching components to see if any are too hot, do it gently, because a bad IC can get hot enough to give a nasty burn if you keep your finger on it too long.

Check to see that all ICs are firmly seated in their sockets and that the ICs have no bent pins. Vibration can cause ICs to work loose in their sockets. A bent pin may make contact for a while, but after heating, cooling, and vibration, it may no longer make contact. Also, inexpensive IC sockets may oxidize with age and no longer make good contact.

Check for broken wires and loose connectors. A thin film of dust, etc. may form on printed circuit board edge connectors and prevent them from making dependable contact. The film can be removed by gently rubbing the edge connector fingers with a clean, nonabrasive pencil eraser. If the microcomputer has ribbon cables, check to see if they have been moved around or stressed. Ribbon cables usually have small wires that are easily broken. If you suspect a broken conductor in a ribbon cable, you can later make an electrical check to verify your suspicions.

3. Checking the Power Supply

From the manual for the microcomputer determine the power supply voltages. Check the supply voltage(s) directly on the appropriate pins of some ICs to make sure the voltage is actually getting there. Check with a scope to make sure the power supplies do not have excessive noise or ripple. One microcomputer that we were called on to troubleshoot had very strange symptoms caused by 2-V peak-to-peak ripple on the 5-V supply.

4. Signal Roll Call

The next step is to make a quick check of some key signals around the CPU of the microcomputer. If the problem is a bad IC, this can help point you toward the one that is bad. First, check if the clock signal is present and at the right frequency. If not, perhaps the clock generator IC is bad. If the microcomputer has a clock, but doesn't seem to be doing anything, use an oscilloscope to check if the CPU is putting out control signals such as RD, WR, and ALE. Also, check the least-significant data bus line to see if there is any activity on the buses. If there is no activity on these lines, a common cause is that the CPU is stuck in a wait, hold, halt, or reset condition by the failure of some TTL devices. To check this out, use the manual to help you predict what logic level should be on each of the CPU input control signals for normal operation. The RDY input of the 8086, for example, should be high for normal operation. If an external logic gate fails and holds RDY low, the 8086 will go on inserting WAIT states forever, and the buses will be held constant. If the 8086 HOLD input is held high or the RST input is held high, the 8086 buses will be floating. Connecting a scope probe to these lines will pull them to ground, so you will see them as lows.

If there is activity on the buses, use an oscilloscope to see if the CPU is putting out control signals such as $\overline{RD}$ and $\overline{WR}$. Also check with your oscilloscope to see if select signals are being generated on the outputs of the ROM, RAM, and port decoders as the system attempts to run its monitor or basic program. If no select signals are being produced, then the address decoder may be bad or the CPU may not be sending out the correct addresses.

After a little practice you should be able to work through the previously described steps quite quickly. If you have not located the problem at this point, the next step for a system with its ICs in sockets is to systematically substitute known good ICs for those in the nonworking system.

5. Systematically Substituting ICs

The easiest case of substitution is that where you have two identical microcomputers, one that works and one that doesn't, and the ICs of both units are in sockets. For this case you can use the working system to test the ICs from the nonworking system. The trick here is to do this in such a way that you don't end up with two systems that do not work! Here's how you do it.

First of all, DO NOT REMOVE OR INSERT ANY ICs WITH THE POWER ON! Now, with the power off, remove the CPU from the good system and put it in a piece of conductive foam. Plug the CPU from the bad system into the now empty socket on the good board and turn on the power. If the good system still works, then probably the CPU is good. Turn off the power and put the CPU back in the bad system. If the good system does not work with the CPU from the bad system, then the CPU is probably bad. Remove it from the good system and bend the pins so that you know it is bad. If the CPU seems bad, you can try replacing it with the CPU you removed from the good system. If you do this, however, it is important to keep track of which IC came from where. To do this we like to mark each IC from the good system with a wide-tip, water-soluble marking pen. We can then rebuild the good system by simply putting back all the marked ICs. The marks on the ICs can easily be removed with a damp cloth.

The procedure from here on is to keep testing ICs from the bad system until you find all of the bad ICs. Make sure to turn the power off before you remove or insert any ICs. Be aware that more than one IC may be bad. It is not unusual, for example, that an AC power-line surge will wipe out several devices in a system. We usually work our way out from the CPU to address latches, buffers, decoders, and memory devices. Often the specific symptoms point you to the problem group of ICs without your having to test every IC in the system. If, for example, the system accesses ROM, but doesn't access RAM, suspect the RAM decoder. If a system uses buffers on the buses, suspect these devices. Buffers are high-current devices and they often fail.

6. Troubleshooting a System with Soldered-in ICs

The approach described in the preceding paragraphs works well if the system ICs are all in sockets and you have two identical systems. However, since sockets add to the cost and unreliability of a system, many small systems put only the CPU and ROMs in sockets. This makes your troubleshooting work harder, but not impossible.

Again, if you have two identical systems, one that works and one that doesn't work, you can attempt to run the monitor or basic system program on each and compare signals on the two. A missing or wrong signal may point you to the bad IC or ICs.

If the system works enough to read some instructions from ROM and execute them, you can replace the monitor or basic system ROM with one that contains diagnostic programs which test RAM and I/O devices. A RAM test routine, for example, might attempt to write all 1's to each RAM location, and then read the memory location to see if the the data was written correctly to that location. If the data read back is not correct, the diagnostic program can stop and in some way indicate the address that it could not write to. If a write of all 1's is successful, then the test routine will try to write all 0's to each memory location. A port test routine might initialize a port for output, and then write alternating 1's and 0's to the port over and over again. With an oscilloscope you can then see if the port device is getting enabled and if the data is getting to the output of the port device. Another port test routine might try to read a byte of data in from a port over and over so that you can again see if the device is getting enabled and if the data is getting through the device to the system data bus. The technique of using program routines to test hardware is a very important one that you will use many times when you are working with microcomputer systems.

Now, suppose that you have localized the problem to a few ICs that are soldered in. If the problem is one that occurs when the unit gets hot, you might try spraying some Freon cold spray on the ICs, one at a time, to see if you can determine which one has a problem. If this does not find the bad IC or the problem is not heat-related, what you do next is to replace these ICs one at a time until the system works correctly. The point we want to stress here is that cost of these few ICs is probably much less that the cost of the time it would take you to determine just which IC is bad, if you do not have specialized test equipment.

To remove an IC from a printed circuit board, DO NOT attempt to desolder pins with a hand-held solder "slurper." Modern multilayer printed circuit boards are quite fragile, and these tools can slip and knock a trace right off the board. Instead, use cutters with narrow tips to cut all the leads of the IC next to the body. Since you are going to throw it out anyway, you don't care if you destroy the IC. With the body of the IC out of the way, you can then gently heat each pin individually and use needle nose pliers to remove it from the PC board. If the hole fills with solder, heat it gently and insert a small wooden toothpick until the solder cools. After you replace each IC, power up the system and see if it now works.

The techniques described in the preceding sections will enable you to troubleshoot many microcomputer systems with a minimum of test equipment. However, specialized test equipment is available to speed up the process and help find complex problems. The following sections describe two of these instruments.

7. Using a Logic Analyzer to Troubleshoot a Microcomputer System

A *logic analyzer* is an instrument which allows you to see the signals on 16 to 64 signal lines at once. With a logic analyzer you can, for example, see the signals on the address bus, data bus, and control bus of a microcomputer. Figure 7-20 shows a picture of a relatively low-cost logic analyzer, the Tektronix 318. Instruments such as this are themselves controlled by internal microprocessors. Small clipleads plug into a pod shown at the bottom of the drawing to get parallel data signals into the analyzer. The model shown only has 16 parallel data inputs. In addition, a scope-type probe can be used to send in serial data such as that sent out from a UART to a modem.

Figure 7-21 shows a functional block diagram of a simple logic analyzer. Since logic analyzers are used to detect and display only 1's and 0's, a comparator is put on each input. The reference input of the comparator is set for the logic threshold of the devices in the system. The signals out of the comparators to the rest of the analyzer are then clear-cut 1's or 0's.

The analyzer takes "snapshots" of the logic levels on each of the data inputs and stores these samples in an

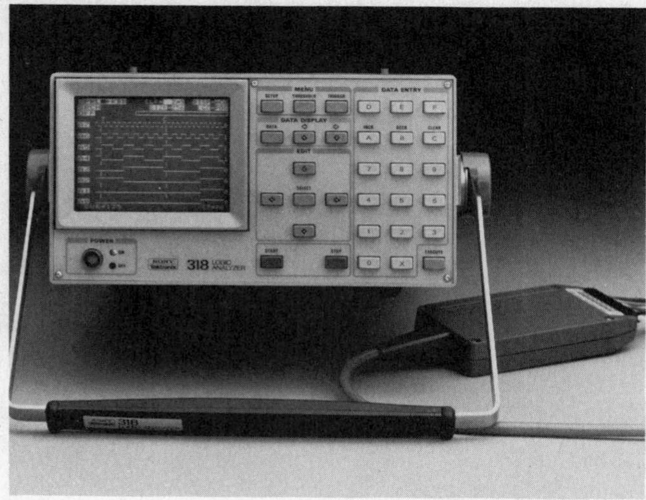

FIGURE 7-20 Tektronix 318 logic analyzer. *(Copyright 1983, Tektronix Inc.)*

internal RAM. Different analyzers store between 256 and 1024 samples for each input channel. A *clock* signal tells the analyzer how often to take samples. As shown by the block diagram in Figure 7-21, an internally produced signal or some external signal can be used to clock the analyzer. If you are using an analyzer to look at 8086 address and data lines, for example, you could use ALE as a clock signal. The analyzer will then take a sample each time the 8086 puts out an address and pulses ALE. The samples stored in the analyzer memory will then represent the sequence of addresses output by the 8086 after some specified *trigger*. As another example, you could clock the analyzer on $\overline{RD}$ from an 8086. After a specified trigger the analyzer will take a sample each time the 8086 does a read operation. In this case the samples stored in the analyzer memory will represent the sequence of data words read in from memory or from ports.

To make precise timing measurements with an analyzer a clock signal from an internal, crystal-controlled oscillator is used. In this case the analyzer will take a sample each time a pulse from the internal clock oscillator occurs. If, for example, you choose an internal clock frequency of 50 MHz, the analyzer will take a sample every 20 ns.

If the analyzer is receiving either an internal or an external clock, it will be continuously taking samples of the input data and storing these samples in the internal RAM. A *trigger* signal tells the analyzer when to display the samples stored in the RAM. As shown by the block diagram in Figure 7-21 some external signal can be used to trigger the analyzer, or the trigger signal can come from a *word recognizer* in the analyzer. A word recognizer compares the binary word on the input signal lines with a word you set with switches or a keyboard. When the two words match, the word recognizer sends out a trigger signal.

Since the analyzer is continuously taking samples, you can set the analyzer for a *pretrigger* display, a *center*

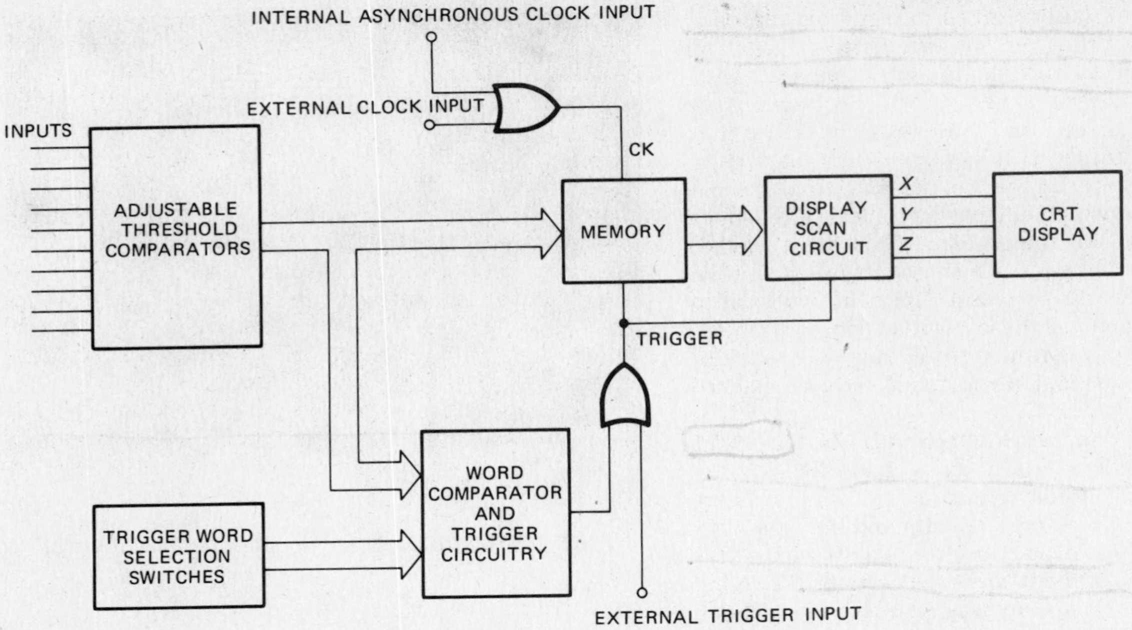

FIGURE 7-21 Logic analyzer block diagram.

trigger display, or a *posttrigger* display. For an analyzer that displays 256 samples, pretrigger means that the display will show the 256 samples that were taken just before the trigger occurred. For center trigger mode, 128 samples taken before the trigger and 128 samples taken after the trigger will be displayed. Posttrigger mode means that the analyzer will take 256 more samples after the trigger and display them.

Figure 7-22 shows some of the formats in which a logic analyzer can display the samples stored in its RAM. The series of displayed data samples is often called a *trace*. The timing diagram format in Figure 7-22*a* is most useful when making time measurements with an internal clock. A binary listing such as that in Figure 7-22*b* is useful for seeing the actual pattern of 1's and 0's on signal lines, but a hexadecimal listing such as that in Figure 7-22*c* makes it easier to recognize if a microcomputer is putting out addresses in the right sequence.

Some analyzers, such as the Tektronix 318, allow you take a series of samples from a functioning system, store these samples in a second memory in the analyzer, and then compare these samples with a series of samples taken from a nonfunctioning system. We have found this feature quite helpful in troubleshooting malfunctioning instruments which have poor documentation.

As we mentioned previously, the 318 can also be used to display a sequence of serial data as shown in Figure 7-22*c*. Note that in this format the analyzer shows the binary, hexadecimal, and the equivalent ASCII code for each of the data bytes taken in.

To summarize then, a logic analyzer takes samples of the signals present on its data inputs each time a clock pulse occurs and stores these samples in an internal RAM. A system signal such as ALE may be used as a clock source. In this case the analyzer is said to be operating in synchronous mode. For precise timing measurements an internal, crystal controlled clock source is used. The group of samples that are actually displayed on the screen is determined by a trigger signal. The trigger signal may come from some external source, or it may be produced by a word recognizer when it finds a specified data word on the parallel signal lines. Now that you have an overview of how a logic analyzer works, here's a few hints on how to use one for troubleshooting an 8086 microcomputer.

Connect the analyzer data inputs to the address and data bus lines from the CPU. For an 8086, connect the external clock input of the analyzer to the 8086 ALE pin. Look at an 8086 timing diagram such as the one in Figure 7-2 to see at which edge of the ALE signal valid addresses are present on the buses. Set the analyzer to clock on this edge. Set the analyzer to trigger on address FFFF0H, the first address output by the 8086 after a reset. Set the analyzer display format for posttrigger display. Tell the analyzer to do a trace and press the 8086 system reset button. The display on the analyzer should show you the sequence of addresses output after a reset. If you have one, use the system monitor listing to see if the displayed sequence is correct. If the sequence is not correct, look for address bits that should change, but don't. The cause of this problem may be the CPU or an address buffer. A common failure mode for buffers is that an input or an output will short to V_{cc} or to ground. This prevents that line from changing.

If the address sequence seems reasonable, connect the analyzer external clock input to the 8086 $\overline{RD}$ pin. Set the analyzer to clock on the positive edge of this signal. Set the format for posttrigger display. Tell the analyzer to do a trace and push the system reset button. The display on the analyzer should show the data transferred

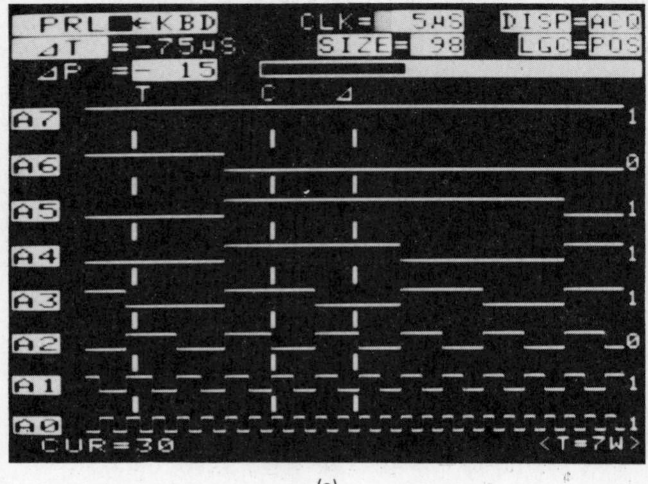

(a)

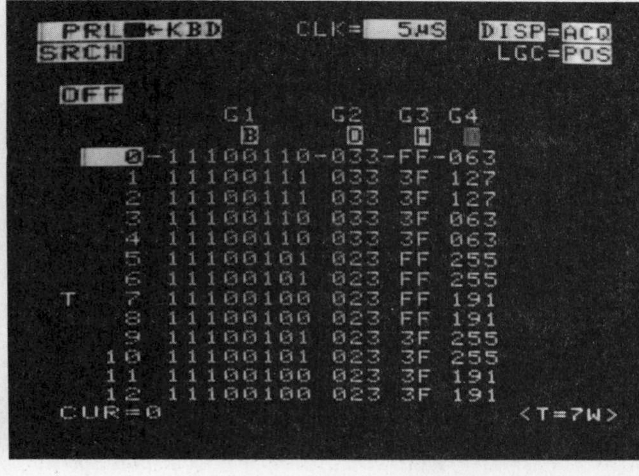

(b)

(c)

FIGURE 7-22 Logic analyzer display formats. *(a)* Parallel timing display. *(b)* Parallel state display. *(c)* Serial data display. *(Tektronix Inc.)*

on AD0–AD15. Again, use the monitor program listing to see if instruction bytes are coming in correctly. To help with this, some analyzers allow you to display the instruction mnemonic that corresponds to the bytes read in. If the data sequence is not correct, again check for stuck bits.

Another important logic analyzer feature you should learn to use is the clock qualifier input. If you switch on this input, the analyzer will only accept clock signals when a specified logic level is present on it. You can use the clock qualifier input to, for example, do a trace of only data read from ports. To do this in an 8086 minimum mode system, you connect the data inputs to the data bus, the $\overline{RD}$ signal to the analyzer clock input, and the 8086 M/$\overline{IO}$ signal to the analyzer clock qualifier input. You set the clock qualifier input to respond to a low. The analyzer will then take samples only when $\overline{RD}$ pulses and M/$\overline{IO}$ are low, as they will be during reads from ports.

We obviously can't describe here all of the ways to use a logic analyzer. If you have one, consult the manual for it to learn some of the finer points of its use. Also, the lab manual that is available for use with this book has some exercises to help you gain more skill with an analyzer. The point here was to show you how to use the analyzer as a "window" into what's going on in a system. By carefully choosing what signals you look at, what signal you clock on, and what word you trigger on, you can often solve difficult problems. For this reason, a logic analyzer is a valuable tool when developing a new microcomputer-based product. However, it is important for you to have a perspective of when to use an analyzer in troubleshooting simple systems that previously worked. Most of the time you can use the techniques described in previous sections to find and fix a problem in less time than it would take you to connect up the logic analyzer and figure out the trace display. If you have an analyzer, however, don't hesitate to use it when the simple techniques don't seem to be getting you anywhere.

8. Other Microcomputer Troubleshooting Equipment

A logic analyzer is a very powerful troubleshooting tool, but to use it effectively you need some detailed knowledge and a program listing for the system that you are trying to troubleshoot. If you are working as a repair technician and have to repair several different types of microcomputer systems with poor documentation to work from, most analyzers then are not too useful. To make your life easier in this case, "smart" instruments such as the Fluke 9010A microsystem troubleshooter have been created.

As you can see from the picture of the 9010A in Figure 7-23, it has a keyboard, a display, and an "umbilical" cable with an IC plug on the end. The unit also contains a minicasette tape recorder. For troubleshooting, the 9010A is used as follows.

The microprocessor in a fully functioning unit is re-

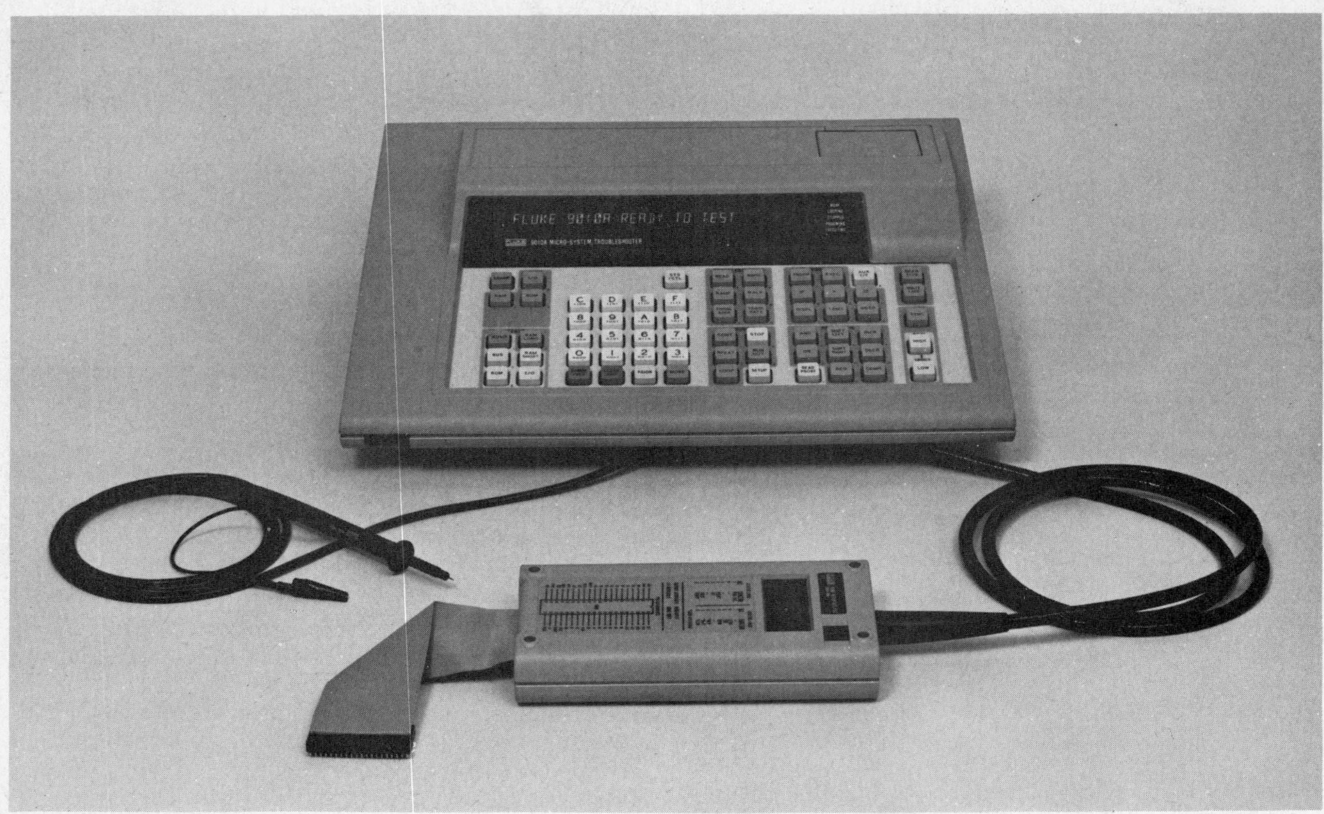

FIGURE 7-23 Fluke 9010A microsystem troubleshooter. *(John Fluke Mfg. Co., Inc.)*

moved, and the plug at the end of the cable is inserted in its place. The learn function of the 9010A is then executed. This function finds and maps ROM, RAM, and I/O registers that can be written into and read from. It also computes signatures (checksums) for blocks of ROM. All of these parameters are stored in the 9010A's RAM and/or on a minicassette tape. The microprocessor on a malfunctioning unit is then removed and the plug at the end of the umbilical cable inserted in its place. An automatic test function is then executed. In this mode the 9010A tests the buses, RAM, ROM, ports, power supply, and clock on the malfunctioning system. Any problem found, such as stuck nodes or adjacent trace short-circuits, is indicated on the display. The results of this test give some good hints as to the source of the problem. Because of its built-in intelligence, the 9010A can be programmed to do other tests as well.

The point of an instrument such as the 9010A is that with it you do not have to be intimately familiar with the programming language and hardware details of a simple microcomputer system in order to troubleshoot it.

IMPORTANT TERMS AND CONCEPTS FROM THIS CHAPTER

If you do not remember any of the terms or concepts in the following list, use the index to find them in the chapter.

Pin functions of 8086:
V_{cc}, $\overline{RD}$, $\overline{WR}$, CLK, ALE, M/$\overline{IO}$, $\overline{LOCK}$, MN/$\overline{MX}$, RESET, NMI, INTR, $\overline{BHE}$, $\overline{DEN}$, DT/$\overline{R}$

8086 RESET response

Maximum and minimum mode of 8086

8086 timing diagram interpretation

State, instruction cycle, machine cycle, wait state, READY signal

Bus activities during read/write

Bidirectional buffer

General functions: 3625, 8284, 8255A, 8251A, 8279, 2716, 2142

SDK-86 schematic: zones, plugs, jacks, wire wraps, resistor packs

Address decoding: ROM decoding, RAM decoding, port decoding

Memory-mapped I/O

Direct I/O

8086, 8088 memory banks

Timing parameters: t_{ACC}, t_{CL}, t_{OE}, t_{CE}, TCLAV, TCLRL, TDVCL

8086 typical clock frequencies

Troubleshooting steps for a simple 8086-based microcomputer

Logic analyzer: clock signal, trigger, trace

REVIEW QUESTIONS AND PROBLEMS

1. From what point on the clock waveform is the start of an 8086 state measured?

2. Why are latches required on the AD0–AD15 bus in an 8086 system?

3. What is the purpose of the ALE signal in an 8086 system?

4. Describe the sequence of events on the 8086 data/address bus, the ALE line, the M/$\overline{\text{IO}}$ line, and the $\overline{\text{RD}}$ line as the 8086 fetches an instruction word.

5. What logic levels will be on the 8086 $\overline{\text{RD}}$, $\overline{\text{WR}}$, and M/$\overline{\text{IO}}$ lines when the 8086 is doing a write to a memory location? A read from a port?

6. What is the major difference between an 8086 operating in minimum mode and an 8086 operating in maximum mode?

7. Describe the response an 8086 will make when its RESET (RST) input is asserted high.

8. Why are buffers often needed on the address, data, and control buses in a microcomputer system?

9. *a.* How is an 8086 entered into a WAIT state?
   b. At what point in a machine cycle does an 8086 enter a WAIT state?
   c. What information is on the buses during a WAIT state?
   d. How long is a WAIT state?
   e. How many WAIT states can be inserted?
   f. Why would you want the 8086 to insert a WAIT state?

10. What are the functions of the 8086 DT/$\overline{\text{R}}$ and $\overline{\text{DEN}}$ signals?

11. What does an arrow going from a transition on one signal waveform to a transition on another tell you?

12. How are wire wrap jumpers indicated on a schematic?

13. What is the meaning of /8 on a signal line on a schematic?

14. Describe the two purposes of address decoders in microcomputer systems.

15. A memory device has 15 address lines connected to it and 8 data outputs. What size words and how many words does the device store?

16. Briefly describe the function of the 8255, 8251A, and 8279 devices in the SDK-86 microcomputer system.

17. A group of signal lines on a schematic have the label *2ZB3* next to them. What is the meaning of this label?

18. What is the difference between a connector identified with a "J" and a connector identified with a "P"?

19. Describe the purpose of the many small capacitors connected between V_{cc} and ground on microcomputer printed circuit boards.

20. A 74LS138 decoder has its three SELECT inputs connected to A12, A13, and A14 of the system address bus. It has $\overline{\text{G2A}}$ connected to A15, $\overline{\text{G2B}}$ connected to $\overline{\text{RD}}$, and G1 connected to +5 V. Use an address decoder worksheet to determine what eight ROM address blocks the decoder outputs will select. Why is $\overline{\text{RD}}$ used as one of the enables on a ROM decoder?

21. Show a memory map for the ROMs in Problem 20.

22. Use an address decoder worksheet to help you draw a circuit to show how another 74LS138 can be connected to select one of eight 1 Kbyte RAMs starting at address 8000H.

23. Why are there actually many addresses that will select one of the port devices connected to the port decoder in Figure 7-10*a*.

24. Describe memory-mapped I/O and direct I/O. Give the main advantage and main disadvantage of each.

25. *a.* Why is the 8086 memory set up as two byte-wide banks?
    b. What logic levels would you find on $\overline{\text{BHE}}$ and A0 when an 8086 is writing a byte to address 04274H? Writing a word to 04274H?
    c. Describe the 8086 bus operations required to write a word to address 04373H.

26. How does the circuitry on the SDK-86 make sure that you cannot accidentally write a byte or word to ROM?

27. Why is some ROM put at the top of the address space in an 8086 system?

28. *a.* Show the truth table you would use for a 3625 PROM decoder to produce $\overline{\text{CS1}}$ signals for 4K × 8 RAMs in an 8086 system. Assume the first RAM starts at address 00000H. Don't forget A0 and $\overline{\text{BHE}}$.
    b. Draw the circuit connections for the 3625 decoder PROM and for two of the 4K × 8 RAMs.

29. Use sheets 5 and 7 of the SDK-86 schematics to help you determine for the SDK-86 what logic levels will be on $\overline{\text{BHE}}$, A0–A19, M/$\overline{\text{IO}}$, $\overline{\text{RD}}$, and $\overline{\text{WR}}$ when a word is read from ports FFF8H and FFF9H. Are these ports memory-mapped or direct? What instruction(s) would you use to do this read operation?

30. *a.* How is the $\overline{\text{OFF BOARD}}$ signal produced on the SDK-86 board?
    b. Describe the purpose of the $\overline{\text{OFF BOARD}}$ signal.

31. Describe how the 8088 memory is configured. Why doesn't the 8088 need a $\overline{\text{BHE}}$ signal?

32. By referring to the 8086 timing diagrams in Figure 7-18*a* and parameters in Figure 7-18*c* determine for the 8086-2:
   a. The maximum clock frequency.
   b. The time between CLOCK going low and $\overline{RD}$ going low.
   c. The time for which memory must hold data on the data bus after CLOCK goes low at the start of T4.
   d. The time that the lower 16 address bits remain on the data bus after ALE goes low.

33. The 27128-25 is a 16K × 8 EPROM with a t_{ACC} of 250 ns maximum, a t_{CE} of 250 ns maximum, and a t_{OE} of 100 ns maximum. Will this device work correctly without WAIT states in an 8-MHz 8086-2 system with circuit connections such as those in the SDK-86 schematics? Assume the address latches have a propagation delay of 12 ns and the decoder has a delay of 30 ns.

34. List the major steps you would take to troubleshoot a microcomputer system such as the SDK-86 which previously worked. Assume all ICs are in sockets.

35. Why is it important to check power supplies with an oscilloscope?

36. Describe how you can keep from mixing up ICs from a good system with those from a bad system when substituting.

37. Write an 8086 routine to test the system RAM in addresses 00200H–07FFH.

38. Write a test routine to output alternating 1's and 0's to port FFFAH over and over. With this routine running you could check with an oscilloscope to see if the port device is getting enabled and is outputting data.

39. Describe the symptoms that an SDK-86 would show for each of the following problems.
   a. Pin 8 of *A*15 in zone *D*5 of schematic sheet 2 is stuck low.
   b. The reset key is stuck on.
   c. None of the outputs of *XA*29 in zone *D*7 of schematic sheet 6 ever goes low.
   d. Pin 6 of *A*3 in zone *A*5 of schematic sheet 5 is stuck low.

40. Draw a block diagram of a simple logic analyzer and briefly describe how it operates. Include in your answer the function of the clock and the function of the trigger.

41. What do you use for a logic analyzer clock when you want to make detailed timing measurements.

42. On what signal and what edge of that signal would you clock a logic analyzer and on what word would you trigger to see in an 8086 system:
   a. The sequence of addresses output after a RESET?
   b. The sequence of instructions read in after a RESET? (Assume the first instruction word is FAH.)
   c. Both the addresses sent out and the words read in?
   d. Most logic analyzers have a clock qualifier input. If this input is used, the logic analyzer will not respond to a clock signal unless a specified logic level is on the qualifier input. You might, for example, connect the M/$\overline{IO}$ to the clock qualifier input and set it for a high to see a trace of data read from memory. What clock qualifier would you use to see a trace of only data read in from ports?

43. How is it possible for a logic analyzer to display data that occurred before the trigger?

CHAPTER

8 Interrupts and Interrupt Service Procedures

Most microprocessors allow normal program execution to be interrupted by some external signal or by a special instruction in the program. When a microprocessor is interrupted, it stops executing its current program and calls a procedure which "services" the interrupt. At the end of the interrupt service procedure, execution is usually returned to the interrupted program. This chapter shows you how the 8086 family members respond to interrupts, how to write interrupt service procedures, and how interrupts are used in a variety of applications.

OBJECTIVES

At the conclusion of this chapter you should be able to:

1. Describe the interrupt response of an 8086 family processor.
2. Initialize an 8086 interrupt vector (pointer) table.
3. Write interrupt service procedures.
4. Describe the operation of an 8254 programmable counter/timer and write the instructions necessary to initialize an 8254 for a specified application.
5. Describe the operation of an 8259A priority interrupt controller and write the instructions needed to initialize an 8259A for a specified application.

8086 INTERRUPTS AND INTERRUPT RESPONSES

Overview

An 8086 interrupt can come from any one of three sources. One source is from an external signal applied to the *nonmaskable interrupt* (NMI) input pin, or the *interrupt* (INTR) input pin. An interrupt caused by a signal applied to one of these inputs is referred to as a *hardware interrupt*.

A second source of an interrupt is execution of the interrupt instruction, INT. This is referred to as a *software interrupt*.

The third source of an interrupt is from some condition produced in the 8086 by the execution of an instruction. An example of this is the divide by zero interrupt. Program execution will automatically be interrupted if you attempt to divide an operand by zero. *Conditional interrupts* such as this are also referred to as software interrupts.

At the end of each instruction cycle the 8086 checks to see if any interrupts have been requested. If an interrupt has been requested, the 8086 responds to the interrupt by stepping through the following series of major actions.

1. It decrements the stack pointer by two and pushes the flag register on the stack.
2. It disables the INTR interrupt input by clearing the interrupt flag in the flag register.
3. It resets the trap flag in the flag register.
4. It decrements the stack pointer by two and pushes the current code segment register contents on the stack.
5. It decrements the stack pointer again by two and pushes the current instruction pointer contents on the stack.
6. It does an indirect far jump to the start of the procedure you wrote to respond to the interrupt.

To summarize these steps, then, the 8086 pushes the flag register on the stack, disables the single step and the INTR input, and does essentially an indirect far call to the interrupt service procedure. Figure 8-1 shows this in diagram form. Note that an IRET instruction at the end of the interrupt service procedure returns execution to the main program.

Now remember from Chapter 5 that when the 8086 does a far call to a procedure, it puts a new value in the code segment register and a new value in the instruction pointer. For an indirect call the 8086 gets the new values for CS and IP from four memory addresses. Likewise, when it responds to an interrupt the 8086 goes to memory locations to get the CS and IP values for the

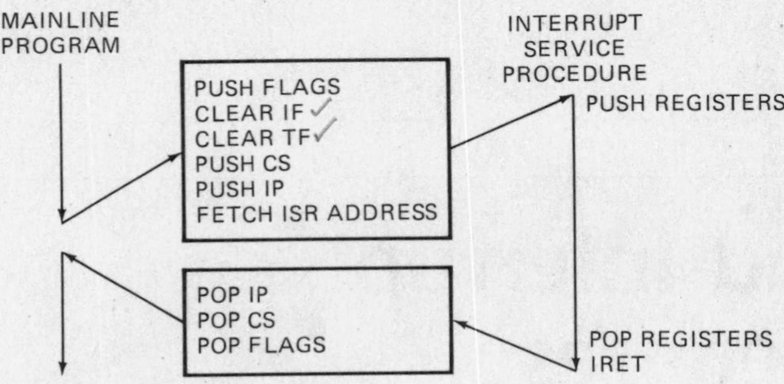

FIGURE 8-1 8086 interrupt response.

start of the interrupt service procedure. In an 8086 system the first 1 Kbyte of memory from 00000H to 003FFH is set aside as a table for storing the starting addresses of interrupt service procedures. Since 4 bytes are required to store the CS and IP values for each interrupt service procedure, the table can hold the starting addresses for up to 256 interrupt procedures. The starting address of an interrupt service procedure stored in this table is often called the *interrupt vector* or the *interrupt pointer*, and the table itself is then referred to as the *interrupt vector table* or the *interrupt pointer table*.

Figure 8-2 shows how the 256 interrupt pointers are arranged in the memory table. Each doubleword interrupt pointer is identified by a number from 0 to 255. Intel calls this number the *type* of the interrupt. The lowest five types are dedicated to specific interrupts such as the divide by zero interrupt and the nonmaskable interrupt which we explain in detail later. The next 27 interrupt types, from 5 to 31, are reserved by Intel for use in future microprocessors. The upper 224 interrupt types, from 32 to 255, are available for you to use for hardware or software interrupts.

When the 8086 responds to an interrupt, it automatically goes to the specified location in the interrupt pointer table to get the starting address of the interrupt service procedure. The 8086, however, does not automatically load the starting address in the pointer table. As we will show later, you have to do this with instructions at the start of your program. Note that the new value for the instruction pointer is put in as the low word of the pointer, and the new value for the code segment register is put in as the high word of the pointer.

Now that you have an overview of how the 8086 responds to interrupts, we can show in detail how one of these interrupts works.

An 8086 Interrupt Response Example—Type 0

Probably the easiest 8086 interrupt to understand is the divide-by-zero interrupt, identified as *type 0* in Figure 8-2. We'll use a type 0 interrupt to show you in detail how an 8086 interrupt works, and how to write a procedure to service an interrupt.

First of all let's refresh your memory about how the 8086 DIV and IDIV instructions work. The 8086 DIV instruction allows you to divide a 16-bit unsigned binary number in AX by an 8-bit unsigned number from a specified register or memory location. The 8-bit result (quotient) from this division will be left in the AL register. The 8-bit remainder will be left in the AH register. The DIV instruction also allows you to divide a 32-bit unsigned binary number in DX and AX by a 16-bit number in a specified register or memory location. The 16-bit quotient from this division is left in the AX register, and the 16-bit remainder is left in the DX register. The 8086 IDIV instruction, in the same manner, allows you to divide a 16-bit signed number in AX by an 8-bit signed number in a specified register, or a 32-bit signed number in DX and AX by a 16-bit signed number from a specified register or memory location.

If the quotient from dividing a 16-bit number is too large to fit in AL or the quotient from dividing a 32-bit number is too large to fit in AX, the result of the division will be meaningless. A special case of this is where an attempt is made to divide a 32-bit number or a 16-bit number by zero. The result of dividing by zero is infinity (actually undefined), which is somewhat too large to fit in AX or AL. Whenever the quotient from a DIV or IDIV operation is too large to fit in the result register, the 8086 will do a type 0 interrupt.

The type 0 response proceeds as follows. The 8086 first decrements the stack pointer by two and copies the flag register to the stack. It then clears the IF and the TF. Next it saves the return address on the stack. To do this the 8086 decrements the stack pointer by two, pushes the CS value of the return address on the stack, decrements the stack pointer by two again, and pushes the IP value of the return address on the stack. The 8086 then gets the starting address of the interrupt service procedure from the type 0 locations in the interrupt pointer table. As you can see in Figure 8-2 it gets the new value for CS from addresses 00002H and 00003H, and the new value for IP from addresses 00000H and 00001H. After the starting address of the procedure is loaded into CS and IP, the 8086 then fetches and executes the first instruction of the procedure.

At the end of the interrupt service procedure an IRET instruction will be used to return execution to the interrupted program. The IRET instruction pops the stored value of IP off the stack and increments the stack pointer by two. It then pops the stored value of CS off the stack and increments the stack pointer again by two. Finally it restores the flags by popping off the stack the values stored during the interrupt response and increments the stack pointer by two. Remember from the previous paragraph that during its interrupt response, the 8086 disables the INTR and single-step interrupt by clearing IF and TF. Now, if the INTR input and/or the trap interrupt were enabled before the interrupt, they will be enabled upon return to the interrupted program. The reason for this is that flags from the interrupted program were pushed on the stack before IF and TF were cleared by the 8086 in its interrupt response. To summarize, then, IRET returns execution to the interrupted program and restores the IF and the TF to the state they were in before the interrupt. Now that we have described the type 0 response, we can show you how to write a program to handle this interrupt.

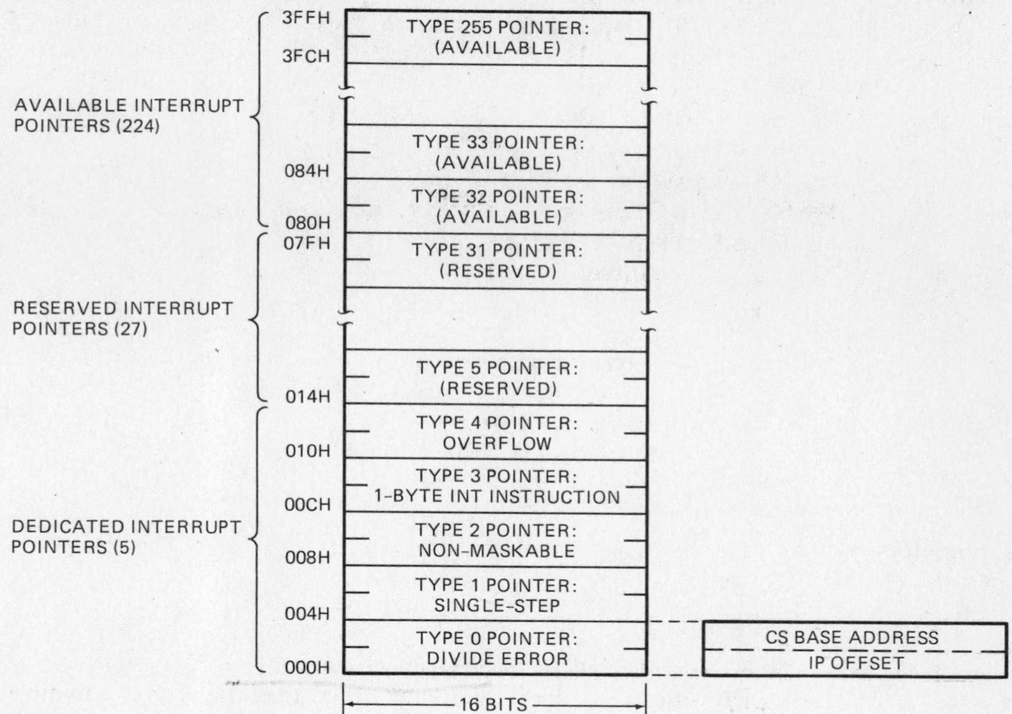

FIGURE 8-2 8086 interrupt pointer table.

An 8086 Interrupt Program Example

DEFINING THE PROBLEM AND WRITING THE ALGORITHM

In the last chapter we were mucking around mostly in hardware, so instead of jumping directly into the program, let's use this example to review how you go about writing any program.

As described in Chapter 3, you start by carefully defining the problem that you want the program to solve or the operations that you want it to perform. Part of this step is to determine the amount and types of data that the program is to work with.

For the example program here we have four word-sized hexadecimal values stored in memory. We want to divide each of these values by a byte-type scale factor to give a byte-type scaled value. If the result of the division is valid, we want to put the scaled value in an array in memory. If the result of the division is invalid (too large to fit in the 8-bit result register), we want to put 0 in the array for that scaled value. Figure 8-3 shows the algorithm for this program in pseudocode. As shown in Figure 8-3*a*, the mainline part of this program gets each 16-bit value from memory in turn and divides that value by the 8-bit scale factor. If the result of the division is too large to fit in the quotient register, AL, then the 8086 will do a type 0 interrupt immediately after the divide instruction finishes.

Figure 8-3*b* shows the algorithm for our type 0 interrupt service procedure. The main function of this procedure is to set a *flag* which will be checked by the mainline program. The flag in this case is not one of the flags in the 8086 flag register. The flag here is a bit in a memory location we set aside for this purpose. In the actual program we give this memory location the name BAD_DIV_FLAG. At the end of the interrupt service procedure we return to the interrupted mainline program.

After the division in the mainline program we check to see if the result of the division is valid. If the result is valid, we store it in the correct place in the scaled values array in memory. If the result is not valid, we leave zero in that place in the scaled values array. The way we actually make the decision whether a result is valid or not is to check the BAD_DIV_FLAG. If the result of the division was too large, then the 8086 will have done a type zero interrupt, and our interrupt service procedure will have set the BAD_DIV_FLAG to a one. If the result of the division is valid, then the 8086 will not do the interrupt, and the BAD_DIV_FLAG will be zero.

The sequence of operations is repeated until all of the values have been scaled. We use a register to keep track of which input value is being operated on at a particular time.

WRITING THE INITIALIZATION LIST

After you have worked out the data structure and the algorithm for a program, the next step is to make an initialization list such as the one shown in Chapter 3. Here is a list for this program.

1. Initialize the interrupt pointer table. In other words, the starting address of our type 0 interrupt service routine must be put in locations 00000H and 00002H.

```
INITIALIZATION LIST

REPEAT
     get INPUT_VALUE
     divide by scale factor
     IF result valid THEN
          store result as scaled value
     ELSE store zero
UNTIL all values scaled
```

(a)

```
Save registers
Set error flag
Restore registers
Return to mainline
```

(b)

FIGURE 8-3 Algorithm for divide by zero program example. *(a)* Mainline program. *(b)* Interrupt service procedure.

2. Set up the data segment where the values to be scaled, the scale factor, the scaled values, and the BAD_DIV_FLAG will be put.
3. Initialize the data segment register to point to the base address of the data segment containing the values to be scaled.
4. Set up a stack to store the return address, since we are essentially calling a procedure.
5. Initialize the stack segment and the stack pointer registers.
6. Initialize a pointer to the start of the data to be scaled, a counter to keep track of how many values we have scaled, and a pointer to the start of the array where we want to put the scaled values.

Once you have the algorithm and the initialization list for a program, the next step is to start writing the instructions for the program, so now let's look at the assembly language program for this problem.

ASSEMBLY LANGUAGE PROGRAM AND INTERRUPT PROCEDURE

Figure 8-4 shows our 8086 assembly language program for the mainline and for the type 0 interrupt service procedure. You can use many of the parts of these when you write your own interrupt programs. To help refresh your memory of the PUBLIC and the EXTRN directives, we have written the mainline program and the interrupt service procedure as two separate assembly modules. Remember, if you are not using an assembler, you can just substitute the actual offsets or numbers for the names used in the example program.

At the start of the mainline program in Figure 8-4*a*, we declare a segment named DATA_HERE for the data that the program will be working with. The WORD directive tells the locator to start this segment on the next available even address. The PUBLIC directive in this statement identifies the segment name as public so it can be referred to in other assembly modules. The input values are words, so we use a DW directive to declare these four values. The scaled values will be bytes, so we use the DB directive to set aside four locations for these. The DUP(0) in the statement initializes the 4-byte locations to all 0's. As the program executes, the results will be written into these locations. SCALE_FACTOR DB 09H sets aside a byte location for the number that we are going to be dividing the input values by. The advantage of using a DB to declare the scale factor, rather than an EQU directive, is that with a DB the value of scale factor can be held in RAM where it can be changed dynamically in the program as needed. If you use a statement such as SCALE_FACTOR EQU 09H to set a value, you have to reassemble the program to change the value.

Part of the 8086 interrupt response is essentially a far call to the interrupt service procedure. In any program that calls a procedure we have to set up a stack to store the return address and parameters passed to and from the procedure. The next section of the program declares a stack segment called STACK_HERE. It also establishes a pointer to the next location above the stack with the statement TOP_STACK LABEL WORD. Remember from the examples in Chapter 5 that this label is used to initialize the stack pointer to the next location after the top of the stack.

The next two parts of the program are necessary because we wrote the main program and the interrupt service procedure as two separate assembly modules. When the assembler reads through a source program, it makes a *symbol table* which contains the segment and offset of all of the names and labels used in the program. The statement PUBLIC BAD_DIV_FLAG tells the assembler to identify the name BAD_DIV_FLAG as public. This means that when the object module for this program is linked with some other object module that declares BAD_DIV_FLAG as EXTRN, the linker will be allowed to

```
page ,132
;8086 PROGRAM
;ABSTRACT:       Program scales some data values by division.
;PROCEDURES:     Uses BAD_DIV, a type 0 interrupt service procedure
;PORTS USED:     None

DATA_HERE       SEGMENT WORD    PUBLIC
        INPUT_VALUES    DW  0035H, 0855H, 2011H, 1359H
        SCALED_VALUES   DB 4 DUP(0)
        SCALE_FACTOR    DB 09H
        BAD_DIV_FLAG    DB 0
DATA_HERE       ENDS
STACK_HERE      SEGMENT STACK
                DW  100 DUP (0)              ; Set up stack of 100 words
        TOP_STACK  LABEL  WORD               ; Pointer to top of stack
STACK_HERE      ENDS

PUBLIC  BAD_DIV_FLAG            ; Make flag available to other modules

INT_PROC_HERE   SEGMENT WORD    PUBLIC
        EXTRN  BAD_DIV:FAR              ; Let assembler know procedure BAD_DIV is
INT_PROC_HERE   ENDS                    ;  in  another assembly module

CODE_HERE       SEGMENT WORD    PUBLIC
        ASSUME CS:CODE_HERE, DS:DATA_HERE, SS:STACK_HERE
START:  MOV  AX, STACK_HERE             ; Initialize stack segment register
        MOV  SS, AX
        MOV  SP, OFFSET TOP_STACK       ; Initialize stack pointer
        MOV  AX, DATA_HERE              ; Initialize data segment register
        MOV  DS, AX
;store the address for the BAD_DIV routine at address 0000:0000
;address 00000-00003 is where type 0 interrupt gets interrupt
;service procedure address. CS at 00002 & 00003, IP at 00000 & 00001
        MOV  AX, 0000
        MOV  ES, AX
        MOV  WORD PTR ES:0002, SEG BAD_DIV
        MOV  WORD PTR ES:0000, OFFSET BAD_DIV
        MOV  SI, OFFSET INPUT_VALUES    ; Initialize pointer for input values
        MOV  BX, OFFSET SCALED_VALUES   ; Point BX at start of result array
        MOV  CX, 0004H                  ; Initialize data value counter
NEXT:   MOV  AX, [SI]                   ; Bring a value to AX for divide
        DIV  SCALE_FACTOR               ; Divide by scale factor
        CMP  BAD_DIV_FLAG, 01H          ; Check if divide produced invalid result
        JNE  OK                         ; No, go save scaled value
        MOV  BYTE PTR [BX], 00          ; Yes, load 0 as scaled value
        JMP  SKIP
OK:     MOV  [BX], AL                   ; Save scaled value
SKIP:   MOV  BAD_DIV_FLAG, 0            ; Reset BAD_DIV_FLAG before doing next
        ADD  SI, 02H                    ; Point at location of next input value
        INC  BX                         ; Point at location for next result
        LOOP NEXT                       ; Repeat until all values done
STOP:   NOP
CODE_HERE       ENDS
        END     START
```

(a)

FIGURE 8-4 8086 assembly language program for divide by zero example.
(a) Mainline. *(b)* Interrupt service procedure.

```
age , 132

;8086 PROCEDURE TO SERVICE DIVIDE BY ZERO INTERRUPT (TYPE 0)

; This procedure sets the LSB of a memory location called BAD_DIV_FLAG,
;  enables INTR, and returns execution to the interrupted program with
;  registers and flags unchanged.

DATA_HERE          SEGMENT WORD PUBLIC
      EXTRN  BAD_DIV_FLAG:BYTE          ; Let assembler know BAD_DIV_FLAG
DATA_HERE          ENDS                 ;  is in another assembly module

PUBLIC  BAD_DIV                         ; Make procedure BAD_DIV available to
                                        ;  other assembly modules

INT_PROC_HERE      SEGMENT WORD PUBLIC  ; Set up a segment for all
                                        ;  interrupt service procedures
BAD_DIV  PROC FAR                       ; Procedure for type 0 interrupt
      ASSUME CS:INT_PROC_HERE, DS:DATA_HERE

      PUSH  AX                ; Save AX of interrupted program
      PUSH  DS                ; Save DS of interrupted program
      MOV   AX, DATA_HERE     ; Load DS value needed here
      MOV   DS, AX
      MOV   BAD_DIV_FLAG, 01  ; Set LSB of BAD_DIV_FLAG byte
      POP   DS                ; Restore DS of interrupted program
      POP   AX                ; Restore AX of interrupted program
      IRET                    ; Return to next instruction in
                              ;  interrupted program

BAD_DIV  ENDP
INT_PROC_HERE      ENDS

      END
```

(*b*)

FIGURE 8-4 (*continued*)

make the connection. Some programmers say that the PUBLIC directive "exports" a name or label.

The other end of this export operation is to "import" labels or names that are defined in other assembly modules. The statement EXTRN BAD_DIV:FAR in our example program, for example, tells the assembler that BAD_DIV is a label of type FAR and that BAD_DIV is defined in some other assembly module. The INT_PROC_HERE SEGMENT WORD PUBLIC and INT_PROC_HERE ENDS statements tell the assembler that BAD_DIV is defined in a segment named INT_PROC_HERE. When the assembler reads these statements it will make an entry in its symbol table for BAD_DIV, and identify it as external. When the object module for this program is linked with the object module for the program where BAD_DIV is defined, the linker will fill in the proper values for the CS and IP of BAD_DIV.

For the actual instructions of our mainline program we declare a code segment with the statement CODE_HERE SEGMENT WORD PUBLIC. The WORD in this statement tells the linker/locator to locate this segment on the first available even address. The PUBLIC in this statement tells the linker that this segment can be joined together (concatenated) with segments of the same name from other assembly modules.

As usual at the start of the code segment we use an ASSUME statement to tell the assembler what logical segments to use for code, data, and stack. After this comes the hopefully familiar instructions for initializing the stack segment register, the stack pointer register, and the data segment register.

The next four instructions are needed to place the address of the BAD_DIV procedure in the type 0 location in the interrupt pointer table. The code segment address for BAD_DIV is stored at 00002 and 00003 and the address of the offset of BAD_DIV at 00000 and 00001. It is necessary to load the interrupt procedure addresses in this way if you are using an SDK-86 board, or the

MASM and Link programs on an IBM PC-type machine. This is because the linker overrides any ORG directives which makes it difficult to put programs at absolute addresses.

Next we initialize SI as a pointer to the first input value with the statement MOV SI, OFFSET INPUT_VALUES. The statement MOV BX, OFFSET SCALED_VALUES then initializes BX as a pointer to the first of the locations we set aside for the 8-bit scaled results.

To keep track of how many values have been scaled we set up the CX register as a counter. The statement MOV CX, 0004H initializes the counter with the number of values we want to scale. This register will be decremented after each input value is scaled. When CX = 0, we know that all values have been scaled.

Finally everything is initialized, and we get to the operations we set out to do. The statement MOV AX, [SI] copies an input value from memory to the AX register where it has to be for the divide operation. The DIV SCALE_FACTOR instruction divides the number in AX by 09H, the value we assigned to SCALE_FACTOR previously with a DB directive. The 8-bit quotient from this division will be put in AL and the 8-bit remainder will be put in AH. If the quotient is too large to fit in AL, then the 8086 will automatically do a type 0 interrupt. For our program here, the 8086 will push the flags on the stack, reset the IF and TF, and push the return address on the stack. It will then go to addresses 0000H and 0002H to get the IP and CS values for the start of BAD_DIV, the procedure we wrote to service a type 0 interrupt. It will then execute the BAD_DIV procedure. Now let's look at the procedure in Figure 8-4*b* and see how it works.

The BAD_DIV procedure starts by letting the assembler know that the name BAD_DIV_FLAG represents a variable of type byte, and that this variable is defined in a segment called DATA_HERE in some other (EXTRN) assembly module. We also tell the assembler that the label BAD_DIV should be made available to other assembly modules (PUBLIC).

Next we declare a logical segment called INT_PROC_HERE. We could have put this procedure in the segment CODE_HERE with the mainline program. However, in system programs where there are many interrupt service procedures, a separate segment is usually set aside for them. What we are doing here, then, is to show you an overall structure that we will fill in as we work our way through the rest of the book.

The statement BAD_DIV PROC FAR identifies the actual start of the procedure, and tells the assembler that both the CS and IP values for this procedure must be saved. The ASSUME statement at the start of the procedure then tells the assembler the names of the segments to use for code and data for this procedure.

Now, an important operation to do at the start of any interrupt service procedure is to push on the stack any registers that you are going to use in the procedure. You can then restore these registers by popping them off the stack just before returning to the interrupted program. The interrupted program will then resume with its registers as they were before the interrupt. In our procedure here we save AX and DS. Since we use the same same data segment, DATA_HERE, in the mainline and in the procedure, you may wonder why we saved DS. The point is that an interrupt service procedure should be written so that it can be used at any point in a program. By saving the DS value of the interrupted program, this interrupt service procedure can be used in a program section that does not use DATA_HERE as its data segment.

The ASSUME statement tells the assembler the name of the segment to use as a data segment, but remember that it does not load the DS register with a value for the start of that segment. The instructions MOV AX, DATA_HERE and MOV DS, AX do this in our procedure.

Finally, we get to the whole point of this procedure with the MOV BAD_DIV_FLAG, 01 instruction. This instruction simply sets the least-significant bit of the memory location we set aside with a DB directive at the start of the mainline program. Note that in order to access this variable by name you have to let the assembler know that it is external, and you have to make sure that the DS register contains the segment base for the segment in which BAD_DIV_FLAG is located.

To complete the procedure we pop the saved registers off the stack and return to the interrupted program. The IRET instruction, remember, is different from the regular RET instruction in that it pops the flag register and the return address off the stack. Note in the source program in Figure 8-4*b* that if you are using an assembler, the procedure must be "closed" with an ENDP directive, and the segment must as usual be closed with an ENDS directive.

Now let's look back in the mainline to see what it does with this BAD_DIV_FLAG. Immediately after the DIV instruction, the mainline checks to see if the BAD_DIV_FLAG is set by comparing it with 01. If the BAD_DIV_FLAG was not set by the type 0 interrupt service procedure, then a jump is made to the MOV [BX], AL instruction. This instruction copies the result of the division in AL to the memory location in SCALED_VALUES pointed to by BX. If BAD_DIV_FLAG was set by a type 0 interrupt, then zero is put in the memory location in SCALED_VALUES and a jump will be made to the MOV BAD_DIV_FLAG, 00 instruction which resets the BAD_DIV_FLAG. Since this jump passes over the MOV [BX], AL instruction, the invalid result of the division will not be copied into one of the locations in SCALED_VALUES.

After putting the scaled value or zero in the array and resetting the flag, we get ready to operate on the next input value. The ADD SI, 02 instruction increments SI by two so that it points to the next 16-bit value in INPUT_VALUES. The INC BX instruction points BX at the next 8-bit location in SCALED_VALUES. The LOOP instruction after these automatically decrements the CX register by one, and, if CX is not then zero, it causes the 8086 to jump to the specified label, NEXT.

The preceding section has shown you how to set up an interrupt pointer table, how to write an interrupt service procedure, and how the 8086 responds to a type 0 interrupt. Now we can discuss some of the other types of 8086 interrupts.

8086 Interrupt Types

The preceding sections used the type 0 interrupt as an example of how the 8086 interrupts function. In this section we discuss in detail the different ways an 8086 can be interrupted, and how the 8086 responds to different types of interrupts. We discuss these in order, starting with type 0, so that you can easily find a particular discussion when you need to refer back to it. However, as you read though this section you should not attempt to learn all of the details of all of the kinds of interrupts at once. Read through all of the kinds to get an overview, and then focus on the details of the hardware-caused NMI interrupt, the software interrupts produced by the INT instruction, and the hardware interrupt produced by applying a signal to the INTR input pin.

DIVIDE-BY-ZERO INTERRUPT—TYPE 0

As we described in the preceding section, the 8086 will automatically do a type 0 interrupt if the result of a DIV operation or an IDIV operation is too large to fit in the destination register. For a type 0 interrupt the 8086 pushes the flag register on the stack, resets the IF and TF, and pushes the return address (CS and IP) on the stack. It then gets the CS value for the start of the interrupt service procedure from address 00002H in the interrupt pointer table, and the IP value for the start of the procedure from address 00000H in the interrupt pointer table.

Since the 8086 type 0 response is automatic and cannot be disabled in any way, you have to account for it in any programs where you use the DIV or IDIV instructions. One way to do this is to in some way make sure the result will never be too large for the result register. We showed one way to do this in the example program in Figure 5-25*b*. In that example you may remember we first make sure the divisor is not zero, and then we do the division in several steps so that the result of the division will never be too large.

Another way to account for the 8086 type 0 response is to simply write an interrupt service procedure which takes the desired action when an invalid division occurs. The advantage of this approach is that you don't have the overhead of a more complex division routine in your mainline program. The 8086 automatically does the checking and only does the interrupt procedure if there is a problem. Remember that when using any interrupts with the 8086 you must in some way load the starting address of the interrupt service procedure in the interrupt pointer table.

SINGLE-STEP INTERRUPT—TYPE 1

In a section of Chapter 3 on debugging assembly language programs we discussed the use of the single-step feature present in some monitor programs and debugger programs. When you tell a system to single-step, it will execute one instruction and stop. You can then examine the contents of registers and memory locations. If they are correct, you can tell the system to go on and execute the next instruction. In other words, when in single-step mode, a system will stop after it executes each instruction, and wait for further direction from you. The 8086 trap flag and type 1 interrupt response make it quite easy to implement a single-step feature in an 8086-based system.

If the 8086 trap flag is set, the 8086 will automatically do a type 1 interrupt after each instruction executes. When the 8086 does a type 1 interrupt it pushes the flag register on the stack, resets the TF and IF, and pushes the CS and IP values for the next instruction on the stack. It then gets the CS value for the start of the type 1 interrupt service procedure from address 00006H, and it gets the IP value for the start of the procedure from address 00004H.

The tasks involved in implementing single step then are: set the trap flag, write an interrupt service procedure which saves all registers on the stack where they can later be examined or perhaps displayed on the CRT, and load the starting address of the type 1 interrupt service procedure into addresses 00004H and 00006H. The actual single-step procedure will depend very much on the system that it is to be implemented on. We do not have space here to show you the different ways to do this. We will, however, show you how the trap flag is set or reset, because this is somewhat unusual.

The 8086 has no instructions to directly set or reset the trap flag. These operations are done by pushing the flag register on the stack, changing the trap-flag bit to what you want it to be, and then popping the flag register back off the stack. Here is the instruction sequence to set the trap flag.

```
PUSHF               ; Push flags on stack
MOV BP,SP           ; Copy SP to BP for use as index
OR [BP+0], 0100H    ; Set TF bit
POPF                ; Restore flag register
```

To reset the trap flag, simply replace the OR instruction in the above sequence with the instruction AND [BP+0], 0FEFFH.

NOTE: We have to use [BP + 0] because BP cannot be used as a pointer without a displacement. See Figure 3-8.

The trap flag is reset when the 8086 does a type 1 interrupt, so the single-step mode will be disabled during the interrupt service procedure.

NONMASKABLE INTERRUPT—TYPE 2

The 8086 will automatically do a *type 2* interrupt response when it receives a low-to-high transition on its NMI input pin. When it does a type 2 interrupt the 8086 will push the flags on the stack, reset TF and IF, and push the CS value and the IP value for the next instruction on the stack. It will then get the CS value for the start of the type 2 interrupt service procedure from address 0000AH, and the IP value for the start of the procedure from address 00008H.

The name *nonmaskable* given to this input pin on the 8086 means that the type 2 interrupt response cannot be disabled (masked) by any program instructions. Because this input cannot be intentionally or accidentally disabled, we use it to signal the 8086 that some condition in an external system must be taken care of.

We could, for example, have a pressure sensor on a large steam boiler connected to the NMI input. If the pressure goes above some preset limit the sensor will send an interrupt signal to the 8086. The type 2 interrupt service procedure we write for this case can turn off the fuel to the boiler, open a pressure relief valve, and sound an alarm.

Another common use of the type 2 interrupt is to save program data in the case of a system power failure. Some external circuitry detects when the ac power to the system fails and sends an interrupt signal to the NMI input. Because of the large filter capacitors in most power supplies, the dc system power will remain for perhaps 50 ms after the ac power is gone. This is more than enough time for a type 2 interrupt service procedure to copy program data to some RAM which has a battery backup power supply. When the ac power returns, program data can be restored from the battery-backed-up RAM and the program can resume execution where it left off. A practice problem at the end of the chapter gives you a chance to write a simple procedure for this task.

BREAKPOINT INTERRUPT—TYPE 3

The type 3 interrupt is produced by execution of the INT 3 instruction. The main use of the type 3 interrupt is to implement a breakpoint function in a system. In Chapter 4 we described the use of breakpoints in debugging assembly language programs. Hopefully you have been using them in debugging your programs. When you insert a breakpoint the system executes the instructions up to the breakpoint, and then goes to the breakpoint procedure. Unlike the single-step feature which stops execution after each instruction, the breakpoint feature executes all the instructions up to the inserted breakpoint and then stops execution.

When you tell most 8086 systems to insert a breakpoint at some point in your program, they actually do it by temporarily replacing the instruction byte at that address with CCH, the 8086 code for the INT 3 instruction. When the 8086 executes this INT 3 instruction it pushes the flag register on the stack, resets TF and IF, and pushes the CS and IP values for the next mainline instruction on the stack. The 8086 then gets the CS value of the start of the type 3 interrupt service procedure from address 0000EH and the IP value for the procedure from address 0000CH. A breakpoint interrupt service procedure usually saves all of the register contents on the stack. Depending on the system, it may then send the register contents to the CRT display and wait for the next command from the user, or in a simple system it may just return control to the user. In this case an examine register command can be used to check if the register contents are correct at that point in the program.

OVERFLOW INTERRUPT—TYPE 4

The 8086 overflow flag, OF, will be set if the signed result of an arithmetic operation on two signed numbers is too large to be represented in the destination register or memory location. For example, if you add the 8-bit signed number 01101100 (108 decimal) and the 8-bit signed number 01010001 (81 decimal), the signed result will be 10111101 (189 decimal). This is the correct result if we were adding unsigned binary numbers, but it is not the correct signed result. For signed operations the 1 in the most-significant bit of the result indicates that the result is negative and in 2's complement form. The result then actually represents −67 decimal, which is obviously not the correct result for adding +108 and +89.

There are two major ways to detect and respond to an overflow error in a program. One way is to put the Jump if Overflow instruction, JO, immediately after the arithmetic instruction. If the overflow flag is set as a result of the arithmetic operation, execution will jump to the address specified in the JO instruction. At this address you can put an error routine which responds in the way you want to the overflow.

The second way of detecting and responding to an overflow error is to put the *Interrupt on Overflow* instruction, INTO, immediately after the arithmetic instruction in the program. If the overflow flag is not set when the 8086 executes the INTO instruction, the instruction will simply function as an NOP. However, if the overflow flag is set, indicating an overflow error, the 8086 will do a *type 4* interrupt after it executes the INTO instruction.

When the 8086 does a type 4 interrupt, it pushes the flag register on the stack, resets the TF and IF, and pushes the CS and IP values for the next instruction on the stack. It then gets the CS value for the start of the interrupt service procedure from address 00012H and the IP value for the procedure from address 00010H. Instructions in the interrupt service procedure then perform the desired response to the error condition. The procedure might, for example, set a "flag" in a memory location as we did in the BAD_DIV procedure in Figure 8-4*b*. The advantage of using the INTO and type 4 interrupt approach is that the error routine is easily accessible from any program.

SOFTWARE INTERRUPTS—TYPE 0—255

The 8086 INT instruction can be used to cause the 8086 to do any one of the 256 possible interrupt types. The desired interrupt type is specified as part of the instruction. The instruction INT 32, for example, will cause the 8086 to do a *type 32* interrupt response. The 8086 will push the flag register on the stack, reset the TF and IF, and push the CS and IP values of the next instruction on the stack. It will then get the CS and IP values for the start of the interrupt service procedure from the interrupt pointer table in memory. The IP value for any interrupt type is always at an address of 4 times the interrupt type, and the CS value is at a location two addresses higher. For a type 32 interrupt, then, the IP value will be put at 4 × 32 or 128 decimal (80H), and the CS value will be put at address 82H in the interrupt pointer table.

Software interrupts produced by the INT instruction have many uses. In a previous section we discussed the use of the INT 3 instruction to insert breakpoints in programs for debugging. Another use of software interrupts is to test various interrupt service procedures. You could, for example, use an INT 0 instruction to send execution to a divide-by-zero interrupt service procedure without having to run the actual division program. As another example, you could use an INT 2 instruction to send execution to an NMI interrupt service procedure. This allows you to test the NMI procedure without needing to apply an external signal to the NMI input of the 8086.

Another important use of software interrupts is to call desired procedures from many different programs in a system. The BIOS in the IBM PC is a good example of this. The IBM PC has in its ROMs a collection of procedures. Each procedure performs some specific function such as reading a character from the keyboard, writing some characters to the CRT, or reading some information from a disk. This collection of procedures is referred to as the *B*asic *I*nput *O*utput *S*ystem or BIOS. The BIOS procedures are called with INT instructions. You can read the BIOS section of the IBM PC technical reference manual to get all of the details of these if you need them, but here's an example of how you might use one of them.

Suppose that, as part of an assembly language program that your are writing to run on an IBM PC, you want to send some characters to the printer. Figure 8-5 is a program which shows how to do this.

Note that the DX, AH, and AL registers are used to pass parameters to the procedure. Also note that the procedure is used for two different operations: initializing the printer port and sending a character to the printer. The operation performed by the procedure is determined by the number passed to the procedure in the AH register. AH = 1 means initialize the printer port, AH = 0 means print the character in AL, and AH = 2 means read the printer status and return it in AH. If an attempt to print a character was not successful for some reason such as the printer not being turned on, not being selected, or being busy, 01 is returned in AH.

The main advantage of calling procedures in this way is that you don't need to worry about the absolute address where the procedure actually resides or about trying to link the procedure into your program. All you have to know is the interrupt type for the procedure and the format for the parameters you need to pass to the procedure. We show some other examples of using BIOS procedures in later chapters.

INTR INTERRUPTS—TYPE 0—255

The 8086 INTR input allows some external signal to interrupt execution of a program. Unlike the NMI input, however, INTR can be masked (disabled) so that it cannot cause an interrupt. If the interrupt flag, IF, is cleared, then the INTR input is disabled. The IF can be cleared at any time with the *clear interrupt* instruction, CLI. If the interrupt flag is set, the INTR input will be enabled. The IF can be set at any time with the *set interrupt* instruction, STI.

When the 8086 is reset, the interrupt flag is automatically cleared. Before the 8086 can respond to an interrupt signal on its INTR input you have to set the IF with an STI instruction. The 8086 was designed this way so that ports, timers, registers, etc. can be initialized before enabling the INTR input. In other words this allows you to get the 8086 ready to handle an interrupt before letting an interrupt in, just as you might want to get yourself ready in the morning with a cup of coffee before turning on the telephone and having to cope with the interrupts it produces.

The interrupt flag is also automatically cleared as part of the response of an 8086 to an interrupt. This is done for two reasons. First, it prevents a signal on the INTR input from interrupting a higher priority interrupt service procedure in progress. You can, however, set the IF with an STI instruction at the start of the procedure if you want an INTR input signal to be able to interrupt a procedure in progress.

The second reason for automatically disabling the INTR input at the start of an INTR interrupt service procedure is to make sure that a signal on the INTR input does not cause the 8086 to continuously interrupt itself. The INTR input is activated by a high level. In other words, whenever the INTR input is high and INTR is enabled, the 8086 will be interrupted. If INTR were not disabled during the first response, the 8086 would be continuously interrupted, and never get to the actual interrupt service procedure. Since the INTR is level-activated, the interrupt signal must remain present until it is recognized by the 8086.

The IRET instruction at the end of the interrupt service procedure restores the flags to the condition they were in before the procedure by popping the flag register off the stack. This will reenable the INTR input. If a high level signal is still present on the INTR input, it will cause the 8086 to be interrupted again. If we do not want the 8086 to be interrupted again by the same input signal, we have to use external hardware to make sure the signal is made low again before we reenable INTR with the STI instruction, or before the end of the INTR service procedure.

When the 8086 responds to an INTR interrupt signal, its response is somewhat different from its response to other interrupts. The main difference is that for an INTR interrupt, the interrupt type is sent to the 8086 from an external hardware device such as the 8259A *priority interrupt controller* which we discuss later in this chapter. An 8086 INTR response proceeds as follows.

The 8086 first does two interrupt acknowledge machine cycles, as shown in Figure 8-6. The purpose of these two machine cycles is to get the interrupt type from the external device. At the start of the first interrupt acknowledge machine cycle the 8086 floats the data bus lines, AD0–AD15. It then sends out an interrupt acknowledge pulse on its $\overline{INTA}$ output pin. This pulse essentially tells the external device, "get ready." During the second interrupt acknowledge machine cycle the 8086 sends out another pulse on its $\overline{INTA}$ output pin. In response to this second $\overline{INTA}$ pulse the external device puts the interrupt type (number) on the lower eight lines of the data bus where it is read by the 8086.

Once the 8086 receives the interrupt type, it pushes the flag register on the stack, clears TF and IF, and pushes the CS and IP values of the next instruction on

```
PAGE, 132
;8086 PROGRAM
;ABSTRACT        : This program sends a string of characters to a
;                  printer from the IBM PC
;REGISTERS USED : CS, SS, DS, BX, AX, CX, DX
;PORTS USED      : printer port 0
;PROCEDURES USED: Calls BIOS printer IO procedure INT 17

STACK_HERE      SEGMENT STACK
        DW      200 DUP(0)      ; set aside 200 words for stack
STACK_TOP       LABEL   WORD    ; assign name to word above stack top
STACK_HERE      ENDS

CHAR_COUNT      EQU     27

DATA_HERE       SEGMENT
                MESSAGE         DB      'HELLO THERE, HOW ARE YOU?'
                MESSAGE_END     DB      0DH, 0AH    ; return & line feed
DATA_HERE       ENDS
CODE_HERE       SEGMENT
                ASSUME CS:CODE_HERE, SS:STACK_HERE, DS:DATA_HERE

        MOV     AX, STACK_HERE  ; initialize stack segment register
        MOV     SS, AX
        MOV     SP, OFFSET STACK_TOP ; initialize stack pointer

        MOV     AX, DATA_HERE   ; initialize data segment
        MOV     DS, AX
        MOV     AH, 01          ; initialize printer port
        MOV     DX, 0           ; to use printer port 0
        INT     17H             ; call procedure to intitialize printer port
        LEA     BX, MESSAGE     ; get to start of message
        MOV     CX, CHAR_COUNT  ; set up a count variable
 AGAIN:
        MOV     AH, 0           ; code to tell procedure to send character
        MOV     AL, [BX]        ; load character to be sent into AL
        INT     17H             ; send character to printer
        CMP     AH, 01H         ; if character not printed then AH =1
        JNE     NEXT
NOT_RDY:STC                     ; set carry to indicate message not sent
        JMP     EXIT            ; leave loop
NEXT:   CLC                     ; clear carry flag to show character is sent
        INC     BX              ; address of next character
        LOOP    AGAIN           ; send the next character
EXIT:   NOP
CODE_HERE ENDS
        END
```

FIGURE 8-5 8086 assembly language program for outputting characters to a printer.

the stack. It then uses the type it read in from the external device to get the CS and IP values for the interrupt service procedure from the interrupt pointer table in memory. The IP value for the procedure will be put at an address equal to 4 times the type number, and the CS value will be put at an address equal to 4 times the type number plus 2, just as is done for the other interrupts.

The advantage of having an external device insert the desired interrupt type is that the external device can "funnel" interrupt signals from many sources into the INTR input pin on the 8086. When the 8086 responds with $\overline{\text{INTA}}$ pulses, the external device can send to the 8086 the interrupt type that corresponds to the source of the interrupt signal. As you will see later the external

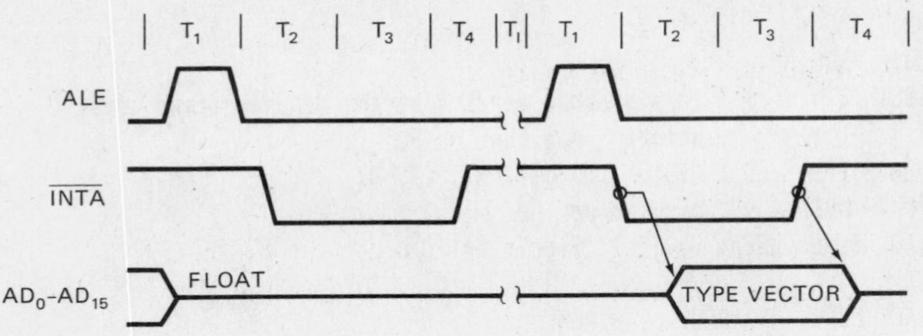

FIGURE 8-6 8086 interrupt acknowledge machine cycles.

device can also prevent an argument if two or more sources send interrupt signals at the same time.

PRIORITY OF 8086 INTERRUPTS

As you read through the preceding discussions of the different interrupt types, the question may have occurred to you, "What happens if two or more interrupts happen at the same time?" The answer to this question is that the highest priority interrupt will be serviced first, and then the next highest priority interrupt will be serviced. Figure 8-7 shows the priorities of the 8086 interrupts as shown in the Intel data book. Some examples will show you what these priorities actually mean.

As a first example, suppose that the INTR input is enabled, the 8086 receives an INTR signal during execution of a divide instruction, and the divide operation produces a divide-by-zero interrupt. Since the internal interrupts such as divide error, INT, and INTO have higher priority than INTR, the 8086 will do a divide error (type 0) interrupt response first. Part of the type 0 interrupt response is to clear the IF. This disables the INTR input and prevents the INTR signal from interrupting the higher priority type 0 interrupt service procedure. An IRET instruction at the end of the type 0 procedure will restore the flags to what they were before the type 0 response. This will reenable the INTR input and the 8086 will do an INTR interrupt response. A similar sequence of operations will occur if the 8086 is executing an INT or INTO instruction and a high level signal arrives at the INTR input.

As a second example of how this priority works, suppose that a rising-edge signal arrives at the NMI input while the 8086 is executing a DIV instruction, and that the division operation produces a divide error. Since the 8086 checks for internal interrupts before it checks for an NMI interrupt, the 8086 will push the flags on the stack, clear TF and IF, push the return address on the stack, and go to the start of the divide error (type 0) service procedure. However, because the NMI interrupt request is not disabled, the 8086 will then do an NMI (type 2) interrupt response. In other words, the 8086 will push the flags on the stack, clear TF and IF, push the return address on the stack, and go execute the NMI interrupt service procedure. When the 8086 finishes the NMI procedure, it will return to the divide error procedure, finish executing that procedure, and then return to the mainline program.

INTERRUPT	PRIORITY
DIVIDE ERROR, INT n, INTO	HIGHEST
NMI	
INTR	
SINGLE-STEP	LOWEST

FIGURE 8-7 Priority of 8086 interrupts. *(Intel Corporation)*

To finish our discussion of 8086 interrupt priorities, let's see how the single step (TRAP or type 1) interrupt fits in. If the trap flag is set, the 8086 will do a type 1 interrupt response after every mainline instruction. When the 8086 responds to any interrupt, however, part of its response is to clear the trap flag. This disables the single-step function, so the 8086 will not normally single-step through the instructions of the interrupt service procedure. In actuality, if the 8086 is in single-step mode when it enters an interrupt service procedure, it will execute the single-step procedure once before it executes the called interrupt procedure. The trap flag can be set again in the single-step procedure if single stepping is desired in the interrupt service procedure.

Now that we have shown you the different types of 8086 interrupts and how the 8086 responds to each, we will show you a few examples of how the 8086 hardware interrupts are used. Other applications of interrupts will be shown throughout the rest of the book.

HARDWARE INTERRUPT APPLICATIONS

Hardware and Software Considerations When Using Interrupts

HARDWARE

Whenever you are going to do some task with an interrupt, there are some important hardware points for you to consider. Among these are:

1. How many interrupt inputs does the microprocessor have?
2. Do these inputs require active high, active low, or edge-active signals to assert them?
3. Do the interrupt inputs have priorities?
4. Is external hardware required to insert a restart instruction or interrupt type, or is this done automatically when the CPU responds to the interrupt?

SOFTWARE

Among the software considerations when you are going to use an interrupt are the following:

1. What instructions are required to unmask/enable the interrupt input you want to use.
2. How are the stack and stack pointer initialized?
3. Does the CPU automatically save flags and register contents when it responds to the interrupt, or do you have to use push instructions at the start of the routine to do this?
4. How can data required by the interrupt service procedure be accessed no matter where in the main program the interrupt occurs?
5. What instructions are required at the end of the procedure to restore main program flags and registers, enable interrupts, and return to the interrupted mainline program.

SIMPLE INTERRUPT DATA INPUT

One of the most common uses of interrupts is to relieve a CPU of the burden of polling. Back in Chapter 4 we showed you how ASCII characters can be read in from an encoded keyboard on a polled basis. Figure 4-13 shows the circuit connections, and Figure 4-14 shows the algorithm and program for this. To refresh your memory, polling works as follows.

The strobe or data ready signal from some external device is connected to an input port line on the microcomputer. The microcomputer uses a program loop to read and test this port line over and over until the data ready signal is found to be asserted. The microcomputer then exits the polling loop and reads in the data from the external device. Data can also be output on a polled basis.

The disadvantage of polled input or output is that while the microcomputer is polling the strobe or data ready signal, it can not easily be doing other tasks. In systems where the microcomputer must be doing many tasks, polling is a waste of time, so interrupt input and output is used. In this case the data ready or strobe signal is connected to an interrupt input on the microcomputer. The microcomputer then goes about doing its other tasks until it is interrupted by a data ready signal from the external device. An interrupt service procedure can read in or send out the desired data and, when finished, return execution to the interrupted program.

For our example here we will connect the keypressed strobe to the NMI interrupt input of the 8086 on an SDK-86. The NMI input is usually reserved for responding to a power failure or some other catastropic condition. However, since we are not expecting any catastropic conditions to befall our SDK-86, we choose to use this input because it does not require an external hardware device to insert the interrupt type as does the INTR input.

Sheet 2 of the SDK-86 schematics in Figure 7-6 shows the circuitry normally connected to the NMI input. This circuitry is designed so that you can cause an NMI interrupt by pressing a key labeled INTR on the hex keypad.

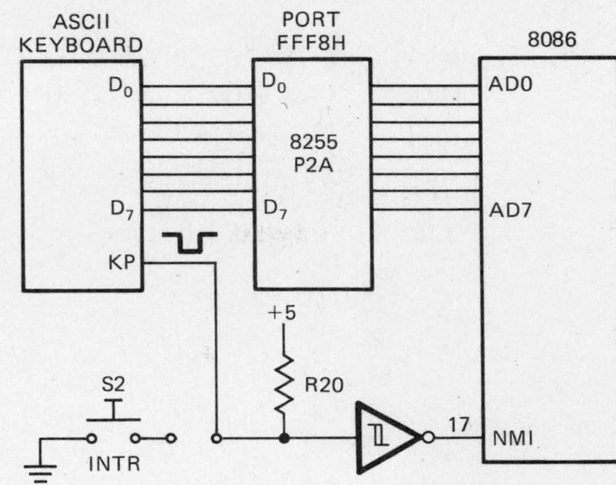

FIGURE 8-8 Circuit modifications for SDK-86 **NMI** input.

When this key is pressed, the input of the 74LS14 inverter will be made low, and the output of the inverter will go high. The low-to-high transition on the NMI input causes the 8086 to automatically do an NMI (type 2) interrupt response.

Figure 8-8 shows how we modified circuitry for our example here. We removed *R*22, a 110-Ω resistor, and *C*33, a 1-μF capacitor, so the keypad switch can no longer cause an interrupt. We then connected an active low strobe line from an ASCII-encoded keyboard directly to the input of *A*21, the 74LS14 inverter. When a key on the ASCII keyboard is pressed, the keyboard circuitry will send out the ASCII code for the pressed key on its eight parallel data lines and it will assert the keypressed strobe line low. The keypressed strobe going low will cause the NMI input of the 8086 to be asserted high. This will cause the 8086 to do a type 2 interrupt. Now let's look at the hardware and software considerations for this interrupt example.

The hardware considerations for this example are quite simply answered. The NMI input requires a low-to-high transition, and, with the circuit connections shown in Figure 8-8, this will be produced when a key on the ASCII keyboard is pressed. Since we are only using one interrupt here, we are not concerned about priorities. In response to its NMI input being asserted, the 8086 automatically does a type 2 interrupt response. No external hardware is needed for the interrupt type.

The software considerations require a little more thought, but their answers are very similar to those for the divide by zero example in a previous section. At the start of the mainline we need to load address 00008H with the IP value for the start of the type 2 procedure, and address 0000AH with the CS value for the start of the procedure. Since any interrupt response uses the stack, we need to set up a stack. Assuming that we are going to read in the ASCII characters from the keyboard and put them in an array in memory, we need to set up a data segment for the array. In the actual code section of the mainline we need to initialize the data segment register, the stack segment register, and the stack pointer register. Figure 8-9*a* shows the instructions for doing all this. Another important thing to do in the start of the mainline program is to initialize a pointer to the start of

```
page ,132
;8086 PROGRAM TO READ CHARACTERS FROM A KEYBOARD
;ABSTRACT:   The mainline of this procedure initializes the interrupt
;            table with the address of the procedure that reads the
;            characters from a keyboard on an interrupt basis.
;PROCEDURES: Uses KEYBOARD
;PORTS USED: None in mainline, FFF8H for keyboard input in KEYBOARD
;
DATA_HERE       SEGMENT WORD    PUBLIC
       ASCII_STRING    DB      100 DUP(0)      ; store for characters
       ASCII_POINTER   DW      OFFSET ASCII_STRING
       CHARCNT         DB      100             ; read 100 characters
       KEYDONE         DB      0               ; =1 if characters all read
DATA_HERE       ENDS
STACK_HERE      SEGMENT STACK
                       DW  100 DUP (0)         ; Set up stack of 100 words
       TOP_STACK  LABEL  WORD                  ; Pointer to top of stack
STACK_HERE      ENDS

PUBLIC  ASCII_POINTER, CHARCNT, KEYDONE        ; Make available to other modules
EXTRN   KEYBOARD:FAR                           ; Procedure in another assembly module

CODE_HERE       SEGMENT WORD    PUBLIC
       ASSUME CS:CODE_HERE, DS:DATA_HERE, SS:STACK_HERE
START: MOV  AX, STACK_HERE             ; Initialize stack segment register
       MOV  SS, AX
       MOV  SP, OFFSET TOP_STACK       ; Initialize stack pointer
       MOV  AX, DATA_HERE              ; Initialize data segment register
       MOV  DS, AX
;store the address for the KEYBOARD routine at address 0000:0008
;address 00008-0000B is where type 2 interrupt gets interrupt
;service procedure address. CS at 0000A & 0000B, IP at 00008 & 00009
       MOV  AX, 0000
       MOV  ES, AX
       MOV  WORD PTR ES:000AH, SEG KEYBOARD
       MOV  WORD PTR ES:0008H, OFFSET KEYBOARD
;simulate larger program.
HERE:  JMP  HERE

CODE_HERE       ENDS
       END
```

(a)

FIGURE 8-9 Reading characters from an ASCII keyboard on interrupt basis. *(a)* Initialization and mainline. *(b)* Interrupt service procedure.

the array where the ASCII characters will be put as they are read in. The statement ASCII_POINTER DW OFFSET ASCII_STRING in the data segment in Figure 8-9*a* sets aside a word location in memory and initializes that location with the offset of the start of the array we declared to put the ASCII characters in. In the procedure we get this pointer, use it to store a character, and increment it to point to the next location in the array. Since this pointer is stored in a named memory location, it can be accessed easily by the procedure, no matter when the interrupt occurs in the mainline program.

The HERE: JMP HERE instruction at the end of the mainline program simulates a complex mainline program that the 8086 might be executing. The 8086 will execute this instruction over and over until an interrupt occurs. When an interrupt occurs the 8086 will service the interrupt and then return to execute the HERE: JMP HERE instruction over and over again until the next interrupt. Note that if we had connected the interrupt signal to the 8086 INTR interrupt input instead of the NMI input, we would have had to enable the INTR input with an STI instruction before the HERE: JMP HERE.

Figure 8-9*b* shows the interrupt service procedure for this example. The comments for the procedure express its algorithm fairly clearly. After saving AX, BX, CX, and DX on the stack, we check to see if all characters have

```
;8086 READ KEYBOARD ON INTERRUPT BASIS PROCEDURE
      ;ABSTRACT  : This procedure reads in ASCII characters from an
      ;          : encoded keyboard on an interrupt basis and stores them
      ;          : in a buffer in memory
      ;SAVES     : all registers used
      ;PORTS USED: input port FFF8H for the keyboard input

      DATA_HERE       SEGMENT WORD    PUBLIC
             EXTRN    ASCII_POINTER:WORD, CHARCNT:BYTE, KEYDONE:BYTE
      DATA_HERE       ENDS

      PUBLIC  KEYBOARD

      CODE_HERE       SEGMENT WORD    PUBLIC
      KEYBOARD        PROC            FAR
             ASSUME CS:CODE_HERE, DS:DATA_HERE

             STI                ; enable 8086 INTR so higher priority
                                ; interrupts can be recognized
             PUSH AX            ; save registers
             PUSH BX
             PUSH CX
             PUSH DX
             CMP  CHARCNT, 00          ; see if all characters read in
             JZ   EXIT                 ; leave if all done
             MOV  BX, ASCII_POINTER    ; get pointer to buffer
             MOV  DX, 0FFF8H           ; point at keyboard port
             IN   AL, DX               ; Read ASCII code
             AND  AL, 7FH              ; Mask parity bit
             MOV  [BX], AL             ; Write character to buffer
             INC  ASCII_POINTER        ; point to next buffer location
             DEC  CHARCNT              ; Check if 100 characters yet
             JNZ  NOTDONE              ; No, clear carry to indicate
             MOV  KEYDONE, 01H         ; Yes, set flag to indicate done
             JMP  EXIT
      NOTDONE:MOV KEYDONE, 00H         ; No, clear keydone flag
      EXIT:   POP DX                   ; restore registers
             POP  CX
             POP  BX
             POP  AX
             IRET
      KEYBOARD        ENDP
      CODE_HERE       ENDS
                      END
```

(*b*)

FIGURE 8-9 (*continued*)

been read. If CHARCNT is zero, then we do not read in any characters. If CHARCNT is not zero, we copy the array pointer from its named memory location, ASCII_POINTER, to BX. We then read in the ASCII character from the port that the keyboard is connected to and mask the parity bit of the ASCII character. The MOV [BX], AL instruction next copies the ASCII character to the memory location pointed to by BX. To get the pointer ready for the read and store operation, we increment the stored pointer with the INC ASCII_POINTER instruction. Finally, our work done, we restore DX, CX, BX, and AX, and return to the mainline program.

Sitting in a HERE: JMP HERE loop waiting for an interrupt signal may not seem like much of an improvement over polling the keypressed strobe. However, in a more realistic program the 8086 would be doing many other tasks between keyboard interrupts. With polling the 8086 would not easily be able to do this.

Using Interrupts for Counting and Timing

COUNTING

As a simple example of the use of an interrupt input for counting, suppose that we are using an 8086 to control a printed-circuit-board-making machine in our computerized electronics factory. Further suppose that we want to detect each finished board as it comes out of the machine and to keep a count of finished boards so that we can compare this count with the number of boards fed in. This way we can determine if any boards were lost in the machine.

To do this count on an interrupt basis, all we have to do is detect when a board passes out of the machine and send an interrupt signal to an interrupt input on the 8086. The interrupt service procedure for that input can simply increment the board count stored in a named memory location.

To detect a board coming out of the machine we use an infrared LED, a phototransistor, and two conditioning gates as shown in Figure 8-10. The LED is positioned over the track where the boards come out, and the phototransistor is positioned below the track. When no board is between the LED and the phototransistor, the light from the LED will strike the phototransistor and turn it on. The collector of the phototransistor will then be low, as will the NMI input on the 8086. When a board passes between the LED and the phototransistor, the light will not reach the phototransistor, and it will turn off. Its collector will go high, and so will the signal to the NMI input of the 8086. The 74LS14 Schmitt trigger inverters are necessary to turn the slow rise-time signal from the phototransistor collector into a signal which meets the rise-time requirements of the NMI input on the 8086. When the 8086 receives the low-to-high signal on its NMI input, it will automatically do a type 2 interrupt response. As we mentioned above, all the type 2 interrupt service procedure has to do in this case is increment the board count in a named memory location and return to running the machine. This same technique can be used to count people going into a stadium, cows coming in from the pasture, or just about any thing else you might want to count.

USING AN INTERRUPT INPUT FOR TIMING APPLICATIONS

In Chapter 4 we showed how a delay loop could be used to set the time between microcomputer operations. In the example there we used a delay loop to let us take in data samples at 1-ms intervals. The obvious disadvantage of a delay loop is that while the microcomputer is stuck in the delay loop, it cannot easily be doing other useful work. In many cases a delay loop would be a waste of the microcomputer's valuable time. For most microcomputer timing, an interrupt approach is much more efficient.

Suppose, for example, that in our 8086-controlled printed circuit board machine we need to check the pH of a solution approximately every 4 minutes. If we used a delay loop to count off the 4 minutes, either the 8086 wouldn't be able to do much else, or we would have some difficult calculations to figure out at what points in the program to go check the pH.

To solve this problem, all we have to do is connect a simple 1-Hz pulse source to an interrupt input as shown in Figure 8-11. This 555 timer circuit is not very accurate, but it is inexpensive, and it is good enough for this application. We connect the timer output to the 8086 NMI input as you might do to demonstrate this concept on an SDK-86 board. The 555 timer will send an interrupt signal to the 8086 NMI input approximately once every second. If we simply count the number of NMI interrupts that occur, we will then know how many seconds have passed.

Here's how the programming is done for this application. In the mainline we set aside a memory location for

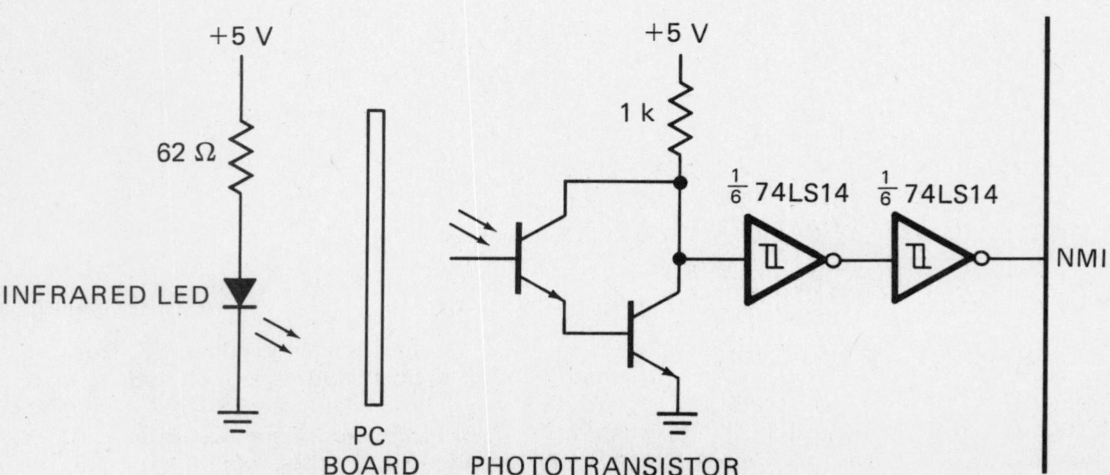

FIGURE 8-10 Circuit for optically detecting presence of an object.

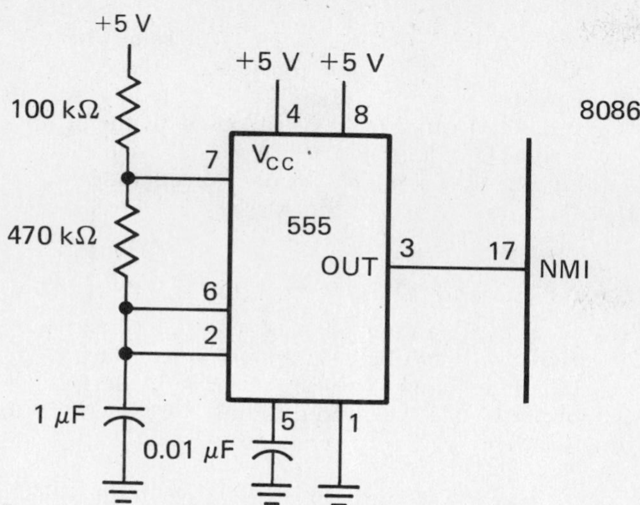

FIGURE 8-11 Inexpensive 1-Hz pulse source for interrupt timing.

the seconds count and initialize that location to the number of seconds that we want to count off. In this case we want 4 minutes, which is 240 decimal or F0H seconds. Each time the 8086 receives an interrupt from the 555 timer, it executes the interrupt service procedure for the NMI interrupt. In this procedure we decrement the seconds count in the named memory location and test to see if the count is down to zero yet. If the count is zero, we know that 4 minutes have elapsed, so we reload the seconds count memory location with F0H and call the procedure which reads the pH of the solution and takes appropriate action if the pH is not correct. If the seconds count is not zero, execution simply returns to the mainline program until the next interrupt from the 555 or from some other source occurs. To help you visualize how this works, Figure 8-12 shows the algorithm for this mainline and procedure. The advantage of this interrupt approach is that the interrupt service procedure only takes a few microseconds of the 8086's time once every second. The rest of the time the 8086 is free to run the mainline program.

USING AN INTERRUPT TO PRODUCE A REAL-TIME CLOCK

Another application using a 1-Hz interrupt input might be to generate a real-time clock of seconds, minutes, and hours. The time from this clock can then be displayed and/or printed out on timecards, etc. To generate the clock a 1-Hz signal is applied to an interrupt input. A seconds count, a minutes count, and an hours count are kept in three successive memory locations. When an interrupt occurs, the seconds count is incremented by one. If the seconds count is not equal to 60, then execution is simply returned to the mainline program. If the seconds count is equal to 60 then the seconds count is reset to zero, and the minutes count is incremented by one. If the minutes count is not 60 then execution is simply returned to the mainline. If the minutes count is 60 then the minutes count is reset to zero, and the

```
INITIALIZE
     INTERRUPT POINTER TABLE
     STACK AND STACK SEGMENT POINTER
     DATA SEGMENT
     SECONDS COUNT TO 240 DECIMAL
WAIT FOR INTERRUPT
```

(a)

```
SAVE REGISTERS
DECREMENT SECONDS COUNT
IF SECONDS COUNT = 0 THEN
     RELOAD SECONDS COUNT WITH 240 DECIMAL
     CALL pH READ PROCEDURE
     RESTORE REGISTERS
     RETURN TO MAINLINE
ELSE RESTORE REGISTERS
     RETURN TO MAINLINE
```

(b)

FIGURE 8-12 Algorithm for pH read at 4-minute intervals. *(a)* Initialization and mainline. *(b)* Interrupt service procedure.

hours count is incremented by one. If the hours count is not 13, then execution is simply returned to the mainline. If the hours count is equal to 13 then it is reset to 1 and execution returned to the mainline. A problem at the end of the chapter asks you to write the algorithm and program for this real-time clock.

The interrupt service routine for the real-time clock can easily be modified to also keep track of other time measurements such as the 4-minute timer shown in the preceding example. In other words, the single interrupt service routine can be used to keep track of several different time intervals. By counting a different number of interrupts or applying a different frequency signal to the interrupt input, this technique can be used to time many different tasks in a microcomputer system.

GENERATING AN ACCURATE TIME BASE FOR TIMING INTERRUPTS

The 555 timer that we used for the 4-minute timer described above was accurate enough for that application, but for many applications, it is not. For more precise timing we usually use a signal derived from a crystal-controlled oscillator such as the processor clock signal. The processor clock signal is stable, but it is obviously too high in frequency to drive a processor interrupt input directly. Therefore, it is divided down with an external counter device to an appropriate frequency for the interrupt input. Most microcomputers have a counter device such as the Intel 8253 or 8254, which can be programmed with instructions to divide an input frequency by any desired number. Besides acting as programmable frequency dividers, these devices have many important uses in microcomputer systems. Therefore, the next section describes how an 8254 operates, how an 8524 can easily be added to an SDK-86 board, and how an 8254 is used in a variety of interrupt applications. Also in the next section we use the 8254 discussion to show you the general procedure for initializing any of the programmable peripheral devices we discuss in later chapters.

A Software-Programmable Timer/Counter, the Intel 8253 and 8254

Because of the many tasks that they can be used for in microcomputer systems, programmable timer/counters are very important for you to learn about. As you read through the following sections, pay particular attention to the applications of this device in systems and the general procedure for initializing a programmable device such as the 8254. Read lightly through the discussions of the different counter modes to become aware of the types of problems that the device can solve for you. You can later dig into the details of these discussions when you have a specific problem to solve.

Another important point to make to you here is that the discussions of various devices throughout the rest of this book are not intended to replace the manufacturers' data sheets for the devices. Many of the programmable peripheral devices we discuss are so versatile that they require almost a small book for each to describe all the details of their operations. The discussions here are intended to introduce you to the devices, show you what they can be used for, and show you enough details about them that you can do some real jobs with them. After you become familiar with using a device in some simple applications, you can read the data sheets to learn further "bells and whistles" that the devices have.

Basic 8253 and 8254 Operation

The Intel 8253 and 8254 each contain three 16-bit counters which can be programmed to operate in several different modes. The 8253 and 8254 devices are pin-for-pin compatible, and they are nearly identical in function. The major differences are:

1. The maximum input clock frequency for the 8253 is 2.6 MHz, the maximum clock frequency for the 8254 is 8 MHz (10 MHz for the 8254-2).
2. The 8254 has a *read-back* feature which allows you to latch the count in all of the counters and the status of the counter at any point. The 8253 does not have this read-back feature.

To simplify reading of this section we will refer only to the 8254. However, you can assume that the discussion also applies to the 8253 except where we specifically state otherwise.

As shown by the block diagram of the 8254 in Figure 8-13, the device contains three 16-bit counters. In some ways these counters are similar to the TTL presettable counters we reviewed in Chapter 1. The big advantage of these counters, however, is that you can load a count in them, start them, and stop them with instructions in your program. The device is then said to be software

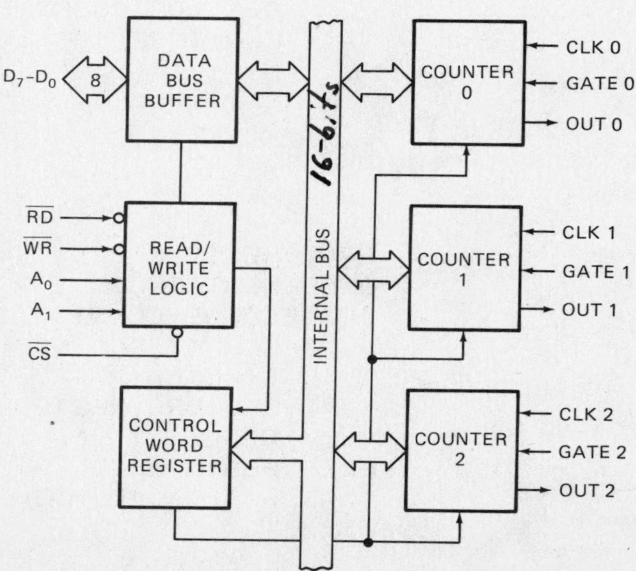

FIGURE 8-13 8254 internal block diagram. *(Intel Corporation)*

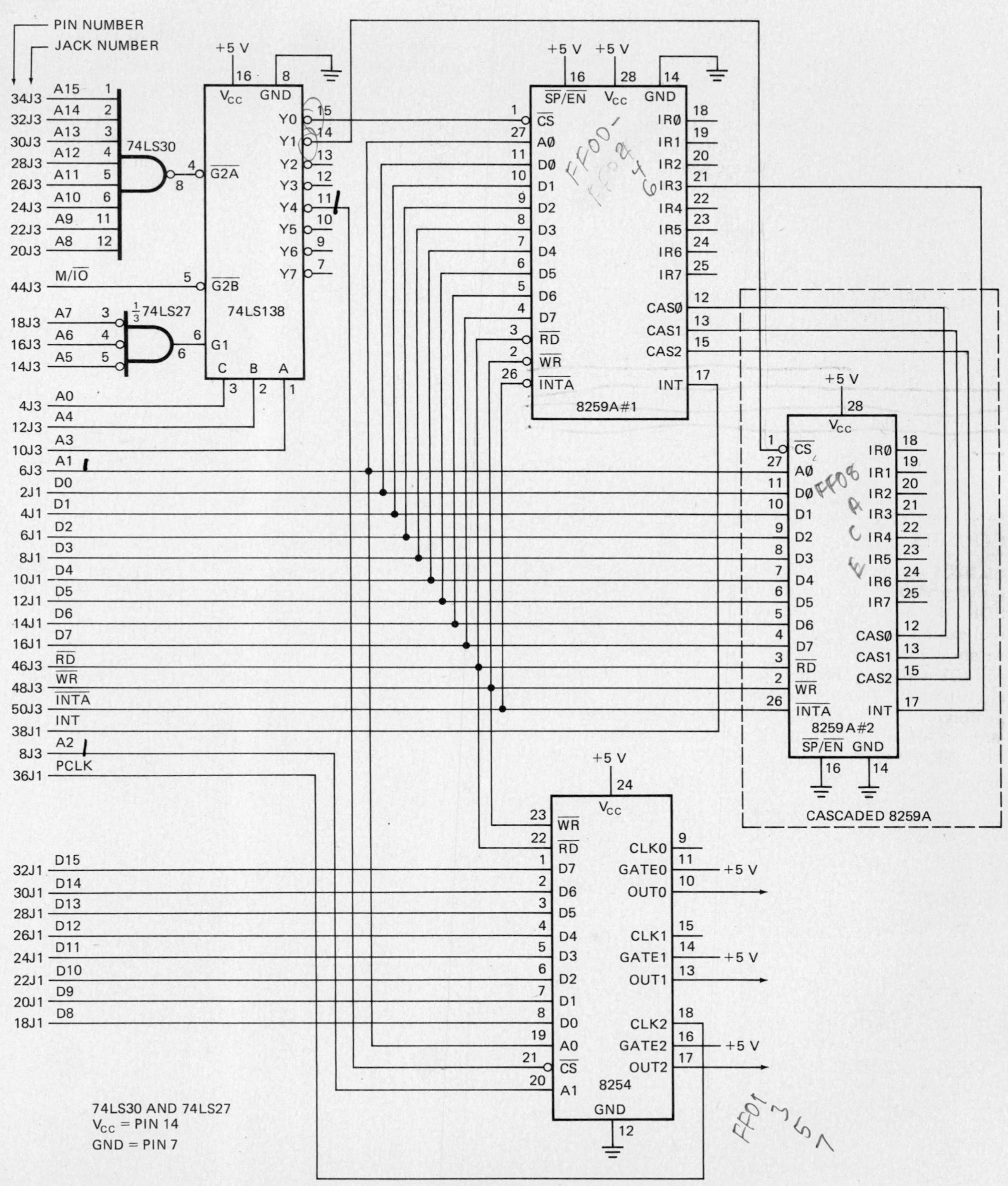

FIGURE 8-14 Circuit showing how to add an 8254 and 8259A(s) to an SDK-86 board.

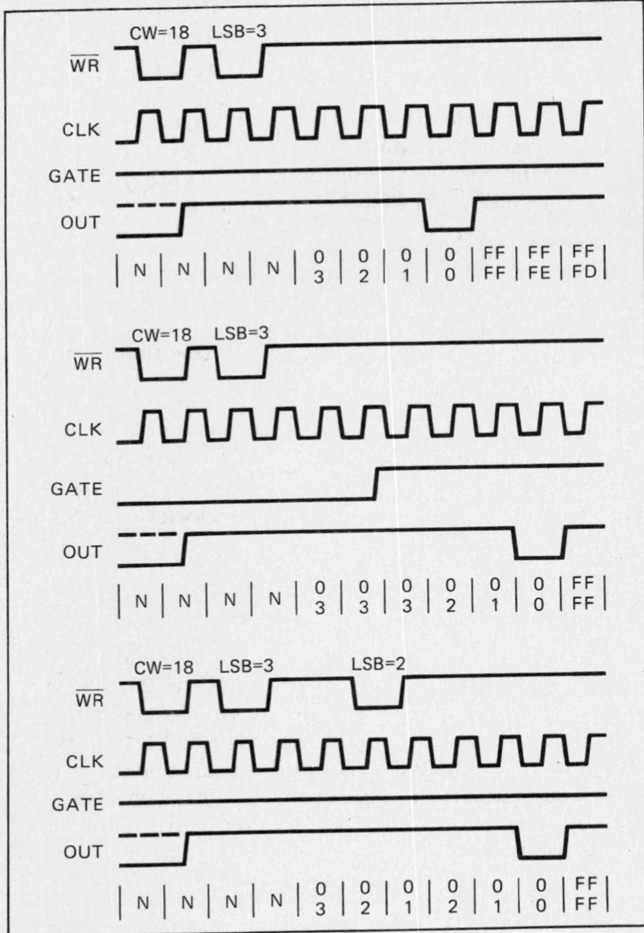

FIGURE 8-24 8254 MODE 4 example timing waveforms. *(Intel Corporation)*

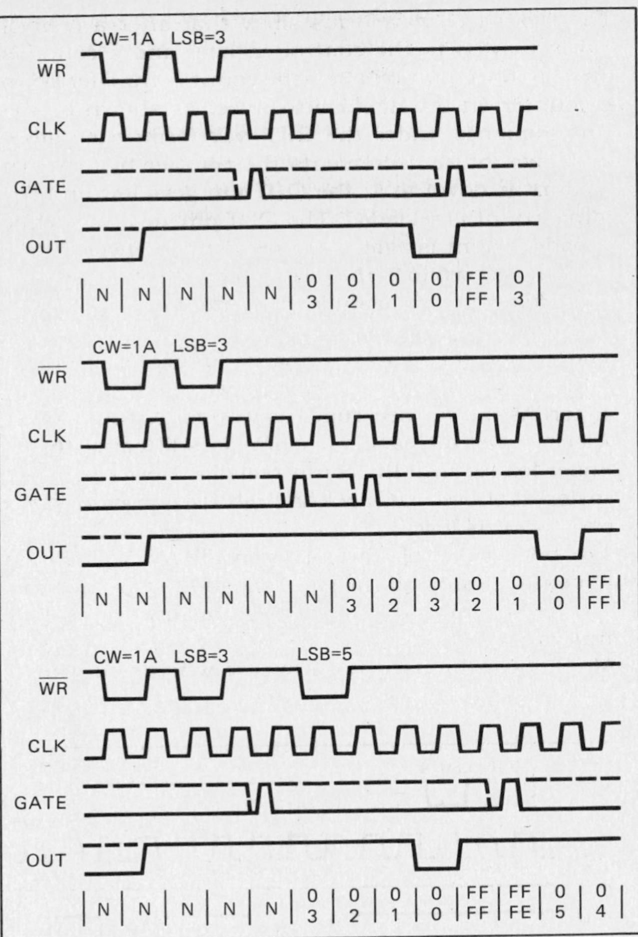

FIGURE 8-25 8254 MODE 5 example timing waveforms. *(Intel Corporation)*

Mode 4 can be used in a case where you want to send out some parallel data on a port, and then after some delay send out a strobe signal to let the receiving system know that the data is available.

MODE 5—HARDWARE-TRIGGERED STROBE

Mode 5 is used where we want to produce a low-going strobe pulse some programmable time interval after a rising-edge trigger signal is applied to the GATE input. This mode is very useful when you want to delay a rising edge signal by some amount of time.

Figure 8-25 shows some example waveforms for a counter operating in mode 5. For a start let's look at the top set of waveforms. As usual we write a control word and the desired count to a counter. As shown by the count sequence under the OUT waveform, however, the count does not get transferred to the counter until the the GATE (trigger) input is made high. When the trigger input is made high the count will be transferred to the counter on the next clock pulse. Succeeding clock pulses will decrement the counter. When the counter reaches zero, the OUT pin will go low for one clock pulse time. The OUT pin will go low $N + 1$ clock pulses after the trigger input goes high.

The second set of waveforms in Figure 8-25 shows that if another trigger pulse occurs during the countdown time, the original count will be reloaded on the next clock pulse and the countdown will start over. The OUT pin will remain high until the count is finally counted down. If trigger pulses continue to come before the countdown is completed, the OUT pin will continue to stay high. Therefore you can use a counter in mode 5 to produce a power fail signal as we showed in the previous discussion of mode 1. Note that for mode 5, however, the OUT pin will be high if the power is on and go low when the power fails.

The bottom set of waveforms in Figure 8-25 shows that if a new count is written to a counter, the new count will not be loaded into the counter until a new trigger pulse occurs.

USING A NONSYSTEM CLOCK WITH 8254 IN MODES 2 AND 3

If you are applying a signal which is not derived from the system clock to the CLK input of an 8254 (not 8253), then a small note in the Intel data sheet indicates that the GATE input of a counter must be pulsed low just after the count is written to the counter. An easy way to do this is to connect the GATE input of the counter to an otherwise unused output port pin. You can then pulse the GATE by outputting a low and then outputting a high to that port pin.

READING THE COUNT FROM AN 8254 COUNTER

For many counter applications we want to be able to read the current count in the counter. Suppose, for example, that we are using an 8254 counter to count the cars coming into a parking lot as we did in our example for mode 0 above. In that case we used the counter to produce an interrupt when the parking lot was full, so we could shut the gate. Now further suppose that as part of a traffic flow study we want to find out how many cars have come into the lot by 7:30 a.m. An interrupt-driven real-time clock procedure can, at 7:30 a.m., call a procedure which reads in the current count from the counter. Since the counter was initially loaded with 1000 decimal and is being counted down as cars come in, we can simply subtract the current count from 1000 to determine how many cars have come in.

The counters in an 8254 have latches on their outputs. When you read the count from a counter, what you are actually reading is the data on the outputs of these latches. These latches are normally enabled during counting so that the latch outputs just follow the counter outputs. If you try to read the count while the counter is counting, the count may change between reading the LSB and the MSB. This may give you a strange count. To read a correct count, then, you must in some way stop the counting or latch the current count on the output of the latches. There are three major ways of doing this.

The first is to stop counting by turning off the clock signal or making the GATE input low with external hardware. This method has the disadvantages that it requires external hardware and that a clock pulse which occurs while the clock is disabled will obviously not be counted.

The second way of reading a stable value from a counter is to latch the current count with a counter latch command, and then read the latched count. A counter is latched by sending a control word to the control register address in the 8254. If you look at the format for the 8254 control word in Figure 8-17 you should see that a counter latch command is specified by making the RW1 and RW0 bits both 0. The SC1 and SC0 bits specify which counter we want to latch. The lower 4 bits of the control word are "don't cares" for a counter latch command word so we usually make them 0's for simplicity. As an example, here is the sequence of instructions you would use to latch and read the LSB and MSB from counter 1 of the 8254 in Figure 8-14. We assume that the counter was already programmed for read/write LSB then MSB when the device was initialized. If the counter was programmed for only LSB or only MSB, then only that byte can be read.

```
MOV  AL, 01000000B ; Counter 1 latch command
MOV  DX, 0FF07H    ; Point at 8254 control registe
OUT  DX, AL        ; Send latch command
MOV  DX, 0FF03H    ; Point at counter 1 address
IN   AL, DX        ; Read LSB of latched count
MOV  AH, AL        ; Save LSB of latched count
IN   AL, DX        ; Read MSB of latched count
XCHG AH, AL        ; Put count in AX
```

When a counter latch command is sent, the latched count is held until it is read. When the count is read from the latches, the latch outputs return to following the counter outputs.

The third method of reading a stable count from a counter is to latch the count with a read-back command. This method is available in the 8254, but not in the 8253. It is essentially an enhanced version of the counter latch command approach described in the preceding paragraphs.

Figure 8-26 shows the format for the 8254 counter read-back command word. It is sent to the same address that other control words are for a particular 8254. The 1's in bits D7 and D6 identify this as a read-back command word. To latch the count on a counter you put a 0 in bit D5 of the control word and put a 1 in the bit position that corresponds to that counter in the control word. The advantage of this control word is that you can latch one, two, or all three counters by putting 1's in the appropriate bits. Once a counter is latched, the count is read as shown in the example program above. After being read, the latch outputs return to following the counter outputs.

If a read-back command word with bit D4 = 0 is sent to an 8254, the status of one or more counters will be latched on the output latches. Consult the Intel data sheet for further information on this latched status.

The preceding sections have shown how 8254 counters can be used to do a wide variety of tasks around microcomputers. Many of these applications produce an interrupt signal which must be connected to an interrupt input on the microprocessor. In the next section we show how a *priority interrupt controller* device, the Intel 8259A, is used to service multiple interrupts.

A0, A1 = 11 $\overline{CS}$ = 0 $\overline{RD}$ = 1 $\overline{WR}$ = 0

D_7	D_6	D_5	D_4	D_3	D_2	D_1	D_0
1	1	$\overline{COUNT}$	$\overline{STATUS}$	CNT 2	CNT 1	CNT 0	0

D_5: 0 = LATCH COUNT OF SELECTED COUNTERS(S)
D_4: 0 = LATCH STATUS OF SELECTED COUNTER(S)
D_3: 1 = SELECT COUNTER 2
D_2: 1 = SELECT COUNTER 1
D_1: 1 = SELECT COUNTER 0
D_0: RESERVED FOR FUTURE EXPANSION; MUST BE 0

FIGURE 8-26 8254 read-back control word format.

Multiple Interrupts and the 8259A Priority Interrupt Controller

Previous sections of this chapter show how interrupts can be used for a variety of applications. In a small system, for example, we might read ASCII characters in from a keyboard on an interrupt basis; count interrupts from a timer to produce a real-time clock of seconds, minutes, and hours; and detect several emergency or job-done conditions on an interrupt basis. Each of these interrupt applications requires a separate interrupt input. If we are working with an 8086, we have a problem here because the 8086 has only two interrupt inputs, NMI and INTR. If we save NMI for a power failure interrupt, this leaves only one interrupt input for all the other applications. For applications where we have interrupts from multiple sources such as this we use an external device called *a priority interrupt controller* (PIC) to "funnel" the interrupt signals into an interrupt input on the processor. In this section we show how a common PIC, the Intel 8259A, is connected in an 8086 system, how it is initialized, and how it is used to handle interrupts from multiple sources.

8259A OVERVIEW AND SYSTEM CONNECTIONS

To show you how an 8259A functions in an 8086 system we first need to review how the 8086 INTR input works. Remember from a discussion earlier in this chapter that if the 8086 interrupt flag is set and the INTR input receives a high signal, the 8086 will:

1. Push the flags on the stack.
2. Clear the IF and TF.
3. Push the return address on the stack.
4. Put the data bus in the input mode.
5. Send out two interrupt acknowledge pulses on its $\overline{\text{INTA}}$ pin. The $\overline{\text{INTA}}$ pulses tell some external hardware device such as an 8259A to send the desired interrupt type to the 8086.
6. When the 8086 receives the interrupt type from the external device, it will multiply that interrupt type by 4 to produce an address in the interrupt pointer table.
7. From that address and the three following addresses the 8086 gets the IP and CS values for the start of the interrupt service procedure. Once these values are loaded into CS and IP, the 8086 will then execute the interrupt service procedure.

Now if you look at the internal block diagram of the 8259A in Figure 8-27, I think you will be able to start seeing how it fits into the INTR operation. First notice the 8-bit data bus and control signal pins in the upper left corner of the diagram. The data bus allows the 8086 to send control words to the 8259A and read a status word from the 8259A. The $\overline{\text{RD}}$ and $\overline{\text{WR}}$ inputs control these transfers when the device is selected by asserting its chip select ($\overline{\text{CS}}$) input low. The 8-bit data bus also allows the 8259A to send interrupt types to the 8086. Next notice the eight interrupt inputs labeled IR0–IR7 on the right side of the diagram. If the 8259A is properly enabled, an interrupt signal applied to any one of these inputs will cause the 8259A to assert its INT output pin high. If this pin is connected to the INTR pin of an 8086 and if the 8086 interrupt flag is set, then this high signal will cause the previously described INTR response.

The $\overline{\text{INTA}}$ input of the 8259A is connected to the $\overline{\text{INTA}}$ output of the 8086. The 8259A uses the first $\overline{\text{INTA}}$ pulse from the 8086 to do some activities which depend on the mode that it is programmed in. When it receives the sec-

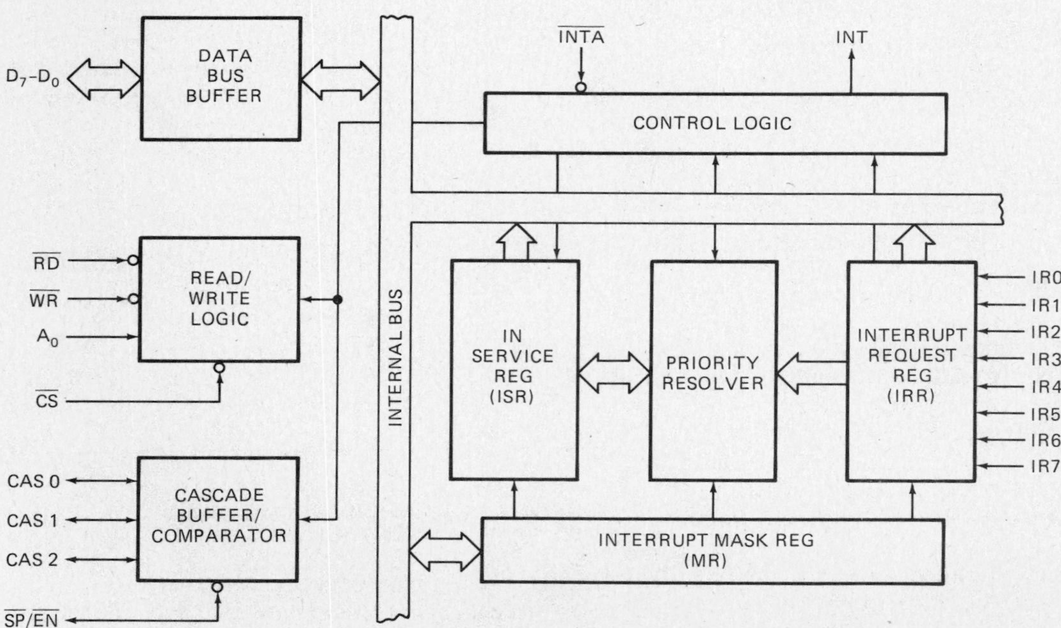

FIGURE 8-27 8259A internal block diagram. *(Intel Corporation)*

ond $\overline{\text{INTA}}$ pulse from the 8086, the 8259A outputs an interrupt type on the 8-bit data bus as shown in Figure 8-6. The interrupt type that it sends to the 8086 is determined by the IR input that received an interrupt signal and by a number you send the 8259A when you initialize it. The point here is that the 8259A "funnels" interrupt signals from up to eight different sources into the 8086 INTR input, and it sends the 8086 a specified interrupt type for each of the eight interrupt inputs.

At this point the question may occur to you, "What happens if interrupt signals appear at, for example, IR2 and IR4 at the same time?" In the *fixed priority mode* that the 8259A is usually operated in, the answer to this question is quite simple. In this mode the IR0 input has the highest priority (most important), the IR1 input the next highest, and so on down to IR7 which has the lowest priority. What this means is that if two interrupt signals occur at the same time, the 8259A will service the one with the highest priority first, assuming that both inputs are unmasked (enabled) in the 8259A.

Now let's look again at the block diagram of the 8259A in Figure 8-27 so we can explain in more detail how the device will respond to multiple interrupt signals. In the block diagram note the four boxes labeled *interrupt request register* (IRR), *interrupt mask register* (IMR), *in-service register* (ISR), and *priority resolver*. The operation of these four functional blocks is quite logical.

The interrupt mask register is used to disable (mask) or enable (unmask) individual interrupt inputs. Each bit in this register corresponds to the interrupt input with the same number. You unmask an interrupt input by sending a command word with a 0 in the bit position that corresponds to that input.

The interrupt request register keeps track of which interrupt inputs are asking for service. If an interrupt input is unmasked, and has an interrupt signal on it, then the corresponding bit in the interrupt request register will be set.

The in-service register keeps track of which interrupt inputs are currently being serviced. For each input that is currently being serviced, the corresponding bit will be set in the in-service register. An example will show how the priority resolver acts as a judge in the middle of all this.

Suppose that IR2 and IR4 are unmasked and that an interrupt signal comes in on the IR4 input. Since IR4 is unmasked, bit 4 of the interrupt request register will be set. The priority resolver will detect that this bit is set and see if any action needs to be taken. To do this it checks the bits in the in-service register (ISR) to see if a higher priority input is being serviced. If a higher priority input is being serviced as indicated by a bit being set for that input in the ISR, then the priority resolver will take no action. If no higher priority interrupt is being serviced, then the priority resolver will activate the circuitry which sends an interrupt signal to the 8086. When the 8086 responds with $\overline{\text{INTA}}$ pulses, the 8259A will send the interrupt type that we specified for the IR4 input when we initialized the device. The 8086 will use the type number it receives to find and execute the interrupt service procedure we wrote for the IR4 interrupt.

Now, suppose that while the 8086 is executing the IR4 service procedure, an interrupt signal arrives at the IR2 input of the 8259A. Since we assumed for this example that IR2 was unmasked, bit 2 of the interrupt request register will be set. The priority resolver will detect that this bit in the IRR is set and make a decision whether to send another interrupt signal to the 8086. To make the decision, the priority resolver looks at the in-service register. If a higher priority bit in the ISR is set, then a higher priority interrupt is being serviced. The priority resolver will wait until the higher priority bit in the ISR is reset before sending an interrupt signal to the 8086 for the new interrupt input. If the priority resolver finds that the new interrupt has a higher priority than the highest priority interrupt currently being serviced, it will set the appropriate bit in the ISR and activate the circuitry which sends a new INT signal to the 8086. For our example here, IR2 has a higher priority than IR4 so the priority resolver will set bit 2 of the ISR and activate the circuitry, which sends a new INT signal to the 8086. If the 8086 INTR input was reenabled with an STI instruction at the start of the IR4 service procedure, as shown in Figure 8-28*a*, then this new INT signal will interrupt the 8086 again. When the 8086 sends out a

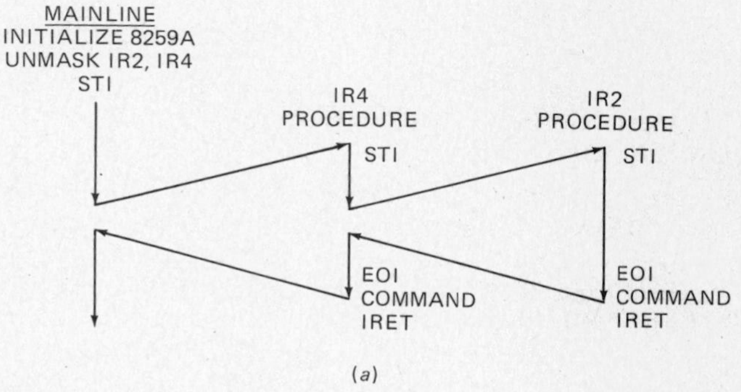

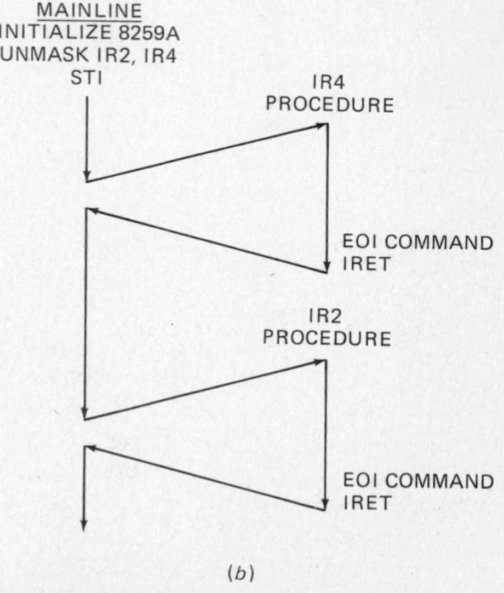

FIGURE 8-28 8259A and 8086 program flow for IR4 interrupt followed by IR2 interrupt. *(a)* Response with INTR enabled in IR4 procedure. *(b)* Response with INTR not enabled in IR4 procedure.

second $\overline{\text{INTA}}$ pulse in response to this interrupt, the 8259A will send it the type number for the IR2 service procedure. The 8086 will use the received type number to find and execute the IR2 service procedure.

At the end of the IR2 procedure we send the 8259A a command word that resets bit 2 of the in-service register so that lower priority interrupts can be serviced. After that, an IRET instruction at the end of the IR2 procedure sends execution back to the interrupted IR4 procedure. At the end of the IR4 procedure we send the 8259A a command word which resets bit 4 of the in-service register so that lower priority interrupts can be serviced. An IRET instruction at the end of the IR4 procedure returns execution to the mainline program. This all sounds very messy, but it is really just a special case of nested procedures. Incidentally, if the IR4 procedure did not reenable the INTR input with an STI instruction, as shown in Figure 8-28*b*, the 8086 would not respond to the IR2-caused INT signal until it finished executing the IR4 procedure. We can't describe all of the possible cases, but the main point here is that the 8086 and the 8259A can be programmed to respond to interrupt signals from multiple sources in almost any way you want them to. Now, before we show you how to initialize and write programs for an 8259A, we will show you more about how it is connected in microcomputer systems.

8259A SYSTEM CONNECTIONS AND CASCADING

Figure 8-14 shows how an 8259A can be added to an SDK-86 board. As shown by the truth table in Figure 8-15, the 74LS138 address decoder will assert the $\overline{\text{CS}}$ input of the 8259A when an I/O base address of FF00H is on the address bus. The A0 input of the 8259A is used to select one of two internal addresses in the device. This pin is connected to system address line A1, so the system addresses for the two internal addresses are FF00H and FF02H. The eight data lines of the 8259A are always connected to the lower half of the 8086 data bus because the 8086 expects to receive interrupt types on these lower eight data lines. $\overline{\text{RD}}$ and $\overline{\text{WR}}$ are connected to the system $\overline{\text{RD}}$ and $\overline{\text{WR}}$ lines. $\overline{\text{INTA}}$ from the 8086 is connected to $\overline{\text{INTA}}$ on the 8259A. The interrupt request signal, INT, from the 8259A is connected to the INTR input of the 8086. The multipurpose $\overline{\text{SP}}/\overline{\text{EN}}$ pin is just tied high because we are only using one 8259A in this system. Since we are not cascading any slave 8259As on the IR inputs, the cascade lines (CAS0, CAS1, and CAS2) can be left open. The eight IR inputs are available for interrupt signals. Unused IR inputs should be tied to ground so that a noise pulse cannot accidentally cause an interrupt. In a later section we will show you how to initialize this 8259A, but first we need to show you how more than one 8259A can be added to a system.

The dashed box on the right side of Figure 8-14 shows how another 8259A could be added to the SDK-86 system to give 15 interrupt inputs. If needed, an 8259A could be connected to each of the eight IR inputs of the original 8259A to give a total of 64 interrupt inputs. Note that since the 8086 has only one INTR input, only one of the 8259A INT pins is connected to the 8086 INTR pin. The 8259A connected directly into the 8086 INTR pin is referred to as the *master*. The INT pin from the other 8259A connects into an IR input on the master. This secondary or *cascaded* device is referred to as a *slave*. Note that the $\overline{\text{INTA}}$ signal from the 8086 goes to both the master and to the slave devices.

Each 8259A has its own addresses so that command words can be written to it and status bytes read from it. For the cascaded 8259A in Figure 8-14, the two system I/O addresses will be FF08H and FF0AH.

The cascade pins (CAS0, CAS1, and CAS2) from the master are connected to the corresponding pins of the slave. For the master these pins function as outputs, and for the slave device they function as inputs. A further difference between the master and the slave is that on the slave the $\overline{\text{SP}}/\overline{\text{EN}}$ pin is tied low to let the device know that it is a slave.

Briefly, here is how the master and the slave work when the slave receives an interrupt signal on one of its IR inputs. If that IR input is unmasked on the slave and if that input is a higher priority than any other interrupt level being serviced in the slave, then the slave will send an INT signal to the IR input of the master. If that IR input of the master is unmasked and if that input is a higher priority than any other IR inputs currently being serviced, then the master will send an INT signal to the 8086 INTR input. If the 8086 INTR is enabled, the 8086 will go through its INTR interrupt procedure and sends out two $\overline{\text{INTA}}$ pulses to both the master and the slave. The slave ignores the first interrupt acknowledge pulse. When the master receives the first $\overline{\text{INTA}}$ pulse, it outputs a 3-bit slave identification number on the CAS0, CAS1, and CAS2 lines. (Each slave in a system is assigned a 3-bit ID as part of its initialization.) Sending the 3-bit ID number enables the slave. When the slave receives the second $\overline{\text{INTA}}$ pulse from the 8086, the slave will send the desired interrupt type number to the 8086 on the eight data lines.

If an interrupt signal is applied directly to one of the IR inputs on the master, the master will send the desired interrupt type to the 8086 when it receives the second $\overline{\text{INTA}}$ pulse from the 8086.

Now that we have given you an overview of how an 8259A operates and how 8259As can be cascaded, the initialization command words for the 8259A should make some sense to you.

INITIALIZING AN 8259A

Earlier in this chapter, when we showed you how to initialize an 8254, we listed a series of steps you should go through to initialize any programmable device. To refresh your memory of these very important steps we will work quickly through them again for the 8259A.

The first step in initializing any device is to find the system base address for the device from the schematic or from a memory map for the system. In order to have a specific example here, we will use the 8259A shown in Figure 8-14. The base address for the 8259A in this system is FF00H.

The next step is to find the internal addresses for the device. For an 8259A the two internal addresses are se-

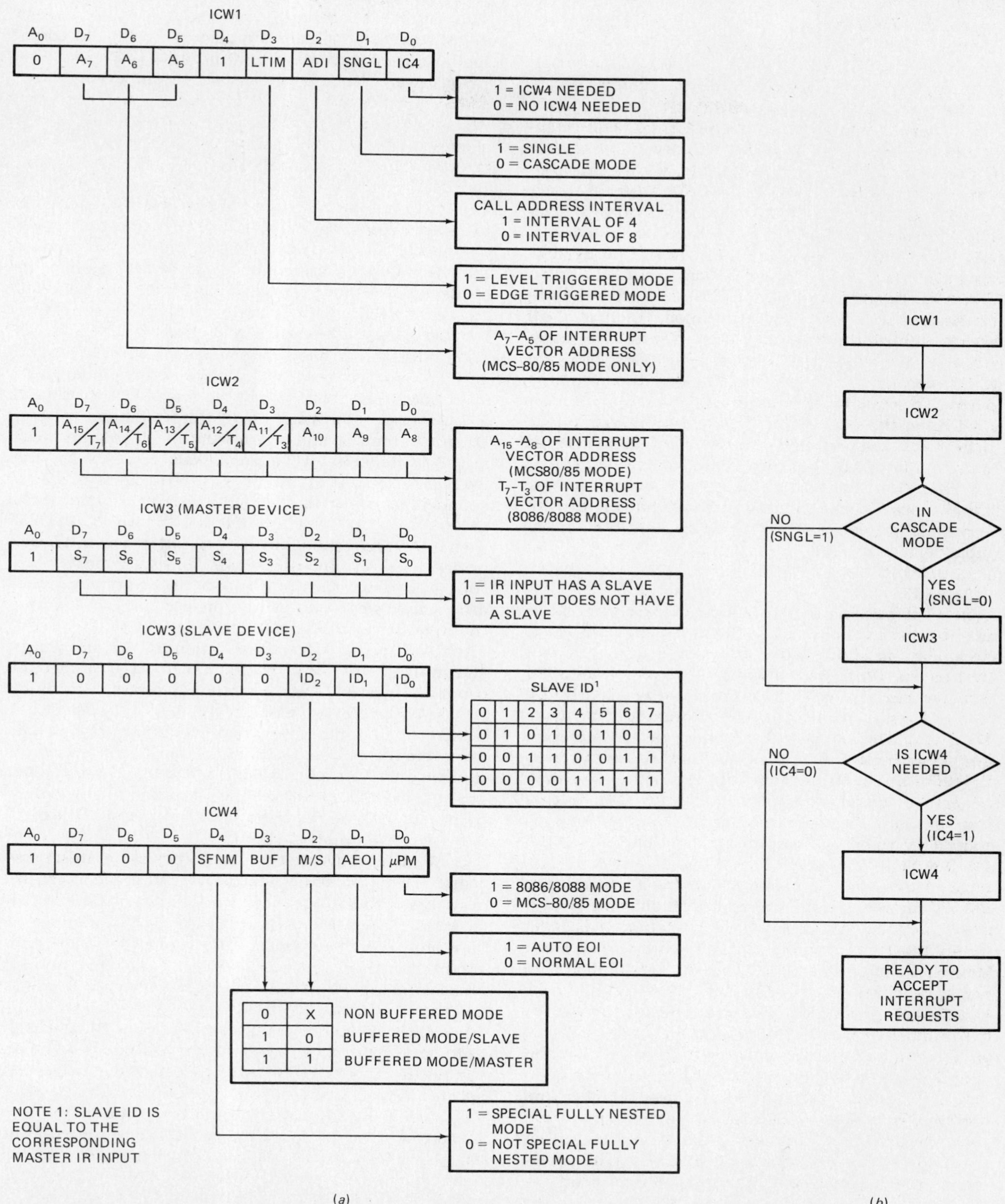

FIGURE 8-29 8259A initialization command word formats and sending order. *(a)* Formats. *(b)* Sending order and requirements. *(Intel Corporation)*

lected by a high or a low on the A0 pin. In the circuit in Figure 8-14 the A0 pin is connected to system address line A1, so the internal addresses correspond to 0 and 2.

Next you add the internal addresses to the base address for the device to get the system address for each internal part of the device. The two system addresses for this 8259A then are FF00H and FF02H.

Now look at Figure 8-29*a* for the format of the command words that must be sent to this device to initialize it. The sight of all of these command words may seem overwhelming at first, but taken one at a time they are quite straightforward. To help you see which initialization command words (ICWs) are needed for various 8259A applications, Figure 8-29*b* shows this in flowchart form. According to this flowchart an ICW1 and an ICW2 must be sent to any 8259A in the system. If the system has any slave 8259As (cascade mode) then an ICW3 must be sent to the master, and a different ICW3 must be sent to the slave. If the system is an 8086, or if you want to specify certain special conditions, then you have to send an ICW4 to the master and to each slave. Now let's look at the formats for the different ICWs.

The first thing to notice about the the ICW formats in Figure 8-29*a* is that the bit labeled A0 on the left end of each of these is not part of the actual command word. This bit tells you the internal address that the control word must be sent to. The A0 = 0 next to ICW1, for example, tells you that ICW1 must be sent to internal address 0, which for our 8259A corresponds to system address FF00H.

The next step in the initialization procedure is to make up the control words. The least-significant bit of ICW1 tells the 8259A whether it needs to look for an ICW4 or not. Since we are using the device in an 8086 system we need to send ICW4. Therefore we make bit D0 a 1. We only want to use one 8259A for now, so we make bit D1 a 1. When used with an 8086, bit D2 is a don't care, so we make it a 0. Bit D3 is used to specify level-triggered mode or edge-triggered mode. In level-triggered mode, service will be requested whenever a high level is present on an IR input. In edge-triggered mode, a signal on an IR input must go from low to high and stay high until serviced. We usually use the edge-triggered mode so that a signal such as a square wave will not cause multiple interrupts. Making bit D3 a 0 does this. Bit D4 has to be a 1. For operation in an 8086 system, bits D5, D6, and D7 are don't cares, so we make them 0's for simplicity. The ICW1 for our example here then is 00010011.

In an 8086 system ICW2 is used to tell the 8259A the type number to send in response to an interrupt signal on the IR0 input. In response to an interrupt signal on some other IR input, the 8259A will automatically add the number of the IR input to this base number and send the result to the 8086 as the type number for that input. Because 8086 interrupt types 0–31 are either dedicated or reserved, type 32 (decimal) is the lowest type number available for us to use. If we send the 8259A an ICW2 of 00100000 binary or 32 decimal, the 8259A will send this number as the type to the 8086 in response to an IR0 interrupt. For an IR1 input the 8259A will send 00100001 binary or 33 decimal and so on for the other IR inputs. In any ICW2 you send the 8259A, the lowest three bits must always be 0's, because the 8259A automatically supplies these bits to correspond to the number of the IR input.

Since we are not using a slave in our example, we don't need to send an ICW3. If you are using a slave 8259A in a system, you have to send an ICW3 to the master to tell it which IR inputs have slaves. The master has to be told this so that it knows for which IR input signals it has to send out a slave ID number on the CAS0, CAS1, and CAS2 lines. You have to send an ICW3 to a slave 8259A to give it an ID number. The ID number you give a slave is equal to the IR input of the master that its INT output is connected to. When the master sends out an ID number on the CAS lines, the slave will recognize its ID number and output the desired type number to the 8086 when it receives an $\overline{\text{INTA}}$ pulse.

For our example here, the only reason we need to send an ICW4 is to let the 8259A know that it is operating in an 8086 system. We do this by making bit D0 of the word a 1. Another interesting bit in this command word is D1, the automatic end-of-interrupt bit. If this bit is set in ICW4, the 8259A will automatically reset the in-service register bit for the interrupt input that is being responded to when the second interrupt acknowledge pulse is received. The effect of this is that the 8259A will then be able to respond to an interrupt signal on a lower priority IR input. In other words, a lower priority interrupt input could then interrupt a higher priority procedure. Since we don't want automatic end of interrupt, the ICW4 for our example here is 00000001.

In addition to the initialization command words shown in Figure 8-29*a*, the 8259A has a second set of command words called *operation command words* or OCWs. These are shown in Figure 8-30. An OCW1 must be sent to an 8259A to unmask any IR inputs that you want it to respond to. For our example here let's assume that we only want to use IR2 and IR3. Since a 0 in a bit position of OCW1 unmasks the corresponding IR input, we put 0's in these two bits and 1's in the rest of the bits. Our OCW1 then is 11110011.

OCW2 is mainly used to reset a bit in the in-service register. This is usually done at the end of the interrupt service procedure, but it can be done at any time in the procedure. The effect of resetting the ISR bit for an interrupt level is that once the bit is reset, the 8259A can then respond to interrupt signals of lower priority. In small systems we usually use the nonspecific end-of-interrupt command word. The OCW2 for this is 00100000. When the 8259A receives this OCW it will automatically reset the in-service register bit for the IR input currently being serviced. If you want to reset a specific ISR bit, you can send the 8259A an OCW2 with 011 in bits D7, D6, and D5, and the number of the ISR bit you want to reset in the lowest 3 bits of the word. You can also use OCW2 to tell the 8259A to rotate the priorities of the IR inputs so that after an IR input is serviced, it drops to the lowest priority. If you are interested, consult the Intel data sheet for more information on this and on the use of OCW3.

Now that we have made up the required ICWs and OCWs the next step is to write the instructions to send these command words to the 8259A.

Figure 8-31 shows an 8086 assembly language program which shows how to initialize an 8259A and combines many of the concepts of this chapter. You can use this program as a pattern for writing programs which service several interrupts. The purpose of this program is to initialize the SDK-86 system in Figure 8-14 for generating a real-time clock of seconds, minutes, and hours from a 1-kHz interrupt signal, and for reading ASCII codes from a keyboard on an interrupt basis. This program assumes that the 2.4576-MHz PCLK signal on the board is connected to the CLK input of 8254 counter 0, the GATE input of the 8254 counter 0 is tied high, and the OUT pin of counter 0 is connected to the IR0 input of

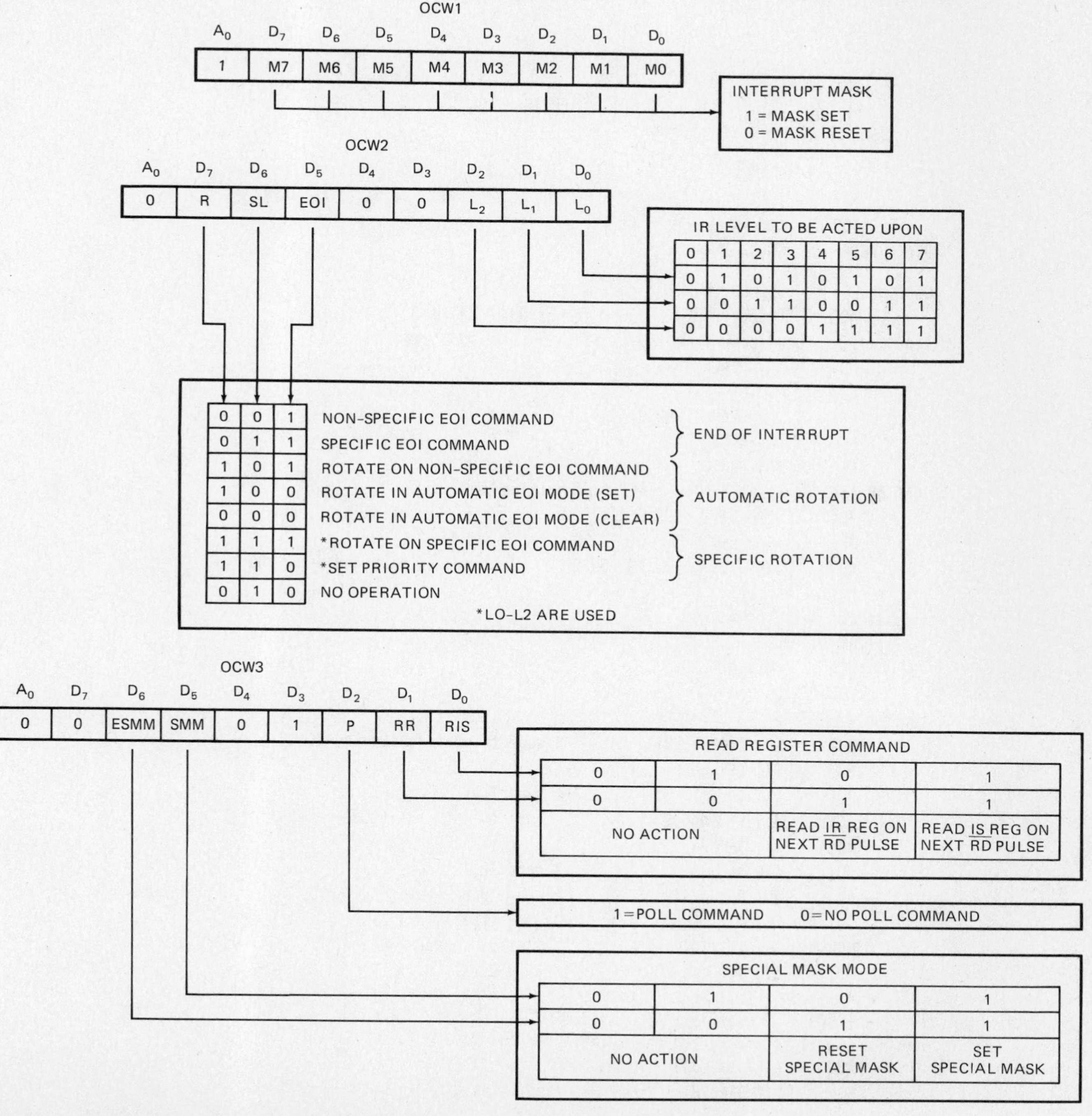

FIGURE 8-30 8259A operational command words. *(Intel Corporation)*

```
page ,132
;8086 PROGRAM FRAGMENT TO SHOW INITIALIZATION OF INTERRUPT JUMP TABLE,
;             8259A, AND COUNTER 0 OF 8254.

AINT_TABLE      SEGMENT WORD    PUBLIC
        TYPE_64         DW      2 DUP(0)        ;reserve space for clock proc addr
        TYPE_65         DW      2 DUP(0)        ;not used in this program
        TYPE_66         DW      2 DUP(0)        ;reserve space for keyboard proc addr
AINT_TABLE      ENDS

DATA_HERE       SEGMENT WORD    PUBLIC
        SECONDS         DB      0
        MINUTES         DB      0
        HOURS           DB      0
        INT_COUNT       DW      03E8H           ;1 kHz interrupt counter
        KEY_BUF         DB      100     DUP(0)  ;Buffer for 100 ASCII chars
DATA_HERE       ENDS

STACK_HERE      SEGMENT                         ; no STACK directive, because
                        DW      100     DUP(0)  ;   will be using EXE2BIN
        TOP_STACK       LABEL   WORD
STACK_HERE      ENDS

CODE_HERE       SEGMENT PUBLIC
        ASSUME CS:CODE_HERE, DS:AINT_TABLE, SS:STACK_HERE
;initialize stack segment register, stack pointer,data segment
        MOV     AX, STACK_HERE
        MOV     SS, AX
        MOV     SP, OFFSET TOP_STACK
        MOV     AX, AINT_TABLE
        MOV     DS, AX
;define the addresses for the interrupt service procedures
        MOV     TYPE_64+2, SEG CLOCK            ; put in clock proc addr
        MOV     TYPE_64,   OFFSET CLOCK
        MOV     TYPE_66+2, SEG KEYBOARD         ; put in keyboard proc addr
        MOV     TYPE_66,   OFFSET KEYBOARD
;initialize data segment
        ASSUME DS:DATA_HERE
        MOV     AX, DATA_HERE
        MOV     DS, AX
;initialize 8259A
        MOV     AL, 00010011B           ; edge triggered, single, ICW4
        MOV     DX, 0FF00H              ; point at 8259A control
        OUT     DX, AL                  ; send ICW1
        MOV     AL, 01000000B           ; type 64 is first 8259A type
        MOV     DX, 0FF02H              ; point at ICW2 address
        OUT     DX, AL                  ; send ICW2
        MOV     AL, 00000001B           ; ICW4, 8086 mode
        OUT     DX, AL                  ; send ICW4
        MOV     AL, 11111010B           ; OCW1 to unmask IR0 and IR2
        OUT     DX, AL                  ; send OCW1

;initialize 8254 counter 0 for 1 kHz output
; 8254 command word for counter 0, LSB then MSB, square wave, BCD
        MOV     AL, 00110111B
        MOV     DX, 0FF07H              ; point at 8254 control addr
```

FIGURE 8-31 Assembly language program showing initialization of 8086, 8259A, and 8254 for real-time clock and keyboard interrupt procedures.

```
          OUT     DX, AL               ; send counter 0 command word
          MOV     AL, 58H              ; Load LSB of count
          MOV     DX, OFF01H           ; point at counter 0 data addr
          OUT     DX, AL               ; send LSB of count
          MOV     AL, 24H              ; load MSB of count
          OUT     DX, AL               ; send MSB of count
;enable interrupt input of 8086
          STI
HERE:     JMP     HERE                 ; wait for interrupt

CLOCK     PROC    FAR
;         :                            ; clock procedure intructions
          MOV     AL, 00100000B        ; OCW2 for non-specific EOI
          MOV     DX, OFF00H           ; address for OCW2
          OUT     DX, AL               ; send OCW2 for end of interrupt
          IRET
CLOCK     ENDP

KEYBOARD PROC     FAR
;         :                            ; keyboard proc intructions
          MOV     AL, 00100000B        ; OCW2 for non-specific EOI
          MOV     DX, OFF00H           ; address for OCW2
          OUT     DX, AL               ; send OCW2 for end of interrupt
          IRET
KEYBOARD ENDP
CODE_HERE ENDS
          END
```

FIGURE 8-31 (*continued*)

the 8259A. The program further assumes that the keypressed strobe from the ASCII keyboard is connected to the IR2 input of the 8259A.

In the program we first declare a segment called AINT_TABLE to reserve space for the pointers to the interrupt procedures. The statement TYPE_64 DW 2 DUP(0), for example, sets aside a word space for the offset of the the type 64 procedure and a word for the segment base of the procedure. Because of the way the IBM MASM, LINK, and EXE2BIN programs work, it is necesssary to do a little trick to get the AINT_TABLE segment located at absolute address 0000:0100H where it must be for the program to work correctly. The trick is simply to give the segment which sets aside space for these pointers a name which alphabetically comes before the names of the other segments in your program, just as we named our segment here AINT_TABLE. When you MASM and LINK your program, the result is a relocatable object code (.EXE) program which the computer will load into any convenient location to run. The .EXE form of the program will not get put at the required absolute locations. To solve this problem you process your .EXE program with a program called EXE2BIN. When run, this program prompts you to put in a segment fixup (absolute starting address) for your program. If you give a segment fixup value of 0010H, EXE2BIN will produce a .BIN file which will load at absolute address 0000:0100H. Since AINT_TABLE is alphabetically first, it will be located starting at this address, which is the correct absolute address for the 8086 type 64 interrupt.

The next thing we do in our program is to declare a data segment and set aside some memory locations for seconds count, minutes count, hours count, and 100 characters read in from the keyboard. After the data segment we set up a stack segment.

At the start of the mainline program we initialize the stack segment register, the stack pointer register, and the data segment register. We will be using interrupt type 64 for a real-time clock and type 66 will point at the start of the procedure that reads ASCII codes from the keyboard. We will not be using a type 65 interrupt in this program. The next four instructions are needed to place the addresses of the clock and keyboard procedures in the type 64 and type 66 locations in the interrupt pointer table. Later we initialize the 8259A so that type 64 corresponds to its IR0 input and type 66 corresponds to its IR2 interrupt. We then ASSUME DS:DATA_HERE and initialize DATA_HERE as the data segment.

For the example here we have chosen type 64 to correspond to an IR0 interrupt, so the needed ICW2 will be 01000000. We then initialize the 8259A with the command words we worked out above and this new ICW2. Note that those command words shown with a 0 as the A0 bit in Figures 8-29 and 8-30 are sent to system address FF00H and those command words shown with a 1 as the A0 bit are sent to system address FF02H.

The next section of the mainline program initializes counter 0 of the 8254 for mode 2, BCD countdown, and read/write LSB then MSB. To produce a 1-kHz signal from the 2.4576-MHz PCLK we then write a count of 2458 to counter 0. This will not give exactly 1 kHz, but it is as close as we can get with this particular input clock frequency. The PCLK frequency for this board was chosen to make baud rate clock frequencies come out exact, not a 1-kHz real-time clock. Larger systems usually have two or more crystal-controlled oscillators to accommodate both.

Finally, after the timer is initialized, we enable the 8086 INTR input with the STI instruction so that the 8086 can respond to INT signals from the 8259A, and wait for an interrupt with the HERE: JMP HERE instruction.

For the two interrupt service procedures we show just the skeletons and the end of interrupt instructions. We leave it to you to write the actual procedures. Note that the procedures must be declared as FAR so that the assembler will load both the IP and the CS in the interrupt pointer table. Remember from a previous discussion that when the 8259A responds to an IR signal, it sets the corresponding bit in the ISR. This bit must be reset at some time during or at the end of the interrupt service procedure so that the priority resolver can respond to future interrupts of the same or lower priority. At the end of our procedures here we do this by sending an OCW2 to the 8259A. The OCW2 of 00100000 that we send tells the 8259A to reset the ISR bit for the IR level that is currently being serviced. This is a nonspecific end of interrupt (EOI) instruction.

This chapter has introduced you to interrupts and some interrupt applications. The following chapters will show you more of this, because much of the interfacing discussed there is done on an interrupt basis.

IMPORTANT TERMS AND CONCEPTS FROM THIS CHAPTER

If you do not remember any of the terms in the following list, use the index to help you find them in the chapter for review.

Interrupt—INTR

Nonmaskable interrupt—NMI

Software interrupts—INT instruction

Interrupt service procedure

Interrupt vector, interrupt pointer

Interrupt vector table, interrupt pointer table

Interrupt type

Divide by zero interrupt—type 0

Single-step interrupt—type 1

Nonmaskable interrupt—type 2

Breakpoint interrupt—type 3

Overflow interrupt—type 4

Software interrupts—type 0–255

INTR interrupts—type 0–255

BIOS

Edge-activated interrupt input

Level-activated interrupt input

Interrupt priority

Hardware interrupts

Software programmable

Programmable timer/counter devices—8253, 8254

Internal addresses

Control words, command words, mode words

8259A priority interrupt controller
- Fixed priority
- In-service register—ISR
- Priority resolver
- Interrupt request register—IRR
- Interrupt mask register—IMR

REVIEW QUESTIONS AND PROBLEMS

1. List and describe in general terms the steps an 8086 will take when it responds to an interrupt.
2. Describe the purpose of the 8086 interrupt pointer table.
3. What addresses in the interrupt pointer table are used for a type 2 interrupt?
4. The starting address for a type 4 interrupt service procedure is 0010:0082. Show where and in what order this address should be placed in the interrupt jump table.
5. Address 00080H in the interrupt jump table contains 4A24H, and address 00082H contains 0040H. To what interrupt type do these locations correspond? What is the starting address for the interrupt service procedure?
6. Briefly describe the condition(s) which cause the 8086 to perform each of the following types of interrupts: type 0, type 1, type 2, type 3, type 4.
7. Why is it necessary at the start of an interrupt service procedure to PUSH all registers used in the procedure and to POP them at the end of the procedure?
8. Why must you use an IRET instruction rather than the regular RET instruction at the end of an interrupt service procedure?

9. Show the assembler directive and instructions you would use to initialize the interrupt pointer table locations for a type 0 procedure called DIV_0_ERROR and a type 2 procedure called POWER_FAIL.

10. Describe the main use of the 8086 type 1 interrupt. Show the assembly language instructions necessary to set the 8086 trap flag.

11. In a system which has battery-backed RAM for saving data in case of a power failure, the stack is often put in the battery-backed RAM. This makes it easy to save registers and critical program data. Assume that the battery-backed RAM is in the address range of 08000H-08FFFH. Write an 8086 power failure interrupt service procedure which:

    Sets an external battery-backed flip-flop connected to bit 0 of port 28H to indicate that a power failure has occurred.

    Saves all registers on the stack.

    Saves the stack pointer value for the last entry at location 8000H.

    Saves the contents of memory locations 00100H–003FFH after the saved stack pointer value at the start of the battery backed memory. (A string instruction might be useful for this.)

    Halts.

    When the power comes back on, the start-up routine can check the power fail flip-flop. If the flip-flop is set, the start-up procedure can copy the saved data back into its operating locations, initialize the stack segment register, and then get the saved SP value from address 08000H. Using this value it can restore the pushed registers and return execution to where the power fail interrupt occurred. This is called a "warm start." If we don't want it to do a warm start, we can reset the flip-flop with an external RESET key so the system does a start from scratch or "cold start."

12. Why is the 8086 INTR input automatically disabled when the 8086 is RESET? How is the 8086 INTR input enabled to respond to interrupts? What instruction can be used to disable the INTR input? Why is the INTR input automatically disabled as part of the response to an INTR interrupt? How does the INTR input automatically get reenabled at the end of an INTR interrupt service procedure?

13. Describe the response an 8086 will make if it receives an NMI interrupt signal during a division operation which produces a divide by zero interrupt.

14. The data outputs of an 8-bit analog-to-digital converter are connected to bits D0–D7 of port FFF9H and the end-of-conversion signal from the A/D converter is connected to the NMI input of an 8086. Write a simple mainline program and an interrupt service procedure which reads in a byte of data from the converter. If the MSB of the data is a 0, indicating the value is in range, add the byte to a running total kept in two successive memory locations. If the MSB of data is 1, showing that the value is out of range, ignore the input. After 100 samples have been totaled, divide by 100 to get the average, store this average in another reserved memory location, and reset the total to zero.

15. Write the algorithm and the program for an interrupt service procedure which turns on an LED connected to bit D0 of port FFFAH on for 25 seconds and off for 25 seconds. The procedure should also turn a second LED connected to bit D1 of port FFFAH on for 1 minute and off for 1 minute. Assume that a 1-Hz interrupt signal is connected to the NMI input of an 8086, and that a high on a port bit turns on the LED connected to it.

16. Write the algorithms for a mainline program and an interrupt service procedure which generate a real-time clock of seconds, minutes, and hours in three memory locations using a 1-Hz signal applied to the NMI input of an 8086. Then write the assembly language programs for the mainline and the procedure. If you are working on an SDK-86 board, there is a procedure in Figure 9-33 that you can add to your program to display the time on the data and address field LEDs of the board. You can use this procedure without needing to understand the details of how it works. To display a word on the data field, simply put the word in the CX register, put 00H in AL, and call the procedure. To display a word on the address field, put the word in CX, 01H in AL, and call the procedure. *HINT*: Clear carry before incrementing a count in AL so that DAA works correctly.

17. In Chapter 5 we discussed using breakpoints to debug programs containing procedures. List the sequence of locations where you would put breakpoints in the example program in Figure 8-9 to debug it if it did not work when you loaded it into memory.

18. Suppose that we add another 8254 to the SDK-86 add-on circuitry shown in Figure 8-14, and that the $\overline{CS}$ input of the new 8254 is connected to the Y5 output of the 74LS138 decoder.

    a. What will be the system base address for this added 8254?
    b. To which half of the 8086 data bus should the eight data lines from this 8254 be connected?
    c. What will be the system addresses for the three counters and the control word register in this 8254?
    d. Show the control word you would use to initialize counter 1 of this device for read/write LSB then MSB, mode 3, and BCD countdown.
    e. Show the sequence of instructions you would use to write this control word and a count of 0356 to the counter.
    f. Assuming the GATE input is high, when does the counter start counting down in mode 3?

g. Assuming initialization as in parts *d* and *f*, and that a 712-kHz signal is applied to the CLK input of counter 1 in mode 3, describe the frequency, period, and duty cycle of the waveform that will be on the OUT pin of the counter.

h. Describe the effect that a control word of 10010000 sent to this 8254 will have.

19. Show the instructions you would use to initialize counter 2 of the 8254 in Figure 8-14 to produce a 1.2-ms-wide STROBE pulse on its OUT pin when it receives a trigger input on its GATE input.

20. Show the instructions needed to latch and read a 16-bit count from counter 1 of the 8254 in Figure 8-14.

21. Describe the sequence of actions that an 8259A and an 8086, as connected in Figure 8-14, will take when the 8259A receives an interrupt signal on its IR2 input. Assume only IR2 is unmasked in the 8259A and that the 8086 INTR input has been enabled with an STI instruction.

22. Describe the use of the CAS0, CAS1, and CAS2 lines in a system with a cascaded 8259A.

23. Describe the response that an 8259A will make if it receives an interrupt signal on its IR3 and IR5 inputs at the same time. Assume fixed priority for the IR inputs. What response will the 8259A make if it is servicing an IR5 interrupt and an IR3 interrupt signal occurs

24. Why is it necessary to send an end-of-interrupt (EOI) command to an 8259A at some time in an interrupt service routine?

25. Show the sequence of command words and instructions that you would use to initialize an 8259A with a base address of FF10H as follows:

edge-triggered; only one 8259A; 8086 system; interrupt type 40 corresponds to IR0 input; normal EOI; nonbuffered mode, not special fully nested mode; IR1 and IR3 unmasked.

CHAPTER

9 Digital Interfacing

The major goal of this chapter and the next is to show you much of the interface circuitry and software needed to control a complex machine such as our printed-circuit-board-making machine or a medical instrument with a microprocessor. We try to show enough detail in each topic so that you can build and experiment with some real circuits and programs. Perhaps you can use some of these to control appliances around your house or solve some problems at work.

OBJECTIVES

At the conclusion of this chapter you should be able to:

1. Describe simple input and output, strobed input and output, and handshake input and output.
2. Initialize a programmable parallel port device such as the 8255A for simple input or output and for handshake input or output.
3. Interpret the timing waveforms for handshake input and output operations.
4. Describe how phonemes are sent to a speech synthesizer on a handshake basis.
5. Describe how parallel data is sent to a printer on a handshake basis.
6. Show the hardware connections and the programs that can be used to interface keyboards to a microcomputer.
7. Show the hardware connections and the programs that can be used to interface alphanumeric displays to a microcomputer.
8. Describe how an 8279 can be used to refresh a multiplexed LED display and scan a matrix keyboard.
9. Initialize an 8279 for a given display and keyboard format.
10. Show the circuitry used to interface high-power devices to microcomputer ports.
11. Describe the hardware and software needed to control a stepper motor.

PROGRAMMABLE PARALLEL PORTS AND HANDSHAKE INPUT/OUTPUT

Throughout the program examples in the preceding chapters, we have used port devices to input parallel data to the microprocessor and to output parallel data from the microprocessor. Most of the available port devices such as the 8255A on the SDK-86 board contain two or three ports which can be programmed to operate in one of several different modes. The different modes allow you to use the device for many common types of parallel data transfer. First we will discuss some of these common methods of transferring parallel data, and then we will show how the 8255A is initialized and used in a variety of I/O operations.

Methods of Parallel Data Transfer

SIMPLE INPUT AND OUTPUT

When you need to get digital data from some simple switch such as a thermostat into a microprocessor, all you have to do is connect the switch to an input port line and read the port. The thermostat data is always present and ready, so you can read it at any time.

Likewise, when you need to output data to a simple display device such as an LED, all you have to do is connect the input of the LED buffer on an output port pin and output the logic level required to turn on the light. The LED is always there and ready, so you can send data to it at any time. The timing waveform in Figure 9-1*a* represents this situation. The crossed lines on the waveform represent the time at which a new data byte becomes valid on the output lines of the port. The absence of other waveforms indicates that this output operation is not directly dependent on any other signals.

SIMPLE STROBE I/O

In many applications valid data is only present on an external device at a certain time and it must be read in

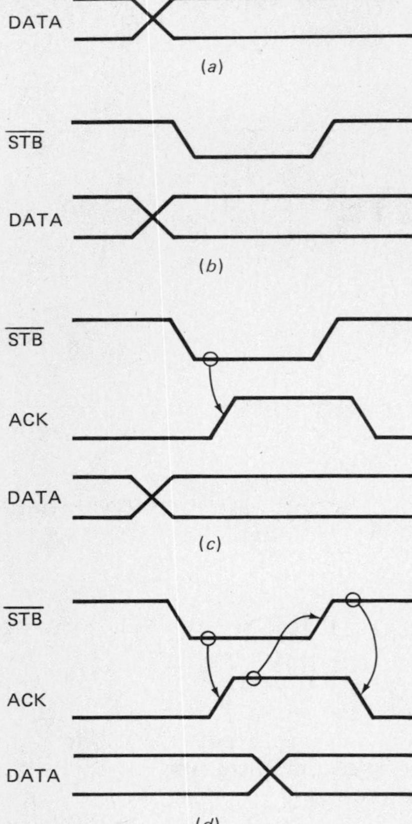

FIGURE 9-1 Parallel data transfer. *(a)* Simple output. *(b)* Simple strobe I/O. *(c)* Single handshake I/O. *(d)* Double handshake I/O.

at that time. An example of this is the ASCII-encoded keyboard shown in Figure 4-13. When a key is pressed on the keyboard, circuitry on the keyboard sends out the ASCII code for the pressed key on eight parallel data lines. The keyboard circuitry then sends out a strobe signal on another line to indicate that valid data is present on the eight data lines. As shown in Chapter 3, you can connect this strobe line to an input port line and poll it to determine when you can input valid data from the keyboard. Another alternative, described in Chapter 8, is to connect the strobe line to an interrupt input on the processor and have an interrupt service routine read in the data when the processor receives an interrupt. The point here is that this transfer is time-dependent. You can only read in data when a strobe pulse tells you that the data is valid.

Figure 9-1*b* shows the timing waveforms which represent this type of operation. The sending device, such as a keyboard, outputs parallel data on the data lines and then outputs an $\overline{\text{STB}}$ signal to let you know that valid data is present.

For low rates of data transfer, such as from a keyboard to a microprocessor, a simple strobe transfer works well. However, for high-speed data transfer this method does not work because there is no signal which tells the sending device when it is safe to send the next data byte. In other words the sending system might send data bytes faster than the receiving system could read them. To prevent this problem a *handshake* data transfer scheme is used.

SINGLE HANDSHAKE I/O

Figure 9-1*c* shows some example timing waveforms for a *handshake data transfer* from a peripheral device to a microprocessor. The peripheral outputs some parallel data and sends an $\overline{\text{STB}}$ signal to the microprocessor. The microprocessor detects the asserted $\overline{\text{STB}}$ signal on a polled or interrupt basis and reads in the byte of data. The microprocessor then sends an acknowledge signal, ACK, to the peripheral to indicate that the peripheral can send the next byte of data. From the viewpoint of the microprocessor, this operation is referred to as a handshake or strobed input.

These same waveforms might represent a handshake output from a microprocessor to a parallel printer. In this case the microprocessor outputs a character to the printer and asserts an $\overline{\text{STB}}$ signal to the printer to tell the printer, "Here is a character for you." When the printer is ready, it answers back with the ACK signal to tell the microprocessor, "I got that one, send me another." We will show you much more about printer interfacing in a later section.

The point of this handshake scheme is that the sending device or system cannot send the next data byte until the receiving device or system indicates with an ACK signal that it is ready to receive the next byte.

DOUBLE HANDSHAKE DATA TRANSFER

For data transfers where even more coordination is required between the sending system and the receiving system, a *double handshake* is used. Figure 9-1*d* shows some example waveforms for a double handshake input from a peripheral to a microprocessor. Perhaps it will help you to follow these waveforms by thinking of them as a conversation between two people. In these waveforms each signal edge has meaning. The sending device asserts its $\overline{\text{STB}}$ line low to ask, "Are you ready?" The receiving system raises its ACK line high to say, "I'm ready." The peripheral device then sends the byte of data and raises its $\overline{\text{STB}}$ line high to say, "Here is some valid data for you." After it has read in the data the receiving system drops its ACK line low to say, "I have the data, thank you, and I await your request to send the next byte of data."

For a handshake output of this type, from a microprocessor to a peripheral, the waveforms are the same but the microprocessor sends the $\overline{\text{STB}}$ signal and the data, and the peripheral sends the ACK signal. In a later section we show how this type of handshake is used to transfer *phoneme* bytes from a microprocessor to a speech-synthesizer device.

For handshake data transfer, a microprocessor can determine when it is time to send the next data byte on a polled or on an interrupt basis. We usually use the interrupt approach because it makes better use of the processor's time. The $\overline{\text{STB}}$ or ACK signals for these handshake transfers can be produced on a port pin by instructions in the program. This method, however, tends to use too much processor time. Therefore, port devices such as the 8255A have been designed so that they can be programmed to automatically manage the handshake operation. For example, the 8255A can be programmed to automatically receive a $\overline{STB}$ signal from a peripheral, send an interrupt signal to the processor, and send the ACK signal to the peripheral at the proper times. The following sections show you how to connect, initialize, and use an 8255A for a variety of applications.

8255A Internal Block Diagram and System Connections

Figure 9-2 shows the internal block diagram of the 8255A. Along the right side of the diagram you can see that the device has 24 input/output lines. Port A can be used as an 8-bit input port or as an 8-bit output port. Likewise, port B can be used as an 8-bit input port or as an 8-bit output port. Port C can be used as an 8-bit input or output port, two 4-bit ports, or to produce handshake signals for ports A and B. We will discuss the different modes for these lines in detail a little later.

Along the left side of the diagram you see the usual signal lines used to connect the device to the system buses. Eight data lines allow you to write data bytes to a port or the control register and to read bytes from a port or the status register under the control of the $\overline{RD}$ and $\overline{WR}$ lines. The address inputs, A0 and A1, allow you to selectively access one of the three ports or the control register. The internal addresses for the device are: port A–00, port B–01, port C–10, control–11. Asserting the $\overline{CS}$ input of the 8255A enables it for reading or writing. The $\overline{CS}$ input will be connected to the output of the address decoder circuitry to select the device when it is addressed.

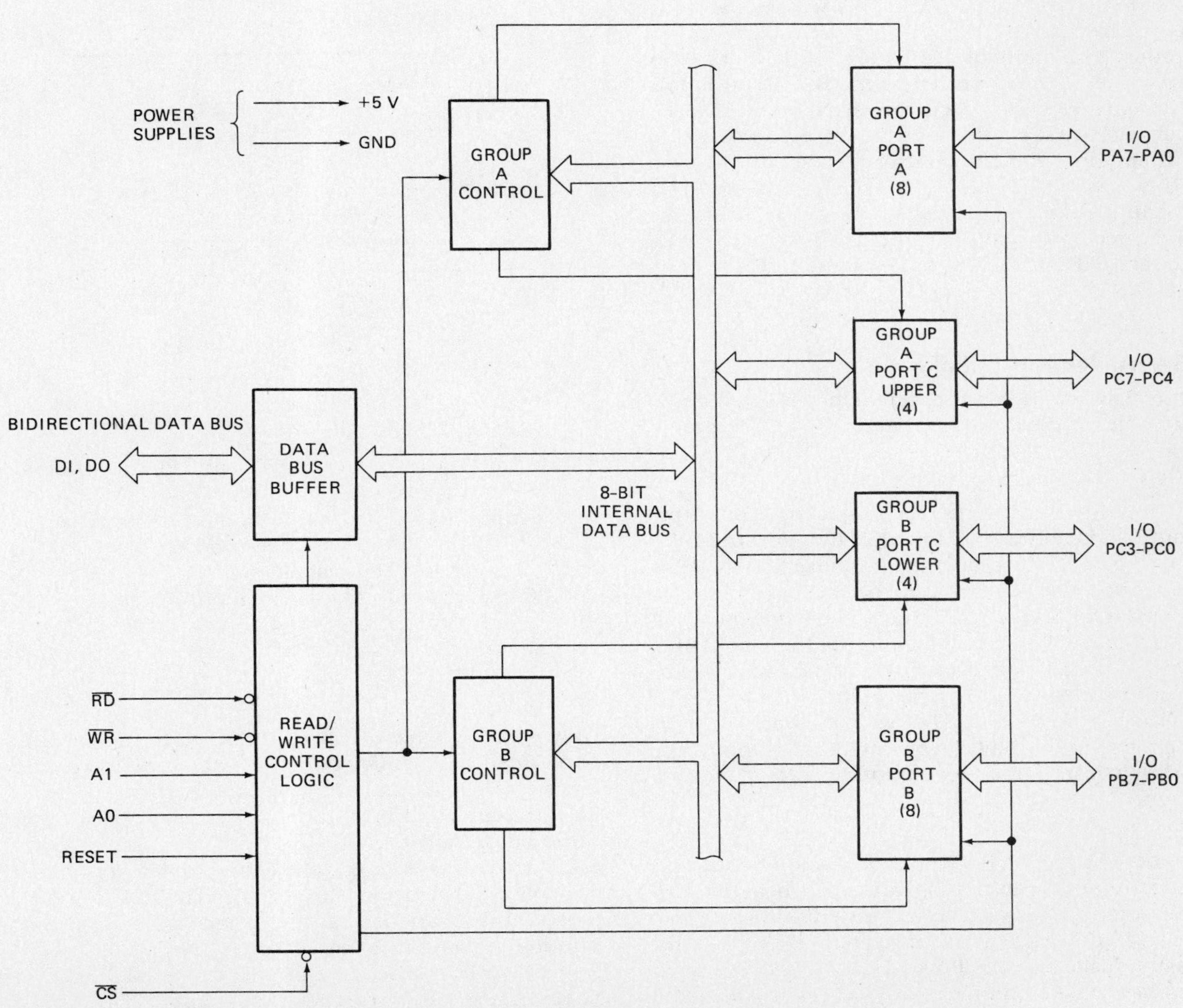

FIGURE 9-2 Internal block diagram of 8255A programmable parallel port device. *(Intel Corporation)*

The RESET input of the 8255A is connected to the system reset line so that, when the system is reset, all of the port lines are initialized as input lines. This is done to prevent destruction of circuitry connected to port lines. If port lines were initialized as outputs after a power-up or reset, the port might try to output into the output of a device connected to the port. The possible argument between the two outputs might destroy one or both of them. Therefore all of the programmable port devices initialize their port lines as inputs when reset.

We discussed in Chapter 7 how two 8255As can be connected in an 8086 system. Take a look at Figure 7-6 (sheet 5) to refresh your memory of these connections. Note that one of the 8255As is connected to the lower half of the 8086 data bus, and the other 8255A is connected to the upper half of the data bus. This is done so that a byte can be transferred by enabling one device, or a word can be transferred by enabling both devices at the same time. According the truth table for the I/O port address decoder in Figure 7-15, the *XA*40 8255A on the lower half of the data bus will be enabled for a base address of FFF8H, and the *XA*35 8255A will be enabled for a base address of FFF9H.

Another point to notice in Figure 7-6 is that system address line A1 is connected to the 8255A A0 inputs, and system address line A2 is connected to the 8255A A1 inputs. With these connections the system addresses for the three ports and the control register in the *XA*40 8255A will be FFF8H, FFFAH, FFFCH, and FFFEH as shown in Figure 7-15. Likewise, the system addresses for the three ports and the control register of the *XA*35 8255A are FFF9H, FFFBH, FFFDH, and FFFFH.

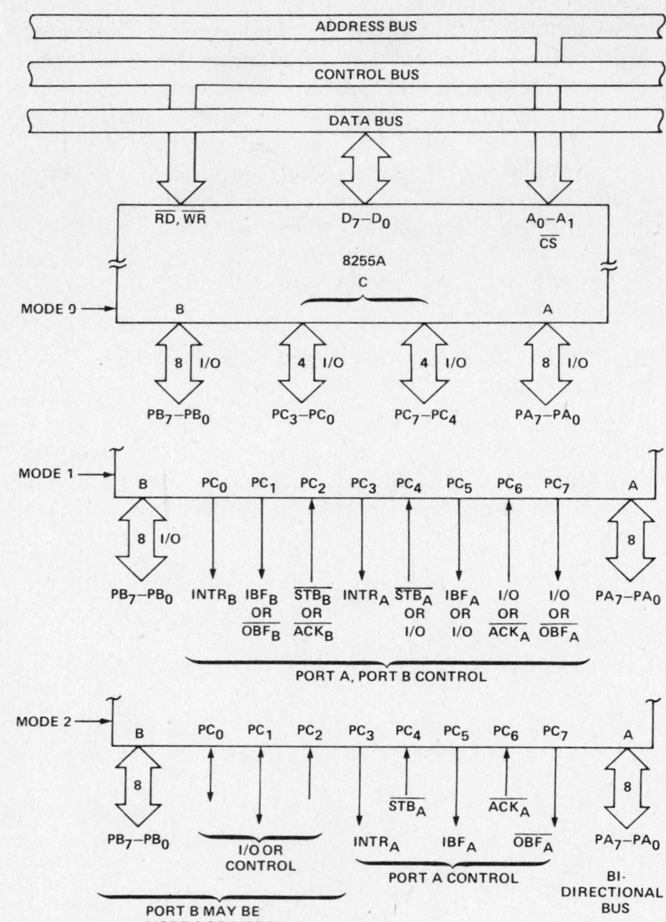

FIGURE 9-3 Summary of 8255A operating modes. *(Intel Corporation)*

8255A Modes and Initialization

Figure 9-3 summarizes the different modes in which the ports of the 8255A can be initialized.

MODE 0

When you want to use a port for simple input or output without handshaking, you initialize that port in MODE 0. If both port A and port B are initialized in MODE 0, then the two halves of port C can be used together as an additional 8-bit port, or they can be used individually as two 4-bit ports. When used as outputs the port C lines can be individually set or reset by sending a special control word to the control register address. Later we will show you how to do this. The two halves of port C are independent, so one half can be initialized as input, and the other half initialized as output.

MODE 1

When you want to use port A or port B for a handshake (strobed) input or output operation such as we discussed in previous sections, you initialize that port in MODE 1. In this mode some of the pins of port C function as handshake lines. Pins PC0, PC1, and PC2 function as handshake lines for port B if it is initialized in MODE 1. If port A is initialized as a handshake (MODE 1) input port, then pins PC3, PC4, and PC5 function as handshake signals. Pins PC6 and PC7 are available for use as input lines or output lines. If port A is initialized as a handshake output port, then port C pins PC3, PC6, and PC7 function as handshake signals. Port C pins PC4 and PC5 are available for use as input or output lines. Since the 8255A is often used in this mode, we show several examples in the following sections.

MODE 2

Only port A can be initialized in MODE 2. In MODE 2, port A can be used for *bidirectional handshake* data transfer. This means that data can be output or input on the same eight lines. The 8255A might be used in this mode to extend the system bus to a slave microprocessor or to transfer data bytes to and from a floppy disk controller board. If port A is initialized in MODE 2, then pins PC3–PC7 are used as handshake lines for port A. The other three pins of port C can be used for I/O if port B is in MODE 0. The three pins will be used for port B handshake lines if port B is initialized in MODE 1. After you work your way through the MODE 1 examples in the following sections you should have little difficulty understanding the discussion of MODE 2 in the Intel data sheet if you encounter it in a system.

Constructing and Sending 8255A Control Words

Figure 9-4 shows the formats for the two 8255A control words. The MSB of the control word tells the 8255A which control word you are sending it. You use the *mode definition control word* format in Figure 9-4*a* to tell the device what modes you want the ports to operate in. For the mode definition control word you put a 1 in the MSB. You use the *bit set/reset control word* format in Figure 9-4*b* when you want to set or reset the output on a pin of port C, or when you want to enable the interrupt output signals for handshake data transfers. The MSB is 0 for this control word. Both control words are sent to the control register address for the 8255A.

As usual, making up a control word consists of figuring out what to put in the eight little boxes one bit at a time. As an example for this device, suppose that you want to initialize the 8255A (*XA*40) in Figure 7-6 as follows: Port B MODE 1 input, port A MODE 0 output, port C upper as inputs, and bit 3 of port C as output. Figure 9-5*a* shows the control word which will program the 8255A in this way. The figure also shows how you should document any control words you make up for use in your programs. Using Figure 9-4*a*, work your way through this word to make sure you see why each bit has the value it does.

As we said previously, the control register address for the *XA*40 8255A is FFFEH. To send a control word then you load the control word in AL with a MOV AL, 10001110B instruction, point DX at the port address with the MOV DX, 0FFFEH instruction, and send the control word to the 8255A control register with the OUT DX, AL instruction.

As an example of how to use the bit set/reset control word, suppose that you want to output a 1 to (set) bit 3 of port C, which was initialized as an output with the mode set control word above. To set or reset a port C output pin you use the bit set/reset control word shown in Figure 9-4*b*. Make bit D7 a 0 to identify this as a bit set/reset control word and put a 1 in bit D0 to specify that you want to set a bit of port C. Bits D3, D2, and D1 are used to tell the 8255A which bit you want to act on. For this example you want to set bit 3, so you put 011 in these three bits. For simplicity and compatibility with future products, make the other three bits of the control word 0's. The result of 00000111B, with proper documentation, is shown in Figure 9-5*b*.

To send this control word to the 8255A simply load it into AL with the MOV AL, 00000111B instruction, point DX at the control register address with the MOV DX, 0FFFEH instruction if DX is not already pointing there, and send the control word with the OUT DX, AL instruction. As part of the application examples in the following sections, we will show you how you know which bit in port C to set to enable the interrupt output signal for handshake data transfer.

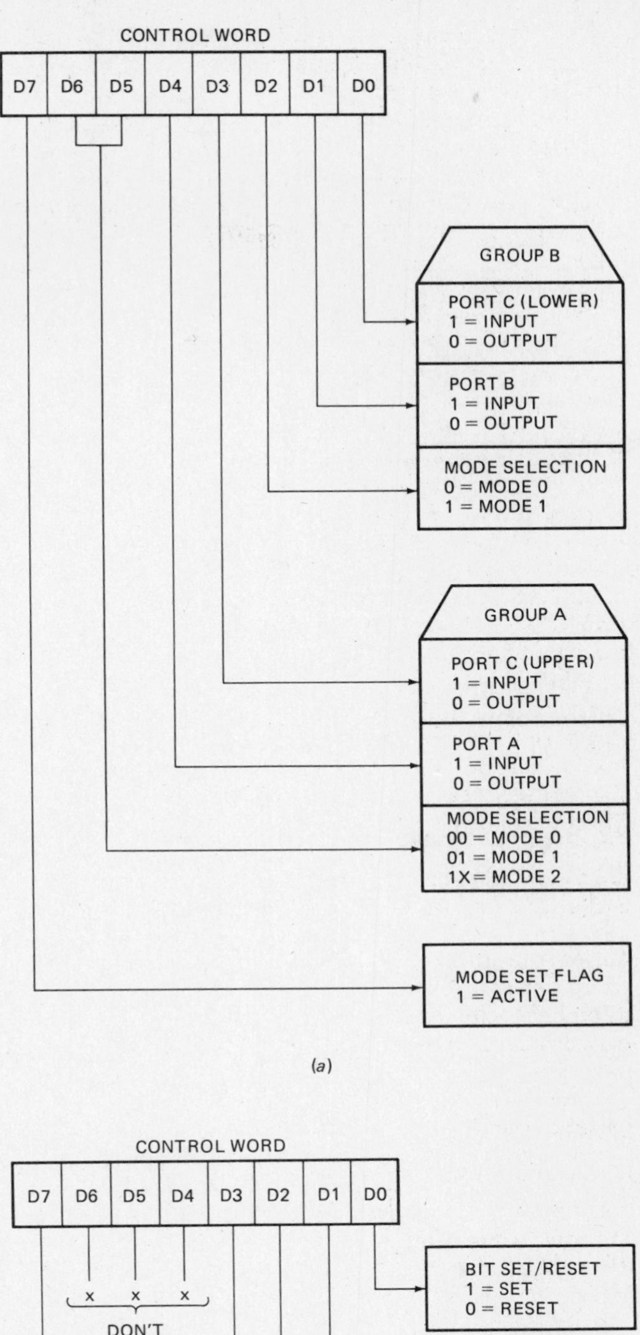

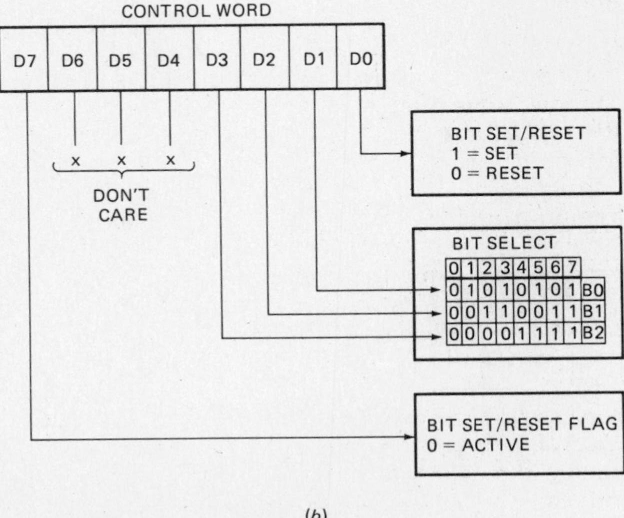

FIGURE 9-4 8255A control word formats. *(a)* Mode set control word. *(b)* Port C bit set/reset control word.

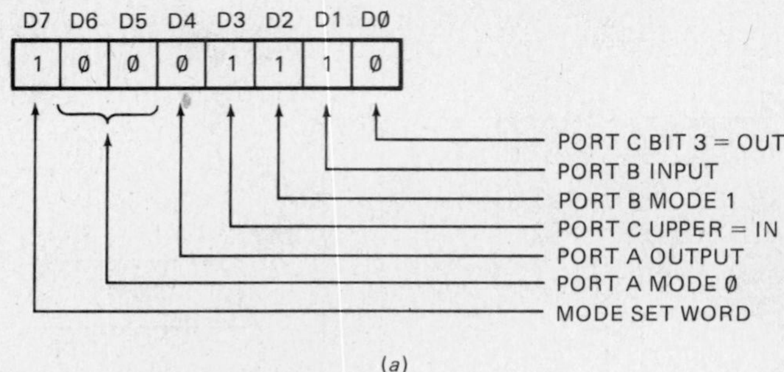

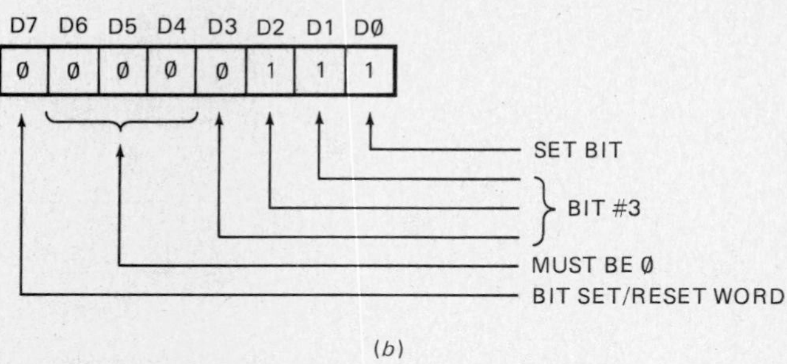

FIGURE 9-5 Control word examples for 8255A. *(a)* Mode set control word. *(b)* Port C bit set/reset control word to set bit 3.

8255A Handshake Application Examples

INTERFACING TO A MICROCOMPUTER-CONTROLLED LATHE

All of the machines in the machine shop of our computer-controlled electronics factory operate under microcomputer control. One example of the machines here is a lathe which makes bolts from long rods of stainless steel. The cutting instructions for each type of bolt that we need to make are stored on a ¾-in wide paper or metal tape. Each instruction is represented by a series of holes in the tape. A tape reader pulls the tape through an optical or mechanical sensor to detect the hole patterns and convert these to an 8-bit parallel code. The microcomputer reads the instruction codes from the tape reader on a handshake basis and sends the appropriate control instructions to the lathe. The microcomputer must also monitor various conditions around the lathe. It must, for example, make sure the lathe has cutting lubricant oil, is not out of material to work on, and is not jammed up in some way. Machines that operate in this way are often referred to as *computer numerical control* or *CNC machines*.

Figure 9-6 shows in diagram form how an 8255A might be used to interface a microcomputer to the tape reader and lathe. In the next chapter we will show you some of the actual circuitry needed to interface the port pins of the 8255A to the sensors and the high-power motors of the lathe. For now we want to talk about initializing the 8255A for this application and analyze the timing waveforms for the handshake input of data from the tape reader.

First you want to make up the control word to initialize the 8255A in the correct modes for this application. To do this start by making a list showing how you want each port pin or group of pins to function. Then put in the control word bits that implement those pin functions. For our example here:

Port A needs to be initialized for handshake input (MODE 1), because instruction codes have to be read in from the tape reader on a handshake basis.

Port B needs to be initialized for simple output (MODE 0). No handshaking is needed here because this port is being used to output simple on or off control signals to the lathe.

Port C, bits PC0, PC1, and PC2 are used for simple input of sensor signals from the lathe.

Port C, bits PC3, PC4, and PC5 function as the handshake signals for the data transfer from the tape reader connected to port A.

Port C, bit PC6 is used for output of the STOP/GO signal to the tape reader.

Port C, bit PC7 is not used for this example.

Figure 9-7 shows the control word to initialize the 8255A for these pin functions. This word will be sent to the control register address as shown above. Now let's talk about how the program for this machine might operate, and how the handshake data transfer actually takes place.

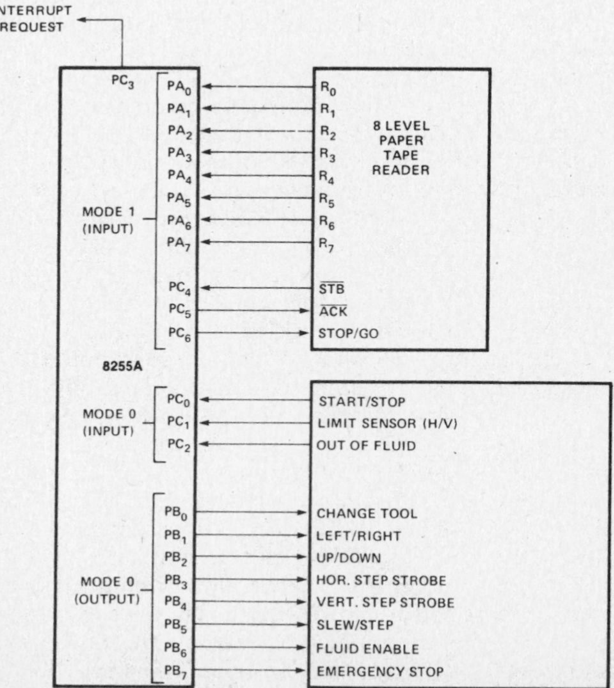

FIGURE 9-6 Interfacing a microprocessor to a tape reader and lathe.

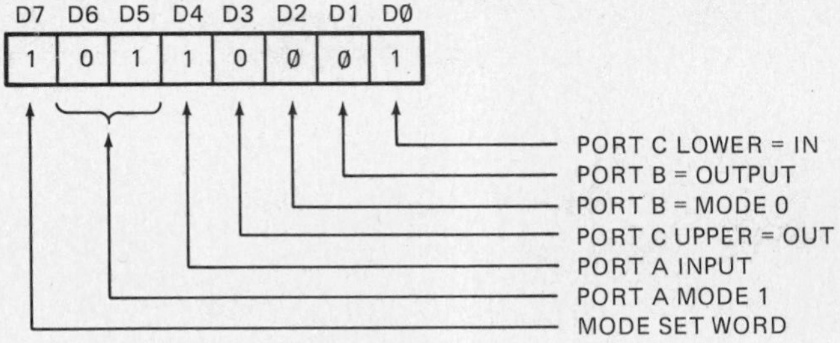

FIGURE 9-7 Control word to initialize 8255A for interface with tape reader and lathe.

After initializing everything, the system would probably read port C bits PC0, PC1, and PC2 to check if the lathe was ready to operate. For any 8255A mode you read port C by simply doing an input from the port C address. Then the microprocessor would output a start command to the tape reader on bit PC6. This is done with a bit set/reset command. Assuming you want to reset bit PC6 to start the tape reader, the bit set/reset control word for this is 00001100. When the tape reader receives the go command, it will start the handshake data transfer to the 8255A. Let's work our way through the timing waveforms in Figure 9-8 to see how the data transfer takes place.

The tape reader starts the process by sending out a byte of data to port A on its eight data lines. The tape reader then asserts its $\overline{STB}$ line low to tell the 8255A that a new byte of data has been sent. In response the 8255A raises its input buffer full (IBF) signal on PC5 high to tell the tape reader that it is ready for the data. When it detects the IBF signal at a high level, the tape reader raises its $\overline{STB}$ signal high again. The rising edge of the $\overline{STB}$ signal has two effects on the 8255A. It first latches the data byte in the input latches of the 8255A. Once the data is latched, the tape reader can remove the data byte in preparation for sending the next data byte. This is shown by the dashed section on the right side of the data waveform in Figure 9-8. Secondly, if the interrupt signal output has been enabled, the rising edge of the $\overline{STB}$ signal will cause the 8255A to output an interrupt request signal to the microprocessor on bit PC3.

The processor's response to the interrupt request will be to go to an interrupt service procedure which reads in the byte of data latched in port A. When the $\overline{RD}$ signal from the microprocessor goes low for this read of port A, the 8255A will automatically reset its interrupt request signal on PC3. This is done so that a second interrupt cannot be caused by the same data byte transfer. When the processor raises its $\overline{RD}$ signal high again at the end of the read operation, the 8255A automatically drops its IBF signal on PC5 low again. IBF going low again is the signal to the tape reader that the data transfer is complete, and that it can send the next byte of data. The time between when the 8255A sends the interrupt request signal and when the processor reads the data byte from port A depends on when the processor gets around to servicing that interrupt. The point here is that this time doesn't matter. The tape reader will not send the next byte of data until it detects that the IBF signal has gone low again. The transfer cycle will then repeat for the next data byte.

After the processor reads in the lathe control instruction byte from the tape reader, it will decode this instruction, and output the appropriate control byte to the lathe on port B of the 8255A. The tape reader then sends the next instruction byte. If the instruction tape is made into a continuous loop, the lathe will keep making the specified parts until it runs out of material. The unused bit of port C, PC7, could be connected to a mechanism which loads in more material so the lathe can continue.

Before we go on there is one more point we have to make about initializing the 8255A for this microcomputer-controlled lathe application. In order for the handshake input data transfer from the tape reader to work correctly the interrupt request signal from bit PC3 has to be enabled. This is done by sending a bit set/reset control word for the appropriate bit of port C. Figure 9-9 shows the port C bit that must be set to enable the interrupt output signal for each of the 8255A handshake modes. For the example here port A is being

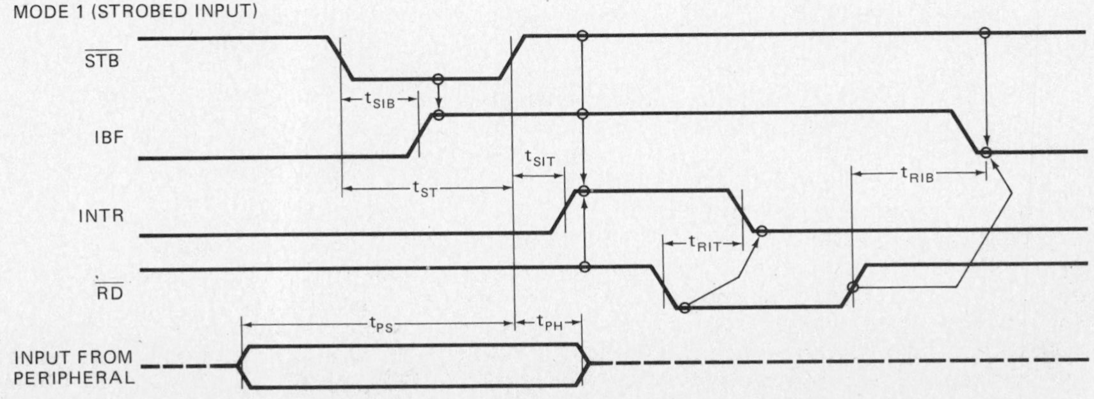

FIGURE 9-8 Timing waveforms for 8255 handshake data input from a tape reader.

FOR MODE 1	PORT C INTERRUPT SIGNAL PIN NUMBER	TO ENABLE INTERRUPT REQUEST SET PORT C BIT
PORT A IN	PC3	PC4
PORT B IN	PC0	PC2
PORT A OUT	PC3	PC6
PORT B OUT	PC0	PC2

FOR MODE 2	PORT C INTERRUPT SIGNAL PIN NUMBER	TO ENABLE INTERRUPT REQUEST SET PORT C BIT
PORT A IN	PC3	PC4
PORT A OUT	PC3	PC6

FIGURE 9-9 Port C bits to set to enable interrupt request outputs for handshake modes.

used for handshake input. According to Figure 9-9, port C bit PC4 must be set to enable the interrupt output for this operation. The bit set/reset control word to do this is 00001001. This bit set/reset control word will be sent to the control address of the 8255A.

Handshake data transfer from the tape reader to the 8255A can be stopped by disabling the 8255A interrupt output on port C pin PC3. This is done by resetting bit PC4 with a bit set/reset control word of 00001000. You will later see another example of the use of this interrupt enable/disable process in Figure 9-17.

As another example of 8255A interrupt output enabling, suppose that you are using port B as a handshake output port. According to Figure 9-9 you need to set port C bit PC2 to enable the 8255A interrupt output signal. The bit set/reset control word to do this is 00000101.

The microcomputer-controlled lathe we have described here is a small example of automated manufacturing. The advantage of this approach is that it relieves humans of the drudgery of standing in front of a machine continually making the same part, day after day. Hopefully society can find more productive use for the human time made available.

A SPEECH SYNTHESIZER INTERFACE—8255A HANDSHAKE OUTPUT

Many microprocessor-based products now recognize spoken commands and speak to you. In Chapter 12 we discuss in detail several methods of producing human speech under microprocessor control. For our example here we chose the *Votrax SC-01A phoneme speech synthesizer* because it is relatively inexpensive, it is easy to program, and it interfaces easily with a microprocessor port on a handshake basis. You may want to build up the circuit shown here and give your programs a voice. The circuit can be connected to one of the 8255As on an SDK-86 board if you have one of these available.

SC-01A OPERATION AND CIRCUIT CONNECTIONS

Figure 9-10*a* shows how an SC-01A speech synthesizer IC can be connected to an 8255A. The SC-01A uses *phonemes* to produce speech. Phonemes are the individual sounds in words. By linking phonemes, you can produce any word. To produce words, phrases, or even sentences, the microcomputer simply has to output a series of phonemes to the SC-01A with the proper timing. A 6-bit binary code sent to the P0–P5 inputs of the SC-01A determines which of its 64 phonemes it will output. An additional two bits sent to the SC-01A's I1 and I2 inputs determine the inflection of the sounded phoneme. A table in the appendix shows the 64 phoneme codes and the phoneme sequence for some example words. To sound a phoneme you send the phoneme and inflection codes for that phoneme and then assert the STB input of the SC-01 high. The SC-01A will then assert its acknowledge/request ($\overline{A}$/R) line low to tell you that it received the phoneme, and it will sound the phoneme. The time required to sound a phoneme ranges from 47 to 250 ms. When the SC-01A finishes sounding the phoneme, it will raise its $\overline{A}$/R line high again to indicate that it is ready for the next phoneme. The variable time it takes to sound a phoneme means that you have to send phonemes to the SC-01A on a handshake basis. You could poll the $\overline{A}$/R line to determine when the SC-01A is ready for the next phoneme, but because of the relatively long time between requests, it is much more reasonable to service the device on an interrupt basis. An 8255A port operating in MODE 1 easily manages the required STB, $\overline{A}$/R, and interrupt signals, so these lines are con-

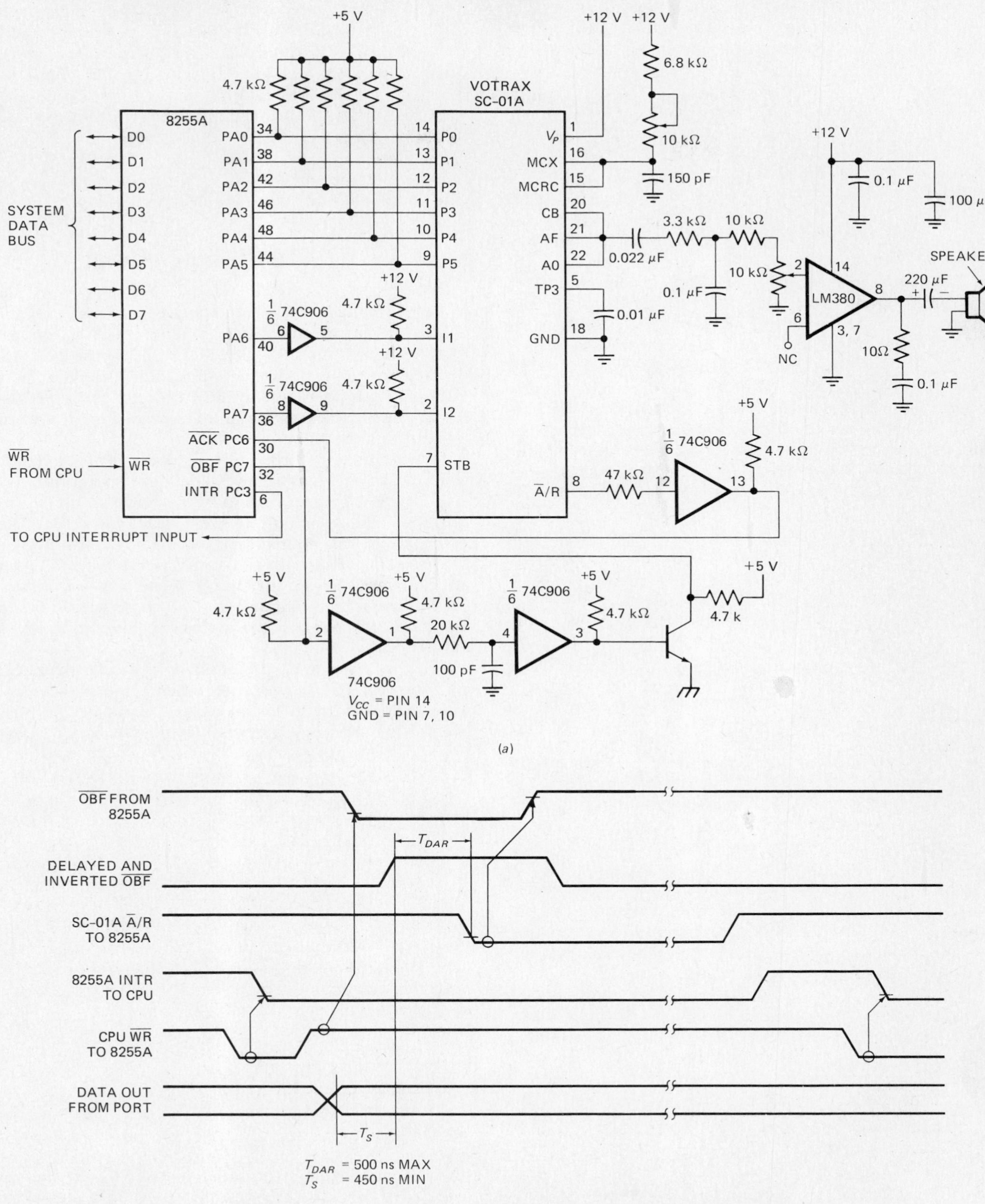

FIGURE 9-10 *(a)* Connection of a Votrax SC-01A speech synthesizer to an 8255A for handshake output of phonemes. *(b)* Timing waveforms for transfer of a phoneme from 8255A to SC-01A on handshake basis. *(Votrax Incorporated)*

nected to the appropriate bits of port C for this mode. Before we go on to the 8255A operation and timing waveforms, here are a few more points about the circuit connections.

The LM380 in Figure 9-10*a* is an audio amplifier which amplifies the signal from the SC-01A so that it can drive a speaker. The resistors and capacitors connected to pins 15 and 16 of the SC-01A determine the internal clock frequency. This clock frequency determines the pitch of the phoneme. Adjust the 10-kΩ potentiometer to get a frequency of about 680 kHz on pin 16 or until you like the pitch of the sounded phonemes. The 74C906 open drain CMOS buffers, between the 8255A PA6–PA7 pins and the I1–I2 pins, convert the 0–5 V range signals from the 8255A to the 0–12 V range signals required by the SC-01A inputs. Likewise, the 74C906 buffer on the $\overline{A}$/R output of the SC-01A converts the 0–12 V range signal from the SC-01A to the 0–5 V range signal required by the 8255A. The STB signal to the SC-01A must come at least 450 ns after the phoneme and inflection codes arrive at the device. The 20-kΩ resistor and the 100-pF capacitor between the two 74C906 buffers on the STB line produce the required delay for this signal. The transistor after the second buffer inverts the $\overline{OBF}$ signal from the 8255A so it has the correct polarity for the SC-01A STB input. It is often necessary to "massage" the handshake strobe signal so that it meets the timing requirements of the receiving device. In our next application example, a printer interface, we show you another way to do this.

PHONEME TRANSFER TIMING WAVEFORMS

Figure 9-10*b* shows the timing waveforms for a handshake output data transfer to the SC-01A. Here's how this works.

When the SC-01 is first powered up it raises its $\overline{A}$/R output high to indicate that it is ready for a phoneme. This causes the 8255A to send an interrupt signal to the processor. In response to the interrupt request the processor does an interrupt service procedure which writes a phoneme and an inflection code to port A of the 8255A. The left edge of the waveforms in Figure 9-10*b* represents the start of the phoneme write operation. During this write operation the $\overline{WR}$ from the 8086 will go low. When the 8255A detects this low, it will automatically reset its interrupt request output on pin PC3. A little later you will see how this was set. Now, when the $\overline{WR}$ signal from the 8086 goes high, the phoneme and inflection codes will be present on the output of the 8255A. $\overline{WR}$ being at a high state causes the 8255A to automatically assert its output buffer full ($\overline{OBF}$) signal low on bit PC7. This signal, inverted and delayed 450 ns by the buffer circuit, arrives at the STB input of the SC-01A. This signal edge says to the SC-01A, "Here is a phoneme for you." In response, the SC-01A drops its $\overline{A}$/R output low to say, "I got the phoneme, thank you." When this falling edge arrives at the 8255A $\overline{ACK}$ input on bit PC6, the 8255A automatically raises its $\overline{OBF}$ signal high again. This edge essentially asks the SC-01A, "May I send you another phoneme?" After the SC-01A finishes sounding the phoneme (47–250 ms later) it raises its $\overline{A}$/R line high again to say, "Send me the next phoneme." When the 8255A $\overline{ACK}$ input receives the rising edge of this $\overline{A}$/R signal, it automatically raises the interrupt request signal on pin PC3 high if that signal has been enabled. If the 8086 interrupt input being used is enabled, the 8086 will go and execute the interrupt service routine that writes a phoneme to port A of the 8255A. Writing a phoneme to the 8255A will cause the 8255A interrupt request output on PC3 to be automatically reset. The handshake sequence then repeats for this phoneme.

8255A INITIALIZATION FOR HANDSHAKE OUTPUT

In order to have specific addresses let's assume the SC-01A is connected to the 8255A, *XA*40, on an SDK-86 board. As shown in Figure 7-15, the port addresses for this device are port P2A—FFF8H, port P2B—FFFAH, port P2C—FFFCH, and P2 control register—FFFEH. Now let's make up the mode control word to send to the 8255A.

For the mode control word we make bit D7 a 1. We want to use port A as a handshake port, so we initialize it in MODE 1 by putting 0 in bit D6 and 1 in bit D5. To initialize port A for output, we put a 0 in bit D4. The other bits in this control word would be determined by the use of port B and the remaining pins of port C. If you are not using these, just make these bits 0's. Figure 9-11*a* shows the resultant control word. We send this mode control word to the control register at address FFFEH.

Since we want to do the handshake data transfer on an interrupt basis, we have to send another control word to enable the interrupt request signal on pin PC3. According to Figure 9-9 we enable this interrupt request

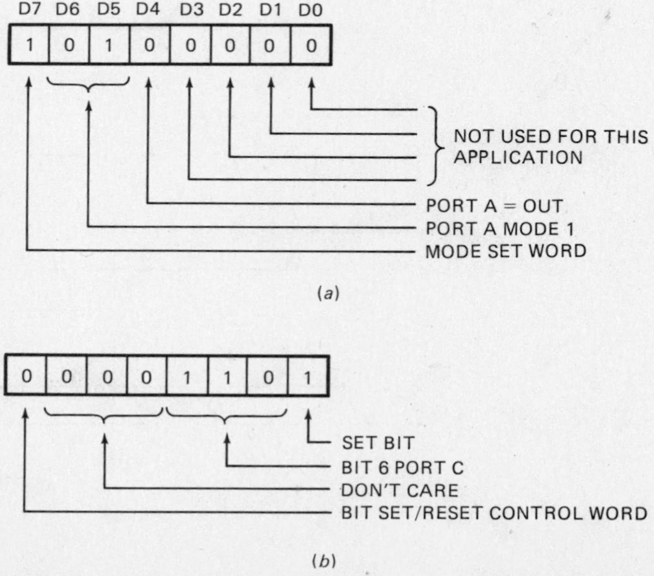

FIGURE 9-11 8255A control words for Votrax SC-01A interface. *(a)* Mode control word for port A, MODE 1. *(b)* Bit set/reset word to enable port A INTR.

by setting bit PC6. Figure 9-11*b* shows the bit set/reset control word to set bit PC6. This control word is also output to the control register at address FFFEH.

PROGRAM NOTES FOR SC-01A MAINLINE AND INTERRUPT PROCEDURE

The major tasks you have to do for the mainline here are:

1. Set up a table containing the sequence of phoneme codes you want to send. Make the last code in the table the no-sound phoneme, FFH, so that you can easily determine when all of the phoneme codes have been sent. As you read out the codes from the table you can then compare each with this *sentinel* value to see if you have reached the end of the table.
2. Initialize, in a memory location, a pointer to the start of the phoneme table.
3. Initialize the interrupt pointer table to point to the start of the interrupt service procedure.
4. Enable and unmask the interrupt input you are using.
5. Initialize the 8255A and enable the 8255A interrupt request output. When the SC-01A is ready for the next phoneme, the 8255A will send an interrupt signal to the 8086.

The 8086 interrupt service procedure must get the table pointer from memory, use the pointer to get the next phoneme from the table, and send the phoneme to the 8255A. The service procedure should then compare the phoneme code to the sentinel value of FFH. If the phoneme code is equal to FFH, then the procedure can simply return to the interrupted program. If the code is not FFH, then the procedure should increment the table pointer to point to the next phoneme, store the pointer back in memory, and do an IRET.

We leave the actual assembly language program for you to write as an exercise at the end of the chapter.

PARALLEL PRINTER INTERFACE—ANOTHER HANDSHAKE OUTPUT EXAMPLE

For most common printers such as the IBM PC printer, the Epson FX-80, and the NEC 8023, the data to be printed is sent to the printer as ASCII characters on eight parallel lines. The printer receives the characters to be printed and stores them in an internal RAM buffer. When the printer detects a carriage return character (0DH), it prints out the first row of characters from the print buffer. When the printer detects a second carriage return it prints out the second row of characters. The process continues until all the desired characters have been printed.

Transfer of the ASCII codes from a microcomputer to a printer must be done on a handshake basis because the microcomputer can send characters much faster than the printer can print them. The printer must in some way let the microcomputer know that its buffer is full, and that it cannot accept any more characters until it prints some out. A common standard for interfacing with parallel printers is the *Centronics Parallel Standard*, named for the company that developed it. In the following sections we show you how a Centronics parallel interface works, and how to implement it with an 8255A.

Centronics Interface Pin Descriptions and Circuit Connections

Centronics-type printers usually have a 36-pin interface connector. Figure 9-12 shows the pin assignments and descriptions for this connector as it is used in the IBM PC printer and the Epson printers. Some manufacturers use one or two pins differently so consult the manual for your specific printer before connecting it up as we show here.

Thirty-six pins may seem like a lot of pins just to send ASCII characters to a printer. The large number of lines is caused by the fact that each data and signal line has its own individual ground return line. For example, as shown in Figure 9-12, pin 2 is the LSB of the data character sent to the printer, and pin 20 is the ground return for this signal. The reason for the individual ground returns is to reduce the chance of picking up electrical noise in the lines. If you are making an interface cable for a parallel printer, these ground return lines should only be connected together and to ground at the microcomputer end of the cable as shown in Figure 9-14. While we are talking about grounds, note that pin 16 is listed as logic ground and pin 17 is listed as chassis ground. In order to prevent large noise currents from flowing in the logic ground wire, these wires should only be connected together in the microcomputer. (This precaution is necessary whenever you connect any external device or system to a microcomputer.)

The rest of the pins on the 36-pin connector fall into two categories, signals sent to the printer to tell it what operation to do and signals from the printer that indicate its status. The major control signals to the printer are $\overline{\text{INIT}}$ on pin 31, which tells the printer to perform its internal initialization sequence and $\overline{\text{STROBE}}$ on pin 1, which tells the printer, "Here is a character for you." Two additional input pins, pin 14 and pin 36 are usually taken care of inside the printer.

The major status signals output from the printer are:

1. The $\overline{\text{ACKNLG}}$ signal on pin 10 which, when low, indicates that the data character has been accepted and the printer is ready for the next character.
2. The BUSY signal on pin 11, which is high if, for some reason such as being out of paper, the printer is not ready to receive a character.
3. The PE signal on pin 12, which goes high if the out-of-paper switch in the printer is activated.
4. The SLCT signal on pin 13 which goes high if the printer is selected for receiving data.
5. The $\overline{\text{ERROR}}$ signal on pin 32 which goes low for a variety of problem conditions in the printer.

SIGNAL PIN NO.	RETURN PIN NO.	SIGNAL	DIRECTION	DESCRIPTION
1	19	$\overline{\text{STROBE}}$	IN	STROBE pulse to read data in. Pulse width must be more than 0.5 μs at receiving terminal. The signal level is normally "high"; read-in of data is performed at the "low" level of this signal.
2	20	DATA 1	IN	These signals represent information of the 1st to 8th bits of parallel data respectively. Each signal is at "high" level when data is logical "1" and "low" when logical "0."
3	21	DATA 2	IN	
4	22	DATA 3	IN	
5	23	DATA 4	IN	
6	24	DATA 5	IN	
7	25	DATA 6	IN	
8	26	DATA 7	IN	
9	27	DATA 8	IN	
10	28	$\overline{\text{ACKNLG}}$	OUT	Approximately 5 μs pulse; "low" indicates that data has been received and the printer is ready to accept other data.
11	29	BUSY	OUT	A "high" signal indicates that the printer cannot receive data. The signal becomes "high" in the following cases: 1. During data entry. 3. In "offline" state. 2. During printing operation. 4. During printer error status.
12	30	PE	OUT	A "high" signal indicates that the printer is out of paper.
13	–	SLCT	OUT	This signal indicates that the printer is in the selected state.
14	–	$\overline{\text{AUTO FEED XT}}$	IN	With this signal being at "low" level, the paper is automatically fed one line after printing. (The signal level can be fixed to "low" with DIP SW pin 2-3 provided on the control circuit board.)
15	–	NC		Not used.
16	–	OV		Logic GND level.
17	–	CHASIS-GND	–	Printer chasis GND. In the printer, the chassis GND and the logic GND are isolated from each other.
18	–	NC	–	Not used.
19-30	–	GND	–	"Twisted-Pair Return" signal; GND level.
31	–	$\overline{\text{INIT}}$	IN	When the level of this signal becomes "low" the printer controller is reset to its initial state and the print buffer is cleared. This signal is normally at "high" level, and its pulse width must be more than 50 μs at the receiving terminal.
32		$\overline{\text{ERROR}}$	OUT	The level of this signal becomes "low" when the printer is in "Paper End" state, "Offline" state and "Error" state.
33	–	GND	–	Same as with pin numbers 19 to 30.
34	–	NC	–	Not used.
35				Pulled up to +5 Vdc through 4.7 k-ohms resistance.
36	–	$\overline{\text{SLCT IN}}$	IN	Data entry to the printer is possible only when the level of this signal is "low." (Internal fixing can be carried out with DIP SW 1-8. The condition at the time of shipment is set "low" for this signal.)

Notes:
1. "Direction" refers to the direction of signal flow as viewed from the printer.
2. "Return" denotes "Twisted-Pair Return" and is to be connected at signal-ground level.
   When wiring the interface, be sure to use a twisted-pair cable for each signal and never fail to complete connection on the return side. To prevent noise effectively, these cables should be shielded and connected to the chassis of the system unit.
3. All interface conditions are based on TTL level. Both the rise and fall times of each signal must be less than 0.2 μs.
4. Data transfer must not be carried out by ignoring the $\overline{\text{ACKNLG}}$ or BUSY signal. (Data transfer to this printer can be carried out only after confirming the $\overline{\text{ACKNLG}}$ signal or when the level of the BUSY signal is "low.")

FIGURE 9-12 Pin connections and descriptions for Centronix-type parallel interface to IBM PC and EPSON FX-100 printers. *(IBM Corporation)*

Figure 9-13 shows the timing waveforms for transferring data characters to an IBM printer using the basic handshake signals. Here's how this works.

Assuming the printer has been initialized, you first check the BUSY signal pin to see if the printer is ready to receive data. If this signal is low, indicating the printer is ready (not busy), you send an ASCII code on the eight parallel data lines. After at least 0.5 μs you assert the $\overline{\text{STROBE}}$ signal low to tell the printer a character has been sent. The $\overline{\text{STROBE}}$ signal going low causes the printer to assert its BUSY signal high. After a minimum time of 0.5 μs the $\overline{\text{STROBE}}$ signal can be raised high again. Note that the data must be held valid on the data lines for at least 0.5 μs after the $\overline{\text{STROBE}}$ signal is made high.

When the printer is ready to receive the next character, it asserts its $\overline{\text{ACKNLG}}$ signal low for about 5 μs. The rising edge of the $\overline{\text{ACKNLG}}$ signal tells the microcomputer that it can send the next character. The rising edge of the $\overline{\text{ACKNLG}}$ signal also resets the BUSY signal from the printer. BUSY being low is another indication that the printer is ready to accept the next character. Some systems use the $\overline{\text{ACKNLG}}$ signal for the handshake, and some systems use the BUSY signal. Now let's see how you can do this handshake printer interface with an 8255A.

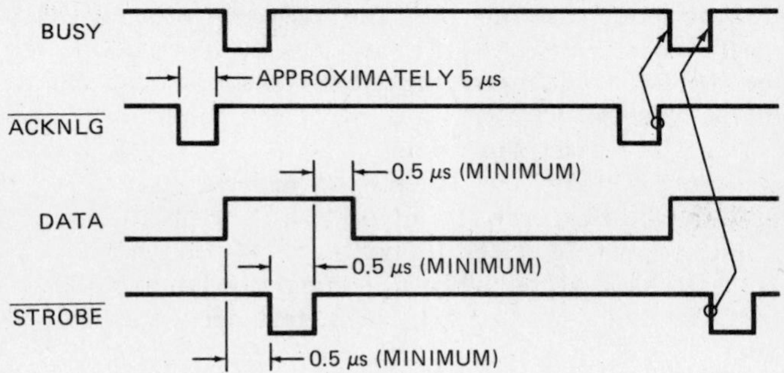

FIGURE 9-13 Timing waveforms for transfer of a data character to a Centronix-type parallel printer such as the IBM-PC or Epson printer. *(IBM Corporation)*

8255A CONNECTIONS AND INITIALIZATION

Figure 9-14 shows the circuit for connecting the Centronics parallel printer signals to an 8255A. We show here the pin connections for the J6 connector on the SDK-86 board so you can easily add this interface if you are working with one.

For this interface circuitry, 74LS07 open-collector buffers are used on the signal and data lines from the 8255A, because the 8255A outputs do not have enough current drive to charge and discharge the capacitance of the connecting cable fast enough. Pull-up resistors for the open-collector outputs of the 74LS07s are built into the printer.

Port B is used for the handshake output data lines. Therefore, as shown in Figure 9-3, bit PC0 functions as the interrupt request output to the 8086. The $\overline{\text{ACKNLG}}$ signal from the printer is connected to the 8255A $\overline{\text{ACK}}$ input on bit PC2. The $\overline{\text{OBF}}$ signal from the 8255A does not have the right timing parameters for this handshake, so PC1 is left unconnected. For this the $\overline{\text{STROBE}}$ input of the printer is connected to bit PC4. The $\overline{\text{STROBE}}$ signal will be generated by a bit set/reset of this pin.

The four printer status signals are connected to port A so the program can read them in, determine the condi-

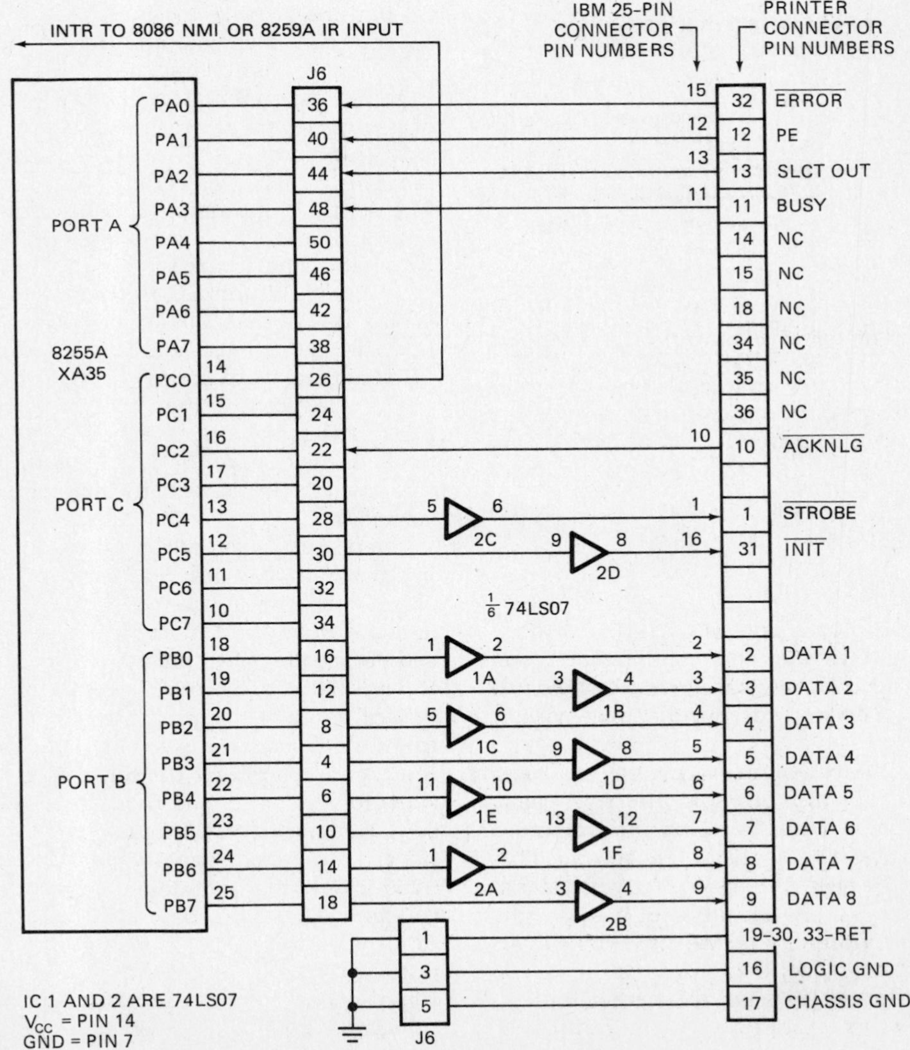

FIGURE 9-14 Circuit for interfacing Centronix-type parallel input printer to 8255A on SDK-86 board.

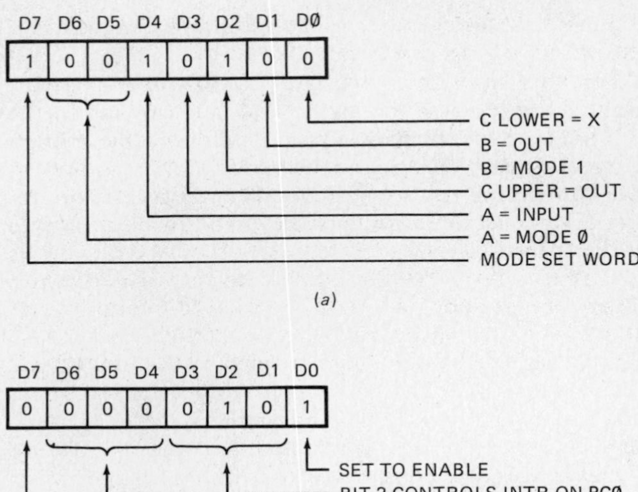

FIGURE 9-15 8255A control words for printer interface. *(a)* Mode control word. *(b)* Bit set/reset control word.

tion of the printer, and send the appropriate messages to the CRT if the printer is not ready.

Finally the $\overline{\text{INIT}}$ input of the printer is connected to bit PC5 so that the printer can be reinitialized under program control. Now let's look at the 8255A control words for this application.

Figure 9-15*a* shows the mode control word to initialize port B in MODE 1 output, port A for MODE 0 input, and the upper 4 bits of port C as outputs. Figure 9-15*b* shows the bit set/reset control word necessary to enable the interrupt request signal on bit PC0 for the handshake. The addresses for the 8255A, *XA*35, on the SDK-86 board are, as shown in Figure 7-15, port P1A—FFF9H, port P1B—FFFBH, port P1C—FFFDH, and control P1—FFFFH. For that system, then, both control words are output to FFFFH.

THE PRINTER DRIVER PROGRAM

Procedures which input data from or output data to peripheral devices such as disk drives, modems, and printers are often called *I/O drivers*. Here we show you one way to write the driver procedure for our parallel printer interface.

The first point to consider when writing any I/O driver is whether to do it on a polled or on an interrupt basis. For the parallel Centronics interface here the maximum data transfer rate is about 1000 characters/second. This means that there is a little less than 1 ms between transfers. If characters are sent on an interrupt basis, many other program instructions can be executed while waiting for the interrupt request to send the next character. Also, when the printer buffer gets full, there will be an even longer time that the processor can be working on some other job while waiting for the next interrupt. This is another illustration of how interrupts allow the computer to do several tasks "at the same time." For our example here assume that the interrupt request from PC0 of the 8255A is connected to the IR6 interrupt input of the 8259A shown in Figure 8-14 so that a clock interrupt, a keyboard interrupt, and the printer interrupt can all be serviced in turn.

Figure 9-16*a* shows the steps you need in the mainline to initialize everything and "call" the printer driver to send a string of ASCII characters to the printer.

At the start of the mainline some named memory locations are set aside to store parameters needed for transfer of data to the printer. The memory locations set aside for passing information between the mainline and the driver procedure are often called a *control block*. In the control block a named location is set aside for a pointer to the address of the ASCII character that is currently being sent. Another memory location is set aside to store the number of characters to be sent. The number in this location will function as a counter so you know when you have sent all of the characters in the buffer. Instead of using this counter approach to keep track of how many characters have been sent, the *sentinel method* we described for handshake output to the SC-01A in Figure 9-10 could have been used. With the sentinel approach you put a *sentinel* character in memory after the last character to be sent out. MSDOS, for example, uses a $ (24H) as a sentinel character for some of its drivers. As you read each character in from memory, you compare it with the sentinel value. If it matches, you know all of the characters have been sent. The sentinel approach and the counter approach are both widely used, so you should be familiar with both.

To get the hardware ready to go, you need to initialize the 8259A and unmask the IR inputs of the 8259A that are used. The 8086 INTR input must also be enabled. Next the 8255A must be initialized by sending it the mode control word shown above. A bit set/reset control word is then sent to the 8255A to make the $\overline{\text{STROBE}}$ signal to the printer high because this is its unasserted level. To make sure the printer is internally initialized, you pulse the $\overline{\text{INIT}}$ line to the printer low for a few microseconds.

When you are actually ready to print some characters in a program, you first read the printer status from port A and check if the printer is selected, not out of paper, and not busy. In a more complete program you could send a specific error message to the display indicating the type of error found. The program here just sends a general error message. If no printer error condition is found, you load the starting address of the string of ASCII characters into the control block location you set aside for this, and load the number of characters to be sent in the reserved location in the control block. Finally, you enable the interrupt request pin on the 8255A. Note that you do not enable this interrupt until you are actually ready to send data. A high on the $\overline{\text{ACKNLG}}$ line from the printer causes the 8255A to output an interrupt request signal. This interrupt request signal goes through the 8259A to the processor and causes it to go to the interrupt service procedure.

Figure 9-16*b* shows the algorithm for the procedure which services this interrupt and actually sends the characters to the printer. After pushing some registers the 8086 INTR input is enabled so that higher-priority interrupts can interrupt this procedure. The string address pointer is then read in from the control block and used to read a character in from the memory buffer to AL. The character in AL is then output to port B of the 8255A.

From here on the program follows the timing diagram in Figure 9-13. After sending the character the program waits at least 0.5 μs, asserts the $\overline{\text{STROBE}}$ input low, waits at least another 0.5 μs and raises the $\overline{\text{STROBE}}$ line high again. The data byte will be latched on the port B output pins until the next character is sent, so the data hold parameter in the timing diagram is satisfied. Sending of the character is now complete, so the next step is to get ready to send another character.

To do this the buffer pointer is incremented by one, and the incremented value is placed back in the control block location. The character counter in the control block is then decremented. If the character counter is not down to zero, there are more characters to send so the EOI command is simply sent to the 8259A, everything popped off the stack, and execution returned to the interrupted program. If the character counter is down to zero, all of the characters have been sent, so the interrupt request output of the 8255A is disabled with a bit set/reset control word to prevent further interrupt

```
Mainline algorithm for printer driver
Initialization
     set up control block
          word for storing pointer to ASCII string
          word for number of characters in string
     initialization control words to 8259A
     unmask 8259A IR6 and any other IR inputs used
     unmask 8Ø86 INTR input
     mode set word to 8255A
     send STROBE high to printer
     initialize printer (pulse init low)
To send ASCII string
     read printer status from port
     if error then
          send error message
          exit
     set print done status bit
     load starting address of string into pointer store.
     load length of string into character counter
     enable 8255A INTR output
     wait for interrupt
```

(a)

FIGURE 9-16 Algorithm for printer mainline and interrupt-based printer driver procedure. *(a)* Mainline steps. *(b)* Printer driver procedure steps.

```
Printer Driver Procedure Algorithm

    save registers

    enable 8086 INTR for higher priority interrupts

    get pointer to string

    get ASCII character from buffer

    send character to printer

    wait 1 usec

    send STROBE low

    wait 1 usec

    send STROBE high

    increment pointer to string

    put pointer back in pointer store

    decrement character count

    if character count = 0 then

         disable 8255A interrupt request output

    send EOI command to 8259A

    restore registers

    return from interrupt procedure
```

(*b*)

FIGURE 9-16 (*continued*)

requests from there. This interrupt source will remain disabled until you want to send another buffer of characters to the printer. Execution then exits from the procedure by sending an EOI command to the 8259A, popping registers, and doing an IRET.

Figure 9-17 shows the pertinent parts of the mainline program and the printer driver procedure. The preceding discussion of the algorithms and the comments with the instructions should make most of these reasonably clear if you work your way through them one step at a time. You have seen many of the pieces in previous programs. One part of the program that we do want to expand and clarify is the generation of the $\overline{\text{STROBE}}$ signal with bit PC3.

In the speech synthesizer example in a preceding section we used external hardware to "massage" the $\overline{\text{OBF}}$ signal from the 8255A so it matched the timing and polarity requirements of the receiving device. Here we generate the strobe directly under software control.

In the mainline we make the $\overline{\text{STROBE}}$ signal on PC4 high by sending a bit set/reset control word of 00001001 to the control register of the 8255A. In the printer driver procedure a character is sent to the printer with the OUT DX, AL instruction. According to the timing diagram in Figure 9-13 we then want to wait at least 0.5 μs before asserting the $\overline{\text{STROBE}}$ signal low. This is automatically done in the program because the instructions required to assert the strobe low take longer than 0.5 μs. The MOV AL, 00001000B instruction requires 4 clock cycles, and the OUT DX, AL instruction requires 8 clock cycles to execute. Assuming a 5-MHz clock (0.2-μs period), these two instructions take 2.4 μs to execute, which is more than required.

Again referring to the timing diagram in Figure 9-13,

```
page ,132
;8086 Printer-driver program
;               This program sets up the 8259A and the 8255A on an SDK-86
;               board so that a message in a buffer can be sent to a
;               printer. The mainline sets up a control block and
;               initializes all variables
;PORTS USED:    SDK-86 ports P1A - FFF9H used to input status of printer
;                            P1B - FFFBH used to output a character
;                            P1C - for handshake signals for port B
;PROCEDURES:    PRINT_IT used to output characters

A_INT_TABLE     SEGMENT WORD
        TYPE_64_69      DW      12 DUP(0)       ; reserved for IR0-IR6
        TYPE_70         DW      2  DUP(0)       ; IR6 interrupt
        TYPE_71         DW      2  DUP(0)       ; IR7 interrupt - not used
A_INT_TABLE     ENDS
DATA_HERE       SEGMENT WORD PUBLIC
        MESSAGE_1       DB      'This is the message from the printer driver!'
                        DB      0DH, 0AH, 0DH    ; return & line-feed for printer
        PRINT_DONE      DB      0
        POINTER         DW      00      ; storage for pointer to MESSAGE_1
        COUNTER         DB      0       ; counter for length of MESSAGE_1
        PRINTER_ERROR   DB      0
DATA_HERE       ENDS
PUBLIC  PRINT_DONE, POINTER, COUNTER, MESSAGE_1
EXTRN   PRINT_IT:FAR
MESSAGE_LENGTH  EQU     47              ; length of MESSAGE_1
STACK_HERE      SEGMENT
                        DW      30 DUP(0)
        STACK_TOP       LABEL   WORD
STACK_HERE      ENDS

CODE_HERE       SEGMENT WORD PUBLIC
        ASSUME CS:CODE_HERE, DS:A_INT_TABLE, SS:STACK_HERE
        MOV     AX, STACK_HERE          ; initialize stack segement
        MOV     SS, AX
        MOV     SP, OFFSET STACK_TOP
        MOV     AX, A_INT_TABLE
        MOV     DS, AX
;set up interrupt table and put in address for printer interrupt subroutine
        MOV     TYPE_70+2, SEG PRINT_IT
        MOV     TYPE_70,   OFFSET PRINT_IT
ASSUME DS:DATA_HERE
        MOV     AX, DATA_HERE           ; set up data segment
        MOV     DS, AX
;initialize 8259A and unmask IR6
        MOV     DX, 0FF00H              ; point at 8259A control address
        MOV     AL, 00010011B           ; ICW1, edge triggered, single, 8086
        OUT     DX, AL                  ; send ICW1
        MOV     DX, 0FF02H              ; point at ICW2 address
        MOV     AL, 01000000B           ; type 64 is first 8259A type
        OUT     DX, AL                  ; send ICW2
```

FIGURE 9-17 8086 assembly language instructions for mainline and printer driver procedure. *(a)* Mainline. *(b)* Procedure.

```
        MOV     AL, 00000001B           ; ICW4, 8086 mode
        OUT     DX, AL                  ; send ICW4
        MOV     AL, 10111111B           ; OCW1 to unmask IR6
        OUT     DX, AL                  ; send OCW1
;initialize 8255A, P1A-mode1 input. P1B-mode0 output. Unused P1C bits-output
        MOV     DX, 0FFFFH              ; control address for 8255A
        MOV     AL, 10010100B           ; control word for above conditions
        OUT     DX, AL                  ; send control word
        STI                             ;unmask 8086 INTR interrupt
;send STROBE high to printer with bit set on PC4
        MOV     AL, 00001001B
        OUT     DX, AL
;initialize printer - pulse INIT low for > 50 useconds (on PC5)
        MOV     AL, 00001101B           ; bit set on PC5
        OUT     DX, AL                  ; send INIT high
        MOV     AL, 00001100B           ; bit reset on PC5,
        OUT     DX, AL                  ; send INIT low
        MOV     CX, 17H                 ; wait > 50 usec
PAUSE1: LOOP    PAUSE1
        MOV     AL, 00001101B           ; bit set on PC5
        OUT     DX, AL                  ; send INIT high again
;read printer status from port A, status OK - AL = XXXX0101
;PA3-BUSY=0, PA2-SLCT=1, PA1-PE=0, PA0-ERROR=1
        MOV     PRINTER_ERROR, 0        ; printer OK so far
        MOV     DX, 0FFF9H              ; point at port A
        IN      AL, DX                  ; get status of printer
        AND     AL, 0FH                 ; upper four bits are not used
        CMP     AL, 00000101B           ; is status OK
        JZ      SEND_IT                 ; send it if OK
;printer not ready, try once more after waiting 20 ms.
        MOV     CX, 16EAH               ; load count for 20ms
PAUSE:  LOOP    PAUSE                   ; and wait
        IN      AL, DX                  ; repeat steps to read status
        AND     AL, 0FH
        CMP     AL, 00000101B
        JZ      SEND_IT                 ; is printer ready yet?
        MOV     PRINTER_ERROR, 01       ; set error code
        JMP     FIN                     ; not ready so terminate send
;set up pointer to message storage and say print not done yet
SEND_IT:MOV     AX, OFFSET MESSAGE_1
        MOV     POINTER, AX
        MOV     PRINT_DONE, 00
        MOV     COUNTER, MESSAGE_LENGTH
;enable 8255A interrupt request output on PC0 by setting PC2
        MOV     DX, 0FFFFH              ; point at port control addr
        MOV     AL, 00000101B           ; bit set word for PC0 intr
        OUT     DX, AL
;wait for an interrupt from the printer
WT:     JMP     WT
FIN:    NOP

CODE_HERE       ENDS
                END
```

(*a*)

FIGURE 9-17 (*continued*)

```
PAGE ,132
;8086 Procedure for printer driver program
;ABSTRACT:      This procedure outputs a character from a buffer to
;               a printer. If no characters are left in the buffer
;               then the interrupt to the 8086 on IR6 of the 8259A
;               is disabled
;PROCEDURES:    None used
;PORTS:         Uses SDK-86 board Port P1B (FFFBH) to output characters
;               Port P1C bits for handshake signals and printer intr
;REGISTERS USED:AX, BX, DX Flags, destroys no registers

PUBLIC  PRINT_IT
DATA_HERE       SEGMENT PUBLIC
        EXTRN   COUNTER:BYTE, POINTER:WORD
        EXTRN   MESSAGE_1:BYTE, PRINT_DONE:BYTE
DATA_HERE       ENDS

CODE_HERE       SEGMENT WORD PUBLIC
PRINT_IT        PROC    FAR
                ASSUME  CS:CODE_HERE, DS:DATA_HERE
                PUSH    AX                  ; save registers
                PUSH    BX
                PUSH    DX
                STI                         ; enable higher interrupts
                MOV     DX, OFFFBH          ; point at port B
                MOV     BX, POINTER         ; load pointer to message
                MOV     AL, [BX]            ; get a character
                OUT     DX, AL              ; send the character to printer
;send printer strobe on PC4 low then high
                MOV     DX, OFFFFH          ; point at port control addr
                MOV     AL, 00001000B       ; strobe low control word
                OUT     DX, AL
                MOV     AL, 00001001B       ; strobe high control word
                OUT     DX, AL
;increment pointer and decrement counter
                INC     BX
                MOV     POINTER, BX
                DEC     COUNTER
                JNZ     NEXT                ; wait for next character?
;no more characters-disable 8255A int request on PC0 by bit reset of PC2
                MOV     AL, 00000100B       ; bit reset word for PC0 interrupt
                OUT     DX, AL
                MOV     PRINT_DONE, 1
NEXT:           MOV     AL, 00100000B       ; OCW2 for non-specific EOI
                MOV     DX, OFF00H          ; point at 8259A control addr
                OUT     DX, AL
                POP     DX                  ; restore registers
                POP     BX
                POP     AX
                IRET
PRINT_IT        ENDP
CODE_HERE       ENDS
                END
```

(*b*)

FIGURE 9-17 (*continued*)

the $\overline{STROBE}$ time low must also be at least 0.5 μs. The MOV AL, 00001001B instruction takes 4 clock cycles and the OUT DX, AL instruction takes 8 clock cycles. With a 5-MHz clock this totals to 2.4 μs, which again is more than enough time for $\overline{STROBE}$ low. In this case creating the $\overline{STROBE}$ signal with software does not use much of the processor's time, so this is an efficient way to do it.

A FEW MORE POINTS ABOUT THE 8255A

Before leaving our discussion of the 8255A we want to show you a little more about how port C is used.

Any bits of port C which are programmed as inputs can be read by simply doing a read from the port C address. You can mask out any unwanted bits of the word read in. If port A and/or port B is programmed in a handshake mode, then some of the bits of a byte read in from port C represent *status information* about the handshake signals. Figure 9-18 shows the meaning of the bits read from port C for port A and/or port B in MODE 1. Here's how you read this diagram. If port B is initialized as a handshake (MODE 1) input port, then bits D0, D1, and D2 read from port C represent the status of the port B handshake signals. Bit D2 will be high if the port B interrupt request output has been enabled. Bit D1 is a copy of the level on the input buffer full (IBF) pin. Bit D0 is a copy of the interrupt request output, so it will be high if port B is requesting an interrupt.

In our previous application examples, we showed how to do handshake data transfer on an interrupt basis to make maximum use of the CPU time. However, in applications where the CPU has nothing else to do while waiting to, for example, read in the next character from some device, then you can save one interrupt input by reading data from the 8255A on a polled basis. To do this for a handshake input operation on port B you simply loop through reading port C and checking bit D1 over and over until you find this bit high. The IBF pin being high means that the input data byte has been latched into the 8255A and can now be read. The timing waveforms for this case are the same as those in Figure 9-9, except that you are not using the interrupt request output from the 8255A.

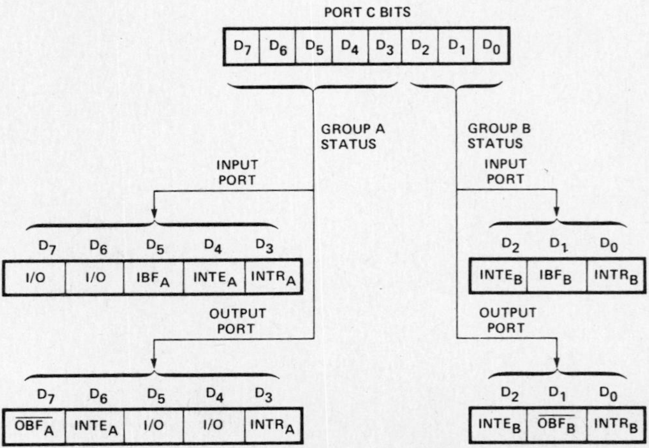

FIGURE 9-18 8255A status word format for MODE 1 input and output operations.

Port C bits not used for handshake signals and programmed as outputs can be written to by sending bit set/reset control words to the control register. Technically, bits PC0–PC3 can also be written to directly at the port C address, but we have found it safer to just use the bit set/reset control word approach to write to all leftover port C bits programmed as outputs.

INTERFACING A MICROPROCESSOR TO KEYBOARDS

Keyboard Types

When you press a key on your computer you are activating a switch. There are many different ways of making these switches. Here's an overview of the construction and operation of some of the most common types.

MECHANICAL KEYSWITCHES

In mechanical switch keys, two pieces of metal are pushed together when you press the key. The actual switch elements are often made of a phosphor-bronze alloy with gold plating on the contact areas. The keyswitch usually contains a spring to return the key to the nonpressed position and perhaps a small piece of foam to help damp out bouncing. Mechanical switches are relatively inexpensive, but they have several disadvantages. First, they suffer from *contact bounce*. A pressed key may make and break contact several times before it makes solid contact. Second, the contacts may become oxidized or dirty with age so they no longer make a dependable connection. Higher-quality mechanical switches typically have a rated lifetime of about 1 million keystrokes.

MEMBRANE KEYSWITCHES

These switches are really just a special type of mechanical switch. They consist of a three-layer plastic or rubber sandwich as shown in Figure 9-19*a*. The top layer has a conductive line of silver ink running under each row of keys. The middle layer has a hole under each key position. The bottom layer has a conductive line of silver ink running under each column of keys. When you press a key you push the top ink line through the hole to contact the bottom ink line. The advantage of membrane keyboards is that they can be made as very thin, sealed units. They are often used on cash registers in fast food restaurants, on medical instruments, and in other messy applications. Lifetime of membrane keyboards varies over a wide range.

CAPACITIVE KEYSWITCHES

As shown in Figure 9-19*b*, a capacitive keyswitch has two small metal plates on the printed-circuit board and another metal plate on the bottom of a piece of foam. When you press the key, the movable plate is pushed closer to the fixed plate. This changes the capacitance between the fixed plates. Sense amplifier circuitry de-

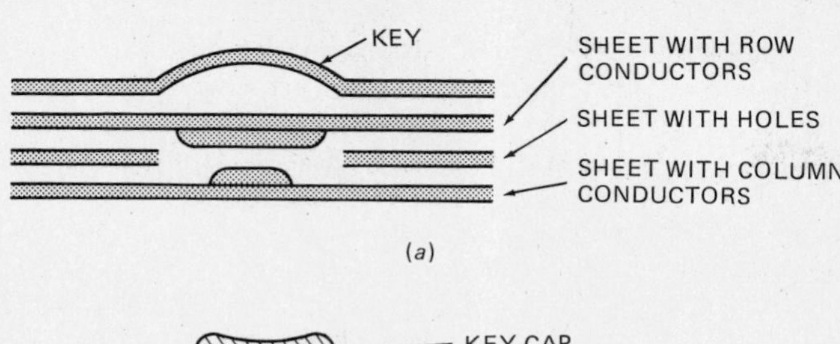

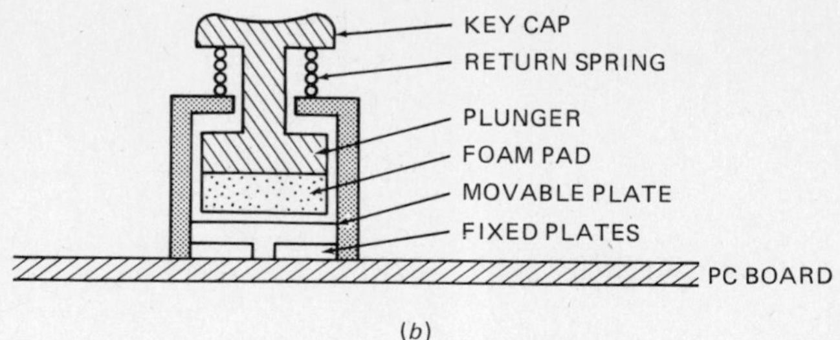

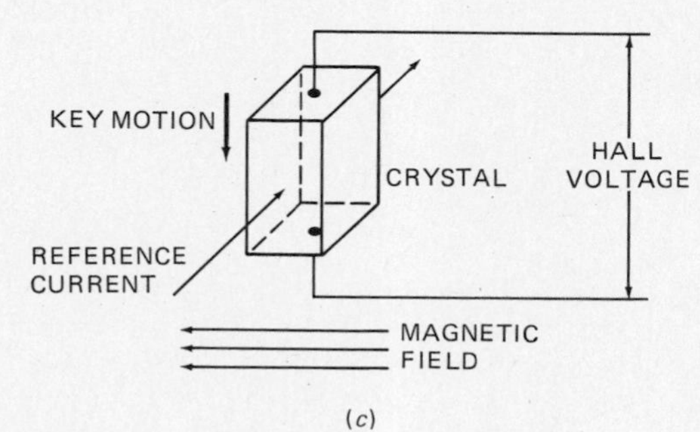

FIGURE 9-19 Key switch types. *(a)* Membrane. *(b)* Capacitive. *(c)* Hall effect.

tects this change in capacitance and produces a logic-level signal that indicates a key has been pressed. The big advantage of a capacitive switch is that it has no mechanical contacts to become oxidized or dirty. A small disadvantage is the specialized circuitry needed to detect the change in capacitance. Capacitive key-switches typically have a rated lifetime of about 20 million keystrokes.

HALL EFFECT KEYSWITCHES

This is another type of switch which has no mechanical contact. It takes advantage of the deflection of a moving charge by a magnetic field. Figure 9-19*c* shows you how this works. A reference current is passed through a semiconductor crystal between two opposing faces. When a key is pressed, the crystal is moved through a magnetic field which has its flux lines perpendicular to the direction of the current flow in the crystal. (Actually it is easier to move a small magnet past the crystal.) Moving the crystal through the magnetic field causes a small voltage to be developed between two of the other opposing faces of the crystal. This voltage is amplified and used to indicate that a key is pressed. Hall effect keyboards are more expensive because of the more complex switch mechanisms, but they are very dependable, and have typical rated lifetimes of 100 million or more keystrokes.

Keyboard Circuit Connections and Interfacing

In most keyboards the keyswitches are connected in a matrix of rows and columns as shown in Figure 9-20*a*. We will use simple mechanical switches for our examples here, but the principle is the same for other types of switches. Getting meaningful data from a keyboard such as this requires doing three major tasks. They are:

1. Detect a keypress.
2. Debounce the keypress.
3. Encode it (Produce a standard code for the pressed key).

The three tasks can be done with hardware, software, or a combination of the two, depending on the application. We will first show you how they can be done with software as might be done in a microprocessor-based grocery scale where the microprocessor is not pressed for time. Later we describe some hardware devices which do these tasks.

Software Keyboard Interfacing

CIRCUIT CONNECTIONS AND ALGORITHM

Figure 9-20*a* shows how a hexadecimal keypad can be connected to a couple of microcomputer ports so our three tasks can be done as part of a program. The rows of the matrix are connected to four output port lines. The column lines of the matrix are connected to four input port lines. When no keys are pressed, the column lines are held high by the pull-up resistors to +5 V. The main principle here is that pressing a key connects a row to a column. If a low is output on a row and a key in that row is pressed, then the low will appear on the column which contains that key and can be detected on the input port. If you know the row and the column of the pressed key, you then know which key was pressed, and can make up any code you want to represent that key. Figure 9-20*b* shows a flowchart for a procedure to detect, debounce, and produce the hex code for a pressed key.

The first step is to output 0's to all of the rows. Next the columns are read and and checked over and over until the columns are all high. This is done to make sure a previous key has been released before looking for the next one. In standard keyboard terminology this is called *two-key lockout*. Once the columns are found to be all high the program enters another loop which waits until a low appears on one of the columns, indicating a key has been pressed. This loop does the detect task for us. A simple 20-ms delay procedure then does the debounce task.

After the debounce time another check is made to see if the key is still pressed. If the columns are all high, then no key is pressed and the initial detection was just a noise pulse or a light brushing past a key. If any of the columns are still low, then the assumption is made that it is a valid keypress.

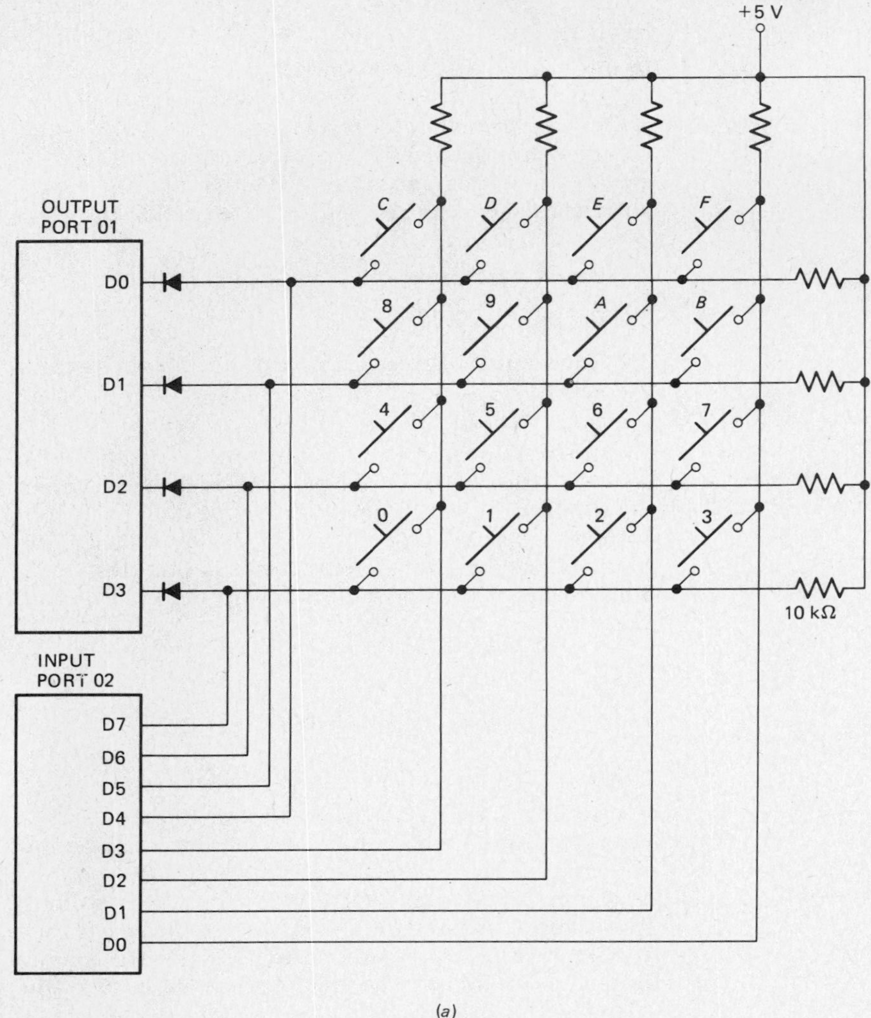

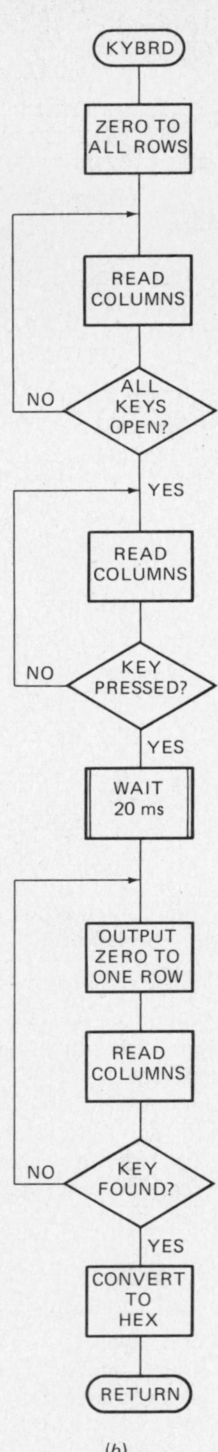

FIGURE 9-20 Detecting a matrix keyboard key-press, debouncing it, and encoding it with a microcomputer. *(a)* Port connections. *(b)* Flowchart for procedure.

The final task is to determine the row and column of the pressed key, and convert this row and column information to the hex code for the pressed key. To get the row and column information, a low is output to one row and the columns are read. If none of the the columns are low, the pressed key is not in that row, so the low is rotated to the next row and the columns are checked again. The process is repeated until a low on a row produces a low on one of the columns. The pressed key is in the row which is low at that time. The byte read in from the input port will contain a 4-bit code which represents the row of the pressed key and a 4-bit code which represents the column of the pressed key. As we show later, this row-column code can easily be converted to hex using a lookup table.

Figure 9-21 shows the assembly language program for this procedure. The detect, debounce, and row-detect parts of the program follow the flowchart very closely and should be easy for you to follow. Work your way down through these parts until you reach the ENCODE label, then continue with the discussion here.

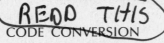

CODE CONVERSION

There are two major ways of converting one code to another in a program. The ENCODE portion of this program uses a *compare* technique, which is important for you to learn, so we will discuss this portion in detail. In a later section on keyboard interfacing with hardware

```
page ,132
;8086 Program to scan and decode a 16 switch keypad
;ABSTRACT :  This program initializes the ports below and then
;            calls a procedure to input an 8-bit value from
;            a 16-switch keypad and encode it.
;PORTS    :  SDK-86 board Port P1A - FFF9H as output, P1B - FFFBH as input
;ROUTINES : Calls KEYBRD to scan and decode 16-switch keypad
;REGISTERS: Uses DS, SS, SP, AX, DX

DATA_HERE       SEGMENT WORD    PUBLIC
TABLE   DB   77H,  7BH,  7DH,  7EH, 0B7H, 0BBH, 0BDH, 0BEH
;             0     1     2     3     4     5     6     7
        DB  0D7H, 0DBH, 0DDH, 0DEH, 0E7H, 0EBH, 0EDH, 0EEH
;            8     9     A     B     C     D     E     F
DATA_HERE       ENDS
STACK_HERE      SEGMENT
                        DW      30      DUP(0)  ; set up stack of 30 words
        TOP_STACK       LABEL   WORD            ; pointer to top of stack
STACK_HERE      ENDS

CODE_HERE       SEGMENT WORD    PUBLIC
                ASSUME  CS:CODE_HERE, DS:DATA_HERE, SS:STACK_HERE
;initialize segment registers
START:          MOV     AX, STACK_HERE
                MOV     SS, AX
                MOV     SP, OFFSET TOP_STACK
                MOV     AX, DATA_HERE
                MOV     DS, AX
; initialize ports, load DX with port control address
                MOV     DX, 0FFFFH
;mode set word, port A as output, mode 0, port B & C input ports, mode 0
                MOV     AL, 10001011B           ; code 8BH
                OUT     DX, AL                  ; Send control word
                CALL    KEYBRD
                NOP
                NOP
;program will continue here with other tasks


;PROCEDURE KEYBRD
;ABSTRACT :  procedure gets a code from a 16-switch keypad and decodes
;           it. It returns the code for the keypress in AL and AH=00. If there
;           is an error in the keypress then it returns AH=01.
;PORTS    : Uses SDK-86 ports P1A - FFF9H as output and P1B - FFFBH as input
;INPUTS   : Keypress from port
;OUTPUTS  : Keypress code or error message in AX
;ROUTINES : None used
;REGISTERS: Destroys AX


KEYBRD  PROC    NEAR
                PUSHF                   ; save registers used
                PUSH    BX
                PUSH    CX
```

FIGURE 9-21 Assembly language instructions for keyboard detect, debounce, and encode procedure.

```
                PUSH    DX
                MOV     AL,.00              ; send 0's to all rows
                MOV     DX, 0FFF9H          ; load output address
                OUT     DX, AL              ; send 0's
;Read columns
                MOV     DX, 0FFFBH          ; load i/p port address
WAIT_OPEN:      IN      AL, DX
                AND     AL, 0FH             ; mask row bits
                CMP     AL, 0FH             ; wait until no keys pressed
                JNE     WAIT_OPEN
;Read columns for keypress
WAIT_PRESS:     IN      AL, DX              ; read columns
                AND     AL, 0FH             ; mask row bits
                CMP     AL, 0FH             ; see if keypressed
                JE      WAIT_PRESS
;Debounce keypress
                MOV     CX, 16EAH           ; delay of 20 ms
DELAY:          LOOP    DELAY
                IN      AL, DX              ; read columns
                AND     AL, 0FH
                CMP     AL, 0FH             ; see if key still pressed
                JE      WAIT_PRESS
;Initialize a row mask with bit 0 low
                MOV     AL, 0FEH
                MOV     CL, AL              ; save mask
NEXT_ROW:       MOV     DX, 0FFF9H          ; put a low on one row
                OUT     DX, AL
                MOV     DX, 0FFFBH          ; read columns & check for low
                IN      AL, DX
                AND     AL, 0FH             ; mask out row code
                CMP     AL, 0FH             ; check for low in a column
                JNE     ENCODE              ; found column, now encode it
                ROL     CL, 01              ; rotate mask
                MOV     AL, CL              ; move mask
                JMP     NEXT_ROW            ; look at next row
;Encode the row/column information
ENCODE:         MOV     BX, 000FH           ; set up BX as a counter
                IN      AL, DX              ; read row and column from port
TRY_NEXT:       CMP     AL, TABLE[BX]       ; compare row/col code with table
                JZ      DONE
                DEC     BX                  ; point at next table entry
                JNS     TRY_NEXT
                MOV     AH, 01              ; pass an error code in AH
                JMP     EXIT
DONE:           MOV     AL, BL              ; hex code for key in AL
                MOV     AH, 00              ; valid-code key in AH
EXIT:           NOP
                POP     DX
                POP     CX
                POP     BX
                POPF
                RET
KEYBRD          ENDP
CODE_HERE       ENDS
                END     START
```

FIGURE 9-21 (*continued*)

we will show you the other major code conversion technique which we call *add and point*.

After the row which produces a low on one of the columns is found, execution jumps to the label ENCODE. The IN AL, DX instruction here reads the row and column codes in from the input port. This 8-bit code read in represents the key pressed. All that has to be done now is to convert this 8-bit code to the simple hex code for the key pressed. For example if you press the D key, you want to exit from the procedure with 0DH in AL.

The conversion is done with the lookup table declared with DBs at the top of Figure 9-21. This table contains the 8-bit keypressed codes for each of the 16 keys. Note that the codes are put in the table in order for the hex code they represent. The principle of the conversion technique we use here is to compare the row and column code read in with each of the values in the table until a match is found. We use a counter to keep track of how far down the table we have to go to find a match for a particular input code. When a match is found, the counter will contain the hex code for the key pressed.

In the program in Figure 9-21 we use the BX register as the counter and as a pointer to one of the codes in the table. To start we load a count of 000FH in BX with the MOV BX, 000FH instruction. The CMP AL, TABLE[BX] after this compares the code at offset [BX] in the table with the row and column code in AL. BX contains 000FH and the code in the table at this offset is the row and column code for the F key. If we get a match on this first compare, we know the F key was pressed, and BL contains the hex code for this key. The hex code in BL is copied to AL to pass it back to the calling program. AH is loaded with 00H to tell the calling program this was a valid keypress, and a return made to the calling program.

If we don't get a match on the first compare, we decrement BX to point to the code for the E key in the table and do another compare. If a match occurs this time, the E key was the key pressed, and the hex code for that key, 0EH, is in BL. If we don't get a match on this compare, we cycle through the loop until we get a match or until the row and column code for the pressed key has been compared with all of the values in the table. As long as the value in BX is zero or above after the DEC BX instruction, the Jump if Not Sign instruction, JNS TRY_NEXT, will cause execution to go back to the compare instruction. If no match is found in the table, BX will decrement from 0 to FFFFH. Since the sign bit is a copy of the MSB of the result after the DEC instruction, the sign bit will then be set. Execution will fall through to an instruction which loads an error code of 01H in AH. We then return to the calling program. The calling program will check AH on return to determine if the contents of AL represent the code for a valid keypress.

ERROR TRAPPING

The concept of detecting some error condition such as "no match found" is called *error trapping*. Error trapping is a very important part of real programs. Even in this simple program, think what might happen with no error trap if two keys in the same row were pressed at exactly the same time. A column code with two lows in it would be produced. This would not match any of the row and column codes in the table. After all of the values in the table were checked, BX would be decremented to FFFFH and AL would then be compared with a value off in memory at offset FFFFH. The cycle would continue until, by chance, the value in a memory location matched the row and column code in AL. The contents of BL at that point would be passed back to the calling routine. The chances are 1 in 256 that this would be the correct value. Since these are not very good odds, it is advisable to put error traps in your programs wherever there is a chance for it to go off to "never-never land" in this way. The error/no-error code can be passed back to the calling program in a register as shown, in a dedicated memory location, or on the stack.

Keyboard Interfacing With Hardware

The previous section described how you can connect a keyboard matrix to a couple of microprocessor ports, and perform the three interfacing tasks with program instructions. For systems where the CPU is too busy to be bothered doing these tasks in software, an external device is used to do them. One example of an MOS device which can do this is the General Instruments AY-5-2376, which can be connected to the rows and columns of a keyboard switch matrix. The AY-5-2376 independently detects a keypress by cycling a low down through the rows and checking the columns just as we did in software. When it finds a key pressed, it waits a debounce time. If the key is still pressed after the debounce time, the AY-5-2376 produces the 8-bit code for the pressed key and sends it out to, for example, a microcomputer port on eight parallel lines. To let the microcomputer know that a valid ASCII code is on the data lines, the AY-5-2376 outputs a strobe pulse. The microcomputer can detect this strobe pulse and read in the ASCII code on a polled basis as we showed in Figure 4-14, or it can detect the strobe pulse on an interrupt basis as we showed in Figure 8-9. With the interrupt method the microcomputer doesn't have to pay any attention to the keyboard until it receives an interrupt signal, so this method uses very little of the microcomputer's time.

The AY-5-2376 has a feature called *two-key rollover*. This means that if two keys are pressed at nearly the same time, each key will be detected, debounced, and converted to ASCII. The ASCII code for the first key and a strobe signal for it will be sent out, then the ASCII code for the second key and a strobe signal for it will be sent out. Compare this with two-key lockout which we described previously in the software method of keyboard interfacing.

CONVERTING ONE KEYBOARD CODE TO ANOTHER USING XLAT

Suppose that you are building up a simple microcomputer to control the heating, watering, lighting, and ventilation of your greenhouse. As part of the hardware, you buy a high-quality, fully encoded keyboard at the local electronics surplus store for a few dollars. When you get the keyboard home you find that it works perfectly, but that it outputs EBCDIC codes instead of the ASCII codes that you want. Here's how you use the 8086 XLAT instruction to easily solve this problem.

First look at Table 1-2 which shows the ASCII and EBCDIC codes. The job you have to do here is convert each input EBCDIC input code to the corresponding ASCII code. One way to do this is the compare technique described previously for the hex-keyboard example. For that method you first put the EBCDIC codes in a table in memory in the order shown in Table 1-2, and set up a register as a counter and pointer to the end of the table. Then enter a loop which compares the EBCDIC character in AL with each of the EBCDIC codes in the table until a match is found. The counter is decremented after each compare so that when a match is found, the count register contains the desired ASCII code. This compare technique works well, but for this conversion it will, on the average, have to do 64 compares before a match is found. The compare technique then is often too time-consuming for long tables. The XLAT method is much faster.

The first step in the XLAT method is to make up in memory a table which contains all of the ASCII codes. You can use the DB assembler directive to do this. Since EBCDIC code is an 8-bit code, the table will require 256 memory locations. The trick here is to put each ASCII code in the table at a displacement equal to the value of the EBCDIC character from the start of the table. For example, the EBCDIC code for uppercase A is C1H, so at offset C1H in the table you put the ASCII code for uppercase A, 41H, as shown in Figure 9-22.

To do the actual conversion, you simply load the BX register with the offset of the start of the table, load the EBCDIC character to be converted in the AL register, and do the XLAT instruction. When the 8086 executes the XLAT instruction, it internally adds the EBCDIC value in AL to the starting offset of the table in BX. Because of the way the table is made up, the result of this addition will be a pointer to the desired ASCII value in the table. The 8086 uses this pointer to copy the desired ASCII character from the table to AL.

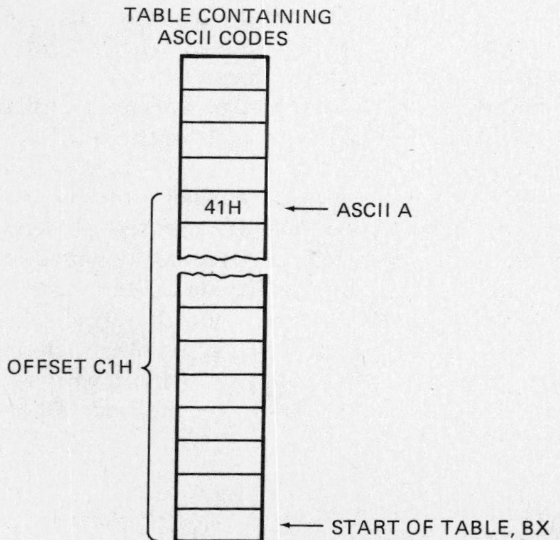

FIGURE 9-22 Memory table setup for using XLAT to convert EBCDIC keycode to ASCII equivalent.

The advantage of this technique is that, no matter where in the table the desired ASCII value is, the conversion only requires execution of two loads and one XLAT instruction. The question may occur to you at this point, "If this method is so fast, why didn't we use it for the hex keypad conversion described earlier?" The answer is that since the row and column code from the hex keypad is an 8-bit code, the lookup table for the XLAT method would require 256 memory locations. Of these 256 memory locations, only 16 would actually be used. This would be a waste of memory, so the compare method is a better choice. It is important for you to become familiar with both code conversion methods, so that you can use the one that best fits a particular application.

DEDICATED MICROPROCESSOR KEYBOARD ENCODERS

Most computers and computer terminals now use detached keyboards with built-in encoders. Instead of using a hardware encoder device such as the AY-5-2376 these keyboards use a dedicated microprocessor. Figure 9-23 shows the encoder circuitry for the IBM PC capacitive-switch matrix keyboard. The 8048 microprocessor used here contains an 8-bit CPU, a ROM, some RAM, three ports, and a programmable timer/counter. A program stored in the on-chip ROM performs the three keyboard tasks and sends the code for a pressed key out to the computer. To cut down the number of connecting wires, the key code is sent out in serial form rather than in parallel form. Some keyboards send data to the computer in serial form using a beam of infrared light instead of a wire.

Note in Figure 9-23 the sense amplifier to detect the change in capacitance produced when a key is pressed. Also note that the 8048 uses a tuned *LC* circuit rather than a more expensive crystal to determine its operating clock frequency.

One of the major advantages of using a dedicated microprocessor to do the three keyboard tasks is programmability. Special function keys on the keyboard can be programmed to send out any code desired for a particular application. By simply plugging in an 8048 with a different lookup table in ROM, the keyboard can be changed from outputting ASCII characters to outputting some other character set.

The IBM keyboard, incidentally, does not send out ASCII codes, but instead sends out a hex "scan" code for each key when it is pressed and a different scan code when that key is released. This double-code approach gives the system software maximum flexibility because a program command can be implemented either when a key is pressed or when it is released.

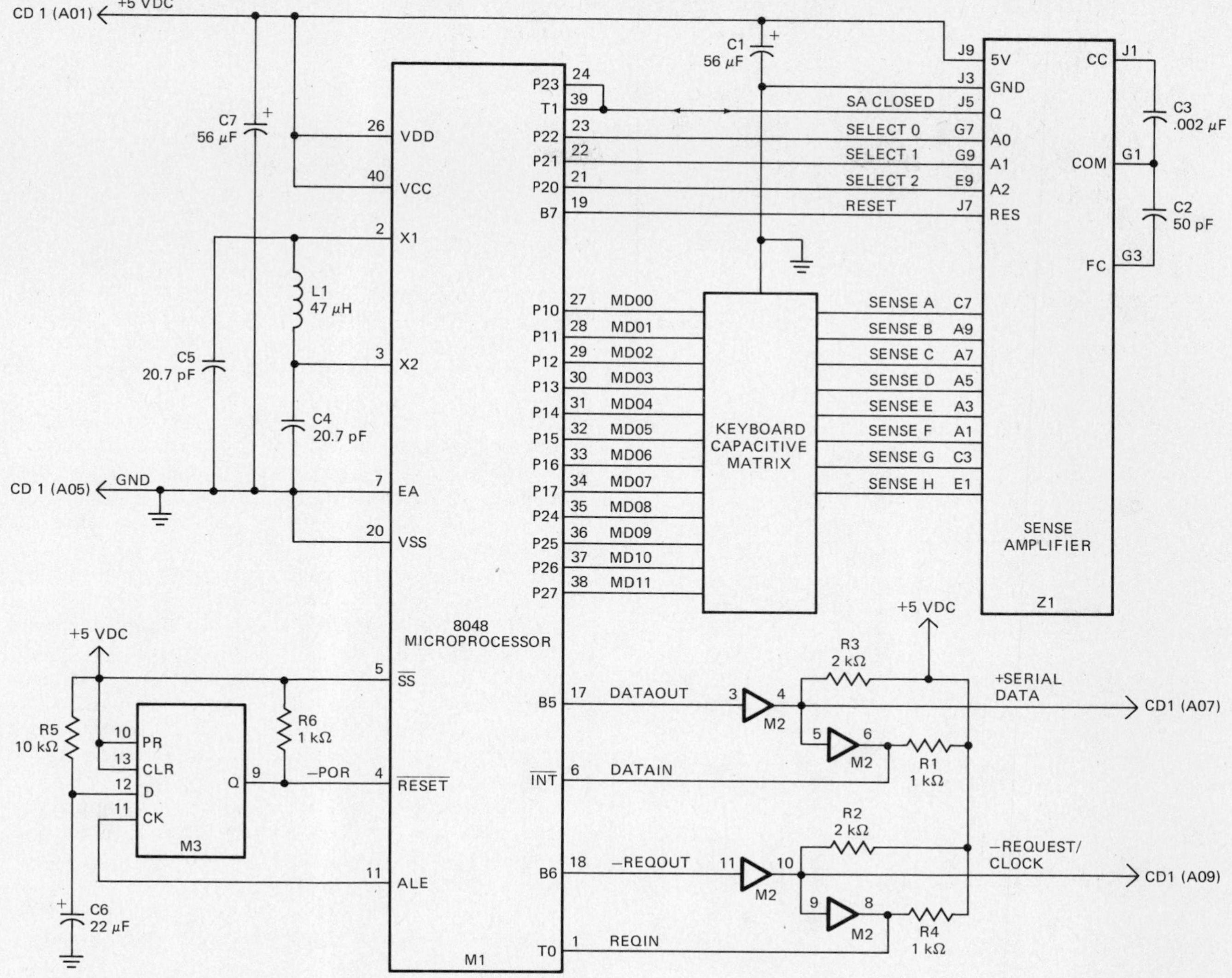

FIGURE 9-23 IBM PC keyboard scan circuitry using a dedicated microprocessor. *(IBM Corporation)*

INTERFACING TO ALPHANUMERIC DISPLAYS

Many microprocessor-controlled instruments and machines need to display letters of the alphabet and numbers to give directions or data values to users. In systems where a large amount of data needs to be displayed, a CRT is usually used to display the data. In a later chapter we show you how to interface a microcomputer to a CRT. In systems where only a small amount of data needs to be displayed, simple digit-type displays are often utilized. There are several technologies used to make these digit-oriented displays, but we only have space here to discuss the two major types. These are *light-emitting diodes* (LEDs) and *liquid-crystal displays* (LCDs). LCD displays use very low power, so they are often used in portable, battery-powered instruments. LCDs however, do not emit their own light, they simply change the reflection of available light. Therefore, for an instrument that is to be used in dim light conditions you have to include a light source for the LCDs, or use LEDs which emit their own light. Starting with LEDs, the following sections show you how to interface these two types of displays to microcomputers.

Interfacing LED Displays to Microcomputers

Alphanumeric LED displays are available in three common formats. For displaying only numbers and hexadecimal letters, simple seven-segment displays such as that shown in Figure 1-6*a* are used.

To display numbers and the entire alphabet, 18-segment displays such as that shown in Figure 9-24*a*, or 5 by 7 dot-matrix displays such as that shown in Figure 9-24*b* can be used. The seven-segment type is the

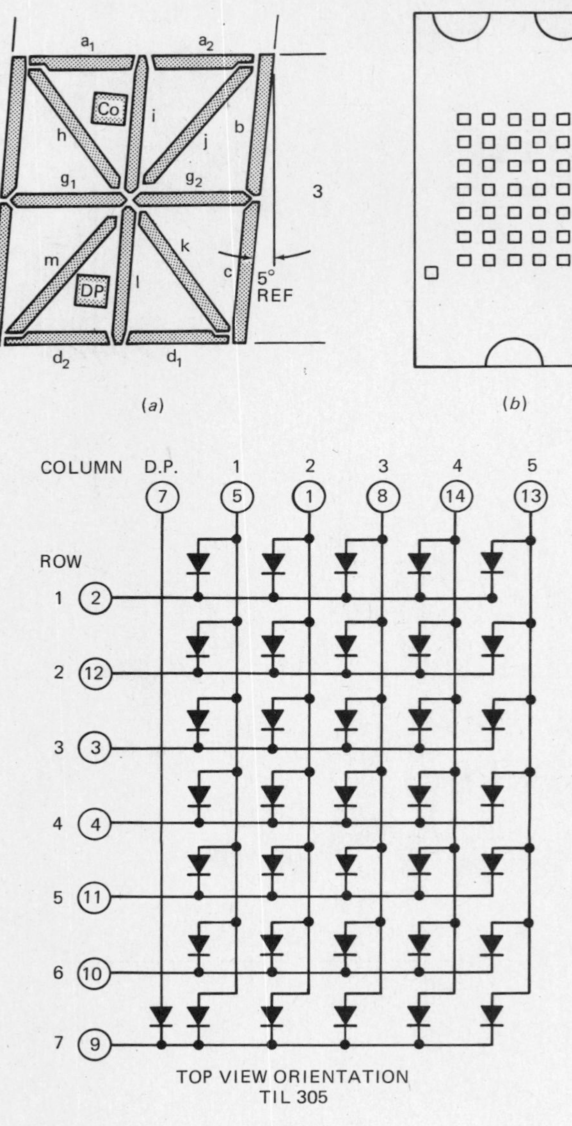

FIGURE 9-24 Eighteen-segment and 5 by 7 matrix LED displays. *(a)* 18-segment. *(b)* 5 by 7 dot-matrix display format. *(c)* 5 by 7 dot-matrix circuit connections.

least expensive, most commonly used, and easiest to interface, so we will concentrate first on how to interface this type. Later we will show the modifications needed to interface to the other types.

STATIC AND MULTIPLEXED DISPLAY CIRCUITS

Figure 9-25 shows a circuit you might use to drive a single, seven-segment, common-anode display. For a common-anode display, a low is applied to a segment to turn it on. When a BCD code is sent to the inputs of the 7447, it outputs lows on the segments required to display the number represented by the BCD code. This circuit connection is referred to as a *static display* because current is being passed through the display at all times. Note that current-limiting resistors are required in series with each segment. Here's how you calculate the value of these resistors.

Each segment requires a current of between 5 and 30 mA to light. Let's assume you want a current of 20 mA. The voltage drop across the LED when it is lit is about 1.5 V. The output low voltage for the 7447 is a maximum of 0.4 V at 40 mA, so assume that it is about 0.2 V at 20 mA. Subtracting these two voltage drops from the supply voltage of 5 V leaves 3.3 V across the current-limiting resistor. Dividing 3.3 V by 20 mA gives a value of 168 Ω for the current-limiting resistor. The voltage drops across the LED and the output of the 7447 are not exactly predictable and the exact current through the LED is not critical as long as we don't exceed its maximum rating. Therefore, a standard value of 150 Ω is reasonable.

The circuit in Figure 9-25 works well for driving just one or two LED digits. However, there are problems if you want to drive, for example, eight digits. The first problem is power consumption. For worst-case calculations, assume that all eight digits are displaying the digit 8 so all seven segments are lit. Seven segments times 20 mA per segment gives a current of 140 mA per digit. Multiplying this by 8 digits gives a total current of 1120 mA or 1.12 A for the the eight digits! A second problem of the static approach is that each display digit requires a separate 7447 decoder, each of which uses, perhaps, another 13 mA. The current required by the decoders and the LED displays might be several times the current required by the rest of the circuitry in the instrument.

To solve the problems of the static display approach, we use a *multiplex* method. A circuit example is the easiest way to explain to you how this multiplexing works. Figure 9-26 shows a circuit you can add to a couple of microcomputer ports to drive some common-anode LED displays in a multiplexed manner. Note that the circuit

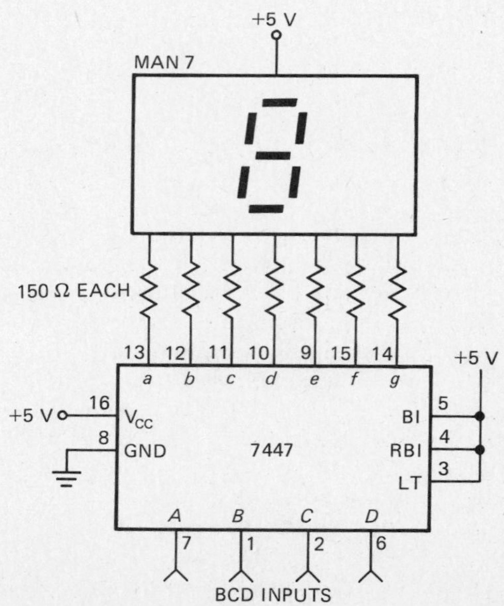

FIGURE 9-25 Circuit for driving single seven-segment LED display with 7447.

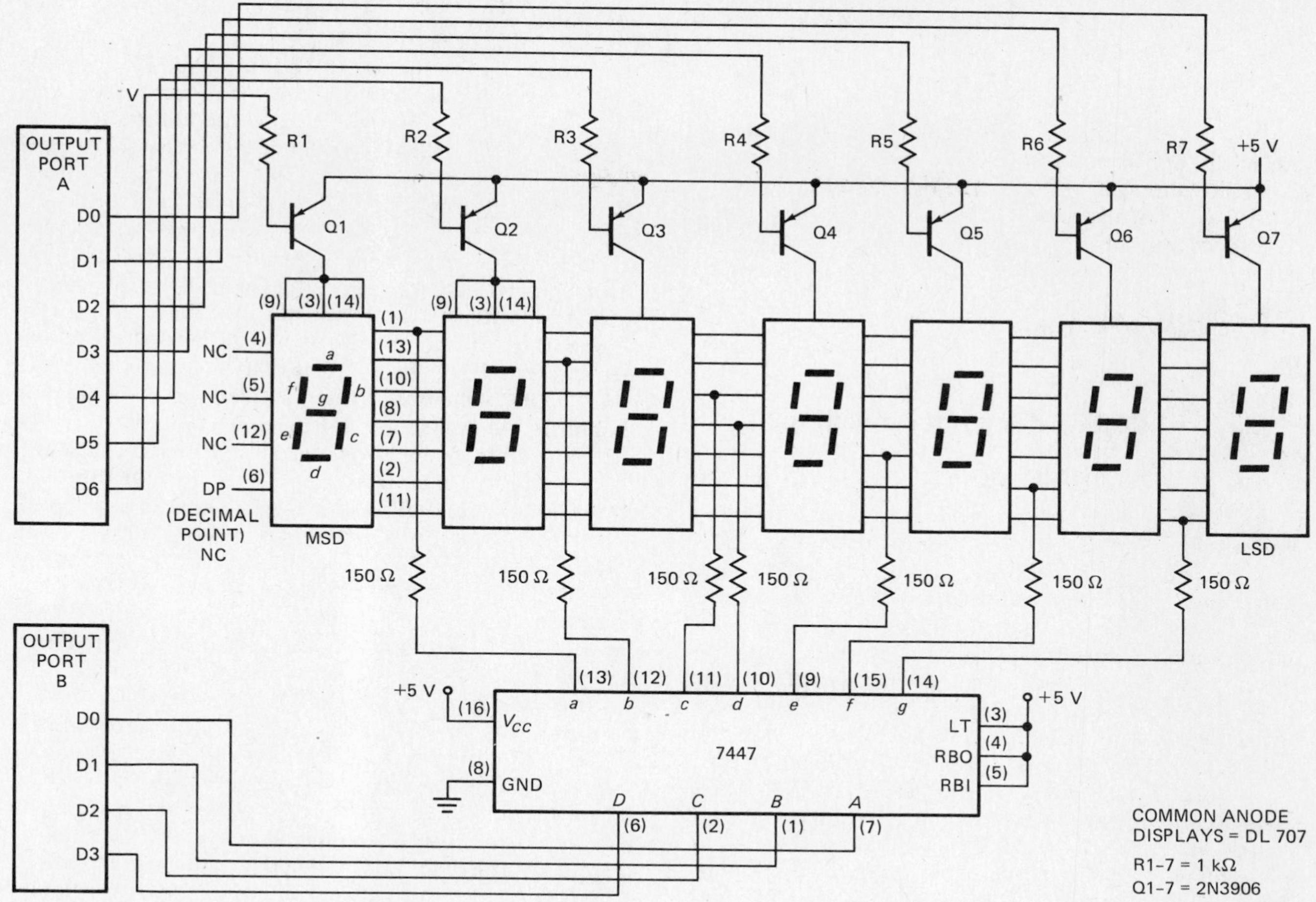

FIGURE 9-26 Circuit for multiplexing seven-segment displays with a microcomputer.

has only one 7447 and that the segment outputs of the 7447 are bused to the segment inputs of all of the digits. The question that may occur to you on first seeing this is, "Aren't all of the digits going to display the same number?" The answer is that they would if all of the digits were turned on at the same time. The trick of multiplexing displays is that the segment information is sent out to all of the digits on the common bus, but only one display digit is turned on at a time. The PNP transistor in series with the common-anode of each digit acts as an on and off switch for that digit. Here's how the multiplexing process works.

The BCD code for digit 1 is first output from port B to the 7447. The 7447 outputs the corresponding seven-segment code on the segment bus lines. The transistor connected to digit 1 is then turned on by outputting a low to that bit of port A. (Remember, a low turns on a PNP transistor.) All of the rest of the bits of port A should be high to make sure no other digits are turned on. After 1 or 2 ms, digit 1 is turned off by outputting all highs to port A. The BCD code for digit 2 is then output to the 7447 on port B, and a word to turn on digit 2 is output on port A. After 1 or 2 ms, digit 2 is turned off and the process repeated for digit 3. The process is continued until all of the digits have had a turn. Then digit 1 and the following digits are lit again in turn. We leave it to you as an exercise at the end of the chapter to write a procedure which is called on an interrupt basis every 2 ms to keep these displays refreshed with some values stored in a table.

With 8 digits and 2 ms per digit you get back to digit 1 every 16 ms or about 60 times a second. This refresh rate is fast enough that, to your eye, the digits will each appear to be lit all of the time. Refresh rates of 40 to 200 times a second are acceptable.

The immediately obvious advantages of multiplexing the displays are that only one 7447 is required, and only one digit is lit at a time. We usually increase the current per segment to between 40 and 60 mA for multiplexed displays so that they will appear as bright as they would if not multiplexed. Even with this increased segment current, multiplexing gives a large saving in power and parts.

NOTE: If you are calculating the current-limiting resistors for multiplexed displays, make sure to check the data sheet for the maximum current rating for the displays you are using.

A disadvantage of the software multiplexing approach shown here is that it puts an additional burden on the CPU. Also, if the CPU gets involved in doing some lengthy task which cannot be interrupted to refresh the display, only one digit of the display will be left lit. An alternative approach to interfacing multiplexed displays to a microcomputer is to use a *dedicated display controller* such as the Intel 8279, which independently keeps displays refreshed and scans a matrix keyboard. In the next section we show you how an 8279 is connected in a circuit, discuss how the 8279 operates, and show you how to initialize an 8279.

Display and Keyboard Interfacing with the 8279

8279 CIRCUIT CONNECTIONS AND OPERATION OVERVIEW

Sheets 7 and 8 of the SDK-86 schematics in Figure 7-6 show the circuit connections for the keypad and the multiplexed seven-segment displays. First let's look at the display circuitry on sheet 8. The displays here are common-anode and each digit has a PNP transistor switch between its anode and the +5-V supply. A logic low is required to turn on one of these switches. Note the 22-μF capacitor between +5 V and ground at the top of the schematic. This is necessary to filter out transients caused by switching the large currents to the LEDs off and on. The segments of each digit are all connected on a common bus. Since these are common-anode displays, a low is needed to turn on a segment. Now let's look at sheet 7 in Figure 7-6 to see how these displays are driven.

The drive for the digit-switch transistors comes from a 7445 BCD to decimal decoder. This device is also known as a one-of-ten-low decoder. When a 4-bit BCD code is applied to the inputs of this device, the output corresponding to that BCD number will go low. For example, when the 8279 outputs 0100 or BCD 4, the 7445 output labeled O4 will go low. In the mode used for this circuit the 8279 outputs a continuous count sequence from 0000 to 1111 over and over. This causes a low to be stepped from output to output of the 7445 in ring counter fashion, turning on each LED digit in turn. Only one output of the 7445 will ever be low at a time, so only one LED digit will be turned on at a time.

The segment bus lines for the displays are connected to the A3–A0 and B3–B0 outputs of the 8279 through some high-current buffers in the ULN2003A. Note that the 22-Ω current-limiting resistors in series with the segment lines are much smaller in value than those we calculated for the static circuit in Figure 9-25. There are two reasons for this. First, there is an additional few tenths of a volt drop across the transistor switch on each anode. Second, when multiplexing displays we pass a higher current through the displays so that they appear as bright as they would if not multiplexed. Here's how the 8279 keeps these displays refreshed.

When you want to display some letters or numbers you write the seven-segment codes for the letters or numbers that you want displayed to a 16-byte RAM inside the 8279. The 8279 then automatically cycles through the process we described previously for sending these codes in sequence to the displays. Figure 9-27 shows the operation in timing diagram form. The 8279 first outputs the binary number for the first digit to the 7445 on the SL0–SL3 lines (Figure 7-6, sheet 7) to turn on the first one of the digit-driver transistors. The lines S0 and S1 in Figure 9-27 represent the SL0 and SL1 lines from the 8279. The 8279 then outputs the seven-segment code for the first digit on the A3–A0 and B3–B0 lines. This will light the first digit with the desired pattern. After 490 μs the 8279 outputs on the A and B lines a code which turns off all of the segments. For the circuit in Figure 7-6, sheet 7, this blanking code will be all zeros (00H). The display is blanked here to prevent "ghosting" of information from one digit to the next when the digit strobe is switched to the next digit. While the displays are blanked, the 8279 sends out the BCD code for the next digit to the 7445 to enable the digit-2 driver transistor. It then sends out the seven-segment code for digit 2 on the A and B lines. This then lights the desired pattern on digit 2. After 490 μs the 8279 blanks the display again and goes on to digit 3. The 8279 steps through all of the digits and then returns to digit 1 and repeats the cycle. Since each digit requires about 640 μs, the 8279 gets back to digit 1 after about 5.1 ms for an 8-digit display and back to digit 1 after about 10.3 ms for a 16-digit display. The time it takes to get back to a digit again is referred to as the *scan time*.

The point is that once you load the seven-segment codes into the internal RAM in the 8279, it automatically keeps the displays refreshed without you having to do anything else in the program. As we will show later, the 8279 can be connected and initialized to refresh a wide variety of displays.

The 8279 can also automatically perform the three tasks for interfacing to a matrix keyboard. Remember from previous discussions that the three tasks involve putting a low on a row of the keyboard matrix and checking the columns of the matrix. If any keys are pressed in that row, a low will be present on the column which contains the key, because pressing a key shorts a row to a column. If no low is found on the columns the low is stepped to the next row and the columns checked again. If a low is found on a column, then, after a debounce time, the column is checked again. If the keypress was valid, a compact code representing the key is constructed. Take a look at the circuit on sheet 7 of Figure 7-6 to see how an 8279 can be connected to do this.

When connected as shown in Figure 7-6, sheet 7, the 74LS156 functions as a one-of-eight-low decoder. In other words, if you apply 011, the binary code for 3, to its inputs, the 74LS156 will output a low on its 2Y3 output. Now remember from the discussion of 8279 display refreshing, that the 8279 is outputting a continuous counting sequence from 0000 to 1111 on its SL0–SL3 lines. This count sequence applied to the inputs of the 74LS156 will cause it to step a low along its outputs. The 74LS156 then puts a low on one row of the keyboard at a time.

The column lines of the keyboard are connected to the

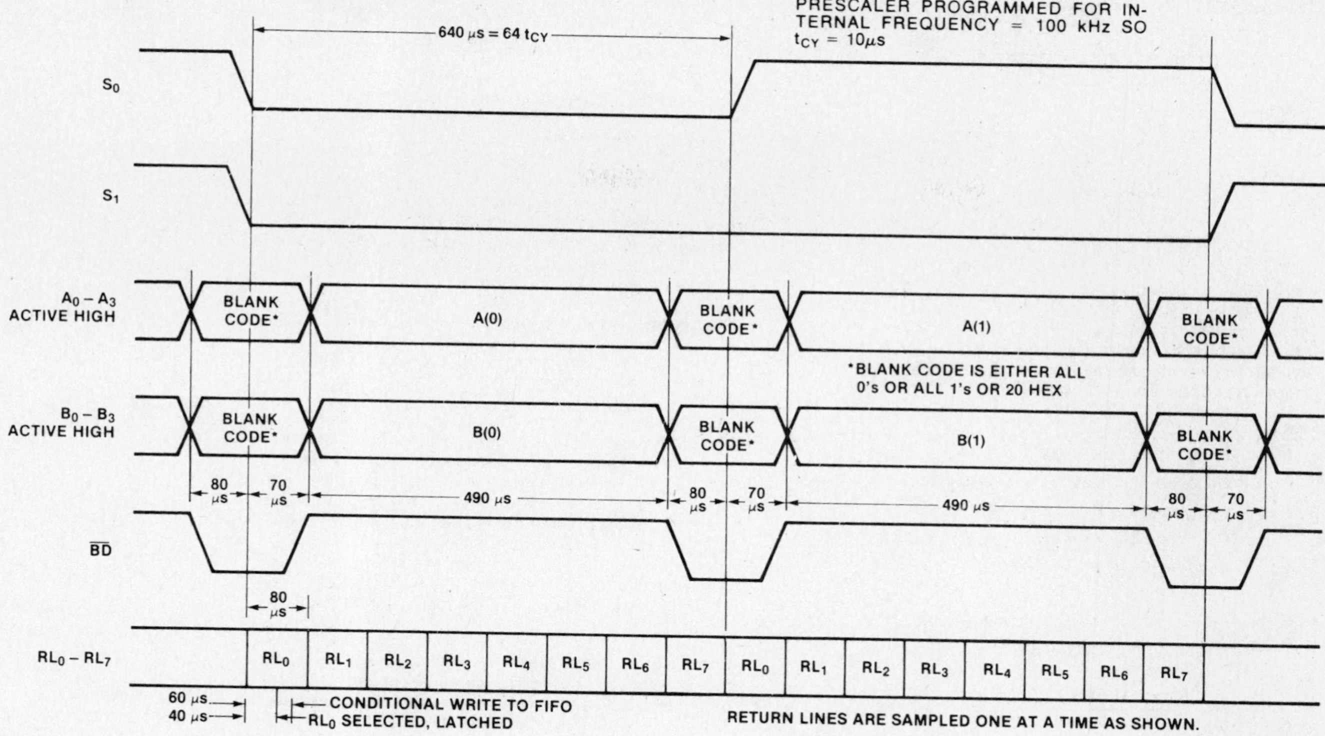

FIGURE 9-27 8279 display refresh timing and keyboard scan timing. *(Intel Corporation)*

return lines, RL0–RL7 of the 8279. As a low is put on each row by the scan-line count and the 74LS156, the 8279 checks these return lines one at a time to see if any of them are low. The bottom line of the timing waveforms in Figure 9-27 shows when the return lines are checked. If the 8279 finds any of the return lines low, indicating a keypress, it waits a debounce time of about 10.3 ms and checks again. If the keypress is still present, the 8279 produces an 8-bit code which represents the key pressed. Figure 9-28 shows the format for the code produced. Three bits of this code represent the number of the row in which it found the pressed key, and another 3 bits represent the column of the pressed key. For interfacing to full typewriter keyboards the shift and control keys are connected to pins 36 and 37 respectively of the 8279. The upper 2 bits of the code produced represent the status of these two keys.

After the 8279 produces the 8-bit code for the pressed key it stores the word in an internal 8-byte *FIFO* RAM. The term FIFO stands for first-in–first-out, which means that when you start reading codes from the FIFO, the first code you read out will be that for the first key pressed. The FIFO can store the codes for up to eight pressed keys before overflowing.

When the 8279 finds a valid keypress, it does two things to let you know about it. It asserts its interrupt request pin, IRQ, high, and it increments a FIFO count in an internal status register. You can connect the IRQ output to an interrupt input and detect when the FIFO has a character for you on an interrupt basis, or you can simply check the count in the status word to determine when the FIFO has a code ready to be read. The point here is that, once the 8279 is initialized, you don't need to pay any attention to it until you want to send some new characters to be displayed, or until it notifies you that it has a valid keypressed code for you in its FIFO. Now that you have an overview of how the 8279 functions, we will show you how to initialize an 8279 to do all of these wondrous things and more.

INITIALIZING AND COMMUNICATING WITH AN 8279

As we have shown before, the first step in initializing a programmable device is to determine the system base address for the device, the internal addresses, and the system addresses for the internal parts. As an example

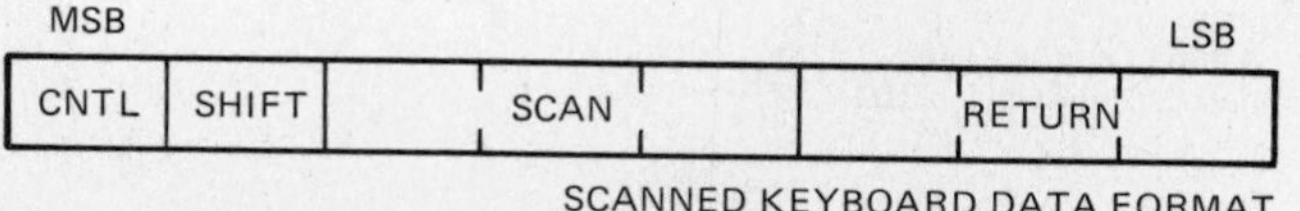

FIGURE 9-28 Format for data word produced by 8279 keyboard encoding.

Keyboard/Display Mode Set

	MSB							LSB
Code:	0	0	0	D	D	K	K	K

Where DD is the Display Mode and KKK is the Keyboard Mode.

DD

0 0 8 8-bit character display — Left entry

0 1 16 8-bit character display — Left entry*

1 0 8 8-bit character display — Right entry

1 1 16 8-bit character display — Right entry

For description of right and left entry, see Interface Considerations. Note that when decoded scan is set in keyboard mode, the display is reduced to 4 characters independent of display mode set.

KKK

0 0 0 Encoded Scan Keyboard — 2 Key Lockout*

0 0 1 Decoded Scan Keyboard — 2-Key Lockout

0 1 0 Encoded Scan Keyboard — N-Key Rollover

0 1 1 Decoded Scan Keyboard — N-Key Rollover

1 0 0 Encoded Scan Sensor Matrix

1 0 1 Decoded Scan Sensor Matrix

1 1 0 Strobed Input, Encoded Display Scan

1 1 1 Strobed Input, Decoded Display Scan

Program Clock

Code:	0	0	1	P	P	P	P	P

All timing and multiplexing signals for the 8279 are generated by an internal prescaler. This prescaler divides the external clock (pin 3) by a programmable integer. Bits PPPPP determine the value of this integer which ranges from 2 to 31. Choosing a divisor that yields 100 kHz will give the specified scan and debounce times. For instance, if Pin 3 of the 8279 is being clocked by a 2 MHz signal, PPPPP should be set to 10100 to divide the clock by 20 to yield the proper 100 kHz operating frequency.

Read FIFO/Sensor RAM

Code:	0	1	0	AI	X	A	A	A	X = Don't Care

The CPU sets up the 8279 for a read of the FIFO/Sensor RAM by first writing this command. In the Scan Keyboard Mode, the Auto-Increment flag (AI) and the RAM address bits (AAA) are irrelevant. The 8279 will automatically drive the data bus for each subsequent read ($A_0 = 0$) in the same sequence in which the data first entered the FIFO. All subsequent reads will be from the FIFO until another command is issued.

In the Sensor Matrix Mode, the RAM address bits AAA select one of the 8 rows of the Sensor RAM. If the AI flag is set (AI = 1), each successive read will be from the subsequent row of the sensor RAM.

Read Display RAM

Code:	0	1	1	AI	A	A	A	A

The CPU sets up the 8279 for a read of the Display RAM by first writing this command. The address bits AAAA select one of the 16 rows of the Display RAM. If the AI flag is set (AI = 1), this row address will be incremented after each following read *or write* to the Display RAM. Since the same counter is used for both reading and writing, this command sets the next read *or write* address and the sense of the Auto-Increment mode for both operations.

Write Display RAM

Code:	1	0	0	AI	A	A	A	A

The CPU sets up the 8279 for a write to the Display RAM by first writing this command. After writing the command with $A_0 = 1$, all subsequent writes with $A_0 = 0$ will be to the Display RAM. The addressing and Auto-Increment functions are identical to those for the Read Display RAM. However, this command does not affect the source of subsequent Data Reads; the CPU will read from whichever RAM (Display or FIFO/Sensor) which was last specified. If, indeed, the Display RAM was last specified, the Write Display RAM will, nevertheless, change the next Read location.

Display Write Inhibit/Blanking

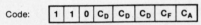

					A	B	A	B
Code:	1	0	1	X	IW	IW	BL	BL

The IW Bits can be used to mask nibble A and nibble B in applications requiring separate 4-bit display ports. By setting the IW flag (IW = 1) for one of the ports, the port becomes marked so that entries to the Display RAM from the CPU do not affect that port. Thus, if each nibble is input to a BCD decoder, the CPU may write a digit to the Display RAM without affecting the other digit being displayed. It is important to note that bit B_0 corresponds to bit D_0 on the CPU bus, and that bit A_3 corresponds to bit D_7.

If the user wishes to blank the display, the BL flags are available for each nibble. The last Clear command issued determines the code to be used as a "blank." This code defaults to all zeros after a reset. Note that both BL flags must be set to blank a display formatted with a single 8-bit port.

Clear

Code:	1	1	0	C_D	C_D	C_D	C_F	C_A

The C_D bits are available in this command to clear all rows of the Display RAM to a selectable blanking code as follows:

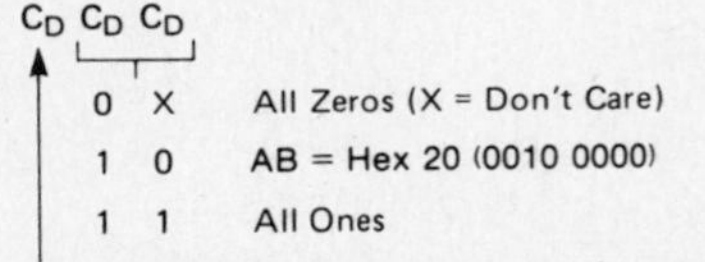

During the time the Display RAM is being cleared (~160 μs), it may not be written to. The most significant bit of the FIFO status word is set during this time. When the Display RAM becomes available again, it automatically resets.

If the C_F bit is asserted ($C_F = 1$), the FIFO status is cleared and the interrupt output line is reset. Also, the Sensor RAM pointer is set to row 0.

C_A, the Clear All bit, has the combined effect of C_D and C_F; it uses the C_D clearing code on the Display RAM and also clears FIFO status. Furthermore, it resynchronizes the internal timing chain.

End Interrupt/Error Mode Set

Code:	1	1	1	E	X	X	X	X	X = Don't care.

For the sensor matrix modes this command lowers the IRQ line and enables further writing into RAM. (The IRQ line would have been raised upon the detection of a change in a sensor value. This would have also inhibited further writing into the RAM until reset).

For the N-key rollover mode — if the E bit is programmed to "1" the chip will operate in the special Error mode. (For further details, see Interface Considerations Section.)

FIGURE 9-29 8279 command word formats and bit descriptions. *(Intel Corporation)* here we will use the 8279 on sheet 7 of Figure 7-6. Figure 7-15*b* shows that the system base address for this device is FFE8H. The 8279 has only two internal addresses which are selected by the logic level on its A0 input, pin 21. If the A0 input is low when the 8279 is selected, then the 8279 is enabled for reading data from it or writing data to it. A0 being high selects the internal control/status registers. For the circuit on sheet 7 of Figure 7-6, the A0 input is connected to system address line A1. Therefore, the data address for this 8279 is FFE8H and the control/status address is FFEAH.

After you have figured out the addresses for a device, the next step is to look at the format for the control word(s) you have to send to the device to make it operate in the mode you want. Figure 9-29 shows the format for the 8279 control words as they appear in the Intel data book. After you use up your 5-minute "freak-out" time we will help you decipher these.

A question that may occur to you when you see all of these control words is, "If the 8279 only has one control register address, how am I going to send it all of these different control words?" The answer to this is that all of the control words are sent to the same control register address, FFEAH for this example. The upper three bits of each control word tell the 8279 which control word is being sent. A pattern of 010 in the upper three bits of a control word, for example, identifies that control word as a "Read FIFO/Sensor RAM" control word.

The first control word you send to initialize the 8279 is the *keyboard/display mode set* word. Keep Figure 9-29 handy as we discuss this and the other control words. The bits labeled DD in the control word specify first of all whether you have 8 digits or 16 digits to refresh. If you have eight or fewer displays, make sure to initialize for 8 digits so the 8279 doesn't spend half of its time refreshing nonexistent displays. The DD bits in this control word also specify the order in which the characters in the internal 16-byte display RAM will be sent out to the digits. In the left entry mode, the seven-segment code in the first address of the internal display RAM will be sent to the leftmost digit of the display. If you want to display the letters AbCd on the 4 leftmost digits of an 8-digit display, then you put the seven-segment codes for these letters in the first four locations of the display RAM as shown in Figure 9-30*a*. Codes put in higher addresses in the display RAM will be displayed on following digits to the right. In the right entry mode, the first code sent to the display RAM is put in the lowest address. This character will be displayed on the rightmost digit of the display. If a second character is written to the display RAM it will be put in the second location in the RAM as shown in Figure 9-30*b*. On the display, however, the new character will be displayed on the rightmost digit, and the previous character will be shifted over to the second position from the right. This is the way that the displays of most calculators function as you enter numbers.

Now let's look at the KKK bits of the mode-set control word. The first choice you have to make here if you are using the 8279 with a keyboard is whether you want *encoded scan* or *decoded scan*. You know that for scanning a keyboard or turning on digit drivers, you need a pattern of stepping lows. In encoded mode the 8279 puts out a binary count sequence on its SL0–SL3 scan lines, and an external decoder such as the 7445 is used to produce the stepping lows. If you only have 4 digits to refresh, you can program the 8279 in decoded mode. In this mode the 8279 directly outputs stepping lows on the four scan lines. The second choice you have to make for this control word is whether you want *two-key lockout*, or *N-key rollover*. In the two-key mode, one key must be released before another keypress will be detected and processed. In the *N*-key rollover mode, if two keys are pressed at nearly the same time, both keypresses will be detected and debounced and their codes put in the FIFO in the order the keys were pressed.

In addition to being used to scan a keyboard, the 8279 can also be used to scan a matrix of switch sensors such as the metal strips and magnetic sensors you see on store windows and doors. In sensor matrix mode the 8279 scans all of the sensors and stores the condition of up to 64 switches in the FIFO RAM. If the condition of any of the switches changes, an IRQ signal is sent out to the processor. An interrupt service procedure can then sound an alarm and turn the dogs loose. The return lines of the 8279 can also function as a strobed input port in much the same way as the 8255A.

The SDK-86 initializes the 8279 for eight-character display, left entry, encoded scan, two-key lockout. See if you can determine the mode-set control word for these conditions. You should get 00000000.

The next control word you have to send the 8279 is

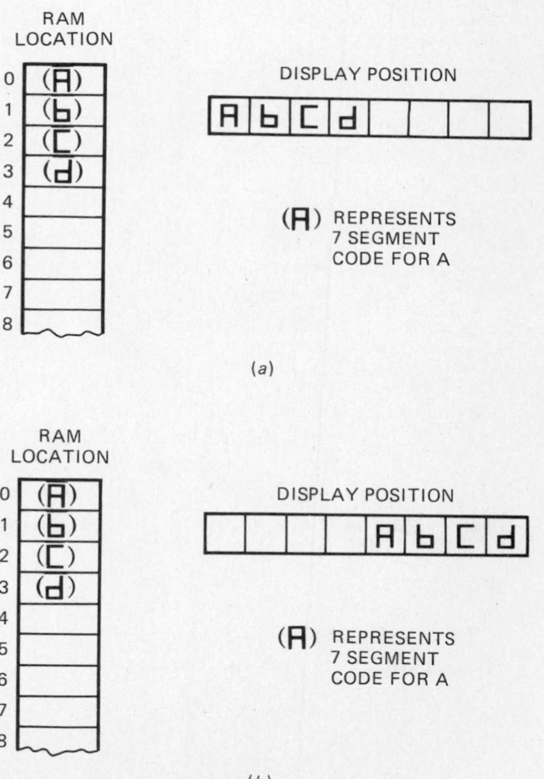

FIGURE 9-30 8279 RAM and display location relationships. *(a)* Left entry. *(b)* Right entry.

the *program-clock word*. The 8279 requires an internal clock frequency of about 100 kHz. A programmable divider in the 8279 allows you to apply some available frequency such as the 2.45-MHz PCLK signal to its clock input and divide this frequency down to the needed 100 kHz. The lower 5 bits of the program clock control word simply represent the binary number you want to divide the applied clock by. For example, if you want to divide the input clock frequency by 24, you send a control word with 001 in the upper 3 bits and 11000 in the lower 5 bits.

The final control word needed for basic initialization is the *clear* word. You need to send this word to tell the 8279 what code to send to the segments to turn them off while the 8279 is switching from one digit to the next. (Refer to Figure 9-27 and its discussion.) In addition to telling the 8279 what blanking character to use during refresh, this control word can be used to clear the display RAM and/or the FIFO at any time. For now we are only concerned with the first function. The lower two bits labeled C_D in the control word in Figure 9-29 specify the desired blanking code. The required code will depend on the hardware connections in a particular system. For the SDK-86 a high from the 8279 turns on a segment, so the required blanking code is all 0's. Therefore you can put 0's in the two C_D bits. The resultant control word is 11000000.

The three control words described so far take care of the basic initialization. However, before you can send codes to the internal display RAM, you have to send the 8279 a *write-display-RAM* control word. This word tells the 8279 that data later sent to the data address should be put in the display RAM, and it tells the 8279 where in the display RAM to put the data byte sent in. Refer to Figure 9-29 for the format of this word. The 8279 has an internal 4-bit pointer to the display RAM. You use the lower 4 bits of this control word to initialize the pointer to the location where you want to write a data byte in the RAM. If you want to write a data byte to the firstlocation in the display RAM, you put 0000 in these bits. If you put a 1 in the auto increment bit, labeled AI in the figure, the internal pointer will be automatically incremented to point to the next RAM location after each data byte is written. To start loading characters in the first location in the RAM and select auto increment, then, the control word is 10010000.

Figure 9-31 shows the sequence of instructions to send the control words we have developed here to the 8279 on the SDK-86 board. Also shown are some instructions to send a seven-segment code to the first location in the display RAM. Note that the control words are all sent to the control address, FFEAH, and the character going to the display RAM is sent to the data address, FFE8H. Also note from sheet 7 of Figure 7-6 that the D0 bit of the byte sent to the display RAM corresponds to segment output B0, and D7 of the byte sent to the display corresponds to segment output A3. This is important to know when you are making up a table of seven-segment codes to send to the 8279.

You now know how to initialize an 8279 and send characters to its display RAM. Two additional points we need to show you are how to read keypressed codes from the FIFO, and how to read the status word. In order to read a code from the FIFO you first have to send a *read FIFO/sensor RAM* control word to the 8279 control address. Figure 9-29 shows the format for this word. For a read of the FIFO RAM, the lower 5 bits of the control word are don't cares, so you can just make them zeros. You send the resultant control word, 01000000, to the control register address and then do a read from the data address. The bottom section of Figure 9-31 shows this.

Now, suppose that the processor receives an interrupt signal from the 8279 indicating that one or more valid keypresses have occurred. The question then comes up, "How do I know how many codes I should read from the FIFO?" The answer to this question is that you read the status register from the control register address before you read the FIFO. Figure 9-32 shows the format for this status word. The lowest 3 bits of the status word indicate the number of valid characters in the FIFO. You can load this number into memory location and count it down as you read in characters. Incidentally, if more than 8 characters have been entered in the FIFO, only the last 8 will be kept. The error-overrun bit, labeled O in the status word, will be set to tell you characters have been lost.

Characters can be read from the 8279 on a polled basis as well as on an interrupt basis. To do this you simply read and test the status word over and over again until bit 0 of the status word becomes a 1. The SDK-86 uses this method to tell when the FIFO holds a keypressed code.

SDK-86 DISPLAY DRIVER PROCEDURE

Figure 9-33 shows an 8086 assembly language procedure to display the contents of the CX register on SDK-86 LED displays. This procedure assumes the 8279 has already been initialized by the SDK-86 monitor program, or as shown in the first part of Figure 9-31. If AL is zero when this procedure is called, the contents of CX will be displayed on the data field LEDs. If AL is not zero then the contents of CX will be displayed on the address field LEDs. There are two main points for you to see in this procedure. The first is the sending of the write-display-RAM control word to the 8279 so we can write to the desired locations in the display RAM. Note that, for the data field, we write a control word of 90H which tells the 8279 to put the next data word sent into the first location in the display RAM. Since the 8279 is initialized for left entry, the first location should correspond to the leftmost display digit. However, if you look at sheet 8 of the SDK-86 schematics you will see that digit 1 (leftmost as far as the 8279 is concerned) is actually the rightmost on the board. This means that, for the SDK-86, the position of a seven-segment code in the display RAM corresponds to its position in the display starting from the right! All you have to do is send the seven-segment code for a number you want to display in a particular digit position to the corresponding location in the display RAM.

The next part of the display procedure to take a close look at is the instructions which convert the four hex

```
INITIALIZATION

MOV  DX, 0FFEAH          ; Point at 8279 control address
MOV  AL, 00000000B       ; Mode set word for left entry,
                         ; encoded scan, 2-key lockout
OUT  DX, AL              ; Send to 8279
MOV  AL, 00111000B       ; Clock word for divide by 24
OUT  DX, AL
MOV  AL, 11000000B       ; Clear display char is all zeros
OUT  DX, AL

SEND SEVEN SEGMENT CODE TO DISPLAY RAM

MOV  AL, 10010000B       ; Write display RAM, first location,
                         ;  auto increment
MOV  DX, 0FFEAH          ; Point at 8279 control address
OUT  DX, AL              ; Send control word
MOV  DX, 0FFE8H          ; Point at 8279 data address
MOV  AL, 6FH             ; Seven segment code for 9
OUT  DX, AL              ; Send to display RAM
MOV  AL, 5BH             ; Seven segment code for 2
OUT  DX, AL              ; Send to display RAM
; .
; .
; .

READ KEYBOARD CODE FROM FIFO

MOV  AL, 01000000B       ; Control word for read FIFO RAM
MOV  DX, 0FFEAH          ; Point at 8279 control address
OUT  DX, AL              ; Send control word
MOV  DX, 0FFE8H          ; Point at 8279 data address
IN   AL, DX              ; Read FIFO RAM
```

FIGURE 9-31 8086 instructions to initialize SDK-86 8279, write to display RAM, and read FIFO RAM.

nibbles in the CX register to the corresponding seven-segment codes for sending to the display RAM. To do this we first shuffle and mask to get each nibble into a byte by itself. We then use a lookup table and the XLAT instruction to do the actual conversion. Note that when making up seven-segment codes for the SDK-86 board, a high turns on a segment, bit D0 of a display RAM byte represents the "a" segment, bit D6 represents the "g" segment, and bit D7 represents the decimal point. Work your way through this section as a review of using XLAT.

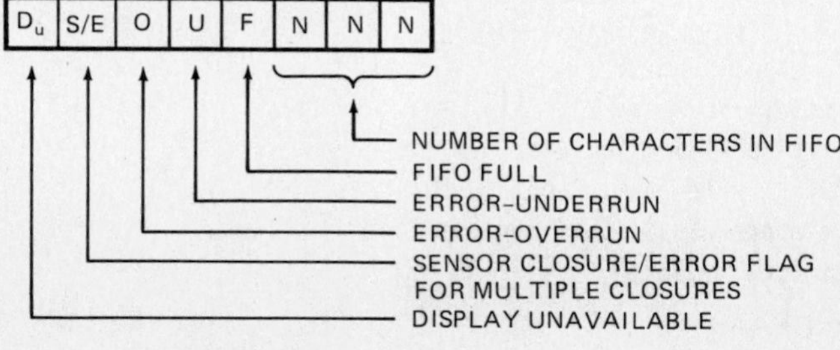

FIGURE 9-32 8279 status word format.

INTERFACING TO 18-SEGMENT AND DOT-MATRIX LED DISPLAYS

In the preceding examples we used an 8279 to refresh some seven-segment displays. The seven-segment codes for each digit were stored in successive locations in the display RAM. To display ASCII codes on 18-segment LED displays you can store the ASCII codes for each digit in the display RAM. (Remember that the A lines are driven from the upper nibble of the display RAM and the B lines are driven by the lower nibble). An external ROM is used to convert the ASCII codes to the required 18-segment codes and send them to the segment drivers. Strobes for each digit driver are produced just as they are for the seven-segment displays in Figure 7-6. The refreshing of each digit then proceeds just as it does for the seven-segment displays.

```
PAGE ,132
;8086 PROCEDURE TO DISPLAY DATA ON SDK-86 LEDs
;ABSTRACT:  This procedure will display a 4-digit hex or BCD number
;           passed in the CX register on LEDs of the SDK-86
;INPUTS:    Data in CX, control in AL.
;           AL =  00H  data displayed in data-field of LEDs
;           AL <> 00H, data displayed in address field of LEDs.
;PORTS:     Uses none
;PROCEDURES:Uses none
;REGISTERS: saves all registers and flags
PUBLIC  DISPLAY
DATA_HERE SEGMENT       WORD    PUBLIC
SEVEN_SEG       DB      3FH, 06H, 5BH, 4FH, 66H, 6DH, 7DH, 07H
                ;        0    1    2    3    4    5    6    7
                DB      7FH, 6FH, 77H, 7CH, 39H, 5EH, 79H, 71H
                ;        8    9    A    b    C    d    E    F
DATA_HERE ENDS
CODE_HERE       SEGMENT WORD    PUBLIC
                ASSUME CS:CODE_HERE, DS:DATA_HERE
DISPLAY PROC    FAR
        PUSHF                           ; save flags
        PUSH DS                         ; save caller's DS
        PUSH AX                         ; save registers
        PUSH BX
        PUSH CX
        PUSH DX
        MOV  BX, DATA_HERE              ; init DS as needed for procedure
        MOV  DS, BX
        MOV  DX, 0FFEAH                 ; point at 8279 control address
        CMP  AL, 00H                    ; see if data field required
        JZ   DATFLD                     ; yes, load control word for data field
        MOV  AL, 94H                    ; no, load address-field control word
        JMP  SEND                       ; go send control word
DATFLD: MOV  AL, 90H                    ; load control word for data field
SEND:   OUT  DX, AL                     ; send control word to 8279
        MOV  BX, OFFSET SEVEN_SEG       ; pointer to seven-segment codes
        MOV  DX, 0FFE8H                 ; point at 8279 display RAM
        MOV  AL, CL                     ; get low byte to be displayed
        AND  AL, 0FH                    ; mask upper nibble
        XLATB                           ; translate lower nibble to 7-seg code
        OUT  DX, AL                     ; send to 8279 display RAM
        MOV  AL, CL                     ; get low byte again
        MOV  CL, 04                     ; load rotate count
        ROL  AL, CL                     ; Move upper nibble into low position
        AND  AL, 0FH                    ; Mask upper nibble
        XLATB                           ; translate 2nd nibble to 7-seg code
        OUT  DX, AL                     ; send to 8279 display RAM
        MOV  AL, CH                     ; Get high byte to translate
        AND  AL, 0FH                    ; Mask upper nibble
        XLATB                           ; Translate to 7-seg code
        OUT  DX, AL                     ; send to 8279 display RAM
        MOV  AL, CH                     ; get high byte to fix upper nibble
        ROL  AL, CL                     ; move upper nibble into low position
        AND  AL, 0FH                    ; mask upper nibble
```

FIGURE 9-33 Procedure to display contents of CX register on SDK-86 LED displays.

```
        XLATB               ; translate to 7-seg code
        OUT  DX, AL         ; 7-seg code to 8279 display RAM
        POP  DX             ; restore all registers and flags
        POP  CX
        POP  BX
        POP  AX
        POP  DS
        POPF
        RET
DISPLAY ENDP
CODE_HERE ENDS
        END
```

FIGURE 9-33 (*continued*)

Refreshing 5 by 7 dot-matrix LED displays is a little more complex, because instead of lighting an entire digit, you have to refresh one row or one column at a time in each digit. Think of how you might do this for one 5 by 7 matrix which has its row drivers connected to one port and its column drivers connected to another port. To display a letter on this matrix you send out the code for the first column to the row drivers and send a code to the column drivers to turn on that column. After a millisecond or so you turn off the first column, send out the code for the second column, and light the second column. You repeat the process until all of the columns have been refreshed and then cycle back to column 1 again. You could use additional ports to drive additional digits, but the number of ports required soon gets too large. To reduce the number of ports required, inexpensive external latches can be used to hold the row codes for each digit. You then write the row codes for the first columns of all the digits to these latches. The columns of all the digits are connected in parallel, so when you output a code to turn on the first column, the first column of each digit will be lit with the code stored in its row latch. The process is repeated for each column until all columns are refreshed, and then started over again.

To further simplify interfacing multidigit dot-matrix LED displays to a microcomputer, Beckman Instruments, Hewlett-Packard, and several other companies make large integrated display/driver devices which require you to send only a series of ASCII codes for the characters you want displayed and one or two strobe signals for each character sent.

Liquid Crystal Display Operation and Interfacing

LCD OPERATION

Liquid crystal displays are created by sandwiching a thin (10- to 12-micron) layer of a liquid-crystal fluid between two glass plates. A transparent, electrically conductive film or backplane is put on the rear glass sheet. Transparent sections of conductive film in the shape of the desired characters are coated on the front glass plate. When a voltage is applied between a segment and the backplane, an electric field is created in the region under the segment. This electric field changes the transmission of light through the region under the segment film.

There are two commonly available types of LCD: *dynamic scattering*, and *field effect*. The dynamic scattering type scrambles the molecules where the field is present. This produces an etched-glass-looking light character on a dark background. Field effect types use polarization to absorb light where the electric field is present. This produces dark characters on a silver-gray background.

Most LCDs require a voltage of 2 or 3 V between the backplane and a segment to turn on the segment. You can't, however, just connect the backplane to ground and drive the segments with the outputs of a TTL decoder as we did the static LED display in Figure 9-25! The reason for this is that LCDs rapidly and irreversibly deteriorate if a steady dc voltage of more than about 50 mV is applied between a segment and the backplane. To prevent a dc buildup on the segments, the segment-drive signals for LCDs must be square waves with a frequency of 30–150 Hz. Even if you pulse the TTL decoder, it still will not work because the output low voltage of TTL devices is greater than 50 mV. CMOS gates are often used to drive LCDs.

Figure 9-34*a* shows how two CMOS gate outputs can be connected to drive an LCD segment and backplane. Figure 9-34*b* shows typical drive waveforms for the backplane and for the on and the off segments. The off (in this case unused) segment receives the same drive signal as the backplane. There is never any voltage between them, so no electric field is produced. The waveform for the on segment is 180° out of phase with the backplane signal, so the voltage between this segment and the backplane will always be +V. The logic for this is quite simple, because you only have to produce two signals, a square wave and its complement. To the driving gates the segment-backplane sandwich appears as a somewhat leaky capacitor. The CMOS gates can easily supply the current required to charge and discharge this small capacitance.

Older and/or inexpensive LCD displays turn on and off too slowly to be multiplexed in the way we do with LED displays. At 0°C some LCDs may require as much as 0.5 seconds to turn on or off. To interface to these types we use a nonmultiplexed driver device. Newer LCDs can turn on and off faster. To reduce the number of connect-

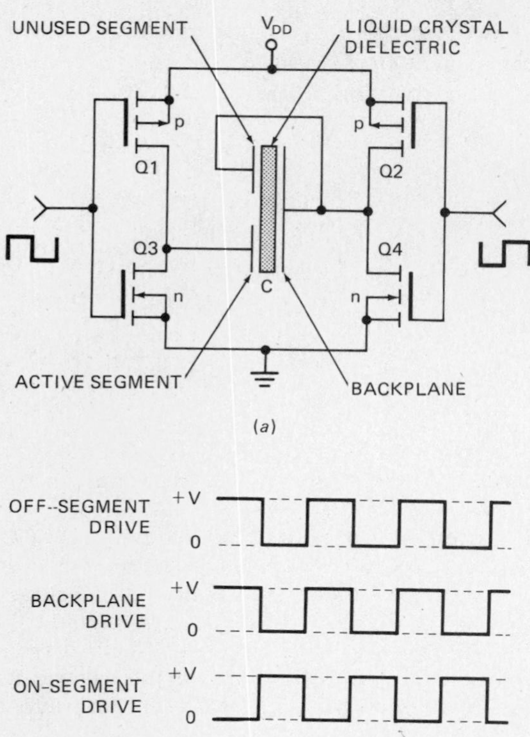

FIGURE 9-34 LCD drive circuit and drive waveforms. *(a)* CMOS drive circuits. *(b)* Segment and backplane drive waveforms.

ing wires when interfacing to these, we use a *triplex* technique. The following sections show you brief examples of each of these.

INTERFACING A MICROCOMPUTER TO NONMULTIPLEXED LCD DISPLAYS

Figure 9-35 shows how an Intersil ICM7211M can be connected to drive a 4-digit, nonmultiplexed, seven-segment LCD display such as you might buy from your local electronics surplus store. The 7211M inputs can be connected to port pins or directly to microcomputer buses as shown. For our example here we have connected the $\overline{CS}$ inputs to the Y2 output of the 74LS138 port decoder that we showed you how to add to an SDK-86 board in Figure 8-14. According to the truth table in Figure 8-15, the device will then be addressable as ports with a base address of FF10H. SDK-86 system address line A2 is connected to the digit-select input (DS2) and system address line A1 is connected to the DS1 input. This gives digit 4 a system address of FF10H. Digit 3 will be addressed at FF12H, digit 2 at FF14H, and digit 1 at FF16H. The data inputs are connected to the lower four lines of the SDK-86 data bus. The oscillator input is left open.

To display a character on one of the digits, you simply put the 4-bit hex code for that digit in the lower 4 bits of the AL register, and output it to the address of that digit. The ICM 7211M converts the 4-bit hex code to the required seven-segment code. The rising edge of the $\overline{CS}$ input signal causes the seven-segment code to be latched in the output latches for the addressed digit. An internal oscillator automatically generates the segment and backplane drive waveforms shown in Figure 9-34*b*.

INTERFACING TO TRIPLEXED LCD DISPLAYS

For many microcomputer-based instruments we want to display letters as well as numbers. To do this we usually use 18-segment digits such as the one shown in Figure 9-24*a*. For 18-segment LED digits we simply bus all of the segment inputs and multiplex the displays as described previously. Current LCD digits, however, cannot be multiplexed in the same way because of their slow switching response time. To reduce the connections required for a set of LCD digits, a compromise approach called *triplexing* has been devised. For triplexing, each digit is built as a matrix of six rows and three columns. Each digit has a 6-bit latch to hold the 6-bit row code for the segments in a column. The row codes are sent to all of the latches and the columns of each digit turned on. After a period of time the row codes for the second column are sent out to the latches. The first column is turned off and the second column turned on. After a period of time the row codes for the third columns are sent out to digits and the third columns turned on. At any given time one of the three columns in each display is activated, which is where the term triplexing comes from. Since only three columns ever need to be refreshed, no matter how many digits are connected, the switching rates are much lower than they are for the LED multiplexing method. The Intersil ICM7233 is an example of a device which contains all of the circuitry needed to drive four triplexed, 18-segment LCD digits. It can be connected directly to a microcomputer bus as we showed for the ICM7211M in Figure 9-35. To display a series of characters all you have to do is output a 6-bit ASCII code for each character to the appropriate digit address in the device. A demonstration kit containing two 7233s, eight 18-segment LCD displays and a PC board is available from Intersil, if you want to add this type of display to something you are building.

INTERFACING MICROCOMPUTER PORTS TO HIGH-POWER DEVICES

As shown for the 8255A in Figure 9-36, the output pins on programmable port devices can typically source only a few tenths of a milliampere from the +5-V supply and sink only 1 or 2 mA to ground. If you want to control some high-power devices such as lights, heaters, solenoids, and motors with your microcomputer, you need to use interface devices between the port pins and the high-power device. This section shows you a few of the commonly used devices and techniques.

INTEGRATED CIRCUIT BUFFERS

One approach to buffering the outputs of port devices is with TTL buffers such as the 7406 hex inverting and 7407 hex noninverting. In Figure 9-14 for example, we

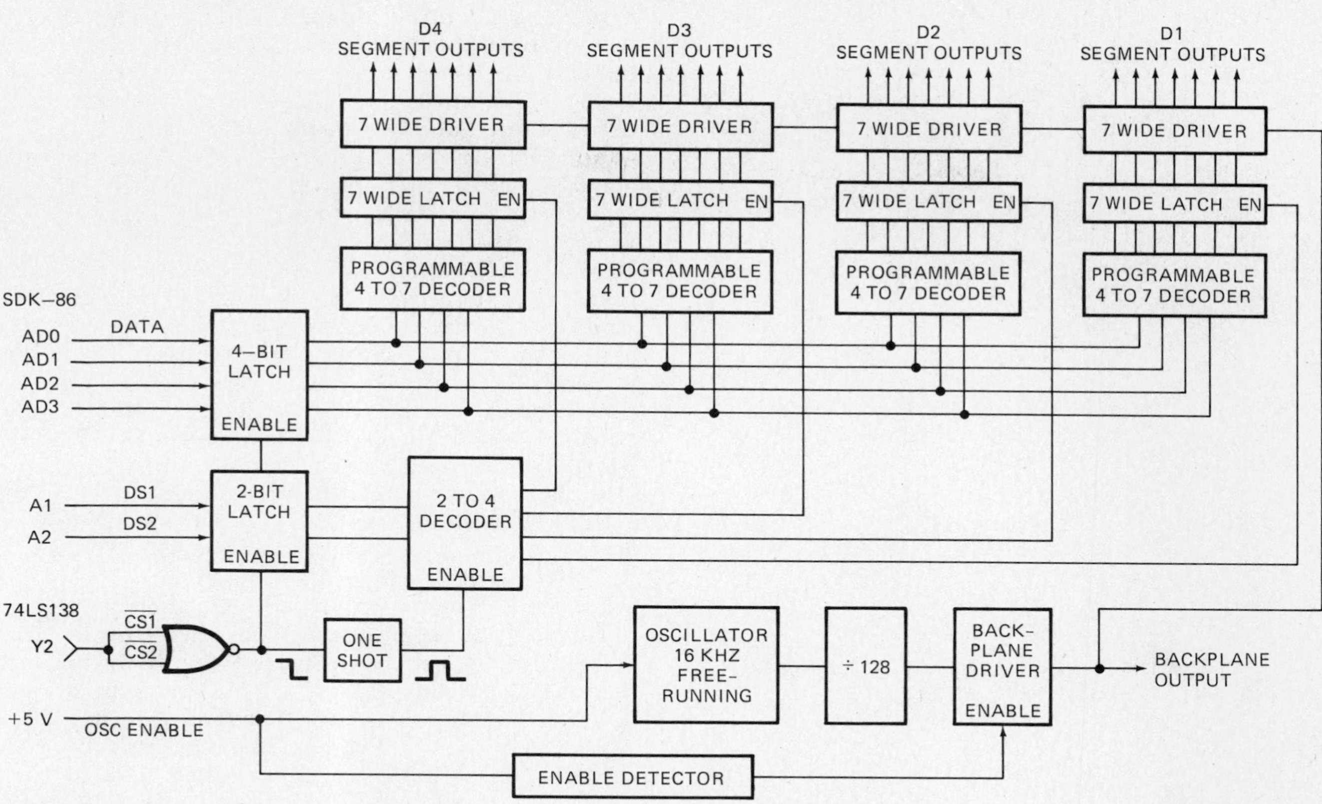

FIGURE 9-35 Circuit for interfacing four LCD digits to an SDK-86 bus using Intersil ICM7211M.

show 74LS07 buffers on the lines from ports to a printer. In an actual circuit the 8255A outputs to the computer-controlled lathe in Figure 9-6 should also have buffers of this type. The 74LS06 and 74LS07 have open collector outputs, so you have to connect a pull-up resistor from each output to +5 V. Each of the buffers in a 74LS06 or 74LS07 can sink as much as 40 mA to ground. You could then drive an LED with each output by simply connecting the LED and a current-limiting resistor in series between the buffer output and +5 V.

Buffers of this type have the advantage that they come six to a package, and they are easy to apply. For cases where you only need a buffer on one or two port pins, you may use discrete transistors.

D.C. CHARACTERISTICS
$T_A = 0°C$ to $70°C$, $V_{CC} = +5\ V \pm 5\%$; GND = 0V

SYMBOL	PARAMETER	MIN.	MAX.	UNIT	TEST CONDITIONS
V_{IL}	INPUT LOW VOLTAGE	−0.5	0.8	V	
V_{IH}	INPUT HIGH VOLTAGE	2.0	V_{CC}	V	
V_{OL} (DB)	OUTPUT LOW VOLTAGE (DATA BUS)		0.45	V	$I_{OL} = 2.5$ mA
V_{OL} (PER)	OUTPUT LOW VOLTAGE (PERIPHERAL PORT)		0.45	V	$I_{OL} = 1.7$ mA
V_{OH} (DB)	OUTPUT HIGH VOLTAGE (DATA BUS)	2.4		V	$I_{OH} = -400\ \mu A$
V_{OH} (PER)	OUTPUT HIGH VOLTAGE (PERIPHERAL PORT)	2.4		V	$I_{OH} = -200\ \mu A$
I_{DAR}[1]	DARLINGTON DRIVE CURRENT	−1.0	−4.0	mA	$R_{EXT} = 750\ \Omega$; $V_{EXT} = 1.5$ V
I_{CC}	POWER SUPPLY CURRENT		120	mA	
I_{IL}	INPUT LOAD CURRENT		±10	μA	$V_{IN} = V_{CC}$ TO 0V
I_{OFL}	OUTPUT FLOAT LEAKAGE		±10	μA	$V_{OUT} = V_{CC}$ TO 0V

NOTE 1: AVAILABLE ON ANY 8 PINS FROM PORT B AND C.

FIGURE 9-36 8255A dc operating characteristics.

FIGURE 9-37 Transistor buffer circuits for driving LED from 8255A port pin. *(a)* NPN. *(b)* PNP.

TRANSISTOR BUFFERS

Figure 9-37 shows some transistor circuits you can connect to microprocessor port lines to drive LEDs or small dc lamps. We will show you how to quickly determine the parts values to put in these circuits for your particular application. First determine how much current you need to flow through the LED, lamp, or other device. For our example here, suppose that we want 20 mA to flow through an LED. Next determine whether you want a logic high on the output port pin to turn on the device or whether you want a logic low to turn on the device. If you want a logic high to turn on the LED, then use the NPN circuit. Now look through your transistor collection to find an NPN transistor which can carry the required current, has a collector-to-emitter breakdown voltage (V_{BCEO}) greater than the applied supply voltage, and can dissipate the power generated by the current flowing through it. We usually keep some inexpensive 2N3904 NPNs and some 2N3906 PNPs on hand for low-current switch applications such as this. Some alternatives are the 2N2222 NPN and the 2N2907 PNP. When you decide what transistor you are going to use, look up its current gain, h_{FE}, on a data sheet. If you don't have a data sheet, assume a value of 50 for the current gain of small-signal transistors such as these. Remember, current gain, or beta as it is commonly called, is the ratio of collector current to the base current needed to produce that current. To produce a collector current of 20 mA in a transistor with a beta of 50 then requires a base current of 20 mA/50 or 0.4 mA. To drive this buffer transistor, then, the output port pin only has to supply the 0.4 mA.

A look at the V_{OH}(PER) specification of the 8255A in Figure 9-36 shows that an 8255A peripheral port pin can only source 200 μA (0.2 mA) of current and still maintain a legal TTL-compatible output voltage of 2.4 V! When you see this specification, you may at first think the port output will not be able to drive the transistor. However, the fact is that the outputs can source more than 0.2 mA, but if they source more than 0.2 mA, the output high voltage will drop below 2.4 V. You don't care about the output high voltage dropping below 2.4 V except in the unlikely case that you are trying to drive a logic gate input off the same port pin as the transistor. The I_{DAR} specification in Figure 9-36 indicates that port B and port C pins can source at least 1.0 mA, but when doing so the output voltage may be as low as 1.5 V. Let's assume an output voltage of 2.0 V for calculating the value of our current-limiting resistor, R_b. The value of this resistor is not very critical as long as it lets through enough base current to drive the transistor. The base of the NPN transistor will be at about 0.7 V when the transistor is conducting, and the output port pin will be at least 2.0 V. Dividing the 1.3 V across R_b by the desired current of 0.4 mA gives an R_b value of 3.25 kΩ. A 2.7-kΩ or 3.3-kΩ resistor will work fine here.

For the PNP circuit in Figure 9-37*b* the output port pin can easily supply the needed drive current. The V_{OL}(PER) specification in Figure 9-36 shows that an output pin can sink at least 1.7 mA and still have an output low voltage no greater than 0.45 V. R_b in Figure 9-37*b* has about 4 V across it. Dividing this voltage by the required 0.4 mA gives an R_b value of 10 kΩ.

When you need to switch currents larger than about 50 mA on and off with an output port line, a single transistor does not have enough current gain to do this dependably. One solution to this problem is to connect two transistors in a Darlington configuration. Figure 9-38 shows how we might do this to drive a small solenoid-controlled valve which controls the flow a chemical into our printed-circuit-board-making machine, or a small solenoid in the print heads of a dot-matrix printer. For the case of the printer solenoid, when a current is passed through the coil of the solenoid, a print wire is

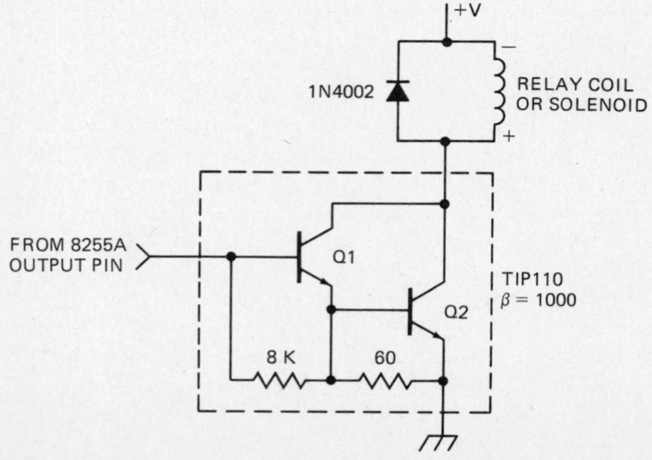

FIGURE 9-38 Darlington transistor used to drive relay coil or solenoid.

forced out. The print wire hits the ribbon against the paper and produces a dot on the paper.

The dotted lines around the two transistors in Figure 9-38 indicate that both devices are contained in the same package. Here's how this configuration works. The output port pin supplies base current to transistor Q1. This base current produces a collector current beta times as large in Q1. The collector current of Q1 becomes the base current of Q2 and is amplified by the current gain of Q2. The result of all this is that the device acts like a single transistor with a current gain of (beta Q1 × beta Q2) and a base-emitter voltage of about 1.4 V. The internal resistors help turn off the transistors. The TIP110 device we show here has a minimum beta of 1000 at 1 A. If we assume that we need 400 mA to drive the solenoid, then the worst-case current that must be supplied by the output port pin is about 400 mA/1000 or 0.4 mA, which it can easily do. If the drive current required for the Darlington is too high for the port output, you can add a resistor from the transistor base to +5 V to supply the added current. The output can easily sink the added current when the output is in the low state. Also another transistor could be added as a buffer between the output pin and the Darlington input. Note that since the V_{BE} of the Darlington is about 2 V, no R_b is needed here. Now let's check out the power dissipation.

According to the data sheet for the TIP110, it comes in a TO-220 package which can dissipate up to 2 W at an ambient temperature of 25°C with no heat sink. With 400 mA flowing through the device it will have a collector-emitter saturation voltage of about 2 V. Multiplying the current of 400 mA times the voltage drop of 2 V gives us a power dissipation of 0.8 W for our circuit here. This is well within the limits for the device. A rule of thumb that we like to follow is, if the calculated power dissipation for a device such as this is more than half of its 25°C no-heat-sink rating, mount the device on the chassis or a heat sink to make sure it will work on a hot day. If mounted on the appropriate heat sink the device will dissipate 50 W at 25°C.

One more important point to mention about the circuit in Figure 9-38 is the reverse-biased diode connected across the solenoid coil. You must remember to put in this diode whenever you drive an inductive load such as a solenoid, relay, or motor. Here's why. The basic principle of an inductor is that it fights against a change in the current through it. When you apply a voltage to the coil by turning on the transistor, it takes a while for the current to start flowing. This does not cause any major problems. However, when you turn off the transistor, the collapsing magnetic field in the inductor keeps the current flowing for a while. This current cannot flow through the transistor because it is off. Instead this current develops a voltage across the inductor with the polarity shown by the + and − signs on the coil in Figure 9-38. This induced voltage, sometimes called inductive "kick," will usually be large enough to break down the transistor if you forget to put in the diode. When the coil is conducting, the diode is reverse-biased so it doesn't conduct. However, as soon as the induced voltage reaches 0.7 V this diode turns on and supplies a return path for the induced current. The voltage across the inductor is clamped at 0.7 V, which saves the transistor.

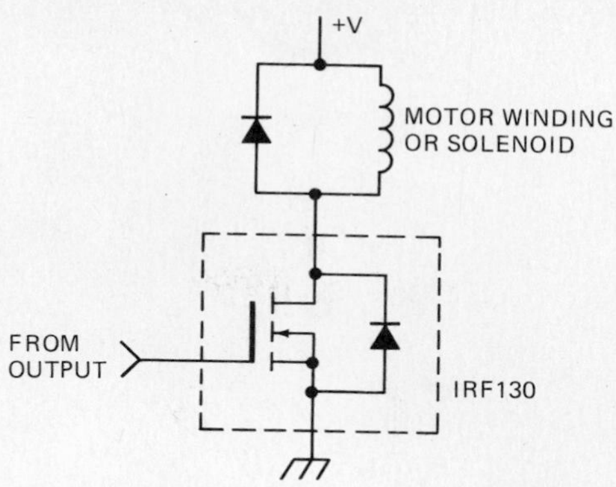

FIGURE 9-39 Power MOSFET circuit for driving solenoid or motor winding.

Figure 9-39 shows how a power MOSFET transistor can be used to drive a solenoid, relay, or motor winding. Power MOSFETS are several times more expensive than bipolar Darlingtons, but they have the advantage that they only require a voltage to drive them. The Motorola IRF130 shown here, for example, only requires a maximum gate voltage of 4 V for a drain current of 8 A. Note that a diode is required across the coil here also.

INTERFACING TO AC POWER DEVICES

To turn 110-V, 220-V, or 440-V ac devices on and off under microprocessor control we usually use *mechanical* or *solid-state relays*. The control circuitry for both of these types of relay is electrically isolated from the actual switch. This is very important because if the 110 V ac line gets shorted to the V_{cc} line of a microcomputer, it usually bakes most of the microcomputer's ICs. Figure 9-40*a* shows a picture of a mechanical relay. This relay has both normally open and normally closed contacts. When a current is passed through the coil of the relay, the switch arm is pulled down, opening the top contacts and closing the bottom set of contacts. The contacts are rated for a maximum current of 25 A, so this relay could be used to turn on a 1 or 2-horsepower motor or a large electric heater in one of the machines in our electronics factory. When driven from a 12-V supply, the coil requires a current of about 170 mA. The circuit shown in Figure 9-38 could easily drive this relay coil from a microcomputer port line.

Mechanical relays, sometimes called contactors, are available to switch currents from milliamps up to several thousand amps. Mechanical relays, however, have several serious problems. When the contacts are opened and closed, arcing takes place between the contacts. This causes the contacts to oxidize and pit just as the ignition points in your car do with age. As the contacts become oxidized they make a higher-resistance contact and may get hot enough to melt. Another disadvantage of mechanical relays is that they can switch on or off at any point in the ac cycle. Switching on or off at a high voltage point in the ac cycle can cause a large amount of electrical noise called electromagnetic interference

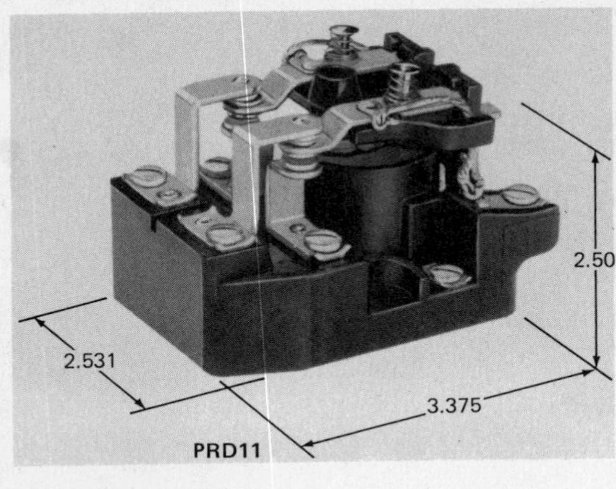

(a)

(b)

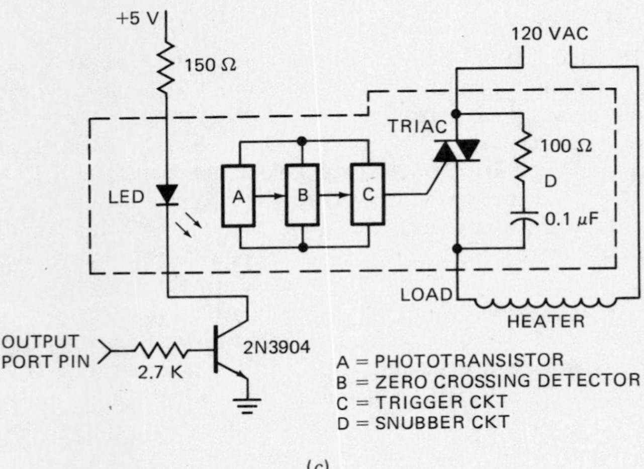

(c)

FIGURE 9-40 Relays for switching large currents. *(a)* Mechanical. *(b)* Solid-state. *(Potter and Brumfield)*. *(c)* Internal circuitry for solid-state relay.

(EMI). The solid-state relays discussed next avoid these problems to a large extent.

Figure 9-40*b* shows a picture of a solid-state relay which is rated for 25 A at 25°C if mounted on a suitable heat sink. Figure 9-40*c* shows a block diagram of the circuitry in the device and its connection from an output port to an ac load.

The input circuit is essentially an LED and a current-limiting resistor. To turn the device on you simply turn on the buffer transistor which pulls the required 11 mA through the internal LED. The light from the LED is focused on a phototransistor connected to the actual output-control circuitry. Since the only connection between the input and the output is a beam of light, there is several thousand volts of isolation between the input circuitry and the output circuitry.

The actual switch in a solid-state relay is a triac which conducts in either direction when triggered. The zero-voltage detector makes sure that the triac is only triggered when the ac line voltage is very close to one of its zero voltage crossing points. If you output a signal to turn on the relay, the relay will not actually turn on until the next time the ac line voltage crosses zero. Triacs automatically turn off when the current through them drops below a small value called the holding current. If the control signal is on, the trigger circuitry will automatically retrigger the triac for each half cycle. If you send a signal to turn off the relay, it will actually turn off the next time the ac current drops to zero. Zero-point switching eliminates most of the EMI that would be caused by switching the triac on at high-voltage points in the ac cycle.

Solid-state relays then have the advantages that they produce less EMI, they have no mechanical contacts to arc, and they are easily driven from microcomputer ports. Their disadvantages are that they are more expensive than an equivalent mechanical relay and there is a voltage drop of a couple of volts across the triac when it is on. Another potential problem with solid-state relays occurs when driving a large inductive load such as a motor. Remember from basic ac theory that the voltage waveform leads the current waveform in an ac circuit with inductance. A triac turns off when the current through it drops to near zero. In an inductive circuit the voltage waveform may be at several tens of volts when the current is at zero. When the triac is conducting it has perhaps 2 V across it. When the triac turns off, the voltage across the triac will quickly jump to several tens of volts. This large dV/dT may possibly turn on the triac at a point you don't want it turned on. To keep the voltage across the triac from changing too rapidly, an *RC snubber* circuit is connected across the triac as shown in Figure 9-40*c*. A system in the next chapter uses a solid-state relay to control an electrical heater.

INTERFACING A MICROCOMPUTER TO A STEPPER MOTOR

A unique type of motor useful for moving things in small increments is the stepper motor. If you have a dot-matrix printer such as the Epson FX-80, look inside and you will probably see one small stepper motor which is used to advance the paper to the next line position, and another small stepper motor which is used to move the print head to the next character position. While you are in there, you might look for a small device containing an LED and a phototransistor which detects when the print head is in the "home" position. Stepper motors are also used to position the read/write head over the desired track of a hard or floppy disk, and to position the pen on X-Y plotters.

Instead of rotating smoothly around and around as

most motors do, stepper motors rotate or "step" from one fixed position to the next. Common step sizes range from 0.9° to 30°. A stepper motor is stepped from one position to the next by changing the currents through the fields in the motor. The two common field connections are referred to as two-phase and four-phase. We will discuss *four-phase steppers* here because their drive circuitry is much simpler.

Figure 9-41 shows a circuit you can use to interface a small four-phase stepper such as the Superior Electric MO61-FD302, IMC Magnetics Corp. Tormax 200, or a similar, nominal 5-V unit to four microcomputer port lines. If you build up this circuit, bolt some small heat sinks on the MJE2955 transistors and mount the 10-W resistors where you aren't likely to touch them.

Since the 7406 buffers are inverting, a high on an output-port pin turns on current to a winding. Figure 9-41*b* shows the switching sequence to step a motor such as this clockwise, as you face the motor shaft, or counterclockwise. Here's how this works. Suppose that SW1 and SW2 are turned on. Turning off SW2 and turning on SW4 will cause the motor to rotate one step of 1.8° clockwise. Changing to SW4 and SW3 on will cause the motor to rotate another 1.8° clockwise. Changing to SW3 and SW2 on will cause another step. After that, changing to SW2 and SW1 on again will cause another step clockwise. You can repeat the sequence until the motor has rotated as many steps clockwise as you want. To step the motor counterclockwise, you simply work through the switch sequence in the reverse direction. In either case the motor will be held in its last position by the current through the coils. Figure 9-41*c* shows the switch sequence that can be used to rotate the motor half-steps of 0.9° clockwise or counterclockwise.

A close look at the switch sequence in Figure 9-41*b* shows an interesting pattern. To take the first step clockwise from SW2 and SW1 being on, the pattern of 1's and 0's is simply rotated one bit position around to the right. The 1 from SW1 is rotated around into bit 4. To take the next step the switch pattern is rotated one more bit position. To step counterclockwise the switch pattern is rotated left one bit position for each step desired. Suppose that you initially load 00110011 into AL and output this to the switches. Duplicating the switch pat-

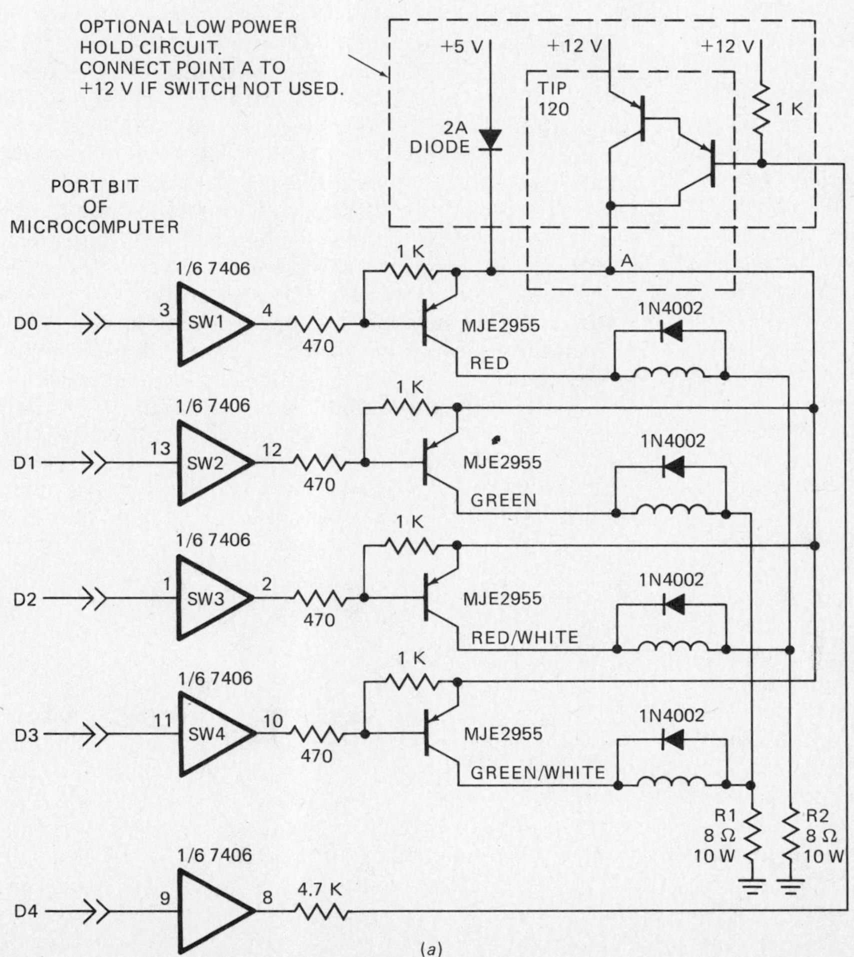

STEP	SWITCH			
	SW4	SW3	SW2	SW1
1	0	0	1	1
2	1	0	0	1
3	1	1	0	0
4	0	1	1	0
1	0	0	1	1

CW ↑↓ CCW

1 = SWITCH ON

(*b*)

EIGHT-STEP INPUT SEQUENCE
(HALF-STEP MODE)

STEP	SW4	SW3	SW2	SW1
1	OFF	OFF	ON	ON
2	OFF	OFF	OFF	ON
3	ON	OFF	OFF	ON
4	ON	OFF	OFF	OFF
5	ON	ON	OFF	OFF
6	OFF	ON	OFF	OFF
7	OFF	ON	ON	OFF
8	OFF	OFF	ON	OFF
1	OFF	OFF	ON	ON

(*c*)

FIGURE 9-41 Four-phase stepper motor interface circuit and stepping waveforms. *(a)* Circuit. *(b)* Full-step drive signal order. *(c)* Half-step drive signal order.

tern in the upper half of AL will make stepping easy. To step the motor clockwise, you just rotate this pattern right one bit position and output it to the switches. To step counterclockwise, you rotate the switch pattern left one bit position and output it. After you output one step code you must wait a few milliseconds before you output another step command, because the motor can only step so fast. Maximum stepping rates for different types of steppers vary from a few hundred steps per second to several thousand steps per second. To achieve high stepping rates the stepping rate is slowly increased to the maximum, then it is decreased as the desired number of steps is approached.

As a stepper motor steps to a new position it tends to oscillate around the new position before settling down. A common software technique to damp out this oscillation is to first send the pattern to step the motor toward the new position. When the motor has rotated part of the way to the new position, a word to step the motor backward is output for a short time. This is like putting the brakes on. The step forward word is then sent again to complete the step to the next position. The timing for the damping command must be determined experimentally for each motor and load.

Before we go on, here are a couple of additional points about the circuit in Figure 9-41*a*, in case you want to add a stepper to your robot or some other project. First of all, don't forget the clamp diodes across each winding to save the transistors from inductive kick. Second, we need to explain the function of the current-limiting resistors, *R*1 and *R*2. The motor we used here has a nominal voltage rating of 5.5 V. This means that we could have designed the circuit to operate with a voltage of about 6.5 V on the emitters of the driver transistors (5.5 V for the motor plus 1 V for the drop across the transistor). For low stepping rates, this would work fine. However, for higher stepping rates and more torque while stepping, we use a higher supply voltage and current-limiting resistors as shown. The point of this is that by adding series resistance, we decrease the *L/R* time constant. This allows the current to change more rapidly in the windings. For the motor we used, the current per winding is 0.88 A. Since only one winding on each resistor is ever on at a time, 6.5 V/0.88 A gives a resistor value of 6.25 Ω. To be conservative we used 8-Ω, 10-W resistors. The optional transistor switch and diode connection to the +5-V supply are used as follows. When not stepping, the switch to +12 V is off so the motor is held in position by the current from the +5 V supply. Before you send a step command, you turn on the transistor to +12 V to give the motor more current for stepping. When stepping is done you turn off the switch to +12 V, and drop back to the +5 V supply. This cuts the power dissipation.

In small printers such as the IBM PC parallel printer, a dedicated microprocessor is used to control the various operations in the printer. In this case the microprocessor has plenty of time to control the print-head and line-feed stepper motors in software as we described above. For applications where the main microcomputer is too busy to be bothered with controlling a stepper directly, a simple one-chip microcomputer or a device such as the Cybernetic Microsystems CY525 stepper controller is used.

OPTICAL MOTOR SHAFT ENCODERS

In order to control the machines in our electronics factory, the microcomputers in these machines often need information about the position, direction of rotation, and speed of rotation of various motor shafts. The microcomputer, of course, needs this information in digital form. The circuitry which produces this digital information from each motor for the microcomputer is called a *shaft encoder*. There are two basic types of shaft encoder, *absolute* and *incremental*. Here's how these two types work.

Absolute Encoders

Absolute encoders attach a binary-coded disk such as the one shown in Figure 9-42 on the rotating shaft. Light sections of the disk are transparent, and dark sections are opaque. An LED is mounted on one side of each track and a phototransistor is mounted on the other side, opposite the LED. Outputs from the four phototransistors will produce one of the binary codes shown in Figure 9-42. The phototransistor outputs can be conditioned with Schmitt-trigger buffers and connected to a microcomputer port. Each code represents an absolute angular position of the shaft in its rotation. With a 4-bit disk, 360° is divided up into 16 parts, so the position of the shaft can be determined to the nearest 22.5°. With an 8-bit disk the position of the disk can be determined to the nearest 360°/256, or 1.4°.

Observe that the codes in Figure 9-42 do not follow a normal binary count sequence. The codes here follow a sequence called *Gray code*. Using Gray code reduces the size of the largest possible error in reading the shaft

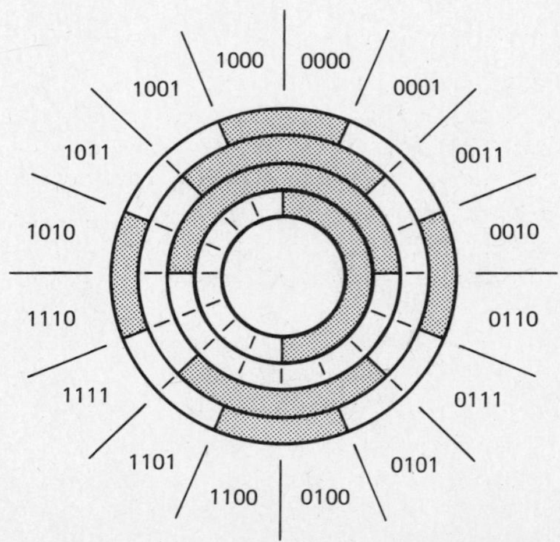

FIGURE 9-42 Gray code optical-encoder disk used to determine angular position of a rotating shaft.

position to the value of the least-significant bit. If the disk used straight binary code, the largest possible error would be the value of the most significant bit. Look at the parallel listings of binary and Gray codes in Table 1-1 to help you see why this is the case.

To start, assume we did have a binary disk and the disk was rotating from position 0111 (7) to position 1000 (8). Now suppose that the detectors pick up the change to 000 on the least-significant 3 bits, but don't pick up the change to 1 on the most-significant bit. The output code would then be 0000 instead of the desired 1000. This is an error equal to the value of the MSB. Now, while this is fresh in your mind, look across the table at the same position change for the Gray code encoder. The Gray code for position 7 is 0100 and the Gray code for position 8 is 1100. Note that only one bit changes for this transition. If you look at the Gray code table closely, you will see that this is the case for all of the transitions. What this means is that if a detector fails to pick up the new bit value during a transition, the resulting code will always be the code for the preceding position. This represents an error equal to the value of the LSB.

If you need to construct a Gray code table for more than 4 bits, a handy method is to observe the pattern of 1's and 0's in Table 1-1, and just extend it. The least-significant-bit column starts with a 0, and then has alternating groups of two 1's and two 0's. The second-most-significant column starts with two 0's and then has alternating groups of four 1's and four 0's. The third column starts with four 0's and has alternating groups of eight 1's and eight 0's. By now you should see the pattern. Try to figure out the Gray code for the decimal number 16. You should get 11000.

Absolute encoding using a Gray code disk has the advantage that each position is represented by a specific code which can be directly read in by the microcomputer. Disadvantages are the multiple detectors needed, the multiple lines required, and the difficulty keeping track of position during multiple rotations.

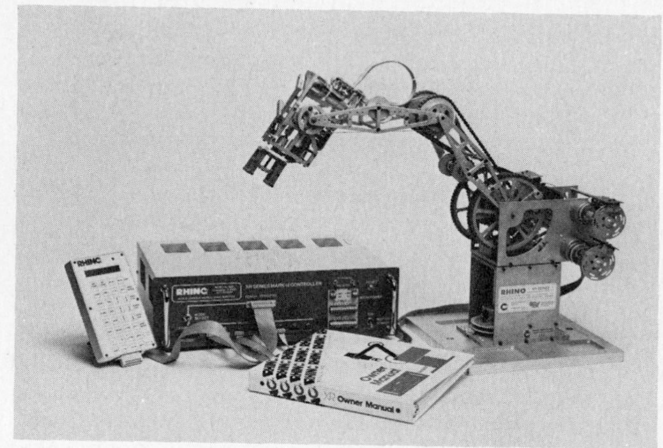

FIGURE 9-43 Rhino XR robotics system. *(Rhino Robots Incorporated)*

Incremental Encoders

An incremental encoder produces a pulse for each increment of shaft rotation. Figure 9-43 shows the Rhino XR-2 robot arm, which uses incremental encoders to determine the position and direction of rotation for each of its motors. For this encoder, a metal disk with two tracks of slotted holes is mounted on each motor shaft. An LED is mounted on one side of each track of holes and a phototransistor is mounted opposite the LED on the other side of the disk. Each phototransistor produces a train of pulses as the disk is rotated. The pulses are passed through Schmitt trigger buffers to sharpen their edges.

The two tracks of slotted holes are 90° out of phase with each other as shown at the top of Figure 9-44. Therefore, as the disk is rotated, the waveforms shown at the bottom of Figure 9-44 will be produced by the phototransistors for rotation in one direction. Rotation in the other direction will shift the phase of the waveforms 180° so that the B waveform leads the A waveform by 90° instead of lagging it by 90°. Now the question is, "How do you get position, speed, and direction information from these waveforms?"

You can determine the speed of rotation by simply counting the number of pulses in the time between two interrupts as we described in Chapter 8. Each track has six holes so six pulses will be produced for each revolution. Some simple arithmetic will give you the speed in revolutions per minute (rpm).

You can determine the direction of rotation with hardware or with software. For the hardware approach connect the A signal to the D input of a D flip-flop, and the B signal to the clock input of the flip-flop. The rising edge of the B signal will clock the level of the A signal at that

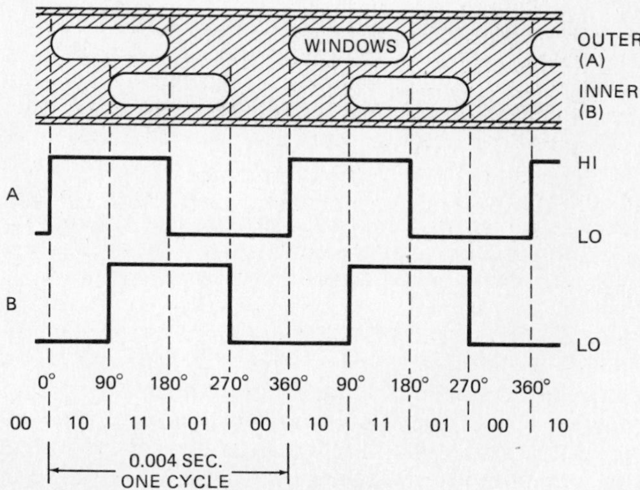

FIGURE 9-44 Optical-encoder disk slot pattern and output waveforms.

point through the flip-flop to its Q output. If you look at the waveforms in Figure 9-44 you should see that the Q output will be high for rotation in the direction shown. You can convince yourself that the Q output will be low for rotation in the other direction. To determine the direction of rotation more directly, you can detect the rising edge of the B signal on a polled or an interrupt basis, and then read the A signal. As shown in the waveforms, the A signal being high represents rotation in one direction, and the A signal being low represents rotation in the opposite direction.

To determine the position of the motor shaft you simply keep track of how many holes the motor has moved from some "home" position. On the Rhino robot arm a small mechanical switch on each axis is activated when the arm is in its starting or "home" position. When you turn on the power, the motor controller/driver box automatically moves the arm to this home position. To move the arm to some new position you calculate the number of holes each motor must rotate to get the arm to that position. For each motor you then send the controller a command which tells it which direction to rotate that motor and how many holes to rotate it. The controller will drive the motor the specified number of holes in the specified direction. If you then manually rotate the encoder wheel or some heavy load moves the arm and rotates the encoder disk, the controller will detect the change in position of the disk and drive the motor back to its specified position. This is an example of digital *feedback control*, which is easily done with a microcomputer. The Rhino controller uses an 8748 single-chip microcomputer to interpret and carry out the commands you send it. Commands are sent to the controller in the serial ASCII form described at the start of Chapter 13.

Incidentally, you may wonder at this point why the designers of the Rhino arm did not use stepper motors such as those we described in a previous section. The answers are: stepper motors are much more expensive than the simple dc motors used; if a stepper motor is forced back a step there is no way to know about it and correct for it unless you have an external encoder. Also the dc motor-encoder approach better demonstrates the method used in large commercial robots.

In the Rhino robot arm each motor drives its section of the arm through a series of gears. Gearing the motor down reduces the force that the motor has to exert, and makes the exact position of the motor shaft less critical. Therefore, for the Rhino, six sets of slots in the encoder disk are sufficient. However, for applications where a much more accurate indication of shaft position is needed, a self-contained shaft encoder such as the Hewlett-Packard HEDS-5000 is attached to the motor shaft. These encoders have two track-encoder disks with 500 tiny radial slits per track. The waveforms produced are the same as those shown for the Rhino encoder in Figure 9-44, but at a much higher frequency for the same motor speed.

Optical encoders in their many different forms are an important part of a large number of microcomputer-controlled machines.

IMPORTANT TERMS AND CONCEPTS FROM THIS CHAPTER

If you do not remember any of the terms in the following list, use the index to help you find them in the chapter for review.

Simple input and output

Simple strobe I/O

Single handshake I/O

Double handshake data transfer

8255A initialization of ports A, B, and C
- MODE 0, MODE 1, MODE 2
- Mode definition control word
- Set/reset control word

Computer numerical control (CNC) machines

VOTRAX SC-01A speech synthesizer
- Phoneme

Centronix parallel standard
- I/O driver
- Control block
- Counters and sentinels

Keyswitches—mechanical, capacitive, Hall effect

Debounce keypress

Two-key lockout, two-key rollover

Code conversion
- Compare
- Add and point, XLAT

Error trapping

LED interfacing
- Static display
- Multiplexed display
- Dedicated display controller
- Scan time

8279
- FIFO
- Encoded and decoded scan
- Keyboard/display mode-set control word
- Clear control word
- Write-display control word

LCD interfacing
- Dynamic scattering
- Field effect
- Backplane
- Triplexing

Relays
- Mechanical

Solid state
Electromagnetic interference
Zero-point switching
RC-snubber circuit
Four-phase stepper motor
Shaft encoders—absolute and incremental
Digital feedback control

REVIEW QUESTIONS AND PROBLEMS

1. Why must data be sent to a printer on a handshake basis?

2. For the double handshake data transfer in Figure 9-1*d*
   a. Indicate which signal is asserted by the sender and which signal is asserted by the receiver.
   b. Describe the meaning of each of the signal transitions.

3. Why are the port lines of programmable port devices automatically put in the input mode when the device is first powered up or reset?

4. An 8255A has a system base address of FFF9H. What are the system addresses for the three ports and the control register for this 8255A?

5. *a.* Show the mode-set control word needed to initialize an 8255A as follows:
   Port A—handshake input
   Port B—handshake output
   Port C—bits PC6 and PC7 as outputs
   b. Show the bit set/reset control word needed to initialize the port A interrupt request and the port B interrupt request.
   c. Show the assembly language instructions you would use to send these control words to the 8255A in Question 4.
   d. Show the additional instruction you need if you want the handshake to be done on an interrupt basis through the IR3 input of the 8259A in Figure 8-14.
   e. Show the instructions you would use to put a high on port C bit PC6 of this device.

6. Describe the exchange of signals between the tape reader, 8255A, and 8086 in Figure 9-6 as a byte of data is transferred from the tape reader to the microprocessor.

7. Why is it more efficient to send phonemes to the SC-01A speech synthesizer in Figure 9-10*a* on an interrupt basis than on a polled basis?

8. If you have an SC-01A speech IC connected to your system as shown in Figure 9-10*a*, write the mainline program and the interrupt procedure to send phonemes to the SC-01A. The mainline can terminate with the HERE: JMP HERE instruction so that it simply waits for interrupts from the 8255A. Use the phoneme table in the appendix to help you make up the table of phonemes for the message "self-test complete."

9. When connecting peripheral devices such as printers, terminals, etc. to a computer, why is it very important to connect the logic ground and the chassis ground together only at the computer?

10. Describe the function and direction of the following signals in a Centronics parallel-printer interface.
    a. $\overline{\text{STROBE}}$
    b. $\overline{\text{ACKNLG}}$
    c. BUSY
    d. $\overline{\text{INIT}}$

11. Modify the printer driver procedure in Figure 9-17 so that it stops sending characters to the printer when it finds a sentinel character of 03H, instead of using the counter approach.

12. Would the software method of generating the $\overline{\text{STROBE}}$ signal to the printer in Figure 9-17 still work if you try to run the program with an 8-MHz 8086?

13. Show the instructions you would use to read the status byte from the 8255A in Question 5.

14. Describe the three major tasks needed to get meaningful information from a matrix keyboard.

15. Describe how the "compare" method of code conversion in Figure 9-21 works.

16. Why is "error trapping" necessary in real programs? Describe how the error trap in the program in Figure 9-21 works.

17. Assume the rows of the circuit shown in Figure 9-45 are connected to ports FFF8H and the 74148 is connected to port FFFAH of an SDK-86 board. The 74148 will output a low on its $\overline{\text{GS}}$ output if a low is applied to any of its inputs. The way the keyboard is wired, the $\overline{\text{A2}}$, $\overline{\text{A1}}$, and $\overline{\text{A0}}$ outputs will have a 3-bit binary code for the column in which a low appears. Use the algorithm and discussion of Figure 9-21 to help you write a procedure which detects a keypress, debounces the keypress, and determines the row number and column number of the pressed key. The procedure should then combine the row code, column code, shift bit and control bit into a single byte in the form: control, shift, row code, column code. The XLAT instruction can then be used to convert this code byte to ASCII for return to the calling program. *HINT*: Use DB directive to make up table of ASCII codes.
    Why is the XLAT approach more efficient than the compare technique for this case?

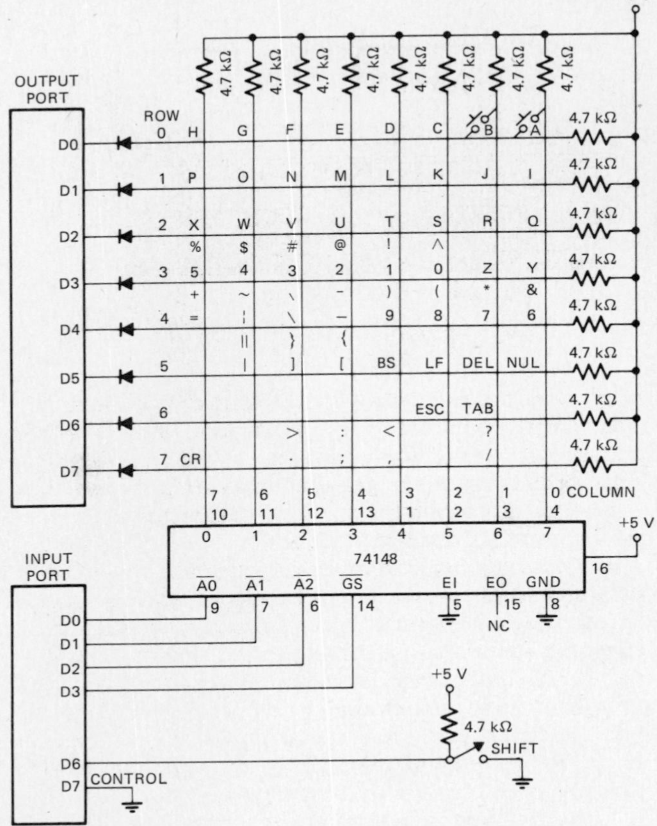

FIGURE 9-45 Interface circuitry for unencoded matrix keyboard for Problem 9-17.

NOTE: For test purposes, the keyboard matrix can be simulated by building the diodes, resistors, and 74148 on a prototyping board and using a jumper wire to produce a "keypress."

18. *a.* Calculate the value of the current-limiting resistor needed in series with each segment of a seven-segment display driven by a 7447, if you want 40 mA per segment.

b. Approximately how much current is being pulsed through each LED segment on the SDK-86 board?

19. *a.* Write the algorithm for a procedure which refreshes the multiplexed LED displays shown in Figure 9-26. Assume the procedure will be called every 2 ms by an interrupt signal to IR4 of an 8259A.

b. Write the assembly language instructions for the display refresh procedure. Since this procedure is called on an interrupt basis, all display parameters should be kept in named memory locations. If you have time, you can add the circuitry shown in Figure 9-26 to your microcomputer so you can test your program.

20. Figure 9-46 shows a circuit for an 8 by 8 matrix of LEDs that you can add to a couple of ports on your microcomputer to produce some interesting displays. The principle here is to output a 1 to port B for each LED you want turned on in the top row and then output a 1 to the D0 bit of port A to turn on that row. After 2 ms, you output the pattern you want in the row to port B and a 1 to bit 1 of port A to turn on the second row. The process is repeated until all rows are done and then started over.

The row patterns can be kept in a table in memory. If you want to display a sequence of letters, you can display the contents of one table for a few seconds, then switch to another table containing the second letter. Using the rotate instruction, you can produce some scrolled displays. *HINT*: The wiring required to build the LED matrix can be reduced by using an IC 5 by 7 dot-matrix LED display such as the Texas Instruments TIL305.

Write the algorithm and program for an interrupt procedure (called every 2 ms) to refresh these displays.

21. You are assigned the job of fixing several SDK-86 boards with display problems. For each of the problems listed below, describe a possible cause of the problem and tell where you would look with an oscilloscope to check out your theory. Use the circuit on sheet 7 of Figure 7-6 to help you.

a. The segment never lights.

b. The leftmost digit of the data field never lights.

c. All of the displays show dim "eights."

22. *a.* Show the command words and assembly language instructions necessary to initialize an 8279 at address 80H and 82H as follows:
16-character display, left entry, encoded-scan keyboard, *N*-key rollover.
1-MHz input clock divided to 100 kHz.
Blanking character FFH.

b. Show the 8279 instructions necessary to write 99H to the first location in the display RAM and autoincrement the display RAM pointer.

c. Show the assembly language instructions necessary to read the first byte from the 8279 FIFO RAM.

d. Determine the seven-segment codes you would have to send to the SDK-86 8279 to display the letters HELP on the data field display. Remember that D0 of the byte sent = B0 and D7 of the byte sent = A3.

e. Show the sequence of instructions you can send to the 8279 of the SDK-86 board to blank the entire display.

23. Write a procedure which polls the LSB of the 8279 status register on the SDK-86 board until it finds a key pressed, then reads the keypressed code from the FIFO RAM to AL and returns.

24. Why must the backplane and segment-line signals be pulsed for LCD displays?

25. Draw a circuit you could attach to an 8255A port B pin to drive a 1-A solenoid valve from a +12-V supply. You want a high on the port pin to turn on the solenoid.

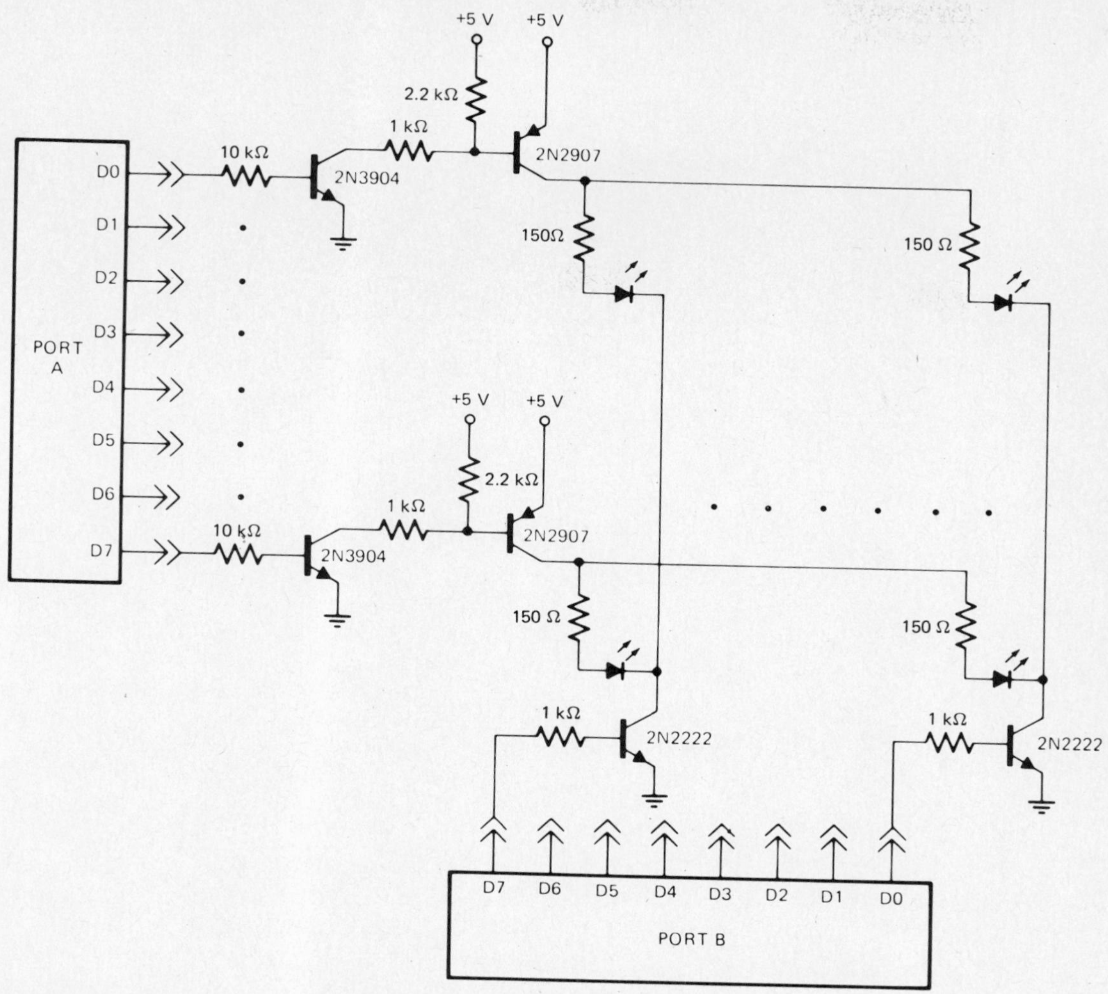

FIGURE 9-46 Eight by eight LED matrix circuitry for Problem 9-20.

26. Why must reverse-biased diodes always be placed across inductive devices when you are driving them with a transistor?

27. What are the major advantages and disadvantages of mechanical relays and solid-state relays.

28. *a.* How is electrical isolation between the control input and the output circuitry achieved in a solid-state relay?

b. Describe the function of the zero-crossing detector used in better-quality solid-state relays.

c. Why is a "snubber circuit" required across the triac of a solid-state relay when you are driving inductive loads?

29. Write the algorithm and the program for an 8086 procedure to drive the stepper motor shown in Figure 9-41. Assume the desired direction of rotation is passed to the procedure in AL (AL = 1 is clockwise, AL = 0 is counterclockwise) and the number of steps is passed to the procedure in CX. Also assume full-step mode as shown in Figure 9-41*b*. Don't forget to delay 20 ms between step commands!

30. *a.* Why is Gray code, rather than straight binary code, used on many absolute-position shaft encoders?

b. If a Gray-code wheel has six tracks and each track represents 1 binary bit, what is its angular resolution?

31. *a.* Look at the encoder disk on the Rhino arm in Figure 9-43. Do the waveforms in Figure 9-44 represent clockwise or counterclockwise rotation of the motor shaft as seen from the gear end of the motor, which is what you care about.

b. Assume the A signal shown in Figure 9-44 is connected to bit D0 and the B signal is connected to bit D1 of port FFF8H. Write a procedure which determines the direction of rotation and passes a 1 back in AL for clockwise and a 0 back in AL for counterclockwise rotation.

c. The dc motors, such as those on the RHINO arms, are rotated clockwise by passing a current through them in one direction and rotated counterclockwise by passing a current through them in the opposite direction. Assume you have a motor controller that responds to a 2-bit control word as follows:

00 = hold   01 = rotate clockwise
11 = hold   10 = rotate counter-clockwise

Write the algorithm and program for a procedure to rotate a motor. The number of holes is passed to the procedure in CX; the direction of rotation is determined by the value in AL. AL = 1 is clockwise, AL = 0 is counterclockwise.

CHAPTER

10 Analog Interfacing and Industrial Control

In order to control the machines in our electronics factory, medical instruments, or automobiles with a microcomputer we need to determine the values of variables such as pressure, temperature, and flow. There are usually several steps in getting an electrical signal which represents the values of these variables, and converting the electrical signals to a digital form that the microcomputer understands.

The first step involves a *sensor* which converts the physical pressure, temperature, or other variable to a proportional voltage or current. The signals from most sensors are quite small, so they must next be amplified, and perhaps filtered. This is usually done with some type of operational-amplifier (op-amp) circuit. The final step is to convert the signal to digital form with an analog-to-digital (A/D) converter. In this chapter we review some op-amp circuits commonly used in these steps, show the interface circuitry for some common sensors, and discuss the operation and interfacing of A/D converters. We also discuss the interfacing of D/A converters and show how all of these pieces are put together in a microcomputer-based scale and a machine-control system.

OBJECTIVES

At the conclusion of this chapter you should be able to:

1. Recognize several common op-amp circuits, describe their operation, and predict the voltages at key points in each.
2. Describe the operation and interfacing of several common sensors used to measure temperature, pressure, flow, etc.
3. Draw circuits showing how to interface D/A converters with any number of bits to a microcomputer.
4. Define D/A data-sheet parameters such as resolution, settling time, accuracy, and linearity.
5. Describe briefly the operation of flash, successive approximation, and ramp A/D converters.
6. Draw circuits showing how A/D converters of various types can be interfaced to a microcomputer.
7. Write programs to control A/D and D/A converters.
8. Describe how feedback is used to control variables such as pressure, temperature, flow, motor speed, etc.
9. Describe the operation of a "time slice" factory control system.

REVIEW OF OPERATIONAL-AMPLIFIER CHARACTERISTICS AND CIRCUITS

Basic Operational Amplifier Characteristics

Figure 10-1*a* shows the schematic symbol for an op amp. Here are the important points for you to remember about the basic op amp. First, the pins labeled +V and −V represent the power supply connections. The voltages applied to these pins will usually be +15 V and −15 V, or +12 V and −12 V. The op amp also has two signal inputs. The amplifier amplifies the difference in voltage between these two inputs by 100,000 or more. The input labeled with a − sign is called the inverting input and the one labeled with the + sign is called the noninverting input. The + and − on these inputs has nothing to do with the power-supply voltages. These signs indicate the phase relationship between a signal applied to that input and the result that signal produces on the output. If for example, the noninverting input is made more positive than the inverting input, the output will move in a positive direction, which is in phase with the applied input signal. Now let's see how much the output changes for a given input signal, and see how an op amp is used as a comparator.

Op-amp Circuits and Applications

OP AMPS AS COMPARATORS

We said previously that the op amp amplifies the difference in voltage between its inputs by 100,000 or more.

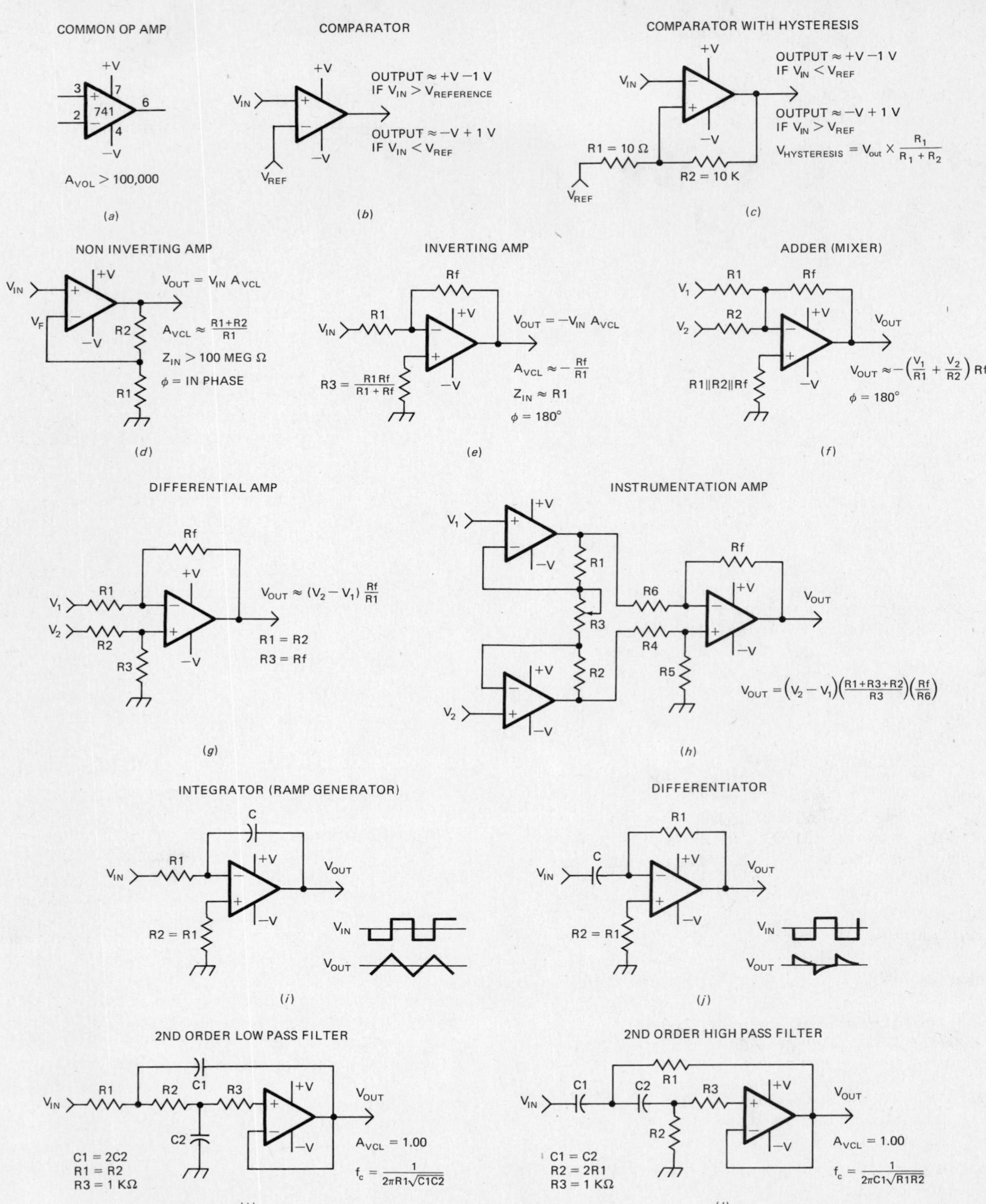

$$V_{HYSTERESIS} = V_{out} \times \frac{R_1}{R_1 + R_2}$$

$$V_{OUT} \approx -\left(\frac{V_1}{R1} + \frac{V_2}{R2}\right) Rf$$

$$V_{OUT} = (V_2 - V_1)\left(\frac{R1+R3+R2}{R3}\right)\left(\frac{Rf}{R6}\right)$$

$$f_c = \frac{1}{2\pi R1\sqrt{C1C2}}$$

$$f_c = \frac{1}{2\pi C1\sqrt{R1R2}}$$

FIGURE 10-1 Overview of commonly used op-amp circuits. *(a)* Common op amp. *(b)* Comparator. *(c)* Comparator with hysteresis. *(d)* Noninverting amp. *(e)* Inverting amp. *(f)* Adder (mixer). *(g)* Differential amp. *(h)* Instrumentation amp. *(i)* Integrator (ramp generator). *(j)* Differentiator. *(k)* Second-order low-pass filter. *(l)* Second-order high-pass filter.

(The number is variable with temperature and from device to device.) Suppose that you power an op amp with +15 V and −15 V, tie the inverting input of the op amp to ground, and apply a signal of +0.01 V dc to the noninverting input. The op amp will attempt to amplify this signal by 100,000 and produce the result on its output. An input signal of 0.01 V times a gain of 100,000 predicts an output voltage of 100 V. The op-amp output, however, can only go positive to a voltage a volt or two less than the positive supply voltage, perhaps 13 V, so this is as far as it goes. Now suppose that you apply a signal of −0.01 V to the noninverting input. The output will now try to go to −100 V as fast as it can. The output, however, can only go to about −13 V, so it stops here.

In this circuit the op amp effectively compares the input voltage with the voltage on the inverting input and gives a high or low output depending on the result of the comparison. If the input is more than a few microvolts above the reference voltage on the inverting input, the output will be high (+13 V). If the input voltage is a few microvolts more negative than the reference voltage, the output will be low (−13 V). An op amp used in this way is called a *comparator*. Figure 10-1*b* shows how a comparator is usually labeled. The reference voltage applied to the inverting input does not have to be ground (0 V). An input voltage can be compared to any voltage within the input range specified for the particular op amp.

As you will see throughout this chapter, comparators have many applications. We might, for example, connect a comparator to a temperature sensor on the boiler in our electronics factory. When the voltage from the temperature sensor goes above the voltage on the reference input of the comparator, the output of the comparator will change state and send an interrupt signal to the microprocessor controlling the boiler. Commonly available comparators such as the LM319 have TTL-compatible outputs which can be connected directly to microcomputer ports or interrupt inputs.

Figure 10-1*c* shows another commonly used comparator circuit. Note in this circuit that the reference signal is applied to the noninverting input, and the input voltage is applied to the inverting input. This connection simply inverts the output state from those in the previous circuit. Note also in Figure 10-1*c* the positive-feedback resistors from the output to the noninverting input. This feedback gives the comparator a characteristic called *hysteresis*. Hysteresis means that the output voltage changes at a different input voltage when the input is going in the positive direction than it does when the input voltage is going in a negative direction. If you have a thermostatically controlled furnace in your house you have seen hysteresis in action. The furnace, for example, may turn on when the room temperature drops to 65°F, and then not turn off until the temperature reaches 68°F. Hysteresis is the difference between the two temperatures. Without this hysteresis the furnace would rapidly be turning on and off if the room temperature were near 68°F. Another situation where hysteresis saves the day is the case where you have a slowly changing signal with noise on it. Hysteresis prevents the noise from causing the comparator output to oscillate as the input signal gets close to the reference voltage.

To determine the amount of hysteresis in a circuit such as that in Figure 10-1*c*, assume $V_{REF} = 0$ V and $V_{OUT} = 13$ V. A simple voltage-divider calculation will tell you that the noninverting input is at about 13 mV. The voltage on the inverting input of the amplifier will have to go more positive than this before the comparator will change states. Likewise, if you assume V_{OUT} is −13 V, the noninverting input will be at about −13 mV, so the voltage on the inverting input of the amplifier will have to go below this to change the state of the output. The hysteresis of this comparator is +13 mV and −13 mV.

NONINVERTING AMPLIFIER OP-AMP CIRCUIT

When operating in open-loop mode (no feedback to the inverting input), an op amp has a very high, but unpredictable, gain. This is acceptable for use as a comparator, but not for use as a predictable amplifier. Figure 10-1*d* shows one way negative feedback is added to an op amp to produce an amplifier with stable, predictable gain. First of all notice that the input signal in this circuit is applied to the noninverting input, so the output will be in phase with the input. Second, note that a fraction of the output signal is fed back to the inverting input. Now, here's how this works.

To start assume that V_{IN} is 0 V, V_{OUT} is 0 V, and the voltage on the inverting input is 0. Now, suppose that you apply a +0.01-V dc signal to the noninverting input. Since the 0.1-V difference between the two inputs will be amplified by 100,000, the output will head towards 100 V as fast as it can. However, as the output goes positive, some of the output voltage will be fed back to the inverting input through the resistor divider. This feedback to the inverting input will decrease the difference in voltage between the two inputs. To make a long story short, the circuit quickly reaches a predictable balance point where the voltage on the inverting input (V_F) is very, very close to the voltage on the noninverting input (V_{IN}). For a 1.0-V dc output this equilibrium voltage difference might be about 10 μV. If you assume that the voltages on the two inputs are equal, then predicting the output voltage for a given input voltage is simply a voltage divider problem. $V_{OUT} = V_{IN}(R1 + R2)/R1$. If $R2$ is 99 kΩ and $R1$ is 1 kΩ, then $V_{OUT} = V_{IN} \times 100$. For a 0.01-V input signal the output voltage will be 1.00 V. The closed-loop gain, A_{VCL}, for this circuit is equal to the simple resistor ratio, $(R1 + R2)/R1$.

To see another advantage of feeding some of the output signal back to the inverting input, let's see what happens when the load connected to the output of the op amp changes and draws more current from the output. The output voltage will temporarily drop because of the increased load. Part of this drop will be fed back to the inverting input, increasing the difference in voltage between the two inputs. This increased difference will cause the op amp to drive its output to correct for the increased load. Feedback which causes an amplifier to oppose a change on its output is called *negative feedback*. Because of the negative feedback, then, the op amp will work day and night to keep its output stabilized and its two inputs at nearly the same voltage! This is probably the most important point you need to know to analyze or troubleshoot an op-amp circuit with negative feedback. Draw a box around this point in your mind so you don't forget it.

The noninverting circuit we have just discussed is used mostly as a *buffer*, because it has a very high *input impedance* (Z_{IN}), and will therefore not load down a sensor or some other device you connect to its input. Bipolar-transistor-input op amps will have an input impedance greater than 100 MΩ. Some op amps such as the National LF356 have a FET input stage so their input impedance is 10^{12} Ω.

INVERTING AMPLIFIER OP-AMP CIRCUIT

Figure 10-1*e* shows a somewhat more versatile amplifier circuit using negative feedback. Note that in this circuit, the noninverting input is tied to ground with a resistor and the signal you want to amplify is sent to the inverting input through a resistor. The output signal will therefore be 180° out of phase with the input signal. Resistor R_f supplies the negative feedback which keeps the two inputs at nearly the same voltage. Since the noninverting input is tied to ground, the op amp will sink or source current to hold the inverting input also at zero volts. In this circuit the inverting input point is referred to as *virtual ground* because the op amp holds it at ground. The voltage gain of this circuit is also determined by the ratio of two resistors. The A_{VCL} for this circuit at low frequencies is equal to $-R_f/R1$. You can derive this for yourself by just thinking of the two resistors as a voltage divider with V_{IN} at one end, zero volts in the middle, and V_{OUT} on the other end. The minus sign in the gain expression simply indicates that the output is inverted from the input. The input impedance (Z_{IN}) of this circuit is approximately $R1$ because the op amp holds one end of this resistor at zero volts.

One additional characteristic we need to refresh in your mind about op-amp circuits before going on to other op-amp circuits is *gain-bandwidth product*. As we indicated previously, an op amp may have an open-loop dc gain of 100,000 or more. At higher frequencies the gain decreases until, at some frequency, the open-loop gain drops to 1. Figure 10-2*a* shows an open-loop voltage gain versus frequency graph for a common op amp such as a 741. The frequency at which the gain is 1 is referred to on data sheets as the *unity-gain bandwidth* or the *gain-bandwidth product*. A common value for this is 1 MHz. The bandwidth of an amplifier circuit with negative feedback times the low-frequency closed-loop gain will be equal to this value. For example, if an op amp with a gain-bandwidth product of 1 MHz is used to build an amplifier circuit with a closed-loop gain of 100, the bandwidth of the circuit (f_c) will be about 1 MHz/100 or 10 kHz, as shown in Figure 10-2*b*.

OP-AMP ADDER CIRCUIT

Figure 10-1*f* shows a commonly used variation of the inverting amplifier described in the previous section. This circuit adds together or mixes two or more input signals. Here's how it works.

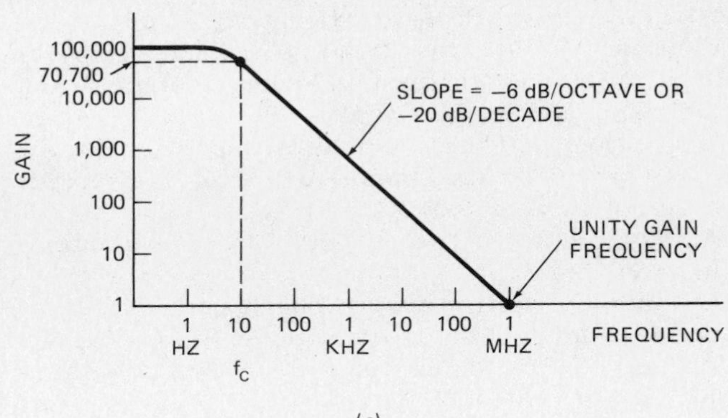

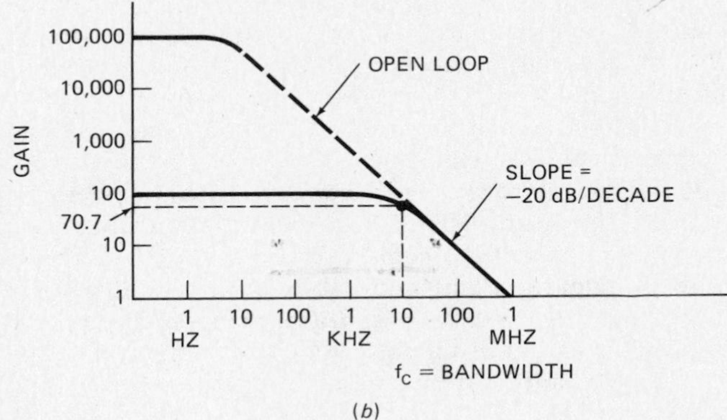

FIGURE 10-2 *(a)* Open-loop gain versus frequency response of 741 op amp. *(b)* Gain versus frequency response of 741 op-amp circuit with closed-loop gain of 100.

Remember from the previous discussion that in an inverting circuit, the op amp holds the inverting input at virtual ground. For the circuit here the input voltage, V_1, produces a current through $R1$ to this point. The input voltage, V_2, causes a current through $R2$ to this point. The two currents add together at the virtual ground, which is commonly called the *summing point* for this circuit. The sum of the two currents is pulled through resistor R_f by the op amp to hold the inverting input at zero volts. The output voltage is then equal to the sum of the currents times the value of R_f, or $(V_1/R1 + V_2/R2) \times R_f$. A circuit such as this is used to "mix" audio signals and to sum binary-weighted currents in a D/A converter. An adder circuit can have several inputs.

SIMPLE DIFFERENTIAL-INPUT AMPLIFIER CIRCUIT

As we will show later, many sensors have two output signal lines with a dc voltage of several volts on each signal line. The dc voltage present on both signal leads is referred to as a *common-mode signal*. The actual signal you need to amplify from these sensors is the few millivolts difference between them. If you try to use a standard inverting or noninverting amplifier circuit to do this, the large dc voltage will be amplified along with the small difference voltage you need to amplify. Figure 10-1*g* shows a simple circuit which, for the most part, solves this problem without using coupling capacitors to block the dc. The analysis of this circuit is beyond the space we have here, but basically the resistors on the noninverting input hold this input at a voltage near the common-mode voltage. The amplifier holds the inverting input at the same voltage. If the resistors are matched carefully, the result is that only the difference in voltage between V_2 and V_1 will be amplified. The output will be a single line which contains only the amplified difference. We say that the common-mode signal has been *rejected*.

AN INSTRUMENTATION AMPLIFIER CIRCUIT

Figure 10-1*h* shows an op-amp circuit used in applications needing a greater rejection of the common-mode signal than is provided by the simple differential circuit in Figure 10-1*g*. The first two op amps in this circuit remove the common-mode voltage and the last op amp converts the result from a differential signal to a signal referenced to ground. Instrumentation amplifier circuits such as this are available in single packages.

AN OP-AMP INTEGRATOR CIRCUIT

Figure 10-1*i* shows an op-amp circuit that can be used to produce linear voltage ramps. A dc voltage applied to the input of this circuit will cause a constant current of $V_{IN}/R1$ to flow into the virtual-ground point. This current flows onto one plate of the capacitor. In order to hold the inverting input at ground, the op-amp output must pull the same current from the other plate of the capacitor. The capacitor is then getting charged by the constant current $V_{IN}/R1$. Basic physics tells you that the voltage across a capacitor being charged by a constant current is a *linear ramp*. Note that because of the inverting amplifier connection, the output will ramp negative for a positive input voltage. Also note that some provision must be made to prevent the amplifier output from ramping into *saturation*.

The circuit is called an integrator because it produces an output voltage proportional to the integral or "sum" of the current produced by an input voltage over a period of time. The waveforms in Figure 10-1*i* show the circuit response for a pulse-input signal.

AN OP-AMP DIFFERENTIATOR CIRCUIT

Figure 10-1*j* shows an op-amp circuit which produces an output signal proportional to the rate of change of the input signal. With the input voltage to this circuit at zero or some other steady dc voltage, the output will be at zero. If a new voltage is applied to the input, the voltage across the capacitor cannot change instantly, so the inverting input will be pulled away from zero volts. This will cause the op amp to drive its output in a direction to charge the capacitor and pull the inverting input back to zero. The waveforms in Figure 10-1*j* show the circuit response for a pulse-input signal. The time required for the output to return to zero is determined by the time constant of *R*1 and *C*.

OP-AMP ACTIVE FILTERS

In many control applications we need to filter out unwanted low-frequency or high-frequency noise from the signals read in from sensors. This could be done with simple *RC* filters, but *active filters* using op amps give much better control over filter characteristics. There are many different filter configurations using op amps. The main points we want to refresh here are the meanings of the terms *low-pass* filter, *high-pass* filter, and *bandpass* filter; and how you identify the type when you find one in a circuit you are analyzing.

A low-pass filter amplifies or passes through low frequencies, but at some frequency determined by circuit values, the output of the filter starts to decrease. The frequency at which the output is down to 0.707 of the low-frequency value is called the *critical frequency* or *break point*. Figure 10-3*a* shows a graph of gain versus frequency for a low-pass filter with the critical frequency (f_c) labeled. Note that above the critical frequency the gain drops off rapidly. For a first-order filter such as a single *R* and *C*, the gain decreases by a factor of 10 for each increase of 10 times in frequency (−20 dB/decade). For a second-order filter the gain decreases by a factor of 100 for each increase of 10 times in frequency.

Figure 10-1*k* shows a common circuit for a second-order low-pass filter. The way you recognize this as a low-pass filter is to look for a dc path from the input to the noninverting input of the amplifier. If the dc path is present, as it is in Figure 10-1*k*, you know that the amplifier can amplify dc and low frequencies. Therefore, it is a low-pass filter with a response such as that shown in Figure 10-3*a*.

For contrast look at the circuit for the second-order high-pass filter in Figure 10-1*l*. Note that in this circuit the dc component of an input signal cannot reach the noninverting input because of the two capacitors in series with that input. Therefore, this circuit will not amplify dc and low-frequency signals. Figure 10-3*b* shows the graph of gain versus frequency for a high-pass filter such as this. Note that the gain-bandwidth product of the op amp limits the high-frequency response of the circuit.

For the low-pass circuit in Figure 10-1*k*, the gain for the flat part of the response curve is 1, or unity, because the output is fed back directly to the inverting input. At the critical frequency, f_c, the gain will be 0.707, and above this frequency the gain will drop off. The critical frequency for the circuit is determined by the equation next to the circuit. The equation assumes that *R*1 and *R*2 are equal, and that the value of *C*1 is twice the value of *C*2. *R*3 is simply a damping resistor. The positive feedback supplied by *C*1 is the reason the gain is only down to 0.707 at the critical frequency rather than down to 0.5 as it would be if we simply cascaded two simple *RC* circuits.

For the high-pass filter, the gain for the flat section of the response curve is also one. Assuming that the two capacitors are equal and the value of *R*2 is twice the value of *R*1, the critical frequency is determined by the formula shown next to Figure 10-1*l*. Again, *R*3 is for damping.

A low-pass filter can be put in series with a high-pass filter to produce a bandpass filter which lets through a desired range of frequencies. There are also many different single amplifier circuits which will pass or reject a band of frequencies.

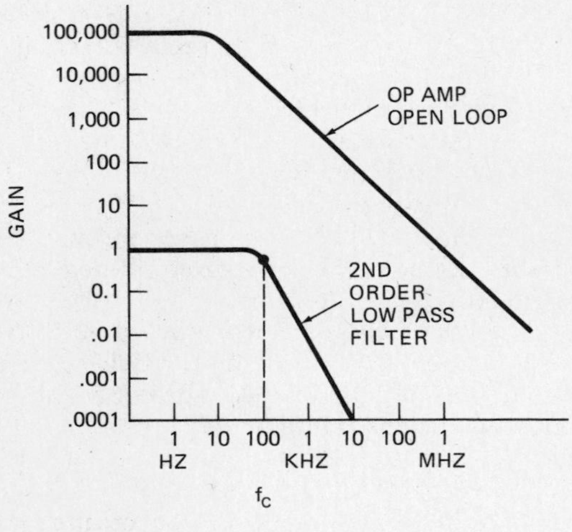

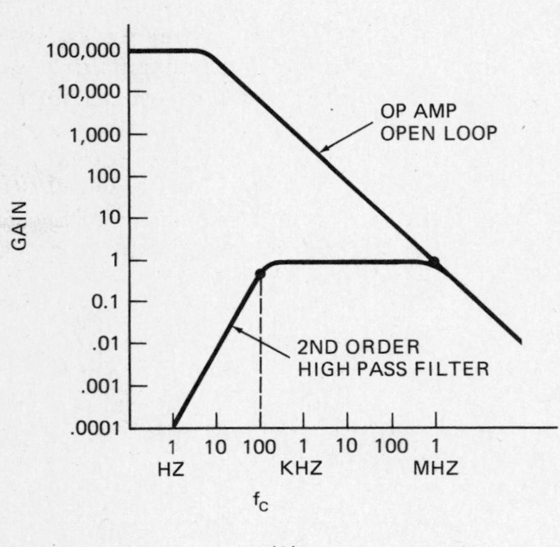

FIGURE 10-3 Gain versus frequency response for second-order low-pass and high-pass filters. *(a)* Low pass. *(b)* High pass.

Now that we have refreshed your memory of basic op-amp circuits we will next discuss some of the different types of sensors you can use to determine the values of temperatures, pressures, position, etc.

SENSORS AND TRANSDUCERS

It would take a book many times the size of this one to describe the operation and applications of all of the different types of available sensors and transducers. What we want to do here is introduce you to a few of these and show how they can be used to get data for microcomputer-based instruments in, for example, our electronics factory.

Light Sensors

One of the simplest light sensors is a light-dependent resistor such as the Clairex CL905 shown in Figure 10-4*a*. A glass window allows light to fall on a zig-zag pattern of cadmium sulfide or cadmium selenide whose resistance depends on the amount of light present. The resistance of the CL905 varies from about 15 MΩ when in the dark to about 15 kΩ when in a bright light. Photoresistors such as this do not have a very fast response time and are not stable with temperature, but they are inexpensive, durable, and sensitive. For these reasons they are usually used in applications where a measurement of the amount of light need not be precise. The devices on top of streetlights which turn them on when it gets dark, for example, contain a photoresistor, a transistor driver, and a mechanical relay as shown in Figure 10-4*b*. As it gets dark, the resistance of the photoresistor goes up. This increases the voltage on the base of the transistor until, at some point, it turns on. This turns on the transistor driving the relay, which in turn switches on the lamp.

Another device used to sense the amount of light present is a photodiode. If light is allowed to fall on a specially constructed silicon diode, the reverse leakage current of the diode increases linearly as the amount of light falling on it increases. A circuit such as that shown in Figure 10-5 can be used to convert this small leakage current to a proportional voltage. Note that in this circuit a negative reference voltage is applied to the noninverting input of the amplifier. The op amp will then produce this same voltage on its inverting input, reverse biasing the photodiode. The op amp will pull the photodiode leakage current through R_f to produce a proportional voltage on the output of the amplifier. For a typical photodiode such as the HP 5082-4203 shown, the reverse leakage current varies from near 0 μA to about 100 μA, so with the 100-kΩ R_f, an output voltage of about 0 V to 10 V will be produced. The circuit will work

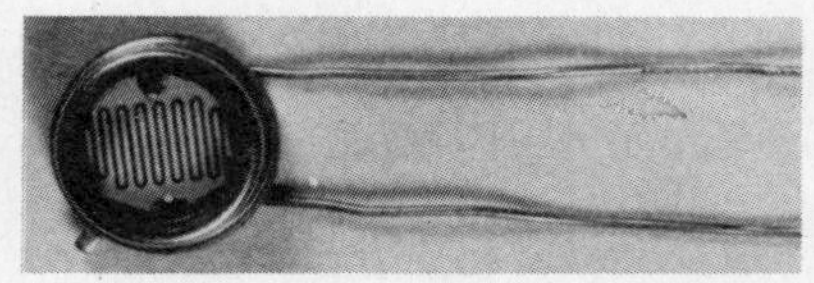

(a)

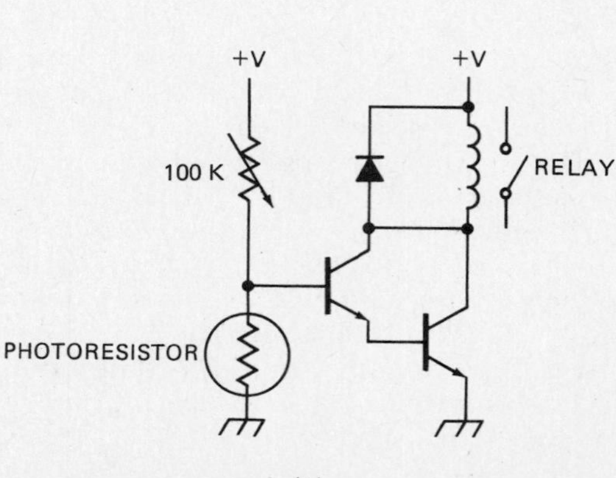

(b)

FIGURE 10-4 *(a)* Cadmium sulfide photocell. *(Clairex Electronics)*. *(b)* Light-controller relay circuit using a photocell.

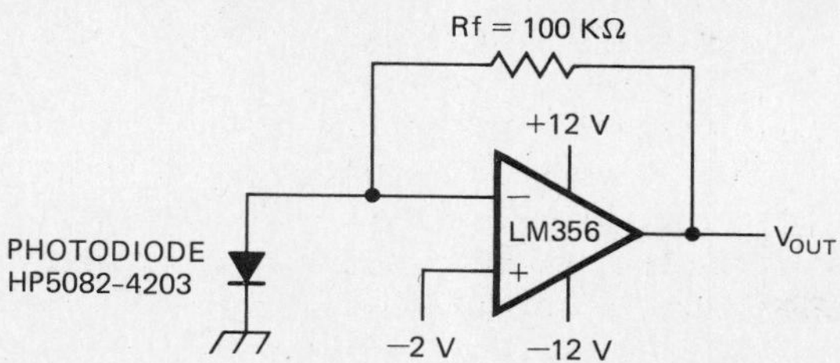

FIGURE 10-5 Photodiode circuit to measure infrared light intensity.

without any reverse bias on the diode, but with the reverse bias, the diode responds faster to changes in light. An LM356 FET input amplifier is used here because it does not require an input bias current.

A photodiode circuit such as this might be used to determine the amount of smoke being emitted from a smokestack. To do this a gallium arsenide infrared LED is put on one side of the smokestack, and the photodetector circuit put on the other. Since smoke absorbs light, the amount of light arriving at the photodetector is a measure of the amount of smoke present. An infrared LED is used here because the photodiode is most sensitive to light wavelengths in the infrared region.

Still another useful light-sensitive device is a solar cell. Common solar cells are simply large, very heavily-doped, silicon PN junctions. Light shining on the solar cell causes a reverse current to flow, just as in the photodiode. Because of the large area and the heavy doping in the solar cell, however, the current produced is milliamperes rather than microamperes. The cell functions as a light-powered battery. Solar cells can be connected in a series-parallel array to produce a solar power supply.

Light meters in cameras, photographic enlargers, and our printed-circuit-board-making machine use solar cells. The current from the solar cell is a linear function of the amount of light falling on the cell. A circuit such as that in Figure 10-5 can be used to convert the output current to a proportional voltage. Because of the larger output current we decrease R_f to a much smaller value, depending on the output current of the cell. We also connect the noninverting input of the amplifier to ground because we don't use reverse biasing with solar cells. The frequency response to light (spectral response) of solar cells has been tailored to match the output of the sun. Therefore, they are ideal in photographic applications where we want a signal proportional to the total light from the sun or from an incandescent lamp.

Temperature Sensors

Again, there are many types of temperature sensors. The two types we discuss here are: semiconductor devices, which are inexpensive and can be used to measure temperatures over the range of −55°C to 100°C, and thermocouples which can be used to measure very low temperatures and very high temperatures.

SEMICONDUCTOR TEMPERATURE SENSORS

The two main types of semiconductor temperature sensors are temperature-sensitive voltage sources and temperature-sensitive current sources. An example of the first type is the National LM35 which we show the circuit connections for in Figure 10-6*a*. The voltage output from this circuit increases by 10 mV for each degree Celsius that its temperature is increased. By connecting the output to a negative reference voltage (V_S) as shown, the sensor will give a meaningful output for a temperature range of −55 to +150°C. You adjust the output to zero volts for 0°C. The output voltage can be amplified to give the voltage range you need for a particular applica-

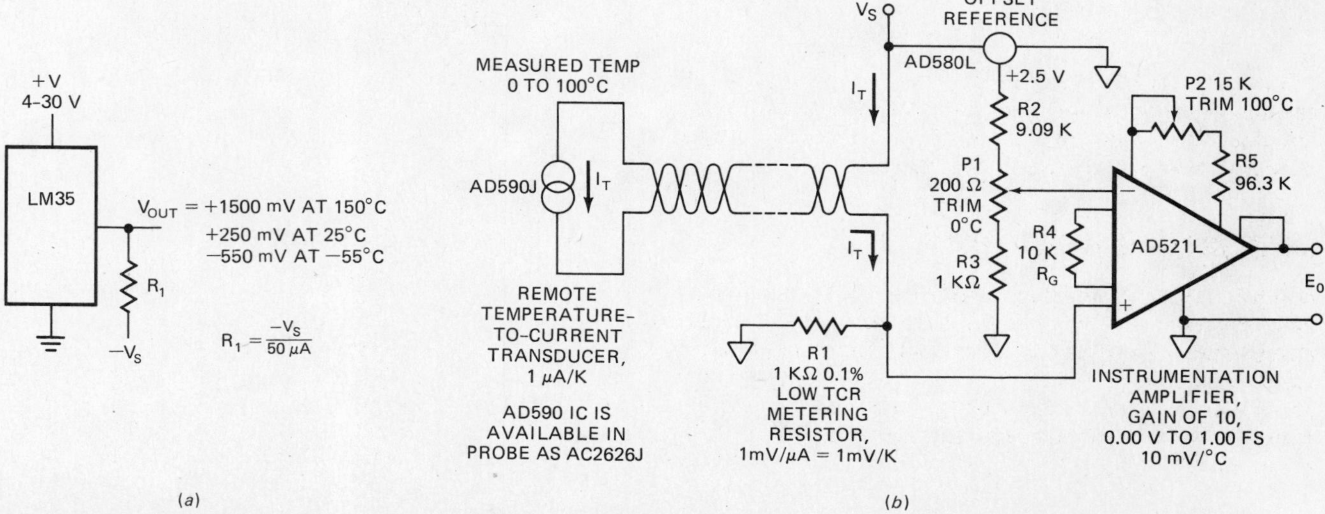

FIGURE 10-6 Semiconductor temperature-sensor circuits. *(a)* LM35 temperature-dependent voltage source. *(b)* AD590 temperature-dependent current source. *(Analog Devices Incorporated)*

tion. In a later section of this chapter we show another circuit using the LM35 temperature sensor. The accuracy of this device is about 1°C.

Another common semiconductor temperature sensor is a temperature-dependent current source such as the Analog Devices AD590. The AD590 produces a current of 1 μA/°Kelvin. Figure 10-6*b* shows a circuit which converts this current to a proportional voltage. In this circuit the current from the sensor (I_T) is passed through an approximately 1-kΩ resistor to ground. This produces a voltage which changes by 1 mV/°Kelvin. The AD580 is a precision voltage reference used to produce a reference voltage of 273.2 mV. With this voltage applied to the inverting input of the amplifier, the amplifier output will be at zero volts for 0°C. The advantage of a current-source sensor is that voltage drops in long connecting wires do not have any effect on the output value. If the gain and offset are carefully adjusted, the accuracy of the circuit in Figure 10-6*b* is ±1°C using an AD590K part.

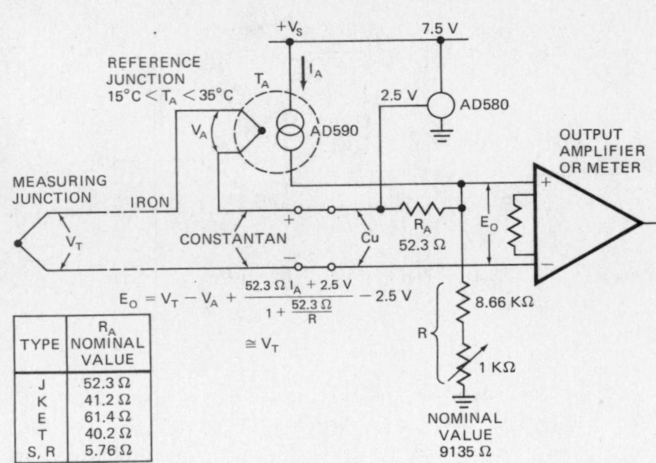

TYPE	R_A NOMINAL VALUE
J	52.3 Ω
K	41.2 Ω
E	61.4 Ω
T	40.2 Ω
S, R	5.76 Ω

FIGURE 10-7 Circuit showing amplification and cold-junction compensation for thermocouple. *(Analog Devices Incorporated)*

THERMOCOUPLES

Whenever two different metals are put in contact, a small voltage is produced between them. The voltage developed depends on the types of metals used and the temperature. Depending on the metals, the developed voltage increases between 7 μV and 75 μV for each degree Celsius increase in temperature. Different combinations of metals are useful for measuring different temperature ranges. A thermocouple junction made of iron and constantan, commonly called a type J thermocouple, has a useful temperature range of about −184 to +760°C. A junction of platinum and an alloy of platinum and 13 percent rhodium has a useful range of 0°C to about 1600°C. Thermocouples can be made small, rugged, and stable; however, they have three major problems which must be overcome.

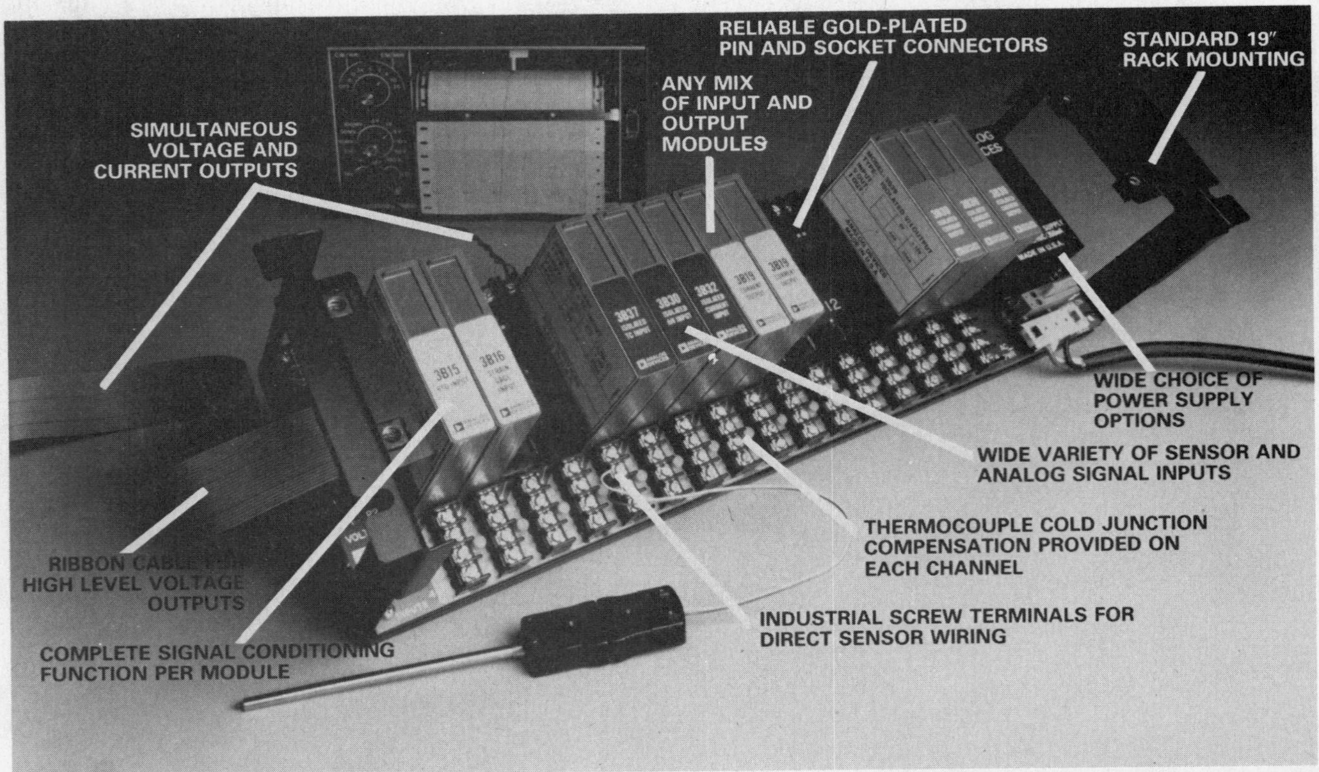

FIGURE 10-8 Packaging of signal-conditioning circuitry for use in industrial environments. *(Analog Devices Incorporated)*

First of these is the fact that the output is very small and must be amplified a great deal to bring it up into the range where it can, for example, drive an A/D converter. Second, in order to make accurate measurements, a second junction made of the same metals must be included in the circuit as a reference. Adding this second junction is referred to as *cold-junction compensation*. Figure 10-7 shows a circuit to amplify the output of a thermocouple and provide cold-junction compensation for a type J thermocouple.

The first thing to notice in the circuit is that the reference junction is connected in the reverse direction from the measuring junction. This is done so that the output connecting wires are both constantan. The thermocouples formed by connecting these wires to the copper wires going to the amplifier will then cancel out. The resultant output voltage will be the difference between the voltages across the two thermocouples. If we simply amplify the output of the two thermocouples, however, there is a problem if the temperature of both thermocouples is changing. The problem is that it is impossible to tell which thermocouple caused a change in output voltage. One cure for this is to put the reference junction in an ice bath or a small oven to hold it at a constant temperature. This solution is usually inconvenient, so instead a circuit such as that in Figure 10-7 is used to compensate electronically for changes in the temperature of the reference junction.

As we discussed in a previous section the AD590 shown here produces a current proportional to its temperature. The AD590 is attached to the reference thermocouple so that they are both at the same temperature. The current from the AD590, when passed through the resistor network, produces a voltage which compensates for changes in the reference thermocouple with temperature. The output amplifier for this circuit is a differential amplifier such as that shown in Figure 10-1*g* or the instrumentation amplifier shown in Figure 10-1*h*.

The third problem with thermocouples is that their output voltages do not change linearly with temperature. This can be corrected with analog circuitry which changes the gain of an amplifier according to the value of the signal. However, when a thermocouple is used with a microcomputer-based instrument, the correction can be easily done using a lookup table in ROM. An A/D converter converts the voltage from the thermocouple to a digital value. The digital value is then used as a pointer to a ROM location which contains the correct temperature for that reading.

For use in industrial environments, circuitry such as that in Figure 10-7 is usually packaged in durable modules and mounted on racks in metal cabinets. Figure 10-8 shows some of the Analog Devices 3B series signal-conditioning modules on a rack-mount panel. The 3B37, for example, is a thermocouple-amplifier module with built in cold-junction compensation. The silver probe in front of the unit is a common type of thermocouple. This rack unit is constructed so that you can plug in the modules you need for a given application. Modules such as these usually have both a voltage output and a current output. Sending a signal as a current has the advantages that the signal amplitude is then not affected by resistance, induced-voltage noise, or voltage drops in a long connecting line. A common range of currents used to represent analog signals in industrial environments is 4 mA to 20 mA. A current of 4 mA represents a zero output, and a current of 20 mA represents the full-scale value. The reason that the current range is offset from zero is so that a current of zero is left to represent an open circuit. The current can be converted to a proportional voltage at the receiving end by simply passing it through a resistor.

Force and Pressure Transducers

To convert force or pressure (force/area) to a proportional electrical signal, the most common methods use *strain gages* and *linear variable differential transformers* (LVDTs). Both of these methods involve moving something. This is why we refer to them as *transducers* rather than as sensors. Here's how strain gages work.

STRAIN GAGES AND LOAD CELLS

A strain gage is a small resistor whose value changes when its length is changed. It may be made of thin wire, thin foil, or semiconductor material. Figure 10-9*a* shows a simple setup for measuring force or weight with strain gages. One end of a piece of spring steel is attached to a fixed surface. A strain gage is glued on the top of the flexible bar. The force or weight to be measured is applied to the unattached end of the bar. As the applied force bends the bar, the strain gage is stretched, increasing its resistance. Since the amount that the bar is bent is directly proportional to the applied force, the change in resistance will be proportional to the applied force. If a current is passed through the strain gage, then the change in voltage across the strain gage will be proportional to the applied force.

Unfortunately, the resistance of the strain-gage elements also changes with temperature. To compensate for this problem two strain-gage elements mounted at right angles as shown in Figure 10-9*b* are often used. Both of the elements will change resistance with temperature, but only element A will change resistance appreciably with applied force. When these two elements are connected in a balanced-bridge configuration as shown in Figure 10-9*c*, any change in resistance of the elements due to temperature will have no effect on the differential output of the bridge. However, as force is applied, the resistance of the element under strain will change and produce a small differential output voltage. The full-scale differential output voltage is typically 2 or 3 mV per volt of applied voltage. For example if 10 V is applied to the bridge, the full-load output voltage will only be 20 or 30 mV. This small signal can be amplified with a differential amplifier or an instrumentation amplifier. The Analog Devices 3B16 module shown in Figure 10-8 provides a 10-V excitation voltage and amplification for the differential output signal for a strain-gage bridge.

Strain-gage bridges are used in many different forms to measure many different types of force and pressure. If

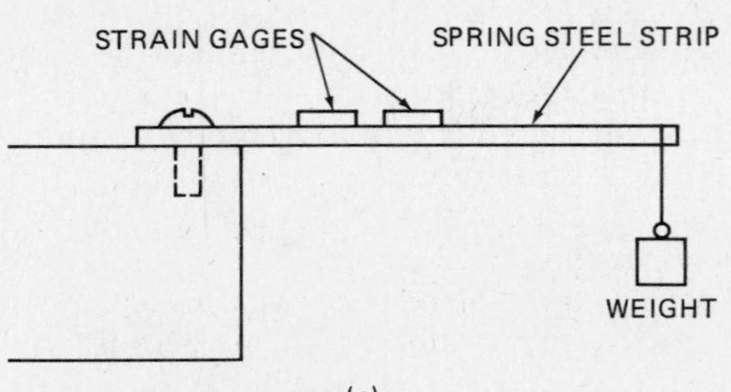

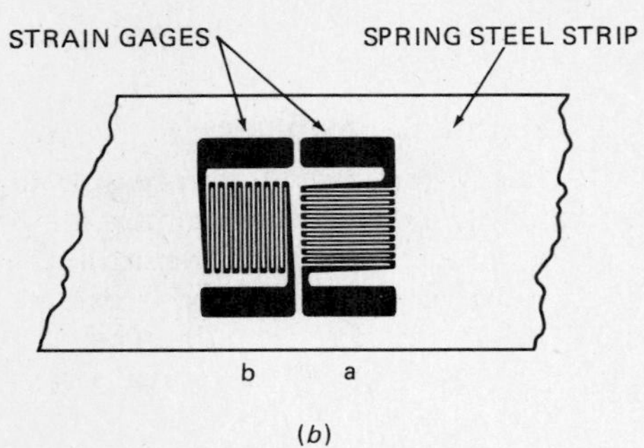

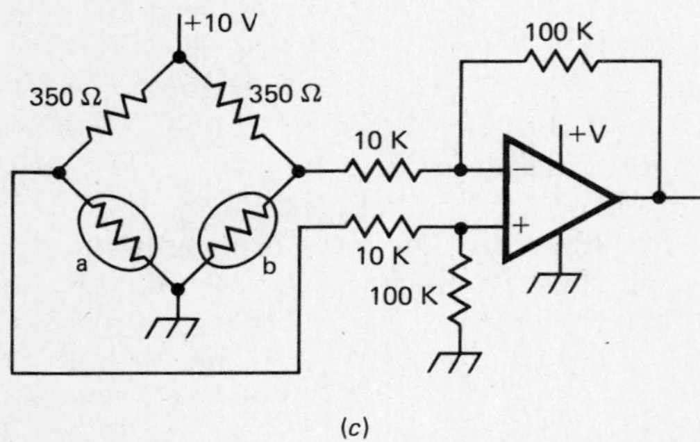

FIGURE 10-9 Strain gauges used to measure force. *(a)* Side view. *(b)* Top view (expanded). *(c)* Circuit connections.

FIGURE 10-10 Photograph of load-cell transducer used to measure weight. *(Transducers, Incorporated)*

FIGURE 10-11 LX1804GBZ pressure transducer. *(Sensym, Inc.)*

the strain-gage bridge is connected to a bendable beam structure as shown in Figure 10-9*a*, the result is called a *load cell* and is used to measure weight. Figure 10-10 shows a 10-lb load cell that might be used in a microprocessor-controlled delicatessen scale or postal scale. Larger versions can be used to weigh barrels being filled, or even trucks.

If a strain-gage bridge is mounted on a movable diaphragm in a threaded housing, the output of the bridge will be proportional to the pressure applied to the diaphragm. If a vacuum is present on one side of the diaphragm, then the value read out will be a measure of the absolute pressure. If one side of the diaphragm is open then the output will be a measure of the pressure relative to atmospheric pressure. If the two sides of the diaphragm are connected to two other pressure sources, then the output will be a measure of the differential pressure between the two sides. Figure 10-11 shows a SENSYM LX1804GBZ pressure transducer which measures pressures in the range of 0 to 15 lb per square inch. A transducer such as this might be used to measure blood pressure in a microcomputer-based medical instrument.

LINEAR VARIABLE DIFFERENTIAL TRANSFORMERS

An *LVDT* is another type of transducer often used to measure force, pressure or position. Figure 10-12 shows the basic structure of an LVDT. It consists of three coils of wire wound on the same form and a movable iron core. An ac excitation signal of perhaps 20 kHz is applied to the primary. The secondaries are connected so that the voltage induced in one opposes the voltage induced in the other. If the core is centered then the induced voltages are equal and they cancel, so there is no net output voltage. If the coil is moved off center, coupling will be stronger to one secondary coil so that coil

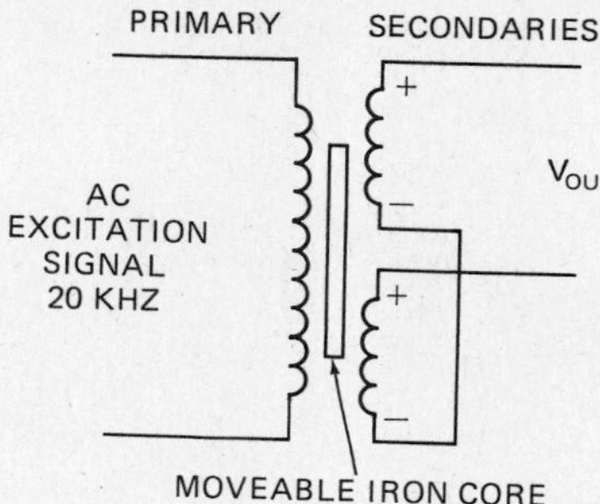

FIGURE 10-12 Linear variable differential transformer (LVDT) structure.

will produce a greater output voltage. The result will be a net output voltage. The phase relationship between the output signal and the input signal is an indication of which direction the core moved from the center position. The amplitude of the output signal is linearly proportional to how far the core moves from the center position.

An LVDT can be used directly in this form to measure displacement or position. If you add a spring so that a force is required to move the core, then the voltage out of the LVDT will be proportional to the force applied to the core. In this form the LVDT can be used in a load cell for an electronic scale. Likewise, if a spring is added and the core of the LVDT attached to a diaphragm in a threaded housing, the output from the LVDT will be proportional to the pressure exerted on the diaphragm. We do not have space here to show the ac-interface circuitry required for an LVDT.

Flow Sensors

If we are going to control the flow rate of some material in our electronics factory, we need to be able to measure it. Depending on the material, flow rate, and temperature, we use different methods.

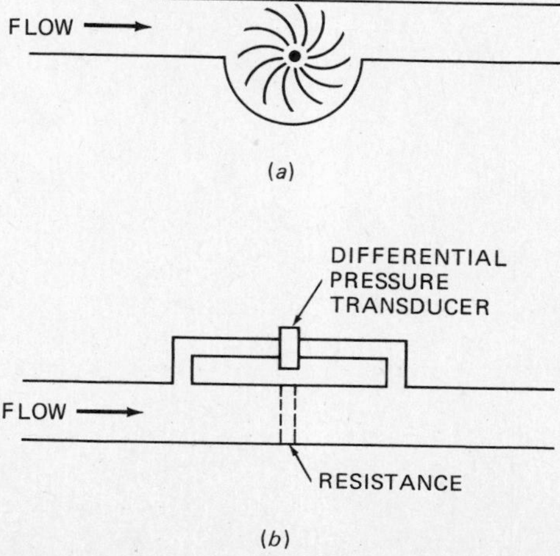

FIGURE 10-13 Flow sensors. *(a)* Paddle wheel. *(b)* Differential pressure.

One method used is to put a paddle wheel in the flow as shown in Figure 10-13*a*. The rate at which the paddle wheel turns is proportional to the rate of flow of a liquid or gas. An optical encoder can be attached to the shaft of the paddle wheel to produce digital information as to how fast the paddle wheel is turning.

A second common method of measuring flow is with a *differential pressure transducer*, as shown in Figure 10-13*b*. A wire mesh or screen is put in the pipe to create some resistance. Flow through this resistance produces a difference in pressure between the two sides of the resistance. The pressure transducer gives an output proportional to the difference in pressure between the two sides of the resistance. In the same way that the voltage across an electrical resistor is proportional to the flow of current through the resistor, the output of the pressure transducer is proportional to the flow of a liquid or gas through the pipe.

Other Sensors

As we mentioned previously, the number of different types of sensors is very large. In addition to the types we have discussed, there are sensors to measure pH, concentration of various gases, thickness of materials, and just about anything else you might want to measure. Often you can use commonly available transducers in creative ways to solve a particular application problem you have. Suppose, for example, that you need to accurately determine the level of a liquid in a large tank. To do this you could install a pressure transducer at the bottom of the tank. The pressure in a liquid is proportional to the height of the liquid in the tank, so you can easily convert a pressure reading to the desired liquid height. The point here is to check out what is available and then be creative.

D/A CONVERTER OPERATION, INTERFACING, AND APPLICATIONS

In the previous sections of this chapter we have discussed how we use sensors to get electrical signals proportional to pressure, temperature, etc. and how we use op amps to amplify and filter these electrical signals. The next logical step would be to show you how we use an A/D converter to get these signals into digital form that a microcomputer can work with. However, since D/A converters are simpler and several types of A/D converter have D/As as part of their circuitry, we will discuss D/As first.

D/A Converter Operation and Specifications

OPERATION

The purpose of a digital-to-analog converter is to convert a binary word to a proportional current or voltage. To see how this is done let's look at the simple op-amp circuit in Figure 10-14. This circuit functions as an adder. Since the noninverting input of the op amp is grounded,

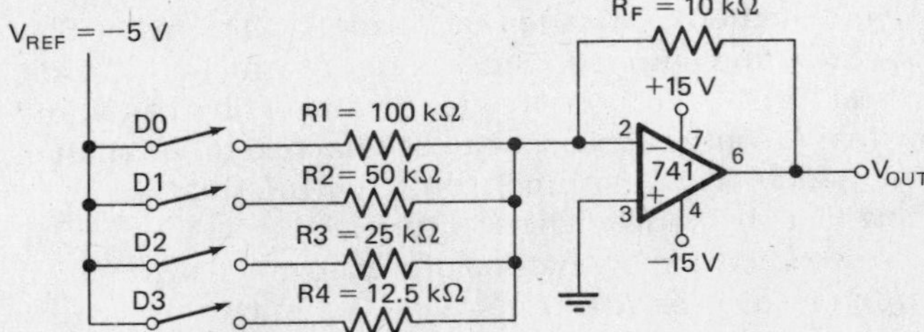

FIGURE 10-14 Simple 4-bit digital-to-analog (D/A) converter.

the op amp will work day and night to hold the inverting input also at zero volts. This point, remember, is referred to as a virtual ground or summing point. When one of the switches is closed a current will flow from the −5-V (V_{REF}) through that resistor to the summing point. The op amp will pull the current on through the feedback resistor to produce a proportional output voltage. If you close switch D0, for example, a current of 0.05 mA will flow into the summing point. In order to pull this current through the feedback resistor, the op amp must put a voltage of 0.05 mA × 10 kΩ or 0.5 V on its output. If you also close switch D1, it will send another 0.1 mA into the summing point. In order to pull the sum of the currents through the feedback resistor, the op amp has to output a voltage of 0.15 mA × 10 kΩ or 1.5 V.

The point here is that the binary-weighted resistors produce binary-weighted currents which are summed by the op amp to produce a proportional output voltage. The binary word applied to the switches produces a proportional output voltage. Technically the output voltage is "digital" because it can only have certain fixed values just as the display on a digital voltmeter can. However, the output simulates an analog signal, so we refer to it as analog. Switch D3 in Figure 10-14 represents the most significant bit, because closing it produces the largest current. Note that since V_{REF} is negative, the output will go positive as switches are closed.

As you see here, the heart of a D/A converter is a set of binary-weighted current sources which can be switched on or off according to a binary word applied to its inputs. Since these current sources are usually inside an IC, we don't need to discuss the different ways the binary-weighted currents can be produced. As shown in Figure 10-14, a simple op-amp circuit can be used to convert the sum of the currents to a proportional voltage if needed.

D/A CHARACTERISTICS AND SPECIFICATIONS

Figure 10-15 shows the circuit for an inexpensive IC D/A converter with an op-amp circuit as a current-to-voltage converter. We will use this circuit for our discussion of D/A characteristics.

The first characteristic of a D/A converter to consider is *resolution*. This is determined by the number of bits in the input binary word. A converter with eight binary inputs such as the one in Figure 10-15 has 2^8 or 256 possible output levels, so its resolution is 1 part in 256. As another example, a 12-bit converter has a resolution of 1 part in 2^{12} or 4096. Resolution is sometimes expressed as a percentage. The resolution of an 8-bit converter then is about 0.39 percent.

The next D/A characteristic to determine is the *full-scale output voltage*. For the converter in Figure 10-15 the current for all of the switches is supplied by V_{REF} through $R14$. The current output from pin 4 of the D/A is pulled through R_o to produce the output voltage. The formula for the output voltage is shown under the circuit in Figure 10-15. In the equation the term $A1$, for example, represents the condition of the switch for that bit. If a switch is closed, allowing a current to flow, put a 1 in that bit. If a switch is open, put a 0 in that bit. As we also show in Figure 10-15, if all of the switches are closed, the output will be (10 V)(255/256) or 9.961 V. Even though the output voltage can never actually get to 10 V, this is referred to as a *10-V output converter*. The maximum output voltage of a converter will always have a value 1 least significant bit less than the named value. As another example of this, suppose that you have a 12-bit, 10-V converter. The value of 1 LSB will be (10 V)/4096 or 2.44 mV. The highest voltage out of this converter when it is properly adjusted will then be (10.0000 − 0.0024) V or 9.9976 V.

Several different binary codes such as *straight binary*, BCD, and *offset binary* are commonly used as inputs to D/A converters. We will show examples of these codes in a later discussion of A/D converters.

The accuracy specification for a D/A converter is a comparison between the actual output and the expected output. It is specified as a percentage of the full-scale

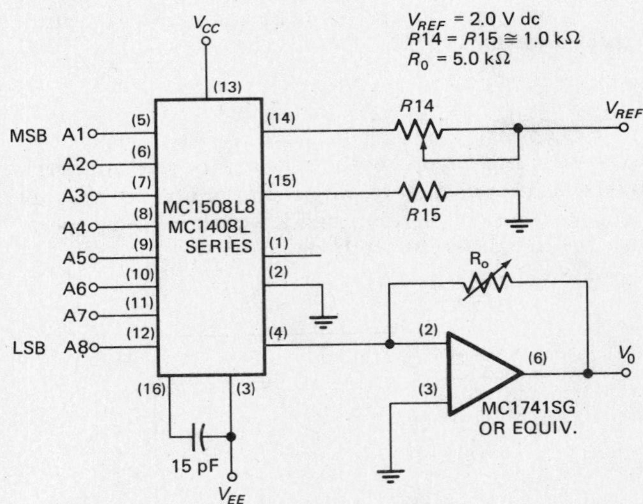

Theoretical V_0

$$V_0 = \frac{V_{REF}}{R14}(R_0)\left\{\frac{A1}{2}+\frac{A2}{4}+\frac{A3}{8}+\frac{A4}{16}+\frac{A5}{32}+\frac{A6}{64}+\frac{A7}{128}+\frac{A8}{256}\right\}$$

ADJUST V_{REF}, $R14$ OR R_0 SO THAT V_0 WITH ALL DIGITAL INPUTS AT HIGH LEVEL IS EQUAL TO 9.961 V

$$V_0 = \frac{2\text{ V}}{1\text{ k}\Omega}(5\text{ k}\Omega)\left\{\frac{1}{2}+\frac{1}{4}+\frac{1}{8}+\frac{1}{16}+\frac{1}{32}+\frac{1}{64}+\frac{1}{128}+\frac{1}{256}\right\}$$

$$= 10\text{ V}\left\{\frac{255}{256}\right\} = 9.961\text{ V}$$

FIGURE 10-15 Motorola MC1408 8-bit D/A with current-to-voltage converter.

output voltage or current. If a converter has a full-scale output of 10 V and ±0.2 percent accuracy, then the *maximum error* for any output will be 0.002 × 10.00 V or 20 mV. Ideally the maximum error for a D/A converter should be no more than ±1/2 of the value of the LSB.

Another important specification for a D/A converter is *linearity*. Linearity is a measure of how much the output ramp deviates from a straight line as the converter is stepped from no switches on to all switches on. Ideally the deviation of the output from a straight line should be no greater than ±1/2 of the value of the LSB to maintain overall accuracy. However, many D/A converters are marketed which have linearity errors greater than that. National Semiconductor, for example, markets the DAC1020, DAC1021, DAC1022 series of 10-bit-resolution converters. The linearity specification for the DAC1020 is 0.05 percent, which is appropriate for a 10-bit converter. The DAC1021 has a linearity specification of 0.10 percent and the DAC1022 has a specification of 0.20 percent. The question that may occur to you at this point is, "What good is it to have a 10-bit converter if the linearity is only equivalent to that of an 8- or 9-bit converter?" The answer to this question is that for many applications the resolution given by a 10-bit converter is needed for small output signals, but it doesn't matter if the output value is somewhat nonlinear for large signals. The price you pay for a D/A converter is proportional not only to its resolution, but also to its linearity specification.

Still another D/A specification to look for is *settling time*. When you change the binary word applied to the input of a converter, the output will change to the appropriate new value. The output, however, may overshoot the correct value and "ring" for a while before finally settling down to the correct value. The time the output takes to get within ±1/2 LSB of the final value is called settling time. As an example, the National DAC1020 10-bit converter has a typical settling time of 500 ns for a full-scale change on the output. This specification is important, because if a converter is operated at too high a frequency, it may not have time to settle to one value before it is switched to the next.

D/A Applications and Interfacing to Microcomputers

D/A converters have many applications besides those where they are used with a microcomputer. In a compact-disk audio player, for example, a 13- or 14-bit D/A converter is used to convert the binary data read off the disk by a laser to an analog audio signal. Most speech-synthesizer ICs contain an D/A converter to convert stored binary data for words into analog audio signals. Here, however, we are primarily interested in the use of a D/A converter with a microcomputer.

The inputs of the D/A circuit (A1–A8) in Figure 10-15 can connected directly to a microcomputer output port. As part of a program you can produce any desired voltage on the output of the D/A. Here's some ideas as to what you might use this circuit for.

As a first example, suppose that you want to build a microcomputer-controlled tester which determines the effect of power-supply voltage on the output voltage of some integrated-circuit amplifiers. If you connect the output of the D/A converter to the reference input of a programmable power supply, or simply add the high-current buffer circuit shown in Figure 10-16 to the output of the D/A, you have a power supply which you can vary under program control. To determine the output voltage of the IC under test as you vary its supply voltage, connect the input of an A/D converter to the IC output, and connect the output of the A/D converter to an input port of your microcomputer. You can then read in the value of the output voltage on the IC.

Another application you might use a D/A and a power buffer for is to vary the voltage supplied to a small resistive heater under program control. Also, the speed of small dc motors is proportional to the amount of current passed through them, so you could connect a small dc motor on the output of the power buffer and control the speed of the motor by the value you output to the D/A. Note that without feedback control the speed of the motor will vary if the load changes. Later we show you how to add feedback control to maintain constant motor speed under changing loads.

So far we have talked about using an 8-bit D/A with a microprocessor. Interfacing an 8-bit converter involves simply connecting the inputs of the converter to an output port, or for some D/As simply connecting the inputs to the buses as you would a port device. Now, suppose that for some application you need 12 bits of resolution, so you need to interface a 12-bit converter. If you are working with a system which has an 8-bit data bus, your first thought might be to connect the lower eight inputs of the 12-bit converter to one output port and the upper four inputs to another port. You could send the lower 8 bits with one write operation, and the upper 4 bits with another write operation. However, there is a potential problem with this approach caused by the time between the two writes. Suppose, for example, that you want to change the output of a 12-bit converter from 0000 1111 1111 to 0001 0000 0000. When you write the lower 8 bits, the output will go from 0000 1111 1111 to 0000 0000 0000. When you write the upper 4 bits, the output will then go back up to the desired 0001 0000 0000. The point here is that for the time between the two writes the output will go to an unwanted value. In

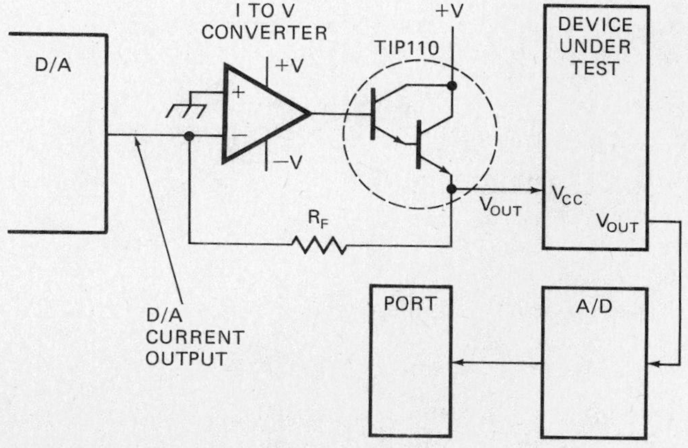

FIGURE 10-16 High-power buffer for D/A output.

many systems this could be disastrous. The cure for this problem is to put latches on the input lines. The latches can be loaded separately and then strobed together to pass all 12 bits to the D/A converter at the same time.

Many currently available D/A converters contain built-in latches to make this easier. Figure 10-17*a* shows a block diagram of the National DAC1230- and DAC1208-type 12-bit converters. Note the internal latches and the register. The DAC1230 series of parts has the upper 4 input bits connected to the lower 4 bits so that the 12 bits can be written with two write operations from an 8-bit port or data bus such as that of the 8088 microprocessor. The DAC1208 series of parts has the upper four data inputs available separately so they can be connected directly to the bus in a system which has a 16-bit data bus, as shown in Figure 10-17*a*. If, for example, you want to connect up a DAC1208 converter to an SDK-86 board, you can simply connect the DAC1208 data inputs to the lower 12 data bus lines, connect the $\overline{CS}$ input to an address decoder output, connect the $\overline{WR1}$ input to the system $\overline{WR}$ line, and tie the $\overline{WR2}$ and $\overline{XFER}$ inputs to ground. The BYTE1/$\overline{BYTE2}$ input is tied high. You then write words to the converter just as if it were a 16-bit port. The timing parameters for the DAC1208 are acceptable for an 8086 operating with a clock frequency of 5 MHz or less. For higher 8086 clock frequencies you would have to add a one-shot or other circuitry which inserts a WAIT state each time you write to the D/A. Here's a few notes about the analog connections for these devices.

These D/A converters require a precision voltage reference. The circuit in Figure 10-17*b* uses a −10.000-V reference. The D/A converters have a current output so we use an op amp, as shown, to convert the output current to a proportional voltage. A FET input amplifier is used, because the input bias current of a bipolar input amp might affect the accuracy of the output. The DAC1208 and DAC1230 have built-in feedback resistors which match the temperature characteristics of the internal current-divider resistors, so all you have to add externally is a 50-Ω resistor for "tweaking" purposes. With a −10.000-V reference as shown, the output voltage will be equal to (the digital input word/4096) × (+10.000 V). Note that the D/A has both a digital ground and an analog ground. To avoid getting digital noise in the analog portions of the circuit, these two should be connected together only at the power supply.

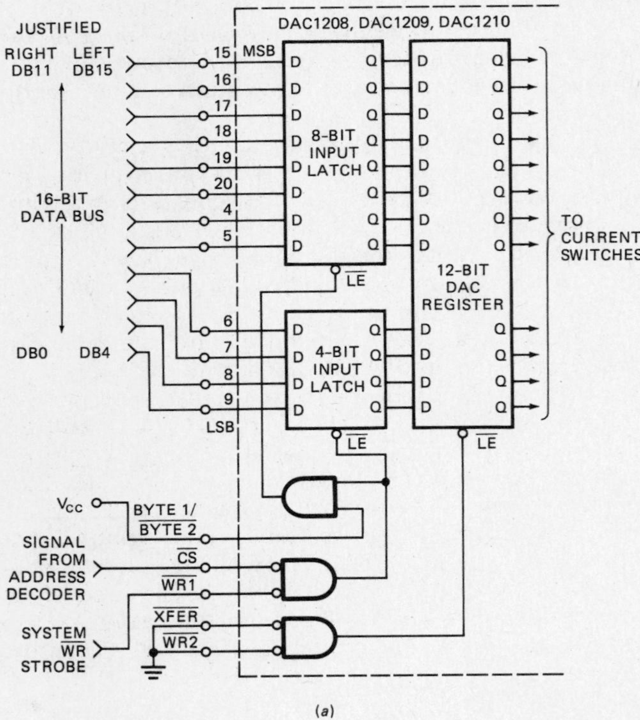

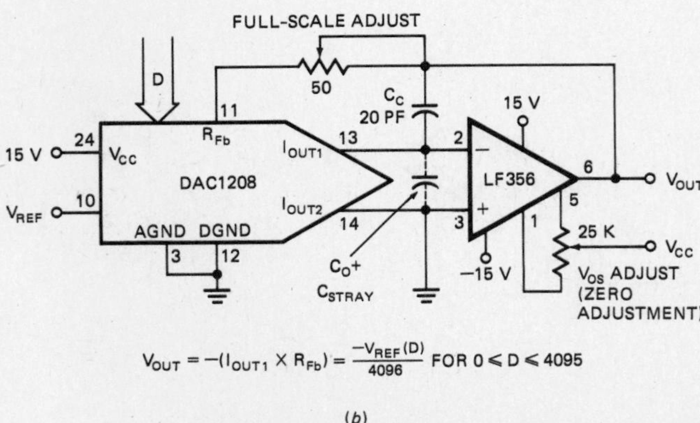

$$V_{OUT} = -(I_{OUT1} \times R_{Fb}) = \frac{-V_{REF}(D)}{4096} \text{ FOR } 0 \leq D \leq 4095$$

(b)

FIGURE 10-17 *(a)* National DAC1208 12-bit D/A input block diagram showing internal latches. *(b)* Analog circuit connections.

A/D CONVERTER TYPES, SPECIFICATIONS, AND INTERFACING

A/D Converter Types

The function of an A/D converter is to produce a digital word which represents the magnitude of some analog voltage or current. The specifications for an A/D converter are very similar to those for a D/A converter. The resolution of an A/D converter refers to the number of bits in the output binary word. An 8-bit converter, for example, has a resolution of 1 part in 256. Accuracy and linearity specifications have the same meanings for an A/D converter as we described previously for a D/A converter. Another important specification for an A/D converter is its *conversion time*. This is simply the time it takes the converter to produce a valid output binary code for an applied input voltage. When we refer to a converter as *high-speed* we mean it has a short conversion time. There are many different ways to do an A/D conversion, but we only have space here to review three commonly used methods, which represent a wide variety of conversion times.

PARALLEL COMPARATOR A/D CONVERTER

Figure 10-18 shows a circuit for a 2-bit A/D converter using *parallel comparators*. A voltage divider sets reference voltages on the inverting inputs of each of the com-

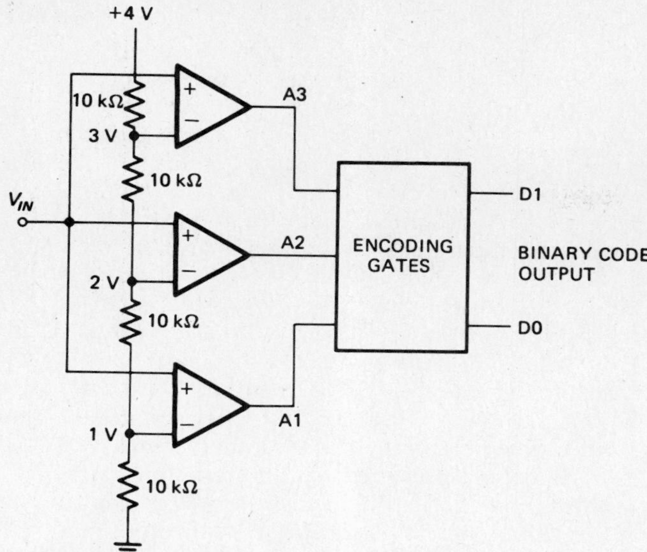

FIGURE 10-18 Parallel comparator A/D converter.

parators. The voltage at the top of the divider chain represents the full-scale value for the converter. The voltage to be converted is applied to the noninverting inputs of all of the comparators in parallel. If the input voltage on a comparator is greater than the reference voltage on the inverting input, the output of the comparator will go high. The outputs of the comparators then give us a digital representation of the voltage level of the input signal. With an input voltage of 2.6 V, for example, the outputs of comparators *A*1 and *A*2 will be high.

The major advantage of a parallel, or *flash*, A/D is its speed of conversion, which is simply the propagation delay time of the comparators. The output code from the comparators is not a standard binary code, but it can be converted with some simple logic. The major disadvantage of a flash A/D is the number of comparators needed to produce a result with a reasonable amount of resolution. The 2-bit converter in Figure 10-18 requires three comparators. To produce a converter with *N* bits of resolution you need $(2^N - 1)$ comparators. In other words for an 8-bit conversion you need 255 comparators, and for a 10-bit flash converter you need 1023 comparators. Single-package flash converters are available from TRW for applications where the high speed is required, but they are relatively expensive. Devices are available which can do an 8-bit conversion in 20 ns.

DUAL-SLOPE A/D CONVERTERS

Figure 10-19*a* shows a functional block diagram of a *dual-slope* A/D converter. This type of converter is often used as the heart of a digital voltmeter because it can give a large number of bits of resolution at a low cost. Here's how the converter in Figure 10-19 works.

To start, the control circuitry resets all of the counters to zero and connects the input of the integrator to the input voltage to be converted. If you assume the input voltage is positive, then this will cause the output of the integrator to ramp negative as shown in Figure 10-19*b*. As soon as the output of the integrator goes a few microvolts below ground, the comparator output will go high. The comparator output being high enables the AND gate and lets the 1-MHz clock into the counter chain. After some fixed number of counts the control circuitry switches the input of the integrator to a negative reference voltage and resets the counters all to zero. With a negative input voltage the integrator output will ramp positive as shown in Figure 10-19*b*. When the integrator output crosses zero volts, the comparator output will drop low and shut off the clock signal to the counters. The number of counts required for the integrator output to get back to zero is directly proportional to the input voltage. For the circuit shown in Figure 10-19*a*, an input signal of +1 V, for example, produces a count of 1000. Because the resistor and the capacitor on the integrator are used for both the input voltage integrate and the reference integrate, small variations in their value with temperature do not have any effect on the accuracy of the conversion.

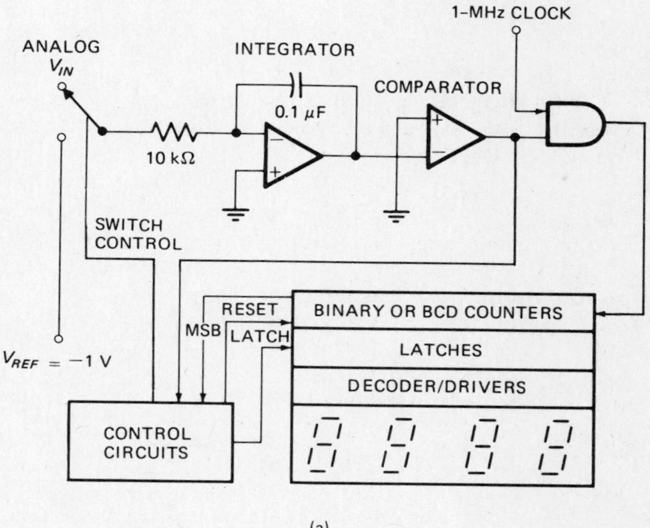

(*a*)

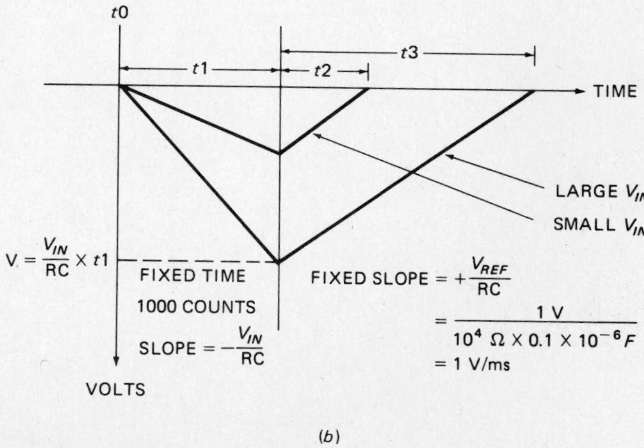

(*b*)

FIGURE 10-19 Dual-slope A/D converter. *(a)* Circuit. *(b)* Integrator output waveform.

Complete slope-type A/D converters are readily available in single IC packages. One example is the Intersil ICL7136 which contains all of the circuitry for a 3½-digit A/D converter and all of the interface circuitry needed to drive a 3½-digit LCD. Another example is the Intersil ICL7135 which contains all of the circuitry for a 4½-digit A/D converter and has a multiplexed BCD output. Note that, because of the usual use of this type of converter, we often express its resolution in terms of a number of digits. The full-scale reading for a 3½-digit converter is 1999, so the resolution corresponds to about 1 part in 2000. A two-chip set, the Intersil ICL8068 and ICL7104-16, contains all of the circuitry for a slope-type 16-bit binary output A/D converter.

The main disadvantage of slope-type converters is their slow speed. A 4½-digit unit may take 300 ms to do a conversion.

SUCCESSIVE-APPROXIMATION A/D CONVERTERS

Figure 10-20 shows a circuit for an 8-bit *successive-approximation* converter which uses readily available parts. The heart of this converter is a successive-approximation register (SAR) such as the MC14549 which functions as follows.

On the first clock pulse at the start of a conversion cycle the SAR outputs a high on its most-significant bit to the MC1408 D/A converter. The D/A converter and the amplifier convert this to a voltage and apply it to one input of a comparator. If this voltage is higher than the input voltage on the other input of the comparator, the comparator output will go low and tell the SAR to turn off that bit because it is too large. If the voltage from the D/A converter is less than the input voltage, then the comparator output will be high, which tells the SAR to keep that bit on. When the next clock pulse occurs, the SAR will turn on the next-most-significant bit to the D/A converter. Based on the answer this produces from the comparator, the SAR will keep or reset this bit. The SAR proceeds in this way on down to the least-significant bit, adding each bit to the total in turn and using the signal from the comparator to decide whether to keep that bit in the result. Only 8 clock pulses are needed to do the actual conversion here. When the conversion is complete the binary result is on the parallel outputs of the SAR. The SAR sends out an end-of-conversion (EOC) signal to indicate this. In the circuit in Figure 10-20 the EOC signal is used to strobe the binary result into some latches where it can be read by a microcomputer. If the EOC signal is connected to the start-conversion (SC) input as shown, then the converter will do continuous conversions. Note in the circuit in Figure 10-20 that the noninverting input of the op amp on the 1408 D/A converter is connected to −5 V instead of to ground. This shifts the analog input range from −5 V to +5 V instead of 0 V to +10 V so that sine-waves and other ac signals can be input directly to the converter to be digitized.

The National ADC1280 is a single-chip 12-bit successive-approximation converter which does a conversion in about 22 μs. Datel and Analog Devices have several 12-bit converters with conversion times about 1 μs.

Several commonly available successive-approximation A/D converters have analog multiplexers on their inputs. The National ADC0816, for example, has a 16-input multiplexer. This allows one converter to digitize any one of 16 input signals. You specify the input chan-

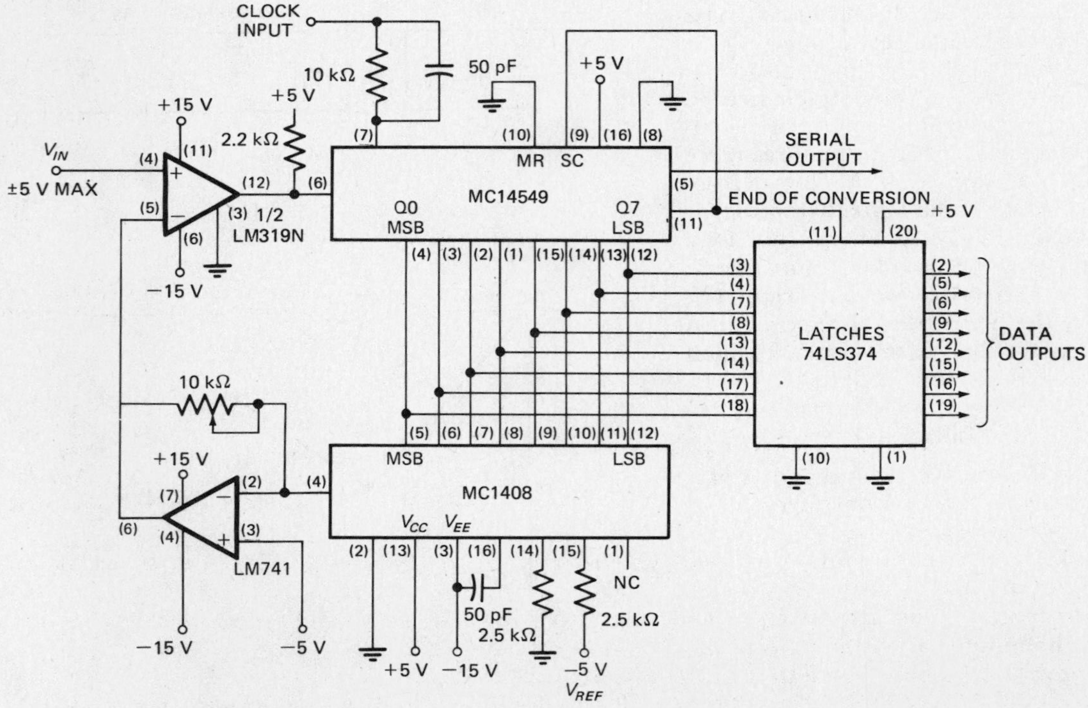

FIGURE 10-20 Successive-approximation A/D converter circuit.

nel you want to digitize with a 4-bit address you apply to the address inputs of the device. An A/D converter with a multiplexer on its inputs is often called a *data acquisition system* or DAS. Later in this chapter we show an application of a DAS in a factory control system.

Before we go on to discuss A/D interfacing, we need to make a few comments about common A/D output codes.

A/D OUTPUT CODES

For convenience in different applications, A/D converters are available with several different, somewhat confusing, output codes. The best way to make sense out of these different codes is to see them all together with representative values as shown in Figure 10-21. The values shown here are for an 8-bit converter, but you can extend them to any number of bits.

For an A/D converter with only a positive input range (*unipolar*) a straight binary code or inverted binary code is usually used. If the output of an A/D converter is going to drive a display, then it is convenient to have the output coded in BCD. For applications where the input range of the converter has both a negative and a positive range (*bipolar*) we usually use offset-binary coding. As you can see in Figure 10-21 the values of 00000000 to 11111111 are simply shifted downward so that 00000000 represents the most negative input value and 10000000 represents an input value of zero. This coding scheme has the advantage that the 2's complement representation can be produced by simply inverting the most-significant bit. Some bipolar converters output the digital value directly in 2's complement form.

UNIPOLAR BINARY CODES

VALUE	10 VOLTS FULL SCALE	BINARY (BIN)	COMPLEMENTARY BINARY (CB)	INVERTED BINARY (IB)	INVERTED COMPLEMENTARY BINARY (ICB)
+FS −1 LSB	9.9609	1111 1111	0000 0000		
+½ FS	5.0000	1000 0000	0111 1111		
+½FS −1 LSB	4.9609	0111 1111	1000 0000		
+1 LSB	0.0391	0000 0001	1111 1110		
ZERO	0.0000	0000 0000	1111 1111	0000 0000	1111 1111
−1 LSB	−0.0391			0000 0001	1111 1110
−½ FS + 1 LSB	−4.9609			0111 1111	1000 0000
−½ FS	−5.0000			1000 0000	0111 1111
− FS + 1 LSB	−9.9609			1111 1111	0000 0000

UNIPOLAR BINARY CODED DECIMAL CODES

VALUE	10 VOLTS FULL SCALE	BINARY CODED DECIMAL (BCD)	COMPLEMENTARY BINARY CODED DECIMAL (CBCD)	INVERTED BINARY CODED DECIMAL (IBCD)	INVERTED COMPLEMENTARY BINARY CODED DECIMAL (ICBCD)
+ FS −1 LSB	9.9	1001 1001	0110 0110		
+½ FS	5.0	0101 0000	1010 1111		
+1 LSB	0.1	0000 0001	1111 1110		
ZERO	0.0	0000 0000	1111 1111	0000 0000	1111 1111
−1 LSB	−0.1			0000 0001	1111 1110
−½ FS	−5.0			0101 0000	1010 1111
−FS +1 LSB	−9.9			1001 1001	0110 0110

BIPOLAR BINARY CODES

VALUE	10 VOLTS FULL SCALE RANGE	OFFSET BINARY (OB)	COMPLEMENTARY OFFSET BINARY (COB)	TWO'S COMPLEMENT (TC)
+FS	5.0000			
+FS −1 LSB	4.9609	1111 1111	0000 0000	0111 1111
+1 LSB	0.0391	1000 0001	0111 1110	0000 0001
ZERO	0.0000	1000 0000	0111 1111	0000 0000
−1 LSB	−0.0391	0111 1111	1000 0000	1111 1111
−FS +1 LSB	−4.9609	0000 0001	1111 1110	1000 0001
−FS	−5.0000	0000 0000	1111 1111	1000 0000

FIGURE 10-21 Common A/D output codes.

Interfacing Different Types of A/D Converters to Microcomputers

INTERFACING TO PARALLEL-COMPARATOR A/D CONVERTERS

In any application where a parallel comparator converter is used, the converter is most likely going to be producing digital output values much faster than a microcomputer could possibly read them in. Therefore, separate circuitry is used to bypass the microprocessor and load a set of samples from the converter directly into a series of memory locations. The microprocessor can later perform the desired operation on the samples. Bypassing the microprocessor in this way is called *direct memory access* or DMA. The basic principle of DMA is that an external controller IC tells the microprocessor to float its buses. When the microprocessor does this, the DMA controller takes control of the buses and allows data to be transferred directly from the A/D converter to successive memory locations. We discuss DMA in detail in the next chapter.

INTERFACING TO SLOPE-TYPE A/D CONVERTERS

Most of the commonly available slope-type converters were designed to drive seven-segment displays in, for example, a digital voltmeter. Therefore, they usually output data in a multiplexed BCD or seven-segment form. Figure 10-23 shows how you can connect the multiplexed BCD outputs of an inexpensive 3½-digit slope converter, the MC14433, to a microprocessor port. In the section of the chapter where Figure 10-23 is located, we use this converter as part of a microcomputer-based scale. The BCD data is output from the converter on lines Q0–Q3. A logic high is output on one of the digit strobe lines, DS1–DS4, to indicate when the BCD code for the corresponding digit is on the Q outputs. The MC14433 converter shown in Figure 10-23 outputs the BCD code for the most-significant digit, and then outputs a high on the DS1 pin. After a period of time it outputs the BCD code for the next-most-significant digit and outputs a high on the DS2 pin. After all 4 digits have been put out, the cycle repeats.

To read in the data from this converter, the principle is simply to poll the bit corresponding to a strobe line until you find it high, read in the data for that digit, and put the data in a reserved memory location for future reference. After you have read the BCD code for one digit, you poll the bit which corresponds to the strobe line for the next digit until you find it high, read the code for that digit, and put it in memory. Repeat the process until you have the data for all of the digits. The A/D converter in Figure 10-23 is connected to do continuous conversions, so you can call the procedure to read in the value from the A/D converter at any time.

Frequency counters, digital voltmeters, and other test instruments often have multiplexed BCD outputs available on their back panel. With the connections and procedure we have just described you can use these instruments to input data to your microcomputer.

INTERFACING A SUCCESSIVE-APPROXIMATION A/D CONVERTER

Successive-approximation A/D converters usually have outputs for each bit. The code output on these lines is usually straight binary or offset binary. You can simply connect the parallel outputs of the the converter to the required number of input port pins and read the converter output in under program control. In addition to the data lines, there are two other successive approximation A/D converter signal lines you need to interface to the microcomputer for the data transfer. The first of these is a START CONVERT signal which you output from the microcomputer to the A/D to tell it to do a conversion for you. The second signal is a STATUS signal which the A/D converter outputs to indicate that the conversion is complete and that the word on the outputs is valid. Here are the program steps you use to get a data sample from the converter.

First you pulse the START CONVERT high for a minimum of 100 ns. You then detect the STROBE signal going low on a polled or interrupt basis. You then read in the digitized value from the parallel outputs of the converter. In a later section of this chapter we show a detailed example of this for the ADC0808 converter.

If you are working with a personal computer such as the IBM PC, there are available a wide variety of multichannel A/D and D/A converter boards which plug directly into the bus connectors of these machines.

A MICROCOMPUTER-BASED SCALE

So far in this book we have shown you how a lot of the pieces of a microcomputer system function. Now it's time to show you how some of these pieces are put together to make a microcomputer-based instrument. The first instrument we have chosen is a "smart" scale such as you might see at the checkout stand in your local grocery store.

Overview of Smart Scale Operation

Figure 10-22 shows a block diagram of our smart scale. A load cell converts the applied weight of, for example, a bunch of carrots to a proportional electrical signal. This small signal is amplified and converted to a digital value which can be read in by the microprocessor and sent to the attached display. The user then enters the price per pound with the keyboard and this price per pound is shown on the display. When the user hits the compute key on the keyboard, the microprocessor multiplies the weight times the price per pound and shows the result on the display. After holding the price display long enough for the user to read it, the scale goes back to reading in the weight value and displaying it. To save the user from having to type the computed price into the cash register, an output from the scale could be connected directly into the cash register circuitry. A speech synthesizer, such as the Votrax SC-01A we described in Chapter 9, could be attached to verbally tell the customer the weight, price per pound, and total price.

Smart scales such as this have many applications other than weighing carrots. A modified version of this scale is used in company mail rooms to weigh packages and calculate the postage required to send them to different postal zones. The output of the scale can be connected to a postage meter which then automatically prints out the required postage sticker. Another application of smart scales is to count coins in a bank or gambling casino. For this application the user simply enters the type of coin being weighed. A conversion factor in the program then computes the total number of coins and the total dollar amount. Still another application of a scale such as this is in packaging items for sale. Suppose, for example, that we are manufacturing woodscrews, and that we want to package 100 of them per box. We can pass the boxes over the load cell on a

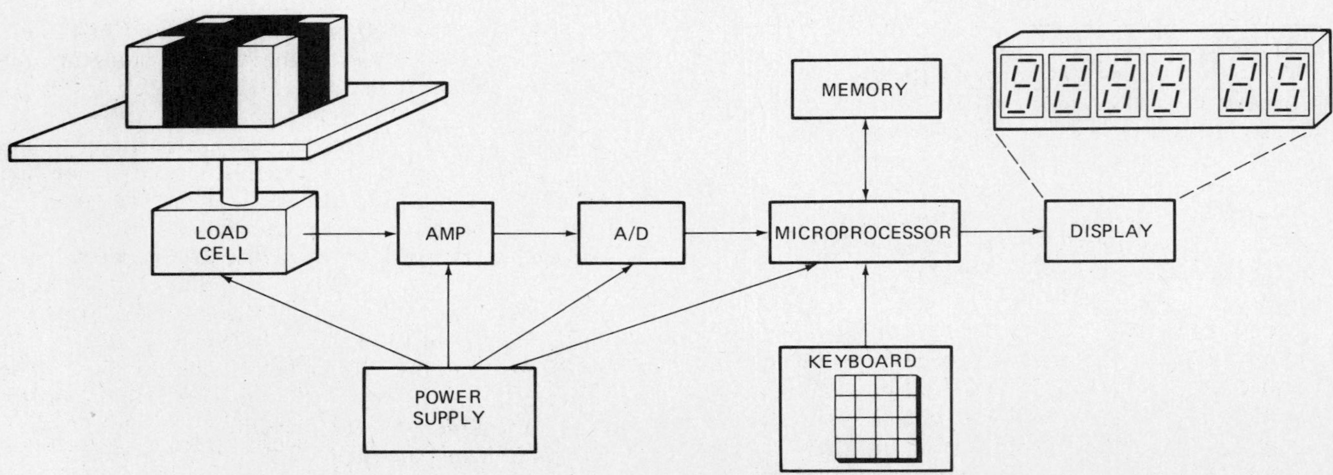

FIGURE 10-22 Block diagram of microcomputer-based smart scale.

conveyor belt and fill them from a chute until the weight, and therefore the count, reaches some entered value. The point here is that the combination of intelligence and some simple interface circuitry gives you an instrument with as many uses as your imagination can come up with.

Smart Scale Input Circuitry

Figure 10-10 shows a picture of the Transducers, Inc. Model C462-10#-10P1 strain-gage load cell we used when we built this scale. We added a piece of plywood to the top of the load cell to keep the carrots from falling off. This load cell has an accuracy of about 1 part in 1000 or 0.01 lb over the 0- to 10-lb range for which it was designed.

As shown in Figure 10-23, the load cell consists of four 350-Ω resistors connected in a bridge configuration. A stable 10.00-V excitation voltage is applied to the top of the bridge. With no load on the cell, the outputs from the bridge are at about the same voltage, 5 V. When a load is applied to the bridge, the resistance of one of the lower resistors will be changed. This produces a small differential output voltage from the bridge. The maximum differential output voltage for this 10-lb load cell is 2 mV per volt of excitation. With a 10.00 V excitation as shown, the maximum differential-output voltage is then 20 mV.

To amplify this small differential signal we use a National LM363 instrumentation amplifier. This device contains all of the circuitry shown for the instrumentation amplifier in Figure 10-1*h*. The closed-loop gain of the amplifier is programmable for fixed values of 5, 100, and 500 with jumpers on pins 2, 3, and 4. We have jumpered it for a gain of 100 so that the 20-mV maximum signal from the load cell will give a maximum voltage of 2.00 V to the A/D converter input. A precision voltage divider on the output of the amplifier divides this signal in half so that a weight of 10.00 lb produces an output voltage of 1.000 V. This scaling simplifies the display of the weight after it is read into the microprocessor. The 0.1-μF capacitor between pins 15 and 16 of the amplifier reduces the bandwidth of the amplifier to about 7.5 Hz. This removes 60 Hz and any high-frequency noise that might have been induced in the signal lines.

The MC14433 A/D converter used here is an inexpensive dual-slope device intended for use in 3½-digit digital voltmeters, etc. Because the load cell changes slowly, a fast converter isn't needed here. The voltage across an LM329 6.9-V precision reference diode is amplified by *IC*4 to produce the 10.00-V excitation voltage for the load cell, and a 2.000-V reference for the A/D. With a 2.000-V reference voltage, the full-scale input voltage for the A/D is 2.000 V. Conversion rate and multiplexing frequency for the converter are determined by an internal oscillator and *R*11. An *R*11 of 300 kΩ gives a clock frequency of 66 kHz, a multiplex frequency of 0.8 kHz, and about four conversions per second. Accuracy of the converter is ±0.05 percent and ±1 count, which is comparable to the accuracy of the load cell. In other words, the last digit of the displayed weight may be off by 1 or 2 counts. As we described in a previous section, the output from this converter is in multiplexed BCD form.

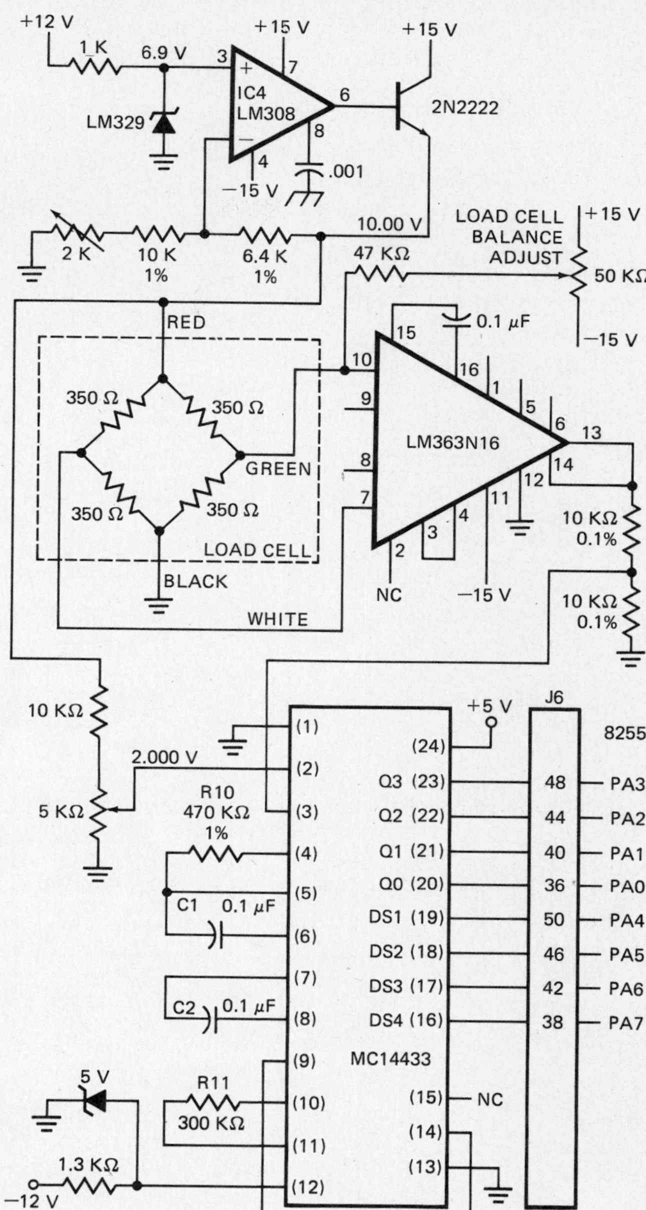

FIGURE 10-23 Circuit diagram for load-cell interface circuitry and A/D converter for smart scale.

An Algorithm for the Smart Scale

Figure 10-24 shows the flowchart for our smart scale. Note that, as indicated by the double-ended boxes in the flowchart, most major parts of the program are written as procedures. The output of the A/D is in multiplexed BCD form as we described in the section on slope-converter interfacing. Therefore, each strobe has to be polled until it goes high, and then the BCD code for that digit can be read in.

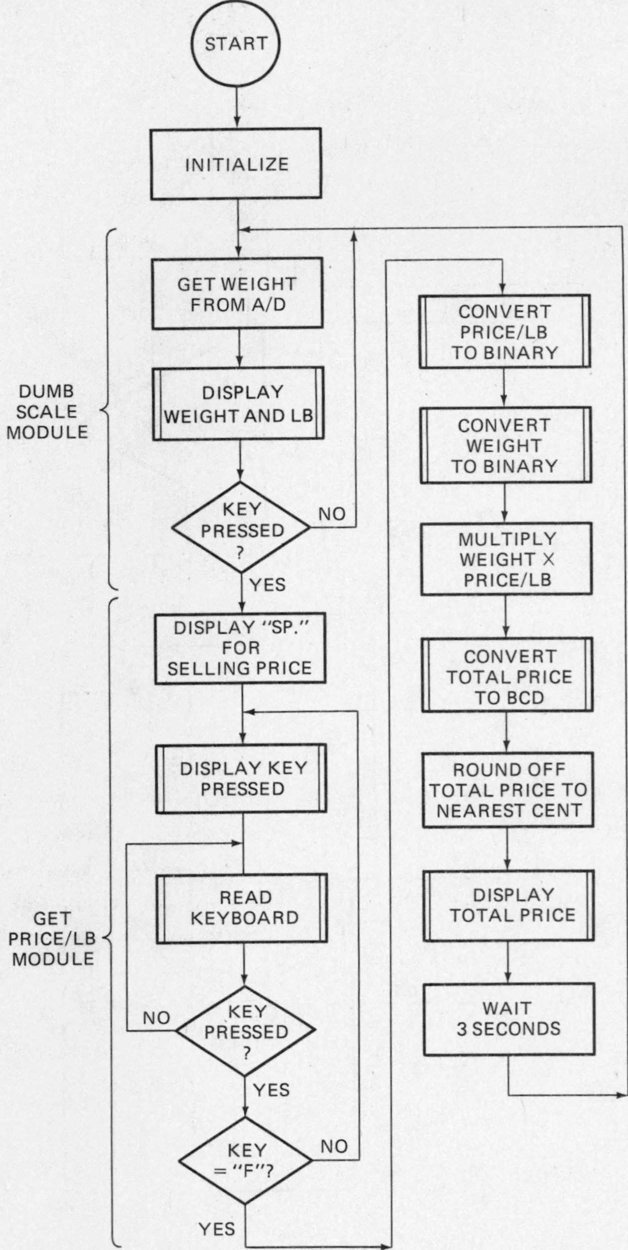

FIGURE 10-24 Flowchart for smart-scale program.

The BCD values read in from the converter are stored in four memory locations. A display procedure accesses these values and sends them to the address field display of the SDK-86. The letters "Lb" are displayed in the data field. After the weight is displayed, a check is made to see if any keys have been pressed by the user. If a key has been pressed, the letters "SP," which represents selling price, are displayed in the address field. Keycodes are read from the 8279 as entered and displayed on the data field display. Keys can be pressed until the desired price per pound shows on the display. The price per pound entered by a user is assembled in a series of memory locations. When a nonnumeric key is pressed, it is assumed that the entered price per pound is correct, and the program goes on to compute the total price.

Computing the price involves multiplying the weight in BCD form times the price per pound in BCD form. It is not easy to do a BCD × BCD multiply directly, so we took an alternate route to get there. Both the weight and the price per pound are converted to binary. The two binary numbers are then multiplied. The binary result of the multiplication is then converted to BCD, rounded off to the nearest cent, and displayed in the data field. The letters "Pr" are displayed in the address field. After a few seconds the program goes back to reading and displaying weight over and over, until a key is pressed.

The Microprocessor-based Scale Program

Figure 10-25 shows the complete program for our microprocessor-based scale. It is important for you not to be overwhelmed by a multipage program such as this. If you use the 5-minute rule, and work your way through this program one module at a time, you should pick up some more useful programming techniques and procedures for your "toolbox."

Three 4-byte buffers set up at the start of the program are used to store the unpacked BCD values of the weight, the price per pound, and the computed total price. These values will be used by the display procedure. Instead of using the display procedure we showed you in Figure 9-33, we used here a more versatile procedure which can display a few letters as well as hex digits. The SEVEN_SEG table in the data segment contains the seven-segment codes for hex digits and these letters. In the display procedure you will see how these codes are accessed.

After initializing everything the program polls the digit strobe for the most-significant digit from the A/D converter. Since this A/D converter is a 3½-digit unit, the MSD can only be a 0 or a 1. The value for this digit is sent in the third bit (bit 2) of the 4-bit digit read in. If this bit is a one, then 01 is loaded into the buffer location. If the bit is a 0, then the value which will access the seven-segment code for a blank (14H) is loaded into the buffer location. Each of the other digit strobes is then polled in turn and the values for those digits read in. When all of the BCD digits for the weight are in the WEIGHT_BUFFER, the display procedure is called to show the weight on the address field.

To use this display procedure you first load a 0 or a 1 into AL to specify data field or address field and a 1 or a 0 in AH to specify a decimal point in the middle of the display, or no decimal point. You then load BX with the offset of a buffer containing codes for the digits to be displayed. A program loop in the display procedure uses the XLAT instruction and the SEVEN_SEG table to convert these codes to the required seven-segment values and send the values to the 8279 display RAM. Note how a 1 is ORed into the seven-segment code for digit 3 when a 1 is in AH passed to the procedure. For displaying the weight, BX is simply loaded with the offset of WEIGHT_BUFFER, AL loaded with 01 to display the

```
Page ,132
;8086 PROGRAM FOR SMART SCALE
;PORTS:       Uses input port P1A - FFF9H
;PROCEDURES: READ_KEY, DISPLAY, PACK, EXPAND, CONVERT2BIN, BINCVT

DATA_HERE SEGMENT        WORD    PUBLIC

WEIGHT_BUFFER  DB  4 DUP(0)              ; Space for unpacked BCD weight
SELL_PRICE     DB  4 DUP(0)              ; Space for unpacked price/pound
PRICE_TOTAL    DB  4 DUP(0)              ; Space for total price to display
BINARY_WEIGHT  DW  0                     ; Space for converted weight
LB             DB  0BH, 10H, 14H, 14H,   ; b, L, blank, blank
S_P            DB  12H, 11H, 14H, 14H,   ; P, S, blank, blank
PR             DB  13H, 12H, 14H, 14H    ; r, P, bblank, blank

SEVEN_SEG       DB      3FH, 06H, 5BH, 4FH, 66H, 6DH, 7DH, 07H
                ;        0    1    2    3    4    5    6    7
                DB      7FH, 6FH, 77H, 7CH, 39H, 5EH, 79H, 71H
                ;        8    9    A    b    C    d    E    F
                DB      38H, 6DH, 73H, 50H, 00H, 76H
                ;        L    S    P    r  blank  H


DATA_HERE ENDS

STACK_HERE SEGMENT
               DW      40 DUP(0)
       STACK_TOP       LABEL   WORD
STACK_HERE       ENDS

CODE_HERE       SEGMENT WORD    PUBLIC
       ASSUME CS:CODE_HERE, DS:DATA_HERE, SS:STACK_HERE
;initialize data & stack segments
START:  MOV     AX, DATA_HERE
        MOV     DS, AX
        MOV     AX, STACK_HERE
        MOV     SS, AX
        MOV     SP, OFFSET STACK_TOP
;8279 initialized at power-up of SDK-86 for 8 character display, left entry
;encoded scan, 2-key lockout.
        MOV     DX, 0FFEAH               ; point at 8279 control address
        MOV     AL, 00H                  ; control word for above conditions
        OUT     DX, AL                   ; send control word
        MOV     AL, 00111000B            ; clock word for divide by 24
        OUT     DX, AL
        MOV     AL, 11000000B            ; Clear display character is all 0's
        OUT     DX, AL

;Dumb scale start
RDWT:   MOV     CX, 04H                  ; Zero out weight buffer
        MOV     BX, OFFSET WEIGHT_BUFFER
NEXT1:  MOV     BYTE PTR[BX], 00H
        INC     BX
        LOOP    NEXT1
        MOV     CX, 04H                  ; Zero out price/pound buffer
```

FIGURE 10-25 Assembly language program for smart scale.

```
        MOV     BX, OFFSET SELL_PRICE
NEXT2:  MOV     BYTE PTR[BX], 00H
        INC     BX
        LOOP    NEXT2
;Get weight from A/D converter and display
        MOV     BX, OFFSET WEIGHT_BUFFER+3      ; MSD Position in weight buffer
        MOV     DX, 0FFF9H              ; Point at A/D port
DS1:    IN      AL, DX                  ; Read byte from A/D
        AND     AL, 10H                 ; Check for MSD strobe high
        JZ      DS1                     ; Loop till high
        IN      AL, DX                  ; Read MSD data from A/D
        AND     AL, 0FH                 ; Mask strobe bits
        CMP     AL, 04H                 ; See if MSD in bit 3 is a one
        JE      LOAD1                   ; Yes, go load 01H in buffer
        MOV     BYTE PTR[BX], 14H       ; No, load code for blank
        JMP     NXTCHR
LOAD1:  MOV     BYTE PTR[BX], 01H
NXTCHR: DEC     BX                      ; Point to next buffer location
DS2:    IN      AL, DX                  ; Poll for digit 2 strobe
        AND     AL, 20H
        JZ      DS2
        IN      AL, DX                  ; Read digit 2 from A/D
        AND     AL, 0FH                 ; Mask strobe bits
        MOV     [BX], AL                ; Digit 2 BCD to buffer
        DEC     BX                      ; Point at next buffer location
DS3:    IN      AL, DX                  ; Poll for digit 3 from A/D
        AND     AL, 40H
        JZ      DS3
        IN      AL, DX                  ; Read digit 3 from A/D
        AND     AL, 0FH                 ; Mask strobe bits
        MOV     [BX],AL                 ; Digit 3 to buffer
        DEC     BX                      ; Point to next buffer location
DS4:    IN      AL, DX                  ; Poll for digit 4 (LSD)
        AND     AL, 80H
        JZ      DS4
        IN      AL, DX                  ; Read digit 4 from A/D
        AND     AL, 0FH                 ; Mask strobe bits
        MOV     [BX], AL                ; Digit 4 BCD to buffer
;Display weight on address field of SDK-86
        MOV     BX, OFFSET WEIGHT_BUFFER   ; Point at stored weight
        MOV     AL, 01H                    ; Specifies address field
        MOV     AH, 01H                 ; Specifies decimal point
        CALL    DISPLAY
        MOV     BX, OFFSET LB           ; Point at Lb string
        MOV     AL, 00                  ; Specifies data field
        MOV     AH, 00                  ; Specifies no decimal point
        CALL    DISPLAY
;Check if key has been pressed
        MOV     DX, 0FFEAH              ; Point at 8279 status address
        IN      AL, DX                  ; Read 8279 FIFO status
        AND     AL, 01H                 ; See if FIFO has keycode
        JNZ     GETKEY                  ; Yes, go read it
        JMP     RDWT                    ; No, go get weight and display
GETKEY: MOV     AL, 01000000B           ; Control word for read FIFO
        OUT     DX, AL                  ; Send to 8279
```

FIGURE 10-25 (*continued*)

```
        MOV     DX, ØFFE8H              ; Point at 8279 data address
        IN      AL, DX                  ; Read code from FIFO
        CMP     AL, Ø9H                 ; Check if legal keycode(number)
        JBE     OK                      ; Go on if below or equal 9
        JMP     RDWT                    ; Else ignore, read weight again

;Read in and display price/pound

OK:     MOV     BX, OFFSET SELL_PRICE   ; Point at price per pound buffer
        MOV     [BX], AL                ; Keycode to buffer
        MOV     AL, ØØ                  ; Specify data field for display
        MOV     AH, Ø1                  ; Specify decimal point
        CALL    DISPLAY
        MOV     BX, OFFSET S_P          ; Point at SP string
        MOV     AL, Ø1                  ; Specify address field
        MOV     AH, ØØ                  ; Specify no decimal point
        CALL    DISPLAY
NXTKEY: CALL    READ_KEY                ; Wait for next keypress
        CMP     AL, Ø9H                 ; See if more price or command
        JA      COMPUTE                 ; Go compute total price
        MOV     BX, OFFSET SELL_PRICE   ; Point at price per pound buffer
        MOV     CL, [BX+2]              ; Shift contents of buffer one
        MOV     [BX+3], CL              ; position left and insert new
        MOV     CL, [BX+1]              ; keycode
        MOV     [BX+2], CL
        MOV     CL, [BX]
        MOV     [BX+1], CL
        MOV     [BX], AL
        MOV     AL, ØØ                  ; Specify data field
        MOV     AH, Ø1                  ; Specify decimal point
        CALL    DISPLAY
        JMP     NXTKEY                  ; Keep reading and shifting keys
                                        ; until command key pressed
;compute total price

COMPUTE:
        MOV     BX, OFFSET WEIGHT_BUFFER        ; Point at weight buffer for pack
        CMP     BYTE PTR[BX+3], 14H     ; See if MSD of weight = Ø
        JNE     NOTZER
        MOV     BYTE PTR[BX+3], ØØ      ; Yes, load Ø in place of blank code
NOTZER: CALL    PACK                    ; Pack BCD weight into word
        CALL    CONVERT2BIN             ; Convert to 16 bit binary in AX
        MOV     BINARY_WEIGHT, AX       ;  and save
        MOV     BX, OFFSET SELL_PRICE   ; Point at price per pound for pack
        CALL    PACK                    ; Pack BCD price into AX for convert
        CALL    CONVERT2BIN             ; Convert price to 16-bit binary in AX
        MUL     BINARY_WEIGHT           ; Price per pound in AX x binary weight
                                        ; total price result in DX:AX
        MOV     BX, AX                  ; Prepare for convert to BCD
        CALL    BINCVT                  ; Packed BCD price result in DX:BX

;round off price to nearest cent and display

        CMP     BL, 49H                 ; Carry set if BL >49H
        MOV     AL, ØØ                  ; Clear AL, keep carry
```

FIGURE 10-25 (*continued*)

```
        ADC     AL, BH                  ; Add any carry to next digit
        DAA                             ; Keep in BCD format
        MOV     BL, AL                  ; Save lower two digits of price
        MOV     AL, 00                  ; Clear AL, save carry
        ADC     AL, DL                  ; Propagate carry to upper digits
        DAA                             ; Keep in BCD form
        MOV     AH, AL                  ; Position upper digits for EXPAND
        MOV     AL, BL                  ; Position lower digits for EXPAND
        MOV     BX, OFFSET PRICE_TOTAL  ; Point at buffer for expanded BCD
        CALL    EXPAND                  ; Unpack BCD for DISPLAY procedure
        MOV     AL, 00                  ; Display total price on data field
        MOV     AH, 01                  ;  with decimal point
        CALL    DISPLAY
        MOV     BX, OFFSET PR           ; Point at price/lb string
        MOV     AL, 01                  ; Display in address field
        MOV     AH, 00                  ; without decimal point
        CALL    DISPLAY
;delay a few seconds
        MOV     CX,0FFFFH               ; Delay a few seconds
CNTDN1: MOV     BX, 000AH
CNTDN2: DEC     BX
        JNZ     CNTDN2
        LOOP    CNTDN1
;go read next weight
        JMP     RDWT                    ; Jump back to dumb scale
;*************************************************************************
;************* procedures used in smart scale program ****************

;PROCEDURE READ_KEY
;ABSTRACT       reads the SDK-86 keyboard - procedure polls the status register
;               of the 8279 on the SDK-86 board until it finds a key pressed.
;               It then reads the keypressed code from the FIFO RAM to AL and exits
;REGISTERS:     Destroys AL - returns with character read in AL

READ_KEY        PROC    NEAR
        PUSH    DX
        MOV     DX, 0FFEAH              ; point at 8279 control address
NO_KEY: IN      AL, DX                  ; get FIFO status
        AND     AL, 00000001B           ; mask all but LSB, high if key in FIFO
        JZ      NO_KEY                  ; loop until a key is pressed
        MOV     AL, 01000000B           ; control word for read FIFO
        OUT     DX, AL                  ; send control word
        MOV     DX, 0FFE8H              ; point at 8279 data address
        IN      AL, DX                  ; read character in FIFO ram
        POP     DX
        RET
READ_KEY ENDP

;8086 PROCEDURE called DISPLAY
;ABSTRACT:  This procedure displays characters on the SDK-86 display
;           The data is sent to the procedure in the following manner:
; AL=0 for data field
; AL=1 for address field
; AH=0 for no decimal point
; AH=1 for decimal point between second & third digit
```

FIGURE 10-25 (*continued*)

```
; BX= offset of buffer containing 7-seg codes of the 4 characters to be displayed

DISPLAY PROC    NEAR
        PUSHF                              ; save flags and registers
        PUSH    AX
        PUSH    BX
        PUSH    CX
        PUSH    DX
        PUSH    SI
        MOV     DX, ØFFEAH                 ; point at 8279 control address
        CMP     AL, ØØH                    ; see if data field required
        JZ      DATFLD                     ; yes, load control word for data field
        MOV     AL, 94H                    ; no, load address-field control word
        JMP     SEND                       ; go send control word
DATFLD: MOV     AL, 9ØH                    ; load control word for data field
SEND:   OUT     DX, AL                     ; send control word to 8279
        MOV     CL, Ø4H                    ; counter for number of characters
        MOV     SI, BX                     ; Free BX for use with XLAT
        MOV     BX, OFFSET SEVEN_SEG       ; pointer to seven-segment codes
        MOV     DX, ØFFE8H                 ; point at 8279 display RAM
AGAIN:  MOV     AL, [SI]                   ; Get character to be displayed
        XLATB                              ; translate to 7-seg code
        CMP     CL, Ø2H                    ; see if digit that gets decimal point
        JNE     MORE                       ; no, go send digit
        CMP     AH, Ø1H                    ; yes, see if decimal point specified
        JNE     MORE                       ; no, go send character
        OR      AL, 8ØH                    ; yes, OR in decimal point
MORE:   OUT     DX, AL                     ; send seven seg codeto 8279 display RAM
        INC     SI                         ; Point to next character
        LOOP    AGAIN                      ; until all four characters sent
        POP     SI
        POP     DX                         ; restore all registers and flags
        POP     CX
        POP     BX
        POP     AX
        POPF
        RET
DISPLAY ENDP

;8Ø86 PROCEDURE PACK
;ABSTRACT: This procedure converts four unpacked BCD digits pointed to by
;          BX to four packed BCD digits in AX
;DESTROYS: AX

PACK  PROC  NEAR
        PUSHF                              ; save flags and registers
        PUSH    BX
        PUSH    CX
        MOV     AL, [BX]                   ; first BCD digit to AL
        MOV     CL, Ø4H                    ; counter for rotate
        ROL     BYTE PTR[BX+1], CL         ; position second BCD digit
        ADD     AL, [BX+1]                 ; first 2 digits in AL
        MOV     AH, [BX+2]                 ; third digit to AH
        ROL     BYTE PTR[BX+3], CL         ; position fourth digit
        ADD     AH, [BX+3]                 ; second two digits now in AH
```

FIGURE 10-25 (*continued*)

```
        POP     BX
        POP     CX
        POPF
        RET
PACK  ENDP

;8086 PROCEDURE EXPAND
;ABSTRACT:      This procedure expands a packed BCD number in AX
;               to 4 unpacked BCD digits in a buffer pointed to by BX

EXPAND  PROC NEAR
        PUSHF
        PUSH    AX
        PUSH    BX
        PUSH    CX
        MOV     [BX],AL                 ; move first 2 BCD digits to buffer
        AND     BYTE PTR[BX],0FH        ; mask off upper digit
        MOV     CL, 04H                 ; counter for rotates
        ROR     AL, CL                  ; position digit 2 in low nibble
        AND     AL, 0FH                 ; mask upper nibble
        MOV     [BX+1], AL              ; digit 2 to buffer
        MOV     [BX+2], AH              ; second 2 BCD digits to buffer
        AND     BYTE PTR[BX+2],0FH      ; mask off upper digit
        ROR     AH, CL                  ; position digit 4 in low nibble
        AND     AH, 0FH                 ; mask upper nibble
        MOV     [BX+3], AH              ; digit 4 to buffer
        POP     CX
        POP     BX
        POP     AX
        POPF
        RET
EXPAND ENDP

;PROCEDURE CONVERT2BIN
;         : This procedure converts a 4 digit BCD number in
;         : the AX register into its BINARY (HEX) equivalent. It
;         : returns the result in the AX register
;SAVES    : FLAG register, BX, DX, CX, DI
;DESTROYS : AX register
        THOU    EQU     3E8H            ; 1000 = 3E8H
CONVERT2BIN PROC        NEAR
        PUSHF                   ; save registers
        PUSH    BX
        PUSH    DX
        PUSH    CX
        PUSH    DI
        MOV     BX, AX          ; copy number into BX
        MOV     AL, AH          ; place for upper 2 digits
        MOV     BH, BL          ; place for lower 2 digits
; split up numbers so that we have one digit in each register
        MOV     CL, 04          ; nibble count for rotate
        ROR     AH, CL          ; digit 1 in correct place
        ROR     BH, CL          ; digit 3 in correct place
        AND     AX, 0F0FH
        AND     BX, 0F0FH       ; mask upper nibbles of each digit
```

FIGURE 10-25 (*continued*)

```
; copy AX into CX so that can use AX for multiplication
        MOV     CX, AX
        MOV     AX, 0000H
; now multiply each number by its place value
        MOV     AL, CH              ; multiply byte in AL * word
        MOV     DI, THOU            ; no immediate multiplication
        MUL     DI                  ; digit 1 * 1000
; result in DX and AX, because BCD digit will not be greater than 9
; the result will only be in AX
; zero DX and add BL because that digit needs no multiplication for
; place value. Then add the result in AX for digit 4
        MOV     DX, 0000H
        ADD     DL, BL              ; add digit 1
        ADD     DX, AX              ; add digit 4
; continue with multiplications
        MOV     AX, 0064H           ; byte * byte result in AX
        MUL     CL                  ; digit 2 * 100
        ADD     DX, AX              ; add digit 3
        MOV     AX, 000AH           ; byte * byte result in AX
        MUL     BH
        ADD     DX, AX              ; add digit 2
        MOV     AX, DX              ; put result in correct place
        POP     DI
        POP     CX
        POP     DX                  ; restore registers
        POP     BX
        POPF
        RET
CONVERT2BIN     ENDP

;8086 PROCEDURE BINCVT
;ABSTRACT: Converts a 24-bit binary number in DL and BX to a
;          packed BCD equivalent in DX:BX
;INPUTS:   DL, BX - 24 BIT BINARY NUMBER
;OUTPUTS:  DX, BX - PACKED BCD RESULT
;CALLS:    CNVT1
;DESTROYS: DX and BX

BINCVT PROC NEAR
        PUSHF                       ; save registers and flags
        PUSH  AX
        PUSH  CX
        MOV   DH, 19H               ; bit counter for 24 bits
        CALL  CNVT1                 ; produce 2 LS BCD digits in CH
        MOV   CL, CH                ; save in CL
        MOV   DH, 19H               ; bit counter for 24 BITS
        CALL  CNVT1                 ; produce next 2 BCD digits in CH
        PUSH  CX                    ; save lower four BCD digits on stack
        MOV   DH, 19H               ; bit counter for 24 bits
        CALL  CNVT1                 ; produce next two BCD digits in CH
        MOV   CL, CH                ; position in CL
        MOV   DH,19H                ; set bit counter for 24 bits
        CALL  CNVT1                 ; produce last two BCD digits in CH
        MOV   DX,CX                 ; position 4 MS BCD DIGITS for return
        POP   BX                    ; 4 LS BCD digits back from stack for RET
```

FIGURE 10-25 (*continued*)

```
        POP   CX
        POP   AX
        POPF
        RET
BINCVT  ENDP

;8086 PROCEDURE CNVT1
CNVT1   PROC  NEAR
        XOR   AL, AL           ; clear AL and carry as workspace
        MOV   CH, AL           ; clear CH
CNVT2:  XOR   AL, AL           ; clear AL and CARRY
        DEC   DH               ; decrement bit counter
        JNZ   CONTINUE         ; do all bits
        RET                    ; done if DH down to zero
CONTINUE:
        RCL   BX, 1            ; BX left one bit, MSB to carry
        RCL   DL, 1            ; MSB from BX to LSB of DL, MSB of DL to carry
        MOV   AL, CH           ; move BCD digit being built to AL
        ADC   AL, AL           ; double AL and add carry from DL shift
        DAA                    ; keep result in BCD form
        MOV   CH, AL           ; put back in CH for next time through
        JNC   CNVT2            ; no carry from DAA, continue
        ADC   BX, 0000H        ; if carry, propogate to BX and DL
        ADC   DL, 00H          ;  for future terms
        JMP   CNVT2            ; continue conversion
CNVT1   ENDP

CODE_HERE ENDS
        END START
```

FIGURE 10-25 (*continued*)

weight in the address field, and AH loaded with 01 to insert a decimal point at the appropriate place.

To display the letters Lb in the data field, BX is loaded with the offset of the string named LB, and the display procedure is called. Again, the XLAT instruction loop converts the codes from the LB string to the required seven-segment codes and sends them out to the 8279 display RAM. The codes in the string named LB represent the offsets from the start of the SEVEN_SEG table for the desired seven-segment codes. For example, the seven-segment code for a P is at offset 12H in the SEVEN_SEG table. Therefore, if you want to display a P, you put 12H in the appropriate location in the the character string in memory. The XLAT instruction will then use the value 12H to access the seven-segment code for P in the SEVEN_SEG table.

After displaying the weight, the program reads the 8279 status register to see if the operator has pressed a key to start entering a price per pound. If no key has been pressed, or if a nonnumeric key has been pressed, the program simply goes back and reads the weight again. If a number key has been pressed, the weight is removed from the address field and the letters SP for "selling price" displayed there. The number entered is put in the SELL_PRICE buffer and displayed on the rightmost digit of the data field. The program then polls the 8279 status register until another keypress is detected. If the pressed key is a numeric key, then the code(s) for the previously entered number(s) will be shifted one location in the buffer to make room for the new number. The new number is then put in the first location in the buffer so that is will be displayed in the rightmost digit of the display. In other words, previously entered numbers are continuously shifted to the left as new numbers are entered. If a mistake is made, the operator can simply enter a 0 followed by the correct price per pound.

If the pressed key is not a numeric key, then this is the signal that the displayed price per pound is correct and that the total price should now be computed. Before the weight and the price/pound can be multiplied, they must each be put in packed BCD form and converted to binary. The PACK procedure converts four unpacked BCD digits in a memory buffer pointed to by BX to a 4-digit packed result in AX. This procedure is simply some masking and moving nibbles. Note how the process is simplified by the ability to rotate the contents of a memory location. Conversion of the packed weight and the packed price per pound is done by the CONVERT2BIN procedure. The algorithm for this procedure is explained in detail in Chapter 5.

For the 8086 a single MUL instruction does the 16 ×

16 binary multiply to produce the total price. Earlier processors required a messy procedure to do this. After the multiplication the total price is in binary form, which is not the form needed for the display procedure. The procedure BINCVT is used to convert the binary total price to packed BCD form. Here's how this procedure works.

In a binary number, each bit position represents a power of 2. An 8-bit binary number, for example, can be represented as

$$b7 \times 2^7 + b6 \times 2^6 + b5 \times 2^5 + b4 \times 2^4 + b3 \times 2^3 + b2 \times 2^2 + b1 \times 2^1 + b0$$

This can be shuffled around and expressed

$$\text{as binary number} = ((((((2b7 + b6)2 + b5)2 + b4)2 + b3)2 + b2)2 + b1)2 + b0$$

where b7 through b0 are the values of the binary bits. If we start with a binary number and do each operation in the nested parentheses in BCD with the aid of the DAA instruction, the result will be the BCD number equivalent to the original binary number.

The procedure in Figure 10-25 produces two BCD digits of the result at a time by calling the subprocedure CNVT1. Figure 10-26 shows a flowchart for the operation of CNVT1. The main principle here is to shift the 24-bit number left one bit position so the MSB goes into the carry flip-flop, then add this bit to twice the previous result. We use the DAA instruction to keep the result of the addition in BCD format. If the DAA produces a carry we add this carry back into the shifted 24-bit number in DL and BX so that it will be propagated into higher BCD digits. After each run of CNVT1 (24 runs of CNVT2), DL and BX will be left with a binary number which is equal to the original binary number minus the value of the two BCD digits produced. You can adapt this procedure to work with a different number of bits by simply calling CNVT1 more or fewer times, and by adjusting the count loaded into DH to be one more than the number of binary bits in the number to be converted. The count has to be one greater because of the position of the decrement in the loop. The temperature-controller procedure in Figure 10-35 shows another example of this conversion.

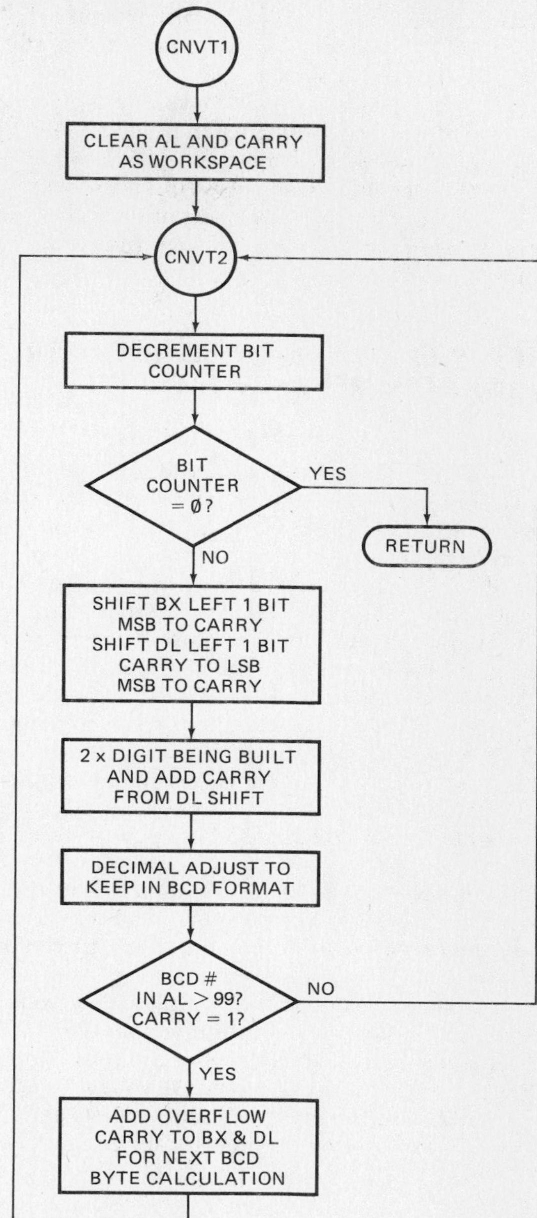

FIGURE 10-26 Flowchart for CNVT1 subprocedure.

The least-significant 2 digits of the BCD value for the total price returned by BINCVT in BL represent tenths and hundredths of a cent. If the value of these two BCD digits is greater than 49H, then the carry produced by the compare instruction and the next two higher BCD digits in BH are added to AL. This must be done in AL, because the DAA instruction, used to keep the result in BCD format, only works on an operand in AL. Any carry from these two BCD digits is propagated on to the upper two digits of the result in DL. After this rounding off, the packed BCD for the total price is left in AX.

In order for the display procedure to be able to display this price, it must be converted to unpacked BCD form and put in four successive memory locations. Another "mask and move nibbles" procedure called EXPAND does this. The DISPLAY procedure is then called to display the total price on the data field. The DISPLAY procedure is called again to display the letters Pr in the address field.

Finally, after delaying a few seconds to give the operator time to read the price, execution returns to the "dumb scale" portion of the program and starts over.

A question that may occur to you when reading a long program such as this is, "How do you decide which parts of the program to keep in the mainline, and which parts to write as procedures?" There is no universal agreement on the answer to this question. The general guidelines we follow are to write a program section as a procedure if: it is going to be used more than once in the program; it is reusable (could be used in other programs); it is so lengthy (more than 1 page) that it clutters up the conceptual flow of the main program; or it is an essentially independent section. The disadvantage of using too many procedures is the time and overhead required for each procedure call. As you write more programs, you will arrive at a balance that feels comfortable to you. The following section shows you another long program example which was written in a highly modular manner so that it can easily be expanded. This example should further help you see when and how to use procedures.

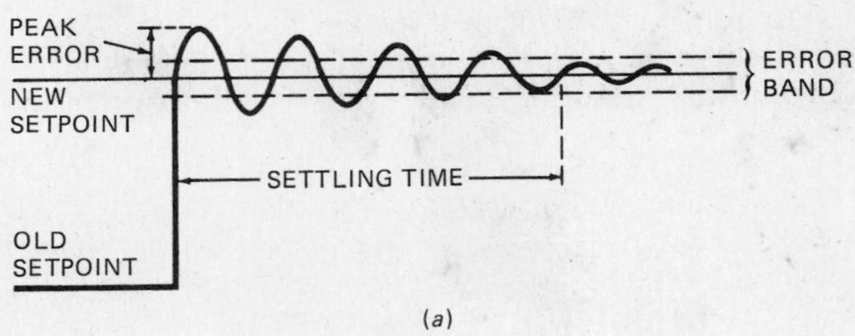

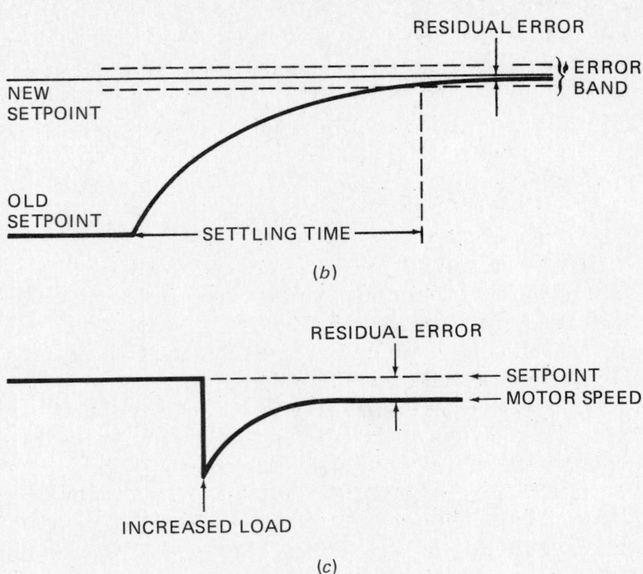

FIGURE 10-28 Overshoot and undershoot of system when setpoint or load is changed. *(a)* Overshoot. *(b)* Undershoot. *(c)* Load change.

A MICROCOMPUTER-BASED INDUSTRIAL PROCESS-CONTROL SYSTEM

Overview of Industrial Process Control

An area in which microprocessors and microcomputers have had a major impact is *industrial process control*. Process control involves first measuring system variables such as motor speed, temperature, the flow of reactants, the level of a liquid in a tank, the thickness of a material, etc. The system is then adjusted until the value of each variable is equal to a predetermined value for that variable called a *set point*. The system controller must maintain each variable as close as possible to its set point value, and it must compensate as quickly and accurately as possible for any change in the system such as an increased load on a motor. A simple example will show the traditional approach to control of a process variable and explain some of the terms used in control systems.

The circuit in Figure 10-27 shows one approach to controlling the speed of a dc motor. Attached to the shaft of the motor is a dc generator, or *tachometer*, which puts out a voltage proportional to the speed of the motor. The output voltage is typically a few volts per 1000 rpm. A fraction of the output voltage from the tachometer is fed back to the inverting input of the power amplifier driving the motor. A positive voltage is applied to the noninverting input of the amplifier as a set point. When the power is turned on, the motor accelerates until the voltage fed back from the tachometer to the inverting input of the amplifier is nearly equal to the set-point voltage. Using negative feedback to control a system such as this is often called *servo control*. A control loop of this type keeps the motor speed quite constant for applications where the load on the motor does not change much. Some hard-disk drive motors and high-quality phonograph turntables use this method of speed control.

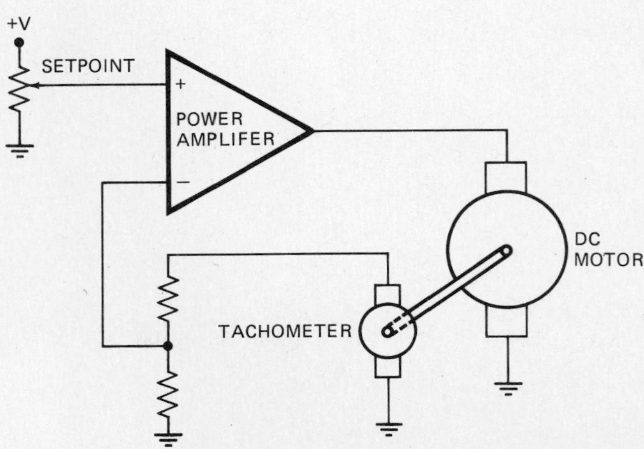

FIGURE 10-27 Circuit for controlling speed of dc motor using feedback from tachometer.

For applications in which the load and/or set point changes drastically, there are several potential problems. The first of these is overshoot when you change the set point, as shown in Figure 10-28*a*. In this case the variable, motor speed for example, overshoots the new set point and bounces up and down for a while. The time it takes the bouncing to settle within a specified error range or error band is called the *settling time*. This type of response is referred to as *underdamped* and is similar to the response of a car with bad shock absorbers when it hits a bump. Figure 10-28*b* shows the opposite situation where the system is overdamped so that it takes a long time for the variable to reach the new setpoint.

Another problem of any real control system is *residual error*. Figure 10-28*c* shows the response of a control system such as the motor speed controller in Figure 10-27 when more load is added on the motor. When the increased load is first added the motor slows down so the voltage out of the tachometer decreases. This increases the voltage difference between the amplifier inputs and causes the amplifier output to increase. Increased amplifier output increases the speed of the motor and thereby the output from the tachometer. When the system reaches equilibrium, however, there is some noticeable difference between the set point and the voltage fed back from the tachometer. It is this difference or residual error which is amplified by the gain of the amplifier to produce the additional drive for the motor. For stability reasons, the gain of many control systems cannot be too high. Therefore, even if you adjust the speed of a motor, for example, to be exactly at a given speed for one load, when you change the load there will always be some residual error between the set point and the actual output.

To help solve these problems, circuits with more complex feedback are used. Figure 10-29 shows a circuit which represents the different types of feedback commonly used. First note in this circuit that the output power amplifier is an adder with four inputs. The current supplied to the summing point of the adder by the set-point input produces the basic output drive current. The other three inputs do not supply any current unless there is a difference between the set point and the feedback voltage from the tachometer. Amplifier 1 is another adder whose function is to compare the set-point voltage with the feedback voltage from the tachometer. Let's assume the two input resistors, $R1$ and $R2$, are equal. Since the set-point voltage is negative and the voltage from the tachometer is positive, there will be no net current through the feedback resistor of the amplifier if the two voltages are equal in magnitude. In other words, if the speed of the motor is at its set-point value, the output of amplifier 1 will be zero, and amplifiers 2, 3, and 4 will contribute no current to the summing junction of the power amp.

Now, suppose that you add more load on the motor, slowing it down. The tachometer voltage is no longer equal to the set-point voltage so amplifier 1 now has some output. This error signal on the output produces three types of feedback to the summing junction of the power amp.

Amplifier 1 produces simple dc feedback proportional to the difference between the set point and the tachometer output. This is exactly the same effect as the voltage divider on the tachometer output in Figure 10-27. *Proportional feedback*, as this is called, will correct for most of the effect of the increased load, but as we discussed before, there will always be some residual error.

The cure for residual error is to use some *integral feedback*. Amplifier 3 in Figure 10-29 provides this type of feedback. Remember from a previous discussion that this circuit produces a ramp on its output whenever a voltage is applied to its input. For the example here the integrator will ramp up or ramp down as long as there is any error signal present on its input. By ramping up and down just a tiny bit about the set point, the integrator can eliminate most of the residual error. Too much integral feedback, however, will cause the output to oscillate up and down.

A third type of feedback called *derivative feedback* is produced by amplifier 4 in Figure 10-29. Integral feed-

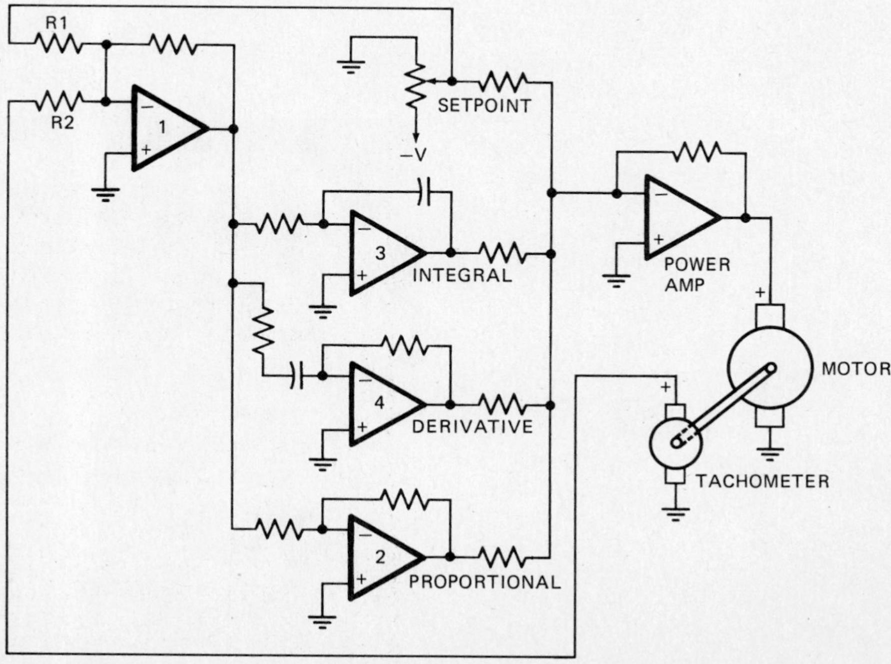

FIGURE 10-29 Circuit showing proportional, integral, and derivative feedback control.

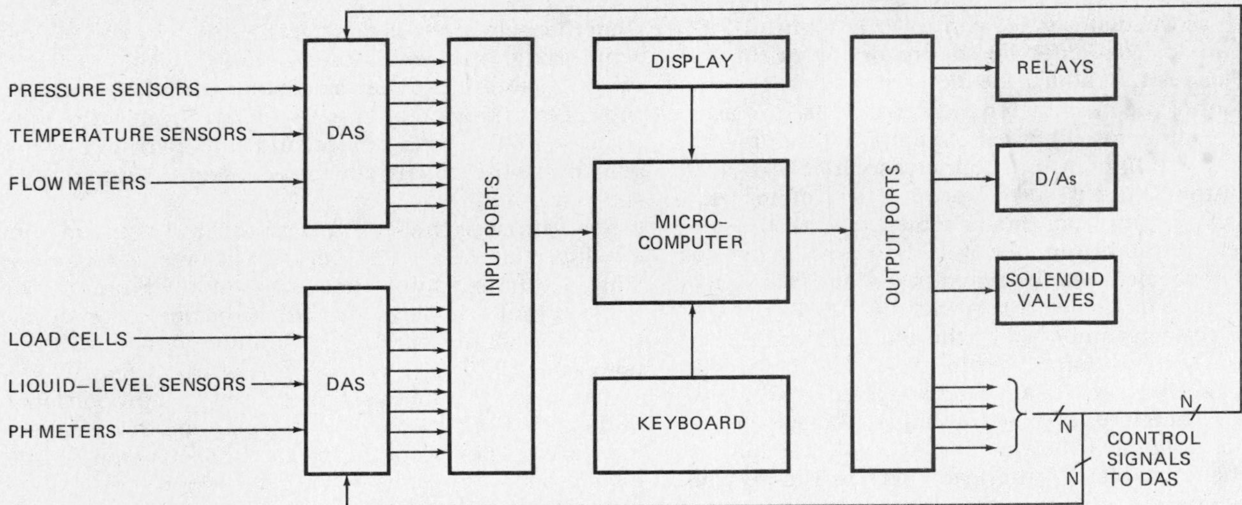

FIGURE 10-30 Block diagram of microcomputer-based process control system.

back discussed in the previous paragraph is slow because the error signal must be present for some time before the integrator has much output. Derivative feedback is a signal proportional to the rate of change of the error signal. If the load on the system is suddenly changed, the derivative amplifier circuit will give a quick shot of feedback to try and correct the error. When the error signal is first applied to the differentiator circuit, the capacitor in series with the input is not charged, so it acts like a short circuit. This initially lets a large current flow so the amplifier has a sizable output. As the capacitor charges, the current decreases, so the feedback from the differentiator decreases. Too much derivative feedback can cause the system to overshoot and oscillate.

The point here is that by using a combination of some or all of these types of feedback, a given feedback-controlled system can be adjusted for optimum response to changes in load or set point. Process control loops that use all three types of feedback are called *proportional integral-derivative* or PID control loops. Because process variables change much more slowly than the microsecond operation of a microcomputer, a microcomputer with some simple input and output circuitry can perform all of the functions of the analog circuitry in Figure 10-29 for several PID loops.

Figure 10-30 shows a block diagram of a microcomputer-based process-control system. Data acquisition systems convert the analog signals from various sensors to digital values that can be read in and processed by the microcomputer. A keyboard and display in the system allow the user to enter set point values and to read the current values of process variables. Relays, D/A converters, solenoid valves, and other actuators are used to control process variables under program direction. A programmable timer in the system determines the rate at which control loops get serviced.

Microcomputer-based process-control systems range from a small programmable controller such as the one shown in Figure 10-31, which might be used to control one or two machines on a factory floor, to a large minicomputer used to control an entire fractionating column in an oil refinery. To show you how these microcomputer-based control systems work, here's an example system you can build and experiment with.

AN 8086-BASED PROCESS-CONTROL SYSTEM

Program Overview

Figure 10-32 shows in flowchart form one way in which the program for a microcomputer-based control system with eight PID loops can operate. After power is turned on, a mainline or *executive program* initializes ports, initializes the timer, and initializes process variables to

FIGURE 10-31 Photograph of Texas Instruments' programmable controller for up to eight PID loops.

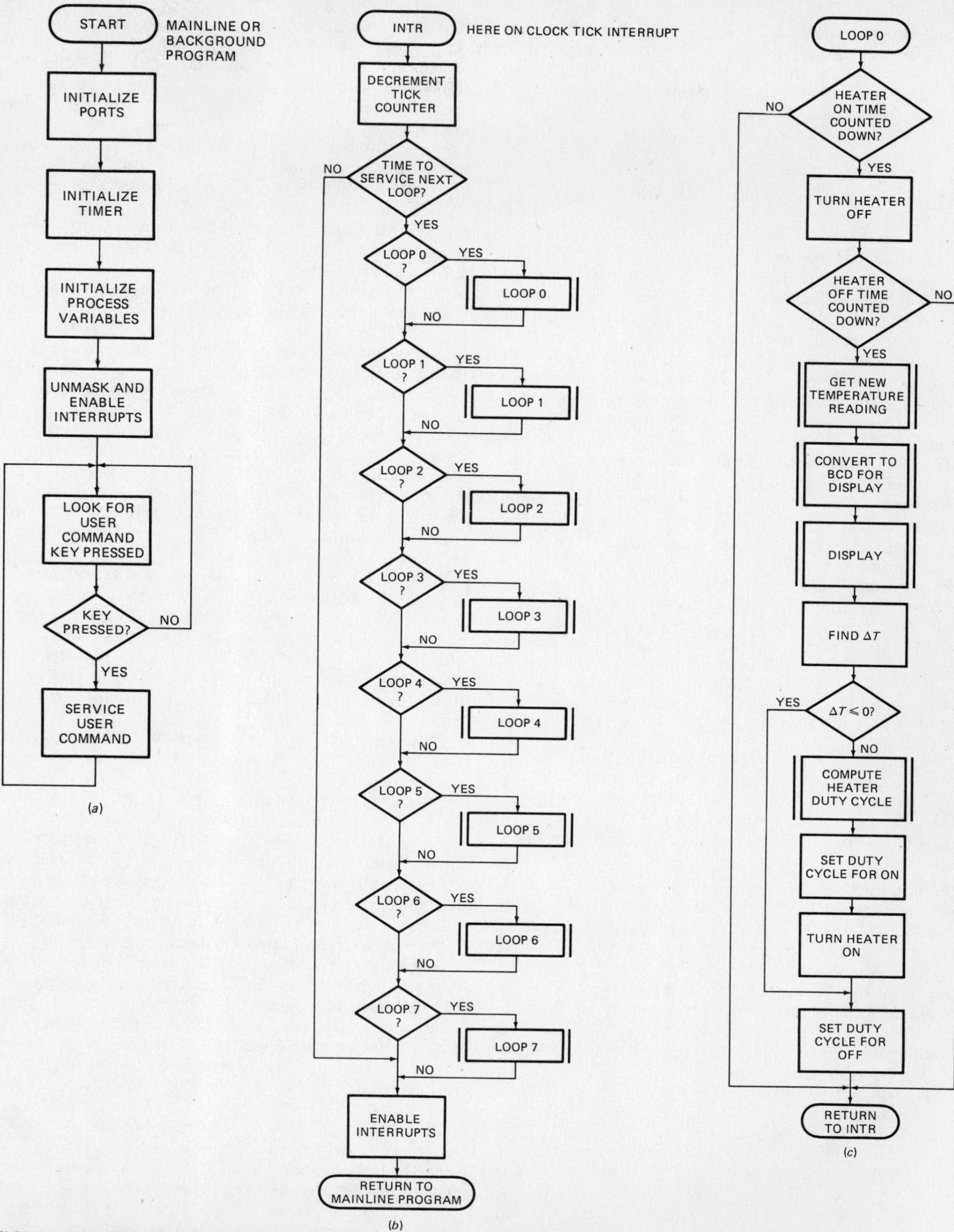

FIGURE 10-32 Flowchart for microcomputer-based process control system. *(a)* Mainline or executive. *(b)* Loop selector. *(c)* Temperature-control loop.

some starting values. The executive program then sits in a loop waiting for a user command from the keyboard or a clock "tick" from the timer. Both the keyboard and the clock are connected to interrupt inputs.

When the microcomputer receives an interrupt from the timer it goes to a procedure which determines whether it is time to service the next control loop. The interrupt procedure does this by counting interrupts in the same way as the real-time clock we described in Chapter 8. For example if you program the timer to produce a pulse every 1 ms, and you want the controller to service another loop every 20 ms, you can simply have the interrupt procedure count 20 interrupts before going on to update the next loop. Once you have counted down 20 interrupts, the program then falls into a decision structure which determines which loop is to be updated next. Every 20 ms a new loop is updated in turn, so with eight loops, each loop gets updated every 160 ms. Note that the microcomputer services each loop at a regular interval instead of simply updating all eight loops, one loop right after another. This is done so that the timing for each loop is independent of the timing for the other loops. A change in the internal timing for one loop then will not affect the timing in the other loops. This system is one type of *time-slice* system, because each loop gets a 20-ms "slice" of time.

The procedures which actually update each control loop are independent of each other. For our example system here we only have space to show the implementation of one loop, the control of the temperature of a tank of liquid in, perhaps, our printed-circuit-board-making machine. You could write other similar control loop procedures to control pH, flow, light exposure timing, motor speed, etc. Figure 10-32*c* shows the flowchart for our temperature-controller loop. We will explain how this works after we have a look at the hardware for the system.

Hardware for Control System and Temperature Controller

To build the hardware for this project we started with an SDK-86 board and added an 8254 programmable timer and an 8259A priority interrupt controller as shown in Figure 8-14. The timer is initialized to produce 1-kHz clock ticks. The 8259A provides interrupt inputs for the clock-tick interrupts and for keyboard interrupts. We built the actual temperature sensing and detecting circuitry on a separate prototyping board and connected it to some ports on the SDK-86 with a ribbon cable. Figure 10-33 shows the added circuitry.

The temperature-sensing element in the circuit is an LM35 precision Centigrade-temperature sensor. The voltage between the output pin and the ground pin of this device will be 0 V at 0°C, and will increase by 10 mV for each increase of 1°C above that. The 300 kΩ resistor connecting the output of the LM35 to −15 V allows the output to go negative for temperatures below 0°C. (If you are operating with ±12-V supplies, use a 240-kΩ resistor.) This makes the circuit able to measure temperatures over the range of −55 to +150°C. For our application here we only use the positive part of the output range, but we thought you might find this circuit useful for some of your other projects. An LM308 amplifies the signal from the sensor by 2 so that the signal uses a greater part of the input range of the A/D converter. This improves the noise immunity and resolution.

The ADC0808 A/D converter used here is an eight-input *data acquisition system*. You tell the device which input signal you want digitized with a 3-bit address you send to the ADC, ADB, and ADA inputs. This eight-input device was chosen so that other control loops could be added later. Some Schmitt-trigger inverters in a 74C14 are connected as an oscillator to produce a 300-kHz clock for the DAS. The voltage drop across an LM329 low-drift zener is buffered by an LM308 amplifier to produce a V_{cc} and a V_{REF} of 5.12 V for the A/D converter. With this reference voltage the A/D converter will have 256 steps of 20 mV each. Since the temperature sensor signal is amplified by 2, each degree Celsius of temperature change will produce an output change of 20 mV or one step on the A/D converter. This gives us a resolution of 1°C, which is about equal to the typical accuracy of the sensor. The advantage of using V_{REF} as the V_{cc} for the device is that this voltage will not have the switching noise that the digital V_{cc} line has. The control inputs and data outputs of the A/D converter are simply connected to SDK-86 ports as shown.

Figure 10-34 shows the timing waveforms and parameters for the ADC0808. Note the sequence in which control signals must be sent to the device. The 3-bit address of the desired input channel is first sent to the multiplexer inputs. After at least 50 ns the ALE input is sent high. After another 2.5 μs the START CONVERSION input is sent high and then low. Then the ALE input is brought low again. When you detect the END OF CONVERSION signal from the A/D converter going high, you can then read in the 8-bit data value which represents the temperature.

To control the power delivered to the heater we used a 25 A, 0-V turn on, solid-state relay such as the Potter-Brumfield unit described in Chapter 9. With this relay we can control a 120- or 240-V ac-powered hot plate or immersion heater. The heater is pulsed on and off under program control. The duty cycle of the pulses determines the amount of heat put out by the heater.

For very low power applications, a D/A converter and a power amplifier could be used to drive the heater. However, in high-power applications this is not very practical, because the power amplifier dissipates as much or more power than the load. For example, when driving a 5000-W heater, the amplifier will dissipate 5000 W or more. The D/A-converter approach has the added disadvantage that it cannot directly use the available ac line voltage.

The driver transistor on the input of the solid-state relay serves three purposes: it supplies the drive for the relay, isolates the port pin from the relay, and holds the relay in the off position when the power is first turned on. Port pins, remember, are in a floating state after a reset. Now that you know how the hardware is connected we can explain how the program for this system works.

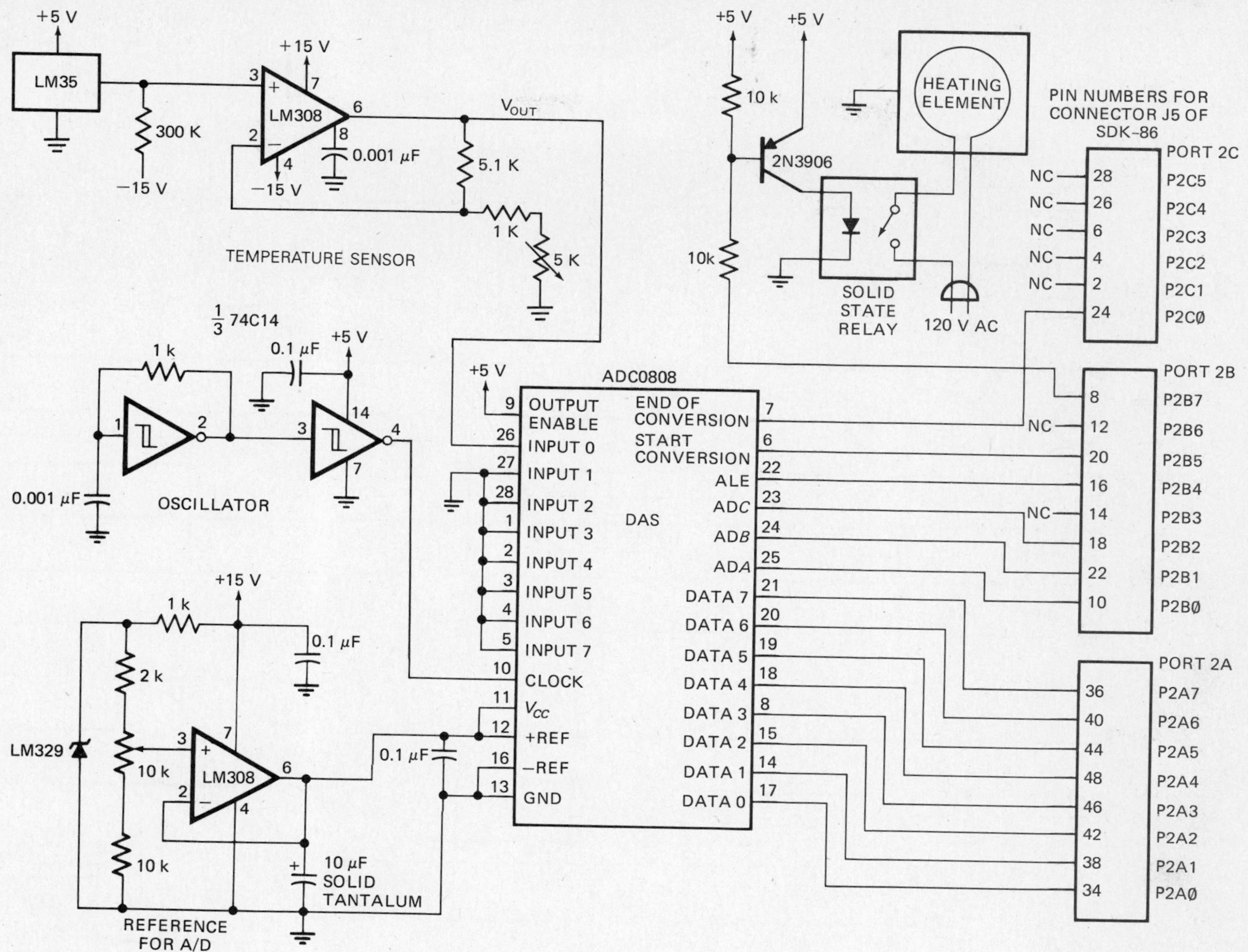

FIGURE 10-33 Temperature-sensing and heater-control circuitry for microcomputer-based controller.

The Controller System Program

THE MAINLINE OR EXECUTIVE SECTION

Figure 10-35 shows the assembly language program for our controller system. Refer to the flowchart in Figure 10-32 as you work your way through this program. The mainline or executive part of the program starts by initializing port FFFAH for output, the 8259A to receive interrupt inputs from the timer and the keyboard, and the 8254 to produce a 1-kHz square wave from its counter 0. We have described all of these operations in detail previously, so we won't dwell on them here. We also initialize here some process variables which we will explain later when they will have more meaning. After enabling the 8086 INTR input with an STI instruction, the program then enters a loop and waits for an interrupt from the user via the keyboard, or from the timer. The keyboard-interrupt procedure would normally contain a command recognizer and subprocedures to implement each of the commands, similar to the way the SDK-86 monitor program is structured. Due to severe space limitations, we do not show here the implementation of the keyboard interrupt procedure which allows the user to change set points, stop a process, or examine the value of process variables at any time.

THE CLOCK-TICK INTERRUPT HANDLER

The next part of the program to discuss is the interrupt procedure which counts clock ticks and decides which process control loop to service. At the start of this procedure we simply decrement an interrupt counter kept in a memory location. In the initialization this counter was set to 20 decimal or 14H. If the counter is not down to zero, execution is simply returned to the wait loop. If the tick counter is now down to zero, the clock tick counter is reset to 20, and one of the loop procedures is called to service the next loop. It is important that this clock tick procedure be reentrant, because if one of the loop procedures takes more than the time between clock ticks (1 ms), the procedure will be reentered before its first

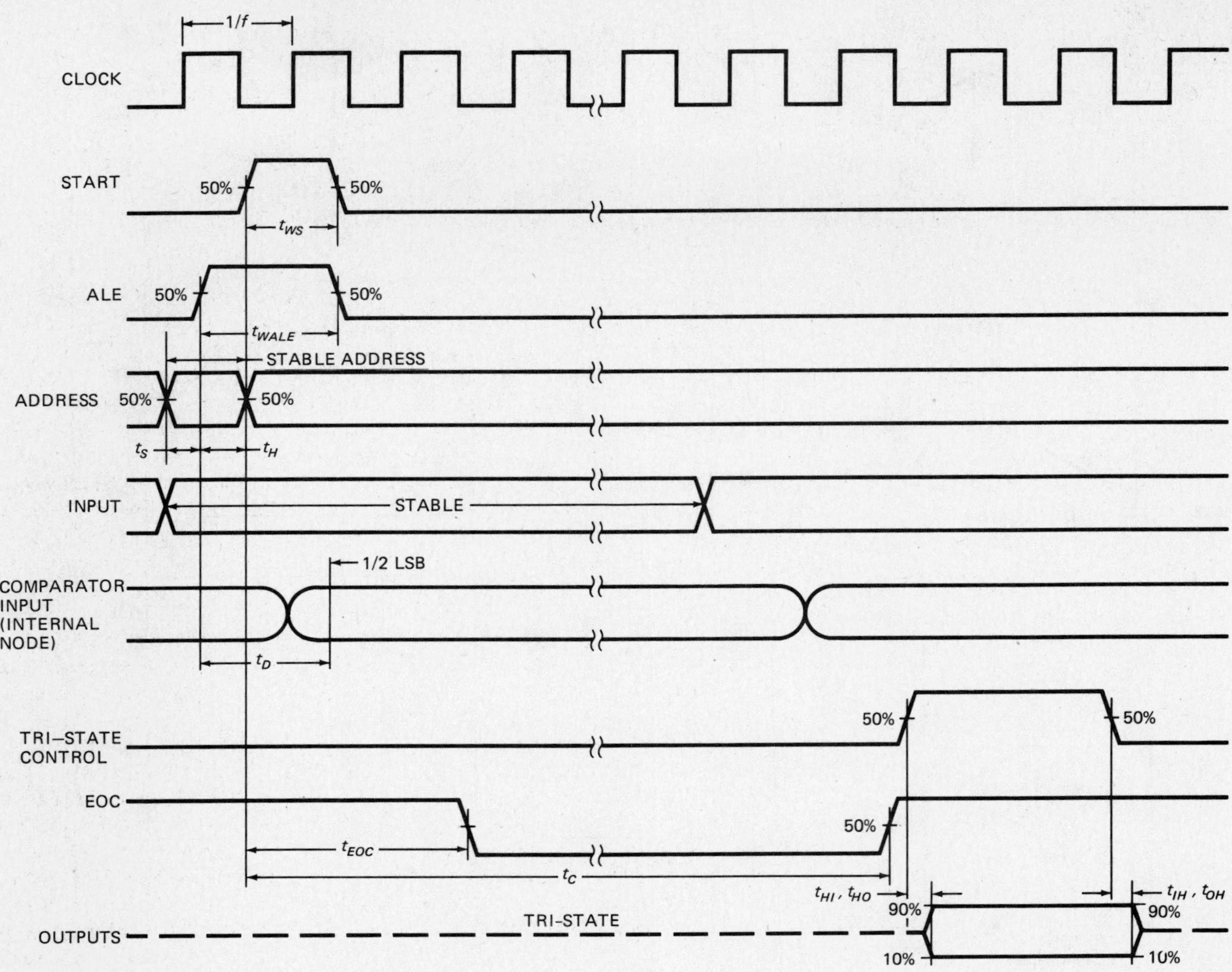

FIGURE 10-34 Timing waveforms for the ADC0808 data acquisition system.

use is completed. The procedure is made reentrant by pushing all registers used in the procedure, and by immediately resetting the clock tick counter to 20. If a loop procedure takes longer than 1 ms and the clock tick procedure is called again, it will just decrement the tick counter and return to the interrupted loop procedure.

The method used here to call the desired loop procedure is an important programming technique. It uses a *call table* to efficiently implement the CASE or nested IF—THEN—ELSE programming structure described in Chapter 3. Here's how it works.

To keep track of which loop should be serviced next, we use a variable called LOOPNUM in memory. During initialization LOOPNUM is loaded with OOH. When it is time to service the first loop, the value in LOOPNUM is loaded into BX. The CALL DWORD PTR LOOP_ADDR_TABLE[BX] instruction then gets a far call address from a table called LOOP_ADDR_TABLE in memory. BX functions as a pointer to the desired address in the table. For the first access BX is zero so the first address in the table is used.

Take a look at how the table of procedure addresses is set up with DD directives at the start of module 2 in Figure 10-35. The names LOOP0, LOOP1, LOOP2, etc. are the names of the procedures to service each of the loops. When this program module is linked and loaded into memory, the instruction pointer and code segment addresses for each of the procedures will be loaded into the table.

When execution returns from one of the loop procedures, 4 is added to LOOPNUM so that execution will go to the next loop in sequence the next time the tick counter is counted down to zero. LOOPNUM must be incremented by four because each address in the call table uses 4 bytes. If all loops have been serviced, LOOPNUM is set back to 0 so LOOP0 will be serviced again. Now let's look at the actual temperature-control loop.

THE TEMPERATURE-CONTROLLER PROCEDURE

As we said previously, the amount of heat output by the heater is controlled by the duty cycle of a pulse waveform

```
page ,132
;8086 PROGRAM FOR CONTROLLER SYSTEM - MODULE 1
;
;ABSTRACT:      This program services eight process control loops on a
;               rotating basis. It is written to run on an Intel SDK-86 board.
;               Timing for the control loops is generated on an interrupt basis
;               by an on-board 8254 timer. Control-loop 0 in the program controls
;               the temperature of a water bath.
;PORTS:         Uses port P2B (FFFAH) as output
;               bits 7 = heater, bit 6,3 = not connected, bit 5 = start conversion
;               bit 4 = ALE,     bit 2,1,0 = channel address
;               Uses port P2A (FFF8H) as data input
;               Uses port P2C (FFFCH) as end-of-conversion input from A/D
;PROCEDURES:    Calls: CLOCK_TICK - interrupt service procedure
;                      KEYBOARD   - interrupt service procedure (empty)

INT_PROC_HERE   SEGMENT WORD    PUBLIC
        EXTRN   CLOCK_TICK:FAR, KEYBOARD:FAR
INT_PROC_HERE   ENDS

PUBLIC  COUNTER, TIMEHI, TIMELO, LOOPNUM, CURTEMP, SETPOINT

AINT_TABLE      SEGMENT WORD    PUBLIC
        TYPE_64         DW      2 DUP(0)        ;reserve space for clock-tick proc addr IR0
        TYPE_65         DW      2 DUP(0)        ;not used in this program - IR1
        TYPE_66         DW      2 DUP(0)        ;reserve space for keyboard proc addr - IR2
AINT_TABLE      ENDS

DATA_HERE       SEGMENT WORD    PUBLIC
        COUNTER         DB      00              ;counter for number of interrupts
        TIMEHI          DB      01              ;heater relay - time on
        TIMELO          DB      01              ;heater relay - time off
        LOOPNUM         DB      00              ;temp storage for loop counter
        CURTEMP         DB      00              ;current temperature
        SETPOINT        DB      60              ;setpoint temperature
DATA_HERE       ENDS

STACK_HERE      SEGMENT
                                                ; no STACK directive because using EXE2BIN
                        DW      40      DUP(0)  ; so can then download code to SDK-86
        TOP_STACK       LABEL   WORD
STACK_HERE      ENDS

CODE_HERE       SEGMENT WORD    PUBLIC
        ASSUME CS:CODE_HERE, DS:AINT_TABLE, SS:STACK_HERE
;initialize stack segment register, stack pointer,data segment
        MOV     AX, STACK_HERE
        MOV     SS, AX
        MOV     SP, OFFSET TOP_STACK
        MOV     AX, AINT_TABLE
        MOV     DS, AX
;define the addresses for the interrupt service procedures
        MOV     TYPE_64+2, SEG CLOCK_TICK       ; put in clock-tick proc addr
        MOV     TYPE_64,   OFFSET CLOCK_TICK
        MOV     TYPE_66+2, SEG KEYBOARD         ; put in keyboard proc addr
        MOV     TYPE_66,   OFFSET KEYBOARD
```

FIGURE 10-35 8086 assembly language program for process control system. *(a)* Module 1—Mainline. *(b)* Module 2—interrupt service procedures. *(c)* Module 3—loop service procedures. *(d)* Module 4—utility procedures.

```
;initialize data segment
        ASSUME DS:DATA_HERE
        MOV     AX, DATA_HERE
        MOV     DS, AX
;initialize port P2B (FFFA) as output - mode 0, P2A & P2C as inputs - mode 0
        MOV     DX, 0FFFEH              ; point DX at port control addr
        MOV     AL, 10011001B           ; mode control word for above conditions
        OUT     DX, AL                  ; send control word
;initialize 8259A
        MOV     AL, 00010011B           ; edge triggered, single, ICW4
        MOV     DX, 0FF00H              ; point at 8259A control
        OUT     DX, AL                  ; send ICW1
        MOV     AL, 01000000B           ; type 64 is first 8259A type (IR0)
        MOV     DX, 0FF02H              ; point at ICW2 address
        OUT     DX, AL                  ; send ICW2
        MOV     AL, 00000001B           ; ICW4, 8086 mode
        OUT     DX, AL                  ; send ICW4
        MOV     AL, 11111110B           ; OCW1 to unmask IR0 only leave IR2 masked
        OUT     DX, AL                  ; because not used & send OCW1
;initialize 8254 counter 0 for 1-kHz output
; 8254 command word for counter 0, LSB then MSB, square wave, BCD
        MOV     AL, 00110111B
        MOV     DX, 0FF07H              ; point at 8254 control addr
        OUT     DX, AL                  ; send counter 0 command word
        MOV     AL, 58H                 ; Load LSB of count
        MOV     DX, 0FF01H              ; point at counter 0 data addr
        OUT     DX, AL                  ; send LSB of count
        MOV     AL, 24H                 ; load MSB of count
        OUT     DX, AL                  ; send MSB of count
;initialize variables
        MOV     SETPOINT, 3CH           ; initialize final temp at 60 deg
        MOV     COUNTER,  14H           ; intialize time counter
        MOV     LOOPNUM,  00H           ; start at first loop
        MOV     TIMEHI,   01H
        MOV     TIMELO,   01H
        MOV     CURTEMP,  00H
;enable interrupt input of 8086
        STI
HERE:   JMP     HERE                    ; wait for interrupt
        NOP                             ; if required, can put more
        NOP                             ; instructions here
        NOP
CODE_HERE ENDS
          END
```

(*a*)

FIGURE 10-35 (*continued*)

sent to the solid-state relay. The time on for the output waveform to the solid-state relay is determined by counting down a value called TIMEHI. The time off for this waveform is determined by counting down a value called TIMELO. At start-up the mainline program initializes TIMEHI and TIMELO to 01H, so that the first time the LOOP0 procedure is called both of these are decremented to 0 and execution falls through to the A/D conversion procedure. This needs to be done so that we have a temperature value to use for computing the duty cycle.

The number of the A/D channel that we want to digitize is passed to the A/D conversion procedure in the BL register. The procedure then sends out this channel number to the A/D converter and generates the control wave forms shown in Figure 10-34 under software control. The binary value for the temperature is returned in AL.

```
PAGE ,132
;MODULE 2 - CONTAINS THE INTERRUPT SERVICE SUBROUTINES

PUBLIC     CLOCK_TICK, KEYBOARD

;tell assembler where to find loop addresses used in this module
DATA_HERE     SEGMENT     WORD     PUBLIC
     LOOP_ADDR_TABLE     DD     LOOP0
                         DD     LOOP1
                         DD     LOOP2
                         DD     LOOP3
                         DD     LOOP4
                         DD     LOOP5
                         DD     LOOP6
                         DD     LOOP7

     EXTRN     COUNTER:BYTE, LOOPNUM:BYTE
DATA_HERE     ENDS

;tell assembler where to find procedures used in this module
CODE_HERE     SEGMENT WORD     PUBLIC
     EXTRN    LOOP0:FAR, LOOP1:FAR, LOOP2:FAR, LOOP3:FAR
     EXTRN    LOOP4:FAR, LOOP5:FAR, LOOP6:FAR, LOOP7:FAR
CODE_HERE     ENDS

INT_PROC_HERE  SEGMENT WORD  PUBLIC  ;segment for interrupt service procedures
     ASSUME    CS:INT_PROC_HERE, DS:DATA_HERE

;8086 INTERRUPT PROCEDURE TO SERVICE PROCESS CONTROL LOOPS
;
;ABSTRACT:   This procedure services calls 1 of 8 process control
;            loops on a rotating basis.
;PORTS USED: none
;PROCEDURES: calls LOOP0,LOOP1,LOOP2,LOOP3,LOOP4,LOOP5,LOOP6,LOOP7
;REGISTERS:  saves all

CLOCK_TICK     PROC     FAR
     PUSH   AX                  ; save registers
     PUSH   BX
     PUSH   DX
     PUSH   DS                  ; save DS of interrupted program
     STI                        ; enable higher interrupts if any
     MOV    AL, 00100000B       ; OCW2 for nonspecific EOI
     MOV    DX, 0FF00H          ; address for OCW2
     OUT    DX, AL
     MOV    AX, DATA_HERE       ; load DS needed here
     MOV    DS, AX
     DEC    COUNTER             ; decrement interrupt counter
     JNZ    EXIT2               ; not zero yet , go wait
     MOV    COUNTER, 20         ; if zero, reset tick counter to 20
     MOV    BH, 00              ; load BX with number of loop to
     MOV    BL, LOOPNUM         ;  service
     CALL   DWORD PTR LOOP_ADDR_TABLE[BX]     ; and service that loop
     ADD    LOOPNUM, 04         ; point at next loop address
     CMP    LOOPNUM, 20H        ; was this the last loop?
     JNE    EXIT2               ; no, exit
```

FIGURE 10-35 (*continued*)

```
      MOV      LOOPNUM, 00       ; yes, get back to first loop
EXIT2:POP      DS                ; restore registers
      POP      DX
      POP      BX
      POP      AX
      IRET
CLOCK_TICK     ENDP


;DUMMY INTERRUPT PROCEDURE TO SERVICE KEYBOARD
KEYBOARD PROC       FAR
                                ; keyboard proc instructions
      MOV      AL, 00100000B     ; OCW2 for non-specific EOI
      MOV      DX, 0FF00H        ; address for OCW2
      OUT      DX, AL            ; send OCW2 for end of interrupt
      IRET
KEYBOARD ENDP

INT_PROC_HERE ENDS
      END
```

(*b*)

```
PAGE ,132
;MODULE 3 - CONTAINS THE PROCEDURES TO SERVICE EACH LOOP
;
DATA_HERE       SEGMENT WORD    PUBLIC
        EXTRN   TIMEHI :BYTE, TIMELO  :BYTE      ; imported into this
        EXTRN   CURTEMP:BYTE, SETPOINT:BYTE      ; module from the mainline
DATA_HERE       ENDS

PUBLIC  LOOP0, LOOP1, LOOP2, LOOP3, LOOP4, LOOP5, LOOP6, LOOP7

CODE_HERE SEGMENT WORD PUBLIC
EXTRN   DISPLAY  : NEAR          ; These procedures can be
EXTRN   A_D_READ : NEAR          ; found in another assembly
EXTRN   BINCVT   : NEAR          ; module which will be linked
CODE_HERE ENDS                   ; with this module & other modules

CODE_HERE       SEGMENT WORD    PUBLIC
        ASSUME  CS:CODE_HERE, DS:DATA_HERE

;8086 PROCEDURE TO SERVICE TEMPERATURE CONTROLLER
;
;ABSTRACT:      This procedure services the temperature controller
;REGISTERS:     Destroys none
;PORTS:         Uses P2B (FFFAH) as output port to turn heater with
;               bit 7.
;CALLS:         DISPLAY, A_D_READ, BINCVT
LOOP0   PROC    FAR
        PUSHF                           ; save registers
        PUSH    AX
        PUSH    BX
        PUSH    CX
        PUSH    DX
        DEC     TIMEHI                  ; decrement time for heater on
```

FIGURE 10-35 (*continued*)

```
          JNZ     EXIT                    ; return to interrupt procedure
          MOV     TIMEHI, Ø1              ; reset time high to fall through value
          MOV     DX, ØFFFAH              ; point at o/p port P2B &
          MOV     AL, 8ØH                 ; turn off heater
          OUT     DX, AL
          DEC     TIMELO                  ; decrement time for heater off
          JNZ     EXIT                    ; return to interrupt procedure
          MOV     BL, ØØ                  ; load channel address (Ø)
          CALL    A_D_READ                ; do A/D conversion
          MOV     CURTEMP, AL             ; save current temperature
          CALL    BINCVT                  ; convert to BCD
          MOV     CL, AL                  ; put result in CX to display
          MOV     CH, ØØ
          MOV     AL, ØØ                  ; temp in data field of SDK-86
          CALL    DISPLAY
          MOV     AL, SETPOINT            ; get setpoint temperature
          SUB     AL, CURTEMP             ; get temperature & subtract from setpoint
          JBE     DONE                    ; heater off if above or equal setpoint
          MOV     DL, AL                  ; save temperature difference
          MOV     AX, ØØ64H               ; compute new TIMELO
          DIV     DL                      ; ØØ64/error, quotient is value
          MOV     TIMELO, AL              ; for new time low
          MOV     TIMEHI, Ø4              ; set time high for 4 loops on
          MOV     AL, ØØ
          MOV     DX, ØFFFAH              ; point at output port
          OUT     DX,AL                   ; turn on heater
          JMP     EXIT
DONE:     MOV     TIMEHI, Ø1H             ; fall through value for time high
          MOV     TIMELO, 7FH             ; long off value for time low
EXIT:     POP     DX                      ; loop serviced - return to
          POP     CX                      ; interrupt service procedure
          POP     BX
          POP     AX
          POPF
          RET
LOOPØ     ENDP

;DUMMY LOOPS HERE
LOOP1     PROC    FAR
;         :                               ; instructions for this loop
          RET
LOOP1     ENDP

LOOP2     PROC    FAR
;         :                               ; instructions for this loop
          RET
LOOP2     ENDP

LOOP3     PROC    FAR
;         :                               ; instructions for this loop
          RET
LOOP3     ENDP

LOOP4     PROC    FAR
;         :                               ; instructions for this loop
          RET
LOOP4     ENDP
```

FIGURE 10-35 (*continued*)

```
LOOP5   PROC    FAR
;       :                                ; instructions for this loop
        RET
LOOP5   ENDP

LOOP6   PROC    FAR
;       :                                ; instructions for this loop
        RET
LOOP6   ENDP

LOOP7   PROC    FAR
;       :                                ; instructions for this loop
        RET
LOOP7   ENDP

CODE_HERE       ENDS
        END
```

(c)

```
PAGE ,132
;MODULE 4 - CONTAINS THE SERVICE PROCEDURES NEEDED BY THE LOOP MODULES

PUBLIC  DISPLAY, A_D_READ, BINCVT ; make procedures available to other modules

DATA_HERE SEGMENT       WORD    PUBLIC
SEVEN_SEG       DB      3FH, Ø6H, 5BH, 4FH, 66H, 6DH, 7DH, Ø7H
                ;        Ø    1    2    3    4    5    6    7
                DB      7FH, 6FH, 77H, 7CH, 39H, 5EH, 79H, 71H
                ;        8    9    A    b    C    d    E    F
DATA_HERE ENDS
CODE_HERE       SEGMENT WORD    PUBLIC
                ASSUME CS:CODE_HERE, DS:DATA_HERE

;8Ø86 PROCEDURE TO DISPLAY DATA ON SDK-86 LEDs
;ABSTRACT:  This procedure will display a 4-digit hex or BCD number
;           passed in the CX register on LEDs of the SDK-86
;INPUTS:    Data in CX, control in AL.
;           AL = ØØH  data displayed in data-field of LEDs
;           AL <> 00H, data displayed in address field of LEDs.
;PORTS:     Uses none
;PROCEDURES:Uses none
;REGISTERS: saves all registers and flags

DISPLAY PROC    NEAR
        PUSHF                       ; save flags
        PUSH DS                     ; save caller's DS
        PUSH AX                     ; save registers
        PUSH BX
        PUSH CX
        PUSH DX
        MOV  BX, DATA_HERE          ; init DS as needed for procedure
        MOV  DS, BX
        MOV  DX, ØFFEAH             ; point at 8279 control address
        CMP  AL, ØØH                ; see if data field required
        JZ   DATFLD                 ; yes, load control word for data field
```

FIGURE 10-35 (*continued*)

```
        MOV  AL, 94H              ; no, load address-field control word
        JMP  SEND                 ; go send control word
DATFLD: MOV  AL, 90H              ; load control word for data field
SEND:   OUT  DX, AL               ; send control word to 8279
        MOV  BX, OFFSET SEVEN_SEG ; pointer to seven-segment codes
        MOV  DX, 0FFE8H           ; point at 8279 display RAM
        MOV  AL, CL               ; get low byte to be displayed
        AND  AL, 0FH              ; mask upper nibble
        XLATB                     ; translate lower nibble to 7-seg code
        OUT  DX, AL               ; send to 8279 display RAM
        MOV  AL, CL               ; get low byte again
        MOV  CL, 04               ; load rotate count
        ROL  AL, CL               ; Move upper nibble into low position
        AND  AL, 0FH              ; Mask upper nibble
        XLATB                     ; translate 2nd nibble to 7-seg code
        OUT  DX, AL               ; send to 8279 display RAM
        MOV  AL, CH               ; Get high byte to translate
        AND  AL, 0FH              ; Mask upper nibble
        XLATB                     ; Translate to 7-seg code
        OUT  DX, AL               ; send to 8279 display RAM
        MOV  AL, CH               ; get high byte to fix upper nibble
        ROL  AL, CL               ; move upper nibble into low position
        AND  AL, 0FH              ; mask upper nibble
        XLATB                     ; translate to 7-seg code
        OUT  DX, AL               ; 7-seg code to 8279 display RAM
        POP  DX                   ; restore all registers and flags
        POP  CX
        POP  BX
        POP  AX
        POP  DS
        POPF
        RET
DISPLAY ENDP

;8086 PROCEDURE TO CONTROL A/D CONVERTER
;
;PORTS:         Port P2A is input from A/D
;               Port P2B, bit 7 = heater, bit 5 = start conversion
;                         bit 4 = ALE     bits 2,1,0 = channel address
;               Port P2C  bit 0 = end of conversion
;INPUTS:        Channel address for A/D in BL
;OUTPUTS:       A/D data in AL
;REGISTERS:     DESTROYS AL & BL

A_D_READ        PROC    NEAR
        PUSHF
        PUSH    DX
        MOV     AL, 80H               ; control for heater off
        OR      AL, BL                ; combine with channel address
        MOV     DX, 0FFFAH            ; point at P2B, output port
        OUT     DX, AL                ; send
        MOV     AL, 90H               ; send ALE, keep heater on
        OR      AL, BL                ; keep channel address on
        OUT     DX, AL
        MOV     AL, 0B0H              ; send start of conversion
```

FIGURE 10-35 (*continued*)

```
        OR      AL, BL              ; keep channel address on
        OUT     DX, AL
        MOV     AL, 80H             ; turn off ALE and start
        OR      AL, BL              ; keep channel address
        OUT     DX, AL
        MOV     DX, 0FFFCH          ; point at port P2C
EOCL:   IN      AL, DX              ; wait for end of conversion
        RCR     AL, 01              ; to go low
        JC      EOCL
EOCH:   IN      AL, DX              ; wait for end of conversion
        RCR     AL, 01              ; to go high
        JNC     EOCH
        MOV     DX, 0FFF8H          ; point at port P2A
        IN      AL, DX              ; read data from A/d
        POP     DX
        POPF
        RET
A_D_READ        ENDP

;BINCVT -       Converts an 8-bit binary number in AL
;                to packed BCD equivalent in AL
;INPUTS:        AL - 8-bit binary number
;OUTPUTS:       AL - packed BCD result

BINCVT  PROC    NEAR
        PUSHF                   ; save registers and flags
        PUSH  CX
        MOV   AH,09H            ; bit counter for 8 bits
        MOV   CL, AL            ; save binary in CL
        MOV   CH, 00            ; clear CH for use as buffer
CNVT2:  XOR   AL, AL            ; clear AL and carry
        DEC   AH                ; decrement bit counter
        JNZ   GO_ON             ; do all bits
        JMP   HOME              ; done if AH down to zero
GO_ON:  RCL   CL,1              ; MSB from CL to carry
        MOV   AL, CH            ; move BCD digit being built to AL
        ADC   AL, AL            ; double AL and add carry from CL shift
        DAA                     ; keep result in BCD form
        MOV   CH, AL            ; put back in CH for next time through
        JMP   CNVT2             ; continue conversion
HOME:   MOV   AL, CH            ; BCD in AL for return
        POP   CX                ; restore registers
        POPF
        RET
BINCVT  ENDP

CODE_HERE  ENDS
        END
```

(*d*)

FIGURE 10-35 (*continued*)

Upon return, the binary value of the temperature is stored in a memory location called CURTEMP for future reference. For testing purposes we wanted to display the temperature on the address field of the SDK-86 display. To do this we convert the binary value for the temperature to a BCD value using a reduced version of the binary-to-BCD procedure from the scale program earlier in this chapter, and the display routine from Chapter 9.

After displaying the current temperature, it is then compared with the set-point temperature to see if the heater needs to be turned on. If the temperature is at or above the set point, TIMEHI is loaded with the fall-through value, and TIMELO with a large number.

If the temperature is below the set point, we could call a procedure, DUTY_CYCLE, which computes the correct values for TIMEHI and TIMELO based on the difference between the set point and the current temperature. A complex PID algorithm might be used for this procedure in a precision system. For our example here, however, we have used simple proportional feedback. To further simplify the calculations a fixed value of 4 was used for TIMEHI. The thinking for the value of TIMELO then goes as follows. If the difference in temperature is large, then TIMELO should be small so the heater is on for a longer duty cycle. If the difference in temperature is small, then the value of TIMELO should be large so the heater has a short duty cycle. Experimentally we found that a good first approximation for our system was (difference in temperature) × TIMELO = 100 decimal (64H). For example, if the difference in temperature is 20° (14H), then 64H/14H gives a value of 5 for TIMELO. The values for TIMEHI and TIMELO are returned in their named memory locations. Upon return to the main loop procedure we send a control word which turns on the heater. Execution then jumps to EXIT.

When execution returns to loop 0 again after 160 ms, TIMEHI will be decremented. If TIMEHI did not decrement to 0, then execution simply adjusts a few things and returns. If TIMEHI is 0 after the decrement, the heater is turned off, and TIMELO is decremented. TIMELO is then decremented every time loop 0 is serviced (every 160 ms) until TIMELO reaches 0. When TIMELO gets counted down to 0, a new A/D conversion is done, and a new feedback value for TIMELO recalculated.

An important point here is that the part of the program that determines the feedback is separate from the rest of the program so it can be easily altered without changing any of the rest of the program. All that needs to be changed in this procedure is the value of TIMEHI, the value of TIMELO, and the rate at which these change in response to a difference in temperature to produce proportional, integral, and derivative feedback control.

TEMPERATURE CONTROLLER RESPONSE

The dotted line in Figure 10-36 shows the temperature versus time response of our system with traditional thermostat control, which is often called *on-off control* or "bang-bang" control. As you can see the temperature overshoots the set point a great deal, and then oscillates around the set-point temperature. The solid line in Figure 10-36 shows the response of the system operating with our temperature-controller program. The initial overshoot was caused by the large thermal inertia of the hot plate we used. The overshoot and the residual error of about 1° could be eliminated by using a more complex feedback algorithm. This example should make you aware of the advantages of computer feedback control.

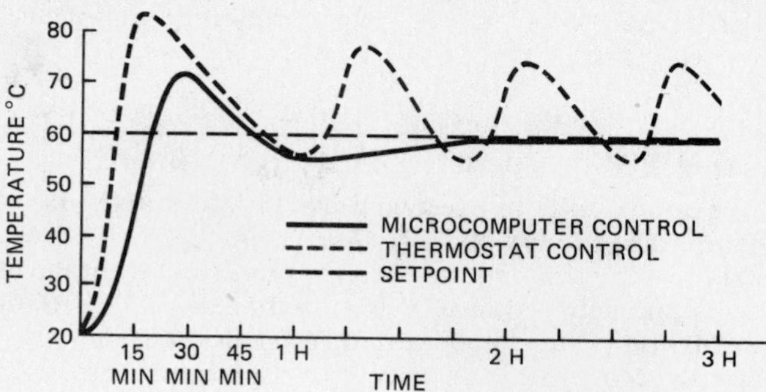

FIGURE 10-36 Temperature versus time responses for thermostat-controlled and microcomputer-controlled heaters.

Robotics

In recent years the term *robot* has become a "buzzword" in the media and in many people's minds. Science fiction movies have helped us form an image of robots as mobile, rational companions. Robots, however, have many forms, and in operation they are simply a special case of feedback control systems such as we described in the previous section. This is why we have not included a chapter dedicated just to robotics. The Rhino robot arm shown in Figure 9-43, for example, uses optical encoders to detect the position of its different joints, motors (actuators) to move each joint to a desired position, and a microcomputer to control the motors based on feedback from the sensors. In large industrial robots such as those that weld or spray-paint cars, the sensors used may also include vision, and the actuators may be hydraulic or pneumatic, but the control principle is the same. Feedback from the various sensors is used to control the output to the actuators.

Most of you have probably used some simple robots around your home without realizing it. One example is an electric garage door opener which starts to open or close when you tell it to, and then stops when a sensor indicates that it is closed or open as desired. Other examples are an automatic clothes washer, a clothes dryer, and a microwave oven with a temperature probe.

The next major section of this chapter is a discussion of how you develop the prototype of a microcomputer-based instrument such as the smart scale or the control system we discussed in the preceding sections.

DEVELOPING THE PROTOTYPE OF A MICROCOMPUTER-BASED INSTRUMENT

The first step in developing a new instrument is to very carefully define exactly what you want the instrument to do. The next step is to decide which parts of the instrument you want to do in hardware, and which parts you want to do in software. You then can decide how you want to do each of these.

For the software, you will break the overall programming job down into modules which can be individually tested and debugged as we have described previously.

For the hardware there are several different approaches you can take.

Using a Microcomputer-Prototyping Board

One approach is to use a commercially available microcomputer-prototyping board such as the SDK-86 we used for the examples in this chapter. An advantage of this approach is that it gives you the basic CPU, RAM, ROM, and ports already tested. You can then easily add any needed timers, priority interrupt controllers, and other interface circuitry. Some of the available prototyping boards such as the SDK-86 have on-board monitor programs which let you load and execute your programs. The major advantage of this approach is that it allows you to quickly get a prototype up and running to see if the instrument is feasible. If the instrument is feasible you can then design a custom hardware board which exactly fits your needs.

Computer-Aided Design Approach

Another approach to creating the needed hardware for the prototype is with a *computer-aided design* or CAD system. This system may be a large and powerful engineering workstation such as those made by Mentor Graphics, or simply an IBM PC-type computer with programs such as the PCAD system from Personal CAD Systems, Inc., Electronic Design Automation Division. The programs on these systems allow you, first of all, to easily design and draw a schematic for your hardware. You can just select the schematic symbol for a part you want to use by number from a large library of common devices in a disk file and bring it on to your CRT screen. You use a "mouse" to move the symbol into position and to draw signal lines connecting it to other symbols. You can move a device around as needed, and the connecting signal lines will follow.

When you get the schematic drawn up, you can then use another program in the CAD system to *simulate* the operation of the circuit. By simulate we mean to "run" the circuit in software. This helps you to find out if the signals are connected correctly, and if timing parameters are acceptable. If the circuit passes simulation, you can make a printout of the schematic on a printer or plotter.

The next step is to design a printed circuit board for your circuit. Another program in the CAD system will, with a little help from you, produce the artwork for the printed-circuit board. Some systems will even produce the control tape for the machine which automatically drills the required holes in the printed circuit board. The time is not too far away when the engineering workstation can be connected directly to the printed-circuit-board-making machine, the machine that gets parts from the warehouse, the machine that stuffs the parts in the printed circuit board, and the machine that does the initial functional tests on the board. This concept, incidentally, is called *computer integrated manufacturing* or CIM and seems to be where the industry is heading, but it isn't quite there yet. Therefore, you still have some work to do when you get the prototype printed circuit board back.

After you stuff the board with the required parts you can power it up and check for hot or otherwise unhappy components. If there are no apparent problems you can proceed to test the board. Probably the best tool to test the board with is an emulator.

Using an Emulator

Figure 3-12 shows a picture of an Applied Microsystems ES 1800 emulator which works with the IBM PC and other compatible computers. Several other companies make similar emulators. The hardware of an emulator consists of control circuitry, memory to store the trace data after each instruction executes, and an "umbilical" cable with a plug at the end of it. To use the emulator you remove the microprocessor from the prototype unit and insert the plug at the end of the umbilical cable in its place. The emulator contains a microprocessor which will actually run your test programs under control of the emulator. The emulator then gives you a window into the operation of the circuitry on the prototype under control of a development system or PC.

The software of the emulator is similar to a powerful monitor program or debugger program. You can use the emulator commands and the system memory to test each part of the prototype. For example, you can write a short program to test the RAM in the prototype, load this program into the system RAM, and run the program under emulator control. To help with debugging, emulators allow you to set breakpoints, examine and change the contents of registers and memory locations, and do a trace which shows the contents of registers after each instruction executes. Some emulators have an additional pod like those used on logic analyzers so that you can do a trace of the sequence of hardware signals on a group of lines to check timing.

An important point here is that, just as we stressed with building programs, the fastest way to get a prototype debugged and operating is one small part at a time. Because problems tend to interact, trying to debug too large a section at a time can be frustrating and time-consuming. Therefore, remove all but the basic CPU group ICs for your first test then keep adding, testing and debugging one section at a time. As you get a hardware section working, you can if you want write and debug the software module which uses or drives that hardware module. To give you a better idea of how to do this development process, we will briefly describe the steps we went through to develop the process-control system discussed earlier in this chapter.

A Product Development Example

For our process-control demonstration system we started with an SDK-86 board because we only wanted to make one unit, and because we did not have CAD equipment and a printed-circuit-board-making machine. For the controller we needed a timer to produce 1-kHz clock ticks and a priority interrupt controller to handle keyboard and clock tick interrupts. We added these two devices and some address decoder circuitry to the SDK-86 as shown in Figure 8-14, and proceeded to test this circuitry with an emulator. To do this we wrote a short program which wrote a byte to the starting address for the timer over and over again. We ran this program with the emulator and with a scope we checked to see if the $\overline{CS}$ input of the timer was getting asserted. It was, so we knew that the address decoding circuitry was working correctly. We then connected the 2.45-MHz PCLK signal to the clock inputs of all three timers in the 8254 and wrote the instructions needed to initialize the three timers for 1-kHz square-wave output. Even though we only need one timer here, it was very little additional work to check the other two for future reference. Hooray, the timers worked the first time, now on to the 8259A PIC.

Testing the 8259A was a little more complex because we had to provide an interrupt signal, initialize the 8259A, initialize the interrupt vector table in low RAM, and provide a location for execution to go to when the PIC received an interrupt. We used the 1-kHz clock tick from the timer as the interrupt signal to the 8259A. For 8259A initialization and the interrupt jump table initialization we used the instructions in the mainline program in Figure 10-35. For the test-interrupt procedure we actually used a real-time clock and display procedure that we developed for examples in previous chapters. We used these so that we could see if the interrupt mechanism was working correctly by watching the displays on the SDK-86 count off seconds. This again shows the advantage of writing programs as separate reusable modules. Note in the program in Figure 10-35 that we initialize the 8259A before we initialize and start the timer. When we first wrote a test program to test an 8259A and an 8254, we did this in the reverse order. When we ran the test program with the emulator, the system would only accept one interrupt and hang up. We did a trace with the emulator and found that execution was returning from the interrupt procedure to the WAIT loop in the mainline program properly, but not recognizing the next interrupt. Careful reading of the 8259A data sheet showed us that we had to initialize the 8259A *before* we started sending it interrupt signals, or it would not respond correctly to the nonspecific EOI command that we used at the end of the interrupt procedure to reset the 8259A's in-service register.

After the interrupt mechanism was working correctly, we wrote the interrupt procedure which implements the decision structure shown in Figure 10-32*b*. Initially we made all eight loops dummy loops to test the basic structure. By inserting breakpoints with the emulator we were able to see if execution was getting to each of the eight loops. When all of this was working, we went on to build and test the temperature-control section.

For the temperature-control section we first built the analog circuitry and tested it. Then we wrote a small program to read the temperature from the A/D converter and display the result on the SDK-86 displays. Initially then, the loop 0 procedure simply read in the temperature, displayed it in binary (hex) form and returned. This worked the first time, so we went on to add the binary-to-BCD conversion routine and run the result with the emulator. This was a previously written and tested module, and when added, the result worked fine.

Next we added a couple of instructions to turn the heater on during one execution of loop 0 and turn the heater off during the next time through loop 0. We then used an oscilloscope to check that the solid-state relay was getting turned on and off correctly.

Finally, we added the actual duty cycle and control instructions, and sat back waiting for the system to heat us up a big container of water for tea.

The actual development cycle will obviously be somewhat different for every instrument developed. The main points here are to develop and test both the hardware and software in small modules. To speed up the debugging process, take the time to learn to use all or most of the power of the emulator and system you are working with.

DIGITAL FILTERS

A section at the start of this chapter showed how op amps can be used to build high-pass and low-pass filter circuits. Filtering of a signal can also be done by taking samples of the signal with an A/D converter, performing mathematical operations on the samples from the A/D converter, and outputting the result to a D/A converter. This approach, referred to as a *digital filter*, can easily produce a response curve which is difficult, if not impossible, to produce with analog circuitry. This digital approach has the further advantage that the filter response can be changed under program control. Digital filters are used in speech synthesizers, satellite image-enhancement systems, and many other applications.

There are two basic types of digital filter, the *finite impulse response* or FIR type and the *infinite impulse response* or IIR type. The basic principle of a digital filter is to operate on the samples as a function of time rather than as a function of frequency as the analog filter does.

Figure 10-37*a* shows a functional diagram of the operation of an FIR-type filter. The box containing Z^{-1} represents a delay of one sample interval. Circles containing an X represent a multiplication operation, and the letters to the left of each circle represent the number that the term will be multiplied by. Y_0 represents the value of the current sample from the A/D, Y_1 represents the value of the previous sample from the A/D, and Y_2 represents the value of the sample before that. Here's how this works. The output value, V, at any time is produced by summing the (current sample × some coefficient) + (the previous sample × some coefficient) + (the sample before that × some coefficient), etc. To do all of this with a microprocessor involves simple operations of saving previous samples, multiplying, and adding. The Intel 2920 microprocessor, which was specifically designed for this type of operation, contains an A/D converter, D/A converter, and an architecture and instruction set which works with the 25-bit numbers required for accurate filter response.

Figure 10-37*b* shows a functional diagram for an IIR digital filter. Here again the blocks containing Z^{-1} rep-

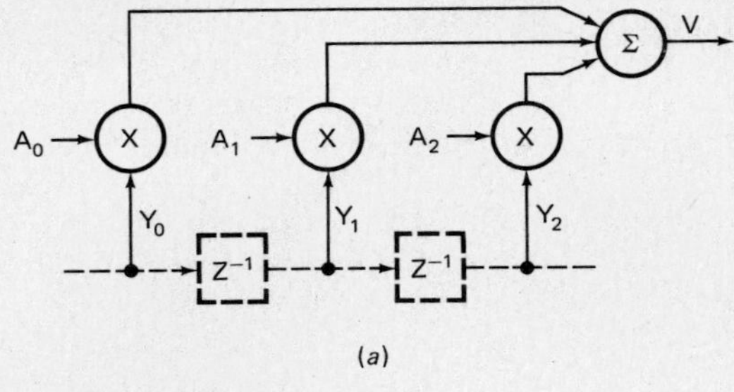

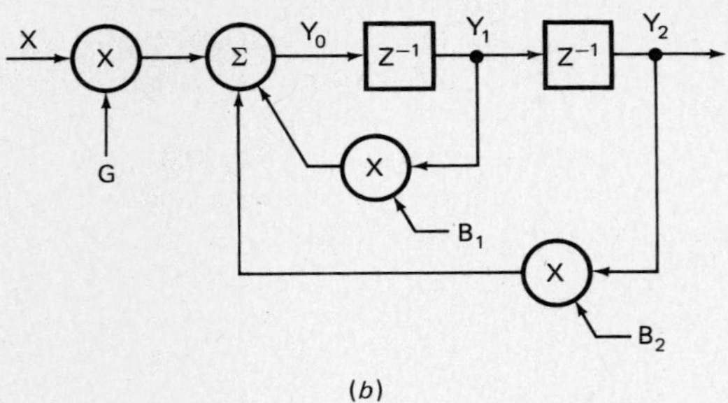

FIGURE 10-37 FIR and IIR digital filter principles. *(a)* FIR. *(b)* IIR.

resent a delay of one sample time. The value of the current sample from the A/D converter is represented by the X at the left of the diagram. The Y_0 point represents the output from the microprocessor to the D/A converter. Note that for an IIR filter it is this output value which is saved to be used in computing feedback terms for future samples. In the FIR type, remember, the samples from the A/D converter were saved directly for future use. The output for an IIR type is produced by summing (the current sample × a calculated coefficient) + (the previous output value × a calculated coefficient) + (the output value before that × a calculated coefficient), etc. The coefficients for both the FIR- and the IIR-type filters are usually calculated using a computer program. FIR filters are easier to design, but they may require many terms to produce a given filter response. IIR filters require fewer stages, but they have to be carefully designed so that they do not become oscillators.

A new type of filter called a *switched capacitor filter* implements digital filtering for simple filter responses without the need for the A/D and D/A converter. An example is the National MF10. In this type of filter an input signal is sampled on a capacitor. The signal is passed on to other capacitors and fractions of the outputs from these capacitors are summed to produce an analog output signal directly. Switched capacitor filters are less expensive, but they do not give the degree of programmability that the microprocessor-based filters do.

IMPORTANT TERMS AND CONCEPTS FROM THIS CHAPTER

If you do not remember any of the terms in the following list, use the index to help you find them in the chapter for review.

Op amp

Comparator

Hysteresis

Noninverting amplifier

Inverting amplifier
  Virtual ground

Gain-bandwidth product

Unity-gain bandwidth

Adder circuit—summing point

Differential amplifier
  Common-mode signal, common-mode rejection

Instrumentation amplifier

Op-amp integrator circuit
  Linear ramp
  Saturation

Op-amp differentiator

Op-amp active filters
  Low-pass filter, high-pass filter, bandpass filter
  Critical frequency or breakpoint
  Second-order low-pass filter, second-order high-pass filter

Light sensor
  Photodiode
  Solar cell

Temperature-sensitive voltage sources

Temperature-sensitive current sources

Thermocouples
  Type J thermocouple
  Cold-junction compensation

Force and pressure transducers
  Strain gage, LVDT, load cell

Flow sensors
  Paddle wheel, differential pressure transducer

D/A converters
  Binary weighted
  Resolution
  Full-scale output voltage
  Maximum error
  Linearity
  Settling time

A/D converters
  Conversion time
  Parallel-comparator A/D converter
  Dual-slope A/D converter
  Successive-approximation A/D converter
  Data acquisition system

A/D output codes
  Unipolar binary code, unipolar BCD code, biopolar binary code

Direct memory access

Set point

Servo control

Settling time, underdamped, overdamped

Residual error

Proportional-integral-derivative control loop, PID

Time slice

On-off control

Robotics

Digital filters
Finite impulse response (FIR), infinite impulse response (IIR)

Switched capacitor filter

Computer-aided design
Simulate

Computer-integrated manufacturing, CIM

Emulator

REVIEW QUESTIONS AND PROBLEMS

1. *a.* A comparator circuit such as the one in Figure 10-1*b* is powered by ±15 V, the inverting input is tied to +5 V, and the noninverting input is at +5.3 V. About what voltage will be on the output of the comparator?
   b. An amplifier circuit, such as the one in Figure 10-1*d*, has an $R1$ of 10 kΩ and an $R2$ of 190 kΩ. Calculate the closed-loop voltage gain for the circuit and the V_{out} that will be produced by a V_{in} of 0.030 V. What voltage would you measure on the inverting input? What would be the gain of the circuit if $R2 = 0\ \Omega$.
   c. An amplifier circuit, such as the one in Figure 10-1*e*, is built with an $R1$ of 15 kΩ and an R_f of 75 kΩ. Calculate the closed-loop voltage gain for the circuit and the output voltage for an input voltage of 0.73 V. What voltage will you always measure on the inverting input of this circuit?
   d. A differential amplifier, such as the one in Figure 10-1*g*, is built with $R1 = R2 = 100$ kΩ and $R_f = R3 = 1$ MΩ. V_1 is 4.9 V and $V_2 = 5.1$ V. Calculate the output voltage and polarity.
   e. Describe the main advantage of the instrumentation amplifier in Figure 10-1*h* over the simple differential amplifier in Figure 10-1*g*.
   f. If the amplifier used in the circuit in Question 1*b* has a gain-bandwidth product of 1 MHz, what will be the closed-loop bandwidth of the circuit?

2. Draw a circuit showing how a light-dependent resistor can be connected to a comparator so the output of the comparator changes state when the resistance of the LDR is 10 kΩ.

3. For the photodiode amplifier circuit in Figure 10-5, what voltage will you measure on the inverting input of the amplifier? Why is it important to use an FET input amplifier for this circuit? Which direction are electrons flowing through the photodiode?

4. In what application might you use a temperature-dependent current device such as the AD590 rather than a temperature-dependent voltage device such as the LM35?

5. Why must thermocouples be cold-junction compensated in order to make accurate measurements? How can the nonlinearity of a thermocouple be compensated for?

6. Why are strain gages usually connected in a bridge configuration? Why do you use a differential amplifier to amplify the signal from a strain-gage bridge?

7. Calculate the full-scale output voltage for the simple D/A converter in Figure 10-14.

8. What is the resolution of a 13-bit D/A converter? If the converter has a full-scale output of 10,000 V, what is the size of each step? What will be the actual maximum output voltage of this converter? What accuracy should this converter have to be consistent with its resolution.

9. Why must a 12-bit D/A converter have latches on its inputs if it is to be connected to 8-bit ports or an 8-bit data bus?

10. Describe the operation of a "flash" type A/D converter. What are its main advantages and disadvantages?

11. For the dual-slope A/D converter in Figure 10-19, what will be the displayed count for an input voltage of 2.372 V? What is the resolution of a 4½-digit slope-type A/D converter expressed in bits?

12. How many clock cycles does a 12-bit successive-approximation A/D converter take to do a conversion on a 0.1-V input signal? On a 5-V input signal? How does this compare with the number of clock cycles required for a 12-bit dual-slope type?

13. *a.* Assume the inputs of the MC1408 D/A converter in Figure 10-20 are connected to an output port on your microcomputer board and the output of the comparator is connected to bit D0 of an input port. Write the algorithm for a procedure to do an A/D conversion by outputting an incrementing count to the output port.
    b. Write an algorithm for a procedure to do the conversion by the successive approximation method. Which method will produce a faster result? If the hardware is available, write the

programs for these algorithms and compare the times by watching the comparator output with an oscilloscope.

14. Show the detailed algorithm for the procedure you would use to read in the data from a multiplexed BCD output A/D converter such as the MC14433 in Figure 10-23 and assemble the value in a 16-bit register for display.

15. The data sheet for an A/D converter indicates that its output is in offset-binary code. If the converter is set up for a range of −5 to +5 V and the output code is 01011011, what input voltage does this represent? How could you convert this code to 2's complement form after you read the code into your microcomputer?

16. Write a procedure to round a 32-bit BCD number in DX:AX to a 16-bit BCD number in DX.

17. For the scale circuitry in Figure 10-23, what voltage should you measure on the inverting input of the LM308 amplifier? What voltages should you measure on the two inputs of the LM363 amplifier with no load on the scale? What voltage should you measure on the output of the LM363 with no load on the scale?

18. The section of the scale program following the label NXTKEY in Figure 10-35 moves some bytes around in memory. Rewrite this section of the program using an 8086 string instruction to do the move operations. Which version seems more efficient in this case?

19. Describe how feedback helps hold the value of some variable, such as a motor speed, constant. Refer to Figure 10-27 in your explanation.

20. What problem in a control loop does integral feedback help solve? Why is derivative feedback sometimes added to a control loop?

21. What is the major advantage of a microcomputer-controlled loop over the analog approach shown in Figure 10-29?

22. Suppose that you want to control the speed of a small dc motor, such as the one in Figure 10-27, with LOOP1 of our microcomputer-based process controller.

a. Show how you would connect the output from the motor's tachometer to the system in Figure 10-33. Also show how you would connect an 8-bit D/A to control the current to the motor.

b. Write a flowchart for the LOOP1 procedure to control the speed of the motor.

c. Describe how a lookup table could be used to determine the feedback value.

23. Describe the major difference in how the feedback is produced in an FIR digital filter and how it is produced in an IIR filter.

24. When developing a prototype, why is it very important to build, test and debug both software and hardware in small modules?

CHAPTER

11 Multiple Microprocessor Systems and Buses

The major point of the first six chapters of this book was to introduce you to structured programming and to writing 8086 assembly language programs. Chapters 7 through 10 introduced you to the hardware of an 8086 minimum-mode system, showed you how to interface a microcomputer to a wide variety of input and output devices, and finally demonstrated how all of these pieces are put together to build a microcomputer-based instrument or simple control system. The major theme of Chapters 11 through 14 is to show you how larger microcomputer systems are built and programmed. As some of the parts of this we show you how large memory banks are added to a system, how multiple processors are used in a system, how you interface to more complex peripherals such as disk drives, and how systems communicate with each other. We also discuss the system programs used to coordinate all of this.

OBJECTIVES

At the end of this chapter you should be able to:

1. Show how an 8086 is connected with a controller device for operation in its maximum mode.
2. Show how a direct memory access (DMA) controller device can be connected in an 8086 system and describe how a DMA data transfer takes place.
3. Describe how large banks of dynamic RAM can be connected in a system and how automatic error-correcting circuitry works with this memory.
4. Describe the added architectural features of the 80186 microprocessor.
5. Show how a coprocessor can be connected to an 8086 or 8088 operating in maximum mode.
6. Describe the operation of the 8087 math coprocessor, and write simple programs for the 8087.
7. Show how several CPU boards can be connected to share a common set of buses, and describe how data is transferred on this common bus.
8. Use a timing diagram to describe how control of the bus is transferred from one CPU board on the bus to another.

THE 8086 MAXIMUM MODE

Many of the circuits shown in this chapter and the following chapters use the 8086 or 8088 in its maximum mode. Therefore, we start this chapter with a discussion of maximum-mode operation.

Figure 11-1*a* shows the pin diagram of the 8086 again. You may remember from our discussion in Chapter 7 that if pin 33, the MN/$\overline{\text{MX}}$ pin is tied high, the 8086 operates in its minimum mode. In minimum mode the 8086 generates control-bus signals directly. Specifically, for pins 24–31, the 8086 in minimum mode generates the signals identified in parentheses in Figure 11-1*a*.

If the MN/$\overline{\text{MX}}$ pin is tied low, the 8086 operates in its maximum mode and pins 24–31 generate the signals named next to the pins in Figure 11-1*a*. In maximum mode the control-bus signals are sent out in coded form on the status lines, $\overline{\text{S0}}$, $\overline{\text{S1}}$, and $\overline{\text{S2}}$. As shown in Figure 11-1*b*, an external controller device such as the Intel 8288 is used to produce the required control-bus signals from these lines. Figure 11-1*b* shows the expanded names for each of the control-bus signals generated by the 8288. Note in Figure 11-1*b* that we use 8282 octal latches to demultiplex the address signals and 8286 bidirectional drivers to buffer the data bus so that it can drive a board full of devices. Figure 11-1c shows the status line codes for each type of machine cycle.

The *request/grant* pins, $\overline{\text{RQ}}/\overline{\text{GT0}}$ and $\overline{\text{RQ}}/\overline{\text{GT1}}$, are used by other devices to tell the 8086 that they want to use the address, data, and control buses. These pins are bidirectional. They operate in a similar way to that in which the HOLD and HLDA pins operate when some other device wants to borrow the buses in an 8086 minimum-mode system. We will show you how these signals work in a later section on the 8087 coprocessor. A signal can be sent out from the 8086 on the $\overline{\text{LOCK}}$ pin under program control (the LOCK prefix) to prevent some other device from taking over the bus during exe-

GND 1
AD14 2
AD13 3
AD12 4
AD11 5
AD10 6
AD9 7
AD8 8
AD7 9
AD6 10
AD5 11
AD4 12
AD3 13
AD2 14
AD1 15
AD0 16
NMI 17
INTR 18
CLK 19
GND 20
40 V_{CC}
39 AD15
38 AD16/S3
37 AD17/S4
36 A18/S5
35 A19/S6
34 $\overline{BHE}$/S7
33 MN/$\overline{MX}$
32 $\overline{RD}$
31 $\overline{RQ}/\overline{GT0}$ (HOLD)
30 $\overline{RQ}/\overline{GT1}$ (HLDA)
29 $\overline{LOCK}$ ($\overline{WR}$)
28 $\overline{S2}$ (M/$\overline{IO}$)
27 $\overline{S1}$ (DT/$\overline{R}$)
26 $\overline{S0}$ ($\overline{DEN}$)
25 QS0 (ALE)
24 QS1 ($\overline{INTA}$)
23 $\overline{TEST}$
22 READY
21 RESET
8086
CPU
40 LEAD

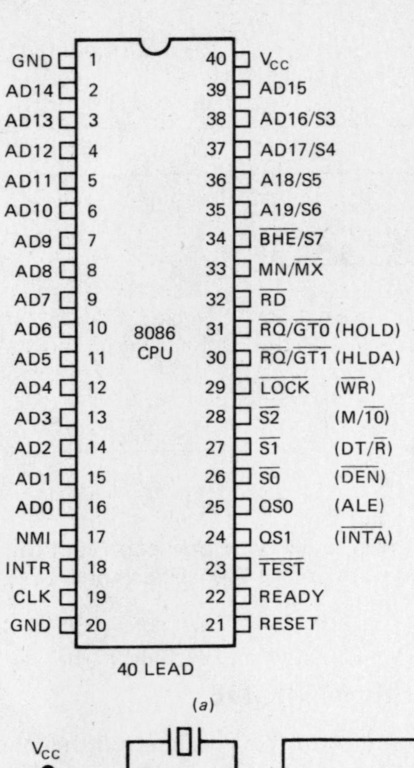

(*a*)

$\overline{S_2}$	$\overline{S_1}$	$\overline{S_0}$	
0 (LOW)	0	0	INTERRUPT ACKNOWLEDGE
0	0	1	READ I/O PORT
0	1	0	WRITE I/O PORT
0	1	1	HALT
1 (HIGH)	0	0	CODE ACCESS
1	0	1	READ MEMORY
1	1	0	WRITE MEMORY
1	1	1	PASSIVE

(*c*)

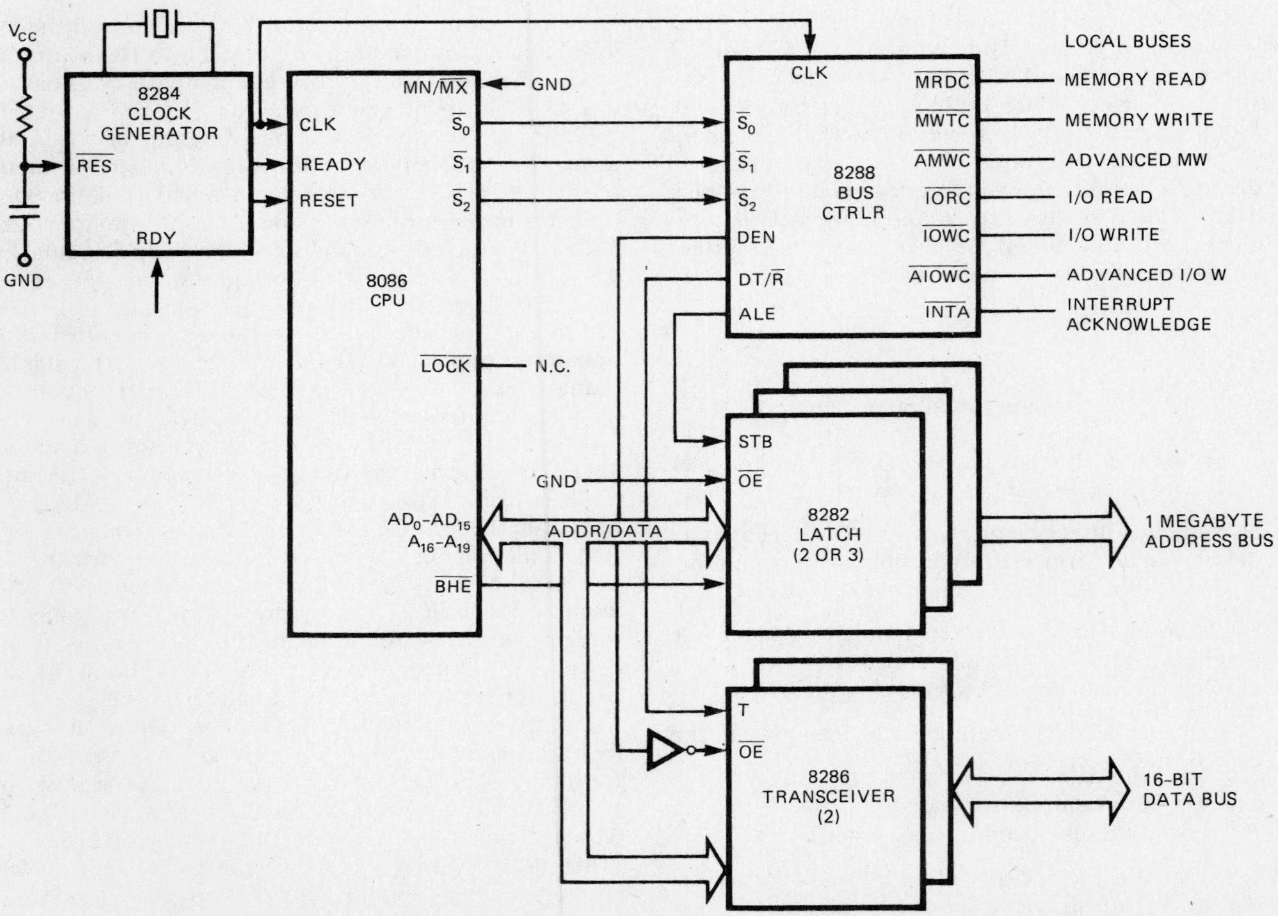

V_{CC}
GND
8284
CLOCK
GENERATOR
$\overline{RES}$
RDY
CLK
READY
RESET
MN/$\overline{MX}$
GND
$\overline{S_0}$
$\overline{S_1}$
$\overline{S_2}$
8086
CPU
$\overline{LOCK}$
N.C.
AD_0-AD_{15}
A_{16}-A_{19}
$\overline{BHE}$
ADDR/DATA
GND
CLK
DEN
DT/$\overline{R}$
ALE
8288
BUS
CTRLR
$\overline{MRDC}$
$\overline{MWTC}$
$\overline{AMWC}$
$\overline{IORC}$
$\overline{IOWC}$
$\overline{AIOWC}$
$\overline{INTA}$
LOCAL BUSES
MEMORY READ
MEMORY WRITE
ADVANCED MW
I/O READ
I/O WRITE
ADVANCED I/O W
INTERRUPT
ACKNOWLEDGE
STB
$\overline{OE}$
8282
LATCH
(2 OR 3)
1 MEGABYTE
ADDRESS BUS
T
$\overline{OE}$
8286
TRANSCEIVER
(2)
16-BIT
DATA BUS

(*b*)

FIGURE 11-1 8086 Revisited. *(a)* 8086 pin diagram. *(b)* Circuit showing 8086 connections for MAX mode operation. *(c)* $\overline{S2}$, $\overline{S1}$, and $\overline{S0}$ codes for 8086 machine cycles. *(Intel Corporation)* cution of a critical instruction. The queue status signals, QS1 and QS0, indicate the operation most recently done to the instruction-byte queue in the 8086 BIU. These signals allow an external device such as the 8087 math coprocessor, which we discuss later in this chapter, to monitor the 8086 queue and read the same instruction bytes as the 8086. Now we will show you some of the ways that a microprocessor can share its buses in minimum mode and in maximum mode.

DIRECT MEMORY ACCESS (DMA) DATA TRANSFER

DMA Overview

Up to this point in the book we have used program instructions to transfer data from ports to memory, or from memory to ports. For some applications, such as transferring data bytes to memory as they are read off a magnetic or optical disk, however, the data bytes are being sent from the disk faster than they can be read in with program instructions. In a case like this we use a dedicated hardware device called a *direct memory access* controller. A DMA controller temporarily borrows the address bus, data bus, and control bus from the microprocessor and transfers the data bytes directly from the port to a series of memory locations. Because the data transfer is handled totally in hardware, it is much faster than it would be if done by program instructions. A DMA controller can also transfer data from memory to a port. Some DMA devices can also do memory-to-memory transfers. Here's an example of how a common DMA controller is connected and used in an 8086 minimum-mode system.

Circuit Connections and Operation of the Intel 8237 DMA Controller

We chose the 8237 DMA controller as the example for this section because it is a commonly used device, and because it is one of the devices you will find if you start poking around inside an IBM PC or PC/AT. However, before we dig into the actual connections and operation of an 8237 circuit, let's take a look at the block diagram in Figure 11-2 to get an overview of how a DMA transfer takes place. The main point to keep in your mind here is simply that the microprocessor and the DMA controller time-share the use of the address, data, and control buses. We have tried to indicate this with the three switches in the middle of the block diagram. Here's how a transfer takes place.

When the system is first turned on, the switches are in the position where the buses are connected from the microprocessor to system memory and peripherals. We initialize all of the programmable devices in the system and go on executing our program until we need to, for example, read a file off a disk. To read a disk file we send a series of commands to the smart disk-controller device, telling it to go find and read the desired block of data from the disk. When the disk controller has the first byte of data from the disk block ready, it sends a *DMA request* (DREQ) signal to the DMA controller. If that input (channel) of the DMA controller is unmasked, the DMA controller will send a *hold-request* (HRQ) to the microprocessor HOLD input. The microprocessor will respond to this input by floating its buses and sending out an *hold-acknowledge* (HLDA) signal to the DMA controller. When the DMA controller receives the HLDA signal it will send out a control signal which throws the three bus switches to their DMA position, disconnecting

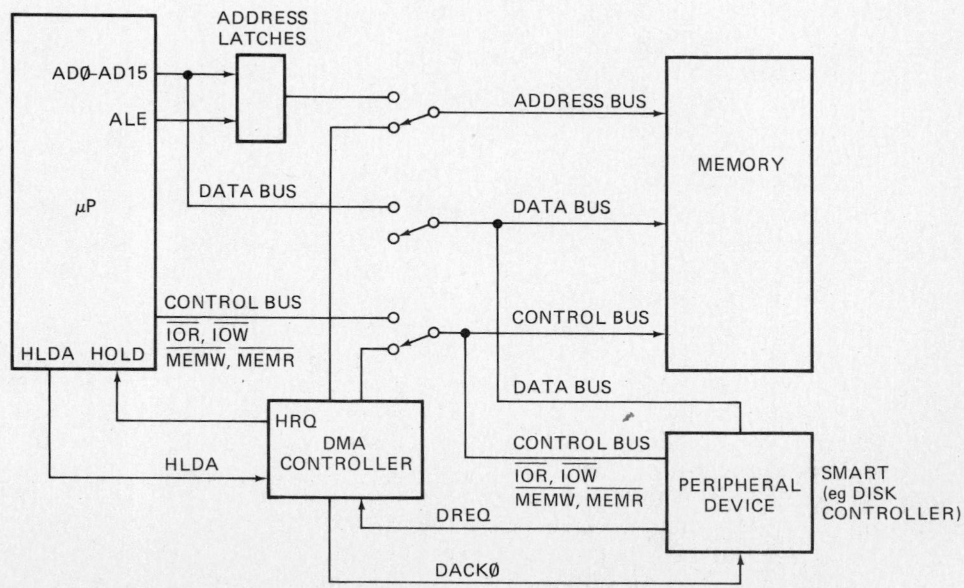

FIGURE 11-2 Block diagram showing how a DMA controller operates in a microcomputer system.

the processor from the buses. The DMA controller then outputs on the address bus the memory address where we want the byte of data from the disk controller to go. Next the DMA controller sends a *DMA-acknowledge* (DACK0) signal to the disk-controller device to tell it to get ready to output the byte. Finally, the DMA controller asserts both the $\overline{\text{MEMW}}$ and the $\overline{\text{IOR}}$ lines on the control bus. Asserting $\overline{\text{MEMW}}$ enables the addressed memory for writing data to it. Asserting $\overline{\text{IOR}}$ enables the disk controller to output the byte of data from the disk on the data bus. The byte of data will then be written to the addressed memory location.

NOTE: For this type of transfer the disk controller chip-select input does not have to be enabled by the port address decoding circuitry as it does for normal reading from and writing to registers in the device. In fact, the normal port-decoding circuitry is disabled during DMA operations to prevent the combination of $\overline{\text{IOR}}$ and the output memory address from turning on unwanted ports.

When the data transfer is complete the DMA controller unasserts its hold-request signal to the processor, and lets the processor take over the buses again until another DMA transfer is needed. The processor then continues executing from where it left off. A DMA transfer from memory to the disk controller would proceed in a similar manner except that the DMA controller would assert the *memory-read* control signal ($\overline{\text{MEMR}}$), and the *output-write* control signal ($\overline{\text{IOW}}$). DMA transfers may be done a byte at a time or in blocks.

Now, to give you more practice working your way through actual microprocessor circuits, let's look at Figure 11-3 to see some of the circuitry we might add to an 8086 system so that we can do DMA transfers to and from a disk controller. This circuitry is simply a more detailed version of the block diagram in Figure 11-2.

The first thing to do in analyzing this schematic is to identify the major devices and relate their function, where possible, to the block diagram. The 8086 and 8284 should be old friends from your exploration of the SDK-86. The 8237 is, of course, the DMA controller, and the 8272 is the floppy-disk controller. We will discuss the operation of the disk controller in the next chapter, but for now all we need to know about it is an overview of how it interacts with the 8237 as we described above. The 8282s in this circuit are octal latches with three-state outputs. They are used here to latch addresses output from either the 8086 or from the DMA controller. These devices are controlled by ALE from the 8086 and by AEN and ADSTB from the DMA controller.

When the power is first turned on, the *address-enable* signal (AEN) from the DMA controller is low. Devices *U*1, *U*2, and *U*4 are then enabled, and the ALE signal from the 8086 gets to the strobe inputs of all three devices. When the 8086 sends out an address and an ALE signal, these three devices will grab the address and send it out on the address-bus lines, A19–A0. This is just as would be done in a simpler 8086 system. Now, when the DMA controller wants to take over the bus, it asserts its AEN output high. This does several things. First, it disables device *U*1 so that address lines A7–A0 no longer come from the 8086 bus. The 8237 directly outputs the lower 8 bits of the memory address for the DMA transfer.

Secondly, AEN, going high, switches the strobe multiplexer so that the strobe for device *U*2 comes from the address strobe output of the 8237. To save pins, the 8237 outputs the upper 8 bits of the memory address for the DMA transfer on its data-bus pins and asserts its ADSTB output high to let you know that this address is present there. At the start of a DMA transfer, then, memory address bits A15–A8 will be sent out by the 8237 and latched on the outputs of *U*2.

Still another effect of AEN going high is to switch the source of address bits A19–A16 from device *U*4 to device *U*3. The DMA controller does not send out these address bits during a DMA transfer, so you have to produce them in some other way. You can either hard-wire the inputs of *U*3 to ground or +5 V to produce a fixed value for these bits, or you can connect these inputs to an output port so you can specify these address bits under program control.

Finally, AEN, going high, switches the source of the control-bus signals from the outputs of the control-bus decoder circuitry to the control-bus signal outputs of the DMA controller. This is necessary because, during a DMA transfer, the 8237 generates the required control-bus signals such as $\overline{\text{MEMW}}$ and $\overline{\text{IOR}}$. Incidentally, the NOR gate decoder circuitry in the upper right corner of the schematic is necessary to produce processor control-bus signals compatible with those from the 8237.

The final part of the circuit in Figure 11-3 to analyze is the two 8286 octal bus transceivers. The disk controller has only an 8-bit data bus output. If we connected these eight lines on the lower eight data bus lines of the 8086 system, the DMA controller could only transfer bytes to even addresses. Likewise, if we connected the disk-controller data outputs on the upper eight data lines of the 8086 system, the DMA controller could only transfer bytes to odd addresses in memory. To solve this problem, we connect the two 8286s as a switch which can route data to/from the disk controller from/to either odd or even addresses in memory. A0 determines which half of the data bus is connected to the eight data pins of the disk controller. Now let's look at the signal flow and timing for this circuit.

A DMA Transfer Timing Diagram

Figure 11-4 shows the sequence of signals that will take place for a DMA transfer in a system such as that in Figure 11-3. Keep a copy of the circuit handy as you work your way down through these waveforms. The labels we have added to each signal should help you. We will pick up where the 8237 asserts AEN high and gains control of the buses. After the 8237 gains control of the bus it sends out the lower 8 bits of the memory address on its A7–A0 pins, and the upper 8 bits of the memory address on its DB0–DB7 pins. The 8237 pulses ADSTB high to latch these address bits in the 8282, and then removes these address bits from the data bus. At about the same time the 8237 sends a DACK signal to the disk controller to tell it to get ready for a data transfer. Now

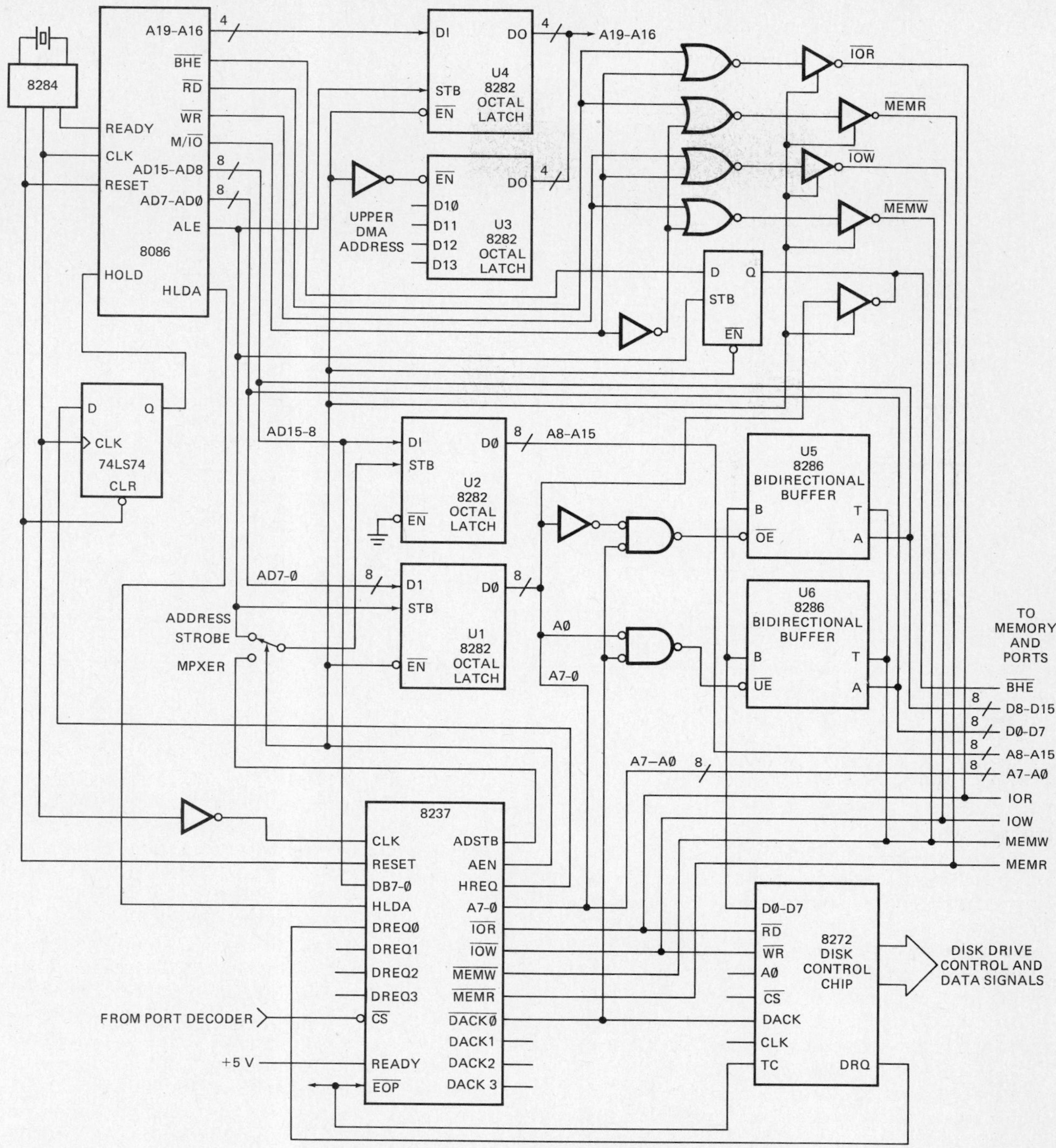

FIGURE 11-3 Schematic for 8086 system with 8237 DMA controller and 8272 floppy-disk controller.

that everything is ready the 8237 asserts two control-bus signals to enable the actual transfer. For a transfer from memory to the disk controller, it will assert MEMR and IOW. For a transfer from the disk controller to memory, it will assert MEMW and IOR. Note that the 8237 does not have to put out an I/O address to enable the disk controller for this transfer. When programmed in DMA mode, the disk controller needs only IOR or IOW to be asserted to enable it for the transfer. Also note that the 8237 will not output a new address on A8–A15 when a second transfer is done, unless those bits have to be changed. This saves time during multiple-byte transfers.

When the programmed number of bytes have been transferred, the DMA controller pulses its end-of-process (EOP) pin low, unasserts its hold request to the 8086, and drops its AEN signal low to release the buses back to the 8086. Now that you have an idea how an 8237 is connected and operates in a system, we will give you an overview of what is involved in initializing it.

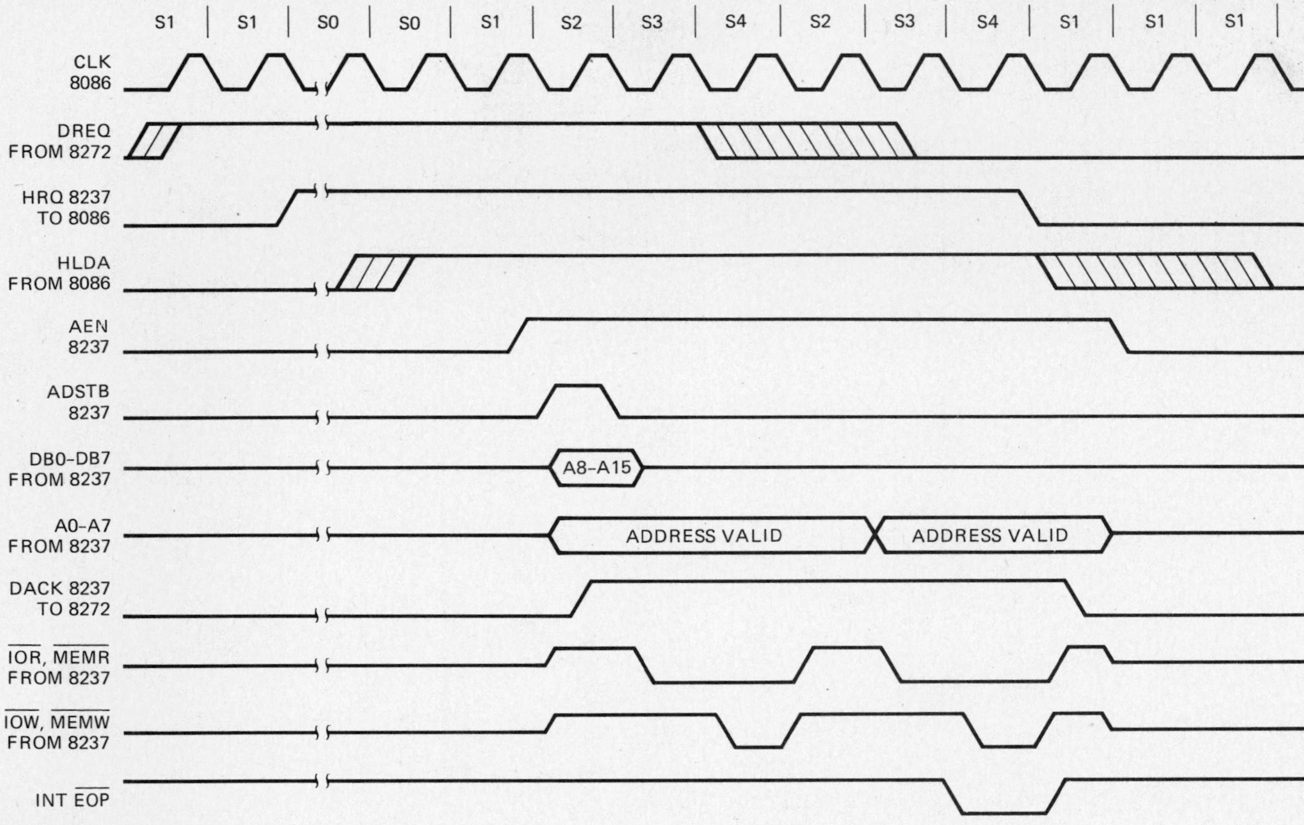

FIGURE 11-4 Timing diagram for 8237 DMA transfer. *(Intel Corporation)*

8237 Initialization Overview

Initializing an 8237 is not difficult, but it does require a fairly large number of bytes. Therefore, we do not have space here to show you a complete initialization. What we can do is give you an overview so that, hopefully, the data sheet will make more sense to you if you do have to initialize one.

As shown by the pin labels on the 8237 in Figure 11-3, the 8237 has four DMA request inputs or *channels*, as they are commonly called. To initialize an 8237 you need to send it a command word which specifies the general operation. You also need to send it mode words, starting transfer addresses, and the number of bytes to be transferred for each channel you are using. Figure 11-5*a* shows the names of the different types of registers used to hold this data in the 8237, the number of bits in each type of register, and how many registers of that type the device has. Register names with a 4 next to them have a register of that type for each channel. Now that you know about all of these registers, the next question is how do you write to or read from all of them.

The 8237 is connected in a system as a port device, so you write initialization words to it just as you would to any other port device. The lower four address bits, A3–A0, together with the input/output read signal, $\overline{\text{IOR}}$, and the input/output write signal, $\overline{\text{IOW}}$, determine which internal register you write to or read from. Figure 11-5*b* shows the internal addresses that you use when sending commands to and reading the status byte, etc. from an 8237. We'll come back to these in a minute. Figure 11-5*c* shows the internal addresses you use when you send or read addresses and counts to/from the 8237. Note that the low byte and the high byte of, for example, the base memory address are written to the same internal address in the 8237. The 8237 keeps track of which byte is being sent or read with an internal first-last flip-flop. If the flip-flop is reset then the 8237 assumes that the byte being sent or read is the least-significant byte. If the first-last flip-flop is set, the 8237 assumes the byte being sent or read is the most significant byte. The first-last flip-flop is automatically toggled after each write to a particular address so you can just write to an internal address twice to send a full 16-bit count. It is important to understand this mechanism so that you remember to keep track of the state of the first-last flip-flop as you send counts and addresses to the device. Also, at the start of the initialization before you read or write any words, it is a good idea to send the device a command which resets the first-last flip-flop. You do this by writing a byte to internal address 1100 as shown in Figure 11-5*b*. The contents of the byte written don't matter, it is the act of writing to the particular address which resets the flip-flop. Here's the order in which you might send initialization words to an 8237. Consult the data sheet in an Intel data book to get the details of each command word.

1. Output a master reset command word to internal address 1101. The actual word written doesn't matter; the command resets the first-last flip-flop.

NAME	SIZE	NUMBER
BASE ADDRESS REGISTERS	16 BITS	4
BASE WORD COUNT REGISTERS	16 BITS	4
CURRENT ADDRESS REGISTERS	16 BITS	4
CURRENT WORD COUNT REGISTERS	16 BITS	4
TEMPORARY ADDRESS REGISTER	16 BITS	1
TEMPORARY WORD COUNT REGISTER	16 BITS	1
STATUS REGISTER	8 BITS	1
COMMAND REGISTER	8 BITS	1
TEMPORARY REGISTER	8 BITS	1
MODE REGISTERS	6 BITS	4
MASK REGISTER	4 BITS	1
REQUEST REGISTER	4 BITS	1

(*a*)

SIGNALS						OPERATION
A3	A2	A1	A0	$\overline{IOR}$	$\overline{IOW}$	
1	0	0	0	0	1	READ STATUS REGISTER
1	0	0	0	1	0	WRITE COMMAND REGISTER
1	0	0	1	0	1	ILLEGAL
1	0	0	1	1	0	WRITE REQUEST REGISTER
1	0	1	0	0	1	ILLEGAL
1	0	1	0	1	0	WRITE SINGLE MASK REGISTER BIT
1	0	1	1	0	1	ILLEGAL
1	0	1	1	1	0	WRITE MODE REGISTER
1	1	0	0	0	1	ILLEGAL
1	1	0	0	1	0	CLEAR BYTE POINTER FLIP/FLOP
1	1	0	1	0	1	READ TEMPORARY REGISTER
1	1	0	1	1	0	MASTER CLEAR
1	1	1	0	0	1	ILLEGAL
1	1	1	0	1	0	CLEAR MASK REGISTER
1	1	1	1	0	1	ILLEGAL
1	1	1	1	1	0	WRITE ALL MASK REGISTER BITS

(*b*)

CHANNEL	REGISTER	OPERATION	SIGNALS							INTERNAL FLIP-FLOP	DATA BUS DB0-DB7
			$\overline{CS}$	$\overline{IOR}$	$\overline{IOW}$	A3	A2	A1	A0		
0	BASE AND CURRENT ADDRESS	WRITE	0	1	0	0	0	0	0	0	A0-A7
			0	1	0	0	0	0	0	1	A8-A15
	CURRENT ADDRESS	READ	0	0	1	0	0	0	0	0	A0-A7
			0	0	1	0	0	0	0	1	A8-A15
	BASE AND CURRENT WORD COUNT	WRITE	0	1	0	0	0	0	1	0	W0-W7
			0	1	0	0	0	0	1	1	W8-W15
	CURRENT WORD COUNT	READ	0	0	1	0	0	0	1	0	W0-W7
			0	0	1	0	0	0	1	1	W8-W15
1	BASE AND CURRENT ADDRESS	WRITE	0	1	0	0	0	1	0	0	A0-A7
			0	1	0	0	0	1	0	1	A8-A15
	CURRENT ADDRESS	READ	0	0	1	0	0	1	0	0	A0-A7
			0	0	1	0	0	1	0	1	A8-A15
	BASE AND CURRENT WORD COUNT	WRITE	0	1	0	0	0	1	1	0	W0-W7
			0	1	0	0	0	1	1	1	W8-W15
	CURRENT WORD COUNT	READ	0	0	1	0	0	1	1	0	W0-W7
			0	0	1	0	0	1	1	1	W8-W15
2	BASE AND CURRENT ADDRESS	WRITE	0	1	0	0	1	0	0	0	A0-A7
			0	1	0	0	1	0	0	1	A8-A15
	CURRENT ADDRESS	READ	0	0	1	0	1	0	0	0	A0-A7
			0	0	1	0	1	0	0	1	A8-A15
	BASE AND CURRENT WORD COUNT	WRITE	0	1	0	0	1	0	1	0	W0-W7
			0	1	0	0	1	0	1	1	W8-W15
	CURRENT WORD COUNT	READ	0	0	1	0	1	0	1	0	W0-W7
			0	0	1	0	1	0	1	1	W8-W15
3	BASE AND CURRENT ADDRESS	WRITE	0	1	0	0	1	1	0	0	A0-A7
			0	1	0	0	1	1	0	1	A8-A15
	CURRENT ADDRESS	READ	0	0	1	0	1	1	0	0	A0-A7
			0	0	1	0	1	1	0	1	A8-A15
	BASE AND CURRENT WORD COUNT	WRITE	0	1	0	0	1	1	1	0	W0-W7
			0	1	0	0	1	1	1	1	W8-W15
	CURRENT WORD COUNT	READ	0	0	1	0	1	1	1	0	W0-W7
			0	0	1	0	1	1	1	1	W8-W15

(*c*)

FIGURE 11-5 8237 registers and internal addresses. *(a)* Internal registers. *(b)* Internal addresses for writing commands and reading status. *(c)* Internal addresses for writing transfer addresses and counts. *(Intel Corporation)*

2. Output a master command word to internal address 1000.

3. Output a mode word for each channel you are using to internal address 1011.

4. Output the starting memory address for the transfer, one byte at a time, to the base register internal address for each channel you are using.

5. Output the number of bytes you want to transfer to the base word count internal address for each channel you are using.

6. Output clear mask command word(s) to unmask the channel(s) you are using.

Each channel of the 8237 can be programmed to transfer a single byte for each request, a block of bytes for each request, or to keep transferring bytes until it receives a wait signal on the EOP input/output. 8237s can be cascaded in a master-slave arrangement to give more input channels. As we said before, the main concept here is that the microprocessor and the DMA controller share the use of the address, data, and control buses.

As another DMA example we will now show you how the IBM PC is designed to allow peripheral boards to interface on a DMA basis.

The IBM PC Expansion Bus and DMA

To continue our evolution toward larger and larger microcomputer systems we will now take a brief look at the IBM PC, which is a multiboard system. Figure 11-6 shows a view of the component side of the main microprocessor board, often called a *motherboard*, for the IBM PC. After you find the ROM, RAM, and microprocessor on this board, note the system expansion slots in the upper left corner. These slots allow you to add the specific function boards you need in your system in addition to the basic CPU board. For example, you may want to add a disk-controller board, a serial-port board, a monochrome- or color-CRT board, a board with additional memory, an A/D-D/A board, or a board which allows your PC to function as a logic analyzer. This "open system" approach lets you easily customize the system for your application and your financial state. Now let's see how these slots connect into the basic system.

Figure 11-7 shows a block diagram for the motherboard of the IBM PC. Start on the left side of the diagram and work your way across it from the 8088 CPU and the 8259A priority-interrupt controller. The next vertical line of devices to the right consists of the address bus buffers, the data bus buffers, and the 8288 bus-controller chip. The bus-controller chip is required because the 8088 is operated in maximum mode. The buses from

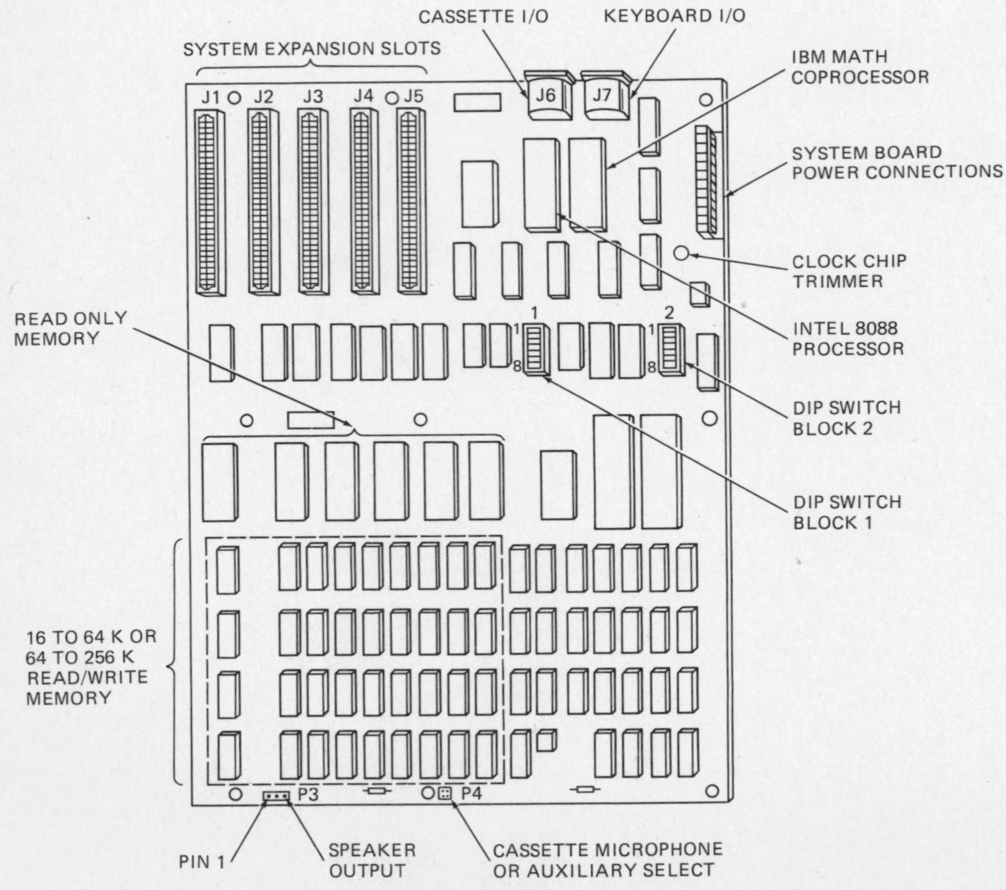

FIGURE 11-6 Component layout diagram for IBM PC motherboard.

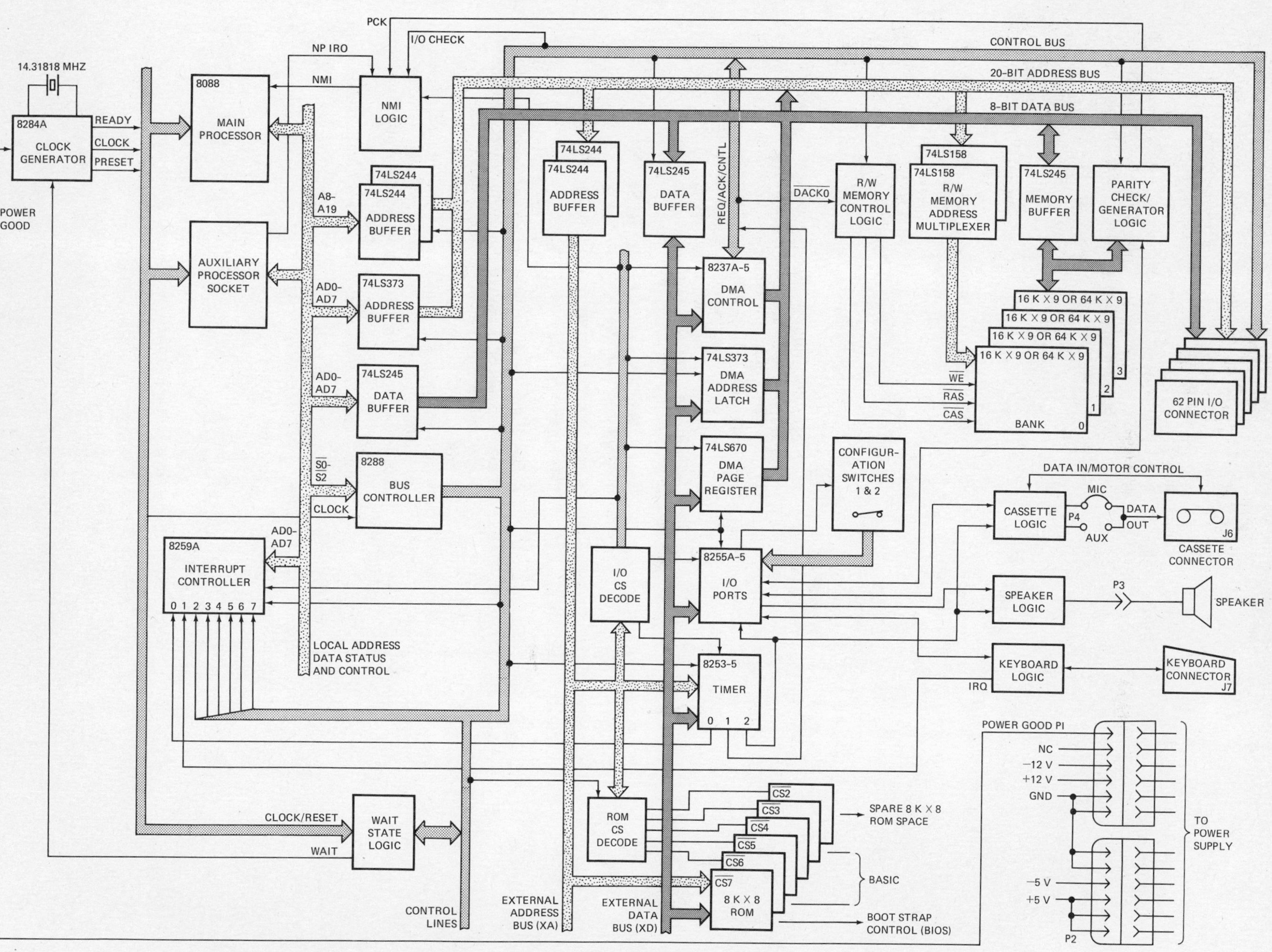

FIGURE 11-7 Block diagram of circuitry on IBM PC motherboard.

these devices go across the drawing and connect to the 62-pin peripheral board connectors. The CPU then can use these buses to communicate directly with the boards in the peripheral expansion slots. Now find the ROM in the lower right, the keyboard logic etc. in the middle right, and the dynamic RAM in the upper right. We will discuss this dynamic RAM later. Finally, take a look at the column of devices which contains the 8237A-5 DMA controller. Starting at the bottom of this column you see an 8253-5 programmable timer which is nearly identical to the 8254 we described in Chapter 8. Just above this is a familiar 8255A-5 programmable port device. Now you are left with just the three devices with DMA in their labels to ponder. The 8237A-5 is, of course, the DMA controller. The 74LS373 just under it is used to grab the upper 8 bits of the DMA address sent out on the data bus by the 8237A-5 during a transfer. This device has the same function as device *U*2 in Figure 11-3. The 74LS670 just below this is used to output bits A16–A19 of the DMA transfer address, the same function performed by *U*3 in the circuit in Figure 11-3. When you have worked your way around the diagram in Figure 11-7 and feel reasonably comfortable with it, take a look at the pin descriptions for the peripheral connectors in Figure 11-8.

The signals shown in Figure 11-8 are bused to all six peripheral connectors. Most of the signals on these connectors should be easily recognizable to you. A + in front of a signal indicates that the signal is active high, and a – indicates that the signal is active low. A0–A19 on the connectors are the 20 demultiplexed address lines, and D0–D7 are the eight data lines. IRQ2–IRQ7 are interrupt request lines which go to the 8259A priority-interrupt controller so that peripheral boards can interrupt the 8088 if necessary. Some other simple signals on the connectors are the power supply voltages; the standard ALE, MEMW, MEMR, IOW, and IOR control-bus signals; and some clock signals.

Finally, we are down to the DMA signals on the expansion connectors. The DMA request pins DRQ1–DRQ3 allow peripheral boards to request use of the buses. A disk controller board, for example, might request a DMA transfer of a block of data from system memory. When the DMA controller gains control of the system buses, it lets the peripheral device or board know by asserting the appropriate DACK0–DACK3 signal. The AEN signal on the connectors is used to gate the DMA address on the bus as we described earlier. When the programmed number of bytes has been transferred, the T/C pin on the connector goes high to let the peripheral know that the transfer is complete. A peripheral board can assert the I/O CH RDY pin on the connector low to cause the 8088 to insert WAIT states until it is ready.

Later you will see many more examples of bus sharing. For our next example we show how dynamic RAM is connected and refreshed in a microcomputer.

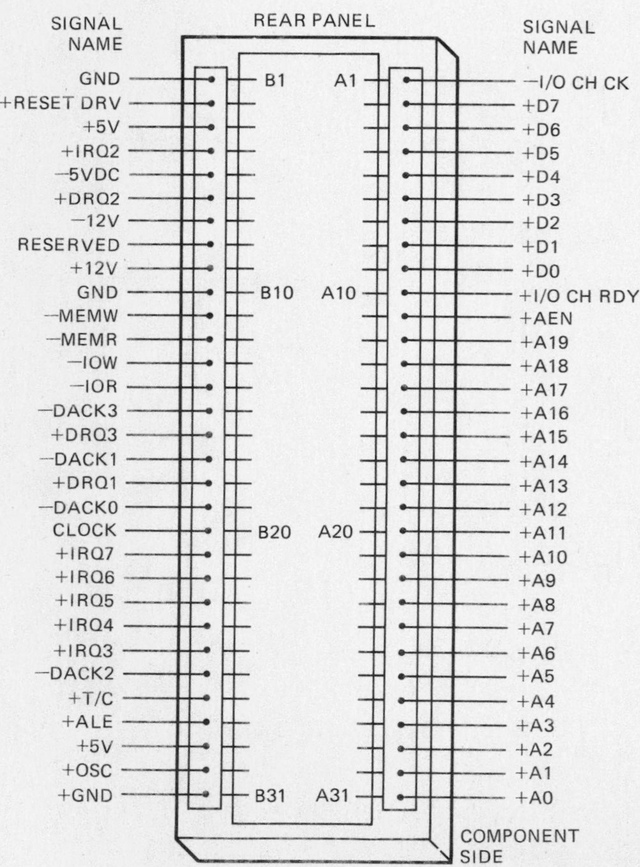

FIGURE 11-8 Pin names and numbers for peripheral slots on IBM PC motherboard.

INTERFACING AND REFRESHING DYNAMIC RAM

Review of Dynamic RAM Characteristics

For small systems such as the SDK-86 where we only need a few kilobytes of RAM we usually use static RAM devices. For larger systems where we want several hundred kilobytes or megabytes of memory we use dynamic RAMs, often called DRAMs. Here's why.

Static RAMs store each bit in an internal flip-flop which requires six or so transistors. DRAMs store bits as a charge or no charge on a tiny capacitor, so they need only one transistor to access the capacitor when you write a bit to it or read a bit from it. The result of this is that DRAMs require much less power per bit, and many more bits can be stored in a given-size chip. The cost per bit of storage is then much less. The disadvantage of DRAMs is that each bit must be refreshed every 2 ms or so because the charge stored on those tiny capacitors tends to change due to leakage. The internal refresh circuitry has to check the voltage level in each storage location; if the voltage is greater than $V_{cc}/2$ then that location is charged to V_{cc}, if the voltage is less than $V_{cc}/2$ then that location is discharged to zero volts. Let's take a look at the pin diagram and timing waveforms for a typical DRAM to see how we read, write, and refresh it.

Figure 11-9 shows the pin diagram for an Intel 51C256H CHMOS DRAM. This device is a 256K by 1 device, so it stores 262,144 words of 1 bit each in its 16-pin package. You can connect eight of these in parallel to store bytes, or 16 in parallel to store 16-bit words. Now, according to the basic rules of address decoding,

Pin	Signal	Pin	Signal
1	A_8	16	V_{SS}
2	D_{IN}	15	$\overline{CAS}$
3	$\overline{WE}$	14	D_{OUT}
4	$\overline{RAS}$	13	A_6
5	A_0	12	A_3
6	A_2	11	A_4
7	A_1	10	A_5
8	V_{DD}	9	A_7

$\overline{RAS}$	ROW ADDRESS STROBE
$\overline{CAS}$	COLUMN ADDRESS STROBE
$\overline{WE}$	WRITE ENABLE
A_0–A_8	ADDRESS INPUTS
D_{IN}	DATA INPUT
D_{OUT}	DATA OUTPUT
V_{DD}	POWER (+5V)
V_{SS}	GROUND

(a)

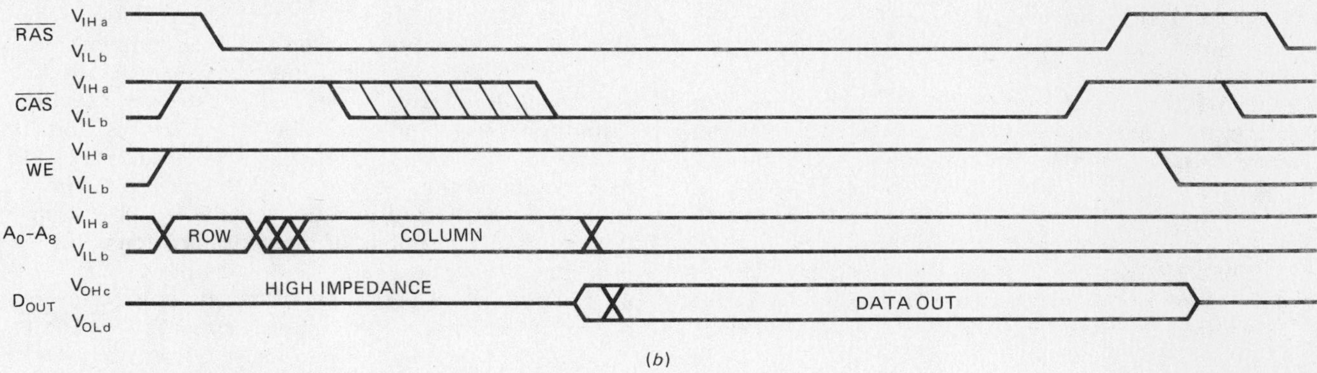

FIGURE 11-9 51C256H CHMOS dynamic RAM. *(a)* Pin diagram. *(b)* Read-operation timing diagram. *(Intel Corporation)*

18 address lines should be required to address one of the 2^{18} words stored in this device. The pin diagram in Figure 11-9*a*, however, shows only nine address inputs, A0–A8. The trick here is that to save pins, DRAMs usually send in the address one-half at a time. A look at the timing diagram for a read operation in Figure 11-9*b* should help you to see how this works.

To read a word from a bank of dynamic RAMs, a DRAM-controller device or other circuitry asserts the write-enable ($\overline{WE}$) pin of the DRAMs high to enable them for a read operation. It then sends the lower half of the address, called the row address, to the address inputs of the DRAMs. The controller then asserts the *row-address-strobe* ($\overline{RAS}$) input of the DRAM low to indicate a row address is present. After the proper timing interval, the controller removes the row address and outputs the upper half of the address, called the column address, to the address inputs of the DRAM. The controller then asserts the *column-address-strobe* ($\overline{CAS}$) inputs of the DRAMs low to indicate that the column address is present. After a propagation delay, the data word from the addressed memory cells will appear on the data outputs of the DRAMs.

The timing diagram for a write cycle is nearly the same except that after it sends out the column address and $\overline{CAS}$, the controller asserts the write-enable ($\overline{WE}$) input low to enable the DRAMs for writing, and asserts a signal which gates the data to be written onto the data inputs of the DRAMs.

The DRAM controller refreshes the cells in the DRAMs by sending out each of the 512 row addresses and pulsing $\overline{RAS}$ low at least every 4 ms. The refresh can be done in either a *burst* mode or in a *distributed* mode. In the burst mode all 512 rows are addressed and pulsed one right after the other every 4 ms. In the distributed mode another row is addressed and pulsed after every 4/512 ms or 7.8 μs. In a particular system you use the mode which will least interfere with the operation of the system. Now that the operation of dynamic RAMs is fresh in your mind, we will show you how you interface banks of DRAMs to an 8086.

Interfacing DRAMs to an 8086

As perhaps you can see from the preceding discussion, the main tasks you have to do to interface a bank of DRAMs to a microprocessor are:

1. To refresh each location at the proper interval.
2. To "funnel" the two halves of the address into the each device with the appropriate $\overline{RAS}$ and $\overline{CAS}$ strobes.
3. To assure that a read or write operation and a refresh operation do not take place at the same time.
4. To provide a read/write control signal to enable data into or out of the devices.

There are several ways to do these tasks.

DRAM Refreshing and Error Checking in the IBM PC

As you can see in Figure 11-7, the IBM PC 256K version has four banks of DRAMs which are 64K by 1 devices. The PC uses a dummy DMA read approach to refresh its

DRAM. Here's how it works. An 8253 timer is programmed to produce a pulse every 15 μs. This pulse is connected into one of the DMA request inputs (DREQ0) of an 8237 DMA controller which has been programmed to read from memory and write to a nonexistent port. When the 8237 DMA controller receives this pulse, it sends a hold request to the 8088 microprocessor. After the 8088 responds with a HLDA signal, the 8237 takes over the buses, sends out a memory address, sends out a memory read signal, and sends out a DMA acknowledge (DACK0) signal. The lower 8 bits of the memory address it sends out goes to the address inputs of all of the DRAMs. The DACK0 signal is used to pulse the $\overline{RAS}$ lines of all of the DRAM banks low at this time. After each DMA operation the current address register in the DMA controller will be automatically incremented or decremented, depending on how the device was programmed. In either case, the next DMA operation will refresh the next row in the DRAMs. If the 8237 is programmed for transfer of 64 Kbytes, start at address 0, increment count after DMA, and autoinitialize, the sequence of addresses sent out will refresh all 256 rows in the DRAMs over and over. One row in each of the banks is then refreshed every 15 μs. With the 4.77-MHz clock used in the IBM PC, a refresh DMA cycle takes about 820 ns every 15 μs, or about 5 percent of the processor's time.

Another point about the DRAM memory banks in the IBM PC is that each bank is 9 bits wide. Eight of these bits make up the data byte being stored, and the ninth bit is a parity bit which is used to detect errors in the stored data. A 74LS280 parity generator/checker circuit generates a parity bit for each byte and stores it in the ninth location as each byte is written to memory. When the 9 bits are read out, the parity is checked by the parity generator checker circuit. If the parity is not correct, an error signal is sent to an 8255 port pin where it can be read by the 8088 microprocessor. When you first turn on the power to an IBM PC or warm boot it by pressing the Ctrl, Alt, and Del keys at the same time, one of the self tests that it performs is to write byte patterns to all of the RAM locations and check if the byte read back and the parity of that byte are correct. If any error is found, an error message is displayed on the screen so you don't try to load and run programs in defective RAM.

A DRAM Controller IC—The Intel 8208

In high-performance systems where we want DRAM refreshing to take up a minimum amount of the processor's time, we usually use a dedicated device which handles all of the refreshing chores without tying up the microprocessor or its buses as the DMA approach does. An example of this type of device is the Intel 8208. Figure 11-10 shows, in block diagram form, how an 8208 can be connected with an 8086 in maximum mode to refresh and control 1 Mbyte of dynamic RAM. The memories here are 256K by 1 devices. As usual for an 8086, the memory array is set up as two banks. Each bank has two blocks containing 8 RAM chips, or 256 Kbytes.

In the system in Figure 11-10 the 8208 takes care of all of the refresh tasks in addition to funneling in addresses from the 8086 for read and write operations as we described previously. One important point to observe here is that the status signals, S0–S3, from the 8086 are connected directly to the control inputs of the 8208. The 8208 decodes these status signals to produce the read and write signals it needs. This means that most of the time the 8086 will be able to read a byte or word from the DRAMs without any WAIT states being required. If the 8208 happens to be in the middle of a refresh cycle when the 8086 tries to read a DRAM location, the 8208 will hold its AACK high and cause the 8086 to insert a WAIT state. The 8086 will then have to wait 1 clock cycle while the 8208 finishes its refresh cycle before it can access the DRAMs. The occasional access conflict here is arbitrated by the controller, and slows the 8086 up less than the DMA approach shown in the previous section.

Another interesting point about the 8208 is that, in order to save pins, it does not connect to the data bus to allow command words to be sent to it for initialization. If the PDI pin is tied to ground, the 8208 will initialize itself in a mode suitable for many applications. For applications where the default mode will not work, the output of a parallel-in–serial-out shift register is connected to the PDI input of the 8208. After a reset the $\overline{WE/PCLK}$ pin outputs a series of pulses. These pulses are used to clock the desired command word from the shift register into the 8208. The desired mode word is simply hardwired on the parallel inputs of the shift register.

Battery Backup of Dynamic RAMs

In Chapter 8 we discussed the use of an 8086 NMI interrupt procedure to save program data in the case of a power failure. In the few milliseconds between the time the ac power goes off and the time the dc power drops below operating levels, the interrupt procedure copies program data to a block of static RAM which has a battery backup power supply. When the system is repowered, the saved data is copied back into the main RAM, and processing takes up where it left off. In larger systems such as the one in Figure 11-10, there may not be time enough to copy all of the important data etc. to another RAM. In this case we simply use a battery backup for the entire RAM array as shown in Figure 11-10.

In this circuit we used CHMOS DRAMs because when these devices are not being accessed for reading, writing, or refreshing, they take only microwatts of power. During battery backup of the DRAMs they must still be refreshed, so the 8208 DRAM controller is also connected to the battery power. The 8208 normally receives its required clock signal from the 8284 clock generator, but since that is a high-current device, we added a CMOS clock generator which will be switched in when the power fails. We use a nickel-cadmium or some other type of battery which can stand the continuous recharging and supply the needed current. The diodes in the circuit prevent the power supply output and the battery from fighting with each other.

In applications where the entire system must be kept running during an ac power outage, we use an *uninterruptible power supply*, UPS, which contains a large battery

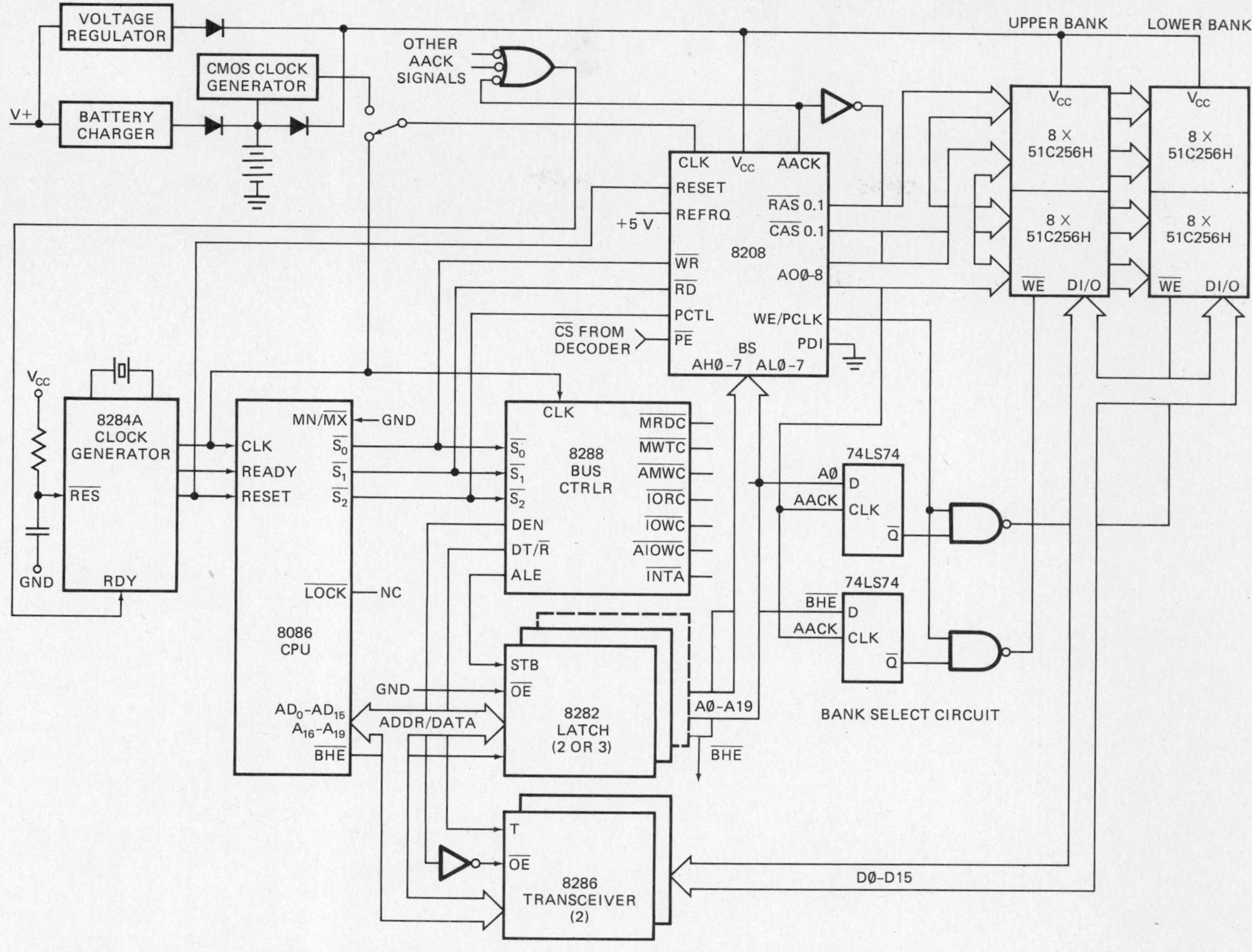

FIGURE 11-10 Circuit for refreshing dynamic RAMs with the 8208 dynamic RAM controller.

and the circuitry needed to convert the battery voltage to the voltage needed by the microcomputer.

Error Detecting and Correcting in RAM Arrays

Data read from RAMs is subject to two types of errors, *hard errors* and *soft errors*. Hard errors are caused by permanent device failure. This may be caused by a manufacturing defect or simply random breakdown in the chip. Soft errors are one-time errors caused by a noise pulse in the system or, in the case of dynamic RAMs, perhaps an alpha particle or some other radiation causing the charge to change on the tiny capacitor on which a data bit is stored. As we add larger and larger arrays of RAMs to a system, the chance of a hard or a soft error occurring increases sharply. This then increases the chance that the entire system will fail. It seems unreasonable that one fleeting alpha particle could possibly cause an entire system to fail. To prevent or at least reduce the chances of this kind of failure, we add circuitry which detects and in some cases corrects errors in the data read out from RAMs. There are several ways to do this, depending on the amount of detection and correction needed.

The simplest method for detecting an error is with a parity bit. As we described previously for the IBM PC, we do this by first determining the parity of, say, an 8-bit data word as it is being written to a memory location. We then generate a parity bit such that the overall parity of the 8 data bits plus the parity bit is, for example, always odd. The generated parity bit for each byte is written into a separate memory device in parallel with the devices containing the data byte. When the data byte and the parity bit are read from memory, we check the parity of the 9 bits together. If the overall parity of these nine is not odd as it should be, then we know that somewhere in the read/write process an error was introduced. If external hardware is being used to generate/check parity, then an output from this circuitry can be used to tell the processor that an error occurred, and that the data is not valid. The processor can then respond appropriately.

One difficulty with a simple parity check is that two errors in a data word may cancel each other. A second problem with simple parity is that it does not tell you

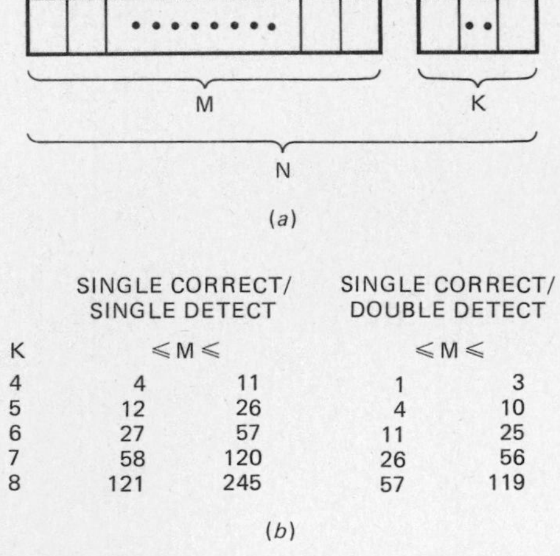

K	SINGLE CORRECT/ SINGLE DETECT ≤M≤		SINGLE CORRECT/ DOUBLE DETECT ≤M≤	
4	4	11	1	3
5	12	26	4	10
6	27	57	11	25
7	58	120	26	56
8	121	245	57	119

(b)

FIGURE 11-11 Error detecting/correcting codes. *(a)* Encoding bits. *(b)* Number of encoding bits for detecting/correcting.

which bit in a word is wrong so that you can correct the error. More complex error detecting/correcting codes (ECCs), often called *Hamming codes* after the man who did some of the original work in this area, permit you to detect multiple-bit errors in a word and to correct at least one bit error. Here's how they work.

As the data word is read in, several encoding bits are generated and stored in memory along with the data word. Figure 11-11*a* shows this in diagram form. The number of encoding bits, *k*, required is determined by the size of the data word, *m*, and the degree of detection/correction required. The total number of bits required for a data word, *n*, is equal to $m + k$. Figure 11-11*b* shows the number of encoding bits needed for different numbers of data bits and different degrees of detection/correction. According to these values, 5 encoding bits are required to detect and correct a single-bit error in a 16-bit data word, so the total number of bits that have to be stored for each word in this case is 21. To give you enough information to correct one error and detect 2 wrong bits in a 16-bit word would require 6 encoding bits.

When you write a word to memory the error detecting/correcting circuitry generates the required encoding bits and writes them to memory along with the data word. The encoding bits, incidentally, are not just tacked on to one end of the data word as a parity bit is. They are interspersed in the data word. When you read a data word from memory, the error detecting/correcting circuitry recalculates the encoding bits for the data word read out. It then exclusive-NORs these encoding bits with the encoding bits that were stored in memory for that data word. The word produced by this operation is known as a *syndrome word*. The encoding bits are generated in such a way that the value of this syndrome word indicates which bit, if any, is wrong in the total word of data word plus encoding bits. The erroneous bit can then be corrected by simply inverting it. Because of hardware implementation tradeoffs, there are actually several different schemes for determining the encoding bits, so if you are working with a RAM system with error correction, consult the manual for it if you need the specific coding. Several available ICs such as the Intel 8206 will automatically detect/correct single bit errors and detect two bit errors in 16-bit data words. The devices can be cascaded to work with up to 80-bit data words.

Now that we have shown you the operation of a DMA controller and the operation of the 8086 in maximum mode, we can introduce you to the 80186 and 80188 microprocessors which have DMA controllers and other peripherals built in.

PROCESSORS WITH INTEGRATED PERIPHERALS—THE 80186 AND 80188

Overview

Figure 11-12*a* shows a block diagram of the internal architecture of the Intel 80186 microprocessor. The architecture and instruction set of the 80188 are identical to those of the 80186 except that the 80188 has only an 8-bit data bus instead of the 16-bit data bus that the 80186 has. With this in mind, we will use 80186 to represent both the 80186 and the 80188 in our discussions here.

The 80186 has the same bus-interface unit and execution unit as the 8086 which we discussed previously, so there is nothing new there for you. Unlike the 8086, however, the 80186 has the clock generator built in so that all you have to add is an external crystal. Also note that the 80186 does not have a pin labeled MN/$\overline{\text{MX}}$. The 80186 is packaged in a 68-pin leadless package as shown in Figure 11-12*b*, so it has enough pins to send out both the minimum-mode type signals $\overline{\text{RD}}$ and $\overline{\text{WR}}$ and the S0–S3 status signals which can be connected to external bus-controller ICs for maximum-mode systems. Now let's look at the four peripheral chip function blocks in the 80186.

First is a priority interrupt controller which has up to four interrupt inputs, INT0, INT1, INT2/$\overline{\text{INTA0}}$, and INT3/$\overline{\text{INTA1}}$ as well as an NMI interrupt input. If the four INT inputs are programmed in their internal mode, then a signal applied to one of them will cause the 80186 to push the return address on the stack and vector directly to the start of the interrupt service procedure for that interrupt. Figure 11-14 shows the interrupt type which corresponds to each of these inputs. The INT2/$\overline{\text{INTA0}}$, and INT3/$\overline{\text{INTA1}}$ pins can be programmed to be used as interrupt inputs as we have just described, or they can be programmed to function as interrupt acknowledge outputs. This mode is used to interface with external 8259As. The interrupt request line from an external 8259A is connected to, for example, the 80186 INT0 input, and the 80186 INT2/$\overline{\text{INTA0}}$ pin is connected to the interrupt acknowledge input of the 8259A. When the 8259A receives an interrupt request, it asserts the INT0 input of the 80186. When the 8259A receives interrupt acknowledge signals from the INT2/$\overline{\text{INTA0}}$ pin, it sends the desired interrupt type to the 80186 on the data bus. This second mode is commonly referred to in the literature as *iRMX mode*, because an 80186 system must have an external 8259A and 8254 if the iRMX operating system is going to be run on it.

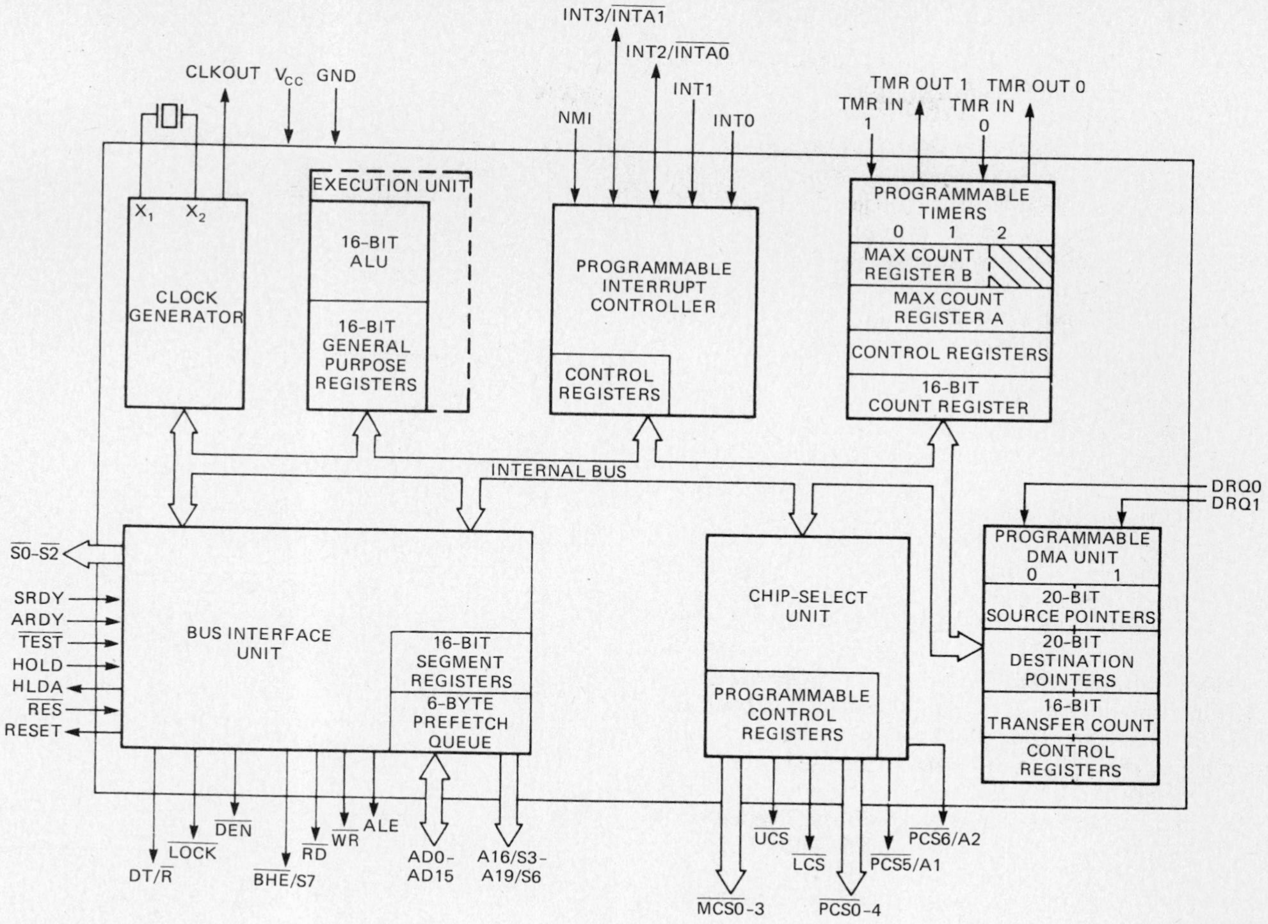

INT3/INTA1
INT2/INTA0
CLKOUT
VCC
GND
INT1
NMI
INT0
TMR OUT 1
TMR OUT 0
TMR IN 1
TMR IN 0
X1
X2
CLOCK GENERATOR
EXECUTION UNIT
16-BIT ALU
16-BIT GENERAL PURPOSE REGISTERS
PROGRAMMABLE INTERRUPT CONTROLLER
CONTROL REGISTERS
PROGRAMMABLE TIMERS
0 1 2
MAX COUNT REGISTER B
MAX COUNT REGISTER A
CONTROL REGISTERS
16-BIT COUNT REGISTER
INTERNAL BUS
DRQ0
DRQ1
S0-S2
SRDY
ARDY
TEST
HOLD
HLDA
RES
RESET
BUS INTERFACE UNIT
16-BIT SEGMENT REGISTERS
6-BYTE PREFETCH QUEUE
CHIP-SELECT UNIT
PROGRAMMABLE CONTROL REGISTERS
PROGRAMMABLE DMA UNIT
0 1
20-BIT SOURCE POINTERS
20-BIT DESTINATION POINTERS
16-BIT TRANSFER COUNT
CONTROL REGISTERS
DT/R
LOCK
DEN
BHE/S7
RD
WR
ALE
AD0-AD15
A16/S3-A19/S6
UCS
LCS
PCS6/A2
PCS5/A1
MCS0-3
PCS0-4

(a)

BOTTOM
HLDA
HOLD
SRDY
LOCK
TEST
NMI
INT0
INT1
VCC
INT2/INTA0
INT3/INTA1
DT/R
DEN
MCS0
MCS1
MCS2
MCS3
52
35
S0
S1
S2
ARDY
CLKOUT
RESET
X2
X1
VSS
ALE/QS0
RD/QSMD
WR/QS1
BHE
A19/S6
A18/S5
A17/S4
A16/S3
UCS
LCS
PCS6/A2
PCS5/A1
PCS4
PCS3
PCS2
PCS1
VSS
PCS0
RES
TMR OUT 1
TMR OUT 0
TMR IN 1
TMR IN 0
DRQ1
DRQ0
18
1
PIN NO. 1 MARK
AD15
AD7
AD14
AD6
AD13
AD5
AD12
AD4
VCC
AD11
AD3
AD10
AD2
AD9
AD1
AD8
AD0

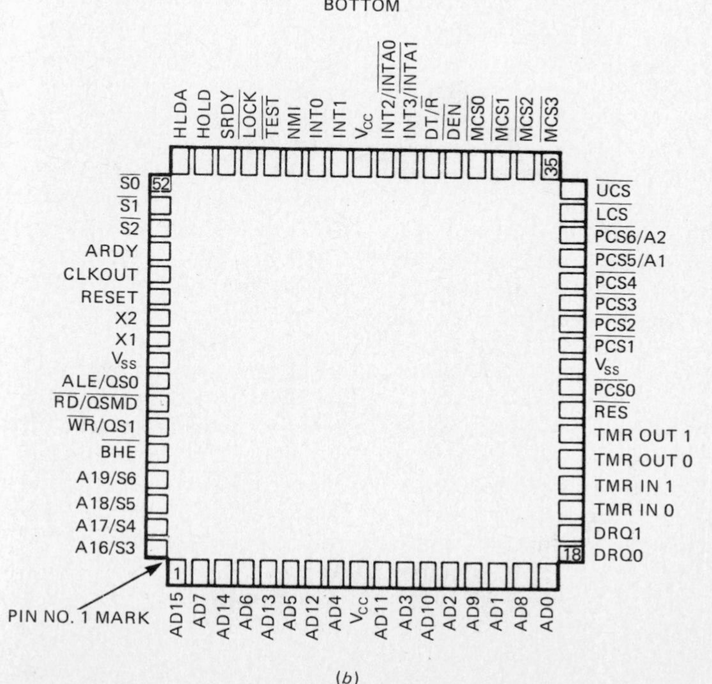

(b)

FIGURE 11-12 80186. *(a)* Internal block diagram. *(b)* Pin diagram. *(Intel Corporation)*

Next to look at in the block diagram is the built-in address decoder, referred to in the drawing as the chip-select unit. This unit can be programmed to produce an active low chip-select signal when a memory address in the specified range or a port address in a specified range is sent out. Six memory address chip-select signals are available: $\overline{LCS}$, $\overline{UCS}$, and $\overline{MCS0–3}$. The *lower-chip-select* signal, $\overline{LCS}$, will be asserted by addresses between 00000H and some address which you specify in a control word. The specified ending address can be anywhere between 1K and 256K. The highest address that will assert the *upper-chip-select* signal, $\overline{UCS}$, is fixed at FFFFFH. The lowest address for this block of memory is again programmable by some bits you put in a control word. The size of the upper memory block can be anywhere between 1K and 256K. Finally, there are four *middle-chip-select* lines, $\overline{MCS0–3}$. Each of these four is asserted by an address in a block of memory in the middle range of memory. Both the starting address and the size of the four blocks can be specified for this middle-range block. The specified size of blocks can be anywhere from 2K to 128K. The memory areas assigned to different chip selects cannot overlap, or two chip-select outputs will be asserted at the same time, possibly damaging some memory devices. The point of this built-in decoder is to select major blocks of memory. External decoders can then be used to select specific groups of memory devices. At the rate memory devices are growing in size, external decoders may soon not be needed.

In addition to producing memory chip-select signals, the 80186 can be programmed to produce up to seven peripheral chip-select signals on its $\overline{PCS0}$–$\overline{PCS4}$, $\overline{PCS5}$/A1, and $\overline{PCS6}$/A2 pins. You program a base address for these I/O addresses in a control word. $\overline{PCS0}$ will be asserted when this base address is output during an IN or an OUT instruction. The other PCS outputs will be asserted by addresses at intervals of 128 bytes above.

Now let's look at the programmable DMA unit in the 80186. As you can see from the block diagram in Figure 11-12, the DMA unit has two DMA request inputs, DRQ0 and DRQ1. These inputs allow external devices such as disk controllers, CRT controllers, etc. to request use of one of the DMA channels as we described earlier in this chapter. For each DMA channel the 80186 has a full 20-bit register to hold the address of the source of the DMA transfer, a 20-bit register to hold the destination address, and a 16-bit counter to keep track of how many words or bytes have been transferred. DMA transfers can be from memory to memory, I/O to I/O, or between I/O and memory.

Finally, let's look at the three 16-bit programmable counter/timers in the 80186. The inputs and outputs of counters 0 and 1 are available on pins of the 80816. These two counters can be used to divide down the frequency of external signals, produce programmed-width pulses, etc. just as you do with the counters in an 8254. You can also internally direct the processor clock to the input of one of these counter inputs by clearing the appropriate bit in a control word. The input of the third counter in the 80186 is internally connected to the processor clock. Because of the way the counters in the 80186 are decremented, counter 2 will be decremented every 4 processor clocks. By setting or clearing the appropriate bits in a control word, you can direct the output of counter 2 to a DMA input, an interrupt input, or the input of counter 1 and/or counter 0.

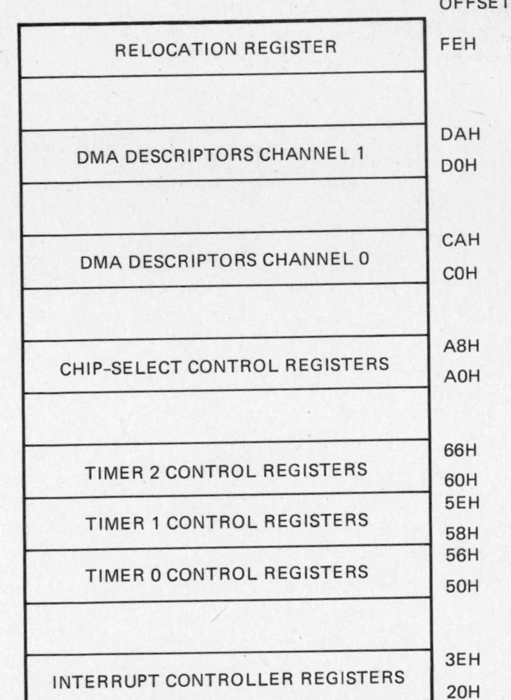

(*a*)

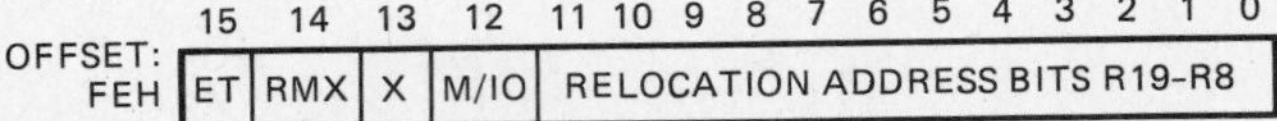

ET = ESC TRAP/NO ESC TRAP (1/0)
M/IO = REGISTER BLOCK LOCATED IN MEMORY / I/O SPACE (1/0)
RMX = MASTER INTERRUPT CONTROLLER MODE / IRMX COMPATIBLE INTERRUPT CONTROLLER MODE (0/1)

(*b*)

FIGURE 11-13 80186 Peripheral control block. *(a)* Control block format. *(b)* Relocation word format. *(Intel Corporation)*

As you can see from the preceding discussion, the 80186 contains many of the peripheral chip functions needed in a medium-complexity microcomputer system. In order to use these integrated peripherals, you have to initialize them just as you do external peripherals. Note in Figure 11-12 that control registers are shown as part of each of the integrated peripherals. These 16-bit control registers are all contained in an internal 256-byte block, as shown in Figure 11-13*a*. After a reset this block will be located at I/O address FF00H. Control and status registers in this block can then be accessed with IN and OUT instructions. This peripheral control block can be relocated to some other address in the I/O space, or to an address in memory by writing the appropriate word to the relocation register in the control block. Figure 11-13*b* shows the format for the word you send to the relocation register. We do not have space here to show and explain all of the control word formats for the

80186. If you have to work with an 80186, you can find the formats for these words in the 80186 data sheet, and work out the control words you need for your particular application on a bit-by-bit basis, just as you do for the separate peripherals. You may also find Intel application note 186, *Introduction to the 80186 Microprocessor*, helpful.

The final points we want to make about the 80186 are the additional instructions and interrupts it has beyond those of the 8086. The 10 additional instructions that the 80186 has are:

ENTER —Enter a procedure
LEAVE —Leave a procedure
BOUND —Check if an array index in a register is in range of array
INS —Input string byte or string word
OUTS —Output string byte or string word
PUSHA —Push all registers on stack
POPA —Pop all registers off stack
PUSH immediate—Push immediate number on stack
IMUL destination register, source, immediate
—Immediate × source to destination
SHIFT/ROTATE destination, immediate
—Shift register or memory contents specified immediate number of times

These instructions are explained in greater detail in Chapter 6 for your reference. Now let's look at the additional built-in interrupt types the 80186 has.

Figure 11-14 shows the names, type numbers, and default priorities for the 80186 internal interrupts. The first five of these should be familiar to you from our discussions of the 8086 internal interrupts. The 80186 will do a type 5 interrupt if an array index number in a register is outside of the specified range for the array when the BOUND instruction executes. It will do a type 6 interrupt if it finds an undefined opcode in the instructions fetched from memory by the BIU. If this interrupt is unmasked, and if the 80186 finds an ESC opcode in the instructions it fetches from memory, the 80186 will do a type 7 interrupt. The additional interrupt types are dedicated to the integrated peripherals as shown.

Now that you have an overview of the relatively sophisticated 80186 microprocessor, our next step is to show you how two or more microprocessors are used in a system. Earlier in this chapter we showed you how a DMA controller, a floppy-disk controller, and a dynamic RAM controller can share the buses of a microprocessor. These devices have some "intelligence," but they are not comparable to the microprocessor in power. In the next section we show you how two or more processors can directly share the address, data, and control buses. Processors which share the local buses in this way are referred to as *coprocessors*.

INTERRUPT NAME	VECTOR TYPE	DEFAULT PRIORITY	RELATED INSTRUCTIONS
DIVIDE ERROR EXCEPTION	0	*1	DIV, IDIV
SINGLE STEP INTERRUPT	1	12**2	ALL
NMI	2	1	ALL
BREAKPOINT INTERRUPT	3	*1	INT
INTO DETECTED OVERFLOW EXCEPTION	4	*1	INTO
ARRAY BOUNDS EXCEPTION	5	*1	BOUND
UNUSED-OPCODE EXCEPTION	6	*1	UNDEFINED OPCODES
ESC OPCODE EXCEPTION	7	*1***	ESC OPCODES
TIMER 0 INTERRUPT	8	2A****	
TIMER 1 INTERRUPT	18	2B****	
TIMER 2 INTERRUPT	19	2C****	
RESERVED	9	3	
DMA 0 INTERRUPT	10	4	
DMA 1 INTERRUPT	11	5	
INT0 INTERRUPT	12	6	
INT1 INTERRUPT	13	7	
INT2 INTERRUPT	14	8	
INT3 INTERRUPT	15	9	

NOTES:
*1. These are generated as the result of an instruction execution.
**2. This is handled as in the 8086.
****3. All three timers constitute one source of request to the interrupt controller. The Timer interrupts all have the same default priority level with respect to all other interrupt sources. However, they have a defined priority ordering amongst themselves. (Priority 2A is higher priority than 2B.) Each Timer interrupt has a separate vector type number.
4. Default priorities for the interrupt sources are used only if the user does not program each source into a unique priority level.
***5. An escape opcode will cause a trap only if the proper bit is set in the peripheral control block relocation register.

FIGURE 11-14 80186 internal interrupt types. *(Intel Corporation)*

A COPROCESSOR—THE 8087 MATH COPROCESSOR

Overview

The instruction set of general-purpose processors such as the 8086 is not optimized to do complex numerical calculations, CRT graphics manipulations, or word processing. Therefore, specialized coprocessors have been developed for these applications. These coprocessors operate in parallel with an 8086-type processor on the same buses and with the same instruction-byte stream. To show you how a coprocessor works, we will use a specific example, the 8087 math coprocessor. If you have an IBM PC type of computer, you can plug an 8087 chip in it directly and run 8087 programs. You can then run the example programs, and write some of your own as you work your way through this chapter.

In many microcomputer programs such as those used for scientific research, engineering, business, and graphics, you need to make mathematical calculations such as computing the square root of a number, the tangent of a number, or the log of a number. Another common need is to do arithmetic operations on very large and very small numbers. There are several ways to do all of this. One way is to write the number-crunching part of the program in a high-level language such as FORTRAN, compile this part of the program, and link in I/O modules written in assembly language. The difficulty with this approach is that programs written in high level languages tend to run considerably slower than programs written in assembly language.

Another way is for you to write an assembly language program which uses the normal instruction set of the processor to do the arithmetic functions. Reference books which contain the algorithms for these are readily available. Our experience has shown that it is often time-consuming to get from the algorithm to a working assembly language program.

Still another approach is to buy a library of floating-point arithmetic object modules from the manufacturer of the microprocessor you are working with or from an independent software house. In your program you just declare a procedure needed from the library as external, call the procedure as required, and link the library to the object code for your program. This approach spares you the labor of writing all the procedures.

In an application where you need a calculation to be done as quickly as possible, however, all of the previous approaches have a problem. The architecture and instruction sets of general-purpose microprocessors such as the 8086 are not designed to work efficiently with mathematical manipulation. Therefore, even highly optimized number-crunching programs run slowly on these general-purpose machines. To solve this problem, special processors, which have architectures and instruction sets optimized for number crunching, have been developed. An example of this type of number-crunching processor is the Intel 8087 math processor. An 8087 is used in parallel with the main microprocessor in a system, rather than serving as a main processor itself. Therefore it is referred to as a *coprocessor*. The major principle here is that the main microprocessor, an 8088 for example, handles the general program execution, and the 8087 coprocessor handles specialized math computations. First we will show you how an 8087 is connected and functions in a system, then we will show you how to program it.

Circuit Connection for an 8087

Figure 11-15 shows the first sheet of the schematics for the 256K version of the IBM PC. We chose this schematic not only to show you how an 8087 is connected in a system with an 8088 microprocessor, but also to show you another way in which schematics for microcomputers are commonly drawn. The more schematics you work your way around, the easier it will get for you.

First in Figure 11-15, note the numbers along the left and right edges of the schematic. These numbers indicate the other sheet(s) that the signal goes to. This is an alternative approach to the zone coordinates used in the schematics in Figure 7-6. In the schematic here the zone coordinates are not needed because all of the input signal lines are extended to the left edge of the schematic, and all of the output signal lines are run to the right edge of the schematic. If you see that an output signal goes to sheet 10, then it is a simple task to scan down the left edge of sheet 10 to find that signal. The wide crosshatched strips in Figure 11-15 represent the address, data, and control buses. From the pin descriptions for the major ICs you know where these signals are produced. You can then scan along the bus to see where various signals get dropped off at other devices. On this type of schematic the buses are always expanded to individual lines where they enter or leave a schematic. Now let's look at how the 8087 is connected.

First note that the multiplexed address-data bus lines, AD0–AD7, go directly from the 8088 to the 8087. The 8088, remember, has the same instruction set as the 8086, but it only has an 8-bit data bus, so all read and writes are byte operations. The upper address lines, A8–A19, also connect directly from the 8088 to the 8087. If you look a little closer at the schematic, you should see that the status lines, $\overline{S2}$, $\overline{S1}$, and $\overline{S0}$, from the 8088 and the queue status lines, QS1 and QS0, from the 8088 also connect directly to the 8087. The 8087 receives the same clock and reset signals as the 8088. Three more connections to the 8087 that you need to pay close attention to are:

First, the request/grant signal, $\overline{RQ}/\overline{GT0}$, from the 8087 is connected to the request/grant pin, $\overline{RQ}/\overline{GT1}$, of the 8088. The way you figure this out from the schematic is to notice that the signal from the 8087 $\overline{RQ}/\overline{GT0}$ pin is labeled just $\overline{RQ}/\overline{GT}$ where it enters the crosshatched bus. Likewise, the label on the signal coming from the crosshatched bus to the $\overline{RQ}/\overline{GT1}$ pin of the 8088 is also just labeled $\overline{RQ}/\overline{GT}$. You know from the fact that the two lines have the same label, they are connected together.

Second, the BUSY signal from the 8087 is connected to the $\overline{TEST}$ input of the 8088. If the 8088 must have the result of some computation that the 8087 is doing before it can go on with its instructions, you tell the 8088 with a WAIT instruction to keep looking at its $\overline{TEST}$ pin until it finds the pin low. A low on the 8087 BUSY output indicates that the 8087 has completed the computation.

Third, the interrupt output, INT, of the 8087 is connected to the nonmaskable interrupt, NMI, input of the 8088. This connection is made so that an error condition in the 8087 can interrupt the 8088 to let it know about the error condition. The signal from the 8087 INT output actually goes through some circuitry on sheet 2 of the schematics and returns to the input labeled NMI on the left edge of Figure 11-15. We do not have room here to show and explain all of the circuitry on sheet 2. The main purposes of the circuitry between the INT output of the 8087 and the NMI input of the 8088 is to make sure that an NMI signal is not present upon reset, to make it possible to mask the NMI input, and to make it possible for other devices to cause an NMI interrupt.

A couple of pins on the 8087 that we aren't concerned with here are the bus-high-enable (BHE) and request/grant1 (RQ/GT1) pins. When the 8087 is used with an 8086, the BHE pin is connected to the system BHE line to enable the upper bank of memory. The RQ/GT1 input is available so that another coprocessor such as the 8089 I/O processor can be connected and function in parallel with the 8087.

As you can see from the preceding discussion, the 8087 is connected very tightly with the 8088. Now let's talk about how the two devices work together.

8087-8088 Cooperation

The point that we need to make about the 8087 is that it is an actual processor with its own, specialized instruction set. Instructions for the 8087 are written in a program as needed, interspersed with the 8088/8086 instructions. To you, the programmer, adding an 8087 to

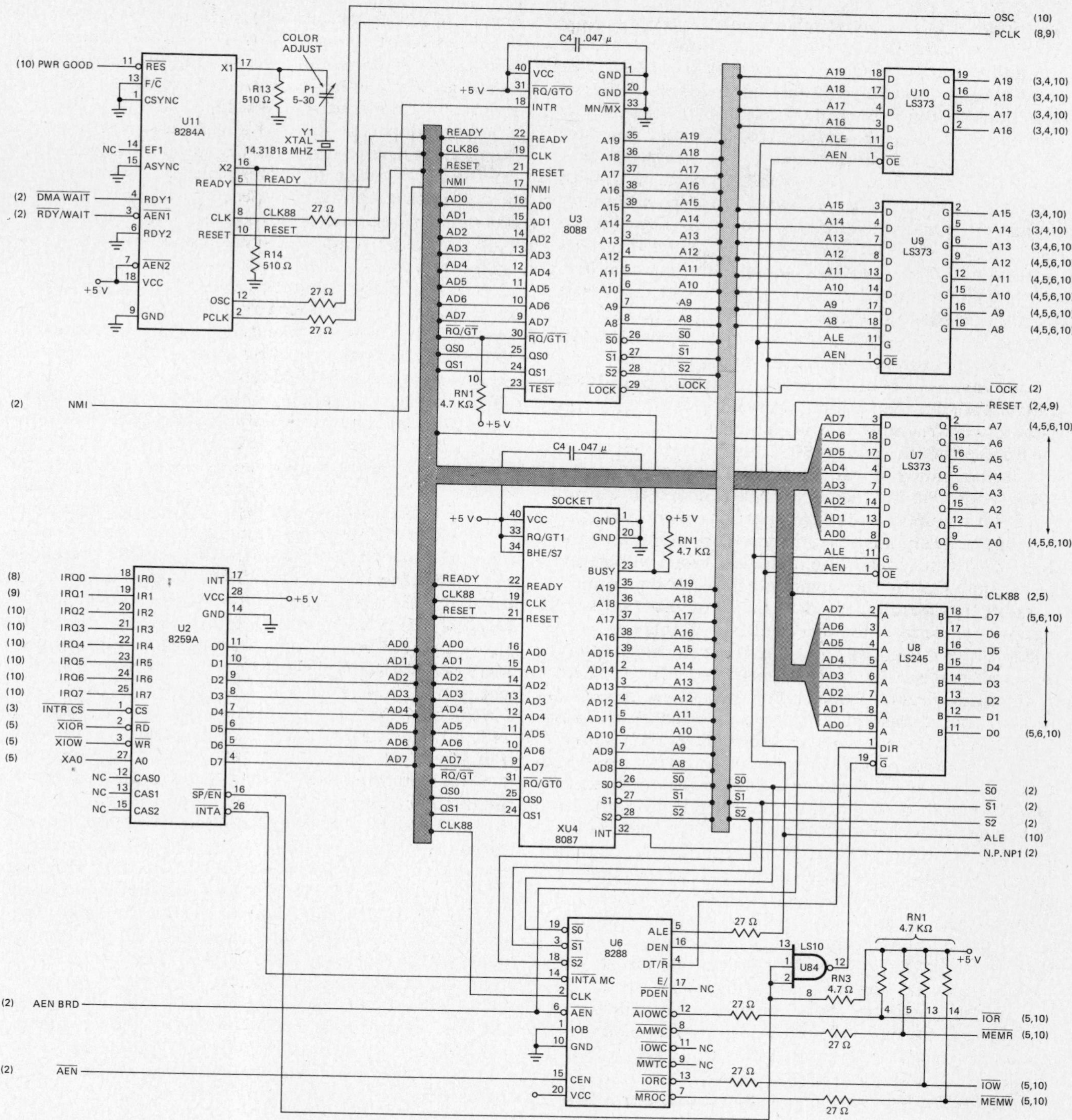

FIGURE 11-15 8088 and 8087 section of IBM PC schematic.

the system simply makes it appear that you have suddenly been given a whole new set of powerful math instructions to use in writing your programs. The opcodes for the 8087 instructions are put in memory right along with the codes for the 8086 or 8088 instructions. As the 8086 or 8088 fetches instruction bytes from memory and puts them in its queue, the 8087 also reads these instruction bytes and puts them in its internal queue. The fact that the status lines and the queue status lines from the 8086 are connected directly to the 8087 allows the 8087 to track the 8086 or 8088 queue in this way. The 8087 decodes each instruction that comes into its queue. When it decodes an instruction from its queue and finds that it is an 8086 instruction, the 8087 simply treats the instruction as an NOP. Likewise, when the 8086 or 8088 decodes an instruction from its queue and finds that it is an 8087 instruction, the 8086 simply treats the instruction as an NOP, or in some cases reads one additional word from memory for the 8087. The point here is that each processor decodes all of the instructions in the fetched instruction byte stream, but only executes its own instructions. The first question that may occur to you is, "How do the two processors recognize 8087 instructions?" The answer is that all of the 8087 instruction codes have 11011 as the most-significant bits of their first code byte. Later we show you how to code 8087 instructions. The synchronous operation of these two processors is an example of a *tightly coupled* multiprocessor system. Now, before we get into the 8087 data types, architecture, and instruction set, let's dig a little more into how the two processors are synchronized during various operations.

One type of cooperation between the two processors that you need to know about is how the 8087 transfers data between memory and its internal registers. When the 8086 or 8088 reads an 8087 instruction that needs data from memory or wants to send data to memory, the 8086 sends out the memory address coded in the instruction and sends out the appropriate memory read or memory write signals to transfer a word of data. In the case of a memory read, the addressed word will be put on the data bus by the memory. The 8087 then simply reads in this word off the data bus. The 8086 or 8088 ignores this word. If the 8087 only needs this one word of data, it can then go on and execute its instruction, However, some 8087 instructions need to read in or write out up to 80-bit words. For these cases the 8086 outputs the address of the first data word on the address bus and outputs the appropriate control signal. The 8087 reads the data word put on the data bus by memory or writes a data word to memory on the data bus. The 8087 then grabs the 20-bit physical address that was output by the 8086 or 8088. To transfer additional words it needs to/from memory, the 8087 then takes over the buses from the 8086. To take over the bus the 8087 sends out a low-going pulse on its $\overline{RQ}/\overline{GT0}$ pin as shown in Figure 11-16. The 8086 or 8088 responds to this by sending another low-going pulse back to the $\overline{RQ}/\overline{GT0}$ pin of the 8087 and by floating its buses. The 8087 then increments the address it grabbed during the first transfer and outputs the incremented address on the address bus. When the 8087 outputs a memory read or memory write signal, another data word will be transferred to or from the 8087. The 8087 continues the process until it has transferred all of the data words required by the instruction to/from memory. When the 8087 is through using the buses for its data transfer, it sends another low-going pulse out on its $\overline{RQ}/\overline{GT0}$ pin to let the 8086 or 8088 know it can have the buses back again. This bus sharing is another example of a DMA-type operation. The $\overline{RQ}/\overline{GT0}$ line is used in a bidirectional mode here to save pins. The key point here then is that the coprocessor, by pulsing the $\overline{RQ}/\overline{GT0}$ input of the host processor, can take over the buses from the *host* or *bus master* processor to transfer data when it needs to. This is another example of a DMA operation.

The next type of synchronization between the host processor and the coprocessor that you need to know about is that required to make sure the 8086 or 8088 host does not attempt to execute the next instruction before the 8087 has completed an instruction. There are two possible problem situations here.

One problem situation is the case where the 8086 needs the data produced by execution of an 8087 instruction to carry out its next instruction. In the instruction sequence in Figure 11-17*a* for example, the 8087 must complete the FSTSW STATUS instruction before the 8086 will have the data it needs to execute the MOV AX, STATUS instruction. Without some mechanism to make the 8086 wait until the 8087 completes the FSTSW instruction, the 8086 will go on and execute the MOV AX, STATUS instruction with erroneous data. We solve this problem by connecting the 8087 BUSY output to the $\overline{TEST}$ pin of the 8086 or 8088, and putting an 8086 WAIT instruction in the program. Here's how it works.

While the 8087 is executing an instruction it asserts its BUSY pin high. When it is finished with an instruction, the 8087 will drop its BUSY pin low. Since the BUSY pin from the 8087 is connected to the $\overline{TEST}$ pin of the 8086 or 8088, the host can check this pin to see if the 8087 is done with an instruction. The 8086 instruction used to check the $\overline{TEST}$ pin is the WAIT instruction. You put the 8086 WAIT instruction in your program after the 8087 FSTSW instruction, as shown in Figure 11-17*b*. (Actually, for reasons we explain later, you should use the 8087 FWAIT instruction which does the same thing.) When the 8086 or 8088 executes the WAIT instruction, it enters an internal loop where it repeatedly checks the logic level on the $\overline{TEST}$ input. The 8086 will stay in this loop until it finds the $\overline{TEST}$ input asserted low, indicating the 8087 has completed its instruction. The 8086 will then exit the internal loop, fetch and execute its next instruction.

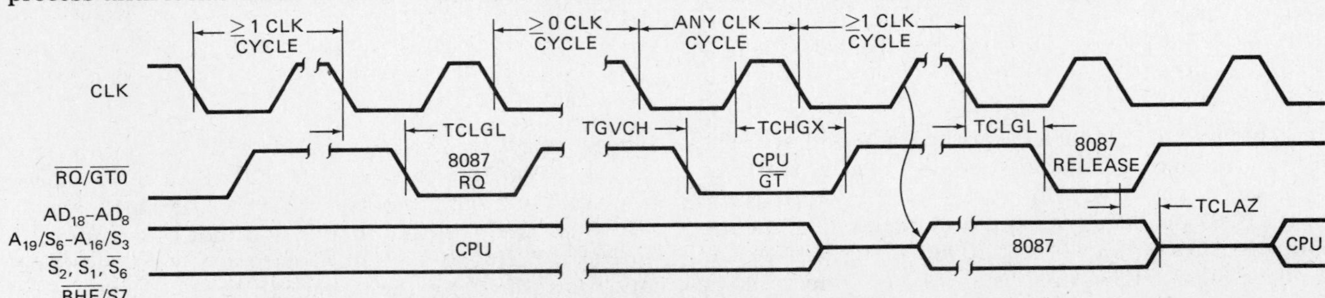

FIGURE 11-16 Signals on 8087 to 8088 $\overline{RQ}/\overline{GT}$ line during bus takeover by 8087 instruction coding formats. (Intel Corporation)

```
FSTSW  STATUS          ; copy 8087 status word to memory
MOV  AX, STATUS        ; copy status word to AX to check bits
```

(a)

```
FSTSW  STATUS          ; copy 8087 status word to memory
FWAIT                  ; wait for 8087 to finish before doing
                       ; next 8086 instruction
MOV  AX, STATUS        ; copy status word to AX to check bits
```

(b)

FIGURE 11-17 Synchronizing 8086 and 8087 instruction execution. (*a*) Code section without needed synchronization. (*b*) Code section with needed FWAIT instruction.

Another execution case where you need synchronization of the host and the coprocessor is the case where a program has several 8087 instructions in sequence. The 8087 can obviously execute only one instruction at a time, so you have to make sure that the 8087 has completed one instruction before you allow the 8086 to fetch the next 8087 instruction from memory. Here again you use the BUSY-$\overline{\text{TEST}}$ connection and the FWAIT instruction to solve the problem. If you are hand coding, you can just put the 8086 WAIT (FWAIT) instruction after each 8087 instruction to make sure that instruction is completed before going on to the next. If you are using an assembler which accepts 8087 mnemonics, the assembler will automatically insert the 8-bit code for the WAIT instruction, 10011011 binary (9BH), as the first byte of the code for the 8087 instruction. You can see an example of this in the code column of the sample program in Figure 11-24 which we discuss later. When the 8086 or 8088 fetches and decodes this code byte, it will enter the internal loop and wait for the $\overline{\text{TEST}}$ input to go low before fetching and decoding the 8087 instruction following this byte. The point here is that by putting the FWAIT instruction after an 8087 instruction in some way, you make sure that one instruction is finished before the next is started.

In the preceding sections we have shown you how two tightly coupled processors can operate essentially as one unit, sharing the same buses, memory, and instruction stream. Because the 8087 math coprocessor which we used as an example in the preceding sections is such a useful and common device, we now want to go on and show you how you can use one. We can't show you all there is to know about the 8087, because it is a fairly complex device. However we can show you enough that if you have an 8087 in your system, you can write a few simple programs for it. We will start with a discussion of the types of numbers that the 8087 is designed to work with.

8087 Data Types

Figure 11-18 shows the formats for the different types of numbers that the 8087 is designed to work with. The three general types are binary integer, packed decimal, and real. We will discuss and show examples of each type individually.

BINARY INTEGERS

The first three formats in Figure 11-18 show different-length binary integer numbers. These all have the same basic format that we have been using to represent signed binary numbers throughout the rest of the book. The most-significant bit is a sign bit which is 0 for positive numbers and 1 for negative numbers. The other 15–63 bits of the data word in these formats represent the magnitude of the number. If the number is negative, the magnitude of the number is represented in 2's complement form. Zero, remember, is considered a positive number in this format, because it has a sign bit of 0. Note also in Figure 11-18 the range of values that can be represented by each of the three integer lengths. When you put numbers in this format in memory for the 8087 to access, you put the least-significant byte in the lowest address.

PACKED DECIMAL NUMBERS

The second type of 8087 data format to look at in Figure 11-18 is the packed decimal. In this format a number is represented as a string of 18 BCD digits, packed two per byte. The most-significant bit is a sign bit which is 0 for positive numbers and 1 for negative numbers. The bits indicated with an X are don't cares. This format is handy for working with financial programs. Using this format you can represent a dollar amount as large as $9,999,999,999,999,999.99, which is probably about what the national debt will be by the year 2000. Again, when you are putting numbers of this type in memory locations for the 8087 to access, the least-significant byte goes in the lowest address.

REAL NUMBERS

Before we discuss the 8087 real number formats, we need to talk a little about real numbers in general.

So far the computations we have shown in this book have used signed integer numbers or BCD numbers. These numbers are referred to as *fixed-point* numbers because they contain no information as to the location of the decimal point or binary point in the number. The

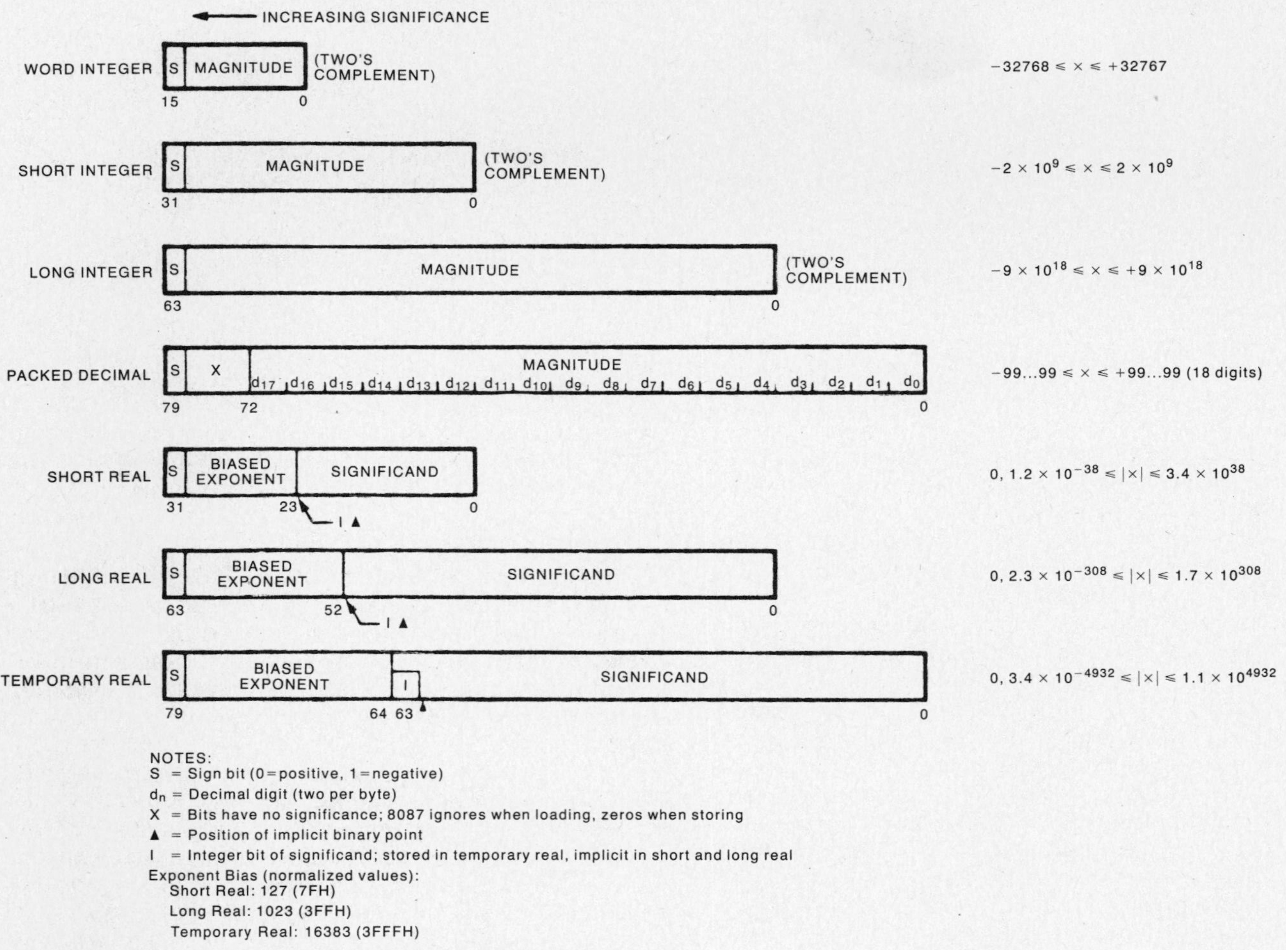

FIGURE 11-18 8087 data formats. (Intel Corporation)

decimal or binary point is always assumed to be to the right of the least-significant digit, so all numbers are represented in this form as whole numbers with no fractional part. A weight of 9.4 lb, for example, is stored in a memory location simply as 10010100 BCD or 01011110 binary. A price of $0.29 per pound is stored in a memory location as 00101001 in BCD or 00011101 in binary. When the binary representation of the weight is multiplied by the price per pound to give the total price, the result is 101010100110 binary, or 2726 decimal. To give the desired display of $2.73, the programmer must round off the result and keep track of where to put the decimal point in the result. For simple numbers such as these from the scale program in Chapter 10, it is not too difficult to do this. However, for a great many applications we need a representation that automatically keeps track of the position of the decimal or binary point for us. In other words we need to be able to represent numbers which have both an integer part and a fractional part. Such numbers are called *real numbers*, or *floating-point numbers*.

There are several different formats for representing real numbers in binary form. The basic principle of all of these, however, is to use one group of bits to represent the digits of the number, and another group of bits to represent the position of the binary point with respect to these digits. This is very similar to the way numbers are represented in scientific notation, so as a lead-in we will refresh your memory about scientific notation.

To convert the number 27,934 to scientific notation you move the decimal point four digit positions to the left and multiply the number by 10^4. The result, 2.7934×10^4, is said to be in scientific notation. As another example, you convert 0.00857 to scientific notation by moving the decimal point three digit positions to the right and multiplying by 10^{-3} to give 8.57×10^{-3}. The process of moving the decimal point to a position just to the right of the most-significant, nonzero digit is called *normalizing* the number. In these examples you can see the digit part, sometimes called the *significand* or the *mantissa*, and the *exponent* part of the representation. When you are working with a calculator or computer, the number of digits you can store for the significand part of the number determines the accuracy or *precision* of the representation. In most cases the real numbers you work with in your computer will be approximations, because to "accurately" represent a number such as π would require an infinite number of digits. The point here is that more digits give more precision, or in other words a better approximation.

The number of digits you can store for the exponent of a number determines the range of magnitudes of numbers you can store in your computer or calculator. The sign of the exponent indicates whether the magnitude of the number is greater than one or less than one. The sign of the significand or mantissa indicates whether the number itself is positive or negative. Now let's see how you represent real numbers in binary form so the 8087 can digest them.

First let's look at the short-real format shown in Figure 11-18. This format, which uses 32 bits to represent a number, is sometimes referred to as *single-precision* representation. In this format 23 bits are used to represent the magnitude of the number, 8 bits to represent the magnitude of the exponent, and 1 bit to indicate whether the number is negative or positive. The magnitude of the number is normalized so that there is only a single one to the left of the binary point. The one to the left of the binary point is not actually present in the representation, it is simply assumed to be there. This leaves more bits for representing the magnitude of the number. You can think of the binary point as being between the bits numbered 22 and 23. The exponent for this format is put in an *offset form*, which means that an offset of 127 (7FH) is added to the 2's complement value of the exponent. This is done so that the magnitude of two numbers can be compared without having to do arithmetic on the exponents first. The sign bit is 0 for positive numbers, and 1 for negative numbers. To help make this clear to you, we will show you how to convert a decimal number to this format.

We chose the number 178.625 for this example because the fractional part converts exactly, and therefore we don't have to cope with rounding at this point. The first step is to convert the decimal number to binary to give 10110010.101 as shown in Figure 11-19. Next normalize the binary number so that only a single one is to the left of the binary point and represent the number of bit positions you had to move the binary point as an exponent as shown in Figure 11-19. The result at this point is 1.0110010101E7. If you now add the bias of

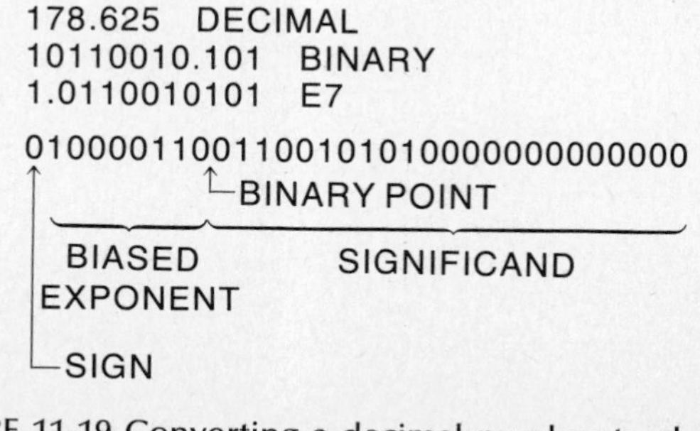

```
178.625   DECIMAL
10110010.101   BINARY
1.0110010101   E7

01000011001100101010000000000000
↑          └BINARY POINT
|└─────────┘└────────────────────┘
| BIASED        SIGNIFICAND
|EXPONENT
|
└SIGN
```

FIGURE 11-19 Converting a decimal number to short-real format.

127 (7FH) to the exponent of 7, you get the biased exponent value of 86H that you need for the short-real representation. The final line in Figure 11-19 shows the complete short-real result. For the significand you put in the binary bits to the right of the binary point. Remember, the 1 to the left of the binary point is assumed. The biased exponent value of 86H or 10000110 binary is put in as bits 23 through 30. Finally, since the number is positive, a 0 is put in bit 31 as the sign bit. The complete result is then 01000011001100101010000000000000 or 4332A000H, which is lengthy, but not difficult to produce.

The long-real format shown in Figure 11-18 uses 64 bits to represent each number. This format is often referred to as *double-precision* representation. This format is basically the same as that of the short-real, except that it allows greater range and accuracy because more bits are used for each number. For long-real, 52 bits are used to represent the magnitude of the number. Again the number is normalized so that only a single 1 is to the left of the binary point. You can think of the binary point as being between the bits numbered 51 and 52. The one to the left of the binary point is not actually put in as one of the 64 bits. For this format, 11 bits are used for the exponent, so the offset added to each exponent value is 1023 decimal or 3FFH. The most significant bit is the sign bit. Our example number of 178.625 will be represented in this long-real or double-precision format as 4066540000000000H. Note in Figure 11-18 the range of numbers that can be represented with this format. This range should be large enough for most of the problems you want to solve with an 8087.

The final format in Figure 11-18 to discuss is the temporary-real format which uses 80 bits to represent each number. This is the format that all numbers are converted to by the 8087 as it reads them in, and it is the format in which the 8087 works with numbers internally. The large number of bits used in this format reduces rounding errors in long chain calculations. To understand what this means, think of multiplying 1234×4567 in a machine that can only store the upper 4 digits of the result. The actual result of 5,635,678 will be truncated to 5,635,000. If you then divide this by 1234 to get back to the original 4567, you get instead 4566 because of the limited precision of the intermediate number.

As you can see in Figure 11-18, the temporary-real format has a sign bit, 15 bits for a biased exponent, and 64 bits for the significand. The offset or bias added to the exponent here is 16,383 decimal or 3FFFH. A major difference in the significand for this format from that for short-reals and long-reals is that the 1 to the left of the binary point after normalization is included as bit 63 in the significand. To express our example number of 178.625 in this form, then, we convert it to binary and normalize it as before to give 1.0110010101E7. This gives us the upper bits of the significand directly as 10110010101. We simply add enough 0's on the right of this to fill up the rest of the 64 bits reserved for the significand. To produce the required exponent, we add the bias value of 3FFFH to our determined value of 7. This gives 4006H or 100000000000110 binary as the value for the exponent. The sign bit is a 0 because the number is positive. Putting all of these pieces together gives4006B2A000000000000H as the temporary-real representation of 178.625. This concludes our initial discussion of the way numbers are represented for the 8087.

The 8087 Internal Architecture

Figure 11-20 shows a block diagram of the 8087. As we described before, the 8087 connects directly on the address, data, and status lines of the 8086 or 8088 so that it can track and decode instructions fetched by the 8086 or 8088 host. The 8087 has a control-word register and a status register. Control words are sent to the 8087 by writing them to a memory location and having the 8087 execute an instruction which reads in the control word from memory. Likewise, to read the status word from an 8087 you have it execute an instruction which writes the status word to memory where you can read or check it with an 8086 instruction. Figure 11-21 shows the formats for the 8087 control and status words. Take a look at these now so you have an overview of the meaning of the various bits of these words. We will discuss the meaning of most of these bits as we work our way through the following sections.

The 8087 works internally with all numbers in the 80-bit temporary-real format which we discussed in the preceding paragraphs. To hold numbers being worked on, the 8087 has a register stack of eight, 80-bit registers labeled (0)–(7) in Figure 11-20. These registers are used as a last-in–first-out stack in the same way the 8086 uses a stack. The 8087 has a 3-bit stack pointer which holds the number of the register which is the current top-of-stack. When the 8087 is initialized, the 3-bit stack pointer in the 8087 is loaded with 000, so register 0 is then the TOS. When the 8087 reads in the first number that it is going to work on from memory, it converts the number to 80-bit temporary-real format if necessary. It then decrements the stack pointer to 111, and writes the temporary-real representation of the number in register number 111 (7). Figure 11-22*a* shows this in diagram form. As shown by the arrow in the figure, you can think of the stack as being wrapped around in a circle so that if you decrement 000 you get 111. Also from this diagram you can see that if you push more than 8 numbers on the stack they wrap around and write over previous numbers. After this write-to-stack operation, register 7 is now the TOS.

In the 8087 instructions the register that is currently the TOS is referred to as ST(0), or simply ST. The register just below this in the stack is referred to as ST(1). By the register "just below," we mean the register that the stack pointer would be pointing to if we popped one number off the stack. For the example in Figure 11-22*a*, register 000 would be ST(1) after the first push.

To help you understand this concept, Figure 11-22*b* shows another example. In this example we have pushed three numbers on the stack after initializing. Register 101 is now the TOS, so it is referred to as ST(0) or just ST. The preceding number pushed on the stack is in register 110, so it is referred to as ST(1). Likewise, the location below this in the stack is referred to as ST(2). If you draw a diagram such as that in Figure 11-22*b*, it is relatively easy to keep track of where everything is in the stack as instructions execute. In a program you can determine which register is currently the ST by simply transferring the status word to memory and checking the bits labeled ST in the status-word format in Figure 11-21*b*. Now let's have a look at the 8087 instruction set.

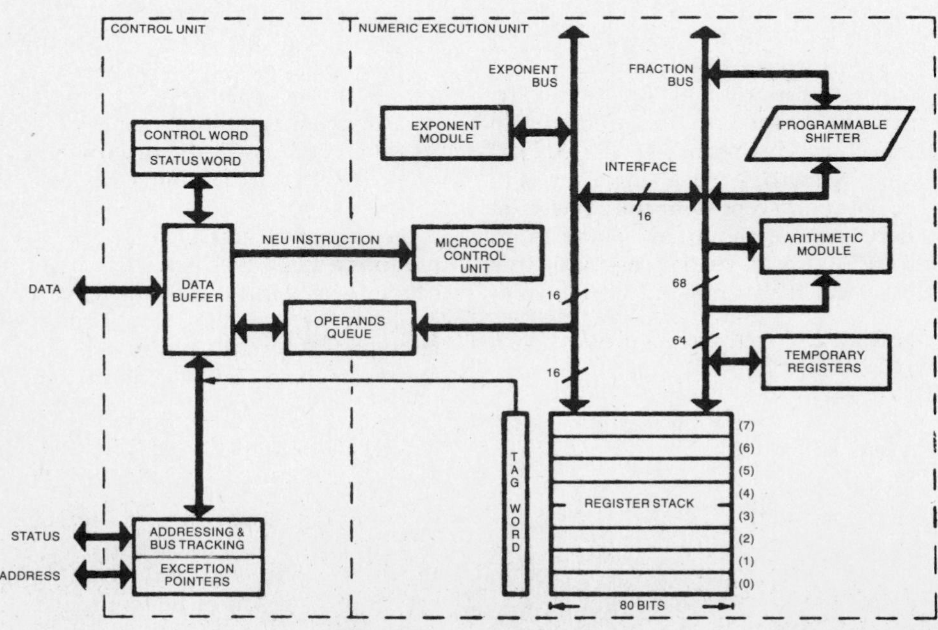

FIGURE 11-20 8087 internal block diagram. (Intel Corporation)

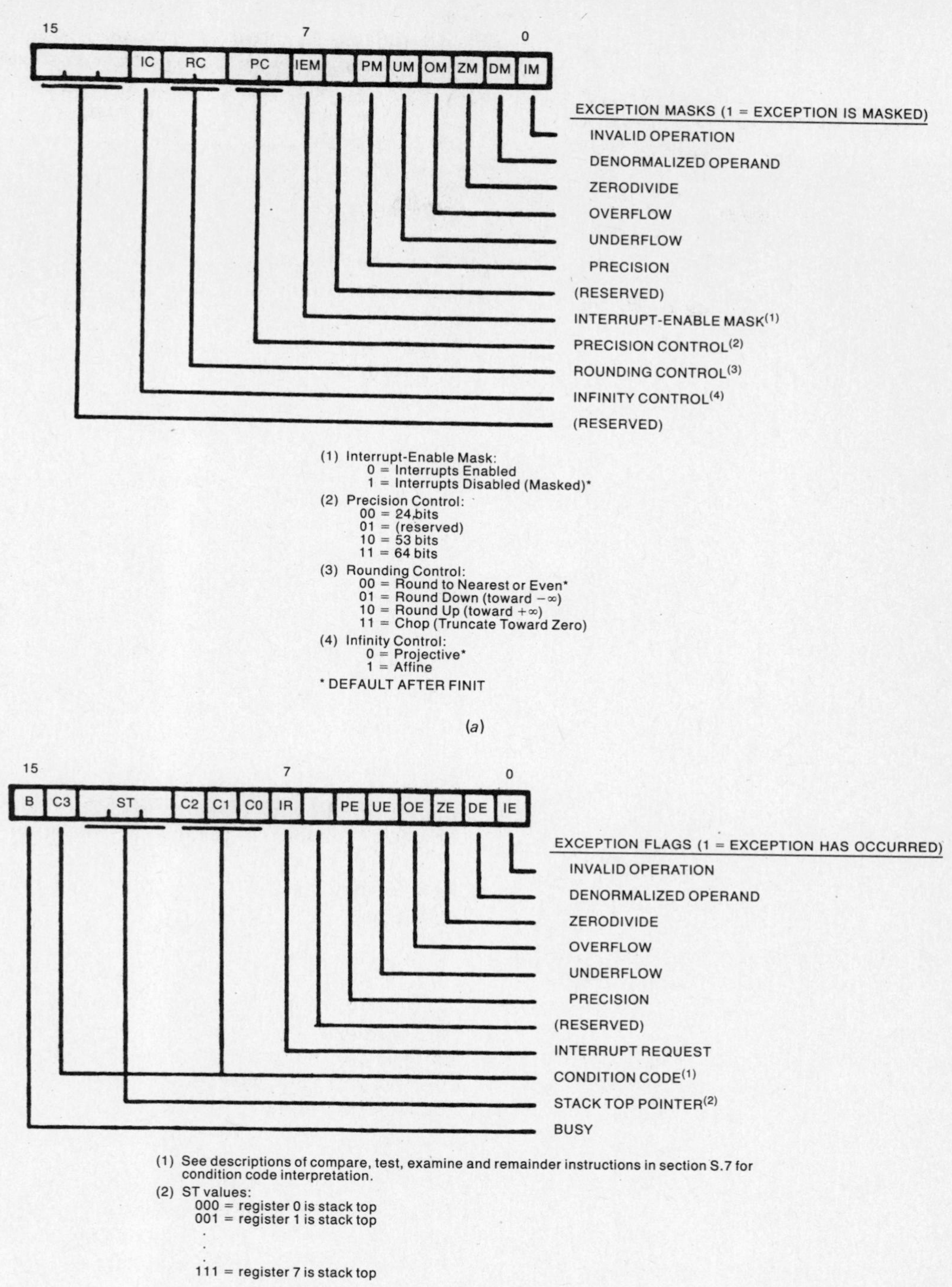

FIGURE 11-21 8087 control and status word formats. *(a)* Control. *(b)* Status. (Intel Corporation)

8087 Instruction Set

8087 INSTRUCTION FORMATS

Before we work our way through the list of 8087 instructions we will use one simple instruction to show you how 8087 instructions are written, how they operate, and how they are coded. Instructions for the 8087 can be written as 8086 ESCAPE (ESC) instructions followed by a number as, for example, ESC 28, or they can be written using specific 8087 mnemonics. For the following discussion we will use the 8087 mnemonics. Later we will show you how to code the instructions as ESC instructions if you don't have an assembler which accepts 8087 mnemonics. The instruction we have chosen to use as an example here is the FADD instruction.

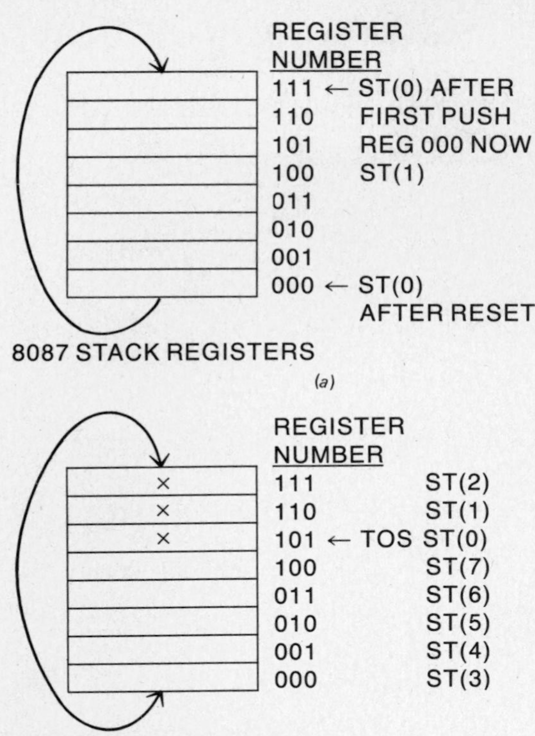

FIGURE 11-22 8087 stack operation. *(a)* Condition of stack after reset and one push. *(b)* Condition of stack after reset and three pushes.

All of the 8087 mnemonics start with an F, which stands for floating point, the form in which the 8087 works with numbers internally. If you look in the Intel data book, you will see this instruction represented as FADD //source/destination, source. This cryptic representation means that the instruction can be written in three different ways.

The // at the start indicates that the instruction can be written without any specified operands as simply FADD. In this case, when the 8087 executes the instruction it will automatically add the number at the top of the stack (ST) to the number in the next location under it in the stack, ST(1). The 8087 stack pointer will be incremented by one so that the register containing the result will be ST.

The word "source" by itself in the expression means that the instruction can be written as FADD source. The source specified here can be one of the stack elements, or a memory location. For example, the instruction FADD ST(2) will add the number from two locations below ST to the number in ST, and leave the result in ST. As another example, the instruction FADD CORRECTION_FACTOR will add a real number from the memory location named CORRECTION_FACTOR to the number in ST and leave the result in ST. The assembler will be able to determine whether the number in memory is a short-real, long-real, or temporary-real by the way that CORRECTION_FACTOR was declared. Short-reals, for example, are declared with the DD directive, long-reals with the DQ directive, and temporary-reals with the DT directive. If you want to add an integer number from memory to ST, you use an instruction such as FIADD CORRECTION_FACTOR. The I in the mnemonic tells the assembler to code the instruction so that the 8087 treats the number read in as an integer.

NOTE: The FIADD instruction only works for a source operand in memory.

The /destination, source in the representation of the FADD instruction means that you can write the instruction with both a specified source and a specified destination. The source can be one of the stack elements, or a number from memory. The destination has to be one of the stack elements. The instruction FADD ST(2), ST(1), for example, will add the number one location down from ST to the number two locations down from ST, and leave the result in ST(2). The instruction FADD ST(3), CORRECTION_FACTOR will add the real number from the memory location named CORRECTION_FACTOR to the contents of the ST(3) stack element.

Another form of the 8087 FADD instruction shown in the data book is FADDP. The P at the end of this mnemonic means to POP. When the 8087 executes this form of the FADD instruction, it will increment the stack pointer by one after it does the add operation. This is referred to as "popping the stack." The instruction FADDP ST(1), ST(4), for example, will add the number at ST(4) to the number at ST(1), and put the result in ST(1). It will then "pop the stack" or, in other words, increment the stack pointer so that what was ST(1) is now ST. This form of the instruction leaves the result at ST where it can easily be transferred to memory. Now let's see how the different forms of this instruction are coded.

CODING 8087 INSTRUCTIONS

The coding templates for all of the 8087 instructions are in the appendix for your reference. You use these templates in the same manner as you do those for the 8086 instructions. For closer reference, Figure 11-23 shows the coding templates for the 8087 FADD instructions in the form shown in the appendix and in expanded form so you can see the individual bits. Note that the figure shows coding for "8087" encoding and for "emulator" encoding. The 8087 encoding represents the codes required by the actual device. The emulator encoding represents the codes needed to call an FADD procedure from an available Intel library of 8086 procedures which perform the same functions as the 8087 instructions. The procedures in this library, written in 8086 code, run much slower, but they allow you to test an 8087 program without having an actual 8087 in the system. We will concentrate here on the codes for the actual 8087 device.

First let's look at the coding for the FADD instruction with no specified operands. This instruction, remember, will add the contents of ST to the contents of ST(1), put the results in ST(1), and then pop the stack so that the result is at ST. The first byte of the instruction code, 10011011, is the code for the 8086 WAIT instruction. Remember from our previous discussion that this in-

Type 1: Stack top and stack element

8087	10011011	11011 d 00	11000(i)
Emulator	11001101	00011 d 00	11000(i)

Type 2: Stack top and memory operand

8087	10011011	11011 m 00	mod 000 r/m
Emulator	11001101	00011 m 00	mod 000 r/m

m = 0 for short real operand; 1 for long real operand

Type 3: Pop stack

8087	10011011	11011110	11000(i)
Emulator	11001101	00011110	11000(i)

8087 Timing (clocks)	**TYPICAL**	**RANGE**
stack element and stack top	85	70-100
stack element, stack top + pop	90	75-105
short real memory and stack top	105+EA	90-120+EA
long real memory and stack top	110+EA	95-125+EA

FADD

Stack top + Stack Element

WAIT	op1	op2 + i

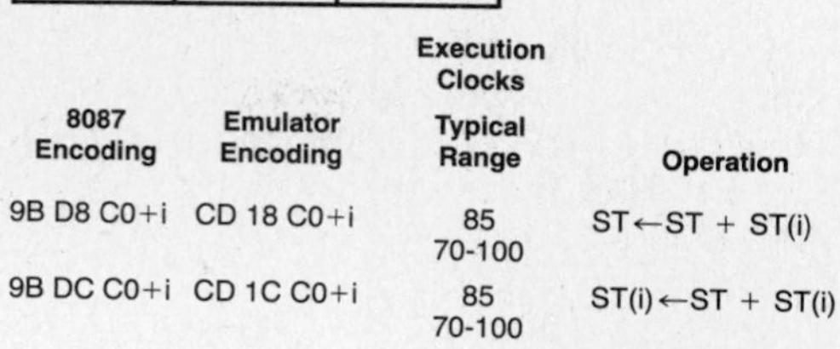

8087 Encoding	Emulator Encoding	Execution Clocks Typical Range	Operation
9B D8 C0+i	CD 18 C0+i	85 70-100	ST←ST + ST(i)
9B DC C0+i	CD 1C C0+i	85 70-100	ST(i)←ST + ST(i)

Stack top + memory operand

WAIT	op1	mod 000 r/m	addr1	addr2

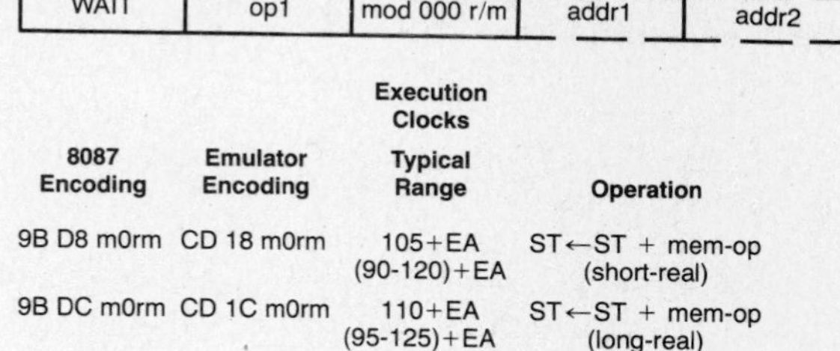

8087 Encoding	Emulator Encoding	Execution Clocks Typical Range	Operation
9B D8 m0rm	CD 18 m0rm	105+EA (90-120)+EA	ST←ST + mem-op (short-real)
9B DC m0rm	CD 1C m0rm	110+EA (95-125)+EA	ST←ST + mem-op (long-real)

FADDP = Add Real and Pop

Stack top + Stack Element

WAIT	op1	op2 + i

8087 Encoding	Emulator Encoding	Execution Clocks Typical Range	Operation
9B DE C1	CD 1E C1	90 75-105	ST(1)←ST + ST(1) pop stack
9B DE C0+i	CD 1E C0+i	90 75-105	ST(i)←ST + ST(i) pop stack

FIGURE 11-23 8087 FADD coding templates. (Intel Corporation)

struction code is put here to make the 8086 and 8087 wait until it has completed a previous instruction before starting this one. The second byte shown is actually the first byte of the 8087 FADD instruction. The 5 most-significant bits, 11011, identify this as an 8087 instruction. The lower 3 bits of the first code byte and the middle 3 bits of the second code byte are the opcode for the particular 8087 instruction. The bit labeled d at the start of these 6 is a 0 if the destination for an FADD ST(N), ST(N) type instruction is ST. The d bit is a 1 if the destination stack element is one other than ST, as it is for the FADD instruction with no specified operands. For the FADD instruction with no specified operands these 6 bits will be 100 000. The two most significant (MOD) bits in the second code byte are ones, because this form of the FADD instruction does not read a number from memory. The least-significant 3 bits of the second instruction byte, represented by an i in the template, indicate which stack element other than ST is specified in the instruction. Since the simple FADD instruction uses ST(1) as a destination, 001 will be put in these bits. Putting all of this together for the FADD instruction with no specified source or destination gives 10011011 11011100 11000001 binary or 9BH DCH C1H as the code bytes.

For a little more practice with this see if you can code the 8087 instruction FADD ST, ST(2). Most of the coding for this instruction is the same as that for the previous instruction. For this one, however, the d bit is a 0 because ST is the specified destination. Also, the R/M bits are 010, because the other register involved in the addition is ST(2). The answer is 9BD8C2H. Now let's try an example which uses memory as the source of an operand for FADD.

For an FADD instruction such as FADD CORRECTION_FACTOR, which brings in one operand from memory and adds it to ST, the memory address can be specified in any of the 24 ways shown in Figure 3-8. For the memory reference form of the FADD instruction the MOD and R/M bits in the second code byte are used to specify the desired addressing mode. FADD CORRECTION_FACTOR represents direct addressing, so the MOD bits will be 00 and the R/M bits will be 110 as shown in Figure 3-8. Two additional code bytes will be used to put in the direct address, low byte first. Since we are not using any of the other stack elements other than ST for this instruction, we don't need the d bit to specify the other stack element. Instead, as shown in Figure 11-23, this bit is labeled m. A 0 in this bit is used to specify a short-real, and a 1 in this bit is used for a long-real. Assuming CORRECTION_FACTOR is declared as a long-real, the code bytes for our FADD CORRECTION_FACTOR instruction will then be 10011011 11011100 00000110 followed by the two bytes of the direct address.

So far in this section we have shown you examples of how some 8087 instructions will be coded out if they are written with 8087 mnemonics and assembled with an assembler that recognizes 8087 mnemonics. If you don't have an assembler with 8087 capability, you can code 8087 instructions as 8086 ESCAPE (ESC) instructions with the help of the 8087 instruction templates in the appendix. Your 8086 assembler should then produce the correct code for them. Here's how you do it.

The 8086 ESC instruction has two basic forms. The first of these, ESC immediate, memory, is used to produce 8087 instructions which bring an operand in from memory or send an operand out to memory. The second form of the escape instruction is ESC immediate, register. This second form is used to produce 8087 instructions which operate only on registers. We'll start with the ESC immediate, memory form.

The coding template for the ESC immediate, memory instruction is 11011xxx MODxxxR/M. The 6 x's in the template represent a 6-bit binary opcode for the desired 8087 instruction. You specify these 6 bits in the ESC instruction as an immediate number. You determine the value for this immediate number by looking at the coding template for the 8087 instructions in the appendix. For example, suppose that you want to use the ESC instruction to produce the FADD CORRECTION_FACTOR instruction. In our discussion of the coding for this instruction above, we determined that if CORRECTION_FACTOR is a long-real, then the binary code for the instruction is 10011011 11011100 00000011 followed by the direct address in the next 2 bytes. The first byte of this is the WAIT instruction. The values for the 6 bits that we are interested in are 100000. Converting this to hex gives 20H, the immediate number you need to put in the ESC instruction. You write the 8086 ESC instruction then as ESC 20H, CORRECTION_FACTOR. When the assembler reads this instruction statement, it will automatically determine the values for the MOD and the R/M bits of the instruction from the reference to the memory location CORRECTION_FACTOR. You can put an 8086 WAIT instruction before the ESC instruction if necessary.

Now we will show you how to write an ESC instruction to produce an 8087 instruction which operates only on internal registers of the 8087. The coding template for this ESC instruction is also 11011xxx MODxxxR/M. The 6 x's again represent the desired 8087 opcode. You get the values for these bits from the 8087 code templates in the appendix. As an example, suppose that you want to get the 8086 assembler to produce the correct code for the 8087 instruction FADD ST, ST(2), which was one of our examples in a previous section. According to the templates in the appendix, the code for this instruction is 10011011 11011<u>000</u> 11<u>000</u>i. The 10011011 at the start is the code for the WAIT instruction. The 6 underlined bits from this code that you use for the immediate number in the ESC instruction are 000 000. The ones in the MOD position of the last code byte indicate that only registers are involved in the operation. The three i bits in this byte must contain the number of the other stack element besides ST that is used in the instruction. For our example here we want the assembler to put in 010 or 2 for these bits, because we are using ST(2). To get the assembler to put in 11 for the MOD bits in the ESC instruction code, you simply put an 8086 register name after the immediate number in the ESC instruction. The register name you use tells the assembler what to put in the 3-bit i field of the instruction. Look at Figure 3-8 to determine the 3-bit codes for each of the 8086 registers. The code of 010 which you need here corresponds to that for the DX register. If you put all of these pieces together, the 8087 FADD ST, ST(2) can be written as the 8086 ESC 00H, DX instruction. Once you see the correspondence here, it is not too difficult to get the 8086 assembler to produce a desired 8087 instruction code. Now that you have an overview of how 8087 instructions are written and coded, we will briefly discuss the operation of the available 8087 instructions.

8087 INSTRUCTION DESCRIPTIONS

The 8087 instruction mnemonics all begin with the letter F which stands for floating point and distinguishes the 8087 instructions from 8086 instructions. We have found that if we mentally remove the F as we read the mnemonic, it makes it easier to connect the mnemonic and the operation performed by the instruction. Here we briefly describe the operation of each of the 8087 instructions so that you can use some of them to write simple programs. As you read through these instructions the first time, don't try to absorb them all, or you probably won't remember any of them. Concentrate first on the instructions you need to get operands from memory into the 8087, simple arithmetic instructions, and the instructions you need to get results copied back from the 8087 to memory where you can use them. Then work your way through the first example program in the next section. After that, read through the instructions again and pay special attention to the transcendental instructions and the load constant instructions. Finally, work your way through the second example program in the next section. We hope that you will find, as we have, that the 8087 is fun to work with. After you play around with some simple programs such as those here, you can go to the Intel literature to get more information about error handling and more complex program examples.

The instructions are grouped here in four functional groups so that you can more easily find the instruction which performs a desired operation. A section in the appendix shows the coding templates and clock cycles for each instruction.

If the 8087 detects an error condition, usually called an *exception*, while it is executing an instruction, it will set the appropriate bit in its status register. After the instruction finishes executing, the status register contents can be transferred to memory with another 8087 instruction. You can then use 8086 instructions to check the status bits and decide what action to take if an error has occurred. Figure 11-21*b* shows the format of the 8087 status word. The lowest 6 bits are the exception status bits. These bits will all be 0's if no errors have occurred. In the instruction descriptions following, we use the first letter of each exception type to indicate the status bits affected by each instruction.

If you send the 8087 a control word which unmasks the exception interrupts as shown in Figure 11-21*a*, the 8087 will also send a hardware interrupt signal to the 8086, when an error occurs. If the 8086 interrupt input is enabled, this allows the 8086 to go directly to an exception handling procedure.

DATA TRANSFER INSTRUCTIONS

Real Transfers

FLD source—Decrements the stack pointer by one and copies a real number from a stack element or memory location to the new ST. A short-real or long-real number from memory is automatically converted to temporary-real format by the 8087 before it is put in ST. Exceptions: I, D. Examples:

```
FLD ST(3)              ; Copies ST(3) to ST
FLD LONG_REAL[BX]      ; Number from memory copied
                       ; to ST
```

FST destination—Copies ST to a specified stack position or to a specified memory location. If a number is transferred to a memory location, the number and its exponent will be rounded to fit in the destination memory location. Exceptions: I, O, U, P. Examples:

```
FST ST(2)              ; Copy ST to ST(2), and
                       ; increment stack pointer
FST SHORT_REAL[BX]     ; Copy ST to memory
                       ; at SHORT_REAL[BX]
```

FSTP destination—Copies ST to a specified stack element or memory location and increments the stack pointer by one to point to the next element on the stack. This is a stack POP operation. It is identical to FST except for the effect on the stack pointer.

FXCH //destination—Exchanges the contents of ST with the contents of a specified stack element. If no destination is specified, then ST(1) used. Exception: I. Example:

```
FXCH ST(5)   ; Swap ST and ST(5)
```

Integer Transfers

FILD source—Integer load. Convert integer number from memory to temporary-real format and push on 8087 stack. Exception: I. Example:

```
FILD DWORD PTR [BX]   ; Short integer from memory
                      ; at [BX]
```

FIST destination—Integer store. Convert number from ST to integer form, and copy to memory. Exceptions: I, P. Example:

```
FIST LONG_INT    ; ST to memory locations
                 ; named LONG_INT
```

FISTP destination—Integer store and pop. Identical to FIST except that stack pointer is incremented after copy.

Packed Decimal Transfers

FBLD source—Packed decimal(BCD) load. Convert number from memory to temporary-real format and push on top of 8087 stack. Exception: I. Example:

```
FBLD MONEY_DUE    ; Ten byte BCD number from
                  ; memory to ST
```

FBSTP destination—BCD store in memory and pop 8087 stack. Pops temporary-real from stack, converts to 10-byte BCD, and writes result to memory. Exception: I. Example:

```
FBSTP TAX   ; ST converted to BCD, sent to memory
```

ARITHMETIC INSTRUCTIONS

Addition

FADD //source/destination, source—Add real from specified source to real at specified destination. Source can be stack element or memory location. Destination must be a stack element. If no source or destination is specified, then ST is added to ST(1) and the stack pointer is incremented so that the result of the addition is at ST. Exceptions: I, D, O, U, P. Examples:

```
FADD ST(3), ST      ; Add ST to ST(3), result in ST(3)
FADD ST,ST(4)       ; Add ST(4) to ST, result in ST
FADD INTEREST       ; Real num from mem + ST
FADD                ; ST + ST(1), pop stack-result at ST
```

FADDP destination, source—Add ST to specified stack element and increment stack pointer by one. Exceptions: I, D, O, U, P. Example:

```
FADDP ST(1)   ; Add ST(1) to ST. Increment stack
              ; pointer so ST(1) becomes ST
```

FIADD source—Add integer from memory to ST, result in ST. Exceptions: I, D, O, P. Example:

```
FIADD CARS_SOLD   ; Integer number from
                  ; memory + ST
```

Subtraction

FSUB //source/destination, source—Subtract the real number at the specified source from the real number at the specified destination and put the result in the specified destination. Exceptions: I, D, O, U, P. Examples:

```
FSUB ST(2), ST    ; ST(2) becomes ST(2) - ST
FSUB CHARGE       ; ST becomes ST - real from memory
FSUB              ; ST becomes (ST(1) - ST)
```

FSUBP destination, source—Subtract ST from specified stack element and put result in specified stack element. Then increment stack pointer by one. Exceptions: I, D, O, U, P. Examples:

```
FSUBP ST(1)   ; ST(1) − ST. ST(1) becomes new ST.
```

FISUB source—Integer from memory subtracted from ST, result in ST. Exceptions: I, D, O, P. Example:

```
FISUB CARS_SOLD   ; ST becomes ST − integer
                  ; from memory
```

Reversed Subtraction

FSUBR //source/destination, source
FSUBRP //destination, source
FISUBR source

These instructions operate the same as the FSUB instructions described above except that these instructions subtract the contents of the specified destination from the contents of the specified source and put the difference in the specified destination. Normal FSUB instructions, remember, subtract source from destination.

Multiplication

FMUL //source/destination, source—Multiply real number from source by real number from specified destination, and put result in specified stack element. See FADD instruction description for examples of specifying operands. Exceptions: I, D, O, U, P.

FMULP destination, source—Multiply real number from specified source by real number from specified destination, put result in specified stack element, and increment stack pointer by one. See FADDP instruction for examples of how to specify operands for this instruction. With no specified operands FMULP multiplies ST(1) by ST and pops stack to leave result at ST. Exceptions: I, D, O, U, P.

FIMUL source—Multiply integer from memory times ST and put result in ST. Exceptions: I, D, O, P. Example:

```
FIMUL DWORD PTR [BX]
```

Division

FDIV //source/destination, source—Divide destination real by source real, result goes in destination. See FADD formats. Exceptions: I, D, Z, O, U, P.

FDIVP destination, source—Same as FDIV, but also increment stack pointer by one after DIV. See FADDP formats. Exceptions: I, D, Z, O, U, P.

FIDIV source—Divide ST by integer from memory, result in ST. Exceptions: I, D, Z, O, U, P.

Reversed Division

FDIVR //source/destination, source
FDIVP destination, source
FIDIVR source
These three instructions are identical in format to the FDIV, FDIVP, and FIDIV instructions above except that they divide the source operand by the destination operand and put the result in the destination.

Other Arithmetic Operations

FSQRT—Contents of ST are replaced with its square root. Exceptions: I, D, P. Example: FSQRT

FSCALE—Scale the number in ST by adding an integer value in ST(1) to the exponent of the number in ST. Fast way of multiplying by integral powers of two. Exceptions: I, O, U.

FPREM—Partial remainder. The contents of ST(1) are subtracted from the contents of ST over and over again until the contents of ST are smaller than the contents of ST(1). In an 8087 program example later in this chapter we show how FPREM is used to reduce a large angle to less than $\pi/4$ so that we can use the 8087 trig functions on it. Exceptions: I, D, U. Example: FPREM

FRNDINT—Round number in ST to an integer. The *round-control* (RC) bits in the control word determine how the number will be rounded. If the RC bits are set for down or chop, a number such as 205.73 will be rounded to 205. If the RC bits are set for up or nearest, 205.73 will be rounded to 206. Exceptions: I, P.

FXTRACT—Separates the exponent and the significand parts of a temporary-real number in ST. After the instruction executes, ST contains a temporary-real representation of the significand of the number and ST(1) contains a temporary-real representation of the exponent of the number. These two could then be written separately out to memory locations. Exception: I.

FABS—Number in ST is replaced by its absolute value. Instruction simply makes sign positive. Exception: I.

FCHS—Complements the sign of the number in ST. Exception: I.

COMPARE INSTRUCTIONS

The compare instructions with COM in their mnemonic compare contents of ST with contents of specified or default source. The source may be another stack element or real number in memory. These compare instructions set the condition code bits C3, C2, and C0 of the status word shown in Figure 11-21*b* as follows:

C3	C2	C0	
0	0	0	ST > source
0	0	0	ST < source
1	0	0	ST = source
1	1	1	numbers cannot be compared

You can transfer the status word to memory with the 8087 FSTSW instruction and then use 8086 instructions to determine the results of the comparison. Here are the different compares.

FCOM //source—Compares ST with real number in another stack element or memory. Exceptions: I, D. Examples:

```
FCOM                  ; Compares ST with ST(1)
FCOM ST(3)            ; Compares ST with ST(3)
FCOM MINIMUM_PAYMENT  ; Compares ST with real
                      ; from memory
```

FCOMP //source—Identical to FCOM except that the stack pointer is incremented by one after the compare operation. Old ST(1) becomes new ST.

FCOMPP—Compare ST with ST(1) and increment stack pointer by 2 after compare. This puts the new ST above the two numbers compared. Exceptions: I, D.

FICOM source—Compares ST to a short or long integer from memory. Exceptions: I, D. Example:
FICOM MAX_ALTITUDE

FICOMP source—Identical to FICOM except stack pointer is incremented by one after compare.

FTST—Compares ST with zero. Condition code bits C3, C2, and C0 in the status word are set as shown above if you assume the source in this case is zero. Exceptions: I, D.

FXAM—Tests ST to see if it is zero, infinity, unnormalized, or empty. Sets bits C3, C2, C1, and C0 to indicate result. See Intel data book for coding. Exceptions: None.

TRANSCENDENTAL (TRIGONOMETRIC AND EXPONENTIAL) INSTRUCTIONS

FPTAN—Computes the values for a ratio of Y/X for an angle in ST. The angle must be expressed in radians, and the angle must be in the range of $0 <$ angle $< \pi/4$.

NOTE: FPTAN does not work correctly for angles of exactly 0 and $\pi/4$. You can convert an angle from degrees to radians by dividing it by 57.295779. An angle greater than $\pi/4$ can be brought into range with the 8087 FPREM instruction. The Y value replaces the angle on the stack, and the X value is pushed on the stack to become the new ST. The values for X and Y are created separately so you can use them to calculate other trig functions for the given angle as we show in an example program later in this chapter. Exceptions: I, P.

FPATAN—Computes the angle whose tangent is Y/X. The X value must be in ST, and the Y value must be in ST(1). Also, X and Y must satisfy the inequality $0 < Y < X < \infty$. The resulting angle expressed in radians replaces Y in the stack. After the operation the stack pointer is incremented so the result is then ST. Exceptions: U, P.

F2XM1—Computes the function $Y = 2^X - 1$ for an X value in ST. The result, Y, replaces X in ST. X must be in the range $0 \leq X \leq 0.5$. To produce 2^X, you can simply add one to the result from this instruction. Using some common equalities you can produce values often needed in engineering and scientific calculations. Here are some examples.

$10^X = 2^{X(\mathrm{LOG}_2 10)}$

$e^X = 2^{X(\mathrm{LOG}_2 e)}$

$Y^X = 2^{X(\mathrm{LOG}_2 Y)}$

FYL2X—Calculates Y times the LOG to the base 2 of X or $Y(\mathrm{LOG}_2 X)$. X must be in the range of $0 < X < \infty$ and Y must be in the range $-\infty < Y < +\infty$. X must initially be in ST and Y must be in ST(1). The result replaces Y and then the stack is popped so that the result is then at ST. This instruction can be used to compute the log of a number in any base, n, using the identity $\mathrm{LOG}_n X = \mathrm{LOG}_n 2(\mathrm{LOG}_2 X)$. For a given n, $\mathrm{LOG}_n 2$ is a constant which can easily be calculated and used as the Y value for the instruction. Exceptions: P.

FYL2XP1—Computes the function Y times the LOG to the base 2 of $(X + 1)$ or $Y(\mathrm{LOG}_2(X + 1))$. This instruction is almost identical to FYL2X except that it gives more accurate results when computing the LOG of a number very close to one. Consult the Intel manual for further detail.

INSTRUCTIONS WHICH LOAD CONSTANTS

The following instructions simply push the indicated constant on the stack. Having these commonly used constants available reduces programming effort.

FLDZ —Push 0.0 on stack
FLD1 —Push +1.0 on stack
FLDPI —Push the value of π on stack
FLD2T —Push LOG of 10 to the base 2 on stack ($\mathrm{LOG}_2 10$)
FLDL2E —Push LOG of e to the base 2 on stack ($\mathrm{LOG}_2 e$)
FLDLG2—Push LOG of 2 to the base 10 on stack ($\mathrm{LOG}_{10} 2$)

PROCESSOR CONTROL INSTRUCTIONS

These instructions do not perform computations. They are used to do tasks such as initializing the 8087, enabling interrupts, writing the status word to memory, etc.

Instruction mnemonics with an N as the second character have the same function as those without the N, but they put a NOP in front of the instruction instead of putting a WAIT instruction there.

FINIT/FNINT—Initializes 8087. Disables interrupt output, sets stack pointer to register 7, sets default status.

FDISI/FNDISI—Disables the 8087 interrupt output pin so that it cannot cause an interrupt when an exception (error) occurs.

FENI/FNENI—Enables 8087 interrupt output so it can cause an interrupt when an exception occurs.

FLDCW source—Loads a status word from a named memory location into the 8087 status register. This instruction should be preceded by the FCLEX instruction to prevent a possible exception response if an exception bit in the status word is set.

FSTCW/FNSTCW destination—Copies the 8087 control word to a named memory location where you can determine its current value with 8086 instructions.

FSTSW/FNSTSW destination—Copies the 8087 status word to a named memory location. You can check various status bits with 8086 instructions and base further action on the state of these bits.

FCLEX/FNCLEX—Clears all of the 8087 exception flag bits in the status register. Unasserts BUSY and INT outputs.

FSAVE/FNSAVE destination—Copies the 8087 control word, status word, pointers, and entire register stack to a named, 94-byte area of memory. After copying all of this the FSAVE/FNSAVE instruction initializes the 8087 as if the FINIT/FNINIT instruction had been executed.

FRSTOR source—Copies a 94-byte named area of memory into the 8087 control register, status register, pointer registers, and stack registers.

FSTENV/FNSTENV destination—Copies the 8087 control register, status register, tag words, and exception pointers to a named series of memory locations. This instruction does not copy the 8087 register stack to memory as the FSAVE/FNSAVE instruction does.

FLDENV source—Loads the 8087 control register, status register, tag word, and exception pointers from a named area in memory.

FINCSTP—Increment the 8087 stack pointer by one. If the stack pointer contains 111 and it is incremented, it will point to 000.

FDECSTP—Decrement stack pointer by one. If the stack pointer contains 000 and it is decremented, it will contain 111.

FFREE destination—Changes the tag for the specified destination register to empty. See the Intel manual for a discussion of the tag word which you usually don't need to know about.

FNOP—Performs no operation. Actually copies ST to ST.

FWAIT—This instruction is actually an 8086 instruction which makes the 8086 wait until it receives a not busy signal from the 8087 to its $\overline{\text{TEST}}$ pin. This is done to make sure that neither the 8086 nor the 8087 starts the next instruction before the preceding 8087 instruction is completed.

8087 Example Programs

PYTHAGORAS REVISITED

As you may remember from back there somewhere in geometry, the pythagorean theorem states that the hypotenuse (longest side) of a right triangle squared is equal to the square of one of the other sides plus the square of the remaining side. This is commonly written as $C^2 = A^2 + B^2$. For this example program we want to solve this for the hypotenuse, C, so we take the square root of both sides of the equation to give $C = \sqrt{A^2+B^2}$. Figure 11-24 shows a simple 8087 program you can use to compute the value of C for given values of A and B. We have shown the assembler listing for the program so you can see the actual codes that are generated for the 8087 instructions. Note, for example, that each of the codes for the 8087 instructions here starts with 9BH, the code for the WAIT instruction whose function we explained before.

At the start of the program we set aside some named memory locations to store the values of the three sides of our triangle, the control word we want to send the 8087, and the status word we will read from the 8087 to check for error conditions. Remember, the only way you can pass numbers to and from the 8087 is by using 8087 instructions to read the numbers from memory locations or write the numbers to memory locations. In this section of the example program the statement SIDE_A DD 3.0 tells the assembler to set aside two words in memory to store the value of one of the sides of the triangle. The decimal point in 3.0 tells the assembler that this is a real number. The assembler then produces the short-real representation of 3.0 (40400000) and puts it in the reserved memory locations. Likewise the statement SIDE_B DD 4.0 tells the assembler to set aside two word locations and put the short-real representation of 4.0 in them. The statement HYPOTENUSE DD 0 reserves a double word space for the result of our computation. When the program is finished, these locations will contain 40A00000, the short-real representation for 5.0.

The actual code section of this program you would normally write as a procedure so that you could call it as needed. To make it simple here we have written it as a stand-alone program. We start by initializing the data segment register to point to our data in memory. We then initialize the 8087 with the FINIT instruction. The notations for the control word in Figure 11-21*a* show the default values for each part of the control word after FINIT executes. For most computations these values give the best results. However, just in case you might want to change some of these settings from their default values, we have included the instructions needed to send a new control word to the 8087. You first load the desired control word in a reserved memory location with the MOV CONTROL_WORD, 03FFH instruction, and then load this word into the 8087 with the FLDCW CONTROL_WORD instruction.

To perform the actual computation, we start in the inside of the equation and work our way outward. FLD SIDE_A brings in the value of the first side and pushes it on the 8087 stack. FMUL ST, ST(0) multiplies ST by ST

```
IBM Personal Computer MACRO Assembler   Version 2.00   Page   1-1
                                                              05-21-85
                         page ,132
                         ;8087 NUMERIC DATA PROCESSOR EXAMPLE PROGRAM
                         ;
                         ;ABSTRACT:      This program calculates the hypotenuse of a right
                         ;               triangle, given SIDE A and SIDE B
                         NAME    PYTHAG

0000                     DATA_HERE       SEGMENT WORD    PUBLIC
0000  00 00 40 40               SIDE_A          DD      3.0     ; set aside space for Side A, short real
0004  00 00 80 40               SIDE_B          DD      4.0     ; set aside space for Side B, short real
0008  00 00 00 00               HYPOTENUSE      DD      0       ; set aside space for result, short real
                                                                ; 5.0 normalized = 40A00000
000C  0000                      CONTROL_WORD    DW      0       ; space for control word
000E  0000                      STATUS_WORD     DW      0       ; space for status  word
0010                     DATA_HERE       ENDS

0000                     CODE_HERE       SEGMENT WORD    PUBLIC
                                ASSUME CS:CODE_HERE, DS:DATA_HERE
                         ;                                                                  ESCAPE CODES
0000  B8 ---- R          START: MOV     AX, DATA_HERE           ; initialize data segment
0003  8E D8                     MOV     DS, AX
0005  9B DB E3                  FINIT                           ; initialize 8087            ESC 1CH, BX

0008  C7 06 000C R 03FF         MOV     CONTROL_WORD, 03FFH     ; put control word in memory
                                                                ; so 8087 can access it, round
                                                                ; to even, mask interrupts
000E  9B D9 2E 000C R           FLDCW   CONTROL_WORD            ; load control to 8087       ESC 0DH,CONTROL_WORD
0013  9B D9 06 0000 R           FLD     SIDE_A                  ; put value of SIDE_A on
                                                                ; stack top                  ESC 08H, SIDE_A
0018  9B D8 C8                  FMUL    ST, ST(0)               ; square SIDE_A              ESC 01H, AX
001B  9B D9 06 0004 R           FLD     SIDE_B                  ; get SIDE_B  stack top      ESC 08H, SIDE_B
0020  9B D8 C8                  FMUL    ST, ST(0)               ; square SIDE_B              ESC 01H, AX
0023  9B D8 C1                  FADD    ST, ST(1)               ; add A squared + B squared  ESC 00H, CX
                                                                ; result at top of stack
0026  9B D9 FA                  FSQRT                           ; take square root of ST
                                                                ; result in ST               ESC 0FH, DX
0029  9B DD 3E 000E R           FSTSW   STATUS_WORD             ; copy status word to memory
                                                                ; where 8086 can access it   ESC 2FH, STATUS_WORD
002E  9B                        FWAIT                           ; wait until status store done
002F  A1 000E R                 MOV     AX, STATUS_WORD         ; bring status to AX to check
                                                                ; for errors
0032  24 BF                     AND     AL, 0BFH                ; mask unneeded bit
0034  75 05                     JNZ     STOP                    ; handle error if found
0036  9B D9 1E 0008 R           FSTP    HYPOTENUSE              ; no error, copy result from
                                                                ; 8087 to memory              ESC 0BH, HYPOTENUSE
003B  90                 STOP:  NOP
003C                     CODE_HERE ENDS
                                END     START
```

FIGURE 11-24 8087 program to compute the hypotenuse of a right triangle.

and puts the result in ST, so ST now has A^2. Next we bring in SIDE_B and push it on the 8087 stack with the FLD SIDE_B instruction, and square it with the MUL ST, ST(0) instruction. ST now contains B^2 and ST(1) now contains A^2. We add these together and leave the result in ST with the FADD instruction. FSQRT takes the square root of the contents of ST and leaves the results in ST. To see if the result is valid, we copy the 8087 status word to the memory location we reserved for it with the FSTSW STATUS_WORD instruction. We then use 8086 instructions to check the six exception status bits to see if anything went wrong in the square root computation. If there were no exceptions (errors), these status bits will all be 0's, and the program will copy the result from ST to the memory location named HYPOTENUSE using the FSTP HYPOTENUSE instruction. We used the POP form of this instruction so that after this instruction the stack pointer is back at the same register as it was when we started. This makes it easier to keep track of which register is ST if necessary.

For the case where our test found an error had occurred, we could have program execution go to an error handling routine instead of simply to the STOP label as we did for this simple example. We have shown the ESC form for each of the instructions to give you more examples of these.

When you feel comfortable with the preceding example, read through the 8087 instruction descriptions again, and then work your way through the next example which shows you how to use the 8087 for working with trig functions.

AN 8087 TRIG FUNCTION EXAMPLE

As our second example of an 8087 program we have chosen to show you how to compute the tangent of a given angle using the 8087 FPTAN instruction. Figure 11-25*a* shows the standard reference triangle we will be using for this example, and the definitions of sine, cosine, and

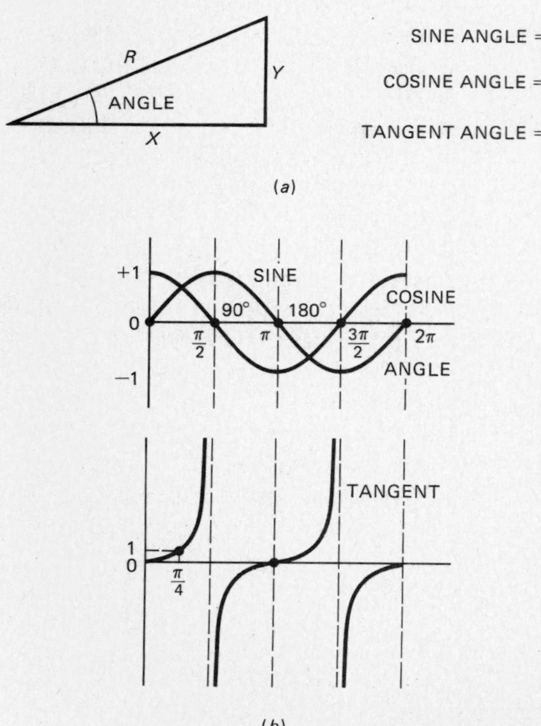

FIGURE 11-25 *(a)* Reference triangle for trigonometry examples. *(b)* Definitions of basic trigonometric functions.

tangent based on this triangle. The 8087 FPTAN instruction does not produce the tangent of a given angle directly, it produces two proportional values which represent Y and X. You then divide the Y value by the X value to produce the actual tangent value. To produce the sine and cosine values for the given angle, you can use these values of X and Y in the relationships shown in Figure 11-25*a*. Here are a few more general comments before we get into the actual program example.

To simplify the internal design of the 8087, the FPTAN instruction was designed to work only with an angle in the range $0 < \text{angle} < \pi/4$ radians (0 to 45°). Figure 11-25*b* shows graphically the values for the sine, cosine, and tangent for angles from 0 to 360°. As you can see there, the values for each function are repetitive. If you compute the values for these functions for the first octant (0–45° or 0–$\pi/4$ radians), you can determine their values for any other octant by using various simple trigonometric equations. The values for the sine of an angle in octant 4 (180 to 225°), for example, are the same as those in octant 0 except that their sign is changed. As another example, the tangent of an angle in octant 1 is equal to 1/(tan (90° − the angle)). The point of all of this is that before you can use the FPTAN instruction to find the Y and X values for an angle, you have to reduce the angle to within the range of 0–$\pi/4$ radians. The 8087 FPREM instruction is used to do this.

The FPREM instruction subtracts $\pi/4$ from ST over and over until the result in ST is less than $\pi/4$. After FPREM executes, ST contains the remainder from these subtractions, and bits C0, C3, and C1 of the status word contain a 3-bit binary number which indicates the number of times $\pi/4$ had to be subtracted from the original angle. The number in these status bits then tells you what octant the original angle was in. You use this octant information to tell you which formula you use to compute the desired value for the angle. For example, suppose that you are computing the sine of an angle, and the status bits tell you that the angle is in octant 4. You then know that you have to change the sign of the result produced by $Y/\sqrt{X^2+Y^2}$ to get the correct sine for the angle, because as shown in Figure 11-25*b*, sines in octant 4 are negative.

Finally, you have to check if the remainder left in ST after the FPREM instruction is zero. You need to do this because the FPTAN instruction will not work for a value of exactly 0 in ST. Now, let's look at our example program in Figure 11-26.

In order to keep this example short so you don't get lost in trigonometric manipulations, we require that the input angle be in the range of 0 to $\pi/2$ radians (0–90°). If you need to expand this example to work with other angles, use the identities from a standard trig text to help you.

In the data segment of the program in Figure 11-26 we set aside memory spaces for the status word and for the values we want to calculate. Since we set aside double word spaces with the DD directive, the 8087 assembler will convert results to short-real format before writing them to these spaces. We also declare here the value of $\pi/4$ which will be used by the FPREM instruction. We could have calculated this value with the 8087, but we

```
IBM Personal Computer MACRO Assembler   Version 2.00    Page    1-1
                                                                05-21-85
                                        page ,132
                                        ;8087 PROGRAM SECTION
                                        ;ABSTRACT       :This program section uses an 8087 to compute the tangent
                                        ;                of an angle in the range of 0<angle<pi/2 radians.
                                        ;                The angle, expressed in radians, is assumed to be in a
                                        ;                memory location named ANGLE.
                                        ;                The program also produces values for Y and X,
                                        ;                the opposite and adjacent sides of a right
                                        ;                triangle with the given angle. These Y and X values can
                                        ;                be used to compute the SINE and COSINE of the given angle.


 0000                                   DATA_HERE SEGMENT WORD
 0000  0000                                     STATUS      DW 0
                                                                                        ; Reserve space for status word
 0002  35 C2 68 21 A2 DA                        PI_OVER_4   DT 3FFEC90FDAA22168C235R    ; Temporary real form for Pi/4
       0F C9 FE 3F
 000C  00 00 00 3F                              ANGLE       DD 0.5                      ; Angle to be processed, 0.5 Radians
 0010  00 00 00 00                              X           DD 0                        ; Space for X value for angle
 0014  00 00 00 00                              Y           DD 0                        ; Space for Y value for angle
                                                                                        ; Normalized results X=3FBC7A43 Y=3F4DEE7A
 0018  00 00 00 00                              TANGENT     DD 0                        ; Space for Tangent of angle 0.5 radians
                                                                                        ; Tan 0.5r = 0.546; normalized = 3F0BDA7B
 001C  00 00 00 00                              SINE        DD 0                        ; Space for SINE of angle
 0020  00 00 00 00                              COSINE      DD 0                        ; Space for COSINE of angle
 0024                                   DATA_HERE ENDS


 0000                                   CODE_HERE SEGMENT WORD
                                                ASSUME CS:CODE_HERE, DS:DATA_HERE


 0000  B8 ---- R                        START:  MOV AX, DATA_HERE       ; Initialize data segment register
 0003  8E D8                                    MOV DS, AX
 0005  9B DB E3                                 FINIT                   ; Initialize 8087
 0008  9B DB 2E 0002 R                          FLD     PI_OVER_4       ; PI/4 to ST from memory
 000D  9B D9 06 000C R                          FLD     ANGLE           ; ANGLE to ST, PI/4 in ST(1)
 0012  9B D9 F8                                 FPREM                   ; Reduce angle to range 0 to pi/4,
                                                                        ; result in ST
 0015  9B DD 3E 0000 R                          FSTSW   STATUS          ; Check status to determine octant
 001A  9B                                       FWAIT
 001B  A1 0000 R                                MOV  AX, STATUS         ; Bring to register to check
 001E  F6 C4 02                                 TEST AH, 00000010B      ; Bit 1 = 0 if octant 0 (0 - pi/4)
                                                                        ; Bit 1 = 1 if octant 1 (pi/4-pi/2)
 0021  74 2A                                    JZ      OCTANT_0        ; If octant 0, go check for 0, do Tangent
 0023  9B D9 E4                                 FTST                    ; Else, Test for result from FREM = 0.
                                                                        ; FPTAN will not work with value of 0
 0026  9B DD 3E 0000 R                          FSTSW   STATUS          ; Status word to memory
 002B  9B                                       FWAIT
 002C  A1 0000 R                                MOV  AX, STATUS         ; Copy to register to check
 002F  F6 C4 40                                 TEST AH, 01000000B      ; Bit 6 = 1 if result from FTST = 0
 0032  75 5B                                    JNZ  ANGLE_45           ; Go load values for ANGLE = 45 degrees
 0034  9B DE E9                                 FSUB                    ; Else subtract angle from pi/4 for octant 1
 0037  9B D9 F2                                 FPTAN                   ; X value put in ST, Y value put in ST(1)
 003A  9B D9 16 0010 R                          FST X                   ; Copy X value to memory for SIN and COS
```

```
003F  9B D9 C9                    FXCH                  ; Swap ST and ST(1) to get Y in ST
0042  9B D9 16 0014 R             FST Y                 ; Copy Y value to memory for SIN and COS
0047  9B DE F9                    FDIV                  ; Divide X value in ST(1) by Y value in ST
                                                        ; To give Tangent for octant 1 angle in ST

004A  EB 67 90                    JMP STORE_TAN
004D                        OCTANT_0:
004D  9B D9 E4                    FTST                  ; Test for result from FREM = 0. FPTAN
                                                        ; will not work with value of 0

0050  9B DD 3E 0000 R             FSTSW    STATUS       ; Status word to memory
0055  9B                          FWAIT
0056  A1 0000 R                   MOV  AX, STATUS       ; Copy to register to check
0059  F6 C4 40                    TEST AH, 01000000B    ; Bit 6 = 1 if result from FTST = 0
005C  75 19                       JNZ  ANGLE_0          ; Go load values for ANGLE = 0
005E  9B D9 F2                    FPTAN                 ; X value put in ST, Y value put in ST(1)
0061  9B D9 16 0010 R             FST X                 ; Copy X value to memory for SIN and COS
0066  9B D9 C9                    FXCH                  ; Swap ST and ST(1) to get Y in ST
0069  9B D9 16 0014 R             FST Y                 ; Copy Y value to memory for SIN and COS
006E  9B D9 C9                    FXCH                  ; Put X back in ST and Y in ST(1)
0071  9B DE F9                    FDIV                  ; Divide Y value in ST(1) by X value in ST
                                                        ; to give Tangent for octant 0 angle in ST

0074  EB 3D 90                    JMP STORE_TAN
0077                        ANGLE_0:
0077  9B D9 E8                    FLD1                  ; Load one in ST
007A  9B D9 1E 0020 R             FSTP COSINE           ; Copy to memory reserved for COSINE
007F  9B D9 EE                    FLDZ                  ; Load zero in ST
0082  9B D9 16 001C R             FST  SINE             ; Copy to memory reserved for SINE
0087  9B D9 16 0018 R             FST  TANGENT          ; Copy to memory reserved for TANGENT
008C  EB 2A 90                    JMP DONE
008F                        ANGLE_45:
008F  9B D9 E8                    FLD1                  ; Load 1 in ST
0092  9B D9 16 0018 R             FST  TANGENT          ; Tangent of 45 degrees is 1
0097  9B D9 E8                    FLD1                  ; ST and ST(1) now 1
009A  9B DE C1                    FADD                  ; ST now = 2
009D  9B DD D1                    FST ST(1)             ; ST(1) now = 2
00A0  9B D9 FA                    FSQRT                 ; ST now = square root of 2
00A3  9B D8 F1                    FDIV  ST, ST(1)       ; ST now = (square root 2)/2 = sin 45
00A6  9B D9 16 001C R             FST  SINE             ; Copy to memory reserved for SINE
00AB  9B D9 16 0020 R             FST  COSINE           ; Copy to memory reserved for COSINE
00B0  EB 06 90                    JMP  DONE
00B3                        STORE_TAN:
00B3  9B D9 16 0018 R             FST TANGENT           ; Copy computed Tangent value to memory
00B8                        DONE:
00B8  90                          NOP
00B9  90                          NOP
00BA  90                          NOP
00BB                        CODE_HERE  ENDS
                                          END START
```

FIGURE 11-26 8087 program to compute the tangent of an angle.

did it this way to show you how temporary-real numbers can be declared with a DT directive.

In the code segment of the program we first initialize the data segment register and the 8087. We then load $\pi/4$ and the angle we want to compute the values for, reduce the angle to within range with the FPREM instruction as described before, and check the status word to determine what octant the angle is in. Remember from our previous example program that you check the 8087 status word by first having the 8087 write the status word to a memory location with the FSTSW STATUS instruction. You then read this status word and check it with 8086 instructions. Since we have limited the input angle to be in either octant 0 or octant 1, we only have to check bit C1 of the status word. To do this we copy the status word to a register with the MOV AX, STATUS instruction, and check bit C1 with the TEST AH, 00000010B instruction. The 8086 TEST instruction, remember, ANDs the specified source and destination. Flags are affected, but the operands are not.

If the result of the TEST was 0, we know the angle is in octant 0, so we jump to the program section which deals with octant 0 angles. If the result of the TEST was not 0, then we know the angle is in octant 1, and process it accordingly. Let's start with how we handle an angle in octant 0.

For an octant 0 angle we first use the 8087 FTST instruction to check if the result left in ST by the FPREM instruction is zero. FTST will not change the contents of ST, but it will affect the flags in the 8087 status register. With the FSTSW STATUS instruction we then copy the 8087 status register out to memory where we can get at it. Bit 6 of the upper byte of the status word will be a 1 after FTST if the value in ST is 0. If we find that ST is zero for an octant 0 angle, we know that the angle is zero. The sine, cosine, and tangent values for 0 are known constants. Therefore, for this case we simply load these values one at a time into the 8087 ST register, and copy them to the appropriate memory locations. The cosine of 0, for example, is 1, so we simply load 1 into ST with the FLD1 instruction and copy this value to memory with the FST COSINE instruction. If we find that the result of FPREM in ST is not 0, we go and compute its tangent ratio with FPTAN.

FPTAN, remember, does not give the value for tangent directly, it gives two numbers whose ratio is equal to the tangent of the angle. We call these two values Y and X as shown in Figure 11-25*a*. This form of result is actually more useful than having just a tangent result, because you can use the X and Y values to compute the sine and cosine of the angle as shown. To save the X and Y values for these computations, we first copy X from ST to memory with the FST X instruction. We then exchange ST and ST(1) with the FXCH instruction. The Y value is now at ST. We copy Y to memory with the FST Y instruction, and then put X and Y back in their original position with another FXCH instruction. To get the actual tangent value we divide the Y in ST(1) by the X in ST with the FDIV instruction. The result of the division is left in ST where we can copy it to memory with an FST TANGENT instruction. Now let's look at how we handle an octant 1 angle.

Again for octant 1, the first thing we have to do is to check if the result left in ST by the FPREM instruction is 0. If it is, we know that the angle is $\pi/2$ or 45°. Again, the sine, cosine, and tangent for this angle are known constants which we can just calculate and load into the reserved memory locations. If the value left in ST by FPREM is not 0, we go on and compute the tangent ratio. The computation in this case is a little less direct.

The formula we use to compute the tangent of an angle in octant 1 is: tangent angle $= 1/(\text{tangent } ((\pi/4) - R)$, where R is the remainder left in ST after FPREM executes. This looks messy, but it is really quite simple because of the way the 8087 works. Since at this point in our calculations R is in ST and $\pi/4$ is in ST(1), we can do the needed subtraction with the FSUB instruction. The result of this subtraction will be in ST. We then use the FPTAN instruction to find the Y and X values for this result. After storing the X and Y values as we do for octant 0, we leave out the final FXCH instruction that we use there. This leaves the X value in ST(1) and the Y value in ST. Therefore, when we do the FDIV instruction, we really are dividing the X value by the Y value. This gives the reciprocal we need to satisfy our equation. The tangent value for the octant 1 angle will then be left in ST where we can copy it to memory with an FST TANGENT instruction. For your reference we have shown the short-real values produced by this program for an angle of 0.5 radians.

Hopefully, by now you have some understanding of how the 8087 works and can write some programs of your own. To debug 8087 programs, you may find it helpful to insert extra store instructions to copy intermediate results out to reserved memory locations where you can get at them to see if they are correct. The extra store instructions can be removed when the program works. If you are going to be writing programs where you need extensive 8087 sections, there are several commercially available 8087 software packages. These packages contain 8087 routines which you can simply link into your assembly or higher level language programs.

MULTIPLE BUS MICROCOMPUTER SYSTEMS

In a previous section of this chapter we discussed how a coprocessor can be connected on the local buses of a microcomputer to increase its computing power. In another section of this chapter we discussed how several different function boards can be connected on the local bus of the IBM PC to customize and extend its capabilities. The amount that you can add to a system using this approach, however, is limited. In both of these cases the coprocessor or peripheral boards borrow the local buses from the main microprocessor on a DMA basis as needed. When the coprocessor or peripheral board is using the buses, the main microprocessor is just sitting in a hold state doing nothing. Therefore, if you add too many DMA operations, you soon start to slow down the main processor. The thought might occur to you to simply add another main processor, another 8086 for example, on the local buses to increase the computing power. Since only one main processor on the local buses could be active at a time, this does not gain anything for you. There are several ways, however, that two or more standard microprocessors can be used in a system.

One major approach is to set up each microprocessor as essentially a stand-alone microcomputer with its own RAM, ROM, ports, and local buses. These separate microcomputer boards then communicate with each other and with shared resources such as a hard disk drive using a separate system bus. Figure 11-27 shows a block diagram of this type of multiprocessor system.

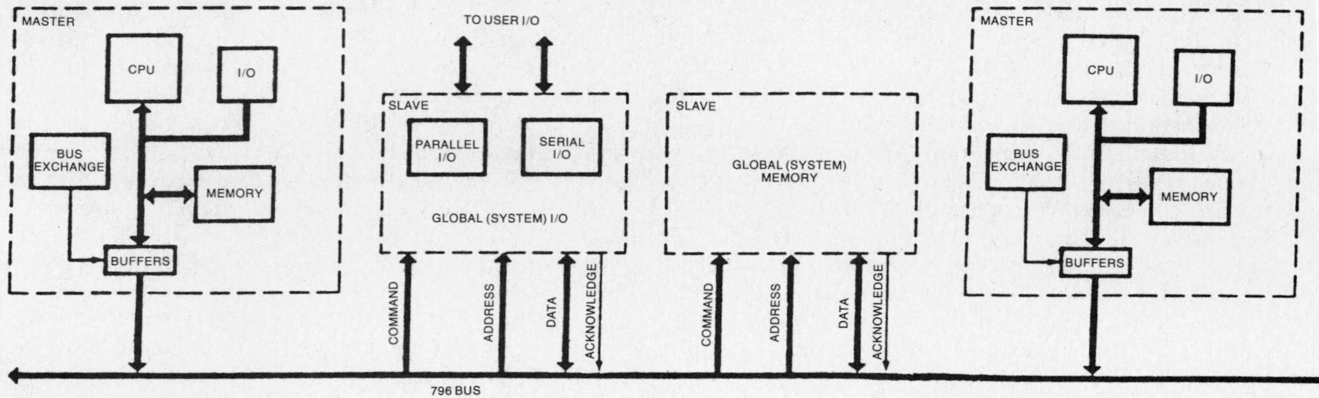

FIGURE 11-27 Multiprocessor bused system. (Intel Corporation)

The principle here is that each processor board can operate independently, fetching and executing its own instructions from its on-board memory, until it needs to access some shared resource such as the system memory, printer, or I/O board. This type of system is often referred to as a *loosely coupled* system. Each board which can take over and use the bus is called a *bus master*. A board which can only be written to or read from is called a *bus slave*.

A question that may occur to you at this point is, "What happens if two or more masters on the system bus try to use the bus at the same time?" The answer to this question is that the system must contain logic which in some way "arbitrates" the dispute and makes sure only one master at a time asserts its control signals on the bus. Later we will show you in detail some ways in which this is done. For now we will start with an overview of a commonly used system bus so you have an idea about how it operates.

The Intel Multibus—IEEE 796 Bus Standard

There are many different microcomputer system buses currently in use. Almost every microprocessor and microcomputer manufacturer has its own bus standard, so it is not possible here to give even a survey of the different ones. We have chosen to discuss the Intel Multibus because several hundred companies make several thousand different boards using this standard, and because it fits in with the devices and systems we are working with in the rest of this book. This bus standard was developed and evolved by Intel and later adopted by IEEE as Bus Standard 796.

The basic IEEE 796 standard defines the signals for two printed circuit board edge connectors, an 86-pin connector referred to as P1 and a 60-pin connector referred to as P2. Figure 11-28 shows the signal names and numbers for these connectors. Figure 11-29 shows a block diagram for part of a single-board computer that might be used as a master on the Multibus. Keep copies of these two figures handy to refer to as we discuss how all of this works.

Whenever you are confronted with a long list of pin names such as that in Figure 11-28, start with the easily recognizable groups of signal lines and work your way down to the toughies. For the Multibus 86-pin P1 connector, start with the power supply and ground connections on pins 1–12 and 75–86. This knocks off 24 pins. Next check out the 16 data lines labeled DATA*–DAT1* on pins 59–74. The * after each of these signal names indicates that these signals are active low (inverted) on the Multibus. Note in Figure 11-29 that there are three sets of buffers on the data lines. Device *A*44, on the left side, buffers the local data bus for the 8-bit peripheral devices. Buffers *A*60 and *A*61 in the right center of the diagram buffer the local data bus for the dual-port RAM. Two bidirectional inverting buffers, *A*69 and *A*89, are used to interface these local RAM data lines to the Multibus. Due to a lack of space, the on-board ROM, ROM data-bus buffers, and ROM decoder are not shown in Figure 11-29.

Next look for the address lines on the Multibus connectors. Sixteen address lines, ADRE*–ADR1*, are on pins 43–58 of the P1 connector. Four more address lines, AD10*–AD13*, are on pins 28, 30, 32, and 34. Four more address lines, ADR14*–ADR17*, are bused on pins 55–58 of the P2 connector. These 24 address lines make it possible for the bus to address up to 16 Mbytes of memory. For many systems we use simple inverting buffers to interface the on-board local bus to these address lines. In some systems, however, we want both the on-board CPU and another master on the bus to be able to access on-board RAM. In this case we use bidirectional buffers on the address lines so that addresses for RAM can be sent from the board to the Multibus, or come from the Multibus to the on-board memory. RAM which is accessible from two directions in this way is called *dual-port RAM*. Note in Figure 11-29 that devices *A*42 and *A*58 are used to buffer the local address bus to the RAM. Bidirectional devices *A*86, *A*87, and *A*88 are used to buffer address lines to and from the Multibus.

Next observe the eight interrupt request lines, INT0*–INT7*, on pins 35–42 of the P1 connector. These lines can be routed to the inputs of a processor or an 8259A on one of the master boards so that a slave board or another master board down the bus can interrupt that master when it needs attention. This is indicated by the wirewrap interrupt jumper matrix in the lower right corner of Figure 11-29.

P1

	Pin	(Component Side)		Pin	(Circuit Side)	
		Mnemonic	Description		Mnemonic	Description
Power Supplies	1	GND	Signal GND	2	GND	Signal GND
	3	+5V	+5Vdc	4	+5V	+5Vdc
	5	+5V	+5Vdc	6	+5V	+5Vdc
	7	+12V	+12Vdc	8	+12V	+12Vdc
	9		Reserved, bussed	10		Reserved, bussed
	11	GND	Signal GND	12	GND	Signal GND
Bus Controls	13	BCLK*	Bus Clock	14	INIT*	Initialize
	15	BPRN*	Bus Pri. In	16	BPRO*	Bus Pri. Out
	17	BUSY*	Bus Busy	18	BREQ*	Bus Request
	19	MRDC*	Mem Read Cmd	20	MWTC*	Mem Write Cmd
	21	IORC*	I/O Read Cmd	22	IOWC*	I/O Write Cmd
	23	XACK*	XFER Acknowledge	24	INH1*	Inhibit 1 (disable RAM)
Bus	25	LOCK*	Lock	26	INH2*	Inhibit 2 (disable PROM or ROM)
Controls and Address	27	BHEN*	Byte High Enable	28	AD10*	
	29	CBRQ*	Common Bus Request	30	AD11*	Address
	31	CCLK*	Constant CLK	32	AD12*	Bus
	33	INTA*	Intr Acknowledge	34	AD13*	
Interrupts	35	INT6*	Parallel	36	INT7*	Parallel
	37	INT4*	Interrupt	38	INT5*	Interrupt
	39	INT2*	Requests	40	INT3*	Requests
	41	INT0*		42	INT1*	
Address	43	ADRE*		44	ADRF*	
	45	ADRC*		46	ADRD*	
	47	ADRA*	Address	48	ADRB*	Address
	49	ADR8*	Bus	50	ADR9*	Bus
	51	ADR6*		52	ADR7*	
	53	ADR4*		54	ADR5*	
	55	ADR2*		56	ADR3*	
	57	ADR0*		58	ADR1*	
Data	59	DATA*		60	DATF*	
	61	DATC*		62	DATD*	
	63	DATA*	Data	64	DATB*	Data
	65	DAT8*	Bus	66	DAT9*	Bus
	67	DAT6*		68	DAT7*	
	69	DAT4*		70	DAT5*	
	71	DAT2*		72	DAT3*	
	73	DAT0*		74	DAT1*	
Power Supplies	75	GND	Signal GND	76	GND	Signal GND
	77		Reserved, Bussed	78		Reserved, bussed
	79	−12V	−12Vdc	80	−12V	−12Vdc
	81	+5V	+5Vdc	82	+5V	+5Vdc
	83	+5V	+5Vdc	84	+5V	+5Vdc
	85	GND	Signal GND	86	GND	Signal GND

P2

	Pin	(Component Side)		Pin	(Circuit Side)	
		Mnemonic	Description		Mnemonic	Description
	1		Reserved, Not Bussed	2		Reserved, Not Bussed
	3		Reserved, Not Bussed	4		Reserved, Not Bussed
	5		Reserved, Not Bussed	6		Reserved, Not Bussed
	7		Reserved, Not Bussed	8		Reserved, Not Bussed
	9		Reserved, Not Bussed	10		Reserved, Not Bussed
	11		Reserved, Not Bussed	12		Reserved, Not Bussed
	13		Reserved, Not Bussed	14		Reserved, Not Bussed
	15		Reserved, Not Bussed	16		Reserved, Not Bussed
	17		Reserved, Not Bussed	18		Reserved, Not Bussed
	19		Reserved, Not Bussed	20		Reserved, Not Bussed
	21		Reserved, Not Bussed	22		Reserved, Not Bussed
	23		Reserved, Not Bussed	24		Reserved, Not Bussed
	25		Reserved, Not Bussed	26		Reserved, Not Bussed
	27		Reserved, Not Bussed	28		Reserved, Not Bussed
	29		Reserved, Not Bussed	30		Reserved, Not Bussed
	31		Reserved, Not Bussed	32		Reserved, Not Bussed
	33		Reserved, Not Bussed	34		Reserved, Not Bussed
	35		Reserved, Not Bussed	36		Reserved, Not Bussed
	37		Reserved, Not Bussed	38		Reserved, Not Bussed
	39		Reserved, Not Bussed	40		Reserved, Not Bussed
	41		Reserved, Bussed	42		Reserved, Bussed
	43		Reserved, Bussed	44		Reserved, Bussed
	45		Reserved, Bussed	46		Reserved, Bussed
	47		Reserved, Bussed	48		Reserved, Bussed
	49		Reserved, Bussed	50		Reserved, Bussed
	51		Reserved, Bussed	52		Reserved, Bussed
	53		Reserved, Bussed	54		Reserved, Bussed
Address	55	ADR16*	Address Bus	56	ADR17*	Address Bus
	57	ADR14*		58	ADR15*	
	59		Reserved, Bussed	60		Reserved, Bussed

All Reserved Pins are reserved for future use and should not be used if upwards compatibility is desired.

FIGURE 11-28 Pin assignments for bus signals on IEEE 796 (Multibus) P1 and P2 connectors. (Intel Corporation)

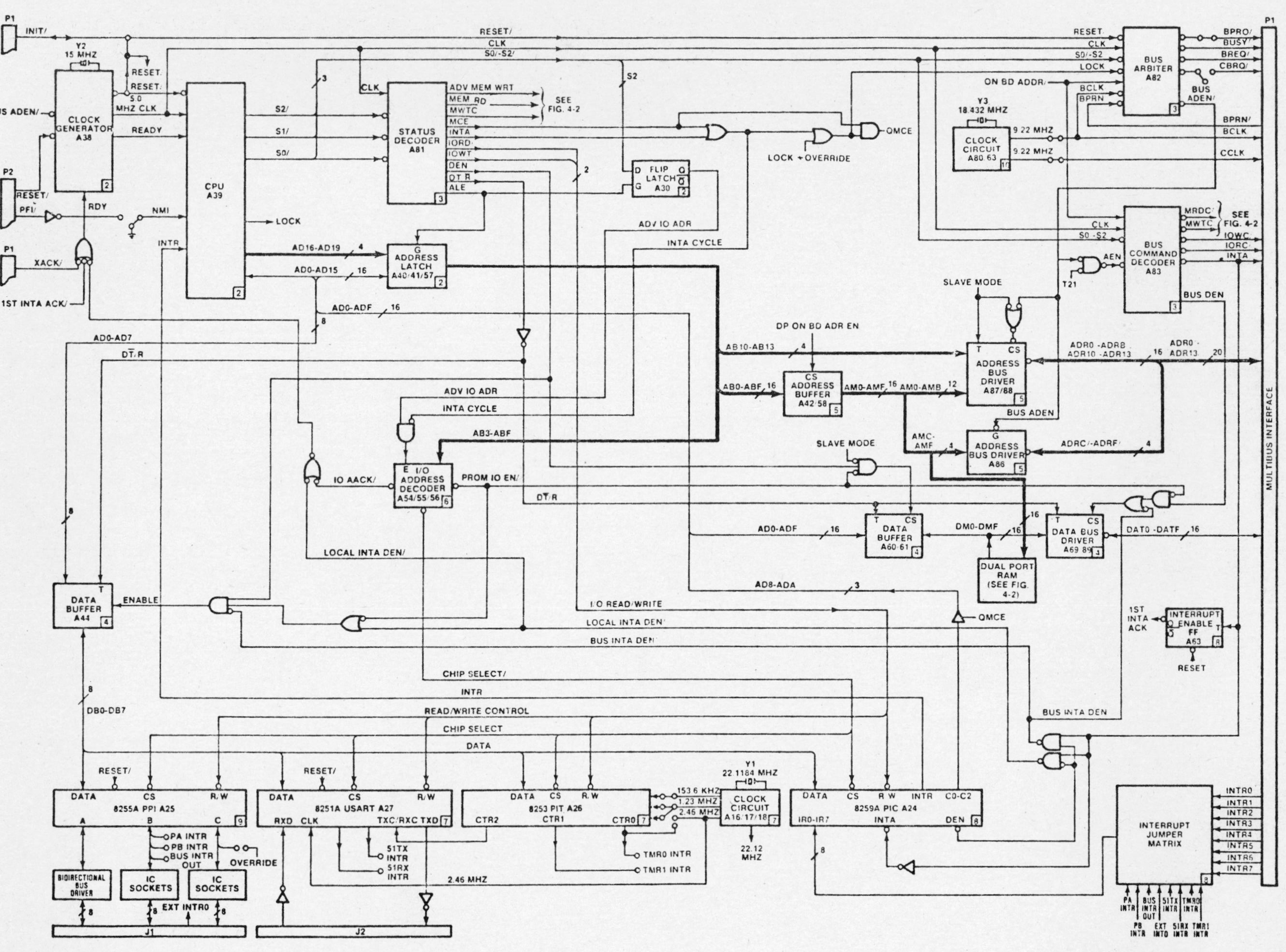

FIGURE 11-29 Block diagram of circuitry on a typical Multibus master board.

Now that we have found the address and data bus connections, let's see how the control-bus read and write signals are produced. The 8086 here is operating in MAX mode so device *A*81, an 8288 controller, is used to produce the control-bus signals for on-board operations. Another 8288, device *A*83 on the right side of the diagram, is used to produce the control-bus signals needed when this board writes to or reads from another board on the Multibus. The control signals produced by this device connect to Multibus pins 19—22 and 33. The transfer of data from, for example, a memory board on the bus to a master is nearly identical to a transfer from local memory to the CPU. The master outputs the desired address on the Multibus, and the controller outputs a memory-read command, MRDC*. The addressed location on the memory board is enabled, and puts its data on the Multibus to be returned to the CPU on the master board which has control of the bus.

The last major group of signals on the Multibus are those which transfer control of the Multibus from one master to another. The signals in this group are BCLK*, BPRN*, BPRO*, BUSY*, BREQ*, and CBRQ*. In our example system in Figure 11-29, these signals are for the most part produced and interpreted by an 8289 bus arbiter, device *A*82, in the upper right corner. In a later section we show you how these signals interact when two masters exchange control of the bus. For now we will make some comments about the few remaining signals on the bus.

The INIT* signal on pin 14 can be used to reset all of the master and slave boards on the bus. It is usually driven by circuitry on the highest priority master. The INTA* signal is produced by the 8288 bus-controller device in response to an interrupt request. An I/O board on the bus, for example, might send an interrupt request on the bus to our master board in Figure 11-29. The master board, when ready, might assert INTA* on the bus to tell an 8259A on the I/O board to send back the desired interrupt type to the master board on the system data bus. The inhibit signals, INH1* and INH2*, on pins 24 and 26, can be used to disable a block of memory in the system. You might, for example, want to have ROM in a particular address space when the system is first turned on, and later have RAM in that address space. These signals can be used to do this. Finally, note the transfer-acknowledge signal, XACK*, on pin 23 of the Multibus. In our example system in Figure 11-29 this signal is connected to the READY input logic of the 8284 in the upper left corner. This connection allows an addressed memory or peripheral on the bus to make the 8086 insert WAIT states until it has accepted or output valid data. Now, we will show you how a master can gain control of the bus.

Arbitrating and Transferring Bus Control

When two or more masters share a bus such as the Multibus, some mechanism must be used to settle the argument when two masters want to use the bus at the same time. The Multibus can use either a serial priority scheme or a parallel priority scheme to do this.

Figure 11-30*a* shows how three masters are connected for the serial priority arbitration scheme. The key here is that, in order for a master board to take over the bus, its bus priority input, BPRN/, must be asserted low. The highest priority master has its BPRN/ input tied to ground, so it can take over the Multibus anytime it needs to. If the highest priority master does not need to use the bus, it will assert its bus priority output, BPRO/, low. This will assert the BPRN/ of the next lower priority master so it can take over the bus if it needs to. If the second priority master does not need to use the bus, it asserts its BPRO/ output low. This enables the lowest priority master to use the bus if it needs to. If a low priority master is using the bus and a higher priority master needs to use the bus, the lower priority master will be allowed to finish transferring its current byte or word, and then the higher priority master will take control.

Figure 11-30*b* shows the connections for a parallel priority scheme. This scheme uses the bus request signals, BREQ/, from each master, and the BPRN/ signals to each master. Here again, the BPRN/ input of a master must be asserted low in order for that master to be able to take control of the Multibus. Here's how this scheme works. When a master needs to use the bus to transfer some data, it asserts its BREQ/ signal. This signal, along with bus-request signals from other masters, goes into the inputs of a priority encoder. The priority encoder will output a 3-bit code which represents the highest numbered input that is asserted low. The 3-bit code from the 74LS148 is connected to the select inputs of a 74LS138 one-of-eight-low decoder. The result of all of this is that the 74LS138 will assert the BPRN/ input of the highest priority master requesting service. When this master finishes its data transfer, it raises its BREQ/ signal high. The 74LS138 will then assert the BPRN/ input of the next highest priority master requesting use of the bus. Now we will show you how bus control gets transferred from one master to another in an orderly manner.

Figure 11-31 shows the signal waveforms for transfer of control of the Multibus from a lower priority master (*A*) to a higher priority master (*B*). Keep a copy of Figure 11-29 handy as we work through these waveforms with you.

The bus-control transfer process starts when the CPU on the higher priority master, *B*, outputs an address which is not decoded on that board. This off-board address causes a signal labeled ON BD ADDR/ to be sent to the system-bus-request input of the 8289 bus arbiter, telling it to attempt to take over the bus. Refer to the top right corner of Figure 11-29 to see how these signals are connected. On the waveforms in Figure 11-31 this signal is referred to as TRANSFER REQUEST/. In response to this request, the 8289 asserts its BREQ/ output low. Assuming we are using a parallel priority scheme as described before, the priority encoder-decoder will then unassert the BPRN/ input of master *A* and assert the BPRN/ input of master *B* as shown in the waveforms.

While master *A* is using the bus for a data transfer, it holds the BUSY/ line on the Multibus low. The BUSY/ line is an open-collector line which any master can pull low when it is using the bus. No other master can actually

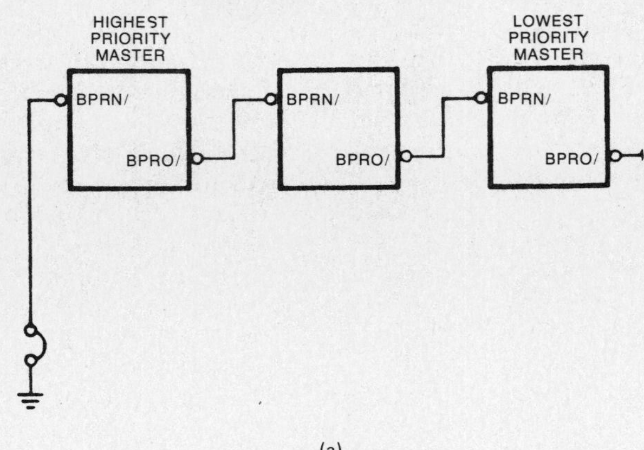

(a)

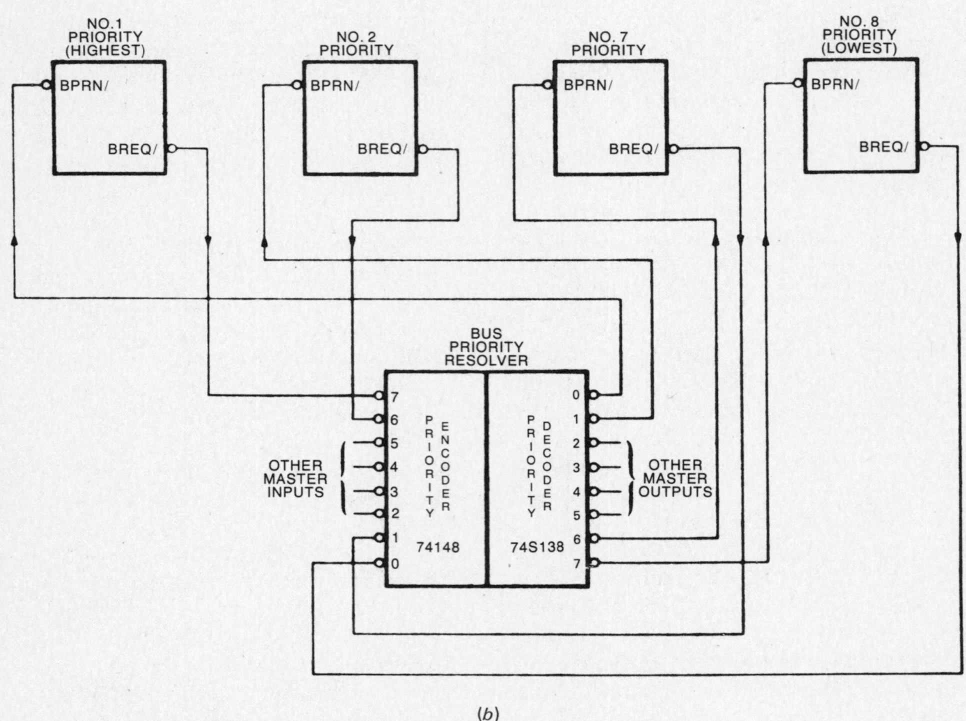

(b)

FIGURE 11-30 Serial and parallel priority resolution circuitry for Multibus systems *(a)* Serial. *(b)* Parallel. (Intel Corporation)

take over the bus until the master currently using the bus releases the BUSY/ line. After master *A* finishes transferring data it disables its address, data, and control buffers connected to the Multibus, and releases the BUSY/ line. Master *B* then pulls the BUSY/ line low to let other masters know that the bus is in use. Master *B* next enables its buffers to output address and control signals on the Multibus for its data transfer. In normal operation a master releases the bus after each byte or word data transfer so that a high priority master cannot prevent lower priority masters from ever having a turn.

In some cases, however, we want a master to be able to transfer several bytes or words of data needed for an instruction without interleaving with other masters. The way this is done is with a bus-lock mechanism. Observe in Figure 11-29 that the bus arbiter device has an input labeled LOCK. If a master has control of the bus, the bus arbiter will hold the BUSY/ line on the Multibus low as long as the LOCK input is asserted. As we described above, this prevents any other masters from taking a turn on the bus. The LOCK signal for the 8289 bus arbiter can come from one of several sources on the board, but the main source we are concerned with here is the LOCK output of the 8086.

Note in Figure 11-29 that, when the 8086 is set to operate in maximum mode, pin 29 outputs a signal

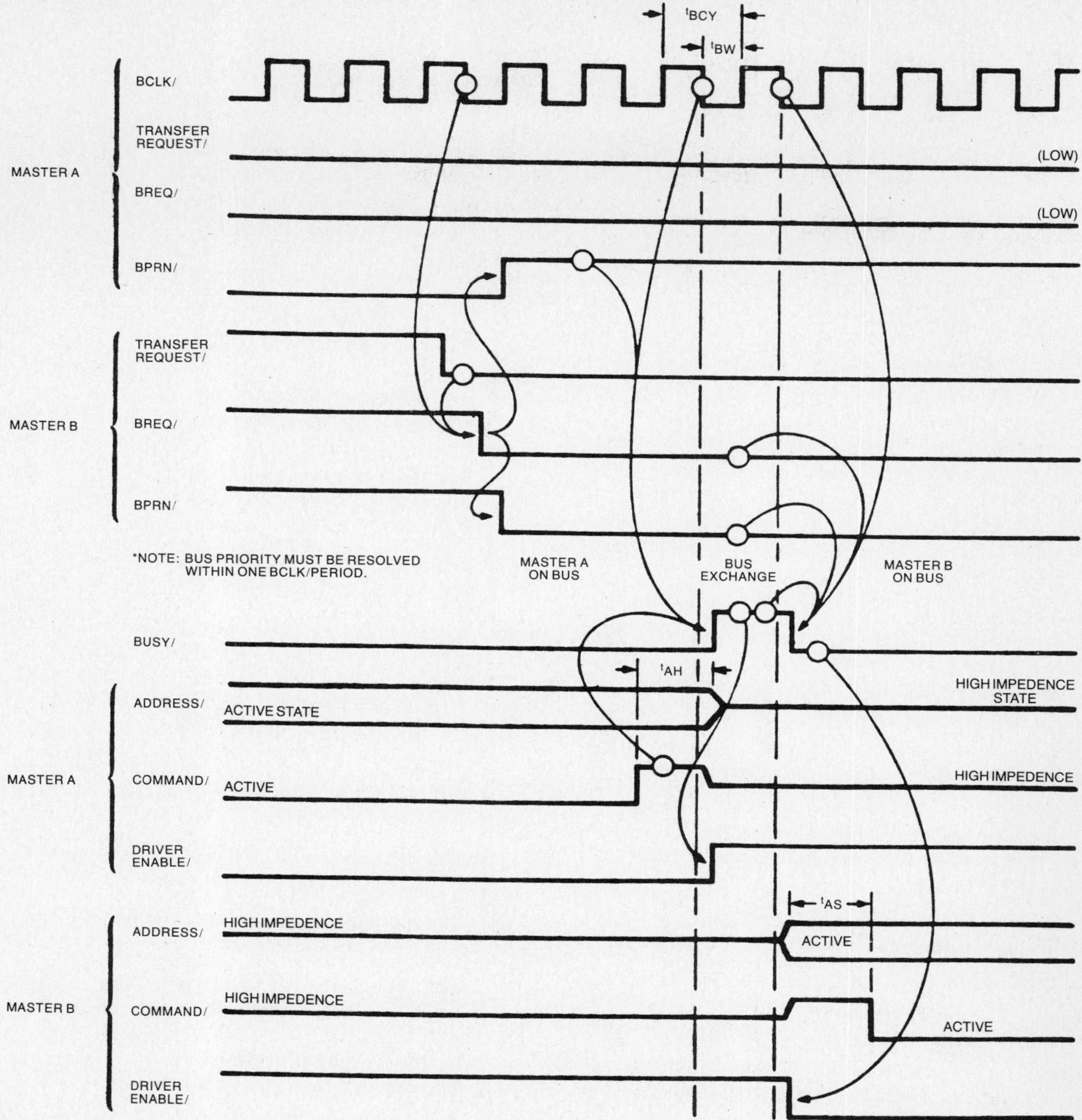

FIGURE 11-31 Signal waveforms for transfer of control of Multibus from a lower priority master to a higher priority master. (Intel Corporation)

called LOCK. The 8086 will assert this signal when it executes an instruction which has a LOCK prefix in front of it. An example of this type of instruction is LOCK XCHG AL, FLAG. When this instruction is assembled, the code for the LOCK prefix, 111000, will be put in before the code for the XCHG instruction. The XCHG instruction takes two bus cycles, one to read in the byte from the memory location named FLAG on a shared memory board, and another to copy AL to the memory location. Without the LOCK mechanism, another master on the Multibus might take over the bus between the two operations and read the old value of FLAG, rather than the new value that you are trying to put there with the XCHG AL, FLAG instruction.

This section has shown you how several processor boards can share a common bus in a harmonious manner. In Chapter 13 we show you how several complete computers can be networked together to communicate and share a common data base.

IMPORTANT TERMS AND CONCEPTS FROM THIS CHAPTER

8086 maximum mode

DMA
  DMA channel
  8237 DMA controller

Motherboard and system expansion slots

DRAM
  Refresh—burst and distributed modes
  $\overline{RAS}$ and $\overline{CAS}$ strobes

8208 DRAM controller IC

Error detecting and correcting
  Hard and soft errors
  Parity check
  Hamming codes
  Syndrome word

80186/80188—integrated peripherals

Tightly coupled multiprocessor system

8087 math coprocessor
  data types and terms
  Word, short, and long integers
  Packed decimals
  Short-, long-, and temporary-reals
  Fixed-point numbers
  Floating-point numbers
  Normalizing
  Significand, mantissa, exponent
  Single- and double-precision representation
  Offset form

8087 control and status words

Multiple bus microprocessor systems
  loosely coupled system
  Intel Multibus—796 bus standard
  Bus master and bus slave

Dual-port RAM

Serial and parallel bus arbitration schemes

REVIEW QUESTIONS AND PROBLEMS

1. Describe how the control-bus signals are produced for an 8086 system operating in maximum mode.
2. Why is DMA data transfer faster than doing the same data transfer with program instructions?
3. Describe the series of actions that a DMA controller will do after it receives a request from a peripheral device to transfer data from the peripheral device to memory.
4. Describe how the 20-bit memory address for a DMA transfer is produced by the circuit in Figure 11-3.
5. Describe the function and operation of devices *U*5 and *U*6 in Figure 11-3.
6. Why are microcomputers such as the IBM PC designed with peripheral expansion slots instead of having functions such as a CRT controller designed into the motherboard?
7. List the series of signals that must occur to read a data word from a dynamic RAM such as the 51C256H.
8. List the major tasks that must be done when using dynamic RAM in a microcomputer system.
9. How does a dynamic RAM controller, in a system such as that in Figure 11-10, arbitrate the dispute that occurs when you attempt to read from or write to a bank of dynamic RAMs while the controller is doing a refresh cycle?
10. Describe how parity is used to check for RAM data errors in microcomputers such as the IBM PC. What is a major shortcoming of the parity method of error detection?
11. When using a Hamming code error detection/correction scheme for DRAMs, how many encoding bits must be added to detect and correct a single-bit error in a 32-bit data word?
12. List the peripheral functions integrated into the Intel 80186 microprocessor.
13. Describe the function of the relocation register in the 80186 peripheral control block.
14. How can you tell from the schematic that the 8088 in Figure 11-15 is configured in maximum mode?
15. Device *U*7 in Figure 11-15 has a signal named AEN connected to its OE input. If, in troubleshooting this system, you find that this signal is not getting asserted, on which schematic sheet would you first look to see how this signal is produced?
16. In what ways are a standard microprocessor and a coprocessor different from each other?
17. *a*. When a coprocessor and a standard processor are connected together in a system such as that in Figure 11-15, why are the $\overline{S2}$–$\overline{S0}$ status lines, the QS1–QS0 lines, the address, and the data lines of the two devices connected directly together?
    b. Where does the 8087 coprocessor in Figure 11-15 get its instructions from?
    c. How does the main processor distinguish its instructions from those for the 8087 as it fetches instructions from memory?
    d. Describe how the 8087 and 8088 work together to load a long-real data item from memory to the 8087 ST.

e. How does the 8087 in Figure 11-15 signal the 8088 that it needs to use the buses?

f. How can you prevent the 8088 in Figure 11-15 from going on with its next instruction before the 8087 has completed an instruction? What hardware connection in Figure 11-15 is part of this mechanism?

18. *a.* Given the decimal number 2435.5625, convert this number to binary, normalized binary, long-real, and temporary-real format.

b. Why are most floating-point numbers actually approximations?

19. *a.* Which 8087 stack register is ST after a reset?

b. Which 8087 stack register will be ST after one data item is read into the 8087?

c. Describe the operation that will be done by the 8087 FADD ST(2), ST(3) instruction.

d. How does the operation of the instruction FADDP ST(2), ST(3) differ from the operation of the instruction in 19*c*?

20. Describe the operation performed by each of the following 8087 instructions.

a. FLD TAX-RATE

b. FMUL INFLATION_FACTOR

c. FSQRT

d. FLDPI

e. FSTSW CHECK_ANSWER

f. FPTAN

21. *a.* Show the binary codes required for each of the instructions in question 20.

b. Why is 9BH, the code for the 8086 WAIT instruction, put in before most of the 8087 instructions?

c. Show the 8086 ESC instructions required to get an 8086 assembler to produce the correct codes for the instructions in question 20.

22. In the example program in Figure 11-24, why did we put a WAIT instruction after the FSTSW STATUS instruction?

23. Using the example program in Figure 11-24, write an 8087 program which computes the volume of a sphere. The formula is $V = \frac{4}{3}\pi R^3$.

24. Describe the function of the FPREM instruction in the example program in Figure 11-26.

25. Extend the example program in Figure 11-26 to calculate the sine and the cosine of the given angle in the range $0 \leq$ ANGLE $< 90°$ ($\pi/2$).

26. What are the advantages of having several microprocessors connected on a common system bus such as the Multibus? What is the major problem that has to be worked out in order for these multiple processors to exist peacefully on the common bus?

27. Name the two schemes used to determine which master on the Multibus gets control when two or more masters request use of the bus at the same time.

28. On board a master, how is the signal produced which tells the bus controller to take over the bus?

29. How can a master keep control of the bus for more than 1 byte or word access if that master is in the middle of some critical program section?

CHAPTER

12 Microcomputer System Peripherals

In the preceding chapters we discussed basic microcomputer systems and some of the programmable peripheral devices used in these systems. In this chapter we expand outward to discuss the hardware and software of system peripherals such as CRT displays, computer vision devices, disk drives, and printers.

OBJECTIVES

1. Describe how characters are produced on a CRT or an LCD screen.
2. Use BIOS calls to display a message on the CRT display of an IBM PC-compatible computer.
3. Describe how bit-mapped and vector graphic displays are produced on a CRT.
4. Describe how computer vision systems produce an image that can be stored in a digital memory.
5. Show in general terms the formats in which digital data is stored on magnetic and optical disks.
6. Describe the operation of disk controller circuitry.
7. Use DOS calls to open, read or write, and close disk files.
8. Describe the mechanism used in several common types of computer printers.
9. Describe how phoneme, formant filters, and linear predictive coding synthesizers produce human-sounding speech from a computer.
10. Describe the basic principle used in speech recognition systems.

MICROCOMPUTER DISPLAYS

Currently there are several different technologies used to display numbers, letters, and graphics for a microcomputer. The most common types are *cathode-ray tubes* (CRTs) and *liquid-crystal displays* (LCDs). In Chapter 9 we discussed the operation of alphanumeric LCD displays and a little later in this chapter we will show how large LCD screens are interfaced to a microcomputer. For now, however, we want to discuss the operation and interfacing of CRT-type displays.

Basic CRT Operation

A CRT is a large, bottle-shaped vacuum tube. The picture tube used in a TV set is an example of a CRT. An electron gun at the rear of the tube produces a beam of electrons which is directed towards the front of the tube. The inside surface of the front of the tube is coated with a phosphor substance which gives off light when it is struck by electrons. The color of the light given off is determined by the particular phosphor used. To produce color displays as in a color TV set, dots of red-, blue-, and green-producing phosphors are put on the inside of the screen in triangle patterns. Separate electron beams are focused on the dots for each color phosphor. By altering the intensity ratio of the three beams we can make the three-dot triangle appear any desired color.

The most common method of producing images on the CRT screen is to sweep the electron beam(s) back and forth across the screen. When the beam reaches the right side of the screen, it is turned off (blanked) and retraced rapidly back to the left side of the screen to start over. If the beam is slowly swept from the top of the screen to the bottom of the screen as it is swept back and forth horizontally, the entire screen appears lighted. When the beam reaches the bottom of the screen, it is blanked and rapidly retraced back to the top to start over. A display produced in this way is referred to as a *raster* display. To produce an image we turn the electron beam on or off as it sweeps across the screen. The trick here is to get the beam intensity or *video information* synchronized with the horizontal and vertical sweeping so that we get a stable display.

Black-and-white TVs in the United States use a horizontal sweep frequency of 15,750 Hz and a vertical sweep frequency of 60 Hz. One sweep of the beam from the top of the screen to the bottom is called a *field*. Sixty fields per second are then swept out. To get better pic-

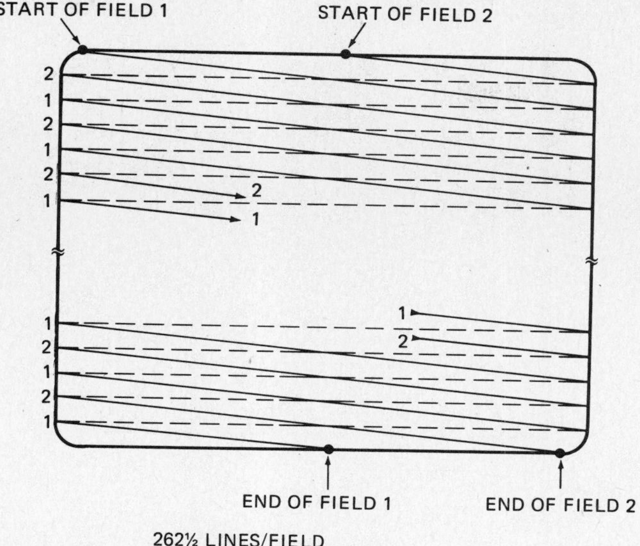

262½ LINES/FIELD
2 FIELDS/FRAME
525 LINES/FRAME FOR 15,750 Hz
HORIZONTAL AND 60 Hz VERTICAL

(*a*)

START OF FIELD

END OF FIELD

260 LINES/FIELD
1 FIELD/FRAME
260 LINES/FRAME FOR
15,600 Hz HORIZONTAL AND
60Hz VERTICAL

(*b*)

FIGURE 12-1 CRT scan patterns. *(a)* Interlaced. *(b)* Noninterlaced.

ture resolution and avoid flicker, TVs use *interlaced scanning*. As shown in Figure 12-1*a*, this means the scan lines for one field are offset and interleaved with those of of the next field. After every other field the scan lines repeat. Therefore, two fields are required to make a complete picture or frame. The frame rate is then 30 frames/second. The beam sweeps 262.5 times horizontally for each vertical sweep.

CRT units used for computer readouts usually have *noninterlaced scanning*, as shown in Figure 12-1*b*. In this case a horizontal sweep rate of 15,600 Hz and a vertical sweep rate of 60 Hz gives 260 sweep lines/field. The field rate and the frame rate are both 60 Hz in this case.

Whether the CRT you are using to display your programs is in a TV set, a video monitor, or a terminal, there are certain basic circuits required to drive the CRT. These are: the vertical oscillator to produce the vertical sweep signal for the beam, the horizontal oscillator to produce the horizontal sweep signal for the beam, and the video amplifier to control the intensity of the electron beam. A unit which contains only this basic drive circuitry is referred to as a *video monitor*. A TV set contains the basic monitor functions plus RF and audio decoding circuitry. A CRT *terminal* contains a keyboard, memory, communication circuitry, and usually a microprocessor to control all of these parts.

The basic CRT drive circuitry for a one-color, or *monochrome*, display requires three input signals to operate properly. It must have horizontal sync pulses to keep the horizontal oscillator synchronized, and vertical sync pulses to keep the vertical oscillator synchronized. Also it must have the video information for each point as the beam sweeps across the screen. All of this must be synchronized so that a particular dot of video information gets displayed at the same point on the screen during each frame. If you have seen a TV picture rolling, or a TV picture with jagged horizontal lines in it, you have seen what happens if the horizontal, vertical, and video information are not synchronized.

When transmitted to a TV set or to a video monitor, the two sync signals and the video information are usually combined into a single signal called *composite video*. Figure 12-2 shows a typical TV-type composite video signal waveform. It is hard to show in a figure, but there is one vertical sync pulse for each 262.5 horizontal sync pulses. The video information is represented by the waveform sections between horizontal sync pulses. For

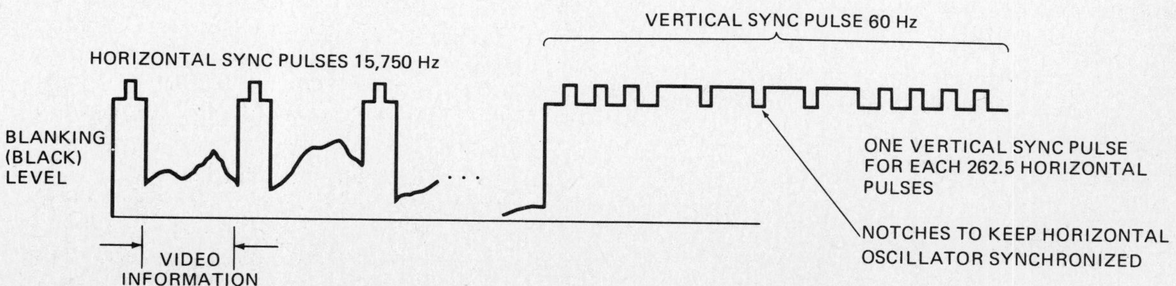

FIGURE 12-2 Composite video waveforms.

these waveforms, a more positive voltage turns the beam off. Therefore, the beam will be *blanked* during the horizontal retrace time represented by the pulse that the horizontal sync pulse sits on top of. The beam will also be blanked during the vertical retrace time. Now let's see how we generate these three signals to display characters on a CRT screen.

Creating a Page of Monochrome Characters on a CRT

Characters or graphics are generated on a CRT screen as a pattern of light and dark dots. To do this we turn the electron beam on and off as it sweeps across the screen. Figure 12-3 shows how this works. The round dots in the figure represent the beam on, and the empty, square boxes represent the beam off. With this dot matrix we can produce a reasonable approximation to any letter or symbol. The more dots used for each character, the better the representation. Common dot-matrix sizes for a character are 5 by 7, 7 by 9, and 7 by 12. The dot patterns for each character we want to display are stored in a ROM called a *character generator* ROM. Figure 12-4 shows the matrix for a Motorola MC6571 character generator. The MC6571 uses a 7 by 9 matrix for the actual character, but it has extra dot rows to leave space between rows of characters and so that lowercase letters can be dropped in the matrix to show descenders correctly. Each dot row in Figure 12-4 represents the pattern of dots for a horizontal scan line of the character. Figure 12-5 shows how the character generator is connected with some RAM, a shift register, and some counters to produce the signals required to display characters on a CRT. Here's how it works.

The ASCII or EBCDIC codes for the characters to be displayed on the screen are stored in a RAM so that they can be changed when you want to display something new on the screen. This RAM is often referred to as the *display RAM* or the *display refresh RAM*. The RAM must contain at least one byte location for each character to be displayed. A common display size is 25 rows of characters with 80 characters in each row. This display then requires about 2 Kbytes of display RAM. A character counter and a row counter are used to address the ASCII codes in this RAM.

To start the display in the upper left corner, the character counter and the row counter outputs are all 0's so

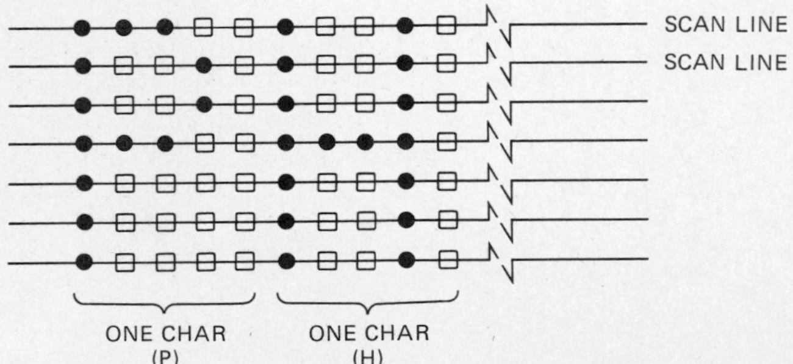

FIGURE 12-3 Producing characters on a CRT screen with dots.

DOT ROW	CAPITAL OR UPPERCASE							SMALL OR LOWERCASE						
0000	0	0	0	0	0	0	0	0	0	0	0	0	0	0
0001	1	1	1	1	1	1	0	0	0	0	0	0	0	0
0010	1	0	0	0	0	0	1	0	0	0	0	0	0	0
0011	1	0	0	0	0	0	1	0	0	0	0	0	0	0
0100	1	0	0	0	0	0	1	1	0	1	1	1	0	0
0101	1	1	1	1	1	1	0	1	1	0	0	0	1	0
0110	1	0	0	0	0	0	0	1	0	0	0	0	1	0
0111	1	0	0	0	0	0	0	1	0	0	0	0	1	0
1000	1	0	0	0	0	0	0	1	1	0	0	0	1	0
1001	1	0	0	0	0	0	0	1	0	1	1	1	0	0
1010	0	0	0	0	0	0	0	1	0	0	0	0	0	0
1011	0	0	0	0	0	0	0	1	0	0	0	0	0	0
1100	0	0	0	0	0	0	0	1	0	0	0	0	0	0
1101	0	0	0	0	0	0	0	0	0	0	0	0	0	0
1110	0	0	0	0	0	0	0	0	0	0	0	0	0	0
1111	0	0	0	0	0	0	0	0	0	0	0	0	0	0

FIGURE 12-4 Dot format for Motorola MC6571 character generator ROM.

the ASCII code for the first character is addressed in the display RAM. The addressed code will be output from the RAM to the data inputs of the character generator ROM. The outputs of a dot row counter are also applied to the character generator. With these two inputs the character generator will output the 7-bit dot pattern for one dot row in the character. For the first scan across the screen the counter will output 0000 so the dot pattern output will be that for dot row 0000 of the character. The output from the character generator is in parallel form. In order to turn the beam on and off at the correct time as it sweeps across the screen, this dot pattern must be in serial form. A simple parallel-to-serial shift register is used to do this conversion. Note that the eighth data input of the shift register is tied to ground so that there is always one dark dot or *undot* between characters. The high-frequency clock used to clock this shift register is called the *dot clock* because it controls the rate at which dot information is sent out to the video amplifier.

After the dots for the first scan line of the first character are shifted out, the character counter is incremented by one. It then points to the ASCII code for the second character in the top row of characters in the display RAM. Therefore the ASCII code for this second character will be output to the character generator ROM. Since the dot line counter inputs to the ROM are still 0000, the ROM will output the dot pattern for the top scan line of the second character in the top row of characters on the screen. When all of the dots for the top scan line of this character are all shifted out, the character counter will be incremented by one again, and the process repeated for the third character in the top row of characters. The process continues until the first scan line for all 80 characters in the top row of characters is traced out.

A horizontal sync pulse is then produced to cause the

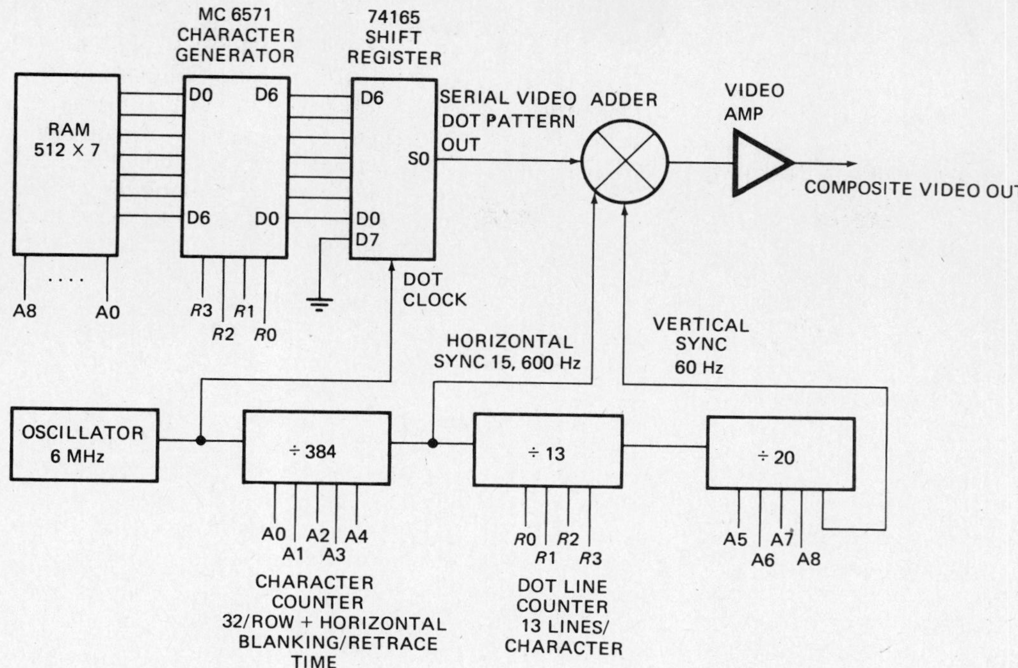

FIGURE 12-5 Block diagram of circuitry to produce dot-matrix character display on CRT.

beam to sweep back to the left side of the screen. After the beam retraces to the left, the character counter is rolled back to zero to point to the ASCII code for the first character in the row again. The dot line counter is incremented to 0001 so that the character generator will now output the dot patterns for the second scan line of each character. After the dot pattern for the second scan line of the first character in the row is shifted out to the video amplifier, the character counter is incremented to point to the ASCII code for the second character in the display RAM. The process repeats until all of the scan lines for one row of characters have been scanned.

The character row counter is then incremented by one. The outputs of the character counter and the character row counter now point to the display RAM address where the ASCII code for the first character of the second row of characters is stored. The process we described for the first row will be repeated for the second row of characters. After the second row of characters is swept out, the process will go on to the third row of characters, and then on to the fourth, and so on until all 16 rows of characters have been swept out.

When all of the character rows have been swept out, the beam is at the lower right corner of the screen. The counter circuitry then sends out a horizontal sync pulse to retrace the beam to the left side of the screen, and a vertical sync pulse to retrace the beam to the top of the screen. When the beam reaches the top left corner of the screen, the whole *screen-refresh* process that we have described will repeat. As we mentioned before, the entire screen must be scanned (refreshed) 30 to 60 times a second to avoid a blinking display. Now let's see what frequencies are involved in each major part of the circuitry.

CRT Display Timing and Frequencies

There are many different horizontal, vertical, and dot clock frequencies commonly used in raster-scan CRT displays. The horizontal sweep frequency is usually in the range of 15–30 kHz, the vertical sweep frequency is usually 50 or 60 Hz, and the dot clock frequency is usually 5–25 MHz. For our first specific example, we will use the frequencies used in the IBM PC monochrome display adapter, which we use as a circuit example in a later section.

The IBM monochrome display adapter produces a display of 25 rows of 80 characters/row. Each character is produced as a 7 by 9 matrix of dots in a 9 by 14 dot space. This means that because clear space is left around each actual character, each character actually uses 9 dot spaces horizontally, and 14 scan lines vertically. The active horizontal display area then is 9 dots/character × 80 characters/line or 720 dots per line. The active vertical display area is 25 rows × 14 scan lines/row or 350 scan lines.

Now, according to the IBM Technical Reference Manual, the monochrome adapter uses a dot clock frequency of 16.257 MHz. This means that the video shift register is shifting out 16,257,000 dots/second. The manual also indicates that the board uses a horizontal sweep frequency of 18,432 lines/second. Multiplying 16,257,000 dots per second by 1/18,432 seconds per line tells you that the board is shifting out 882 dots/line. Just above we showed you that the active display area of a line is only 720 dots. The extra 162 dot times actually present are required to give the beam time to get from the right edge of the active display to the right edge of the screen, retrace to the left edge of the screen, and sweep to the left edge of the active display area. This large number of extra dot times is necessary because most monitors have a large amount of *overscan*. This means that the beam is actually swept far off the left and right sides of the screen so that the portion of the sweep actually displayed is linear.

The manual for the display adapter indicates that the frame rate is 50 Hz. In other words the beam sweeps from the top of the screen to the bottom and back again 50 times/second. To see how many horizontal lines are in each frame, you can divide the 18,432 lines/second by 50 frames/second to give 369 scan lines/frame. As we showed above, the active vertical display area is 350 lines, so this gives 19 extra scan line times for the beam to get to the bottom of the screen, retrace to the top of the screen, and get to the start of the active display area again. Note that the dot clock, horizontal sweep frequency, and vertical sweep frequency must all be related to each other so that the display is synchronized.

Another point we need to make here concerns the bandwidth required by a video amplifier or monitor to clearly display a given number of dots per line. For our example here, the dot clock frequency is 16.257 MHz. This means that the dot shift register is shifting out 16,257,000 dots/second. If we are shifting out alternating dots and undots, then the waveform on the serial output pin of the shift register will be a square wave with a frequency of half that of the dot clock or 8.1285 MHz. In order to produce a clear display with this many dots per line, then, the video amplifier in the monitor connected to the display adapter must have a bandwidth of at least 8 MHz. In other words, the circuitry in the monitor must be able to turn on and off fast enough so that dots and undots don't smear together.

This bandwidth requirement is the reason that normal TV sets connected to computers cannot display high-resolution 80-character lines for word processing, etc. In order to filter out the sound subcarrier and the color subcarrier, the bandwidth of TV video amplifiers is limited to about 3 MHz. When using a TV as a readout device for a microcomputer, then, we usually limit the display to a smaller number of dots per character, and to 40 characters/line. A CRT monitor used for displaying characters or graphics should have a bandwidth greater than one-half the dot clock frequency.

A final point we want to make about CRT timing is how often the display-refresh RAM has to be accessed. As the circuitry scans one line of the display, it has to access a new character in RAM after each 9 dots are shifted out, assuming 9 dots horizontally per character. Dividing the dot clock frequency of 16.257 MHz by 9 dots/character tells you that characters are read from RAM at a rate of 1,806,333 characters/second, or one character every 553 ns! Next we will show you how programmable CRT display controllers are used to produce a desired display.

CRT Controller ICs and Circuits

In addition to the chain of counters shown in Figure 12-5, considerable other circuitry is needed to produce horizontal blanking pulses, vertical blanking pulses, a cursor, scrolling, and highlighting for a CRT display. Several manufacturers offer CRT controller ICs that contain different amounts of the required circuitry. The two devices we discuss here are the Intel 8275 and the Motorola 6845.

THE INTEL 8275 CRT CONTROLLER

Figure 12-6 shows, in block diagram form, how an 8275 controller is connected with other circuitry to produce

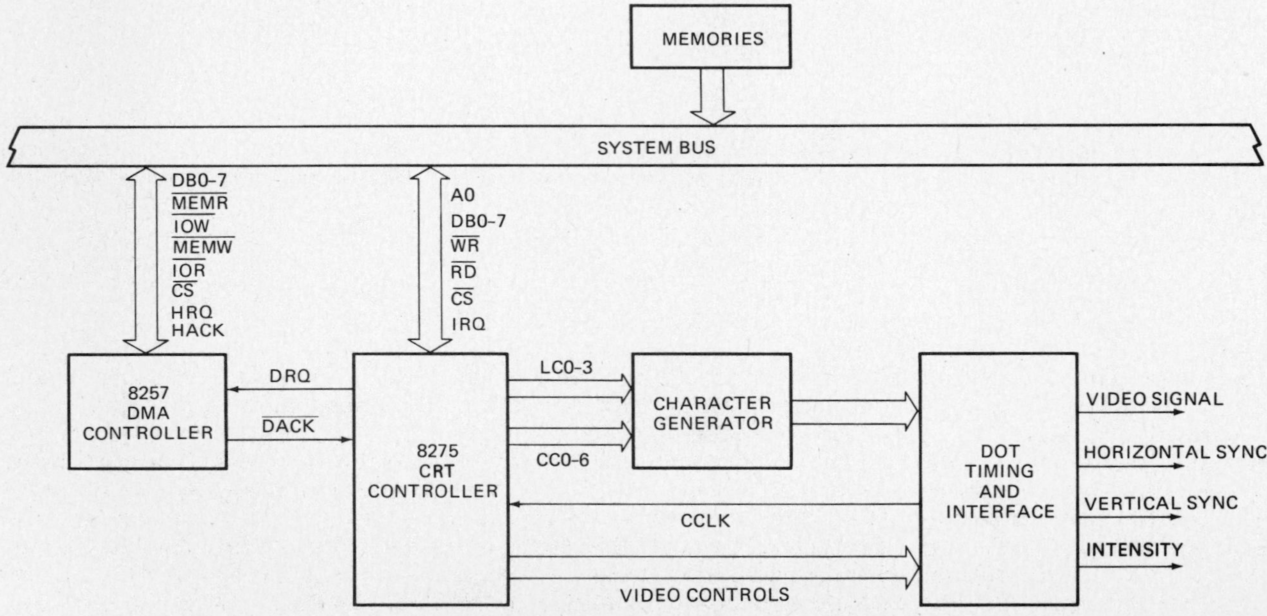

FIGURE 12-6 Block diagram showing connections of Intel 8275 CRT controller in a microcomputer system.

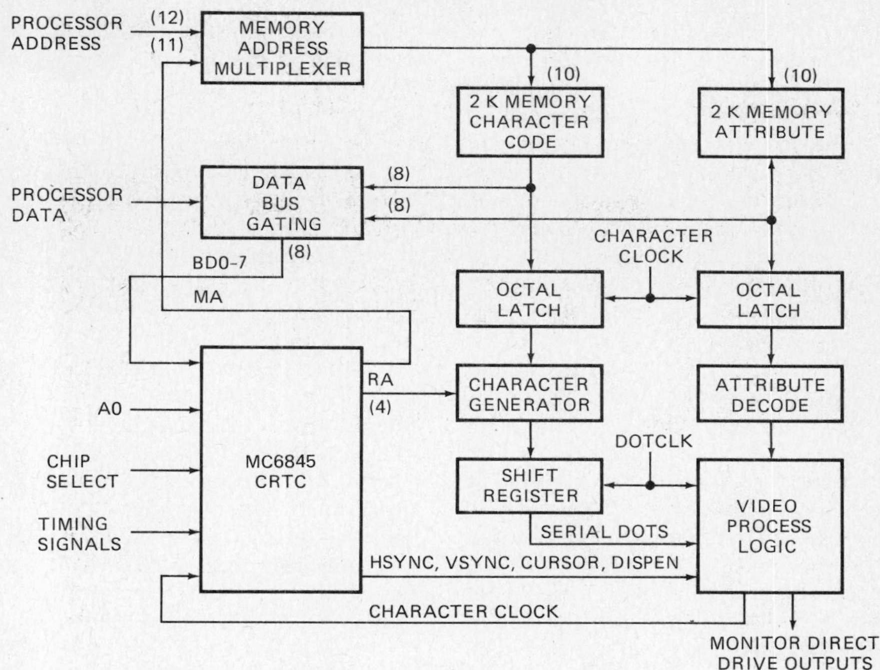

FIGURE 12-7 IBM monochrome display adapter board block diagram.

the drive signals for a CRT monitor. The 8275 contains a row counter which can be programmed for a display of 1 to 64 rows, a character counter which can be programmed for a display of 1 to 80 characters/row, and a scan line counter which can be programmed for 1 to 16 scan lines/character. The 8275 also has an 80-byte buffer to hold the ASCII characters for the row currently being displayed and an 80-byte buffer to hold the ASCII characters for the next row of characters to be displayed.

For the system in Figure 12-6 the page of characters to be displayed is stored in a buffer in the main microprocessor memory. While the 8275 is using the contents of one of its 80-byte buffers to refresh a row of characters on the screen, it fills the other 80-byte buffer from the main memory on a DMA basis. To do this it sends a DMA request signal (DREQ) to the 8257 DMA controller. The DMA controller sends a DMA request signal to, for example, the HOLD input of an 8086. When the 8086 sees the request signal, it floats its buses and sends a hold acknowledge signal. As we described in Chapter 11, the DMA controller then sends out the memory address and control signals needed to transfer the characters from memory to the 8275 buffer. The DMA approach uses only a small percentage of the microprocessor's time and, since the *display page* is located in the main memory, new characters are easily written to it.

The character generator is left out of the controller so that a ROM for any desired character set can be used. The dot clock and the dot shift register are also external because of the high frequencies involved in that part of the circuit. The 8275 produces vertical and horizontal sync signals, but external circuitry is used to massage the timing of these signals to correspond with the video information from the dot shift register. Now we will show you another CRT controller approach.

THE MOTOROLA 6845 CRT CONTROLLER

The 6845 CRT controller chip performs most of the 8275 functions discussed in the previous section, but it interfaces with the display refresh RAM in a very different way. The 6845 is used in both the monochrome display adapter board and the color/graphics monitor adapter boards for the IBM PC, so we will use some circuitry from these boards to show you how it works.

Figure 12-7 shows a block diagram for the IBM PC monochrome display adapter board. Take a look at this figure and see what parts you recognize from our previous discussions. You should quickly find the CRT controller, character generator, and dot shift register. Next, find the 2 Kbyte memory where the ASCII codes for the characters to be displayed are stored. To the right of this memory is another 2 Kbyte memory used to store an attribute code for each character. An attribute code specifies how the character is to be displayed. For example, with an underline or with increased or decreased intensity. As you may have observed, it is common practice to display a menu at reduced intensity so it does not distract from the main text on the screen.

Now observe that there is a multiplexer in series with the address lines going to the character and attribute memories. This is done so that either the CPU or the CRT controller can access the display-refresh RAM. The 6845 has 14 address outputs, so it can address up to 16 Kbyte display and attribute locations. To keep the display refreshed, the 6845 sends out the memory address for a character code and an attribute code. The character clock signal latches the code from memory for the character generator and the attribute code for the attribute decode circuitry. The character clock also increments the address counter in the 6845 to point to the next character code in memory. The next character clock transfers the next codes to the character generator and attribute decoder. The process cycles through all of the characters on the page and then repeats. Now, when you want to display some new characters on the screen, you simply have the CPU execute some instructions which write the ASCII codes for the new characters to the appropriate address in the display RAM. When the address decoding circuitry detects a display RAM address, it produces a signal which toggles the multiplexers so that the CPU has access to the display RAM. The question that probably occurs to you at this point is, "What happens if the 6845 and the CPU both want to access the display RAM at the same time?" There are several solutions to this problem. One solution is to allow the CPU to access the RAM only during horizontal and/or vertical retrace times. Another solution is to interleave 6845 accesses and CPU accesses. This is how it is done in the IBM board. The character clock signal going to the 6845 and the multiplexers allows the CPU to access the RAM during one half of the clock signal and the 6845 to access the RAM during the other half of the clock signal. If the CPU tries to access the display RAM during the controller's half of the character clock cycle, a not-ready signal from the CRT controller board will cause the processor to insert WAIT states until the half of the character clock signal when it can access the display refresh RAM.

6845 INTERNAL REGISTERS AND INITIALIZATION

Figure 12-8 shows the pin diagram and labels for the 6845. We will take a brief look at these pin functions, and then discuss the internal registers so we can show you how the device is initialized.

The function of most of the pins should be easily recognizable to you from the block diagram in Figure 12-7. Ground is on pin 1, +5 V is on pin 20, and a reset input is on pin 2. The 6845 sends out the display RAM address of the character currently being scanned on the MA0–MA13 lines. On the RA0–RA4 pins the 6845 sends out the number of the character scan line currently being scanned to the character generator. A character clock signal which changes state when it is time for the controller to access the next character in memory is connected to the 6845 CLK input. The horizontal and vertical sync output signals on pins 39 and 40 are produced by dividing down this CLK input signal. The 6845 has eight data inputs, D0–D7, which connect to the system data bus so that initialization words can be written to the device and status words read from the device, just as with any of the other peripheral devices we have discussed. The 6845 will be enabled for a read or write on its data bus when its CS input is asserted low. The R/$\overline{W}$ is asserted high for a read and low for a write. The processor clock, or a signal derived from it, is applied to the E input of the 6845 to synchronize data transfers in or out on the data lines. As seen from the processor, the 6845 has two internal addresses, a control address selected when RS is low and a data address selected when the RS input is high. We will tell you more about this after we talk briefly about the few remaining pins.

The Cursor output pin will be asserted high when the controller is displaying the cursor. This signal can be combined with signals from the attribute decoder to cause the cursor to blink or to be highlighted, depending on attributes stored for the cursor location.

The Display Enable output pin will be asserted when the 6845 is scanning the active display area of the screen. This signal can be used to produce blanking pulses during horizontal and vertical retrace times. In a system that accesses the display RAM during retrace times, this signal can be used to tell the CPU when it can access the display RAM.

When the light pen strobe input, LPSTB, is made to go from low to high, the current refresh address will be latched in two registers inside the 6845.

The 6845 has a register bank of 19 registers which are used to set and to keep track of display counts during display refreshing. Figure 12-9 shows the function of each of these registers. Even if you are not going to be programming a 6845, it is worth taking a look at this figure so you have an idea of the types of parameters you specify for a CRT controller chip such as the 6845.

The 6845 has only two internal I/O addresses which are selected by the RS input. When the RS input is low, the internal address register is selected. When the RS input is high, one of the 18 internal data registers is selected. In order to access one of the internal data registers, you first have to write the number (address) of that register to the address register with RS low, and then write the data to the 6845 with RS high. RS is usually tied to a system address line so that you just write the address word to one address, perhaps 3B4H, and the data word to another address, perhaps 3B5H.

The standard way to initialize all of these parameters for a 6845 in a system is to use a program loop of the form:

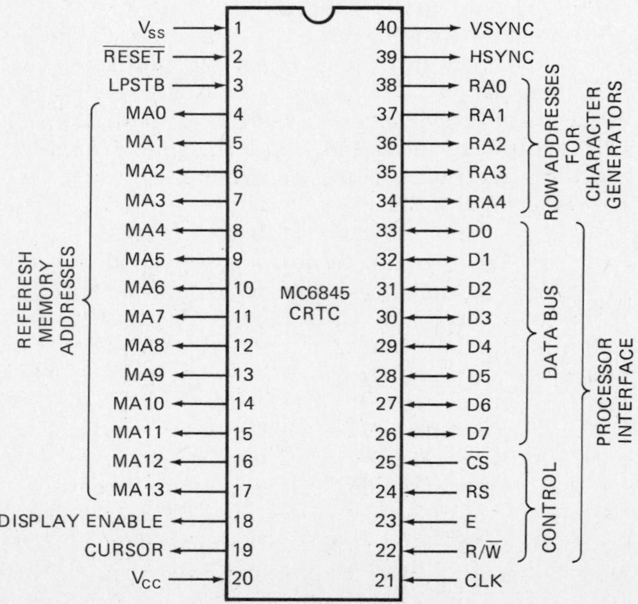

FIGURE 12-8 Motorola MC6845 CRT controller pin names.

RS	Register number	Function
0	X	Holds number of data register to write to.
1	0	Total number of horizontal character times +1, including retrace.
1	1	Number of horizontal characters displayed.
1	2	Character number when horizontal-sync pulse is produced. Determines horizontal display position.
1	3	Width of horizontal-sync pulse in character times.
1	4	Total number of vertical character rows-1, including vertical retrace.
1	5	Adjusts vertical timing to get exactly 50 or 60 Hz.
1	6	Number of vertical character rows displayed.
1	7	Vertical row number when vertical-sync pulse produced. Controls vertical position on screen.
1	8	Sets controller for interlaced or non-interlaced scanning.
1	9	Number of horizontal scan lines-1 per character row.
1	10	Starting scan line for the cursor and cursor blink rate.
1	11	Ending scan line for the cursor.
1	12	Starting address (high byte) for character to be put out after vertical retrace. Determines which character row from buffer appears at top of screen. Change this value to scroll display.
1	13	Low byte of first row starting address.
1	14	High byte of current cursor address.
1	15	Low byte of current cursor address in display RAM.
1	16	High byte of display RAM address when LPSTR occurs.
1	17	Low byte of display RAM address when LPSTR occurs.

FIGURE 12-9 MC6845 internal register functions.

REPEAT
    Output a data register number to the 6845 internal address register (RS = 0).
    Output parameter byte for that register to data register address (RS = 1).
UNTIL all required registers of the 18 are initialized.

Before we start the next section on computer graphics, let's take a brief look at how you can use the IBM PC BIOS procedures to display characters on the CRT screen.

Using the IBM PC INT 10H to Display Characters on the CRT

If you are working on an IBM PC it is quite easy to display characters on the CRT as part of your program by using the BIOS routines in ROM. In Chapter 8 we showed you how to use the BIOS INT 17H procedure to send characters to a printer. To use the BIOS procedures you load the parameters required by the procedure into registers specified for that procedure in the IBM Technical Reference Manual, and then execute the INT # instruction that accesses that procedure. You can use the BIOS INT 10H procedure for 15 different functions related to the CRT display. Some of these functions are: set display mode, set cursor position, scroll page up, scroll page down, set color palette, write dot, and write character to screen. You specify the function you want by loading the number for that function in the AH register before executing the INT 10H instruction. To write a character to the screen you simply load AH with 14 decimal, load AL with the character you want to display, and then execute the INT 10H instruction. Another BIOS procedure that you might want to use with this one is the INT 16H procedure which you can use to read characters from the keyboard. If you load AH with 0 and execute the INT 16H instruction, the ASCII code for the next key pressed on the keyboard will be left in the AL register after the procedure executes. Coupling the two INT procedures lets you read in characters from the keyboard and display them on the CRT.

RASTER SCAN CRT GRAPHICS DISPLAYS

The previous section of this chapter showed you how a monochrome display of alphanumeric characters can be produced on a CRT screen. In this section we show you how we produce a picture or graphics display. The two major methods of producing a graphics display are the *bit-mapped raster scan* approach, and the *vector graphics* approach. We'll explore the raster approach first.

Figure 12-5 shows a block diagram of some simple circuitry that can be used to create a display of characters on a CRT screen by turning the electron beam on and off as it is scanned across the screen. Characters are produced as a series of dots and undots on the screen. The ASCII codes for the page of characters to be displayed are stored in a display-refresh RAM. The dot patterns for each scan line of each character are stored in a character generator ROM. Now, suppose that we leave the character generator out of this circuit and connect the outputs of the RAM directly to the inputs of the dot shift register. And further suppose that instead of storing the ASCII codes for characters in the RAM, we store the dot patterns we want for each eight dots of a scan line in successive memory locations. When a byte is read from the RAM and loaded into the shift register, the stored dot pattern will be shifted out to the CRT beam to produce the desired pattern of dots for that section of a scan line on the screen. The next RAM byte will hold the dot pattern for the next 8 dots on a scan line, etc. Operating in this mode, each bit location in memory corresponds to a dot location on the screen. The entire screen then can be thought of as a matrix of dots. Each dot can be programmed to be on or off by putting a one or a zero in the corresponding bit location in RAM. A graphics display produced in this way is known as a *bit-mapped raster scan display*. Each dot or in some cases block of dots is called a *picture element*. Most people shorten this to *pixel* or *pel*. For our first example let's assume a pixel is 1 dot.

Now, suppose that we want a graphics display of 640 pels horizontally by 200 pels vertically. This gives a total of 200 × 640 or 128,000 dots on the screen. Since each dot corresponds to a bit location in memory, this means that we have to have at least 128,000 bits or 16 Kbytes of RAM to hold the pel information for just one display screen. Compare this with the 2 Kbytes needed for each page of an 80 by 24 character display. As we will show you a little later, producing a color graphics display with a large number of pels increases the memory requirements even further.

Now that you have a picture of a raster graphics screen as a large matrix of dots, the question that may occur to you is, "How do I draw a rocket ship or other picture on the screen?" One method is to program each of the 128,000 dots to be on or off as required to produce the desired display. This method works, but it is somewhat analogous to handprinting copies of the Bible, a very tedious process. To make your life easier, many graphics programs are now available. These programs allow you to create a complex graphics display, dump the display to a printer, store the display on a disk, or include the display in another program you are writing. These graphics programs contain graphics routines or *primitives* which allow you to draw lines, draw arcs, draw three-dimentional figures, shade in areas, set up "windows," etc. Often these programs work with a *mouse*. A mouse in this case is a device which moves a cursor around the CRT screen when you move it around on the desk next to your computer. To draw a straight line between two points, for example, you move the cursor to the point on the screen where you want one end of the line and press a button on the mouse. You then move the cursor to the point on the screen where you want the other end of the line, and press a button on the mouse again. The graphics program then computes the coordinates for the other points on the line and puts 1's in the appropriate locations in the display RAM to draw in the line. By moving the cursor around on the screen and pressing buttons on the mouse at the appropriate times, you can quickly create some elaborate graphics displays. If you have not had a chance to play with a computer that has these graphics capabilities, do not pass go, proceed directly to your nearest computer store and experiment with a graphics program on the Apple Macintosh or IBM PC.

CRT TERMINALS

Several times previously in this book we have used the term CRT terminal. You may have used a CRT terminal to communicate with a minicomputer or mainframe computer. In addition to the basic CRT drive circuitry, a terminal contains a keyboard so you can talk to it, the CRT-refresh RAM and controller to keep the display refreshed, and a UART to communicate to and from a computer. Most CRT terminals now have one or more built-in microprocessors to coordinate keyboard, display, and communications functions. A major advantage of using a microprocessor instead of dedicated logic here is that key functions and communications parameters can be changed to match a given computer by simply typing a few keystrokes. A device from National Semiconductor, the NS456, contains a microprocessor-based CRT controller, a keyboard interface, a UART, and most of the other functions needed for a graphics/character CRT terminal.

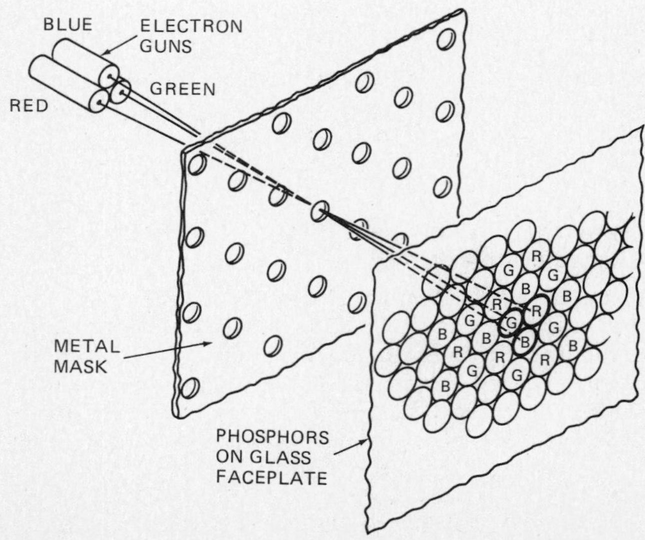

FIGURE 12-10 Three-color phosphor dot pattern used to produce color on a CRT screen.

I	R	G	B	COLOR
0	0	0	0	BLACK
0	0	0	1	BLUE
0	0	1	0	GREEN
0	0	1	1	CYAN
0	1	0	0	RED
0	1	0	1	MAGENTA
0	1	1	0	BROWN
0	1	1	1	WHITE
1	0	0	0	GRAY
1	0	0	1	LIGHT BLUE
1	0	1	0	LIGHT GREEN
1	0	1	1	LIGHT CYAN
1	1	0	0	LIGHT RED
1	1	0	1	LIGHT MAGENTA
1	1	1	0	YELLOW
1	1	1	1	HIGH INTENSITY WHITE

FIGURE 12-11 Sixteen colors produced by different combinations of red, blue, and green beams at normal and at increased intensity.

RASTER SCAN COLOR GRAPHICS

Monochrome graphics displays get boring after a while, so let's see how you can get some color in the picture.

To produce a monochrome display we coat the inside of the tube with a single phosphor which produces the desired color light when bombarded with electrons from a single electron gun at the rear of the tube. To produce a color CRT display we apply red, green, and blue phosphors to the inside of the tube, and bombard these three different phosphors with three separate electron beams. One approach is to have dots of the three phosphors in a triangular pattern as shown in Figure 12-10. The dots are close enough together so that to your eye they appear as a single dot. By changing the intensity ratio of the three beams we can make the three-part dot appear any color we want, including black and white. If all three beams are off, the dot is of course black. If the beams are turned on in the ratio of 0.30 RED, 0.59 GREEN, and 0.11 BLUE, then the dot will appear white. The overall intensity of the three beams, often represented with the letter I or the letter Y determines whether the dot will be a light or a dark shade of the color. Figure 12-11 shows 16 colors that can be produced by simply turning on or off different combinations of the red, blue, and green beams. A 1 in the I bit means that the overall intensity of the beam is increased to lighten the color as shown. If we drive the color guns and the intensity with the output of a D/A converter instead of simply on or off signals, we can produce a much wider variety of colors. A 2-bit D/A converter on each of the color signals and the intensity signal, for example, gives 256 color variations. In order to produce a display with a large number of pixels and a large number of colors, a large memory is needed. As we discuss a common color graphics adapter in the next section, we will show you some of the tradeoffs involved in this.

The IBM PC Color/Graphics Adapter Board

As a real system example here we will use the IBM PC color/graphics adapter board whose block diagram is shown in Figure 12-12.

This board again uses the Motorola MC6845 CRT controller device to do the overall display control. It produces the sequential addresses required for the display-refresh RAM, the horizontal sync pulses, and the vertical sync pulses as we described in a previous section. The 16 Kbyte display-refresh RAM is *dual-*

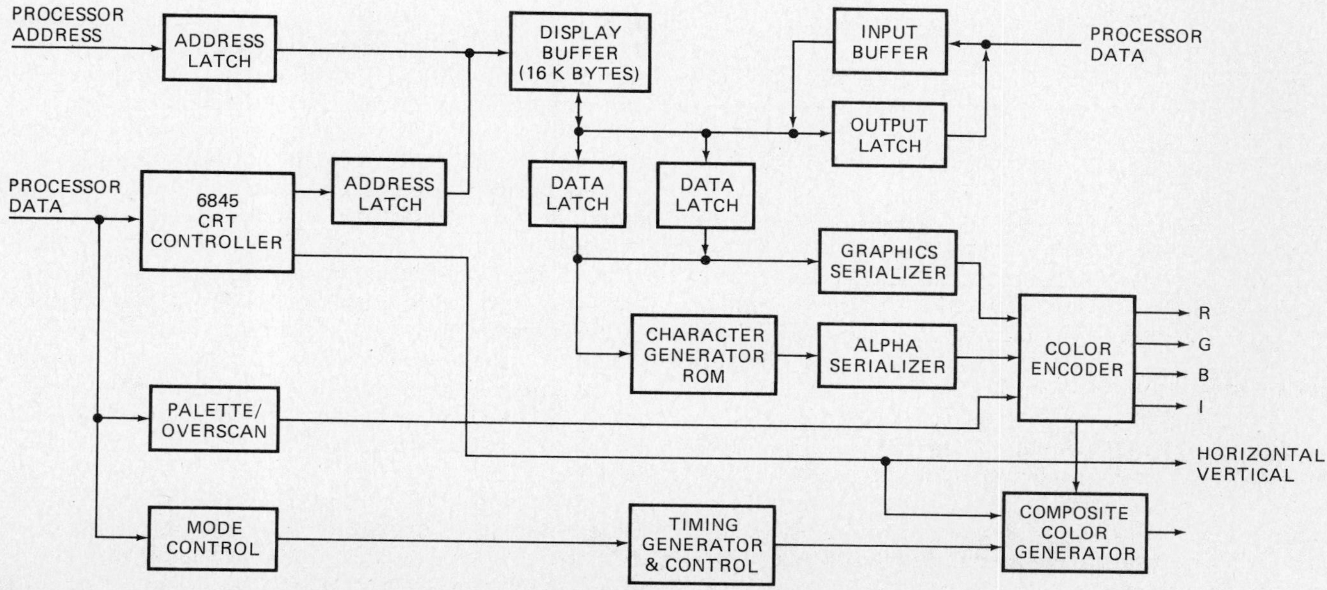

FIGURE 12-12 IBM PC color graphics adapter board block diagram.

ported. This means that it can be accessed by either the system processor or the CRT controller on a time-share basis as we also described previously. A little later we will show you how display information is stored in RAM for various display modes.

This adapter board can operate in either a character mode or a graphics mode. In the character mode it uses a character generator ROM and a single shift register (alpha serializer) to produce the serial dot information for display scan lines. When operating in a color graphics mode, the board uses separate shift registers (graphics serializer) to produce the dot information for each of the color guns and for the overall intensity.

As you can see by the signals shown in the lower right corner of Figure 12-12, the adapter board is designed to drive either of the two common types of color monitor. One type, commonly called an RGB monitor, has separate inputs for each of the required signals, red, green, blue, intensity, horizontal sync, and vertical sync. The other type of color monitor is called a *composite color monitor* because all of the required signals are combined on a single line. Color TV sets used as color monitors for computers require a composite video signal if they have a direct video input, or they require a radio-frequency signal modulated with the composite video signal if they do not have a direct video input. Later we will show you how we produce a composite color video signal from the separate signals. Now let's look at how the display information is stored in the display-refresh RAM for various display modes.

In the character or alphanumeric mode each character is represented by two bytes in the display-refresh RAM in the format shown in Figure 12-13*a*. This is the same format as the monochrome adapter board. The upper byte contains the 8-bit ASCII code for the character to be displayed. The lower byte contains an attribute code which you use to specify the character color (foreground) and the background color for the character.

DISPLAY-CHARACTER CODE BYTE								ATTRIBUTE BYTE							
7	6	5	4	3	2	1	0	7	6	5	4	3	2	1	0

(*a*)

ATTRIBUTE FUNCTION	ATTRIBUTE BYTE							
	7	6	5	4	3	2	1	0
	B	R	G	B	I	R	G	B
	FG	BACKGROUND			FOREGROUND			
NORMAL	B	0	0	0	1	1	1	1
REVERSE VIDEO	B	1	1	1	1	0	0	0
NONDISPLAY (BLACK)	B	0	0	0	1	0	0	0
NONDISPLAY (WHITE)	B	1	1	1	1	1	1	1

I = HIGHLIGHTED FOREGROUND (CHARACTER)
B = BLINKING FOREGROUND (CHARACTER)

(*b*)

FIGURE 12-13 Data storage formats for IBM color graphics board operating in alphanumeric mode. *(a)* Character byte and attribute byte. *(b)* Attribute byte format.

7	6	5	4	3	2	1	0
C1	C0	C1	C0	C1	C0	C1	C0
FIRST DISPLAY PEL		SECOND DISPLAY PEL		THIRD DISPLAY PEL		FOURTH DISPLAY PEL	

C1	C0	FUNCTION
0	0	DOT TAKES ON THE COLOR OF 1 of 16 PRESELECTED BACKGROUND COLORS
0	1	SELECTS FIRST COLOR OF PRESELECTED COLOR SET 1 OR COLOR SET 2
1	0	SELECTS SECOND COLOR OF PRESELECTED COLOR SET 1 OR COLOR SET 2
1	1	SELECTS THIRD COLOR OF PRESELECTED COLOR SET 1 OR COLOR SET 2

COLOR SET 1	COLOR SET 2
COLOR 1 IS GREEN COLOR 2 IS RED COLOR 3 IS BROWN	COLOR 1 IS CYAN COLOR 2 IS MAGENTA COLOR 3 IS WHITE

FIGURE 12-14 Data storage format for medium-resolution graphics mode of IBM PC color adapter board.

The intensity bit, I, in the attribute byte allows you to specify normal intensity or increased intensity for a character. The bit patterns used to produce different colors with the RGB and I bits are shown in Figure 12-13*b*. The B bit in the attribute byte allows you to specify that a character will be blinked. Only 4 Kbytes of the display RAM are needed to hold the character and attribute codes for an 80 character by 25 row display.

For displaying graphics, the adapter board can be operated in three different modes: low resolution, medium resolution, and high resolution. Higher resolution means more pixels in the display. We will use these three modes to show you the tradeoffs between number of colors, resolution, and memory requirements.

We often use the low-resolution mode when we are using a color TV set or a composite video monitor as a display device, because this mode requires less video amplifier bandwidth than high-resolution modes. In this low-resolution mode each pel is 2 dot times horizontally and 2 dot times vertically, so the picture is actually being made with larger blocks. The display consists of 100 rows of pels with 160 pels in each row. The total number of pels is then 16,000. The color and intensity for each pixel is specified by the I, R, G, and B bits in the lower half of a byte in the display RAM. Since 4 bits are being used to specify color and intensity, a pel can be any one of 16 colors. Since a byte is used to store the information for each pel, all 16 Kbytes of the display RAM are used to display the 100 by 160 pel display.

In the medium-resolution mode each pel is a single dot. The display consists of 200 rows of pels with 320 pels in each row, or a total of 64,000 pels. The 16 Kbytes of display refresh RAM corresponds to 16 Kbits × 8 or

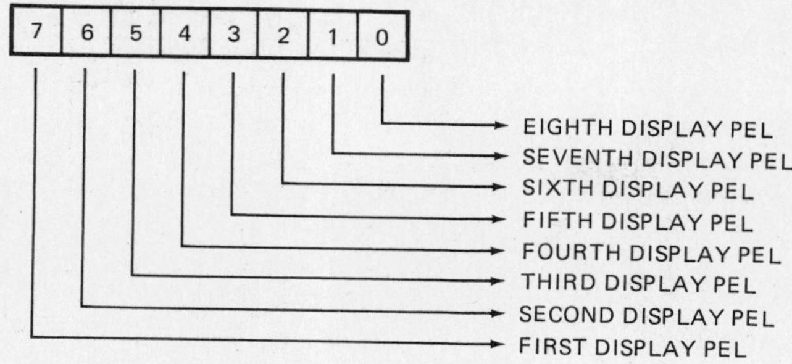

FIGURE 12-15 Data storage format for high-resolution graphics mode of IBM PC color graphics adapter board.

128 Kbits. Dividing the number of pels into the number of bits available for storage tells you that in this mode there are only 2 bits per pel available to store color information. With 2 bits we can specify only one of four colors for each pel. As you can see, increasing the resolution of the display has reduced the number of colors that can be specified with a given amount of memory. Figure 12-14 shows the format in which the pel information is stored in RAM bytes and the meaning of the bits in these bytes. The background color is selected by outputting a control byte through port 3D9H to the palette circuit shown on the left edge of Figure 12-12. Consult the IBM Technical Reference Manual for more details if you need them.

In the high-resolution graphics mode the IBM color graphics adapter board displays 200 rows of pels with 640 pels in each row, or a total of 128,000 pels. Since the 16 Kbyte refresh RAM contains 128,000 bits, this corresponds to 1 bit per pel. Therefore, you can only specify for each bit whether it is on or off. In other words, in this high-resolution mode you are limited to a black-and-white display, because there are no bits left to specify colors. Figure 12-15 shows the format in which pel data is stored in display RAM bytes for high-resolution displays. Here again we want to point out that if you want to produce color graphics displays as part of your programs, the best approach is probably to buy one of the commercially available graphics packages. These programs allow you to produce the figures you want with a mouse or with drawing instructions rather than specifying the bit values for each pixel.

As you should see by now, the limiting factor for color graphics displays is the amount of memory you are willing to devote to the display. Some high-resolution displays used in engineering work stations have a display of 1000 by 1000 pels with 16 colors. A display such as this requires about 500 Kbytes of high-speed-refresh RAM.

For each of the graphics formats above, data for a pel is read from the display RAM and converted to separate R, G, B, and I signals. These signals, along with the horizontal and vertical sync signals, can be sent directly to an RGB-type monitor. Before they can be sent to a composite video-type monitor these signals must be put together in a single signal. Here's how we do it.

Producing a Composite Color Video Signal

In order to produce a composite color signal from the R, G, B, and sync signals, we can't just add all the signals together. Instead, the approach we use is based on the NTSC standards for color television signals. Figure 12-16 shows in diagram form the somewhat complex method used to put the pieces together.

As a first step, the red, the green, and the blue signals are combined in the ratios shown to produce a signal proportional to the overall intensity or *luminance*. If horizontal and vertical sync pulses are added to this signal, the result is a monochrome composite video signal identical to that we described earlier in this chapter. This signal will produce a monochrome display on either a monochrome monitor or a color monitor.

To develop the correct color signals we pass the luminance signal through a 1.5-MHz low-pass filter and then an inverter. The filter is required to comply with FCC bandwidth rules if this signal is going to be sent out as part of a TV signal modulation. The inverted luminance signal, −Y, is then added to the red signal to produce

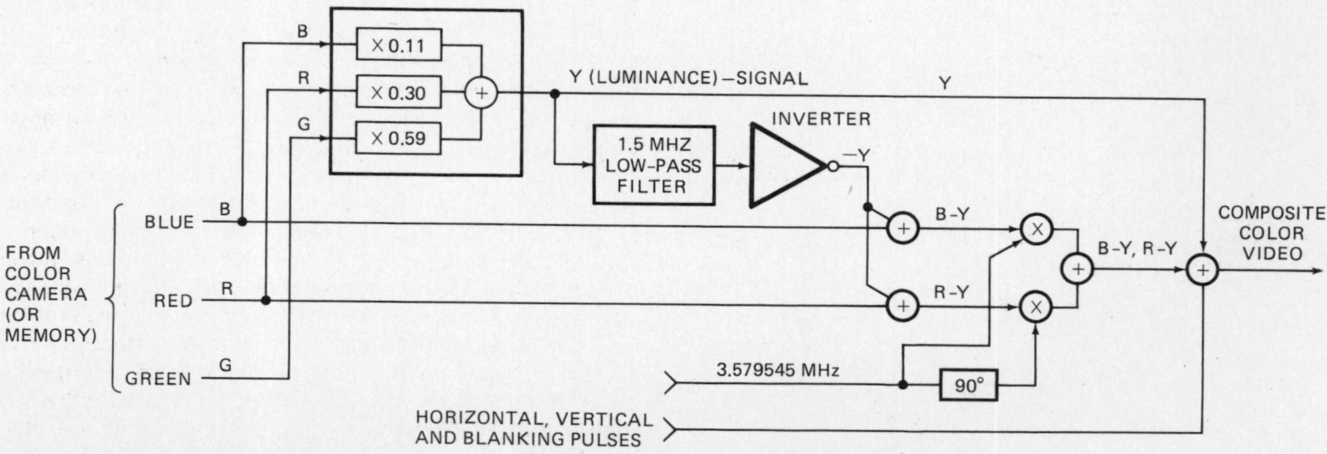

FIGURE 12-16 Block diagram of circuitry used to produce composite color video signal.

R − Y, and it is added to the blue signal to produce B − Y. The reason we do this is probably not obvious to the casual observer, but this scheme reduces the number of separate signals which have to be sent. Here's how it works. The Y, R − Y, and B − Y signals are sent as part of the color TV signal or as part of the composite video signal. In the receiver the Y signal is added to the R − Y signal to reconstruct the red signal. The Y signal is added to the B − Y signal to reconstruct the blue signal. Since the Y signal is composed of red, green, and blue, the red signal and the blue signal are subtracted from the Y signal to reconstruct the green signal. Because of all this we don't have to send a separate green signal. Now that you have an idea why we do all of this, let's continue the story of a composite color video signal.

The key to the next step is a stable 3.579545-MHz signal produced by a crystal oscillator. The B − Y signal is used to modulate this signal, and the R − Y signal is used to modulate a portion of this 3-MHz signal whose phase has been shifted by 90°. The two modulated 3.579545-MHz signals are then added together. The result is sometimes called the *chroma* signal, because it contains the color information.

Now, to produce the color composite video signal we simply add the horizontal sync pulses, the vertical sync pulses, the Y signal, and this chroma signal together as shown in Figure 12-16. When the composite video monitor receives this signal, it will separate all of the pieces again.

To produce a composite signal which can be fed into the antenna input of a color TV set, we usually use a chroma modulator device such as the Motorola MC1372 shown in Figure 12-17. This device produces the 3.579545-MHz color carrier frequency, and it produces the chroma signal from the R − Y and B − Y signals. The device also produces a radio-frequency carrier at the frequency for standard TV channel 3 or 4 and modulates this carrier signal with the Y, R − Y, B − Y, and sync information. When a color TV set receives this modulated signal, it demodulates the signal and separates the various parts. Because it has to filter out the remnants of the 3.579545-MHz color carrier frequency, the bandwidth of a composite color monitor or a color TV is limited to less than 3 MHz. As we explained in the section of the chapter on monochrome displays, this limits the resolution, and makes it difficult to display 80-character lines or detailed graphics on standard TV displays. Now that we have beat raster scan displays into the ground, we will show you how vector scan displays work.

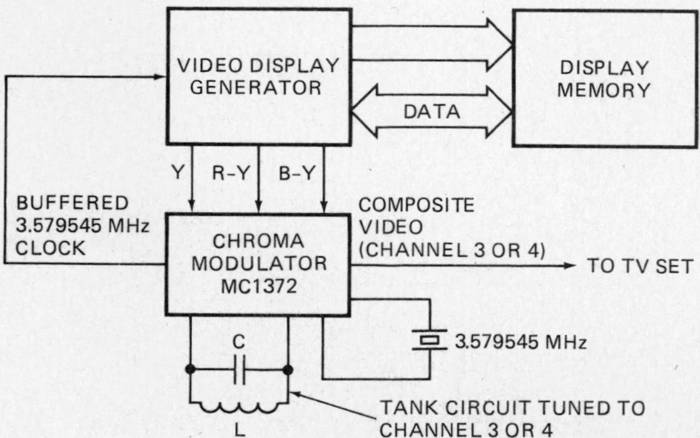

FIGURE 12-17 Motorola MC1372 used to produce color video signal compatible with a standard TV channel.

VECTOR SCAN CRT DISPLAYS

A raster scan CRT display scans the electron beam over the entire screen and turns the beam on and off to produce a light or dark spot at each point in the scan. For certain CRT display applications such as computer-aided design workstations where the display consists mostly of background and an array of straight lines, it seems wasteful to sweep the beam back and forth over the entire screen. Also diagonal lines drawn on a raster scan display look like stair steps if you look closely at them, because of the rigid placement of the pixels on the screen.

A vector graphics scheme solves both of these problems by directly tracing out only the desired lines on the CRT. In other words, if we want a line connecting point A with point B on a vector graphics display, we simply drive the beam-deflection circuitry with a signal which causes the beam to go directly from point A to point B. If we want to move the beam from point A to point B without showing a line between the points, we can blank the beam as we move it. To draw a line on the CRT, then, we simply tell the beam how far to move and in what direction to move across the CRT. The name vector graphics comes from the fact that in physics a quantity which has magnitude and direction is called a vector.

The question that may occur to you at this point is, "How do you tell the beam where to move on the screen?" One way to direct the beam is by connecting a D/A converter to the horizontal deflection circuitry and another D/A converter to the vertical deflection circuitry. The values input to the two D/A converters then determine the position of the beam on the screen. If we use 10-bit D/A converters, we can direct the beam to one of 1024 positions horizontally and one of 1024 positions vertically. This is equivalent in resolution to a 1K by 1K raster display. Color displays can be produced by using a three-beam, three-phosphor CRT and moving the three beams together as we described for the raster scan color display.

The next question that may occur to you is, "If this scheme is so simple, why don't we use it for all CRT graphics displays?" The answer is that a vector display works well where the information we want to display is mostly straight lines, but it does not work well for displays that have many curves and large shaded areas. When using a vector graphics system, we draw, for example, a circle by drawing many short vectors around in a circle. The circle is then made up of short line segments or points. The number of vectors you can draw on the screen is limited by the fact that you have to go back and redraw each vector 60 times a second to keep the display refreshed. Some current vector graphics systems can draw 150,000 short vectors 60 times a second, but for complex images you soon run out of vectors. The point here is that no one display technique or technology has all of the marbles at this point in time. Here's another display technology that has some advantages for portable instruments and computers.

ALPHANUMERIC/GRAPHICS LCD DISPLAYS

In Chapter 9 we discussed how LCDs work and how they can be used to display numbers and letters as individual digits. To make a screen-type display the liquid crystal elements are constructed in a large X-Y matrix of dots. The elements in each row are connected together, and the elements in each column are connected together. An individual element is activated by driving both the row and the column that contain that element. LCD elements cannot be turned on and off fast enough to be scanned one dot at a time in the way that we scan a CRT display. Therefore, we apply the data for one dot line of one character, or for an entire line, to the X axis of the matrix, and activate that dot row of the matrix. For a graphics display we wait a short time, then we deactivate that dot row, apply the data for the next dot row to the X axis, and activate that dot row. We continue the process until we get to the bottom of the display and then start over at the top of the screen. For large LCDs the matrix may be divided into several blocks of perhaps 40 dot lines each. Since each block of dot rows can be refreshed individually, this reduces the speed at which each liquid crystal element must be switched in order to keep the entire display refreshed. Large LCDs usually come with the multiplexing circuitry built in so that all you have to do is send the display data to the unit in the format specified by the manufacturer for that unit. We should soon see color LCDs for use with computers.

COMPUTER VISION

For many applications we need a microcomputer to be able to "see" its environment or perhaps a part that the machine it controls is working on. As part of a microcomputer-controlled security system, for example, we might want the microcomputer to "look" down a corridor to see if any intruders are present. In an automated factory application we might want a microcomputer-controlled robot to "look" in a bin of parts, recognize a specified part, pick up the part, and mount the part on an engine being assembled. There are several mechanisms we can use to allow a computer to see. The first one we will discuss uses sound waves.

Ultrasonic Vision

Bats "see" in the dark by emitting sound waves that are above the human hearing range or *ultrasonic*. A bat sends out ultrasonic pulses, and on the basis of the time it takes for echoes to return, determines how far it is from obstacles. Some Polaroid cameras use the same mechanism to determine the distance to an object being photographed. The camera then uses the distance information to automatically focus the camera lens.

The major parts of the range finder circuitry used in these cameras, including a printed circuit board, is available as a kit from Texas Instruments. With one of these kits and some simple circuitry you can add this type of vision to your microcomputer. Figure 12-18*a* shows a block diagram for the circuitry on the experimental board, and Figure 12-18*b* shows the major waveforms for one cycle of operation. A cycle starts when the VSW input is pulsed high. The transmitter section then sends out a "chirp" of 56 pulses through the transducer. The output is called a chirp because the 56 pulses step through four frequencies, 60 kHz, 57 kHz, 53 kHz, and 50 kHz to avoid absorption problems that might occur with just one frequency. This transmission is represented by the XLG signal in Figure 12-18*b*.

After the pulses are sent out, the circuitry is switched so that the transducer functions as a receiver. When the echo of the sound waves returns to the transducer it produces an analog electrical signal out of the transducer. A programmable-gain amplifier amplifies this echo and converts it to a digital pulse shown as the FLG signal in Figure 12-18*b*. The time it took the ultrasonic signal to go out to the target and return then is the time between the first rising edge of XLG and the rising edge of the FLG signal.

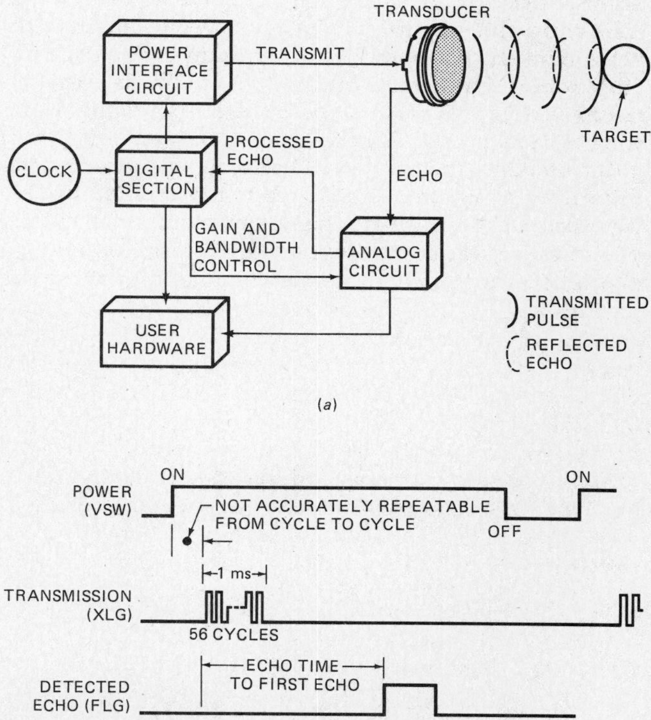

FIGURE 12-18 Polaroid ultrasonic range finder. *(a)* Block diagram of interface circuitry. *(b)* Major signal waveforms.

You can measure this time in any one of several ways. One way is to start a counter with the rising edge of XLG, and stop the counter with the rising edge of FLG. the number left in the counter then is the number of clock pulses required for the signal to go out to the target and back. To get the total time for the trip, you can multiply the number of clock pulses counted by the period of the clock pulses. Divide this time by 2 to get the actual time to the target. Since sound travels at about 1 foot in 0.888 ms, you can easily convert the transit time to an equivalent distance. An exercise in the laboratory manual written to accompany this book shows you more about all of this.

A simple ultrasonic range finder such as we have described here could be mounted in a mobile robot. By scanning the rangefinder back and forth the robot could determine a clear path through a series of obstacles, or detect when someone intrudes into its space. The range finder we described has a range of about 35 feet, and a resolution of about ⅛ inch when looking at a flat surface perpendicular to the sound waves. For applications where we need greater resolution or to recognize the shapes of objects, we use optical vision devices with our microcomputer.

Video Cameras and Computers

Cameras used in TV stations and for video recorders use a special vacuum tube called a *vidicon*. A light-sensitive coating on the inside of the face of the vidicon is swept horizontally and vertically by a beam of electrons. The beam is swept in the same way as the beam in a TV set displaying the picture will be swept. The amount of beam current that flows when the beam is at a particular spot on the vidicon is proportional to the intensity of the light that falls on that spot. The output signal from the vidicon for each scan line then is an analog signal proportional to the amount of light falling on the points along that scan line. This signal is represented by the waveform between the horizontal sync pulses in Figure 12-2. In order to get this analog video information into a digital form that a computer can store and process, we have to pass it through an A/D converter. For a color camera we need an A/D converter on each of the three color signals. Each output value from an A/D converter then represents a dot of the picture. The number of bits of resolution in the A/D converter will determine the number of intensity levels stored for each dot.

Standard video cameras and the associated digitizing circuitry are relatively expensive, so they are not cost-effective for many applications. In cases where we don't need the resolution available from a standard video camera we often use a CCD camera.

CCD Cameras

Charge-coupled devices or CCDs are constructed as long shift registers on semiconductor material. Figure 12-19 shows the structure for a CCD shift register section. As you can see, the structure consists of simply a *P*-type substrate, an insulating layer, and isolated gates. If a gate is made positive with respect to the substrate, a

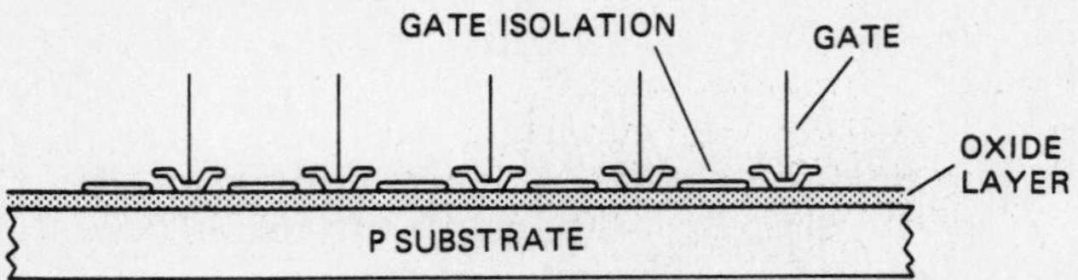

FIGURE 12-19 Basic structure of charge-coupled device used in CCD video cameras.

"potential well" is created under that gate. What this means is that, if a charge of electrons is injected into the region under the gate, the charge will be held there. By applying a sequence of clock signals to the gates, this stored charge can be shifted along to the region under the next gate. In this way a CCD can function as an analog or a digital shift register.

To make an image sensor, several hundred CCD shift registers are built in parallel on the same chip. A photodiode is doped in under every other gate. When all of the gates with photodiodes under them are made positive, potential wells are created. A camera lens is used to focus an image on the surface of the chip. Light shining on the photodiodes causes a charge proportional to the light intensity to be put in each well which has a diode. These charges can be shifted out to produce the dot-by-dot values for the scan lines of a picture. Improved performance can be gained by alternating nonlighted shift registers with the lighted ones. Information for a scan line is shifted in parallel from the lighted register to the dark, and then shifted out serially.

The video information shifted out from a CCD register is in discrete samples, but these samples are analog because the charge put in a well is simply a function of the light shining on the photodiode. To get the video information into a form that can be stored in memory and processed by a microcomputer, it must be passed through an A/D converter, or in some way converted to digital. For many robot applications and surveillance applications, a black-and-white image with no gray tones is all we need. In this case the video information from the CCD registers can simply be passed through a comparator to produce a 1 or a 0 for each dot of the image. CCD cameras have the advantages that they are smaller in size, more rugged, less expensive, and easier to interface to computer circuitry than vidicon-based cameras. Next we describe an inexpensive type of camera which produces digital video information directly.

OPTICRAM Cameras

Figure 12-20 shows a picture of the Micron Eye camera produced by Micron Technology in Boise, Idaho. This camera is relatively inexpensive, interfaces easily to common microcomputers, and has enough resolution for simple robot-type applications.

The heart of this camera is a 64 Kbit dynamic RAM with a glass cover instead of the usual metal lid. A lens on the front of the camera is used to focus the image directly onto the surface of the dynamic RAM. Here's how it works.

FIGURE 12-20 Micron Eye optic RAM video camera with interface board for IBM PC. *(Micron Technology Inc.)*

The 65,536 storage cells of dynamic RAM are arranged in two arrays of 128 by 256 cells each. Each cell functions as a pel. There is a dead zone of about 25 cell widths between the two arrays. If the two arrays are used together, this dead zone has to be taken into account.

Remember now that data is stored in dynamic RAMs as a charge on a tiny capacitor. Dynamic RAMs have to be refreshed because the charge gradually changes due to leakage. If you shine a light on a dynamic RAM cell, the charge changes faster than it would without the light. To use the dynamic RAM as an image sensor, then, we start by charging up all of the cells to a logic 1 level. After some amount of time we read the logic level on each cell. A cell which still contains a logic 1 represents a dark spot, and a cell which has dropped to a logic 0 represents a light spot. The logic levels can be read out of the OPTICRAM and stored directly in a microcomputer memory for processing. The sensitivity of the camera to light can be adjusted by changing the time between when you charge up all the cells and when you read out the logic levels on the cells. For brighter light conditions, use a shorter time, etc.

Available with the Micron Eye are printed circuit boards which contain circuitry to interface the camera to common microcomputers such as the IBM PC, the APPLE, and the Commodore 64. With these boards installed you can display images on the CRT screen, adjust display parameters under program control, and save images on a disk. Once you get the bit pattern for an image into memory, you can then experiment with programs which attempt to recognize the image of, for example, a square in the image.

Figure 12-21 shows an example of what a little vision can do for a robot. The Sumitomo Electric Company robot shown here can play an organ using both hands on the keys and both feet on the pedals. It can press up to 15 keys per second. The robot can play selections from memory when verbally told to do so. Using its vision it can read and play songs from standard sheet music. The robot uses seventeen 16-bit microprocessors and fifty 8-bit controllers to control all of its activities.

If you think some about what is involved in recognizing complex visual shapes, in all of their possible orientations, with a computer program, it should give you a

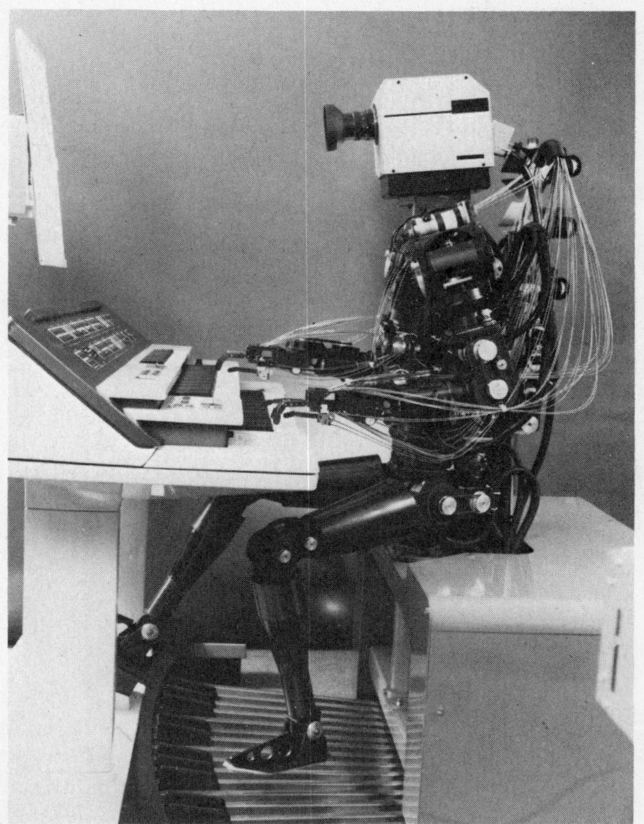

FIGURE 12-21 Organ-playing robot developed by Sumitomo Electric Company.

new appreciation for the pattern recognition capabilities of the human eye-brain system.

Another area where the human brain excels is in that of data storage. Only very recently have the devices used to store computer data approached the capacity of the human brain. In the next section we look at how some of these mass data storage systems operate, and how they are interfaced to microcomputers.

MASS DATA STORAGE SYSTEMS

Since the ROM and RAM in a computer cannot possibly hold all of the programs that we might want to run and all of the data that we might want to analyze, a computer system needs some other form of data storage which can hold massive amounts of data, is nonvolatile, can be updated, and has relatively low cost per bit of storage. The most common devices used for mass data storage are magnetic tape, floppy magnetic disks, hard magnetic disks, and optical disks. Magnetic tapes are used mostly for backup storage, because the access time to get to data stored in the middle of the tape is usually too long to be acceptable. Therefore, in our limited space here we will concentrate on the three types of disk storage.

FLOPPY DISK DATA STORAGE

Floppy Disk Overview

Figure 12-22 shows a picture of a typical floppy disk enclosed in its protective envelope. The common sizes for disks are 8, 5.25, and 3.5 inches. The disk itself is made of Mylar and coated with a magnetic material. The Mylar disk is only a few thousanths of an inch thick, thus the name floppy. When the disk is inserted in a drive unit, a spindle clamps in the large center hole and spins the disk at a constant speed of perhaps 300 or 360 rpm.

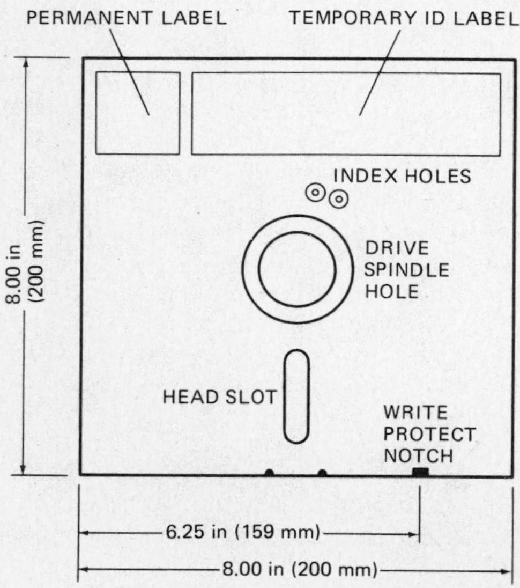

FIGURE 12-22 Floppy disk in protective envelope.

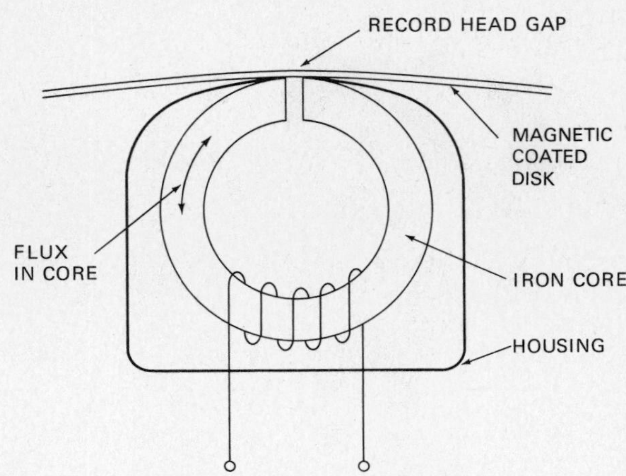

FIGURE 12-23 Magnetic disk read/write head.

Data is stored on the disk in concentric, circular tracks, rather than in a spiral track as it is on a phonograph record. A read/write head contacts the disk through the racetrack-shaped slot to read from or write to the disk. Figure 12-23 shows a diagram of a read/write head. In the write mode a current passing through the coil in the head creates a magnetic flux in the iron core of the head. A gap in the iron core allows the magnetic flux to spill out and magnetize the magnetic material on the disk. Once a region on the disk is magnetized in a particular direction, it retains that magnetism. The polarity of the magnetized region is determined by the direction of the current through the coil. We will say more about this later.

Data can be read from the disk with the same head. Whenever the polarity of the magnetism changes as the track passes over the gap in the read/write head, a small voltage, typically a few millivolts, is induced in the coil. An amplifier and comparator are used to convert this small signal to standard logic levels.

The write-protect notch in a floppy disk envelope can be used to protect stored data from being written over, as the knock-out plastic tabs on audiotape cassettes are. An LED and a phototransistor can indicate whether the notch is present and disable the write circuits if it is.

An index hole punched in the disk indicates the start of the recorded tracks. An LED and a phototransistor are used to detect when the index hole passes.

Disk Drive and Head Positioning

The motor used to spin the floppy disk is usually a dc motor whose speed is precisely controlled by negative feedback as we described in Chapter 10. In most systems this speed will be held constant at all times. Typically it takes about 250 ms for the motor to start up after a start motor command.

The most common method of positioning the read/write head over a desired track is with a stepper motor. A lead screw or a let-out–take-in steel band, such as that

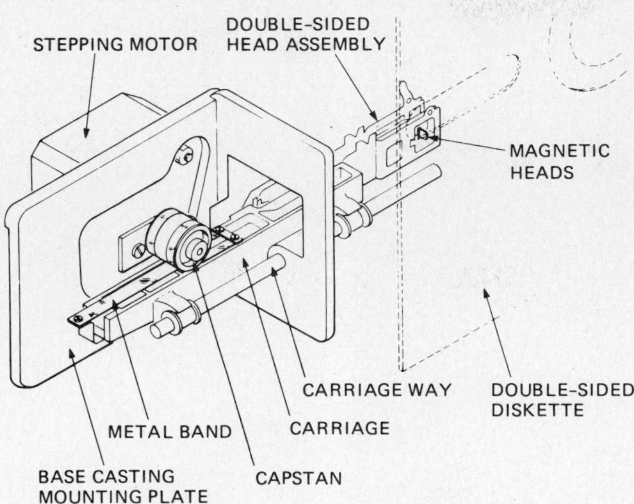

FIGURE 12-24 Head positioning mechanism for floppy disk drive unit. *(Shugart Corporation)*

shown in Figure 12-24, converts the rotary motion of the stepper motor to the linear motion needed to position the head over the desired track on the disk. As the stepper motor in Figure 12-24 rotates, the steel band is let out on one side of the motor pulley, and pulled in on the other side. This slides the head along its carriage.

To find a given track, the motor is usually stepped to move the head to track zero near the outer edge of the disk. The motor is then stepped the number of steps required to move the head to the desired track. Typically it takes a few hundred milliseconds to position the head over a desired track.

Once the desired track is found, the head must be pressed against the disk or *loaded*. Typically it takes about 50 ms to load the head and allow it time to settle against the disk.

Floppy Disk Data Formats and Error Detection

As we said previously, floppy disks come in several standard sizes. Larger disks tend to have more data tracks than smaller disks, but there is no one standard number of tracks for any size disk; 8-in disks typically have about 77 tracks/side, 5.25-in disks about 40 tracks/side, and the new 3.5-in disks in hard plastic envelopes about 80 tracks/side. Single-sided drives record data tracks on only one side of the disk. Double-sided drives use two read/write heads to store data on both sides of the disk. The data tracks on floppy disks are divided into sectors. There are two different methods of indicating the start of sectors: *hard sectoring* and *soft sectoring*. Hard-sectored 8-in disks typically have 32 additional index holes spaced equally around the disk. Each hole signals the start of a sector. The index hole photodetector is used to detect these sector holes.

Soft-sectored disks have only the one index hole which indicates the start of all of the tracks. The sector format is established by bytes stored on the track. Most newer systems use soft sectoring because it is more reliable than hard sectoring.

The actual digital data is stored on floppy disks in many different formats, so we can't begin to show you all of them. To give you a general idea, we will use an old standard, the IBM 3740 format, which is the basis of most current formats. Figure 12-25 shows how bytes are written to a track in this format.

In the 3740 format a track has three types of fields. An *index field* identifies the start of the track. *ID fields* contain the track and sector identification numbers for each of the 26 data sectors on the track. Each of the 26 sectors also contains a *data field* which consists of 128 bytes of data plus two bytes for an error-checking code. As you can see, in addition to the bytes used to store data, many bytes are used for identification, synchronization, error checking, and buffering between sectors. One type of separator used here is called a *gap*. A gap is simply a region which contains no data. Gaps are provided to separate fields, so that the information stored in one field can be changed without altering an adjacent field.

Address marks shown at several places in this format are special bytes which have an extra clock pulse recorded along with their D2 data bit. Address marks are used to identify the start of a field. The four types of address mark are: index, ID, data, and deleted data.

Two bytes at the end of each ID field and 2 bytes at the end of each data field are used to store *checksums* or *cyclic redundancy characters*. These are used to check for errors when the ID and the data are read out. A data checksum, for example, is produced by adding up all of the data bytes and keeping only the least-significant 2 bytes of the result. These 2 bytes are then recorded after the data bytes. When the data is read, it is readded and the sum is compared with the recorded checksum bytes. If the two sums are equal, then the data was probably read out correctly. If the sums do not agree, then another attempt can be made to read the data. If, after several tries, the sums still do not compare, then a disk read error can be sent out to the CRT.

Instead of using a checksum, most disk systems use a cyclic redundancy character or CRC method. There are actually several similar techniques using CRC. Here's one way to give you the idea. To produce the 2 CRC bytes the 128 data bytes are treated as a single large binary number and are divided by a constant number. The 16-bit remainder from this division is written in after the data bytes as the CRC bytes. When the data bytes and the CRC bytes are read out, the CRC bytes are subtracted from the data string. The result is divided by the original constant. Since the original remainder has already been subtracted, the remainder of the division should be zero if the data was read out correctly. Higher-quality systems usually write data to a disk and immediately read it back to see if it was written correctly. If an error is detected, then another attempt can be made. If 10 write attempts are unsuccessful, then the operator can be prompted to throw out the disk, or the write can be directed to another sector on the disk.

The IBM 3740 format we have been describing is referred to as *single density*. An 8-in disk in this format has one index track and 76 data tracks. Since each track has 26 sectors with 128 data bytes in each sector,

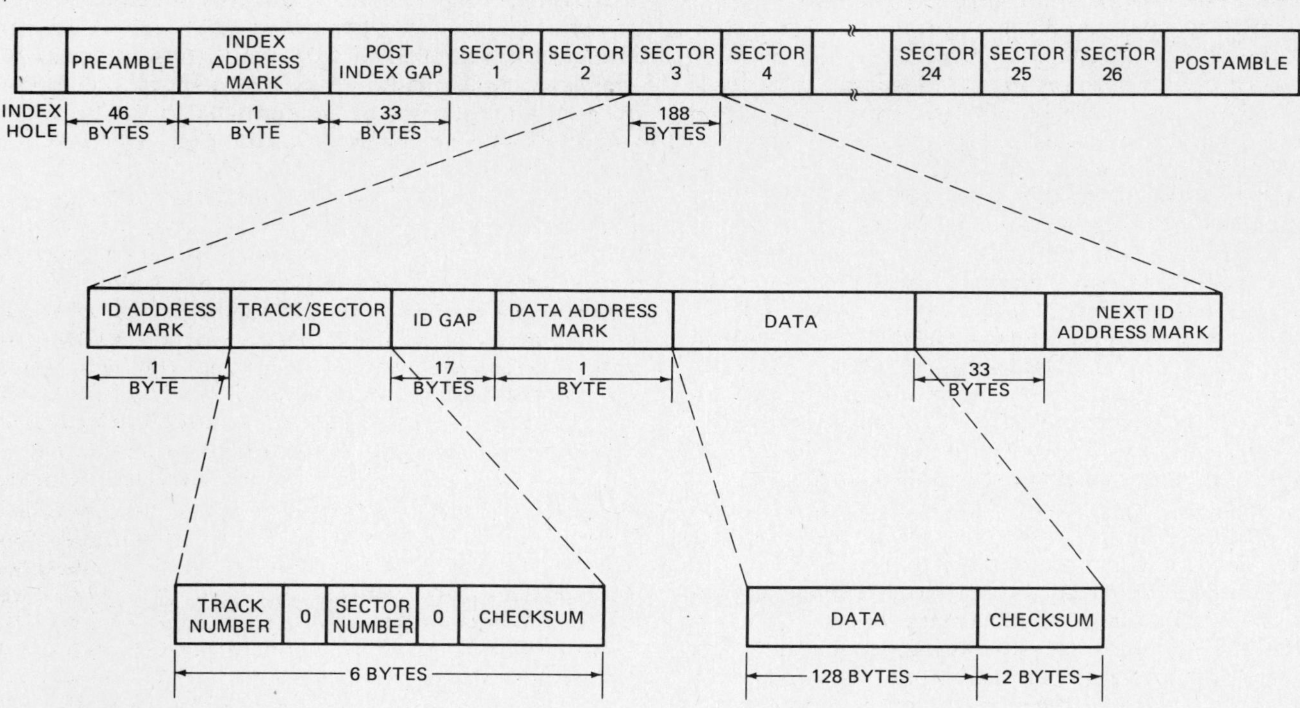

FIGURE 12-25 IBM 3740 floppy disk soft-sectored track format (single density).

the total is about 250 Kbytes. If we use both sides of the disk we get about 500 Kbytes. To increase the storage capacity even further, most systems use *double-density* recording. Double-density recording uses a different clock and data bit pattern to pack twice as many sectors in a track. Now let's look at how data bits are actually recorded on floppy disks.

Recorded Bit Formats – FM and MFM

A "one" bit is represented on magnetic disks as a change in the polarity of the magnetism on the track. A "zero" bit is represented as no change in the polarity of the magnetism. This form of recording is often called *non-return-to-zero* or NRZ recording, because the magnetic field is never zero on a recorded track. Each point on the track is always magnetized in one direction or the other. The read head produces a signal when a region where the magnetic field changes passes over it. As you read through the next section, keep in mind that what we show in the waveforms as a pulse simply represents a change in magnetic polarity on the disk.

Figure 12-26 shows how bits are stored on a disk track in single-density format. This format is often called *frequency modulation*, FM, or F2F recording. Note that there is a clock pulse, C, at the start of each bit cell in this format. These pulses represent the basic frequency. A 1 is written in a bit cell by putting in a pulse, D, between the clock pulses; a 0 is represented by no pulse between the clock pulses. Putting in the data pulses modifies the frequency, thus the name frequency modulation.

The recorded clock pulses are required to sychronize the readout circuits. The actual distance, and therefore time, between data bits read from an outer track is longer than it is for data bits read from an inner track. A circuit called a *phase-locked loop* adjusts its frequency to that of the clock pulses and produces a signal which

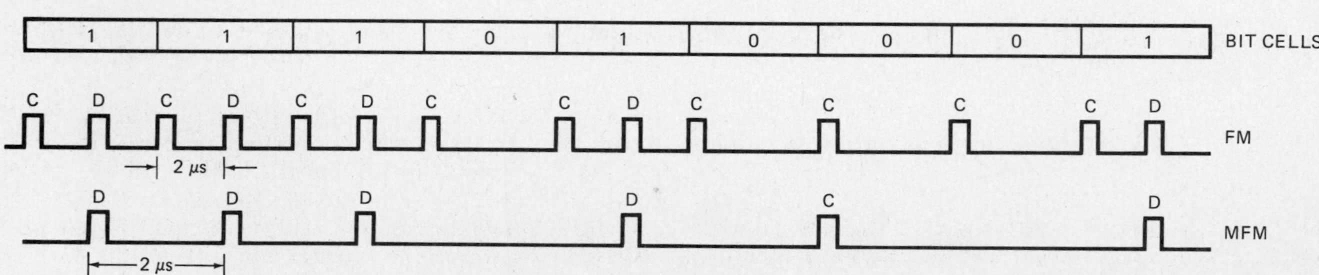

FIGURE 12-26 FM and MFM recording formats for magnetic disks.

tells the read circuit when to check for a data bit. Recording clock information along with data information not only makes it possible to accurately read data from different tracks, but it also reduces the chances of a read error caused by small changes in disk speed.

A disadvantage of standard F2F recording is that a clock pulse and the data bit are required to represent each data bit. Since bits can only be packed just so close together on a disk track without interfering with each other, this limits the amount of data that can be stored on a track in this format. To double the amount of data that we can store on a track we use the *modified frequency modulation* or MFM recording format shown as the second waveform in Figure 12-26. The basic principle of this format is that both clock pulses and "one" data pulses are used to keep the phase-locked loop and read circuitry synchronized. A clock pulse is not put in unless data pulses do not happen to come often enough in the data bytes to keep the phase-locked loop locked. Clock bits are put at the start of the bit cell and data bits are put in the middle of the bit cell time. A clock bit will only be put in, however, if the data bit in the previous cell was a 0, and the data bit in the current bit cell is also a 0. Since this format has in all cases only one pulse per bit cell, a bit cell can be half as long, or in other words, twice as many of them can be packed into a track. This is the way that double-density recording is achieved in the IBM PC and other common microcomputers. For a 5.25-in double-density recorded disk, data bits will be read out at about 250,000 *bits*/s. Incidentally, a new disk recording technology called *perpendicular* or *vertical* recording should allow 4 to 8 times as much data to be put on a given-size disk. With perpendicular recording the tiny magnetic regions are oriented perpendicular to the disk surface instead of parallel to it as they are for standard disks.

Now that we have shown you how digital data is stored on floppy disks, we will show you the circuitry required to interface a floppy disk drive to a microcomputer.

A Floppy Disk Controller – the Intel 8272A

As you can probably tell from the preceding discussion, writing data to a floppy disk and reading the data back requires coordination at several levels. One level is the motor and head drive signals. Another level is the actual writing and reading at the bit level. Still another level is interfacing with the rest of the circuitry of a microcomputer. Doing all of this coordination is a full-time job, so we use a specially designed floppy disk controller to do it. As our example device here we will use the Intel 8272A controller, which is equivalent to the NEC μPD765A controller used in the IBM PC. It is easier to find data sheets and application notes for the 8272A, if you need further information.

8272 SIGNALS AND CIRCUIT CONNECTIONS

Figure 11-3 showed you how an 8272A controller can be connected in an 8086-based microcomputer system. Also in Chapter 11 we discussed in detail how data can be transferred to and from a floppy disk controller on a DMA basis. Now we want to take a closer look at the controller itself to show you the types of signals it produces and how it is programmed.

To start, take a look at the block diagram of the 8272A in Figure 12-27. The signals along the left side of the diagram should be readily recognizable to you. The data bus lines, $\overline{\text{RD}}$, $\overline{\text{WR}}$, A0, RESET, and $\overline{\text{CS}}$ are the standard peripheral interface signals. The DRQ, $\overline{\text{DACK}}$, and INT signals are used for DMA transfer of data to and from the controller. To refresh your memory from Chapter 11, here's a review of how the DMA works. When a microcomputer program needs some data off the disk, it sends a series of command words to registers inside the controller. The controller then proceeds to read the data from the specified track and sector on the disk. When the controller reads the first byte of data from a sector, it sends a DMA request, DRQ, signal to the DMA controller. The DMA controller sends a hold request signal to the HOLD input of the CPU. The CPU floats its buses and sends a hold acknowledge signal to the DMA controller. The DMA controller then sends out the first transfer address on the bus and asserts the $\overline{\text{DACK}}$ input of the 8272 to tell it that the DMA transfer is underway. When the number of bytes specified in the DMA initialization has been transferred, the DMA controller asserts the TERMINAL COUNT input of the 8272. This causes the 8272 to assert its interrupt output signal, INT. The INT signal can be connected to a CPU or 8259A interrupt input to tell the CPU that the requested block of data has been read in from the disk to a buffer in memory. The process would proceed in a similar manner for a DMA write-to-disk operation.

Now let's work our way through the drive control signals shown in the lower right corner of the 8272 block diagram in Figure 12-27. Reading through our brief descriptions of these signals should give you a better idea of what is involved in the interfacing to the disk drive hardware. Note the direction of the arrow on each of these signals.

The READY input signal from the disk drive will be high if the drive is powered and ready to go. If, for example, you forget to close the disk drive door, the READY signal will not be asserted.

The WRITE PROTECT/TWO SIDE signal indicates whether the write protect notch is covered when the drive is in the read or write mode. When the drive is operating in track-seek mode, this signal indicates whether the drive is two-sided or one-sided.

The INDEX signal will be pulsed when the index hole in the disk passes between the LED and phototransistor detector.

The FAULT/TRACK 0 signal indicates some disk drive problem condition during a read/write operation. During a track-seek operation this signal will be asserted when the head is over track 0, the outermost track on the disk.

The DRIVE SELECT output signals, DS0 and DS1, from the controller are sent to an external decoder which uses these signals to produce an enable signal for one to four drives.

The MFM output signal will be asserted high if the controller is programmed for modified frequency modu-

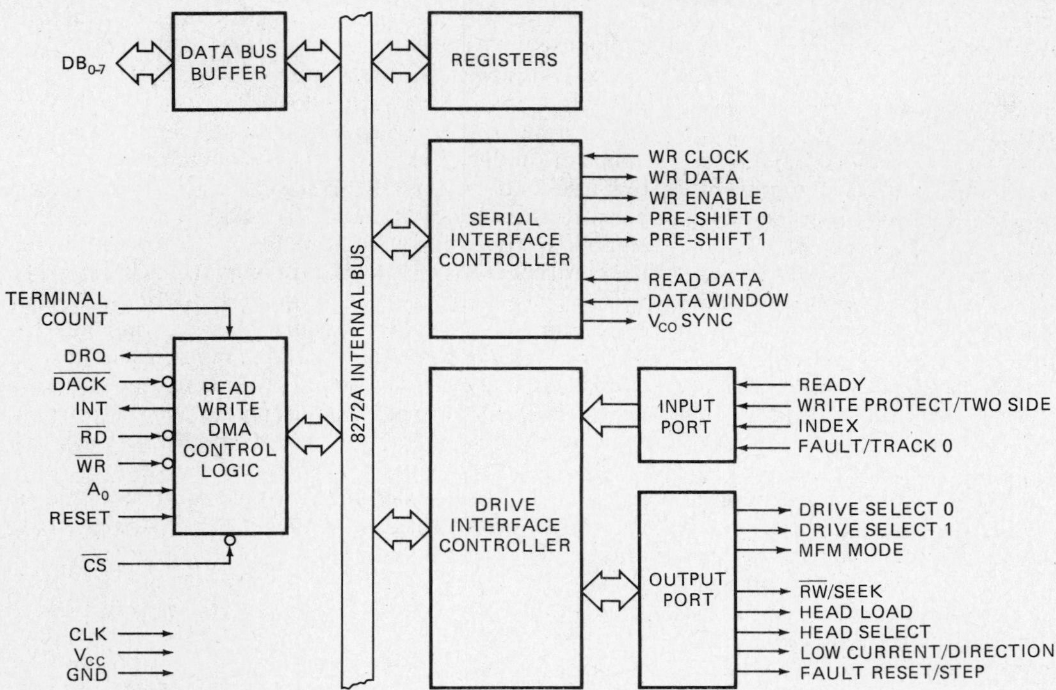

FIGURE 12-27 INTEL 8272A floppy disk controller block diagram.

lation, and low if the controller is programmed for standard frequency modulation (FM).

The $\overline{RW}$/SEEK signal is used to tell the drive to operate in read-write mode or in track-seek mode. Remember, some of the other controller signals have different meanings in the read-write mode than they do in the seek mode.

The HEAD LOAD signal is asserted by the controller to tell the drive hardware to put the read/write head in contact with the disk. When interfacing to a double-sided drive, the HEAD SELECT from the controller is used along with this signal to indicate which of the two heads should be loaded.

During write operations on inner tracks of the disk the LOW CURRENT/DIRECTION signal is asserted by the controller. Because the bits are closer together on the inner tracks, the write current must be reduced to prevent recorded bits from splattering over each other. When executing a seek-track command this signal pin is used to tell the drive whether to step outward toward the edge of the disk or inward toward the center.

The FAULT RESET/STEP output signal is used to reset the fault flip-flop after a fault has been corrected when doing a read or write command. When the controller is carrying out a track-seek command, this pin is used to output the pulses which step the head from track to track.

Now that we have led you quickly through the drive interface signals, let's take a look at the 8272A signals used to read and write the actual clock and data bits on a track. To help with this, Figure 12-28 shows a block diagram of the circuitry between these pins and the read/write head.

Remember from our discussion of FM and MFM recording that clock information is recorded on the track with the data information. We use the clock bits to tell us when to read the data bits. The V_{CO} SYNC signal from the controller tells an external phase-locked loop circuit to synchronize its frequency with that of the clock pulses being read off the disk. (In the case of MFM recording, the data bits are also part of the signal the PLL locks on). The output from the phase-locked loop circuitry is a DATA WINDOW signal. This signal is sent to the controller to tell it where to find the data pulses in the data stream coming in on the READ DATA input.

For writing pulses to the disk, the story is a little more complex. External circuitry supplies a basic WR CLOCK signal at a frequency of 500 kHz for FM and 1 MHz for

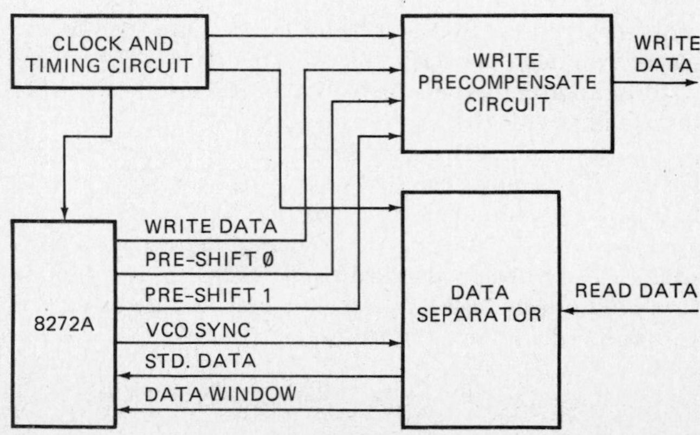

FIGURE 12-28 Block diagram of external circuitry used with Intel 8272A floppy disk controller for reading and writing serial data.

MFM recording. The 8272 outputs the serial stream of clock bits and data bits that are to be written to the disk on its WR DATA pin. During a write operation the 8272 asserts its WR ENABLE signal to turn on the external circuitry which actually sends this serial data to the read/write head. Now, data bits written in MFM on a disk will tend to shift in position as they are read out. A "one" bit, for example, will tend to shift toward an adjacent "zero" bit. This shift could cause errors in readout unless it were compensated for. The PRE-SHIFT 0 and PRE-SHIFT 1 signals from the controller go to external circuitry which shifts bits forward or backward as they are being written. The bits will then be in the correct position when read out.

8272 COMMANDS

The 8272 can execute 15 different commands. Each of these commands is sent to the data register in the controller as a series of bytes. Consult an 8272 data sheet to find the formats for these commands if you need them. After a command has been sent to the 8272, it carries out the command, and returns the results to status registers in the 8272, and/or to the data register in the 8272. To give you an overview of the commands you get to send to an 8272, we list them here with a short description for each.

SPECIFY	—Initialize head load time, head step time, DMA/non-DMA.
SENSE DRIVE STATUS	—Return drive status information.
SENSE INTERRUPT STATUS	—Poll the 8272 interrupt signal.
SEEK	—Position read/write head over specified track.
RECALIBRATE	—Position head over track 0.
FORMAT TRACK	—Write ID field, gaps, and address marks on track.
READ DATA	—Load head, read specified amount of data from sector.
READ DELETED DATA	—Read data from sectors marked as deleted.
WRITE DATA	—Load head, write data to specified sector.
WRITE DELETED DATA	—Write deleted data address mark in sector.
READ TRACK	—Load head, read all sectors on track.
READ ID	—Return first ID field found on track.
SCAN EQUAL	—Compare sector of data bytes read from disk with data bytes sent from CPU or DMA controller until strings match. Set bit in status register if match.
SCAN HIGH OR EQUAL	—Set flag if data string from disk sector greater than or equal to data string from CPU or DMA controller.
SCAN LOW OR EQUAL	—Set flag if data string from disk sector is less than or equal to data string from CPU or DMA controller.

Working out a series of commands for a disk controller such as the 8272 on a bit-by-bit basis is quite tedious and time-consuming. Fortunately, you usually don't have to do this, because in most systems, you can use higher level procedures to read from and write to a disk. In the next section we show you some of the software used to interface to disk drives.

Disk Drive Interface Software

There are several different software levels at which you can interact with a disk drive. One level is directly at the controller level. The next level up is at the BIOS level. A still higher and easier-to-use level is at the disk operating system (DOS) level. Using the IBM PC as an example we will show you in the following sections how to interface your programs with a disk drive using the BIOS approach and the DOS approach.

BIOS Level Floppy Disk Interfacing

In previous discussions we have shown you how to use IBM BIOS procedures to interface with the keyboard, the CRT, and a printer. BIOS procedures, remember, are called with the INT (type) instruction. Figure 12-29 shows the header for the BIOS INT 13H procedure which allows you to interact with disk drives. To give you an idea of what is involved in using this procedure, read through the list of parameters you must pass to it for different operations. As you can see from the header, when using this procedure, you have to specify the particular track and sector(s) that you want to read or write. You have to set up a buffer in memory and pass a pointer to the start of the buffer. Also, you have to set up a table in memory that contains the numbers of tracks and sectors you have recorded data on. The point here is that, yes, you can use this BIOS procedure to interact with a disk by loading registers with the indicated parameters and executing the INT 13H instruction. However, to use an old cliche, it is not a very user friendly way to do it. An easier way to interface your programs with the disk drive is to use DOS procedures. Here's how you do this.

Disk Operating System (DOS) Interfacing

DISK OPERATING SYSTEM OVERVIEW

First of all, let's clarify some terms for you. An *operating system* is simply a program or collection of programs which allows you to format disks, execute programs, create disk files, write data to files, read data from files,

```
LINE  SOURCE

         JMZ        K65                  ; DO ANOTHER CYCLE
         POP        AX                   ; RECOVER CONTROL
         OUT        KB_CTL.AL            ; OUTPUT THE CONTROL
         JMP        K27
;-------------------------------------------------------------------------------
:        ROS CHECKSUM SUBROUTINE         :
;-------------------------------------------------------------------------------
ROS_CHECKSUM    PROC     HEAR            ; NEXT_ROS_MODULE
         MOV        CX,8192              ; NUMBER OF BYTES TO ADD
ROS_CHECKSUM_CNT:                        ; ENTRY FOR OPTIONAL ROS TEST
         XDR        AL,AL
C26:
         ADD        AL,DS:[BX]
         INC        BX                   ; POINT TO NEXT BYTE
         LOOP       C26                  ; ADD ALL BYTES IN ROS MODULE
         OR         AL,AL                ; SUM = 0?
         RET
ROS_CHECKSUM    ENDP

; -- INT 13 ---------------------------------------------------------------------
; DISKETTE I/O                                                                 :
;        THIS INTERFACE PROVIDES ACCESS TO THE 5 1/4" DISKETTE DRIVES          :
; INPUT                                                                        :
;        (AH) = 0  RESET DISKETTE SYSTEM                                       :
;                  HARD RESET TO NEC, PREPARE COMMAND, RECALL REQUIRED         :
;                  ON ALL DRIVES                                               :
;        (AH) = 1  READ THE STATUS OF THE SYSTEM INTO (AL)                     :
;                  DISKETTE_STATUS FROM LAST OPERATION IS USED                 :
;                                                                              :
; REGISTERS FOR READ/WRITE/VERIFY/FORMAT                                       :
;        (DL)—DRIVE NUMBER (0-3 ALLOWED, VALUE CHECKED)                        :
;        (DH)—HEAD NUMBER (0-1 ALLOWED, NOT VALUE CHECKED)                     :
;        (CH)—TRACK NUMBER (0-39, NOT VALUE CHECKED)                           :
;        (CL)—SECTOR NUMBER (1-8, NOT VALUE CHECKED,                           :
;                      NOT USED FOR FORMAT)                                    :
;        (AL)—NUMBER OF SECTORS ( MAX = 8, NOT VALUE CHECKED, NOT USED         :
;                           FOR FORMAT)                                        :
;        (ES:BX)—ADDRESS OF BUFFER ( NOT REQUIRED FOR VERIFY)                  :
;                                                                              :
;        (AH) = 2  READ THE DESIRED SECTORS INTO MEMORY                        :
;        (AH) = 3  WRITE THE DESIRED SECTORS FROM MEMORY                       :
;        (AH) = 4  VERIFY THE DESIRED SECTORS                                  :
;        (AH) = 5  FORMAT THE DESIRED TRACK                                    :
;                  FOR THE FORMAT OPERATION, THE BUFFER POINTER (ES.BX)        :
;                  MUST POINT TO THE COLLECTION OF DESIRED ADDRESS FIELDS      :
;                  FOR THE TRACK. EACH FIELD IS COMPOSED OF 4 BYTES,           :
;                  (C,H,R,N), WHERE C = TRACK NUMBER, H = HEAD NUMBER,         :
;                  R = SECTOR NUMBER, N = NUMBER OF BYTES PER SECTOR           :
;                  (00 = 128, 01 = 256, 02 = 512, 03 = 1024). THERE MUST BE ONE :
;                  ENTRY FOR EVERY SECTOR ON THE TRACK. THIS INFORMATION       :
;                  IS USED TO FIND THE REQUESTED SECTOR DURING READ/WRITE      :
;                  ACCESS.                                                     :
;                                                                              :
; DATA VARIABLE—DISK_POINTER                                                   :
;        DOUBLE WORD POINTER TO THE CURRENT SET OF DISKETTE PARAMETERS         :
; OUTPUT                                                                       :
;        AM = STATUS OF OPERATION                                              :
;                  STATUS BITS ARE DEFINED IN THE EQUATES FOR                  :
;                  DISKETTE_STATUS VARIABLE IN THE DATA SEGMENT OF THIS        :
;                  MODULE.                                                     :
;        CY = 0    SUCCESSFUL OPERATION (AH = 0 ON RETURN)                     :
;        CY = 1    FAILED OPERATION (AH HAS ERROR REASON)                      :
;        FOR READ/WRITE/VERIFY                                                 :
;                  DS,BX,DX,CH,CL PRESERVED                                    :
;                  AL = NUMBER OF SECTORS ACTUALLY READ                        :
;                  ***** AL MAY NOT BE CORRECT IF TIME OUT ERROR OCCURS        :
;        NOTE:     IF AN ERROR IS REPORTED BY THE DISKETTE CODE, THE           :
;                  APPROPRIATE ACTION IS TO RESET THE DISKETTE, THEN RETRY     :
;                  THE OPERATION, ON READ ACCESSES, NO MOTOR START DELAY       :
;                  IS TAKEN, SO THAT THREE RETRIES ARE REQUIRED ON READS       :
;                  TO ENSURE THAT THE PROBLEM IS NOT DUE TO MOTOR              :
;                  START-UP.                                                   :
;-------------------------------------------------------------------------------
        ASSUME  CS:CODE,DS:DATA,ES:DATA
        ORS     0EC59H
DISKETTE_IO     PROC  FAR
        STI              ; INTERRUPTS BACK ON
```

FIGURE 12-29 Header for IBM BIOS INT 13H procedure for interfacing with floppy disk drives.

communicate with system peripherals such as modems and printers, etc. As we will discuss in Chapter 14, some operating systems allow several users to share a CPU on a time-share basis. The term *disk operating system* or DOS means that the operating system resides on a disk and is loaded into memory and executed when you turn on or reset the system. The term *file* in this case refers to a collection of related data accessible by name. The principle is the same as having a named file folder in an office file cabinet.

Using DOS to format disks, write files, and read files relieves you of the burden of keeping track of the individual tracks and sectors. DOS does all of this for you. Now, before we show you how to use DOS procedure calls, we will briefly show you how DOS keeps track of where it puts everything.

Boot record—variable size
First copy of file allocation table—variable size
Second copy of file allocation table—variable size
Root directory—variable size
Data area

FIGURE 12-30 IBM PC DOS format for floppy disks.

Figure 12-30 shows the "housekeeping" information that IBM PC DOS puts on the first track of a disk to do this. The basic structure for these parts is put on a disk when it is formatted with a DOS format command. As files are created and written to the disk, the relevant information for each file is put in the directory and tables.

The boot record in the first sector of the first track indicates whether the disk contains the DOS files needed to load DOS into RAM and run it. Loading DOS and running it is commonly referred to as "booting" the system.

The directory on the disk contains a 32-byte entry for each file. Let's take a quick look at the use of these bytes to get an overview of the information stored for each file.

Byte number (decimal)

- 0-7 Filename
- 8-10 Filename extension
- 11 File attribute
  - 01H – read only
  - 02H – hidden file
  - 04H – system file
  - 08H – volume label in first 11 bytes, not filename
  - 10H – file is a subdirectory of files in lower level of hierarchical file tree
  - 20H – file has been written to and closed
- 12-21 Reserved
- 22-23 Time the file was created or last updated
- 24-25 Date the file was created or last updated
- 26-27 Starting cluster number – DOS allocates space for files in *clusters* of one or more adjacent sectors in size.
- 28-31 Size of the file in bytes

DOS uses the first *file allocation table* or FAT to keep track of which clusters on a disk are currently being used for each file, and which clusters are still available. The FAT is part of the link between a filename and the actual track and sector numbers where that file is stored. The second FAT is simply a copy of the first, included for backup purposes.

Most current microcomputer operating systems, IBM PC DOS 2.1 and later versions for example, allow you to set up a *hierarchical file structure*. In this structure you have one main or *root* directory which resides in the directory of the disk as shown in Figure 12-30. This root directory can contain the names of program or data files. The root directory can also have the names of *subdirectories* of files. Each subdirectory can also refer directly to program or data files, or it can refer to lower subdirectories. The point here is that this structure allows you to group similar files together, and to avoid going through a long list of filenames to find a particular file you need. To get to a file in a lower level directory, you simply specify the *path* to that file. The path is the series of directory names that you go through to get to that file.

USING IBM PC DOS CALLS IN YOUR PROGRAMS

As we said previously, DOS is largely a collection of procedures which you can call from your programs, similar to the way you call BIOS procedures. Many disk operating systems and earlier versions of PC DOS require you to construct a *file control block* or FCB in order to access disk files from your programs. The format of a file control block differs from system to system, but basically the FCB must contain among other things, the name of the file, the length of the file, the file attribute, and information about the blocks in the file. Version 2.0 and later versions of PC DOS simplify calling DOS file procedures by letting you refer to a file with a single 16-bit number. This number is called the *file handle* or *token*. You simply put the file handle for a file you want to access in a register, and call the DOS procedure. DOS then constructs the FCB needed to access the file. The question that may occur to you at this point is, "How do I know what the file handle is for a file I want to access on a disk?" The answer is that to get the file handle for a disk file you simply call a DOS procedure which returns the file handle in a register. You can then pass the file handle to the procedure that you want to call to access the file. PC DOS treats external devices such as printers, the keyboard, and the CRT as files for read and write operations. These devices are assigned fixed file handles by DOS as follows: 0000 – keyboard, 0001 – CRT, 0002 – error output to CRT, 0003 – serial port, 0004 – printer. The point here is that file handles make it easy for you to access files. There are more examples of calling DOS procedures in Figure 13-24, but here are a few to get you started.

Each DOS function (procedure) has an identification number. To call a DOS function you put the function number in the AH register, put any parameters required by the procedure in other registers, and then execute the INT 21H instruction. For example, DOS function call 40H can be used to print a string. To use this procedure set up the registers as follows:

1. Load the function number, 40H, into the AH register.
2. Load the DS register with the segment base of the segment which contains the string.
3. Load the DX register with the offset of the start of the string.
4. Load the CX register with the number of bytes to write.

5. Load the BX register with the fixed file handle for the printer, 0004H.

Then, to call the DOS procedure, execute the INT 21H instruction. Note that the DOS function allows you to send an entire string to the printer, rather than just a single character at a time as the BIOS INT 17H does.

As another example, the DOS 0AH function will read in a string from the keyboard and put the string in a buffer pointed to by DS:DX. Characters will also be displayed on the CRT as they are entered on the keyboard. The function terminates when a carriage return is entered. To use this function, first set up a buffer in the data segment with the DB directive. The first byte of the buffer must contain the maximum number of bytes the buffer can hold. The 0AH call will return the actual number of characters read in the second byte. The function does not require you to pass it a file handle, because the file handle is implied in the function.

To leave a program and return to the DOS command level, you can use the DOS 4AH call. Load AL with 00, AH with 4CH, and execute the INT 21H instruction.

As a final example here, we will show you how DOS calls can be used to open a file, read data from a file into a buffer in memory, and close the file. Opening a file means copying the file parameters from the directory to a file control block in memory and marking the file as open. Closing a file means updating the directory information for the file and marking the file closed. To open a file and get the file handle we use DOS function call 3DH. For this call DS:DX must point to the start of an *ASCIIZ* string which contains the disk drive number, the path, and the filename. An ASCIIZ string is a string of ASCII characters which has a byte of of all 0's as its last byte. Also AL must contain an access code which indicates the type of operation that you want to perform on the file. Use an access code of 00 for read only, 01 for write only, and 02 for read and write. Again, to actually call the function, you load 3DH into AH and execute the INT 21H instruction. The handle for the opened file is returned in the AX register. The first part of Figure 12-31 shows how these pieces are put together.

To read a file we use function call 3FH. For this call BX must contain the file handle and CX the number of bytes to read from the file. DS:DX must point to the buffer location in RAM that the data from the file will be read into. To do the actual call we load 3FH into AH and do an INT 21H instruction. After the file is read, AX contains the number of bytes actually read from the file.

To close the file we load function number 3EH into AH, load the file handle into BX, and execute the INT 21H instruction. The last half of Figure 12-31 shows the instructions you can use to read and close a file. Watch for some more examples in Figure 13-24. Consult the IBM DOS Technical Reference Manual for the details of all of the available function calls.

RAM DISKS

Currently available for most microcomputers are programs which allow you to set aside an area of RAM in

```
;8086 Program fragment
;ABSTRACT:      This code shows how to use DOS functions to
;               open a file, read the file contents into a buffer
;               in memory, and close the file
;
; point at start of buffer containing file name
     MOV   DX, OFFSET FILE_NAME ; and move pointer over
     ADD   DX, 02H              ; string length bytes
     MOV   AL, 00               ; open file for read
     MOV   AH, 3DH              ; and get file handle
     INT   21H
     MOV   BX, AX               ; save file handle in BX
     PUSH  BX                   ; and push for future use
     MOV   CX, 2048             ; set up maximum read
; point at memory buffer reserved for disk file contents
     MOV   DX, OFFSET FILE_BUF
     MOV   AH, 3FH              ; read disk file
     INT   21H
     POP   BX                   ; get back file handle for close
     PUSH  AX                   ; save file length returned by
                                ; 3FH function call
     MOV   AH, 3EH              ; close disk file
     INT   21H
; use the file now stored in memory
```

FIGURE 12-31 Instruction sequence to open a disk file and get file handle, read file contents to a buffer in memory, and close file using IBM PC DOS function calls.

such a way that it appears to DOS as simply another disk drive. In an IBM PC that has two actual drives, A: and B:, the installed RAM disk becomes C:. You can copy files to and from this RAM disk by name just as you would for any other drive. Here's the point of this. Suppose you are using Wordstar to edit program files. Most of the time when you execute a Wordstar command the system must go and get the code for that command from the Wordstar system disk and load it into memory before it can execute the command. This makes you spend a lot of time waiting. If you load all of the Wordstar files into the RAM disk, they can then be accessed much faster because there is no mechanical access time. The advantage of configuring the RAM as a disk drive is that the software can be accessed just as if it were on a disk.

MAGNETIC HARD DISK DATA STORAGE

The floppy disks that we discussed in the previous section have the advantage that they are relatively inexpensive and removable. The distance between tracks, and therefore the amount of data that can be stored on floppy disks, is limited to a large extent by the flexibility of the disks. The rate at which data can be read off a disk is limited by the fact that a floppy disk can only be rotated at 300 or 360 rpm. To solve these problems, we use a hard disk system like the one in Figure 12-32.

The disks in a hard disk system are made of a metal alloy, coated on both sides with a magnetic material. Hard disks are more dimensionally stable. This means that they can be spun at higher speed, and that tracks and the bits on the tracks can be put closer together. In most cases the hard disks are permanently fastened in the drive mechanism and sealed in a dust-free package, but some systems do have removable enclosed disks. Common hard disk sizes are 3.5, 5.25, 8, 10.5, 14, and 20 in. To increase the amount of storage per drive, several disks may be stacked with spacers between. A read-write head is used for each disk surface. Current technology allows 3 to 10 Mbytes per 5.25-in disk, 5 to 20 Mbytes per 8-in disk, 30 to 50 Mbytes per 10-in disk, and 40 to 100 Mbytes per 14-in disk.

FIGURE 12-32 Multiple-platter hard disk memory system.

Rigid disks are rotated at 1000 to 3600 rpm. This high speed not only makes it possible to read and write data faster, it also creates a thin cushion of air that floats the read-write head 10 μin off the disk. Unless the head *crashes*, it never touches the recorded area of the disk, so wear is minimized. When data is not being read or written, the head is retracted to a *parking zone* where no data is recorded. Hard disks must be kept in a dust-free environment, because the diameter of dust and smoke particles may be 10 times the distance the head floats off the disk. If dust does get into a hard disk system, the result will be the same as that which occurs when a plane does not fly high enough to get over some mountains. The head will crash and perhaps destroy the data stored on the disk.

Hard disk drives are often referred to as Winchesters. Legend has it that the name came from an early IBM dual-drive unit with a planned storage of 30 Mbytes/drive. The 30-30 configuration apparently reminded someone of the famous rifle, and the name stuck.

In some hard disk drives the read-write heads are positioned over the desired track by a stepper motor and a band actuator as we described for the floppy disk drive. Other hard disk drives use a *linear voice coil* mechanism to position the read-write heads. This mechanism uses feedback control, such as that we described in Chapter 10, to control the position of what is essentially a linear motor. The feedback system adjusts the position of the head over the desired track until the strength of the read signal is a maximum.

Most hard disk drives record data bits on a disk track using the MFM method we described in the floppy disk section of this chapter. As with floppy disks, there is no real standard for the format in which the data is recorded. Most systems format a track in a manner similar to that shown for floppy disks in Figure 12-25. The hard disk drive unit used in the IBM PC XT, for example, uses two double-sided hard disks with 306 tracks on each disk surface. On disk drives with more than one recording surface, tracks are often referred to as *cylinders*, because if you mentally connect same numbered tracks on the two sides of a disk or on different disks, the result is a cylinder. The cylinder number then is the same as the track number. On the PC XT hard disk, each track has 17 sectors with 512 bytes in each sector. This adds up to about 10 Mbytes of data storage. Data is read out at 5 M*bits*/s, which is about 10 times faster than the readout rate for double-density floppy disks.

To interface a hard disk drive to a microcomputer system we use a dedicated controller device such as the Intel 82064, which operates similarly to the 8272 floppy disk controller we described previously in this chapter. An added feature of this controller is the ability to record either CRC words or error-correcting code words with each data sector.

From a software standpoint, writing files to and reading files from a hard disk is very similar to the same operations for a floppy disk. To DOS the hard disk appears for the most part as simply another drive. One difference is that a hard disk is often divided into *parti-*

tions so that groups of programs can be separated from each other. Partitions function essentially as separate disks. An operating system loaded from one partition, for example, cannot accidentally destruct another operating system stored in another partition. The only way to get to the other partition in many systems is to reboot the system into that partition.

Another term encountered in connection with hard disks is *file server*. A file server is a hard disk system which has its own CPU and operating system. The unit is usually a major part of a computer network. The function of the file server is to manage the access to and use of files stored on the disk by other systems on the network.

To prevent data loss in the event of a head crash, hard disk files are backed up on some other medium such as floppy disks or magnetic tape. The difficulty with using floppy disks for backup is the number of disks required. Backing up a 10 Mbyte hard disk with 360 Kbyte floppies requires 30 disks and considerable time shoving disks in and out. Many systems now use a high-speed magnetic tape system for backup. A typical streaming tape system, as these high-speed systems are often called, can dump or load the entire contents of a 10 Mbyte hard disk to a single tape in a few minutes. The next technology we discuss here, optical disks, can store even larger amounts of data on a single drive unit than magnetic hard disks can.

OPTICAL DISK DATA STORAGE

Optical disks are probably familiar to you from their use as laser video disks and compact audio disks. Higher quality versions of the same type of disk can be used to store very large quantities of digital data for computers. One currently available unit, the Shugart Optimem 1000, for example, stores up to a total of 1 gigabyte (1000 Mbytes) of data on one side of a single 12-in disk. This amount of storage corresponds to about 400,000 pages of text. In addition to their ability to store large amounts of data, optical disks have the advantages that they are relatively inexpensive, immune to dust, and in most cases, removable. Also, since data is written on the disk and read off the disk with the light from a tiny laser diode, the read/write head does not have to touch the disk. The laser head is held in position above the disk, so there is no disk wear, and the head cannot crash and destroy the recorded data as it can with magnetic hard disks.

The actual drive and head positioning mechanisms for optical disk drives are very similar to those for magnetic hard disk drives. A feedback system is used to precisely control the speed of the motor which rotates the disk. Some units spin the disk at a constant speed of 700 to 1200 rpm. Other systems such as those based on the compact disk (CD) audio format adjust the rotational speed of the disk so that the track passes under the head with a constant linear velocity. In this case the disk is rotated more slowly when outer tracks are read. Some optical disk systems record data in concentric tracks as magnetic disks do. The CD disk systems and some other systems record data on a single spiral track as a phonograph record does. A linear voice coil mechanism with feedback control is used to precisely position the read head over a desired track or section of the track. The head positioning must be very precise, because the tracks on an optical disk are so close together. The 24-μin-wide tracks on the Optimem 1000 disks, for example, are only 70 μin between centers. This spacing allows 40,000 tracks to be put on the disk. For the Optimem 1000 the average access time to a track is 150 ms, and data is read out at 5 Mbits/s. The disk sizes currently available in different systems are 4.72 (the compact audio disk size), 5.25, 12, and 14 in. Optical disk systems are available in three basic types: read only, write once/read, and read/write.

Read only systems allow only prerecorded disks to be read out. A disk which can only be read from is often referred to as an optical ROM or OROM. Examples of this type are the 4.7-in audio compact disks.

Write-once/read systems allow you to write data to a disk, but once the data is written, it cannot be erased or changed. Once data is written, you can read it out as many times as you want. Write-once systems are sometimes referred to by the name DRAW, which stands for *direct read after write*.

Read/write optical disk systems, as the name implies, allow you to erase recorded data and write new data on a disk. The recording materials and the recording methods are different for these different types of systems.

Disks used for read-only and write-once/read systems are coated with a substance which will be altered when a high-intensity laser beam is focused on it with a lens. The principle here is similar to using a magnifying glass to burn holes in paper as you may have done in your earlier days. In some systems the focused laser light actually produces tiny pits along a track to represent 1's. In other systems a special metal coating is applied to the disk over a plastic polymer layer. When the laser beam is focused on a spot on the metal, heat is transferred to the polymer, causing it to give off a gas. The gas given off produces a microscopic bubble at that spot on the thin metal coating to represent a stored 1. Both of these recording mechanisms are irreversible, so once written, the data can only be read. Data can be read from this type of disk using the same laser diode used for recording, but at reduced power (a system might, for example, use 25 mW for writing, but only 5 mW for reading). In some systems, such as the one in Figure 12-33, a separate laser is used for reading. The laser beam is focused on the track and a photodiode used to detect the beam reflected from the data track. A pit or bubble on the track will spread the laser beam light out so that very little of it reaches the photodiode. A spot on the track with no pit or bubble will reflect light to the photodiode. Read-only and write-once systems are less expensive than read/write systems, and for many data storage applications the inability to erase and rerecord is not a major disadvantage.

For the most common read/write optical disk system the disks are coated with an exotic metal alloy which has the required magnetic properties. The read/write head in this type of system has a laser diode and a coil of wire.

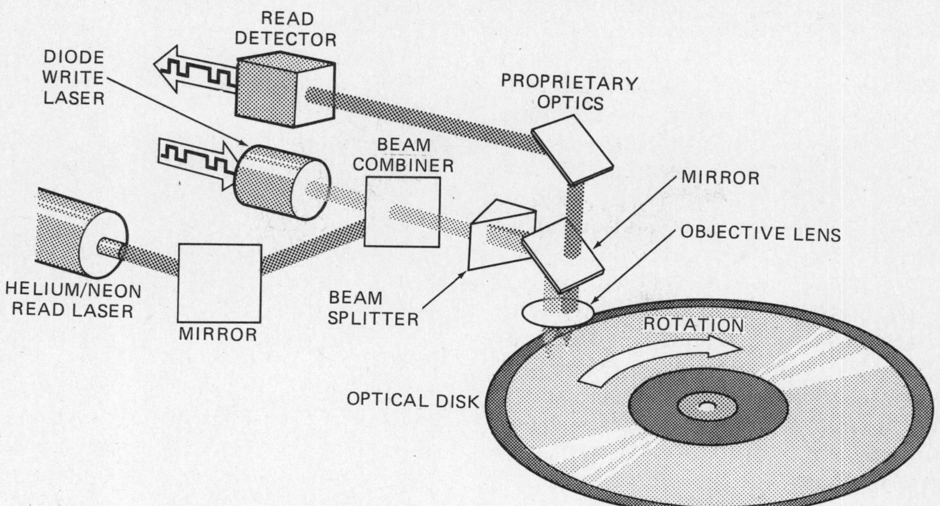

FIGURE 12-33 Read/write mechanism for optical disks.

A current is passed through the coil to produce a magnetic field perpendicular to the disk. At room temperature the applied vertical magnetic field is not strong enough to change the horizontal magnetization present on the disk. To record a 1 at a spot in a data track, a pulse of light from the laser diode is used to heat up that spot. Heating the spot makes it possible for the applied magnetic field to flip the magnetic domains around at that spot and create a tiny vertical magnet. To read data from the disk, polarized laser light is focused on the track. When the polarized light reflects from one of the tiny vertical magnets representing a 1, its plane of polarization is rotated a few degrees. Special optical circuitry can detect this shift and convert the reflections from a data track to a data stream of 1's and 0's. A bit is erased by turning off the vertical magnetic field and heating the spot corresponding to that bit with the laser. When heated with no field present, the magnetism of the spot will flip around in line with the horizontal field on the disk. Other techniques for producing read/write disks are now being researched intensely because of the promise this form of data storage has.

Data is stored on optical disks in several different formats. Figure 12-34 shows the format in which digital data is stored on the 4.7-in audio compact disks.

As shown in Figure 12-34*a*, data is stored serially in one long spiral track, starting near the center of the disk. The track is divided into blocks, each containing 2 Kbytes of actual data. Figure 12-34*b* shows the format for each block. Note that a considerable number of bytes in each block are used for header, synchronization, and error-detecting/correcting codes. Extensive error detection/correction is necessary to bring the error rate down to that of magnetic disks. The position of each block on the track is identified with coordinates of minutes, seconds, and block number. As shown in Figure 12-34*a*, a second represents 75 blocks numbered 0–74. A minute represents 60 seconds, or a total of 4500 blocks. The entire disk represents one hour or 270K blocks. Note that although data can be read out from the disk at 150

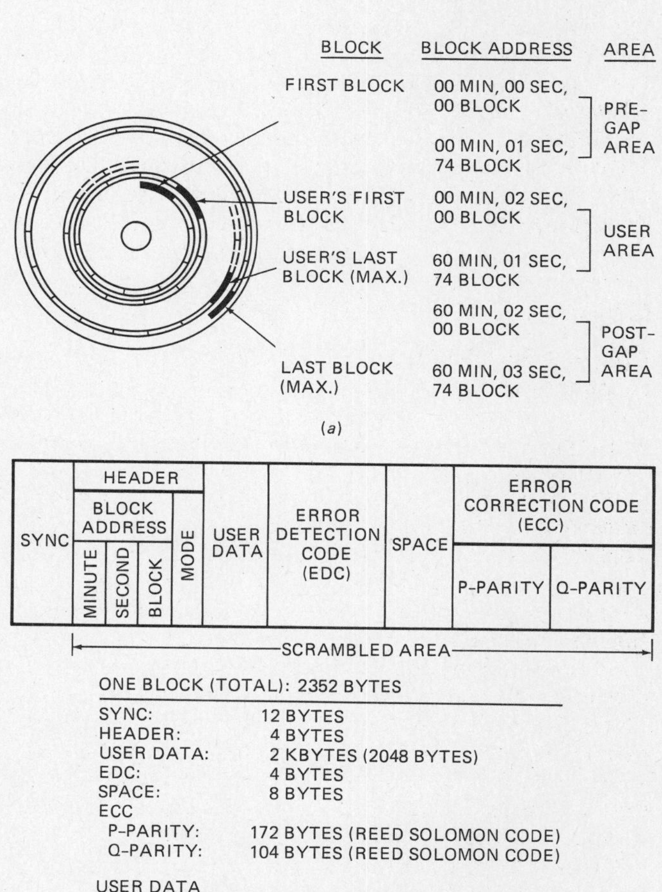

FIGURE 12-34 Industry-wide data structure for audio compact disk (CD) optical disks. *(a)* Disk format. *(b)* Track format. (*Electronic Engineering Times*, March 25, 1985)

Kbytes/s (about 3 times the rate for floppy disks), the disk contains so much data that it takes an hour to read out all of the data on the disk. Also note that a large area at the start of the track and a large area at the end of the track are used as gaps. In all, about half of the total area on an optical disk is used for synchronization, identification, and error correction. This is not a big drawback because of the immense amount of data that can be stored on the disk.

There are currently available several "jukebox" optical disk systems, which contain up to 256 disks. Typically it takes only a few seconds to access a disk. The potentially low cost of a few cents per megabyte and the hundreds of gigabytes of data storage possible for optical disk systems may change the whole way our society transfers and processes information. The contents of a sizable library, for example, can be stored on a few disks. Likewise, the entire financial records of a large company may be able to be kept on a single disk. "Expert" systems for medical diagnosis or legal defense development can use a massive data base stored on disk to do a more thorough analysis. Engineering workstations can use optical disks to store drawings, graphics, or IC-mask layouts. The point here is that optical disks bring directly to your desktop computer a massive data base that previously was only available through a link to large mainframe computers, or in many cases was not available at all. Perhaps the distribution of data made possible by optical disks will reduce the need for printers which we discuss in the next section.

PRINTER MECHANISMS

Many different mechanisms and techniques are used to produce printouts or "hard" copies of programs and data. This section is intended to give you an overview of the operation and tradeoffs of some of the common printer mechanisms. We start with those that mechanically hit the paper in some way.

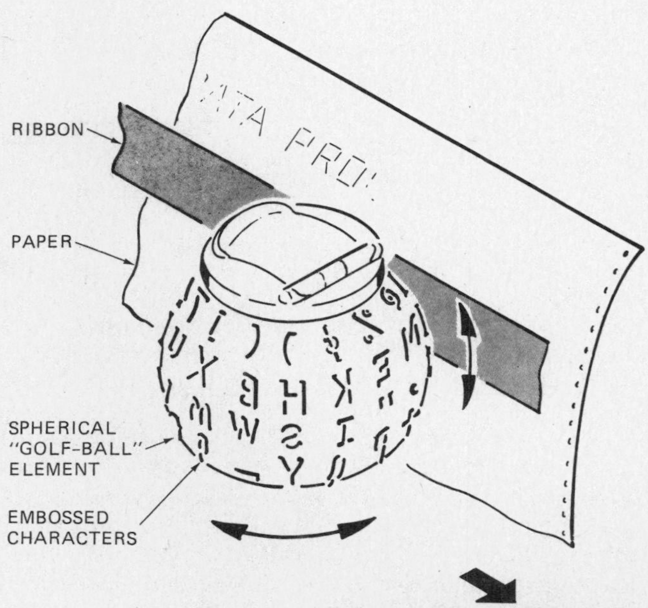

FIGURE 12-35 IBM Selectric printer mechanism. (Data Products Corporation)

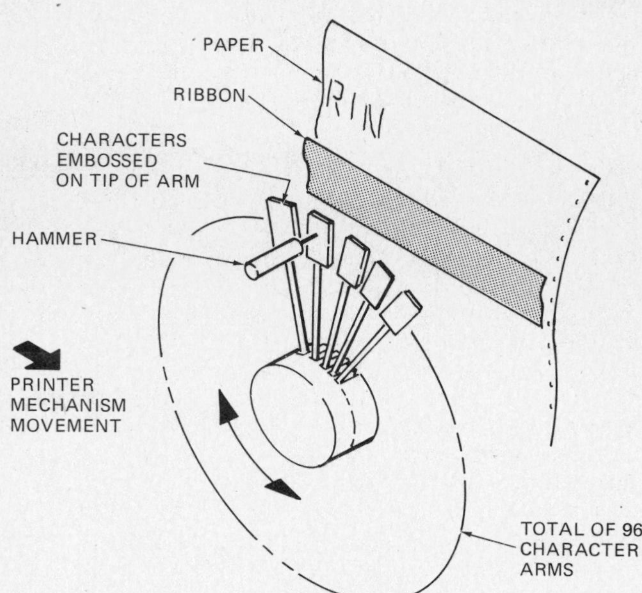

FIGURE 12-36 Daisy-wheel printer mechanism. (Data Products Corporation)

Formed Character Impact Printers

This category of printers function in the same way as a typewriter. In fact the unofficial standard of comparison for print quality is the print produced by the "spinning golf ball" IBM Selectric typewriter.

IBM SELECTRIC MECHANISM

To refresh your memory, Figure 12-35 shows how this works. The entire character set is present as raised type around a sphere. The bottom of the sphere is connected to the drive mechanism. By shifting the ball up or down, rotating it, and tilting it, the character to be printed can be precisely positioned over the desired spot on the paper. When the ball is hit against the ribbon, the letter is printed on the paper. The head is moved across the paper to print a string of characters. Selectric typewriters can be interfaced to computers to do printouts.

The advantages of the Selectric mechanism are the excellent print quality and the fact that the *font* can be changed by simply changing the sphere. Font is the name used to refer to the character set of a printer. The disadvantages of this mechanism are: it is mechanically complicated, noisy, and can only print about 14 characters per second (cps).

DAISY-WHEEL PRINTERS

Figure 12-36 shows a drawing of a daisy-wheel printer mechanism. Here the raised letters are attached at the ends of spokes of a wheel. To print a letter the wheel is rotated until the desired letter is in position over the paper. A solenoid-driven hammer then hits the "petal" against the ribbon to print the letter.

The advantages of the daisy-wheel mechanism are: high print quality, interchangeable fonts, and print speed up to 55 cps. Print quality is not quite as good as that produced by the spinning golf ball.

DRUM, BAND, AND CHAIN PRINTERS

A daisy-wheel produces good quality print, but for massive data output from large mini and mainframe computers, 55 cps is not nearly fast enough. For these systems *drum*, *band*, or *chain* type line printers are used. Figure 12-37 shows a diagram of how a drum type is constructed. A rapidly spinning drum has a complete raised character set constructed around the drum for each character position across the paper. To print characters, magnetically driven hammers in each character position hit the paper and ribbon against the spinning drum. An entire line of characters can be printed during each rotation of the drum. Some drum printers can print 2000 lines/min. If you assume 80 characters per line, this corresponds to 2700 cps. However, print lines may be wavy, fonts are not easily changed, and the noise level is high.

In a band printer several raised character sets are constructed on a metal band which is rapidly pulled across a line position behind the paper. Each character position has a magnetically driven hammer such as those shown for the drum printer. When the desired character is under a hammer, the hammer is fired. This hits the ribbon and paper against the letter on the band and prints the character. Some band printers can print up to 2000 lines/min. Print quality is acceptable, fonts are easily changed, and the noise level is high.

Chain printers operate like band printers, except that the character sets are held in a metal or rubber chain and rotated across the paper along a print line. Another variation of this type of printer is the *train* printer which rotates metal slugs with characters on them around in a track across the paper. These mechanisms also produce print speeds up to 2000 lines/min and the font is changeable, but they are noisy and the print mechanism tends to wear out.

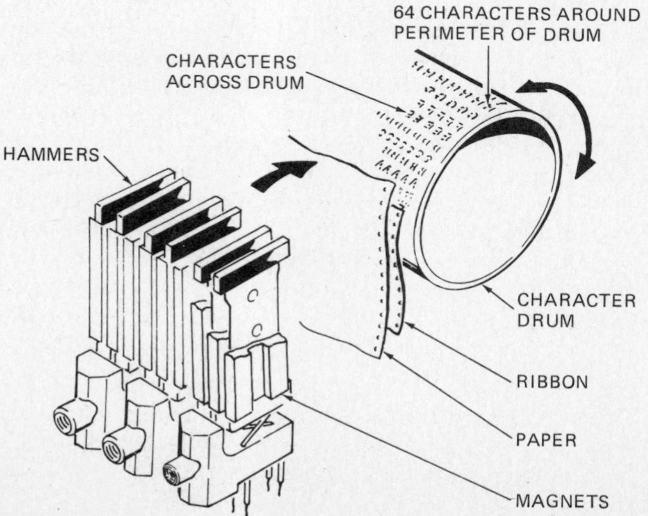

FIGURE 12-37 Drum printer mechanism. (Data Products Corporation)

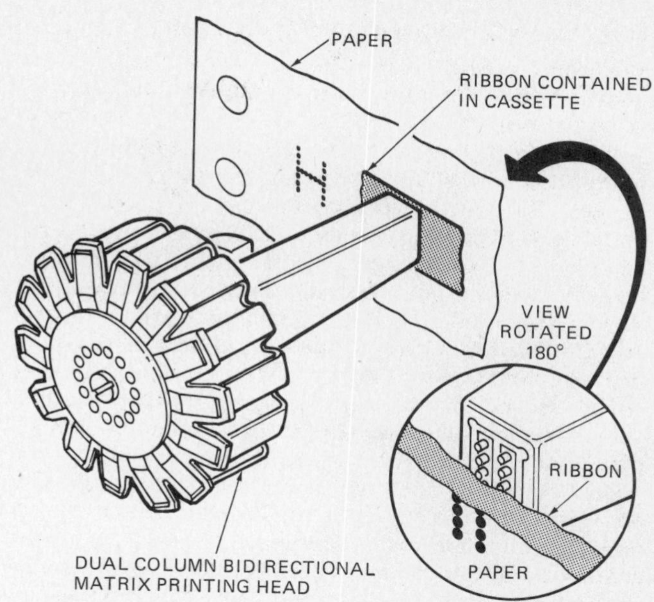

FIGURE 12-38 Impact dot-matrix printer mechanism. (Data Products Corporation)

Dot-Matrix Impact Print Mechanisms

Figure 12-38 shows an impact-type dot-matrix print head. Characters are printed as a matrix of dots. Thin print wires driven by solenoids at the rear of the print head hit the ribbon against the paper to produce dots. The print wires are arranged in a vertical column so that characters are printed out one dot column at a time as the print head is moved across a line. Early dot-matrix print heads had only seven print wires, so print quality of these units was not too good. Currently available dot-matrix printers use 9, 14, 18, or even 24 print wires in the print head. Using a large number of print wires and/or printing a line twice with the dots for the second printing offset slightly from those of the first, produces print that is difficult to tell from that of a Selectric or daisy wheel.

Unlike the formed character printers, dot-matrix printers can also print graphics. To do this the dot pattern for each column of dots is sent out to the print head solenoids as the print head is moved across the paper. The principle is similar to the way we produce bit-mapped raster graphics on a CRT screen. By using different color ribbons and making several passes across a line, some dot-matrix impact printers allow you to print color graphics. Most dot-matrix printers now contain one or more microprocessors to control all of this.

Print speeds for dot-matrix impact printers range up to 350 cps. Some units allow you to use a low-resolution mode of 200 cps for rough drafts, a medium resolution mode of 100 cps for finish copy, or 50 cps for near-letter-quality printing. A big advantage of dot-matrix impact printers is their ability to change fonts or print graphics under program control.

Dot-Matrix Thermal Print Mechanisms

Most thermal printers require paper which has a special heat-sensitive coating. When a spot on this special paper is heated, the spot turns dark. Characters or graphics are printed with a matrix of dots. There are two main print head shapes for producing the dots. For one of these the print head consists of a 5 by 7 or 7 by 9 matrix of tiny heating elements. To print a character the head is moved to a character position and the dot-sized heating elements for the desired character turned on. After a short time the heating elements are turned off and the head is moved to the next character position. Printing then is done one complete character at a time.

The second print head configuration for thermal dot-matrix printers has the heating elements along a metal bar which extends across the entire width of the paper. There is a heating element for each dot position on a print line, so this type can print an entire line of dots at a time. The metal bar removes excess heat. Characters and graphics are printed by stepping the paper through the printer one dot line at a time. A few thermal printers can print up to 400 lines/min.

Some of the newer thermal printers have the heat-sensitive material on a ribbon instead of on the paper. When a spot on the ribbon is heated, a dot of ink is transferred to the paper. This approach makes it possible to use standard paper, and by switching ribbons, to print color graphics as well as text.

The main advantage of thermal printers is their low noise. Their main disadvantages are: the special paper or ribbon is expensive, printing carbon copies is not possible, and most thermal printers with good print quality are slow.

Spark Gap Printers

These printers use a special paper that looks and feels somewhat like aluminum foil. When a spot on the paper is "zapped" with a high voltage, the outer coating at that point is burned off, exposing a dark layer underneath. Characters are printed as a matrix of dots. These printers are often used to print out movie theater tickets because they can print out as many as 2000 cps. Most of the disadvantages relate to the paper which is expensive, difficult to handle, not very durable, and does not produce very good print quality.

Laser and Other Xerographic Printers

These printers operate on the same principle as most office copy machines, such as Xerox machines. The basic approach is to first form an image of the page that is to be printed on a photosensitive drum in the machine. Powdered ink, or "toner," is then applied to the image on the drum. Next the image is electrostatically transferred from the drum to a sheet of paper. Finally the inked image on the paper is "fused," usually with heat.

In a Xerox machine the image on the photosensitive drum is simply a copy of an "original" produced with a camera lens. A more computer-compatible method of producing an image on the photosensitive drum is with a laser. Turning a laser on and off as it is swept back and forth across the drum produces an image in about the same way that an image is produced on a raster scan CRT. Figure 12-39 shows a diagram of how this is done. The rotating mirror sweeps the laser beam across the rotating drum. A modulator controlled by a microcomputer turns the laser beam on or off to produce dots. After the image is inked and transferred to the paper, the drum is cleaned and is ready for the next page.

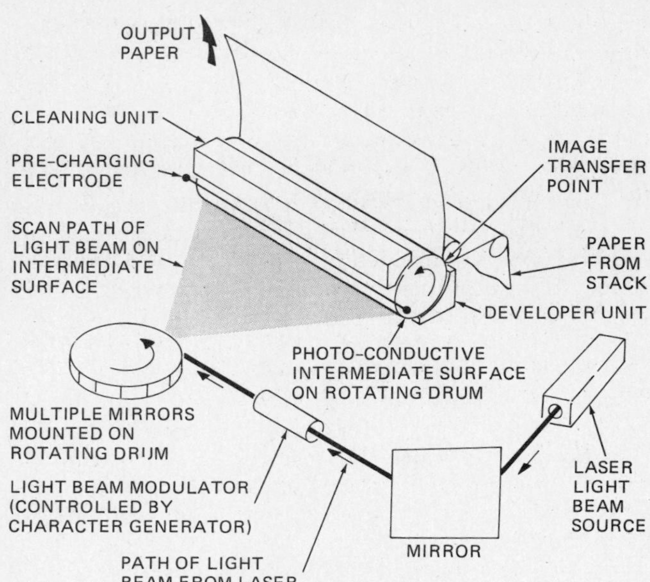

FIGURE 12-39 Laser printer mechanism. (Data Products Corporation)

An alternative to the photosensitive drum is a magnetically sensitive drum used in some units. An image is written on this magnetic drum in the same way that data is recorded on magnetic disks. Magnetized ink particles are then applied to the drum, transferred to the paper, and fused.

Laser and other xerographic printers have the advantages of very high print quality (text and graphics can easily be printed on the same page), very high print speeds (up to 20,000 lines/min), ability to use standard paper, and relatively quiet operation. They have the disadvantages that the copies "look like Xerox copies," the machines are very expensive, and the machines require a lot of maintenance.

Ink-Jet Printers

Still another type of printer that uses a dot-matrix approach to produce text and graphics is the ink jet. Early ink-jet printers used a pump and a tiny nozzle to send out a continuous stream of tiny ink globules. These ink globules were passed though an electric field which left them with an electrical charge. The stream of charged ink globules was then electrostatically deflected to produce characters on the paper in the same way that the electron beam is deflected to produce an image on a CRT screen. Excess ink was deflected to a gutter and returned to the ink reservoir. Ink-jet printers are relatively quiet, and some of these electrostatically deflected ink-jet printers can print up to 45,000 lines/min. Several disadvantages, however, prevented them from being used more widely. They tend to be messy and difficult to keep working well. Print quality at high speeds is poor and multiple copies are not possible.

Newer ink-jet printers use a variety of approaches to solve these problems. Some, such as the HP Thinkjet, use ink cartridges which contain a column of tiny heaters. When one of these tiny heaters is pulsed on, it caused a drop of ink to explode onto the paper. Others, such as the IBM Quietwriter, for example, use an electric current to explode microscopic ink bubbles from a special ribbon directly onto the paper. These last two approaches are really hybrids of thermal and ink-jet technologies. They can produce very near letter-quality print at speeds comparable to those of slower dot-matrix impact printers. A disadvantage of some ink-jet printers is that they require special paper for best results.

SPEECH SYNTHESIS AND RECOGNITION WITH A COMPUTER

In a great many cases it is very convenient for a computer to communicate verbally with a user. Some examples of the use of computer-created speech are talking games, talking cash registers, and text-to-speech machines used by blind people. Other examples are medical monitor systems that give verbal warnings and directions when some emergency condition exists. This use demonstrates some of the major advantages of speech readout. The verbal signal attracts more attention than a simple alarm, and the user does not have to search through a series of readouts to determine the problem.

Adding speech recognition circuitry to a computer so that it can interpret verbal commands from a user also makes the computer much easier to use. The pilot of a rocket ship or space shuttle, for example, can operate some controls verbally while operating other controls manually. (It probably won't be too long before we eliminate the verbal/manual link and control the whole ship directly from the brain, but that is another story, perhaps in the next book.) Voice entry systems are also useful for handicapped programmers and other computer users. We will first describe for you the different methods used to create speech with a computer, and then describe speech recognition methods.

Speech Synthesis Methods

There are several common methods of producing speech from a computer. The tradeoffs between the different methods are speech quality and the number of bits that must be stored/sent for each word. In other words, the higher the speech quality you want, the more bits you have to store in memory to represent each word, and the faster you have to send bits to the synthesizer circuitry. All of the common methods of speech synthesis fall into two general categories: waveform modification, and direct digitization. In order to explain how the waveform modification approaches work we need to talk briefly about how humans produce sounds.

WAVEFORM MODIFICATION SPEECH SYNTHESIS

Some sounds, called voiced sounds, are produced by vibration of the vocal cords as air passes from the lungs. The frequency of vibration or *pitch*, the position of the tongue, the shape of the mouth, and the position of the lips determine the actual sound produced. The vowels A and E are examples of voiced sounds. Another type of sound, called unvoiced sounds, in speech are produced by modifying the position of the tongue and the shape of the mouth as a constant stream of air comes from the lungs. The letter S is an example of this type of sound. A third type of sound, the nasal sounds called *fricatives*, consist of a mixture of voiced and unvoiced sounds. In electronic terms then the human vocal system consists of a variable-frequency signal generator as the source for voiced sounds, a "white" noise signal source for unvoiced sounds, and a series of filters which modify the outputs from the two signal sources to produce the desired sounds. Figure 12-40 shows this in block diagram form.

The three main approaches to implementing this model electronically are *linear predictive coding* or LPC, *formant*, and *phoneme*. These methods differ mostly in the type of filter used, and in how often the filter characteristics are updated.

LPC synthesizers, such as that in the Texas Instruments "Speak and Spell," use a digital filter such as we described in Chapter 10 to modify the signals from a pulse and a white noise source. For this type of filter the parameters that must be sent from the microcomputer are the coefficients for the filter and the pitch for the pulse source. Remember from the discussion in Chapter 10 that for a digital filter, the current output value is computed or "predicted" as the sum of the current input value and portions of previous input values. A high-quality LPC synthesizer may require as many as 16 Kbits/s. One difficulty with most LPC devices has been that complex computer equipment and programs had to be used to analyze a spoken word and determine the series of coefficients required to produce that word. Usually the IC manufacturer did this for a fee, and produced a ROM with the parameters for a particular vocabulary. The General Instruments SP1000, however, has now simplified this process somewhat.

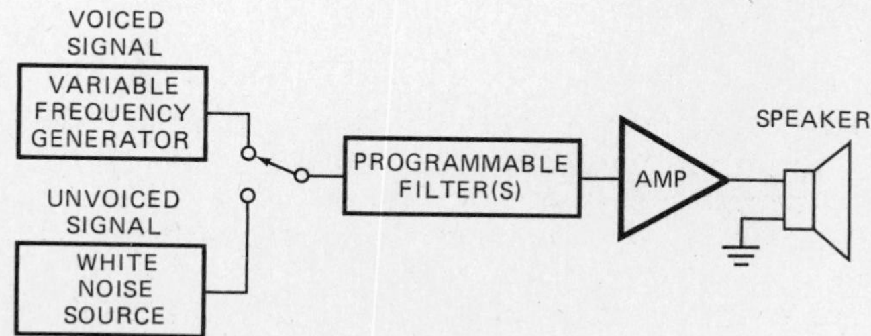

FIGURE 12-40 Electronic model of human vocal tract.

The SP1000 can function as an LPC speech processor, an LPC speech recognizer, and an LPC speech synthesizer under the control of a microcomputer. In learn mode the device generates LPC coefficients for spoken words. The microcomputer reads these coefficients from the SP1000, and stores them in memory. To operate in recognition mode the SP1000 is used to generate the coefficients for the unknown word. These coefficients are then compared with those of known words in memory to identify the unknown word. For use as a speech synthesizer the SP1000 is switched to talk mode and the coefficients for the desired word are sent to it by the microcomputer. Consult the General Instruments data sheet for more information about this interesting device.

The formant approach uses several resonant or *formant* filters to massage the signals from a variable-frequency signal source and a white-noise source. Figure 12-41 shows how the frequencies of these formant filters might be arranged for a male and for a female voice. For this type of system the parameters that must be sent from the computer are the pitch of the variable-frequency signal, the center frequency for each formant filter, and the bandwidth of each formant filter. The data rate for direct formant synthesis is only about 1 Kbit/s, but the parameters must again be determined with complex equipment. It is then not easy to develop a custom vocabulary for a specific application. A phoneme approach solves this problem and requires a still lower data rate, at the expense of lower speech quality.

Phonemes are fragments of words. An example of a phoneme speech synthesizer is the Votrax SC-01 which we described in Chapter 9. In the case of the SC-01 you get it to sound one of its 64 phonemes by sending it a 6-bit binary code from a computer port. When the SC-01 finishes sending the phoneme, it asserts a REQUEST signal which indicates that it is ready for the next phoneme. Words are produced by sending a series of phoneme codes. In addition to the 6-bit phoneme code, an additional 2 bits can be sent to specify rising, falling, or flat inflection for each phoneme. Inside the SC-01A, the 6-bit phoneme code is used to control the characteristics of some formant filters as described in the previous paragraph. Since only one code is sent out for a relatively long period of speech, the required bit rate is only about 70 bits/s. However, the long period between codes gives less control over waveform details, and therefore

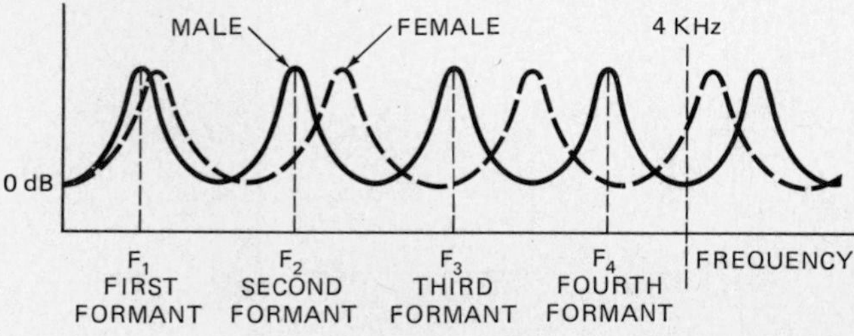

FIGURE 12-41 Filter responses for formant speech synthesizer.

sound quality. A phoneme synthesizer has a mechanical sound. One big advantage of phoneme synthesizers is that you can make up any message you want by simply putting together a sequence of phoneme codes. Another example of a phoneme synthesizer is the SSI263 from Silicon Systems, Inc.

DIRECT DIGITIZATION SPEECH SYNTHESIS

This method produces the highest-quality speech, because it is essentially just a playback of digitally recorded speech. To start, the word you want the computer to speak is spoken clearly into a microphone. The output voltage from the microphone is amplified and applied to the input of perhaps a 12-bit A/D converter. One approach at this point might be to simply store the A/D samples for the word in a ROM and read the values out to a D/A converter when you want the computer to speak the word. The difficulty with this approach is that, if the samples are taken often enough to produce good speech quality, a lot of memory is required to store the samples for a word. To reduce the amount of memory required, several speech compression algorithms are used. These algorithms are too complex to discuss here, but the basic principles involve storing repeated waveforms only once, taking advantage of symmetry in waveforms, and not storing values for silent periods. To further reduce the memory required for direct digital speech, some systems use differential or *delta* modulation. In these systems only a 3-bit or 4-bit code, representing how much a sample has changed from the last sample, is stored in memory instead of storing the complete 12-bit value. Since audio signals change slowly, this is very acceptable. Even with compression, however, direct digital speech requires considerable memory and a bit rate as high as 64 Kbits/s. The OKI Semiconductor MSM5218RS is an example of a device which functions in this way. In record mode it can be used with an A/D converter to produce the differential codes for a spoken word. In play mode the device produces speech from applied codes using an internal 10-bit D/A converter. Another example of a direct digital system is the National Semiconductor *Digitalker*. For further information, consult the data sheets for these devices.

Speech Recognition

Speech recognition is considerably more difficult than speech synthesis. The process is similar to trying to recognize human faces with a computer vision system. The first step in speech recognition is to train the system, or in other words produce templates for each of the words that the system needs to recognize, and store these templates in memory. To produce a template for a word, the intended user speaks the word several times into a microphone connected to the system. The system then determines several parameters or *features* for each repetition of the word and averages them to produce the actual template.

Different systems extract different parameters to form the template. Figure 12-42 shows a block diagram for

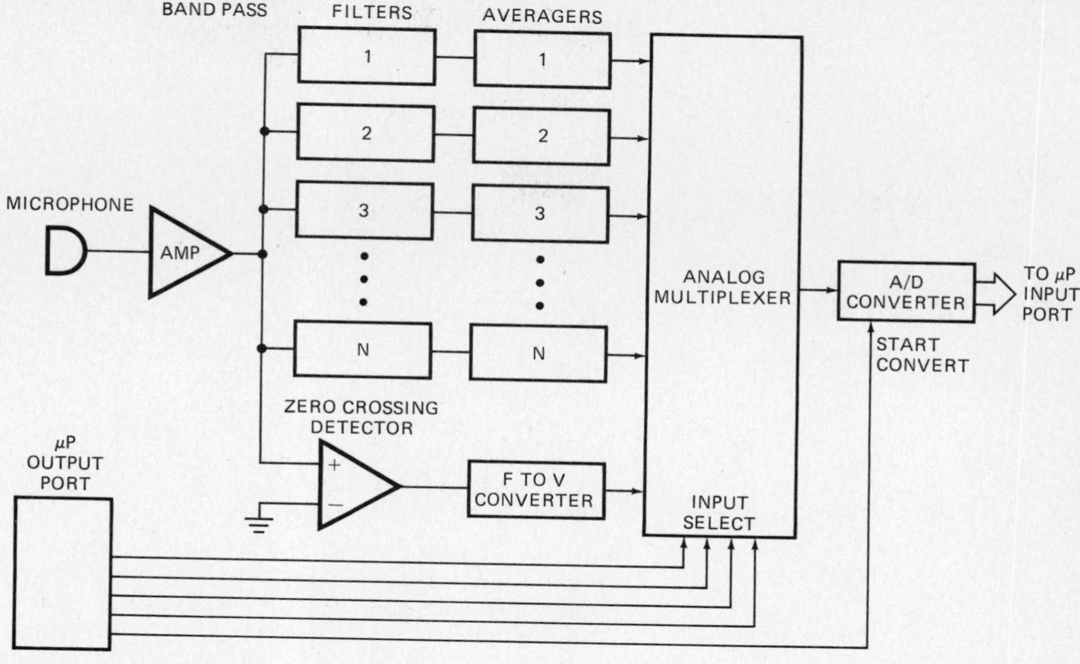

FIGURE 12-42 Block diagram of one type of speech recognition system.

one of the most common methods. This method uses a set of formant filters with their center frequencies adjusted to match those of the average speaker. The output amplitudes of these formant filters are averaged to produce a signal proportional to the energy in each of the frequency bands. Also used are one or more zero-crossing detectors to give basic frequency information. The pulse train from the zero-crossing detector is converted to a proportional voltage, so it can be digitized along with the outputs from the formant averagers.

Now, when a word is spoken, samples of each of the features are taken and digitized at evenly spaced intervals of 10–20 ms during the duration of the word. The features are stored in memory. If this is a training run, this set of samples will be averaged with others to form the template for the word. If this is a recognition run, this set of features will be compared with the templates stored in memory. The best match is assumed to be the correct word. Currently none of the available voice recognition systems is 100 percent accurate. The most accurate systems are those that only work with the speaker who trained them and those that only work with isolated words. However, considerable progress is being made in this area. The VPC 2000 from VOTAN Inc., for example, is a speech recognition unit which plugs into IBM PC-compatible computers and can recognize continuous phrases. It also has a built in voice-activated telephone dialing and answering service. Another PC-compatible unit, the VocaLink from Interstate Voice Products, permits the programming of up to 240 spoken commands to control standard PC software such as word processors and business programs. Perhaps the HAL 9000 is not too far away.

IMPORTANT TERMS AND CONCEPTS FROM THIS CHAPTER

CRT operation
- raster display
- field
- interlaced scanning
- frame

Video monitor

CRT terminal

Horizontal and vertical sync pulses

Composite video

Character generator

Display refresh RAM
- Dot, undot
- dot clock
- overscan

Display page

Attribute code

Bit-mapped raster scan CRT graphics display
- picture element—pixel—pel

Mouse

Composite color monitor

Luminance signal

Chroma signal

Vector-scan CRT displays

Alphanumeric/graphics liquid crystal displays (LCDs)

Computer vision
- ultrasonic vision
- video cameras—vidicon
- CCD cameras
- OPTICRAM cameras

Floppy disks
- hard and soft sectoring
- index holes
- index, ID, and data fields, gaps, address marks

Checksums

Cyclic redundency character

Single and double density

FM and MFM recording

File allocation table

Hierarchical file structure

Root directory and subdirectory

File control block

File handle

ASCIIZ

RAM disk

Hard disk systems
- cylinders
- partitions

Optical disk systems
- OROM
- DRAW

Printer mechanisms
- IBM Selectric
- daisy wheel
- drum, band, and chain
- dot-matrix impact and dot-matrix thermal
- spark gap
- laser and xerographic
- ink jet

Speech synthesis
- pitch, unvoiced sounds, and fricatives
- linear predictive coding, formant, phoneme
- direct digitization

Speech recognition

REVIEW QUESTIONS AND PROBLEMS

1. With the help of a simple drawing explain how a noninterlaced raster is produced on a CRT.

2. Use a simple drawing to help you describe how a display of the letter X is produced on a noninterlaced raster-scan CRT display.

3. Refer to Figure 12-5 to help you answer the following questions.
- *a.* What is the purpose of the RAM in this circuit?
- *b.* At what point(s) in displaying a frame do the address inputs of this RAM get changed?
- *c.* At what point(s) in displaying a frame do the R0–R3 address inputs of the character generator ROM get changed?
- *d.* What is the purpose of the shift register on the output of the character generator ROM?
- *e.* Why is one input of the shift register tied to ground?
- *f.* At what point(s) in displaying a frame are horizontal sync pulses produced?
- *g.* At what point(s) in displaying a frame are vertical sync pulses produced?
- *h.* List the three components of a composite video signal.

4. A CRT display is designed to display 24 character rows with 72 characters in each row. The system uses a 7 by 9 character generator in a 9 by 12 dot matrix. Assuming a 60-Hz noninterlaced frame rate, three additional character times for horizontal overscan, and 120 additional scan lines for vertical overscan, answer the following questions.
- *a.* Total number of character times/row
- *b.* Total number of scan lines/frame
- *c.* Horizontal frequency (number of lines/second)
- *d.* Dot-clock frequency (dots/second)
- *e.* Minimum bandwidth required for video amplifier
- *f.* Time between RAM accesses

5. The IBM PC color adapter board uses a 14-MHz dot clock frequency, a 15.750-kHz horizontal scan rate, and a 60-Hz frame rate. Characters are produced in an 8 by 8 dot matrix. There are 80 characters/row and 25 rows/frame.
- *a.* What is the total number of dot times per scan line?
- *b.* How many dot times then are left for horizontal overscan?
- *c.* What is the total number of scan lines per frame including overscan?
- *d.* How many scan lines then are left for vertical overscan?

6. Describe how a DMA controller is used with a CRT controller such as the 8275 to keep a CRT display refreshed.

7. How does the CRT display system in Figure 12-7 arbitrate the dispute that occurs when the 6845 CRT controller and the microprocessor both want to access the display RAM at the same time.

8. Write a program which uses the IBM BIOS procedures to read a string of characters entered from the keyboard, put the key codes in a buffer in memory, and display the characters for the pressed keys on the CRT.

9. How much memory is required to store the pel data for a bit-mapped display of 640 by 480?

10. What is the difference between a CRT monitor and a CRT terminal?

11. Describe how three electron beams are used to produce all possible colors on a color CRT screen.

12. How much memory is required to store the pel data for a 512 by 512 display where each pel can be any one of 16 colors?

13. Describe how a composite color video signal is produced from the red, blue, green, and sync signals. Include in your answer the function of the 3.579545-MHz signal.

14. Describe how a vector graphics CRT display system produces a display of a triangle on the screen. What is the major problem with the vector approach to CRT graphics?

15. The inputs of an 8-bit D/A converter are connected to port FFF8H of a microcomputer and the output of the D/A converter is connected to the *X* axis of an oscilloscope. The inputs of another 8-bit D/A converter are connected to port FFFAH of a microcomputer, and the output of this D/A is connected to the *Y* axis of the oscilloscope. Write a program which uses these D/A converters to display a square on the screen of the oscilloscope. Then modify the program so that the square enlarges after each 100 refreshes.

16. Describe the methods used by CCD and OPTICRAM cameras to produce visual images which can be stored in computer memory.

17. How is the read/write head for a disk drive moved into position over a specified track?

18. What additional information besides the actual data is recorded on each track of a soft-sectored floppy disk? Describe the purpose of the CRC bytes included with each block of data recorded on the disk.

19. Why must clock bits be recorded along with data bits on floppy disks? Under what conditions will a clock pulse be inserted in a bit cell when recording data on a disk in MFM format?

20. List the major types of information contained in the directory of a magnetic disk formatted by a DOS. If a data file requires several clusters on a disk, how does a DOS keep track of where the pieces of the file are located.

21. What is meant by the term *hierarchical file structure*? What is a major advantage of this type of file structure?

22. Write a program which uses the IBM PC DOS function calls to read in a string containing your name from the keyboard to a buffer in memory, and sends the string to a printer. Remember to use the DOS 4CH function call to return to DOS at the end of the program.

23. Explain why magnetic hard disks can store much more data than floppy disks, and why data can be written or read out much faster from hard disks.

24. Why must hard disks be operated in a dust-free environment?

25. Two terms often encountered in hard disk system manuals are *cylinder* and *partition*. Define and tell the difference between these two terms.

26. Describe how stored data is read from optical disks. What advantages does this readout method have over that used for hard magnetic disks?

27. Describe how data bits are recorded in magneto-optic read/write optical disk systems and in DRAW optical disk systems.

28. A human brain can store about 10^{10} bits of data and has an access time in the order of about a second. Compare these parameters with those of an optical disk system such as the Optimem 1000.

29. Describe the operation of the print mechanism for each of the following types of printer. Also give an advantage and a disadvantage for each type.
    a. Spinning golf ball
    b. Daisy wheel
    c. Drum
    d. Chain or band
    e. Dot matrix
    f. Thermal
    g. Laser
    h. Ink jet

30. Draw a block diagram of a waveform modification type of speech systhesizer. Describe the operation of the LPC, formant, and phoneme types of speech synthesizer that use this model.

31. What are the major differences between an LPC speech synthesizer and a formant speech synthesizer?

32. Describe the operation of a direct digitization speech synthesizer. What is the major advantage and the major disadvantage of this type?

CHAPTER

13 Data Communication and Networks

In Chapter 2 we discussed "computerizing" an electronics factory. What this means is that computers are integrated into all of the operations of the factory, and that each person in the company has access to a computer. The company may have a large centrally located mainframe computer, several supermicrocomputers that serve groups of users, individual computer engineering workstations, and portable computers spread around the world with the salespeople. In order for all of these computers to work together, they must be able to communicate with each other in an organized manner. In this chapter we show you some of the devices, signal standards, and systems used for communication with and between computers.

OBJECTIVES

At the end of this chapter you should be able to:

1. Show and describe the meaning of the bits in the format used for sending asynchronous serial data.
2. Describe the use of the major signals in the RS-232C standard.
3. Show how to connect RS-232C equipment directly or with a "null-modem" connection.
4. Initialize a common UART for transmitting serial data in a specified format.
5. Use the IBM PC BIOS and DOS procedures to send and receive serial data.
6. Describe several voltage, current, and light (fiber-optic) signal methods used to transmit data.
7. Describe the three types of modulation commonly used by modems.
8. Show the formats for a byte-oriented protocol and for a bit-oriented protocol used in synchronous serial data transmission.
9. Draw diagrams to show the common computer network configurations.
10. Describe how data is transmitted on an Ethernet system.
11. Describe how data is transmitted in a token-passing ring system.
12. Show the major signal groups for the GPIB (IEEE 488) bus, describe how bus control is managed, and how data is transferred on a handshake basis for the GPIB.

ASYNCHRONOUS SERIAL DATA COMMUNICATION

Introduction and Overview

Serial data communication is a somewhat difficult subject to approach, because you need pieces of information from several different topics in order for each part of the subject to really make sense. To make this approach easier, we will first give an overview of how all the pieces fit together and then describe the details of each piece later in specific sections. A problem with this subject is that it contains a great many terms and acronyms. To help you absorb all of these, you may want to make a glossary of terms as you work your way through the chapter.

Within a microcomputer data is transferred in parallel, because that is the fastest way to do it. For transferring data over long distances, however, parallel data transmission requires too many wires. Therefore, data to be sent long distances is usually converted from parallel form to serial form so that it can be sent on a single wire or pair of wires. Serial data received from a distant source is converted to parallel form so that it can easily be transferred on the microcomputer buses. Three terms often encountered in literature on serial data systems are *simplex*, *half-duplex*, and *full-duplex*. A simplex data line can transmit data only in one direction. An earthquake sensor sending data back from Mount St. Helens or a commercial radio station are examples of simplex transmission. Half-duplex transmission means that communication can take place in either direction between two systems, but can only occur in one direction at a time. An example of half-duplex transmission is a two-way radio system, where one user always listens while the other talks because the receiver circuitry is turned off during transmit. The term full-duplex means that each system can send and receive data at the same time. A normal phone conversation is an example of a full-duplex operation.

Serial data can be sent *synchronously* or *asynchronously*. For synchronous transmission, data is sent in blocks at a constant rate. The start and end of a block are identified with specific bytes or bit patterns. We discuss synchronous data formats in a later section of this chapter. For asynchronous transmission, each data character has a bit which identifies its start and 1 or 2 bits which identify its end. Since each character is individually identified, characters can be sent at any time (asynchronously), in the same way that a person types on a keyboard at different rates.

Figure 13-1 shows the bit format often used for transmitting asynchronous serial data. When no data is being sent, the signal line is in a constant high or *marking* state. The beginning of a data character is indicated by the line going low for 1 bit time. This bit is called a *start* bit. The data bits are then sent out on the line one after the other. Note that the least-significant bit is sent out first. Depending on the system, the data word may consist of 5, 6, 7, or 8 bits. Following the data bits is a parity bit which, as we explained in Chapter 11, is used to check for errors in received data. Some systems do not insert or look for a parity bit. After the data bits and the parity bit, the signal line is returned high for at least 1 bit time to identify the end of the character. This always-high bit is referred to as a *stop bit*. Some systems use 2 stop bits. For future reference note that the efficiency of this format is low, because 10 or 11 bit times are required to transmit a 7-bit data word such as an ASCII character.

The term *baud rate* is used to indicate the rate at which serial data is being transferred. Baud rate is defined as 1/(the time for a bit cell). If a bit time is 3.33 ms, for example, the baud rate is 1/(3.33 ms), or 300 Bd. There is an almost unavoidable, but incorrect, tendency to refer to this as 300 bits/s. In some cases, the two do correspond, but in other cases 2 to 4 actual data bits are encoded within one transmitted bit time, so data bits per second and baud do not correspond. Commonly used baud rates are 110, 300, 1200, 2400, 4800, 9600, and 19,200 Bd.

To interface a microcomputer with serial data lines the data must be converted to and from serial form. A parallel-in–serial-out shift register and a serial-in–parallel-out shift register can be used to do this. Also needed, for some cases of serial data transfer, is handshaking circuitry to make sure that a transmitter does not send data faster than it can be read in by the receiving system. There are available several programmable LSI devices which contain most of the circuitry needed for serial communication. A device such as the National INS8250, which can only do asynchronous communication, is often referred to as a *universal asynchronous receiver-transmitter* or *UART*. A device such as the Intel 8251A, which can be programmed to do either asynchronous or synchronous communication, is often called a *universal synchronous-asynchronous receiver-transmitter* or *USART*.

Once the data is converted to serial form it must in some way be sent from the transmitting UART to the receiving UART. There are several ways in which serial data is commonly sent. One method is to use a current to represent a 1 in the signal line and no current to represent a 0. We discuss this *current loop* approach in a later section. Another approach is to add line drivers on the output of the UART to produce a sturdy voltage signal. The range of each of these methods, however, is limited to a few thousand feet.

For sending serial data over long distances the standard telephone system is a convenient path, because the wiring and connections are already in place. Standard phone lines, often referred to as *switched lines* because any two points can be connected together through a series of switches, have a bandwidth of only about 300 to 3000 Hz. Therefore, for several reasons, digital signals of the form shown in Figure 13-1 cannot be sent directly over standard phone lines. (NOTE: Phone lines capable of carrying digital data directly can be leased, but these are somewhat costly, and limited to the specific destination of the line.)

The solution to this problem is to convert the digital signals to audio-frequency tones, which are in the frequency range that the phone lines can transmit. The device used to do this conversion and to convert transmitted tones back to digital information is called a *modem*. The term is a contraction of modulator-demodulator. In a later section of this chapter we discuss the operation of some common types of modems. For now, take a look at Figure 13-2 which shows how two modems can be connected to allow a remote terminal to communicate with a distant mainframe computer over a phone line. Modems and other equipment used to send serial data over long distances are known as *data communication equipment* or DCE. The terminals and

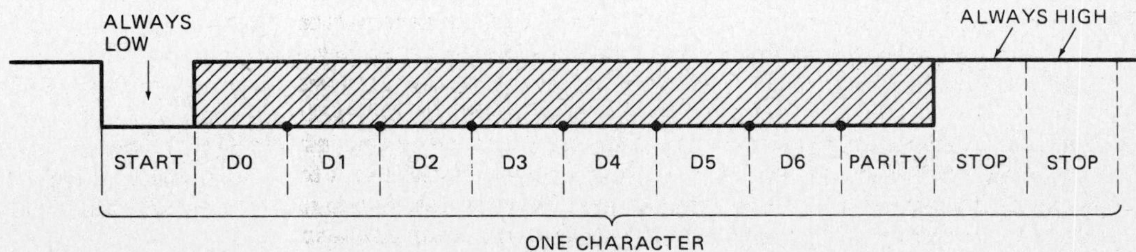

FIGURE 13-1 Bit format used for sending asynchronous serial data.

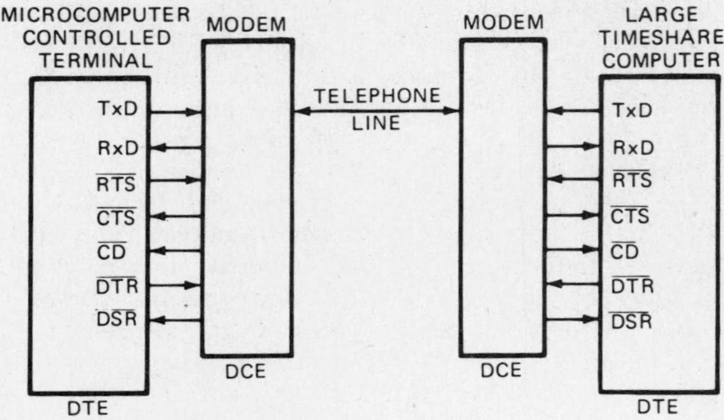

FIGURE 13-2 Digital data transmission using modems and standard phone lines.

computers that are sending or receiving the serial data are referred to as *data terminal equipment* or DTE. The signal names shown in Figure 13-2 are part of a serial data communications standard called RS-232C, which we discuss in detail in a later section. For now you just need enough of an overview so that the signals and initialization of the 8251A described in the next section make sense to you. Note the direction arrowheads on each of these signals. Here is a sequence of signals that might occur when a user at a terminal wants to send some data to the computer.

After the terminal power is turned on and the terminal runs any self-checks, it asserts the *data-terminal-ready* ($\overline{\text{DTR}}$) signal to tell the modem it is ready. When it is powered up and ready to transmit or receive data, the modem will assert the *data-set-ready* ($\overline{\text{DSR}}$) signal to the terminal. Under manual control or terminal control the modem then dials up the computer.

If the computer is available, it will send back a specified tone. Now, when the terminal has a character actually ready to send, it will assert a *request-to-send* ($\overline{\text{RTS}}$) signal to the modem. The modem will then assert its *carrier-detect* ($\overline{\text{CD}}$) signal to the terminal to indicate that it has established contact with the computer. When the modem is fully ready to transmit data, it asserts the *clear-to-send* ($\overline{\text{CTS}}$) signal back to the terminal. The terminal then sends serial data characters to the modem. When the terminal has sent all the characters it needs to, it makes its $\overline{\text{RTS}}$ signal high. This causes the modem to unassert its $\overline{\text{CTS}}$ signal and stop transmitting. As we show later, a similar handshake occurs between the modem and the computer at the other end of the data link. The important point at this time is that a set of handshake signals are defined for transferring serial data to and from a modem.

Now that you have an overview of asynchronous serial data, modems, and handshaking, we will describe the operation of a typical device used to interface a microcomputer to a modem or other device which requires serial data.

A Serial Interface Device—The Intel 8251A

Since the 8251A is used as the serial port on SDK-86 boards, on the IBM PC synchronous communication board, and on many other boards, we will use it as an example here.

SIGNALS AND SYSTEM CONNECTIONS

Figure 13-3 shows a block diagram and the pin descriptions for the 8251A. Figure 7-6, sheet 9, shows how an 8251A is connected on the SDK-86 board. Keep copies of these two handy as you work your way through the following discussion.

As shown in the SDK-86 schematic, the eight parallel lines, D7–D0, connect to the system data bus so that data words and control/status words can be transferred to and from the device. The *chip-select* ($\overline{\text{CS}}$) input is connected to an address decoder so the device is enabled when addressed. The 8251A has two internal addresses, a control address which is selected when the C/$\overline{\text{D}}$ input is high, and a data address which is selected when the C/$\overline{\text{D}}$ input is low. For the SDK-86 the control/status address is FFF2H and the data read/write address is FFF0H. The RESET, $\overline{\text{RD}}$, and $\overline{\text{WR}}$ lines are connected to the system signals with the same names. The clock input of the 8251A is usually connected to the system clock to synchronize internal operations with system operations. In the case of the SDK-86 the clock input is connected to the 2.45-MHz PCLK signal because it is related to the system clock, but at a frequency the 8251A can handle.

The signal labeled TxD on the upper right corner of the 8251A block diagram is the actual *serial-data* output. The pin labeled RxD is the *serial-data* input. The additional circuitry connected to the TxD pin on the SDK-86 board is needed to convert the TTL logic levels from the 8251A to current loop or RS-232C signals. The circuitry connected to the RxD pin performs the opposite conversion. We will discuss current loop and RS-232C signal standards a little later.

The shift registers in the UART require clocks to shift the serial data in and out. $\overline{\text{TxC}}$ is the *transmit shift-register clock* input, and $\overline{\text{RxC}}$ is the *receive shift-register clock* input. Usually these two inputs are tied together so they are driven by the same clock frequency. Look at Figure 7-6, sheet 9, to see how a variety of clock signals are produced from a 74LS393 counter. A wirewrap jumper is installed to select the desired $\overline{\text{TxC}}$ and $\overline{\text{RxC}}$. The frequency of the applied clock signal must be 1, 16, or 64 times the transmit and receive baud rate, depending on the mode in which the 8251A is initialized. Using a clock frequency higher than the baud rate allows the receive shift register to be clocked at the center of a bit time rather than at a transition. This reduces the chance of noise at a transition causing a read error.

The 8251A is *double-buffered*. This means that one character can be loaded into a holding buffer while another character is being shifted out of the actual transmit shift register. The TxRDY output from the 8251A will go high when the holding buffer is empty and another character can be sent from the CPU. The TxEMPTY pin

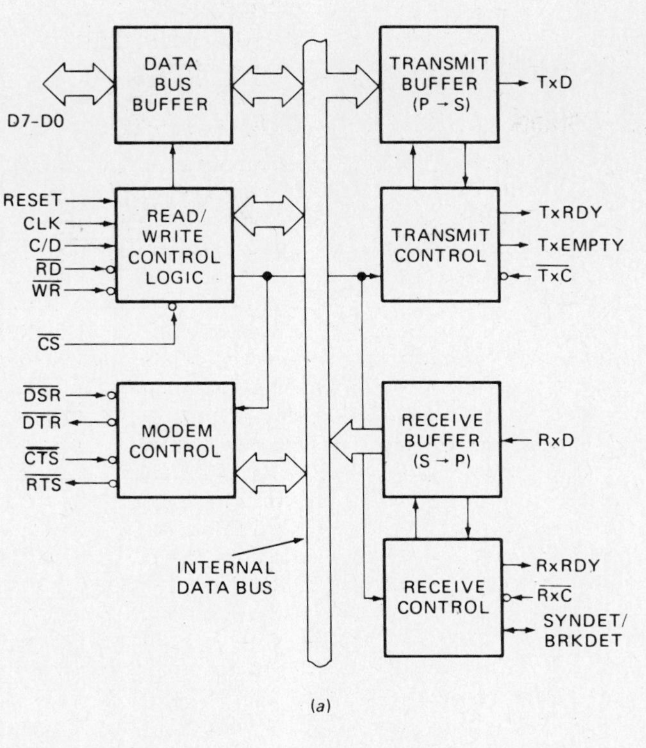

8251 Pin Functions

Pin Name	Pin Function
D7–D0	Data bus (8 bits)
C/$\overline{D}$	Control or data is to be written or read
$\overline{RD}$	Read data command
$\overline{WR}$	Write data or control command
$\overline{CS}$	Chip select
CLK	Clock pulse (TTL)
RESET	Reset
$\overline{TxC}$	Transmitter clock
TxD	Transmitter data
$\overline{RxC}$	Receiver clock
RxD	Receiver data
RxRDY	Receiver ready (has character for CPU)
TxRDY	Transmitter ready (ready for char. from CPU)
$\overline{DSR}$	Data set ready
$\overline{DTR}$	Data terminal ready
SYNDET/BD	Sync detect/break detect
$\overline{RTS}$	Request to send data
$\overline{CTS}$	Clear to send data
TxEMPTY	Transmitter empty
V_{CC}	+5-V supply
GND	Ground

(b)

FIGURE 13-3 Block diagram and pin descriptions for the Intel 8251A USART. *(a)* Block diagram. *(b)* Pin descriptions. *(Intel Corp.)*

on the 8251A will go high when both the holding buffer and the transmit shift register are empty. The RxRDY pin of the 8251A will go high when a character has been shifted into the receiver buffer and is ready to be read out by the CPU. Incidentally, if a character is not read out before another character is shifted in, the first character will be overwritten and lost.

The *sync-detect/break-detect* (SYNDET/BD) pin has two uses. When the device is operating in asynchronous mode, which we are interested in here, this pin will go high if the serial data input line, RxD, stays low for more than 2 character times. This signal then indicates an intentional break in data transmission, or a break in the signal line. When programmed for synchronous data transmission this pin will go high when the 8251A finds a specified sync character(s) in the incoming string of data bits.

The four signals connected to the box labeled MODEM CONTROL in the 8251A block diagram are handshake signals which we described in a previous section.

INITIALIZING AN 8251A

To initialize an 8251A you must send first a mode word and then a command word to the control register address for the device. Figure 13-4 shows the formats for these words and for the 8251A status word which is read from the same address. Baud rate factor, specified by the two least-significant bits of the mode word, is the ratio between the clock signal applied to the $\overline{TxC}$-$\overline{RxC}$ inputs and the desired baud rate. For example, if you want to use a $\overline{TxC}$ of 19,200 Hz and transmit data at 1200 Bd, the baud rate factor is 19,200/1200 or 16 ×. If bits D0 and D1 are both made 0's, the 8251A is programmed for synchronous data transfer. In this case the baud rate will be the same as the applied $\overline{TxC}$ and $\overline{RxC}$. The other three combinations for these 2 bits represent asynchronous transfer. A baud rate factor of one can only be used for asynchronous transfer if the transmitting system and the receiving system both use the same $\overline{TxC}$ and $\overline{RxC}$. The character length specified by bits D2 and D3 in the mode word includes only the actual data bits, not the start bit, parity bit or stop bit(s). If parity is disabled, no parity bit is inserted in the transmitted bit string. If the 8251A is programmed for 5, 6, or 7 data bits, the extra bits in the data character byte read from the device will be 0's.

After you send a mode word to an 8251A, you must then send it a command word. A 1 in the least-signifi-

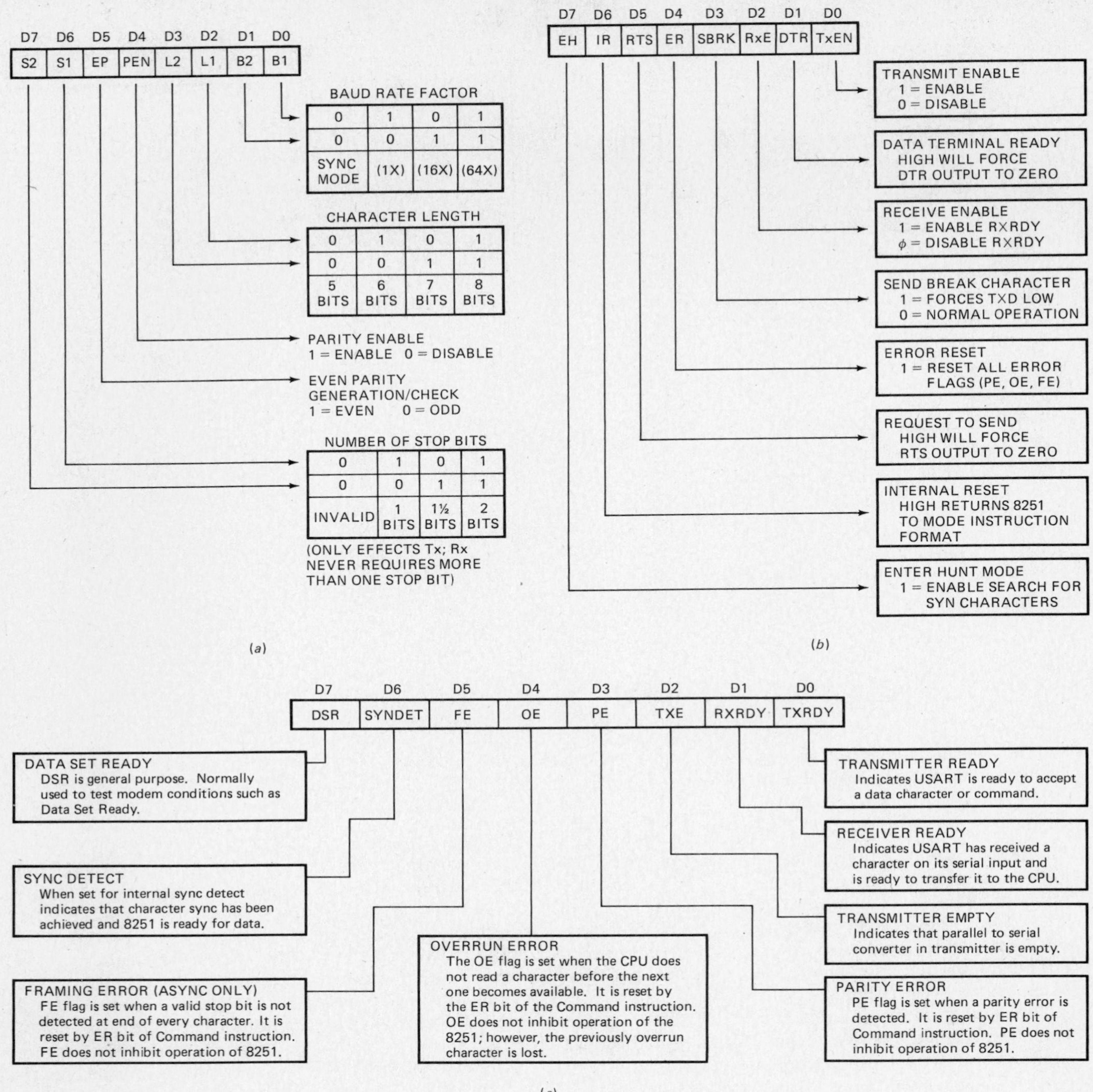

FIGURE 13-4 Format of 8251A mode, command, and status words. *(a)* Mode word. *(b)* Command word. *(c)* Status word. *(Intel Corp.)*

cant bit of the command word enables the transmitter section of the 8251A and the TxRDY output. When enabled, the 8251A TxRDY output will be asserted high if the $\overline{\text{CTS}}$ input has been asserted low, and the transmitter holding buffer is ready for another character from the CPU. The TxRDY signal can be connected to an interrupt input on the CPU or an 8259A, so that characters to be transmitted can be sent to the 8251A on an interrupt basis. When a character is written to the 8251A data address, the TxRDY signal will go low and remain low until the holding buffer is again ready for another character. Putting a 1 in bit D1 of the command word will cause the $\overline{\text{DTR}}$ output of the 8251A to be asserted low. As we explained before, this signal is used to tell a modem that a terminal or computer is operational. A 1 in bit D2 of the command word enables the RxRDY output pin of the 8251A. If enabled, the RxRDY pin will go high when the 8251A has a character in its receiver buffer ready to be read. This signal can be connected to an interrupt input so that characters can be read in on an interrupt basis. The RxRDY output is reset when a character is read from the 8251A.

Putting a 1 in bit D3 of the command word causes the 8251A to output a character of all 0's, which is called a break character. A break character is sometimes used to indicate the end of a block of transmitted data. Sending a command word with a 1 in bit D4 causes the 8251A to reset the parity, overrun, and framing error flags in the 8251A status register. The meanings of these flags are explained in Figure 13-4*c*. A 1 in bit D5 of the command word will cause the 8251A to assert its request-to-send ($\overline{RTS}$) output low. This signal, remember, is sent to a modem to ask whether the modem and the receiving system are ready for a data character to be sent.

Putting a 1 in bit D6 of the command word causes the 8251A to be internally reset when the command word is sent. After a software reset command is sent in this way, a new mode word must be sent. Later we will show you how this is used.

The D7 bit in the command word is only used when the device is operating in synchronous mode. A command word with a 1 in this bit position tells the 8251A to look for specified sync character(s) in a stream of bits being shifted in. If the 8251A finds the specified sync character(s), it will assert its SYNDET/BD pin high. We will discuss this more in the synchronous data communication section of this chapter.

Figure 13-5 shows an example of the instruction sequence you can use to initialize an 8251A. This sequence is somewhat lengthy for two reasons. First, the

```
;8086 Instructions to initialize the 8251A on an SDK-86 board
        MOV   DX, OFFF2H          ; point at command register address
        MOV   AL, 00H             ; send 0's to guarantee device is in
        OUT   DX, AL              ; the command instruction format before
        MOV   CX, 2               ; the RESET command is issued
D0:     LOOP  D0                  ; and delay after sending each command
        OUT   DX, AL              ; instruction.
        MOV   CX, 2
D1:     LOOP  D1
        OUT   DX, AL
        MOV   CX, 2
D2:     LOOP  D2
        MOV   AL, 40H             ; Send internal reset command to
        OUT   DX, AL              ; return device to idle state
        MOV   CX, 2               ; Load delay constant
D3:     LOOP  D3                  ; and delay
        MOV   AL, 11001110B       ; Load mode control word and send it

; 1 1 0 0 1 1 1 0       Mode Word
;  \ \ \ \ \ \ \_\______baud rate factor of 16x
;   \ \ \ \ \_\_________character length of 8 bits
;    \ \ \_\____________parity disabled
;     \_\_______________2 stop bits

        OUT   DX, AL
        MOV   CX, 2               ; and delay
D4:     LOOP  D4
        MOV   AL, 00110111B       ; Load command word and send it
        OUT   DX, AL

; 0 0 1 1 0 1 1 1      Command Word
; \ \ \ \ \ \ \ \_____Transmit enable
;  \ \ \ \ \ \ \______Data terminal ready, DTR will output 0
;   \ \ \ \ \ \_______Receive enable
;    \ \ \ \ \________Normal operation
;     \ \ \ \_________Reset all error flags
;      \ \ \__________RST output 0, request to send
;       \ \___________Do not return to mode instruction form
;        \____________Disable hunt mode
```

FIGURE 13-5 Instruction sequence for 8251A initialization.

8251A does not always respond correctly to a hardware reset on power-up. Therefore, a series of software commands must be sent to the device to make sure it is reset properly before the desired mode and command words are sent. The device is put into a known state by writing 3 bytes of all 0's to the 8251A control register address, and then it is reset by sending a control word with a 1 in bit D6. After this reset sequence the desired mode and control words can be sent to the 8251A. The 8251A distinguishes a command word from a mode word by the order they are sent to the device. After reset, a mode word must be sent to the command address. Any words sent to the command address after the mode word will be treated as command words until the device is reset.

The second factor which lengthens this initialization is the *write-recovery* time T_{RV} of the 8251A. According to the data sheet the 8251A requires a worst case recovery time of 16 cycles of the clock signal connected to the CLK input. On the SDK-86 board the PCLK signal, which is the same as the processor clock frequency, is connected to the CLK input of the 8251A. Therefore, for the SDK-86 board, the required write-recovery time corresponds to 16 processor clock cycles. What all this means is that you have to delay this many clock cycles between successive initialization byte writes to the 8251A. A simple way to produce the required delay and some extra is to load CX with 0002 and count it down with the LOOP instruction. The MOV CX, 0002 instruction takes 4 clock cycles, the first execution of the LOOP instruction takes 17 clock cycles, and the last execution of the LOOP instruction takes 5 cycles. The 8 cycles required for the OUT instruction, which writes the control words, also count as part of the time between writes, so the sum of all these is more than enough. When writing data characters to an 8251A you don't have to worry about this recovery time, because a new character will not be written to the 8251A until the previous character has been shifted out. This shifting, of course, requires much more time than T_{RV}.

The comments in Figure 13-5 explain the meanings of the bits in the mode and control words used in this example. Once the 8251A is initialized as shown, new control words can be sent at any time to, for example, reset the error flags. Now let's look at how characters are sent to and read from an 8251A.

SENDING AND RECEIVING CHARACTERS WITH AN 8251A

Data characters can be sent to and read from the 8251A on an interrupt basis or on a polled basis. To send characters on an interrupt basis the TxRDY pin of the 8251A is connected to an interrupt input on the processor or an 8259A priority interrupt controller. The transmitter and the TxRDY output are enabled by putting a 1 in bit D0 of the control word sent to the 8251A during initialization. When the $\overline{\text{CTS}}$ input of the 8251A is asserted low, and the 8251A buffer is ready for a character, the TxRDY pin will go high. If the processor and 8259A interrupt path is enabled, the processor will go to an interrupt service procedure which writes a data character to the 8251A data address. Writing the data character causes the 8251A to reset its TxRDY output until the buffer is again ready to receive a character. A counter can be used to keep track of how many characters have been sent.

In a similar manner characters can be read from an 8251A on an interrupt basis. In this case the RxRDY output of the 8251A is connected to an interrupt input of the processor or an 8259A, and this output is enabled by putting a 1 in bit D2 of the command word sent during initialization. When a character has been shifted into the 8251A, and the character is in the receiver buffer ready to be read, the RxRDY pin will go high. If the interrupt chain through the 8259A and the processor is enabled, the processor will go to an interrupt procedure which reads in the data character. Reading a data character from the 8251A causes it to reset the RxRDY output signal. This signal will stay low until another character is ready to be read.

To send characters to an 8251A on a polled basis, the 8251A status register is read and checked over and over until the TxRDY bit (D0) is found to be a 1. In some systems you also want to check bit D7 of the status register to make sure the $\overline{\text{DSR}}$ input of the 8251A has been asserted by a signal from, for example, a modem. When the required bit(s) of the status register are all high, a data character is then written to the 8251A. Figure 13-6*a* shows the instruction sequence needed to do this. Note that the status register has the same internal address as the control register. Also note that both an AND and a CMP operation must be done to determine when the two desired bits are both high. Writing a data character to the 8251A resets the TxRDY bit in the status register.

Reading a character from the 8251A on a polled basis is a similar process, except that the RxRDY bit (D1) of the status register is polled to determine when a character is ready to be read. When bit D1 is found high, a character is read in from the 8251A data address. Figure 13-6*b* shows the instruction sequence for this. Status register bits D3, D4, and D5 can be checked to see if a parity error, overrun error, or framing error has occurred. If an error has occurred, a message to retransmit the data can be sent to the transmitting system.

The next step in our journey into serial data communications is to discuss the signal standards used to connect the serial inputs and outputs of UARTS to modems and other serial devices.

SERIAL DATA TRANSMISSION METHODS AND STANDARDS

Aside from drum beats in the jungle, one of the earliest forms of serial data communication was the telegraph. In a telegraph pressing a key at one end of a signal line causes a current to flow through the line. When this current reaches the receiving end of the line, it activates a solenoid (sounder) which produces a sound. Letters and numbers are sent using the familiar Morse code or some other convenient code. After a hundred years or so the telegraph key and sounder evolved into the teletypewriter. A teletypewriter terminal has a typewriter-style keyboard so that the user can simply press a key to send a desired letter or number. A teletype terminal also has a print mechanism which prints out characters as they

```
; Instructions for transmitting data using an SDK-86 8251A
; using polling method

         MOV   DX, 0FFF2H          ; point at control register address
TEST1:   IN    AL, DX              ; read status
         AND   AL, 10000001B       ; and check status of
;                 \______\_________data set ready & transmit ready
         CMP   AL, 10000001B       ; is it ready?
         JNE   TEST1               ; continue to poll if not ready
         MOV   DX, 0FFF0H          ; otherwise point at data address
         MOV   AL, DATA_TO_SEND    ; load data to send
         OUT   DX, AL              ; and send it
```

(a)

```
; Instructions for receiving data with an SDK-86 8251A
; using polling method

         MOV   DX, 0FFF2H          ; point at control register address
TEST2:   IN    AL, DX              ; read status
         AND   AL, 00000010B       ; and check status of RxRdy
         JZ    TEST2               ; continue to poll if not ready
         MOV   DX, 0FFF0H          ; otherwise point at data address
         IN    AL, DX              ; get data
```

(b)

FIGURE 13-6 Instruction sequences for transmitting and receiving with an 8251A on a polled basis. *(a)* Transmit. *(b)* Receive.

are received. Most teletypes use a current to represent a 1 and no current to represent a 0. We start this section by briefly describing the old current-loop standards, and then go on to newer methods.

20- and 60-mA Current Loops

In teletypewriters or other current signal systems some manufacturers use a nominal current of 20 mA to represent a 1, or mark, and no current to represent a 0. Other manufacturers use a nominal current of 60 mA to represent a 1 and no current to represent a 0.

NOTE: The actual current in a specific system may be considerably different from the nominal value.

Sheet 9 of Figure 7-6 shows circuitry which can be used to interface current type signals with the TTL input and output of an 8251A USART on the SDK-86 board. With the jumpers in place as shown, a high on the TxD output of the 8251A will produce a low on the PNP transistor. This will turn the transistor on and cause a positive current to flow out the TTY TX line. Inside a teletypewriter this current flows through an electromagnet and back to the TTY TX RET. To help you visualize this, think of a coil of wire connected between pins 13 and 25 of J7 in the drawing. The current then flows on to −12 V through *R*2 to complete the path. To send a data bit, the teletypewriter opens or closes a switch in a current path. The current for this path in the SDK-86 circuitry is supplied from +5 V through *R*10 to the TTY RX RET line. Think of the key mechanism of the teletypewriter as a simple switch connected between pins 24 and 12 of J7 on the circuit. When the switch is closed the current flows back on the TTY RX line and through *R*3 to −12 V. The current flowing through *R*3 will produce a legal TTL high logic level on the input of the 74LS14 inverter. This high signal passes through two inverters and produces a high on the RxD input of the 8251A.

The circuit as shown in Figure 7-6 is set up for full-duplex operation because the transmit circuit and the receive circuit are independent of each other. In this case, a character sent to the SDK-86 will not be printed out on the teletypewriter until it is echoed back from the SDK-86. This is sometimes referred to as *echoplex* mode. If jumper W17 is installed, the system will operate in half-duplex mode. In this mode a character will be printed out directly as it is typed on the keyboard. However, data cannot be sent and received at the same time because typed characters will be interspersed with characters sent from the SDK-86. We will leave it to you to trace the current paths for this half-duplex mode. Now we will go on to a more common signal standard which uses voltages.

RS-232C Serial Data Standard

OVERVIEW

In the 1960s as the use of time-share computer terminals became more widespread, modems were developed so that terminals could use phone lines to communicate with distant computers. As we stated earlier, modems and other devices used to send serial data are often referred to as *data communication equipment* or DCE. The terminals or computers that are sending or receiving the data are referred to as *data terminal equipment* or DTE. In response to the need for signal and handshake standards between DTE and DCE, the Electronic Industries Association (EIA) developed EIA standard *RS-232C*. This standard describes the functions of 25 signal and handshake pins for serial data transfer. It also describes the voltage levels, impedance levels, rise and fall times, maximum bit rate, and maximum capacitance for these signal lines. Before we work our way through the 25 pin functions, we will take a brief look at some of the other hardware aspects of RS-232C.

RS-232C specifies 25 signal pins and it specifies that the DTE connector should be a male, and the DCE connector should be a female. A specific connector is not given, but the most commonly used connectors are the DB-25P male and the DB-25S female shown in Figure 13-7. When you are wiring up these connectors, it is important to note the order in which the pins are numbered.

The voltage levels for all RS-232C signals are as follows. A logic high, or mark, is a voltage between −3 V and −15 V under load (−25 V no load). A logic low or space is a voltage between +3 V and +15 V under load (+25 V no load). Voltages such as ±12 V are commonly used.

RS-232C TO TTL INTERFACING

Obviously a USART such as the 8251A is not directly compatible with these signal levels. Sheet 9 of the SDK-86 schematics in Figure 7-6 shows one way to interface TTL signals of the 8251A to RS-232C signal levels. If the jumpers shown are removed and the jumpers shown in the jumper table under CRT are inserted, the circuit will produce and accept RS-232C signals. (NOTE: This is the jumpering needed to prepare the SDK-86 board for downloading programs from an IBM PC or other computer.) Here's an example of how it works.

With a jumper between the points numbered 7 and 8, a high on the TxD output of the 8251A produces a high on the base of the transistor, which turns it off. With points numbered 9 and 10 jumpered, the CR TX line will then be pulled to −12 V which is a legal high or marking condition for RS-232C. A low on the TxD output of the 8251A will turn on the transistor and pull the CR TX line to +5 V, which is a legal low or space condition for RS-232C.

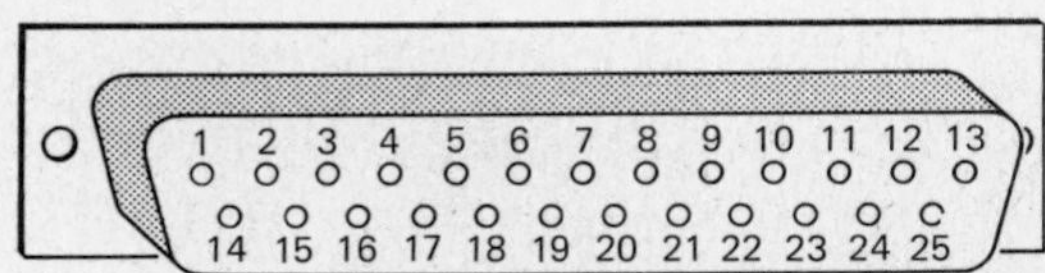

FIGURE 13-7 DB-25P connector often used for RS-232C connections.

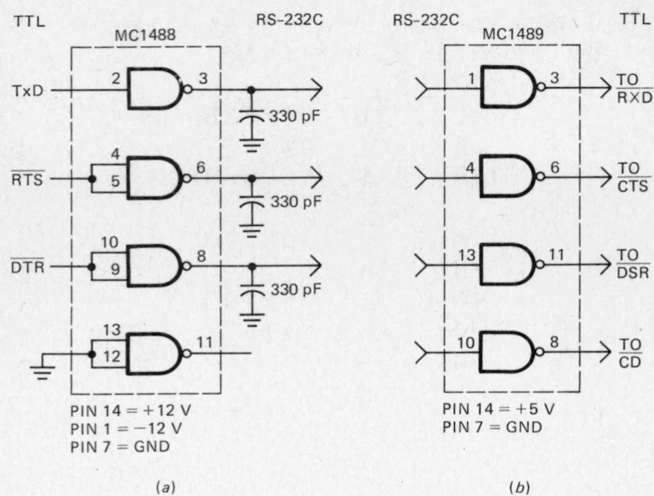

FIGURE 13-8 TTL to RS-232C and RS-232C to TTL signal conversion. *(a)* MC1488 used to convert TTL to RS-232C. *(b)* MC1489 used to convert RS-232C to TTL.

Another, more standard way to interface between RS-232C and TTL levels is with MC1488 quad TTL-to-RS-232C drivers and MC1489 quad RS-232C-to-TTL receivers shown in Figure 13-8. The MC1488s require + and − supplies, but the MC1489s require only +5 V. Note the capacitor to ground on the outputs of the MC1488 drivers. To reduce cross talk between adjacent wires the rise and fall times for RS-232C signals are limited to 30 V/μs. Also note that the RS-232C handshake signals such as $\overline{RTS}$ are active low. Therefore, if one of these signals is asserted, you will find a positive voltage on the actual RS-232C signal line when you check it during troubleshooting. Now let's look at the RS-232C pin descriptions.

RS-232C SIGNAL PINS

Figure 13-9 shows the signal names, signal direction, and a brief description for each of the 25 pins defined for RS-232C. For most applications only a few of these pins are used, so don't get overwhelmed. Here are a few additional notes about these signals.

First note that the signal direction is specified with respect to the DCE. This convention is part of the standard. We have found it very helpful to put arrowheads on all signal lines as shown in Figure 13-2 when we are drawing circuits for connecting RS-232C equipment.

Next observe that there is both a chassis ground (pin 1) and a signal ground (pin 7). To prevent large ac-induced ground currents in the signal ground these two should be connected together only at the power supply in the terminal or the computer.

The TxD, RxD, and handshake signals shown with common names in Figure 13-9 are the ones most often used for simple systems. We gave an overview of their use in the introduction to this section of the chapter, and will discuss them further in a later section of the chapter on modems. These signals control what is called the *primary* or *forward* communications channel of the

PIN NUMBER	COMMON NAME	RS-232-C NAME	DESCRIPTION	SIGNAL DIRECTION ON DCE
1		AA	PROTECTIVE GROUND	—
2	TXD	BA	TRANSMITTED DATA	IN
3	RXD	BB	RECEIVED DATA	OUT
4	$\overline{RTS}$	CA	REQUEST TO SEND	IN
5	$\overline{CTS}$	CB	CLEAR TO SEND	OUT
6	$\overline{DSR}$	CC	DATA SET READY	OUT
7	GND	AB	SIGNAL GROUND (COMMON RETURN)	—
8	$\overline{CD}$	CF	RECEIVED LINE SIGNAL DETECTOR	OUT
9		—	(RESERVED FOR DATA SET TESTING)	—
10		—	(RESERVED FOR DATA SET TESTING)	—
11			UNASSIGNED	—
12		SCF	SECONDARY REC'D. LINE SIG. DETECTOR	OUT
13		SCB	SECONDARY CLEAR TO SEND	OUT
14		SBA	SECONDARY TRANSMITTED DATA	IN
15		DB	TRANSMISSION SIGNAL ELEMENT TIMING (DCE SOURCE)	OUT
16		SBB	SECONDARY RECEIVED DATA	OUT
17		DD	RECEIVER SIGNAL ELEMENT TIMING (DCE SOURCE)	OUT
18			UNASSIGNED	—
19		SCA	SECONDARY REQUEST TO SEND	IN
20	$\overline{DTR}$	CD	DATA TERMINAL READY	IN
21		CG	SIGNAL QUALITY DETECTOR	OUT
22		CE	RING INDICATOR	OUT
23		CH/CI	DATA SIGNAL RATE SELECTOR (DTE/DCE SOURCE)	IN/OUT
24		DA	TRANSMIT SIGNAL ELEMENT TIMING (DTE SOURCE)	IN
25			UNASSIGNED	—

FIGURE 13-9 RS-232C pin names and signal descriptions.

modem. Some modems allow communication over a *secondary* or *backward* channel which operates in the reverse direction from the forward channel and at a much lower baud rate. Pins 12, 13, 14, 16, and 19 are the data and handshake lines for this backward channel.

Pins 15, 17, 21, and 24 are used for synchronous data communication. We will tell you a little more about these in the section of the chapter on modems. Next we want to show you some of the tricks in connecting up RS-232C "compatible" equipment.

CONNECTING UP RS-232C EQUIPMENT

A major point we need to make right now is that you can seldom just connect together two pieces of equipment, described by their manufacturers as RS-232C compatible, and expect them to work the first time. There are several reasons for this. To give you an idea of one of the reasons, suppose that you want to connect the terminal in Figure 13-2 directly to the computer rather than through the modem-modem link. The terminal and the computer probably both have DB-25 type connectors so that, other than a possible male-female mismatch, you might think you could just plug the terminal cable directly into the computer. To see why this doesn't work, hold your fingers over the modems in Figure 13-2 and refer to the pin numbers for the RS-232C signals in Figure 13-9. As you should see, both the terminal and the computer are trying to output data (TxD) from their number 2 pins to the same line. Likewise, they are both trying to input data (RxD) from the same line on their number 3 pins. The same problem exists with the handshake signals. RS-232C drivers are designed so that connecting the lines together in this way will not destroy anything, but connecting outputs together is not a productive relationship. A solution to this problem is to make an adapter with two connectors so that the signals cross over as shown in Figure 13-10*a*. This crossover connection is often called a *null modem*. We have again put arrowheads on the signals in Figure 13-10*a* to help you keep track of the direction for each. As you can see in the figure, the TxD from the terminal now sends data to the RxD input of the computer. Likewise, the TxD from the computer now sends data to the RxD input of the computer as desired. The handshake signals also are crossed over so that each handshake output signal is connected to the corresponding input signal.

A second reason that you can't just plug RS-232C compatible equipment together and expect it to work is that a partial implementation of RS-232C is often used to communicate with printers, plotters, and other computer peripherals besides modems. These other peripherals may be configured as DCE or as DTE. Also, they may use all, some, or none of the handshake signals. As an example of this, suppose that we want to connect the RS-232C port on the IBM PC asynchronous communication board to the serial port on the SDK-86 so that we can download object-code programs.

The IBM PC asynchronous board is configured as DTE, so TxD is on pin 2, RxD on pin 3, $\overline{RTS}$ on pin 4, $\overline{CTS}$ on pin 5, $\overline{DTR}$ on pin 20, $\overline{DSR}$ on pin 6, and carrier detect ($\overline{CD}$) on pin 8. In order for the IBM board to be able to transmit and receive, its $\overline{CTS}$, $\overline{DSR}$, and $\overline{CD}$ inputs must be asserted. The BIOS software asserts the $\overline{DTR}$ and $\overline{RTS}$ outputs. Now take another look at sheet 9 of the SDK-86 schematics in Figure 7-6 to see how the data and handshake signals are connected there.

For communicating with RS-232C type equipment, the SDK-86 board is jumpered as shown in the jumper

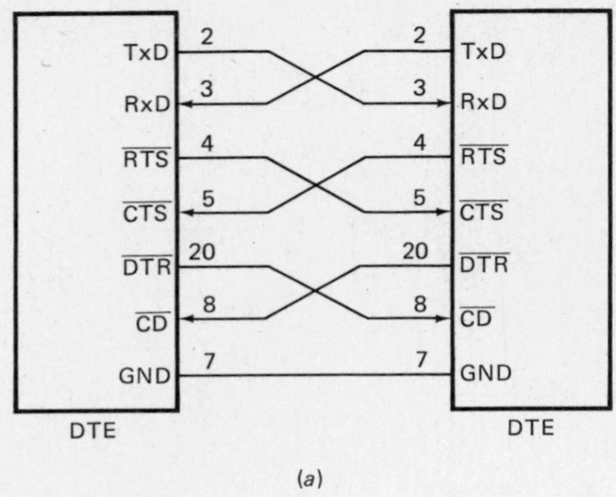

(*a*)

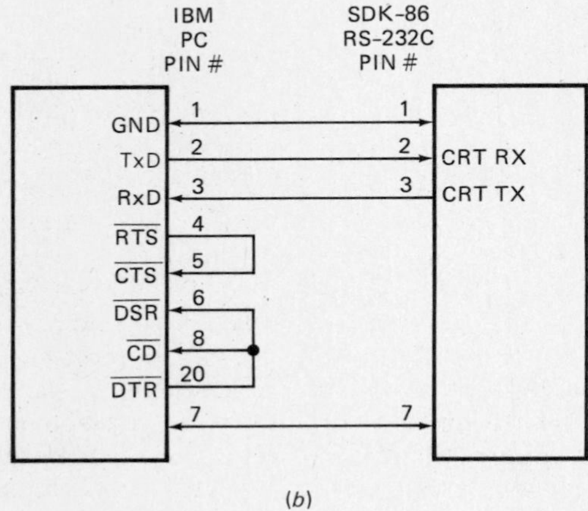

(*b*)

FIGURE 13-10 Nonmodem RS-232C connections. *(a)* Null modem for connecting two RS-232C data-terminal-type devices. *(b)* IBM PC serial port to SDK-86 RS-232C connection.

table column labeled "stand alone CRT." The output data on CRT TX then connects to pin 3 of connector J7, a DB-25S–type connector. This corresponds to the RxD on the IBM connector, so no crossover is needed. Likewise, the CRT RX of the SDK corresponds to the TxD of the IBM board, so this is also a straight-through connection. The handshake signals here are another story.

The $\overline{RTS}$ of the SDK-86 is simply looped into the $\overline{CTS}$ so $\overline{CTS}$ will automatically be asserted when $\overline{RTS}$ is asserted by the 8251A. Therefore, neither of these signals is available for external handshaking. The $\overline{DTR}$ output of the 8251A on the SDK board is used for a teletypewriter function, and does not connect to the normal RS-232C $\overline{DTR}$ pin number, so it is not available either. The $\overline{DSR}$ input of the 8251A is connected to the RxD input so that it will be asserted when a start bit comes in on the serial data line, but this line is also not available for handshaking with external devices. The problem here then is that the SDK-86 is not set up to supply the handshake signals needed by the IBM PC serial board. Figure 13-10*b* shows the connections we make to solve this problem so the PC can talk to the SDK-86. The PC $\overline{RTS}$ line on pin 4 is jumpered on the connector to its $\overline{CTS}$ line on pin 5, so that $\overline{CTS}$ will automatically be asserted when $\overline{RTS}$ is asserted. Pins 6, 8, and 20 are also jumpered together on the connector so that when the PC asserts its $\overline{DTR}$ output on pin 20, the $\overline{DSR}$ input and the $\overline{CD}$ input will automatically be asserted. These connections do not provide for any hardware handshaking. They are necessary just to get the PC and the SDK-86 to talk to each other.

The point here is that whenever you have to connect RS-232C "compatible" devices such as terminals, serial printers, etc., get the schematic for each and work your way through the connections one pin at a time. Make sure that an output on one device goes to the appropriate input on the other device. Sometimes you have to look at the actual drivers and receivers on the schematic to determine which pins on the connector are outputs and which are inputs. This is necessary because some manufacturers label an output pin connected to pin 3 as RxD, indicating that this signal goes to the RxD input of the receiving system.

RS-422A, RS-423A, and RS-449

A major problem with RS-232C is that it can only transmit data reliably about 50 ft [16.4 m] at its maximum rate of 20,000 Bd. If longer lines are used, the transmission rate has to be drastically reduced. This limitation is caused by the open signal lines with a single common ground that are used for RS-232C.

A newer standard, *RS-422A* specifies that each signal will be sent differentially over two adjacent wires in a ribbon cable or a twisted pair of wires as shown in Figure 13-11*a*. Differential signals are produced by differential line drivers such as the MC3487 and translated back to TTL levels by differential line receivers such as the MC3486. Data rates for this standard are 10 MBd for a distance of 50 ft [16.4 m] or 100,000 Bd for a distance of 4000 ft [1220 m]. The higher transmission rate of RS-422A is possible because the differential lines are terminated by resistors so they act as transmission lines instead of simply open wires. A further advantage of differential signals is that any common-mode electrical noise induced in the two lines will be rejected by the differential line receiver. For RS-422A a logic high or mark is indicated by the B signal line being more positive than the A signal line. A logic low or space is indicated by the A signal line being more positive than the B signal line. The voltage difference between the two lines must be greater than 0.4 V, but not greater than 12 V. The common-mode voltage on the signal lines must be in the range of −7 V to +7 V.

Another EIA standard intended to solve the speed and distance problems of RS-232C is *RS-423A*. This standard specifies a low impedance single-ended signal instead of the differential signal of RS-422A. The low-impedance signal can be sent over 50-Ω coaxial cable and terminated at the receiving end to prevent reflections. Figure 13-11*b* shows how an MC3487 driver and MC3486 receiver can be connected to produce the required signals. A logic high in this standard is represented by the A line being between 4 and 6 V negative with respect to the B line (ground), and a logic low is

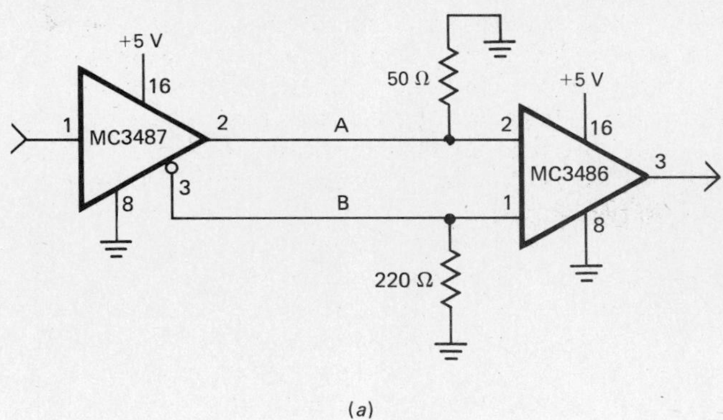

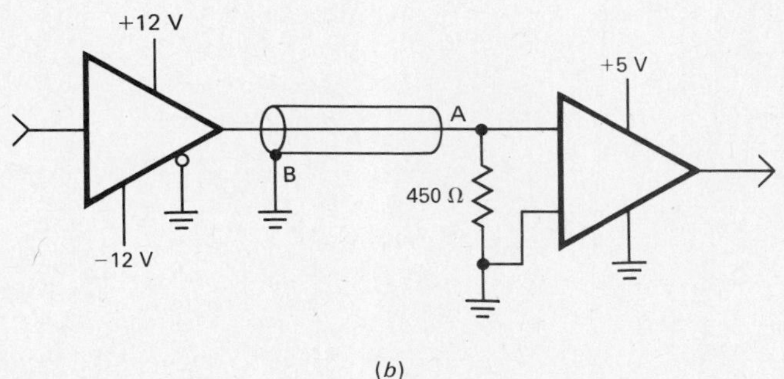

FIGURE 13-11 RS-422A and RS-423A drivers and receivers. *(a)* MC3487 driver and MC3486 receiver used for RS-422A differential signals. *(b)* MC3487 driver and MC3486 receiver used for RS-423A signal on coax cable.

represented by the A line being 4–6 V positive with respect to ground.

The RS-422A and RS-423A standards do not specify connector pin numbers or handshake signals the way that RS-232C does. An additional EIA standard called *RS-449* does this for the two. RS-449 specifies 37 signal pins on a main connector and 9 additional pins on an optional connector. The signals on these connectors are a superset of the RS-232C signals so adapters can be used to interface RS-232C equipment with RS-449 equipment. Still another EIA standard, *RS-366*, incorporates signals for automatic telephone dialing with modems.

Telephone Circuits and Systems

A large amount of the communication between users and computers and between different computers takes place over telephone lines in some form. In this section we give you an introduction to the terminology and operation of phone lines, and then discuss how different types of modems send and receive data over telephone lines.

In the case where digital data needs to be transferred only between two fixed points, *broadband* lines can be leased from telephone or other companies. Depending on the type of line leased, digital data can be directly sent and received at rates from 10 Kbits/s to several megabits per second on these lines. However, in cases where digital data needs to be transferred to many different locations, or where the amount of data to be transferred does not warrant the cost of a leased line, standard (switched) phone lines are used. As we indicated in a previous section, the bandwidth of standard phone lines is limited to 300 Hz–3 kHz, so modems must be used to convert digital data to tones that it can be sent over standard telephone lines, and to convert the tones back to digital data at the receiving end of the phone line. Before we can explain how modems interact with phone lines, we need to look at some telephone circuitry.

Figure 13-12 shows some generic circuitry for *plain old telephone service* or POTS, that many of us are still stuck with. A POTS system uses a rotary dial and electromechanical ringer. Newer systems use *dual-tone multifrequency* (DTMF or touch-tone) dialing and electronic ringers, but the line connections we are interested in here are the same.

The circuitry to the left of the first vertical line in Figure 13-12 is contained in the telephone. The circuitry between the two dotted vertical lines may be located in a *private branch exchange*, or PBX, if the phone is part of a multiphone system in a large building. It may be located in a centralized building if the phone is that of a single subscriber connected directly to the phone lines. Note that for a simple system such as this, only two wires are required to connect the phone to the PBX or local exchange. To send and receive the signals over long distances, however, the two-wire signal must be converted into separate send and receive signals. This must be done so that amplifiers or *repeaters* can be put in each signal path. The conversions back and forth between two-wire signals and four-wire signals is done by a device called a *hybrid coil*. Now let's see how this works and pick up some more terminology.

Let's assume that the phone handset is in its cradle, or *on-hook*, to start. At this point, then, switches *S*1 and *S*2 are open, and *S*3 is closed. To ring up the phone, an ac voltage of 48 V or 96 V rms is sent from the local exchange or PBX to the phone. This voltage activates the ringer mechanism. When the phone handset is lifted off-hook, switches *S*1 and *S*2 close, and switch *S*3 opens. Closing *S*1 and *S*2 causes a direct current to flow from the 48-V dc supply. Circuitry in the PBX or in the local exchange detects this direct current and turns off the ringing signal within about 200 ms. The process is referred to as a *ring trip*. Incidentally, the ring and tip names on the signal lines in Figure 13-12 refer to the parts of the old-fashioned phone plug connected to that signal line. Closing *S*1 and *S*2 also allows the voice signals to get in and out of the phone. As you talk into the phone, the induction coil feeds back part of the transmitted voice signal to the receiver so you can tell how loud you are talking. Now let's see what happens when you make a call.

Again when the handset is lifted off-hook a direct current is produced in the wires to the PBX or local exchange. The PBX or local exchange returns a dial tone to let you know that it is alive and ready to serve you. As you turn the rotary dial to dial a number, switches *S*4 and *S*5 open and close as the dial passes each number.

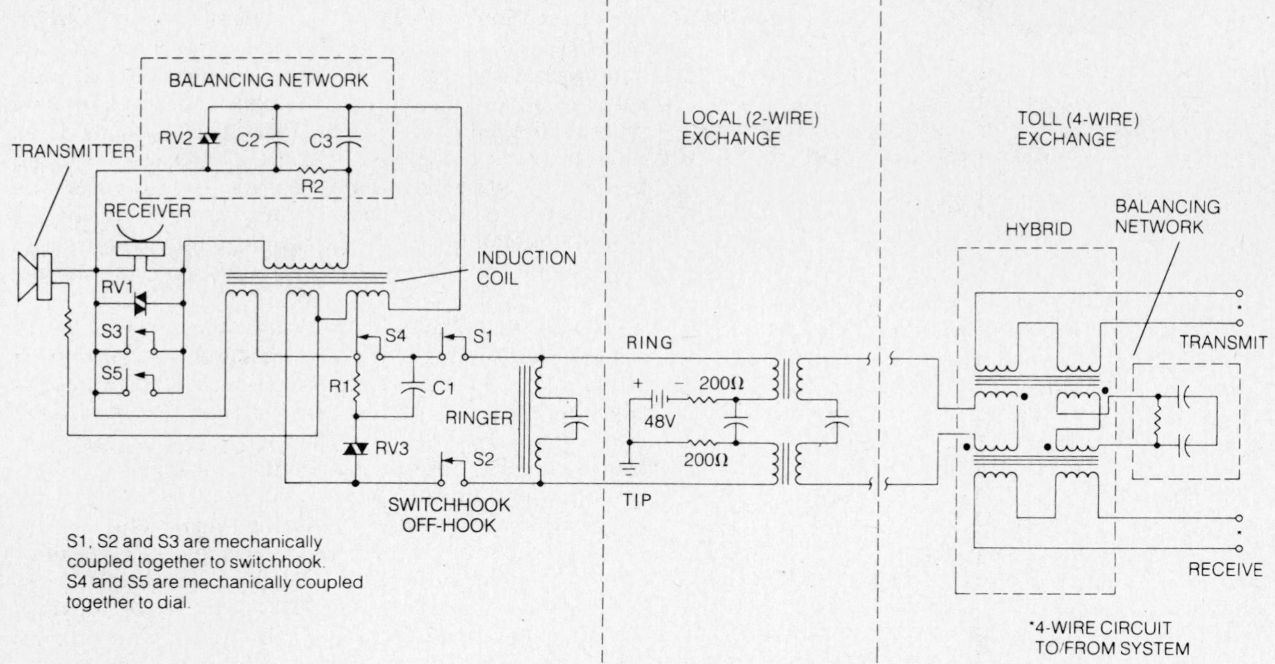

FIGURE 13-12 Circuitry and line connections for standard rotary-dial telephone. *(Texas Instruments, Inc.)*

This produces a series of pulses equal to the desired number. Switching circuitry in the local exchange uses the series of pulses to start finding a path to the dialed phone. *Dual-tone frequency-modulation* or DTFM telephones produce a mixture of two tones for each number button pushed. Circuitry in the PBX or the local exchange decodes these tones to get the required number information. In either case when all the desired numbers have been entered, the local exchange attempts to complete the connection. If the dialed unit is unavailable, the local exchange returns a busy signal to your phone.

An important point here is that any circuit or system that is going to be connected to standard phone lines must be approved by the FCC. This regulation is intended to prevent untested devices from damaging the phone system or creating a shock hazard.

The next topic we want to discuss here is one way that analog phone signals are converted to digital form so that they can be more efficiently sent over long distances.

CODECs, TDM, and PCM

Because digital signals have much better noise immunity than analog signals, analog signals are often converted to digital signals with an A/D converter for transmission over long distances. A D/A converter at the destination uses the received binary codes to reconstruct a replica of the original analog signal. Sending analog signals such as phone signals as a series of binary codes is called *pulse-code modulation* or PCM. The A/D converter that produces the binary codes in this application is usually called a *coder* and the D/A converter that reconstructs the analog signal from the pulse codes is referred to as a *decoder*. Since both a coder and a decoder are needed for two-way communication, they are often packaged in the same IC. This combined coder and decoder is called a *codec*. Common examples of codecs are the Intel 2910A and the Intel 2911A-1. These devices each contain a sample-and-hold circuit on the analog input, an 8-bit A/D converter, an 8-bit D/A converter, and appropriate control circuitry.

Normal A/D converters are linear, which means that the steps are the same size over the full range of the converters. The A/D converters used in codecs are nonlinear. They have small steps for small signals and large steps for large signals. In other words, for signals near the zero point of the A/D converter, it only takes a small change in the signal to change the code on the output of the A/D. For a signal near the full scale of the converter, a large change in the input signal is required to produce a change in the output binary code. This nonlinearity of the A/D converter is said to *compress* the signal, because it reduces the dynamic range of the signal. Compression in this way greatly improves the accuracy for small signals where it is needed, without going to a converter with more bits of resolution. The D/A in the codec is nonlinear in the reverse manner, so that when the binary pulse codes are converted to analog, the result is *expanded* to duplicate the original waveform. A codec which has this intentional nonlinearity is often referred to as a *compander* or a *companding codec*. The two most common ways of changing the size of the steps as the signal gets larger are called the *μ LAW*, and the *A LAW*. Consult the Intel 2910A data sheet for more infor-

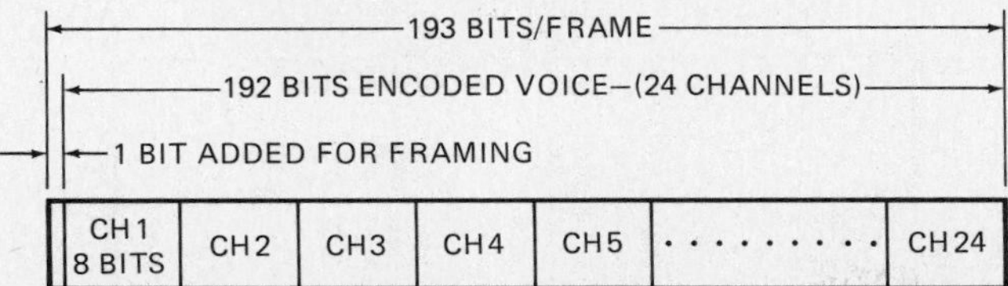

FIGURE 13-13 Frame format for time-domain-multiplexed data from codec.

mation about a μ-LAW device, and the Intel 2911A-1 data sheet for more information about an A-LAW device.

In most systems the output of the codec A/D is not simply sent on a wire by itself, it is multiplexed with the outputs of many other codecs in a manner known as *time-division multiplexing*, TDM. There are several different formats used. A simple one will give you the idea of how it's done.

One of the first TDM systems was the T1 or DS-1 system which multiplexes 24 PCM voice channels onto a single wire. For this system an 8-bit codec on each channel samples and digitizes the input signal at an 8-kHz rate. The 8-bit codes from the codecs are sent to a multiplexer which sends them out serially, one after the other. One set of bits from each of the 24 codecs plus a framing bit is referred to as a frame. Figure 13-13 shows the format of a frame for this system. The framing bit at the start of each frame toggles after each frame is sent. It is used to keep the receiver and the transmitter synchronized and for keeping track of how many frames have been sent. After it sends the framing bit, the multiplexer sends out the 8-bit code from the first codec, then sends out the 8-bit code from the next codec, and so on until the codes for all 24 have been sent out. At specified intervals the multiplexer sends out a frame which contains synchronization information and signaling information. This does not seriously affect the quality of the transmitted data.

Since the multiplexer is sending out 193-bit frames at a rate of 8000 per second, the data rate on the wire is 193×8000, or 1.544 Mbits/s. A newer system, known as T4M or DS-4 multiplexes 4032 channels onto a single coaxial cable or optic fiber. The bit rate for this system is 274.176 Mbits/s.

Telephone companies transmit long-distance phone signals over high-speed digital lines, and all local phone service may eventually be converted to a wideband digital system known as the *integrated services digital network* or ISDN. For now, however, the bandwidth of each standard user channel is still only about 4 kHz. Until this "weak link" is removed we still have to use modems to communicate with computers over standard phone lines. The next section shows how modems operate.

Modems

MODULATION METHODS

As we described in a previous section, a modulator-demodulator, or modem, sends digital 1's and 0's over standard phone lines as modulated tones. The frequency of the tones is within the bandpass of the lines. The three major forms of modulation used are *amplitude*, *frequency-shift keying* (FSK), and *phase-shift keying* (PSK).

To produce amplitude modulation, a single-frequency tone of perhaps 387 Hz is turned on to represent a 1 and turned off to represent a 0 as shown in Figure 13-14*a*. Amplitude modulation is only used for very low speed reverse channel transmission because of its poor noise rejection characteristics. A temporary change in line resistance, for example, might drop the amplitude of the 1 signal below the threshold of the detector, and the data would appear to be all 0's.

Frequency-shift keying uses one tone to represent a 0 and another tone to represent a 1 as shown in Figure 13-14*b*. In order to allow full-duplex communication, four different frequencies are often used. An old standard, the Bell 103A, 300-Bd FSK modem, for example, uses 2025 Hz for a 0 and 2225 Hz for a 1 in one direction, and 1070 Hz for a 0 and 1270 Hz for a 1 in the other direction. Another standard, the Bell 202 modem, permits half-duplex communication at 1200 Bd. The 202 uses 1200 Hz to represent a 0 and 1700 Hz to represent a 1 for the main channel. Different versions of the 202 may also have either a 5 bit/s amplitude-modulated back channel, or a 150 bit/s FSK back channel which uses 387 Hz for a 0 and 487 Hz for a 1.

LSI has made it possible to build an FSK modem with very few parts. Figure 13-15 shows a circuit diagram for a modem which uses the Advanced Micro Devices Am 7910 device. The 7910 can be programmed to operate in a Bell 103 compatible mode, Bell 202 compatible mode, or in a mode compatible with one of several other standards. It uses A/Ds, D/As, and the digital filter techniques we described in Chapter 10 to synthesize and filter all of the data signals. The circuit in Figure 13-15 is connected to a terminal or microcomputer through a stand-

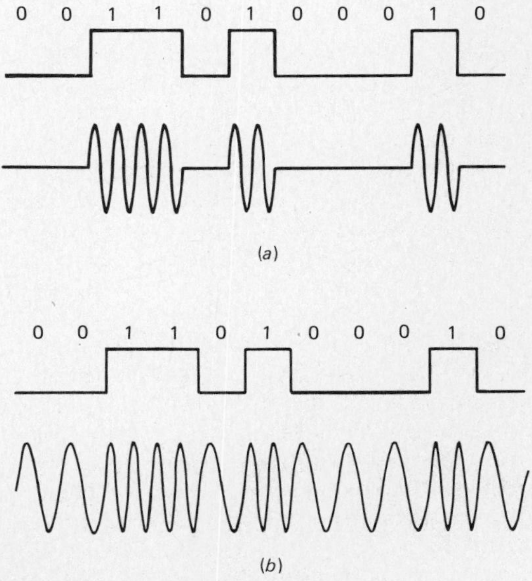

FIGURE 13-14 Modem modulation methods. *(a)* Amplitude. *(b)* Frequency-shift keying (FSK).

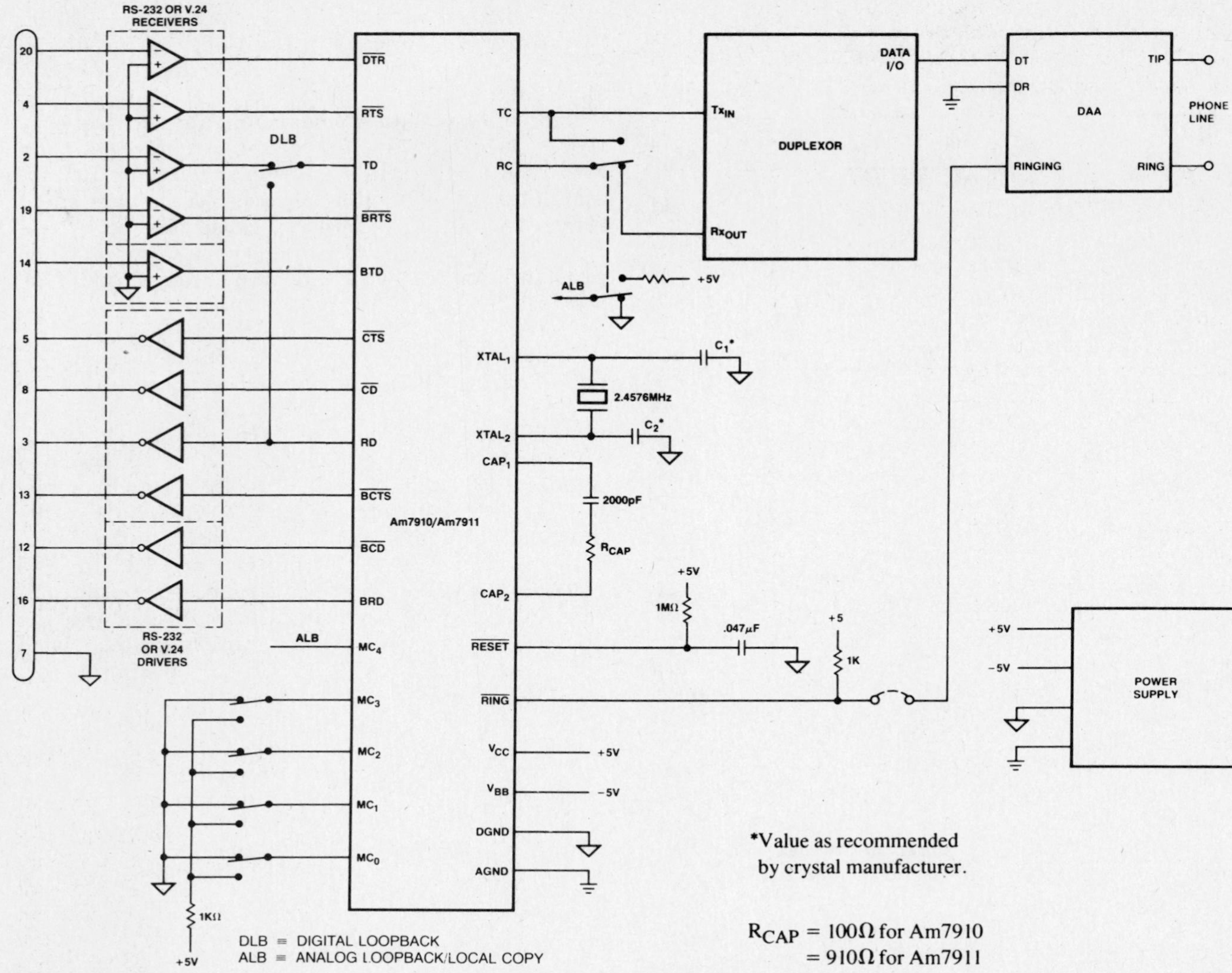

FIGURE 13-15 FSK modem circuit using AM7910 modem chip. *(Advanced Micro Devices)*

ard RS-232C interface. Signal names on the 7910 which start with a B are the back channel signals. The 7910 inputs labeled MC0–MC4 are used to program the operating mode for the device. These can be connected to manual switches as shown, or in a microcomputer system where the data and handshake signals are connected directly to the UART, these lines could be connected to a port so that the operating mode could be changed under program control.

FSK-modulated data is sent out from the 7910 on the pin labeled TC and received on the pin labeled RC. The duplexer puts the transmitted signal on the common signal line and taps off the received signal from the common signal line. Remember from a previous discussion that data is sent and received on the same wire for a standard two-wire phone service. The box labeled DAA in Figure 13-15 is the *data access arrangement* circuitry which actually interfaces the signals with the phone lines. It is this circuitry that must conform to the provisions of FCC rules section 68. Several integrated packages are available which contain a duplexer and sophisticated DAA circuitry. One of these is the CH1810 from Cermetek Microelectronics, Inc. Note in Figure 13-15 that the DAA circuitry provides a RINGING signal to the 7910 when the modem is being called.

Two important features of the modem circuit in Figure 13-15 are the *analog loopback* (ALB) and the *digital loopback* (DLB) which are used for testing. The analog loop mode is used to test the modem locally. When the ALB switch in the middle of Figure 13-15 is in the up position, the FSK-modulated data will be routed back into the FSK input. A software test procedure can then compare the incoming data with the transmitted data to see if the modem is a 7910 and the connecting circuitry is working correctly. The digital loopback is used to check the operation of the modem from some remote location. When the DLB switch in Figure 13-15 is in the down position, data received from the phone line will be retransmitted back to the sending system. The sending system can then compare the sent and returned data to see if the data link is operating correctly.

On a standard two-wire phone line FSK modulation is

limited to half-duplex operation at 1200 Bd. (With a four-line service, full-duplex operation at 1200 bits/s is possible.) For higher bit rates and full-duplex operation on standard phone service, phase-shift modulation is used.

PHASE-SHIFT MODULATION VARIATIONS

In the simplest form of *phase-shift modulation*, the phase of a constant-frequency sine-wave carrier of perhaps 1700 Hz is shifted by 180° to represent a change in the data from a 1 to a 0 or from a 0 to a 1. Figure 13-16*a* shows an example of this. As the digital data changes from a 0 to a 1, near the left edge of the figure, the phase of the signal is shifted by 180°. When the data changes from a 1 to a 0, the phase of the carrier is again shifted by 180°. For the next section of the digital data where the data stays 0 for 3 bit times, the phase of the carrier is not changed. Likewise, in a later section of the waveform where the data remains at a one level for 2 bit times, the phase of the carrier is not changed. The phase of the carrier then is only shifted by 180° when the data line changes from a 1 to a 0 or from a 0 to a 1.

The simple phase-shift modulation shown in Figure 13-16*a* has no real advantage over FSK as far as maximum bit rate etc. are concerned. However, by using additional phase angles besides 180°, 2 or 3 bits can be sent in 1 baud time. Two bits sent in 1 baud time are called *dibits*, and 3 bits sent in 1 baud time are called *tribits*. Here's how dibits and tribits are encoded.

For dibit encoding, each pair of bits in the data stream is treated together, and referred to as a dibit. The value of these two bits determines the amount that the phase of the carrier will be shifted. Figure 13-16*b* shows the angle that the phase of the carrier will be shifted for the four possible values of a dibit. If, for example, the value of 2 bits taken together is 01, the phase of the carrier will be shifted 90° to represent that dibit. The trick here is that the phase of the carrier only has to shift once for each two transmitted bits. Remember from a previous discussion that baud rate is the rate at which the carrier is changing. In this case it is not the same as the number of bits per second. Bell 212A type modems use this scheme to transmit 1200 bits/s at a baud rate of only 600 Bd. Two carrier frequencies, 1200 Hz and 2400 Hz, are used to permit full-duplex operation.

For tribit encoding, the data stream is divided into groups of three bits each, called tribits. Figure 13-16*c* shows one possible set of angles that the phase of the carrier might be shifted to represent the eight different values that the tribit can have. The Bell 208 modem uses this tribit scheme to transmit data at 4800 bits/s.

Another similar scheme which makes it possible to transmit data at 9600 bits/s over conditioned standard phone lines encodes 4 bits in each baud time and is called *quaternary amplitude modulation* (QAM). This scheme uses eight different angles to represent three of the bits in each group of four, and two different amplitudes to represent the fourth bit in each quadbit. A baud rate of 2400 Bd and 4 bits/Bd produces a data rate of 9600 bits/s.

Dibit and tribit phase-shift modulation permits higher data rates on phone lines, but detecting this type of phase-encoded data presents some unique problems. We will use a dibit example to describe these problems and how they are solved. Remember from our previous discussion that, in a dibit system, the value of a dibit is represented by shifting the phase of a carrier signal some specified number of degrees from a reference phase. In order to detect the amount of phase shift, the receiver and the transmitter must be using the same reference phase. This would be easy if we could just run another wire to carry a synchronizing clock signal. Since this is not easily done, the synchronizing signal must in some way be included with the data. The carrier signal itself cannot be used directly, because we want to measure the phase of that signal.

The solution to this problem is to use transitions in the transmitted signal to synchronize a phase-locked loop oscillator in the receiver. In order for this to work, two factors must be included in the transmitted data. First of all, the system must be operated synchronously rather than asynchronously, so that data, sync, or null characters are always being received by the receiver. Secondly, the transmitted data must have enough transitions at regular intervals to keep the phase-locked loop locked in the desired phase. The transmitted data from the USART may not have enough transitions in it to satisfy this second condition, so a special circuit called a *scrambler* in the transmitter puts any required extra transitions in the signal. The scrambler usually consists of a shift register with feedback. The output from the

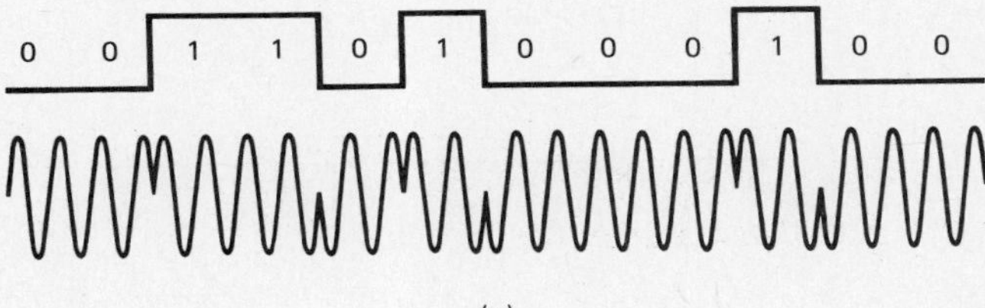

(*a*)

GRAY CODE DIBIT VALUE	DEGREES OF PHASE SHIFT
00	0
01	90
11	180
10	270

(*b*)

GRAY CODE DIBIT VALUE	DEGREES OF PHASE SHIFT
001	22.5
000	67.5
010	112.5
011	157.5
111	202.5
110	247.5
100	292.5
101	337.5

(*c*)

FIGURE 13-16 Phase-shift modulation (PSK). (*a*) Waveforms for simple phase-shift modulation. (*b*) One common set of phase shifts used to represent four possible dibit combinations. (*c*) One common set of phase shifts used to represent the eight possible tribit combinations.

scrambler is then used to modulate the phase of the carrier. When the carrier signal reaches the receiver, the signal is demodulated to produce a signal of 1's and 0's. This signal is then passed through a descrambler which reverses the scrambling process and outputs the original data.

MODEM HANDSHAKING

Many of the currently available modems, such as the Hayes Smartmodem 1200 that we use with our IBM PC, contain a dedicated microprocessor. The built-in intelligence allows these units to automatically dial a specified number with either tones or pulses, and redial the number if it is found busy or doesn't answer. When a smart modem makes contact with another modem, it will automatically try to set its transmit circuitry to match the baud rate of the other modem. It can be set to automatically answer a call after a programmed number of rings so that you can access your computer from a remote location. Some CRT terminals now come with a smart modem which allows the user to establish voice contact and then switch over to digital data communication.

After a modem dials up another modem, a series of handshake signals takes place. The handshake signals may be generated by hardware in the modem or by software in the system connected to the modem. The handshake sequence is similar for most of the Bell compatible modems, so we will use the Bell 202 as an example.

Figure 13-17 shows the data and handshake waveforms for a 202 modem as produced by the AM7910 single-chip modem described in the FSK section previously. Keep a copy of the circuit diagram in Figure 13-15 handy as you work your way through the waveforms here.

The modem which makes a call is usually referred to as the *originate* modem, and the modem which receives the call is usually referred to as the *answer* modem. In the following discussion we will use the terms *calling modem* and *called modem*, respectively, to agree with the labels on the waveforms in Figure 13-17.

At the left side of the waveforms, a call is being made from one modem to another. Assuming that the $\overline{\text{DTR}}$ of the called modem is asserted, the ringing signal on the line will cause the DAA circuitry to assert the *ringing input* ($\overline{\text{RI}}$) of the 7910. In response to this the 7910 will send out a silent period of about 2 seconds to accommodate billing signals, and then it will send out an answer tone of 2025 Hz to the calling modem for 2 seconds. If the $\overline{\text{DTR}}$ and the $\overline{\text{RTS}}$ of the calling modem are asserted indicating that data is ready to be sent, the calling modem then puts a tone of 2225 Hz (mark) on the line

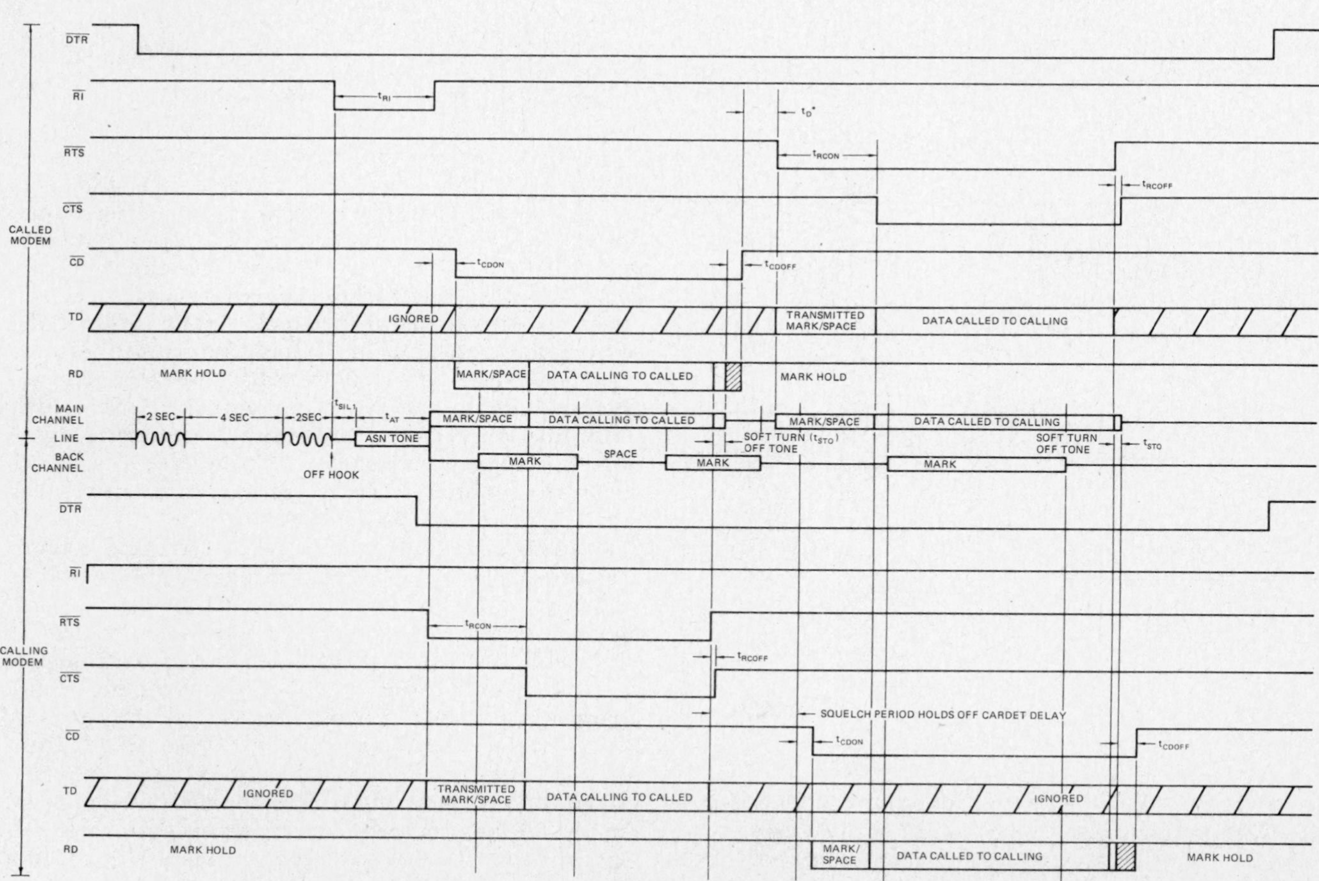

FIGURE 13-17 Handshake signal sequence for Bell type 202 FSK modem using AM7910 modem chip.

for 8 ms to let the called modem know that contact is complete. In response to this mark the called modem asserts its *carrier detect* output ($\overline{CD}$) to enable the receiving UART. The calling modem then sends data until its $\overline{RTS}$ input is released by the computer or terminal sending the data. While it is receiving data on the main channel, the called modem can send data to the calling modem on the 5 bit/s back channel. Releasing $\overline{RTS}$ causes the modem to release $\overline{CTS}$ to the sending computer, and remove the carrier from the line. The called modem senses the loss of the carrier and unasserts its carrier detect, $\overline{CD}$ signal.

Now, if the called system is to send some data back to the calling system on the main channel, it asserts the $\overline{RTS}$ input to its modem. The called modem sends a marking tone to the calling modem for 8 ms. The calling modem asserts its $\overline{CD}$ output to its UART. The called modem then sends data to the calling modem on the main channel until its $\overline{RTS}$ input is unasserted by the called system, indicating no more data to send. While the called modem is transmitting on the main channel, the calling modem can transmit over the back channel if necessary. For a full-duplex system the handshake is similar, but the data rates are equal in both directions.

MODEM STANDARDS

Two organizations are responsible for most of the current standards regarding modems. In the United States most modems follow one of the Bell Telephone standards. Examples of these de facto standards are the Bell types 103, 202, 208, and 212A which we have used as examples in this section. Throughout much of the rest of the world modems follow one of the standards of the *Comité Consultatif Internationale Téléphonique et Télégraphique* (CCITT), which is part of the International Telecommunications Union. CCITT standards which relate to modems start with a V. Examples are the V.26, which is a 2400 bit/s modem, and the V.27, which is a 4800 bit/s modem. In the next section we discuss a means of data communication that may make modems obsolete.

Fiber-Optic Data Communication

INTRODUCTION

All of the data communication methods we have discussed so far use metallic conductors. The systems we describe here transfer data through very thin glass or plastic fibers with a beam of light and have no conducting electrical path. Therefore, they are called *fiber-optic* systems. Figure 13-18 shows the connections for a basic fiber-optic data link you can build and experiment with.

The light source here is a simple infrared LED. Higher performance systems use an *infrared injection laser diode* (ILD) or some other laser driven by a high-speed, high-current driver.

NOTE: If you are working on a fiber-optic system you should never look directly into the end of the fiber to see

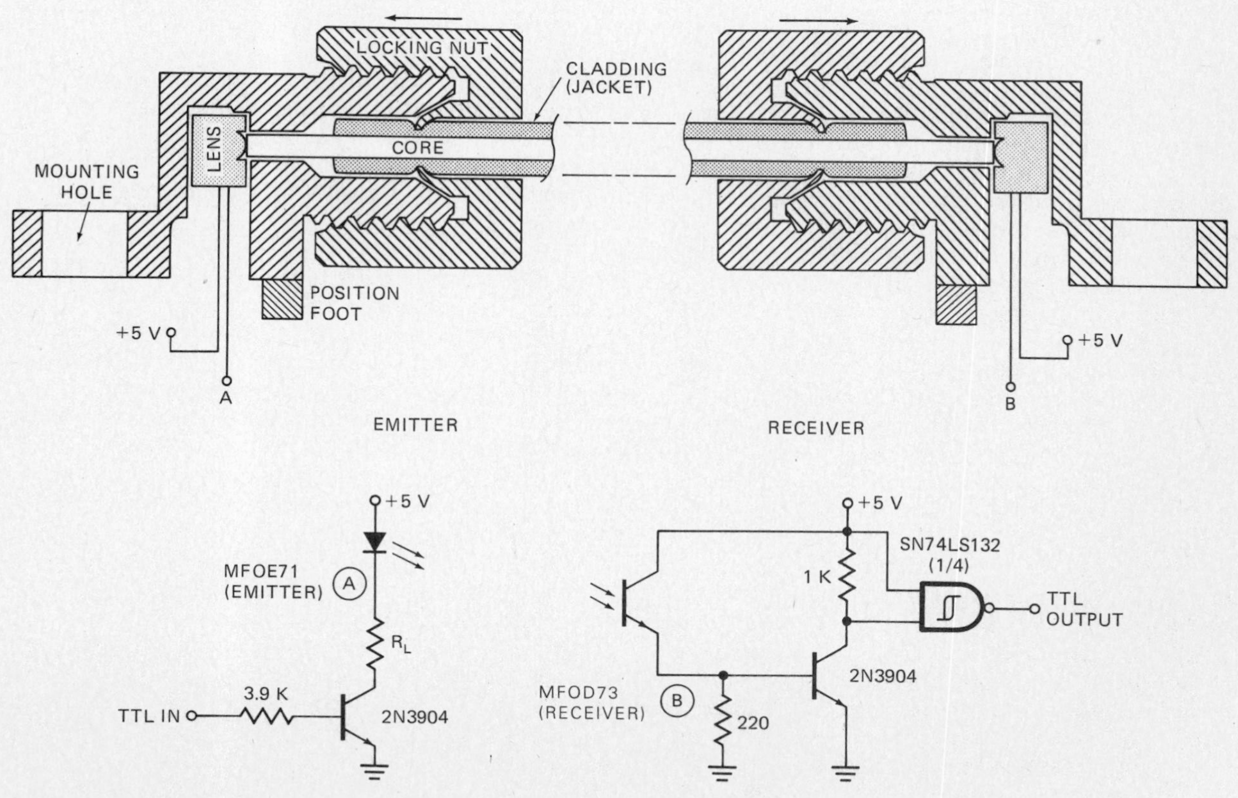

FIGURE 13-18 Diagram of simple fiber-optic data link.

if the light source is working, because the light beam from some laser diodes is powerful enough to cause permanent eye damage. Use a light meter, or point the cable at a nonreflecting surface to see if the light source is working.

Digital data is sent over the fiber by turning the light beam on for a 1 and off for a 0. Data rates for some currently available systems are as high as a gigabit per second. Current systems use one of three light wavelengths, 0.85 μm, 1.3 μm, or 1.500 μm. These wavelengths are used because the absorption of light by the optical fibers is minimum at these wavelengths.

The fibers used are made of special plastic or glass. Depending on the desired operating mode, bandwidth, and transmitting distance, different diameter fibers are used. Fiber diameters used range from 2–1000 μm. As shown in Figure 13-19*e*, the fiber-optic cable consists of three parts. The optical-fiber core is surrounded by a *cladding* material which is also transparent to light. We will explain the function of this cladding later. The cable is enclosed in a sheath which protects the cladding and does not allow external light to enter.

To convert the light signal back into an electrical signal at the receiving end, Darlington photodetectors such as the MFOD73 shown in Figure 13-18, p-i-n FET devices, or avalanche photodiodes (APDs) are used. APDs are more sensitive and operate at higher frequencies, but the circuitry for them is more complex. A Schmitt trigger is usually used on the output of the detector to "square up" the output pulses. Now that you have an overview of an optical-fiber link, we will briefly discuss some of the optics involved.

THE OPTICS OF FIBERS

The path of a beam of light going from a material with one optical density to a material of different optical density depends on the angle at which the beam hits the boundary between the two materials. Figure 13-19 shows the path that will be taken by beams of light at various angles going from an optically dense material such as glass to a less dense material such as a vacuum or air. If the beam hits the boundary at a right angle, it will go straight through as shown in Figure 13-19*a*. When a beam hits the boundary at a small angle away from the perpendicular or *normal*, it will be bent away from the normal when it goes from the more dense to the less dense, as shown in Figure 13-19*b*. A light beam going in the other direction would follow the same path. A quantity called the *index of refraction* is used to describe the amount that the light beam will be bent. Using the angle identifications shown in Figure 13-19*b*, the index of refraction, n, is defined as the (sine of angle B)/(sine of angle A). A typical value for the index of refraction of glass is 1.5. The larger the index of refraction, the more the beam will be bent when it goes from one material to another.

Figure 13-19*c* shows a unique situation that occurs when a beam going from a dense material to a less dense material hits the boundary at a special angle called the *critical angle*. The beam will be bent so that it travels parallel to the boundary after it enters the less dense material.

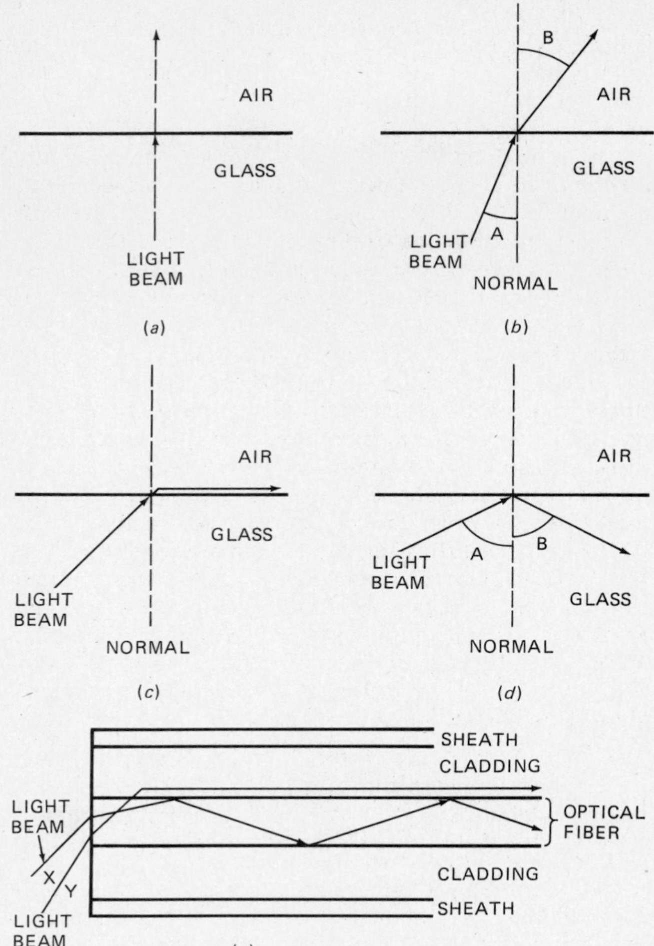

FIGURE 13-19 Light-beam paths for different angles of incidence with boundary of material leaving a lower optical density. *(a)* Right angle. *(b)* Angle less than critical angle. *(c)* At critical angle. *(d)* Angle greater than critical angle. *(e)* Angle greater than critical angle in optical fiber.

A still more interesting situation is shown in Figure 13-19*d*. If the beam hits the boundary at an angle greater than the critical angle, it will be totally reflected from the boundary at the same angle on the other side of the normal. This is somewhat like skipping stones across water. In this case the light beam will not leave the more dense material.

To see how all of this relates to optical fibers, take a look at the cross-sectional drawing of an optical fiber in Figure 13-19*e*. If a beam of light enters the fiber parallel to the axis of the fiber, it will simply travel through the fiber. If the beam enters the fiber so that it hits the glass-cladding layer boundary at the critical angle, it will travel through the fiber optic cable in the cladding layer as shown for beam *Y* in Figure 13-19*e*. However, if the beam enters the cable so that it hits the glass-cladding layer boundary at an angle greater than the critical angle, it will bounce back and forth between the walls of the fiber as shown for beam *X* in Figure 13-19*e*. The glass or plastic used for fiber-optic cables has very low absorption, so the beam can bounce back and forth along the fiber for several feet or miles without excessive attenuation.

MULTIMODE AND SINGLE-MODE FIBERS

If an optical fiber has a diameter many times larger than the wavelength of the light being used, then beams which enter the fiber at different angles will arrive at the other end of the fiber at slightly different times. The different angles of entry for the beams are referred to as *modes*. A fiber with a diameter large enough to allow beams with several different entry angles to propagate through it is called a *multimode* fiber. Since multimode fibers are larger, they are easier to manufacture, are easier to manually work with, and can use inexpensive LED drivers. However, the phase difference between the output beams in multimode fibers causes problems at high data rates. One partial solution to this problem is to dope the glass of the fiber so that the index of refraction decreases toward the outside of the fiber. Light beams travel faster in the region where the index of refraction is lower, so beams which take a longer path back and forth through the faster outer regions tend to arrive at the end of the fiber at the same time as those that take a shorter path through the slower center region.

A better solution to the phase problems of the multimode fiber is to use a fiber that has a diameter only a few times the wavelength of the light being transmitted. Only beams very nearly parallel to the axis of the fiber can be transmitted then. This is referred to as *single-mode* operation. Single-mode systems currently available can transmit data a distance of over 30 km at a rate of nearly 1 Gbit/s. An experimental system developed by AT&T multiplexes 10 slightly different wavelength laser beams onto one single-mode fiber. The system can transmit data at an effective rate of 20 Gbit/s over a distance of 68 km without amplification.

One of the main problems with single-mode fibers is the difficulty in making low-loss connections with the tiny fibers. Another difficulty is that in order to get enough light energy into the tiny fiber, relatively expensive laser diodes or other lasers rather than inexpensive LEDs must be used.

FIBER-OPTIC CABLE USES

Fiber-optic transmission has the advantages that the signal lines are much smaller than the equivalent electrical signal lines, the signal lines are immune to electrical noise, and signals can be sent much longer distances without repeater amplifiers. A large number of fibers can be put in a single cable. One of the first major uses of fiber-optic transmission systems has been for carrying large numbers of phone conversations across oceans and throughout cities. The specifications of currently available fiber-optic systems are impressive, but relatively primitive as compared to the possiblities shown by laboratory research. In the future it is possible that the high data rate of fiber-optic transmission may make picture phones a household reality, replace TV cables, replace satellite communication for many applications, replace modems, and provide extensive computer networking.

ASYNCHRONOUS COMMUNICATION SOFTWARE ON THE IBM PC

In a previous section of this chapter we discussed how asynchronous serial data can be sent or received with an 8251A on a polled or an interrupt basis. Any serial communication at some point has to get down to that level of hardware interaction. However, when you are working in a microcomputer system which has a DOS and BIOS available, you can often add serial communication capability to a program without getting down to this hardware level. To help you see how to decide which software level to use for a given application, we will show you how we developed a simple terminal emulator program and a program which downloads object code files from the IBM PC to an SDK-86 board.

A Terminal Emulator Using DOS Function Calls and BIOS Calls

As a first step in developing the SDK download program we decided to write a simple terminal emulator program. A terminal emulator program, when run, makes the PC act like a dumb CRT terminal. Characters typed on the keyboard are sent out on an RS-232C line to a modem or some other RS-232C compatible equipment, and characters coming into the PC on an RS-232C line are displayed on the CRT.

Whenever you want to write a system program such as this, you should first see what DOS function calls are available to do all or part of the job for you. There are several reasons for this approach. First, DOS function calls are usually very easy to use because they do not

```
INIT COM1
REPEAT
     IF CHARACTER READY IN UART THEN
          READ CHARACTER
          SEND TO CRT
     IF KEYPRESSED ON IBM KEYBOARD THEN
          READ KEY
          SEND TO SERIAL PORT
UNTIL FOREVER
```

FIGURE 13-20 Algorithm for simple terminal emulator program.

require you to have extensive knowledge of the hardware details. Second, programs written at the DOS level are much more likely to run correctly on another "compatible" system. If you are going to be writing system programs for the IBM PC, you should get a copy of the *DOS Technical Reference Manual*.

If you need some operation that is not provided by a DOS function call, then the next step is to check the available BIOS procedures in the *IBM PC Technical Reference Manual*. Finally, if neither DOS or BIOS has the functions you need, you invoke the 5-minute rule, and then dig into the Technical Reference Manual to find the pieces you need to write the functions yourself. First, we will show you an example using DOS and BIOS calls, and then an example which manipulates the hardware directly to obtain greater performance.

Figure 13-20 shows the algorithm for our terminal emulator program. Let's see which parts of the algorithm can be done with DOS, and which must be done with BIOS.

The relevant DOS function calls are:

Function Call 2—The character in DL is sent to the CRT and the cursor is advanced one position.

Function Call 3—Waits for a character to be received in the serial port, then returns character in AL.

Function Call 4—The character in DL is output to the serial port.

Function Call 8—Waits for a key to be pressed on the keyboard, and then returns the ASCII code for the key in AL.

Function call 2 looks useful for sending a character to the CRT, and function call 4 looks useful for sending a character to the serial port. However, the keyboard call and the serial-read call will not work because they both sit in loops waiting for input. In other words, if you call function 8, execution will not return from that function until a key is pressed on the keyboard. If execution is in the function 8 loop, characters coming into the serial port will not be read. What is needed here are procedures which allow polling to go back and forth between the keyboard and the serial port receiver. Also needed is the least painful way to initialize the serial port. Let's see what BIOS has to offer.

Figure 13-21*a* shows the header for the IBM PC BIOS, INT 14H procedure. This procedure will do one of four functions, depending on the value passed to it in the AH register. If AH = 0 when the procedure is called, the byte in AL is used to initialize the serial port device as shown. If AH = 1, then the character in AL will be sent out from the serial port. Likewise, if AH = 2, then a character will be read in from the serial port and left in AL. Finally, if AH = 3 when the procedure is called, the status of the serial port will be returned in AH and AL. The first of these four options solves the initialization problem. The last (AH = 3) supplies most of the solution for the problem of determining when the UART has a character

```
RS232_IO
    THIS ROUTINE PROVIDES BYTE STREAM I/O TO THE COMMUNICATIONS
    PORT ACCORDING TO THE PARAMETERS:
    (AH) = 0  INITIALIZE THE COMMUNICATIONS PORT
              (AL) HAS PARAMETERS FOR INITIALIZATION

    7       6       5       4        3       2        1       0
    ----- BAUD RATE --    -PARITY--        STOPBIT   --WORD LENGTH--
      000–110             X0–NONE            0–1        10–7 BITS
      001–150             01–ODD             1–2        11–8 BITS
      010–300             11–EVEN
      011–600
      100–1200
      101–2400
      110–4800
      111–9600

    ON RETURN, CONDITIONS SET AS IN CALL TO COMMO STATUS (AH = 3)
    (AH) = 1  SEND THE CHARACTER IN (AL) OVER THE COMMO LINE
              (AL) REGISTER IS PRESERVED
              ON EXIT, BIT 7 OF AH IS SET IF THE ROUTINE WAS UNABLE
                  TO TRANSMIT THE BYTE OF DATA OVER THE LINE.
                  IF BIT 7 OF AH IS NOT SET, THE REMAINDER OF AH
                  IS SET AS IN A STATUS REQUEST, REFLECTING THE
                  CURRENT STATUS OF THE LINE.
    (AH) = 2  RECEIVE A CHARACTER IN (AL) FROM COMMO LINE BEFORE
                  RETURNING TO CALLER
              ON EXIT, AH HAS THE CURRENT LINE STATUS, AS SET BY
                  THE STATUS ROUTINE, EXCEPT THAT THE ONLY BITS
                  LEFT ON ARE THE ERROR BITS (7,4,3,2,1)
                  IF AH HAS BIT 7 ON (TIME OUT) THE REMAINING
                  BITS ARE NOT PREDICTABLE.
                  THUS, AH IS NON ZERO ONLY WHEN AN ERROR
                  OCCURRED.
    (AH) = 3  RETURN THE COMMO PORT STATUS IN (AX)
              AH CONTAINS THE LINE STATUS
              BIT 7 = TIME OUT
              BIT 6 = TRANS SHIFT REGISTER EMPTY
              BIT 5 = TRANS HOLDING REGISTER EMPTY
              BIT 4 = BREAK DETECT
              BIT 3 = FRAMING ERROR
              BIT 2 = PARITY ERROR
              BIT 1 = OVERRUN ERROR
              BIT 0 = DATA READY
              AL CONTAINS THE MODEM STATUS
              BIT 7 = RECEIVED LINE SIGNAL DETECT
              BIT 6 = RING INDICATOR
              BIT 5 = DATA SET READY
              BIT 4 = CLEAR TO SEND
              BIT 3 = DELTA RECEIVE LINE SIGNAL DETECT
              BIT 2 = TRAILING EDGE RING DETECTOR
              BIT 1 = DELTA DATA SET READY
              BIT 0 = DELTA CLEAR TO SEND

    (DX) = PARAMETER INDICATING WHICH RS232 CARD (0,1 ALLOWED)

DATA AREA RS232_BASE CONTAINS THE BASE ADDRESS OF THE 8250 ON THE
    CARD LOCATION 400H CONTAINS UP TO 4 RS232 ADDRESSES POSSIBLE
    DATA AREA LABEL RS232_TIM_OUT (BYTE) CONTAINS OUTER LOOP COUNT
    VALUE FOR TIMEOUT (DEFAULT = 1)
OUTPUT
    AX MODIFIED ACCORDING TO PARMS OF CALL
    ALL OTHERS UNCHANGED
```

(*a*)

```
KEYBOARD I/O
    THESE ROUTINES PROVIDE KEYBOARD SUPPORT
INPUT
    (AH) = 0  READ THE NEXT ASCII CHARACTER STRUCK FROM THE KEYBOARD
              RETURN THE RESULT IN (AL), SCAN CODE IN (AH)
    (AH) = 1  SET THE Z FLAG TO INDICATE IF AN ASCII CHARACTER IS
              AVAILABLE TO BE READ.
              (ZF) = 1—NO CODE AVAILABLE
              (ZF) = 0—CODE IS AVAILABLE
              IF ZF = 0, THE NEXT CHARACTER IN THE BUFFER TO BE READ
              IS IN AX, AND THE ENTRY REMAINS IN THE BUFFER
    (AH) = 2  RETURN THE CURRENT SHIFT STATUS IN AL REGISTER
              THE BIT SETTINGS FOR THIS CODE ARE INDICATED IN
              THE EQUATES FOR KB_FLAG
OUTPUT
    AS NOTED ABOVE, ONLY AX AND FLAGS CHANGED
    ALL REGISTERS PRESERVED
```

(*b*)

FIGURE 13-21 Header for IBM PC BIOS calls. *(a)* INT 14 serial communication procedure. *(b)* INT 16 keyboard access procedure.

```
;TERMINAL EMULATOR PROGRAM FOR SDK-86
; This program sends characters entered on the IBM PC to the COM1
; serial port at 600 baud, and displays characters received from the
; COM1 serial port on the CRT.
PAGE ,132

STACK_HERE       SEGMENT STACK
                 DW 100 DUP(0)
       STACK_TOP LABEL WORD
STACK_HERE ENDS

CODE_HERE        SEGMENT
       ASSUME CS:CODE_HERE, SS:STACK_HERE

START:  MOV  AX, STACK_HERE      ; Initialize stack segment
        MOV  SS, AX
        MOV  SP, OFFSET STACK_TOP; Initialize stack pointer
        MOV  AH, 00              ; Initialize COM1
        MOV  DX, 0000            ; Point at COM1
        MOV  AL, 01100111B       ; 600 Bd, no parity, 2 stop,8-bit
        INT  14H                 ; via BIOS INT 14H
        STI                      ; Enable interrupts
CHKAGN: MOV  DX, 0000            ; Point at COM1
        MOV  AH, 03              ; Check for character from SDK
        INT  14H
        TEST AH, 01H             ; See if char waiting in UART
        JNZ  RDCHAR              ; If char, read it
        JMP  KYBD                ; else, go look for keypress
RDCHAR: MOV  AH, 02              ; Read character
        INT  14H                 ; from UART to AL
        MOV  DL, AL              ; Character to DL for DOS call
        MOV  AH, 02H             ; DOS call number for CRT display
        INT  21H                 ; Do DOS call
KYBD:
        MOV  AH, 1               ; Check if key has been pressed
        INT  16H                 ;  using BIOS call
        JNZ  RDKY                ; If keypress, read key code
        JMP  CHKAGN              ; else look for more from SDK
RDKY:   MOV  AH, 0               ; Read key code
        INT  16H                 ; using BIOS call
        MOV  DX, 0000H           ; Point at COM1 serial port
        MOV  AH, 01
        INT  14H                 ; Send character to UART with BIOS
        JMP  CHKAGN              ; Go look for another char from UART
                                 ; or from keyboard

CODE_HERE ENDS
END START
```

FIGURE 13-22 Simple 300/600-Bd terminal emulator program.

ready to be read. Bit 0 of the status byte returned in AH will be set if the UART contains a character ready to be read. If a character is ready, it can be read in and sent to the CRT. If no character is present, the program can go check to see if a key on the keyboard has been pressed.

Figure 13-21*b* shows the header for the IBM PC BIOS, INT 16H procedure which accesses the keyboard. As you can see in the figure, this procedure supplies three different functions, depending on the value passed to it in AH. AH = 0 returns the code for a pressed key in AL. AH = 1 returns the zero flag = 0 if a key has been pressed and the code is available to be read. AH = 2

```
INITIALIZE EVERYTHING
  REPEAT
    IF KEY PRESSED THEN
       READ KEY
       IF KEY = Q THEN
            QUIT
       ELSE IF KEY = L THEN
              DOWNLOAD BINARY FILE FROM DISK TO SDK-86
            ELSE SEND CHARACTER FOR PRESSED KEY TO SDK-86
    IF UART BUFFER HAS CHARACTER THEN
       SEND CHARACTER TO CRT
  UNTIL QUIT
```

(a)

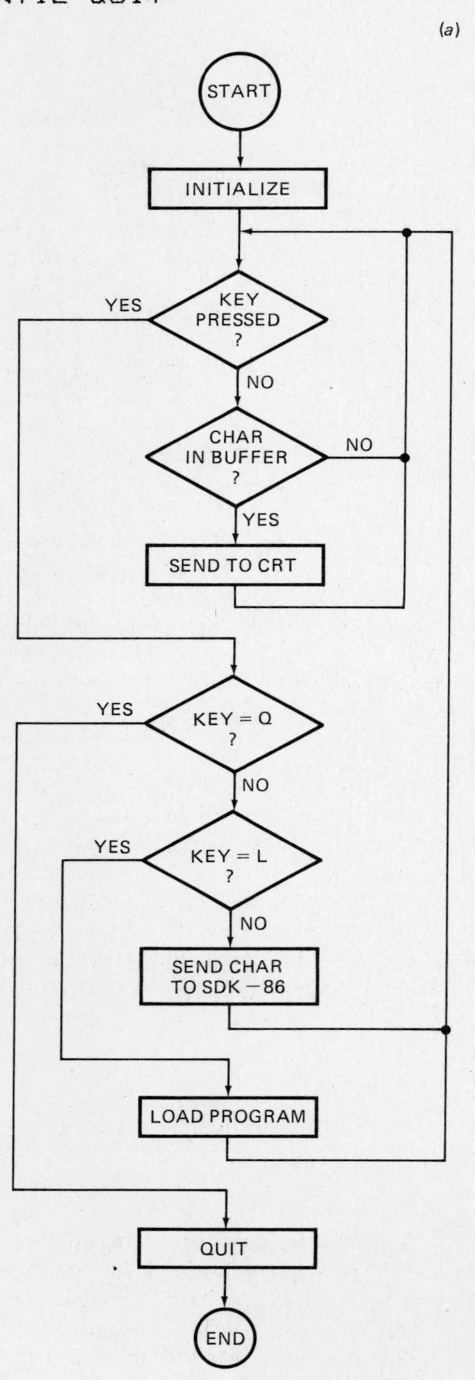

(b)

FIGURE 13-23 Algorithm for download program. *(a)* Pseudocode. *(d)* Flowchart.

causes the procedure to return the shift status in AL. Bit D6 of this byte will be set if the shift key is depressed. Calling the INT 16 procedure with AH = 1 solves the problem of polling the keyboard without sitting in a loop the way the DOS function call does. The zero flag can simply be checked upon return from the INT 16 procedure, and if no key is ready, execution can go check the UART again. If a key code is ready, it can be read in with a DOS call or another INT 16 call and sent to the UART.

Figure 13-22 shows a simple terminal emulator program which uses the procedures we have described. The program follows the algorithm almost line by line. Remember from previous chapter examples that BIOS procedures are called directly by an INT (number) instruction, and DOS calls are done by putting the function number in AH and doing an INT 21H instruction.

The program in Figure 13-22 works well at 300 Bd or 600 Bd. You can connect the serial port on an IBM-compatible computer to the serial port of an SDK-86 board as shown in Figure 13-10*b* and use this program to communicate with the board. However, if you try to use the program at 1200 or 2400 Bd, the first character of each line of characters received from the SDK-86 or other source will be lost. It took some work to figure out why this is the case, because with a processor as fast as the 8088 in the IBM PC, even 4800-Bd communication should be no problem. The problem is in the procedure which sends a character to the CRT. After a carriage return is sent to the CRT, the display on the screen is scrolled up one line. To avoid flicker, however, the screen is not scrolled until the next frame update. Since the frame rate for the monochrome display is 50 Hz, the return from the display procedure may take as long as 20 ms. One or more characters that come in during this time will be lost. The next section shows how we solved this problem in a high-speed download program.

IBM PC to SDK-86 Download Program

The main purpose of the program described in this section is to allow the binary codes for programs developed on an IBM PC compatible computer to be downloaded through an RS-232C link to an SDK-86 board. The program also functions as a dumb terminal so that downloaded programs can be run, memory contents displayed, and registers examined by typing the appropriate keys on the computer keyboard. Figure 13-23 shows the overall algorithm for the program. The main difference between this algorithm and the one for the dumb terminal in Figure 13-20 is the addition of the actions when the letter Q or the letter L is typed. However, we implemented the algorithm in a different way in order to solve the speed problem described in the previous section and to show you some very important programming techniques.

Figure 13-24 shows the complete program. The data segment declared at the start of the program contains buffers, flags, and the messages used in the program. We will refer to these as needed throughout the discussion. The mainline part of the program which follows this is only a little over a page long and consists mostly of various initializations. Four procedures, SERIAL_IN, CHK_N_DISPLAY, XMIT, and LOAD_IT, are used to do most of the work. After we give an overview, we will explain in detail how each of these five parts work.

OVERVIEW

The procedure SERIAL_IN reads in characters received from the SDK-86 by the IBM serial board on an interrupt basis and puts the characters in a buffer. The procedure CHK_N_DISPLAY, when called, checks the buffer to see if it contains any characters. If the buffer contains a character, the procedure sends it to the CRT. If the buffer is empty, the procedure simply returns. Now, take a look at the mainline section of the program starting at the label THERE, to see how these two procedures, together with XMIT and LOAD_IT implement the algorithm in Figure 13-23.

After interrupts are enabled, the BIOS INT 16 procedure is used to see if a key on the PC has been pressed. If a key has been pressed, then the BIOS INT 16 procedure is called again to read in the code for the pressed key. An IF—THEN—ELSE decision structure is then used to quit the program and return to DOS, go download a binary file, or simply send the character to the SDK-86. If the first call of the BIOS INT 16 procedure does not indicate that a key has been pressed, then the CHK_N_DISPLAY procedure is called. If the UART interrupt procedure, SERIAL_IN, has read in a character from the SDK and put it in the buffer, this procedure will send the character to the CRT and return to the mainline. If there is no character in the buffer, CHK_N_DISPLAY will simply return to the mainline. Once back in the mainline, execution loops back to again see if a key on the PC has been pressed. The interrupt and buffer approach used to read and hold the characters coming in from the SDK solves the timing problem we described for the program in Figure 13-22. Here's how.

The problem with operating the program in Figure 13-22 at over 600 Bd is that characters which come into the UART while the INT 10H procedure is scrolling the CRT display are missed. The program in Figure 13-24 reads characters from the UART on an interrupt basis. Even if the PC is in the middle of the INT 10H procedure or some other procedure when the UART has a character ready, the interrupt procedure will read the character and put it in the buffer. When execution loops back around to the CHK_N_DISPLAY procedure again, the character will then be read from the buffer and sent to the display. The XMIT procedure is used at several places in the program to send characters to the UART for transmission to the SDK.

The LOAD_IT procedure, which is called when the user presses the L key on the PC, prompts the user to enter the name of a binary file, converts the binary file to a form the SDK can digest, and sends the result to the SDK through the UART. Now let's look at the details of the initialization and the four procedures.

INITIALIZATION

The UART used on the IBM asynchronous communications adapter board is an INS8250. If the board is configured as system serial port COM1, the interrupt output from this device is connected to the IR4 input of an 8259A priority interrupt controller on the main PC board of the IBM computer. The major part of the initialization here involves getting the 8250 initialized and setting up the interrupt mechanism. Remember from previous discussions that when an 8259A receives an interrupt on an IR input that is unmasked, it sends a specified interrupt type to the processor. The 8259A is initialized by the BIOS so that type 8 will be sent for an IR0 input. Therefore, for an IR4 signal from the UART, the 8259A will send type 0CH to the processor. The processor multiplies the type number by 4 and goes to that address to get the starting address of the service procedure for that interrupt. The recommended way of putting the IP and CS values for the procedure in these absolute memory locations is with the DOS function call 25H. To use this call, the interrupt type number is put in AL, the CS value in the DS register, and the IP value in the DX register as shown in Figure 13-24.

The 8259A itself is mostly initialized by the BIOS when the system is turned on. However, since the UART is connected to IR4 of the 8259A, that input has to be unmasked. To do this the current contents of the 8259A interrupt mask register are read in from address 21H. The bit corresponding to IR4 is then ANDed with a 0 to unmask the interrupt, and the result sent back to the interrupt mask register. Using this approach saves the system environment. It is important to do this rather than just sending out a control word directly, so that you don't disable other system functions. In this system, for example, the system clock tick is connected to IR0 and the keyboard is connected to IR1, so these would be disabled if you accidentally put 1's in these bits of the control word.

Initializing the 8250 UART is next. Figure 13-25 shows the internal addresses and the bit formats for the control words we need here. The first part of the initialization is the baud rate, parity, and stop bits. Since this step requires several words to be sent, we simply used the BIOS INT 14H procedure to do it. (NOTE: We initialize the 8250 here for 4800 Bd, so the baud-rate jumper on the SDK-86 must be set for this baud rate.)

The next task we need to do here is enable the desired interrupt circuitry in the 8250. In order to do this, the DLAB bit of the line control word must first be made a 0. Note that this is done by reading in the line control

```
;TERMINAL EMULATOR AND DOWNLOAD PROGRAM FOR SDK-86
;This program allows an IBM PC compatible computer to operate as a 4800-Bd
; dumb terminal for use with an SDK-86 board. The program also allows
; binary files to be downloaded from a disk in the PC to RAM in the SDK-86
; through the COM1 serial port on the PC.
PAGE ,132

DATA_HERE  SEGMENT
SIGN_ON         DB 'SDKDMP PROGRAM',0DH,0AH
                DB '  BY DOUGLAS V. HALL',0DH,0AH
                DB 'COPYRIGHT - McGraw-Hill Book Co.,1986',0DH,0AH
                DB 0DH,0AH
                DB 'Press RESET key on SDK-86 to get Monitor prompt.'
                DB 0DH,0AH,0DH,0AH,24H
QUEUE           DB 1000 DUP(0)  ; Circular buffer
HEAD_POINTER    DW 0            ; Next character to read out of queue
TAIL_POINTER    DW 0            ; Next location to put char in queue
CHAR_COUNTER    DB 0            ; Used to count number of char sent to CRT

TIME_OUT_MESS   DB ' Transmit Timeout - Check Hardware ',     0DH, 0AH
PROMPT          DB ' Please type in binary filename',         0DH, 0AH
                DB ' Filename format is d:path filename.bin', 0DH, 0AH
                DB  24H         ; String terminator

FILE_NAME       DB  40 DUP(0)   ; Space for user entered filename

ERR_MESS_POINTERS  DW   0       ; Dummy, no ERR_MESS0
                DW   OFFSET ERR_MESS1
                DW   OFFSET ERR_MESS2
                DW   OFFSET ERR_MESS3

ERR_MESS1       DB 'INVALID FUNCTION NUMBER', 0DH, 0AH, 24H
ERR_MESS2       DB 'FILE NOT FOUND', 0DH, 0AH, 24H
ERR_MESS3       DB 'PATH NOT FOUND', 0DH, 0AH, 24H

FILE_BUF        DB 2048 DUP(0)  ; Buffer for bin file read from disk

HEADER          DB 53H,20H,30H,30H,30H,30H,3AH,30H
                DB 31H,30H,30H,2CH              ; SDK-86 Substitute Command

DATA_HERE  ENDS

STACK_HERE SEGMENT STACK
                DW 400H DUP(0)
       STACK_TOP  LABEL WORD
STACK_HERE ENDS

CODE_HERE SEGMENT
       ASSUME CS:CODE_HERE, DS:DATA_HERE, SS:STACK_HERE

START: MOV  AX, STACK_HERE     ; Initialize stack segment
       MOV  SS, AX
       MOV  SP, OFFSET STACK_TOP; Initialize stack pointer
       MOV  AL, 0CH            ; Initialize interrupt vector for UART
       MOV  BX, SEG SERIAL_IN  ; using DOS function call 25H
```

FIGURE 13-24 Program to download object code programs from IBM PC to SDK-86 and allow PC to function as a "dumb" terminal for the SDK-86.

```
        MOV  DS, BX
        MOV  DX, OFFSET SERIAL_IN
        MOV  AH, 25H
        INT  21H
        MOV  AX, DATA_HERE      ; Initialize DS register
        MOV  DS, AX
        MOV  HEAD_POINTER, 0    ; Initialize circular buffer pointers
        MOV  TAIL_POINTER, 0
;unmask 8259A IR4
        IN  AL, 21H             ; Read 8259A IMR
        AND  AL, 0ECH           ; Unmask IR4
        OUT  21H, AL
;initialize 8250 UART baud rate,etc.
        MOV  AH, 00             ; Initialize COM1
        MOV  DX, 0000           ; Point at COM1
        MOV  AL, 11000111B      ; 4800 Bd,No parity,2 stop,8-bit
        INT  14H                ;  via BIOS INT 14H
;enable 8250 RxRDY interrupt
        MOV  DX, 03FBH          ; Point at 8250 line control port
        IN   AL, DX             ; Read in line control word
        AND  AL, 7FH            ; Set DLAB = 0
        OUT  DX, AL             ; Send line control word back out
        MOV  AL, 01H            ; Value to enable RxRDY interrupt
        MOV  DX, 03F9H          ; Point at interrupt enable register
        OUT  DX, AL             ; Enable RxRDY interrupt
        MOV  AL, 0BH            ; Assert 8250 OUT2, RTS, DTR byte
        MOV  DX, 03FCH          ; Point at modem control reg in 8250
        OUT  DX, AL             ; Send to 8250
        STI                     ; Enable 8086 interrupts
;main program starts here
        MOV  DX, OFFSET SIGN_ON ; Send sign on message to CRT
        MOV  AH, 09H            ;  with DOS call
        MOV  BH, 0
        INT 21H
;look for response from SDK
THERE:  MOV  AH, 1              ; Check if key has been pressed
        INT  16H
        JNZ  RDKY               ; If keypress, go read key code
        CALL CHK_N_DISPLAY      ; See if char in circular buffer from
                                ; UART and send it to CRT if there
        JMP  THERE              ; Go look for keypress or char from UART
RDKY:   MOV  AH, 0              ; Read key code
        INT  16H
        CMP  AL, 51H            ; See if quit commnad
        JNE  NXCHK              ; No,  go check if load command
        JMP  QUIT               ; Yes, go exit to DOS
NXCHK:  CMP  AL, 4CH            ; Check if load command
        JNE  SENDIT             ; No, go send char to SDK
        CALL LOAD_IT            ; Yes, go load file
        JMP  THERE              ; Go wait for next command
SENDIT: CALL XMIT               ; Char not Q or L, send char to SDK-86
        JMP  THERE              ; Go wait for next command
QUIT:   IN   AL, 21H
        OR   AL, 10H            ; Mask UART interrupt
        OUT  21H, AL            ;  to prevent it from disrupting DOS
```

Figure 13-24 (*continued*)

```
        MOV  AL, 0              ; Exit to DOS using DOS function call 4CH
        MOV  AH, 4CH
        INT  21H
        NOP

SERIAL_IN PROC FAR
        STI                     ; Interrupts back on for keyboard, etc
        PUSH AX
        PUSH BX
        PUSH DX
        PUSH DI
        PUSH DS                 ; Save DS of interrupted program
        MOV  AX, DATA_HERE      ; Install DS needed here
        MOV  DS, AX
        MOV  DX, 03F8H          ; Receiver buffer address for 8250
        IN   AL, DX             ; Read character
        MOV  DI, TAIL_POINTER   ; Get current tail pointer value
        INC  DI                 ; Point to next storage location
        CMP  DI, 1000           ; Compare with queue length to see if time
                                ;  to wrap around
        JNE  FULCHK             ; No, go check if queue full
        MOV  DI, 00             ; Yes, set DI for wraparound to start
FULCHK: CMP  DI, HEAD_POINTER   ; Check for full queue
        JE   NO_MORE            ; Full, return without writing char
        MOV  BX, TAIL_POINTER   ; Not full, point at location to put char
        MOV  QUEUE[BX], AL      ; Character to circular buffer
        MOV  TAIL_POINTER, DI   ; Tail pointer to next location
NO_MORE:
        MOV  AL, 20H            ; Non-specific End Of Interrupt command
        OUT  20H, AL            ;  to 8259A
        POP  DS
        POP  DI
        POP  DX
        POP  BX
        POP  AX
        IRET
SERIAL_IN  ENDP

CHK_N_DISPLAY PROC NEAR
        PUSH BX
        IN   AL, 21H
        OR   AL, 10H            ; Disable 8259A IR4 during critical region
        OUT  21H, AL            ;  by masking bit 4 of int mask register
        MOV  DI, HEAD_POINTER
        CMP  DI, TAIL_POINTER   ; Is queue empty ?
        JE   NOCHAR             ; Yes, just return
        MOV  AL, QUEUE[DI]      ; No, get char from queue to AL
        INC  DI                 ; Point DI at next byte in queue
        CMP  DI, 1000           ; See if time to wrap pointer around
        JNE  OK                 ; No, go on
        MOV  DI, 00             ; Yes, wrap pointer around
OK:     MOV  HEAD_POINTER, DI   ; Store new pointer value
        PUSH AX                 ; Save character in AL on stack
        IN   AL, 21H
        AND  AL, 0ECH           ; Enable IR4 interrupt so new char in 8250
```

Figure 13-24 (*continued*)

```
        OUT  21H, AL            ;   can interrupt INT 10H
        POP  AX                 ; Get character back from stack
        MOV  AH, 14             ; Use BIOS INT 10H procedure to send to CRT
        MOV  BH, 0
        INT  10H                ; Send char to CRT
        DEC  CHAR_COUNTER       ; Decrement count of char to be sent to CRT
NOCHAR: IN   AL, 21H
        AND  AL, 0ECH           ; End of critical region. Enable IR4 by
                                ;  unmasking bit 4 in IMR of 8259A so new
        OUT  21H, AL            ;  char in UART can interrupt
        POP  BX
        RET
CHK_N_DISPLAY ENDP

;Send character in AL to COM1 serial port after checking if
; handshake signals asserted
; INPUTS:  character in AL
; OUTPUTS: character in AL, CY flag set if xmitter not ready

XMIT PROC NEAR
        PUSH BX
        PUSH CX
        PUSH DX
        PUSH AX                 ; Save char
        MOV  CX,0
RECHK:  MOV  DX, 03FEH          ; Check CTS and DSR asserted
        IN   AL, DX
        AND  AL, 30H
        CMP  AL, 30H
        JNE  NOT_READY
        MOV  DX, 03FDH          ; Check if transmitter buffer ready
        IN   AL, DX
        AND  AL, 20H
        JZ   NOT_READY
        POP  AX                 ; Get character back
        MOV  DX, 03F8H          ; Send to UART
        OUT  DX, AL
        CLC                     ; Clear carry to indicate char sent
        JMP  DONE
NOT_READY:
        LOOP RECHK              ; Check for status ready CX times
        MOV  DX, OFFSET TIME_OUT_MESS   ; If still not ready
        MOV  AH, 09H                    ;  send error message
        MOV  BH, 0
        INT  21H
        STC                     ; Set carry to indicate xmitter not ready
        POP  AX                 ; Restore registers
DONE:   POP  DX
        POP  CX
        POP  BX
        RET
XMIT    ENDP

;LOAD_IT - Down-load procedure
```

Figure 13-24 (*continued*)

```
; Prompts user to enter name of binary file, then reads file from disk
;  to a buffer in memory. The file is converted to the ASCII character form
;  required by the SDK-86, and sent to an SDK-86 board via the COM1 serial
;  port. Replies from the SDK-86 are displayed on the CRT as received.

LOAD_IT PROC NEAR
        PUSH BX
        MOV  DX, OFFSET PROMPT   ; Send message to CRT telling user
        MOV  AH, 09H             ;  to enter filename with DOS function
        MOV  BH, 0               ;  call 09H
        INT  21H                 ;
        MOV  DX, OFFSET FILE_NAME; Point at filename buffer
        MOV  FILE_NAME, 40       ; Make first byte of buffer = max chars
        MOV  AH, 0AH             ; DOS function call number to
        INT  21H                 ;  read in filename from keyboard
        MOV  BL, FILE_NAME+1     ; Get length of file name from buffer
        ADD  BL, 02              ; Add 2 to reach carriage return at end
        MOV  BH, 00              ; BX now has offset of CR at end of file name
        MOV  FILE_NAME[BX], 00   ; Replace 0DH at end of file name with 00H
        MOV  DX, OFFSET FILE_NAME; Point at start of file name buffer
        ADD  DX, 02H             ; Move pointer over string length bytes
        MOV  AL, 0               ; Open file for read
        MOV  AH, 3DH             ;  and get file handle with DOS 3DH call
        INT  21H
; Check for file error
        JNC  FILEOK              ; No carry, file opened properly
        ROL  AX, 1               ; Multiply error code in AX by 2
        MOV  BX, AX                     ; Copy to BX for use as pointer
        MOV  DX, ERR_MESS_POINTERS[BX]  ; Get pointer to desired error
        MOV  BH, 0                      ; message from table to DX
        MOV  AH, 09H             ; Use DOS function call 09 to send
        INT  21H                 ;  error message to CRT
        MOV  DL, 0DH             ; Send carriage return to CRT
        MOV  AH, 02H             ;  with DOS function call 02H
        INT  21H
        JMP  EXIT1               ; Return to look for next command from user
; Read binary file from disk to buffer in memory
FILEOK: MOV  BX, AX              ; File handle to BX
        PUSH BX                  ; Save file handle for file close
        MOV  CX, 2048            ; Set maximum number of char to read
        MOV  DX, OFFSET FILE_BUF ; Point at buffer to store char read in
        MOV  AH, 3FH             ; Read disk file
        INT  21H
        POP  BX                  ; Get back file handle for close
        PUSH AX                  ; Save length of file returned by 3FH
        MOV  AH, 3EH             ; Close disk file with DOS 3EH call
        INT  21H
;SEND SUBSTITUTE COMMAND TO SDK86
        MOV  BX, OFFSET HEADER   ; Point at string buffer
        MOV  CX, 000CH           ; Number of characters to send to SDK
NEXT1:  MOV  AL, [BX]            ; Get a character to be sent
TRY2:   CALL XMIT                ; Character to COM1
        JC   EXIT1
        INC  BX                  ; Pointer to next location in buffer
        LOOP NEXT1               ; Loop until all sent
        MOV  CHAR_COUNTER, 11H   ; Number of characters to send to CRT
```

Figure 13-24 (*continued*)

```
MORE1:  CALL CHK_N_DISPLAY       ; Characters to CRT
        DEC  CHAR_COUNTER        ; See if all sent
        JNZ  MORE1
;SEND FIRST CODE BYTE TO SDK86
        POP  AX                  ; Get back length of file
        MOV  CX, AX              ; Use CX as counter
        MOV  BX, OFFSET FILE_BUF ; Point at start of object code file
NXTCHR: MOV  DL, [BX]            ; Get a character from file buffer
        AND  DL, 0F0H            ; Mask lower nibble
        ROR  DL, 1               ; Move to lower nibble position
        ROR  DL, 1
        ROR  DL, 1
        ROR  DL, 1
        CMP  DL, 0AH             ; Convert to ASCII
        JAE  ADD37
        ADD  DL, 30H
        JMP  SEND1
ADD37:  ADD  DL, 37H
SEND1:  MOV  AL, DL              ; Position character for send
        CALL XMIT                ; Send upper nibble of byte to SDK
        JC   EXIT1
        MOV  DL, [BX]            ; Get char again and make ASCII for
        AND  DL, 0FH             ;  low nibble
        CMP  DL, 0AH
        JAE  ADDHI
        ADD  DL, 30H
        JMP  SEND2
ADDHI:  ADD  DL, 37H
SEND2:  MOV  AL, DL              ; Position for send
        CALL XMIT                ; Send ASCII for low nibble to SDK
        JC   EXIT1
        DEC  CX                  ; Check if all bytes sent
        JZ   EXIT                ; Yes, done, send carriage return
        MOV  AL, 2CH             ; Else load comma
        CALL XMIT                ; Send to SDK
        JC   EXIT1
        MOV  CHAR_COUNTER, 0EH   ; Number of characters to send to CRT
MORE2:  CALL CHK_N_DISPLAY       ; SDK echo message to CRT
        CMP  CHAR_COUNTER, 0     ; See if all of message sent to CRT
        JNE  MORE2
        INC  BX                  ; Point to next byte in binary file
        JMP  NXTCHR              ; Send next code byte
EXIT:   MOV  AL, 0DH             ; Load carriage return
        CALL XMIT                ; Send to SDK
EXIT1:  POP BX
        RET                      ; Go look for SDK answer and next command
LOAD_IT  ENDP

CODE_HERE ENDS
END START
```

Figure 13-24 (*continued*)

word, resetting the desired bit, and sending the word out again. This preserves the previous state of the rest of the bits in the line control register. As shown in Figure 13-25*b*, with DLAB = 0, a control word which enables the enable-receive line status interrupt can be sent to the interrupt enable register at address 03F9H. As shown in Figure 13-25*b*, the 8250 has four different conditions which can be enabled to assert the interrupt output when true. In cases where multiple interrupts are used, the interrupt identification register can be

I/O DECODE (IN HEX)		REGISTER SELECTED	DLAB STATE
PRIMARY ADAPTER	ALTERNATE ADAPTER		
3F8	2F8	TX BUFFER	DLAB=0 (WRITE)
3F8	2F8	RX BUFFER	DLAB=0 (READ)
3F8	2F8	DIVISOR LATCH LSB	DLAB=1
3F9	2F9	DIVISOR LATCH MSB	DLAB=1
3F9	2F9	INTERRUPT ENABLE REGISTER	DLAB=X
3FA	2FA	INTERRUPT IDENTIFICATION REGISTERS	DLAB=X
3FB	2FB	LINE CONTROL REGISTER	DLAB=X
3FC	2FC	MODEM CONTROL REGISTER	DLAB=X
3FD	2FD	LINE STATUS REGISTER	DLAB=X
3FE	2FE	MODEM STATUS REGISTER	DLAB=X

(*a*)

INTERRUPT ENABLE REGISTER (IER)

HEX ADDRESS 3F9 DLAB = 0

BIT 7 6 5 4 3 2 1 0

- 0: 1 = ENABLE DATA AVAILABLE INTERRUPT
- 1: 1 = ENABLE TX HOLDING REGISTER EMPTY INTERRUPT
- 2: 1 = ENABLE RECEIVE LINE STATUS INTERRUPT
- 3: 1 = ENABLE MODEM STATUS INTERRUPT
- 4: = 0
- 5: = 0
- 6: = 0
- 7: = 0

(*b*)

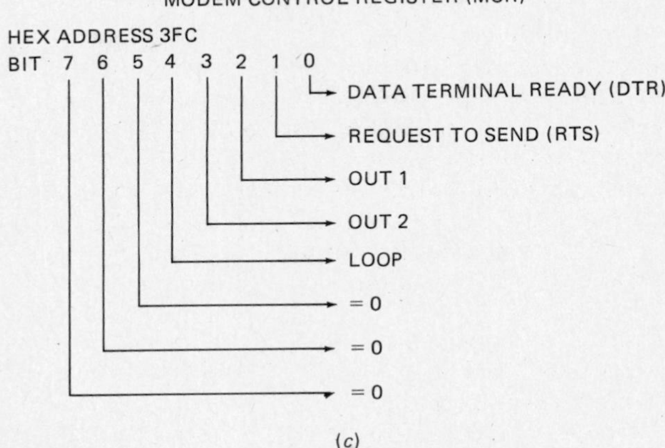

(*c*)

LINE STATUS REGISTER (LSR)

HEX ADDRESS 3FD

BIT 7 6 5 4 3 2 1 0

- 0: DATA READY (DR)
- 1: OVERRUN (OR)
- 2: PARITY ERROR (PE)
- 3: FRAMING ERROR (FE)
- 4: BREAK INTERRUPT (BI)
- 5: TRANSMITTER HOLDING REGISTER EMPTY (THRE)
- 6: TX SHIFT REGISTER EMPTY (TSRE)
- 7: = 0

(*d*)

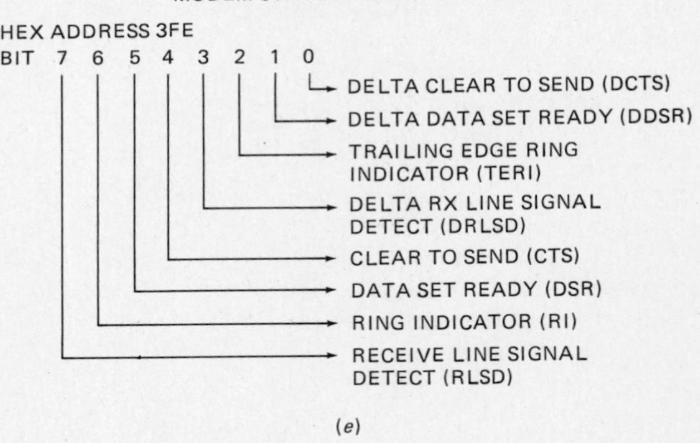

(*e*)

FIGURE 13-25 8250 internal addresses, registers, and control words. *(a)* System addresses. *(b)* Interrupt enable register. *(c)* Modem control register. *(d)* Line status register. *(e)* Modem status register.

read to determine the source of an interrupt. For this application we are only using the enable receive line status interrupt, so a 1 is put in that bit. The final step in the 8250 initialization is to assert the $\overline{RTS}$, $\overline{DTR}$, and $\overline{OUT2}$ output signals. As shown by the circuit connections in Figure 13-10*a*, asserting $\overline{RTS}$ is necessary to assert the $\overline{CTS}$ input so the UART can transmit. Likewise, asserting $\overline{DTR}$ is necessary to assert the $\overline{DSR}$ and $\overline{CD}$ inputs of the UART. The $\overline{OUT2}$ signal from the 8250 must be asserted in order to enable a three-state buffer which is in series with the interrupt signal from the 8250 to the 8259A.

When you are working out an initialization sequence such as this, read the data sheet carefully, and check out the actual hardware circuitry for the system you are working on. We missed the $\overline{OUT2}$ connection the first time through, but a second look at the schematic for the communications board showed that it was necessary to assert this signal. Now let's see how the procedure which reads characters from the UART works.

THE SERIAL_IN PROCEDURE

The purpose of this interrupt procedure is to read characters in from the UART and put them in a buffer. Note that since this is an interrupt procedure which can occur at any time, it is important to save the DS register of the interrupted program and load the DS register with DATA_HERE, the value needed for this procedure.

The buffer used here is a special type of queue called a *circular buffer*. Figure 13-26 attempts to show how this works. One pointer, called the TAIL_POINTER, is used to keep track of where the next byte is to be written to the buffer. Another pointer called the HEAD_POINTER is used to keep track of where the next character to be read from the buffer is located. The buffer is circular because, when the tail pointer reaches the highest location in the memory space set aside for the buffer, it is "wrapped around" to the beginning of the buffer again. The head pointer follows the tail pointer around the circle as characters are read from the buffer. Two checks are made on the tail pointer before a character is written to the buffer.

First the tail pointer is brought into a register and incremented. This incremented value is then compared with the maximum number of bytes the buffer can hold. If the values are equal, the pointer is at the highest address in the buffer, so the register is reset to zero. After the current character is put in the buffer, this value will be loaded into TAIL_POINTER to wrap around to the lowest address in the buffer again.

Second, a check is made to see if the incremented value of the tail pointer is equal to the head pointer. If the two are equal, it means that the current byte can be written, but that the next byte would be written over the byte at the head of the queue. In this case we simply return to the interrupted program without writing the current character into the buffer. Actually this wastes a byte of buffer space, but it is necessary to do this so that the pointers have different values for this buffer-full condition than they do for the buffer-empty condition.

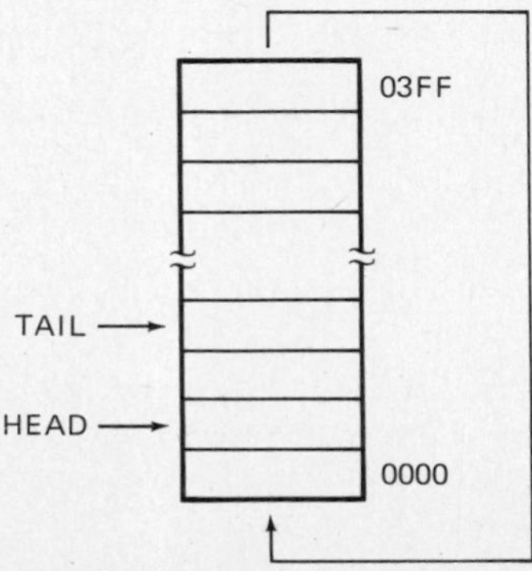

FIGURE 13-26 Diagram showing how circular buffer pointers wrap around at the top of allocated buffer space.

The buffer-empty condition is indicated when the head pointer is equal to the tail pointer. If the buffer is not full, the character read in from the UART is written to the buffer, and the pointer to the next available location in the buffer is transferred from the register to the memory location called TAIL_POINTER. Finally, before returning, an end-of-interrupt command must be sent to the 8259A to reset bit 4 of the interrupt mask register.

To summarize the operation of a circular buffer, then, bytes are put in at the tail pointer location and read out from the head pointer location. The buffer is considered full when the tail pointer reaches one less than the head pointer. An empty buffer is indicated by head pointer equal to tail pointer.

THE CHK_N_DISPLAY PROCEDURE

The main purpose of this procedure is to read a character from the circular buffer and send it to the CRT with the BIOS INT 10H procedure. In order to make sure the procedure operates correctly under all conditions, however, we mask the IR4 interrupt in the 8259A right at the start so that an interrupt from the UART cannot call the SERIAL_IN procedure while CHK_N_DISPLAY is using the head and tail pointers. This is necessary to prevent the SERIAL_IN procedure from altering the values of the pointers in the middle of CHK_N_DISPLAY's use of them and causing the CHK_N_DISPLAY procedure to make the wrong decisions about whether the buffer is empty, for example. The group of instructions which you need to protect from interruption is called a *critical region*. It is important to keep critical regions as short as possible so that interrupts need not be masked for unnecessarily long times. Note that we masked the IR4 interrupt input of the 8259A rather than disable the processor interrupt. This was done so that the keyboard and the timer interrupts, which have nothing to do with the critical region in this procedure, can keep running.

Once the critical region is safe, a check is made to see if there are any characters in the buffer. If not, the 8259A IR4 input is unmasked, and execution returned to the calling program. If a character is available in the buffer, the character is read out and the head pointer updated to point to the next available character. If the pointer is at the top of the space allotted for the buffer, the pointer will be wrapped around to the start of the buffer again. As soon as the character is read out from the buffer and the pointers updated, an interrupt from the UART cannot do any damage, so we unmask IR4. The BIOS INT 10H procedure is then used to send the character to the CRT. If a UART interrupt occurs during the INT 10H procedure, the SERIAL_IN procedure will read the character from the UART and return execution to the INT 10H procedure. This short interruption produces no noticeable effect on the operation of the INT 10H procedure, and it makes sure no characters from the UART are missed. After the INT 10H procedure finishes, a character-sent counter is decremented and execution is returned to the calling program. This counter counts the number of characters actually sent to the CRT rather than just the number of times the CHK_N_DISPLAY procedure is called. This allows the procedure to be called over and over again until a given number of characters are sent to the CRT.

THE XMIT PROCEDURE

After first checking to see if the handshake signals and the transmitter buffer are ready, this procedure sends a character to the 8250 UART. The status of the $\overline{DSR}$ input and the $\overline{CTS}$ input are available as bits 5 and 4 respectively, of the modem status word of the 8250. For an IBM PC with the serial board configured as COM1, the address of this register will be 03FEH. The transmitter-buffer-ready status bit of the 8250 is available as bit 5 of the line status register at address 03FDH. This bit will be high when a character can be sent to the internal buffer for transmission. Rather than having the program hang in a loop checking the status signals forever, if any one of them is not ready, we send an error message and exit after a specified number of tries. The CX register is loaded with the desired number of tries, and counted down after each loop through the status check. After the error message is sent to the CRT with the DOS 09H function call, the carry flag is set to indicate that a character could not be sent. Execution is then returned to the section of the program from which XMIT was called. After each call of XMIT in the program, a JC instruction is used to send execution back to look for the next user command if the transmitter was not ready for some reason.

THE LOAD_IT PROCEDURE

In response to a filename entered by the user, this procedure reads a binary file from disk to a buffer in memory, converts each byte to the form needed for sending to the SDK, and sends the result to the SDK-86. SDK responses are displayed on the CRT.

At the start of the procedure, DOS function call 09H is used to send a prompt message to the user on the CRT. DOS function call 0AH is then used to read in the filename entered by the user on the computer keyboard. To use this call the DX register must point to the start of a buffer in memory where the characters are to be put. The first byte of the buffer must contain the maximum number of characters that you want to be read in. The function call terminates when the user enters a carriage return. The second byte of the buffer then holds the number of characters actually read in, not including the carriage return.

The next task in the procedure is to open the named binary file for reading with the DOS 3DH function call. Before this can be done, however, the carriage return at the end of the filename in the buffer must be changed to 00H. To do this we get the number of characters read from the second byte in the buffer, and use it to construct a pointer to the carriage return in the buffer. That location is then loaded with 0's.

If an error is detected while trying to open the file, the DOS 3DH function call will return the carry flag set, and an error number in AX. We multiply the error number by 2 and use it as a pointer to a table which contains the offsets of the error messages for some of the errors. As a refresher on the use of address tables, work your way through how the pointer gets to DX for the 09H function call which is used to display the error message. If the file was opened correctly, then the binary file is read in from a disk with the DOS function call 3FH, and the file is closed with the DOS function call 3EH as we described in Chapter 12.

The next section of the procedure sends the substitute command to the SDK-86 to get it ready to receive the binary file. The SERIAL_IN interrupt procedure will read the echo of the command sent back from the SDK and put it in the circular buffer. To display this echo on the CRT, we load CX with the number of characters in the echo message, and enter a loop which calls the CHK_N_DISPLAY procedure over and over until all of the SDK response is sent to the CRT. Now comes the bit-fiddling section of the procedure.

The SDK-86 requires that each nibble of a program code byte be sent in as the corresponding ASCII character. The code byte 3AH for example must be sent as 33H (ASCII 3), followed by 41H (ASCII A). You can work your way through this section to see how the conversion is done if you need to use it in some other program. After the ASCII characters for each code byte are sent, the ASCII code for a comma is sent as required by the SDK-86. The SERIAL_IN procedure reads in the SDK reply and puts it in the circular buffer. A loop containing a call to the CHK_N_DISPLAY procedure is used to send the SDK reply to the CRT. After the ASCII codes for the final byte are sent to the SDK, a carriage return is sent to the SDK to terminate the substitute command. Execution then returns to the mainline program and then to the section of the program which waits for the user to enter another command.

CONCLUSION

This program was written to do a specific job and to demonstrate some important programming concepts. Space limitation prevented us from making the program as "friendly" as we would have liked it to be. Instructions could be added, for example, to allow the desired baud rate to be entered by the user from the keyboard. Hopefully you can use some of the techniques shown here in your own programs. In the next section we show you how to call assembly language procedures from higher level language programs.

Calling Assembly Language Procedures from High Level Language Programs

Programs which need to do a lot of bit-fiddling and hardware manipulation are usually written in assembly language because this level gives direct hardware control. However, business, scientific, and other programs which involve mostly manipulating large amounts of data are usually written in a higher level language such as BASIC, Pascal, or C. For programs such as communications programs, which involve both types of operation, the main program is usually written in a high level language, and assembly language procedures are called to do the bit fiddling as needed. The intent of this section is to give you an overview of how to write and call these procedures. However, we first have to briefly discuss the two ways that high level language programs are converted into machine code and executed, interpreting and compiling.

Figure 13-27*a* shows in flowchart form how an interpreter program executes a high level language program. The interpreter reads a high level language statement of the source program, translates that statement to machine code and, if it doesn't need information from another instruction, executes the code for that statement immediately. It then reads the next high level language source statement, translates it, and executes it. BASIC programs are often executed in this way.

The advantage of using an interpreter is that if an error is found, you can just correct the source program and immediately rerun it. The major disadvantage of the interpreter approach is that an interpreted program runs 5 to 25 times slower than the same program will run after being compiled. The reason is that with an interpreter each statement must be translated to machine code every time the program is run. In other words, the translation time is part of the execution time.

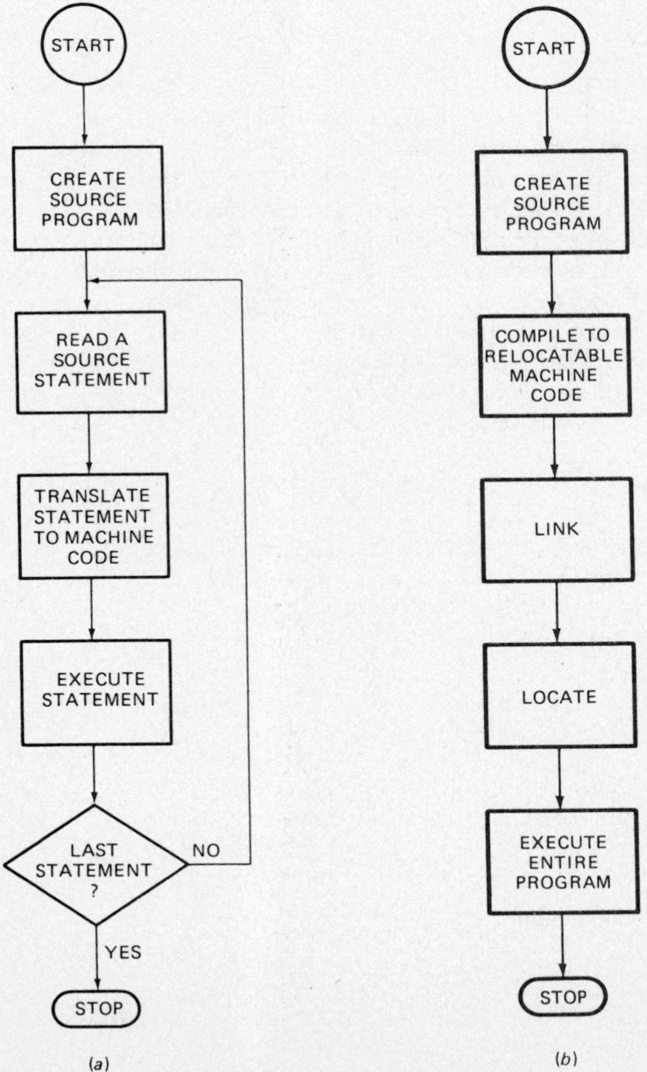

FIGURE 13-27 Comparison of compiler and interpreter operation. *(a)* Interpreter. *(b)* Compiler.

Figure 13-27*b* shows how a compiler fits into the translation-execution process. A compiler program reads through the entire high-level language source program, and in two or more passes through it, translates it all to a relocatable machine code version. Before the program can be run, however, this relocatable object code version must be linked with any other required object modules from the system library, a user library, or assembly language procedures. The output file from the linker is then located, which means that it is given absolute addresses so that it can be loaded into memory. Finally the located program is loaded into memory. Some systems, incidentally, combine two or more of the link, locate, and load functions in a single program. Once the located program is loaded into memory, the entire program can be run without any further translation. Therefore, it will run much faster than it would if executed by an interpreter. The major disadvantage of the compiler approach is that when an error is found, it usually must be corrected in the source program and the entire compile-load sequence repeated.

Calling assembly language procedures from an interpreted high level language is quite messy, especially in the case of multiple procedures, because of the way the interpreter uses memory. If you are working with IBM PC Microsoft BASIC, consult Appendix C of the *IBM BASIC Reference Manual* to see how to do it for that language. We recommend the compiler approach for most hybrid programs, because of the obvious execution speed advantage and the ease with which assembly language modules can be called.

Calling assembly language procedures in compiled programs is much simpler, because the object modules produced by the assembler can be simply linked with object modules produced by the compiler and object modules from libraries. The major task when using assembler-created modules with compiler-created modules is to make sure the modules can find and communicate with each other. Since common Pascal, C, and BASIC compilers use similar conventions to do this, we will use the Microsoft BASIC compiler conventions as an example here.

The BASIC call statement has the format CALL numvar (var1, var2, var3, . . ., varN). For compiled BASIC programs numvar is the name of the assembly language procedure being called. When the BASIC program and the assembly language module are linked, the linker will establish the required connection between the call and the named procedure. Var1, var2, var3, etc. represent the names of variables which are being passed to or from the assembly language procedure. Numeric variables or string variables can be passed to or from an assembly language procedure.

Figure 13-28*a* shows a simple BASIC program which inputs a line of characters from the keyboard, calls an assembly language procedure to make sure all letters in the string are upper case, and then outputs the resultant string to the CRT. The program terminates when

```
10 REM This program inputs a string of characters from the keyboard,
11 REM   converts any lowercase letters to upper case, and outputs
12 REM   the resulting string to the CRT
13 REM  Procedures called: UCASE
14
100 LINE INPUT Q$
110 CALL UCASE(Q$)
120 PRINT Q$
130 IF Q$<>"END" THEN 100
140 END
```

(a)

```
; This procedure is intended to be called from an interpreted
;  or compiled BASIC program.
; The procedure converts any lower case ASCII characters in an
;  input string to upper case and returns the result as the same string.

        PUBLIC  UCASE
;Segment name 'CODE' required for complier compatibility
CODE    SEGMENT   PUBLIC  'CODE'
        UCASE PROC FAR
                ASSUME CS:CODE
        PUSH BP             ; Save old BP
        MOV  BP,SP          ; Set up second stack pointer
        MOV  BX,[BP+6]      ; Pointer to string descriptor from stack
                            ;  add 2 to displacement for each word
                            ;  pushed on stack in addition to BP
        MOV  CX,[BX]        ; Length of string from memory to CX as counter
;       MOV  CL,[BX]        ; For IBM interpreted BASIC string length 1byte
        MOV  BX,[BX+2]      ; Offset of start of string from descriptor
                            ;  displacement in instruction=1 for
                            ;  IBM interpreted BASIC
NEXT:   MOV  AL,[BX]        ; Get byte from string
        CMP  AL,61H         ; Check if lower case
        JB   OK
        CMP  AL,7AH
        JA   OK             ; No, leave as is
        SUB  AL,20H         ; Yes, convert to upper case
OK:     MOV  [BX],AL        ; Put back in string
        INC  BX             ; Increment pointer to next char
        LOOP NEXT           ; Repeat until all string done
        POP  BP             ; Restore old BP
        RET  2              ; Return and increment stack pointer over
                            ;  string descriptor passed on stack
UCASE   ENDP
CODE    ENDS
        END
```

(b)

FIGURE 13-28 Integration of high-level language and assembly language programs. *(a)* BASIC calling program. *(b)* Assembly language procedure called.

END followed by a carriage return is entered. The CALL instruction here calls a procedure called UCASE and passes the "hooks" needed for the procedure to access the string named Q$. Before we can discuss the actual assembly language procedure, we need to show you how BASIC passes these parameters to the procedure on the stack.

The left side of Figure 13-29 shows the contents of the top few locations of the stack after the CALL executes. The top 2 words on the stack contain the IP and the CS

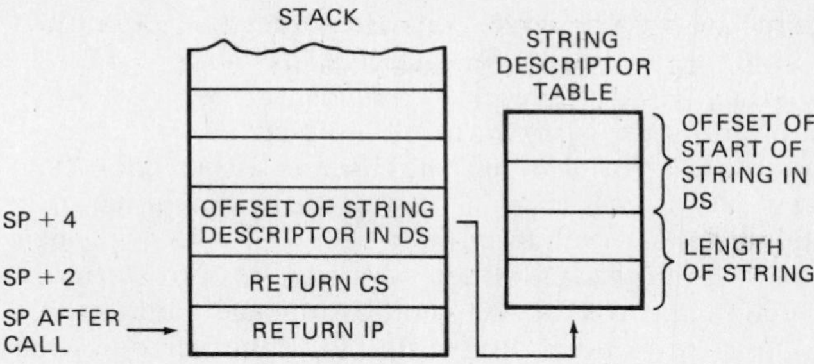

FIGURE 13-29 Stack after assembly language procedure call showing pointer to string variable descriptor table passed by calling program.

of the return address. The next word in the stack contains the offset (in the data segment) of a 4-byte *descriptor* for the string passed to the procedure. As shown in the right side of Figure 13-29 the lower 2 bytes of the descriptor contain the length of the string. The upper 2 bytes of the descriptor contain the offset of the actual string in the data segment. In other words, the offset passed on the stack for the string is a pointer to a table which contains the length of the string and the actual location of the string. When a simple nonstring variable is passed to a procedure, the offset in the stack points directly to a word location which contains the offset of the actual variable in the data segment. Once you know where the offset for a variable or a descriptor is stored in the stack, it is a simple matter to access the variable in your assembly language program.

Figure 13-28*b* shows how this is done. The BP register is first saved on the stack, and then the value in the stack pointer copied to it. Since a value in the BP register is added to the stack segment base to produce a physical address, BP can now function as a second pointer into the stack. After BP is pushed on the stack, the offset of the string descriptor that we need will be 6 bytes up in the stack. The instruction MOV BX, [BP + 6] then brings the string descriptor offset from the stack to BX. The MOV CX, [BX] instruction then uses this offset to bring the length of the string into CX for use as a counter. The MOV BX, [BX + 2] instruction then brings the offset of the start of the string from the descriptor table to BX where it can be used to access the elements in the string. The next section of the program runs through a simple check and fix-if-necessary loop until all of the string elements have been processed. In this case, the results of the processing are passed back to the calling program in the same string as the data was passed in. Finally, the initial BP is restored and execution returned to the calling program. Note that the RET 2 instruction is used to increment the stack pointer after the return. This is done to move the stack pointer over the variable offset that was passed to the procedure on the stack. If this is not done to balance the stack, the stack may grow downward in memory over the program. For each variable passed to the procedure, add 2 to the return number. It is not necessary to push the flags and the general-purpose registers used in the procedure, because this is done as part of the call statement. The registers and flags are restored upon return if the correct number is used with the RET instruction. If you are not sure they are pushed by the call statement in a particular high level language, it won't hurt anything to push and pop them in the procedure.

Combining assembly language procedures with high level language programs is a powerful programming technique. Hopefully, this section has shown you that it is not a difficult one if done in a compiler environment.

SYNCHRONOUS SERIAL DATA COMMUNICATION AND PROTOCOLS

Introduction

Most of the discussion of serial data transfer up to this point in the chapter has been about asynchronous transmission. For asynchronous serial transmission a start bit is used to identify the beginning of each data character, and at least one stop bit is used to identify the end of each data character. The transmitter and the receiver are effectively synchronized on a character-by-character basis. Since a total of 10 bits must be sent for each 8-bit data character, 20 percent of the transmission time is wasted. A more efficient method of transferring serial data is to synchronize the transmitter and the receiver, and then send a large block of data characters one after the other. No start or stop bits are then needed for individual data characters, because the receiver automatically knows that every 8 bits received after synchronization represents a data character. When a block of data is not being sent through a synchronous data link, the line is held in a marking condition. To indicate the start of a transmission the transmitter sends out one or more unique characters called *sync characters*, or a unique bit pattern called a *flag*, depending on the system being used. The receiver uses the sync characters or the flag to synchronize its internal clock with that of the receiver. The receiver then shifts in the data characters following and converts them to parallel form so they can be read in by a computer. Higher-speed data links or digital communication channels usually use synchronous transmission.

Now, remember from a previous section that a hardware level set of handshake signals is required to transmit asynchronous or synchronous digital data over phone lines with modems. In addition to this handshaking, a higher level of coordination, or *protocol*, is required between transmitter and receiver to assure the orderly transfer of data. A protocol in this case is an agreed set of rules concerning the form in which the data is to be sent. There are many different serial data protocols. The two most common that we discuss here are the IBM *binary synchronous communications protocol*, or BISYNC, and the *high-level data link control protocol*, or HDLC.

Binary Synchronous Communication Protocol—BISYNC

BISYNC is a referred to as a *byte-controlled protocol* (BCP), because specified ASCII or EBCDIC characters (bytes) are used to indicate the start of a message and to handshake between the transmitter and the receiver. Incidentally, even in a full-duplex system, BISYNC only allows data transfer in one direction at a time.

Figure 13-30 shows the general message format for BISYNC. For our first cycle through this we will assume that the transmitter has received a message from the receiver that it is ready to receive a transmission. If no message is being sent, the line is in an "idle" condition with a continuous high on the line. To indicate the start of a message, the transmitting system sends 2 or more previously agreed upon sync characters. For example, a sync character might be the ASCII 16H. As we said before, the receiver uses these sync characters to synchronize its clock with that of the transmitter. A header may then be sent if desired. The header contents are usually defined for a specific system and may include information about the type, priority, and destination of the message that follows. The start of the header is indicated with a special character called *start-of-header* (SOH), which in ASCII is represented by 01H.

After the header, if present, the beginning of the text portion of the message is indicated by another special character called *start-of-text* (STX), which in ASCII is represented by 02H. To indicate the end of the text portion of the message, an *end-of-text* (ETX) character or an *end-of-block* (ETB) character is sent. The text portion may contain 128 or 256 characters (different systems use different-size blocks of text). Immediately following the ETX character, 1 or 2 block check characters (BCC) are sent. For systems using ASCII, the BCC is a single byte which represents complex parity information computed for the text of the message. For systems using EBCDIC a 16-bit *cyclic redundancy check* is performed on the text part of the message and the 16-bit result sent as 2 BCCs. The point of these BCCs is that the receiving system can recompute the value for them from the received data and compare the results with the BCCs sent from the transmitter. If the BCCs are not equal, the receiver can send a message to the transmitter, telling it to send the message again. Now let's look at how messages are used for data transfer handshaking between the transmitter and the receiver.

To start let's assume that we have a remote "smart" terminal connected to a computer with a half-duplex connection. Further, let's assume that the computer is in the receive mode. Now, when the brain in the terminal determines that it has a block of data to send to the computer, it first sends a message with the text containing only the single character ENQ (ASCII 05H), which stands for *enquiry*. The terminal then switches to receive mode to await the reply from the computer. The computer reads the ENQ message, and, if it is not ready to receive data, it sends back a text message containing the single character for *negative acknowledge*, NAK (ASCII 15H). If the receiver is ready, it sends a message containing the *affirmative acknowledge*, ACK, character (ASCII 06H). In either case, the computer then switches to receive mode to await the next message from the terminal. If the terminal received a NAK, it may give up, or it may wait a while and try again. If the terminal received an ACK, it will send a message containing a block of text and ending with a BCC character(s). After sending the message, the terminal switches to receive mode and awaits a reply from the computer as to whether the message was received correctly. The computer meanwhile computes the BCC for the received block of data and compares it with the BCC sent with the message. If the two BCCs are not equal, the computer sends a NAK message to the terminal. This tells the terminal to send the message again, because it was not received correctly. If the two BCCs are equal, then the computer sends an ACK message to the terminal, which tells it to send the next message or block of text. In a system where multiple blocks of data are being transferred, an ACK 0 message is usually sent for one block, an ACK 1 message sent for the next, and an ACK 0 again sent for the next. The alternating ACK messages are a further help in error checking. In either case, after the message is sent the computer switches to receive mode to await a response from the terminal.

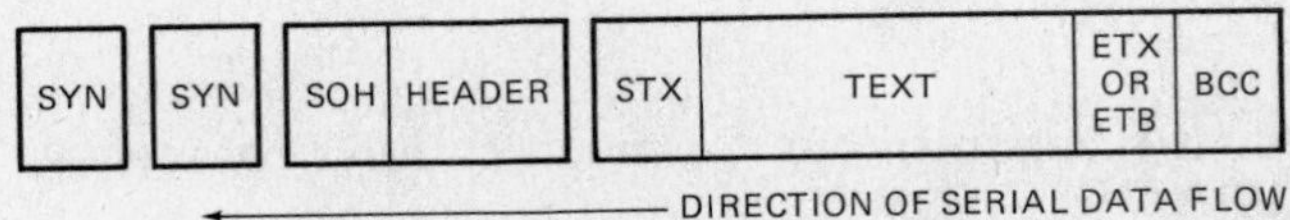

FIGURE 13-30 General message format for BISYNC.

One major problem with this protocol is that the transmitter must stop after each block of data is transferred, and wait for an ACK or NAK signal from the receiver. Due to the wait and line turnaround times, the actual data transfer rate may be only half of the theoretical rate predicted by the physical bit rate of the data link. The HDLC protocol discussed in a later section greatly reduces this problem. Next we want to return to the Intel 8251A USART and give you a brief look at how it is used for BISYNC communication.

Using the Intel 8251A USART for BISYNC Communication

As shown in Figure 13-5, we initialize an 8251A by first getting its attention, sending it a mode word, and then sending it a command word. To initialize the 8251A for synchronous communication, 0's are put in the least-significant 2 bits of the mode word. The rest of the bits in the mode word then have the meanings shown in Figure 13-31. Most of the bit functions should be reasonably clear from the descriptions in the figure, but a couple need a little more explanation.

Bit 6 of the mode word specifies the SYNDET pin on the 8251A to be an input or an output. The pin is programmed to function as an input if external circuitry is used to detect the sync character in the data bit stream. When programmed as an output, this pin will go high when the 8251A has found one or more sync characters in the data bit stream.

Bit 7 of the mode word is used to specify whether 1 sync character, or a sequence of 2 different sync characters is to be looked for at the start of a message.

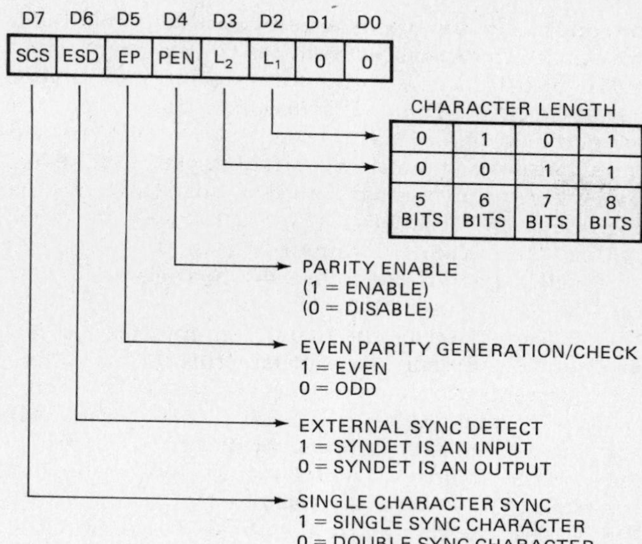

FIGURE 13-31 8251A mode word for synchronous communication.

To initialize an 8251A for synchronous operation:

1. Send a series of nulls and a software reset command to the control address as shown at the start of Figure 13-5.
2. Send a mode word based on the format in Figure 13-31 to the control address.
3. Send the desired sync character for that particular system to the control address of the 8251A.
4. If a second sync character is needed, send it to the control address.
5. Finally, send a command word to the control address to enable the transmitter, enable the receiver, and enable the device to look for sync characters in the data bit stream coming in on the RxD input.

The format for the command word is shown in Figure 13-32. Now, let's examine how the 8251A participates in a synchronous data transfer. As you work your way through this section, try to keep separate in your mind the parts of the process that are done by the 8251A and the parts that are done by software at one end of the link or the other.

To start, let's assume the 8251A is in a terminal which has blocks of data to send to a computer as we described earlier in this section. Further assume that the computer is in receive mode waiting for a transmission from the terminal, and that the 8251A in the terminal has been initialized and is sending out a continuous high on the TxD line.

An I/O driver routine in the terminal will start the transfer process by sending a sync character(s), SOH character, header characters, STX character, ENQ character, ETX character, and BCC byte to the 8251A, one after the other. The 8251A sends the characters out in synchronous serial format (no start and stop bits). If, for some reason such as a high-priority interrupt, the CPU stops sending characters while a message is being sent, the 8251A will automatically insert sync characters until the flow of data characters from the CPU resumes.

After the ENQ message has been sent, the CPU in the terminal awaits a reply from the computer through the RxD input of the 8251A. If the 8251A has been programmed to enter hunt mode by sending it a control word with a 1 in bit 7, it will continuously shift in bits from the RxD line and check after each shift if the character in the receive buffer is a sync character. When it finds a sync character, the 8251A asserts the SYNDET pin high, exits the hunt mode, and starts the normal data read operation. When the 8251A has a valid data character in its receiver buffer, the RxRDY pin will be asserted, and the RxRDY bit in the status register will be set. Characters can then be read in by the CPU on a polled or an interrupt basis.

When the CPU has read in the entire message, it can determine whether the message was a NAK or an ACK. If the message was an ACK, the CPU can then send the actual data message sequence of characters to the 8251A. Handshake and data messages will be sent back and forth until all of the desired block of data has been

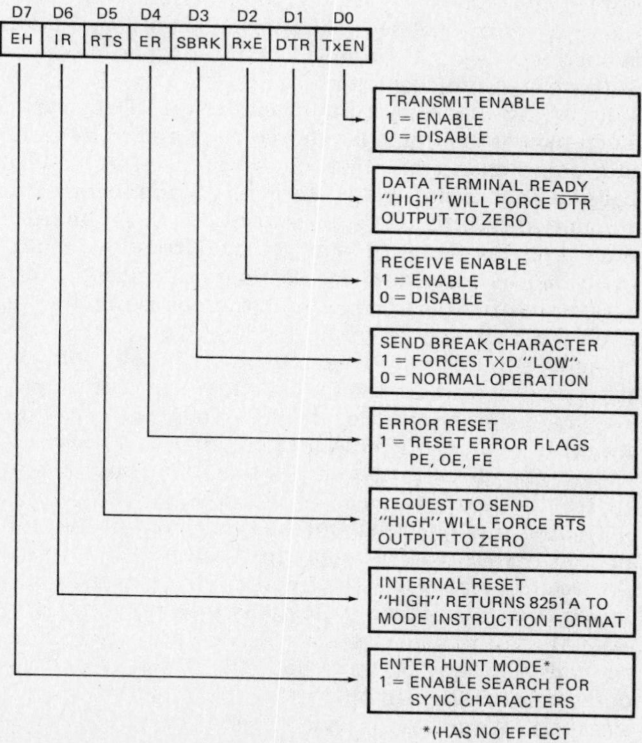

FIGURE 13-32 8251A command-word format for synchronous operation.

sent to the computer. In the next section we discuss another protocol used for synchronous serial data transfer.

High-level Data Link Control (HDLC) and Synchronous Data Link Control (SDLC) Protocols

The BISYNC protocol, which we discussed in the previous section only works in half-duplex mode, has difficulty accurately transmitting pure binary data such as object code for programs, and is not easily adapted to serving multiple units sharing a common data link. In an attempt to solve these problems, the *International Standards Organization* (ISO) proposed the *high level data link control protocol* (HDLC) and IBM developed the *synchronous data link control protocol* (SDLC). The standards are so nearly identical that, for the discussion here, we will treat them together under the name HDLC and indicate any significant differences as needed.

As we said previously, BISYNC is referred to as a byte-controlled protocol because character codes or bytes such as SOH, STX, and ETX are used to mark off parts of a transmitted message or act as control messages. HDLC is referred to as a *bit-oriented protocol* (BOP) because messages are treated simply as a string of bits, rather than a string of characters. The group of bits which make up a message is referred to as a *frame*. The three types of frames used are: information or *I frames*, supervisory control sequences or *S frames*, and command/response or *U frames*. The three types of frames all have the same basic format.

Figure 13-33*a* shows the format of an HDLC frame. Each part of the frame is referred to as a *field*. A frame starts and ends with a specific bit pattern, 01111110, called a *flag* or *flag field*. When no data is being sent, the line idles with all 1's, or continuous flags. Immediately after the flag field is an 8-bit address field which contains the address of the destination unit for a control or information frame, and the source of the response for a response frame.

Figure 13-33*b* shows the meaning of the bits in the 8-bit control field for each of the three types of frames. We don't have the space or the desire to explain here the meaning of all of these. A little later we will, however, explain the use of the Ns and Nr bits in the control byte for an information frame.

The information field, which is only present in information frames, can have any number of bits in HDLC protocol, but in SDLC the number of bits has to be a multiple of 8. In some systems as many as 10,000 or 20,000 information bits may be sent per frame. Now, the question may occur to you, "What happens if the data contains the flag bit pattern, 01111110?" The answer to this question is that a special hardware circuit modifies the bit stream between flags so that there are never more than 5 ones in sequence. To do this the circuit monitors the data stream and automatically stuffs in a zero after any series of 5 ones. A complementary circuit in the receiver removes the extra zeros. This scheme allows any type of characters or data to be sent without the problems BISYNC has in this area.

The next field in a frame is the 16-bit *frame check sequence* (FCS). This is a cyclic redundancy word derived from all of the bits between the beginning and end flags, but not including 0's inserted to prevent false flag bytes. This CRC value can be recomputed by the receiving system to check for errors.

Finally, a frame is terminated by another flag byte. The ending flag for one frame may be the starting flag for another frame.

In order to describe the HDLC data-transfer process, we first need to define a couple of terms. HDLC is used for communication between two or more systems on a data link. One of the systems or *stations* on the link will always be set up as a controller for the link. This station is called the *primary station*. Other stations on the link are referred to as *secondary stations*.

Now, suppose that a primary station, a computer for example, wants to send several frames of information to a secondary station such as another computer or terminal. Here's how a transfer might take place.

The primary station starts by sending an S frame containing the address of the desired secondary station and a control word which inquires if the receiver is ready. The secondary station then sends an S frame which contains the address of the primary station and a con-

FRAME

BEGINNING FLAG 01111110 8 BITS	ADDRESS 8 BITS	CONTROL 8 BITS	INFORMATION ANY NUMBER OF BITS	FRAME CHECK 16 BITS	ENDING FLAG 01111110 8 BITS

(*a*)

BITS IN CONTROL FIELD

HDLC FRAME FORMAT	7	6	5	4	3	2	1	Ø
I-FRAME (INFORMATION TRANSFER COMMANDS/RESPONSES)	Nr	Nr	Nr	P/F	Ns	Ns	Ns	Ø
S-FRAME (SUPERVISORY COMMANDS/RESPONSES)	Nr	Nr	Nr	P/F	S	S	Ø	1
U-FRAME (UNNUMBERED COMMANDS/RESPONSES)	M	M	M	P/F	M	M	1	1

SENDING ORDER – BIT Ø FIRST, BIT 7 LAST

NS THE TRANSMITTING STATION SEND SEQUENCE NUMBER, BIT 2 IS THE LOW-ORDER BIT.

P/F THE POLL BIT FOR PRIMARY STATION TRANSMISSIONS, AND THE FINAL BIT FOR SECONDARY STATION TRANSMISSIONS.

Nr THE TRANSMITTING STATION RECEIVE SEQUENCE NUMBER, BIT 6 IS THE LOW-ORDER BIT.

S THE SUPERVISORY FUNCTION BITS

M THE MODIFIER FUNCTION BITS

(*b*)

FIGURE 13-33 *(a)* Format of HDLC frame. *(b)* Meaning of bits in 8-bit control field for a frame.

trol word which indicates its ready status. If the secondary station receiver was ready, the primary station then sends a sequence of information frames. The information frames contain the address of the secondary station, a control word, a block of information, and the FCS words. For all but the last frame of a sequence of information frames, the P/F bit in the control byte will be a 0. The 3 Ns bits in the control byte will contain the number of the frame in the sequence.

Now, as the secondary station receives each information frame, it reads the data into memory and computes the frame check sequence for the frame. For each frame in a sequence that the secondary station receives correctly, it increments an internal counter. When the primary station sends the last frame in a sequence of up to seven frames, it makes the P/F bit in the control byte a 1. This is a signal to the secondary station that the primary station wants a response as to how many frames were received correctly. The secondary station responds with an S frame. The Nr bits in the control word of this S frame contain the sequence number of the last frame that was received correctly plus 1. In other words, Ns represents the number of the next expected frame. The primary station compares Ns − 1 with the number of frames sent in the sequence. If the two numbers do not agree, the primary station knows that it must retransmit some frames, because they were not all received correctly. The Nr number tells the primary station which frame number to start the retransmission from. For example, if Nr is 3, the primary station will retransmit the sequence of frames starting with frame 3. If the sequence of frames was received correctly, another series of frames can be sent if desired. Actually, since HDLC operates in full duplex, the receiving station can be queried after each frame is sent to see if the previous frame was received correctly. A similar series of actions takes place when a secondary station transmits to a primary station or to another secondary station.

One advantage of this HDLC scheme is that the transmitter does not have to stop after every short message for an acknowledge as it does in BISYNC protocol. True, several frames may have to be resent in case of an error, but in low error rate systems, this is the exception. As we will show in the next section, HDLC is used along with some higher level protocols to allow communication between a wide variety of systems.

One final point to make here is how HDLC protocol is implemented with a microcomputer. At the basic hardware level, a standard USART cannot be used because of the need to stuff and strip 0 bits. Instead, specially designed parts such as the Intel 8273 HDLC/SDLC protocol controller are used. Devices such as this automatically stuff and strip the required 0 bits, generate and check frame-check sequence words, and produce the interface signals for RS-232C. The devices interface directly to microcomputer buses.

The actual control of which station uses the data link at a particular time and the formatting of frames is done by the system software. The next section discusses how several systems can be connected together or "networked" so they can communicate with each other.

LOCAL AREA NETWORKS

Introduction

The objective of this section is to show you how several computers can be connected together to communicate with each other and to share common peripherals such as printers and large disk drives. We will start with simple cases and progress to the type of network that might be used in the computerized electronics factory we described in an earlier chapter.

To communicate between a single terminal and a nearby computer, a simple RS-232C connection is sufficient. If the computer is distant, then a modem and phone line or a leased phone line is used, depending on the required baud rate. Now, for a more difficult case, suppose that we have in a university building 100 terminals that need to communicate with a distant computer. We could use 100 phone lines with modems, but this seems quite inefficient. One solution to this problem is to run wires from all of the terminals to a central point in the building, and then use a multiplexer or *data concentrator* of some type to send all of the communications over one wideband line. Either time-domain multiplexing or frequency-division multiplexing can be used. A demultiplexer at the other end of the line reconstructs the original signals.

As another example of computer communication, suppose that we have several computers in one building or a complex of buildings that need to communicate with each other. Our computerized electronics factory is an example of this situation. What is needed in this case is a high-speed network, commonly called a *local area network* or *LAN*, connecting the computers together. We start our discussion of LANs by showing you some of the basic connection configurations.

LAN Connection Configurations

The different ways of physically connecting devices on a network with each other are commonly referred to as *topologies*. Figure 13-34 shows the five most common topologies and some other pertinent data about each, such as examples of commercially available systems which use each type.

In a *star topology* network, a central controller coordinates all communication between devices on the network. The most familiar example of how this works is probably a private automatic branch exchange, or PABX, phone system. In a PABX all calls from one phone on the system to another or to an outside phone are routed through a central switchboard. The new digital PABX systems allow direct communication between computers within a building at baud rates up to perhaps 100 kBd.

In the *loop topology*, one device acts as a controller. If a device wants to communicate with one or more other devices on the loop, it sends a request to the controller. If the loop is not in use, the controller enables the one device to output, and the other device(s) to receive. The GPIB or IEEE488 bus described in the last section of this chapter is an example of this topology.

TOPOLOGY	TYPICAL PROTOCOLS	TYPICAL NO. OF NODES	TYPICAL SYSTEMS
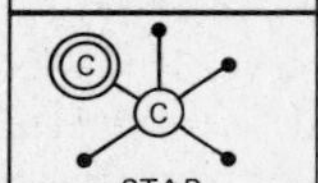 STAR	RS-232C OR COMPUTER	TENS	PABX, COMPUTER μC CLUSTERS
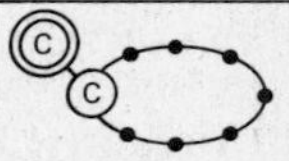 LOOP	SDLC	TENS	IBM 3600/3700, μC CLUSTERS
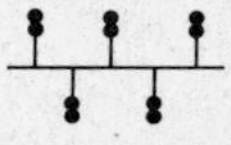 COMMON BUS	CSMA/CD OR CSMA WITH ACKNOWLEDGMENT	TENS TO HUNDREDS PER SEGMENT	ETHERNET, NET/ONE, OMNINET, Z-NET μC CLUSTERS
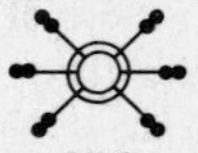 RING	SDLC HDLC (TOKEN PASSING)	TENS TO HUNDREDS PER CHANNEL	PRIMENET, DOMAIN, OMNILINK μC CLUSTERS
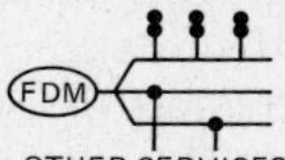 FDM OTHER SERVICES BROADBAND BUS	CSMA/CD RS-232C & OTHERS PER CHANNEL	TWO TO HUNDREDS PER CHANNEL	WANGNET, LOCALNET M/A-COM

• TERMINAL
DISTRIBUTED CONTROL
(C) LOCAL CONTROLLER
((C)) MULTINETWORK CONTROLLER
(FDM) FREQUENCY DIVISION MULTIPLEX

FIGURE 13-34 Summary of common computer network topologies.

In the *common-bus topology*, control of the bus is spread among all of the devices on the bus. The connection in this type of system is simply a wire (usually but not always a coaxial cable) which any number of devices can be tapped into. Any device can take over the bus to transmit data. Data is transmitted in fixed-length blocks called *packets*. Two devices are prevented from transmitting at the same time by a scheme called *carrier sense, multiple access with collision detection*, or CSMA/CD. This is discussed in detail in a later section on Ethernet.

In a *ring network*, the control is also distributed among all of the devices on the network. Each device on the ring functions as a repeater, which means that it simply takes in the data stream and passes the data stream on to the next device on the ring if it is not the intended receiver for the data. Data always circulates around the ring in one direction. Any device can transmit on the ring. A *token* is one common way used to prevent two or more devices from transmitting at the same time. A token is a specific lone byte such as 01111111 which is circulated around the ring when no device is transmitting. A device must possess the token in order to transmit. When a device needs to transmit, it removes the token from the bus, thus preventing any other devices from transmitting. After transmitting one or more packets of data, the transmitting device puts the token back on the ring so another device can grab it and transmit. We discuss this more in a later section.

The final topology we want to discuss here is the *tree* structured network which often uses broadband transmission. Before we can really explain this one, we need to introduce you to a couple of terms commonly used with networks. In some networks such as Ethernet, data is transmitted directly as digital signals at a rate of 10M bits/s. With this type of signal, only one device can transmit at a time. This form of data transmission is often referred to as *baseband* transmission, because only one basic frequency is used. The other common form of data transmission on a network is referred to as *broadband* transmission. Broadband transmission is based on a frequency-division multiplexing scheme such as that used for community antenna television (CATV) systems. The radio-frequency spectrum is divided up into 6-MHz-bandwidth channels.

A single device or group of devices can be assigned one channel for transmitting and another for receiving. Each channel or pair of channels is considered a branch on the tree. Special modems are used to convert digital signals to and from the modulated radio-frequency signals required. The multiple channels and the 6-MHz bandwidth of the channels in a broadband network allow voice, data, and video signals to be transmitted at the same time throughout the network. This is an advantage over baseband systems which can only transmit one digital data signal at a time, but the broadband system is much more expensive.

Network Protocols

In order for different systems on a network to communicate effectively with each other, a series of rules or protocols must be agreed upon and followed by all of the devices on the network. The International Standards Organization, in an attempt to bring some order to the chaos of network communication, has developed a standard called the *open systems interconnection* (OSI) model. This model is not a rigid standard. It is a seven-layer hierarchy of protocols as shown in Figure 13-35. This layered approach structures the design tasks and makes it possible to change, for example, the actual hardware used to transmit the data without changing the other layers. We will use a common network operation, electronic mail, to explain to you the function of the upper-layers model.

Electronic mail allows a user on one system on a network to send a message to another user on the same system or on another system. The message is actually sent to a "mailbox" in a hard-disk file. Each user on the network periodically checks a personal mailbox to see if it contains any messages. If any messages are present, they can be read out and then deleted from the mailbox.

The *application layer* of the OSI protocol specifies the general operation of network services such as electronic mail, access to common data bases, and access to common peripherals. For our example, this layer of the protocol dictates how you go about invoking the electronic mail function of the network.

The *presentation layer* of the OSI protocol governs the programs which convert messages to the code and format that will be understood by the receiver. For our electronic mail message this layer might involve translating a message from ASCII to EBCDIC, or perhaps from English to French.

	LAYER NUMBER	FUNCTION
APPLICATION	7	SELECTS APPROPRIATE SERVICE FOR APPLICATIONS
PRESENTATION	6	PROVIDES CODE CONVERSION, DATA REFORMATTING
SESSION	5	COORDINATES INTERACTION BETWEEN END-APPLICATION PROCESSES
TRANSPORT	4	PROVIDES END-TO-END DATA INTEGRITY AND QUALITY OF SERVICE
NETWORK	3	SWITCHES AND ROUTES INFORMATION
DATA LINK	2	TRANSFERS UNITS OF INFORMATION TO OTHER END OF PHYSICAL LINK
PHYSICAL	1	TRANSMITS BIT STREAM TO MEDIUM

FIGURE 13-35 ISO open system interconnect model for network communications.

The *session layer* of the OSI protocol establishes and terminates logical connections on the network. This layer is responsible for opening and closing named files, and for translating a user name into a physical network address. Electronic mail allows you to specify the intended receiver of a message by name. It is the responsibility of this layer of the protocol to make the connection between the name and the network address of the named receiver.

The *transport layer* of the protocol is responsible for making sure a message is transmitted and received correctly. An example of the operation of this protocol layer is the ACK or NAK handshake used in BISYNC transmission after the receiver has checked to see if the data was received correctly. For electronic mail, the message can be written to the addressed mailbox and then read back to make sure it was sent correctly.

The *network layer* of the protocol is only used in multichannel systems. It is responsible for finding a path through the network to the desired receiver by switching between channels. The function of this layer is similar to the function of postal mail routing which finds a route to get a letter from your house to the addressed destination.

The *data link layer* of the OSI model includes the framing of the data in terms of packet size and address information, the means used to check errors (parity or CRC), the handshake signals between the transmitter and the receiver, etc. The HDLC protocol described earlier in this chapter is an example of the type of transmission factors involved in this layer.

The *physical layer* of the OSI model is the lowest level. This layer is used to specify the connectors, cables, voltage levels, bit rates, modulation methods, etc. RS-232C is an example of a standard which falls in this layer of the model.

Now we will take a more detailed look at the operation of a very widespread "common-bus" network, Ethernet. Ethernet is a trademark of Xerox Corporation.

Ethernet

The *Ethernet network standard* was originally developed by Xerox Corporation. Later Xerox, DEC, and Intel worked on defining the standard sufficiently so that commercial products for implementing the standard were possible. It has now been adopted, with slight changes, as the IEEE802.3 standard.

Physically, Ethernet is implemented in a common-bus topology with a single 50-Ω coaxial cable. Data is sent over the cable using baseband transmission at 10 Mbits/s. Data bits are encoded using Manchester coding as shown in Figure 13-36. The advantage of this coding is that each bit cell contains a signal transition. A system that wants to transmit data on the network first checks for these transitions to see if the network is currently busy. If the system detects no transitions, then it can go ahead and transmit on the network.

Figure 13-37 shows how a very simple Ethernet is set up. The backbone of the system is the coaxial cable. Terminations are put on each end of the cable to prevent signal reflections. Each unit is connected into the cable with a simple tee-type tap. A transmitter-receiver, or *transceiver*, sends out data on the coax, receives data from the coax, and detects any attempt to transmit while the coax is already in use. The transceiver is connected to an interface board with a 15-pin connector and four twisted-wire pairs. The transceiver cable can be as long as 15 m. The interface board, as the name implies, performs most of the work of getting data on and off the network in the correct form. The *interface board* assembles and disassembles data frames, sends out source and destination addresses, detects transmission errors, and prevents transmission while some other unit on the network is transmitting.

The method used by a unit to gain access to the network is *CSMA/CD*. Before a unit attempts to transmit on the network, it looks at the coax to see if a carrier (Manchester code transitions) is present. If a carrier is present, the unit waits some random length of time and then tries again. When the unit finds no carrier on the line, it starts transmitting. While it is transmitting, it

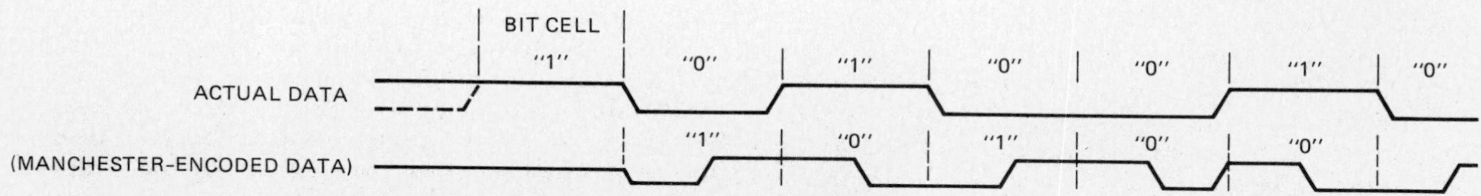

FIGURE 13-36 Manchester encoding used for Ethernet data bit stream. Note that encoded data has a transition at center of each data bit cell time.

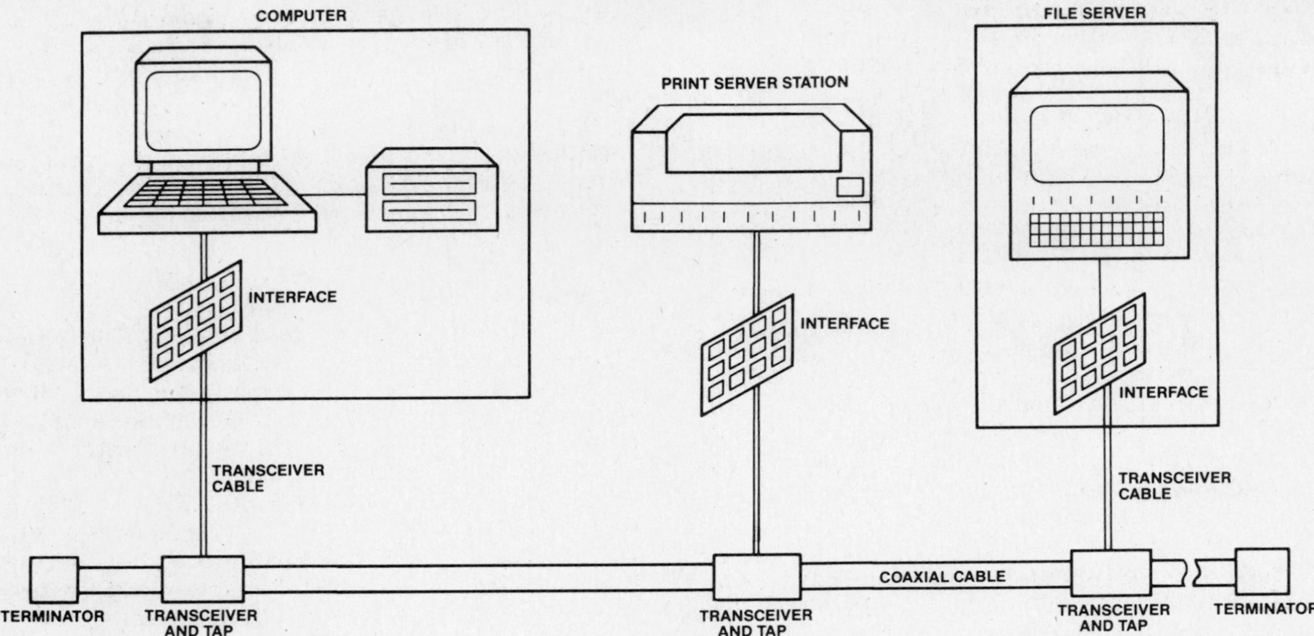

FIGURE 13-37 Very simple Ethernet system.

also monitors the line to make sure no other unit is transmitting at the same time. The question may occur to you at this point, "If a unit cannot start transmitting until it finds no carrier on the coax, how can another unit be transmitting at the same time?" The answer to this question involves propagation delay. Since transceivers can be as much as 2500 m apart, it may take as long as 23 μs for data transmitted from one unit to reach another unit. In other words, one unit may start transmitting before the signal from a transmitter that started earlier reaches it. Two units transmitting at the same time is referred to as a *collision*. When a unit detects a collision, it will keep transmitting long enough that all transmitting stations detect that a collision has occurred. All of the units then stop transmitting and try again after a random period of time. The term "multiple access" in the CSMA/CD name means that any unit on the network can attempt to transmit. No central controller decides which unit has use of the network at a particular time. Access is gained by any unit using the mechanism we have just described. The maximum number of units that can be connected on a single Ethernet is 1024. For further information about how an interface board is built, consult the data sheets for the Intel 82586 LAN coprocessor, and the data sheet for the Intel 82501 Ethernet serial interface.

Incidentally, a file server such as the one shown in Figure 13-37 is a "smart" hard-disk system which manages file access requests by other systems on the network. A print server is a "smart" printer which queues up print requests from other systems on the network.

Token-Passing Rings

Token-passing ring networks solve the multiple access problem in an entirely different way from the CSMA/CD approach described for Ethernet. As the name implies, systems are connected in series around a ring. Data always travels in one direction around the ring. Unlike the passive taps used in an Ethernet system, however, each active station on a token ring receives data, examines it to see if the data is addressed to it, and retransmits the data to the next station on the ring. A bypass relay is used to shunt data around defective or inactive units. Data is sent around the ring at perhaps 4–5Mbits/s in HDLC or SDLC frames which we described in an earlier section of the chapter on synchronous transmission. Any station on the network can use the network.

A token is a byte of data with an agreed-upon, unique bit pattern such as 01111111. If no station is transmitting, this token is circulated continuously around the ring. When a station needs to transmit, it withdraws the not-busy token, changes it to a busy token of perhaps 01111110, and sends the busy token on around the ring. The transmitting unit then sends a frame of data around the ring to the intended receiver(s). When the transmitting station receives the busy token back again, it reads it in, and sends out the not-busy token again. The transmitting station also pulls the transmitted data off the ring as it returns, so it can't circulate around again. As soon as a transmitting station releases the not-busy token again, the next station on the loop can grab the token and transmit on the network. The first station that transmitted cannot transmit again until the not-busy token works its way around the ring. This gives all units on the network a chance to transmit in a "round-robin" manner. (NOTE: Some token ring networks use tokens with priority bits so that one station can transmit again if necessary before a lower-priority station gets a turn.)

Two questions occurred to us the first time we read about token-passing rings; perhaps these same two questions may have occurred to you. The first question is, "How does a station on the network tell the bit pattern for a token from the same bit pattern in the data frame?" The answer to this question is bit-stuffing, the same technique that is used to prevent the flag bit pattern from being present in the data section of an HDLC frame. A hardware circuit in the transmitter alters the data stream so that certain bit patterns are not present. Another hardware circuit in the receiver reconstructs the original data.

The second question is, "What happens if the not-busy token somehow gets lost going around the ring?" A couple of different approaches are used to solve this problem. One approach uses a timer in each station. When a station has a frame to transmit, it starts a timer. If the station does not detect a token in the data stream before the timer counts down, it assumes that the token was lost, and sends out a new token. Another approach used by IBM sets up one station as a network monitor. If this station does not detect a token within a prescribed time, it clears any leftover data from the ring and sends out a new not-busy token.

Token-passing ring networks have the disadvantage that more complex hardware is required where each station connects to the network. The receive and transmit circuitry at the connection, however, acts as a repeater which maintains signal quality throughout the network. Since signals only travel in one direction around the ring, this topology is ideally suited for fiber-optic transmission, which allows high data rates and long distances between repeaters. IEEE802.5 standard describes a token-passing ring network. Texas Instruments is currently offering the TI TMS380 chip set which implements a token-passing ring microcomputer interface.

In the next section we discuss a somewhat different type of network which is used to connect instruments with a computer to form an integrated test and measurement system.

The GPIB, HPIB, IEEE488 Bus

The *general-purpose interface bus* (GPIB), also known as the *Hewlett-Packard interface bus* and the *IEEE488 bus* is not intended for use as a computer network in the same way that the Ethernet and token rings are used. It was developed by Hewlett-Packard to interface smart test instruments with a computer.

The standard describes three types of devices that can be connected on the GPIB. First is a *listener*, which can receive data from other instruments or from the controller. Examples of listeners are printers, display devices, programmable power supplies, and programmable signal generators. The second type of device defined is a *talker*, which can send data to other instruments. Examples of talkers are tape readers, digital voltmeters, frequency counters, and other measuring equipment. A device can be both a talker and a listener. The third type of device on the bus is a *controller*, which determines who talks and who listens on the bus.

Physically the bus consists of a 24-wire cable with a connector such as that shown in Figure 13-38*a* on each end. Actually, each end of the cable has both a male connector and a female connector, so that cables can daisy-chain from one unit to the next on the bus. Instruments intended for use on a GPIB usually have some switches which allow you to select the 4-bit address that the instrument will have on the bus. Standard TTL signal voltage levels are used.

As shown in Figure 13-38*b*, the GPIB has eight bidirectional data lines. These lines are used to transfer data, addresses, commands, and status bytes among as many as 8 or 10 instruments.

The GPIB also has five bus management lines which function basically as follows. The *interface clear* line (IFC), when asserted by the controller, resets all devices on the bus to a starting state. It is essentially a system reset. The *attention* (ATN) line, when asserted (low), indicates that the controller is putting a universal command or an address-command such as "listen" on the data bus. When the ATN line is high, the data lines contain data or a status byte. *Service request* (SRQ) is similar to an interrupt. Any device that needs to transfer data on the bus asserts the SRQ line low. The controller then polls all the devices to determine which one needs service. When asserted by the system controller, the *remote enable* (REN) signal allows an instrument to be controlled directly by the controller rather than by its front panel switches. The *end or identify* (EOI) signal is usually asserted by a talker to indicate that the transfer of a block of data is complete.

Finally, the bus has three handshake lines that coordinate the transfer of data bytes on the data bus. These are *data valid* (DAV), *not ready for data* (NRFD), and *not data accepted* (NDAC). These handshake signals allow devices with very different data rates to be connected together in a system. A little later we will show you how this handshake works. First we will give you an overview of general bus operation.

Upon power-up the controller takes control of the bus and sends out an IFC signal to set all instruments on the bus to a known state. The controller then proceeds to use the bus to perform the desired series of measurements or tests. To do this the controller sends out a series of commands with the ATN line asserted low. Figure 13-38*c* shows the formats for the combination command-address codes that a controller can send to talkers and listeners. Bit 8 of these words is a don't-care, bits 7 and 6 specify which command is being sent, and bits 5 through 1 give the address of the talker or listener to which the command is being sent. For example, to enable (address) a device at address 04 as a talker, the controller simply asserts the ATN line low and sends out a command-address byte of X1000100 on the data bus. A listener is enabled by sending out a command-address byte of $X01A_5A_4A_3A_2A_1$, where the lower 5 bits contain the address that the listener has been given in the system. When a data transfer is complete, all listeners are turned off by the controller sending an unlisten command, X0111111. The controller turns off the talker by sending an untalk command, X1011111. *Universal commands* sent by the controller with bits 7, 6, and 5 all 0's will go to all listeners and talkers. The lower 4 bits of these words specify one of 16 universal commands.

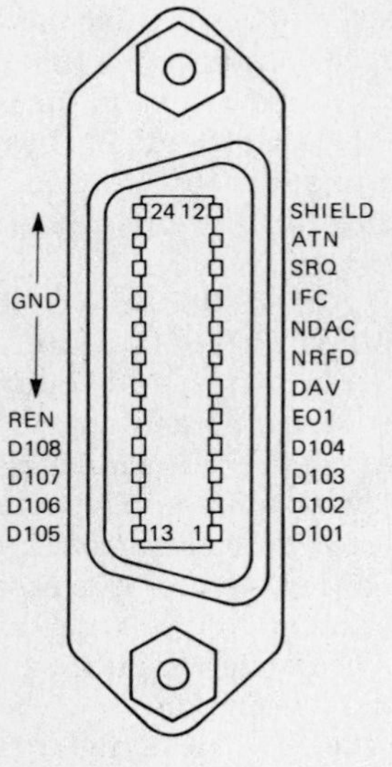

24 12
SHIELD
ATN
SRQ
IFC
NDAC
NRFD
DAV
EO1
D104
D103
D102
D101
GND
REN
D108
D107
D106
D105
13 1

(a)

DEVICE A
ABLE TO TALK, LISTEN AND CONTROL
(E. G., CALCULATOR)
DEVICE B
ABLE TO TALK AND LISTEN
(E. G., DIGITAL VOLTMETER)
DEVICE C
ONLY ABLE TO LISTEN
(E. G., SIGNAL GENERATOR)
DEVICE D
ONLY ABLE TO TALK
(E. G., TAPE READER)
DATA BUS
(8 SIGNAL LINES)
DATA BYTE TRANSFER CONTROL
(3 SIGNAL LINES)
GENERAL INTERFACE MANAGEMENT
(5 SIGNAL LINES)
} DIO 1 . . . 8
DAV
NRFD
NDAC
IFC
ATN
SRQ
REN
EOI

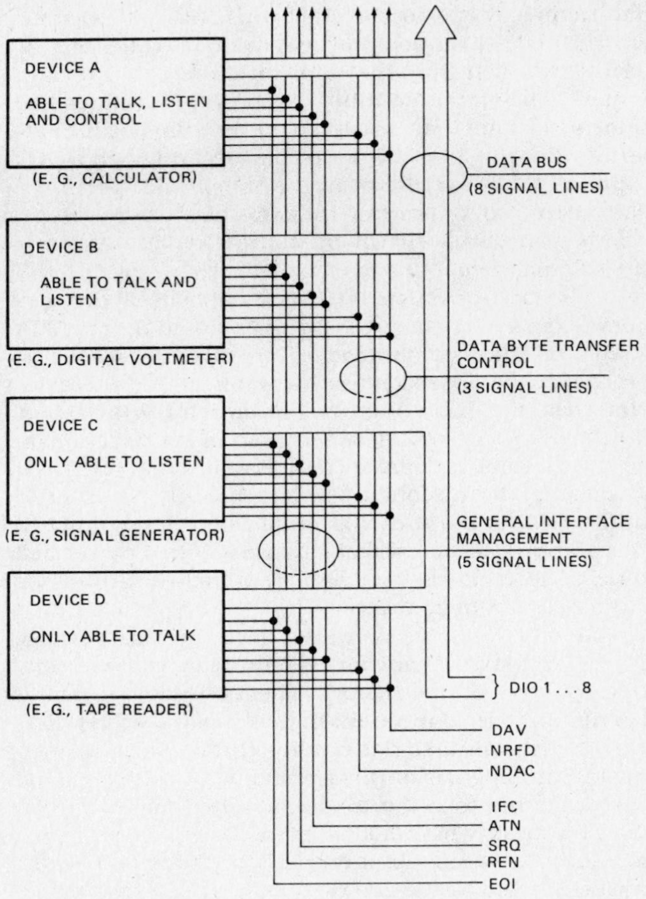

(b)

CODE								
D8	D7	D6	D5	D4	D3	D2	D1	MEANING
X	0	0	0	B4	B3	B2	B1	UNIVERSAL COMMANDS
X	0	1	A5	A4	A3	A2	A1	LISTEN ADDRESSES
X	0	1	1	1	1	1	1	UNLISTEN COMMAND
X	1	0	A5	A4	A3	A2	A1	TALK ADDRESSES
X	1	0	1	1	1	1	1	UNTALK COMMAND
X	1	1	A5	A4	A3	A2	A1	SECONDARY COMMANDS
X	1	1	1	1	1	1	1	IGNORED

CODE FOR TYPE OF COMMAND (D7, D6)

NOTES: THESE CODES ARE ONLY VALID WHEN ATN IS LOW. ADDRESS 11111 CANNOT BE USED FOR A LISTENER OR A TALKER.

(c)

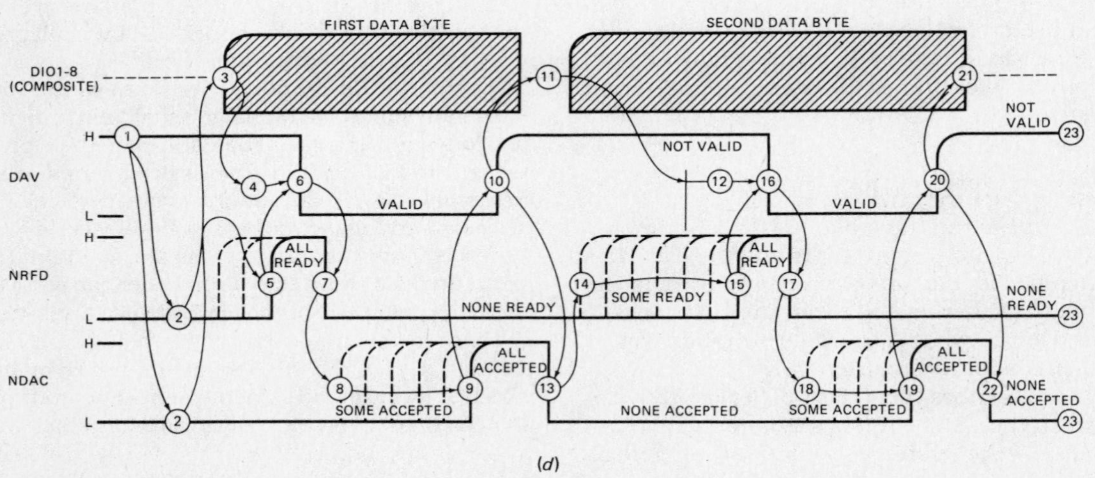

(d)

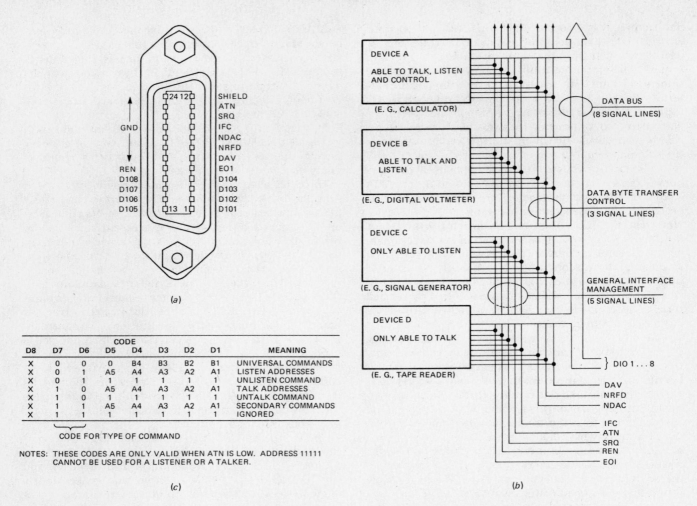

FIGURE 13-38 GPIB pins, signal lines, and waveforms. *(a)* Connector. *(b)* Bus structure. *(c)* Command formats. *(d)* Data transfer handshake waveforms.

Periodically while it is using the bus, the controller checks the SRQ line for a service request. If the SRQ line is low, the controller polls each device on the bus one after another (serial), or all at once (parallel), until it finds the device requesting service. A talker such as a DVM, for example, might be indicating that it has completed a series of conversions and has some data to send to a listener such as a chart recorder. When the controller determines the source of the SRQ, it asserts the ATN line low and sends listener address commands to each listener that is to receive the data and a talk address command to the talker that requested service. The controller then raises the ATN line high, and data is transferred directly from the talker to the listeners using a double-handshake-signal sequence.

Figure 13-38*d* shows the sequence of signals on the handshake lines for a transfer of data from a talker to several listeners. The DAV, NRFD, and NDAC lines are all open-collector. Therefore, any listener can hold NRFD low to indicate that it is not ready for data, or hold NDAC low to indicate that it has not yet accepted a data byte. The sequence proceeds as follows. When all listeners have released the NRFD line (5 in Figure 13-38*d*), indicating that they are ready (not not-ready), the talker asserts the DAV line low to indicate that a valid data byte is on the bus. The addressed listeners then all pull NRFD low and start accepting the data. When the slowest listener has accepted the data, the NDAC line will be released high (9 in Figure 13-38*d*). The talker senses NDAC becoming high and unasserts its DAV signal. The listeners all pull NDAC low again, and the sequence is repeated until the talker has sent all of the data bytes it has to send. The rate of data transfer is determined by the rate at which the slowest listener can accept the data.

When the data transfer is complete, the talker pulls the EOI line in the management group low to tell the controller that the transfer is complete. The controller then takes control again and sends an untalk command to the talker. It also sends an unlisten command to turn off the listeners, and continues to use the bus according to its internal program.

A standard microprocessor bus can be interfaced to the GPIB with dedicated devices such as the Intel 8291 GPIB talker-listener, and 8292 GPIB controller. The importance of the GPIB is that it allows a microcomputer to be connected with several test instruments to form an integrated test system.

IMPORTANT TERMS AND CONCEPTS FROM THIS CHAPTER

Serial data communication
- simplex, half-duplex, full-duplex
- synchronous, asynchronous
- marking state, spacing state
- start bit, stop bit
- baud rate

UART, USART, DTE, DCE

20- and 60-mA current loops

RS-232C, RS-422A, RS-423A, RS-449 serial data standards

Telephone circuits and systems
- leased and switched lines
- POTS, DTMF, PBX
- repeater, hybrid-coil, ring trip

CODECs, TDM, and PCM

Modems
- FSK, PSK
- analog and digital loopback (ALB and DLB)
- dibit, tribit
- quaternary amplitude modulation (QAM)

Fiber-optic data communication
- index of refraction, critical angle
- Multimode and single-mode fibers

Circular buffer

Critical region

Compiler and interpreter

Descriptor

Binary synchronous communications protocol (BISYNC)
- byte-controlled protocol (BCP)
- cyclic redundancy check

HDLC,SDLC protocols
- bit-oriented protocol (BOP)
- frame, field, flag
- frame check sequence (FCS)

Local area network (LAN)

Star, loop, ring, common-bus, broadband-bus (tree) topologies
- token
- baseband and broadband transmission

Electronic mail

Open system interconnection model (OSI)
- presentation, session, transport, network, data link, physical layers

Ethernet
- transceiver
- collision
- CSMA/CD

Token-passing rings

GPIB, HPIB, IEEE 488 bus standard
- listener, talker, controller

REVIEW QUESTIONS AND PROBLEMS

1. Draw a diagram showing the bit format used for asynchronous serial data. Label the start, stop, and parity bits. Use numbers to indicate the order of the data bits.

2. A terminal is transmitting asynchronous serial data at 1200 Bd. What is the bit time? Assuming 7 data bits, a parity bit, and 1 stop bit, how long does it take to transmit one character?

3. What is the main difference between a UART and a USART?

4. Define the term modem and explain why a modem is required to send digital data over standard switched phone lines.

5. Describe the functions of the $\overline{DSR}$, $\overline{DTR}$, $\overline{RTS}$, $\overline{CTS}$, TxD, and RxD signals exchanged between a terminal and a modem.

6. What frequency transmit clock (TxC) is required by an 8251A in order for it to transmit data at 4800 Bd with a baud rate factor of 16.

7. *a.* Show the bit pattern for the mode word and the command word that must be sent to an 8251A to initialize the device as follows: baud rate factor of 64, 7 bits/character, even parity, 1 stop bit, transmit interrupt enabled, receive interrupt enabled, $\overline{DTR}$ and $\overline{RTS}$ asserted, error flags reset, no hunt mode, no break character.
   b. Show the sequence of instructions required to initialize an 8251A at addresses 80H and 81H with the mode and command words you worked out in part *a*.
   c. Show the sequence of instructions that can be used to poll this 8251A to determine when the receiver buffer has a character ready to be read.
   d. How can you determine whether a character received by an 8251A contains a parity error?
   e. What frequency transmit and receive clock will this 8251A require in order to send data at 2400 Bd?
   f. What other way besides polling does the 8251A provide for determining when a character can be sent to the device for transmission? Describe the additional hardware connections required for this method.

8. Draw a flowchart showing how asynchronous serial data can be sent from a port line using a software routine.

9. Give the signal voltage ranges for a logic high and for a logic low in the RS-232C standard.

10. Describe the problem that occurs when you attempt to connect together two RS-232C devices that are both configured as DTE. Draw a diagram which shows how this problem can be solved.

11. Why are the two ground pins on an RS-232C connector not just jumpered together?

12. What symptom will you observe if the wire connected to pin 5 of an RS-232C terminal is broken?

13. Explain why systems which use the RS-422A or RS-423A signal standards can transmit data over longer distances and at higher baud rates than RS-232C systems.

14. Describe the function of the hybrid coil in Figure 13-12.

15. Describe the operation of a codec. Why are codecs designed with nonlinear response?

16. How does an FSK modem represent digital 1's and 0's in the signal it sends out on a phone line? How does an FSK modem perform full-duplex communication over standard phone lines?

17. Draw a waveform to show the signal that a simple phase-shift keying (PSK) modem will send out to represent the binary data 011010100.

18. *a.* Draw a diagram which shows the construction of a fiber-optic cable, and label each part.
    b. Identify two types of devices which are used to produce the light beam for a fiber-optic cable and two devices which are commonly used to detect the light at the receiving end of the fiber.
    c. Why should you never look into the end of a fiber optic cable to see if light is getting through?
    d. Describe the difference between a multimode fiber and a single-mode fiber. Give a major advantage and a major disadvantage of each type.
    e. What are the major advantages of fiber-optic cables over metallic conductors?

19. Using IBM PC BIOS and DOS calls, write an assembly language program which reads characters from the keyboard and puts them in a buffer until a carriage return is entered. The characters should be displayed on the CRT as entered. When a carriage return is entered, the contents of the buffer should be sent out the COM1 serial port.

20. The SDK-86 will only accept uppercase letters as commands. The SDK-86 download program in Figure 13-24 would be friendlier if you did not have to remember to press the caps lock key on the IBM. Write an assembly language routine that will convert a letter entered in lowercase to uppercase without affecting entered uppercase letters or numbers. Show where you would insert this section of code in the program in Figure 13-24.

21. Describe the operation of a circular buffer. Include in your answer the function of the tail pointer, the head pointer, and how the buffer-full and buffer-empty conditions are detected.

22. Why is it necessary to disable the UART interrupt input of the 8259A during part of the CHK_N_DISPLAY procedure in Figure 13-24?

23. Why, when changing a bit in a control word or interrupt mask word, should you not alter the other bits in the word? Show the assembly language instructions you would use to unmask IR5 of an 8259A at base address 80H without changing the interrupt status of any other bits.

24. Describe the major difference between the way that an interpreter translates a high level language program and the way that a compiler does the translation. Give a major advantage and a major disadvantage of each approach.

25. Show how the CALL statement in Figure 13-28*a* would be modified to pass two additional parame-

ters, A2 and B3, to the assembly language procedure. Show the assembly language instructions that you would add to the procedure to bring the actual value of A2 into the CX register. Assume the order of the passed parameters is Q$, A2, B3. Describe the function of the string descriptor table during a procedure call.

26. Why is synchronous serial data communication much more efficient than asynchronous communication?

27. If an 8251A is being used in synchronous mode for a BISYNC data link, what additional initialization word(s) must be sent to the device. How does the 8251A detect the start of a message? How does the 8251A indicate that is has found the start of a message? How does the receiving station in a BISYNC link indicate that it found an error in the received data?

28. How is the start of a message frame indicated in a bit-oriented protocol such as HDLC? How does an HDLC system prevent the flag bit pattern from appearing in the data part of the message? How does the receiver in an HDLC system tell the transmitter that an error was found in a transmitted frame?

29. Draw simple diagrams which show the five common network topologies. For each topology identify one commercially available system which uses it.

30. What is the difference between a baseband network and a broadband network?

31. List the seven layers of the ISO open systems model. Which of these layers is responsible for assembling messages into frames or packets? Which layer is responsible for making sure the message was transmitted and received correctly?

32. *a.* Describe the topology, physical connections, and signal type used in Ethernet.
    b. Describe the method used by a unit on an Ethernet to gain access to the network for transmitting a message.
    c. What response will a transmitting station make if it finds that another station starts transmitting after it starts? What is the term used to refer to this condition?

33. Describe the method used by a unit on a token-passing ring to take control of the network for transmitting a message frame. What is the advantage of this scheme over the method used in Ethernet?

34. How can a token ring network recover if the token is lost while being passed around the ring?

35. *a.* For what purpose was the GPIB designed?
    b. Give the names for the three types of devices which the GPIB defines.
    c. List and briefly describe the function of the three signal groups of the GPIB.
    d. Describe the sequence of handshake signals that take place when a talker on a GPIB transfers data to several listeners. How does this handshake scheme make it possible for talkers and listeners with very different data rates to operate correctly on the bus?

CHAPTER

14 Operating Systems, the 80286 Microprocessor, and the Future

As we told you in an earlier chapter, a general-purpose operating system in its simplest form is a program which allows a user to create, print, copy, delete, display, and in other ways work with files. It also allows a user to load and execute other programs. The operating system insulates the user from needing to know the intricate hardware details of the system in order to use it. Up to this point in the book we have only referred to single-user operating systems such as the IBM PC DOS. To round out the book we now want to give you an overview of multiuser/multitasking operating systems, and an introduction to the 80286 microprocessor. The 80286 (used in the IBM PC/AT and its clones) has advanced features which make it suitable as the CPU in a multitasking system. Finally, in this chapter we discuss a few directions in which microcomputer evolution seems to be heading.

OBJECTIVES

At the conclusion of this chapter you should be able to:

1. Describe the difference between time-slice scheduling and preemptive priority-based scheduling.
2. Define the terms blocked, task queue, deadlock, deadly embrace, critical region, semaphore, kernel, memory management unit, and virtual memory.
3. Describe two methods that can be used to protect a critical region of code.
4. Show with assembly language instructions how a semaphore can be used to accomplish mutual exclusion.
5. Describe the major features of the UNIX operating system and define the terms kernel, pipe, and shell.
6. List and describe the types of "objects" used in the RMX 86 operating system.
7. List and describe the states that an RMX task can be in.
8. Describe the mechanism used to schedule tasks in RMX 86.
9. List some of the differences between UNIX and RMX 86.
10. Draw a block diagram of the internal structure of the 80286.
11. List the major hardware and software features that the 80286 microprocessor has beyond those of the 8086.
12. Show how the 80286 constructs physical addresses in its real address mode and in its protected virtual address mode.
13. Describe how the 80286 uses descriptor tables and call gates to control memory access.
14. Define the term "demand-paged virtual memory" and describe briefly how the 80386 produces a physical address in paged mode.

OPERATING SYSTEM CONCEPTS AND TERMS

Multiuser/Multitasking Operating System Overview

Newer 16-bit and 32-bit microprocessors are designed to be used as the CPU in multiuser/multitasking microcomputer systems. Therefore, to understand how these processors operate, you need to understand some of the terms and concepts of operating systems.

In Chapter 2 we discussed how several terminals can be connected to a single CPU and operated on a time-share basis. An operating system which coordinates the actions of a time-share system such as this is referred to as a *multiuser* operating system. The basic principle of a time-share system is that the CPU services one terminal for a few milliseconds, then services the next for a few milliseconds, and so on until all of the terminals have had a turn. It cycles through all of the terminals over and over, fast enough that each user seems to have the complete attention of the CPU. The program or section of a program which services each user is referred to as a *task* or *process*. A multiuser operating system then, can also be referred to as *multitasking*, but this term is more often used when referring to real-time industrial-control operating systems. With the addition of a user interface, the factory controller program in Figure 10-35 would be an example of a very simple real-time multitasking operating system.

The multiple tasks that are to be executed by a CPU must in some way be scheduled so that they execute properly. This part of the operating system is called the *scheduler, dispatcher*, or *supervisor*. There are several different methods of scheduling tasks, but we are mainly interested in two of them.

The first method is the *time-slice* method which we discussed previously. In this approach the CPU executes one task for perhaps 20 ms, then switches to the next task. After all tasks have had their turn, execution returns to the first. The UNIX operating system, which we discuss in detail later, uses this scheduling approach for a multiple-user system. The advantage of the time-slice approach in a multiuser system is that all users are serviced at approximately equal time intervals. As more users are added, however, each user gets serviced less often, so each user's program takes longer to execute. This is referred to as *system degradation*. In industrial-control operating systems this variable time between services is often not acceptable, so a different scheduling method is used.

The second scheduling method we are interested in is *preemptive priority-based scheduling*. In this approach an executing low priority task can be interrupted by a higher priority task. When the high priority task finishes executing, execution returns to the low priority task. This approach is well suited to some control applications because it allows the most important tasks to be done first. Priority interrupt controllers such as the 8259A are often used to set up and manage the task service requests. The Intel RMX 86 operating system, which we discuss later, uses priority-based scheduling.

In addition to scheduling, multitasking operating systems have several other considerations which have to be taken into account. The next section discusses some of these.

Problems Encountered in Building Multitasking Operating Systems

There are a great many operating system variations, and many different ways of solving various problems in an operating system. What we have tried to do in this section is use simple enough examples to illustrate the basic problems without getting lost in all of the possible variations.

PRESERVING THE ENVIRONMENT

The first problem to be solved in a multitasking system is to preserve the registers, data, and return address (environment) of each task when execution is switched to another task. This is necessary so that the task can be restarted correctly. The usual way of preserving the environment is to keep it on a stack. Often the operating system keeps a separate stack for each task. Current processors such as the 80186 and 80286 have the ENTER and LEAVE instructions to make it easy to save and restore the environment. Any procedures used in a multitasking system have to be reentrant.

ACCESSING RESOURCES

The second problem encountered in a multitasking system is assuring that tasks have orderly access to resources such as printers, disk drives, etc. As one example of this, suppose that a user at a terminal needs to read a file from a hard disk and print it on the system printer. Obviously the file cannot be read in from the disk and printed in one of the 20-ms time slices allotted to the terminal service, so several provisions must be made to gain access to the resources and hang on to them long enough to get the job done properly. A flag or *semaphore* in memory is used to indicate whether the disk drive is in use by another task or not. Likewise, another semaphore is used to indicate whether the printer is in use. If a task cannot access a resource because it is busy, the task is said to be *blocked*. Now, rather than making the user type in a print command over and over until the disk drive and the printer are available, most operating systems of this type set up queues of tasks waiting for each resource. When one task finishes with a resource, it resets the semaphore for that resource. The next task in the queue can then set the semaphore, to indicate the resource is busy, and use the resource.

In order to keep track of the state of a task, a block of data called a *process control block, process header*, or *process descriptor* is set up by the operating system for each task. Part of the information contained in the process control block is the progress of the read disk and print job. To simplify the disk and printer queues, all that needs to be put in these queues are pointers to the process control blocks of tasks that are waiting for access. This is similar to the way a pointer to a string descriptor table is passed to a procedure, rather than passing the string itself, as shown in Figure 13-29. Incidentally, most systems use a separate I/O processor to actually handle disks, printers, and other slow resources, so that these do not load down the main processor.

Another problem situation in a multitasking system can occur when two tasks need the same two resources, for example, a disk drive and a printer. Suppose that one task gains access to the disk drive and sets its semaphore to indicate that the disk drive is busy at the end of its time slice. The next task finds the disk busy, so its request goes on the queue. However, suppose that the second task finds the printer not busy, so it sets the printer semaphore to indicate it has control of the printer, and goes on about its business. When execution returns to the first task, it will try to access the printer so it has both the disk drive and the printer it needs. However, it finds the printer busy, so its request is put on the printer queue. The situation here is that each task controls a resource that the other needs in order to proceed. Therefore, neither can proceed. This condition is called *deadlock* or *deadly embrace*. The problem can be solved in a number of ways. One way is to link the printer and the disk drive together under one semaphore so that the two resources are accessed with a single action. Another more practical approach is to set up a hierarchy among the tasks, so that if deadlock occurs, the higher priority task can gain access to all of the resources it needs.

Still another interesting problem can occur in a multitasking operating system when two or more users attempt to read and change the contents of some memory locations at the same time. As an example, suppose that an airline ticket reservation system is operating on a time-slice basis. Now, further suppose that one user examines the memory location which represents a seat on a plane and finds the seat empty, just before the end of its time slice. Another user on the system can then, in its time slice, examine the same memory location, find it empty, mark it full, and print out a reservation confirmation on the CRT. When execution returns to the first user, it has already checked the seat during its previous time slice, so it marks the seat full, and prints out a reservation confirmation on the CRT. The two people assigned to the same seat may make nasty remarks about computers unless this problem is solved.

The section of a program where the value of a variable is being examined and changed must be protected from access by other tasks until the operation is complete. The section of code which must be protected is called a *critical region*. A technique called *mutual exclusion* is used to prevent two tasks from accessing a critical region at the same time. In the CHK_N_DISPLAY procedure in Figure 13-24 we showed one way in which a critical region can be protected from an interrupt procedure by simply masking the interrupt. In a time-slice system, however, a semaphore is used to provide mutual exclusion.

Figure 14-1 shows how this can be done with 8086 assembly language instructions. The instruction sequence is the same for each task. If task 1 needs to enter a critical section of code, it first loads the semaphore value for critical-region-busy into AL. The single instruction, XCHG AL, SEMAPHORE, then swaps the byte in AL with the byte in the memory location named SEMAPHORE. It is important to do this in one instruction so that the time-slice mechanism cannot switch to another task halfway through the exchange and cause our airline problem.

After the semaphore is read in Figure 14-1, it is compared with the busy value. If the critical region is busy, execution will remain in a wait loop for as many time slices as are required for the critical region to become free. If the semaphore value is a 0, indicating not busy, then execution enters the critical region. The XCHG instruction has already set the semaphore to indicate the critical region is busy. After execution of the critical region finishes, the MOV SEMAPHORE,00 instruction resets the semaphore to indicate that the critical region is

```
;Instructions for accessing critical region of code protected by
; semaphore - User 1

       MOV   AL, 01           ; Load semaphore value for region busy
HOLD:  XCHG  AL, SEMAPHORE    ; Swap and set semaphore
       CMP   AL, 01           ; Check if region busy
       JE    HOLD             ; Yes, loop until not busy
                              ; No, enter critical region of code
;Instructions which access critical region inserted here.
       MOV   SEMAPHORE, 00    ; Reset semaphore to make critical
                              ;  region available to other users.
```

```
;Instructions for accessing critical region of code protected by
; semaphore - User 2

       MOV   AL, 01           ; Load semaphore value for region busy
HOLD:  XCHG  AL, SEMAPHORE    ; swap and set semaphore
       CMP   AL, 01           ; Check if region busy
       JE    HOLD             ; Yes, loop until not busy
                              ; No, enter critical region of code
;Instructions which access critical region inserted here.
       MOV   SEMAPHORE, 00    ; Reset semaphore to make critical
                              ;  region available to other users.
```

FIGURE 14-1 8086 assembly language instruction sequences showing how a semaphore can be used to provide mutual exclusion for a critical region.

no longer busy. Task 2 can then swap the semaphore and access the critical region when needed. The semaphore functions in the same way as the "occupied" sign on a restroom of a plane or train. If you mentally try interrupting each sequence of instructions at different points, you should see that there is no condition where both tasks can get into the critical region at the same time.

In an Intel multibus system a problem could still result if the semaphore were located on a different board from the CPU. The XCHG instruction takes 2 bus cycles, so a task on another master could take over the bus and access the semaphore between the 2 bus cycles. This problem is solved by putting the LOCK prefix in front of the XCHG instruction. The LOCK prefix causes the 8086 to assert a hardware signal which can be used to maintain control of the bus as we described in Chapter 11. In the next section we look at some other ways that an operating system must protect various data and code areas that it uses.

The Need for Protection

Most single-user operating systems do little to prevent user programs from "tromping on" the code or data areas of the operating system. The usual results of this and Murphy's law are that an incorrect address in a user program will cause it to write over critical sections of the operating system. The system then "locks up," and the only way to get control again is to reboot the system. In a multitasking system this is intolerable, so several methods are used to protect the operating system.

The major method is to construct the operating system in two or more *layers*. Figure 14-2*a* shows an "onionskin" diagram for a two-layer operating system. The basic principle here is that the inner circle represents the code and data areas used by the operating system. The outer layer represents the code and data areas of user programs or tasks that are being run under control of the operating system. The inner layer is protected because user programs can only access operating system resources through very specific mechanisms rather than a simple, accidental call or jump. The Motorola MC68000 family of microprocessors is designed to accommodate a two-level structure such as this. The MC68000 has two modes of operation, user and supervisory. Certain privileged instructions which affect the operating system can only be executed when the processor is in supervisory mode.

The AT&T UNIX™ operating system, which we discuss in the next major section of the chapter, is an example of a three-layer operating system. Figure 14-2*b* shows the three layers for UNIX. The innermost layer, or *kernel*, contains the major operating system functions such as the scheduler. The middle layer or *shell* contains the command line interpreter, which translates user-entered commands to a sequence of kernel operations. The shell level is the user-interface level. The outer layer contains application programs such as data base management programs. It also contains utilities such as editors, compilers, etc. which programmers can use to write more application programs.

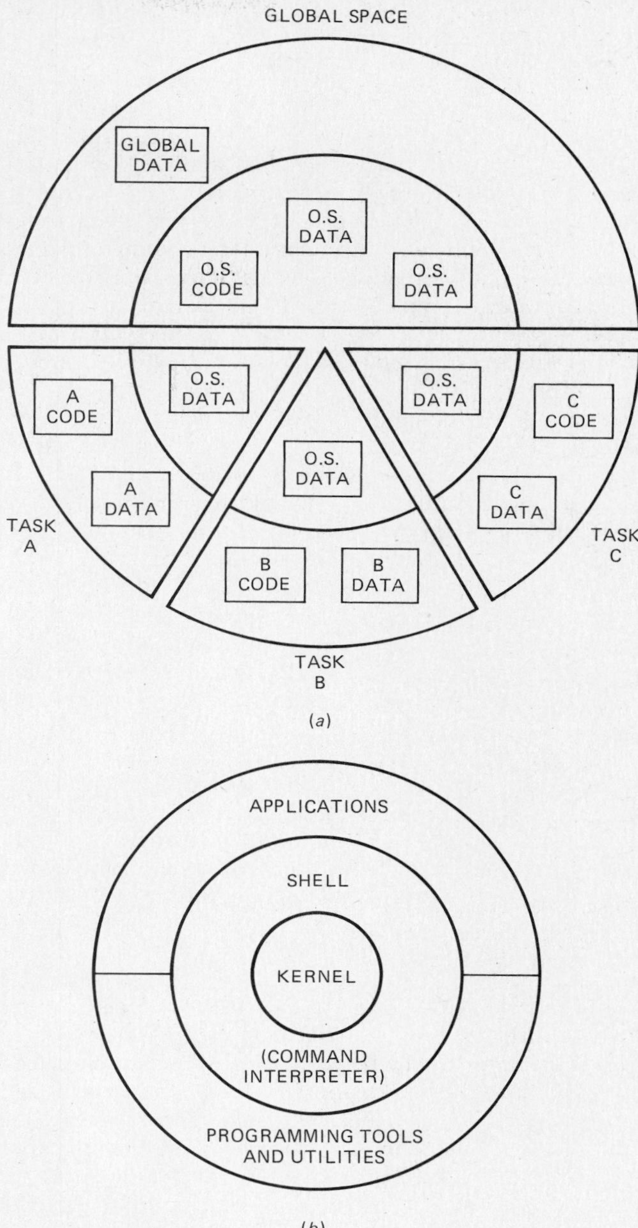

FIGURE 14-2 "Onionskin" diagrams for multitasking operating systems. *(a)* Operating system with two levels of protection. *(b)* Operating system with three levels, e.g., UNIX.

Other systems use even more levels of protection. The Intel 80286 processor has designed into its hardware a mechanism which allows up to four levels of protection to be built into an operating system running on it.

In addition to protecting itself from being tromped on by executing tasks, an operating system should provide some way of protecting tasks from each other. Throughout the rest of this chapter we will be showing you how protection layers are actually implemented, and how tasks can be protected from each other. To start this, we need to introduce you to the concepts of memory management.

Memory Management

There are two major reasons why memory must be specifically managed in a multitasking operating system. The first reason is that the physical memory is usually not large enough to hold all of the operating system and all of the application programs that are being executed by the multiple users. The second reason is to make sure that executing tasks do not access protected areas of memory. Memory management can be done totally by the operating system or with the aid of hardware called a *memory management unit* or MMU. Before we get into the operation of an MMU, we want to give you a little background on methods used to solve the limited memory problem.

A common problem, especially in older, single-user systems, is that the physical memory is not large enough to hold, for example, an assembler and the program being assembled. The traditional solution to this problem is to write the assembler in modules, and use an *overlay* scheme. When the assembler is invoked, the executive module of the assembler is loaded into memory, and reserves an additional memory space called the *overlay area*. The assembler then reads through the source program. When it reaches a point where it needs a particular module, it reads that module, referred to as an *overlay*, from the disk into the overlay area reserved in memory. When the assembler reaches a point where it needs another overlay, it reads the overlay from the disk, and loads it into the same overlay area in memory. The overlay approach is commonly used and works well for specific cases such as the assembler example we used here, but it is not flexible enough for multitasking systems.

Another approach traditionally used to expand the available memory in a microcomputer is *bank switching*. A system which has only 16 address lines can directly address only 64 Kbytes of memory. As shown in Figure 14-3, however, the addition of some simple selection hardware allows the system to access up to eight memory "banks" of 64 Kbytes each. The hardware is configured so that when the power is turned on, the system is using bank 0. To switch to bank 1, a byte which turns off bank 0 and turns on bank 1 is output to the selection port. Execution then proceeds in bank 1. In practice, some system-dependent tricks are often necessary to get execution smoothly from one bank to another, but the approach does help overcome the memory limits designed into the processor.

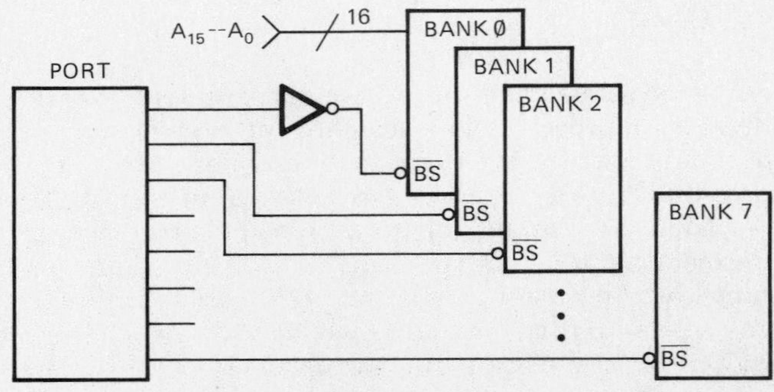

FIGURE 14-3 Block diagram showing how microcomputer memory can be expanded with bank switching.

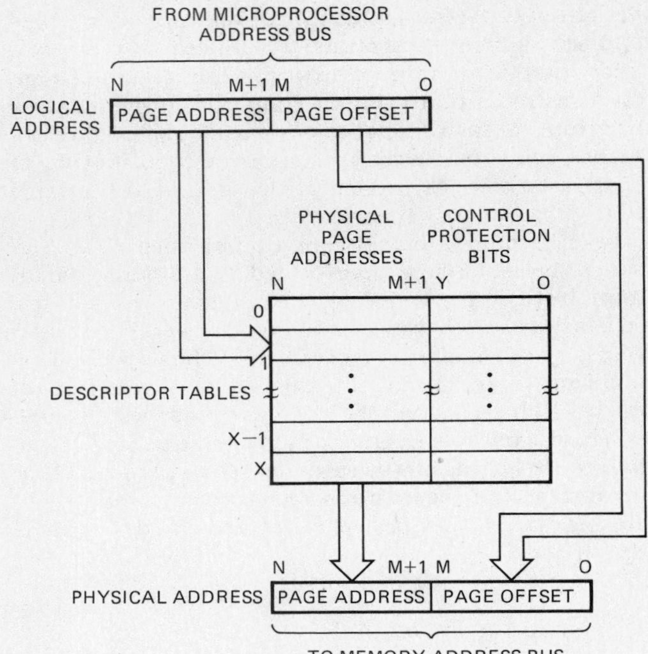

FIGURE 14-4 Block diagram showing operation of a memory management unit.

To use bank switching in a multiuser system, each user's program might be assigned to a bank. The difficulty with this is that a copy of the operating system kernel must be kept in each bank, the actual memory available for each user is still limited to 64 Kbytes, and users cannot easily share code or data. Thus memory is not very efficiently used. Also, protection is not as easily implemented as it is in the MMU approaches we discuss next.

MMUs

To reduce the burden of memory management on the operating system, most microprocessor manufacturers now have hardware memory management devices available. The device may be built into the processor as it is in the 80286, or be available separately. In either case the MMU is functionally positioned between the processor and the actual memory as shown in Figure 14-4. The major function of the MMU is to translate logical program addresses to physical memory addresses. We will explain how it does this, but first let's clarify what is meant, in this case, by logical address and physical address.

When you write an assembly language program, you usually refer to addresses by name. The addresses you work with in a program are called *logical addresses*, because they indicate the logical positions of code and data. An example of this is the 8086 instruction, JNZ NEXT. The label NEXT represents a logical address that execution will go to if the zero flag is not set. When an

8086 program is assembled, each logical address is represented with a 16-bit offset and a 16-bit segment base. The 8086 BIU then produces the actual physical memory address by simply adding these two parts together as explained many times previously.

When a program is assembled or compiled to run on a system with an MMU, each logical address is also represented by two components, but the components function differently. In a segment-oriented system the upper component is referred to as a *segment selector*, and the lower component is referred to as the *offset*. In a page-oriented system the upper component is referred to as the *page address*, and the lower component is referred to as the *page offset*.

In the segment case the MMU uses the upper component, a segment selector for example, to access a *descriptor* in a table of descriptors in memory, rather than just adding it to the offset in the lower component. A descriptor is a series of memory locations that contains the physical base address for a segment, the privilege level of the segment, and some control bits. As an example, let's assume the selector has 14 address bits and 2 privilege-level bits. The 14 address bits in the selector can select any one of 16,384 descriptors in the descriptor table. If the offset component of the logical address has 16 bits, then each segment can contain 64 Kbytes. Since each descriptor points to a segment, the logical address space for our example system here is 65,536 bytes/segment × 16,384 segments, or about 1 gigabyte. What this means is that the operating system can function as if a gigabyte of memory were available. Now let's see how this relates to the actual semiconductor memory.

Physically the MMU may have perhaps 24 address lines so it can only address 16 Mbytes of physical memory. The question that may immediately come to mind here is, "How can the operating system function as if there were a gigabyte of memory, when the maximum physical memory that the system can have is 16 Mbytes?" The answer to this question is that the physical memory, whatever its actual size, is simply a holding place for the segments currently being used by the operating system or user programs.

When the MMU receives a logical address from the CPU, it checks to see if that segment is currently in the physical memory. If the segment is present in physical memory, the MMU adds the offset component of the address to the segment base component of the address from the segment descriptor to form the physical address. It then outputs the physical address to memory on the memory address bus. If the MMU finds that the segment specified by the logical address is not in memory, it sends an interrupt signal to the CPU. In response to the interrupt, the CPU reads the desired code or data segment from a disk or other secondary storage, and loads it into the physical memory. The MMU then computes and outputs the physical address as described above. The operation is semiautomatic, so other than a slight delay, the operating system or other program is not aware that the segment had to be loaded. The gigabyte of logical address space that is available to programs is called *virtual memory* and the logical address in this type of system is usually called the *virtual address*. The term virtual refers to something that appears to be present but actually isn't.

When the CPU or smart MMU wants to load a segment from secondary storage into physical memory, it must first make space for it in the physical memory. Depending on the system, it may do this by compacting the segments already present and changing the descriptors to point to the new physical locations, or by swapping the segment being brought in with one currently in physical memory. To help in deciding which segment to swap back to memory, most systems use some bits in the descriptor to keep track of how many times the sector has been used. A low-use segment is the most likely candidate to swap back to memory. Most systems also have a *dirty bit* in each descriptor. This bit will be set if the contents of a segment have been changed. If the dirty bit is set, a segment must be swapped back to secondary storage if its space is needed. If the dirty bit is not set, then the segment has not been altered. The copy of the segment in secondary storage is still correct, so the segment can just be overwritten. This eliminates one write-to-disk operation.

Another term often found in MMU data sheets is the term *hit rate*. Hit rate refers to the percentage of the time that the segment required at a particular time is present in the physical memory. In a well-structured system the hit rate may be 85–90 percent.

The use of a descriptor table to translate logical addresses to physical addresses has another major advantage besides making virtual memory possible. The selector component of each address contains 1 or 2 bits which represent the privilege level of the program section requesting access to a segment. The descriptor for each segment also contains 1 or 2 bits which represent the privilege level of that segment. When an executing program attempts to access a segment, the MMU can compare the privilege level in the selector with the privilege level in the descriptor. If the selector has the same or greater privilege, then the MMU allows the access. If the selector privilege is lower, the MMU can send an interrupt signal to the CPU indicating a privilege-level violation. The indirect method of producing physical addresses then gives a method of providing privilege levels and protecting program sections such as the operating system kernel.

In most segment-oriented systems the segments swapped in and out of physical memory are quite large. The disadvantages of these large segments are the time required to load them and the compaction that often must be done to make space for a segment in physical memory. The method described next helps solve this problem.

The second major memory management approach currently used is called *demand-paged virtual memory*. In this approach the virtual memory is mapped as fixed-length pages of perhaps 4 Kbytes in length. The two components of the virtual address are called the page address and the page offset. The page offset, as the name implies, contains the offset of a desired byte within a page. The page address is used as a pointer to a descriptor table just as the selector is in the segmentation approach. The descriptors function in about the same way here that they do in the segmentation scheme. When a demanded page is found to be not present in the physical memory, the MMU or the CPU swaps it in. The typically smaller and fixed length of the pages makes the swapping operation much easier.

Before we summarize and go on to the next topic, we need to explain one more term commonly used with MMUs. For some MMUs the descriptor table is stored in a part of the main physical memory. Other MMUs have a built-in, high-speed memory called a *cache* (pronounced "cash"). The descriptors for the currently used segments or pages are kept in the cache memory so that they can be accessed much more quickly than they could if they were in the main memory. The descriptors for pages not currently being used are kept in a table in main memory. If the descriptor for a required page is not present in the cache, then it is read in from the descriptor table in main memory. The descriptor is then used to read in the required page.

To summarize then, MMUs translate logical program addresses to physical addresses with an indirect method through a descriptor table. This indirect approach makes possible a virtual address space much larger than the physical address space. The indirect approach also makes it possible to protect a memory segment or page from access by a program section with a lower privilege level. You will meet all of these concepts again in a later section which describes the operation of the 80286 microprocessor. First, however, we want to give you overviews of UNIX, a common multiuser operating system, and RMX 86, a common real-time multitasking operating system.

THE UNIX OPERATING SYSTEM

The purpose of this section is to show you the structure, terminology, and overall operation of the UNIX operating system, so you can see how it relates to multiuser microcomputer systems. If you are going to be working with UNIX, there are available several books which show with step-by-step examples how to use it.

History

In 1969 Ken Thompson, a researcher at Bell Laboratories, decided to write some system programs that would make it easier to develop other programs. Over the next few years, with the help of another researcher, Dennis Richie, these programs evolved into a powerful multiuser operating system. The original versions were written in assembly language for a DEC PDP-7 minicomputer, but when the value of the operating system became obvious, there was a strong desire to write versions for other machines. Adapting an assembly language program to run on another machine with a different CPU means rewriting the whole thing. To help solve this portability problem, Dennis Richie developed a high level language called C. This language has much of the capability of assembly language to work with hardware and twiddle bits, but it also allows a programmer to write high level language structured programs. Adapting a high level language program to run on a different machine involves rewriting the I/O sections as needed by the hardware of the new machine, and compiling the high level language program to the machine code for the new machine. By 1972 a version of UNIX written in C was operating successfully on the DEC PDP-11 computer.

In the following years Western Electric, a parent company of Bell Laboratories, licensed the source code of UNIX to several universities where it underwent further evolution. A commonly available enhanced version was developed at the University of California at Berkeley. The evolution also continued at Bell Labs. In 1979 version 7 was released, and later versions III and V were released by Western Electric.

Unfortunately, the basic structure of UNIX is easy to understand and alter. Therefore, each group using UNIX tended to extend and modify it to fit its specific needs or prejudices. Furthermore, due to licensing difficulties with Western Electric, commercial companies developing UNIX-like operating systems developed their own proprietary versions. The result of all of this is that there are many different versions of UNIX-type operating systems in use. Hopefully, the current efforts to work out a standard will be successful.

UNIX Operating System Structure

As shown in Figure 14-2*b*, the UNIX operating system consists of three layers. The innermost, most privileged layer, or kernel, contains a process scheduler, a hierarchal file structure, and mechanisms for processes to communicate with each other. The middle layer of the operating system, called the shell, is the layer that a user interfaces with. This layer contains the command interpreter which decodes and carries out user-entered commands. The outermost layer contains programming tools such as editors, assemblers, compilers, debuggers, etc., and application programs such as an accounting package. Let's take a closer look at how each of these layers function, and how they operate together.

OPERATIONS OF THE KERNEL

The UNIX operating system was designed to allow several users to share a CPU on a time-slice basis. Each user program is referred to as a *process*. One of the major functions of the kernel is to schedule and service the needs of processes. To do this the kernel keeps two tables in memory.

One of these, the *process table*, contains information about the state of each process. Among other things the entry in the process table contains the location of the process in memory, the length of the process, the identification number of the process, the identification of the user, and whether the process is active or blocked.

The second type of table maintained by the kernel is called a *user table*, or a *per-process segment*. The user table contains pointers to the data, files, and directories currently being used by the process.

When a user or process is added to the system, the kernel creates a process table entry and a user table for that process. The length of the process table is fixed for each system, so only this number of processes can be present in the system at one time. A process can create a subprocess, called a *child process*. When a child process is created, an entry is made in the process table for it, and a user table created for it. When any process is removed from the system, its process table entry and user table are removed to make room for another process.

At any given instant in time, only one process can actually be running since there is only one CPU to run processes on. All of the other processes are *suspended*. Processes essentially compete with each other for service. The scheduler in the kernel determines which process is to be run at a given time. The scheduling mechanism works as follows.

An external clock signal interrupts the CPU 50 or 60 times a second to produce the basic time slices. The interrupt procedure which services this clock interrupt checks the process table entries for each process to determine which process should be run next. The decision as to which process to run is based on several factors. The first factor is whether the process is ready to run or blocked. A process may be blocked or *put to sleep* if it has to wait for: an input or output operation to complete, a child process to complete, a signal from some other process, an external interrupt signal, or some fixed amount of time before continuing. A sleeping process will not be given a turn until the waited-for event occurs and the process is marked as active (ready to run).

A second factor used to determine which active process should be serviced next is how recently each process has been serviced. An active process which has recently had a turn will have a lower priority than an active process which has not recently had a turn because it just became unblocked or was just *swapped in* from disk. Because there is usually not room enough in memory to store all of the suspended processes, some of them are *swapped out* to secondary storage such as a disk. The scheduler decides which processes to swap so that all processes get serviced as needed.

A second major function of the UNIX kernel is to maintain the system file structure. Unix uses a hierarchical file structure as shown in Figure 14-5. This structure is sometimes called a tree structure because it looks like an inverted tree. The highest level in the hierarchy is the root directory. This directory contains the names of system files and the names of subdirectories. A directory in UNIX is simply a file which contains the name of the directory above it in the hierarchy, and names of files or directories below it in the hierarchy. The directory above a file or directory is often referred to as the *parent* directory.

A user logged on to the system is given a directory, under a directory labeled usr in Figure 14-5, under the parent directory. The user can then create subdirectories or files under this directory. To refer to other files or directories in the system, a user specifies the directory path to it. For example, a user whose directory is at point 2 in Figure 14-5 can refer to the file at point 8 as

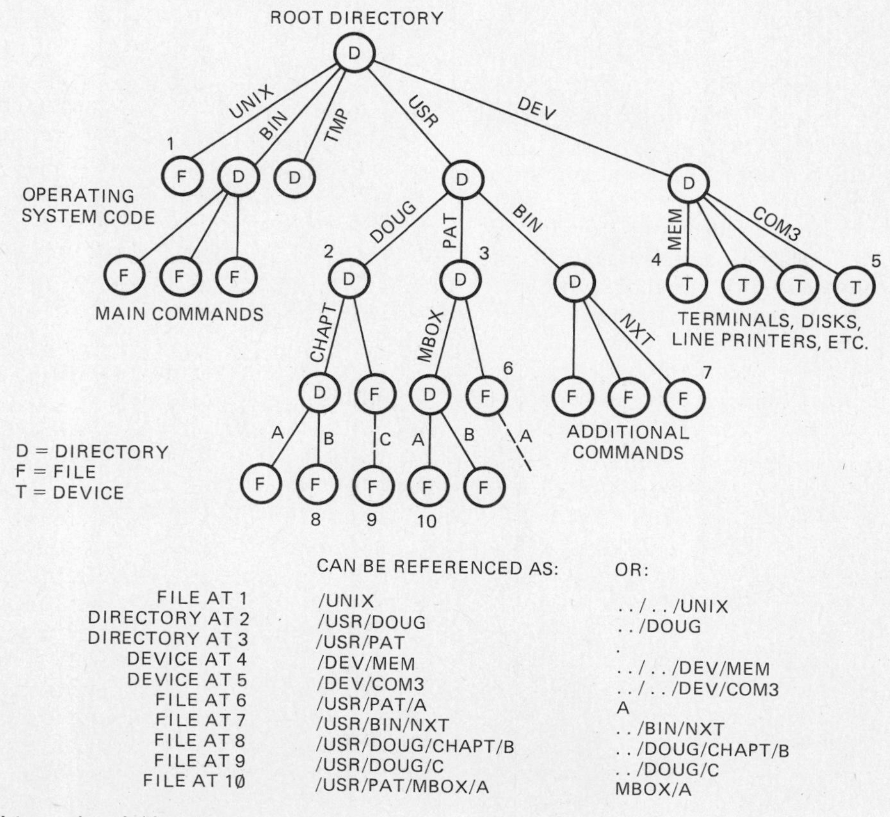

FIGURE 14-5 UNIX hierarchical file structure.

/usr/doug/chapt/b. The name of a parent directory is often represented simply by two periods, so ../doug/chap/b can also be used to refer to the file at point 8 in, for example, a copy command. Figure 14-5 shows some other examples of how files, directories, and input/output devices are referred to in this type file structure.

In addition to names, the directory entry for each file and subdirectory contains a 2-byte *inode* number. The inode number identifies the position of the inode for that file or directory in a table of inodes kept by the operating system kernel. An inode is similar to a file control block, which we discussed in chapter 12. It contains the type of the file, the length of the file, the location of the file, the identification number of the owner, and the times the file was created, modified, and last accessed. The kernel uses inodes to manipulate files, but normally a user only has to be concerned with the file names.

Still another function of the kernel is to provide a means of communication between processes. The two methods it provides are *signals* and *pipes*. Signals are software interrupts generated by one process to tell another process to stop what it is doing, respond to the signal, and then go on with what it was doing. Signals can also be generated by user commands such as an abort command, or by processing errors such as a divide by zero error.

A pipe is a mechanism for passing the output data from one program directly to another program as input. We will discuss how a pipe is used later. Now that you have an overview of some of the kernel functions, let's take a look at some of the shell functions.

THE UNIX SHELL

As we said before, the shell layer of UNIX is the level at which a user usually interacts with the system. The shell executes user commands and programs. It calls kernel procedures as needed to do this. The UNIX command shell has some interesting features that we want to acquaint you with.

The first feature of the shell to discuss is how it handles I/O. At the user level, UNIX essentially treats I/O devices as files in a directory called dev as shown in Figure 14-5. A modem connected to the system at point 5 in the system, for example, can be referred to simply as /dev/com3. Devices are opened, read from or written to, and closed just as other files are. When a process is created, it has three files already open for use. The three are referred to as *standard input*, *standard output*, and *error output*. Standard input usually means the keyboard on the user's terminal. Standard output and error output usually mean the CRT on the user's terminal.

What this means is that when a user enters a command, which requires input, the input will be taken from the keyboard unless otherwise specified. Likewise a command that produces output data will send it to the user's CRT unless some other destination is indicated. The UNIX command ls, for example, will send a simple list of the user's directory to the CRT on the user's terminal. However, input data or output data can be *redirected* to other devices or files. The < and the > symbols are used to indicate redirection. For a user at point 3 in Figure 14-5, the command ls /usr/doug > /dev/com3, for example, reads the directory of /usr/doug and sends it to the device named com3, instead of to the user's CRT. The command sort −d < /usr/pat > lpr will alphabetically sort the directory /user/pat and send the result to the line printer. Note that UNIX commands are entered in lowercase letters.

Another feature of the UNIX shell which we mentioned previously is the pipe command. The pipe command allows output data from one program to be passed directly as input data to another program. The unique feature of a pipe is the way that the data is passed between the two. In most other systems data is passed from one program to another through files. One program processes some data and puts the results in a file. When the first program is done, a second program may access the file, further process the data, and put its results in another file which can be accessed by another program or command. The command ls −l > myfile, for example, might be used to produce a long listing (including subdirectories etc.) of a user's directory and put it in a file called myfile. The command sort −d < myfile might then be used to sort the directory listing in the file in alphabetical order, and display the result on the user's CRT. The pipe command makes it possible to do both the list and the sort operations without the need for an intermediate file to pass the data between the two commands. The single command ls −l ¦ sort −d can be used to do this. The dashed vertical line ¦ in the middle of the command indicates that the two commands are to be piped together. When a UNIX user issues a command to pipe two programs together, the kernel makes a connection so that the output from the first program is fed directly to the second program *as it is produced*. The pipe feature is often used with programs called *filters*. A filter is a program which simply performs some operation on a stream of input data and outputs the results. Some common types of filters are programs that format data into columns, sort data in various ways, and translate from one file format to another. As another example of how this is used, suppose that a user on the system shown in Figure 14-5 at point 2 wants to sort a directory alphabetically and send the result to the line printer. The simple command sort −d < /usr/doug ¦ lpr will do this. The designated output for the lpr command is the line printer, so no redirection is needed.

Another useful feature of the UNIX command shell allows a user to execute two commands concurrently. As an example of how this capability might be used, suppose that a programmer wants to assemble and print the listing of one program module, while editing a second module. The terms *foreground* and *background* are often used to describe the way in which the two processes are executing. For our example here, the compiling and printing will be done in the background while editing is done in the foreground. A command followed by an & (ampersand) indicates that the command should be carried out in the background mode. The sort and print command from the previous paragraph, for example, can be run as a background process by simply entering the command sort −d < /usr/doug ¦ lpr &.

The kernel actually does the background command by

creating a new process for it. The initial user process is referred to as the parent process and the new process is referred to as the child process. The parent process may be put to sleep until the child process finishes, or the parent process and the child process can compete for time slices and execute concurrently as we described in the example above.

The UNIX shell also provides a simple way to execute a series of commands over and over again. The commands to be executed are simply written into a named file using the editor. The resulting file is called a *shell file*. The shell file can be executed with the single command sh followed by the name that was given to the shell file.

One final feature of the UNIX shell and kernel that we want to describe is *spooling*. Spooling is a mechanism that allows users to send files off to get printed without worrying about whether the printer is available at that particular moment. Incidentally, the term spool stands for *simultaneous peripheral operation on line*. Here's how it works. A user sends a file off to the spooler with the lpr command. The file to be printed and another short file containing information about the file are put in a dedicated directory called /usr/lpd. Writing a file in this directory causes a special printer program called the *printer demon* to start running and print the file. The printer demon program does this by stealing small amounts of time between other operations. If the printer is busy, then the print request is queued up behind other print requests and eventually gets printed. The main point here is that while all of this printing is going on, users can go on editing, compiling, or executing other programs. Now we will take a brief look at the programs and utilities that are included in the outermost UNIX layer.

The UNIX Utilities/Application Layer

Utilities are software tools used to develop, write, compile, debug, and document programs. Because UNIX has been around for so many years, there are a great many utilities available for it. Among these are several powerful editors, programs which format text for typesetting machines, compilers for many high level languages, and a host of debuggers. For just about any function that a programmer or writer might want, there is probably a UNIX utility which does it. There are also a large number of application programs which will run under UNIX. Application programs, in contrast to utilities, are self-contained or "canned" programs. Examples of application programs are accounting packages, data base management packages, and computer-aided engineering design packages.

Some of the advantages of UNIX are its portability to new systems, the shell features we described previously, and the large number of utilities available for it. However, UNIX has various shortcomings, some of which have been remedied in later versions and in newer UNIX-like operating systems. One problem is that a user can load down the system with multiple background programs, fill a disk with files, and even crash the system. Also, a full UNIX system requires 8–10 Mbytes of disk space, which makes it more difficult to implement on small systems such as personal computers. Another major problem is that the basic time-slice approach of UNIX, which works well for a time-share system, responds too slowly for many real-time control applications. For these applications, an operating system such as Intel's RMX 86, which we describe in the next section, is used.

THE INTEL RMX 86 OPERATING SYSTEM

The UNIX operating system, described in the preceding section, is designed to allow several users to develop programs or run application programs on a time-share basis. UNIX and similar operating systems are usually sold to users as complete packages which can simply be configured to the hardware of a particular system and run. The time-slice approach of UNIX works well for a multiuser time-share system, but it does not respond fast enough and does not have a suitable priority setup for many real-time control systems. Several companies offer operating systems more suitable to the needs of real-time control systems. One example is the Intel RMX 86 operating system.

RMX 86 is a "building block" operating system. It is primarily intended to assist OEMs (original equipment manufacturers) in building custom control systems to sell to end users. Therefore, RMX 86 consists of a group of highly structured functional modules and utilities from which a system designer can chose the required functions. The purpose of this section of the chapter is to introduce you to the structure, terminology, and scheduling used in this common operating system.

RMX 86 Structure

Figure 14-6 shows an onionskin diagram of the basic structure of RMX 86. At the center is the *nucleus*, which corresponds to the kernel in UNIX. The nucleus consists mostly of a few dozen procedures which system developers can call as needed to implement a desired end user application program. This is indicated in Figure 14-6 by the fact that the user application section of the diagram extends all the way to the nucleus. The nucleus is the only software module required in a system. All of the other modules shown in Figure 14-6 are optional.

The *basic input/output system* contains device drivers to interface the system to disk drives, UARTS, keyboards, multiple CRT terminals, parallel printers, and other devices. The *extended input/output system*, or *EIOS*, contains higher level I/O routines which include built-in buffering. The application loader allows user programs to be loaded from disk into memory to be run. The *human interface* part of the system corresponds roughly to the shell in a UNIX system. It decodes and carries out user-entered commands. The basic human interface comes with commands for working with disk files, but other commands can be added as needed for a particular application. The final piece of the puzzle

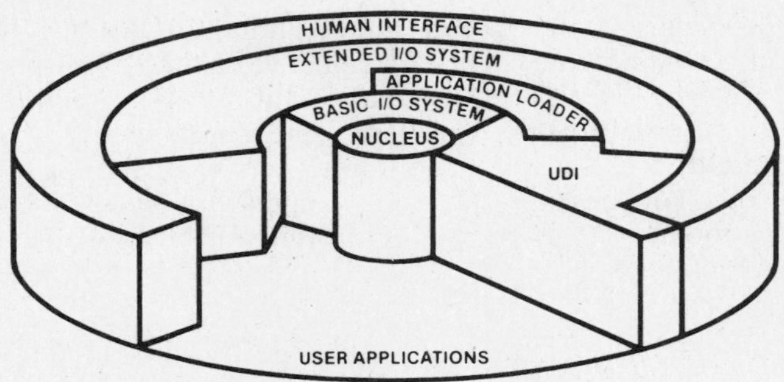

FIGURE 14-6 "Onionskin" diagram of Intel RMX 86 operating system.

shown in Figure 14-6 is the *universal development interface* or *UDI*. This software module, when added to the basic system, allows program development tools such as editors, assemblers, compilers, linkers, etc. to be loaded and run. Other software modules are also available. The point here is that software modules can be included, added to, or left out to produce a wide variety of custom operating systems. Now let's look a little closer to see how RMX 86 provides for multitasking.

RMX 86 Objects

The basic building blocks for RMX 86 programs are called *objects*. Objects are program structures which are created and manipulated by calls to procedures in the nucleus. The major object types are tasks, jobs, segments, mailboxes, regions, and semaphores. We will briefly describe each of these types, and then show how they are used.

Tasks in RMX 86 are equivalent to processes described previously. Tasks are the only active type of object. As a task executes, it manipulates the other types of objects by calling procedures in the nucleus. Tasks compete with each other for CPU time. Tasks are scheduled for execution on a preemptive, priority basis. We will talk about this more later, but basically what it means is that if several tasks are ready to run, the task which has been assigned the highest priority will be run first.

A *job* in RMX 86 is a logical environment in which tasks and other objects reside. A job usually corresponds to an application. The system initially has one job called the *root job* and a task that can be used to create other jobs. Tasks use system calls to create jobs. When a job is created, it is given a memory pool. From this memory pool tasks can create child jobs and other objects as needed. Figure 14-7 shows a simple diagram to illustrate this hierarchy.

A *segment* in RMX 86 is a contiguous block of memory, 16 to 64 Kbytes in size. When a task requests a segment, the requested memory is taken from the memory pool of the job which contains that task.

A *mailbox* is an object used to pass objects from one task to another. The object being passed through a mailbox is usually referred to as a message. What is actually passed through the mailbox is not the object itself, but a 16-bit *token* which represents the object. When each object is created, it is assigned a unique 16-bit number called a token. This approach is similar to the "file handle" approach used in some PC DOS function calls. Tasks can create mailboxes, delete mailboxes, send message tokens to mailboxes, and receive message tokens from mailboxes. A mailbox has two queues, one for tasks that are waiting to receive a message (object), and the other for objects that have not yet been received by their destination task. If a task attempts to receive a message, and there is no message in the mailbox, the task may be *put to sleep* for a while to wait for the message. This mechanism can be used to make one task wait at a mailbox until another task is finished before it starts.

A *region* in RMX 86 is one mechanism that can be used to prevent two or more tasks from accessing shared data at the same time. A task can create a region, delete a region, receive control, or send control of a region. If a task has received control of a region (has the token for it), no other task can access the region, until the task "sends control" of it (releases the token for it) back to the operating system. A region then is usually used to provide mutual exclusion for a collection of data shared by two tasks. To provide mutual exclusion for a single variable or protect a critical region of code, a simpler way is to use a semaphore.

A *semaphore* in its simplest case is simply a 1-bit flag used to indicate that a resource is busy. Figure 14-1 shows an example of how a simple semaphore can be set up to do this. In RMX 86 a semaphore is a *counter*. A task can create a semaphore, delete a semaphore, send units to the semaphore, and receive units from a semaphore. For a simple case such as that shown in Figure 14-1, a semaphore can be created and sent one unit. When a task wants to access the variable protected by the semaphore, it is made to receive one unit from the semaphore. If the variable is not busy, then the semaphore will contain one unit. The task can receive that unit and access the variable. If any other tasks that access that variable are made to receive one unit before accessing the variable, then once one task has received the unit, no other tasks can access it. This is because there is no unit in the semaphore for the other tasks to receive. When a task has finished with a shared variable

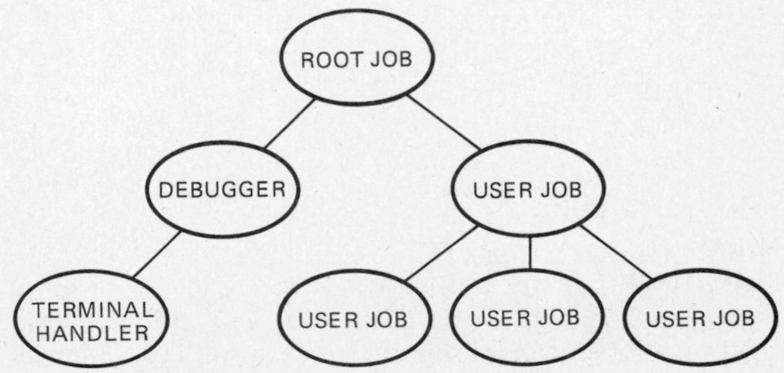

FIGURE 14-7 RMX 86 hierarchy of jobs.

or critical region, it sends one unit to the semaphore to release the variable so other tasks can access it. All of this is the same principle as the example in Figure 14-1 described with a different vocabulary. The fact that a semaphore can have values other than 0 or 1 allows it to be used to synchronize two tasks. For example, a task can be written to send one unit to a semaphore each time it executes. A second task can be made to wait at the semaphore until it is able to receive a specified number of units from the semaphore.

In addition to the defined object types, a programmer can create custom objects. Now that we have given you an overview of the types of objects that RMX 86 works with, we will describe how RMX 86 handles task execution.

RMX 86 Task Execution

Real-time control systems usually must respond to asynchronous requests for service in a manner that makes sure the most important request gets serviced first. In an RMX 86 system each service for a request is set up as a task. When an RMX 86 task is created, it is assigned a priority number between 0 and 255. The lower the number the higher the priority. Numbers between 0 and 127 are used for interrupt tasks. In addition to the built-in 8086 interrupt types, RMX 86 supports a single or several cascaded 8259A priority interrupt controllers for multiple hardware interrupts. Priority numbers between 128 and 255 are used for software tasks. RMX 86 schedules the execution of tasks on a preemptive priority basis. This means that if two or more tasks are ready to run, the task which has been assigned the highest priority will be executed first. This task will execute until it finishes, or until it reaches a point where it needs some resource which is not yet available. If a higher priority task becomes ready while a task is executing, the executing task will be preempted (put to sleep), and the higher priority task will be executed.

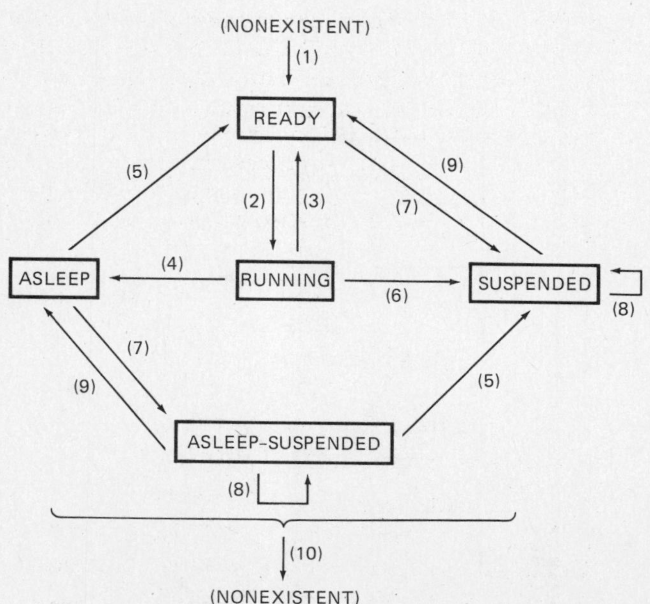

FIGURE 14-8 RMX 86 task state diagram.

Figure 14-8 shows an RMX 86 *task state diagram* which is often used to summarize the different states a task can be in, and the conditions necessary to go from one state to another. As we work our way around through the numbers in the figure, try to develop some intuitive feel for how it all works.

1. When a task is created, it is placed in the ready state. A task is created, remember, by a call to a procedure in the nucleus.
2. A task enters the running state when it has a higher priority than any other ready task, or it has been waiting longer than another ready task of the same priority.
3. A task is returned to the ready state when a task with a higher priority becomes ready and preempts it.
4. A task goes from the running state to the asleep state if:
   a. The task puts itself to sleep with a sleep system call. A task can put itself to sleep for a specified amount of time and then return to the ready state.
   b. The task must wait for a semaphore, a message, or a region in order to proceed.
5. Note that there are two number 5's on Figure 14-8. A task will go from the asleep state to the ready state or from the asleep-suspended state to the suspended state if:
   a. The time specified in the sleep call has expired.
   b. The semaphore, message, or region that the task was waiting for becomes available.
   c. The task's waiting time limit expires without the object that the task was waiting for becoming available.
6. A task goes from the running state to the suspended state when it does a suspend-task system call or a wait-for-interrupt system call.
7. A task in the ready state will be suspended when another task suspends it by calling the suspend-task procedure from the nucleus.
8. A task remains in a suspended state or an asleep-suspended state until the resume-task nucleus procedure has been called as many times as the suspend-task procedure was called for the task.
9. A task in the suspended state will return to the ready state, and a task in the asleep-suspended state will return to the asleep state when the resume-task system call has been done as many times for the task as the suspend-task system call. Another case where a task may exit from a sus-

pended state is when an interrupt that the task was waiting for occurs.

10. A task can be deleted with the delete-task system call.

A question that might occur to you at this point is, "If RMX 86 tasks are executed on a priority basis, how can a multiuser capability be included in an RMX 86 based system?" The answer to this question is that a clock tick can be used to produce an interrupt every 20 ms or so. The interrupt service procedure for that interrupt can then cycle around to a different terminal after each interrupt.

The final point we want to make here about RMX 86 is how a designer goes about using it to develop a custom system program. The design steps usually follow a sequence such as:

1. Define the system requirements.
2. Break the overall system into logical jobs.
3. Carefully define the functions of each job.
4. Determine the data structures needed for each job.
5. Determine whether jobs need to communicate or share resources.
6. Break down each job into tasks.
7. Write the algorithms for each task, including any needs for shared resources, synchronization, or communication between tasks.
8. Write the system initialization modules which set up the jobs, tasks, segments, regions, and semaphores using nucleus calls.
9. Write and test the program code for each task using system calls to define and manipulate "objects" as needed.
10. Integrate and test the completed system.

In the next section of this chapter we introduce you to the Intel 80286 microprocessor, which was designed to be used as the CPU in a multitasking system with virtual memory capability.

THE INTEL 80286 MICROPROCESSOR

We started this chapter with an introduction to some of the needs of multitasking/multiuser operating systems such as protection, mutual exclusion, and virtual memory capability. Later sections gave brief overviews of UNIX, a common multiuser operating system, and of RMX 86, a common real-time multitasking operating system. The Intel 80286 microprocessor was designed to serve as the CPU in a multitasking microcomputer system such as those we have described. The IBM PC/AT and its clones, as well as several other common systems capable of multitasking operation, use the 80286 as their CPU.

After a brief introduction to the internal architecture, signals, and hardware connections of the 80286, we will show you how memory management, task switching, and protection are done with the features built into the device.

80286 Architecture, Signals, and System Connections

Figure 14-9 shows an internal block diagram for the 80286. Note that the 80286 contains four separate processing units.

The *bus unit* (BU) in the device performs all memory and I/O reads and writes. When the BU is not using the buses for other operations, it prefetches instruction bytes and puts them in a 6-byte prefetch queue. When a

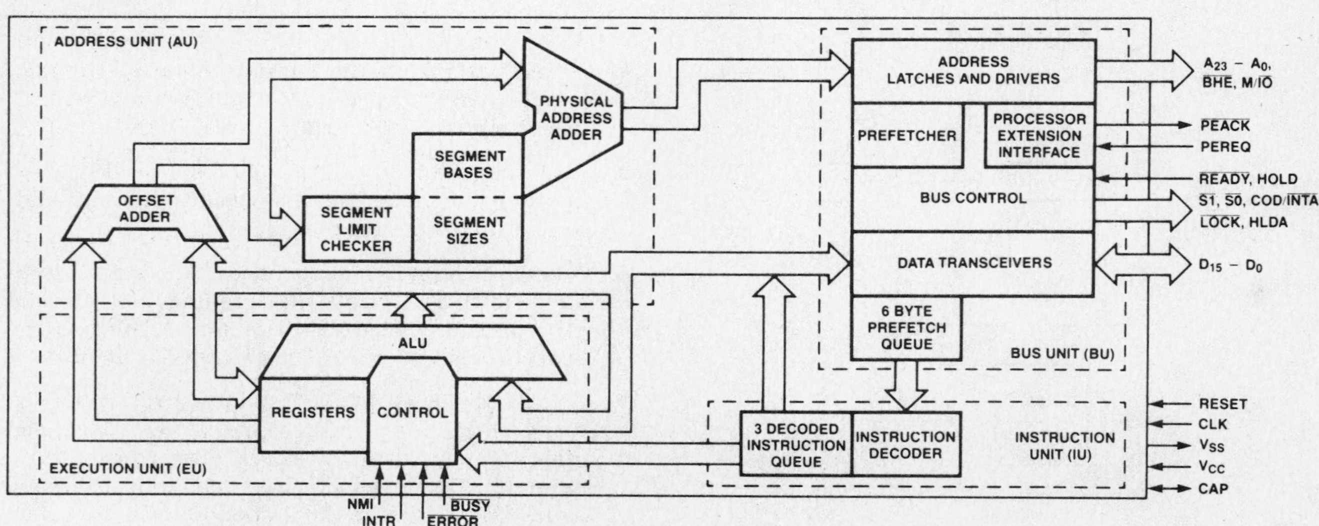

FIGURE 14-9 Internal block diagram of Intel 80286 microprocessor.

jump or call instruction executes, the BU will dump the queue and start filling it from the destination address. The BU also controls transfer of data to and from processor extension devices such as the 80287 math coprocessor.

The *instruction unit* (IU) fully decodes up to three prefetched instructions and holds them in a queue where the execution unit can access them. This is a further example of using pipelining to speed up the operation of a processor.

The *execution unit* (EU) sequentially executes instructions it receives from the instruction unit. It contains a set of index, pointer, and general-purpose registers identical to those of the 8086. In addition to a flag register like that of the 8086, the 80286 also has a 16-bit machine status word register which we will discuss later. The execution unit directs the BU to access memory or I/O operands as needed.

The *address unit* (AU) computes the physical addresses that will be sent out to memory or I/O by the BU. The 80286 can operate in one of two memory addressing modes, *real address mode* or *protected virtual address mode*. When programmed to operate in the real address mode, the address unit computes addresses with a segment base and an offset component just as the 8086 does. The familiar CS, DS, SS, and ES registers are used to hold the base addresses for the segments currently in use. The instruction pointer holds the offset of the currently addressed code byte in the code segment, and the stack pointer register holds the offset of the top of the stack. The maximum physical address space in this mode is 1 Mbyte, just as it is for the 8086.

When programmed to operate in *protected virtual address mode* (PVAM), the address unit functions as a complete memory management unit (MMU). In this address mode the 80286 uses all 24 address lines to access up to 16 Mbytes of physical memory. It is this mode which provides the protection and virtual memory capability desirable in multitasking operating systems. We will discuss this mode in detail in a later section.

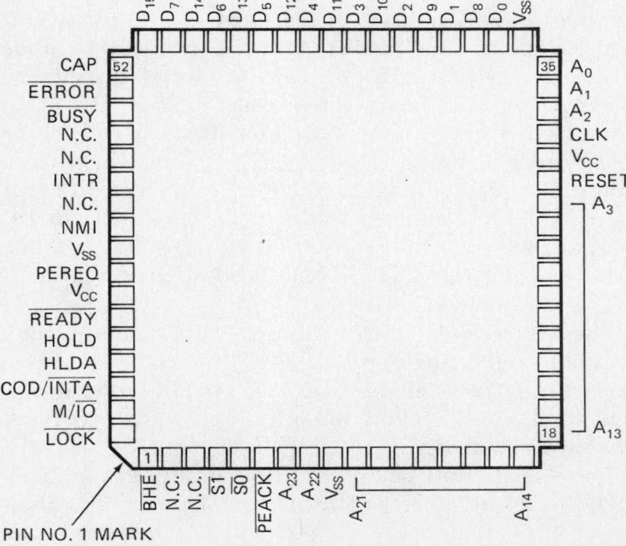

FIGURE 14-10 Pin diagram for 80286 microprocessor.

The 80286 is packaged in a 68-pin ceramic flat-pack as shown in Figure 14-10. Figure 14-11 shows how an 80286 is connected with some other components to form a simple system. Keep these figures handy as we work our way around the pins of the 80286. Many of the signals of the 80286 should be familiar to you from our discussion of the 8086 signals in Chapter 7.

An external 82284 clock generator is required to produce a single-phase clock signal for the 80286. The 82284 also synchronizes RESET and $\overline{READY}$ signals with the clock signal for the 80286.

The 80286 has a 16-bit data bus and a 24-bit nonmultiplexed address bus. Having the address lines available directly speeds up processing and simplifies the hardware. The 24-bit address bus allows the processor to access 16 Mbytes of physical memory. External buffers are used on both the address and the data bus.

Memory for the 80286 is set up as an odd bank and an even bank, just as it is for the 8086. The even bank will be enabled when A0 is low, and the odd bank will be enabled when $\overline{BHE}$ is low. To access an aligned word, both A0 and $\overline{BHE}$ will be low.

From a control standpoint, the 80286 functions similarly to an 8086 operating in maximum mode. Status signals $\overline{S0}$, $\overline{S1}$, and M/$\overline{IO}$ are decoded by an external 82288 bus controller to produce the control bus, read, write, and interrupt acknowledge signals.

Some other familiar pins on the 80286 should be the HOLD input which is used to request use of the buses for DMA operations, and the hold acknowledge (HLDA) output which is used to tell the DMA controller that the buses are available. An 8259A priority interrupt controller can be connected to the 80286 INTR interrupt input to funnel in external hardware interrupts. The interrupt acknowledge output ($\overline{INTA}$) from the 82288 tells the 8259 to send the desired interrupt type to the processor on the data bus. The nonmaskable interrupt (NMI) input, the $\overline{READY}$ input, and the $\overline{LOCK}$ output pins function the same as they do with the 8086.

After the RESET input has been held high for the required time and then made low, the 80286 will begin executing in the real address mode at address FFFFF0H. The internal registers will be initialized as follows: flag word—0002H, machine status word—FFF0H, IP—FFF0H, CS register—F000H, DS register—0000, ES register—0000H, SS register—0000.

A new pin function on the 80286 is the CAP pin. In order to operate at maximum speed, the substrates of the MOS devices in the 80286 must be biased with a negative voltage. This negative voltage is produced from the +5-V supply by a bias generator on the 80286. The external capacitor connected to the CAP pin filters this bias voltage. Note the polarity of the capacitor.

A second new pin here is the COD/$\overline{INTA}$ pin. This is a type of status signal output which can be used with M/$\overline{IO}$ to produce early control bus signals. COD/$\overline{INTA}$ will be asserted low for interrupt acknowledge, memory data read, or memory data write signals. It will be high for I/O read, I/O write, or memory instruction read machine cycles.

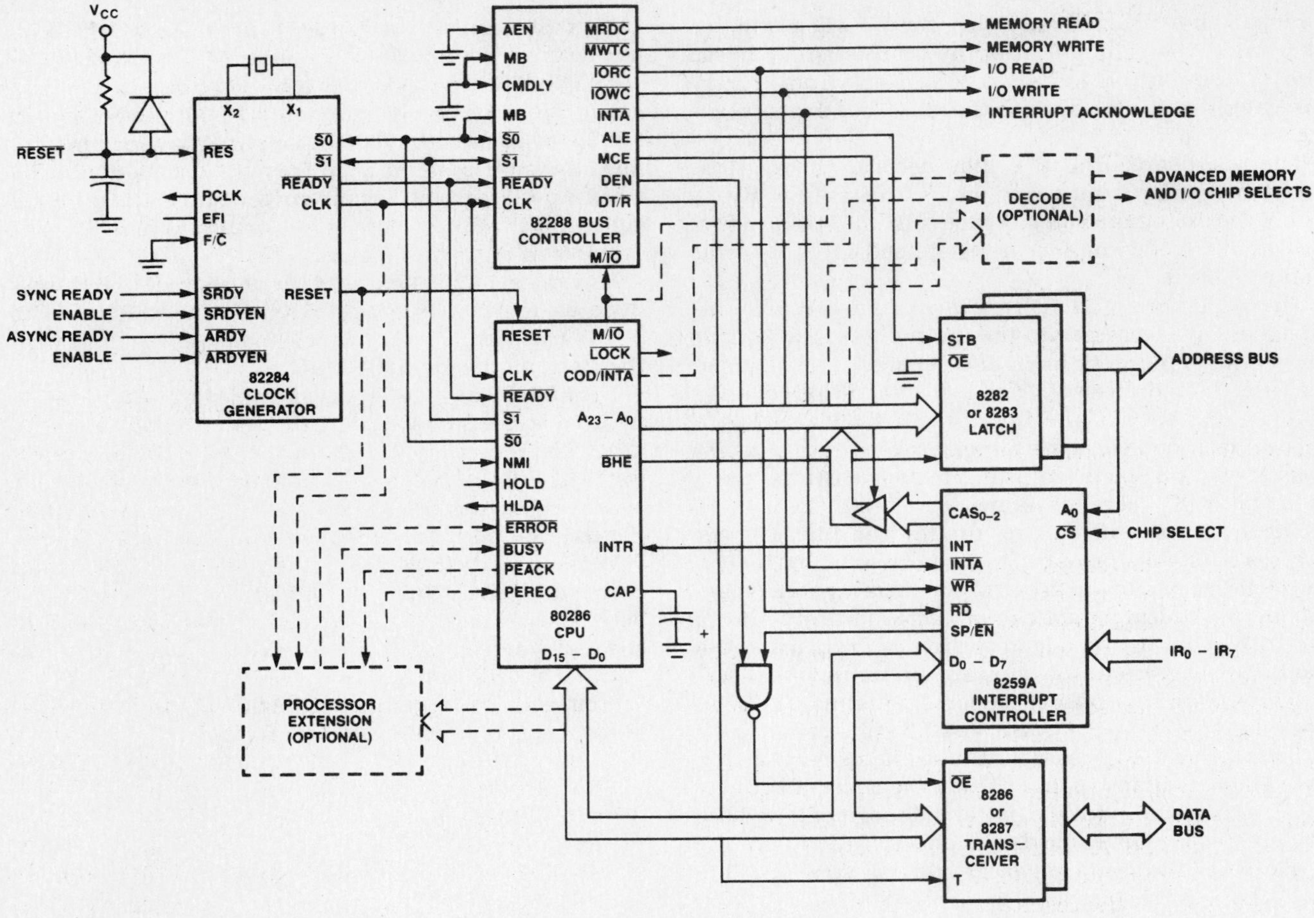

FIGURE 14-11 Circuit connections for simple 80286 system. *(Intel)*

The final four signal pins we need to discuss here are used to interface with processor extensions (coprocessors) such as the 80287 math coprocessor. The *processor extension request* (PEREQ) input pin will be asserted by a coprocessor to tell the 80286 to perform a data transfer to or from memory for it. When the 80286 gets around to do the transfer, it asserts the *processor extension acknowledge* ($\overline{\text{PEACK}}$) signal to the coprocessor to let it know the data transfer has started. Data transfers are done through the 80286 in this way so that the coprocessor uses the protection and virtual memory capability of the MMU in the 80286. The $\overline{\text{BUSY}}$ signal input on the 80286 functions the same as it does on the 8086. When the 80286 executes the WAIT instruction, it will remain in a WAIT loop until it finds the $\overline{\text{BUSY}}$ signal from the coprocessor high. If a coprocessor finds some error during processing, it will assert the $\overline{\text{ERROR}}$ input of the 80286. This will cause the 80286 to automatically do a type 16H interrupt call. An interrupt service procedure can be written to make the desired response to the error condition.

The machine cycle waveforms for the 80286 are very similar to those of the 8086 that we showed and discussed in earlier chapters. You should be able to work your way through them in the Intel 80286 data sheets if you need that type of information. In the limited space we have for the remainder of this section, we want to concentrate on the operation of the 80286 in its real address mode and in its protected virtual address mode.

The 80286 Real Address Mode

After an 80286 is reset, it starts executing in its real address mode. This mode is referred to as real because physical memory addresses are produced directly by adding an offset to a segment base just as the 8086 does. In this mode the 80286 can address up to 1 Mbyte of physical memory. As you will see later, the virtual address mode computes addresses in a very different way. In the real address mode, an 80286 functions essentially as a "souped up" 8086. Here are some of the ways in which the 80286 is enhanced when operating in real address mode.

The 80286 will directly execute 8086 machine code programs with only minor modifications to them. However, due to the extensive pipelining and other hardware improvements, the 80286 will execute most programs several times faster.

The instruction set of the 80286, in real address mode, is a "superset" of the 8086 instructions as illustrated by Figure 14-12. The 80286 in real address mode executes all of the 8086 instructions; the additional in-

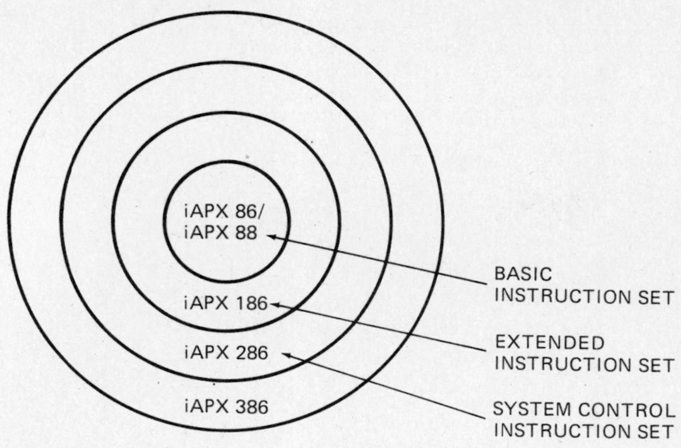

FIGURE 14-12 Relationship of 80386, 80286, 80186, and 8086 instruction set.

structions of the 80186 such as ENTER, LEAVE, and BOUND; and a few instructions used to switch the 80286 from real address mode to virtual address mode. In a later section we will show the additional instructions the 80286 can execute in its virtual address mode.

The 80286 has several additional built-in interrupt types as shown in Figure 14-13. For your reference we have included here a brief explanation of the cause of each of the interrupt types; some of these may not make much sense until we dig a little deeper into the operation of the 80286. As with the 8086, when an interrupt occurs, the 80286 multiplies the interrupt type number by 4 and goes to the resulting address in the interrupt vector table to get the CS and IP values for the interrupt procedure. In real address mode the interrupt vector table is in the first 1 Kbyte of memory. As we show later, the interrupt vector table has no fixed physical address in memory in the virtual address mode.

The 80286 was designed to be upward-compatible from the 8086 and, except for the integrated peripherals, from the 80186, so that the huge amount of software developed for these could be easily transported to the 80286. Previously debugged modules can then be integrated with new program modules written to take advantage of the advanced features of the 80286. Let's take a look at how some of these advanced features work.

FUNCTION	INTERRUPT NUMBER
DIVIDE ERROR EXCEPTION	0
SINGLE STEP INTERRUPT	1
NMI INTERRUPT	2
BREAKPOINT INTERRUPT	3
INTO DETECTED OVERFLOW EXCEPTION	4
BOUND RANGE EXCEEDED EXCEPTION	5
INVALID OPCODE EXCEPTION	6
PROCESSOR EXTENSION NOT AVAILABLE EXCEPTION	7
INTERRUPT TABLE LIMIT TOO SMALL	8
PROCESSOR EXTENSION SEGMENT OVERRUN INTERRUPT	9
INVALID TASK STATE SEGMENT	10
SEGMENT NOT PRESENT	11
STACK SEGMENT OVERRUN OR NOT PRESENT	12
SEGMENT OVERRUN EXCEPTION	13
RESERVED	14,15
PROCESSOR EXTENSION ERROR INTERRUPT	16
RESERVED	17-31
USER DEFINED	32-255

FIGURE 14-13 80286 interrupt types.

The 80286 Protected Virtual Address Mode

The major features of the *protected virtual address mode*, PVAM, of the 80286 that we want to discuss in this section are memory management, protection, task switching, and interrupt processing. We will work our way through these in order, but first we want to make some general comments about how an 80286 is switched to PVAM when an operating system running on it is booted.

After the 80286 is reset, it initially operates in real address mode. This mode is usually used to initialize peripheral devices, load the main part of the operating system from disk into memory, load some registers, enable interrupts, and enter the PVAM. The PVAM is entered by setting the protection enable bit of the *machine status word* (MSW) in the 80286. Figure 14-14*a* shows the format for the MSW. Bit 0 of this word is the

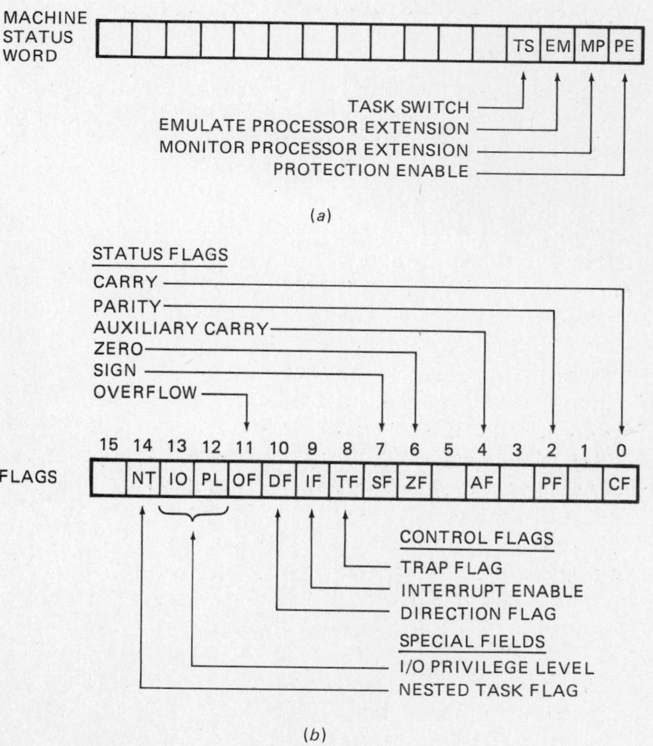

FIGURE 14-14 80286 machine status word and flag word. *(a)* Machine status word. *(b)* Flag word.

protection enable bit we are interested in here. Bits 1, 2, and 3 are used, for the most part, to indicate whether a processor extension (coprocessor) is present or not. Bits are changed in the MSW by loading the desired word in a register or memory location and executing the *load machine status word* (LMSW) instruction. Once the PVAM is entered by executing the LMSW instruction, the only way to get back to real address mode is by resetting the system. The 80286 was designed this way so that a "clever" programmer could not switch the system back into real address mode to defeat the protection schemes in PVAM. The final step to get the 80286 operating in PVAM is to execute an intersegment jump to the start of the main system program. This jump is necessary to flush the queue because the queue functions differently in PVAM. Now that we have the 80286 in PVAM, let's see how it manages memory and does all of those other wondrous things.

The 80286 Memory Management Scheme

Just as with the 8086, the basic building blocks of memory management in PVAM are logical segments. The segments probably should be referred to as virtual segments, because they may not all be present in physical memory at the same time. Unlike 8086 segments, however, segments for the 80286 can be any length from 1 byte to 64 Kbytes. A size or *limit* is given to each segment when it is created. Defining the length of segments in this way makes more efficient use of memory,

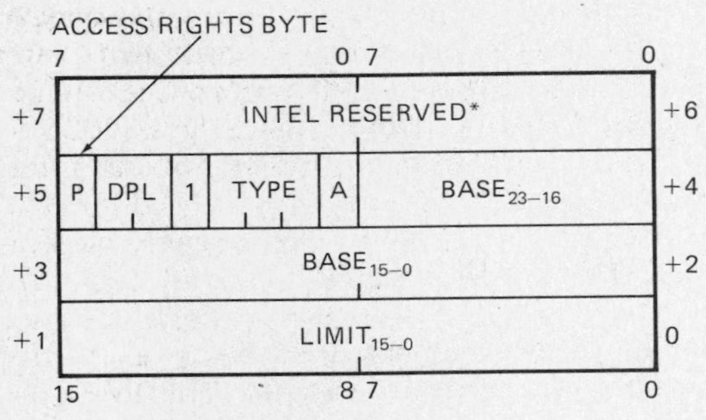

P = PRESENT
DPL = DESCRIPTOR PRIVILEGE LEVEL
TYPE = SEGMENT TYPE AND ACCESS INFORMATION
A = ACCESSED

*MUST BE SET TO 0 FOR COMPATIBILITY WITH iAPZ 386

(*a*)

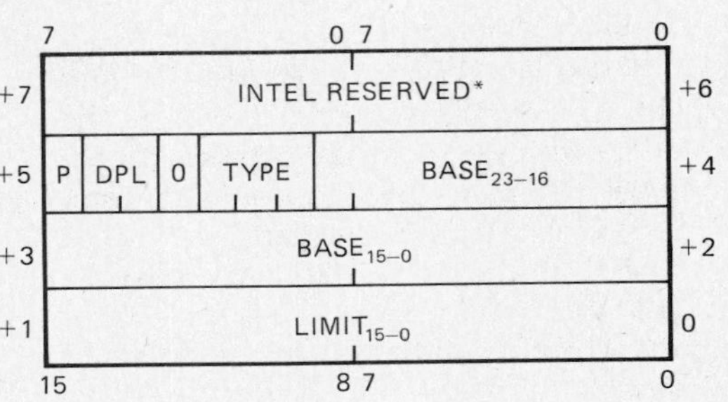

P = PRESENT
DPL = DESCRIPTOR PRIVELEGE LEVEL
TYPE = TYPE OF SPECIAL DESCRIPTOR (INCLUDES CONTROL AND SYSTEM SEGMENTS)

0 = INVALID DESCRIPTOR
1 = AVAILABLE TASK STATE SEGMENT
2 = LDT DESCRIPTOR
3 = BUSY TASK STATE SEGMENT
4-7 = CONTROL DESCRIPTOR
8→F = INVALID DESCRIPTOR

*MUST BE SET TO 0 FOR COMPATIBILITY WITH iAPX 386

(*b*)

BIT	NAME	DESCRIPTION
7	PRESENT	1 MEANS PRESENT AND ADDRESSABLE IN REAL MEMORY; 0 MEANS NOT PRESENT. SEE SECTION 11.3.
6, 5	DPL	2-BIT DESCRIPTOR PRIVILEGE LEVEL, 0 TO 3.
4	SEGMENT	1 MEANS SEGMENT DESCRIPTOR; 0 MEANS CONTROL DESCRIPTOR.
FOR SEGMENT = 1, THE REMAINING BITS HAVE THE FOLLOWING MEANINGS:		
3	EXECUTABLE	1 MEANS CODE, 0 MEANS DATA.
2	C OR ED	IF CODE, CONFORMING: 1 MEANS YES, 0 NO. IF DATA, EXPAND DOWN: 1 YES, 0 NO—NORMAL CASE.
1	R OR W	IF CODE, READABLE: 1 MEANS READABLE, 0 NOT. IF DATA, WRITABLE: 1 MEANS WRITABLE, 0 NOT.
0	ACCESSED	1 IF SEGMENT DESCRIPTOR HAS BEEN ACCESSED, 0 IF NOT.

(*c*)

FIGURE 14-15 Descriptor and access byte formats. *(a)* Code or data segment descriptor format. *(b)* Control descriptor format. *(c)* Access byte format for code and data segment descriptors.

and makes it possible for the 80286 to check if a memory access accidentally goes outside of the bounds of a segment. The segments currently being used by a task or program are kept in physical memory. In PVAM all 24 address lines are active, so 16 Mbytes of physical memory can be accessed. Segments not currently being used are swapped out from physical memory to secondary storage such as a hard disk, and then swapped back into physical memory as needed. When you write programs for the 80286 in PVAM, you refer to segments by the names you give them, just as you do in 8086 programs. For example, if you want to use a segment named ACCOUNTS_IN as the current data segment, you can do this with the simple instructions: MOV AX, ACCOUNTS_IN, and MOV DS,AX. When the 80286 in PVAM executes these two instructions, it will automatically point at the segment ACCOUNTS_IN as the current data segment. If the segment ACCOUNTS_IN is not currently present in physical memory, an interrupt will be produced. The service routine for this interrupt will load the segment from disk to physical memory and return execution to the interrupted program. To summarize, then, the MMU translates the logical (virtual) addresses for segments used in programs to the actual physical addresses of the segments in memory. The MMU also has a mechanism for detecting if a named segment is not present in physical memory, and interrupting the program to get the segment into physical memory.

DESCRIPTORS

When a program is assembled and made ready for execution in PVAM, a unique, 8-byte quantity called a *descriptor* is produced for each segment. Figure 14-15*a* and Figure 14-15*b* show the formats for the two major types of descriptors, segment and system control. For now we will concentrate on the characteristics of segment descriptors.

The least-significant 2 bytes of a descriptor (bytes 0 and 1) contain the length, or *limit*, of the segment in bytes. This limit value is used by the MMU to produce an interrupt if an attempt is made to access a location beyond the end of a segment. Bytes 2, 3, and 4 of a descriptor contain the 24-bit base address where the segment is, or will be located in the 16 Mbyte physical address space. Byte 5 of a descriptor, the access byte, contains information about the privilege level, access, and type of the segment. To give you an idea of the kind of information contained in the access byte of a descriptor, Figure 14-15*c* summarizes the meanings of the bits in the access bytes of code segment and data segment descriptors. For now, just skim through the descriptions to get an overview. We will say more about the meanings of these bits later. Bytes 6 and 7 of a descriptor are filled with 0's for the 80286. These bytes were included in the descriptor format for upward compatibility with the 80386 microprocessor.

DESCRIPTOR TABLES

The descriptors for an 80286 system are kept in tables in memory and read into the processor as needed. There

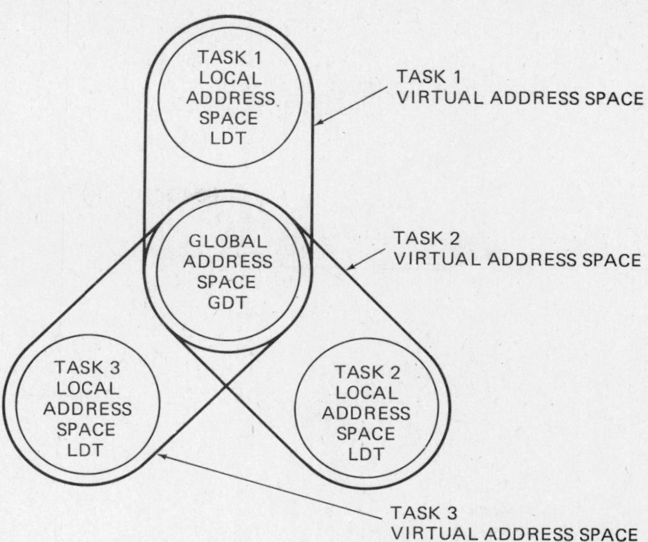

FIGURE 14-16 Diagram showing how tasks can share memory mapped by the global descriptor table, but be isolated from each other by having their own local descriptor tables. *(Intel)*

are two major categories of descriptor table, global and local. A system can have only one global descriptor table. The *global descriptor table* contains, among other things, the segment descriptors for the operating system segments and the descriptors for segments which need to be accessed by all user tasks. A *local descriptor table* is set up in the system for each task or closely related group of tasks. Figure 14-16 shows, in diagram form, how this works. Tasks share a global descriptor table and the memory area defined by the descriptors in it. Each task has its own local descriptor table and memory area defined by the descriptors in it. Because each task has its own local descriptor table, tasks are protected from each other. A four-level protection scheme which we discuss a little later can be used to protect the operating system kernel descriptors in the global descriptor table from unauthorized access by user tasks.

ACCESSING SEGMENTS

Before going on, let's review where we are at in our discussion of PVAM. The major building block of programs in PVAM are segments. Each segment has associated with it an 8-byte descriptor which contains the length, starting address, and access rights for that segment. Segment descriptors for programs are kept in a local descriptor table or in the global descriptor table in memory. To complete the general picture of how segment descriptors are used, we simply need to show you how the 80286 keeps track of where the descriptor tables are in memory, how it accesses a descriptor that corresponds to a named segment, and how it produces the physical address for a word or byte in a segment in memory.

The 80286 keeps the base addresses and limits for the descriptor tables currently in use in internal registers.

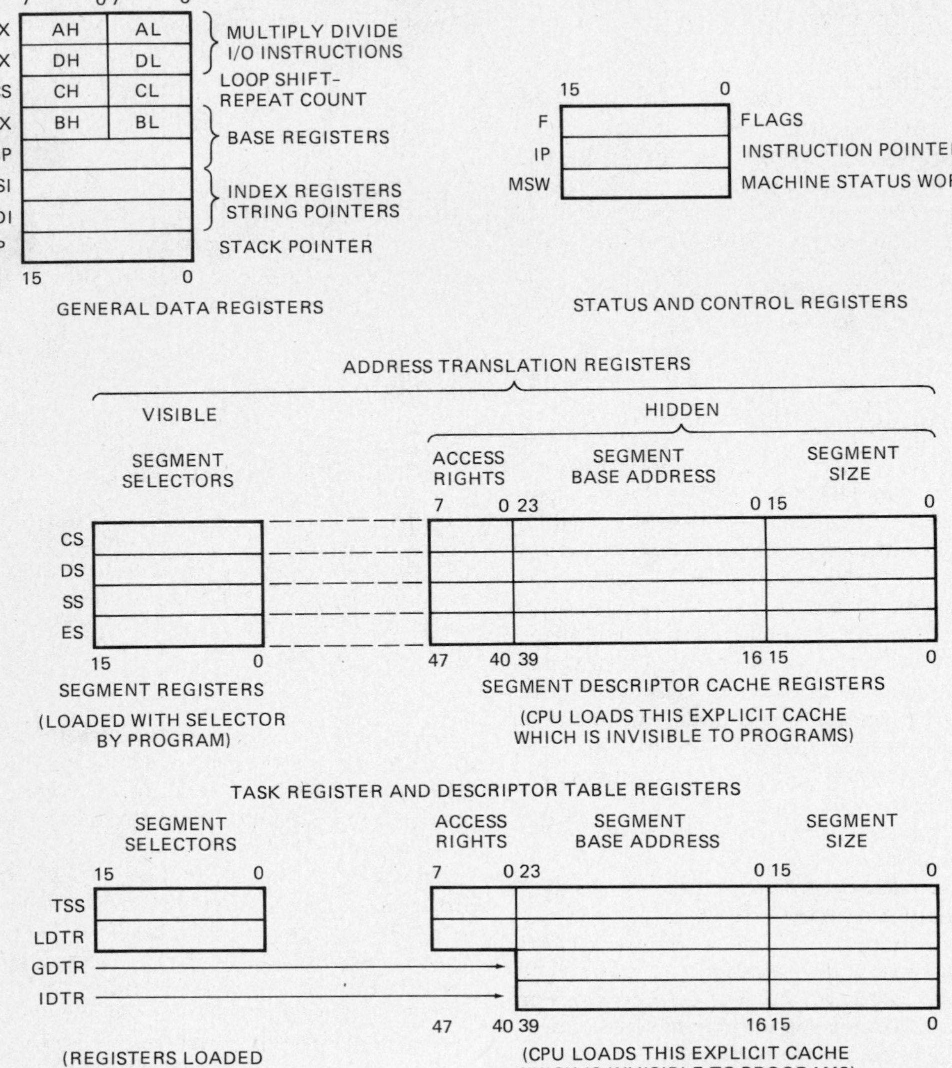

FIGURE 14-17 80286 complete register set.

Figure 14-17 shows the complete register set of the 80286. The *global descriptor table register* (GDTR) contains the 24-bit base address and limit for the table containing the global address space descriptors. This register is initialized with the LGDT instruction when the system is booted.

The *local descriptor table register* (LDTR) in the 80286 contains the base address and limit of the local descriptor table for the task currently being executed. The LLDT instruction is used to load this register when the system is booted. The LLDT instruction can only be executed by programs executing at the highest privilege level. Therefore, unless a task is operating at the highest privilege level, it cannot intentionally or maliciously access the local descriptor table of another task. Task switching is often handled by the operating system kernel which, of course, operates at the highest priority level.

Each local descriptor table is actually a named segment which has its own unique descriptor. The descriptors for the local descriptor tables in the system are kept in the global descriptor table. This sounds more complex than it really is, so let's see if we can clarify it. For example, when the operating system does a task switch, the new local descriptor table descriptor is read from the global descriptor table and loaded into the LDTR register in the 80286. As the new task executes, it then uses the descriptors in the local descriptor table pointed to by the LDT register to access the segments it needs. In later sections we will explain the function of the *task register* (TSS or TR) and the *interrupt descriptor table register* (IDTR) shown in Figure 14-17. The next step in our explanation here is to show how a descriptor in a descriptor table is accessed.

SELECTORS

When a program is assembled and prepared for execution on an 8086 or on an 80286 operating in real address mode, each named segment is given a 16-bit base

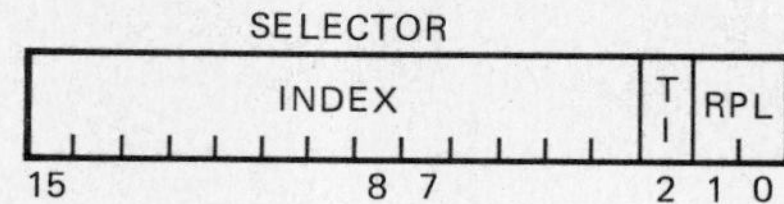

BITS	NAME	FUNCTION
1–0	REQUESTED PRIVILEGE LEVEL (RPL)	INDICATES SELECTOR PRIVILEGE LEVEL DESIRED
2	TABLE INDICATOR (TI)	TI = 0 USE GLOBAL DESCRIPTOR TABLE (GDT) TI = 1 USE LOCAL DESCRIPTOR TABLE (LDT)
15–3	INDEX	SELECT DESCRIPTOR FROM TABLE

FIGURE 14-18 Segment selector format.

address. Offsets in program instructions are added to this segment base address to produce a physical address, as we have described many times before. When a program is assembled for execution on an 80286 in PVAM, instead of being directly assigned a base address, each segment is assigned a 16-bit *selector*. Figure 14-18 shows the format for segment selectors. The upper 13 bits of a selector contain the number of the descriptor in a descriptor table. This part of the selector is referred to as an index because the value in these bits, when internally multiplied by 8, points at the descriptor for that segment in a descriptor table. (The index value is multiplied by 8 because each descriptor requires 8 bytes in the descriptor table.) If the *table indicator* bit (bit 2) of the selector is a 0, then the upper 13 bits will index a segment descriptor in the global descriptor table. If the TI bit of the selector is a 1, then the upper 13 bits of the selector will index a segment descriptor in a local descriptor table. This is a form of indirect addressing. The selector points to a descriptor location in a descriptor table, and the descriptor at that location contains the actual base address and other information about the desired segment. This may seem to be a roundabout way to get to the start of a segment, but it is this indirect approach which allows several forms of protection to be built into the 80286. The least-significant 2 bits of a selector, the *requested privilege level* or RPL bits, are part of the built-in protection. We will explain 80286 protection mechanisms after we finish discussing the basic addressing scheme.

ADDRESS TRANSLATION REGISTERS AND PHYSICAL ADDRESSES

For an 8086 or a 80286 operating in real address mode the base addresses for the currently used segments are kept in the CS, DS, SS, and ES registers in the processor, where they can be used to produce physical addresses. For the 80286 operating in PVAM, descriptors must be brought in from descriptor tables in memory to registers in the 80286, where they can be used for producing and checking physical addresses. Figure 14-17 shows the *segment address translation registers* which hold the descriptors for the currently used segments. These are usually referred to simply as segment registers with names the same as those of the 8086. However, the registers have an added 48-bit hidden part, and they are used differently.

When a segment register is loaded in a PVAM program, the selector for that segment is loaded into the the selector portion of the indicated address translation (segment) register. For example, the instructions MOV AX,ACCOUNTS_IN and MOV DS,AX will load the selector for the segment ACCOUNTS_IN into the selector portion of the DS address translation register. When the selector is loaded into the DS register, the 80286 will automatically get the descriptor pointed to in a descriptor table by that selector and put the lower 6 bytes of the descriptor in the 48-bit hidden descriptor part of the DS address translation register. This part of the DS address translation register is referred to as hidden because it cannot be directly accessed by program instructions. If the TI bit of the selector is a 0, then the index part of the selector will be multiplied by 8 and added to the global descriptor table base address in the global descriptor table register to produce the physical address where the descriptor is located. If the TI bit in the selector is a one, then the index part of the selector will be multiplied by 8 and added to the local descriptor base address held in the local descriptor table register to produce the physical address of the DS descriptor in the local descriptor table. The left side of Figure 14-19 shows how this works. The main points are that the descriptor table registers hold the 24-bit physical starting addresses for the global and local descriptor tables. The 13-bit index part of a selector is multiplied by 8 and added to one of these bases to produce the physical address of the descriptor which corresponds to that selector. When a selector is loaded into the visible part of the segment register, the 80286 automatically computes the physical address of the corresponding descriptor, and loads that descriptor into the hidden part of the segment register. The next point to consider is how the physical address for a code or data byte within a segment is produced.

Each virtual memory address for an 80286 operating in PVAM is represented by two components, a 16-bit selector and a 16-bit offset, similar to the way that 8086 addresses are represented as two 16-bit components. As we explained in the previous paragraphs, however, the selector points to a descriptor for the segment which contains that address. When the selector for a segment is loaded into the visible part of an address translation register such as DS, the lower 6 bytes of the segment descriptor will be loaded into the hidden part of the address translation register. As shown in Figure 14-19, the 24-bit physical base address for the segment is part of the descriptor that is loaded in. The actual physical address of an addressed byte or word is produced by adding the 16-bit offset part of the original virtual address directly to the segment base address in the hidden part of the address translation register. The right side of Figure 14-19 shows in diagram form how this works. NOTE: The 24-bit segment base in the address translation register is NOT shifted left four bit positions before the add as is done when producing physical addresses in an 8086.

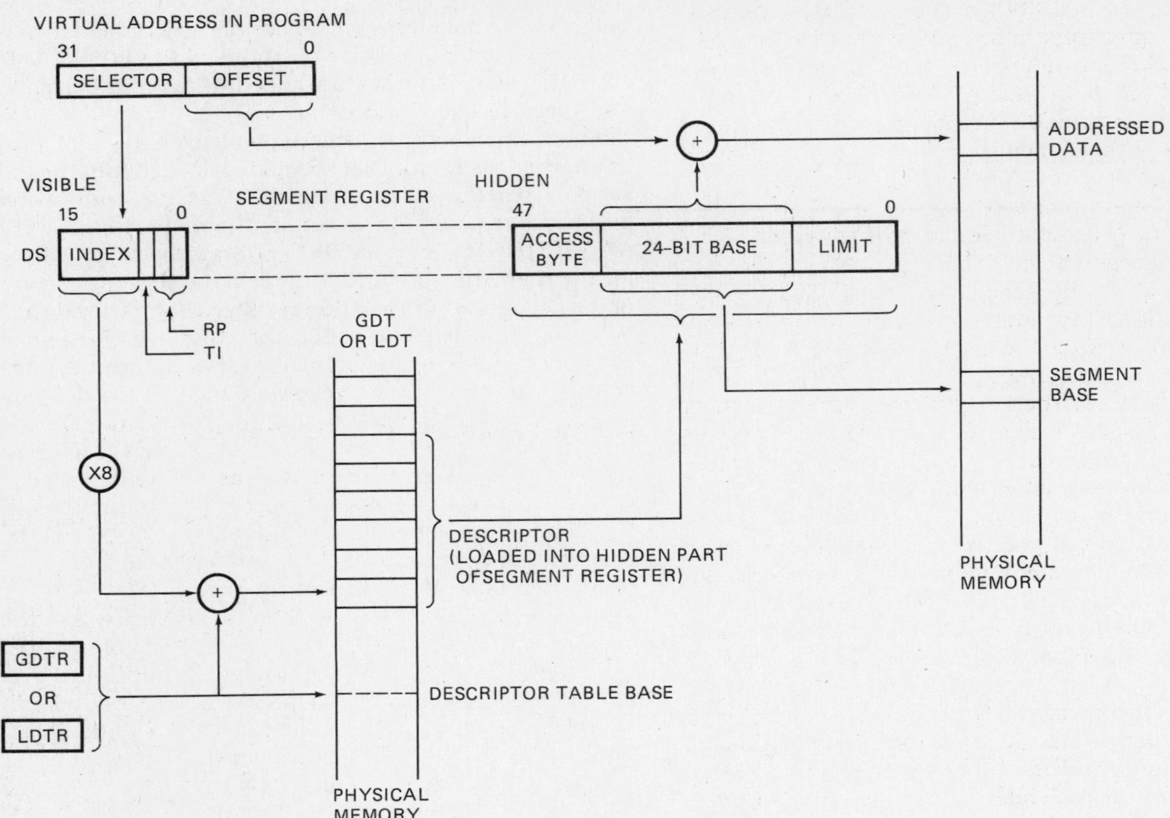

FIGURE 14-19 80286 translation of 32-bit virtual address to 24-bit physical address.

To summarize all of this, then, each address in PVAM is represented by a 32-bit virtual address consisting of a 16-bit selector and a 16-bit offset. To access a segment, the selector for that segment is loaded into the visible part of the appropriate segment register in the 80286. The 80286 then automatically multiplies the index value in the upper 13 bits of the selector by 8 and adds the result to a descriptor table base address in its GDT register or its LDT register. The 80286 then fetches the segment descriptor from the resultant address in a descriptor table and loads it into the hidden part of the segment register. The 24-bit segment base address, loaded in as part of the descriptor, is added directly to the offset part of the virtual address to produce the physical address of the desired byte or word. In a system which always runs the same program, the physical base addresses in descriptors are fixed by program development tools when the program is built. In a general-purpose system which runs many different programs, the physical base addresses in descriptors may be changed by the operating system when a program is loaded into memory to be run. This is done so that the program can be loaded into available memory without disturbing programs or tasks already present. In a dynamic system such as this, the selectors do not need to be changed, only the base addresses in the descriptors. This is one advantage of addressing segments indirectly through selectors and descriptors. In the next section we discuss how this indirect access to memory makes it possible to establish privilege levels and protection.

80286 Protection Mechanisms

The 80286 operating in PVAM has mechanisms to protect system software from user programs, protect user tasks from each other, and generally protect regions of memory from accidental access. All of these mechanisms depend in some way on the contents of descriptors. The overall principle here is that information in segment descriptors is used to check every attempt to access memory to see if the attempt is valid. If the attempt is valid, then the access is allowed. If the access is not valid, then an error interrupt is produced. Let's take another look at the descriptor formats in Figure 14-15*a* and the access rights byte definition in Figure 14-15*c*, so we can discuss how some of this protection works. First we will discuss some of the ways in which regions of memory are protected from accidental access.

When an attempt is made to load a segment selector into a segment register, the 80286 automatically makes several checks. First of all, it checks to see if the descriptor table indexed by the selector contains a valid descriptor for that selector. If a valid descriptor is not present, then an interrupt is produced. If a valid descriptor is present, the limit, base, and access rights byte of the descriptor are loaded into the hidden part of the segment register. The 80286 then checks to see if the segment for that descriptor is present in physical memory. If it is not present, as indicated by the P bit in the access rights byte of the descriptor, an interrupt is produced. The service procedure for this interrupt can swap the segment into physical memory and return execution to the interrupted program. The 80286 also checks to see if the segment descriptor is of the right type to be loaded into the specified segment register. The descriptor for a read-only data segment, for example, cannot be loaded into the SS register, because a stack must be able to be written to. A descriptor for a code segment which does not allow reading cannot be loaded into the DS register.

After a segment selector and descriptor are loaded into a segment register, further checks are made each time a location in the actual segment is accessed. An attempt to write to a code segment or a read-only data segment, for example, will cause an error. Furthermore, the limit value contained in the segment descriptor is used to check that an address produced by program instructions does not fall outside the limit defined for the segment. For example, an effective address produced by a memory reference in an instruction might, because of some error, give an offset which exceeds the limit for a segment.

User tasks are protected from each other in an 80286 PVAM system by the fact that one task cannot access descriptors in the local descriptor table for another task. When execution is switched from one task to another, the LDT register is loaded with the base address of the local descriptor table for the new task by instructions operating at a high privilege level. Instructions in the user task, operating at a lower privilege level, cannot change the contents of the LDT register.

System software, such as the operating system kernel, is protected from corruption in several ways. One way we have already mentioned is that code segments cannot be written to. The second and most important way is with privilege levels. Figure 14-20 illustrates how an 80286 PVAM system can be set up with four privilege levels. As you can see, the operating system kernel is assigned a privilege level of 0, which is the highest privilege level. Privilege level 1 might contain system services such as BIOS procedures and file handling procedures. Custom utilities and user application programs operate at lower (higher-numbered) privilege levels. The privilege level of a code or data segment is inserted as bits 5 and 6 of the access byte of the segment descriptor, when the program is built. These 2 bits are referred to as the *descriptor privilege level* or DPL. When a task executes, it executes at a specified privilege level. The privilege level of the executing task is contained in the least-significant 2 bits of the selector currently in the CS register (see Figure 14-18). This privilege level is referred to as the *current privilege level* or CPL. When an attempt is made to access, for example, a data segment by loading its selector and descriptor into the DS register, the DPL from the descriptor is compared with the CPL. If the DPL is lower (a higher number) or the same as the the CPL, the descriptor will be loaded and the access allowed. If the task attempts to access a segment with a higher DPL (lower number), an error interrupt will be produced. The point here then is that a task cannot directly access a segment which has a higher DPL.

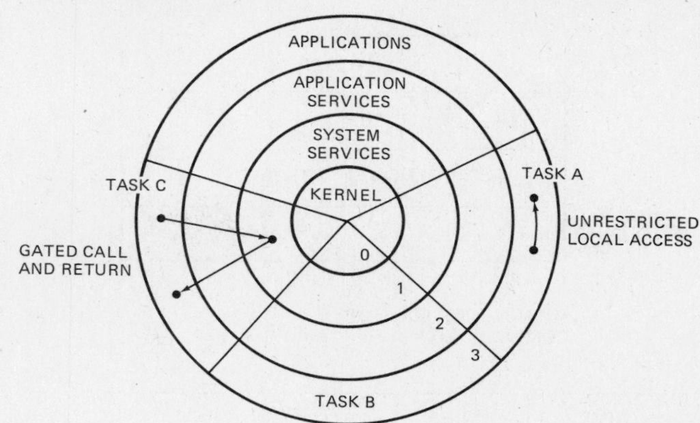

FIGURE 14-20 80286 use of privilege levels in PVAM.

The question that might come to mind at this point is, "If a task cannot access a segment with a higher DPL, how can user programs access operating system kernel, BIOS, or utilities procedures in segments which have higher DPLs?" The answer to this is that a procedure in a segment at a higher privilege level cannot be called directly, but it can be called through a special structure called a *gate*. There are four types of gates: call, trap, interrupt, and task. Figure 14-21 shows the format for gate descriptors. For now, we will just describe how a call gate operates.

As you can see in Figure 14-21, a gate is simply a special type of descriptor. Gate descriptors can be put in the GDT or a LDT, just as segment and other descriptors are. When a program does a call to a far procedure, the selector for a call gate is loaded into the CS register, and the call gate descriptor is loaded into the hidden part of the CS register. If you compare the call gate descriptor in Figure 14-21 with the segment descriptor in Figure 14-15*a*, you will see that the call gate descriptor does not directly contain the 24-bit base address of the segment containing the procedure called. The call gate descriptor instead contains a selector which points to the segment containing the called procedure. If the call is determined to be valid, then the selector from the call gate and the corresponding segment descriptor will be loaded into the CS register. The called procedure will then execute. In other words, the call is done indirectly through the call gate descriptor rather than directly through a descriptor to the segment containing the procedure.

This indirect approach permits another level of checking before access to the procedure in the higher privileged segment is allowed. The privilege level of the calling program is compared with the privilege level of that specified in the call gate. If the privilege level of the calling program is lower than the privilege level specified in the call gate, the access will not be allowed. If, for example, the DPL in the call gate descriptor is 2, a level 2 program can use the call gate to call a privilege level 1 procedure, but a level 3 program cannot. Another advantage of the indirect call gate approach is that user

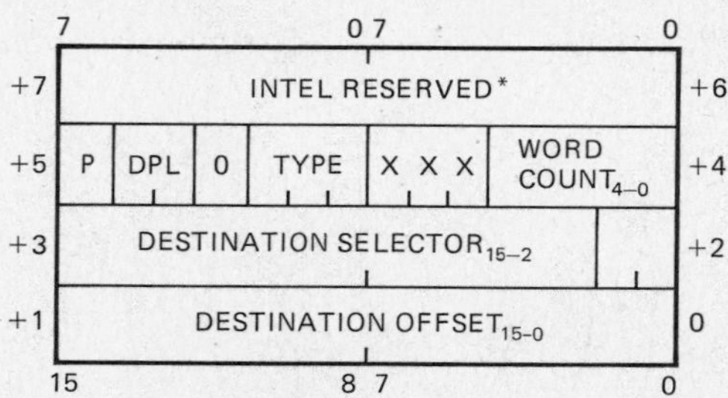

NAME	VALUE	DESCRIPTION
TYPE	4 5 6 7	CALL GATE TASK GATE INTERRUPT GATE TRAP GATE
P	0 1	DESCRIPTOR CONTENTS ARE NOT VALID DESCRIPTOR CONTENTS ARE VALID
DPL	0-3	DESCRIPTOR PRIVILEGE LEVEL
WORD COUNT	0-31	NUMBER OF WORDS TO COPY FROM CALLERS STACK TO CALLED PROCEEDURES STACK. ONLY USED WITH CALL GATE.
DESTINATION SELECTOR	16-bit SELECTOR	SELECTOR TO THE TARGET CODE SEGMENT (CALL, INTERRUPT OR TRAP GATE) SELECTOR TO THE TARGET TASK STATE SEGMENT (TASK GATE)
DESTINATION OFFSET	16-bit OFFSET	ENTRY POINT WITHIN THE TARGET CODE SEGMENT

FIGURE 14-21 80286 gate descriptor format and gate descriptor access byte format.

programs cannot accidentally enter higher privileged segments at just any old point. If they are going to enter at all, they must enter at the specific points contained in the call gate descriptors. In the next section we discuss how the 80286 does task switching and uses task gates.

Task Switching and Task Gates

Each task in a PVAM system has a 22-word *task state segment* (TSS) associated with it. A TSS holds copies of all registers and flags, the selector for the task's LDT, and a link to the TSS of the previously executing task. Descriptors for each task state segment are kept in the global descriptor table. A *task register* (TR) in the 80286 holds the selector and the task state segment descriptor for the currently executing task. The *load task register* (LTR) instruction can be used to initialize the task register to the task state segment for a particular task. During a task switch the task register is automatically loaded with the selector and descriptor for the new task.

A task switch may be done in any one of four ways:

1. A long jump or call instruction contains a selector which points at a task state segment descriptor. The call instruction is used if a return to the previously executing task is desired. A jump instruction is used if a return is not desired.
2. An IRET instruction is executed with the NT bit in the flag word equal 1. The return address is contained in the TSS.
3. The selector in a long jump or call instruction points to a task gate. In this case the selector for the destination TSS is in the task gate. The indirect mechanism here is similar to that we described above for call gates, and has the same advantages regarding privilege levels and protection.
4. An interrupt occurs, and the interrupt vector points to a task gate descriptor.

The point here is that once the task state segments and the rest of the structure are set up, normal program instructions such as CALL, JUMP, and IRET are used to accomplish a task switch. The next point we want to discuss here is how the 80286 handles interrupts in PVAM.

80286 Interrupt Handling in PVAM

An 8086 or an 80286 operating in real address mode uses the first 1 Kbyte of memory as an interrupt vector table. The CS and the IP values for up to 256 interrupt types are put in this table as we explained in Chapter 8. When operating in PVAM the 80286 can also handle up to 256 interrupts but, in order to provide protection, it is done with descriptors. An *interrupt descriptor table* (IDT) is set up in memory. The base address, access byte, and limit for the interrupt descriptor table are held in a special *interrupt descriptor table register* in the 80286. The interrupt descriptor table can be located anywhere in memory. When an interrupt occurs, the interrupt type is multiplied by 8 and used as a selector to point to the desired descriptor in the interrupt descriptor table.

The descriptors in the interrupt descriptor table are gates. They can be interrupt gates, trap gates, or task gates. Interrupt and trap gates are used to handle interrupts with procedures in the same task. A task gate is used if the interrupt handling procedure is in another task. The only difference between an interrupt gate and a trap gate is that an interrupt gate is used to go to a procedure with interrupts disabled, and a trap gate is used to get to an interrupt procedure with interrupts enabled. Interrupt gates and trap gates have the same format as the call gates described in a previous section. Incidentally, in 80286 data books the term *exception* is often used for interrupts which are caused by errors during execution of an instruction. The term interrupt is reserved for interrupts caused by some event external to the executing program.

In summary, then, the PVAM interrupt response proceeds as follows. The interrupt descriptor table register in the 80286 holds the base address of the interrupt descriptor table in memory. When an interrupt occurs, the interrupt type is multiplied by 8 and added to the

IDT register to index a gate descriptor in the IDT. The gate descriptor contains a selector for the segment which holds the interrupt service procedure, and the offset of the procedure in that segment. If the access is valid, the selector from the gate descriptor is loaded into the visible part of the CS register, and the segment descriptor pointed to by the selector is loaded into the hidden part of the CS register. This is essentially the same indirect process that we described for the operation of call gates.

As you should see by now, the key to understanding the 80286 PVAM is to think of segments, descriptors to define the characteristics of the segments, selectors to point at desired segment descriptors, and 80286 registers to hold the selectors and descriptors for the descriptor tables and segments currently in use. Now that you have an overview of how the 80286 operates in PVAM, we want to briefly introduce you to the 80286 instructions which are used for PVAM.

80286 Instructions for PVAM

The following brief descriptions are intended to introduce you to the instructions that the 80286 has beyond those of the 80186. For further details, consult Intel's 80286 Assembly Language Programming Manual.

CTS—Clear task-switched flag in machine status word

LGDT—Load global descriptor table register from memory

SGDT—Store global descriptor table register contents in memory

LIDT—Load interrupt descriptor table register from memory

LLDT—Load selector and associated descriptor into LDTR

SLDT—Store selector from LDTR in specified register or memory

LTR—Load task register with selector and descriptor for TSS

STR—Store selector from task register in register or memory

LMSW—Load machine status register from register or memory

SMSW—Store machine status word in register or memory

LAR—Load access rights byte of descriptor into register or memory

LSL—Load segment limit from descriptor into register or memory

ARPL—Adjust requested privilege level of selector (down only)

VERR—Determine if segment pointed to by selector is readable

VERW—Determine if segment pointed to be selector is writable

In the remaining sections of this chapter we show you some of the directions microprocessor evolution is heading beyond the 80286.

NEW DIRECTIONS

Microprocessor evolution has been proceeding very rapidly in the last few years, and the rate of evolution seems to be increasing. Throughout this book we have tried to point out some of the directions this evolution has been taking. One area of evolution has been from batch-processing computer systems to time-share and multitasking systems. Another direction has been to distributed processing systems linked together in networks such as we described in Chapter 13. Also, the development of optical disk storage makes available, at each user's desk, more data than was previously available at many large mainframe computers. The overall direction of evolution is toward microcomputers with greater screen resolution, more memory capability, larger data words, and higher processing speeds. We will use the remainder of this chapter to introduce you to some developing areas: the Intel 80386 32-bit microprocessor, parallel processing, RISC machines, and optical computers.

The Intel 80386 32-bit Microprocessor

The 80386 microprocessor is a logical extension of the 80286 we discussed in the preceding section to a 32-bit machine. Remember that the 80286 in PVAM can address up to 8192 virtual memory segments of 64 Kbytes each. The 80286 then has a virtual address space of 1 gigabyte. Virtual memory segments are swapped in from disk storage to as much as 16 Mbytes of physical memory, addressed with 24 address lines. In order to operate with maximum efficiency, a processor working with virtual memory should have an addressing capability equivalent to the size of the secondary storage. As the capacity of optical disk storage units passes the 10-gigabyte mark, processors with greater addressing range than the 80286 are needed. Also, in the eternal quest for speed, processors which use more pipelining and work with wider data words are needed. Here's how the 80386 attempts to answer these needs.

First of all, the 80386 is more highly pipelined than the 80286. Figure 14-22 shows a block diagram of the functional processors within the 80386. Instruction fetching, instruction decoding, instruction execution and memory management are all carried out in parallel. As shown in Figure 14-12, the 80386 instruction set is a superset of that of the other members of the 8086 family. Figure 14-23 shows the register set of the 80386. All of the general-purpose registers can be used for bytes, words, or long words. Long registers are referred to in instructions by simply putting an L in front of the register name, as in the instruction MOV LAX, 7FF0845BH.

Secondly, the 80386 has a 32-bit data bus and produces a full 32-bit nonmultiplexed address bus. This

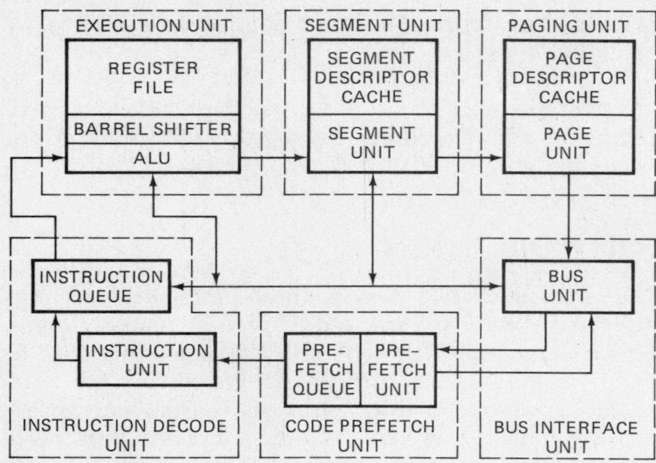

FIGURE 14-22 Intel 80386 internal block diagram showing separate processing units.

32-bit address bus allows it to address 2^{32}, or about 4 gigabytes of physical memory. The 80386 memory management unit allows it to address 2^{46}, or about 64 terabytes of virtual memory. The 80386 can be operated in one of two memory management modes, *paged mode* and *nonpaged mode*. In nonpaged mode the MMU operates very similarly to that of the 80286. Virtual addresses are represented with a selector component and an offset component as they are with the 80286. The selector component is used to index a descriptor in a descriptor table. The descriptor contains the 32-bit physical base address for the desired segment. The offset part of the virtual address is added to the base address from the descriptor to produce the actual physical address as we described in previous sections. The offset part of a virtual address can be 16 or 32 bits, so segments can be as large as 4 gigabytes, rather than being limited to 64 Kbytes as they are for the 80286. In nonpaged mode, named segments are swapped into physical memory as needed. For very large programs, a pure segment approach is not efficient because the whole segment has to be swapped in, even if only a very small part of the segment is needed. To solve this problem, the 80386 can be operated in paged mode.

When operated in paged mode, the 80386 switches the paging unit in after the segment unit. The paging unit allows memory pages of perhaps 4 Kbytes each to be swapped in and out from disk. The principle here is that only the pages that are actually needed from a large segment have to be swapped in. This type of operation is often called *demand-paged virtual memory*. The 80386 paging unit inserts another layer of address computation after adding a base address from a descriptor and an offset. Figure 14-24 shows how this works.

The 32-bit address produced by adding a base address from a descriptor and an offset is referred to as a *linear address*. Components of this linear address are used as pointers to two levels of paging tables. The first level is the page table directory which contains the base addresses of all of the page tables for the system. The second level is the actual page tables. Page tables contain the addresses of each page in the system.

To summarize the operation of an 80386 in paging mode, then, task and memory protection are provided by descriptor tables and the segment unit, just as they are for an 80286 operating in PVAM. The paging unit allows small, fixed-length pages to be swapped into physical memory as needed. In systems with very large segments this is more efficient than swapping in an entire segment. When coupled with optical disk storage, devices such as the 80386 will make it possible to have much of the power of a mainframe computer on your desk. In the next section we discuss how several proces-

31 — 16	15 — 8:7 — 0	
	AH AX AL	EAX
	BH BX BL	EBX
	CH CX CL	ECX
	DH DX DL	EDX
	SI	ESI
	DI	EDI
	BP	EBP
	SP	ESP
	286 REGISTER SET	

15 — 0	
CS	286 SEGMENT REGISTERS
DS	
SS	
ES	
FS	
GS	

31 — 0	
	IP
	FLAGS
	GDTR
	LDTR
	IDTR
	TR
	CRØ
	CR1
	CR2
	CR3

FIGURE 14-23 Intel 80386 registers.

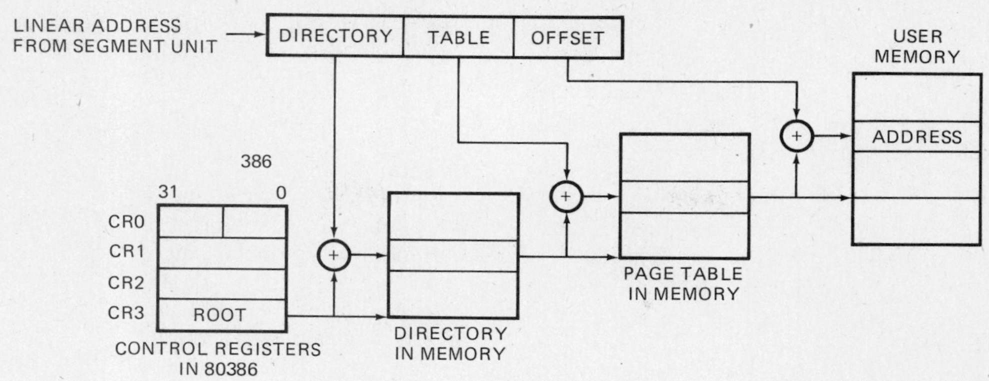

FIGURE 14-24 Linear address from 80386 segment unit is converted to 32-bit physical address by two-level paging mechanism. *(Intel)*

sors such as the 80286 or 80386 can be connected in parallel to produce a "supercomputer."

Parallel Processing

Some computer jobs such as analyzing weather data, modeling the response of complex drugs, or creating the graphics for high-tech science fiction movies require a type of computer commonly called a *supercomputer*. These supercomputers typically work with 64-bit data words, address large amounts of memory, and execute hundreds of millions of instructions per second. The processing speed of these supercomputers is usually expressed in millions of instructions per second (MIPS) or in millions of floating-point operations per second (megaflops). An example of a floating-point operation is adding together two numbers expressed in floating-point form. One current supercomputer, the X-MP2 from Cray Research, Inc. is capable of about 500 megaflops. Depending on configuration, the X-MP2 costs between $9 million and $12 million. The high price of supercomputers is caused by the fact that in order to achieve their great speed, they have to use large quantities of expensive, state-of-the-art discrete components. Less expensive LSI components are not nearly fast enough for a supercomputer with a traditional one- or two-processor architecture. One solution to this problem is to build a system using many LSI processors which operate in parallel or *concurrently*. Each processor can then work on a part of the overall problem that the computer is analyzing.

There are several different ways of connecting processors in parallel. In Chapter 11 we discussed how several microprocessors can operate in parallel on an Intel Multibus. The difficulty with a simple bus structure such as this is that processors compete for shared resources such as memory. If one processor is using the bus, others must wait. This slows down the overall processing speed. One of the more efficient multiprocessor architectures is the hypercube topology developed by Seitz and Fox at Caltech. A diagram of this topology is shown in Figure 14-25. Each node in the system consists of a complete processing unit with the ability to communicate with other units. The number of nodes can be expanded to give the power and speed needed to handle the problem the computer is being used to solve. Each processor unit is typically connected to its nearest neighbors as shown.

Intel has produced the iPSC family of commercial products based on the hypercube topology. The three currently available versions have 32, 64, and 128 nodes. Figure 14-26 shows the components contained on the processor board for each node. Each node is a complete microcomputer with an 80286 processor, 80287 math coprocessor, 500 Kbytes of RAM, 64 Kbytes of ROM, and interface circuitry. The procesor board also has an Intel 82586 Ethernet coprocessor to control communications with other nodes. Each processor has seven 10 Mbit/s lines to communicate with other processors and one 10 Mbit/s line to communicate with a central controller. The Intel systems use an Intel 286/310 minicomputer as the central controller for the hypercube. The advantage of this structure is that each processor has enough

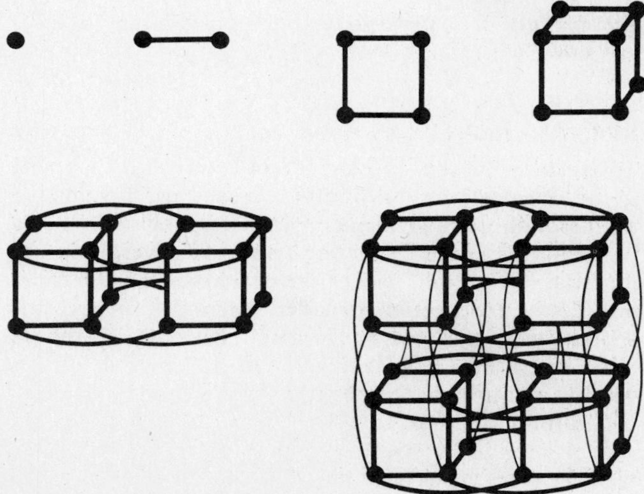

FIGURE 14-25 Hypercube multiprocessor topologies for 1 to 32 nodes.

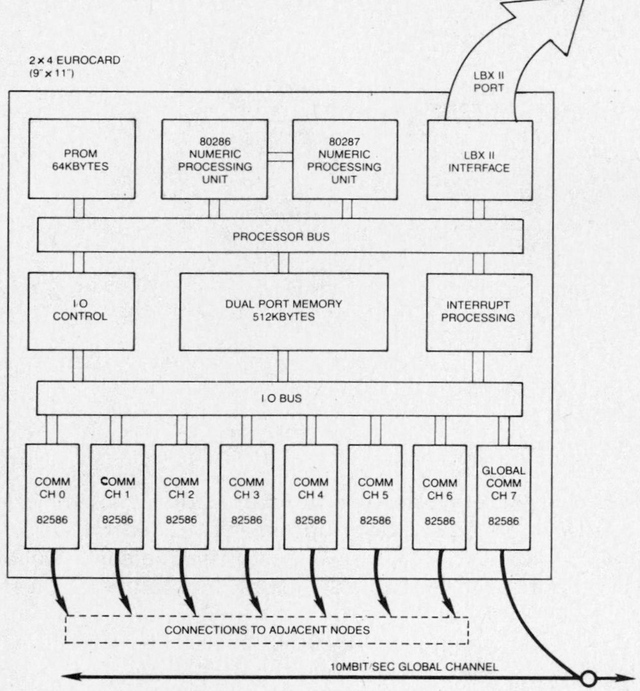

FIGURE 14-26 Block diagram of Intel iPSC hypercube node processor board.

memory to operate independently, and communication between processors can take any one of several routes, instead of being limited to a single bus. Current systems operate at 2–10 Mflops, which puts them in the low end of the supercomputer range. However, because common LSI components are used, the cost is much less than that of an equivalent single-processor supercomputer. Adding more nodes should produce faster systems in the future because parallel processors eliminate much of the "bottleneck" caused by a single serial processor. Another method currently being developed to speed up the operation of processors is to streamline their instruction set.

RISC Machines

The term RISC stands for *reduced instruction set computer*. By designing a microprocessor instruction set with only simple logical and arithmetic instructions, the processor can operate faster. There are several reasons for this. First of all, fewer instructions mean a simpler and faster instruction decoder. Secondly, instruction sequences can be written to most efficiently do the desired operation. The tradeoff here, of course, is that writing a program requires more work on the part of the programmer.

Optical Computers

So far in this book the microcomputer devices we have discussed use electrical currents or voltage levels to represent logic levels. In the final section of this chapter we want to introduce you to experimental computers which use light beams to represent logic levels and switch logic devices on and off. The basic principle is to let a light beam represent a logic 1 and no beam represent a logic 0 just as is done in simple fiber-optic digital signal transmission systems. Logic gates in an optical computer transmit a beam when switched on and block the light beam when switched off. The logic gates themselves are switched on and off by a light beam shining on them. In other words, logic levels are represented by light or no light, logic gate switches are controlled by the presence or absence of a light beam, and the connecting links between optical logic gates are light beams.

One advantage of optical logic gates and computers is that signals can easily be sent to many elements in parallel. This may lead to their use in parallel processor systems. Another major advantage of optical logic gates is their switching speeds. Even though current optical logic gates are quite primitive, switching speeds are in the picosecond range. Optics researchers believe that switching speeds of a few femtoseconds (10^{-15} seconds) are possible. Optical computers may be able to run with clocks of several hundred MHz. A major disadvantage of current optical devices is the relatively large amount of power they require. Hopefully, further research will realize the potential of this technology.

EPILOGUE

This book has only been able to show you a small view of where microcomputer electronics is and where it seems to be evolving. Hopefully it has given you enough of a start that you can proceed on your own and enjoy playing a part in the continuing evolution. As you are faced with learning some new and seemingly difficult material, remember the 5-minute rule and the old saying "Grapevines and people bear the best fruit on new growth."

IMPORTANT TERMS AND CONCEPTS FROM THIS CHAPTER

Multiuser, multitasking

Scheduler

Time-slice and preemptive priority-based scheduling

Semaphore

Process control block

Deadlock

Critical region

Application programs

Utilities

Memory management

Overlay

Bank switching

Descriptor table

Virtual memory

Demand-paged virtual memory

Cache

UNIX

Kernel
- process and user tables
- child process
- parent process
- inode number
- signal
- pipe

Shell
- standard input and output, error output
- redirection
- spooling

RMX 86
- nucleus
- modules
- basic I/O systems
- extended I/O systems
- human interface
- universal development interface

Objects
- tasks, jobs, segments, mailboxes, regions, semaphores

Task states

80286
- bus, instruction, execution, and address units
- real address mode
- protected virtual address mode (PVAM)
- descriptor
- global and local descriptor tables
- selector
- segment address translation register (segment register)
- privilege level
- descriptor and current privilege levels
- task state segment
- interrupt, trap, and task gates

80386
- paged and nonpaged mode
- demand-paged virtual memory

Parallel processing
- parallel or concurrent operation
- hypercube topology

RISC machine

Optical computer

5-minute rule

Grapevine

REVIEW QUESTIONS AND PROBLEMS

1. List and briefly describe the two types of scheduling commonly used in multiuser/multitasking operating systems.
2. Suppose that two users in a time-share computer system each want to print out a file. How can the system be prevented from printing lines from one file between lines of the other file?
3. Define the term "deadlock" and describe one way it can be prevented.
4. Define the term "critical region" and show with 8086 assembly language instructions how a semaphore can be used to protect a critical region.
5. The UNIX operating system is set up as a "three-layer" operating system. What is the major reason why it is configured as layers? Identify and describe the function of each of the three layers.
6. Describe how an overlay scheme is used to run programs such as compilers which are too large to be loaded into physical memory all at once.
7. Define the term "virtual memory," and use Figure 14-4 to help you briefly describe how a logical address is converted to a physical address by a memory management unit using a descriptor table. What action will the MMU take if it finds that a requested segment is not present in physical memory? What is another major advantage of the indirect addressing provided by descriptor tables, besides the ability to address a large amount of virtual memory?
8. How does a UNIX scheduler determine which active process to service next?
9. Define the term "hierarchial file structure" as used in the UNIX operating system. What is the advantage of this type file structure over a simple list type?
10. In a UNIX system, input or output can be "redirected." Explain briefly what this means.
11. What is meant by the term "piping" in a UNIX system. What symbol is used to indicate a pipe?
12. A programmer was heard to say that she "sent the file off to the print spooler before going to lunch." What did she mean by this statement?
13. For what types of applications was the RMX 86 operating system designed? Compare the scheduling method of RMX 86 with that of UNIX.

14. List the four major processing units in an 80286 microprocessor and briefly describe the function of each.

15. The data sheet for a computer which uses the 80286 as its CPU indicates that the 80286 is operated in its "real address mode." What does this mean?

16. How is an 80286 switched from real address mode to protected virtual address mode operation? How can it be switched back to real address mode operation?

17. Explain the term "virtual memory." How much virtual memory can an 80286 address? How much physical memory can an 80286 address?

18. Why is the length of the segment included in the descriptor for the segment? How does the 80286 keep track of where the global descriptor table and the currently used local descriptor table are located in memory?

19. Give the names of the two parts of an 80286 PVAM virtual address. Using Figure 14-19, describe how a 32-bit virtual address for a data segment location in a task's local memory is translated to the actual 24-bit physical address. How would this translation be different if the memory location were in the global memory area?

20. How are tasks in an 80286 system protected from each other?

21. How can operating system kernel procedures and data be protected from access by application programs in an 80286 system?

22. In an 80286 system a task operating at a level 2 privilege can in a special way call a procedure at a higher privilege level. Describe briefly the mechanism that is used to make this access.

23. The 80286 maintains a task state segment for each active task in a system. How are these task state segments accessed?

24. List three major advances that the 80386 microprocessor has over the 80286.

25. What are the major advantages of using parallel processors such as is done in the Intel hypercube, instead of using a single fast processor.

26. What factor makes optical computers an inviting technology?

BIBLIOGRAPHY

Because of the technical level of this book, the major sources of further information on the topics discussed are manufacturers' data books, application notes, and articles in current engineering periodicals. With the foundation provided here, you should be able to comfortably read these materials. Listed below, by chapter, are some materials you may find helpful. Following the chapter listings is a list of periodicals which we have found to be particularly helpful in keeping up with the latest advances in microcomputer evolution and applications. Most of these periodicals have articles which review the basic principles of a particular area of electronics and then discuss the latest developments in that area.

Chapter 1

Hall, Douglas V., *Microprocessors and Digital Systems*, 2d ed., McGraw-Hill, Inc., New York, 1983.

Chapters 2–6

Mick, John, and Jim Brick, *Bit-Slice Microprocessor Design*, McGraw-Hill, Inc., New York, 1980.

Myers, Glendford J., *Digital System Design with LSI Bit-Slice Logic*, John Wiley and Sons, New York, 1980.

A History of Microprocessor Development at Intel, Intel Article Reprint/AR-173, Intel Corporation, Santa Clara, Calif.

8086/8087/8088 Macro Assembly Language Reference Manual for 8086-Based Development Systems, Intel Corporation, Santa Clara, Calif., 1980.

Microsystem Components Handbook Microprocessors and Peripherals, vols. 1 and 2, Intel Corporation, Santa Clara, Calif., 1985.

iAPX 86/88, 186/188 User's Manual Programmer's Reference, Intel Corporation, Santa Clara, Calif. 1983.

Staff of Microsoft, *Macro Assembler*, IBM Corp., 1981.

Chapters 7 and 8

Microsystem Components Handbook Microprocessors and Peripherals, vols. 1 and 2, Intel Corporation, Santa Clara, Calif., 1985.

SDK-86 MCS-86 System Design Kit User's Guide, Intel Corporation, Santa Clara, Calif., 1981.

8086 System Design, Application Note, Intel Corporation/AP-67, Intel Corporation, Santa Clara, Calif.

Chapter 9

Microsystem Components Handbook Microprocessors and Peripherals, vols. 1 and 2, Intel Corporation, Santa Clara, Calif. 1985.

Technical Reference Manual, IBM Corp., 1983.

SC-01 Speech Synthesizer Data Sheet, Votrax, Troy, Mich., 1980.

Dorf, Richard C., *Robotics and Automated Manufacturing*, Reston Publishing Company, Reston, Va., 1983.

Hall Effect Manual, 2d ed., Helipot Division of Beckman Instruments, Inc., Fullerton, Calif. 1964.

AMF Potter & Brumfield Catalog, Potter & Brumfield, Princeton, Ind., 1984.

Optoelectronics Designer's Catalog, Hewlett-Packard, Palo Alto, Calif., 1985.

Interfacing Liquid Crystal Displays in Digital Systems, Application Note AN-B, Beckman Instruments, Inc., Scottsdale, Ariz., 1980.

Hot Ideas in CMOS Data Book, GE-Intersil, Cupertino, Calif., 1984.

Optoelectronics Device Data Book, DL118R1, Motorola Semiconductor Products Inc., Phoenix, Ariz. 1983.

Power Mosfet Selector Guide and Cross Reference, SG56R4, Motorola Semiconductor Products Inc., Phoenix, Ariz., 1983.

Sandhu, H.S., *Hands-On-Introduction to ROBOTICS—The Manual for the XR-Series Robots*, Rhino Robots, Champaign, Ill., 1983.

Slo-Syn DC Stepping Motors Catalog, DCM1078, Superior Electric Company, Bristol, Conn., 1979.

Auslander, David M., and Paul Sagues, *Microprocessors for Measurement and Control*, Osborne/McGraw-Hill, Berkeley, Calif., 1981.

Allocca, John A., and Allen Stuart, *Transducers Theory and Applications*, Reston Publishing Company, Inc., Reston, Va., 1984.

Seippel, Robert G., *Transducers, Sensors, and Detectors*, Reston Publishing Company, Inc., Reston, Va., 1983.

Johnson, Curtis D., *Process Control Instrumentation Technology*, 2d ed., John Wiley & Sons, New York, 1982.

Hunter, Ronald P., *Automated Process Control Systems Concepts and Hardware*. Prentice-Hall, Englewood Cliffs, N.J., 1978.

Sheingold, Daniel H. (ed), *Transducer Interfacing Handbook—A Guide to Analog Signal Conditioning*, Analog Devices, Inc., Norwood, Mass. 1981.

Analog Devices 3B Industrial Control Series Data Sheet, Analog Devices, Inc., Norwood, Mass., 1981.

Chapter 11

8086/8087/8088 Macro Assembly Language Reference Manual for 8086-Based Development Systems, Intel Corporation, Santa Clara, Calif. 1980.

iAPX 86/88, 186/188 User's Manual Programmer's Reference, Intel Corporation, Santa Clara, Calif., 1983.

Error Detecting and Correcting Codes, Application Note AP-46, Intel Corporation, Santa Clara, Calif., 1979.

Introduction to the 80186 Microprocessor, Application Note AP-186 Intel Corporation, Santa Clara, Calif., 1983.

Multibus Handbook, Intel Corporation, Santa Clara, Calif., 1983.

Multibus Interfacing, Application Note AP-28A, Intel Corporation, Santa Clara, Calif., 1979.

Getting Started With the Numeric Data Processor, Application Note AP-113, Intel Corporation, Santa Clara, Calif., 1981.

Chapter 12

Raster Graphics Handbook, Conrac Corporation, Covina, Calif., 1980.

Lesea, Austin, and Rodnay Zaks, *Microprocessor Interfacing Techniques*, 2d ed., Sybex Inc., Berkeley, Calif., 1977.

CRT Terminal Design Using the Intel 8275 and 8279, Application Note AP-32, Intel Corporation, Santa Clara, Calif., 1977.

An Intelligent Data Base System Using the 8272, Application Note AP-116, Intel Corporation, Santa Clara, Calif., 1981.

Intel SBC 202 Double Density Diskette Controller Hardware Reference Manual, Intel Corporation, Santa Clara, Calif., 1977.

Chapter 13

LAN Components User's Manual, Intel Corporation, Santa Clara, Calif., 1984.

Data Acquisition Telecommunications Local Area Networks 1983 Data Book, Advanced Micro Devices, Inc., Sunnyvale, Calif., 1983.

Data Communications — A User's Handbook, Racal-Vadic, Sunnyvale, Calif.

Stallings, William, *Local Networks — An Introduction*, Macmillan, New York, 1984.

Friend, George E., et al., *Understanding Data Communications*, Texas Instruments, Dallas, 1984.

Fike, John L., and George E. Friend, *Understanding Telephone Electronics*, Texas Instruments, Dallas, 1984.

McNamara, John E., *Technical Aspects of Data Communication*, Digital Equipment Corporation, Maynard, Mass., 1977.

Smartmodem 1200 Hardware Reference Manual, Hayes Microcomputer Products, Inc., Norcross, Ga., 1983.

AM7911 FSK Modem Product Specification, Advanced Micro Devices, Sunnyvale, Calif., 1983.

EIA Standard RS-422, Electrical Characteristics of Balanced Voltage Digital Interface Circuits, Electronic Industries Association, Engineering Department, Washington, 1975.

EIA Standard RS-232-C, Interface Between Data Terminal Equipment and Data Communication Equipment Employing Serial Binary Data Interchange, Electronic Industries Association, Engineering Department, Washington, 1969.

Using the 8273 SDLC/HDLC Protocol Controller, Application Note AP-36, Intel Corporation, Santa Clara, Calif., 1978.

Essentials of Data Communications, Tektronix Inc., Beaverton, Ore., 1978.

Designer's Guide to Fiber Optics, EDN Magazine, Cahners Publishing Company, Boston, 1978.

Fiber Optic Applications in Electrical Substations, IEEE 83TH0104 PWR, IEEE Service Center, Piscataway, N.J., 1983.

Improving Measurements in Engineering and Manufacturing – HP–1B, Hewlett-Packard, Palo Alto, Calif., 1976.

Using the 8292 GPIB Controller, Application Note AP-66, Intel Corporation, Santa Clara, Calif., 1980.

The AM7990 Family Ethernet Node, Advanced Micro Devices, Sunnyvale, Calif., 1983.

Chapter 14

iRMX 86 Introduction and Operator's Reference Manual, Intel Corporation, Santa Clara, Calif., 1984.

Kaisler, Stephen H., *The Design of Operating Systems for Small Computer Systems*, John Wiley & Sons, New York, 1983.

Multiprogramming with the iAPX 88 and iAPX 86 Microsystems, Application Note AP-106, Intel Corporation, Santa Clara, Calif., 1980.

ASM286 Assembly Language Reference Manual, Intel Corporation, Santa Clara, Calif., 1983.

Gauthier, Richard: *Using the UNIX System*, Reston Publishing Company, Inc., Reston, Va., 1981.

Lumuto, Ann Nicols and Nico Lomuto: *A UNIX Primer*, Prentice-Hall, Englewood Cliffs, N.J., 1983.

Christian, Kaare, *The UNIX Operating System*, John Wiley & Sons, New York, 1983.

Introduction to the iAPX 286, Intel Corporation, Santa Clara, Calif., 1985.

iAPX 286 Operating Systems Writer's Guide, Intel Corporation, Santa Clara, Calif., 1983.

iAPX 286 Hardware Reference Manual, Intel Corporation, Santa Clara, Calif., 1983.

iAPX 286 Programmer's Reference Manual, Intel Corporation, Santa Clara, Calif., 1983.

iAPX 386 High Performance 32-bit Microcomputer Product Preview, Advance Information, Intel Corporation, Santa Clara, Calif.

Periodicals

BYTE. ISSN 0360-5280. Byte Publications, Inc., 70 Main Street, Peterborough, New Hampshire 03458.

EDN. ISSN 0012-7515. Cahners Publishing Co., Boston, Mass.

Electronic Design. USPS-172-080. Hayden Publishing Co., Rochelle Park, N.J.

Electronics. ISSN 0013-5070, McGraw-Hill, Inc., New York.

Instruments and Control Systems. ISSN 0164-0089. Chilton Company, Radnor, Pa.

Mini-Micro Systems. ISSN 0364-9342. Cahners Publishing Co. Boston, Mass.

Electronic Engineering Times. ISSN 0192-1541. Electronic Engineering Times, Manhasset, N.Y.

intel

iAPX 86/10
16-BIT HMOS MICROPROCESSOR

8086/8086-2/8086-1

- **Direct Addressing Capability 1 MByte of Memory**
- **Architecture Designed for Powerful Assembly Language and Efficient High Level Languages.**
- **14 Word, by 16-Bit Register Set with Symmetrical Operations**
- **24 Operand Addressing Modes**
- **Bit, Byte, Word, and Block Operations**
- **8 and 16-Bit Signed and Unsigned Arithmetic in Binary or Decimal Including Multiply and Divide**
- **Range of Clock Rates:**
  5 MHz for 8086,
  8 MHz for 8086-2,
  10 MHz for 8086-1
- **MULTIBUS™ System Compatible Interface**
- **Available in EXPRESS**
  - Standard Temperature Range
  - Extended Temperature Range

The Intel iAPX 86/10 high performance 16-bit CPU is available in three clock rates: 5, 8 and 10 MHz. The CPU is implemented in N-Channel, depletion load, silicon gate technology (HMOS), and packaged in a 40-pin CerDIP package. The iAPX 86/10 operates in both single processor and multiple processor configurations to achieve high performance levels.

Figure 1. iAPX 86/10 CPU Block Diagram

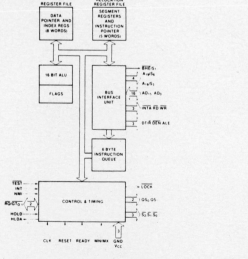

Figure 2. iAPX 86/10 Pin Configuration

Table 1. Pin Description

The following pin function descriptions are for iAPX 86 systems in either minimum or maximum mode. The "Local Bus" in these descriptions is the direct multiplexed bus interface connection to the 8086 (without regard to additional bus buffers).

Symbol	Pin No.	Type	Name and Function
AD_{15}-AD_0	2-16, 39	I/O	**Address Data Bus:** These lines constitute the time multiplexed memory/IO address (T_1) and data (T_2, T_3, T_W, T_4) bus. A_0 is analogous to $\overline{BHE}$ for the lower byte of the data bus, pins D_7-D_0. It is LOW during T_1 when a byte is to be transferred on the lower portion of the bus in memory or I/O operations. Eight-bit oriented devices tied to the lower half would normally use A_0 to condition chip select functions. (See $\overline{BHE}$.) These lines are active HIGH and float to 3-state OFF during interrupt acknowledge and local bus "hold acknowledge."
A_{19}/S_6, A_{18}/S_5, A_{17}/S_4, A_{16}/S_3	35-38	O	**Address/Status:** During T_1 these are the four most significant address lines for memory operations. During I/O operations these lines are LOW. During memory and I/O operations, status information is available on these lines during T_2, T_3, T_W, and T_4. The status of the interrupt enable FLAG bit (S_5) is updated at the beginning of each CLK cycle. A_{17}/S_4 and A_{16}/S_3 are encoded as shown. This information indicates which relocation register is presently being used for data accessing. These lines float to 3-state OFF during local bus "hold acknowledge."
$\overline{BHE}/S_7$	34	O	**Bus High Enable/Status:** During T_1 the bus high enable signal ($\overline{BHE}$) should be used to enable data onto the most significant half of the data bus, pins D_{15}-D_8. Eight-bit oriented devices tied to the upper half of the bus would normally use $\overline{BHE}$ to condition chip select functions. $\overline{BHE}$ is LOW during T_1 for read, write, and interrupt acknowledge cycles when a byte is to be transferred on the high portion of the bus. The S_7 status information is available during T_2, T_3, and T_4. The signal is active LOW, and floats to 3-state OFF in "hold." It is LOW during T_1 for the first interrupt acknowledge cycle.
$\overline{RD}$	32	O	**Read:** Read strobe indicates that the processor is performing a memory of I/O read cycle, depending on the state of the S_2 pin. This signal is used to read devices which reside on the 8086 local bus. $\overline{RD}$ is active LOW during T_2, T_3 and T_W of any read cycle, and is guaranteed to remain HIGH in T_2 until the 8086 local bus has floated. This signal floats to 3-state OFF in "hold acknowledge."
READY	22	I	**READY:** is the acknowledgement from the addressed memory or I/O device that it will complete the data transfer. The READY signal from memory/IO is synchronized by the 8284A Clock Generator to form READY. This signal is active HIGH. The 8086 READY input is not synchronized. Correct operation is not guaranteed if the setup and hold times are not met.
INTR	18	I	**Interrupt Request:** is a level triggered input which is sampled during the last clock cycle of each instruction to determine if the processor should enter into an interrupt acknowledge operation. A subroutine is vectored to via an interrupt vector lookup table located in system memory. It can be internally masked by software resetting the interrupt enable bit. INTR is internally synchronized. This signal is active HIGH.
$\overline{TEST}$	23	I	**$\overline{TEST}$:** input is examined by the "Wait" instruction. If the $\overline{TEST}$ input is LOW execution continues, otherwise the processor waits in an "Idle" state. This input is synchronized internally during each clock cycle on the leading edge of CLK.

A_{17}/S_4	A_{16}/S_3	Characteristics
0 (LOW)	0	Alternate Data
0	1	Stack
1 (HIGH)	0	Code or None
1	1	Data
S_6 is 0 (LOW)		

$\overline{BHE}$	A_0	Characteristics
0	0	Whole word
0	1	Upper byte from/ to odd address
1	0	Lower byte from/ to even address
1	1	None

Table 1. Pin Description (Continued)

Symbol	Pin No.	Type	Name and Function
NMI	17	I	**Non-maskable interrupt:** an edge triggered input which causes a type 2 interrupt. A subroutine is vectored to via an interrupt vector lookup table located in system memory. NMI is not maskable internally by software. A transition from a LOW to HIGH initiates the interrupt at the end of the current instruction. This input is internally synchronized.
RESET	21	I	**Reset:** causes the processor to immediately terminate its present activity. The signal must be active HIGH for at least four clock cycles. It restarts execution, as described in the Instruction Set description, when RESET returns LOW. RESET is internally synchronized.
CLK	19	I	**Clock:** provides the basic timing for the processor and bus controller. It is asymmetric with a 33% duty cycle to provide optimized internal timing.
V_{CC}	40		**V_{CC}:** +5V power supply pin.
GND	1, 20		**Ground**
MN/$\overline{MX}$	33	I	**Minimum/Maximum:** indicates what mode the processor is to operate in. The two modes are discussed in the following sections.

The following pin function descriptions are for the 8086/8288 system in maximum mode (i.e., MN/$\overline{MX}$ = V_{SS}). Only the pin functions which are unique to maximum mode are described; all other pin functions are as described above.

Symbol	Pin No.	Type	Name and Function
$\overline{S_2}$, $\overline{S_1}$, $\overline{S_0}$	26-28	O	**Status:** active during T_4, T_1, and T_2 and is returned to the passive state (1,1,1) during T_3 or during T_W when READY is HIGH. This status is used by the 8288 Bus Controller to generate all memory and I/O access control signals. Any change by $\overline{S_2}$, $\overline{S_1}$, or $\overline{S_0}$ during T_4 is used to indicate the beginning of a bus cycle, and the return to the passive state in T_3 or T_W is used to indicate the end of a bus cycle. These signals float to 3-state OFF in "hold acknowledge." These status lines are encoded as shown.
$\overline{RQ}/GT_0$, $\overline{RQ}/GT_1$	30, 31	I/O	**Request/Grant:** pins are used by other local bus masters to force the processor to release the local bus at the end of the processor's current bus cycle. Each pin is bidirectional with $\overline{RQ}/GT_0$ having higher priority than $\overline{RQ}/GT_1$. $\overline{RQ}/GT$ has an internal pull-up resistor so may be left unconnected. The request/grant sequence is as follows (see Figure 9): 1. A pulse of 1 CLK wide from another local bus master indicates a local bus request ("hold") to the 8086 (pulse 1). 2. During a T_4 or T_1 clock cycle, a pulse 1 CLK wide from the 8086 to the requesting master (pulse 2), indicates that the 8086 has allowed the local bus to float and that it will enter the "hold acknowledge" state at the next CLK. The CPU's bus interface unit is disconnected logically from the local bus during "hold acknowledge." 3. A pulse 1 CLK wide from the requesting master indicates to the 8086 (pulse 3) that the "hold" request is about to end and that the 8086 can reclaim the local bus at the next CLK. Each master-master exchange of the local bus is a sequence of 3 pulses. There must be one dead CLK cycle after each bus exchange. Pulses are active LOW. If the request is made while the CPU is performing a memory cycle, it will release the local bus during T_4 of the cycle when all the following conditions are met: 1. Request occurs on or before T_2. 2. Current cycle is not the low byte of a word (on an odd address). 3. Current cycle is not the first acknowledge of an interrupt acknowledge sequence. 4. A locked instruction is not currently executing.

$\overline{S_2}$	$\overline{S_1}$	$\overline{S_0}$	Characteristics
0 (LOW)	0	0	Interrupt Acknowledge
0	0	1	Read I/O Port
0	1	0	Write I/O Port
0	1	1	Halt
1 (HIGH)	0	0	Code Access
1	0	1	Read Memory
1	1	0	Write Memory
1	1	1	Passive

Table 1. Pin Description (Continued)

Symbol	Pin No.	Type	Name and Function
			If the local bus is idle when the request is made the two possible events will follow: 1. Local bus will be released during the next clock. 2. A memory cycle will start within 3 clocks. Now the four rules for a currently active memory cycle apply with condition number 1 already satisfied.
$\overline{LOCK}$	29	O	**$\overline{LOCK}$:** output indicates that other system bus masters are not to gain control of the system bus while $\overline{LOCK}$ is active LOW. The $\overline{LOCK}$ signal is activated by the "LOCK" prefix instruction and remains active until the completion of the next instruction. This signal is active LOW, and floats to 3-state OFF in "hold acknowledge."
QS_1, QS_0	24, 25	O	**Queue Status:** The queue status is valid during the CLK cycle after which the queue operation is performed. QS_1 and QS_0 provide status to allow external tracking of the internal 8086 instruction queue.

QS_1	QS_0	CHARACTERISTICS
0 (LOW)	0	No Operation
0	1	First Byte of Op Code from Queue
1 (HIGH)	0	Empty the Queue
1	1	Subsequent Byte from Queue

The following pin function descriptions are for the 8086 in minimum mode (i.e., MN/$\overline{MX}$ = V_{CC}). Only the pin functions which are unique to minimum mode are described; all other pin functions are as described above.

Symbol	Pin No.	Type	Name and Function
M/$\overline{IO}$	28	O	**Status line:** logically equivalent to S_2 in the maximum mode. It is used to distinguish a memory access from an I/O access. M/$\overline{IO}$ becomes valid in the T_4 preceding a bus cycle and remains valid until the final T_4 of the cycle (M = HIGH, IO = LOW). M/$\overline{IO}$ floats to 3-state OFF in local bus "hold acknowledge."
$\overline{WR}$	29	O	**Write:** indicates that the processor is performing a write memory or write I/O cycle, depending on the state of the M/$\overline{IO}$ signal. $\overline{WR}$ is active for T_2, T_3 and T_W of any write cycle. It is active LOW, and floats to 3-state OFF in local bus "hold acknowledge."
$\overline{INTA}$	24	O	**$\overline{INTA}$** is used as a read strobe for interrupt acknowledge cycles. It is active LOW during T_2, T_3 and T_W of each interrupt acknowledge cycle.
ALE	25	O	**Address Latch Enable:** provided by the processor to latch the address into the 8282/8283 address latch. It is a HIGH pulse active during T_1 of any bus cycle. Note that ALE is never floated.
DT/$\overline{R}$	27	O	**Data Transmit/Receive:** needed in minimum system that desires to use an 8286/8287 data bus transceiver. It is used to control the direction of data flow through the transceiver. Logically DT/$\overline{R}$ is equivalent to $\overline{S_1}$ in the maximum mode, and its timing is the same as for M/$\overline{IO}$. (T = HIGH, R = LOW.) This signal floats to 3-state OFF in local bus "hold acknowledge."
$\overline{DEN}$	26	O	**Data Enable:** provided as an output enable for the 8286/8287 in a minimum system which uses the transceiver. $\overline{DEN}$ is active LOW during each memory and I/O access and for INTA cycles. For a read or $\overline{INTA}$ cycle it is active from the middle of T_2 until the middle of T_4, while for a write cycle it is active from the beginning of T_2 until the middle of T_4. $\overline{DEN}$ floats to 3-state OFF in local bus "hold acknowledge."
HOLD, HLDA	31, 30	I/O	**HOLD:** indicates that another master is requesting a local bus "hold." To be acknowledged, HOLD must be active HIGH. The processor receiving the "hold" request will issue HLDA (HIGH) as an acknowledgement in the middle of a T_1 clock cycle. Simultaneous with the issuance of HLDA the processor will float the local bus and control lines. After HOLD is detected as being LOW, the processor will LOWer the HLDA, and when the processor needs to run another cycle, it will again drive the local bus and control lines. The same rules as for $\overline{RQ}/GT$ apply regarding when the local bus will be released. HOLD is not an asynchronous input. External synchronization should be provided if the system cannot otherwise guarantee the setup time.

FUNCTIONAL DESCRIPTION

GENERAL OPERATION

The internal functions of the iAPX 86/10 processor are partitioned logically into two processing units. The first is the Bus Interface Unit (BIU) and the second is the Execution Unit (EU) as shown in the block diagram of Figure 1.

These units can interact directly but for the most part perform as separate asynchronous operational processors. The bus interface unit provides the functions related to instruction fetching and queuing, operand fetch and store, and address relocation. This unit also provides the basic bus control. The overlap of instruction pre-fetching provided by this unit serves to increase processor performance through improved bus bandwidth utilization. Up to 6 bytes of the instruction stream can be queued while waiting for decoding and execution.

The instruction stream queuing mechanism allows the BIU to keep the memory utilized very efficiently. Whenever there is space for at least 2 bytes in the queue, the BIU will attempt a word fetch memory cycle. This greatly reduces "dead time" on the memory bus. The queue acts as a First-In-First-Out (FIFO) buffer, from which the EU extracts instruction bytes as required. If the queue is empty (following a branch instruction, for example), the first byte into the queue immediately becomes available to the EU.

The execution unit receives pre-fetched instructions from the BIU queue and provides un-relocated operand addresses to the BIU. Memory operands are passed through the BIU for processing by the EU, which passes results to the BIU for storage. See the Instruction Set description for further register set and architectural descriptions.

MEMORY ORGANIZATION

The processor provides a 20-bit address to memory which locates the byte being referenced. The memory is organized as a linear array of up to 1 million bytes, addressed as 00000(H) to FFFFF(H). The memory is logically divided into code, data, extra data, and stack segments of up to 64K bytes each, with each segment falling on 16-byte boundaries. (See Figure 3a.)

All memory references are made relative to base addresses contained in high speed segment registers. The segment types were chosen based on the addressing needs of programs. The segment register to be selected is automatically chosen according to the rules of the following table. All information in one segment type share the same logical attributes (e.g. code or data). By structuring memory into relocatable areas of similar characteristics and by automatically selecting segment registers, programs are shorter, faster, and more structured.

Word (16-bit) operands can be located on even or odd address boundaries and are thus not constrained to even boundaries as is the case in many 16-bit computers. For address and data operands, the least significant byte of the word is stored in the lower valued address location and the most significant byte in the next higher address location. The BIU automatically performs the proper number of memory accesses, one if the word operand is on an even byte boundary and two if it is on an odd byte boundary. Except for the performance penalty, this double access is transparent to the software. This performance penalty does not occur for instruction fetches, only word operands.

Physically, the memory is organized as a high bank (D_{15}-D_8) and a low bank (D_7-D_0) of 512K 8-bit bytes addressed in parallel by the processor's address lines

A_{19} - A_1. Byte data with even addresses is transferred on the D_7-D_0 bus lines while odd addressed byte data (A_0 HIGH) is transferred on the D_{15}-D_8 bus lines. The processor provides two enable signals, $\overline{BHE}$ and A_0, to selectively allow reading from or writing into either an odd byte location, even byte location, or both. The instruction stream is fetched from memory as words and is addressed internally by the processor to the byte level as necessary.

Memory Reference Need	Segment Register Used	Segment Selection Rule
Instructions	CODE (CS)	Automatic with all instruction prefetch.
Stack	STACK (SS)	All stack pushes and pops. Memory references relative to BP base register except data references.
Local Data	DATA (DS)	Data references when: relative to stack, destination of string operation, or explicitly overridden.
External (Global) Data	EXTRA (ES)	Destination of string operations: Explicitly selected using a segment override.

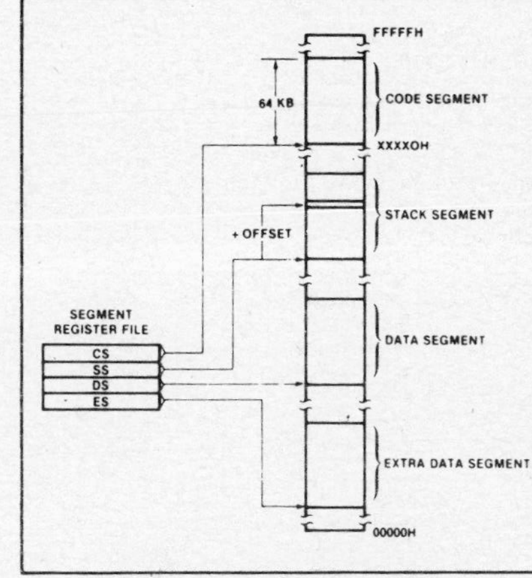

Figure 3a. Memory Organization

In referencing word data the BIU requires one or two memory cycles depending on whether or not the starting byte of the word is on an even or odd address, respectively. Consequently, in referencing word operands performance can be optimized by locating data on even address boundaries. This is an especially useful technique for using the stack, since odd address references to the stack may adversely affect the context switching time for interrupt processing or task multiplexing.

Certain locations in memory are reserved for specific CPU operations (see Figure 3b.) Locations from address FFFF0H through FFFFFH are reserved for operations including a jump to the initial program loading routine. Following RESET, the CPU will always begin execution at location FFFF0H where the jump must be. Locations 00000H through 003FFH are reserved for interrupt operations. Each of the 256 possible interrupt types has its service routine pointed to by a 4-byte pointer element consisting of a 16-bit segment address and a 16-bit offset address. The pointer elements are assumed to have been stored at the respective places in reserved memory prior to occurrence of interrupts.

RESET BOOTSTRAP PROGRAM JUMP — FFFFFH, FFFF0H
INTERRUPT POINTER FOR TYPE 255 — 3FFH, 3FCH
INTERRUPT POINTER FOR TYPE 1 — 7H, 4H
INTERRUPT POINTER FOR TYPE 0 — 3H, 0H

Figure 3b. Reserved Memory Locations

MINIMUM AND MAXIMUM MODES

The requirements for supporting minimum and maximum iAPX 86/10 systems are sufficiently different that they cannot be done efficiently with 40 uniquely defined pins. Consequently, the 8086 is equipped with a strap pin (MN/$\overline{MX}$) which defines the system configuration. The definition of a certain subset of the pins changes dependent on the condition of the strap pin. When MN/$\overline{MX}$ pin is strapped to GND, the 8086 treats pins 24 through 31 in maximum mode. An 8288 bus controller interprets status information coded into $\overline{S_0}$,$\overline{S_1}$,$\overline{S_2}$ to generate bus timing and control signals compatible with the MULTIBUS™ architecture. When the MN/$\overline{MX}$ pin is strapped to V_{CC}, the 8086 generates bus control signals itself on pins 24 through 31, as shown in parentheses in Figure 2. Examples of minimum mode and maximum mode systems are shown in Figure 4.

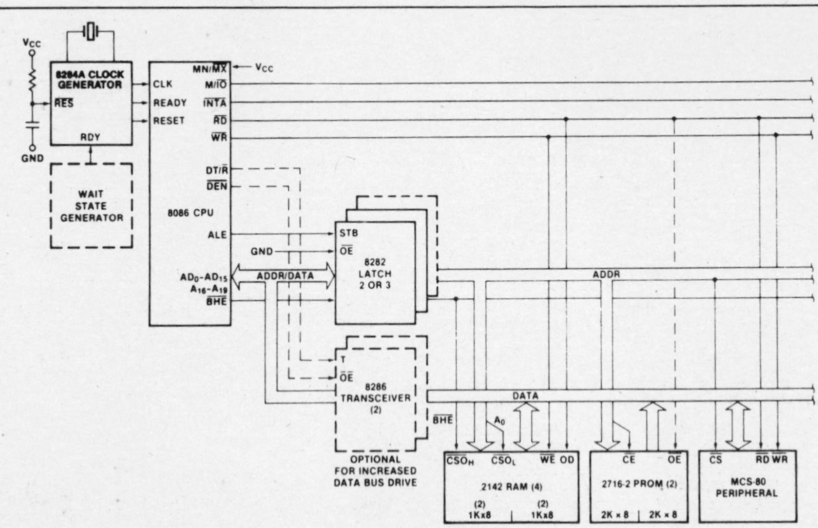

Figure 4a. Minimum Mode iAPX 86/10 Typical Configuration

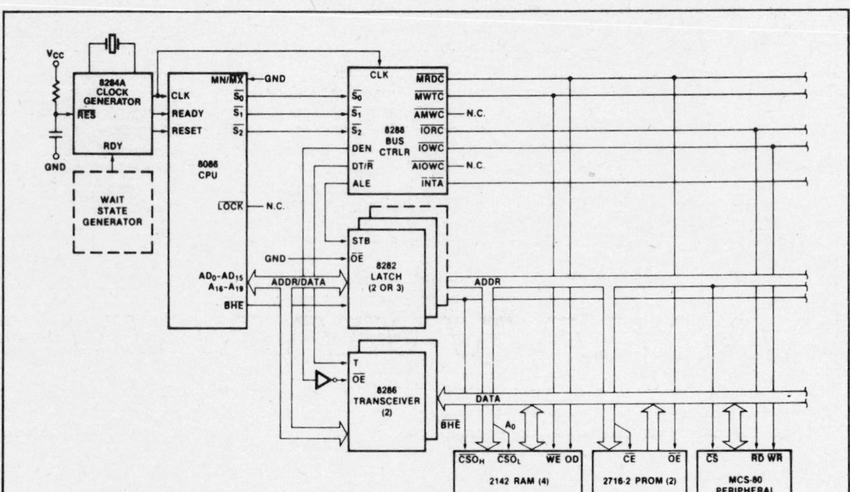

Figure 4b. Maximum Mode iAPX 86/10 Typical Configuration

BUS OPERATION

The 86/10 has a combined address and data bus commonly referred to as a time multiplexed bus. This technique provides the most efficient use of pins on the processor while permitting the use of a standard 40-lead package. This "local bus" can be buffered directly and used throughout the system with address latching provided on memory and I/O modules. In addition, the bus can also be demultiplexed at the processor with a single set of address latches if a standard non-multiplexed bus is desired for the system.

Each processor bus cycle consists of at least four CLK cycles. These are referred to as T_1, T_2, T_3 and T_4 (see Figure 5). The address is emitted from the processor during T_1 and data transfer occurs on the bus during T_3 and T_4. T_2 is used primarily for changing the direction of the bus during read operations. In the event that a "NOT READY" indication is given by the addressed device, "Wait" states (T_W) are inserted between T_3 and T_4. Each inserted "Wait" state is of the same duration as a CLK cycle. Periods can occur between 8086 bus cycles. These are referred to as "Idle" states (T_I) or inactive CLK cycles. The processor uses these cycles for internal housekeeping.

During T_1 of any bus cycle the ALE (Address Latch Enable) signal is emitted (by either the processor or the 8288 bus controller, depending on the MN/$\overline{MX}$ strap). At the trailing edge of this pulse, a valid address and certain status information for the cycle may be latched.

Status bits $\overline{S_0}$, $\overline{S_1}$, and $\overline{S_2}$ are used, in maximum mode, by the bus controller to identify the type of bus transaction according to the following table:

$\overline{S_2}$	$\overline{S_1}$	$\overline{S_0}$	CHARACTERISTICS
0 (LOW)	0	0	Interrupt Acknowledge
0	0	1	Read I/O
0	1	0	Write I/O
0	1	1	Halt
1 (HIGH)	0	0	Instruction Fetch
1	0	1	Read Data from Memory
1	1	0	Write Data to Memory
1	1	1	Passive (no bus cycle)

Status bits S_3 through S_7 are multiplexed with high-order address bits and the $\overline{BHE}$ signal, and are therefore valid during T_2 through T_4. S_3 and S_4 indicate which segment register (see Instruction Set description) was used for this bus cycle in forming the address, according to the following table:

S_4	S_3	CHARACTERISTICS
0 (LOW)	0	Alternate Data (extra segment)
0	1	Stack
1 (HIGH)	0	Code or None
1	1	Data

S_5 is a reflection of the PSW interrupt enable bit. S_6=0 and S_7 is a spare status bit.

I/O ADDRESSING

In the 86/10, I/O operations can address up to a maximum of 64K I/O byte registers or 32K I/O word registers. The I/O address appears in the same format as the memory address on bus lines A_{15}-A_0. The address lines A_{19}-A_{16} are zero in I/O operations. The variable I/O instructions which use register DX as a pointer have full address capability while the direct I/O instructions directly address one or two of the 256 I/O byte locations in page 0 of the I/O address space.

I/O ports are addressed in the same manner as memory locations. Even addressed bytes are transferred on the D_7-D_0 bus lines and odd addressed bytes on D_{15}-D_8. Care must be taken to assure that each register within an 8-bit peripheral located on the lower portion of the bus be addressed as even.

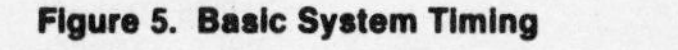

Figure 5. Basic System Timing

EXTERNAL INTERFACE

PROCESSOR RESET AND INITIALIZATION

Processor initialization or start up is accomplished with activation (HIGH) of the RESET pin. The 8086 RESET is required to be HIGH for greater than 4 CLK cycles. The 8086 will terminate operations on the high-going edge of RESET and will remain dormant as long as RESET is HIGH. The low-going transition of RESET triggers an internal reset sequence for approximately 10 CLK cycles. After this interval the 8086 operates normally beginning with the instruction in absolute location FFFF0H (see Figure 3B). The details of this operation are specified in the Instruction Set description of the MCS-86 Family User's Manual. The RESET input is internally synchronized to the processor clock. At initialization the HIGH-to-LOW transition of RESET must occur no sooner than 50 μs after power-up, to allow complete initialization of the 8086.

NMI may not be asserted prior to the 2nd CLK cycle following the end of RESET.

INTERRUPT OPERATIONS

Interrupt operations fall into two classes; software or hardware initiated. The software initiated interrupts and software aspects of hardware interrupts are specified in the Instruction Set description. Hardware interrupts can be classified as non-maskable or maskable.

Interrupts result in a transfer of control to a new program location. A 256-element table containing address pointers to the interrupt service program locations resides in absolute locations 0 through 3FFH (see Figure 3b), which are reserved for this purpose. Each element in the table is 4 bytes in size and corresponds to an interrupt "type". An interrupting device supplies an 8-bit type number, during the interrupt acknowledge sequence, which is used to "vector" through the appropriate element to the new interrupt service program location.

NON-MASKABLE INTERRUPT (NMI)

The processor provides a single non-maskable interrupt pin (NMI) which has higher priority than the maskable interrupt request pin (INTR). A typical use would be to activate a power failure routine. The NMI is edge-triggered on a LOW-to-HIGH transition. The activation of this pin causes a type 2 interrupt. (See Instruction Set description.)

NMI is required to have a duration in the HIGH state of greater than two CLK cycles, but is not required to be synchronized to the clock. Any high-going transition of NMI is latched on-chip and will be serviced at the end of the current instruction or between whole moves of a block-type instruction. Worst case response to NMI would be for multiply, divide, and variable shift instructions. There is no specification on the occurrence of the low-going edge; it may occur before, during, or after the servicing of NMI. Another high-going edge triggers another response if it occurs after the start of the NMI procedure. The signal must be free of logical spikes in general and be free of bounces on the low-going edge to avoid triggering extraneous responses.

MASKABLE INTERRUPT (INTR)

The 86/10 provides a single interrupt request input (INTR) which can be masked internally by software with the resetting of the interrupt enable FLAG status bit. The interrupt request signal is level triggered. It is internally synchronized during each clock cycle on the high-going edge of CLK. To be responded to, INTR must be present (HIGH) during the clock period preceding the end of the current instruction or the end of a whole move for a block-type instruction. During the interrupt response sequence further interrupts are disabled. The enable bit is reset as part of the response to any interrupt (INTR, NMI, software interrupt or single-step), although the

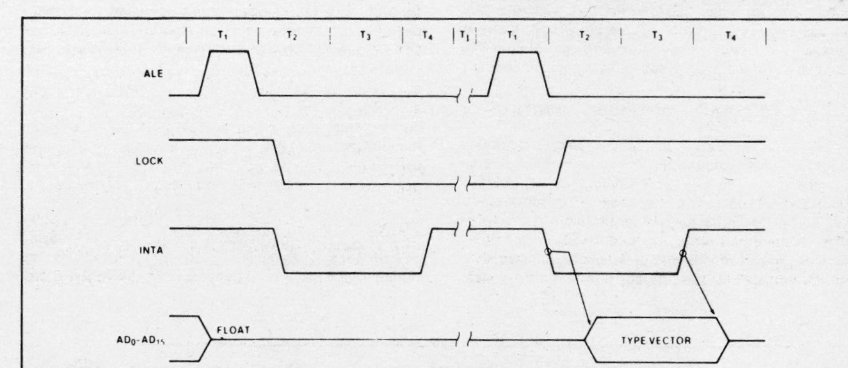

Figure 6. Interrupt Acknowledge Sequence

FLAGS register which is automatically pushed onto the stack reflects the state of the processor prior to the interrupt. Until the old FLAGS register is restored the enable bit will be zero unless specifically set by an instruction.

During the response sequence (figure 6) the processor executes two successive (back-to-back) interrupt acknowledge cycles. The 8086 emits the LOCK signal from T_2 of the first bus cycle until T_2 of the second. A local bus "hold" request will not be honored until the end of the second bus cycle. In the second bus cycle a byte is fetched from the external interrupt system (e.g., 8259A PIC) which identifies the source (type) of the interrupt. This byte is multiplied by four and used as a pointer into the interrupt vector lookup table. An INTR signal left HIGH will be continually responded to within the limitations of the enable bit and sample period. The INTERRUPT RETURN instruction includes a FLAGS pop which returns the status of the original interrupt enable bit when it restores the FLAGS.

HALT

When a software "HALT" instruction is executed the processor indicates that it is entering the "HALT" state in one of two ways depending upon which mode is strapped. In minimum mode, the processor issues one ALE with no qualifying bus control signals. In Maximum Mode, the processor issues appropriate HALT status on $\overline{S}_2\overline{S}_1\overline{S}_0$ and the 8288 bus controller issues one ALE. The 8086 will not leave the "HALT" state when a local bus "hold" is entered while in "HALT". In this case, the processor reissues the HALT indicator. An interrupt request or RESET will force the 8086 out of the "HALT" state.

READ/MODIFY/WRITE (SEMAPHORE) OPERATIONS VIA LOCK

The $\overline{\text{LOCK}}$ status information is provided by the processor when directly consecutive bus cycles are required during the execution of an instruction. This provides the processor with the capability of performing read/modify/write operations on memory (via the Exchange Register With Memory instruction, for example) without the possibility of another system bus master receiving intervening memory cycles. This is useful in multiprocessor system configurations to accomplish "test and set lock" operations. The $\overline{\text{LOCK}}$ signal is activated (forced LOW) in the clock cycle following the one in which the software "LOCK" prefix instruction is decoded by the EU. It is deactivated at the end of the last bus cycle of the instruction following the "LOCK" prefix instruction. While $\overline{\text{LOCK}}$ is active a request on a RQ/GT pin will be recorded and then honored at the end of the LOCK.

EXTERNAL SYNCHRONIZATION VIA TEST

As an alternative to the interrupts and general I/O capabilities, the 8086 provides a single software-testable input known as the $\overline{\text{TEST}}$ signal. At any time the program may execute a WAIT instruction. If at that time the $\overline{\text{TEST}}$ signal is inactive (HIGH), program execution becomes suspended while the processor waits for $\overline{\text{TEST}}$ to become active. It must remain active for at least 5 CLK cycles. The WAIT instruction is re-executed repeatedly until that time. This activity does not consume bus cycles. The processor remains in an idle state while waiting. All 8086 drivers go to 3-state OFF if bus "Hold"is entered. If interrupts are enabled, they may occur while the processor is waiting. When this occurs the processor fetches the WAIT instruction one extra time, processes the interrupt, and then re-fetches and re-executes the WAIT instruction upon returning from the interrupt.

BASIC SYSTEM TIMING

Typical system configurations for the processor operating in minimum mode and in maximum mode are shown in Figures 4a and 4b, respectively. In minimum mode, the MN/$\overline{\text{MX}}$ pin is strapped to V_{CC} and the processor emits bus control signals in a manner similar to the 8085. In maximum mode, the MN/$\overline{\text{MX}}$ pin is strapped to V_{SS} and the processor emits coded status information which the 8288 bus controller uses to generate MULTIBUS compatible bus control signals. Figure 5 illustrates the signal timing relationships.

AX	AH	AL	ACCUMULATOR
BX	BH	BL	BASE
CX	CH	CL	COUNT
DX	DH	DL	DATA
	SP		STACK POINTER
	BP		BASE POINTER
	SI		SOURCE INDEX
	DI		DESTINATION INDEX
	IP		INSTRUCTION POINTER
	$FLAGS_H$	$FLAGS_L$	STATUS FLAGS
	CS		CODE SEGMENT
	DS		DATA SEGMENT
	SS		STACK SEGMENT
	ES		EXTRA SEGMENT

Figure 7. iAPX 86/10 Register Model

SYSTEM TIMING — MINIMUM SYSTEM

The read cycle begins in T_1 with the assertion of the Address Latch Enable (ALE) signal. The trailing (low-going) edge of this signal is used to latch the address information, which is valid on the local bus at this time, into the 8282/8283 latch. The $\overline{\text{BHE}}$ and A_0 signals address the low, high, or both bytes. From T_1 to T_4 the M/$\overline{\text{IO}}$ signal indicates a memory or I/O operation. At T_2 the address is removed from the local bus and the bus goes to a high impedance state. The read control signal is also asserted at T_2. The read ($\overline{\text{RD}}$) signal causes the addressed device to enable its data bus drivers to the local bus. Some time later valid data will be available on the bus and the addressed device will drive the READY line HIGH. When the processor returns the read signal to a HIGH level, the addressed device will again 3-state its bus drivers. If a transceiver (8286/8287) is required to buffer the 8086 local bus, signals DT/$\overline{\text{R}}$ and $\overline{\text{DEN}}$ are provided by the 8086.

A write cycle also begins with the assertion of ALE and the emission of the address. The M/$\overline{\text{IO}}$ signal is again asserted to indicate a memory or I/O write operation. In the T_2 immediately following the address emission the processor emits the data to be written into the addressed location. This data remains valid until the middle of T_4. During T_2, T_3, and T_W the processor asserts the write control signal. The write ($\overline{\text{WR}}$) signal becomes active at the beginning of T_2 as opposed to the read which is delayed somewhat into T_2 to provide time for the bus to float.

The $\overline{\text{BHE}}$ and A_0 signals are used to select the proper byte(s) of the memory/IO word to be read or written according to the following table:

$\overline{\text{BHE}}$	A0	CHARACTERISTICS
0	0	Whole word
0	1	Upper byte from/ to odd address
1	0	Lower byte from/ to even address
1	1	None

I/O ports are addressed in the same manner as memory location. Even addressed bytes are transferred on the D_7–D_0 bus lines and odd addressed bytes on D_{15}–D_8.

The basic difference between the interrupt acknowledge cycle and a read cycle is that the interrupt acknowledge signal ($\overline{\text{INTA}}$) is asserted in place of the read ($\overline{\text{RD}}$) signal and the address bus is floated. (See Figure 6.) In the second of two successive INTA cycles, a byte of information is read from bus lines D_7–D_0 as supplied by the interrupt system logic (i.e., 8259A Priority Interrupt Controller). This byte identifies the source (type) of the interrupt. It is multiplied by four and used as a pointer into an interrupt vector lookup table, as described earlier.

BUS TIMING—MEDIUM SIZE SYSTEMS

For medium size systems the MN/$\overline{\text{MX}}$ pin is connected to V_{SS} and the 8288 Bus Controller is added to the system as well as an 8282/8283 latch for latching the system address, and a 8286/8287 transceiver to allow for bus loading greater than the 8086 is capable of handling. Signals ALE, DEN, and DT/$\overline{\text{R}}$ are generated by the 8288 instead of the processor in this configuration although their timing remains relatively the same. The 8086 status outputs ($\overline{S}_2$, $\overline{S}_1$, and $\overline{S}_0$) provide type-of-cycle information and become 8288 inputs. This bus cycle information specifies read (code, data, or I/O), write (data or I/O), interrupt acknowledge, or software halt. The 8288 thus issues control signals specifying memory read or write, I/O read or write, or interrupt acknowledge. The 8288 provides two types of write strobes, normal and advanced, to be applied as required. The normal write strobes have data valid at the leading edge of write. The advanced write strobes have the same timing as read strobes, and hence data isn't valid at the leading edge of write. The 8286/8287 transceiver receives the usual T and OE inputs from the 8288's DT/$\overline{\text{R}}$ and DEN.

The pointer into the interrupt vector table, which is passed during the second INTA cycle, can derive from an 8259A located on either the local bus or the system bus. If the master 8259A Priority Interrupt Controller is positioned on the local bus, a TTL gate is required to disable the 8286/8287 transceiver when reading from the master 8259A during the interrupt acknowledge sequence and software "poll".

ABSOLUTE MAXIMUM RATINGS*

Ambient Temperature Under Bias ....0°C to 70°C
Storage Temperature ....−65°C to +150°C
Voltage on Any Pin with
Respect to Ground ....−1.0 to +7V
Power Dissipation ....2.5 Watt

**NOTICE: Stresses above those listed under "Absolute Maximum Ratings" may cause permanent damage to the device. This is a stress rating only and functional operation of the device at these or any other conditions above those indicated in the operational sections of this specification is not implied. Exposure to absolute maximum rating conditions for extended periods may affect device reliability.*

D.C. CHARACTERISTICS

(8086: T_A = 0°C to 70°C, V_{CC} = 5V ± 10%)
(8086-1: T_A = 0°C to 70°C, V_{CC} = 5V ± 5%)
(8086-2: T_A = 0°C to 70°C, V_{CC} = 5V ± 5%)

Symbol	Parameter	Min.	Max.	Units	Test Conditions
V_{IL}	Input Low Voltage	−0.5	+0.8	V	
V_{IH}	Input High Voltage	2.0	V_{CC}+0.5	V	
V_{OL}	Output Low Voltage		0.45	V	I_{OL}=2.5 mA
V_{OH}	Output High Voltage	2.4		V	I_{OH}=−400 μA
I_{CC}	Power Supply Current: 8086 8086-1 8086-2		340 360 350	mA	T_A=25°C
I_{LI}	Input Leakage Current		±10	μA	0V ≤ V_{IN} ≤ V_{CC}
I_{LO}	Output Leakage Current		±10	μA	0.45V ≤ V_{OUT} ≤ V_{CC}
V_{CL}	Clock Input Low Voltage	−0.5	+0.6	V	
V_{CH}	Clock Input High Voltage	3.9	V_{CC}+1.0	V	
C_{IN}	Capacitance of Input Buffer (All input except AD_0-AD_{15}, $\overline{RQ}/\overline{GT}$)		15	pF	fc=1 MHz
C_{IO}	Capacitance of I/O Buffer (AD_0-AD_{15}, $\overline{RQ}/\overline{GT}$)		15	pF	fc=1 MHz

A.C. CHARACTERISTICS

(8086: T_A = 0°C to 70°C, V_{CC} = 5V ± 10%)
(8086-1: T_A = 0°C to 70°C, V_{CC} = 5V ± 5%)
(8086-2: T_A = 0°C to 70°C, V_{CC} = 5V ± 5%)

MINIMUM COMPLEXITY SYSTEM TIMING REQUIREMENTS

Symbol	Parameter	8086		8086-1 (Preliminary)		8086-2		Units	Test Conditions
		Min.	Max.	Min.	Max.	Min.	Max.		
TCLCL	CLK Cycle Period	200	500	100	500	125	500	ns	
TCLCH	CLK Low Time	118		53		68		ns	
TCHCL	CLK High Time	69		39		44		ns	
TCH1CH2	CLK Rise Time		10		10		10	ns	From 1.0V to 3.5V
TCL2CL1	CLK Fall Time		10		10		10	ns	From 3.5V to 1.0V
TDVCL	Data in Setup Time	30		5		20		ns	
TCLDX	Data in Hold Time	10		10		10		ns	
TR1VCL	RDY Setup Time into 8284A (See Notes 1, 2)	35		35		35		ns	
TCLR1X	RDY Hold Time into 8284A (See Notes 1, 2)	0		0		0		ns	
TRYHCH	READY Setup Time into 8086	118		53		68		ns	
TCHRYX	READY Hold Time into 8086	30		20		20		ns	
TRYLCL	READY Inactive to CLK (See Note 3)	−8		−10		−8		ns	
THVCH	HOLD Setup Time	35		20		20		ns	
TINVCH	INTR, NMI, $\overline{TEST}$ Setup Time (See Note 2)	30		15		15		ns	
TILIH	Input Rise Time (Except CLK)		20		20		20	ns	From 0.8V to 2.0V
TIHIL	Input Fall Time (Except CLK)		12		12		12	ns	From 2.0V to 0.8V

A.C. CHARACTERISTICS (Continued)

TIMING RESPONSES

Symbol	Parameter	8086		8086-1 (Preliminary)		8086-2		Units	Test Conditions
		Min.	Max.	Min.	Max.	Min.	Max.		
TCLAV	Address Valid Delay	10	110	10	50	10	60	ns	
TCLAX	Address Hold Time	10		10		10		ns	
TCLAZ	Address Float Delay	TCLAX	80	10	40	TCLAX	50	ns	
TLHLL	ALE Width	TCLCH−20		TCLCH−10		TCLCH-10		ns	
TCLLH	ALE Active Delay		80		40		50	ns	
TCHLL	ALE Inactive Delay		85		45		55	ns	
TLLAX	Address Hold Time to ALE Inactive	TCHCL−10		TCHCL−10		TCHCL−10		ns	
TCLDV	Data Valid Delay	10	110	10	50	10	60	ns	*C_L = 20-100 pF for all 8086 Outputs (In addition to 8086 self-load)
TCHDX	Data Hold Time	10		10		10		ns	
TWHDX	Data Hold Time After WR	TCLCH−30		TCLCH−25		TCLCH−30		ns	
TCVCTV	Control Active Delay 1	10	110	10	50	10	70	ns	
TCHCTV	Control Active Delay 2	10	110	10	45	10	60	ns	
TCVCTX	Control Inactive Delay	10	110	10	50	10	70	ns	
TAZRL	Address Float to READ Active	0		0		0		ns	
TCLRL	$\overline{RD}$ Active Delay	10	165	10	70	10	100	ns	
TCLRH	$\overline{RD}$ Inactive Delay	10	150	10	60	10	80	ns	
TRHAV	$\overline{RD}$ Inactive to Next Address Active	TCLCL−45		TCLCL−35		TCLCL−40		ns	
TCLHAV	HLDA Valid Delay	10	160	10	60	10	100	ns	
TRLRH	$\overline{RD}$ Width	2TCLCL−75		2TCLCL−40		2TCLCL−50		ns	
TWLWH	$\overline{WR}$ Width	2TCLCL−60		2TCLCL−35		2TCLCL−40		ns	
TAVAL	Address Valid to ALE Low	TCLCH−60		TCLCH−35		TCLCH−40		ns	
TOLOH	Output Rise Time		20		20		20	ns	From 0.8V to 2.0V
TOHOL	Output Fall Time		12		12		12	ns	From 2.0V to 0.8V

NOTES:
1. Signal at 8284A shown for reference only.
2. Setup requirement for asynchronous signal only to guarantee recognition at next CLK.
3. Applies only to T2 state. (8 ns into T3).

A.C. TESTING INPUT, OUTPUT WAVEFORM

INPUT/OUTPUT

2.4 / 0.45 — 1.5 ← TEST POINTS → 1.5

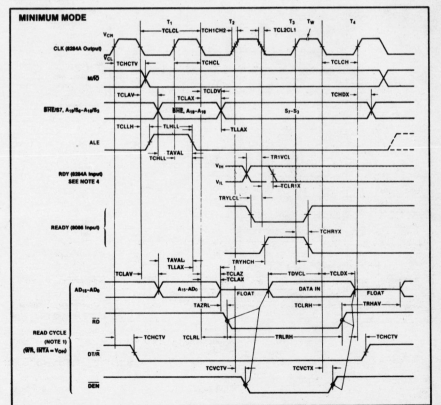

A.C. TESTING: INPUTS ARE DRIVEN AT 2.4V FOR A LOGIC "1" AND 0.45V FOR A LOGIC "0". TIMING MEASUREMENTS ARE MADE AT 1.5V FOR BOTH A LOGIC "1" AND "0".

A.C. TESTING LOAD CIRCUIT

DEVICE UNDER TEST — C_L = 100 pF

C_L INCLUDES JIG CAPACITANCE

WAVEFORMS

MINIMUM MODE

WAVEFORMS (Continued)

MINIMUM MODE (Continued)

NOTES:
1. All signals switch between V_{OH} and V_{OL} unless otherwise specified.
2. RDY is sampled near the end of T_2, T_3, T_W to determine if T_W machines states are to be inserted.
3. Two INTA cycles run back-to-back. The 8086 LOCAL ADDR/DATA BUS is floating during both INTA cycles. Control signals shown for second INTA cycle.
4. Signals at 8284A are shown for reference only.
5. All timing measurements are made at 1.5V unless otherwise noted.

A.C. CHARACTERISTICS

MAX MODE SYSTEM (USING 8288 BUS CONTROLLER) TIMING REQUIREMENTS

Symbol	Parameter	8086		8086-1 (Preliminary)		8086-2 (Preliminary)		Units	Test Conditions
		Min.	Max.	Min.	Max.	Min.	Max.		
TCLCL	CLK Cycle Period	200	500	100	500	125	500	ns	
TCLCH	CLK Low Time	118		53		68		ns	
TCHCL	CLK High Time	69		39		44		ns	
TCH1CH2	CLK Rise Time		10		10		10	ns	From 1.0V to 3.5V
TCL2CL1	CLK Fall Time		10		10		10	ns	From 3.5V to 1.0V
TDVCL	Data in Setup Time	30		5		20		ns	
TCLDX	Data In Hold Time	10		10		10		ns	
TR1VCL	RDY Setup Time into 8284A (See Notes 1, 2)	35		35		35		ns	
TCLR1X	RDY Hold Time into 8284A (See Notes 1, 2)	0		0		0		ns	
TRYHCH	READY Setup Time into 8086	118		53		68		ns	
TCHRYX	READY Hold Time into 8086	30		20		20		ns	
TRYLCL	READY Inactive to CLK (See Note 4)	−8		−10		−8		ns	
TINVCH	Setup Time for Recognition (INTR, NMI, $\overline{TEST}$) (See Note 2)	30		15		15		ns	
TGVCH	$\overline{RQ}/\overline{GT}$ Setup Time	30		12		15		ns	
TCHGX	$\overline{RQ}$ Hold Time into 8086	40		20		30		ns	
TILIH	Input Rise Time (Except CLK)		20		20		20	ns	From 0.8V to 2.0V
TIHIL	Input Fall Time (Except CLK)		12		12		12	ns	From 2.0V to 0.8V

NOTES:
1. Signal at 8284A or 8288 shown for reference only.
2. Setup requirement for asynchronous signal only to guarantee recognition at next CLK.
3. Applies only to T3 and wait states.
4. Applies only to T2 state (8 ns into T3).

A.C. CHARACTERISTICS (Continued)

TIMING RESPONSES

Symbol	Parameter	8086		8086-1 (Preliminary)		8086-2 (Preliminary)		Units	Test Conditions
		Min.	Max.	Min.	Max.	Min.	Max.		
TCLML	Command Active Delay (See Note 1)	10	35	10	35	10	35	ns	
TCLMH	Command Inactive Delay (See Note 1)	10	35	10	35	10	35	ns	
TRYHSH	READY Active to Status Passive (See Note 3)		110		45		65	ns	
TCHSV	Status Active Delay	10	110	10	45	10	60	ns	
TCLSH	Status Inactive Delay	10	130	10	55	10	70	ns	
TCLAV	Address Valid Delay	10	110	10	50	10	60	ns	
TCLAX	Address Hold Time	10		10		10		ns	
TCLAZ	Address Float Delay	TCLAX	80	10	40	TCLAX	50	ns	
TSVLH	Status Valid to ALE High (See Note 1)		15		15		15	ns	
TSVMCH	Status Valid to MCE High (See Note 1)		15		15		15	ns	
TCLLH	CLK Low to ALE Valid (See Note 1)		15		15		15	ns	
TCLMCH	CLK Low to MCE High (See Note 1)		15		15		15	ns	
TCHLL	ALE Inactive Delay (See Note 1)		15		15		15	ns	C_L = 20-100 pF for all 8086 Outputs (in addition to 8086 self-load)
TCLMCL	MCE Inactive Delay (See Note 1)		15		15		15	ns	
TCLDV	Data Valid Delay	10	110	10	50	10	60	ns	
TCHDX	Data Hold Time	10		10		10		ns	
TCVNV	Control Active Delay (See Note 1)	5	45	5	45	5	45	ns	
TCVNX	Control Inactive Delay (See Note 1)	10	45	10	45	10	45	ns	
TAZRL	Address Float to Read Active	0		0		0		ns	
TCLRL	RD Active Delay	10	165	10	70	10	100	ns	
TCLRH	RD Inactive Delay	10	150	10	60	10	80	ns	
TRHAV	RD Inactive to Next Address Active	TCLCL−45		TCLCL−35		TCLCL−40		ns	
TCHDTL	Direction Control Active Delay (See Note 1)		50		50		50	ns	
TCHDTH	Direction Control Inactive Delay (See Note 1)		30		30		30	ns	
TCLGL	GT Active Delay	0	85	0	45	0	50	ns	
TCLGH	GT Inactive Delay	0	85	0	45	0	50	ns	
TRLRH	RD Width	2TCLCL−75		2TCLCL−40		2TCLCL−50		ns	
TOLOH	Output Rise Time		20		20		20	ns	From 0.8V to 2.0V
TOHOL	Output Fall Time		12		12		12	ns	From 2.0V to 0.8V

intel iAPX 86/10

WAVEFORMS

MAXIMUM MODE

READ CYCLE

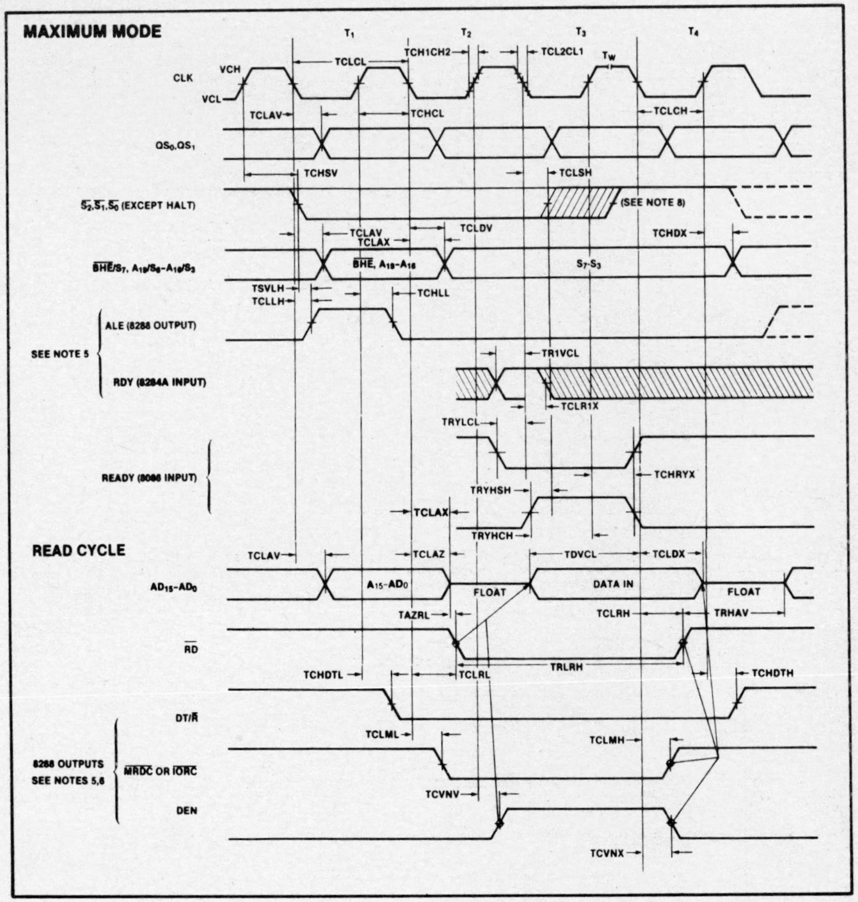

WAVEFORMS (Continued)

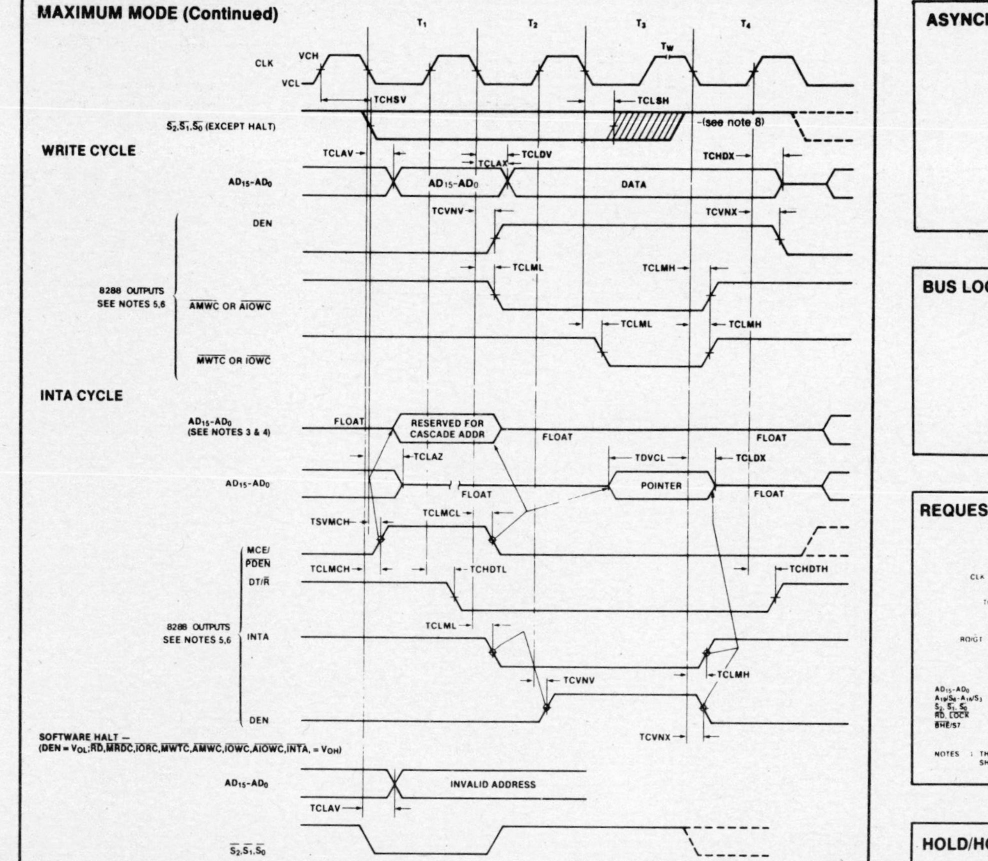

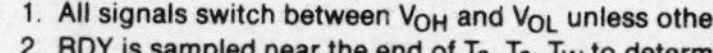

NOTES:
1. All signals switch between V_{OH} and V_{OL} unless otherwise specified.
2. RDY is sampled near the end of T_2, T_3, T_W to determine if T_W machines states are to be inserted.
3. Cascade address is valid between first and second INTA cycle.
4. Two INTA cycles run back-to-back. The 8086 LOCAL ADDR/DATA BUS is floating during both INTA cycles. Control for pointer address is shown for second INTA cycle.
5. Signals at 8284A or 8288 are shown for reference only.
6. The issuance of the 8288 command and control signals ($\overline{MRDC}$, $\overline{MWTC}$, $\overline{AMWC}$, $\overline{IORC}$, $\overline{IOWC}$, $\overline{AIOWC}$, $\overline{INTA}$ and DEN) lags the active high 8288 CEN.
7. All timing measurements are made at 1.5V unless otherwise noted.
8. Status inactive in state just prior to T_4.

iAPX 86/10

WAVEFORMS (Continued)

ASYNCHRONOUS SIGNAL RECOGNITION

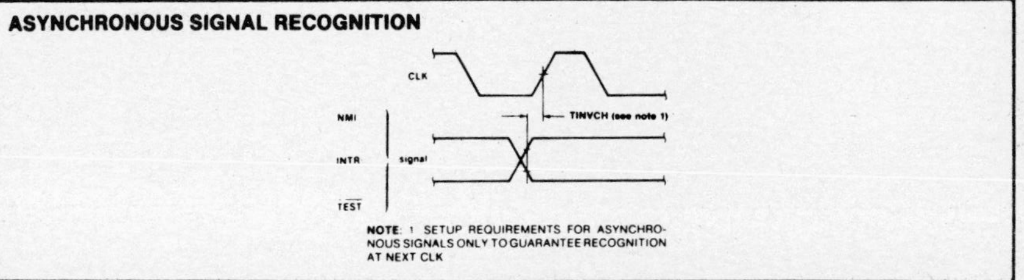

BUS LOCK SIGNAL TIMING (MAXIMUM MODE ONLY)

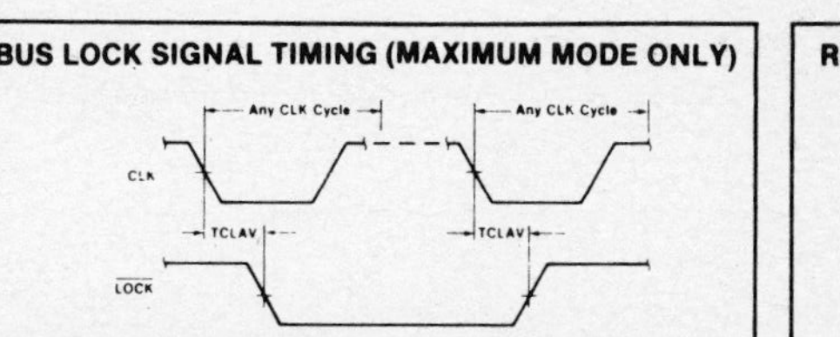

RESET TIMING

REQUEST/GRANT SEQUENCE TIMING (MAXIMUM MODE ONLY)

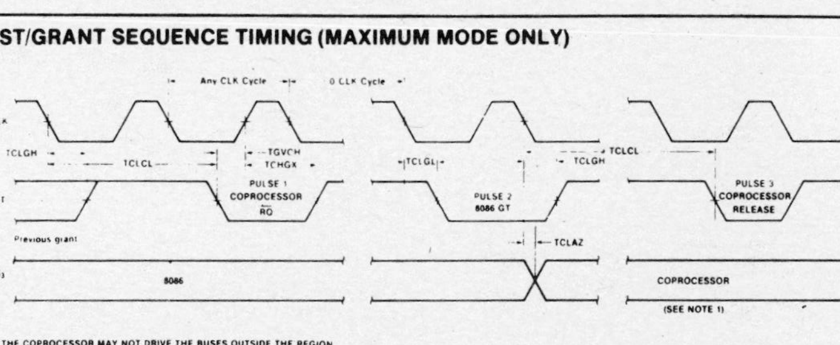

HOLD/HOLD ACKNOWLEDGE TIMING (MINIMUM MODE ONLY)

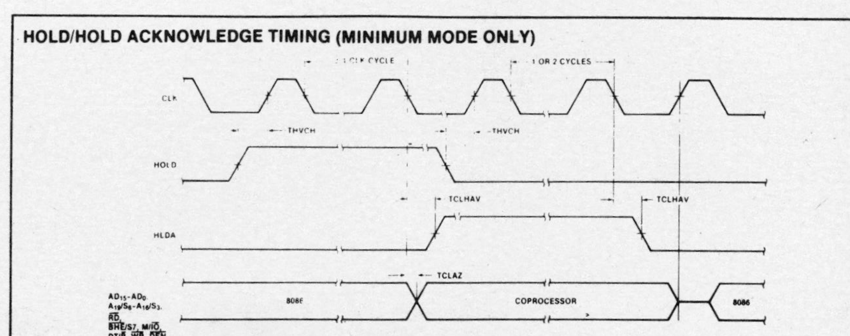

intel

IAPX 86/10

Table 2. Instruction Set Summary

DATA TRANSFER

MOV = Move:	76543210	76543210	76543210	76543210
Register/memory to/from register	100010dw	mod reg r/m		
Immediate to register/memory	1100011w	mod 000 r/m	data	data if w 1
Immediate to register	1011w reg	data	data if w 1	
Memory to accumulator	1010000w	addr-low	addr-high	
Accumulator to memory	1010001w	addr-low	addr-high	
Register/memory to segment register	10001110	mod 0 reg r/m		
Segment register to register/memory	10001100	mod 0 reg r/m		
PUSH = Push:				
Register/memory	11111111	mod 110 r/m		
Register	01010 reg			
Segment register	000 reg 110			
POP = Pop:				
Register/memory	10001111	mod 000 r/m		
Register	01011 reg			
Segment register	000 reg 111			
XCHG = Exchange:				
Register/memory with register	1000011w	mod reg r/m		
Register with accumulator	10010 reg			
IN = Input from				
Fixed port	1110010w	port		
Variable port	1110110w			
OUT = Output to				
Fixed port	1110011w	port		
Variable port	1110111w			
XLAT = Translate byte to AL	11010111			
LEA = Load EA to register	10001101	mod reg r/m		
LDS = Load pointer to DS	11000101	mod reg r/m		
LES = Load pointer to ES	11000100	mod reg r/m		
LAHF = Load AH with flags	10011111			
SAHF = Store AH into flags	10011110			
PUSHF = Push flags	10011100			
POPF = Pop flags	10011101			

ARITHMETIC

ADD = Add:	76543210	76543210	76543210	76543210
Reg/memory with register to either	000000dw	mod reg r/m		
Immediate to register/memory	100000sw	mod 000 r/m	data	data if s w 01
Immediate to accumulator	0000010w	data	data if w 1	
ADC = Add with carry:				
Reg/memory with register to either	000100dw	mod reg r/m		
Immediate to register/memory	100000sw	mod 010 r/m	data	data if s w 01
Immediate to accumulator	0001010w	data	data if w 1	
INC = Increment:				
Register/memory	1111111w	mod 000 r/m		
Register	01000 reg			
AAA = ASCII adjust for add	00110111			
DAA = Decimal adjust for add	00100111			
SUB = Subtract:				
Reg/memory and register to either	001010dw	mod reg r/m		
Immediate from register/memory	100000sw	mod 101 r/m	data	data if s w 01
Immediate from accumulator	0010110w	data	data if w 1	
SBB = Subtract with borrow				
Reg/memory and register to either	000110dw	mod reg r/m		
Immediate from register/memory	100000sw	mod 011 r/m	data	data if s w 01
Immediate from accumulator	0001110w	data	data if w 1	

DEC = Decrement:	76543210	76543210	76543210	76543210
Register/memory	1111111w	mod 001 r/m		
Register	01001 reg			
NEG Change sign	1111011w	mod 011 r/m		
CMP = Compare:				
Register/memory and register	001110dw	mod reg r/m		
Immediate with register/memory	100000sw	mod 111 r/m	data	data if s w 01
Immediate with accumulator	0011110w	data	data if w 1	
AAS ASCII adjust for subtract	00111111			
DAS Decimal adjust for subtract	00101111			
MUL Multiply (unsigned)	1111011w	mod 100 r/m		
IMUL Integer multiply (signed)	1111011w	mod 101 r/m		
AAM ASCII adjust for multiply	11010100	00001010		
DIV Divide (unsigned)	1111011w	mod 110 r/m		
IDIV Integer divide (signed)	1111011w	mod 111 r/m		
AAD ASCII adjust for divide	11010101	00001010		
CBW Convert byte to word	10011000			
CWD Convert word to double word	10011001			

LOGIC

	76543210	76543210	76543210	76543210
NOT Invert	1111011w	mod 010 r/m		
SHL/SAL Shift logical/arithmetic left	110100vw	mod 100 r/m		
SHR Shift logical right	110100vw	mod 101 r/m		
SAR Shift arithmetic right	110100vw	mod 111 r/m		
ROL Rotate left	110100vw	mod 000 r/m		
ROR Rotate right	110100vw	mod 001 r/m		
RCL Rotate through carry flag left	110100vw	mod 010 r/m		
RCR Rotate through carry right	110100vw	mod 011 r/m		
AND = And:				
Reg/memory and register to either	001000dw	mod reg r/m		
Immediate to register/memory	1000000w	mod 100 r/m	data	data if w 1
Immediate to accumulator	0010010w	data	data if w 1	
TEST = And function to flags, no result:				
Register/memory and register	1000010w	mod reg r/m		
Immediate data and register/memory	1111011w	mod 000 r/m	data	data if w 1
Immediate data and accumulator	1010100w	data	data if w 1	
OR = Or:				
Reg/memory and register to either	000010dw	mod reg r/m		
Immediate to register/memory	1000000w	mod 001 r/m	data	data if w 1
Immediate to accumulator	0000110w	data	data if w 1	
XOR = Exclusive or:				
Reg/memory and register to either	001100dw	mod reg r/m		
Immediate to register/memory	1000000w	mod 110 r/m	data	data if w 1
Immediate to accumulator	0011010w	data	data if w 1	

STRING MANIPULATION

	76543210
REP = Repeat	1111001z
MOVS = Move byte/word	1010010w
CMPS = Compare byte/word	1010011w
SCAS = Scan byte/word	1010111w
LODS = Load byte/wd to AL/AX	1010110w
STOS = Stor byte/wd from AL/A	1010101w

Mnemonics ©Intel, 1978

intel

IAPX 86/10

Table 2. Instruction Set Summary (Continued)

CONTROL TRANSFER

CALL = Call:	76543210	76543210	76543210
Direct within segment	11101000	disp-low	disp-high
Indirect within segment	11111111	mod 010 r/m	
Direct intersegment	10011010	offset-low	offset-high
		seg-low	seg-high
Indirect intersegment	11111111	mod 011 r/m	
JMP = Unconditional Jump:			
Direct within segment	11101001	disp-low	disp-high
Direct within segment-short	11101011	disp	
Indirect within segment	11111111	mod 100 r/m	
Direct intersegment	11101010	offset-low	offset-high
		seg-low	seg-high
Indirect intersegment	11111111	mod 101 r/m	
RET = Return from CALL:			
Within segment	11000011		
Within seg adding immed to SP	11000010	data-low	data-high
Intersegment	11001011		
Intersegment, adding immediate to SP	11001010	data-low	data-high
JE/JZ = Jump on equal/zero	01110100	disp	
JL/JNGE = Jump on less/not greater or equal	01111100	disp	
JLE/JNG = Jump on less or equal/not greater	01111110	disp	
JB/JNAE = Jump on below/not above or equal	01110010	disp	
JBE/JNA = Jump on below or equal/not above	01110110	disp	
JP/JPE = Jump on parity/parity even	01111010	disp	
JO = Jump on overflow	01110000	disp	
JS = Jump on sign	01111000	disp	
JNE/JNZ = Jump on not equal/not zero	01110101	disp	
JNL/JGE = Jump on not less/greater or equal	01111101	disp	
JNLE/JG = Jump on not less or equal/greater	01111111	disp	

	76543210	76543210
JNB/JAE Jump on not below/above or equal	01110011	disp
JNBE/JA Jump on not below or equal/above	01110111	disp
JNP/JPO Jump on not par/par odd	01111011	disp
JNO Jump on not overflow	01110001	disp
JNS Jump on not sign	01111001	disp
LOOP Loop CX times	11100010	disp
LOOPZ/LOOPE Loop while zero/equal	11100001	disp
LOOPNZ/LOOPNE Loop while not zero/equal	11100000	disp
JCXZ Jump on CX zero	11100011	disp
INT Interrupt		
Type specified	11001101	type
Type 3	11001100	
INTO Interrupt on overflow	11001110	
IRET Interrupt return	11001111	

PROCESSOR CONTROL

	76543210	76543210
CLC Clear carry	11111000	
CMC Complement carry	11110101	
STC Set carry	11111001	
CLD Clear direction	11111100	
STD Set direction	11111101	
CLI Clear interrupt	11111010	
STI Set interrupt	11111011	
HLT Halt	11110100	
WAIT Wait*	10011011	
ESC Escape (to external device)	11011xxx	mod x x x r/m
LOCK Bus lock prefix	11110000	

Footnotes:

AL = 8-bit accumulator
AX = 16-bit accumulator
CX = Count register
DS = Data segment
ES = Extra segment
Above/below refers to unsigned value.
Greater = more positive;
Less = less positive (more negative) signed values
if d = 1 then "to" reg; if d = 0 then "from" reg
if w = 1 then word instruction; if w = 0 then byte instruction

if mod = 11 then r/m is treated as a REG field
if mod = 00 then DISP = 0*, disp-low and disp-high are absent
if mod = 01 then DISP = disp-low sign-extended to 16 bits, disp-high is absent
if mod = 10 then DISP = disp-high: disp-low
if r/m = 000 then EA = (BX) + (SI) + DISP
if r/m = 001 then EA = (BX) + (DI) + DISP
if r/m = 010 then EA = (BP) + (SI) + DISP
if r/m = 011 then EA = (BP) + (DI) + DISP
if r/m = 100 then EA = (SI) + DISP
if r/m = 101 then EA = (DI) + DISP
if r/m = 110 then EA = (BP) + DISP*
if r/m = 111 then EA = (BX) + DISP
DISP follows 2nd byte of instruction (before data if required)

*except if mod = 00 and r/m = 110 then EA = disp-high: disp-low.

if s:w = 01 then 16 bits of immediate data form the operand.
if s:w = 11 then an immediate data byte is sign extended to form the 16-bit operand.
if v = 0 then "count" = 1; if v = 1 then "count" in (CL)
x = don't care
z is used for string primitives for comparison with Z.F FLAG.

SEGMENT OVERRIDE PREFIX

0 0 1 reg 1 1 0

REG is assigned according to the following table:

16-Bit (w = 1)	8-Bit (w = 0)	Segment
000 AX	000 AL	00 ES
001 CX	001 CL	01 CS
010 DX	010 DL	10 SS
011 BX	011 BL	11 DS
100 SP	100 AH	
101 BP	101 CH	
110 SI	110 DH	
111 DI	111 BH	

Instructions which reference the flag register file as a 16-bit object use the symbol FLAGS to represent the file:

FLAGS = X:X:X:X:(OF):(DF):(IF):(TF):(SF):(ZF):X:(AF):X:(PF):X:(CF)

Mnemonics © Intel, 1978

APPENDIX B

8086/8088 Instructions

Notes for 8086/8088 Instructions

The individual instruction descriptions are shown by a format box such as the following:

Opcode	m/op/r/m	- - -	- - -	Data	- - -

These are byte-wise representations of the object code generated by the assembler and are interpreted as follows:

- Opcode is the 8-bit opcode for the instruction. The actual opcode generated is defined in the "Opcode" column of the instruction table that follows each format box.
- m/op/r/m is the byte that specifies the operands of the instruction. It contains a 2-bit mode field (m), a 3-bit register field (op), and a 3-bit register or memory (r/m) field.
- Dashed blank boxes following the m/op/r/m box are for any displacement required by the mode field.
- Data is for a byte of immediate data.
- A dashed blank box following a Data box is used whenever the immediate operand is a word quantity.

Operand Summary

"reg" field Bit Assignments:

Word Operand	Byte Operand	Segment
000 AX	000 AL	00 ES
001 CX	001 CL	01 CS
010 DX	010 DL	10 SS
011 BX	011 BL	11 DS
100 SP	100 AH	
101 BP	101 CH	
110 SI	110 DH	
111 DI	111 BH	

Second Instruction Byte Summary

mod xxx r/m

mod	Displacement
00	DISP = 0*, disp-low and disp-high are absent
01	DISP = disp-low sign-extended to 16-bits, disp-high is absent
10	DISP = disp-high: disp-low
11	r/m is treated as a "reg" field

r/m	Operand Address
000	(BX) + (SI) + DISP
001	(BX) + (DI) + DISP
010	(BP) + (SI) + DISP
011	(BP) + (DI) + DISP
100	(SI) + DISP
101	(DI) + DISP
110	(BP) + DISP*
111	(BX) + DISP

DISP follows 2nd byte of instruction (before data if required).

*except if mod = 00 and r/m = 110 then EA = disp-high: disp-low.

Flags

AF: AUXILIARY CARRY — BCD
CF: CARRY FLAG
DF: DIRECTION FLAG (STRINGS)
IF: INTERRUPT ENABLE FLAG
OF: OVERFLOW FLAG (CF SF)
PF: PARITY FLAG
SF: SIGN FLAG
TF: TRAP (SINGLE STEP FLAG)
ZF: ZERO FLAG

Instructions that reference the flag register file as a 16-bit object use the symbol FLAGS to represent the file:

15 8 0

X	X	X	X	OF	DF	IF	TF	SF	ZF	X	AF	X	PF	X	CF

X = Don't Care

Segment Override Prefix

0 0 1 reg 1 1 0

Timing: 2 clocks

Use of Segment Override

Operand Register	Default	With Override Prefix
IP (code address)	CS	Never
SP (stack address)	SS	Never
BP (stack address or stack marker)	SS	BP + DS or ES, or CS
SI or DI (not incl. strings)	DS	ES, SS, or CS
SI (implicit source addr for strings)	DS	ES, SS, or CS
DI (implicit dest addr for strings)	ES	Never

Operand Address (EA) Timing (Clocks):

Add 4 clocks for word operands at ODD ADDRESSES.
Immed Offset = 6
Base (BX, BP, SI, DI) = 5
Base + DISP = 9
Base + Index (BP + DI, BX + SI) = 7
Base + Index (BP + SI, BX + DI) = 8
Base + Index (BP + DI, BX + SI) + DISP = 11
Base + Index (BP + SI, BX + DI) + DISP = 12

AAA = ASCII Adjust for Addition

Opcode

Opcode	Clocks	Operation
37	4	adjust AL, flags, AH

AAD = ASCII Adjust for Division

Long——Opcode

Opcode	Clocks	Operation
D5,0A	60	Adjust AL, AH prior to division

AAM = ASCII Adjust for Multiplication

Long——Opcode

Opcode	Clocks	Operation
D4,0A	83	Adjust AL, AH after multiplication

AAS = ASCII Adjust for Subtraction

Opcode

Opcode	Clocks	Operation
3F	4	adjust AL, flags, AH

ADC = Integer Add with Carry

Memory/Reg + Reg

Opcode	mod reg r/m	- - -	- - -

	Opcode	Clocks	Operation
Byte	12	3	Reg8 ← CF + Reg 8 + Reg8
	12	9+EA	Reg8 ← CF + Reg8 + Mem8
	10	16+EA	Mem8 ← CF + Mem8 + Reg8
Word	13	3	Reg16 ← CF + Reg16 + Reg16
	13	9+EA	Reg16 ← CF + Reg16 + Mem16
	11	16+EA	Mem16 ← CF + Mem16 + Reg16

Immed to AX/AL

Opcode	Data	- - -

	Opcode	Clocks	Operation
Byte	14	4	AL ← CF + AL + Immed8
Word	15	4	AX ← CF + AX + Immed16

Immed to Memory/Reg

Opcode	mod 010 r/m			Data	

	Opcode	Clocks	Operation
Byte	80	4	Reg8 ← CF + Reg8 + Immed8
	80	17+EA	Mem8 ← CF + Mem8 + Immed8
Word	81	4	Reg16 ← CF + Reg16 + Immed16
	81	17+EA	Mem16 ← CF + Mem16 + Immed16
	83	4	Reg16 ← CF + Reg16 + Immed8
	83	17+EA	Mem16 ← CF + Mem16 + Immed8

ADD = Integer Addition

Memory/Reg + Reg

Opcode	mod reg r/m		

	Opcode	Clocks	Operation
Byte	02	3	Reg8 ← Reg8 + Reg8
	02	9+EA	Reg8 ← Reg8 + Mem8
	00	16+EA	Mem8 ← Mem8 + Reg8
Word	03	3	Reg16 ← Reg16 + Reg16
	03	9+EA	Reg16 ← Reg16 + Mem16
	01	16+EA	Mem16 ← Mem16 + Reg16

Immed to AX/AL

Opcode	Data	

Opcode	Clocks	Operation
04	4	AL ← AL + Immed8
05	4	AX ← AX + Immed16

Immed to Memory/Reg

Opcode	mod 000 r/m			Data	

	Opcode	Clocks	Operation
Byte	80	4	Reg8 ← Reg8 + Immed8
	80	17+EA	Mem8 ← Mem8 + Immed8
Word	81	4	Reg16 ← Reg16 + Immed16
	81	17+EA	Mem16 ← Mem16 + Immed16
	83	4	Reg16 ← Reg16 + Immed8
	83	17+EA	Mem16 ← Mem16 + Immed8

AND = Logical AND

Memory/Reg with Reg

Opcode	mod reg r/m		

	Opcode	Clocks	Operation
Byte	22	3	Reg8 ← Reg8 AND Reg8
	22	9+EA	Reg8 ← Reg8 AND Mem8
	20	16+EA	Mem8 ← Mem8 AND Reg8
Word	23	3	Reg16 ← Reg16 AND Reg16
	23	9+EA	Reg16 ← Reg16 AND Mem16
	21	16+EA	Mem16 ← Mem16 AND Reg16

Immed to AX/AL

Opcode	Data	

	Opcode	Clocks	Operation
Byte	24	4	AL ← AL AND Immed8
Word	25	4	AX ← AX AND Immed16

Immed to Memory/Reg

Opcode	mod 100 r/m			Data	

	Opcode	Clocks	Operation
Byte	80	4	Reg8 ← Reg8 AND Immed8
	80	17+EA	Mem8 ← Mem8 AND Immed8
Word	81	4	Reg16 ← Reg16 AND Immed16
	81	17+EA	Mem16 ← Mem16 AND Immed16

CALL = Call

Within segment or group, IP relative

Opcode	DispL	DispH

Opcode	Clocks	Operation
E8	19	IP ← IP + Disp16—(SP) ← return link

Within segment or group, Indirect

Opcode	mod 010 r/m		

Opcode	Clocks	Operation
FF	16	IP ← Reg16—(SP) ← return link
FF	21+EA	IP ← Mem16—(SP) ← return link

Inter-segment or group, Direct

Opcode	offset	offset	segbase	segbase	segbase

Opcode	Clocks	Operation
9A	28	CS ← segbase IP ← offset

Inter-segment or group, Indirect

Opcode	mod 011 r/m		

Opcode	Clocks	Operation
FF	37+EA	CS ← segbase IP ← offset

CBW = Convert Byte to Word

Opcode

Opcode	Clocks	Operation
98	2	convert byte in AL to word in AX

CLC = Clear Carry Flag

Opcode

Opcode	Clocks	Operation
F8	2	clear the carry flag

CLD = Clear Direction Flag

Opcode

Opcode	Clocks	Operation
FC	2	clear direction flag

CLI = Clear Interrupt Enable Flag

Opcode	Clocks	Operation
FA	2	clear interrupt flag

CMC = Complement Carry Flag

Opcode

Opcode	Clocks	Operation
F5	2	complement carry flag

CMP = Compare Two Operands

Memory/Reg with Reg

Opcode	mod reg r/m		

	Opcode	Clocks	Operation
Byte	38	3	flags ← Reg8 - Reg8
	38	9+EA	flags ← Reg8 - Mem8
	3A	9+EA	flags ← Mem8 - Reg8
Word	39	3	flags ← Reg16 - Reg16
	39	9+EA	flags ← Reg16 - Mem16
	3B	9+EA	flags ← Mem16 - Reg16

Immed to AX/AL

Opcode	Data	

	Opcode	Clocks	Operation
Byte	3C	4	flags AL - Immed8
Word	3D	4	flags AX - Immed16

Immed to Memory/Reg

Opcode	mod 111 r/m			Data	

	Opcode	Clocks	Operation
Byte	80	4	flags ← Reg8 - Immed8
	80	10+EA	flags ← Mem8 - Immed8
Word	81	4	flags ← Reg16 - Immed16
	81	10+EA	flags ← Mem16 - Immed16
	83	4	flags ← Reg16 - Immed8
	83	10+EA	flags ← Mem16 - Immed8

CWD = Convert Word to Doubleword

Opcode

Opcode	Clocks	Operation
99	5	convert word in AX to doubleword in DX:AX

DAA = Decimal Adjust for Addition

Opcode

Opcode	Clocks	Operation
27	4	adjust AL, flags, AH

DAS = Decimal Adjust for Subtraction

Opcode

Opcode	Clocks	Operation
2F	4	adjust AL, flags, AH

DEC = Decrement by 1

Word Register

Opcode + reg

Opcode	Clocks	Operation
48+reg	2	Reg16 ← Reg16 - 1

Memory/Byte Register

Opcode	mod 001 r/m		

	Opcode	Clocks	Operation
Byte	FE	3	Reg8 ← Reg8 - 1
	FE	15+EA	Mem8 ← Mem8 - 1
Word	FF	15+EA	Mem16 ← Mem16 - 1

DIV = Unsigned Division

Memory/Reg with AX or DX:AX

Opcode	mod 110 r/m		

	Opcode	Clocks	Operation
Byte	F6	80-90	AH,AL ← AX / Reg8
	F6	(86-96)+EA	AH,AL ← AX / Mem8
Word	F7	144-162	DX,AX ← DX:AX / Reg16
	F7	(150-168)+EA	DX,AX ← DX:AX / Mem16

ESC = Escape

Opcode + i	mod xxx r/m		

Opcode	Clocks	Operation
D8+i	8+EA	data bus ← (EA)
D8+i	2	data bus ← (EA)

HLT = Halt

Opcode

Opcode	Clocks	Operation
F4	2	halt operation

IDIV = Signed Division

Memory/Reg with AX or DX:AX

Opcode	mod 111 r/m		

	Opcode	Clocks	Operation
Byte	F6	101-112	AH,AL ← AX / Reg8
	F6	(107-118)+EA	AH,AL ← AX / Mem8
Word	F7	165-184	DX,AX ← DX:AX / Reg16
	F7	(171-190)+EA	DX,AX ← DX:AX / Mem16

IMUL = Signed Multiplication

Memory/Reg with AL or AX

Opcode	mod 101 r/m		

	Opcode	Clocks	Operation
Byte	F6	80-98	AX ← AL*Reg8
	F6	(86-104)+EA	AX ← AL*Mem8
Word	F7	128-154	DX:AX ← AX*Reg16
	F7	(134-160)+EA	DX:AX ← AX*Mem16

IN = Input Byte, Word

Fixed port

Opcode	Port

	Opcode	Clocks	Operation
Byte	E4	10	AL ← Port8
	E5	10	AX ← Port8

Variable port

Opcode

	Opcode	Clocks	Operation
Word	EC	8	AL ← Port16(in DX)
	ED	8	AX ← Port16(in DX)

INC = Increment by 1

Word Register

Opcode + reg

Opcode	Clocks	Operation
40+reg	2	Reg16 ← Reg16 + 1

Memory/Byte Register

Opcode	mod 000 r/m		

	Opcode	Clocks	Operation
Byte	FE	3	Reg8 ← Reg8 + 1
	FE	15+EA	Mem8 ← Mem8 + 1
Word	FF	15+EA	Mem16 ← Mem16 + 1

INT / INTO = Interrupt

Opcode	type

Opcode	Clocks	Operation
CC	52	Interrupt 3
CD	51	Interrupt 'type'
CE	53 or 4	Interrupt4 if FLAGS.OF=1, else NOP

IRET = Return from Interrupt

Opcode

Opcode	Clocks	Operation
CF	24	Return from interrupt

J*cond* = Jump on Condition

Operation

```
if condition is true then do;
   sign-extend displacement to 16 bits;
   IP ← IP + sign-extended displacement;
   end if;
```

Format

Opcode	Disp

Opcode	Clocks	Operation	*cond* =
77	16 or 4	jump if above	JA
73	16 or 4	jump if above or equal	JAE
72	16 or 4	jump if below	JB
76	16 or 4	jump if below or equal	JBE
72	16 or 4	jump if carry set	JC
74	16 or 4	jump if equal	JE
7F	16 or 4	jump if greater	JG
7D	16 or 4	jump if greater or equal	JGE
7C	16 or 4	jump if less	JL
7E	16 or 4	jump if less or equal	JLE
76	16 or 4	jump if not above	JNA
72	16 or 4	jump if neither above nor equal	JNAE
73	16 or 4	jump if not below	JNB
77	16 or 4	jump if neither below nor equal	JNBE
73	16 or 4	jump if no carry	JNC
75	16 or 4	jump if not equal	JNE
7E	16 or 4	jump if not greater	JNG
7C	16 or 4	jump if neither greater nor equal	JNGE
7D	16 or 4	jump if not less	JNL
7F	16 or 4	jump if neither less nor equal	JNLE
71	16 or 4	jump if no overflow	JNO
7B	16 or 4	jump if no parity	JNP
79	16 or 4	jump if positive	JNS
75	16 or 4	jump if not zero	JNZ
70	16 or 4	jump if overflow	JO
7A	16 or 4	jump if parity	JP
7A	16 or 4	jump if parity even	JPE
7B	16 or 4	jump if parity odd	JPO
78	16 or 4	jump if sign	JS
74	18 or 6	jump if zero	JZ
E3	18 or 6	jump if CX is zero (does not test flags)	JCXZ

JMP = Jump

Within segment or group, IP relative

[Opcode] [DispL] [DispH]

Opcode	Clocks	Operation
E9	15	IP ← IP + Disp16
EB	15	IP ← IP + Disp8 (Disp8 sign-extended)

Within segment or group, Indirect

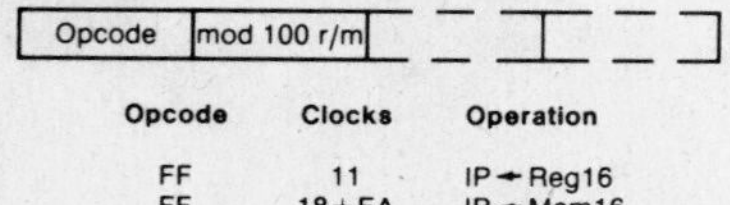

Opcode	Clocks	Operation
FF	11	IP ← Reg16
FF	18+EA	IP ← Mem16

Inter-segment or group, Direct

[Opcode] [offset] [offset] [segbase] [segbase]

Opcode	Clocks	Operation
EA	15	CS ← segbase IP ← offset

Inter-segment or group, Indirect

[Opcode] [mod 101 r/m] [– –] [– –]

Opcode	Clocks	Operation
FF	24+EA	CS ← segbase IP ← offset

LAHF = Load AH from Flags

[Opcode]

Opcode	Clocks	Operation
9F	4	copy low byte of flags word to AH

LDS/LES = Load Pointer to DS/ES and Register

[Opcode] [mod reg r/m] [– –] [– –]

Opcode	Clocks	Operation
C4	16+EA	dword pointer at EA goes to reg16 (1st word) and ES (2nd word)
C5	16+EA	dword pointer at EA goes to reg16 (1st word) and DS (2nd word)

LEA = Load Effective Address

[Opcode] [mod reg r/m] [– –] [– –]

Opcode	Clocks	Operation
8D	2+EA	Reg16 ← EA

LOCK = Assert Bus Lock

[Opcode]

Opcode	Clocks	Operation
F0	2	assert the bus lock next instruction

LOOP*xx* = Loop Control

[Opcode] [Disp]

Opcode	Clocks	Operation	*xx* =
E1	18 or 6	dec CX; loop if equal and CX not 0	LOOPE
E0	19 or 5	dec CX; loop if not equal and CX not 0	LOOPNE
E1	18 or 6	dec CX; loop if zero and CX not 0	LOOPZ
E0	19 or 5	dec CX; loop if not zero and CX not 0	LOOPNZ
E2	17 or 5	dec CX; loop if CX not 0	LOOP

MOV = Move Data

Memory/Reg to or from Reg

[Opcode] [mod reg r/m] [– –] [– –]

	Opcode	Clocks	Operation
Byte	88	9+EA	Mem8 ← Reg8
	88	2	Reg8 ← Reg8
	8A	8+EA	Reg8 ← Mem8
Word	89	9+EA	Mem16 ← Reg16
	89	2	Reg16 ← Reg16
	8B	8+EA	Reg16 ← Mem16

Direct-Addressed Memory to or from AX/AL

[Opcode] [AddrL] [AddrH]

	Opcode	Clocks	Operation
Byte	A0	10	AL ← Mem8
	A2	10	Mem8 ← AL
Word	A1	10	AX ← Mem16
	A3	10	Mem16 ← AX

Immed to Reg

[Opcode] [Data] [– –]

	Opcode	Clocks	Operation
Byte	B0+reg	4	Reg 8 ← Immed8
Word	B8+reg	4	Reg16 ← Immed16

Immed to Memory/Reg

[Opcode] [mod 000 r/m] [– –] [– –] [Data] [– –]

Opcode	Clocks	Operation
C6	4	Reg8 ← Immed8
C6	10+EA	Mem8 ← Immed8
C7	4	Reg16 ← Immed16
C7	10+EA	Mem16 ← Immed16

Memory/Reg to or from SReg

[Opcode] [mod sreg r/m] [– –] [– –]

	Opcode	Clocks	Operation
Word	8C	9+EA	Mem16 ← SReg
	8C	2	Reg16 ← SReg
	8E	8+EA	SReg ← Mem16
	8E	2	SReg ← Reg16

MUL = Unsigned Multiplication

Memory/Reg with AL or AX

[Opcode] [mod 100 r/m] [– –] [– –]

	Opcode	Clocks	Operation
Byte	F6	70-77	AX ← AL*Reg8
	F6	(76-83)+EA	AX ← AL*Mem8
Word	F7	118-133	DX:AX ← AX*Reg16
	F7	(124-139)+EA	DX:AX ← AX*Mem16

NEG = Negate an Integer

Memory/Reg

Opcode	mod 011 r/m

	Opcode	Clocks	Operation
	F6	3	Reg8 ← 00H - Reg 8
	F7	3	Reg16 ← 0000H - Reg16
	F6	16+EA	Mem8 ← 00H - Mem8
	F7	16+EA	Mem16 ← 0000H - Mem16

NOP = No Operation

Opcode

Opcode	Clocks	Operation
90	3	no operation

NOT = Form One's Complement

Memory/Reg

Opcode	mod 010 r/m

	Opcode	Clocks	Operation
Byte	F6	3	Reg8 ← 0FFH - Reg8
	F6	16+EA	Mem8 ← 0FFH - Mem8
Word	F7	3	Reg16 ← 0FFFFH - Reg16
	F7	16+EA	Mem16 ← 0FFFFH - Mem16

OR = Logical Inclusive OR

Memory/Reg with Reg

Opcode	mod reg r/m

	Opcode	Clocks	Operation
Byte	0A	3	Reg8 ← Reg8 OR Reg8
	0A	9+EA	Reg8 ← Reg8 OR Mem8
	08	16+EA	Mem8 ← Mem8 OR Reg8
Word	0B	3	Reg16 ← Reg16 OR Reg 16
	0B	9+EA	Reg16 ← Reg16 OR Mem16
	09	16+EA	Mem16 ← Mem16 OR Reg16

Immed to AX/AL

Opcode	Data

Opcode	Clocks	Operation
0C	4	AL ← AL OR Immed8
0D	4	AX ← AX OR Immed16

Immed to Memory/Reg

Opcode	mod 001 r/m		Data

	Opcode	Clocks	Operation
Byte	80	4	Reg8 ← Reg8 OR Immed8
	80	17+EA	Mem8 ← Mem8 OR Immed8
Word	81	4	Reg16 ← Reg16 OR Immed16
	81	17+EA	Mem16 ← Mem16 OR Immed16

OUT = Output Byte, Word

Fixed port

Opcode	Port

	Opcode	Clocks	Operation
Byte	E6	10	Port8 ← AL
	E7	10	Port8 ← AX

Variable port

Opcode

	Opcode	Clocks	Operation
Word	EE	8	Port16 (in DX) ← AL
	EF	8	Port16 (in DX) ← AX

POP = Pop a Word from the Stack

Word Memory

Opcode	mod 000 r/m

Opcode	Clocks	Operation
8F	17+EA	Mem16 ← (SP)++

Word Register

Opcode + reg

Opcode	Clocks	Operation
58+reg	8	Reg16 ← (SP)++

Segment Register

Opcode + SReg

Opcode	Clocks	Operation
07+SReg	8	SReg ← (SP)++

POPF = Pop the TOS into the Flags

Opcode

Opcode	Clocks	Operation
9D	8	FLAGS ← (SP)++

PUSH = Push a Word onto the Stack

Memory/Reg

Opcode	mod 110 r/m

Opcode	Clocks	Operation
FF	16+EA	—(SP) ← Mem16

Word Register

Opcode + reg

Opcode	Clocks	Operation
50+reg	11	—(SP) ← Reg16

Segment Register

Opcode + SReg

Opcode	Clocks	Operation
06+SReg	10	—(SP) ← SReg

PUSHF = Push the Flags to the Stack

Opcode

Opcode	Clocks	Operation
9C	10	—(SP) ← FLAGS

RCL = Rotate Left Through Carry

Memory or Reg by 1

Opcode	mod 010 r/m

	Opcode	Clocks	Operation
Byte	D0	2	rotate Reg 8 by 1
	D0	15+EA	rotate Mem8 by 1
Word	D1	2	rotate Reg 16 by 1
	D1	15+EA	rotate Mem16 by 1

Memory or Reg by count in CL

Opcode	mod 010 r/m

	Opcode	Clocks	Operation
Byte	D2	8+4/bit	rotate Reg8 by CL
	D2	20+EA+4/bit	rotate Mem8 by CL
Word	D3	8+4/bit	rotate Reg16 by CL
	D3	20+EA+4/bit	rotate Mem16 by CL

RCR = Rotate Right Through Carry

Memory or Reg by 1

Opcode	mod 011 r/m

	Opcode	Clocks	Operation
Byte	D0	2	rotate Reg8 by 1
	D0	15+EA	rotate Mem8 by 1
Word	D1	2	rotate Reg16 by 1
	D1	15+EA	rotate Mem16 by 1

Memory or Reg by count in CL

Opcode	mod 011 r/m

	Opcode	Clocks	Operation
Byte	D2	8+4/bit	rotate Reg8 by CL
	D2	20+EA+4/bit	rotate Mem8 by CL
Word	D3	8+4/bit	rotate Reg16 by CL
	D3	20+EA+4/bit	rotate Mem16 by CL

REP*x* = Repeat Prefix

Opcode

Opcode	Clocks	Operation	REP*x* =
F3	2	repeat next instruction until CX=0	REP
F3	2	repeat next instruction until CX=0 or ZF=0	REPE REPZ
F2	2	repeat next instruction until CX=0 or ZF=1	REPNE REPNZ

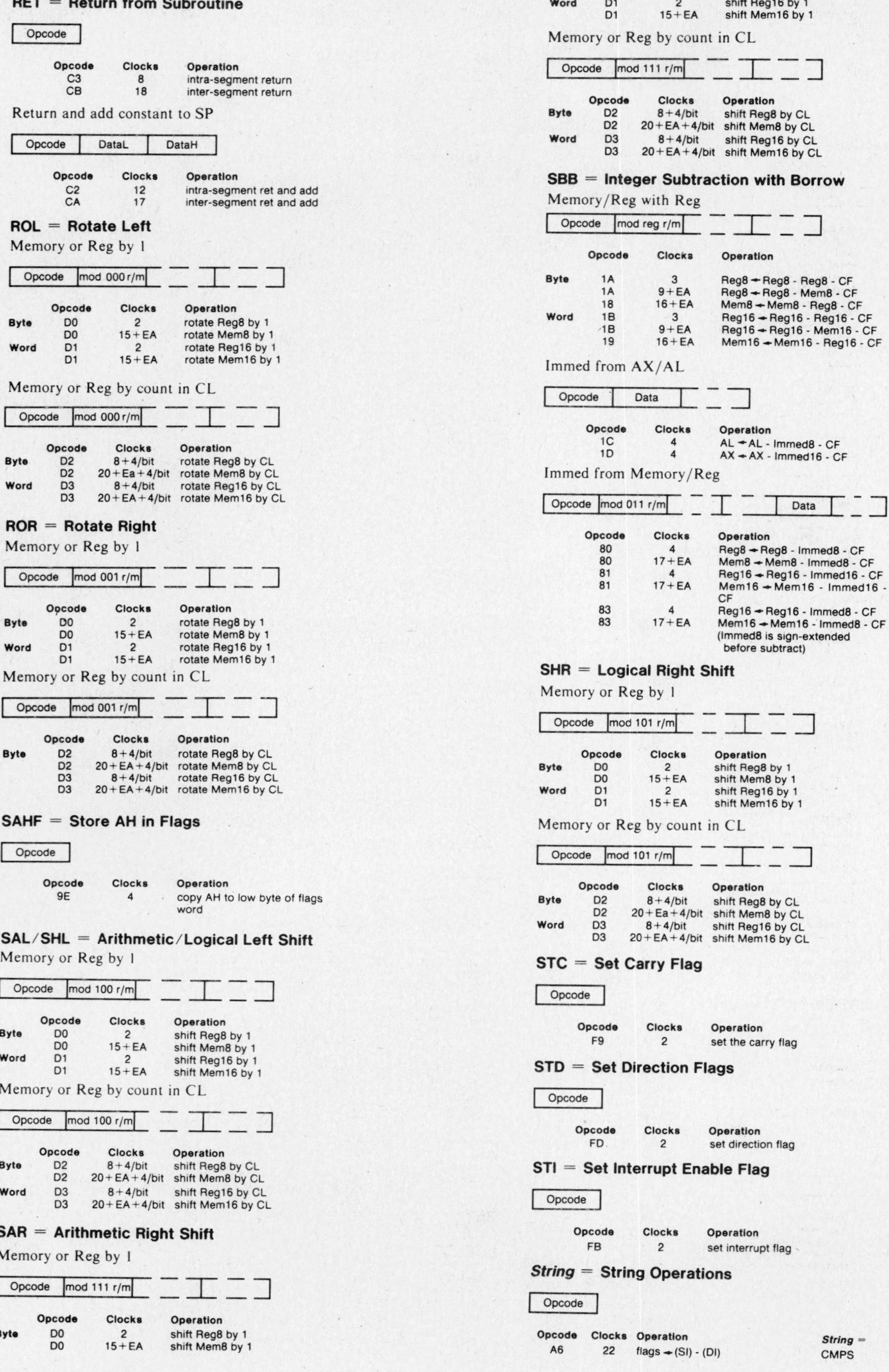

RET = Return from Subroutine

[Opcode]

	Opcode	Clocks	Operation
	C3	8	intra-segment return
	CB	18	inter-segment return

Return and add constant to SP

[Opcode | DataL | DataH]

	Opcode	Clocks	Operation
	C2	12	intra-segment ret and add
	CA	17	inter-segment ret and add

ROL = Rotate Left

Memory or Reg by 1

[Opcode | mod 000 r/m | — — | — —]

	Opcode	Clocks	Operation
Byte	D0	2	rotate Reg8 by 1
	D0	15+EA	rotate Mem8 by 1
Word	D1	2	rotate Reg16 by 1
	D1	15+EA	rotate Mem16 by 1

Memory or Reg by count in CL

[Opcode | mod 000 r/m | — — | — —]

	Opcode	Clocks	Operation
Byte	D2	8+4/bit	rotate Reg8 by CL
	D2	20+Ea+4/bit	rotate Mem8 by CL
Word	D3	8+4/bit	rotate Reg16 by CL
	D3	20+EA+4/bit	rotate Mem16 by CL

ROR = Rotate Right

Memory or Reg by 1

[Opcode | mod 001 r/m | — — | — —]

	Opcode	Clocks	Operation
Byte	D0	2	rotate Reg8 by 1
	D0	15+EA	rotate Mem8 by 1
Word	D1	2	rotate Reg16 by 1
	D1	15+EA	rotate Mem16 by 1

Memory or Reg by count in CL

[Opcode | mod 001 r/m | — — | — —]

	Opcode	Clocks	Operation
Byte	D2	8+4/bit	rotate Reg8 by CL
	D2	20+EA+4/bit	rotate Mem8 by CL
	D3	8+4/bit	rotate Reg16 by CL
	D3	20+EA+4/bit	rotate Mem16 by CL

SAHF = Store AH in Flags

[Opcode]

	Opcode	Clocks	Operation
	9E	4	copy AH to low byte of flags word

SAL/SHL = Arithmetic/Logical Left Shift

Memory or Reg by 1

[Opcode | mod 100 r/m | — — | — —]

	Opcode	Clocks	Operation
Byte	D0	2	shift Reg8 by 1
	D0	15+EA	shift Mem8 by 1
Word	D1	2	shift Reg16 by 1
	D1	15+EA	shift Mem16 by 1

Memory or Reg by count in CL

[Opcode | mod 100 r/m | — — | — —]

	Opcode	Clocks	Operation
Byte	D2	8+4/bit	shift Reg8 by CL
	D2	20+EA+4/bit	shift Mem8 by CL
Word	D3	8+4/bit	shift Reg16 by CL
	D3	20+EA+4/bit	shift Mem16 by CL

SAR = Arithmetic Right Shift

Memory or Reg by 1

[Opcode | mod 111 r/m | — — | — —]

	Opcode	Clocks	Operation
Byte	D0	2	shift Reg8 by 1
	D0	15+EA	shift Mem8 by 1
Word	D1	2	shift Reg16 by 1
	D1	15+EA	shift Mem16 by 1

Memory or Reg by count in CL

[Opcode | mod 111 r/m | — — | — —]

	Opcode	Clocks	Operation
Byte	D2	8+4/bit	shift Reg8 by CL
	D2	20+EA+4/bit	shift Mem8 by CL
Word	D3	8+4/bit	shift Reg16 by CL
	D3	20+EA+4/bit	shift Mem16 by CL

SBB = Integer Subtraction with Borrow

Memory/Reg with Reg

[Opcode | mod reg r/m | — — | — —]

	Opcode	Clocks	Operation
Byte	1A	3	Reg8 ← Reg8 - Reg8 - CF
	1A	9+EA	Reg8 ← Reg8 - Mem8 - CF
	18	16+EA	Mem8 ← Mem8 - Reg8 - CF
Word	1B	3	Reg16 ← Reg16 - Reg16 - CF
	1B	9+EA	Reg16 ← Reg16 - Mem16 - CF
	19	16+EA	Mem16 ← Mem16 - Reg16 - CF

Immed from AX/AL

[Opcode | Data | — —]

	Opcode	Clocks	Operation
	1C	4	AL ← AL - Immed8 - CF
	1D	4	AX ← AX - Immed16 - CF

Immed from Memory/Reg

[Opcode | mod 011 r/m | — — | — — | Data | — —]

	Opcode	Clocks	Operation
	80	4	Reg8 ← Reg8 - Immed8 - CF
	80	17+EA	Mem8 ← Mem8 - Immed8 - CF
	81	4	Reg16 ← Reg16 - Immed16 - CF
	81	17+EA	Mem16 ← Mem16 - Immed16 - CF
	83	4	Reg16 ← Reg16 - Immed8 - CF
	83	17+EA	Mem16 ← Mem16 - Immed8 - CF (Immed8 is sign-extended before subtract)

SHR = Logical Right Shift

Memory or Reg by 1

[Opcode | mod 101 r/m | — — | — —]

	Opcode	Clocks	Operation
Byte	D0	2	shift Reg8 by 1
	D0	15+EA	shift Mem8 by 1
Word	D1	2	shift Reg16 by 1
	D1	15+EA	shift Mem16 by 1

Memory or Reg by count in CL

[Opcode | mod 101 r/m | — — | — —]

	Opcode	Clocks	Operation
Byte	D2	8+4/bit	shift Reg8 by CL
	D2	20+Ea+4/bit	shift Mem8 by CL
Word	D3	8+4/bit	shift Reg16 by CL
	D3	20+EA+4/bit	shift Mem16 by CL

STC = Set Carry Flag

[Opcode]

	Opcode	Clocks	Operation
	F9	2	set the carry flag

STD = Set Direction Flags

[Opcode]

	Opcode	Clocks	Operation
	FD	2	set direction flag

STI = Set Interrupt Enable Flag

[Opcode]

	Opcode	Clocks	Operation
	FB	2	set interrupt flag

***String* = String Operations**

[Opcode]

Opcode	Clocks	Operation	*String* =
A6	22	flags ← (SI) - (DI)	CMPS

A7	22	flags ← (SI) - (DI)	CMPS
A4	18	(DI) ← (SI)	MOVS
A5	18	(DI) ← (SI)	MOVS
AE	15	flags ← (DI) - AL	SCAS
AF	15	flags ← (DI) - AX	SCAS
AC	12	AL ← (SI)	LODS
AD	12	AX ← (SI)	LODS
AA	11	(DI) ← AL	STOS
AB	11	(DI) ← AX	STOS

SUB = Integer Subtraction

Memory/Reg with Reg

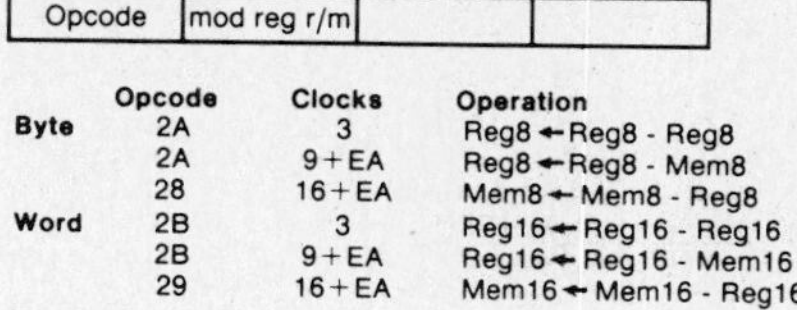

Opcode | mod reg r/m | |

	Opcode	Clocks	Operation
Byte	2A	3	Reg8 ← Reg8 - Reg8
	2A	9+EA	Reg8 ← Reg8 - Mem8
	28	16+EA	Mem8 ← Mem8 - Reg8
Word	2B	3	Reg16 ← Reg16 - Reg16
	2B	9+EA	Reg16 ← Reg16 - Mem16
	29	16+EA	Mem16 ← Mem16 - Reg16

Immed to AX/AL

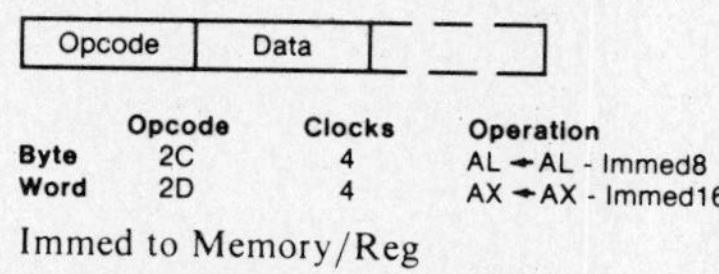

Opcode | Data |

	Opcode	Clocks	Operation
Byte	2C	4	AL ← AL - Immed8
Word	2D	4	AX ← AX - Immed16

Immed to Memory/Reg

Opcode | mod 101 r/m | | | Data |

	Opcode	Clocks	Operation
Byte	80	4	Reg8 ← Reg8 - Immed8
	80	17+EA	Mem8 ← Mem8 - Immed8
Word	81	4	Reg16 ← Reg16 - Immed16
	81	17+EA	Mem16 ← Mem16 - Immed16
	83	4	Reg16 ← Reg16 - Immed8
	83	17+EA	Mem16 ← Mem16 - Immed8

TEST = Logical Compare

Memory/Reg with Reg

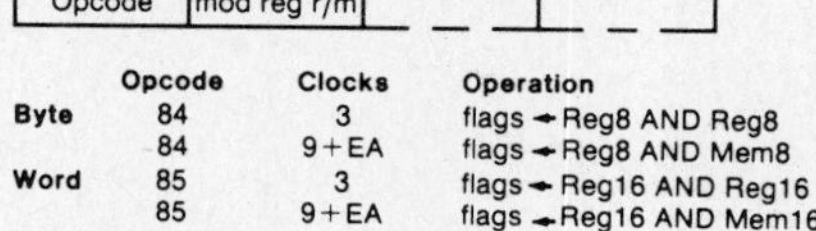

Opcode | mod reg r/m | |

	Opcode	Clocks	Operation
Byte	84	3	flags ← Reg8 AND Reg8
	84	9+EA	flags ← Reg8 AND Mem8
Word	85	3	flags ← Reg16 AND Reg16
	85	9+EA	flags ← Reg16 AND Mem16

Immed to AX/AL

Opcode | Data |

	Opcode	Clocks	Operation
Byte	A8	4	flags ← AL AND Immed8
Word	A9	4	flags ← AX AND Immed16

Immed to Memory/Reg

Opcode | mod 000 r/m | | | Data |

	Opcode	Clocks	Operation
Byte	F6	5	flags ← Reg8 AND Immed8
	F6	11+EA	flags ← Mem8 AND Immed8
Word	F7	5	flags ← Reg16 AND Immed16
	F7	11+EA	flags ← Mem16 AND Immed16

WAIT = Wait While TEST Pin Not Asserted

Opcode

Opcode	Clocks	Operation
9B	3+5n	none

XCHG = Exchange Memory/Register with Register

Memory/Reg with Reg

Opcode | mod reg r/m | |

	Opcode	Clocks	Operation
Byte	86	4	Reg8 ↔ Reg8
	86	17+EA	Mem8 ↔ Reg8
Word	87	4	Reg16 ↔ Reg16
	87	17+EA	Mem16 ↔ Reg16

Word Register with AX

Opcode + Reg

Opcode	Clocks	Operation
90+Reg	3	AX ↔ Reg16

XLAT XLATB = Table Look-up Translation

Opcode

Opcode	Clocks	Operation
D7	11	replace AL with table entry

XOR = Logical Exclusive OR

Memory/Reg with Reg

Opcode | mod reg r/m | |

	Opcode	Clocks	Operation
Byte	32	3	Reg8 ← Reg8 XOR Reg8
	32	9+EA	Reg8 ← Reg8 XOR Mem8
	30	16+EA	Mem8 ← Mem8 XOR Reg8
Word	33	3	Reg16 ← Reg16 XOR Reg16
	33	9+EA	Reg16 ← Reg16 XOR Mem16
	31	16+EA	Mem16 ← Mem16 XOR Reg16

Immed to AX/AL

Opcode | Data |

Opcode	Clocks	Operation
34	4	AL ← AL XOR Immed8
35	4	AX ← AX XOR Immed16

Immed to Memory/Reg

Opcode | mod 110 r/m | | | Data |

	Opcode	Clocks	Operation
Byte	80	4	Reg8 ← Reg8 XOR Immed8
	80	17+EA	Mem8 ← Mem8 XOR Immed8
Word	81	4	Reg16 ← Reg16 XOR Immed16
	81	17+EA	Mem16 ← Mem16 XOR Immed16

186 INSTRUCTIONS

Notes for iAPX 186 Instructions

These instructions can be used only if the MOD186 control is specified. When MOD186 is specified, clocks for all instructions are as stated under "Clocks for MOD186 Operation."

BOUND = Check Array Against Bounds

Opcode | ModRM | |

Opcode	Operation
62	if Reg16<Mem16 at EA, or Reg16>Mem16 at EA+2 then INTERRUPT 5

ENTER = High Level Procedure Entry

Opcode | DataL | DataH | Level

Opcode	Operation
C8	build new stack frame

IMUL = Signed Multiplication

Mem/Reg* Immediate to Reg

Opcode | ModRM | | | Data |

Opcode	Operation
6B	Reg 16 ← Reg 16 * Immed 8
6B	Reg 16 ← Reg 16 * Immed 8
6B	Reg 16 ← Mem 16 * Immed 8
69	Reg 16 ← Reg 16 * Immed 16
69	Reg 16 ← Reg 16 * Immed 16
69	Reg 16 ← Mem 16 * Immed 16

LEAVE = High Level Procedure Exit

Opcode

Opcode	Operation
C9	release current stack frame and return to prior frame.

POPA = Pop All Registers

Opcode

Opcode	Operation
61	restore registers from stack

PUSH = Push a Word onto the Stack

Word Immediate

Opcode	Data		

Opcode	Operation
6A	—(SP) ← Immed8 (sign extended)
68	—(SP) ← Immed16

PUSHA = Push All Registers

Opcode

Opcode	Operation
60	save registers on the stack

RCL = Rotate Left Through Carry

Mem or Reg by Immed8

Opcode	ModRM*				count

*—(Reg field = 011)

Opcode	Operation
C0	rotate Reg8 by Immed8
C0	rotate Mem8 by Immed8
C1	rotate Reg16 by Immed8
C1	rotate Mem16 by Immed8

RCR = Rotate Right Through Carry

Mem or Reg by Immed8

Opcode	ModRM*				count

*—(Reg field = 011)

Opcode	Operation
C0	rotate Reg8 by Immed8
C0	rotate Mem8 by Immed8
C1	rotate Reg16 by Immed8
C1	rotate Mem16 by Immed8

ROL = Rotate Left

Mem or Reg by Immed8

Opcode	ModRM*				count

*—(Reg field = 000)

Opcode	Operation
C0	rotate Reg8 by Immed8
C0	rotate Mem8 by Immed8
C1	rotate Reg16 by Immed8
C1	rotate Mem16 by Immed8

ROR = Rotate Right

Mem or Reg by Immed8

Opcode	ModRM*				count

*—(Reg field = 001)

Opcode	Operation
C0	rotate Reg8 by Immed8
C0	rotate Mem8 by Immed8
C1,	rotate Reg16 by Immed8
C1	rotate Mem16 by Immed8

SAL/SHL = Arithmetic/Logical Left Shift

Mem or Reg by immediate count

Opcode	ModRM*				count

*—(Reg field = 100)

Opcode	Operation
C0	rotate Reg8 by Immed8
C0	rotate Mem8 by Immed8
C1	rotate Reg16 by Immed8
C1	rotate Mem16 by Immed8

SAR = Arithmetic Right Shift

Mem or Reg by Immed8

Opcode	ModRM*				count

*—(Reg field = 111)

Opcode	Operation
C0	rotate Reg8 by Immed8
C0	rotate Mem8 by Immed8
C1	rotate Reg16 by Immed8
C1	rotate Mem16 by Immed8

SHR = Logical Right Shift

Mem or Reg by Immed8

Opcode	ModRM*				count

*—(Reg field = 101)

Opcode	Operation
C0	rotate Reg8 by Immed8
C0	rotate Mem8 by Immed8
C1	rotate Reg16 by Immed8
C1	rotate Mem16 by Immed8

String = String Operations (INS/OUTS)

Opcode

Opcode	Clocks	Operation
6E	INS	(DI) ← port(DX)
6F	INS	(DI) ← port(DX:DX+1)
6C	OUTS	port(DX) ← (SI)
6D	OUTS	port(DX:DX+1) ← (SI)

8087 INSTRUCTIONS

Notes for 8087 Instructions

The individual instruction descriptions are shown by a format box such as the following:

WAIT	op1	m/op/r/m	addr1	addr2

These are the byte-wise representations of the object code generated by the assembler and are interpreted as follows:

- WAIT is an 8086 wait instruction, NOP or emulator instruction.
- op1 is the opcode, possibly taking two bytes.
- m/op/r/m byte (middle 3-bits is part of the opcode).
- addr1 and addr2 are offsets of either 8 or 16 bits.

For integer functions, m = 0 for short-integer memory operand; 1 for word-integer memory operand.
For real functions, m = 0 for short-real memory operand; 1 for longreal memory operand.
i = stack element index.
If mod = 00 then DISP = 0 , disp-lo and disp-hi are absent.
If mod = 01 then DISP = disp-lo sign-extended to 16 bits, disp-hi is absent.
If mod = 10 then DISP = disp-hi; disp-lo.
If mod = 11 then r/m is treated as an ST(i) field.

If r/m = 000 then EA = (BX)+(SI)+DISP
If r/m = 001 then EA = (BX)+(DI)+DISP
If r/m = 010 then EA = (BP)+(SI)+DISP
If r/m = 011 then EA = (BP)+(DI)+DISP
If r/m = 100 then EA = (SI)+DISP
If r/m = 101 then EA = (DI)+DISP
If r/m = 110 then EA (BP)+DISP*
If r/m = 111 then EA = (BX)+DISP
*Except if mod = 000 and r/m = 110 then EA = disp-hi; disp-lo.

ST(0) = Current stack top
ST(i) = i[th] register below stack top
d = Destination
0 — Destination is ST(0)
1 — Destination is ST(i)
P = Pop
0 — No pop
1 — Pop ST(0)
R = Reverse
0 — Destination (op) source
1 — Source (op) destination

For FSQRT:	$-0 \leq ST(0) \leq +\infty$
For FSCALE:	$-2^{15} \leq ST(1) < +2^{15}$ and ST(1) integer
For F2XM1:	$0 \leq ST(0) \leq 2$
For FYL2X:	$0 \leq ST(0) < \infty$ $-\infty < ST(1) < +\infty$
For FYL2XP1:	$0 < \vert ST(0) \vert < (2-\sqrt{2})/2$ $-\infty \leq ST(1) < \infty$
For FPTAN:	$0 \leq ST(0) < \pi/4$
For FPATAN:	$0 \leq ST(0) < ST(1) < +\infty$

F2XMI = Compute 2^x — 1

WAIT	op1	op2

8087 Encoding	Emulator Encoding	Execution Clocks Typical Range	Operation
9B D9 F0	CD 19 F0	500 310-630	ST ← 2ST-1

FABS = Absolute Value

WAIT	op1	op2

8087 Encoding	Emulator Encoding	Execution Clocks Typical Range	Operation
9B D9 E1	CD 19 E1	14 10-17	ST ← |ST|

FADD = Add Real

Stack top + Stack element

WAIT	op1	op2 + i

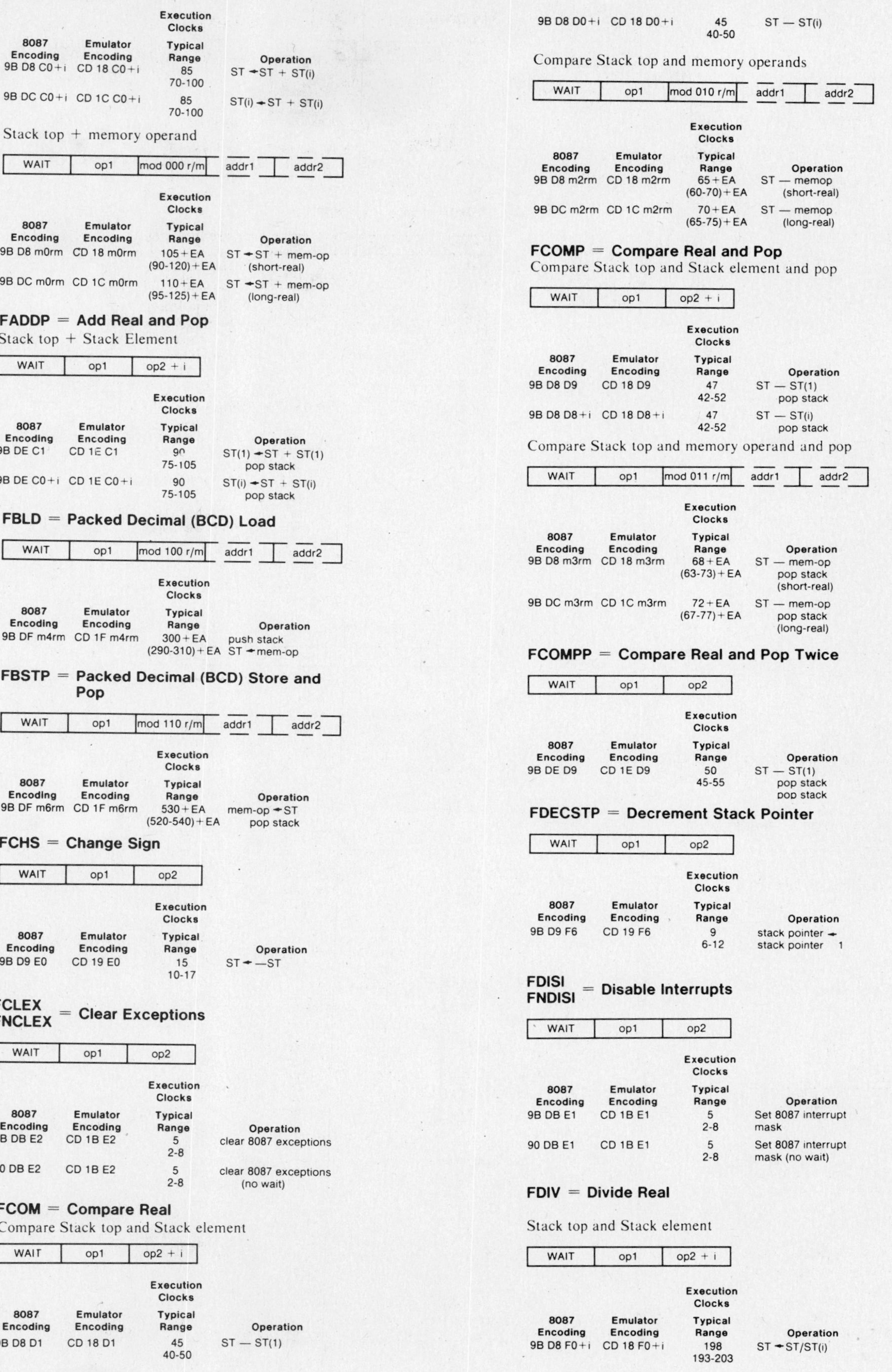

8087 Encoding	Emulator Encoding	Execution Clocks Typical Range	Operation
9B D8 C0+i	CD 18 C0+i	85 70-100	ST ← ST + ST(i)
9B DC C0+i	CD 1C C0+i	85 70-100	ST(i) ← ST + ST(i)

Stack top + memory operand

WAIT	op1	mod 000 r/m	addr1	addr2

8087 Encoding	Emulator Encoding	Execution Clocks Typical Range	Operation
9B D8 m0rm	CD 18 m0rm	105+EA (90-120)+EA	ST ← ST + mem-op (short-real)
9B DC m0rm	CD 1C m0rm	110+EA (95-125)+EA	ST ← ST + mem-op (long-real)

FADDP = Add Real and Pop

Stack top + Stack Element

WAIT	op1	op2 + i

8087 Encoding	Emulator Encoding	Execution Clocks Typical Range	Operation
9B DE C1	CD 1E C1	90 75-105	ST(1) ← ST + ST(1) pop stack
9B DE C0+i	CD 1E C0+i	90 75-105	ST(i) ← ST + ST(i) pop stack

FBLD = Packed Decimal (BCD) Load

WAIT	op1	mod 100 r/m	addr1	addr2

8087 Encoding	Emulator Encoding	Execution Clocks Typical Range	Operation
9B DF m4rm	CD 1F m4rm	300+EA (290-310)+EA	push stack ST ← mem-op

FBSTP = Packed Decimal (BCD) Store and Pop

WAIT	op1	mod 110 r/m	addr1	addr2

8087 Encoding	Emulator Encoding	Execution Clocks Typical Range	Operation
9B DF m6rm	CD 1F m6rm	530+EA (520-540)+EA	mem-op ← ST pop stack

FCHS = Change Sign

WAIT	op1	op2

8087 Encoding	Emulator Encoding	Execution Clocks Typical Range	Operation
9B D9 E0	CD 19 E0	15 10-17	ST ← —ST

FCLEX / FNCLEX = Clear Exceptions

WAIT	op1	op2

8087 Encoding	Emulator Encoding	Execution Clocks Typical Range	Operation
9B DB E2	CD 1B E2	5 2-8	clear 8087 exceptions
90 DB E2	CD 1B E2	5 2-8	clear 8087 exceptions (no wait)

FCOM = Compare Real

Compare Stack top and Stack element

WAIT	op1	op2 + i

8087 Encoding	Emulator Encoding	Execution Clocks Typical Range	Operation
9B D8 D1	CD 18 D1	45 40-50	ST — ST(1)
9B D8 D0+i	CD 18 D0+i	45 40-50	ST — ST(i)

Compare Stack top and memory operands

WAIT	op1	mod 010 r/m	addr1	addr2

8087 Encoding	Emulator Encoding	Execution Clocks Typical Range	Operation
9B D8 m2rm	CD 18 m2rm	65+EA (60-70)+EA	ST — memop (short-real)
9B DC m2rm	CD 1C m2rm	70+EA (65-75)+EA	ST — memop (long-real)

FCOMP = Compare Real and Pop

Compare Stack top and Stack element and pop

WAIT	op1	op2 + i

8087 Encoding	Emulator Encoding	Execution Clocks Typical Range	Operation
9B D8 D9	CD 18 D9	47 42-52	ST — ST(1) pop stack
9B D8 D8+i	CD 18 D8+i	47 42-52	ST — ST(i) pop stack

Compare Stack top and memory operand and pop

WAIT	op1	mod 011 r/m	addr1	addr2

8087 Encoding	Emulator Encoding	Execution Clocks Typical Range	Operation
9B D8 m3rm	CD 18 m3rm	68+EA (63-73)+EA	ST — mem-op pop stack (short-real)
9B DC m3rm	CD 1C m3rm	72+EA (67-77)+EA	ST — mem-op pop stack (long-real)

FCOMPP = Compare Real and Pop Twice

WAIT	op1	op2

8087 Encoding	Emulator Encoding	Execution Clocks Typical Range	Operation
9B DE D9	CD 1E D9	50 45-55	ST — ST(1) pop stack pop stack

FDECSTP = Decrement Stack Pointer

WAIT	op1	op2

8087 Encoding	Emulator Encoding	Execution Clocks Typical Range	Operation
9B D9 F6	CD 19 F6	9 6-12	stack pointer ← stack pointer 1

FDISI / FNDISI = Disable Interrupts

WAIT	op1	op2

8087 Encoding	Emulator Encoding	Execution Clocks Typical Range	Operation
9B DB E1	CD 1B E1	5 2-8	Set 8087 interrupt mask
90 DB E1	CD 1B E1	5 2-8	Set 8087 interrupt mask (no wait)

FDIV = Divide Real

Stack top and Stack element

WAIT	op1	op2 + i

8087 Encoding	Emulator Encoding	Execution Clocks Typical Range	Operation
9B D8 F0+i	CD 18 F0+i	198 193-203	ST ← ST/ST(i)

8087 Encoding	Emulator Encoding	Execution Clocks Typical Range	Operation
9B DC F8+i	CD 1C F8+i	198 193-203	ST(i) ← ST(i)/ST

Stack top and memory operand

WAIT	op1	mod 110 r/m	addr1	addr2

8087 Encoding	Emulator Encoding	Execution Clocks Typical Range	Operation
9B D8 m6rm	CD 18 m6rm	220+EA (215-225)+EA	ST ← ST/mem-op (short-real)
9B DC m6rm	CD 1C m6rm	225+EA (220-230)+EA	ST ← ST/mem-op (long-real)

FDIVP = Divide Real and Pop

WAIT	op1	op2 + i

8087 Encoding	Emulator Encoding	Execution Clocks Typical Range	Operation
9B DE F9	CD 1E F9	202 197-207	ST(1) ← ST(1)/ST pop stack
9B DE F8+i	CD 1E F8+i	202 197-207	ST(i) ← ST(i)/ST pop stack

FDIVR = Divide Real Reversed

Stack top and Stack element

WAIT	op1	op2 + i

8087 Encoding	Emulator Encoding	Execution Clocks Typical Range	Operation
9B D8 F8+i	CD 18 F8+i	199 194-204	ST ← ST(i)/ST
9B DC F0+i	CD 1C F0+i	199 194-204	ST(i) ← ST/ST(i)

Stack top and memory operand

WAIT	op1	mod 111 r/m	addr1	addr2

8087 Encoding	Emulator Encoding	Execution Clocks Typical Range	Operation
9B D8 m7rm	CD 18 m7rm	221+EA (216-226)+EA	ST ← mem-op/ST (short-real)
9B DC m7rm	CD 1C m7rm	226+EA (221-231)+EA	ST ← mem-op/ST (long-real)

FDIVRP = Divide Real Reversed and Pop

WAIT	op1	op2 + i

8087 Encoding	Emulator Encoding	Execution Clocks Typical Range	Operation
9B DE F1	CD 1E F1	203 198-208	ST(1) ← ST/ST(1) pop stack
9B DE F0+i	CD 1E F0+i	203 198-208	ST(i) ← ST/ST(i)

FENI / FNENI = Enable Interrupts

WAIT	op1	op2

8087 Encoding	Emulator Encoding	Execution Clocks Typical Range	Operation
9B DB E0	CD 1B E0	5 2-8	clear 8087 interrupt mask
90 DB E0	CD 1B E0	5 2-8	clear 8087 interrupt mask (no wait)

FFREE = Free Register

WAIT	op1	op2 + i

8087 Encoding	Emulator Encoding	Execution Clocks Typical Range	Operation
9B DD C0+i	CD 1D C0+i	11 9-16	TAG(i) masked empty

FIADD = Integer Add

WAIT	op1	mod 000 r/m	addr1	addr2

8087 Encoding	Emulator Encoding	Execution Clocks Typical Range	Operation
9B DA m0rm	CD 1A m0rm	125+EA (108-143)+EA	ST ← ST + mem-op (short integer)
9B DE m0rm	CD 1E m0rm	120+EA (102-137)+EA	ST ← ST + mem-op (word integer)

FICOM = Integer Compare

WAIT	op1	mod 010 r/m	addr1	addr2

8087 Encoding	Emulator Encoding	Execution Clocks Typical Range	Operation
9B DA m2rm	CD 1A m2rm	85+EA (78-91)+EA	ST — mem-op (short integer)
t9B DE m2rm	CD 1E m2rm	80+EA (72-86)+EA	ST — mem-op (word integer)

FICOMP = Integer Compare and Pop

WAIT	op1	mod 011 r/m	addr1	addr2

8087 Encoding	Emulator Encoding	Execution Clocks Typical Range	Operation
9B DA m3rm	CD 1A m3rm	87+EA (80-93)+EA	ST — mem-op pop stack (short integer)
9B DE m3rm	CD 1E m3rm	82+EA (74-88)+EA	ST — mem-op pop stack (word integer)

FIDIV = Integer Divide

WAIT	op1	mod 110 r/m	addr1	addr2

8087 Encoding	Emulator Encoding	Execution Clocks Typical Range	Operation
9B DA m6rm	CD 1A m6rm	236+EA (230-243)+EA	ST ← ST/mem-op (short integer)
9B DE m6rm	CD 1E m6rm	230+EA (224-238)+EA	ST ← ST/mem-op (word integer)

FIDIVR = Integer Divide Reversed

WAIT	op1	mod 111 r/m	addr1	addr2

8087 Encoding	Emulator Encoding	Execution Clocks Typical Range	Operation
9B DA m7rm	CD 1A m7rm	237+EA (231-245)+EA	ST ← mem-op/ST (short integer)
9B DE m7rm	CD 1E m7rm	230+EA (225-239)+EA	ST ← mem-op/ST (word integer)

FILD = Integer Load

Word Integer or Short Integer

WAIT	op1	mod 000 r/m	addr1	addr2

8087 Encoding	Emulator Encoding	Execution Clocks Typical Range	Operation
9B DB m0rm	CD 1B m0rm	56+EA (52-60)+EA	push stack ST ← mem-op (short integer)
9B DF m0rm	CD 1F m0rm	50+EA (46-54)+EA	push stack ST ← mem-op (word integer)

Long Integer

WAIT	op1	mod 101	addr1	addr2

8087 Encoding	Emulator Encoding	Execution Clocks Typical Range	Operation
9B DF m5rm	CD 1F m5rm	64+EA (60-68)+EA	push stack ST ← mem-op (long integer)

FIMUL = Integer Multiply

WAIT	op1	mod001 r/m	addr1	addr2

8087 Encoding	Emulator Encoding	Execution Clocks Typical Range	Operation
9B DA m1rm	CD 1A m1rm	136 + EA (130-144) + EA	ST ← ST * mem-op (short integer)
9B DE m1rm	CD 1E m1m	130 + EA (124-138) + EA	ST ← ST * mem-op (word integer)

FINCSTP = Increment Stack Pointer

WAIT	op1	op2

8087 Encoding	Emulator Encoding	Execution Clocks Typical Range	Operation
9B D9 F7	CD 19 F7	9 6-12	stack pointer ← stack pointer + 1

FINIT FNINIT = Initialize Processor

WAIT	op1	op2

8087 Encoding	Emulator Encoding	Execution Clocks Typical Range	Operation
9B DB E3	CD 1B E3	5 2-8	initialize 8087
90 DB E3	CD 1B E3	5 2-8	initialize 8087 (no wait)

FIST = Integer Store

WAIT	op1	mod 010 r/m	addr1	addr2

8087 Encoding	Emulator Encoding	Execution Clocks Typical Range	Operation
9B DB m2rm	CD 1B m2rm	88 + EA (82-92) + EA	mem-op ← ST (short integer)
9B DF m2rm	CD 1F m2rm	86 + EA (80-90) + EA	mem-op ← ST (word integer)

FISTP = Integer Store and Pop

Short Integer or Word Integer

WAIT	op1	mod 011 r/m	addr1	addr2

8087 Encoding	Emulator Encoding	Execution Clocks Typical Range	Operation
9B DB m3rm	CD 1B m3rm	90 + EA (84-94) + EA	mem-op ← ST pop stack (short integer)
9B DF m3rm	CD 1F m3rm	88 + EA (82-92) + EA	mem-op ← ST pop stack (word integer)

Long Integer

WAIT	op1	mod 111	addr1	addr2

8087 Encoding	Emulator Encoding	Execution Clocks Typical Range	Operation
9B DF m7rm	CD 1F m7rm	100 + EA (94-105) + EA	mem-op ← ST pop stack (long integer)

FISUB = Integer Subtract

WAIT	op1	mod 100 r/m	addr1	addr2

8087 Encoding	Emulator Encoding	Execution Clocks Typical Range	Operation
9B DA m4rm	CD 1A m4rm	125 + EA (108-143) + EA	ST ← ST — mem-op (short integer)
9B DE m4rm	CD 1E m4rm	120 + EA (102-137) + EA	ST ← ST — mem-op (word integer)

FISUBR = Integer Subtract Reversed

WAIT	op1	mod 101 r/m	addr1	addr2

8087 Encoding	Emulator Encoding	Execution Clocks Typical Range	Operation
9B DA m5rm	CD 1A m5rm	125 + EA (109-144) + EA	ST ← mem-op — ST (short integer)
9B DE m5rm	CD 1E m5rm	120 + EA (103-139) + EA	ST ← mem-op — ST (word integer)

FLD = Load Real

Stack element to Stack top

WAIT	op1	op2 + i

8087 Encoding	Emulator Encoding	Execution Clocks Typical Range	Operation
9B D9 C0 + i	CD 19 C0 + i	20 17-22	T, ← ST(i) push stack ST ← T,

Memory operand to Stack top
Short Integer or Long Integer

WAIT	op1	mod 000 r/m	addr1	addr2

8087 Encoding	Emulator Encoding	Execution Clocks Typical Range	Operation
9B D9 m0rm	CD 19 m0rm	43 + EA (38-56) + EA	push stack ST ← mem-op (short integer)
9B DD m0rm	CD 1D m0rm	46 + EA (40-60) + EA	push stack ST ← mem-op (long integer)

Temp Real

WAIT	op1	mod 101	addr1	addr2

8087 Encoding	Emulator Encoding	Execution Clocks Typical Range	Operation
9B DB m5rm	CD 1B m5rm	57 + EA (53-65) + EA	push stack ST ← mem-op (temp real)

FLD1 = Load + 1.0

WAIT	op1	op2

8087 Encoding	Emulator Encoding	Execution Clocks Typical Range	Operation
9B D9 E8	CD 19 E8	18 15-21	push stack ST ← 1.0

FLDCW = Load Control Word

WAIT	op1	mod 101 r/m	addr1	addr2

8087 Encoding	Emulator Encoding	Execution Clocks Typical Range	Operation
9B D9 m5rm	CD 19 m5rm	10 + EA (7-14) + EA	processor control word ← mem-op

FLDENV = Load Environment

WAIT	op1	mod 100 r/m	addr1	addr2

8087 Encoding	Emulator Encoding	Execution Clocks Typical Range	Operation
9B D9 m4rm	CD 19 m4rm	40 + EA (35-45) + EA	8087 environment ← mem-op

FLDL2E = Load Log_2e

WAIT	op1	op2

8087 Encoding	Emulator Encoding	Execution Clocks Typical Range	Operation
9B D9 EA	CD 19 EA	18 15-21	push stack ST ← log_2e

FLDL2T = Load $Log_2 10$

WAIT	op1	op2

8087 Encoding	Emulator Encoding	Execution Clocks Typical Range	Operation
9B D9 E9	CD 19 E9	19 16-22	push stack ST ← $\log_2 10$

FLDLG2 = Load $\log_{10} 2$

WAIT	op1	op2

8087 Encoding	Emulator Encoding	Execution Clocks Typical Range	Operation
9B D9 EC	CD 19 EC	21 18-24	push stack ST ← $\log_{10} 2$

FLDPI = Load π

WAIT	op1	op2

8087 Encoding	Emulator Encoding	Execution Clocks Typical Range	Operation
9B D9 EB	CD 19 EB	19 16-22	push stack ST ← π

FLDZ = Load + 0.0

WAIT	op1	op2

8087 Encoding	Emulator Encoding	Execution Clocks Typical Range	Operation
9B D9 EE	CD 19 EE	14 11-17	push stack ST ← 0.0

FMUL = Multiply Real

Stack top and Stack element

WAIT	op1	op2 + i

8087 Encoding	Emulator Encoding	Execution Clocks Typical Range	Operation
9B D8 C8+i	CD 18 C8+i	138 130-145	ST ← ST · ST(i)
9B DC C8+i	CD 1C C8+i	138 130-145	ST(i) ← ST(i) — ST

Stack top and memory operand

WAIT	op1	mod 001 r/m	addr1	addr2

8087 Encoding	Emulator Encoding	Execution Clocks Typical Range	Operation
9B D8 m1rm	CD 18 m1rm	118+EA (110-125)+EA	ST ← ST · mem-op (short real)
9B DC m1rm	CD 1C m1rm	161+EA (154-168)+EA	ST ← ST · mem-op (long real)

FMULP = Multiply Real and Pop

WAIT	op1	op2 + i

8087 Encoding	Emulator Encoding	Execution Clocks Typical Range	Operation
9B DE C9 + i	CD 1E C9+i	142 134-148	ST(i) ← ST(i) · ST pop stack

FNOP = No Operation

WAIT	op1	op2

8087 Encoding	Emulator Encoding	Execution Clocks Typical Range	Operation
9B D9 D0	CD 19 D0	13 10-16	ST ← ST

FPATAN = Partial Arctangent

WAIT	op1	op2

8087 Encoding	Emulator Encoding	Execution Clocks Typical Range	Operation
9B D9 F3	CD 19 F3	650 250-800	T_1 ← arctan (ST(1)/ST) pop stack ST ← T_1

FPREM = Partial Remainder

WAIT	op1	op2

8087 Encoding	Emulator Encoding	Execution Clocks Typical Range	Operation
9B D9 F8	CD 19 F8	125 15-190	ST ← REPEAT (ST — ST(1))

FPTAN = Partial Tangent

WAIT	op1	op2

8087 Encoding	Emulator Encoding	Execution Clocks Typical Range	Operation
9B D9 F2	CD 19 F2	450 30-540	Y/X ← TAN (ST) ST ← Y push stack ST ← X

FRNDINT = Round to Integer

WAIT	op1	op2

8087 Encoding	Emulator Encoding	Execution Clocks Typical Range	Operation
9B D9 FC	CD 19 FC	45 16-50	ST ← nearest integer (ST)

FRSTOR = Restore Saved State

WAIT	op1	mod 100 r/m	addr1	addr2

8087 Encoding	Emulator Encoding	Execution Clocks Typical Range	Operation
9B DD m4rm	CD 1D m4rm	202+EA (197-207)+EA	8087 state ← mem-op

FSAVE
FNSAVE = Save State

WAIT	op1	mod 110 r/m	addr1	addr2

8087 Encoding	Emulator Encoding	Execution Clocks Typical Range	Operation
9B DD m6rm	CD 1D m6rm	202+EA (197-207)+EA	mem-op ← 8087 state
90 DD m6rm	CD 1D m6rm	202+EA (197-207)+EA	mem-op ← 8087 state (no wait)

FSCALE = Scale

WAIT	op1	op2

8087 Encoding	Emulator Encoding	Execution Clocks Typical Range	Operation
9B D9 FD	CD 19 FD	35 32-38	ST ← ST · $2^{ST(1)}$

FSQRT = Square Root

WAIT	op1	op2

8087 Encoding	Emulator Encoding	Execution Clocks Typical Range	Operation
9B D9 FA	CD 19 FA	183 180-186	ST ← $\sqrt{ST}$

FST = Store Real

Stack top to Stack element

WAIT	op1	op2 + i

8087 Encoding	Emulator Encoding	Execution Clocks Typical Range	Operation
9B DD D0+i	CD 1D D0+i	18 15-22	ST(i) ← ST

Stack top to memory operand

WAIT	op1	mod 010 r/m	addr1	addr2

8087 Encoding	Emulator Encoding	Execution Clocks Typical Range	Operation
9B D9 m2rm	CD 19 m2rm	87+EA (84-90)+EA	mem-op ← ST (short-real)
9B D0 m2rm	CD 1D m2rm	100+EA (96-104)+EA	mem-op ← ST (long-real)

FSTCW FNSTCW = Store Control Word

WAIT	op1	mod 111 r/m	addr1	addr2

8087 Encoding	Emulator Encoding	Execution Clocks Typical Range	Operation
9B D9 m7rm	CD 19 m7rm	15+EA (12-18)+EA	mem-op ← processor control word
90 D9 m7rm	CD 19 m7rm	15+EA (12-18)+EA	mem-op ← processor control word (no wait)

FSTENV FNSTENV = Store Environment

WAIT	op1	mod 110 r/m	addr1	addr2

8087 Encoding	Emulator Encoding	Execution Clocks Typical Range	Operation
9B D9 m6rm	CD 19 m6rm	45+EA (40-50)+EA	mem-op ← 8087 environment
90 D9 r6rm	CD 19 m6rm	45+EA (40-50)+EA	mem-op ← 8087 environment (no wait)

FSTP = Store Real and Pop

Stack top to Stack element

WAIT	op1	op2 + i

8087 Encoding	Emulator Encoding	Execution Clocks Typical Range	Operation
9B DD D8+i	CD 1D D8+i	20 17-24	ST(i) ← ST pop stack

Stack top to memory operand

WAIT	op1	mod 011 r/m	addr1	addr2

Long Real or Short Real

8087 Encoding	Emulator Encoding	Execution Clocks Typical Range	Operation
9B D9 m3rm	CD 19 m3rm	89+EA (86-92)+EA	mem-op ← ST pop stack (short-real)
9B DB m3rm	CD 1B m3rm	102+EA (98-106)+EA	mem-op ← ST pop stack (long-real)

Temp Real

WAIT	op1	mod 111 r/m	disp-lo	disp-hi

8087 Encoding	Emulator Encoding	Execution Clocks Typical Range	Operation
9B DD m7rm	CD 1D m7rm	55+EA (52-58)+EA	mem-op ← ST pop stack (temp-real)

FSTSW FNSTSW = Store Status Word

WAIT	op1	mod 111 r/m	addr1	addr2

8087 Encoding	Emulator Encoding	Execution Clocks Typical Range	Operation
9B DD m7rm	CD 1D m7rm	15+EA (12-18)+EA	mem-op ← 8087 status word
90 DD m7rm	CD 1D m7rm	15+EA (12-18)+EA	mem-op ← 8087 status word (no wait)

FSUB = Subtract Real

Stack top and Stack element

WAIT	op1	op2 + i

8087 Encoding	Emulator Encoding	Execution Clocks Typical Range	Operation
9B D8 E0+i	CD 18 E0+i	85 70-100	ST ← ST — ST(i)
9B DC E8+i	CD 1C E8+i	85 70-100	ST(i) ← ST(i) — ST

Stack top and memory operand

WAIT	op1	mod 100 r/m	addr1	addr2

8087 Encoding	Emulator Encoding	Execution Clocks Typical Range	Operation
9B D8 m4rm	CD 18 m4rm	105+EA (90-120)+EA	ST ← ST — mem-op (short-real)
9B DC m4rm	CD 1C m4rm	110+EA (95-125)+EA	ST ← ST — mem-op (long-real)

FSUBP = Subtract Real and Pop

WAIT	op1	op2 + i

8087 Encoding	Emulator Encoding	Execution Clocks Typical Range	Operation
9B DE E9	CD 1E E9	90 75-105	ST(1) ← ST(1) — ST pop stack
9B DE E8+i	CD 1E E8+i	90 75-105	ST(i) ← ST(i) — ST pop stack

FSUBR = Subtract Real Reversed

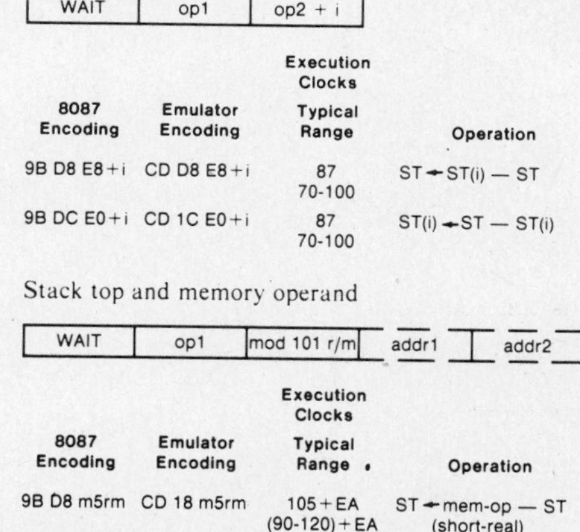

Stack top and Stack element

WAIT	op1	op2 + i

8087 Encoding	Emulator Encoding	Execution Clocks Typical Range	Operation
9B D8 E8+i	CD D8 E8+i	87 70-100	ST ← ST(i) — ST
9B DC E0+i	CD 1C E0+i	87 70-100	ST(i) ← ST — ST(i)

Stack top and memory operand

WAIT	op1	mod 101 r/m	addr1	addr2

8087 Encoding	Emulator Encoding	Execution Clocks Typical Range	Operation
9B D8 m5rm	CD 18 m5rm	105+EA (90-120)+EA	ST ← mem-op — ST (short-real)
9B DC m5rm	CD 1C m5rm	110+EA (95-125)+EA	ST ← mem-op — ST (long-real)

FSUBRP = Subtract Real Reversed and Pop

WAIT	op1	op2 + i

8087 Encoding	Emulator Encoding	Execution Clocks Typical Range	Operation

8087 Encoding	Emulator Encoding	Execution Clocks Typical Range	Operation
9B DE E1	CD 1E E1	90 75-105	ST(1) ← ST — ST(1) pop stack
9B DE E0+i	CD 1E E0+i	90 75-105	ST(i) ← ST — ST(i) pop stack

FTST = Test Stack Top Against + 0.0

WAIT	op1	op2

8087 Encoding	Emulator Encoding	Execution Clocks Typical Range	Operation
9B D9 E4	CD 19 E4	42 38-48	ST ← ST — 0.0

FWAIT = (CPU) Wait While 8087 Is Busy

WAIT

8087 Encoding	Emulator Encoding	Execution Clocks Typical Range	Operation
9B	90	3+5n 3+5n	8086 wait instruction

FXAM = Examine Stack Top

WAIT	op1	op2

8087 Encoding	Emulator Encoding	Execution Clocks Typical Range	Operation
9B D9 E5	CD 19 E5	17 12-23	set condition code

FXCH = Exchange Registers

WAIT	op1	op2 + i

8087 Encoding	Emulator Encoding	Execution Clocks Typical Range	Operation
9B D9 C8	CD 19 C8	12 10-15	T_1 ← ST(1) ST(1) ← ST ST ← T_1
9B D9 C8+i	CD 19 C8+i	12 10-15	T_1 ← ST(i) ST(i) ← ST ST ← T_1

FXTRACT = Extract Exponent and Significand

WAIT	op1	op2

8087 Encoding	Emulator Encoding	Execution Clocks Typical Range	Operation
9B D9 F4	CD 19 F4	50 27-55	T_1 ← exponent (ST) T_2 ← significand (ST) ST ← T_1 push stack ST ← T_2

FYL2X = Compute Y · Log_2 X

WAIT	op1	op2

8087 Encoding	Emulator Encoding	Execution Clocks Typical Range	Operation
9B D9 F1	CD 19 F1	950 900-1100	T_1 ← ST(1) · $\log_2$ (ST) pop stack ST ← T_1

FYL2XP1 = Compute Y · Log_2 (X + 1)

WAIT	op1	op2

8087 Encoding	Emulator Encoding	Execution Clocks Typical Range	Operation
9B D9 F9	CD 19 F9	850 700-1000	T_1 ← ST + 1 T_2 ← ST(1) · $\log_2 T_1$ pop stack ST ← T_2

INDEX